Arizona Breeding Bird Atlas

This book is published with the assistance
of the Arizona Game and Fish Department
and funding from the Wildlife Conservation
Restoration Program.

Arizona Breeding Bird Atlas

Edited by
Troy E. Corman and Cathryn Wise-Gervais

UNIVERSITY OF NEW MEXICO PRESS | ALBUQUERQUE

Copy Editor: Gregory McNamee

Layout and Design: Roberta Dobolek

Production Coordinator: Melissa Tandysh

Map Design and Production: Matt Alderson, Cathryn Wise-Gervais

Graph Production: Cathryn Wise-Gervais

Contributing Authors: Annalaura Averrill-Murray, Robert Bradley, Bill Burger, Greg Clark, Troy E. Corman, James Driscoll, Daniel L. Fischer, Peter Friederici, Bill Grossi, Chuck LaRue, Margie J. Latta, Jennifer L. Martin, Tracy McCarthey, Gale Monson, Amanda Moors, Linden Piest, Norm Shrout, Suzanne Sitko, John Spence, Cathryn Wise-Gervais

Cover Art: Narca Moore-Craig

Photographers: George Andrejko, Fran Barbano, Rick and Nora Bowers, Jim Burns, Greg Clark, Troy Corman, Henry Detwiler, Richard Ditch, James Driscoll, Dan Fischer, Bob Miles, Pat O'Brien, Richard Ockenfels, Chris Parish, Todd Pringle, Earle Robinson, Gary Rosenberg, Brian Small, Alexander Smith, Noel and Helen Snyder, Bruce Taubert

Text Reviewers: Roy Jones, Susan Schuetze, David Stejskal, Mark Stevenson

Project Coordinator: Troy E. Corman

Computer and Data Managers: Annalaura Averill-Murray, David Felley, Tracy McCarthey, Dale Ward, Cathryn Wise-Gervais

Arizona Breeding Bird Atlas Field Crew Members: Seth Ames, Annalaura Averill-Murray, Gwen Bauluss, Mike Collins, Troy Corman, Tami Denette, David Felley, Aaron Flesch, Peter Friederici, David Griffin, Megan Hall, Charley Land, Margie Latta, Tracy McCarthey, John McGehee, Lisa Miller, Karen Newlon, Judy Putera, Karen Short, Benny Thatcher, Bryant Ward, and Cathryn Wise-Gervais

---

Printed in China by Everbest Printing Company Ltd. through Four Colour Imports, Ltd.
10 09 08 07 06 05 1 2 3 4 5

Library of Congress Cataloging-in-Publication Data

The Arizona breeding bird atlas / edited by Troy E. Corman and Cathryn Wise-Gervais.
p. cm.
Includes bibliographical references and index.
ISBN 0-8263-3379-6 (cloth : alk. paper)
1. Birds—Arizona. 2. Birds—Arizona—Geographical distribution.
3. Birds—Arizona—Geographical distribution—Maps.
I. Corman, Troy E. II. Wise-Gervais, Cathryn.
QL684.A6A75 2005
598'.09791—dc22

2005002023

Acknowledgments

The Arizona Breeding Bird Atlas project and this book were made possible from support from the W-95-M Federal Aid in Wildlife Restoration Act (Pittman-Robertson Act), Arizona's Nongame Wildlife Check-off, and by generous grants and other funding sources from:

Arizona Game and Fish Department Heritage Fund
National Fish and Wildlife Foundation
Partnerships For Wildlife
U.S. Fish and Wildlife Service
Wildlife Conservation Restoration Program
Bureau of Land Management
The Nature Conservancy
U.S. Bureau of Reclamation
U.S. Forest Service

Jones & Stokes provided funds for computer programming and database transfer to Microsoft Access.

The following dedicated folks served as Regional Coordinators during the project, helping organize fieldwork, recruit volunteers, and review completed data forms:

Arizona Strip: Mike Herder
Flagstaff: Terry Blows, Elaine Morrall
Huachuca: Jack Whetstone
KOFA: George Morrison, Ron Kearns
North Kaibab: John Spence
Phoenix East: Bob Bradley
Prescott: Carl Tomoff
Tohono O'odham: B. June Babcock, Greg Clark
White Mountains: Sue Sitko, Brian Heap
Chiricahua: Arnold Moorhouse
Hopi and Navajo West: Chuck LaRue
Kingman: Rick Hibbard
Navajo East: David Mikesic
Payson: Cathy Taylor
Phoenix West: Bill Grossi
Safford: Erin Bibles, Jim Gacey
Tucson: Deborah Bieber
Yuma: Bob and Susanna Henry

Field surveys were made possible with the generous cooperation of both public and private landowners and managers as well as through the cooperation of many Native American tribes and nations. Our gratitude to the following tribes and nations for permitting atlas surveys on their lands:

Colorado River Indian Tribes
Hualapai Tribe
Navajo Nation
Tohono O'odham Nation
Hopi Tribe
Kaibab Paiute Tribe
San Carlos Apache Tribe
Zuni Tribe

Many thanks to the Arizona Game and Fish Department personnel who facilitated good landowner relations: Bill Burger, Dan Groebner, Susi MacVean, Lin Piest, Mike Pruss, Tim Snow and Richard Winstead, and many Wildlife Managers, including John Bacourn, Bob Barsh, Bob Birkeland, Mark Brown, Mark Clark, Kyle Cooper, Tom Finley, Joe Hall, Winford Hooe, Bill Ough, Scott Paulsen, Tim Pender, Bob Posey, Bob Price, Don Rinker, David Rippeto, Mark Severson, Jimmie Simmons, Darren Tucker, Daniel Urquidez Jr., Shawn Wagner, Jon Wangnild, and John Windes. Our apologies to anyone we may have overlooked.

The following individuals were also instrumental in acquiring local site and regional access to conduct atlas surveys:

Barry M. Goldwater Range: Bob Barry, David Blockland, David Mendez
Buenos Aires National Wildlife Refuge: Sally Gall
Cabeza Prieta National Wildlife Refuge: Laura Thompson-Olais
Fort Huachuca: Sheridan Stone
Grand Canyon National Park: Jim Petterson, Della Synder
Lake Mead National Recreation Area: Kent Turner, Bill Pelle
Organ Pipe Cactus National Monument: Tim Tibbitts
Pima Community Resources: Amy Loughner
Ray-Asarco Mine Complex: Neil Gambell
San Tans Regional Park: Bob Ingram
Silverbell Mine: Cathy Arnold
Yuma Proving Grounds: Valerie Morrill, Junior Kearns

We thank Leo Drum for all-terrain vehicle training of field crew members and to Bob Miles, Roberta Dobolek, and Heidi Vasiloff for Atlas newsletter layout and design.

Finally, a special word of appreciation is due to the nonbirding family members of Atlas project volunteers (Appendix A). Without their understanding and cooperation, this monumental endeavor would not have been possible.

DEDICATION

To all the field workers who made the Arizona Breeding Bird Atlas project and this publication possible.

Contents

FIGURES AND TABLES	viii
FOREWORD	ix
INTRODUCTION — ORGANIZATION AND METHODS	1
Arizona Atlas History, Organization, and Funding	1
Methodology	2
Limitations and Biases	9
Summary of Results	10
GEOGRAPHY, CLIMATE, AND HABITATS OF ARIZONA	19
A BRIEF HISTORY OF ARIZONA ORNITHOLOGY	44
SPECIES ACCOUNTS	48
Species account Overview	48
Species Accounts	49–588
SUPPLEMENTAL SPECIES ACCOUNTS	590
Rare and Local Nesting Species	590
Possible and Probable Nesting Species	595
Historical Nesting Species	600
APPENDICES	604
A. List of Atlas Volunteers	605
B. Arizona Breeding Bird Atlas Project Funding	609
C. Common and Scientific Plant Names Used in the Text	610
D. Cowbird Brood Parasitism	612
LITERATURE CITED	614
INDEX OF ENGLISH BIRD NAMES	633
ATLAS AUTHOR BIOGRAPHIES	635

Figures and Tables

Figure 1. Priority Block Selection 2
Figure 2. Arizona Breeding Bird Atlas Regions 3
Figure 3. Arizona General Land Ownership 8
Figure 4. Arizona Breeding Bird Atlas Effort: Blocks Initiated 11
Figure 5. Arizona Breeding Bird Atlas Effort: Blocks Completed 11
Figure 6. Arizona Breeding Bird Atlas Survey Status 12
Figure 7. Species Richness by Topographic Map 15
Figure 8. Nest Data Locations 17
Figure 9. Arizona Topography 20
Figure 10. Biotic Communities of Arizona 21
Figure 11. PRISM 1971-2000 Average Annual Precipitation in Arizona 23
Figure 12. Significant Riparian Areas 25
Figure 13. Selected Arizona Cities and Towns 26
Figure 14. Dams, Lakes, and Water Impoundments 28

Table 1. Breeding Criteria and Definition of Codes 5
Table 2. Habitat Codes 6
Table 3. Abundance Codes 7
Table 4. Annual Survey Effort 1993-2000 11
Table 5. Top Twenty Species-Rich Priority Blocks 13
Table 6. Breeding Bird Species Detected on Priority Blocks, but Confirmed Only Outside Blocks 14
Table 7. Confirmed Breeding Bird Species Not Detected on Priority Blocks 14
Table 8. Confirmed and Potential Breeding Bird Species Reported by County 14
Table 9. Most Frequently Reported Breeding Birds in Arizona 16
Table 10. New Breeding Bird Species for Arizona 18

Foreword by Gale Monson

The Arizona Breeding Bird Atlas is designed to depict the distribution of breeding birds in the period primarily from 1993 to 2000. It is meant to be repeated every twenty years or so in order to give continuity to the process. We can see the value in this—to enable us to view changes in the density as well as the composition of our breeding bird populations for any given physiographic unit of measurement that do not change location over time. Although historical bird distributional information is far from complete, Atlas data can be compared to historical records and accounts to have a better understanding of bird distributional changes that have and continue to occur in Arizona. With the Atlas information in hand, we can better contemplate the pre-1993 records. Having a background of bird studies that began in Arizona in 1934 and includes most parts of the state, I hope that my observations, recollections, and experiences may be of interest to readers. Naturally, I cannot run the whole gamut, but I can offer a sampling.

During the summers of 1939 and 1940, I would drive my rattley International pickup on old US 80 from Tucson to near Bisbee without ever being out of earshot of the mystical, plaintive song of Cassin's Sparrows. The windows were rolled down to mitigate the heat, and I never drove the pickup faster than 50 mph, so hearing conditions were good (this was before the advent of air conditioning). It was thought at the time, since no nests or young were ever found, that Cassin's Sparrows left their breeding grounds in the Great Plains to come to Arizona with their fledged young to take advantage of the abundance of food produced by the summer rains. This theory was controverted when Bob Ohmart found a nest in 1965; later, other observers found more nests. But the abundance of Cassin's Sparrows in 1939 and 1940 was surely far greater than in any year since then. These years were ones of good rainfall, indicating an important relationship of sparrows to rainfall that I believe is a given.

In 1939, the closely related Botteri's Sparrow was actually thought to be extirpated from the state, since there were no records since 1900. When I collected specimens in Cochise County of birds I thought were Cassin's Sparrows, although they had a totally different song, and showed them to Allan Phillips, he literally pounced on them and proclaimed them to be Botteri's. But a post-1900 nest was not found until 1967, again by the selfsame Ohmart. I would pause here to pay my respects to the late Allan Phillips as one who brought his intellect to bear on the entire subject of Arizona ornithology. He lived and breathed Arizona birds, spent all of his waking hours on the subject until he emigrated to Old Mexico about 1957, and had little patience with the observations of dilettante birders. There is no questioning that he was the preeminent Arizona ornithologist of the twentieth century. Sad to say, today he is almost forgotten and many birders would not recognize his name. I deem it a privilege to have associated with him and to have learned much Arizona ornithology from him.

I was witness to the arrival of the Great-tailed Grackle in 1935 at Safford, and to the European Starling in 1946 (I took the first specimen in the state from an athel tamarisk in my front yard at Parker on the Colorado River). A species that was incredibly numerous in farmlands and grasslands statewide until the 1950s is the Horned Lark. Not only that, but there appeared to be much fluctuation in numbers, and contraction and expansion of its breeding range, according to the amount of annual rainfall. Still another species that has seen a large drop-off in numbers, although not in territory, in the last fifty years or so is the Loggerhead Shrike.

Nowhere has the habitat changed and many birds' occurrences simultaneously changed than along the Colorado River following the construction by the Bureau of Reclamation of massive dams beginning with Hoover (Boulder) Dam in 1936, then Parker Dam, Imperial Dam, Davis Dam, and finally Glen Canyon Dam, all straddling the river and also the Arizona state line. The resultant stilling of the river waters immediately caused the deposition of large amounts of silt (almost entirely sand), especially in the reaches of Parker and Imperial dams. The result was a change in channels and the blocking-off of entrances to backwaters, some of them quite large—Topock Marsh and Martinez and Ferguson lakes, for example. Areas immediately above Imperial Dam and at the head of Lake Havasu filled in, creating beautiful cattail and bulrush stands with areas of open water. Breeding colonies of Western and Clark's Grebes have since become established. The Bill Williams River delta went from an open stand of Bermuda grass, willows, arrowweed, and screwbean mesquite threaded by a small stream to a large, sterile stand of cattails.

The Bureau of Reclamation recognized that sand deposits at the head of Topock Gorge would cause unwanted spreading of the river bottom and rising river levels (threatening the town of Needles) from the Gorge to Davis Dam. Therefore, they resorted to dredging a deepwater channel from Needles to Topock, creating a huge dry spoil bank and nearly sealing off Topock Marsh, which, having no freshwater infusion, became increasingly unproductive. This marsh is a localized area of less than a hundred acres, at least from 1946 until 1954, consisted of a drowned mesquite thicket in several feet of water. The dead mesquites served as a substrate to support a concentration of nests of several species, including Great and Snowy Egrets, Double-crested Cormorants, Great Blue Herons, Black-crowned Night-Herons, Harris's Hawks, and Great Horned Owls.

Considering the breeding distribution expansion and/or contraction of various avian species in the state, I could go on and on. In many cases, the underlying causes for individual species distribution change are not at all difficult to ascertain and are often a combination of more than one factor. Most are based on the many human-altered environments in the state, but some are related to wildfires, drought, flooding, and changing climate. Although it is all enough to make one's head swim, the Atlas publication strives to make some sense of it all.

It is gratifying to note that bird nomenclature follows the only possible authority, that of the American Ornithologists' Union Check-List. The species accounts are written in an easily understandable format, are well-done, and authoritative. Acclaim to the writers.

Gale Monson
Albuquerque, New Mexico
July 2003

Introduction

Cathryn Wise-Gervais and Troy E. Corman

When its organizers and volunteers initiated the Arizona Breeding Bird Atlas (ABBA) project in 1993, they faced a formidable task. Never before had Arizona's birds been surveyed comprehensively on a statewide basis, and the state itself offered significant logistical challenges: Arizona is generally sparsely populated away from its large cities; much of the terrain is rugged, remote, and difficult to access; and more than a quarter of the state is made up of Native American tribal lands, requiring close coordination with numerous tribes. Despite these and other obstacles, atlas participants dove headfirst into the challenge and completed the basic surveys during the 2000 field season.

The primary goal of the ABBA was to provide a breeding distribution "snapshot" for each of Arizona's nesting bird species at the end of the twentieth century. Bird populations are constantly changing because of varying environmental factors that are often influenced directly or indirectly by human activities. Data collected and compiled serve as a baseline against which to judge future range expansions and contractions within the state. These data also provide a wealth of natural history information previously lacking or poorly known for many of Arizona's birds. The ABBA provides a central breeding bird database that is available to land managers, biologists, policymakers, ecologists, and other interested parties when responding to proposed land management changes, as well as avian population evaluations and recommendations for conservation. In addition, we hope that the atlas text will be a regularly used resource for the birding community, educators, and students, and that it will encourage a greater appreciation for the natural history, ecology, and distribution of the vast avian life found within Arizona.

Organizers planned the ABBA as a ten-year project, divided into an eight-year survey period followed by two years of data synthesis and writing. Not surprising, the project expanded outside of these original predictions and required an extra season of very local cleanup surveys and another year for compilation and writing. During the primary eight years of fieldwork, dedicated participants collected data on approximately 97 percent of the survey areas and established many noteworthy records. These include new national and state breeding records, new distribution information, and numerous early and late nesting records for many species.

ORGANIZATION AND METHODS

Arizona Atlas History, Organization, and Funding

In March 1986, Duane Shroufe, the Arizona Game and Fish Department's (AGFD) director, was the first to suggest the idea of conducting a statewide Arizona Breeding Bird Atlas. The AGFD Nongame Branch staff, including Terry B. Johnson, Branch Chief, discussed the feasibility of such an endeavor. Then in February 1987, three active birders in Arizona, Rick Bowers, Barny Dunning, and Jeff Price, contacted Johnson to rekindle discussion on this subject and to investigate the role AGFD envisioned for the project. This group had already made plans to conduct preliminary atlas block surveys during the nesting season later that same year to gain a better understanding of what would be expected for such an undertaking. Even though the vision was strongly supported, at the time financial funding was not readily available to initiate such a monumental endeavor.

In November 1990, Arizona voters overwhelmingly approved a public initiative to allocate up to ten million dollars from the Arizona Lottery to be transferred annually to the AGFD. This newly acquired funding was to be used for the conservation of sensitive species and their habitats (including property acquisition), habitat evaluations and protection, public access, urban wildlife, and environmental education. Shroufe and Johnson now had the financial backing for initiating the atlas project through what became the AGFD Heritage Fund. During the fall of 1992, Troy Corman became the ABBA project coordinator, and the foundation of the project was organized in preparation for the first official field season in the spring of 1993.

The ABBA project was coordinated by the AGFD, but many additional financial supporters came on board through the life of the project. Other funding partners included the U.S. Bureau of Land Management (BLM), the National Fish and Wildlife Foundation, the U.S. Bureau of Reclamation, the U.S. Fish and Wildlife Service, the U.S. Forest Service, and The Nature Conservancy (see appendix B for monetary contribution by funding agency). Throughout the project, the AGFD Heritage Fund and the annual in-kind contribution from volunteer survey and travel hours were used as nonfederal matches for these grants and agreements. Along with annual funding, BLM also donated two full sets of Arizona 7.5-minute topographical maps for project use. Project partners had access to regional bird data as they became available, and thus benefited directly from atlas surveys before the project was completed. In addition, agency biologists and representatives occasionally accompanied surveyors in the field or provided logistical support when needed.

Methodology

Priority Block Sampling

Because of size (Arizona is the sixth-largest U.S. state), many logistical challenges, and the relatively limited volunteer workforce, the project's leaders quickly determined that full atlas survey coverage was not practical for Arizona. The ABBA grid survey design closely followed the atlasing protocols set forth by the North American Ornithological Atlas Committee (NORAC) in 1990. Like many other prior state atlases, ABBA was based on U.S. Geological Survey topographic maps covering 7.5 minutes of latitude and longitude. Even though they were often outdated, these maps, often referred to as quadrangles or simply quads, were ideal for atlasing purposes, depicting topographic relief, roads, trails, water sources, and other important features. Project staff divided each quad map into six approximately ten-square-mile sectors as shown in figure 1. One of these sectors was then randomly selected as the "priority block" with the roll of a die, and it served as the basic sampling unit of the atlas survey. Therefore, approximately one-sixth of the state was designated to be surveyed. It was determined that 1899 quad maps contained enough area in Arizona for a priority block. To prevent clustering, priority blocks were randomly relocated when the initially selected block fell adjacent to another one. Priority blocks were also moved whenever possible if private landowners or Native American tribes denied access, if surveyors encountered significant geographic barriers, or if the block fell over restricted or dangerous areas at military installations. Project staff moved a total of thirty-five blocks for these reasons.

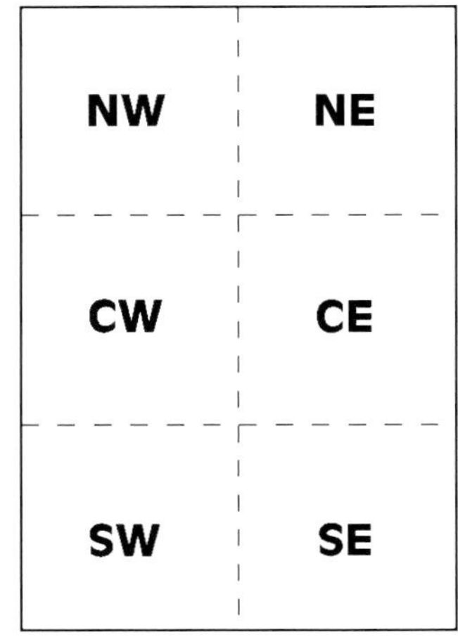

Figure 1: Priority Block Selection. Each quad map contained six sectors. One priority block was selected randomly from these.

Casual Observations

The process of randomly selecting priority blocks to be surveyed often excluded several unique habitats and other areas of high ornithological interest within a quad map. As an example, many of Arizona's limited rivers and streams support critically important and often relatively narrow riparian habitats. These areas in turn support a unique assemblage of birds not found in the adjacent drier and typically much more widespread deserts and uplands. Random priority-block designations often missed such local habitats. By broadening the scope of atlas surveys to include such areas, project organizers expected to obtain records for locally occurring and underrepresented species, and thus to be better able to define breeding ranges of uncommon species. As a means to this end, ABBA organizers developed an atlas data category for sightings made outside of priority blocks known as "casual observations." From 1993 to 1997, atlasers were encouraged to report only confirmed breeding sightings obtained outside priority blocks as casual observations. In 1998, after six years of data collection, the definition of a casual observation was expanded to include any reports of suspected or confirmed nesting species outside priority blocks. These casual observation data are considered supplemental and appear on distribution maps only if the species was not detected on the priority block for a particular quad map. Casual observation records were included in breeding-phenology and habitat-use descriptions for all species and have proved especially valuable for nocturnal species, riparian, marsh, and other water-oriented species, as well as for localized breeders.

The ABBA staff also incorporated species-specific survey results into the atlas casual observation database. Throughout the ABBA project period, many state, federal, tribal, university, and private agencies conducted species-specific surveys and nest monitoring in Arizona. These include surveys for Bald Eagle, Northern Goshawk, Peregrine Falcon, Black Rail, Clapper Rail, Ferruginous Pygmy-owl, Spotted Owl, Elegant Trogon, Yellow-billed Cuckoo, Buff-breasted Flycatcher, and Willow Flycatcher. Many of these species are local, secretive, and not easily detected. Likewise, specialized avian studies that focused more time and attention to relatively small geographic areas effectively added considerable data for rare or difficult-to-detect species. Specialized surveys occasionally occurred on priority blocks; in these rare instances, these data were added to priority-block species lists. Additional information collected while conducting species-specific surveys was also useful to the atlas project. For example, Spotted Owl surveyors often recorded other owl and nightjar species they detected during surveys. Compilation of this local data helped delineate the breeding distribution of these species in the state and resulted in more accurate distribution maps.

Regional Coordination

Although the ABBA was certainly an interagency project, volunteers conducted more than half of the fieldwork. To ease volunteer coordination, ABBA organizers divided the state into twenty geographic regions (figure 2) based on quad map boundaries. A regional coordinator knowledgeable about the birds of the area was appointed to act as volunteer liaison for seventeen of these regions. The remaining three atlas regions encompassed tribal areas and were coordinated by project staff. The number of priority blocks in each ABBA region ranged from 18 to 182 but averaged approximately 95 blocks. These volunteer regional coordinators played an important role as they recruited volunteers, assigned blocks, helped with logistical issues, provided the first round of quality control for submitted data, and forwarded field cards and forms to the atlas staff office at the end of each field season. Some of these outstanding folks had few qualified or interested volunteer helpers and took it upon themselves to survey

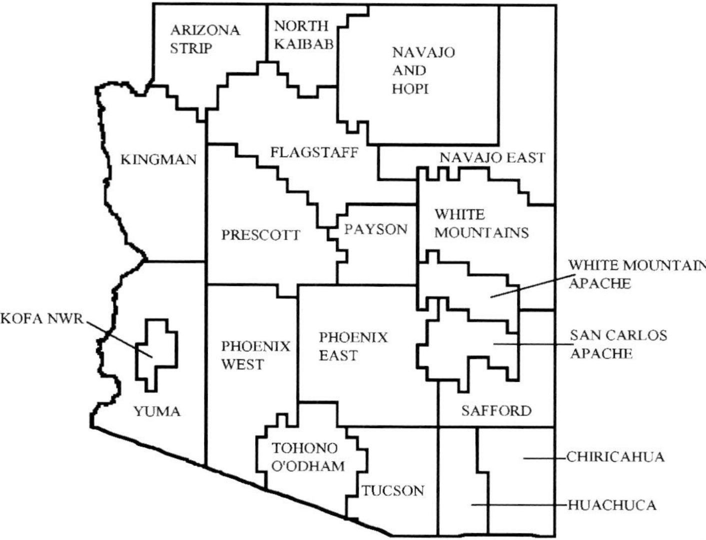

Figure 2. Arizona Breeding Bird Atlas Regions

many of the blocks in their assigned region. One regional coordinator even helped survey blocks in an adjacent region once surveys had been completed in his region. Regional coordinators and their volunteers were invaluable to the project, and their enthusiasm and perseverance carried the atlas endeavor to successful completion.

Field Methods

Project staff produced an ABBA handbook outlining atlas protocols and describing the abbreviated codes to be used on the field cards and on other atlas forms. Field cards, ABBA handbooks, and other specialized forms served to standardize data collection and were distributed to volunteers when they were assigned one or more priority blocks. Project staff also provided at least one workshop per year, at which volunteers were instructed in atlas survey protocols, interpretation of breeding bird behavior, and in nest-finding techniques. Volunteers were instructed to submit one field card for each block surveyed per year, even if they did not complete work on their block(s).

Volunteers were directed to visit their blocks several times during the breeding season and for each visit, list the date, hours surveyed, and hours spent traveling to and from their blocks. It was estimated that the average block required approximately twenty-five hours to survey for birds. The actual time spent on a block varied considerably, however, based on the atlasers' skill level, the block's habitat diversity, and on the accessibility of the block. Atlasers attempted to visit each habitat type present on their block, and to pay special attention to any springs, seeps, or other water sources depicted on their maps. Some low habitat-diversity blocks required only a matter of hours to complete; in contrast, high-diversity blocks and those with a wide range of elevations required many more visits at various periods throughout the breeding season. The elevation range within priority block boundaries was quite variable. Some relatively flat desert blocks contained less than 10 ft (3 m) elevation change, while the Mount Graham block encompassed a range of over 5300 ft (1615 m).

Atlasers: Volunteers and Field Crews

The ABBA project would not have been possible without dedicated volunteers, and so recruitment was an ongoing process. The atlas staff gave presentations at Audubon and Wildlife Society meetings to inform others about the project and to recruit volunteers. Atlas supporters received project updates in the ABBA newsletter and in newspaper and magazine articles. The ABBA newsletters contained statewide and regional status reports, promotions for upcoming events, helpful hints for completing data forms, and many articles from volunteers and field crew members. Articles often ranged from memorable atlas experiences and anecdotes to focus species and avian nesting behavior. Volunteers who completed five or more survey blocks were recognized in the project newsletter at regular intervals. In addition to the newsletter, the ABBA staff attempted to pique volunteer interest over the years by offering group atlasing events called "blockbusters." Blockbusting events focused a group of atlasers on a single block for a day or weekend. If the event occurred during the peak of breeding season, the block was often completed through this effort.

In addition to volunteers, the atlas staff hired small field crews, and these proved vital to the project. These crews consisted of four, occasionally five, full-time wildlife biologists who worked for approximately four to five months surveying blocks. However, thanks to an increase in annual funding during the final full field season in 2000, there were eight crew members surveying their way across Arizona's varied landscapes. Field crews typically split into two-person teams and focused on blocks that were difficult to access either physically or politically, were in remote areas, were located in areas that had few atlasers, or were simply of little interest to others due to low habitat and bird diversity. For political and liability reasons, it was often easier to gain access for field crews on military and tribal lands than it was for the volunteers. As a result, field crews often focused their survey efforts on these lands. Field crews were provided vehicles and some field equipment, and typically had rigorous schedules working and camping for eight to nine consecutive days in many far reaches of the state, often where few if any avian biologists had ever explored.

Survey Objectives and Timing

The basic objective of priority block surveys was simply to find each bird species that nests within the confines of the survey area, and then to confirm breeding for as many of these as possible. However, the objective of detecting every nesting species within a block is unrealistic if not impossible with limited numbers of surveyors. From 1993 to 1995, atlasers wishing to complete a block were required to document 80 percent or more of the anticipated breeding species and to obtain a 50 percent confirmation rate of those species. Statewide progress was exceedingly slow, so in 1996, the atlas staff lowered the target confirmation rate to 25 percent. By the end of the 1999 field surveys, the atlas coordinator was able to reasonably predict which breeding species should occur in given habitats and time frames based on prior knowledge gained from similar surveyed blocks in adjacent areas. Therefore, during the 2000 field season, the atlas coordinator considered blocks complete when approximately 80 percent or more of the anticipated species were detected, even when less than 25 percent of those species were confirmed. In this respect, the last year of atlas surveys resembled British and Irish atlas projects, in that atlasers shifted their focus from obtaining a set confirmation rate to gathering a species list that was as complete as possible.

The timing and peak period for conducting atlas surveys in Arizona's diverse landscapes was quite variable and was determined by the location, elevation, and the habitat being surveyed. Many resident desert birds begin nesting in mid- to late winter and reach a peak in nesting in March and April, just as migrant species arrive in the area to begin their nesting cycle. Few surveys were conducted in lowland desert regions before late February or early March and most mid- to high-elevation blocks were not initiated before early May. As nesting activity wanes in July for much of the desert and central and northern mountainous regions of the state, Arizona's "second spring" begins. This is most notable in the southeastern quarter of the state as subtropical moisture is pulled up from Mexico from early July through early September, increasing the humidity and frequency of afternoon and evening thunderstorms. Owing to the typical bountiful rains during this period, many avian species take advantage of increased lush vegetative growth and subsequent elevated prey density by either initiating a second nesting or actually beginning their first breeding activity of the year. Nesting activity for many bird species in this region continues well into September and occasionally later, although this is well after most atlas surveys had ended in mid-August.

Breeding Codes

Atlasers reported each detected bird's status by using one of four breeding category codes based on NORAC (1990) standards (table 1). Nonbreeding migrants or vagrants were simply listed as "observed." Birds suspected of breeding in an area were either listed as "possible" for birds seen or heard in potential breeding habitat, "probable" for birds engaging in behaviors that suggested they were nesting (courtship, territorial aggression, and the like), or "confirmed" indicating that atlasers obtained evidence that the bird was actually nesting. Each of these categories was further divided into twenty-one breeding activity codes to describe an observation. For example, an atlaser who discovered a nest with eggs would use the NE code to indicate "nest with eggs" under the "confirmed" category. The visit dates were also noted for all breeding codes listed on the field card for each species detected. These corresponding dates and breeding activity codes greatly contributed to our understanding of each species' breeding phenology in Arizona.

Table 1: Breeding Criteria and Definition of Codes

Observed (OB)

Code **Description**

O Nonbreeder or migrant **observed** in block during breeding season, but not believed to be breeding. Use this for species in unlikely breeding habitat and with no indication of breeding. This could apply to ducks summering on an urban or sewage settling pond with no breeding habitat or a Great Blue Heron foraging when no heronry exists on the block. (Note: Observations designated with this code were not included in distribution maps.)

Possible (PO)

Code **Description**

Species observed or identified by vocalizations in suitable nesting habitat during its breeding season. Also use this code for those species that do not have true songs (owls, woodpeckers, corvids, raptors, and the like). Use this for birds seen in likely breeding habitat, such as a Western Tanager in a pon derosa pine forest. Be especially cautious during the migration period of birds, which may be passing through or birds that may linger on wintering areas. Some wintering species may be present in late winter and early spring in the desert, while some resident species have commenced breeding.

X **Singing male** present in suitable nesting habitat during its breeding season. If you hear that same tanager singing, code it X (though if you hear it singing on a second trip, see if it qualifies as probable).

Probable (PR)

Code **Description**

P **Pair** observed in suitable habitat during its breeding season. If you see a male and female of the same species in proper breeding habitat, use this code. Note that some birds (e.g., ducks) are often paired during migration.

S Permanent territory presumed through **song** at same location on at least two occasions seven or more days apart. If the Western Tanager mentioned above was heard singing twice in the same place a week apart, code it S.

T Permanent territory presumed through defense of breeding territory (chasing individuals of the same species). One male American Robin chasing anoth er falls under this code. **Caution**: some species, especially raptors and hummingbirds, exhibit territorial behavior in defense of feeding areas, favorite perches, and the like while wintering or migrating.

C **Courtship** behavior or **copulation** between a male and female. This includes courtship displays or food exchange.

N Visiting probable **nest site**, but no further evidence obtained. This applies to a bird that consistently flies into the same likely nest site but provides insufficient behavior for upgrading to confirmed. This is especially useful for cavity-nesters.

A **Agitated** behavior or anxiety calls of adult, indicating nest site or young in the vicinity. Two birds circling above your head or a Northern Goshawk dis tress call falls into this category. Do not include agitation induced by "pishing" or using taped calls.

B Nest **building** by Verdins and some species of wrens (Cactus, Bewick's, House, and Marsh) or excavation of cavities by woodpeckers. Woodpeckers and other cavity excavators usually make only one nest hole, but use other holes for roosting; some species of wrens and Verdins will build several nests before a female selects one, and unmated males do this, too.

Confirmed (CO)

Code **Description**

CN Bird seen **carrying nesting** material (e.g., sticks, grass, mud, cobwebs). This applies for all species except some species of wrens (Cactus, Bewick's, House, Marsh) and Verdins.

NB **Nest building** seen at the actual nest site, excluding some species of wrens (Cactus, Bewick's, House, Marsh), woodpeckers, and Verdins.

DD **Distraction displays**, defense of unknown nest or young or injury feigning. Used if an adult bird is seen trying to lead people away from nest or young. Commonly seen in most ground nesters, this is the typical Killdeer broken-wing act. This also includes active defense, such as a Cooper's Hawk diving at you, but it does not include agitated behavior (A under Probable).

UN **Used nest** or eggshells found. Unless carefully identified, use this only for unmistakable eggshells and nests used during the atlas period. Magpie nests, for example, are very characteristic, but if you are unsure, do not use this code. Do not use this code for species that build multiple nests in a breeding season, such as Verdins and Cactus Wrens. Do not collect the nest, because some species roost in them all year and it is illegal to collect nests or eggs (Migratory Bird Treaty Act).

FL Recently **fledged** young of altricial species incapable of sustained flight or downy young of precocial species restricted to the natal area by dependence on adults or by limited mobility. A duck brood on an isolated pond merits this code, but note that barely fledged blackbirds and swallows may fly considerable distances. The presence of young cowbirds confirms both the cowbird and the host.

ON **Occupied nest** indicated by adult entering or leaving nest site in circumstances indicating an occupied nest, including those in high trees, cliffs, cavities, and burrows where the contents of the nest and incubating or brooding adult cannot be seen.

CF Adults seen **carrying food**, excluding raptors, corvids (e.g. jays, ravens, crows, nutcrackers, magpies), roadrunners, shrikes, and kingfishers. These birds often carry food some distance before eating it themselves, so be very cautious when using this code.

FY Adults **feeding** recently fledged **young**. Young cowbirds begging food confirm both the cowbird and the host.

FS Adult carrying **fecal sac**. Many passerines keep their nests clean by carrying fecal sacs away from the nest.

NE **Nest** with **eggs** found. Unless you see the adult, the same warnings under the UN code apply here. Cowbird eggs confirm both the cowbird and the host.

NY **Nest** with **young** seen or heard. Use when you actually see the young or, as with most cavity nesters, if you only hear the young. A cowbird chick in the nest confirms both the cowbird and the host.

Habitat Codes

For a landlocked state, Arizona has a tremendous diversity of distinct habitats. Atlasers standardized their data collection by using abbreviated codes to indicate the habitats they visited while conducting surveys on their block. These codes are listed and described in table 2 below. Habitat characterizations were largely derived from *Biotic Communities of the Southwest*, edited by David E. Brown (1994).

ABBA habitat codes were divided into seven main habitat landscapes: tundra, forest, scrublands, grasslands, desertlands, wetlands, and urban/agricultural areas, and these were further divided into forty habitat types, each indicated by a three-letter code. Habitat data collected for each species across their range in Arizona added considerably to our understanding of their distributional limits and habitat preferences. These data will also help planners and land managers assess the effects of changing land management for each species. Although atlasers were instructed to choose one habitat code containing the majority of the listed plant species found on the block, observers often had to use two codes to describe more accurately the habitat composition where each bird species was found. Only the first habitat code listed was used in the habitat graphs presented by species in the Species Account section, and sometimes atlas staff made minor changes in the order of these to reflect actual habitat usage more accurately.

Table 2: Habitat Codes

Tundra	
TAL	Alpine Tundra: alpine meadow, boulder field, talus (above 11,000 ft)
Forests and Woodlands	
Montane Forests	
FSC	Subalpine Conifer Forest: Engelmann and blue spruce, subalpine (corkbark) fir
FMP	Ponderosa Pine Forests: primarily pure ponderosa pine
FPO	Ponderosa–Gambel's Oak Forest
FMM	Mixed Conifer Forests: Douglas fir, white fir, ponderosa pine, often some aspen and Gambel's oak
FMA	Aspen Forest: >50 percent pure aspen
Cold-Temperate (Great Basin) Conifer Woodlands	
FPJ	Pinyon Pine–Juniper Woodland
FPP	Pinyon Pine–Juniper Woodland with scattered ponderosa pine
Madrean Woodlands	
FME	Madrean Evergreen Woodland: Madrean evergreen oaks, juniper, pinyon pine
FMO	Madrean Pine–Oak Woodland: evergreen oaks, juniper, Chihuahuan pine, Apache pine, ponderosa pine (only in southeastern Arizona mountain ranges)
Scrublands	
SSS	Subalpine Scrub: dwarfed Engelmann spruce, bristlecone pine, dwarf juniper
SIC	Interior Chaparral: shrub live oak, manzanita, mountain-mahogany, cliffrose
Grasslands	
GSA	Subalpine Grasslands
GMM	Montane Meadow Grassland
GGB	Cold-Temperate (Great Basin) Grassland: scattered pinyon pine and juniper
GPL	Plains Grassland: predominantly flat and open continuous grassland, primarily 5000–7500 ft (1524–2286 m) in elevation (northern Arizona)
GSD	Semiarid Grassland, often with scattered sotol, agaves, burroweed, snakeweed, yucca, mesquite
GSS	Sonoran Savanna Grassland: scattered mesquite, ironwood, paloverde
Desertlands	
DGB	Cold-Temperate (Great Basin) Desertscrub: sagebrush, blackbrush, shadscale
DMO	Mojave Desertscrub: Joshua tree, creosote bush, saltbush
DCH	Chihuahuan Desertscrub: creosote bush, tarbush, whitethorn acacia, soaptree yucca
Sonoran Desertscrub	
DSL	Lower Colorado River Biome: scattered mesquite, creosote bush, white bursage, brittlebush, saltbush. Typically very few or lacking saguaros
DSU	Arizona Upland Biome: paloverde, ironwood, mesquite, catclaw, acacia, saguaro, cholla, barrel cactus, prickly pear, creosote bush, jojoba, crucifixion thorn
Wetlands	
WAB	Arctic-Boreal Wetlands: scrub willow, alder
WMR	Montane Riparian Wetlands: cottonwood, maple, box elder, alder, willow, some Gambel's oak, ponderosa pine, Douglas fir, white fir, and aspen
WGB	Cold–Temperate (Great Basin) Riparian Wetlands: cottonwood, scrub willow, Russian olive, tamarisk (saltcedar)
WMC	Marshlands, cienegas, ponds, and lake edges: bulrush, sedges, pondweeds, cattail, duckweed, saltgrass
WIR	Interior Riparian Deciduous Forests and Woodlands: sycamore, cottonwood, willow, ash, walnut, bigtooth maple, hackberry, cypress, juniper, oak
WRS	Riparian Scrubland: common reed, willow, seepwillow, arrowweed, tamarisk (saltcedar)
WSD	Sonoran Riparian Deciduous Forest and Woodlands: primarily cottonwood, willow, mesquite, tamarisk (saltcedar), some ash, walnut, and hackberry
WSO	Sonoran Oasis Woodlands: California fan palm
WSR	Sonoran Riparian Scrubland (dry wash): mesquite, paloverde, ironwood, burrobush, desert broom, quailbush, desert willow
WAR	Altered Riparian: primarily tamarisk (saltcedar) or Russian olive–dominated drainages
Urban/Agricultural	
URS	Residential: ornamental plantings, yards, residential ponds, lakes, and canals
UPG	Parks: city parks planted to grass and trees, golf courses, cemeteries
UIN	Industrial: downtowns, commercial districts, warehouses, little vegetation
ARU	Rural: scattered farm buildings, shelterbelts, wastewater ponds, canals, pastures, feedlots, and earthen livestock tanks
ACW	Cultivated Woodlands: orchards, tree farms
ACR	Cropland: grain fields, hay fields, cotton fields, etc.
ABG	Barren Ground: plowed fields, disturbed areas, fallow fields (tumbleweeds, etc.)

Abundance Codes

Abundance estimates, although rough, can sometimes be a useful component of breeding bird atlases. Imagine if John James Audubon had noted only "the Passenger Pigeon is present" rather than estimating that in one flock more than 300 million birds flew by him each hour. Atlasers were directed to estimate the *total number* of breeding pairs of each species on the entire priority block, rather than count the birds actually seen or confirmed (table 3). To do this, observers had to determine the amount of suitable nesting habitat on the block, then estimate nesting density. Although this process was rather coarse, it did provide an idea of a block's bird density.

Table 3: Abundance Codes

Code	Description	Example
A1	One breeding pair in block	Eared Trogon in Ramsey Canyon
A2	2–10 breeding pairs in block	Great Horned Owls along San Pedro River
A3	11–100 breeding pairs in block	Great Blue Heronry
A4	101–1000 breeding pairs in block	Cactus Wren in cholla-dominated desert
A5	> 1000 breeding pairs in block	House Finches or Inca Doves in residential Phoenix

Nocturnal Surveys

Weather permitting, the ABBA field crews conducted nocturnal surveys in areas with suitable owl habitat. Volunteers were also encouraged but not required to conduct these specialized surveys on their blocks. However, volunteers were not able to survey for Spotted Owl and Ferruginous Pygmy-Owl because surveys for federally listed species require permits and special training.

Nocturnal surveyors selected audiotaped calls of different species based on the specific location and elevation of their block and played the calls after sunset or prior to first morning light. Each series of vocalizations was followed by a silent period during which observers listened and watched for responses. Some nocturnal surveyors did not use taped calls, but simply listened and watched for owls and nightjars. Even atlasers who did not conduct night surveys detected nocturnal species occasionally by incidentally flushing birds from their daytime roosts.

Land Ownership and Access

Arizona land ownership falls into five broad categories: private property, federal public land, state trust land, military installations, and Native American tribal lands (figure 3). Project staff or individual atlasers obtained the necessary permits or made logistical arrangements with these entities to secure access into most of the survey areas. Private lands account for approximately 17.5 percent of the state's landmass. Volunteers were encouraged to use Arizona Game and Fish Department (AGFD) regional personnel as liaisons when contacting landowners for access to private lands, and to acquire written documentation that permission was granted whenever possible. AGFD wildlife managers were often the most familiar with private landowners and atlas staff often relied heavily on contact information from these individuals to request access to conduct atlas surveys for both field crews and volunteers.

Access on military installations, especially those with desert bombing and target practice ranges, often took close coordination with military personnel. Frequently, the "safe windows" to conduct atlas surveys within these restricted desert areas occurred only during a narrow range of dates each spring.

As noted before, more than a quarter of Arizona lies within Native American lands. Atlasers obtained permits to conduct surveys on Native American lands, and this process was different for each tribe or nation. It was sometimes as simple as submitting a proposal requesting access. For others it often first involved conducting slide presentations summarizing all aspects of the atlas project at tribal council meetings, followed by additional presentations to individual district councils within the tribe. Most tribes were very accepting to the idea, while several refused any involvement with the project.

Owing to restrictions, the field crews and a handful of volunteers completed the majority of surveys on Native American tribal lands. In some cases, tribal representatives accompanied atlasers during the surveys. The lands of the Tohono O'odham Nation were the single exception to this. Volunteers conducted all surveys within this large desert area through the coordinated efforts of B. June Babcock, Greg Clark, and Tim Price. In exchange for survey access, Greg Clark provided the tribe with educational materials pertaining to the birds of the Tohono O'odham Nation, including a compact disc with common bird songs/calls he recorded and the name of the bird in both O'odham and English.

Figure 3

Arizona General Land Ownership

Nest Site Data

To acquire additional nesting information for many of Arizona's breeding birds, field crews and several volunteers documented nest-site characteristics at many active nests they discovered while conducting surveys from 1994 to 2001. In accordance with a data form and protocol prepared by atlas staff (McCarthey et al. 1994; Averill-Murray et al. 1997), observers were instructed to use great care collecting these data to minimize disturbance at the nest. At most nests, data could be collected in a matter of minutes, leaving the adult birds to resume their normal nesting duties quickly. Information collected at nest sites included location of nest (UTM coordinates, elevation), habitat type, nesting substrate (plant species, cliff, human-made structures, etc.), nest and substrate height dimensions, status (number or presence of eggs/young), and cowbird parasitism. Atlasers were required to estimate measurements in some cases (i.e., extremely tall nest substrates). Measurements were taken in meters but are presented in the text in both metric and standard English formats for the reader's convenience.

Project Administration and Data Processing

The Arizona Breeding Bird Atlas project coordinator and several other full-time atlas staff biologists at the AGFD's Nongame Branch in Phoenix were the primary administrators of the atlas project. All data management, storage, and coordination were conducted from this facility.

At the end of each field season, atlasers submitted their data to their regional coordinators for preliminary review. As local experts, regional coordinators were generally familiar with local breeding bird communities and with the abilities of individual volunteers. Regional coordinators then forwarded all data to the atlas project office. Once there, the atlas project coordinator made final reviews of the field cards and casual observation forms. Notes were made on the data forms if important information was missing, errors were noted, or questions arose from the submitted data. Atlas staff would then make all efforts to contact the atlaser either by phone, email, or letter requesting additional information or clarifications. Once the data was approved, atlas staff would enter all information into the atlas database. The atlas staff entered the bulk of the data annually from September to December and produced an annual atlas progress report summarizing the existing data for cooperating entities.

The atlas staff began preparing for the next field season in January by compiling volunteer packets and hiring seasonal field crew members. This was also the period when regional coordinators periodically met with the atlas project coordinator to discuss progress, future changes, challenges, and concerns. Regional coordinators were annually given printed data summaries for each priority block within their region. The data printouts helped coordinators organize their efforts and provided some quality control.

Even though a number of review steps prevented the incorporation of erroneous information in the atlas database, errors did occur. Many errors surfaced while querying the database or during preparation of species distribution maps. These were often corrected soon after discovery, with database changes occurring throughout the compilation and preparation of this publication.

LIMITATIONS AND BIASES

Atlasers encountered several factors outside their control that influenced atlas survey outcomes. Although every effort has been made to address these issues, readers should keep the following factors in mind while evaluating a given species range in Arizona.

Land Access

Lengthy efforts by the AGFD to obtain permission to survey on White Mountain Apache, Havasupai, or Gila River Indian Community tribal lands were ultimately unsuccessful. As a result, project staff moved blocks to alternate quad sectors off tribal land whenever possible or surveyed only portions of these blocks not on tribal land. There were thirty priority blocks on White Mountain Apache tribal lands alone, and many of these included significant high elevation habitats. This large unsurveyed area is readily visible on many species distribution maps. Surveys in this area occurred on eight blocks that were moved off tribal land and on four others that were surveyed only on portions of blocks that fell outside tribal boundaries. There were three blocks on Havasupai tribal land, and two of these were moved and surveyed by the hired field crew. Of the ten blocks on the Gila River Indian Community tribal land, atlasers surveyed four of these by visiting only portions of blocks not on tribal land. Atlasers also collected casual observations outside this tribe's boundaries near four other blocks.

Many private landowners were very supportive of the atlas project. However, some individuals, especially within the Little Colorado River valley, were reluctant to grant access or denied access for surveys altogether. Additionally, one very large ranch in northwestern Yavapai County refused access, which kept atlas surveys from being conducted on four entire 7.5 min. topographic maps. Reasons for this varied, but one reoccurring concern was the potential for endangered species discovery, even in areas with poor habitat and low bird species diversity. Only partial surveys could be conducted on some priority blocks owing to private and leased land access issues. In any case, readers should be aware that a species' absence from a given area might be due to lack of survey effort rather than due to a true dearth of birds.

Atlaser Skill Level

Arizona Breeding Bird atlasers were a diverse group of extremely hard-working and dedicated individuals. As with any other body of volunteers, however, birding skills and abilities ranged widely, as did physical condition. Although ABBA staff and regional coordinators sought to ensure that individuals assigned to blocks both knew what they were getting themselves into and were up to the task, situations did arise in which blocks needed to be reassigned or additional instruction given. One large inconsistency between individuals was hearing ability and the observer's familiarity with birdcalls and songs. Whenever possible, the atlas field crew visited blocks suspected to contain more species than were reported by volunteers but these cleanup visits were not always possible.

Inconsistencies also existed in the data-reporting realm. Despite coaching by regional coordinators and atlas staff, some individuals had difficulty identifying and properly reporting habitat, breeding, and abundance codes. These measures could sometimes be quite subjective, so questionable reports were verified by phone or letters when possible.

Database Limitations

The ABBA database was originally developed to accept only one record per species on a priority block. As atlasers "upgraded" their species, the dates listed for previous sightings were lost. For example, "nest with young" is considered a higher code than "nest with eggs." If an atlaser discovered a Verdin nest with eggs one year and a Verdin nest with young the following year, the nest with eggs record would be lost. This glitch did not affect distribution maps inasmuch as the species would still be shown as "confirmed," but it did decrease breeding phenology graph accuracy, especially for uncommon species. The ABBA casual observation database accepted multiple records for the same species, even within the same sector, so some of the missing data from priority blocks were recaptured there.

Timing of Surveys

In general, the peak breeding period for birds in much of Arizona is from mid-May to late June. However, this is too late for many desert nesting species and too early for those species that do not initiate nesting until the beginning of the late summer monsoon season. Therefore, the peak period for conducting atlas surveys is quite variable depending on the elevation, habitat, and region of the state. In fact, some southeastern Arizona blocks that contained habitats ranging from desert and grassland to forested mountain canyons needed to be periodically surveyed between early April and August to acquire a full suite of species that breed there through the course of the season. For those atlasers with multiple blocks, they were sometimes forced to visit blocks at less than optimum time due to time constraints. If surveys were conducted too early or late, some migratory breeding species would be missing and present a false picture of the block's species composition.

Variability in Annual Precipitation

Annual rainfall often played a significant part in the species observed breeding, the habitats selected for breeding, and often species abundance. Arizona experienced two above-normal precipitation years (1993 and 1998), five below-normal years, and one near-normal precipitation year (2000) during the primary atlas period. Abundant winter and spring rains produced lush, resource-rich conditions throughout much of southern and western Arizona for the 1993 and 1998 breeding seasons. This allowed some birds to nest in areas that would under normal circumstances be considered marginal habitat. As noted previously by Monson and Phillips (1981), atlasers reported several instances of Western Meadowlarks and Horned Larks nesting in southwestern desert flats during wet years. Additionally, atlasers encountered Barn Swallows nesting in new locations during high precipitation years, probably because of increased mud availability. Northern Mockingbirds and Phainopeplas were more conspicuous in desert areas and lingered in lowland deserts longer than in typical or dry years.

Forty percent of Long-eared Owl records were obtained in 1998, likely due to the increased quality of suitable habitat and increased prey availability. Plentiful rains also permitted birds to nest earlier in the season than possible in dry to normal years. For example, the earliest nests with young for both Loggerhead Shrike and Northern Mockingbirds were reported in 1998 (both on 1 March). These annual fluctuations were problematic for atlas surveys because species such as Northern Mockingbirds were often absent in dry years from the same lowland deserts that they had nested in during wet years. As a result, block profiles could and did vary tremendously between wet, dry, and normal years. In addition, peak nesting periods that differed from year to year made determining the optimal time to visit lowland desert blocks difficult. During dry years, many atlasers endured fairly fruitless early spring trips to desert areas that revealed little nesting activity. Such blocks ended up with misleadingly sparse species lists if no follow-up visits were made.

SUMMARY OF RESULTS

Atlaser Effort

From 1993 to 2000, a total of 710 individuals surveyed on ABBA priority blocks, including hired field crew personnel (appendix A). Each priority block was assigned to a single person, and this individual was considered the "primary atlaser" for that block, but could enlist the assistants of other field helpers. Over the course of the atlas, many blocks had to be reassigned to new surveyors for a myriad of reasons. It was not uncommon for a block to change hands several times, and in these cases, the ABBA staff assigned the primary atlaser status to the party that completed the most work on the block. A total of 276 individuals (not including field crews) were named primary atlasers, and 422 helpers assisted them. Our deepest appreciation goes to every ABBA surveyor.

During the eight official survey years, volunteers completed 57 percent of atlas fieldwork and hired field crews completed the remainder. Twenty-two biologists worked one or more years on the hired field crews, and their names are also listed in appendix A. These individuals surveyed over 790 blocks and completed survey work on more than 663 blocks during the atlas period. These figures are approximate because volunteers may have also worked on some of these blocks, but the field crews had been designated the primary surveyor. Conversely, the field crews worked on many blocks that had volunteers named as primary atlasers. Volunteers were designated primary atlasers on 1044 blocks and completed surveys on 945 of these.

Volunteers donated approximately 41,000 hours surveying priority blocks and 18,000 hours traveling to and from atlas blocks (representing approximately 506,000 miles on their personal vehicles). If we assigned a $10 per hour value to volunteer labor and $.35 per mile driven by volunteers, this effort equates to approximately $767,000.

Annual Effort Summaries

Volunteer atlaser and hired field crew efforts varied considerably between years, as one might expect (table 4; figures 4 and 5). Atlasers initiated the most blocks midway through the project. After this point, it is likely that volunteers focused on revisiting blocks rather than starting new ones. The number of completed blocks rose yearly, except in 1998. More blocks were completed in 2000 than in any other year owing to the protocol change that eliminated the need to obtain a set confirmation rate. As mentioned previously, blocks surveyed in 2000 were considered complete once a comprehensive species list was obtained. As a result, blocks were completed more quickly than in previous years. In addition, there were eight individuals on the hired field crews in 2000, instead of the usual four. The crew was able to divide into four two-person teams and maximize survey coverage. At the conclusion of the 2000 field season, the ABBA project coordinator reviewed all incomplete blocks from all years, and blocks with comprehensive species lists were designated as complete.

Atlasers spent the most hours surveying and traveling and drove the most miles in 1994. These figures may represent a surge in volunteer involvement beyond the first year of surveys, during which atlasers logged the fewest survey and travel hours and drove the fewest miles.

Table 4. Annual Survey Effort 1993–2000

	1993	1994	1995	1996	1997	1998	1999	2000	Total
Blocks Initiated	196	217	170	300	265	202	219	265	1834
Blocks Completed	15	95	193	214	243	227	246	375	1608
Hours Surveyed[1]	4027	7956	7247	7362	6539	5076	6639	6891	51,737
Miles Traveled[2]	41,159	83,968	67,192	66,896	63,416	58,623	61,952	62,397	505,603
Travel Hours[3]	1483	3519	2051	2085	2253	1941	2328	2459	18,119

[1] Number of hours atlasers (volunteers and ABBA field crew) spent surveying priority blocks.
[2] Number of miles volunteers traveled to and from priority blocks
[3] Number of hours volunteers spent traveling to and from priority blocks

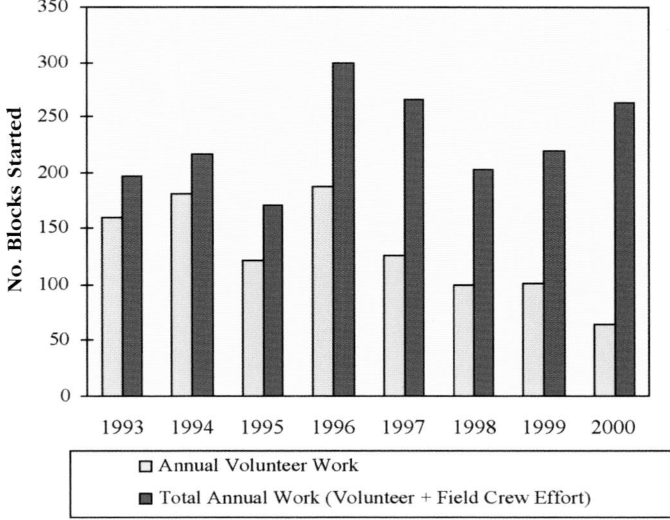

Figure 4. Arizona Breeding Bird Atlas Annual Survey Effort: Blocks Initiated

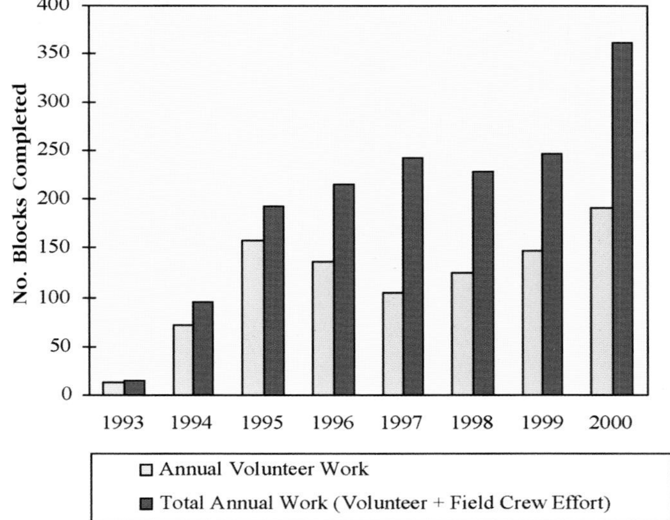

Figure 5. Arizona Breeding Bird Atlas Annual Survey Effort: Blocks Completed

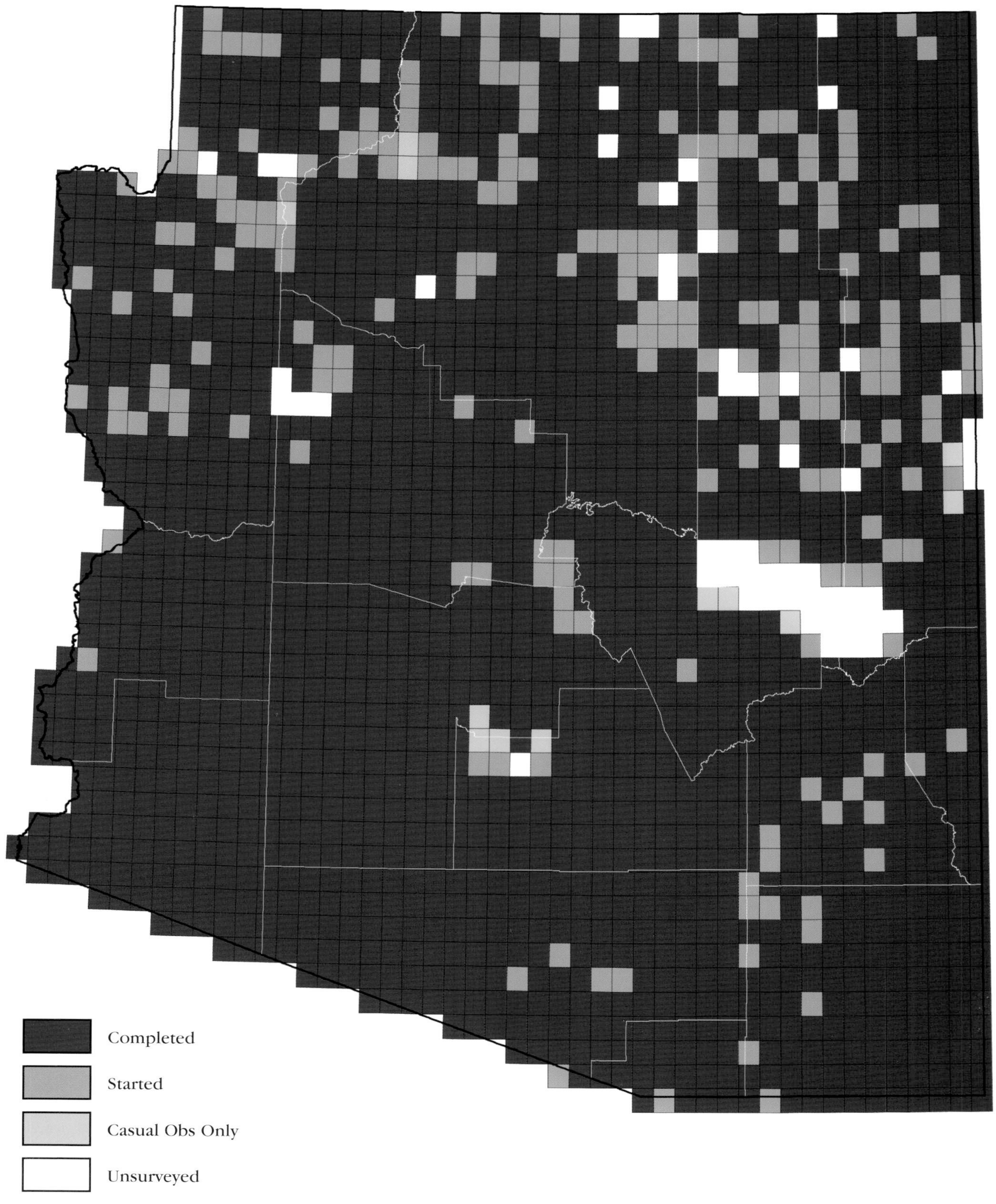

Figure 6. Arizona Breeding Bird Atlas Survey Status

Priority Block Coverage

Atlasers initiated surveys on 1834 (97 percent) of the 1899 priority blocks during the atlas period, and completed surveys on 88 percent of the blocks initiated (figure 6). Approximately 2 percent of the unsurveyed blocks were inaccessible to atlasers due to some private landowners and Native American tribes refusing access to conduct surveys, and the inability to move these blocks to alternate locations. For example, the White Mountain Apache Tribe denied all survey access, and the lack of data from this sizable reservation is quite conspicuous on many distribution maps. Based on the range of elevations, varied topography, and evidence from surveys conducted adjacent to these tribal lands, nearly two hundred species of birds likely breed on this habitat-diverse reservation. In addition, access permits to conduct atlas surveys could not be obtained from the smaller Gila River Indian and Havasupai tribal lands. Although both the Hopi and Navajo tribes were very supportive of the atlas project and allowed surveys, atlasers simply ran out of time to survey every block in this expansive region of the state. Some of these areas had very low habitat and bird diversity, and field crews chose to focus their efforts in more productive areas. Other unsurveyed areas included portions of private and state leased land in the Kingman, Prescott, and White Mountains regions.

Atlasers failed to complete surveys on 12 percent of initiated priority blocks for a variety of reasons. In order to maximize survey coverage, especially toward the end of the atlas period, atlas staff placed a higher priority on visiting new blocks rather than on revisiting areas that had been previously surveyed. Some atlasers required a great deal of persuasion before they were willing to abandon "old" blocks in favor of unsurveyed areas. On the other hand, some blocks were exceedingly difficult to access and atlasers were reluctant to abuse themselves and their vehicles on return trips to such areas. In some cases, atlasers intended to complete their blocks but became ill, moved out of state, or had different priorities, despite their best intentions.

As a result of these extensive surveys, the ABBA database contains over 76,000 individual records for 362 species of birds on priority blocks. Of these bird species, 60 were considered migrants or nonbreeders and 283 were confirmed breeding during the atlas period in Arizona. Of the confirmed breeding species, atlasers actually confirmed 263 (93 percent) of them on priority blocks. The remaining 20 species were only confirmed breeding outside designated priority blocks.

As expected, species richness between priority blocks varied considerably. Atlasers reported the highest number of breeding species (106) on the Patagonia priority block and detected the fewest breeding species (2) on the sparsely vegetated Cameron NE block (Horned Lark and Rock Wren). Table 5 lists the twenty priority blocks with the most breeding species. Both field crews and atlasers spent an average of thirty-one hours on the 1608 priority blocks completed. They located an average of thirty-seven potential breeding species per block for all blocks completed and obtained an average confirmation rate of 41.5 percent for completed blocks.

Table 5. Top Twenty Species-Rich Priority Blocks

Priority Block Name	County	# of Breeding Species	# of Confirmed Species	Confirmtion Rate	Min. Elevation (ft)	Max. Elevation (ft)	Total Survey Hours
Patagonia	Santa Cruz	106	70	66.0	3880	4894	147
Stanford Canyon	Cochise	91	45	49.4	5182	7386	83
Cochise Head	Cochise	87	34	39.1	4560	8113	96
Guadalupe Canyon	Cochise	87	56	64.4	4174	5331	111
Portal	Cochise	86	52	60.5	5000	7360	57
Kitt Peak	Pima	85	49	57.4	3400	6880	66
Imperial Reservoir	Yuma	81	35	43.2	196	411	158
Bismarck Mesa	Yavapai	81	62	77.7	3650	4264	163
Chiricahua Peak	Cochise	80	47	58.8	5710	8370	142
Wickenburg	Maricopa	80	44	55.0	1941	2624	64
Pinal Ranch	Gila	79	21	26.6	3425	6675	22
Helvetia	Pima	79	51	64.6	3840	6284	220
Prescott	Yavapai	79	70	88.6	4975	6178	32
Mount Baldy	Apache	78	40	50.6	9164	10360	45
College Peaks	Cochise	78	46	59.0	4367	6282	50
Luna Lake	Apache	78	45	57.7	7925	9911	30
Lewis Springs	Cochise	77	48	62.3	3975	4470	25
Winkelman	Pinal	77	34	44.2	1900	2520	31
Kirkland	Yavapai	77	67	87.0	4110	5560	75
Gisela	Gila	76	55	72.4	2830	4300	74

Despite the best efforts of atlas surveyors, several bird species known to breed in Arizona were not confirmed breeding on atlas priority blocks. In general, these birds are either very local breeders or have secretive nesting habits. Atlasers located 10 species in suitable breeding habitat on priority blocks that were only confirmed breeding outside these survey blocks (table 6). Ten additional species were confirmed breeding in Arizona during the atlas period, but were never reported on any priority blocks (table 7).

Table 6. Breeding Bird Species Detected on Priority Blocks but Confirmed Only Outside Blocks

- White-faced Ibis
- Mississippi Kite
- Northern Harrier
- Chukar
- Black Rail
- Mountain Plover
- Long-billed Curlew
- Whiskered Screech-Owl
- White-eared Hummingbird
- Gray Jay

Table 7. Confirmed Breeding Bird Species Not Detected on Priority Blocks

- Monk Parakeet
- Berylline Hummingbird
- American Pipit
- Hammond's Flycatcher
- Flame-colored Tanager
- Rose-breasted Grosbeak
- White-crowned Sparrow
- Streak-backed Oriole
- American Goldfinch
- Orange Bishop

Casual Observations

As noted earlier, bird records outside priority blocks are often referred to as casual observations. Many atlasers and nearly one hundred additional individuals that never conducted atlas surveys submitted casual observation data. These records added valuable distribution information for localized breeding birds as well as for those species occurring in easily overlooked habitats. Riparian and wetland birds would have been woefully underrepresented in the atlas had priority block data been used alone, as the randomly selected priority blocks regularly excluded narrow, linear riparian habitats. In fact, casual observation sightings often comprised the majority of total atlas data obtained for rare or local birds. For example, the atlas database contains 162 potential breeding records for Yellow-billed Cuckoo, and 69 percent of these are casual observations. In this case, casual observations have more than doubled the number of records obtained for this species. Additionally, surveyors were able to collect casual observation data on twelve topographic quadrangle maps that had inaccessible priority blocks, thereby increasing total survey coverage.

The atlas database contains over 7850 casual observation records for 300 species, including over 3200 breeding confirmation records for 263 species. As previously mentioned, 263 species were also confirmed breeding on priority blocks, but this number is purely coincidental.

In summary, atlasers reported a total of 376 bird species, both on and off blocks. Of these, 302 were considered potential breeders with 283 actually confirmed breeding during the atlas period. Of the 19 unconfirmed potential breeders, nine species had previously been documented nesting in Arizona. These were the Least Grebe, American Wigeon, Northern Shoveler, Canvasback, Ring-necked Duck, Buff-collared Nightjar, Eared Quetzal, Bobolink, and Pine Grosbeak.

Species Richness

The species richness on a statewide basis is depicted in figure 7, and notable areas of high species diversity include portions of southeastern Arizona, areas along the Mogollon Rim, and locations within the White Mountains region. Atlas data also reveal high bird-species diversity intermittently along major rivers, including the Colorado, Gila, San Pedro, and Verde, and also along Oak Creek and at the Bill Williams River delta. In addition, high species diversity was reported in mountainous areas in the Prescott vicinity, at Mount Trumbull within the Arizona Strip region, and in the Chuska Mountains on Navajo tribal lands.

On a county basis, atlas data revealed that the highest breeding-species diversity is found in Cochise and Coconino counties with 207 species each. Yuma County is in the most arid region of the state; therefore, it was not unexpected that it contained the fewest potentially breeding bird species (table 8).

Table 8. Confirmed and Potential Breeding Bird Species Reported by County

County	Number of Breeding Species
Apache	199
Cochise	207
Coconino	207
Gila	177
Graham	194
Greenlee	173
La Paz	112
Maricopa	149
Mohave	187
Navajo	168
Pima	199
Pinal	167
Santa Cruz	176
Yavapai	182
Yuma	107

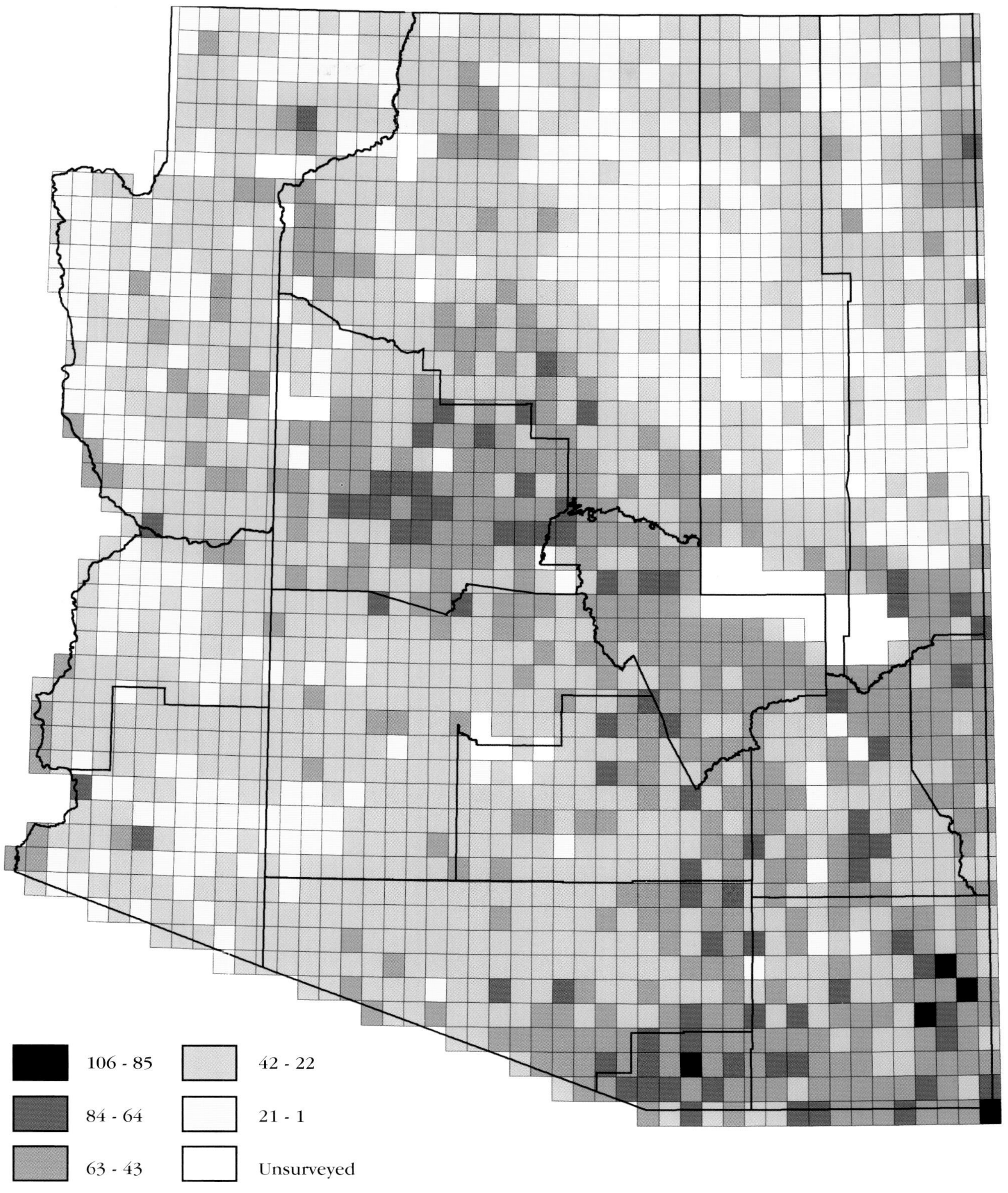

Figure 7. Species Richness by Topographic Map.
Each square represents one 7.5-minute topographic map. Species totals include bird reported both on and off priority blocks.

Most Frequently Recorded Birds

Bird species that breed in the greatest diversity of habitats are typically the most widespread and frequently detected on atlas blocks. In Arizona, the Mourning Dove topped the list, with atlasers reporting this species on 1674 of the 1834 priority blocks visited (91 percent). Table 9 lists the twenty most frequently reported breeding species. These totals represent possible, probable, and confirmed breeding records only.

Table 9. Most Frequently Reported Breeding Birds in Arizona

Bird Species	Number of Priority Blocks	Percentage of Blocks Surveyed	Number of Quads
Mourning Dove	1674	91	1767
Ash-throated Flycatcher	1530	83	1595
House Finch	1483	81	1580
Common Raven	1444	79	1511
Red-tailed Hawk	1335	73	1438
Northern Mockingbird	1321	72	1364
Black-throated Sparrow	1262	69	1313
Brown-headed Cowbird	1235	67	1320
Rock Wren	1120	61	1168
American Kestrel	1068	58	1112
Gambel's Quail	1001	55	1077
Turkey Vulture	984	54	1025
Say's Phoebe	967	53	1032
Cactus Wren	928	51	982
Loggerhead Shrike	915	50	948
Phainopepla	882	48	939
Verdin	882	48	925
Great Horned Owl	873	48	964
Bewick's Wren	822	45	875
Western Kingbird	818	45	886

Nocturnal Surveys

Atlasers conducted at least partial nocturnal surveys on 1263 priority blocks across the state, which accounts for approximately 67 percent of blocks where atlas surveys were initiated. Observers reported twelve breeding species of owls and five breeding species of nightjars in Arizona. It is not urprising that the most commonly reported owl species, Great Horned Owl and Western Screech-Owl, are those that have the largest ranges in Arizona (see respective species accounts). The owls and nightjars most frequently recorded on priority blocks (number of blocks on which species was found divided by number of initiated blocks) were the Great Horned Owl (48 percent), Common Poorwill (41 percent), Lesser Nighthawk (28 percent), Western Screech-Owl (27 percent), and Common Nighthawk (26 percent).

Several owl species were not well represented in the atlas database because surveys were often conducted too late in the season. This was particularly apparent with forest species that breed at higher elevations such as Northern Saw-whet, Flammulated, and Northern Pygmy-Owls. These owls call most readily from March through mid-May, even earlier for the Northern Saw-whet. As nesting activity commences, paired owls call infrequently and are often difficult to detect through the summer as their efforts are focused on tending broods. Most nocturnal surveys at high elevation were unfortunately conducted after late May during visits to document the majority of other forest nesting birds.

Nest Site Measurements

Atlasers took at least partial measurements and other easily noted information at 3507 nests of 184 species. These were collected on 814 topographic quads statewide (figure 8). Only the atlas field crew and a few specially trained volunteer collected nest measurements, so few nest data are from southeastern Arizona and from other parts of the state surveyed primarily by volunteers. It was not always possible for field crews to measure all the desired variables at a given nest, but observers were able to obtain some or all measurements for 10 or more nests of seventy species. Atlas staff calculated nest height median values for species with a sample size greater than five. Medians were used instead of means because data were not normally distributed and the variables were often measured, but higher placed nests and tree heights were regularly estimated. Medians are more resistant than means to effects of extreme outliers and may be more appropriate for variables that are both measured and estimated (L. Allison, personal communication).

Arizona Breeding Bird Atlas nest data are especially valuable because they were collected in Arizona. Many published natural history and breeding ecology resources for birds are often compiled from other parts of a species' range, where different subspecies may have been studied. Information collected for the atlas project on breeding phenology and nest site characteristics will greatly expand the natural history information available for both common and rare species. Even with common species, many natural history aspects are unique to a geographical location in the state. This local information is more useful to Arizona land and wildlife management agencies when making land-management recommendations.

Atlas Highlights

Undoubtedly, the most notable discoveries during the atlas period were of confirmed nesting records for two species that were new not only for Arizona but also for the United States. In 1993, during the first year of atlas project, Streak-backed Orioles were unexpectedly discovered nesting along the lower San Pedro River near Dudleyville, and a pair of Ruddy Ground-Doves was found with a fledgling near Wickenburg.

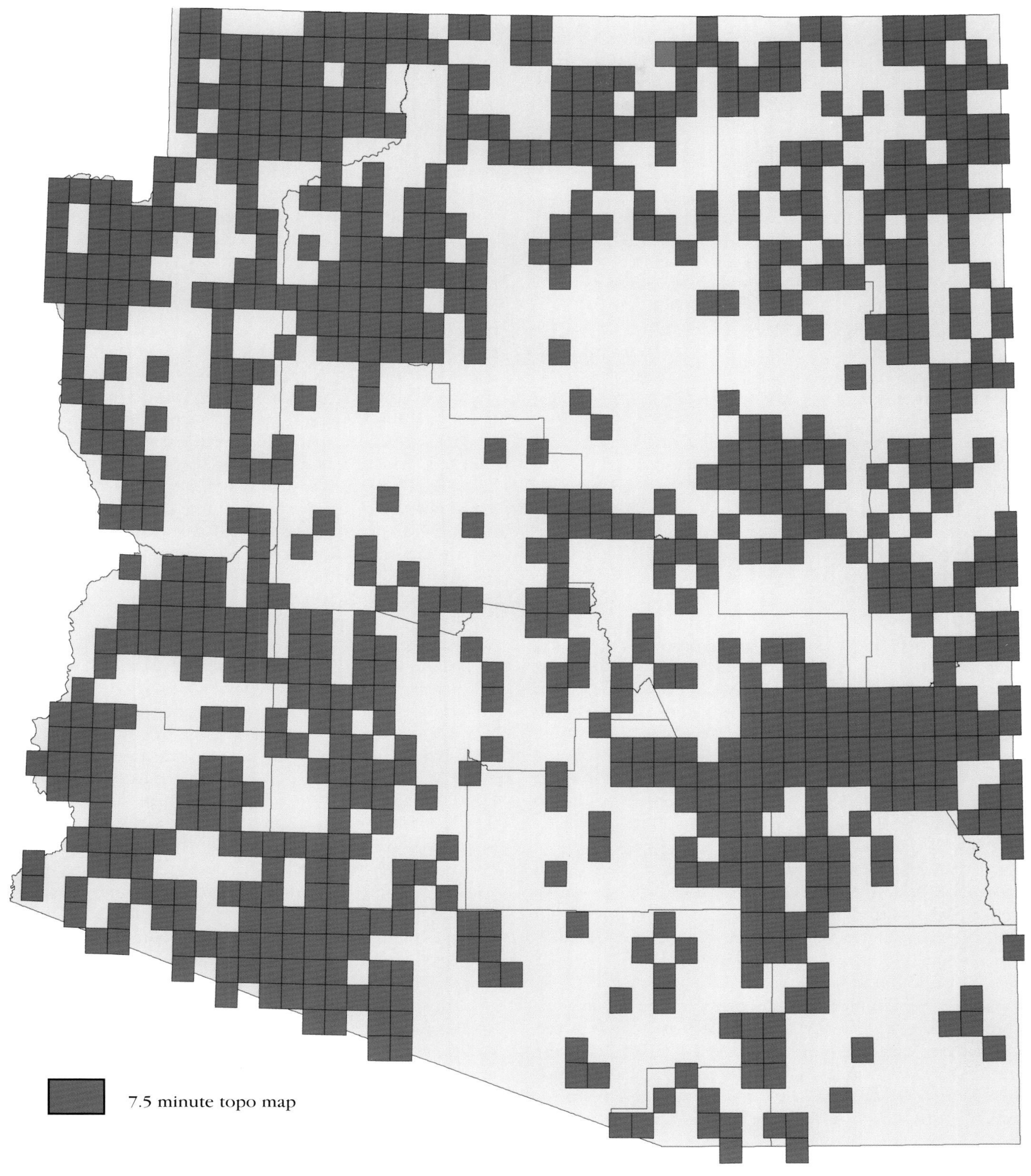

Figure 8. Nest Data Locations

In addition to these, eight species were encountered nesting or at least attempting to nest for the first time in Arizona during the atlas period (table 10). These include several exotic species: Eurasian Collared-Dove, Monk Parakeet, and Orange Bishop. Some new nesting species were anticipated to be finally confirmed breeding in the state such as the Mountain Plover, Winter Wren, and White-faced Ibis, while others were not, like the Long-billed Curlew and Scissor-tailed Flycatcher.

Table 10. New Breeding Bird Species for Arizona

Species	Year	First Location
Ruddy Ground-Dove	1993	Near Wickenburg
Streak-backed Oriole	1993	Near Dudleyville
Long-billed Curlew	1993	Near Eagar
Scissor-tailed Flycatcher	1995	South of Winkelman
Mountain Plover	1996	Near Springerville
Winter Wren	1999	Near Christopher Creek
White-faced Ibis	2000	Cibola NWR
Eurasian Collared-Dove	2000	Eagar
Monk Parakeet	2000	Casa Grande
Orange Bishop	2000	North Phoenix

One of the many benefits of conducting a statewide breeding bird atlas is collecting data from many remote and rugged regions of the state where few if any avian surveys have ever been conducted. Arizona is blessed with many of these wonderful and often breathtaking areas, which are not typically visited by birders or avian researchers. As a result, atlasers obtained new breeding location records for numerous species, sometimes extending their breeding ranges considerably. One little-known area is the Arizona Strip region in northwestern Arizona, which encompasses the lands north of the Colorado River and west of the Kaibab Plateau. Here atlasers revealed that many sagebrush species such as the Sage Thrasher, Sage Sparrow, and Brewer's Sparrow are fairly widespread, along with Crissal Thrashers. There were few, if any previously published breeding records for these species in this corner of the state. Similar exiting finds were discovered in other remote landscapes in the north, particularly those on the Hualapai, Hopi, and Navajo tribal lands where access is often limited or restricted.

Atlasers encountered many other species that were more widespread than expected in Arizona, such as the Pyrrhuloxia, Gray Flycatcher, Dusky Flycatcher, and Gray Vireo. Even very local and isolated nesting species such as MacGillivray's Warbler and Winter Wren were discovered in several new areas. Although many new discoveries undoubtedly came to light because observers were looking for birds in remote areas for the first time, other species are steadily expanding their range to the north and northwest. This includes species that were once primarily considered southeastern Arizona specialties such as the Gray Hawk, Zone-tailed Hawk, Northern Beardless-Tyrannulet, Dusky-capped Flycatcher, Sulphur-bellied Flycatcher, Tropical Kingbird, and Hepatic Tanager. During the atlas period, several bird species that were once only rare or casual visitors from Mexico have become much more regular and widespread in the southeast, with increasing nesting records. These include several hummingbird species (White-eared, Lucifer, and Berylline), Black-capped Gnatcatcher, Rufous-capped Warbler, and Flame-colored Tanager. Time will tell if these welcome trends continue.

Breeding populations of birds are increasing elsewhere in Arizona as well, such as Double-crested and Neotropic Cormorants, Least Bitterns, and Cattle Egrets in southern Arizona. In central and northern regions, atlas data revealed Wood Ducks, Ospreys, Belted Kingfishers, and Tree Swallows have obviously expanded their breeding range in the state. In fact, the kingfisher was once a species of concern for Arizona, but owing primarily to our findings it is no longer considered so.

Although obviously not considered atlas highlights, compiled data revealed some species are not doing well in Arizona. These findings may act as early warnings and encourage future study to determine the reason for these declines and provide recommendations for reversing these negative trends. Apparently declining Arizona species include Buff-breasted Flycatcher, American Dipper, and Evening Grosbeak. Other nesting species in Arizona such as the Eastern Bluebird, Gray Jay, Grasshopper Sparrow, and Pine Grosbeak may also be declining, and this is especially alarming with their small, local populations. Atlas data also revealed the widespread Prairie Falcon could be facing a downward trend in Arizona, possible partly due to the increase of nesting pairs of Peregrine Falcons. Several historical Prairie Falcon eyries have recently been usurped by the more aggressive Peregrine. Populations of Montezuma Quail are apparently fairly stable in southeastern Arizona, but those to the north could be extirpated outside the small populations remaining in the White Mountains region. The reasons for bird population declines are many and often complex. Even the steady warmer climate changes that have been documented during the past hundred years could be partly to blame for not only the declines but also population increases and northward range expansions of many bird species (Price and Root 2001).

Atlas fieldwork established a wealth of baseline information for which we can now compare future changes in avian distribution in Arizona. It is unfortunate such information was not available during the past century so we would have a clearer picture on the obvious changes that have taken place across Arizona varied landscapes. Even with scattered historical accounts, it is difficult to envision how Arizona's deserts, grasslands, riparian woodlands, and forests appeared 150 years ago, let alone the density and diversity of the birdlife that once inhabited them.

Geography, Climate, and Habitats of Arizona

John R. Spence and Troy E. Corman

Arizona is known for its breathtaking vistas and amazingly diverse vegetative communities. These communities in turn support a rich assortment of avian life, with more than three hundred bird species known to have nested within the state's boundaries. The vegetation of Arizona comprises a complex mosaic of different plant communities arranged in a nonrandom pattern on the physical landscape of the state. Many factors interact to produce the vegetation of Arizona, with the principal elements being climate, topography, aspect, soils, geology, the presence of year-round (perennial) water, and historical disturbances such as fires. Proximity to other floristic regions can also influence the composition of vegetation in Arizona. Elevations in the state range from 75 ft (23 m) where the Colorado River flows into Mexico to 12,633 ft (3851 m) on the top of Humphreys Peak in the San Francisco Mountains (figure 9). All these factors foster a remarkable variety of plant communities, from subtropical desertscrub to alpine tundra (figure 10).

Several biogeographic provinces enter Arizona from surrounding regions, including four of the five major deserts of North America. In fact, much of the upland division of the Sonoran Desert occurs within the borders of Arizona. Five major provinces occur in the state, the Colorado Plateau, Sonoran Desert, Mojave Desert, Chihuahuan Desert, and Madrean Region. Because of the state's diverse topography and climates ranging from subtropical to arctic-alpine, some of the most important and pioneering work on vegetation zonation and climate in the deserts and mountains of the western United States was conducted in Arizona (Merriam 1890; Whittaker and Niering 1965; Brown 1982). First the various biogeographic provinces, and then the vegetation patterns on the landscape of Arizona, are discussed. Finally, more detailed habitat information is provided for each principal plant community. The following treatments are modified from the extensive analysis and discussions in Brown (1982) and McLaughlin (1986, 1989).

Biogeography

The *Colorado Plateau* is found in the northern and eastern third of the state, with elevations generally above 4000 ft (1219 m). The southern boundary is the Mogollon Rim. The western boundary is less defined, but it includes northern Yavapai County, eastern Mohave County, and much of the Arizona Strip region north of the Grand Canyon. It is characterized by flat-lying mesas and scattered laccolithic and volcanic mountains and north–south trending sandstone monoclines. The Colorado River flows from east to west across the western Colorado Plateau, carving out numerous deep canyons, including the Grand Canyon. Topographic and substrate diversity is high. Because of its generally high elevations, the Colorado Plateau has cold winters and is often called a cold desert. Vegetation consists of mixtures of grass and low shrub-dominated vegetation at lower elevations, extensive pinyon pine–juniper woodlands at moderate elevations, and forests and various shrub and grass-dominated vegetation at the highest elevations. These higher-elevation forests are related to those in the mountains of central and northern Utah, Colorado, and New Mexico. The southern Rocky Mountains of southern Colorado and New Mexico extend into east-central Arizona in an area known as the White Mountains. Volcanic in origin, they support extensive forest, meadow, and grassland communities related to the vegetation of both the southern Colorado and New Mexico mountain ranges and the Colorado Plateau. Small areas at the summits of the highest peaks support subalpine scrub or krummholz, and areas of talus alpine–like vegetation above timberline.

The *Sonoran Desert* region occurs in the southern and western portions of the state and continues southward into Sonora, Mexico. Most of this desert lies at elevations below 4000 ft (1219 m), although isolated mountains may rise higher. This region is part of the Basin and Range Physiographic Province of the interior western United States, with isolated mountain ranges separated by broad valleys fringed by bajadas. Several major rivers flow, or once flowed, across this desert region, including the Gila, Salt, and Verde, which intermittently support tall stands of broadleaf riparian trees and a rich avian community. The lower Colorado River bisects the Sonoran Desert in half along the Arizona-California border. The climate is subtropical, with hot summer and cool winters, but only short periods of below-freezing temperatures and little snowfall. Desert areas receiving the most precipitation often contain vegetation that is an almost luxurious mix of drought resistant shrubs, trees, and large cacti. Drier and hotter areas in the lower valleys and along the Colorado River consist primarily of monotonous expanses of low shrubs, especially creosotebush. Numerous dry washes that typically only flood after heavy rains meander throughout the region, supporting denser and taller thickets of thorny small tree and shrub species. These narrow dry wooded corridors often support the highest density of breeding birds in desert localities and are equally important to migratory birds traveling through this arid landscape.

The *Mojave Desert* is very similar to the Sonoran Desert, sharing many plant species. Many biogeographers place the two together into an expanded Sonoran Desert. The border between the two is somewhat vague, but is typically placed somewhere in the area of the Mohave Mountains–Lake Havasu City area south of I-40. The Mojave

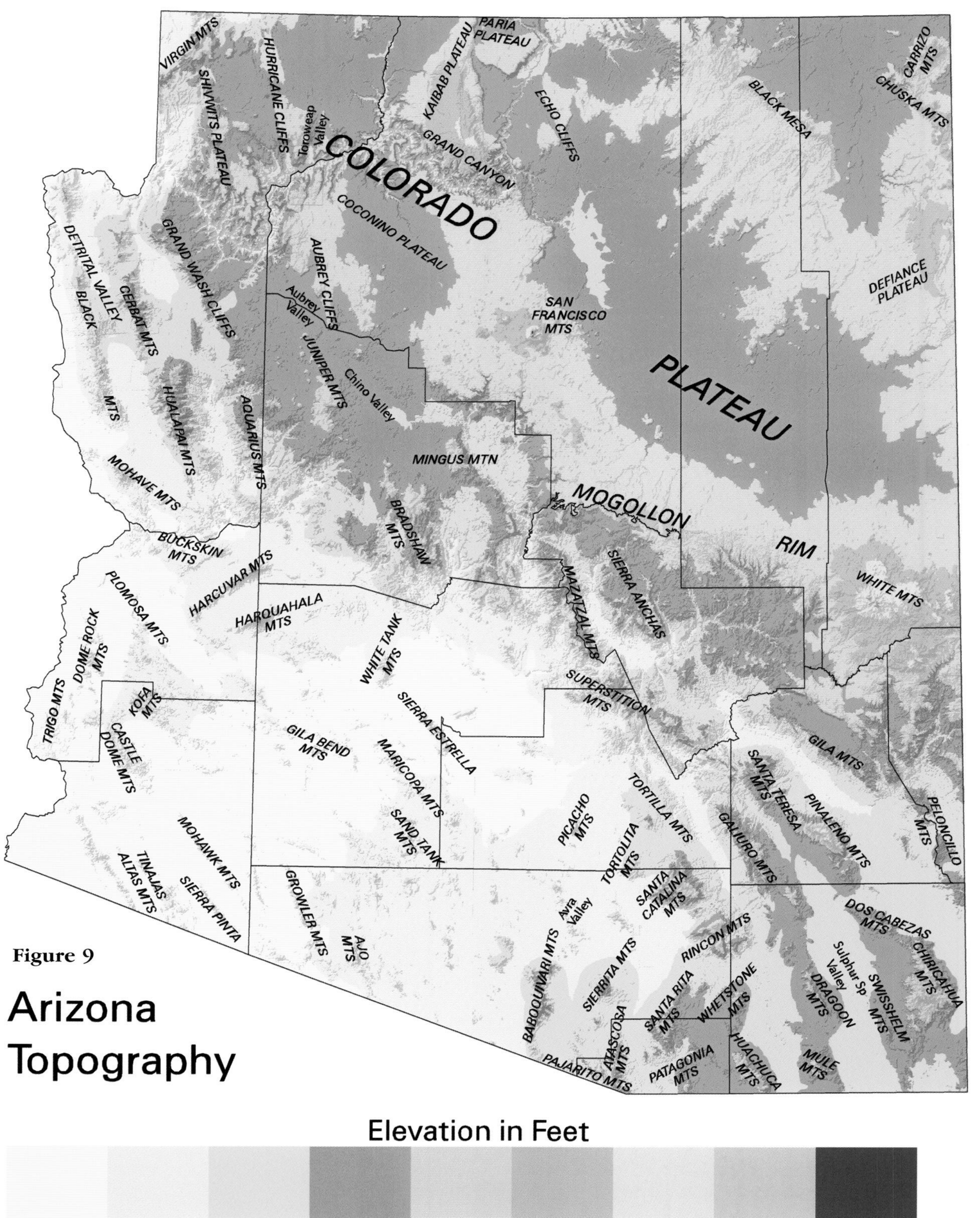

Figure 9

Arizona Topography

Elevation in Feet

<1500 1500 3000 4500 6000 7500 9000 10500 12000 >12000

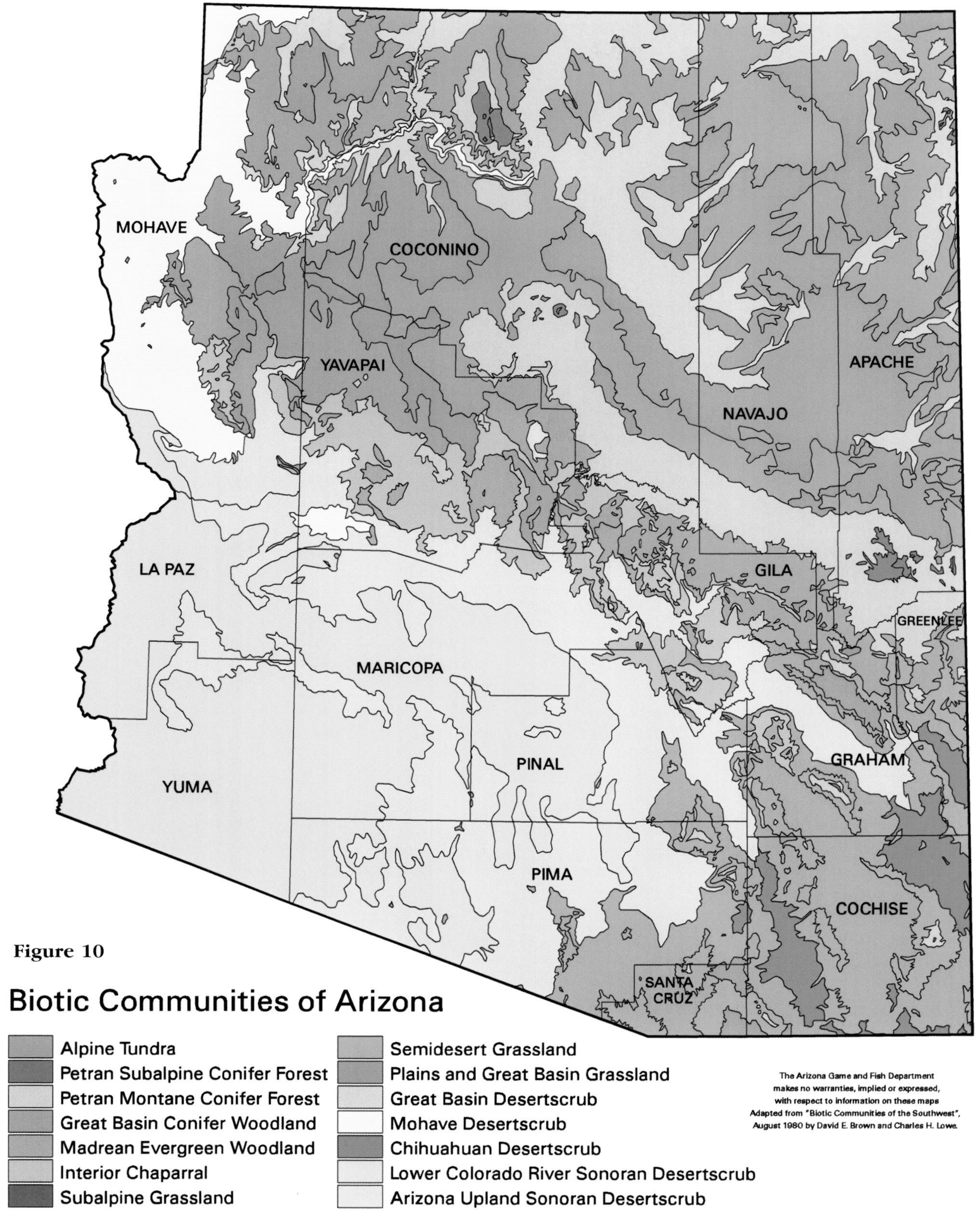
MOHAVE
COCONINO
YAVAPAI
APACHE
NAVAJO
LA PAZ
GILA
GREENLEE
MARICOPA
PINAL
GRAHAM
YUMA
PIMA
COCHISE
SANTA CRUZ
Alpine Tundra
Petran Subalpine Conifer Forest
Petran Montane Conifer Forest
Great Basin Conifer Woodland
Madrean Evergreen Woodland
Interior Chaparral
Subalpine Grassland
Semidesert Grassland
Plains and Great Basin Grassland
Great Basin Desertscrub
Mohave Desertscrub
Chihuahuan Desertscrub
Lower Colorado River Sonoran Desertscrub
Arizona Upland Sonoran Desertscrub
The Arizona Game and Fish Department makes no warranties, implied or expressed, with respect to information on these maps Adapted from "Biotic Communities of the Southwest", August 1980 by David E. Brown and Charles H. Lowe.

Figure 10

Biotic Communities of Arizona

Desert is typically found in drier and somewhat higher elevations to the north of the Sonoran Desert, at elevations above 1000 ft (305 m). Like the Sonoran Desert, it is part of the Basin and Range, with mountains bordering long broad valleys. The Colorado River flows through the Mojave Desert from the Grand Wash Cliffs west and then south toward Lake Havasu City. The vegetation and some avian influences of this desert are also very apparent on the dry, lower slopes within the Grand Canyon. Because winters are colder and freezing temperatures and snow occur fairly regularly in winter, the climate is considered warm-temperate rather than tropical. The Mojave Desert is characterized by vast expanses of creosotebush at lower elevations, with blackbrush and Joshua tree communities above. The mountains support pinyon pine–juniper woodlands and interior chaparral on their upper slopes, while small stands of coniferous forest occur very locally at the highest elevations.

The *Chihuahuan Desert* enters the state in the far southeastern corner, within the area dominated by the Madrean "sky island" mountains. It is found at elevations below about 4500 ft (1372 m) in Arizona, primarily in the valleys between the Dragoon and Huachuca Mountains along the San Pedro River, and in the San Simon River Valley north and east of the Chiricahua Mountains. The desert is considered warm-temperate, for it is high enough in elevation to have cold winters with some snow, but also hot summers. It is primarily within the Basin and Range region, with broad plains and valleys separating the mountain ranges. Vegetationally, the Chihuahuan Desert is characterized by semiarid grasslands and desertscrub. In addition to expanses of creosotebush at the lowest elevations, whitethorn acacia, and tarbush are also characteristic shrubs. Perennial grasslands are widespread and include a variety of grama grasses, tobosa, three-awns, and sacatons or dropseeds. Numerous forbs and small cacti occur, but large cacti are lacking. Soaptree and other yucca species, stool, and nolina species are common in the scrub and grasslands and form part of the unique character of this desert landscape.

Finally, the *Madrean* region, including the isolated sky island mountains, is found in the southeastern part of the state and extends in a band up to and across the center of the state below the Mogollon Rim northwest to Yavapai County. The diverse vegetation within this region includes many plant communities that are more widespread in the mountains and foothills of northern Mexico. Consequently, this region supports many avian species that primarily occur nowhere else in the United States and is therefore a frequent destination for visiting birders. The southeastern "sky islands" are a series of north–south trending mountain ranges that rise thousands of feet above the surrounding valleys and Chihuahuan desertscrub and grassland. These mountains support a diverse array of forested communities, from evergreen oak-pinyon-juniper woodlands on their lower slopes, to extensive and widespread pine–oak forests on most major ranges, up to high elevation mixed coniferous forests and even some subalpine spruce–fir on the Pinaleno Mountains. A second phase of Madrean vegetation occurs as a band of chaparral across the state below the Mogollon Rim, extending as far north as the Virgin Mountains in the extreme northwest corner of Arizona. This community consists of low dense scrub vegetation adapted to fire. Although structurally different from the southeastern Madrean region, this vegetation shares many species with the mountains of northern Mexico and southeastern Arizona.

Vegetation Ecology and Historical Changes

At the largest scale of the American Southwest including Arizona, vegetation is largely controlled by climate. The climate in much of the state is in turn determined largely by the topography and mountainous landscape (orographic effects), with precipitation generally increasing and temperature generally decreasing as the elevation climbs (figure 11).

Precipitation in the state occurs primarily during two seasons, with winter rains or snow occurring for several days when cold fronts move down from the Gulf of Alaska across the Pacific Ocean eastward into Arizona. Summer rains, particularly between July and September, occur when moisture is pumped up from the Gulf of Mexico and generally occur as regular afternoon and evening thunderstorms that are often heavy but of short duration. This period is often referred to as the monsoon season and typically follows an extended dry period. These welcome rains stimulate new growth of grasses, forbs, and other plants, and particularly influence plant communities in southeastern Arizona, where the monsoon season is sometimes known as the "second spring." The breeding season of many grassland and other bird species in this region is closely tied to this humid, wet period and stimulates other species to attempt second or third broods. Occasionally dissipating tropical storms move north through the Gulf of California, bringing extensive precipitation in the fall. Typically, Arizona's driest months are May and June, with many regions often receiving no precipitation during this period.

At low elevations, warm-temperate to subtropical climates prevail, with hot summers and cool but not cold winters. Precipitation is generally low and highly variable from year to year. This combination has produced the well-known Sonoran and Mojave Deserts, with their distinctive plant communities. At higher elevations, primarily in northern and eastern regions of the state, cooler and more predictable climates give rise to different shrub, forest, and woodland communities. Zonation is pronounced in many regions of Arizona, with desertlike vegetation at the lowest elevations, with semiarid grasslands and then Madrean evergreen woodlands of pinyon pines, junipers, and oaks at higher elevations. As elevation increases further, forest communities dominated by taller and larger pines appear, and finally mixed coniferous forests and aspen occur in the coolest and wettest climates high elevation mountains. At the summits of the highest mountains, primarily on the San Francisco Peaks, low-growing alpine tundra occurs where conditions are cold year-round, with strong winds and somewhat drier climates than just down slope in the dense forests.

Although climate is the principal controlling factor in the development and distribution of the vegetation, other factors often become important at the local and regional

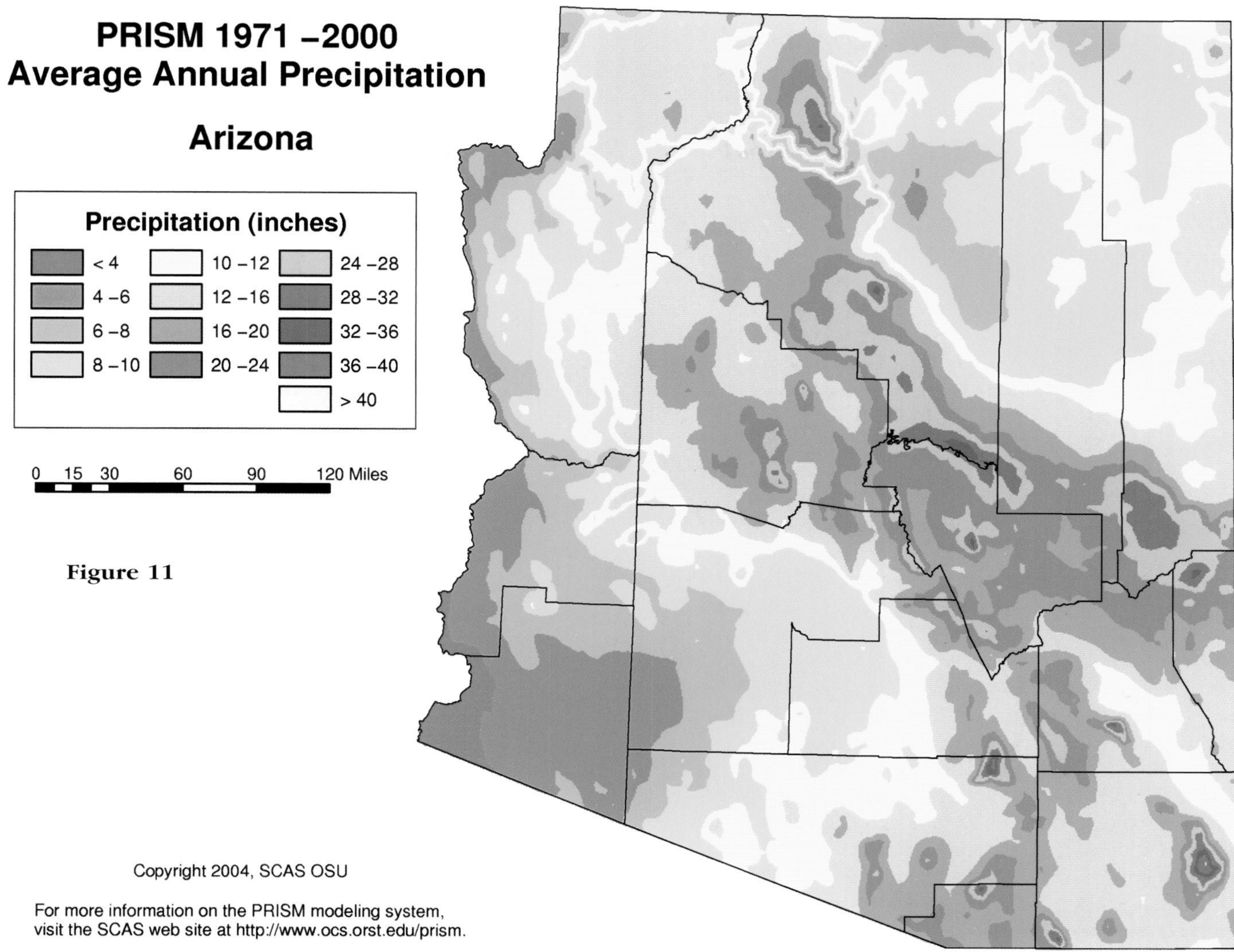

Figure 11

levels. Slope aspect often determines the composition and distribution of plant communities on mountains, plateaus, and higher mesas through local climate control. Slopes with north or east aspects tend to be cooler and moister compared with slopes on south and west aspects. At the same elevation, a cooler north-facing slope may be dominated by pinyon pine–juniper woodland, while the adjacent warmer south-facing slope may support a desert shrub community including saguaros. The angle of the slope may also contribute to the types of plants found. Steeper unstable slopes often support more open herbaceous vegetation that can respond more rapidly to landslides and other mass movements than woody plants.

Since most plants derive their water and nutrient needs from the soil they are rooted in, soil characteristics are extremely important. Soil texture, depth, and chemistry are all significant factors, and are largely determined by the kind of parent material, weathering processes, the slope steepness, and amount of time (aging). Differences in soils and the vegetation they support can be gradual or abrupt. An example of gradual change is bajada vegetation of the Sonoran and Mojave Deserts, which can extend down slope for miles. Soil texture and water-holding capacity change very gradually along these bajadas, producing gradual and almost imperceptible changes in the distributions of plants. Upper slopes are rockier and have coarser soils that tend to have more available water, and are favored by species with relatively higher water needs, such as saguaros. Lower bajada slopes consist of finer materials with less available water, and tend to be vegetated by more drought tolerant shrubs such as creosotebush (Robichaux 1999). In some areas, abrupt changes in soil occur because of sharply contrasting underlying parent materials. For example, in central Arizona infertile and fine-textured limestone soils derived from lake deposits support distinctive plant communities of shrubs and forbs, while adjacent vegetation on volcanic or metamorphic-derived soils support typical Sonoran vegetation dominated by creosotebush and paloverde (Anderson 1996). The chaparral shrub communities below the Mogollon Rim are typically found on poorly developed and coarse-textured soils, while adjacent pinyon pine–juniper woodlands occur on better-developed, fine-textured soils. Deep sandy sites such as dunes tend to hold water better than other soils, and often support grasslands and other types of herbaceous vegetation (Bowers 1982). On the Colorado Plateau, where windblown sand accumulates in swales and along drainages, various distinctive sand-shrub and grassland communities occur, while adjacent slopes and uplands may be vegetated by blackbrush or shadscale desertscrub.

Most of Arizona is arid, with available water only occurring seasonally. Very different and lush vegetation occurs where water is available year-round, such as at springs and along rivers, steams, ponds, and lakes (figure 12). The change from the drier "upland" vegetation to wetland communities is often very abrupt. These wetlands support highly diverse plant and avian communities with many bird species that are strongly dependent on these limited habitats. Riparian zones along streams and rivers support mosaics of woodlands, shrublands, and lush herbaceous vegetation. True wet meadows or wetlands with hygric organic soils are rare in Arizona, but include the cienegas of the southeast and wet meadows and boggy areas in the mountains at higher elevations (Hendrickson and Minckley 1984).

Fire is an important agent of change in the natural plant communities of Arizona. Most high-elevation coniferous forests in the state have evolved with a natural regime of recurring fires, ignited by summer thunderstorm activity. The interval between fires in these forests varied from as little as three to five years in open ponderosa pine savanna to more than one hundred years in moist subalpine spruce-fir. Some plant species are dependent on recurring fires to maintain their populations. One of the most important of these is aspen, which grows quickly after a fire, but then declines in health and density over time with the encroachment of more fire-sensitive species. Eventually, the aspen clones will die out in the absence of further fires. Large ponderosa pines are fire-adapted as well, with thick bark that resists the cool low-intensity fires that historically occurred. Even Gambel's oaks, which often occur in ponderosa pine and other conifer forests, regenerate rather quickly from trunks and roots after fire. Natural fires are less common in semiarid and arid shrub and grassland communities. Generally, fires in these communities favor grasses and other herbaceous species over shrubs or smaller trees. In hot desert communities in the Sonoran, Mojave, and Chihuahuan deserts, fire was apparently rare prior to human occupation. Many of the woody and succulent species are very fire-sensitive and are eliminated with frequent fires. The saguaro, for example, is highly sensitive and can be easily killed by fire. The more lush and moist wetland and riparian communities of Arizona also rarely experienced natural fires.

With the arrival of humans, fire ecology changed in many areas of Arizona. The original human inhabitants used fire for a variety of reasons, among them to drive game animals and increase plant resources. Although the use of fire by American Indians in Arizona is not well known, it is likely that fires were set in many grassland and open forest communities. With the arrival of Europeans, fire became less frequent owing to fire-suppression policies. Without fire, many communities saw the encroachment of fire-sensitive woody species such as spruces, firs, pinyon pines, junipers, and numerous woody shrubs. This may have caused the decline of several open forest birds, including the very locally distributed Buff-breasted Flycatcher. Dense thickets of trees and shrubs have developed, and when fires did occur they were hotter and more destructive than the natural fires of the pre-settlement period. Ironically, in some areas fire frequency has increased even with fire-suppression policies. In the Sonoran Desert, fires have increased since the middle 1950s despite fire suppression, probably because of the widespread invasion of the desert by exotic annuals such as red brome (Schmid and Rogers 1988). This grass produces abundant flammable litter in wet years that is easily ignited when conditions dry out in spring and summer. In general, fire and climate are strongly linked in Arizona. With the state's variable climate, fuel builds up during wet years, in turn increasing fire frequency and severity during drought years. These cycles of fire and climate can have major and often disastrous consequences for vegetation, bird life, and people, as the massive Arizona fires of 2002 demonstrated.

The accelerated American colonization and settlement of Arizona in the late 1800s and early 1900s has produced major changes in the vegetation of the state, greater than any since the waning of the ice ages 12,000 years ago. In addition to changing the role of fire in shaping Arizona vegetation, settlement has caused changes in vegetation as a result of water developments, livestock grazing, urbanization, agriculture, recreation, timber harvesting and wood collecting, mining, and introduction of exotics. Some areas of Arizona have completely lost their native vegetation to urbanization and agriculture (figure 13). Other localized areas have been severely degraded by pollution from power plants and smelters (e.g., Wood and Nash 1976). Although much of the state's vegetation cover is still intact, it has been altered by more than a century of human activities. Habitat alteration has negatively affected many bird species while benefiting others.

Livestock grazing has changed the composition of many grasslands, with a decline in perennial grasses and an increase in shrubs and exotics being most evident. Semiarid grasslands in particular have been extensively altered by grazing and may have been an important factor that resulted in the extirpation of the Aplomado Falcon in Arizona. Much of this community has been converted to shrublands dominated by mesquite, catclaw acacia, creosotebush, and prickly pear.

Although overgrazing in the period from about 1880 to 1930 has been blamed as the primary cause of loss of grasslands in Arizona, a warming trend since the late 1800s has favored shrub species over grasses (McClaran and VanDevender 1995). Many of these conversions from grasslands to shrublands are irreversible as the climate has changed, and increased erosion has stripped the landscape of the deeper better-developed soils favored by grasses. Livestock grazing has also affected forest and woodland communities, often by allowing increased establishment of tree species and declines in understory herbaceous vegetation. The expansion of pinyon pine–juniper woodlands into shrub and grass vegetation, well

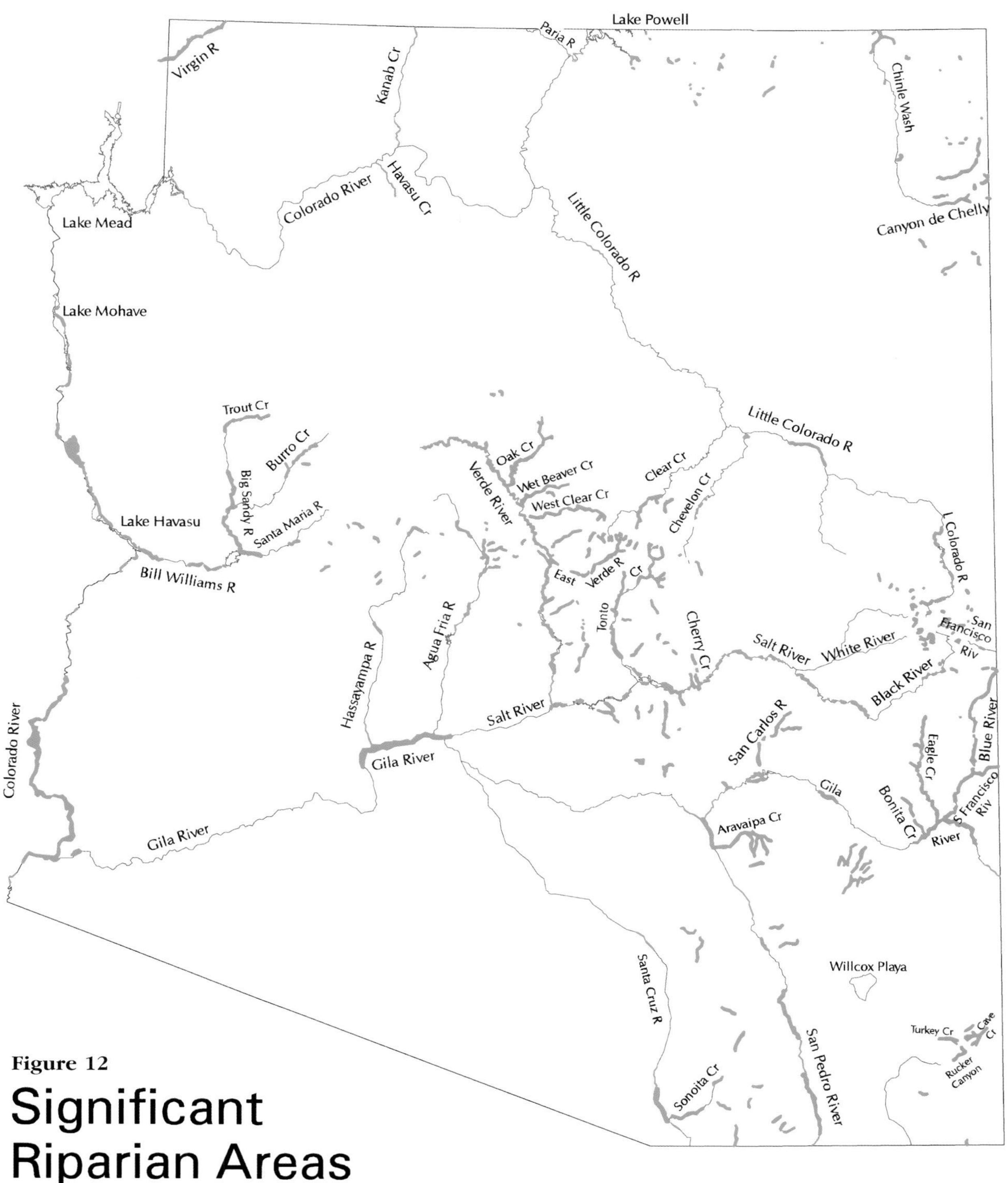

Figure 12

Significant Riparian Areas

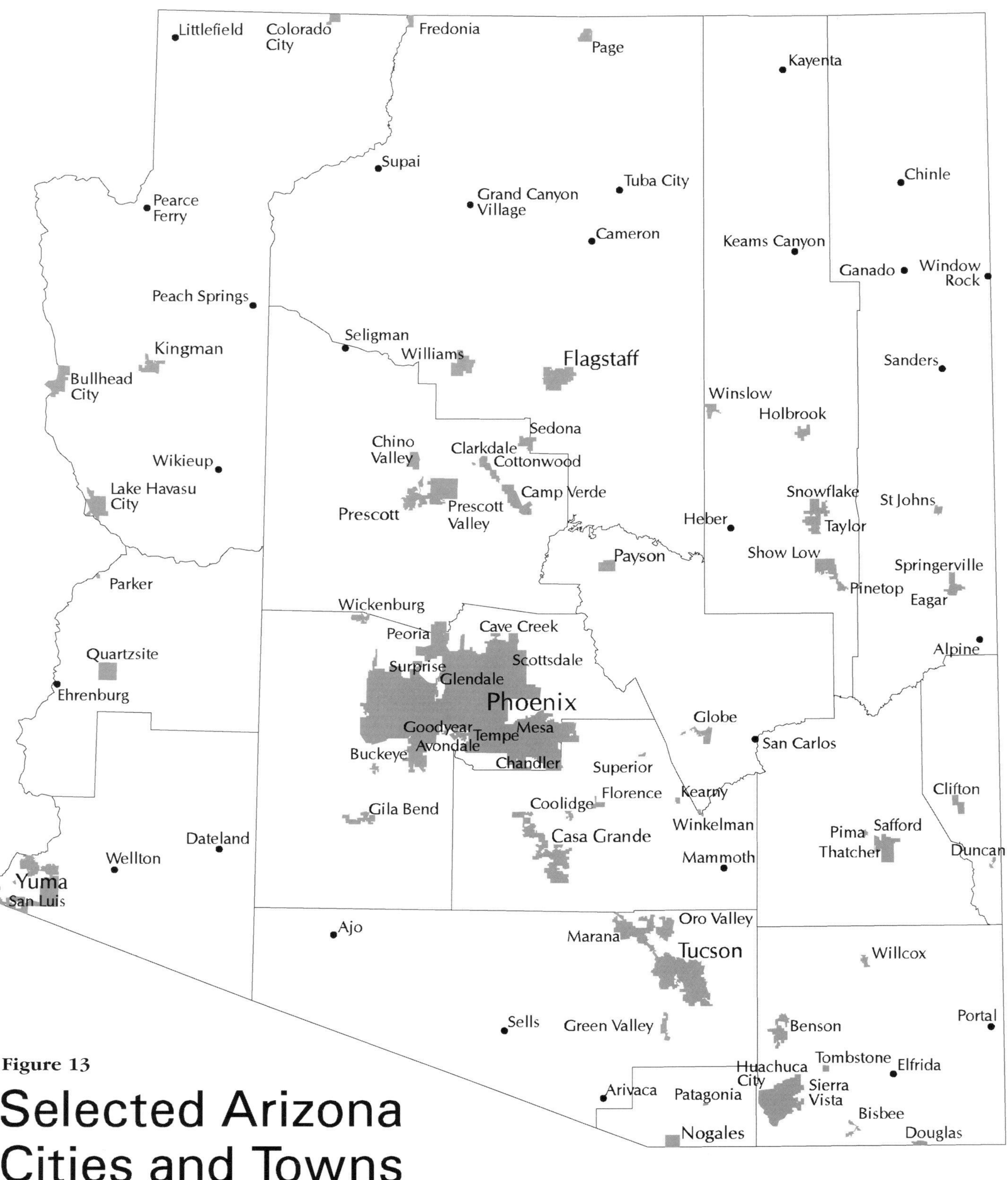

Figure 13

Selected Arizona Cities and Towns

documented in Arizona (Hastings and Turner 1965), is probably a result of grazing, along with fire suppression and climate change.

Timber harvesting has had a major impact on the coniferous forests of Arizona. Extensive logging in the twentieth century eliminated much of the original old-growth forests. The large ponderosa pine forests along the Mogollon Rim were originally much more open and savanna-like, with scattered large fire-resistant trees. Most of these trees were removed, and because of fire suppression, dense thickets of smaller trees have replaced them. These communities are prone to more and much hotter fires than the original pine forests. Timber harvesting has also occurred in mixed-conifer forests on the mountains, and even in subalpine spruce–fir forests. In addition to logging, wood collection and snag removal have also occurred on a large scale. Around Flagstaff, both legal and illegal collection of the large old-growth Gambel's oak has greatly reduced their abundance in the forests. In many pine forests, Flammulated Owls commonly use these oaks for roosting and nesting. Large dead standing snags are often collected for firewood, thus reducing the snag densities in the forests and the density of many cavity-nesting birds. Once a common component of lowland drainages in southern Arizona, the large mesquite (woodlands) bosques have also been nearly eliminated by fuelwood cutting, agriculture conversion, and reductions in local water tables.

Recreation is becoming increasingly common in Arizona's natural landscapes. Although many recreational impacts are minimal, some kinds of activities can have major long-lasting consequences. Off-road vehicle use can cause serious damage to vegetation, especially in sensitive areas such as high elevation wet meadows and desert landscapes. In many cases, decades are needed for vegetation to recover from such use, and there are many areas of the Sonoran and Mojave deserts that have been seriously affected by off-road vehicle use.

Because of the need for water in the arid Southwest, water developments such as dams, spring diversions, canals, and groundwater pumping are very common (figure 14). Dams create reservoirs that drown canyon vegetation, thus eliminating important riparian and wetland habitats. Water pumping and diversions can lower water tables and reduce spring flows, in turn reducing or eliminating wetland communities. Extensive groundwater pumping around Phoenix and Tucson has not only eliminated much of the natural vegetation but has also even caused the land to collapse in some areas. On the other hand, in some instances dams can create new bird habitat, such as the extensive marshlands that are now inhabited by nesting rails and grebes. With the construction of Glen Canyon Dam on the Colorado River, a new lush riparian zone developed downstream through the Grand Canyon. Many native bird species took advantage of this new riparian vegetation, colonizing the Grand Canyon region (Carothers and Brown 1991).

With the arrival of Europeans in the state, exotic plant species from Europe and Asia also began to appear. Early exotics included species such as Russian thistle and various ornamental trees, while more recently species such as the exotic bromes, Russian knapweed, and tamarisk (saltcedar) have spread across the state. Russian olive has also become a common component of many drainages in northern Arizona. Although some exotic plants do not cause much harm to natural vegetation in Arizona, other species are serious pests, and have major impacts on native species. Tamarisk invades and alters many riparian communities in Arizona, particularly those already stressed by water developments and livestock grazing. This species can alter the soil where it occurs, making it so salty that few other species can survive. Tamarisk also readily burns and creates extensive fires that often kill the remaining native cottonwood and willow stands that so many riparian birds depend upon. These burned drainages are typically replaced by monotypic stands of tamarisk that quickly sprouts from trunks. Brome grasses, including rip-gut, red, and cheatgrass, can dominate arid and semiarid landscapes, creating fire cycles that kill native species and cause downward spiral of degradation that ultimately eliminates most native species from areas where they are abundant. Many other exotic species are just now invading Arizona and its natural vegetation, and the future may hold new scourges that seriously affect native species and communities.

Arizona Bird Habitats

Many diverse habitats and plant communities exist among Arizona's nearly 73 million acres. Some habitats are widespread and encompass extensive areas, while others are rare, local, and declining. Vegetation type and structure exert a major influence on the distribution of birds across the state. However, so do other habitats that contain little or no vegetation, but still contain their own unique set of breeding birds. One good example are the bar rock faces, cliffs, and sheer canyon walls that are home to the Peregrine Falcon, White-throated Swift, and Canyon Wren. Of course, where specific habitat communities meet they often merge with one another forming transition zones or ecotones. These areas are frequently difficult to place within a single specific vegetation community.

The following thirty-one general habitat descriptions are for the most common vegetation community categories used by atlasers while surveying. One or more photographs are included for each to help the reader visualize the vegetation diversity being described. Several specific or very local habitats were occasionally lumped within these general descriptions for convenience. General habitat descriptions are categorized into seven specific vegetation landscapes: tundra, forests and woodlands, scrublands, grasslands, desertlands, wetlands, and urban/agriculture. The habitat name is followed by one to as many as four three-letter Atlas Habitat Codes, which atlasers placed on field cards to describe where each bird species was detected while conducting surveys on their block.

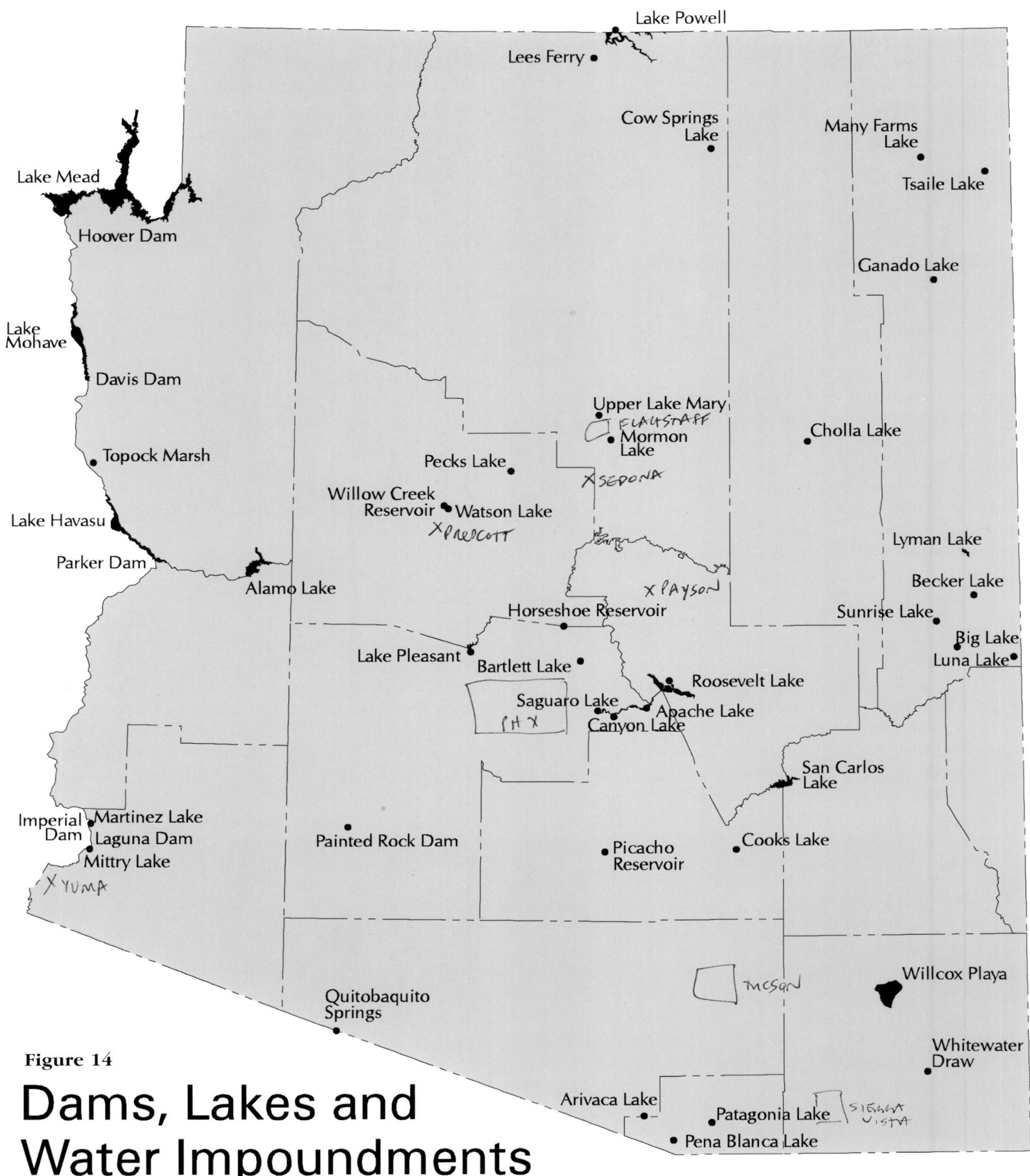

Figure 14

Dams, Lakes and Water Impoundments

TUNDRA

Alpine Tundra (TAL)
Biogeographic Provinces: Colorado Plateau
Climate: alpine
Elevation Zone: >11,500 ft (>3505 m)

TROY CORMAN

Description: Low matted vegetation consisting of grasses, forbs, and low shrubs growing on slopes and talus among boulders. Common species include golden avens and alpine sedges, along with tufted hairgrass, spike Trisetum, alpine fescue, Sibbaldia, and fleabane daisies. Cover can vary from high in swales and late snowmelt areas to scattered plants among boulders. This community is adjacent to and forms mosaics with the subalpine scrub community (SSS). Important natural disturbances include storm events, soil creep, and rockslides.

Status and distribution: Alpine tundra is one of the rarest communities in Arizona, restricted to a few thousand acres above timberline on the San Francisco Peaks near Flagstaff and Mount Baldy in the White Mountains. This tundra community is extremely isolated from the similar communities in the Rocky Mountains and comprises the only patches of alpine tundra for more than 200 miles (322 km) in all directions. The closest tundra to the San Francisco Peaks is in the mountains of central New Mexico. Some recreational activity and past sheep grazing has affected this community.

FORESTS AND WOODLANDS

Subalpine Spruce-Fir Forest (FSC)
Biogeographic Provinces: Colorado Plateau, Madrean
Climate: subalpine
Elevation Zone: 8500–11,500 ft (2591–3505 m).

Description: Lush moist forests dominated by Engelmann spruce, subalpine fir, and corkbark firs. The trees form a rather open to closed canopy reaching up to 75 ft (22.9 m) tall. Aspen is an occasional associate. The forest floor and clearings are often covered with ferns, mosses, and lichens. Shrubs are common, and include species of blueberries, whortleberry, common juniper, honeysuckle, snowberry, kinnikinnik, and Oregon grape. In drier rockier areas, bristlecone pine and limber pine dominate, with a sparse rocky understory of grasses, forbs, and shrubs. Blue spruce and various willow and alder species can be found in wetter environments along streams. The climate of these subalpine forests is harsh, with a short growing season, intense solar radiation, wind, and freezing temperatures. Precipitation is higher than in other forest communities. Adjacent communities include the subalpine scrub (SSS), alpine tundra (TAL), and the mixed-conifer (FMM) and aspen (FMA) forests. Important natural disturbances include intense winter storms, snowmelt patterns, native ungulate grazing, and occasionally fire.

TROY CORMAN

Status and Distribution: Subalpine spruce–fir forests occur as isolated islands in six regions of the state. Extensive stands occur on the Kaibab Plateau, and in the San Francisco and White Mountains. Smaller stands occur in the Pinaleno and Chiricahua mountains of southeastern Arizona and in the Chuska Mountains of the northeast. Fire suppression, livestock grazing, and logging have altered many stands of subalpine forests. Recreational activities and associated development increasingly threaten these forests.

Ponderosa Pine Forest (FMP)
Biogeographic Provinces: Colorado Plateau, Madrean, Mojave
Climate: montane
Elevation: 6000–8500 ft (1829–2591 m)

Description: Forests composed almost entirely of ponderosa pine, with an herbaceous or shrubby understory. Other tree species that can occur as scattered individuals include white fir, Douglas fir, aspen, New Mexico locust, and Gambel's oak. The aspect and climate of these forests is rather open and dry. Grasses often dominate the understory, including Arizona fescue, mountain muhly, nodding brome, fringed brome, junegrass, muttongrass, and squirreltail. Shrubs tend to be sparse, rarely forming dense thickets, and include Fendler buckthorn, creeping mahonia, currants, and snowberries. Examples of this community in southern Arizona include the five-needled variety of ponderosa pine, southwestern white pine, Apache pine, Chihuahuan pine, and alligator juniper. Original ponderosa pine forests prior to logging and fire suppression were open and parklike, with scattered large trees. Where fire suppression has occurred, dense thickets of "dog hair" pine can form, often choking out understory species. Adjacent communities to ponderosa pine forests include mixed-conifer (FMM) and aspen (FMA) forests, and lower elevation pinyon pine–juniper and oak scrub (FPJ and FPP). Scattered clearings occur, comprising the montane meadow–grassland community (GMM). Important natural disturbances in these pine forests include fire, drought, bark beetle infestations, and native ungulate grazing.

GEORGE ANDREJKO

Status and Distribution: Ponderosa pine forests are one of the most widespread forest communities in the southwest. The largest ponderosa pine–dominated forest in the world stretches from the San Francisco Mountains–Flagstaff area south and east along the Mogollon Rim into New Mexico. Extensive stands also occur on the Kaibab Plateau. Most of the higher mountains and plateaus in the state harbor stands of this community as well. Threats to ponderosa pine forests include high-intensity destructive fires, improper grazing practices, and timber harvesting. Urban sprawl and recreational activities are also causing impacts in some areas.

Ponderosa Pine–Gambel's Oak Forest (FPO)
Biogeographic Provinces: Colorado Plateau, Madrean
Climate: montane
Elevation: 6500–8500 ft (1981–2591 m)

Description: Forests composed almost entirely of ponderosa pine, with an understory of Gambel's oak and other shrubs. Other species that can occur as scattered individuals include Douglas fir, aspen, and New Mexico locust. The aspect and climate of these forests is more closed and moister than pure ponderosa pine forests. Gambel's oak can occur as dense shrubby thickets or as individuals scattered small trees. Shrubs other than the oak tend to be sparse, rarely forming dense thickets, and include Fendler buckthorn, creeping mahonia, currants, and snowberries. Where fire suppression has occurred, dense thickets of "dog hair" pine and Gambel's oak can form. Adjacent communities include mixed-conifer (FMM) and aspen (FMA) forests, and lower elevation pinyon–juniper and oak scrub (FPJ and FPP). Scattered clearings occur, comprising the montane meadow–grassland community (GMM). Important natural disturbances are similar to pure ponderosa pine forests.

TROY CORMAN

Status and Distribution: Ponderosa pine–Gambel's oak forests occur primarily in the northern part of the state along the Mogollon Rim, Kaibab Plateau, and the San Francisco Mountains. However, most mountains in the state harbor stands of this community as well. Threats to these forests include high-intensity destructive fires owing to past fire-suppression activity, improper grazing practices, and timber harvesting. Illegal fuelwood cutting of Gambel's oaks is an increasing threat. Urban sprawl and recreational activities are also causing impacts in some areas.

Mixed-Conifer Forest (FMM)
Biogeographic Provinces: Colorado Plateau, Madrean
Climate: montane
Elevation Zone: 8000–9500 ft (2438–2896 m)

BOB MILES

Description: These dense conifer forests are composed primarily of Douglas fir, white fir, aspen, blue spruce, and ponderosa pine. These forests form a wide band between the drier pine forests (FMP and FPO) at lower elevations and the wetter subalpine spruce–fir (FSC) forests at higher elevations. Tree composition varies from almost pure stands of Douglas fir to mixtures of several tree species. Southwestern white pine occurs in stands in the sky island mountains of southeastern Arizona. The understory is generally sparsely developed because of the dense canopy, and consists of forbs, grasses, and low shrubs, with occasional Gambel's oak, Rocky Mountain maple, and New Mexico locust. Other common shrubs include snowberry, mountain lover, and common juniper. Meadows of grasses, forbs, and low shrubs form in clearings resulting from wind blowdowns and fires. Aspen (FMA) often form pure stands within the mixed conifer forests. Important natural disturbances include wind, fire, and native ungulate grazing.

GEORGE ANDREJKO

Status and Distribution: Mixed-conifer forests are widespread in northern and central Arizona in the San Francisco Mountains, Kaibab Plateau, and White Mountains and higher elevations along the Mogollon Rim. Elsewhere they are found in smaller stands at higher elevations and locally on cooler north-facing slopes and in canyons of many smaller ranges and higher plateaus. This includes most of the higher mountains of southeastern Arizona such as the Pinaleno, Chiricahua, Santa Rita, Santa Catalina, and Huachuca ranges. Threats to these forests include major fires resulting from past fire suppression policies, timber harvesting, recreational activities, and to a lesser extent livestock grazing and elk browsing.

Aspen Forest (FMA)
Biogeographic Provinces: Colorado Plateau, Madrean
Climate: montane
Elevation: 8000–10,000 ft (2438–3048 m)

TROY CORMAN

Description: Deciduous forests dominated by quaking aspen. These forests are often moist and highly diverse, with a rich and well-developed understory of numerous shrub, grass, and forb species. Common shrubs include snowberry, honeysuckle, gooseberry, wild rose, and New Mexico locust. Numerous grasses occur, of which the most important are bromes, wheatgrass, and bluegrass. Forbs are often especially diverse, with numerous species of sunflowers, geraniums, mints, lupines, and bracken fern comprising a tall herbaceous layer. Aspen forests occur primarily in association with either mixed-conifer forests (FMM) or subalpine spruce–fir forests (FSC), and less so in ponderosa pine forests (FMP). Important natural disturbances include fire, native ungulate browsing and grazing, and diseases.

Status and Distribution: The largest aspen forests are found in northern Arizona in the San Francisco Mountains, Kaibab Plateau, and White Mountains and in locally dispersed at higher elevations along the Mogollon Rim. Elsewhere they are fairly widespread in scattered smaller stands in higher mountain ranges and plateaus of eastern, central, and northern Arizona. Because aspen is a fire-adapted species, fire-suppression policies have caused a general decline in the health and abundance of aspen, with many stands dying out and being replaced by mixed-conifer forests (FMM) of Douglas fir and white fir. Other threats include logging, recreational activities, and overgrazing (and browsing) by elk and domestic livestock.

Pinyon Pine–Juniper Woodland (FPJ)
Biogeographic Provinces: Colorado Plateau, Madrean, Mojave
Climate: cold-temperate
Elevation: 4000–7500 ft (1219–2286 m)

GEORGE ANDREJKO

Description: An open woodland of relatively short conifers, with an understory that can vary from grasses, shrubs, or virtually no vegetation depending on elevation, aspect, slope, and soil type. The dominant species are two-needled (Colorado) pinyon pine and one of series of juniper species, either Utah juniper, one-seed juniper, or alligator juniper. Gambel's oak can be an important component on the Colorado Plateau and evergreen oaks below the Mogollon Rim. Common shrubs associated with the woodlands include roundleaf buffaloberry, Utah serviceberry, big sagebrush, and skunkbush. At higher elevations this habitat merges with scattered ponderosa pine (FPP), particularly in canyons and drainages that support stringers of scattered ponderosa pine at the lower elevation limits of these trees. Recent drought conditions and subsequent bark beetle infestations in Arizona have caused the loss of many isolated and lower elevation stands of ponderosa pine and even the more drought-resistant pinyon pine and juniper. Fire is another important natural disturbance in this community.

TROY CORMAN

Status and Distribution: One of the most widespread and common communities in the state, these woodlands occur throughout much of northern and central Arizona as well as in the White Mountains region and the southeastern sky island country. In the Sonoran Desert and Mojave Desert regions these woodlands are very rare, restricted to a few ranges such as the Black, Poachie, and Mohave mountains. Most examples of this community have been altered by livestock grazing, fire suppression, past chaining, and fuelwood cutting. Exotic plant species often invade altered pinyon–juniper woodlands and can alter community dynamics.

Mexican Evergreen Woodland (FME)
Biogeographic Provinces: Madrean
Climate: warm-temperate
Elevation: 4000–7200 ft (1219–2195 m)

Description: Typically open, but occasionally heavily canopied woodlands of various species of evergreen oaks, including Emory, netleaf, Arizona white, silverleaf, and Mexican blue, along with Mexican pinyon pine and oneseed and alligator junipers. The groundcover and openings between the trees are usually dominated by a grass or grass-forb cover, with relatively few shrubs in most examples. In some sites, shrub species of brickelbush, buckwheats, and indigobushes can be common. Common grasses include blue, sideoats, hairy gramas, and muhly grasses. The rare relict Arizona cypress occurs in isolated stands of this community off the Mogollon Rim. On drier mountain slopes, chaparral (SIC) association shrubs such as manzanita and mountain mahogany occur among scattered oaks. These oak woodlands transition into semiarid grasslands (GSD) on lower slopes where the trees often become more scattered or are concentrated as stringers along typically dry foothill drainages. Natural disturbances include fire and drought.

TROY CORMAN

GEORGE ANDREJKO

Status and Distribution: These woodlands are widespread in the mountains and foothills of southeastern Arizona. The northernmost stands of this community occur in canyons and on mountain slopes south and west of the Mogollon Rim in central Arizona to western Yavapai County. Threats to these woodlands include devastating wildfires owing to past fire-suppression efforts, fuelwood cutting, recreational activities, livestock grazing, and urban development.

Madrean Pine–Oak Woodland (FMO)
Biogeographic Provinces: Madrean
Climate: cold-temperate
Elevation Zone: 5000–8200 ft (1524–2499 m)
Description: These woodlands comprise various pine and evergreen oak species. Important tree species include Apache pine, Chihuahuan pine, and Arizona pine. The latter is a distinct variety of ponderosa pine occurring in southeastern Arizona south into Mexico. Common

TROY CORMAN

understory species include silverleaf oak, netleaf oak, Emory oak, alligator juniper, Mexican pinyon pine, and Arizona madrone. Natural disturbances include periodic fire events and drought.

Status and Distribution: Widespread in the highlands of northern Mexico, this woodland extends primarily north only into the higher mountains of southeastern Arizona. The largest stands of Madrean pine–oak woodlands can be found in the Santa Catalina, Pinaleno, Santa Rita, Huachuca, and Chiricahua ranges, but it also occurs locally along several north-flowing drainages of the Dragoon and Patagonia mountains. Nearly all Arizona examples of this vegetative community are within the Coronado National Forest. Threats to these woodlands include devastating wildfires owing to past fire-suppression efforts, recreational development and activities, and livestock grazing.

SCRUBLANDS

Subalpine Scrub (SSS)

Biogeographic Provinces: Colorado Plateau
Climate: subalpine
Elevation: 10,000–11,500 ft (3508–3505 m)

TROY CORMAN

Description: This unique vegetative community is a band of dwarfed trees, shrubs, and herbaceous plants occurring above the subalpine spruce–fir and grassland communities and below alpine tundra. Subalpine scrub is an ecotonal region that is often called krummholz. Dwarf trees and shrub forms of Engelmann spruce, subalpine fir, limber pine, and bristlecone pine occur as scattered clumps, gradually becoming smaller and further apart as elevation increases to timberline. Common juniper, scrub willows, and currants typically occur around the tree islands, while numerous grasses, sedges, and forbs characteristic of tundra and subalpine grassland form a dense low herbaceous cover between the woody plants. In some cases on steep slopes, boulders predominate, with scattered shrubs and trees growing from among them. This scrub type is floristically quite rich, but is limited in extent by gradients of wind, moisture, and elevation. On some mountain slopes it can occur across an elevation range of several hundred meters, while on other slopes is consists of a narrow band, often only tens of meters wide, between tundra and other subalpine communities. Snowfall and snow depth, wind and mass wasting events on steep slopes are common natural disturbances.

Status and Distribution: This "elfin woodland" occurs over a very limited extent on the highest mountains in the state. Subalpine scrub is primarily restricted locally to the White Mountains and San Francisco Peaks region in Arizona. Current threats include past and present livestock and native ungulate grazing, climate change, and recreational activities and development.

Interior Chaparral (SIC)

Biogeographic Provinces: Madrean, Mojave, Sonoran
Climate: warm-temperate
Elevation: 3500–7500 ft (1067–2286 m)

ARIZONA GAME AND FISH DEPT.

TROY CORMAN

Description: This is a rather arid habitat of low, often dense scrub of numerous primarily evergreen shrubs. Common species include scrub live oak, manzanita, mountain mahogany, silktassel, cliffrose, and desert ceanothus. In some areas, crucifixion thorn becomes locally dominant. Cacti and yuccas are often present, and grasses are sometimes locally common, including sideoats and hairy grama, and three-awn. Occasionally scattered pinyon pines and junipers are found in the chaparral scrub. Pinyon pine–juniper woodlands (FPJ) and open ponderosa pine forests (FMP) commonly occur adjacent to chaparral vegetation. At lower elevations adjacent communities include the Sonoran upland desertscrub (DSU), Mojave desertscrub (DMO), and semiarid grassland (GSD). Fire is an important natural disturbance in chaparral communities.

Status and Distribution: Chaparral associations are distributed south of the Colorado Plateau (below the Mogollon Rim) from near the Pinaleno Mountains north and west to the Hualapai Mountains near Kingman, then reappearing north of Lake Mead in the Virgin Mountains and other ranges in the extreme northwest of the state. Threats include invasion of exotics plants, altered fire frequencies, inappropriate livestock gazing, and soil erosion on steeper slopes.

GRASSLANDS

Montane Meadow–Grassland (GMM)
Biogeographic Provinces: Colorado Plateau, Madrean
Climate: montane
Elevation: 6500–8500 ft (1981–2591 m)

Description: Damp meadows and openings in montane forests, dominated by typically low-growing grasses and forbs. Cover can vary from extremely high in wetter sites to more open with extensive bare ground in drier sites. Common species include Arizona fescue, brome grasses, yarrow, muhly grasses, and a wide variety of low growing forbs. Shrubs, including bitterbrush, rabbitbrush, and sagebrush can become important in disturbed sites and around forest edges. Species richness, especially of forbs, can be very high. Montane meadows occur within the montane forest communities, including ponderosa pine (FMP), ponderosa pine–Gambel's oak (FPO), mixed conifer forests (FMM), and aspen forest (FMA). Upslope, these meadows grade into the very similar subalpine grasslands (GSA). Important natural disturbances include fire and native ungulate grazing.

Status and Distribution: Widespread grassland community, but scattered and isolated in the montane forests of most mountains in Arizona above 7000 ft (2134 m), probably covering less than 100,000 acres in total. Montane meadow–grasslands are particularly well developed on the Kaibab Plateau, the extensive ponderosa pine forests from Flagstaff southeast above the Mogollon Rim, and in the White Mountains. This community has been severely altered by human activities, including livestock grazing, fire suppression, exotic plant invasions, recreational activities, and rural and urban development, especially around Flagstaff and in the White Mountains.

Subalpine Grassland (GSA)
Biogeographic Provinces: Colorado Plateau, Madrean
Climate: subalpine
Elevation: 8500–11,500 ft (2591–3505 m)

Description: Vegetation consisting primarily of low growing bunch and turf grasses, mostly less than 3 ft (0.9 m) in height. Perennial forbs are common in most examples, and low-growing shrubs occasionally occur. Important species include Arizona fescue, alpine timothy, tufted hairgrass, yarrow, and species of aster, sedge, fleabanes, cinquefoil, and clovers. In low-lying swales where water pools early in the season after snowmelt, a dense grasslike sward of sedges and rushes can develop. Bitterbrush often co-occurs with the grasses and forbs. Species richness can be very high, with slope, aspect, and moisture status determining which species dominate. Subalpine grasslands are adjacent to and form mosaics with subalpine conifer forest (FSC), alpine tundra (TAL), and subalpine scrub (SSS). Downslope they grade into the very similar montane meadow–grassland (GSA). Important natural disturbances include water erosion, drought, and native ungulate grazing.

GEORGE ANDREJKO

GEORGE ANDREJKO

Status and Distribution: This grassland community is restricted to high elevations primarily in the San Francisco, White, Chuska, and Pinaleno mountains, and on the Kaibab Plateau. Subalpine grasslands have been extensively altered in the past by heavy livestock grazing and continue to threaten this community, along with elk grazing and increasing recreational activities.

Cold-temperate (Great Basin) Grassland (GGB)
Biogeographic Provinces: Colorado Plateau
Climate: cold-temperate
Elevation Zone: 4000–7500 ft (1219–2286 m)

Description: This community contains a mixed grass-shrub (steppelike) vegetation that in some places has been invaded in recent years by pinyon pine–juniper woodlands. Most examples of this community have been strongly altered by livestock grazing. Originally, this community consisted of a variety of bunch and sod grasses, including Indian ricegrass, needle and thread, dropseeds, galleta, muhly, and blue grama, with scattered shrubs and forbs. Common shrubs include sand sagebrush, Mormon tea, yuccas, rabbitbrush, and Vanclevea. Differences in grass and shrub composition are related to variations in soil type, texture, and depth. With extensive grazing since the 1800s, the grasses have declined while many shrub species, including the invasive snakeweeds, have increased in abundance and have come to dominate over large expanses. Climate warming and fire restrictions have also allowed trees, primarily junipers, to invade down slope into these altered grasslands. In some areas a savanna-like landscape of grasses and junipers develops. Adjacent communities include cold-temperate desertscrub (DGB), pinyon pine–juniper woodlands (FPJ), and various riparian wetlands. In the western Colorado Plateau, cold-temperate grasslands are often adjacent to lower-elevation Mojave desertscrub (DMO). Important disturbances include drought, wind, cool grass fires, and native ungulate grazing.

GEORGE ANDREJKO

Status and Distribution: This grassland–shrub community is widespread on the central and northern regions of the Colorado Plateau, mostly below 6000 ft (1829 m), but with scattered examples up into the pinyon pine–juniper woodlands. To the east this community transitions into a much more distinctive plains-type grassland (GPL). Most of this grassland has been altered by extensive livestock grazing and now contains a higher percentage of low woody shrubs.

Plains Grassland (GPL)
Biogeographic Provinces: Colorado Plateau, Madrean (locally)
Climate: cold-temperate
Elevation Zone: 5000–7500 ft (1524–2286 m)

TROY CORMAN

Description: Often extensive grass-dominated community with relatively few shrubs or forbs. This community is very similar to the cold-temperate (Great Basin) grassland but differs in having a stronger influence from the summer monsoons and in being more like a true grassland in aspect, with some species present that are typical of the shortgrass prairies to the east, particularly buffalograss. Other common grasses include blue and sideoats grama, galleta, various muhly grasses, three-awns, and dropseeds. The shrubs present include rabbitbrush, Mormon tea, sand sagebrush, yuccas, and sand (shinnery) oak. Differences in grass and shrub composition are related to variations in soil type, texture, and depth. With extensive grazing since the 1800s, the grasses have declined while the shrubs have increased in abundance and have come to dominate in some areas. Important natural disturbances are primarily the same as for cold-temperate grasslands.

Status and Distribution: This grassland is widespread in eastern and central sections of the Colorado Plateau, mostly below 6500 ft (1981 m). To the west and north this community grades into a cold-temperate grassland (GGB), including south to Chino Valley in northern Yavapai County. This community also occurs locally in southeastern Arizona, with the best examples being the Sonoita and San Rafael grasslands. Adjacent communities include cold–temperate desertscrub (DGB), pinyon–juniper woodlands (FPJ), Chihuahuan desertscrub (DCH), semiarid grasslands (GSD), and various riparian wetlands. Extensive livestock grazing has significantly altered these grasslands.

Semiarid Grassland (GSD) and
Sonoran Savannah Grassland (GSS)
Biogeographic Provinces: Madrean, Chihuahuan, Sonoran
Climate: warm-temperate
Elevation Zone: 3000–5500 ft (914–1676 m)

GEORGE ANDREJKO

Description: These are shrub-grassland–dominated communities with a variety of annuals, woody shrubs, small trees, cacti, and other succulents. Grasses are often patchily distributed among bare ground and scattered shrubs. Originally, this grassland was composed of a variety of numerous perennial bunch grasses of which black grama and tobosa were the most common. In periodically flooded areas of southeastern Arizona, such as grassy swales, floodplain bottoms, and canyon mouths, these grasslands are often dominated by giant sacaton. A rich array of shrubs and succulents are often present, such as mesquite, whitethorn and catclaw acacias, tarbush, creosotebush, agaves, nolina, stool, and soaptree and other yuccas. Similar Sonoran savannah grasslands are very locally distributed and often contain scattered trees from Sonoran desertscrub associations, including paloverde, ironwood, and mesquite. With long-term livestock grazing, much of this grassland has been converted to low-growing sod grasses such as curly mesquite and annuals, while the numerous shrubs, cacti, and yuccas have increased in abundance and in many areas dominate the original grassland region. Important natural disturbances include wind, drought, fire, and native ungulate grazing.

GEORGE ANDREJKO

Status and Distribution: These grasslands are common and widespread in the valleys of southeastern Arizona, where this arid community is adjacent to Chihuahuan desertscrub (DCH) and Mexican evergreen woodlands (FME). Semiarid grasslands are also found in disjunct stands north to the San Carlos Apache tribal land and northwest to Cottonwood-Clarkdale and even into eastern Mohave County in the Hualapai Valley north of Kingman. In these regions, this community often transitions into Sonoran desertscrub (DSU), Mojave desertscrub (DMO), and interior chaparral (SIC). Sonoran savannah grasslands are found primarily in the upper Altar Valley of south-central Arizona. Much of this habitat has been altered by inappropriate livestock grazing practices, exotic plant invasion, and agricultural development. Other current threats to this community include fire suppression activity, urban development, and increasing recreational activities.

DESERTLANDS

Cold-temperate (Great Basin) Desertscrub (DGB)
Biogeographic Provinces: Colorado Plateau
Climate: cold-temperate
Elevation Zone: 4000–7000 ft (1219–2134 m)

Description: Arid landscapes where most precipitation falls as rain and snow during winter storms. This desertscrub association is characterized by open vegetation consisting of short to medium height shrubs from 2 to 7 ft (0.6–2.1 m), in particular blackbrush, shadscale, sagebrush, Mormon tea, rabbitbrush, and prickly pear. Elevation, aspect, and soil type determine which species or combination of species dominates. This community is extremely variable in composition, and supports many additional shrub and subshrub species. Annuals, perennial forbs, and perennial grasses often form an important herbaceous layer, particularly at higher elevations. Extensive monotonous expanses of blackbrush and shadscale are found at lower elevations, with very few others species present. Big sagebrush becomes important at higher elevations on deep loamy soils. Low blackish crusts composed of bacteria, fungi, algae, lichens, and mosses often cover the ground between the shrub canopies. The exotics red brome, cheatgrass, and Russian thistle are often abundant in degraded vegetation. The principal natural disturbances include drought, wind, and water erosion.

TROY CORMAN

GEORGE ANDREJKO

TROY CORMAN

Status and distribution: This widespread and common community is found throughout northern Arizona on the Colorado Plateau, and at higher elevations above the creosotebush community on the mountains of northwest Arizona in the Mojave Province. Most examples of this community have been altered to a greater or lesser extent by livestock grazing activities since the late 1800s. Other threats include urban development and exotic plant invasion, which create unnaturally frequent fire regimes.

Mojave Desertscrub (DMO)
Biogeographic Provinces: Mojave
Climate: warm-temperate
Elevation Zone: 1000–5000 ft (304–1524 m)

Description: Precipitation for this generally hot and arid landscape falls primarily as rain during winter storms. This desertscrub community generally contains open and sparse low-growing vegetation dominated by creosotebush, blackbrush, and desert holly, mostly under 6 ft (1.8 m) tall. Joshua tree is the only tall woody species, reaching heights of 25 ft (7.6 m). At lower elevations, low monotonous expanses of creosotebush and desert holly occur, while at higher elevations creosotebush drops out and Joshua tree and blackbrush dominate. Slopes often support a rich mixture of various additional species, including prickly pear and cholla cacti, barrel cactus, black grama, and numerous shrubs. After wet winters, the open areas between shrubs are carpeted with numerous annual wildflowers. Red brome is an abundant annual exotic in much of the Mojave. Adjacent communities include pinyon pine–juniper woodlands (FPJ) and interior chaparral (SIC) at higher elevations, and Sonoran desertscrub (DSL and DSU) to the south. Principal natural disturbances include drought and wind and water erosion.

BOB MILES

Status and Distribution: This desertscrub community is widespread in northwestern Arizona from the Utah border to the north slopes of the Mohave Mountains, mostly west of the Grand Wash Cliffs and Hualapai Mountains. An extension of this desertscrub extends up the Colorado River into the Grand Canyon. Recent threats to this community include mining activities, local urban development, off-road vehicles, overgrazing by livestock and feral ungulates, invasion by exotic plants, and recurring fires fueled by red brome.

GEORGE ANDREJKO

Chihuahuan Desertscrub (DCH)
Biogeographic Provinces: Chihuahuan
Climate: warm-temperate
Elevation: 3200–4800 ft (975–1463 m)

Description: This desertscrub community receives most of its minimal annual rainfall during the late summer monsoon season, but is occasionally soaked by winter storms. An open low-growing scrub community dominated by creosotebush occurs in the lower and flatter areas of this desert. Other shrubs include tarbush, whitethorn acacia, soaptree yucca, ocotillo, and mesquite. The mesquite typically forms clumps where deeper sandy soils occur. A variety of forbs and cacti occur around and under the shrubs. On rocky slopes a diverse community of shrubs and succulents occur, including catclaw, coldenia, ocotillo, graythorn, and numerous species of agave, nolina, sotol, and yucca. A few grasses occur, primarily species such as tobosa and black grama from the semiarid grasslands. Red brome is a common exotic annual. In the bottoms of many of the valleys, playas occur, where water often ponds for several months following winter rains. Areas around the playas often support dense grasslands of tobosa, sacatons, and scattered shrubs. Saline margins are vegetated by saltgrass, and succulents such as iodine bush and seepweed. Adjacent communities include primarily the semiarid grassland (GSD), as well as linear strips of riparian woodlands including lowland Sonoran deciduous woodlands (WSD) and desert dry washes (WRS). Common natural disturbances include drought, wind erosion, and occasional severe freezes.

TROY CORMAN

GEORGE ANDREJKO

Status and Distribution: This vegetative community is limited in extent in southeastern Arizona, primarily within the upper San Pedro, San Simon, and upper Gila River valleys. However, some vegetative characteristics of this habitat transition in other areas as well, including near Douglas and the Cienega Creek drainage west of Benson. Greatest threats to this community include inappropriate livestock grazing practices, soil erosion, and urban development.

Sonoran Desertscrub: Lower Colorado River (DSL)
Biogeographic Provinces: Sonoran
Climate: subtropical
Elevation Zone: 100–1800 ft (30–549 m), but to near 3000 ft (914 m) on some desert mountain peaks

GEORGE ANDREJKO

GEORGE ANDREJKO

Description: The lowest and driest portions of the Sonoran Desert are characterized by large monotonous expanses of creosotebush and white bursage. Limited precipitation occurs primarily as rain during winter storms, which are often followed by annual wildflowers carpets covering the desert floor. Late summer monsoon precipitation is typically much more sparse and local compared to its influence to the east. Dry washes are common throughout the region, and support stands of small trees adapted to drought, such as honey mesquite, ironwood, blue paloverde, desert willow, chuparosa, burrobush, and catclaw acacia. Extensive sand dune areas occur in several localities. Sandy soils elsewhere are often dominated by saltbush. Rocky slopes are vegetated by a variety of cacti, shrubs and grasses, including prickly pear, chollas, ocotillo, brittlebush, and big galleta. This community is the lowest in elevation in Arizona, and is generally adjacent to the Arizona upland desertscrub (DSU) and Mojave desertscrub (DMO). Common disturbances include drought and wind erosion.

Status and Distribution: This widespread, but increasingly threatened community, is distributed in southwestern Arizona, extending north to around Topock along the Colorado River, and east to Phoenix and Florence in the Gila River valley. Extensive areas around Phoenix and westward have been eliminated or severely altered because of urban and agricultural expansion. Other recent threats to this community include the invasion of exotic species and the spread of fire, off-road vehicle activity, browsing by feral ungulates, and groundwater depletion.

Sonoran Desertscrub: Arizona Uplands (DSU)
Biogeographic Provinces: Sonoran
Climate: subtropical
Elevation: 1200–3600 ft (366–1097 m)

Description: A rather lush desert community of large cacti, small thorny trees, shrubs, and annuals that receives most of its precipitation during periodic winter storms and the late summer monsoon period. Common cacti include saguaro, prickly pear, cholla, barrel, and, locally, organ pipe cactus and numerous small species. The many small trees are mostly in the legume family, and include paloverde, catclaw acacia, ironwood, and mesquite, as well as ocotillo. At the highest elevations, crucifixion thorn becomes common. Other common shrubs include creosotebush, white bursage, jojoba, and brittlebush. In spring, numerous annual wildflowers often occupy the spaces between the woody species and cacti. Perennial grasses are uncommon, but the invasive annual red brome is often locally abundant. This community is adjacent to the lower elevation Colorado River desertscrub (DSL), and merges at higher elevations with pinyon pine–juniper woodlands (FPJ), interior chaparral (SIC), and semiarid grasslands (GSD). Important natural disturbances include native ungulate grazing, drought, wind, and winter freezes.

GEORGE ANDREJKO

GEORGE ANDREJKO

Status and Distribution: Widespread and common in southern and western portions of Arizona. This community is typically found on slopes and mesas above the lower-elevation valley floors. Currently, the Arizona uplands are under serious threat because of major suburban sprawl around Phoenix, Tucson, and other growing towns. The presence of invasive plant species, of which red brome is of particular concern, has introduced a fire regime into the desert vegetation that native species cannot cope with. Paloverdes, saguaros, and other cacti are particularly vulnerable. Other threats include livestock grazing, off-road and other recreational activity, and illegal collecting of many cacti species.

WETLANDS

Cold-temperate (Great Basin) Riparian Wetlands (WGB)

Biogeographic Provinces: Colorado Plateau
Climate: cold-temperate
Elevation: 4000–7000 ft (1219–2134 m)

TROY CORMAN

Description: Riparian communities comprised of mixtures of shrubs and trees, with or without herbaceous understories. Common native species include Fremont cottonwood, Goodding willow, coyote willow, seepwillows, and rabbitbrush. Other native shrubs that are less common include apache plume, desert olive, western redbud, netleaf hackberry, skunkbush, and yellow willow. The exotic tamarisk (saltcedar) and Russian olive are often present. In areas lacking heavy flooding or livestock grazing, a dense herbaceous cover can develop, consisting of rushes, sedges, horsetails, and various grasses. With persistent flooding or grazing, this herbaceous layer is often reduced or eliminated, and the woody vegetation becomes more restricted in distribution to channel margins. Occasional small pools and beaver ponds within the riparian zone occur, supporting wetlands with cattails and rushes. These riparian communities tend to occur as thin linear strips through adjacent upland communities, in particular pinyon pine–juniper woodlands (FPJ), cold-temperate grasslands (GGB), and cold-temperate desertscrub (DGB). Where they form continuous riparian zones extending in higher and lower elevation zones, they tend to intergrade with montane riparian wetlands. The most significant natural disturbances in these communities are flooding and beaver activity.

Status and Distribution: An uncommon and scattered community associated with rivers, streams, and springs throughout the Colorado Plateau. Almost all examples of cold-temperate riparian wetlands have been severely altered or in many cases eliminated by human activity, ranging from inappropriate livestock grazing practices to various kinds of flood control, water diversions, and dam projects. In some examples, the exotics Russian olive and tamarisk have taken over the riparian vegetation, often forming pure stands. Other invasive weeds such as Russian knapweed and ravenna grass also threaten these communities.

Montane Riparian Wetlands (WMR)

Biogeographic Provinces: Colorado Plateau, Madrean
Climate: montane
Elevation: 6500–9500 ft (1981–2896 m)

GREG CLARK

TROY CORMAN

Description: Lush and cool, densely shrubby or forested communities along drainages and often high-gradient canyons at higher elevations. These communities are dominated by one or more of a variety of trees, including alder, narrowleaf cottonwood, boxelder, bigtooth maple, Gambel's oak, aspen, blue spruce, white fir, and Douglas fir. Other common understory shrubs and vines include Arizona grape, thicket creeper, chokecherry, dogwood, New Mexico locust, water birch, and various willow species. A lush herbaceous layer comprised of numerous forbs, sedges, ferns, and grasses are usually found. These riparian communities tend to occur as thin linear strips through adjacent montane forests, in particular ponderosa pine (FMP and FPO), mixed conifer (FMM), and aspen (FMA) forests. Where they form continuous riparian zones extending in higher and lower elevation zones, they tend to intergrade with subalpine wetlands (WAB), and cold-temperate riparian (WGB) zones and wetlands below. The most significant natural disturbances in these communities are flooding, native ungulate browsing, drought, and beaver activity.

Status and Distribution: These riparian communities are widespread, but of limited extent in the forested mountains, plateaus, and mesas of eastern, central, and northern Arizona. This includes higher mountain ranges of the southeast. Many have been significantly altered by timber harvesting activity, wildfires owing to fire-suppression efforts, recreational activity, and livestock and native ungulate grazing.

Arctic-Boreal Wetlands (WAB)
Biogeographic Provinces: Colorado Plateau
Climate: subalpine-alpine
Elevation: 8000–11,500 ft (2438–3505 m)

TROY CORMAN

GEORGE ANDREJKO

Description: This is a low-growing shrubby and herbaceous riparian community associated with streams and springs, usually dominated by scrub willows including Geyer and Bebb willows, and other deciduous shrubs, such as currants and thinleaf alder. Blue spruce and aspen are often common species adjacent to the wetland communities, but rarely occur in them. Dense herbaceous vegetation typically occurs under and around the shrubs, dominated by species of sedge, Juncus, and numerous grasses and forbs. Adjacent communities include the subalpine forest (FSC), subalpine scrub (SSS), and subalpine grasslands (GSA). Winter snowpack depth, snowmelt patterns, and freezing winter wind are controlling factors in these communities. They are also influenced by beaver activity and native ungulate browsing.

Status and Distribution: Very limited in distribution in Arizona, this riparian community is most widespread in the White Mountains region and sparingly in the San Francisco Mountains. Most examples of this rare habitat are seriously threatened by elk and livestock browsing and grazing, and locally by recreational activity.

Marshlands and Cienegas (WMC)
Biogeographic Provinces: all
Climate: all
Elevation: 75–9500 ft (21–2896 m)

GEORGE ANDREJKO

PAT O'BRIEN

GEORGE ANDREJKO

TROY CORMAN

Description: Diverse open, wetland community, often containing dense emergent moisture dependent plants species. Commonly occurring plants include cattails, bulrushes, and sedges that depending on water depth, may cover the entire water surface or only along the shallower shoreline of the water feature. Commonly found along lakes, ponds, reservoirs, irrigation ditches, canals, or slower sections of rivers and streams. The most significant natural disturbances in these communities are drought, flooding, native ungulate grazing, and beaver activity.

Status and Distribution: Typically relying on open shallow water sources, this diverse community can be found nearly statewide within most habitats occurring in the state. Current threats include livestock and native ungulate grazing, water diversions, ground water depletion, off-road travel, and urbanization. This vegetative community has both been lost and created through human activity. New wetlands have become established behind dams on rivers or at ponds and lakes constructed in rural and urban settings including at wastewater treatment facilities.

Interior Riparian Deciduous Woodlands (WIR)
Biogeographic Provinces: Madrean, Sonoran
Climate: warm-temperate
Elevation Zone: 3000–6000 ft (914–1829 m)

TROY CORMAN

TROY CORMAN

Description: This riparian community is a rich mixed-deciduous woodland, with numerous tree and shrub species typically found in mountain foothills and canyons. Arizona sycamore is the characteristic tree in this diverse community, but other common species include Arizona walnut, Fremont cottonwood, velvet ash, and various willows. Many other woody species are occasionally present, including Arizona cypress, Arizona alder, netleaf hackberry, boxelder, Texas mulberry, bigtooth maple, narrowleaf cottonwood, and chokecherry. Common understory species include smooth sumac, Arizona grape, bracken fern, and the exotic Himalayan blackberry. This habitat often merges with montane riparian woodlands (WMR) at higher elevations and Sonoran riparian deciduous woodlands (WSD) at lower elevations. Natural disturbances include drought, flash-flooding, and native ungulate grazing.

Status and Distribution: Commonly occurring riparian community at mid-elevations in perennial and intermittent drainages south and west of the Mogollon Rim, and in southeastern Arizona. Often found in moderately high gradient, rocky, or boulder-strewn drainages. Threatened by groundwater depletion, inappropriate livestock grazing, recreational activity and development, and wildfires owing to fire-suppression activities in adjacent habitats.

Sonoran Riparian (Desert Dry Wash) Scrubland (WSR)
Biogeographic Provinces: Sonoran, Mojave, Chihuahuan, Madrean
Climate: subtropical to warm temperate
Elevation: 100–4500 ft (30–1372 m)

TROY CORMAN

Description: Frequently known as dry washes or arroyos, this important arid riparian community is found within lowland desert drainages that typically contain flowing water only for very short periods immediately following infrequent heavy rains. Many of these drainages may only flow for a few hours annually. This community often contains many of the same low- to medium-height woody species found in the adjacent desertscrub communities; however, the vegetation typically becomes much denser and the trees obtain a greater height. Commonly occurring trees include mesquite, paloverde, ironwood, and, locally, netleaf hackberry at higher elevations. Other frequent woody shrubs are wolfberry, graythorn, catclaw acacia, desert hackberry, desert willow, desert broom, and saltbush. Natural disturbances typically include flash flooding, soil erosion, and drought.

Status and Distribution: Found braiding their way through lowland desert landscapes, this dry riparian community is most widespread and developed in Sonoran desertscrub associations (DSL and DSU) in southwestern Arizona. However, similar vegetated and structured communities also occur along dry washes to the north in Mojave desertscrub (DMO) and to the east in Chihuahuan desertscrub (DCH). Upper elevation limits grade into semi-arid grasslands (GSD) of central and southeastern Arizona. Locally, these vegetative communities are seriously threatened by urban development and expansion, wild burrow browsing, inappropriate livestock grazing practices, and off-road travel. Fire has also been introduced into this community through the introduction of exotic grasses such as red brome with serious consequences.

Sonoran Riparian Deciduous Woodlands (WSD)
Biogeographic Provinces: Sonoran, Mojave, Chihuahuan, Madrean
Climate: subtropical to warm temperate
Elevation: 100–4500 ft (30–1372 m)

TROY CORMAN

GEORGE ANDREJKO

TROY CORMAN

Description: Deciduous lowland woodlands associated with perennial streams, rivers, cienegas, and springs, as well as along the shorelines of ponds and lakes. This community consists primarily of relatively narrow corridors of medium to relatively large trees typically dominated by Fremont cottonwood, Goodding willow, and various species of mesquite. Although cottonwood and willow occur primarily only along the immediate perennial channels, large floodplain areas with subsurface water are sometimes dominated by open to moderately dense stands of mesquite, and are frequently referred to as mesquite "bosques." A variety of smaller trees and shrubs occur in association with the dominant species, including seepwillow, velvet ash, Mexican elderberry, and netleaf hackberry. Many exotic species occur in this community as well, and in some cases this riparian community becomes so altered that the dominant native species disappear. Common exotics include tamarisk, red brome, Bermuda grass, and Schismus. Where this habitat enters mountain foothills and lower canyons, Arizona sycamore becomes a regular component. The most common natural disturbances are flooding and drought.

Status and Distribution: Although originally widespread along lowland perennial drainages in otherwise arid desert landscapes of southern and western Arizona, these lush, riparian woodlands have declined dramatically since European colonization. Most examples of this community have been destroyed or heavily altered by human activities, including dam construction, water diversions, groundwater depletion, logging, fuelwood cutting, fire, inappropriate livestock grazing practices, urbanization, off-road travel, and other recreational activities. Most remaining stands are relatively small, isolated, and intermittently distributed, with the largest and most continuous groves occurring along the San Pedro River in southeastern Arizona.

Altered Riparian (WAR)
Biogeographic Provinces: all
Climate: subtropical, warm-temperate, cold-temperate
Elevation Zone: 75–6500 ft (23–1981 m)

TROY CORMAN

Description: This is a severely disturbed or altered riparian zones dominated by the exotic tamarisk (saltcedar). This species tends to form dense monotypic stands, often excluding most other native species. The ground cover is typically open, in part because of the dense salty leaf litter, and is dominated by exotic grasses, such as red and ripgut bromes and cheatgrass. Tamarisk invades following some form of disturbance, generally one that alters riparian flows, such as dam construction, groundwater depletion, or other kinds of water diversions. Livestock overgrazing can also favor the establishment and spread of tamarisk. It is also fire-adapted, and repeated burns encourages denser and thicker growth while at the same time reducing or eliminating the more fire-sensitive native species such as cottonwoods and willows. In undisturbed riparian zones where natural flooding still occurs, tamarisk is not common, although it is often present. In some areas at higher elevations, the exotic Russian olive also occurs as a codominant and in some areas in dominant dense stands.

Status and Distribution: Although originally brought in for erosion control, tamarisk has escaped and now dominates much of the riparian landscape in the American Southwest. It is gradually moving north and up slope as it adapts to colder conditions, and is found in riparian sites throughout Arizona below 7000 ft (2134 m). Common disturbances in this community include fire, livestock grazing, and water development and diversion projects.

URBAN/AGRICULTURE

Urban and Residential (URS, UPG, UIN)

Biogeographic Provinces: all
Climate: all
Elevation: 100–9500 ft (30–2896 m)

TROY CORMAN

GREG CLARK

GEORGE ANDREJKO

Description: Complex landscapes with a highly diverse, frequently introduced flora. This includes major cities, small towns, and suburban neighborhoods with structurally diverse human dwellings, buildings, bridges, and roads. Much of the land is covered in concrete and asphalt, particularly in highly developed downtown districts with little vegetation. Other areas include residential yards, parks, and golf courses containing manicured grass, gardens, and shade trees sometimes scattered around manmade canals, ponds, and lakes. Because of frequent human activity, reduced native vegetation, and other factors, breeding avian diversity is typically low in such settings and generally favors more adaptable species of birds.

Status and Distribution: Unlike most of the native habitats in Arizona, the urban and residential landscape is rapidly expanding in the state as human populations grow. Even with this growth however, it is estimated that these manmade habitats still account for only one percent of the state's landmass.

Rural and Agricultural (ARU, ACW, ACR, ABG)

Biogeographic Provinces: all
Climate: all
Elevation: 100–8000 ft (31–2438 m)

GEORGE ANDREJKO PHOTOS

Description: Rural landscapes come in many varieties in Arizona and range from isolated ranches with scattered buildings, corrals, pastures, and shade trees to extensive farmland with their monoculture fields, canals, irrigation ditches, ponds, shelterbelts, and livestock feedlots. Wastewater treatment facilities with their associated ponds are also included under this broad category. Most of Arizona agricultural lands are found in desert river valleys and are irrigated, but extensive canal systems allow crops to be grown in many regions that had previously been arid desertscrub landscapes. Pesticide and herbicide use is high in these regions and irrigation runoff locally carries some of these chemicals into river drainages contaminating fish and other aquatic animals in several areas. Common crops in these areas included alfalfa, grains, sorghum, and cotton. Many vegetables are also grown during the mild winter climate in southwestern regions of the state. Turf and tree farms for urban landscaping are increasing in several regions. Common orchard crops include citrus, pecan, and, locally, apple.

Status and Distribution: Rural and agricultural lands encompass approximately two million acres or approximately three percent of Arizona. However, near larger metropolitan areas, agricultural lands and orchards are rapidly being converted to housing developments, golf courses, warehouses, power plants, and other developed areas.

A Brief History of Arizona Ornithology

Dan L. Fischer

Long before the boundaries of what we now know as Arizona were defined, first as a territory in 1863 and then as a state in 1912, explorers and naturalists began noting the birds in this arid, rugged, and spectacular landscape. In 1540–1542, the first recorded bird observations began with an entrada, or exploration, led by Francisco Vasquez de Coronado on his march northward from colonial New Spain in quest of the so-called Seven Cities of Cibola (Winship 1893). From these rather scant observations, many naturalists and scientists have followed in succession to provide a rich and interesting knowledge of the birds within the region.

Early Exploration (1840–1900)

In the mid-1840s, the United States expanded its boundaries westward through conquests thereby requiring the lands to be surveyed and mapped. Congress authorized military expeditions to determine the new boundaries, find railroad routes, assess geological wealth, and document the region's biotic resources. The expedition parties usually included surgeons who often served as naturalists collecting and cataloging biological specimens they encountered. Several talented and capable members of the army also participated in these activities until the surrender of Geronimo and his band in 1886.

In the mid-nineteenth century, two men, John Cassin of the Academy of Natural Sciences of Philadelphia and Spencer Baird of the Smithsonian Institution, greatly influenced the early development of American ornithology through their field and taxonomic work. Cassin and Baird also named most of the specimens secured by the naturalists working in the West, including Arizona. Baird was especially instrumental in recommending the placement with various military units of individuals who were very interested in the task of collecting specimens. Many of these field collectors have birds named in their honor, as do military men who engaged in scientific research while performing their duties, such as Lt. James William Abert, in whose honor Baird named the Abert's Towhee.

The first American naturalists to enter Arizona accompanied the troops during the territorial expansion and subsequent military action of the United States against Mexico under the command of Col. Stephen W. Kearny and the Army of the West in 1846. While on that expedition, which continued into southern California, Lt. William H. Emory noted birds along the Gila River. In 1851, Dr. Samuel Washington Woodhouse (1853), serving as naturalist on Lt. Lorenzo Sitgreaves's expedition in search of a wagon route down the Zuni and Colorado Rivers, recorded many birds, including a new swift, the White-throated Swift. In 1853–1854, the type specimen of this swift was obtained in Arizona by two naturalists working together, Dr. Caleb Burwell Rowan Kennerly and the German artist Baldwin Möllhausen, on the Whipple Railroad Survey as they followed a similar route west through northern Arizona along the thirty-fifth parallel (Kennerly 1859). In addition, they also discovered the Cassin's Finch on Pueblo Creek and the Gila Woodpecker on the Bill Williams Fork before they crossed the Colorado River.

In 1854, another railroad survey arrived from San Diego at Fort Yuma and continued east along the thirty-second parallel under the command of Lt. John Parke. After crossing the Colorado River, they continued upstream along the Gila River to the Pima villages, then past Picacho Peak to Tucson. From there they continued eastward crossing the San Pedro River, the Willcox Playa, and on through Apache Pass at the extreme north end of the Chiricahua Mountains. Dr. Adolphus Lewis Heermann (1859) served as naturalist recording and collecting many birds through this southern region of Arizona, which at that time was still Mexico.

The Gadsden Treaty in 1853 added lands south of the Gila River to U.S. holdings and, with subsequent land purchases, determined the present southern border of Arizona. Under the command of Maj. W. H. Emory, several surveyor-naturalists worked the southern Arizona border portion of the survey, where they documented the rich bird life (Baird 1859).

The next army expedition that contributed to Arizona ornithology was most unusual for the Southwest, a steamboat exploration of the Colorado River. In 1857–1858, Lt. Joseph C. Ives, with Möllhausen as naturalist, undertook a journey on the Explorer through the Colorado River delta to Fort Yuma, where they preceded upstream more than three hundred miles before leaving the river to journey east to Fort Defiance (Baird 1860). Then in 1861 at Fort Mojave, located just north of the Needles on the Colorado River, Dr. James G. Cooper discovered two new birds, Lucy's Warbler and Elf Owl (Cooper 1861). The Cooper's Ornithological Society bears this naturalist's name.

From 1863 to 1865, Dr. Elliott Coues, an army surgeon posted at Fort Whipple near Prescott, became one of the most prolific and appealing writers of Western ornithology. He discovered and secured many new species in Arizona. *Birds of the Colorado Valley* (1878), which is much larger in scope than the title implies, is among several of his contributions. Dr. Edward Palmer, an English naturalist serving as surgeon with the army, also collected during the same period while at Fort Whipple. In 1866, Palmer continued collecting after being transferred to Camp Lincoln (later named Camp Verde), located on the middle Verde River, and later to Camp Grant, situated at the junction of Arivaipa Creek and the San Pedro River.

As a young German emigrant, Charles Emil Bendire entered the army as an enlisted man and served at Fort Buchanan in southeastern Arizona, where he developed a serious interest in birds. Returning as an officer to Camp Lowell near Tucson in 1871–1873, he discovered Bendire's Thrasher and Rufous-winged Sparrow. As an oologist, Bendire was also the first to collect the eggs of the birds he had discovered in addition to those of the Crissal Thrasher and Lucy's Warbler (Bendire 1892, 1895).

Henry Wetherbee Henshaw (1875), working on the geographic and geological explorations and surveys under Lt. George M. Wheeler in 1873 and 1874, recorded birds in portions of eastern Arizona. His first trip included Fort Apache and south to Fort Bowie. His trip of the following year extended from these forts to Camp Crittenden north of the Huachuca Mountains and east of the Santa Rita Mountains and then to Camp Lowell at Tucson. On his return, he became the first naturalist to climb the high coniferous forest of the Graham (Pinaleno) Mountains.

Ten years later, Dr. Edgar A. Mearns (1886, 1890), posted at Fort Verde, explored some of the central and northern areas of Arizona Territory, including the Mogollon Rim and Grand Canyon regions. His observations and collections of Arizona's birds constitute a thorough, complete picture of the birdlife of this region when it was largely unsettled and undeveloped (Brown et al. 1987). He also became the first naturalist to climb the highest of the San Francisco Peaks. Then, in 1892–1894, Mearns returned and collected extensively during the United States–Mexico International Boundary Commission Survey.

Among the several early ornithologists working during the late nineteenth century was Frank Stephens, who beginning in 1876, undertook collecting trips into the deserts and mountains of southern Arizona. He became the first naturalist to investigate the birdlife in the higher elevations of the Chiricahua Mountains. In 1881, William Earl Dodge Scott began four years of collecting in the vicinity of Tucson, the Santa Catalina Mountains, and the nearby San Pedro River. He was quick to note that many birds of the mountainous southwest have seasonal altitudinal or vertical movements similar to a north and south migration.

In 1889, C. Hart Merriam, a scientist working on the San Francisco Peaks for the U.S. Department of Agriculture, developed his "life zone" concept in which the altitudinal succession of mountain biota is primarily due to climatic conditions. His work extended to the adjacent forests of the Colorado Plateau, the Grand Canyon, and the Painted Desert regions (Merriam 1890). A founder of the American Ornithologists' Union, he later became the first chief of the U.S. Office of Economic Mammalogy and Ornithology, which later became the Biological Survey, and ultimately the U.S. Fish and Wildlife Service (USFWS).

After meeting with visiting naturalist Edward W. Nelson in southern Arizona, Herbert Brown, who later became Arizona's first resident ornithologist, began seriously collecting nest, bird, and egg specimens. From 1885 to 1911, he assembled specimens from the Tucson, Yuma, and the lower Colorado River regions. His experiences before and during his birding exploits varied from prospector and newspaper editor, to clerk of the Superior Court of Pima County and Superintendent of the Yuma Territorial Prison. He was a founder and the first curator of the University of Arizona's museum, and his bird specimens have formed the nucleus of the collections.

Regional Perspective (Post-1900)

Middle Gila River Valley

With a growing population at the beginning of the twentieth century, Arizona experienced increased demands on its natural environment, especially to grasslands, rivers, and streams. These demands often caused dramatic and destructive changes from which the ecosystems never fully recovered. One river receiving a devastating ecological setback was the Gila, which crosses southern Arizona from east to west. In 1901, George Breninger was the first to compile a list of birds on the middle Gila River located on the Pima (Gila River) Indian Reservation. In 1907, as the demise of this riverine system began to unfold, M. French Gilman, a schoolteacher, also recorded the bird

Herbert Brown investigating an Elf Owl's nest.
(From *Bird-Lore*, 1915)

life and their nesting habits for eight years, thereby establishing a base from which a historic perspective could develop. From 1963 to 1983, Amadeo M. Rea, who, in addition to teaching for five years at tribal schools, studied and revealed the severity of impacts on the birdlife and river environs in his book *Once a River* (1983).

Lower Colorado River Valley

Joseph Grinnell, a University of California professor, after having floated the lower Colorado River, initiated the basis for a historic study of the avifauna on another unrestricted and free flowing pristine stream in "An Account of the Mammals and Birds of the Lower Colorado Valley" (1914). Gale Monson, serving as a manager of several U.S. Fish and Wildlife Refuges on or near the river, contributed greatly to the knowledge of the birds in the region from 1943 to 1962. In addition to observing birds there, he witnessed many destructive environmental changes as they were occurring. Over seven decades following Grinnell and after extensive alterations had occurred to the river and riparian-gallery forests through damming, clearing, straightening, and channeling, a study of the status of the river's bird life was undertaken. The results of this comprehensive effort along the two-hundred-mile river stretch north of Yuma was *Birds of the Lower Colorado River Valley* (1991) by Kenneth V. Rosenberg, Robert D. Ohmart, William C. Hunter, and Bertin W. Anderson. Their common interest in this study stems from their association with Arizona State University.

Southeastern Arizona

At the turn of the century, Harry S. Swarth, although primarily associated with California institutions, began working in the southeastern region of the state and wrote "Birds of the Huachuca Mountains" (1904). Beginning in 1935 and returning from Ohio for eight separate seasons, Herbert Brandt observed the nesting birds in the southeastern corner of the state. Many of his personal experiences with birds were noted as he explored the lower deserts, drainages, grasslands, foothills, and high mountains in *Arizona and Its Bird Life* (1951).

For three summers starting in 1951, Joe T. Marshall Jr. studied the woodlands of mixed pines and oaks of the higher mountains of southeastern Arizona, including those extending south into the Sierra Madre Occidental of Mexico. Within this woodland belt, Marshall determined behavior and breeding status of the birds in a classic scientific study entitled "Birds of Pine-Oak Woodland in Southern Arizona and Adjacent Mexico" (1957). From 1958 and continuing for more than three decades, Seymour H. Levy explored and noted many new accounts of birds occurring and nesting within the southern regions of the state.

Northeastern Arizona

The isolated northeast corner of the state received little attention until the summers of 1933 to1938 by members of the Rainbow Bridge–Monument Valley Expedition under the direction of the National Park Service. The ornithological investigations were conducted by Angus M. Woodbury and Henry Norris Russell and later published in "Birds of the Navajo Country" (1945). For thirty years

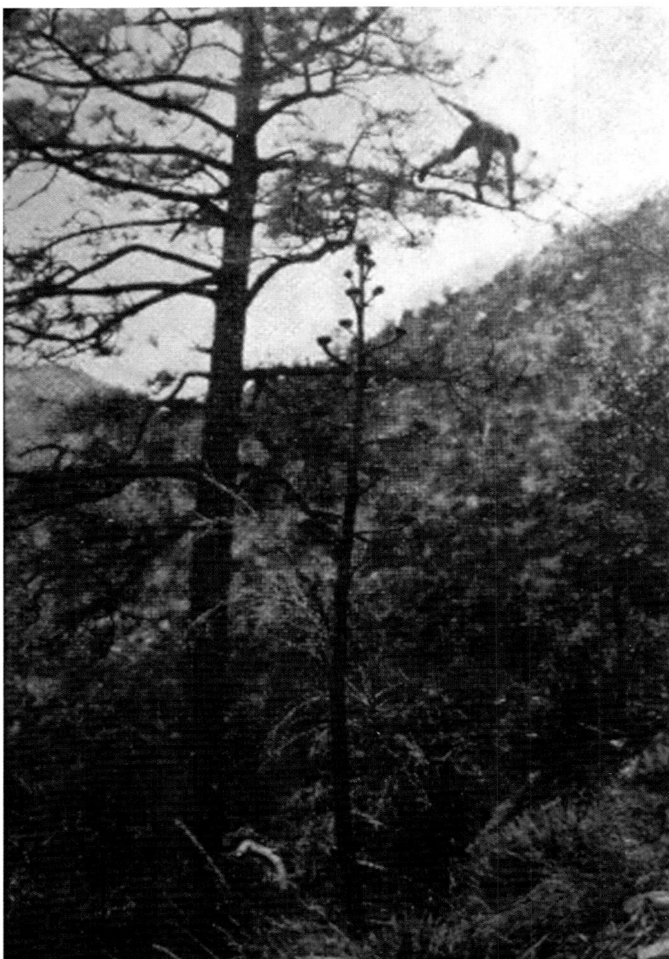

Francis C. Willard collecting an active Buff-breasted Flycathcher nest in the Huachuca Mountains in May 1907. (From *Condor*, 1923)

beginning in the early 1970s, Charles T. LaRue and later Brad Jacobs explored the mountains and canyons of this vast region and documented the birdlife within the tribal lands of northeastern Arizona. Jacobs later wrote an account of the region at large in *Birding on the Navajo and Hopi Reservation* (1986). During the late 1980s, LaRue, then an employee of Peabody Coal Company, studied the birds around the mine, resulting in "Birds of Northern Black Mesa, Arizona" (1994).

Grand Canyon Region

To the west, the U.S. Biological Surveys sponsored the Edward W. Nelson expedition of 1909 to study birds and mammals in remote areas of the Grand Canyon, including the Kaibab Plateau and Arizona Strip region. The Grand Canyon was designated a national park in 1919, sparking additional regional avian studies. *Grand Canyon Birds* (1986), by Bryan T. Brown, Steven W. Carothers, and R. Roy Johnson, presents a thorough regional focus on one of the great natural wonders including its diverse bird community amid a great variety of habitats. The three scientists authoring this ornithology and ecological study of the canyon, in addition to their considerable field experience, have all held positions with the National Park Service.

Bird Checklists in Arizona

Harry Swarth's "A Distributional List of the Birds of Arizona" (1914) was the first attempt to determine the bird species occurring within the entire state. This account documented 362 species and subspecies found within Arizona. It also included a large bibliography on the subject. Anders H. Anderson (1933), in combination with his fieldwork, updated the state list of birds in 1932, which then stood at 397 species. Anderson compiled *A Bibliography of Arizona Ornithology* (1972). This included a listing of the great volume of ornithological literary titles with annotations about this interesting subject through 1970.

The most definitive work on the avifauna in the state to this date has been *The Birds of Arizona* (1964) by Allan Phillips, Joe Marshall, and Gale Monson, which includes 423 species. The most experienced field ornithologists and scientists in Arizona, Phillips and Marshall were professors at the University of Arizona, while Monson worked for the U.S. Fish and Wildlife Service. Their collaboration brought forth the first species accounts of the birds including their distribution and status for the entire state. A smaller companion book, *Annotated Checklist of the Birds of Arizona* (1981) by G. Monson and A. Phillips, updated the status of 475 species of birds documented in the state, and including the notes and observations of many other field observers.

The Arizona Bird Committee, organized by Steven Speich in 1972, updates bird records and maintains the "Field Checklist of the Birds" for the state. The current edition (2002) includes 523 species and is the result of a review and evaluation of submitted observations undertaken by a committee of eight volunteer members elected to four-year terms.

Recent Efforts of Education and Concern (1970–2001)

Many prominent Arizona ornithologists and biologists have received instruction through the years from several outstanding professors, including Robert D. Ohmart at Arizona State University, Russell P. Balda at Northern Arizona University, Charles T. Vorhies and Steven M. Russell at the University of Arizona, and Carl Tomoff at Prescott College. Research by the universities and private groups cooperating with governmental agencies has reinforced and identified the need and urgency for studying birds and habitat associations in the deserts, forests, grasslands, and especially riparian areas across the state.

Concern over habitat loss and the serious reduction of some species has also become a major focus of many private organizations and governmental agencies. Through county, state, and federal legislation, several parks, monuments, refuges, and designated conservation areas have been established to help conserve Arizona's natural heritage. Additionally, private organizations have set aside sensitive areas that are essential to and, in some cases, even a last resort for bird protection. Monitoring and protecting of federally endangered species or the reintroduction of extirpated species have been major concerns of the Arizona Game and Fish Department (AGFD) and the USFWS. A great many biologists have aided in these efforts.

Including the important publications noted earlier in this chapter, many other authors have added significantly to our knowledge of Arizona birds. David E. Brown, a past supervisor with the AGFD, and author of several books, wrote *Arizona Wetlands and Waterfowl* (1985). In addition to species accounts, the book depicts the limit of surface-water resources in this arid state as it pertains to habitat requirements necessary for successfully managing nesting and migratory waterfowl species. Brown followed with *Arizona Game Birds* (1989). Several regional guidebooks have enabled us to enjoy birds through specified locations in the field. Artists have also inspired our appreciation and enjoyment of birds by beautifully portraying them in their natural settings. Numerous photographers have skillfully captured stunning bird images that are often artistic and have proved important for verification of records.

The Arizona Breeding Bird Atlas provides an overview of the distribution of the state's nesting birds at the end of the twentieth century. This project also establishes a baseline against which to compare future range changes. The atlas represents a major effort whereby volunteer birders, researchers, and professionals alike have voiced an interest, concern, and active participation in gaining knowledge about the distribution and nesting phenology of Arizona's marvelous and diverse avifauna.

In looking back to the mid-nineteenth century, Spencer F. Baird directed his field associates, as they explored the pristine western regions, to determine the "nidification" or the breeding habits of our native birds. The documentation of nesting phenology has continued as a major focus of this invaluable and significant project. Perhaps those who have participated in the atlas or have otherwise taken an interest in Arizona's birds will pause to reflect with the same "enthusiasm" that Elliot Coues shared at Fort Whipple in the 1860s. In his writing, Coues expressed "a sort of charitable pity for the rest of the poor world, who are not ornithologists, and have not the chance of pursuing the science in Arizona."

Species Accounts Overview

Most of this publication is devoted to the breeding birds of Arizona and includes a summary of the data that were collected for each species during the primary atlas period from 1993 to 2000. As noted earlier, it also includes information from very local reports and limited surveys conducted in 2001. There are 270 full species accounts, one for each bird species for which observers obtained three or more potential breeding records during the course of the atlas project. Fourteen additional species were confirmed breeding in Arizona during this period, but they were noted in only one or two locations. These are discussed in a supplemental chapter immediately following the main body of species accounts. This supplemental chapter also includes eighteen species that fell under breeding classes of possible or probable breeders, but for which confirmed nesting information was not obtained during the atlas period. Eight of these species had previously been documented nesting in the state. The final accounts are of fifteen species that were previously reported nesting at least once in Arizona, but that were not suspected of nesting in the state during the atlas period. Overall, 307 species of birds had been confirmed nesting or at least attempting to nest in Arizona through the end of 2001. These include several nonnative species and one species (White-tailed Hawk) that should best be designated as a hypothetical breeding species for the state.

The full species account text consists of three sections: Habitat, Breeding, and Distribution and Status. In the Habitat section, authors summarize the vegetative communities and topography that atlasers reported for the given species and often compare these with historical reports and other relevant studies. If sufficient atlas data were obtained, a habitat graph is presented depicting the most commonly reported habitat types. For species found in numerous vegetative communities, only the ten most frequently reported habitats are displayed, owing to space constraints. If only one or two records were reported in several single habitats, these are often lumped together under the category "other habitats."

The Breeding section is divided into several components for each species, including the basic timing of migration and nesting in Arizona using both atlas and prior published information. The authors provide basic information on the breeding biology of each species to help put atlas results into context and to stimulate interest of the reader in the diverse nesting habits of Arizona's avifauna. For most species, determining the incubation period and days to fledge was beyond the scope of the atlas project. When available, this information was compiled from reputable sources, and complete references are provided. This section also notes where certain basic nesting aspects of a particular species are poorly known or lacking. This, we hope, will encourage some enthusiastic biologist or researcher in the state to conduct studies that will eventually uncover some of these avian secrets.

For species with greater than ten confirmed records that are not in the "FL" or "UN" categories, a breeding phenology graph is provided. Unless otherwise noted, this graph does not include fledgling sightings for several reasons. Fledglings are generally easy to observe and appear toward the end of a bird's breeding cycle, which would produce an inaccurate peak on the graph. In addition, fledglings can vary considerably in age and may make the breeding season appear longer than it actually is. However, records of adult birds observed feeding fledglings were often included in the phenology graph, inasmuch as they indicate some continued parent dependency. Fledgling records are included on graphs for many waterbirds and gallinaceous species, however, as the vast majority of confirmations for these birds were dependent "FL" records. Graphs that included fledgling records are clearly marked.

The Distribution and Status section of the species accounts provides an overview of the given species' broad geographic range, as well as of the past and present distribution of the bird in Arizona. Authors also indicate the relative status of the bird in the state, if known. Although determining the status of many species of birds falls outside of the scope of the atlas project, data from other sources such annual Breeding Bird Survey (BBS) routes were sometimes used and cited.

DISTRIBUTION MAPS

Among the most important visual aspects of any breeding bird atlas project are the species distribution maps that are produced by using atlas data. Each colored square shown on species maps represents one 7.5-minute topographic map. These squares indicate that the species was detected and determined to be at least potentially nesting on that particular quad map, either on or outside the priority block. The three breeding classes (possible, probable, and confirmed) are shown on the distribution maps. If a species was located both on and outside the priority block, the breeding class obtained on the priority block is shown. For example, if an Ash-throated Flycatcher was confirmed breeding outside a priority block and also recorded as a possible breeder on the priority block, the possible record would be displayed. If there was no record of the Ash-throated Flycatcher on the priority block, but the species was noted outside the block on the same quad, then the casual observation (off-block) would be displayed.

Although it may seem unfortunate that the entire topographic map locations are shown on the maps rather than the exact block locations, this measure was necessary to protect sensitive bird species. Many private landowners and Native American tribes also appreciated the fact that only general location information would be shared.

The block and topographic quad statistics appear with each distribution map, charting the number and percentage of priority blocks in which observers reported the species, broken down by each breeding level or class. It also denotes the number of quads in which the species was determined to be breeding or potentially breeding in Arizona. Owing to off-block records and casual observations, the second number is routinely higher.

Species names and sequence follow the American Ornithologists' Union Check-list of North American Birds, 7th ed. (1998), and its supplements through 2004.

Arizona Breeding Bird Atlas

Species Accounts

Black-bellied Whistling-Duck

by Troy E. Corman *Dendrocygna autumnalis*

Oddly built, but still strikingly handsome, Black-bellied Whistling-Ducks are rather tame and locally an easily observed species in southeastern Arizona. Their behavior of frequently perching and nesting high in trees, as well as nocturnal feeding habits adds to the unique nature of these dapper long-legged ducks.

JIM BURNS

HABITAT

In Arizona, the Black-bellied Whistling-Duck prefers the shallow edges of lakes, oxbow ponds, wetlands, and slow flowing rivers and creeks. Aquatic habitats with overhanging trees and shrubs such as Fremont cottonwood, willow, and velvet mesquite are especially favored. More than 50 percent of atlas records were from marshes and pond ($n = 25$). This species is often discovered perched on trees and stumps over the water or resting in the shade along the shoreline. They also frequently roost in much more open situations such as wastewater settling ponds, residential lakes, irrigation catchments, and dairy sump ponds where an additional 32 percent of atlas records were noted. Fewer Black-bellied Whistling-Duck observations came from riparian woodlands dominated by cottonwood, willow, and sycamore. One requirement in Arizona appears to be the nearby presence of agriculture lands or irrigated pastures (Brown 1985). These ducks feed primarily at night and in Arizona have been observed in Bermuda grass pastures and in fields of alfalfa, sorghum, and corn (Brown 1985).

BREEDING

During the atlas period, wintering Black-bellied Whistling-Ducks were primarily noted only in the greater Phoenix areas, with flocks occasionally numbering greater than 100

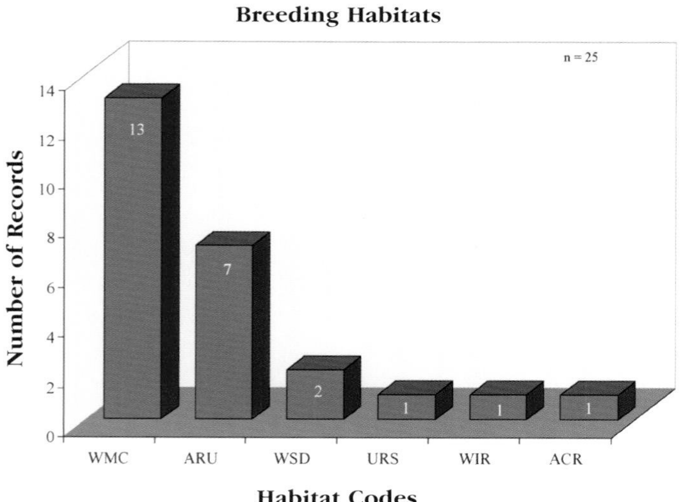

individuals. As the breeding season approaches, mated pairs of Black-bellied Whistling-Duck leave wintering concentration flocks. These ducks typically begin arriving in southern Arizona in April. The nesting season is lengthy in Arizona, with young ducklings observed as early as May and as late as 16 October (Brown 1985). Likely due to the secretive nature of nesting Black-bellied Whistling-Ducks, nests with eggs are rarely reported in Arizona. Atlasers observed dependent fledglings from 30 May–18 September indicating egg laying begins as early as late April. But most duck broods were observed in July, suggesting May and June as peak egg-laying months. Young downy broods occasionally observed into mid-October would also suggest egg laying into at least early September. Atlasers may have missed later nesting activity since most atlas surveys had ended by mid-August.

Post-breeding dispersal of Black-bellied Whistling-Ducks in Arizona occurs from August-October, when individuals and small groups are often found well away from nesting areas. Just prior to their southward migration, these ducks sometimes congregate in large numbers. Concentrations of 200–250 individuals have been noted near Nogales in October and early November.

Black-bellied Whistling-Ducks frequently nest in natural tree cavities, and in Arizona these include cottonwoods and willows. They also nest in large tree forks and on the ground in dense scrub. In Texas, Bolen (1967) found these ducks also readily use nest boxes when provided. In the greater Phoenix area, where potential nesting trees are particularly lacking, most pairs nest on the ground. Here they favor small, densely vegetated islands built in residential lakes and wetlands constructed at wastewater facilities. The vegetation on these islands often consists of impenetrable stands of large, four-wing saltbush, arrowweed, seep willow, or shrubby velvet mesquite.

Unlike so many other duck species, the nests are not lined with down, and the 9–18 eggs are directly placed in a shallow scrape in wood debris in the tree cavity, on the ground, or a shallow nest bowl of woven grass (Bent 1925,

James and Thompson 2001). Tree nests have been documented as high as 20 ft (6.1 m) above the ground (James and Thompson 2001). Also, unlike many other duck species, both the male and female alternate incubation bouts that last approximately 24 hours each (James and Thompson 2001). The eggs are incubated for approximately 28 days (Bolen et al. 1964). Young are capable of flight between 56–63 days old, but remain with parents up to four months after fledging (James and Thompson 2001).

DISTRIBUTION AND STATUS

The range of the Black-bellied Whistling-Duck extends from southern Arizona, Texas, and Louisiana south locally to northern Argentina. Only the most northern populations appear to be migratory. The first evidence of this duck nesting in Arizona was a pair observed with 16 newly hatched ducklings near Tucson on 13 September 1949. Prior to that year, there were only two records of this duck in Arizona; both of those were near Tucson (Phillips et al. 1964). Numbers and distribution have gradually increased in Arizona ever since. Black-bellied Whistling-Ducks are now considered locally common during the summer as far north as the greater Phoenix area where they were first found nesting in Peoria in 1969 (Monson and Phillips 1981).

Atlasers documented Black-bellied Whistling-Ducks nesting locally at elevations from approximately 900–4500 ft (274–1372 m) in Arizona. In the Phoenix area, atlasers noted this duck only along the southern edge of eastern Maricopa County from the Gilbert–Chandler area west along the Salt–Gila rivers valley to Tolleson and Avondale. These rural suburbs are currently located adjacent to agricultural areas required for feeding by these ducks. Yet many agricultural fields are rapidly being converted to housing and business developments, so future use of these areas may be limited.

Atlasers also confirmed Black-bellied Whistling-Ducks nesting locally in the San Pedro River valley from Mammoth north to Dudleyville and near Hereford north to St. David. In Santa Cruz County, atlasers observed adults with ducklings along Sonoita Creek near Patagonia and within the upper Santa Cruz River drainage near Nogales north to Rio Rico. Although Black-bellied Whistling-Duck pairs were observed along this river north to Amado and as far west as Arivaca Cienega on the Buenos Aires National Wildlife Refuge. In the Sulphur Springs Valley, these ducks were detected only near Douglas. In the past, Black-bellied Whistling-Ducks nested irregularly in several areas near Tucson, at Picacho Reservoir, and at Cluff Ranch near Pima, Graham County (Phillips et al. 1964, Brown 1985). During the atlas period, however, they were not observed at the latter two locations, and only pairs were noted during the breeding season in the Tucson and Marana areas.

Black-bellied Whistling-Duck populations appear to be stable or slightly increasing in Arizona. Their overall distribution in the state has changed little in the past 20 years, but numbers have increased locally. Northern populations increased dramatically during the atlas period, while some edge localities are no longer occupied, primarily due to loss of foraging, nesting, or roosting habitat. Brown (1985) noted that whistling-ducks are easily shot in Arizona. If the birds are in an area open to hunting, the entire population may be killed on the opening day of the waterfowl season. Brown suggested having a closed season on these ducks or at least a delay in the opening of the waterfowl season until October 15. Fortunately, many of Arizona's whistling-ducks currently roost during the day on private land or residential areas closed to hunting. Productivity of these fine ducks may also be enhanced by the installation of nest boxes where natural cavity abundance is low.

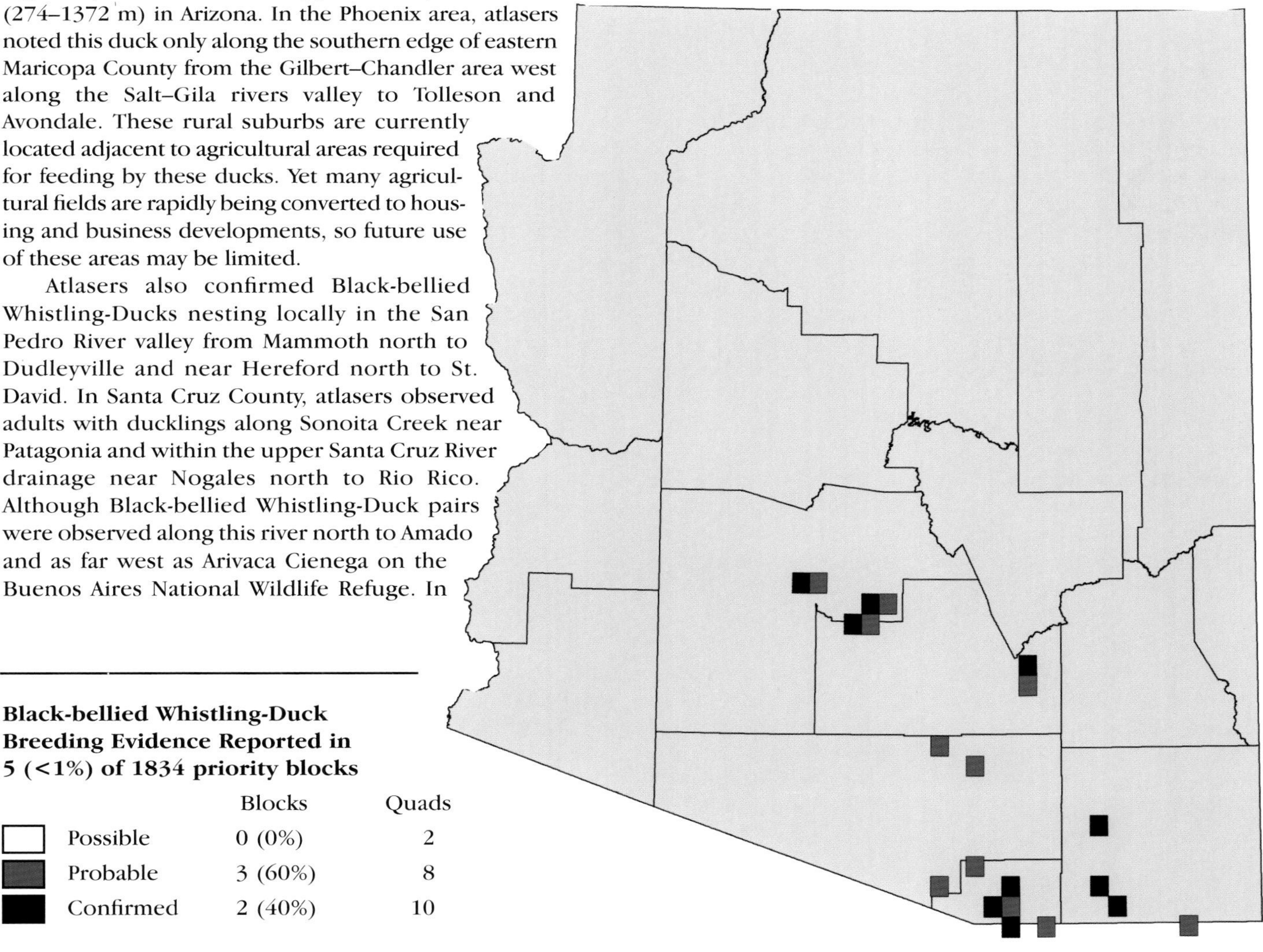

Black-bellied Whistling-Duck Breeding Evidence Reported in 5 (<1%) of 1834 priority blocks

	Blocks	Quads
Possible	0 (0%)	2
Probable	3 (60%)	8
Confirmed	2 (40%)	10

Canada Goose

by Bill Grossi and Troy E. Corman *Branta canadensis*

One of the most recognizable and widespread of waterfowl in North America, Canada Geese are frequently noted in literature as harbingers of seasonal change. These geese readily attract attention with their distinctive resonant honking calls as migrating flocks wing their way across the sky in characteristic "V" formation.

JIM BURNS

HABITAT

In Arizona, Canada Geese are known primarily as migrants and local winter residents along rivers, lakes, ponds, and reservoirs, especially those near agricultural areas throughout the state. The local introduced breeding populations in Arizona occur in similar habitat and most records noted by atlasers were in high elevation wetland habitats consisting of marshes, ponds, and lake edges near subalpine meadows and other similar open grasslands. Aquatic vegetation in these areas often includes stands of cattails, bulrush, and sedge. Canada Geese prefer open areas where their visibility is unobstructed by vegetation. Most occupied breeding habitat consists of open bodies of water with easy shoreline access for goslings and an abundance of low growing sedge, grasses, and other semiaquatic plants for foraging (Mowbray et al. 2002). Arizona's small urban population nest near residential lakes and ponds, and forage on the adjacent manicured grass of lawns, parks, and golf courses, much to the dismay of some local residents.

BREEDING

In Arizona, spring migration of Canada Geese often begins in February with few remaining in the state after mid-March, but occasionally into early May. Pair bonding usually does not occur until the geese are 2–3 years old. Canada Geese are well known for their long-term pair bonds, typically lasting until death. In the White Mountains of Arizona, these geese usually arrive in early March already paired and begin selecting nest sites when snow is still on the ground (Brown 1985). In Arizona, the timing of nesting for Canada Geese apparently depends on climate and elevation. All atlas confirmed breeding records of Canada Geese were noted by the presence of downy young. Atlasers noted the small resident population in Scottsdale produced young by 16 April, suggesting egg-laying initiation in late February or early March. The earliest observation of adults with small goslings in populations north of the Mogollon Rim was noted on 5 May. This would suggest egg-laying initiation in late March or early April for these higher elevation populations. Atlasers noted adults with goslings through 28 July. In Arizona, a few migrant Canada Geese may begin arriving in late September, but most are not observed until mid-October or even November.

Canada Geese nests are typically on the ground, on drier, slightly elevated sites near water and are especially fond of protected islands (Mowbray et al. 2002). The female selects the site, while accompanied by her mate. Nesting materials include dried grass, forbs, moss, and other nearby vegetation to which down is added as incubation begins. Nearby vegetation is often incorporated into the nest throughout the laying process (Mowbray et al. 2002) and down is not added until the second or third egg is laid (Brakhage 1965). The adults are territorial around the nest site and will defend their nest forcefully if threatened. Only the female incubates the typical clutch of 4–7 eggs (range 2–10), which hatch in approximately 25–28 days (Mowbray et al. 2002). Her mate remains in the vicinity of the nest throughout incubation and occasionally joins her during incubation breaks to bathe, drink, and feed (Mowbray et al. 2002).

The female Canada Goose broods her young at the nest for 1–2 days, and, during their first week after hatching, continues to brood them away from the nest in cold, wet, or windy weather (Mowbray et al. 2002). The young are precocial, and while under the watchful eyes of both parents, fledge in 7–9 weeks (Ehrlich 1988). However, the young typically remain with the parents as a family group throughout the first year. Due to the lengthy nesting and rearing process, Canada Geese are typically single brooded, but they will renest in 14–20 days following early nest failure in some lower latitude populations (Atwater 1959).

DISTRIBUTION AND STATUS

Canada geese are made up of several races of varying size and shape that breed across North America, from Alaska and Canada south to central United States. These geese also nest locally in southern United States, primarily from past introduction efforts. Throughout their range, Canada Geese exhibit perhaps the most extreme differences in body size of any bird species, with subspecies that are among the largest and smallest of all geese (Mowbray 2002).

Phillips et al. (1964) made no mention that Canada Geese ever nested in Arizona. They described them as uncommon to common migrants and local winter residents in the state. From 1966–1968, the Arizona Game and Fish Department acquired goslings of the Great Basin (Moffitt's) subspecies of Canada Geese from Utah, Nevada, Wyoming, and Washington (Brown 1985). These birds were raised and transplanted to Carnero Lake, Merlin Slough, and Geneva Reservoir in the White Mountains. At about the same time, pinioned Canada Geese from Utah were released at Red Lake on the Arizona–New Mexico border on Navajo tribal lands (Krausman 1990). In 1970, the first documented breeding of Canada Geese in Arizona occurred at Becker Lake (Brown 1985). Since that time breeding has been documented at many other locations in the White Mountains region. Canada Geese also nest regularly at Red Lake north of Window Rock and have nested at Tsaile Lake and other nearby lakes on Navajo Tribal lands (Jacobs 1986). In this region, atlasers only confirmed these geese nesting at Many Farms Lake.

Atlasers found the distribution of Canada Geese remains relatively small and local in the state, but possibly expanding. Most of these geese breed above the Mogollon Rim. In the White Mountains region, atlasers documented these geese nesting at elevations from approximately 6900–9100 ft (2103–2774 m) from Green's Peak to near Hannagan Meadow. In the past, Canada Geese have also nested in appropriate habitat on the adjacent White Mountain Apache tribal lands (Krausman 1990) as far west as McNary and beyond. Unfortunately, permission to conduct atlas surveys on these tribal lands could not be obtained. Atlasers also confirmed Canada Geese nesting near Mormon Lake southeast of Flagstaff, and Scholtz Lake southeast of Williams.

The most recent publications which describe the breeding status of Canada Geese in Arizona (Brown 1985, Krausman 1990), consider them established, but express doubts whether the birds can significantly increase their numbers at higher elevations due to scarcity of wetlands, over-hunting, and disturbance from recreationalists. Correspondingly, as drought conditions gripped Arizona during much of the atlas period, breeding habitat was greatly reduced as many shallow lakes and marshes eventually dried.

Canada Geese have been nesting in the greater Phoenix area since at least 1992 (Witzeman et al. 1997) and atlasers confirmed them nesting locally in the Scottsdale–Paradise Valley area. The source of these urban nesting birds is unknown but possibly from several pairs introduced in the 1980s to lakes at Turf Paradise in northwest Phoenix. Unconfirmed reports of local summering birds at lakes and ponds in nearby Sun City, may also indicate possible nesting.

Canada Geese provide nationwide hunting opportunities, which are important from a social and economic standpoint. This may have been a reason for introducing the birds to Arizona. However, burgeoning Canada Geese populations in many urban areas around the country have become serious nuisances and are locally causing habitat and agriculture damage. It is unknown if the current resident urban population in the greater Phoenix area will persist and grow into a problem as well.

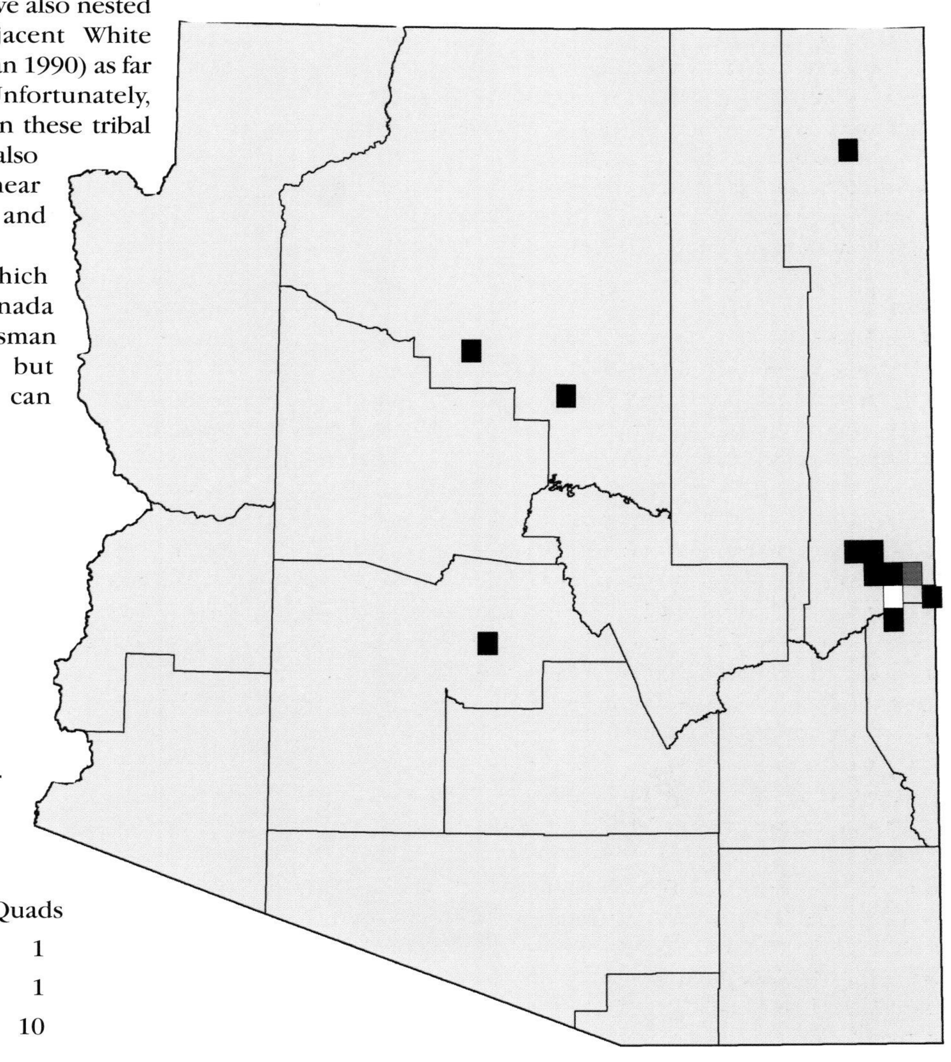

Canada Goose Breeding Evidence Reported in 5 (<1%) of 1834 priority blocks

	Blocks	Quads
Possible	1 (20%)	1
Probable	0 (0%)	1
Confirmed	4 (80%)	10

Wood Duck

by Troy E. Corman *Aix sponsa*

With amazing speed and agility, Wood Duck pairs thread their way through riparian woodlands enroute to their lofty nest tree cavities. Found nesting in Arizona only relatively recently, the gaudy, iridescent drake is a stunningly beautiful duck. He is often found resting or preening from a low limb or log above a serene wooded pond or stream.

JIM BURNS

HABITAT

Across their range, Wood Ducks prefer wooded, freshwater habitats with an abundance of cover. In Arizona, these attractive ducks nest along permanent ponds, marshes, and lakes, as well as slower sections of streams and rivers lined by large trees for nesting. Dominant riparian trees within their limited breeding range in Arizona are Arizona sycamore, Fremont cottonwood, velvet ash, Goodding willow, and Arizona alder. Whenever possible, Wood Ducks avoid large areas of open water, preferring the cover along shaded edges among downed timber and water-tolerant shrubs including buttonbush and young willows. Areas of emergent wetland vegetation are also frequently encountered at Wood Duck nesting locations in Arizona and include cattails, bulrush, and watercress. Vegetative cover and an abundant aquatic plant and invertebrate food base close to nesting sites are essential for successful rearing of broods (Hepp and Bellrose 1995).

BREEDING

Throughout Arizona, Wood Ducks are most frequently encountered in the fall and winter, but typically remain sparse and local in their distribution. Although during winter and early spring, concentrations of 50–100+ individuals have recently been observed near breeding areas along the upper Verde River. Away from nesting areas, spring migrants are primarily observed from late March and April, with stragglers in May and rarely into early June. Most Wood Ducks are paired by winter and a male defending his mate was observed briefly chasing another drake on 2 April. Due to their fairly recent nesting status in Arizona and very local distribution, atlasers collected little nesting information. Based on the dates of several atlas and other observations of duckling broods, egg laying is initiated by late March to mid-April in Arizona. Atlasers observed downy ducklings by 5 May. Most young broods in the state are noted in May, but a female with small ducklings was observed on 19 June. The latest confirmation during the atlas was an observation of a hen with her brood on 26 July. In Arizona, early fall migrants are noted by late September, with a notable increase in observations in October and November.

Breeding Habitats

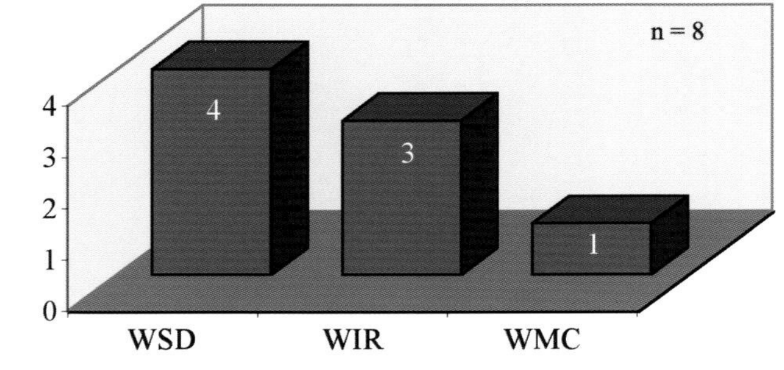

Habitat Codes

These small ducks are typically tree cavity nesters and the male accompanies the female in search of the nest, but he plays no role in selection (Bellrose 1976). Most cavities suitable for Wood Ducks develop when branches break and permit subsequent heart rot of the trunk (Soulliere 1990). In Arizona, the few nests discovered have been in Arizona sycamore or Fremont cottonwood. One brood near Camp Verde was also hatched from a nest box placed in the middle of a small wooded pond. No nesting cavities were discovered by altasers, but of 375 nests measured in eastern North America, the average cavity height was 23.9 ft (7.3 m) and ranged from 2–56.8 ft (0.6–17.3 m) above the ground or water surface (Soulliere 1990).

Once selected, the female lines the nest with down taken from her breast beginning about midway through egg-laying (Hepp and Bellrose 1995). Most clutches contain 9–12 eggs, but egg dumping is common in this species and it is not unusual to find 20+ eggs in a single nest. One brood observed near the Page Springs Fish Hatchery on 6 May 2001 contained 14 ducklings (R. Radd pers. comm.). Only the female incubates the eggs, which hatch in approximately 30 days. Cool ambient temperatures, frequent disturbance of the females, and large clutches may lengthen the incubation period (Hepp et al. 1990). Ducklings usually leap from the nest cavity in the morning approximately 24 hours after hatching. The young are coaxed from the nest after a short period of calling by the female below. The broods frequently travel long distances immediately after leaving the nest, with some known to move as much as 3 mi (4.8 km) within the first two days (Smith and Flake 1985). The length of time hens stay with their broods averages 4–5 weeks, but can range to 8 weeks (Hepp and Bellrose 1995). Wood Ducks frequently renest if earlier attempts have failed and southern populations regularly produce two broods in a single breeding season.

DISTRIBUTION AND STATUS

Wood Ducks nest throughout the eastern United States and southern Canada. They nest quite locally in the Great Plains, arid Southwest, and Great Basin regions of the United States and more commonly in the Pacific northwest south through California. Phillips et al. (1964) considered Wood Ducks a rare visitor nearly statewide in Arizona, with records primarily in fall and winter. Wood Duck observations in Arizona steadily increased through the 1970s including the number of mid-summer records. This also coincided well with a significant increase of Wood Duck detections on Breeding Bird Survey routes in North America from 1966–1987 (Sauer and Droege 1990). They were first found nesting in Arizona on Peck's Lake near Clarkdale on 11 July 1975 when a hen with two young was observed (Brown 1985). Wood Ducks were later discovered nesting near Camp Verde, when a female was observed with nine newly hatched ducklings on 29 May 1981. In 1984, Wood Ducks were also confirmed nesting along Granite Creek near Prescott and along lower Oak Creek near Cornville and Page Springs (Witzeman and Stejskal 1984). Breeding season records within the lower Colorado River Valley include a pair at Imperial National Wildlife Refuge on 25 June 1977 and a pair observed among flooded cottonwoods at the Bill Williams River delta on 12 May 1982 (Rosenberg et al. 1991).

Atlasers found Wood Ducks nesting only in Yavapai County at elevations ranging primarily from 3100–5150 ft (945–1570 m), locally down to 2150 ft (655 m). Most observations came from the upper Verde River from Clarkdale, Cottonwood, Bridgeport, and downstream to Camp Verde. This includes adjacent Peck's Lake and Tavasci Marsh. One hen with larger ducklings was also discovered as far downstream on the Verde River to near the Sycamore Creek confluence just upstream of Horseshoe Reservoir. Atlasers frequently reported nesting Wood Ducks along lower Oak Creek from near Sedona, and especially near Page Springs and Cornville. When water levels are sufficient, atlasers also found Wood Ducks nesting periodically along Granite Creek near Watson Lake just north of Prescott.

Atlas data suggests that Arizona's nesting Wood Duck population has steadily increased and expanded during the past two decades. There are many other seemingly appropriate nesting locations in central and southern Arizona that may some day harbor future broods of these splendid little ducks.

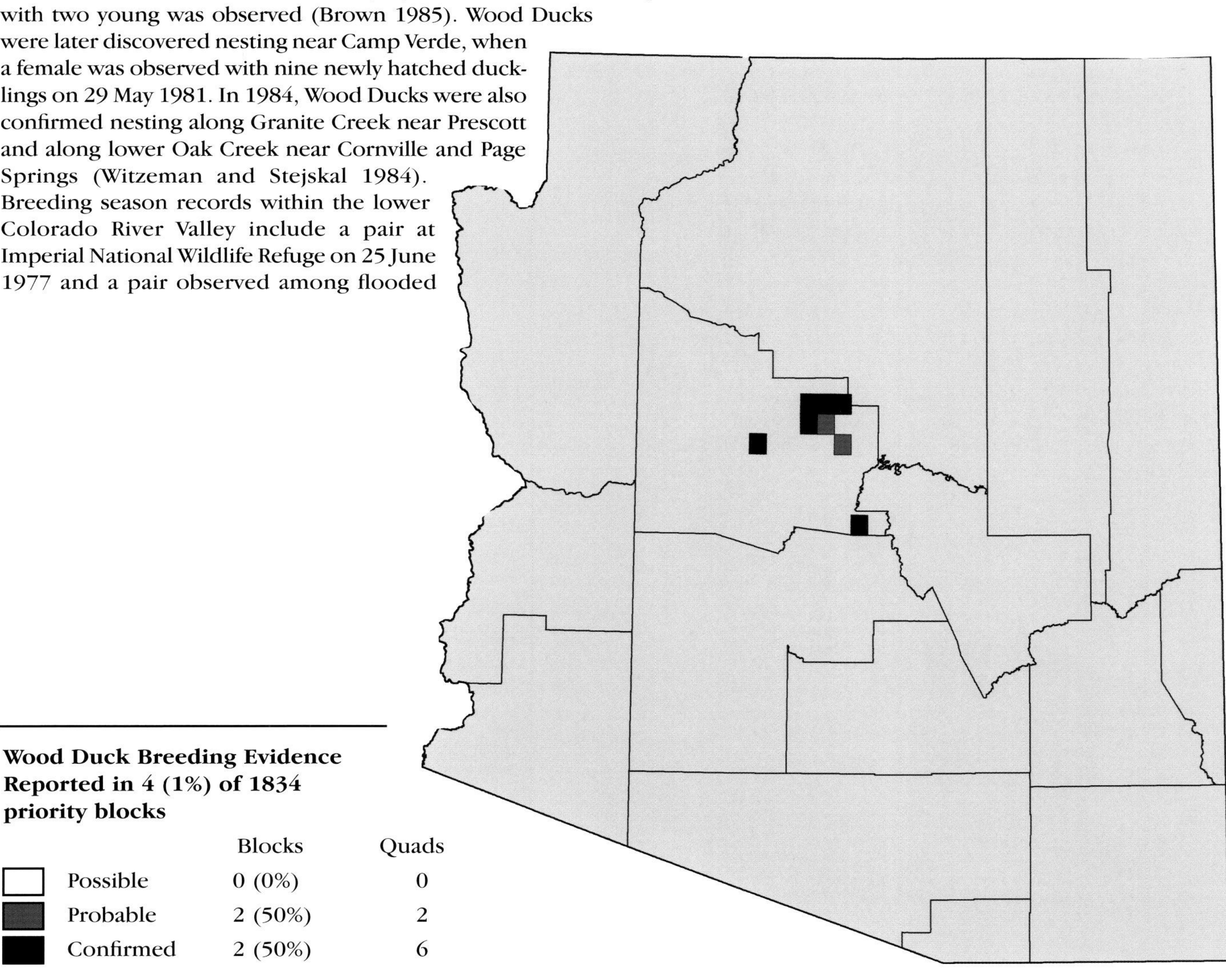

Wood Duck Breeding Evidence Reported in 4 (1%) of 1834 priority blocks

	Blocks	Quads
Possible	0 (0%)	0
Probable	2 (50%)	2
Confirmed	2 (50%)	6

Gadwall

by Linden Piest *Anas strepera*

Despite the lack of bright plumage colors displayed by males of most other ducks, Gadwalls are often referred to as "handsome" because of their intricate patterns of speckling and fine barring. Their diet tends to be more vegetarian than most other dabbling ducks, and they prefer to feed in deeper water with an abundance of aquatic plants.

BRUCE TAUBERT

HABITAT

Gadwalls in North America nest primarily in seasonal and semi-permanent marshes in prairies, parklands, and sub-Arctic deltas (Leschak et al. 1997). In Arizona, the species nests mostly at mid and high-elevations where it can find its preferred combination of productive marshes and lake edges in proximity to dense nesting cover on uplands or islands. Atlasers reported nearly 96 percent of all observations of Gadwalls from this habitat (*n* = 23). Hardstem bulrush or sedge usually dominates wetland vegetation at occupied locations in Arizona (Brown 1985). Gadwalls favor islands for nesting and have benefited from islands constructed for this purpose in the Apache–Sitgreaves National Forest. Vegetation availability and density are greater considerations for nest site selection than species composition (Bellrose 1980). In Arizona, vegetation at Gadwall nests studied in and near the White Mountains was primarily tall wheatgrass or beaked sedge (Piest 1982, Piest and Sowls 1985). Brood-rearing habitat consists of emergent vegetation such as cattails, bulrush, or sedge to provide escape cover, and open water with submerged vegetation providing food for the ducklings (Leschack et al 1997).

BREEDING

In regions where water remains open, Gadwalls are locally common winter residents in Arizona. Spring migration begins in February and March, with late migrants into early May or even later. Pair formation occurs during fall migration (Leschack et al. 1997), earlier than in most other species of dabbling ducks. Gadwalls arrive on their nesting grounds approximately one month prior to nesting. An atlaser reported an adult with ducklings on 13 May along the lower Colorado River, suggesting local nesting may begin by early April at lower elevations in Arizona. If the identity of this brood was correct, this is much earlier than reported by others (Leschack et al. 1997). Elsewhere in the state however, most evidence suggests nesting activity begins in May or later. At higher elevations, where most Gadwalls in the state nest, atlasers noted hens with ducklings from 7 June–26 July. A study in the White Mountains found the peak of nesting there to occur in June and July, later than for other dabbling ducks (Piest 1982). Early migrants typically begin arriving in nonbreeding areas of Arizona by mid-August.

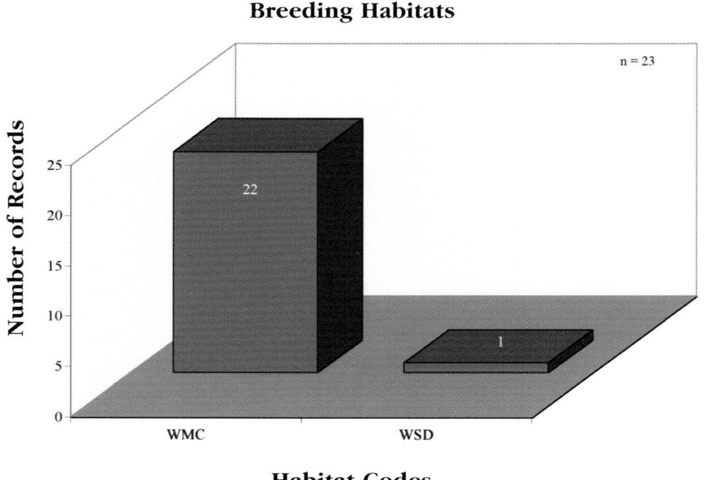

Nests are typically within 500 ft (152 m) of water or, when on islands, within a few yards depending on island size and density of nests (Leschack et al. 1997). Gadwalls are more selective of secure nesting sites than other ducks, preferring islands over adjacent uplands and typically in dense brush, forbs, and grasses in dry areas (Bellrose 1980, Hines and Mitchell 1983). As a result of these preferences, nest success of this species often exceeds that of all other dabbling ducks (Bellrose 1980).

Leschack et al. (1997) compiled much of the following natural history information. Only the Gadwall hen incubates the average clutch of 10 eggs, which can range from 7–12. Males occasionally remain near the female during the 26 days she is incubating, but most males desert their mate after the clutch is completed. Gadwall broods depart the nest within 24–36 hours after hatching, following the hen to nearby brood-rearing habitat. Young are capable of flight in approximately 50 days, but they may remain with the hen for an additional week or more. Renesting usually occurs if the first clutch is destroyed, but there are no reports of two broods being raised.

DISTRIBUTION AND STATUS

Gadwalls occur over much of the middle latitudes of North America and Eurasia. In western United States, they breed south to California, Arizona, and New Mexico. In North America, this duck nests primarily within the Great Plains, Great Basin, and prairie parklands. Arizona is at the southwest limit of it nesting range, and nesting here occurs only sparingly. This is evidenced by the fact that atlasers recorded only 11 confirmations for this species, 5 of which were casual observations.

Prior to the Atlas project, Gadwalls were known to nest at high elevation marshes in the White Mountains (Piest 1982), the Mogollon Rim near Show Low (Piest and Sowls 1985), and Anderson Mesa near Flagstaff (Myers 1982). Elsewhere in the state, Gadwalls have previously been noted nesting sparsely and irregularly in the lower Colorado River Valley at Topock Marsh and below Imperial Dam (Rosenberg et al 1991), and Pipe Spring National Monument (Monson 1981).

During the atlas, most confirmed records were from high elevation lakes and marshes in the White Mountain region. Elsewhere, duckling broods were detected at Martinez Lake at an elevation of 196 ft (60 m) and at previously unreported locations near Prescott, Safford, and Nogales. Most Gadwall observations during the atlas were at elevations from approximately 5000–9200 ft (1524–2804 m) north of the Mogollon Rim. Jacobs (1986) also noted that these ducks nest quite commonly at most of the larger lakes on Navajo Tribal lands and specifically documented them nesting at Ganado, Moaning, and Tsaile lakes. Within this region, atlasers observed Gadwall pairs or individuals at Many Farms, Ganado, and Cow Springs lakes.

More thorough surveys of wetlands and lakes on the Colorado Plateau (north of the Mogollon Rim) in Arizona may reveal Gadwalls are sparse yet a more widespread nesting species than atlas data suggest.

Drought or near-drought conditions plagued Arizona during much of the atlas and nesting habitat conditions may have been inadequate during years when local surveys were conducted. Several successive years of low precipitation greatly reduced the available nesting habitat, as many lakes and marshes previously occupied by Gadwalls dried during the nesting season.

Wetlands that support Gadwall nesting in Arizona are located primarily on public lands and hence receive a measure of protection from development. Habitat deterioration, though, can result from subnormal precipitation and runoff, reservoir depletion to satisfy downstream water users, and overgrazing by livestock and elk. Gadwalls respond well to habitat improvements that include the creation of nesting islands and the establishment of dense nesting cover. Their high nesting success and their tendency for adult and first-year hens to return to previous nesting areas can result in a rapid response to new or improved habitats (Duebbert 1966). Numbers of Gadwall nests at Pintail Lake near Show Low, which was created in 1979 from treated sewage and included densely-vegetated nesting islands, increased from 7 in 1980 to 53 in 1982 (Piest and Sowls 1985).

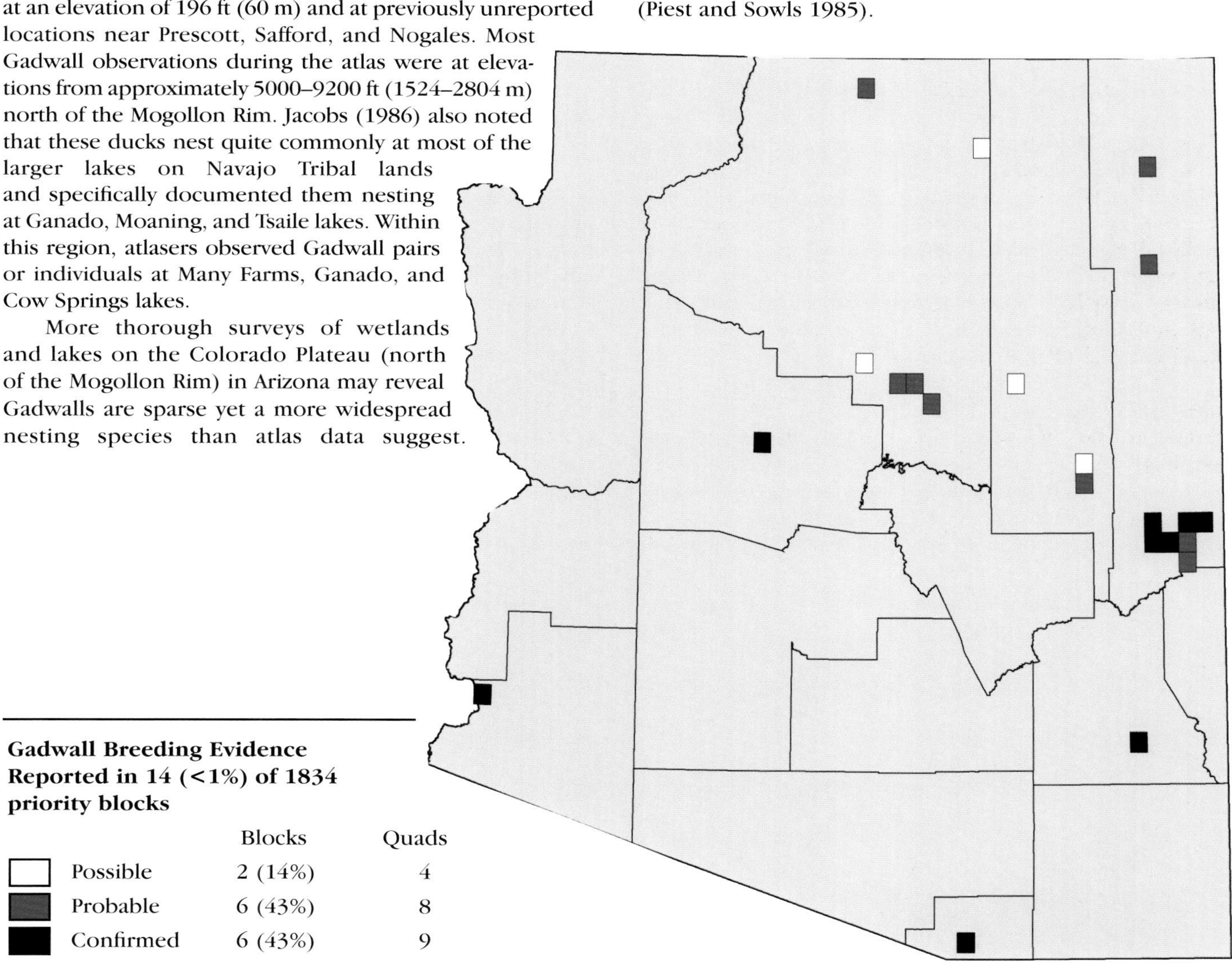

Gadwall Breeding Evidence Reported in 14 (<1%) of 1834 priority blocks

	Blocks	Quads
Possible	2 (14%)	4
Probable	6 (43%)	8
Confirmed	6 (43%)	9

Mallard

by Troy E. Corman *Anas platyrhynchos*

The most widespread nesting duck in Arizona, breeding Mallards come in two distinct races in the state. The darker Mexican Ducks (*A.p. diazi*) are primarily residents in southeastern Arizona, where they usually greatly outnumber typical Mallards during the nesting season.

GEORGE ANDREJKO

HABITAT

Most wetland habitats in Arizona can harbor nesting Mallards. Important breeding habitat requirements include nearby dense vegetation in which to conceal their nests and shallow water with and abundance of food and cover for brooding ducklings. As expected, atlasers encountered Mallards most commonly (41 percent of all records) in aquatic habitats with marshes, including cienegas, and shorelines of lakes, ponds, rivers, and streams ($n = 229$). An additional 17 percent of the observations were reported from rural aquatic habitats, such as stock ponds, earthen tanks, wastewater ponds, drainage ditches, canals, and irrigation runoff ponds. Drainages and ponds dominated by thickets and stands of Fremont cottonwood, Gooding willow, mesquite, and seepwillow also accounted for 12 percent of the atlas records. Other habitat supporting nesting Mallards included drainages dominated by Arizona sycamore or tamarisk and in urban lakes and ponds.

Along with rivers and streams, Mexican Ducks and their broods were also found at cienegas, alkali ponds, and man-made stock ponds basically surrounded by semiarid grasslands. Occasionally within the upper San Pedro River valley, Mexican Ducks, presumably in search of nest sites, have been observed wandering along dusty, back roads through upland habitat of creosote and dry washes more than 0.5 mi (0.8 km) from the nearest water.

BREEDING

Mallards are common wintering ducks throughout Arizona where water remains open. Mexican Ducks move around locally through the year, but they tend not to be as migratory as typical Mallards. Due to their limited seasonal movements, many Mexican Duck pairs bond or rebond by as early as September, prior to the arrival of the majority of the typical Mallards. That many Mexican Ducks are paired by early fall tends to help reproductively isolate them from typical Mallards which pair later in the fall and winter (Brown 1985), although hybrids are frequently observed. The earliest confirmation noted by atlasers was the observation of a typical Mallard hen with ducklings along the lower Salt River southwest of Phoenix on 7 April. This suggests incubation initiation no later than early March. The earliest confirmation for Mexican Ducks was a nest with eggs discovered on 25 April south of Safford. Based on atlas data, peak nesting activity for most Mallard population in Arizona occurs from early May through mid-June, slightly later at higher elevations. Atlasers reported adults with dependent young as late as 21 August. In the Sulphur Springs Valley, Mexican Ducks with downy ducklings have been observed as late as mid-September (Swarbrick 1975), which is well past when most atlas surveys had ended.

After a nesting territory is established, the pair reconnoiters a nest site by flying low over the terrain (Bellrose 1976). The nest is usually constructed on the ground within 328 ft (100 m) of the water's edge and is typically concealed in or under dense vegetation (Brown 1985). Marsh vegetation including cattails, bulrushes, and sedges approximately 24 in. (60 cm) high appears to be preferred nesting sites in

Mallard Breeding Habitats

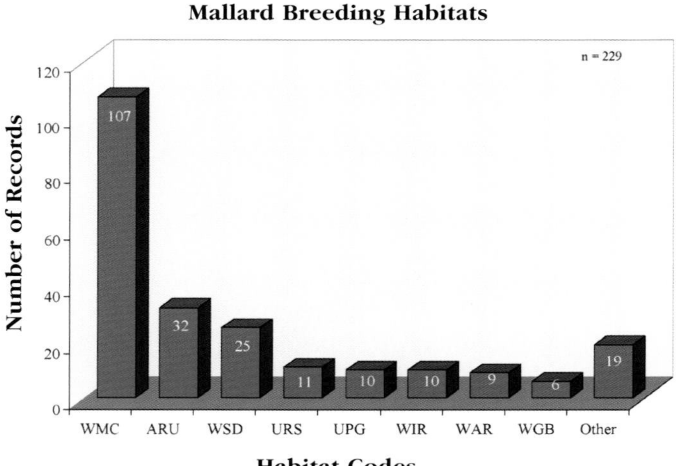

Mallard Breeding Phenology

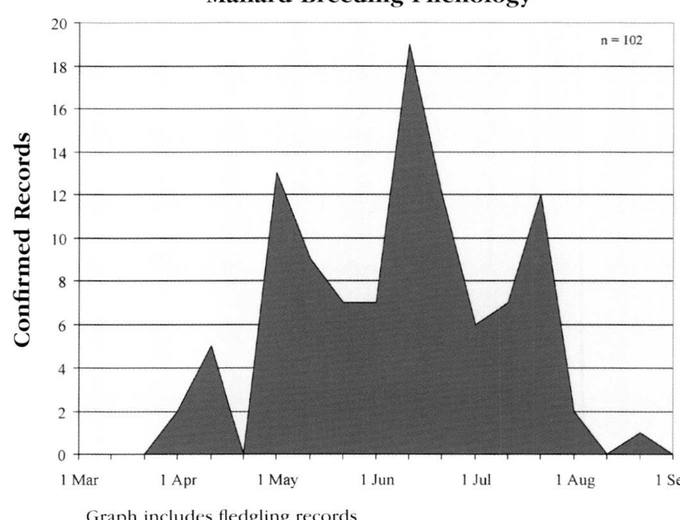

Graph includes fledgling records

Mexican Duck

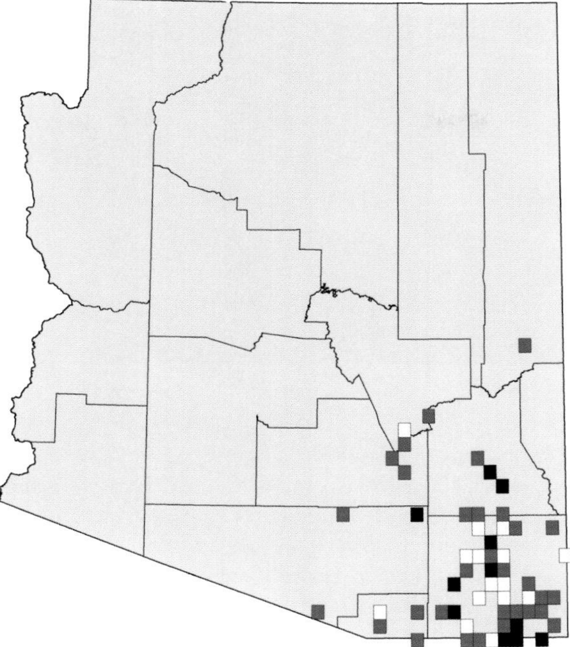

valleys. Mexican Ducks had also been found nesting along the upper San Pedro River, the San Raphael Valley, and in the White Mountains (Brown 1985).

Atlasers found Mallards nesting locally in appropriate habitat throughout Arizona, at elevations ranging from 80–9500 ft (24–2896 m). The concentration of records in and around the greater Phoenix area may be influence by some feral domestic stock. Nesting Mallards were found more regularly during the atlas project along the lower Colorado River and locally within the upper Grand Canyon, than the previous casual nesting status would suggest (Brown et al. 1987, Rosenberg et al. 1991). Drought conditions in Arizona throughout much of the atlas period often greatly reduced the availability of nesting sites for Mallards and other ducks. This was especially true above the Mogollon Rim as many shallow lakes and ponds the waterfowl depended on eventually dried.

Atlasers reported Mexican Ducks throughout much of Cochise County, north into Graham County in the San Simon River drainage and along the Gila River to at least Thatcher. Mexican Ducks were also discovered fairly regularly along the lower San Pedro River to its confluence with the Gila River at Winkelman, and then up the Gila River and at one location along the San Carlos River. This race was reported as far west as the Buenos Aires National Wildlife Refuge, in Tucson, and near Marana.

Arizona (Brown 1985). Typical clutch size for Mallards is 8–10 eggs (range 1–13), which the female incubates for approximately 28 days (Drilling et al. 2002). Ducklings remain with the hen until they can fly in approximately 52–70 days (Drilling et al. 2002). Typically only one brood is produced per season. Mallards will commonly renest if earlier nesting attempts fail.

DISTRIBUTION AND STATUS

In North America, Mallards breed from Alaska and Canada, south through western United States and in the East, south to Oklahoma and through the Ohio River valley to Virginia. Mexican Ducks breed from southern Arizona and New Mexico to central Mexico. Phillips et al. (1964) noted that typical Mallards breed on suitable ponds throughout Arizona, locally in the lower Colorado River Valley, and formally near Phoenix. Mallards were also common summer residents on the Mogollon Plateau, north on Navajo Tribal lands to Kayenta and probably east in the Lukachukai Mountains. Monson and Phillips (1981) described the breeding distribution of the Mexican Duck as a local resident in southeastern Arizona in the Sulphur Springs (from Willcox south), San Simon, and San Bernardino

Mallard

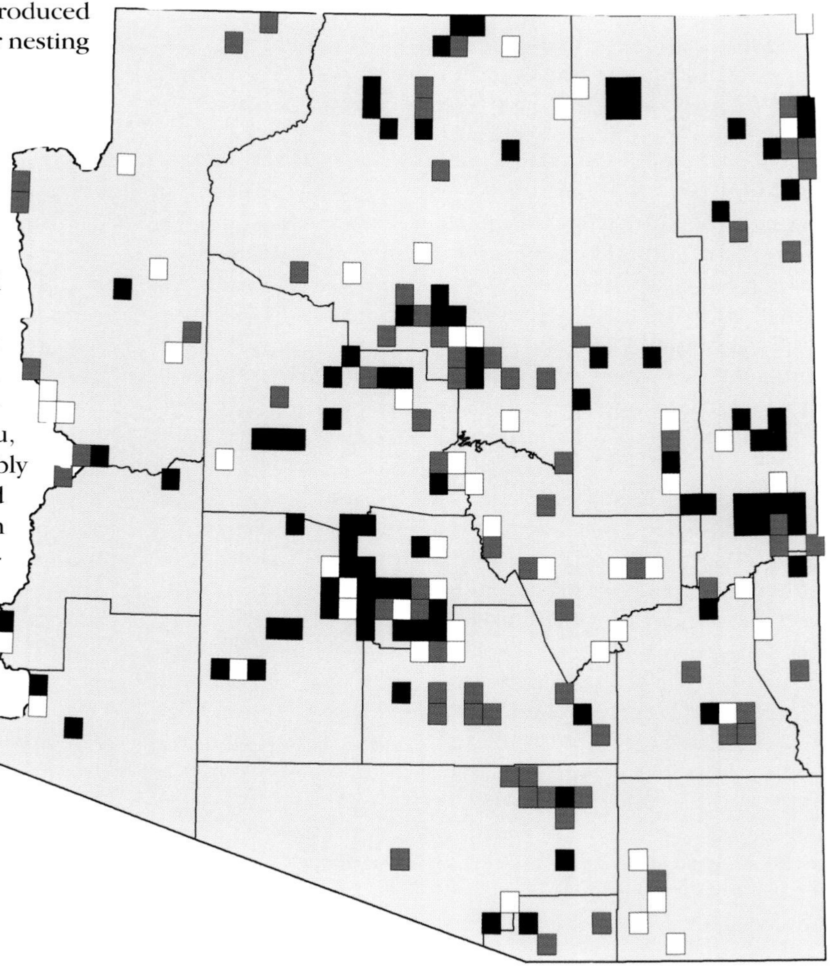

Mallard Breeding Evidence Reported in 170 (9%) of 1834 priority blocks

	Blocks	Quads
Possible	41 (24%)	51
Probable	61 (36%)	69
Confirmed	68 (40%)	88

Blue-winged Teal

by Cathryn Wise-Gervais *Anas discors*

Blue-winged Teal are small, attractive ducks that prefer warm climates, and most individuals migrate south of the United States for the fall and early winter months. These petite ducks are the least common of the teal in Arizona and forage in very shallow water, primarily on invertebrates and seeds. Unlike other dabbling ducks, Blue-winged Teal rarely "upend."

HABITAT

Throughout their range, Blue-winged Teal are most commonly observed in shallow freshwater locations. All atlas sightings were noted in marshes, ponds, and lake edges dominated by stands of cattails, bulrush, reeds, sedges, and other aquatic plants. These teal favor shallow ponds with abundant invertebrates and early in the spring pairs mostly use temporary and seasonal wetlands but later shift to semi-permanent wetlands (Swainson et al. 1974). This species is considered a "prairie nester" that favors wetlands adjacent to open grassy areas for nesting. Blue-winged Teal are closely related to Cinnamon Teal and the two select similar breeding habitats. During migration, Blue-winged Teals moving through Arizona can be observed in various wetland habitats, including on irrigation storage ponds and at wastewater treatment facilities.

BREEDING

In Arizona, northbound Blue-winged Teals typically begin arriving by mid-February, but occasionally by early January (Monson and Phillips 1981). Peak passage is in March and April, with stragglers observed into mid-May. Like other small dabbling ducks that breed in North America, Blue-winged Teal pair on their wintering grounds or as they initiate migration in early spring (Rohwer et al. 2002).

Due to their local breeding status in Arizona there is little information on Blue-winged Teals nesting biology in the state. In 1983, a pair was reported with ducklings on 10 May at a pond near the Salt River in Phoenix (Witzeman et al. 1997), indicating nest initiation in early to mid-April. If accurate, this was a highly unusual lowland nesting record for Arizona and an exceptionally early nesting date for the species. Across their range, Blue-winged Teal egg dates range from late April through late August, with a peak from mid-May through mid-July (Rohwer et al. 2002). Prior to the atlas, a study in the White Mountains reported that the earliest nest initiation date for Blue-winged Teal was not until 11 June, with broods observed into August (L. Piest pers. comm.). The only confirmed atlas record for Blue-winged Teals was a sighting of a brood on 25 July. Otherwise, these teals were noted in suitable breeding habitat from 4 June–26 July. Fall migration dates for this species have been difficult to ascertain because females and eclipse plumaged males closely resemble the more commonly encountered Cinnamon Teal (Rosenberg et al. 1991). In Arizona, some early migrants have been observers in early to mid-July, but most begin to pass through from mid-August through October, with stragglers noted into November.

Blue-winged Teal nests are typically well-concealed structures comprised of dried grasses and finer materials such as down. Nests are often covered from above by arching vegetation (Glover 1956), and are typically placed in upland sites, sometimes a considerable distance from water (Rohwer et al. 2002). The female Blue-winged Teal prospects for nest sites 1–3 days prior to laying the first egg and most nests are constructed on the first day of laying (Rohwer et al. 2002).

The average clutch size for Blue-winged Teals is 10 eggs (range 6–14), and females incubate these for approximately 23–24 days (Rohwer et al. 2002). Male Blue-winged Teal abandon their mates toward the end of the incubation period (Kaufman 1996). Upon hatching, the brood may remain in the nest for up to 24 hours, but some broods depart as soon as the ducklings dry (Rohwer et al. 2002). The young are precocial and are able to swim and feed themselves almost immediately. Most hens attend to their broods until the ducklings are near the flight stage of 35–44 days of age (Rohwer et al. 2002). Before this time, the female will perform broken-wing displays to distract predators and humans from her young. Blue-winged Teal rear only one brood per season, but will renest if earlier attempts have failed. It is of interest that Blue-winged Teal groups migrating in fall often consist only of young birds, indicating that migration routes are inherent rather than learned (Kaufman 1996).

DISTRIBUTION AND STATUS

Blue-winged Teals breed throughout Canada, eastern Alaska, as well as in the northern and central United States. In the southwest, this species nests regularly in New Mexico, west Texas, and only sparingly in Arizona. Mearns (1890) observed Blue-winged Teals in May and June on lakes above the

Mogollon Rim where he suspected them of breeding. Prior to the atlas, this rare teal had also been documented nesting in the White Mountains (Goldman 1926, Fleming 1959, Piest 1981), on Anderson Mesa southwest of Flagstaff (Myers 1982), and once in Chino Valley (Monson and Phillips 1981).

Atlasers encountered few Blue-winged Teals in appropriate nesting habitat. All were in east-central Arizona at elevations ranging from 5000–9000 ft (524–2743 m), and half of atlas records were from the White Mountain region from near Eagar to Big Lake. Atlasers also observed a pair of Blue-winged Teal at Pintail Lake north of Show Low, where they have nested in the past (Piest and Sowls 1985).

Atlasers did not report Blue-winged Teal at several locations north of the Mogollon Rim that previously had small nesting populations, including on Anderson Mesa. It is likely that although the birds may have been present, they were missed due to the difficulty in separating female and their broods from the much more common Cinnamon Teal. At Pintail Lake, Piest and Sowls (1985) found that based on censuses of breeding pairs, approximately 4 percent of 189 Cinnamon Teal nests they located from 1980–1982 were likely Blue-winged Teal nests. As with other waterfowl in Arizona, drought conditions throughout much of the atlas period probably limited nesting and brood-rearing habitat greatly as well. In North Dakota, Stewart and Kantrud (1974) found that in dry years when temporary and seasonal wetlands are greatly reduced, breeding-pair density of Blue-winged Teals dropped dramatically.

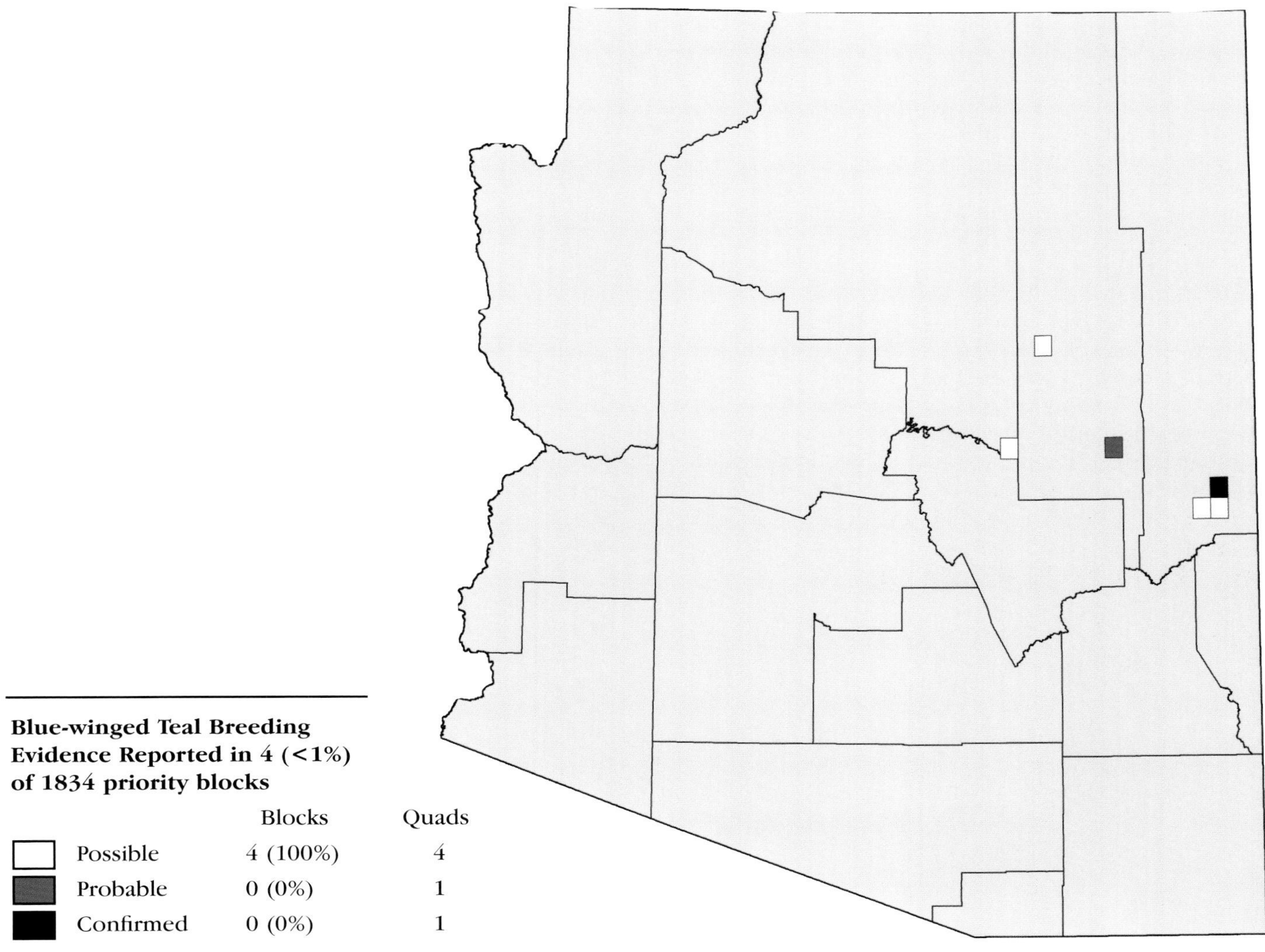

Blue-winged Teal Breeding Evidence Reported in 4 (<1%) of 1834 priority blocks

	Blocks	Quads
Possible	4 (100%)	4
Probable	0 (0%)	1
Confirmed	0 (0%)	1

Cinnamon Teal

by Cathryn Wise-Gervais *Anas cyanoptera*

These short distance migrants are named for the ruby-eyed drake's rich chestnut plumage. Cinnamon Teal are one of the earliest "spring" arrivals in southern Arizona, typically appearing in mid-winter. Most of these ducks migrate south in early fall, so are not hunted as often as other teal species.

JIM BURNS

HABITAT

This attractive dabbling duck is found in a wide variety of freshwater wetlands with well-developed stands of emergent vegetation. In general, Cinnamon Teal spend much of their time in shallower areas, foraging and loafing among flooded and wetland vegetation. In Arizona, the breeding density of Cinnamon Teal is determined by wetland size and habitat diversity (Gammonley 1996). Atlasers reported 77 percent of all records from marshes and ponds, as well as from the shores of lakes, reservoirs, and slow-moving rivers with stands of cattail, bulrush, sedge, and other aquatic plants (n = 58). Similarly, Gammonley (1996) noted that adults with ducklings use seasonal and semipermanent wetlands with abundant emergent cover to rear their broods. Another 13 percent of records were from rural settings including vegetated wastewater ponds, canals, and irrigation holding ponds. Only a few Cinnamon Teal observations were from drainages with young stands of cottonwood and willow or dominated by exotic tamarisk.

BREEDING

Some Cinnamon Teal pairs begin arriving in southern Arizona by early January, with numbers steadily increasing through February and March. These teal continue to migrate northward into mid-May. Cinnamon Teals form pairs on their wintering grounds or during migration. The actual timing of nest initiation varies considerably with latitude, elevation, and annual weather conditions (Gammonley 1996). In Arizona studies, Myers (1982) and Piest (1981) found the earliest nest initiation for Cinnamon Teals in mid-April, with nesting activity continuing through early August. The earliest atlas confirmation for this species was a hen with ducklings on 21 May. By backdating this brood, we can estimate a nest initiation period in late April, in keeping with the finding of Myers and Piest. The limited data obtained during the atlas period suggests that the peak breeding period for Cinnamon Teal in Arizona is from mid- to late June. Myers (1982) reported that the peak nesting initiation time on Anderson Mesa southeast of Flagstaff was the last week in June, with most broods hatching from early July through mid-August. The latest dependent brood reported by atlasers was on 12 August. In Arizona, early southbound migrants appear in late July, peak in August and early September, and only stragglers are noted after early October.

Cinnamon Teal nest in grass clumps or in grass-like emergent vegetation such as tall wheatgrass, foxtail barley, spikerush, bulrush, three-square, and saltgrass (Brown 1985). The female selects the nest site, which is usually close to water. Atlasers did not locate any active Cinnamon Teal nests, but during another Arizona study, researchers found that 44 percent (n = 57) of the Cinnamon Teal nests they located were less than 33 ft (10 m) from water (Myers 1982). The female builds the nest by scraping a hollow depression, then lining it with dead grasses and other materials (Palmer 1976). Nests are often placed amidst dry or dead vegetation that provide good cover from all sides.

The typical Cinnamon Teal clutch in Arizona consists of 8 eggs, with a range of 4–12 eggs (Myers 1982). Males typically abandon their mates by the third week of incubation and have no role in caring for the female or young (Oring 1964). Females incubate for between 21 and 25 days, but take short breaks to feed, generally in the afternoon (Gammonley 1996). When flushed from the nest, females will perform a distraction display by calling loudly and feigning injury (Gammonly 1996). The young usually leave the nest within 24 hours of hatching and can feed themselves the first day by pecking food items from the water's surface. The ducklings fledge at approximately 49 days old, but remain close to the hen until this time (Gammonly 1996).

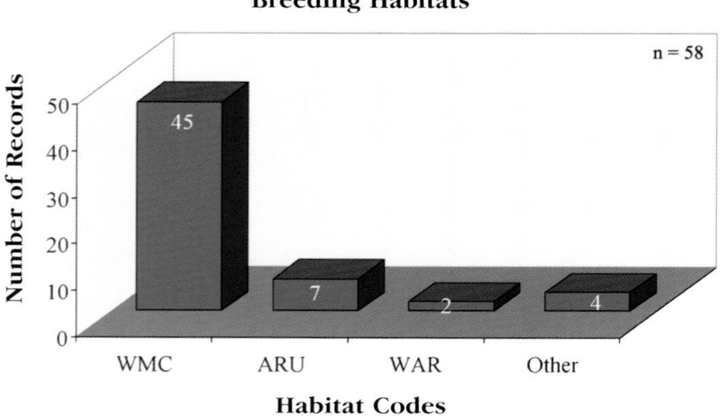

Breeding Phenology

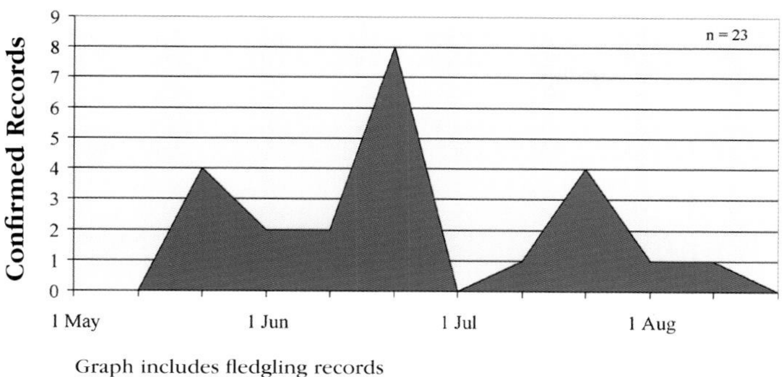

Graph includes fledgling records

DISTRIBUTION

Cinnamon Teal are found throughout western North America and there are disjunct breeding races in South America. Northern populations breed from central Alberta south through the central highlands of Mexico, and from eastern Colorado to the Pacific coast.

In Arizona, Cinnamon Teals are found nesting at a fairly wide range of elevations. Brown (1985) noted that most breeding activity in Arizona occurs primarily above the Mogollon Rim, on the San Francisco Plateau, in the White Mountains, and sparsely southward (Swarbrick 1975, Monson and Phillips 1981). Brown further commented that nests south and west of the Mogollon Rim are unusual. Atlasers confirmed Cinnamon Teals nesting in many region of Arizona, suggesting these duck have the potential to nest nearly statewide. Atlasers confirmed these teal nesting at elevations ranging from approximately 120 ft (37 m) near Yuma to 9300 ft (2835 m) in the White Mountains.

Atlasers verified that Cinnamon Teal continue to breed above the Mogollon Rim south and east of Flagstaff and regularly in the White Mountains region. Rosenberg et al. (1991) described these teal as sparse breeders along the lower Colorado River and adjacent lower Gila River from Parker south. Rosenberg et al. also suggested that Cinnamon Teal have bred successfully at Cibola National Wildlife Refuge since 1981, but atlasers did not find them there during the nesting season. Along the Colorado River, atlasers confirmed only Cinnamon Teal nesting near Yuma; potential nesting pairs were noted elsewhere in this area north to Imperial National Wildlife Refuge.

Cinnamon Teal are considered common summer residents on Navajo Tribal lands and are known to nest locally in the Chuska Mountains (Jabobs 1986). Atlasers confirmed their nesting status in the Chuska Mountains and obtained several early summer records from large lakes in this region including Cow Springs, Many Farms, and Ganado. Nesting remains unconfirmed at these regular summering locations, but more intensive surveys may reveal them nesting here in small numbers.

Atlasers confirmed that these attractive teals nest widely in the general Prescott region and locally in the Arlington Valley of the Gila River. Cinnamon Teal are apparently sparse and irregular nesters throughout southeastern Arizona, with breeding documented prior to the atlas at Willcox, Arivaca, and the Empire Cienega (Tucson Audubon Society 1995).

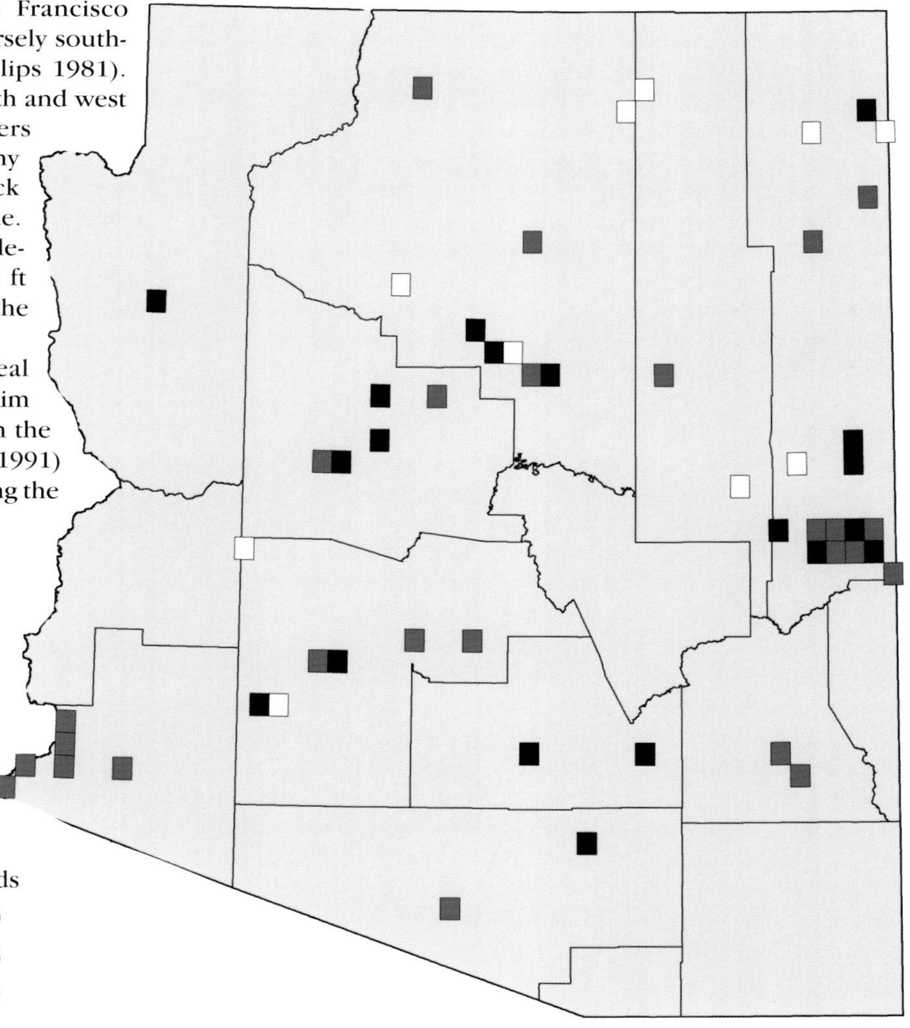

Cinnamon Teal Breeding Evidence Reported in 45 (2%) of 1834 priority blocks

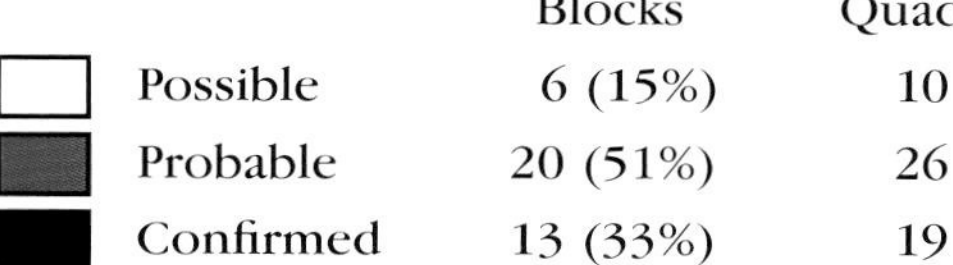

	Blocks	Quads
Possible	6 (15%)	10
Probable	20 (51%)	26
Confirmed	13 (33%)	19

Northern Pintail

by Linden Piest *Anas acuta*

BRUCE TAUBERT

The long and slim proportions of the Northern Pintail and its namesake plumage feature give this duck a strikingly elegant appearance whether on the wing or the water. It is one of our earliest nesting ducks and its arrival at high-elevation marshes signals winter's reluctant end and the beginning of another spring in Arizona's pine country.

HABITAT

Found on almost any body of water during migration and winter, intermittent high-elevation wetlands are preferred for nesting by Northern Pintails in Arizona (Myers 1982). Atlasers noted all records of this species in marshes and lake shores with an abundance of wetland vegetation. In the Flagstaff region, marshes used for brood-rearing by these ducks are typified by emergent plants such as hardstem bulrush, common spikerush, and smartweeds interspersed with some areas of open water. In the White Mountains, Northern Pintails nest at high elevation lakes and marshes, which are typically fairly small or comprise the shallow portions of larger lakes. Principal emergent plant species are beaked sedge, hardstem bulrush, northern mannagrass, and common spikerush. Wetlands at these elevations in Arizona are similar to those preferred by Northern Pintails much farther north in the United States and Canada. These northern habitats can be characterized as open country with shallow, seasonal, or intermittent wetlands with emergent vegetation and low upland cover (Austin and Miller 1995).

BREEDING

Since Northern Pintails winter throughout much of Arizona, it is difficult to determine when spring migrants begin passing through. Yet pairs and small groups begin appearing on non-wintering bodies of water in mid-January and February. They are infrequently observed in southern Arizona after mid-May and nonbreeders are noted occasionally throughout the summer. In Arizona, Northern Pintails begin arriving on their high elevation nesting grounds by late March and April (Brown 1985). Nest construction and egg-laying begins in early April in Arizona and peaks in May and June (Myers 1982, Piest 1982). Most broods are observed from early May through July. These dates are only a week or two earlier than those reported from across a remarkably wide portion of the species' North American range (Austin and Miller 1995). The only confirmed atlas record was a hen with ducklings observed on 25 June. Early fall migrants in Arizona—typically drakes and unsuccessful hens—begin appearing away from nesting areas by mid- to late July with a peak passage in late August and September.

Nests are always located on the ground, or rarely in vegetation over water (Austin and Miller 1995). In contrast to many other species of ducks, Northern Pintails select nest sites with low or sparse vegetation, sometimes on bare earth in stubble fields (Bellrose 1980). Meadows of residual grass or sedge are typical, but they may also nest in small patches of brush or dense cover, and a wide variety of vegetation types are used across its breeding range (Austin and Miller 1995). Little is known of nest site selection in Arizona, though Piest (1985) found 44 nests at Pintail Lake (a man-made wastewater marsh near Show Low) on islands dominated by dense stands of tall wheatgrass and yellow sweet clover. But Northern Pintails usually avoid islands and shorelines, preferring to nest on mainland uplands. They nest farther from water than other ducks. In shortgrass prairies, Duncan (1987) found most nests between 0.6–1.2 mi (1–2 km) from water, but some nests were nearly 2 mi (3.2 km) away from brood-rearing areas.

The female Northern Pintail constructs the nest and incubates her clutch of 3–12 eggs from 22–24 days (Austin and Miller 1995). Mean clutch size varies little, ranging only from 6.9 to 8.0 in multiple studies across its range (Austin and Miller 1995). Male Northern Pintails abandon their mates in early incubation and begin congregating in flocks in early to mid-June. Drakes typically depart the immediate breeding area by late June or mid-July (Austin and Miller 1995). Ducklings are led from the nest as soon as their down has dried. Because nests are often far from water, long overland movements of ducklings to wetland brood-rearing areas are common (Austin and Miller 1995). Hens attend their broods for 4–6 weeks following hatching and usually abandon their young when they are capable of flight. Flight stage is reached in 36–57 days. Only one brood is produced per season, but females may renest if the first clutch is destroyed (Bellrose 1980). Renesting after loss of nest seems related to availability and stability of wetlands, with the proportion of adults renesting greatest in years of good wetland condition and low to nonexistent in years of dry conditions (Austin and Miller 1995).

DISTRIBUTION AND STATUS

Northern Pintails are one of the most widespread species of waterfowl in the world. This species is circumpolar in its nesting distribution and winters as far south as Colombia, the south Pacific, Phillipines, India, and central Africa. These ducks breed across vast areas of northern North America with key areas in Alaska and the Prairie Pothole Region of south-central Canada and north-central United States (Bellrose 1980). Breeding populations from Arizona and southern California represent the southern extent of its breeding range. Nearly all nesting records of Northern Pintails in Arizona are from elevations ranging from approximately 5600–9300 ft (1707–2835 m).

Northern Pintails were confirmed nesting during the atlas project only on White Mountain Reservoir near Mount Baldy. Probable and possible breeding locations were recorded sparingly from above the Mogollon Rim at Mormon Lake southeast of Flagstaff east to Show Low and the White Mountain region. These records reflect the previous knowledge of this species' distribution. Northern Pintails were known to nest regularly in moderate numbers on Anderson Mesa near Flagstaff and more sparingly across the Mogollon Plateau and the White Mountains (Brown 1985). Jacobs (1986) also noted Northern Pintails nesting irregularly on Navajo Tribal lands at Ganado, Moaning, Tsaile, and Wheatfields lakes. The only observations of Northern Pintails nesting below the Colorado Plateau are single records near Wilcox Playa and in the Prescott region (Monson and Phillips 1981). Phillips et al. (1964) suggested this species became a more common nester in Arizona between 1920–1960.

Undoubtedly, Northern Pintails are a more widespread nesting species in northern Arizona during years of normal or above normal precipitation. Due to below normal precipitation plaguing Arizona throughout much of the atlas period, many wetlands previously occupied by nesting Northern Pintails were dried completely. Therefore, atlas data may reflect more of this elegant duck's breeding distribution in the state during prolonged drought conditions.

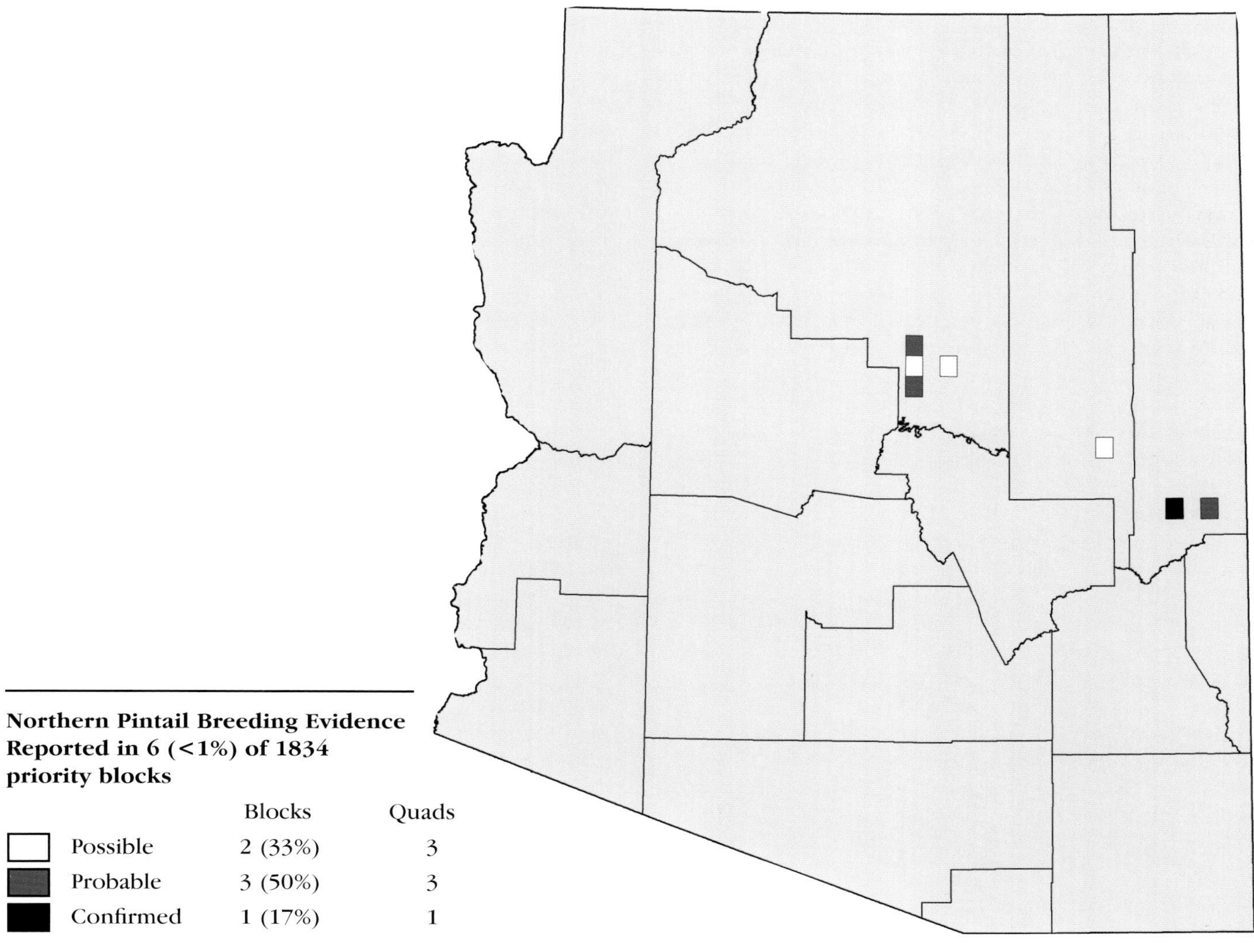

Northern Pintail Breeding Evidence Reported in 6 (<1%) of 1834 priority blocks

	Blocks	Quads
Possible	2 (33%)	3
Probable	3 (50%)	3
Confirmed	1 (17%)	1

Green-winged Teal

by Linden Piest *Anas crecca*

Perhaps an illusion resulting from their diminutive size, Green-winged Teals give the impression of being particularly fast and agile on the wing. These little dabbling ducks are one of the rarest of Arizona's nesting waterfowl, but they are widespread and common fall and winter visitors and are among the ducks most frequently taken by hunters.

BRUCE TAUBERT

HABITAT

In Arizona, Green-winged Teals nest almost exclusively at mid- or high elevation lakes or marshes. They are probably attracted to wetlands at these elevations because of the similarity of habitats there to those within their primary breeding range much farther north in the parklands of Canada. Johnsgard (1975) noted that Green-winged Teal reach their highest breeding density in wooded ponds of northern deciduous parklands often containing aspen. Atlasers found these ducks using similar habitat at beaver ponds and wetlands in mountains and on higher forested plateaus. Dominant vegetation often included sedge, thinleaf alder, and various species of scrub willows. Beyond this, habitat preferences of Green-winged Teal in Arizona are poorly known. Piest and Sowls (1985) found these teal also nesting regularly at a wastewater marsh surrounded by scattered juniper and grasslands near Show Low where, like several other duck species, they were apparently attracted by nesting islands and abundant aquatic invertebrates. Elsewhere in North America, Green-winged Teal occupy diverse habitats but generally prefer small and shallow permanent ponds near woodlands with fairly dense herbaceous nesting cover nearby. Ponds with an abundance of emergent vegetation are preferred to open water (Johnsgard 1978).

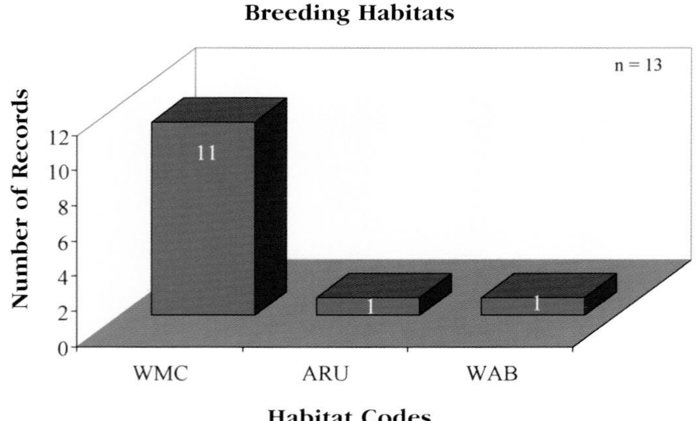

BREEDING

In Arizona, northward migration for Green-winged Teal begins by late January or February, with a peak in March and stragglers regularly into May. Their arrival in breeding areas in Arizona is unknown, but likely occurs soon after the lakes and ponds thaw in late February or March. As with most other species of ducks, Green-winged Teal typically arrive already paired and atlasers noted pairs in seemingly appropriate nesting habitat by mid-May. In Arizona, early nest initiation is in late April, while peak activity is not until late May at mid-elevations and mid- to late June at higher elevations (Piest 1982). Numbers of active nests, therefore, probably peak in June and July, respectively. The only confirmed atlas record was a hen performing a distraction display on 28 July, suggesting a brood nearby. These dates are similar to those reported elsewhere, mostly from northern parts of the continent (Johnson 1995). Some fall-migrating Green-winged Teal begin to appear in Arizona by early to mid-August, with a peak passage in September and October. Winter numbers continue to build into December as more northern localities freeze.

Nests are located on the ground, typically in sedge meadows, grasslands, brush thickets, or woods near a lake, pond, or slough (Bellrose 1980). But this duck is occasionally found nesting far from water, concealed at the base of some shrub, log, or clump of tree saplings. Nests are placed under heavy vegetative cover and are well concealed compared to nests of other dabbling ducks (Johnson 1995). Little is known of nest site selection in Arizona. Of the 53 nests that Piest and Sowls (1985) discovered at Pintail Lake, 36 were on islands dominated by dense stands of tall wheatgrass and yellow sweet clover, and 17 were on upland areas, mostly under low-hanging branches of Utah junipers.

The hen Green-winged Teal constructs the nest and adds nest material during egg-laying, but down is not added until incubation begins (Johnson 1995). Clutch size is known to range from 5–16, with a mean of 8.6 (Bellrose 1980). The drake usually abandons the hen as she incubates the eggs for approximately 20–23 days (Johnson 1995). The ducklings are brooded, lead to foraging areas, and defended from potential predators by the female for an unknown period, but the young are capable of flight in about 35 days, the fastest growth rate of all ducks (Ehrlich et al. 1988). Only one brood is raised to fledging per year, but females may lay replacement clutches if eggs or young broods are lost (Johnson 1995).

DISTRIBUTION AND STATUS

Green-winged Teals nest widely across most of Canada, Alaska, and the northern United States. Unlike most other species of ducks, Green-winged Teals breed more commonly in river deltas and forest wetlands of western Canada and Alaska than they do in the prairie pothole region of the central continent (Johnson 1995). Arizona represents the southern extreme of the breeding range of this hardy, Arctic-tending species. Previous reports indicated Green-winged Teal nested sparsely and locally in the White Mountains and in the higher elevations above the Mogollon Rim to near Flagstaff (Monson and Phillips 1981, Brown 1985).

Atlasers confirmed Green-winged Teal nesting only in the higher elevations of the Chuska Mountains in extreme northeastern Arizona. Probable and possible breeding locations were recorded from scattered lakes and ponds across the northeasterly portion of the state, primarily in the White Mountains, but also on the Defiance and Kaibab plateaus. Most atlas records were at elevations ranging from 7000–9300 ft (2134–2835 m). Although prior to the atlas they were confirmed nesting locally as low as 6350 ft (1935 m) at Pintail Lake near Show Low (Piest and Sowls 1985).

Appropriate habitat continues to exist in the higher elevations above the Mogollon Rim. The near lack of records in this region was surprising. This may have been a result of drought conditions throughout most of the atlas period, which caused shallow lakes and ponds to dry up. These teal had previously been confirmed nesting at several lakes in and around Anderson Mesa southeast of Flagstaff (Myers 1982). Documentation is lacking for Green-winged Teal nesting below 6000 ft (1829 m) in Arizona and summer records at lower elevations likely pertain to nonbreeding individuals. Therefore, possible nesting records noted near Buckeye (Monson and Phillips 1981) and near Arivaca (Fleming 1959) remain questionable.

As noted previously, atlas data suggest Green-winged Teal still remain a sparse nesting species in Arizona. The state's limited nesting population may also greatly fluctuate on an almost annual basis due to varying water levels and the subsequent quality of appropriate nesting habitat. Many of the smaller, isolated wooded lakes and ponds preferred for nesting by this hardy, little duck remained unsurveyed because they fell outside the designated atlas block. Additional nesting localities would likely be found if more specific surveys were conducted in the forested regions of the Colorado Plateau during normal precipitation years.

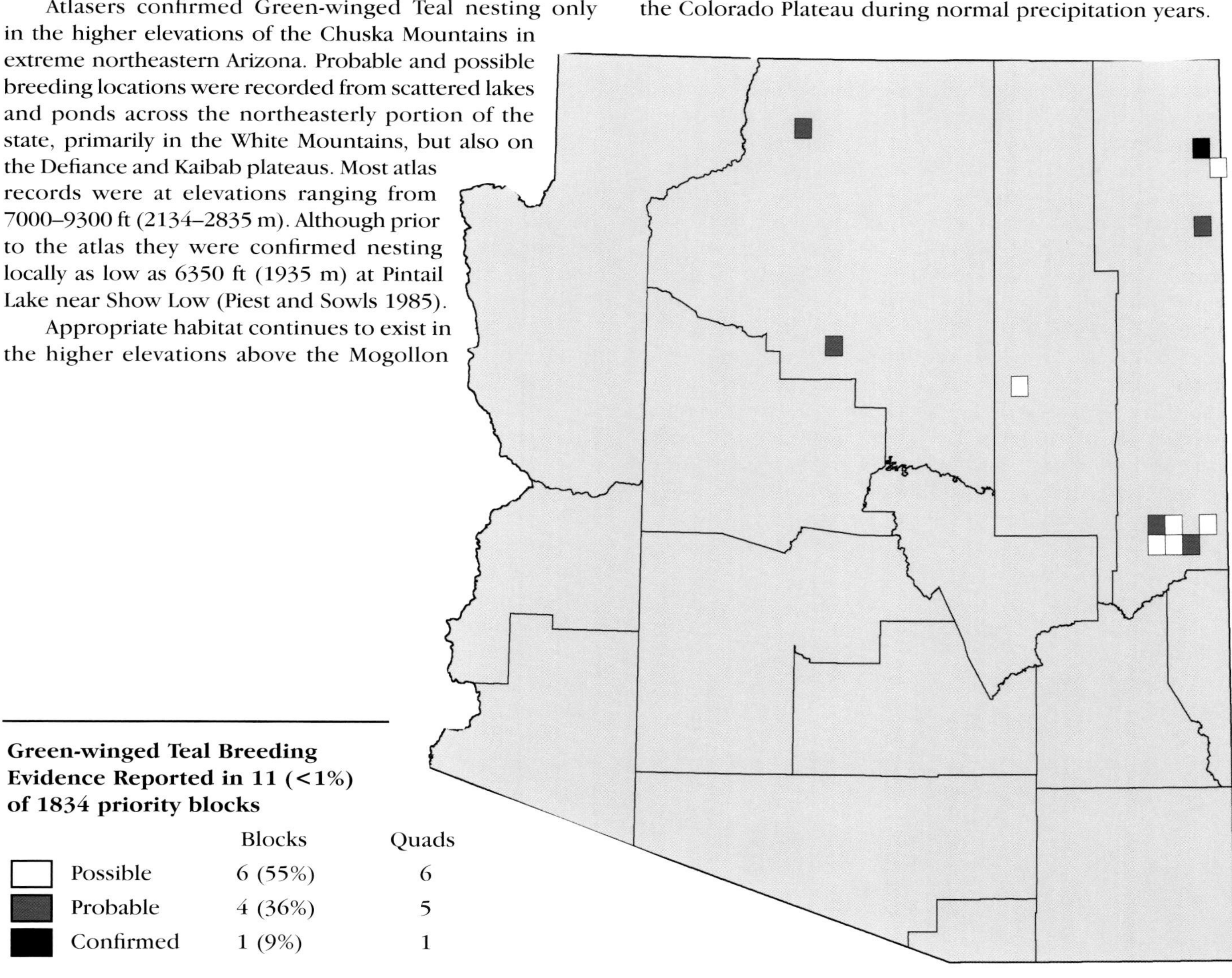

Green-winged Teal Breeding Evidence Reported in 11 (<1%) of 1834 priority blocks

	Blocks	Quads
Possible	6 (55%)	6
Probable	4 (36%)	5
Confirmed	1 (9%)	1

Redhead

by Bob Bradley *Aythya americana*

Arizona's most numerous breeding diving duck, Redheads are notorious for frequently laying their eggs in the nests of other ducks, including other species. These ducks are highly omnivorous, feeding on seeds, tubers, algae, and invertebrates, which they acquire not only by diving, but also by tipping and dabbling in the shallows like a puddle duck.

BRUCE TAUBERT

HABITAT

Redheads are not too particular when it comes to water bodies they inhabit in Arizona. As with other diving ducks, they prefer deep water such as open ponds, lakes, reservoirs, and rivers during migration and winter. Breeding habitats in the state typically include areas of dense, wetland vegetation. Therefore, it was not too surprising when atlasers noted Redheads approximately 86 percent of the time in marshes, ponds, and lake edges with stands of cattails, hardstem bulrush, and sedge (n = 21). Most observations were from higher elevation, semipermanent wetlands, often near larger, deeper marshes or permanent lakes. Many of Arizona's nesting Redheads occupy wetlands that are highly dependent on snowmelt and thus show great annual variability in water depth, sometimes drying completely following a series of extremely low precipitation years. In the Sonoran Desert, atlasers also found these ducks nesting once on a golf course pond in a residential area and at a small lake primarily surrounded by dense tamarisk.

BREEDING

Since Redheads can be found wintering throughout Arizona where water remains free of ice, it is difficult to determine when breeders first arrive in nesting areas. Elsewhere, these ducks begin departing wintering grounds in late January and February, with most individuals migrating northward by mid March (Woodin and Michot 2002). In Arizona, Brown (1985) states that Redheads arrive on their nesting grounds at higher elevations shortly after the ice disappears, typically in March or April at the latest. But they may not initiate nesting until late May or even June (Myers 1982). The earliest confirmed nesting record during the atlas was the discovery of a pair and brood of 9 ducklings at Rio Verde on 30 May, suggesting nest initiation in late April. This timing is similar to other southern Redhead nesting locations in North America. In Arizona, hens are noted with ducklings throughout much of the summer. The latest broods observed during the atlas were on 30 July. Although some past observations in Arizona suggest late nesting attempts are initiated in early July or later with broods of dependent young noted throughout August and even into September (Goldman 1926, Phillips et al. 1964, Myers 1982). A few fall migrating Redheads begin appearing away from nesting areas by early August in Arizona, but most do not arrive until September or October.

Brown (1985) finds that most nest sites in Arizona are in emergent vegetation and over water, especially in stands of hardstem bulrush and cattails. Redheads rarely nest on the ground and then invariably within 10 ft (3.3 m) of the water in emergent marsh vegetation (Myers 1982). Elsewhere, they are also known to nest on isolated islands (Woodin and Michot 2002). The female is solely responsible for constructing the solidly woven nest and incubating the average clutch of 7–8 eggs (Woodin and Michot 2002). The hen generally begins adding down feathers a few days prior to the onset of incubation, which lasts 24–25 days (Woodin and Michot 2002). Male Redheads usually abandon their mate near the onset of incubation, leaving the hen to tend the brood for 6–8 weeks (Low 1945), although some broods may be deserted as early as 3 weeks.

The Redhead demonstrates facultative brood parasitism to a greater extent than any other North American duck (Woodin and Michot 2002). These ducks commonly lay eggs in other Redhead nests, as well as most other duck species nesting in the area. A female can choose to lay eggs in other duck nests before laying a clutch she incubates or simply parasitizes another duck nest without producing a clutch of her own (Woodin and Michot 2002). Sorenson (1991) found that in some populations, Redhead hens lay

Breeding Habitats

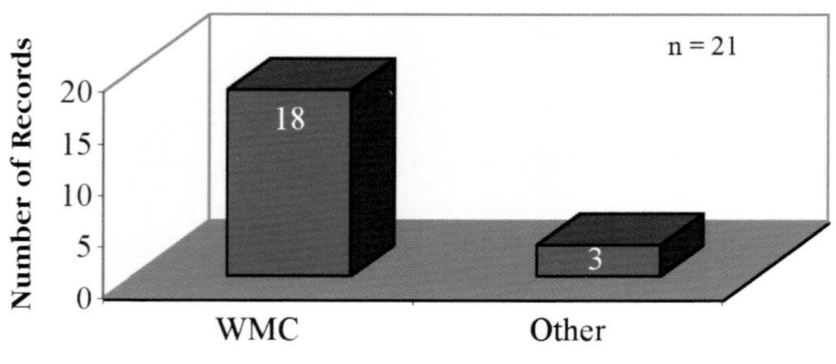

up to 75 percent of their eggs in nests other than their own, and up to 50 percent of Redhead ducklings grow up in "foster" broods. This practice is so skillfully undertaken by Redheads that it enables them to maximize reproduction with minimum energy cost (Sorenson 1991).

DISTRIBUTION AND STATUS

Redheads breeds only in North America, primarily in the Prairie Pothole region of the Great Plains of Canada and the United States, and in the intermountain marshes of the West. These ducks also nest locally east in the Great Lakes region and south to Texas, New Mexico, Arizona, and California. There are disjunct populations in Alaska and central Mexico. In Arizona, Redheads are known to nest most consistently north of the Mogollon Rim, with only a few scattered and irregular nesting records elsewhere in the state including Picacho Reservoir, lower Colorado River Valley, and Sulphur Springs Valley (Phillips et al. 1964, Myers 1982, Brown 1985). On Navajo tribal lands, Jacobs (1986) also found this duck nesting commonly at Ganado and Tsaile lakes.

During the atlas, Redheads were found nesting at a wide range of elevations from 460 ft (140 m) along lower Colorado River at Topock Marsh to near 9300 ft (2835 m) in the White Mountains. According to Brown (1985) these ducks are a common nesting species on the more permanent water bodies above the Mogollon Rim during years of favorable water conditions. Atlasers had similar findings, with observations of Redheads regularly at lakes and marshes in the White Mountains from near Show Low to the New Mexico border at Luna Lake. Near Flagstaff, possible nesting Redheads were noted at Mormon Lake and Lower Lake Mary although these ducks undoubtedly also continue to inhabit many of the other nearby smaller lakes in this region as previously noted by Myers (1982).

On Navajo tribal lands, atlasers confirmed Redheads nesting in the Lukachukai and Chuska mountains region and noted scattered pairs at Ganado and Many Farms lakes, as well as ponds on Black Mesa. To the south, single broods were found below Painted Rock Dam and at Rio Verde near the lower Verde River. Redhead pairs were also noted at Picacho Reservoir where this duck was found nesting in the late 1950s (Phillips et al. 1964).

Some unconfirmed atlas records may pertain to nonbreeding individuals or pairs, but based on past and atlas data, these ducks potentially nest at least irregularly almost anywhere in the state. More intense surveys of lakes, ponds, and marshes on the Colorado Plateau (north of the Mogollon Rim) would likely reveal these intriguing diving ducks to be more widespread breeders than atlas data suggest. This would especially be true if surveys were conducted under more favorable climate conditions. Surveyors were challenged throughout much of the atlas period by drought conditions, which led to record low water levels and eventual complete drying of many potential nesting areas.

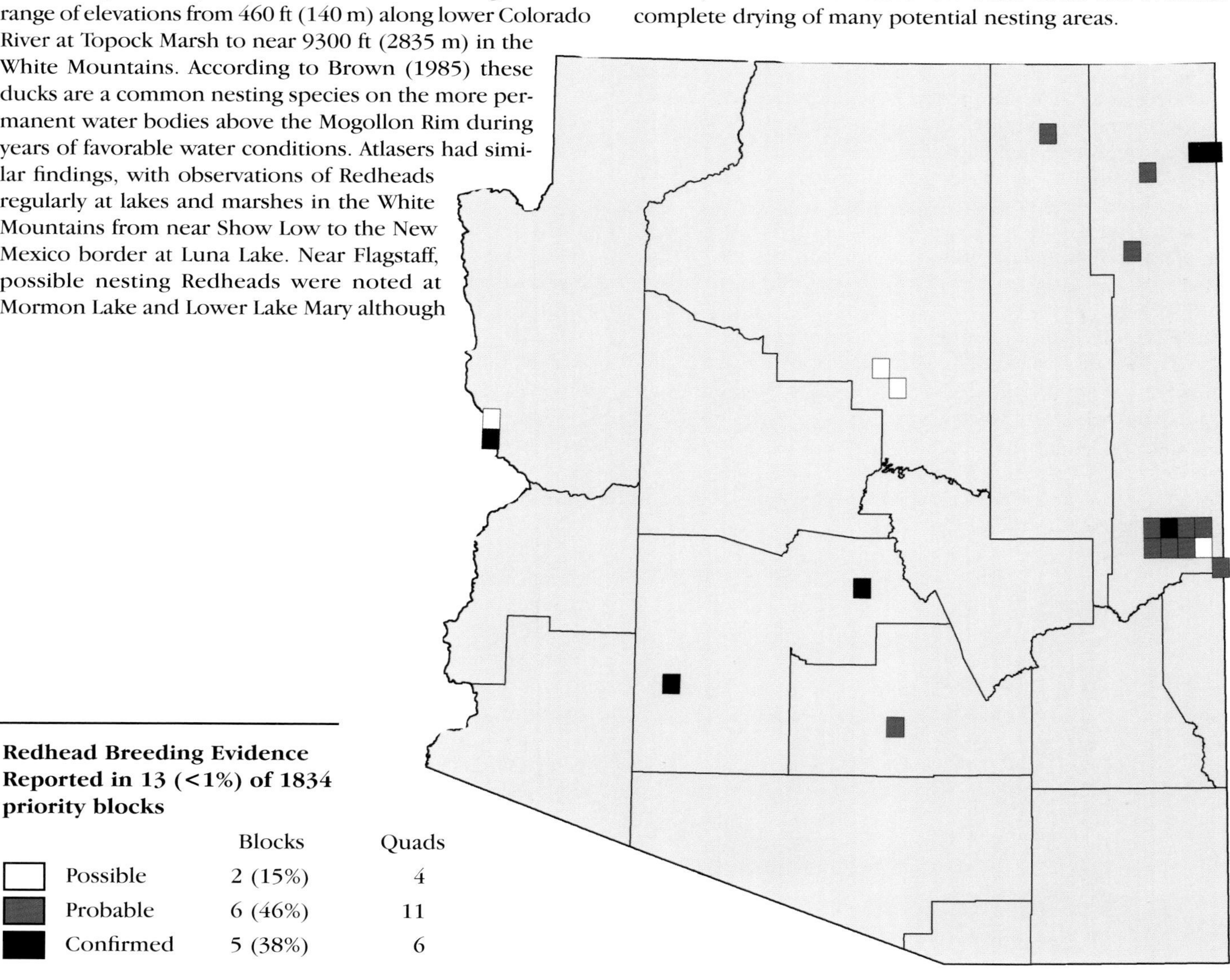

Redhead Breeding Evidence Reported in 13 (<1%) of 1834 priority blocks

	Blocks	Quads
Possible	2 (15%)	4
Probable	6 (46%)	11
Confirmed	5 (38%)	6

Common Merganser

by Troy E. Corman *Mergus merganser*

Reaching their most southern breeding limits in Arizona, Common Mergansers prefer the state's cooler and more remote stream drainages in which to nest and rear their young. Often nesting in tree cavities within their breeding range to the north, most evidence suggests cliff ledges are the nesting site of choice for these large, hardy ducks in Arizona.

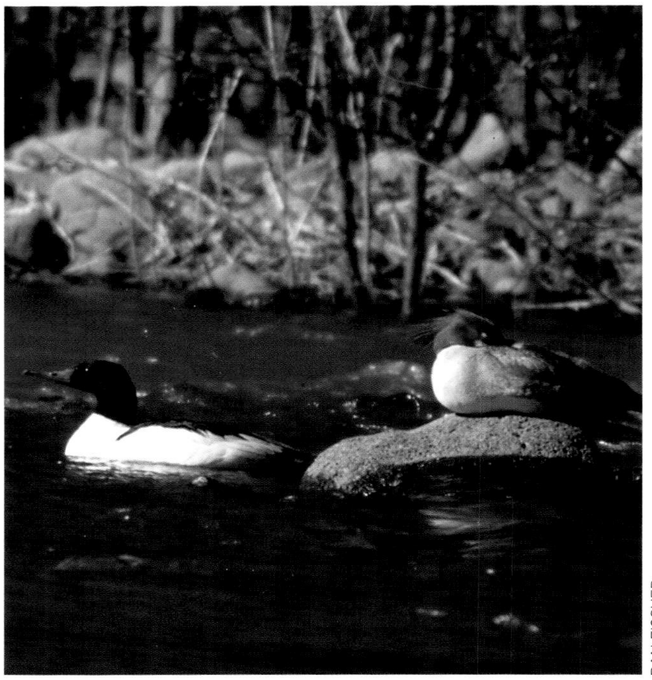
DAN FISCHER

HABITAT

In Arizona, Common Mergansers primarily nest and raise their ducklings along cool, clear, perennial creeks and rivers, occasionally on reservoirs. Atlasers encountered this duck 42 percent of the time from upper mountain drainages flowing through forests of ponderosa pine, Douglas fir, Gambel's oak, box elder, and maples (n = 24). An additional 25 percent of atlas records were from lower elevations along wooded drainages dominated by Fremont cottonwood, willow, and velvet mesquite. Common Mergansers also nest along foothill and canyon drainages dominated by Arizona sycamore and Arizona alder, where five observations were reported. In Arizona, these ducks often nest along smaller wooded streams—then move their broods downstream to larger drainages with an abundance of fish.

BREEDING

Common Mergansers winter fairly commonly throughout southern and western Arizona, and more locally in the north on open rivers, lakes, and reservoirs where they often congregate near dam spillways. Courtship displays and pair bonding occur on their wintering grounds or soon after they arrive in their nesting area (Palmer 1976). In Arizona, spring migration is primarily in February and March with stragglers through April and occasionally into May. Due to their local and secretive nesting habits, atlasers had little opportunity in locating Common Merganser nests. All confirmed atlas records pertain to adults with ducklings. The earliest observation of ducklings reported by atlasers was on 4 May along Oak Creek near Page Springs. This would suggest egg laying no later than the last two weeks of March. Phillips et al. (1964) also report on a family group of 15 young estimated to be approximately three days old at the confluence of Sycamore Creek and Verde River north of Clarkdale on 2 May 1954. Flightless young were reported through17 July and atlasers noted the latest family group on 8 August along the Blue River. Common Mergansers typically do not return to wintering areas of Arizona until late October or November.

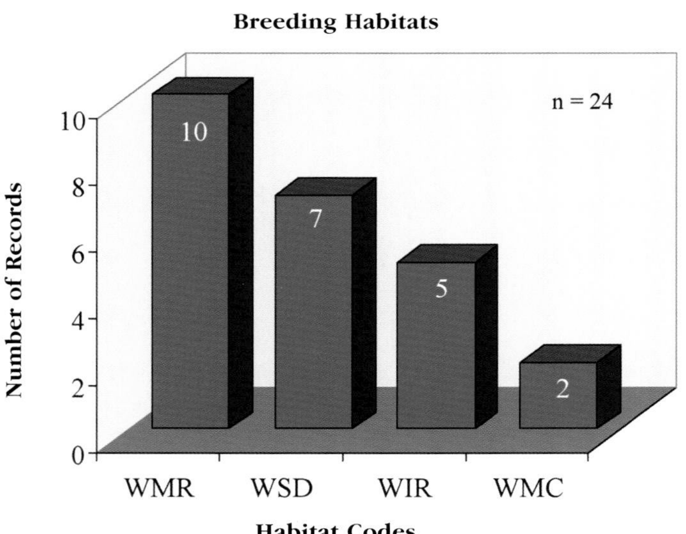

Few nests of the Common Merganser have ever been reported in Arizona, but Phillips et al. (1964) noted that they nest on cliff ledges. Across their range, however, they also nest in tree cavities, nest boxes, in cut banks, streamside thickets, and even in boulder-covered slopes and abandoned buildings (Bent 1923). Some nesting locations are used year after year. Females construct and maintain their nests, scraping a shallow depression that is lined with cavity debris, feathers, and sometimes grasses.

Common Mergansers typically lay 9–12 eggs to a clutch, but this can range from 6–17 (Bent 1923). Since the eggs are laid at a rate of 1.5 days per egg, there is a quite lengthy laying period of 2–3 weeks for most clutches (Mallory and Metz 1999). The drake typically abandons his mate once the eggs are laid, leaving the females to perform the duties of incubation and care for the ducklings (Bent 1923). Incubation starts when the clutch is completed and varies from 28–35 days (Mallory and Metz 1999). The young can remain in the nest cavity for 24–48 hours after hatching and then depart with the female to the nearest brooding-rearing stream (Palmer 1976). The young leap from high cavities and cliffs to join the calling female below. Broods typically stay with the female for 30–50 days after hatching and can fly when they are 60–75 days old (Mallory and Metz 1999).

DISTRIBUTION AND STATUS

One of the most widespread mergansers, Common Mergansers are found throughout much of the northern hemisphere. In North America, they nest from the boreal forest tree line of central Alaska and Canada, south to northern Pennsylvania in the East. From the Rocky Mountain region west, they are found south locally to central Arizona and New Mexico. Phillips et al. (1964) noted Common Mergansers as a fairly common resident of drainages flowing south and west of the Mogollon Rim and White Mountain region, west to the upper Verde Valley. Brown (1985) also noted broods of mergansers from the upper and middle Verde River drainage, east to the upper Gila and Black river drainages. Even though 20–40 Common Mergansers annually spend the spring and summer along the Colorado River between Glen and Marble canyons, there is no indication that these birds are breeding at this location (C. LaRue, personal communication).

Atlasers found Common Mergansers throughout much of their previously known breeding distribution within Arizona, thus confirming their breeding at elevations ranging from 2840–6700 ft (866–2042 m). Pairs were observed locally on lakes as high as 9100 ft (2774 m). The most western observations came from the upper Verde River east of Paulden and along Oak Creek near Page Springs. Common Mergansers were found on the Verde River downstream to below the East Verde River confluence. Atlasers confirmed Common Mergansers with broods on Tonto Creek and within the Salt River Canyon. Atlsers also occasionally observed Common Mergansers pairs above the Mogollon Rim, such as at Mormon Lake and White Mountain Reservoir that could pertain to nonbreeding individuals. However, a brood was observed at Blue Ridge Reservoir confirming these duck do nest at least locally north of the Mogollon Rim. The only Gila River observation came from the Gila Box, which is near the tributaries of Eagle and Bonita creeks, where this species has nested in the past. Common Mergansers were most commonly found along tributaries draining south and west from the White Mountains, such as the Blue and Black rivers. This merganser undoubtedly nests within the White Mountain Apache Tribal lands along tributaries of the White, Black, and upper Salt rivers. Unfortunately, data are lacking for these tribal lands due to the inability to gain permission to conduct atlas surveys in this diverse region of the state.

Many Common Mergansers were likely missed by typical atlas surveys due to their secretive nature during the nesting and brooding stages. During this period they often stay close to shoreline vegetation and boulders. Surveys rarely involved river float trips through more remote sections of streams where these ducks often rear their broods. It should also be noted that since females often move their broods gradually downstream to larger rivers in Arizona, observations of females with older ducklings may not have nested specifically within the block where they were observed by atlasers.

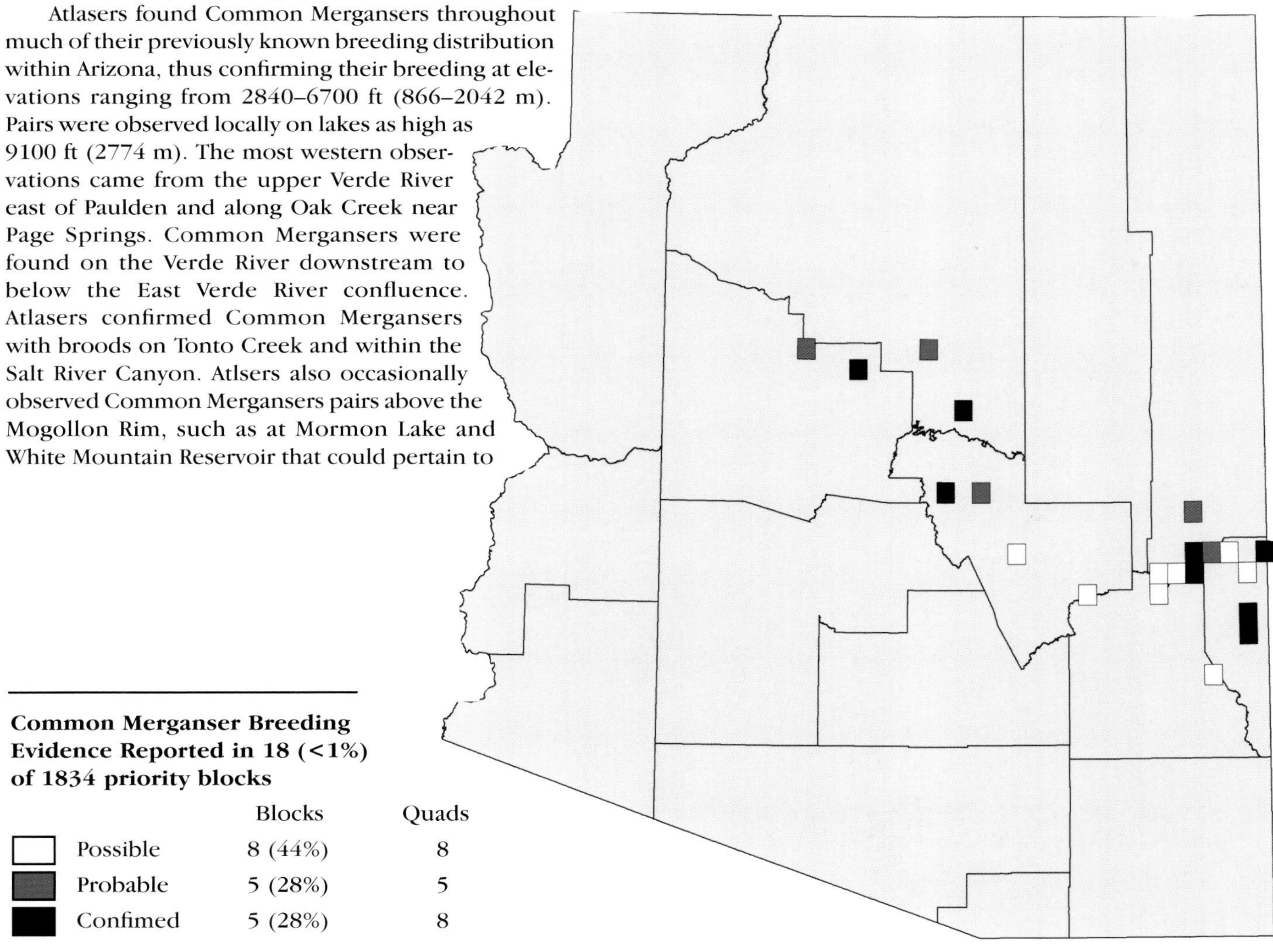

Common Merganser Breeding Evidence Reported in 18 (<1%) of 1834 priority blocks

	Blocks	Quads
Possible	8 (44%)	8
Probable	5 (28%)	5
Confimed	5 (28%)	8

Ruddy Duck

by Cathryn Wise-Gervais *Oxyura jamaicensis*

With tails raised stiffly skyward, courting male Ruddy Ducks thump their bright blue bills rapidly against their chests. This amusing process produces small pond ripples and bubbles, and often concludes in a peculiar croak. Unlike most migratory waterfowl, Ruddy Ducks do not initiate courtship and acquire mates until they reach their nesting grounds.

JIM BURNS

HABITAT

In Arizona, Ruddy Ducks will occupy a wide variety of open aquatic habitats during winter and migration, but prefer those containing dense emergent vegetation for nesting. Nearly 88 percent of all atlas records of Ruddy Ducks were noted in ponds and marshes, as well as edges of lakes, reservoirs, and slow flowing sections of rivers ($n = 40$). No matter at what elevation or adjacent upland habitat was present, these occupied habitats were all characterized as having some open water coupled with dense stands of cattails, bulrush, sedges, or other aquatic plants. Atlasers found Ruddy Ducks from lowland wetlands in the Sonoran Desert to permanent or semipermanent lakes and ponds surrounded by subalpine meadows. Atlasers also found these small ducks nesting locally in marshy canals, stock ponds, and in agricultural irrigation holding ponds. In addition, Ruddy Ducks seem especially fond of habitat-enhanced wastewater treatment ponds with typical emergent vegetation.

BREEDING

Some populations of Ruddy Ducks reside in Arizona, while others begin migrating northward in March and April. The unique courtship displays of this little, stiff-tailed duck commence soon after their arrival to breeding areas. In lowland areas, atlasers first reported courtship behavior on 26 March, noted ducklings by 18 April, and observed fresh broods through 26 August. These dates indicate that lowland birds initiate incubation for early nests no later than the final week of March. At higher elevations in Arizona, egg laying typically begins in mid-May and the earliest downy brood was not noted until 14 June. Nests remained hidden from atlasers and all confirmations were of duckling broods. Most records were obtained in midsummer, from mid-June through late July, but observers reported several late duckling broods on 25 and 27 September, well after most atlasing efforts had ended. In Arizona, migrants typically begin appearing away from nesting localities in early to mid-August and some continue passing through into December.

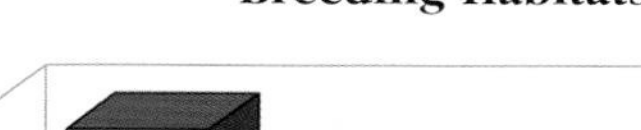

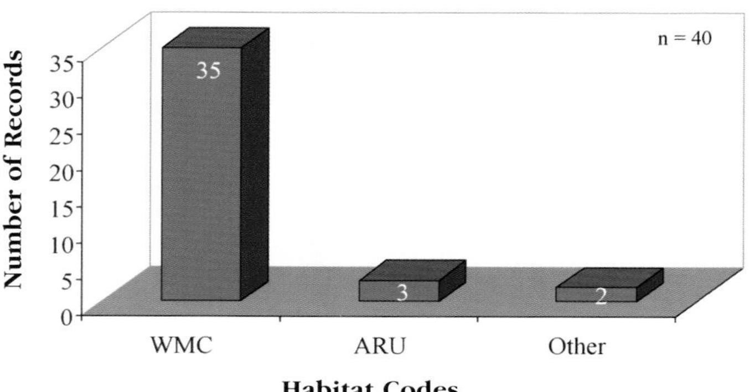

Ruddy Duck nests are typically well concealed in tall emergent vegetation and nests are often floating platforms anchored to cattails or bulrush. Other nesting substrates in Arizona include patches of sedge (Goldman 1926) and on small islands in dense stands of tall wheatgrass (Piest and Sowls 1985). Nests consist of marsh plant materials that the females weave together and build above the water level. They will continue to add nest material to elevate the nest platform in response to rising water levels (Brua 2002). Ruddy Ducks will occasionally cover their nests from above by pulling stems over them (Low 1941) and will sometimes use abandoned coot, grebe, or other duck nests instead of building their own (Brua 2002).

The typical Ruddy Duck clutch consists of 6–8 eggs (range 3–13), but this species is notorious for dumping eggs in other Ruddy Duck nests as well as in other species' nests including Redheads and Canvasbacks. Therefore, higher numbered clutches may pertain to egg dumping by other females. Like most other ducks, the male typically abandons the female during incubation, which lasts for approximately 24 days (Brua 2002). Most female Ruddy Ducks abandon their broods in 2–4 weeks, well before the ducklings can fly in 6–7 weeks (Brua 2002). Throughout their temperate range in North America, Ruddy Ducks likely produce only one brood, but in southern Arizona two broods are possible given the 4–5 month nesting season noted during the atlas.

DISTRIBUTION AND STATUS

Ruddy Ducks breed primarily throughout the interior western and prairie pothole regions of North America from the Northwest Territories south through Baja and southern Mexico. These stiff-tailed ducks also breed

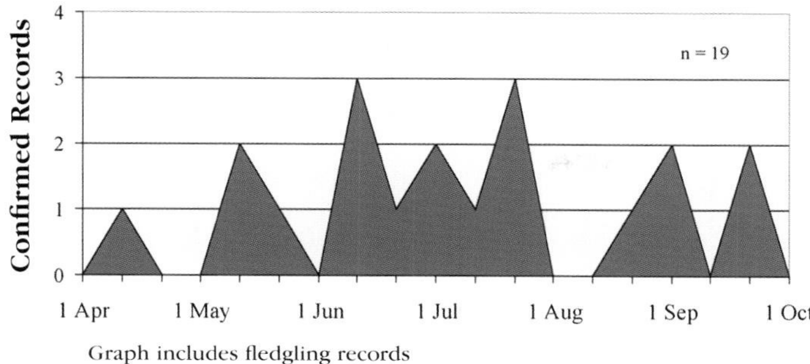

Graph includes fledgling records

locally in south Texas, the Great Lakes region, and in the West Indies (Brua 2002).

The earliest accounts of Ruddy Ducks presumably nesting in Arizona were from Mearns (1890) who noted them preparing to breed above the Mogollon Rim at Mormon, Stoneman, and other lakes north to the general Flagstaff area. Phillips et al. (1964) and Monson and Phillips (1981) described these small ducks as nesting regularly only on the Mogollon Plateau and locally elsewhere including on the lower Colorado River, in the Pipe Springs National Monument, around the Phoenix area, and in southeastern Arizona near Tucson and Arivaca Junction.

Atlasers found that Ruddy Ducks are capable of breeding locally throughout much of Arizona where appropriate habitat exists naturally or is created. In fact, atlasers discovered these little ducks nesting sparsely, but in many more widespread locations in the state than previous literature suggested. Ruddy Ducks were confirmed or suspected of nesting at elevations ranging from 150 ft (46 m) near Mittry Lake to near 9300 ft (2835 m) at White Mountain Reservoir. Along the lower Colorado River, atlasers noted them nesting near Parker and Imperial Reservoir. Atlasers also frequently observed Ruddy Ducks in the many lakes and ponds in the White Mountain region.

In northeastern Arizona, Jacobs (1986) noted that Ruddy Ducks were locally fairly common breeders on Navajo and Hopi tribal lands, including at Tsaile Lake, Ganado Lake, and at Many Farms Spring. Atlasers also found Ruddy Ducks nesting in Pasture Canyon near Tuba City, and at Cow Springs Lake. Atlasers noted courtship at a man-made pond on Black Mesa but did not confirm breeding at this location. In southeastern Arizona, atlasers found that Ruddy Ducks were a sparse and local nesting species in several areas including Willcox, Whitewater Draw, and on the east side of the Chiricahua Mountains at Willow Tank. These ducks were also found regularly in appropriate habitat at many ponds in the Thatcher–Safford area.

Statewide, atlasers found many new nesting locations at wastewater treatment ponds containing dense stands of emergent vegetation, even when these ponds were isolated and surrounded by agriculture, grasslands, or desertscrub. Additional breeding areas of these little, adaptable ducks will likely be established in Arizona as more wastewater facilities continue the trend of creating wetlands and using emergent and submergent vegetation as natural filtering systems.

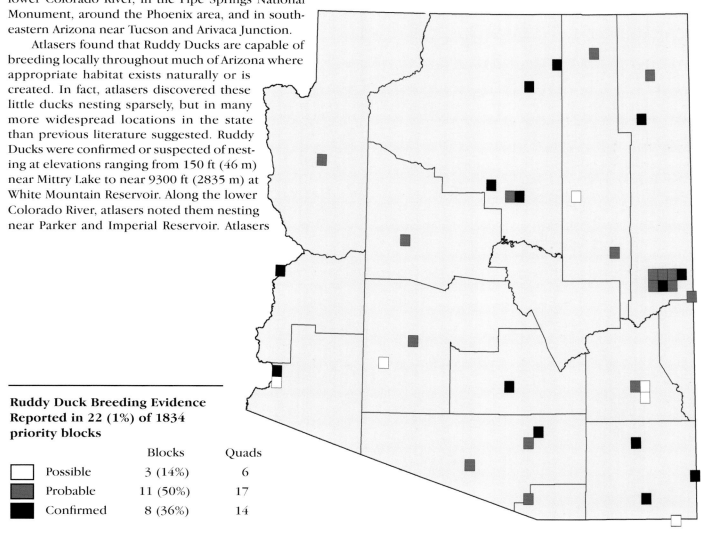

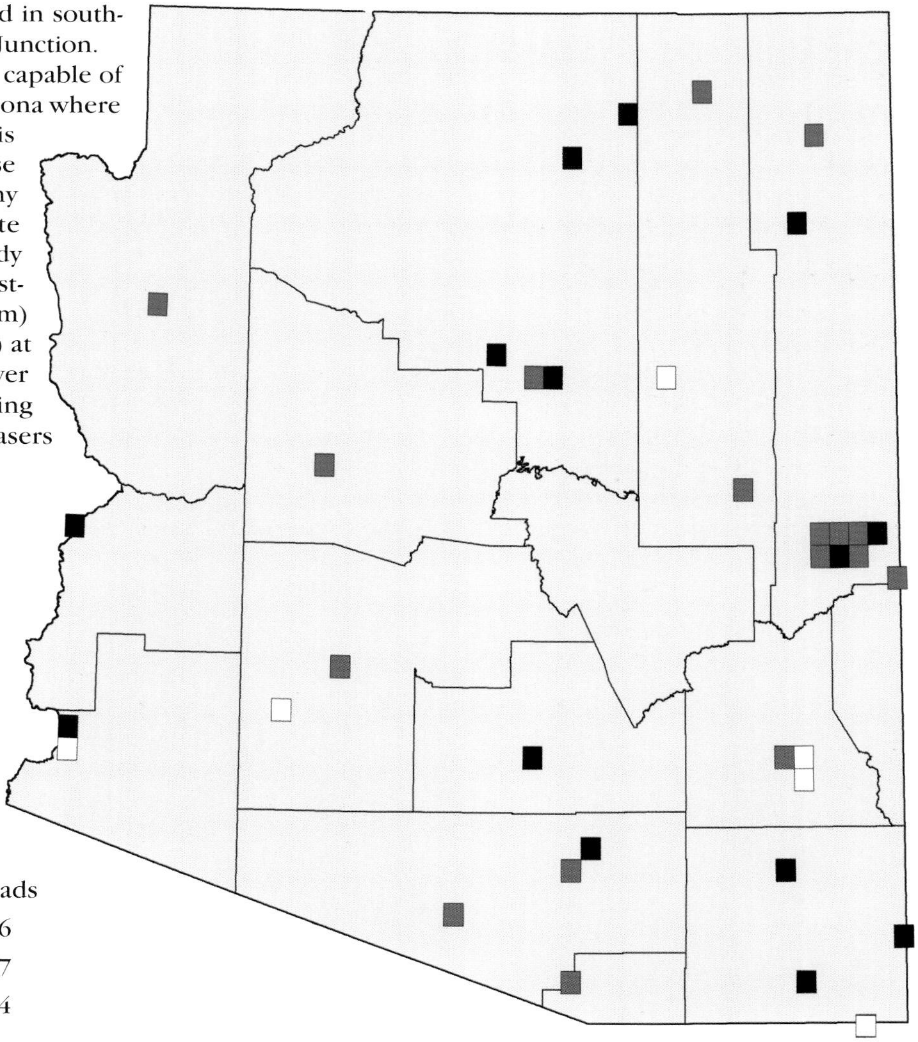

Ruddy Duck Breeding Evidence Reported in 22 (1%) of 1834 priority blocks

	Blocks	Quads
Possible	3 (14%)	6
Probable	11 (50%)	17
Confirmed	8 (36%)	14

Chukar

by Troy E. Corman *Alectoris chukar*

An introduced game bird of rugged, arid lands of northern Arizona, Chukars inhabit some of the most remote and often difficult to access regions of the state. There is some indication that the local distribution of these striking partridges is steadily increasing in Arizona, likely from established populations in Utah.

JIM BURNS

HABITAT

Chukars typically occupy steep, arid habitats that are infrequently visited by the average birder in Arizona. Their world is a land of steep hillsides, dry canyons, rock outcrops, cliffs, and talus slopes (Brown 1989). In Arizona, their preferred habitat typically consists of rocky terrain with sparse vegetation, but often include big sagebrush, rabbitbrush, ephedra, bunch grasses, various annuals (both native and exotic), and sometimes a scattering of junipers. Nearly 78 percent of all atlas records were from a mixture of open cold-temperate desertscrub and grasses. Many fewer records of these wary partridges were from Mojave desertscrub and open juniper stands. Water in this otherwise arid environment is an important component of Chukar habitat. During hot summer months, the distribution of adults and chicks depends largely on the availability of water (Christensen 1996). Isolated springs, perennial drainages, and artificial water sources, such as guzzlers, earthen livestock tanks, and even deep within abandoned mines suffice for their required daily visits. Seeds of annuals become staple food for these partridges during the summer, and Brown (1989) notes that if exotic annuals such as filaree, Russian thistle, and cheatgrass are lacking in an area, so are populations of Chukar.

BREEDING

Because of their relatively isolated distribution in Arizona, Chukars have received minimal attention by hunters and even less so by birders. Also, owing to the Chukars preferred inhospitable environment, practically no breeding information was collected during the atlas period. In Nevada, Christensen (1970) noted that covey break-up and pair formation takes place between late February and mid-March. But during drought years when food is limited, pairing may be restricted to only a small portion of the population, with the remaining birds staying in coveys (Christensen 1996). Once birds are paired and establish a territory, males become aggressive and fight with other males that enter their nesting territory (Christensen (1996). Egg laying and incubation begin in late March and usually continues into mid-April, with most hatching in late May and early June, the driest time of year in Arizona (Brown 1989). The only confirmed breeding reported during the atlas was of an adult with young on 4 July south of Littlefield. During wet years with abundant food sources, Chukars are persistent renesters. If the first attempt fails, it is not uncommon to see downy young in late August (Christensen 1996). Yet during drought years when resources are low, there are few renesting attempts (Brown 1989).

Chukar nests are difficult to find and are located on rocky, brush-covered mountain and canyon slopes, well hidden by rocks and brush (Christensen 1970). The nest is merely a depression scratched in the ground and lined with dry grasses and breast feathers (Christensen 1954). The female incubates the 8–15 (range to 21) eggs for approximately 24 days (Machie and Buechner 1963). The precocial young leave the nest soon after hatching and are brooded primarily by the female (Christensen 1996). Male Chukars often remain with their mates until all rearing duties are complete (Christensen 1970). Either parent may feign being crippled in an attempt to lure an intruder away from eggs or downy young (Brown 1989). The young reach the size of adults by 12 weeks and remain in coveys with adults and other young until pairing begins in late winter or early spring (Alkon 1982; Christensen 1996).

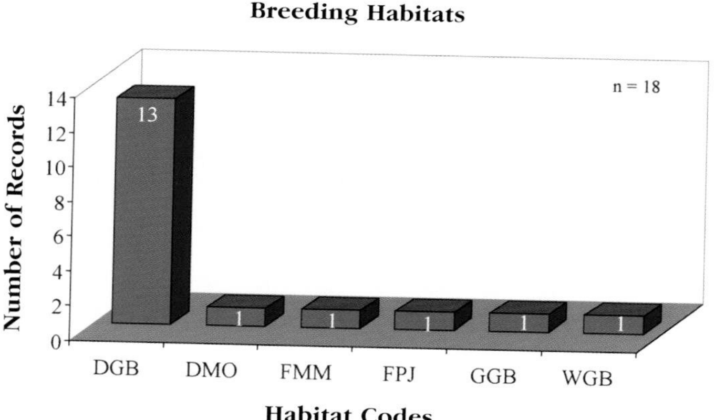

DISTRIBUTION AND STATUS

Native to southern Asia, Chukars have been successfully introduced as game species in western North America, New Zealand, and the Hawaiian Islands. Most established populations are found in the Great Basin region from southern British Columbia and Montana south to western Colorado, extreme northern edge of Arizona, and locally in southern California.

In Arizona, private releases of this partridge were conducted as early as 1941 (Brown 1989). The Arizona Game and Fish Commission released almost ten thousand Chukars from the Cluff Ranch Game Farm near Pima at twenty-nine different locations in eastern and central Arizona between 1946 and 1949 (Brown 1989). Most of these releases were unsuccessful, and after evaluating Chukar habitat in adjacent states, Webb (1958) recommended the Snake Gulch area near Kanab Creek as the most suitable Arizona locale. The last attempt to establish this exotic game bird by the Arizona Game and Fish Department was in 1963 (Webb and Robeck 1963). Brown (1989) reported that the only populations of Chukars established in Arizona are restricted to the Kanab Creek drainage in the Arizona Strip region, Cataract Canyon northeast of Williams, and the Paria Canyon drainage northwest of Lees Ferry. The latter birds are believed to be the result of growing populations just to the north in Utah (Brown 1989). Chukars are also still occasionally seen in the southern end of the Toroweap Valley from introductions in the Mt. Trumbull area in the 1960s (Brown et al. 1987). On Navajo tribal land, they were also established along the slopes of northern and eastern Black Mesa from birds released near Chilchinbito in 1958 (LaRue 1994).

Atlasers and Arizona Game and Fish Department Wildlife Managers reported Chukars throughout their previously described established distribution within the state at elevations ranging from approximately 3000 to 6600 ft (914–2012 m). These game birds were also detected locally at several new locations such as the eastern edge of the Hualapai tribal lands, northeast of Bitter Springs along Echo Cliffs, west of Colorado City, within the Virgin Mountains south of Littlefield, and in Navajo Canyon north of Kaibito. A private release of Chukar near Lazy Boy Spring near Oatman, Mohave County accounts for the small nesting population there. Additional Chukar populations undoubtedly exist in other remote and rugged localities in the northwest region of the state where visits by atlasers were few or lacking. Drought conditions throughout much of the atlas period likely reduced population sizes of these partridge, lowering the probability of being detected during surveys.

As noted by Christenson (1970) on studies he conducted in Nevada, the size of Chukar populations are determined by the amount and timing of spring precipitation and the number of adults surviving from the previous year. Christenson also suggested that almost no young are produced during drought years. Because cheatgrass and other exotic annuals increase with grazing and range fires, heavy grazing practices are not detrimental to Chukars and in fact greatly assist in their establishment and success (Brown 1998). Habitat management is limited to water development and improvement of existing water sources (Christenson 1970).

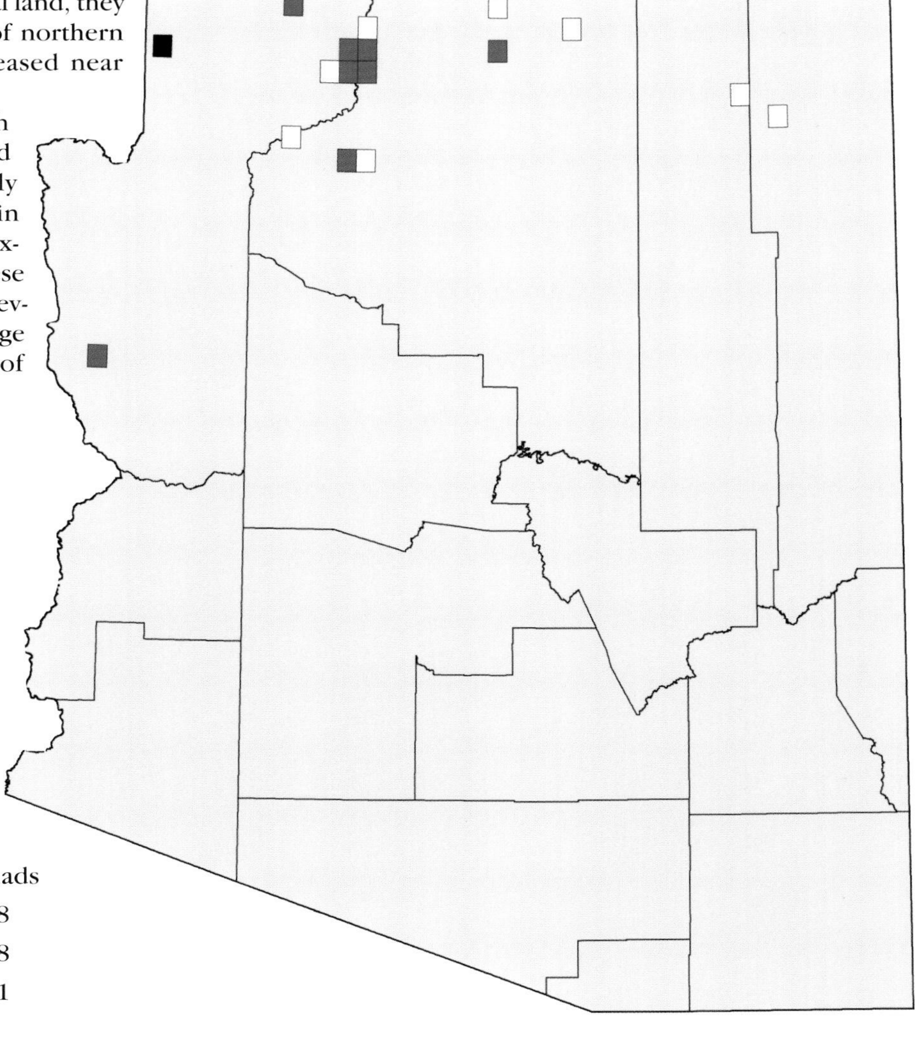

Chukar Breeding Evidence Reported in 10 (<1%) of 1834 priority blocks

	Blocks	Quads
Possible	8 (80%)	8
Probable	2 (20%)	8
Confirmed	0 (0%)	1

Ring-necked Pheasant

by Linden Piest *Phasianus colchicus*

BRIAN SMALL

One of the gaudiest members of the state's avifauna, a male Ring-necked Pheasant can be mistaken for no other species. In Arizona, these splendid birds are scarce, local, and seldom observed. Unless forewarned by the cock's distinctive crow, one is never prepared for an encounter; the occasion is often accompanied by a momentary feeling of disbelief.

HABITAT

Ring-necked Pheasants in Arizona are entirely restricted to irrigated agricultural areas and adjacent brushy habitats within humid river valleys. The remainder of Arizona is simply too dry to sustain any race of pheasant (Brown 1989). These game birds are further restricted to those few areas that provide the suitable combination of temperature, humidity, cover, and food. All atlas records were reported from either irrigated cropland, primarily grains and alfalfa, or in the adjacent fence rows, brushy ditches, or field edges containing thickets of arrowweed, mesquite, and saltbush. Habitat near Yuma also includes mature citrus trees with an understory of irrigated grasses. A proximity to densely vegetated river bottoms, sumps, drains, or other wetlands is essential (Brown 1989). Elsewhere in North America, this species is associated mostly with cultivated lands interspersed with grassy ditches, hedges, marshes, woodland borders, and brushy groves (Giudice and Ratti 2001).

BREEDING

Due to their very limited distribution in Arizona, no nesting studies of Ring-necked Pheasant have been conducted in the state. Therefore, very little is known about the breeding phenology of these birds in Arizona. Inferences about timing can be drawn, however, from studies elsewhere and from the timing of calling in Arizona. Male Ring-necked Pheasants in Arizona begin calling and establishing territories in March and April (Brown 1989). Atlasers reported calling birds through 24 April. Male Ring-necked Pheasants typically attract 1–3 hens to their territory, which he typically abandons soon after the last female begins to nest (Taber 1949). Mating most likely begins in early April and nest initiation probably peaks in late April or early May. Hatching is estimated to peak in late May and continue through June (Brown 1989). Atlasers reported Ring-necked Pheasant hens with young from 3 June to 4 July. These dates appear to be only slightly earlier than those average dates reported throughout the remaining portions of the North American range, primarily much farther north. Ring-necked Pheasants are persistent renesters when a nest is destroyed, allowing for laying and hatching dates to span over several months (Clark and Bogenschutz 1999).

Female Ring-necked Pheasants construct their nests on the ground under the canopy of tall grasses, weeds, or shrubs. Few nests of these pheasants have ever been found in Arizona, and none were discovered during the atlas period. Brown (1989) observed, however, that "the herbaceous understories of Bermuda grass and exotic forbs found within the humid confines of mature citrus groves are among the more productive nesting sites in Arizona." Elsewhere in North America, nesting is often concentrated in areas with residual cover, including roadsides, fence lines, ditches, rights-of-way, wetlands, and hay fields (Giudice and Ratti 2001).

The clutch size of Ring-necked Pheasants usually consists of 7–15 (Baicich and Harrison 1997) and clutches greater than 18 likely pertain to the laying efforts of two females (Cramp and Simmons 1980). Incubation is by the female and lasts an average of 23–24 days (Johnsgard 1999). Young leave the nest within a few hours of hatching and are capable of short flights in 7–12 days (Cramp and Simmons 1980). The young Ring-necked Pheasants become independent in about 70–80 days. Most evidence suggests hens raise only 1 brood per year (Giudice and Ratti 2001).

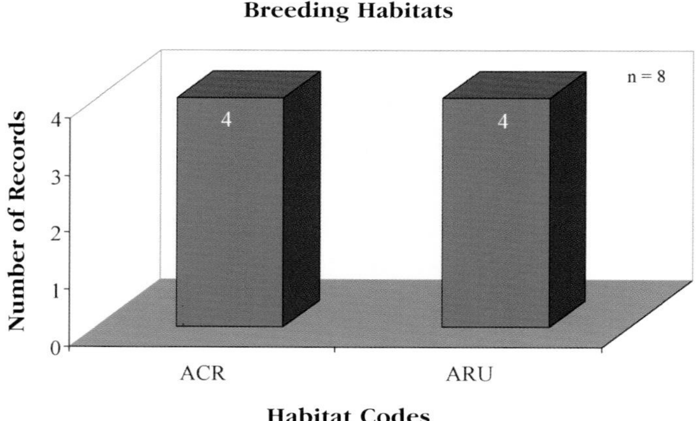

DISTRIBUTION AND STATUS

North American populations of Ring-necked Pheasants are a result of the introduction and blending of a multitude of the 34 recognized subspecies that are native to broad areas of Asia. These game birds are distributed widely across the Great Plains and Midwest north to extreme southern Canada and more patchily in the West and Northeast. Ring-necked Pheasants are apparently intolerant of high springtime temperatures and are therefore mostly absent from the south. In Arizona, Ring-necked Pheasants were introduced through private and state efforts widely and often from 1912 to 1972. Introductions in the latter years were primarily of the Afghan white-winged race, which was thought to be better adapted to arid conditions. This race predominates in most of Arizona's existing pheasant populations (Brown 1989). Ring-necked Pheasants around Yuma, however, originated from populations in Baja California and California and appear to be predominantly of Ring-necked origin.

Introduction efforts of Ring-necked Pheasants into Arizona were largely unsuccessful. Populations became established only near Yuma, the upper Gila River valley from Geronimo to the New Mexico state line, the Virgin River valley near Littlefield, the Verde River valley between Camp Verde and Clarkdale, and near Mesa (Brown 1989). Escapes from game farms or dog trials, and illegal releases, probably continue to this day and may account for ephemeral populations in some areas.

Atlasers reported Ring-necked Pheasants at elevations ranging from 80 to 3600 ft (24–1097 m), with the largest population continuing to exist south of Yuma. This population is also the only one sufficiently productive to sustain a firearms hunting season in Arizona. Call count surveys, however, indicate that even this population has declined substantially since the early 1980s, particularly in citrus orchards where changes in insecticide types are suspected to be a factor (R. Henry, personal communication). Elsewhere, these pheasants were observed near Littlefield and within the upper Gila River valley only near Duncan. Ring-necked Pheasants were not detected further east in the Gila River valley, but much of their preferred habitat in this region is on private land and not well surveyed. Atlasers did detect individual pheasants within the Verde River valley near Camp Verde, Page Springs, and Cottonwood. So few remain in these areas, however, that some populations may not have survived through the end of the atlas period (R. Radd, personal communication). Recent population declines of these splendid game birds in localities established since the 1940s may be related to the prolonged drought during the atlas period and lower than normal humidity levels during the critical breeding season.

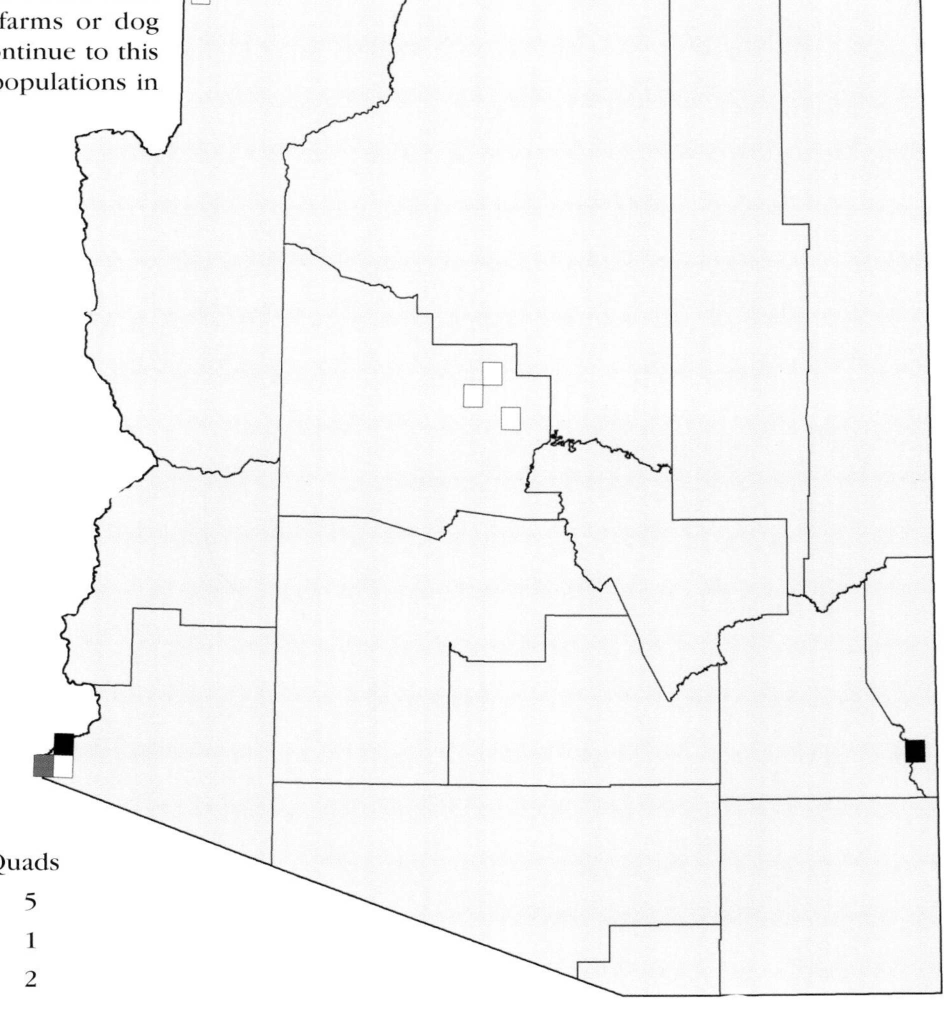

Ring-necked Pheasant Breeding Evidence Reported in 4 (<1%) of 1834 priority block

	Blocks	Quads
Possible	1 (25%)	5
Probable	1 (25%)	1
Confirmed	2 (50%)	2

Blue Grouse

by Bob Bradley *Dendragapus obscurus*

The largest grouse in western North America, the Blue Grouse reaches its southern limits in higher elevation forests in central Arizona. It is also the only grouse with mood-indicating combs. The bare skin above the eyes of courting males rapidly changes basic color from yellow to red at peak courtship.

JIM BURNS

HABITAT

In Arizona, Blue Grouse have previously been reported primarily in subalpine forests of Engelmann spruce, cork bark fir, and quaking aspen (Brown 1989). However, atlasers noted Blue Grouse in this habitat in only 17 percent of all observations (*n* = 24). These grouse were more commonly reported in slightly lower elevation mixed-conifer forests containing Douglas fir, white fir, blue spruce, ponderosa pine, and aspen where 63 percent of all records were noted. Many of the latter localities likely contained trees and shrubs from both habitats, however. Atlasers also reported Blue Grouse on few occasions in primarily pure ponderosa pine forests, ponderosa pine–Gambel's oak, and primarily pure aspen forests. The forest ground cover is often comprised of low shrubs, primarily common juniper, and a variety of ferns, forbs, and grasses (Brown 1989). Blue Grouse hens with broods have also been observed in subalpine meadow grasslands in Arizona, but they were not reported in this habitat during the atlas period. Although Blue Grouse are known to move upslope in winter and downslope to breed, this behavior has not been observed in Arizona (Phillips et al. 1964).

BREEDING

In Arizona, male Blue Grouse that are two or more years old leave their winter roosts as soon as the snow melts to establish a strutting, or breeding territory (Brown 1989). These territories are claimed in early April in Arizona when wing fluttering and "hooting" displays commence. Territories are defended from other males well into June (LeCount 1970). However, atlasers noted aggressive behavior by males as late as 20 July. On that date a male grouse suddenly dropped onto a trail directly in front of an atlaser and began pecking at her hiking boots. Even a head dowsing from a water bottle did not seem to phase his assertive advances (C. Wise-Gervais, personal communication).

Few atlas surveys were conducted in the high elevation habitats Blue Grouse prefer before mid-May; therefore, the earliest calling male grouse was not reported until early June. The cocks are strongly attached to display areas and are likely to return to them each year. Display areas are usually small 1–2 ac (0.4–0.8 ha) openings or clearings on a mountain ridge or slope (Brown 1989). Human-made clearings for fire and radio towers are frequently used in Arizona as display grounds. Blue Grouse hens, apparently not tied to a particular breeding area, move up and down the slope and are intercepted and displayed to by the males (Brown 1989). Peak mating activity takes place in Arizona during the last week of May and the first week of June (LeCount 1970). While Blue Grouse males remain in their territories to attract other females, the hens begin nest site selection, nest building, egg laying, and incubation, with no help from her suitor.

The nest of a Blue Grouse is a shallow scrape or depression on the ground, lined with grass and pine needles, and often partially concealed by exposed tree roots, fallen branches, bunches of grass, or shrubbery (Brown 1989). The mean clutch size varies from year to year but can range from 5 to 10. With their limited range and relatively low abundance in Arizona, it was not surprising that atlasers were unable to find any nests with eggs. All confirmations during the atlas period were of hens with dependent young. Based on the fact that most chicks in Arizona hatch between 15 June and 15 July (Brown 1989) and the typical incubation period is approximately 26 days, eggs are laid in late May and June. Atlasers reported hens with young from 1 July to 1 August. The chicks begin feeding their first day and are usually independent of the hen after

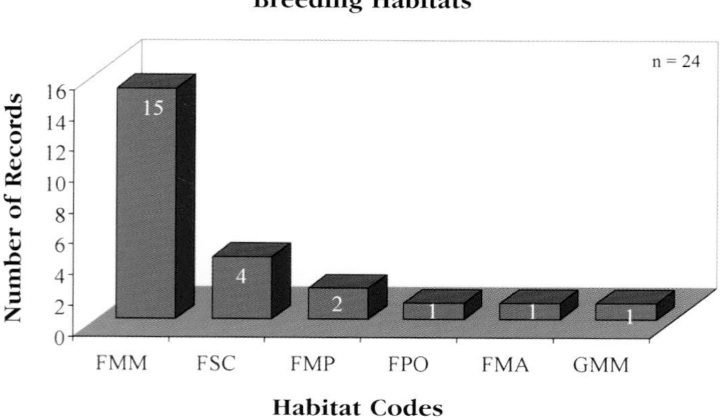

about three weeks (Brown 1989). Forb and grass cover are extremely important for young broods, and LeCount (1970) found that females with broods avoided areas with cover less than 12 in. (30.5 cm) in height. There is but one brood per year, but a second nest is sometime initiated 14–15 days after the first nest is destroyed, even late in incubation (Zwickel and Lance 1965).

DISTRIBUTION AND STATUS

Blue Grouse are endemic to the mountainous regions of western North America from Yukon Territory, south into California, Arizona, and New Mexico. These grouse occupy a wide range of breeding habitats throughout their distribution from sea level to about 12,000 ft (3658 m) in elevation. In Arizona, Blue Grouse are almost entirely confined to subalpine forests and meadow regions at elevations above 8500 ft (2591 m). Earlier accounts noted Blue Grouse as common to fairly common in the White Mountain region of Arizona (Mearns 1890), and less common along the North Rim of the Grand Canyon and in the Chuska Mountains of northern Apache County (Phillips et al. 1964). First noted in the San Francisco Peaks by Merriam (1890), these grouse were apparently never common in this mountain range, with the last report in 1910. From 1975 to 1978, approximately 40 Blue Grouse were captured in the White Mountains and released in the San Francisco Peaks area in an effort to reestablish this species (Brown 1989). This transplant effort was considered successful by the early 1980s.

Atlasers found Blue Grouse throughout their historical range at elevations from 7900 to 10,300 ft (2408–3139 m). However, they likely occur locally to above 11,000 ft (3353 m) in Arizona. Atlasers confirmed this species in the White Mountains, Kaibab Plateau, and the San Francisco Mountains region. In the latter, they were found as far northwest as Kendrick Peak.

Additional observations were made of Blue Grouse in the Chuska and Carrizo mountains in the extreme northeast. Phillips (1964) and Brown (1989) had previously not reported Blue Grouse from the latter mountain range. It should also be noted that Blue Grouse undoubtedly continue to occur in the higher elevations of eastern White Mountain Apache tribal lands where access permission to conduct atlas surveys was not granted. Also due to their relatively low abundance in Arizona and their propensity to hold their position until closely approached, many individuals likely went undetected during typical atlas surveys. When flushed, however, they often fly to a nearby exposed low branch or upslope fallen tree to stare back at the intruder. This seemingly tame behavior has led to its sometime being known as the "fool hen."

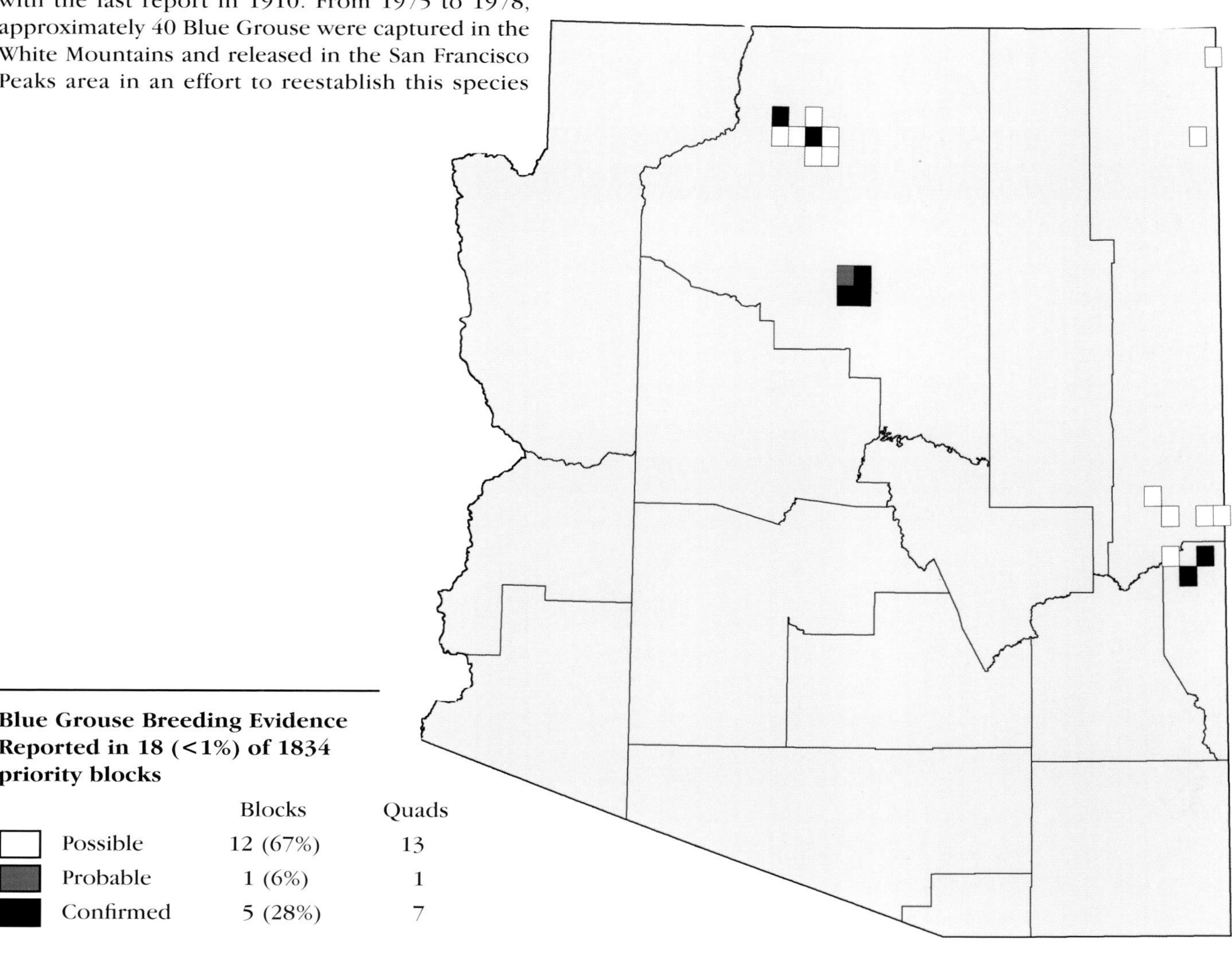

Blue Grouse Breeding Evidence Reported in 18 (<1%) of 1834 priority blocks

	Blocks	Quads
Possible	12 (67%)	13
Probable	1 (6%)	1
Confirmed	5 (28%)	7

Wild Turkey

by Amanda Moors *Meleagris gallopavo*

According to an Apache creation legend, the tail tip of the Wild Turkey was lightened from ocean foam during a great flood. The black, white, and russet tail feathers are a distinctive decoration on the ceremonial dress of crown dancers during the Sunrise Dance, still among the centerpoints of traditional Apache religion today.

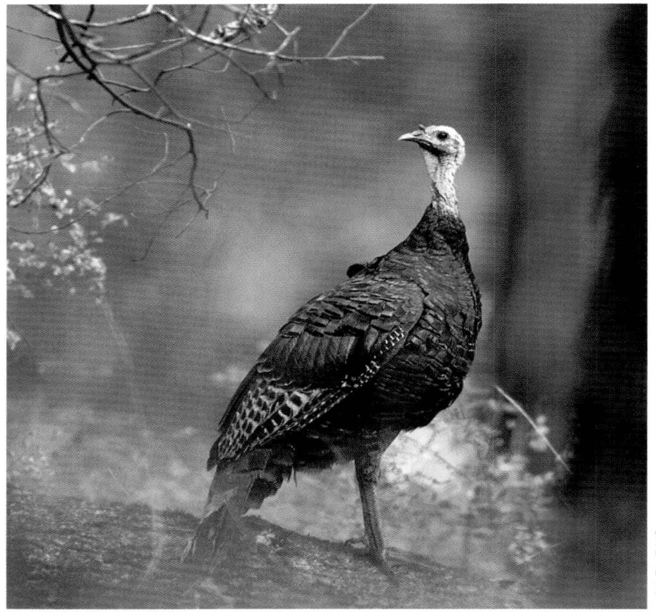
JIM BURNS

HABITAT

Wild Turkeys are a wary game species found throughout many of the forested regions of Arizona, especially in pine forests with a mix of meadows, oak, and juniper. Nearly 25 percent of all atlas records were from forests dominated by ponderosa pine and Gambel's oak (n = 116). Another 22 percent were from either pure ponderosa pine stands or those with a pinyon pine–juniper understory. Atlasers reported another 19 percent of Wild Turkey observations from mixed-conifer forests containing various species of firs, pines, and aspen. Atlasers also noted these large birds in forested drainages containing a mixture of conifers and deciduous trees. In southeastern Arizona, Wild Turkeys were regularly noted in evergreen oak woodlands, Madrean pine–oak forests, and sycamore dominated drainages. Atlasers frequently observed Wild Turkeys foraging in the early morning or evening in forest clearings and at the edge of alpine meadows with an abundance of grasses and other low herbaceous vegetation. Large ponderosa pines or other large trees on steep slopes are used for roosting at night. Locally, riparian areas with large sycamores or cottonwoods also provide good turkey roosts.

BREEDING

Throughout most of the highlands of Arizona, the breeding season of Wild Turkeys is initiated in late March when the males begin strutting and gobbling to entice the females into breeding and to intimidate potential rivals (Brown 1989). This activity continues into late April and early May when the hens begin to incubate their clutches. The only nest with eggs found by atlasers was on 10 June. Courtship and nesting activity begins approximately a month earlier in southeastern Arizona and in populations at lower elevations. Most Wild Turkey breeding confirmations during the atlas pertains to hens with young (poults) including a very early observation on 1 April in extreme southeastern Arizona. The earliest northern Arizona record of poults was noted on 5 May, although the vast majority was reported between 2 June and 2 August.

Wild Turkeys primarily nest in forested habitat, often on steep slopes and in areas with good horizontal and overhead vegetative cover (Wakeling 1991; Wakeling and Shaw 1994). Females build a nest on the ground next to (or even inside) a downed log, within low vegetation, among rocks, or at the base of a bush or tree. The only nest found during the atlas was nestled in a dense clump of sapling Gambel's oaks. An average of 8–12 eggs are laid in approximately a two-week period and incubation takes 26–28 days beginning with the last egg laid (Brown 1989; Eaton 1992). During the laying period, the hen provides no protection for eggs and may even travel as far as 2 mi (3.2 km) away between egg-laying visits (B. Wakeling, personal communication). These game birds will renest if the egg clutch is lost to predation (Eaton 1992).

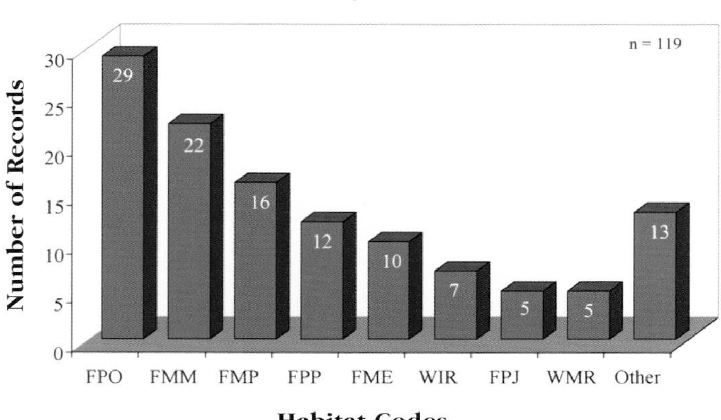

DISTRIBUTION AND STATUS

Wild Turkeys consist of six subspecies found from the extreme southern edge of Canada to central Mexico (Eaton 1992). These large birds are fairly common in appropriate habitat throughout the eastern United States, but they are less common and in scattered populations in the West (Eaton 1992). The more local distribution in the West is primarily the result of transplant efforts, some of which have extended the range of the Wild Turkey.

In Arizona, Wild Turkeys were historically widespread and abundant residents of nearly all forested regions,

Breeding Phenology

Confirmed Records

n = 34

8 7 6 5 4 3 2 1 0

1 Mar | 1 Apr. | 1 May | 1 June | 1 July | 1 Aug.

Graph includes fledgling records

excluding north of the Colorado River and on the Hualapai Mountains (Phillips et al. 1964). In the southeast, populations ranged from the Baboquivari Mountains east to the New Mexico border including within the wooded riparian zones of the upper Santa Cruz and San Pedro rivers (Davis 1982). Many populations of Wild Turkey in Arizona were already on the decline by the 1880s, especially in southeastern Arizona. Phillips et al. (1964) and Brown (1989) detail the historical decrease and the history of reestablishment efforts of Wild Turkeys in Arizona. The exact cause of population declines is unknown, but it may have been related to unregulated hunting, grazing, logging, and perhaps disease (Brown 1989). The distribution of Wild Turkeys in Arizona has been extended beyond their historical range by releases north of the Colorado River on the Kaibab Plateau and in forested mountains within the Arizona Strip region (Brown 1989).

Merriam's (*merriami*) and Gould's (*mexicana*) Turkeys are currently found in Arizona where atlasers noted them between 3800 and 9300 ft (1158–2835 m). The latter subspecies is found only in a few southeastern mountain ranges. Gould's Turkeys were successfully reestablished into the Huachuca Mountains in 1983 and 1987 and into the Galiuro Mountains in 1994 and 1997 (Wakeling et al. 2001). Atlasers also detected Wild Turkeys locally in the Santa Catalina Mountains and western Chiricahua Mountains. Wild Turkeys were not found in the Pinaleno, Pinal, Baboquivari, Santa Rita, and Rincon mountains during the atlas period, where they were found historically (Brown 1989). These birds were also confirmed breeding in the southern Peloncillo Mountains, including Guadalupe Canyon, and at San Bernardino National Wildlife Refuge. However, it is unknown if these turkeys are pure Gould's or of domestic stock from Sonora and New Mexico.

Atlas surveys revealed Wild Turkeys occur throughout the Mogollon Rim and White Mountain regions northwest to near Williams and Flagstaff. Isolated populations exit within the eastern Hualapai tribal lands and in the Arizona Strip region in the higher elevations of the Shivwits Plateau and in the Mount Trumbull and Mount Logan area. Few Wild Turkeys were found on the South Rim of the Grand Canyon, but these large birds were frequently encountered on the Kaibab Plateau. On Navajo tribal lands, atlasers noted Wild Turkeys in the Carrizo, Lukachukai, and Chuska Mountains south to the Defiance Plateau.

The outlook for the Wild Turkey in Arizona is good. Based on recent successes, efforts are likely to succeed in getting Gould's Turkeys reestablished in additional southeastern mountain ranges (B. Wakeling, personal communication).

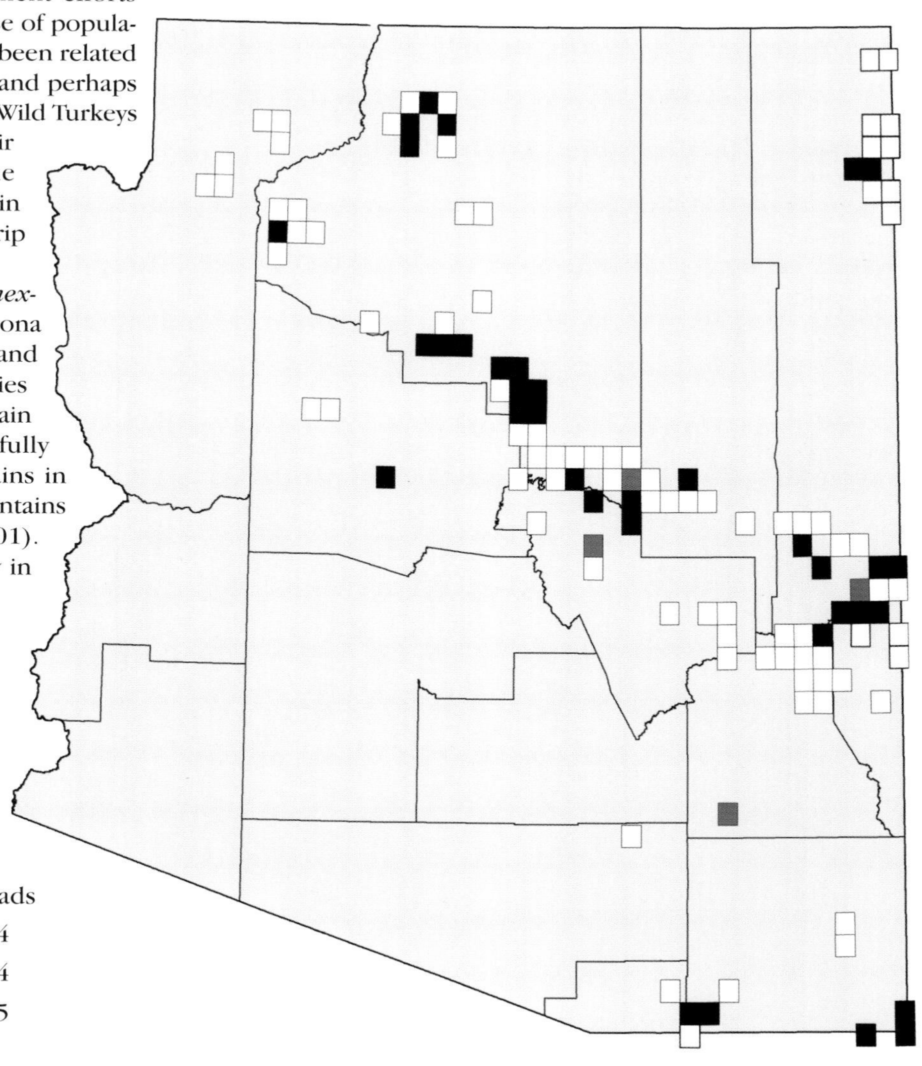

Wild Turkey Breeding Evidence Reported in 101 (6%) of 1834 priority blocks

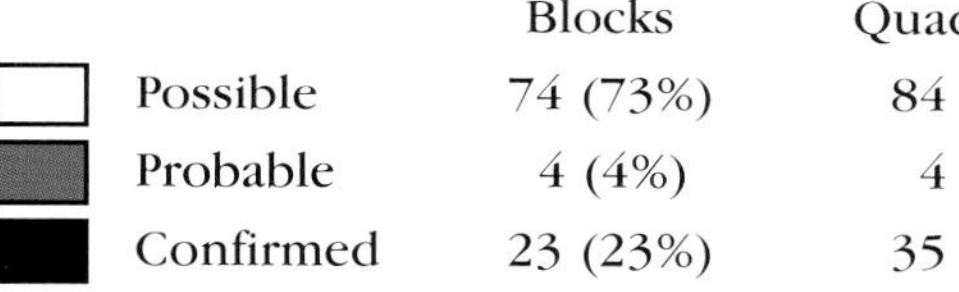

	Blocks	Quads
Possible	74 (73%)	84
Probable	4 (4%)	4
Confirmed	23 (23%)	35

Scaled Quail

by Cathryn Wise-Gervais *Callipepla squamata*

Also known as blue quail, and nicknamed "cotton-top" for their white-tipped crests, Scaled Quail are attractive birds that prefer to run from predators than to flush. This characteristic, as well as their handsome appearance, makes them a popular game species. Although favoring open country, these quail require some cover, be it tall grass or low brush.

JIM BURNS

HABITAT

Scaled Quail favor dry, open grasslands punctuated with low-growing shrubs such as burroweed, snakeweed, cacti, and widely scattered low, shrubby mesquite. These birds generally avoid dense vegetation, preferring instead open rolling hills, low ridges, and mesas (Brown 1989), with less than 50 percent ground cover. Atlasers reported Scaled Quail in 13 habitat types, but observers obtained 53 percent of records in semiarid grasslands characterized by mixed grasses, soaptree yucca, various cacti, and mesquite (n = 125). An additional 16 percent of the records were from Chihuahuan Desert areas comprised of yucca, prickly pear, creosote bush, and acacia. Atlasers reported most of the Scaled Quail detected within the Little Colorado River valley in a mixture of Plains grassland and open desert scrublands with scattered cacti, saltbush, sand sagebrush, and other low shrubs. Observers reported many fewer observations in adjacent open Sonoran Desert scrublands and agricultural areas, but found that Scaled Quail were a familiar sight at old homesteads or ranches, as well as at the edges of crop fields surrounding these. Where their range overlaps in Arizona, Scaled Quail are generally found in more open country than the more numerous, desert scrub inhabiting Gambel's Quail.

BREEDING

Arizona's Scaled Quail are permanent residents that make at most short seasonal movements in search of food. Pair formation typically occurs from late February through March, with nest initiation in normal precipitation years in late April and May (Brown 1989). But nesting is often postponed during dry years until summer monsoons begin in July or August (Brown 1989). The earliest confirmed Scaled Quail record during the atlas was a nest with eggs discovered on 5 May, although atlasers noted adults with young as early as 10 May indicating egg laying initiation by mid-April. Although atlasers obtained 61 breeding confirmations for Scaled Quail, they found only two other nests with eggs with the latest on 8 August. All other confirmed records were of adults with young, and the majority of these were located after 1 July (37 of 61). Atlasers noted adults with young through 12 September. Brown (1989) also noted that downy young may be seen as late as mid-September and even into October, which is well after typical atlas surveys ended. Second broods are rare, even in good years, but these quail will renest if their first attempt fails (Brown 1989).

Scaled Quail nests are a simple shallow depression on the ground lined with grass and leaves (Brandt 1951), usually in a protected and well-shaded situation. Nests are often constructed under dense grasses, forbs, woodpiles, junk (including abandoned vehicles and farm machinery), cholla, prickly pear, or other spiny shrubs (Bent 1932; Schemnitz 1994). Brown (1989) suggested that the male assists with nest construction and will occasionally take over incubation duties if the female disappears. Although atlasers found three Scaled Quail nests, no detailed notes were gathered at these, so nest specifics are not available. The typical Scaled Quail clutch averages 12–13 eggs but can regularly range from 9 to 16, with extremes of 5–22 (Schemnitz 1961). Incubation is mainly by the female and lasts for approximately 22–23 days (Schemnitz 1994). The chicks hatch ready to accompany their parents. Scaled Quail males often perch on low shrubs or posts and act as sentinels while the female and young feed or loaf nearby (Schemnitz 1994).

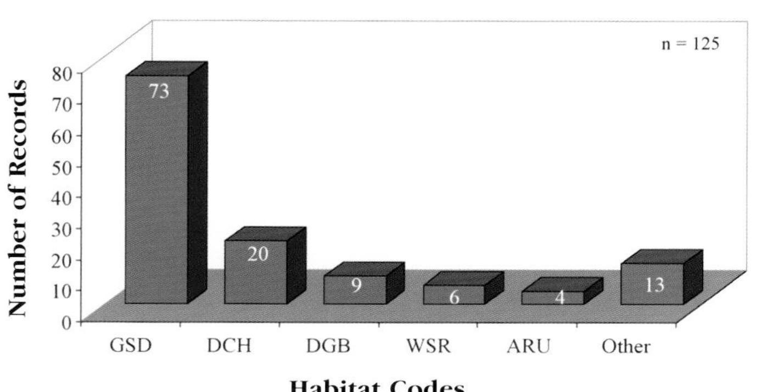

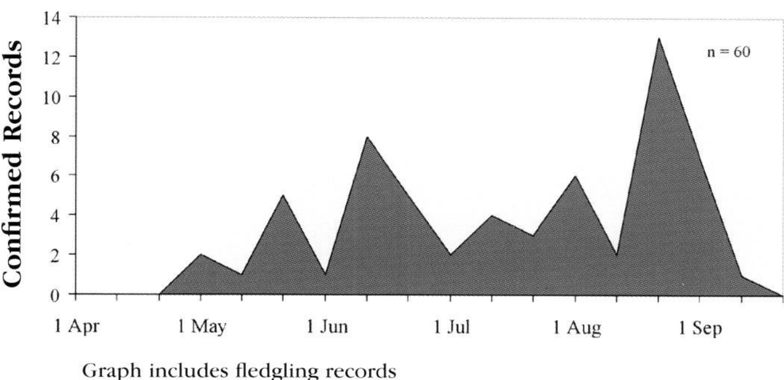

Graph includes fledgling records

DISTRIBUTION AND STATUS

Scaled Quail, or "Cotton-tops" are found throughout the grasslands of western Texas, southeastern Colorado, New Mexico, and eastern Arizona. A large percentage of their range is south of the border in Mexico, specifically in northeast Sonora, Chihuahua, Durango, and south to Hidalgo (Howell and Webb 1995).

Arizona's southern and northern populations of Scaled Quail are neatly divided into two subspecies with *C. s. pallida* in the south and *C. s. hargravei* in the north (Brown 1989). Phillips et al. (1964) suggested that the small population in the upper Little Colorado River drainage may have been introduced, but there is no evidence to support this. Prior accounts reported that Scaled Quail were common to abundant in southeastern Arizona, from San Carlos Apache tribal lands and the Baboquivari Mountains eastward (Swarth 1914; Phillips et al. 1964). Prior to 1925, Scaled Quail were reported to the northwest in the Tonto Basin north of Roosevelt Lake, along the lower Salt River, and near Picacho Peak (Bendire 1892; Swarth 1914). Today, these areas offer little suitable Scaled Quail habitat, and this birds' range has contracted as a result.

In southeastern Arizona, atlasers found Scaled Quail at elevations ranging from 2800 to 5000 ft (853–1524 m) and in east-central Arizona from 5200 to 6700 ft (1584–2042 m). Atlasers found the most western populations of these quail on Tohono O'odham tribal lands in the northwestern foothills of the Baboquivari Mountains. The northern limits of the southeastern Arizona race of Scaled Quail include the upper Aravaipa Valley, lower San Simon River drainage, and just north of Duncan. A seemingly isolated population continues to exist just northeast of San Carlos. Atlasers encountered Scaled Quail as far west in the Little Colorado River valley as just north of Joseph City and as far north as Greasewood on Navajo tribal lands. These quail were not detected near Springerville as noted by Brown (1989) but were found in open Plains grasslands near Saint Johns. Atlasers also encountered Scaled Quail in the Red Rock Valley just northeast of the Chuska Mountains, adjacent to known populations on Navajo tribal lands in northwestern New Mexico (C. LaRue, personal communication).

Atlas data suggest that populations of Scaled Quail have continued to contract in southeastern Arizona, especially at the northern edges of their range. These declines are probably due to habitat modification of open grassland resulting in either increased shrubby vegetation and less open space favoring Gambel's Quail, or complete loss of native grasses. Low annual precipitation during the atlas period undoubtedly also negatively affected these edge populations.

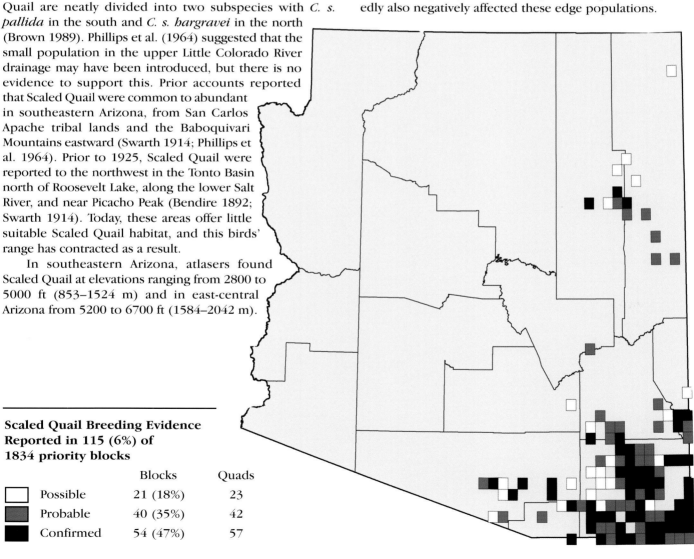

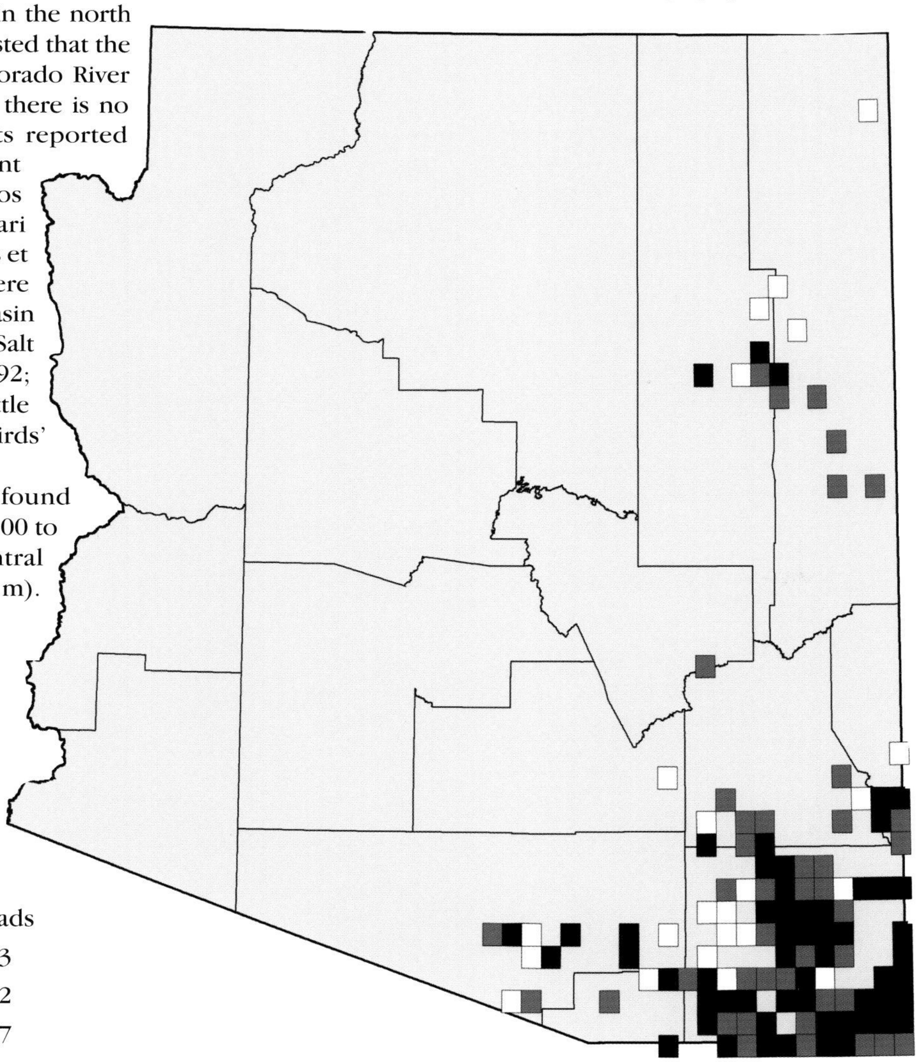

Scaled Quail Breeding Evidence Reported in 115 (6%) of 1834 priority blocks

	Blocks	Quads
Possible	21 (18%)	23
Probable	40 (35%)	42
Confirmed	54 (47%)	57

California Quail

by Troy E. Corman *Callipepla californica*

Prior to atlas efforts, few individuals other than local residents knew there was a small thriving population of California Quail in Arizona. Also known as the "Valley Quail," the descendants of these attractive birds have been surviving on their own for forty years, primarily in the seclusion of private property.

HABITAT

Within their native range, California Quails occupy a diverse array of habitats including chaparral, grassland edges, riparian woodlands, and open foothill forests. The locally introduced population in Arizona inhabits an area that combines several native and human-altered habitats that provide the necessary requirements for their survival. Sources of water are an imported aspect of California Quail habitat and within their limited range in the state, this is obtained from a small perennial river drainage and nearby springs. Additional water sources in the area include adjacent brush-lined irrigation ditches, canals, and ponds. Scattered cottonwoods, Russian olive, and thickets of coyote willow characterize the narrow and open riparian woodlands. An abundant shrub layer in the area provides shelter and consists of dense thickets dominated by four-winged saltbush, raspberry, wild rose, and skunkbush. Various grasses and forbs cover the banks and open lower slopes of the drainage, while the upper slopes are rocky and dry with scattered junipers. Distributed locally throughout the valley are small agricultural fields, pastures, ranches, and homesteads supporting exotic shrubs and shade trees.

BREEDING

California Quails typically remain in coveys of varying size throughout the nonbreeding season. From elevated perches, male California Quail can begin advertising calling in March, reaching a peak intensity in May (Calkins et al. 1999). Calling activity declines in June, but may continue periodically through August (Genelly 1955). Pairing typically occurs in the early spring and complete covey breakup likely occurs sometime in May in Arizona. Brown (1989) noted California Quails in Arizona were paired in mid-April, but were still in coveys at that time. Atlasers reported paired birds from 28 May through 20 July. The nesting phenology of Arizona's population has not been studied, but it likely begins in May or June. Across their North American range, the eggs of most California Quails hatch from late May through late July (Calkins et al. 1999). The only confirmed atlas record was of a pair observed with several young on 1 August near Lyman Lake.

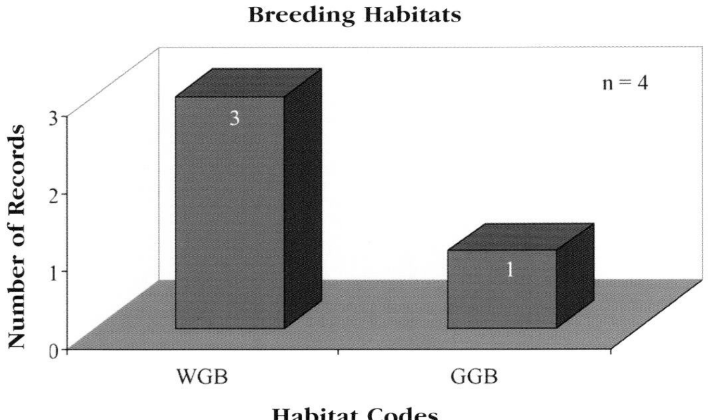

Restricted access within the small range of the California Quail in Arizona greatly limited natural history information that could be gained from atlas surveys. Therefore, much of the following breeding information was gleaned from data compiled by Calkins et al. (1999). Most studies indicate the female California Quail selects the site and constructs the well concealed nest. Nests are usually on the ground and consist of a shallow depression lined with dry vegetation. California Quail nests are constructed under the low canopy of a tree, shrub, weed, or grass clump, as well as under other objects such as rocks, logs, overhanging dirt banks, or boards.

As with many quail, clutch sizes of California Quail can be quite varied between locations and years. Most clutches contain 11–17 eggs, but can range from 1 to 26, with larger clutches likely from multiple females dumping eggs in the same nest. Incubation begins after the entire clutch is laid and is typically performed by the female, while the male acts as a nearby sentinel. Incubation lasts from 22 to 23 days, and the young begin following the parents around soon after hatching. For the first two weeks, chicks are incapable of adequate temperature regulation, and the female broods them at night and during inclement weather to prevent chilling. Fledglings are fully independent at three months of age when fall coveys begin to form. Typically only one brood is reared per year, but females may hatch two broods during favorable years (Francis 1965). Earlier broods are cared for by the male, while the female initiates a second clutch 2–3 weeks following hatching of the first brood.

DISTRIBUTION AND STATUS

California Quails are native to the west coast of North America from southern Oregon, south through Baja California, and inland to western Nevada. They have been widely introduced elsewhere in western North America and the World. In Arizona, California Quail were introduced to the upper Little Colorado River valley near Springerville, Apache County by a local game farm in 1960 (Brown 1989). These quail were originally obtained from Oregon. Eventually California Quail spread down the Little Colorado River to Lyman Lake State Park and up this drainage and the Nutrioso Creek tributary to the approximate boundary of the Apache–Sitgreaves National Forest (Brown 1989).

Atlasers documented the distribution of California Quails to be restricted to the Richville Valley of the Little Colorado River drainage at elevations ranging from 5900 to 6200 ft (1798–1890 m). They were previously reported to at least 7100 ft (2164 m) along Nutrioso Creek east of Springerville (Brown 1989). These quail inhabit the Little Colorado River drainage from approximately 10 mi (16 km) north of Springerville, downstream to below Lyman Lake and north to near Salado. The availability of water and the abundance of dense brushy cover likely limit populations of California Quail in this region.

In Arizona, California Quail populations were found primarily on private property, which greatly restricted access for conducting atlas surveys. Atlasers were often forced to survey the adjacent, more arid State Land in place of the fertile privately owned river valley these birds prefer. Therefore, more thorough surveys may reveal these colorful, introduced quail as more widespread in this region than atlas data indicate.

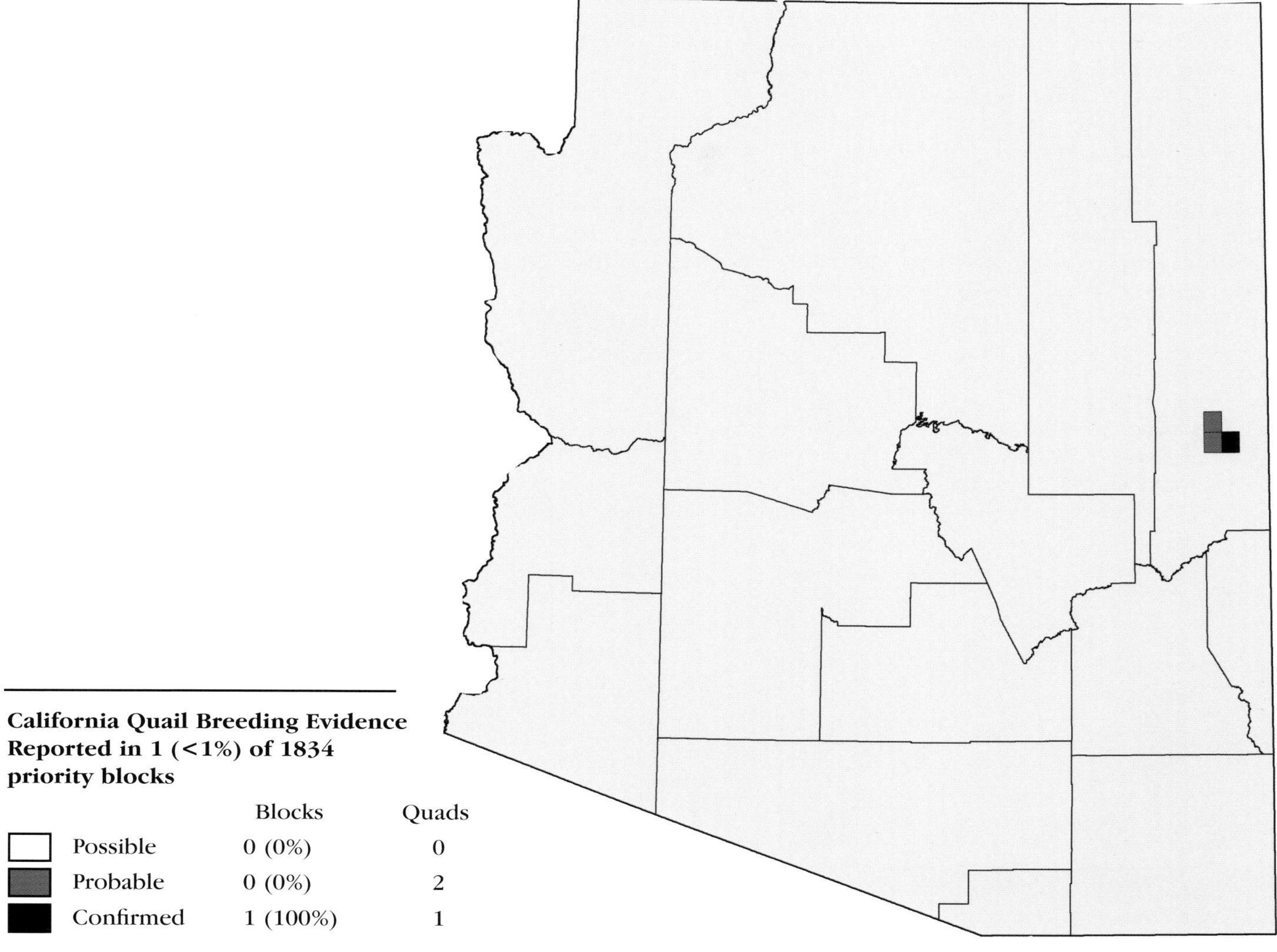

California Quail Breeding Evidence Reported in 1 (<1%) of 1834 priority blocks

	Blocks	Quads
Possible	0 (0%)	0
Probable	0 (0%)	2
Confirmed	1 (100%)	1

Gambel's Quail

by Cathryn Wise-Gervais *Callipepla gambelli*

Gambel's Quail have long been the most popular game bird in Arizona, but win favor with non-hunters as well due to their delightful antics and tame nature. Numbers of these gregarious quail can fluctuate widely from year to year due primarily to food availability based on winter precipitation levels.

HABITAT

This well-known icon of the Southwest favors river valleys and brushy washes in the Sonoran, Mojave, and Chihuahuan deserts (Brown et al. 1998). Atlasers reported the adaptable Gambel's Quail in no less than 31 habitat types with most having some desert influences. Nearly 30 percent of atlas records were from well-vegetated Sonoran Desert uplands characterized by an abundance of thorny legume trees, shrubs, saguaros, and other cacti (n = 1029). An additional 17 percent of Gambel's Quail records were from the adjacent dry desert washes of mesquite, paloverde, and ironwood. Atlasers obtained 10 percent of records in semiarid grasslands containing scattered sotol, agave, acacia, and mesquite. These quail were also regularly reported in suburban and rural areas containing desert vegetation, along the edges of riparian woodland and cultivated lands, and in shrubby grasslands. Generally found below 5400 ft (1650 m), this species avoids pinyon–juniper woodlands and dense chaparral habitats (Brown 1989), although atlasers did regularly encounter this quail at the lower edges of these communities. They also avoid the open, exposed plains favored by Scaled Quail, selecting instead brushy areas that offer both a variety of food and escape cover.

BREEDING

In Arizona, Gambel's Quail begins pair formation in February although courtship can begin as early as January in suburban areas or near other reliable food and water sources. The peak calling of males coincides with the height of reproductive condition and egg incubation, typically in mid-April and early May, but calling and nesting activity may be delayed for months by winter drought (Brown et al. 1998). In a north Phoenix residential area, atlasers reported fledglings as early as 1 March, thereby indicating the initiation of egg laying by late January or early February in this instance. More normally, early egg laying begins in March—occasionally in late February, with fledglings appearing in April through August. Atlasers located the latest Gambel's Quail nest with eggs on 11 July and reported fledglings as late as 7 September.

It is unclear if the Gambel's Quails' lengthy breeding season is due to delayed nesting, renesting attempts, or double-brooding as conflicting evidence exists over this (Brown et al. 1998). It is known that the Gambel's Quail diet changes seasonally, and the consumption of fresh vegetable matter in late winter/early spring brings males into reproductive condition. Because the availability of fresh annuals corresponds directly with breeding phenology (Hungerford 1964), the birds may fail to nest or even form pairs in the driest years (MacGregor and Inlay 1951).

Female Gambel's Quail select a nest site that is commonly on the ground under a tree or shrub or within a clump of prickly pear. She will then build the nest by forming a twig-bordered scrape and lining this with grass, leaves, and feathers (Gorsuch 1934). The average Gambel's Quail clutch consists of 10–12 eggs, although nests in dry years may contain <5 eggs and nests with >15 likely pertain to egg dumping by a second female (Brown et al. 1998). Incubation is usually by the female and takes between 21 and 23 days from the date of the last egg laid (Bent 1932). Males stay nearby, however, and will resume incubation if the female disappears (Gorsuch 1934). For the first few days after hatching, both sexes brood the young vigilantly, since

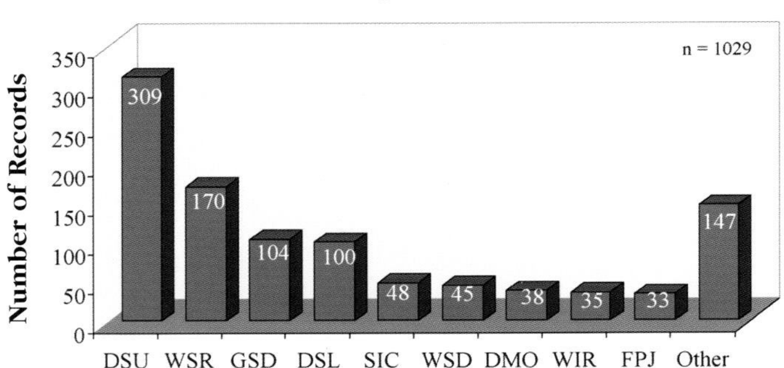

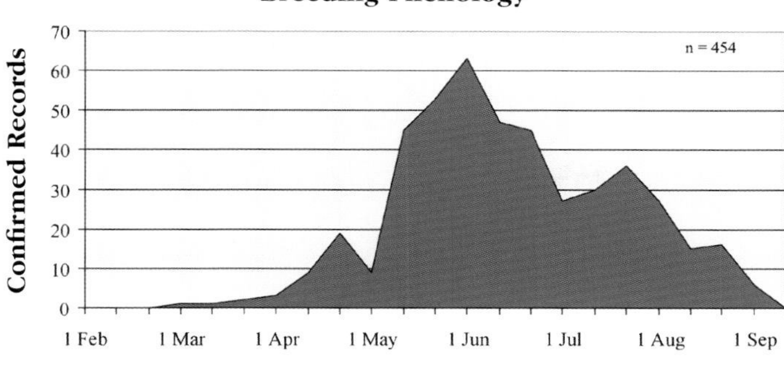

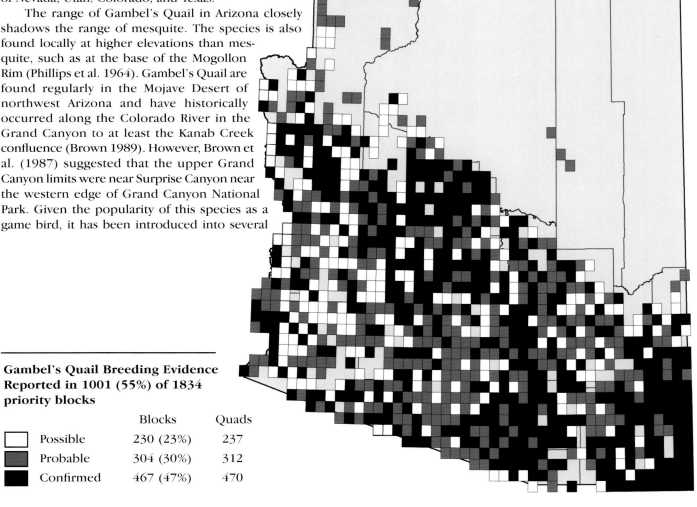

Graph includes fledgling records

the chicks cannot thermoregulate and will burrow into the body feathers of adults for warmth (Brown et. al 1998). Gambel's Quail hens are more involved with chick feeding activities while males spend more time as predator sentinels (Brown et al. 1998).

DISTRIBUTION AND STATUS

Gambel's Quail are the only gallinaceous bird native to the Sonoran Desert and this is the heart of their range (Brown et al. 1998). This quails' range extends from Arizona into northwest Sonora, southeast California, and western New Mexico, as well as sparingly into the adjacent states of Nevada, Utah, Colorado, and Texas.

The range of Gambel's Quail in Arizona closely shadows the range of mesquite. The species is also found locally at higher elevations than mesquite, such as at the base of the Mogollon Rim (Phillips et al. 1964). Gambel's Quail are found regularly in the Mojave Desert of northwest Arizona and have historically occurred along the Colorado River in the Grand Canyon to at least the Kanab Creek confluence (Brown 1989). However, Brown et al. (1987) suggested that the upper Grand Canyon limits were near Surprise Canyon near the western edge of Grand Canyon National Park. Given the popularity of this species as a game bird, it has been introduced into several locations throughout the state including at House Rock Valley, Pipe Springs National Monument, and near Holbrook, Snowflake, and Vernon (Brown 1989).

Atlasers found Gambel's Quail throughout most of their historic range as well as in several of the release locations. Although Brown (1989) considered the introduced populations along the Little Colorado River absent by 1988, atlasers located Gambel's Quail near the town of Leupp on Navajo tribal lands, as well as near Winslow and Hibbard. Atlasers also found Gambel's Quail within the Toroweap Valley on the Arizona Strip, as well as in the upper Kanab Creek drainage near Fredonia and at nearby Pipe Springs National Monument. Atlasers did not locate these quail in the Grand Canyon corridor, although the birds were thought to occur here as recently as 1988 (Brown 1989). Atlasers were not given permission to conduct atlas surveys within Havasupai tribal land; therefore, it is unknown if the native populations in Cataract Canyon and Havasu Creek continue to persist. Brown et al. (1987) suggested that this population was either greatly reduced or had disappeared. Gambel's Quail are known to expand their range slightly during good years, then contract during drought or other difficult periods. Such may be the case in the Grand Canyon region, and the birds may appear in this area periodically.

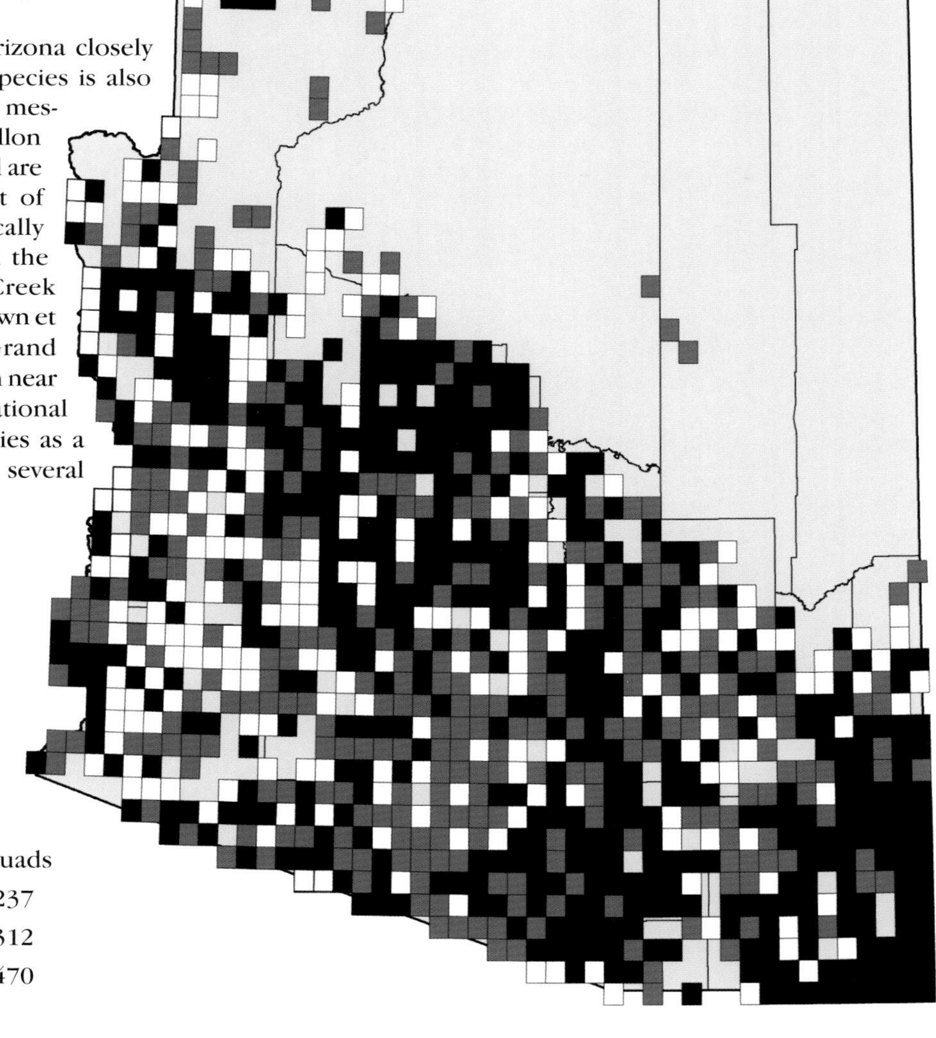

Gambel's Quail Breeding Evidence Reported in 1001 (55%) of 1834 priority blocks

	Blocks	Quads
Possible	230 (23%)	237
Probable	304 (30%)	312
Confirmed	467 (47%)	470

Northern Bobwhite

by Cathryn Wise-Gervais *Colinus virginianus*

RICHARD OCKENFELS

Described by ornithologists as "nearly mythical" in occurrence, the rarely encountered Northern (Masked) Bobwhite was extirpated from Arizona entirely by 1900 due to intense grazing pressure coupled with drought. Fortunately, due to the concerted efforts of many organizations and individuals, there is an encouraging outlook for locally reestablishing this striking quail in Arizona.

HABITAT

The Masked (*ridgwayi*) subspecies of Northern Bobwhite is associated with open savanna grasslands within dry-tropical scrub found in river bottoms, level valleys, and plains (Kuvlesky et al. 1997). These birds favor areas of lush, dense grass mixed with herbaceous plants and scattered semiarid shrubs such as catclaw acacia, mimosa, and velvet mesquite (McLaughlin 1992). Observers obtained only four Masked Bobwhite records during the atlas period, and all records were in semiarid to open savanna grassland habitats characterized by tall mixed grasses with scattered acacia and mesquite. Further, complex native grass mixtures coupled with a climate providing substantial monsoon rains characterize both historical and present-day habitats (Brown and Ellis 1977). Masked Bobwhite are most often encountered in grasslands containing a variety of native forbs and grasses including giant sacaton, three awns, tanglehead, vine mesquite, and several grama species (Brown 1989). The widespread loss of native grasses in southern Arizona by 1900 spelled disaster for Masked Bobwhites, and the monotonous cover of introduced buffelgrass and Lehmann lovegrass do not provide suitable habitat for these quail (Russell and Monson 1998).

BREEDING

Masked Bobwhites are a sedentary species and are behaviorally similar to the widespread eastern Northern Bobwhite races but require high humidity for breeding. Therefore in the arid Southwest, these quail typically delay nesting until the late summer monsoon period. Although Masked Bobwhites are known to breed occasionally in early spring after abundant winter rains, atlasers did not report this. Masked Bobwhites remain in coveys until early June and males usually begin giving their distinctive "bobwhite" call until seasonal rains begin in July (Brown 1989). Atlasers first located birds on breeding territory (presumed by males calling regularly from the same area) on 25 July. Biologists on the Buenos Aires National Wildlife Refuge observed calling males from 27 June through 28 August in 2001, with the peak of activity occurring in early August (M. Honeycutt, personal communication), which coincides with the peak of nesting activity. During studies in adjacent Sonora, calling reached a peak from mid- to late August, with individuals heard calling into late September (Tomlinson 1972). Atlasers noted calling Masked Bobwhite on 6 August and reported a pair of birds on 12 August. Atlasers also sighted adults with young on 8 September; this was the only breeding confirmation obtained for this species. The hatching period in northern Sonora reaches a peak in early to mid-September, but can range from late July to early November (Tomlinson 1972)

Like other races, Masked Bobwhites nest on the ground, concealed by dense grass (Brown 1989). Nests are comprised of grasses and dead vegetation, and these materials are sometimes woven into an arch above the nest (Brennan 1999). Clutches consist of 12–14 eggs (range 5–15) and incubation takes approximately 23 days. Masked Bobwhite chicks eat almost entirely insects and are led to food by parents (Brennan 1999).

DISTRIBUTION AND STATUS

Brown (1989) described the historical range of Masked Bobwhite as limited to plains and river valleys in northern Sonora and extreme south-central Arizona from 500 to 3850 ft (152–1174 m). In Arizona, these birds were found only in the Altar Valley east of the Baboquivari Mountains and in the upper Santa Cruz River valley south of Tucson (Phillips et al. 1964). Unverified historical reports from the Huachuca and Whetstone Mountains were probably misidentified Montezuma Quail, as Masked Bobwhites are not known to use high elevation grasslands (Phillips et al. 1964).

A combination of persistent livestock overgrazing and a series of droughts in the 1890s denuded Masked Bobwhite habitat and the birds probably disappeared entirely from Arizona by the turn of the century (Brown 1904). Reintroduction efforts began prior to 1950 but were unsuccessful due to limited knowledge of the birds' natural history and habitat requirements. This species is difficult to study given its secretive nature: It would rather walk than fly, is silent for most of the year, and often hunkers down rather than flushing. After nearly 15 years of researching the birds in Sonora, biologists established the Buenos Aires National Wildlife Refuge (BANWR) in 1985 with the primary goal of supporting a sustainable population of these birds. Atlasers reported Masked Bobwhite on only four adjacent quad maps in the Altar Valley within the BANWR. In Arizona, Masked Bobwhites undoubtedly occur only within this refugium; the remaining populations in Sonora, Mexico are found only on a few ranches south of Benjamin Hill.

The Masked Bobwhite was among the original fauna listed as endangered by the United States government after the passage of the Endangered Species Conservation Act of 1969. Researchers agree that both habitat protection and proper grazing practices are essential for the reestablishment of the Masked Bobwhite in Arizona (Carroll et al. 1994). Biologists at the BANWR monitor the birds as closely as possible by conducting call-counts from early June through the end of August. There are 20 transects on the refuge and they are sampled 4 to 5 times per year. Additionally, researchers attempt to trap the birds to determine if breeding is occurring in the wild. By the end of the atlas period, biologists estimated that there were 300-500 birds in the wild on BANWR, and each year several 100 birds produced in the on-site captive breeding program were being released into the wild.

Management recommendations include continuing and improving the current monitoring program. Managers should also carefully monitor range and water resources to provide for the best possible conditions for the birds, given their extreme sensitivity to fluctuations in rainfall from year to year (Camou-Luders et al. 1999). Lastly, managers should maintain the genetic diversity of Arizona's captive population, possibly by translocating wild Mexican birds to BANWR and into the captive breeding program (Kuvlesky 1997).

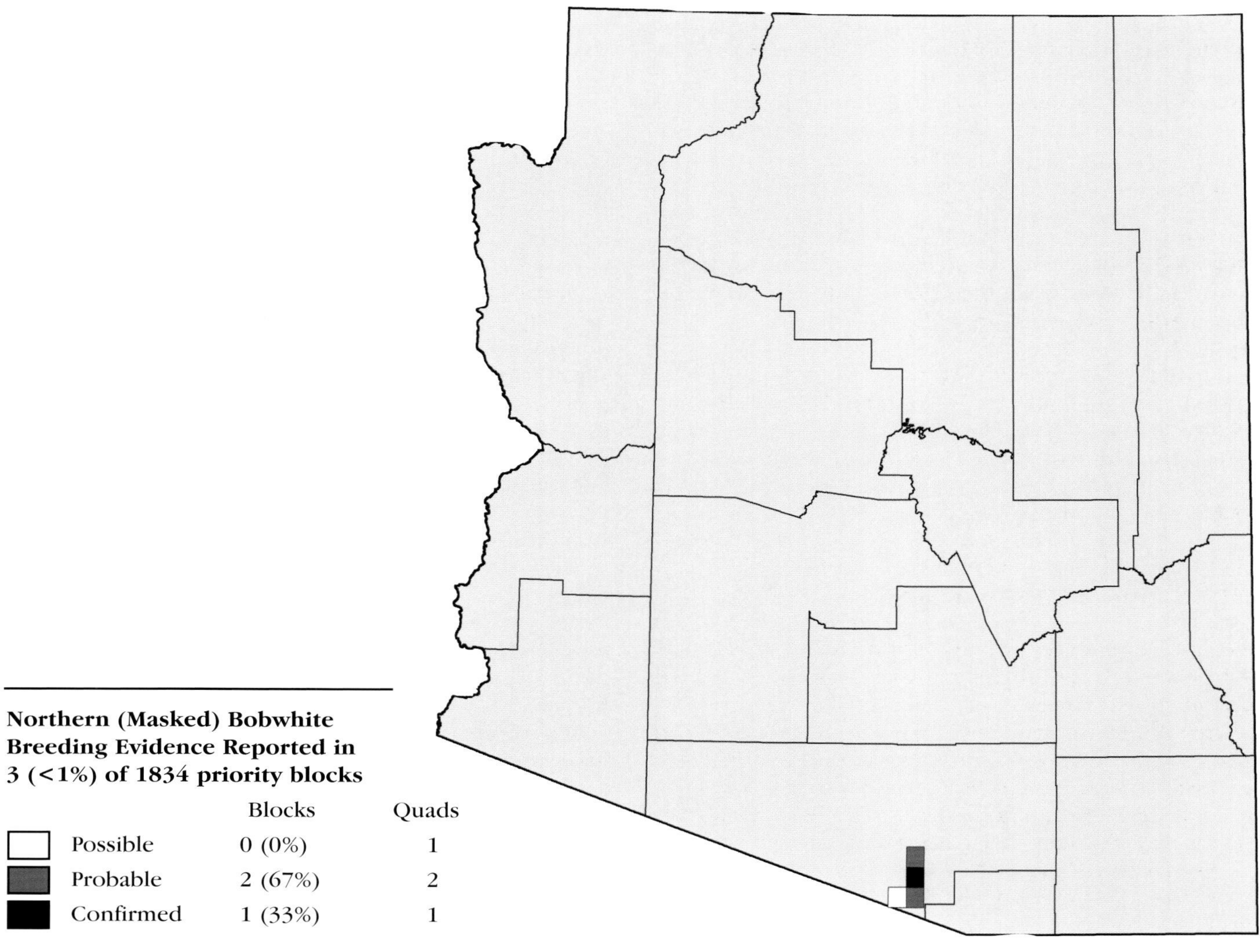

Montezuma Quail

by Troy E. Corman *Cyrtonyx montezumae*

The strikingly gaudy plumage of the male Montezuma Quail overshadows the beautifully cryptic coloration of his mate. These stocky, retiring quail are masters at remaining undetected on the grassy, wooded slopes they prefer. They maintain their invisibility by freezing with the slightest hint of danger only to explode startlingly into the air from one's feet.

RICK AND NORA BOWERS

HABITAT

Occurring in many different open woodland habitats in Arizona, Montezuma Quail rely heavily on an understory of grass and forbs. Atlasers reported this secretive ground dweller most frequently (43 percent of all observation) from Madrean evergreen oak woodlands containing alligator juniper and several oaks including Emory, Arizona White, netleaf, and Mexican blue ($n = 54$). An additional 13 percent of atlas records were reported from adjacent semiarid grasslands where open oak woodlands meet scattered velvet mesquite and agave. Montezuma Quail were also frequently encountered in Madrean pine-oak woodlands where open Apache, Chihuahuan, and ponderosa pines have an understory of various evergreen oaks, juniper, pinyon, and Arizona madrone. Northern and higher elevation populations were detected most often in canyons and near drainage dominated by cottonwood-willow, Arizona sycamore, or Douglas fir, maple, and various pines. These quail were also noted occasionally at the edge of alpine meadows.

BREEDING

Male Montezuma Quails call infrequently in late winter and spring, but routinely do not call consistently until the summer monsoon period begins in late June or July. In Arizona, calling by the males peaks in August and ceases by October (Stromberg 2000). Pairs begin forming in Arizona in late February or March (Bishop 1964). The first pair reported by atlasers was on 8 April. Even though some early observations of adults with fledglings have been noted by 14 June in Arizona (Sutton and Phillips 1942), most confirmed nesting records are later. Atlasers reported the earliest confirmation on 7 July when an adult was observed with young. This would suggest initiation of incubation no later than mid-June. Confirmed atlas records were spread throughout the late summer and fall, without any significant peak. Nesting activity closely coincides with the initiation of summer rains and is often postponed until August if monsoon activity is poor. In Arizona, most broods are observed in August and September, well after most atlas surveys have been conducted. However, atlasers observed broods as late as 18 October and Stromberg (2000) reported that unusually late nests with eggs are occasionally discovered in early October.

The factors that trigger nesting appear to be related to increasing humidity and a switch in the Montezuma Quails' diet to newly emerged vegetative growth and insects (Brown 1989). Nests are constructed on the ground, often completely covered by rooted grasses, forbs, or leafy saplings (Wallmo 1954). Many nests are also under additional cover of fallen logs or adjacent to large trees or rocks (Wallmo 1954). Nest sites range from cool, moist canyon bottoms to hot, semiarid grassy and chaparral covered slopes (Brown 1989).

The female Montezuma Quail incubates the average clutch of 11 eggs, which can range from 6 to 16 (Brown 1989). Eggs hatch in approximately 25 days, and both parents brood the young in the nest for at least a day after hatching, before abandoning the nest (Wallmo 1954). When broods are disturbed, both parents feign injury or flutter near source of disturbance while young scatter and run to dense cover (Brown 1989). The hen may attempt to renest if the first clutch is lost, but second broods are not produced.

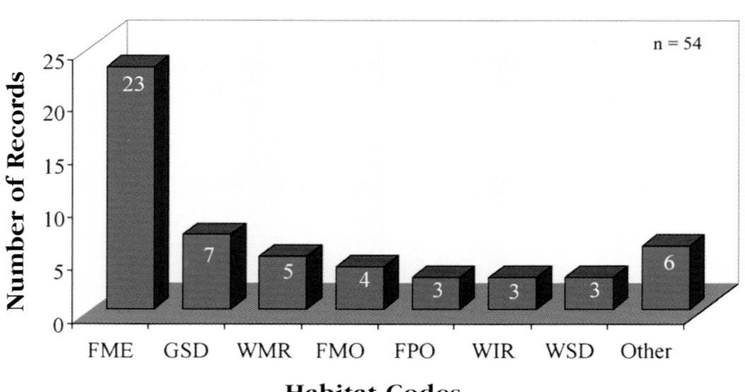

DISTRIBUTION AND STATUS

Montezuma Quail are found from the central highlands of southern Mexico, north to southeastern Arizona, New Mexico, and locally in western Texas. Historical accounts

Breeding Phenology

Confirmed Records

3
2
1
0

n = 14

1 Jun 1 Jul 1 Aug 1 Sep 1 Oct

Graph includes fledgling records

described this quail as having a spotty distribution throughout southeastern Arizona mountains, north to the White and Mogollon mountains (Swarth 1909). The most western record came from the vicinity of Fort Whipple near Prescott (Coues 1866) and the most northern observations were from the San Francisco Mountains near Flagstaff (Beale 1858). Phillips et al. (1964) reported that this quail no longer occurred north of the Pinal Mountain or northwest of the White Mountain region. Brown (1989) noted that the Montezuma Quail was rare on Tonto National Forest, where they were previously reported as locally common (Hargrave 1940). However, these quail were still irregularly reported as far north as 33 mi (53 km) south–southeast of Flagstaff in 1966 and near Camp Verde in 1970 (Monson and Phillips 1981).

Atlas data suggest a continued contraction of the Montezuma Quails northwest distribution in Arizona. Their central Arizona distribution has always been spotty, and loss and alteration of habitat is due to many years of prolonged drought, inappropriate grazing practices, and forest fire suppression likely contributed to the extirpation of these isolated populations.

Atlasers detected Montezuma Quail within a significant range of elevations, from near 3800 ft (1158 m) at Buenos Aires National Wildlife Refuge to 9170 ft (2795 m) in the White Mountains. Monson and Phillips (1981) noted that this quail has been observed as high as 10,000 ft (3048 m) in the White Mountains on the slopes of Mount Baldy.

In east-central Arizona, the most western atlas record was on San Carlos Apache tribal lands, just south of the Black River above the Deer Creek confluence. In the White Mountains, Montezuma Quail were found near Mount Baldy, South Fork of the Little Colorado River, and Sipes White Mountain Wildlife Area. Several records also came from the upper Black River and then south to east of Clifton.

The densities of Montezuma Quail in southeastern mountain ranges along the Mexican border, have always been higher than those to the north and in central Arizona. Atlasers encountered this quail in the southern Peloncillo and Chiricahua Mountains, west to the Baboquivari Mountains. They were not reported in the Santa Catalina Mountains during the atlas period, but were found in the nearby Rincon Mountains. Similarly, atlasers encountered them locally in the Pinaleno Mountains, but did not find them in the Galiuro and Pinal mountains where they have occurred in the past. It is important to note, however, that typical atlas surveys could easily miss this rather quiet, skulking quail. This is especially true in the more northern populations where densities of these quail are low.

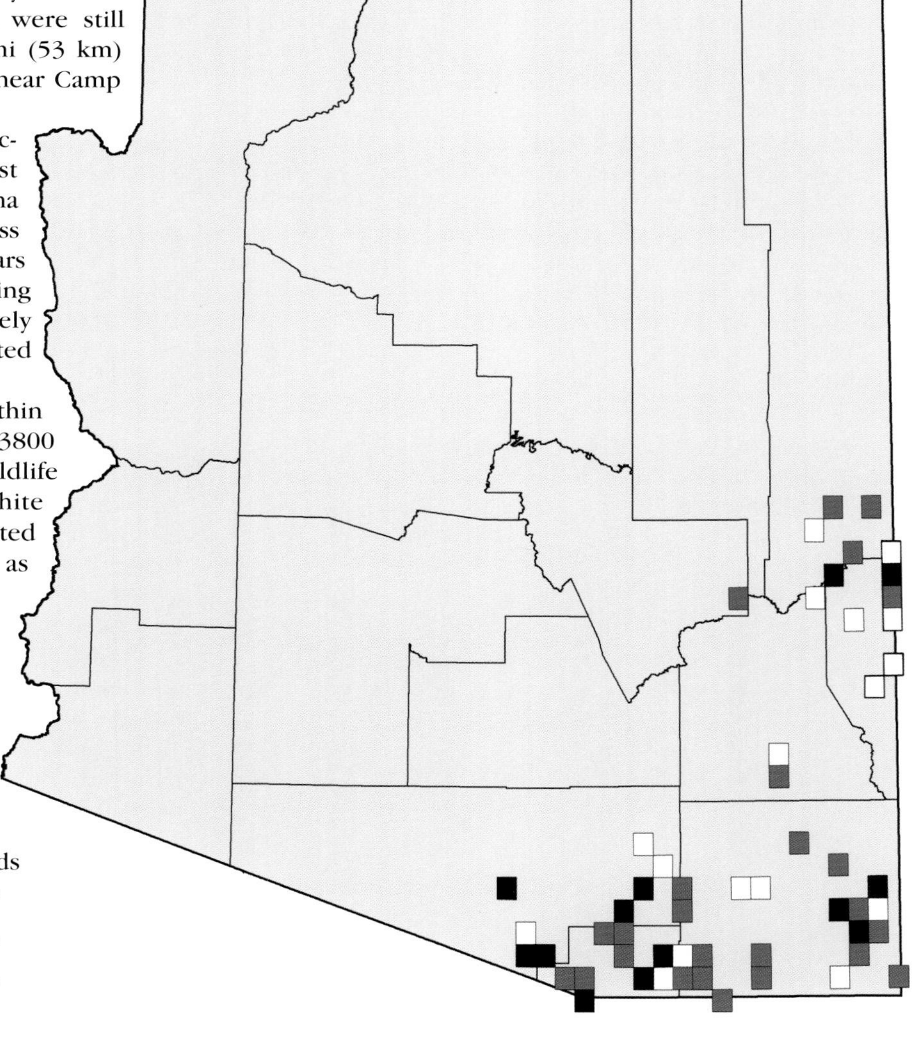

Montezuma Quail Breeding Evidence Reported in 47 (3%) of 1834 priority blocks

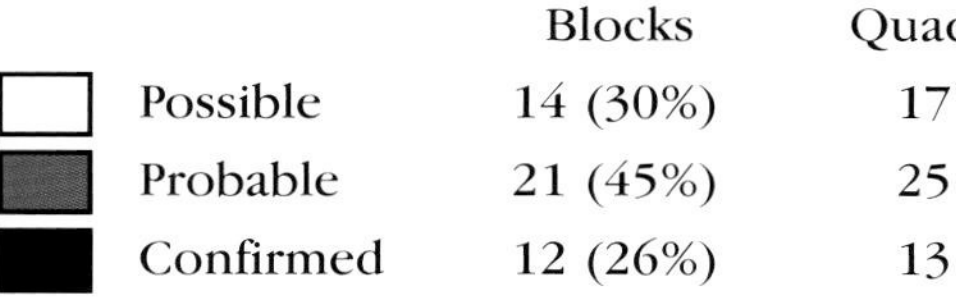

	Blocks	Quads
Possible	14 (30%)	17
Probable	21 (45%)	25
Confirmed	12 (26%)	13

Pied-billed Grebe

by Cathryn Wise-Gervais *Podilymbus podiceps*

Never underestimate the small but aggressive Pied-billed Grebe. This bird, the most widespread and solitary grebe in North America, often lurks in reeds with only its head visible. This petite bully submerges slowly, surfaces unexpectedly, and nips at floating ducks from below to drive them away.

JIM BURNS

HABITAT

Arizona's Pied-billed Grebes nest in a variety of settings, but all are similar in that each provides marshy wetlands with emergent vegetation, especially cattails and bulrush. These solitary grebes tolerate being in close proximity to human development and are equally common on residential and wastewater ponds, as well as on sluggish rivers and high mountain lakes. Atlasers reported Pied-billed Grebes in eight habitat types, but 80 percent of records were in marshland-cienega associations (n = 86). These wetlands occur at most elevations and can be surrounded by considerably different habitat types. Atlasers reported many fewer records in each of the remaining habitats, including cottonwood–willow associations, agricultural settings with irrigation ponds, and urban and suburban parks with ornamental plantings. In all settings, Pied-billed Grebes are equally found foraging in open water or near the cover of floating and emergent vegetation. Rarely seen in flight, Pied-billed Grebes typically escape danger by diving and skulking from the intruder (Bent 1919).

BREEDING

Pied-billed Grebes are local residents in southern and western Arizona, and maintain pair bonds throughout the winter (Muller and Storer 1999). In fact, atlas data suggest that this grebe may breed locally throughout the year at lower elevations. In the Phoenix area, Pied-billed Grebes begin nest building as early as December and observers reported adults with very small young on 12 January in Tempe. The Pied-billed Grebes' breeding season is more contracted in northern Arizona, as the birds usually do not arrive in higher elevation areas until March or April. The earliest high elevation breeding confirmation was an occupied nest at Nelson Reservoir on 11 June. Atlasers obtained the majority of Pied-billed Grebe breeding records between March and September; these data suggest that breeding activity of these grebes in Arizona peaks in mid-July. The latest high elevation breeding confirmation was a nest with eggs near Nutrioso on 28 July, but the breeding cycle continues well into fall in low elevation areas. Atlasers observed an adult with dependent young on 22 November at a Tucson park. The fact that both the earliest and latest breeding were obtained in urban areas indicates that the species benefits from the stable resources available near human developments. It is likely that breeding occurs much more frequently both earlier and later than atlas data show, but such incidents were not detected because they fell outside the typical field survey period. Fall migration in Arizona typically extends from August to December.

Although atlasers did not measure or take detailed notes at any active Pied-billed Grebe nests, it is likely that the species behaves similarly in Arizona as in the rest of their range. Like other grebes, Pied-billeds construct floating raftlike nests comprising vegetation anchored either to the wetland bottom or to growing plants (Muller and Storer 1999). Unlike other nesting grebe species in Arizona, Pied-billed Grebe nests are typically concealed among wetland vegetation and are never in a colonial setting with others of its kind. The male often constructs a platform while establishing his territory early in the breeding season. The pair may later construct the nest together on this platform or select another nesting site (Muller and Storer 1999).

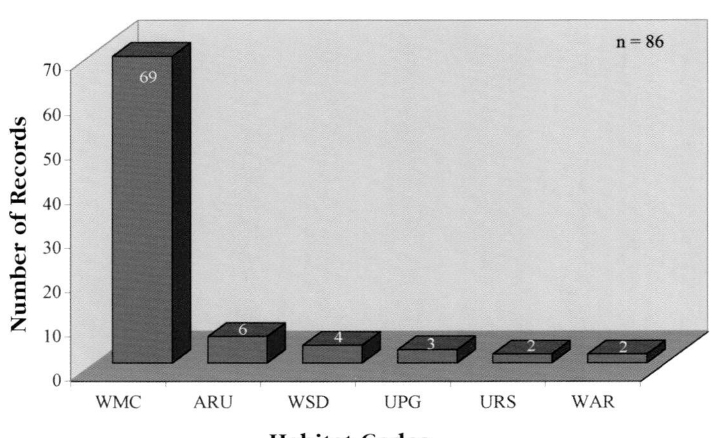

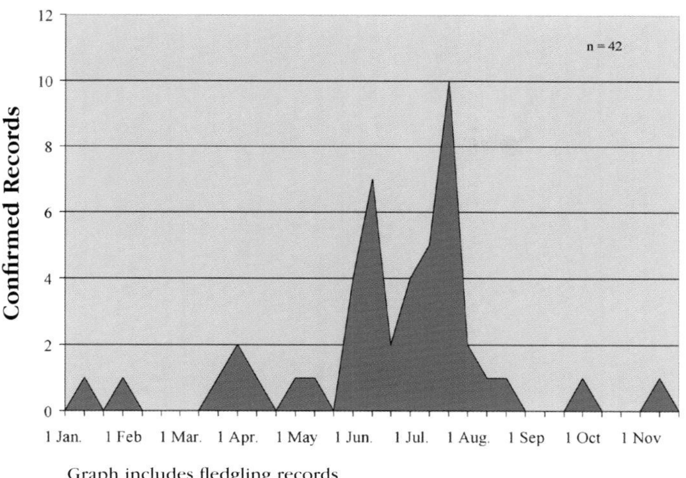

Graph includes fledgling records

Pied-billed Grebes typically lay 5–7 eggs (range 3–10). The male and female share incubation duties, but it is the female that incubates immediately after the eggs are laid and at hatching (Muller and Storer 1999). Incubation takes 21–27 days, then both sexes feed and brood the young and will carry them on their backs while swimming. Adults feed young for approximately 5 weeks and will usually rear 1–2 broods per season (Muller and Storer 1999).

DISTRIBUTION AND STATUS

Pied-billed Grebes breed from central Canada to southern Mexico. While many northern populations are migratory, those in the south and warmer areas of the west are resident. They are locally uncommon to common residents in western and southern Arizona, and are more numerous and widely dispersed in winter from the influx of northern migrants (Rosenberg et al. 1991).

Earlier accounts of nesting Pied-billed Grebes noted that they are scattered throughout Arizona where appropriate wetlands are found (Phillips et al. 1964). Atlas data verified this spotty statewide distribution, and atlasers regularly encountered these grebes in suitable habitat at elevations from 100 to 9200 ft (30–2804 m). Pied-billed Grebes were frequently seen along the lower Colorado River from Topock Marsh south to Gadsden, and they were also commonly reported on open-water portions of the Gila River from Tolleson to Yuma. Elsewhere in the state, these grebes were noted primarily on isolated lakes and ponds with wetland vegetation. At higher elevations, Pied-billed Grebes were also regularly encountered in the White Mountains and atlasers recorded nine adjoining quads south of Springerville. Atlasers reported other high elevation sightings for this bird at mountain lakes south of Flagstaff, including Kinnicknick, White Horse, and Mormon lakes. Due to the local and limited distribution of their preferred habitat, Pied-billed Grebes were detected less frequently in southeastern and northern Arizona.

Given the regularity with which atlasers encountered Pied-billed Grebes, it would seem that this species is fairly stable in Arizona, although more quantitative analysis is necessary to verify this. It is encouraging to note that Pied-billed Grebes have been able to maintain healthy populations in Arizona, even in the face of rapid development and the historical loss of natural wetlands. This success is likely due in part to the bird's flexibility in habitat choice and its ability to take advantage readily of even small artificial wetlands surrounded by desert, agriculture, or urban development.

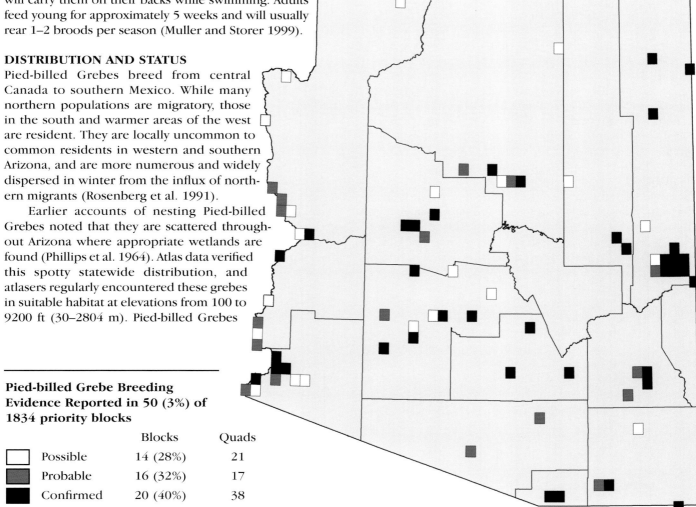

Pied-billed Grebe Breeding Evidence Reported in 50 (3%) of 1834 priority blocks

	Blocks	Quads
Possible	14 (28%)	21
Probable	16 (32%)	17
Confirmed	20 (40%)	38

Eared Grebe

by Cathryn Wise-Gervais *Podiceps nigricollis*

During the breeding season, the ruby-eyed Eared Grebe commands attention with its beautiful golden head plumes and elaborate courtship and nest-selection displays. Both adults take part in these shows, which consist of distinctive postures and vocalizations. These gregarious grebes forage in open water and feed on a wide variety of aquatic insects and crustaceans.

DAN FISCHER

HABITAT

Eared Grebes generally nest in more open situations than other grebes, and prefer shallow bodies of water with sparse emergent vegetation. Cullen et al. (1999) further noted that these grebes rarely nest in wetlands with fish and typically select areas with an abundance of macroinvertebrates. Due to their preference for shallower water, Eared Grebe nesting areas tend to vary considerably from year to year, based on the local effects of seasonal and annual fluctuations in water level (Boe 1992). Observers detected relatively few Eared Grebe nesting areas during the atlas period, and these were primarily at high-elevation marshes and along shallow sections of ponds, lakes, and reservoirs. Many of these sites were ephemeral or became dry occasionally and therefore lacked fish. Eared Grebes generally shun the wetlands immediately adjacent to forests and woodlands, preferring instead nesting areas that are surrounded by open grasslands in Arizona. Eared Grebes also typically avoid tall cattail and bulrush stands, and prefer nesting sites in shallow patchy sedge or flooded grassy areas. They will also nest in slightly deeper water where there is an abundance of low floating or submergent vegetation.

BREEDING

By early March, Eared Grebes begin departing from wintering areas that including western and southern Arizona. Peak passage is from mid-April and early May, with stragglers into early June. Arizona's nesting populations usually arrive in breeding areas in May and are thought to form pair bonds within the first few weeks of their arrival (Cullen et al. 1999). Nest construction at higher elevations in Arizona typically begins in late May; atlasers observed adults on nests beginning on 9 June. However, the few odd lowland nesting efforts in Arizona appear to begin slightly earlier. Just prior to the atlas in 1992, Eared Grebe nests with eggs were noted by mid-May at Willcox and an adult with three nearly grown young were found on 31 May on tribal lands of the Gila River Indian Community (Witzeman et al. 1997). The latter observation suggests the initiation of nesting activity by late April. Atlasers reported occupied nests (presumably with eggs) through 25 July. Newly hatched chicks have been observed as late as 1 August and the latest breeding record obtained during the atlas period was of adults with dependent young on 14 August. In Arizona, Eared Grebes begin to stray from nesting areas by mid-August, with numbers increasing through the fall and stragglers reported into December.

Although Eared Grebes can form large breeding colonies in the hundreds of pairs, they usually nest singly or in small groups in Arizona. Most nesting locations in the state contain fewer than 30 pairs. Eared Grebe pairs work together to construct a somewhat flimsy floating nest, comprised of both rotten and green vegetation (Cullen et al. 1999). Nests are anchored to emergent stems, low floating plants, or submergent vegetation (Cullen et al. 1999). Early nests are placed in a group and act as a nucleus for colony development (McAllister 1958). Nesting material is periodically added throughout incubation.

Unless otherwise noted, the following natural history information was taken from Cullen et al. (1999). Eared Grebes typically lay 2–4 eggs, but can range from 1 to 5, with larger clutches likely indicating brood parasitism by other females. The whole nest remains waterlogged; the lower half of each egg is always wet. The adults will cover eggs with vegetation for concealment, particularly if they are leaving the nest for any length of time (Bent 1919). Incubation by both parents begins as soon as the first egg is laid and takes approximately 21 days. Young hatch asynchronously and move from the nest cup to the parent's back after hatching until all eggs have hatched. Young are back-brooded for the first week, typically carried by one parent and fed by the other. It is uncommon for chicks more than 20 days old to receive parental care and parents often leave the breeding wetlands before their young can fly. Pairs will usually rear a single brood each year, but they will renest if earlier attempts have failed.

DISTRIBUTION AND STATUS

Eared Grebes breed not only in North America, but also over a large area of Europe, east to China, and locally in

Africa and northern South America. In western North America, these grebes nest from southern Canada south through the Great Plain to Arizona, New Mexico, and California, with a disjunct population in central Mexico.

Mearns (1890) first reported Eared Grebes nesting in central Arizona above the Mogollon Rim at such places as Stoneman, Mormon, and other lakes near Flagstaff. The grebes were also found nesting in several locations in the White Mountains such as at Big Lake (Goldman 1926) and were possibly nesting in the upper Verde Valley near Clarkdale at Peck's Lake (Phillips et al. 1964). Atlasers confirmed that Eared Grebes continue to nest at least occasionally near Flagstaff at Mormon and Kinnikinik lakes and at several lakes and reservoirs in the White Mountain region. As with most prior accounts, atlasers found these grebes breeding primarily north of the Mogollon Rim at elevations ranging from 7000 to 9200 ft (2134–2804 m). Prior to the atlas period, one pair was reported nesting as low as 1100 ft (335 m) at a large irrigation-holding pond surrounded by Sonoran desert scrub, but this was an unusual occurrence.

Elsewhere in Arizona, Eared Grebe breeding activity has been much more sporadic, and this is probably because of annual fluctuating water levels. These grebes were found nesting at Watson Lake near Prescott in 1976 (Monson and Phillips 1981) and not again until the atlas in 2001. On Navajo tribal lands, Monson and Phillips (1981) found Eared Grebes nesting near the Chuska Mountain. Jacobs (1986) observed possibly as many as ten pairs each nesting at Ganado and Moaning Lake in 1985. Atlasers found pairs occupying Ganado Lake, but they were unable to confirm nesting during this period. Eared Grebes nested at Willcox in 1992 and again during the atlas period in 1993. Although nesting was suspected again at this location in 1995, atlasers could find no evidence that these fickle grebes nested at Willcox again through the remainder of the atlas period.

Since the numbers and locations of nesting Eared Grebes vary annually in Arizona, it is difficult to determine any significant population trends for the state. Through much of the atlas period, drought or near drought conditions played havoc with Arizona's water birds, including the Eared Grebe. Many lakes and ponds harboring nesting Eared Grebes in the early 1990s were completely dry during the last half of the atlas period.

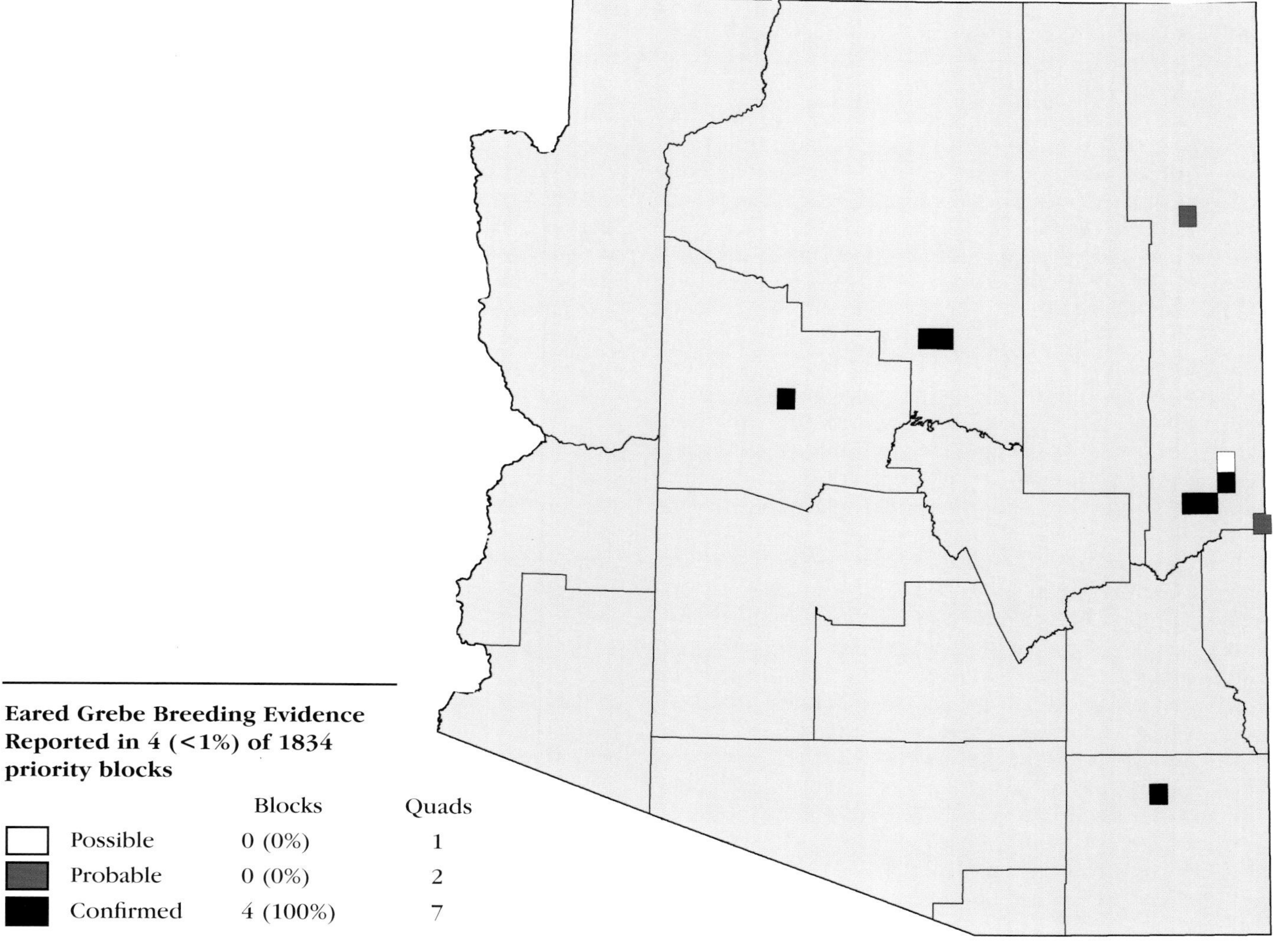

Eared Grebe Breeding Evidence Reported in 4 (<1%) of 1834 priority blocks

Western Grebe

by Cathryn Wise-Gervais *Aechmophorus occidentalis*

Also known as the "Swan Grebe," the Western Grebe's striking appearance and distinctive courtship rituals characterize this graceful, long-necked bird. With wings slightly extended and bill angled upward, the two courting birds in unison lift their bodies out of the water and rapidly scamper across the lake surface, culminating only seconds later in a dramatic forward dive.

HABITAT

In Arizona, most Western Grebes breed in lakes and reservoirs that contain open areas and an abundance of emergent vegetation, such as cattails and bulrush. Emergent vegetation provides Western Grebes with nesting substrate and cover, and blocks wind and waves. However, atlasers also found Western Grebes nesting locally in flooded tamarisk that lacked emergent vegetation. These gregarious birds require fairly large areas of open water that act as arenas for their intricate aquatic courtship displays. In Arizona, boaters and water-skiers often covet these open water areas as well, and human disturbance during the nesting season can be problematic.

Western Grebes select fish-rich waters during the breeding season. This preference ensures that a stable food source will be available for their young. It is not uncommon for large colonies of Western Grebes to be active one year in a given location then abandon the area in later years. This selection process is dictated by local conditions such as water level and quality and food abundance (Storer and Nuechterlein 1992).

BREEDING

Because of wintering and resident populations of Western Grebes on larger lakes and reservoirs in western and central Arizona, it is challenging to determine when spring migration begins. In northern Arizona, early migrants arrive in mid-March and continue arriving through late May. Along the lower Colorado River, courtship dances typically begin in February and March and are observed regularly into May. Courtship consists of an elaborate array of behaviors including pointing, shaking, bobbing, and the infamous rushing activity that should be witnessed first hand to be truly appreciated. Less well known is the "weed dance" in which both sexes collect organic material underwater then swim toward each other while paddling and lifting their bodies nearly out of the water.

Following atlas surveys, it has become clear that some Western Grebes may nest at any time of year along the lower Colorado River. Although Rosenberg et al. (1991) noted adults with downy broods from July through November, atlas records have greatly extended this period. In particular, observers noted an adult Western Grebe with a downy chick riding on its back on 1 January at Imperial National Wildlife Refuge. Atlasers also observed adults feeding young on 19 April at Topock Marsh, indicating that this nest was initiated no later than mid-March. Nesting records continued through May and June locally along the Colorado River, and atlasers noted nest with eggs on 31 July at Bill Williams River Delta.

The vast majority of atlas breeding records were obtained from mid-April through July, although this may reflect when most atlasing surveys were conducted. In northeastern Arizona, most observations of adults with broods are from late May through June (C. LaRue, personal communication). Late Western Grebe nesting records during the atlas included adults with dependent young on 28 August at Painted Rock Reservoir and at Ganado Lake on 4 September. Early fall migrants in Arizona typically do not appear until early October with passage continuing well into December.

Unless otherwise noted, the following nesting ecology information is from Storer and Nuechterlein (1992). Western Grebe nests are constructed by both sexes and consist of coarse stems to provide stability and wet vegetation to bind the dry materials. Nests are sufficiently completed in 1–3 days to hold eggs, but are added to continuously, especially during the first week. In Arizona, sites are typically in stands of cattail or bulrush, but preference is based on water depth >10 in. (25.4 cm) rather than by plant species. In fact, atlasers found Western Grebes nesting in flooded tamarisk clumps at Ganado Lake. Western Grebes nest in colonies and usually place nests >6.5 ft (2 m) apart (Lindvall and Low 1982). Typical clutches consist of 2–4 eggs (range 1–6) and are incubated almost constantly for 22–24 days. Both sexes incubate and will sometimes cover the eggs with nesting material between shifts. After hatching, the adults brood the chicks on their backs both in the nest and in water and can even dive shallowly with their tiny passengers on board. Parental care lasts approximately 6–8 weeks. Western Grebes are known to produce only one brood per season, but they will renest if earlier attempts fail.

DISTRIBUTION AND STATUS

Western Grebes are found throughout much of the western United States, southern Canada, and central Mexico. Their appearance depends on the availability of large, fish-rich lakes or reservoirs; so as water levels fluctuate from year to year, so do the local Western Grebe numbers. Most Western Grebe populations migrate to the Pacific coast or to larger unfrozen lakes and reservoirs during the winter, but Mexican and some southwestern United States populations are residents. In Arizona, Western Grebes nesting on the Colorado Plateau migrate south during the winter, while grebes along the lower Colorado River are residents.

The Western Grebe is a fairly recent breeding species in Arizona, where it was first found nesting on Lake Havasu in 1966 following the establishment of wetland vegetation at the north end of this reservoir (Rosenberg et al. 1991). These grebes have nested regularly in this area ever since. By the early 1980s, Western Grebes were also found occasionally nesting at Topock Marsh and very irregularly at the ephemeral Painted Rock Reservoir (Monson and Phillips 1981; Rosenberg et al. 1991). On Navajo tribal lands, these grebes were found nesting at Red Lake north of Window Rock in 1985 (Jacobs 1986) and Cow Springs Lake in 1989 and 1991 (C. LaRue, personal communication).

The local distribution of nesting Western Grebes in Arizona continues to expand in the state. Atlasers documented these elegant grebes breeding within a wide range of elevations in Arizona, from 181 ft (55 m) at Imperial Reservoir to 7100 ft (2164 m) at Mormon Lake. Along the lower Colorado River, atlasers noted that these grebes not only continue to nest at Lake Havasu and Topock Marsh, but also at Bill Williams River Delta and at Cibola and Imperial National Wildlife Refuges. After the flooding of Painted Rock Reservoir in 1993, at least one pair was observed nesting there. Atlasers also confirmed Western Grebes nesting at Mormon and Kinnikinick lakes southwest of Flagstaff and on Navajo tribal lands at Many Farms and Ganado lakes. Observers did note Western Grebes with nesting Clark's Grebes at Becker's Lake near Springerville, but did not confirm them breeding at this location.

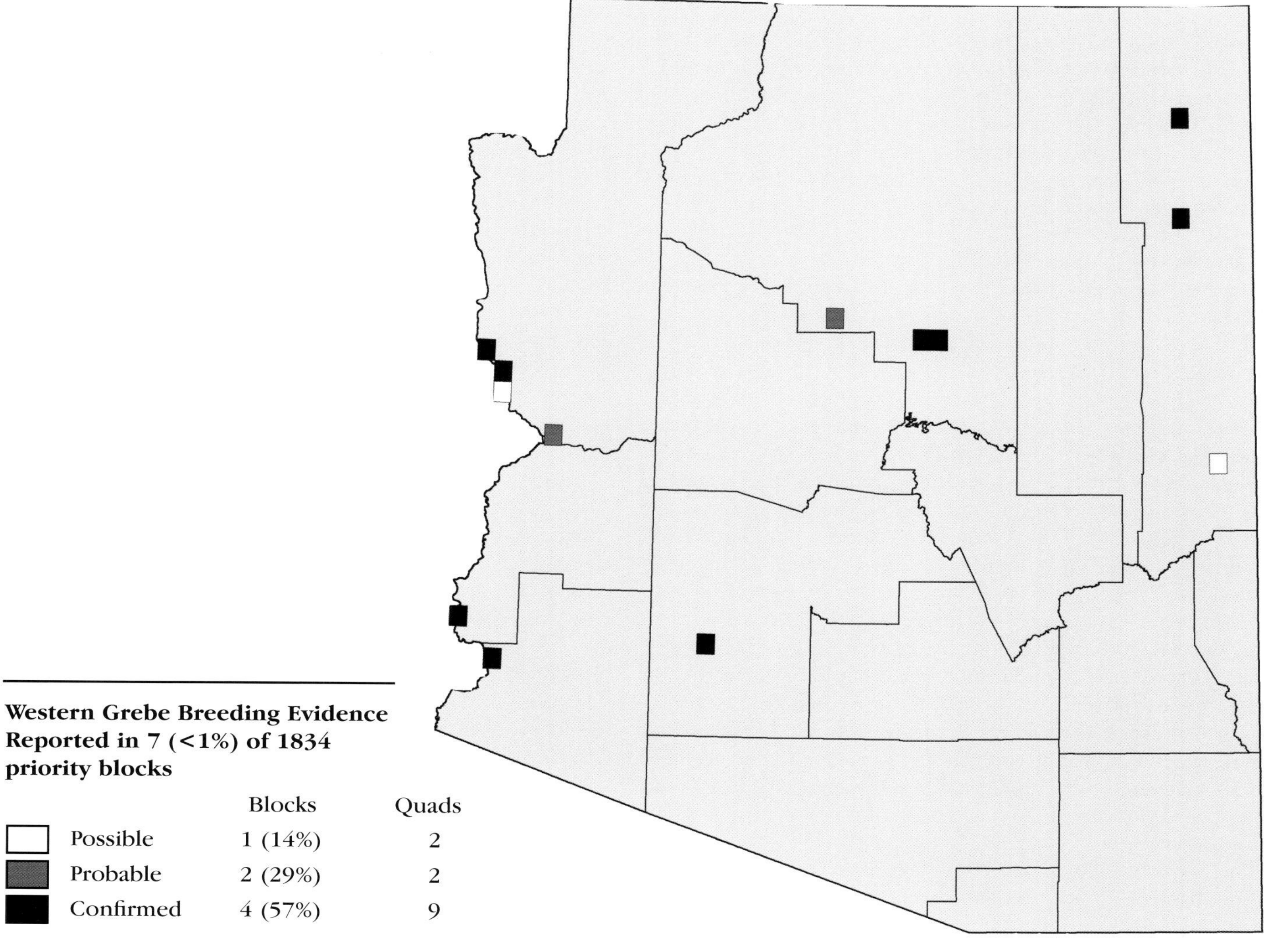

Western Grebe Breeding Evidence Reported in 7 (<1%) of 1834 priority blocks

Clark's Grebe

by Cathryn Wise-Gervais *Aechmophorus clarkii*

Physical differences such as facial pattern and bill color, as well as markedly different calls allows Western and Clark's Grebes to select mates of their own species even though the birds elaborate courtship rituals are identical. Prior to diving, Clark's Grebes will sometimes peer into the water with eyes below the surface, looking for prey such as fish and crustaceans.

JIM BURNS

HABITAT

Although Clark's Grebes associate more closely with their own species both on the breeding and wintering grounds, mixed flocks of Western and Clark's Grebes are common as the two species select nearly identical habitats in Arizona. The fact that, until 1985, the two species were considered mere variants of the Western Grebe has left scant information on the Clark's Grebe in Arizona. Like Western Grebes, atlasers noted Clark's breeding areas offering both large areas of open water for aquatic courtship displays and feeding, and emergent or flooded vegetation for nest cover. Wetland vegetation at occupied locations in Arizona typically consists of cattails and/or bulrushes, but other flooded vegetation may sometimes be used. One study found that Clark's Grebes generally forage farther from shore and in deeper water than do Western Grebes (Nuechterlein and Buitron 1989), but this relationship is unclear at refuges where the shallowest areas are often far from shore (Ratti 1985).

BREEDING

Like their Western counterpart, Clark's Grebes are resident and most abundant on the larger lakes and reservoirs of the Colorado River, but wintering populations elsewhere in the state appear to be much smaller and are distinctly outnumbered by the Western Grebe. The spring migration period of Clark's Grebes is not fully understood in Arizona, but migrants have been noted from late February through May. Courtship displays of resident populations can begin by February and atlasers noted courting activity continuing at least into mid-May. The earliest confirmed atlas record was of an adult Clark's Grebe feeding a chick at Topock Marsh on 18 April. Several other late April observations of adults with chicks from upper Lake Mead to Havasu National Wildlife Refuge indicate that nesting activity commenced by mid-March at the latest. Breeding populations of Clark's Grebes along the Colorado River continue nesting throughout the summer. Atlasers reported a late nest with eggs on 31 July at the Bill Williams River Delta and an occupied nest on 23 August at Topock Marsh. This indicates that some adults will have dependent young well into September.

In northeastern Arizona, atlasers noted nest building by 2 June, but adults with chicks on 9 June would suggest nesting activity beginning in early May at the latest. Atlas records of adults with young continue through August in this region of the state. A pair of Clark's Grebes and their brood was also observed at Ganado Lake on the amazingly late date of 15 October 1997, well after atlasing surveys had ended and migration was well underway. A few fall migrants begin passing through Arizona by late August (occasionally earlier) and continue through November.

The following nesting ecology information was taken from data compiled by Storer and Nuechterlein (1992). Clark's Grebe nest site selection is highly social, with initial nests serving as epicenters from which colony grows outward. Both sexes construct the nest, and in Arizona nests are typically placed in emergent vegetation such as bulrushes or cattails. Clark's Grebe clutches usually consist of 2–3 eggs (range 1–5) and the nest is guarded and defended vigorously by both members of the pair against other grebes. Additional eggs are often laid in unattended or abandoned nests, and "dump" nests with more than usual number of eggs are common. Both parents take turns incubating the eggs for a period of 23–24 days. The Clark Grebe pair often will continue adding nesting material through incubation, especially if weather conditions have diminished the structure. Upon hatching, the chicks leave the nest on the parent's backs, sometimes abandoning the last egg, even though viable. Parents take turns back-brooding and feeding the young, and parental care lasts approximately 8 weeks. The pair may split-brood when the young are half-grown. Most evidence suggests that only one brood is produced per season, but renesting following failure is common.

Rosenberg et al. (1991) noted that some Clark's Grebes nested along with Western Grebes on the north end of Lake Havasu, then toted their newly hatched chicks south approximately 31 mi (50 km) to the Bill Williams River arm of the lake. All Western Grebes and the remaining Clark's Grebes in the population stayed near where they nested. Now that some Clark's Grebes are nesting at the Bill Williams River delta, it is unknown if such arduous journeys continue.

DISTRIBUTION AND STATUS

Clark's Grebes are found sympatrically with Western Grebes throughout much of the western United States. However, Clark's Grebes are less widespread than their Western counterparts as a result of their being more local and less abundant at the northern and eastern edge of their range; they appear only locally in extreme southern Canada (Kaufman 1996). On the central plateau of Mexico, Howell and Webb (1995) noted that Clark's Grebes are more numerous than Western Grebes in the northern and central regions of the plateau. Clark's Grebes are resident along the lower Colorado River, and nesting populations in northeastern Arizona are migratory.

Prior to the atlas, Clark's Grebes were only reported nesting on Lake Havasu along the Colorado River (Rosenberg et al. 1991) and beginning in 1988, at Many Farms Lake on Navajo tribal lands (C. LaRue, personal communication). During the atlas, this grebe was confirmed nesting at several other locations within Arizona and may indicate steadily growing populations. Some nesting areas in northeastern Arizona were not occupied every year, however, during the atlas period due to lower water levels.

Atlasers confirmed Clark's Grebes nesting at elevations ranging from approximately 220 ft (67 m) near Cibola National Wildlife Refuge to 7100 ft (2164 m) at Mormon Lake southeast of Flagstaff. Atlasers found the highest concentration of Clark's Grebes on the lower Colorado River at Lake Havasu and Topock Marsh. These grebes were discovered nesting for the first time at the upper end of Lake Mead (1995) and at Bill Williams River National Wildlife Refuges (2001). Clark's Grebes were also suspected of nesting farther south on Imperial National Wildlife Refuge.

In northeastern Arizona, Clark's Grebes were noted breeding at Many Farms and Ganado lakes on Navajo tribal lands. Lastly, atlasers confirmed Clark's Grebe breeding at Becker Lake near Springerville where they had previously not been confirmed nesting. Additional White Mountain lakes would seem ideal for both nesting Western and Clark's Grebes; if populations continue to expand these elegant grebes may periodically nest in these areas as well.

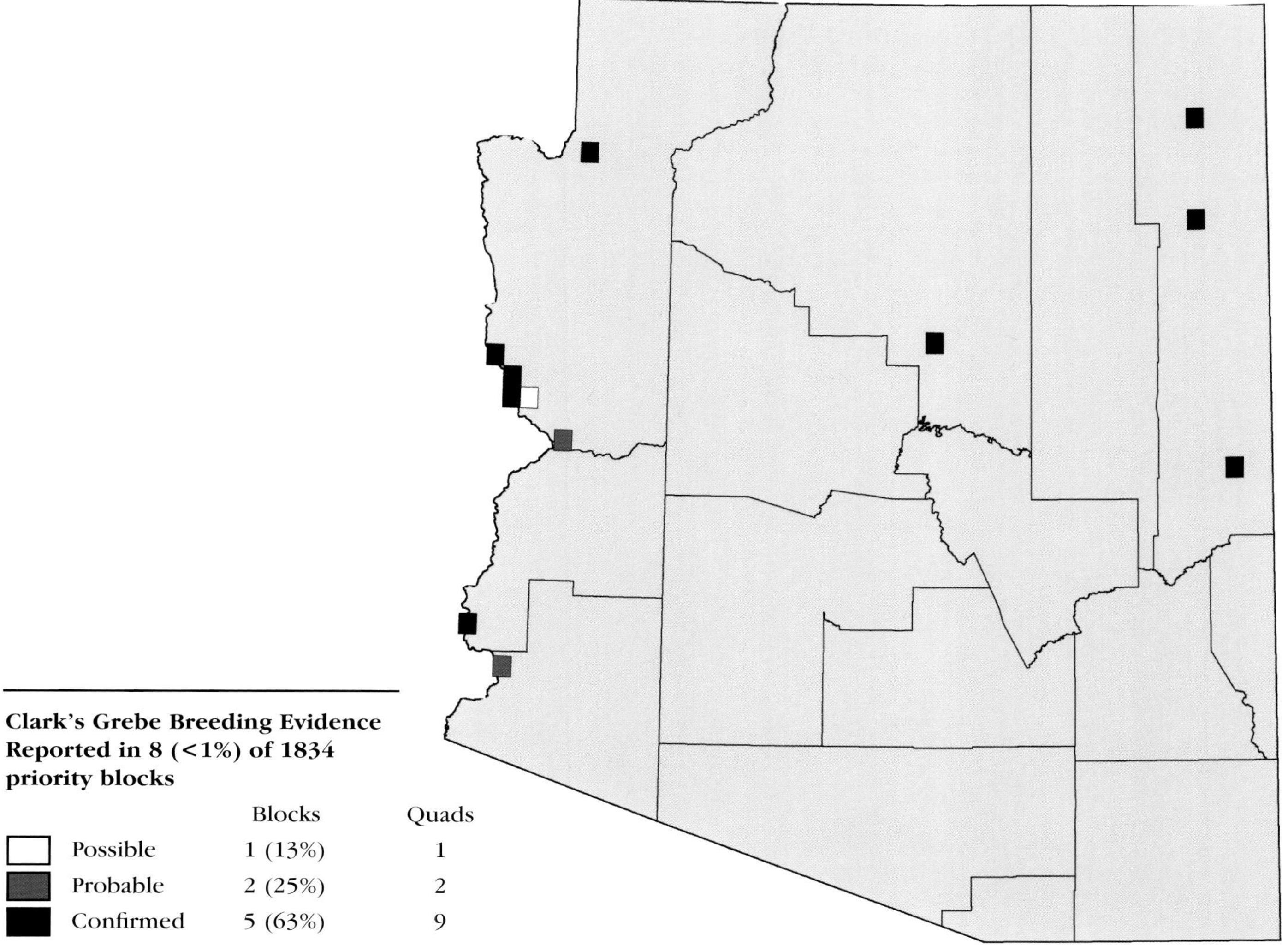

Double-crested Cormorant

by Troy E. Corman *Phalacrocorax auritus*

Expert anglers, Double-crested Cormorants are a local but increasing nesting species in Arizona. Their nesting colonies are typically exposed and often active throughout the relentless summer heat. These large, web-footed waterbirds spend much of their time preening or perched in the sun with wings extended in an effort to dry their waterlogged feathers.

JIM BURNS

HABITAT

Double-crested Cormorants are typically found in or near large, open bodies of water. In Arizona these include larger ponds, slow-moving rivers, lakes, reservoirs, and other artificial impoundments. Atlasers reported 63 percent of all observations from open water near wetland habitat and another 32 percent were from cottonwood-, willow-, or tamarisk-dominated shorelines (n = 19). When not foraging, cormorants rest and dry their feathers on exposed sand or cobble bars, small islands, rocks, trees, snags, stumps, or other objects in or close to the water. Nesting colonies are established at sites safe from ground predators and receive little human disturbance. They are typically close to foraging areas. Most Double-crested Cormorants forage in relatively shallow, open water less than 26 ft (8 m) deep (Hatch and Weseloh 1999), and much to Arizona anglers' dismay, their habitats include mountain lakes and residential ponds stocked with fish.

BREEDING

Double-crested Cormorants from farther north and at higher elevations augment resident populations in southern and western Arizona during the winter. It is unknown when they first arrive at breeding locations at higher elevations in northern Arizona, but migration typically begins in March and can continue into May. Nest-building activity has been observed as early as 15 January along the Gila River below Painted Rock Dam. The earliest confirmed atlas record was a nest with young on 1 April, suggesting egg laying by at least late February or early March. Nests were occupied by 15 May at one higher elevation lake near Williams. Nests with young were reported as late as 7 August at the colony below Painted Rock Dam. These cormorants normally first breed at three years of age (Potter 1998) and nonbreeding individuals and small groups can be found away from nesting areas throughout the summer in Arizona. This makes it difficult to determine when true fall migration begins. Peak passage appears to be in September or October, however.

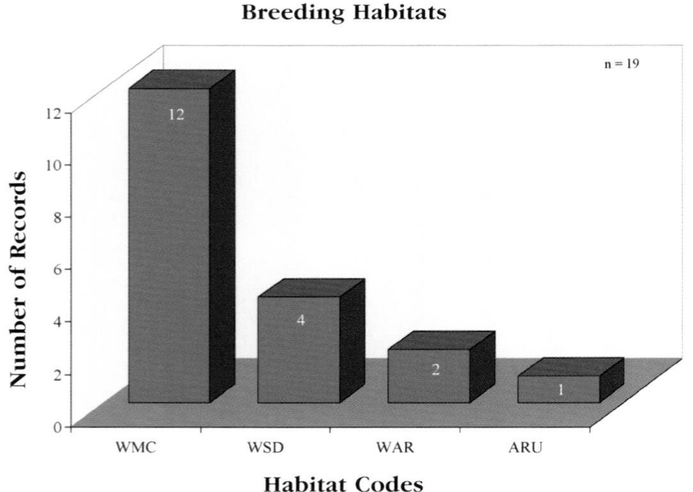

In Arizona, Double-crested Cormorants nest in colonies consisting of 5–50 nests. The nests are often used annually so long as water levels, food availability, and disturbance do not drastically change. Both members of the pair help to build the nest with the male collecting most of the material, while the female remains to build and guard the nest from stick-thieving neighbors (Hatch and Weseloh 1999). In Arizona, lower nests are constructed on islands in small trees or shrubs, as well as in flooded snags 3–8 ft (0.9–2.4 m) above the ground or water. Otherwise, nests are usually placed 40–60 ft (12.1–18.2 m) high in live or dead trees. Atlasers found Double-crested Cormorants nesting in Fremont cottonwoods, tamarisk, mesquite, ponderosa pine, and eucalyptus, often in and around active Great Blue Heron rookeries. Most nest locations afford little shade for the incubating adults and nestlings. Considerable tree damage can eventually occur at repeatedly used nesting colonies. Lemmon et al. (1994) noted the accumulation of cormorant droppings and the behavior of stripping leaves for nest material may kill trees within 3–10 years.

Most Double-crested Cormorant clutches consist of 3–4 eggs, but this can range from 1 to 7 (Mitchell 1977). Both parents help incubate the eggs which hatch in 25–28 days (Hatch and Weseloh 1999). Cormorants often continue adding new nest material throughout incubation and while chicks are small (Hatch and Weseloh 1999). The young are well feathered when they are 3–4 weeks old and typically depart the nest in 6–8 weeks to begin joining their parents in swimming and flying excursions (Hatch and Weseloh 1999). Double-crested Cormorants will readily renest if the first clutch is destroyed, but true second broods are rarely documented (Hatch and Weseloh 1999).

DISTRIBUTION AND STATUS

Double-crested Cormorants are the most widespread cormorant in North America. They nest locally along both coasts from Alaska and Newfoundland, south to Mexico and Florida. These cormorants also nest locally in the interior of the continent in widely spaced, disjunct populations where appropriate nesting and feeding areas occur. Like many other areas of North America, nesting Double-crested cormorant populations have steadily increased in Arizona. Early descriptions noted this cormorant nesting locally only along the lower Colorado River (Phillips et al. 1964). Double-crested Cormorants were considered fairly common local breeders in secluded backwaters at Topock Marsh and Imperial National Wildlife Refuge (Rosenberg et al. 1991). In 1968, a few nests were also discovered at San Carlos Reservoir and at the ephemeral Painted Rock Reservoir in 1979–1980 (Monson and Phillips 1981).

Atlasers discovered Double-crested Cormorants nesting in several additional locations within the state and recorded them at elevations ranging from 460 ft (140 m) at Topock Marsh to 6740 ft (2054 m) at Scholz Lake southeast of Williams. The year following the atlas project, several pairs of Double-crested Cormorants were discovered nesting at 8220 ft (2500 m) in a ponderosa pine snag along River Reservoir near Greer (M. Stevenson, personal communication). These cormorants have been found nesting up to 9000 ft (2743 m) in Colorado (Potter 1998). That nearby lakes are routinely stocked with trout during the spring and summer likely enticed this colony to become established. Elsewhere in the north, they were confirmed nesting at Telephone Lake north of Show Low, Willow Creek Reservoir near Prescott, and near the mouth of Lake Mead. Atlasers also found this cormorant nesting at Lake Pleasant near the inflow of the Agua Fria River and two locations near Roosevelt Lake. During early atlas surveys, Double-crested Cormorants were found nesting near Painted Rock Dam on the Gila River and at Picacho Reservoir, but both of these colonies had been abandoned by the end of the atlas period due to the eventual lack of water.

Extensive foraging and nesting habitat exists for Double-crested Cormorants along the lower Salt and middle Gila rivers of Maricopa County where this and the Neotropic Cormorant have recently become permanent residents in varying numbers and locations. However, the current rate of illegal shooting and recreational disturbance could be too high for establishing nesting colonies in this area. The number of cormorant nesting colonies in Arizona is expected to increase and this progress should be closely monitored. Double-crested Cormorants frequently move into already established Great Blue Heron rookeries. In several Colorado locations, as the number of nesting pairs of cormorants increased, the number of occupied nests of herons markedly decreased over time (Potter 1998).

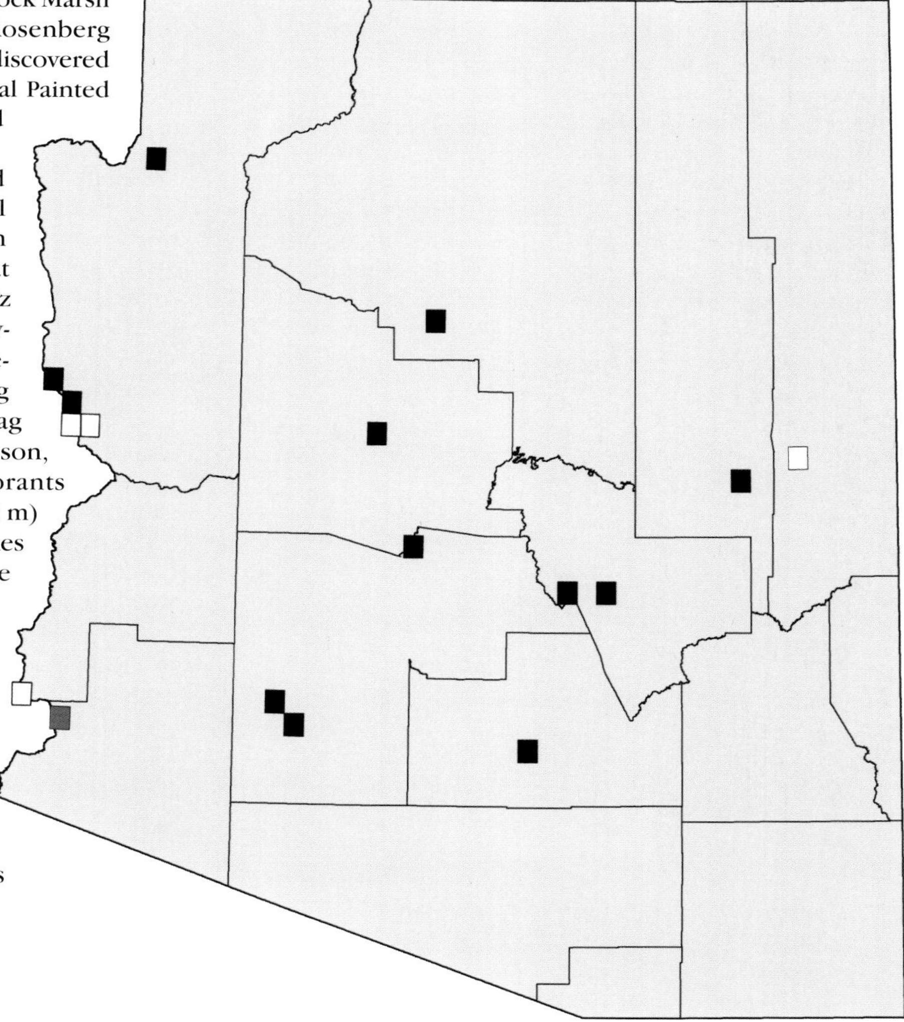

Double-crested Cormorant Breeding Evidence Reported in 10 (<1%) of 1834 priority blocks

	Blocks	Quads
Possible	3 (30%)	4
Probable	1 (10%)	1
Confirmed	6 (60%)	11

Least Bittern

by Troy E. Corman *Ixobrychus exilis*

Nestled among the cattails in their marshy haunts, the diminutive Least Bittern frequently goes unnoticed unless one is familiar with its soft, cooing calls or loud, rail-like outbursts. With careful observation along wetland edges, however, these stealthy herons can be viewed, often with their feet firmly grasping emergent vegetation and legs split to each side in a seemingly uncomfortable stance.

RICK AND NORA BOWERS

HABITAT

The attractive Least Bittern is at home in marshy wetlands throughout its range. In Arizona, these bitterns are found most often in larger marshes with dense, tall growth of emergent vegetation interspersed with areas of open water. Cattails are especially favored, but stands of bulrush are also used (Rosenberg et al. 1991). Atlasers noted this species inhabiting marshes along rivers, ponds, lake edges, and less frequently along irrigation canals and runoff ditches in nearby agricultural area. They are often associated with stable water regimes and deeper water that helps create the wetland edge effect especially favored by these tiny, secretive herons. With their small size and highly compressed trunk, these birds slip easily and surprisingly swiftly through dense, emergent vegetation (Gibbs et al. 1991). They forage for aquatic prey by stalking along branches and reeds, or by clinging to clumps of vegetation above deep water (Weller 1961).

BREEDING

Because of its secretive nature and local distribution, the true migratory status of Least Bitterns in Arizona is incomplete. In much of southwestern Arizona at elevations below 1000 ft (305 m), extensive cattail stands often harbor Least Bitterns throughout the year. Away from this region of the state, migrating Least Bittern are infrequently detected in the spring from mid-April through May. Resident bitterns likely begin breeding earlier than migratory populations, with males initiating their cooing calls in March and April. Atlasers reported a fledgling near Laguna Dam on the Colorado River on 24 May, which suggests nest building by late March or early April and egg laying later in April. Not surprising, few nests were actually found during the atlas period, but one nest held three nestlings on 6 June and a late nest with recently fledged young nearby was discovered on 27 July.

There appears to be some postbreeding dispersal, as some individuals begin to appear at nonbreeding locations in Arizona by at least mid-July. Numbers or at least their detectability diminishes after mid-September. Least Bitterns are rarely observed during the late fall and winter months in the state, but their true status is often revealed at this time by a loud and rapid, short series of "cacks" emanating from the wetlands. This call is not well known and apparently pertains only to western population of Least Bitterns, fooling many, including the author, to initially incorrectly identify the noisemaker as a wintering Clapper Rail!

The nest of a Least Bittern is often cleverly concealed among wetland vegetation. Weller (1961) noted that nest construction is primarily performed by the male and continues throughout incubation. Nests are typically built 6–30 in. (15–76 cm) above the water in dense, tall stands of emergent or woody vegetation (Gibbs et al. 1992; Weller 1961). Nesting material can range from dried cattail leaves, bulrush, sticks, or grasses (Bent 1926). Surrounding vegetation is often pulled down to construct the nesting platform and the stalks, stems, and sticks are arranged on top to create the bowl (Weller 1961).

Both parents incubate the eggs, which begins soon after the first or second egg is laid (Weller 1961). Typical clutches consist of 4–5 eggs (range 2–7) and hatch asynchronously in 17–20 days (Bent 1926; Weller 1961). The agile young begin clambering at 5 days old, but normally they do not leave the nest permanently until 13–15 days (Gibbs et al. 1992). The parents may provide food up to 30 days after hatching (Palmer 1962). Some evidence suggests

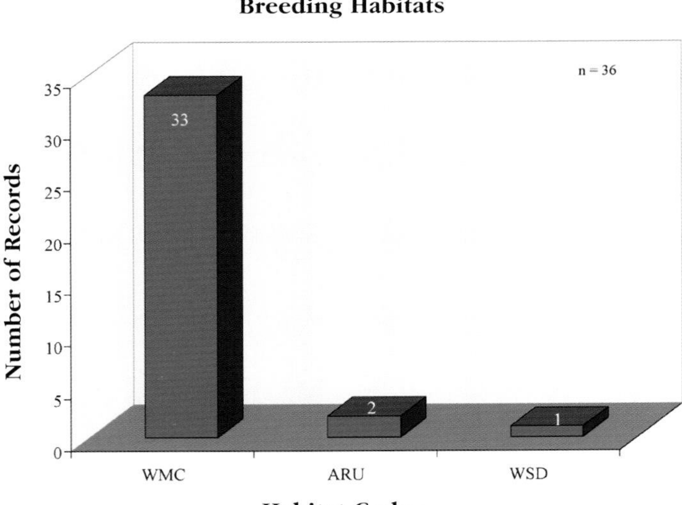

that two broods may be produced in a season (Weller 1961), and would seem quite possible with their lengthy nesting season in Arizona.

DISTRIBUTION AND STATUS

Like their habitat, Least Bitterns have a discontinuous distribution. Most populations in eastern North America are migratory. Here they breed from extreme southern Canada, south through the Gulf States and eastern Great Plains. In the West, they are found in isolated populations from Oregon south. There are resident populations from southern California and Arizona, south to South America.

Previous accounts in Arizona, considered Least Bitterns an uncommon resident in the lower Colorado River valley and a rare summer resident in marshy areas of central Arizona (Phillips et al. 1964). Later, Monson and Phillips (1981) noted this species as fairly common along the Salt River near Phoenix, and possibly nesting at Picacho Reservoir. Along the lower Colorado River, Rosenberg et al. (1991) mention that even though visual encounters with this secretive species are rare, an observer familiar with its calls will appreciate its true abundance there. In some larger marshes, Rosenberg et al. estimated one bittern per 2.5 ac (1 ha).

Least Bitterns were found throughout much of their historical range in Arizona during the atlas project and were discovered nesting in additional isolated locations at elevations from 170 to 3880 ft (52–1183 m). Within the lower Colorado River valley, they existed in marshes from Yuma north to Topock and up the extreme lower Gila River to near Tacna. Sizable populations were discovered during the atlas in marshes along the Salt River near its confluence with the Gila River and then down the Gila River through the Arlington Valley to just above Gillespie Dam. Much of the wetland habitats within this area were destroyed during winter flooding in 1993, but they made a remarkable recovery by the end of the atlas period. Indeed, the acreage of cattail and bulrush marsh along these river stretches was eventually much greater than prior to the flooding. New nesting locations discovered during the atlas include Tavaci Marsh near Clarkdale and Patagonia Lake State Park. In Graham County, Least Bitterns were also discovered nesting in many scattered wetlands in the vicinity of Thatcher and Safford, including Roper Lake State Park and nearby scattered ponds south to Dankworth Lake. Possible breeding records of calling males also came from marshes at Lake Pleasant near the inflow of the Agua Fria River, Arivaca, and Agua Caliente Park east of Tucson.

Many Least Bittern populations in Arizona are found on National Wildlife Refuges or state managed properties where they are relatively protected. The recent surge in interest of creating wetlands at wastewater treatment facilities in Arizona may eventually help expand breeding populations within the state. Along the lower Salt River, wetlands created near existing populations of Least Bitterns were colonized rapidly.

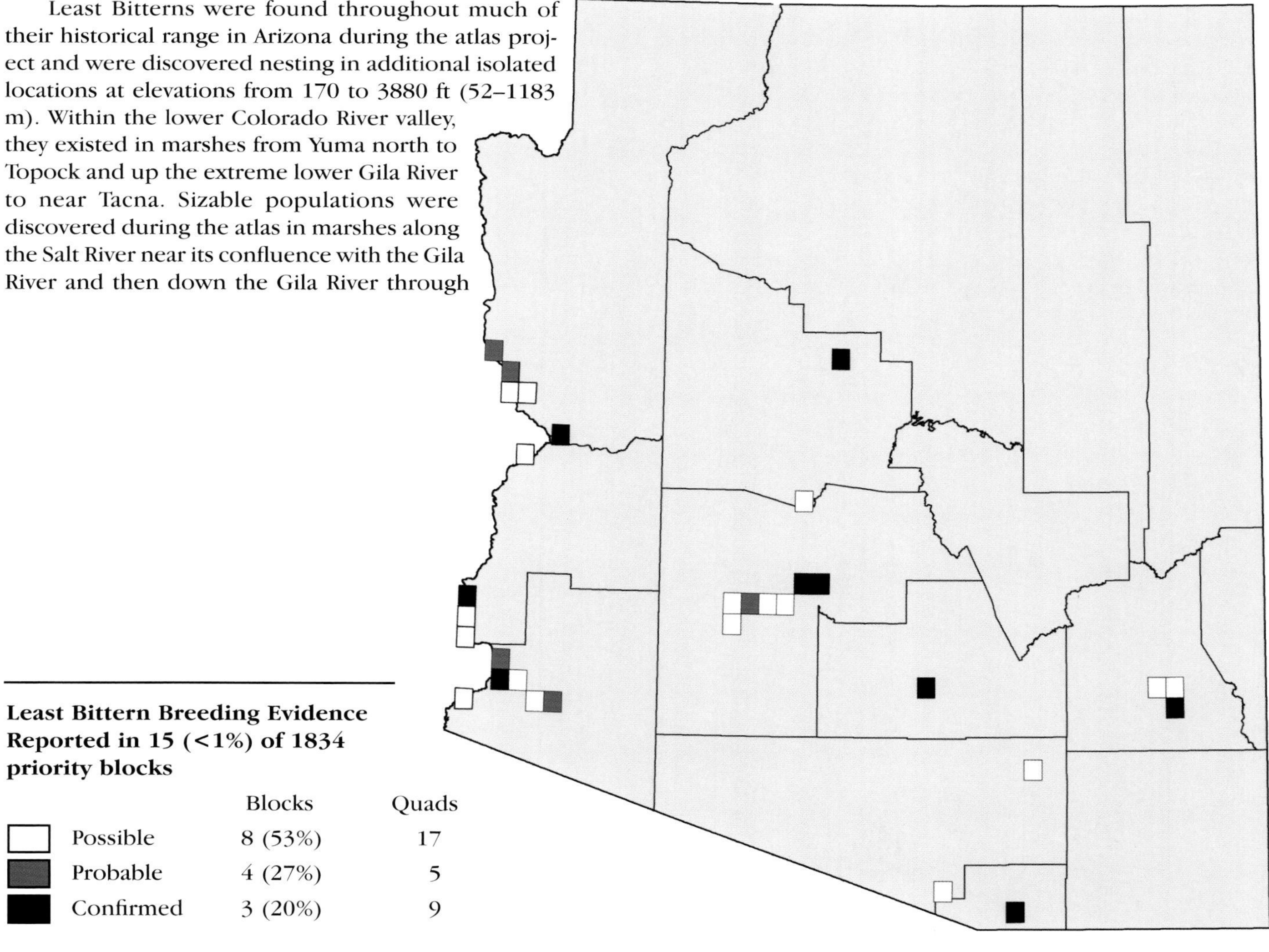

Least Bittern Breeding Evidence Reported in 15 (<1%) of 1834 priority blocks

	Blocks	Quads
Possible	8 (53%)	17
Probable	4 (27%)	5
Confirmed	3 (20%)	9

Great Blue Heron

by Margie J. Latta *Ardea herodias*

With an eerie elegance and incredible patience the Great Blue Heron stands motionless in shallow water, waiting for the key moment to thrust its spearlike bill at unsuspecting prey below. The most widespread and familiar of all North American herons, it is known by locals and fishermen by many colloquial names such as big cranky and long john.

BRUCE TAUBERT

HABITAT

Highly adaptable, Great Blue Herons are encountered in a wide variety of water environments throughout Arizona. These large herons occupy rivers, streams, lakes, and reservoirs, as well as urban ponds, canals, golf courses, and agricultural fields at various elevations from the lower Sonoran Desert to open ponderosa pine forests. Nearly 40 percent of atlas records were from lowland riparian areas containing Fremont cottonwood and willow; another 15 percent were in slightly higher elevation drainages dominated by Arizona sycamore (n = 113). Atlasers reported an additional 22 percent of their observations in cattail wetlands and drainages dominated by exotic tamarisk. Great Blue Herons prefer shallow areas where riparian and wetland habitat exists and fish and other large aquatic prey are abundant. These herons are most commonly seen wading in shallow water searching for prey or flying methodically overhead. In Arizona, they often can be found in periodically flooded agricultural fields where displaced rodents are easy prey.

BREEDING

Great Blue Herons are year-round residents in much of Arizona. Populations nesting in the lowland deserts typically initiate breeding activity by mid-January or mid-February and 1–2 months later at higher elevations. Initial nesting activity often pertains to males returning to previous nesting locations, selecting a nest from the previous year, and guarding it from newcomers. This is followed by elaborate courtship displays from the nest of choice in attempts to attract a mate. At lower elevation in Arizona, egg laying can begin by late February or March. Atlasers noted nests with young by 1 April, suggesting egg laying by at least early March. Even in lowland desert areas, atlasers noted nests with young well into July and early August. The latest nest with young during the atlas period was reported on 5 August. Atlas data, however, reveal the peak nesting period in April and May.

Elsewhere, Great Blue Herons are typically social nesters with heronries sometimes containing several hundred pairs. Likely in response to limited resources in Arizona, these herons have never been found nesting in such large numbers and will often nest in smaller colonies or isolated pairs (Phillips et al. 1964). Heronries in Arizona rarely exceed more than 50 pairs, with most containing fewer than 25 active nests.

Heronries are usually built close to available foraging habitat and to areas difficult for predators to reach (Butler 1992). This heron uses many different substrates in which to support their large nests in Arizona. Nests generally are constructed near the top of the tallest trees, from 30 to 70 ft (9.1–21.3 m) high, which can be live or dead and frequently include cottonwood, sycamore, and at higher elevations, ponderosa pine. But on small islands free of predators, atlasers noted Great Blue Herons nesting in tamarisk less than 10 ft (3 m) above the ground. In urban and rural areas they are especially fond of nesting in eucalyptus and palm trees, locally in citrus groves, and they have also nested in mesquite and paloverde near fish farms. Along the Bill Williams arm of Lake Havasu, Great Blue Herons previously bred on an island, where nests were constructed on protected rock outcrops and occasionally saguaros (Rosenberg et al. 1991). Recently, single pairs have even built nests on

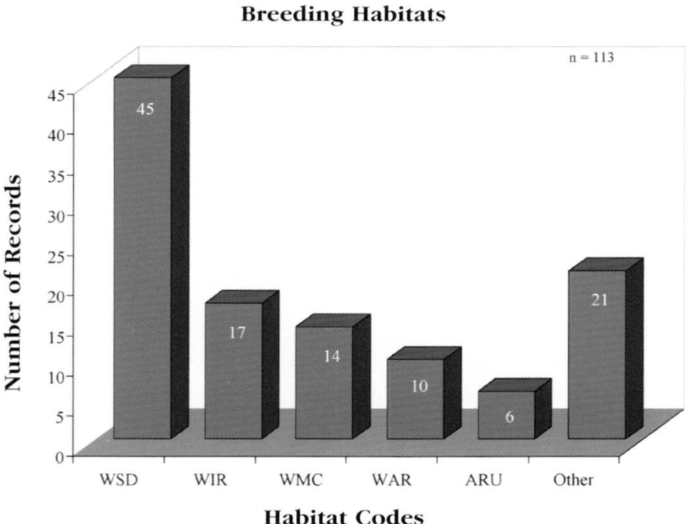

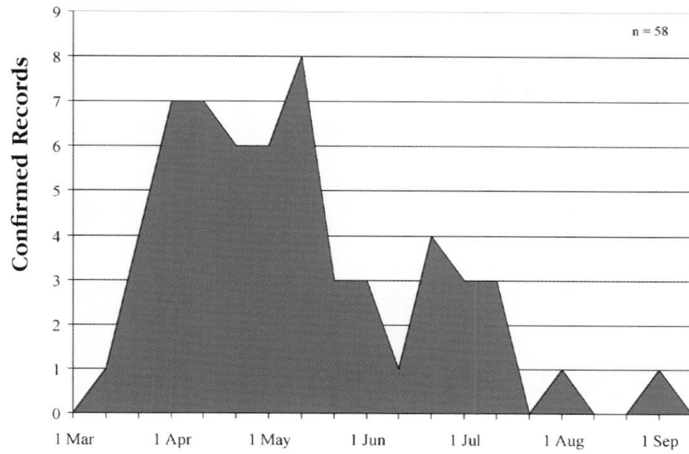

the top of cellular phone towers near favorite foraging areas. In Arizona, they will sometimes share the nesting trees with egrets, night-herons, cormorants, and at one Verde River site, a pair of Bald Eagles! New nests are often a tenuous collection of sticks lined with finer vegetation. Yet many nests are reused year after year, making older nests much larger and sturdier (Butler 1992).

Although mostly monogamous, Great Blue Herons select a new mate each year (Butler 1992). Full clutches consist of 3–5 (range 2–7) eggs. Incubation is shared by both members of the pair and typically lasts 25–29 days (Butler 1992). Young herons are capable of flight at approximately 60 days old. However, nestlings usually do not depart the nest until they are 65–90 days old (Butler 1992).

DISTRIBUTION AND STATUS

Great Blue Herons are ubiquitous throughout much of North America from coastal Alaska and southern Canada south through much of Mexico and the West Indies. In Arizona, the breeding distribution of Great Blue Herons is limited by perennial water sources and the availability of food and nest substrates. Atlasers confirmed these large herons nesting at elevations from approximately 100 ft (30 m) along the lower Colorado River south of Yuma to near 8000 ft (2438 m) in the White Mountain region.

Atlasers noted Great Blue Herons as fairly common throughout much of the state south and west of the Mogollon Rim. These large herons were previously reported nesting locally along the Colorado River north to the Boulder Dam area, along the Gila River and associated streams throughout southern and central Arizona, and at Roosevelt Lake (Phillips et al. 1964). Historically, breeding was unconfirmed north of the Mogollon Rim. But perennial artificial lakes and reservoirs stocked with fish have allowed this species to establish small, local colonies. Above the Mogollon Rim, atlasers found nesting herons near several lakes south of Williams, Mormon Lake, Blue Ridge Reservoir, Woods Canyon Lake, Telephone Lake near Show Low, and Luna Lake east of Alpine. Atlasers also found Great Blue Herons nesting regularly in scattered heronries along the Verde, middle Gila, lower Salt, and upper San Pedro rivers. A few pairs were also found nesting during the atlas period as far north as the Colorado River near Lees Ferry and eastern Lake Mead.

In larger and ever expanding metropolitan areas, such as Phoenix and Tucson, atlasers noted urban lakes and canals are apparently providing sufficient food resources to entice Great Blue Herons to nest nearby. Heronries are appearing with increased frequency in such settings, which emphasizes this bird's adaptability.

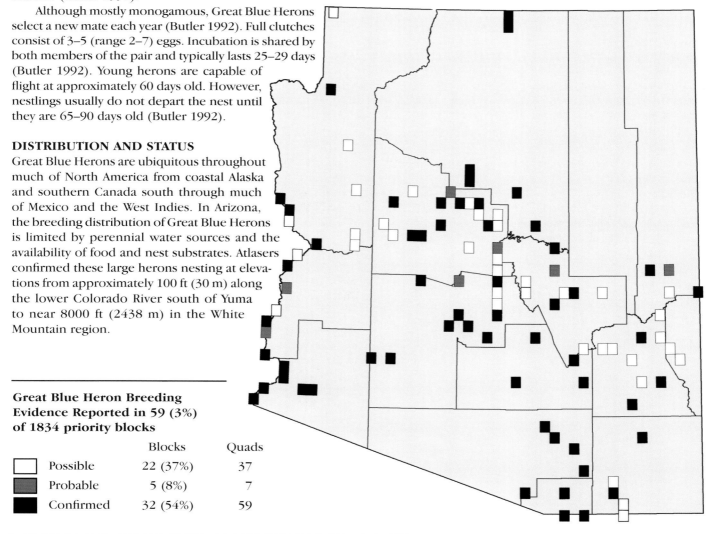

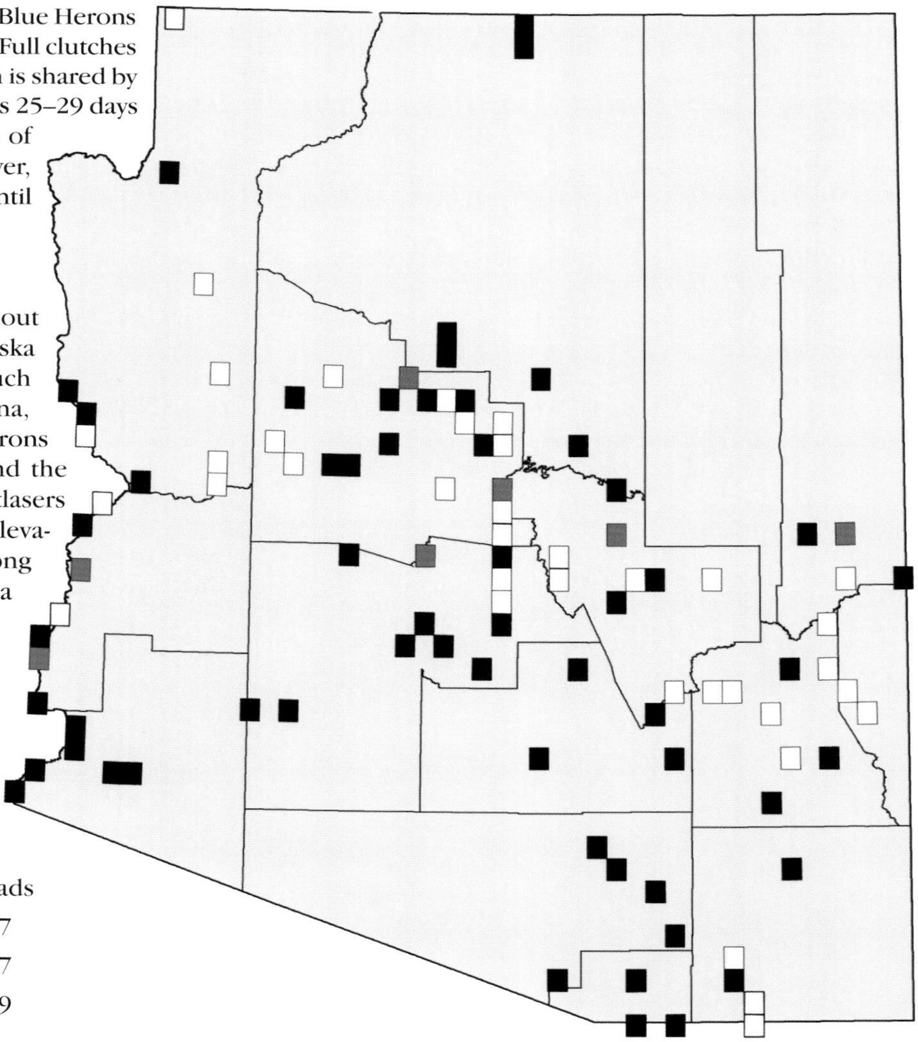

Great Blue Heron Breeding Evidence Reported in 59 (3%) of 1834 priority blocks

	Blocks	Quads
Possible	22 (37%)	37
Probable	5 (8%)	7
Confirmed	32 (54%)	59

Great Egret

by Cathryn Wise-Gervais *Ardea alba*

In the early twentieth century, plume hunters persecuted Great Egrets relentlessly to obtain specialized breeding display feathers called aigrettes. The species was nearly decimated by the millinery trade, a situation that helped spur the creation of conservation laws and organizations. As a result, this slender, snowy-plumaged bird appears today on the logo of the National Audubon Society.

BRUCE TAUBERT

HABITAT

Great Egrets are aquatic habitat generalists that range wide; as such, atlasers reported these stately egrets in 10 habitat types in Arizona. Thirty-four percent of sightings were noted in lowland riparian areas characterized by cottonwood, willow, mesquite, and tamarisk (n = 29). Marshes, ponds, lakeshores, and slower sections of rivers accounted for 17 percent of observation, which included stands of emergent vegetation such as cattails, bulrush, sedges, and other aquatic plants. Atlasers also reported these adaptable birds along exotic tamarisk-dominated waterways. Great Egrets often inhabit nearby agricultural and rural areas where they frequently forage in irrigated croplands, stock ponds, canals, sump ponds, and at wastewater facilities. Rural nesting locations accounted for several records from citrus orchards and palm groves. Atlasers also reported Great Egrets foraging locally in urban areas including residential lakes, ponds, canals, and golf courses.

BREEDING

Within their breeding range along the lower Colorado and Gila River valleys, Great Egrets are year-round residents. Elsewhere in Arizona, these egrets migrate through the state from March to May, and occasionally into early June. Atlasers obtained only 12 confirmed breeding records for this species, so breeding chronology for Great Egrets in Arizona remains somewhat unclear. Nest construction begins by late March or early April in Arizona. Some nests contain eggs by early to mid-April. Atlasers reported the earliest nest with young on 14 May, but it is likely that some occupied nests with undetermined contents contain young by early May. Nests with young were reported through 18 July, suggesting parental dependence continuing into early to mid-August. Away from nesting areas in Arizona, early migrants and postbreeding dispersing individuals are typically noted by late June or July, but stragglers have been observed through early November.

Great Egrets nest communally, often with other species of egrets, herons, and occasionally cormorants. If habitat conditions do not change and the birds remain undisturbed, most nesting locations are used year after year. Nests in Arizona are typically located in trees or tall shrubs, with lower nests often on protected islands or in dense thickets over water. In Arizona, Great Egrets have been noted nesting in cottonwood, willow, tamarisk, mesquite, citrus trees, and both fan and date palms.

Male Great Egrets initiate construction of the nest prior to pair formation. Alone or with assistance from his mate, complete the building process (Mock 1978). Clutches usually contain 3 eggs, but they can range from 1 to 6, which are incubated by both sexes (McCrimmon 2001). Bent (1926) described incubating adults as "indifferent or indolent." Both sexes spend considerable time standing over the eggs rather than sitting on them. The incubation period lasts for approximately 26 days (Maxwell and Kale 1977) then both parents brood and feed the nestlings. After approximately 3 weeks, the young leave the nest initially by climbing on nearby branches, but return to the nest to be fed (McCrimmon et al. 2001). By 49–56 days, the young are capable of flying over open space from perch to perch, particularly when pursuing parents for food (Pratt and Winkler 1985). Great Egrets produce only one brood per year, but

Breeding Habitats

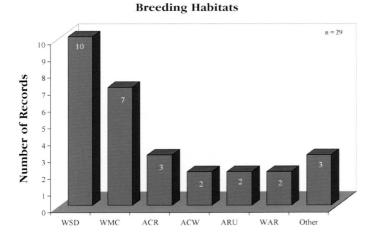

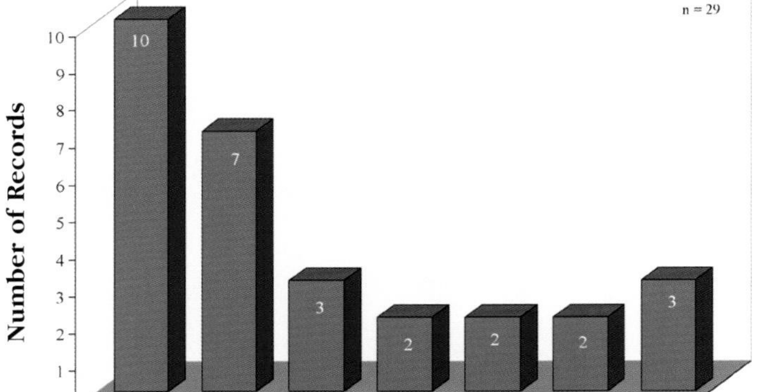

additional clutches are laid if earlier eggs or young are lost (McCrimmon et al. 2001).

DISTRIBUTION AND STATUS

Despite being hunted nearly to extinction by plume hunters at the turn of the century, the adaptable Great Egret made a wide ranging recovery once it received protected status and not only reoccupied but also expanded the northern reaches of its former range (McCrimmon et al. 2001). Great Egrets have a nearly worldwide distribution, but in North America they breed along both coasts in the United States and Mexico and are widespread in the Mississippi River drainage and elsewhere in the southeast. In the interior west, nesting populations are local and widely scattered.

In Arizona, Swarth (1914) suggested that Great Egrets were likely only migrants with records from the Colorado, Gila, and San Pedro rivers. However, in a few decades, populations of this egret were observed year-round along the lower Colorado River, where the first evidence of nesting was noted in 1947 at Topock Marsh (Monson 1948). By the 1980s, Great Egrets were considered fairly common residents and local breeders along the lower Colorado River (Rosenberg et al. 1991). On the Gila River, below Painted Rock Dam, winter and summer records also began to increase during the 1970s and 1980s, and these egrets began nesting there in 1991 (Witzeman et al. 1997). Populations of Great Egrets continued to expand along the lower Gila River and adjacent Salt River, and became common year-round residents by the end of the atlas period.

Atlasers confirmed Great Egrets nesting at elevations of approximately 80 ft (24 m) along the Colorado River near Gadsden to 1530 ft (466 m) at Picacho Reservoir. These egrets occurred on the Colorado River as far north as Topock Marsh during the nesting period, but atlasers failed to confirm breeding in this area. Along the lower Gila River, Great Egrets were discovered nesting near Tacna, below Painted Rock Dam, and at one locality near the Gila Bend Canal west of Paloma. Unfortunately, some nesting localities that were active during the beginning of the atlas, had been abandoned by the end of the period due to lowering water levels and eventual lakebed drying. Abandoned areas included nest sites below Painted Rock Dam and at Picacho Reservoir.

Atlasers were unable to confirm breeding Great Egrets elsewhere in Maricopa County. But the number of resident birds greatly increased each year along the lower Salt River near Phoenix and downstream along the Gila River in the Arlington Valley to Gillespie Dam. This trend indicated the probability that additional undiscovered nesting locations were in this area. Most evidence suggests that the distribution and abundance of nesting Great Egrets will continue to expand in Arizona, especially within the Gila and lower Salt River drainages. Future plans to create additional wetland and reestablish native riparian vegetation within this region will likely encourage this positive trend. In the greater Phoenix area, these adaptable and stately egrets are also now becoming resident at urban ponds and lakes stocked with fish, and such birds may eventually nest on nearby islands or in adjacent shade trees.

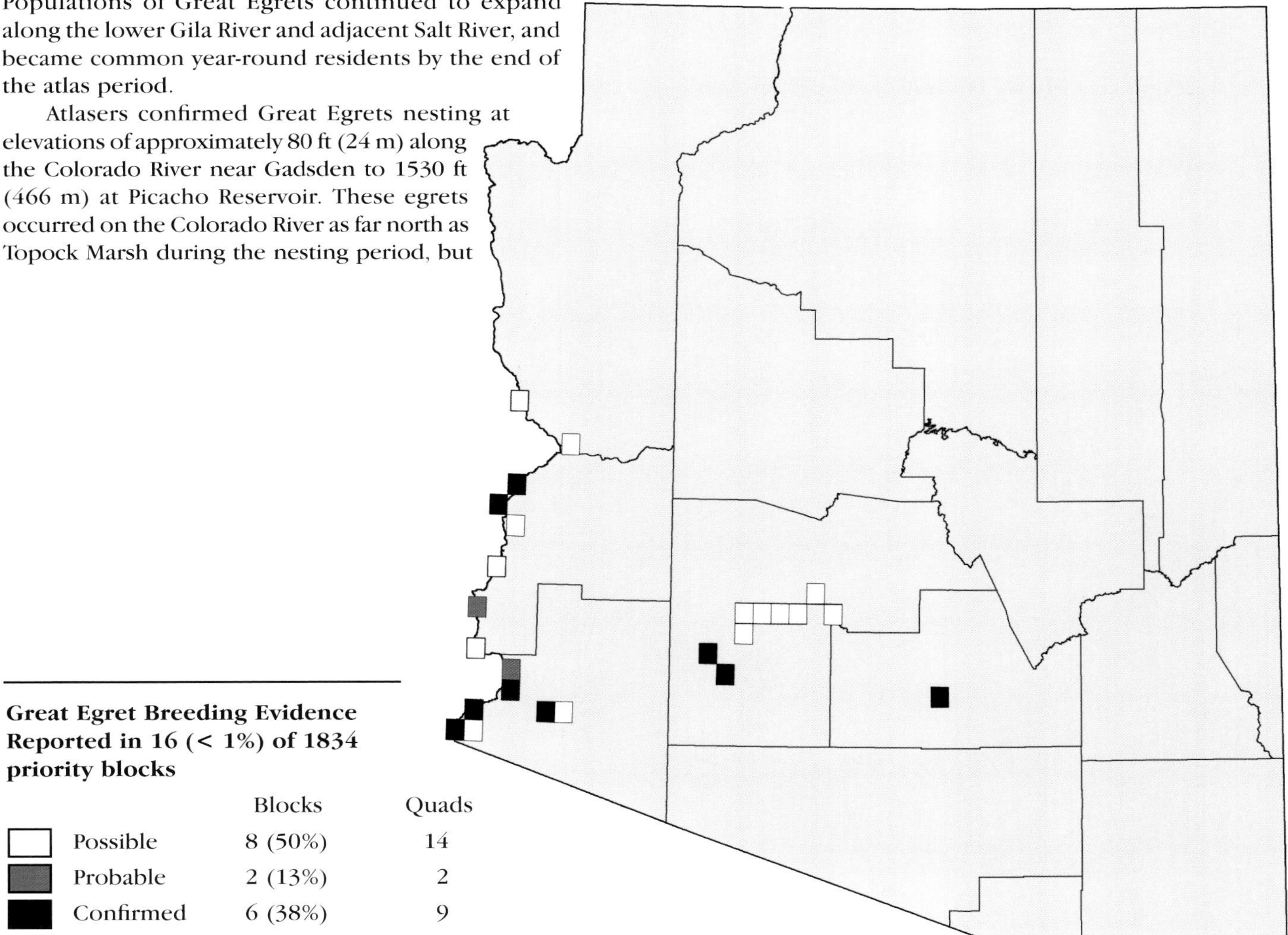

Great Egret Breeding Evidence Reported in 16 (< 1%) of 1834 priority blocks

	Blocks	Quads
Possible	8 (50%)	14
Probable	2 (13%)	2
Confirmed	6 (38%)	9

Snowy Egret

by Bill Burger *Egretta thula*

Hunted commercially for their delicate recurved back plumes and extirpated from many areas near the turn of the twentieth century, Snowy Egrets have rebounded and are now locally common in many American wetlands. These active, golden-footed birds possess a delicate elegance not shared by the other two nesting egrets in Arizona.

HABITAT

Across their range, Snowy Egrets inhabit many different aquatic habitats. In Arizona, these energetic egrets forage along the shallow protected backwaters of lakes, rivers, canals, or other wetlands and roost in nearby trees and shrubs. Approximately 24 percent of Snowy Egret records collected during the atlas were from marshes or similar habitat along the shorelines of ponds, lakes, and rivers (n = 25). Another 24 percent of the records were from open lowland riparian woodlands along drainages consisting primarily of Fremont cottonwood, willow, tamarisk, and mesquite. Tamarisk-dominated drainages and impoundments also held their share of these egrets. In rural and residential areas, Snowy egrets were found foraging along runoff ponds, irrigation ditches, canals, wastewater ponds, urban lakes, golf course ponds, and occasionally in irrigated fields. Nesting habitat in Arizona also includes rural stands of palm trees and citrus orchards.

BREEDING

In Arizona, Snowy Egrets are primarily resident along the lower Gila and Colorado River valleys. Elsewhere in the state, migrants appear in the south by mid-March and in the north by early April with stragglers into early June or later. Breeding phenology data for Snowy Egrets in Arizona are sparse, but during the atlas some nests were occupied by 8 April and may have hatched eggs by that time. One rookery near Yuma contained 10 occupied nests by early April, but had increased in size to an estimated 120 nests by late May (L. Piest, personal communication). By 9 June some of these nests contained small downy young, while others held young near fledging. During the atlas, nests with young were observed through 22 July, with some late nesting activity likely continuing into early August. Snowy Egrets are well known for postbreeding dispersal, and observation across Arizona increase from late July through September, with stragglers into late October.

The male Snowy Egret often collects much of the nesting material, which the female then uses to construct the nest (Palmer 1962). Known nests in Arizona have been constructed in citrus trees, date palms, fan palms, Fremont cottonwood, tamarisk, and velvet mesquite. Locally, these egrets were also found nesting in tall bulrushes and cattails wetlands, which appears to be the nesting habitat of choice in Colorado (Ryder 1998). Nest height is generally correlated with vegetation height, averaging about 5.6–10.5 ft (1.7–3.2 m) in various studies across their range (Parsons and Master 2000), although some of Arizona's tree nests are greater than 30 ft (9.1 m) high. Nests are often aggregated in suitable areas and in Arizona are generally in mixed-species colonies. Nesting sites in Arizona are shared with one or more of the following: Cattle Egrets, Great Egrets, Great Blue Herons, Black-crowned Night-Herons, and Double-crested Cormorants.

Parsons and Master (2000) review the breeding and nesting specifics of Snowy Egrets. Males perform elaborate and quite vocal bonding and courtship displays at the nest. A Stretch display, wherein the male pumps his elaborate body plumes up and down while pointing his bill skyward and vocalizing, is most common. The clutch size of Snowy Egrets is generally 3–5 eggs (range 2–6), which are laid at

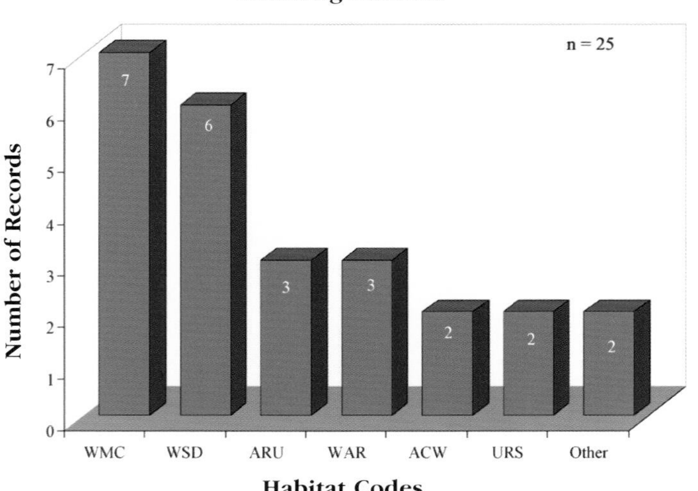

intervals of one about every two days. Incubation is shared by both members of the pair and typically begins when the first or second egg is laid. Incubation continues for 22–24 days. Once the pair stops brooding the nestlings (in approximately 10 days), the energetic youngsters begin moving to nearby branches, but they return to the nest to be fed. Both sexes feed the young. Fledglings begin dispersing from nesting areas when they are 7–8 weeks old. Renesting by Snowy Egrets will occur if the first attempt fails, but second broods have not been reported.

DISTRIBUTION AND STATUS

Arizona represents only a small portion of a Snowy Egret's breeding range, which extends coastally from the United States south to South America and locally inland. Distribution of Snowy Egrets has undergone major changes since the late nineteenth century (Parsons and Master 2000). Numbers and distribution were drastically reduced between about 1880 and 1910 by the taking of adults for feathers used in the millinery trade. After legal protection was provided in 1913–1916, Snowy Egret numbers increased and their range expanded into previously occupied areas and beyond.

Coinciding with this history, there were few records of Snowy Egrets in Arizona prior to 1900 (Swarth 1914), and Grinnell (1914) had not noted this species during their travels along the lower Colorado River in the spring of 1910. But by the 1940s these egrets had become resident along the Colorado River and were found nesting at Topock Marsh in 1947 (Monson 1948). This rookery grew to 141 nests in 1950, but was abandoned by 1953 (Rosenberg et al. 1991). Prior to the atlas period, Snowy Egrets were also found nesting sporadically on Imperial National Wildlife Refuge (Rosenberg et al. 1991), once at Picacho Reservoir in 1973 (Monson and Phillips 1981), and along the Gila River below Painted Rock Dam beginning in 1991 (Witzeman et al. 1997).

Atlasers found Snowy Egrets nesting locally only within the lower Colorado and Gila River valleys at elevations primarily from 120 to 1000 ft (37–305 m), and locally up to 2860 ft (872 m). Along the Colorado River, atlasers confirmed these egrets nesting near Mittry Lake and several locations near Yuma. Snowy Egrets were also suspected of nesting on Imperial, Bill Williams River, and Havasu National Wildlife Refuges, as well as the Colorado River Indian tribal lands.

Along the Gila River, Snowy Egrets continued nesting below Painted Rock Dam through 1996. This site was abandoned in 1997, however, as water levels dropped and the lake below the dam eventually dried. Another smaller rookery was established nearby on the western edge of Paloma Ranch in 1998 within a dense stand of mesquite along an irrigation runoff pond. This rookery slowly grew through the end of the atlas period. In 2001—the final cleanup year of the atlas—Snowy Egrets were also discovered breeding within the upper Gila River valley near Thatcher, Graham County, and in 2002, a small breeding colony was documented along the Salt River on the Tempe–Mesa border. Large numbers of these egrets were found throughout the spring and summer in other sections of the Gila River, strongly suggesting nearby breeding. Such areas of likely breeding included southwest of Phoenix from near the Salt River confluence, downstream through the Arlington Valley to Gillespie Dam, and near the inflow to San Carlos Reservoir.

Most evidence suggests that the breeding range of Snowy Egrets has greatly expanded in Arizona. This trend is expected to continue. Protection and enhancement of healthy wetlands in the state would likely benefit this and other species.

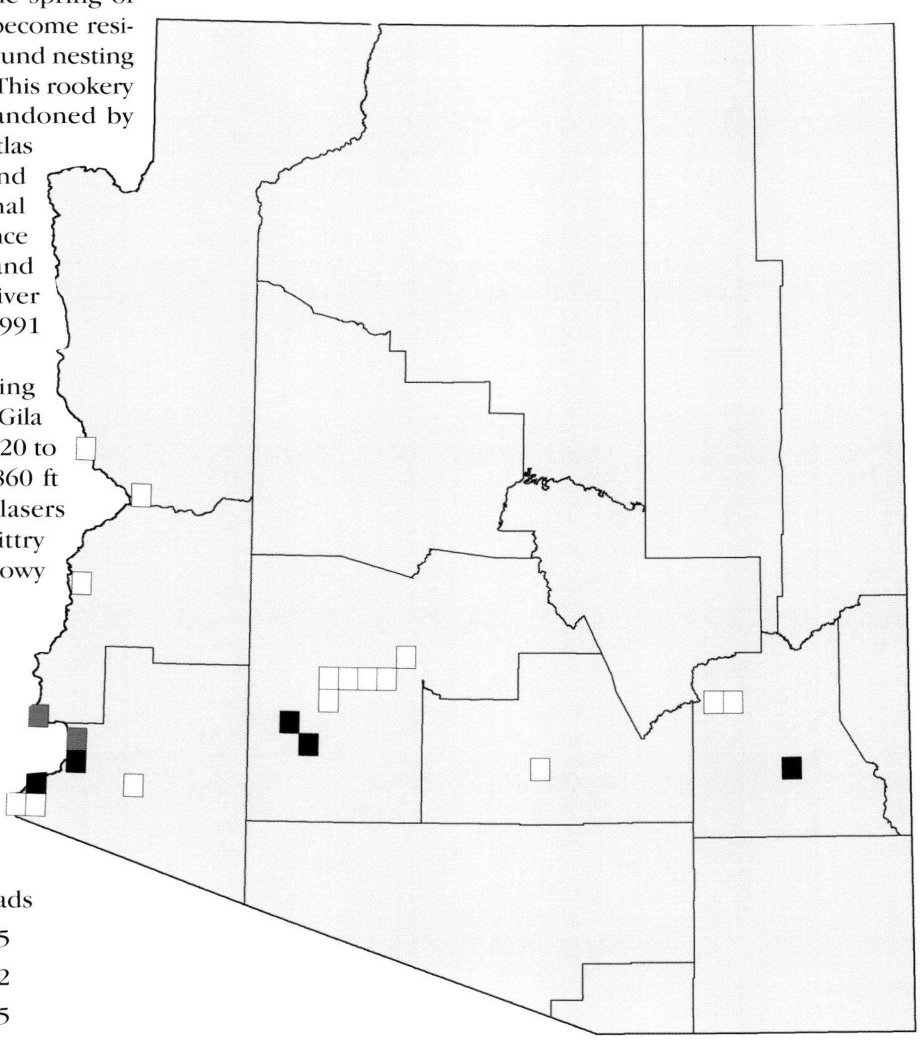

Snowy Egret Breeding Evidence Reported in 13 (<1%) of 1834 priority blocks

	Blocks	Quads
Possible	8 (62%)	15
Probable	2 (15%)	2
Confirmed	3 (23%)	5

Cattle Egret

by Cathryn Wise-Gervais *Bubulcus ibis*

Cattle Egrets rapidly colonized much of the Western Hemisphere. Today flocks of these stocky egrets are locally observed wandering through Arizona's agricultural fields. Named for their close association with bovine species, these birds were once believed to pick ticks off large mammals. They are now known to feast instead on insects disturbed by grazing animals or machines.

JIM BURNS

HABITAT

Considered the most terrestrial heron (Telfair 1994), Cattle Egrets use a wide variety of habitats, with foraging and nesting areas differing markedly from each other. Atlasers obtained only 14 potential breeding records for this species, and eight of these were in land-based habitats used as foraging areas. In Arizona, Cattle Egrets forage in varying sized flocks in rural areas containing pastures, cultivated land, fallow fields, and occasionally at landfills. These birds can also be found along the edges of weedy ponds or irrigation ditches. Nesting habitat in the state is also quite variable and includes tamarisk or mesquite thickets along irrigation runoff ponds and ditches; bulrush and cattail filled wastewater treatment ponds, citrus orchards, and rural stands of date palms. Cattle Egrets are often in close association with livestock, but they also follow farm machinery, such as mowers or cutters through alfalfa, hay, and grain fields. Telfair (1994) suggested that it seems unlikely that Cattle Egrets would breed successfully in areas where cattle or other livestock were absent or scarce. But foraging in agricultural fields (without livestock) appears to be much more prevalent in Arizona.

BREEDING

In most nesting areas of Arizona, Cattle Egrets are primarily resident. Yet elsewhere in the state these gregarious egrets begin arriving in mid-March, with stragglers passing through into mid-June or later. During the atlas, some Cattle Egrets nests were noted as occupied as early as 8 April. The number of nests at this location, however, continued to increase into May. Nests with eggs were not reported during the atlas period, but based on observations of nests with young by 25 May, the eggs were likely laid in mid- to late April. Atlasers reported dependent fledglings by mid-June, and noted the latest nest with young on 18 July. But some Cattle Egret nests in Arizona remain active through early August and possibly later (T. Corman, personal communication). Due to postbreeding dispersal northward, it is difficult to determine the initiation of fall migration in Arizona. In northeastern Arizona, records span from late July to early December, with the highest counts in September (C. LaRue, personal communication).

Breeding Habitats

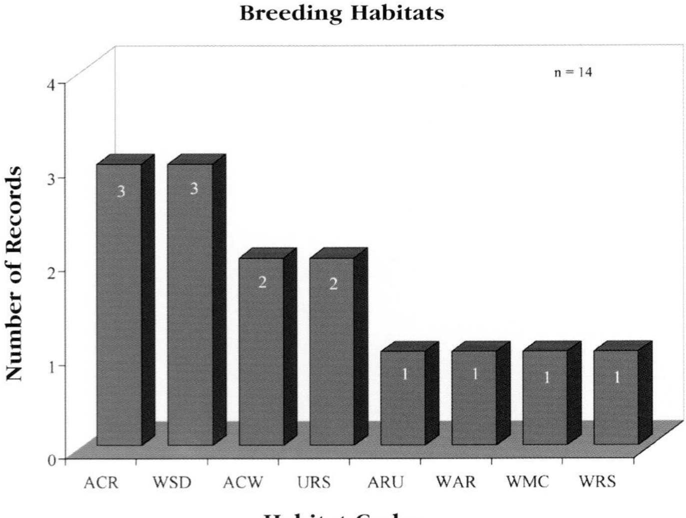

Cattle Egrets nest in active, multispecies rookeries and occupy vacant or abandoned sites rather then displace nesting birds (Telfair 1994). Although most rookeries contain several different species of egrets and herons in Arizona, several large rookeries near Yuma contain 65–90 percent Cattle Egret nests (L. Piest, personal communication). Individual nests vary considerably in substrate, height, and canopy cover. In Arizona, Cattle Egrets have nested in tamarisk, velvet mesquite, bulrush, date palm, and various citrus trees. Although atlasers did not measure Cattle Egret nest heights, data from Texas suggest that nests are generally placed 3 ft (0.9 m) below the nest substrate canopy (Telfair 1994).

The following nesting ecology information was taken from Telfair (1994). Cattle Egret nests are shallow, saucer-shaped stick structures, constructed by both sexes. Females typically lay 3–4 eggs (range 1–9) and several factors affect the number of eggs laid. Both adults incubate their eggs conscientiously for about 24 days (range 21–26 days). Nestlings are easily overheated during the first week and are faithfully shaded from the sun for the first 10 days after hatching. When the young are between 14 and 21 days old they frequently leave the nest but remain nearby where they perch on branches and beg for food. The chicks are gregarious and peaceful except at feeding time when rivalry is fierce. Young grow rapidly and leave the nest by age 30 days. They are independent of their parents by 45 days of age and often travel great distances during postbreeding dispersal. Cattle egrets will renest following nest failure early in the breeding season, but only one brood is likely produced per year.

DISTRIBUTION

In the late 1800s, Cattle Egrets probably crossed the Atlantic Ocean from the west coast of Africa to coastal northeastern South America (Telfair 1994). Of course the origin of New World Cattle Egrets cannot be known for certain (Arendt 1988), but birds are still observed crossing the Atlantic, suggesting that this species is still dispersing from Africa (Telfair 1994).

Cattle Egrets are now widespread throughout South, Central, and North America. They colonized the United States from east to west beginning in 1941 and have been confirmed breeding in most of the lower 48 states (Telfair 1994). That Cattle Egrets dispersed throughout much of North America in 30–40 years gives good insight into the extremely mobile and adaptable nature of these birds. The Cattle Egrets' breeding range is continuous along the southeastern coast and the Mississippi drainage, but otherwise locations are fairly scattered and isolated. In the West, resident populations are primarily found in southeastern California, southern Arizona, and adjacent Mexico.

Cattle Egrets were not reported in Arizona until 1966, when an injured bird was found near Phoenix in early December (Monson and Phillips 1981). These egrets had reached the Colorado River by 1970 and were suspect of breeding near Cibola National Wildlife Refuge and Dome Valley by the early 1980s (Rosenberg et al. 1991). Cattle Egrets were first confirmed breeding in Arizona in 1991, when as many as 700 nests were discovered in a lemon grove on the southwest side of Yuma. However, the landowner noted that the rookery had been there for the prior three years. The rookery had moved to an orange grove east of Somerton in 1996 and by June 1999 an estimated 900 active nests were noted at this location (L. Piest, personal communication).

Atlasers documented Cattle Egrets breeding at elevations from 100 to 2860 ft (30–872 m). During the atlas period, Cattle Egrets were confirmed breeding locally within the lower Colorado River valley from Parker to Somerton. In the Gila River valley, atlasers noted nesting activity at Painted Rock Dam and at one location on Paloma Ranch west of Gila Bend. In 1994, atlasers confirmed Cattle Egrets nesting in a residential area of Ocotillo southwest of Phoenix and in 2001, observers discovered several pairs of Cattle Egrets nesting with Snowy Egrets well to the east in Thatcher, Graham County. Cattle Egrets have also been suspected of nesting in the Arlington Valley and near the confluence of the Salt and Gila rivers since 1990 (Witzeman et al. 1997). Atlasers noted these egrets in both areas during the nesting season, often in high breeding plumage, which further suggests nearby nesting.

Populations of this gregarious heron are expected to increase in Arizona, and their breeding range will probably expand as well. These increases will likely occur despite the anticipated loss of some nesting rookeries as housing and urban developments replace their agricultural foraging areas.

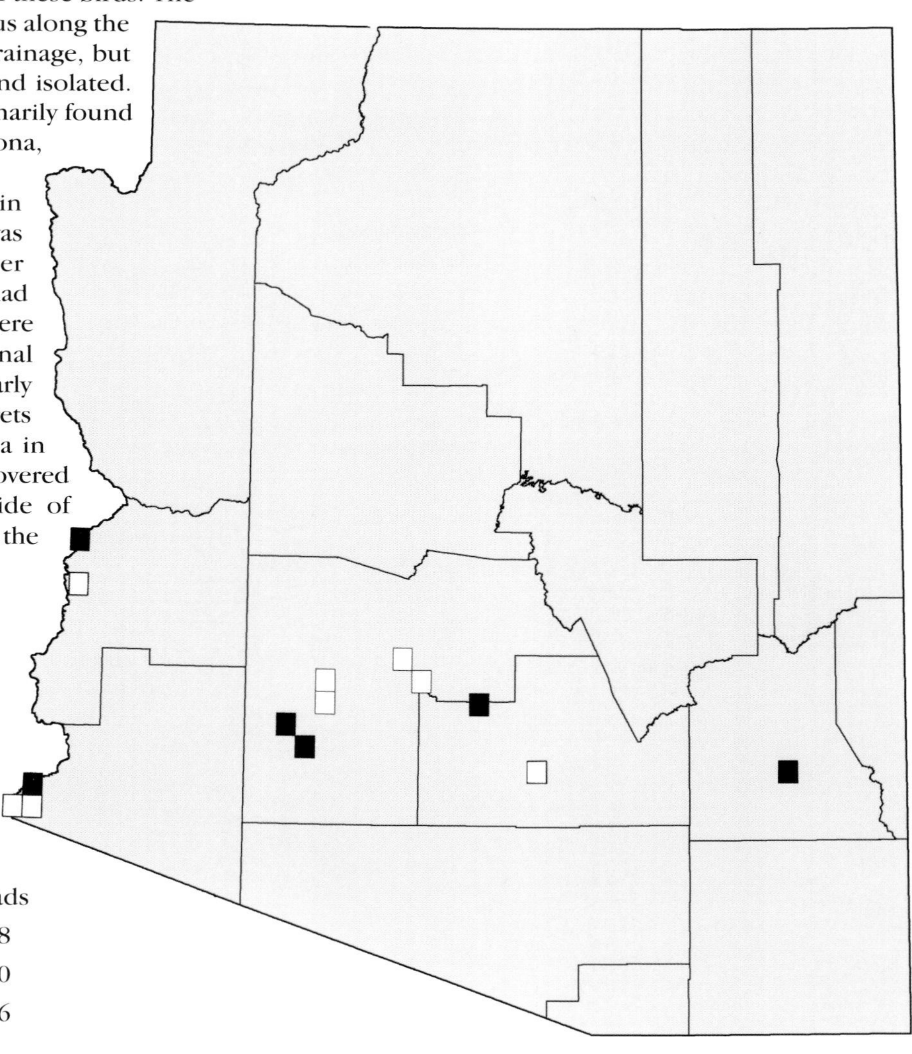

Cattle Egret Breeding Evidence Reported in 8 (<1%) of 1834 priority blocks

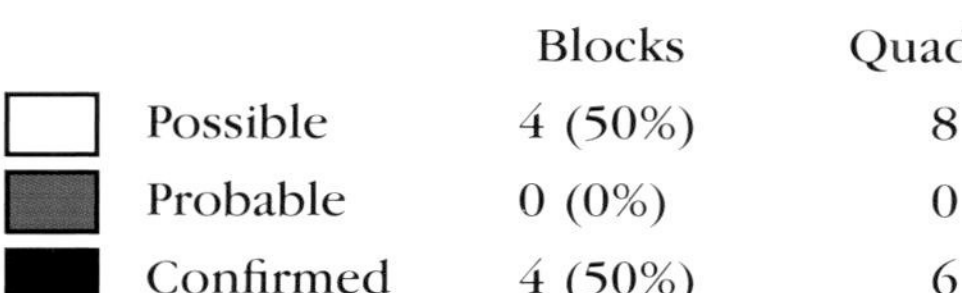

	Blocks	Quads
Possible	4 (50%)	8
Probable	0 (0%)	0
Confirmed	4 (50%)	6

Green Heron

by Cathryn Wise-Gervais *Butorides virescens*

The Green Heron is a resourceful fisherman that will lure small fish to the surface by using bait such as small twigs, leaves, insects, and other materials. This heron tosses the lures into the water then dines on the fish that come to investigate. Although common, the Green Heron's cryptic coloration and secretive habits render it easy to miss by the casual observer.

RICHARD DITCH

HABITAT

In Arizona, Green Herons are typically birds of brushy marshlands and riparian corridors, but also use artificial waterways. Atlasers reported this species in 11 habitat types, and the most commonly reported of these was cottonwood–willow riparian woodlands (35 percent of potential breeding records; $n = 107$). Marshes, ponds, lakeshores, and slow sections of rivers accounted for an additional 26 percent of records, which often included stands of cattails, bulrush, and other dense wetland vegetation. An additional 13 percent of Green Heron records were from tamarisk-dominated waterways or along foothill drainages with sycamore, cottonwood, willow, and ash. These adaptable herons also occur regularly in rural and urban settings in Arizona, where they occupy vegetated canals, ponds, and lakes at wastewater treatment facilities. They are also found at ponds in agricultural areas, golf courses, parks, and lakeside residential developments. Green Herons usually hunt and rest in areas with dense vegetation, and their plumage color enables them to blend inconspicuously with such surroundings. Despite this predilection, the birds are occasionally observed foraging in the open near favorite fishing areas (Davis and Kushlan 1994).

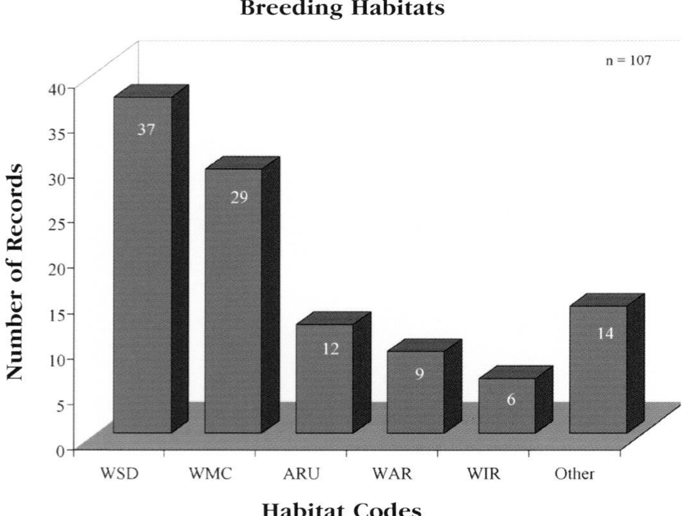

BREEDING

In Arizona, migrant Green Herons begin appearing in March and April, with stragglers still passing through into June. Arizona's resident populations can initiate breeding quite early in the lowlands. Atlasers reported an agitated pair of Green Herons on 17 April and obtained the first breeding confirmation of adults carrying nesting materials on 23 April. However, observers reported the first fledglings on 29 April, indicating that this pair began nesting by early to mid-March. Atlasers obtained only 31 confirmations for this secretive heron, but the limited data suggest that breeding activities peak in late June. Nests with young were reported through 7 July, but atlasers observed adults feeding fledglings through 28 August at higher elevations. In Arizona, fall migration can begin by mid-August and continue into October.

Unlike many other wading species, Green Herons are not gregarious birds so pairs nest alone or occasionally in loose colonies. The males select the secluded and typically well-shaded nest site and will sometimes use old nests or dismantle them to reuse sticks (Davis and Kushlan 1994). Nests are placed in a variety of trees, and the birds seem to select sites based on foliage density rather than by specific tree species. Nests are typically on a limb suspended above the water and common nest substrates in Arizona include tamarisk, willow, and cottonwood. Atlasers did not measure any Green Heron nests but figures taken from other parts of North America range from 0.0 to 32.8 ft (0–10 m), with rare height records of 65.6 ft (20 m) or more (Davis and Kushlan 1994).

Typical Green Heron clutches consist of 3–5 eggs, and both parents incubate these for 19–21 days (Davis and Kushlan 1994). After hatching, both adults feed the young and will stand over them to shade them for the sun if the nest is in an exposed location. The young remain in the nest for 16–17 days and take their first flights at 21–22 days of age (Meyerriecks 1962). It is not known how long the parents will continue feeding the fledglings, but some researchers estimate that the birds reach independence by age 30–35 days (Davis and Kushlan 1994). Green Herons typically rear one brood per year, especially in the northern latitudes. Second broods have been noted, however,

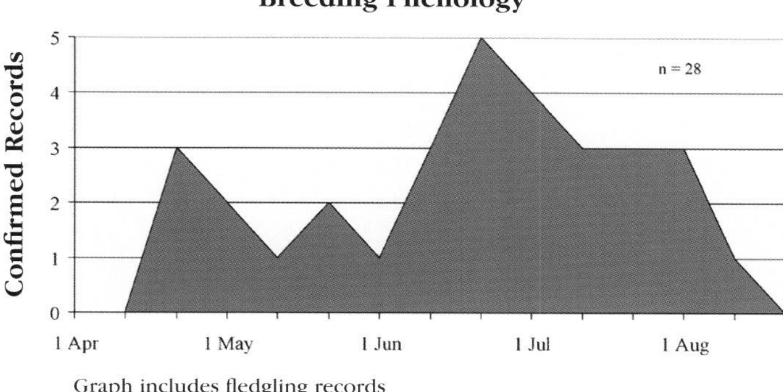

Graph includes fledgling records

and which is quite possible with the lengthy nesting season atlas data revealed in Arizona. Green Herons will also certainly renest if their initial attempt fails (Meyerriecks 1962).

DISTRIBUTION

Green Herons breed throughout the lowlands of North and Central America, from the eastern United States and adjacent Canada to eastern Colorado. These birds are also found in the Pacific coast states and provinces from southwestern British Columbia south. Populations in the Interior West and in the Southwest are much more local.

Phillips et al. (1964) described the Green Heron's prior breeding range in Arizona as encompassing riparian areas south and west of the Mogollon Plateau. Atlasers found most Green Herons within the same general region at elevations ranging from 80 to 5200 ft (24–1585 m). Although few records have been obtained for this species above the Mogollon Rim, atlasers discovered a Green Heron pair nesting in a Gambel's oak in Lakeside at 6740 ft (2054 m). This successful nest fledged young on 28 August. Prior to the atlas, the only other confirmed record on the Colorado Plateau was a pair carrying food to a nest hidden in dense tamarisk at Cow Springs Lake on 30 June 1988 (C. LaRue, personal communication).

Green Herons remain rare summer visitors along the Colorado River in the Grand Canyon, including Glen Canyon, with no evidence of nesting (Brown et al. 1987). During the atlas, one Green Heron was noted near 205 Mile Rapid and an individual spent May through July 1997 near Lees Ferry. Other isolated northern Arizona atlas records included sightings near Truxton, and at the confluence of Beaver Dam Wash and the Virgin River near Littleton.

Rosenberg et al. (1991) considered the species a common resident in the southern portion of the lower Colorado River and less common in the northern valley. Atlasers found this species fairly regularly from Cibola National Wildlife Refuge south, including on the lower Gila River upstream to Tacna, and from Topock Marsh to the Bill Williams River National Wildlife Refuge.

Researchers have had difficulties determining population trends for this solitary and somewhat secretive species. Limited Breeding Bird Survey data available for Green Herons suggest slight increases, especially in central and eastern regions (Davis and Kushlan 1994). Atlasers regularly reported Green Herons in suitable habitats throughout their previously described range in Arizona, indicating some degree of stability. Loss and degradation of riparian and wetland areas have probably affected the bird on local levels however.

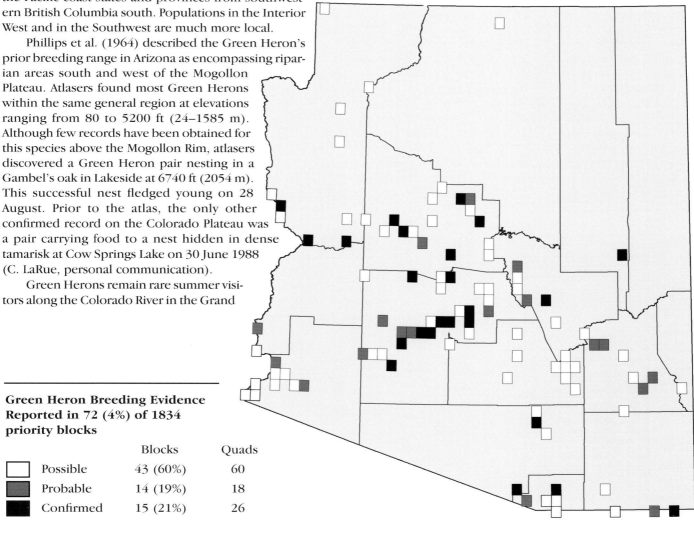

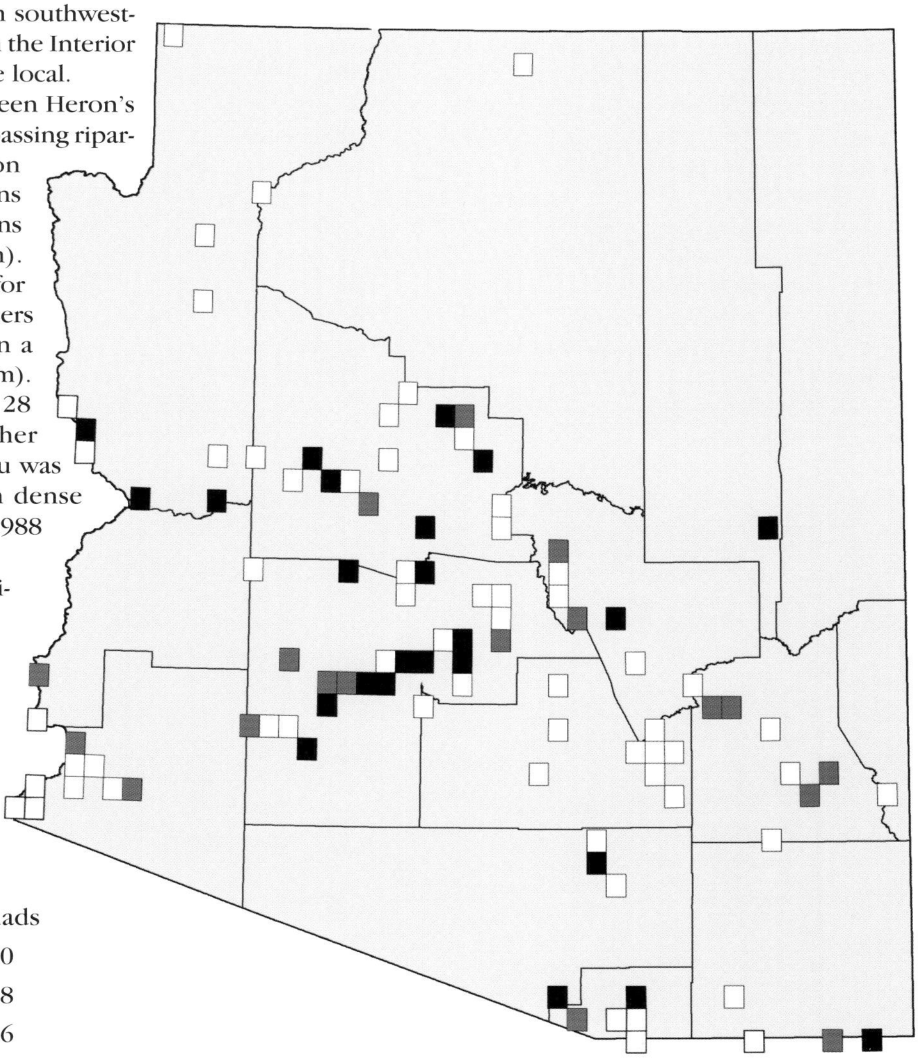

Green Heron Breeding Evidence Reported in 72 (4%) of 1834 priority blocks

	Blocks	Quads
Possible	43 (60%)	60
Probable	14 (19%)	18
Confirmed	15 (21%)	26

Black-crowned Night-Heron

by Cathryn Wise-Gervais *Nycticorax nycticorax*

The handsome Black-crowned Night-Heron appears at dusk, often announcing itself with a characteristic "quawk." The heron's Latin name means "night raven" and refers to this corvid-like sound. Although these unique herons roost gregariously and nest colonially, they are solitary foragers and defend individual feeding territories.

RICHARD DITCH

HABITAT

Black-crowned Night-Herons use a wide variety of aquatic habitats throughout their extensive range. In Arizona, most are found roosting and nesting in wetland vegetation or riparian trees and shrubs, and nocturnal foraging often occurs in more open areas nearby. Atlasers reported 33 percent of all potential breeding records in marshes, lake edges, and ponds characterized by aquatic vegetation such as cattails and bulrushes (n = 64). Another 22 percent of night-heron sightings were noted in lowland deciduous riparian areas dominated by cottonwood, willow, tamarisk, and mesquite, and 11 percent of records were in tamarisk-dominated drainages.

Atlasers also sighted nearly 21 percent of these adaptable herons in urban or rural settings. These included lakes, ponds, and canals at parks, golf courses, waste water facilities, and residential areas. In rural areas these herons were occasionally found roosting and nesting in orchards and in vegetation along irrigation runoff ponds and stock tanks.

BREEDING

In Arizona, Black-crowned Night-Herons are primarily resident within the lower Colorado, Salt, and Gila River valleys, but elsewhere they begin migrating to nesting areas in early to mid-March. Northbound migration peaks in April, with some stragglers still passing through into early June. Males begin building or refurbishing nests soon after they arrive, and this coincides with courtship and pair formation (Davis 1986). Males can become quite aggressive and display vigorously at the onset of the breeding season. These displays are thought to provide social stimulation to other birds to initiate breeding (Davis 1993). Atlasers first reported a pair of birds on 20 March, but did not report nest building until 21 April. However, atlasers did report adults with fledglings on 25 April indicating that Black-crowned Night-Herons can initiate nesting at lower elevations as early as late March. Observers obtained the majority of confirmed records for this species in May–June, but reported nests with young as late as 18 July. It is likely that these late records were renesting attempts after failure, as second broods are uncommon (Parsons and Burger 1981). In Arizona, migrants and postbreeding wanderers begin appearing in July, with numbers increasing in August and early September. Most Black-crowned Night-Herons have left nontraditional wintering areas in the state by mid-October.

Black-crowned Night-Herons are gregarious at all seasons and nest colonially (Davis 1993). In fact, in Arizona, night-herons frequently nest with egrets and other species of herons. Since the former tends to nest earlier and feeds nocturnally, competition for food resources is minimized (Davis 1993). Black-crowned Night-Herons nest in a wide variety of substrates and during the atlas they were found nesting in Goodding willow, Fremont cottonwood, velvet mesquite, bulrush, cattails, and several exotic trees such as tamarisk, date palms, and fan palms. Nests can be placed either near tree forks or toward the end of branches and are equally common in the open or deep in the foliage. Black-crowned Night-Herons will also reuse their old nests as well, or use the abandoned nests of other heron species.

Male Black-crowned Night-Herons initiate nest building or refurbishing by acquiring sticks and presenting them ceremoniously to the female. The female then weaves the

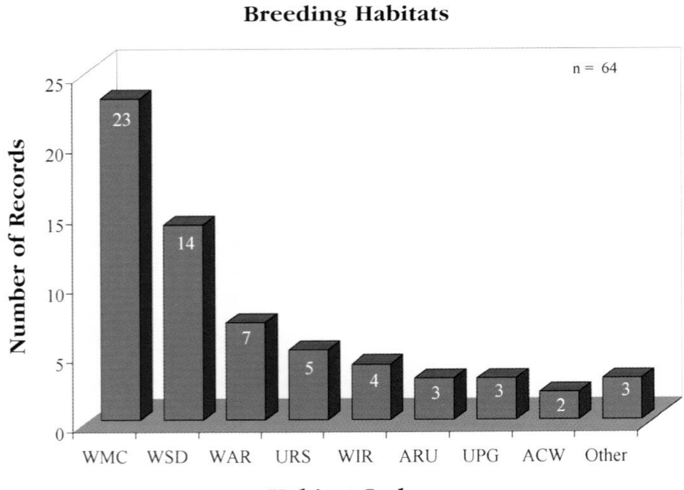

Breeding Phenology

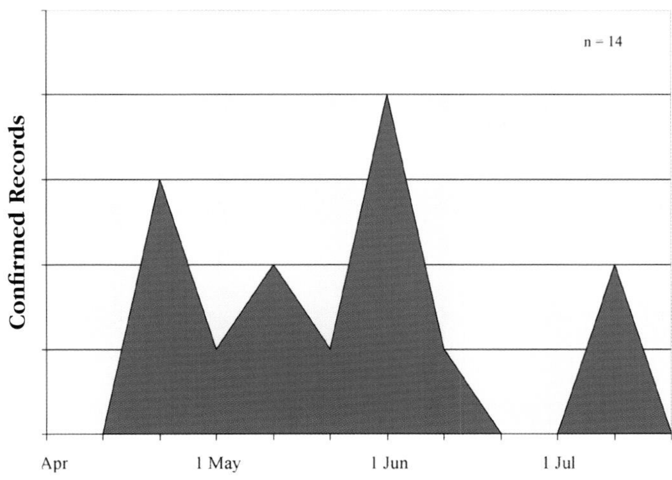

materials into place. Females typically lay 3–4 eggs (range 3–5) and begin the 23–26 day incubation period as soon as the first egg is laid (Hancock and Kushlan 1984). Both parents incubate and the young hatch asynchronously. Nestlings begin clambering on limbs around the nest after only about 2 weeks. The young are capable of flight when they are 6–7 weeks old, at which time they begin following adults to foraging areas (Palmer 1962).

DISTRIBUTION AND STATUS

Black-crowned Night-Herons are one of the most widespread herons in the world, nesting on every continent except Australia and Antarctica. This cosmopolitan species nests widely throughout the United States and into south-central Canada and Mexico. In Arizona, earlier accounts noted Black-crowned Night-Herons as residents in the lower Colorado River valley and nesting at least historically on the Salt and Verde rivers (Phillips et al. 1964). Monson and Phillips (1981) also noted these herons were resident near the confluence of the Salt and Gila rivers and nested occasionally elsewhere.

Atlas surveys revealed that Black-crowned Night-Herons are a much more widespread nesting species in Arizona than previous literature suggested. Most atlas records were at low elevations below 5100 ft (1554 m), primarily along the Colorado, Gila, lower Salt, and Verde rivers, but some breeding records were also obtained in high elevation areas. Black-crowned Night-Herons were confirmed nesting locally above the Mogollon Rim and in the White Mountains from 6700 to 7400 ft (2042–2256 m). Atlasers also reported birds as high as 8200 ft (2499 m) near Greer, but did not confirm breeding in this area. Black-crowned Night-Herons were found nesting sparsely in southeastern Arizona. Appropriate habitat does not appear to be lacking in this region and this paucity of records is rather perplexing. Atlasers did obtain several confirmations in the Thatcher-Safford area, however. It was not surprising that Black-crowned Night-Herons were absent from northeastern Arizona because there is limited appropriate nesting habitat and food resources for the birds in this region.

The apparent increase in the abundance and distribution of nesting Black-crowned Night-Herons in Arizona parallels population trends elsewhere in the United States (Davis 1993). These adaptable night prowlers are very tolerant of humans and their habitat changes. They readily take advantage of suburban lakes and ponds stocked with fish, roosting during the day in nearby exotic shade trees. Since the birds are high on the food chain and are widely distributed throughout the country, they make excellent environmental indicators (Davis 1993).

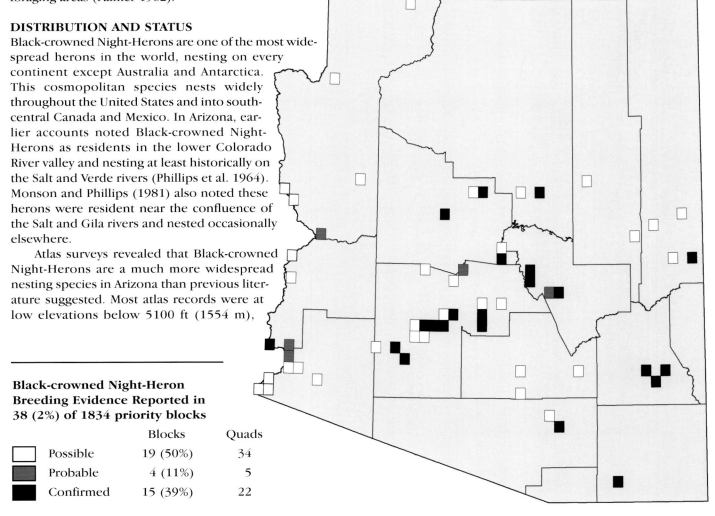

Black-crowned Night-Heron Breeding Evidence Reported in 38 (2%) of 1834 priority blocks

	Blocks	Quads
Possible	19 (50%)	34
Probable	4 (11%)	5
Confirmed	15 (39%)	22

Black Vulture

by Troy E. Corman *Coragyps atratus*

Opportunistic Black Vultures are relative newcomers to Arizona, where they were first reported in 1920. They are often observed soaring in large numbers and frequently rely on the meeker Turkey Vulture to locate carrion. By sheer numbers, these mobsters quickly displace the unfortunate original finder at the carcass.

DAN FISCHER

HABITAT

Black Vultures are found in a wide variety of habitats across their extensive range, but in Arizona, atlasers reported approximately 69 percent of all records in Sonoran desert scrub habitat (n = 42). Typically these vultures were found in areas with an abundance of saguaros and larger trees including ironwood, paloverde, and mesquite, but were occasionally found in sparsely vegetated desert regions as well. In sharp contrast to their distribution and density south of Arizona, this vulture is most abundant where human populations are sparse. Locally, Black Vultures were also found near riparian woodlands, dense washes, semi-arid grasslands, and in rural settings including small towns, agricultural fields, and pecan orchards. They especially seem to favor relatively flat open areas where they are equally at home on the ground or roosting on some elevated perch such as a tree, saguaro, telephone pole, or transmission tower. During the breeding season these vultures also roost and nest on steep, sparsely vegetated arid mountains, canyon walls, and rock outcrops.

Black Vultures depend primarily on carrion, especially large mammals such as domestic livestock. The bulk of their diet in Arizona likely consists of road kills or open range cattle and horses that succumb to starvation or thirst in the inhospitable desert. They are also sometimes found feeding on dead fish at pond and lake edges. Unlike Turkey Vultures, Black Vultures rely on sight and not olfaction to locate carcasses (Stager 1964). They routinely monitor the foraging activities of Turkey Vultures and quickly join them at newly discovered carrion (Buckley 1999). The anatomy of the Black Vulture has evolved for social feeding at larger carcasses, feeding rapidly, and reaching satiation quickly (Rea 1998).

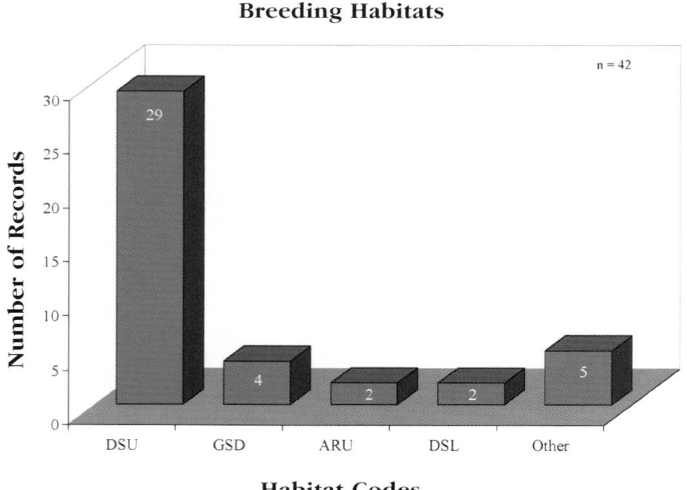

BREEDING

Most populations of Black Vultures are resident in Arizona, with some local dispersal to adjacent areas, especially in fall and winter. There is little information available on the breeding biology and chronology of Black Vultures in Arizona. Only four active nests had been reported in the state prior to the atlas (Rea 1998). Like Turkey Vultures, the resident population likely includes a high proportion of nonbreeding immatures.

Black Vultures appear to mate for life and clearly associate with their mates more than with other adults (Rabenold 1986). During the atlas, courtship behavior was reported as early as 1 March at Organ Pipe Cactus National Monument. However, courtship also likely takes place in January and February, prior to the initiation of most atlas surveys. In Arizona, eggs are typically laid in early spring, with egg dates reported between 20 March and 19 April (Monson and Phillips 1981). The only nest found during the atlas period was in a shallow, rocky outcrop cave near Patagonia, overlooking Sonoita Creek (R. Hoyer, personal communication). It contained two eggs on 4 April. Nestlings have been reported as early as 10 April at Organ Pipe Cactus National Monument. Therefore, based on the length of incubation, egg laying was initiated no later than 3 March. Most fledging in Arizona likely takes place in late June through July.

Black Vultures choose a dark, secluded location in which to lay their eggs, which entails no nest construction. The few nests discovered in Arizona have been in rocky outcrops and small, shallow, arid mountain caves where the eggs are placed directly on the bare ground. Weeks before nesting begins, pairs of Black Vultures may spend long periods perching conspicuously near prospective nest sites (Jackson 1983). This may enable the birds to assess a site's quality and freedom from disturbance (Stewart 1983). Successful nest sites are often used by the same pair year after year (Jackson 1988).

Black Vultures typically lay two eggs and both parents share incubation equally, taking twenty-four-hour shifts (Stewart 1974). The incubation period is 38–39 days (Stewart 1974). The young grow relatively slowly and take first flight when they are 75–80 days old (Stewart 1974; Jackson 1988). The parents continue to feed the young long after they have fledged, sometimes up to eight months (Rabenold 1986). Black Vultures are known to replace egg clutches 3–5 weeks after loss of first clutch, often in or near the original nest (Jackson 1983).

DISTRIBUTION AND STATUS

Black Vultures nest throughout South and Central America, north through much of Mexico. In the United States they are resident in the Southeast, from central Texas northeast to Pennsylvania and New York. In the West, they are only found nesting in south-central Arizona.

First reported in Arizona on Tohono O'odham tribal land in June 1920, Black Vulture numbers and distribution in the state steadily increased thereafter (Phillips et al. 1964). By 1928, these vultures were considered resident in portions of Arizona. However, a nest with eggs was not found until 1967 (Monson and Phillips 1981). They were noted since the mid-1960s as far north as the Gila River Indian Community lands, with most observation near the confluence of the Santa Cruz and Gila rivers (Rea 1983). Small flocks were observed in this area through the end of the atlas period. Monson and Phillips (1981) described the Black Vultures Arizona range primarily within the Santa Cruz River drainage north to Picacho Peak area and west to Organ Pipe Cactus National Monument.

Atlasers noted Black Vultures throughout much of their previously described range at elevations from approximately 1000 ft (305 m) near the confluence of the Santa Cruz and Gila Rivers in Maricopa County to 4000 ft (1219 m) near Patagonia. Atlas data reveal these vultures to be sparse to locally uncommon from Organ Pipe Cactus National Monument east to Nogales and Patagonia. The highest concentration of reports was on the Tohono O'odham tribal lands at the center of their distribution within Arizona. Atlasers found Black Vultures throughout the nesting season as far northeast as Florence and north to the edge of the Estrella and White Tank mountains in Maricopa County. A pair of courting Black Vultures in mid-March 1995 remained through at least April in the White Tank Mountains area, which strongly suggests nesting. They became resident in the general vicinity of Laveen and near the Salt and Gila rivers confluence during the mid-1990s. Black Vultures populations in Arizona, appear to be relatively stable or slightly increasing.

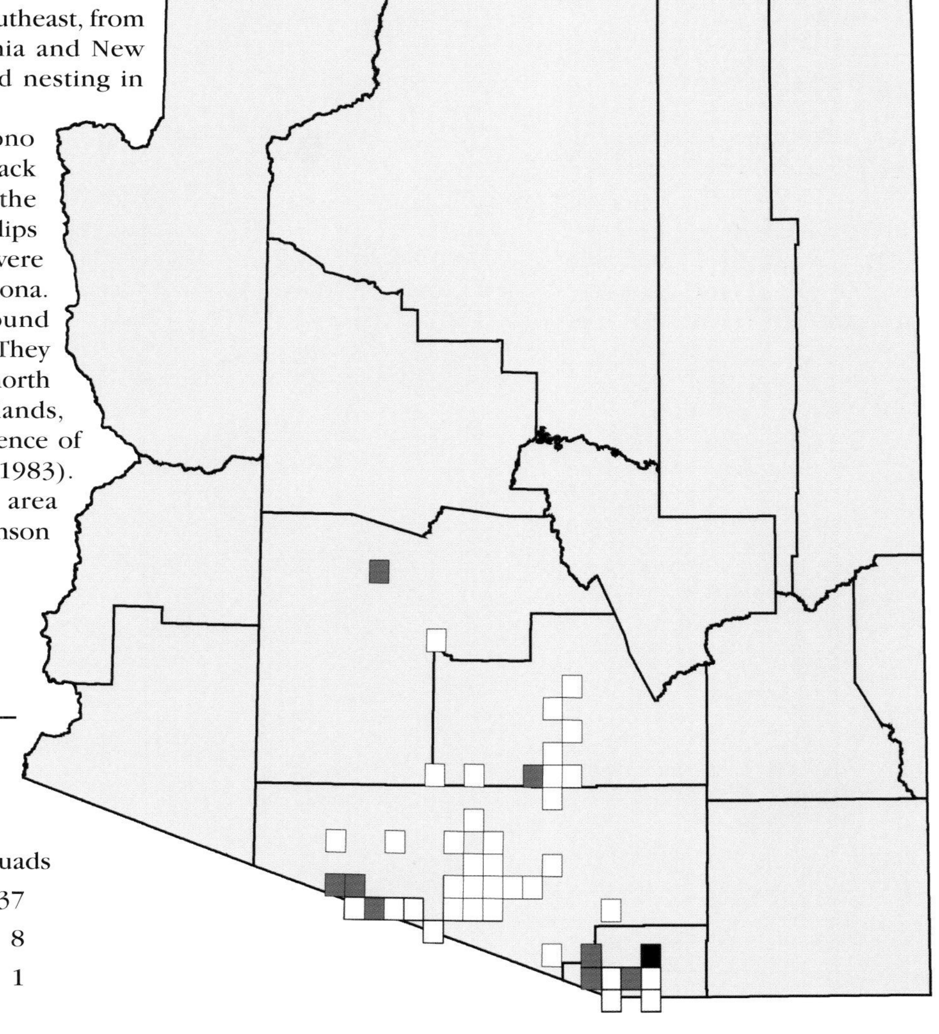

Black Vulture Breeding Evidence Reported in 42 (2%) of 1834 priority blocks

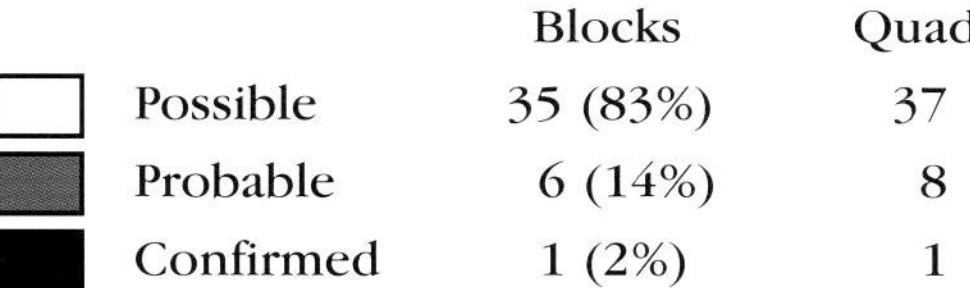

	Blocks	Quads
Possible	35 (83%)	37
Probable	6 (14%)	8
Confirmed	1 (2%)	1

Turkey Vulture

by Troy E. Corman *Cathartes aura*

What the Turkey Vulture lacks in close-up attractiveness and land-based agility, is compensated by grace on the wing as they soar effortlessly on thermal upwellings. Their many unique adaptations and secretive nesting habits also add a little intrigue to a very familiar and commonly observed species.

RICHARD DITCH

HABITAT

Turkey Vultures can be observed soaring over any habitat and at most elevations in Arizona. More than 50 percent of all atlas records of these vultures were in Sonoran desertscrub or pinyon pine–juniper habitats (n = 950). However, this likely pertains to a much greater percentage of these habitats in Arizona as opposed to specific preferences by Turkey Vultures. Atlasers also commonly noted these vultures over grasslands and forested mountain ridges. These vultures are frequently observed perched singly or in small groups (<50), but larger groups of 100 or more often form at roosts during migration. Favored perch sites such as rocky outcrops, cliffs, canyon walls, transmission towers, telephone poles, and tall trees usually afford commanding views, dawn sunbathing opportunities, and easier access to thermals. Communal roosts are used daily and can be recognized by extensively white washed perch sites with many molted feathers below.

BREEDING

Turkey Vultures begin migrating north into Arizona sometimes as early as late January with a peak passage in March. Throughout North America, active nest have been documented from late March–late June, with likely replacement nests active until mid-September (Kirk and Mossman 1998).

Breeding Habitats

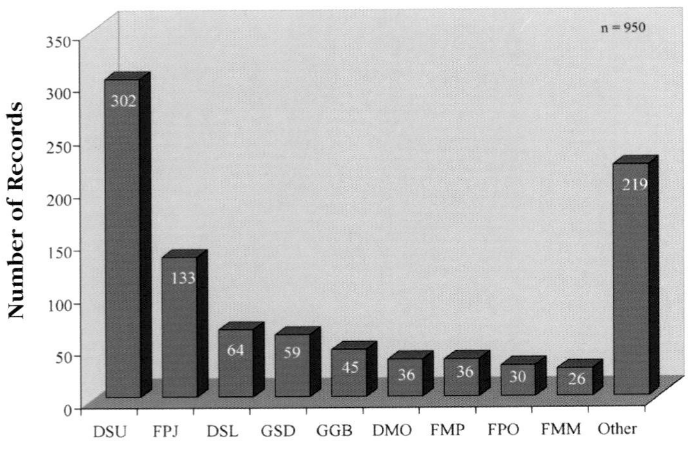

There is very little prior breeding information available on Turkey Vultures in Arizona. Phillips et al. (1964) noted that in the desert, copulation had been observed as early as Feb. and two nests with eggs were found at Picacho Peak, Pinal County on 28 April and 17 May (Hana 1961). As widespread as they are in Arizona, only sixteen active Turkey Vulture nests were found during the atlas period. The earliest confirmed atlas record was a nest with young on 17 April, indicating the initiation of egg laying was during the first week of March or earlier. Nearly half of the nests documented during the atlas occurred in June. The latest active nest contained young on 6 August. Fall migration for Turkey Vultures begins by late August, peaking in late September and October, with stragglers into early December.

The most important requirement of nest site selection by Turkey Vultures appears to be isolation from human disturbance (Kirk and Mossman 1998). Once found, there are many instances of vultures using the same nest site repeatedly over the years (Kirk and Mossman 1998). In Arizona, relatively few nests have been found, but most have been discovered in difficult to reach locations, including rock outcrops, caves, steep boulder-strewn slopes, rocky ridges, abandoned mines, and ancient Native American ruins such as cliff dwellings and granaries. During the atlas, one nest with young was also located on the ground next to a fallen ponderosa pine near Lakeside.

Kirk and Mossman (1998) compiled much of the following natural history information. Turkey Vultures do not construct a nest and typically 2 eggs (range 1–3) are laid in a scrape on the ground in a secluded location. Both parents incubate about equally with changeover occurring probably only once daily and usually in the morning. Incubation continues from 38 to 41 days, and young are capable of flight when they are between 65 and 90 days old. Only one brood is produced per year, but they will renest if first attempts fail early in the nesting stage.

Primarily an opportunistic and solitary scavenger of dead animals, Turkey Vultures prefer relatively fresh carrion and likely feed most often on animals found within a day or two of death (Rea 1998). Unlike most birds, this species has an excellent sense of smell, and uses both sight and

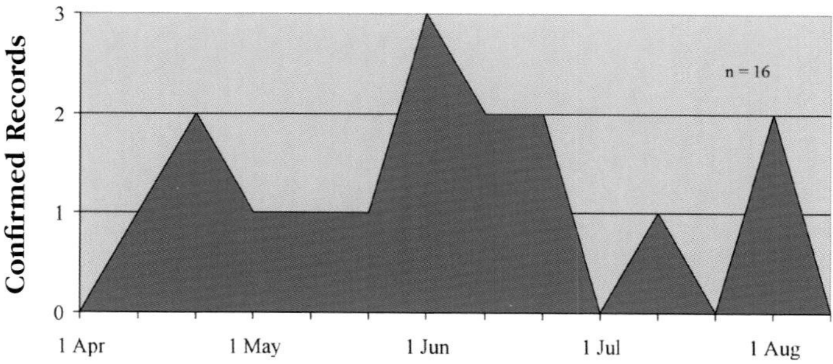

smell in locating food. It frequently finds concealed food by approaching from downwind (Lemon 1991; Stager 1964). With their superior olfactory senses, Turkey Vultures often find food sources first and the more aggressive Black Vultures will then follow and sometimes displace them (Kirk and Mossman 1998).

DISTRIBUTION AND STATUS

Turkey Vultures breeding range is extensive from southern Canada south to the southern tip of South America. In Arizona, Turkey Vultures are uncommon winter residents in lowland Sonoran desert regions primarily below 1000 ft (305 m) elevation. This includes the lower Colorado River valley south of Parker and southwest of Phoenix in the Gila River drainage and adjacent rural areas. A study of Turkey Vulture subspecies (Rea 1983) has shown that probably all the birds that summer and breed in Arizona (April–October) vacate the state in winter and that wintering individuals are members of a larger subspecies from the northern part of the continent (Rea 1998).

During the breeding season, Turkey Vultures are commonly observed throughout the state. Although, as the atlas map depicts, they are more sparsely distributed in the northeast. Clearly, Turkey Vultures occur and likely nest throughout much of the White Mountain Apache tribal lands as they do in all surrounding areas. However, permission to conduct atlas surveys on these lands could not be obtained, thus the lack of records there.

It is important to note that many Turkey Vultures observed in Arizona during the summer are nonbreeders. These vultures may take five years to reach sexual maturity (Dexter 1998; Rea 1998). Therefore, the distribution map may exaggerate the number of possible breeding localities in the state. Although as previously mentioned, this vulture has been found nesting in many diverse habitats and elevations throughout the state. Because breeding behavior is so infrequently observed in Turkey Vultures, atlasers found it very difficult to distinguish between breeding and nonbreeding individuals. This is also compounded by the fact that vultures often cover large areas (far greater than an atlas block) during their feeding excursions (Dexter 1998).

Tolerant of human activity and adaptable in its diet and choice of nest sites, Turkey Vultures have fared well in our changing landscapes (Kirk and Mossman 1998). Populations in the state are considered fairly stable and there are no immediate concerns for this species.

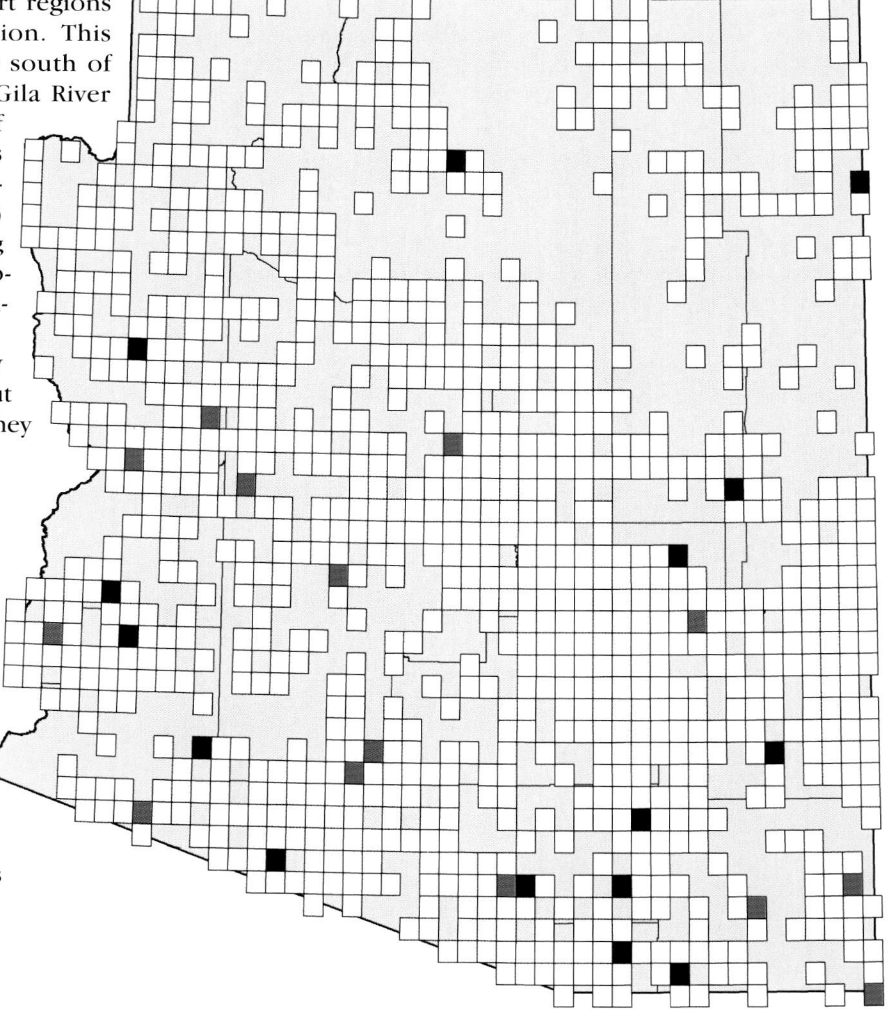

Turkey Vulture Breeding Evidence Reported in 984 (54%) of 1834 priority blocks

	Blocks	Quads
Possible	957 (97%)	972
Probable	14 (1%)	14
Confirmed	13 (1%)	15

Osprey

by James T. Driscoll *Pandion haliaetus*

One of the most widespread birds of prey in the world, Ospreys are specialized fish-eating raptors that are quite efficient in capturing their quarry. When foraging territories overlap, Arizona's other fish-eating raptor, the Bald Eagle, often takes advantage of the smaller Osprey's superiority in obtaining prey by readily pirating their meal soon after capture.

JIM BURNS

HABITAT

In Arizona, Ospreys are typically observed near open bodies of water-containing fish, including artificial impoundments such as urban lakes, canals, and fish hatchery ponds. Nearly 40 percent of all atlas records were from wetlands and shorelines of ponds, lakes, reservoirs, and rivers in several different habitats (n = 29). An additional 18 percent were from along montane drainages containing a mixture of ponderosa pine, Douglas fir, cottonwood, maple, boxelder, alder, and willow. Nesting sites are common in tall trees or built structures, and atlasers reported another 21 percent of Osprey observations in either ponderosa pine or mixed conifer–dominated forests. Recently, several breeding pairs of Ospreys have also reoccupied Sonoran Desert riparian habitat along rivers dominated by Fremont cottonwood and Goodding willow woodlands.

BREEDING

Although some Ospreys regularly winter in Arizona along the lower Colorado, Gila, Verde, and Salt rivers, migrants begin heading to northern nesting areas by late February or early March, peaking in mid-April. Nest construction of the few resident lower elevation pairs has been observed as early as December with egg laying by late March. The remainder of Arizona's nesting populations are at much higher elevations, and atlasers noted them occupying established nests by late March or early April. Due to Osprey's lofty nests, atlasers were unable to determine when eggs were laid at higher elevations, but (Vahle et al. 1988) noted most nests in Arizona contain eggs by mid- to late April. Atlasers noted nests with young by late June, although in Arizona, eggs typically begin hatching in late May and early June (Dodd and Vahle 1998). The latest nest with young reported was noted on 25 August. Migrant Ospreys begin appearing away from nesting areas in Arizona by early August, with peak passage in mid-September and continuing through late October.

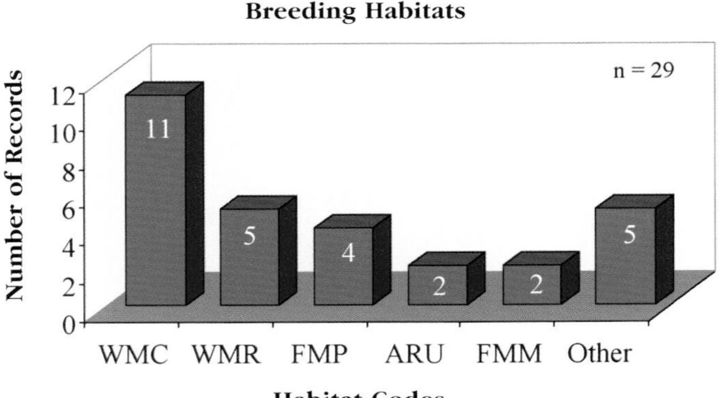

The bulky, stick nests of Ospreys are placed in a conspicuous location, and in Arizona, most nests are constructed atop large ponderosa pine snags or on a large sturdy side branch (Dodd and Vahle 1998). In the absence of large pine snags in Arizona, the adults will occasionally place their large, bulky stick nests on artificial structures, such as power poles, cell phone towers, and topped live pines with platforms. Osprey pairs typically reused the same nest, with new material added each year. Consequently, nest structures can become quite large over time.

Typical Osprey egg clutches consist of 3 eggs, but this can range from 1 to 4 (Brown and Amadon 1989). One clutch is laid per year. The female does most of the incubating, while the male provides food for both the female and young throughout the breeding attempt. Incubation lasts 38–43 days, and the nestlings remain in the nest for 7–9 weeks (Ehrlich et al. 1988). Following initial nest departure, fledglings often return to the nest or nearby perches for an additional 1–3 weeks to feed on fish the parents continue to provide (Poole et al. 2002). At higher elevations, Arizona's Osprey productivity has been documented at or near 1.5 young per active nest (Vahle and Beatty 1995). Unfortunately, recent nesting attempts along lowland rivers in the Sonoran Desert have failed to fledge young.

Breeding Phenology

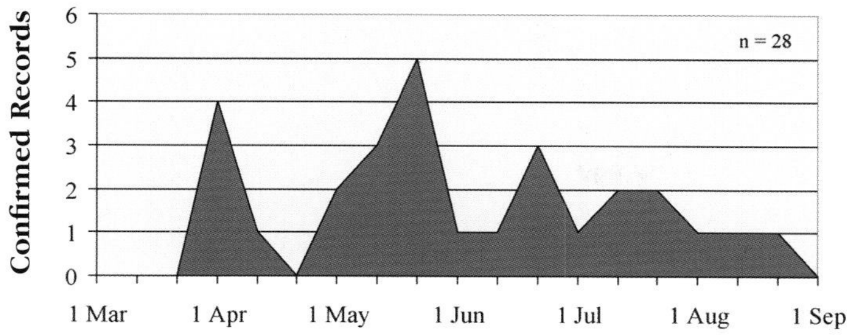

DISTRIBUTION AND STATUS

The Osprey is one of a few raptor species that retains a nearly worldwide distribution. The species is common inland and in coastal regions in the northern hemisphere, and limited to the coastal areas of the southern hemisphere (Grossman and Hamlet 1988). In North America, Ospreys breed throughout southern and western Canada, Alaska, south along the Atlantic Coast through Florida, and west to Louisiana. They also breed locally in the western United States south to Arizona and New Mexico. Disjunct nesting populations in Mexico are primarily restricted to coastal areas (Poole et al. 2002).

Ospreys in Arizona were historically considered rare (Swarth 1914), and later were noted as local nesting species along rivers just below the Mogollon Rim (Phillips et al. 1964). These unique raptors also nested until 1951 near the confluence of the Verde and Salt rivers (Monson and Phillips 1981).

Atlas data revealed the distribution, and the density of nesting Ospreys in Arizona continues to increase steadily. Most of the state's Ospreys were found nesting along the Mogollon Rim at elevations ranging from 6000 to 8300 ft (1829–2530 m). Elsewhere, a pair was found nesting at Lynx Lake near Prescott at 5550 ft (1692 m). During the atlas, nesting Ospreys also began an attempt to reestablish themselves along Sonoran Desert rivers near Phoenix at elevations ranging from 975 to 1500 ft (297–457 m). Beginning in 1996, an Osprey pair attempted nesting near Granite Reef Dam on the Salt River where they have not nested in over 40 years. Another nest was discovered being built near the dry Agua Fria River, a few miles upstream of its confluence with the Gila River in 2000. Competition with nesting Bald Eagles may limit their success along the Salt and lower Verde rivers. Arizona Bald Eagle populations increased 40 percent over the past twelve years, and they may be locally outcompeting Osprey for Arizona's limited fish resources.

Atlasers found the highest concentrations of nesting Ospreys were in Apache and Coconino National Forests. However, Dodd and Vahle (1998) reported 33 percent of Arizona's nesting osprey population (not included in the atlas data) occurs along the White River and its tributaries on White Mountain Apache tribal lands, an area not available for access by atlasers. With this and other survey information, an estimated 55–60 breeding areas exist in Arizona. As in Bald Eagles, however, the significant factor affecting Arizona osprey populations is most likely the availability and abundance of fish, and adequate locations to construct their nests.

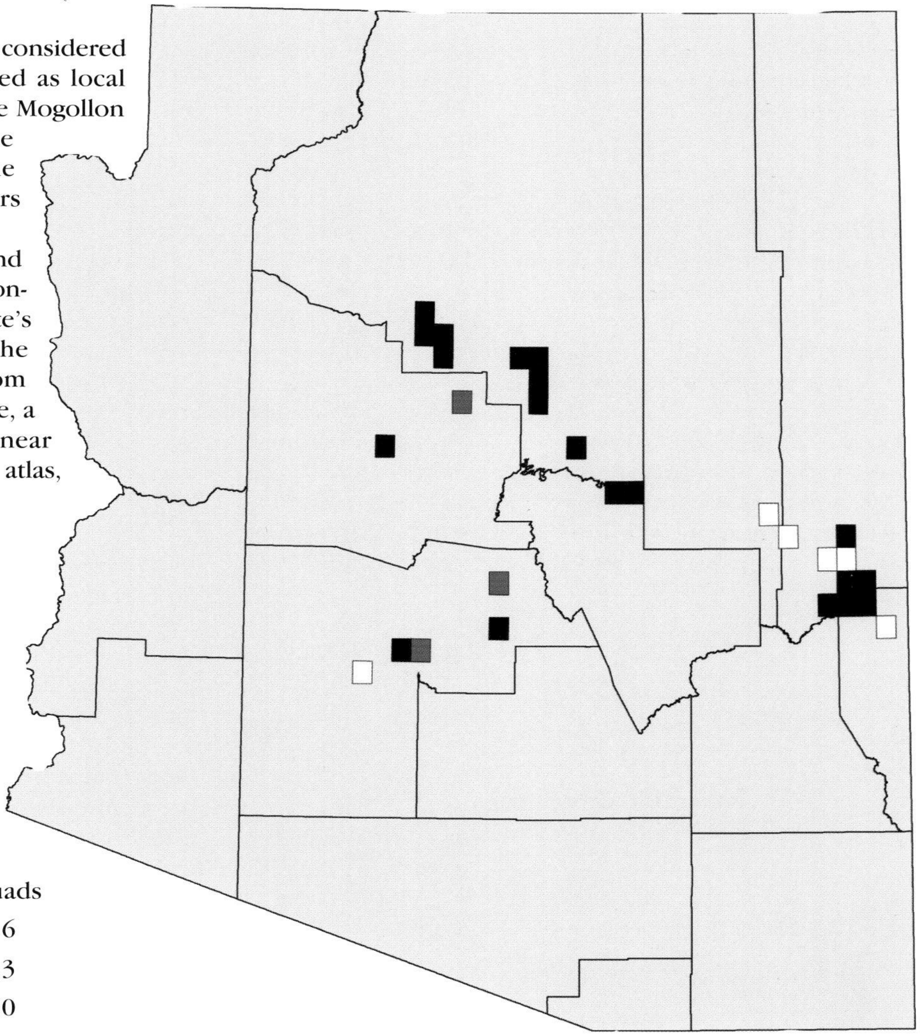

Osprey Breeding Evidence Reported in 9 (<1%) of 1834 priority blocks

	Blocks	Quads
Possible	4 (50%)	6
Probable	0 (0%)	3
Confirmed	5 (50%)	20

White-tailed Kite

by Troy E. Corman *Elanus leucurus*

Often observed hovering over grasslands or fields, White-tailed Kites have a pure elegance that is matched by few other raptors in Arizona. These graceful birds are a recently welcomed addition to the state's breeding avifauna. For a resident species, they have a seemingly nomadic nature and often remain unreliable in their whereabouts from one season to the next.

HELEN AND NOEL SNYDER

HABITAT

In Arizona, White-tailed Kites prefer open habitats with flat to gently rolling terrain and an abundance of low, herbaceous cover found in grasslands, agricultural areas, and wetlands. Habitat also includes some trees or tall shrubs for perching and nesting. Most grassland observations come from semiarid grasslands with scattered velvet mesquite, paloverde, or soaptree yucca. Atlasers also found them using the edges of cottonwood–willow lined drainages, cienegas, dry washes, and Madrean evergreen oak stringers adjacent to open grasslands. Nearly 46 percent of all records were in or adjacent to irrigated agricultural areas where they foraged over fallow or cultivated fields, especially alfalfa and grains, and nested in isolated trees or groves (n = 23). Several nests each were also found in pecan orchards and in Sonoran desert habitats.

BREEDING

White-tailed Kites are basically nonmigratory, but likely in response to prey availability these raptors make unpredictable seasonal movements throughout southern Arizona. If habitat and prey abundance do not change, however, some pairs remain year round on their breeding territory (Dunk 1995). In Arizona, courtship activity and pair bonding begins during the winter. Atlasers observed a White-tailed Kite pair copulating on 12 February. Courtship displays, performed by the male and sometimes by a pair, include flutter flights in which the wings are held at a shallow angle and flapped with short strokes, often appearing vibrated (Dunk 1995). The earliest confirmation was of a nest with a recently hatched nestling on 30 March. This would suggest nest construction in February and egg laying no later than the last week of February. Atlasers observed White-tailed Kites nest building through 23 May. However, nest building activity has been observed in Arizona as late as 5 August with nests with eggs on 12 August (Gatz et al. 1985). If successful, the young from the latter nest would not have fledged until mid-October. The latest occupied nest reported by atlasers was discovered on 7 July, with fledglings reported through 6 August. There were too few confirmed atlas records to indicate any peak nesting period during White-tailed Kites' seemingly lengthy nesting season in Arizona.

Both members of a pair contribute to nest construction, sometimes with the male collecting nesting material and the female then arranging the twigs (Dunk 1995). Nest substrate and height are quite variable with nest height records ranging from 3 to 60 ft (0.9–18.3 m) above the ground and with construction taking 1–4 weeks to complete (Faanes and Howard 1987). Atlasers only measured two White-tailed Kite nests, both exposed to the elements. One nest was in a nearly dead pecan tree 41 ft (12.5 m) above the ground and the other was a highly unusual nest placed near the top of a cane cholla only 7.5 ft (2.3 m) high. The latter nest was in a mixture of semiarid grassland and Sonoran desertscrub, adjacent to irrigated agricultural fields. Atlasers also found them nesting in Fremont cottonwood, velvet mesquite, and paloverde. Gatz (1998) compiled reports of them also nesting in netleaf hackberry and Emory oak in Arizona.

Only the female White-tailed Kite incubates the typical clutch of 4–5 eggs, but clutch size can range from 2 to 6 and may be related to prey density (Stendall 1972). The incubation period can range from 30 to 32 days (Hawbecker 1942), and the young fledge when they are 35–40 days old

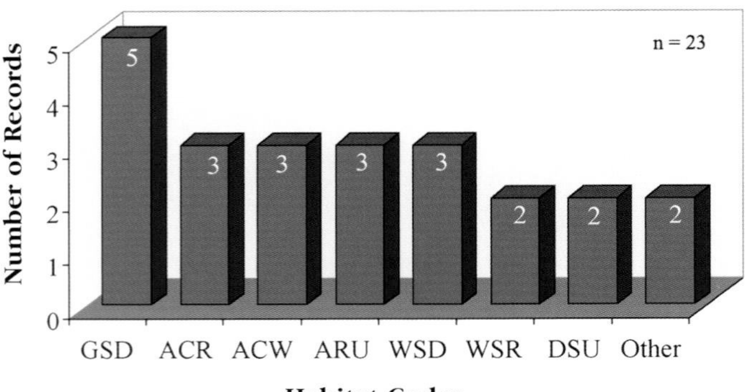

(Gatz 1998). The adults continue feeding the fledglings for 1–2 months following nest departure (Dunk 1995). White-tailed Kites are among the few diurnal raptors that regularly raise two broods in a single year (Gatz 1998). This is very possible with the lengthy nesting season in Arizona.

DISTRIBUTION AND STATUS

White-tailed Kites nest regularly along the Pacific slope from Washington, south through California, and northern Baja California, then east through southern Arizona, New Mexico (recently), Texas, and Florida. South of the United States they nest in disjunct populations through Mexico, and Central and South America. Even though there were several sight observations of White-tailed Kites in Arizona prior to the mid-1960s (Phillips et al. 1964), this elegant raptor did not become annually reported in the state until after the early 1970s (Monson and Phillips 1981). The first nesting attempt in Arizona was documented in 1983 south of Casa Grande (Gatz et al. 1985). Observations of nesting and the distribution of the White-tailed Kite in Arizona have increased ever since.

Atlasers found White-tailed Kites to be irregularly local residents throughout southern Arizona at elevations ranging from 200 to 4400 ft (61–1341 m). The only concentration of records during the atlas came from the Buenos Aires National Wildlife Refuge. However, several records came from agricultural areas between Chandler and Marana and along the middle Gila River valley between Phoenix and Gila Bend. Atlasers discovered White-tailed Kites nesting for the first time in the agricultural areas of the Centennial Wash drainage from Aguila in northwestern Maricopa County, southwest to Salome, La Paz County. Atlasers observed pairs and courtship at both Cibola and Imperial National Wildlife Refuges along the lower Colorado River and it is only a matter of time before this raptor is confirmed nesting in this valley. The most unusual nesting locality was a pair discovered nesting in the Sonoran Desert within the Cabeza Prieta National Wildlife Refuge where an occupied nest was found in a paloverde near Jose Juan Tank and San Cristobal Wash in 1994 (D. Griffin, personal communication). A follow-up visit several weeks later revealed the nest abandoned and egg shells fragments below the nest.

Some White-tailed Kite pairs were resident in an area for only one to several years, only to have them disappear and the locality not occupied again during the atlas period. This nomadic existence in Arizona makes it difficult to estimate population size and status from one year to the next. Yet most evidence suggests that the number of nesting pairs of these adaptable raptors will continue to ebb and flow in the state likely in response to annual levels of rainfall and local prey availability.

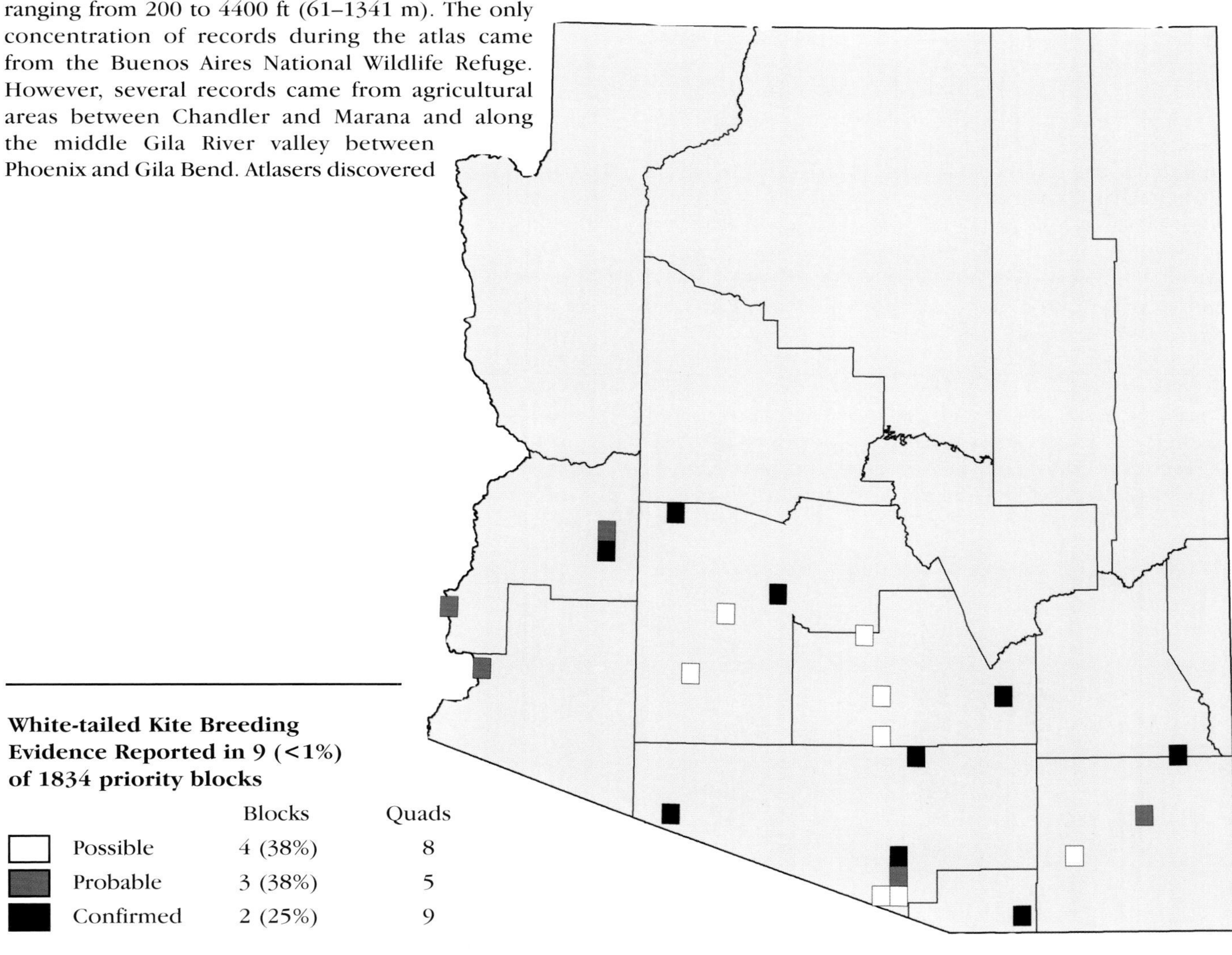

White-tailed Kite Breeding Evidence Reported in 9 (<1%) of 1834 priority blocks

	Blocks	Quads
Possible	4 (38%)	8
Probable	3 (38%)	5
Confirmed	2 (25%)	9

Mississippi Kite

by Troy E. Corman *Ictinia mississippiensis*

Sleek, graceful raptors, Mississippi Kites favor tall groves of cottonwoods in their limited distribution in Arizona. With rapid swoops, they capture flying cicadas and dragonflies, which they quickly devour on the wing. Their effortless soaring often takes them to great heights, leaving the observer with a mere speck that soon disappears.

DAN FISCHER

HABITAT

Mississippi Kites use a wide variety of habitats for nesting throughout their range, but the small population in Arizona is primarily restricted to lowland riparian woodlands. Atlasers reported 15 of the 17 observations of this kite from Fremont cottonwood-dominated habitats. Tall, decadent stands of cottonwoods appear to be favored by this kite, especially those adjacent to large open areas such as agricultural fields and deserts. In Arizona, nesting habitat for Mississippi Kites consists of cottonwoods taller than 50 ft (15.2 m), typically arranged in open groves or scattered clumps (Glinski and Ohmart 1983). Favored cottonwood stands often have an abundance of dead limbs for perching in the upper canopy and are frequently surrounded by dense thickets of tamarisk and velvet mesquite (Glinski and Ohmart 1983). The strong association to cottonwoods and tamarisk could be related to the principal prey of Mississippi Kites in Arizona, the Apache cicada, which is especially abundant in this habitat (Glinski and Ohmart 1984). Atlasers also noted Mississippi Kites nesting in stands of tall athel tamarisk growing in and along a golf course. Prior to the atlas, this kite was also discovered nesting in a pecan orchard surrounded by large expanses of open country (Glinski 1998).

BREEDING

In Arizona, Mississippi Kites begin to arrive in early to mid-May, and casually as early as late April. Courtship flights and pairing soon follow, and atlasers observed nest building activity as early as 16 May. Atlasers were unable to determine nests with eggs; however, Glinski (1998) noted eggs are usually laid in early June. Atlasers reported occupied nests from 22 May to 27 July, with most records prior to late June. Atlaser observed several instances of adults carrying nesting material or building nests in July, which may pertain to the fact that late in the nesting season some single yearlings and adults may build nests that are not completed (Rolfs 1973). In Arizona, nests with downy young have been observed by 28 June, thereby suggesting egg laying by the last week of May. Most eggs, however, hatch around the first week of July, nestlings fledge by mid-August, and adults can be found feeding their young well into late August (Glinski 1998). Mississippi Kites begin to depart nesting areas in August, with stragglers casually observed to mid-September.

Mississippi Kites often nest in loose colonies. Both adults share in nest construction, which may involve a few days or greater than two weeks (Parker 1999). Nearly all nests in Arizona are constructed in Fremont cottonwood. However, they have also nested in athel tamarisk and pecan trees. The small nests of Mississippi Kites are often constructed of freshly snapped leafy limbs of cottonwoods, which are placed in well-shaded crotches in the upper canopy. The height of the single cottonwood nest measured by atlas field crews was 50.2 ft (15.3 m) above the ground. Parker (1974) measured 63 nests in cottonwoods in the Great Plains that ranged in height of 47.2–57.7 ft (14.4–17.6 m).

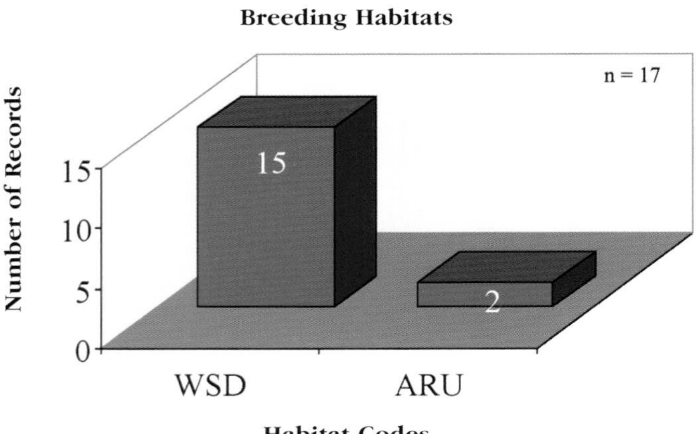

Mississippi Kites typically lay clutches containing only two eggs (rarely 1 or 3), which both adults incubate for approximately 30 days (Glinski 1998). Both parents deliver food and feed nestlings, which begin to branch when 25 days old, and fledge in 30–35 days (Parker 1974; Glinski and Ohmart 1983). The adults continue to feed the vocal fledglings for at least 15–20 days following nest departure

(Rolfs 1973). Mississippi Kites only produce one brood a year, but they may renest after failure early in nesting stage (Parker 1999).

DISTRIBUTION AND STATUS

Wintering in South America, Mississippi Kites are long distant neotropical migrants that are known to breed only in the United States. Although recent observation suggest they may also nest locally in northern Chihuahua, Mexico. Disjunct nesting populations are found in the southeast north to Virginia, west through the southern Great Plains to southeastern Colorado and eastern Arizona.

Mississippi Kites are relatively recent additions to Arizona's avifauna. They were first discovered in the state along the lower San Pedro River in 1970, where Levy (1971) estimated as many as ten nesting pairs. Johnson and Carothers (1976) reported on evidence suggesting 1–2 nesting pairs of kites along the Verde River in central Arizona near Camp Verde from 1970 to 1973. A pair of Mississippi Kites also nested successfully in 1976 along the lower Verde River just north of the Ft. McDowell tribal lands in Maricopa County (Monson and Phillips et al. 1981). In 1983, a nesting pair of Mississippi Kites was discovered in a pecan orchard northwest of Marana, Pima County (Glinski 1998). But the only consistent nesting population remains along the lower San Pedro River and immediate adjacent Gila River. Monson and Phillips (1981) noted this kites distribution from near Redington downstream to Winkelman and then down the Gila River to near Kearny.

Atlasers found Mississippi Kites as locally fairly common throughout their previously described nesting range along the San Pedro and adjacent Gila rivers. During the atlas, the elevational limits of most nesting Mississippi Kites were from 1750 to 3680 ft (533–1122 m). This kite was also found nesting farther south along the San Pedro River than previously noted. Nesting was confirmed near Cascabel and as far south as Saint David. On the Gila River, they were found nesting downstream of the San Pedro River confluence to Kelvin and individuals were found upstream to the Dripping Springs Wash confluence northeast of Winkelman.

In 2001, during the final cleanup year of atlas surveys, one or more of these kites were noted near Chino Valley, Yavapai County from early June through mid-August, including a pair with a fledgling on 18 July (C. Tomoff, personal communication). This nesting occurred at approximately 4700 ft (1433 m) in elevation. During the atlas period, Mississippi Kites were also reported at several more northern locations, although there was no evidence of nesting activity at these sites. These May through August observations of kites came from Prescott, Big Sandy River near Wikieup, and Flagstaff. Since their initial discovery in Arizona, Mississippi Kites have periodically wandered and occasionally nested north of their San Pedro River stronghold. The factors leading to the irruptions are unknown, and few of these outlying localities are ever occupied by these graceful raptors the following year.

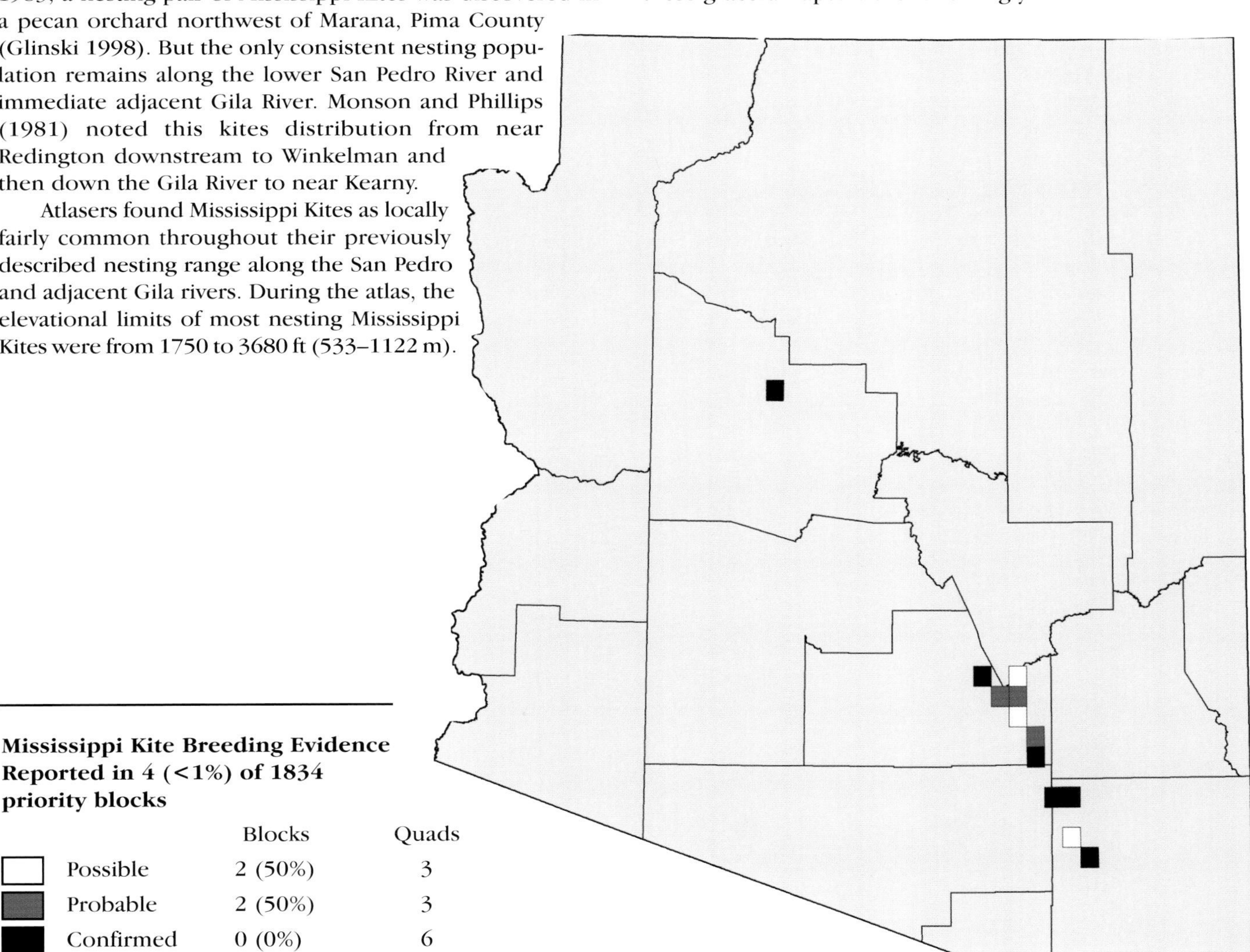

Mississippi Kite Breeding Evidence Reported in 4 (<1%) of 1834 priority blocks

	Blocks	Quads
Possible	2 (50%)	3
Probable	2 (50%)	3
Confirmed	0 (0%)	6

Bald Eagle

by James T. Driscoll *Haliaeetus leucocephalus*

A familiar and easily recognized species, many people are surprised to learn there is an isolated thriving population of desert-nesting Bald Eagles in Arizona. As elsewhere across their range, these stately raptors have made a remarkable recovery in the state since the post World War II use of DDT.

HABITAT

Breeding Bald Eagles are found near lakes, reservoirs, and perennial rivers throughout central Arizona, where they perch in large riparian trees, pines, or on cliffs. Occupied breeding areas typically contain inaccessible substrates in which to construct their nests and nearby foraging areas with an abundance of prey items. Of Arizona's 41 known breeding areas (some irregularly occupied) during the atlas period, 68 percent were located along lowland desert riparian corridors irregularly dominated by cottonwoods, willows, or sycamores. Many of these were near large reservoirs. An additional 20 percent were in pinyon pine/juniper–dominated areas and 12 percent were in ponderosa pine forests (Koloszar and Driscoll 2001).

BREEDING

Bald Eagles nesting in Arizona typically stay within their breeding areas throughout the year, but wintering populations usually head north out of the state in February and March. As with other southern populations, they begin breeding in midwinter to correspond with the spawn of their major prey item, fish. Bald Eagles conduct courtship and nest building activities from November to February. Most eggs are laid from mid-December to March, with chicks hatching from mid-January through April. Nestlings in Arizona are known to fledge from April to mid-June (Hunt et al. 1992). Studies have found that many of Arizona fledgling Bald Eagles journey north in June–July to cooler localities in the Pacific Northwest, Intermountain West, and Canada. These juveniles return in late August and September, just before the 300+ wintering Bald Eagles begin arriving in October.

In Arizona, Bald Eagle pairs construct their large, bulky stick nests either on cliffs and pinnacles, or in large cottonwoods, willows, sycamores, and ponderosa pines. The average tree nest is 52.5 ft (16 m) above the ground (Hunt et al. 1992), which is typically placed within 1 mi (1.6 km) of a riparian corridor. Since bald eagles will reuse and build upon the same structure annually, their nests can become large. Arizona's population of Bald Eagles is the only population to use cliff structures as nesting substrate (Hunt et al. 1992).

Bald Eagle clutches consist of 1–3 eggs, and both adults share incubation duties. Incubation lasts an average of 35 days, and the nestlings remain in the nest for approximately 12 weeks. The male typically conducts most of the foraging once the nestlings hatch, while the female defends the nest from intruders. The adults continue to feed the fledgling for approximately 45 days, at which time most young begin their journey north. During the atlas period, productivity of Bald Eagles in Arizona averaged 0.74 young per occupied nest. Only one brood is produced per year, but they will occasionally renest if the clutch is lost early during incubation.

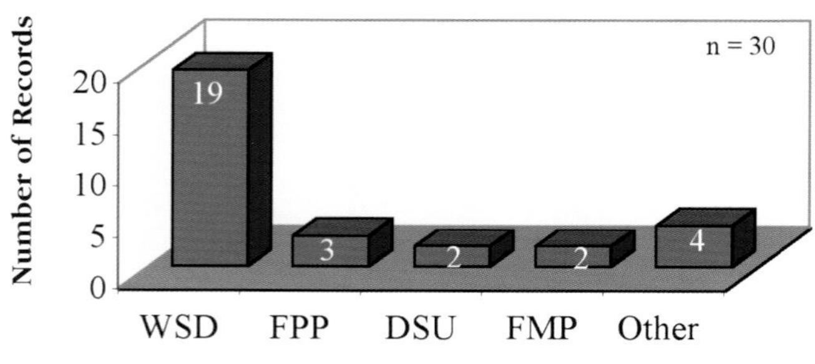

DISTRIBUTION AND STATUS

Bald Eagles breed only in North America from Alaska and Canada south through Florida and into Baja California and Sonora. Habitat alterations, persecution for feathers, and the use of DDT nearly eliminated the species. After the protection against persecution in 1940, and the ban of DDT in 1973, the Bald Eagle has recovered to the point where biologists are considering delisting the species (USFWS 1999).

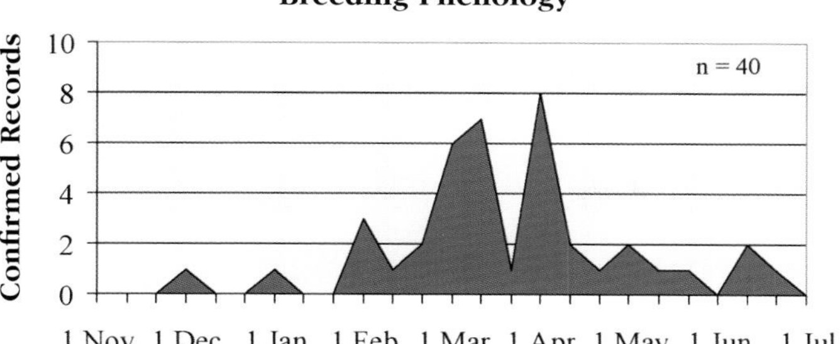

Bald Eagles were first documented nesting in Arizona in the 1880s at Stoneman Lake south of Flagstaff (Mearns 1890). Phillips et al. (1964) considered it an uncommon resident about lakes and streams of the White Mountain region and rarer west down the Salt River and to the Flagstaff region. When the species was listed as Endangered in 1978, only ten breeding pairs were known in Arizona, located along the Salt and Verde rivers near Phoenix. However, due to increased survey efforts and management practices directed at conserving the population during the atlas period, the number of breeding pairs in Arizona steadily grew from 26 to 37.

Arizona Bald Eagle breeding populations have been monitored extensively during the past 25 years and atlas efforts provided little new information. Specific Bald Eagle nest monitoring and survey data collected during the atlas period were incorporated and used to define the breeding distribution in the state. The highest concentration of breeding areas continues to occur along the lower Verde River, although nesting pairs also bred upstream as far as Perkinsville. Bald Eagles also nest regularly along the Salt River from near the confluence of the Verde River upstream to include tributaries on White Mountain Apache tribal lands. Elsewhere, these eagles nest on the Gila River near Coolidge Dam, up the nearby San Carlos River, as well as at Alamo Lake and upper Lake Pleasant.

Bald Eagles established new nesting areas during the atlas. Unfortunately, several of these were active for only 1–3 years before being abandoned. These include breeding areas near Camp Verde, Becker Lake near Springerville, and near the confluence of the Gila and San Pedro rivers. By the end of the atlas period the only remaining active breeding area above the Mogollon Rim was near Luna Lake in the White Mountains at an elevation of 8000 ft (2438 m). Otherwise, Arizona's nesting Bald Eagles were found at lower elevations of 1200–6580 ft (366–2006 m).

Studies have revealed that the Arizona Bald Eagle population is biologically isolated. In 15 years, only one Bald Eagle from another state has bred in Arizona, and, similarly, only one Bald Eagle hatched in Arizona has traveled to another state to breed. Although Bald Eagle numbers are higher than ever recorded in Arizona, the risk of loosing the breeding population still exists. Nesting habitat is decreasing in the most productive areas. Human populations, recreational pressures, and developments in or near the best breeding habitat are increasing. Also, mortality from shooting, monofilament entanglement, and heat stress continue to affect population expansion. Arizona's Bald Eagle population has improved because of intensive management, cooperation among many agencies, and broad public support.

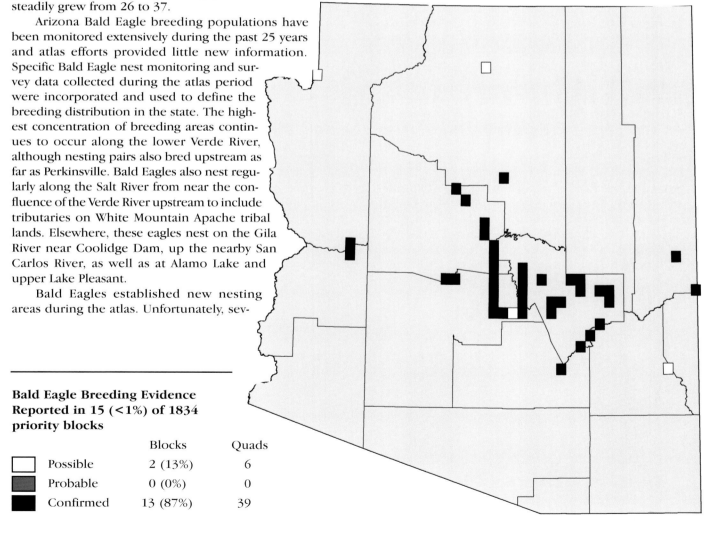

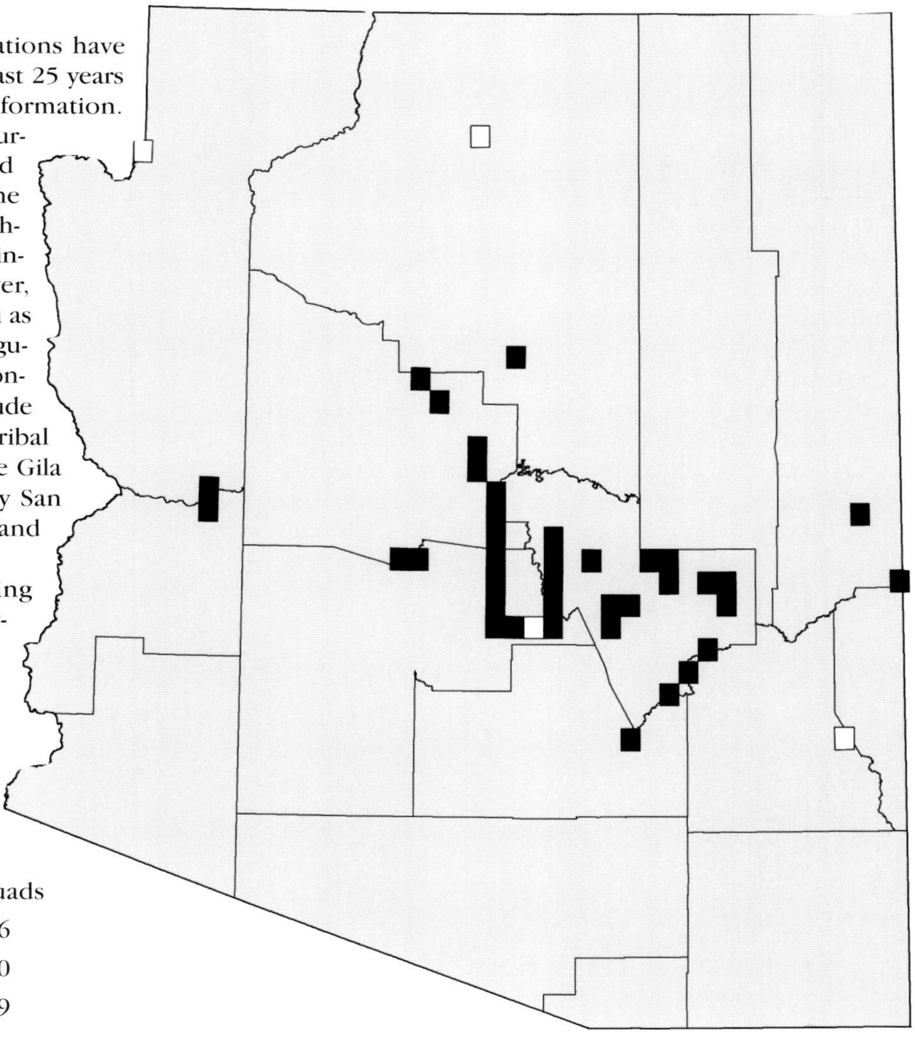

Bald Eagle Breeding Evidence Reported in 15 (<1%) of 1834 priority blocks

	Blocks	Quads
Possible	2 (13%)	6
Probable	0 (0%)	0
Confirmed	13 (87%)	39

Northern Harrier

by Cathryn Wise-Gervais *Circus cyanus*

Formerly known as the "Marsh Hawk," these slender, long-winged raptors are commonly observed flying low and buoyantly over wetlands, agricultural regions, and other open country areas in search of prey. Few Northern Harrier nests have been discovered in Arizona, and little is known regarding their breeding habitat selection in the state.

HELEN AND NOEL SNYDER

HABITAT

Across their North American range, Northern Harriers nest primarily in wetlands, agricultural areas, grasslands, and low brushy country. These medium-sized hawks rarely perch in trees, preferring instead fence posts, rocks, low vegetation, or the ground (Snyder 1998). Most of Arizona's few nesting records are from marshes or cienegas containing bulrush, cattails, sedge, and grasses, and the only confirmed nesting record reported during the atlas was in wetland vegetation. Atlasers also reported Northern Harriers in extensive plains grasslands, semiarid grasslands, cold-temperate desertscrub, and active farm fields. Several Northern Harrier nests discovered prior to the atlas were in grasslands and agricultural fields. These seemingly diverse habitats are similar in that they all offer undisturbed open areas with dense vegetation growth (MacWhirter and Bildstein 1996).

BREEDING

Northern Harriers commonly winter in Arizona, with the highest concentrations of birds found in agricultural and grassland areas. Most harriers have migrated to more northern breeding areas by mid-April, with stragglers lingering into mid-May and occasionally later. Northern Harriers presumably arrive on Arizona breeding grounds in March and April. Courtship flight activity was not observed during the atlas, but consists of a sky dance performed primarily by the male, but occasionally by both sexes high in the air (MacWhirter and Bildstein 1996). During the atlas, courtship feeding was observed on 24 March (Mikesic and Duncan 2000). Simmons et al. (1987) reported that courtship feeding of females can begin as much as 3 weeks (but at least 1 week) prior to egg laying. Atlasers reported Northern Harriers in suitable breeding habitat from 16 May to 1 July, and the only active nest discovered during the atlas period contained eggs on 5 May. This record falls well within the published egg-laying dates for Arizona and New Mexico from 27 April to 9 June (Mikesic and Duncan 2000). Occasionally, early southbound migrants begin appearing in mid- to late July or early August, but most birds do not reach their wintering grounds until after August.

Both Northern Harrier adults work together to construct the nest, and these structures are typically placed on the ground in tall grass, wetland vegetation, or similar cover (Snyder 1998). At most nest sites, even many of those in dryland habitats, a disproportionate number of nests are located in wet areas (MacWhirter and Bildstein 1996). Only one active nest was discovered during the atlas period and this structure was made entirely of bulrush and placed within the marsh vegetation (Mikesic and Duncan 2000). Prior to the atlas, one Arizona nest was discovered in an irrigated alfalfa field.

A typical Northern Harrier clutch consists of 4–6 eggs (range 2–10) and incubation takes 30–32 days (Snyder 1998). The female will begin brooding eggs after laying two or more, so these will hatch together and the remainder will hatch asynchronously (Snyder 1998). When food availability is low, the younger and weaker birds will not survive. The male provides most of the food for the newly hatched young and will often transfer prey items to his mate in mid-air (MacWhirter and Bildstein 1996) or he will drop food near the nest. The female then tears and actually feeds the young. The young hawks are able to leave the nest at 2 weeks of age and will walk to alternate resting platforms, forming narrow trails (MacWhirter and Bildstein 1996). The fledglings accomplish

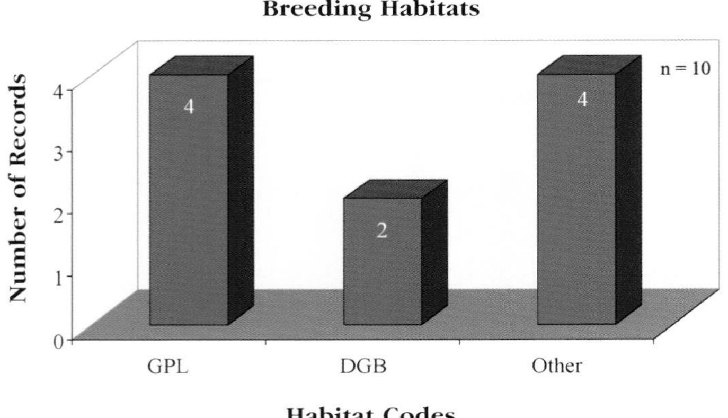

sustained flight in approximately 33 days (range 29–37) but continue to be fed by parents until they are 6.5–9.5 weeks old (MacWhirter and Bildstein 1996).

DISTRIBUTION AND STATUS

Northern Harriers have an extensive summer range in North America and breed from Alaska and Canada south through the Great Plains to northern New Mexico and Texas. This species is found throughout the north Atlantic states, as well as in the Midwest. Northern Harriers are also encountered along the Pacific coast from northern Washington to northern Baja California. This raptor also breeds in Europe and Asia where it is known as the Hen Harrier.

In Arizona, Northern Harriers are opportunistic in their breeding habits, taking advantage of favorable conditions capriciously at best (Snyder 1998). Mikesic and Duncan (2000) researched the breeding history of Northern Harriers in Arizona and listed only seven confirmed and three suspected nesting sites scattered throughout the state from 1872 to 1998. Most breeding activity has been noted in eastern Arizona, but a nest with eggs was discovered in Cunningham Wash northwest of Hope, La Paz County on 27 April 1980 (Millsap 1981). A nest with young was also found in central Arizona near Dugas, Yavapai County, on 26 May 1983. This nest was in an alfalfa field and contained five feathered but flightless young. Unfortunately, this nest was discovered after two of the young had been inadvertently killed by farm machinery while harvesting the crop (K. Williams, personal communication).

In Arizona, Northern Harriers may linger late or arrive early during migration and are rather secretive at nest sites. As a result, atlasers were often unsure of the breeding status of the Northern Harriers they encountered while surveying. During data analysis, final conclusions were based on the observation date and habitat. Atlasers reported a total of 111 Northern Harrier observations while conducting surveys, including sightings made both on and outside priority blocks. Of these, only ten were considered potential breeding records, including the one confirmed record.

Atlasers obtained potential Northern Harrier breeding records at elevations ranging from 3200 to 6000 ft (975–1829 m). Prior to the atlas, Northern Harriers were confirmed nesting in Arizona at elevations ranging from 1300 to 7000 ft (396–2134 m).

During the atlas, southeastern Arizona observations included a pair of birds seen on 25 June in the semiarid grasslands northwest of the Santa Rita Mountains and a single harrier observed near wetlands south of Safford on 6 June. It is much more challenging to determine the status of the single individual Northern Harriers observed in Coconino and Mohave counties during the presumed nesting period. Some of these observations may pertain to late migrants or nonbreeding summering individuals.

The single Northern Harrier breeding confirmation for the atlas was a nest with eggs located in 1998 at Hugo Meadows (Mikesic and Duncan 2000). This nest was located in an alkaline marsh near the confluence of the Little Colorado River and Chevelon Creek, southeast of Winslow.

Additionally, atlasers observed an individual near Clear Creek, approximately 12 mi (19.3 km) southwest of Hugo Meadows, suggesting that additional nesting areas may be found in the Little Colorado River drainage. Despite the sparse number of breeding observations, Mikesic and Duncan (2000) believe that nesting Northern Harriers may be more common in Arizona than current records reveal. Breeding Harriers could be escaping detection due to their secretive nesting habits and extremely local and often remote summer distribution.

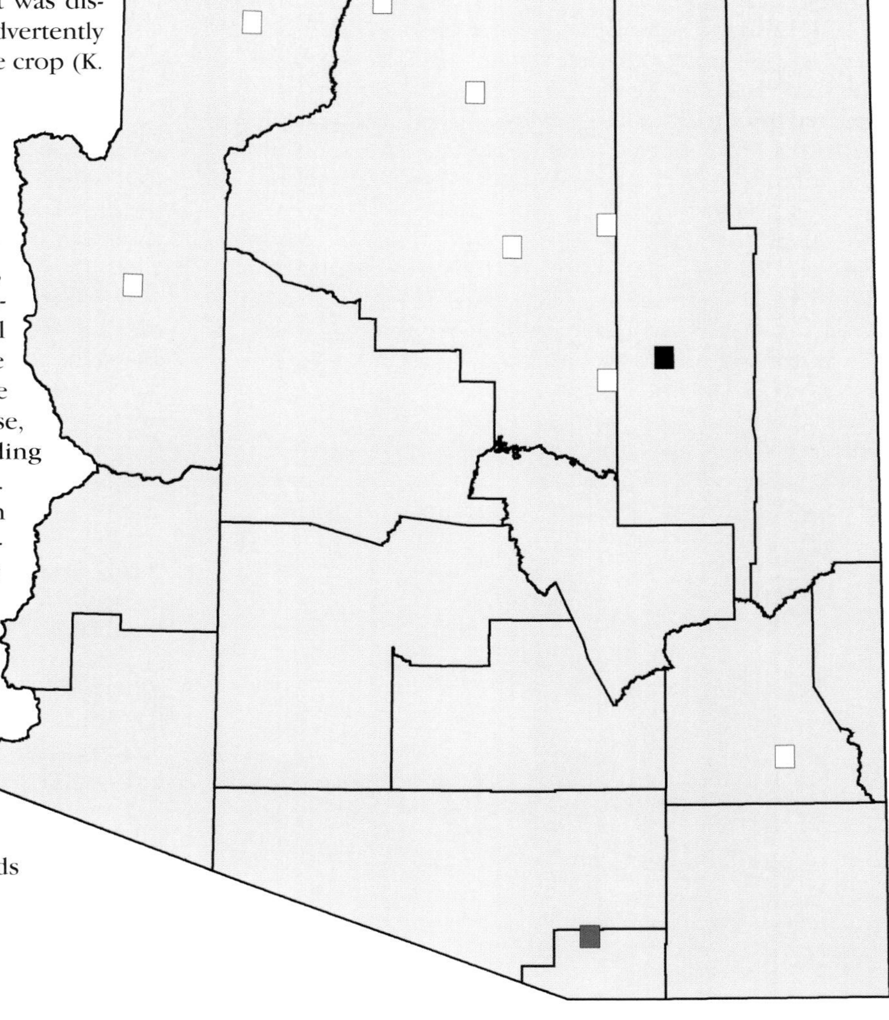

Northern Harrier Breeding Evidence Reported in 9 (<1%) of 1834 priority blocks

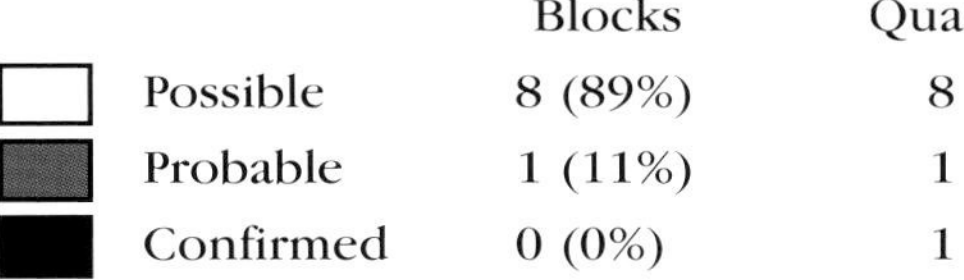

	Blocks	Quads
Possible	8 (89%)	8
Probable	1 (11%)	1
Confirmed	0 (0%)	1

Sharp-shinned Hawk

by Cathryn Wise-Gervais *Accipiter striatus*

Sharp-shinned Hawks feed almost entirely on small birds, and this agile and accomplished hunter is quite certainly a songbird's worst nightmare. Petite and feisty, these slight, fast-flying forest hawks exhibit the largest size difference between sexes in all Arizona's raptors, with females often being nearly twice as heavy as males.

HELEN AND NOEL SNYDER

HABITAT

Most Sharp-shinned Hawks nesting in Arizona inhabit high-elevation forested mountains and drainages, and these often have a deciduous tree component. These raptors favor impenetrably dense conifer stands for nesting, to the point that even these highly maneuverable birds take a beating both coming and going to their brushy citadels (Snyder and Snyder 1998). Atlasers observed potentially breeding Sharp-shinned Hawks in 11 habitat types, and the most commonly reported of these was mixed-conifer forests containing various firs, pines, and aspen (24 percent of records; $n = 62$). Observers also obtained a total of 34 percent of the records in ponderosa pine-dominated forests, including those with Gambel's oak or pinyon juniper components. Atlasers reported nearly 15 percent of Sharp-shinned Hawk records in montane riparian areas characterized by pines, fir, cypress, walnut, oaks, alder, and maple. Few records were obtained from spruce-fir forests and Madrean pine-oak woodlands, but this may reflect the limited distribution of these two habitats in Arizona. In addition, atlasers detected several northern Arizona Sharp-shinned Hawks in dense, multistructured pinyon pine woodlands where nesting has been documented in the past.

BREEDING

Sharp-shinned Hawks are fairly common winter residents throughout the mid- and lower elevations of Arizona, and are often observed helping themselves to feathered treats at backyard bird feeding stations during this time. These small *Accipiters* begin their northward migration in late March and early April, and few birds remain in Arizona's lowlands by May. Pair formation begins soon after arrival on the breeding grounds and courtship flights consists of both birds soaring, calling, and diving steeply (Bildstein and Mayer 2000). In Arizona, Sharp-shinned Hawks are the last Accipiter to initiate breeding activity, with nest construction typically beginning in late April or early May (Snyder and Snyder 1998). Atlasers reported the first occupied nest on 30 April and the first nest with eggs was noted on 14 May. In Arizona, nestlings are typically observed from mid-June through July, and atlasers reported nests with young from 2 to 25 July. During the atlas, fledgling reports ranged from 17 July to 10 August. A few Sharp-shinned Hawks begin appearing away from nesting areas in late August, but these raptors are not regularly encountered in lowlands until after mid-September.

Sharp-shinned Hawks nest in both conifers and deciduous trees, and build their nests in a dense area of the tree, so it is well-camouflaged from below. As a result, Sharp-shinned Hawk nests can be quite difficult to locate, and observers reported only four during the atlas period. These were located in Engelmann spruce, white fir, bigtooth maple, and Gambel's oak, but Arizona's Sharp-shinned Hawks are also known to nest in ponderosa pine, Douglas fir, and occasionally in pinyon pine and Rocky Mountain juniper (LaRue 1994). Bildstein and Meyer (2000) reported nests heights for this species to range from 8 to 62 ft (2.4–19 m). Heights of the four nests measured during the atlas ranged from 10.8 to 19.7 ft (3.3–6 m), but little can be inferred from such a small sample size.

Male and female sharp-shinned Hawk adults bring materials to the nest site, but the female does most of the nest building (Palmer 1988). The typical Sharp-shinned Hawk clutch consists of 4–5 eggs (range 3–8) and the female does most if not all incubation for approximately 30–32 days (Platt 1976; Reynolds and Wight 1978). During

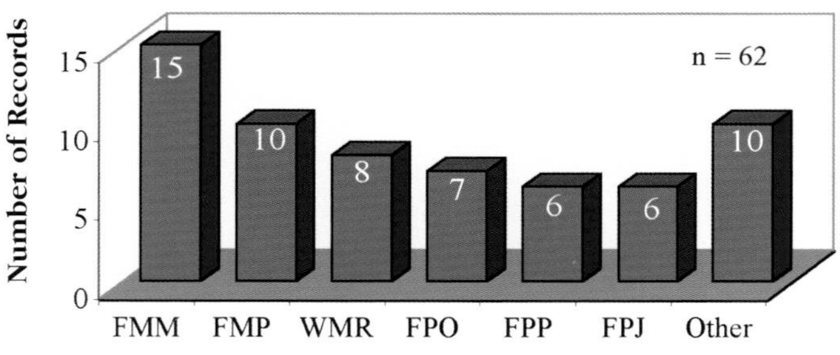

nest building and incubation, male Sharp-shinned Hawks provide their mates with food 3–4 times per day (Snyder and Snyder 1998). The female remains at the nest for approximately the first two weeks after the chicks hatch, and the male provides all the food for the female and the young during this period (Snyder and Wiley 1976). Although the male delivers the food, it is the female that actually feeds the nestlings through nest departure in approximately 4 weeks (Snyder and Snyder 1998). Fledglings usually remain near the nest and depend on their parent for an additional 3.5 weeks following nest departure (Bildstein and Meyer 2000).

DISTRIBUTION AND STATUS

Sharp-shinned Hawks occur throughout most of North America, either in the winter, summer or both. These raptors breed from central Alaska and Canada south through the highlands of Mexico and locally to northern Argentina. In eastern North America, Sharp-shinned Hawks nest primarily south through New England, the upper Midwest, and the Appalachian regions.

Swarth (1914) suggested that Sharp-shinned Hawks probably breed in small numbers in Arizona's higher mountains but noted only one published breeding record. Later authors considered Sharp-shinned Hawks as generally uncommon breeders in Arizona's eastern mountains, and rare and local nesters in the southeast (Phillip et al. 1964). More recent accounts accurately suggest that the Sharp-shinned Hawk breeding range in Arizona closely resembles that of the Northern Goshawk (Snyder and Snyder 1998) and includes higher, forested mountains statewide.

Atlasers indeed located Sharp-shinned Hawks within the previously described range primarily at elevations between 6500 and 9800 ft (1981–2987 m). Yet these slender forest raptors were noted nesting locally down to 5600 ft (1707 m) in cool, heavily wooded mountain drainages of southeastern Arizona. Sharp-shinned Hawks are still a sparse nesting species in the southeastern sky islands with atlas records in the Huachuca, Pinaleno, and Chiricahua mountains. Prior to the atlas, this raptor had also been found nesting in the Santa Catalina, Santa Rita, and possibly the Mule mountains (Phillips et al. 1964; Monson and Phillips 1981), but atlasers did not report birds from these ranges.

To the north, atlasers observed Sharp-shinned Hawks throughout the Mogollon Rim region from the White Mountains northwest to Flagstaff and Williams. In Yavapai County, atlasers reported potentially nesting Sharp-shinned Hawks in the Bradshaw, Juniper, and Mingus mountains. Sharp-shinned Hawks were also regularly reported on the Kaibab Plateau and west locally to Mount Trumbull, Mount Dellenbaugh, and Hualapai tribal lands. Surveys conducted on Navajo and Hope tribal lands also revealed these raptors nesting on Black Mesa and nearby Tsegi Canyon drainage, as well as from the Carrizo Mountains south to the Defiance Plateau.

Observers obtained few Sharp-shinned Hawk records in southern Navajo and eastern Gila counties, in part due to the inability to gain survey access on White Mountain Apache tribal lands. In addition, Sharp-shinned Hawks are more secretive than other Accipiters nesting in Arizona, and are easily missed when conducting atlas surveys. As a result, there are undoubtedly more nesting localities in Arizona than atlas efforts revealed.

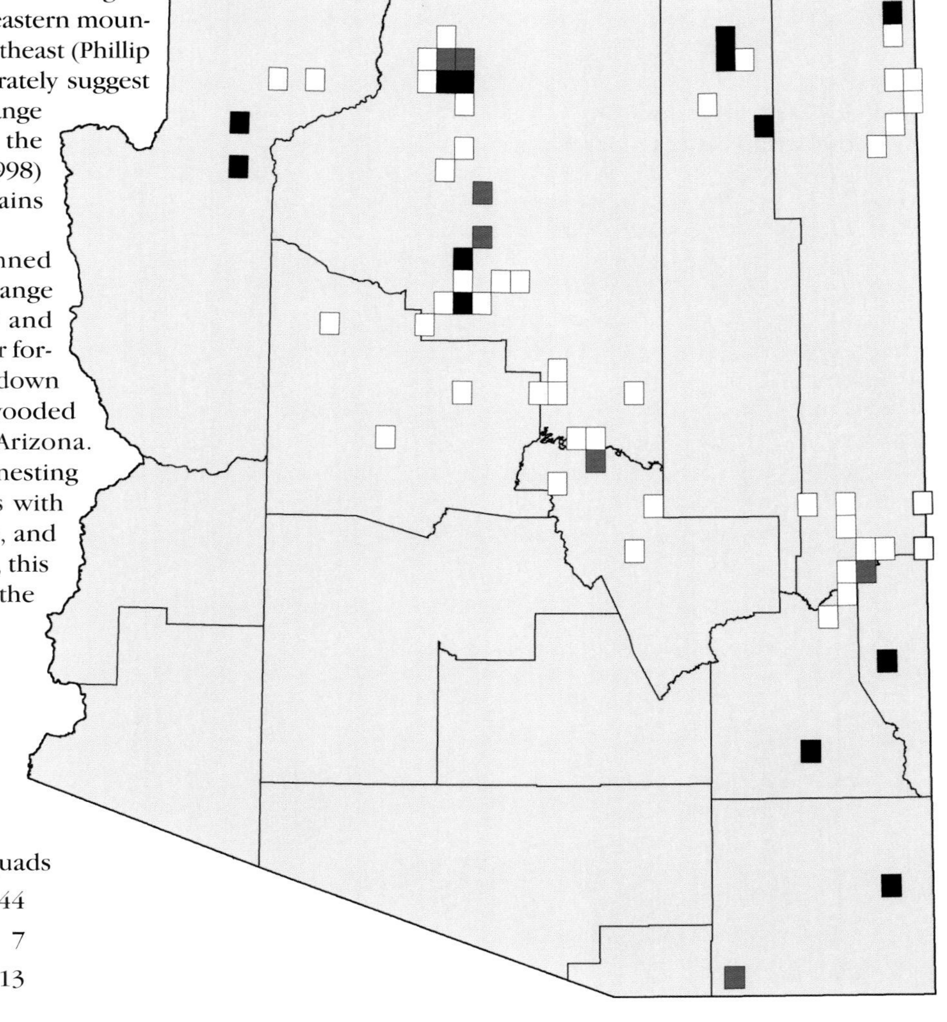

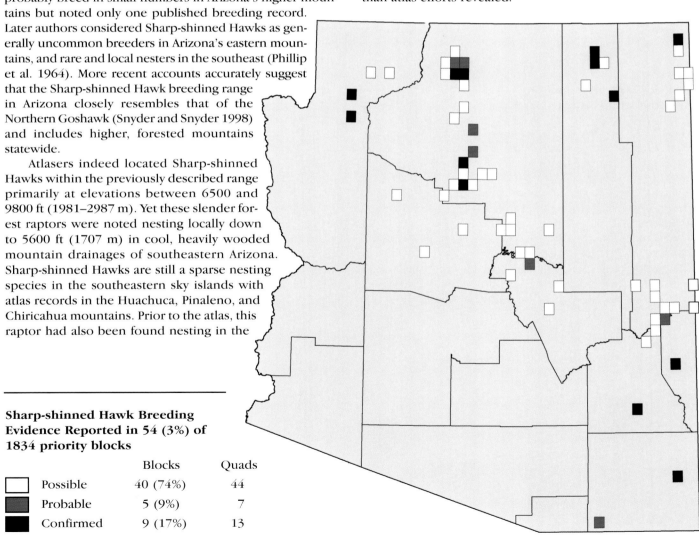

Sharp-shinned Hawk Breeding Evidence Reported in 54 (3%) of 1834 priority blocks

	Blocks	Quads
Possible	40 (74%)	44
Probable	5 (9%)	7
Confirmed	9 (17%)	13

Cooper's Hawk

by Cathryn Wise-Gervais *Accipiter cooperii*

Clever and agile, Cooper's Hawks are resourceful raptors and make use of a variety of wooded habitats and prey animals. This opportunistic predator uses surprise to their advantage, darting out at potential prey from hidden perches. Old timers knew this raptor as the "chicken hawk," as the birds would occasionally snatch barnyard poultry.

HELEN AND NOEL SNYDER

HABITAT

These medium-sized woodland hawks occupy a wider variety of habitats and occur over a broader range of elevations than either the Sharp-shinned Hawk or Northern Goshawk. As a result, Cooper's Hawks are the most commonly encountered *Accipiter* in Arizona, and atlasers reported them in 25 habitat types, but predominantly found them in low- to mid-elevation riparian woodlands. During the atlas, approximately 22 percent of all Cooper's Hawk records were from lowland riparian areas along drainages, canyons, and even some isolated desert foothill springs (n = 379). These areas were typically characterized by large deciduous trees such as cottonwood, willow, ash, and mesquite. Atlasers also regularly documented Cooper's Hawks nesting in sycamore-dominated drainages (19 percent of records), and in forested areas including pinyon-juniper woodlands, ponderosa pine forests, and evergreen oak woodlands (8 percent of records in each). Observers reported fewer records from mixed-conifer and ponderosa pine–Gambel's oak forests. These raptors are tolerant of some human disturbance and habitat fragmentation, and nest locally in several urban settings with large trees. During the atlas period, atlasers reported eleven potential breeding records for Cooper's Hawks in urban and rural areas.

BREEDING

The many Cooper's Hawks that winter in the lowlands of Arizona migrate to nesting areas in March and April. Generally, Cooper's Hawk breeding initiation dates are closely related to elevation, with lowland birds beginning the nesting cycle earlier than their high-elevation compatriots. In Arizona, banded females have been observed on breeding territories year-round, but males and young of the year are thought to disperse in the fall and winter (Milsap 1981). Pair formation probably occurs in early March in most of the bird's range, and atlasers observed Cooper's Hawks nest building by late March. However, atlasers also reported three nests with young between 9 and 23 April. All were in riparian areas of the Sonoran Desert below 1700 ft (518 m) in elevation. This would suggest that the eggs were laid in late February or early March, much earlier than previously documented for the species. Atlas data reveal that the peak nesting period in Arizona was from mid-May to late June. However, atlasers encountered some active Cooper's Hawk nests into late summer. The latest active nest contained young on 27 August northwest of Show Low. These raptors begin appearing away from nesting areas in late August with migrants continue to pass through into November.

Cooper's Hawks are not particular in their nest tree selection and will use a wide variety of both native and exotic trees. In urban Tucson, most Cooper's Hawks nests are in eucalyptus and aleppo pines (J. Mannan, personal communication). Territories often contain several old nests, and the pair usually alternates between these from year to year (Snyder and Snyder 1998). During the atlas, most Cooper's Hawk nests were noted in Fremont cottonwoods, but they were also found in Arizona sycamore, Arizona alder, boxelder, netleaf hackberry, ponderosa pine, juniper, Douglas fir, and various species of oaks. Of 16 nests measured during the atlas, the median height was 30 ft (9.1 m) and ranged from 20 to 66 ft (6.1–20.1 m).

Both sexes bring sticks and twigs to their selected site and often build the new nest directly on top of an old one. Cooper's Hawks line the nest with bark (Bent 1937) and will use some greenery in the nest cup, but not nearly as much as is used by Northern Goshawk (Snyder and Snyder 1998). Eggs are laid every three days until a complete clutch of four eggs is obtained (range 3–5), and incubation takes 34–35 days (Snyder and Snyder 1998). Incubation duty is performed almost entirely by the female, while the male

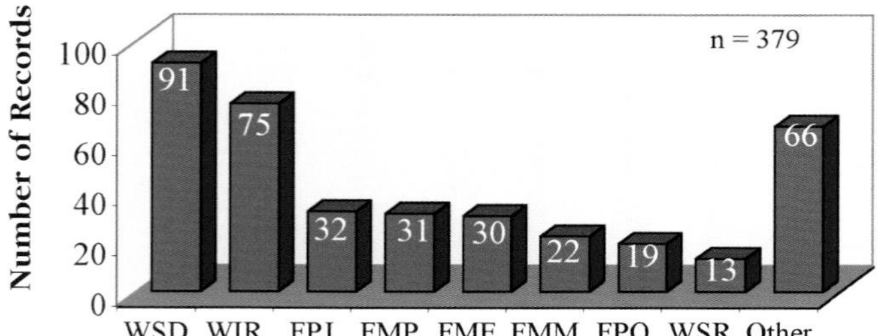

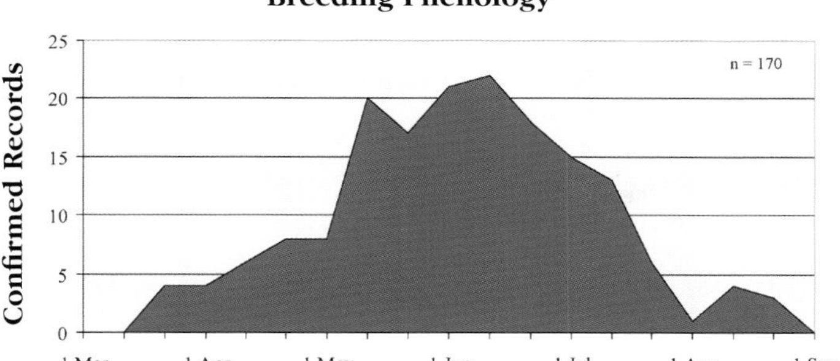

provides food for both his mate and the young after they hatch. The female alone broods and feeds the young for the first 14 days, then assists with hunting. Young fledge at approximately 31 days in Arizona (Milsap 1981) but will often return to the nest site for an additional week or so to roost and to be fed (Rosenfield and Bielefeldt 1993).

DISTRIBUTION AND STATUS

The Cooper's Hawks' breeding range includes most of the lower 48 states and extends slightly into northern Mexico and southern Canada (Snyder and Snyder 1998). Earlier accounts considered Cooper's Hawks to be fairly common summer residents throughout much of Arizona, but stated that the birds were more frequently observed during winter or migration (Phillips et al. 1964). Atlasers confirmed Cooper's Hawks nesting over a wide elevation range in Arizona, from approximately 650 to 8500 ft (198–2591 m). Found in wooded areas nearly statewide, these hawks were most frequently encountered along timbered drainages south of the Mogollon Rim and in southeastern mountain ranges. During the breeding season, they were largely absent only from the lowland deserts and treeless regions of the Colorado Plateau. The lack of records from below the Mogollon Rim on the White Mountain Apache tribal lands pertain to the inability to gain approval to conduct atlas surveys there. Atlas data suggest that Cooper's Hawks undoubtedly breed throughout this region.

Observers first located breeding Cooper's Hawks in the greater Tucson area in the early 1990s. The birds have been found nesting in and near Tucson reliably since then, although densities vary depending on resources, primarily large trees (J. Mannan, personal communication). However, no such phenomenon has been noted in the Phoenix area, despite the availability of mature ornamentals and abundant food sources. It is likely that Cooper's Hawks breed sporadically along the lower Colorado River where suitable habitat exists. Atlasers obtained one potential breeding record along this river south of Ehrenberg. Cooper's Hawks have previously been confirmed breeding near Picacho, Parker, Topock, and at the Bill Williams River delta (Rosenberg et al 1991), but observers did not locate birds in any of these areas during the atlas period.

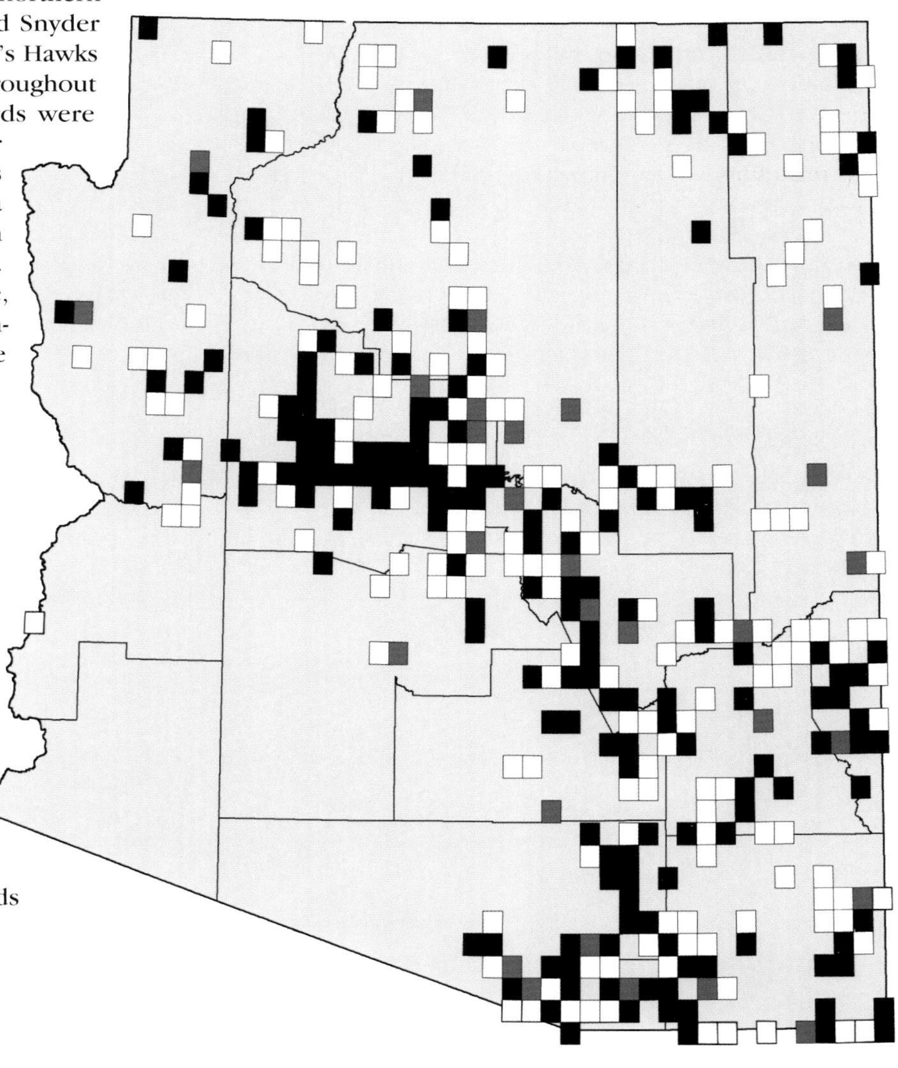

Cooper's Hawk Breeding Evidence Reported in 335 (18%) of 1834 priority blocks

	Blocks	Quads
Possible	155 (47%)	177
Probable	29 (9%)	30
Confirmed	150 (45%)	173

Northern Goshawk

by Cathryn Wise-Gervais *Accipiter gentilis*

The Northern Goshawk is a handsome raptor inhabiting deep forests. Here, its large size, loud cackling cries, and swift, unanticipated dives will intimidate the bravest of souls venturing near a nest tree. Unfortunately, potential conflicts between this raptor's livelihood and timber harvesting activities have led to much heated controversy in Arizona.

HELEN AND NOEL SNYDER

HABITAT

In Arizona, Northern Goshawks favor cool forests of tall pine, fir, and/or spruce, including the adjacent conifer dominated drainages. Atlasers found these impressive raptors in 10 habitat types, but reported 41 percent of potential breeding records in pure ponderosa pine forests ($n = 90$). Atlasers reported an additional 26 percent of records in mixed-conifer forests comprised of Douglas fir, white fir, ponderosa pine, and aspen, and 17 percent of sightings in ponderosa pine–Gambel's oak associations. In the mountains of southeastern Arizona, observers also noted Northern Goshawks nesting frequently in Madrean pine-oak woodlands dominated by Chihuahuan, Apache, and ponderosa pine forests, with a scattered evergreen oak and juniper understory. Fewer observations came from spruce-fir and ponderosa-and pinyon pine–dominated habitats. Most inhabited forests commonly include tall trees with an open canopy allowing unobstructed flights but still offer enough cover to reduce nest predation and provide a cool environment (Reynolds et al. 1982).

BREEDING

Northern Goshawks in Arizona are primarily resident, although some will move into lower elevations in winter when food resources become scarce (Millsap 1981). Northern Goshawks typically initiate breeding earlier than other North American Accipiters and can begin nest building in March and egg-laying in April (Snyder and Snyder 1998). In northern Arizona, females lay eggs slightly later than this, in late April to early May (Reynolds et al. 1994). Atlasers observed occupied nests as early as 1 May, and reported the earliest nest with young on 9 June. Atlas data reveal that breeding activity peaks in June, and the earliest fledging data obtained during the atlas period was 17 June. This early fledging date would suggest egg laying no later than mid-April and nestlings by mid-May. Observers reported the latest nest containing young on 27 July and sighted fledglings as late as 18 August.

Northern Goshawks often nest in more open forests than those inhabited by the other two Accipiters in Arizona (Snyder and Snyder 1998). Their bulky nests are generally built in the largest trees available and are placed in the lower one-third of the substrate or right below the canopy (Reynolds et al 1982). In Arizona, most nests are constructed in ponderosa pine, but they can also be found in other pines, firs, and occasionally aspen. Observers measured only three nests during the atlas period, two in ponderosa and one in Apache pine. These nests ranged in height from 47 to 69 ft (14.3–21 m). Pairs will often reuse old nests and the female does most of the construction or repair work on the structure (Squires and Reynolds 1997). Discriminating females have been observed taking more than five minutes choosing a particular nest stick (Squires and Reynolds 1997). Additionally, the female will line the nest bowl with greenery, often fresh conifer sprigs, and continue periodically adding this material through the nestling stage. As a result, some Arizona nests have been described as "shaggy green carpets" (Snyder and Snyder 1998).

These raptors lay a typical clutch consisting of 3 eggs (range 2–4, rarely 5) and incubation typically takes 30–35 days (Squires and Reynolds 1997), sometimes longer due to cooler temperatures and inclement weather. Females incubate primarily, but males may assist for brief periods. Once the young have reached 9–12 days of age, the adults

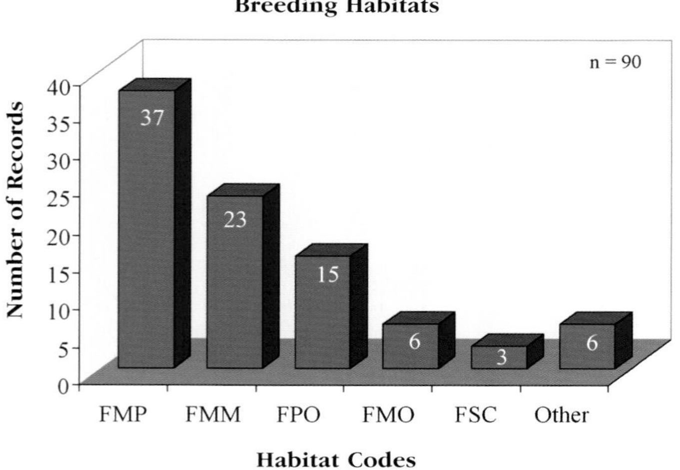

Breeding Phenology

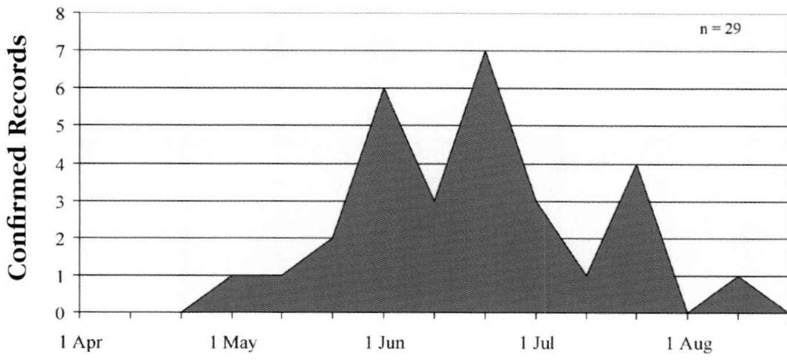

(particularly the female) will vigorously defend the nest, and this species is considered the most aggressive nest-defending raptor in North America (Snyder and Snyder 1998). Young fledge in approximately 5–6 weeks (Boal 1994), after first moving to branches near the nest. Even after fledging, the young remain fully dependent on their parents for an additional 4–5 weeks (Snyder and Snyder 1998).

DISTRIBUTION AND STATUS

Northern Goshawks are found in many forested regions throughout the Northern Hemisphere. In North America they occur from tree lines in Canada and Alaska, south to Virginia in the East and to the highlands of western Mexico in the West. Some authorities believe that there are two subspecies of Northern Goshawks breeding in Arizona, but this has been debated over the years. The pale *atricapillus* race is found throughout most of the state and much of North America. However, populations in the mountains of southeastern Arizona and adjacent Mexico are noted as larger and darker *apache* race (Phillips et al. 1964). Populations of the latter race may be imperiled, as Snyder and Snyder (1998) found the number of active territories in Arizona has declined by nearly 50 percent by the mid-1990s.

Historically Northern Goshawks were found in limited numbers throughout eastern and central Arizona's forested habitats (Phillips et al. 1964), except on the Kaibab Plateau where they could have been considered common. The Kaibab Plateau population once possessed one of the highest nesting densities throughout the species' geographic range but has declined in recent years (Crocker-Bedford and Chaney 1988).

Atlaser efforts and specific Northern Goshawk surveys conducted by others during the atlas period reveal that these impressive raptors still occur to some extent in most of the heavily forested regions of the state. Most were found nesting at elevations between 6000 and 9500 ft (1829–2896 m) and locally outside this range. Atlasers found these raptors locally on Navajo tribal lands at such locations as northern Black Mesa, Chuska Mountains, and the Defiance Plateau. Atlasers also discovered this species nesting sparingly within the Arizona Strip region on isolated forested mountains. Northern Goshawks undoubtedly nest at least locally throughout the forested regions of White Mountain Apache and adjacent San Carlos Apache tribal lands, but access to conduct atlas surveys on the former were never granted.

Although Northern Goshawk populations were not affected by organophosphate poisoning as significantly as other raptors, they have suffered markedly from timber harvesting activities, especially in the western states (Snyder and Snyder 1998). Individuals concerned about population declines petitioned to list Northern Goshawk as endangered in 1991, but the petition was denied and all efforts to overturn this decision have also failed.

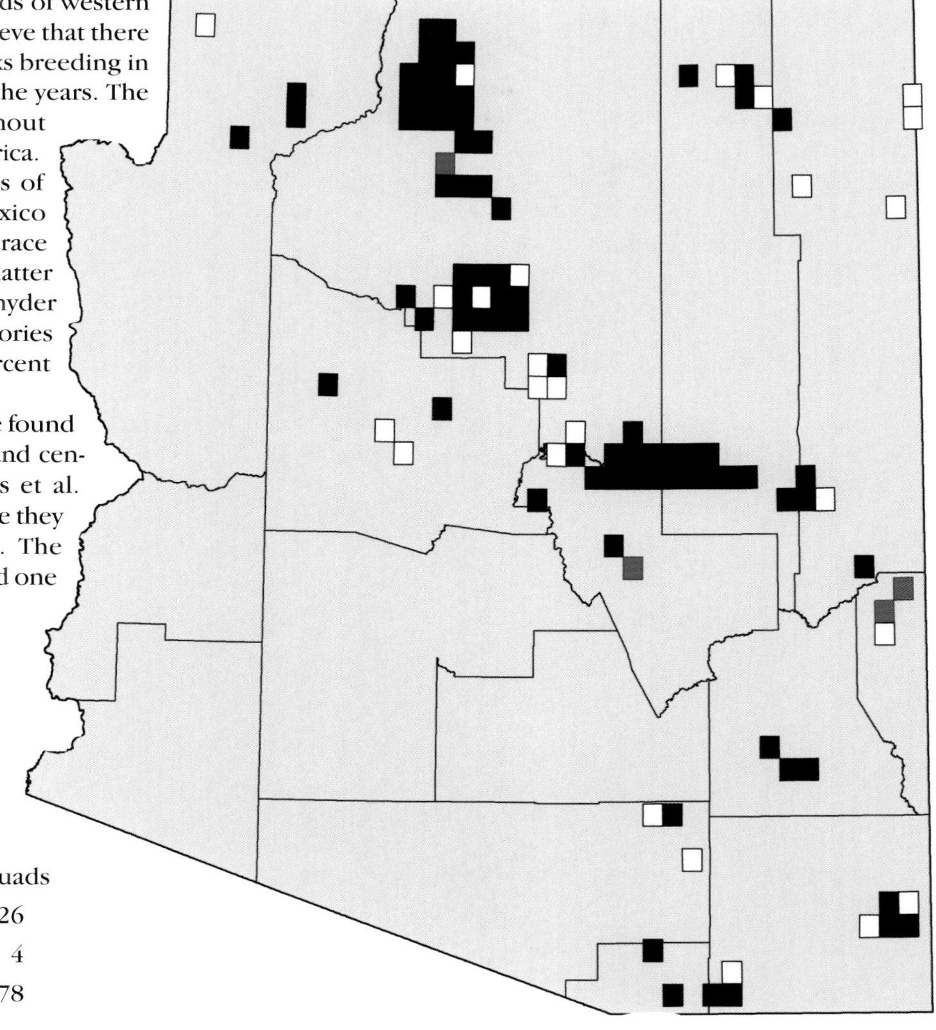

Northern Goshawk Breeding Evidence Reported in 56 (3%) of 1834 priority blocks

	Blocks	Quads
Possible	21 (38%)	26
Probable	4 (7%)	4
Confirmed	31 (55%)	78

Gray Hawk

by Troy E. Corman *Asturina nitida*

With shrill whistles and loud cries, the handsome Gray Hawk is sometimes first observed as it sails effortlessly on silvery wings above its riparian woodland territory. At other times these delicately barred raptors are discovered perched within the canopy watching intently for unwary lizards, their preferred prey in Arizona.

HELEN AND NOEL SNYDER

HABITAT

In Arizona, Gray Hawks nest almost exclusively along lowland riparian areas. Atlasers noted these attractive raptors most frequently along perennial and intermittent drainages dominated with tall groves of Fremont cottonwood and Goodding willow, typically with adjacent stands of velvet mesquite. Nearly 73 percent of the records were reported in this habitat (n = 55). Most of the remaining Gray Hawk observations were in riparian woodlands containing Arizona sycamore, often with a mixture of cottonwoods and willows. Locally, atlasers also found these hawks nesting along drier drainages dominated by netleaf hackberry, velvet ash, Arizona walnut, and Madrean evergreen oaks. Historically in Arizona, they also nested in the extensive mesquite bosques where the trees routinely attained heights >50 ft (15.2 m), a rare sight these days.

BREEDING

Arizona's Gray Hawks are primarily neotropical migrants that typically begin to arrive in the state during the third week of March, exceptionally as early as 11 March (Phillips et al. 1964). Territoriality and courtship behaviors are initiated soon after. Atlasers observed nest building or nest repairing activity in April and early May. Gray Hawks typically return to the same territory year after year, and either add layers of fresh leafy branches to the nest from the previous year or construct a new nest nearby (Bibles 1999).

Due to the nest height and location, atlasers were unable to report nests with eggs. However, Glinski (1998) noted that egg-laying typically occurs during the first half of May in Arizona. Atlasers reported nests with young from 6 June through 31 July. Most young leave the nest by mid- to late July. Prior to the atlas, an extremely late renesting attempt was noted along the San Pedro River near Saint David. Two recently fledged young were discovered near a nest on 13 September 1989, where both fledglings remained as late as 16 October (Krueper 1999). Based on nesting phenology, the eggs of this late nesting would have been laid in late June or early July and likely pertained to a renesting attempt. Most Gray Hawks depart Arizona by late September or early October, although a few have recently been found wintering.

Gray Hawks typically place their nests in the upper third of one of the taller trees in an area and are constructed by both adults (Glinski 1998). Recent nest heights in Arizona average 63 ft (19.2 m) and ranged from 46.6 to 103.3 ft (14.2–31.5 m) above the ground (Bibles et al. 2002). In Arizona, most Gray Hawk nests are discovered in Fremont cottonwood, but atlasers also noted them in velvet ash, Arizona sycamore, and several species of Madrean evergreen oaks. Within the mesquite bosques that historically extended for miles along the flood plain of the Santa Cruz River south of Tucson, Gray Hawks also once nested in tall velvet mesquite and netleaf hackberry only 30–40 ft (9.1–12.2 m) above the ground (Bent 1937).

The female Gray Hawk incubated the 2–3 eggs for approximately 33 days and the nestlings remain in the nest for an additional 5–6 weeks (Glinski 1998). However, nestlings frequently move to adjacent branches a few days prior to fledging (Bibles et al. 2002). Both parents continue to feed the fledglings for an additional month or two following nest departure (Snyder and Snyder 1991).

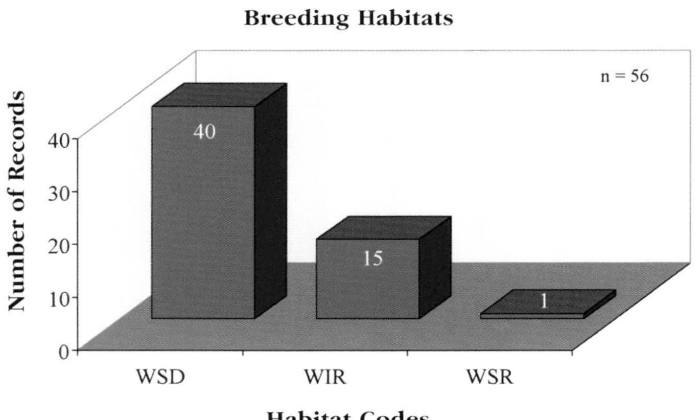

DISTRIBUTION AND STATUS

Barely entering the United States in southern Arizona, New Mexico, and Texas, this small, tropical raptor is widespread and common south of the Mexico border to northern Argentina. The status of Gray Hawks in Arizona has changed considerably during the past century. Phillips et al. (1964) stated that it was formerly a fairly common summer resident

Breeding Phenology

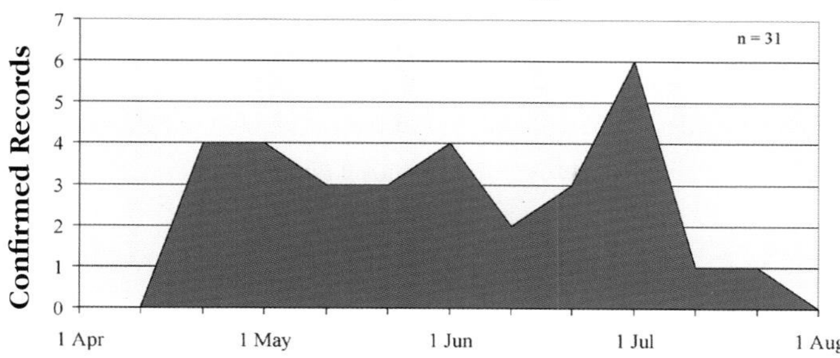

in southeastern Arizona primarily along the Santa Cruz River drainage north to Tucson. Much of their nesting habitat along the Santa Cruz River had been lost by the early 1900s, especially in Pima County, where numbers of Gray Hawks diminished. But small numbers still ranged west to Arivaca, north to Aravaipa Creek, and east to the upper San Pedro River and San Bernardino Ranch, east of Douglas (Phillips et al. 1964). By the mid-1900s, Gray Hawk numbers began to increase in other parts of southeastern Arizona. During the 1970s they were considered fairly common once again with nesting as far north as Dudleyville along the lower San Pedro River (Monson and Phillips 1981).

Gray Hawk numbers and their distribution in Arizona steadily increased through the atlas period. They were found nesting at elevations from 1950 to 5000 ft (594–1524 m). Atlasers found this raptor to be locally common along sections of the San Pedro River with perennial flow from the Mexico border to Saint David and then again from Cascabel to Winkelman. Sizable populations were also found along Cienega Creek northeast of Sonoita and along Sonoita Creek near Patagonia downstream to below Patagonia Lake. Atlasers also noted that Gray Hawks were the most abundant raptor along the Santa Cruz River from Rio Rico to near Amado.

During the atlas, Gray Hawks were documented nesting farther north than they had been. Agitated pairs were found on the Gila River upstream of Winkelman to below Coolidge Dam and along the San Carlos River near Peridot. The most northern confirmed record was of an occupied nest along Pinal Creek just southeast of Roosevelt Lake, Gila County. An atlaser also found an agitated individual north of there along Cherry Creek east of the Sierra Ancha. In the extreme southeast, Gray Hawks were confirmed nesting on the San Bernardino National Wildlife Refuge and in Guadalupe Canyon. The most western nesting record came from the Buenos Aires National Wildlife Refuge in Brown Canyon on the eastern slope of the Baboquivari Mountains.

As more riparian areas are protected and conservatively managed in Arizona, the number of Gray Hawk nesting territories will likely continue to expand steadily, especially to the north along perennial drainages and their tributaries. Some nesting territories, however, have recently been lost due to wildfires, local urban development, and groundwater depletion from drought and groundwater pumping for increasing human populations.

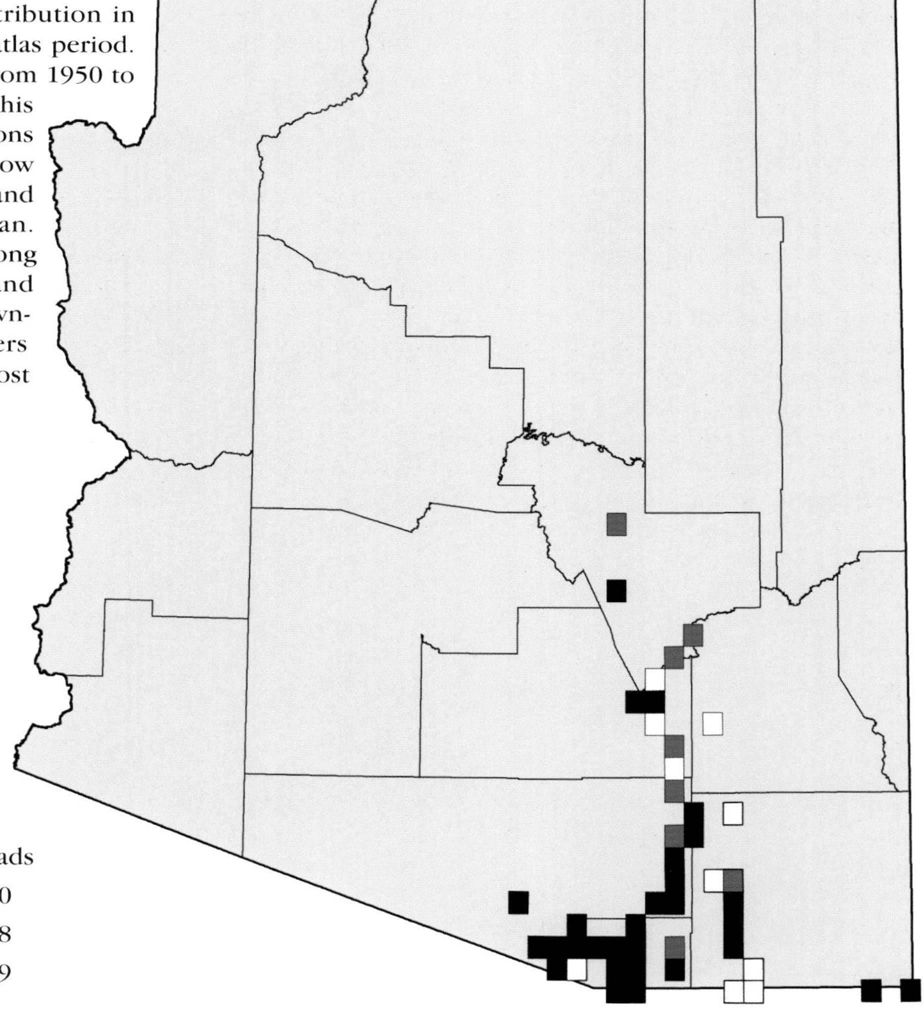

Gray Hawk Breeding Evidence Reported in 29 (2%) of 1834 priority blocks

	Blocks	Quads
Possible	5 (17%)	10
Probable	5 (17%)	8
Confirmed	19 (66%)	29

Common Black-Hawk

by Troy E. Corman *Buteogallus anthracinus*

Frequently flushed from the edge of a watercourse, Common Black-Hawks are typically found in or near riparian woodlands. Visitors are instantly aware when they enter the territory of these dark, streamside guardians, for they readily proclaim their discontent with a distinctive series of high, shrill whistles.

HELEN AND NOEL SNYDER

HABITAT

In Arizona, Common Black-Hawks are riparian obligate raptors, nesting primarily along perennial drainages with mature gallery forests of broadleaf deciduous trees. They especially favor continuous flowing steams less than 8 in. (20.3 cm) deep with low to moderate gradients and riffles, runs, and pools (Schnell 1998). Ideal hunting conditions include an abundance of low, streamside perches such as exposed boulders, logs, and branches (Schnell 1994). They occur less frequently along intermittent flowing drainages with scattered perennial pools. More than 90 percent of all atlas records were reported from two main riparian habitats along rivers, creeks, and streams (n = 89). Arizona sycamore dominated drainages accounted for 53 percent of all records. Other dominant trees in these drainages often included Arizona alder, Fremont cottonwood, Arizona cypress, and Arizona walnut. At lower elevations where Fremont cottonwood was the dominant tree, nesting Common Black-Hawks were noted less frequently. Nearly 37 percent of all atlas records were reported in this habitat, which often included Goodding willow, velvet ash, tamarisk, and velvet mesquite. Atlasers found this raptor to be sparse at higher elevation canyon drainages where scattered Arizona sycamore and Arizona alder grew among ponderosa pines and Douglas fir.

BREEDING

In southeastern regions of the state, Common Black-Hawks typically begin to arrive in breeding areas by early to mid-March. Nevertheless, a few early individuals reach central Arizona by the third week of February. The pair often returns to the same territory where aerial displays begin immediately after arrival and continue interspersed with courtship feeding (Schnell 1994). Common Black-Hawks frequently select the same nest used in previous years and add a new surface layer. Atlasers reported nest building as early as 16 March, and this activity continues until the eggs are laid in mid-April (Schnell 1994). Occupied nests were reported by 22 April, suggesting incubation. Atlasers noted nests with young from 29 May to 25 July and the first fledgling was observed by 12 July. The last confirmed record was of an adult feeding a fledgling on 13 August. Common Black-Hawks may initiate fall migration by late August, with a peak in late September through mid-October (Schnell 1994). A few individuals may linger into late October and early November.

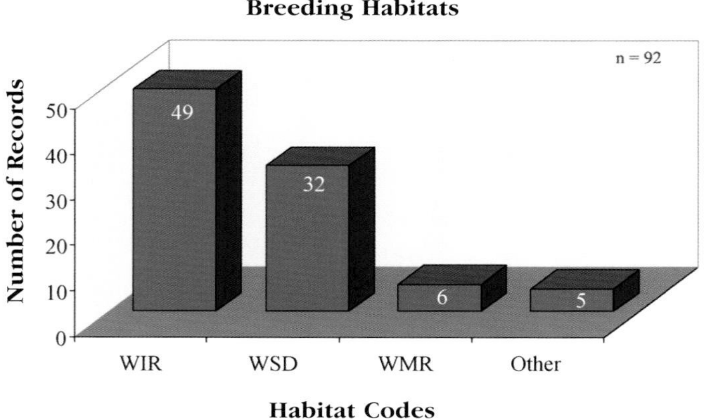

Most Common Black-Hawk nests are well shaded and usually constructed in the crotch of the main trunk (Schnell 1994). However, atlasers did note several nests built on top of mistletoe clumps that were much less shaded. In Arizona, most nests are built in Fremont cottonwoods and Arizona sycamore, which are the largest trees in the habitats they prefer. Of the nine nests measured by atlas field crews, one was in a velvet ash and the remaining were evenly distributed between cottonwood and sycamore. In Arizona, nests have also been found in Arizona walnut, Arizona alder, Goodding willow, ponderosa pine, Douglas fir, and historically in velvet mesquite (Bent 1937; Schnell 1994). The mean height of nests measured during the atlas was 35.4 ft (10.8 m) and ranged from 27.9 to 45.9 ft (8.5–14 m). However, of 152 Arizona Common Black-Hawk nests measured by Schnell (1994), the mean nest height was 58.7 ft (17.9 m) with a range of 29.5–98.4 ft (9–30 m).

Both parents share in the incubation of the 1–2 eggs, which hatch between 37 and 39 days (Schnell 1979; Millsap

Breeding Phenology

Confirmed Records

n = 42

1 Mar | 1 Apr | 1 May | 1 Jun | 1 Jul | 1 Aug

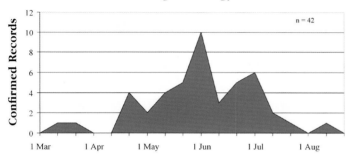

1981). The young leave the nest and often perch on nearby branches when they are 40–50 days old (Schnell 1994). The young are dependent on the adults for food for an additional 1.5–2 months following nest departure (Schnell 1998).

DISTRIBUTION AND STATUS

This tropical raptor is primarily a resident from northern South America to central Mexico. More northern populations are migratory, which include southwestern Utah, Arizona, New Mexico, and locally in Texas. Phillips et al. (1964) considered Common Black-Hawks a regular summer resident in southeastern and central Arizona, as far northwest as the Big Sandy drainage. Monson and Phillips (1981) considered this raptor fairly common and noted them also occurring in the Virgin River drainage in the extreme northwest. By 1980, Monson and Phillips also noted a decline of nesting observations in southeastern Arizona, primarily south of the Galiuro Mountains where Common Black-Hawks nested along Sonoita Creek until 1976 and along the Santa Cruz River south of Tucson in 1922.

Schnell (1998) noted that the distribution of Common Black-Hawks in Arizona is patchy because of the scarcity of suitable nesting habitat. Schnell also observed that during years of high rainfall, nests are established in new areas, but these may be used only irregularly. Atlasers found this raptor nesting at elevations from 1800 to 6200 ft (549–1890 m) and foraging as high as 7000 ft (2133 m). During the atlas, Common Black-Hawks were found primarily in waterways draining the Mogollon Plateau, east to the Verde, Big Sandy, and Santa Maria river drainages. The atlas distribution map does not reflect that these raptors undoubtedly also nest regularly within the upper Salt, White, and Black River drainages on White Mountain Apache tribal lands. Unfortunately, atlasers were unsuccessful in acquiring access to conduct surveys in this vast region.

Common Black-Hawk numbers have apparently increased along the lower San Pedro River, where they had historically only nested along smaller, perennial side streams of this drainage system. An active nest was found on this river as far south as near San Manuel. Another active nest was discovered in the Chiricahua Mountains during the atlas and these raptors were found nesting once again along Sonoita Creek below Patagonia Lake. Atlasers also noted that this species continues to nest near the confluence of Beaver Dam Wash and Virgin River in extreme northwestern Arizona.

Atlasers encountered Common Black-Hawks fairly frequently where appropriate habitat continues to exist. The unfortunate introduction of crayfish to Arizona's waterways has played havoc on populations of many native aquatic species, although they have been added to the broad diets of these shadowy, tropical raptors.

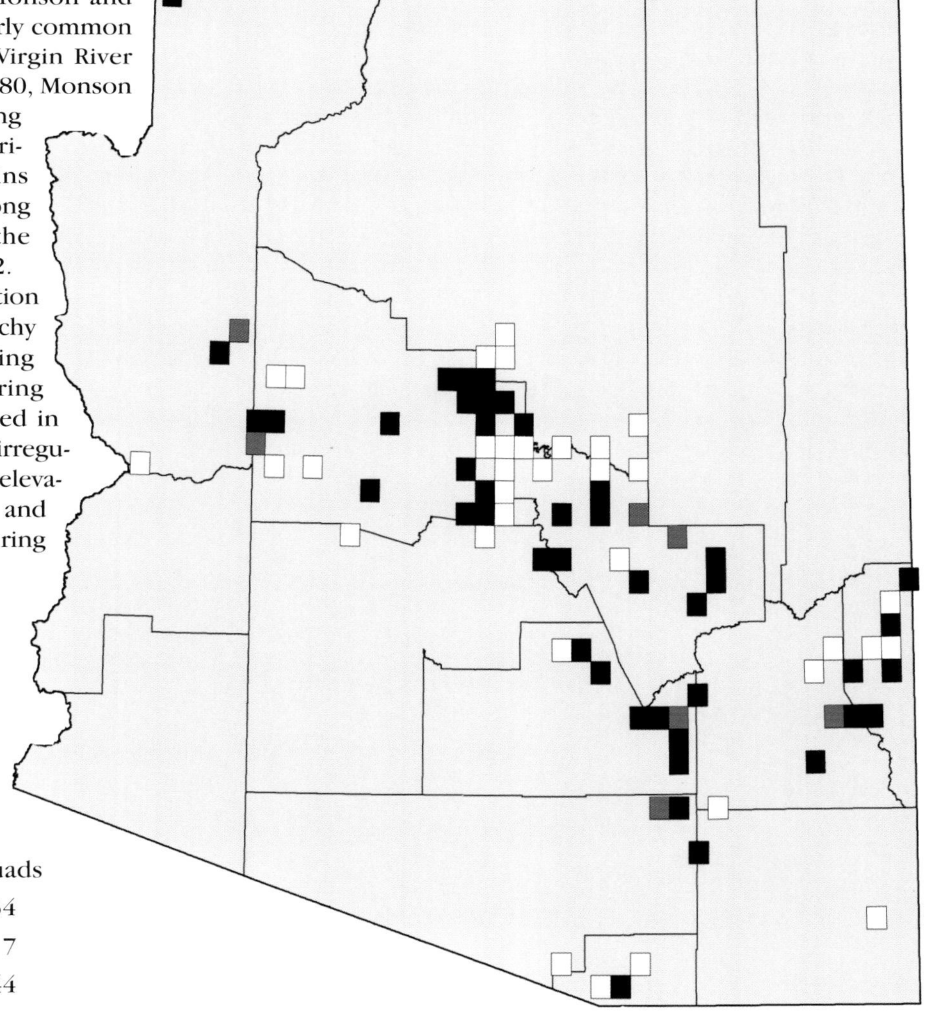

Common Black-Hawk Breeding Evidence Reported in 57 (3%) of 1834 priority blocks

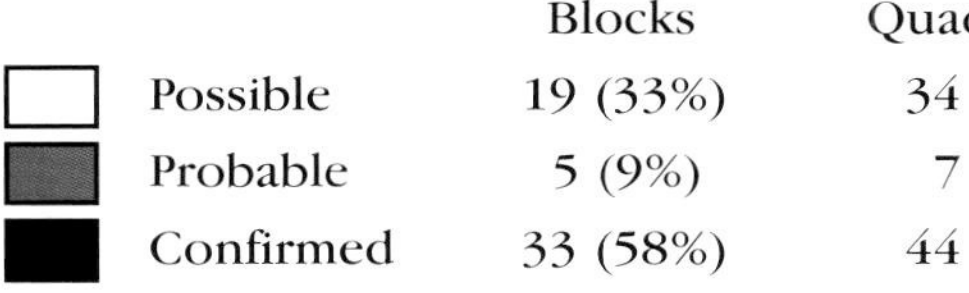

	Blocks	Quads
Possible	19 (33%)	34
Probable	5 (9%)	7
Confirmed	33 (58%)	44

Harris's Hawk

by Troy E. Corman *Parabuteo unicinctus*

Often found perched in groups of three or more individuals, Harris's Hawks have many bizarre yet fascinating social and behavioral attributes, including one of the most sophisticated cooperative hunting tactics ever documented in birds. These large, handsome hawks are also the only raptors in Arizona that are occasionally found nesting throughout the year.

DAN FISCHER

HABITAT

In Arizona, Harris's Hawks can be found inhabiting a variety of arid, open country environments, although Millsap (1981) suggested that access to some open water may be an important factor in habitat selection. Atlasers reported 60 percent of all records of this raptor in complex Sonoran desertscrub communities where large, many-armed saguaros are plentiful and trees such as velvet mesquite, paloverde, and ironwood are common (n = 136). Locally these raptors were found in semiarid grasslands where taller and denser vegetation grows along washes and earthen tanks. Along perennial rivers and streams within desert landscapes, Harris's Hawks were noted occupying the edge of riparian areas dominated by Fremont cottonwood, willow, and mesquite. Within the past several decades these raptors have also steadily increased as a nesting resident in and around some rural and urban communities with tall trees. Atlasers reported 17 percent of all Harris's Hawk records in these settings and noted them nesting in orchards, city parks, cemeteries, golf courses, and even in residential neighborhoods in the greater Tucson and Phoenix areas.

BREEDING

Harris's Hawks are primarily resident. When prey abundance remains high in Arizona, nesting activity has been observed throughout the year (Radke and Klimosewski 1977; Dawson 1998). However, during the atlas period, nesting activity was reported from late January through late June, which compares well with the typical nesting period reported by Dawson (1998). The earliest confirmed nesting activity during the atlas was a pair observed nest-building on 29 January. In Arizona, Harris's Hawks often begin to construct nests about 5 weeks prior to egg laying (Mader 1975). The earliest nest with young was reported on 1 March, suggesting the eggs were laid by at least late January. Atlas data reveal a peak nesting period from mid-April to mid-May; however, this may also reflect when atlasers were conducting most of their surveys in desert regions. The latest reported occupied Harris's Hawk nest contained young on 29 June.

Breeding Habitats

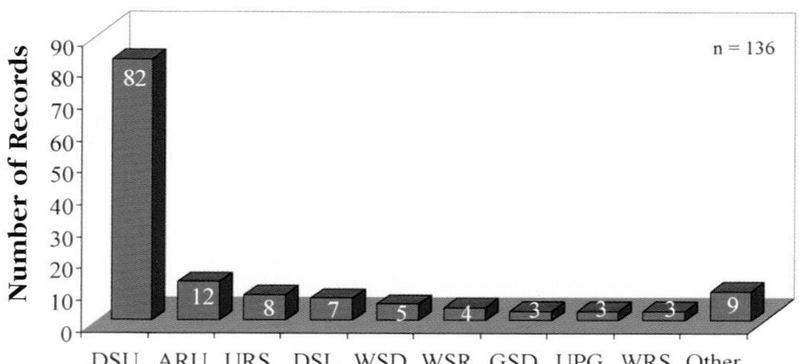

Habitat Codes

Unlike most raptors, Harris's Hawks are often quite social during the breeding season, and one or more individual may be observed helping the parents through the entire nesting cycle. Breeding groups remain united throughout the year and during the nesting season, they stay within their territories and exclude trespassers (Dawson and Mannan 1991). Breeding groups can contain up to seven hawks that work together to build a nest and raise young (Dawson and Mannan 1989). Many groups suspend all breeding when prey levels are low and breeding as much as possible (up to 3 broods) in good years (Mader 1978; Bednarz 1995).

Atlasers found Harris's Hawks often construct their nests in saguaros, paloverde, mesquite, and, less often, isolated stands of Fremont cottonwood. In desert trees, many nests were constructed on top of large mistletoe clumps. In urban and rural environments, transmission towers and tall, exotic trees such as eucalyptus, aleppo pines, pecans, and various palms also suffice. Mader (1975) and Whaley (1986) notes nests are typically placed 14.4–20.7 ft (4.4–6.3 m) high, but they also documented nests in urban areas as high as 49–70 ft (14.9–21.3 m).

Most clutches contain 2–3 eggs (range 1–7), which are incubated primarily by the female for 29–34 days (Dawson 1998). Nestlings fledge in approximately 45 days and the young hawks remain with their parents for at least

Breeding Phenology

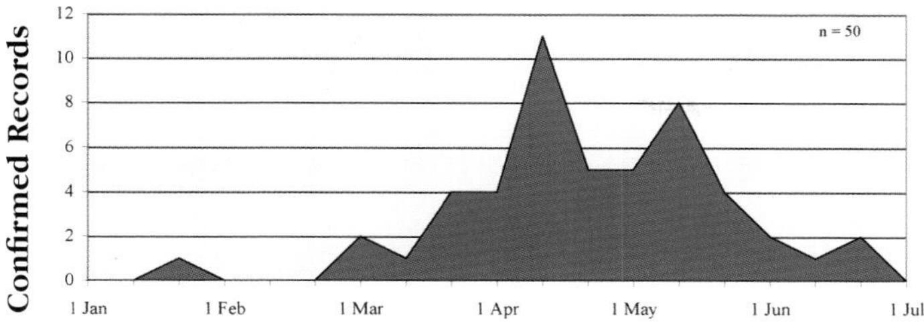

4 months before venturing off (Dawson 1998). Some offspring remain with the parental group for up to 4 years, however, and help raise successive broods before leaving to nest elsewhere (Dawson and Mannan 1991).

DISTRIBUTION AND STATUS

Harris's Hawks have an exceptionally large range from southeastern California, Arizona, New Mexico, and Texas south to central Chile and Argentina. Prior Arizona range descriptions noted these raptors as local along the lower Colorado River north to at least Topock, east to Superior, Florence, and Tucson, then south to the Mexico border including Tohono O'odham tribal lands and Organ Pipe Cactus National Monument (Phillips et al. 1964). By 1961, the population along the Colorado River disappeared due to unknown causes, except at Topock Marsh, where a small population persisted until 1964 (Rosenberg et al. 1991). Rea (1983) reported that this raptor was primarily extirpated from the Gila River Indian Community once the Gila River no longer flowed through their lands and the cottonwoods disappeared. During the 1980s, family groups, active nests, and individual Harris's Hawks began to appear in various locations in Cochise County, especially in the San Simon and Sulphur Springs valleys.

Atlasers found Harris's Hawks to be generally uncommon, but locally common throughout much of its south-central historical range where their distribution closely follows the more densely vegetated Sonoran Desert regions. These raptors were also found northwest to near Wikieup, in southern Yavapai County near Congress, and along the Verde River to near Camp Verde. Breeding populations continued locally in Cochise County, and a few individuals were also found in nearby Graham County in the Thatcher-Safford area.

During the atlas period, most Harris's Hawks were found at elevations ranging from 850 to 4150 ft (259–1265 m). In 1978, a ten-year reestablishment effort began at lower elevations along the lower Colorado River by the University of California–Santa Cruz Predatory Bird Research Group. With support from the Bureau of Land Management, more than 100 individuals were hacked and released, which likely produced most of the individuals found in this area during the atlas project (S. Henry, personal communication). But numbers quickly declined once the efforts ended in the late 1980s.

Harris's Hawk populations are most threatened by habitat alteration and loss. Although urban sprawl continues to reduce prime habitat, the species' range in Arizona has been steadily increasing since Whaley (1986) surveyed the population in the mid-1970s (Dawson 1998). Additionally, the adaptability of Harris's Hawks to nest in urban areas offers some hope of mitigating habitat loss to development, but unfortunately electrocution claims the lives of many urban hawks as they perch on utility poles (Dawson 1998).

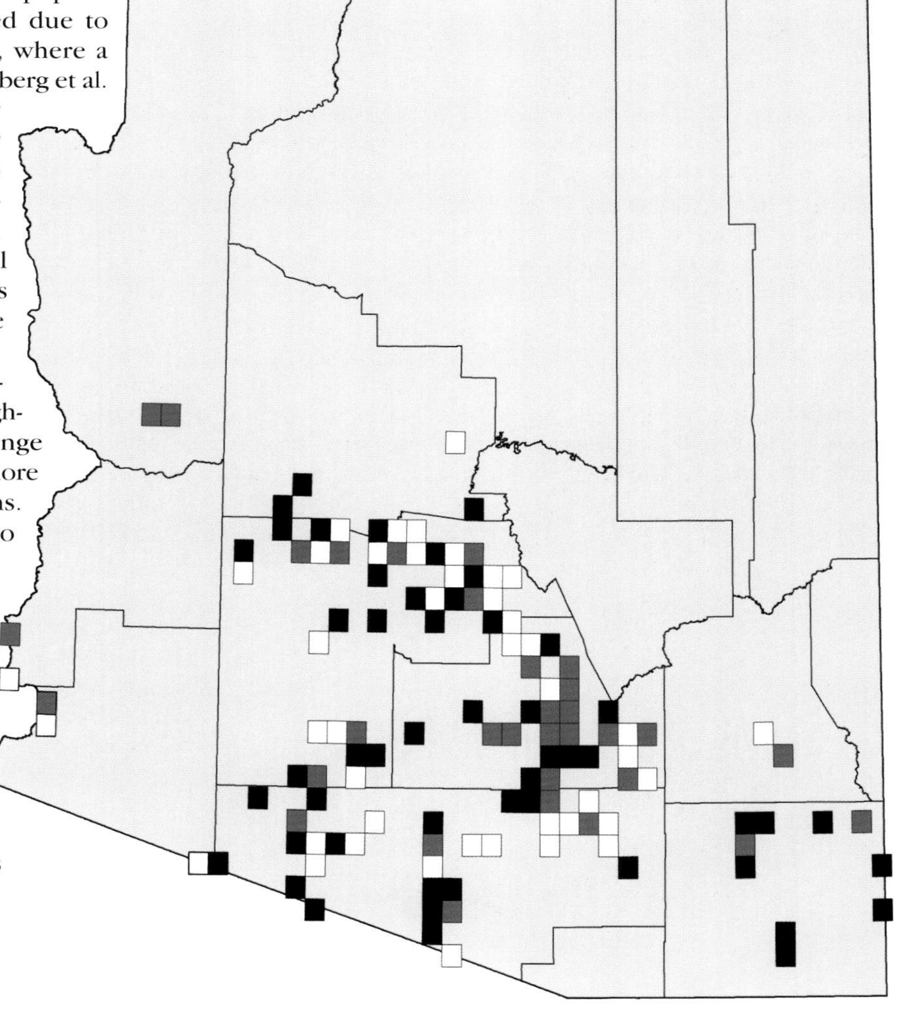

Harris's Hawk Breeding Evidence Reported in 111 (6%) of 1834 priority blocks

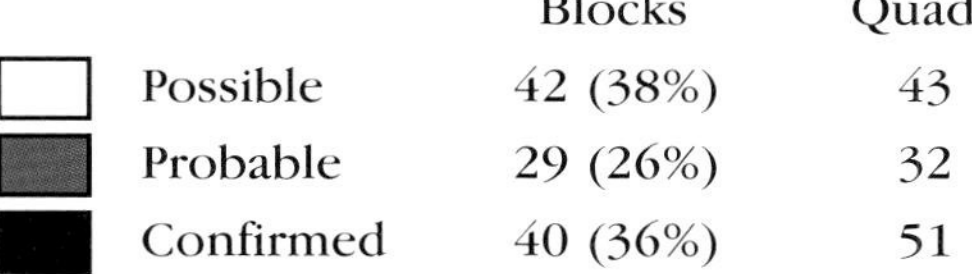

	Blocks	Quads
Possible	42 (38%)	43
Probable	29 (26%)	32
Confirmed	40 (36%)	51

Swainson's Hawk

by Cathryn Wise-Gervais *Buteo swainsoni*

One sure sign of spring is the return of Swainson's Hawks to the windswept grasslands of Arizona. These attractive hawks are opportunistic predators; moreover their diets change considerably throughout the year. When nesting, these raptors prey primarily on small mammals and reptiles, and then switch predominantly to large insects during migration and on their wintering grounds.

HELEN AND NOEL SNYDER

HABITAT

Swainson's Hawks are most frequently encountered in a variety of open grasslands and similar structured grain or alfalfa croplands. In Arizona, these raptors can be surprisingly flexible in habitat choice—often they select areas containing scattered trees, tall shrubs, or a riparian corridor edge for roosting, nesting, and perching. Although atlasers reported Swainson's Hawks in 25 different habitat types, 46 percent of records were obtained in semiarid grasslands, primarily in southeastern Arizona (n = 165). This habitat type is often characterized by scattered sotol, yucca, mesquite, and juniper. The second most commonly reported habitat was a mixture of grassland and Chihuahuan desertscrub with creosote, tarbush, whitethorn acacia, and scattered mesquite (8 percent of records), and 7 percent of atlas records were from rural areas with pastures, agricultural fields, shelterbelts, outbuildings, and stock tanks. Atlasers also found Swainson's Hawks foraging and occasionally nesting in a variety of other habitats including Sonoran desertscrub with some grassland component, riparian woodland edges, and open conifer stands near subalpine grasslands.

BREEDING

Swainson's Hawks are long-distance neotropical migrants that usually begin arriving in Arizona in mid-March and exceptionally early as late February. Peak numbers pass through Arizona in April and early May, with stragglers occasionally reported into early June. Atlasers noted the first paired birds on 29 March and the first occupied nest on 16 April. The earliest Swainson's Hawk nest with eggs was noted on 28 April, and atlas data suggest that most eggs are laid between late April and late May. Atlas data also reveal a slight peak in breeding activity in late May and early June, with a surge of nests with young noted from mid-July to early August, especially in southeastern populations. The latest active nest documented during the atlas period was found on 11 August and fledglings were reported through 4 September. In Arizona, a few Swainson's Hawks begin appearing in nonbreeding agricultural areas by mid-July, but most birds do not begin migrating south until late August and September, when large flocks or "kettles" of 50–100+ individuals can be observed.

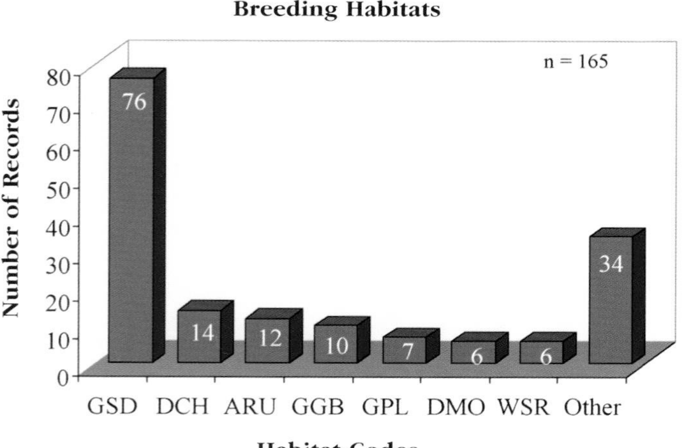

Swainson's Hawks typically select a solitary, conspicuous tree or tall shrub for nesting (England et al. 1997) and will often return to the same nest site each year (Glinski and Hall 1998). In southeastern Arizona, most nests are placed in velvet mesquite, but also regularly in soaptree yucca. Statewide, however, Swainson's Hawks are known to use a wide variety of trees and shrubs for nesting including western soapberry, Joshua tree, netleaf hackberry, paloverde, and occasionally even in a cholla or saguaro (Glinski and Hall 1998). Atlasers measured six Swainson's Hawk nests during the atlas period, two nests were in catclaw acacia, and one nest each in Fremont cottonwood, Utah juniper, tamarisk, and in an unidentified shrub. In the Hualapai Valley north of Kingman, Glinski and Hall (1998) reported nest substrates were fairly short and nest height ranges from 6 to 14 ft (1.8–4.3 m). Nests measured during the atlas period had a median nest height of 10.7 ft (3.3 m) and ranged from 8.2 to 18.7 ft (2.5–5.7 m).

Swainson's Hawk nests are bulky masses of sticks constructed and refurbished by both sexes. Additionally, both adults will bring fresh green sprigs for lining the nest (England et al. 1998). Clutch size varies from 1 to 4 eggs (usually 2–3) and incubation takes 34–35 days (Fitzner 1980; Bednarz 1988). The female does most of the incubating but the male will cover the eggs for brief intervals while the

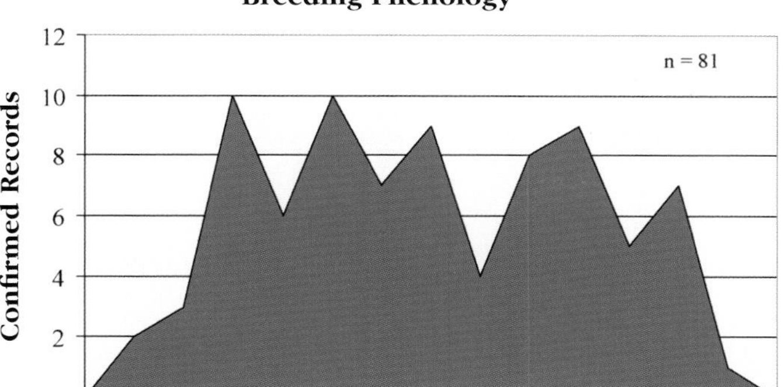

female forages and preens away from the nest (England et al. 1997). At age 27–33 days, the young Swainson's Hawks begin venturing to nearby limbs and typically take their first flight at 38–46 days old (England et al. 1997). Fledglings depend on their parents for food for an additional 3–5 weeks (Fitzner 1980).

DISTRIBUTION AND STATUS

Swainson's Hawks are long-distance migrants with some populations traveling annually from central Canada to Argentina, a distance of over 12,400 mi (nearly 20,000 km) round trip (England et al. 1997). During the breeding season, they range primarily from the Great Plains region of south-central Canada south through central and western United States to northern Mexico.

Phillips et al. (1964) noted that Swainson's Hawks were common summer residents in eastern Arizona and sparsely distributed throughout the central portions of the state and possibly to eastern Mohave County. On Navajo tribal lands, they were seen in migration and were documented occasionally nesting in cottonwoods (Woodbury et al. 1945). Sparse northern historical records may reflect observer bias and the fact that few early ornithologists visited northern Arizona (Glinski and Hall 1998).

Atlas data verify that Swainson's Hawks were still common in southeastern Arizona west to the Altar Valley and north locally to San Carlos Apache tribal lands. However, these hawks had been nesting sparingly as far west as Sells on the Tohono O'odham tribal lands (Phillips et al. 1964). Atlasers also documented significant numbers of this raptor nesting in the Hualapai and Detrital valleys in Mohave County. Swainson's Hawks were also detected nesting locally on the Coconino Plateau north of Seligman and in Chino Valley. Atlasers found evidence of nesting at elevations from approximately 1900 ft (580 m) near Marana to 9200 ft (2800 m) in large alpine meadows of the White Mountains and Kaibab Plateau. Swainson's Hawks were also discovered still nesting sparingly in the southwest corner of Navajo and Hopi tribal lands and up the Little Colorado River drainage to near Petrified Forest National Park.

Although Swainson's Hawks were encountered throughout most of their known historical breeding range in Arizona, they are still considered a species of management concern due to their close grassland association. Most of the native grasslands in Arizona have been significantly altered or lost to inappropriate grazing practices, fire suppression, as well as conversion to agriculture and housing developments. This habitat loss undoubtedly reflects an equal reduction in the abundance and breeding distribution of these attractive prairie raptors.

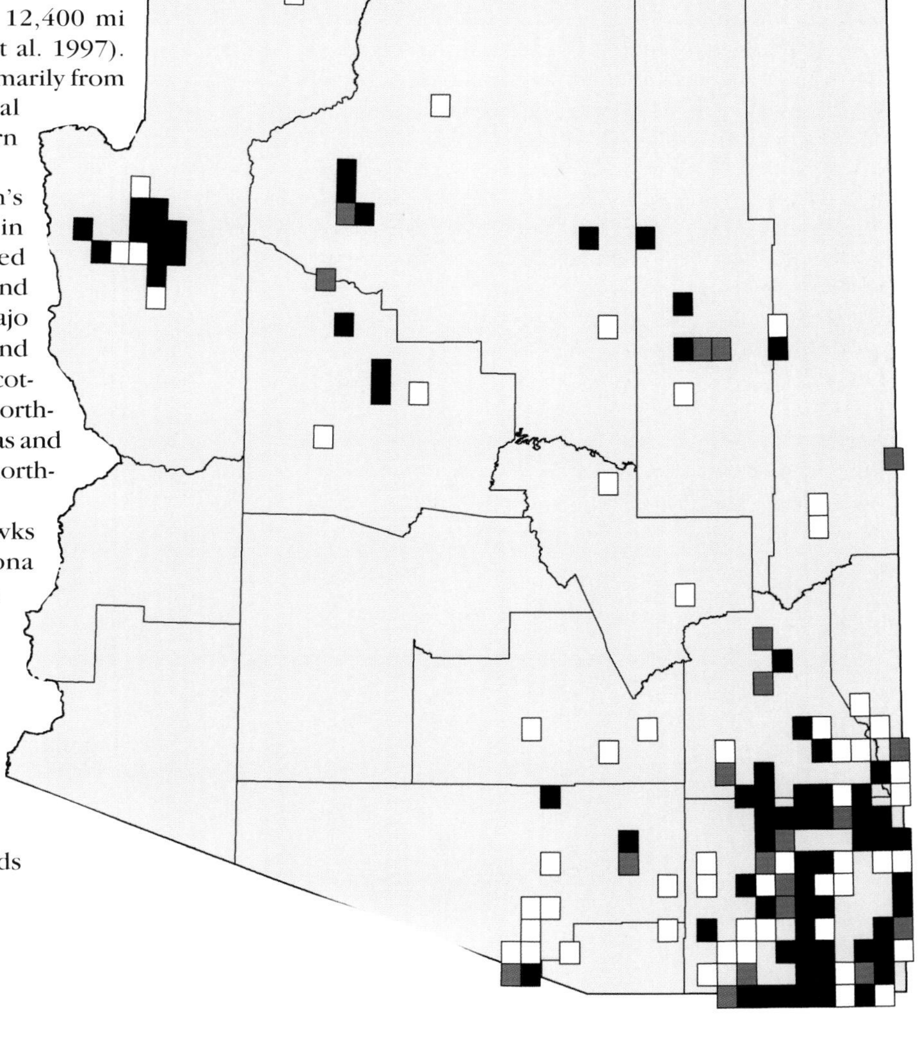

Swainson's Hawk Breeding Evidence Reported in 126 (7%) of 1834 priority blocks

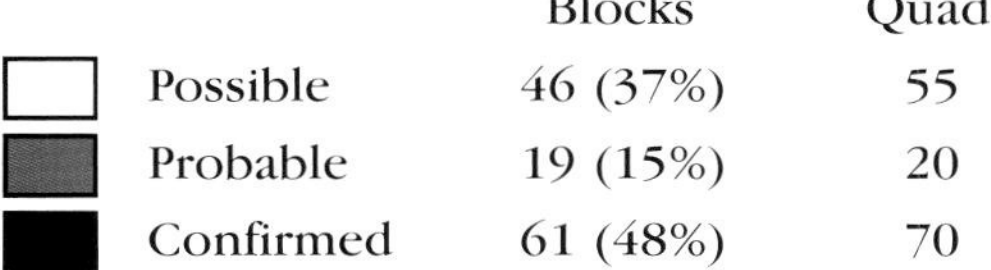

	Blocks	Quads
Possible	46 (37%)	55
Probable	19 (15%)	20
Confirmed	61 (48%)	70

Zone-tailed Hawk

by Troy E. Corman *Buteo albonotatus*

A closer look at the many thermal riding Turkey Vultures soaring through Arizona skies, may sometimes reveal a black impostor. Easily overlooked by the casual observer, Zone-tailed Hawks have become a fairly common tropical raptor in Arizona; their range has steadily advanced northward in the state in the past 50 years.

HELEN AND NOEL SNYDER

HABITAT

In Arizona, Zone-tailed Hawks nest from high elevation forests down to lowland riparian areas and locally, even along dry desert washes. These raptors also forage over many adjacent open habitats including grasslands, deserts, and along cliff faces and rocky ridges. More than 53 percent of all atlas records were from riparian woodlands dominated by Arizona sycamore (31 percent) or Fremont cottonwood (22 percent; n = 192). Other frequently occurring tree species in the cottonwood-dominated drainages included mesquite, Arizona ash, Goodding willow, and netleaf hackberry. In the sycamore-lined canyons and mountain foothill drainages inhabited by these raptors, bigtooth maple, alligator juniper, Arizona cypress, and various evergreen oaks also regularly occur. Furthermore, Zone-tailed Hawks were found nesting in Madrean evergreen oak and pinyon-juniper woodlands. At higher elevations, atlasers regularly observed this hawk nesting in ponderosa pine forests, Madrean pine-oak woodlands, and sparsely up to mixed conifer forests. Atlasers also found them locally nesting along larger, more wooded dry washes of the Sonoran Desert, where blue paloverde and velvet mesquite grew to heights greater than 25 ft (7.6 m).

BREEDING

Although recently noted wintering in limited numbers in the lowlands of southern Arizona, most Zone-tailed Hawks begin to arrive in mid-March, occasionally earlier. The earliest observation reported by atlasers was on 16 March. These raptors frequently return to the same nest year after year, often initiating nest repair and courtship soon after their arrival. Nest building activity was reported as early as 1 April and an adult was observed carrying nesting material as late as 7 May. Atlasers reported an occupied nest by 15 April and a nest with eggs by 18 April. Snyder (1998) noted that in Arizona most eggs are laid in mid- to late April. The earliest nest with young reported by atlasers was on 2 June and the latest was 26 July. A fledgling reported on 28 June would be slightly early, with the next reported fledgling on 10 July. In Arizona, July and August are the typical fledging months (Snyder 1998). Most Zone-tailed Hawks have departed Arizona by mid- to late September, but the species is occasionally reported into November.

In Arizona, Zone-tailed Hawks usually construct their nest in a sturdy crotch in the upper third, often upper quarter, of one of the tallest trees in an area. Atlasers found most nests in Fremont cottonwood and Arizona sycamore, but also in Douglas fir, Emory oak, juniper sp., blue paloverde, and various pines including ponderosa, Chihuahuan, and Apache. Atlasers noted several nests placed on top of mistletoe clumps and many were fully exposed to the sun and elements. The atlas field crews measured ten nests with a median height of 42.3 ft (12.9 m) and a range of 17.4–75.1 ft (5.3–22.9 m). In Arizona, some nests in cottonwoods have been estimated to be greater than 100 ft (30.5 m) high (Bent 1937).

A typical Zone-tailed Hawk clutch consists of 1–2, rarely 3 eggs (Bent 1937). The eggs are incubated for 28–34 days by both adults, but primarily by the female (Johnson et al. 2000). Most prey items are brought to the nest by the male and fed to the nestlings by the female (Kennedy et al. 1995). The young depart the nest when they are between 41 and 53 days old (Johnson et al. 2000). There is little information

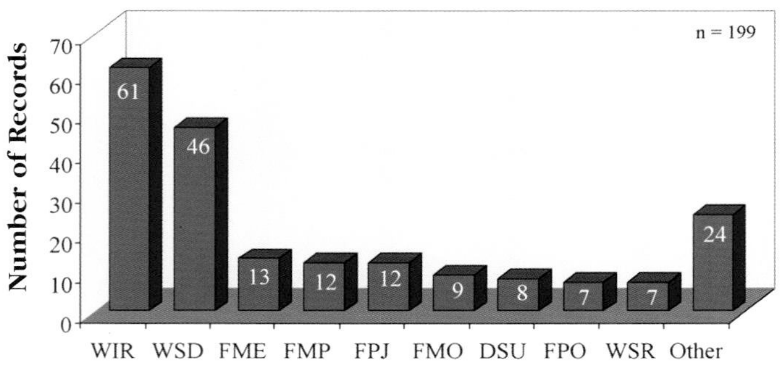

Breeding Phenology

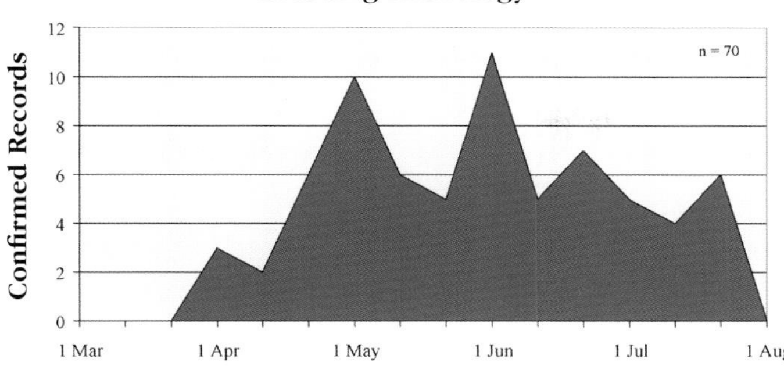

on the length of time that adults feed the fledglings, but they have been observed delivering prey several weeks following nest departure (Snyder and Glinski 1988). Only one brood is produced per year, although Zone-tailed Hawks may renest if the first attempt fails early in the incubation period (Johnson et al. 2000).

DISTRIBUTION AND STATUS

Zone-tailed Hawks are primarily tropical raptors that nest from Arizona, New Mexico, and Texas, south through the central highlands of northern Mexico. South of there, nesting populations are local and discontinuous to central South America. Phillips et al. (1964) considered Zone-tailed Hawks as fairly common summer residents in northwestern, central, and southeastern Arizona. By the mid-1900s, these raptors were reported nesting in the northwest to the Hualapai and Juniper mountains and in southeastern Arizona, north to the Pinaleno Mountains. This species formally nested along drainages in Tucson and near the mouth of the Bill Williams River (Monson and Phillips 1981).

Atlasers documented this raptor's continued breeding range expansion to the north and northwest. Zone-tailed Hawks were found nesting at elevations that ranged from 1780 to 7800 ft (542–2377 m). But they have nested as low as 475 ft (145 m) near the mouth of the Bill Williams River (Rosenberg et al. 1991). Atlasers found them to be fairly common in southeastern Arizona, north to along the entire southern edge of the Mogollon Rim, including Oak Creek Canyon north of Sedona. Breeding regularly in cottonwoods along the lower San Pedro River, Zone-tailed Hawks remain unexplainably absent along the upper reaches of this drainage where the habitat appears ideal.

During the atlas, Zone-tailed Hawks were also found near Williams and confirmed nesting along the South Rim of the Grand Canyon. North of the Grand Canyon, the species was observed near Mount Logan and Mount Dellenbaugh, and the first active Kaibab Plateau nest was discovered south of Big Springs. In western Mohave County, atlasers also found this species nesting in the Cerbat Mountains near Mount Tipton. Surveys in Hualapai tribal lands produced a nesting pair near Fraziers Well in western Coconino County and several other observations to the west.

Phillips et al. (1964) suggested that Zone-tailed Hawks may also nest irregularly in Sonoran desertscrub of western Pima County. Atlasers were finally able to confirm nesting along several well-vegetated washes in Organ Pipe Cactus National Monument and within the Tohono O'odham tribal land. These included Kuakatch Wash north of the Ajo Mountains and Siovi Shuatak Wash north of Menagers Lake. Several other nesting season observations in this area included Growler Wash south of Ajo and Anegam Wash northwest of Gu Achi.

Zone-tailed Hawk Breeding Evidence Reported in 143 (8%) of 1834 priority blocks

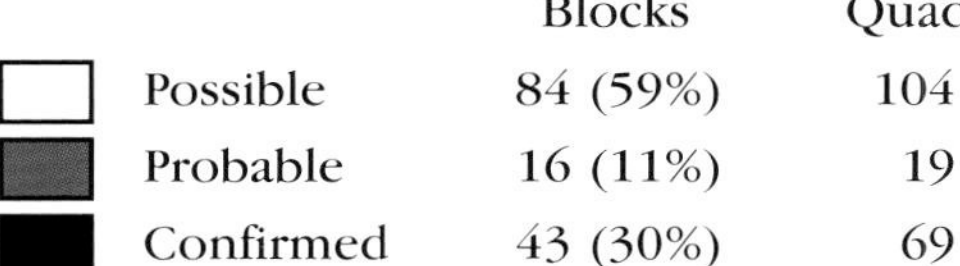

	Blocks	Quads
Possible	84 (59%)	104
Probable	16 (11%)	19
Confirmed	43 (30%)	69

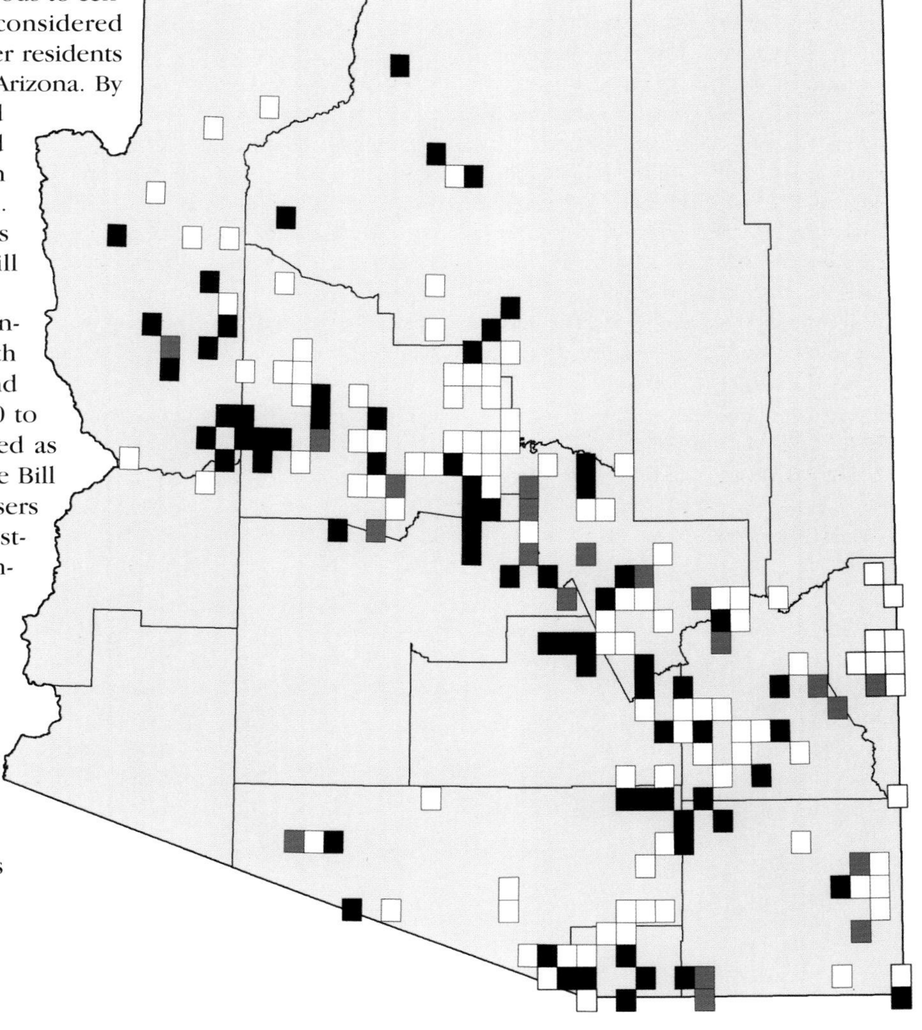

Red-tailed Hawk

by Cathryn Wise-Gervais *Buteo jamaicensis*

When sunlit from above, the rusty tail of these heavy-bodied hawks provides observers with an unmistakable field mark. Whether soaring lazily above open fields or perching boldly on a pole or fence post, Red-tailed Hawks are common and conspicuous raptors throughout Arizona's many varied landscapes.

BRUCE TAUBERT

HABITAT

Red-tailed Hawks require only the basics when it comes to breeding habitat selection: open areas for hunting coupled with scattered nesting sites and perches. As a result, these robust hawks inhabit diverse landscapes offering these features, including deserts, open woodlands, and grasslands, as well as agricultural and suburban areas. Red-tailed Hawks are opportunistic in their feeding habits, and it is this flexibility that enables them to occur in such a wide variety of habitats. These adaptable hawks are able to shift quickly from one prey source to another based on relative availability. In keeping with this, atlasers located Red-tailed Hawks in nearly every habitat in Arizona, except for in the densest forests and in the driest, most desolate desert extremes. Of the 1384 Red-tailed Hawk records obtained by atlasers that included habitat type information, 27 percent were in Sonoran desert uplands and 11 percent were in pinyon pine–juniper woodlands. These two are also the most widespread habitat types in the state, so it is likely that birds were making use of available space rather than selecting for these habitats directly. Although Monson (1998) noted Red-tailed Hawks to be four times as common in lower Sonoran and Chihuahuan deserts than elsewhere in the state, atlas abundance data were inconclusive on this.

BREEDING

Wintering Red-tailed Hawks increase Arizona's resident population dramatically, as do the northbound spring migrants that typically pass through the state in March and April. Resident Red-tailed Hawks remain in pairs year-round, and they begin courtship activities in early winter in lowland deserts and late winter and early spring at higher elevations. Courtship consists of acrobatic flights in which both adults scream and soar, sometimes grappling in mid-air with talons locked (Bent 1937). Males will often fly above females with legs dangling down. Mader (1978) reported some desert Red-tailed Hawks begin nest refurbishing or construction as early as late December and Millsap (1981) reported on an early egg date of 15 January. Few atlas surveys were conducted prior to mid-February and the first nest building activity was reported on 23 February. Atlasers detected occupied nests by 27 February and a nest with eggs on 4 March. However, a nest discovered with young on 11 March indicated egg-laying initiation no later than early February. Egg laying is presumably postponed for a month or more at higher elevations in the state, which is similar to elsewhere in North America. In Arizona, Red-tailed Hawk breeding activity peaks in late April through early May—observers located the latest nest with young on 28 July. Red-tailed Hawks begin migrating south in September and continue through October or later.

As elsewhere, Red-tailed Hawks in Arizona will nest in a wide variety of substrates including trees, saguaros, cliffs, and many artificial structures. Regardless of the specific substrate, sites usually provide a commanding view of the surrounding area. Atlasers acquired measurements from 63 Red-tailed Hawk nests, in no less than 14 substrates. Most nests (28) were in saguaros, 13 were on cliffs, and 9 were in juniper. The remaining nests were in pinyon pine, ponderosa pine, cottonwood, oak, paloverde, tamarisk, and several other tree species. Additionally, two nests were located in transmission towers. The lowest nest recorded was only 8.9 ft (2.7 m) above the ground.

Red-tailed Hawk pairs have a high degree of site fidelity and will return to nests used in the past, sometimes refurbishing more than one of these before making a final selection (Bent 1937). The pair constructs or repairs the nest together, but the female spends more time than the male lining the nest (Preston and Beane 1993). Red-tailed Hawks

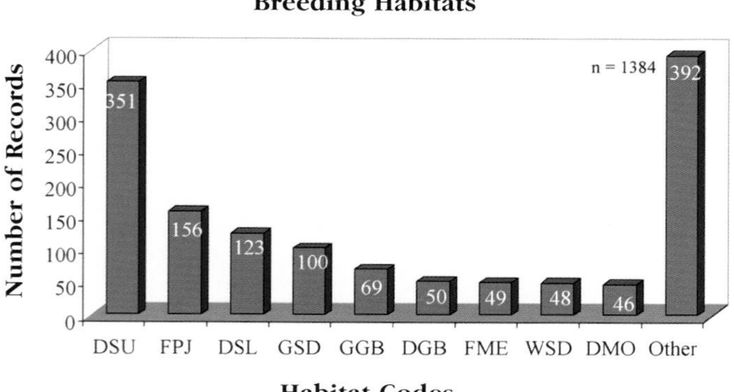

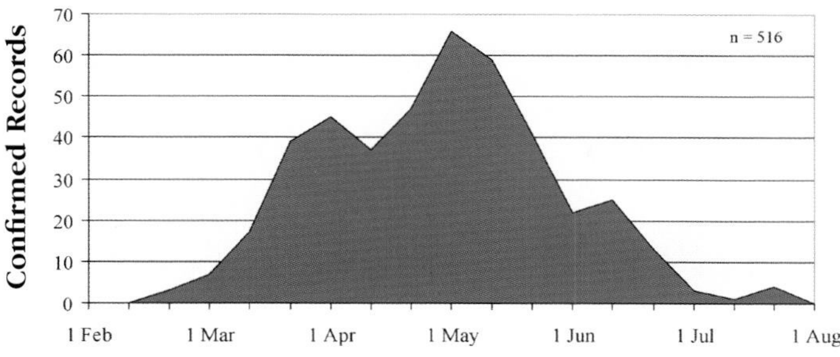

usually lay 2–3 eggs (range 1–5) that are incubated by both parents, but primarily by the female for approximately 28–31 days (Bent 1937; Hardy 1939). The male brings food to the female and newly hatched young, but the female will also hunt (Bent 1937; Austing 1964; Wiley 1975). The female broods the young until the oldest nestling reaches 30–35 days old and the young typically leave the nest by 46 days (Preston and Beane 1993). Juveniles begin capturing small prey 6–7 weeks after fledging, but continue receiving food from parents for at least another week (Johnson 1986).

DISTRIBUTION AND STATUS

Red-tailed Hawks are probably the most widespread and commonly observed bird of prey in the West. These familiar raptors breed from Alaska and Canada south throughout the United States, West Indies, much of Mexico, and locally to Panama.

Red-tailed Hawks have always been considered common and widespread in Arizona (Swarth 1914; Phillips et al. 1964), and were the most commonly reported raptor during the atlas period. Observers located this species in suitable breeding habitat on 73 percent of all blocks visited and confirmed breeding at elevations ranging from 170 to 9200 ft (30–2804 m). Red-tailed Hawks undoubtedly nest sparingly throughout the White Mountain Apache tribal lands but atlasers were unable to verify this, as the tribe did not permit surveys. As a result, the boundary of these tribal lands is clearly delineated on the accompanying distribution map as the bird occurs in all the surrounding areas. Red-tailed Hawks were predictably sparse or absent from some of the most desolate patches of lowland deserts in the lower Gila River and Yuma vicinity, perhaps due to a paucity of prey or nesting sites. On the Colorado Plateau, atlasers also encountered these raptors much less frequently than expected throughout much of Navajo and Hopi tribal lands and adjacent Little Colorado River drainage. This may be related to lower hawk densities in this region of the state where they are much more easily missed while conducting the 1- or 2-day atlas surveys.

Due to their adaptable nature, Red-tailed Hawks escape many of the deleterious circumstances that have led to the decline of more specialized species. They are tolerant of human disturbance and land alterations and are considered by some to be more numerous now than in recent years (Monson 1998).

Red-tailed Hawk Breeding Evidence Reported in 1335 (73%) of 1834 priority blocks

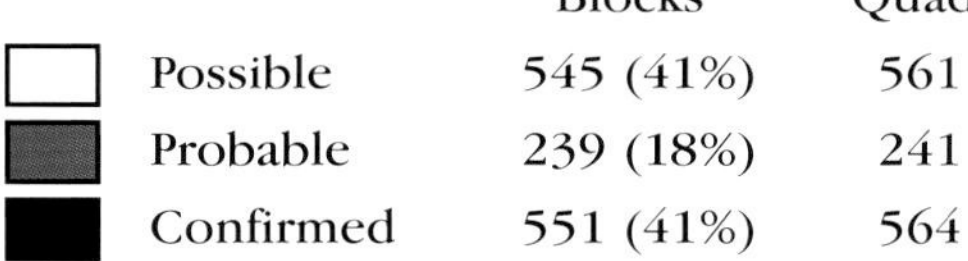

	Blocks	Quads
Possible	545 (41%)	561
Probable	239 (18%)	241
Confirmed	551 (41%)	564

Ferruginous Hawk

by Troy E. Corman *Buteo regalis*

Truly handsome raptors of open, expansive country, Ferruginous Hawks are at home on grasslands and sparse sagebrush deserts. Never considered common as a nesting species in Arizona, these large, pale hawks typically choose more remote and undisturbed locations in which to nest.

GREG CLARK

HABITAT

During the nesting season in Arizona, Ferruginous Hawks prefer open, flat to gently rolling landscapes and are typically found in various grassland associations. Atlasers noted 66 percent of all observations in cold-temperate grasslands containing various grasses and a mixture of low woody shrubs such as snakeweed and big sagebrush (n = 32). Most occupied habitats include nearby slopes or knolls of widely scattered junipers. Another 25 percent of Ferruginous Hawk observation came from plains grasslands that generally contain fewer woody shrubs and trees. Sagebrush-shrouded deserts and open pinyon pine–juniper woodlands accounted for the remaining observations. Although frequently noted foraging over agricultural lands during the winter, these large raptors were not observed using this habitat during the birds' nesting season.

BREEDING

Ferruginous Hawks are fairly common winter residents throughout much of Arizona, with spring migration starting in mid-February. In Utah, pair formation occurs from late February to early March (Smith and Murphy 1973). Some of Arizona's nesting pairs, though, may remain mated throughout the year and move to their breeding areas by March. Atlasers did not observe courtship behavior and nest building and refurbishing activity, but this likely takes place in March, prior to when most atlas surveys were conducted in northern Arizona. The earliest confirmed record by atlasers was of a nest with young found on 14 May. This suggests that egg laying is no later than mid-April. Nests with eggs have been found as early as mid-March in Utah (Smith and Murphy 1973) and 15 April in Arizona (Jacot 1934). Atlasers found a nest with one egg and a newly hatched chick as late as 31 May, and if successful, this brood would have likely fledged sometime in mid-July. Atlasers discovered most of the nests with young in June, with the latest noted on 29 June. Fledglings were reported through late July. Ferruginous Hawks begin to return to southern Arizona by late September or early October.

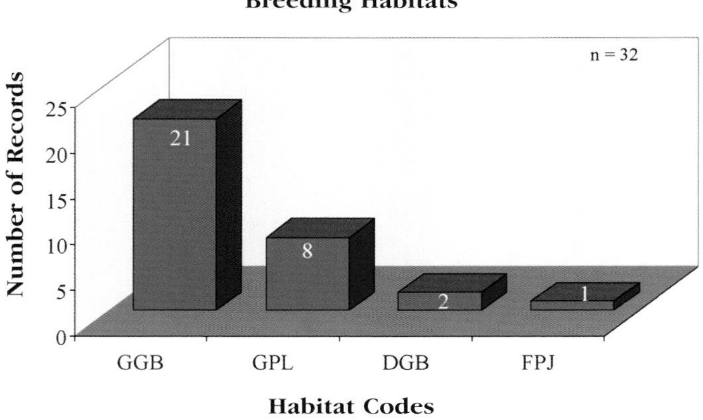

Throughout their range, Ferruginous Hawk pairs construct their nests on a variety of substrates. In Arizona, nests have primarily been discovered in isolated junipers with a commanding view of their territory. The few remaining active nests on Navajo tribal lands in Arizona are found on cliffs and difficult to access rocky outcrops (D. Mikesic, personal communication). Of the nine nests measured by atlasers, all were centered at or near the top of either Utah or one-seeded junipers that provided no protection from the elements. The median height of these nests was 14.1 ft (4.3 m) with a range of 8.2–26.2 ft (2.5–8.0 m). Nests are frequently reused for many years with additional material added each year. Older Ferruginous Hawk nests can become quite large structures, and one active nest measured by atlasers in a juniper snag had an impressive outside height of 6.9 ft (2.1 m).

Most Ferruginous Hawk clutches consist of 2–4 eggs, but this can range from 1 to 6 depending on prey abundance (Smith and Murphy 1978; Smith et al. 1981). Both members of a pair help incubate the eggs for approximately 32–33 days. Yet females perform more incubation duties while males provide most of the food (Bechard and Schmutz 1995). The male continues to deliver most of the food to the nestlings, but the female actually feeds the young until they fledge in 38–50 days (Bechard and Schmutz 1995). Fledglings remain dependent on the parents for several weeks following nest departure (Blair and Schitoskey 1982).

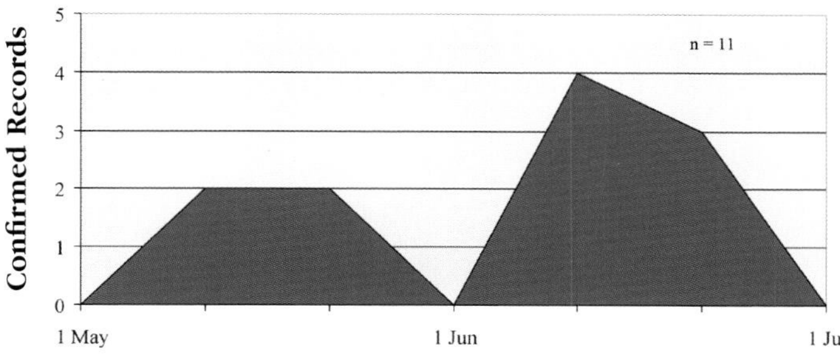

DISTRIBUTION AND STATUS

Ferruginous Hawks nest in western North America from south-central Canada, south through the Great Basin and western Great Plains states to northern Arizona and New Mexico. The first documented Arizona nest of this regal raptor was found in 1926 in the Williamson Valley, approximately 25 mi (40.2 km) northwest of Prescott (Jacot 1934). Phillips et al. (1964) described the Ferruginous Hawk as an uncommon but a widely distributed summer resident of grassy plains of northern Arizona. Irregular and local summer records of this raptor in the grasslands of southeastern Arizona prior to 1950, also suggested that they nested there in limited numbers. By 1980, this hawk was considered an uncommon to sparse nesting species in northern Arizona, and no longer nesting near Prescott or in southeastern Arizona (Monson and Phillips 1981).

Atlasers found nesting Ferruginous Hawks occupying a fairly narrow range of elevations, from 4700 to 6400 ft (1433–1951 m). The center of Arizona's nesting population was found to be in and around the Coconino Plateau from Seligman north. Atlasers also discovered a fair concentration of these raptors in the Arizona Strip region of northwestern Arizona, west of Kanab Creek toward Colorado City. Atlasers did not find any evidence of nesting Ferruginous Hawks in the Hualapai Valley, north of Kingman, where a lone pair nested prior to the atlas (R. Hall, personal communication). However, an individual was observed nearby in appropriate nesting habitat on Hualapai tribal land northwest of Peach Springs.

East of Williams, Ferruginous Hawk populations appear to be much more local and widespread, with the only group of records occurring just south and west of Winslow. Only a handful of these hawks continue to nest on Navajo tribal lands within Chinle Valley and near Hopi Buttes (D. Mikesic, personal communication). The most southeastern atlas record was of an individual southwest of Lyman Lake in southern Apache County.

Prairie dogs were likely important in determining the historical breeding distribution of the Ferruginous Hawk in Arizona (Glinski 1998). Coupled with loss of habitat, the widespread extirpations of these rodents has greatly reduced the hawk's nesting distribution. Ferruginous Hawks are also sensitive to human activity around their nests. Many researchers have found that nesting success for these impressive raptors depends heavily on the degree of remoteness of nesting sites from developed areas (Snyder and Snyder 1991).

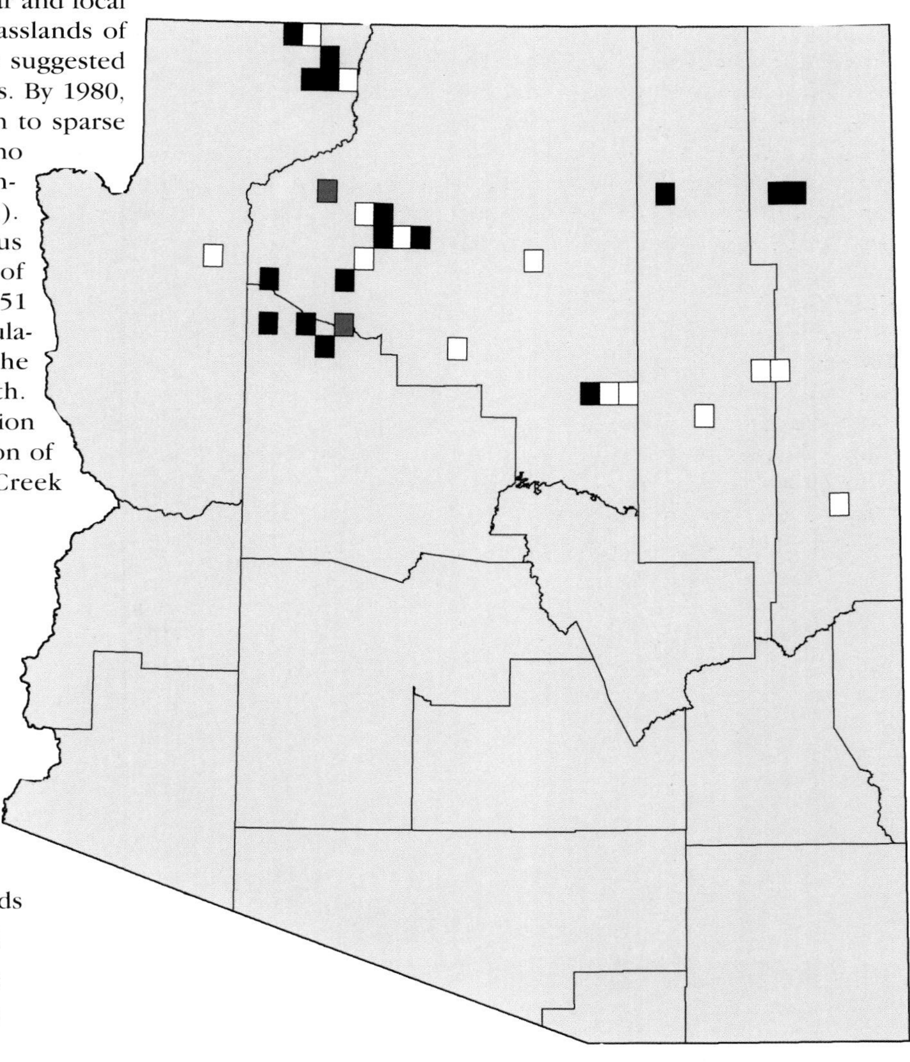

Ferruginous Hawk Breeding Evidence Reported in 22 (1%) of 1834 priority blocks

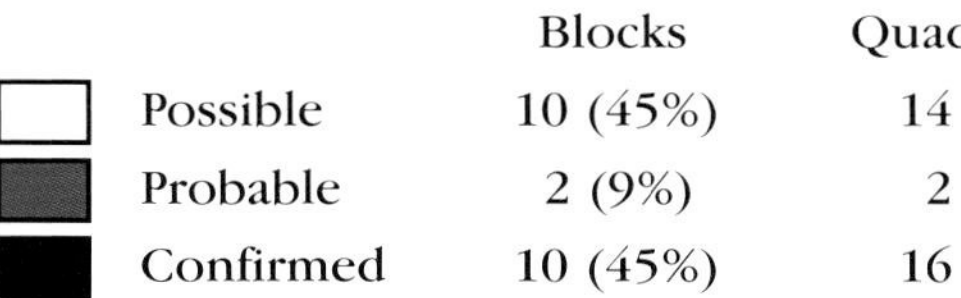

	Blocks	Quads
Possible	10 (45%)	14
Probable	2 (9%)	2
Confirmed	10 (45%)	16

Golden Eagle

by James T. Driscoll *Aquila chrysaetos*

The largest of Arizona's avian predators, Golden Eagles are named for the rich hues of their nape and crown. Ambassadors of wilderness and remote, rugged regions, these impressive raptors remain sparse or absent where human disturbance is frequent. Golden Eagles are well known for subduing large prey; however, most of their diet consists of ground squirrels, rabbits, and prairie dogs.

DAN FISCHER

HABITAT

Less restrictive than their white-headed counterpart, Golden Eagles are found nesting in a wide variety of Arizona habitats from arid desert scrub to open conifer forests. No matter what habitat they choose in the state, topography features include tall cliffs or canyons in which to construct a nest and nearby large open areas to forage for prey. As this species is cautious of humans, the level of human activity in conjunction with areas of high rabbit populations are likely the determining factors in nest placement.

Atlas surveys revealed 21 percent of the reported Golden Eagles were in pinyon pine–juniper woodlands and an additional 15 percent were noted in Sonoran desertscrub landscapes (*n* = 212). Other habitats frequently occupied by Golden Eagles during the atlas included Madrean evergreen oak woodlands, semiarid grasslands, chaparral, and landscapes dominated by big sagebrush. Golden Eagles are generalists, however, and are documented nesting in most open habitats across the state.

BREEDING

Most Golden Eagles nesting in Arizona are primarily residents, remaining within or near their home range throughout the year. Home range size for these eagles can be quite extensive and depends on the amount of available food and foraging areas near the nest. However, in certain areas where large prey populations exist, home ranges of adjacent Golden Eagle pairs may overlap and breeding densities may be higher.

The nesting season of Golden Eagles is prolonged, extending more than 6 months from the time eggs are laid until young reach independence (Kochert et al. 2002). In Arizona, Golden Eagles perform impressive aerial courtship displays near their nests in January and February, but courtship displays can be observed in almost any month (Brown and Amadon 1968). Egg laying in the state can begin as early as February in the lower elevations and as late as April in higher country. Atlasers first noted occupied nests by mid-March and a nest contained eggs by 30 March. However, a nest containing young on 7 April would indicate that the eggs were laid by late February. The earliest fledgling reported during the atlas was on 14 May and the latest nest with young was reported on 12 June. Glinski (1998) noted that May and June are the main months for young Golden Eagles in Arizona to first take wing. Some eaglets at higher elevations are occasionally observed in the nest through late July, however.

In Arizona, cliff ledges are the most common nesting substrate used by Golden Eagles, but they will also use tall trees (esp. ponderosa pine), junipers, rock outcrops, and in rare cases, transmission towers (Glinski et al. 1998). Nests are typically huge structures composed mainly of large and small branches. Since Golden Eagles will reuse and build upon the same nest structure annually, their nests can become large. Adults will often build on two or three nest structures within their territory before choosing the one in which to lay their eggs. This behavior can lead to cliff nests that are over 12 ft (3.7 m) wide and 5 ft (1.5 m) high, with a weight that prohibits this from occurring in tree nests.

Golden Eagles normally lay only 2 eggs, but this can range from 1 to 3 (DeGroot 1928). Incubation lasts 41–45 days, with the female assuming most of the duties (Kochert

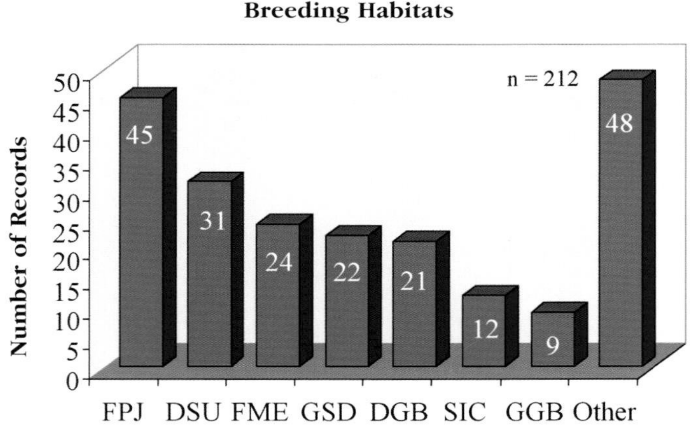

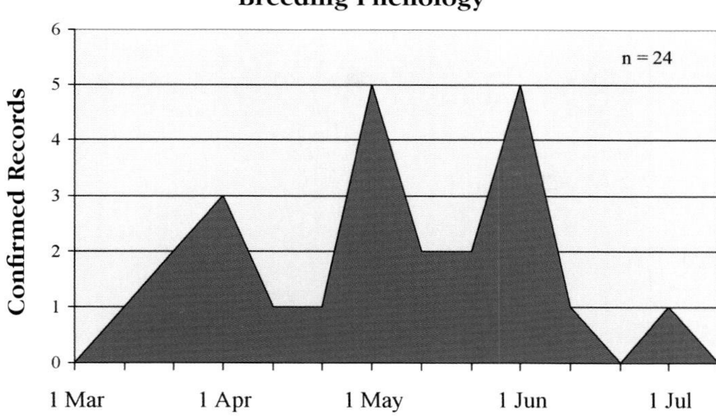

et al. 2002). The male will supply the female with food, or will take over incubation while the female forages. Normal nest productivity averages 0.78 young fledged per occupied nest (Hunt et al. 1995). Nestlings fledge at 65–70 days, and typically spend the next three months in the natal area before dispersing (Brown and Amadon 1968).

Golden eagles pairs commonly refrain from laying eggs in some years, particularly when prey, especially rabbits, are scarce. Therefore, the number of young that Golden Eagles produce each year largely depends on a combination of weather and prey population cycles (Kochert et al. 2002).

DISTRIBUTION AND STATUS

Golden Eagles occur throughout the entire northern hemisphere, including northern Africa. In North America, these raptors primarily breed in the West from Alaska and Canada south to central Mexico. However, remnant populations still exist in northeastern Canada and very locally in the southern Appalachian Mountains (Kochert et al. 2002).

In Arizona, Swarth (1914) described Golden Eagles as fairly common residents of the higher mountain ranges in the north, as well as the eastern half of the state. Later, Phillips et al. (1964) noted these eagles as sparingly distributed through the state in all mountainous regions. Phillips et al. further stated that these eagles are probably as common in Arizona as in any part of the world, and they even inhabit the extremely arid mountains in the southwest corner of the state.

Atlasers noted Golden Eagles throughout their previously described range from approximately 1300 to 9000 ft (396–2743 m). These impressive raptors were fairly regularly encountered in the mountains and plateaus of northern, central, and southeastern Arizona, but were notably sparse or lacking in heavily forested regions of the state. Golden Eagles were detected much less frequently within the lower Colorado River valley and the lower Gila River drainage where they nest sparingly only in the higher desert mountain ranges.

Arizona has many remote and rugged regions favored by Golden Eagles, but access to conduct atlas surveys in these regions was often very limited. This may help explain the surprising few atlas records of these eagles within the Grand Canyon where inaccessible nesting cliffs are in abundance. The secretive nature of these large raptors likely limits their detection. There are undoubtedly many more breeding areas in Arizona than atlas data revealed. There appears to be no outstanding threats to Golden Eagles in Arizona; however, urban encroachment and increased recreational activity may soon begin affecting some local breeding areas. A long-term population monitoring study is needed to determine population numbers and trends.

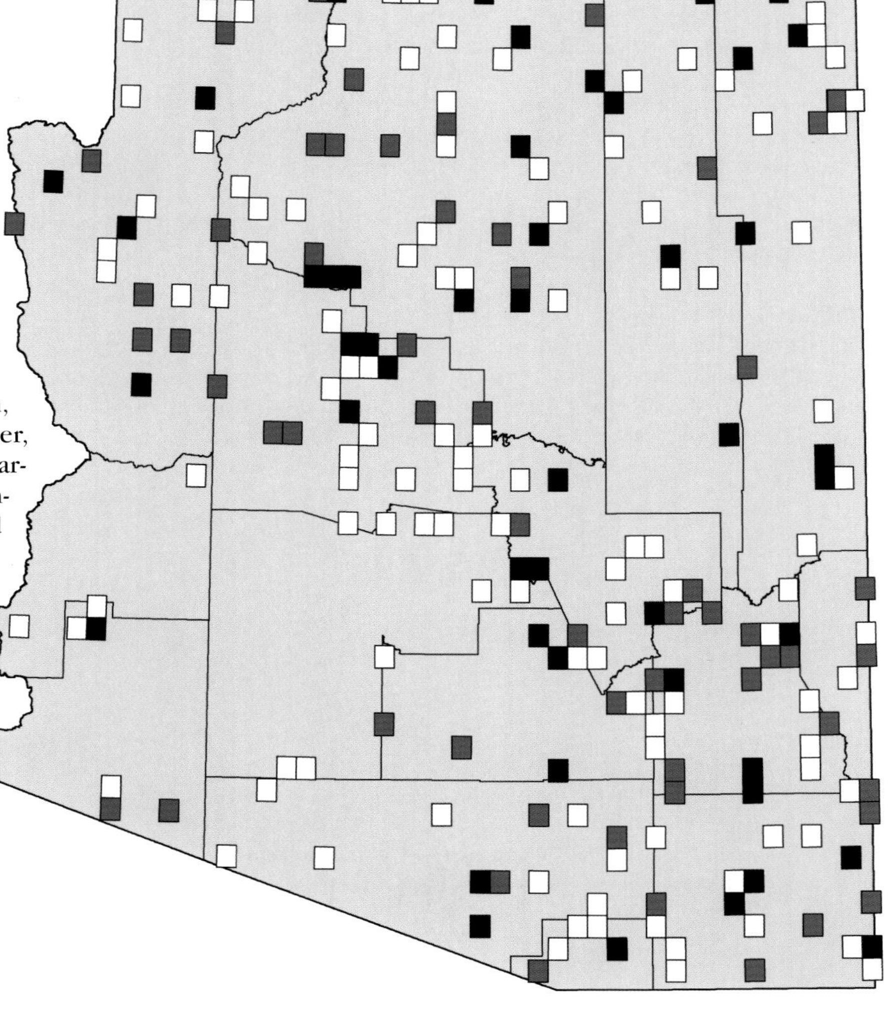

Golden Eagle Breeding Evidence Reported in 187 (10%) of 1834 priority blocks

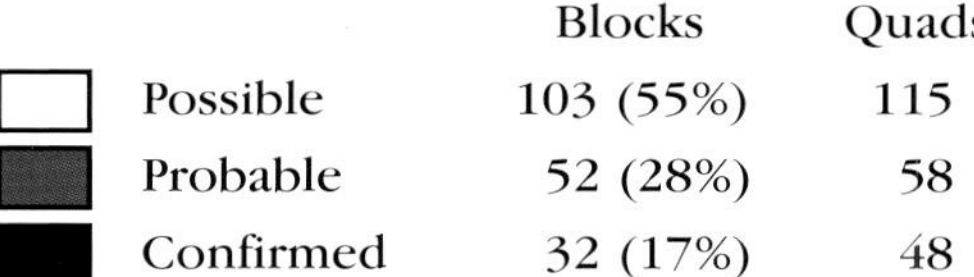

	Blocks	Quads
Possible	103 (55%)	115
Probable	52 (28%)	58
Confirmed	32 (17%)	48

Crested Caracara

by Troy E. Corman *Caracara cheriway*

Distributed locally and seldom observed in Arizona, Crested Caracaras are unique among the other raptors within the state. Spending much of their time on or near the ground, these handsome, long-legged birds often locate their carrion prey by watching where vultures concentrate. They also capture live prey, and the remains at some Arizona nests reveal that horned lizards are a frequent meal.

DAN FISCHER

HABITAT

Crested Caracaras occur in a wide range of habitats and elevations across their extensive range. But they are restricted primarily to flat or gently rolling Sonoran Desert habitats in Arizona. Atlasers reported nearly 86 percent of all atlas observations of this raptor in well vegetated, Sonoran desertscrub dominated landscapes with an abundance of large saguaros, ironwood, paloverde, and velvet mesquite ($n = 29$). The few other atlas reports were from observations of caracaras on telephone poles and saguaros in nearby small, rural Native American communities and near the denser vegetation along washes and isolated earthen stock tanks. Levy (1998) suggested that perhaps the caracaras are attracted to these locations by the numerous dead livestock often found around the only water source available for miles. In Arizona, it seems that caracaras are always found in reasonably close proximity to water (Levy 1988).

BREEDING

In Arizona, Crested Caracaras are primarily resident; however individuals, especially juveniles, are found irregularly wandering north and east of their nesting range within the state. Morrison (1996) concluded that the adults are extremely site faithful, remaining on territory year-round.

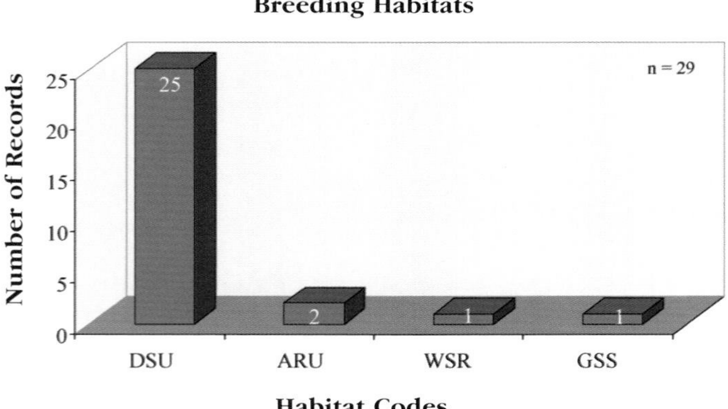

Limited nesting information was collected during the atlas project, and much of what we know about the phenology and breeding behavior of the Crested Caracara in Arizona comes from studies conducted by Levy (1988). Adult pairs remain together throughout the year within their breeding territory. Nest building or nest repair activity often begins in mid-March. In Arizona, nests with eggs have been found from late March to late June, with a peak in April and May. The only nest with eggs discovered by atlasers was on 17 May. Nests with young are noted from late April through early August.

The heights of Crested Caracara nests were not measured by atlasers, but Levy (1988) noted that nests in Arizona are almost invariably in the lower swirl of arms of a saguaro, typically 8–14 ft (2.4–4.3 m) in height, rarely as high as 18.5 ft (5.6 m). The nest is frequently well hidden and below the highest level of the canopy of the surrounding trees. Nests are often used is successive years and frequently become quite large as new material is added each season (Bent 1937). Levy (1988) also found that most active nests were 5–10 mi (8–16 km) apart; however, two pairs successfully fledged young from a nest less than a mile apart.

The typical Crested Caracara clutch consists of 2 eggs, but occasionally only 1 and rarely 3 eggs are laid (Levy 1988). Both parents share the duty of incubation, which lasts from 30 to 33 days (Dickinson 1996). The young begin standing on adjacent branches and nest supports approximately 1 week prior to fledging (Dickinson 1996). Levy (1988) noted that young Crested Caracaras in Arizona typically fledge when they are 5–6 weeks old, while Dickinson (1996) reported nest departure of young in Texas did not happen until they were 7–8 weeks old. Both parents feed the young for at least two months after fledging and most permanent departure from the natal territory occurs at 4–6 months of age (Morrison 1996). Only one brood is produced per year in Arizona, but two broods have been documented in Florida and suspected elsewhere (Morrison 1996). Crested Caracaras will renest if earlier attempts have failed and in Florida, the time between failure and the second clutch is estimated at 4–6 weeks (Morrison 1996).

DISTRIBUTION AND STATUS

Crested Caracaras are primarily a resident raptor from southern Florida, southeastern Texas, and south-central Arizona, south to northern South America. Based on historical records, the early status and breeding distribution of caracaras in Arizona is largely unknown. Phillips et al. (1964) considered the Crested Caracara as resident in small numbers on Tohono O'odham (formally Papago) tribal lands, and Monson (1981) noted that Crested Caracaras were considerably more common in southern Arizona prior to 1920. However, based on a compilation of all records, Levy (1998) concluded that caracaras were never more numerous than they are now. This is especially true of nesting populations. Only two nests have ever been found outside of the Tohono O'odham tribal lands. One nest was discovered near Three Points (Robles Junction) in 1964 and the other along Olsen Wash north of Oracle Junction in 1988 (Levy 1988). The latter nest, may have been active since at least 1986 and an adult had been observed in this area since 1980. Crested Caracaras were formally once thought to be resident and nesting at Tucson. The only evidence of this were several May and June records and eggs collected by H. Brown near Tucson in 1889. Yet a reexamination of these eggs revealed that they were not eggs of the Crested Caracara (Levy 1988).

Levy (1998) suggested that Crested Caracara may have expanded their breeding range north from Sonora recently into the Tohono O'odham tribal lands. The introduction of cattle to this typically poor grazing range gave caracaras a fairly stable food source in the form of dead livestock from starvation and thirst. Extensive surveys conducted by Levy (1988) found that breeding caracaras appear to be restricted to the south central part of the Tohono O'odham tribal lands. He estimated that the entire population consisted of 20–25 breeding pairs.

During the nesting season, atlasers found Crested Caracaras within the Tohono O'odham tribal lands at elevations from 1600 to 3000 ft (488–914 m). Atlasers encountered this raptor from the vicinity of Menagers Lake, east to San Miguel and then north to Quijotoa (Covered Wells) and Sells. Atlasers also found caracaras further north and northwest on tribal lands than noted by Levy (1988). The most western observation was in the upper Aguirre Valley north of Schuchk and the more northern records came from near Ventana, Gu Achi (Santa Rosa), North Komelik, and east of the Santa Rosa Mountains.

Unlike many other raptors, the Sonoran Desert nesting Crested Caracara is a difficult species to detect. They are mostly silent, infrequently soar as do vultures and hawks, and spend much of their time on or near the ground (Levy 1988). Coupled with their relatively low densities in Arizona, these unique raptors are fairly easy to miss during typical atlas surveys.

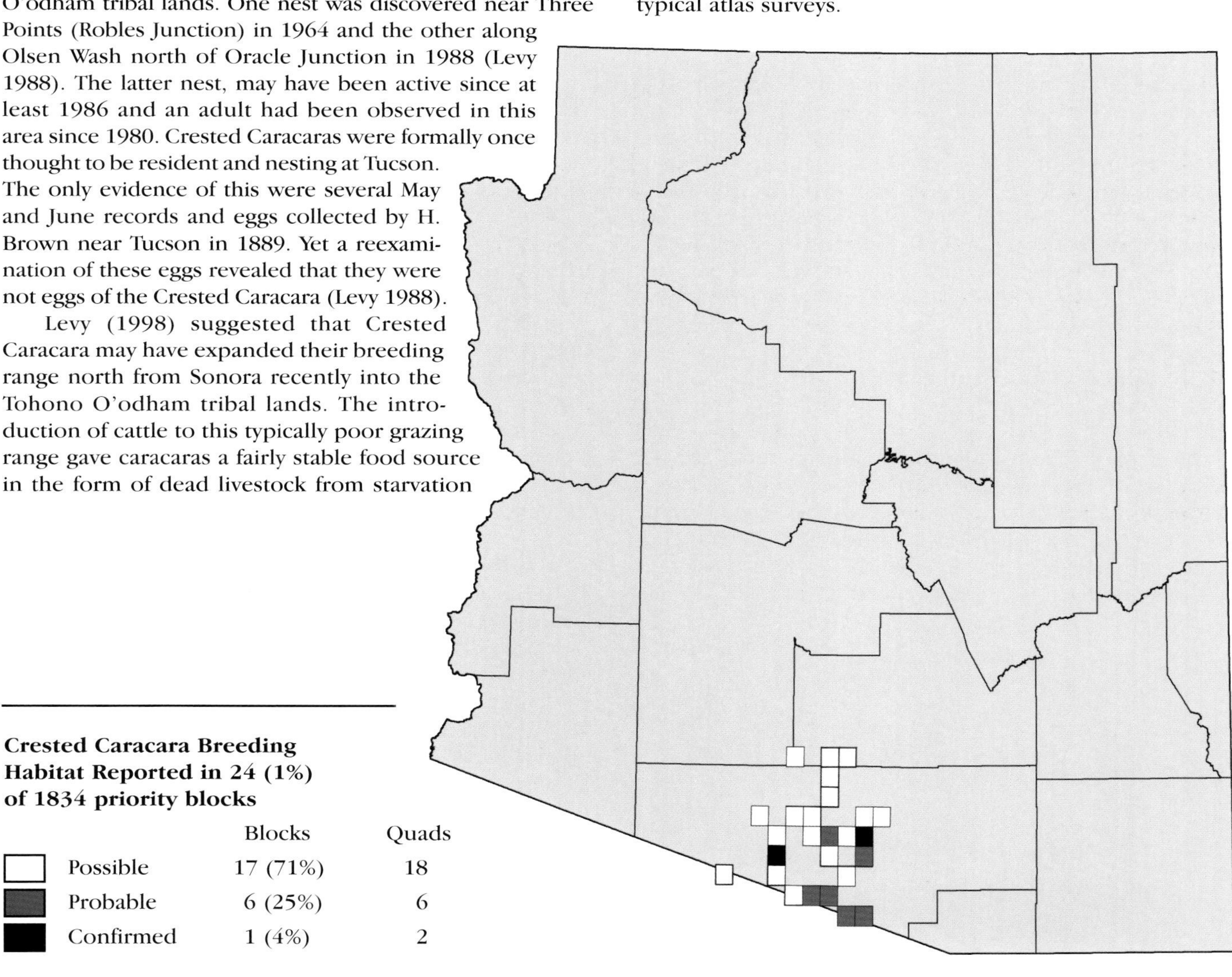

Crested Caracara Breeding Habitat Reported in 24 (1%) of 1834 priority blocks

	Blocks	Quads
Possible	17 (71%)	18
Probable	6 (25%)	6
Confirmed	1 (4%)	2

American Kestrel

by Cathryn Wise-Gervais *Falco sparverius*

Tiny and fierce, American Kestrels are the smallest and most numerous falcon in North America. Colorful and buoyant on the wing, this species often hovers in place while watching for prey activity below and are more likely to hunt in this fashion in areas lacking perches such as trees, utility lines, or fences.

DAN FISCHER

HABITAT

Although American Kestrels are encountered over a wide range of habitats, these birds distinctly favor open settings with scattered trees or other structures for perching and nesting. Such areas include deserts, grasslands, agricultural areas, and suburban parks, as well as riparian and forest edges. Atlasers reported American Kestrels in 34 habitat types, illustrating this species' adaptive nature. Thirty-two percent of the potential breeding records for this species were in Sonoran desertscrub, typically characterized by large saguaros and scattered legume trees and shrubs (*n* = 1077). Eleven percent of records were reported in open pinyon pine–juniper woodlands, and the remaining records were in diverse habitat types including semiarid grasslands, subalpine meadows, open coniferous forests, aspen stand edges, riparian woodlands, and residential areas. In addition, Arizona's American Kestrels regularly occur in landscapes that lack large trees or cacti for nesting. Under these circumstances, atlasers reported the birds nesting in holes in steep cut banks along washes and roads, or in cliff faces and canyon walls.

BREEDING

American Kestrels are found year round in most of Arizona, but migrants from the north augment winter populations in the southern and western regions of the state. Migrants move north primarily from late February through April. In nonmigratory or partially migratory populations, pairs sometimes remain associated during the winter (Smallwood and Bird 2002) and desert nesting pairs can initiate breeding as early as late winter. Observers reported the earliest occupied nests on 21 March and discovered a nest containing young on 26 March. This record indicates that egg laying occurred by mid- to late February. The earliest fledglings were noted on 3 May. At higher elevations, nesting begins by late March or April and atlasers reported American Kestrel nests with eggs as late as 2 June. Observers also reported nests with young through 19 July, and occupied nests through 24 July. Atlas data suggest a gradual increase in breeding activity from late March to the peak breeding time of late June. Activity then dropped precipitously. Atlasers reported the latest record of adults feeding young on 11 August, and they observed fledglings as late as 16 August. In Arizona, American Kestrels' migration typically begins in August and continues through October (Phillips et al. 1964).

American Kestrels are cavity nesters that will take up residence in a wide array of substrates. In Arizona, most nests are found in natural holes and in old woodpecker cavities in trees and saguaros, but these small falcons also commonly nest in cutbank burrows or in shallow cavities on cliffs, often at considerable heights. In some urban and rural areas, American Kestrels nest on shelves under the dried fronds of untrimmed palm trees, in nest boxes, and occasionally in small covered pockets in buildings. Atlasers measured 19 American Kestrel nest cavities in five substrates: cliffs and cutbanks (11), ponderosa pine snags (3), cottonwoods (2), junipers (2), and saguaro (1). The median nest substrate height was 30.1 ft (9.2 m) and the median nest height was 19.7 ft (6 m).

American Kestrels do not add nesting materials to their nest cavity but instead lay their 4–5 eggs directly on the cavity floor (Smallwood and Bird 2002). The female incubates for approximately 30 days (range 26–32) with some to little assistance from the male (Bird and Palmer 1988). The female

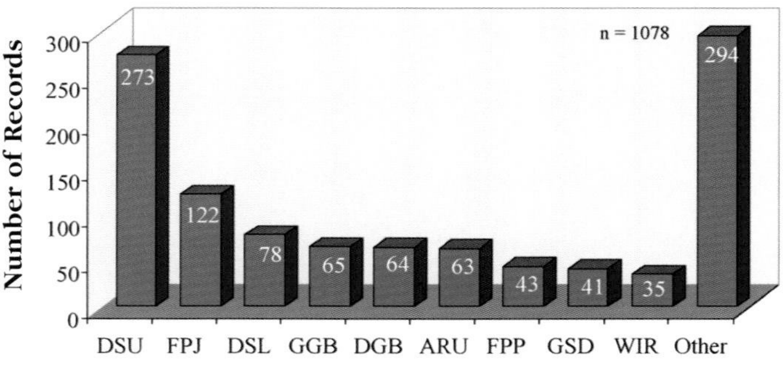

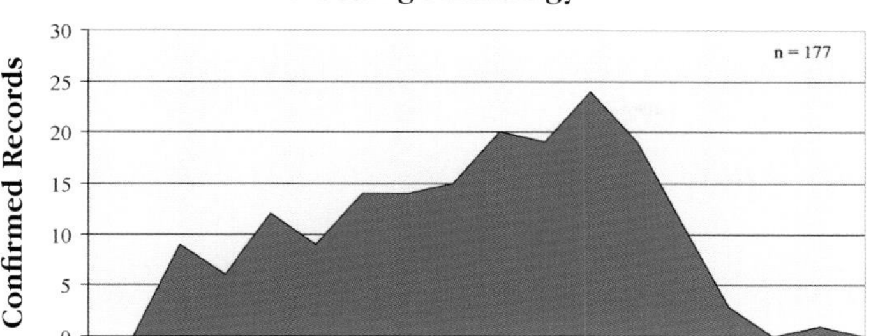

also broods the young exclusively for the first 7–10 days after hatching, while the male provides all the food for his mate and nestlings (Smallwood and Bird 2002). After this time, the female will assist with hunting duties. The young typically fledge by 28–31 days of age but continue receiving food from parents for at least 12 days after nest departure (Bird and Palmer 1988). Adults usually rear one brood per year but two broods are not uncommon, particularly in the southern portions of the birds' range.

DISTRIBUTION AND STATUS

American Kestrels are one of the most widespread nesting raptors in the Western Hemisphere. Their breeding range includes much of North America from Alaska and Canada south through Central and South America. But the range of these raptors is not continuous; 17 subspecies have been recognized (Smallwood and Bird 2002).

In Arizona, prior accounts described American Kestrels as nesting commonly throughout the state (Swarth 1914). Later observers, however, did note that these raptors were notably uncommon to rare as a breeding species in the lowland deserts of extreme western Arizona (Phillips et al. 1964; Rosenberg et al. 1991).

Atlasers had similar findings, as American Kestrels were regularly encountered in suitable breeding habitat nearly statewide at elevations ranging from approximately 100 to 9500 ft (30–2896 m). As noted by others, these raptors were more sparsely distributed in the driest deserts of western Arizona, as well as in the semiarid grasslands of the southeast. In northern Arizona, American Kestrels were encountered infrequently during atlas surveys within the immediate Grand Canyon region, where Brown et al. (1987) reported them as fairly common. Atlasers also found that these little falcons were sparingly distributed in the flat and treeless Little Colorado River drainage. Based on the regularity of detections in surrounding areas, American Kestrels undoubtedly also breed throughout the more open and less forested regions of unsurveyed White Mountain Apache tribal lands.

Population trends of American Kestrels in Arizona are largely unknown, but the frequency with which observers reported this species within their prior known range indicates that these adaptable raptors are fairly stable in the state. As one might expect, activities such as timber harvesting and clearing land for agriculture have increased available American Kestrel habitat in Arizona, and balance habitat loss due to urbanization, wild fires, and increasing incidents of vehicle collisions (Mills 1998).

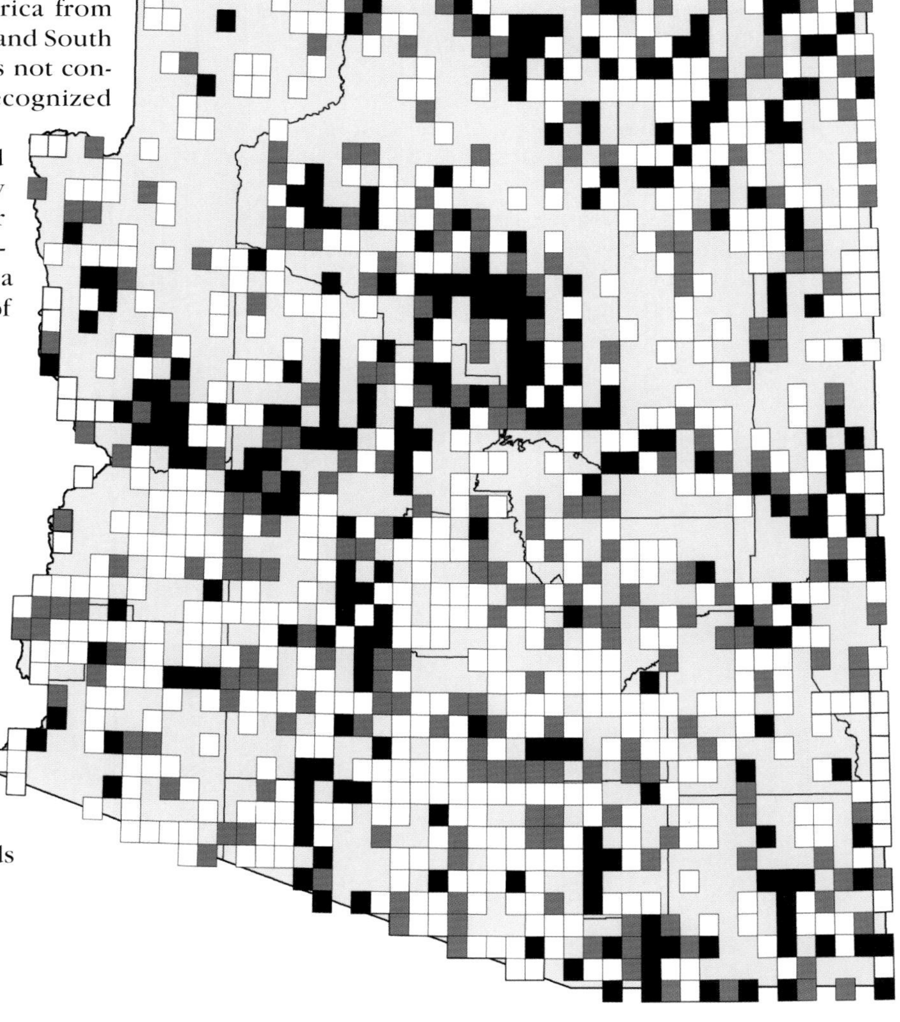

American Kestrel Breeding Evidence Reported in 1067 (58%) of 1834 priority blocks

	Blocks	Quads
Possible	572 (54%)	579
Probable	244 (23%)	248
Confirmed	251 (24%)	259

Peregrine Falcon

by Bill Burger *Falco peregrinus*

Occurring nearly worldwide, Peregrine Flacons are well-known for their great speed and agility in capturing prey on the wing. Population declines during the mid-1900s from the effects of pesticides have now been reversed and these impressive raptors are frequently observed patrolling the skies surrounding the numerous cliffs and canyons in Arizona.

JIM BURNS

HABITAT

Habitat vegetation is not as important as is topographic relief and prey base abundance in determining occupancy of an area by nesting Peregrine Falcons. Arizona's countless cliffs, canyon walls, and towering rock spires afford these falcons nesting sites and awe-inspiring vantage points to watch for prey. Atlasers reported Peregrine Falcons in 22 different habitat types primarily encompassing various forests, deserts, and wetlands. Nearly 48 percent of all atlas records were reported from forested regions from pinyon pine–juniper and evergreen oaks to ponderosa pine and mixed conifer (n =144). Peregrines are adapted for hunting in open areas, so within woodlands or forests the habitat actually used is the open sky above the treetops. Another 33 percent of the records were primarily from cold-temperate desertscrub containing sagebrush and other low shrubs, as well as Sonoran desertscrub near water. Many of Arizona's breeding sites are near rivers or other water sources, corresponding to a higher prey base in such areas. Unlike Prairie Falcons, few Peregrines nest in Sonoran and Mojave desert mountain ranges away from large water features.

BREEDING

Some of Arizona's Peregrine Falcons remain near nesting cliffs year round, while others move to lowlands or migrate south to spend the winter. Glinski (1998) noted that these falcons return to their breeding cliffs in Arizona from mid-February to mid-March. Atlasers reported courtship displays and pair formation beginning in early March. The earliest Peregrine Falcon nest with eggs reported by atlasers was on 15 April, but occupied nests were noted as early as 13 March in lowland deserts suggesting earlier egg laying. In Arizona, eggs are typically laid from mid-March to mid-May (Glinski 1998). Atlasers reported nestlings from 1 May to 8 July, with fledglings through 16 August. Some Peregrine Falcons in Arizona begin to appear in lowlands by late July or August. However, peak migration through Arizona, likely from more northern populations, is from early September through October.

In Arizona, all known Peregrine Falcon eyries have been on cliff faces, canyon walls, spires, and occasionally on steep rocky ridges or mountain outcrops. Males often explore many ledges, pockets, crevices, or small caves and usually make several shallow scrapes or bowls prior to the female making the final selection (Ponton 1983). Glinski (1998) reports on one Peregrine Falcon pair in Arizona that nested in an abandoned Golden Eagle nest placed on a ledge. Nest sites are often used year-after-year, or alternate sites within a breeding area may be used in intermittent years. Within the Grand Canyon were Peregrine Falcons reach their highest nesting density, Brown (1991) found the average distance between eyries was 4.2 mi (6.8 km), with a minimum distance of 1.8 mi (2.9 km).

Female Peregrine Falcons often become lethargic approximately 5 days before egg-laying (White et al. 2002). These falcons lay a typical clutch consisting of 3–4 eggs (range 2–6). The female does most of the incubation but the male may incubate up to one-third of the daylight hours (Enderson et al. 1973). Incubation is about 33–35 days, occasionally longer if there are lengthy or frequent periods of interrupted incubation (White et al. 2002). Most nestlings fledge within 35–42 days (Newton 1979; Glinski 1998), but remain dependent on the parents for more than 5 weeks following nest departure (White et al. 2002). There is usually only one clutch, although a replacement clutch is often laid within 14 days if the first is lost (Newton 1979; White et al. 2002).

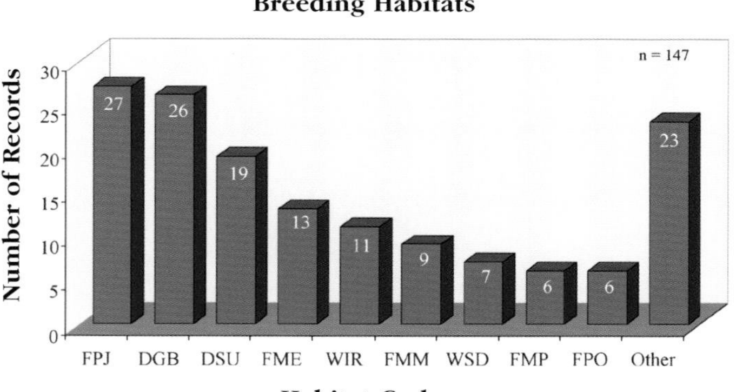

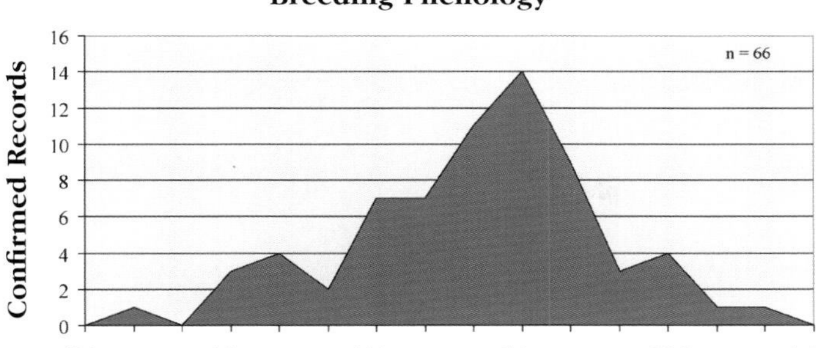

DISTRIBUTION AND STATUS

The breeding range of Peregrine Falcons is nearly worldwide in disjunct populations consisting of at least 18 subspecies. In North America, these falcons breed from Alaska and Canada south to western Mexico, including Baja California.

Likely due to their preference for remote and often inaccessible locations, the historical abundance and distribution of Peregrine Falcons in Arizona were never really known. Merriam (1890) considered these falcons as apparently common in the mountains of central Arizona. Phillips et al. (1964) later noted Peregrine Falcons as a rare nesting raptor at cliffs throughout the state, but also suggested they were increasing as a nesting species by 1939. It is largely unknown how much influence pesticide contaminants had on Arizona's nesting Peregrine Falcons during the mid-1900s, but it was obvious that populations were once again increasing by the mid-1980s (Glinski 1998).

Atlasers documented Peregrine Falcons nesting over a wide range of elevations in the state from 460 ft (140 m) within Topock Gorge along the lower Colorado River close to 9000 ft (2743 m) near Greer in the White Mountains. The greatest concentration of breeding Peregrine Falcons in Arizona are within the Grand Canyon region, where Snyder and Snyder (1991) reported that recent surveys had revealed a population there that may exceed 150 pairs. Atlasers surveying in this vast, remote area also regularly documented these falcons from Lake Powell to Lake Mead. Peregrine Flacons were also frequently encountered along the Mogollon Rim from the upper Verde River drainage and Sedona area to the New Mexico border. Atlasers also revealed a sizable population in the mountains and canyons of southeastern Arizona and northern Navajo and Hopi tribal lands. The only notable voids in breeding distribution throughout Arizona are the extremely hot and dry southwestern deserts and much of the relatively flat country encompassing the Little Colorado River drainage.

Peregrine Falcons are doing well in Arizona as evidenced by both atlas and specific species surveys conducted during the atlas period. Ward (1992) reported 179 known Peregrine Falcon breeding areas in Arizona. Glinski (1998) indicated there were over 200 breeding pairs in Arizona. This falcon's distribution had likely not changed much in the past century, but breeding density had increased in some areas. Recent Arizona Game and Fish Department estimates suggest that there could be as many as 300 or more occupied breeding areas in the state, as many remote areas, particular in the Grand Canyon region, still remain incompletely surveyed.

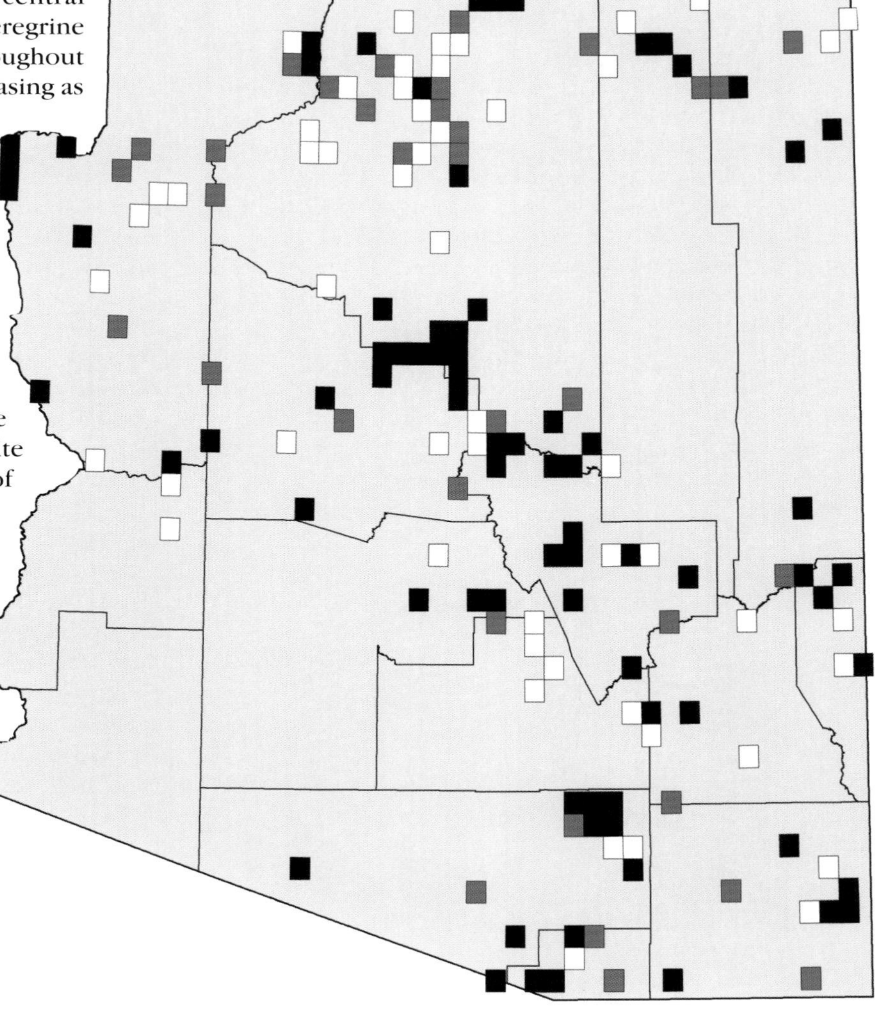

Peregrine Falcon Breeding Evidence Reported in 90 (5%) of 1834 priority blocks

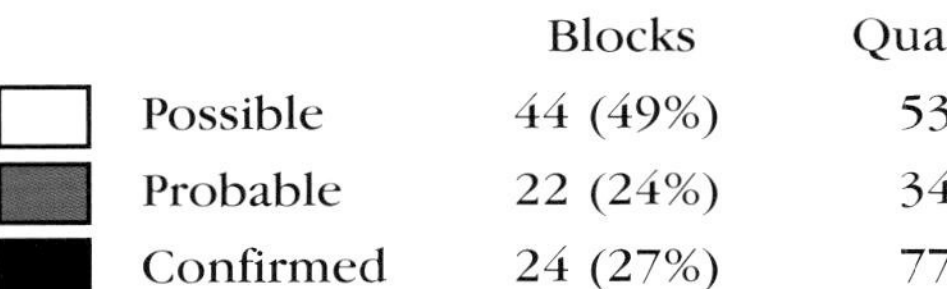

	Blocks	Quads
Possible	44 (49%)	53
Probable	22 (24%)	34
Confirmed	24 (27%)	77

Prairie Falcon

by Amanda Moors *Falco mexicanus*

True master of speed and aerial acrobatics, Prairie Falcons prey on both small mammals and birds. Their subtle plumage hues are often quite similar to the cliffs and canyon walls they frequently inhabit. Typically only heard near breeding areas, these impressive raptors are often first detected by loud wailing and shrill cackling vocalizations.

HELEN AND NOEL SNYDER

HABITAT

Prairie Falcons are primarily raptors of deserts and grasslands in Arizona, where they often prefer more arid, open, and less vegetated habitats than do similar Peregrine Falcons. The two species do, however, inhabit many of the same areas in Arizona, even occasionally nesting on the same cliff face (Dawson 1998). Millsap (1981) reported that these falcons in west-central Arizona preferred foraging areas with vegetative cover averaging less than 3.3 ft (1 m) tall. Open foraging areas and availability of suitable nesting cliffs are primary features that determine use of an area by Prairie Falcons. Atlasers found these raptors most often associated with Sonoran desertscrub, which accounted for more than 50 percent of all atlas records (n = 115). Another 22 percent of the records were from a combination of cold-temperate desertscrub and grasslands, often dominated by a mixture of grasses, sagebrush, and other low growing shrubs. Nesting areas were also regularly reported near pinyon pine–juniper and Madrean evergreen oak woodlands. Occasionally these falcons were discovered nesting on cliffs and rocky ridges at higher elevations where they foraged over scattered alpine grasslands surrounded by pine and mixed- conifer forests.

BREEDING

Prairie Falcons can be found throughout the year in Arizona, with a noticeable population influx during the fall and winter to open grasslands and agricultural areas. Nesting activity can begin quite early in the southwestern desert regions of Arizona. Atlasers reported adults near nesting cliffs as early as 15 January and courtship on 15 February. However, during the atlas project a nest was discovered with young approximately 10 days old on 10 March, indicating early egg laying in late January. Prairie Falcons in these desert mountain ranges generally begin nesting up to a month before those in more northern Arizona localities (T. Tibbitts, personal communication). The earliest fledgling reported by atlasers in the southwest desert region was on 1 May.

Elsewhere in Arizona, Prairie Falcons typically arrive on their breeding territories in February or early March, with most egg clutches laid in March and April, occasionally into early May (Dawson 1998). Atlas data reveal the majority of nests with young from early May to mid-June, and the latest active nest contained chicks on 29 June.

Prairie Falcons nest almost exclusively on ledges and within crevices and potholes of cliffs, canyon walls, and rocky ridges. However, they do not hesitate using the old stick nests of other cliff nesting raptors and ravens (Steenhof 1998). Many Prairie Falcon nest sites can be found on much shorter cliffs than sites typically selected by Peregrine Falcons (Millsap 1981; Dawson 1998). Dawson (1998) monitored one desert nest that was only half-way up a 60-ft (18.3-m) cliff. Atlasers estimated the height of three nests and found the cliffs to average 98.4 ft (30 m) high, with nests generally in the middle of the cliff. In desert mountain ranges, Millsap (1981) noted the average distance between Prairie Falcon eyries was approximately 6.5 mi (10.5 km), but where ledges were scarce he note pairs nesting as close as 492 ft (150 m).

In Arizona, typical Prairie Falcon clutches consist of 3–5 eggs (Millsap 1981), which are laid in a shallow scrape on the floor of the chosen eyrie. The incubation period ranges from 29 to 33 days (Dawson 1998) and is typically conducted primarily by the female, but the male sometimes shares the responsibility (Steenhof 1998). Prairie Falcon nestlings typically depart the nest in approximately 38 days (range 29–47) and the parents continue to feed the fledglings for an additional 4–5 weeks (Steenhof 1998).

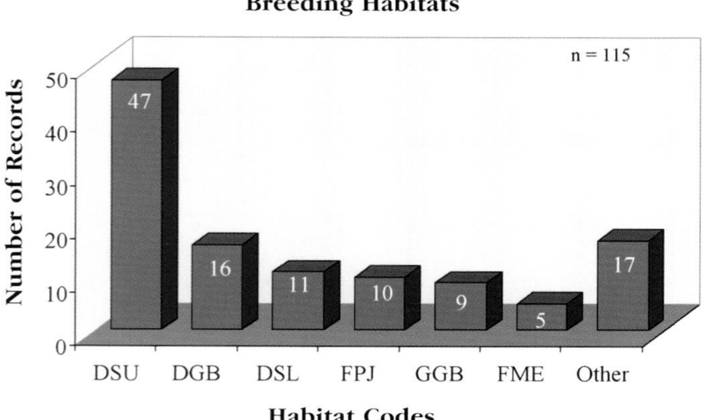

Breeding Phenology

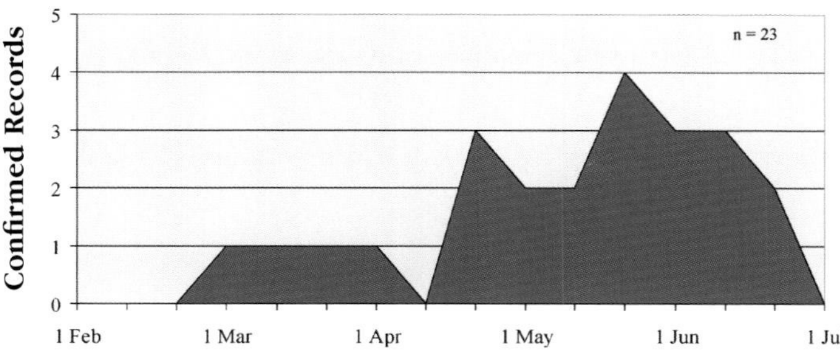

DISTRIBUTION AND STATUS

Based on prehistoric records, it appears that Prairie Falcons have not significantly changed their range since the Pleistocene (Steenhof 1998). These raptors breed in western North America from southwestern Canada south to northern Mexico and from California to the western Great Plains region. Prairie Falcons are more of a "wanderer" than a true migrant. After the breeding season, these falcons shift to open wintering areas, but they do not necessarily fly south as do many other falcons (Dunne et al. 1988). These seasonal movements probably reflect changes in food availability (Steenhof 1998; Dunne et al. 1988).

Over the years, various authors have described the Prairie Falcon as fairly common to scarce residents throughout Arizona (Swarth 1914; Phillips et al. 1964; Monson and Phillips 1981). Similarly, atlasers found Prairie Falcons nesting in appropriate habitat throughout the state at elevations ranging from approximately 500 to 9000 ft (152–2743 m). However these falcons are occasionally discovered nesting at higher elevations in the state. Dawson (1998) found an active nest in the White Mountains of Arizona at 10,500 ft (3200 m).

Atlas data reveal a significant concentration of Prairie Falcon records in the arid Sonoran Desert mountain ranges in the southwestern quarter of the state. It may be notable that Peregrine Falcons are sparse or lacking as a nesting species in this region. Another concentration of records came from the Colorado Plateau in the northeast corner of the state. In southeastern Arizona and along the Mogollon Rim region, Prairie Falcons appear to nest sparingly, while Peregrine Falcons are much more frequently encountered. Atlasers undoubtedly missed detecting many Prairie Falcons while conducting surveys as many arid, remote, and rugged locations were never accessed or were visited too late in the season.

Prairie Falcon populations seem to be fairly stable in Arizona with good reproductive success (Millsap 1981), although some evidence suggests that Peregrine Falcons are replacing these falcons at some localities. This was first noted in the 1940s in southern Arizona (Phillips et al. 1964). During the decline of the Peregrine Falcons in the 1970s, many Peregrine eyries may have become inhabited by Prairie Falcons. As the Peregrine recovery continues, these two species will probably be in more conflict, perhaps with the Peregrine regaining control of some sites.

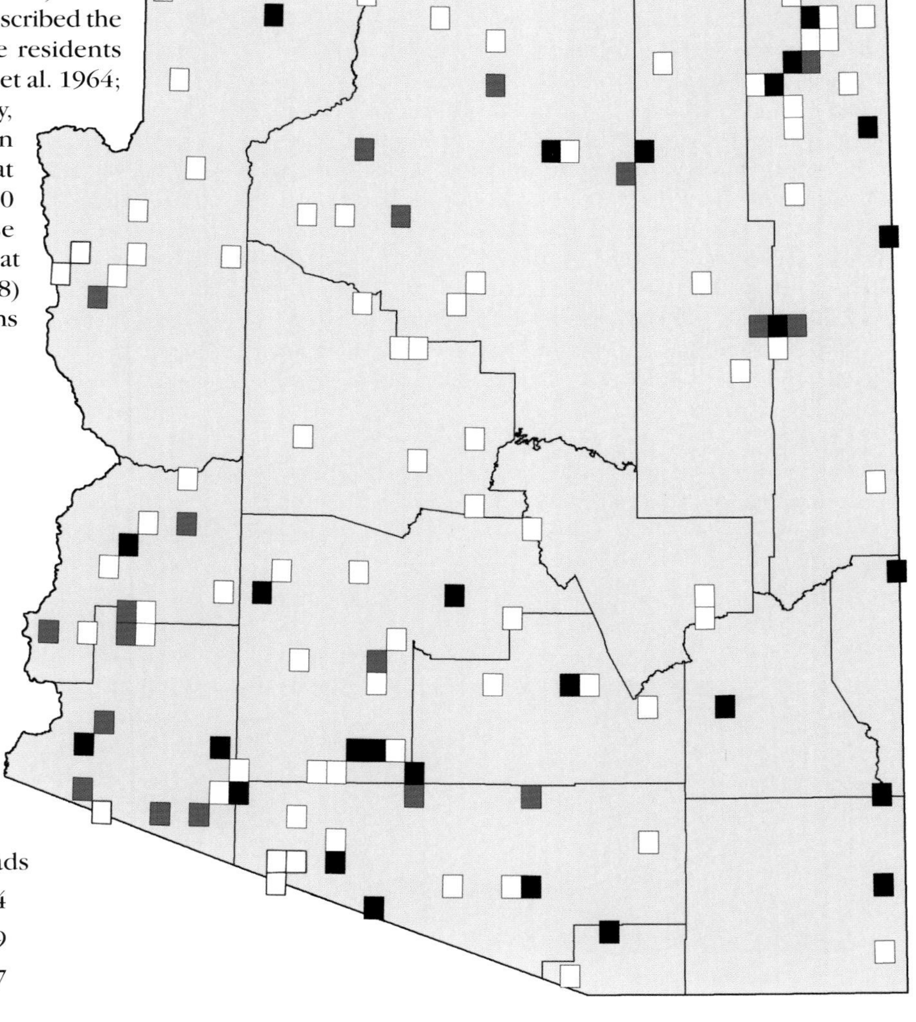

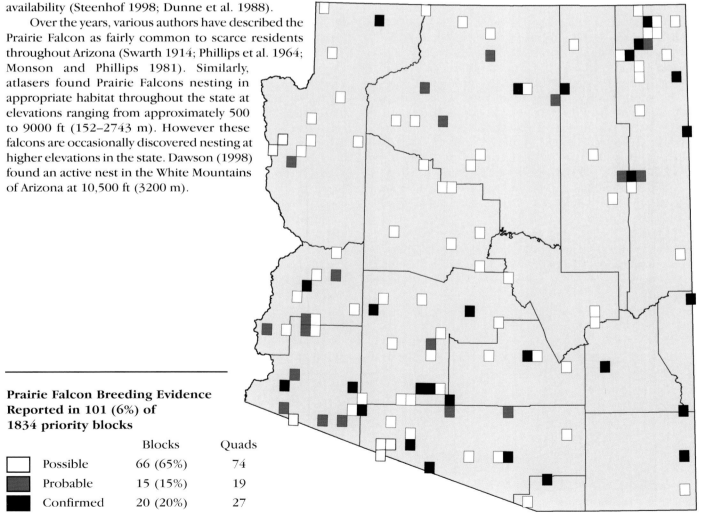

Prairie Falcon Breeding Evidence Reported in 101 (6%) of 1834 priority blocks

	Blocks	Quads
Possible	66 (65%)	74
Probable	15 (15%)	19
Confirmed	20 (20%)	27

Black Rail

by Troy E. Corman *Laterallus jamaicensis*

In Arizona, the peculiar "kickee-doo" calls of the tiny and secretive Black Rail can be heard emanating only from deep within a precious few shallow marshes of the lower Colorado River valley. And even here, very few lucky observers ever get a chance to glimpse this diminutive wetland skulker.

DAN FISCHER

HABITAT

Across their range, Black Rails can be found in a variety of wetlands, which include both salt and freshwater marshes, wet meadows, and flooded grassy vegetation (Eddleman et al. 1994). In Arizona, the extremely local California subspecies (*coturniculus*) is restricted to wetlands with shallow, stable water levels, gently sloping shorelines, and vegetation dominated by dense, fine-stemmed emergent plants, especially threesquare bulrush (Repking and Ohmart 1977). Atlasers and researchers conducting specific Black Rail surveys described eight of the nine occupied locations within this habitat. Threesquare bulrush is most common in shallow water or saturated soil situations on gentle slopes; hence, the association between this plant and the Black Rail may simply reflect similar microhabitat requirements (Conway et al. 2002). Other vegetation significantly more common at Arizona occupied sites includes Fremont cottonwood, seepwillow, tamarisk, saltgrass, and arrowweed (Conway et al. 2002). In contrast, deeper-water wetlands containing cattail, common reed, or California bulrush were used much less frequently by Black Rails (Flores and Eddleman 1991; Conway et al. 2002). Flores and Eddleman (1995) suggested that shallow water less than 1.2 in. (3 cm) deep, proximity to cover-type edges, and vegetation height best predict the habitat used in Arizona.

BREEDING

In Arizona, resident Black Rails can be heard delivering their unique territorial calls from late February into July, although the "kickee-doo" call is heard less often after June (Conway et al. 2002). California Black Rails call almost exclusively at twilight or during the day, and rarely at night. This is a sharp contrast to most of the eastern U.S. populations, among which nocturnal calling predominates (Eddleman et al. 1994).

Black Rails typically construct a well-concealed nest bowl in the center of a vegetation clump at or near the upper limits of marsh vegetation (Flores and Eddleman 1993). The nest usually includes a woven canopy of dead or living vegetation. Dominant emergent plants at or near nest site are used to construct the nest and an interesting trait is a ramp of dead vegetation that leads from the substrate to the entrance on one side of the nest (Eddleman et al. 1994). The few nests discovered in Arizona were constructed of cattails and spikerush and were found between 19 April and 23 July (Flores and Eddleman 1993), although nesting may begin as early as March. Most of Arizona's nests are found in April and May, with hatching noted from early May to late July. The only confirmed Black Rail record during the atlas period was of an agitated adult pair with calling chicks on 19 July 2000.

In Arizona, the clutch size for Black Rails ranges from 3 to 7 eggs (Flores and Eddleman 1993). Both parents take the responsibility of incubation, which lasts 17–20 days, and the chicks leave the nest within 24 hours of hatching (Flores and Eddleman 1993). The family returns to the nest area the first several nights after hatching, and there is some evidence to suggest that the parents may split the brood for foraging and brooding (Eddleman et al. 1994). There is apparently no information on how long the chicks are tended by the parents. Circumstantial evidence suggests that Black Rails lay replacement clutches if earlier attempts have failed or may even have second clutches after the first broods have fledged (Flores and Eddleman 1993).

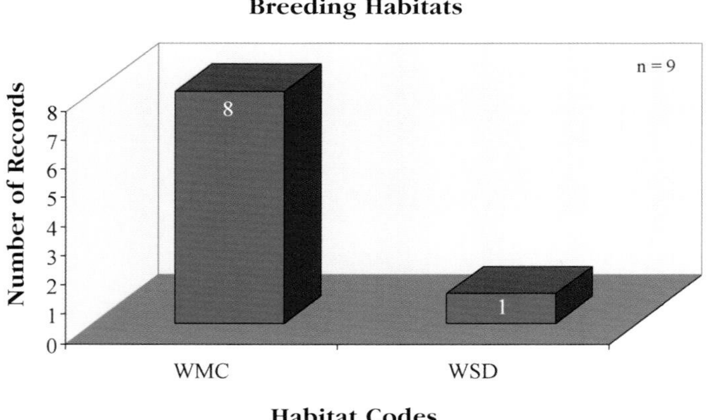

DISTRIBUTION AND STATUS

Black Rail breeding distribution is very spotty and disjunct, with the eastern U.S. populations ranging from the Great Plains to New England and south along the East and Gulf Coast. It is also found sparingly in Mexico, the Caribbean,

Central America, and South America. Northern and interior populations are migratory. The resident western populations are extremely isolated in California, southwestern Arizona, and adjacent northwestern Mexico.

First detected along the Colorado River below Imperial Dam during the summer of 1969 (Monson and Phillips 1981), the California Black Rail was detected at five locations between Mittry and Martinez lakes during surveys conducted in the early 1970s (Repking 1975). By 1982, a small population had also become established along the lower Bill Williams River (Rosenberg et al. 1991).

Atlasers and researchers detected Black Rails in most prior reported locations at elevations between 150 and 600 ft (46–183 m), with Mittry Lake and Bill Williams River National Wildlife Refuge containing the bulk of Arizona's limited populations (Conway et al. 2002). In 2000, researchers conducting specific surveys for Black Rails discovered a previously unknown population containing fourteen calling birds near the border of the Bill Williams River National Wildlife Refuge and Planet Ranch. During the atlas period, these birds were also detected in Imperial and Havasu National Wildlife Refuges, as well as one location on Colorado River Indian tribal lands. A surprising record came from within the Grand Canyon near the Spencer Canyon confluence with the Colorado River (river mile 246) where a presumed unpaired male called from a marsh during the spring through fall of 1998 and 1999 (Conway et al. 2002).

Water level fluctuations in many marshes along the Colorado River likely limit the number of viable populations that can become established in Arizona. Repking and Ohmart (1977) noted that Black Rails are present in the main stem of the Colorado River only at Imperial Reservoir because the large amount of water above Imperial Dam results in more stable levels relative to emergent marshes upriver.

In 2000, Conway et al. (2002) conducted surveys for Black Rails within the lower Colorado River valley in California and Arizona. These thorough surveys detected only 100 individuals, of which 62 were in Arizona. Degradation and elimination of suitable wetland habitat has caused considerable decline in California Black Rail populations and significant reduction in its distribution (Conway et al. 2002). These rails have relatively narrow habitat breadth and require very stable, shallow water emergent marshland conditions (Flores and Eddleman 1991). Goals listed in the Lower Colorado River Multi-Species Conservation Plan for the Black Rail include the enhancement of existing habitat, restoration of unsuitable habitat, and the establishment of additional breeding locations within the lower Colorado River area (Conway et al. 2002). It is hoped that this document will encourage land managers in the area to provide the much-needed management and attention this unique species deserves. The Black Rail's apparent high level of productivity and juvenile dispersal capabilities may enable relatively quick colonization of new habitats in the region.

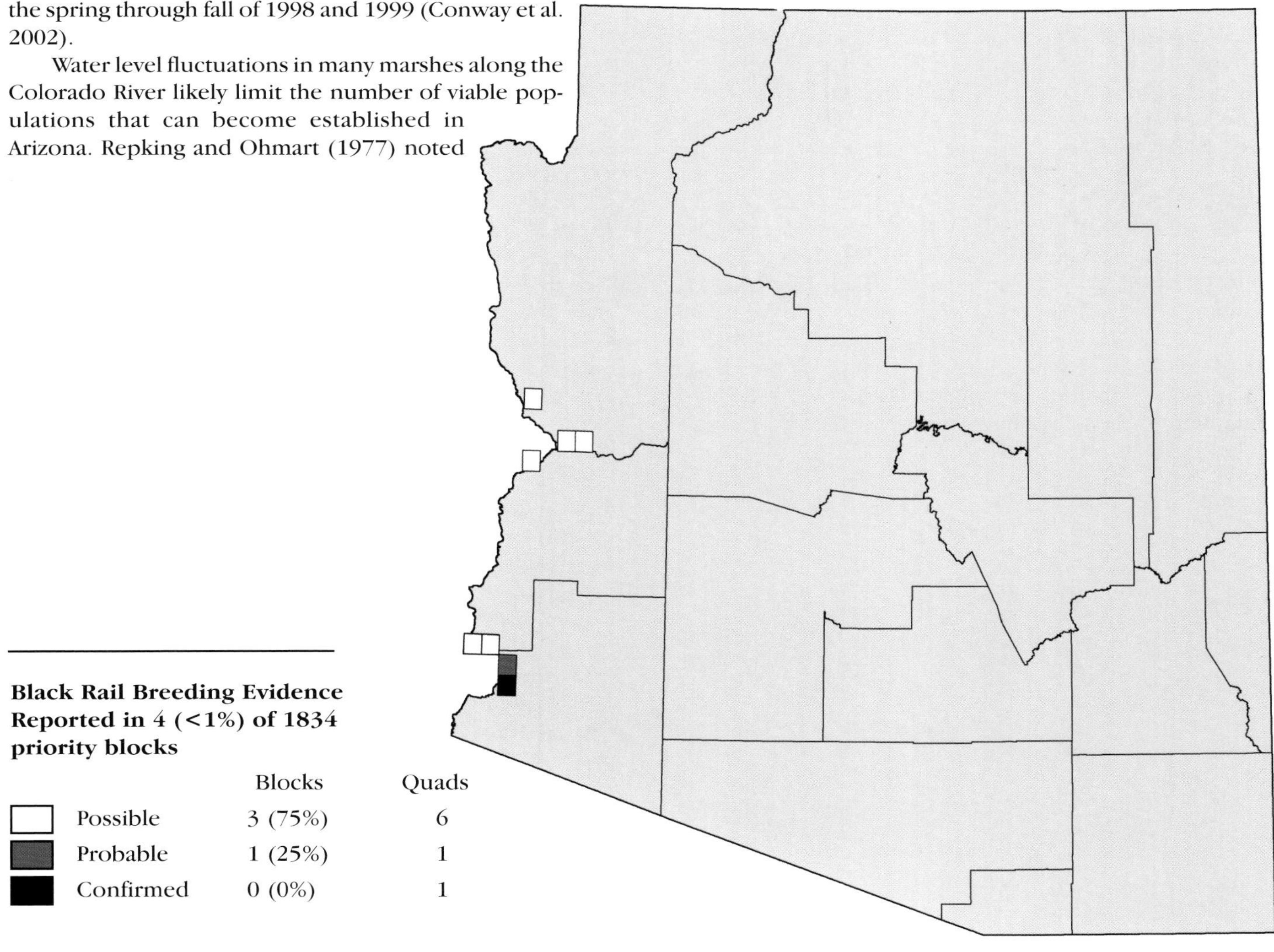

Black Rail Breeding Evidence Reported in 4 (<1%) of 1834 priority blocks

	Blocks	Quads
Possible	3 (75%)	6
Probable	1 (25%)	1
Confirmed	0 (0%)	1

Clapper Rail

by Cathryn Wise-Gervais *Rallus longirostris*

Clapper Rails are fairly common in coastal salt marshes and in mangrove swamps throughout their range. However, the race in Arizona is unique in that Clapper Rails also nest in freshwater marshes, where they commonly feed on introduced crayfish. Seldom observed, these attractive rails are usually detected by their many loud clattering calls.

HABITAT

In Arizona, the Yuma (*yumanensis*) Clapper Rail uses freshwater marshes, often dominated by cattails, bulrushes, and sedges (Eddleman and Conway 1998). However, the presence of emergent cover seems more important to the birds than the specific plant species present or the size of the marsh (Anderson and Ohmart 1985). Atlasers reported all but one Clapper Rail record in marshes and stands of emergent vegetation along ponds, reservoirs, canals, ditches, and sections of slow-flowing rivers (n = 29). The one remaining record was in riparian scrubland consisting of reeds, willow, and tamarisk. Arizona's birds typically occupy cattails and bulrushes, but these rails will also inhabit tall stands of marsh-purslane, sedge, and other aquatic plants. Conway et al. (1993) concluded that these rails used densely vegetated marshes with shallow water for nesting and that a variety of mixed age stands of emergent vegetation containing shallow open-water pools were selected for year-round use.

BREEDING

Unlike many other races, Yuma Clapper Rails are believed to be mostly sedentary year-round, inasmuch as radio telemetry studies along the lower Colorado River have not confirmed migration (Eddleman 1989; Conway 1990). However, researchers have suggested that some if not most Clapper Rails along the Gila River do migrate out of their breeding areas in the winter. Migration could possibly be induced in these populations because of the slightly higher elevations and cooler winter temperatures, reducing food availability. Along the lower Colorado River, males can begin advertising as early as February and March (Eddleman and Conway 1998). However, observers have noted that populations along the Gila River (and possibly other locations as well) often delay calling and territory establishment until mid-April or later, with a peak in calling activity noted in late May (Todd 1986; B. Burger, personal communication). Further, observations of individual Clapper Rails in April and May at an isolated desert spring and in a residential Phoenix neighborhood suggest that the birds are migratory in some regions of the state.

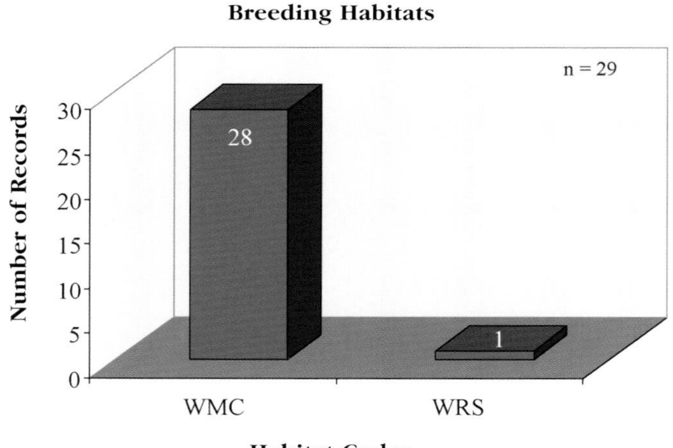

In Arizona, the Clapper Rail's nesting season is lengthy, extending from March through August. Eddleman (1989) reported the earliest Arizona nest with eggs on 13 March, but he further noted that most eggs are laid in May. Observers first reported birds in suitable breeding habitat on 21 April but obtained only one confirmed breeding record during the atlas period. This sighting was of an adult carrying food on 27 May. Rail surveyors have determined that the first broods are generally produced around mid-May in Arizona, but some early broods are noted by mid-April. Subsequent surveys on the Gila River after the atlas period yielded sightings of fledglings on 25 June and downy young in early July (B. Burger and T. Hildebrandt, personal communication). In addition, Eddleman (1989) reported nests with eggs into late July and dependent young into early September, indicating a rather protracted breeding season. Although it is likely that less than 50 percent of *yumanensis* birds renest in midsummer, second broods are common for saltwater Clapper Rails because food availability remains more constant (Todd 1986).

The Clapper Rail male builds the nest, a bulky platform of dry marsh vegetation, and typically places the structure in dense cover along shorelines with shallow water (Eddleman and Conway 1998). The female sometimes deposits eggs in the nest before the structure is complete. The birds will fortify the nest with additional vegetation in times of high water and will occasionally build alternate nest platforms for use by their fledglings (Eddleman and Conway 1998).

The average Yuma Clapper Rail clutch consists of 6 eggs (range 5–8), and both sexes incubate for 23 to 28 days (Eddleman and Conway 1998). Incubation often begins with the first eggs laid so that young hatch asynchronously (Meanley 1985). One parent cares for the first hatched chicks while the other continues incubating (Kozicky and Schmidt 1949). Chicks are independent of parents approximately six weeks after hatching (Adams and Quay 1958).

DISTRIBUTION AND STATUS

Clapper Rails are found in many coastal areas of the United States south to Brazil, and many subspecies are recognized (Eddleman and Conway 1998). Historically, Clapper Rails were known to occur in Arizona only along the lower Colorado River from Yuma north to the Bill Williams River delta (Phillips et al. 1964). By the mid-1960s these rails had expanded northward to Topock Marsh, and since the early 1970s they have been found on the Gila River near Tacna and Phoenix (Monson and Phillips 1981). Monson and Phillips also reported that since the mid-1970s, Clapper Rails have occupied both the wetlands at Picacho Reservoir and those along the lower Salt River near the Verde River confluence.

Atlas and annual Clapper Rail survey data show that these birds still occur throughout most of their previously described range in the state, and are found at elevations ranging from approximately 100 to 1000 ft (30–305 m) and very locally to 1500 ft (457 m). Within the lower Colorado River valley, these rails were detected as far north as Havasu National Wildlife Refuge, including Topock Marsh, and south locally to the Colorado River Indian tribal lands. Clapper Rails were also found fairly regularly from Cibola National Wildlife Refuge south to the international border and then up the Gila River to just above Tacna. Elsewhere on the Gila River, these rails were detected primarily from Gillespie Dam in the Arlington Valley upstream to the Salt River confluence. Clapper Rails were also noted at Picacho Reservoir through the mid-1990s, although this reservoir was completely dry by the end of the atlas period. Except for near the Gila River confluence, Clapper Rails were not detected along the Salt River during the atlas period.

The Yuma Clapper Rail is one of three endangered Clapper Rail subspecies. This designation was made owing to the limited distribution of their habitat and perceived small population size (Eddleman 1989). Throughout the atlas period, Clapper Rail surveyors in Arizona detected approximately 300 individuals annually in the state (L. Fitzpatrick, personal communication). Much of the existing lower Colorado River wetland habitat is protected within state or federal wildlife refuges. Despite concerns regarding increasing levels of selenium along the lower Colorado River, Clapper Rail numbers seem to be stable to increasing.

Yuma Clapper Rail management recommendations include continued population monitoring, managing wetlands based on the assumption that the birds are present year-round, avoiding rapid water level fluctuation during nesting season, and restoring and maintaining wetlands in the Colorado River delta (Eddleman and Conway 1998). Wastewater facility managers should be encouraged to create ponds and habitat adjacent to flood plains with rail populations (Latta et al. 1999). In addition, aggressive wetland management should include periodic burning to maintain uneven aged, emergent plant communities favored by the birds (Eddleman and Conway 1998).

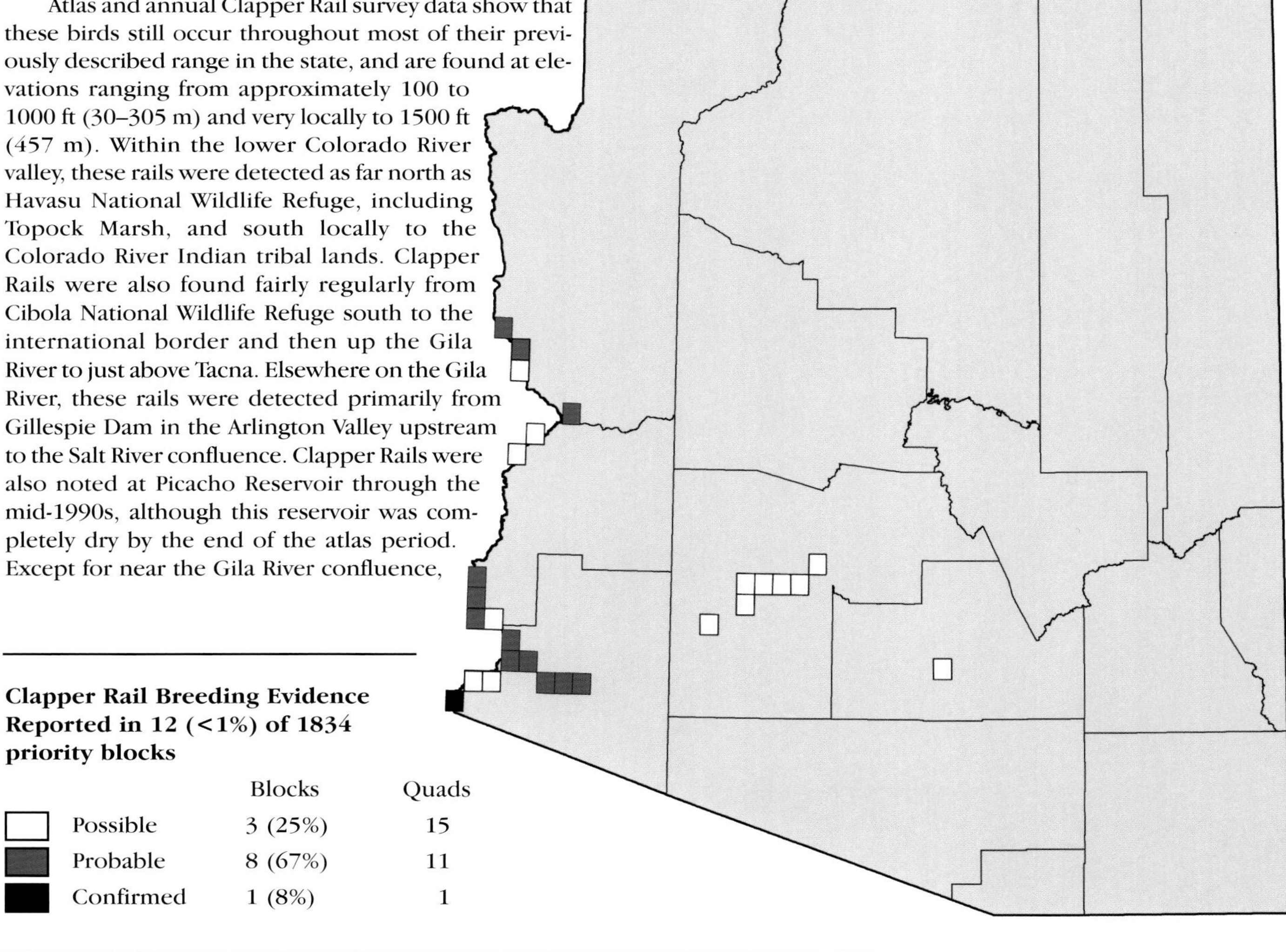

Clapper Rail Breeding Evidence Reported in 12 (<1%) of 1834 priority blocks

	Blocks	Quads
Possible	3 (25%)	15
Probable	8 (67%)	11
Confirmed	1 (8%)	1

Virginia Rail

by Bill Burger *Rallus limicola*

The phrase "thin as a rail" refers to the laterally compressed bodies of Virginia and other rail species, an adaptation that allows them to move easily through the dense marshland vegetation they typically inhabit. Owing to their secretive nature, these rich rufous-colored birds are seldom seen, and much about their natural history remains poorly known.

JIM BURNS

HABITAT

Virginia Rails are typically detected by their distinctive, periodic outbursts emanating from deep within marshland vegetation. In Arizona, 89 percent of atlas records of this rail were from marshes, cienegas, or wetlands along ponds, lakes, and slower reaches of rivers (n = 48). The remaining detections were from wastewater ponds containing stands of emergent vegetation, high-elevation willow and alder wetlands, and montane riparian wetlands. Cattails or bulrushes are dominant in most localities used by Virginia Rails, although areas with tall, coarse grasses and sedges are also inhabited. Shallow water, emergent cover, and substrate with high invertebrate abundance are thought to be the most important features of Virginia Rail habitat (Conway 1995). Conway also describes Virginia Rails as being most common in freshwater wetlands with upright emergent vegetation interspersed with open water and mudflats and/or matted vegetation. These rails prefer marshes in early stages of succession to those stands with high stem densities and large amounts of residual vegetation. Vegetation height is not considered important as long as there is adequate overhead cover (Conway 1995).

BREEDING

Virginia Rails breed sparsely in appropriate habitat throughout much of Arizona, and migrants increase fall and winter populations in the state. Spring migration in Arizona is difficult to determine but likely occurs between March and early May. Timing of breeding activities specific to Arizona also remains poorly understood. Atlas fieldwork resulted in eleven confirmed breeding records of Virginia Rails. Fledglings were confirmed on ten occasions with dates between 1 May and 11 July, and an adult carrying food was seen as late as 21 July. However, Rosenberg et al. (1991) reported downy young at the Bill Williams River delta as early as 28 March, indicating some nest building and egg laying occurs in Arizona by late February or early March. Southbound migration for Virginia Rails is also poorly known, but migrants begin arriving in or passing through Arizona by mid-August and continue well into the fall as food availability decreases and wetlands begin to freeze in more northern areas.

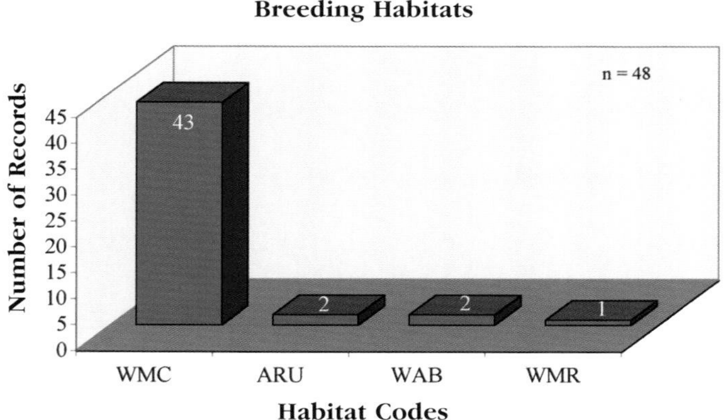

No Virginia Rail nests were documented during atlas fieldwork, although Goldman (1926) described a nest at Big Lake in the White Mountains that contained 12 eggs on 20 June 1915. The nest was in a sedge-dominated marsh and was constructed approximately 5 in. (12.7 cm) above shallow water. Conway (1995) reports nests are generally in robust emergent vegetation of various species, although frequently in cattails or bulrush. Nests are well concealed, often with a vegetative canopy above the nest bowl, slightly submerged to about 5.9 in. (15 cm) above water level.

Conway (1995) compiled the following Virginia Rail breeding information from various sources and studies. Both sexes construct the nest, which is usually completed within a week, but with material sometimes added throughout laying and incubation. Up to five additional "dummy" nests may be built near the active nest and are probably used for feeding, brooding, resting, or as alternatives in case of nest flooding, destruction, or predation. Clutch sizes of 4–13 eggs have been documented, with a mean of 8. Incubation is 18–20 days; both parents incubate, but females apparently contribute more time. Virginia Rail chicks usually leave the nest within 3–4 days as they follow their parents on foraging excursions. Young are capable of foraging independently within 7 days, but adults continue to feed young for 4 weeks or longer. Evidence suggests second broods in some areas.

DISTRIBUTION AND STATUS

Virginia Rails breed in suitable habitats from southern Canada and across the northern United States, south primarily

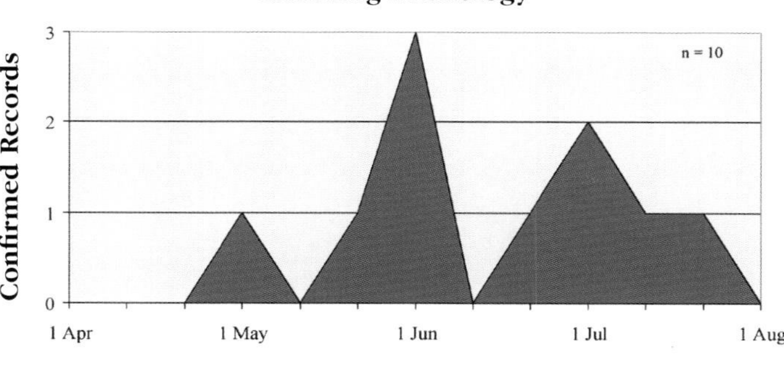

Graph includes fledgling records

through the western states into Arizona, New Mexico, and southern California. Resident populations also exist in Mexico, Guatemala, and South America. In Arizona, Phillips (1964) describes Virginia Rails as a summer resident in marshes from the White Mountains down into the middle elevations of the state, possibly to the lowlands of Maricopa County. During the 1970s, these rails were also found nesting within the lower Colorado and adjacent Gila River valleys, as well as possibly in southeastern Arizona marshes at San Bernardino Ranch and St. David (Monson and Phillips 1981; Rosenberg et al. 1991).

Atlas data suggest that Virginia Rails breed sparsely in areas of suitable habitat throughout most of Arizona at elevations ranging from approximately 120 to 9000 ft (37–2743 m). Within the Colorado River valley, atlasers detected these rails primarily from Topock Marsh south to just below Yuma. Virginia Rails were also found in marshes at the confluence of Beaver Dam Wash and the Virgin River and near the mouth of Spencer Canyon within the Grand Canyon. In central Arizona, these rails were detected at several locations within the upper Verde River drainage downstream to Tavasci Marsh, near Kirkland, and at the Kachina Wetlands near Flagstaff. Atlasers also noted Virginia Rails in many areas of the White Mountains from Luna Lake west to Show Low and north to the vicinity of Saint Johns. These rails were more widespread as a nesting species in southeastern Arizona than earlier accounts suggested, with records coming from Picacho Reservoir, within the lower San Pedro River valley at Cook's Lake and Bingham Cienega, the vicinity of Thatcher-Safford, Empire Cienega, Arivaca Cienega, and Nogales.

Other than at a marsh near Moenave, Virginia Rails were not detected within Navajo and Hopi tribal lands during atlas surveys. However, Jacobs (1986) noted several of these rails occupying wetlands at the Tsaile wastewater ponds, and preliminary evidence suggests they may also breed within Pasture Canyon near Tuba City (C. LaRue, personal communication).

There is little population trend data for Virginia Rails in Arizona. However, populations in the lower Colorado River valley apparently increased during the late 1970s (Rosenberg et al. 1991). Local nesting populations have also been discovered in new regions of the state, perhaps reflecting increased protection and enhancement of marshlands and creation of new wetlands at wastewater facilities.

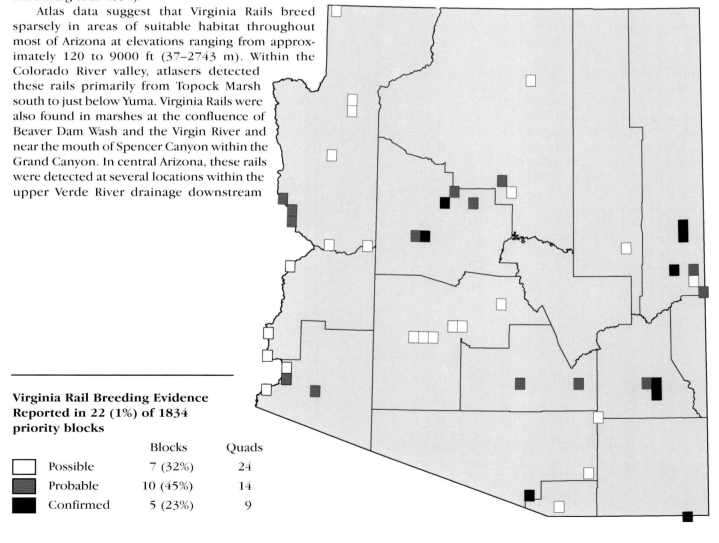

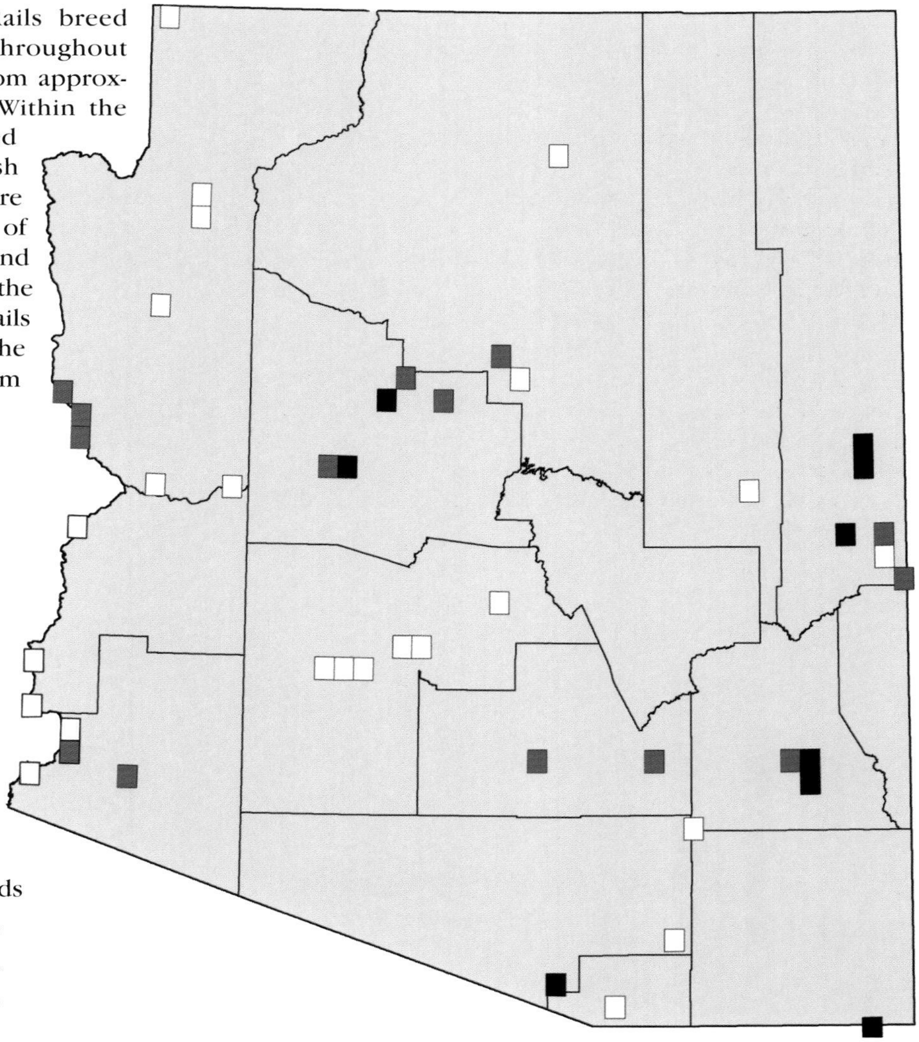

Virginia Rail Breeding Evidence Reported in 22 (1%) of 1834 priority blocks

	Blocks	Quads
Possible	7 (32%)	24
Probable	10 (45%)	14
Confirmed	5 (23%)	9

Sora

by Norm Shrout *Porzana carolina*

The most widely distributed of North American rails, Soras are also the most frequently viewed of the reclusive rail species occurring in Arizona. These rails often inhabit the same marshlands as Virginia Rails, but competition between the two is likely reduced because the predominant diet of each is quite different.

JIM BURNS

HABITAT

Soras are observed in almost any marshy or flooded dense vegetation during migration in Arizona. However, these secretive birds closely associate with permanent or semipermanent wetland habitats for breeding and wintering. Atlasers report Soras inhabiting marshlands dominated primarily by dense stands of cattail, bulrush, and sedge. Nearly 94 percent of all atlas detections were from marshes, cienegas, and wet meadows, as well as the edges of ponds, lakes, and slower sections of rivers (n = 29). Several other atlas observations were noted at wastewater ponds with emergent vegetation and at wetlands with a cottonwood and willow overstory. Soras prefer relatively shallow marshes and wetland shorelines where water level instability produces diverse mosaics of fine and robust emergent vegetation (Melvin and Gibbs 1996). These short-billed rails will also forage over deeper water in search of seeds and invertebrates when substrates such as floating and partially submerged residual vegetation are available.

BREEDING

More widespread and abundant during the fall and winter, Arizona's Sora populations are primarily migratory, although several wetlands in the state are inhabited throughout the year. In Arizona, Sora migration may begin by late March or early April with stragglers through early May. The timing of arrival to higher elevation breeding areas in the state is uncertain, but it likely occurs in April as emergent vegetation begins to flourish. Atlasers observed Soras in suitable breeding habitat as early as 3 April, although Conway (1990) noted that Soras in Arizona can occupy their wintering grounds as late as 7 May. This fact complicates the determination of some individuals as potential breeders or simply late migrants. Few nests of Soras have ever been documented in Arizona, and the only confirmation of breeding during the atlas was from observations of dependent young. Atlasers reported adult Soras with young by 2 June, indicating nest building by late April or early May. In Arizona, most eggs are likely laid between early May and early July. Goldman (1926) reported on three nests with eggs found from 14 to 21 June at Big Lake in the White Mountains. The latest confirmed record during the atlas was a fledgling noted on 4 August. Southbound migration of Soras in Arizona begins early, with regular reports of individuals in southern nonbreeding areas by mid-July. Migration apparently peaks in September as the densities of Soras increases in wintering areas of the state.

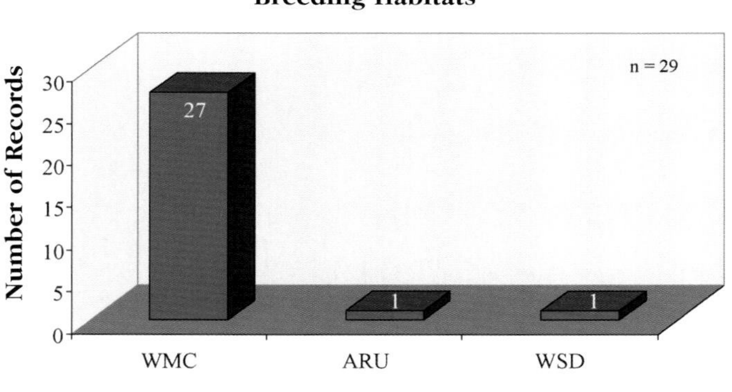

Preferred nest sites for the Sora appear to be within dense stands of cattails and/or sedges, especially near borders between vegetation types or patches of open water (Melvin and Gibbs 1996). Goldman (1926) discovered several nests at approximately 9000 ft (2743 m) elevation in Arizona and all were constructed in tufts of sedge approximately 6 in. (15.2 cm) above the surface of the water. A typical Sora nest is built with a ramp leading up to it and an overhead canopy made by bending surrounding vegetation, then tucking it into the nest rim on the opposite side (Walkinshaw 1940).

Melvin and Gibbs (1996) provided the following compilation of information on Sora nesting phenology from various sources. Nest building begins with a crude pile of vegetation onto which the first egg is laid. Soras typically lay a large clutch of 8–11 eggs (range 5–16) in conjunction with nest building. Incubation usually commences after the first few eggs are laid, causing eggs to hatch asynchronously. Both parents begin sharing incubation duties lasting from 16 to 22 days. The first Sora chicks hatched are frequently brooded by one adult nearby, while the other parent continues to incubate. First flight and independence of parents occurs at approximately 4 weeks of age, but juveniles may remain with parents for several additional weeks. Most evidence suggests that Soras normally rear one brood per year, and occasionally two, but will regularly renest if earlier efforts have failed.

DISTRIBUTION AND STATUS

The breeding range of Soras extends from southeastern Alaska east to Newfoundland, then south in the East through Pennsylvania and the Midwest. In the West, the known southern breeding limits include Arizona, New Mexico, and central California. This rail nested at least formally as far south as northwestern Baja California (Howell and Webb 1995). In Arizona, Soras are described as common breeders at marshes in the north and more locally in central regions of the state (Phillips et al. 1964). Some of the earliest accounts regarding this species were from Mearns (1890), who noted these rails as abundant in May and presumably breeding north of the Mogollon Rim at Mormon and Stoneman lakes. Nesting has been confirmed as far south as southeastern Maricopa County, and additional reports suggest that these rails may have bred at Picacho Reservoir (Monson and Phillips 1981). Soras winter commonly at marshes within the lower Colorado River valley and in much of southeastern Arizona, where summer records are few and breeding has yet to be determined (Monson and Phillips 1981; Rosenberg et al. 1991).

During atlas surveys, potential breeding records of Soras ranged in elevation from approximately 740 to 9250 ft (225–2819 m). Lower elevation records were primarily from the extensive marshes in the Gila River and immediately adjacent Salt River downstream through the Arlington Valley to Gillespie Dam. During the atlas period, these rails were also detected at Cook's Lake near the lower San Pedro River and were confirmed nesting at the Boyce Thompson Arboretum in 1993.

Farther north, atlasers detected Soras at Tavasci Marsh and Page Springs, as well as in the Flagstaff region southeast to Mormon Lake. Another concentration of atlas records was noted in the White Mountain region from Show Low east to Luna Lake and north to the many springs and wetlands around St. Johns. Soras undoubtedly also nest within the adjacent White Mountain Apache tribal lands, but information is lacking because of the denial of access to conduct atlas surveys there.

Soras were not detected during atlas surveys on Navajo and Hopi tribal lands, although Woodbury and Russell (1945) reported a chick in the marshes of Pasture Canyon near Tuba City. Jacobs (1986) also reported as many as eight of these rails throughout much of May 1986 at the emergent-filled wastewater ponds at Tsaile. The span of dates and number of individuals would suggest nesting activity at this location. Specific wetland bird surveys that included the many local and isolated marshes of northern Arizona, especially those within the Mogollon Rim and White Mountain regions, would undoubtedly reveal many additional nesting localities for these secretive little rails.

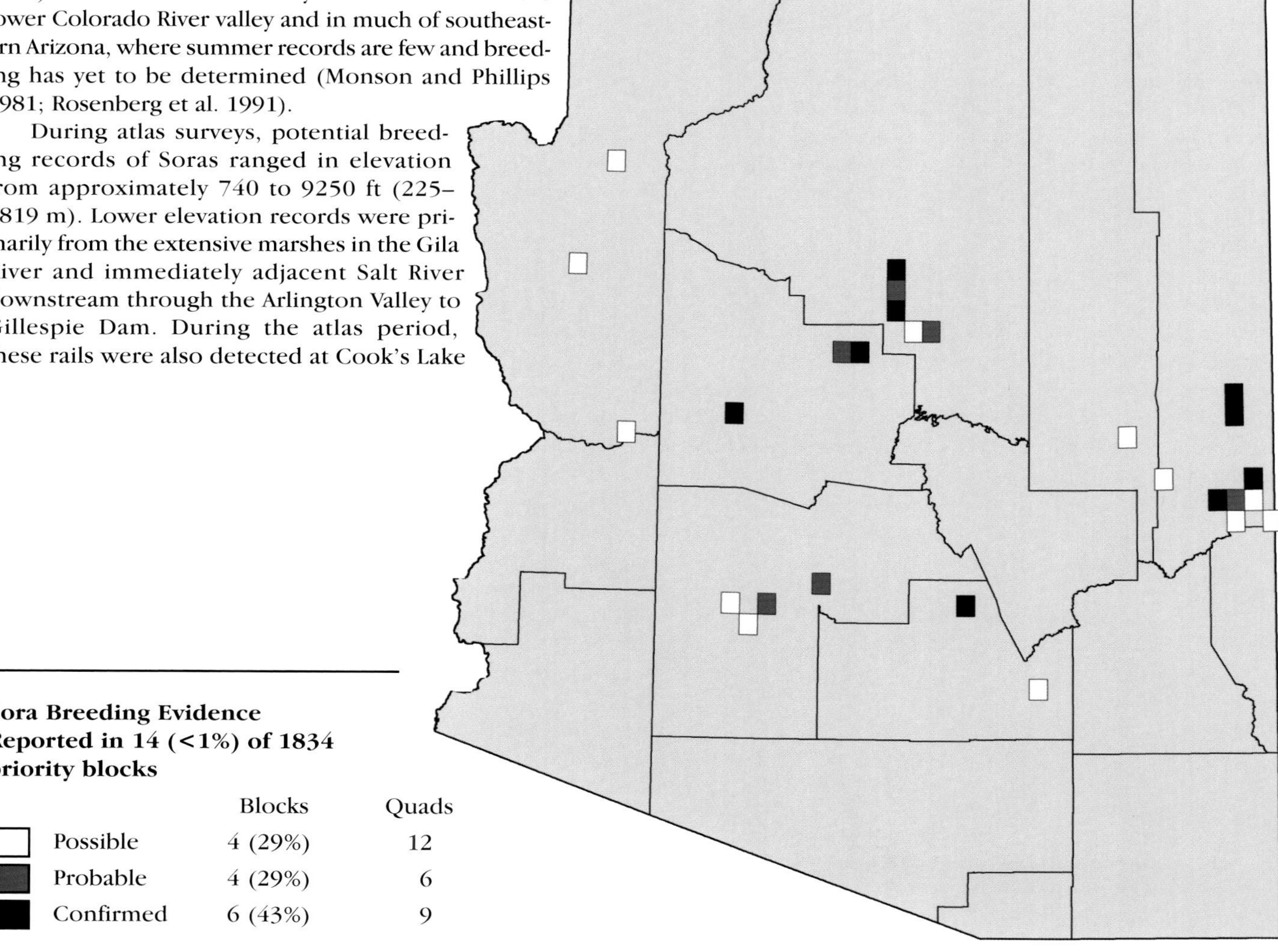

Sora Breeding Evidence Reported in 14 (<1%) of 1834 priority blocks

	Blocks	Quads
Possible	4 (29%)	12
Probable	4 (29%)	6
Confirmed	6 (43%)	9

Common Moorhen

by Cathryn Wise-Gervais *Gallinula chloropus*

Common Moorhens are somewhat retiring, and are content to forage and loaf in or near dense wetland vegetation, only occasionally venturing into open water. Despite their shyness, this species is fairly easy to observe, as it is locally common and widespread in many of Arizona's lowland marshes.

HABITAT

Common Moorhens are adaptable birds that are found nearly worldwide, often seen alongside American Coots. Common Moorhens are more selective than coots when choosing breeding habitat, however, and generally require shallower water and denser marsh vegetation than their close relative. Atlasers reported Common Moorhens in seven habitat types, but 76 percent of records were in marsh-cienega settings of cattail, bulrush, and other emergent vegetation (n = 55). Eleven percent of sightings were in rural aquatic environments containing stands of emergent vegetation. These included reservoirs, livestock ponds, drainage ditches, and wastewater ponds. Several records were obtained in cottonwood, willow, tamarisk, or common reed-dominated wetlands, such as those formed in the backwaters of many desert rivers. The birds were also found nesting locally in emergent vegetation at residential lakes and ponds.

BREEDING

Arizona's Common Moorhens are primarily year-round residents, although individuals may make some local movements in April and May. Evidence suggests that northern populations in the state and those at elevations above approximately 3000 ft (914 m) are at least partially migratory (T. Corman, personal communication). Beginning in late winter, Common Moorhens engage in rather conspicuous courtship and territorial displays including allopreening and chasing. Atlasers observed nest building as early as 23 March and reported dependent chicks on 25 April, indicating initiation of egg laying in late March or early April. Only two nests with eggs were discovered during the atlas period, and observers reported these on 1 May and 19 June. Most of the 32 breeding confirmations obtained for this species were of dependent young, and this factor makes determining the peak time of egg laying difficult. Atlas data illustrate that Common Moorhens breed in Arizona from mid-March through late August, with a peak in activity from June to early July. Atlasers observed Common Moorhens nest building as late as 17 August, but the fate of this late breeding attempt is unknown. This record suggests that Common Moorhen breeding activity may possibly continue into September. Atlasers reported adults feeding young through 27 August. Migrant or dispersing Common Moorhens are occasionally noted in nonbreeding areas of Arizona from late August to November.

Common Moorhens pairs regularly construct their nest in a secluded location of the marsh, but are commonly within one meter from the edge of open water (Abbott 1907). Nests are typically anchored and constructed of nearby emergent vegetation and often have ramps leading down to the water (Helm et al. 1987). In addition to the nesting platform, Common Moorhens often construct nearby display and brooding structures as well (Helm et al. 1987).

The following natural history information is from numerous studies compiled in Bannor and Kiviat (2002). Common Moorhens typically lay 5–10 eggs, although females regularly lay eggs in other hens' nests, producing larger clutches. Both sexes incubate the eggs for 20–22 days. Incubation is initiated anytime during egg laying; therefore, Common Moorhen chicks hatch asynchronously and move about the nest soon after. Both parents feed and care for the chicks for 3–5 weeks, and the young are capable of flight by age 40–50 days. These prolific wetland birds produce two or more broods per year and often begin renesting within days of fledging young. Siblings from early broods will often assist in rearing later clutches.

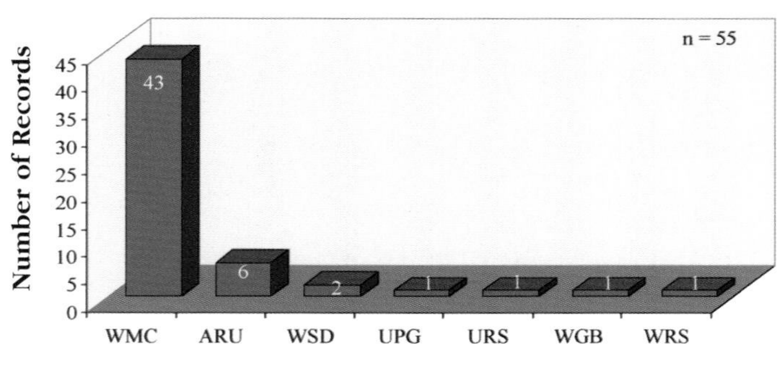

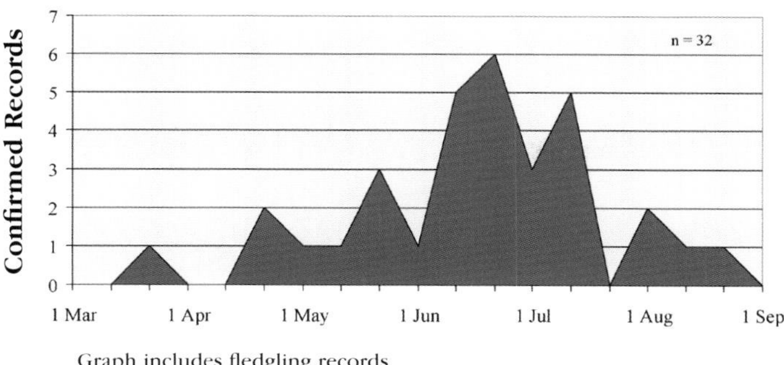

Graph includes fledgling records

DISTRIBUTION AND STATUS

The Common Moorhen is a widespread species occurring throughout most of the Western Hemisphere, Europe, northern Africa, and southern Asia. In North America, it breeds locally throughout the eastern United States and adjacent Canada. By comparison, Common Moorhen populations are much more dispersed and localized in the West from northern Utah and California's Central Valley south into Mexico, possibly owing to arid conditions and limited habitat. Phillips et al. (1964) described Arizona's Common Moorhens as fairly common residents in the cattail and bulrush marshes along the lower Colorado River and found them locally in the central and southern regions of the state. In addition, this species was reported as far north as Chino Valley in 1976 (Monson and Phillips 1981). Along the lower Colorado River, Rosenberg et al. (1991) considered Common Moorhens to be a common and locally abundant resident throughout the valley, but noted that numbers seemed to decrease in winter north of Parker.

Atlasers confirmed Common Moorhens breeding throughout much of their previously described Arizona range at elevations from approximately 90 to 4500 ft (27–1372 m). Atlasers regularly encountered Common Moorhens along the lower Colorado River from Fort Mojave tribal lands south to the Mexican border and up the Gila River to Tacna. Farther north, these birds were found very locally at wetlands within the lower Grand Canyon and at the confluence of the Virgin River and Beaver Dam Wash near the Utah border. In central Arizona, Common Moorhens were confirmed nesting in Chino Valley and in the upper Verde River valley at Page Springs and at Tavasci Marsh. These birds were also regularly reported in marshes along the Gila River and in the adjacent lower Salt River from approximately Gillespie Dam upstream to Tempe.

Atlasers encountered Common Moorhens locally at isolated locations throughout southeastern Arizona. Observers obtained only one cluster of records in this region, and this was in the Thatcher and Safford area. Elsewhere in the southeast, these birds were reported at isolated wastewater ponds on Tohono O'odham tribal lands near Pisinimo and Sells east to marshes in the upper San Pedro River valley and the San Bernardino National Wildlife Refuge.

Although Common Moorhen populations in Arizona were initially reduced through loss of wetland habitat during the first half of the 1900s, these birds are strong colonizers when local conditions are suitable (Rea 1983). These wary birds quickly inhabited the emergent vegetation of recently established ponds at several wastewater facilities in southern and central Arizona.

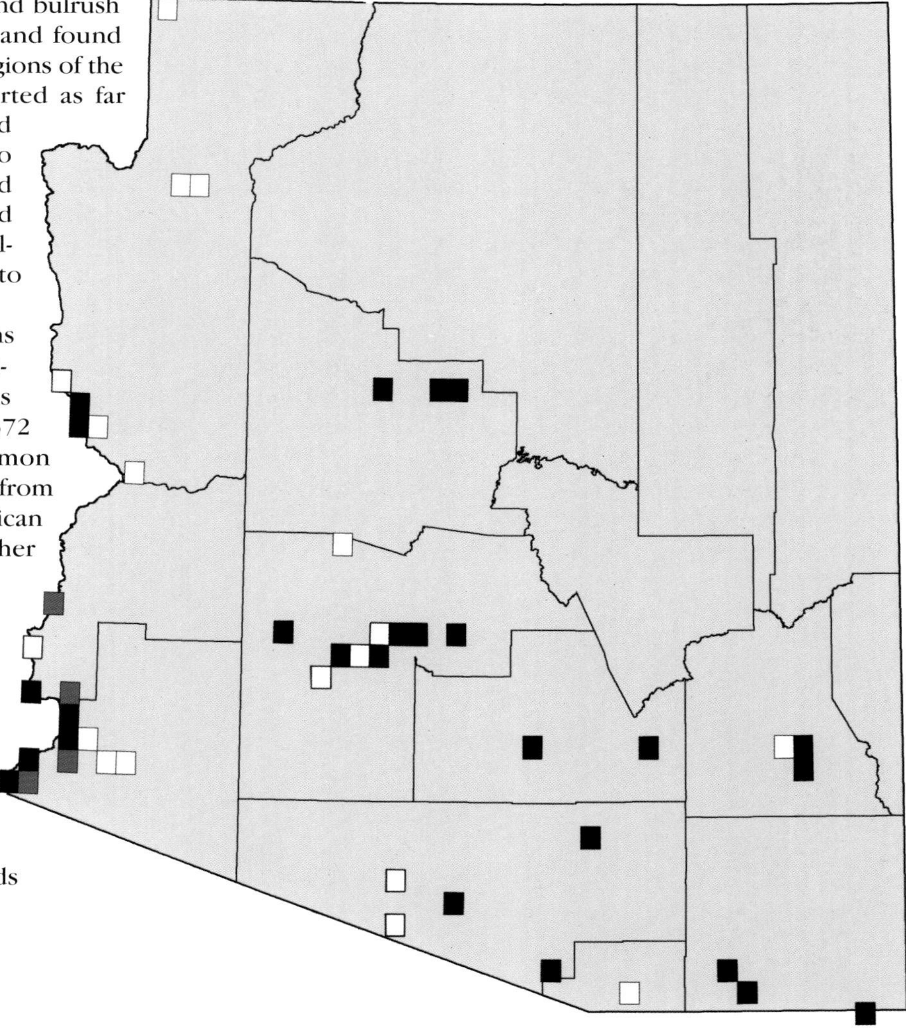

Common Moorhen Breeding Evidence Reported in 26 (1 %) of 1834 priority blocks

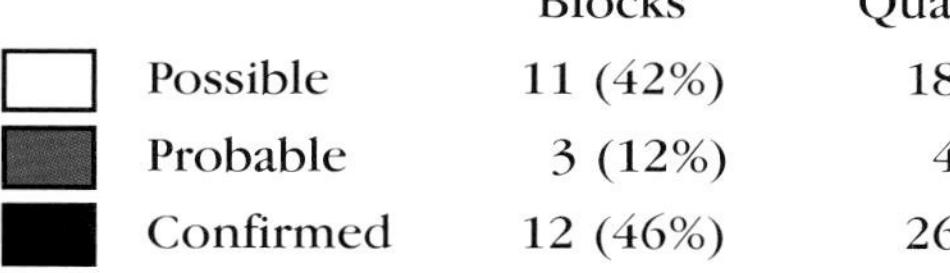

	Blocks	Quads
Possible	11 (42%)	18
Probable	3 (12%)	4
Confirmed	12 (46%)	26

American Coot

by Greg S. Clark *Fulica americana*

Thanks to their gregarious aquatic habits and aggressive nature, American Coots are the most conspicuous members of the rail family. Their territorial defense displays are many and can be quite entertaining to observe. With a variety of loud cackles and croaks, they readily intimidate and charge after trespassing coots, as well as other species swimming nearby.

JIM BURNS

HABITAT

American Coots are strongly associated with food-rich wetlands that provide a mix of open water and marsh vegetation (Rosenberg et al. 1991), especially during the breeding season. These birds typically inhabit permanent and semipermanent water bodies and are detected less frequently in seasonal ponds or those with regularly changing water levels. Atlasers reported 71 percent of American Coot observations from marshes, as well as the edges of ponds, lakes, reservoirs, and slow-flowing rivers with dense emergent vegetation (n = 126). Characteristic plants often include bulrushes, cattails, and sedges, but flooded willows, tamarisk, reeds, and grasses are also occasionally used. An additional 14 percent of atlas records were obtained in rural settings that included wastewater treatment ponds, irrigation runoff impoundments, farm ponds, and canals. Fewer than 10 percent of records were in other habitat types including cottonwood-willow–dominated riparian areas and urban lakes and ponds.

BREEDING

Many American Coots in Arizona are migratory birds that winter in the state in large numbers and begin passing northward in February and March. However, portions of many lower-elevation populations are year-round residents that initiate nesting activity early. The earliest breeding confirmation reported by atlasers was nest building on 29 March, although American Coots were also noted with young by 5 April, indicating egg laying by early March in some areas. In general, these birds tend to initiate nesting activity 3–5 weeks later at high elevations. In Arizona, the nesting activity of coots likely peaks in May and early June, as atlasers reported most adults with young from mid-June to late July. During the atlas period, adults with dependent young were noted as late as 3 September. In Arizona, the number of American Coots begins to increase in August, suggesting some migratory movement, although the largest concentrations are not noted until mid-October.

American Coots build as many as 7–9 platform structures from dead emergent vegetation in early spring. The female performs most of the construction with early platforms used for displaying and copulating, while one or two later structures are built for the eggs and brooding young (Gullion 1954). The foundation typically floats in 1–4 ft (0.3–1.2 m) of water and is anchored to surrounding plants (Harrison 1979). The nest is usually concealed within dense stands of living or dead emergent vegetation, although often near open water (Gullion 1954). Fredrickson (1970) suggested that American Coots may delay nesting until sufficient cover has grown.

American Coots typically lay 8–12 eggs, although Phillips et al. (1964) reported the normal clutch consists of 5–12 at nests on the Mogollon Plateau. Clutches much larger than 12 are likely the result of an additional female laying in the nest (Gullion 1954). Both members of the nesting pair incubate, although the male performs a greater share of the incubation period of 23–26 days (Gullion 1954). Incubation typically begins after the first several eggs are laid, leading to asynchronous hatching over several days or as long as a week. Older chicks often leave the nest with one parent, typically the female, while the other adult remains to defend and incubate the unhatched eggs (Gullion 1954). The adults continue feeding the young for approximately 60–70 days (Brisbin and Mowbray 2002). Typically only one brood is produced per year, although two successful broods have been produced in some southern U.S. populations (Gullion 1954; Hill 1986).

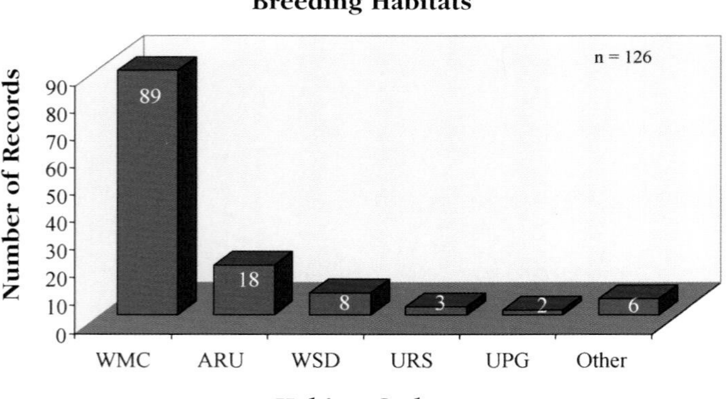

DISTRIBUTION AND STATUS

American Coots are resident throughout much of western and southern United States and Mexico. Migrants extend

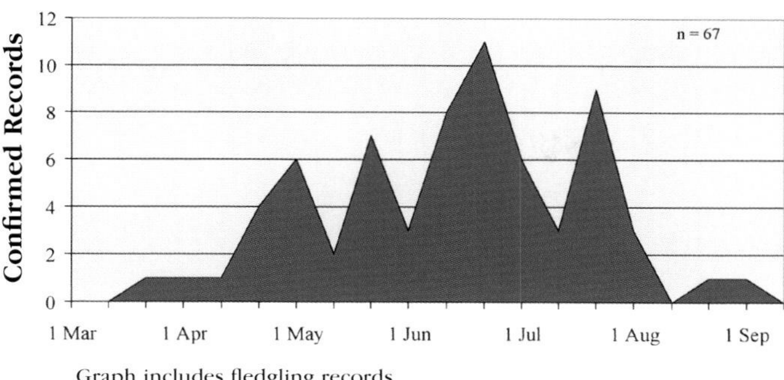

north to breed in northern United States and Canada as well. In Arizona, Phillips et al. (1964) described American Coots as breeding commonly nearly statewide where appropriate wetlands had become established. Atlasers also reported these familiar waterbirds throughout much of the state over a wide range of elevations from approximately 100 to 9300 feet (30–2835 m).

Rosenberg (1991) reported that American Coots were common to abundant along the lower Colorado River, where Grinnell (1914) encountered very few individuals in the spring of 1910. Rosenberg et al. speculated that construction of dams and other water-harnessing changes has benefited American Coots within this river valley, and atlas data support this theory. Atlasers found these birds on most blocks surveyed along the Colorado River from the Havasu National Wildlife Refuge to the Mexican border and along the adjacent lower Gila River.

Atlasers noted American Coots regularly nesting in urban and rural areas in and around the greater Phoenix area, including near the confluence of the Salt and Gila rivers downstream to Painted Rock Reservoir. In comparison, this species was noted only locally in the Tucson area, but fairly regularly elsewhere in appropriate habitat in southeastern Arizona.

North of the Mogollon Rim, atlasers found American Coots breeding from Williams to Mormon Lake area and in much of the White Mountains region. These waterbirds undoubtedly also nest within the adjacent White Mountain Apache tribal lands where atlas surveys were not permitted. American Coots were not detected in the Little Colorado River valley downstream of St. Johns, but were confirmed nesting locally at appropriately vegetated lakes and ponds on Navajo and Hopi tribal lands.

The locations and quantity of marsh habitat available to American Coots for breeding in Arizona has changed considerably over the past century. Many of Arizona's native wetland habitats were lost as major rivers were dammed, streams were diverted, and cienegas dried because of groundwater pumping. However, many new constructed habitats have appeared during this period, including at wastewater treatment facilities, urban lakes, golf course ponds, agricultural impoundments, and reservoirs. Atlasers also discovered that American Coots will quickly colonize new wetlands as they develop and many ponds isolated by miles of open desert, grassland, or agricultural fields are readily occupied by one or more pairs of these birds.

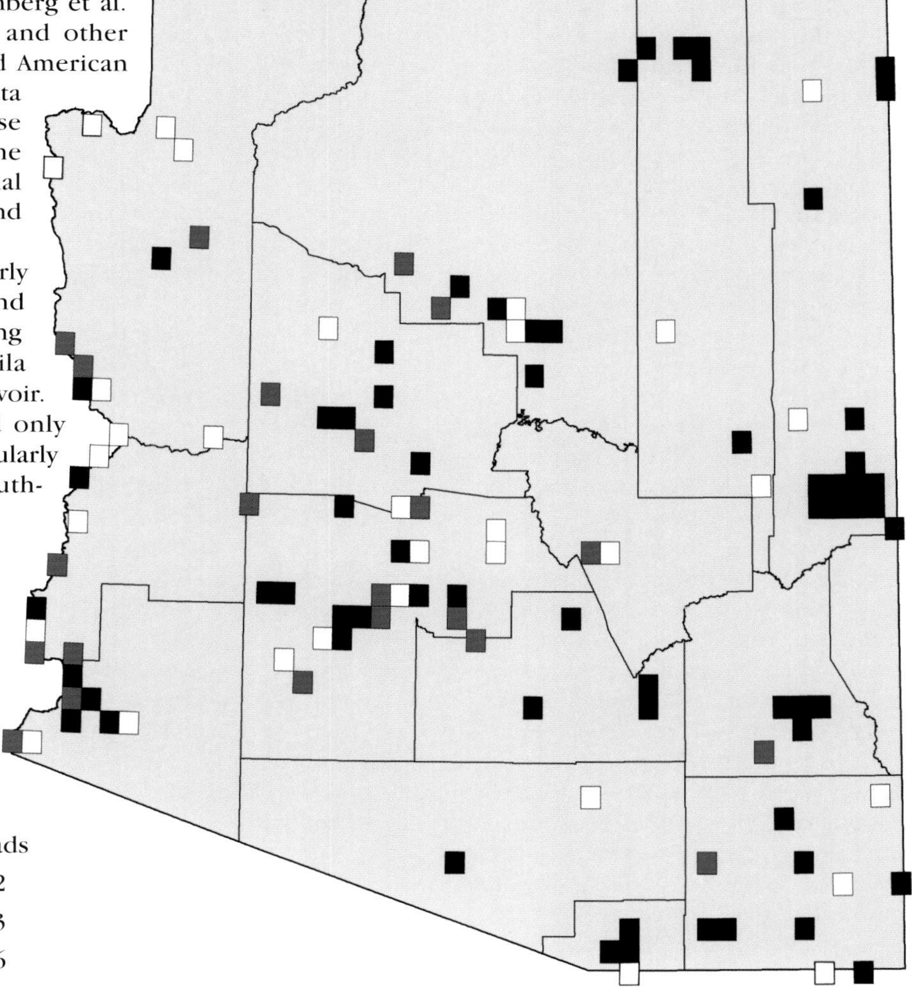

American Coot Breeding Evidence Reported in 84 (5%) of 1834 priority blocks

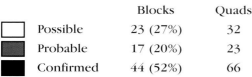

	Blocks	Quads
Possible	23 (27%)	32
Probable	17 (20%)	23
Confirmed	44 (52%)	66

Snowy Plover

by Cathryn Wise-Gervais *Charadrius alexandrinus*

The Snowy Plover's pale plumage matches the sandy soil or barren ground it typically inhabits, enabling these birds to disappear seamlessly into their surroundings. Although these lovely little shorebirds can raise as many as three broods per season, most populations remain small and localized in the United States.

BURCE TAUBERT

HABITAT

Throughout much of their North American range, Snowy Plovers select sparsely vegetated, sandy soil habitats for nesting, and these are primarily near water. These birds breed most commonly along coastal sandy beaches, lagoons, and salt evaporation ponds but are also found inland at saline lakes and reservoirs (Page et al. 1995). Arizona's Snowy Plovers choose some of the most inhospitable environments in the state for nesting, including sparsely vegetated alkali flats and the drying shores of shallow water impoundments. Even though open water is typically nearby, many of these landscapes lack plants, rocks, and other topographic relief and thereby offer little to no protection from the sun or wind (Ryser 1985). Snowy Plovers are rare and somewhat irregular breeders in Arizona, and this is probably because of the ephemeral nature of their preferred habitats near water. Instead, these plovers are more commonly observed as migrants along open shorelines, mudflats, or on the sandbars of reservoirs, ponds, and rivers. Atlasers reported only four potential breeding records for this species during the atlas period. Two observations were from the barren shorelines of alkali lakes or ponds and two were from the extensive dry mudflats of shallow, receding reservoirs.

BREEDING

Arizona's Snowy Plovers typically begin arriving in early April, but are occasionally reported as early as late March. These plovers continue to migrate north through the spring, with stragglers in late May and early June. Snowy Plover breeding phenology varies geographically, with resident coastal populations initiating nesting activity one or more months prior to migratory interior populations. Female plovers choose from displaying males soon after arrival on the breeding territory. There have been very few published accounts documenting confirmed nesting activity of these plovers in Arizona, and atlasers did not report birds in suitable breeding habitat until 2 May. The only confirmed breeding records obtained during the atlas period was a nesting pair with eggs and a separate nearby pair with chicks on 10 July northwest of Gila Bend.

Because Snowy Plovers prefer flat, open country, their nests are rather conspicuous and are prone to predation as well as to destruction by the elements or by human activities. The species will readily renest after failed attempts and researches have documented as many as six attempts in a single season (Page et al. 1995). As a result, the species can have a rather protracted breeding season. Most nesting activity in Arizona probably takes place from late May through July, but adults with dependent young are probably present into August. Breeding records in Arizona prior to the atlas included adult pairs noted by early to mid-June and downy young by early to mid-July (J. Witzeman, personal communication.). In Arizona, southbound migrants are observed from late June through mid-November, with primary passage from mid-July through early September.

Male Snowy Plovers initiate nest building by creating several scrapes in the soil or choosing shallow depressions from which the female selects one for egg laying (Page et al. 1995). The pair typically lines the nest with small bits of debris, and this activity continues through incubation (Page et al. 1995). Nests are often placed near a conspicuous point of reference such as small rocks or bits of wood and can be located up to 500 ft (152 m) from water (Nelson 1998). These landmarks rarely provide much protection from the elements (Purdue 1976b), so nest structures are short-lived and are seldom reused for subsequent broods (Page et al. 1995).

Snowy Plover clutches generally consist of 3 eggs (range 2–5), and both sexes incubate (Warriner et al. 1986; Paton 1995). In warm climates such as Arizona, these plovers often stand over the eggs or sit on them after wetting their belly feathers, activities thought to prevent the eggs from overheating (Purdue 1976a). The incubation period varies with location and season, averaging 26–28 days but ranging from 24 to 32 (Warriner et al. 1986). Chicks leave the nest to forage within hours after the last egg hatches but still require periodic brooding (Page et al. 1995). In western North America, female Snowy Plovers often desert their first mate by the sixth day after hatching and go in search of another, ready to start and rear another brood (Page et al. 1995). This leaves the males to brood and defend the young until they fledge in 29–47 days (Warriner et al. 1986).

DISTRIBUTION AND STATUS

Snowy Plovers are cosmopolitan shorebirds that occur in North and South America, Europe, Africa, and Asia (Page et al. 1995). In North America, these plovers occur along the Pacific and Gulf coasts, as well as inland at isolated locations throughout the West. Interior populations are found from central Texas and Kansas west to California and north irregularly to southern Saskatchewan. Snowy Plovers were first discovered nesting in Arizona near Willcox in 1972 and at Painted Rock Reservoir near Gila Bend in 1974 (Monson and Phillips 1981). There have not been any confirmed nesting records near Willcox since the early 1980s, although observers have irregularly reported summering Snowy Plovers at this location ever since the original sighting.

During the atlas period, observers confirmed Snowy Plovers nesting only at Painted Rock Reservoir in 1993, following extremely high levels of fall and winter precipitation. Before the atlas period, Snowy Plovers were also detected nesting at this ephemeral reservoir in 1974 and 1980 (Witzeman et al. 1997). Both records were obtained following wet winters. Painted Rock Dam was constructed on the Gila River in 1959 primarily to alleviate periodic flooding of downstream agricultural lands and property. Although Painted Rock Reservoir is typically dry throughout the year, this large, relatively shallow basin is capable of becoming an enormous inland desert "sea" during high-precipitation years. At these times, it can measure approximately 6 mi (9.7 km) at its widest and nearly 20 mi (32.2 km) in length. As water is released from the dam throughout the spring and summer, many miles of mudflats are exposed along the reservoir shorelines. These areas become attractive to nesting Snowy Plover, especially as sections of these mudflats dry. Following the nesting activity in 1993, this reservoir remained dry throughout the remainder of the atlas period. However, observers suspect that these plovers nested along the receding smaller lake immediately below the dam in 1995.

Atlasers also observed potential nesting Snowy Plovers at a pond near the western edge of the Willcox Playa near Cochise and at ponds just south of Willcox where nesting has been confirmed in the past. It is possible that Snowy Plovers still nest in these areas but were missed by observers, as few individuals visited these locations during the birds' peak nesting period. The Snowy Plover's breeding season typically corresponds with the hottest part of the year, and most observers avoid sun-baked alkali flats at this time. As a result, some potential nesting locations in the state have never been visited during the appropriate period. For example, the typically dry Willcox Playa and larger ephemeral ponds in the adjacent alkali flats could host Snowy Plovers in wet years, but have never been thoroughly surveyed. Access to these military owned areas is also limited and restricted.

Rosenberg et al. (1991) also speculated that Snowy Plovers could nest locally within the lower Colorado River valley if suitable shoreline existed and was protected from human disturbance. Dry Lake, southwest of Holbrook, is another potential Snowy Plover nesting area, but this private property has never been surveyed for this or any other potential nesting shorebird species.

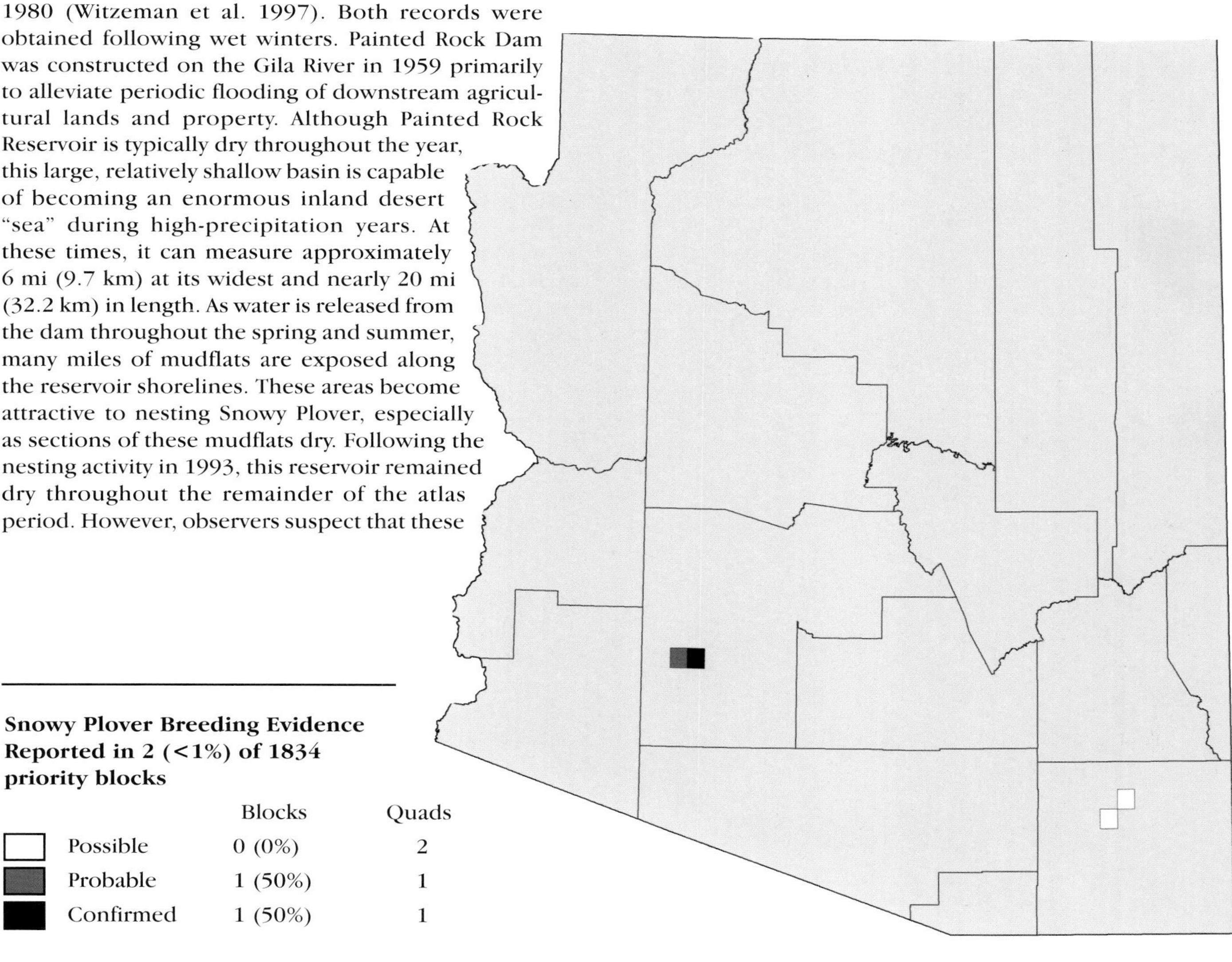

Killdeer

by Jennifer L. Martin *Charadrius vociferus*

Killdeers are charming noisy plovers and are by far the most widespread nesting shorebird in Arizona. Often heard well before they are seen, the loud, distinctive "kill-dee" call is a very familiar sound across the state. These adaptable birds often thrive where humans have created open habitats that include nearby water sources.

RICHARD DITCH

HABITAT

Though Killdeers are technically shorebirds, they are not confined to coasts or shorelines. In the arid southwest, these conspicuous birds prefer open terrain including turf farms, mudflats, or bare ground often in association with permanent water or irrigated agricultural lands. Nearly 35 percent of all atlas records were from rural areas including heavily grazed pastures, wastewater ponds, irrigation runoff impoundments, and stock ponds (n = 460). Atlasers also found that in many remote locations in Arizona, this species now regularly nests along the shores of earthen catchment tanks created for watering range livestock and wildlife. An additional 30 percent of atlas Killdeer records were reported from marshes; shorelines of lakes, ponds, and rivers; and in open riparian areas dominated by willow, cottonwood, and/or tamarisk. In more urban Arizona settings, these familiar plovers frequent canals, airports, road shoulders, lawns, golf courses, and many other open flat areas with short grass or gravel.

BREEDING

In Arizona, there are both resident and migratory populations of Killdeer, with spring migration beginning in February and continuing into April. In southern Arizona, Killdeer nesting activity begins in March and approximately a month later at higher elevations and in northern locations. During the atlas period, the earliest nest discovered with eggs was on 18 March, although downy young noted on 11 April would suggest the initiation of egg laying by at least early March. On a flat, gravel-roofed building in Phoenix, Demaree (1975) observed a nest with eggs on 3 March. Across Arizona, atlas data reveal a notable peak in nesting activity for this plover between early May and early June. Killdeer breeding activity quickly tapers off after mid-June in Arizona, although nests with eggs were discovered as late as 13 July and downy young were observed into early August. Monson and Phillips (1981) reported Killdeer with downy young in Tucson as late as 28 October, well after typical atlasing surveys had ended in mid-August. Local densities of Killdeer begin to build in mid-July in Arizona indicating the likely initiation of fall migration. Peak buildup periods are variable from one year to the next, but can range from mid-August to mid-October depending on the locality in the state.

Nesting on the ground, Killdeer prefer open areas with sparse to no vegetation and often select nest sites that are raised slightly above the surrounding area (Jackson and Jackson 2000). This may be to avoid flooding of the nest and/or as a better vantage point to watch for potential predators. Both sexes make several shallow scrapes in the earth during the 7–10 days before selecting one for egg laying (Jackson and Jackson 2000). Killdeer typically lay 4 (rarely 3 or 5) eggs (Jackson and Jackson 2000). Both sexes incubate the eggs with the female frequently incubating during the day and the male at night (Warnock and Oring 1996). The incubation period typically lasts from 22 to 29 days, and the chicks can be heard peeping at least 2 days before hatching (Jackson and Jackson 2000).

Killdeer hatchlings are precocial and usually leave the nest when all chicks are hatched and dry, which takes from three hours to one day (Jackson and Jackson 2000). Adult Killdeer are not known to feed young, but rather lead chicks to nearby wet feeding areas and cover in the form of scattered low vegetation (Jackson and Jackson 2000). Sexes share the responsibility of tending the chick for 3–4 weeks. This includes performing their trademark distraction displays in which birds attempt to draw potential predators away from the nest or young by feigning a broken wing and emitting distress calls. The young are capable of sustained

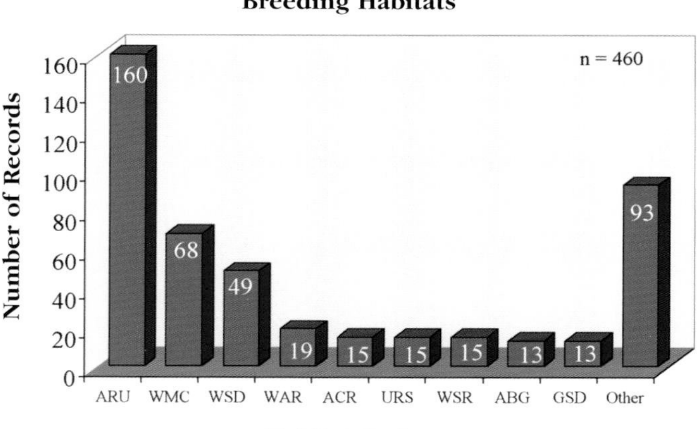

Breeding Phenology

Confirmed Records

25
20
15
10
5
0

n = 115

1 Mar 1 Apr 1 May 1 Jun 1 Jul

flight by 20–31 days (Demaree 1975; Lenington 1980). In Arizona, Killdeer typically have one to two broods per year (Phillips et al. 1964).

DISTRIBUTION AND STATUS

The ubiquitous Killdeer's breeding range extends from southeastern Alaska to Newfoundland and south to central Mexico. In Arizona, these plovers have always been considered common and conspicuous residents nearly statewide (Swarth 1914; Phillips et al. 1964). Killdeer become locally abundant during migration and winter in southern and western Arizona, although some hardy individuals remain during the colder months north of the Mogollon Rim (Phillips et al. 1964).

Atlas data support earlier accounts that Killdeers continue to breed throughout much of the state over a wide range of elevations. Nesting activity was documented from approximately 90 ft (27 m) along the lower Colorado River to 9300 ft (2835 m) on the shores of subalpine lakes in the White Mountains. Killdeer were most frequently detected in urban and rural areas of central and southeastern Arizona and along the Colorado and Gila rivers.

Away from irrigated agricultural lands, atlasers found Killdeers nesting very sparsely in the more arid regions of western and southwestern Arizona, where even the earthen tanks often dry up during much of the breeding season. The scarcity of records in extreme northern and northeastern Arizona likely owes to limited water sources and irrigated lands. Most nesting activity scattered throughout these arid landscapes occurs along lakes, wastewater ponds, and the earthen catchment tanks. Not unexpectedly, these plovers were also lacking in the most heavily forested and steep mountainous regions of the state. However, Killdeer were regularly detected at higher-elevation lakes and ponds in open forest and grasslands just north of the Mogollon Rim.

Native nesting habitats used by Killdeer have undoubtedly decreased in Arizona since 1900, primarily because of water diversions, dams, and other water uses. The resulting decreased water table has reduced perennial flow of many of Arizona's drainages. However, the Killdeers' tolerance of human activities has allowed them to expand their breeding distribution in Arizona by using human-made water sources, unlike many less fortunate and less adaptable water-dependent species.

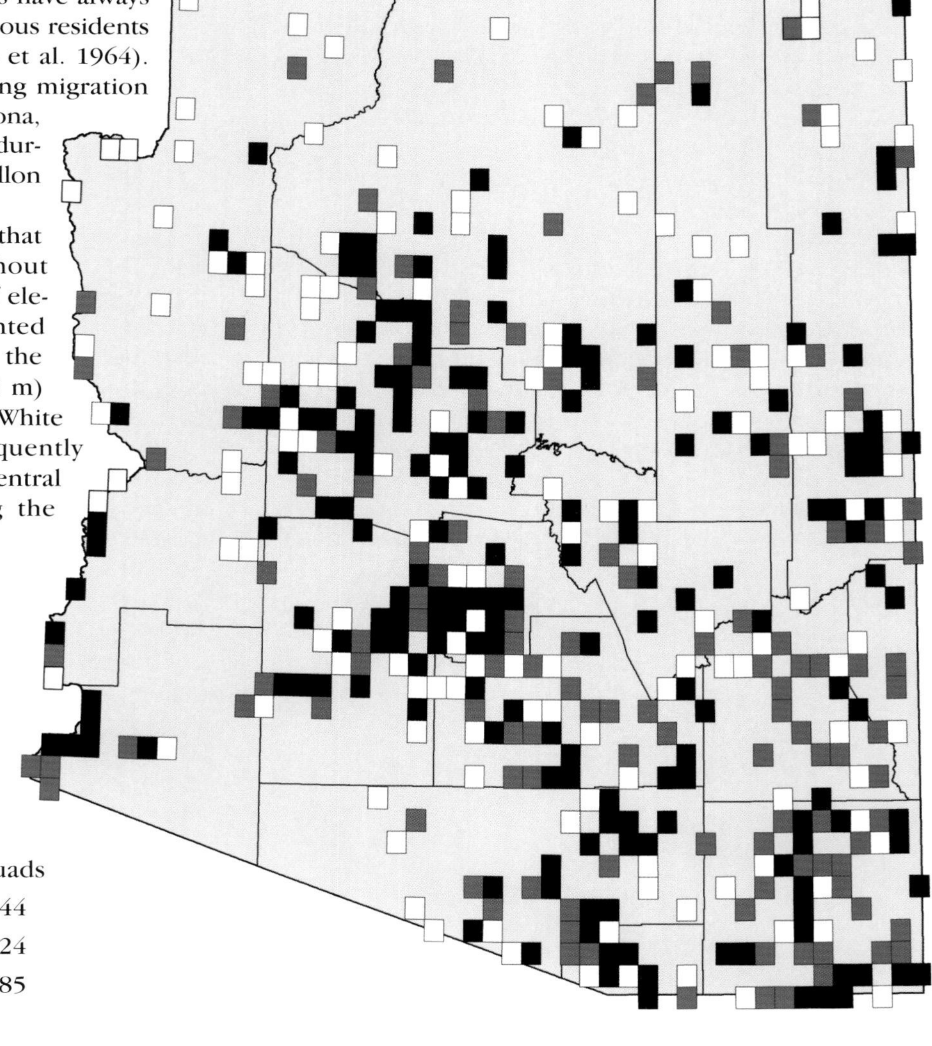

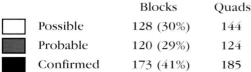

Killdeer Breeding Evidence Reported in 421 (23%) of 1834 priority blocks

	Blocks	Quads
Possible	128 (30%)	144
Probable	120 (29%)	124
Confirmed	173 (41%)	185

Black-necked Stilt

by Troy E. Corman *Himantopus mexicanus*

Affectionately referred to as "pond poodles" because of their loud and often endless yapping calls when disturbed, Black-necked Stilts are distinctive and familiar shorebirds. When a perceived predator approaches, several nesting pairs become quite noisy and highly animated. The varied distraction displays often including ground wing flapping, crouching, and short hopping flights.

BRUCE TAUBERT

HABITAT

Nesting Black-necked Stilts prefer open, shallow watered areas, with or without low emergent vegetation. Most nesting sites in Arizona are found along shallow artificial ponds and lakes in rural and urban areas where the water level remains relatively constant. Atlasers reported 42 percent of their observations from rural habitats, including livestock and agricultural runoff ponds (n = 43). Black-necked Stilts also appear to favor settling ponds at wastewater treatment facilities. An additional 26 percent of atlas records were from wetlands and the shores of ponds, lakes, and rivers. Black-necked Stilts were found nesting locally along shallow urban ponds, especially those constructed with low, isolated islands that are often used for nesting.

BREEDING

In Arizona, Black-necked Stilts winter annually primarily only in the Salt and Gila River valleys in the greater Phoenix area and near Tucson. Migrants begin moving north in early to mid-March, with stragglers observed into early June. These attractive shorebirds initiate courtship and nest building activity in March and April in Arizona. Atlasers reported agitated pairs by 3 April and nests with eggs have been found as early as 14 April. However, atlasers observed adults with young as early as 21 April indicating egg laying by the last week of March. Atlas data suggest a peak in nesting activity from early May to early June. Black-necked Stilt nests with eggs are observed through early July and dependent young are noted through mid-August in Arizona. Early migrants begin to appear in nonbreeding areas of the state by late June and numbers continue to build throughout August and into September. Most migrants have moved south by mid-October, with stragglers reported irregularly through early December.

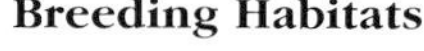

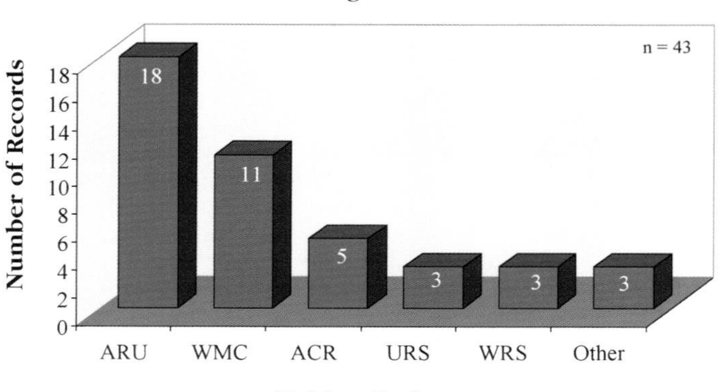

Stilt nests are constructed by either parent and consist of a shallow scrap on the ground or on top of partially submerged debris. Nests are typically very exposed, with little evidence of concealment for the incubating adult. Atlasers discovered nests on earthen pond dikes, low islands, vegetated river sandbars, mats of vegetative debris, and tiny islands of drying wastewater sludge. If water rises, nests are built up by both parents, who place dead vegetation and other debris beneath the nest lining (Robinson et al. 1999).

Both Black-necked Stilt parents share in the duty of incubating the typical clutch of 4 eggs, but clutches can range from 2 to 5 (Grant 1982). Incubation may begin as soon as the first egg is laid, but it depends on local ambient temperatures (Robinson et al. 1999). In very hot environments such as Arizona, incubation behaviors serve to cool eggs rather than to warm them, with the parents soaking belly feathers in water before sitting on nest to facilitate evaporative cooling and to maintain nest humidity (Robinson et al. 1999). The eggs hatch in approximately 25 days, although incubation can range from 21 to 30 days (Robinson et al. 1999). The chicks stay in the nest less than 24 hours after the last chick has hatched, and then broods are led to areas of shallow water with vegetation for cover (Robinson et al. 1999). The young are capable of sustained flight when they are 27–31 days old (Sordahl 1980), but remain with one or both parents well beyond this time (Wetmore 1925). Black-necked Stilts typically only produce one brood per year, but many of these exposed nests are lost to coyotes and other ground predators, and renesting attempts are frequent.

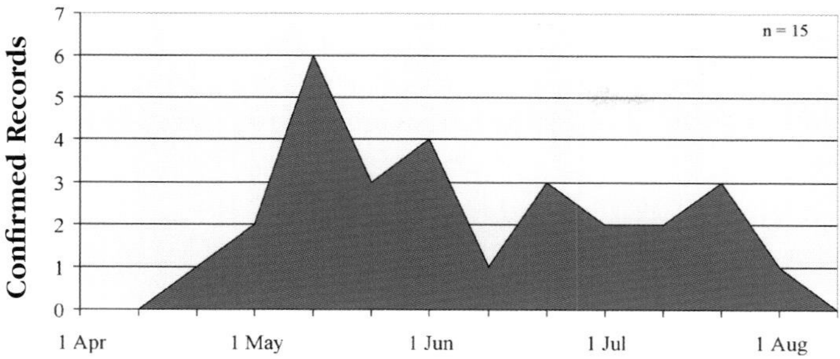

DISTRIBUTION AND STATUS

Black-necked Stilts nest in many disjunct breeding populations in North America. This includes most western U.S. states and locally along the Gulf and Atlantic coast from New Jersey south. They also nest in Hawaii and south into the Caribbean, Mexico, and in Central America and northern South America. Based on historical accounts, the nesting distribution of Black-necked Stilts in Arizona has increased primarily through human-caused habitat alterations. Black-necked Stilts were previously known to breed locally along the lower Colorado River, probably at Picacho Reservoir, and formerly on the San Pedro River (Phillips et al. 1964). By 1980, Monson and Phillips (1981) noted this shorebird as also nesting locally in Phoenix and at least irregularly in Chandler, Tucson, and Painted Rock Reservoir. After a review of nesting records along the lower Colorado River, Rosenberg et al. (1991) considered Black-necked Stilts to be rare, irregular, and local breeders.

Atlasers discovered Black-necked Stilts nesting primarily at elevations between 90 and 2300 ft (27–701 m). One exception was the observation of a pair performing distraction displays at 4900 ft (1493 m) near the confluence of Chevelon Creek and the Little Colorado River, just south of Hibbard, Navajo County, on 17 June 1997.

Along the lower Colorado River, atlasers confirmed the nesting of Black-necked Stilts from Imperial National Wildlife Refuge south to near the international border. Stilts have been previously found nesting locally along the Colorado River north to Headgate Rock Dam, just upstream of Parker (Rosenberg et al. 1991). Atlasers also found these shorebirds potentially nesting along the lower Gila River upstream to near Wellton.

Atlasers discovered the vast majority of Arizona nesting Black-necked Stilts within the lower Salt, middle Gila, and lower Santa Cruz River valleys. This includes the adjacent urban and agricultural areas of Tucson, Marana, Eloy, Casa Grande, and Picacho Reservoir. In the Phoenix area, Black-necked Stilts were found nesting from Chandler, Higley, and Mesa, west to Sun City, Tolleson, and Avondale. These birds were found nesting farther west from Buckeye, through the Arlington Valley, and locally down the Gila River valley to Painted Rock Dam. Additional isolated records include pairs observed during appropriate nesting period near Willcox and Ganado.

The distribution of nesting Black-necked Stilts in Arizona is expected to increase as the human population continues to expand, requiring additional wastewater treatment facilities to be constructed. The current effort to restore and enhance wetlands and riparian areas within the lower Salt, Gila, and Santa Cruz River valleys may also favor this unique shorebird.

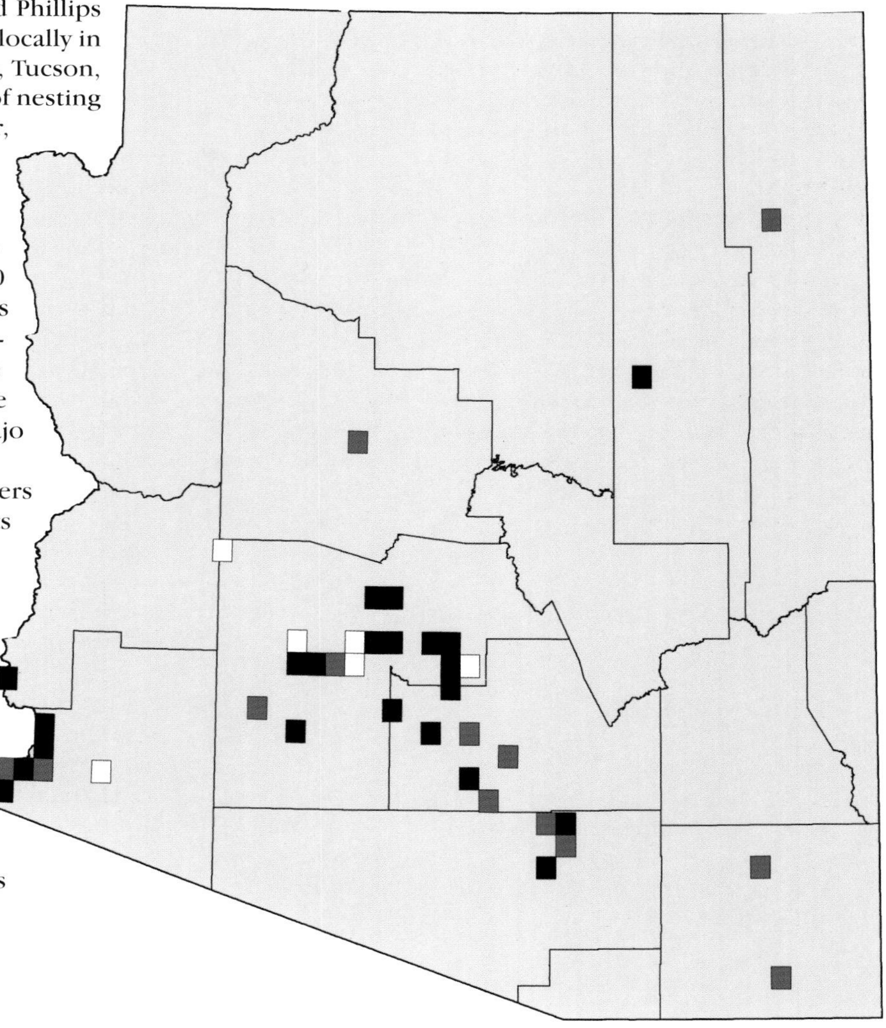

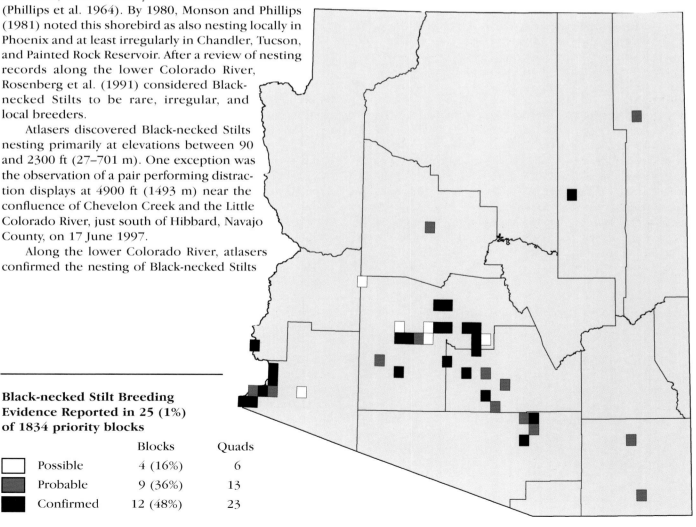

Black-necked Stilt Breeding Evidence Reported in 25 (1%) of 1834 priority blocks

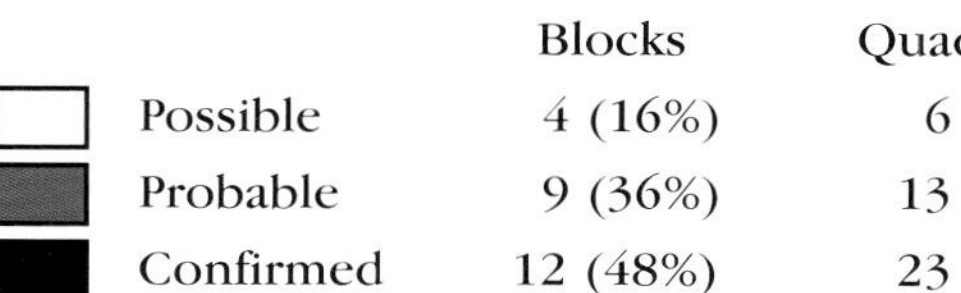

	Blocks	Quads
Possible	4 (16%)	6
Probable	9 (36%)	13
Confirmed	12 (48%)	23

American Avocet

by Troy E. Corman *Recurvirostra americana*

Swinging their heads from side to side, American Avocets use their slender, upturned bills to filter tiny invertebrates from shallow water. These large, attractive shorebirds are devoted and protective parents when nests or chicks are approached too closely. Unsuspecting intruders are soon confronted with intimidation tactics that include loud cries and swift flight dives.

BRUCE TAUBERT

HABITAT

Throughout the year, American Avocets prefer open, shallow bodies of water with sparse to no vegetation. In Arizona, several artificial and natural impoundments are especially favored by these bold shorebirds for nesting. Atlasers noted 67 percent of all records at artificial water impoundments consisting primarily of settling ponds at wastewater treatment facilities (n = 26). However, American Avocets also nest locally at irrigation runoff ponds, aquifer recharge basins, and large earthen livestock tanks. Another 22 percent of atlas records were reported from mudflats along reservoirs, lakes, and ponds with receding water levels, alkali ponds, and locally along lowland rivers with sandbars and small, bare islands.

BREEDING

In Arizona, spring migration for American Avocets begins by late February or early March, with a noticeable peak in April and stragglers occasionally noted into early June. Courtship behavior and pairing probably occurs before and during migration as many individuals arrive in nesting areas already paired (Wolfe 1931). Atlasers reported the earliest breeding behavior of a copulating pair on 19 April. During the atlas period, the earliest nests with eggs and downy young were noted on 6 May. Adults tending downy young on this date would indicate that some egg laying is initiated no later than early to mid-April. Atlas data reveal a peak nesting period for American Avocets in mid-May, although the sample size was relatively low. Atlasers observed adults with flightless young through 24 July, and adult avocets were noted performing distraction displays as late as 10 August. Fall migration in Arizona can be quite protracted, with southbound migrants appearing in nonbreeding areas by mid-June (Rosenberg et al. 1991). Peak passage is variable with a strong late push often noted in October. Stragglers are frequently observed into November and occasionally into early December. American Avocets are casual to rare winter residents in southern Arizona.

American Avocets nest on the ground in a shallow depression they construct. The pair jointly selects the nest site and scrape out the depression, which may remain bare or fully lined with bits of nearby debris or vegetation (Robinson et al. 1997). Lining of the nest often continues throughout incubation (Gibson 1971). American Avocets choose exposed nest sites with little or no vegetation. In Arizona, frequently chosen nest locations include small islands, mudflats, or at the edge or top of an earthen dike surrounding a water impoundment. Both parents and neighboring pairs defend nests and young with noisy flight dives and several different distraction displays.

Unless otherwise noted, much of the following breeding information comes from Robinson et al. (1997). The full clutch size of an American Avocet is 3–4 eggs, with most clutches containing 4. Both adults share the responsibility of incubating the eggs until they hatch in 23–30 days. In Arizona, where ambient temperatures are very warm during the nesting period, the first eggs begin developing immediately after being laid, without parental incubation. Also in hot environments, the incubation behaviors of the adults cool rather than warm the eggs, with parents regularly soaking their belly feathers in water before sitting on the nest to

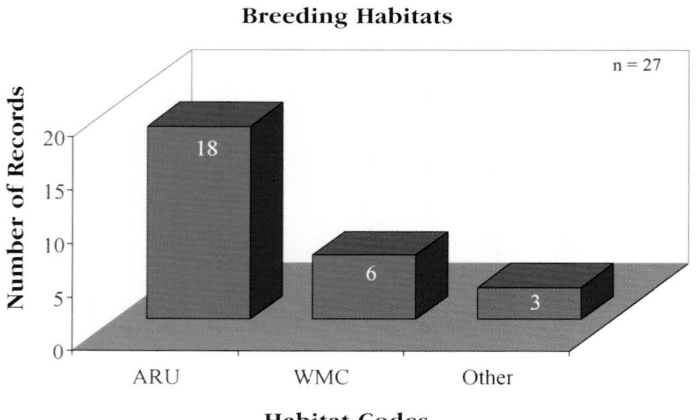

Breeding Phenology

Confirmed Records (0–9); 1 Apr, 1 May, 1 Jun, 1 Jul, 1 Aug; n = 20

Graph includes fledgling records

facilitate evaporative cooling. Entire broods typically hatch over a 1–2 day period, sometimes longer, and the chicks remain in the nest no more than 24 hours after the hatching of the last sibling. Chicks feed themselves but are attended by both parents for a minimum of 3–4 weeks, when they are capable of sustained flight (Gibson 1971). Most evidence suggests American Avocets produce only one brood per year, but they will quickly renest if earlier efforts fail. Gibson (1971) observed two pairs that completed laying 4 eggs only 8 days following loss of their earlier clutches.

DISTRIBUTION AND STATUS

American Avocets breed primarily in disjunct populations of western North America from the northern Great Plains region of southern Canada, south to Texas and west to California. They are also known to nest in central Mexico and recently along the Atlantic coast. Fairly common to common migrants statewide, avocets were not known to breed in Arizona until 1965, when they were found nesting near Willcox (Monson and Phillips 1981). During the following decade, American Avocets were also found nesting very locally in Phoenix, Chandler, and Tucson (Monson and Phillips 1981). In northern Apache County, Jacobs (1986) reported on observations of adults with young at Chinle in 1982 and nearby Moaning Lake in 1985.

Atlasers found American Avocets nesting locally, but in many more localities than previously reported at elevations ranging from 530 ft (162 m) near Painted Rock Dam to 5750 ft (1753 m) at the wastewater treatment facility at Petrified Forest National Park. In southern Arizona, half of the known breeding locations were found in Maricopa County in the greater Phoenix area west through the Arlington Valley. Nesting was noted irregularly along the Santa Cruz River near Tucson. Avocets were also confirmed nesting in Cochise County at Whitewater Drawl near McNeal and along settling ponds near Douglas and Paul Spur. On San Carlos Apache tribal land, atlasers documented the shorebirds nesting at Bonita Tank and possibly nesting at another earthen livestock tank. American Avocets were documented nesting very sparingly north of the Mogollon Rim, but included Many Farms Lake on Navajo tribal lands and at wastewater facilities at Page and nearby Wahweap along Lake Mead.

When conditions are favorable, American Avocets readily take advantage of temporarily available habitat, nesting on exposed mudflats that may be present one year but not the next. In the early 1990s, territorial and displaying avocets were observed along the ephemeral Painted Rock Reservoir northwest of Gila Bend. The year following the atlas, American Avocets were also confirmed breeding at Roosevelt Lake for a first Gila County nesting record. These attractive shorebirds undoubtedly nest locally at additional rural and wastewater treatment facilities ponds that were never visited by atlasers.

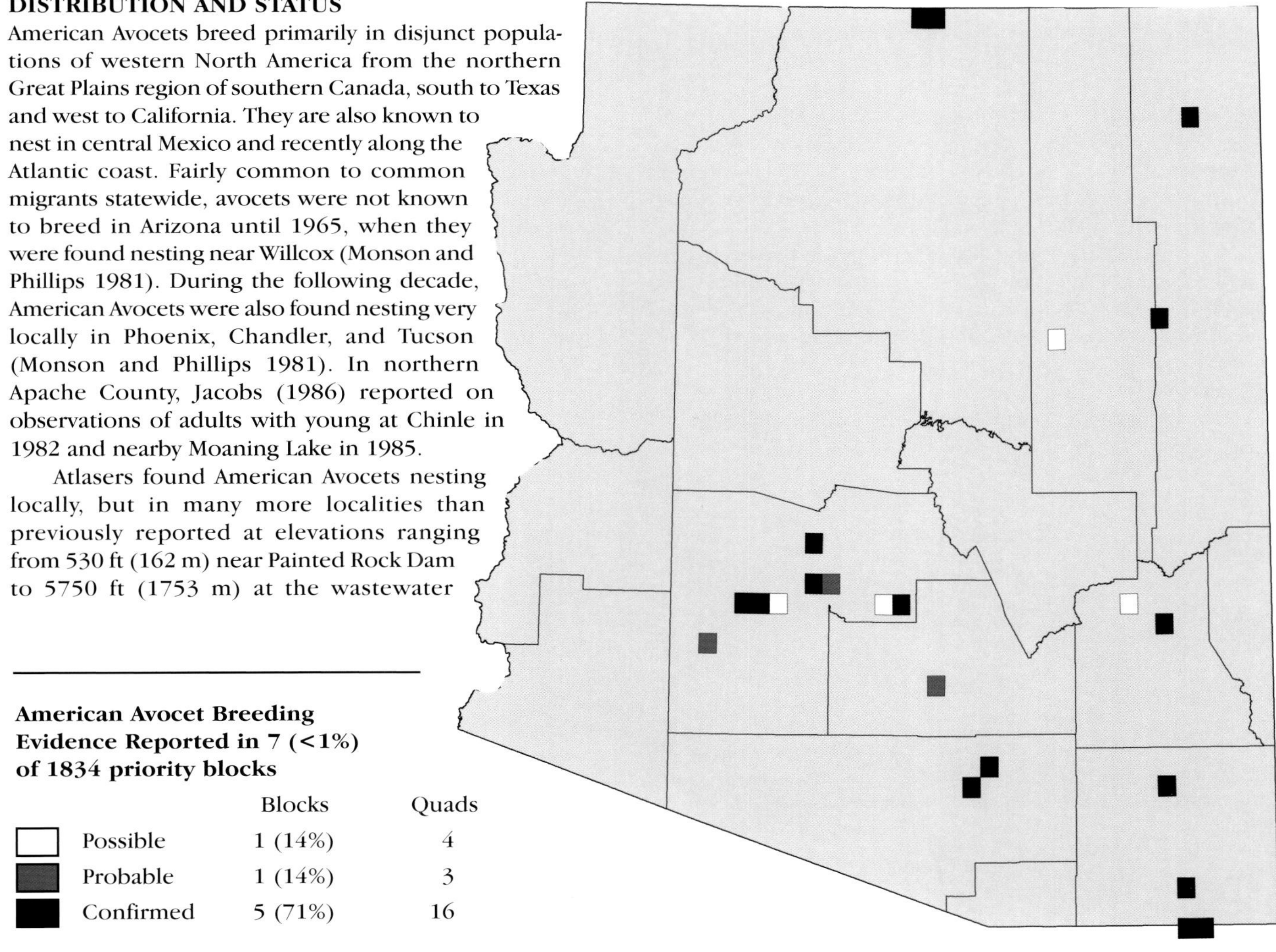

American Avocet Breeding Evidence Reported in 7 (<1%) of 1834 priority blocks

	Blocks	Quads
Possible	1 (14%)	4
Probable	1 (14%)	3
Confirmed	5 (71%)	16

Spotted Sandpiper

by Cathryn Wise-Gervais *Actitis macularia*

The Spotted Sandpiper is one of the most familiar and widespread of Arizona's nesting shorebird species. These well-named birds are frequently observed foraging on the rocky shorelines of rivers and lakes and can be easily identified from a distance by their spotted breasts and bobbing gait.

HABITAT

Migrating Spotted Sandpipers can inhabit almost any natural or human-made aquatic habitat in Arizona, but the birds are more selective when choosing nesting habitat. Typical breeding areas offer a combination of shoreline for foraging, semi-open habitat for nesting, and patches of dense vegetation for brood cover (Oring et al. 1983). In Arizona, elevation, temperature, and vegetation structure is apparently more important than what dominant plant species is present. Atlasers reported these sandpipers in nine habitat types, and 34 percent of records were from marsh edges, ponds, lakes, and reservoirs with various wetland vegetation (n = 53). Atlasers reported 25 percent of records in open montane riparian drainages with scattered coniferous and deciduous trees and shrubs, and obtained 19 percent of records in low elevation drainages dominated by either cottonwood-willow or Arizona sycamore. Fewer Spotted Sandpiper records were reported along drainages dominated by willow–Russian olive associations and high-elevation alder and scrub willows. Observers also regularly encountered Spotted Sandpipers within the Grand Canyon along the Colorado River in patches of tamarisk, arrowweed, coyote willow, seepwillow, and common reed.

BREEDING

In Arizona, Spotted Sandpipers begin spring migration as early as late March or early April, but peak passage is not until mid-May. Determining early spring migration dates in Arizona is complicated by the fact that these birds commonly winter at elevations below 3200 ft (975 m). Unlike many other shorebirds, female Spotted Sandpipers often arrive on the breeding grounds to establish territories 4–5 days prior to the males (Oring et al. 1997). Atlasers first reported Spotted Sandpipers in suitable breeding habitat on 2 April and observed paired birds on 29 April. Observers obtained the earliest confirmed record of adults with chicks on 15 May, indicating that this pair had laid eggs by late April. Surveyors made this nesting observation in the Grand Canyon near the confluence of the Little Colorado River. Spotted Sandpipers are typically present in this area year-round. Atlasers obtained only 12 breeding confirmations for this species throughout the state, but from the limited data it would appear that most egg laying occurs in May and June, and that the peak period for dependent chicks is from mid-June to mid-July. The latest active nest was found on 25 June, and fledgling Spotted Sandpipers were reported as late as 18 July. Atlasers reported agitated adults on 6 August, suggesting the possibility of dependent young nearby. In Arizona, the first southbound migrant Spotted Sandpipers are noted by early July, but peak passage is in August, and stragglers continue into November.

Spotted Sandpipers typically nest within 300 ft (91.4 m) of water, under shade-providing foliage (Oring et al. 1997). Atlasers measured only one Spotted Sandpiper nest near Greer, and this was on the ground under the canopy of grasses. Females or males will attract mates by making nest scrapes and as part of pair formation, adults begin nest building shortly after the pair encounters one another (Oring et al. 1997). The female will then lay her 4-egg clutch, and she may assist with incubation or leave this chore to her mate. Female Spotted Sandpipers are often polyandrous and many find new mates after laying a clutch or soon after the first brood hatches (Oring et al. 1997). In other circumstances, the female will be monogamous and assist in raising the brood.

Incubation takes approximately 21 days, and the chicks leave the nest within hours of hatching. The young feed themselves but are brooded by the male, and occasionally by the female, especially for the first three days (Oring et al. 1997). The young are capable of flight by approximately

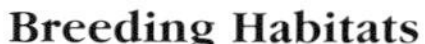

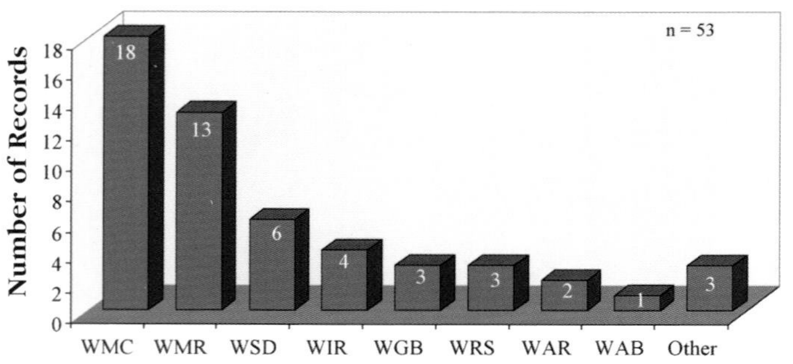

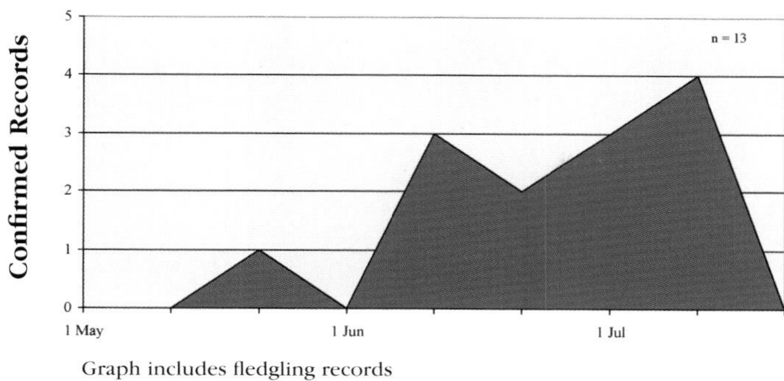

Graph includes fledgling records

18 days, but are tended by the adult for at least 4 weeks (Nice 1962). Spotted Sandpipers commonly raise more than one brood per season.

DISTRIBUTION AND STATUS

Spotted Sandpipers have the most widespread breeding range of any North American sandpiper. In the East they are found south from Canada to North Carolina and Missouri, and in the West they occur from Alaska south to central Arizona. This species can utilize a broad array of both aquatic habitats and elevations, and Bent (1929) reported these birds breeding from sea level to over 14,000 ft (4267 m).

The Spotted Sandpiper's breeding distribution in Arizona has always included the White Mountains region, as well as above and below the Mogollon Rim, where atlasers encountered the species fairly frequently. Although Mearns (1890) suggested that Spotted Sandpipers nested to 10,000 feet in the San Francisco Mountains, Phillips et al. (1964) refuted this. In central Arizona, atlasers reported Spotted Sandpipers at altitudes ranging from approximately 3250 to 9000 ft (990–2743 m), with the lower elevation records from the Gila Box area. In Yavapai County, Spotted Sandpipers were confirmed nesting near Prescott and locally along the Verde River to below the Verde Hot Springs. These sandpipers undoubtedly breed throughout most of the White Mountain Apache tribal lands but is not represented in atlas data because the tribe declined survey access.

In contrast, in the northwest corner of the state Spotted Sandpipers were confirmed or suspected of nesting at lower elevations between 1200 and 3100 ft (366–945 m). These records were all within narrow or high-walled canyons, such as in the Virgin River Gorge or within the Grand and Glen Canyon corridor of the Colorado River. Spotted Sandpiper eggs are more susceptible to heat damage than to cold (Oring et al. 1997), likely limiting their low elevation nesting distribution in Arizona.

In northeastern Arizona, Spotted Sandpipers were detected only near Shonto during atlas surveys. This location is near the Tsegi Canyon area where Woodbury and Russell (1945) documented this sandpiper nesting. Although habitat in several drainages on the Defiance Plateau, including upper Canyon de Chelly, and in the Chuska Mountains would appear appropriate for nesting, these sandpipers escaped detection in this region during atlas surveys.

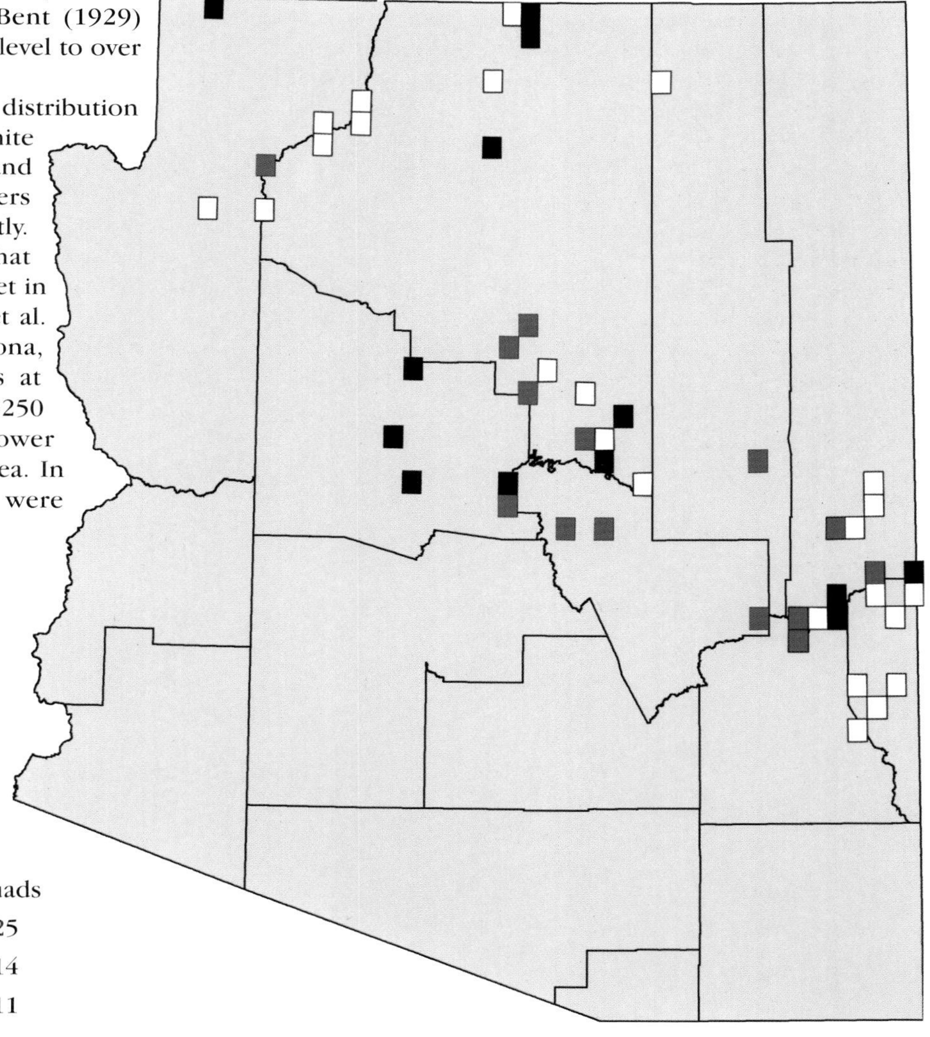

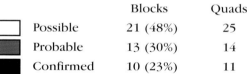

Spotted Sandpiper Breeding Evidence Reported in 44 (2%) of 1834 priority blocks

	Blocks	Quads
Possible	21 (48%)	25
Probable	13 (30%)	14
Confirmed	10 (23%)	11

Wilson's Snipe

by Troy E. Corman *Gallinago delicata*

Relying on cryptic coloration and wetland vegetation, Wilson's Snipes typically crouch and freeze when danger is perceived. Contradictory to their many secretive life activities, during the nesting season individual Wilson's Snipes are regularly observed roosting on very exposed stumps or fence posts within their territory.

HABITAT

During winter and migration in Arizona, Wilson's Snipes use almost any damp to shallow wet habitats with moist organic soil and nearby vegetative cover. This includes streamsides, lake and pond edges, marshes, flooded fields, and even isolated springs and seeps in otherwise arid locations. Reaching the southern edge of their breeding distribution in Arizona, Wilson's Snipes have been found nesting primarily at higher elevations in wet mountain meadows and moist areas along streams or lakes. Vegetation typically includes a dense cover of low-growing sedges, rushes, and/or grasses, but taller cattails or scattered scrub willows are often nearby. Johnson and Ryder (1977) described the most suitable nesting locations contain shallow and stable water levels, interspersed with patches of saturated but not necessarily flooded soil and vegetation. Studies in Wyoming revealed a mean water depth of approximately 1.4 in. (35 mm) in nesting areas (Mueller 1999).

BREEDING

In appropriate habitat, Wilson's Snipe winters fairly commonly throughout western and southern Arizona. North of the Mogollon Rim, snipes are very sparse and local winter residents where wetlands and seeps remain unfrozen. Spring migration begins by late February, reaching northern Arizona by early March. Few individuals remain in Arizona after late April. Male Wilson's Snipes begin performing winnowing flights immediately upon their arrival on breeding grounds, which is 10–14 days prior to the arrival of the females (Mueller 1999). The tremulous winnowing sound is produced by airflow over outstretched outer tail feathers during swift flight dives. These flights are most commonly conducted in the early evening after sunset, but can be occasionally heard throughout the day or night (Mueller 1999). Winnowing flights are mostly given by males and are considered an aggressive behavior for territorial defense, but also may act to attract mates (Mueller 1999). Winnowing activity peaks in May and greatly decreases or completely ceases when females begin to incubate. Atlasers detected a winnowing snipe on 26 June. In Colorado, winnowing snipe are reported from 12 April to 9 August (Levad 1998).

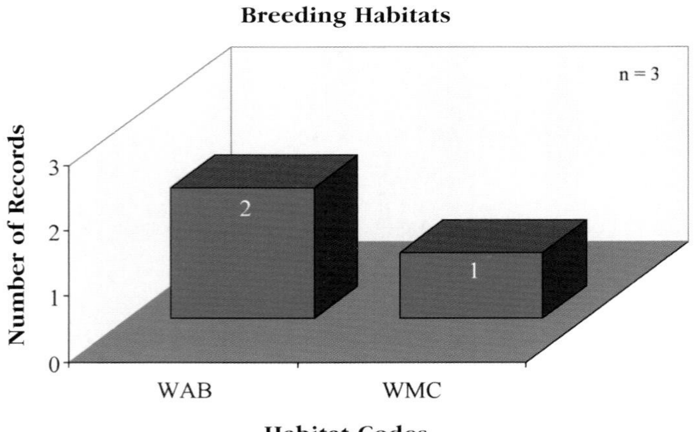

With Arizona's limited Wilson's Snipe breeding detections, the timing of nesting is poorly known in the state. On 1 July 1993, atlasers discovered the first and only Wilson's Snipe nest with eggs ever found in Arizona. In Colorado, where breeding snipe are much more common and widespread, nests with eggs have been found from 21 May to 21 July (Levad 1998). This would suggest that Arizona's clutch was a second nesting attempt after earlier efforts failed or the first nesting attempt of a yearling. Yearling Wilson's Snipes are known to breed later in the season than older birds, sometimes as much as two months later (Tuck 1972). The only other confirmed evidence of Wilson's Snipe nesting in Arizona was of a fledgling not fully grown collected near Springerville on 5 July 1936 (Phillips et al. 1964). During the Colorado Breeding Bird Atlas, fledglings were noted through 5 August (Levad 1998). In Arizona, a few Wilson's Snipes appear in nonbreeding areas by late July or early August, but most are not observed in southern Arizona until early or mid-September.

Nests of Wilson's Snipe are typically on the ground, well concealed in grass, sedge, or other vegetation and not easily observed from above. The woven nest is constructed by the female and is unusually elaborate for a shorebird (Tuck 1972). Placement of the nest is typically very close or even surrounded by water and often in tussocks of grass or sedge, sometimes overhung by larger woody shrub (Tuck 1972). The nest in Arizona was in an open, wet meadow of 10–12 in. (25–30 cm) tall grass and sedge several feet from clumps of Geyer willow.

Clutches typically consist of 4 eggs, occasionally fewer, and are incubated by the female for 18–20 days (Mueller 1999). Upon hatching, the male often leaves the nest with the first two hatched chicks and the female with the remaining two (Tuck 1972). There is apparently no further contact between the mates, with each rearing their reduced broods until the chicks are dependent in 19–20 days (Tuck 1972). The average period for females to lay replacement clutches after loss of clutch or small young was 14 days (Green 1988). Most evidence suggests that only one brood is produced per year (Mueller 1999).

DISTRIBUTION AND STATUS

Wilson's Snipe breeds throughout much of Alaska and Canada, south to West Virginia in the East and northern California and New Mexico in the West. It has been found nesting irregularly and locally south to northern Baja California and central Arizona. Prior to the atlas, Wilson's Snipe had been confirmed nesting in Arizona only once near Springerville in 1936. These snipe have been reported very irregularly in midsummer in this region ever since. This includes four seen and heard winnowing near Springerville on 9–10 June 1990 (P. Lehman and S. Finnegan, personal communication).

Atlasers discovered Wilson's Snipe nesting very locally and possibly irregularly at elevations ranging from 6720 to 8900 ft (2048–2713 m). This is well within the range snipe nests were found during the Colorado Breeding Bird Atlas, from 6000 to 10,000 ft (1829–3048 m) in elevation (Levad 1998). Winnowing snipe were noted over wetlands near Mountainaire south of Flagstaff in June 1993. The nest with eggs was discovered near the headwaters of the San Francisco River near Alpine, and an individual was observed in appropriate nesting habitat along Mexican Hay Lake southwest of Eagar on 20 July 1997.

Wilson's Snipe are known to be very susceptible to changing local conditions, and during dry years they may occur in greatly reduced number or be entirely absent from locations where they were nesting commonly the year prior (Leberman 1992). This could help explain the very erratic reports of nesting activity of this shorebird in Arizona. Two of the three breeding records obtained of Wilson's Snipe during the atlas were in 1993, which was the wettest year of the entire atlas period. The majority of atlas surveys were conduct during years with below normal precipitation, greatly limiting the chances of detecting this local nesting species.

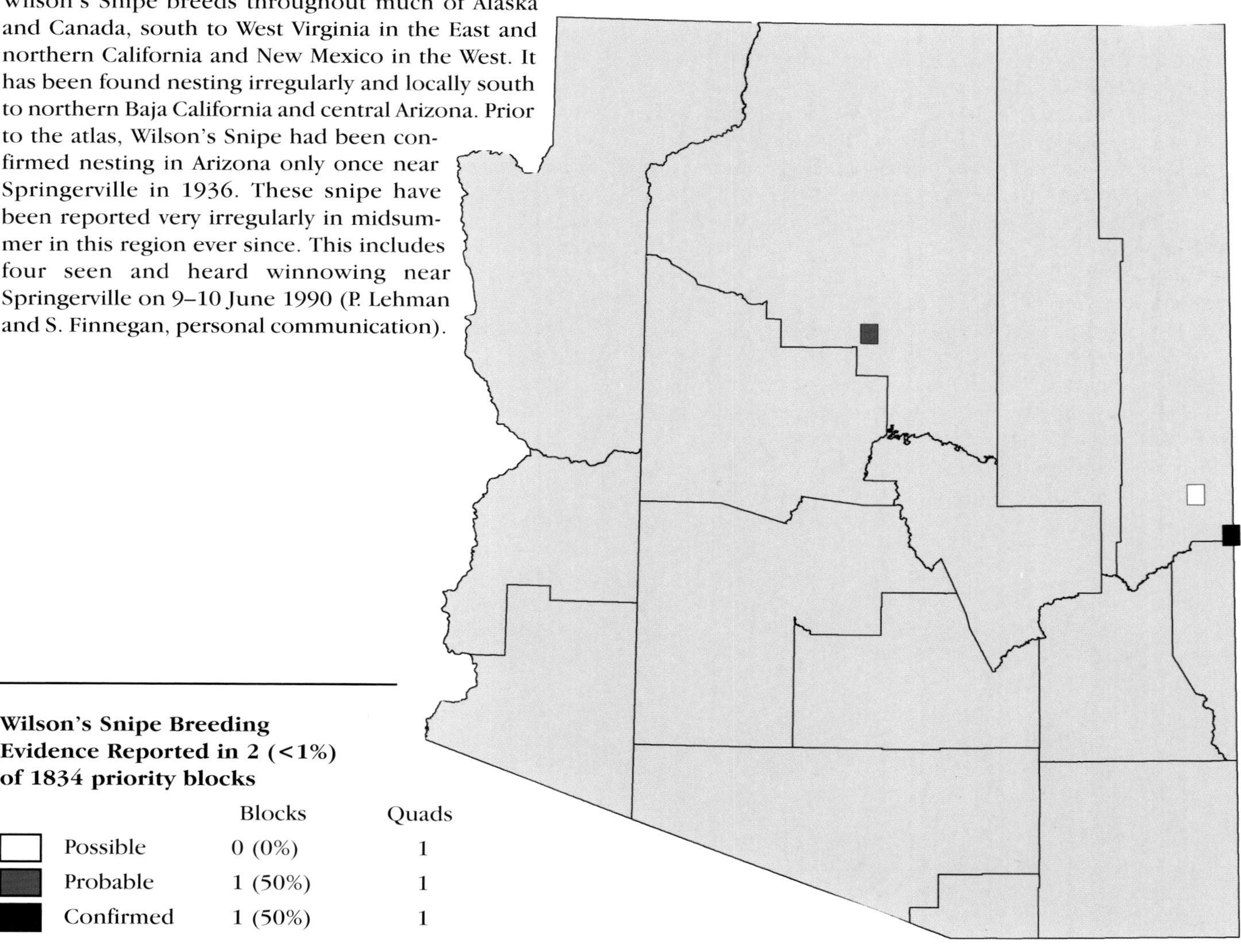

Wilson's Snipe Breeding Evidence Reported in 2 (<1%) of 1834 priority blocks

	Blocks	Quads
Possible	0 (0%)	1
Probable	1 (50%)	1
Confirmed	1 (50%)	1

Rock Pigeon

by Cathryn Wise-Gervais *Columba livia*

Settlers first introduced Rock Pigeons to the New World in the early seventeenth century, and an extensive colonization of the continent soon followed. Few birds have been as thoroughly studied as these familiar pigeons, and much of our understanding of basic avian physiology, flight mechanics, and navigation is owed to this species.

RICHARD DITCH

HABITAT

Rock Pigeons are closely associated with human developments, including towns, parks, and agricultural landscapes. In their native settings, this species nests along the seashore on airy cliffs and in rocky crevices or caves. In urban areas, feral Rock Pigeons commonly nest on high-rise buildings, billboards, and other constructed artifacts. Atlasers reported this species in eleven different habitat types, but 52 percent of potential breeding records were from residential areas including suburban yards, city parks, and golf courses (n = 112). The second most commonly reported setting for this species was rural and agricultural areas, including feedlots, pastures, cropland, and outbuildings (31 percent of records). Only a few observations were obtained in the remaining habitats, including industrial areas and commercial districts. Observers reported a few Rock Pigeons sightings in Sonoran desertscrub habitats, and these birds were near dwellings, highway overpasses, or farm buildings.

BREEDING

Rock Pigeons are resident throughout North America and can theoretically breed year-round in much of their range. Breeding activity in cold climates is triggered by bright, sunny weather independent of temperature, and although fewer winter nesting attempts are made and these are typically less successful than in summer, this behavior persists at least as far north as Canada (Johnston 1992). Atlas surveys did not typically begin until late February or early March, and the first Rock Pigeon–occupied nest was not reported until 17 March. Atlasers reported dependent fledglings as late as 13 August, but nesting activity in Arizona has previously been noted well into the fall. This species undoubtedly breeds successfully throughout the year in many of Arizona's urban and rural communities, but observers missed these late records because atlas surveys typically ended in late August or early September. Observers obtained only 36 confirmed records for Rock Pigeons, not including fledgling sightings. Although most confirmations were reported in mid-April, this time period may correspond more closely to the peak of surveys conducted in high Rock Pigeon concentration areas such as near Phoenix and Tucson, rather than to an actual peak in nesting activity.

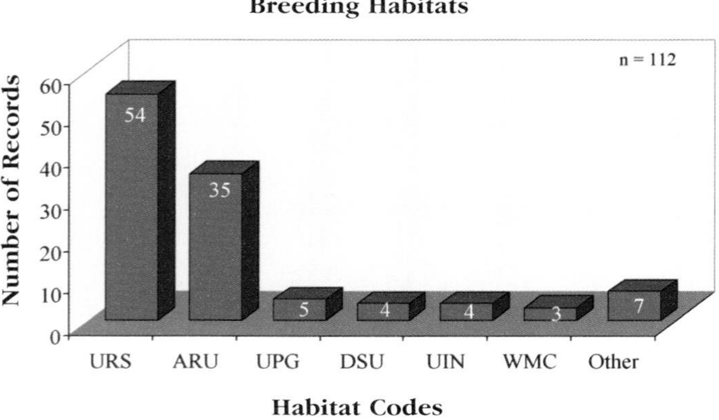

Rock Pigeons nest in a wide variety of settings, usually under an overhang of some sort that provides cover from above. In urban settings, Rock Pigeons in Arizona commonly nest on high-rise buildings, bridges, parking garages, billboards, and other elevated structures. In desert regions of the state, Rock Pigeons also commonly nest on the covered eaves of homes and in untrimmed palm trees. These birds select flat surfaces for nest construction, and will even nest on the ground, such as in the corner of an abandoned building (Johnston 1992). Atlasers did not measure any Rock Pigeons nests, but this species is known to nest from ground level to over 100 ft (30.5 m) high on cliffs or buildings (Johnston 1992). Females typically perch on the nest site while males provide nesting materials such as small twigs. Females tuck the materials around them, and the final nest has a messy appearance. Successful nest sites are often used annually, and three to five broods are typically raised in the same nest during a single year. For each nesting attempt, adult Rock Pigeons simply add additional materials over the top of their first nest, covering fecal matter and even dead nestlings (Johnston 1992).

Rock Pigeons lay clutches of 2 eggs and incubate these for about 19 days (Johnston 1992). Both sexes incubate and feed the young regurgitated "crop milk" exclusively for the

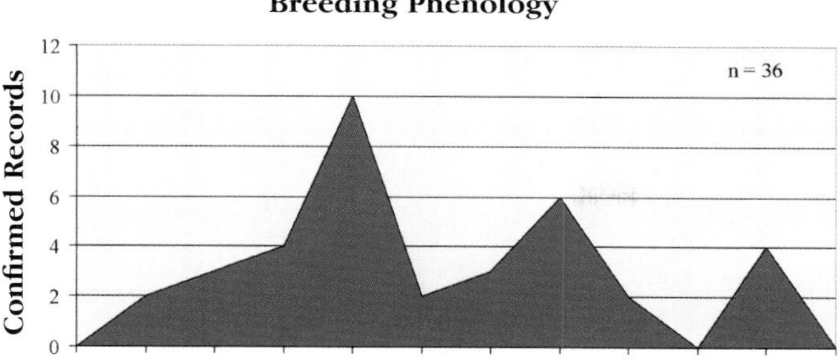

first few days. The parents introduce seeds by day 5, and present the adult diet after day 9 (Johnston 1992). The young fledge at approximately 25–32 days in the summer and at about 45 days in the winter (Johnston 1992). Brood overlap is common in the summer (Burley 1980), so fledging of the first brood can occur after the next clutch is laid (Johnston 1992).

DISTRIBUTION AND STATUS

Humans have either intentionally or accidentally introduced Rock Pigeons to many regions of the world, and today the species is found on a discontinuous basis at cities and towns throughout North America from coast to coast. Rock Pigeons are found north to southern Canada and south throughout Central and South America. The birds are absent from wilderness areas and dense forests, but do occur at mid- to high elevations in developed areas. In Arizona, atlasers reported Rock Pigeons on priority blocks from elevations of approximately 90 ft south of Somerton to 7200 ft in Flagstaff (27–2195 m).

Rock Pigeons are considered common in residential, rural, and agricultural areas throughout much of southern and western Arizona (Rosenberg et al. 1991; Tucson Audubon Society 1995; Witzeman et al. 1997). This familiar pigeon's preferred habitat is scattered, however, and is much more limited in the northern half of the state, including on Navajo and Hopi tribal lands. Atlasers noted Rock Pigeons in most of the larger towns and cities that were surveyed in Arizona. However, many priority blocks fell outside the urban habitats preferred by these pigeons, so atlasers sometimes missed this bird during typical atlas surveys. Further, few atlasers submitted casual observation reports for Rock Pigeons, given the bird's status as an exotic and often unwanted species. As a result, many known urban populations of Rock Pigeons were not included in the atlas database. These omissions are obvious on the bird's distribution map and include areas around Page, Kingman, Prescott, Winslow, Globe, Safford, and Clifton. Observers noted the highest concentration of Rock Pigeons near Phoenix and, to a lesser extent, along the I-10 corridor to Tucson.

Although Rock Pigeons are an exotic species, there seems to be little competition between them and Arizona's native birds, largely because of the Rock Pigeon's close association with humans. The species is somewhat habitat limited in that respect, but undoubtedly these pigeons will soon follow any new developments in previously unsettled terrain.

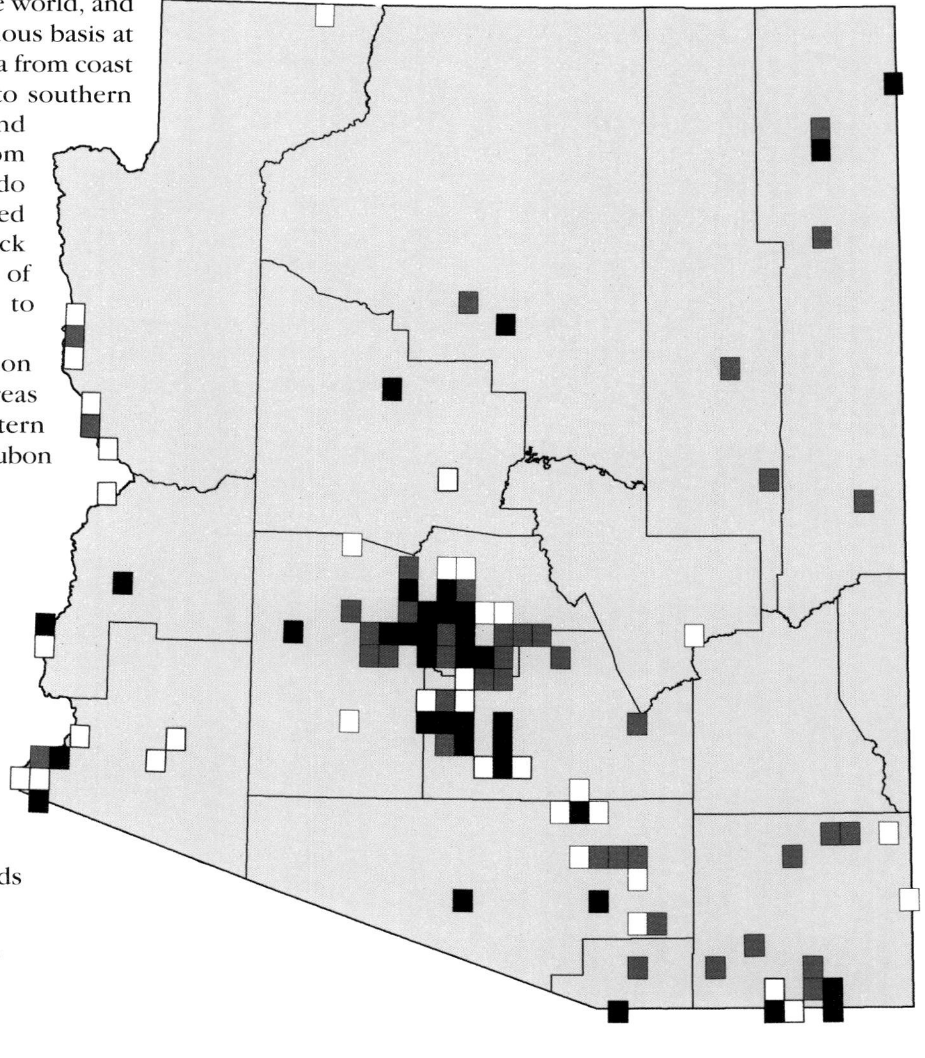

Rock Dove Breeding Evidence Reported in 97 (5%) of 1834 priority blocks

	Blocks	Quads
Possible	32 (33%)	35
Probable	32 (33%)	40
Confirmed	33 (34%)	35

Band-tailed Pigeon

by Jennifer L. Martin *Patagioenas fasciata*

Light on the wing, quick and maneuverable, the distribution of Band-tailed Pigeons in Arizona can be quite erratic and unpredictable from one year to the next. The daily, far-ranging sojourns of these nomadic montane birds are often based on the location of mast crops such as pine nuts, acorns, and berries.

GARY ROSENBERG

HABITAT

In Arizona, Band-tailed Pigeons are typically encountered on forested mountains and higher plateaus, often descending to lower slopes and foothill riparian areas to forage. Strong flyers, these pigeons will often travel in small flocks as much as 20 mi (32 km) per day and drop several thousand feet in elevation to visit good foraging areas (Brown 1989). For nesting in Arizona, atlasers reported 43 percent of Band-tailed Pigeon observations from either mixed conifer–dominated forests with Douglas fir, white fir, and ponderosa pine or in forests of ponderosa pine with a Gambel's oak understory (n = 148). Atlasers reported fewer observations from pure ponderosa pine forests or in pinyon pine–juniper woodlands. In fact, Band-tailed Pigeons went unreported in many areas of the state dominated by these two dryer habitats. In southeastern Arizona, this species is often observed in Madrean pine–oak forest, where Apache, Chihuahua, and ponderosa pines occur with scattered evergreen oaks and junipers. Also in the southeast and locally below the Mogollon Rim, Band-tailed Pigeons were reported from Madrean evergreen oak woodlands. Very few Band-tailed Pigeons were noted in subalpine spruce/fir forests, where Brown (1989) noted this pigeon breeding in low numbers.

BREEDING

Most populations of Band-tailed Pigeons in Arizona are migratory, moving south to spend the winter months in Mexico. However, when food supplies are sufficient, a few winter irregularly in southeastern Arizona mountain ranges and rarely elsewhere. Early northbound migrants begin arriving in southern regions of the state by late March or early April. These pigeons typically do not arrive in northern Arizona much before late April or early May, and even in the southeast flocks are regularly encountered foraging on fruit in lowland riparian areas into late May or later.

The earliest Band-tailed Pigeon pair reported by atlasers was on 8 April. Some pigeons arrive on the breeding grounds already paired while others commence with cooing and courtship flights soon after arrival (Brown 1989). Atlasers reported the first nest with eggs on 26 May, although a nest found with young on 3 June would indicate egg laying by mid-May at the latest. One earlier account reported a nest containing an egg on 2 April in southern Arizona (Fitzhugh 1974). Although early nesting records in the state are frequently questioned, both the migration and nesting activity of these pigeons appear to be quite irregular and unpredictable (Phillips et al. 1964). The latest confirmed record was an adult feeding a fledgling on 1 September. Few nests were found during the atlas and peak nesting activity was difficult to surmise. However, atlas data are consistent with prior findings, which identified most of Arizona's Band-tailed Pigeons nesting between late May and mid-September (Neff 1947, Fitzhugh 1974). Very late nesting activity in Arizona is indicated by a nest with a squab on 10 October in the Huachuca Mountains (Monson and Phillips 1981), and nests with pin-feathered young and another with a recently laid egg on 24–25 October in the White Mountains (Phillips et al. 1964). It is difficult to determine when fall migration begins, but if food sources are in short supply most Band-tailed Pigeons have departed the state by the end of September, with few remaining past mid-October (Brown 1989).

Nest platform construction may take 6 days, typically placed at a height of 18–35 ft (5.5–10.7 m) above ground

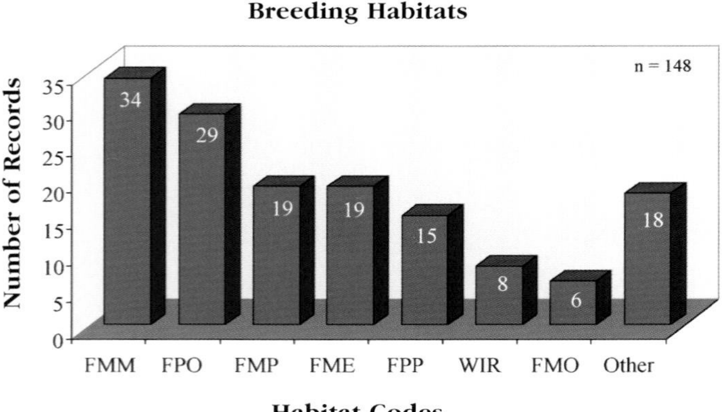

Breeding Phenology

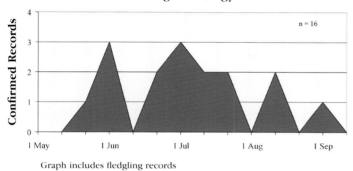

Confirmed Records (0–4); n = 16; 1 May, 1 Jun, 1 Jul, 1 Aug, 1 Sep

Graph includes fledgling records

in various species of firs, pines, and oaks (Brown 1989). The typical one egg clutch is incubated for 18–22 days (Neff 1947). Squabs grow quickly and may move to nearby limbs after 15 days, but do not truly fledge until they are 24–29 days old (Keppie and Braun 2000). Both parents attentively share incubation, brooding, and feeding duties (Keppie and Braun 2000). If food availability continues, this cycle will be repeated from one to three times per year (Gutierrez et al. 1975).

DISTRIBUTION AND STATUS

Band-tailed Pigeons are relatively widespread, breeding from western North America south to Argentina. North of Mexico, these pigeons breed from southwestern British Columbia south through California and in the interior from Utah and Colorado south. In Arizona, Band-tailed Pigeons have always been considered common summer residents of forested mountains throughout much of the state (Swarth 1914; Phillips et al. 1964), although recent declines have been noted.

Atlasers found Band-tailed Pigeons to be uncommon to locally common at elevations from 4800 to 9400 ft (1463–2865 m). Brown (1989) reported that most breeding pairs in Arizona occur at from 5500 to 7500 ft (1676–2286 m). Although Phillips et al. (1964) noted there were no known records of Band-tailed Pigeons in northeastern Arizona, Jacobs (1986) later described them as nesting on Navajo tribal lands in the Chuska and Carrizo mountains. Atlasers also documented Band-tailed Pigeons in these mountain ranges, as well as locally to the south on the Defiance Plateau. In northwestern Arizona, atlas surveys revealed these pigeons nesting at the higher elevations of Hualapai tribal lands and within the Arizona Strip region. In Grand Canyon National Park, Band-tailed Pigeons were regularly encountered on the North Rim but went undetected on the drier South Rim, where they previously had been noted (Brown et al. 1987).

Atlasers found Band-tailed Pigeons immediately above and below the Mogollon Rim, northwest to Williams and the San Francisco Peaks area. These pigeons undoubtedly occur throughout the White Mountain Apache tribal lands and the absence of records is due to land access constraints. In Yavapai County, atlasers documented Band-tailed Pigeons from the Bradshaw Mountains north to the Juniper Mountains.

Atlas surveys in southeastern Arizona confirmed Band-tailed Pigeons in all the higher-elevation mountain ranges as far west as the Baboquivari Mountains. These large pigeons were also discovered in some of the smaller ranges containing limited habitat such as the Winchester and Santa Teresa mountains, but were not found in the Mule Mountains, where nesting had been documented in the past (Phillips et al. 1964).

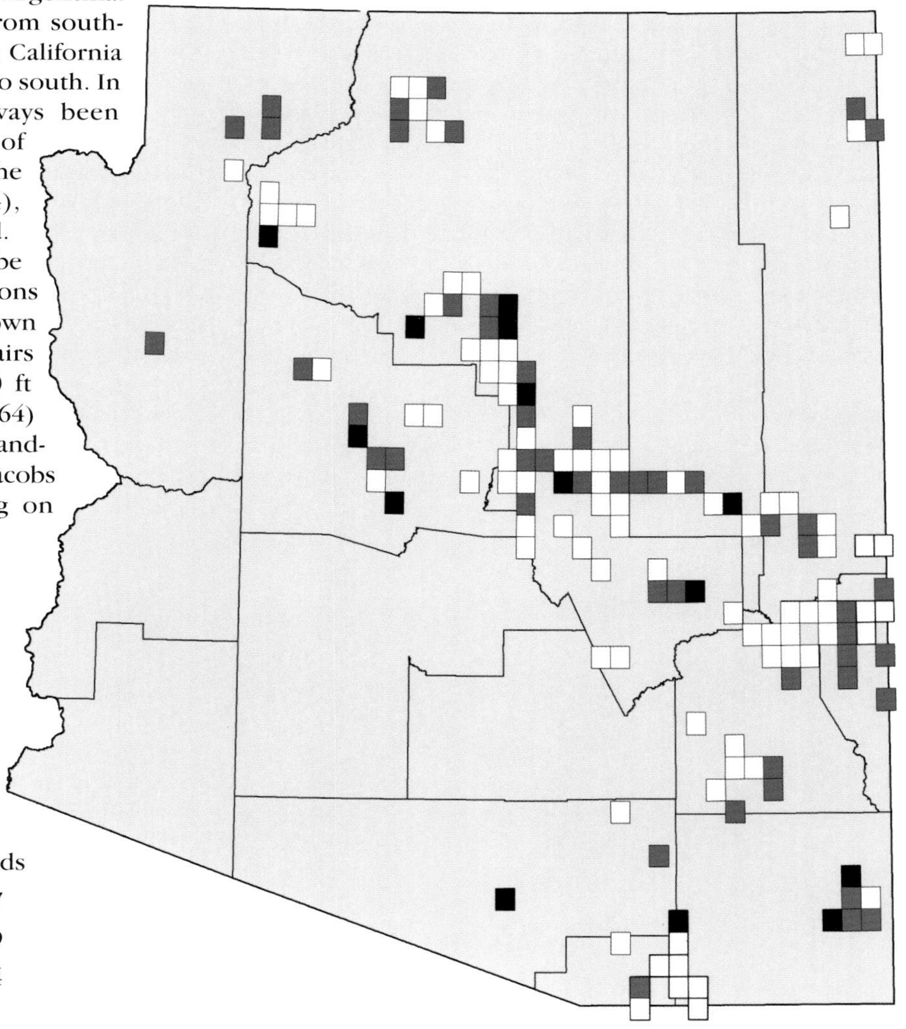

Band-tailed Pigeon Breeding Evidence Reported in 136 (7%) of 1834 priority blocks

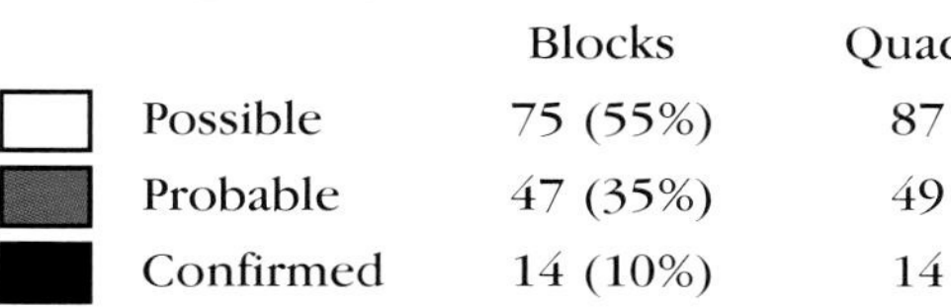

	Blocks	Quads
Possible	75 (55%)	87
Probable	47 (35%)	49
Confirmed	14 (10%)	14

Eurasian Collared-Dove

by Troy E. Corman *Streptopelia decaocto*

First appearing in Arizona near the end of the atlas period, Eurasian Collared-Doves are rapidly establishing satellite populations in small towns and communities across the state. These large, prolific doves are predicted to become common and familiar fixtures to backyards and neighborhoods in North America, much as they have in Europe.

JIM BURNS

HABITAT

Eurasian Collared-Doves appear to thrive best near human habitations in residential suburbs, shaded parks, small towns, and rural communities. These doves typically remain sparsely distributed or lacking in the adjacent city centers or other highly urbanized areas. They also seem to shun densely forested areas away from areas heavily influenced by human activity, and they will likely not adapt well to Arizona's vast desert regions. During the atlas period, observers noted these doves most frequently in residential parks and neighborhoods with an abundance of large shade trees and open ground, such as yards, gardens, and fields. They were also observed at the edges of golf courses and woodlands. Several records were from isolated ranches and farms, which included tall shade trees or shelterbelts with irrigated lawns, ornamental plantings, pastures, and/or agricultural lands. Especially in the early morning hours, Eurasian Collared-Doves are often observed conspicuously perched on television antennas, buildings, bare tree limbs, power poles, or telephone wires. As they have elsewhere, these dove will likely become frequent visitors to many backyard feeding stations.

BREEDING

Where nesting populations become established, Eurasian Collared-Doves are permanent residents. However, young birds may disperse long distances, thus aiding in the spread of populations (Kaufman 1996). Through much of the winter and nesting season, these doves are heard calling and are observed performing flight displays and territory chases. During the atlas period, observers noted Eurasian Collared-Doves nest building as early as 6 March. They have since been confirmed nesting by early February in Prescott (C. Tomoff, personal communication). The earliest nest with young was noted on 24 March. Nesting attempts continue throughout the spring and summer. Courtship activity was noted through 8 September, and an adult was observed feeding a fledgling on 25 September. The latest confirmed record was a nest with two large nestlings on 28 October, which were observed near but out of the nest by 4 November. Nesting activity will likely be documented throughout the year in Arizona.

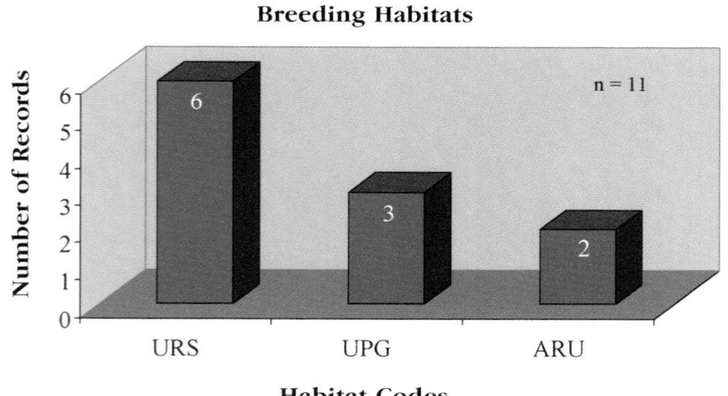

Like many other doves in Arizona, the nest of the Eurasian Collared-Dove is a thin platform of fine twigs and plant stems. Females construct the nest from material brought to her by the male (Baicich and Harrison 1997). Nest heights were not measured during the atlas, but elsewhere nests have ranged from 6 to 70 ft (1.8–21.3 m) above the ground, with most placed 10–40 ft (3.0–12.2 m) high (Kaufman 1997). Eurasian Collared-Dove nests are typically placed in trees, frequently in conifers, and rarely on building ledges (Baicich and Harrison 1997). In Arizona, nests have been found in pinyon pine and several different exotic trees including Aleppo pine, elm, athel tamarisk, and possibly in a palm.

Eurasian Collared-Doves typically lay 1–2 eggs, and the pair shares the incubation duty, which lasts approximately 14–16 days (Baicich and Harrison 1997). Both parents feed the young, which depart the nest in 15–20 days (Kaufman 1997). Fledglings are tended for several additional days before leaving the natal area. When food is predictable and persistent, Eurasian Collared-Doves are very prolific, often successfully fledging three to six broods per year (Cramp 1985). In Europe, Robertson (1990) noted that when food is abundant, these doves frequently start a new clutch while still attending to dependent fledglings and sometimes while young are still in the nest. Like other doves, they often use the same nest for multiple broods, sometimes rotating between one or two other nests during the year.

DISTRIBUTION AND STATUS

Smith (1987) and Romagosa and McEneaney (1999) describe the ever-increasing distribution of Eurasian Collared-Doves. This Old World species is believed to be native to India, Sri Lanka, and Myanmar. It expanded into Turkey and the Balkans in the sixteenth century, either by natural dispersal or by human introduction. In the early 1900s, Eurasian Collared-Doves began their impressive range expansion across Europe to the west and northwest, reaching Great Britain by 1955 and Spain by 1974. In the early 1970s the doves were inadvertently introduced to the Bahamas, where they soon expanded to adjacent islands. Eurasian Collared-Doves likely arrived in southeastern Florida from the population in the Bahamas in the early 1980s and quickly expanded to the north and northwest, reaching eastern Colorado and New Mexico by 1995.

Eurasian Collared-Doves arrived in Arizona near the end of the atlas period. The first observation of these doves in the state was also the first confirmed nesting record. In early March 2000, they were found constructing a nest in Eagar, Apache County. Several months later, these doves were observed in other small eastern Arizona towns, including Snowflake and Ganado. By the end of that year, Eurasian Collared-Doves were also discovered in pairs or small flocks at Roper Lake State Park south of Safford, near Willcox, and as far northwest as Fredonia near the Utah border. Not surprising, additional localities were discovered in 2001, during the final cleanup year of the atlas. These included Pima and Thatcher in Graham County, Pearce and Hereford in Cochise County, Palo Verde in Maricopa County, and Cameron in Coconino County.

During the atlas period, nesting Eurasian Collared-Doves were found at elevations ranging from 840 to 7100 ft (256–2164 m). Eventually, these adaptable and hardy doves will likely establish nesting populations near the lower elevation extreme in southwestern Arizona, but the upper elevation limit is left unknown. They have already successfully overwintered in the state at just above 7000 ft (2134 m) in a residential area within open ponderosa pine forests.

Studies suggest that Eurasian Collared-Doves disperse mainly in spring and primarily westward, perhaps because of saturation of local nesting locations (Smith 1987). They often appear several hundred miles from the nearest known nesting site, with backfilling eventually occurring in suitable areas (Smith 1987). Like the House Sparrow and European Starling, these exotic doves will surely become a common nesting species in suburban and rural communities throughout much of Arizona. No one knows what the eventual affects these aggressive doves will have on Arizona's indigenous avifauna. There are already concerns that the Eurasian Collared-Dove may become a serious competitor for native nesting doves in small towns and communities.

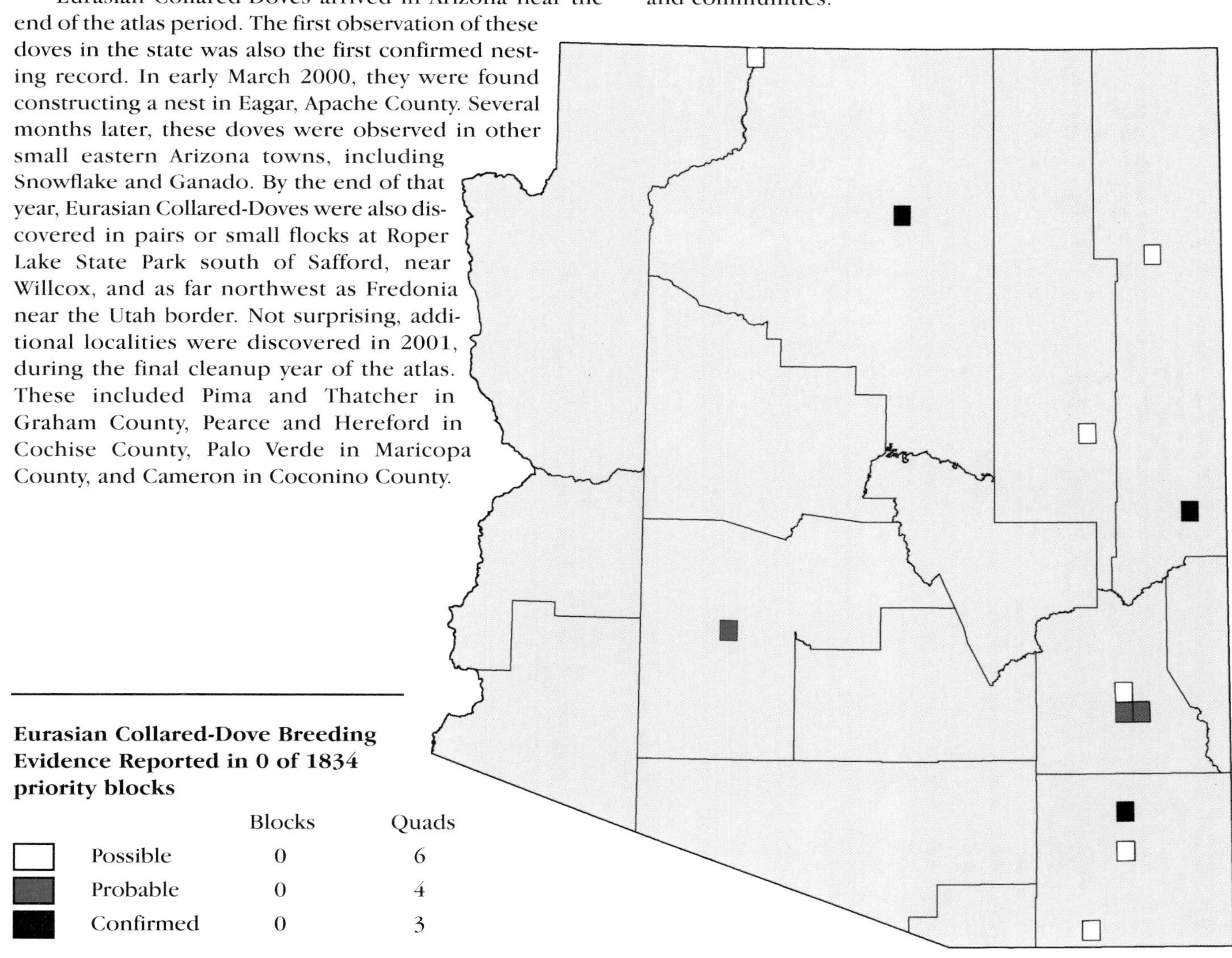

Eurasian Collared-Dove Breeding Evidence Reported in 0 of 1834 priority blocks

	Blocks	Quads
Possible	0	6
Probable	0	4
Confirmed	0	3

White-winged Dove

by Marjorie J. Latta *Zenaida asiatica*

The familiar "who-cooks-for-you" song of the White-winged Dove resonates throughout the riparian thickets of the Sonoran Desert. During peak breeding season their deafening decibels often make other bird species seem altogether absent. One of Arizona's most important migratory pollinators, this "cactus pigeon" plays an important role in the pollination of saguaro flowers.

BRUCE TAUBERT

HABITAT

In Arizona, White-winged Doves are largely habitat generalists. Atlasers noted them in twenty-three different habitat types that ranged from various desertscrub, brushy grasslands, and riparian woodlands to urban and agricultural areas. These doves are most widespread in the Sonoran Desert uplands where saguaros are in abundance and adjacent dry washes contain lush growth of mesquite, ironwood, and paloverde. Nearly 49 percent of all White-winged Dove atlas records were noted in these two habitats (n = 777). This is compared to only 9 percent of the records in the more arid lower Sonoran Desert biome, where saguaros are sparse or lacking. These doves reach their highest nesting density in lowland riparian woodlands of cottonwood, willow, mesquite, and exotic tamarisk that meander their way through desertscrub and agricultural areas. This habitat accounted for an additional 11 percent of atlas records. White-winged Doves also range up into mountain foothills, where atlasers noted them in riparian woodlands dominated by sycamore and lower levels of Madrean evergreen oak woodlands. In rural towns and cities, these doves sing and nest among the many native and exotic tree plantings of residential parks and neighborhoods.

BREEDING

Locally, small numbers of White-winged Doves winter in residential areas of southern Arizona. However, the bulk of Arizona's population is migratory with early individuals arriving in mid-February or early March in the southeast, not reaching western and central Arizona until the first few days of April. Singing commences immediately upon their arrival, and nesting activity shortly follows. In southeastern Arizona, atlasers observed early nesting building by mid- to late March, and early fledglings can be found by late April. This is when saguaros begin blooming and the more northern and western populations initiate construction of their first nests. Atlas data reveal a strong peak of nesting activity from early May to early June. However, nesting for some pairs continues through the summer, and atlasers noted nests with young as late as 27 August and recent fledglings into early September. Phillips et al. (1964) noted nests with young as late as 15 September. Small flocks of White-winged Doves can be seen winging their way to foraging areas in July and huge numbers regularly build in August, especially in agricultural areas near riparian woodlands. There is a mass exodus in late August, and most White-winged Doves have left Arizona by early September, with few remaining after early October.

Female White-winged Doves construct their nest platforms in 2–5 days from material often provided by her mate (Schwertner et al. 2002). Of twenty-three nests measured by atlasers, the mean height above the ground was 8.7 ft (2.7 m) and ranged from 5.9 to 13.8 ft (1.8–4.2 m). Brown (1989) noted that most nests are between 10 and 40 ft (3.3–12.2 m) above the ground. White-winged Doves exhibit little preference for the tree species used to support their nests. In the Sonoran Desert, atlasers found them nesting primarily along dry washes in mesquite, paloverde, ironwood, catclaw acacia, and desert hackberry. Along lowland riparian areas, nests were commonly found in tamarisk, willow, mesquite, cottonwood, and netleaf hackberry. Locally, White-winged Doves nest in high densities, with several thousand nests concentrated in larger tamarisk

Breeding Habitats

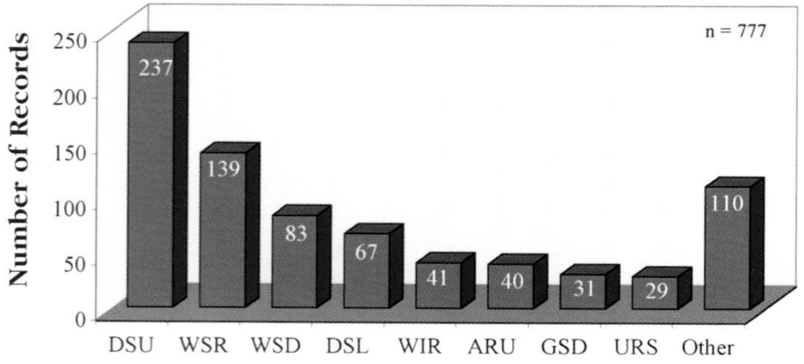

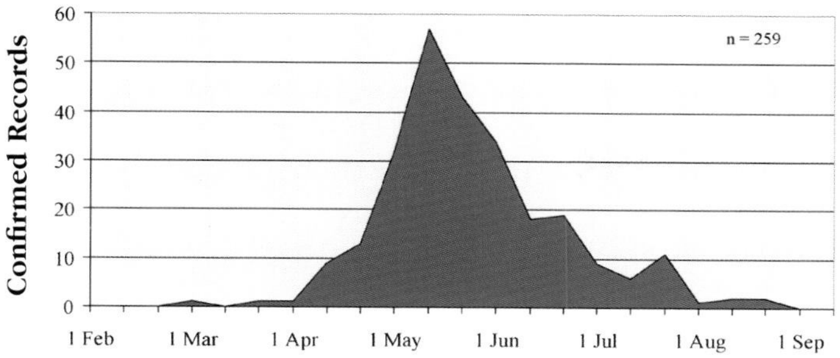

thickets adjacent to agricultural areas (Phillips et al. 1964; Brown 1989). In many areas, this habitat has replaced the extensive mesquite bosques that once existed along the broad floodplains of lowland rivers and where these doves once nested in huge numbers (Phillips et al. 1964).

Typically 2 (range 1–3) eggs are laid and incubated by both members of the pair, with male White-winged Doves incubating during the heat of the day and females from mid-afternoon through early morning (Brown 1989). Incubation lasts between 13 and 14 days, with young fledging between 13 and 18 days after hatching (Neff 1940). Brown (1989) suggested that most desert-nesting White-winged Doves only produced one brood per season, but in areas were the food resources remain high, such as along river valleys near agriculture and in urban areas, two or more broods are produced. Second broods are also likely produced in southeastern Arizona during the late summer monsoon season, where many late-season atlas nesting records were obtained.

DISTRIBUTION AND STATUS

White-winged Doves have an extensive range from southeastern California, southern Nevada, Arizona, New Mexico, Texas, and Florida, south to Central America. Most of the population north of Mexico is migratory. The more abundant, widespread, and highly migratory western Arizona population is tied closely to the distribution of the Sonoran Desert, and specifically the range of the saguaro. However, they breed north to Truxton, Mohave County, and up the Verde River valley to above Clarkdale, outside the range of this large cactus. White-winged Doves in much of southeastern Arizona, roughly east of the Sonoran Desert, are less migratory (Brown 1989) and may be the source of Arizona's local wintering populations.

There is little doubt that White-winged Doves have increased their breeding range to the north and northwest in Arizona since the 1870s (Phillips et al. 1964). This northern expansion is attributed to an increase in human settlement, bringing cultivated grains and the availability of other food sources when native resources were limited or absent (Brown 1989).

Atlasers found White-winged Doves to be abundant throughout most of their previously described distribution in the state at elevations ranging from 100 to 5000 ft (30–1524 m) and locally higher in foothill canyons. Atlas data suggest that the range of these attractive doves in Arizona may still be expanding north. White-winged Doves were reported sparingly north to Lake Mead, and nesting was suspected to near 7000 ft (2134 m) in the Springerville-Eagar area by the end of the atlas period. Records have recently increased in the vicinity of Page as well, with spring observations from 28 April to 20 May and summer observations from 21 July to 13 September (C. LaRue, personal communication). However, nesting has not been confirmed at this location, and these observations may be related to drought conditions and reduced food supply within their normal range to the south.

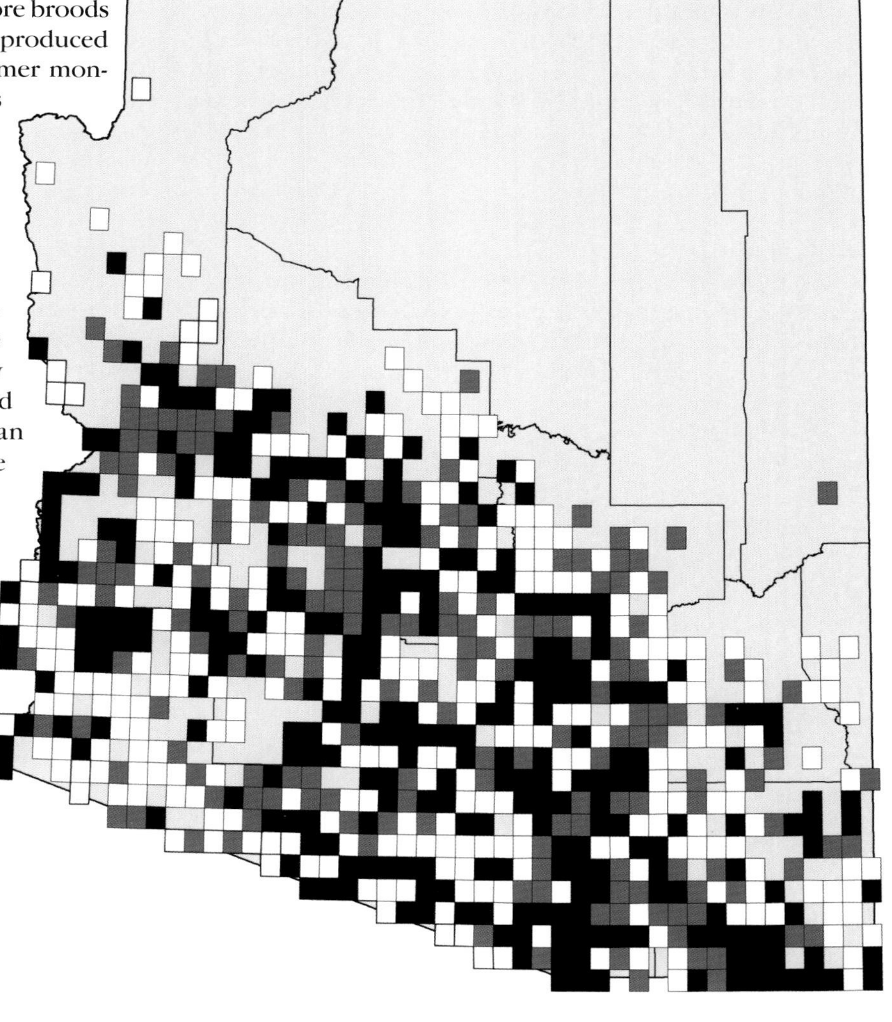

White-winged Dove Breeding Evidence Reported in 743 (41%) of 1834 priority blocks

	Blocks	Quads
Possible	295 (40%)	303
Probable	179 (24%)	183
Confirmed	269 (36%)	275

Mourning Dove

by Greg S. Clark *Zenaida macroura*

The Mourning Dove reigns as the most widespread and likely the most abundant breeding bird in Arizona. Whether flying effortlessly beside your vehicle at freeway speeds, or greeting the new day outside your bedroom window with its low-pitched song, this adaptable melancholy songster is found nearly everywhere.

RICHARD DITCH

HABITAT

Mourning Doves feed almost exclusively on seeds and have adapted to locations where this food source is plentiful. In Arizona, atlasers reported these doves most regularly in desertscrub, shrubby grasslands, and open woodlands. Of the forty habitats designated for use by atlasers in Arizona, Mourning Doves were confirmed breeding in all but seven primarily high-elevation habitats. The majority of atlas records were from Sonoran desertscrub associations, including vegetated dry washes, as well as pinyon pine–juniper woodlands. These habitats represented 47 percent of all atlas records for these doves (n = 1712). However, this is undoubtedly influenced more by the fact that these are the most widespread habitats in the state than as a true preference by the adaptable Mourning Dove. These doves were regularly encountered in lowland riparian areas including timbered drainages, springs, and mesquite bosques and were also found commonly on blocks containing rural and urban habitats. Mourning Doves typically avoid heavily wooded areas, but atlasers reported them nesting sparingly in open ponderosa pine forests.

BREEDING

Mourning Doves occur year-round throughout much of Arizona, although numbers greatly decrease north of the Mogollon Rim in late fall and winter. Spring migrants begin arriving in northern Arizona by late March and early April, with a peak passage in late April. In southern Arizona, the somber song of the Mourning Dove can be heard by midwinter. These doves have been observed nesting every month of the year in southern Arizona (Phillips et al. 1964), with some urban nesting beginning by late January. The earliest confirmed record reported during the atlas was a nest with eggs on 4 February. However, most early nesting records were noted after early March, likely reflecting the period when most spring atlasing efforts began. Atlas data reveal a peak in nesting activity from late April to late May. Although cooing and the majority of nesting efforts often cease by mid-August in Arizona (Brown 1989), atlasers documented Mourning Dove nests with eggs through September 18. Some nesting activity does continue fairly regularly into early October and occasionally into December, well after atlasing surveys had ended. In Arizona, Mourning Doves begin dispersing by mid-August, with peak migration in early to mid-September.

Breeding Habitats

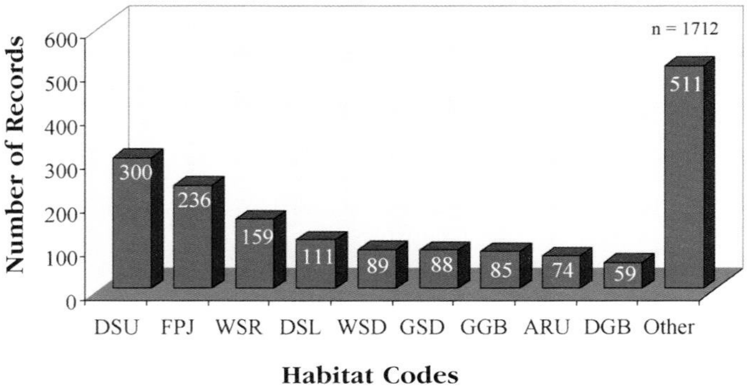

Mourning Doves are noted for flimsy nest construction and adaptable nest locations. The male provides the nest material and the female loosely constructs the nest platform. Nest site selection is seemingly endless for this species and ranges from precarious places on tree limbs to above building signs or parked vehicles. Atlasers also found nests on rock outcrops, cliff ledges, shelves in abandoned buildings, and occasionally on the ground. Many ground nests are found at the base of a shrub, grass tussock, or rock and often on the side of a slope. In desert areas, nests are frequently placed in cholla, either nestled in the cactus arms or atop abandoned thrasher or Cactus Wren nests. Of 231 nests measured by atlas field crews, nearly 58 percent were discovered in common desert trees or shrubs consisting of various species of cholla, paloverde, mesquite, and ironwood. At higher elevations, several species of juniper accounted for an additional 12 percent of the records. The median height for all nests (n = 231) was 5.5 ft (1.7 m) and ranged from 0 to 23 ft (0–7 m).

Mourning Doves typically lay clutches of 2 eggs, and nests discovered with 3–4 eggs pertain to laying by more than one female (Mirarchi and Baskett 1994). Both parents

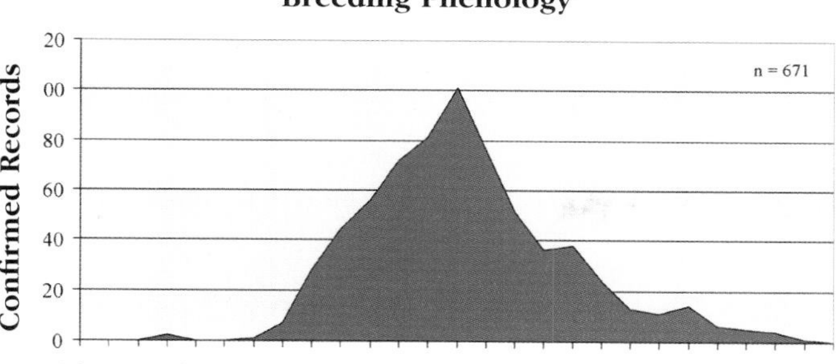

incubate the eggs for 13–14 days, with the male generally incubating from midmorning to late afternoon and the female through the evening and early morning (Mirarchi and Baskett 1994). In desert regions, the eggs are actually cooled by transfer of heat to the adult (Walsberg and Voss-Roberts 1983). Nestlings are fed primarily crop milk from both adults for the first 3–4 days and gradually switched to regurgitated seeds when fledging is completed at 13–15 days. The male, almost alone, feeds the fledglings for approximately 12 days following nest departure (Mirarchi and Baskett 1994), while the female often initiates the next clutch.

Mourning Doves are characterized as champions of multiple brooding among North American birds, typically producing two to three broods and occasionally as many as six per year (Ehrlich et al. 1988). Many successful nests are reused for additional broods, and approximately 30 days are necessary between initiation of one clutch and initiation of the next (Mirarchi and Baskett 1994).

DISTRIBUTION AND STATUS

Widespread in North America, Mourning Doves breed from southern Canada south through Mexico and then locally to Panama. These adaptable birds have greatly benefited from human activity, especially the conversion of densely forested areas to more open lands. Nearly all the Arizona literature describes Mourning Doves as common to abundant in open country statewide. However, Brown (1989) suggests these doves are not evenly distributed throughout the state and noted the highest breeding densities in southern regions.

Atlas data reveal Mourning Doves nesting at elevations from approximately 80 ft (24 m) along the lower Colorado River south of Somerton to over 9000 ft (2743 m) in the White Mountains region. Atlasers found these doves absent primarily only at higher altitudes and in the most heavily forested areas, although the total lack of records on White Mountain Apache tribal lands pertains to the inability to acquire access to conduct surveys there.

Nesting Mourning Doves were also absent in more desolate desert localities where food and water are often lacking. Successful nesting in some of the more arid and sparsely vegetated regions of the Sonoran and Mojave deserts may only be possible following winters with above average precipitation. The availability of surface water on a daily basis is critical for desert-nesting Mourning Doves (Rosenberg et al. 1991), which will travel many miles in the early morning and early evening to acquire it. In Arizona's many arid landscapes, creation of earthen water-catchment tanks for livestock and wildlife has undoubtedly greatly benefited these doves. Mourning Doves were often sparsely distributed in many drier regions of northern Arizona and regularly went undetected by atlas surveys on priority blocks. However, low densities in this region may have been influenced by drought conditions during much of the atlas period.

Mourning Dove Breeding Evidence Reported in 1673 (91%) of 1834 priority blocks

	Blocks	Quads
Possible	384 (23%)	389
Probable	437 (26%)	442
Confirmed	852 (51%)	858

Inca Dove

by Troy E. Corman *Columbina inca*

Typically associating with human habitations, the charming Inca Dove is infrequently encountered away from such altered landscapes. Lightheartedly known as the Doomsday Dove, their melancholy whistled "no hope" is repeated over and over. This incessant call can even be heard throughout the heat of summer days when most other birds fall silent.

HABITAT

Inca Doves strongly associate with the urban and rural life humans have created in arid or semiarid regions of Arizona. Typically, the larger the city or town, the more abundant this dainty dove becomes. Inca Doves are familiar backyard birds at feeding stations and birdbaths in well-established residential areas, as well as in city parks and gardens where 44 percent of all atlas records were reported (n = 129). These doves often concentrate in areas with a mixture of open space, such as lawns, alleys, or vacant lots with higher densities of shade trees and shrubs. Inca Doves are frequently observed perched on roofs, block walls, or telephone lines or on grassy lawns where they forage and sunbathe (flopped to one side with one wing extended). Although typically less abundant, Inca Doves were also regularly found in more rural localities (30 percent of all atlas records). In these areas, Inca Doves are often encountered around scattered buildings at isolated ranches or farms, along irrigated agricultural areas, and in small rural communities, including Native American villages. These doves were occasionally found at the edges of lowland riparian areas and brushy washes away from human habitations, but even these were usually within a few miles of established populations.

BREEDING

Inca Doves are primarily resident in Arizona, where they nest nearly throughout the year, at least during warmer winters (Phillips et al. 1964). The distinctive calls of these little doves can also be heard year-round, although calling increases in January as the primary nesting season commences. Atlasers reported these little doves nesting continuously from mid-February through mid-August, with most breeding records falling in April and May. However, nesting activity has been reported at least into November (Phillips et al. 1964), and the lack of fall and winter atlas records undoubtedly reflects the fact that most atlasing surveys ended by the end of August and few began before late February.

These doves are not especially choosy in nest site selection, with many nests placed near houses or other structures in a wide variety of exotic or native trees and shrubs. Inca Dove nests have been found from 0.7 to 53 ft (0.2–16 m) above the ground (Cornell nest record cards in Mueller 1992) and can range from well shaded to fully exposed. Exposed nest sites include palm fronds, cacti (especially saguaro arms), limbs of dead trees, and even on top of home television antennas.

Female Inca Doves construct the shallow nest platform in approximately three days. However, the male gathers much of the material and, through an important ritual, presents each to the female after climbing on her back (Johnston 1960). These doves frequently use their nests more than once during the breeding season, often over consecutive years, and with use the nest often becomes covered with excrement helping to bind the material and deepening the cup (Johnston 1960). Phillips et al. (1964) noted that this persistent nesting species can produce four to five successful broods per season in Arizona.

The Inca Dove pair shares the duty of incubating the 2-egg clutch for 13–15 days (Anderson and Anderson 1948) and is often reluctant to flush from the nest during this period (Mueller 1992). Both parents feed the nestlings through the 12–16 day nestling stage (Mueller 1992) and for an additional week after fledging (Johnston 1960). Inca Doves will often start building a new nest or refurbishing the old within 1 or 2 days following nest departure of the previous brood (Anderson and Anderson 1948).

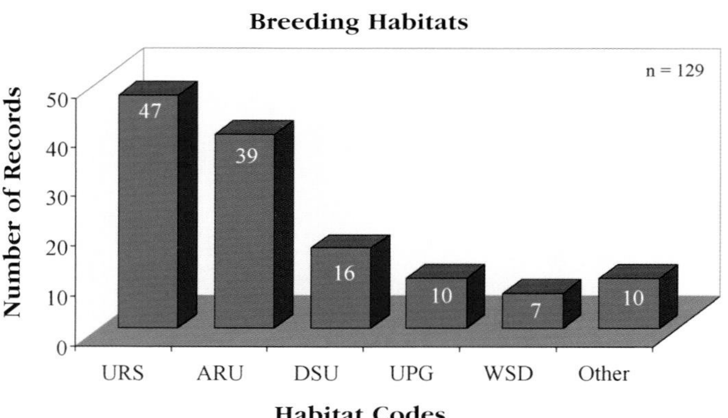

DISTRIBUTION AND STATUS

Inca Doves are found from southeastern California and the southern tip of Nevada, east to southern Oklahoma, south

Breeding Phenology

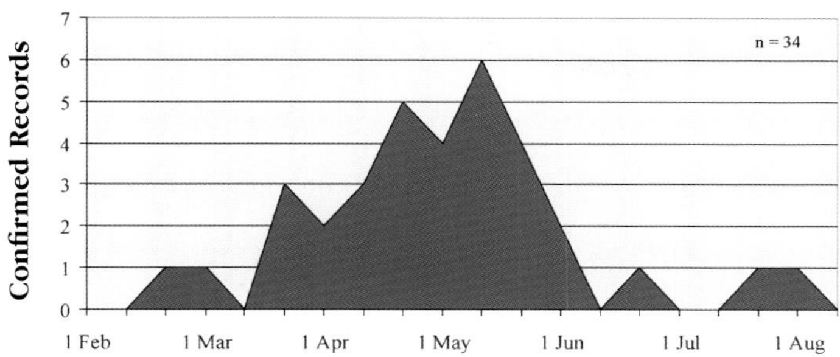

through most of Mexico and into Central America. Before 1870, these doves were thought to have been absent in Arizona and were first found nesting near Tucson and Tubac in 1872 (Phillips et al. 1964). The distribution of Inca Doves continued to expand in the state, as more towns and cities grew and more desert habitat was changed to irrigated agricultural lands. On Gila River Indian Community lands, Rea (1983) reported these doves to be common at many tribal villages and cluster of houses. They were first reported locally along the lower Colorado River in the 1940s, north to the Bullhead City area by 1970 (Monson and Phillips 1981). They remain fairly common local residents in Parker and Bullhead City and are rare in the Yuma area (Rosenberg et al. 1991).

During the atlas period, Inca Doves were found throughout much of their previously described breeding range in Arizona at elevations ranging from approximately 100 ft (30 m) near Yuma to 5400 ft (1646 m) in Bisbee. These doves were most consistently found in the greater Phoenix metropolitan area and down the I-10 corridor to Tucson. Atlasers helped document their continued 120-year range expansion in Arizona with observations of pairs in the extreme northwestern corner near Littlefield and Beaver Dam Wash. In central Arizona, they were found as far north as Cottonwood and Sedona, and in the southeast, as far north as Safford and Clifton. At many smaller towns, tribal villages, and isolated ranches, Inca Doves were likely missed because atlasers tended to keep their distance from human habitations where these birds frequently congregate. Inca Doves are sensitive to cold and northward range expansion should eventually be limited by their inability to tolerate colder winter temperatures (Mueller 1992).

With their ability to thrive near human habitations, Inca Dove populations are expected to expand as cities and towns continue to grow. However, urban life does pose threats to these unwary doves, and domestic cats find them easy prey. Also, there is some speculation that the recent decrease in abundance of Inca Doves in Tucson could be related to the establishment and exponential increase of nesting Cooper's Hawks in that city since 1990.

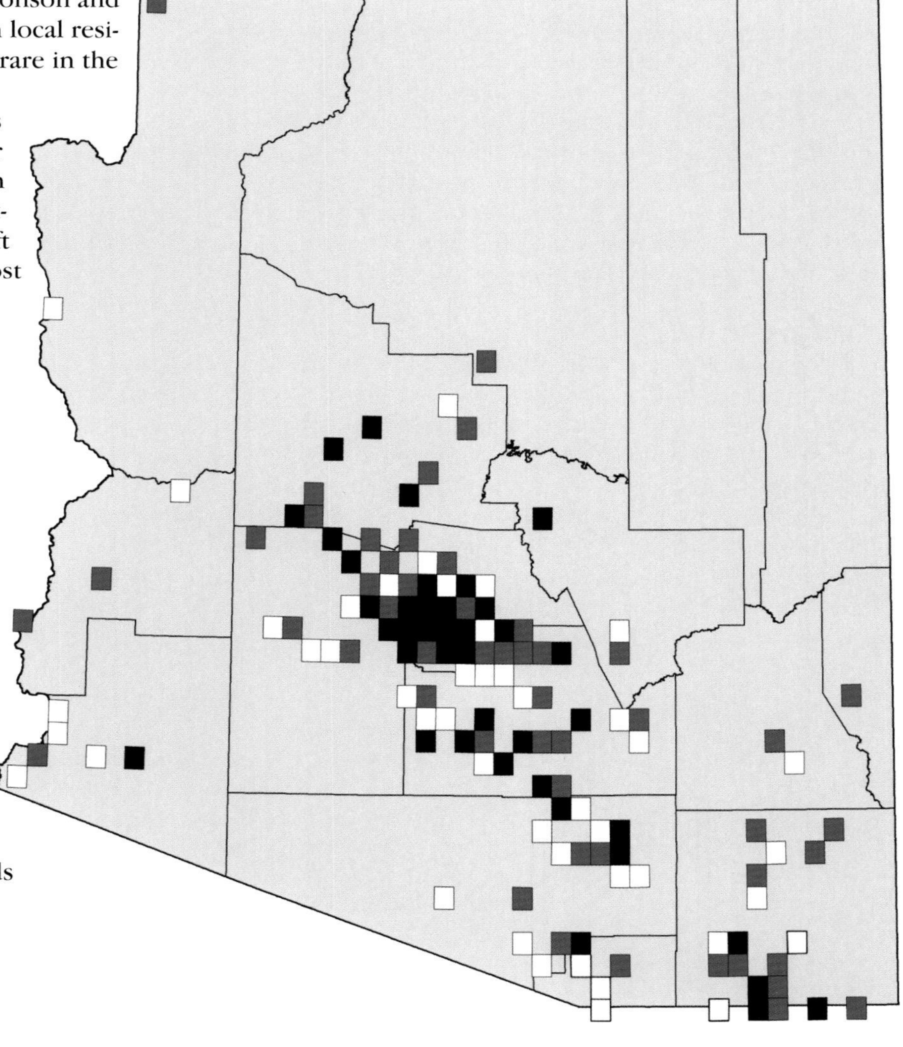

Inca Dove Breeding Evidence Reported in 115 (6%) of 1834 priority blocks

	Blocks	Quads
Possible	34 (30%)	45
Probable	44 (38%)	51
Confirmed	37 (32%)	40

Common Ground-Dove

by Troy E. Corman *Columbina passerina*

Often quite inconspicuous when compared to other doves, the little Common Ground-Dove is well named for it is typically discovered on or near the ground. Frequently remaining motionless when first disturbed, this sparrow-sized dove's presence is often revealed with a quick whir of wings as they hastily retreat into nearby dense cover of low shrubs and brush.

HABITAT

Common Ground-Doves prefer open or edge brushy habitats near washes, drainages, and human modified areas. Nearly 26 percent of all atlas records were from agriculture and rural settings including brushy borders of irrigated fields and pastures, shelterbelts, weedy ditches, and dense vegetation around ponds and farm buildings (n = 113). Lowland riparian areas made up another 22 percent of the atlas observations, which often included open Fremont cottonwood and willow woodlands with a dense understory or edge of seepwillow, mesquite, and sometimes tamarisk. Slightly fewer records came from dense Sonoran desertscrub thickets and washes, especially those near earthen stock tanks. Very locally, atlasers reported Common Ground-Doves in watered residential areas and various irrigated orchards and tree farms, especially citrus and pecan.

BREEDING

In Arizona, Common Ground-Doves are basically resident, but they become more common in summer. Evidence suggests that these doves have some sensitivity to cold temperatures, and they are likely a short-distance migrant in Arizona, with a portion of the population moving south or to slightly lower elevation in late fall and winter. Pairs remain together throughout the year, and nesting activity can begin as early as February near Yuma (Phillips et al. 1964). The earliest atlas record was of a fledgling observed near Yuma on 17 April. This would suggest nest building by mid-March and egg laying by late March. Common Ground-Doves continue nesting through out the summer and often into the fall. Atlasers reported nest building as late as 29 July and fledgling into August. There are frequent observations of Common Ground-Doves in Arizona nesting into September and even October (Phillips et al. 1964; Rosenberg et al. 1991), which is well after most atlas surveys have ended.

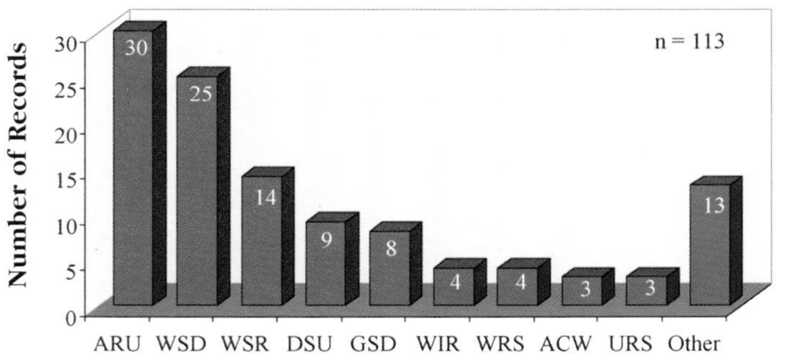

The Common Ground-Dove pair shares the duty of nest construction, which is a small, frail collection of grasses and twigs and easily overlooked (Nicholson 1937). Nest construction occurs rapidly, often in only 3–4 days (Bowman 2002). Birds frequently nest on the ground in eastern North America, but this habit appears to be rare in western populations (Bent 1932). Most nests in Arizona are placed on a low tree or shrub fork, often near water, and are usually 3–7 ft (0.9–2.1 m) above the ground, rarely above 10 ft (3.3 m). The nest supporting substrate can be quite variable. In Arizona, nests are frequently found in mesquite, willow, and Mexican elderberry (Phillips et al. 1964; Rosenberg et al. 1991), but have also been found in Fremont cottonwood, cholla, prickly pear, various citrus, pecan, tamarisk, and other exotic trees and shrubs (Brandt 1951).

As with many other doves, a full Common Ground-Dove clutch consists of 2 eggs, which are incubated by both parents for 12–14 days (Nicholson 1937). The male stops calling during incubation and early nestling period, but often begins again near fledging in preparation for another brood (Nicholson 1937). Both parents feed the nestlings, which grow rapidly and fledge in 12–14 days (Bowman 2002). The parents often renest within 2–3 weeks, so young are presumably independent within this period (Bowman 2002).

Common Ground-Doves are prolific nesters, and, with their protracted nesting period from late winter through early fall, are capable of producing three to four broods per

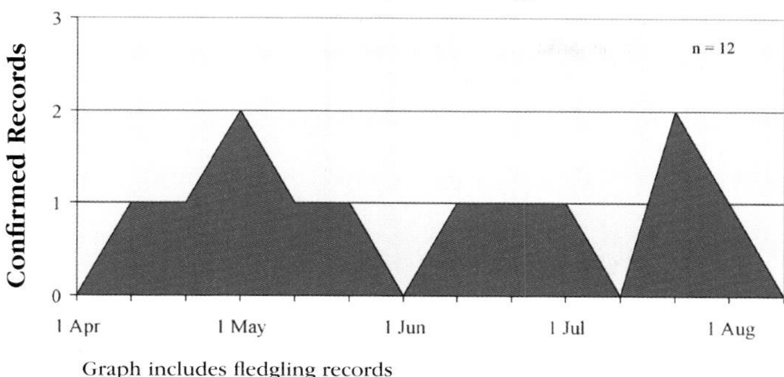

Graph includes fledgling records

season (Bent 1932, Bowman and Woolfenden 1997), although as many as six have been reported (Bowman 2002). As with most doves and pigeons, the number of broods successfully reared is rather low, and is likely less than three broods per year (Bowman 2002). They may reuse their nests consecutively up to four times in one season (Nicholson 1937).

DISTRIBUTION AND STATUS

Common Ground-Doves are resident from southern California, Arizona, Texas, and east to South Carolina, south through Mexico and Caribbean to Ecuador and eastern Brazil. In southeastern and much of central Arizona, Common Ground-Doves have been described as uncommon and inconspicuous summer residents and noticeably less common in winter (Phillips et al. 1964). Populations in the lower Colorado and Gila river drainage appear to fluctuate little throughout the year where they have been described as fairly common, but local residents (Rosenberg et al. 1991; Witzeman et al. 1997). Phillips et al. (1964) also suggested that the distribution of Common Ground-Dove in Arizona appeared to be increasing.

Atlasers reported Common Ground-Doves at elevations that range from approximately 100 to 5000 ft (30–1524 m). The doves were found much more frequently within Tohono O'odham tribal land than previous literature suggested. They were also found in the upper Sulphur Springs Valley, where Monson and Phillips (1981) noted they did not breed. Common Ground-Doves were detected by atlasers for the first time in the San Simon Valley and confirmed nesting near Artesia, south of Safford, and near Thatcher, Graham County. Other northern records came from near Globe, along Tonto Creek just north of Roosevelt Lake, and near Wickenburg.

Unlike the similar sized Inca Dove, Common Ground-Doves are typically absent in urbanized areas of Arizona, preferring small rural communities and agricultural areas on the outskirts of larger towns and cities. The main exception to this is in and around Yuma where these little doves are typically observed more often than the city-loving Inca Dove. North of Yuma, however, these little doves were detected much less frequently within the lower Colorado River valley than expected, with the most northern record coming from near Topock Marsh. Common Ground-Doves were also not detected in several historical nesting locations near Phoenix and Tucson, likely through loss of habitat from expanding urbanization.

Common Ground-Doves are often so inconspicuous that they were easily overlooked during atlas surveys. This is especially true if the observer is not familiar with this dove's low, unobtrusive, monotonous call, which in many areas is heard much more frequently than the birds are seen.

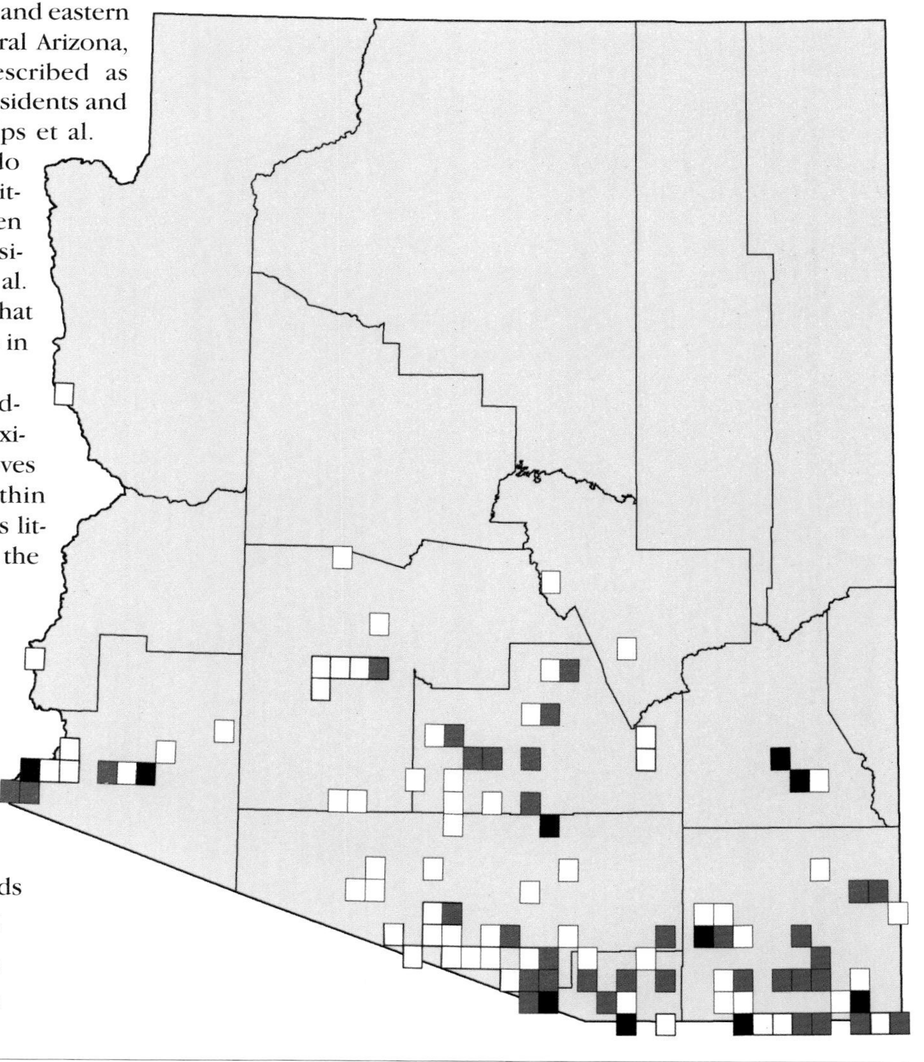

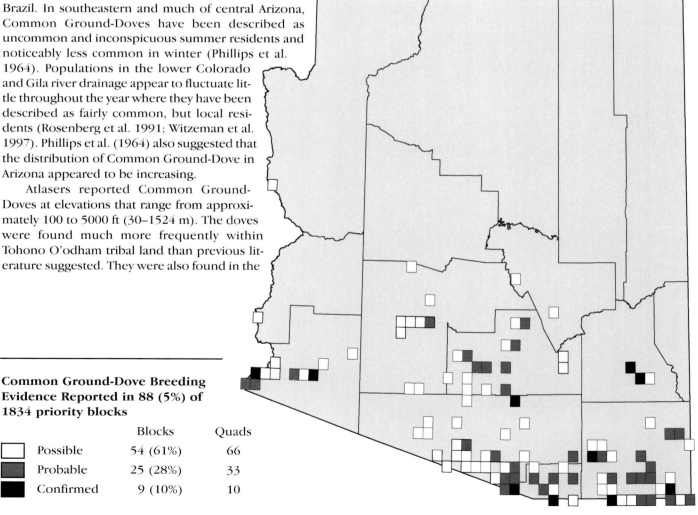

Common Ground-Dove Breeding Evidence Reported in 88 (5%) of 1834 priority blocks

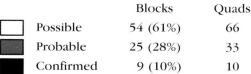

	Blocks	Quads
Possible	54 (61%)	66
Probable	25 (28%)	33
Confirmed	9 (10%)	10

Ruddy Ground-Dove

Troy E. Corman *Columbina talpacoti*

RICHARD DITCH

The fairly recent arrival of Ruddy Ground-Doves in the Southwest emulates the appearance of Inca Doves in Arizona more than a century ago. These little rusty doves are often found alone or in small groups, but when noted associating with other species, they appear to prefer the earlier pioneering Inca, to the smaller Common Ground-Dove.

HABITAT

Ruddy Ground-Doves are found in a wide variety of open and edge habitats in humid areas throughout their range. They seem to prefer a mixture of bare ground and short grassy or weedy vegetation for foraging, especially along roadsides, pastures, agricultural areas, clearings, forest edges, and towns. During the atlas, Ruddy Ground-Doves were found most frequently near irrigated rural settings including edges of fields, canals, ditches, ponds, orchards, yards, ranch buildings, and exotic tree and shrub plantings. These doves were also detected along lowland riparian areas consisting of Fremont cottonwood, willow, and velvet mesquite. Often remaining motionless on the ground when first disturbed, Ruddy Ground-Doves retreat to nearby dense vegetation if approached too closely. Like Inca Doves, they roost gregariously amid dense foliage (Stiles and Skutch 1989). On cool mornings in Arizona, these doves are also frequently observed sunning in the open on or near the ground.

BREEDING

Ruddy Ground-Doves are primarily resident throughout their range south of the United States. However, individuals and small groups begin to appear in Arizona in late September and are often observed through the winter, with most departing by late March. During the atlas period, a few individuals and pairs began to linger through the spring. In Arizona, obvious Ruddy Ground-Dove pairs have been observed performing courtship activity, including allopreening by mid- to late March. During the atlas, these doves were heard calling in April and May, likely indicating initiation of the nesting period. Near Alamos in southern Sonora, Ruddy Ground-Doves have been observed copulating in early April (Russell and Monson 1998).

The only confirmed Ruddy Ground-Dove atlas record began with an observer hearing a calling bird on 1 May 1993 at the Hassayampa River Preserve near Wickenburg, Maricopa County. A bird was still calling at this location during a second visit on 15 May, when a pair of adult Ruddy Ground-Doves was discovered with a fledgling (J. Hentz, personal communication) and later observed feeding this fledgling on 19 May. This would suggest that nest construction began no later than mid-April and egg laying in late April. It is unknown if June through August observations of other individuals and pairs in southern Arizona also pertain to nearby nesting activity. However, the possibility does exist, as this period is outside the typical season for postbreeding fall observations. It is also very possible that the number of summering pairs of Ruddy Ground-Doves in Arizona has been sufficiently small and local that additional nesting activity has been overlooked. There is little available information on the nesting period of the Ruddy Ground-Dove in northern Mexico, but Gibbs et al. (2001) suggest that in tropical regions of Mexico and Central America, they nest nearly year-round.

The nests of Ruddy Ground-Doves have been described as frail to fairly substantial shallow platform of twigs, leaves, and grass (Hilty and Brown 1986; Gibbs et al. 2001). In Central America, nests are typically placed 3–10 ft (0.9–3.0 m), rarely as low as 1 ft (0.3 m), above the ground in a dense shrub, tree, cactus, or vine tangle (Stiles and Skutch 1989). However, some nests have been noted to near 23 ft (7 m) above the ground (Gibbs et al. 2001).

Little has been written on the breeding habits of the Ruddy Ground-Dove, and the following nesting information was taken from information compiled by Gibbs et al. (2001). Like the Common Ground-Dove, they lay 2 white eggs, which are incubated for approximately 11–13 days. Both adults feed the squabs, which fledge after 10–14 days. Ruddy

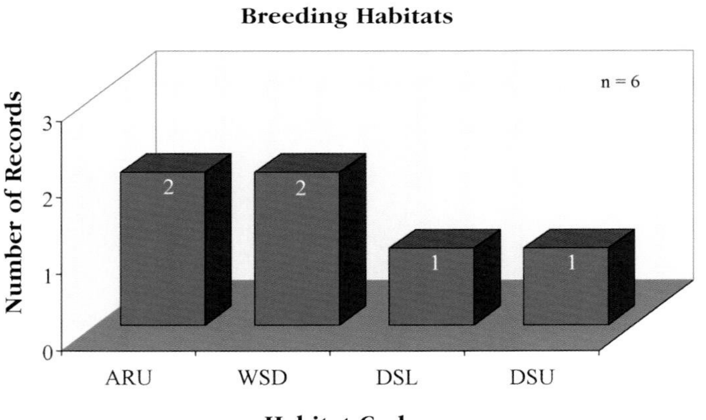

Ground-Doves produce multiple broods during the year and will use the same nest several times if earlier attempts were successful. The interval from the time the first brood fledges to the initiation of the next clutch can range from 2 to 33 days. The parents continue feeding the young doves for an unknown period following nest departure.

DISTRIBUTION AND STATUS

Ruddy Ground-Doves are considered common to abundant throughout their range from the Pacific and Atlantic slopes of northern Mexico, south to central Argentina. In many tropical countries, the distribution of these doves has significantly increased with the extensive clearing of forests for agriculture, grazing, and timber harvesting (Gibbs et al. 2001).

In western North America, Ruddy Ground-Doves began spreading north from southern Sinaloa, Mexico, during the 1970s (Howell and Webb 1995), arriving in southern Sonora by the early 1980s (Russell and Monson 1998). This is the same period this dove began appearing in Arizona, with the first state record in October 1981 near Phoenix (Witzeman et al. 1997). New Mexico and California both received their first Ruddy Ground-Dove records in October 1994. Ruddy Ground-Doves remained casually reported throughout southern Arizona through the late 1980s, at which time observations began to increase greatly. Since the early 1990s, Ruddy Ground-Dove has become a rare but regular fall and winter resident in small numbers.

During the atlas, spring and summer observations of Ruddy Ground-Doves were found at elevations ranging from 680 to 4050 ft (207–1234 m). Breeding confirmation of these doves in Arizona in 1993 was the first evidence of nesting in the United States. That same year, a pair was noted on 6 May near Picacho Reservoir, Pinal County, and a male was observed calling during a several week period through 27 May along the Verde River, just north of Ft. McDowell Yavapai tribal lands in Maricopa County. During the atlas period, other possible breeding records were suggested with individuals and pairs observed from late April through late August. These included observations near Marana, Painted Rock Dam, along the upper San Pedro River east of Sierra Vista, and near the town of Maricopa.

Even though the vast majority of Ruddy Ground-Dove records and numbers of individuals continue to occur in fall and winter, these doves have now been found every month of the year in Arizona. Late spring and summer observations of these doves are also on the increase within the state. Time will tell if Ruddy Ground-Doves will follow the path of the Inca Dove more than a century ago to become a resident and regular nesting species in Arizona.

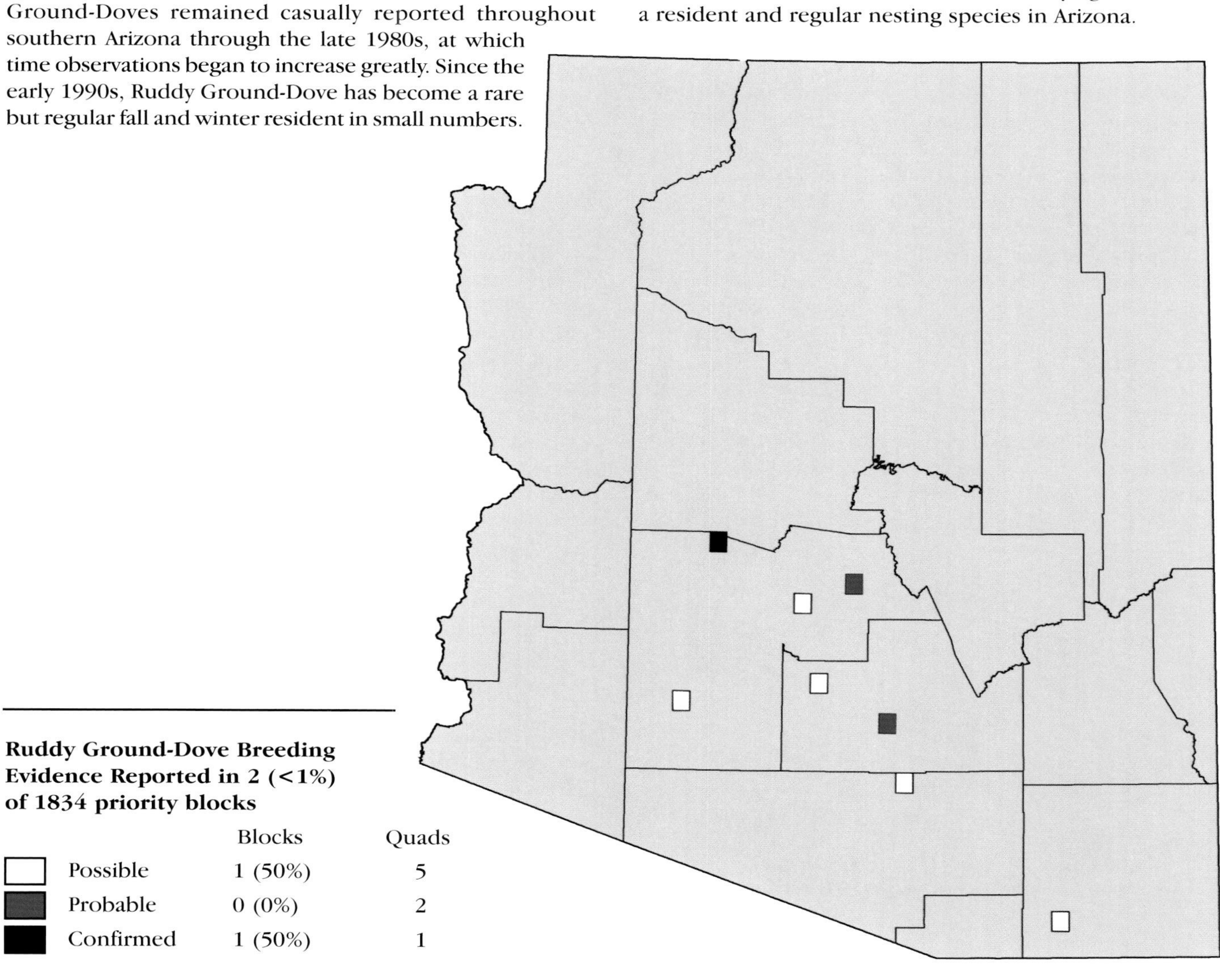

Ruddy Ground-Dove Breeding Evidence Reported in 2 (<1%) of 1834 priority blocks

	Blocks	Quads
Possible	1 (50%)	5
Probable	0 (0%)	2
Confirmed	1 (50%)	1

Peach-faced Lovebird

by Troy E. Corman *Agapornis roseicollis*

Cute, colorful, and often entertaining little backyard exotics, Peach-faced Lovebirds are locally fairly well established in and around the greater Phoenix metropolitan area. Fortunately, there has been little evidence of negative competition of these diminutive parrots on native birds nesting in desert urban settings.

FRAN BARBANO

HABITAT

Native to dry, open country including wooded savannas, palm groves, and arid mountain slopes (Forshaw 1989), exotic Peach-faced Lovebirds in Arizona have been primarily found among the nonnative plantings in desert urban and residential neighborhoods. They seem to shun the adjacent native Sonoran Desert habitats, likely because of the lack of appropriate food and reliable sources of water. Even in their native arid lands, these lovebirds are highly dependent on water sources. Atlasers reported 92 percent of all observations from residential areas, with vegetation ranging from primarily exotic shrubs and tree to a mixture of some natives, including mesquite, paloverde, and saguaro. These birds apparently prefer older established neighborhoods with many tall shade trees and palms. Peach-faced Lovebirds are regular visitors to many backyard water and feeding stations, but have also been observed feeding on cactus fruit, apples, palm fruit, and various seed pods.

BREEDING

In their native Africa, Peach-faced Lovebirds have been observed nesting in February and March, where they nest in cliff crevices and buildings, or more commonly in communal nests of Social Weavers (*Philetairus socius*) (Forshaw 1989). In Arizona, most nesting activity is apparently initiated in April or May. Based on most observations, eggs are likely laid from April-June. Peach-faced Lovebird nestlings have been found in May and June, and newly fledged young have been reported from mid-June through early July. Nests with eggs and newly hatched young found on 18 June would likely have fledged the last week of July or in early August. Adults with 2–3 fledglings have also been observed at backyard feeding stations in December and early April (C. Lam, personal communication.), suggesting that some nesting activity may occur irregularly throughout the year in these urban desert settings.

In Arizona, Peach-faced Lovebirds typically nest in groups. Nests have been placed among the dead leaves of untrimmed fan palms, in saguaros with multiple cavities, and under roof tiles. Some nesting colonies in Phoenix have become rather large. On 18 June 1999, several untrimmed palm trees were removed from a recently purchased home in east Mesa that contained a nesting colony of 25–40 adult Peach-faced Lovebirds (D. Marthaler, personal communication). After the trees toppled, nearly 90 eggs and nestlings were discovered on the ground and in the pool. The young from these nests ranged in age from three days to six weeks.

When available, palm fronds are commonly used for nest construction, but other leaves, grasses, small branches, and bark are also used. Lovebirds soften sections of palm fronds by methodically chewing as they pass them back and forth through the bill. Short pieces of the palm frond are then stuck among the tail, wing, and rump feathers. With the load safely tucked, the adult then flies to the nest site and weaves the material into a rather elaborate cup-shape nest.

In captivity, Peach-faced Lovebirds lay 3–8 eggs, which are incubated primarily by the female for approximately 23 days (Teitler 1988). Both parents feed the nestlings until they fledge in approximately 5–6 weeks. The fledglings begin eating some on their own soon after departing from the nest, but the adults will continue feeding them, typically for less than a week (Teitler 1988). Adult plumage is acquired when the young are about 4 months of age and

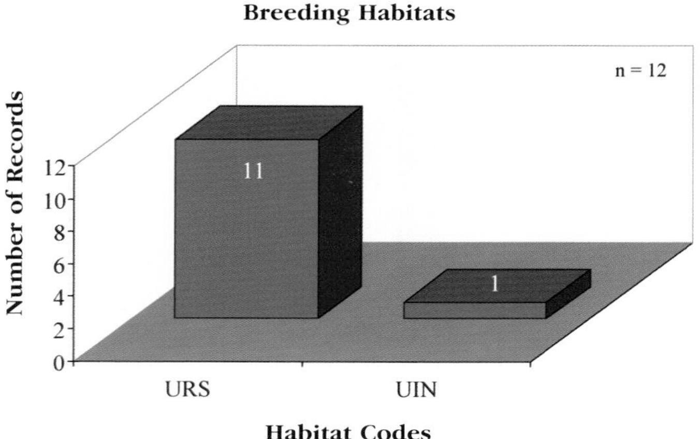

lovebirds are reproductively mature before they are a year old. In the wild, Peach-faced Lovebirds probably regularly produce two broods per year.

DISTRIBUTION AND STATUS

Peach-faced Lovebirds are native to the subdeserts of southwestern Africa from sea level up to 5250 ft (1600 m), including Angola, Namibia, and northwestern South Africa in north Cape Province (Clements 2000). The earliest account of free-ranging Peach-faced Lovebirds in the Phoenix area were of small flocks already established near the border of Mesa and Apache Junction when a home owner moved there in 1987 (M. Moore, personal communication). It was not until the mid-1990s that local flocks and colonies of lovebirds were discovered throughout the eastern half of the greater Phoenix metropolitan area.

Atlasers and interested homeowners reported Peach-faced Lovebirds well established in several locations as far east as Apache Junction. Lovebirds were reported at one location near Guadalupe and sizable populations were also discovered in Mesa and Tempe, but they were not observed in nearby newer neighborhoods of Chandler and Gilbert to the south. Newly established housing developments may not have the abundant tall shade trees and other vegetation preferred by these parrots. Atlasers found established populations in Scottsdale and they have been reported as far north as the Cave Creek–Carefree area. However, the latter location may have been from more local releases. Peach-faced Lovebirds flocks have been reported in east and north Phoenix, including the communities of Sunnyslope, Moon Valley, and Paradise Valley. By the end of the atlas period, there were surprisingly very few records of these lovebirds west of Interstate 17 or south of U.S. 60. However, as lovebird populations continue to grow and expand, it is expected that these residential communities will also eventually have established colonies of these little green, screeching parrots.

Away from the Phoenix area, several Peach-faced Lovebirds were reported visiting home feeding stations near Punkin Center along Tonto Creek in Gila County in 2000. However, it is unknown if this is an established population. In 2000 as well, Peach-faced Lovebirds were observed regularly visiting feeding stations in two separate locations in and around Tucson. One was near the entrance to Saguaro National Park East and the other in central Tucson. Nesting was confirmed at the latter site, when a pair of adults was photographed feeding four fledglings in early July 2001 (C. Lam, personal communication).

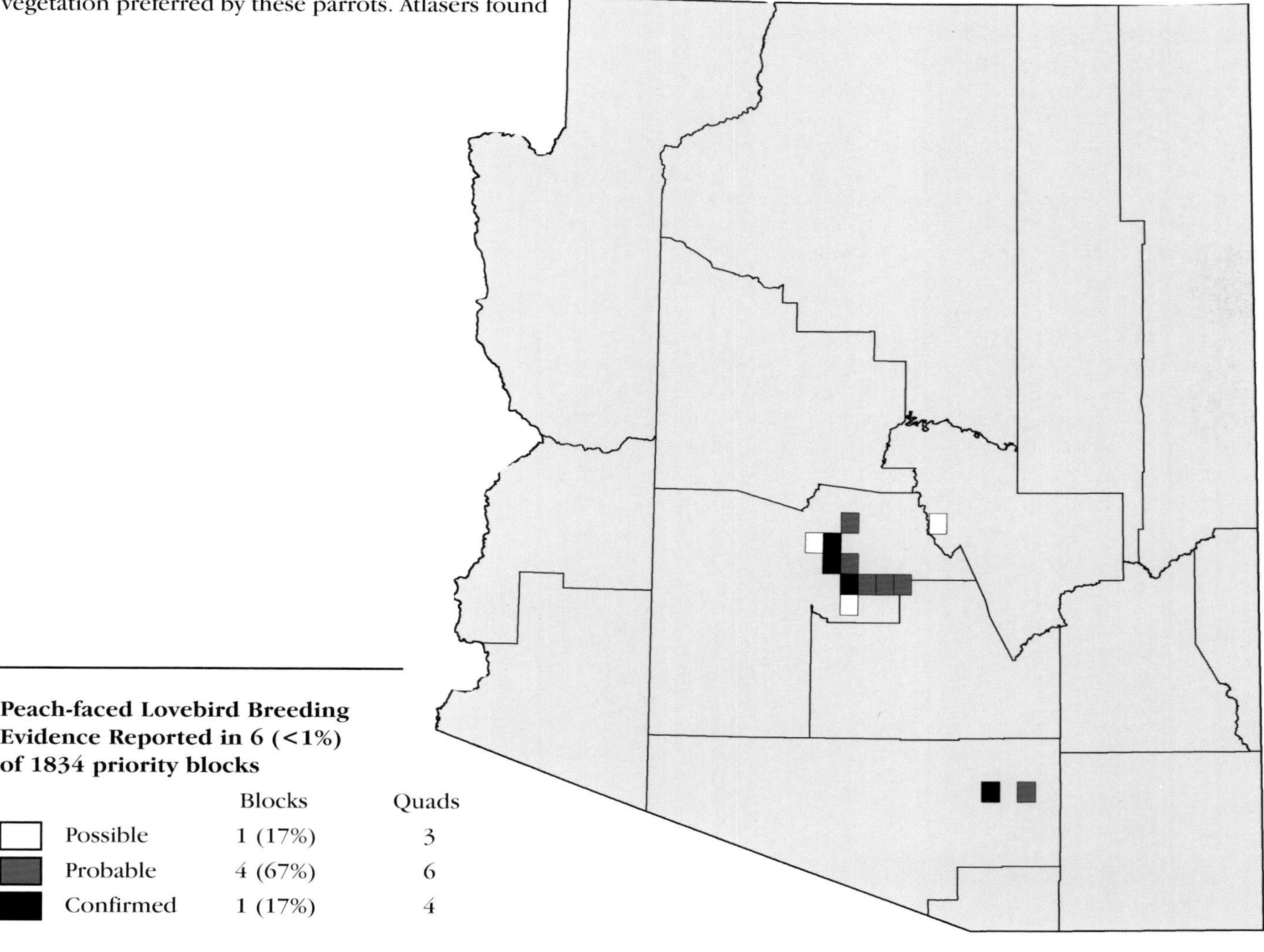

Peach-faced Lovebird Breeding Evidence Reported in 6 (<1%) of 1834 priority blocks

	Blocks	Quads
Possible	1 (17%)	3
Probable	4 (67%)	6
Confirmed	1 (17%)	4

Yellow-billed Cuckoo

by Troy E. Corman *Coccyzus americanus*

RICH AND NORA BOWERS

From deep within its high, leafy domain, the distinctive stuttering call of the Yellow-billed Cuckoo is heard much more often than the bird is actually seen. When perched, it frequently remains motionless, except for the very slow, mechanical tilting of the head as it carefully inspects the leaves and upper branches for its favorite prey.

HABITAT

In the arid Southwest, Yellow-billed Cuckoos are primarily restricted to densely wooded rivers and streams and damp thickets with relatively high humidity. Even though this habitat is much reduced in Arizona, these cuckoos can still be found locally along lowland drainages where stands of multistructured native riparian woodlands occur. Atlasers reported 68 percent of Yellow-billed Cuckoo observations from lowland riparian woodlands, often containing a variable combination of Fremont cottonwood, willow, velvet ash, Arizona walnut, mesquite, and tamarisk (n = 132). In southeastern Arizona, these cuckoos are also found nesting along intermittent drainages with dense stands of velvet mesquite and netleaf hackberry. Yellow-billed Cuckoos are infrequently encountered along higher and narrower mountain drainages where Arizona sycamore or Arizona alder become the dominant riparian trees, although approximately 18 percent of records were from lower reaches of this habitat, where cottonwoods are also commonly present.

BREEDING

In Arizona, Yellow-billed Cuckoos are the latest "spring" migrants to arrive on their breeding grounds. A few individuals arrive in mid- to late May, but the majority does not arrive until mid-June, with late migrants occasionally straggling into early July. Atlasers noted an occupied nest on 21 June and a nest with eggs by 25 June. In Arizona, the earliest egg date reported is 15 June (Bent 1940); however, peak-nesting activity typically occurs from July to early August (Howe 1986; Corman and Magill 2000). Nesting activities continue through August and frequently into September, especially in southeastern Arizona. This is likely in response to the increased food resources and higher humidity associated with the seasonal late summer rains. In Arizona, occupied nests have been reported as late as 26 August; the latest confirmed report during the atlas was an adult observed carrying a fecal sac on 18 September, suggesting a nest with young nearby. Yellow-billed Cuckoos are occasionally noted feeding young through the end of September in Arizona. Late breeding activity was undoubtedly missed as most atlas surveys ended by mid- to late August, when fall migration typically begins for this species. Few Yellow-billed Cuckoos remain in Arizona after mid-September, with stragglers casually reported into mid-October.

In Arizona, most Yellow-billed Cuckoo nests have been located in willows, but nests have also been discovered in cottonwood, sycamore, alder, mesquite, hackberry, and tamarisk. The nest is frequently placed on horizontal limbs and branches of trees or taller shrubs and usually concealed by surrounding foliage (Hughes 1999). In Arizona, nests range in height from 4 to 55 ft (1.2–16.8 m), although the average is approximately 19 ft (5.8 m) above the ground (Corman and Magill 2000; Halterman 2001). Nests are constructed by both adults and are loose, flat platforms of dry twigs and often lined with bark and leaves (Hughes 1999).

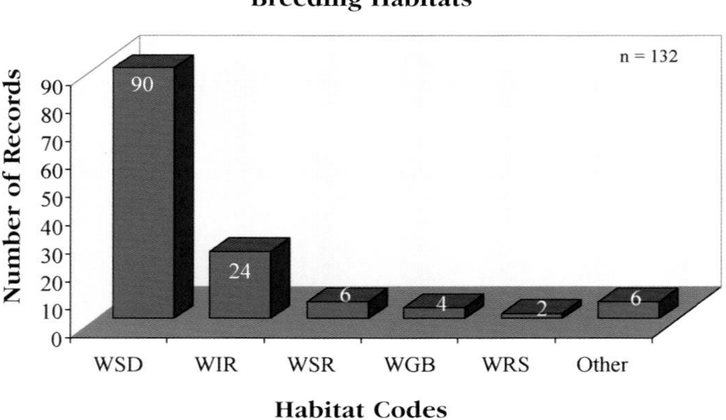

Yellow-billed Cuckoo clutches typically consist of 2–3 (range 1–5) eggs, and both parents share incubation duties of 9–11 days (Hamilton and Hamilton 1965; Potter 1980). The young hatch asynchronously and are in the nest for an extremely short period, averaging only 7–9 days (Potter 1980). Cuckoo young are unable to fly at nest departure, but they are quite capable of awkwardly clambering over limbs and leafy branches in pursuit of adults with food. The young have often left the nest vicinity after only a day (Potter 1980) and obtain the ability of sustained flight when approximately 3 weeks of age (Hughes 1999). Yellow-billed Cuckoos typically produce one or two broods per

Breeding Phenology

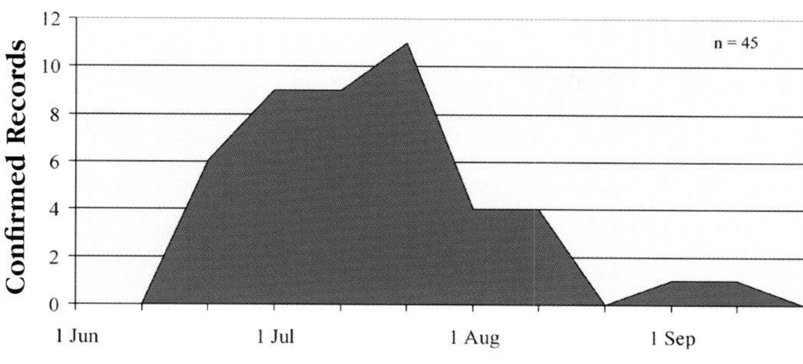

season, although many late nests may simply pertain to efforts following failed earlier attempts. This may be especially true for western populations whose nesting season is limited to only 2–3 months.

DISTRIBUTION AND STATUS

Yellow-billed Cuckoos are neotropical migrants that winter primarily in South America (American Ornithologists' Union 1998). These cuckoos breed throughout the eastern and central United States and southern edge of Canada, south to northern Mexico, and locally west of the Continental Divide to California. It is a sparse migrant throughout Arizona, but it is rarely observed away from riparian habitats. Historically, Yellow-billed Cuckoos were often listed as a common breeding species within extensive riparian forests throughout Arizona (Swarth 1905; Visher 1910; Phillips et al. 1964). These often dense woodlands once extended for many miles along the lower Colorado, Gila, Salt, Verde, Santa Cruz, and San Pedro river valleys. However, these natural plant communities today bear little resemblance to what they were historically (Rosenberg et al. 1991).

Atlasers and specific Yellow-billed Cuckoo surveyors encountered these birds nesting primarily in western, central, and southeastern Arizona along perennial drainages below 5000 ft (1524 m) elevation. Conversely, a few pairs were found nesting to 6950 ft (2118 m) along the upper Little Colorado River near Springerville and even in exotic shade trees within the community of St. Johns, Apache County. Because of the general lack of appropriate nesting habitat in northeastern Arizona, atlas data concur with Phillips et al. (1964) that this species is very local there.

Atlas and specific surveys revealed that Yellow-billed Cuckoos could still be found along most of the twenty-five drainages where they were reported historically. Unfortunately, however, just like their preferred habitat, they are much more local in distribution. The highest concentrations in the state were found along the Agua Fria, San Pedro, upper Santa Cruz, and Verde River drainages and Cienega and Sonoita creeks.

Like many species that depend on riparian habitat in the arid southwest, the breeding distribution and number of Yellow-billed Cuckoos has declined significantly in the past eighty years. In Arizona, these population declines have been most dramatic along the Gila and lower Colorado rivers. Declines are primarily caused by native riparian habitat loss through degradation and fragmentation from decreased water tables, replacement by nonnative trees, inappropriate grazing practices, and poor river management. There is still much to learn about specific habitat requirements of this unique riparian species in Arizona.

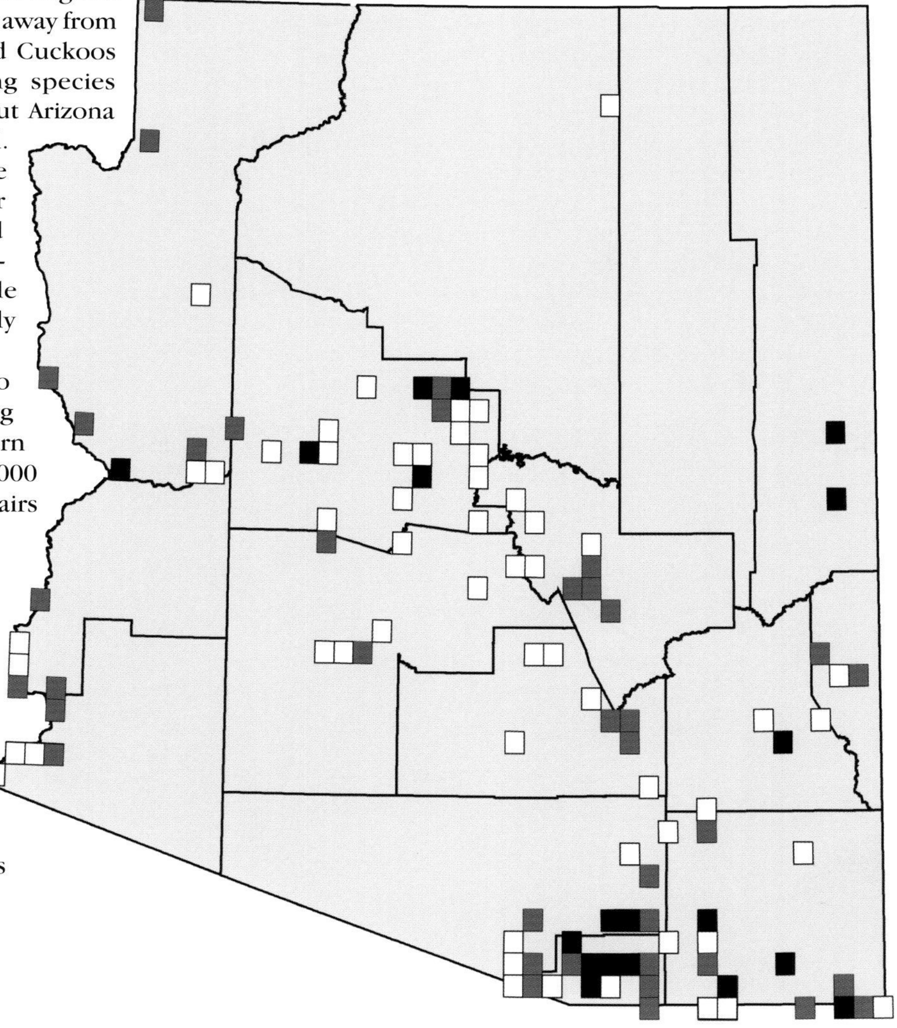

Yellow-billed Cuckoo Breeding Evidence Reported in 50 (3%) of 1834 priority blocks

	Blocks	Quads
Possible	21 (42%)	53
Probable	19 (38%)	39
Confirmed	10 (20%)	22

Greater Roadrunner

by Annalaura Averill-Murray

Geococcyx californianus

Greater Roadrunners are one of Arizona's most distinctive desert dwellers. These unique birds have a curious appearance, with large, zygodactyl feet that leave characteristic "X" footprints in the sand, and have amazed human observers with their speed and agility. From trapping sleeping rattlesnakes to helping lost travelers and warding off evil spirits, this is a bird steeped in legend.

DAN FISCHER

HABITAT

Greater Roadrunners in Arizona are most frequently found in open, arid country with scattered cacti, shrubs, or low trees. During the atlas period, 46 percent of Greater Roadrunner observations were from Sonoran desertscrub and adjacent dry washes (n = 716), including areas with scattered mesquite, creosotebush, paloverde, saguaro, and other leguminous trees and cacti. An additional 14 percent of atlas records were from semiarid grasslands where scattered mesquite and acacia are often interspersed with yucca, agave, cacti, and grasses. Atlasers found Greater Roadrunners in almost every low-elevation habitat type surveyed, including agricultural lands and low- to medium-density residential areas with open space and some native vegetation such as washes, golf course edges, and parks. At middle elevations, these birds were also found nesting in open pinyon-juniper and Madrean evergreen oak woodlands, as well as drier slopes heavily influenced with chaparral vegetation. Atlasers did not find Greater Roadrunners in high-elevation coniferous forests, where individuals are known to wander occasionally in late summer (Monson and Phillips 1981).

BREEDING

The descending, melancholy cooing of the male Greater Roadrunner is most often heard in the early morning, and in lowland deserts can be heard starting in late winter. Atlasers reported this distinctive call through late August

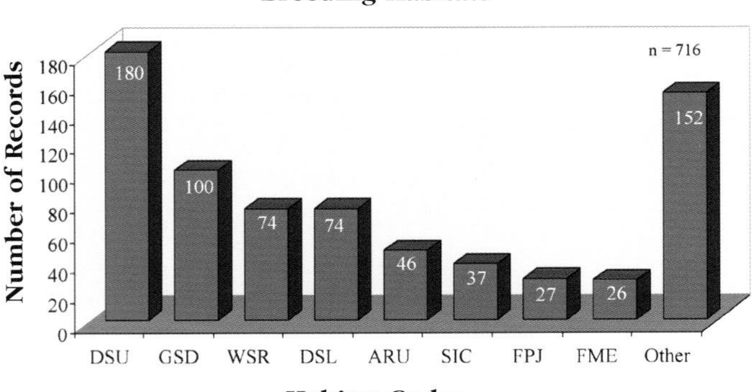

indicating a lengthy breeding season. In southern Arizona, the Greater Roadrunner has a bimodal nesting season, with first broods initiated in spring and second broods initiated in late summer after the start of the monsoon season (Ohmart 1973). Breeding attempts likely correlate with insect and lizard densities. During the atlas, the earliest nest with eggs was found on 4 March and the earliest nest with young on 18 March, indicating that egg laying was initiated in late February or earlier. Atlas data reveal a peak in nesting activity from early April through mid-May. A second small peak in breeding confirmations occurred in August, but many late-season nesting attempts were likely missed as atlasers shifted surveys to higher-elevation habitats. Late nesting records included nest building on 27 August and a nest with eggs on 9 September.

Greater Roadrunners perform elaborate courtship and copulatory displays, including stick and food offerings, prancing, and tail wagging. The male mounts the female by leaping up to a meter in the air while holding a food offering in his bill (Hughes 1996). A shallow, compact nest of thorny sticks is built almost entirely by the female and is lined with softer materials (Baicich and Harrison 1997). Greater Roadrunner nests are often located near the center of a cactus, thorny shrub, or small tree and are frequently adjacent to an open area to allow adults easy access to and from the nest (Hughes 1996; Webster and DeStefano 2001). During the atlas, nesting substrate was recorded for 26 Greater Roadrunner nests found statewide, with the majority of nests in mesquite (46 percent) and paloverde (19 percent). Ohmart (1973) found cholla cactus to be the most common nesting substrate for this species near Tucson, and 15 percent of nests during the atlas period were in a cholla. Additionally, Greater Roadrunners in Arizona will nest in nonnative vegetation planted near residences, businesses, and parks. Atlas data show nest height ranging from 3.3 to 12.5 ft (1.0–3.8 m, n = 24) with a median nest height of 4.9 ft (1.5 m).

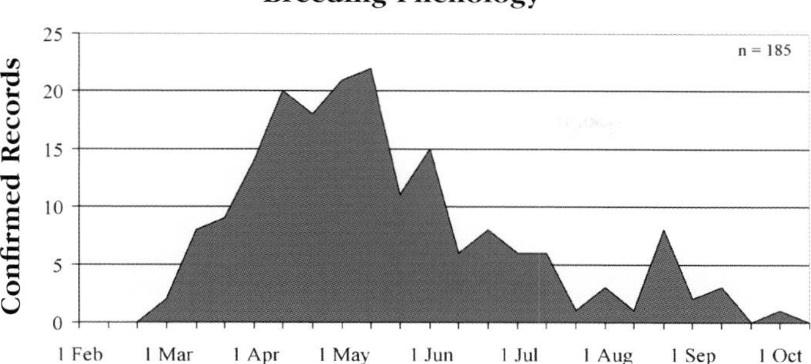

Roadrunners typically lay 3–6 eggs (range 2–13), although larger clutches may result from egg "dumping" by one or more females (Sutton 1940; Hughes 1996). Eggs are laid at irregular intervals, and incubation often begins with the first egg (Baicich and Harrison 1997). Consequently, eggs and young of various stages occur in the same nest. Both sexes incubate and brood, though only the male incubates at night (Hughes 1996). Eggs hatch at approximately 20 days, and young remain in the nest for 14–25 days after hatching. Young are independent 30–40 days after fledging (Whitson 1975; Hughes 1996).

DISTRIBUTION AND STATUS

Greater Roadrunners are year-round residents of much of the southwestern and south-central United States, Baja California, and northern and central Mexico (Hughes 1996). Atlasers found Greater Roadrunners to be uncommon to fairly common throughout southern, west-central, and western Arizona but generally scarce north of the Mogollon Rim. Nesting elevational limits during the atlas ranged from 80 to 6200 ft (24–1890 m), although individuals occasionally wander to over 7500 ft (2286 m) in the state.

In northwestern Arizona, atlasers documented Greater Roadrunners infrequently in the Arizona Strip region west to the Toroweap Valley. Brown et al. (1987) considered this species uncommon within the Grand Canyon corridor, especially west of Havasu Canyon, and rare upstream to Phantom Ranch. Greater Roadrunners went unreported in this region during the atlas period, although nesting was confirmed to the northeast at Page.

On Navajo and Hopi tribal lands, Jacobs (1986) considered Greater Roadrunners to be resident in very small numbers, an observation supported by atlas records. Based on a concentration of records, Phillips et al. (1964) suggested that Greater Roadrunners might nest within the Little Colorado River valley between Holbrook and Saint Johns. Atlasers found Greater Roadrunners to be uncommon in this region, although three nests with young were documented on three separate blocks near Saint Johns. Access was limited within the upper Little Colorado River drainage by private property restrictions, and this species could be more common than atlas data suggest. Other atlas records along this drainage include occurrences north of Winslow and near Cameron.

The Greater Roadrunner's range expanded northward and eastward in the United States during the twentieth century (Hughes 1996). Contributing factors may include the invasion of shrubby plant species following land clearance and overgrazing (Allen 1950). Although populations in Arizona appear to be stable, Breeding Bird Survey data indicate a slight declining trend rangewide. These unique birds have been extirpated from several counties in California, coinciding with extensive agricultural and residential development (Hughes 1996).

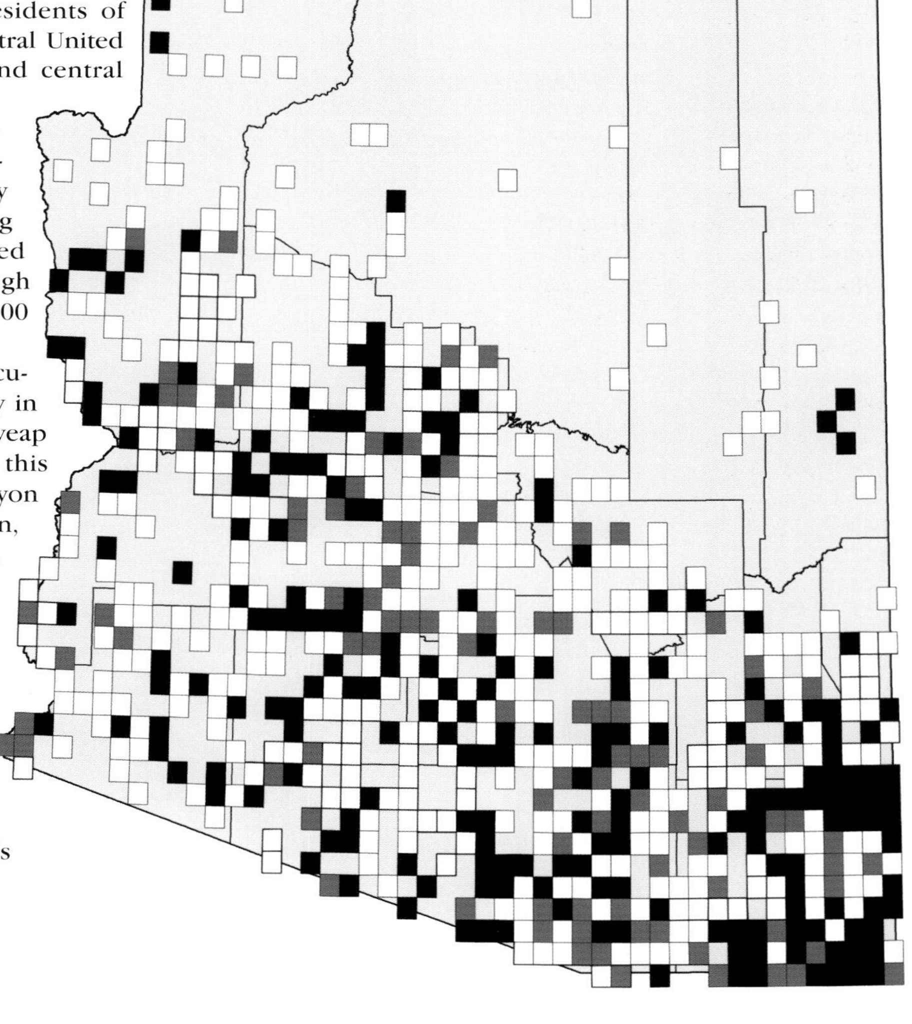

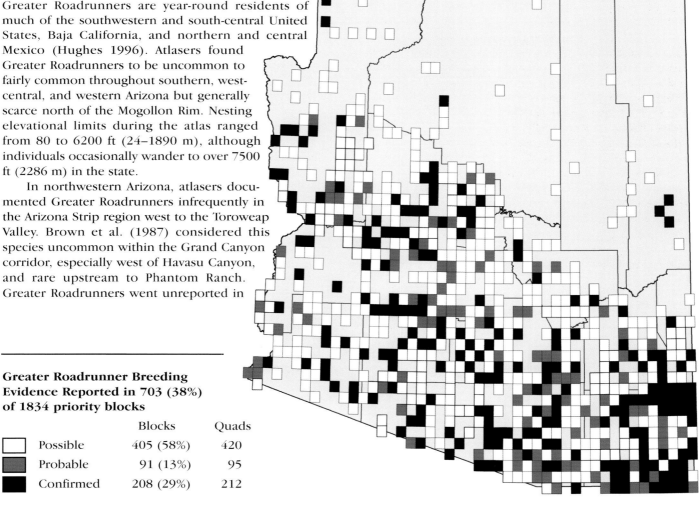

Greater Roadrunner Breeding Evidence Reported in 703 (38%) of 1834 priority blocks

	Blocks	Quads
Possible	405 (58%)	420
Probable	91 (13%)	95
Confirmed	208 (29%)	212

Barn Owl

by Cathryn Wise-Gervais *Tyto alba*

The ghostly Barn Owl is primarily nocturnal and relies heavily on keen hearing to locate prey. These owls hunt like silent spirits, but at other times they fill the night air with keening screeches. Their heart-shaped facial discs are unmistakable field marks that earned the bird the nickname of "monkey-faced owl."

JIM BURNS

HABITAT

Barn Owls are found in a variety of habitats but generally prefer open country that offers scattered nesting and roosting sites. Atlasers reported Barn Owls in eighteen habitat types across Arizona. Nearly 21 percent of all atlas records were from Sonoran Desert uplands, and another 13 percent were from the adjacent wooded dry washes (n = 161). Atlasers reported 17 percent of records in rural and agricultural areas with pastures, dense shade trees, and outbuildings, and approximately 15 percent in lowland riparian woodlands containing cottonwood, willow, and tamarisk. Barn Owls were also reported in urban settings, grasslands, trees near cultivated fields, and open pinyon-juniper woodlands. Barn owls are well known for their habit of roosting and nesting in structures such as barns, abandoned buildings, bridges, and church steeples. In Arizona, they also commonly use caves, cliff ledges, adits, and mineshafts as well as cavities in trees and burrows in cutbanks. In the latter, they have occasionally excavated their own burrows (Marti 1992). Barn Owls typically avoid high elevations and dense forests.

BREEDING

Most of Arizona's Barn Owls are year-round residents but will make local movements during the winter. The birds are generally on their breeding grounds by late winter, and courtship activities such as chasing flights begin at this time. In central Utah, courtship was observed as early as January, approximately one month before egg laying (Smith et al. 1974). Arizona birds probably follow a similar timeline, but atlas data are lacking because most field surveys were not initiated until late February. Millsap (1998) reported egg dates in Arizona from early February to early May. The earliest Barn Owl nest located during the atlas period contained eggs on 10 April. Atlas data suggest that the peak breeding period statewide is from late April through late May. The latest confirmation was a nest with young found on July 24.

Barn Owls engage in a "nest-showing" behavior in which the male flies in and out of a site while calling repeatedly. It is thought that both sexes select the nest site and the female constructs a shallow depression sometimes made of shredded pellets on the floor of a cavity, mine, cave, or building (Marti 1992). They readily use nest boxes where provided, and in Arizona desert cities and rural communities they will also commonly nest behind the mass of dead fronds of untrimmed palms and on the duff collected in large athel tamarisks.

Egg clutches usually consist of 4–7 (range 3–11) eggs (Baičich and Harrison 1997), and incubation begins with the first egg and lasts approximately 32 days (Marti 1992). Females incubate and brood young exclusively. The male brings food to the nest, but only the female actually feeds the young, and by day 14 the female begins to hunt as well (Marti 1992). This bird's hunting prowess is well known, and adults have been documented bringing up to six mice to the nest in a thirty-five-minute period (Bunn et al. 1982). Owlets leave the nest at age 50–55 days but usually stay in the vicinity of home for several weeks after fledging (Smith et al. 1974). Barn Owls usually rear one brood but under good conditions, can bring off two or even three broods per year (Whitmer and Patrick 1987).

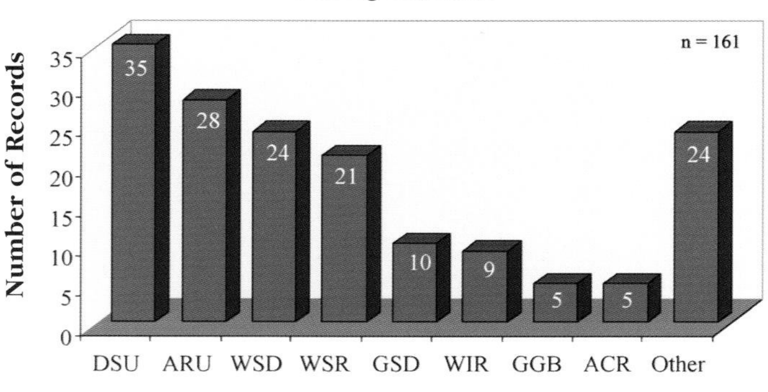

DISTRIBUTION AND STATUS

Barn Owls are the most widespread of all owl species (Burton 1984) and are found on every continent except Antarctica. In the Western Hemisphere, these owls are fairly common to uncommon residents throughout much of the United States and south through South America. There is some debate regarding the Barn Owl's migratory habits, but most

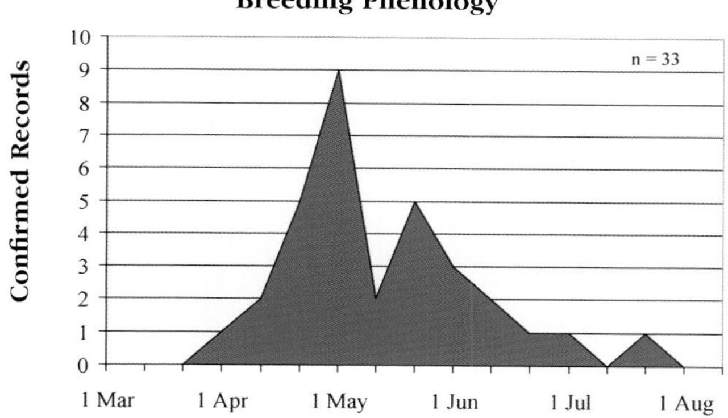

researchers believe that the birds are generally sedentary (Marti 1992). In Arizona, these owls may move to lower elevations for the winter, and northern birds may move into our state during the coldest months (Milsap 1998). To compound the migration question, young birds commonly disperse widely from the natal site, and such movements can be mistaken for migration (Marti 1992).

Phillips et al. (1964) described Barn Owls as fairly common in open country in southern and western Arizona, but believed the species to be rare in the lowland deserts in the southwest portion of the state. In contrast, Millsap (1998) regularly found these owls in desert regions of western Pima and Maricopa counties in the early 1980s. Atlasers had similar findings as Millsap and regularly located Barn Owls in the western deserts both in agricultural settings and in open country, where they frequented mines, dense trees, and cutbank cavities. Fewer individuals were discovered in the lower and drier desert regions of La Paz and Yuma counties. Atlasers encountered Barn Owls on many blocks in southeastern Arizona, but the species was infrequently detected within the upper San Pedro River valley.

Barn Owls are sparse and irregular summer residents in Arizona north of the Mogollon Rim where observations are few and actual breeding records are rare (Phillips et al. 1964; Jacobs 1986). Atlas data reflect these earlier observations, and additional records indicate that this species is more numerous on Navajo tribal lands east of the Chuska Mountains in New Mexico than in Arizona (C. LaRue and P. Ryan, personal communication). Brown et al. (1987) could find no records for this owl within the Grand Canyon region, although atlasers confirmed a nesting pair under a small bridge southwest of Fredonia.

Barn Owl abundance often varies annually, presumably due to prey availability. This variance as well as this owl's nocturnal habits and preference for inaccessible roost sites make determining Barn Owl status and population trends in Arizona difficult.

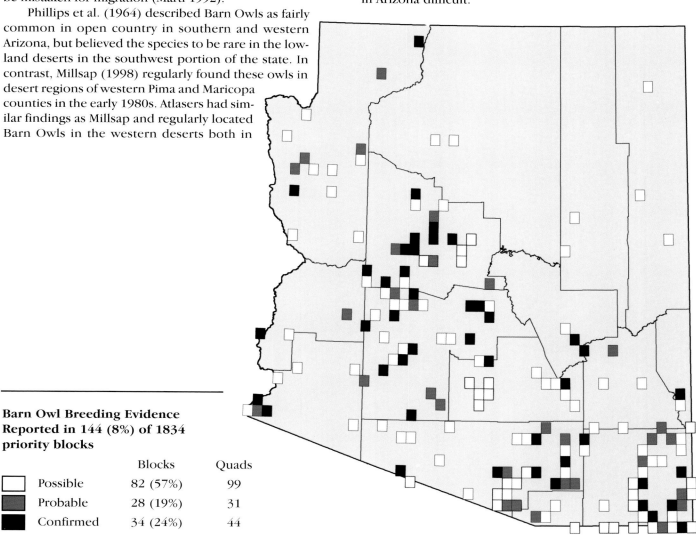

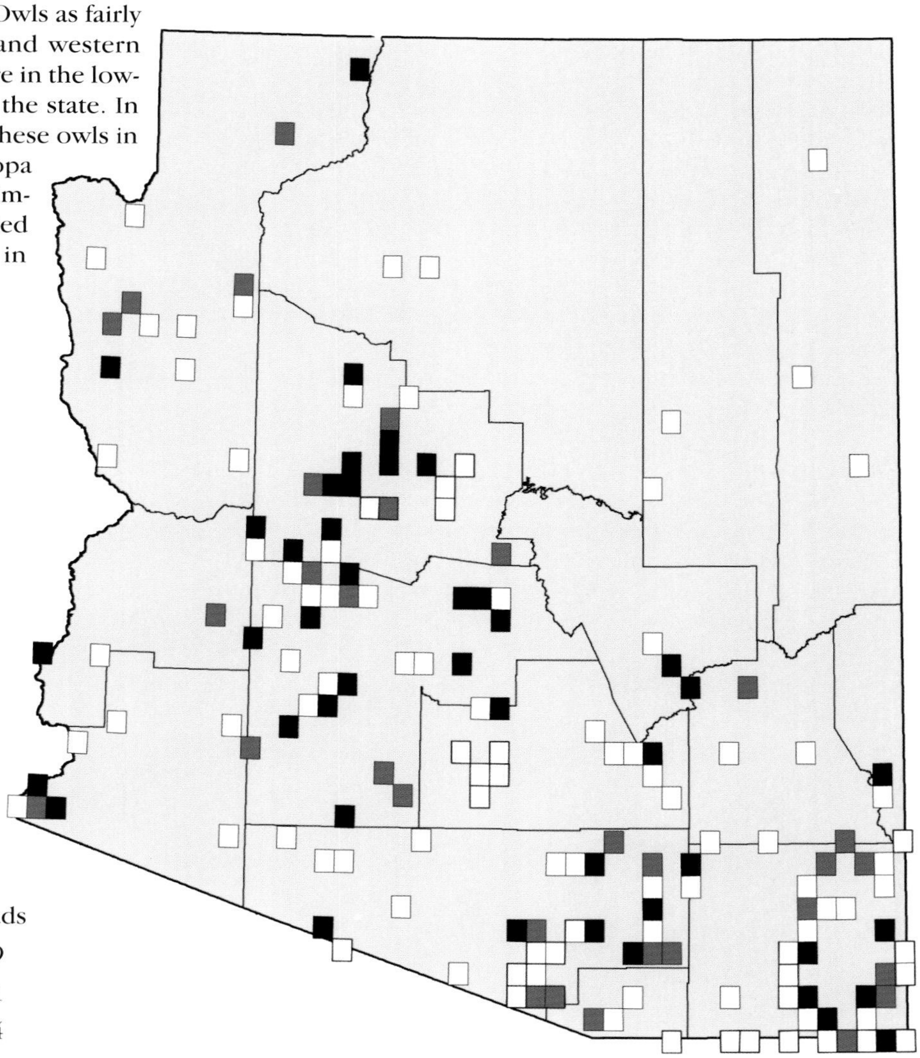

Barn Owl Breeding Evidence Reported in 144 (8%) of 1834 priority blocks

	Blocks	Quads
Possible	82 (57%)	99
Probable	28 (19%)	31
Confirmed	34 (24%)	44

Flammulated Owl

by Cathryn Wise-Gervais *Otus flammeolus*

The lovely and gentle-looking Flammulated Owl dwells primarily in ponderosa pine forests and is the only small owl in Arizona with dark eyes. These petite owls are strictly nocturnal and eat primarily insects, especially moths. Flammulated Owls occupy small territories, and populations can be considerably dense in suitable habitat.

HELEN AND NOEL SNYDER

HABITAT

Flammulated Owls are closely associated with dry coniferous forests throughout their range. In Arizona, such forests are typically dominated by mature ponderosa pines. In general, these owls prefer old growth forests for nesting and foraging (Reynolds and Linkhart 1998). Ponderosa pine forests with scattered stands of large Gambel's oaks are especially favored and account for 28 percent of all atlas records (n = 83). These owls were also noted in primarily pure ponderosa pine forests (22 percent of records) and in higher-elevation mixed-conifer forests with various pines, Douglas fir, white fir, and aspen (21 percent). Flammulated Owls were reported less frequently in pinyon-juniper woodlands within scattered stands of ponderosa pines. In southeastern Arizona mountain ranges, atlasers also regularly encountered Flammulated Owls in Madrean pine-oak forests and in lower canyon drainages containing Madrean evergreen oak–Arizona cypress associations. These small owls require an abundance of natural or abandoned cavities in snags, large dead limbs, or live trees in which to select a nest site.

BREEDING

Flammulated Owls are neotropical migrants that return to southern Arizona in mid-March, occasionally as early as 2 March, and by early to mid-April in the northern portion of the state. Males presumably arrive first and begin establishing territories that are advertised by near-constant calling (Reynolds and Linkhart 1998). Females arrive on the breeding grounds begging to be fed, and males begin courtship feeding immediately. Together the pair selects a nest cavity from within the male's territory. Once the nest tree is selected, the female will remain in close proximity to it for the entire breeding sequence (Reynolds and Linkhart 1998).

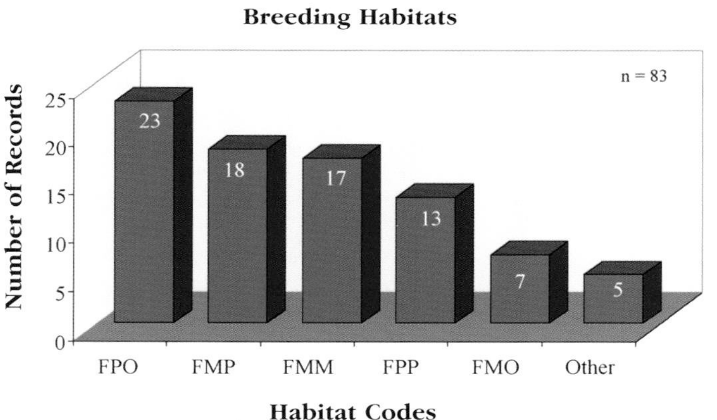

Flammulated Owls begin laying eggs by early to mid-May in southern Arizona (Bent 1938) and several weeks later in northern regions of the state. Atlasers discovered the first occupied nest on 30 May, and the only nest with eggs was reported in a Gambel's oak on 25 June. Apparently these owls will often nest in Gambel's oak cavities, even when suitable ponderosa pine is available (T. Corman, personal communication). The reason for this preference is not known. Eggs begin hatching by early June (Bent 1938) and the latest atlas breeding record was a nest with young found on 7 July. Fledging is believed to occur rangewide from late June to early August (McCallum 1994). In Arizona, southbound migration for the Flammulated Owls begins in August, but peak passage is in late September or October (Balda et al. 1975), with stragglers still traveling into November.

Flammulated Owls nest in natural cavities or abandoned woodpecker holes, favoring those created by Northern Flickers and sapsuckers (McCallum 1994). In Arizona, these small owls are known to nest in Gambel's oak, ponderosa pine, quaking aspen, Arizona cypress, and Arizona sycamore. Flammulated Owls will use nest boxes when provided and can sometimes evict secondary cavity nesters such as bluebirds (McCallum 1994). Atlasers measured one low nest with an egg in a Gambel's oak that was only 6.2 ft (1.9 m) above the ground. Most Arizona nests range in height from 10 to 40 ft (3.0–12.2 m), although one nest was reported to be approximately 100 ft (30.5 m) above the ground in a ponderosa pine (Lesh et al. 1994).

Nests are generally unlined, although sometimes nesting material persists from previous tenants (McCallum 1994). Females lay 2–3 eggs (range 2–4) and incubate these exclusively for 21 to 24 days (McCallum 1994) while being fed by the male. After hatching, the male brings food to the nest and this is probably fed to young by the female, as is typical with owls. Owlets fledge by 25 days of age but are still fed by the adults for an additional 25 to 32 days before dispersing from the natal area (Linkhart and Reynolds 1987).

DISTRIBUTION AND STATUS

Flammulated Owls breed patchily throughout western North America from southern British Columbia and Montana, through the Intermountain West and Southwest to southern Mexico. The bird's winter range and habits are poorly understood (McCallum 1994).

Flammulated Owls are considered the most abundant owl in ponderosa pine–dominated mountain ranges throughout Arizona (Phillips et al. 1964). Atlasers noted this species at elevations primarily between 6000 and 9200 ft (1829–2804 m) and nesting locally down to 5200 ft (1585 m) in cooler, forested canyons. Atlas data for these small forest owls are relatively limited in southeastern Arizona, and this species is likely more widespread in this region than the atlas range map indicates. Flammulated Owls undoubtedly continue to nest in the Rincon, Pinal, and Galiuro mountains, as well as in more localities in the Pinaleno Mountains.

During the atlas period, Flammulated Owls were not detected in many forested areas of Arizona, undoubtedly because of the timing of the atlas surveys. One study in Arizona found that nesting Flammulated Owls become much quieter after early to mid-June when the males begin providing food for the newly hatched young (Lesh et al. 1994). Nocturnal surveys conducted after this period could easily miss the species. Reynolds and Linkhart (1998) suggest that since these owls are so tied to mature ponderosa pine and mixed-conifer forests, simply identifying mountains containing these forests will specify most of their range within the state. Similarly, Flammulated Owls undoubtedly occur throughout much of the White Mountain Apache tribal lands, but atlas surveys were not conducted in this area.

On Navajo tribal lands, these owls were detected on Black Mesa and the Defiance Plateau and in the Chuska Mountains, but were not reported in the nearby Lukachukai and Carrizo Mountains where they have occurred in the past (Jacobs 1986). Many atlas surveys in these mountain ranges were conducted in late summer during a period when these owls often fall silent. Similarly, they were not detected in the Hualapai Mountains during the atlas period, despite previous records of them there (Phillips et al. 1964).

The rangewide status of this small owl is poorly understood. Despite the possibility of dense populations occurring in localized areas of prime habitat, the Southwestern Region of the U.S. Forest Service (Arizona and New Mexico) placed Flammulated Owls on their "sensitive species" list. This designation ensures that managers closely analyze the possible effects of forest management activities on the species' populations and habitats (Reynolds and Linkhart 1998). Specific threats to owls include the loss of mature trees and snags to timber harvesting, fuel wood cutting (especially oaks), and wildfires. Other threats include the reduction of prey items resulting from insecticide use and the transformation of naturally open woodland to forests choked with young trees due to fire suppression (Reynolds and Linkhart 1998). These unnaturally dense woodlands hinder the foraging ability of Flammulated Owls and may adversely affect nesting success.

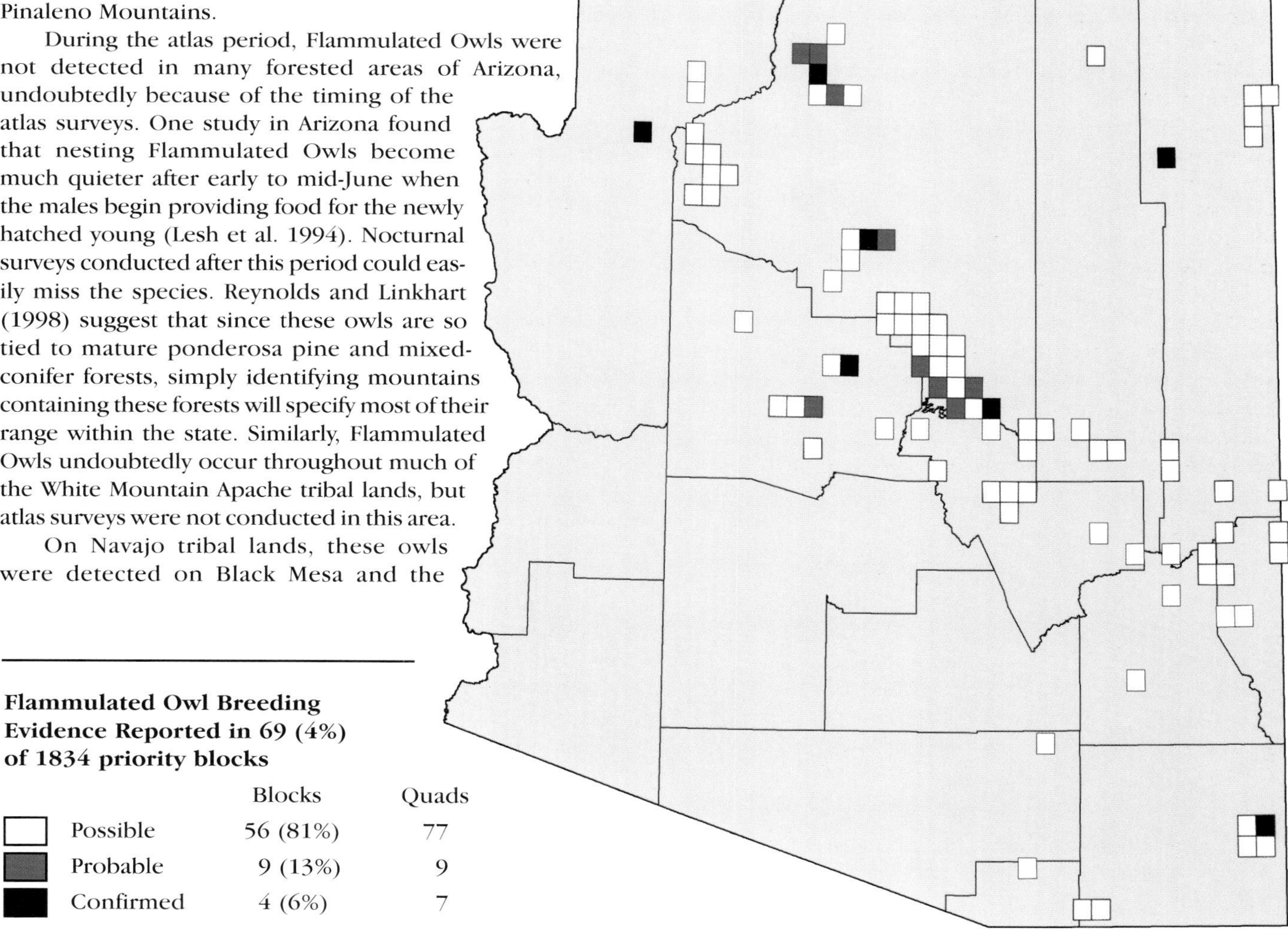

Flammulated Owl Breeding Evidence Reported in 69 (4%) of 1834 priority blocks

	Blocks	Quads
Possible	56 (81%)	77
Probable	9 (13%)	9
Confirmed	4 (6%)	7

Western Screech-Owl

by Cathryn Wise-Gervais *Megascops kennicottii*

Arizona's Western Screech-Owls are attractive but unassuming woodland dwellers that are most commonly detected by their "bouncing ball" call. Aggressive for its small size, this petite owl will ferociously defend breeding territory even from larger birds such as Great Horned Owls.

BRUCE TAUBERT

HABITAT

According to Marshall (1957), the Western Screech-Owl "is at home in any kind of woodland," and atlas data certainly support this statement. Atlasers reported Western Screech-Owls in 22 habitat types, including Sonoran Desert uplands of saguaro, ironwood, and paloverde (29 percent of records), the adjacent densely wooded dry washes (15 percent of records), and in pinyon-juniper woodlands (14 percent of records; n = 524). These owls are also commonly found in lowland wooded drainages dominated by cottonwood-willow, sycamore, or mesquite (18 percent of records), as well as in the lower and more open edges of Madrean evergreen oak woodlands characterized by mixed oaks, juniper, and pinyon pine (5 percent of records). Atlasers reported a handful of Western Screech-Owl records in woodlands with scattered ponderosa pine, but these owls generally avoid heavily timbered, high-elevation forest areas. In southeastern Arizona, Western and Whiskered screech-owls locally occur sympatrically where lower-elevation oaks and riparian areas transition into the denser Madrean oak woodlands and pine-oak forests favored by the latter (Marshall 1957).

BREEDING

Western Screech-Owls are nonmigratory and are often found in pairs throughout the year. Courtship typically begins in January and February, during which time the males will begin calling more frequently. Pairs will perch together with feathers touching and will allopreen (Cannings and Angell 2001). Male Western Screech-Owls bring food to the females and will even entice them to potential nest sites with edible gifts. Atlasers located the first occupied nest on 13 March and the first nest with young on 10 April, indicating that some pairs initiate egg laying by the first week of March or earlier. Atlasers also noted the first fledgling Western Screech-Owls on 25 April, suggesting egg laying by late February. Atlas data reveal a peak in breeding activity for these owls in late April through late May. The latest occupied nest was detected on 13 June; however, atlasers observed fledglings through early August and reported adults feeding fledglings on 10 August. Only 8 percent of atlas records were breeding confirmations, indicating that these owls are fairly secretive near their nest sites.

Western Screech-Owls nest in abandoned woodpecker holes (especially those of flickers) or in natural cavities. These small owls select cavities with entrances very near their body size, probably to reduce the chances of predation by larger animals (Cannings and Angell 2001). In Arizona, Western Screech-Owls will nest in most tree species large enough to support an adequate cavity. In the Sonoran Desert these owls especially favor cavities constructed by Gilded Flickers in saguaros. Also, these owls regularly take advantage of nest boxes and locally nest under the dead fronds of untrimmed palm trees in rural and suburban settings in Arizona. Selected nest cavities are typically 4–30 ft (1.2–9.1 m) above the ground (Bowers 1998).

Western Screech-Owls usually lay 3–5 (range 2–7) eggs (Cannings and Angell 2001), which the female incubates for 33 to 34 days (Gehlbach 1994). The male provisions the female during the entire breeding sequence, and only when the young are approximately 3 weeks old will the female begin to assist with hunting for the family (Sumner 1929). Approximately 10 days before fledging, the owlets begin climbing to the cavity entrance and peering out (Cannings

Breeding Habitats

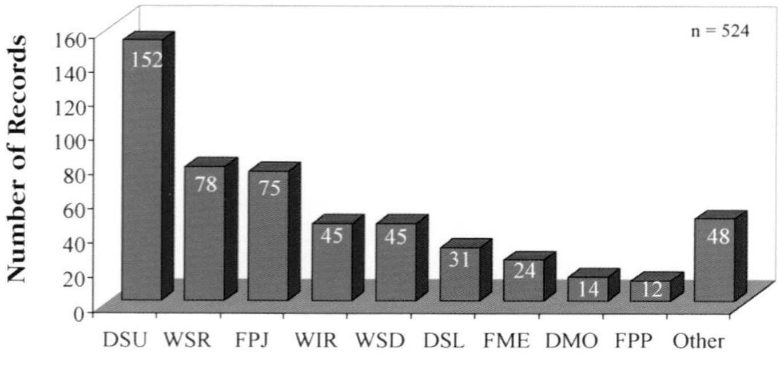

Breeding Phenology

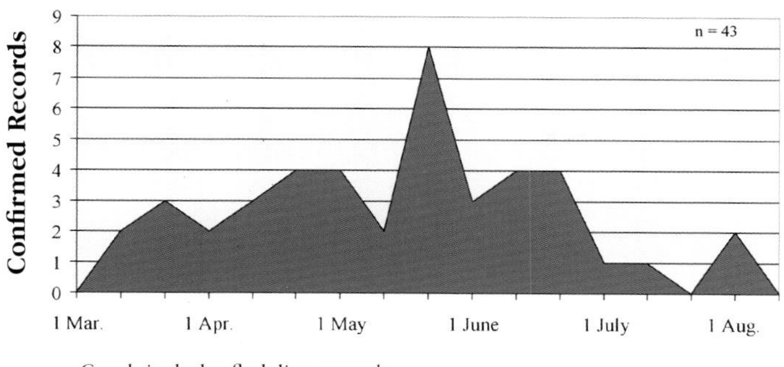

Graph includes fledgling records

and Angell 2001). Fledging occurs at approximately 28 days (Ehrlich et al. 1988), but owlets remain near the adults and the nest site for approximately five weeks after nest departure (Cannings and Angell 2001). If disturbed, the parents will perform distraction displays or bill snapping to attract attention away from their young (Cannings and Angell 2001).

DISTRIBUTION AND STATUS

Western Screech-Owls are one of the most common owls found in western North America. They occur from the coastal areas of southern Alaska and western Canada southeast through eastern Colorado and western Texas to central Mexico. In Arizona, atlasers noted these owls throughout much of the state primarily at elevations from 180 to 6500 ft (55–1981 m). Locally, Western Screech-Owls were detected at higher elevations to just above 7500 ft (2286 m) on dry mountain slopes with pinyon-juniper woodlands. These owls are typically absent from higher elevations dominated by taller conifers.

Previous literature considered these little owls as common throughout Arizona except in the northeast where they were considered scarce (Swarth 1914; Phillips et al. 1964). Atlasers generally found that Western Screech-Owls were much more common in southern and central regions of the state than north of the Mogollon Rim. In the southern lowlands, these owls were notably scarce only in primarily treeless habitats including grassland, extensive agricultural lands, and sparsely vegetated desert areas. Rosenberg et al. (1991) described Western Screech-Owls as fairly common resident throughout the lower Colorado River valley. However, these owls went undetected on many surveyed atlas blocks in this region. Within this vast valley, populations of these owls have undoubtedly been greatly reduced with the loss of large cottonwood, willow, and mesquite-dominated riparian groves during the past century.

During the atlas period, Western Screech-Owls were rather uncommon in northwestern Arizona and as noted by others, were found less frequently in the northeast. However, these owls were detected much more regularly in the latter region than prior literature suggested. On Navajo and Hopi tribal lands, these owls were most widespread in and around Black Mesa. Despite their extensive range, Western Screech-Owls are relatively inconspicuous except during periods of persistent hooting, such as during full moon evenings in late winter and spring. Atlasers most commonly detected this species by hearing its call or by flushing a roosting bird.

Although Western Screech-Owl populations seem to be stable in the United States, little is known of their status in Mexico. Habitat destruction is the greatest threat facing Western Screech-Owls (Bowers 1998), and these birds are also prone to collisions with vehicles owing to their ability to live in close proximity to humans.

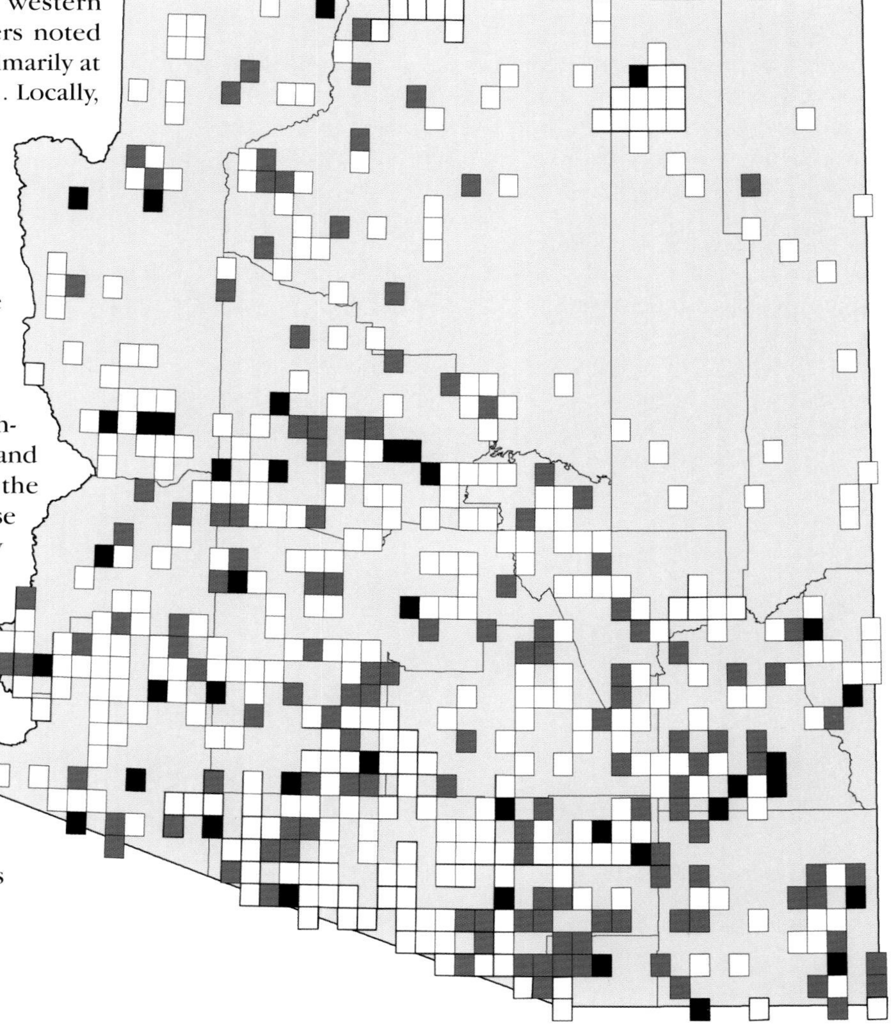

Western Screech-Owl Breeding Evidence Reported in 504 (27%) of 1834 priority blocks

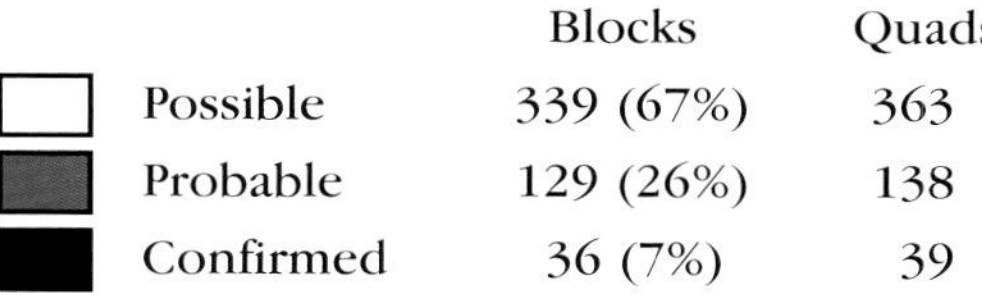

	Blocks	Quads
Possible	339 (67%)	363
Probable	129 (26%)	138
Confirmed	36 (7%)	39

Whiskered Screech-Owl

by Cathryn Wise-Gervais *Megascops trichopsis*

Considered one of southeastern Arizona's specialty birds, Whiskered Screech-Owls draw birders from all over the country and beyond. Few observers are able to discern this owl's characteristically smaller feet or bristly "whiskers," however, and instead will recognize the Whiskered Screech-Owl by its distinctive Morse code calls.

JIM BURNS

HABITAT

Whiskered Screech-Owls reach the northern edge of their range in the forested canyons, slopes, and ridges of the sky island mountains in southeastern Arizona. Within these ranges, these small owls are closely associated with several habitats containing dense stands of Madrean evergreen oaks. They typically select habitats containing extensive oak woodlands with an abundance of medium to large-sized trees and dense screening foliage (Marshall 1957; Monson 1998). In fact, atlasers obtained 40 percent of potential breeding records for Whiskered Screech-Owls in extensive stands of Madrean oak woodlands characterized primarily by various species of evergreen oaks (n = 29). Observers reported an additional 33 percent of records in mountain drainages dominated by Arizona sycamores, but also containing dense oaks, scattered pines, Arizona cypress, and alligator juniper. All remaining Whiskered Screech-Owl records were from Madrean pine-oak forests containing stands of Apache, Chihuahuan, and some ponderosa pine, with an understory of mixed evergreen oaks, juniper, and madrone. Marshall (1957) noted that the highest densities of these owls are reached in this habitat. In general, Whiskered Screech-Owls prefer higher elevations and denser forests than do Western Screech-Owls (Marshall 1957); however, the two species can occasionally be found together.

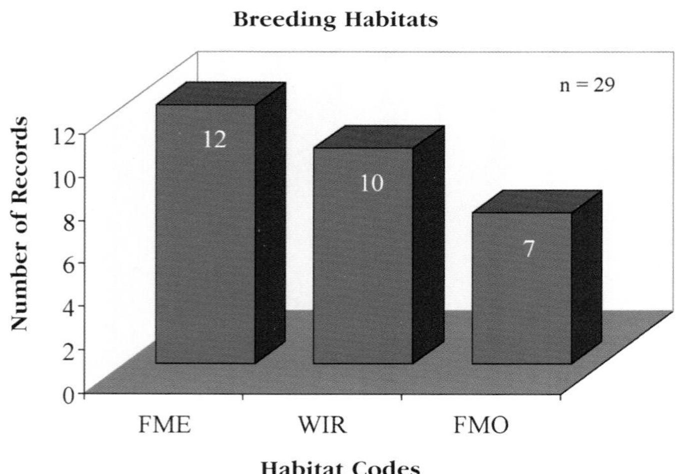

BREEDING

Whiskered Screech-Owls are nonmigratory and remain paired throughout the year. These owls begin calling in late February (Monson 1998), and courtship activities begin in mid-March. The earliest atlas records were of paired Whiskered Screech-Owls observed on 7 and 16 April. Researchers in Arizona have reported that Whiskered Screech-Owls can lay eggs as early as 10 April (Gehlbach and Gehlbach 2000), with most initial clutches laid from mid-April to early May (Bent 1938; Brandt 1951). Replacement clutches are typically laid from late May to early June (Gehlbach and Gehlbach 2000). Observers obtained only five confirmed records for Whiskered Screech-Owls, and the earliest of these was a sighting of an adult feeding fledged young on 7 June. This date would suggest that in this instance, eggs were laid in late April or early May, in keeping with prior published breeding dates. Researchers in southeastern Arizona also reported Whiskered Screech-Owl nestlings in mid-May to early July, and the appearance of fledglings from early June through July (Gehlbach and Gehlbach 2000). For comparison, the latest breeding confirmation made during the atlas period was of adults with dependent fledglings on 21 July.

Observers did not report any active Whiskered Screech-Owl nests and until relatively recently, little study has focused on the breeding biology of this species. Female owls will select a nest site from the available natural and woodpecker constructed cavities in the male's relatively small territory. The clutches of 2–4 eggs are laid directly on the accumulated debris at the bottom of the cavities approximately 17–36 ft (5.2–11.0 m) above the ground (Gehlbach and Gehlbach 2000). In many southeastern Arizona mountain canyons, Whiskered Screech-Owls nest most commonly in Arizona sycamore, often in natural cavities (Gehlbach and Gehlbach 2000). However, the nests of these owls have also been found in Arizona cypress, Chihuahuan pine, alligator juniper, walnut, and Arizona white or other evergreen oaks (Bent 1936; Brandt 1951; Gehlbach and Gehlbach 2000). In Arizona, this species nests locally in telephone poles, and rarely in nest boxes. One recent study in southeastern Arizona noted more nests in natural cavities than those constructed by woodpeckers, primarily Northern Flickers (Gehlbach and Gehlbach 2000).

The female Whiskered Screech-Owl incubates her eggs for approximately 26 days while being fed by the male (Gehlbach and Gehlbach 2000). Both sexes bring food to and brood the young for approximately one month (Gehlbach and Gehlbach 2000). After this time, the female will fly from the nest and coax the owlets out by whistling. Parental care continues for four or more weeks following nest departure.

DISTRIBUTION AND STATUS

These nonmigratory owls are found from southeastern Arizona and the adjacent Peloncillo Mountains of New Mexico south to northern Nicaragua (Monson 1998). Whiskered Screech-Owls are described as locally common to abundant in southeastern Arizona's border mountains from the Baboquivari Mountains in the west, north to the Santa Catalina Mountains, and east to the Chiricahua Mountains (Phillips et al. 1964; Monson and Phillips 1981). During the atlas, these owls were detected primarily at elevations from 5000 to 7600 ft (1524–2316 m). However, atlasers found them locally down to 3800 ft (1158 m) in Sycamore Canyon in the Pajarito Mountains.

During the atlas period, observers regularly found Whiskered Screech-Owls in most of their previously described and easily accessible breeding areas. Additionally, atlasers documented the owls in two new ranges by detecting calling birds in the Galiuro Mountains and finding a pair in the Mule Mountains. Monson (1998) predicted Whiskered Screech-Owls occurred in both of these seldom-explored ranges. The owl detected in the Galiuro Mountains is now the northernmost record obtained for this species, but it was hardly surprising given the quality of the available habitat in this rugged range. Atlasers verified that potential suitable habitat for Whiskered Screech-Owls also exists in Reiley Canyon on the north slope of the nearby Winchester range. Unfortunately, observers were unable to conduct nocturnal surveys in this small range because of time constraints. Monson (1998) also postulated that the birds may occur in small numbers in the Dragoon Mountains and reported them in the Whetstone and Peloncillo Mountains, but most atlasers were unable to conduct nocturnal surveys in the limited habitat available in these relatively dry ranges. Marshall (1956) found Whiskered Screech-Owls to be conspicuous residents in the pine-oak forests of the Rincon Mountains, and they likely continue to occur in this range. However, undoubtedly because of limited nocturnal surveys, these owls went unreported in this rugged and roadless mountain range during the atlas period.

The U.S. Forest Service administers most of the Whiskered Screech-Owl habitat in Arizona since much of it falls within the Coronado National Forest (Monson 1998). For this reason, it is imperative that Forest management plans address concerns germane to this locally occurring species, such as human disturbance and habitat alteration. Since this species is highly sought by visiting birders, it is locally prone to harassment by playback tapes, flash photography, and, unbelievably, by visitors pounding on trees to produce nesting adults. Limiting both the use of tape recorders and the size of birding groups in sensitive and frequently visited areas will clearly benefit these owls.

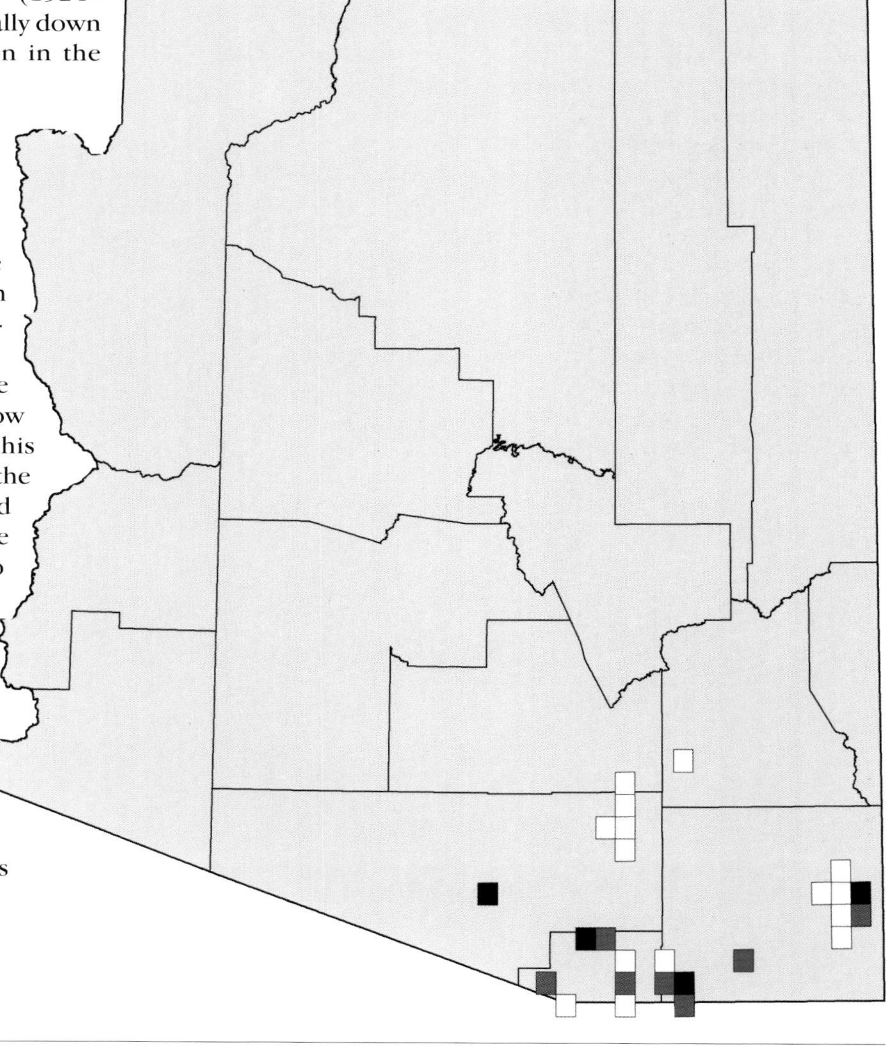

Whiskered Screech-Owl Breeding Evidence Reported in 18 (<1%) of 1834 priority blocks

	Blocks	Quads
Possible	11 (61%)	16
Probable	5 (28%)	7
Confirmed	2 (11%)	4

Great Horned Owl

by Cathryn Wise-Gervais *Bubo virginianus*

The unmistakable silhouette of the Great Horned Owl, nicknamed "Winged Tiger" for its strength and nocturnal hunting prowess, is a common early evening sight on bare trees and telephone poles throughout Arizona. The considerable size and crepuscular habits of this predator make it one of the easiest owls to observe.

HABITAT

Great Horned Owls are found in a wide variety of habitats and in fact, no other North American owl makes use of such a vast array of situations. These owls are equally common in agricultural lands, open woodlands and orchards, deserts, riparian areas, and even suburban neighborhoods. In areas with few trees, Great Horned Owls regularly occupy canyon walls, cutbanks, and cliffs. This remarkable flexibility in habitat selection is due to the opportunistic feeding habits of this bird, whose prey size spans from insects and scorpions to domestic cats and jackrabbits (Johnsgard 1988; Houston et al. 1998). Even with the Great Horned Owl's varied use of habitats, 42 percent of all atlas records were characteristically described as in Sonoran Desert landscapes, including the adjacent wooded dry washes (n = 909). This can be compared to only 10 percent of records in pinyon-juniper woodlands, an equally widespread habitat in Arizona. However, these lower rates of detection may be related to the fact that nocturnal surveys in these mid-elevation woodlands were often conducted later in the season, when the owl's calling frequency is greatly reduced. Regardless, it may be of more use to mention areas not favored by this owl, namely high-elevation, multistructured forests. Great Horned Owls seldom use dense forests, preferring open hunting areas.

BREEDING

Great Horned Owl pairs frequently remain on the same territory year-round (Houston et al. 1998), and in Arizona often initiate nightly hooting and courtship by late fall or early winter. The male will cock his tail, drop his wings, and expand his white throat bib while calling to the female. She will respond vocally and will also assume this chickenlike posture. The pair will often duet the classic owl hooting sound, with the male's call being slightly lower in pitch (Houston et al. 1998). Nesting often immediately follows the courtship period, and the earliest Arizona nests were located on 5 and 31 January, both containing nestlings. Atlasers also reported the earliest fledgling owls on 2 February. These records suggest that at least some Great Horned Owl pairs begin egg laying by early December or even earlier. Forty-eight percent of Arizona's nesting activity records were reported in April (n = 129), however, with peak activity between late March and early May. Atlasers reported the latest nest with young on 29 June, and this likely pertained to a renesting attempt after earlier efforts failed. Great Horned Owls are typically single-brooded (Marti 1969), and most young have departed the nest by mid-May in Arizona.

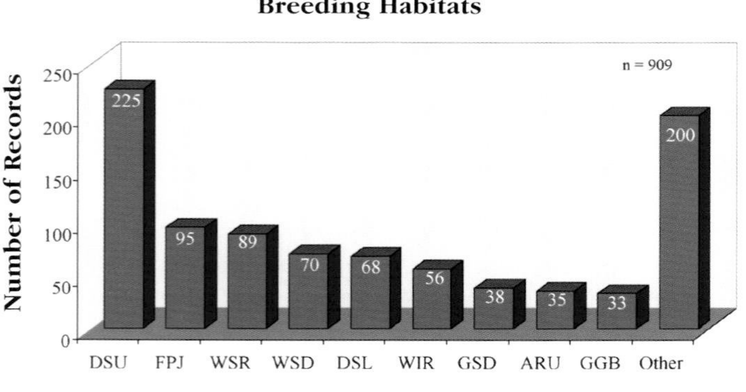

It is not known which sex selects the actual nest site, but it is presumed that the male Great Horned Owl chooses and defends the breeding territory (Houston et al. 1998). Most Great Horned Owls in Arizona select old stick nests of raptors, ravens, and occasionally herons placed in almost any tree, saguaro, or other elevated substrate. Atlasers also found these owls nesting under bridges and on rock outcrops, cliffs, and cutbanks, sometimes lacking a previous stick nest structure. Other nest locations include old buildings, cavities in trees, and on rare occasions, even on the ground (Houston et al. 1998).

In the Sonoran Desert, some Great Horned Owl nests can contain 6 eggs, although 2–3 is the more common number (Dawson 1998). Like other owls, the female alone

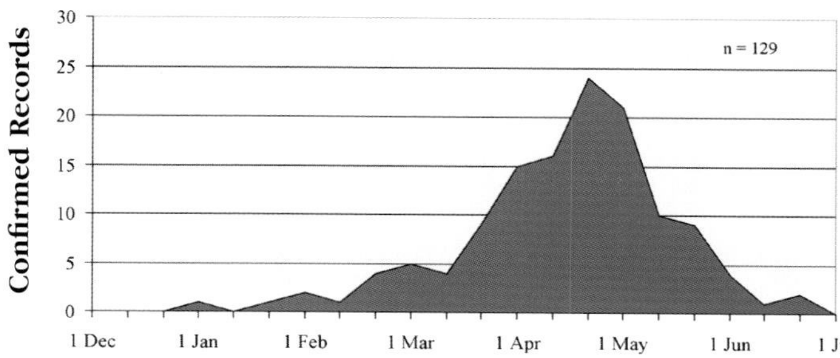

incubates and closely broods the young. Data compiled from various studies by Houston et al. (1998) indicate that incubation lasts from 30 to 37 days and begins with the first egg laid. The owlets hatch asynchronously and siblings may kill the youngest and weakest, especially during food shortages (Houston et al. 1998). The male will bring food to the nest, which the female then tears into bits and feeds to owlets. The young typically leave the nest at 5–7 weeks of age but are incapable of sustained flight for several weeks following nest departure (Dawson 1998). Fledglings will remain near the parents all summer, and some will continue begging for food even four to five months after leaving the nest (Houston et al. 1998).

DISTRIBUTION AND STATUS

Great Horned Owls are found throughout North America, thanks to their extraordinary habitat and diet flexibilities. This species becomes rare or absent in the hot, humid zones of Central and northern South America, but occurs in the cooler altitudes of South America and is more widespread in the southern half of that continent (Houston et al. 1998). These large, adaptable owls are described as fairly common throughout Arizona (Swarth 1914; Phillips et al. 1964). Great Horned Owls were also regularly noted statewide during the atlas period at elevations ranging from approximately 90 ft (27 m) along the lower Colorado River to 9800 ft (2987 m) at the open edges of mixed-conifer and spruce-fir forests in the White Mountains region.

Historically, these owls were believed to be largely absent from the unbroken forests high in the mountains of central-southern Arizona (Phillips et al. 1964), inasmuch as these areas are too heavily timbered for the birds' liking. Atlasers regularly found birds in these areas, however, undoubtedly because more patches of open terrain from timber harvesting activities and other habitat alterations in the past forty years. During the atlas, Great Horned Owls were noted as scarce or absent in relatively flat, treeless landscapes such as extensive agricultural areas, grasslands, and sparsely vegetated deserts.

Given the stability of Great Horned Owl populations throughout Arizona, no special conservation measures are warranted, although education programs clarifying this owl's beneficial habits may help enable suburban and rural owls to coexist more peaceably with humans. The owls have few natural enemies, and human-caused mortality, such as vehicle collisions, power pole electrocution, and widespread illegal shooting, poses the greatest threats to these impressive predators.

Great Horned Owl Breeding Evidence Reported in 873 (48%) of 1834 priority blocks

	Blocks	Quads
Possible	567 (65%)	591
Probable	134 (15%)	139
Confirmed	172 (20%)	188

Northern Pygmy-Owl

by Troy E. Corman *Glaucidium gnoma*

For their size, Northern Pygmy-Owls are feisty diurnal owls that do not hesitate to take prey that outweigh themselves two to one. The densities of these little owls are noticeably higher among the oaks and pines of some southeastern Arizona mountain ranges, which some authorities consider as a distinct species based on vocalizations and smaller size.

HABITAT

Northern Pygmy-Owls occur in most forested regions of Arizona, typically at higher elevations than Ferruginous Pygmy-Owls. During atlas surveys, these owls were found in many different habitats, with none significantly more frequently reported than others. However, nearly 59 percent of all atlas records were from tall pine- and/or oak-dominated forests (n = 74). In the southeast, these included dense Madrean evergreen oak woodlands or Madrean pine-oak forests, which typically have an overstory of Chihuahuan, Apache, and some ponderosa pines. In central and northern Arizona, these little owls were regularly reported in pure ponderosa pine forests and those with a Gambel's oak understory, and less frequently in denser woodlands of pinyon pine–juniper. Atlasers also frequently encountered this species in the adjacent wooded mountain drainages and canyons, especially those dominated by various conifers, Arizona sycamore, or Arizona cypress. Northern Pygmy-Owls were detected less often at higher elevations in mixed conifers with Douglas fir and aspen, as well as in spruce-fir associations. Although lower detection rates in these forests could pertain to the fact that many atlas surveys at these elevations were conducted in late spring and summer, when these owls are typically less vocal. Northern Pygmy-Owls are commonly observed watching for potential prey along the edge of forest clearings and within burned areas.

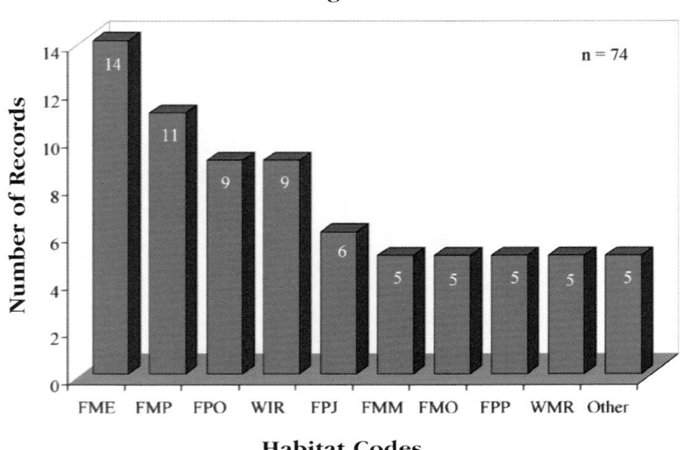

BREEDING

Northern Pygmy-Owls are primarily resident in Arizona, but some individuals regularly move to slightly lower elevations into adjacent habitats during the winter, especially within wooded foothill drainages. Males begin to establish nesting territories in February and March (Jones 1991), with pair formation likely established soon after. Atlasers reported the first detected pair on 26 March. Northern Pygmy-Owl pairs select nest cavities by late April or early May, earlier if the nest was used in previous years (Monson 1998). Atlasers found it difficult to confirm nesting activity of this owl, and therefore the peak nesting period could not be determined. Unlike several other small owls, nests are difficult to locate because females are reluctant to appear at the nest cavity entrance when the tree is tapped (Holt and Petersen 2000). The earliest confirmed record was of an occupied cavity on 10 May. In Arizona, nests with eggs have been found from 26 April to 12 June (Brandt 1951). The earliest fledgling reported by atlasers was observed being fed by an adult on 5 June, suggesting egg-laying initiation in early to mid-April, and fledglings were reported through late July.

Northern Pygmy-Owls typically use old woodpecker cavities in snags or live trees for nesting, although they occasionally use natural cavities as well. In Arizona, nests have been found in various conifers, oaks, sycamores, and aspens (Brandt 1951; Monson 1998). Atlasers did not measure the height of any nesting cavities, but Monson (1998) reported nests are frequently discovered from 8 to 20 ft (2.4–6.1 m) above the ground, exceptionally as high as 55 ft (16.8 m) in an Arizona sycamore (Brandt 1951).

Only the female Northern Pygmy-Owl incubates the typical clutch of 3–4 eggs (range 2–7), but the male brings her food while she incubates (Monson 1998). The precise incubation length is not known for this owl, but extrapolation from hatching dates suggests about 28 days (Holt and Norton 1986). The male continues providing food for the female and the nestlings for approximately the first ten days after the eggs begin to hatch, at which time the female begins to hunt (Holt and Norton 1986). However, most evidence suggests that only the female feeds the nestlings. Nestlings fledge rather quickly at approximately 3–4 weeks of age (Holt and Petersen 2000) and are fed by the adults for three or more additional weeks following nest departure (Rashid 1999).

DISTRIBUTION AND STATUS

Northern Pygmy-Owls are resident in western North America from extreme southeastern Alaska, south through California, Arizona, and the Rocky Mountains. South of the United States, these owls are found through the highlands of Mexico to southern Honduras. These small owls have been described as uncommon to fairly common in eastern and central Arizona, west to the Pajarito Mountains, Prescott, and the South Rim of the Grand Canyon (Phillips et al. 1964; Monson and Phillips 1981). Monson (1998) noted that Northern Pygmy-Owls are scarce in northern Arizona, and seemingly suitable habitat apparently goes unpopulated. Likewise, Marshall (1957) was confounded by the rarity of this owl in the Santa Catalina Mountains, especially when compared to significantly higher densities in similar mountain ranges to the south and southeast.

Atlasers found Northern Pygmy-Owls fairly widespread but generally sparsely distributed across forested regions of northern, central, and eastern Arizona. Only in extreme southeastern Arizona did atlasers find this little fierce-eyed owl with any regularity. Northern Pygmy-Owls are known to nest over a wide elevational range in Arizona, from 3600 to 10,500 ft (1097–3200 m). The lower elevations pertain to a sizable population in Sycamore Canyon in the Pajarito Mountains near the Mexico border. Higher-elevation nesting records include dependent fledglings noted in the White Mountains on the Engelmann spruce- and fir-shrouded upper slopes of Mount Baldy.

Atlasers expanded the Northern Pygmy-Owl's southeastern Arizona range slightly to the west to include the Baboquivari Mountains. Similarly, they were found west in the Four Peaks area of the Mazatzal Mountains in northeastern Maricopa County. These owls were found much farther west in northern Arizona than previously described, including Mohave County at such locations as the Hualapai Mountains, Mount Logan, and Mount Dellenbaugh. On Navajo tribal lands, atlasers detected Northern Pygmy-Owls on Black Mesa, in the Chuska Mountains, and several locations on the Defiance Plateau within upper Canyon de Chelly National Monument.

As with most forest owls, many nesting Northern Pygmy-Owls went undetected in Arizona because of the timing when most higher-elevation atlas surveys were conducted. The peak vocal period for the male's territorial song is in March and April, which often ceases abruptly after the onset of incubation in April or May (Jones 1991). High-elevation surveys were routinely not initiated until after early May. These owls were also undoubtedly missed along the Mogollon Rim within White Mountain Apache tribal lands, where access to conduct atlas surveys was not granted.

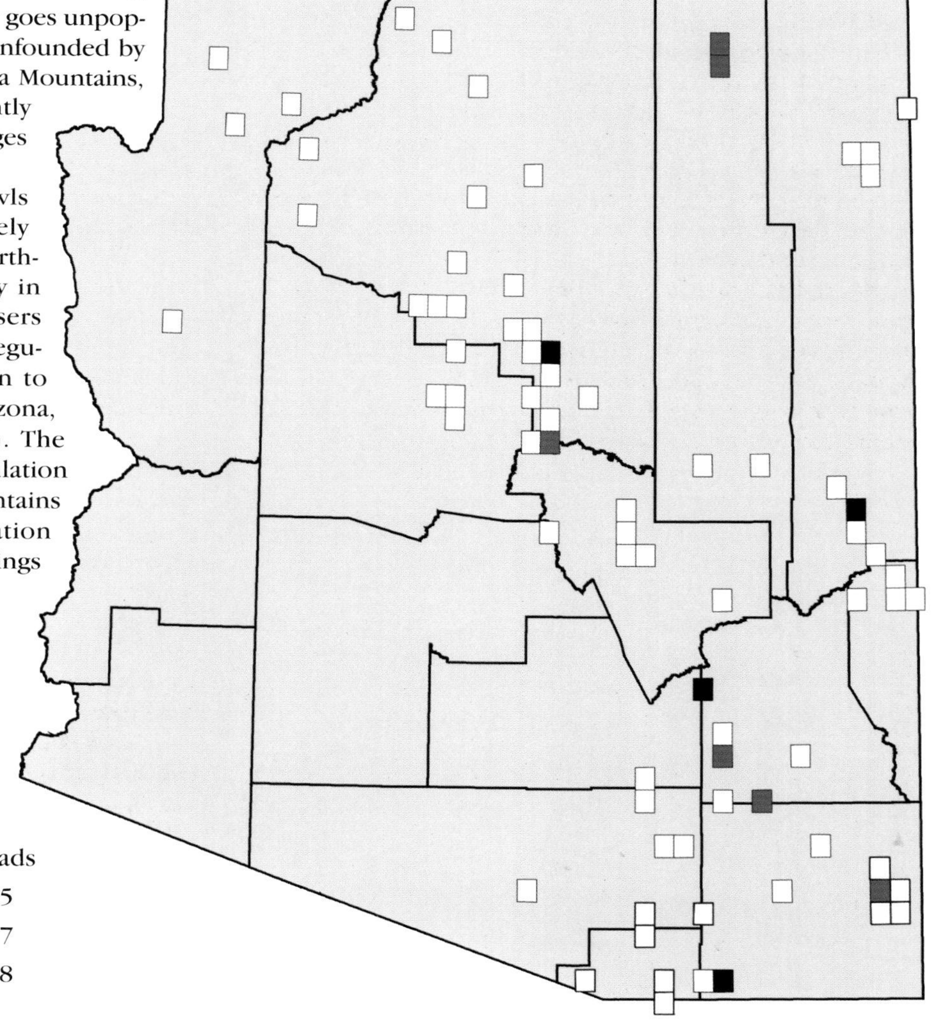

Northern Pygmy-Owl Breeding Evidence Reported in 61 (3%) of 1834 priority blocks

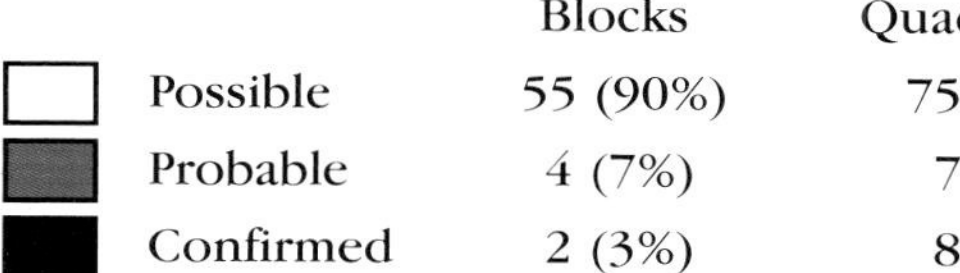

	Blocks	Quads
Possible	55 (90%)	75
Probable	4 (7%)	7
Confirmed	2 (3%)	8

Ferruginous Pygmy-Owl

by Troy E. Corman *Glaucidium brasilianum*

At the northern edge of their range, Ferruginous Pygmy-Owls are highly sought after in Arizona, not only by birders but also by researchers monitoring the local populations of this endangered and controversial species. Frequently mobbed by its avian neighbors, this small, diurnal owl nervously twitches its long, reddish-barred tail when it is agitated.

BOB MILES

HABITAT

Throughout their extensive range, Ferruginous Pygmy-Owls occupy a vast array of habitats from arid desertscrub and thornforests to humid riparian woodlands and lush tropical rainforests. In Arizona however, these small, local owls are currently found primarily in well-vegetated Sonoran desertscrub and the adjacent densely wooded dry washes. Typical vegetation in these habitats often includes higher densities of saguaros and large thorny trees such as ironwood, paloverde, and velvet mesquite. In fact, during the atlas period approximately 92 percent of all Ferruginous Pygmy-Owl records were reported within these two habitats (n = 36). These owls also locally occur in adjacent semi-urban and rural localities where larger tracts of native desert vegetation are still intact. Before the 1950s, most Arizona accounts suggested Ferruginous Pygmy-Owls reached their highest densities along perennial drainages with extensive and continuous riparian woodlands of Fremont cottonwood–Goodding willow and in the nearby mesquite bosques. However, these owls are now infrequently reported in the few, isolated native riparian woodland stands remaining within their current range. Recent evidence suggests that vegetation structure and the availability of nest cavities is more important to this owl than vegetation composition (Cartron et al. 2000).

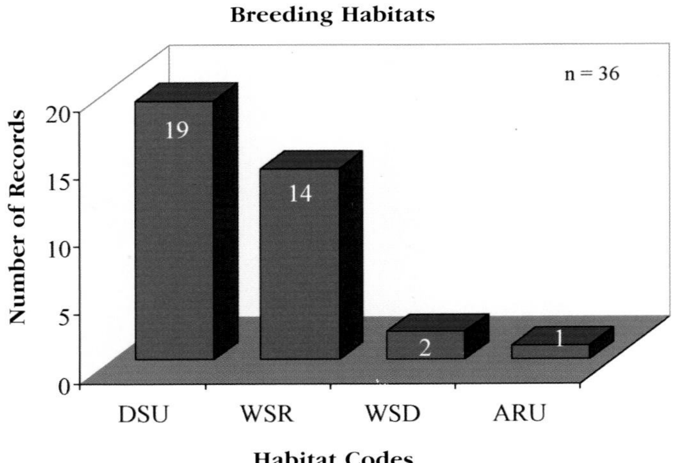

BREEDING

Ferruginous Pygmy-Owls are primarily resident throughout their range and in Arizona will often initiate their characteristic territorial calls and searching for potential nest sites in February. This is approximately two months prior to egg laying (Proudfoot and Johnson 2000). Atlasers reported paired individuals by 25 March, although copulation has been observed as early as 9 March (D. Abbate, personal communication). Most evidence indicates these owls typically lay eggs in April and May, and later egg clutches may pertain to renesting efforts following a failed earlier attempt (Proudfoot and Johnson 2000). Occupied Ferruginous Pygmy-Owl nests were noted by 18 April, and the earliest fledging date reported during the atlas was on 20 May. The latter date suggests that these eggs were laid in late March or early April and hatched by late April. During the atlas period, Ferruginous Pygmy-Owl nests with young were noted as late as 22 July, and fledglings were reported through 25 August.

During a recent eight-year period in Arizona, biologists documented 42 of 44 Ferruginous Pygmy-Owl nests in abandoned woodpecker cavities in saguaros (D. Abbate, personal communication). In Arizona, these owls have also nested in cottonwood, paloverde, mesquite, willow, and ash (Breninger 1898; Gilman 1909; Millsap and Johnson 1988). Selected nest cavities are typically 13–20 ft (4–6.1 m) above the ground, but can range from approximately 6.5 to 40 ft (2–12.2 m) high (Proudfoot and Johnson 2000). No nesting material is collected, and the owls will even remove nest material left from previous occupants in favor of a bare cavity (Proudfoot 1996).

Ferruginous Pygmy-Owls typically lay 3–5 eggs (range 2–7), which the female incubates for 23 to 28 days and then broods the young exclusively during their first week (Proudfoot 1996). The male brings food to the female during incubation and lures her from the nest cavity by calling (Proudfoot and Johnson 2000). Young fledge approximately 21–29 days after hatching but remain dependent on adults for 6 to 7 weeks following nest departure (Proudfoot and Johnson 2000). Recent fledglings are considerably smaller than the adults, are incapable of sustained flight, and often roost in the densest cover available within the territory, with exotic trees near urban settings and ironwoods especially favored. Young Ferruginous Pygmy-Owls disperse from their natal areas approximately 45–65 days following nest departure (D. Abbate, personal communication).

DISTRIBUTION AND STATUS

Ferruginous Pygmy-Owls are permanent residents from extreme south-central Arizona and south Texas to the southern tip of South America. These owls were formerly described as quite common and fairly numerous as far north as New River in northern Maricopa County, along the Salt River and Gila River near Phoenix, and as far down the Gila River as near Agua Caliente (Fisher 1893; Breninger 1898; Gilman 1909). The known historical boundaries included southern Yuma County (Phillips et al. 1964) and east along the Gila River to at least Geronimo, Graham County (Johnson et al. 2000). Since the early 1900s, the Ferruginous Pygmy-Owl's numbers have been greatly reduced, and its distribution has contracted considerably, especially since 1950 (Monson and Phillips 1981; Johnson et al. 2000). There have been no confirmed Ferruginous Pygmy-Owl records in Yuma County since 1955 (Monson and Phillips 1981) and in Maricopa County since 1971 (Johnson and Simpson 1971).

During the atlas period, Ferruginous Pygmy-Owls were documented nesting at elevations between 1330 and 4018 ft (405–1225 m) in Arizona (D. Abbate, personal communication). Historically, however, this owl was collected as low as 450 ft (137 m) along the Gila River and has been detected to nearly 4200 ft (1280 m) on foothill slopes. Atlasers and specific owl surveyors found this local species from southern Pinal County near Oracle Junction and northern Tohono O'odham tribal land south to Arivaca and Sasabe west to Organ Pipe Cactus National Monument. Prior to the atlas project, there were surprisingly no records for Ferruginous Pygmy-Owl within Tohono O'odham tribal lands. Because of its endangered status, atlasers were not permitted to conduct call surveys for this species, including on these tribal lands, and those few detected were found while conducting typical atlas surveys. The extensive and often near pristine conditions of the deserts and washes within Tohono O'odham tribal lands undoubtedly hold many more Ferruginous Pygmy-Owls than the atlas distribution map indicates.

At the very edge of their northern distribution, the relative instability of peripheral populations may help explain why the primarily tropical Ferruginous Pygmy-Owl experienced a population decline in Arizona (Johnson et al. 2000). However, while biogeography may have played an important role, it is generally recognized that loss of habitat was one, if not the primary underlying factor leading to their decline in Arizona (Johnson et al. 1979; Johnson et al. 2000). Early accounts suggested the continuous corridors of floodplain woodlands of towering cottonwood, willow, and mesquite that once covered hundreds of miles of southern Arizona's waterways may have supported sizable Ferruginous Pygmy-Owl populations (Cartron et al. 2000). Much of this optimal habitat is now gone, and what remains is in relatively small, isolated locations well away from currently known populations of this essentially nonmigratory owl.

The current status of Ferruginous Pygmy-Owls in Arizona will remain unclear until the center of their distribution in the state, the Tohono O'odham tribal lands, is thoroughly surveyed. Fueled by exotic grasses, the ever-increasing Sonoran Desert wildfires are a great concern because these intense fires frequently kill the saguaros and larger desert trees this species depend on. Urban sprawl will also continue to alter currently occupied habitat of this little intriguing owl.

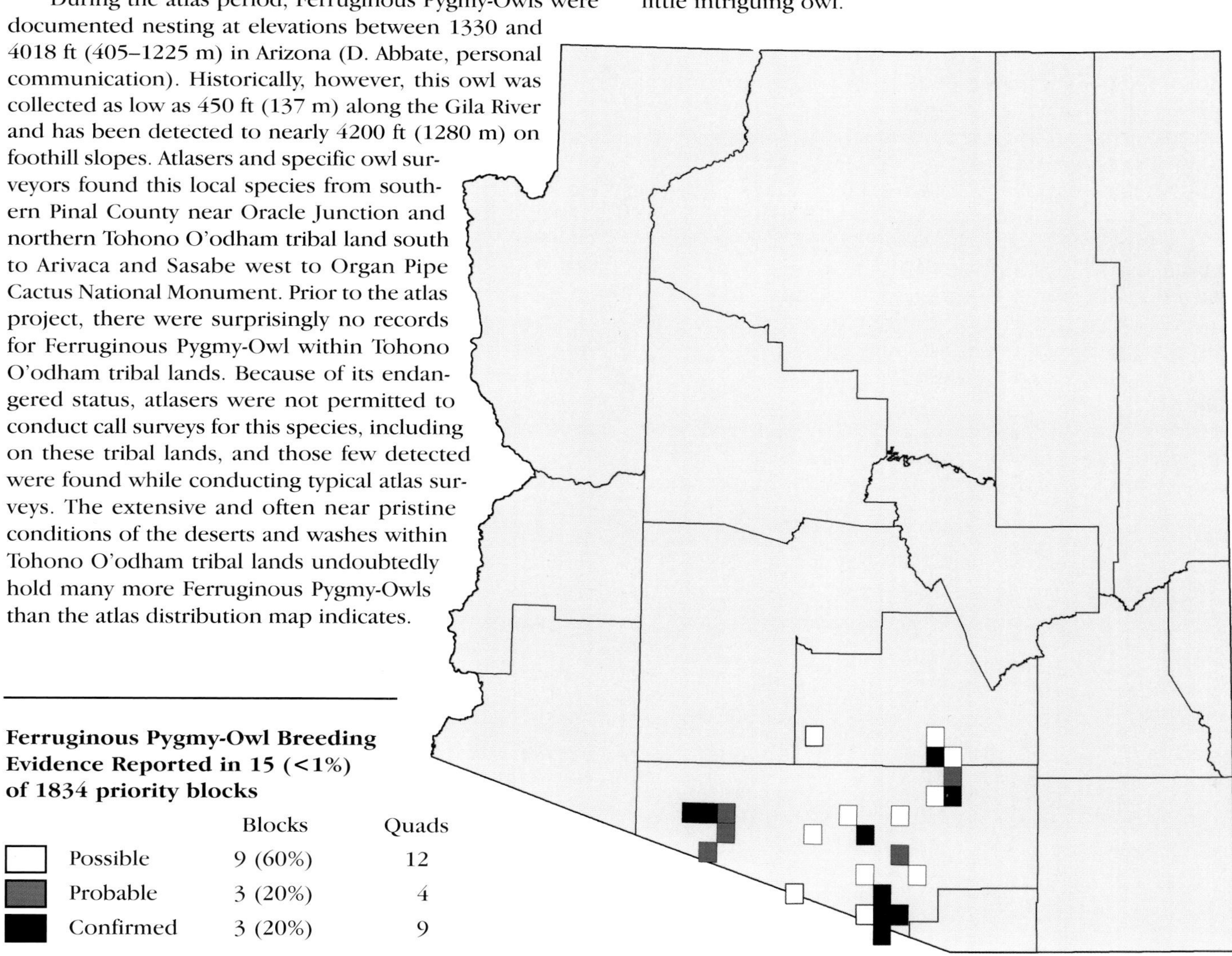

Ferruginous Pygmy-Owl Breeding Evidence Reported in 15 (<1%) of 1834 priority blocks

	Blocks	Quads
Possible	9 (60%)	12
Probable	3 (20%)	4
Confirmed	3 (20%)	9

Elf Owl

by Cathryn Wise-Gervais *Micrathene whitneyi*

The appropriately named Elf Owl is the smallest owl worldwide. Common in Arizona, Elf Owls are capable of astonishingly loud calls, sounds that have been likened to a yipping puppy. Although these birds are decidedly nocturnal, they can occasionally be observed foraging for insects at dusk or before dawn.

BRUCE TAUBERT

HABITAT

Traditional habitat descriptions have probably overemphasized the Elf Owl's association with the Sonoran Desert and its characteristic saguaros (Johnsgard 1988), because, in reality, the birds occur in many other types of woody vegetation. Atlasers reported 62 percent of Elf Owl records in open Sonoran Desert landscapes, typically in areas with an abundance of saguaros and scattered thorny trees such as paloverde, ironwood, and mesquite (n = 335). These owls were reported less frequently in the nearby densely wooded dry washes (6 percent of records) and lowland riparian woodlands of cottonwood, willow, and mesquite (8 percent of records), where Western Screech-Owls commonly occur. Elf Owls were also infrequently encountered in the drier lower elevations of the Sonoran Desert, where saguaros are sparse or absent. At higher elevations, atlasers noted 11 percent of Elf Owl records in foothill canyons dominated by Arizona sycamore. In southeastern Arizona's mountain ranges, many sycamore drainages containing Elf Owls often contained Madrean evergreen oak woodlands on the lower slopes. Preferred habitats are generally cavity-rich, and owl density is correlated to the relative abundance of nest holes (Henry and Gehlbach 1999). Elf Owls habituate to humans and will breed adjacent to suburban and rural localities if cavities and native foraging areas are available.

BREEDING

Elf Owls typically begin arriving in desert nesting areas of Arizona in mid-March, occasionally as early as late February, but often do not arrive in higher-elevation canyons until mid-April. The birds call most frequently from late March to mid-May during pair formation and territory establishment (Henry 1998). Atlasers first reported Elf Owls in suitable breeding habitat on 13 March and noted paired birds beginning on 31 March. Egg laying typically occurs in early May, although clutches have been detected as early as mid-April in Arizona. Atlasers also noted the first fledglings on 21 May, which suggests that some egg-laying initiation is in late March or early April. The latest nest with young was observed on 7 July, and fledglings were reported through 15 August. These later nests probably pertain to replacement clutches since these tiny owls are single-brooded and will renest if earlier efforts fail (Henry and Gehlbach 1999). Atlasers last reported Elf Owls in suitable breeding areas on 4 September, but fall migration typically occurs from late August through September and casually after mid-October.

Elf Owls nest in natural and woodpecker-constructed cavities in substrates such as saguaro, mesquite, cottonwood, and willow in lowland areas. Within wooded mountain canyons, these owls frequently select sycamore, walnut, cypress, evergreen oak, and even an occasional pine or telephone pole in which to nest. Male Elf Owls appear to select the nesting cavity (Henry 1998). Pairs can nest in the same tree or cacti as other avian species, and will help cooperatively protect the nest tree from predators by helping to mob nocturnal intruders (Henry and Gehlbach 1999). Atlasers measured few Elf Owl nests, but prior studies found that cavity height in saguaros averages approximately 19.7 ft (6 m) with a range of 10–36 ft (3–11 m) above the ground (Goad and Mannan 1987). In wooded mountain canyons, Ligon (1968) reported Elf Owl nest heights in sycamores averaging higher at approximately 33 ft (10 m) and ranging from 16.4 to 59 ft (5–18 m).

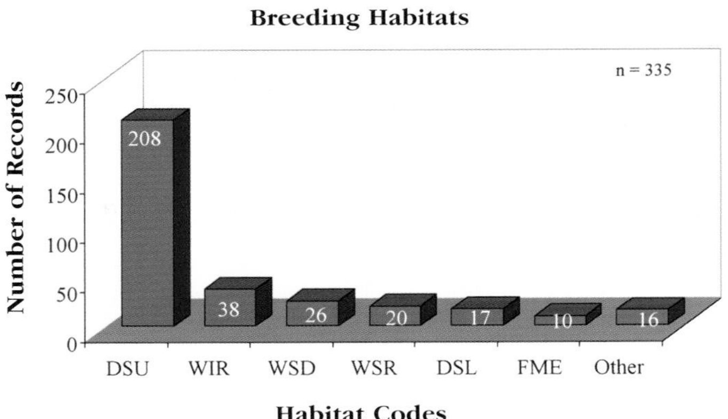

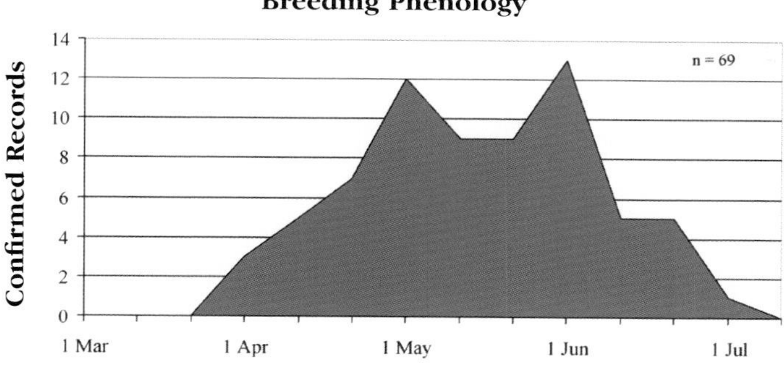

Although Elf Owls typically prefer a bare cavity, they will sometimes lay eggs on top of nest material left by previous tenants (Henry and Gehlbach 1999). Bent (1937) noted that these owls usually lay 3 eggs (range 2–5), and the female incubates these exclusively for 21 to 24 days (Henry and Gehlbach 1999). Throughout the incubation and brooding periods, the male provides most of the food for the female and young. The female assists feeding the nestlings at 2–3 weeks, and the young fledge at 28–32 days after hatching (Henry and Gehlbach 1999). The owlets will continue to beg from parents following nest departure, but it is unknown how long they actually depend on parents for food.

DISTRIBUTION AND STATUS

Elf Owl populations that nest in the United States are migratory and winter along the Pacific Slope of Mexico. These owls breed from the lower Colorado River valley of California (where extremely local), east through southern Arizona, southwestern New Mexico, and western and southern Texas. The breeding distribution in adjacent Mexico is unclear, but includes Sonora, northern Sinaloa, southern Baja California, and regions immediately south of Texas populations (Howell and Webb 1995).

Early accounts noted that Elf Owls occurred commonly throughout the lowlands of southern Arizona and within the lower Colorado River valley north to Topock and Fort Mojave (Swarth 1914). These owls were later described as scarce to rare within the lower Colorado River valley (Phillips et al. 1964) primarily due to dramatic habitat loss in both California and Arizona (Halterman et al. 1989; Rosenberg et al. 1991). During the atlas period, Elf Owls were only reported from the Bill Williams River delta region of the valley, although small, remnant populations may well have been overlooked.

Atlasers noted Elf Owls at elevations ranging from approximately 470 to 5600 ft (143–1707 m). These owls were found as far north as along Oak Creek Canyon near Sedona, where Phillips et al. (1964) reported this species as casual. Otherwise, atlas data reveal the northern limits of Elf Owls in Arizona from the Big Sandy River drainage north of Wikieup to northwest of Prescott and southeast through San Carlos Apache tribal lands to just north of Clifton.

The most significant threat to Elf Owls in Arizona is habitat loss from urban sprawl and increasing Sonoran Desert wildfires. Atlas data reveal that these owls regularly occur in the Tucson vicinity but are absent in many areas immediate to Phoenix, including agricultural areas. Unless more effort is made to preserve natural desert landscapes, especially those with tall saguaro stands, Elf Owls will ontinue to disappear from urban edges.

Elf Owl Breeding Evidence Reported in 313 (17%) of 1834 priority blocks

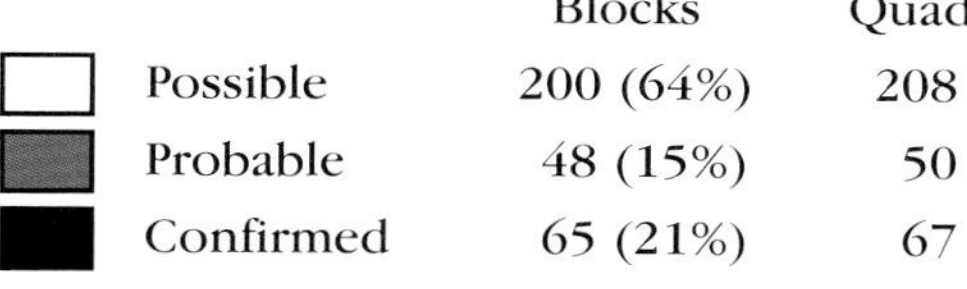

	Blocks	Quads
Possible	200 (64%)	208
Probable	48 (15%)	50
Confirmed	65 (21%)	67

Burrowing Owl

by Jennifer L. Martin *Athene cunicularia*

The long-legged Burrowing Owl is an anomaly in its family because of its crepuscular nature and subterranean lifestyle. These amiable owls are tolerant of humans and can often be observed boldly perching on a fencepost or vigilantly watching from the mouth of a burrow.

RICHARD DITCH

HABITAT

In the western United States, Burrowing Owls are found in flat, open, low-stature grasslands, sparsely vegetated desertscrub, and edges of human disturbed lands. These owls rely primarily on fossorial mammals, such as prairie dogs and ground squirrels, to provide suitable nest burrows. In addition to burrows, the owls also require unobstructed perching locations and make good use of dirt mounds, fences, or other nearby elevated objects. In Arizona, these preferences allow Burrowing Owls to be frequent inhabitants of grazed grasslands scattered throughout the state, and 35 percent of all atlas records were reported from semiarid, plains, and Cold-temperate desert grasslands (n = 104). Human influenced lands account for another 33 percent of the records and include fallow fields, bladed areas for future development, irrigation and canal embankments, as well as the edges of agricultural lands, airports, golf courses, and other open disturbed areas. Atlasers encountered 20 percent of these owls locally inhabiting sparsely vegetated Sonoran and Cold-temperate desertscrub areas.

BREEDING

Arizona has both resident and migratory populations of Burrowing Owls. In northern regions of the state, these owls begin arriving on nesting ground in mid- to late March. Upon arrival, individual males and pairs renovate burrows for use and begin courtship and territorial behavior (Haug et al. 1993). Atlasers first reported occupied burrows on 25 March. Egg-laying dates were not documented during the atlas owing to the bird's underground nesting habits. However, resident populations in the Tucson area typically initiate egg laying from mid-March to early April (C. Conway, personal communication). The earliest observation of young Burrowing Owls was noted on 10 May, suggesting egg laying by late March or earlier. Atlas data reveal a peak in nesting activity between late May and early July. Atlasers reported adult Burrowing Owls feeding young through 29 July, and fledglings were noted through 2 September. Fall migration begins by September and possibly earlier, with few Burrowing Owls remaining in northern Arizona after mid-October.

Arizona Burrowing Owls primarily refurbish abandoned burrows dug by ground squirrels, badgers, kangaroo rats, and prairie dogs, although they will readily use artificial burrows where these mammals are limited. Both male and female owls continue to maintain their burrows throughout most of the breeding season, through the year for nonmigratory populations (Haug et al. 1993). Preferred nest sites are often characterized by an abundance of burrows surrounded by bare ground or short grass, with several elevated perches nearby to watch for prey and predators.

Burrowing Owls most commonly lay 7–9 eggs (range 4–11) and are incubated entirely by the females, presumably beginning with the first egg laid (Thomsen 1971; Martin 1973). The eggs hatch following a 27–30 day incubation period (Henny and Blus 1981), and only the female broods the young for the first week or so after hatching (Haug et al. 1993). The male Burrowing Owl provides most of the food items for the female and young during the incubation and brooding period (Haug et al. 1993). The owlets open their eyes and begin to show evasive behavior at 5 days, when they also begin to respond to nest disturbance with the unique rattlesnake buzzing vocalization (Haug et al. 1993). When the young are approximately 14 days old, they begin to appear at the mouth of the burrow in anticipation of the returning adults with food (Johnsgard 1988). The young owls fledge at approximately 40–45 days (Landry 1979). Burrowing Owls typically nest once per year, but replacement clutches with fewer eggs than the first clutch are often laid if the earlier clutch is lost (Bent 1938).

Breeding Habitats

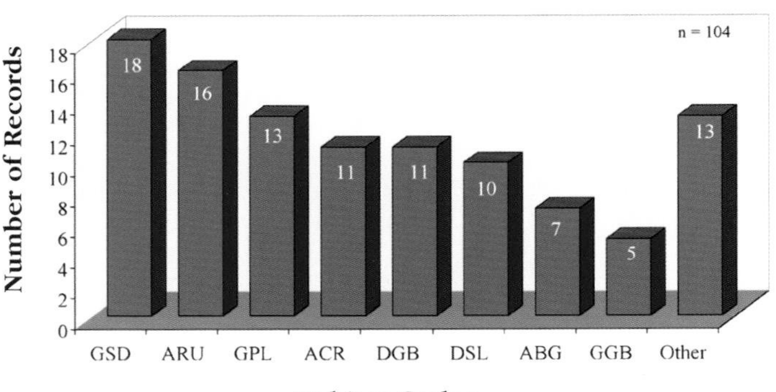

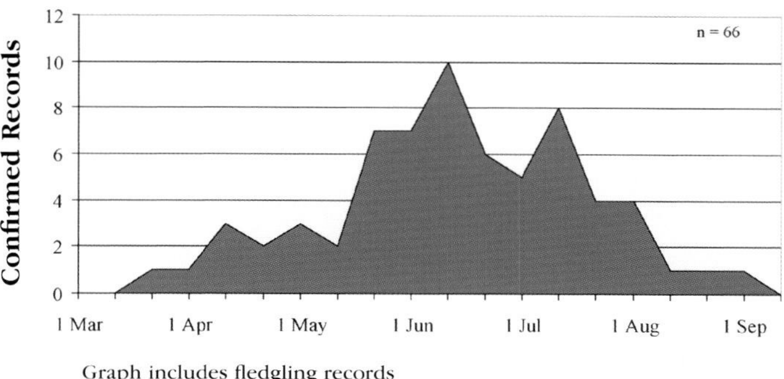

DISTRIBUTION AND STATUS

Burrowing owls have a widespread, but sporadic range in western North America from eastern Washington and the southern prairie provinces of Canada south locally through Central and South America. This owl is also resident in Florida and many Caribbean islands. Swarth (1914) described Burrowing Owls as generally common where prairie dogs are established in the valleys of northeastern and southeastern Arizona and decidedly rare and sparingly distributed elsewhere in the state. By the mid-1900s, these owls were noted as local, and rare to uncommon in Arizona, except in agricultural areas around Phoenix and Yuma where they were still fairly common (Phillips et al. 1964; Monson and Phillips 1981). Burrowing Owls are regionally described as fairly common in the northeast on Navajo and Hopi tribal lands (Jacobs 1986) and within the lower Colorado River valley (Rosenberg et al. 1991), and uncommon and declining in southeastern Arizona (Tucson Audubon Society 1995).

During the atlas period, Burrowing Owls were found nesting generally throughout the state where favorable habitat remains. These unique owls were confirmed nesting at elevations ranging from approximately 100 ft (30 m) near Gadsden to 6600 ft (2012 m) in a prairie dog colony near Flagstaff. Most observations of Burrowing Owls in Arizona were from local and widely scattered localities. However, some concentration areas did emerge such as in the Yuma region and in the Detrital and Hualapai valleys north of Kingman. In the northeast, these owls were frequently encountered from approximately Winslow northeast to near Polacca and in the Chinle Valley. In southern Arizona, concentrations of Burrowing Owl records were noted in Cochise County primarily east of the San Pedro River and from Phoenix down the I-10 corridor to Marana.

Large-scale extirpation of burrowing mammals has had a severe impact on Burrowing Owl populations in the West. In Arizona, prairie dog poisoning has extirpated black-tailed prairie dogs in the southeast and greatly decreased Gunnison's prairie dog numbers and range in the north. Burrowing Owl habitat has also been reduced as development has eliminated burrows. Fortunately, these amiable owls are tolerant of some human activity, and recent efforts to provide artificial burrows and relocate displaced owls in Arizona have been successful.

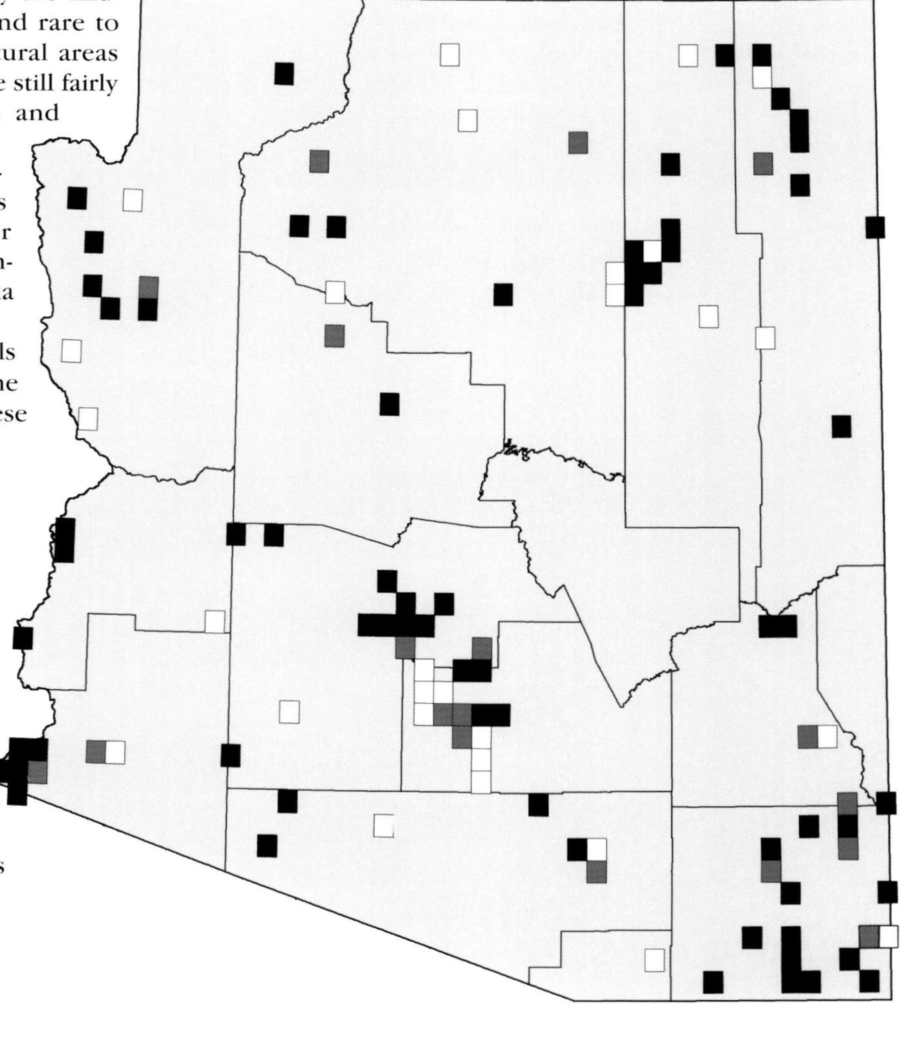

Burrowing Owl Breeding Evidence Reported in 79 (4%) of 1834 priority blocks

	Blocks	Quads
Possible	19 (24%)	28
Probable	14 (18%)	18
Confirmed	46 (58%)	67

Spotted Owl

by Cathryn Wise-Gervais *Strix occidentalis*

Spotted Owls are typically associated with old-growth forests, so management practices for this species can be quite controversial. Named for its spotted head and underparts, this calm, brown-eyed owl can often be approached closely by quiet observers.

HABITAT

Spotted Owls prefer cool, densely vegetated areas and use a variety of forest stand conditions (Gutierrez et al. 1995). Atlasers reported Spotted Owls in eight forested habitats and found that habitat selections were often based on geographic location in the state. In the Mogollon Rim region of central Arizona, the birds were reported most often in forests and along drainages of old-growth mixed conifers comprising Douglas and white fir, ponderosa pine, and Gambel's oak. Approximately 45 percent of all atlas records were in this habitat (n = 73). On Navajo tribal lands, these owls seem to prefer similar vegetation, but in steep, sparsely wooded canyons. Spotted Owls in southeastern Arizona use a wide variety of forest habitats, but were most often found in narrow shady canyons in Madrean evergreen oak woodlands (12 percent of records) or in Madrean pine-oak woodlands containing Apache and Chihuahuan pines (10 percent of records). Fewer observations were obtained in ponderosa pine–dominated forests or in wooded canyon bottoms with sycamore. In general, selected forests are unevenly aged and offer dense canopy (Ganey and Balda 1994). Spotted owls are less able to dissipate metabolic heat than Great Horned Owls and as a result, will seek out cooler environs (Ganey 1998).

BREEDING

Spotted Owls are primarily resident, although some individuals periodically move to lower elevations during the winter or even migrate relatively short distances to acquire prey (Gutierrez et al. 1995). Migrant birds typically leave their breeding areas in October and return in late February or March, when courtship begins (Ganey and Balda 1989; Willey 1993). Atlasers first reported Spotted Owls in suitable breeding habitat on 17 March and found a pair of birds on 7 April. The earliest breeding confirmation obtained during the atlas period was of an occupied nest, located on 16 May. Observers reported dependent fledglings on 20 May, however, suggesting that these birds laid eggs by mid- to late March. Arizona's Spotted Owls typically lay eggs in early April, with eggs hatching in early May (Ganey 1998). Nests with young were noted as late as 28 June. Atlasers reported most confirmed records in late July, and many late-season observations were of dependent fledglings.

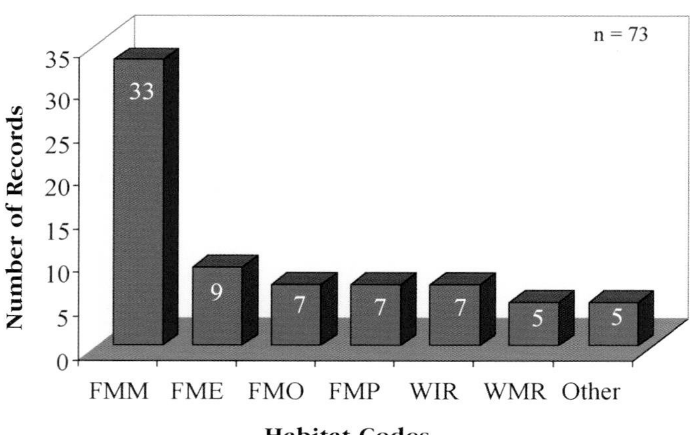

Spotted Owls nest in existing structures. In Arizona these include cliff ledges, small caves, tree cavities, debris piles in trees, and old stick nests (Ganey 1998). Mexican Spotted Owls use cliff nests more often than the other subspecies (Gutierrez et al. 1995).

The female Spotted Owl becomes sedentary approximately two week before egg laying and is fed by the male during this time. If he cannot adequately provide for her, she will not lay eggs (Ganey 1998). These owls nest sporadically and sometimes skip years, probably in response to prey availability (Ganey 1998). Typical clutches consist of 1–2 eggs (rarely 3), and the female incubates exclusively for approximately 30 days (Ganey 1998). During incubation and the early brooding period, the male provides all the food for his mate and the young, but after about 10 days of brooding the female will leave the nest more frequently to assist with hunting. Although the owlets usually cannot fly when they leave the nest at one month of age, they will actively climb or glide between trees. Both adults continue providing food for the young and will roost near them for 60 to 90 days after fledging (Gutierrez et al. 1995).

DISTRIBUTION AND STATUS

Spotted Owls are found from southwestern British Columbia south to central Mexico. The Mexican subspecies (*lucida*) occurs from southern Utah and Colorado south to

Breeding Phenology

Confirmed Records (0–9); 1 May, 1 Jun, 1 Jul, 1 Aug, 1 Sep; n = 29

Graph includes fledgling records

isolated locations in western Texas and in the Sierra Madre in Mexico. Atlasers encountered these owls generally at elevations from 5000 to 9500 ft (1524–2896 m), but also found them nesting locally down to approximately 3700 ft (1128 m) in areas such as in Sycamore Canyon in the Pajarito Mountains of Pima County.

Spotted Owl distribution in Arizona is patchy and reflects the availability of appropriate habitats. Atlasers had difficulties detecting this owl because the randomly selected atlas blocks often missed the bird's localized habitats and few volunteers were permitted to use taped calls to detect this federally threatened species. To increase the accuracy of the distribution map, atlas data were supplemented with records from specific owl surveys conducted during the atlas period.

In Arizona, Spotted Owls have typically been characterized as uncommon residents in heavily forested mountains and higher plateaus of central and eastern regions of the state (Phillips et al. 1964). During the atlas period, these owls were documented in most forested mountain of southeastern Arizona, including locally in the smaller and seldom visited Galiuro, Patagonia, Santa Teresa, Whetstone, and Winchester ranges. With widespread breeding records in the White Mountains and then along the Mogollon Rim region from west of Heber to the Flagstaff area, atlas and specific Spotted Owl survey data suggest that these owls undoubtedly occur on White Mountain Apache and adjacent San Carlos Apache tribal lands as well. Spotted Owl survey data for these tribal lands were not available for the atlas map preparation, however. Atlasers helped delineate local distribution on Navajo tribal lands, with records on Black Mesa, within the Tsegi Canyon drainage, at Canyon de Chelly, and in the Chuska Mountains. Atlasers also obtained the first record of this species in the Carrizo Mountains.

Spotted Owls were historically found in the isolated Hualapai Mountains (Phillips et al. 1964), but recent surveys have failed to find them there. Similarly, these owls have previously been irregularly reported within the Grand Canyon region and went undetected during the atlas period. However, subsequent surveys below the North and South Rims have discovered more than fifty Spotted Owls in isolated side drainages with deep ravines and narrow, convoluted canyons (C. Jurgensen, personal communication).

Because of significant losses of historical habitat and population declines, the U.S. Fish and Wildlife Service listed the Mexican Spotted Owl as a threatened subspecies in 1993. Current management recommendations serve to identify and protect key locations of prime breeding habitat, but more research is needed to understand further this unique owl's demographics.

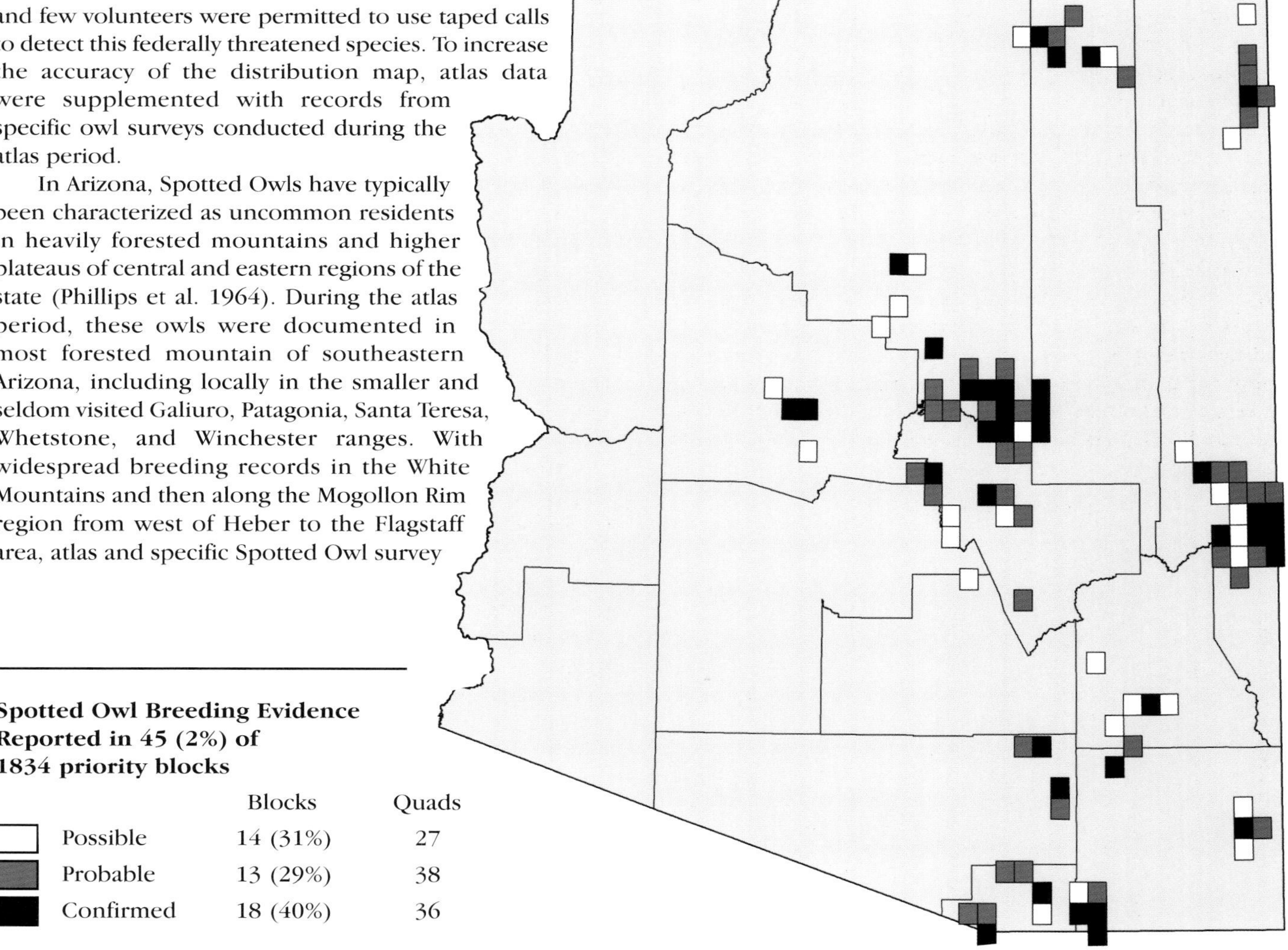

Spotted Owl Breeding Evidence Reported in 45 (2%) of 1834 priority blocks

	Blocks	Quads
Possible	14 (31%)	27
Probable	13 (29%)	38
Confirmed	18 (40%)	36

Long-eared Owl

by Peter Friederici *Asio otus*

Slender and distinctively colored, Long-eared Owls are unpredictable and seldom observed in Arizona, although they can become locally common when prey is abundant. These medium-sized owls are often located at night by their barking and low hooting vocalizations, or when unexpectedly flushed from daytime roosts.

DAN FISCHER

HABITAT

Long-eared Owls are nomadic breeders in Arizona, but they are most often found nesting where groves or woodlands abut open areas that are used for foraging (Marks et al. 1994). Such woodlands do not need to be extensive. In Arizona, Long-eared Owls have been found nesting in most habitats from lowland deserts and riparian woodlands to high-elevation mixed-conifer forests. The essential factor for the occurrence of these owls appears to be high prey abundance, and Long-eared Owls materialize when and where rodent populations boom (Millsap 1989). Atlasers reported 36 percent of all potential breeding records from pinyon-juniper woodlands; another 8 percent of records were from similar Cold-temperate desert grasslands with scattered pinyon pine and juniper (n = 66). Ponderosa pine–dominated forests accounted for 11 percent of atlas records, and another 9 percent were reported from lowland riparian woodlands dominated by cottonwood, willow, and mesquite. Fewer Long-eared Owl atlas records were obtained from such varied habitats as mixed-conifer forests, Sonoran desertscrub including wooded dry washes, and stands of exotic trees such as tamarisk and Russian olive near agricultural areas.

BREEDING

In Arizona, evidence has suggested that some Long-eared Owls often nest near their communal winter roosts, which are determined by high prey abundance within a given area (Millsap 1998). Pair formation presumably begins at winter roosts from January through March, or soon after the roost disbands (Marks et al. 1994). Courtship behavior was noted in April and May at a roost monitored on the Cabeza Prieta National Wildlife Refuge (Cutler et al. 1996). In one western Arizona study where fourteen active nests were located, egg laying occurring in mid- to late March, with young departing the nest between mid-May and early June (Millsap 1998). Earlier nesting activity was documented during the atlas when a nest with young was located in mixed-conifer forests on 23 March, indicating egg laying by at least late February. Atlasers also noted other high-elevation nests with young as late as 29 and 30 June, with fledging through early August. These later nests may reflect renesting efforts following failed earlier attempts. During the nonbreeding season, Long-eared Owls can be found singly or in concentrations of thirty or more birds in habitats similar to breeding areas (Millsap 1998). In Arizona, these communal roosts are typically observed from November to March, although Cutler et al. (1996) reported some individuals from one desert roost were present from late August until early May.

Long-eared Owls do not build their own nests, but instead typically reuse nests of ravens and raptors in almost any tree or substrate, including saguaros and cliffs. In Arizona, they have also been observed nesting on the broken tops of saguaros, woodrat middens in mesquite trees, and flood debris piles in tamarisks (Millsap 1998). Elsewhere, the species has been observed nesting on the ground and on dwarf mistletoe "witches' brooms" in conifers (Marks et al. 1994). Only ten nests were located during the atlas; the remainder of breeding confirmations came by observing fledglings, often accompanied by adults. Only two of these nests were measured, both in abandoned Common Raven nests approximately 21 ft (6.4 m) high in large Utah junipers. Millsap (1998) noted that western Arizona nests were in areas rarely frequented by humans and ranged in height from 7 to 40 ft (2.1–12.2 m), with most nests 10–20 ft (3–6 m) aboveground.

Female Long-eared Owls select a nest and do all incubating (Marks et al. 1994). Clutch size is typically 4–5 in

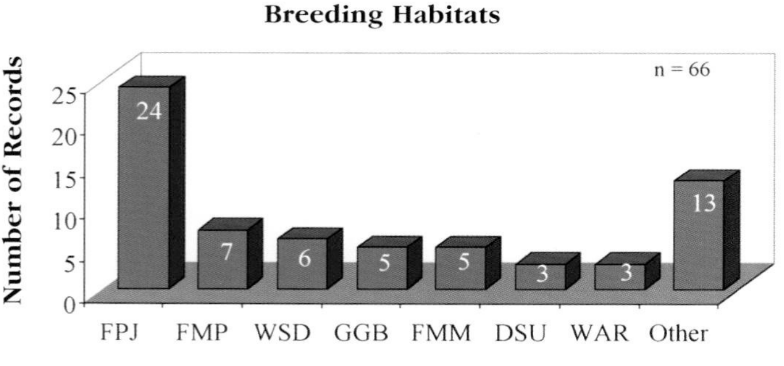

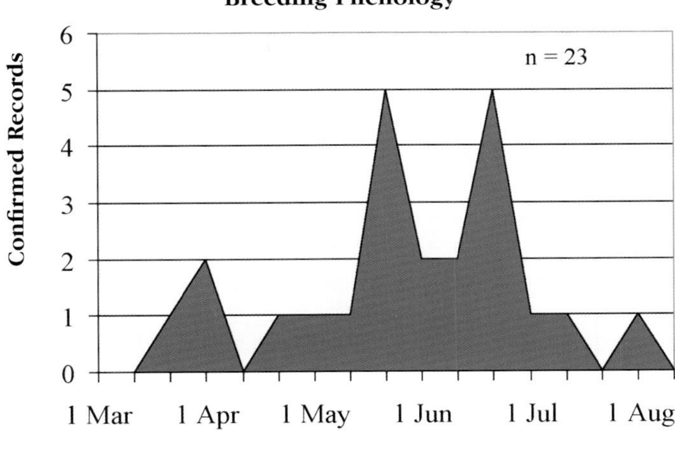

Graph includes fledgling records

Arizona (Millsap 1998). Eggs hatch asynchronously, so family groups typically consist of both downy and feathered young. Juveniles usually leave the nest before they can fly, and these "branchers" roost in the nest tree or nearby trees. "Branching" takes place about 3 weeks after hatching and flight begins at about 5 weeks, although some young are fed until they are 10–11 weeks old (Marks et al. 1994). Long-eared Owls sometimes respond to human intrusion through agitated flight, bill snapping, or vocalizations even in daylight; often, though, adults merely flush quietly from the nest area.

DISTRIBUTION AND STATUS

Long-eared Owls breed through much of the Northern Hemisphere south to Africa and various islands. In North America these owls breed primarily from southern Canada south to extreme northern Mexico, but are rare and irregular nesters in central and eastern U.S. south of Iowa and Pennsylvania (Marks et al. 1994). The species is generally considered a sparse and irregular year-round resident of Arizona (Phillips et al. 1964), but their annual nomadic wanderings makes true residency status difficult to determine. Arizona Long-eared Owl observations increase during the fall and winter, suggesting influxes of northern migrants.

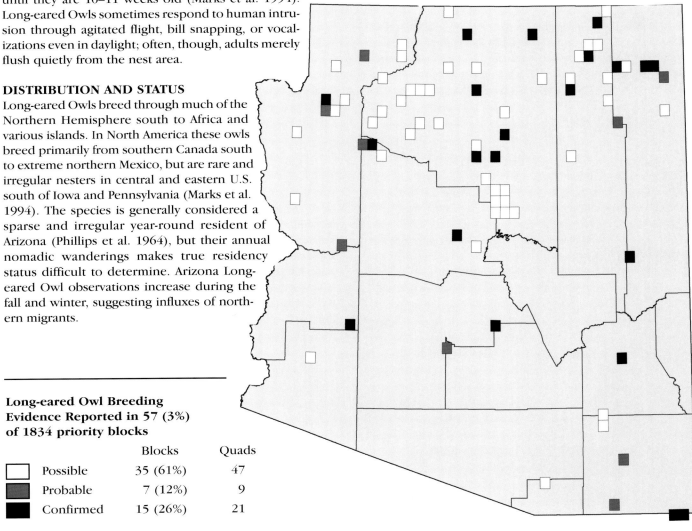

As noted before, wintering and breeding distribution appears to track closely local abundance of small rodent prey (Millsap 1998). In pinyon-juniper woodlands, for example, Long-eared Owls may become much more common and widespread in years immediately following heavy pinyon nut crops that support dense rodent populations. Several studies in western desert regions of Arizona found that winter diets consisted of at least 75 percent kangaroo rats (Millsap 1981; Brown 1995; D. Griffin, personal communication).

During the atlas period, Long-eared Owls were reported at elevations from approximately 850 to 8000 ft (258–2438 m). These owls have previously been documented during the nesting season at elevations as low as 200 ft (61 m) within the lower Colorado River valley (Rosenberg et al. 1991) and as high as 9625 ft (2933 m) in the White Mountains (R. Duncan, personal communication).

Though most of the Long-eared Owl atlas records occurred in northern Arizona, historical and atlas data strongly suggest that this habitat generalist can potentially be found nesting anywhere in the state. These owls are found nowhere regularly in Arizona and typically nest in an area for only one (occasionally two) years, then vanish as prey populations fall (Millsap 1998). Many intriguing questions remain regarding this nomadic owl.

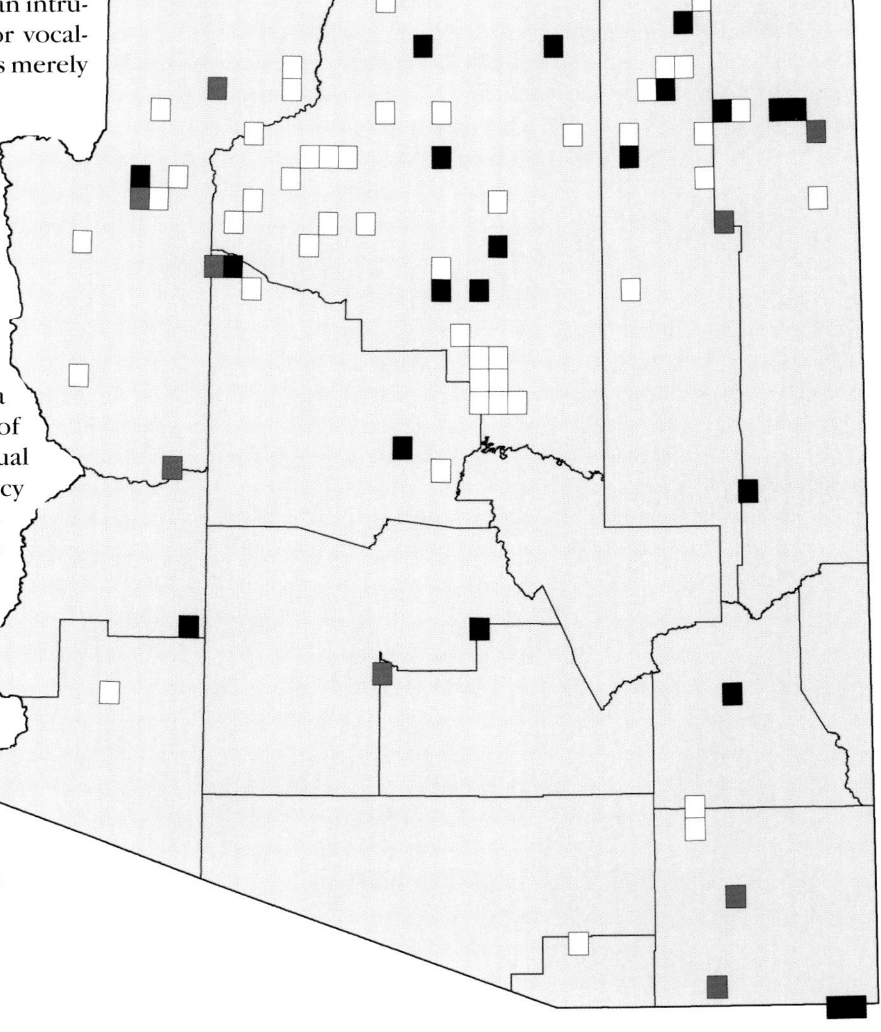

Long-eared Owl Breeding Evidence Reported in 57 (3%) of 1834 priority blocks

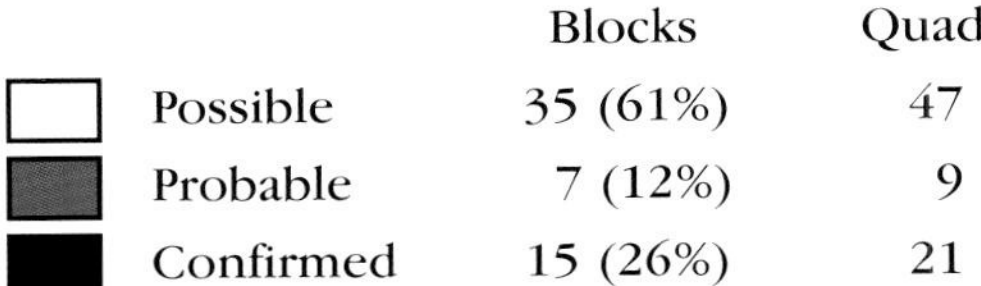

	Blocks	Quads
Possible	35 (61%)	47
Probable	7 (12%)	9
Confirmed	15 (26%)	21

Northern Saw-whet Owl

by Cathryn Wise-Gervais *Aegolius acadicus*

JIM BURNS

Northern Saw-whet Owls were named for a loud, squeaky call that has been likened to the sound of a saw being sharpened. Their more familiar rhythmic whistles are far more pleasing to the ear. Although it is believed to be fairly common, surprisingly little is known of this species' habits.

HABITAT

In western North America, nesting Northern Saw-whet Owls generally prefer coniferous forests, often with some deciduous component. Only thirty-six potential Northern Saw-whet Owls breeding records were obtained during the atlas period, and these were reported in six forested habitat types. Approximately 54 percent of all records were in mixed-conifer forests typically characterized by Douglas and white fir, ponderosa pine, Gambel's oak, and quaking aspen (n = 24). Three additional records were reported in cool, forested montane drainages, often containing various combinations of fir, pine, maple, oak, alder, and aspen. These owls were also reported in forests dominated by ponderosa pine, although those with a scattered Gambel's oak understory acquired more records than pure pine. Similarly, these owls were occasionally found nesting in the taller and denser woodlands of pinyon pine and juniper, including those with scattered ponderosa pine. In southeastern Arizona, several Northern Saw-whet Owls were reported in canyons or on higher mountain slopes were Douglas fir and ponderosa pine mix with a Madrean pine-oak forest containing Apache and Chihuahuan pines. These owls also nest in Arizona's limited subalpine forests of Engelmann spruce, blue spruce, and subalpine fir, especially if these forests are interspersed with occasional aspen groves.

BREEDING

Many Northern Saw-whet Owls are present on their breeding grounds year-round, while other individuals migrate south or to lower elevations during fall and winter. In Arizona, resident males begin their familiar advertising calls by late January or February. Calling often continues into early April but typically ends soon after the females begin to incubate. Few active Northern Saw-whet Owl nests have ever been documented in Arizona, and their breeding phenology in Arizona remains somewhat of a mystery. Elsewhere within their range, these owls typically lay eggs from early March to May, and our earliest confirmed atlas records were occupied nests located on 26 March and 15 April. Northern Saw-whet Owl fledglings were reported as early as 26 May during the atlas, suggesting egg laying initiation by mid- to late March. All remaining confirmed atlas records for this species pertain to fledgling observations through early July.

The number of migrating Northern Saw-whet Owls fluctuates annually but in general, migration is more pronounced in the eastern United States (Cannings 1993). In Arizona, most lowland observations are noted from November to March, but are not reported every year. During high irruption years when this species is present in the deserts and other lowland localities, many individuals are brought to wildlife rehabilitators in severely weakened conditions due to starvation, suggesting low prey availability in typical wintering areas.

Northern Saw-whet Owls usually nest in old woodpecker holes, particularly those of Northern Flickers (Cannings 1993). The birds favor nest cavities in live or dead conifers and especially in quaking aspen. In northeastern Arizona, active nest cavities have also been noted in Gambel's oak and in Rocky Mountain juniper (C. LaRue, personal communication). These owls are known to use nest boxes in other parts of the country, but this has not been documented in Arizona. Throughout the Northern Saw-whet Owl's breeding range, nest cavity height has been reported from 14 to 60 ft (4.3–18.3 m) above the ground (Baicich and Harrison 1997).

Following cavity selection by the female Northern Saw-whet Owl, nest duties are neatly divided between the pair.

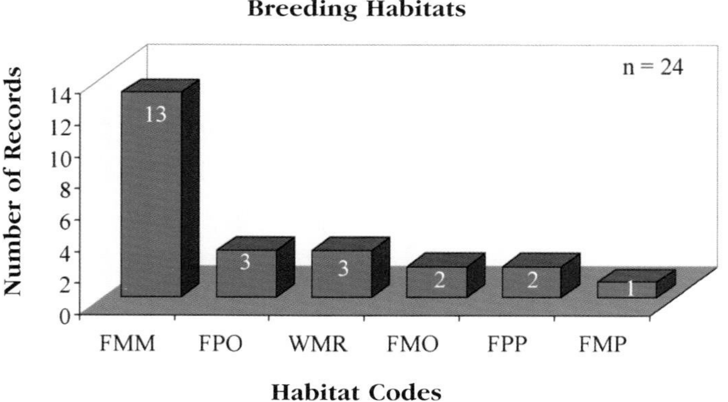

The female incubates and broods exclusively while the male provisions the sitting female and the nestlings with all food. Typically, 5–6 eggs (range 4–7) are laid and are incubated for 27 to 29 days (Cannings 1987). Incubation begins with the first egg laid, so young hatch asynchronously, yet leave the nest within a few days of each other. Fledging occurs 27–34 days after hatching (Baicich and Harrison 1997) and the owlets continue to be fed for at least a month following nest departure (Cannings 1993). Unlike many other owl species in Arizona, Northern Saw-whet Owl fledglings can fly reasonably well immediately after leaving the nest (Cannings 1993).

DISTRIBUTION AND STATUS

Northern Saw-whet Owls are sporadic in their distribution range wide, and can be common in a given area one year and absent in subsequent years, possibly reflecting this owls exploitation of irruptive small mammals populations (C. LaRue, personal communication). This species breeds in forested regions from southern Canada and northern United States south locally through the Appalachian Mountains to North Carolina. In the West, these owls breed from southeastern Alaska and the Rocky Mountain region south through the mountains of California, Arizona, and New Mexico. The species also breeds uncommonly in the highlands of Mexico south to Oaxaca (Howell and Webb 1995).

Phillips et al. (1964) considered the Northern Saw-whet Owl's status in eastern and central Arizona as "resident, perhaps fairly common," but unclear owing to few summer records and because of the bird's erratic appearance. Atlasers had hoped to unravel further its mysterious distribution in Arizona, but they were curtailed by the typical timing of surveys. Because snow and closed roads made such areas inaccessible, atlas surveys within higher-elevation forests were often not conducted until May or June, when nesting Northern Saw-whet Owls often fall silent and become difficult to detect.

More evidence of how widespread Northern Saw-whet Owls may be in central and northern Arizona was revealed during Spotted Owl surveys conducted in the early 1990s. Often initiated by April, these surveys regularly detected incidental calling Northern Saw-whet Owls. Similarly timed Boreal Owl surveys conducted just prior to the atlas in the White Mountains and San Francisco Mountain region also detected many territorial calling Northern Saw-whet Owls (R. Duncan, personal communication).

Atlasers reported Northern Saw-whet Owls at elevations from approximately 5500 ft (1676 m) in cool forested canyons to over 9300 ft (2835 m) on mountain ridges. Territorial individuals have also been heard calling at 10,800 ft (3292 m) in the White Mountains and at similar elevations on the San Francisco Peaks (R. Duncan, personal communication).

In light of all Arizona records, Northern Saw-whet Owls are undoubtedly a widespread breeding species in the Mogollon Rim region from Williams and Flagstaff to the White Mountains. Observers discovered this species within Navajo tribal lands on Black Mesa, near Betatakin Ruins National Monument, and within the Chuska Mountains. Northern Saw-whet Owls have also been noted nesting on the Defiance Plateau (C. LaRue, personal communication). Elsewhere in northern Arizona, these owls were previously confirmed nesting on the Kaibab Plateau and the South Rim of the Grand Canyon (Phillips et al. 1964). Northern Saw-whet Owls are reported more irregularly in southeastern mountain ranges than farther north, and during the atlas period they were noted in the Chiricahua, Santa Catalina, and Santa Rita mountains. Nesting was confirmed for the first time in the last range.

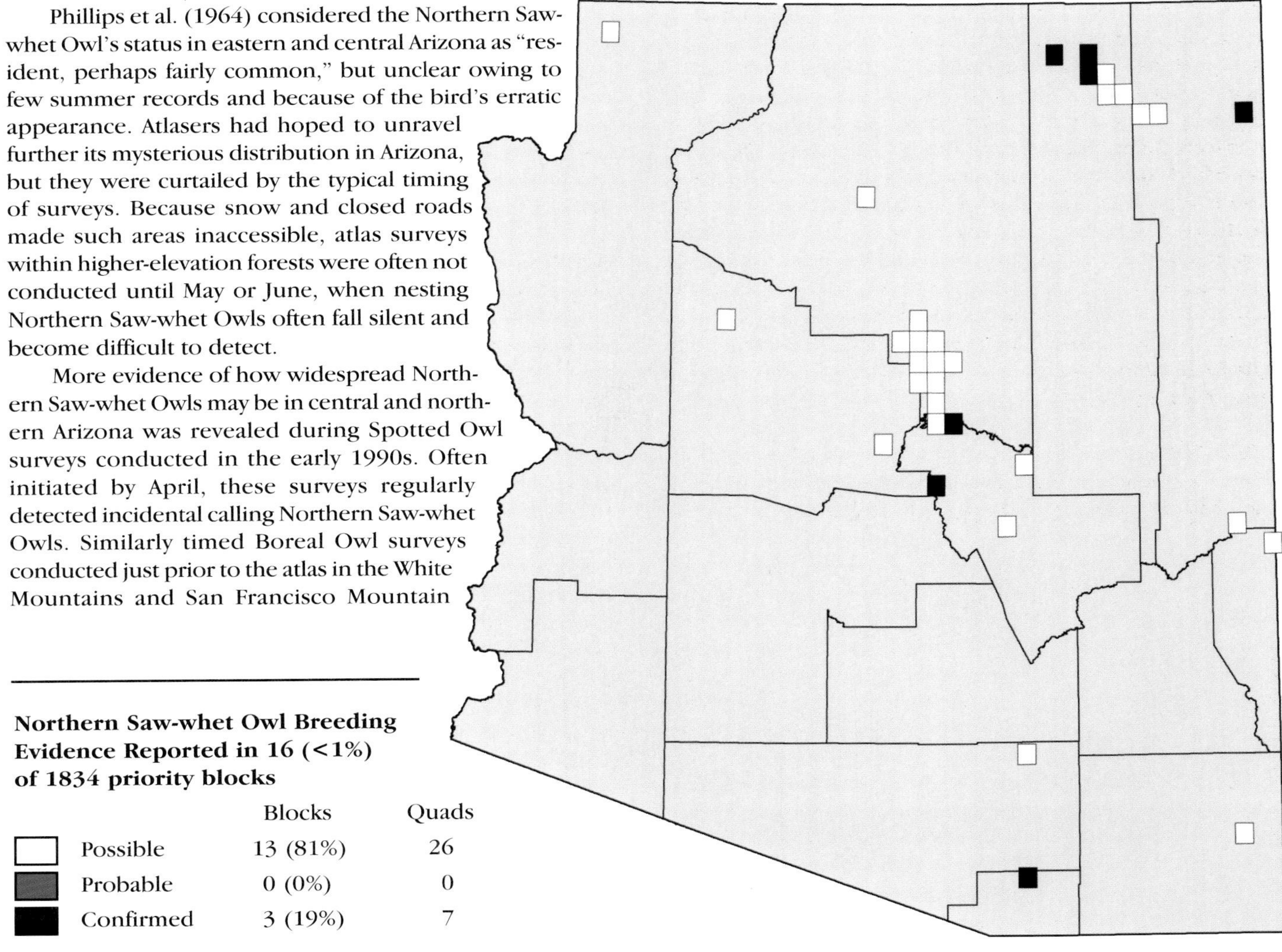

Northern Saw-whet Owl Breeding Evidence Reported in 16 (<1%) of 1834 priority blocks

	Blocks	Quads
Possible	13 (81%)	26
Probable	0 (0%)	0
Confirmed	3 (19%)	7

Lesser Nighthawk

by Cathryn Wise-Gervais *Chordeiles acutipennis*

RICHARD DITCH

Lesser Nighthawks are graceful aerial acrobats. Formerly known as "trilling nighthawks" for their distinctive purring call, they often begin their evening hunting forays soon after sunset and commonly pursue flying insects attracted to tall neighborhood lights. Consequently, they are the most frequently observed Arizona nightjar.

HABITAT

Lesser Nighthawks are amazingly well adapted to temperature extremes and nest in some of the hottest and most inhospitable landscapes in Arizona. These birds are commonly encountered nesting in arid lowlands, deserts, and in sparsely vegetated valleys and washes, but they will use a wide variety of open country for foraging. Atlasers reported Lesser Nighthawks in twenty-two habitat types, but 52 percent of the records were in Sonoran desertscrub–dominated areas ($n = 542$). Observers also reported 13 percent of Lesser Nighthawk records in semiarid grasslands characterized by scattered sotol, agave, yucca, and snakeweed. Far fewer records were reported in the remaining habitat types, including desert washes, dry riverbeds, lowland riparian corridors of cottonwood and willow, and agricultural areas. In addition, Lesser Nighthawks can journey far in their search for food and water and are often observed foraging above unsuitable nesting habitats such as suburban neighborhoods and above open bodies of water, including backyard swimming pools. Locally in southeastern Arizona, Lesser Nighthawks are found sympatrically with Common Nighthawks where the denser and extensive grasslands favored by the latter merge with the less vegetated semiarid grasslands and Chihuahuan desertscrub.

BREEDING

Lesser Nighthawks typically begin returning to the lower Colorado River valley in early March (Rosenberg et al. 1991) and mid- to late March elsewhere in Arizona. Courtship displays are conducted near the ground and consist of the male displaying his white throat patch while flying closely after the female (Miller 1937). This pursuit behavior is accompanied by an odd vocal repertoire of trills, chucks, and coos produced by the male. Observers reported the earliest Lesser Nighthawk courtship activity on 1 April and located the first nest with eggs on 29 April. Most nesting activity was noted in May and June, however, and the latest nest with eggs was found on 17 July. Atlasers noted trilling and courtship behavior continuing into late July and early August, especially in southeastern Arizona. Lesser Nighthawks commonly perform distraction displays to divert attention away from nest sites or fledglings; atlasers witnessed nine such events, from 10 May to 16 July. Observers regularly encountered Lesser Nighthawks in suitable breeding habitat throughout August and into September, and fledglings were observed as late as 9 September. Arizona's Lesser Nighthawks typically migrate south for the winter, following the supply of insects, and most leave the state by mid-October or early November. During mild winters, small numbers linger into December and occasionally later, especially within the lower Gila and Colorado River valleys.

Lesser Nighthawks nest on the ground, typically on a patch of pebbly substrate either in full sun or in partial shade beneath a shrub. The female selects the nest site and may fashion a sort of scrape to hold her cryptically colored eggs, or she may lay them on undisturbed ground. Atlasers took notes at four Lesser Nighthawk nests containing two eggs each. Two nests were in the open, and two were under creosote.

Lesser Nighthawks usually lay their 2-egg clutches on consecutive days, and the females incubate exclusively, although their mates will remain nearby. Incubation typically lasts for 18 to 19 days (Pickwell and Smith 1938) and the female must devote her full attention to this activity to prevent the eggs from reaching lethally high temperatures. The female Lesser Nighthawk will regulate her body temperature by gular fluttering (panting) and will shade the eggs with her body and wings. These nighthawks are known to sometimes roll the eggs a short distance into the shade, only to return them to the original location

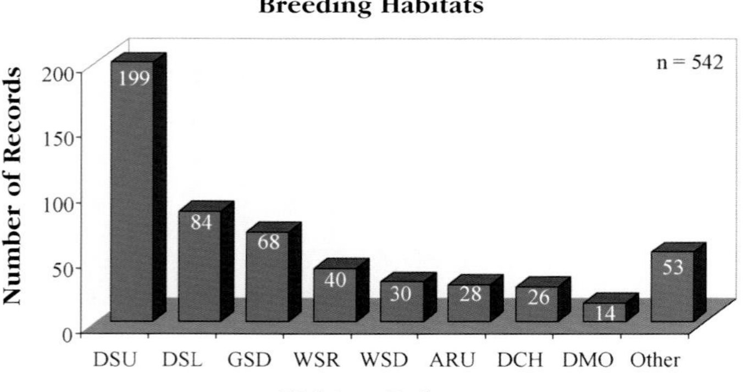

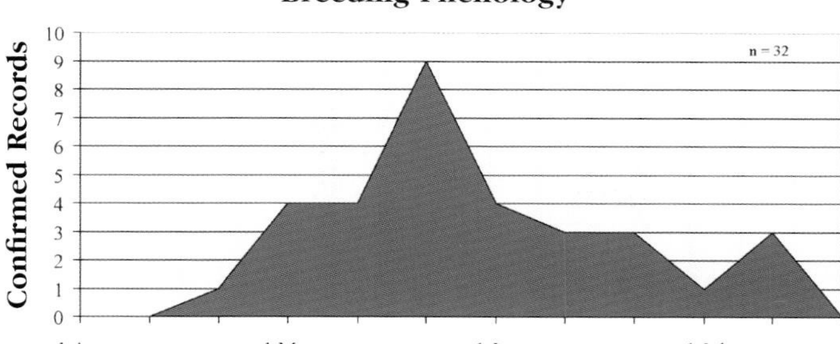

later in the day (Woods 1924; Latta and Baltz 1997). Chicks are semiprecocial at hatch and are able to crawl short distances within 1–2 days. The young are fed primarily by the male but are brooded by the female (Pickwell and Smith 1938). The young can take short flights when they are approximately three weeks old and are capable of sustained flight only a few days later (Latta and Baltz 1997).

DISTRIBUTION AND STATUS

Lesser Nighthawks are found from California's Central Valley and southeastern deserts, southeast through southern portions of Nevada, Arizona, New Mexico, and Texas. South of central Mexico, these birds are found in disjunct breeding regions to Peru and Brazil. Lesser Nighthawks have been described as common to abundant throughout the southern and western desert regions of Arizona, but were considered sparse in Yuma County away from the Colorado and Gila River valleys (Phillips et al. 1964).

Atlasers noted Lesser Nighthawks throughout their previously described range (including much of Yuma County) at elevations primarily below 4500 ft (1372 m) and locally to 5200 ft (1585 m). In western Arizona, these nighthawks were found north to the Hualapai Valley, in the lower Grand Canyon region, and in the Virgin River area near Littlefield. In 1975, Lesser Nighthawks were also found near Wupatki National Monument northeast of Flagstaff (Monson and Phillips 1981). During the atlas, this species was found again near Wupatki National Monument and down the Little Colorado River drainage to Cameron. Observers noted birds at new locations near Supai, Page, and west of Tuba City near Moenave. Lesser Nighthawks were noted in central Arizona north to the upper Verde River valley near Perkinsville. Atlasers found these nighthawks in appropriate habitat throughout much of southeastern Arizona as far north as the upper Gila River valley near Clifton.

According to long-term analysis (1966–1991) of Breeding Bird Survey data, Lesser Nighthawk populations in the United States appear to be increasing significantly (Latta and Baltz 1997). These nighthawks are adaptable and take advantage of insects attracted to irrigated lands, open artificial water sources, and elevated lights near nesting areas. However, this close proximity to humans increases threats to these acrobatic flyers including vehicle collisions and insecticide poisoning in agricultural areas.

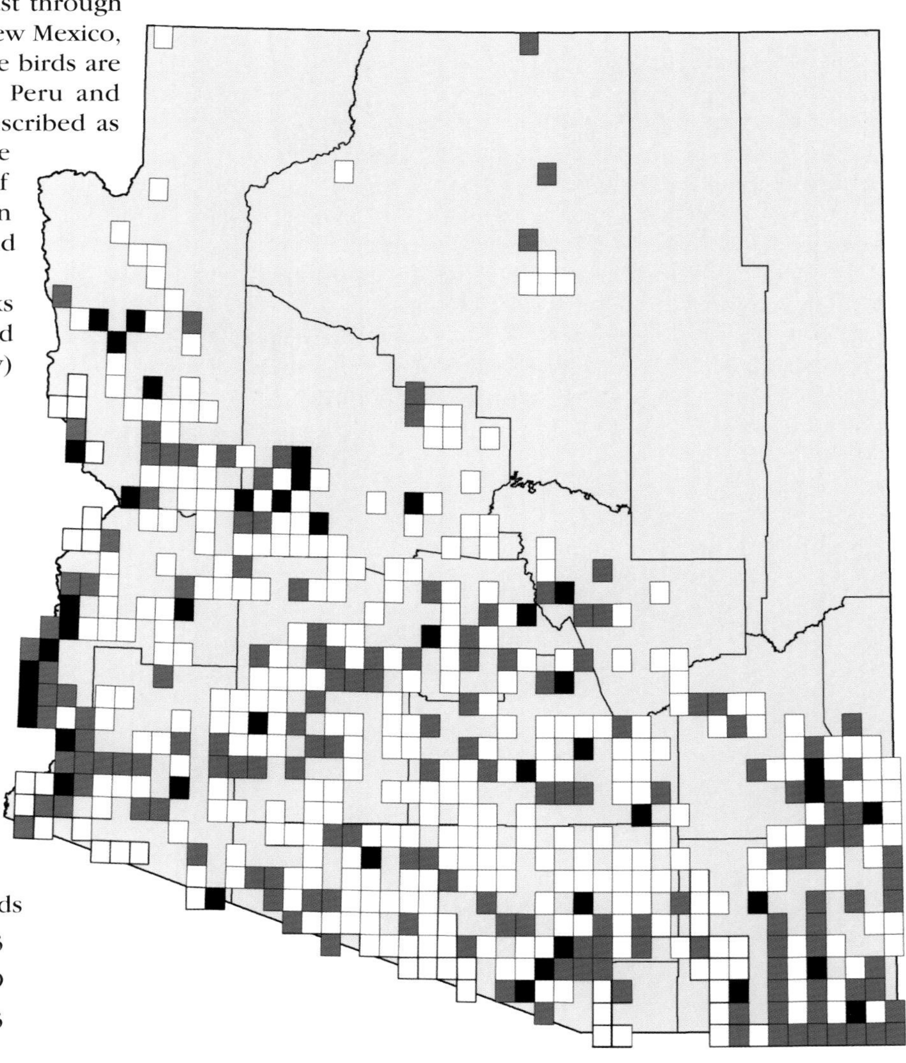

Lesser Nighthawk Breeding Evidence Reported in 518 (28%) of 1834 priority blocks

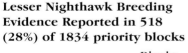

	Blocks	Quads
Possible	323 (62%)	343
Probable	154 (30%)	159
Confirmed	41 (8%)	423

Common Nighthawk

by Cathryn Wise-Gervais *Chordeiles minor*

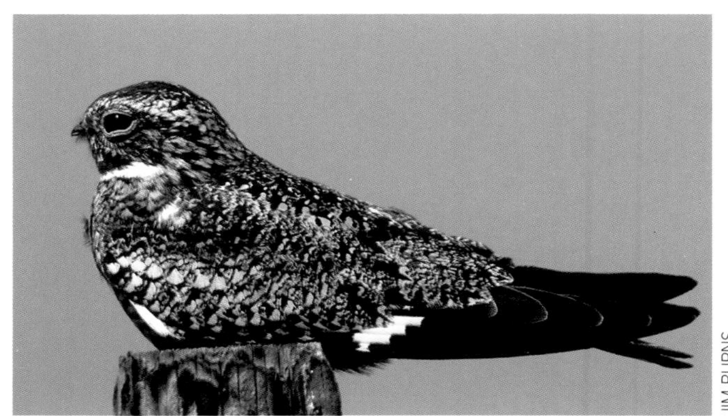

JIM BURNS

Probably best known for their dramatic booming courtship flights and distinctive "preent" call, Common Nighthawks have the widest range of any North American nightjar. This species may hunt by night or by day, but despite their prevalence across the United States, little is known of the cryptic "bullbat."

HABITAT

Across their range, Common Nighthawks are found in a wide variety of habitats, but prefer open areas such as those found in sparse woodlands, forest clearings, grasslands, and agricultural or suburban areas. Atlasers found this species in twenty-seven habitat types; the most frequently reported of these (38 percent of 464 observations) was pinyon-juniper woodland, one of the most prevalent habitats in northern Arizona. It is possible this wide-ranging species was simply making use of available open country rather than actively selecting the pinyon-juniper habitat type. However, an additional 21 percent of Common Nighthawk observations were noted in the adjacent Cold-temperate desert grasslands with scattered pinyon pine and juniper or Cold-temperate desertscrub dominated by sagebrush, blackbrush, shadscale, and other low woody shrubs. Approximately 17 percent of records were from habitats containing ponderosa pine, from almost pure open stands to those associated with Gambel's oak or pinyon-juniper woodlands. In southeastern Arizona, Common Nighthawks were most often reported from semiarid grasslands and Madrean evergreen oak woodlands, as well as in the expansive plains grasslands near Sonoita and San Raphael Valley.

BREEDING

Despite the Common Nighthawk's extensive range across the continent, little is known of its natural history. The species typically appears on Arizona breeding grounds later than most other migrants, with first arrivals typically appearing in early to mid-May. Atlasers first reported Common Nighthawks in suitable breeding habitat on 7 May, but the species was not reported regularly in northern Arizona until late May or early June. Nesting activity often begins soon after arrival and the earliest breeding confirmation obtained during the atlas period was of an adult performing a distraction display on 27 May. This activity suggested an early nest likely containing eggs. Atlasers reported the first Common Nighthawk nest with eggs on 16 June, but a nest with young was noted on 27 June, indicating that egg laying occurred by at least early June. The latest nest with eggs was reported on 3 July, and this pair may have renested after a failed attempt or perhaps was starting a second brood. Fledgling nighthawks were reported through 22 July, but an agitated adult was noted as late as 15 August. This individual was probably responding in this manner due to dependent young nearby. Fall migrants begin to congregate in mid- to late August in Arizona, with peak passage in September and stragglers still traveling into mid-October.

Common Nighthawks' cryptic coloration serves them well during the nesting period, as these odd little birds typically nest on the ground out in the open. This species has also taken to nesting on flat gravel roofs in urban or suburban areas, although this behavior has not been reported in Arizona. Atlasers described three Common Nighthawk nests, and all were at ground level. One nest was in the open, one was under sagebrush, and the last was under a juniper.

Female Common Nighthawks are thought to select the nest site (Rust 1947), and have been documented returning to the same nest for up to four consecutive years (Bent 1940). These nighthawks do not constructed nests, but instead lay their eggs directly on the ground substrate, which can range from soil, gravel, sand, or bare rock to forest litter such as rotten wood, leaves, or pine needles (Bent 1940). In forested regions, nesting is often limited to clearings, rock outcrops, or burned areas. Locally, nests sites also include the flat tops of stumps and fence posts (Bent 1940). The typical Common Nighthawk clutch consists of two eggs and the female incubates these primarily, but will leave them briefly in the evening to feed (Rust 1947). Researchers

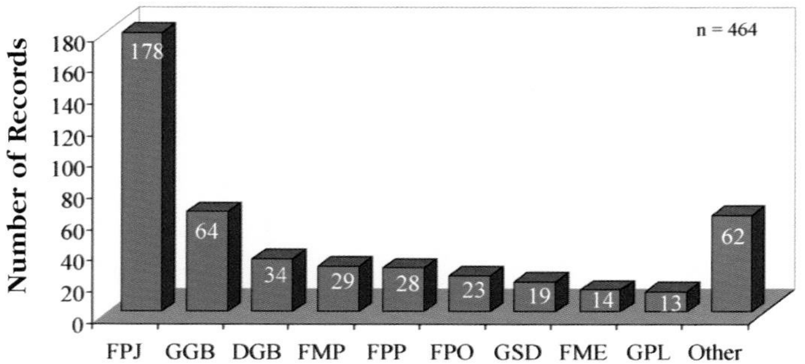

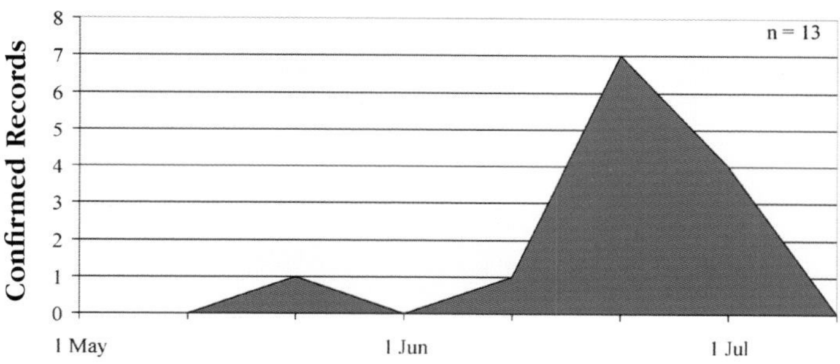

have documented females turning their bodies to match the axis of the sun's rays for maximum warmth during incubation, and they will also move the eggs to nearby shade to prevent overheating (Weller 1958). Incubation takes approximately 18 days, after which males feed the young while females may possibly begin their second brood, although second broods are poorly documented.

Young Common Nighthawks typically attempt their first flight at approximately 18 days of age and can fly well by 25 to 30 days (Rust 1947). It is unknown how long the adults continue to feed the young after fledging, but the young are capable of feeding themselves by day 25 and are last seen with parents when approximately one month of age (Bent 1940).

DISTRIBUTION AND STATUS

Common Nighthawks nest primarily from central Canada and throughout most of the United States, but are absent in the arid deserts of the Southwest and lowlands of California. This species also breeds locally south through Mexico, Central America, and possibly extreme northern South America.

In Arizona, atlasers noted Common Nighthawks from approximately 4200 to 9200 ft (1280–2804 m). These nighthawks have previously been described as common summer residents of northern and central Arizona, and local and uncommon in the southeast (Phillips et al. 1964). In southeastern Arizona, Monson and Phillips (1981) noted this species occurring from the Pajarito Mountains east to at least the Mule Mountains. They may breed irregularly in the Chiricahua Mountains, and several observations were made prior to the atlas period in Pinery Canyon. Atlasers also obtained several Common Nighthawk records along the southern and western edges of the Chiricahua Mountains but were unable to verify breeding. However, given the number of locations and observations of "booming" individuals throughout the summer from late May through mid-August, breeding seems likely. Atlasers also noted Common Nighthawks in the southeast as far west as Kitt Peak in the Quinlan Mountains.

In northern and central Arizona, Common Nighthawks were regularly reported throughout their historical range. Atlas data reveal that the primary southern edge of this species' breeding range extended from the Truxton-Valentine area and Bradshaw Mountains to the Sierra Ancha, San Carlos Apache tribal lands, and near Clifton-Guthrie. With atlas records practically surrounding the White Mountain Apache tribal lands, this species undoubtedly breeds throughout much of this unsurveyed area of the state.

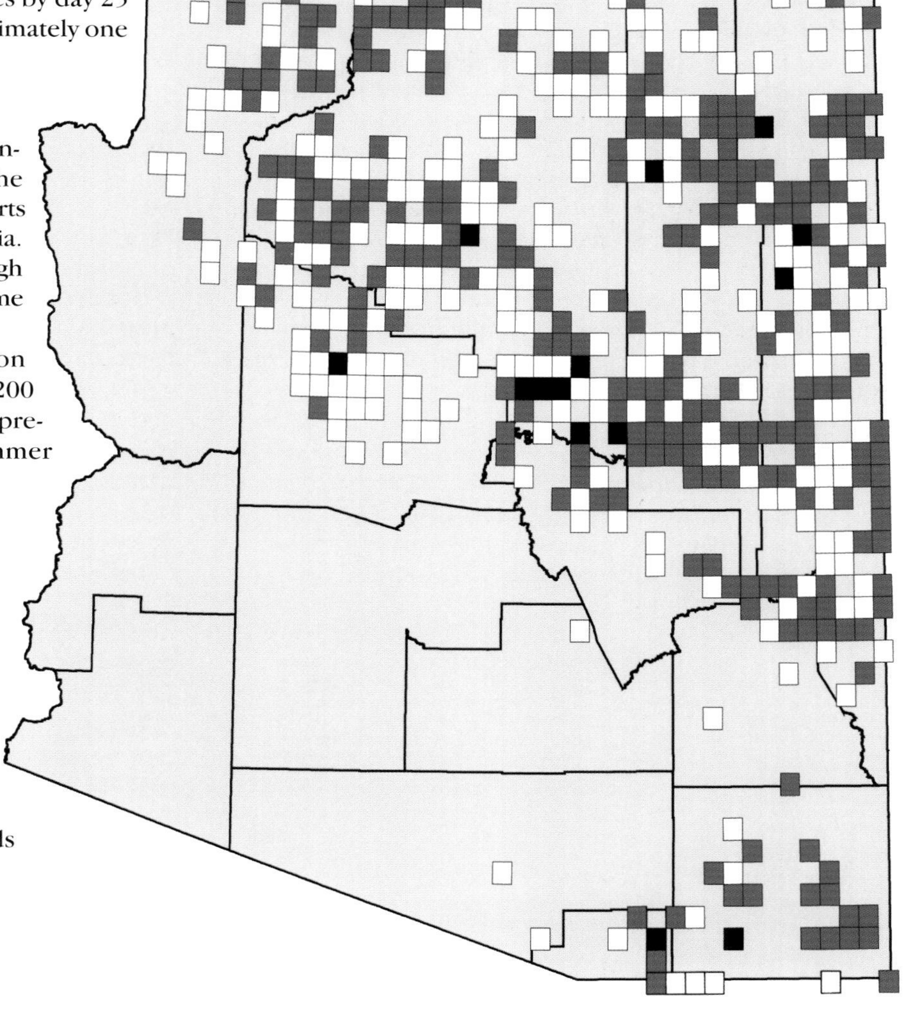

Common Nighthawk Breeding Evidence Reported in 478 (26%) of 1834 priority blocks

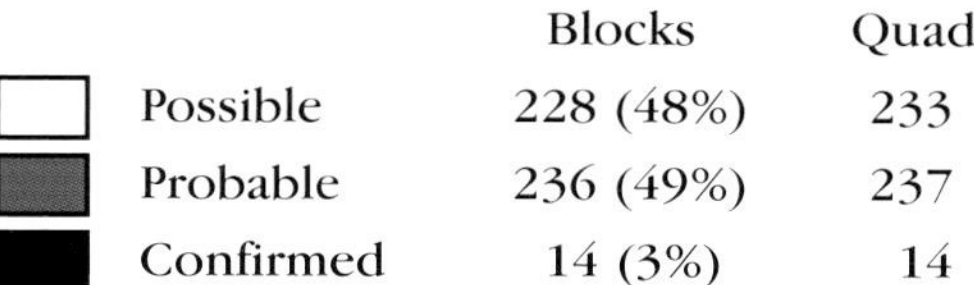

	Blocks	Quads
Possible	228 (48%)	233
Probable	236 (49%)	237
Confirmed	14 (3%)	14

Common Poorwill

by Annalaura Averill-Murray

Phalaenoptilus nuttallii

Known as Hőlchoko, or "the sleeping one," to the Hopi Indians, the Common Poorwill is able to lower its body temperature and metabolism rate for extended periods of time in response to poor environmental conditions. Indeed, these small nightjars are well suited to life in arid locales, where weather extremes and low water availability necessitate efficient use of resources.

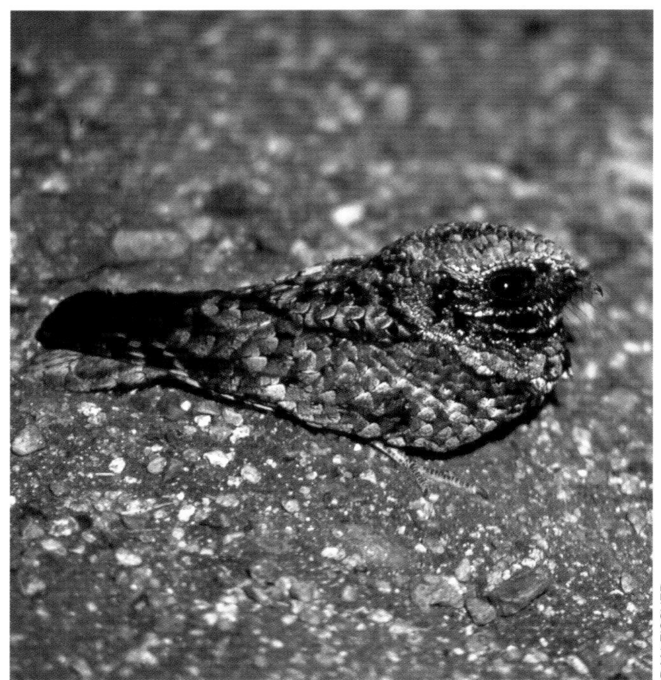
DAN FISCHER

HABITAT

Common Poorwills are birds of arid and semiarid country and were found over a wide range of vegetation communities surveyed during the atlas. In Arizona, atlasers primarily encountered this species in desert and dry woodland settings, typically in rocky and often sloping terrain. Nearly 32 percent of all atlas records were from the Arizona Upland subdivision of the Sonoran Desert, an area characterized by an abundance of saguaro and leguminous trees including mesquite, ironwood, paloverde, and acacia (*n* = 749). An additional 7 percent of atlas records were noted in the sparsely vegetated and extremely dry Lower Colorado River subdivision of the Sonoran Desert. At higher elevations, pinyon pine–juniper woodlands accounted for 16 percent of atlas records, with another 8 percent from semiarid grasslands typified by patchy grassy areas with scattered shrubs, yucca, agave, and cacti. In central and southeastern Arizona, atlasers regularly encountered Common Poorwills inhabiting the open Madrean oak woodlands characterized by various evergreen oaks, juniper, and pinyon pine (8 percent of all records). Approximately 11 percent of atlas records were evenly distributed between arid slopes dominated by chaparral, sagebrush and other Cold-temperate desert shrubs, and Chihuahuan desertscrub. Common Poorwills were infrequently detected in heavily human-modified areas and were recorded on only one atlas block that fell within the city-residential classification. While this species is found within more open parts of pine and fir forests throughout the state, it is absent from heavily forested areas (Phillips et al. 1964) and was only recorded on fourteen high-elevation montane forest blocks.

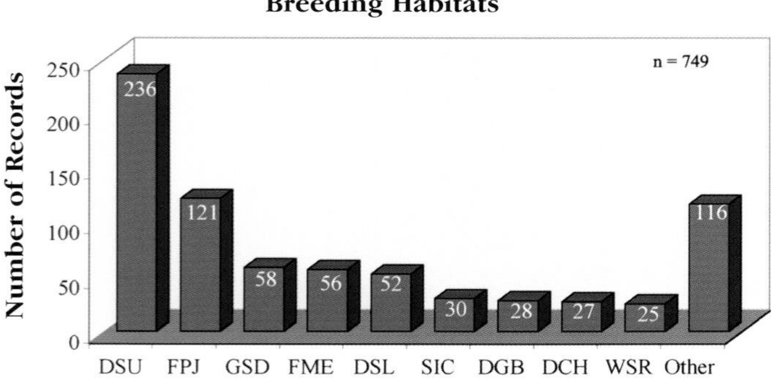

BREEDING

The breeding biology and migratory patterns of this highly cryptic, crepuscular, and nocturnal species is not well understood. Some Common Poorwill populations are likely migratory, especially in the north including northern Arizona. Other individuals may only migrate along altitudinal gradients to overwinter at lower elevations (Bent 1940; Csada and Brigham 1992).

In southern Arizona, Common Poorwills typically begin calling in mid-March, occasionally in February, and in northern regions of the state as early as mid-April. The earliest atlas record was a calling individual on 20 February. Breeding likely occurs from March through August in the southern part of the species' range and late May through September in the north (Cleere 1998). Bent (1940) reported five nests with eggs from Arizona ranging in dates from 2 May to 2 August, but noted egg clutches as early as 22 March in California. During the atlas, there were few confirmed breeding records (*n* = 18) for Common Poorwill. The earliest nest with eggs was discovered on 8 May; however, fledglings noted on 2 June indicate that egg laying began no later than mid- to late April. The latest breeding confirmations were a nest with eggs on 28 June and recently fledged young on 15 August. The fall migration period for this species is difficult to determine, but likely occurs from September through early November. Some Common Poorwills winter in southern and western Arizona by "hibernating," that is, becoming torpid for a prolonged period (Monson and Phillips 1981; Rosenberg et al. 1991).

Breeding Phenology

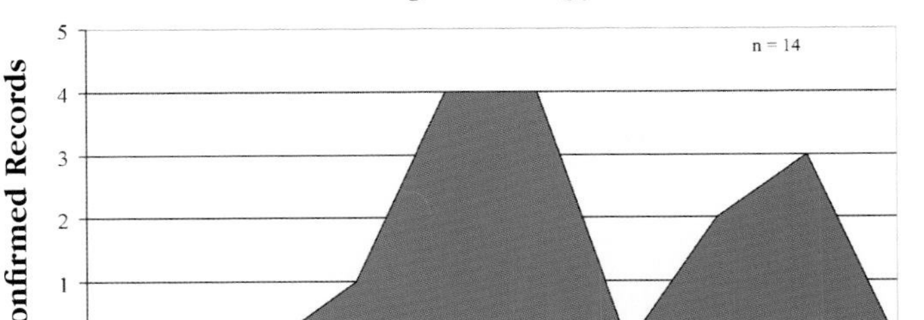

Eggs are laid directly on the ground or in a small scrape, often partially shaded by a shrub, rock, or log (Bent 1940; Csada and Brigham 1992). Four nest sites were described during the atlas period with one nest near a skunkbush and another near a large Utah juniper. Protective vegetation was not noted at the other two nests. Both sexes incubate the clutch of 2 eggs for 20 to 21 days, and the semiprecocial chicks fledge 20–23 days after hatching (Csada and Brigham 1992). Two broods are often raised per year (Baicich and Harrison 1997). Adults may move eggs and nestlings short distances if the nest site is disturbed. Nestlings will also occasionally move themselves short distances (less than 1 m) to take advantage of nearby shade or to avoid wet areas (Swenson and Hendricks 1983).

DISTRIBUTION AND STATUS

Common Poorwills breed from southwestern Canada south through central and western United States into Baja California and central Mexico (Csada and Brigham 1992). In Arizona, Phillips et al. (1964) described these small nightjars as common summer residents in appropriate habitat statewide, but noted them as uncommon in the southwest and rare at higher elevations. During the atlas, these nightjars were noted at elevations primarily between 200 and 7000 ft (61–2134 m), and locally to 9200 ft (2804 m) in montane meadow grasslands of the White Mountains.

Atlasers documented Common Poorwills occurring throughout much of southern and western Arizona, though these nightjars were detected less frequently than expected north of the Mogollon Rim, including Navajo and Hopi tribal lands. Phillips et al. (1964) reported this species absence where dense forests and level plains occur, and atlas data also reveal their scarcity in extensive agricultural and urban areas. As noted by Rosenberg et al. (1991), atlasers frequently documented Common Poorwills in the foothill and mountain slopes surrounding the lower Colorado River valley. However, the species remains locally abundant along the immediate lower Colorado and Bill Williams rivers, but only where cliffs and rocky slopes abound.

Common Poorwills are likely more abundant than previously thought. Their cryptic coloration, habit of sitting tight until closely approached, and crepuscular/nocturnal activity patterns make them difficult to detect during typical bird surveys (Csada and Brigham 1992). Because of the period of the day when Breeding Bird Surveys are conducted, population trend information remains questionable for this species (Csada and Brigham 1992).

Common Poorwills may be negatively affected by urban growth, as evidenced by the negligible number of occurrences on urban and residential atlas blocks. These birds commonly roost and forage along roads in Arizona; consequently, many individuals die annually from vehicular collisions. In heavily wooded and forested regions of Arizona, past timber-harvesting activity and recent massive wildfires have undoubtedly created new open habitats for the Common Poorwill, at least temporarily.

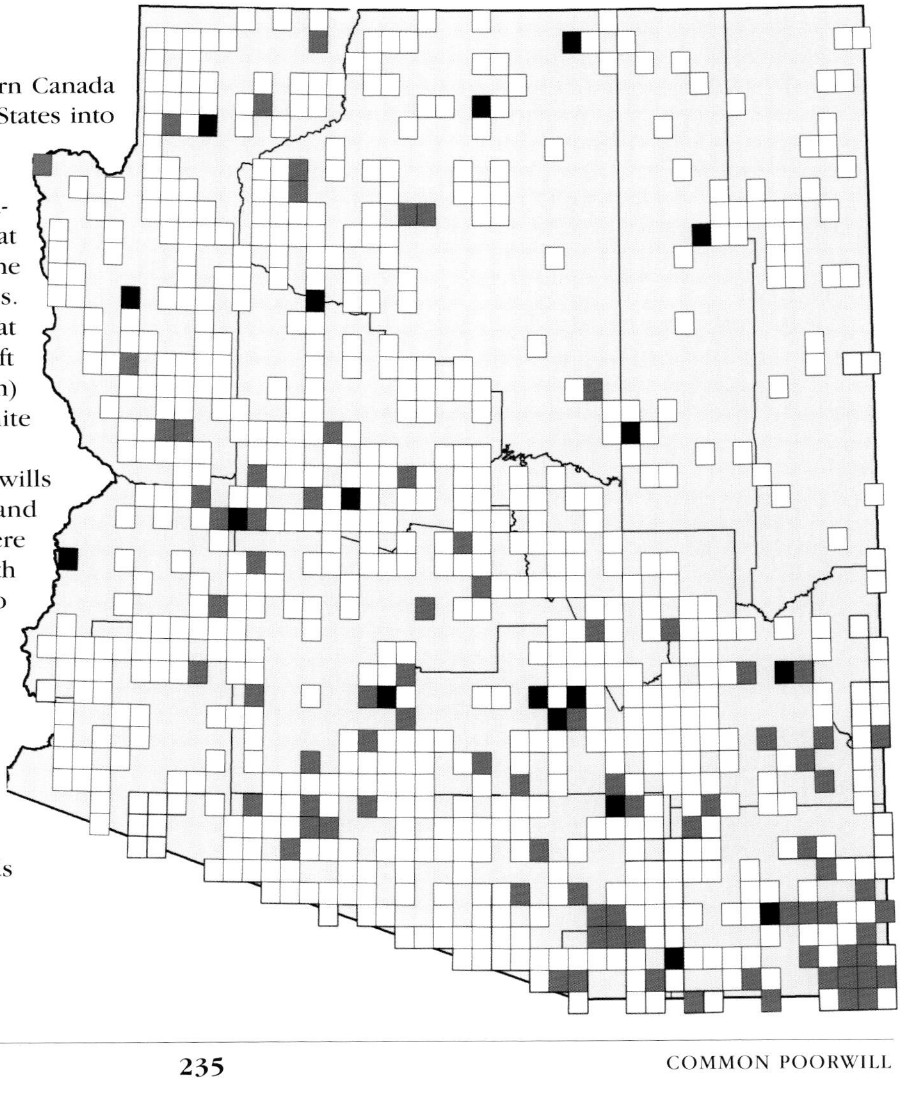

Common Poorwill Breeding Evidence Reported in 745 (41%) of 1834 priority blocks

	Blocks	Quads
Possible	644 (86%)	660
Probable	83 (11%)	83
Confirmed	18 (2%)	18

Buff-collared Nightjar

by Troy E. Corman *Caprimulgus ridgwayi*

Easily identified by their unique twilight serenades, Buff-collared Nightjars are not easy to observe. Many visitors make the summer evening treks to the few readily accessible locations in Arizona, but the nightjars are infrequently glimpsed. The breeding habits of these secretive, poorly studied nocturnal birds remain largely a mystery.

HABITAT

Throughout their range, Buff-collared Nightjars are found in a diverse array of elevations and habitats from desertscrub to pine-oak woodlands (Bowers and Dunning 1997). However, at the northern edge of their range, their selection of habitats is much more restricted. In Arizona, these nightjars are detected most frequently in or near open arid canyons or ravines with steep to moderate slopes. Drainage bottoms are often dry and rocky and dominated by thorny, short-statured trees and shrubs including velvet mesquite, netleaf hackberry, and various acacias. Of the Buff-collared Nightjar records obtained during the atlas period, 67 percent were noted along foothill dry washes in Sonoran desertscrub or semiarid grasslands. The remaining nightjar detections were noted near intermittent flowing drainages with scattered Arizona sycamore and/or Fremont cottonwood, with adjacent nearby thickets of hackberry, mesquite, or Madrean evergreen oaks.

BREEDING

Most evidence suggests northern populations of Buff-collared Nightjars, including those in Arizona, are migratory. The arrival time of individuals in Arizona can be quite variable from one year to the next and is based on when birds are first detected calling. Some years, the distinctive song of these nightjars has been heard by mid-April, but not until mid-May in others (Bowers and Dunning 1997). However, on 29 March 1997, atlasers tape-recorded calling birds on the west side of the Baboquivari Mountains, which is the earliest this species has ever been detected in Arizona. During the breeding season, Buff-collared Nightjars call for approximately forty minutes beginning soon after the first hint of morning light and then again at dusk (Johnston and Hardy 1959). Notably on bright, moonlit evenings, they sometimes sing intermittently throughout the night (Bowers and Dunning 1997).

Breeding evidence is difficult to collect for nocturnal species, and it was not surprising that atlasers collected little information for this sparsely distributed nightjar. Buff-collared Nightjars have only been confirmed nesting in Arizona and the United States only two times. Prior to the atlas period, a copulating pair was observed as early as 18 May in Guadalupe Canyon. In southern Sonora, where this species may be resident, four nests with eggs were collected between 20 May and 16 June (Short 1974), but Russell and Monson (1998) noted that Buff-collared Nightjars likely nest from April into July. On 20 June 1982, an individual in California Gulch was observed performing a broken-wing display (D. Danforth, personal communication), suggesting a nest nearby. A pair produced two young by mid-July in McCleary Wash near Madera Canyon in 1985 (E. Harper and M. Janos, personal communication). It is difficult to determine when Buff-collared Nightjars begin migrating south, but they have been heard calling as late as mid-August in Arizona, with the latest observation on 28 August along the lower San Pedro River near Cook's Lake (Monson and Phillips 1981).

Few Buff-collared Nightjar nests have ever been described and much of their breeding biology remains unknown. They do not construct a nest and the 2-egg clutch is typically placed in the shade, directly on the ground or leaf litter (Rowley 1962). Like other members of the genus *Caprimulgus*, it is presumed the female incubates the eggs for approximately 20 days (Harrison 1979). If danger threatens, the adult tending the nest or young may feign injury

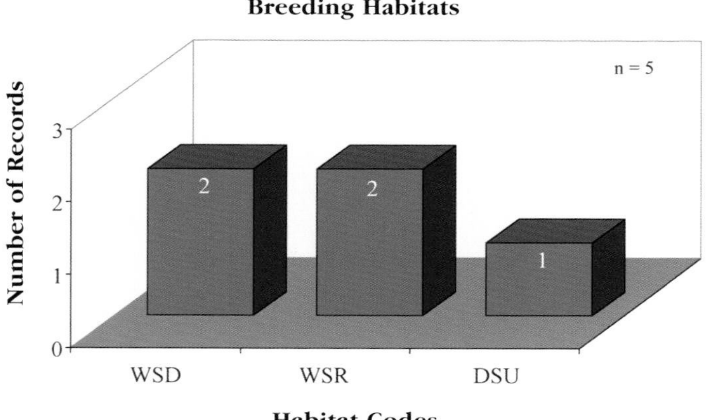

in an attempt to lure intruders away (Kaufman 1996). It is unknown the age of the young when they take their first flight or how many broods are produced each year, but one to two broods are likely.

DISTRIBUTION AND STATUS

Buff-collared Nightjars are primarily resident on the Pacific slope of Mexico from southern Sonora to Oaxaca and locally south to Honduras (Howell and Webb 1995). In Sonora, Russell and Monson (1998) considered these nightjars fairly common to common during the spring and summer. Populations north of southern Sonora and ranging into southeastern Arizona and southwestern New Mexico are presumed to be migratory. The first Buff-collared Nightjar in Arizona was discovered in 1960, when Levy (1962) found it in Guadalupe Canyon, Cochise County. Periodic reports of these nightjars continued in Guadalupe Canyon and one was heard along Sonoita Creek near Patagonia in 1971 (Monson and Phillips 1981). Buff-collared Nightjars were found in Catalina State Park north of Tucson beginning in 1978 (Monson and Phillips 1981). In the early 1980, detections of these nightjars increased, with 1–3 individuals as far north as lower Aravaipa Canyon, Pinal County and as far west as the Baboquivari Mountains, Pima County (Bowers and Dunning 1997).

Most of the Buff-collared Nightjar observations during the atlas were acquired through casual observation reports and not through atlas efforts. During the atlas period, nightjars were found at elevations ranging from 3000 to 4600 ft (914–1402 m). However, in the past they have been noted as low as 2640 ft (805 m) near Aravaipa Canyon. Buff-collared Nightjars were detected very locally and in small numbers only in Santa Cruz and eastern Pima County. Specifically during the atlas period, these nightjars were noted as far north as Romero Canyon near Catalina State Park, south to the foothills of the Santa Rita Mountains in Chino Canyon, McCleary Wash below Madera Canyon, and north of Greaterville. To the west they were found near California Gulch and the mouth of Sycamore Canyon in the Atascosa-Pajarito Mountains. Several Buff-collared Nightjars were also noted on the Buenos Aires National Wildlife Refuge along Arivaca Creek northwest of Arivaca and in Brown Canyon on the eastern slope of the Baboquivari Mountains. Atlasers detected the most western population on Tohono O'odham tribal lands in Mulberry Canyon on the west slope of the Baboquivari Mountains.

Buff-collared Nightjars were not detected during the atlas period in lower Aravaipa Canyon and in Guadalupe Canyon, where they were routinely reported through 1990. They were last detected in the New Mexico portion of Guadalupe Canyon in 1985 (S. O. Williams, personal communication). In Arizona, these nightjars are often found inhabiting remote, rugged desert canyons infrequently visited by birders, especially during the proper time of day and season to detect them. Therefore, Buff-collared Nightjars undoubtedly exist at additional locations within Arizona. As far as known, populations remain small and very local with only one to five calling individuals per site. Many locations have remained occupied for several years before being abandoned, only to become active again years later. This is to be expected for a species at the extreme edge of its breeding range.

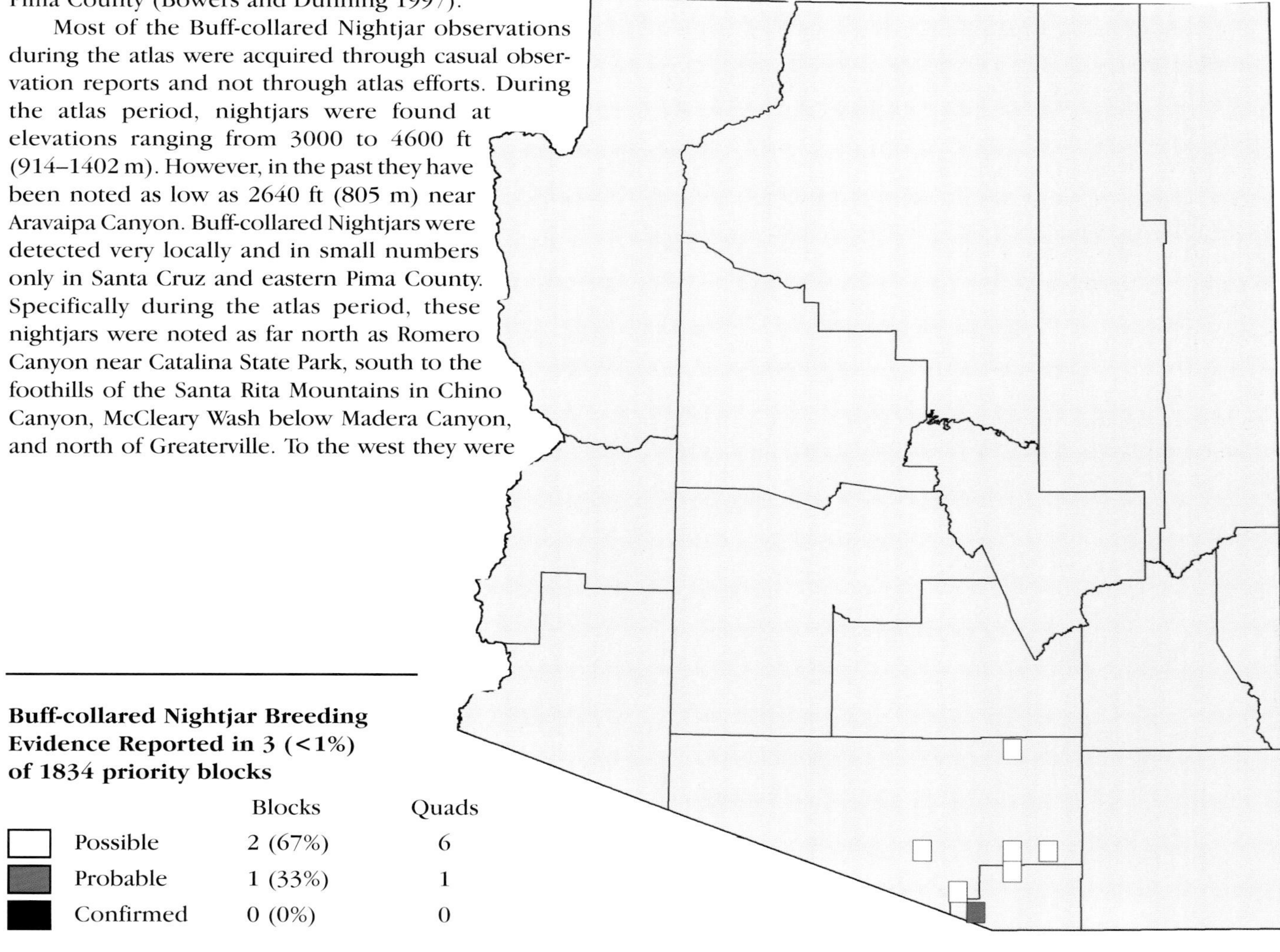

Buff-collared Nightjar Breeding Evidence Reported in 3 (<1%) of 1834 priority blocks

	Blocks	Quads
Possible	2 (67%)	6
Probable	1 (33%)	1
Confirmed	0 (0%)	0

Whip-poor-will

by Troy E. Corman *Caprimulgus vociferus*

Echoing from wooded canyons and mountain ridges, the loud and often persistent serenade of the Whip-poor-will is a comforting sound at nightfall. Many scientists believe that Stephen's or Western Whip-poor-wills of the Southwest, with their slower and hoarser voices and unmarked white eggs, are a separate species from eastern populations.

HABITAT

In Arizona, Whip-poor-wills inhabit cool, often densely forested mountain slopes and canyons typically with some deciduous tree component. Specific nesting habitat for these nightjars is often described as timbered, rocky ravines and ledges or on steep slopes among scattered rock outcrops near forested canyon bottoms (Blackford 1953). Forty-three percent of all atlas records were evenly divided between ponderosa pine forests with a Gambel's oak understory and in Madrean evergreen oak woodlands (n = 56). Whip-poor-wills were also reported from higher-elevation mixed-conifer forests containing various pines, firs, aspen, and Gambel's oak and from southeastern Arizona's Madrean pine-oak woodlands with Apache and Chihuahuan pines. These vociferous nocturnal birds also favor wooded mountain drainages and were regularly noted in canyons dominated by Arizona sycamore and evergreen oaks, as well as in cooler, higher montane drainages often containing bigtooth maple, Gambel's oak, alder, and scattered pines and firs. Blackford (1953) commented on this bird's preference for deep drainages, where the acoustics of the steep slopes and canyons amplify their resounding calls (Marshall 1957).

BREEDING

Whip-poor-will populations in the United States are migratory. In Arizona, this nightjar typically begins arriving in the southeast by early to mid-April and early May in central regions of the state. The familiar "whip-poor-will" call of the males is often repeated consistently to establish territories and attract mates, and presumably begins soon after arrival on the breeding grounds. Some studies of eastern populations suggest pairing occurs within two weeks of their arrival (Cink 2002). In Arizona, Bent (1940) reported egg clutches of these nightjars from 3 May to 8 August, although Brandt (1951) noted most clutches are laid from late May through the middle of July, with an apparent peak in early June. The only Whip-poor-will nest reported with eggs during the atlas period was on 29 May, although a nest with young on 10 June would indicate egg laying by mid- to late May. Nests with young have been reported as late as 28 July, but some young likely remain in the nest through at least early August. Atlasers heard calling Whip-poor-wills as late as 4 September. Most Whip-poor-wills in Arizona have migrated south by the end of September, with stragglers noted into mid-October. There are few winter records for Arizona.

There is little information on nest site selection by Whip-poor-wills, but females have been flushed from the eventual nest site only 1–2 days prior to egg laying (Cink 2002). Nests are not constructed; instead, eggs are typically placed directly on a bed of dried leaves or other forest litter. In Arizona, many nests are found on forest slopes above drainages and often next to or slightly under overhanging rocks with nearby fallen, leafless branches or small shrubs (Bent 1940).

Typical Whip-poor-will clutches consist of 2 eggs, which the pair incubates for 19 to 21 days (Bent 1940; Babcock 1975). Recent evidence suggests that these birds may synchronize nesting activity with lunar cycles, with hatching centered on the full moon, which allows parents to forage longer to supply the increased demand of food (Mills 1986). Incubating adults often rely on their cryptic coloration to conceal the nest and eggs, and do not flush until the intruder is within several feet (Cink 2002). Both

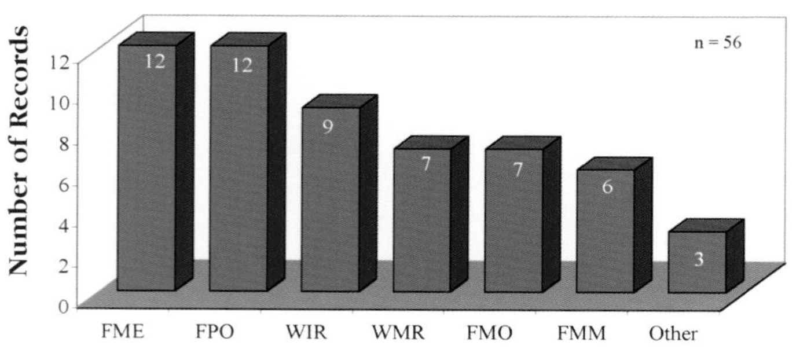

members of the pair brood and feed nestlings for approximately the first week, at which time the chicks are moved to nearby denser cover and are fed primarily by the male (Cink 2002). During this period the female often initiates a second 2-egg clutch nearby, leaving the male to rear the first brood through fledging in approximately 20 days (Cink 2002). Young Whip-poor-wills may accept food from parents at 30 days of age, even though they are capable of feeding themselves by this time (Mills 1986).

DISTRIBUTION AND STATUS

In eastern North America, Whip-poor-wills breed from southern Canada south through the northern edge of the Gulf Coast states. Western populations breed locally in mountains of southern California and Nevada, southeast through Arizona, central New Mexico, western Texas, and south through the highlands of Mexico and northern Central America.

Whip-poor-wills were historically described as fairly common summer residents in southeastern Arizona mountain ranges (Swarth 1914) and by the 1930s had been detected north to the Bradshaw Mountains and Sierra Ancha (Bent 1940). More recently, Whip-poor-wills have been noted north and northwest to central Arizona in the Hualapai Mountains (Phillips et al. 1964), as well as in the Bill Williams and White mountains (Monson and Phillips 1981). Brown et al. (1986) reported of individuals calling during the summers of 1971 and 1982 at Swamp Point on the North Rim of Grand Canyon National Park.

Atlasers found Whip-poor-wills to be rather common between 5500 and 9200 ft (1676–2804 m) throughout the higher mountain ranges of southeastern Arizona, and locally down to 3800 ft (1158 m) in Sycamore Canyon in the Pajarito Mountains. These nightjars were less common and local north to the southern slope and drainages of the White Mountain region and even more local northwest along and on the Mogollon Rim to near Flagstaff and Bill Williams Mountain. Whip-poor-wills undoubtedly nest in the canyons and on ridges of the White Mountain Apache tribal lands, where access to conduct atlas surveys was not granted.

Atlas surveys confirmed the Whip-poor-wills continued occurrence in the isolated Hualapai Mountains and of calling individuals at the North Rim of Grand Canyon National Park. Few birders visit the latter area of the state; given irregular reports of Whip-poor-wills in this area since the early 1970s, this species may be found to be of local but regular occurrence here. This is especially true with the apparent range expansion of this species to the north-northwest in the past forty years, including several localities in southern Nevada and California (Cink 2002).

Whip-poor-will numbers in Arizona appear stable with evidence that populations are still expanding. This could be related to many years of fire suppression, which allowed for patches of dense undergrowth often favored by this species. However, recent large catastrophic forest fires in central Arizona and local prescribed burns to help reduce understory density could initially be detrimental to expanding populations.

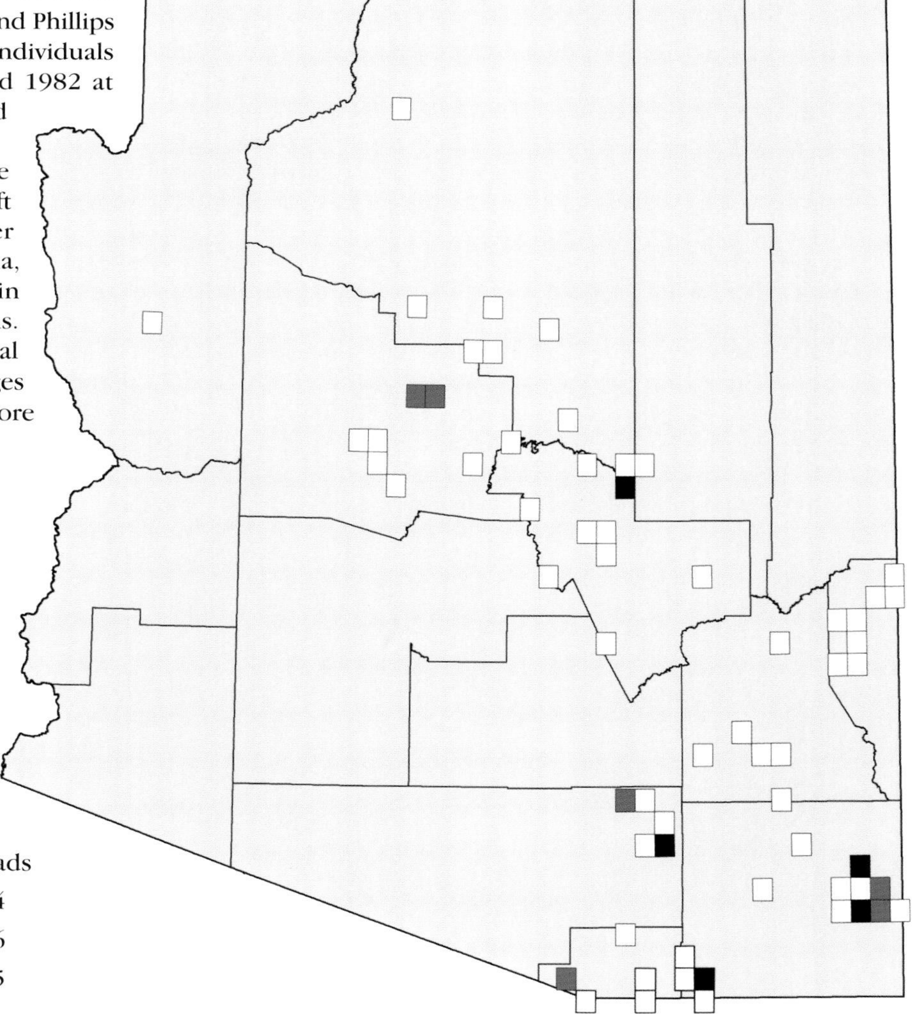

Whip-poor-will Breeding Evidence Reported in 46 (3%) of 1834 priority blocks

	Blocks	Quads
Possible	40 (87%)	54
Probable	3 (7%)	6
Confirmed	3 (7%)	5

White-throated Swift

by Cathryn Wise-Gervais *Aeronautes saxatalis*

Climbers are familiar with this long-winged cliff dweller's rapid, erratic flight and tinkling chatter. The genus name of this accomplished aerial acrobat means "sky sailor" and accurately describes the bird's on-the-wing lifestyle. White-throated Swifts eat high-flying insects exclusively and may become torpid in roosts during cold and inclement weather.

JIM BURNS

HABITAT

Highly social, White-throated Swifts are found statewide in conjunction with steep canyon walls, cliffs, pinnacles, and ridgelines offering blank expanses of open rock. These birds occupy a wide variety of habitats and elevation ranges, and all are related only in the availability of nearby cliffs with adequate nesting and roost sites. Atlasers observed these gregarious birds in twenty-five different habitat types, and the two most frequently reported habitats were also the two most widespread in the state. Observers reported 22 percent of records in Sonoran Desert uplands and 19 percent in pinyon-juniper woodlands (n = 542). These birds are likely making use of the available steep rocky topography they favor rather than selecting these habitats for vegetation type. Atlasers reported fewer than 10 percent of records in each of the remaining habitat categories, including various desertscrubs, chaparral, Madrean evergreen oak woodlands, conifer forests, and wooded drainages. White-throated Swifts spend most of their time in the air and can often be seen foraging on updrafts created by nearby mountains and canyons (Ryan and Collins 2000), and even among tall buildings in Phoenix and Tucson. This species can also fly considerable distances to forage and are seen above habitats that would not be suitable for nesting, including above agricultural lands, open deserts, and grasslands (Monson and Phillips 1981).

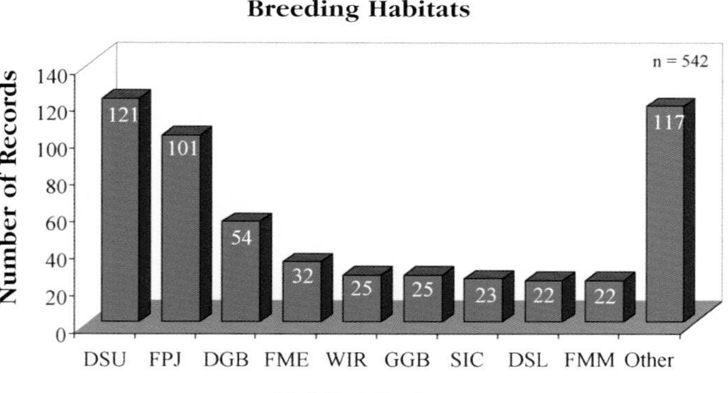

BREEDING

White-throated Swifts are primarily resident in southern and western Arizona but are migratory in the north, where they typically begin arriving in mid-March. Atlasers first reported White-throated Swifts in potential breeding habitat on 15 January in southern Arizona, and on 26 March in the north. Atlasers noted courting birds from 9 March to 14 July. Courtship activities included the dramatic "courtship fall" in which pairs cling together and may plunge several hundred meters in a tight spiral, only to separate just before striking the ground (Ryan and Collins 2000). White-throated Swifts will also copulate in midair and engage in vigorous chases. Observers reported occupied nests from 31 March to 10 August. Given these swifts' lofty, cliff-dwelling habits, it is not surprising most atlas breeding confirmations were noted as occupied nests (79 percent of 92 confirmations). Surveyors generally could not determine the contents of these, but did locate a nest containing young on 8 April. By backdating this southern Arizona record, we estimate that eggs in this nest were laid by early March. These birds begin nesting one or more months later in northern Arizona, and atlasers reported nests with young through 14 July, but atlas data suggest that statewide breeding activity peaks from late May through June. White-throated Swifts generally begin migrating south through Arizona in late August, with peak passage in late September and late migrants still traveling through the end of October.

Typical Arizona nest sites are deep within narrow fissures and crevices on cliffs and canyon walls, as well as behind large, hanging rock slabs that are often accessed from below. White-throated Swifts are faithful to traditional nesting and roosting sites and accumulated layers of streaky white wash are often quite evident below favored slabs or crevices. Large sites are often shared with several other nesting pairs, but these otherwise gregarious swifts also nest singly in Arizona on smaller rock outcrops, buildings, stadiums, and bridges. White-throated Swifts build their nests of various soft items by fastening these materials together with sticky saliva and attaching the structure to a vertical wall or ledge, occasionally in cavities and Cliff Swallow

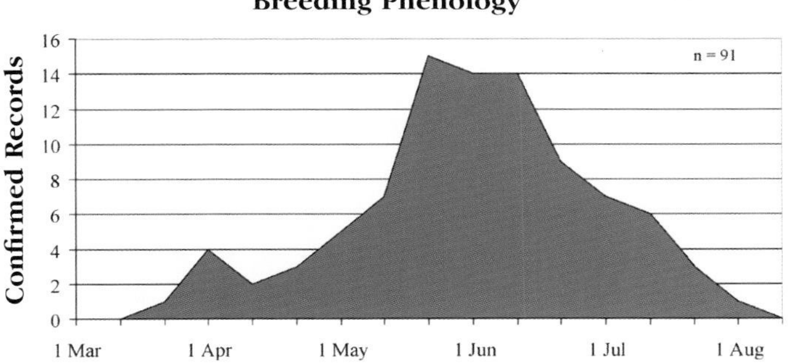

nests (Bent 1940; Pitelka 1944). There is also evidence that old nests are sometimes refurbished and reused (Rett 1946). Some nests sites in Arizona are more than 1000 ft (305 m) high on cliffs, but atlasers measured one nest only 37 ft (11.3 m) above the ground.

There is relatively little information on the nesting biology of White-throated Swifts, for active nests are generally difficult to observe and access. The female begins sitting on the nest before egg laying, to add and adjust materials on the structure (Bent 1940). She eventually lays 4–5 eggs (range 3–6), and incubation lasts approximately 24 days (Ryan and Collins 2000). It is not clear which parent incubates or if it is a shared duty, although both adults feed the young. In one study, the young fledged at 40 to 46 days (Ryan and Collins 2000), but it is unknown how long parental care continues after fledging.

DISTRIBUTION AND STATUS

White-throated Swifts breed from northeastern Washington, east through northern Idaho and Montana and south throughout the western United States into parts of central Mexico and Central America. As previously mentioned, these birds were noted nesting at a wide range of elevations in Arizona, primarily from 350 to 7200 ft (107–2195 m), and possibly to 9000 ft (2743 m) or higher.

Boyle (1998) reported that atlasers in Colorado observed White-throated Swifts nesting above timberline on cliffs and rocky peak tops over 11,000 ft (3353 m), and similar habitat exits in the San Francisco Peaks of Arizona.

White-throated Swifts have always been considered common throughout the canyon country and mountainous regions of Arizona (Swarth 1914), except in the southwestern portion of the state, where they were believed to nest only at the Kofa and Castle Dome mountains and at Parker Dam (Phillips et al. 1964). Atlasers commonly encountered this species in Yuma and La Paz Counties, however, and obtained several confirmed breeding records away from the historical strongholds. White-throated Swifts were easiest to confirm in the open, sandstone cliff country of northeastern Arizona, where atlasers could readily observe forays to and from nest sites. These swifts were generally absent in much of the relatively flat landscape within the Little Colorado River valley east of Cameron, but occurred locally in the upper side canyons. White-throated Swifts undoubtedly breed along the entire exposed southern edge of the Mogollon Rim escarpment. However, atlasers did not survey a large section of this area on White Mountain Apache tribal lands.

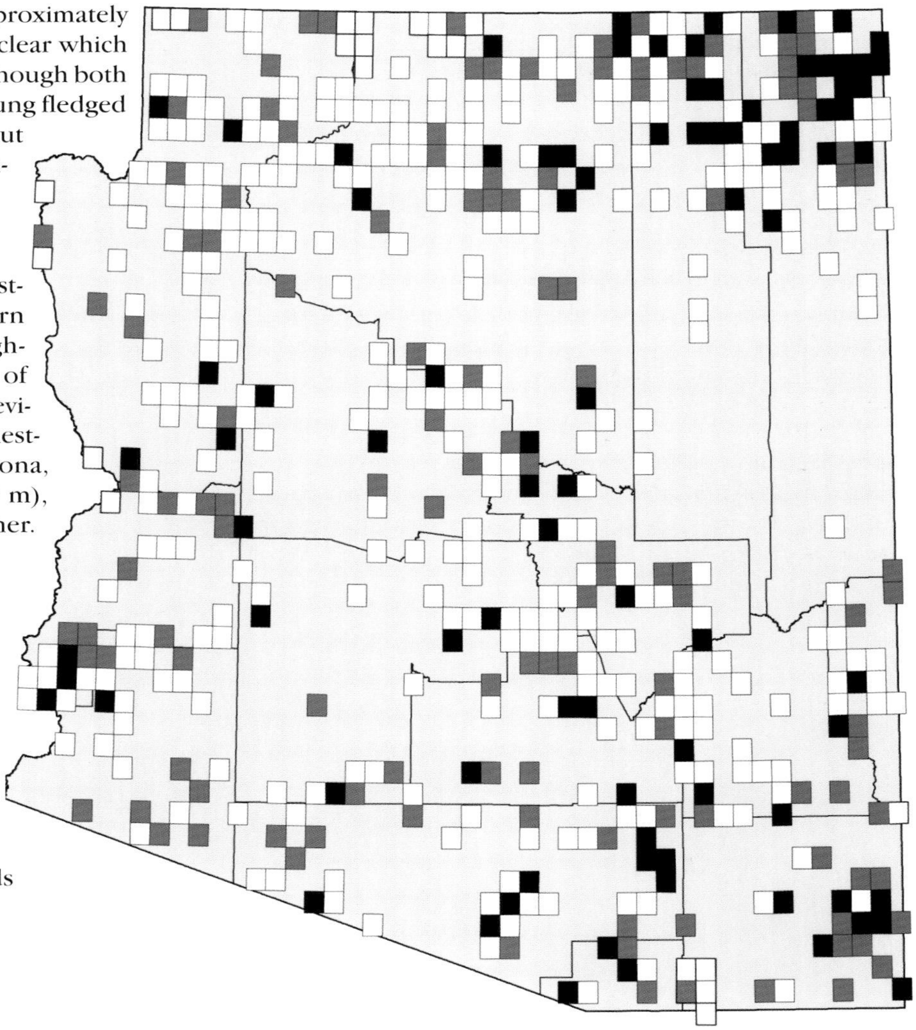

White-throated Swift Breeding Evidence Reported in 529 (29%) of 1834 priority blocks

	Blocks	Quads
Possible	324 (61%)	338
Probable	122 (23%)	127
Confirmed	83 (16%)	90

Broad-billed Hummingbird

by Troy E. Corman *Cynanthus latirostris*

DAN FISCHER

Caught in just the right light, an adult male Broad-billed Hummingbird can be an almost breathtaking experience. Feisty birds, they are often observed jousting for a position at their favorite feeder, or being the first to investigate a whistled imitation of an owl call.

HABITAT

Throughout their range in Mexico, Broad-billed Hummingbirds can be found in a wide array of habitats from lowland arid thorn or humid tropical forests to pine-oak covered mountain slopes. Habitat selection is a little less diverse in Arizona, with these attractive hummingbirds occurring most frequently in or near broadleaf riparian woodlands. Approximately 62 percent of all atlas records were reported from perennial drainages dominated by Arizona sycamore or Fremont cottonwood (n = 77). At higher elevations, these hummingbirds confine most of their activities to mountain and foothill canyon bottoms with sycamore, Arizona walnut, alligator juniper, and various Madrean evergreen oaks. At lower elevations, Broad-billed Hummingbirds were most often noted from cottonwood, willow, or mesquite–dominated woodlands along drainages, lakes, ponds, and springs. These flashy hummingbirds also regularly occur in mesquite bosques and heavily wooded washes containing large velvet mesquite and netleaf hackberry. Broad-billed Hummingbirds are often common visitors to feeding stations in or adjacent to preferred habitat, including some residential and rural backyards, gardens, and parks with exotic plantings.

BREEDING

Typically a very sparse and local winter resident, most of Arizona's Broad-billed Hummingbirds are migratory, with males arriving first in late February or early March. Courtship begins soon after the females arrive and nesting can begin as early as mid-March in Arizona. This is especially true in lower foothill drainages near Tucson, where small numbers of these hummingbirds are now resident. The earliest nesting record reported during the atlas period was of a nest with one egg and a newly hatched chick on 4 April. A female Broad-billed Hummingbird was noted feeding a fledgling as early as 27 April. Most atlas nesting records fall between early April and mid-May, although the sample size was low (n = 19). Atlasers reported the latest nesting record on 22 July, when a female was observed collecting downy nesting material. This would suggest nesting well into August. Most adult males depart Arizona by late August, while the majority of females and juveniles migrate south by mid-September, with stragglers into October (Powers and Wethington 1999).

Female Broad-billed Hummingbirds typically construct their rather messy looking nests less than 6.6 ft (2 m) from the ground (Powers and Wethington 1999). Long strands of cobwebs, fine bark strips, grasses, and dried leaves are often attached to the sides and bottom of the nest, which often dangle several inches below. This makes their nests rather unique and easily identified when compared to those of other hummingbird species breeding in Arizona. Atlas field crews measured only two nests. One was in a hopbush 3.6 ft (1.1 m) high, the other in an exotic Texas persimmon 6.2 ft (1.9 m) above the ground. The average height of 33 nests measured by Baltosser (1989) in Guadalupe Canyon in southwestern New Mexico was 3.6 ft (1.1 m). In Arizona, nests have also been found on the lower branches or saplings of Goodding willow, Fremont cottonwood, Arizona sycamore, netleaf hackberry, and velvet mesquite. Atlasers noted this species constructing a nest on top of the remains of the nest from the previous year.

Female Broad-billed Hummingbirds incubate the typical clutch of two eggs for 15 to 19 days (Powers and

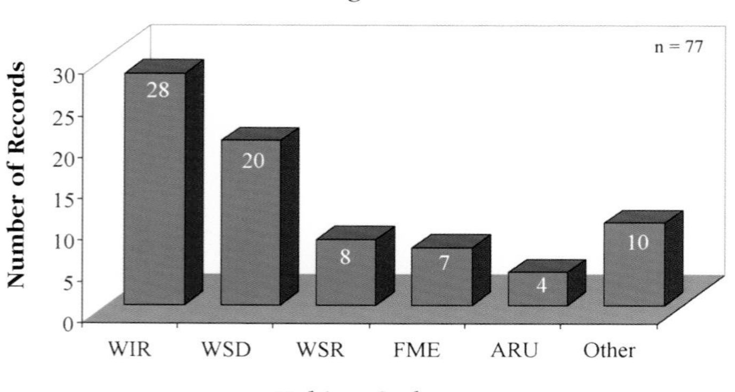

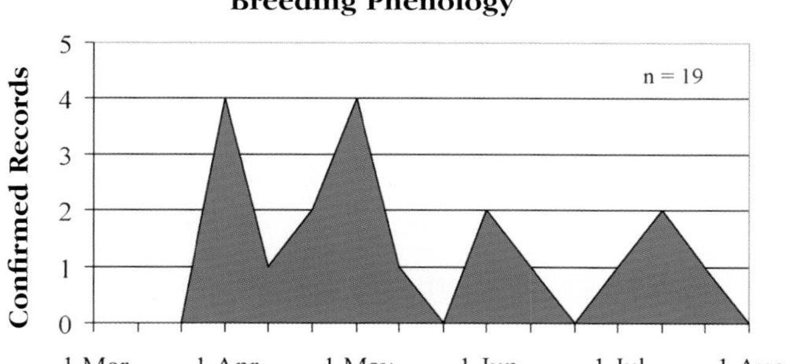

Wethington 1999). Nestlings remain in the nest for approximately 20 to 26 days and the female continues to feed them for an additional 1 to 2 weeks after fledging (Powers and Wethington 1999). Broad-billed Hummingbirds typically attempt two broods per year in Arizona, which coincide with peak nectar availability in spring and then again during the late summer monsoon period (Baltosser 1989).

DISTRIBUTION AND STATUS

Resident throughout much of central Mexico north to southeastern Sonora, breeding populations of Broad-billed Hummingbirds farther north are primarily migratory. They breed as far north as southeastern Arizona, southwestern New Mexico, and locally and irregularly in western Texas. In Arizona, Phillips et al. (1964) described Broad-billed Hummingbirds as common summer residents from Guadalupe Canyon in the extreme southeast, west along the Mexico border to the Baboquivari Mountains, and north to at least the Santa Catalina Mountains. Monson and Phillips (1981) also noted this hummingbird nesting north to the Galiuro Mountains and once in northeast Phoenix in 1980.

Atlasers found Broad-billed Hummingbirds at elevations ranging from 1700 ft (518 m) along the Gila River downstream of Kearny to 5800 ft (1768 m) in Miller Canyon, Huachuca Mountains. The center of abundance of Broad-billed Hummingbirds in Arizona is from the western slope of the Baboquivari Mountains, east to Patagonia, and north to the Santa Catalina Mountain foothill drainages primarily above 3000 ft (914 m) elevation. Within this zone, they are often quite common and frequently dominate local feeders. Outside this area, their abundance drops dramatically. This is especially true in Cochise County, except possibly in Guadalupe Canyon, where they remain rather common. Even though they are a sparse nesting species in Cochise and Pinal counties, Broad-billed Hummingbirds were found by atlasers to be much more widespread in these counties than previously noted. In Cochise County they were found as far northeast as the Dos Cabezas Mountains. Atlasers found it ranges sparingly north along the lower San Pedro River and adjacent Gila River and along lower Aravaipa Creek. Broad-billed Hummingbirds likely nest along the perennial drainages in southern Galiuro Mountains, where they are common visitors at feeder at the Muleshoe Ranch Preserve. An individual was also observed in the Gila River Box of Graham County during atlas surveys.

As early as 1947, Broad-billed Hummingbirds had been irregularly observed at the Boyce Thompson Arboretum near Superior (Phillips et al. 1964). Assumed to be nesting for many years, these hummingbirds were finally confirmed breeding there in 1982. During the atlas period, they were reported there annually, and nesting was also confirmed. Like many other primarily Mexican hummingbirds, evidence suggests that the breeding distribution of Broad-billed Hummingbirds in Arizona is steadily expanding northward.

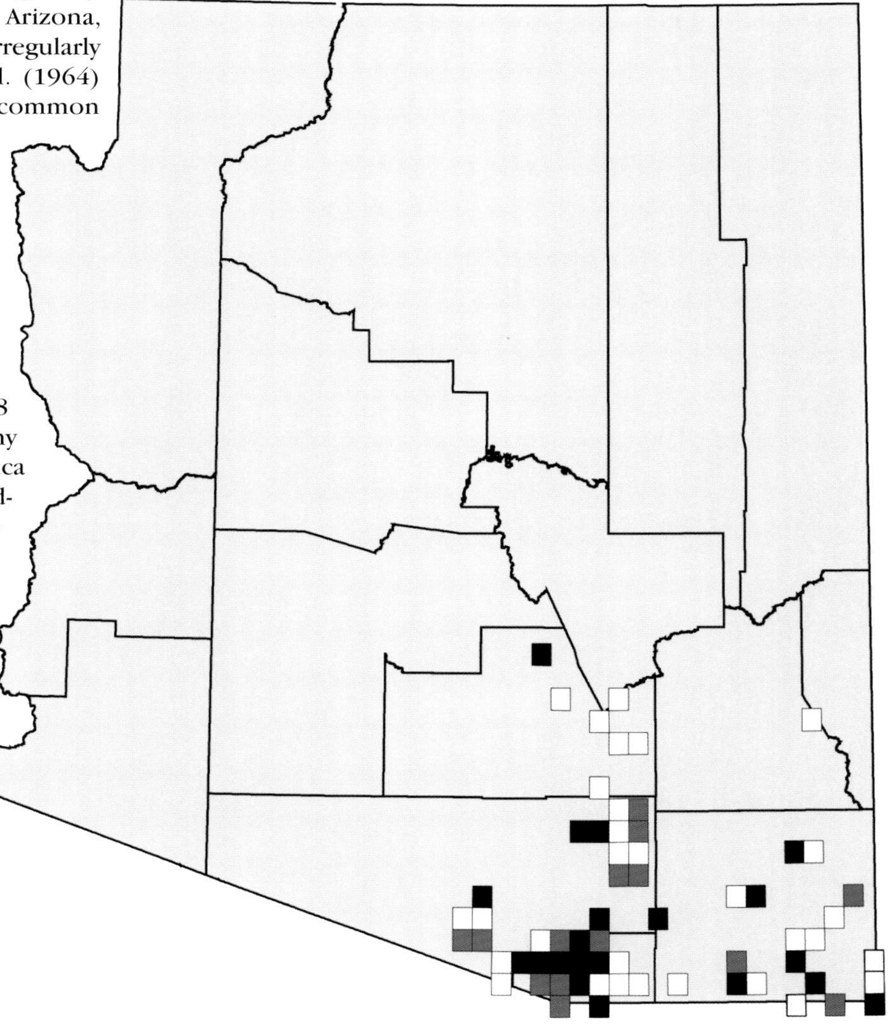

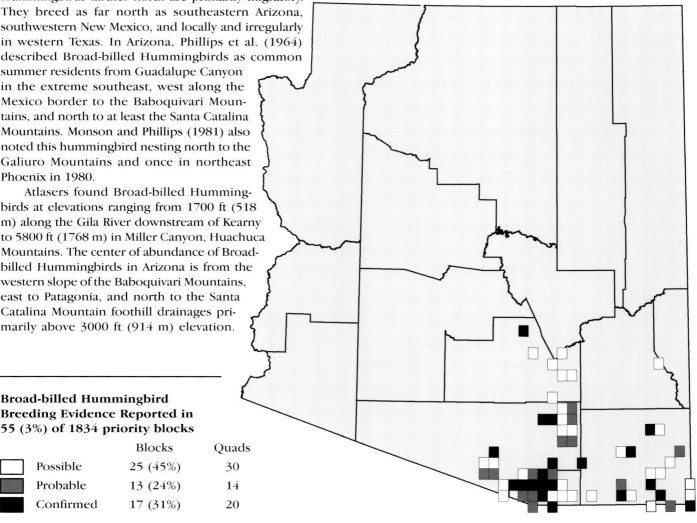

Broad-billed Hummingbird Breeding Evidence Reported in 55 (3%) of 1834 priority blocks

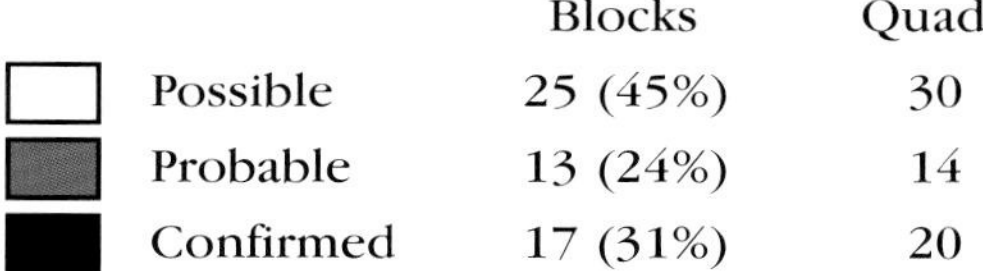

	Blocks	Quads
Possible	25 (45%)	30
Probable	13 (24%)	14
Confirmed	17 (31%)	20

White-eared Hummingbird

by Troy E. Corman *Hylocharis leucotis*

In all plumages, the broad, snow-white head stripe easily identifies the colorful White-eared Hummingbird. Observations of these little mountain gems in southeastern Arizona are rare enough that they are highly sought after by visiting birders. Patience is generally needed, however, for their daily visits to feeding stations are typically infrequent.

JIM BURNS

HABITAT

In Mexico, White-eared Hummingbirds favors shrubby undergrowth of pine-oak and Madrean evergreen oak forests in highlands, and are often common at patches of flowers along roadsides and in clearings (Johnsgard 1983; Howell 2002). These hummingbirds occupy similar habitat in Arizona, where they are found primarily in cool, forested mountain canyons and along shrubby clearings on mountain slope and drainages, especially those recovering from forest fires and other disturbances. Localities frequented by White-eared Hummingbirds in Arizona often include a variety of both broadleaf and coniferous trees. These may include Arizona sycamore, bigtooth maple, Gambel's oak, various Madrean evergreen oaks, New Mexico locust, Douglas fir, Chihuahuan pine, and ponderosa pine.

BREEDING

Typically the earliest White-eared Hummingbirds in Arizona appear in mid-April, but during the atlas period, they were occasionally reported as early as mid-March. However, most individuals are observed after the beginning of May. Males sing from mid-levels in the forest canopy, often from inside a shrub or tree and not necessarily from a prominent perch (Howell 2002). Two nests discovered during the atlas period were likely initiated in mid- to late June, which may suggest second nesting attempts inasmuch as these hummingbirds often arrive several months earlier in Arizona.

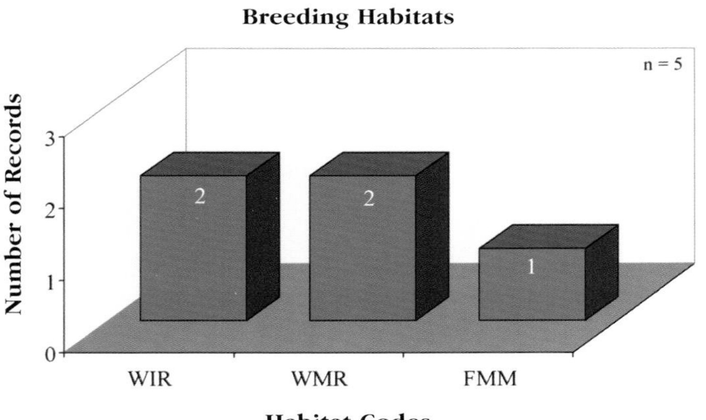

Howell and Webb (1995) noted this hummingbird nested from March to August in northern and central Mexico. However, fewer individuals occur in Arizona during the spring period and may limit earlier nesting activity. In Arizona, the earliest nest with small young was discovered on 13 July, suggesting egg laying in late June. Another nest fledged young in mid-August. In Arizona, juveniles typically appear at feeding stations in July and August. Most White-eared Hummingbirds have departed Arizona by late August or early September, with stragglers casually reported through late September and into October. Very few individuals have lingered through late fall and winter.

Female White-eared Hummingbirds often construct the deep, rounded nest on slender twigs of shrubs or small deciduous trees at a heights ranging from 4 to 25 ft (1.2–7.6 m) above the ground (Baicich and Harrison 1997). Johnsgard (1983) noted that a lengthy 15–20 days are required to build the nest. The only nest described in Arizona was approximately 4 ft (1.2 m) high in a Gambel's oak and largely protected from above by a cluster of oak leaves. Another Arizona nest was placed in a thorny shrub, possibly New Mexico locust, at a similarly low height.

The following breeding biology is from information compiled by Johnsgard (1983). The typical clutch of White-eared Hummingbirds consists of 2 eggs that are incubated by the female for 14 to 16 days. The young are brooded by the female for approximately the first 18 days after hatching. Nestlings depart the nest when they are 23–28 days old and are fed by the female for several additional weeks. One female was observed occasionally still feeding a 40-day-old fledgling, even though she was incubating her second clutch of eggs.

DISTRIBUTION AND STATUS

White-eared Hummingbirds breed from north-central Nicaragua through the highlands of Mexico to the mountains of southeastern Arizona. Populations north of southern

Sonora are primarily migratory. Although some of the northern populations may simply move to lower elevations during the winter. In Sonora, Russell and Monson (1998) described White-eared Hummingbirds as an uncommon summer resident in woodlands and forests above approximately 4600 ft (1402 m).

In Arizona, White-eared Hummingbirds are considered a rare summer visitant to higher southeastern mountain ranges, north to the Santa Catalina Mountains and east to the Chiricahua Mountains (Phillips et al. 1964). The bird was first collected in 1894 in Arizona, but there were not authentic records in the state after 1940 until they were rediscovered in some numbers in the Chiricahua Mountains in July 1961. The number of White-eared Hummingbirds visiting Arizona fluctuates almost annually, but since the mid-1980s, they have become rare but regular summer visitor to feeding stations in canyons on the eastern slope of the Huachuca Mountains, with multiple individuals reported annually. These attractive hummingbirds likely occur annually in the Chiricahua Mountains as well, but fewer individuals are reported from this range. Fewer observations may owe to the lack of frequently monitored feeding station at the higher elevations this species prefers. White-eared Hummingbirds remain very irregularly reported in the Santa Rita and Santa Catalina mountains. Breeding was first confirmed in Arizona at Ramsey Canyon, Huachuca Mountains in July 1989 when two recently fledged young appeared at feeders there. However, occupied nests in the state were not discovered until July 1996 near Comfort Spring in upper Carr Canyon, Huachuca Mountains. Another nest was found in July 2001 in Greenhouse Canyon, a tributary of the Cave Creek drainage in the Chiricahua Mountains (R. Taylor, personal communication).

During the atlas period, White-eared Hummingbirds were noted visiting feeding stations at elevations as low as 4900 ft (1494 m) in Madera Canyon, Santa Rita Mountains. However, most of Arizona's summering White-eared Hummingbirds are detected above 5500 ft (1676 m) and were noted as high as 8400 ft (2560 m) in the Santa Catalina Mountains. The two nests discovered during the atlas period were at elevations between 7200 and 7600 ft (2195–2316 m). Many additional nest records would be needed to determine if White-eared Hummingbirds are selecting to breed at these higher elevations in Arizona.

In the Huachuca Mountains, most observations during the atlas period came from Miller, Carr, Ramsey, and occasionally Sawmill canyons. The vast majority of White-eared Hummingbird records in the Chiricahua Mountains were obtained within the Cave Creek drainage, likely due to the higher concentration of observers and feeding stations there. Based on the availability of appropriate habitat, this hummingbird is likely a sparse, but widespread summer resident in the Chiricahua Mountains. Atlasers also detected an individual in a remote area near Cochise Head northeast of Chiricahua National Monument. Most notable during the atlas, was the observation of an adult male and a female White-eared Hummingbird just west of Turkey Flat in the Pinaleno Mountains in June 1997. These observations were the first for this mountain range, although these hummingbirds could simply be overlooked due to the significantly reduced number of observers in the Pinaleno Mountains. Monitoring feeders at the summer communities of Turkey Flat and Old Columbine may reveal that White-eared Hummingbirds are much more regular in this mountain range.

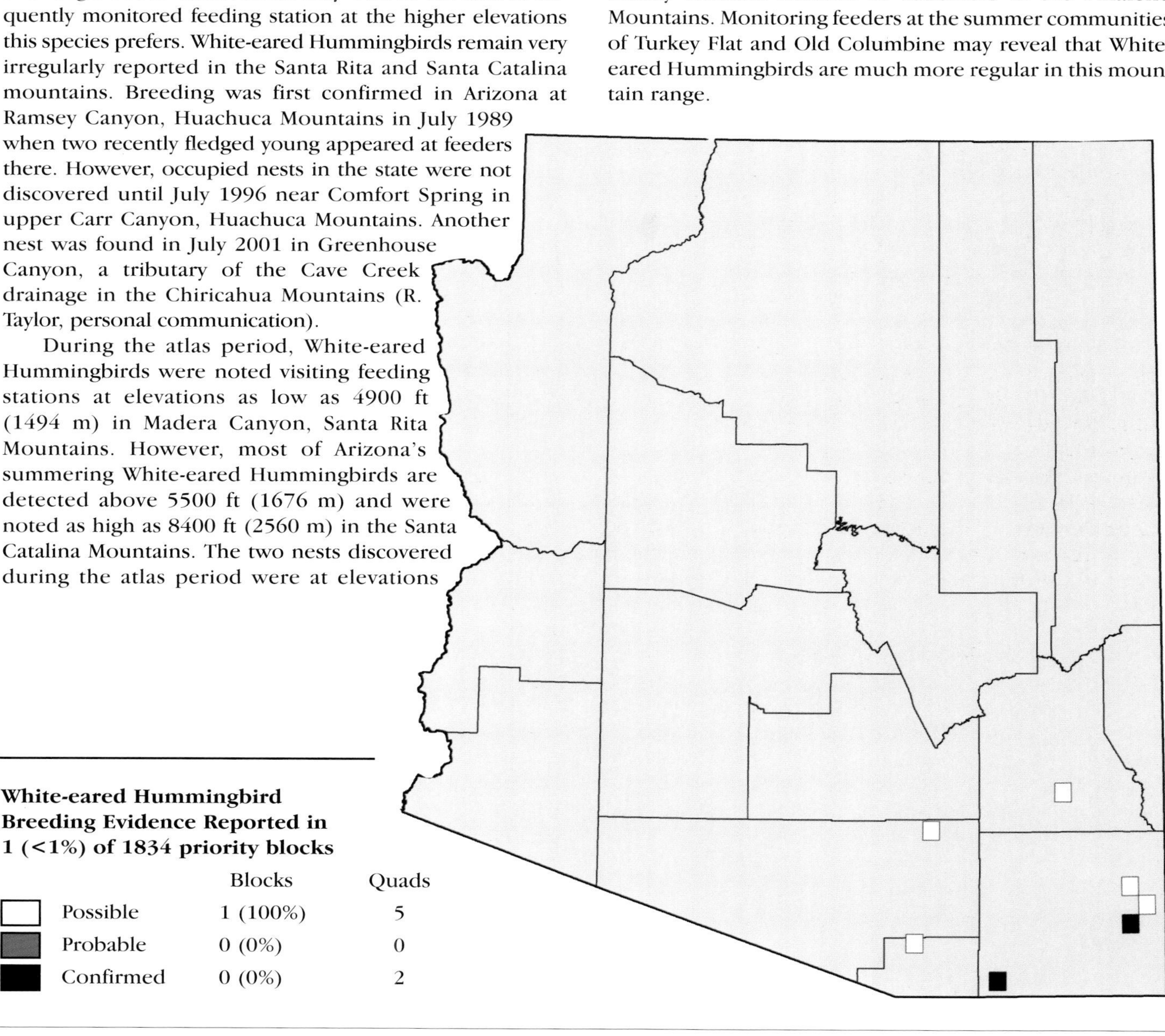

White-eared Hummingbird Breeding Evidence Reported in 1 (<1%) of 1834 priority blocks

	Blocks	Quads
Possible	1 (100%)	5
Probable	0 (0%)	0
Confirmed	0 (0%)	2

Berylline Hummingbird

by Troy E. Corman *Amazilia beryllina*

RICK AND NORA BOWERS

Like several other Mexican hummingbirds that reach their most northern limits in the mountains of southeastern Arizona, records of the Berylline Hummingbird have steadily increased in the last decade. Observations remain rare enough, however, that these rufous-winged, emerald hummingbirds are still highly prized by visiting birders.

HABITAT

Found in a variety of habitats where they are more common in Mexico, Berylline Hummingbirds appear to have a more restricted habitat preference at the northern edge of their range. In Arizona, most observations and nests occur in or near cool and often damp forested mountain canyons adjacent to pine-oak woodlands. During the atlas period, this rare hummingbird was found nesting primarily along perennial and intermittent drainages dominated by Arizona sycamore, bigtooth maple, various Madrean evergreen oaks, alligator juniper, and Arizona walnut. Berylline Hummingbirds have also been discovered nesting in the transition zone of sycamore-lined drainages and Madrean pine-oak woodlands that also contain a scattering of Chihuahuan pine, Apache pine, and Douglas fir. Within these canyons, they are frequently observed visiting feeding stations, but also favor patches of blooming thistle and other flowers in forest openings and edges.

BREEDING

Most of the few Berylline Hummingbirds that frequent Arizona each year do not arrive until May, although some early individuals arrive by mid- to late April. In Arizona, nesting activity has been observed in late spring, with nest building by mid-May and egg laying by late May. However, the majority of Arizona's nesting records fall during the typical monsoon period from late June through mid-August, with most nesting activity in July. Similarly, Russell and Monson (1998) noted numbers of territorial and singing Berylline Hummingbirds in southeastern Sonora in late July, as well as observing a female carrying nesting material. Like several other hummingbird species in southeastern Arizona, the peak nesting period for Berylline Hummingbirds likely corresponds to the increased availability of mountain wildflowers and insects following the initiation of the late summer rainy season. Atlasers reported the latest occupied nest on 19 August, but a nest with a nearly fledged nestling was noted in Ramsay Canyon as late as 3 September. In 1984, an even later Berylline Hummingbird nest was discovered in Chiricahua National Monument, which fledged two young on 14–15 September (S. Williams, personal communication). Few Berylline Hummingbirds have lingered in Arizona after late September.

There is very little information on the nesting habits of migratory populations of Berylline Hummingbirds. In Arizona, most of the few nests discovered have been on the outer, and often horizontal, branches of Arizona sycamore, less often in Arizona cypress. South of the border, nests have also been noted low in shrubs and from 16.4 to 49.2 ft (5–15 m) high in oaks and pines (Johnsgard 1983). Two nests measured in sycamores in Arizona ranged in height from approximately 18 to 24.6 ft (5.5–7.5 m) above the ground (Anderson and Monson 1981).

The female constructs the nest in a fairly shaded location and typically lays 2 eggs. The incubation period for Berylline Hummingbirds is not precisely known, but is suggested to be approximately 15–18 days as it is with similar sized hummingbirds (Kaufman 1996). Only the female feeds the nestlings, which depart the nest in about 20–25 days. She continues feeding the fledglings for an unknown period following nest departure. Berylline Hummingbirds have been observed renesting soon after an earlier brood had been lost to predators or weather. Due to the relatively short late summer nesting period, this hummingbird likely produces only one brood per year in Arizona. However, with the occasional spring nesting, two successful broods are possible.

DISTRIBUTION AND STATUS

Berylline Hummingbirds are found primarily as a common to fairly common resident in the highlands and foothills of the Pacific Slope and interior of Mexico from Sonora south (Howell and Webb 1995). These hummingbirds also occur south to El Salvador and Honduras. The extreme northern populations, including much of Sonora, are considered at least partially migratory and likely account for the few individual that move into the mountains of southeastern Arizona and accidentally to Texas.

The first observation of the Berylline Hummingbird north of Mexico was discovered in Madera Canyon, Santa Rita Mountains in June 1964 (Monson and Phillips 1981). This was followed by an individual in Ramsey Canyon, Huachuca Mountains in 1967 and in Cave Creek Canyon, Chiricahua

Mountains in 1971. The first documented nesting attempt was in the latter location in 1976 and Berylline Hummingbirds successfully nested in Ramsey Canyon in 1978 (Monson and Phillips 1981). As mentioned earlier, this hummingbird also nested once at Chiricahua National Monument.

During the atlas, all information obtained for the Berylline Hummingbird was collected from casual observations from atlasers and others. This hummingbird was most consistently observed at feeders from 4880 to 5800 ft (1487–1768 m), but has been noted occasionally visiting patches of flowers to near 7300 ft (2225 m). Most nesting records continue to come from the Huachuca Mountains in Ramsey Canyon, but observations of this rare hummingbird continue to increase in nearby Miller Canyon. Berylline Hummingbird was also noted nesting in upper Cave Creek Canyon in the Chiricahua Mountains in 1995 and observed only occasionally in the Santa Rita Mountains, where it has visited feeding stations in Madera Canyon. There are still no nesting records for the latter mountain range.

The status of Berylline Hummingbird in Arizona has changed little, other than going from a casual to become a sparse, almost annual summer visitor during the atlas period. Nesting observations have also steadily increased. However, by the end of the atlas period, several hybrid hummingbirds began appearing at feeders in the Huachuca Mountains that showed characteristics of Berylline Hummingbird. Superficially resembling a large Berylline, most observers felt these individuals in Ramsey, Miller, and Ash canyons were from crosses with Magnificent Hummingbirds. Some of these hybrids returned in successive years, but it is unknown if they are capable of producing offspring. Hybridization will likely continue to occur in southeastern Arizona as long as the summer population of Berylline Hummingbirds remains to just a few scattered individuals each year.

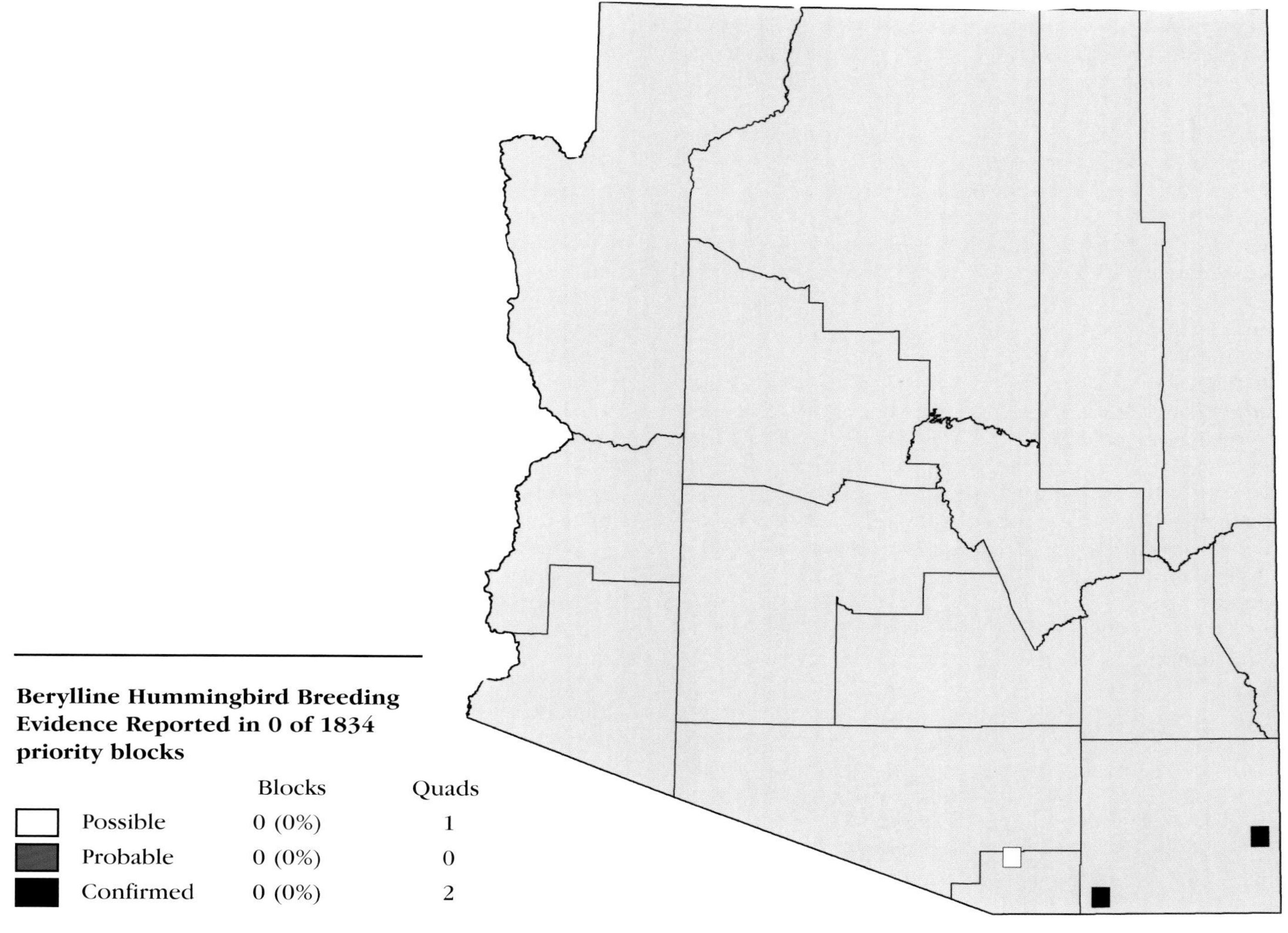

Berylline Hummingbird Breeding Evidence Reported in 0 of 1834 priority blocks

	Blocks	Quads
Possible	0 (0%)	1
Probable	0 (0%)	0
Confirmed	0 (0%)	2

Violet-crowned Hummingbird

by Troy E. Corman *Amazilia violiceps*

With their larger size, red bill, and snow-white underparts, Violet-crowned Hummingbirds are one of the easier to identify hummingbirds in Arizona. This distinctive hummingbird has been noted as quite aggressive and energetic, and is frequently observed chasing other hummingbirds.

JIM BURNS

HABITAT

Basically a riparian obligate in Arizona, Violet-crowned Hummingbirds are most frequently observed in desert foothill drainages and lower mountain canyons with an abundance of tall broadleaf trees, with a strong preference for Arizona sycamore. Actually, drainages containing sycamore accounted for twelve of the nineteen atlas observations of this hummingbird. Other trees often found in drainages frequented by Violet-crowned Hummingbirds include Arizona walnut, Fremont cottonwood, Goodding willow, Arizona ash, alligator juniper, and various Madrean evergreen oaks. Occasionally, atlasers encountered these hummingbirds nesting very locally and in limited numbers along cottonwood or evergreen oak dominated drainages that lacked sycamores. Violet-crowned Hummingbirds will forage in more open situations at nearby flowering agave, yucca, and other desert shrubs, but they typically stay close to woodland edges and areas of dense vegetation (Williamson 2001). In or adjacent to favored habitats, Violet-crowned Hummingbirds will often become regular visitors to residential feeding stations.

BREEDING

In Arizona, Violet-crowned Hummingbirds have become increasingly regular in recent years as a very sparse winter visitors to feeding stations. However, most Violet-crowns are migratory, with early arrivals typically appearing in Arizona by early March, but occasionally by early February. There is also a noticeable increase in observations of these hummingbirds in June, suggesting an influx just prior to the summer rainy period.

Atlas data indicate there is some Violet-crowned Hummingbird nesting activity in spring, with the earliest occupied nest reported on 30 May. However, in 2003, the female of a pair that had wintered near Bisbee was observed collecting nesting material on 5 March (S. Williamson, personal communication). The vast majority of nesting records in Arizona are concentrated during the late summer monsoon season. Nesting activity increases in early July, with atlasers reporting several individuals nest building or incubating from 1 to 16 July. Compilation of Violet-crowned Hummingbird nesting records in Arizona (n = 28) suggests that peak nesting activity is from 1 July through 10 August. Atlasers documented incubating females as late as 13 September. Near Bisbee, nests with young have been known to fledge as late as 24 September (T. Woods, personal communication). Most Violet-crowned Hummingbirds have departed Arizona by late September, with stragglers reported at feeders through November, and locally through the winter.

In Arizona, most Violet-crowned Hummingbird nests have been found high in Arizona sycamores. However, they have also be found in Arizona white oak, various other species of evergreen oaks, and once a few feet above the ground on a seed pod of a fallen dried agave stalk. Nest heights were not measured by atlas field crews; however, Zimmerman and Levy (1950) noted nests ranging in height from 23 to 39.4 ft (7–12 m) in Guadalupe Canyon, and nests have also been found as low as 6 ft (1.8 m) above the ground (Baicich and Harrison 1997). Their often lichen-covered nests are typically placed on a horizontal limb, often with a large overhanging leaf for a roof (Baicich and Harrison 1997). As in most hummingbirds, the typical clutch is two eggs. There is apparently little information on the length of incubation, nestling stage, or fledgling dependency of adult for this hummingbird. It is also

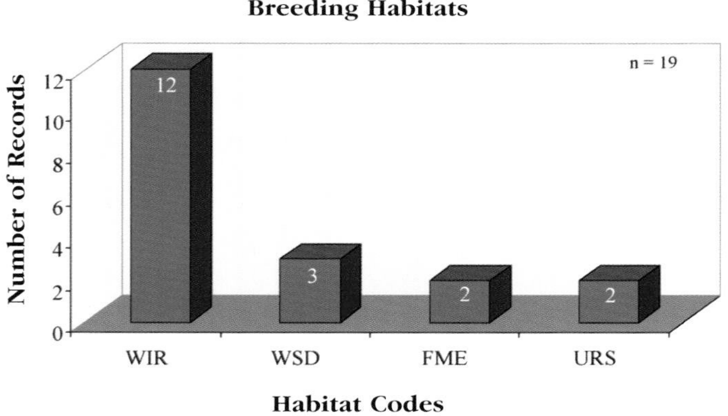

Breeding Phenology

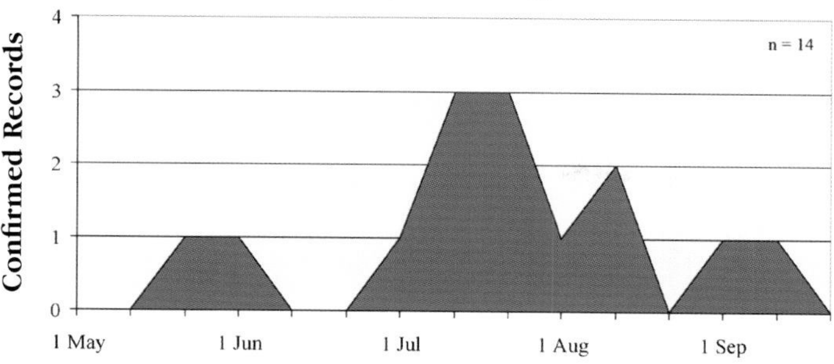

unknown how many broods are produced per year, but they will readily renest if earlier attempts fail. One individual near Bisbee, lost her clutch and nest to a storm and was found incubating two eggs at a new nest only ten days later (C. Melton, personal communication).

DISTRIBUTION AND STATUS

Primarily a Mexican species, Violet-crowned Hummingbirds are resident from central Mexico north along the Pacific slope to southern Sonora. They are primarily only summer residents north to southeastern Arizona and extreme southwestern New Mexico. There were only two records of Violet-crowned Hummingbirds in Arizona prior to 1948. One specimen each had been collected in the Chiricahua and Huachuca (4 July 1905) mountains. Levy (1958) observed as many as six individuals in Guadalupe Canyon during July 1957. He collected an adult female with a recent brood patch, suggesting nesting. Violet-crowned Hummingbirds were confirmed nesting in Guadalupe Canyon in Arizona and New Mexico during fieldwork in 1959 (Zimmerman and Levy 1960). Observations of this hummingbird have steadily increased since. They were noted as rare along Sonoita Creek and in the Huachuca Mountains, but were becoming nearly annual in the Chiricahua Mountains (Phillips et al. 1964). By 1980, Violet-crowned Hummingbirds were considered uncommon in summer from the Portal area and Guadalupe Canyon in the extreme southeast, west to the Santa Rita Mountains and Patagonia region (Monson and Phillips 1981).

During the atlas, Violet-crowned Hummingbirds were found nesting locally at elevations from 3850 to 5800 ft (1173–1768 m). Atlasers noted Violet-crowned Hummingbirds to be most abundant in Guadalupe Canyon, in the Mule Mountains near Bisbee, and along Sonoita Creek near Patagonia. They remain sparse annual summer visitors to feeding stations in the Chiricahua, Huachuca, and Santa Rita mountains. During the atlas period, they were also confirmed nesting at Portal in the Chiricahua Mountains, and for the first time in French Joe Canyon in the Whetstone Mountains and along Silver Creek northeast of Douglas. Atlasers also noted Violet-crowned Hummingbirds during the nesting season along the upper San Pedro River, in Sabino Canyon in the Santa Catalina Mountains, and as far west as Brown Canyon in the Baboquivari Mountains, suggesting additional possible nesting localities.

As the number of summer observation of Violet-crowned Hummingbird have steadily increased in Arizona during the past forty years, their year-round status has also greatly changed. Numbers are now arriving much earlier in the spring than they have in the past, spring nesting records are on the increase, and many more individuals are now lingering at feeders well into the fall. The number of locations in southeastern Arizona that host Violet-crowned Hummingbirds through the winter has also greatly increased recently. At some local feeding stations, these showy hummingbirds have becoming almost annual residents.

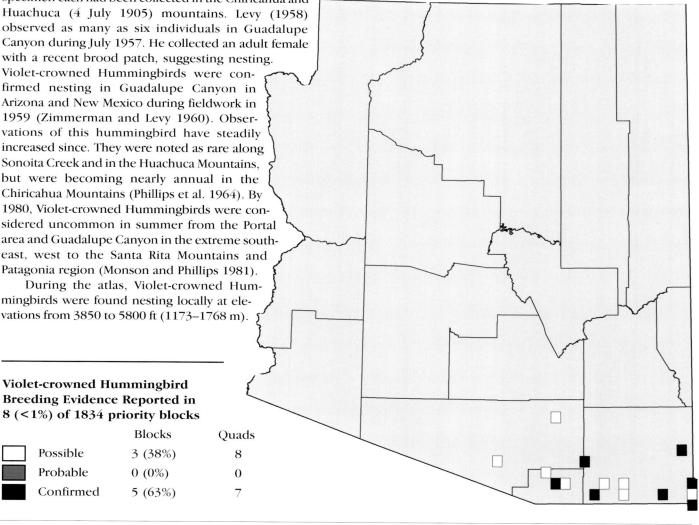

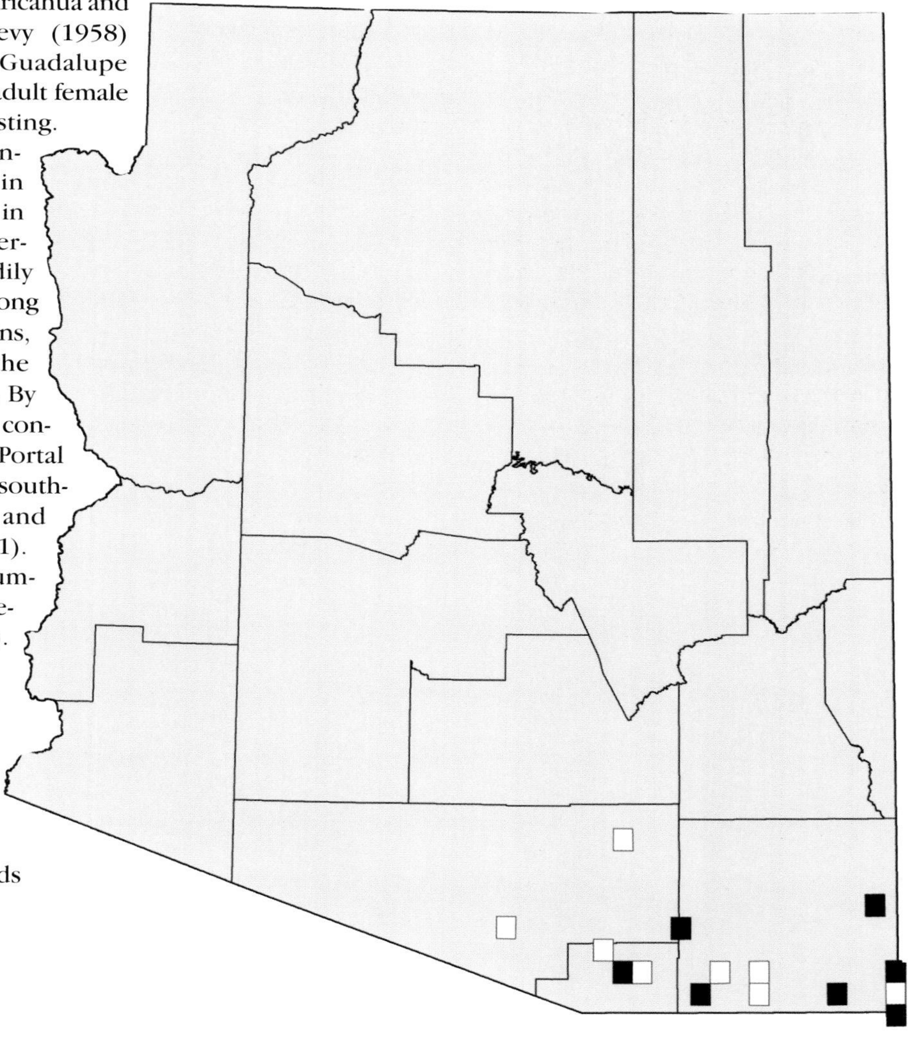

Violet-crowned Hummingbird Breeding Evidence Reported in 8 (<1%) of 1834 priority blocks

	Blocks	Quads
Possible	3 (38%)	8
Probable	0 (0%)	0
Confirmed	5 (63%)	7

Blue-throated Hummingbird

by Cathryn Wise-Gervais *Lampornis clemenciae*

DAN FISCHER

Blue-throated Hummingbirds are the largest hummingbirds in Arizona and are unmistakable at feeders, inasmuch as their robust size sets them apart from most of the other buzzing sprites. Named for the male's sparkling gorget, this highly aggressive hummingbird's loud and monotonous "tseep" call is distinctive and is often heard during territorial chases.

HABITAT

Blue-throated Hummingbirds are found primarily in Arizona's forested mountains, where they favor cool, moist canyons that typically offer perennial or intermittent stream flow. These noisy hummingbirds appear to reach their highest density in areas where sycamore dominated drainages merge with Madrean pine-oak forests, and observers obtained most atlas records in such areas. Characteristic vegetation in Blue-throated Hummingbird habitat includes a combination of Arizona sycamore, bigtooth maple, Arizona madrone, and various evergreen oaks, with scattered Arizona cypress, alligator juniper, Apache pine, and Douglas fir. Atlasers also noted some Blue-throated Hummingbirds nesting locally at slightly lower elevations near the mouth of several canyons. Habitats in these warmer and more open areas typically consisted of scattered large sycamore, cypress, and Madrean evergreen oaks, and were invariably near feeding stations at private residences. Although Blue-throated and Magnificent Hummingbirds coexist in canyons, Blue-throated Hummingbirds are typically lacking on the higher-elevation slopes and ridges that Magnificent Hummingbirds often inhabit.

BREEDING

Although a few Blue-throated Hummingbirds now winter annually at several feeding stations in Arizona, most individuals are migratory and begin appearing on their breeding grounds by early to mid-March. These hummingbirds can initiate nest building by early April, and egg laying has been recorded as early as 17 April in Arizona (Williamson 2000). However, most birds lay their first clutches in late April or early May (Willard 1911; Phillips et al. 1964). Observers reported very few active nests during the atlas period, but Blue-throated Hummingbirds in Arizona are known to rear as many as three broods per year, with second clutches usually laid in early June–early July, and third clutches laid in late July–early August (Williamson 2000). Observers located the latest active nest reported during the atlas period on 5 August, and this nest contained eggs when discovered. Late nesting activity can continue into the fall, as indicated by a nest reported in the Huachuca Mountains that contained a nestling near fledging on 8 September (Willard 1913). Blue-throated Hummingbirds generally begin migrating south to Mexico wintering grounds in late August or early September, with most individuals departing by mid- to late October.

As with other hummingbird species, the female Blue-throated builds the nest, incubates the eggs, and cares for young without male assistance. Blue-throated Hummingbirds have a unique preference among hummingbird species in Arizona, for they typically select nest sites offering cover from above, such as is provided by sheltered rock ledges, overhanging stream banks, entrances to caves, under building eaves, bridges, or within abandoned structures (Williamson 2000). Several nests have been discovered over mountain streams and one unique Arizona nest sites was behind a small dripping waterfall in which the female was often doused with water upon entering or exiting the nest. Nest heights were not measured during the atlas period, but most nests are placed rather low, typically between 4 and 14 ft (1.2–4.3 m) above the ground (Baicich and Harrison 1997). Females commonly reuse their protected nests during the same season and often over several years with new nesting material added after each brood. Over time, Blue-throated Hummingbird nests can become quite tall, and researchers have documented nests that stood nearly 10 inches (25 cm) high (Williamson 2000).

Blue-throated Hummingbird clutches typically consist of two eggs and the females incubate these for 17 to 18 days (Johnsgard 1983). Females care for nestlings, which begin exercising their wings approximately 20 days after hatching and typically fledge in 24–26 days (Williamson 2000). Fledglings will sometimes perch together, but will frequently

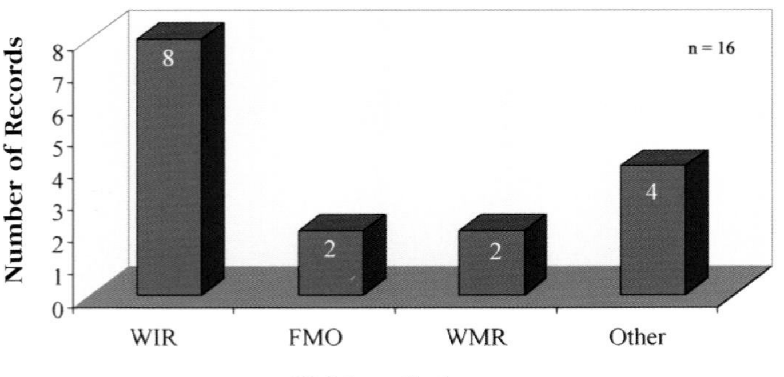

separate and are tended individually by the female for an unknown period (Williamson 2000). If the female initiates the next brood, she or her mate may aggressively drive the fledglings off (Williamson 2000). As noted earlier, Blue-throated Hummingbirds have a lengthy nesting season and often attempt to rear 2–3 broods per year.

DISTRIBUTION AND STATUS

Primarily a Mexican species, Howell and Webb (1995) describe Blue-throated Hummingbirds as occurring fairly commonly in the highlands of Mexico south to Oaxaca, typically at elevations ranging from 5904 to 9840 ft (1800–3000 m). Basically migratory at the northern edge of their range in the southwestern United States, these hummingbirds are found locally in several mountain ranges in western Texas, southern New Mexico, and southeastern Arizona. Atlasers reported Blue-throated Hummingbirds in canyons primarily at elevations from 5100 to 8400 ft (1554–2560 m) and found them nesting locally down to 4800 ft (1463 m) such as in Portal.

Blue-throated Hummingbirds are not numerous in Arizona, but are encountered regularly at several locations in southeastern Arizona, most notably in several moist canyons in the Huachuca, Santa Rita, and Chiricahua mountains (Monson and Phillips 1981). In the Huachuca Mountains, these hummingbirds are found nesting primarily in several cooler drainages on the eastern slope, basically from Huachuca Canyon south to Miller Canyon. Atlasers reported Blue-throated Hummingbirds only in Madera and Florida canyons within the Santa Rita Mountains. However, infrequently visited drainages on the eastern slope, such as upper Gardner and Cave canyons, may also harbor these hummingbirds, especially during wetter summers. Atlasers found Blue-throated hummingbirds in many canyons in the Chiricahua Mountains from Chiricahua National Monument south to upper Price Canyon.

Phillips et al. (1964) reported only two records of Blue-throated Hummingbirds in the Santa Catalina Mountains, but observations began to increase in the late 1970s at feeders in Summerhaven (Monson and Phillips 1981). Within this range during the atlas period, these hummingbirds were only reported coming to cabin feeding stations in Willow Canyon (B. Bickel, personal communication). Although Blue-throated Hummingbirds have yet to be confirmed nesting within this mountain range, these and past records of both males and females throughout the late spring and summer, strongly suggesting local nesting. Atlasers discovered Blue-throated Hummingbirds in the Pinaleno Mountains where they had not been previously documented. One individual was noted in Ash Canyon and both males and females were coming to feeders at Turkey Flat. More intensive surveys in the Pinaleno Mountains will undoubtedly reveal Blue-throated Hummingbirds nesting at least locally in several infrequently visited cool drainages such as in or near Ash, Jacobson, and Wet canyons. Atlasers also noted a Blue-throated Hummingbird in the Dragoon Mountains at Cochise Stronghold, but nesting habitat is very limited within this dry range.

Catastrophic wildfires within favored canyons appear to be the largest threat to Blue-throated Hummingbird populations in Arizona. These hummingbirds are very tolerant of some human influences within their range, and readily take advantage of feeding stations and certain attributes of nearby buildings and other structures for nest placement. Marshall (1957) noted that the distribution and abundance of Blue-throated Hummingbird can be negatively affected by drought and subsequent reduced availability of certain flowers. During such stressful periods, nearby feeding stations may become very important to these adaptable hummingbirds.

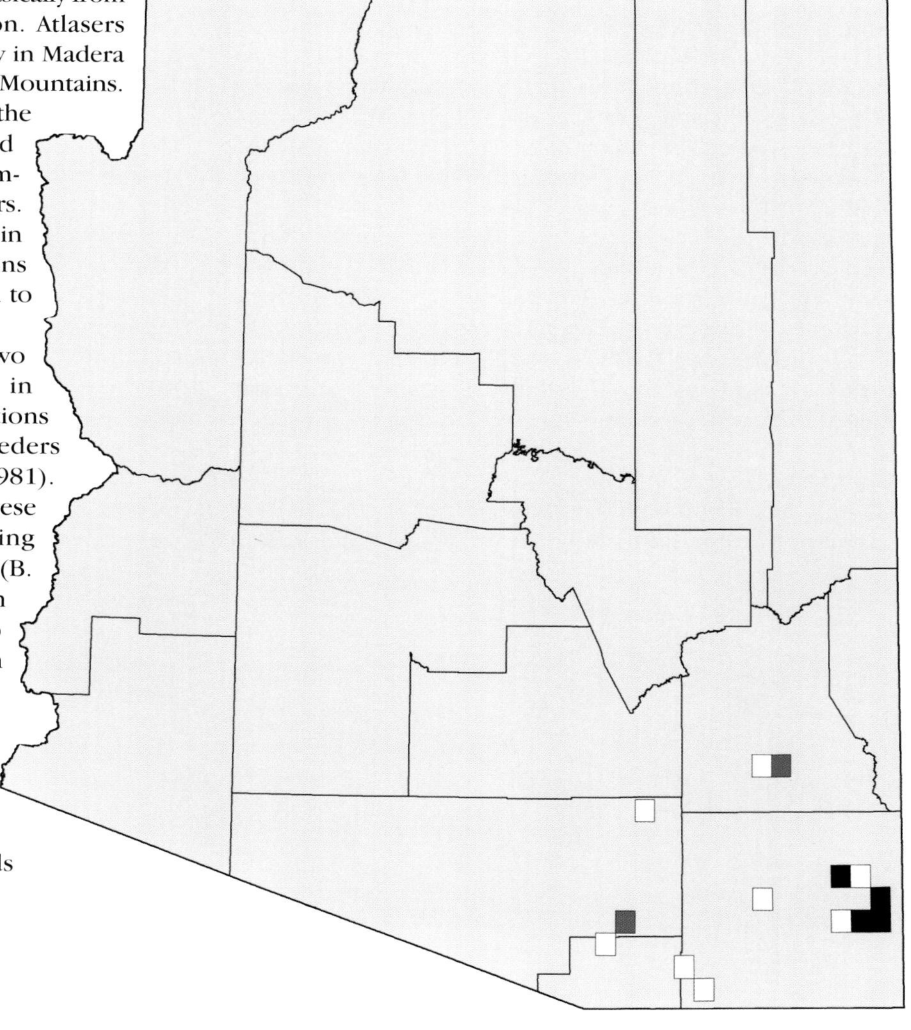

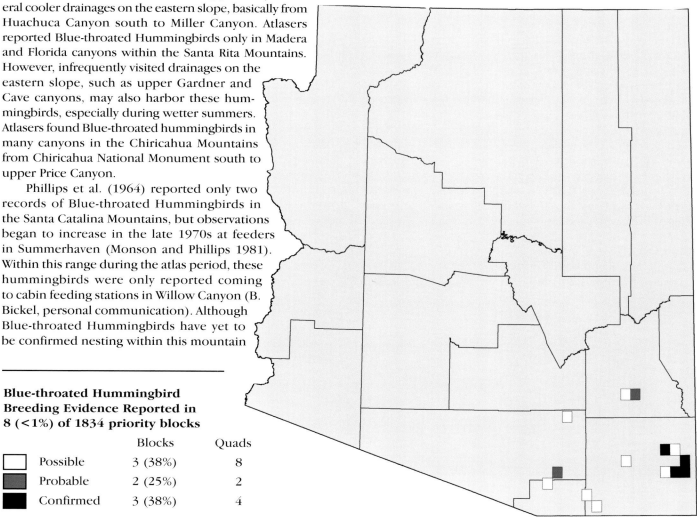

Blue-throated Hummingbird Breeding Evidence Reported in 8 (<1%) of 1834 priority blocks

	Blocks	Quads
Possible	3 (38%)	8
Probable	2 (25%)	2
Confirmed	3 (38%)	4

Magnificent Hummingbird

by Troy E. Corman *Eugenes fulgens*

Living up to its name, the male Magnificent Hummingbird is a true crowd-pleaser at popular feeding stations in southeastern Arizona. When this large, dark hummingbird turns in perfect light, an observer is briefly blessed with a sudden electric flash of purple and brilliant turquoise-green.

DAN FISCHER

HABITAT

In Arizona, Magnificent Hummingbirds prefer the cool, shaded canyons on which the similar sized Blue-throated Hummingbird is so dependent. However, these hummingbirds are also frequently found well away from such drainages on forested mountain slopes and ridges. More than 60 percent of all atlas records were reported from Madrean pine-oak forests in southeastern Arizona and cooler mixed-conifer associations at higher elevations or localities farther north (n = 23). The former habitat typically consists of ponderosa, Chihuahuan, and Apache pines, with an understory of various Madrean evergreen oaks, alligator juniper, and scattered Arizona madrone. The mixed-conifer forests these hummingbirds inhabit often include uneven aged stands of ponderosa pine, Douglas fir, white fir, and scattered quaking aspen. Atlasers also noted Magnificent Hummingbirds in cool canyons and drainages with a mixture of pines, oaks, Arizona cypress, Arizona sycamore, and bigtooth maple. Many fewer observations were from ponderosa pine-Gambel's oak associations and pure Madrean oak woodlands. Even during the nesting season, these hummingbirds will often descend to lower canyon feeding stations, dominated primarily by evergreen oaks and scattered sycamores. However, most nests are discovered at higher elevations in canyons and on conifer-shrouded slopes.

BREEDING

Magnificent Hummingbirds winter locally and in very sparse numbers at year-round feeding stations in several mountain canyons of southeastern Arizona. However, most of Arizona's population is migratory and typically begin to appear in early to mid-March. Nest building can begin by early April and likely incubating females have been noted on nests as early as 13 April in Arizona. A fledgling reported by atlasers on 19 May would appear slightly early, but a fledgling was captured as early as 26 May in Arizona (Powers 1996). Confirmed atlas records were too few to determine a peak period of nesting activity; however, most nests are discovered in June and July. The latest confirmation collected by atlasers was an adult feeding a fledgling on 9 July. However, nests with young ready to fledge have been observed as late as 3 September in the Santa Rita Mountains (S. Johnson, personal communication). Dispersing or southbound Magnificent Hummingbirds are noted away from nesting areas in early August and numbers begin to decrease at favorite feeding stations by mid-October, with few remaining into November.

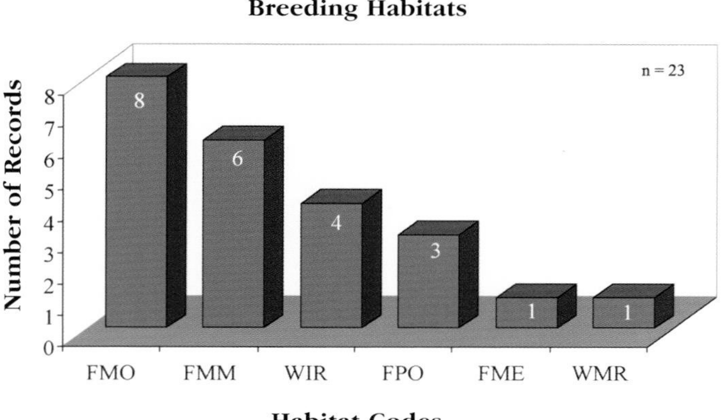

Magnificent Hummingbirds are considered a secretive nesting species, which could help explain why atlasers were unsuccessful in locating nests. In Arizona, nests have been found in ponderosa pine, Chihuahuan pine, Douglas fir, Arizona walnut, Arizona sycamore, and bigtooth maple (Bent 1940; Brandt 1951). The nest height is quite variable and has been reported from 10 to 55 ft (3–16.8 m) above the ground (Bent 1940; Harrison 1979; Baicich and Harrison 1997), although most are typically above 20 ft (6.1 m; Powers 1996) and much higher than Blue-throated Hummingbird nests.

Like other hummingbird species, only the female Magnificent constructs the nest, which is generally placed 6.5–10 ft (2–3 m) away from the trunk and often overhanging a stream or drainage (Powers 1996). Only two eggs are laid and incubated by the female for approximately 16 to 18 days (Harrison 1979; Powers 1996). There is little information on how long nestlings remain in the nest, but it likely ranges between 24 and 29 days, as it is for the similar sized Blue-throated Hummingbird. There is no information on the number of broods produced per season, but based on the lengthy nesting season in Arizona, two and possibly three broods would not be unexpected.

DISTRIBUTION AND STATUS

The Magnificent Hummingbird is primarily a resident in much of its range, but most of the more northern nesting populations withdraw south in the fall. These hummingbirds nest from southeastern Arizona, southwestern New Mexico, and locally in extreme southwestern Texas, south through the higher mountains of Mexico and disjunct populations to western Panama. Phillips et al. (1964) described Magnificent Hummingbirds as fairly common summer resident in Mountains of southeastern Arizona, north to the Pinaleno and Santa Catalina Mountains, possibly as far north as the Sierra Ancha, Gila County. Since 1973, this hummingbird has been found farther north in limited numbers at feeders in the White Mountains, especially near Greer, and occasionally to Flagstaff (Monson and Phillips 1981). Both male and female Magnificent Hummingbirds were present near the North Rim Grand Canyon Ranger Station every summer from 1976 through at least 1981 and were likely nesting nearby (Brown et al. 1987). In Arizona, these impressive hummingbirds are more abundant and widespread and occur in more habitats than Blue-throated Hummingbirds. Unlike the latter bird, Magnificent Hummingbirds are also much more likely to wander to feeding stations north of their southeastern Arizona stronghold.

Atlasers noted Magnificent Hummingbirds at elevations primarily between 5200 and 9000 ft (1585–2743 m), and locally down to approximately 4800 ft (1463 m) near Portal. In southeastern Arizona, atlasers found these hummingbirds to be fairly common to locally common at feeding stations in the Chiricahua, Huachuca, Santa Rita, Santa Catalina, and Pinaleno Mountains. Observations of these hummingbirds significantly decrease away from feeders. Atlasers also noted this hummingbird for the first time on the north slope of the Winchester Mountains in Reiley Canyon. Marshall (1956) reported Magnificent Hummingbirds locally in the Rincon Mountains, and they likely continue to exist in this difficult-of-access range. Seemingly appropriate habitat also exists in the infrequently visited nearby Galiuro Mountains, but preliminary surveys during the atlas did not detect them there.

Observations of Magnificent Hummingbirds north of southeastern Arizona have greatly increased since 1980 and are detected primarily at feeding stations. However, these hummingbirds remain very locally distributed, typically few in number, and nesting has been suspected, but not confirmed. Atlasers reported them in the Pinal Mountains, Gila County, and coming to feeders in the White Mountains near Greer, southeast of Nutrioso, and near Luna Lake. Atlasers also reported both male and female Magnificent Hummingbirds through several successive summers within Oak Creek Canyon northeast of Sedona near the confluence with its West Fork. The most northern atlas records were from Flagstaff and near Big Springs on the western slope of the Kaibab Plateau.

According to historical and atlas data, Magnificent Hummingbirds have likely become very sparse but annual breeding species from the White Mountain region, northwest along the Mogollon Rim to Flagstaff. The tremendous increase of hummingbird feeders during the past two decades at summer homes, campgrounds, and forested residential areas within this region may help support the increase spread of these large, impressive hummingbirds.

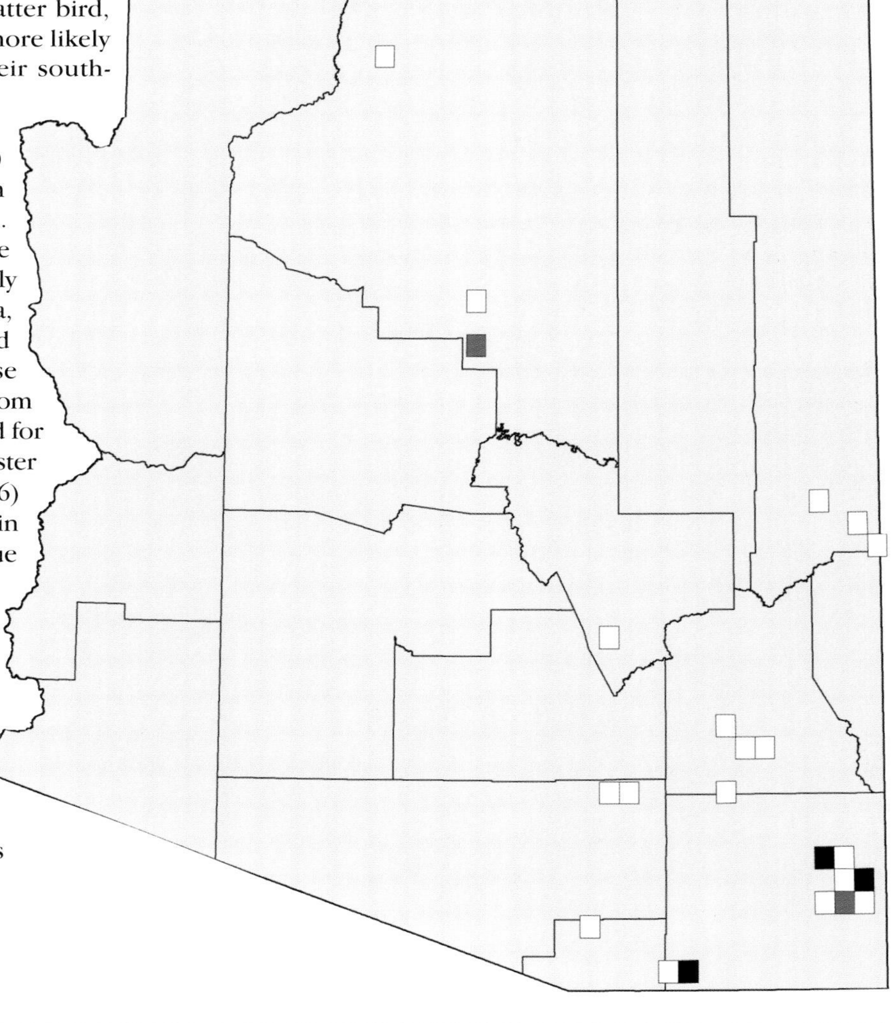

Magnificent Hummingbird Breeding Evidence Reported in 10 (<1%) of 1834 priority blocks

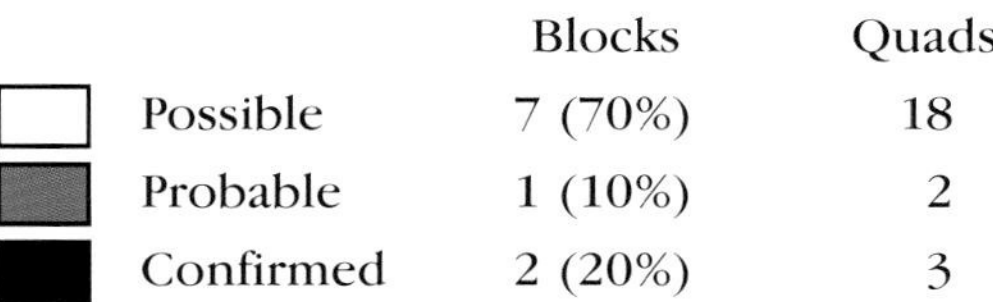

	Blocks	Quads
Possible	7 (70%)	18
Probable	1 (10%)	2
Confirmed	2 (20%)	3

Lucifer Hummingbird

by Troy E. Corman *Calothorax lucifer*

The distinctly curved bill and long narrow tail of the little Lucifer Hummingbird are unique traits separating it from other hummingbirds in Arizona. Much to the delight of local residents and visiting birders, this showy sprite is becoming a more frequent visitor to several southeastern Arizona feeding stations.

HABITAT

Unlike most hummingbirds in Arizona, Lucifer Hummingbirds prefer open, arid landscapes, especially those with scattered flowering plants such as agave, yucca, ocotillo, penstemon, and paintbrush. Occupied nesting habitats in the state often consist of dry brushy to sparsely vegetated rocky canyon slopes, foothill washes, and dryer woodland edges. Most atlas observations of these sparsely distributed hummingbirds were in or near open arid washes containing scattered netleaf hackberry, velvet mesquite, hopbush, and catclaw acacia. Lucifer Hummingbirds were found almost as frequently on the adjacent rocky slopes with scattered patches of various grasses, agave, yucca, sotol, beargrass, ocotillo, and cholla. Several records were noted from the edges of intermittent drainages with small stands of Fremont cottonwood with scattered mesquite, hackberry, and other arid shrubs. This hummingbird was also reported in mountain foothills with scattered Madrean evergreen oaks, although most of these records were from feeders. Lucifer Hummingbirds do visit feeding station in drainages dominated by Arizona sycamore or in Madrean evergreen oak and pine-oak forests at slightly higher elevations. However, many of these observations occur later in the summer and may pertain to postbreeding individuals.

BREEDING

A very sparse visitant and even rarer breeder in Arizona, some Lucifer Hummingbirds begin to arrive in late March or early April. T. Parker reported his discovery of a Lucifer Hummingbird nest in Guadalupe Canyon on 20 May 1973 (Monson and Phillips 1981). This remained the only nesting report for Arizona before the atlas period. Observations of Lucifer Hummingbirds continued to increase throughout the atlas period and four nests were reported. The earliest nest with eggs discovered during the atlas period was on 27 April 1997 in Chino Canyon, Santa Rita Mountains. Atlasers found a nest with young in Portal, Chiricahua Mountains on 25 May 1994. Occupied nests were also found in the Mule Mountains near Bisbee in 1999 and on 26 June 1999 near Leslie Canyon, Swisshelm Mountains. The latter nest would suggest nesting activity continuing at least into early or mid-July. Late nesting records just west of Big Bend National Park in Texas include young fledging on 31 July and a nest with recently laid eggs on 2 August (Pulich and Pulich 1963). In Arizona, Lucifer Hummingbird observations increase at feeding stations in July and August, possibly owing to postbreeding dispersal of adults and juveniles, with some individuals remaining through much of September and casually to mid-October.

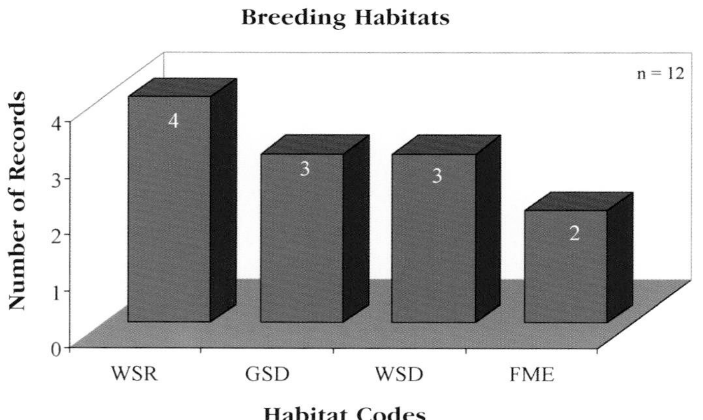

Female Lucifer Hummingbirds often construct their nest in fairly exposed locations on steep arid slopes of canyons and foothills from 1.6 to 9.8 ft (0.5–3 m) above the ground (Pulich and Pulich 1963; Scott 1994). In Arizona, nests have been found in netleaf hackberry, desert hackberry, and Arizona sycamore. In Arroyo Cajon Bonito in extreme northwestern Sonora and less than 10 mi (16 km) from Arizona, they have also been found nesting in ash (Russell and Monson 1998). In Texas, Lucifer Hummingbirds frequently nest on dead agave stalks, cholla, and ocotillo (Scott 1994), which are all very prevalent within their preferred habitat in Arizona.

Possibly unique to Lucifer Hummingbirds is the male's frequent performance of elaborate courtship displays above the females while she sits on the nest, most frequently during the period of nest construction or egg laying (Scott 1994). This behavior has not been observed so consistently in other hummingbird species (Scott 1994).

As in other hummingbird species, incubation, nestling, and fledgling care phases are lengthy in Lucifer Hummingbird and total 7–8 weeks to complete (Scott 1994). Females incubate the 2-egg clutches from 15 to 16 days and feed the nestlings, which typically depart the nest in 20–23 days (Scott 1993). Female Lucifer Hummingbirds continues to care for the fledglings for an additional 2 to 3 weeks, which is sometimes combined with construction of a new nest and incubation of a second clutch (Scott 1993). In Texas, Scott (1994) noted that second clutches were typically produced only during years when nectar sources remain in good supply.

DISTRIBUTION AND STATUS

Lucifer Hummingbirds breed primarily on the arid plateau and mountain slopes of central and northern Mexico, barely entering the United States to breed in western Texas, southwestern New Mexico, and southeastern Arizona (Scott 1994). In southeastern Arizona, this hummingbird had gone from casual with only two historical records (Phillips et al. 1964) to rare, but becoming almost annual at specific location by the early 1970s (Monson and Phillips 1981). The first Arizona nest was found in Guadalupe Canyon in the extreme southeast in 1973 and observations and distribution increased to include the Chiricahua, Huachuca, and Santa Rita mountains, and once west to the Pajarito Mountains (Monson and Phillips 1981).

Throughout the atlas period, the distribution and annual observations of Lucifer Hummingbirds continued to increase steadily in southeastern Arizona. Atlasers confirmed this species nesting at elevations from 3800 ft (1158 m) in Chino Canyon to just over 5000 ft (1524 m) near Bisbee. Lucifer Hummingbirds were also reported regularly as high as 5800 ft (1768 m) at feeding stations in the Huachuca Mountains. The most northern record was an individual observed by atlasers in the Peloncillo Mountain foothills near the Greenlee and Cochise county borders. These small hummingbirds were also observed in several locations in the Mule Mountains, French Joe Canyon in the Whetstone Mountains, and west to Brown Canyon in the Baboquivari Mountains. Lucifer Hummingbirds are regularly observed locally at feeding stations near Sonoita during the spring and summer and recently in Patagonia.

Like several other typically Mexican species of hummingbirds that historically were casual and irregularly recorded in southeastern Arizona, Lucifer Hummingbirds have recently become regular visitors at several locations and more nesting records are expected. Although the arid foothill slopes preferred by the Lucifer Hummingbird are not in short supply in southeastern Arizona, relatively few individuals are observed away from established feeding stations. This may in part reflect the reluctance of most observers to spend any amount of time in such rugged and often inhospitable habitat, especially during this hummingbird's summer nesting period. With closer scrutiny, observers may find the little Lucifer Hummingbird to be a local, but much more regular and widespread nesting species in the state.

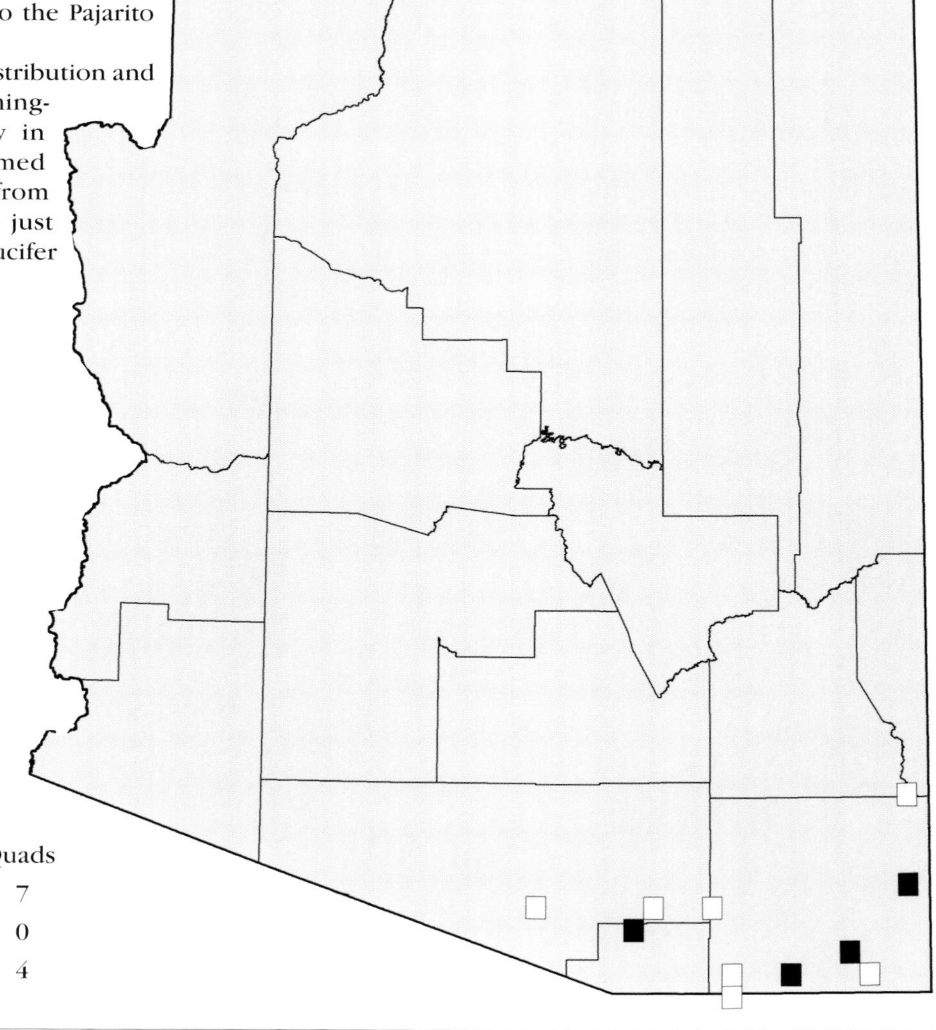

Lucifer Hummingbird Breeding Evidence Reported in 5 (<1%) of 1834 priority blocks

	Blocks	Quads
Possible	4 (80%)	7
Probable	0 (0%)	0
Confirmed	1 (20%)	4

Black-chinned Hummingbird

by Cathryn Wise-Gervais *Archilochus alexandri*

Black-chinned Hummingbirds are Arizona's most common and widespread hummingbird and are important pollinators statewide. Males perform dramatic courtship flights and have sparkling violet gorgets that can appear black in poor light. These birds often overwhelm feeding stations in southern Arizona, especially during late summer migration.

BRUCE TAUBERT

HABITAT

Black-chinned Hummingbirds are basically habitat generalists that breed in a variety of settings and generally only avoid landscapes consisting of dry open deserts and heavily forested high-elevation areas. Atlasers reported these hummingbirds in twenty-two habitat types, and 16 percent of records were from pinyon-juniper woodlands (n = 656). Researchers have found that Black-chinned Hummingbirds often prefer canyons or wooded drainages to other habitat types, particularly in the drier areas of the West (Baltosser and Russell 2000). In keeping with this, atlasers reported Black-chinned Hummingbirds in eight riparian habitats, and nearly 38 percent of the records were from cottonwood-willow-mesquite associations (including mesquite bosques), sycamore-dominated drainages, and in the more densely wood dry washes containing netleaf hackberry and mesquite. Black-chinned Hummingbirds were also common inhabitants of shaded backyards, gardens, parks, and other irrigated areas in residential and rural communities. In addition, Black-chinned Hummingbirds were found nesting regularly in such diverse habitats as disturbed riparian systems dominated by exotic tamarisk or Russian olive, Madrean evergreen oak woodlands, and even chaparral-covered slopes.

BREEDING

Male Black-chinned Hummingbirds typically arrive on their Arizona breeding grounds between early and late March, although at lower elevations these birds begin arriving in late February. Females arrive soon after and elaborate courtship activities quickly commence, often involving dive and shuttle displays. Atlasers first reported Black-chinned Hummingbirds engaging in courtship and territorial defense activities on 28 March, and observed nest building on 1 April. However, nest building has been noted as early as 21 March in Arizona (Baltosser and Russell 2000), and atlasers reported the earliest nest containing two eggs on 3 April. Atlas data reveal a peak nesting period for Black-chinned Hummingbirds from late April through late May, although nests with eggs were discovered as late as 27 July and nests with young through 10 August. The latest atlas confirmation was of an adult feeding a fledgling on 4 September, suggesting nests with young well into August. In Arizona lowlands, male Black-chinned Hummingbirds begin disappearing from their breeding grounds in early July, and at higher elevations, the males leave in late July to early August, weeks before the females and fledglings depart (Baltosser and Russell 2000). Southbound migration peaks in late August and early September, with a noticeable decline in Arizona by mid-September. Most Black-chinned Hummingbirds have departed the state by mid-October, with individuals occasionally lingering at lowland feeders to early November.

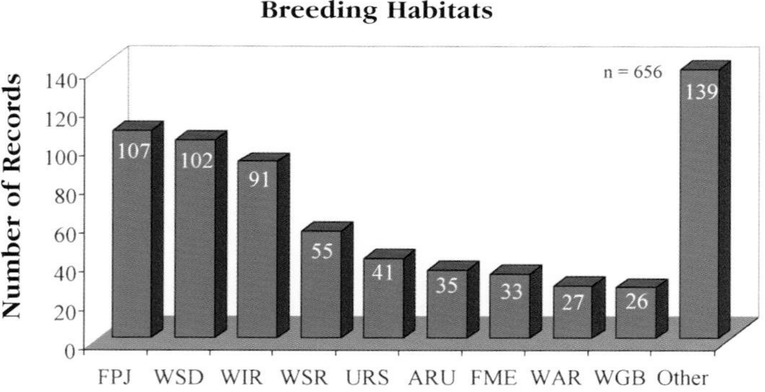

Female Black-chinned Hummingbirds are not very particular in their nest site selection, and use a variety of plant species. Atlasers recorded measurements at 51 nests, in 23 tree or shrub species, although 60 percent of nests were discovered in various species of hackberry (13), junipers (8), evergreen oaks (6), and cottonwoods (4). Additional nests were found in sycamore, alder, willow, maple, and pinyon pine, as well as in exotic plants including tamarisk, Russian olive, and ornamental olive. These hummingbirds were also discovered nesting in relatively low shrubs such as seepwillow, arrowweed, and sumac. Nests were found from 3 to 23 ft (0.9–7 m) above the ground, with a median value of 7.4 ft (2.3 m).

Female Black-chinned Hummingbirds typically lay 2-egg clutches, and incubation takes 12–16 days (Baltosser

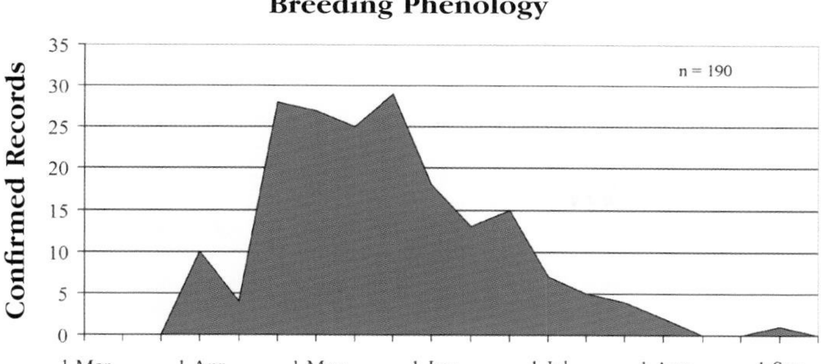

and Russell 2000). The young remain in the nest for approximately 21 days and do not return once they depart the nest, although the female will continue to feed the fledglings for one or more weeks (Baltosser and Russell 2000). Black-chinned Hummingbirds often produce 2 broods per season and commonly renest if earlier attempts fail (Baltosser and Russell 2000).

DISTRIBUTION AND STATUS

Black-chinned Hummingbirds breed through the interior of western North America from southern British Columbia south to central Mexico (Baltosser and Russell 2000). These hummingbirds also nest in California along the southern coastline and in the Central Valley. This species is considered the western counterpart of the Ruby-throated Hummingbird, and the breeding ranges of these two overlap only in central Texas. In Arizona, Black-chinned Hummingbirds are found nesting over a wide range of elevations, and atlasers reported the species from approximately 100 ft (30 m) within the lower Colorado River valley to nearly 7700 ft (2347 m) on dry, pinyon-juniper covered slopes.

Black-chinned Hummingbirds have always been considered a common summer resident in Arizona's deciduous woodlands at low to middle elevations (Swarth 1914; Phillips et al. 1964). Atlasers found these hummingbirds to be widespread in the southeast and northwest to central Arizona along drainages and woodlands below the Mogollon Rim. As earlier observers have noted, these hummingbirds were generally absent as a nesting species in the lowland Sonoran and Mojave deserts of the west and southwest away from wooded riparian areas or residential neighborhoods. However, preliminary data during the atlas period suggest that following wet winters, limited numbers of Black-chinned Hummingbirds may nest locally in deserts at isolated earthen tanks surrounded by dense stands of mesquite. They can also be found along large, heavily wooded washes following winters with above normal precipitation. These adaptable hummingbirds may take advantage of these periodically lush areas and the abundant early spring desert wildflowers.

Along the Colorado River within the Grand Canyon, Black-chinned Hummingbirds have increased thanks to tamarisk thickets that have become established since the construction of the Glen Canyon Dam (Brown 1992). These hummingbirds are now considered one of the most abundant breeding birds within the canyon (Brown et al. 1987). Elsewhere in northern Arizona, Black-chinned Hummingbirds also occurred regularly in most pinyon-juniper woodlands, although not as abundantly as they occur farther south.

The adaptable Black-chinned Hummingbird may gradually expand its breeding distribution in the state as agricultural lands, grasslands, and deserts are transformed to irrigated residential areas with an abundance of shade trees and available feeding stations. In residential areas, however, the slightly larger and more aggressive Anna's Hummingbird will also continue expanding urban populations, increasing competition at feeders.

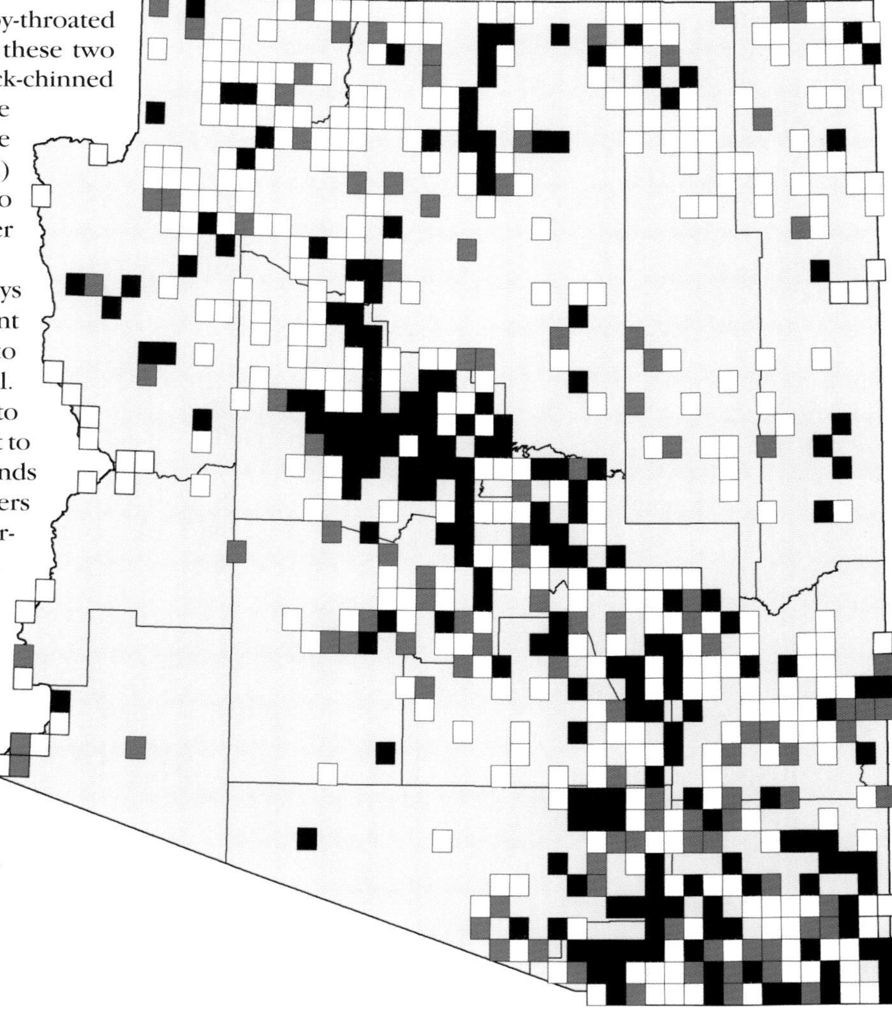

Black-chinned Hummingbird Breeding Evidence Reported in 612 (33%) of 1834 priority blocks

	Blocks	Quads
Possible	325 (53%)	349
Probable	101 (17%)	109
Confirmed	186 (30%)	201

Anna's Hummingbird

by Troy E. Corman *Calypte anna*

BRUCE TAUBERT

A feisty bully at the feeder, the adaptable Anna's Hummingbird has relatively only recently become resident in many Arizona desert towns and cities. Anna's Hummingbirds are much more vocal than other hummingbirds, and their high, squeaky songs are commonly heard throughout the year. Even the local Northern Mockingbirds now add it to their substantial repertoire.

HABITAT

Anna's Hummingbirds can be found breeding in a wide array of habitats in southern and central Arizona, although most nests are detected within riparian woodlands or among the shaded, exotic plantings of cities, towns, and smaller communities. Lowland drainages with cottonwood, willow, and mesquite woodlands, as well as sycamore-lined canyons and drainages accounted for 33 percent of all atlas records (n = 211). An additional 27 percent of Anna's Hummingbird records were reported from watered residential neighborhoods, often with an abundance of exotic shade trees, shrubs, flowers, and nectar feeders. Typically avoiding open desert landscapes for nesting, these hummingbirds were reported infrequently in Sonoran Desert associations and generally only when adjacent to suburban or rural communities. In late spring and early summer, some Anna's Hummingbirds were found nesting at higher elevations on mountain slopes consisting of Madrean evergreen oak woodlands, and chaparral, or, locally, even in ponderosa pine–Gambel's oak forests.

BREEDING

The seasonal movement of Anna's Hummingbirds in Arizona is complex and not well understood. Some urban populations of Anna's Hummingbirds are resident, while an influx of nonbreeders arrives during mid- to late summer, including in mountain foothills and canyons. Wintering populations move into lowland towns, cities, and wooded riparian areas in the fall and migrate presumably west of Arizona in late winter to breed. To complicate the matter, during winters with above-average rainfall in southern Arizona, many "wintering" Anna's Hummingbirds apparently take advantage of the subsequent lush growth of desert forbs and wildflowers. During these infrequent wet winters, large numbers can be found nesting in riparian areas, including mesquite bosques and larger, heavily wooded dry washes.

Anna's Hummingbirds are one of the earliest breeding species in Arizona. Courtship can begin in fall with nests with eggs and young regularly noted in December, sometimes as early as mid-October. This is all well before (or after) most atlasing surveys were typically conducted. The first confirmed atlas records were of a female nest building on 7 January followed by an adult feeding a fledgling on 22 February. Atlas data suggest peak nesting activity from mid-March through mid-May. However, this could reflect the fact that atlas survey activity was concentration during this period and many winter nesting records were undoubtedly missed. Atlasers reported nests with young as late as 30 June and an adult feeding a fledgling through 22 July. Several early August nesting reports were obtained, although additional Arizona nesting evidence in late summer is needed, for these few may pertain to misidentified hummingbirds.

Atlas field crews measured the height of seven Anna's Hummingbird nests that ranged from 8.2 to 25.6 ft (2.5–7.8 m); however, some urban nests in Phoenix have been discovered more than 50 ft (15.2 m) high in eucalyptus and Aleppo pine. Atlasers found nests in many different trees including velvet mesquite, alligator juniper, Arizona sycamore, Fremont cottonwood, ponderosa pine, and many urban exotic trees and shrubs.

Typical Anna's Hummingbirds clutches consist of 2 eggs, which are sometimes laid prior to completion of nest construction (Russell 1996). The female incubates the eggs

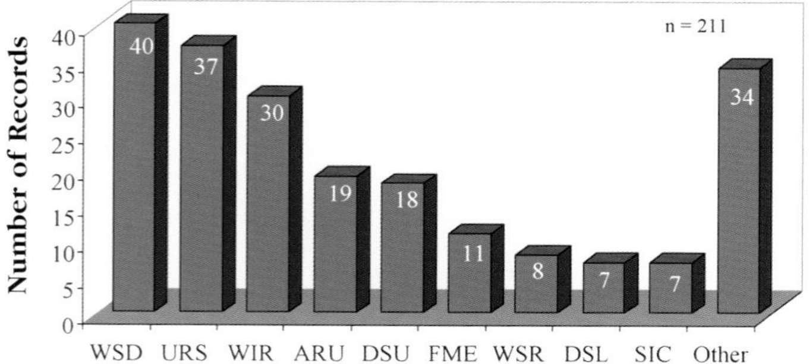

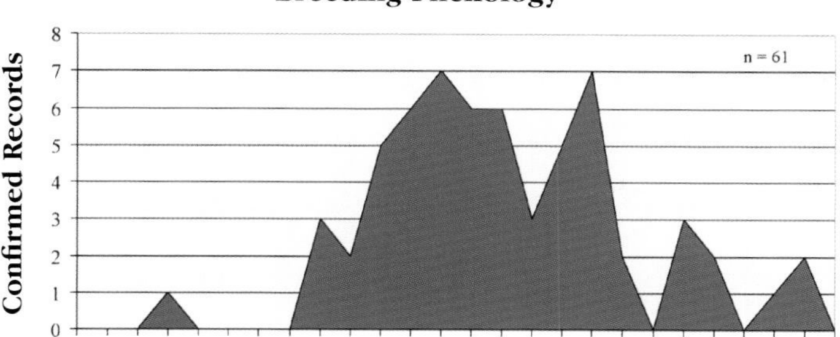

for 14 to 19 days (Russell 1996) and the young fledge in 23–26 days (Kelly 1955; Maender et al. 1996). A minimum of two broods are raised per season, with the female often starting construction of the second nest while still feeding fledglings (Maender et al. 1996). Several nests monitored in Tucson revealed the first eggs of the second clutch were laid only 5–6 days after the first brood had fledged (Maender et al. 1996).

DISTRIBUTION AND STATUS

Historically only breeding in California and northern Baja California, Anna's Hummingbirds now nest north to southwestern British Columbia and east into southern Arizona. The distribution and status of Anna's Hummingbirds in Arizona has changes considerably within the past forty years. Before 1960, this hummingbird was considered primarily only a fall and winter visitor in small numbers to southern Arizona (Phillips et al. 1964). The first documented nesting in the state was in Yuma in March 1962. As towns and cities with their exotic plantings grew, so did the nesting populations of Anna's Hummingbirds. These birds were found nesting in Phoenix by 1964 (Witzeman et al. 1997) and as far up the Colorado River as the Bill Williams River by 1977 (Rosenberg et al. 1991). Some populations were thought to be resident in Arizona by 1971; however, there were still apparently no records east of Tucson and the Huachuca Mountains between late December and late August (Monson and Phillips 1981). Atlasers discovered Anna's Hummingbirds nesting at elevations from approximately 100 ft (31 m) near Yuma to 6400 ft (1951 m) in the Pinal Mountains.

The combination of extensive nonnative plantings and widespread use of nectar feeders has undoubtedly played a major role in expanding populations of Anna's Hummingbirds (Russell 1996). These birds are now common residents in Phoenix and Tucson, where they compete with Black-chinned Hummingbirds. Atlasers noted Anna's Hummingbirds nesting most consistently in the Prescott region and in the Verde River valley as far upstream as Cottonwood and Clarkdale, and then south through the greater Phoenix and Tucson areas. Elsewhere in southeastern Arizona, Anna's Hummingbirds were found nesting in several locations in the Baboquivari Mountains, and locally east to Bisbee, Portal, and Safford. These hummingbirds were found in the lower Colorado River valley as far north as Bullhead City and at several localities within the lower Grand Canyon. Anna's Hummingbirds were also noted north to the base of the Mogollon Rim to Christopher Creek, Strawberry, and Sedona.

Some of the unconfirmed records noted on the accompanying map may pertain to nonbreeding visitors and migrants. However, there is still much to learn about the complexities of seasonal movements, migration, and breeding distribution of Anna's Hummingbirds in Arizona. As urban areas expand and more lowland riparian habitats are protected, the status and distribution of these adaptable birds will continue to adjust dynamically.

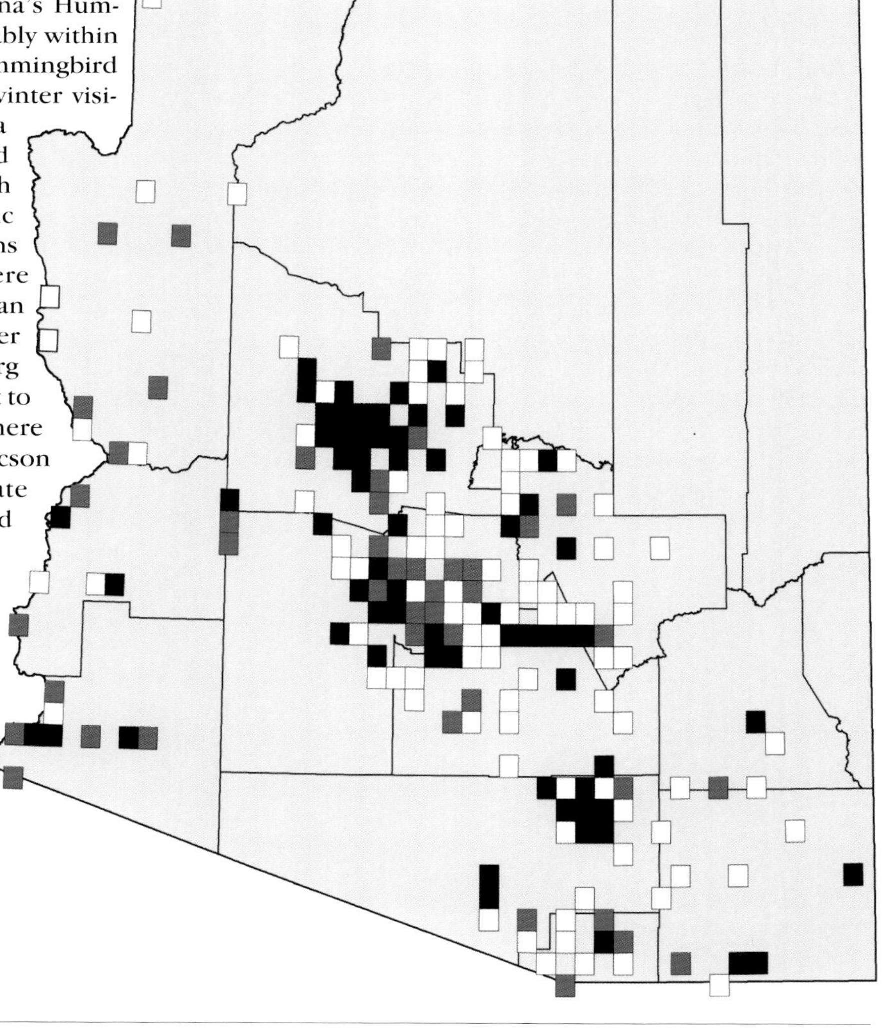

Anna's Hummingbird Breeding Evidence Reported in 181 (10%) of 1834 priority blocks

	Blocks	Quads
Possible	82 (45%)	94
Probable	40 (22%)	43
Confirmed	59 (33%)	65

Costa's Hummingbird

by Troy E. Corman *Calypte costae*

When chuparosa begins to bloom in early winter, male Costa's Hummingbirds initiate their desert nesting season with high, shrill whistles and elaborate, circular courtship displays. By late spring, when the relentless desert sun has shriveled their nectar resources, most of these hummingbirds have left for unknown destinations.

BRUCE TAUBERT

HABITAT

Costa's Hummingbirds are Arizona's smallest breeding birds, which nest primarily in Sonoran and Mojave desertscrub associations where they prefer dry washes, canyons, and rocky slopes. Approximately 33 percent of all atlas records were reported from well-vegetated Sonoran Desert uplands, with only 13 percent noted from the more arid, sparsely vegetated Sonoran Desert lowlands (n = 595). Desert washes are especially favored for nesting and accounted for an additional 30 percent of Costa's Hummingbirds records during the atlas. Trees, cacti, and shrubs in these occupied localities typically include several or most of the following species: paloverde, mesquite, ironwood, acacia, creosote, ocotillo, jojoba, and saguaro. Nesting areas are often associated where chuparosa, ocotillo, and other tubular flowering desert plants abound (Scott 1994). Many of the late season nesting records came from higher-elevation springs and intermittent foothill drainages where young scattered velvet ash, Fremont cottonwood, and even Arizona sycamore mixed with typical chaparral and desertscrub vegetation. During the nesting period, Costa's Hummingbirds infrequently venture far from desert habitats or at least desert landscaped neighborhoods. These hummingbirds generally avoid the lush, exotic plantings and irrigated urban life favored by Anna's and Black-chinned hummingbirds. Atlas data also reveal a general avoidance of extensive, irrigated agricultural lands.

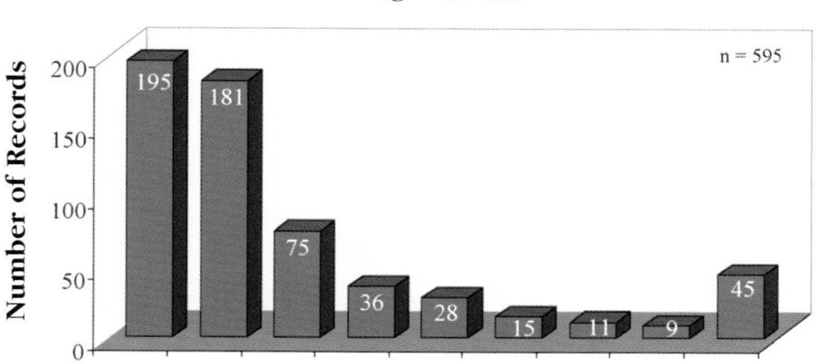

BREEDING

Even though some Costa's Hummingbirds are resident, most of the breeding populations begin to arrive in mid- to late October, with numbers building into early winter just prior to the Sonoran Desert bloom. In Arizona, nest construction can begin by mid-January. Atlas data suggest that egg laying usually begins in February, exceptionally as early as 20 January. Nesting activity peaks from mid-March to mid-April, although atlasers discovered nests with eggs as late as 9 June in Sonoran desertscrub. Clutches initiated after mid-April in Sonoran desertscrub likely pertain to second clutches (Baltosser and Scott 1996). Nesting activity drops considerably after mid-May with few nesting records into late June. Several early July atlas nesting records may pertain to misidentified hummingbirds. Most Costa's Hummingbirds have left the desert regions by late May, when some individuals were found nesting locally at slightly higher elevations on lower mountain slopes and along open canyon drainages. Some evidence also suggests that many Costa's Hummingbirds migrate west to summer or possibly nest again in chaparral and coastal scrub in California and northern Baja California.

Female Costa's Hummingbirds construct a loose, shallow nest, which in desert situations is in relatively open vegetation subject to much sun and heat, although January and February nests face the possibility of near-freezing temperatures at night (Baltosser and Scott 1996). Atlasers measured the height of 125 Costa's Hummingbird nests in 21 plant species and the average height was nearly 6 ft (1.8 m) above the ground with a range of 1.6–15.5 ft (0.5–4.7 m). An overwhelming 68 percent of the nests were placed in blue or foothill paloverdes. Other frequently used species include ironwood, jojoba, catclaw acacia, and canyon ragweed. Interestingly, only two nests were located in mesquite, and several late season nests were in Utah Juniper on an arid, brushy hillside with very scattered trees.

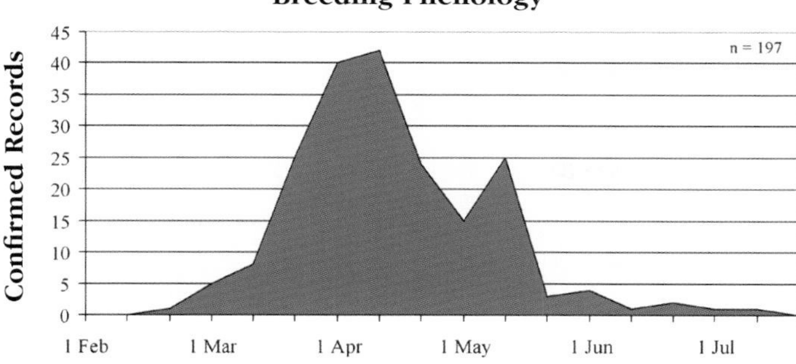

Equally surprising were two nests found on 20 May in young velvet ash where one of the nests with eggs was actually placed over a pool of water! This date and location would suggest the Black-chinned Hummingbird, were it not for the distinct dry ticking call of the attending female.

Female Costa's Hummingbirds incubate their typical 2-egg clutches for approximately 16 days, but this can range from 15 to 18 days (Baltosser and Scott 1996). Females tend the nestlings exclusively for 20 to 23 days and then at least for an additional week after fledging (Baltosser and Scott 1996). Replacement clutches following failure may be common, but true second clutches are rare or at least poorly documented (Baltosser and Scott 1996).

DISTRIBUTION AND STATUS

Costa's Hummingbirds breed from southern California, southern Nevada, and extreme southwestern Utah south through Sonora and Baja California. The easternmost nesting area is in extreme southwestern New Mexico. Costa's Hummingbirds have always been considered a common breeding species in the deserts of central and western Arizona (Swarth 1914; Phillips et al. 1964). Monson and Phillips (1981) noted that beginning in the mid-1970s, these hummingbirds were found nesting in Guadalupe Canyon in the extreme southeastern corner of the state. By the mid-1980s, Costa's Hummingbirds were also found regularly in early spring within the Grand Canyon in desertscrub just above the riparian zone at least as far upstream as Phantom Ranch (Brown et al. 1986).

Atlasers found Costa's Hummingbirds nesting at an approximate elevation of 100 ft (30 m) near Yuma to above 4700 ft (1433 m) on arid mountain foothills. However, during the summer, nonbreeding individuals have been noted at much higher elevations, such as a male above 7800 ft (2377 m) in the Santa Catalina Mountains (Monson and Phillips 1981). Atlasers found Costa's Hummingbirds to be most common in the Sonoran Desert regions of central and southwestern Arizona, especially following wet winters. These hummingbirds were less common in the Mojave Desert region in northwestern Arizona and sparser still in the southeast in Graham and Cochise Counties. During the atlas period, Costa's Hummingbirds were detected intermittently within the Grand Canyon as far upstream as Lees Ferry. Nesting is suspected but has not been documented within the Grand Canyon.

The greatest threats to Costa's Hummingbirds in Arizona are desert wildfires and urban sprawl. Introduced drought-resistant grass to the Sonoran Desert fuels fires that can eliminate native plants such as cacti and trees that are not fire-adapted. These wildfires often kill paloverde and other nesting trees over large areas (Baltosser and Scott 1996). Unlike Anna's, Costa's Hummingbirds have not embraced urban life in most areas such as Phoenix and Tucson, although many artificially watered, desert landscaped properties and feeders become locally important resources during drought years.

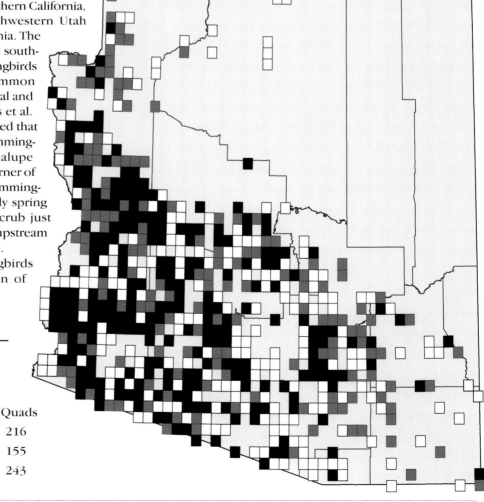

Costa's Hummingbird Breeding Evidence Reported in 595 (32%) of 1834 priority blocks

	Blocks	Quads
Possible	202 (34%)	216
Probable	154 (26%)	155
Confirmed	239 (40%)	243

Broad-tailed Hummingbird

by Bill Grossi and Troy E. Corman *Selasphorus platycercus*

Broad-tailed hummingbirds are the most common high-elevation breeding hummingbird in Arizona. These birds can be found at lower elevations during migration, when males are most often detected by their "wing trill." Produced during flight, this unique sound is the result of specialized flight feathers and makes the male's presence obvious.

HABITAT

Often detected foraging among patches of wildflowers along mountain streams or forest clearings, Broad-tailed Hummingbirds breed in coniferous forests and oak woodlands throughout eastern and northern Arizona. Atlasers reported 42 percent of all records in forests with ponderosa pine, including those with an understory of Gambel's oak or where the pines were scattered among pinyon-juniper woodlands (n = 309). These hummingbirds were also found nesting sparingly in taller and denser stands of pure pinyon pine–juniper, where approximately 16 percent of atlas records were reported. At higher elevations, 14 percent of Broad-tailed Hummingbirds atlas records were noted in mixed-conifer forests containing various pines, Douglas fir, white fir, and quaking aspen. Although relatively limited habitats in Arizona, these hummingbirds were common inhabitants of spruce-fir forests and montane meadows. Breeding records were also noted in a wide variety of upper elevation riparian habitats, especially those containing a mixture of pines, firs, oaks, maples, and sycamore. In southeastern Arizona, Broad-tailed Hummingbirds were commonly found in Madrean pine-oak forests and down nearby canyons of evergreen oak woodlands and sycamore, especially those containing feeding stations.

BREEDING

Spring migration for male Broad-tailed Hummingbirds begins early in southeastern Arizona deserts and foothills, with the first few individuals sometimes arriving by mid-February, especially following wet winters. Typical migration begins in March, peaks in April, with stragglers still passing through in early June. Atlasers first reported Broad-tailed Hummingbirds in appropriate breeding habitat by 2 April with territorial and courtship behavior by 15 April. Some early nest building can begin by late April in Arizona and atlasers discovered the first occupied nest by 27 April. Waser (1976) noted the breeding and nest initiation period for Broad-tailed Hummingbirds often coincides with peak flowering of nectar sources, which can vary between years by as much as two weeks based on weather and snowmelt (Calder and Calder 1992). Atlas data reveal Broad-tailed Hummingbird nesting activity increasing during late May and peaking in June to early July. Atlasers reported male Broad-tailed Hummingbirds engaging in courtship behavior through 17 July, although the latest nest with young was reported on 20 July and fledglings through 20 August. Adult males begin departing breeding areas in late July and early August, with few remaining in Arizona after early September (Calder and Calder 1992). Female and juvenile Broad-tailed Hummingbirds linger longer and can be found visiting feeding stations in southeastern Arizona through early to mid-October, rarely later.

Heat conservation is important for these tiny mountain birds. Female Broad-tailed Hummingbirds typically select nest sites with an overhanging branch or other natural structure (Calder 1973). Females construct most nests in 4–5 days, and nests have been reused in subsequent years by the original builder and successive breeders, suggesting a common criterion for site selection (Calder and Calder 1992). Nest heights vary greatly and the seven nests measured during the atlas ranged in height from 2.6 ft (0.8 m) in a Rocky Mountain maple to above 30 ft (9.2 m) in a Douglas fir. Other nest trees documented during the atlas included blue spruce, Engelmann spruce, ponderosa pine, and pinyon pine, although Arizona nests have also been

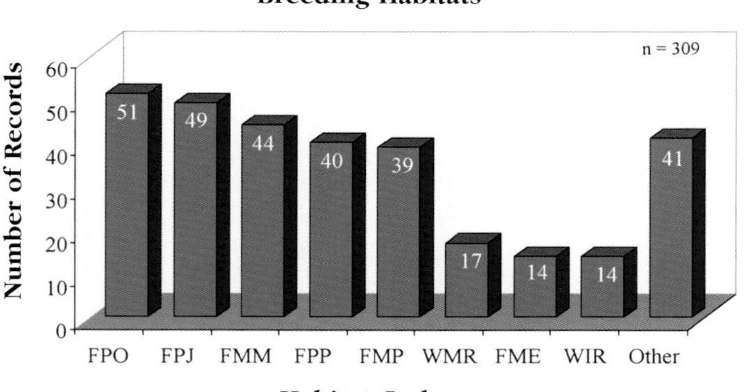

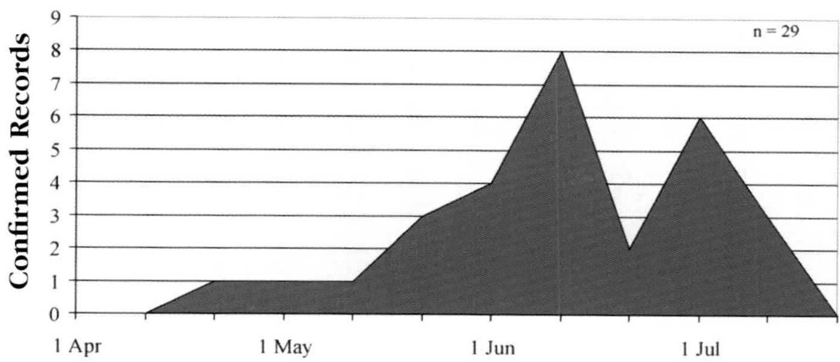

noted in quaking aspen, Gambel's oak, and various Madrean evergreen oaks.

As with other Arizona hummingbirds, the typical Broad-tailed clutch consist of 2 eggs, and all incubation is by the female for 16 to 19 days (Calder and Calder 1992). Fledgling stage is attained in 21–26 days (Ehrlich 1988). The period of fledgling dependency on females is unknown, but is assumed to be 1–2 weeks following nest departure, as with hummingbirds of similar size. It takes approximately 6 weeks from nest building to fledging, and only one nest per season is possible at higher elevations and northern localities (Calder and Calder 1992). However, two broods per season have been documented and are very likely with Arizona's lengthier nesting season.

DISTRIBUTION AND STATUS

Broad-tailed Hummingbirds are resident in the mountains from Guatemala to northern Mexico, and breeding populations are migratory north through the Rocky Mountains to southern Montana and west through forested regions of Nevada and east-central California (Calder and Calder 1992). These hardy hummingbirds have always been considered common summer residents of most forested mountains and plateaus in Arizona (Swarth 1914; Phillips et al. 1964).

The distinctive trilling wings of the male Broad-tailed Hummingbird allowed atlasers to detect this species on atlas blocks easily, although the nesting activity of the more reclusive female was infrequently observed. Atlasers documented these birds nesting at elevations from approximately 5200 to 9500 ft (1585–2896 m). Broad-tailed Hummingbirds were found nesting to over 10,700 ft (3261 m) in Colorado (Boyle 1998), and individuals undoubtedly nest to at least this elevation in the White Mountain and San Francisco Peaks regions of Arizona.

In southeastern Arizona, Broad-tailed Hummingbirds were noted in several infrequently visited ranges such as the Galiuro and Santa Teresa mountains and as far west as Kitt Peak in the Quinlan Mountains. These hummingbirds are common throughout the Mogollon Rim region, where they often overwhelm feeding stations from the White Mountains to the Flagstaff and Williams areas, then north to the Kaibab Plateau. With Broad-tailed Hummingbird atlas records practically encircling the White Mountain Apache tribal lands, there is little doubt that this species occurs throughout most of this unsurveyed region of the state. Atlasers confirmed this species nesting as far northwest as the Virgin Mountains in the Arizona Strip region and in the Hualapai Mountains, but were not detected in the smaller Cerbat Mountains northwest of Kingman.

Calder and Calder (1992) suggested the popularity of feeding stations, such as in the mountains of Arizona, may help maintain unnaturally large population of Broad-tailed Hummingbirds, especially in times of flower scarcity such as drought. Nesting activity may also begin earlier in the spring in areas were these "artificial nectar" sources abound.

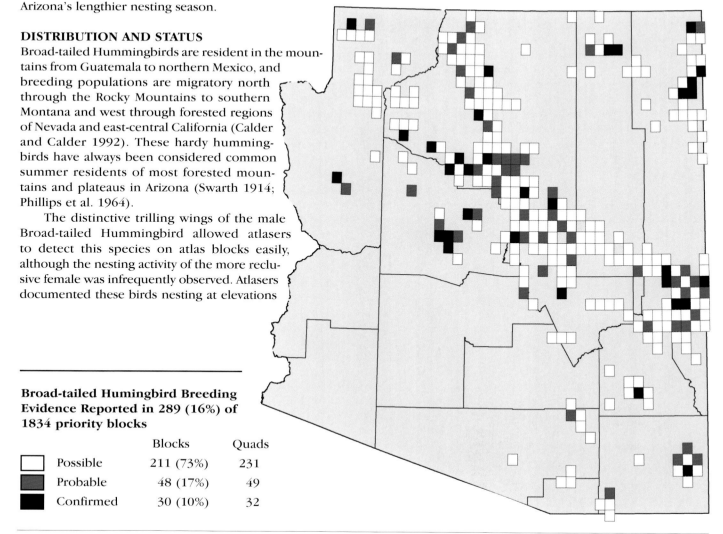

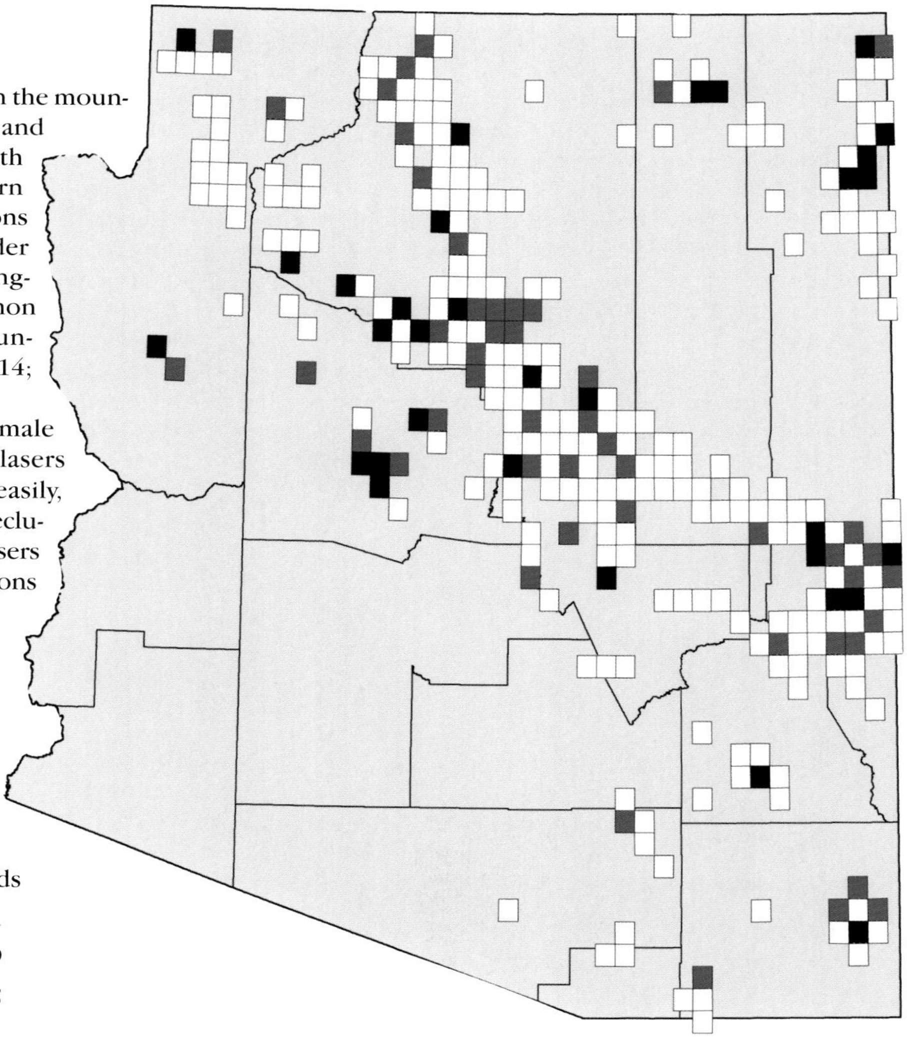

Broad-tailed Humingbird Breeding Evidence Reported in 289 (16%) of 1834 priority blocks

	Blocks	Quads
Possible	211 (73%)	231
Probable	48 (17%)	49
Confirmed	30 (10%)	32

Elegant Trogon

by Troy E. Corman *Trogon elegans*

Along sycamore-lined canyons in the mountains of southeastern Arizona, anticipation rapidly escalates for many visiting birders when they first hear the peculiar steady and repetitive call of the Elegant Trogon. An observer's first view of these showy, exotic-looking birds is a memory not soon forgotten.

BRUCE TAUBERT

HABITAT

Nesting in Mexico from tropical deciduous and arid thornscrub forest up to pine and pine-oak woodlands, Elegant Trogons narrow their preferences considerably in southeastern Arizona. Most nesting pairs inhabit forested mountain canyons were large sycamores merge with Madrean pine-oak woodlands. Approximately 70 percent of Elegant Trogon records during the atlas were from this habitat (n = 27) and typically included some or most of the following tree species: Arizona sycamore, various species of evergreen oaks, Apache pine, Chihuahuan pine, Douglas fir, alligator juniper, Arizona cypress, Arizona madrone, and bigtooth maple. However, a few occupied canyons at lower elevations such as in the Pajarito Mountains only contain sycamores, typically with slopes and side drainages dominated by scattered stands of evergreen oaks, pinyon pine, and juniper. These flashy birds nest most abundantly in canyons with perennial or intermittent water flow (Taylor 1980), although this is not a requirement and they have been found spending significantly more time foraging in the drier upland pine-oak than in riparian areas (Hall 1996). Atlasers noted the remaining Elegant Trogon atlas records from Madrean pine-oak forests lacking sycamores or from evergreen oak-dominated woodlands.

BREEDING

Most Elegant Trogons in Arizona are migratory and may be paired upon arrival on breeding grounds in early to mid-April, while others court and form bonds after arrival (Taylor 1994; Hall and Karubian 1996). Atlasers collected limited nesting data on this local species. However, these unique birds have been fairly intensively studies by others in Arizona, prior to and during the atlas period. The pair spends much time during April and early May in selecting a nesting cavity. Most eggs are laid in May and June, with later clutches, especially in July, likely pertaining to renesting efforts following earlier failed attempts. Hall and Karubian (1996) conducted surveys and monitored Elegant Trogon nests in the early part of the atlas period and noted nests with eggs from 11 May to 1 August. Nestlings were first noted on 2 June, although later nests still contained young as late as 20 August. Atlasers reported the first fledgling being fed by an adult on 19 June. Elegant Trogon family groups are often encountered into early September in Arizona, although numbers drop significantly after mid-September, with few remaining after October. A few individuals winter nearly annually in Arizona, often in riparian areas at slightly lower elevations.

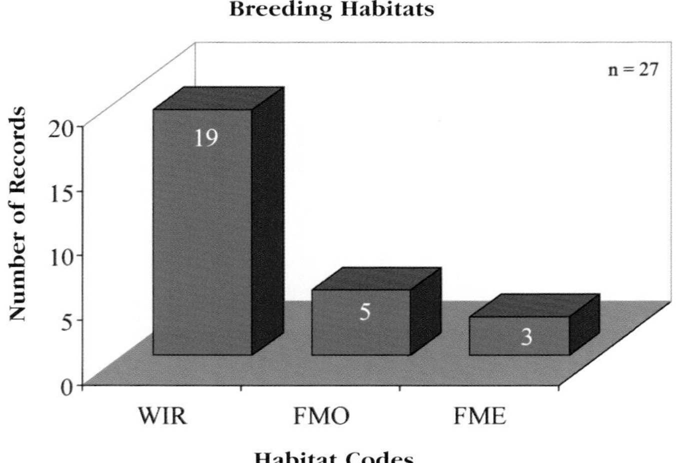

Elegant Trogons use secondary and natural cavities in both live and dead trees for nesting, with a high percentage of them using cavities previously constructed by Northern Flickers. The male initially selects the nest site and then may spend days or even weeks coaxing the finicky female in accepting the cavity (Hall and Karubian 1996). Sycamore cavities are by far the nest site of choice for Elegant Trogons in Arizona, but they have also nested in silverleaf and Arizona white oaks, as well as Apache, Chihuahuan, southwestern white, and ponderosa pines. From measurements taken from 21 nests by R. C. Taylor, nest cavity height averages 25 ft (7.5 m) with a range of 8–49 ft (2.4–14.9 m). Elegant Trogons do not construct a nest and lay their eggs on debris accumulated at the bottom of the cavity.

The typical Elegant Trogon clutch consists of 2–4 eggs (Bent 1940), with 2-egg clutches fairly frequent in Arizona (Taylor 1980). Both adults equally share the duty of incubation with an estimated average length of 19 days, but ranging from 17 to 21 days (Hall and Karubian 1996). Both parents brood nestlings the first week and feed the young through nest departure in 15–17 days after hatching (Hall and Karubian 1996). Elegant Trogon parents continue to feed fledglings for nearly a month (Kunzmann et al. 1998) and may split the brood, with each tending 1–2 different young (Taylor 1980; Kunzmann et al. 1998).

DISTRIBUTION AND STATUS

Primarily a tropical species, Elegant Trogons are only migratory in the most northern reaches of their range in southeastern Arizona and northern Sonora. The species is then basically resident south to Oaxaca, with some individuals descending to slightly lower elevations during the winter. Resident populations are also found from southeastern Guatemala south to northwestern Costa Rica.

Earlier records suggest that the distribution and numbers of Elegant Trogon in southeastern Arizona has steadily increased during the past century. First collected in Arizona by Lt. H. C. Benson in the Huachuca Mountains in 1885 (Bent 1940), the Elegant Trogon was also collected by Dr. Mearns in June 1892 on the eastside of the San Luis Mountains northeast of Sasabe (Bendire 1895). These trogons were not observed in the Santa Rita Mountains until 1918 (Bailey 1923) and spread to the Chiricahua Mountains after 1940 (Monson and Phillips 1981). Elegant Trogons were first discovered in Sycamore Canyon, Pajarito Mountains, in 1966, although these birds did not become regular there until 1972 (Monson and Phillips 1981). Russell and Monson (1998) noted that migratory populations of Elegant Trogons in northern Sonora and southeastern Arizona, infrequently reach the higher breeding density obtained in resident populations to the south.

In Arizona, Elegant Trogons nest locally and uncommonly between 3650 and 6300 ft (1113–1920 m), although they have also been observed foraging above 7000 ft (2134 m). Atlasers documented that these trogons continue to breed in select canyons of the Chiricahua, Huachuca, and Santa Rita mountains. Elegant Trogons were also confirmed nesting in Sycamore Canyon, Pajarito Mountains, and an atlaser discovered a pair nesting for the first time in nearby Peña Blanca Canyon as well. Elegant Trogons have not been documented nesting in the more arid Patagonia Mountains; however, atlasers discovered territorial calling males in late May and early July in two pine-oak drainages within this little explored mountain range.

Elegant Trogons are occasionally discovered in adjacent mountain ranges during migration and postbreeding dispersal, including the Baboquivari, Rincon, and Santa Catalina mountains. Northern extralimital records include Aravaipa Canyon northeast of Mammoth, Pinal County, and north of Carefree, Maricopa County (Witzeman et al. 1997).

Elegant Trogon populations in Arizona appear relatively stable or slightly increasing. The loss of sycamores and adjacent pine-oak woodlands to drawdown of water tables or catastrophic wildfires are of serious concern. Although Hall (1996) found the average distance to campgrounds, buildings, and trails did not vary significantly between successful and unsuccessful nests; local disturbance at nest sites by photographers and overzealous birders with tapes during the nesting period remains one of the greatest issues. Unfortunately, the public pressure for additional recreational opportunities in the Coronado National Forest, where nearly all U.S. nesting Elegant Trogons reside, has meant an increase in parking and other facilities to accommodate more people. Higher concentrations of hikers on trails through trogon territories during critical periods could lead to an increase in nest failures due to desertion at or before the incubation stage.

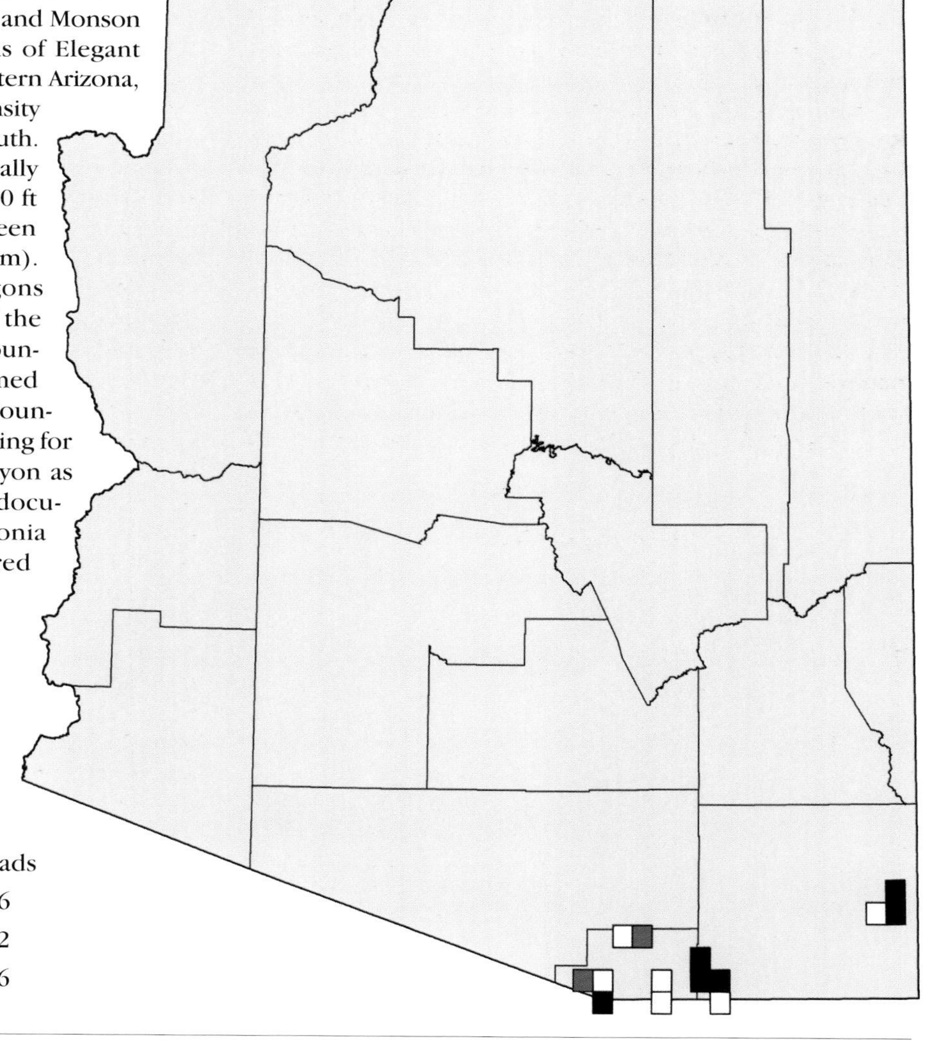

Elegant Trogon Breeding Evidence Reported in 6 (<1%) of 1834 priority blocks

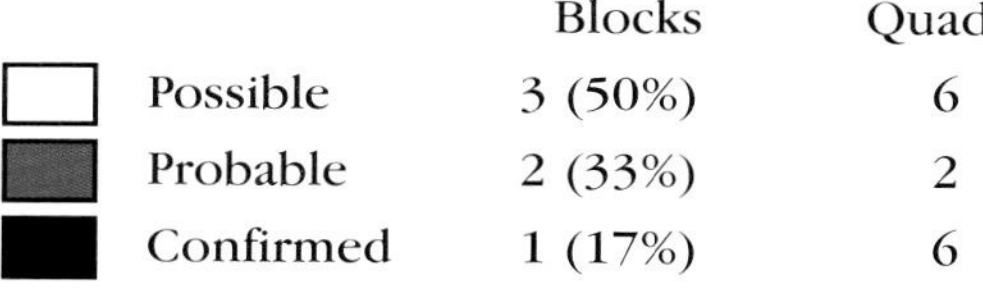

	Blocks	Quads
Possible	3 (50%)	6
Probable	2 (33%)	2
Confirmed	1 (17%)	6

Belted Kingfisher

by Troy E. Corman *Ceryle alcyon*

The loud and distinctive rattling call of Belted Kingfishers usually announces their presence along lakes and perennial drainages, well before they are actually observed. Territories of these alert birds usually contain several favorite exposed perches from which they scan for aquatic prey and defend vigorously against would-be intruders.

RICK AND NORA BOWERS

HABITAT

In Arizona, Belted Kingfishers can be found along relatively clear, perennial sources of water where aquatic prey is in abundance. During the summer, these include lakes, ponds, rivers, creeks, and marshlands with at least some open water. These water sources can be found in a wide array of habitats, but the availability of suitable nesting sites and the clarity of nearby water bodies to allow for successful foraging are likely important factors determining their occurrence in an area (Hamas 1994). Most atlas records were obtained from middle- and high-elevation drainages, including 38 percent from montane mountain riparian areas containing scattered pines, firs, alder, willow, cottonwood, and other deciduous trees ($n = 47$). An additional 23 percent of Belted Kingfisher records were reported from drainages containing Arizona sycamore and 17 percent from cottonwood-willow–dominated drainages. These kingfishers typically avoid turbid waters and may temporarily vacate traditional foraging areas muddied by flooding and storm runoff. During migration and winter, Belted Kingfishers in Arizona can also be found along constructed aquatic habitats such as canals, urban ponds, stock tanks, fish hatcheries, irrigation ditches, and wastewater effluent channels.

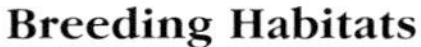

Breeding Habitats

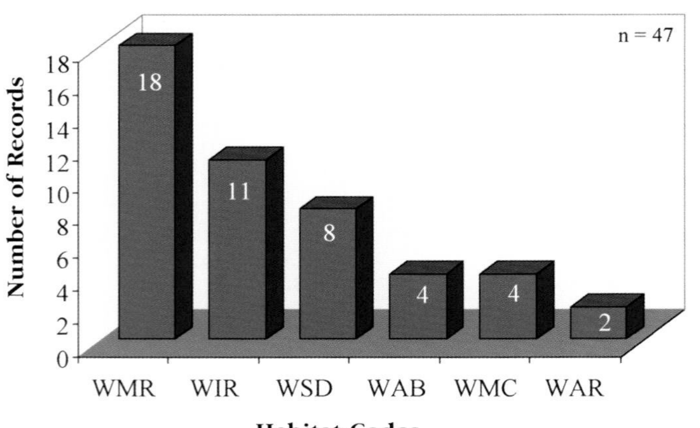

BREEDING

Some regions of Arizona are inhabited by Belted Kingfishers throughout the year, while the species is only a summer resident at higher elevations. Spring migration in the state begins in March or early April, with stragglers in northern regions through mid-May. Belted Kingfisher pairs may form in resident populations by late winter and nest site selection likely occurs during courtship (Hamas 1994). These birds can initiate nest construction at some locations in the state by March. In Arizona, a nest with young reported on 24 April would suggest that egg laying likely began by late March. Confirmed atlas records were too few to determine any peaks in nesting activity, although atlasers reported nests with young through 14 July and fledglings into early August. Later active nests may pertain to renesting efforts following failed earlier attempts. Belted Kingfishers in Arizona begin appearing away from nesting areas by late July and are widespread by the end of August and early September. The availability of unfrozen water with aquatic prey defines the northern winter distribution of these birds, and few remain after mid-November at higher and northeastern Arizona locations.

Belted Kingfishers typically nest near water in burrows that the pair excavates in earthen banks lacking much vegetation (Hamas 1994). In Arizona, these birds were also noted using road cuts away from water and one nest was in a natural red-rock cliff cavity. Nests are sometimes used in subsequent years (Hamas 1994). Burrows are usually constructed 14–25 in. (36–64 cm) below the top of the bank and typically range from approximately 3 to 8 ft (0.9–2.4 m) in length, rarely longer (Hamas 1994).

No nesting material is collected and the eggs are laid directly on the ground in a slightly larger chamber at the end of the burrow. Clutch size usually consists of 5–8 eggs, although reference to 11–14 eggs or young in a single nest (Bent 1940) suggests that two females may sometimes lay in the same nest (Hamas 1994). Both sexes incubate for 22 to 24 days (Bent 1940; Skutch 1945), with the females remaining in the burrow through the night and the male relieving her early in the morning (Hamas 1994). Fledglings depart from the burrow 27–29 days after hatching and are fed

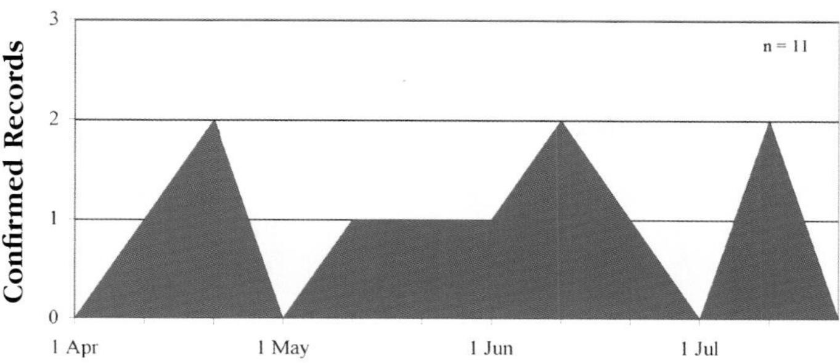

by the parents for an additional 3 weeks, though not regularly (Hamas 1994). There is little evidence to suggest that Belted Kingfishers produce more than one brood per year.

DISTRIBUTION AND STATUS

Belted Kingfishers breed through much of North America north of Mexico, but nesting much more locally in the arid southwest. Phillips et al. (1964) stated that although there were early July records of Belted Kingfishers near Lakeside in 1949 and at the confluence of Sycamore Creek and the Verde River in 1954, there was no good evidence of nesting in Arizona in the present century. However, Bendire (1895) reported that they nested in the 1890s in southern Arizona, and Rea (1983) noted that they likely nested along the Gila River near Komatke, Maricopa County, before 1929. In May 1980 a nest with young was discovered near Cottonwood (Monson and Phillips 1981), and Belted Kingfishers have been irregularly reported nesting in this region of the upper Verde River drainage ever since.

Atlas surveys concluded that nesting Belted Kingfishers are much more widespread along central Arizona drainages than previous records suggested. Atlasers revealed these kingfishers to be uncommon and local, but apparently increasing as a nesting species. Most records were obtained along the Verde, Black, and upper Little Colorado River drainages from Chino Valley and Prescott east to above and below the Mogollon Rim through the White Mountain region. Atlasers confirmed breeding at elevations between 3500 and 9000 ft (1067–2743 m) with midsummer records of individuals down to 2000 ft (610 m) on the Verde River. Probable breeding took place at lower than normal elevation at 1300 ft (396 m), when a pair was observed in late May and June 1993 along the Salt River above Granite Reef Dam. These kingfishers undoubtedly also breed along drainages in eastern Gila and southern Navajo counties within the White Mountain Apache tribal lands, where permission to conduct atlas surveys could not be obtained.

Breeding populations of Belted Kingfishers have apparently greatly increased in central Arizona during the past two decades, although earlier nesting efforts likely went undetected. These kingfishers are particularly sensitive to disturbance when nesting and may avoid habitats that are regularly frequented by humans (Hamas 1994). The unfortunate introduction of crayfish to most of Arizona's waterways may have actually contributed to the expanding nesting population of Belted Kingfishers in the state.

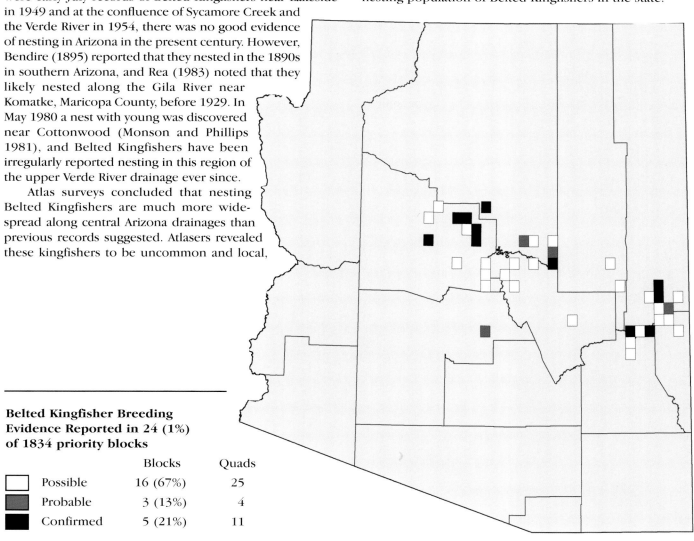

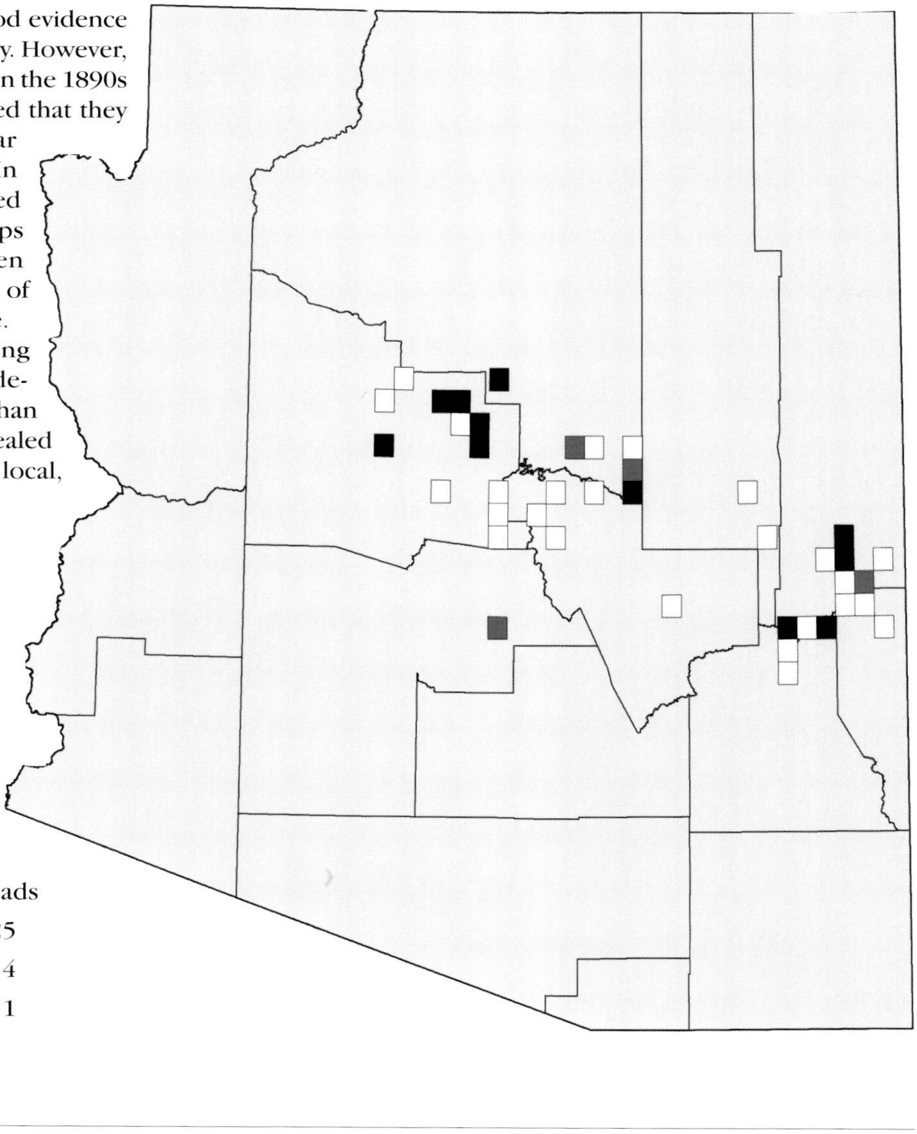

Belted Kingfisher Breeding Evidence Reported in 24 (1%) of 1834 priority blocks

	Blocks	Quads
Possible	16 (67%)	25
Probable	3 (13%)	4
Confirmed	5 (21%)	11

Green Kingfisher

by Troy E. Corman *Chlorocervle americana*

With its disproportionately large bill, the inconspicuous Green Kingfisher appears too delicately balanced as it frequently teeters forward on its preferred low perches. A series of dry "tick" notes along the edge of a wooded stream or pond often alerts the observer to the presence of this little emerald angler.

HABITAT

Green Kingfishers in Arizona frequent a variety of relatively shallow, clear aquatic habitats, which include the edges of perennial and intermittent stream pools, oxbows, ponds, and marshes. During the atlas period, nearly all Green Kingfisher observations were noted along lowland, floodplain drainages with riparian woodlands or less frequently along narrow foothill creeks. Vegetation typically consists of Fremont cottonwood, Goodding willow, seepwillow, and velvet mesquite, and only locally where Arizona sycamore and other deciduous trees merged with this habitat. Green Kingfishers often inhabit watered localities with little to no current that are heavily vegetated with low overhanging twigs and branches from which they can scan for aquatic prey below. Favorite foraging perches are typically within 6 ft (1.8 m) of the water surface (Oberholser 1974), and often much lower. Their primary fishing technique is a period of intense downward peering, followed by abrupt and almost vertical dives into the water (Russell and Monson 1998). Frequented perches also include exposed roots in cut banks or upon rocks, stumps, and other debris within the pond or drainage. When startled or traveling from one perch to another, Green Kingfishers frequently fly very low, often only inches above the water surface.

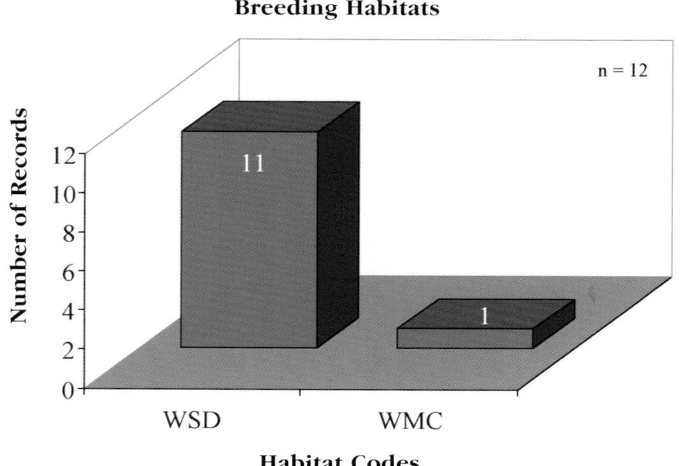

BREEDING

Green Kingfishers are primarily nonmigratory and defend foraging areas from others of their kind throughout the nonbreeding season. There is little information on the timing of pair formation, but nesting Green Kingfisher pairs defend territories along drainages, maintaining a good distance from other pairs (Kaufman 1996). Although a pair may normally forage along a 0.5 mi (0.8 km) or more of flowing water, some have been observed occupying no more than half that distance along productive streams in Sonora, Mexico (Russell and Monson 1998). Atlas data suggest that these little kingfishers nest between March and July in Arizona, with adults observed entering burrows as early as 18 March and as late as 1 June. The earliest fledglings reported during the atlas period, was an adult pair observed tending two young on 13 May. The latest confirmation reported by observers was adults feeding fledged young on 15 August, which would suggest nesting in July. There is little evidence to indicate more than one successful brood per year, therefore, June and July nesting records may pertain to renesting efforts following failed earlier attempts. Late summer nesting attempts in Arizona may not be as successful due to typically heavy seasonal rains during this period. The subsequent heavy monsoon runoff frequently swells drainages, with the potential of flooding some nests and increasing the difficulty in securing aquatic prey in the turbid waters.

Green Kingfisher pairs share the duties of constructing the 2–3 ft (0.6–1 m)-long nest burrow by using their two forward-facing, partially fused toes to move dirt behind as they excavate the tunnel with their sturdy bills (Moskoff 2002). Nest burrows are typically placed in vertical dirt banks, usually 5–8 ft (1.5-2.4 m) above a river or stream (Bent 1940). However, in Sonora, an active burrow was only 15 in. (38 cm) above the water surface (Russell and Monson 1998). Unlike with other North American kingfishers, overhanging vegetation or exposed roots often help conceal burrow entrances (Harrison 1979).

Usually 4–5 (range 3–6) white eggs are laid on the bare ground in a slightly enlarged chamber at the end of the burrow (Bent 1940). Both Green Kingfisher parents share the responsibility of incubation, which lasts 19–21 days (Gilliard 1958). The female incubates during the night and is periodically relieved by the male during the day (Moskoff 2002). The young leave the nesting burrow when they are 26–27 days old and are fed by the parents for up to 4 weeks following nest departure (Bent 1940). Skutch (1983) noted a juvenile was chased from its parents' territory 29 days after leaving the nest.

DISTRIBUTION AND STATUS

Green Kingfishers are resident from central Texas and southeastern Arizona south to northern Chile and central Argentina (American Ornithologists' Union 1998). Russell and Monson (1998) noted that this kingfisher was fairly common in southern Sonora and uncommon in the north. Historically, this species was considered primarily a casual to rare fall and winter visitor to southeastern Arizona north to Tucson and Benson (Phillips et al. 1964), with the first specimen secured along the upper San Pedro River near Fairbank in February 1910 (Willard 1910). Coues's (1866) reports of several Green Kingfishers seen in September 1865 along the Colorado River between Fort Mojave and Yuma have been questioned, although a male was reported at Topock Marsh in late March 1988 (Rosenberg et al. 1991). Monson and Phillips (1981) also later noted several spring and summer records in southeastern Arizona.

In the mid-1980s, observations of Green Kingfisher began to increase along the upper San Pedro River, including during the summer months. By July 1987, there was evidence of nesting, however the first confirmed breeding record in Arizona occurred on 3 June 1988 when a pair was observed repeatedly entering a bank cavity under a root tangle north of Hwy. 90. By 16 July, this pair was observed feeding at least two fledglings. Numbers of Green Kingfishers in southeastern Arizona continued to increase steadily through the early and mid-1990s. During this period, this kingfisher's status had been elevated to a rare to almost uncommon local resident on the upper San Pedro River south of Charleston and on the Santa Cruz River north of Nogales, as well as along Sonoita, Cienega, and Arivaca creeks. Green Kingfishers were confirmed nesting regularly during the atlas period only along the upper San Pedro River between Hereford and Charleston and irregularly along Sonoita Creek near Patagonia and below Patagonia Lake. Most nesting season observations of Green Kingfishers in Arizona have been found in a narrow elevation range from 3500 to 4300 ft (1067–1311 m).

After 1996, observations of Green Kingfisher in Arizona quickly began to decline, and very few individuals were being reported by the end of the atlas period. Explanations for such sudden declines are difficult to determine, but could be related to drought conditions that began to grip the southwest (including Sonora) during this period. Even without habitat loss or alteration, this species' distribution in the state may continue to expand and shrink, as is often the case for many species at the edge of their distributional limits (Krueper 1999). Maintaining breeding populations of Green Kingfishers in Arizona may therefore be difficult owing to these periodic range contractions. Reducing riparian and upland grazing to maintain and enhance cottonwood-willow regeneration, bank stability, and to decrease sediment load during runoff would greatly benefit this and other species (Latta et al. 1999). Similarly, reducing water diversions and groundwater withdrawal to maintain perennial stream flow would also help sustain prey abundance for these unique little kingfishers.

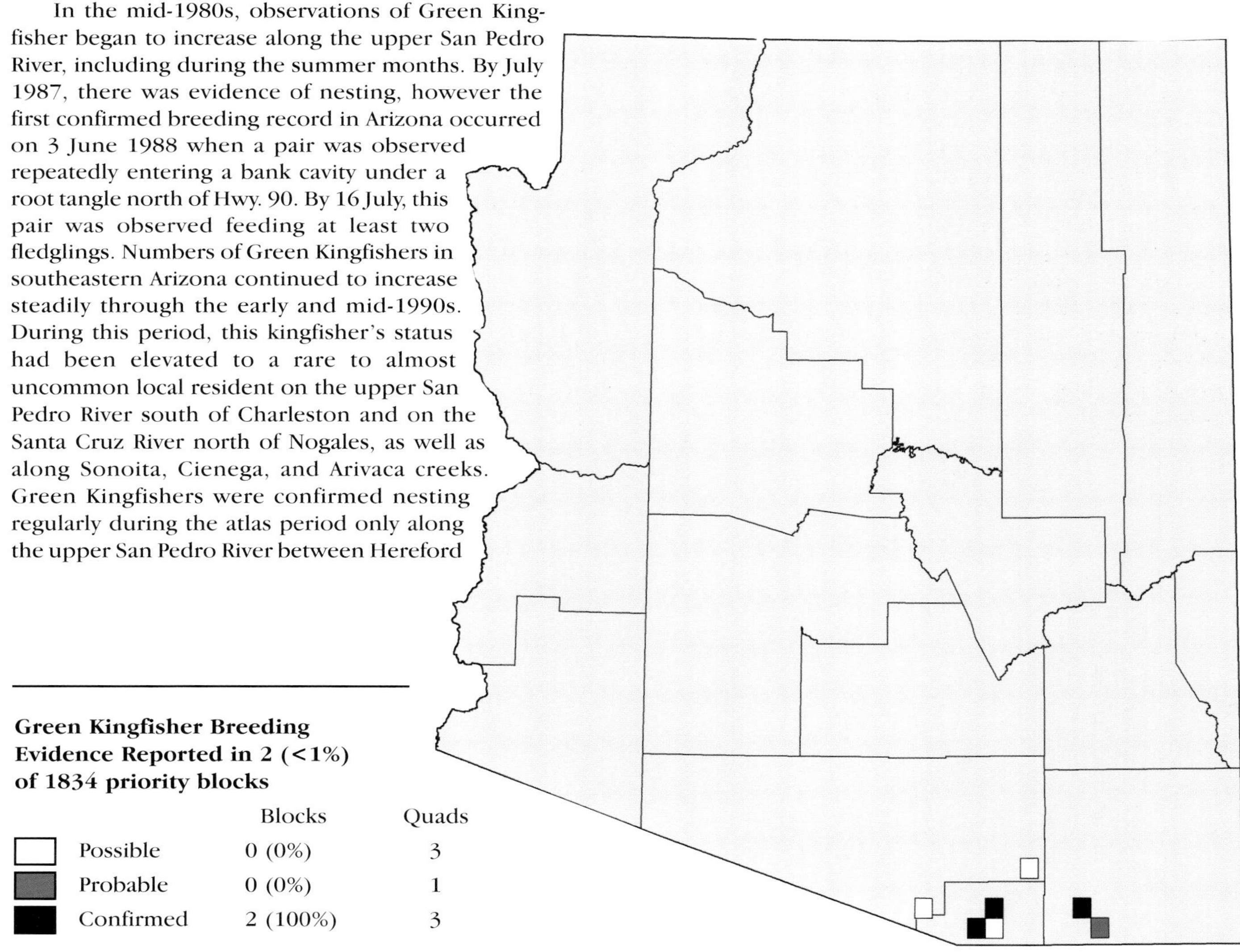

Green Kingfisher Breeding Evidence Reported in 2 (<1%) of 1834 priority blocks

	Blocks	Quads
Possible	0 (0%)	3
Probable	0 (0%)	1
Confirmed	2 (100%)	3

Lewis's Woodpecker

by Cathryn Wise-Gervais *Melanerpes lewis*

Unlike other Arizona woodpeckers, the unique Lewis's Woodpecker flies like a jay and often flycatches with surprising agility. Unmistakable owing to its pink belly and iridescent dark green upperparts, Lewis's Woodpecker eats primarily insects in the summer and shifts to a diet of acorns and other nuts in winter.

GARY ROSENBERG

HABITAT

In Arizona, nesting Lewis's Woodpeckers are closely associated with open ponderosa pine or riparian woodlands and seek out settings offering a brushy understory, open foraging areas, and snags for perching. These requirements are often met in recently burned forests, and Lewis's Woodpeckers are among a suite of birds known to thrive in these recovering landscapes. Atlasers obtained fifty-two potential breeding records for Lewis's Woodpeckers in fifteen habitat types. Of these, 50 percent were from primarily pure, open ponderosa pine forests and from ponderosa pine–Gambel's oak associations. Observers noted fewer Lewis's Woodpeckers in pinyon pine–juniper woodlands that had scattered ponderosa pine. These somewhat adaptable woodpeckers favor the open-pine-forest edge habitat often associated with some residential and smaller rural communities, and twelve of the atlas records were noted in such settings. Lewis's Woodpeckers in urban areas often visit fruit trees, especially apple, and are frequently observed flycatching from telephone poles. Atlasers also found these woodpeckers nesting locally among open cottonwood stands along lakes and drainages, as well as in aspen groves along mountain meadows.

Lewis's Woodpeckers disperse irregularly during the nonbreeding seasons. In Arizona, they can be found in native oaks and pinyon pines, as well as in lowland rural areas among stands of pecans and palms. Historically, they occasionally congregated in areas numbered into the hundreds (Phillips et al. 1964), but the size of these nomadic winter flocks in Arizona has declined significantly during the past century. Since the mid-1980s, such flocks have rarely exceeded 15–20 individuals.

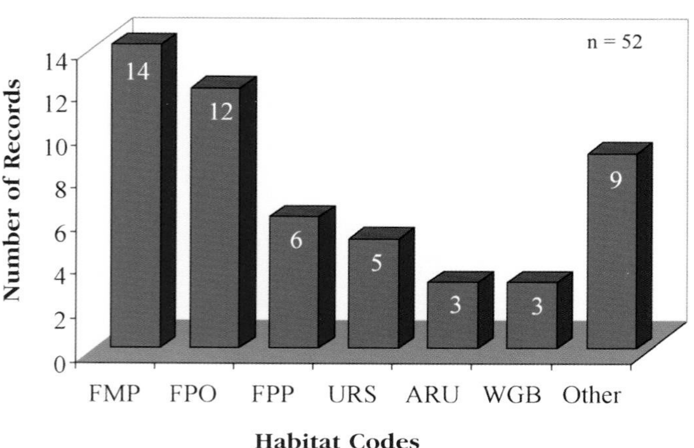

BREEDING

Many Lewis's Woodpeckers reside year-round on their Arizona breeding grounds, while others disperse irregularly and these individuals will linger in the lowlands to mid-April and occasionally into mid-May. There is some evidence to support long-term or permanent pairing for resident populations (Bock 1970). Atlasers first reported paired birds in suitable breeding habitat in late March and early April. The earliest confirmed record was an occupied nest on 9 May. Tobalske (1997) noted that some Lewis's Woodpeckers at the southern edge of their range and at lower elevations begin to lay and incubate in mid-April, with a peak in May. Atlasers obtained twenty-four confirmed breeding records for this species, including fledgling sightings. Although observers were unable to determine any Lewis's Woodpecker nests with eggs during the atlas period, they did locate five nests containing young from 12 June to 30 July. However, the first fledgling was noted on 20 June, indicating nest with young by mid- to late May. The latest confirmed breeding record was of adults feeding fledged young on 10 August. In Arizona, Lewis's Woodpeckers begin to appear away from nesting areas by early September, but most migrants arrive in October or November.

Lewis's Woodpeckers commonly nest in the abandoned nest holes constructed by other large woodpeckers or in natural cavities (Bock 1970). The pair may construct their own cavity, though, often in the trunk or sizable branch of large dead or dying trees (Tobalske 1997). These birds have a high degree of nest site fidelity and will return to the same cavity in subsequent years (Bock 1970). In Arizona, most nests have been discovered in ponderosa pines or cottonwoods. Observers took nest height measurements at only two active nests located during the atlas period; one of

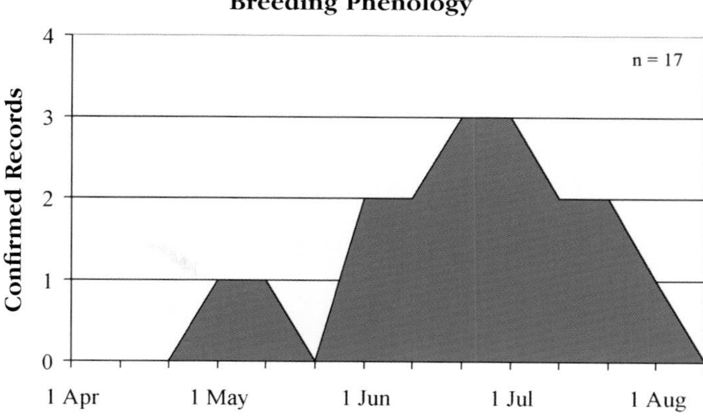

these was in a narrowleaf cottonwood at 25.3 ft (7.7 m) above the ground, and the second was in a quaking aspen at 19.7 ft (6 m).

Lewis's Woodpeckers typically lay 6–7 eggs (range 5–9; Bent 1939) and both sexes incubate these for approximately 12 to 16 days (Bock 1970). The pair both feed the nestlings insects almost exclusively, but only the male broods the young at night (Bock 1970). The young fledge at 28–34 days of age but remain around the nest and beg for food for at least 10 days following nest departure (Bock 1970). Lewis's Woodpeckers raise only one brood per season.

DISTRIBUTION AND STATUS

Lewis's Woodpeckers breed rather locally in the western United States from southwestern British Columbia and Montana south to central California, Arizona, and New Mexico. Atlasers reported Lewis's Woodpeckers, nesting from approximately 6200 to 8900 ft (1890–2713 m), and they obtained a possible breeding record at 5500 ft (1676 m) near Young in Gila County.

Most previous observers considered Lewis's Woodpeckers a fairly common, but local resident of open transition zone parks in the San Francisco Mountains area and in the forests surrounding Lakeside in the White Mountains (Phillips et al. 1964; Monson and Phillips 1981). Although these woodpeckers were described as more sparsely distributed north and east of these locations, Jacobs (1986) noted them as common at the southern edge of the Tunitcha Mountains near Tsaile and Wheatfield Lake on Navajo tribal lands. Atlasers found that Lewis's woodpeckers were more widespread in the northeast, with observations from the Chuska Mountains south to the Defiance Plateau and locally on Black Mesa. In addition, atlasers made a rather intriguing summer observation of a Lewis's Woodpecker pair near Ganado in open pinyon pine–juniper woodlands.

Atlasers were unable to locate these woodpeckers on the North Rim of the Grand Canyon or in the Mount Trumbull area where they had been noted nesting in the past (Brown et al. 1987). Observers did find Lewis's woodpeckers nesting near the South Rim of the Grand Canyon as well as south through the San Francisco Mountains region to near Happy Jack. Lewis's Woodpeckers were also regularly encountered in the White Mountains south to Hannagan Meadow and locally northwest along the Mogollon Rim to Heber. Lewis's Woodpeckers doubtlessly breed in adjacent portions of White Mountain Apache tribal lands, but atlasers were unable to conduct surveys on this reservation.

There is still much to learn about the breeding distribution of these unique woodpeckers in Arizona. Lewis's Woodpeckers can be almost common in one locality, but totally absent from neighboring open forests seemingly offering very similar habitat.

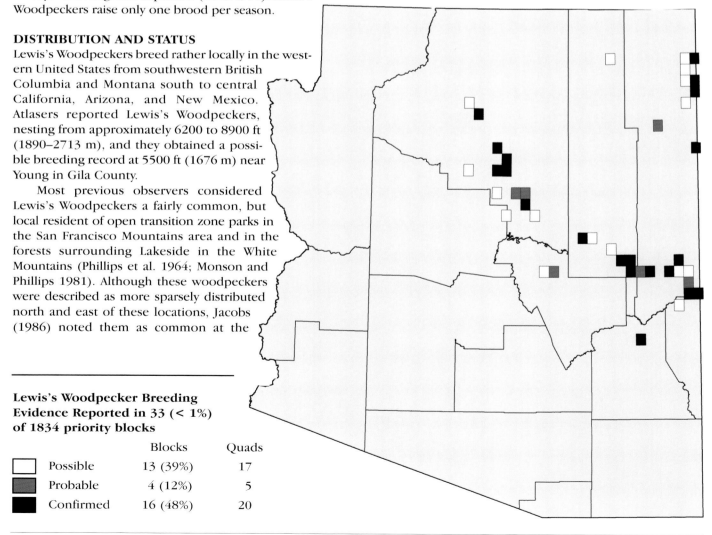

Lewis's Woodpecker Breeding Evidence Reported in 33 (< 1%) of 1834 priority blocks

	Blocks	Quads
Possible	13 (39%)	17
Probable	4 (12%)	5
Confirmed	16 (48%)	20

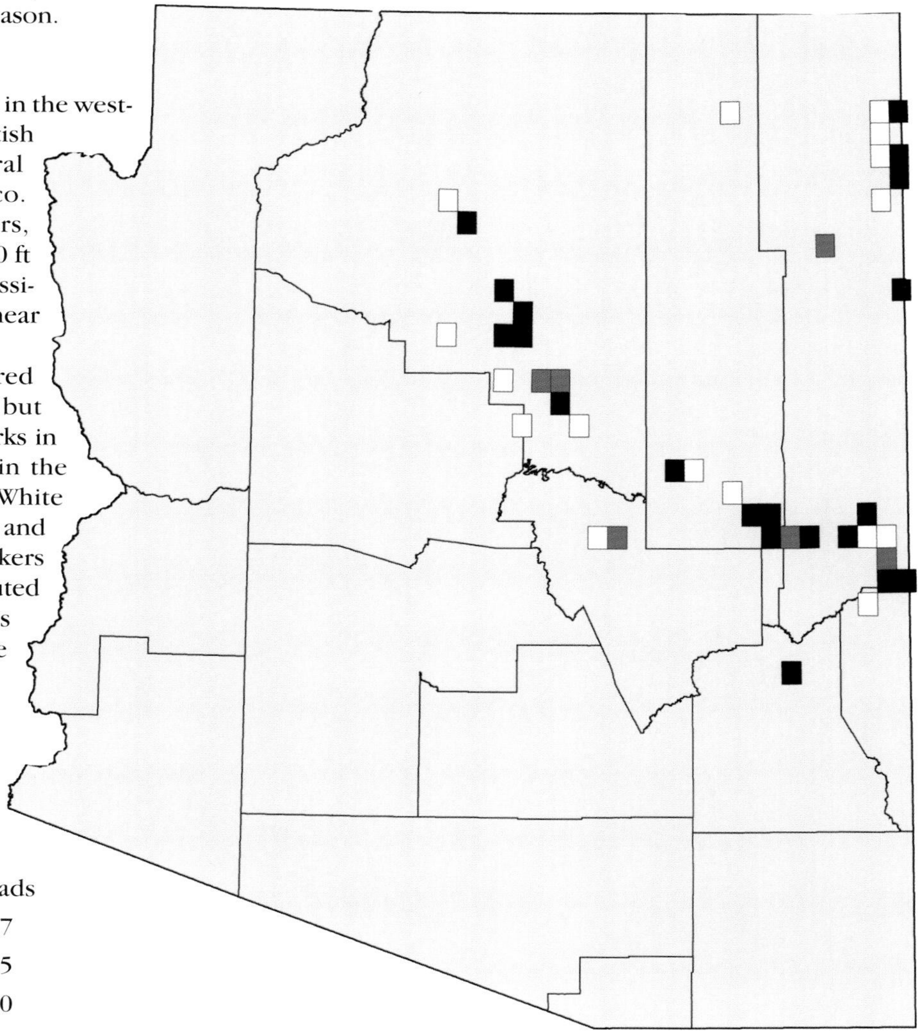

Acorn Woodpecker

by Cathryn Wise-Gervais *Melanerpes formicivorus*

JIM BURNS

The Acorn Woodpecker's clownlike appearance, raucous cries, and distinctive granary trees have long intrigued scientists and casual observers alike. Researchers once believed that acorns were stored as "insect larvae nurseries," but they now know that the larvae typically pupate and leave the dried acorn before the woodpeckers consume the nut.

HABITAT

As their name suggests, Acorn Woodpeckers are closely associated with oaks and typically occur in or near forests and woodlands containing these trees. Atlasers obtained 238 potential breeding records for this species and of these, 24 percent were in ponderosa pine–Gambel's oak associations. Approximately 32 percent of atlas records were evenly distributed between sycamore- and oak-dominated riparian corridors and in Madrean evergreen oak woodlands. Fewer Acorn Woodpecker records were obtained in primarily pure ponderosa pine forests or in pinyon-juniper woodlands containing scattered ponderosa pine. These woodpeckers were also noted in limited numbers in mixed conifer forests with firs, pines, aspen, and Gambel's oak statewide, and were common inhabitants of the Madrean pine-oak forests of southeastern Arizona. This gregarious species often perches and roosts in snags or in the outer dead branches of tall trees. These provide not only good hunting and resting spots, but acorn storage space as well. Although the preferred diet of these birds is comprised primarily of insects, the birds collect and store acorns zealously, often placing these in closely spaced, individually drilled holes.

BREEDING

Acorn Woodpeckers are Arizona residents but will wander irregularly during food shortages. These movements sometimes take individuals to lower deserts, occasionally even during the nesting season, and likely explain the summering pair noted in Tempe in 2000. In most populations, Acorn Woodpecker pairs remain together on their breeding territory throughout their lives (Koenig et al. 1995). Observers reported paired birds as early as 8 April and noted occupied nests by 13 April. As with most woodpeckers, the timing of egg laying is difficult to surmise, although backdating can help determine this. Atlasers noted adults feeding a fledgling by 16 May, indicating clutch initiation by early April. Atlas data reveal nests with young from mid-April through late July. Adults were observed feeding fledglings as late as 16 August, but atlas data suggest that the peak breeding period for Acorn Woodpeckers in Arizona is from mid-May through mid-July. Stacey and Bock (1978) reported that in Arizona, Acorn Woodpeckers typically delay breeding until late June and the onset of the monsoon season. Statewide atlas surveys suggest this might not be true of all populations and that more study is needed.

Acorn Woodpeckers exhibit a variety of mating systems throughout their range. These woodpeckers are generally cooperative breeders, and form groups consisting of 1–7 breeding males that compete for mating with 1–3 females that lay eggs in the same nest cavity (Koenig et al. 1995). Some populations are monogamous, however, and no evidence of joint nesting has been obtained in Arizona (Stacey and Bock 1978; Stacey and Ligon 1987).

Acorn Woodpeckers are not particular in nest site selection, and although they will occasionally nest in live trees, they usually excavate cavities in any snag or large dead limb available. Selected nest sites may be used repeatedly for many years and may or may not be placed in granaries (Koenig et al. 1995). In Arizona, the majority of nests are excavated in sycamore or various species of pines and oaks, although cottonwoods, ash, and power poles are commonly used locally. Heights of Acorn Woodpecker nest cavities are extremely variable and range between 6 and 59 ft (1.8–18 m)

Breeding Habitats

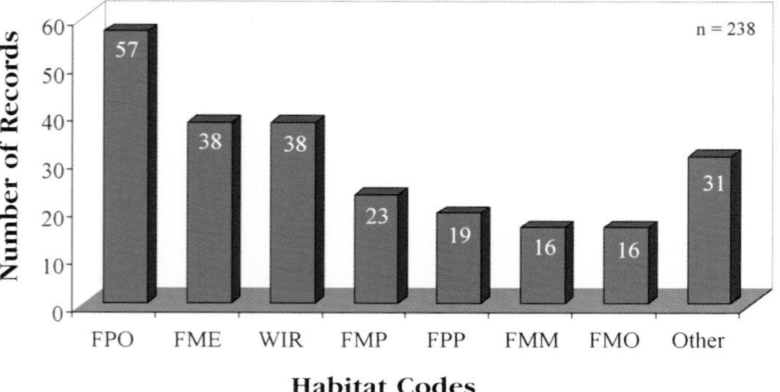

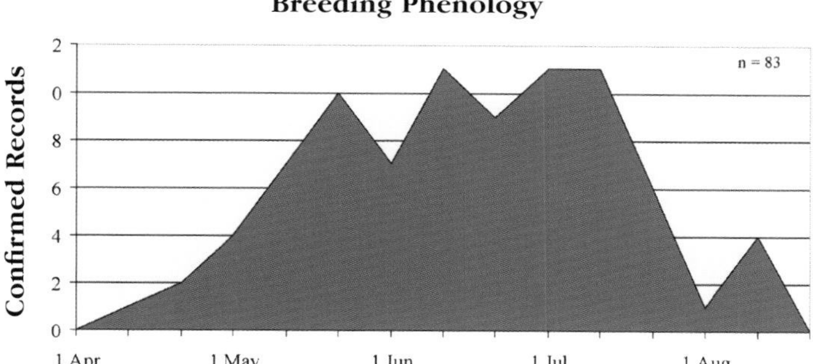

above the ground (Bent 1939; Koenig et al. 1995). During the atlas period, observers measured only three nests, one each in aspen, ponderosa pine, and Arizona sycamore. These nests ranged in height from 11.8 to 32.1 ft (3.6–9.8 m).

Acorn Woodpecker clutches typically consists of 5 eggs (range 3–7), but as many as 10 eggs have been found in multiple-female nests (Bent 1939). Incubation begins when the second to last egg is laid and both sexes incubate for 11 to 12 days (Baicich and Harrison 1997). Both sexes (or all adult group members in cooperative settings) brood and feed the chicks and fledging occurs at approximately 30–32 days after hatching (Koenig et al. 1995). Fledgling Acorn Woodpeckers may continue to be fed for 3 to 4 months after leaving the nest. Depending on the abundance of local food sources, the adults typically produce 1–2, and occasionally 3, broods per season (Koenig et al. 1995).

DISTRIBUTION AND STATUS

Acorn Woodpeckers are residents throughout their range, from Oregon south to Baja California, and from Arizona, southwestern Colorado, and New Mexico south through inland Mexico and locally to Columbia. Acorn Woodpeckers have always been considered common in oak woodlands throughout the state, but were noted as scarce or irregular in the extreme north and in the Baboquivari Mountains (Swarth 1914; Phillips et al. 1964). The birds occur in a wide variety of elevations, and in Arizona, atlasers confirmed Acorn Woodpeckers breeding from approximately 3800 to 8500 ft (1158–2591 m).

Atlas data reveal that these woodpeckers were most common and widespread in southeastern and central Arizona. Acorn Woodpeckers were regularly encountered within the entire Mogollon Rim region and the species undoubtedly occurs throughout much of the White Mountain Apache tribal lands based on atlas records that practically encircle this unsurveyed area. The species distribution continues northwest to Williams and Flagstaff. Populations were much more local west and north of Yavapai County, and atlasers encountered the birds in the Hualapai Mountains and eastern Hualapai tribal lands.

Brown et al. (1987) considered Acorn Woodpeckers rare to uncommon and possibly irregular residents in the Grand Canyon region. Atlasers documented local populations on both the South and North Rim of the Grand Canyon, as well as in the higher elevations of the Shivwits Plateau such as on Mount Dellenbaugh. Elsewhere in the Arizona Strip region, Acorn Woodpeckers were encountered near Mount Trumbull and Mount Logan.

During the atlas period, Acorn Woodpeckers were sparsely distributed on Navajo tribal lands on the Defiance Plateau and at the southern edge of the Chuska Mountains. However, Jacobs (1986) described them as a fairly common resident in the latter range. Acorn Woodpeckers are known to be good colonizers and now inhabit a chained pinyon-juniper woodland containing oaks and scattered ponderosa pines on northern Black Mesa (LaRue 1994).

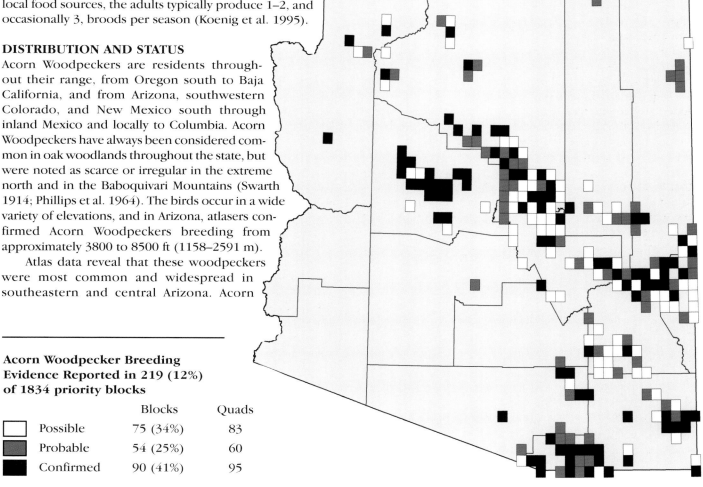

Acorn Woodpecker Breeding Evidence Reported in 219 (12%) of 1834 priority blocks

	Blocks	Quads
Possible	75 (34%)	83
Probable	54 (25%)	60
Confirmed	90 (41%)	95

Gila Woodpecker

by Bob Bradley *Melanerpes uropygialis*

Named for the river along which they were first discovered, Gila Woodpeckers are noisy denizens of the Sonoran Desert and adjacent habitats, and make their presence known to any intruder. Many desert residents owe their cozy cavity homes to these common and industrious woodpeckers.

BRUCE TAUBERT

HABITAT

Gila Woodpeckers are widespread inhabitants of Sonoran desertlands containing tall saguaros and are almost as common in the adjacent timbered drainages and residential shade trees. Obtaining their greatest abundance in Sonoran Desert uplands, observers reported 54 percent of Gila Woodpecker atlas records in areas with an abundance of saguaros, paloverde, mesquite, and ironwood (n = 661). Significantly fewer (12 percent) were noted in the more arid and sparsely vegetated Sonoran Desert lowlands, where saguaros are typically few or lacking. The higher density of larger trees along desert dry washes also attracts this species and accounted for an additional 7 percent of atlas records. Gila Woodpeckers are not restricted by the distribution of saguaros and are common nesters among lowland riparian woodlands dominated by Fremont cottonwood, Goodding willow, and mesquite. These woodpeckers are also found along lower mountain foothill drainages where Arizona sycamores intersperse with lowland riparian woodland trees. More adaptable than other desert woodpeckers, Gila Woodpeckers commonly nests among the exotic trees and isolated saguaros found in highly residential and rural settings.

BREEDING

Gila Woodpeckers are a resident species and can often be found in pairs throughout the year. Courtship and territoriality often escalates in mid-February with early nesting activity initiated by March. Atlasers reported the first occupied nest by 12 March, and early clutches must be laid during this period, based on the discovery of the first nest with young on 31 March. The earliest Gila Woodpecker fledgling was noted being fed by an adult on 21 April. Atlas data reveal a significant peak in nesting activity from mid-April to late May, with a steady decline thereafter. Gila Woodpeckers regularly produce two and sometimes three broods in the same nest per season (Gilman 1915; Phillips et al. 1964). Nests with young and occupied nests were reported through late July and adults were observed feeding fledged young as late as 16 August.

Both members of the pair help excavate the nest cavity (Bent 1939), and when available, saguaros are apparently the nesting substrate of choice for Gila Woodpeckers. During the atlas period thirty-eight nests were identified as to substrate, and 87 percent were noted in this tall cactus. Cavities excavated in saguaros are typically not used for several months to allow for the inner pulp of the cactus to form a solid casing around the cavity and must therefore be constructed outside the lengthy nesting season (Short 1982). The relative height of nest cavities in saguaros is inversely related to the cactus height and ranges from 12 to 35 ft (3.7–10.7 m) above the ground (Gilman 1915; Kerpez and Smith 1990).

Gila Woodpeckers use a wide array of trees when nesting in other habitats in Arizona. Cottonwood, willow, sycamore, and ash are commonly used for nesting in riparian woodlands. In urban and rural setting, these woodpeckers also construct nests in palms, eucalyptus, athel tamarisk, mulberry, and other exotic shade trees (Rosenberg et al. 1991). Mesquite is rarely used for nesting because of the difficulty in excavating cavities in its harder wood (Brush et al. 1983). In riparian woodlands, nests are often in tall snags or dead limbs and have been noted from 5 to 46 ft (1.5–14 m) above the ground (Gilman 1915; Rosenberg et al. 1991).

Breeding Habitats

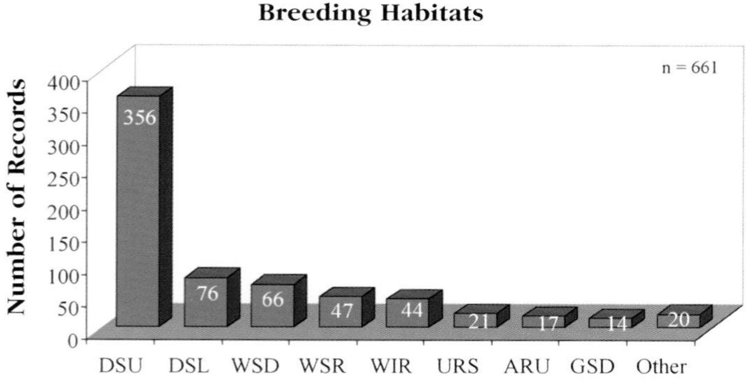

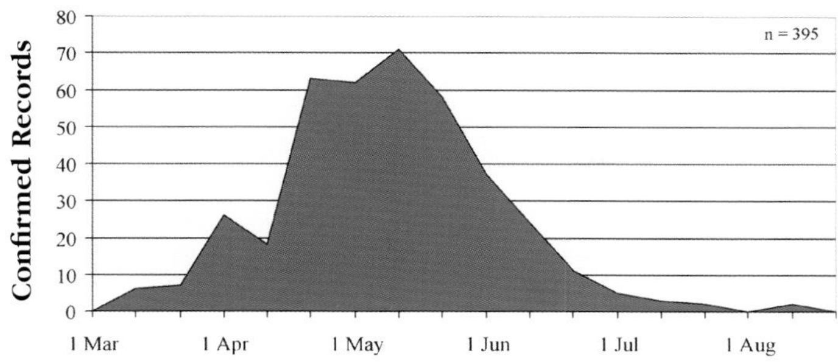

The typical clutch size for Gila Woodpeckers is 3–5 eggs but can range between 2 and 7 (Edwards and Schnell 2000). Incubation is shared by both parents (Hensley 1959), and it takes 12–14 days for the eggs to hatch (Bent 1939; Ehrlich et al 1988). The young fledge at approximately 4 weeks of age (Kaufman 1996), and the pair continues feeding fledglings for an unknown period after nest departure. Rosenberg et al. (1991) noted that family groups from the first brood often remain together as adults attend their second nest.

DISTRIBUTION AND STATUS

In the United States, Gila Woodpeckers occur primarily in the southern half of Arizona and range sparingly into extreme southeastern California, southern Nevada, and southwestern New Mexico. These woodpeckers also range south into Baja California and on the Pacific slope of Mexico to Jalisco and Aguascalientes (Howell and Webb 1995). Gila Woodpeckers have always been described as a common resident in the Lower Sonoran Zone of southern and western Arizona, north in the lower Colorado River valley to at least Fort Mojave (Swarth 1914; Phillips et al. 1964).

Atlasers reported Gila Woodpeckers at elevations from approximately 150 to 4800 ft (46–1463 m). These woodpeckers have apparently extended their distribution along several rivers and their tributaries during the past century, taking advantage of riparian deciduous woodlands. This includes the Verde River north to Clarkdale, lower Oak Creek Canyon, and up the Agua Fria River to near Mayer. This species was also detected in Chino Valley.

Rosenberg et al. (1991) considered Gila Woodpeckers to be locally common within the lower Colorado River valley where tall trees remain. Atlasers reported these woodpeckers as far north as Havasu National Wildlife Refuge near Topock Marsh. Elsewhere in northwestern Arizona, atlasers documented Gila Woodpeckers north to near Oatman and through the Big Sandy River drainage, including Trout Creek.

These woodpeckers were sparsely distributed and often missed on survey blocks in extensive agricultural areas, such as along sections of the middle and lower Gila River valley, as well as south of Parker. As noted by Phillips et al. (1964), Gila Woodpeckers were also much more locally distributed in Cochise, Graham, and Greenlee counties.

In or near urban and rural areas, Gila Woodpeckers are heavily victimized by European Starlings, which aggressively evict the woodpeckers from their nest cavities, sometimes removing the eggs, and thus causing the woodpecker to abandon the nest (Rosenberg et al. 1991). These woodpeckers are also threatened by loss of native habitat due to urban sprawl and increasing desert wildfires that often kill saguaros.

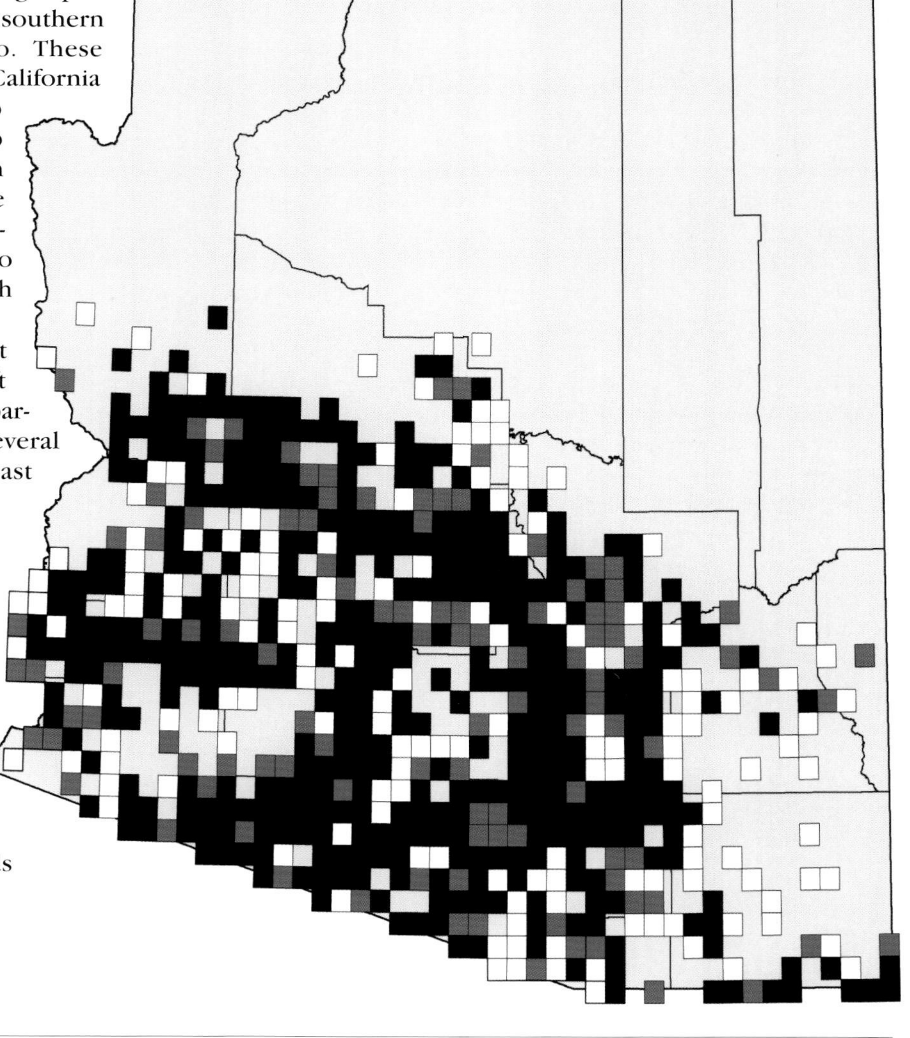

Gila Woodpecker Breeding Evidence Reported in 638 (35%) of 1834 priority blocks

	Blocks	Quads
Possible	145 (23%)	158
Probable	104 (16%)	107
Confirmed	389 (61%)	392

Williamson's Sapsucker

by Marjorie J. Latta and Troy E. Corman

Sphyrapicus thyroideus

The plumage dimorphism between the male and female Williamson's Sapsucker is so strikingly different, they were considered two distinct species for nearly twenty-five years following their discovery in the 1850s. This uniquely attractive woodpecker was named after Lieutenant Robert Stockton Williamson, an early railroad surveyor on the West Coast.

HABITAT

Throughout their breeding range, Williamson's Sapsuckers occupy coniferous forests, often with some deciduous-tree component, especially quaking aspen. Of the 67 atlas records, 52 percent were in cool, mixed conifer forests that often contain Douglas fir, white fir, limber pine, ponderosa pine, and quaking aspen. An additional 30 percent of atlas records were noted in primarily pure ponderosa pine or ponderosa pine–Gambel's oak forests. Although Conway and Martin (1993) considered these sapsuckers preferred cool, montane drainages over ridgetops on the Mogollon Rim, atlasers only reported five records from this habitat. Fewer records were obtained from pure aspen stands and higher-elevation spruce-fir forests, but this could pertain to the relative limited acreage of these habitats, compared to others forested habitats in Arizona. On basis of foraging preferences, Williamson's Sapsuckers tend to select sites in areas close to conifer-dominated forests with some aspens, while Red-naped Sapsuckers choose aspen-dominated areas (Smith 1982).

BREEDING

In central Arizona, some Williamson's Sapsuckers remain in or near nesting areas throughout the year, while other populations move south or to lower elevations. These woodpeckers begin arriving on their breeding territories by late February or March in Arizona. However, in southern Arizona, stragglers remain into April and occasionally into early May. Males arrive 1–2 weeks prior to the females, and nest cavity excavation begins within 3 weeks of the female's arrival (Short 1982). Atlasers noted nest with young on 4 May, suggesting the initiation of egg laying by mid- to late April. Of 148 Williamson's Sapsucker nests monitored on the Mogollon Rim, the first egg for the first clutch was laid from 27 April to 30 May with a median date of 14 May (Dobbs et al. 1997). The latest active nest discovered during the atlas was one with young on 8 July, suggesting a renesting attempt following earlier season nest failure. Atlas data reveal a peak breeding period from mid-June to early July. However, confirmed nesting records during the atlas were relatively few, and this peak may more closely reflect when most atlasing efforts were conducted in this woodpecker's preferred habitat. In Arizona, postbreeding dispersal of Williamson's Sapsuckers to adjacent lower elevation habitats, such as riparian areas and pinyon pine–juniper woodlands, can begin by mid- to late July. Early migrants have been occasionally noted in southeastern Arizona mountain ranges by mid- to late August (Phillips et al. 1964).

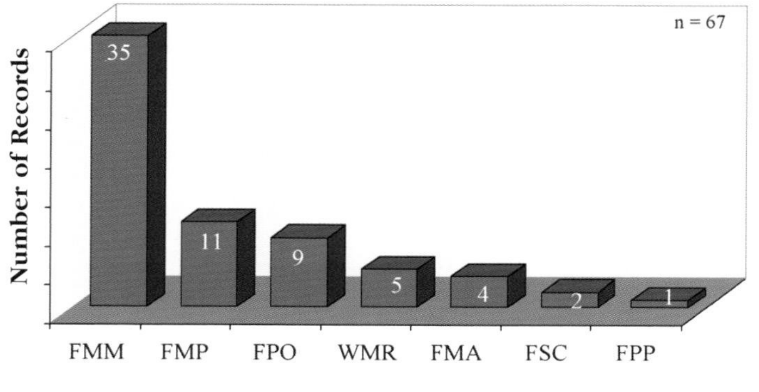

Even though Williamson's Sapsuckers forage most frequently in ponderosa pine and other conifers in Arizona, they apparently prefer to nest in aspen snags. Of 202 nests monitored on the Mogollon Rim, 98.5 percent were in quaking aspen, and 85.4 percent of the aspens were dead (Dobbs et al. 1997). In Arizona, nests have also been found in ponderosa pine and Douglas fir. Nest excavation is conducted over a 3–4 week period and is done predominantly by the male; however, females in Arizona have been observed excavating periodically (Dobbs et al. 1997). Nests heights typically range from 10 to 55 ft (3.3–16.8 m) above the ground (Travis 1992). The median nest cavity height of four nests measured by atlasers was 23.3 ft (7.1 m).

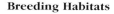

Breeding Phenology

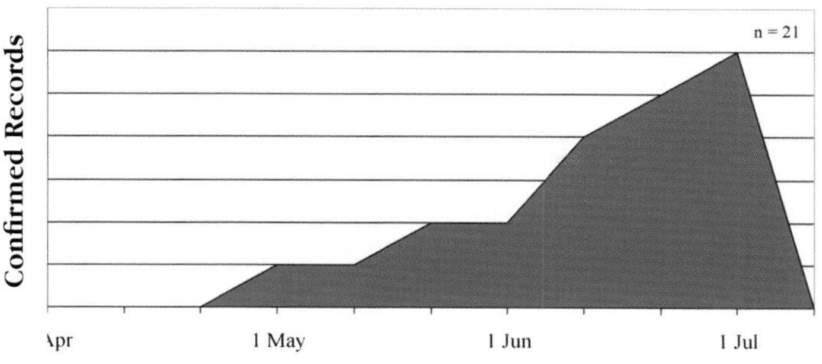

The average clutch size for Williamson's Sapsucker is 4–6 eggs, but occasionally ranges from 3 to 7 (Bent 1939; Martin and Li 1992). Both parents share the 12–14 day incubation duty, which begins before the clutch is complete (Crockett and Hansley 1977). Nestlings will typically fledge in 31–32 days (range 26–33) after hatching (Martin and Li 1992). Adult sapsuckers quickly disperse after young leave the nest, and males often abandon the young 1–2 days before they fledge (Dobbs et al. 1997). Second broods are unrecorded for Williamson's Sapsuckers, but some pairs will renest if the first attempt fails early (Dobbs et al. 1997).

DISTRIBUTION AND STATUS

The disjunct breeding range of Williamson's Sapsuckers is confined to mountainous regions of western North America, primarily from southern British Columbia south to California, central Arizona, and New Mexico. In Arizona, Phillips et al. (1964) considered these woodpeckers as fairly common to common summer residents in forests with aspen from the Mogollon Rim northward. Atlasers documented Williamson's Sapsuckers nesting throughout much of their previously noted range at elevations from approximately 7000 to 9700 ft (2134–2957 m).

In the Grand Canyon region, Brown et al. (1987) noted Williamson's Sapsuckers as uncommon summer residents only on the Kaibab Plateau. Atlasers found Williamson's Sapsuckers to be much more widespread and in higher density than Red-naped Sapsuckers on the Kaibab Plateau. During the atlas, this species was also detected to the west at Mount Trumbull and Mount Logan within the Arizona Strip region.

On Navajo tribal land, atlasers only confirmed this sapsucker in the Chuska and adjacent Lukachukai mountains. Williamson's Sapsuckers likely also breed in the Carrizo Mountains to the north, but this remote mountain range was not thoroughly surveyed. The few surveys in this range were conducted during late summer, when many individuals may have already dispersed to lower elevations. La Rue (1994) also noted Williamson's Sapsuckers as an irregular nesting species in cooler canyons of Black Mesa, but only one individual was detected there during atlas surveys.

Atlas surveys revealed Williamson's Sapsuckers nesting from the San Francisco Mountains region, including Kendrick Peak, south and east through most of the higher elevations of the Mogollon Rim and throughout the White Mountains. The breeding distribution of this sapsucker undoubtedly continues into the White Mountain Apache tribal lands. Unfortunately, this is not reflected on the atlas range map because permission to gain access and conduct atlas surveys on these tribal lands was not granted. Atlasers also did not detect this species on Bill Williams Mountains, south of Williams, where it had been noted nesting in the past (Monson and Phillips 1981).

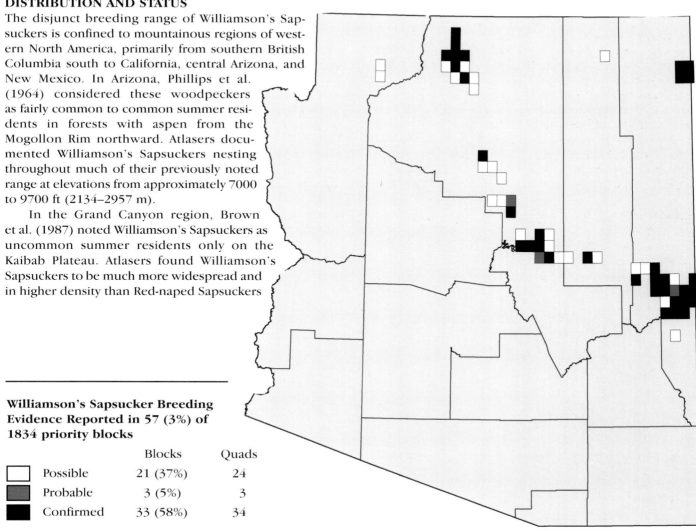

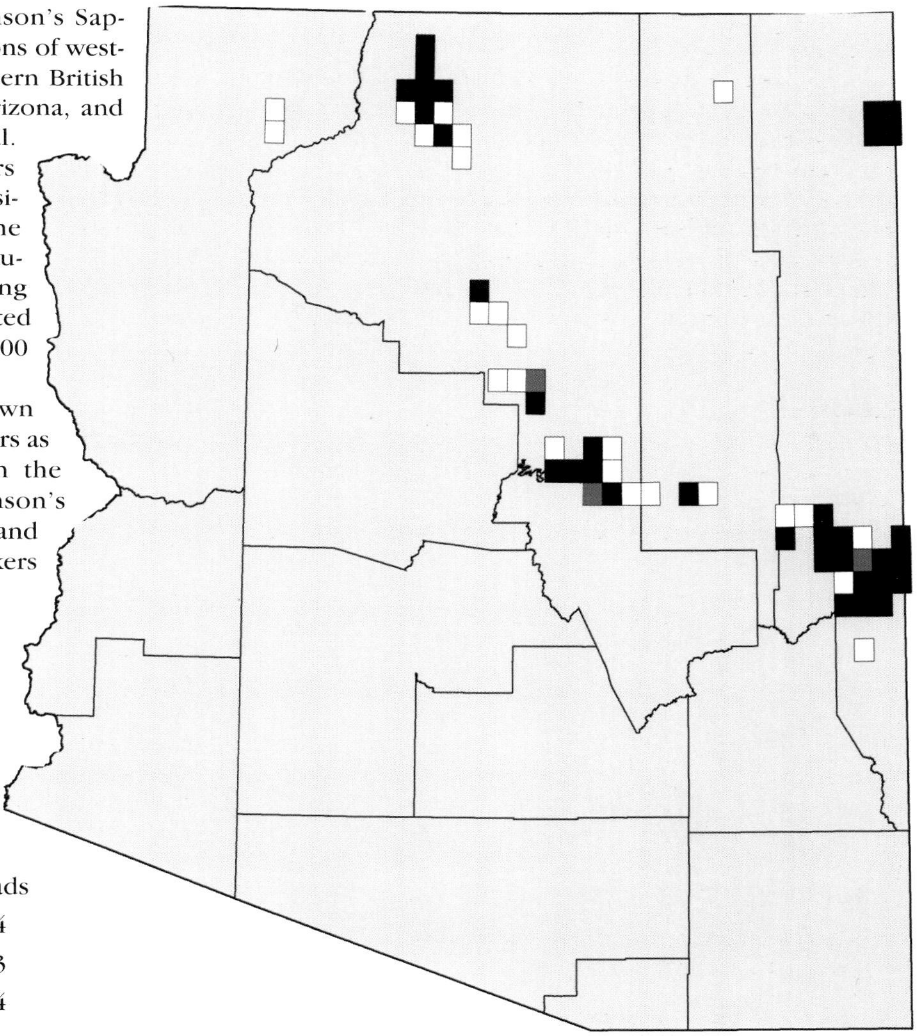

Williamson's Sapsucker Breeding Evidence Reported in 57 (3%) of 1834 priority blocks

	Blocks	Quads
Possible	21 (37%)	24
Probable	3 (5%)	3
Confirmed	33 (58%)	34

Red-naped Sapsucker

by Suzanne Sitko and
Troy E. Corman

Sphyrapicus nuchalis

Many forest birds and other wildlife unknowingly owe a debt of gratitude to the Red-naped Sapsucker for their construction of nest cavities and sap wells. Many of our forests would not be the same without this unobtrusive yet delightfully multifunctional species, truly an important part of the web of life.

RICHARD DITCH

HABITAT

Mixed conifer forests and their adjacent montane drainages accounted for 67 percent of all Red-naped Sapsucker atlas records. These forested habitats often contain a diversity of firs and pines, as well as aspen and other hardwoods such as maple and riparian woody vegetation (n = 39). Only four atlas records were reported in ponderosa pine–Gambel's oak vegetation type, suggesting this widespread habitat is not preferred for nesting. Somewhat surprising were the relatively few Red-naped Sapsucker records obtained in aspen-dominated forests or spruce-fir-aspen associations. However, this might reflect the limited and often spotty distribution of these habitats and the fact they are often interspersed within larger stands of mixed conifer forests. Forest edges, alder-willow riparian complexes, and cut or burned forests that have induced reestablishment of early seral aspen stands are other habitats used by Red-naped Sapsuckers for foraging and nesting. The deciduous component of this sapsucker's habitat should be emphasized, inasmuch as sap-producing hardwoods are the mainstay of the Red-naped Sapsucker's diet and nesting habitat.

BREEDING

Spring migration begins early for Red-naped Sapsuckers in Arizona, with some individuals noted dispersing from traditional wintering areas in February or early March. However, Phillips et al. (1964) suggested that migration can begin by late January in Arizona, with some males arriving on breeding grounds to establish territories in late March or early April and lingering migrants continuing to pass through Arizona into late April and occasionally mid-May. Atlasers noted the earliest pair of Red-naped Sapsuckers on 15 April and the first occupied nest by 7 May. In Arizona, egg laying is initiated in early to mid-May, with young produced by late May and early June. Red-naped Sapsucker nests with young were discovered through 17 July with fledglings reported into early August. Red-naped Sapsuckers migrate south or descend to lower elevations to winter in southern Arizona's deciduous, riparian, and oak woodlands, as well as orchards and other exotic trees in residential areas. Few migrants are detected in southern wintering grounds before early September, with peak passage in October and late individuals still migrating into December.

After forming pair bonds in early spring, male Red-naped Sapsuckers excavate most of the nest cavity, taking 6 days to 4 weeks to complete (Howell 1952, Walters et al. 2002). These sapsuckers often construct a new cavity each year, frequently in the same tree as previous years, or occasionally nest in old cavities (DeGraaf et al. 1991; Walters et al. 2002). Red-naped Sapsuckers prefer live aspens when available, especially those afflicted by heartrot fungus, which facilitates excavation labor and leaves the nest cavity encased in the surrounding harder wood (Ehrlich et al. 1988). In conifer-dominated forests, Red-naped Sapsuckers often choose dead trees in which to construct the nest cavity (Terres 1996; McClelland and McClelland 2000). Measurements were taken at four Red-naped Sapsucker nests during atlas surveys, three in aspen and one in a ponderosa pine snag. The height of these nests ranged from 8 to 14 ft (2.4–2.3 m).

Red-naped Sapsuckers typically lay 4–5 eggs (range 3–7) and are incubated by both sexes, with the male doing

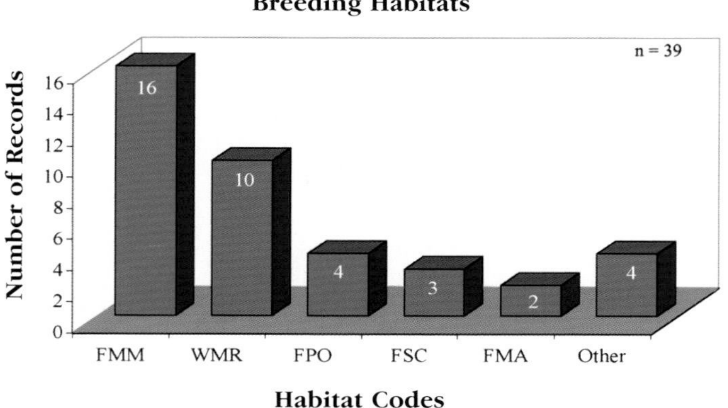

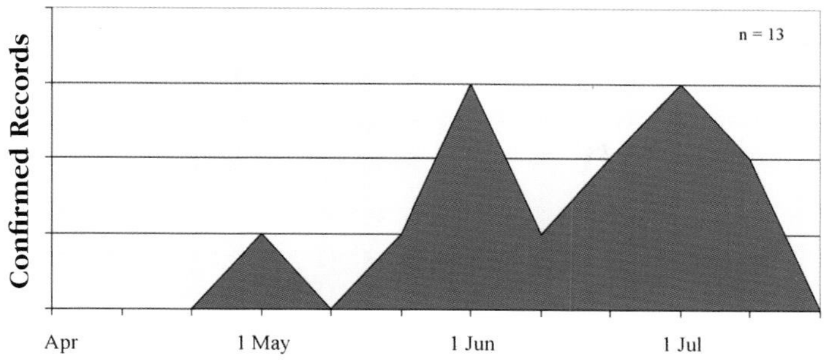

so at night (Ehrlich et al. 1988, Walters et al. 2002). Eggs are incubated for 12 to 13 days, and both parents brood the chick for the first six days after hatching (Howell 1952). The young are fed by both parents and fledge in 23–32 days (Walters et al. 2002). The young are fed irregularly by the parents following nest departure and are able to feed on their own almost immediately (Howell 1952; Tobalske 1992). Red-naped Sapsucker pairs produce only one brood per season, but will sometimes renest if an earlier attempt failed (Walters et al. 2002).

DISTRIBUTION AND STATUS

Red-naped Sapsuckers are rather common summer residents between the Sierra Nevada and Rocky Mountain ranges from central British Columbia south to central Arizona and New Mexico, and rarely western Texas. In the past, this sapsucker has been described breeding most commonly in Arizona on the Kaibab Plateau, locally on the Mogollon Rim, and in the White Mountains region including the Blue Range (Phillips et al. 1964; Monson and Phillips 1981). Red-naped Sapsuckers were considered sparse breeders elsewhere in Arizona.

Arizona atlas surveys revealed Red-naped Sapsuckers nesting at elevations ranging from 6850 to 9800 ft (2088–2987 m). These sapsuckers were most widespread in the White Mountains region from the upper Blue River drainage and Luna Lake west to near Lakeside. Atlasers were not granted access to conduct surveys on White Mountain Apache tribal lands; however, forest habitats on this reservation undoubtedly hold additional breeding populations. On the Mogollon Rim, these sapsuckers were noted along upper snowmelt drainages from approximately Chevelon Creek to East Clear Creek.

Monson and Phillips (1981) reported Red-naped Sapsuckers nesting irregularly in the Bradshaw and Hualapai mountains, but atlasers were unable to document this species in these ranges. Additionally, previous nest records from Mount Trumbull and on the South Rim of the Grand Canyon (Brown et al. 1987) were not verified during the atlas period. However, atlasers found Red-naped Sapsuckers fairly regularly on blocks adjacent to these areas at higher elevations of the Kaibab Plateau.

On Navajo tribal lands, Jacobs (1986) noted that there were several records of Red-naped Sapsuckers in the Chuska Mountains, probably nesting in interspersed conifer-aspen stands. Atlasers confirmed these sapsuckers nesting on four blocks in the Chuska and nearby Lukachukai Mountains. Red-naped Sapsuckers were also discovered nesting locally on the Defiance Plateau and on northern Black Mesa.

The primary threat to nesting Red-naped Sapsuckers in Arizona is the gradual decline of mature aspen stands as well as the loss of nearby willow-alder groves adjacent to water sources. Patch cuts and burns, which promote early seral regrowth of aspen, are management actions that may assist in conserving these sapsuckers.

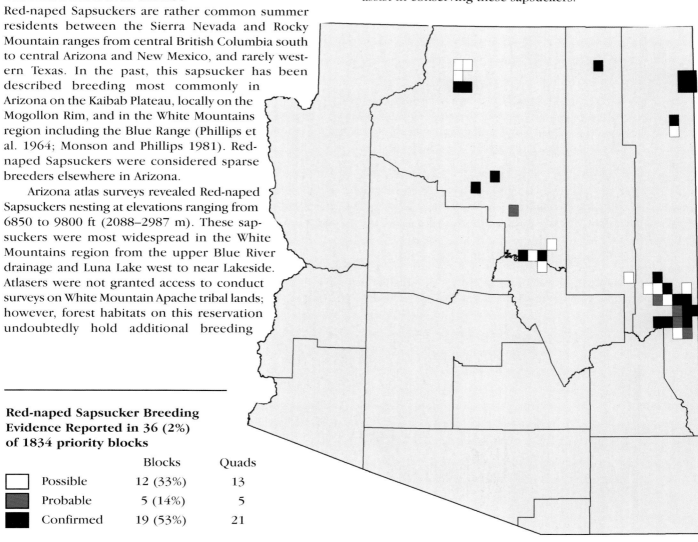

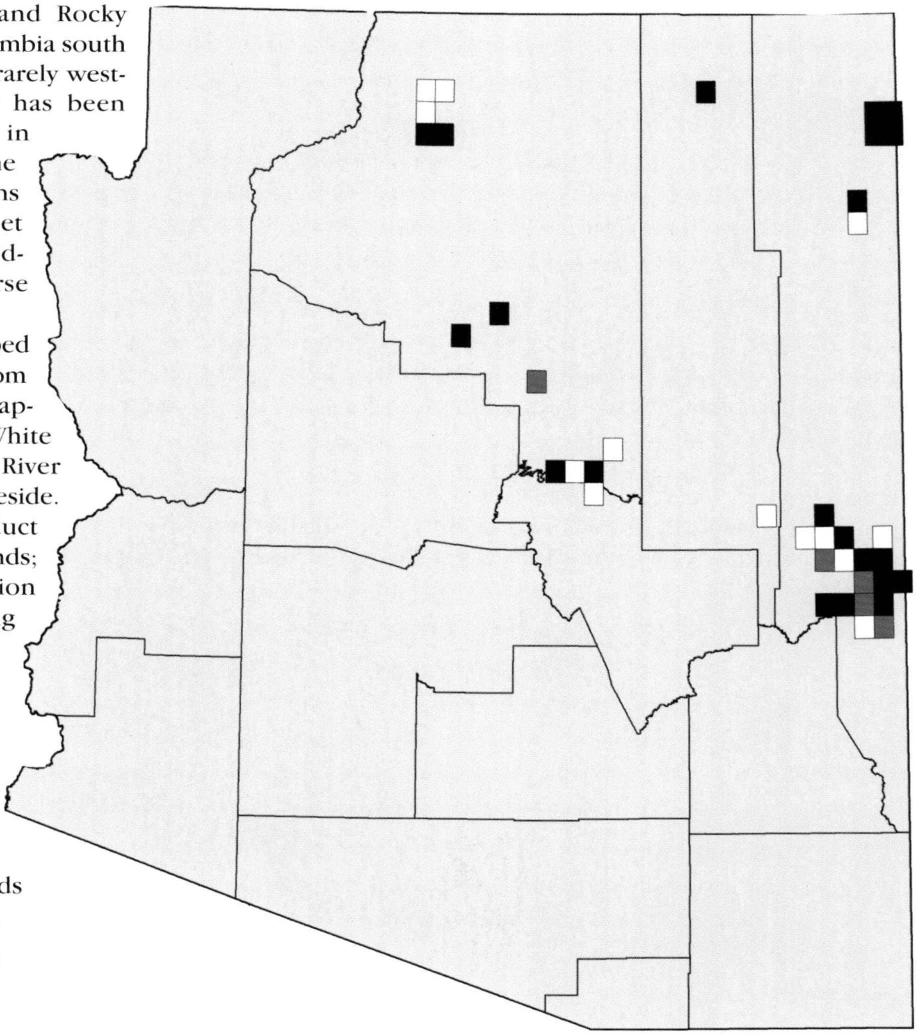

Red-naped Sapsucker Breeding Evidence Reported in 36 (2%) of 1834 priority blocks

	Blocks	Quads
Possible	12 (33%)	13
Probable	5 (14%)	5
Confirmed	19 (53%)	21

Ladder-backed Woodpecker

by Tracy D. McCarthey *Picoides scalaris*

Historically known as "Cactus Woodpeckers," Ladder-backeds are Arizona's most widespread and frequently encountered nesting woodpecker. The characteristic whinny of these small woodpeckers is commonly heard in many desert and arid regions of the state. One limiting factor appears to be the availability of tree or similar-sized trunks for nesting cavities.

GEORGE ANDREJKO

HABITAT

Ladder-backed Woodpeckers occur in low- to-mid elevation habitats in Arizona from arid desertscrub to riparian and pinyon-juniper woodlands. Atlasers reported this species most commonly in Sonoran Desert and dry wash associations, and these habitats accounted for 54 percent of all records (n = 824). An additional 10 percent of atlas records were noted in lowland riparian woodlands (including mesquite bosques) containing cottonwood, willow, ash, and mesquite. Ladder-backed Woodpeckers were also fairly frequent inhabitants of semiarid grassland with scattered mesquite, acacia, yucca, and agave. Fewer records were obtained in foothill drainages dominated by sycamore or the adjacent lower mountain slopes with evergreen oaks and pinyon-juniper woodlands. These small woodpeckers were also detected nesting locally in chaparral scrublands, stands of Joshua trees, and Mojave and Chihuahuan desert washes. Ladder-backed Woodpeckers were found much less frequently in urban and residential habitats than the more adaptable desert dwelling Gila Woodpecker.

BREEDING

Primarily resident throughout their range in Arizona, Ladder-backed Woodpeckers acquire mates from late January to March (Short 1971), with cavity excavation occurring soon after. Nesting begins relatively early and atlasers reported the first occupied nest on 30 March. Early nests in Arizona likely contain eggs by late March based on newly hatched young in a nest on 11 April (Grinnell 1914). Similarly, Ladder-backed Woodpeckers were noted carrying food by 16 April, likely indicating a nest with young nearby. The first fledgling was observed being fed by an adult on 6 May. Atlasers were able to document peak breeding activity as occurring from late April through late May, with a noticeable drop by early June (n = 148). Adults were observed feeding fledglings as late as 4 August.

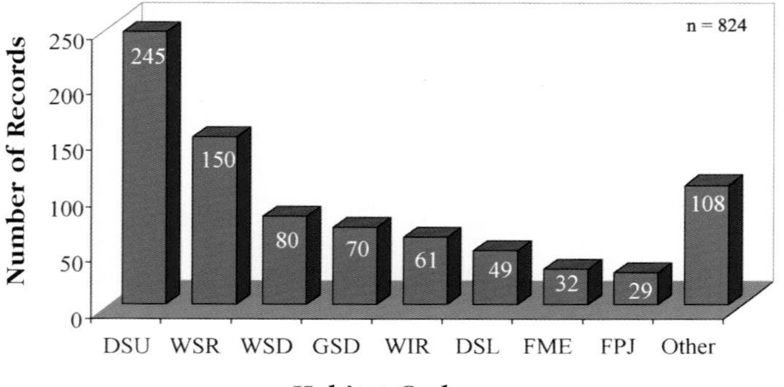

Gilman (1915) noted that Ladder-backed Woodpeckers will construct their nests in any suitable tree or shrub. During the atlas period, Ladder-backed Woodpecker nests were found most commonly in both live and dead paloverde trees (both blue paloverde and foothill paloverde). Multiple nests were also placed in mesquites and willows and in the large dead inflorescence stalks of agaves. Single nests were found in Arizona walnut and, in the northwest corner of the state, a Joshua tree. Other Arizona nests have been found in cottonwood, hackberry, ironwood, sycamore, juniper, old fence posts, and occasionally even in large jumping cholla trunks (Gilman 1915; Short 1982). In Sonora, Mexico, Ladder-backed Woodpeckers also use desert willows, saguaros, and acacias (Russell and Monson 1998) for nesting trees, which are likely utilized in Arizona as well. The nest cavity is likely excavated by both sexes, but primarily the male (Short 1982). Atlas field crews only located and measured ten nests, which ranged from 3 to 18 ft (0.9–5.5 m), with a mean nest height of 9.5 ft (2.9 m). This is similar to the cavity heights from 2 to 29.5 ft (0.6–9.0 m) given in Lowther (2001). Cavity entrances of Ladder-backed Woodpecker nests are typically placed on the underside of large curving branch, unless it was in an agave stalk.

Typically, Ladder-backed Woodpeckers lay 4–5 eggs, rarely 6–7 (Bent 1939), although clutch size appears to decrease to 2–3 eggs farther south into Mexico and Central America (Lowther 2001). Both adults incubate the eggs for an average of 13 days (Baicich and Harrison 1997) There is little known about parental care in Ladder-backed

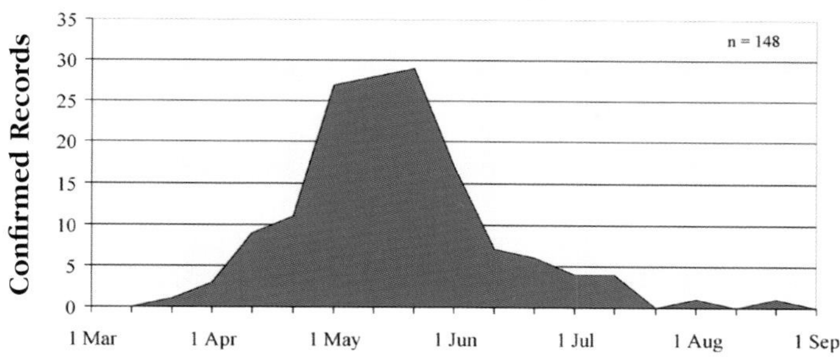

Woodpeckers; however, Baicich and Harrison (1997) list both parents as feeding the young. There is no information as to the length of the nestling period, but Ladder-backed Woodpeckers are thought to have only one brood per season (Lowther 2001).

DISTRIBUTION AND STATUS

Ladder-backed Woodpeckers are residents throughout the southwestern United States from southeastern California, southern Nevada, Arizona, New Mexico, and western Texas. In addition, their range extends south throughout Mexico and locally in isolated populations in northern Central America.

Prior literature considered Ladder-backed Woodpeckers to be common residents in southern Arizona north to the Virgin River valley in the northwest and to the base of the Mogollon Rim in the east (Swarth 1914; Phillips et al. 1964). This woodpecker is absent throughout the northeast corner of the state, primarily east of the Kaibab Plateau and north of the Mogollon Rim. Atlas surveys revealed little change from these earlier findings but helped delineate range limits in the Arizona Strip region of the northwest to areas primarily west of the Shivwits Plateau. Atlasers noted Ladder-backed Woodpeckers at elevations primarily from 100 to 4800 ft (30–1463 m), but locally to 5600 ft (1707 m).

Brown et al. (1987) described Ladder-backed Woodpeckers as rare residents at lower elevations in the western half of the Grand Canyon region, with most observations in riparian woodlands in Havasu Canyon and below the South Rim at Indian Gardens. Atlasers were unable to document these woodpeckers as far east in this region as Indian Gardens. However, Ladder-backed Woodpeckers were found north into Kanab Creek drainage (including along Hack Canyon), in the Toroweap Valley east of Mt. Trumbull, and well south of the Grand Canyon in the Cataract and Havasu Creek drainages.

Although atlas data indicate that Ladder-backed Woodpeckers are widespread inhabitants of the Mojave Desert regions of northwestern Arizona, populations are apparently more sparsely distributed and may reflect a limited number of nest substrates. Similarly, this species was infrequently encountered in the drier, sparsely vegetated Sonoran Desert. Creosote and smaller shrubs frequently dominate these areas, providing little in the way for constructing cavities.

Breeding Bird Survey census data show no significant trend for Ladder-backed Woodpeckers in the United States. Although common throughout most of their range in Arizona, local populations are threatened by human-made habitat alterations and possibly by increasing desert wildfires. Atlas data clearly indicate that these small woodpeckers are largely absent in the expansive agricultural regions of the lower Santa Cruz and Gila River valleys, as well as in large urban centers such as Phoenix. Widespread urbanization will continue to affect adversely the habitat available for this small desert woodpecker.

Ladder-backed Woodpecker Breeding Evidence Reported in 817 (45%) of 1834 priority blocks

	Blocks	Quads
Possible	410 (50%)	424
Probable	207 (25%)	208
Confirmed	200 (24%)	202

Downy Woodpecker

by Troy E. Corman *Picoides pubescens*

Arizona's smallest woodpecker, the dainty Downy is a sparse open forest resident in the state, easily overlooked among the aspens and pines. Following forest fires or prolonged periods of drought, populations of these little woodpeckers temporarily increase during subsequent bark beetle outbreaks.

HABITAT

Downy Woodpeckers inhabit a variety of forests and woodlands across their range. These woodpeckers prefer forests with a deciduous tree component and are very infrequently observed in pure conifer stands. In Arizona, atlasers noted 51 percent of all observation in either mixed conifer forests or nearby mountain drainages containing quaking aspen, Douglas fir, white fir, ponderosa pine, and scattered stands of Gambel's oak and maple (n = 57). Another 18 percent were observed in ponderosa pine stands with a heavy Gambel's oak understory. Almost pure ponderosa pine forests accounted for only eight Downy Woodpecker atlas records, and fewer were noted in spruce-fir and pinyon pine–juniper stands with scattered ponderosa pine. Although frequently nesting and foraging in forests stands dominated by variable age classes of aspens in the West, this habitat is very locally distributed in Arizona and often interspersed among conifer forests. This might help explain the very few atlas records there. Downy Woodpeckers commonly forage in deciduous saplings and dense shrub stands, and atlasers encountered these birds along high-elevation drainages with thickets of scrub willow and thinleaf alder.

BREEDING

Throughout most of their range, Downy Woodpeckers are considered basically permanent residents. However, dispersing individuals in Arizona appear at some lower elevations riparian areas well away from nesting locations from mid-September through early May. Pair formation usually takes place in early spring and atlasers noted the earliest pair on 5 April. Cavities are constructed approximately two weeks prior to egg laying (Jackson 1976). The earliest confirmed atlas record was a nest with young discovered on the Mogollon Rim on 15 May, suggesting egg-laying initiation by late April. Undoubtedly due to their low abundance in Arizona, few active nests were discovered during the atlas period. However, nests with young were noted through 8 June, and adults carrying food were observed through 11 June. Fledgling Downy Woodpeckers were encountered from early June through late July.

Nest cavity excavation by Downy Woodpeckers may begin at multiple sites before the final site is chosen (Jackson and Ouellet 2002). Typical nests sites are in a dead stub of a living or dead tree and characteristically in wood with an advanced stage of heartrot (Jackson 1976). Nest cavities are constructed new each year, with the 16–20 day effort equally shared by both members of the pair (Ritchison 1999). Nest cavity entrances are characteristically on the underside of a tree stub or limb that leans from vertical (Jackson 1976). In Arizona, many nests are discovered in quaking aspen, but they have also been found in Gambel's oak, bigtooth maple, and pinyon pine. Of the two nests measured during the atlas, one was in an aspen snag 53 ft (16.3 m) above the ground and the other in a limb snag of a live pinyon pine approximately 18 ft (5.5 m) above the ground. The mean height of three nest cavities in aspen above the Mogollon Rim in Arizona was 44.3 ft (13.5 m) above the ground (Li and Martin 1991).

Downy Woodpeckers lay a typical clutch of 4–5 eggs, but this can range from 3 to 8 (Bent 1939). The male incubates and broods the young at night, sharing this responsibility with the female during the day (Jackson and Ouellet 2002). The incubation period is rather short at 12 days, and

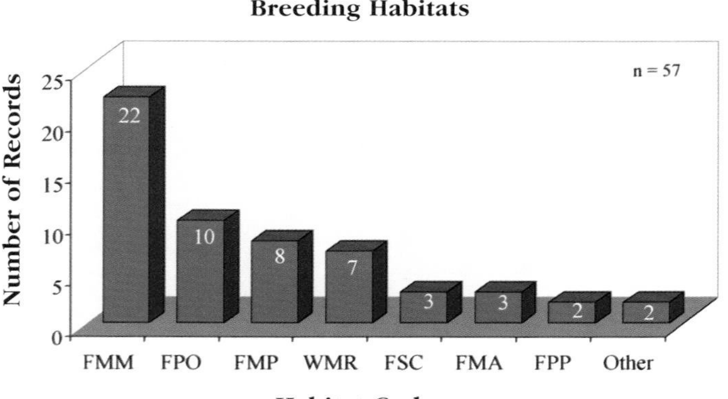

both parents feed the nestlings through fledging at 20–25 days (Kaufman 1996). Approximately 2–3 days before fledging, the noisy nestlings crowd the inside entrance of the cavity, at which time the eager nestlings can often be viewed by observers below (Jackson and Ouellet 2002). Parental care of Downy Woodpecker fledglings extends at least three weeks following nest departure (Jackson and Ouellet 2002). There is little evidence suggesting more than one brood is produced per year, and later nesting activity likely pertains to renesting following failed earlier attempts.

DISTRIBUTION AND STATUS

Although Downy Woodpeckers breed from Alaska and central Canada south through most of the United States, this bird is much more abundant and widespread in the eastern deciduous forests than it is in the West's conifer-shrouded mountains. These woodpeckers are resident throughout the eastern United States, west to eastern Texas, and south in the West to southern coastal California, central Arizona, and south-central New Mexico. From Bent (1939), Major Bendire (1895) wrote that Dr. Edgar A. Mearns reported that Downy Woodpeckers breed sparingly throughout the ponderosa pine region of Arizona, ranging up into the spruce-fir zone of the San Francisco Peaks, and considered it the rarest of the woodpeckers found in the state. Phillips et al. (1964) noted Downy Woodpeckers as sparse residents from the White Mountains, Sierra Ancha, and San Francisco Mountains northward. Downy Woodpeckers had also been found nesting occasionally in cool canyons of the Shonto Plateau north of Black Mesa, such as in Betatakin Canyon (Woodbury and Russell 1945).

Atlaser efforts revealed Downy Woodpeckers were a little more widespread than previous literature suggested, but they remain sparsely distributed and nowhere numerous. These small woodpeckers were encountered breeding at elevations ranging from 6200 to 9500 ft (1890–2896 m), and possibly nesting even higher in the White and San Francisco mountains regions.

Downy Woodpeckers were found sparingly throughout much of the higher elevations of the Kaibab Plateau, including the North Rim of the Grand Canyon. The most western observation during the atlas was from Black Rock Mountain, just east of the Virgin Mountains in the Arizona Strip region. On Navajo tribal lands, a pair of Downy Woodpeckers was noted in northern Black Mesa where they are known to nest only occasionally (LaRue 1994) and throughout the Chuska Mountains.

Atlasers detected these woodpeckers in the San Francisco Mountains and west locally to Bill Williams Mountain south of Williams. Downy Woodpeckers were also noted nesting along the Mogollon Rim southwest to the White Mountains region, where they appear to reach their highest density in the state. Atlas data reveal Downy Woodpeckers inhabiting forests surrounding the eastern half of the White Mountain Apache tribal lands, where access to conduct atlas surveys was not granted. This species undoubtedly nests throughout much of the higher elevations of these tribal lands. Populations of Downy Woodpeckers continue to exist in the Sierra Ancha range in Gila County north to the vicinity of Young. The most southern atlas records for this species were from northeastern San Carlos Apache tribal lands within the Natanes Mountains near Point of Pines.

The distribution and status of Downy Woodpeckers in Arizona has apparently changed little during the past century. It will be interesting to see what effect the recent widespread forest wildfires and bark beetle outbreak will have on this and other woodpecker populations in the state.

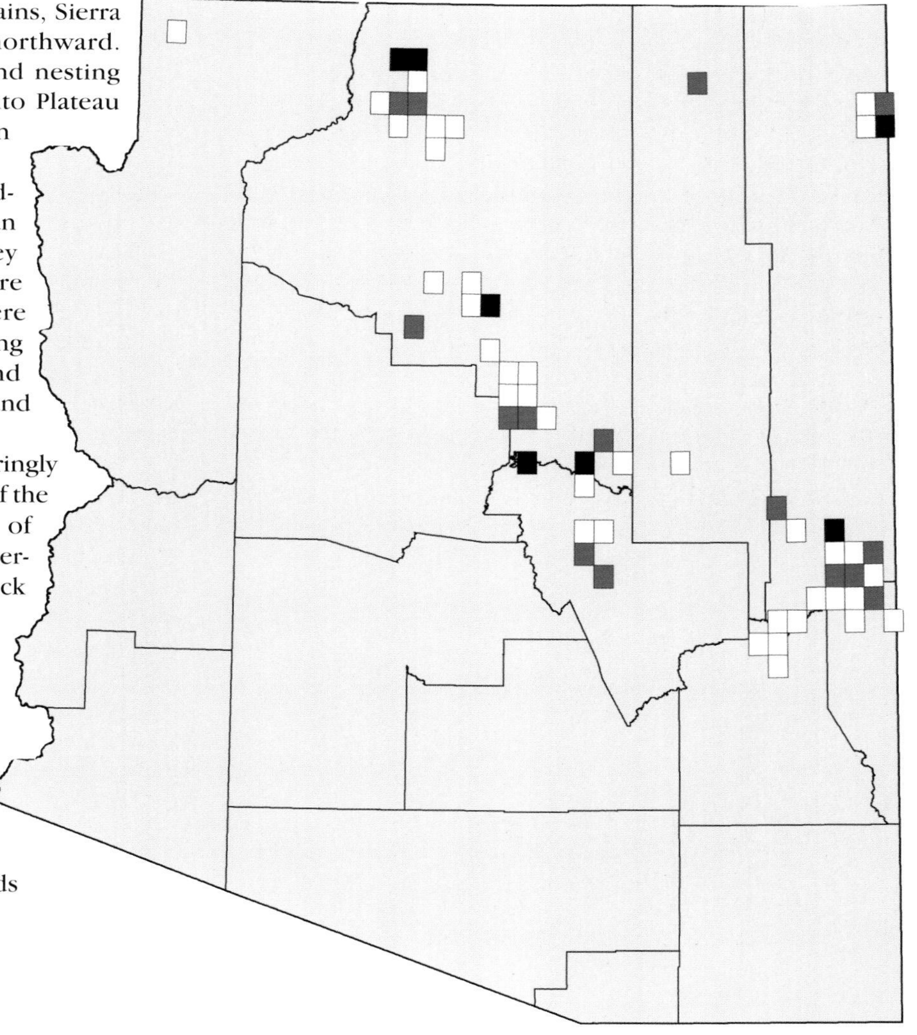

Downy Woodpecker Breeding Evidence Reported in 50 (3%) of 1834 priority blocks

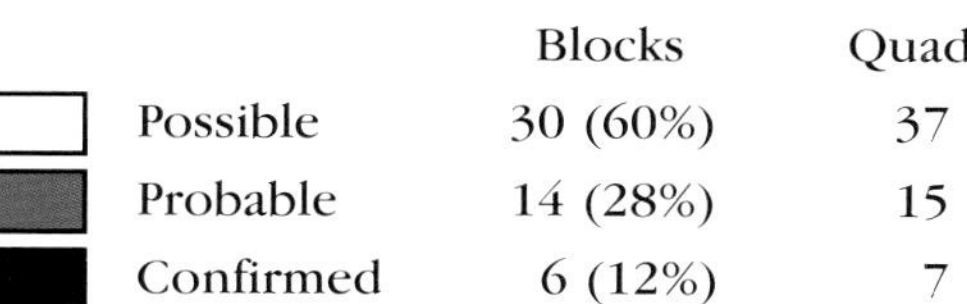

	Blocks	Quads
Possible	30 (60%)	37
Probable	14 (28%)	15
Confirmed	6 (12%)	7

Hairy Woodpecker

by Bill Grossi and Troy E. Corman *Picoides villosus*

Hairy Woodpeckers are the common, black-and-white woodpecker of Arizona's coniferous forests. They spend most of their days busily searching for wood-boring insects, constantly grooming forest trees and thus helping to keep injurious insects at bay. In fact, local Hairy Woodpecker populations increase during periods of bark beetle infestations.

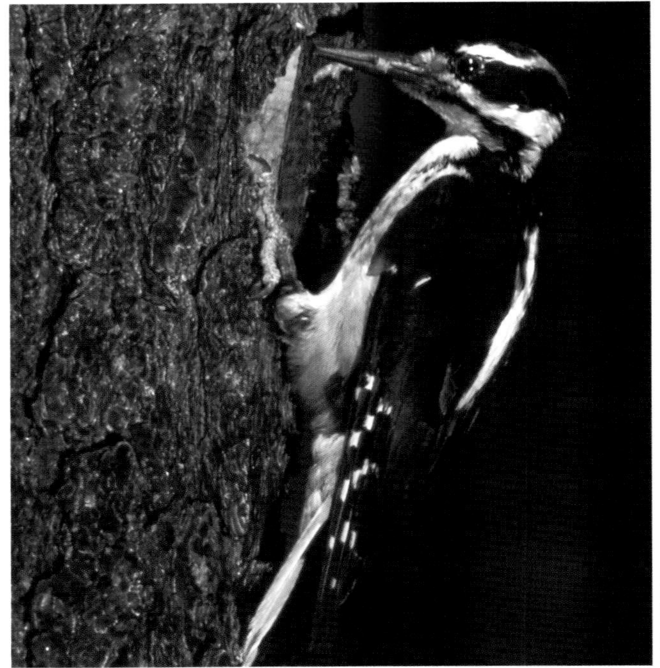
DAN FISCHER

HABITAT

Widespread in mature deciduous forests of eastern North America, Hairy Woodpeckers are primarily birds of coniferous forests and woodlands in Arizona. Atlasers reported 89 percent of records from coniferous-dominated areas, where they reach their highest densities in tall timbered forests (n = 362). Although these woodpeckers are less abundant in pinyon pine–juniper woodlands, this widespread vegetative community accounted for 30 percent of all atlas records. This habitat is not used for nesting in southeastern Arizona. Approximately 40 percent of records were from forests with a heavy ponderosa pine component, from almost pure stands to those with a Gambel's oak or pinyon pine–juniper association. Hairy Woodpeckers are also frequent inhabitants of mixed conifer forests often containing Douglas fir, white fir, ponderosa pine, and aspen. This cooler forest association attributed to 15 percent of all atlas records. Atlasers also regularly encountered these woodpeckers in the relatively limited aspen and spruce-fir vegetative communities. Fewer records were obtained from the adjacent drainages and canyons with a strong deciduous component such as sycamore, alder, maple, and occasionally cottonwood in the north.

BREEDING

Hairy Woodpeckers are typically considered resident birds in Arizona, although there is some movement to slightly lower-elevation drainages in fall and winter. Apparently, some individuals remain paired throughout the year, while others typically form pairs by March. Hairy Woodpeckers characteristically begin nest cavity construction 2–3 weeks prior to egg laying (Jackson 1976). Atlasers first noted this species at a cavity on 27 April and reported an occupied nest by 7 May. Hairy Woodpeckers were observed carrying food by 14 May, but an adult feeding a fledgling on 17 May would suggest that some egg laying may begin by early April. Atlas data reveal a peak in nesting activity from late May to mid-June (n = 73). Some nesting efforts continue through July, with a late nest containing young discovered on 29 July and fledglings noted into mid-August. In July and August, some Hairy Woodpeckers apparently descend with their fledged broods into nearby wooded mountain canyons (Marshall 1957).

Once the pair bond is made, both adults excavate the nest hole, which takes from 1 to 3 weeks depending on the hardness of the wood (Bent 1939). Although Hairy Woodpeckers were most commonly found in coniferous forest habitats, atlas nest data suggest the use of deciduous trees as well as pines for nest holes. Of six nest records, two were in quaking aspen and one was in Gambel's oak. The other three records were all in ponderosa pines, two of which were snags. The cavity height is often related to overall tree height (Jackson et al. 2002). The six nest measurement records suggest a nest hole median height of 15.5 ft (4.7 m) with a range from about 4.6 to 36 ft (1.4–11 m).

Hairy Woodpeckers typically excavate a new cavity each year and lay the eggs on a bed of new wood chips. Occasionally old cavities are used, but in either case, no material is brought into the nest. Egg laying begins 1–14 days following the completion of the nest cavity (Jackson et al. 2002). Both birds incubate the typical clutch of 4 eggs

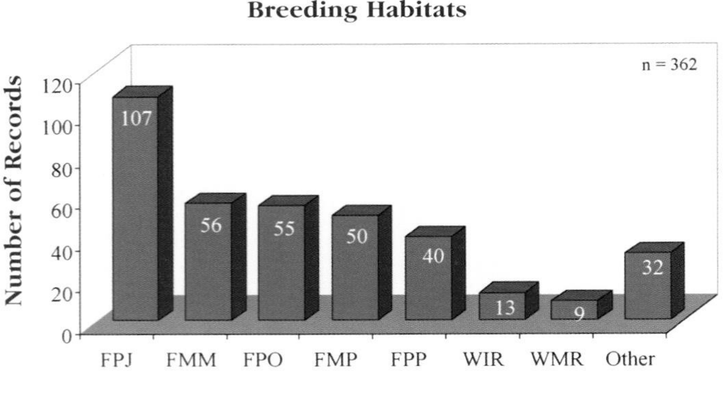

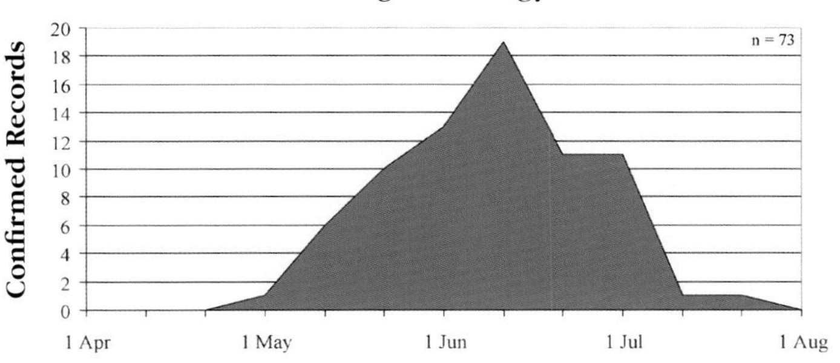

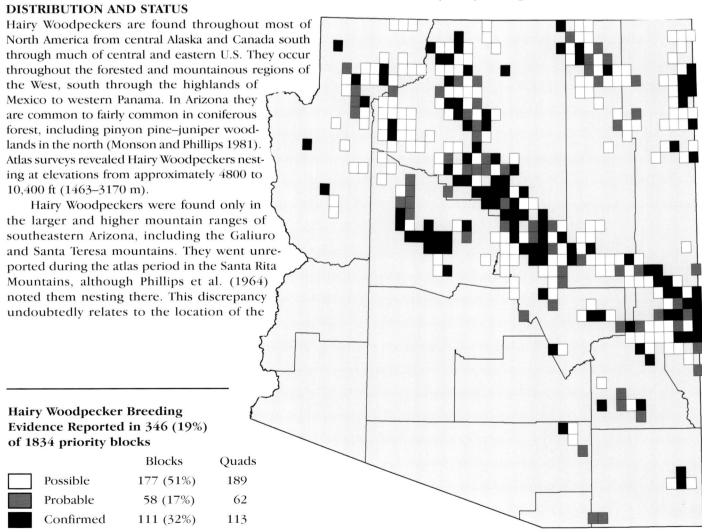

(range 3–7), which hatch in 11–15 days (Burns 1915; Lawrence 1967). The parents make constant trips back and forth to the nest hole to feed the nestlings, which fledge in about 4 weeks (Lawrence 1967; Kilham 1979). The nestlings begin noisily greeting their returning parents at the cavity entrance approximately 3–4 days before nest departure (Jackson et al. 2002). Fledglings remain dependent on parents for 3 to 4 weeks (Bent 1939; Jackson et al. 2002). Only one brood is produced per year, but they will renest if earlier efforts fail.

DISTRIBUTION AND STATUS

Hairy Woodpeckers are found throughout most of North America from central Alaska and Canada south through much of central and eastern U.S. They occur throughout the forested and mountainous regions of the West, south through the highlands of Mexico to western Panama. In Arizona they are common to fairly common in coniferous forest, including pinyon pine–juniper woodlands in the north (Monson and Phillips 1981). Atlas surveys revealed Hairy Woodpeckers nesting at elevations from approximately 4800 to 10,400 ft (1463–3170 m).

Hairy Woodpeckers were found only in the larger and higher mountain ranges of southeastern Arizona, including the Galiuro and Santa Teresa mountains. They went unreported during the atlas period in the Santa Rita Mountains, although Phillips et al. (1964) noted them nesting there. This discrepancy undoubtedly relates to the location of the surveyed priority blocks, and this woodpecker likely continues to nest in unsurveyed forests at higher elevations of this range.

Widespread in the White Mountains and Mogollon Rim regions of Arizona, Hairy Woodpeckers undoubtedly breed throughout most of the adjacent unsurveyed White Mountain Apache tribal lands. They were encountered all through the high country of the Navajo and Hopi tribal lands as noted by Jacobs (1986). Atlasers documented the western limits of Hairy Woodpecker distribution in several isolated ranges such as the Hualapai, Cerbat, and Virgin mountains.

The fact that Hairy Woodpeckers were typically encountered on most surveyed atlas blocks containing appropriate habitat, suggest some populations stability. It is unknown how the widespread loss of mature conifer forests and woodlands to recent devastating wildfires and drought induced bark beetle outbreaks will have on local Arizona populations of these woodpeckers. It is important these forest woodpeckers remain plentiful as they are among the most useful birds due to their constant search for and consumption of insects known to cause damage to trees. Their old excavate nest cavities are also commonly used by numerous secondary cavity nesting birds and other wildlife.

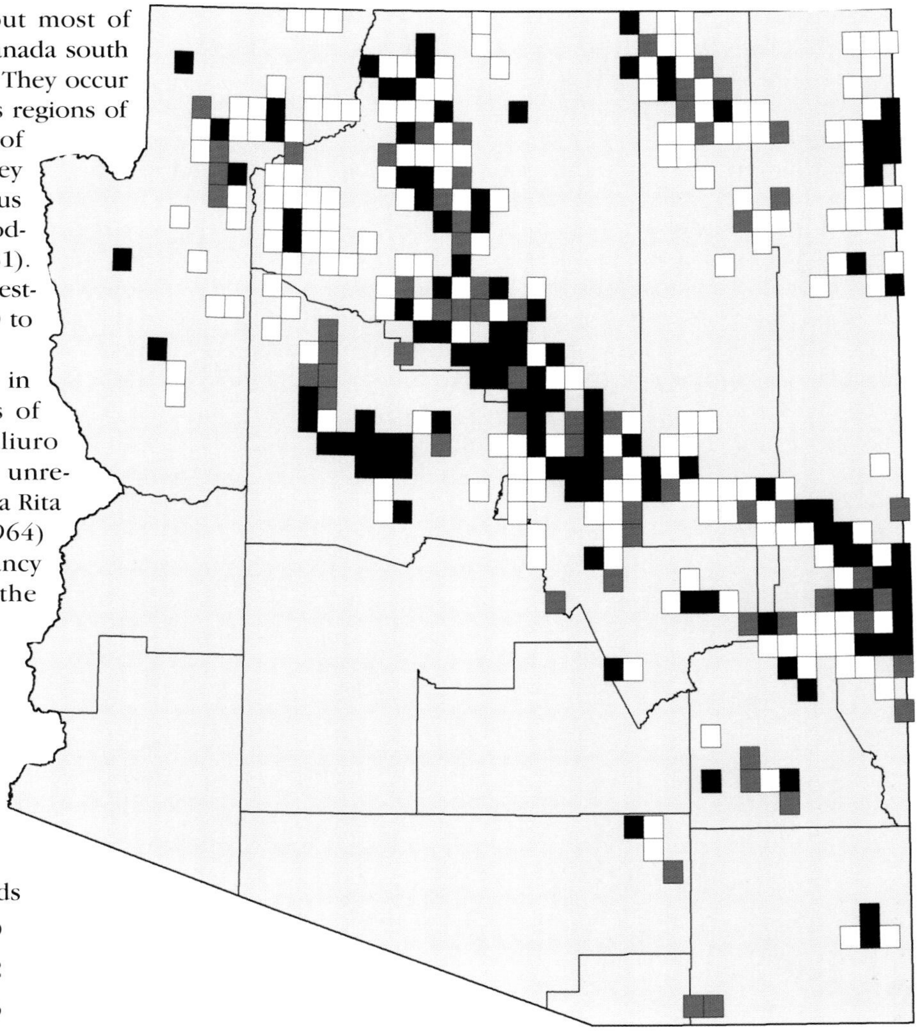

Hairy Woodpecker Breeding Evidence Reported in 346 (19%) of 1834 priority blocks

	Blocks	Quads
Possible	177 (51%)	189
Probable	58 (17%)	62
Confirmed	111 (32%)	113

Arizona Woodpecker

by Troy E. Corman *Picoides arizonae*

Rather quiet and easily overlooked among the evergreen oaks they prefer, Arizona Woodpeckers are typically secretive around the nest, especially during incubation. This could help explain why the breeding biology of this primarily Mexican woodpecker has been little studied in the state and much remains to be determined.

DAN FISCHER

HABITAT

Arizona Woodpeckers occur in several forested habitats in southeastern Arizona, with Madrean evergreen oaks an important and common component of all. Atlasers noted this woodpecker most frequently (49 percent of all atlas records) in the extensive oak woodlands that cover much of the lower and middle slopes of sky island ranges ($n = 42$). These woodlands consist primarily of various species of evergreen oaks, such as Emory, silverleaf, Arizona white, wavyleaf, and Mexican blue. This includes the stringers of oaks that finger their way down dry foothill drainages into semiarid grasslands. Arizona Woodpeckers were also regularly encountered in the adjacent mountain canyons and drainages dominated with oaks and Arizona sycamore. Other common trees in these canyons often include Arizona walnut, Fremont cottonwood, alligator juniper, and Arizona cypress. At slightly higher elevations, Arizona Woodpeckers occur in Madrean pine-oak woodlands where Chihuahuan, Apache, and ponderosa pine have an open understory of evergreen oaks, Arizona madrone, and juniper. These woodpeckers were reported less frequently in higher mountain drainages containing pines, Douglas fir, bigtooth maple, and scattered evergreen oaks, where encounters with Hairy Woodpeckers are much more common.

BREEDING

Even though they are sometimes encountered at slightly lower elevations during the winter, Arizona Woodpeckers are basically a resident species whose nesting habits have been little studied. In Arizona, these woodpeckers are noisier and more conspicuous during pair formation or pair bond renewal, which often occurs in or before March (Johnson et al. 1999). Nest construction has been observed from 15 April through 10 May (Bent 1939; Johnson et al. 1999).

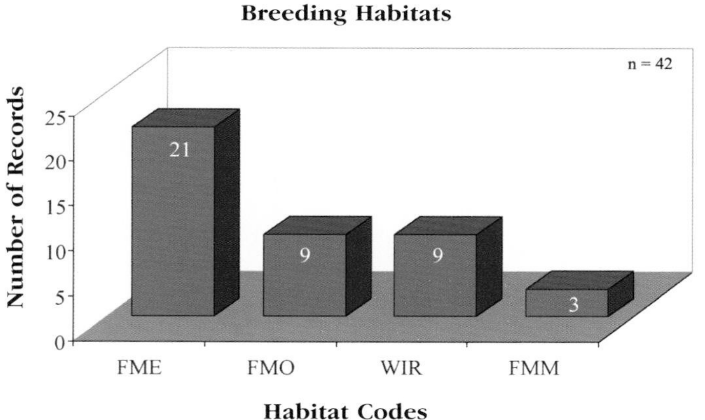

Arizona Woodpecker nests with eggs are difficult to locate because of the quite, secretive nature of this species during incubation (Johnson et al. 1999). Consequently, atlasers discovered very few active nests. The first occupied nest was reported on 18 April. At this nest, the adults were observed switching places for lengthy stays, suggesting incubation. Prior limited data in Arizona indicate that eggs are typically laid in mid-April through mid-May (Bent 1939); however, a freshly excavated cavity ready for eggs was found as late as 10 June by Brandt (1951). Atlasers reported the first nest with young on 28 May. However, a nest with small, naked young was found on 14 May (Bendire 1895) and adults have been observed carrying food into a cavity as early as 7 May. The earliest fledgling noted by atlasers was on 7 June and was observed being fed by an adult. Ligon (1961) noted nestlings near fledging stage on 28 June, and some late initiated nests may not fledge until mid-July.

Arizona Woodpeckers construct a new nest cavity each year, which are frequently excavated in dead trees or limbs. Atlasers noted nest cavities in various evergreen oaks and Arizona sycamore. Several earlier accounts suggested this woodpecker prefers Arizona walnut in which to construct cavities due to this trees softer wood (Brandt 1951). They have also been found nesting in bigtooth maple, Fremont cottonwood, and an agave stalk (Bent 1939). In Arizona, the height of nest cavities has ranged from 7.9 to 50 ft (2.4–15.2 m), but most are typically found at heights from 15 to 20 ft (4.6–6.1 m) above the ground (Baicich and Harrison 1997). Brandt (1951) located an exceptionally low nest in the trunk of a small apple tree, where the cavity entrance was only 2 ft (0.6 m) high.

The incubation of the 3–4 eggs is by both parents and may last for 14 days, although some suggest that the incubation period is probably several days shorter as with other similar woodpeckers (Bent 1939; Johnson et al. 1999). Once incubation begins, it is nearly continuous with the incubating woodpecker not departing the cavity until its mate had returned and given the "nest-relief" vocalization (Johnson et al 1999). Nestlings are fed by both parents, which fledge when they are 24–27 days old (Johnson et al. 1999). Young Arizona Woodpeckers begin foraging for themselves approximately four days following nest departure, but they depend on parents for food for 2 to 3 weeks after fledging (Johnson et al. 1999). Most evidence suggests that only one brood is produced per season and later active nests may pertain to renesting efforts after a failed earlier attempt.

DISTRIBUTION AND STATUS

Arizona Woodpeckers are resident from southeastern Arizona and extreme southwestern New Mexico, south on the Pacific Slope of Mexico and adjacent interior to Jalisco and Michoacan (Howell and Webb 1995). Earlier accounts considered these woodpeckers an uncommon to fairly common resident in mountains of southeastern Arizona, from the Baboquivari Mountains in the west, north to the Santa Catalina and Pinaleno mountains (Swarth 1914; Phillips et al. 1964).

Atlasers found Arizona Woodpeckers throughout their previously described range primarily at elevations from 4500 to 7500 ft (1372–2286 m). However, these woodpeckers nest locally down to just below 3900 ft (1189 m) along Sycamore Canyon in the Pajarito Mountains. Arizona Woodpeckers were found throughout the Chiricahua, Huachuca, and Patagonia mountains, but went oddly undetected in the oak-covered slopes of the Mule Mountains north of Bisbee. This species was also not found in the smaller Whetstone Mountain range where they had been reported in the past (Smith 1908). However, atlas surveys were not conducted in the wooded higher elevations of this rugged range, where Arizona Woodpeckers may still occur. Similarly, these woodpeckers were confirmed breeding only near Kitt Peak in the Quinlan Mountains, but additional unsurveyed oak woodlands exist to the south, especially around Baboquivari Peak.

Atlasers discovered Arizona Woodpeckers in several mountain ranges where they had previously not been reported, including the rugged and seldom-visited Galiuro Mountains. In the northwestern corner of this mountain range, Arizona Woodpeckers were found near Norton Spring and then along Ash Creek on the southeastern slopes. Phillips et al. (1964) reported a previous winter record in the southern Galiuro Mountains. Atlasers also found these woodpeckers to be fairly common within the heavily wooded Reiley Creek drainage on the north slope of the nearby Winchester Mountains.

The status and distribution of Arizona Woodpeckers in the state have changed little. Devastating wildfires and possibly reduced groundwater tables in canyons are likely the greatest threats to local populations of these little, brown-backed woodpeckers.

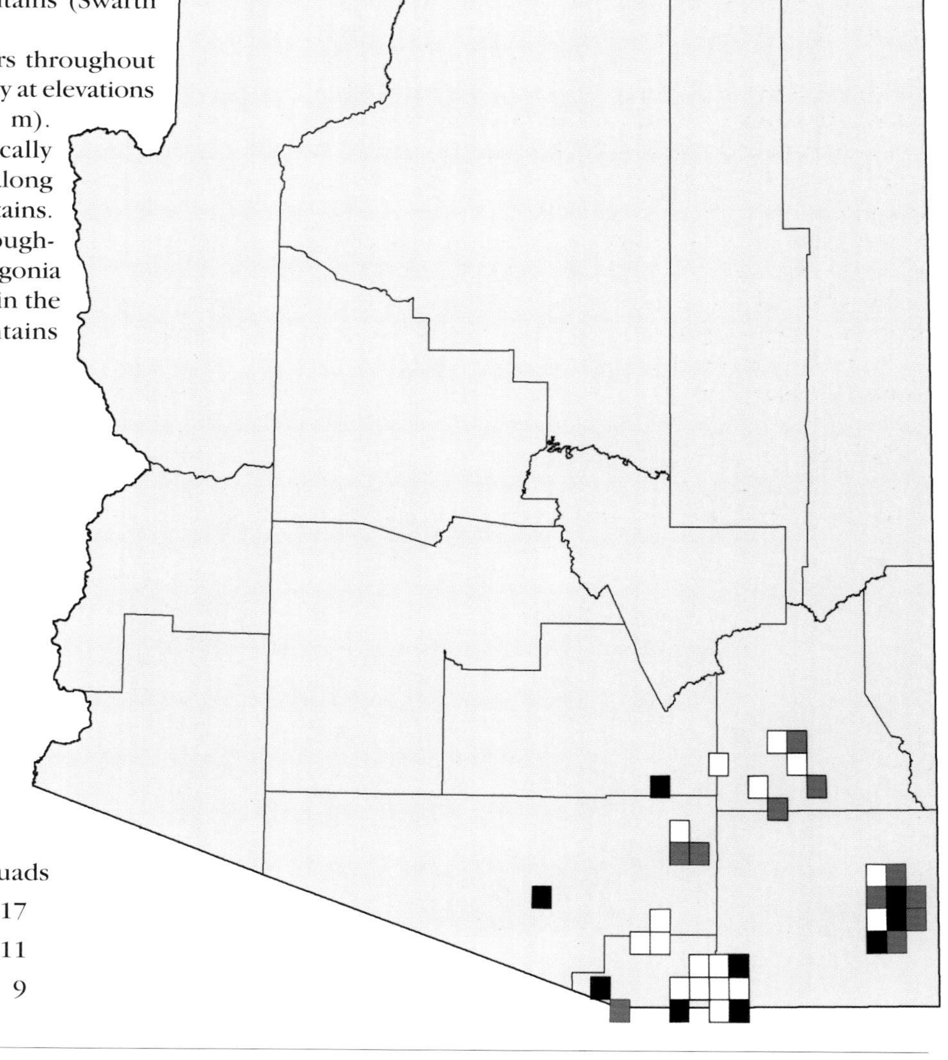

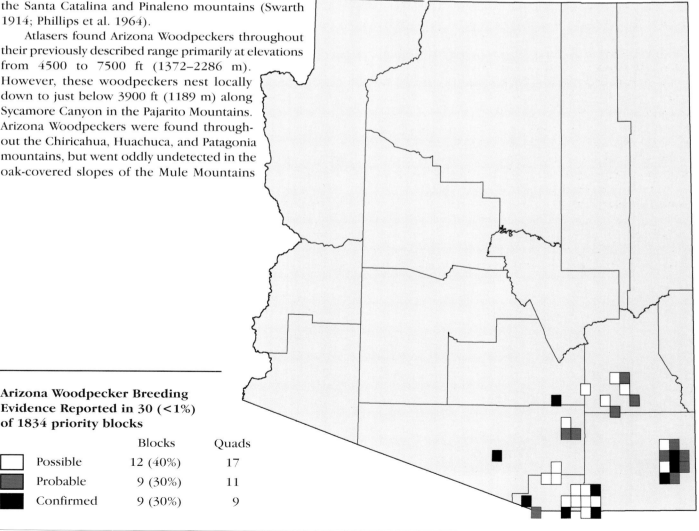

Arizona Woodpecker Breeding Evidence Reported in 30 (<1%) of 1834 priority blocks

	Blocks	Quads
Possible	12 (40%)	17
Probable	9 (30%)	11
Confirmed	9 (30%)	9

American Three-toed Woodpecker

by Troy E. Corman *Picoides dorsalis*

Quiet, retiring, and easily overlooked, American Three-toed Woodpeckers can be surprisingly tame and approachable when they are finally located. This fire-adapted woodpecker is closely associated with spruce and fir in Arizona, where it is often found flaking the bark from dead or dying trees as it searches for its primary food, bark beetle larvae.

RICK AND NORA BOWERS

HABITAT

American Three-toed Woodpeckers are found in boreal and higher elevation montane coniferous forests in Arizona. These unique woodpeckers reach their highest abundance in the state in forests dominated by Engelmann spruce, blue spruce, and subalpine fir. However, this habitat is very limited in Arizona and only accounted for 16 percent of all atlas records (n = 37). Approximately 65 percent of American Three-toed Woodpecker atlas records were obtained at slightly lower elevations in the more widespread mixed conifer associations and similar forested montane drainges. Dominant trees in these habitats typically contain white fir, Douglas fir, limber pine, ponderosa pine, and quaking aspen. Locally and less frequently, American Three-toed Woodpeckers can be found in adjacent ponderosa pine forests, especially after fires or insects have killed large numbers of trees. Generally sparsely distributed in forests, this species is well known for moving into disturbed forests 1–2 years after being ravaged by fire, disease, or insects (Hutto 1995; Leonard 2001). Here these woodpeckers often remain to nest in higher densities for several years taking advantage of the abundant food resources.

American Three-toed Woodpecker's predominant foraging method of scaling and flaking bark from the trunks of dead and dying conifers enable it to expose the larvae in which it depends (Koplin 1969). Through these efforts, these woodpeckers often gradually remove all bark from a dead tree, which characteristically collects as a large heap around the base of the trunk.

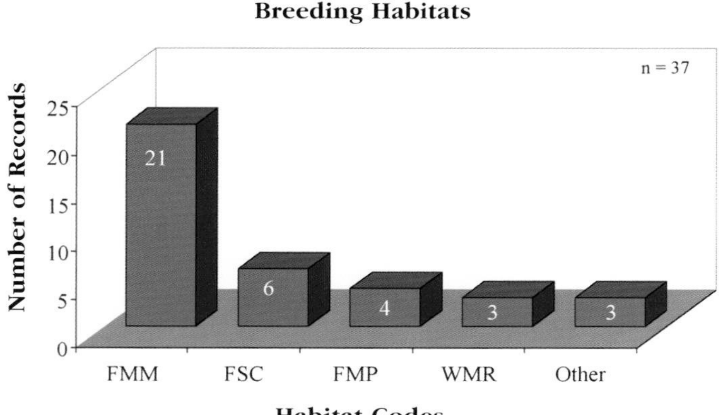

BREEDING

Although some individuals wander into adjacent habitats following fires or descent to slightly lower elevations during the winter, American Three-toed Woodpeckers are basically resident in Arizona. Drumming on dead branches and stumps by these woodpeckers is used to establish territories and pair formation, and may begin as early as March (Leonard 2001). Territories are established by the males, and are often reused by pairs each year (Camp 1985). Fast drumming is used in response to drumming of other American Three-toed Woodpeckers and most likely used in aggressive territorial displays. Slow drumming by both sexes is used mainly between members of a pair and serves mostly as location signals or to initiate breeding encounters (Short 1974).

Due to the retiring nature of American Three-toed Woodpeckers and their limited distribution in Arizona, few active nests were located during the atlas period. However, egg laying likely begins in early May or before as an adult was observed carrying food on 29 May. During the atlas period, the latest nest with young reported was on 27 June, although nests with young have been observed as late as 18 July in Arizona. Similarly, American Three-toed Woodpeckers were noted feeding fledglings from 18 June to 24 July, but this activity has been observed as late as early August in the state.

Nest cavities are constructed by both members of the pair in trunks of coniferous snags and live trees, and less frequently in aspen (Smith 1992; Leonard 2001). Conifer species chosen for nesting are not well documented in Arizona but likely include Engelmann spruce, subalpine fir,

Douglas fir, and ponderosa pine, with a preference for snags over live trees. The nest cavity height can range from 5 to 40 ft (1.5–12.2 m) above the ground (Bent 1939).

Typical American Three-toed Woodpecker clutches contain 4 eggs (range 3–7) and are incubated by both sexes for 11 to 14 days (Bent 1939; Short 1982). There is little information on the length of the nestling period for this woodpecker, but nestlings depart the cavity at 22–26 days for a closely related species, and both parents continue feeding the fledglings for an additional 1–2 months (Cramp 1985). These woodpeckers produce only one brood per year (Leonard 2001).

DISTRIBUTION AND STATUS

American Three-toed Woodpeckers can be found year-round from Alaska through much of the forested regions of Canada, locally south to northern New York and in the Rocky Mountains south to Arizona and New Mexico. In Arizona, Phillips et al. (1964) considered these woodpeckers an uncommon resident in boreal zones from the White Mountains, San Francisco Mountains, and on the Kaibab Plateau. This species was first noted in the Chuska Mountain on Navajo tribal lands in 1980 (Monson and Phillips 1981). Beginning in the late 1980s, American Three-toed Woodpeckers were discovered nesting locally near cool, snowmelt drainages above the Mogollon Rim (T. Martin, personal communication). During the winter in Arizona, some individuals occasionally descend to slightly lower elevations and into adjacent areas where they do not breed, such as the South Rim of the Grand Canyon (Brown et al. 1987). These irregular movements may pertain to dispersing juveniles and attributed to low prey abundance within normal range or to overpopulation following an insect outbreak (Short 1982).

Atlas surveys reconfirmed American Three-toed Woodpeckers throughout their previously described range in Arizona and helped delineate the extent of their distribution at each location. Atlasers found this species at elevations primarily from 7300 to 11,000 ft (2225–3353 m), but locally down to 6500 ft (1981 m). American Three-toed Woodpeckers were also reported west to the Williams area, such as on Sitgreaves Mountain and southwest of White Horse Lake. On the Mogollon Rim, these woodpeckers were found from north of Pine, east to near Chevelon Creek. Atlasers noted these woodpeckers in the White Mountain region from just west of Green's Peak, south to the Blue Range. However, the distribution of these woodpeckers in the White Mountain undoubtedly extends west into the eastern half of the higher elevations of the White Mountain Apache tribal lands. Unfortunately, due to the inability to gain permission to conduct surveys on these lands, the distribution map does not reflect this species' full range within this region.

In Arizona, American Three-toed Woodpecker populations appear to be fairly stable with no obvious loss in distribution within the state. However, modern forestry practices use fire suppression, salvage logging (cutting of burned trees), and suppression logging (cutting of insect infested trees), all of which reduce or remove the dead and dying trees on which this species depends (Leonard 2001). Despite these practices, populations of these fire-adapted birds are expected to increase temporarily due to the widespread forest wildfires and bark beetle outbreaks that recently occurred within their Arizona range.

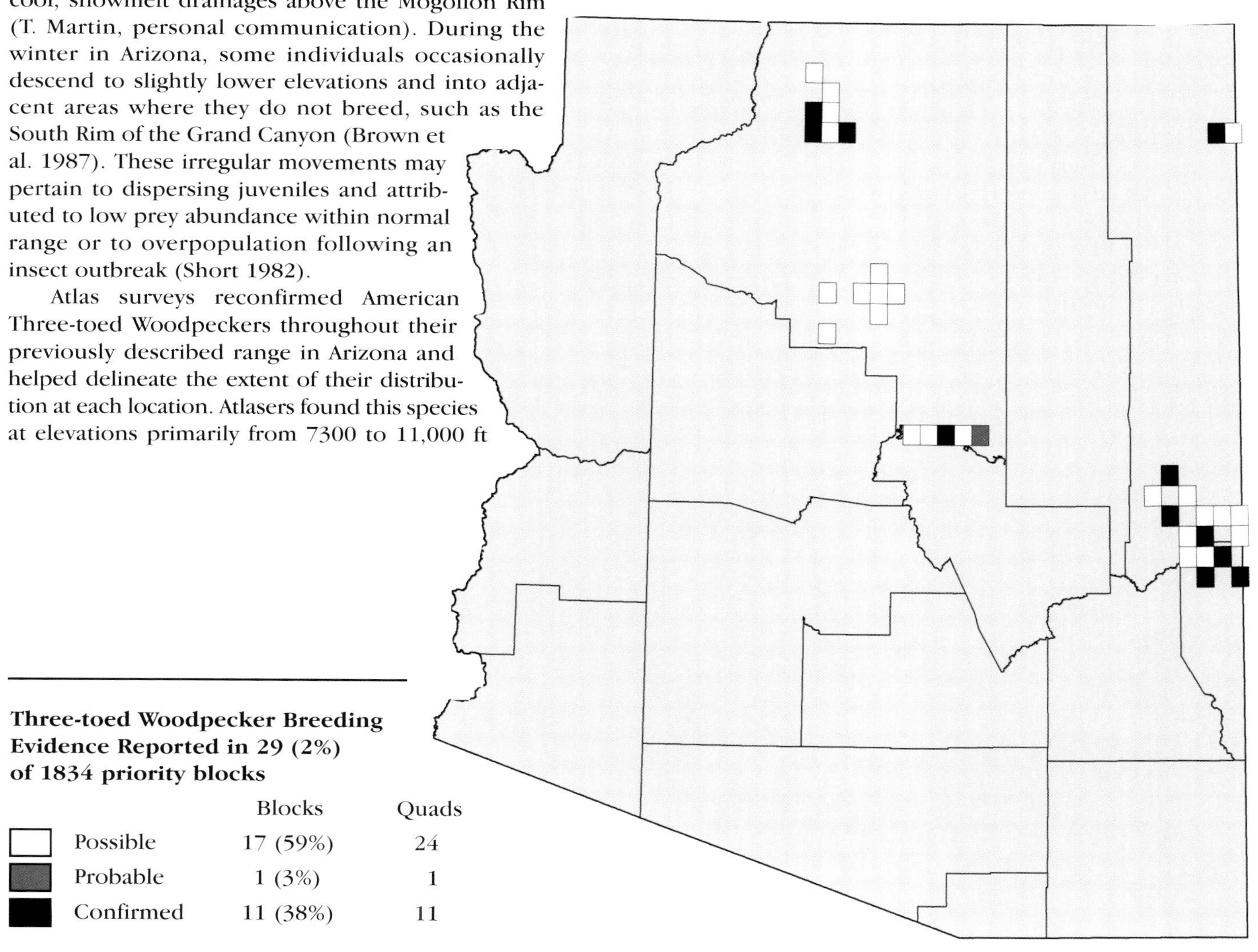

Three-toed Woodpecker Breeding Evidence Reported in 29 (2%) of 1834 priority blocks

	Blocks	Quads
Possible	17 (59%)	24
Probable	1 (3%)	1
Confirmed	11 (38%)	11

Northern Flicker

by John R. Spence *Colaptes auratus*

The loud and imperious call of a Northern Flicker is a common sound in the forests and woodlands of Arizona. Unique traits for a woodpecker include ground-foraging habits and a diet often consisting predominantly of ants. These woodpeckers are considered a keystone species, as they excavate cavities that are subsequently used by many other species.

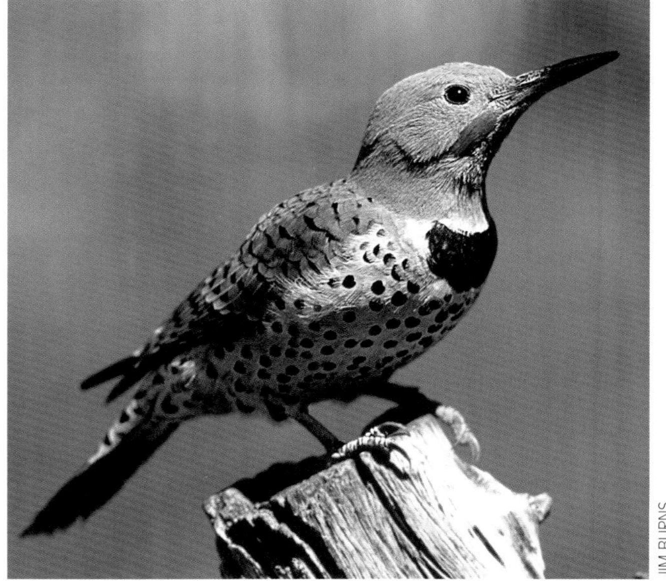

HABITAT

Northern Flickers were detected by atlasers in more habitat than any of the other woodpeckers of Arizona. They reach their highest densities in open coniferous and aspen forests in the state, especially were large snags are abundant. Because they are ground foragers, they also require some clearings where their favorite food items such as ants are most common. Northern Flickers were detected most frequently (62 percent of all records) in forests and woodlands containing pinyon and/or ponderosa pine (n = 522). In taller forests, they prefer the more open ponderosa pine and drier phases of mixed conifer forests rather than denser and moister spruce-fir habitats. Flickers are opportunistic breeders, and were also detected in twenty-one additional habitats in the state, ranging from riparian forests with tall sycamore or cottonwoods to urban neighborhoods. In the mountains of southeastern Arizona they were also encountered in Madrean pine-oak forests, especially where the larger Apache, Chihuahuan, and ponderosa pines occurred.

BREEDING

Northern Flickers begin departing their Arizona lowland wintering areas in early March with few remaining after mid-April. This is approximately the same period when these birds usually arrive on their breeding grounds in the state. Courtship behavior is often protracted and complex, with numerous displays between the pair as well as with intruders. Once paired, nest building begins in April and continues through May. Most active nests in Arizona were found in May or June, although there is one record of an occupied nest in late March and three records from late April, all at relatively low elevations. Egg-laying initiation is difficult to determine for Northern Flickers, but likely begins by at least early May based on atlas records of young by 14 May. Peak breeding in the state is typically from late May through late June, although nests with young were found as late as July 22. These flickers were reported feeding fledglings through 30 July and atlasers noted fledglings into mid-August. Although some Northern Flickers begin arriving in nonbreeding lowland areas of Arizona by mid-September, most individuals are not noted until after early or mid-October.

Northern Flicker nests are typically excavated in snags or less often dead or dying sections of live trees. Cavities used in previous years are sometimes selected for breeding (Moore 1995) and a few atlas nests were discovered in natural tree cavities. Of 19 Northern Flicker tree nests measured during the atlas, most were in ponderosa pine (6), juniper species (6), quaking aspen (5), and less commonly cottonwood (2). Several other active nests found during the atlas were in cutbanks of washes and in the wall of a cabin, and one was reported possibly nesting in a natural cliff cavity. The median height of 21 nest cavities measured by atlas field crews was 14.8 ft (4.5 m) and ranged from 4.6 to 49.2 ft (1.4–15.0 m). Tree species and nest heights in Arizona are typical compared with data on Northern (Red-shafted) Flicker's from other regions of North America.

Both Northern Flicker sexes excavate the nest cavity for 1 to 2 weeks, although the male typically does more of the work (Moore 1995). Egg laying commences soon after the nest is completed. Most clutches consists of 6–8 eggs, but varies from 3 to 12 (Moore and Koenig 1986). Incubation is by both adults and takes about 10–11 days, while young

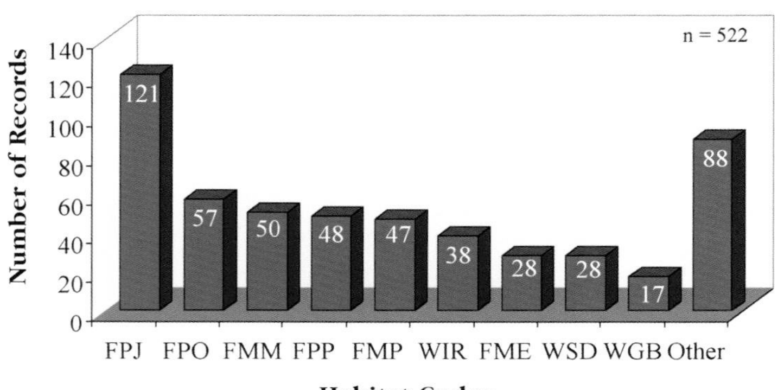

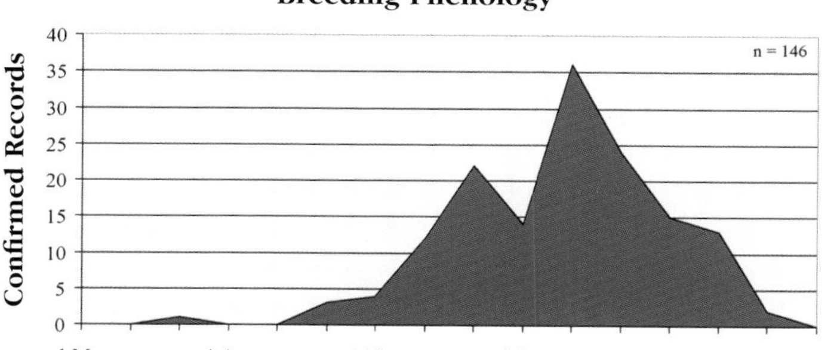

fledge about 24–27 days after hatching (Moore 1995). Both adults brood the hatchlings and feed the young. Northern Flickers typically only produce one brood a year and very rarely two. Flicker nestlings are extremely vocal, sounding somewhat like a colony of honeybees. Duncan (1990) has made the intriguing argument that this is a form of Batesian mimicry to help deter predation by squirrels.

DISTRIBUTION AND STATUS

Northern Flickers are the most widespread woodpeckers breeding in North America. The yellow-shafted subspecies occurs in the eastern part of the continent as well as throughout the boreal forests of Canada and Alaska. The red-shafted subspecies breeds from southern Alaska through British Columbia and throughout the mountains of the western U.S. and Mexico. A rather broad hybrid contact zone occurs east of the Rocky Mountains from Alberta to New Mexico.

Northern Flickers always have been considered common and widespread summer residents in most forested regions of northern and eastern Arizona (Swarth 1914; Phillips et al. 1964). These large, noisy woodpeckers were easily detected by atlasers and were noted on most surveyed blocks containing trees large enough to support their cavities. Atlasers documented Northern Flickers nesting at elevations primarily from above 4000 ft (1219 m), and reaching up to about 11,000 ft (3353 m). However, this species nests locally down into lowland riparian woodlands to below 3400 ft (1036 m), where they occasionally hybridize with Gilded Flickers. Hybrid zones include the upper San Pedro, Santa Cruz, and Agua Fria River drainages; Cienega Creek; and near Camp Verde (Phillips et al. 1964).

In southeastern Arizona, Northern Flickers were found in most mountain forests and down into oak and lowland riparian woodlands west to approximately Sasabe. These flickers were oddly not found nesting in the oak and sycamore-lined drainages of the Baboquivari Mountains or even in the higher-elevation oak woodlands at Kitt Peak.

Northern Flickers were found fairly consistently along the Mogollon Rim northward. In fact, atlas records nearly encompass the White Mountain Apache tribal lands, where atlas surveys could not be conducted. In the Mojave Desert–influenced region of northwestern Arizona, these flickers were rather sparsely distributed to the higher mountain ranges including the Cerbat Mountains.

Northern Flickers are common and widespread in North America, but Breeding Bird Survey data have shown that the species has declined in most parts of its range. Reasons include urbanization and alteration of habitat, removal of snags, and possible competition for nest cavities where European Starlings are plentiful.

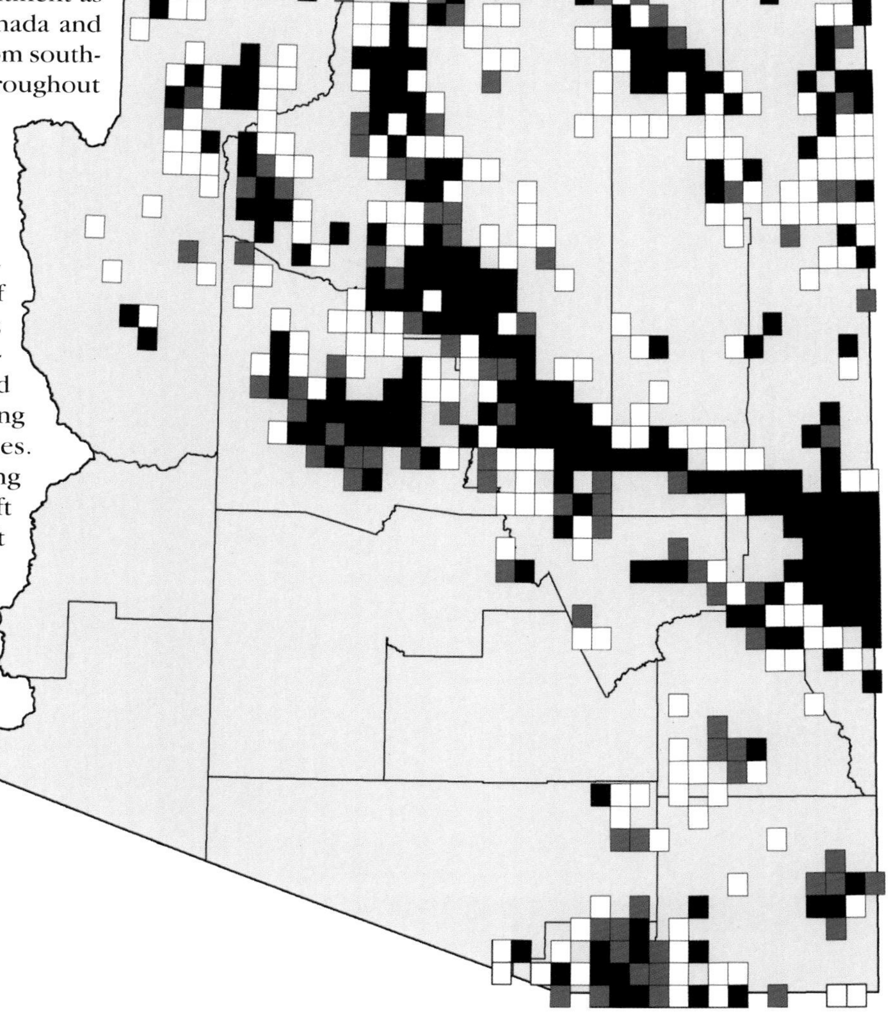

Northern Flicker Breeding Evidence Reported in 502 (27%) of 1834 priority blocks

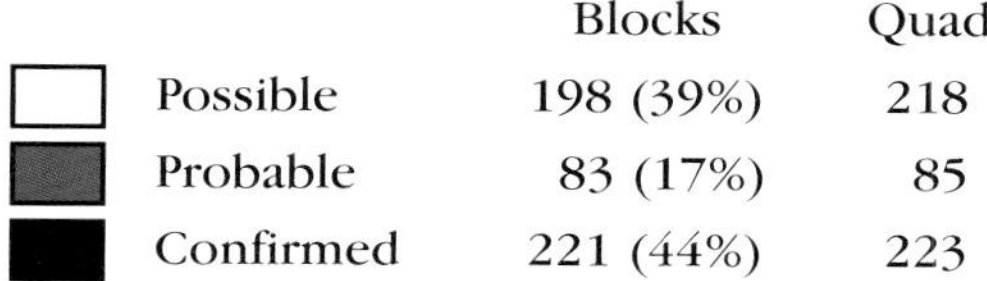

	Blocks	Quads
Possible	198 (39%)	218
Probable	83 (17%)	85
Confirmed	221 (44%)	223

Gilded Flicker

by Troy E. Corman *Colaptes chrysoides*

With flashing golden underwings, Gilded Flickers are often observed as they alight atop a saguaro in their Sonoran Desert domain. Smaller and paler than Northern Flickers, their abandoned saguaro nest cavities are used extensively for nesting and roosting by many other avian desert dwellers from flycatchers and martins to kestrels and owls.

BRUCE TAUBERT

HABITAT

Gilded Flickers have a close affinity with the Sonoran Desert and the majestic saguaro that symbolizes its arid landscapes. In fact, these flickers reach their greatest abundance where this large cactus is in high density. Therefore, it was not surprising to find 83 percent of 505 Gilded Flicker atlas records either in the Sonoran Desert uplands (65 percent) or in the more sparsely vegetated Sonoran Desert lowlands (18 percent). The reduced number of observations in the latter habitat undoubtedly pertains to many fewer saguaros in this drier desert. Significantly fewer records were also reported from the adjacent wooded desert dry washes, as well as the Sonoran riparian woodlands containing tall stands of Fremont cottonwood and Goodding willow. When saguaros are nearby, these two habitats are used more commonly for foraging than nesting. Atlasers also found Gilded Flickers infrequently inhabiting Mojave desertscrub and semiarid grasslands. Unlike Gila Woodpeckers, these flickers typically shy away from more densely populated urban and rural neighborhoods, even where saguaros are included in residential landscaping.

BREEDING

Unlike the Northern Flicker, Gildeds are primarily a resident species and seldom wander far from typical nesting habitat. These flickers may begin constructing nest cavities in saguaros three or more months prior to nesting. This allows the cacti enough time to seal off the open wound with dense scar tissue that surrounds the inside of the cavity. Atlasers noted courtship and pairing activity beginning in February and continuing into early March. The first occupied nest reported by atlasers was on 12 March. The first nest with young was noted on 3 April, which would suggest egg laying beginning in early to mid-March. Based on atlas data, peak nesting activity for Gilded Flickers in Arizona is between mid-April and mid-May. Bent (1939) noted the latest nest with freshly laid eggs was collected on 11 June. The latest nest with young reported by atlasers was on 2 July.

Gilman (1915) found that approximately 90 percent of Gilded Flickers nest in saguaros, with the remainder in Fremont cottonwoods and Goodding willow. They have also been observed occasionally nesting in tall honey mesquite near the Colorado River (Rosenberg et al. 1991). Of the 19 nests in saguaros measured by atlasers, the mean nest cavity entrance height was 15.4 ft (4.7 m) with a range of 5.9–24.6 ft (1.8–7.5 m). Other studies found 20.3 ft (6.2 m) to be the average nest height in saguaros (Kerpez and Smith 1990).

Both sexes participate in cavity excavation, but males typically play the dominant role (Moore 1995). Gilman (1915) noted that Gilded Flickers typically lay 3–5 eggs, which is a significantly smaller clutch size than for the Northern Flicker. Incubation typically takes 11 days, and the pair shares the responsibility (Moore 1995). The nestlings are fed by both parents and fledge when they are 21–27 days old (Moore 1995). Most evidence suggests that flickers produce only one brood per season, however, they will renest if earlier attempts fail (Moore 1995). Conversely, Rosenberg et al. (1991) reported that Gilded Flickers raise two broods per season with young fledging in late May and then again in early July.

DISTRIBUTION AND STATUS

Gilded Flickers are found from southern Arizona and extreme southeastern California, south into much of Baja California and northwestern Sinaloa. Phillips et al. (1964)

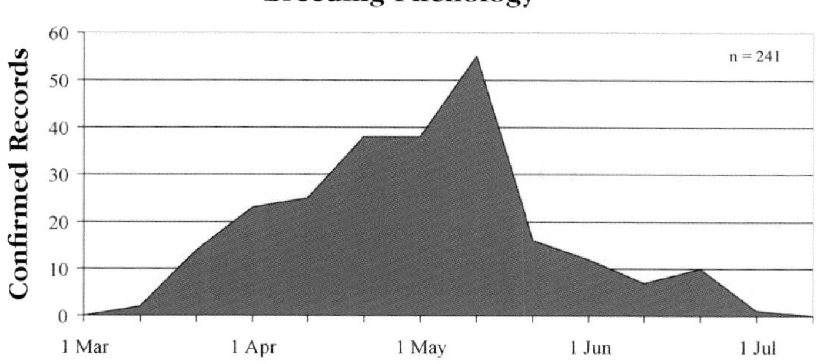

considered Gilded Flickers to be common residents in south-central Arizona, and more sparsely distributed west to the Colorado River valley and north to the Big Sandy and Santa Maria river drainages. Within the Bill Williams River delta, these flickers were noted as still fairly common (Rosenberg et al. 1991). However, in the remainder of the Colorado River valley, Rosenberg et al. also noted this flicker as rather rare with only scattered pairs persisting at Fort Mojave (at least formerly), the Colorado River Indian tribal lands, Cibola and Imperial National Wildlife Refuges, and between Imperial and Laguna Dams. Gilded Flickers were historically more common and widespread throughout this river valley (Grinnell 1914; Swarth 1914), where this flicker associated with both saguaro- and cottonwood-dominated forests.

During the atlas, Gilded Flickers were primarily found at elevations ranging from 200 to 3200 ft (61–975 m), although locally they were found in riparian areas to 4600 ft (1402 m). Individuals observed at these higher elevations along the upper Santa Cruz and San Pedro rivers may pertain to a hybrid zone with the Northern Flicker. Hybrid populations occur mainly in riparian woodlands along drainages flowing from the mountains and grasslands into the Sonoran Desert and tend to have more plumage characteristics of Gilded Flicker (Moore 1995).

Atlasers commonly encountered Gilded Flickers in the southwestern corner of the state east to the lower San Pedro River. Farther east, these flickers were sparingly distributed up the Gila River drainage to approximately the Safford vicinity and along the San Pedro River to the Mexico border. Gilded Flickers were also found in the Salt River Canyon upstream to the western edge of the White Mountain Apache tribal lands. Atlasers confirmed this flicker nesting on the Verde River upstream to near the Fossil Creek confluence and to the northwest to near Oatman. Gilded Flickers were reported very locally north into the Mojave Desert within the Detrital Valley, near Meadville, and one location north of the Colorado River, just west of the Grand Wash Cliffs. This species had previously not been reported north of Kingman.

Gilded Flickers were noticeably absent from many highly developed blocks in the greater Phoenix and adjacent agricultural areas. As noted before, these flickers do not adapt well to urban life. As towns and cities continue to grow in the Sonoran Desert, the distribution of the Gilded Flicker will likely continue to contract. Devastating desert wildfires, which are now fueled by exotic grasses and often kill the large saguaros on which this species depends, constitute another serious threat.

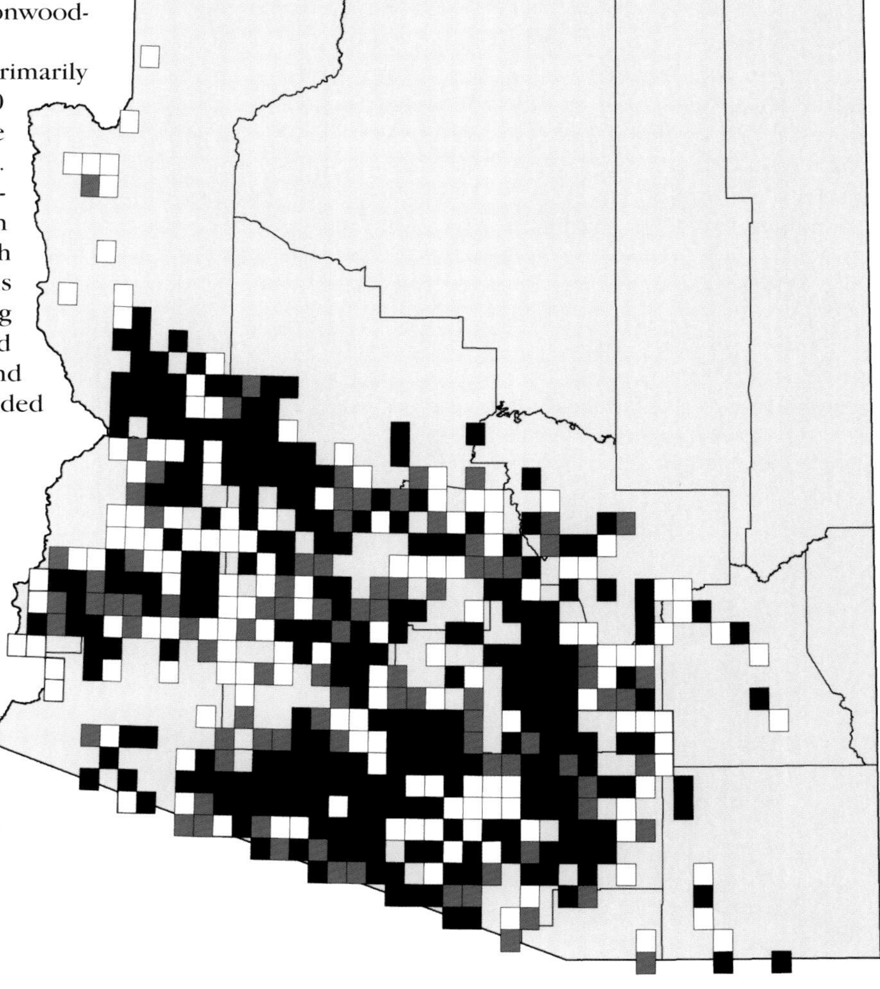

Gilded Flicker Breeding Evidence Reported in 503 (27%) of 1834 priority blocks

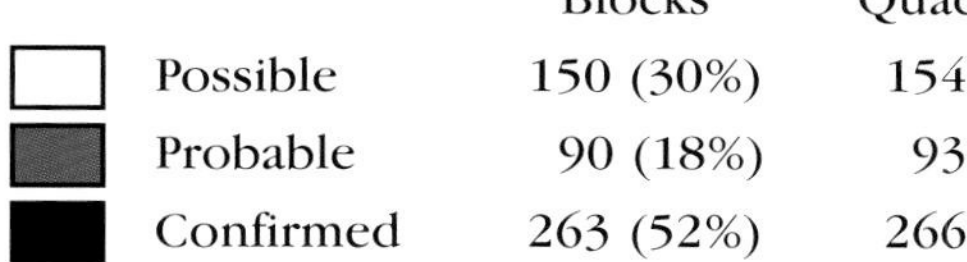

	Blocks	Quads
Possible	150 (30%)	154
Probable	90 (18%)	93
Confirmed	263 (52%)	266

Northern Beardless-Tyrannulet

by Troy E. Corman *Camptostoma imberbe*

Northern Beardless-Tyrannulets are diminutive tropical flycatchers that range north into lowland riparian areas of southeastern Arizona. Unless the observer is familiar with their song and calls, these retiring birds with their unique nesting habits frequently go unnoticed as they glean insects from tree foliage and branches.

DAN FISCHER

HABITAT

In southeastern Arizona, Northern Beardless-Tyrannulets primarily inhabit fairly open riparian woodlands, including lower canyons and heavily wooded dry washes. Surface water is frequently found near occupied locations, but is not a requirement for this tropical species. Atlasers reported most of their observations (43 percent) from lowland riparian woodlands composed of Fremont cottonwood and Goodding willow stands (n = 69). Many occupied riparian locations include an understory of velvet mesquite and locally tamarisk. An additional 25 percent of records were noted at slightly higher elevations in drainages and lower canyons where Arizona sycamore and occasionally nearby evergreen oaks are dispersed among scattered cottonwood, willow, ash, mesquite, and hackberry. Northern Beardless-Tyrannulets commonly inhabit the nearby drier mesquite bosques that frequently cover the upper floodplain. Correspondingly, these little flycatchers were found fairly regularly in intermittent foothill drainages and dry washes with stands of tall netleaf hackberry and mesquite. A few pairs were also encountered nesting in native vegetation at the edge of several urban parks with grass and scattered exotic trees.

BREEDING

Although locally resident, most Northern Beardless-Tyrannulets are migratory in Arizona and return to breeding areas in early to mid-March. Territorial singing begins soon after these small flycatchers arrive. The earliest nest building activity reported during the atlas period was on 12 April, although nest construction has been noted as early as 2 April in Arizona. Northern Beardless-Tyrannulets typically lay first egg clutches in mid- to late April and based on atlas data, the peak nesting period is roughly from early May through late June. An adult was observed feeding a fledgling as early as 15 May. These tropical flycatchers have a lengthy nesting season in Arizona. Atlasers noted nest construction as late as 18 July and an occupied nest on 1 August. Phillips et al. (1964) reported an individual carrying nesting material on 4 August, which, if successful, would suggest that some later nests may not fledge until late August or early September. Although regularly wintering in limited numbers at some lower elevation locations within Arizona, most Northern Beardless-Tyrannulets have departed the state by late September.

Apparently only the female Northern Beardless-Tyrannulet constructs the uniquely placed nest in 4–9 days (Cornell Nest Record Program data); however, the male occasionally accompanies her to the site (Brandt 1951). In Arizona, most nests are constructed near the top or within old, bulky tent caterpillar web clusters or less frequently in mistletoe clumps. These unsightly clusters typically consist of a dense mass of webbing, leaves, and twigs, which are regularly observed dangling from branches of Fremont cottonwood and Goodding willow. Accordingly, the majority of Northern Beardless-Tyrannulet nests in Arizona have been discovered in these trees. Atlasers also found them nesting in similar caterpillar web masses in Arizona sycamore, velvet ash, netleaf hackberry, and velvet mesquite. On two occasions, atlasers also found Northern Beardless-Tyrannulets nesting in masses of flood debris consisting mostly of dry leaves and mud, which had been caught on the limbs of young trees during prior high water events. Both of the latter nests were relatively low, having been constructed only 3.9 and 5.2 ft (1.2 and 1.6 m) above the ground. Nests in

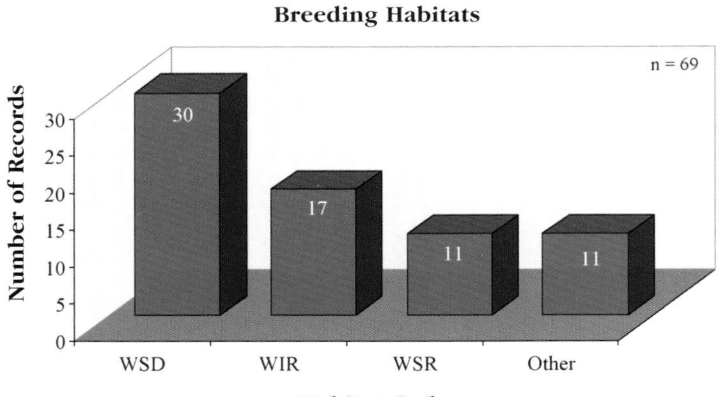

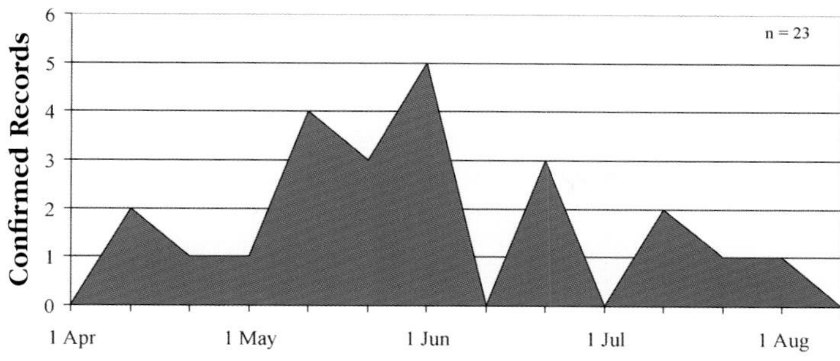

Arizona have previously been reported from 6.5 to 50 ft (2–12 m) high (Bent 1942; Anderson and Anderson 1948). The well-concealed nest is typically domed over and generally not visible from below (Brandt 1951).

Judging by nest records collected by Cornell, the 1–3 egg clutches are incubated by the female for approximately 14 to 16 days. Northern Beardless-Tyrannulet nestlings are fed by both parents, and, a nest in Texas suggests, fledge when they are only 12 days old (Brush 1999). Two or three broods are produced each year in Arizona, with the female sometimes constructing a second nest while the male feeds the fledglings from the first brood (Cornell Nest Record Program data).

DISTRIBUTION AND STATUS

Northern Beardless-Tyrannulets are primarily a resident species from Costa Rica north to the southern tip of Texas and Sonora. Most of the populations in southeastern Arizona and southwestern New Mexico are migratory, withdrawing slightly south during the winter. Phillips et al. (1964) considered this species a fairly common summer resident, north to the confluence of the Gila and San Pedro rivers, and from Guadalupe Canyon in the extreme southeast, west to the western foothill drainages of the Baboquivari Mountains. In recent years, Northern Beardless-Tyrannulets have become almost annual spring and summer visitors as far north as the Boyce Thompson Arboretum near Superior. Elsewhere, they have wandered irregularly north during the breeding season to Maricopa County along the lower Verde and Hassayampa rivers, but nesting has not been documented at these outposts.

Atlas data suggest that the general breeding distribution of the Northern Beardless-Tyrannulet has changed little since the mid-1900s. These small flycatchers were discovered nesting at elevations from 1920 ft (585 m) along the Gila River near Winkelman to 4600 ft (1402 m) in foothill drainages of the Santa Rita Mountains.

Northern Beardless-Tyrannulets were found nesting along nearly the entire length of the San Pedro River and its wooded tributaries, including Aravaipa Creek upstream to Klondyke and Muleshoe Ranch Preserve. They were also frequently encountered along Arivaca Creek, Sonoita Creek, and upper Santa Cruz River north to Amado. They were regularly encountered in wooded foothill drainages of the Baboquivari, Atascosa, Santa Rita, and Santa Catalina mountains, but remain largely absent from similar, but slightly higher elevated drainages of the Huachuca and Chiricahua mountains.

Atlasers confirmed these birds nesting at new locations as far northwest as Cluff Ranch south of Pima and along Markham Creek northeast of Ft. Thomas. However, in the past they have been found in nearby Bonita Creek near its confluence with the Gila River. These records suggest a more widespread breeding distribution in Graham County than previously thought and further investigation would undoubtedly reveal additional locations in this under surveyed county.

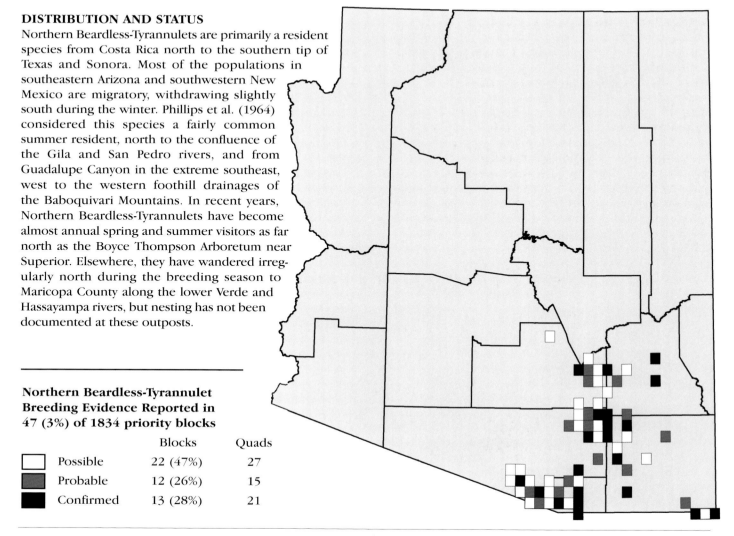

Northern Beardless-Tyrannulet Breeding Evidence Reported in 47 (3%) of 1834 priority blocks

	Blocks	Quads
Possible	22 (47%)	27
Probable	12 (26%)	15
Confirmed	13 (28%)	21

Olive-sided Flycatcher

by Cathryn Wise-Gervais *Contopus cooperi*

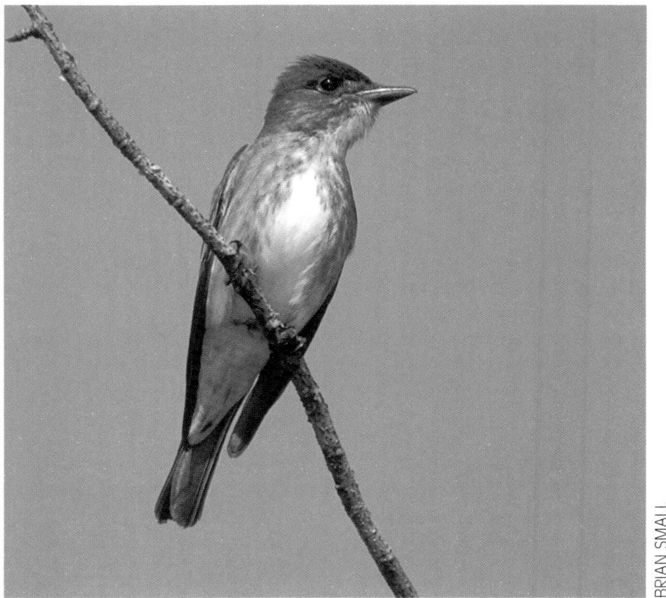

Few would guess that the unassuming Olive-sided Flycatcher undergoes one of the longest migrations of neotropical songbirds, with some wintering south to the Andes. Their distinctive "quick three beers" song is typically delivered from a lofty exposed perch, where they also keep an alert vigil for bees, a favored prey.

HABITAT

Olive-sided Flycatchers prefer coniferous forests offering tall prominent trees and snags from which to hunt insects. In general, this species prefers forest edge habitats and is more commonly encountered in open to semi-open forest stands than in closed canopy forests (Altman and Sallabanks 2000). They also commonly occur along the natural forest edge created by montane streams, lakes, and beaver ponds, where snags are often present and insect densities are often higher. Olive-sided Flycatchers frequently use burned areas and some studies have shown them to be more common in these than in adjacent unburned land (Overturf 1979). Atlasers reported Olive-sided Flycatchers in seven habitat types, and four of these contained a strong ponderosa pine component. Observers most commonly reported the birds in open mixed conifer forests of Douglas fir, White fir, ponderosa pine, and scattered quaking aspen stands (39 percent; $n = 56$). Additionally, atlasers reported 27 percent of potential breeding records in pure ponderosa pine forests and 13 percent in ponderosa pine–Gambel's oak associations. These birds were noted very infrequently in the drier pinyon-juniper woodlands that contained scattered ponderosa pine. Olive-sided Flycatchers often occur in open or edge spruce-fir forests elsewhere within their breeding range and the few atlas records may partially be explained by the limited distribution of this habitat in Arizona.

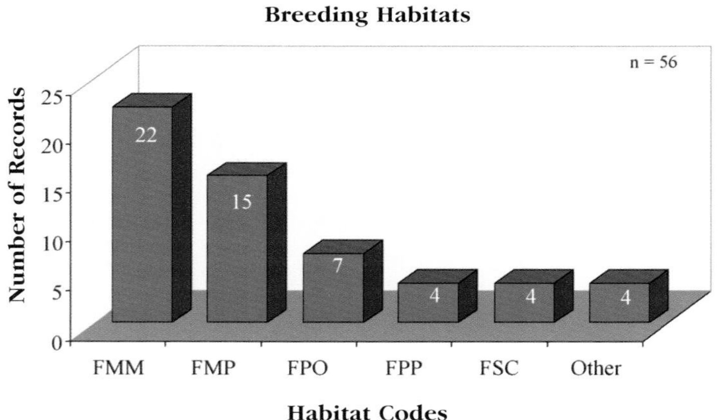

BREEDING

Olive-sided Flycatchers begin arriving in Arizona by mid-April and appear on their breeding grounds between late April and mid-May. Migrants continue to pass through the state regularly into early June and occasionally later. Females arrive slightly later than the males, and pair formation begins soon after (Altman and Sallabanks 2000). Atlasers first reported a pair of birds in suitable breeding habitat on 27 April. From a few early June atlas nesting records, nest construction could begin by mid-May in Arizona with early clutches laid in late May. However, most of the few confirmed atlas records for Olive-sided Flycatcher were in July. These later nests are not surprising, inasmuch as egg laying can occur late at higher elevations. Bent (1942) reported egg clutches as late as 20 July in Colorado, and Altman (1999) noted a late clutch on 29 July in Oregon with the latest young fledging on 30 August. Atlasers discovered a nest with young on 1 August and reported these flycatchers in suitable breeding habitats through 14 August. Migrating Olive-sided Flycatchers are rarely reported in Arizona before mid-August. Peak migration is in early September, with most birds departing southern Arizona by late September and rarely into early October.

Olive-sided Flycatchers will nest in a wide variety of coniferous trees, as well as in Gambel's oak and less commonly in aspen or cottonwood (Altman and Sallabanks 2000). The female selects the nest site and indicates her choice by "bellying down" into the foliage as if molding the interior of a nest (Altman and Sallabanks 2000). Sites are typically on a horizontal limb, well away from the trunk and often beneath another limb that provides some concealment and protection from the elements. Nests are loose, open cup structures and are placed within a wide range of heights. Nests in the western U.S. mountains are generally placed higher than nests in other parts of the bird's range, and Altman and Sallabanks (2000) noted nest heights ranging from 4.9 to 111.5 ft (1.5–34 m), with one exceptionally high California nest reported nearly 200 ft (60 m) above the ground (Head 1903). Atlasers measured only three Olive-sided Flycatcher nests, two in Engelmann spruce and one in Douglas fir. These ranged in height from 42.6 to 60.7 ft (13–18.5 m).

Female Olive-sided Flycatchers construct their nests in 5–10 days, with little to no assistance from the male (Wright 1997). Typical clutches consist of 3–4 eggs (range 2–5) and are incubated by the female for approximately 14 to 16 days (Altman 1999). Both sexes will then feed the nestlings but only the female will brood (Altman and Sallabanks 2000). The young fledge in 17–23 days (Altman 1999) and continue to receive food from the adults for an additional 10 to 17 days after nest departure (Altman and Sallabanks 2000). These flycatchers regularly renest if early attempts have failed. Olive-sided Flycatchers are relatively late migrants and have one of the longest reproductive periods of any passerine bird; thus double-clutching after a successful brood in unlikely (Altman and Sallabanks 2000).

DISTRIBUTION AND STATUS

Olive-sided Flycatchers breed throughout Canada and most of Alaska and south along the Pacific coast to northern California. They also nest in higher mountain ranges in the West to northern Baja California and central Arizona and New Mexico. Eastern populations commonly breed as far south as upstate New York and northern Michigan, and very locally in the Appalachian Mountains farther south.

In Arizona, Swarth (1914) described Olive-sided Flycatchers as common summer residents in higher mountain ranges north of the Mogollon Rim. Later accounts noted these birds as a fairly common nesting species in the state within the prior described range, extending west to the Kaibab Plateau and Bill Williams Mountain, and possibly south to the Sierra Ancha, Gila County (Phillips et al. 1964; Monson and Phillips 1981). In Arizona, atlasers documented Olive-sided Flycatcher in appropriate nesting habitat at elevations from approximately 6900 to 10,000 ft (2103–3048 m).

In the Grand Canyon region, Brown et al. (1987) considered these flycatchers as only an uncommon nesting species on the North and South Rims. Similarly, atlas surveys revealed that Olive-sided Flycatchers were sparsely distributed on the Kaibab Plateau and within the Mount Trumbull area. They were confirmed nesting on Navajo tribal lands in the Chuska Mountains during the atlas and found possibly nesting in the nearby Lukachukai Mountains. Within this region, atlasers also found Olive-sided Flycatchers locally distributed on the Defiance Plateau. These birds were most commonly encountered in the San Francisco Mountains area and within the White Mountain region, south to the Blue Range. This species undoubtedly breed on the adjacent unsurveyed White Mountain Apache tribal lands as well.

Olive-sided Flycatcher populations are declining throughout their range (Altman and Sallabanks 2000). They respond positively to landscapes altered by fire or some timber harvesting practices, activities that have increased throughout the birds range. Given this, it is possible the birds are being adversely affected by some element on their wintering grounds (Altman and Sallabanks 2000). As a result, this species is one of the priority species of conservation concern throughout most of its range. Management recommendations include studying these robust flycatchers on their wintering grounds in an attempt to determine possible causes of declines, and preserving snags and some tall trees during timber harvesting or fire management activities.

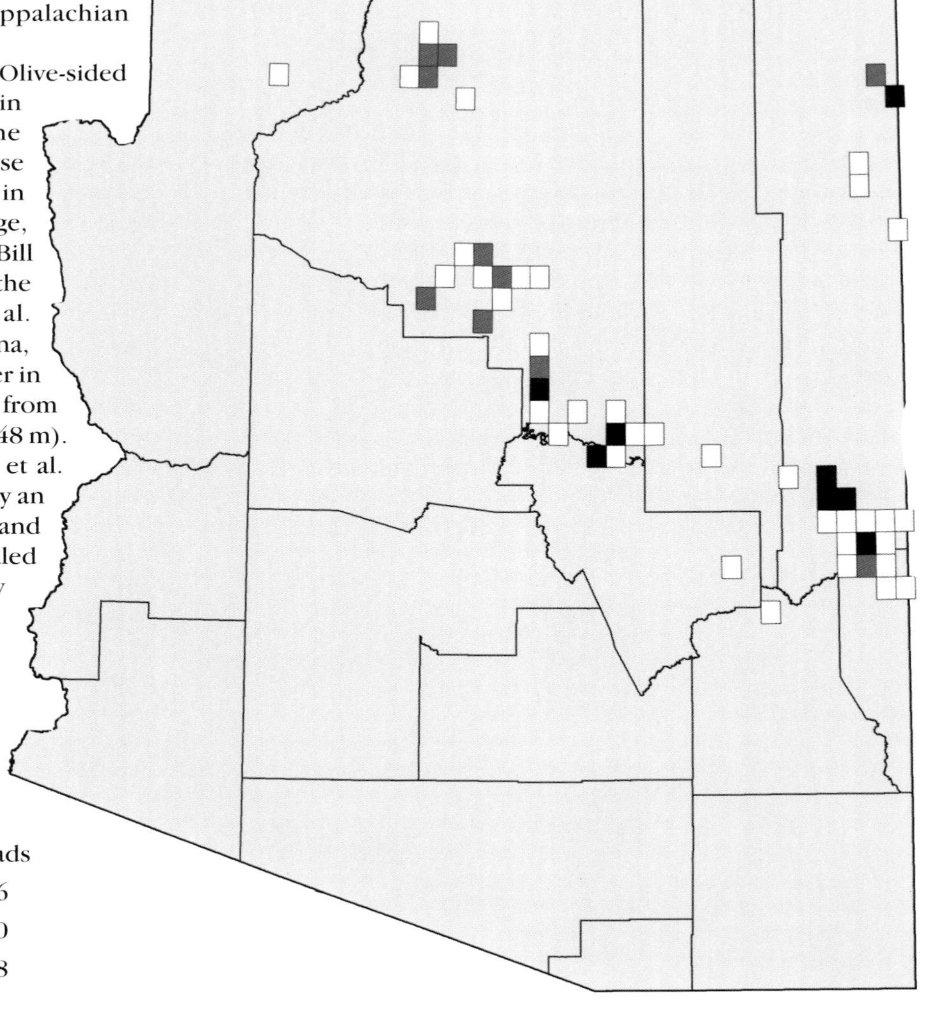

Olive-sided Flycatcher Breeding Evidence Reported in 49 (3%) of 1834 priority blocks

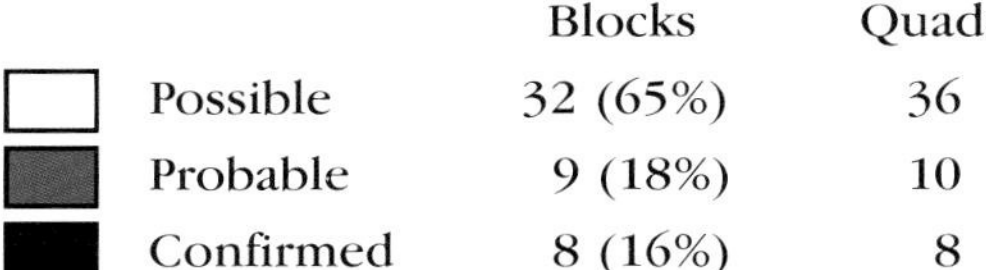

	Blocks	Quads
Possible	32 (65%)	36
Probable	9 (18%)	10
Confirmed	8 (16%)	8

Greater Pewee

by Cathryn Wise-Gervais *Contopus pertinax*

The Greater Pewee's distinctive "ho-say, ma-ree-ah" song is an unmistakable component of southeastern and central Arizona's pine forests. Like other pewees, these birds perch on exposed dead branches, then sally out to catch flying insects with a loud bill-snap. Greater Pewees will then habitually return to the same perch to repeat the process.

RICK AND NORA BOWERS

HABITAT

Arizona's Greater Pewees are typically found on mountain slopes, in steep-sided canyons, and near open pine-oak forests and woodlands. This species selects settings that offer tall pines from which they typically sing and forage from mid-height branches (Marshall 1957). Atlasers observed Greater Pewees in eight habitat types, with the most frequently reported of these being ponderosa pine forests with a Gambel's oak and/or Madrean evergreen oak understory. This is the most commonly used habitat within their central Arizona range and accounted for 33 percent of all atlas records for this flycatcher (n = 40). In southeastern Arizona mountains, these pewees were most frequently encountered in Madrean pine-oak woodlands with tall stands of Chihuahuan, Apache, and ponderosa pines. Observers also found Greater Pewees where this habitat transitions in canyons containing Arizona sycamore and walnut, and approximately 28 percent of atlas records were obtained within these two habitats. Observers located fewer Greater Pewees in the more open mixed conifer and pure ponderosa pine forests, and in the adjacent forested drainages. Marshall (1957) noted that these large pewees often spend the day in riparian shade and spread into surrounding pine-oak in early morning and late afternoon; when actively feeding and singing.

BREEDING

In southeastern Arizona, Greater Pewees begin arriving in late March and early April and are heard delivering their unique whistled song by mid- to late April. Pair formation and nest building can commence almost immediately. Atlasers first reported Greater Pewees collecting nesting material on 3 May. Published nesting dates suggest that these birds lay eggs in mid- to late May through mid-July and have young in the nest from late May through late July (Chace and Tweit 1999). Atlas data coincide with these dates, inasmuch as our earliest record of adults feeding dependent fledglings was obtained on 8 June and the latest nest with young was on 12 July. Fledglings were noted being fed through 20 July, although this activity likely continues into early August. Fall migration is not well understood in Arizona, but Greater Pewees begin appearing away from nesting areas in August and the birds generally depart southern Arizona by late September or early October. Individual Greater Pewees are occasionally found wintering in southern Arizona lowlands.

Greater Pewee nests are typically placed on a horizontal limb at a branch fork and are often in the upper half or third of the tree (Chace and Tweit 1999). Nests are sometimes covered with lichen and spider webs making them cryptic and difficult to locate. Greater Pewees vigorously defend nest sites and other birds nesting in or near their nest tree benefit from this large flycatchers' protection against jays, woodpeckers, and squirrels (Howard 1904). Their most common nest trees in Arizona are ponderosa and Apache pines, with fewer nests in Douglas fir, Arizona sycamore, and various species of oaks. The height of three Greater Pewee nests measured by atlasers in ponderosa pine, Gambel's oak, and netleaf oak, ranged from 18 to 36 ft (5.5–11 m) above the ground, but little can be inferred from such a small sample size. For comparison, Chance and Tweit (1999) reported a mean nest height of approximately 38 ft (11.6 m) for 19 nests measured in the Huachuca Mountains.

Greater Pewees typically lay clutches of 3–4 eggs (range 2–4), and the female incubates these for an unknown period, although likely approximately 14 days as with other *Contopus* flycatchers. Conflicting evidence exists regarding parental care and whether males assist in feeding the nestlings (Chace and Tweit 1999). It is also not known how

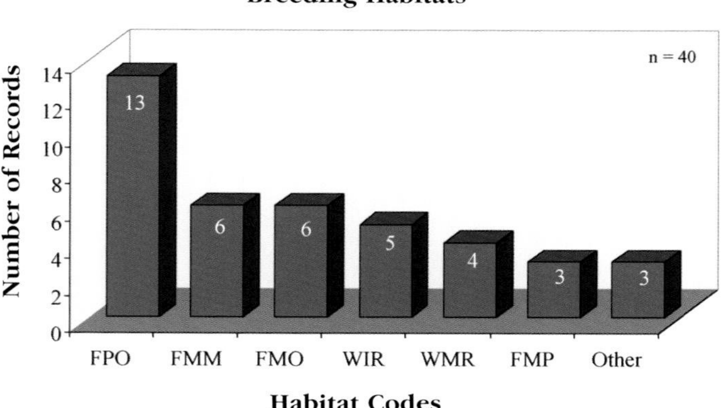

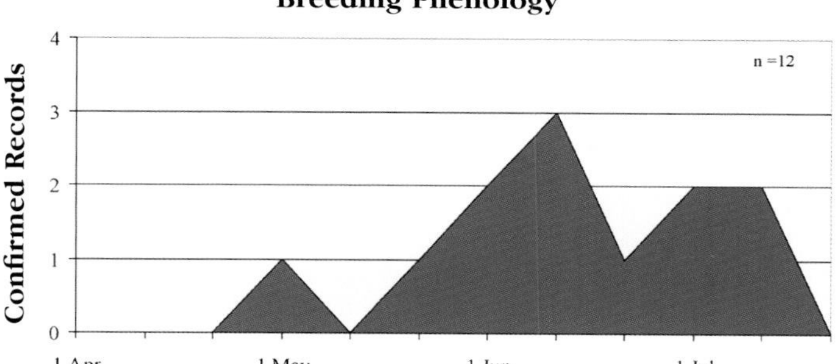

long the young stay in the nest or how long parental care continues after the young fledge. The young are barely able to fly immediately following nest departure and are fed by both parents (Bent 1942). Most evidence suggests only one brood is produced per season, although renesting is common if an earlier attempt is unsuccessful.

DISTRIBUTION AND STATUS

Greater Pewees are primarily Mexican birds, and their occurrence in Arizona and western New Mexico marks the northern edge of their range. They are year-round residents in central and southern Mexico and occur as far south as northern Nicaragua. Atlasers reported Greater Pewees in Arizona at elevations from approximately 5500 to 8400 ft (1676–2560 m).

Atlas data reveal that Greater Pewees continue to occupy the pine-oak country of southeastern and central Arizona previously described by Swarth (1914) and Phillips et al. (1964). Atlasers found that these pewees were most commonly encountered in southeastern Arizona mountain ranges and were much less common and more locally distributed to the north. In southeastern Arizona, Greater Pewees were found in most of the higher elevated ranges containing pines including the Rincon Mountains. Atlasers also discovered them nesting in the smaller and drier Whetstone and Santa Teresa mountains, and with more surveys, these large pewees will likely be found in the seldom-visited higher elevations of the Galiuro Mountains.

Greater Pewees were detected in several other small mountain ranges south of the Mogollon Rim, including the Pinal, Sierra Ancha, and Mazatzal. They were found sparingly north to the southern slope of the Mogollon Rim but were not detected above it, where another large pewee, the Olive-sided Flycatcher nests. Greater Pewees undoubtedly regularly breed on adjacent White Mountain Apache tribal land, but atlasers were unable to verify this due to survey access issues. They were found nesting northwest to forests just south of Prescott and on Mingus Mountain west of Cottonwood, and the westernmost atlas records were of birds in appropriate nesting habitat in the Juniper and Hualapai Mountains.

Compared to historical records, the distribution and abundance of Greater Pewee has apparently changed little other than possibly expanding to several mountain ranges in west-central Arizona. There are many unanswered questions pertaining to this species' general breeding biology and this feisty pewee would greatly benefit from even basic natural history and habitat requirement studies.

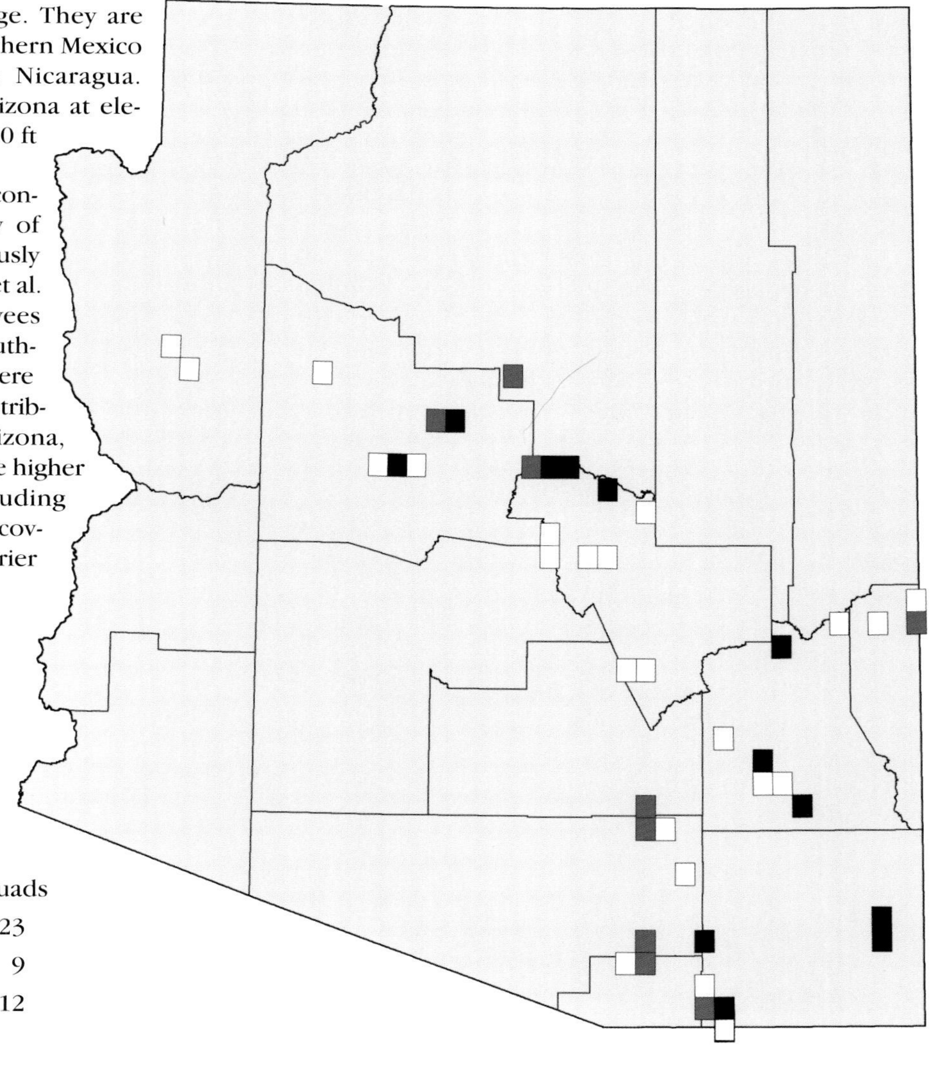

Greater Pewee Breeding Evidence Reported in 26 (1%) of 1834 priority blocks

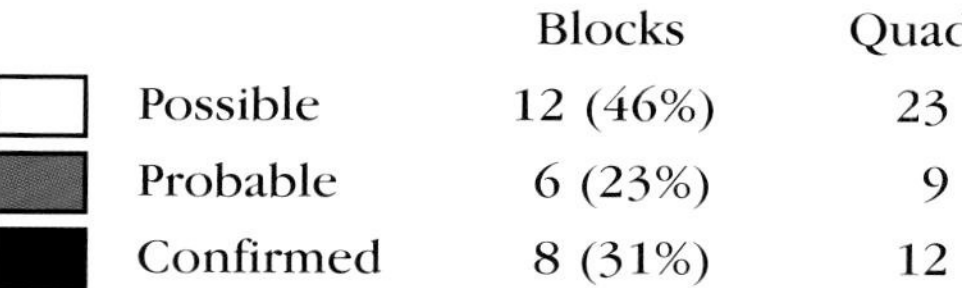

	Blocks	Quads
Possible	12 (46%)	23
Probable	6 (23%)	9
Confirmed	8 (31%)	12

Western Wood-Pewee

by Cathryn Wise-Gervais *Contopus sordidulus*

Owing to their wider selection of forested habitats, Western Wood-Pewees are much more common and widespread in the state than Arizona's other two larger pewees combined. These familiar woodland birds select a favorite perch from which to watch and wait for flying insects and deliver their rather woeful "pee-yee" song.

DAN FISCHER

HABITAT

As their name suggests, Western Wood-Pewees prefer wooded areas but will use a wide array of settings offering vertical structure. Such areas include open coniferous forests and forest edges, as well as oak and riparian woodlands. Atlasers reported a total of 417 potential breeding records for Western Wood-Pewees in twenty-one habitat types. Of these, 23 percent were in foothill and canyon drainages containing sycamore and often including scattered cottonwood, ash, and oak. An additional 10 percent of records were from cottonwood-willow gallery stands, although these lowland riparian woodlands were not used for nesting below approximately 3400 ft (1036 m). Atlasers reported nearly 25 percent of records in primarily pure ponderosa pine forests and ponderosa pine–Gambel's oak associations. These birds also occurred rather sparingly (17 percent of records) in the taller and denser woodlands of pinyon pine–juniper, including areas where these stands included scattered ponderosa pine. In southeastern Arizona mountain ranges, these small pewees nest commonly in Madrean pine-oak forests and less frequently on the lower evergreen oak-covered slopes where tree stature typically does not reach the height preferred by these flycatchers. Although encountered locally in open mixed conifer forests, aspen groves, spruce-fir forests, and along montane riparian drainages, relatively few atlas records were obtained in these higher elevation habitats. Generally, Western Wood-Pewees select either open woodlands or the edge of denser stands that offer snags or dead limbs and open areas for foraging (Bemis and Rising 1999).

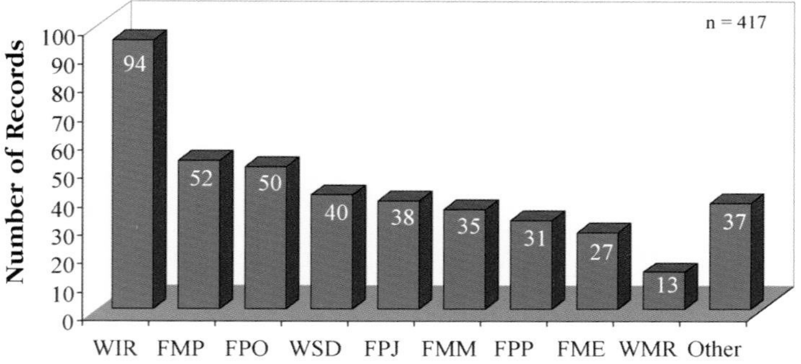

BREEDING

Western Wood-Pewees are infrequently observed in southern Arizona prior to the first week of April, and typically do not become common until May when they also arrive in northern Arizona. Late migrants are commonly observed through mid-June in Arizona. Atlasers reported the first paired birds on 3 May and the earliest nest building activity was noted on 19 May. However, atlasers discovered a nest with young on 25 May, indicating nest building by late April and egg laying by early May. Western Wood-Pewees typically place their nests high in trees making the determination of nest contents difficult. As a result, atlasers commonly reported active nests but were usually unable to determine nest contents. Statewide atlas data suggest that the peak breeding period for Western Wood-Pewees is from early June through early July, with a sharp decline thereafter. Atlasers found the latest nest with eggs on 11 July and observed adults feeding fledglings through 26 August. Late summer breeding records are likely renesting efforts following earlier failed attempts, inasmuch as this species is known to raise only one brood per year (Bemis and Rising 1999). Fall migration can begin by late July in Arizona and is well underway by mid-August, peaking in September, with few individuals remaining after mid-October.

Observers measured the heights of twenty-two Western Wood-Pewee nests, and two of these were in snags. The most commonly reported nest trees were ponderosa pine and Gambel's oak. Other nest trees included Arizona white oak, alligator juniper, aspen, sycamore, cottonwood, box elder, and walnut. The median nest height was 16 ft (4.9 m) and ranged from 6.6 to 40.0 ft (2–12.2 m).

Female Western Wood-Pewees build substantial, well-camouflaged cup nests, usually placed on forks of horizontal limbs a fair distance form the trunk. The typical

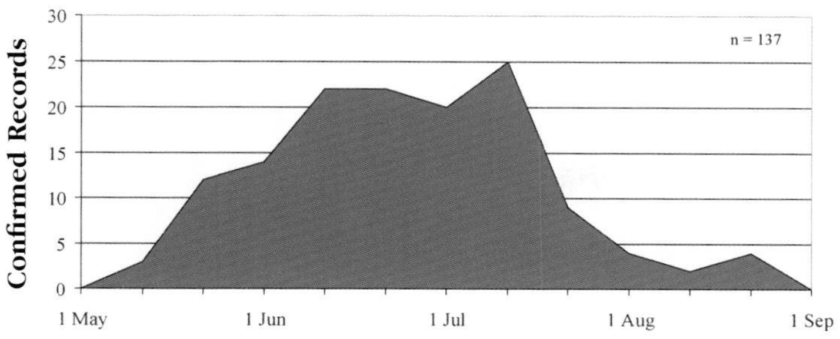

clutch consists of 3 eggs (range 2–4), and the female incubates these without male assistance for 12 to 13 days (Ehrlich et al. 1988). Both parents feed the youngsters and these fledge at 14–18 days of age (Bemis and Rising 1999).

Western Wood-Pewees are considered an infrequent Brown-headed Cowbird host (Friedman and Kiff 1985). Atlasers reported two incidents of cowbird brood parasitism, and both records were fairly late in the breeding season. One report was of a nest with eggs on 11 July, and the other was of adult pewees feeding a cowbird fledgling on 5 August.

DISTRIBUTION AND STATUS

Western Wood-Pewees breed throughout western North America from eastern Alaska to southwestern Manitoba, then south through the highlands of Mexico to Honduras. These neotropical migrants winter in South America and annually travel farther south than any other of Arizona's nesting passerines (Phillips et al. 1964). In Arizona, these flycatchers are not found nesting in woodlands at either high or low elevation extremes, and atlasers confirmed this species breeding on priority blocks from approximately 3400 to 9400 ft (1036–2865 m).

Western Wood-Pewees have previously been described as common summer residents in woodlands and forests of eastern, central, and northern Arizona (Swarth 1914; Phillips et al. 1964). Atlas data strongly support this status and distribution. In southeastern Arizona, atlasers encountered these flycatchers throughout all forested mountain ranges west to the Baboquivari Mountains and down into some cottonwood-willow associations such as the upper San Pedro River. However, they were not found nesting within this drainage downstream of Saint David even though extensive riparian woodlands existed. These limits may pertain to higher average summer temperature at lower elevations in this area.

On Navajo and Hopi tribal lands in northeastern Arizona, the breeding status and distribution of Western Wood-Pewees has always been unclear (Phillips et al. 1964; Jacobs 1986). LaRue (1994) noted that they appeared uncharacteristically sparse as a breeding bird on Black Mesa, considering the available habitat. Atlasers confirmed these birds nesting on the Defiance Plateau north to the Chuska Mountains and found them nesting locally in the Navajo Creek drainage.

Atlasers commonly encountered Western Wood-Pewees along the Mogollon Rim, and the bird undoubtedly breeds regularly on White Mountain Apache tribal lands. Western Wood-Pewee atlas records clearly encircle this unsurveyed section of the state.

Although atlas data cannot provide much insight into population trends, atlasers did encounter the species regularly throughout its historic range. Still, Breeding Bird Survey data suggest a significant declining trend for this species in Arizona.

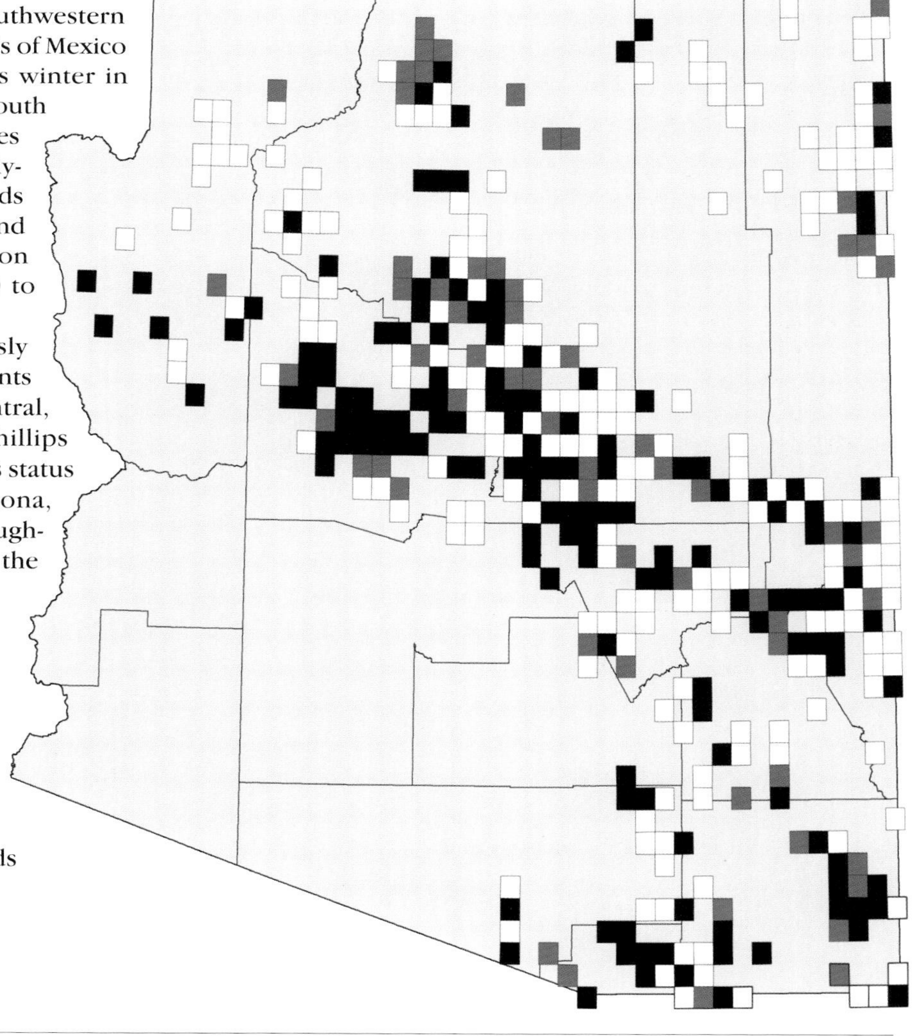

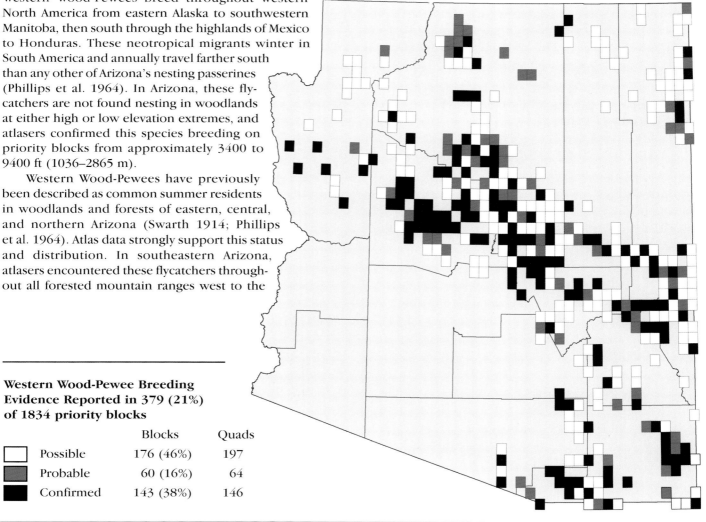

Western Wood-Pewee Breeding Evidence Reported in 379 (21%) of 1834 priority blocks

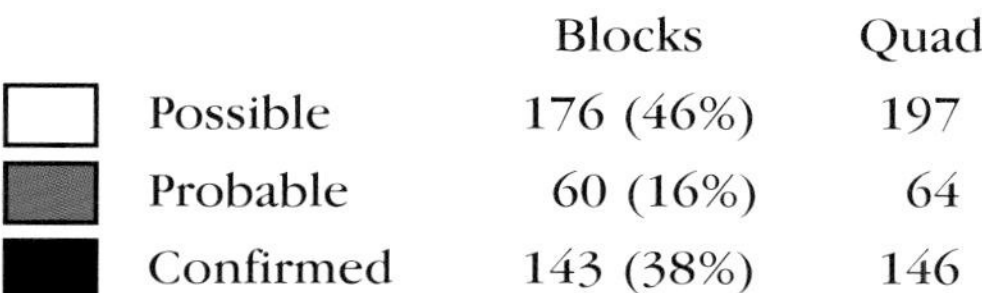

	Blocks	Quads
Possible	176 (46%)	197
Probable	60 (16%)	64
Confirmed	143 (38%)	146

Willow Flycatcher

by Tracy McCarthey *Empidonax traillii*

ALEXANDER SMITH

In Arizona, the Willow Flycatcher is a rare inhabitant of an equally rare habitat—dense riparian woodlands. Its preferred habitats are often so impenetrable and the bird so nondescript that knowing its unique sneezy "fitz-bew" song is often crucial in locating and identifying it.

HABITAT

Nesting Willow Flycatchers in Arizona primarily occur in lowland riparian woodlands and thickets. Historically, this flycatcher once thrived along lowland riparian drainages dominated by extensive Fremont cottonwood and Goodding willow gallery forests. The dense understory vegetation in these forests often included buttonbush, seepwillow, ash, mesquite, and saplings of taller trees. Willow Flycatchers are still most common in habitats containing these native tree species (54 percent of 59 atlas period records), but often the understory plant component has been replaced, or at least includes stands of exotic tamarisk. Fortunately, Willow Flycatchers have been able to breed successfully within some local pure and mixed tamarisk habitats. Approximately 29 percent of all nesting records of these flycatchers during the atlas period were noted in tamarisk or tamarisk dominated drainages. A very small, local population also exists at a few high-elevation drainages, with Geyer and Bebb willow thickets interspersed with thinleaf alder, accounting for five atlas records. Willow Flycatchers are rarely found in sycamore-dominated woodlands, which typically have higher stream gradients, where intermittent flash floods remove the dense understory vegetation favored by this flycatcher.

BREEDING

In Arizona, Willow Flycatchers begin to arrive on territory in late April, peaking in May, with stragglers still regularly passing through in mid-June. The first nest building activity in Arizona usually begins about 15 May, although nest building has been observed as early as 8 May and nests with eggs by 12 May. The first peak of nesting activity is in mid-June, with nesting activity typically delayed by 1–2 weeks in higher elevation. A second breeding peak, coinciding with second nesting attempts, occurs in mid-July. Up to four renesting attempts have been documented for a single female at a low elevation site in central Arizona (Paradzick et al. 2000). Double-brooding (renesting after a successful first nesting attempt) is rather rare but has been documented in the state. Some late nesting attempts continue well into August, with one monitored nest noted hatching eggs on 30 August and containing young through 11 September. In Arizona, Willow Flycatchers typically begin migrating south by late July, with a peak in early September and stragglers through mid-October.

Willow Flycatcher nests at low elevation in Arizona are now most commonly built in tamarisk. During the atlas period, 87 percent (n = 1457) of Willow Flycatcher nests were found in tamarisk, with the remaining primarily in willow (11 percent), buttonbush (1 percent), and cottonwood (less than 1 percent). Nests at higher elevations are built primarily in Geyer willow. Females alone build a well-formed cup, placed in the crotch of a vertical branch, often near the trunk and often in the densest band of vegetation. In grassy areas, especially near high elevation meadows, nests typically have extensive amounts of grasses dangling from the bottom of the nest. Willow Flycatcher nest heights at low elevations averages approximately 15 ft (4.6 m) and range from 4.8 to 38.7 ft (1.5–11.8 m), but nests range from 3 to 10 ft (1–3 m) in height at high-elevations sites. Clutch size is typically 3, but can range from 1-4 eggs. During the atlas period, nests with eggs were found from 19 May to 17 August. Females incubate the eggs for 11 to 14 days, and both parents tend the nestlings, which fledge approximately 10–15 days later (Rourke et al. 1999). Willow Flycatcher pairs continue to feed fledglings for 1 to 2 weeks following nest departure.

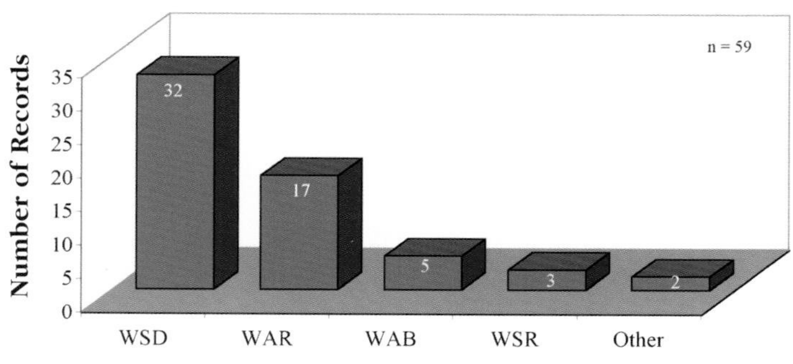

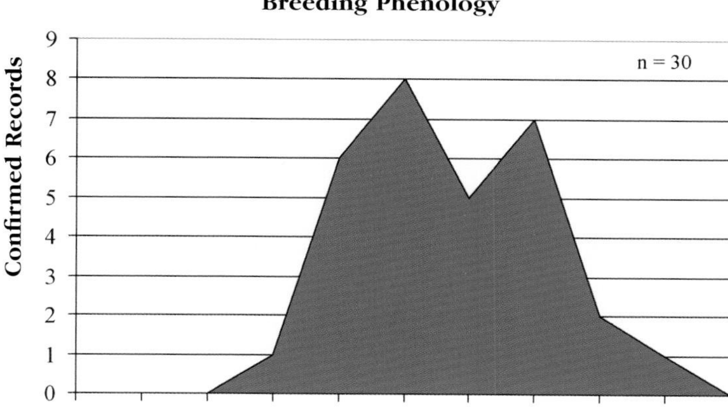

DISTRIBUTION AND STATUS

The Willow Flycatcher is a widely distributed summer resident of much of the United States and southern Canada (Brown 1988). There are four recognized subspecies of Willow Flycatchers. The southwestern (*extimus*) subspecies is the breeding race in Arizona, which also breeds in southern California, New Mexico, southern Nevada, southern Utah, southwestern Colorado, and possibly extreme northern Mexico.

Historically, Willow Flycatchers were considered a fairly common to locally common nesting species along perennial drainages throughout the lower valleys of Arizona (Swarth 1914), but Phillips et al. (1964) noted that their numbers and distribution had been reduced. The current estimated rangewide population of the southwestern race is only 1,800–2000 individuals. In Arizona, fewer than 600 birds are estimated to occur.

Owing to the local and often clumping nature of Willow Flycatcher populations in Arizona, few nesting locations were discovered by atlasers. Therefore, to portray accurately the breeding distribution of this flycatcher in the state, the atlas project relied heavily on results from specific surveys for Willow Flycatchers and casual observations during the atlas period. Willow Flycatcher surveyors noted that this species nests very locally along most of the major perennial drainages below 4000 ft (1219 m) elevation such as the Colorado, lower Big Sandy, Bill Williams, Gila, Santa Maria, Salt, San Pedro, and Verde rivers. They were also found nesting locally from 7900 to 8330 ft (2408–2539 m) elevation along the upper Little Colorado and San Francisco rivers, but have not been documented in the middle elevations between 4000 and 7000 ft (1219–2134 m). The largest populations of Willow Flycatchers occur along the Gila River (from the New Mexico border to the confluence with the San Pedro), the lower San Pedro River, and the lower Salt River (at the inflow to Roosevelt Lake).

Southwestern Willow Flycatchers were federally listed as an endangered species in 1995, primarily because of losses in habitat resulting in a suspected loss in population size. Additionally, they have experienced productivity losses due to cowbird nest parasitism. They only occur in the densest riparian vegetation, so any increases in urbanization or hydrology changes, which lead to a decrease in vegetation density, will result in diminished flycatcher populations. The best management recommendation for recovering Willow Flycatcher populations is to restore natural hydrologic regimes and dense riparian habitats.

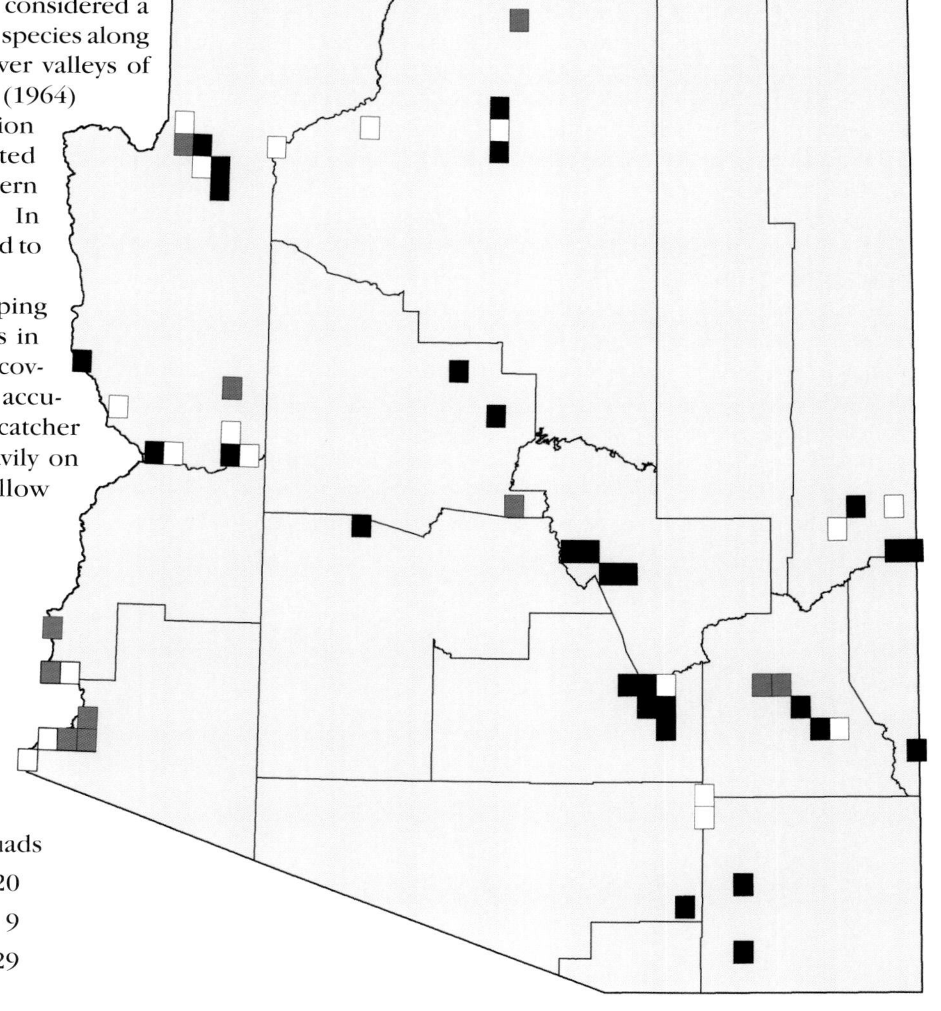

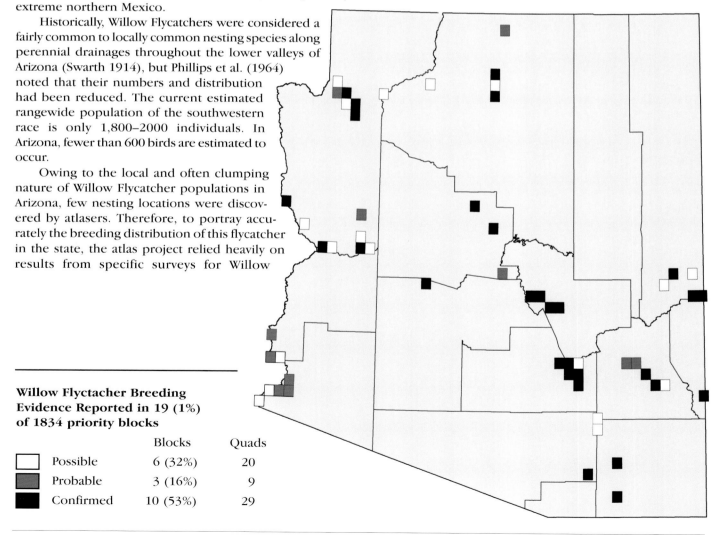

Willow Flyctacher Breeding Evidence Reported in 19 (1%) of 1834 priority blocks

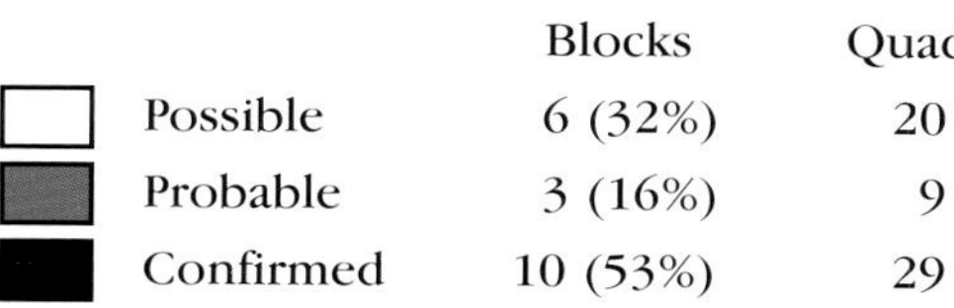

	Blocks	Quads
Possible	6 (32%)	20
Probable	3 (16%)	9
Confirmed	10 (53%)	29

Gray Flycatcher

by Cathryn Wise-Gervais *Empidonax wrightii*

Gray Flycatchers favor drier woodland habitats in both their summer and winter homes than do other Arizona members of this confusing genus. Identification is also aided by their characteristic habit of flicking their tail downward several times upon alighting. They are short-distant migrants and are the most frequently encountered wintering Empidonax flycatcher in Arizona.

HABITAT

Arizona's breeding Gray Flycatchers are most commonly found in arid pinyon pine-juniper woodlands, especially in association with big sagebrush, mountain mahogany, and other similar shrubs. In fact, during the atlas period, observers reported 75 percent of potential breeding records for Gray Flycatcher in pinyon pine-juniper woodlands, including those with scattered ponderosa pine (n = 366). These birds prefer large stands of trees with an abundance of pinyon pine and juniper, and observers reported them only infrequently in grasslands and desertscrub where these trees are few and scattered (7 percent of records). Below the Mogollon Rim, observers also encountered Gray Flycatchers nesting in woodlands comprised of Madrean evergreen oaks, pinyon pine, and juniper. Fewer observations were from open ponderosa pine forests with or without Gambel's oak where the birds occasionally overlap with Dusky Flycatchers. Gray Flycatchers are generally found at lower elevations, however, and prefer more arid conditions. Several atlas records were also obtained along the wooded edges of chaparral-covered slopes.

BREEDING

Gray Flycatchers begin migrating north from their Mexico and southern Arizona wintering grounds in late March and early April. Some lingering individuals continue to pass through the state into mid-May, occasionally later in the north. They begin arriving on their Arizona breeding grounds in mid-April. Atlasers first reported Gray Flycatchers in suitable breeding habitat on 13 April and observed a mated pair on 27 April. The earliest nesting record obtained during the atlas period was of birds carrying nesting material on 3 May. Across their range, Gray Flycatchers are known to lay eggs from late May to late June and have young in the nest from early June to mid-August (Sterling 1999). Atlasers reported the first nest with young on 28 May, indicating the eggs were laid by early to mid-May, slightly earlier than the published egg dates. Atlas data suggest that peak Gray Flycatcher breeding occurs in Arizona from early June to mid-July, but atlasers reported nest building as late as 20 July and adults feeding fledged young as late as 14 August. Observers reported Gray Flycatchers in suitable breeding habitat through 28 August. Although a few early fall migrants can occasionally be found in late July or early August, they are not expected until mid-August in southern Arizona. Peak passage is in September with migrants still arriving on their southern Arizona wintering ground well into October.

Within their pinyon pine-juniper woodland domain in Arizona, Gray Flycatchers apparently select juniper as the tree of choice for constructing their nests. Of 33 nests discovered and measured during atlas surveys, 67 percent were in four species of junipers. Only 6 nests were in pinyon pine, 3 in ponderosa pine, and 1 each was in Douglas fir and Emory oak. All nests ranged in height from 3 to 15 ft (0.9–4.7 m), with a median of 3.6 ft (1.8 m).

Female Gray Flycatchers construct well-camouflaged cup nests and generally place these near the tree trunk or in the crotch of branches attached to the trunk (Sterling 1999). Nests can be virtually invisible to observers because of juniper bark strips that cover the abode and because female Gray Flycatchers are notorious for sitting tightly during incubation and brooding. They will sometimes feign injury near the nest when disturbed by humans (Sterling 1999).

Gray Flycatchers typically lay 3–4 eggs per clutch (Baicich and Harrison 1997) and will usually rear two broods per season if resources allow. The female incubates

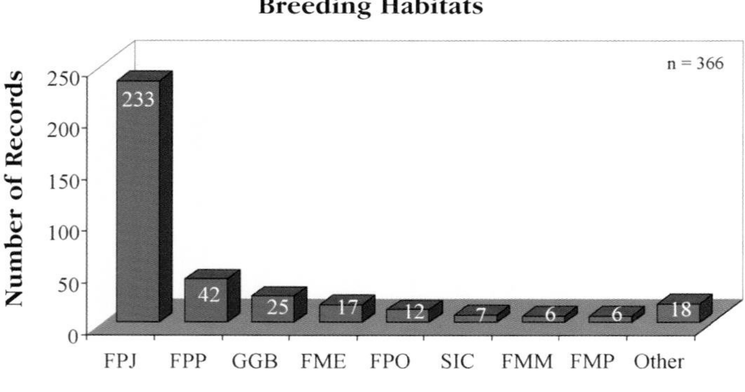

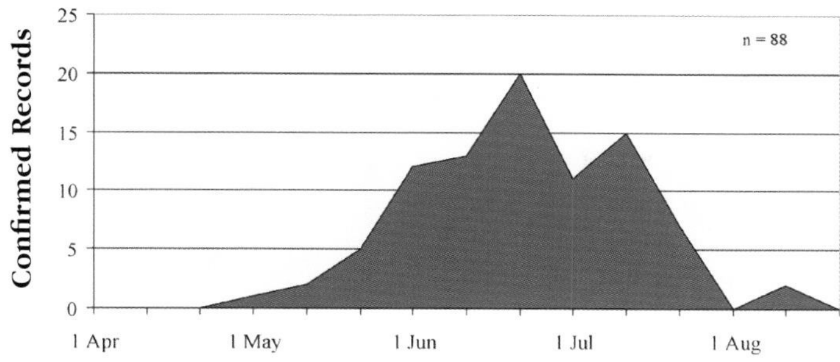

the eggs, but both sexes share the formidable task of feeding the young. The young obtain parental care for approximately 16 days in the nest and for about 2 weeks following fledging (Russell and Woodbury 1941).

DISTRIBUTION AND STATUS

Gray Flycatchers breed as far north as southern British Columbia and south primarily throughout the Great Basin Region to Arizona and New Mexico. They nest very locally in southern California and west Texas. As an uncommon winter resident in southern Arizona, they are often strongly associated with open mesquite bosques and edge areas of adjacent riparian woodlands.

Prior Arizona literature describes Gray Flycatchers as common summer residents of pinyon pine-juniper associations primarily from the Mogollon Rim north and west to the Juniper Mountains (Phillips et al 1964). Atlasers regularly documented these birds throughout this region of the state as well as much farther west and south at elevations from approximately 4300 to 7600 ft (1311–2316 m). Other than records of birds nesting at Ft. Apache (Phillips et al. 1964), Gray Flycatchers were unknown to nest below the Mogollon Rim. However, atlasers encountered them nesting throughout the extensive pinyon pine–juniper woodlands below the Mogollon Rim from Strawberry, Payson, and the Sierra Ancha southeast through San Carlos Apache tribal lands to the Big Lue Mountains east of Clifton. Gray Flycatchers undoubtedly also nest regularly in the adjacent White Mountain Apache tribal lands, where permits to conduct atlas surveys could not be obtained.

Atlasers also discovered isolated pockets of Gray Flycatchers in the foothills of the Pinal and northern Galiuro mountains east to the Santa Teresa Mountains. The birds were also confirmed nesting at the southern end of the Pinaleno Mountains. Surprisingly, two breeding records were obtained even farther south within the southern foothills of the Chiricahua Mountains. One of the latter records was of an adult feeding a recent fledgling incapable of sustained flight.

Likely owing to the paucity of prior avian research in northwestern Arizona, observers extended the known breeding distribution of Gray Flycatchers considerably within this region of the state. Observers obtained breeding records in many areas including on the slopes of the Kaibab Plateau, throughout most of the Arizona Strip region, and south from the Strip through the Aquarius Mountains and into the Bradshaw Mountains.

Breeding Bird Survey data (1966–1995) indicate an overall, rangewide population increase for Gray Flycatchers (Peterjohn et al. 1996). Arizona populations of these hardy flycatchers should be closely monitored, however, inasmuch as extensive stands of pinyon pine and juniper have recently succumbed to drought and subsequent bark beetle infestations.

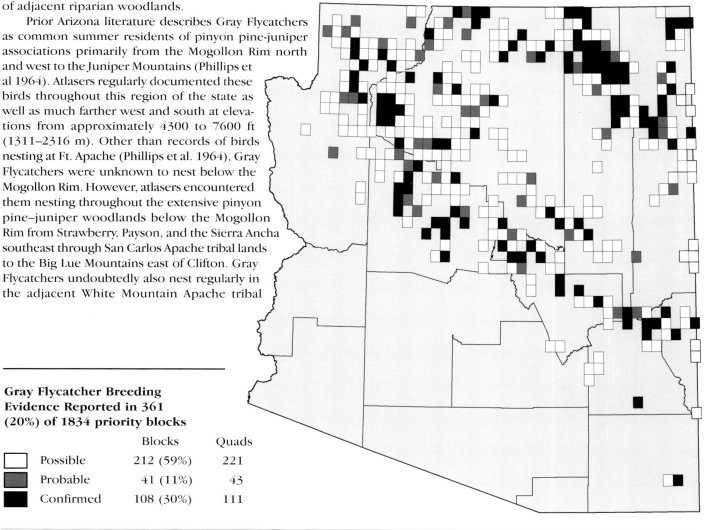

Gray Flycatcher Breeding Evidence Reported in 361 (20%) of 1834 priority blocks

	Blocks	Quads
Possible	212 (59%)	221
Probable	41 (11%)	43
Confirmed	108 (30%)	111

Dusky Flycatcher

by Cathryn Wise-Gervais *Empidonax oberholseri*

Although there is some local overlap in nesting habitat selections among Arizona's Empidonax flycatchers, the Dusky Flycatcher favors woodlands offering a deciduous component. They breed only at higher elevations, and atlasers encountered these small birds over a much wider distribution in northern Arizona than previous literature suggested.

HABITAT

Arizona's Dusky Flycatchers are mountain dwellers during the breeding season and favor a variety of shrubby woodlands and riparian thickets that offer deciduous vegetation. Atlasers discovered that Dusky Flycatchers are commonly associated with Gambel's Oak either in pure stands or in conjunction with conifers, and this oak connection had previously been overlooked in Arizona. These birds were most often encountered in montane scrub thickets of Gambel's oak and in dense young aspen groves that often become established following fires or timber harvesting activities. Atlasers reported Dusky Flycatchers in nine habitat types, and 35 percent of these records were in ponderosa pine–Gambel's oak associations (n = 54). Observers also reported the birds in open mixed-conifer forest with an abundance of young firs, Gambel's oak, and aspen (24 percent), and in montane riparian zones comprising mixed conifers and deciduous trees (15 percent). In the higher elevations, Dusky Flycatchers were typically encountered along boreal riparian thicket of thinleaf alder, Geyer willow, and other shrubby trees.

BREEDING

Although wintering rather locally and in limited numbers in lowland riparian woodlands of southeastern Arizona, Dusky Flycatchers begin migrating north through the state in late March and early April. They reach their Arizona breeding grounds by late April and early May, with males arriving approximately one week before the females (Sedgwick 1993) presumable to establish territories. Atlasers reported Dusky Flycatchers in suitable breeding habitat on 1 May, and first reported a pair of birds on 17 May. Dusky Flycatchers were observed carrying nesting material on 26 May, and atlasers located the earliest nest with eggs on 1 June. Sedgwick (1993) reported that nest building typically begins in late May to early June, in keeping with atlas data, but that sometimes cool, rainy weather will cause a week or more lag in breeding activity between nest construction and egg laying. Atlas data suggest that most nests contain young from mid-June to mid-July, and observers reported adults feeding fledglings from 7 to 25 July. Dusky Flycatchers were noted in suitable breeding habitat through 14 August, although early southbound migrants are often observed by early August in Arizona. Peak passage for these flycatchers in the state is in September, with lingering migrants noted to late October or early November.

Dusky Flycatchers use a variety of trees for nesting in Arizona including Gambel's Oak, Geyer willow, thinleaf alder, chokecherry, aspen, and young Douglas fir (LaRue 1994). Atlasers discovered one Dusky Flycatcher nests in a young Gambel's oak thicket, only 2.8 ft (0.9 m) above the ground. In Montana, Sedgwick (1993) found that Dusky Flycatchers placed nests at a mean height of 4.9 ft (1.5 m) and ranged from 2.3 to 11.4 ft (0.7–3.5 m) above the ground. Occupied nest patches typically have a large percentage of foliage cover and high densities of small trees (Kelly 1993).

The female Dusky Flycatcher handles much of the early nesting activity including constructing the tightly woven nest and incubating the 3–4 eggs for 15 to 16 days (Bent 1942). She also may engage in several distraction displays if the nest is disturbed. Males sometimes feed the incubating females, and will assist feeding the nestlings (Sedgwick

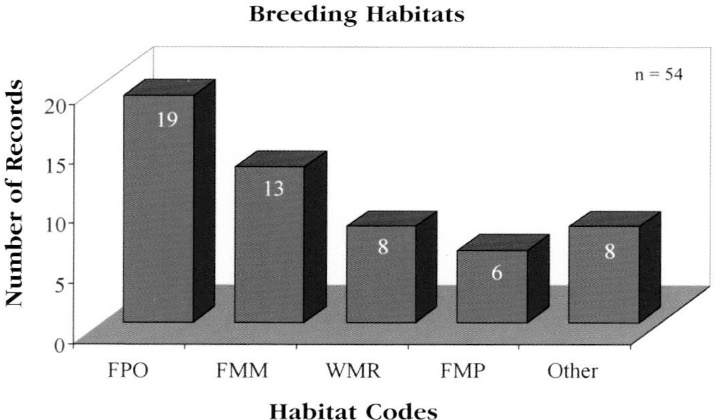

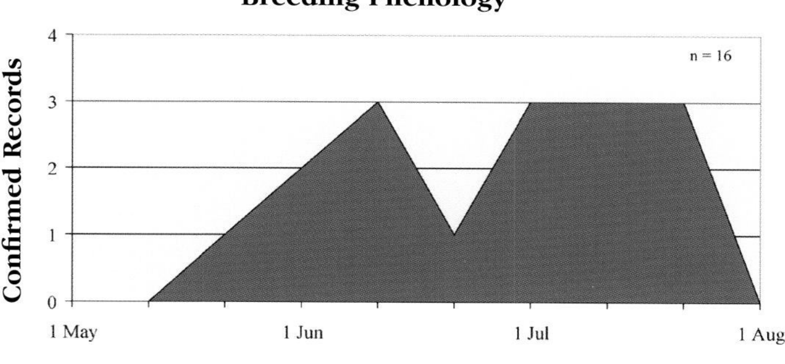

1993). The young remain in the nest for 15 to 20 days and will often huddle together on the same branch soon after fledging (Sedgwick 1993). The young birds are largely dependent on their parents for 2 to 3 weeks after leaving the nest (Sedgwick 1993).

DISTRIBUTION AND STATUS

Dusky Flycatchers breed only in western North America from southwestern Yukon, south to central Arizona, New Mexico, and northern Baja California. Likely due to the difficulty in identification, Swarth (1914) described Dusky Flycatchers as a fairly common migrant in eastern Arizona, but noted there were no authentic breeding records. By the mid-1960s, these flycatchers were only known to breed in the White Mountains region, locally in the San Francisco Mountains area, and possibly on the Kaibab Plateau (Phillips et al. 1964). In the early 1980s, they were also found summering and presumably breeding in the Chuska Mountains and Carrizo Mountains on Navajo tribal lands, as well as confirmed nesting on Black Mesa (Jacobs 1986; LaRue 1994).

Atlas data revealed that Dusky Flycatchers are distributed much more widely in Arizona than previously thought, at elevations ranging from approximately 6000 to 9400 ft (1829–2865 m). In the White Mountains, they were found most commonly in the upper Little Colorado River drainage near Mount Baldy and near Greer, as well as in the Nutrioso Creek and upper Black River drainages. The species undoubtedly also nests on the adjacent White Mountain Apache tribal lands, where access to conduct atlas surveys could not be obtained. Dusky Flycatchers were sparsely distributed along the Mogollon Rim with a concentration of records from Apache Maid Mountain north to upper Oak Creek and the Mormon Lake area. Westward, these flycatchers were discovered nesting locally in the Hualapai Mountains.

Nearly 70 percent of Dusky Flycatcher atlas records were from mountain ranges and higher plateaus along the northern edge of the state. Numerous records were obtained on Navajo tribal lands in the Tsegi Canyon drainage and Black Mesa, and from Carrizo Mountains south through the Defiance Plateau, including upper Canyon de Chelly. The Kaibab Plateau produced many records as well, and these flycatchers were regularly encountered on recovering burned ridges and steep upper slopes of the plateau. Higher isolated mountain ranges within the Arizona Strip region were also found to harbored local populations of Dusky Flycatchers.

Atlas data revealed that this species was fairly common in suitable habitat. Preferring fairly early successional thickets of Gambel's oak and aspen, Dusky Flycatchers probably benefit from some timber harvesting practices, and their distribution may increase in Arizona as forests begin to recover from recent widespread and devastating wildfires.

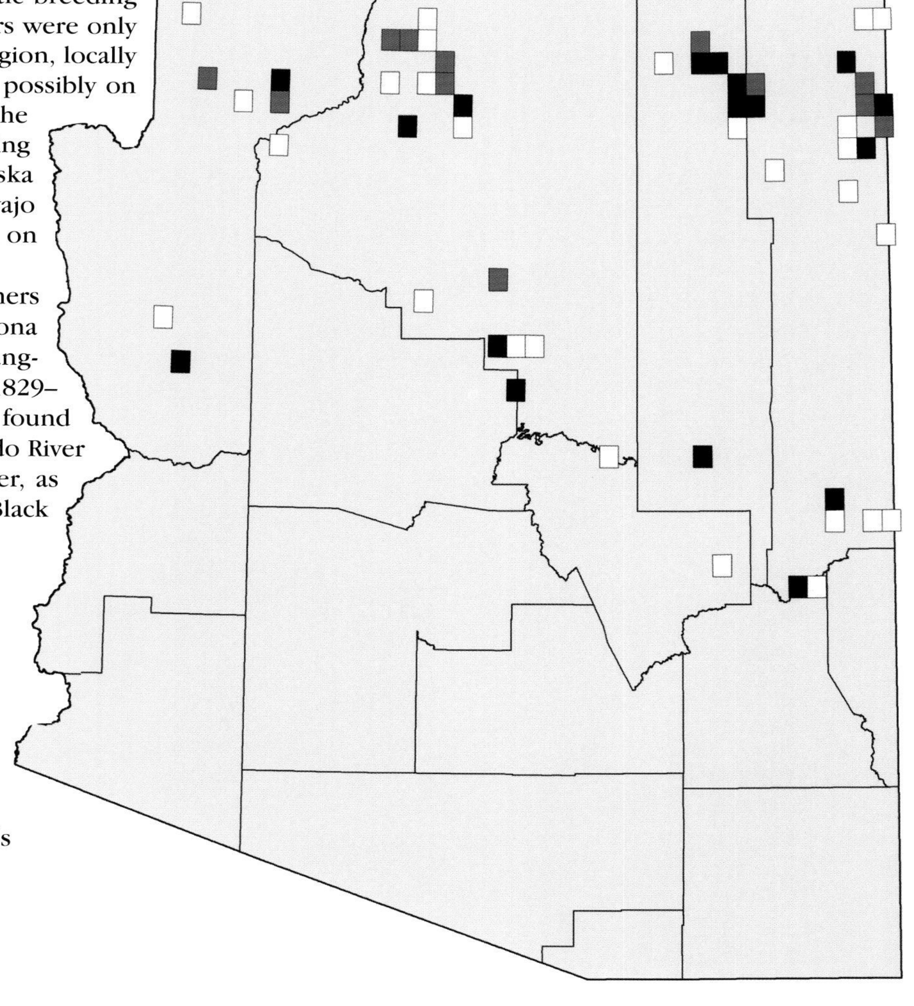

Dusky Flycatcher Breeding Evidence Reported in 48 (3%) of 1834 priority blocks

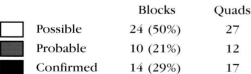

	Blocks	Quads
Possible	24 (50%)	27
Probable	10 (21%)	12
Confirmed	14 (29%)	17

Cordilleran Flycatcher

by Cathryn Wise-Gervais *Empidonax occidentalis*

When ornithologists split the Western Flycatcher into two species, they selected names that described each of the new species' ranges. The Spanish word cordillera means "parallel mountain ranges," referring to the bird's preference for higher elevations of the Intermountain West. In contrast, Pacific-slope Flycatchers are found coastally.

HABITAT

In Arizona, Cordilleran Flycatchers prefer cool forested mountains and higher plateaus, and are most abundant in the moist, shady canyons and steep drainages that incise these landscapes. Atlasers reported these flycatchers in fourteen vegetative communities, with 30 percent of atlas records in mixed conifer forests often containing Douglas fir, white fir, ponderosa pine, and aspen (n = 158). Twenty percent of records were in forested montane drainages characterized by firs, pines, aspen, Gambel's oak, maple, and other deciduous trees, and another 13 percent were in ponderosa pine–Gambel's oak associations. Cordilleran Flycatchers were noted only locally in the drier pure ponderosa pine forests. In southeastern Arizona, they were also found frequently nesting in canyons where Madrean pine-oak forests containing Chihuahuan, Apache, and ponderosa pines merge with Arizona sycamore and evergreen oak woodlands. Only a few atlas records were obtained in aspen groves and spruce-fir forests, but this may pertain to the limited distribution of these habitats in Arizona, inasmuch as such areas are commonly used elsewhere within the bird's range. Away from canyons and drainages, available nest sites can be a limiting factor for these shelf-nesting flycatchers.

BREEDING

Most evidence suggests that Cordilleran Flycatchers typically do not arrive on Arizona breeding grounds until late April or early May when males begin to sing. Western-type flycatchers detected earlier, beginning in mid-March, are generally presumed to be migrating Pacific-slope Flycatchers. Atlasers first detected paired Cordilleran Flycatchers on 11 May and located the earliest occupied nest in southern Arizona on 19 May, the period when early egg laying begins. In central and northern Arizona, nesting activity is initiated approximately 1–2 weeks later, with the first clutches laid by late May or early June (T. Martin, personal communication). Atlas data suggest that Cordilleran Flycatcher nesting activity peaks from early June to early July. Atlasers reported nests with young through 5 August and observed adults feeding fledged young through 14 August. These birds were observed in suitable breeding habitat through 27 August, but may linger longer in some areas. Cordilleran Flycatchers begin migrating south in late August, with peak passage by mid-September and a few lingering individuals remaining in Arizona into October.

Cordilleran Flycatchers are somewhat flexible in nest site selection, but they typically choose settings that provide a ledge and overhead cover. Nest sites in Arizona include rock crevices or ledges, cave entrances, stream banks, natural tree cavities, among root mass of upturned trees, and frequently on sections of pealing bark of logs laying horizontally over small drainages. Resourceful birds, they often take advantage of covered shelves on cabins, outhouses, bridges, and other structures. Atlasers collected measurements at 18 Cordilleran Flycatcher nests from many of the above substrates and the median height of these was 4.6 ft (1.4 m) and ranged from 2.0 to 26.2 ft (0.6–8 m). Previous studies in the snowmelt drainages on the Mogollon Rim identified many of the same nesting substrates for 646 nests, and of these 46 percent were in aspen (T. Martin, personal communication). The mean nest height for 472 of these nests was 15 ft (4.6 m), a value considerably higher than that obtained by atlasers, and ranged from 0.7 to 29.5 ft (0.2–9 m) above the ground.

Female Cordilleran Flycatchers construct the nest in 5–6 days and incubate the 3–4 eggs (range 2–5) without male assistance (Lowther 2000). The mean incubation period for ten clutches monitored in Arizona was 13.6 days (T. Martin, personal communication), but likely ranges from 13 to 16 days, as with Pacific-slope Flycatchers. Both

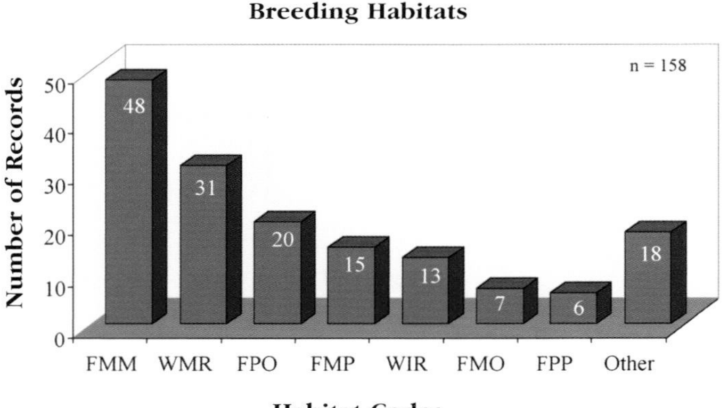

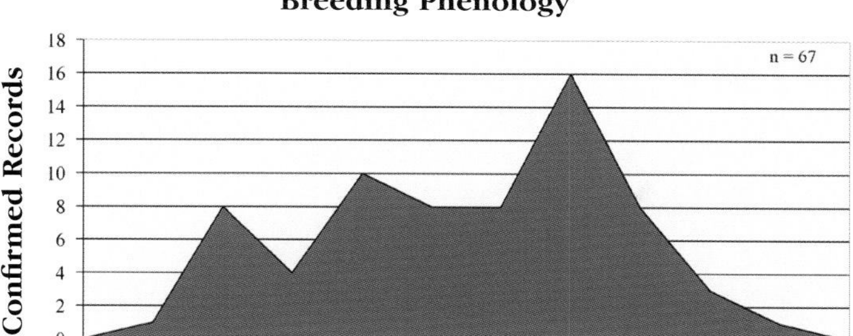

adults feed the young, first during the 14–18 day nestling period and then during the 2–3 weeks following nest departure (Davis et al. 1963). Some evidence suggests the species may occasionally rear two broods per year.

DISTRIBUTION AND STATUS

Cordilleran Flycatchers breed in the Intermountain West from central Alberta south through the highlands of Mexico to Oaxaca. Prior to the atlas project, Cordilleran Flycatchers were known to breed in higher mountain ranges in southeastern Arizona, north to the White Mountains and along the Mogollon Rim to the Williams and Flagstaff areas (Phillips et al. 1964). They were also found in the higher forested mountains and plateaus on Navajo and Hopi tribal lands (Jacobs 1986, LaRue 1994).

Atlasers commonly encountered the species throughout most of the previously described range as well as in several new locations at elevations from approximately 5200 to 9800 ft (1585–2987 m). In southeastern Arizona, these flycatchers were found in most of the larger and wetter ranges, but, surprisingly, were not reported in the Santa Rita Mountains. However, this may be because few observers submitted casual observation records for this local nesting species there. Elsewhere, Cordilleran Flycatchers were found sparingly in several smaller ranges, including the Whetstone, Dragoon, Winchester, and Santa Teresa mountains.

Cordilleran Flycatchers were previously reported as absent as a nesting species in the drier forested ranges of northwestern Arizona, including on the Kaibab Plateau (Phillips et al. 1964). However, atlasers discovered them nesting locally at isolated springs along the Kaibab Plateau's western and southeastern rims. Additionally, they were encountered nesting regularly in northeastern Arizona on Black Mesa north to the Tsegi Canyon drainage and from the Carrizo Mountains south to the Defiance Plateau, including in upper Canyon de Chelly.

Although observers were unable to conduct atlas surveys on White Mountain Apache tribal lands, Cordilleran Flycatchers undoubtedly nest along the entire Mogollon Rim regions of these tribal lands. In Yavapai County, these flycatchers were encountered fairly regularly in the Bradshaw Mountains, on Mingus Mountain, and in the forests around Prescott, northwest to the Santa Maria and Juniper mountains. Atlasers also confirmed Cordilleran Flycatchers nesting in the isolated Hualapai Mountains to the west.

Although there are few data documenting Cordilleran Flycatcher population trends in Arizona, atlasers regularly encountered this species throughout their historic range, indicating some degree of stability. Furthermore, some researchers consider Cordilleran Flycatcher populations in ponderosa pine forests throughout the Southwest to be greater at present than in presettlement times (Brawn and Balda 1988).

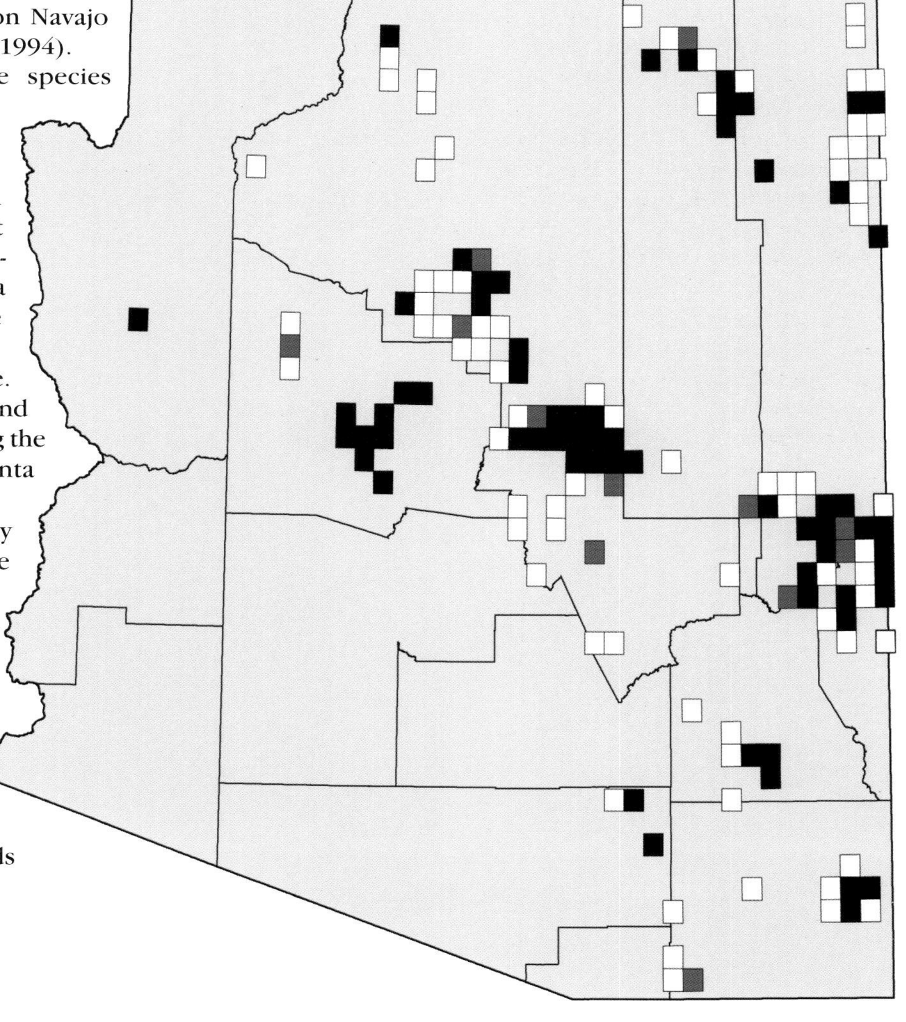

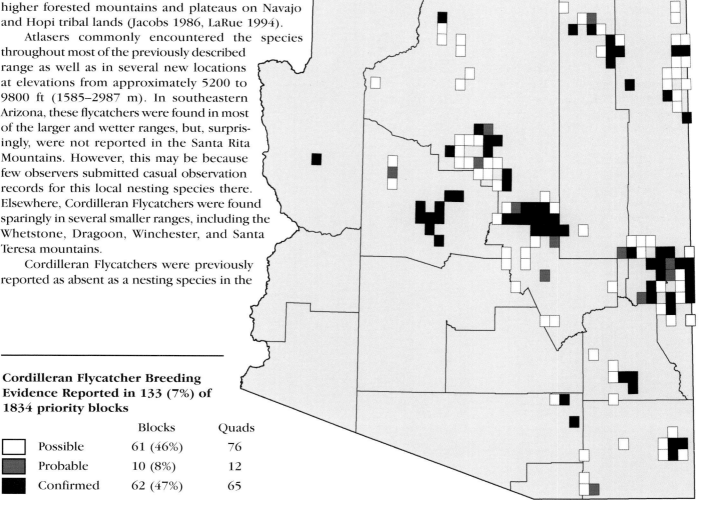

Cordilleran Flycatcher Breeding Evidence Reported in 133 (7%) of 1834 priority blocks

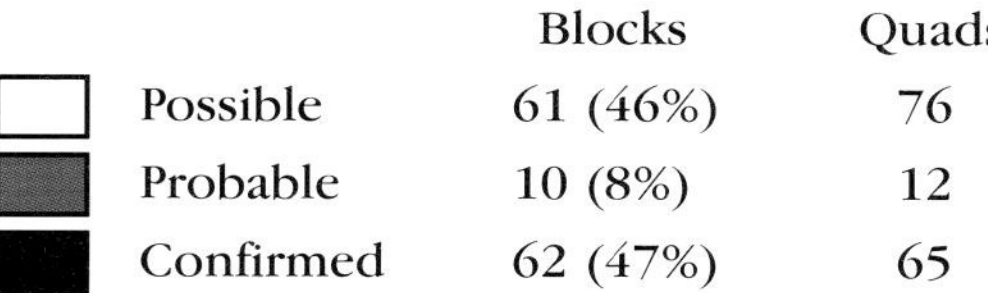

	Blocks	Quads
Possible	61 (46%)	76
Probable	10 (8%)	12
Confirmed	62 (47%)	65

Buff-breasted Flycatcher

by Troy E. Corman *Empidonax fulvifrons*

The tiniest of the Empidonax flycatchers in North America, Buff-breasted Flycatchers delight many birders who visit the few mountain canyons and gentle woodland slopes they now inhabit in southeastern Arizona. This local and diminutive bird frequently forages near forest openings, where it is easily observed and identified by its rich, ocher breast.

DAN FISCHER

HABITAT

Found in a variety of open woodlands and forest edge habitats in Mexico, Buff-breasted Flycatchers associate closely with Madrean pine-oak woodlands in southeastern Arizona. They frequently occupy areas that are characterized by relatively wide, gently sloping mountain drainages with open canopy forests of Chihuahuan, Apache, and sometimes ponderosa pines. Understories are also rather open and often consist of various Madrean evergreen oaks and pine saplings with scattered grasses and forbs (Martin and Morrison 1999). Arizona Sycamore, alligator juniper, and Arizona madrone are also commonly found in areas frequented by these flycatchers. Locally, they are also encountered foraging and singing at the edges of forest burns and recent surveys detected them breeding at higher elevations on broad ridge tops (Conway and Kirkpatrick 2001). Buff-breasted Flycatchers typically return to the same forest and canyon stands each year, leaving many nearby areas that offer seemingly similar ecological conditions vacant. Breeding localities often contain 2–4 adjacent nesting pairs, each defending an extraordinarily small territory (Marshall 1957).

BREEDING

Buff-breasted Flycatchers are rather short-distance migrants at the northern edge of their range, and typically begin to arrive in their Arizona nesting localities by late March or early April. However, on occasion they can arrive as early as 16 March (S. Healy, personal communication). Nest building can begin as early as mid-April, although most nests are constructed in May and June. Bowers and Dunning (1994) noted that there was often a lag period of 5–16 days between completing construction of the nest and laying the first egg. This elapse period was unrelated to inclement weather. Most Buff-breasted Flycatchers in Arizona lay eggs between early May and early August, occasionally as early as late April. The latest nest with young reported during the atlas period was 15 August. Most Buff-breasted Flycatchers in Arizona have left their breeding grounds by mid-September, with some stragglers reported through late September and occasionally into early October.

Nest site selection is by both members of the pair, although the female is the sole builder of the nest, which she completes in approximately 5–10 days (Willard 1923b; Bowers and Dunning 1994). In southeastern Arizona, Buff-breasted Flycatchers nest primarily in Chihuahuan and Apache pines (Martin and Morrison 1999); nests have also been noted in ponderosa pine, Douglas fir, Arizona white oak, Arizona sycamore, bigtooth maple, alligator juniper, and Arizona walnut (Lusk 1901; Willard 1923b; Bowers and Dunning 1994). The average nest height for Arizona populations is approximately 25 ft (7.6 m) and ranges from 6.5 to 46 ft (2–14 m) above the ground (Bowers and Dunning 1994; Martin and Morrison 1999). The camouflaged nests are frequently constructed next to the trunk and directly under an overhanging branch or other cover, which has been known to impede cowbird nest parasitism (Bowers and Dunning 1984). However, other nests have been constructed in more open situations farther out on limbs, sometime on or near pinecones (Lusk 1901; Willard 1923b).

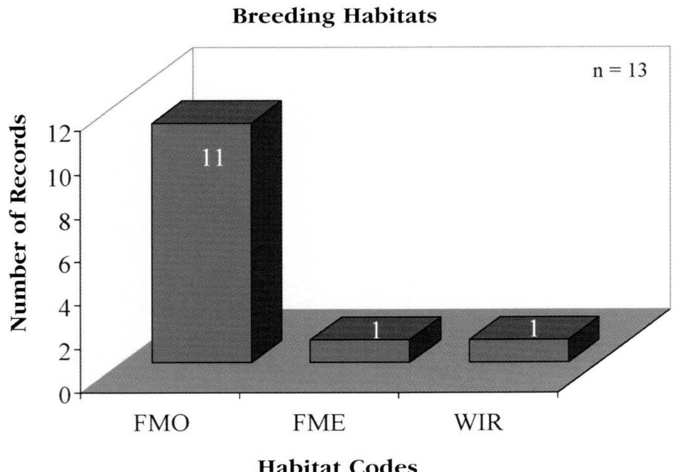

Buff-breasted Flycatcher clutches typically consist of 3–4 eggs, but can range from 2 to 5 (Lusk 1901; Willard 1923b). The female is the sole incubator, which takes 14–16

days and both parents feed nestlings, with fledging occurring from 15 to 17 days (Bowers and Dunning 1994). Evidence suggests that most pairs produce only one brood per year. However, they will continue nesting attempts until successful or until it is too late in the season, and one pair was noted initiating five nests in one season (Bowers and Dunning 1994).

DISTRIBUTION AND STATUS

Buff-breasted Flycatchers currently nests from southeastern Arizona and locally in southwestern New Mexico and west Texas south to central Honduras. Only the northern populations in the United States and northern Sonora are truly migratory; however, they are altitudinal migrants through much of their range (Bowers and Dunning 1994).

Early ornithologists of the 1880s and into the early 1900s reported that Buff-breasted Flycatchers were locally a fairly common bird in the Santa Catalina, Santa Rita, Huachuca, and Chiricahua mountains (Lusk 1901; Willard 1923b; Monson 1972). Historically they were also collected as far north as central Arizona near Prescott, as well as Fort Apache in Navajo County; however, their numbers and distribution have decreased markedly in Arizona since 1920 (Phillips et al. 1964).

During the atlas period, atlasers and researchers noted the local Buff-breasted Flycatcher nesting fairly commonly only in specific drainages of the Chiricahua and Huachuca Mountains. However, territorial birds were also discovered very locally in the Santa Rita, Rincon, and Santa Catalina mountains, where they are no longer reported annually and may only breed occasionally. Buff-breasted Flycatchers were encountered nesting in the Huachuca Mountains as low as 5380 ft (1640 m) in lower Garden Canyon and detected as high as 8450 ft (2575 m) near Pat Scott Peak on the Crest Trail (Conway and Kirkpatrick 2001).

Researchers detected a significant population decline of Buff-breasted Flycatcher in Arizona between surveys conducted in 1995–96 and 2000 (Martin and Morrison 1999; Conway and Kirkpatrick 2001). After their surveys in 2000, they estimated that Arizona's breeding population consisted of fewer than 75 individuals. Theories for these declines are many and include breeding habitat loss and modification by recreational development and unregulated livestock grazing. Phillips et al. (1964) and many others since have also speculated that fire suppression has created unfavorable foraging and breeding conditions in much of this flycatcher's historical distribution in Arizona through increased density of understory vegetation. Fire suppression has also caused catastrophic fires, which have consumed historical breeding locations. Conversely, fires may create new open habitats and future surveys may reveal additional breeding pairs establishing themselves adjacent to recovering burned forests in southeastern Arizona.

Additionally, several small populations of Buff-breasted Flycatchers are currently found in or near Coronado National Forest campgrounds. These localities often have artificially elevated densities of jays, which in turn have led to a tremendous increase in the number of flycatcher nests that are predated (Morrison and Martin 1997). It has also been suggested that intense birding pressures (e.g., daily visits, tape playing) could be detrimental to the nesting success of frequently visited local populations in Arizona (Bowers and Dunning 1994). Willard (1923b) and others noted that if these tiny flycatchers are disturbed during nest construction, they will often abandon their efforts and build elsewhere.

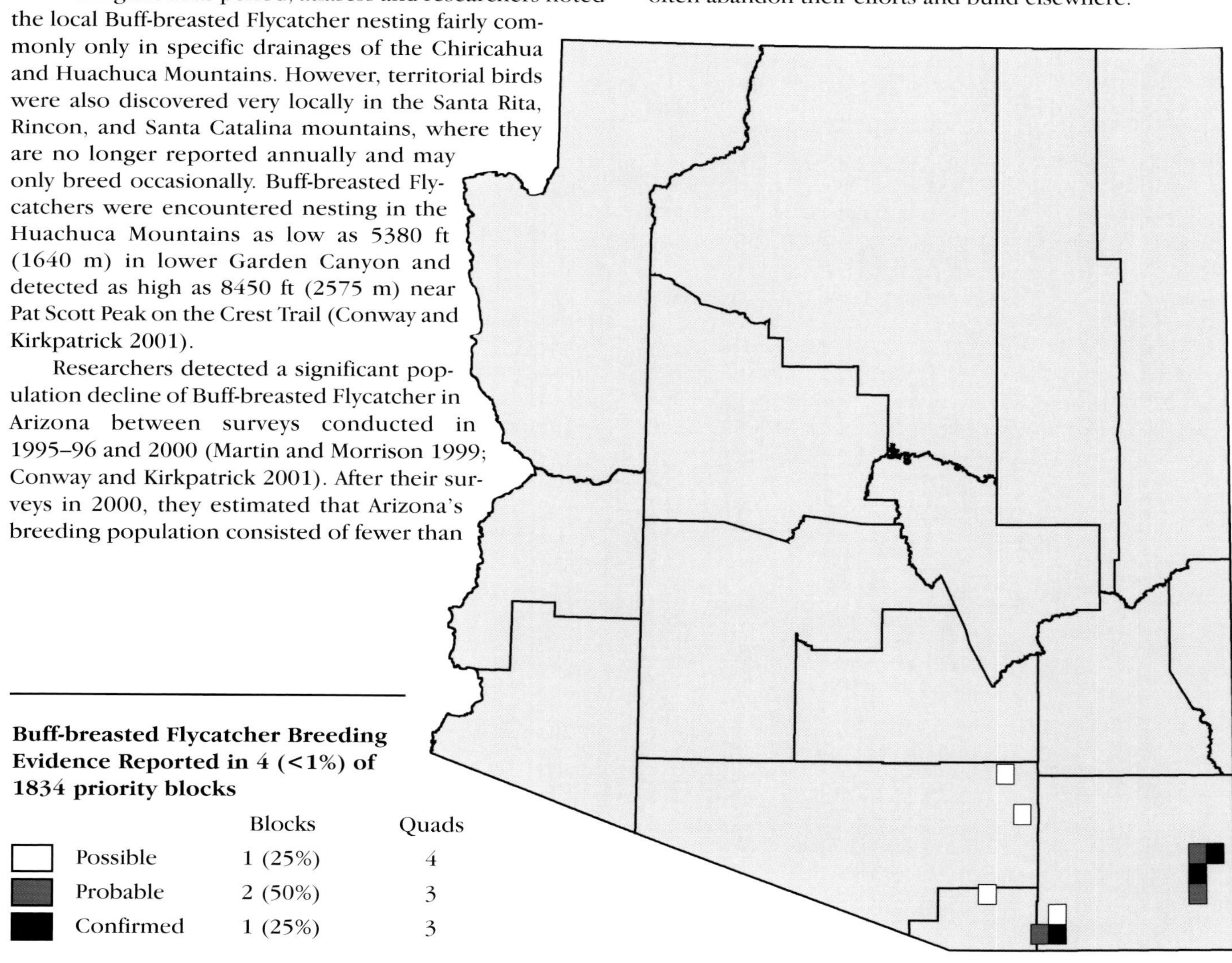

Buff-breasted Flycatcher Breeding Evidence Reported in 4 (<1%) of 1834 priority blocks

	Blocks	Quads
Possible	1 (25%)	4
Probable	2 (50%)	3
Confirmed	1 (25%)	3

Black Phoebe

by Cathryn Wise-Gervais *Sayornis nigricans*

Both the Black Phoebe's unmistakable black-and-white plumage and its close association with water set this bird apart from Arizona's other flycatchers. This handsome bird is practically a fixture along many streams and waterways, where it will give a distinctive "cheep" call while flying erratically after insects.

RICHAARD DITCH

HABITAT

Black Phoebes are common inhabitants along many of Arizona's perennial waterways from marshes, rivers, and mountain streams to manmade canals, ponds, and reservoirs. In fact, the birds are seldom encountered away from water sources and will nest almost anywhere they can find covered areas adjacent to water. Atlasers observed Black Phoebes in twenty-six habitat types, and most commonly reported the bird in lowland riparian woodlands characterized by cottonwood, willow, and mesquite (28 percent; n = 422). An additional 23 percent of records were from foothill drainages and canyons containing Arizona sycamore and other deciduous trees. Rural and manmade water features accounted for 12 percent of Black Phoebe atlas records and included canals, dams, drainage ditches, and stock ponds. Atlasers obtained fewer records from marshes and similar wetland settings, as well as along drainages dominated by exotic tamarisk. Although Black Phoebes are not typically considered high-elevation riparian birds, observers reported them in some open forested montane drainages containing a mixture of firs, pines, alder, oaks, and other trees.

BREEDING

In Arizona, Black Phoebes can be found year-round at many watered lowland localities and are short-distance or altitudinal migrants in others. Residents establish pairs in late winter while migrants pair up soon after arrival on breeding ground in early spring. The earliest confirmed atlas record was a nest with young discovered on the early date of 17 March. This record indicates that some lowland birds initiated nest building by at least mid-February and egg laying by late February. Atlas data reveal that Black Phoebe nesting activity continues to increase through the spring, with a peak from late April to late May, coinciding well with California nesting data (Wolf 1997). Nesting efforts continue well into the summer, however, with observers reporting nests with eggs through 3 July and nest with young to 14 July. Atlasers reported adults feeding fledged young through 29 July. Dispersing individual Black Phoebes regularly begin appearing in nonbreeding areas by mid-July (occasionally earlier) in Arizona and are widespread by August. They occasionally linger in northern Arizona through late October or early November.

Black Phoebes have a knack for nesting in unique and quite diverse locations, although common characteristics include proximity to water and mud, and some sort of protective overhead covering. When such sites are available, nests are often placed over water and natural locations in Arizona, including the downstream side of river boulders, cliff overhangs, rocky outcrops, and even hollow tree cavities. Manmade structures are now also commonly used such as under bridges, canal regulators, road culverts, wells, dams, and outbuildings. Atlasers took at least partial measurements at twenty-seven Black Phoebe nests statewide, with sixteen placed on cliffs, rocks, or solid streambanks and three under bridges. Six nests were placed on buildings including an outhouse, shed, and a dilapidated shack. The remaining nests were placed on a variety of manmade artifacts including within a well, under a pump covering, and on a concrete basin at a fish hatchery. Atlasers found that lower nests were typically placed over water and higher nests over ground. The median nest height was 5.2 ft (1.6 m), but ranged widely from 0.5 to 49.2 ft (0.2–15 m).

Female Black Phoebes construct their nests of mud and grass and have a strong tendency to refurbish old nests, which often takes significantly less time to complete (Wolf 1997). Typical clutches consist of 4 eggs (range 1–6), and both sexes have been observed incubating (Bent 1942). Incubation takes approximately 17 days (range 15–18), and

Breeding Habitats

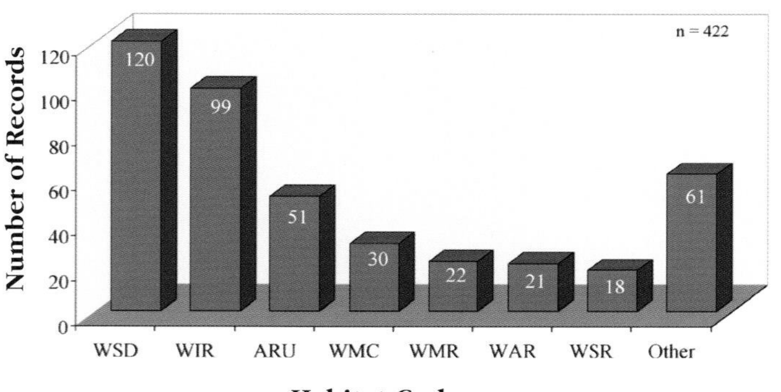

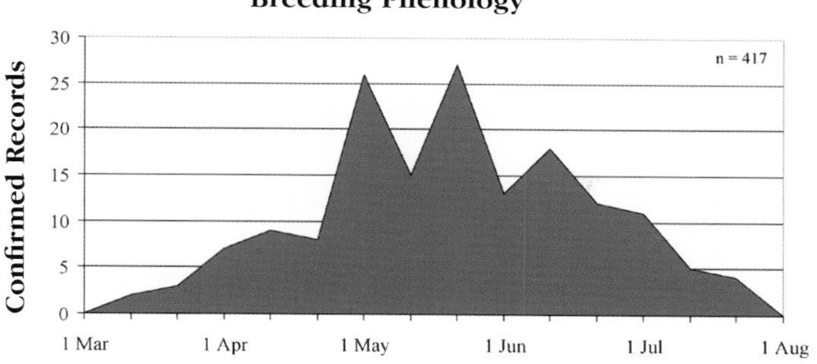

both sexes provide food for the nestlings (Wolf 1997). The young fledge at 18–21 days of age and become independent from their parents in 7–11 days (Wolf 1997). Black Phoebes regularly raise two broods per season, so the female may leave her first fledged brood early to begin incubating her second clutch.

DISTRIBUTION AND STATUS

Black Phoebes breed from southwestern Oregon south within coastal ranges through Baja California. In the southwest interior, they breed primarily in Arizona, New Mexico, and western Texas, and only locally in adjacent Nevada, Utah, and Colorado. These birds are then resident south through the highlands of Mexico to northern South America.

Swarth (1914) described Black Phoebes as irregularly distributed in southern Arizona, and nowhere very common. Phillips et al. (1964) later considered the species as breeding commonly in central and southeastern Arizona, and local and uncommon above the Mogollon Rim, within the Grand Canyon, and along the lower Colorado River. Apparently these birds expanded as a nesting species into the Prescott region in the very early 1900s (Phillips et al. 1964). Atlas data suggest that further distributional changes have occurred during the past thirty or so years.

Atlasers found that Black Phoebes were still most common at permanent water sources in southeastern and central Arizona. In addition, observers confirmed these birds nesting in many other regions of the state at elevations from approximately 90 to 9300 ft (27–2834 m). Atlasers obtained breeding records in several new areas. They were found nesting locally in several agricultural regions within the lower Gila and Santa Cruz River valleys along canals and larger irrigation channels. Black Phoebes are able to nest at some of these new locations because of recent water development activities. Black Phoebes were noted intermittently along the lower Colorado River, but basically throughout the entire length of the Grand Canyon upstream to Lake Powell. They were also discovered nesting within the adjacent Little Colorado River Gorge below Cameron and upper Navajo Creek and Piute Canyon on Navajo tribal lands. Local populations of Black Phoebes were encountered within the Virgin River Gorge in extreme northwestern Arizona.

Along the Mogollon Rim and in the White Mountains, Black Phoebes were confirmed nesting along more of the creeks draining the north slope than previous literature suggested. This includes the upper Little Colorado River drainage north to Saint Johns. They undoubtedly also nest commonly along the many creek and river drainages within the White Mountain Apache tribal lands, where atlas surveys could not be conducted.

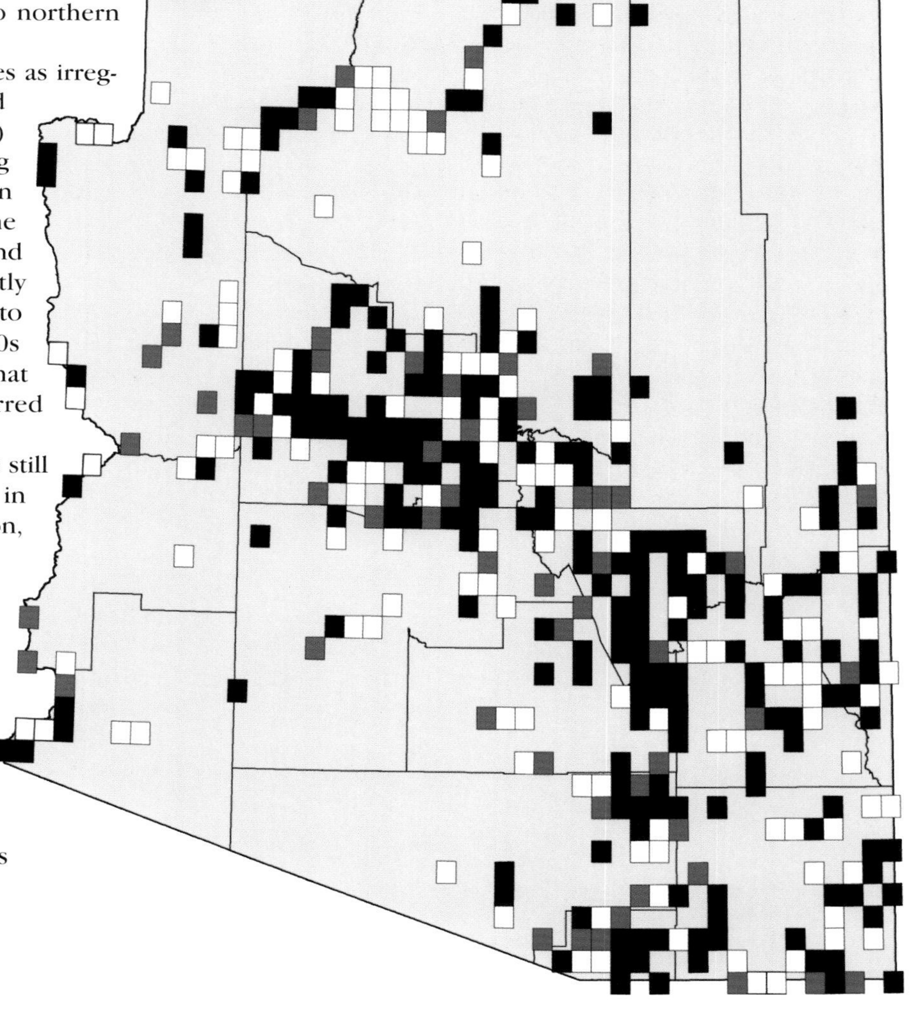

Black Phoebe Breeding Evidence Reported in 331 (18%) of 1834 priority blocks

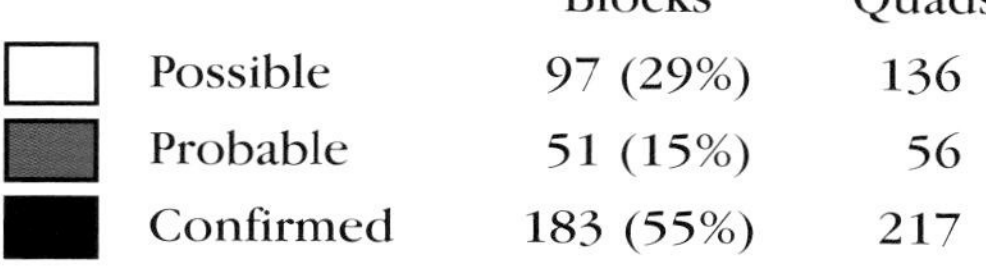

	Blocks	Quads
Possible	97 (29%)	136
Probable	51 (15%)	56
Confirmed	183 (55%)	217

Say's Phoebe

by Tracy McCarthey *Sayornis saya*

Owing to their open country living and adaptable nature, Say's Phoebes are one of the most widespread flycatchers in Arizona. Their plaintive melancholy call is a familiar sound in many windswept regions of the West, where suitable nesting structures range from rock ledges and mine adits to abandoned buildings and rusting vehicles.

DAN FISCHER

HABITAT

Say's Phoebes find the many open and diverse landscapes of Arizona quite attractive with deserts, grasslands, and rural/agricultural areas especially favored. Within such habitats, the need for a suitable covered ledge for nest placement is the primary limiting factor. They were found in nearly 90 percent of the atlas habitat types. Approximately 38 percent of all atlas records for this flycatcher were evenly distributed between rural/agricultural areas and Sonoran desertscrub associations (n = 993). Rural settings typically include ranches, farms, and abandoned homesteads that provide old building and other structures used for nesting. Similar structures are used in the Sonoran Desert landscapes as well as on cliff ledges, shallow cutbank cavities, and within mineshafts and adits. Cold desertscrub and adjacent grassland habitats accounted for an additional 17 percent of the records. Even open stands of pinyon pine and juniper frequently attract these flycatchers in Arizona. These adaptable birds nest in open urban areas as well, including residential parks, golf courses, schoolyards, and ballparks. Unlike the other phoebes, Say's Phoebes are commonly found nesting in areas far from the nearest water source and made possible due to the limited use of mud in their nest construction (Schukman and Wolf 1998).

BREEDING

Say's Phoebes are year-round residents in southern and western Arizona, where pairing can occur by February. This is also the period when migrants begin to arrive in northern breeding areas of the state, with most arriving by the end of March or early April. In Arizona, nest construction can begin by late February, with early egg laying in early or mid-March. Atlasers noted a Say's Phoebe carrying nesting material on 1 March and observed an occupied nest by 10 March. Nests with eggs were not reported until 28 March, but a nest with young on 31 March indicates egg laying by at least the second week of that month. Statewide atlas records revealed Say's Phoebe nesting activities peak from late April to early June with a steady decline after that. Atlasers reported the latest nests with young on 18 July, although adults were observed feeding a fledgling as late as 15 August, suggesting even later nesting activity. Phillips et al. (1964) also reported one active Tucson nest that contained large nestlings in late September. In Arizona, Say's Phoebes begin to disperse to nonbreeding areas in July or August and southern populations steadily increase through late fall as large numbers begin arriving from breeding areas north of the state.

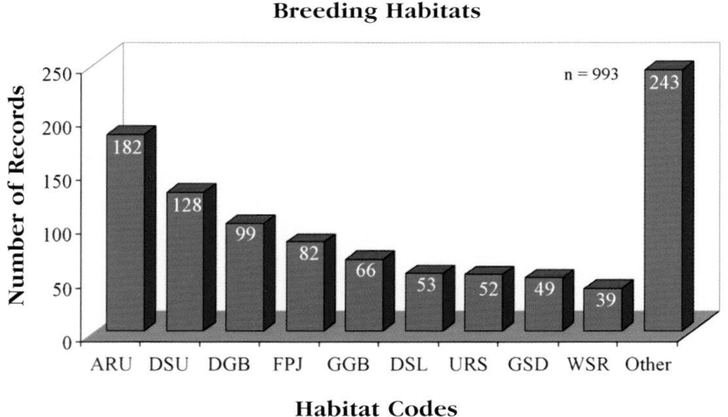

Apparently, the Say's Phoebe pair investigates nest sites together, with the female occasionally demonstrating nest (side-to-side) movements (Schukman and Wolf 1998). Although little direct evidence exists, nest construction is presumed to be undertaken solely by the female. Nests are placed on a sheltered, horizontal ledge in a variety of natural and manmade crevices. As noted earlier, Say's Phoebes rarely use mud in nest construction.

In Arizona, natural nest sites included caves, and crevices or sheltered ledges on cliff faces, rock walls, or shallow dirt cavities in arroyo cuts. One nest discovered was built on a possible Barn Swallow nest, which appears to be common behavior for Say's Phoebes (Bent 1942). They frequently build new nests on top of their own old nests, as well, with the female also frequently relining the nest in between broods or while the nest is active. Typical manmade

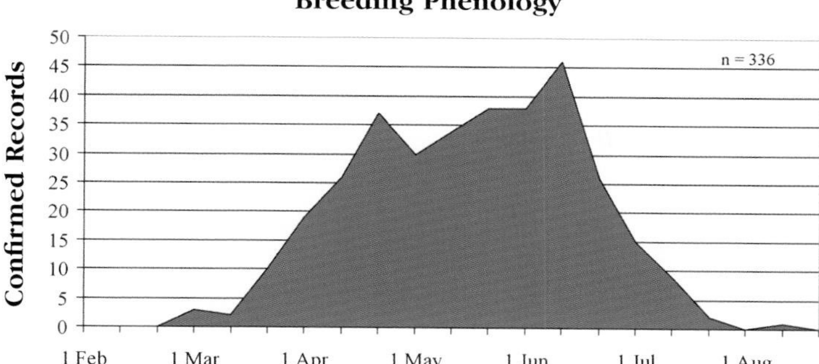

structures used for nesting in Arizona include mine shafts and adits; abandoned buildings and vehicles; and bridges or railroad trestles. Atlasers measured the height of 74 nests (55 percent in natural sites). These nests ranged in height from 0.6 to 98.4 ft (0.17–30 m), with a mean of 8.5 ft (2.6 m).

The typical Say's Phoebe clutch size is 4–5 eggs, but can range from 3 to 6 and rarely 7 (Schukman and Wolf 1998). Incubation period is from 12 to 18 days, and the young fledge in 14–21 days (Schukman and Wolf 1998). Both parents feed the young, although the male may take over much of the fledgling duties while the female initiates the next clutch. Most evidence suggests Say's Phoebes frequently double-brood and occasionally triple-brood within a single nesting season.

DISTRIBUTION AND STATUS

Say's Phoebes are summer resident in western North America in Alaska and the Yukon, and then from southern Canada and western Great Plains region south to central Mexico (generally west of the Hundredth Meridian). In Arizona, they nest basically statewide in appropriate habitat and appear to be limited only by suitable nesting substrates and open areas for foraging. Atlasers found breeding Say's Phoebes at elevations ranging from 100 to 8200 ft (30–2499 m) and nesting possibly to at least 8800 ft (2682 m).

Say's Phoebes have always been described as a fairly common to common breeding bird about cliffs and man-made structures throughout less densely wooded parts of Arizona to approximately 6500 ft (1981 m), and locally higher (Swarth 1914; Phillips et al. 1964). Atlas data reveal a similar conclusion, although they were documented breeding extensively above this elevation and were detected in every habitat except dense forests, alpine tundra, and heavily urbanized areas. During the atlas, the largest gap in the Say's Phoebe's Arizona distribution occurs in the forested areas of the Mogollon Rim and White Mountains. Some of this gap, however, occurs on White Mountain Apache tribal lands, where permission was denied for atlas surveys and thus a lack of data there. Say's Phoebes were also sparsely distributed in some relatively flat desert and grassland areas lacking suitable nesting structures.

Say's Phoebe populations appear to be stable and even slightly expanding in some areas. Human expansion into rural areas has undoubtedly benefited this species by inadvertently providing nesting sites on building and other man-made structures. Forests and woodlands have also been cleared and chained in Arizona, providing even more open landscape for this adaptable flycatcher.

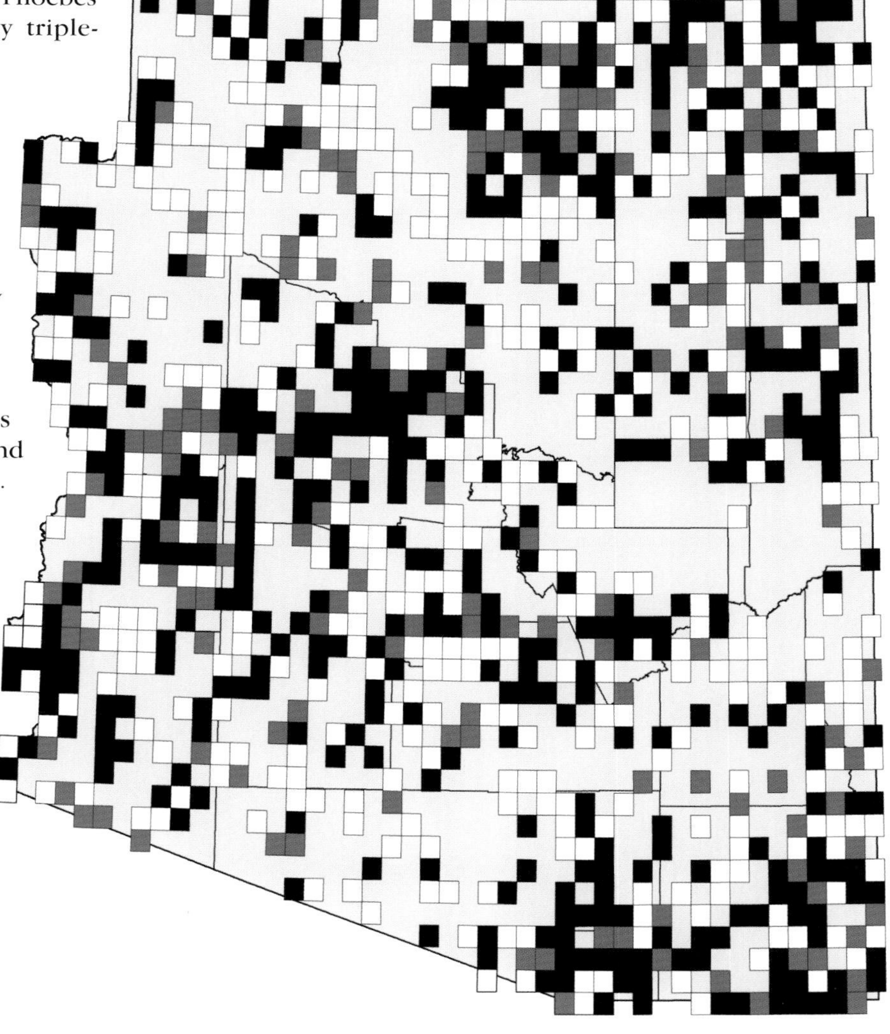

Say's Phoebe Breeding Evidence Reported in 964 (53%) of 1834 priority blocks

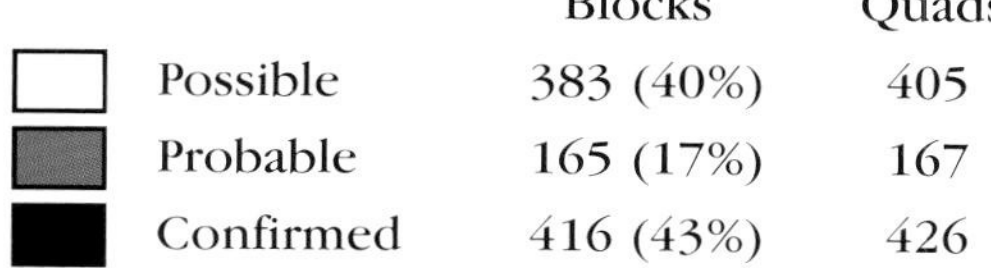

	Blocks	Quads
Possible	383 (40%)	405
Probable	165 (17%)	167
Confirmed	416 (43%)	426

Vermilion Flycatcher

by Annalaura Averill-Murray and Troy E. Corman

Pyrocephalus rubinus

The genus name for the Vermilion Flycatcher means "fire-head," which aptly describes the males. In the spring and summertime, these bright red birds can be observed high above the canopy, singing with their chest puffed out, tail lifted and fanned, and wings fluttering before they drop vertically to alight on a nearby perch.

DAN FISCHER

HABITAT

In Arizona, Vermilion Flycatchers typically breed in broadleaf riparian woodlands and mesquite bosques, often in the vicinity of water. This species is not generally found in areas with a dense canopy and thick understory, preferring open areas for foraging and nesting (Wolf and Jones 2000). During the atlas, 27 percent of potential breeding records (n = 297) were from mesquite-cottonwood-willow riparian woodland; 11 percent from drainages characterized by sycamore, cottonood, walnut, and ash; and 17 percent from heavily wooded dry washes containing large stands of mesquite and paloverde, as well as netleaf hackberry at slightly higher elevations. They were noted less frequently in the adjacent Sonoran desertscrub and semiarid grasslands. Vermilion Flycatchers are somewhat adaptable, and 20 percent of atlas records were noted nesting in rural settings, including stands of trees at ranches, farm houses, pasture edges, and along farm and stock ponds. Locally they were also found nesting at residential parks and golf courses with mesquite and other native shade trees.

BREEDING

Although a fairly widespread wintering species in southern Arizona, much of the state's breeding population of Vermilion Flycatchers is migratory. Males arrive on the breeding grounds first, beginning in early to mid-February prior to tree leaf-out, and both sexes are common by early March (Phillips et al. 1964). Nest construction can begin by late February in Arizona and these early nests may pertain to resident populations. In the lower Colorado River valley, where nesting habitat is likely limited, overwintering males secure a mate and breed earlier than migratory males, avoiding intense territorial disputes that can delay nesting by several weeks (Rosenberg et al. 1991). Atlasers confirmed nesting from mid-March (nest building on 19 March) through early August (nestlings on 1 August), with a peak in activity between late April and late June (n = 125). Earlier nesting records include a nest with eggs on 4 March (Bent 1946). The fall migration period in Arizona is not well understood, but it may begin by mid-August, with a noticeable decline of individuals by mid-September. Although some individuals overwinter on their breeding grounds, most have departed by mid-October.

Female Vermilion Flycatchers typically build their shallow cup nest on a horizontal branch fork free of leaves (Wolf and Jones 2000). Although nests are fairly exposed from above, the cryptic nature of the structure makes them difficult to detect. During the atlas, nest site substrates were described for nineteen nests, with the majority (42 percent) in mesquite. Other nests were found in Goodding willow, Fremont cottonwood, Arizona walnut, Arizona sycamore, ash, desert willow, acacia, and paloverde. Nest height ranged from 5 to 40 feet (1.5–12.2 m) with a median height of 10.5 ft (3.2 m; n = 18). Females incubate their typical clutch of 3 (range 2–4) eggs for 14 to 15 days, and both parents tend the nestlings until they fledge 14–16 days after hatching (Baicich and Harrison 1997). There is apparently little information on the fledgling dependency period. Pairs will raise one or two broods per season (Wolf and Jones 2000), potentially three (Archer 1996).

Atlasers found Vermilion Flycatchers feeding fledgling Brown-headed Cowbirds on two occasions. High parasitism rates (21 percent; n = 39) have been recorded for this

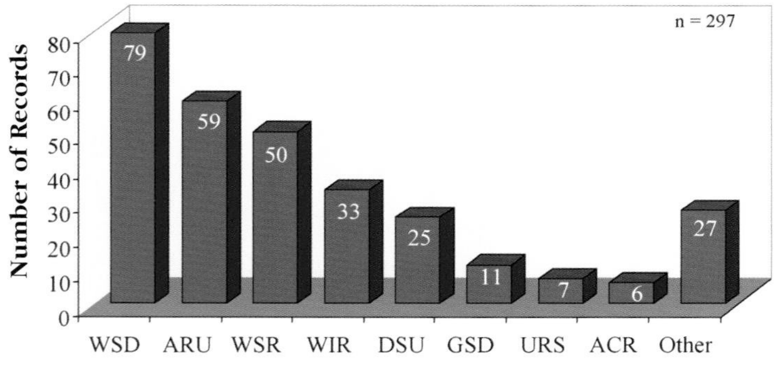

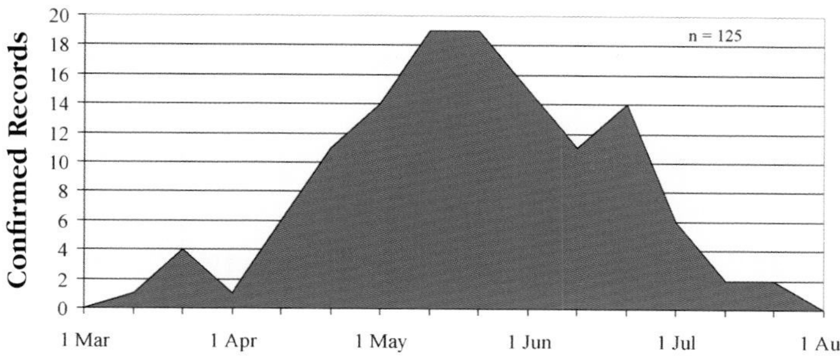

species in central Arizona and Sonora, Mexico (Carothers 1974) and Texas (19 percent; n = 27; Archer 1996).

DISTRIBUTION AND STATUS

In North America, Vermilion Flycatchers breed throughout much of Mexico north locally into southern California and southern Nevada, and more commonly east through central Arizona and southern New Mexico to central Texas. They also occasionally nest in Oklahoma and southwestern Utah (Wolf and Jones 2000).

Vermilion Flycatchers are described as common and often conspicuous summer residents in southeastern and central Arizona, including lower valleys of the state south of the Mogollon Rim (Phillips et al 1964). During the atlas period, they were noted ranging in elevation from 200 to 5400 ft (61–1646 m). Atlas data reveal local concentrations along major drainages such as the Gila, Salt, Verde, Agua Fria, Santa Cruz, and San Pedro rivers. They were also found regularly to west-central Arizona along the Hassayampa, Bill Williams, Santa Maria, and Big Sandy river systems, and north locally to near Valentine along Truxton Wash. As noted by Rosenberg et al. (1991), atlasers found Vermilion Flycatchers to be a local breeder along the lower Colorado River. Although occasionally observed within the Grand Canyon region, the species is not known to breed there (Brown et al. 1987). Phillips et al. (1964) noted a near-absence of this species in the southwestern corner of Arizona during summer; however, atlasers produced several records for this area, including along the lower Gila River and along larger washes on the Cabeza Prieta National Wildlife Refuge and Barry M. Goldwater Range. Atlasers did not find this flycatcher in the extreme northwestern corner of Arizona along the Virgin River, as previously reported (Monson and Phillips 1981).

Permits to conduct atlas surveys on White Mountain Apache tribal lands could not be obtained; therefore, atlasers were unable to verify continued nesting of these flycatchers at Ft. Apache as reported by Phillips et al. (1964). Atlasers also recorded a male Vermilion Flycatcher performing display flights on 17 June 1997 just west of Joseph City in Navajo County. Prior to this, a pair was reported in Snowflake, Navajo County, in April 1964 (Phillips et al. 1964).

To judge by Breeding Bird Survey data, Vermilion Flycatcher numbers have increased slightly in southern Arizona (Wolf and Jones 2000). However, due to the loss of mesquite bosques and other native riparian trees within the lower Colorado River valley and locally elsewhere, their abundance and distribution has been considerably reduced during the past fifty years (Rosenberg et al. 1991). Additionally, the locally high concentration of cowbirds in southwestern riparian areas may have a deleterious effect on local Vermilion Flycatcher populations.

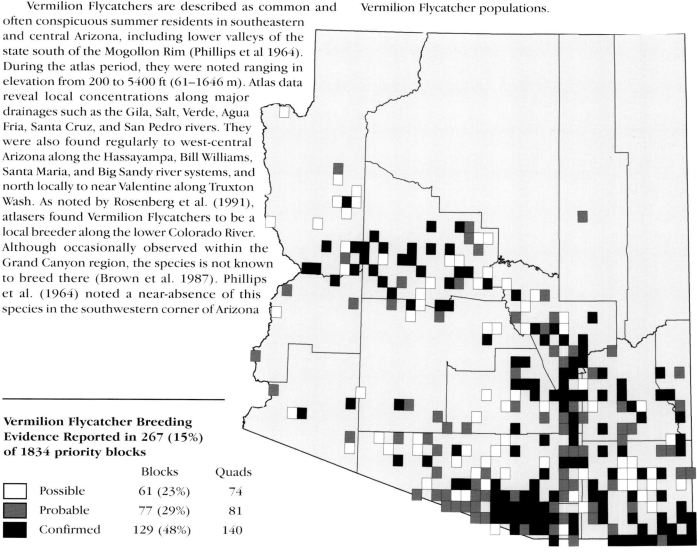

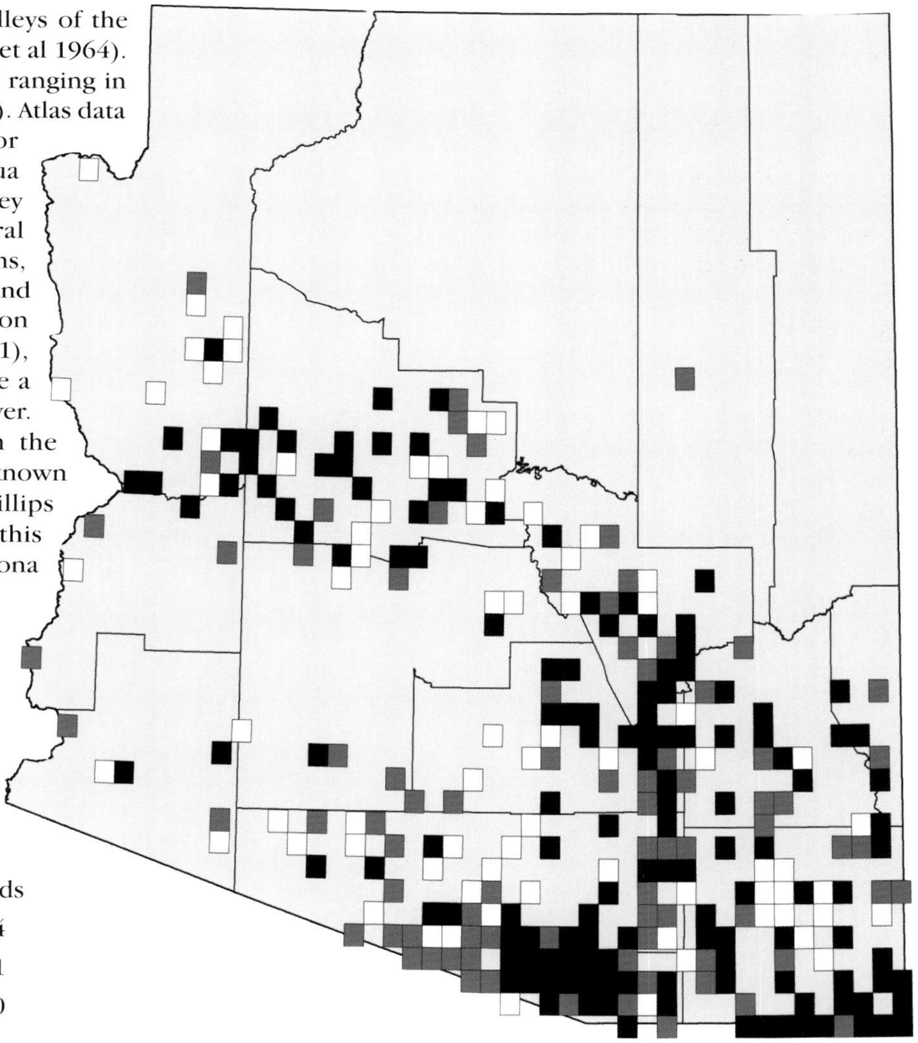

Vermilion Flycatcher Breeding Evidence Reported in 267 (15%) of 1834 priority blocks

	Blocks	Quads
Possible	61 (23%)	74
Probable	77 (29%)	81
Confirmed	129 (48%)	140

Dusky-capped Flycatcher

by Cathryn Wise-Gervais *Myiarchus tuberculifer*

Formerly known as the Olivaceous Flycatcher, the Dusky-capped Flycatcher has more than thirteen subspecies that are found throughout the American tropics. Small and inconspicuous, this *Myiarchus* flycatcher prefers dense foliage and is more often heard than seen. In fact, this bird's mournful whistled call is frequently heard throughout southeastern Arizona's oak woodlands.

HABITAT

Dusky-capped Flycatchers generally prefer densely wooded slopes and canyons with large trees and avoid areas dominated entirely by conifers (Marshall 1957). In Arizona, Dusky-capped Flycatchers are most commonly encountered in dense woodlands containing evergreen oaks and in the adjacent sycamore-lined drainages. Atlasers reported this species in six habitat types, and obtained 35 percent of potential breeding records in wooded canyons and foothill drainages characterized by large to medium Arizona sycamore, cottonwood, ash, and walnut, often with a Madrean evergreen oak influence ($n = 72$). An additional 26 percent of Dusky-capped Flycatcher records were in Madrean evergreen oak woodlands primarily comprising various species of oaks with scattered alligator junipers and pinyon pines. At higher elevations, atlasers frequently encountered these flycatchers (18 percent of records) in Madrean pine-oak woodlands of Chihuahuan, Apache and ponderosa pines intermixed with evergreen oaks and alligator juniper. Locally, Dusky-capped Flycatchers also nest within cottonwood-willow–dominated riparian woodlands and accounted for 17 percent of atlas records. Several of the more northern records were obtained in ponderosa pine–Gambel's oak associations.

BREEDING

Dusky-capped Flycatchers typically begin arriving on Arizona breeding grounds in early April and exceptionally in late March, but most do not arrive until mid-April. Pairing and early nesting activity begins soon after their arrival. Although atlasers obtained 25 confirmed records for this species, very few active nests were located. Atlasers first reported a pair of Dusky-capped Flycatchers in suitable breeding habitat on 8 April, and found the first occupied nest on 28 April. Nests with young were detected as early as 23 May, suggesting egg laying by late April or early May. The earliest fledglings noted were observed being fed by adults on 8 June. Atlas data suggest a peak in breeding activity from mid-May to early June, but the sample size for this estimate is quite small ($n = 19$). Some Dusky-capped Flycatcher breeding activity can continue into late summer, and observers noted adults feeding fledglings on 10 August. Swarth (1904) reported one very late nesting pair feeding a fledgling on 3 September in the Huachuca Mountains. Typically these flycatchers are among the first migrants to leave their summering grounds, with numbers dropping after the end of July and few remaining in their Arizona haunts by mid- to late August. However, individuals occasionally linger into early October.

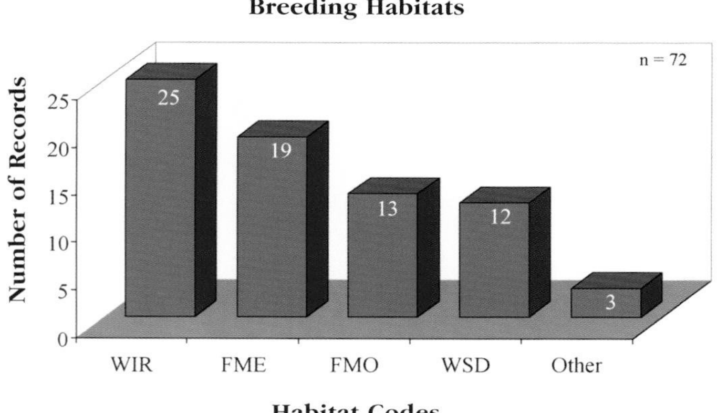

Little is known of Dusky-capped Flycatcher breeding biology. Like other *Myiarchus* flycatchers, these birds are cavity-nesters that take up residence in old woodpecker holes or in natural cavities. This species will also use nest boxes when available (Brandt 1951). Dusky-capped Flycatchers tend to select cavities that are both fairly high in trees and are protected by substantial cover. Nests in Arizona have been reported in sycamore, ash, walnut, maple, juniper, and various species of evergreen oaks (Tweit and Tweit 2002). The fact that Dusky-capped Flycatchers call infrequently near nesting cavities contributes to the difficulty involved in finding their high, well-concealed nests. Observers measured the height of only two Dusky-capped Flycatcher nests during the atlas period, one in sycamore and one in netleaf oak, both at 13.8 feet (4.2 m) above the ground. Tweit and Tweit (2002) determined the mean

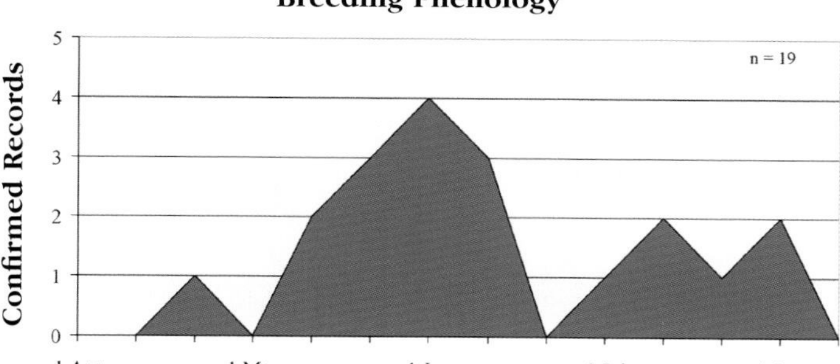

height for 27 Arizona nests was 20.3 feet (6.2 m) and ranged from 5.9 to 49.2 feet (1.8–15 m).

Presumably, only the female Dusky-capped Flycatcher constructs the nest. A typical clutch consists of 3–4 eggs (range 3–5) and the female incubates these for approximately 13 to 15 days (Tweit and Tweit 2002). Both adults feed the young, which fledge in approximately 14 days (Skutch 1960). It is unknown how long parental care continues after cavity departure. Although Dusky-capped Flycatchers have been observed laying replacement clutches when broods are lost to predation or other causes, they are not known to raise two successful broods per year (Tweit and Tweit 2002).

DISTRIBUTION

Dusky-capped Flycatchers are the most widespread *Myiarchus* flycatcher and occur throughout many regions of the American tropic, as far south as northern Argentina. This species reaches the northern edge of their breeding range in Arizona and as a result, their numbers can fluctuate widely from year to year (Phillips et al. 1964). Elsewhere in the United States, Dusky-capped Flycatchers are found within a small portion of southwest New Mexico and possibly irregularly in western Texas.

In Arizona, the summer distribution of Dusky-capped Flycatcher has progressively moved northward in limited numbers since the early 1900s. Swarth (1914) considered them most common in the Huachuca and Santa Rita mountains, but also noted them occurring in the Chiricahua and Santa Catalina ranges. They were later found nesting irregularly north to the Pinaleno Mountains and west to the Baboquivari Mountains (Phillips et al. 1964). By 1980, Dusky-capped Flycatcher records had increased northward to the Pinal Mountains near Globe with individual observations in the Superstition Mountains, Maricopa County, and Christopher Creek northeast of Payson (Monson and Phillips 1981).

Atlasers encountered Dusky-capped Flycatchers to be fairly widespread and locally common in most oak and some riparian woodlands of southeastern Arizona north to the Pinaleno, Galiuro, and Santa Catalina mountains. Elevational limits of these records range from approximately 3700 to 6800 ft (1128–2073 m). North of this stronghold, however, these flycatchers were much more sparsely distributed and typically found in limited numbers. They were detected locally in the Big Lue, Natanes, and Pinal mountains and in the Sierra Ancha north to Young. The most northern potential breeding record was of several pairs and individuals observed along upper Fossil Creek within the Fossil Springs Wilderness north of Strawberry.

Northern Dusky-capped Flycatcher records were in a region of the state where appropriate breeding habitat is common and widespread, but seldom visited by birders or biologists familiar with the species. Undoubtedly, additional nesting pairs of these unobtrusive flycatchers were overlooked during atlas surveys.

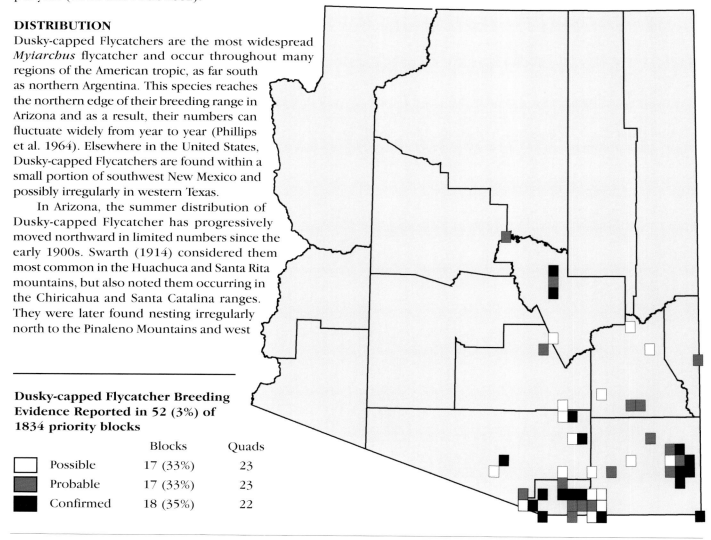

Dusky-capped Flycatcher Breeding Evidence Reported in 52 (3%) of 1834 priority blocks

	Blocks	Quads
Possible	17 (33%)	23
Probable	17 (33%)	23
Confirmed	18 (35%)	22

Ash-throated Flycatcher

by Cathryn Wise-Gervais *Myiarchus cinerascens*

If early spring finds you in the Arizona desert, listen at dawn for the whistled song of the Ash-throated Flycatcher. No bright plumage or kingbird-style machismo here; just subtle, pleasing colors and a well-proportioned build. This strong-billed species captures insects with an audible "snap" that can be likened to the tap of an old-fashioned typewriter.

JIM BURNS

HABITAT

The slender Ash-throated Flycatcher is a familiar bird in most of Arizona's arid and semiarid landscapes from lowland deserts and riparian woodland edges to pinyon pine and juniper covered mountain slopes. These birds are found statewide, primarily in open country that offers scattered trees or structures providing nest cavities. Atlasers reported this species in no less than thirty-three habitat types, suggesting a great deal of flexibility in habitat selection. As with many of Arizona's species that occur nearly statewide, the two most frequently reported habitat types were also the two most prevalent. Sonoran desertscrub accounted for 29 percent of atlas records for this species, and pinyon pine-juniper woodlands another 19 percent (n = 1536). Given this, it is likely that Ash-throated Flycatchers simply make use of what is available, not selecting any specific habitat component. Other commonly reported habitats included wooded desert dry washes and mesquite bosques (10 percent of records), as well as semiarid grasslands with scattered trees and shrubs (5 percent of records). Observers encountered the birds less frequently in cottonwood-willow and open Madrean evergreen oak woodlands. Ash-throated Flycatchers also commonly occur in Chihuahuan and Mojave desertscrub associations, especially among the larger trees in dry washes.

BREEDING

Although Ash-throated Flycatchers winter locally and in limited numbers in southern Arizona, migrants typically begin arriving in late February and early March to this region of the state. They often do not arrive until mid- to late April in northern Arizona. Atlasers reported the first pairs investigating nest cavities by 10 March and noted the earliest occupied nests on 16 March. Observers first reported nests with eggs on 10 April, but discovered a nest with young on 6 April indicates egg-laying initiation by at least the third week of March. Analysis of these data suggest that Ash-throated Flycatchers initiate nesting soon after arrival on their breeding grounds, with a peak in activity in late April and early May and a second, slightly lower peak in mid-June, possibly pertaining to second broods and renesting attempts (n = 572). Atlasers reported the latest nest with young on 6 August and dependent fledglings through 31 August. As widespread as this species is in Arizona, it is difficult to determine when fall migration begins. Northeastern Arizona populations make an abrupt departure in August with few remaining into early September (C. LaRue, personal communication). Migrants continue to pass through the lowlands of western Arizona regularly through October and into November (Rosenberg et al. 1991).

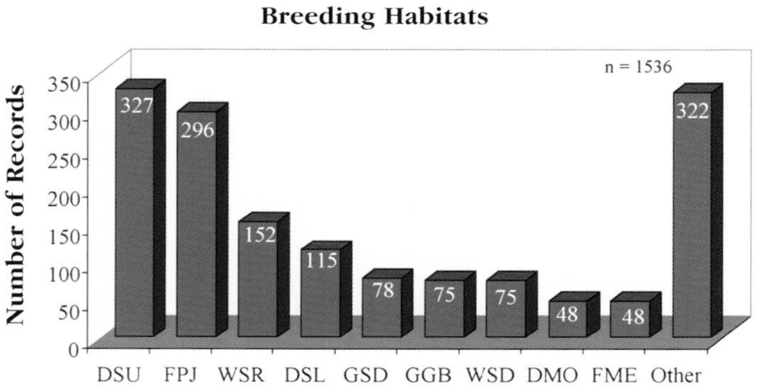

Like other *Myiarchus* species, Ash-throated Flycatchers are cavity nesters and will apparently build their domicile in almost any available and appropriately sized natural, woodpecker-constructed, or human-made cavity. They have even been known to nest in old Cactus Wren structures. Observers measured the height of eighty-two Ash-throated Flycatcher nests and 84 percent were in trees and saguaros. Other nests were in cliff cavities, fence posts, and metal pipes. The author documented one nesting attempt in a cavity within a crumbling and unstable sandstone rock turret that closely resembled a child's sandcastle. The most commonly reported trees were juniper of various species (26 nests), saguaro (10 nests), two species of paloverde (10 nests), and mesquite (6 nests). Other trees

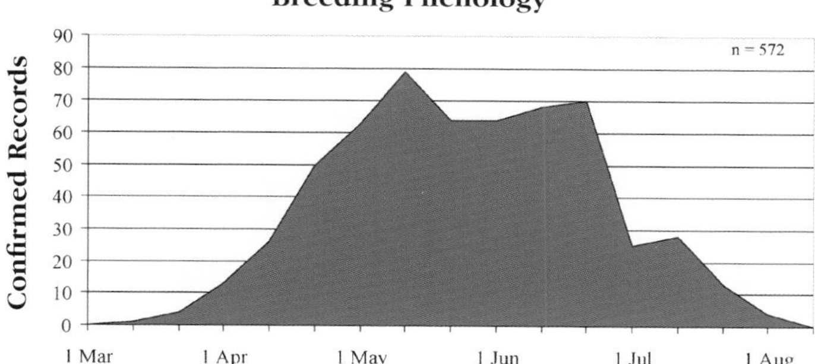

reported included ironwood, pinyon pine, sycamore, cottonwood, and walnut. The median height for the 82 nests measured was 6.9 ft (2.1 m) and ranged from 1.6 to 49.2 ft (0.5–15 m). During the atlas period, one observer noted an adult Ash-throated Flycatcher feeding nestlings in a cavity approximately 300 ft (91.4 m) up a 1000 ft (305 m)-high cliff in Glen Canyon (C. LaRue, personal communication).

Most evidence suggests that the female Ash-throated Flycatcher lines the nest cavity with soft materials before laying her clutch of 4–5 eggs (range 3–7; Cardiff and Dittmann 2002). The female incubates the eggs for approximately 14 to 16 days, and both sexes feed the young, which depart the cavity at 13–17 days of age (Cardiff and Dittmann 2002). The parents continue to feed the fledglings for 1 to 2 weeks following nest departure. Ash-throated Flycatchers are reported to produce two broods per season within the lower Colorado River valley (Brush 1983; Rosenberg et al. 1991), but data are lacking elsewhere within their range.

DISTRIBUTION AND STATUS

Widely distributed in western North America, Ash-throated Flycatchers breed from central Texas and Colorado west to the Pacific Coast, and from central Washington to central Mexico. Because of their flexibility in habitat and nest site selection, Ash-throated Flycatchers are easily the most numerous and widespread flycatcher in Arizona. They have typically been described as common to abundant summer residents throughout the deserts and open woodlands of the state (Swarth 1914; Phillips et al. 1964).

Quite vocal during the breeding season, Ash-throated Flycatchers were often found in fairly high densities allowing observers to easily detect and confirm the species on atlas blocks. Atlasers documented this species nesting primarily at elevations below 6800 ft (2073 m) and locally on drier mountain slopes to 7700 ft (2347 m).

Encountered regularly throughout southern and western Arizona, Ash-throated Flycatchers were notably absent in heavily forested and higher elevation regions such as within the White Mountains and along the Mogollon Rim to Flagstaff. However, the species undoubtedly continues to breed within sections of the White Mountain Apache tribal lands where atlas surveys could not be conducted. Atlas data also reveal that Ash-throated Flycatchers were sparse or absent as a nesting species over large regions of the Navajo and Hopi tribal lands, where the landscape is relatively flat and offers little vegetation.

Although this species was common in many habitats surveyed statewide, it was markedly absent from urban and most suburban neighborhoods. Like several other desert birds, Ash-throated Flycatchers do not persist once housing or industrial developments move into natural areas.

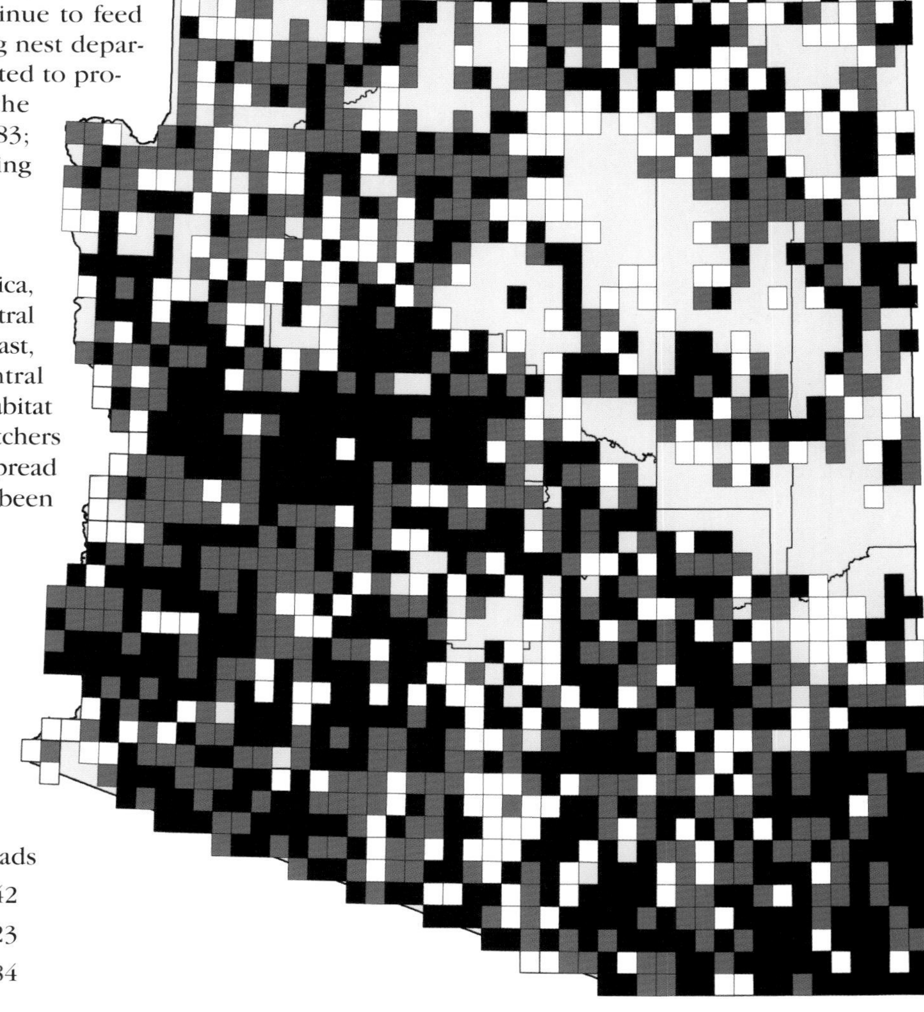

Ash-throated Flycatcher Breeding Evidence Reported in 1529 (83%) of 1834 priority blocks

	Blocks	Quads
Possible	328 (21%)	342
Probable	521 (34%)	523
Confirmed	680 (44%)	684

Brown-crested Flycatcher

by Cathryn Wise-Gervais *Myiarchus tyrannulus*

Brown-crested flycatchers are familiar birds along Arizona's desert rivers and in dense saguaro forests. Almost as aggressive as kingbirds, these large flycatchers give distinctive calls and are generally quite vocal on their breeding grounds. Although they eat primarily insects, they have also been observed capturing lizards and even hummingbirds.

JIM BURNS

HABITAT

Brown-crested Flycatchers prefer relatively lush wooded landscapes where nest cavities and productive foraging areas are plentiful. Brown-crested Flycatchers appear to select somewhat contradictory nesting habitats in Arizona, as they are most commonly found in both Sonoran desertscrub and lowland riparian woodlands. Although atlasers reported Brown-crested Flycatchers in seventeen habitat types, nearly 80 percent of records were obtained in only three of them ($n = 349$). Observers reported 42 percent of records in Sonoran Desert uplands containing dense saguaro stands and an abundance of various legume trees, and 20 percent of records in perennial drainages with tall stands of cottonwood and willow. Seventeen percent of records were obtained in foothill and lower mountain canyons with Arizona sycamore. Atlasers obtained fewer atlas records from sparsely vegetated Sonoran desertscrub and from the adjacent heavily wooded dry washes. Where appropriate habitat is limited, such as along the lower Colorado River valley, Brown-crested Flycatchers are also known to nest locally in the tall shade trees of residential parks and neighborhoods (Rosenberg et al. 1991).

BREEDING

Brown-crested Flycatchers begin arriving on their Arizona breeding grounds in mid- to late April. However, they do not become widespread until May. It is not surprising that the birds initiate breeding activities soon after this, as daytime temperatures in desert areas climb rapidly. Atlasers first observed Brown-crested Flycatchers in suitable breeding habitat on 17 April and reported the earliest occupied nest on 23 April. Observers detected the earliest nest with young on 11 May and noted an adult carrying a fecal sac on 13 May. These records suggest some early egg laying is initiated in late April. Brandt (1951) determined a clutch of four eggs he collected near Tucson had been laid by 1 May. Atlas data suggest that Brown-crested Flycatcher breeding activity peaks from mid-May through mid-June, but observers regularly confirmed the birds breeding into August. Atlasers reported the latest nest with young on 19 July, and observed adults feeding two fledglings on 28 August, slightly later than expected. Brown-crested Flycatchers generally begin migrating south very early, often by late July or early August, with few remaining after mid-August. Lingering individuals are occasionally observed into late September and exceptionally to early October (Phillips et al. 1964).

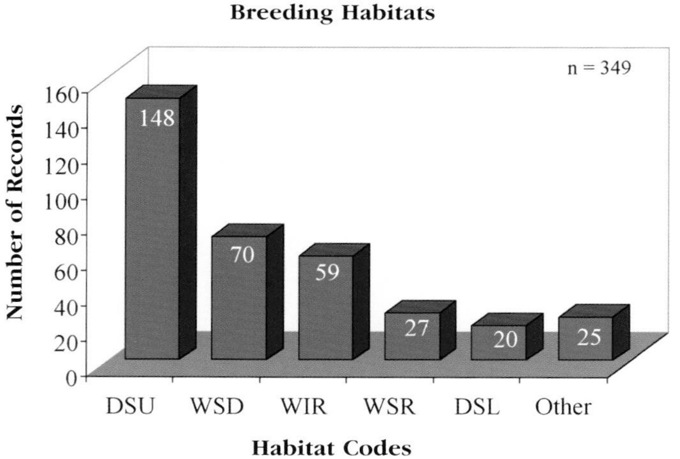

Although they will nest in some natural cavities, Brown-crested Flycatchers often select nest sites excavated by Gila Woodpeckers and Gilded Flickers. In Arizona, most documented nests are in saguaros, cottonwoods, willows, and sycamore. Observers took measurements at only three Brown-crested Flycatcher nests during the atlas period, two in cottonwoods and one in a saguaro. Nest heights for these ranged from 14.4 to 55 ft (4.4–16.8 m). Prior Arizona nests reported in Cardiff and Dittmann (2000) ranged in height from approximately 8 to 49 ft (2.4–15 m).

It is unclear if nest construction is performed by both members of the Brown-crested Flycatcher pair or only by the female. A typical clutch consists of 3–5 eggs in Arizona (Bent 1942), and the female incubates these for approximately 14 to 15 days (Baicich and Harrison 1997). The

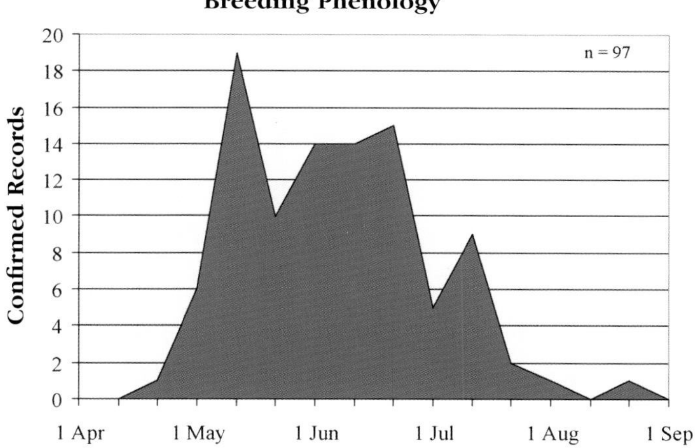

young spend approximately 12–18 days in the nest before fledging, and are fed by both parents during this period (Baicich and Harrison 1997). Brown-crested Flycatchers raise only one brood per season but may renest if their first attempt fails (Cardiff and Dittmann 2000).

DISTRIBUTION AND STATUS

Brown-crested Flycatchers reach the northern edge of their breeding range primarily in southern Texas and central Arizona, but also locally in adjacent New Mexico, Nevada, Utah, and California. They also nest widely south to northern Costa Rica and also in northeastern South America.

Phillips et al. (1964) considered Arizona's Brown-crested Flycatchers to be common summer residents in central and southeastern Arizona, and only locally distributed along the lower Colorado River. In 1966, they were also discovered nesting in extreme northwestern Arizona along lower Beaver Dam Wash near the confluence of the Virgin River (Wauer 1968). Atlas data support these earlier findings and document Brown-crested Flycatchers at elevations from approximately 100 to 5400 ft (30–1646 m) in Arizona.

There were apparently few records of Brown-crested Flycatcher within the lower Colorado River valley prior to the 1950s, but local numbers increased substantially through the 1980s (Rosenberg et al. 1991). Faced with massive riparian habitat reduction during this period, the sudden appearance and increase of this flycatcher is quite perplexing (Rosenberg et al. 1991). Although previously reported within Mohave Valley north of Topock Marsh, atlasers did not detect this species within the lower Colorado River valley north of Lake Havasu.

During the atlas period, Brown-crested Flycatchers were largely absent west of Organ Pipe Cactus National Monument and Gila Bend, probably due to a paucity of saguaros. They were widely reported in eastern Arizona to approximately the San Pedro River drainage. These flycatchers were then more sparingly distributed east to New Mexico, although still fairly common at some localities.

In central Arizona, Atlasers regularly encountered Brown-crested Flycatchers north along the Verde River to at least Perkinsville and into Oak Creek Canyon north of Sedona. To the west, they were found within the Big Sandy, Santa Maria, and Bill Williams River watersheds. During the atlas period, observers discovered a local concentration of these flycatchers within the Grand Canyon, primarily along a 10-mile (16 km) section of the river just above the Parashant Canyon confluence (J. Spence, personal communication). Lacking appropriate tree cavities, cliff nesting is suspected here.

Brown-crested Flycatcher populations appear to be fairly stable in Arizona, although habitat loss is a continued concern. These aggressive birds are largely absent in modified agriculture and residential landscapes.

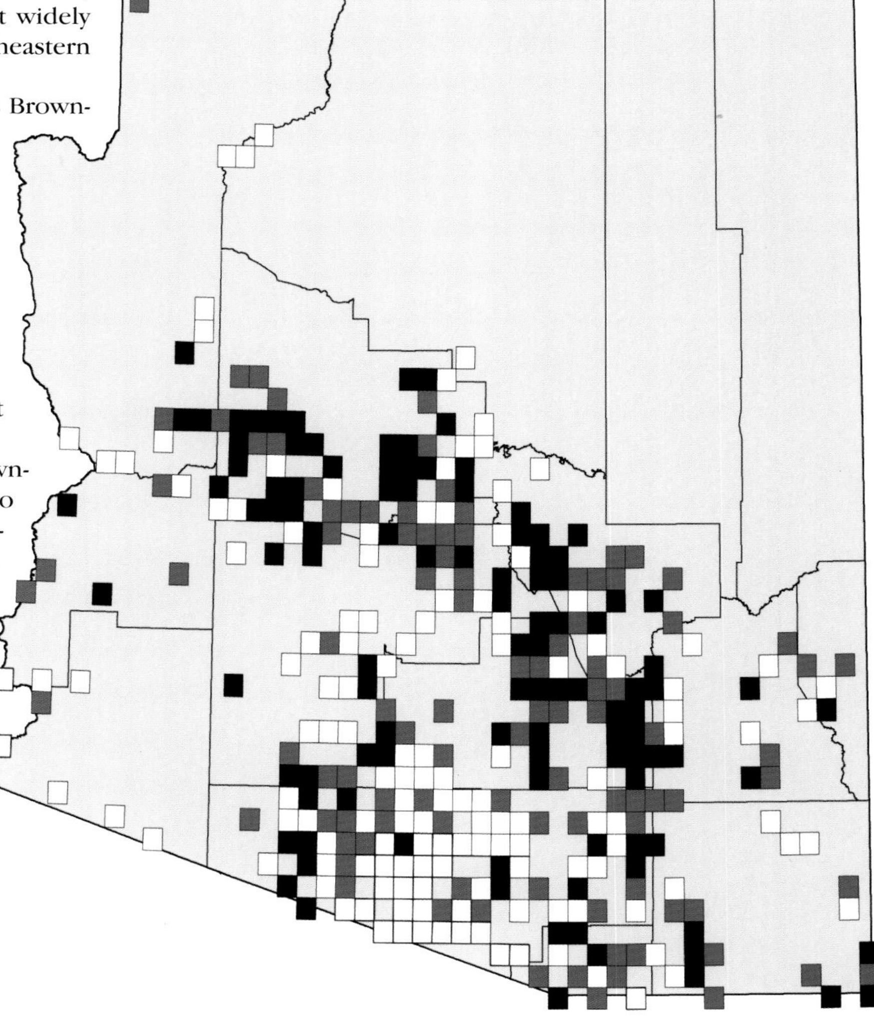

Brown-crested Flycatcher Breeding Evidence Reported in 328 (18%) of 1834 priority blocks

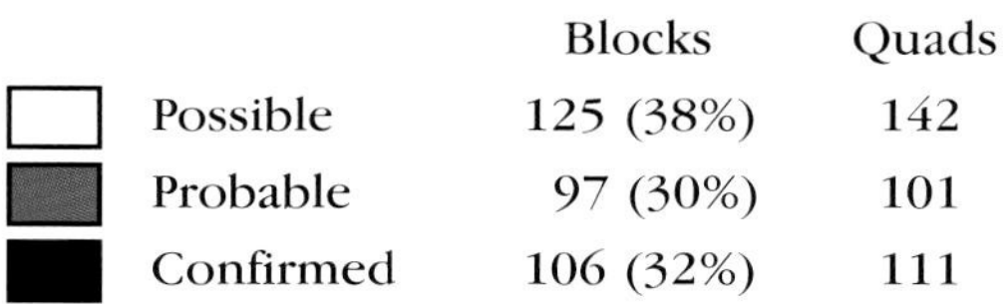

	Blocks	Quads
Possible	125 (38%)	142
Probable	97 (30%)	101
Confirmed	106 (32%)	111

Sulphur-bellied Flycatcher

by Troy E. Corman *Myiodynastes luteiventris*

Within the sycamore-lined canyons of southeastern Arizona mountains, many birders are delighted by the sights and sounds of the almost exotic Sulphur-bellied Flycatcher. Even with their loud, shrill, squeeze-toy calls and boldly striped pattern, these splendid tropical birds can be difficult to view high in the leafy canopy they often occupy.

HABITAT

Occupying many forested tropical habitats throughout their range, Sulphur-bellied Flycatchers in Arizona are confined primarily to nesting in drainages with tall, broadleaf riparian woodlands. However, individuals and pairs frequently travel up adjacent dry drainages or ascend slopes to forage in pines and oaks (Marshall 1957). Atlasers reported 80 percent of Sulphur-bellied Flycatcher observation in canyons and drainages dominated or at least containing Arizona sycamore (n = 35). Fremont cottonwood, Arizona walnut, velvet ash, and various evergreen oaks also frequently occupy the lower mountain drainages these flycatchers prefer. At higher elevations in southeastern Arizona this species was often found in or near canyons were Madrean pine-oak forests of evergreen oaks and Chihuahuan and Apache pine merge with sycamore-maple associations. At more northern locations in Arizona, Sulphur-bellied Flycatchers were also encountered nesting in cool canyons with Arizona alder, Gambel's oak, box elder, Arizona sycamore, and very scattered conifers.

BREEDING

In Arizona, Sulphur-bellied Flycatchers typically do not begin to arrive on breeding territories until mid-May, exceptionally as early as 27 April. Some of Arizona's locations are left unoccupied until early June. Noisy courtship activity and pairing begin soon after arrival. Atlasers observed an adult investigating cavities as early as 21 May and nest building activity as early as 25 May. Atlasers did not report nest with eggs, but noted occupied nest cavities by 10 June. The earliest completed clutch of eggs reported in Arizona was discovered on 3 June (Brandt 1951). Bent (1942) noted Arizona egg dates from 20 June to 15 August, and atlas data suggest a slight peak of nesting activity in mid-July. The earliest nest with young reported by atlasers was on 17 June, which, if correct, is exceptionally early. The latest nest with young reported during the atlas was on 10 August. However, Howard (1899) reported finding a nest in Arizona with recently hatched young on the late date of 28 August. Atlasers observed adults feeding a fledgling as late as 10 September near Bisbee. Most Sulphur-bellied Flycatchers have departed Arizona by mid-September, with stragglers lingering as late as 3 October.

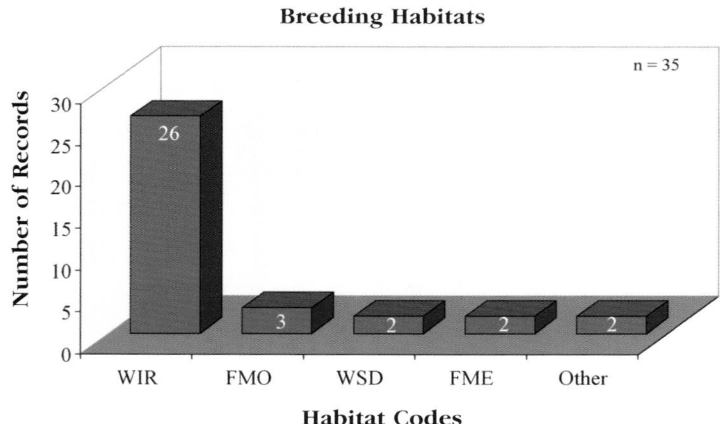

In Arizona, female Sulphur-bellied Flycatchers typically construct their nests in sycamore cavities, which are often used in successive years (Swarth 1904). They frequently use natural cavities but also those constructed by flickers, and they have been known to use nest boxes in Arizona (Ligon 1971). The only nesting cavity height measured by atlas crews was 17.4 ft (5.3 m) above the ground. This is lower than other measured Arizona nests, which ranged from 22.3 to 49.2 ft (6.8–15 m) in height (Howard 1899; Ligon 1971). The cavity is sometimes filled with sticks and other debris until it is within a few inches of the top of the cavity threshold, allowing the incubating female a commanding view (Brandt 1951). Conversely, Howard (1899) found nests nearly 1 ft (0.3 m) below the cavity entrance. In Arizona, the nest bowl is often constructed using the dried, curved petioles of Arizona walnut leaves (Bent 1942), which may suggest a preference for canyons and drainages with both sycamore and walnut.

Female Sulphur-bellied Flycatchers incubate the 3–4 eggs (range 2–5) for approximately 16 days, and the nestlings fledge in 16–18 days (Ligon 1971). The length of time

Breeding Phenology

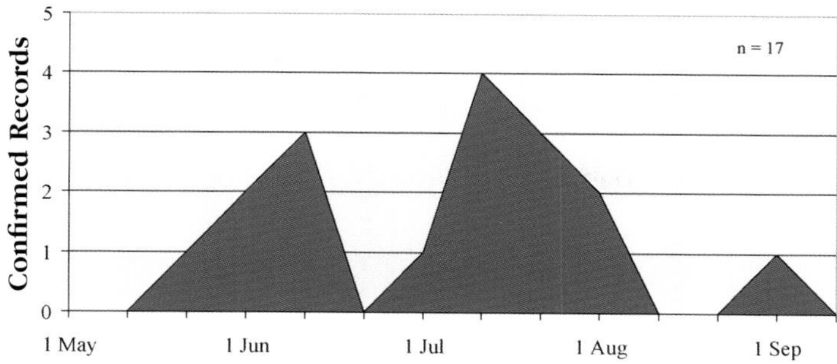

fledglings are dependent on adults is unknown, and there is little evidence suggesting more than one brood per season. Friedmann and Kiff (1985) reports of one Sulphur-bellied Flycatcher egg clutch in Arizona that contained a single Bronzed Cowbird egg.

DISTRIBUTION AND STATUS

Sulphur-bellied Flycatchers are primarily tropical birds that nest from southeastern Arizona and northeastern Mexico south to northern Costa Rica. They winter in northern South America. By the early 1900s, Sulphur-bellied Flycatchers had been found in the Santa Rita, Chiricahua, and Huachuca mountains of extreme southeastern Arizona (Swarth 1914). Phillips et al. (1964) noted this flycatcher as a fairly common summer resident in canyons of not only these ranges, but to the north in the Santa Catalina and Pinaleno mountains. Later, Monson and Phillips (1981) reported additional locations suggesting a range expansion. They were found as far west as the eastern slope of the Baboquivari Mountains, and locally north to the Sierra Ancha in central Gila County. Atlasers documented that Sulphur-bellied Flycatchers continue to nest in a few canyons on the eastern slope of the Sierra Ancha.

Atlasers noted Sulphur-bellied Flycatchers to be locally fairly common throughout much of their prior range in southeastern Arizona and a very sparse, local summer resident north of Pima and Cochise counties. This flycatcher was typically found nesting at elevations from 4500 to 6000 ft (1372–1829 m), locally as low as 3640 ft (1109 m) in Sycamore Canyon in the Pajarito Mountains. However, Swarth (1904) reported Sulphur-bellied Flycatchers in the Huachuca Mountains up to 7500 ft (2286 m).

During the atlas, Sulphur-bellied Flycatchers were discovered in several locations away from prior reported localities. These included several canyons within the Mule, Rincon, and Galiuro Mountains. Farther north, atlasers encountered this species for the first time on San Carlos tribal lands in the Natanes Mountains northwest of Point of Pines and south of San Carlos Reservoir. An individual was observed investigating tree cavities near the base of the Mogollon Rim along Christopher Creek, and a calling Sulphur-bellied Flycatcher was found along Fossil Creek west of Strawberry. The most northern breeding record came from a pair confirmed nesting in 1997 in Oak Creek Canyon near the confluence with its West Fork north of Sedona. A pair of Sulphur-bellied Flycatchers returned to this location each subsequent year through the atlas period.

These additional atlas records suggest the continued steady northern range expansion of Sulphur-bellied Flycatchers in Arizona. Likewise, there are numerous infrequently visited sycamore-lined drainages and canyons south of the Mogollon Rim that undoubtedly harbor additional pairs of these squealing tropical flycatchers.

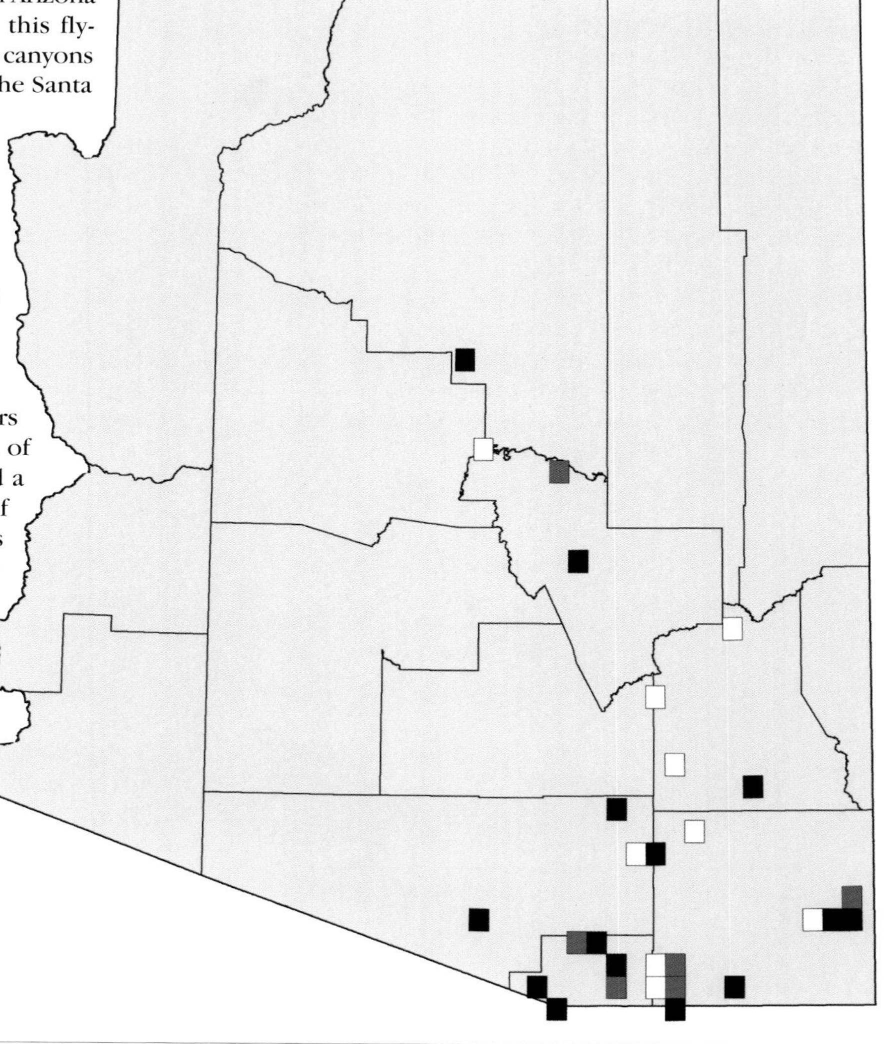

Sulphur-bellied Flycatcher Breeding Evidence Reported in 15 (<1%) of 1834 priority blocks

	Blocks	Quads
Possible	4 (27%)	9
Probable	4 (27%)	6
Confirmed	7 (47%)	14

Tropical Kingbird

by Troy E. Corman *Tyrannus melancholicus*

Always on guard, Tropical Kingbirds typically choose high, exposed perches where they watch for intruding rivals or from which to mob raptors that enter their territory. Unless the observer is familiar with its calls, this splendid kingbird is easily overlooked among the much more common Western and Cassin's kingbirds.

RICK AND NORA BOWERS

HABITAT

Nesting in a wide diversity of habitats throughout their extensive range, Tropical Kingbirds primarily inhabit lowland riparian woodlands in Arizona. Nearly 60 percent of all atlas records were reported along perennial drainages and ponds containing tall, decadent stands of Fremont cottonwood and Goodding willow (n = 22). Understory vegetation often consists of velvet mesquite, tamarisk, and seepwillow, as well as sapling stands of cottonwood and willow. This is a woodland edge species in Arizona, often selecting smaller groves or riparian corridor edges. Tropical Kingbirds typically avoid the closed canopy of the interior forest. They especially favor the tops of larger cottonwoods with many exposed, dead limbs for perching and foraging. Several occupied locations in Arizona consist of several large trees at the edge of a cienega or marshy pond containing cattails, bulrush, or buttonbush. Locally, Tropical Kingbirds were also found nesting in tall athel tamarisk at a golf course and in abandoned pecan orchards, where many of the tree crowns were dead.

BREEDING

Tropical Kingbirds typically begin to return to Arizona in early May, exceptionally as early as 24 April. Territorial defense and pairing begin soon after arrival. Atlasers reported these birds constructing nests by 24 May; however, an older record reported nest building as early as 19 May (Phillips et al. 1964). Because of the typical lofty nest location of Tropical Kingbirds, atlasers were unable to determine nests with eggs. Although the earliest nest with young reported during the atlas was on 16 June, which would indicate egg-laying initiation no later than the last few days of May. This also corresponds well with several atlas observations of occupied nests from 26 May to 6 June. The latest occupied nest reported by atlasers was on 23 July, and adults were observed feeding fledged young as late as 19 August. However, adults have been observed feeding very large nestlings at the Arivaca Cienega on the late date of 4 September (M. Stevenson, personal communication). Fall migration begins in August, with most Tropical Kingbirds having departed Arizona by early to mid-September, casually to early October.

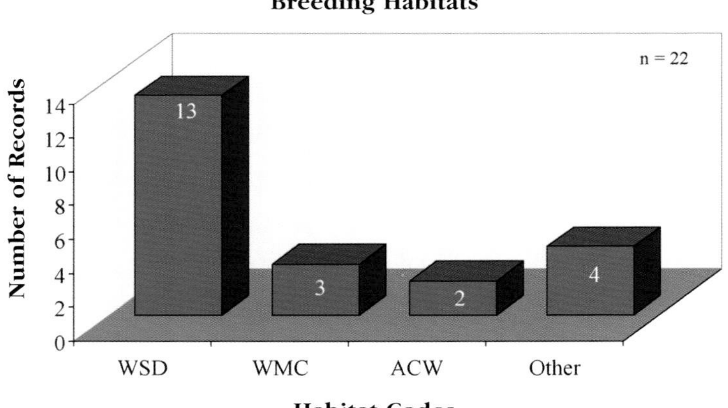

In Arizona, female Tropical Kingbirds typically construct their nests in the upper quarter of tall trees. Most nests are discovered on crotches of outer limbs of Fremont cottonwoods, often near exposed perches. Frequently located on dead limbs, the nests are often very conspicuous and exposed to the elements. In Arizona, Tropical Kingbirds are especially found of constructing their nests on the tops of dense mistletoe clumps. As previously mentioned, atlasers also found them nesting in tall, exotic athel tamarisk and pecan trees. Of three nests in cottonwoods measured by atlas field crews, the mean height was 47.9 ft (14.6 m) with a range of 38–60 ft (11.6–18.3 m).

The female typically incubates the clutch of 2–4 eggs for approximately 15–16 days (Skutch 1954), while the male usually remains near the nest and defends it (Stouffer and Chesser 1998). The young fledge when they are 18–19 days old, and the adults continue feeding them for at least two weeks following nest departure (Skutch 1960). There is no evidence suggesting Tropical Kingbirds produce more than one brood per season; however, they will renest if prior attempts have failed (Stouffer and Chesser 1998).

DISTRIBUTION AND STATUS

Tropical Kingbirds have an extensive range from southeastern Arizona and south Texas to central Argentina. Only the

Breeding Phenology

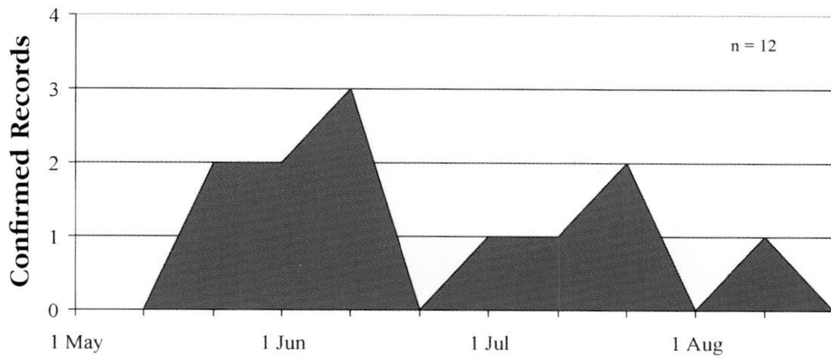

most northern and southern populations appear to be migratory. First found in Arizona near Tucson in 1905, this kingbird was not noted again until it was found nesting south of Tucson in 1938 (Phillips 1940). In the 1950s, Tropical Kingbirds were also found nesting along the Santa Cruz River as far south as Nogales, and an isolated pair was observed nest building along the Salt River east of Phoenix in 1956 (Simpson and Werner 1958; Phillips et al. 1964). Their nesting distribution continued to expand in Arizona, with the discovery of birds near the lower San Pedro River at Cook's Lake in 1975, the San Bernardino Ranch by 1976, and Arivaca by 1977 (Monson and Phillips 1981). By 1985, scattered nesting pairs of Tropical Kingbirds were found along the lower San Pedro River from Dudleyville to near San Manuel.

Atlasers found Tropical Kingbirds nesting throughout much of their historical range in Arizona. Supporting their continued steady range expansion, this kingbird was also discovered nesting in many new locations in the state during the atlas. Tropical Kingbirds were confirmed breeding at elevation from 1100 to 4050 ft (335–234 m) in Arizona. The lowest elevation was of a pair nest building at Quitobaquito Springs at Organ Pipe Cactus National Monument in 2000. The success of this pair was unknown. J. Taylor reported another pair of Tropical Kingbirds at Fortuna Pond just northeast of Yuma on 19 June 1994 at an elevation of 150 ft (46 m). The highest elevation was along the upper San Pedro River south of Highway 90, where a pair successfully fledged young in 1993. Tropical Kingbirds continued to nest at this location throughout the atlas period.

Atlasers also encountered this kingbird nesting locally and uncommonly along the lower San Pedro and adjacent Gila rivers from Winkelman south to Cascabel. During the atlas period, they were also discovered nesting in the Santa Cruz River valley near Marana north to a pecan grove just south of the Pinal Air Park. The northernmost record during the atlas period was of a nesting pair that successfully fledged at least one young at the Hassayampa River Preserve near Wickenburg in 2001.

Based on their history in the state, the nesting distribution of Tropical Kingbirds is expected to continue expanding in Arizona. Observations in the state suggest that territory site fidelity is apparently strong in this species. There are several isolated nesting localities in Arizona where pairs return annually, particularly at sites where they have successfully fledged young.

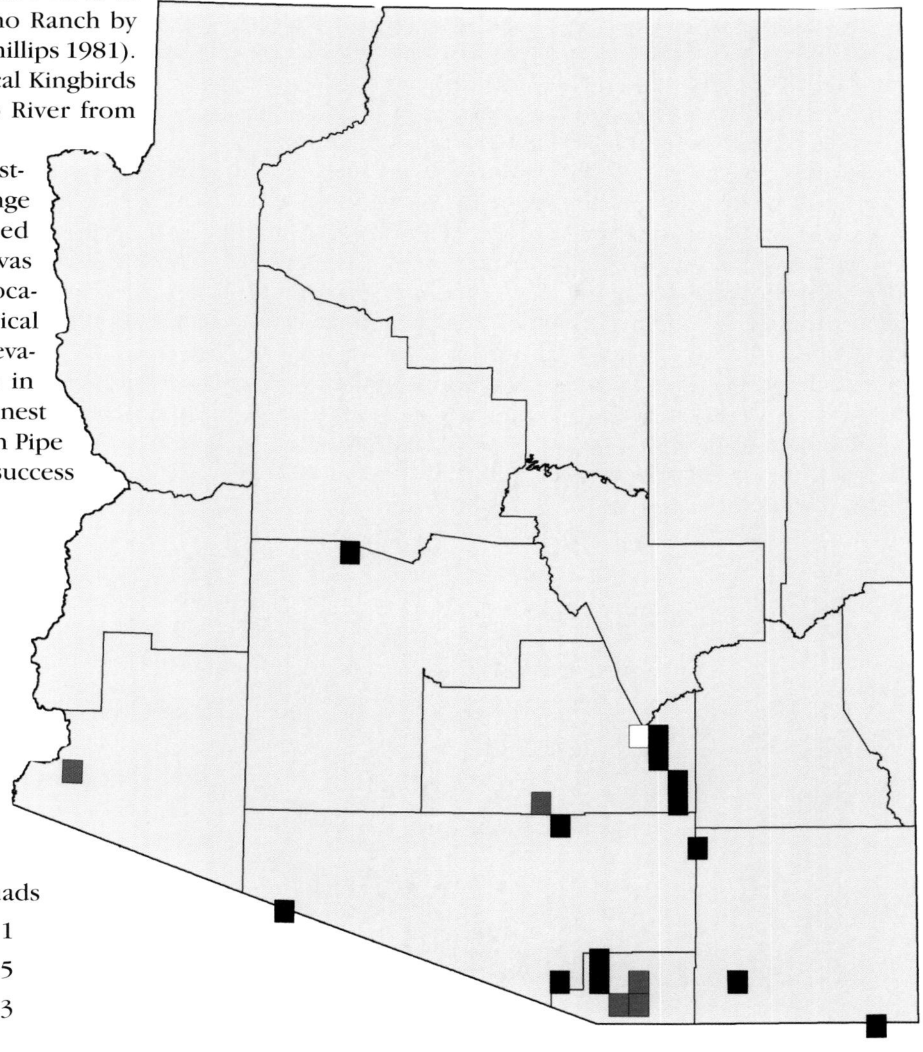

Tropical Kingbird Breeding Evidence Reported in 5 (<1 %) of 1834 priority blocks

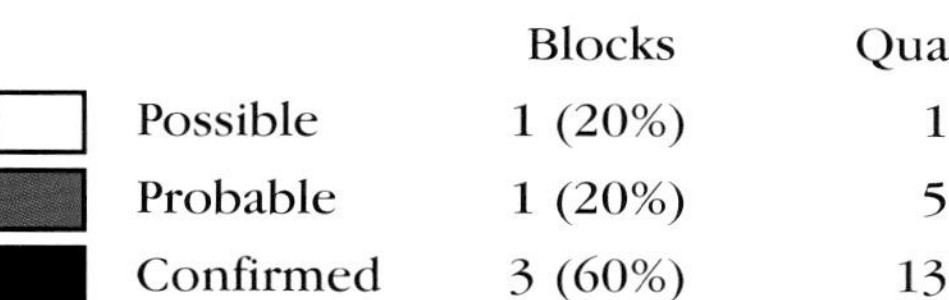

	Blocks	Quads
Possible	1 (20%)	1
Probable	1 (20%)	5
Confirmed	3 (60%)	13

Cassin's Kingbird

by Cathryn Wise-Gervais *Tyrannus vociferans*

JIM BURNS

The rapid and forceful "come here, come-here, come-here!" call of the Cassin's Kingbird is a familiar and unmistakable sound in Arizona's open, mid-elevation woodlands. These large and excitable flycatchers share many habitats with the similar Western Kingbird, and they chatter and hunt from exposed perches, making them easy to observe.

HABITAT

Cassin's Kingbirds require good cover coupled with open areas for foraging but are otherwise habitat generalists. Atlasers reported Cassin's Kingbirds in thirty habitat types, with most (38 percent of 648 records) occurring in pinyon pine–juniper woodlands and in the adjacent grasslands with scattered junipers. Observers also reported the birds in forested canyons and foothill drainages containing Arizona sycamore, cottonwood, walnut, and oaks (12 percent of atlas records) and in lowland riparian woodlands with tall Fremont cottonwoods and willows (10 percent of records). Cassin's Kingbirds are fairly adaptable, and they were found near human developments as well. Observers reported 8 percent of Cassin's Kingbird records in rural areas such as among scattered shade trees around ranches, farm buildings, roadside rests, and at stock ponds. Fewer atlas records were obtained from semiarid grasslands with scattered tree groves and in Madrean evergreen oak woodlands. At higher elevations, these kingbirds were also found in woodlands containing pinyon pine–juniper with scattered ponderosa pine and in southeastern Madrean pine-oak with Apache and Chihuahuan pines. Cassin's Kingbirds prefer larger tree stands and regularly nest at higher elevations than Western Kingbirds but the two species overlap frequently and can even nest in the same tree.

Breeding Habitats

n = 648

Habitat Codes	FPJ	WIR	GGB	WSD	ARU	FME	GSD	FPP	Other
Number of Records	181	78	64	62	53	27	27	25	131

BREEDING

Cassin's Kingbirds begin arriving in southeastern Arizona in early to mid-March, but typically do not appear in the central or northern portions of the state until mid- to late April. They start their breeding cycle soon after arrival. Atlasers first reported Cassin's Kingbirds in suitable breeding habitat on 28 March and noted an individual constructing a nest on 8 April. Based on atlas data, some early nests contain eggs by mid- to late April. Observers reported an adult feeding nestlings by 1 May and fledglings by 19 May. Statewide atlas surveys revealed a peak breeding period from mid-May to mid-June (n = 255), but nesting activity continues well after this date. Atlasers noted nests with young and occupied nests through 8 August, and adults were observed feeding fledgling through 1 September. Although Cassin's Kingbirds typically raise one brood per year, they will renest if the first clutch is lost (Blancher and Robertson 1984). Considered the hardiest of Arizona's kingbirds, most depart the state by late September or early October, but individuals often linger into November. Locally, small numbers of these kingbirds have only recently begun to overwinter in southeastern Arizona regularly.

Cassin's Kingbirds nest in a variety of trees in Arizona and often return to the same tree stand to nest in subsequent years (Tweit and Tweit 2000). They nest much less frequently on power poles than do Western Kingbirds. Atlasers took measurements at fifty-five Cassin's Kingbird nests in eight tree types, including Utah and one-seeded juniper species (49 percent of nests), pinyon pine (20 percent of nests) and sycamore (16 percent of nests). The remaining nests were found in ponderosa pine, cottonwood, Gambel's oak, evergreen oak species, and ash. The median nest height was 13.2 ft (4 m), the range from 5.0 to 55.8 ft (1.8–17 m). Interesting studies have found that Cassin's Kingbirds will nest significantly closer to Western

Breeding Phenology

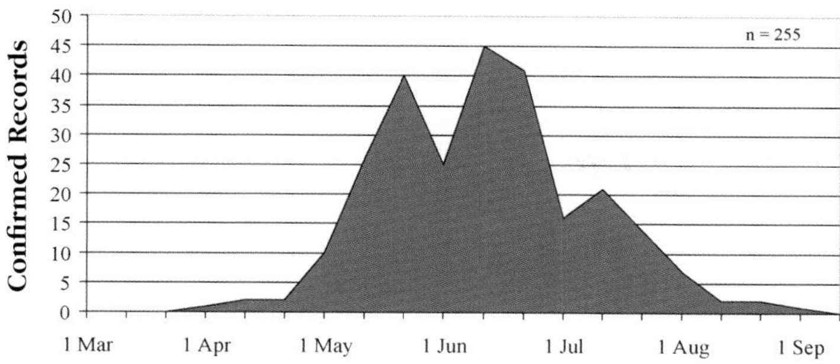

Kingbird nests than to other Cassin's Kingbirds (Blancher and Robertson 1984).

Female Cassin's Kingbirds construct the nest and incubate the 3–4-egg (range 2–6) clutch, while the male closely guards and aggressively defends the nest from intruders (Tweit and Tweit 2000). Incubation takes approximately 14–16 days, and once eggs hatch, both parents will feed the young. Nestling Cassin's Kingbirds depart the nest when they are a little more than 2 weeks old but continue to be fed by adults for several additional weeks (Tweit and Tweit 2000). There is no convincing evidence of Cassin's Kingbirds producing more than one brood per season, but the lengthy nesting season in southern Arizona (April–August) would suggest the possibility.

DISTRIBUTION AND STATUS

The breeding distribution of Cassin's Kingbirds is fairly limited in western North America with several disjunct populations. They are found in California's coastal ranges and valleys from Alameda County south to northern Baja California. To the east, they nest sparingly along the western edge of the Great Plains region from Montana south to Colorado. Their breeding range also includes much of the southwest from southern Nevada, Utah, and New Mexico, south to southern Mexico.

These noisy, conspicuous kingbirds have always been described as common summer residents of eastern, central, and northern Arizona (Swarth 1914; Phillips et al. 1964) and atlas data concur with these prior findings. During the atlas, Cassin's Kingbirds were noted primarily at elevations from 1900 to 7500 ft (579–2286 m), but observers discovered them nesting locally down to 860 ft (262 m) along the Bill Williams River.

Atlasers encountered Cassin's Kingbirds throughout southeastern Arizona, primarily east of the Sonoran Desert dominated region of the state. However, they were found nesting commonly among cottonwood-willow woodlands adjacent to Sonoran desertscrub along the upper Santa Cruz and lower San Pedro River drainages. These kingbirds also nested historically in similar woodlands that previously occurred in the Tucson vicinity along the Santa Cruz River and Rillito Creek (Bendire 1895). Cassin's Kingbirds were found regularly north to the southern slope of the Mogollon Rim and sparingly along the Rim. They undoubtedly also breed in the adjacent White Mountain Apache tribal lands, but atlas data are lacking for this area.

In central and northern Arizona, Cassin's Kingbirds were widespread and fairly common inhabitants of most pinyon pine–juniper woodlands east of Mojave desertscrub and locally in open ponderosa pine forests. Within this region, they were primarily absent as a breeding species only in expansive treeless areas and in higher-elevation forests. Other than some local habitat loss, little threatens Arizona populations of these aggressive kingbirds.

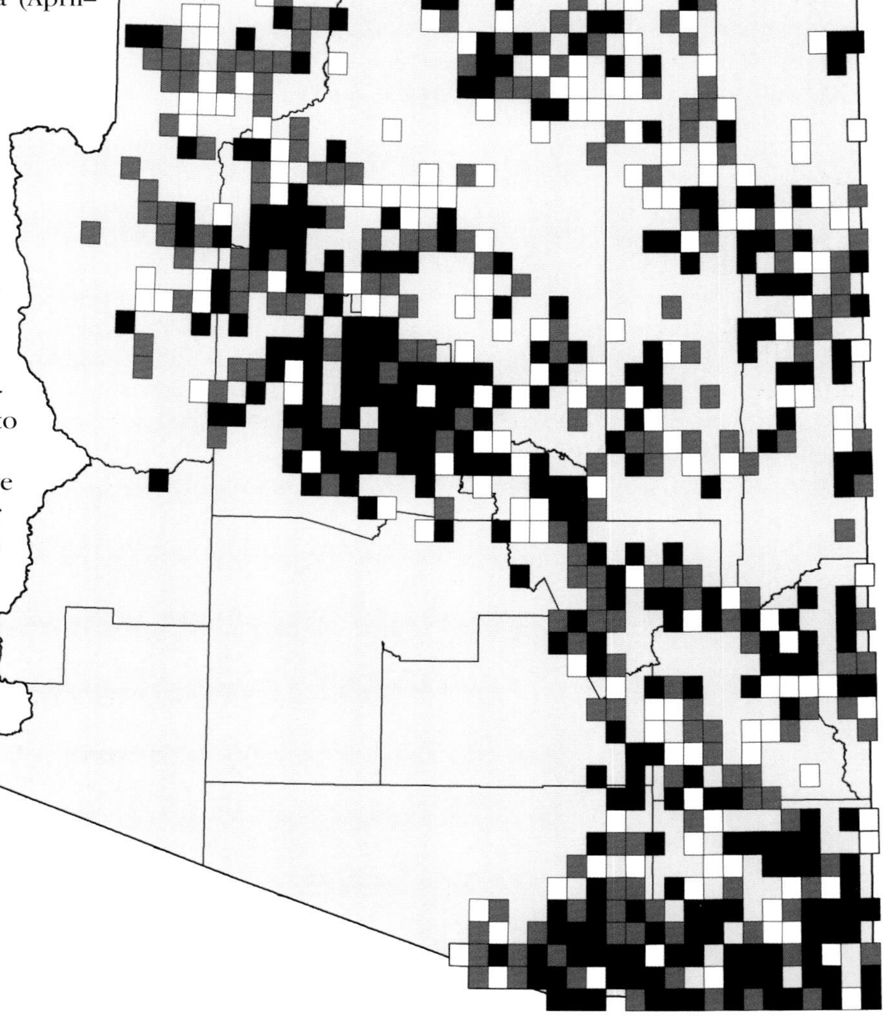

Cassin's Kingbird Breeding Evidence Reported in 623 (34%) of 1834 priority blocks

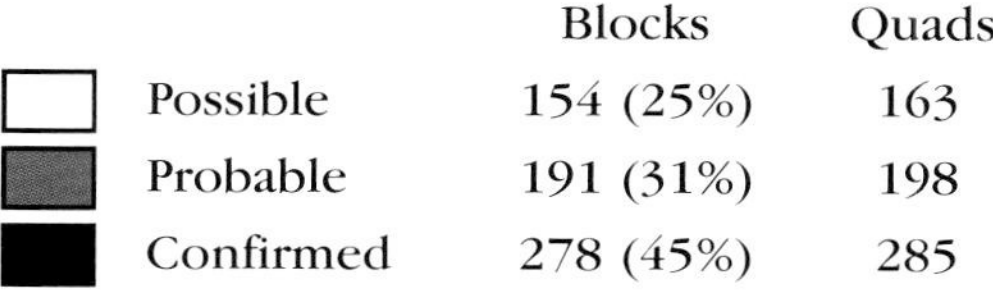

	Blocks	Quads
Possible	154 (25%)	163
Probable	191 (31%)	198
Confirmed	278 (45%)	285

Thick-billed Kingbird

by Troy E. Corman *Tyrannus crassirostris*

Often loud, conspicuous birds, Thick-billed Kingbird pairs seemingly bicker with one another and their neighbors exuberantly throughout the day, and are especially vocal at dawn and dusk. Their uniquely sudden and clear noisy calls carry amazingly well through the large riparian woodland trees they prefer.

HENRY DETWILER

HABITAT

Although inhabiting a wide variety of timbered landscapes in Mexico, Thick-billed Kingbirds in Arizona are primarily encountered among riparian gallery woodlands along perennial or intermittent creeks and rivers. Most occupied drainages have broader flood plains and these large kingbirds are seldom found nesting in the steeper and often narrower mountain canyons. During the atlas, they were most often detected in or near riparian woodland edges and clearings containing large Arizona sycamores and/or Fremont cottonwoods. However, Thick-billed Kingbirds will also forage nearby on the open brushy slopes. Other commonly occurring trees in occupied sites include netleaf hackberry, Goodding willow, velvet mesquite, Arizona walnut, velvet ash, and locally tamarisk. In drainages without tall sycamores, these kingbirds typically frequent decadent cottonwood stands that are laden with clumps of mistletoe often used for nest placement. Thick-billed Kingbirds were also found nesting locally in tall cottonwoods surrounding manmade ponds.

BREEDING

A few Thick-billed Kingbirds begin to arrive in Arizona in mid-April, but are not expected much before early May. They performed courtship flights and other pairing behavior shortly after arriving, which often includes wing fluttering, tail quivering, and much vocalization. Nest construction in Arizona can begin by mid- to late May and atlasers reported an individual nest building on 24 May. Owing to their lofty nest, it is difficult to determine when eggs are first laid, although based on observation of nest with young in Arizona, some nests contain eggs by early to mid-June. Atlasers discovered nests with young from 29 June to 2 August. However, nests with young have been observed near Patagonia as late as 25 August, with the fledglings still being tended by the parents into the second week of September (R. Baxter, personal communication). This suggests egg laying into early August. Most Thick-billed Kingbirds in Arizona have migrated south by mid-September with a few stragglers lingering into late September and occasionally into early October. This kingbird is considered a casual fall to early spring visitor within the lower Colorado River valley, with dates spanning 5 August–12 March (Rosenberg et al. 1991; H. Detwiler, personal communication).

Although there is no direct evidence for Thick-billed Kingbirds, as with other kingbirds it is assumed that only the female undertakes nest construction. They typically build their nests very high in trees and often at fairly exposed locations, including on dead limbs. Nests are frequently constructed on outer branches or near tree crowns in sycamores, netleaf hackberry, and Fremont cottonwoods, occasionally in velvet ash. When nesting in cottonwoods, Thick-billed Kingbirds often select live or dead mistletoe clumps, possibly for added support of their rather flimsy nests. In Arizona, most nests are constructed higher than 35 ft (10.7 m) above the ground; however, the four nests measured during the atlas project ranged from 20 to 69 ft (6.1–21 m). Baltosser (1980) measured the height of eight nests constructed in sycamores in Guadalupe Canyon, southwestern New Mexico, that ranged from 34.4 to 59 ft (10.5–18.0 m) above the ground. Even though their nests are often placed inconspicuously high, they are generally easy to locate because during nest construction and incubation, the male and female routinely greet each other at the nest with much noisy vocalization and wing fluttering. The nests are surprisingly thin and frail, unlike the typically compact, well-built nests of most other North American kingbirds (Zimmerman 1960). Nests are constructed in

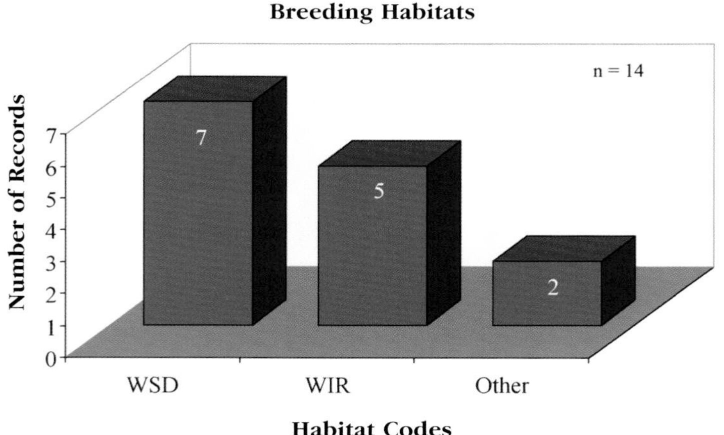

such a way that the rim of nests often appears bristly, with an unfinished appearance (Zimmerman 1960).

As with other kingbird species, most recent observations suggest only female Thick-billed Kingbirds incubate the typical clutch of 3–5 eggs (Lowther 2002). There is practically no information available on the length of time for incubation and nestling stages, which is suspected to be approximately 15–18 days for each. Both parents feed the nestlings and like other kingbirds, defend the nest and young vigorously from potential predators that wander into their territory. In Arizona, some evidence suggests that on occasion Thick-billed Kingbirds may successfully rear two broods in one season.

DISTRIBUTION AND STATUS

Thick-billed Kingbirds breed primarily from southeastern Arizona and extreme southwestern New Mexico south to Oaxaca, Mexico (Howell and Webb 1995). Populations north of Sonora migrate south in winter. Even though Thick-billed Kingbirds were known to nest in extreme northern Sonora just south of Nogales as early as 1929, they were not actually found in Arizona and the United States until 1958. That year, they were discovered nesting in Guadalupe Canyon in the extreme southeast corner of the state (Levy 1959) and have nested there ever since. In 1962, they were also found nesting along Sonoita Creek near Patagonia (Phillips et al. 1964) and their numbers and distribution have steadily increased in Arizona since these early discoveries.

Atlasers found this kingbird to be locally fairly common in many of the locations that were mentioned in Monson and Phillips (1981) including near Arivaca, Nogales, Patagonia, Sycamore Canyon in the Pajarito Mountains, and Guadalupe Canyon. Atlasers also found them in new locations such as along Sonoita Creek below Patagonia Lake Dam, at Kino Springs northeast of Nogales, near Tubac, and in Skeleton Canyon in the Peloncillo Mountains. A pair of Thick-billed Kingbirds spent the summer of 1994 near the Southwestern Research Station in Cave Creek Canyon, Chiricahua Mountains. At 5400 ft (1646 m), this is the highest elevation they have been reported in the State. Most Arizona nesting records occur from 3500 to 4200 ft (1067–1280 m).

At the northern edge of their range, Thick-billed Kingbirds were much more widespread along the lower San Pedro River than previous literature suggested. A pair of these kingbirds was first confirmed nesting near Cook's Lake in 1980 (Monson and Phillips 1981). They were encountered locally along the San Pedro River from near Cascabel north to Dudleyville, where the lowest elevation nesting record was collected at 2020 ft (616 m).

With populations of Thick-billed Kingbirds in Arizona appearing to be stable or even slowly increasing, it is rather perplexing that this species has not been found nesting along the upper San Pedro River south of Benson. This section of the drainage is positioned between the three populations within the state and the habitat and elevation would seem ideal. One possible theory for their absence is the lack of mistletoe clumps in the extensive stands of cottonwoods along the upper San Pedro River. Often used for nest placement elsewhere, the growth of mistletoe may be suppressed along the immediate river corridor by the lengthier winter season of below freezing temperatures annually endured at this location. During the atlas period these loud and excitable kingbirds were also not found in several infrequently occupied nesting locations such as Brown Canyon in the Baboquivari Mountains and Madera Canyon in the Santa Rita Mountains.

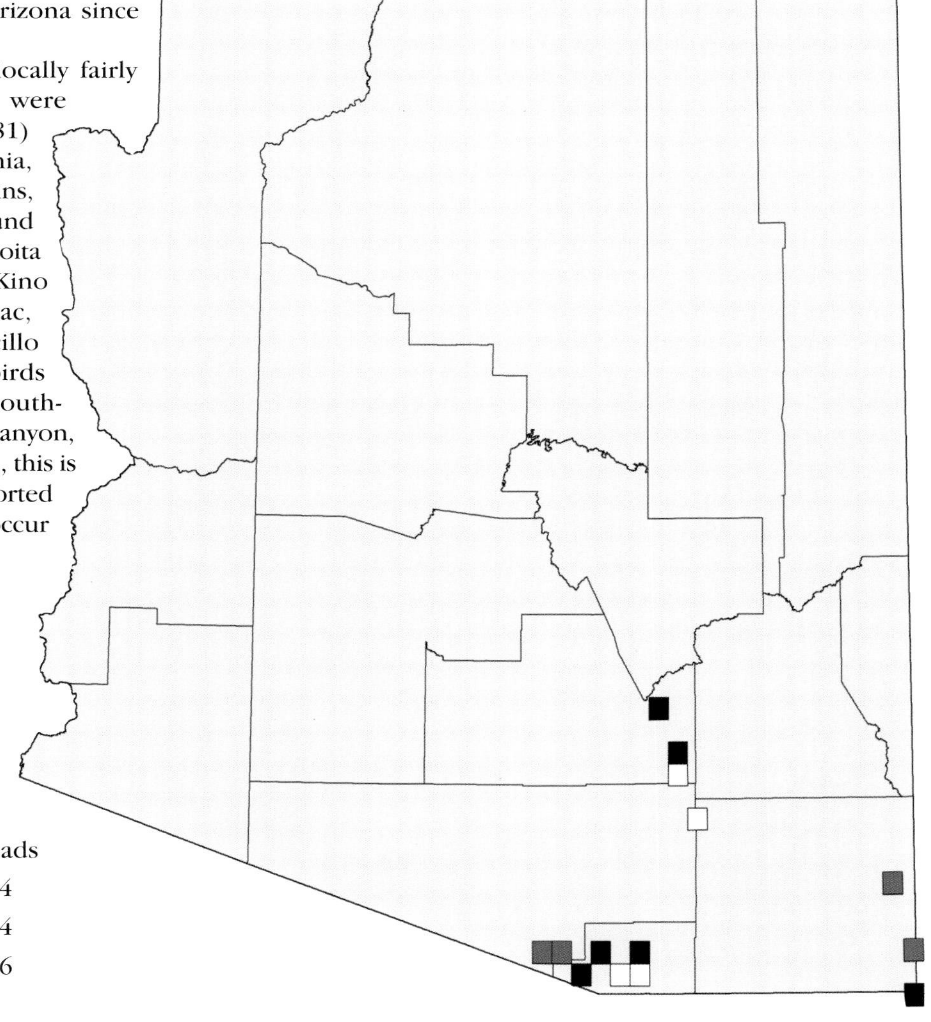

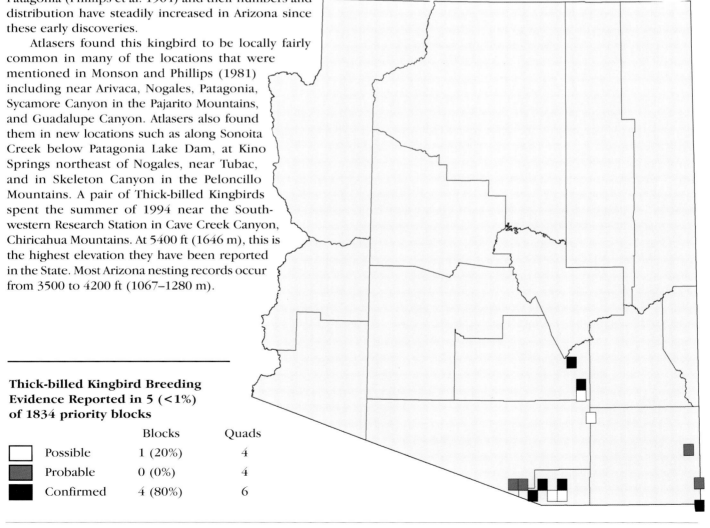

Thick-billed Kingbird Breeding Evidence Reported in 5 (<1%) of 1834 priority blocks

	Blocks	Quads
Possible	1 (20%)	4
Probable	0 (0%)	4
Confirmed	4 (80%)	6

Western Kingbird

by Cathryn Wise-Gervais *Tyrannus verticalis*

Whether perched on a telephone line or in hot pursuit of insects or intruding birds, Western Kingbirds are generally raucous and conspicuous and are readily identifiable by their white outer tail feathers. This aggressive species is a familiar sight in Arizona's open country, where Western Kingbirds frequently assault much larger birds in defense of nest or territory.

HABITAT

Western Kingbirds are quite adaptable birds that prefer open landscapes with scattered trees or at a minimum utility lines and poles for perching and nesting. The birds use a variety of habitats meeting these criteria from deserts and grasslands to woodlands edges and residential neighborhoods. Atlasers reported these kingbirds in thirty habitat types, with nearly 14 percent of records obtained from Sonoran desertscrub typically containing tall saguaros, scattered trees, and roadside utility lines (n = 837). An additional 13 percent of the records were from open pinyon pine–juniper woodlands and in the adjacent grasslands with scattered junipers. Western Kingbirds will also take advantage of manmade open space, and atlasers obtained 12 percent of records in rural and agricultural areas containing cultivated fields, shade trees, windbreaks, and isolated trees near stock or farm ponds. Similarly, Western Kingbirds are at home in the open semiarid grasslands (12 percent of records), where they often nest in isolated trees or among the dense branching of tall agave or yucca flower stalks. Observers found that other commonly used habitats included open riparian woodland edges, dry desert washes with scattered tall trees, and even in suburban areas with parks, ball fields, and golf courses. Although Western Kingbirds are found nesting at lower elevations and in more open terrain than Cassin's Kingbirds, the two species overlap widely, especially in pinyon-juniper woodlands and in riparian areas.

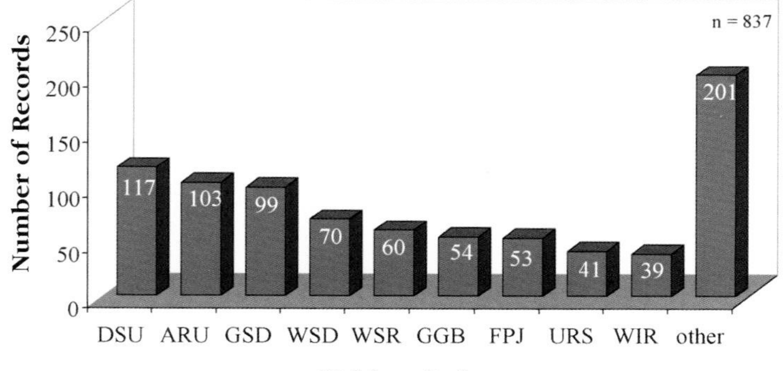

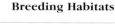

BREEDING

Western Kingbirds arrive on their Arizona breeding grounds in early spring when temperatures have warmed and insect activity has increased. They typically begin arriving in mid-March (occasionally earlier) in southern Arizona and not until mid-April in the north. Atlasers first reported paired birds in suitable breeding habitat on 22 March. Early nest construction can begin by late March or early April in Arizona and atlasers reported the earliest occupied nest on 8 April. Some occupied nests undoubtedly contain eggs by at least mid-April based on a nest with young detected on 30 April. Atlas data suggest that statewide breeding activity peaks from early May to mid-June. Atlasers reported occupied nests through 1 August and adults feeding dependent young through 23 August. Western Kingbirds can begin southbound migration as early as late July, but most travel south from September to early October, with few individuals remaining after late October.

Although Western Kingbird males are often involved in nest sites selection, females construct the nest alone in a wide variety of natural and manmade substrates. Atlasers collected measurements at sixty-two Western Kingbird nests, with most discovered in juniper (23 nests), cottonwood (9 nests), and Joshua trees (7 nests). Active nests were also found in Arizona sycamore, Arizona walnut, hackberry, mesquite, pinyon pine, tall agave/yucca flower stalks, tamarisk, Siberian elm, fan palms, and other ornamental tree species. One nest was photographed within the crown of flowers on a saguaro arm and five nests were discovered in tall cholla stands, all within San Carlos Apache tribal lands. In areas where tall trees are sparse or lacking, Western Kingbirds have an affinity for nesting among the crossbeams or on transformers on utility poles, as well as on windmills.

The median height of these Western Kingbird nests was 14.8 ft (4.5 m) and ranged from 4.1 to 55.8 ft (1.3–17.0 m), with lower nests in cholla noted above. Atlasers also noted

Breeding Phenology

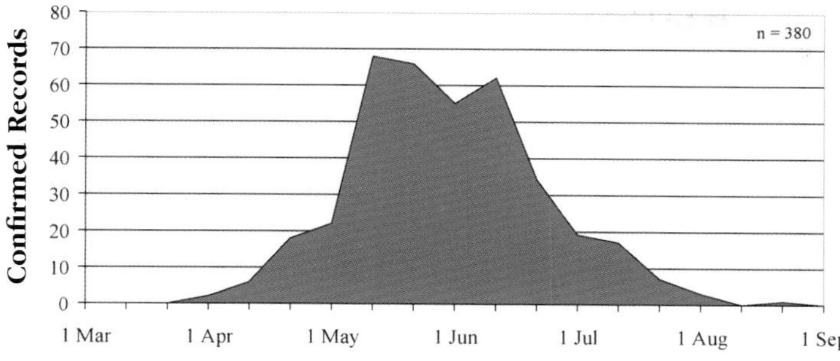

several extremely lofty nests more than 100 ft (30.5 m) high on lattice transmission towers. Analysis of these data suggests that Western Kingbirds typically place their nests in the top third of the nest tree or structure. This placement provides the birds with a commanding view of their surroundings and also gives some cover from predators and from the elements.

Western Kingbird nests are bulky structures, and within this messy assemblage 4 eggs (range 3–7; Bent 1942) are typically laid and incubated by the female for approximately 12 to 14 days (Bendire 1895). During this period, males often perch nearby guarding the nest and territory from intruding birds. Both sexes feed the nestlings, and the young fledge at 13–19 days of age (Bendire 1895; Gamble and Bergin 1996). Parental care continues for 2 to 3 weeks following nest departure (Gamble and Bergin 1996).

Western Kingbirds are considered rare Brown-headed Cowbird hosts, and they are known to eject cowbird eggs (Rothstein 1975). Atlasers reported one such attempt when a broken cowbird egg was found below an active kingbird nest.

DISTRIBUTION AND STATUS

Western Kingbirds are true to their name and typically are found nesting west of the Mississippi River. This species breeds in diverse habitats from southern Canada to Sonora, Mexico. The status and distribution of Western Kingbird in Arizona has been previously described as a common summer resident in most open terrain at elevations below the transition to ponderosa pine forests, but local in the north (Phillips et al. 1964). Atlas data reveal similar findings. Though they were found statewide, Western Kingbirds were more sparsely distributed north of the Mogollon Rim than were Cassin's Kingbirds.

Because of the Western Kingbird's relatively high abundance in open landscapes and propensity for boldly perching on utility lines, fences, and scattered trees, atlasers had little trouble in detecting them on atlas blocks. Atlasers confirmed these kingbirds nesting at elevations from approximately 100 to 6500 ft (30–1981 m), but were also noted very locally to just above 7000 ft (2134 m). They were commonly encountered within the extensive agricultural and rural regions of the lower Colorado, Gila, and Santa Cruz River valleys, but were sparingly distributed in the adjacent desert landscapes.

These adaptable birds have benefited from many human altered landscapes in Arizona. The introduction of the ubiquitous utility pole has undoubtedly allowed Western Kingbirds to nest in historically unoccupied areas. These testy birds should have little trouble continuing their widespread reign over the ravens and raptors that venture too close to their nesting territories.

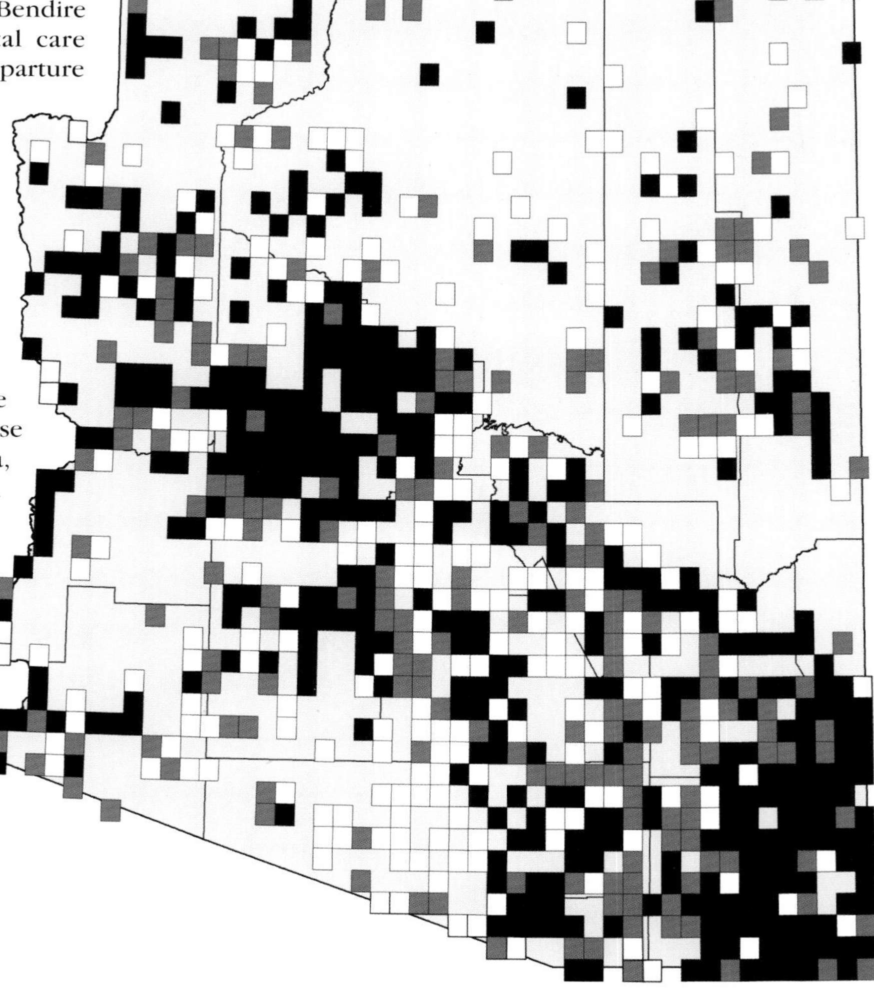

Western Kingbird Breeding Evidence Reported in 818 (45%) of 1834 priority blocks

	Blocks	Quads
Possible	226 (28%)	239
Probable	193 (24%)	201
Confirmed	399 (49%)	411

Rose-throated Becard

by Troy E. Corman *Pachyramphus aglaiae*

Thanks to their quiet, retiring nature, combined with their very local distribution in southeastern Arizona, Rose-throated Becards are prized by birders. Although they often stay hidden high in tree foliage, a little quiet patience observing their large, bulky nests will frequently afford a view of this stocky, bullheaded bird.

DAN FISCHER

HABITAT

Rose-throated Becards are tropical birds that migrate north in very limited numbers to nest extremely locally just north of the Mexican border. Within Arizona, they are primarily encountered in tall, shady riparian woodlands along small perennial or intermittent mountain foothill drainages and canyons. Occupied nesting locations typically consist of large Arizona sycamore, Fremont cottonwood, and velvet ash. The understory often contains scattered stands of velvet mesquite, netleaf hackberry, and tree saplings. These inconspicuous birds frequently forage high in the canopy and construct their nests near forest edges or clearings. In southern Sonora, where Rose-throated Becards are more common, they can also be found in tropical thornscrub and tropical deciduous forests (Russell and Monson 1998).

BREEDING

Rose-throated Becards generally begin to arrive in Arizona in mid- to late May, exceptionally in early May. Site fidelity is strong, and individuals and pairs often return to the same territory and frequently construct nest in the same tree, if not the same limb (Brandt 1951). Nesting activity begins soon after they arrive on territory, with atlasers observing nest building as early as 21 May. Rose-throated Becards can begin laying eggs by early June in Arizona, and most eggs are laid in June and July. Observers reported adults carrying food into their nest in July and early August, but fledglings were not noted. Likely pertaining to earlier failed attempts, atlasers have observed nest building activity in July and early August. Some active nests in Arizona are lost to strong wind gusts during summer monsoon storms. Although fall migration can begin by August in Arizona, Rose-throated Becards are frequently present through mid-September, with stragglers into late October. There are few winter records in the state, when Rose-throated Becards sometimes join roving foraging flocks of other species.

Both members of the Rose-throated Becard pair help construct the surprisingly large and unique nest, although the female often does most of the work. Construction typically takes more than two weeks (Baicich and Harrison 1997) and may continue during laying and incubation (Skutch 1969). Interestingly, both unmated males and females have also been observed solitarily constructing nests in Arizona and recently three adults (including two males) were reported constructing a single nest. In Arizona, nests are most frequently placed 15–60 ft (4.6–18.3 m) above the ground, suspended from the ends of slender, dangling limbs of large sycamores and cottonwoods, much less frequently in ash. The nest is large, 12–30 in. (30–76 cm) long, globular, and rather messy in appearance, and swings freely with the slightest breeze (Brandt 1951; Baicich and Harrison 1997). The nest is constructed of many layers of various plant materials; especially long, inner bark strips of cottonwoods, dry grasses, and dead leaves. In Arizona, nests are often adorned with dangling sycamore seed balls. The actual nest entrance and shallow nest cavity is place in the lower quarter of the nest and is well padded with much softer plant material (Brandt 1951).

Only the female Rose-throated Becard incubates the 3–4 (range 3–6) eggs (Baicich and Harrison 1997). The length of incubation is apparently unknown; however, there is some evidence to suggest that incubation begins after the first egg is laid (Brandt 1951). The young are fed by both parents and fledge after 19 days (Baicich and Harrison 1997). There is no evidence to suggest more than one successful brood is produced during a year; however, the parents will quickly begin constructing a new nest if an earlier brood is lost (Brandt 1951).

DISTRIBUTION AND STATUS

The breeding range of Rose-throated Becard extends from southeastern Arizona and south Texas to western Panama. Only the extreme northern populations (north of southern Sonora) withdraw south after the nesting season (Howell and Webb 1995).

Before 1947, there was only one accidental record for the Rose-throated Becard in Arizona when an individual was collected in the Huachuca Mountains on 20 June 1888 (Phillips et al. 1964). In 1947, it was found nesting in Arizona along Sonoita Creek near Patagonia along with a number of inactive nests from the previous year. The first nest with eggs in Arizona was collected at this location on 19 June 1948 (Brandt 1951). Since 1955, Rose-throated Becards have been found nesting fairly regularly, but very locally and in fluctuating numbers in a few specific drainages and canyons near the Sonora border. In the late 1950s inactive nests were found in Guadalupe Canyon in the extreme southeastern corner of the state and an unmated male built a nest near Tucson (Phillips et al. 1964). In 1968, a lone male also began to construct a nest in the Huachuca Mountain in lower Ramsey Canyon (Krueper 1999). Strays have also been found in Madera and Box canyons in northern Santa Rita Mountains, along the upper San Pedro River, and as far north as upper Aravaipa Canyon, Graham County (Monson and Phillips 1981, Krueper 1999).

Between 1975 and 1987, Rose-throated Becards were noted as a locally fairly common nesting species along Arivaca Creek, Pima County with no fewer than four active nests, with a maximum of seven in 1985 (G. Monson, personal communication). However, by 1990 there was only one active nest along the creek, and none were found along this drainage during the atlas period.

Rose-throated Becard nesting activity has been observed at elevations primarily between 3400 and 4500 ft (1036–1372 m) in Arizona, occasionally to above 5000 ft (1524 m) in lower mountain canyons. During the atlas period, nesting Rose-throated Becards were only reported in Santa Cruz County with the most consistent location along Sonoita Creek near Patagonia. Although even here there were several years that they were absent or only unmated individuals were known to be present. Individuals were also periodically reported during the summer in nearby Harshaw Canyon, Patagonia Mountains. In 1993–94, atlasers located four pairs of Rose-throated Becards with nests along lower Sycamore Canyon, Pajarito Mountains. The birds were not reported in this canyon during the latter half of the atlas period. Like many other primarily tropical species at the northern edge of their range, populations of Rose-throated Becards will likely continue to fluctuate in southern Arizona, where they are considered a locally rare nesting species.

The number of nesting pairs of Rose-throated Becards in Arizona has apparently declined in the last ten to twenty years. However, it is difficult to monitor and manage for a species whose small, borderland breeding populations often fluctuate drastically every few years. Modifying riparian grazing to maintain and enhance sycamore and cottonwood regeneration and reducing groundwater withdrawal to maintain perennial stream flow would benefit this and other riparian obligate species.

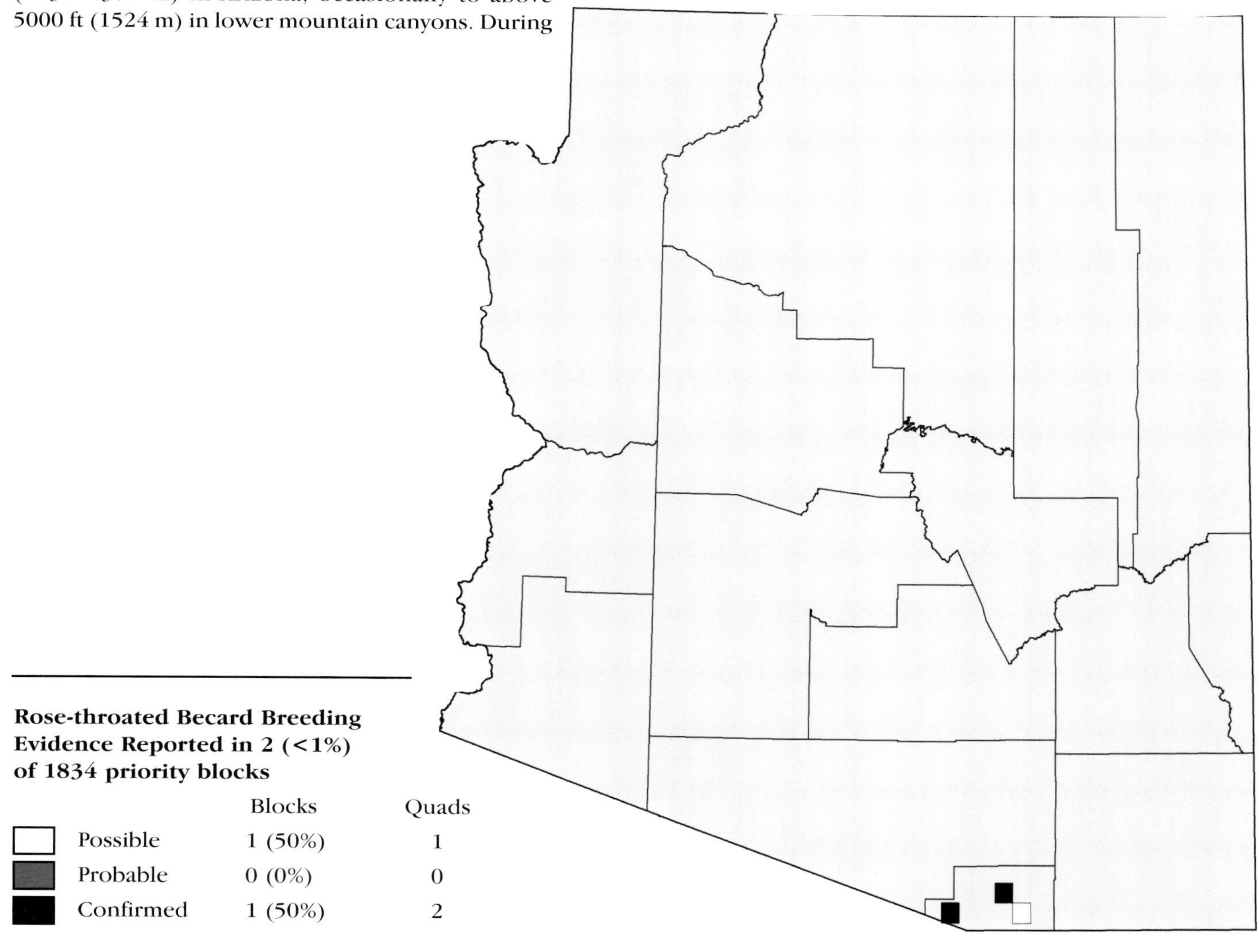

Rose-throated Becard Breeding Evidence Reported in 2 (<1%) of 1834 priority blocks

	Blocks	Quads
Possible	1 (50%)	1
Probable	0 (0%)	0
Confirmed	1 (50%)	2

Loggerhead Shrike

by Cathryn Wise-Gervais *Lanius ludovicianus*

The Loggerhead Shrike's habit of impaling prey is actually an adaptation that allows these relatively small birds to eat like raptors without possessing strong talons. This unique behavior has earned these handsome birds the nickname "butcher-bird." Their odd name refers to the birds' large head relative to their body.

RICHARD DITCH

HABITAT

Loggerhead Shrikes are found in a variety of open and relatively flat to gently rolling habitats and favor areas offering thorny trees and shrubs. Given this preference, it is not surprising that most atlas records were obtained in desert country where thorny plants are the rule rather than the exception. Atlasers reported Loggerhead Shrikes in twenty-five habitat types, and a total of 38 percent of records were in Sonoran desertscrub, including the more arid and sparsely vegetated lower Sonoran Desert regions ($n = 911$). Such areas are typically characterized by paloverde, ironwood, catclaw acacia, and mixed cacti. Observers reported 11 percent of records in semiarid grasslands featuring scattered mesquite, acacia, agave, and yucca. In northern Arizona, most Loggerhead Shrikes (22 percent of records) were encountered nesting in very open juniper woodlands or in the adjacent cold-temperate grasslands and desertscrub. These habitats typically offer rolling terrain of low-growing grasses and shrubs such as blackbrush, greasewood, and sagebrush with very scattered junipers. Loggerhead Shrikes were frequently encountered in Mojave and Chihuahuan desertscrub–influenced areas, and also can be found in rural and agricultural edge areas. In absence of thorny shrubs, the birds often use barbed wire instead for impaling and storing their prey items.

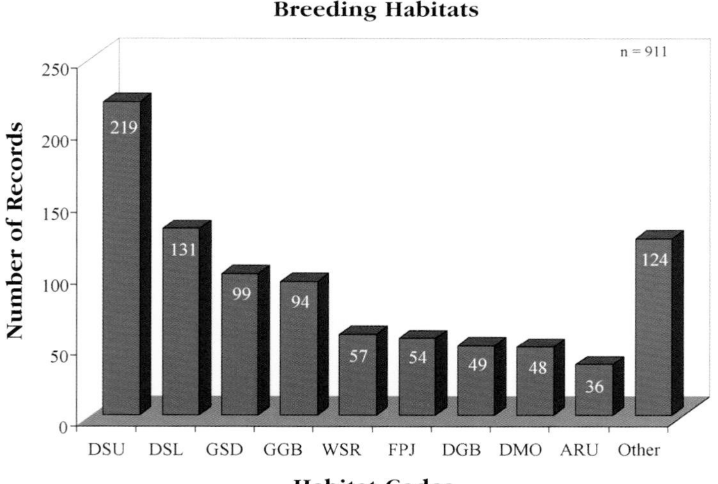

BREEDING

Loggerhead Shrikes are basically Arizona residents, although numbers decrease in the north and increase in the south during the winter. Migrants pass through the state primarily in March–April and then again in August–September. Researchers believe that resident pairs stay together year round (Yosef 1996). As would be expected, the birds initiate breeding activities earlier in lowland desert areas than in high-elevation country, and desert-dwelling Loggerhead Shrikes are one of the first passerines to nest in early spring. Atlasers observed a pair of Loggerhead Shrikes nest building on 17 February and located an occupied nest on this same date. However, atlasers also discovered a nest with young on 1 March and noted the first fledglings on 10 March, indicating egg laying by early February. Statewide atlas data reveal a spring peak of nesting activity between late March and late April, and then a lesser summer peak from late May to late June ($n = 241$). This suggests that some Loggerhead Shrikes produce two broods per year in Arizona, as noted elsewhere within their range. Atlasers observed nests with young through 18 July and feeding fledglings through 27 July. Agitated adults were noted as late as 12 August, suggesting some parental dependency through this period.

Both Loggerhead Shrike adults bring nesting materials to a nest site they select together, but the female does most of the nest building (Yosef 1996). They typically select dense, often spiny bushes or short trees for nesting, and these probably provide cover from predators and some protection from the elements. Atlasers took measurements at ninety-six Loggerhead Shrike nests in nineteen different substrates. Thirty-six percent of these were constructed in paloverde, 16 percent were in ironwood, 8 percent were in juniper, and 7 percent were in mistletoe clumps (in paloverde, oak, or mesquite). Other less frequently reported plants were mesquite, catclaw acacia, saguaro skeletons, tamarisk, cholla, Joshua tree, oak, barberry, Aleppo pine, saltbush, greasewood, yucca, crucifixion thorn, and other shrubs. Atlas data reveal a median nest height of 5.6 ft (1.7 m), with a range of 0.7–24.6 ft (0.2–7.5 m). For comparison, researchers in Colorado reported an average nest height of 6.6 ft (2.0 m) for this species (Porter et al. 1975).

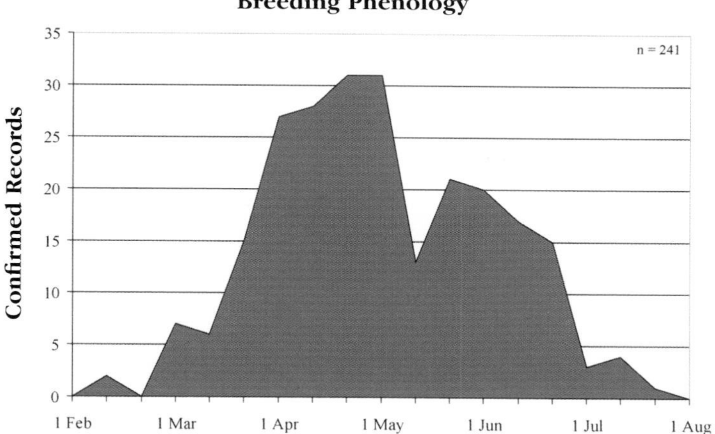

Based on atlas data, Loggerhead Shrikes typically lay 4–5 eggs (range 1–7) in Arizona (n = 82). Only the female incubates, and incubation lasts for 15–17 days (Yosef 1996). The male feeds the female while she is on the nest and for the first 4–5 days after the young hatch. The female then transfers food brought to her by the male to the young beneath her (Yosef 1996). As the young grow, the male spends more time feeding them directly until they leave the nest in approximately 16–18 days (Yosef 1996). In the southern United States, sedentary Loggerhead Shrikes commonly attempt to raise two broods and sometimes a third (Yosef 1996).

DISTRIBUTION AND STATUS

Loggerhead Shrikes are found coast to coast in North America. They breed from central Canada south through Mexico and throughout most states west of the Mississippi River and south of Pennsylvania, but many populations in the upper Midwest and northeast are local and declining. Most prior Arizona literature considered Loggerhead Shrikes fairly common summer residents in open areas statewide, but primarily absent from "brushless grassland" (Phillips et al. 1964). Atlasers located and confirmed Loggerhead Shrikes breeding statewide except in regions that were heavily wooded or had relatively high topographic relief. Loggerhead Shrikes are also generally found only at low to middle elevations in Arizona, and atlasers noted them on priority blocks from approximately 100 to 7100 ft (30–2164 m).

Loggerhead Shrikes were widespread and commonly encountered breeding in the sparsely vegetated deserts of western Arizona. However, they were sparingly distributed and often missed entirely in the more heavily vegetated Sonoran Desert region from approximately the Tohono O'odham tribal lands to Tucson and the lower San Pedro River. Loggerhead Shrike density is likely lower in the more wooded deserts, and therefore the birds may have been missed in these areas during atlas surveys.

The distribution of Loggerhead Shrikes in Arizona has likely expanded to some extent as brush, shrubs, and junipers have invaded many of the states grasslands due to inappropriate grazing practices and fire suppression efforts. Also in some northern regions, pinyon pine–juniper woodlands have been cleared or at least opened creating additional nesting and foraging habitats. Although Saurer et al. (1995) reported a significant declining trend in Arizona from 1966–1989, these hook-beaked passerines remain relatively common in the state's arid and diverse open landscapes.

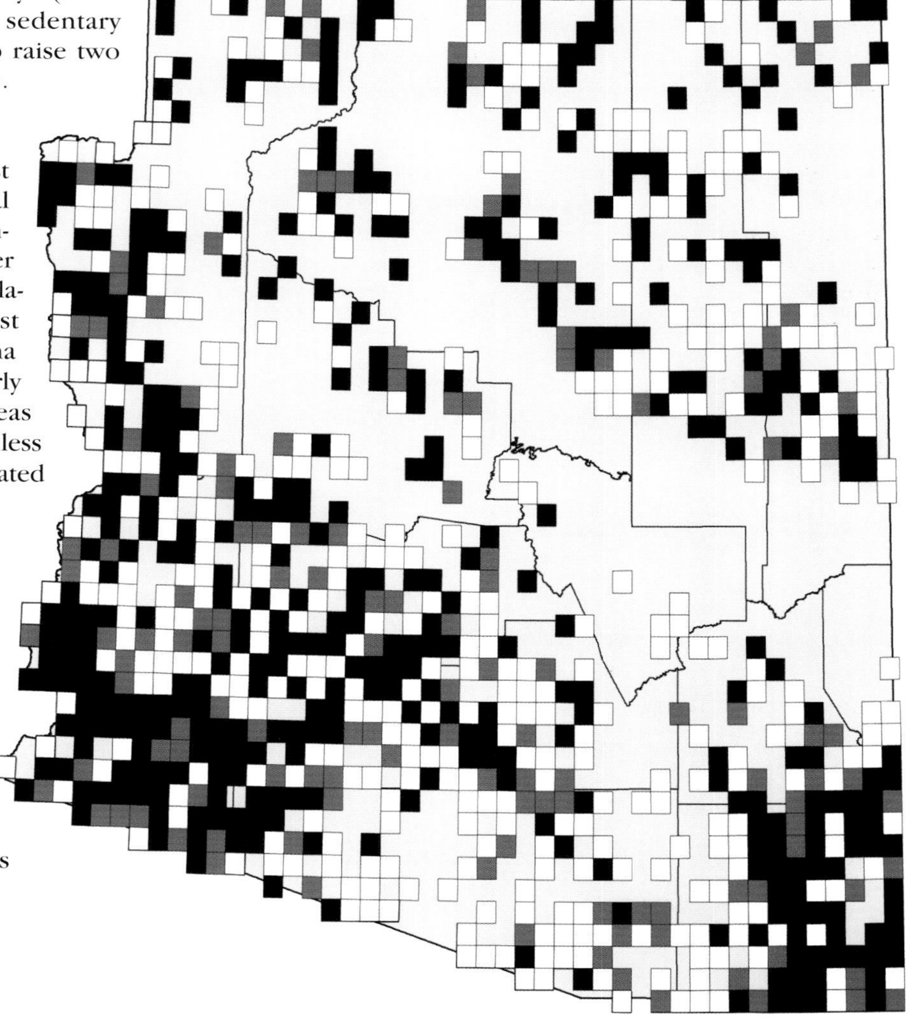

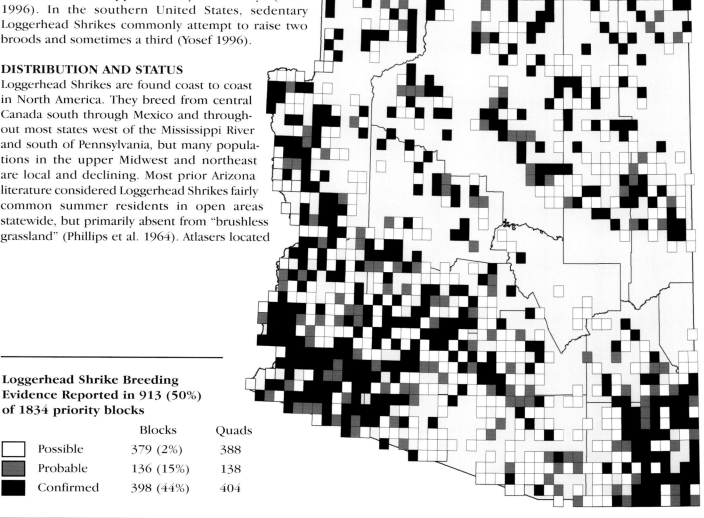

Loggerhead Shrike Breeding Evidence Reported in 913 (50%) of 1834 priority blocks

	Blocks	Quads
Possible	379 (2%)	388
Probable	136 (15%)	138
Confirmed	398 (44%)	404

Bell's Vireo

by Annalaura Averill-Murray and Troy E. Corman

Vireo bellii

These thorny-thicket dwellers are Arizona's smallest vireos, but what they lack in size they make up for in character. During the spring and summer, the querulous song of the Bell's Vireo can be heard emanating from dense undergrowth and streamside vegetation throughout much of southern and central Arizona.

DAN FISCHER

HABITAT

In Arizona, Bell's Vireos are associated with dense, shrubby vegetation and woodland edges, especially those with a mesquite component. These vireos were reported in eighteen vegetation communities during atlas surveys, indicating a great deal of flexibility in habitat choice. They were frequently encountered near perennial or intermittent drainages and other water sources with remnant cottonwood-willow stands and a well-developed understory of seepwillow, mesquite, and occasionally tamarisk (28 percent of 461 records). Additionally, Bell's Vireos readily inhabit drier thickets in Arizona. During the atlas, this species was commonly found in mesquite bosques and in larger, heavily wooded desert washes with dense stands of paloverde, ironwood, mesquite, and/or netleaf hackberry (41 percent of records). Only 12 percent of atlas records were from lower foothill drainages and canyons containing sycamore, and few vireos were found in tamarisk thickets or along ditches and shrubby edges of irrigated farmland.

BREEDING

An early migrant, Bell's Vireos begin arriving on their Arizona breeding grounds in early to mid-March and are common and widespread by April. Males rigorously court females, chasing potential mates through vegetation and deliberately colliding with them in midair (Nolan 1960, Barlow 1962). Nesting activity can begin soon after pairing. Although egg laying typically begins in early April, atlasers reported the first nest with eggs on 25 March. Atlas data reveal a strong peak in nesting activity from late April to late May in Arizona, with some early broods fledging by 21 April. However, Bell's Vireos have a lengthy breeding season in the state with nesting efforts continuing throughout the summer. Atlasers reported a nest with young on 8 August and adults feeding dependent fledglings through 19 September, well after typical atlas surveys had ended. The initiation of fall migration in Arizona is difficult to determine, but Bell's Vireo numbers begin to decrease by early September and most have departed for their wintering grounds by early October. They are rarely noted into November and there are few winter records in Arizona.

Bell's Vireo pairs build small, hanging cup nests that are typically suspended from the terminal fork of low branches and placed within small canopy openings (Nolan 1960; Barlow 1962). During the atlas, 40 nests were found in 15 different plant species, with the majority (37.5 percent) in mesquite. Other commonly used species were graythorn, desert hackberry, and juniper. Although only one nest was found in tamarisk during the atlas, it was the most common nesting substrate along the lower Bill Williams River from 1994 to 1997 (Averill-Murray et al. 1999) and in the Colorado River in the Grand Canyon from 1982 to 1985 (Brown 1993). Atlas data show nest height ranging from 1.6 to 10.8 ft (0.5–3.3 m) with a median nest height of 3.9 ft (1.2 m).

The usual Bell's Vireo clutch consists of 4 eggs (range 3–5), and both adults incubate for approximately 14 days (Baicich and Harrison 1997). Although females likely incubate and brood more often than males, both sexes participate in raising the young, including feeding nestlings (10–12 days) and fledglings (20–30 days; Nolan 1960; Brown 1993). Bell's Vireos typically raise two broods per year (Baicich and Harrison 1997), occasionally as many as four (Franzreb 1989).

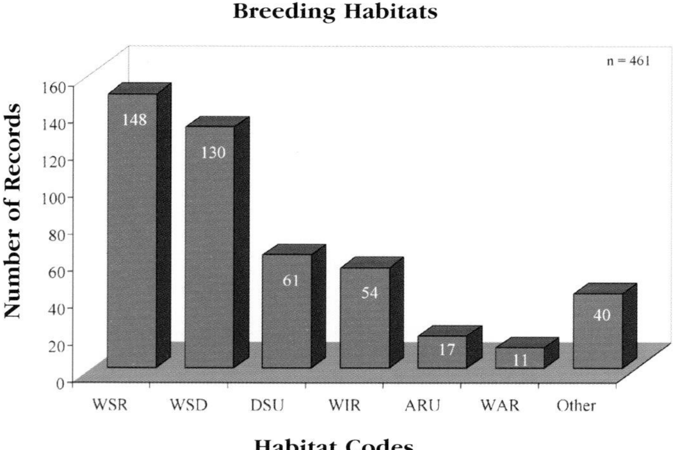

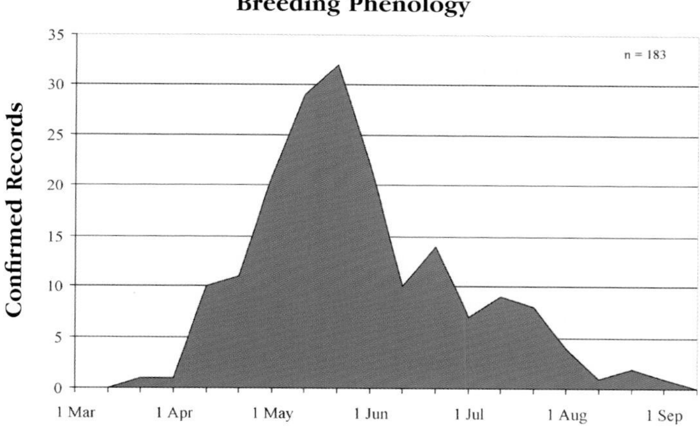

The Bell's Vireo is a common host for Brown-headed Cowbirds and was one of the most frequently observed host species during the atlas. Atlasers reported nineteen incidents of cowbird brood parasitism from 15 April to 25 August. Early Bell's Vireo nests often escape parasitism if initiated well in advance of the onset of cowbird egg laying in mid- to late April.

DISTRIBUTION AND STATUS

Bell's Vireos breed in the central United States from North Dakota east to Indiana and south through Texas to northern Mexico. They also breed from southern California and Nevada southeast through southern New Mexico. The Arizona Bell's Vireo, one of four subspecies, is the breeding race found in Arizona. Atlasers found this vireo a common and widespread summer resident of southeastern and central Arizona, as did Swarth (1914) and Phillips et al. (1964). These vireos were encountered within most lowland river drainages, including the San Francisco River north of Clifton, the Salt River Canyon to the White Mountain Apache tribal lands, and up the Verde River to near Perkinsville. They were sparsely distributed in the deserts west of Ajo and Gila Bend, along the Colorado River, and along the Virgin River drainage in extreme northwestern Arizona. Although atlasers typically found Bell's Vireos at elevations from 160 to 4800 ft (49–1463 m), nests were discovered to 5120 ft (1561 m).

Before the construction of Glen Canyon Dam in 1963, Bell's Vireos were a rare and localized summer resident along the Colorado River within the Grand Canyon below Whitmore Wash (Brown et al. 1987). They have since expanded their range at least 144 mi (232 km) up the Colorado River concomitant with an increase in riparian vegetation created by operations at Glen Canyon Dam (Brown et al. 1983). During the atlas period, Bell's Vireos were documented locally as far upstream as Lees Ferry and the Navajo Creek arm of Lake Powell.

Bell's Vireo numbers have recently declined in parts of their range, but overall Arizona numbers appear to be stable or slightly increasing (Robbins et al. 1986). Once considered abundant along the entire lower Colorado River valley, Bell's Vireo populations have declined markedly since 1950 and they are now only common in remnant cottonwood-willow-mesquite stands along the Bill Williams River (Rosenberg et al. 1991; Averill-Murray et al. 1999). The primary cause of Bell's Vireo population declines in the Southwest is habitat loss: the destruction of riparian and mesquite woodlands resulting from flood control and damming projects, agricultural and urban development, and inappropriate grazing practices (Rosenberg et al. 1991; Brown 1993).

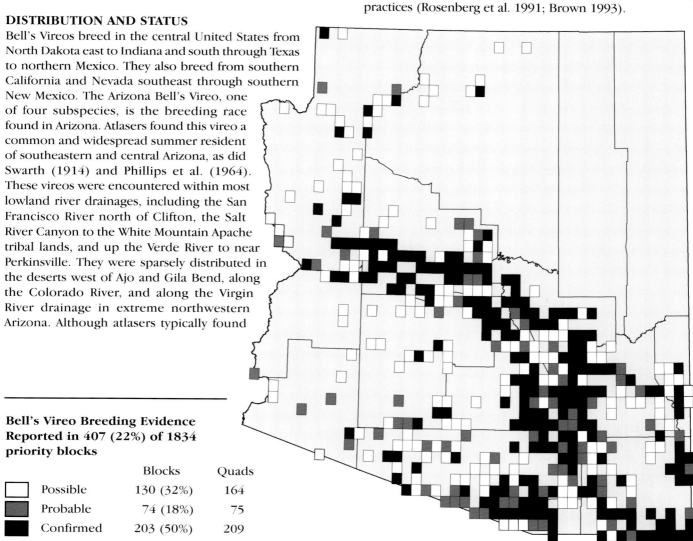

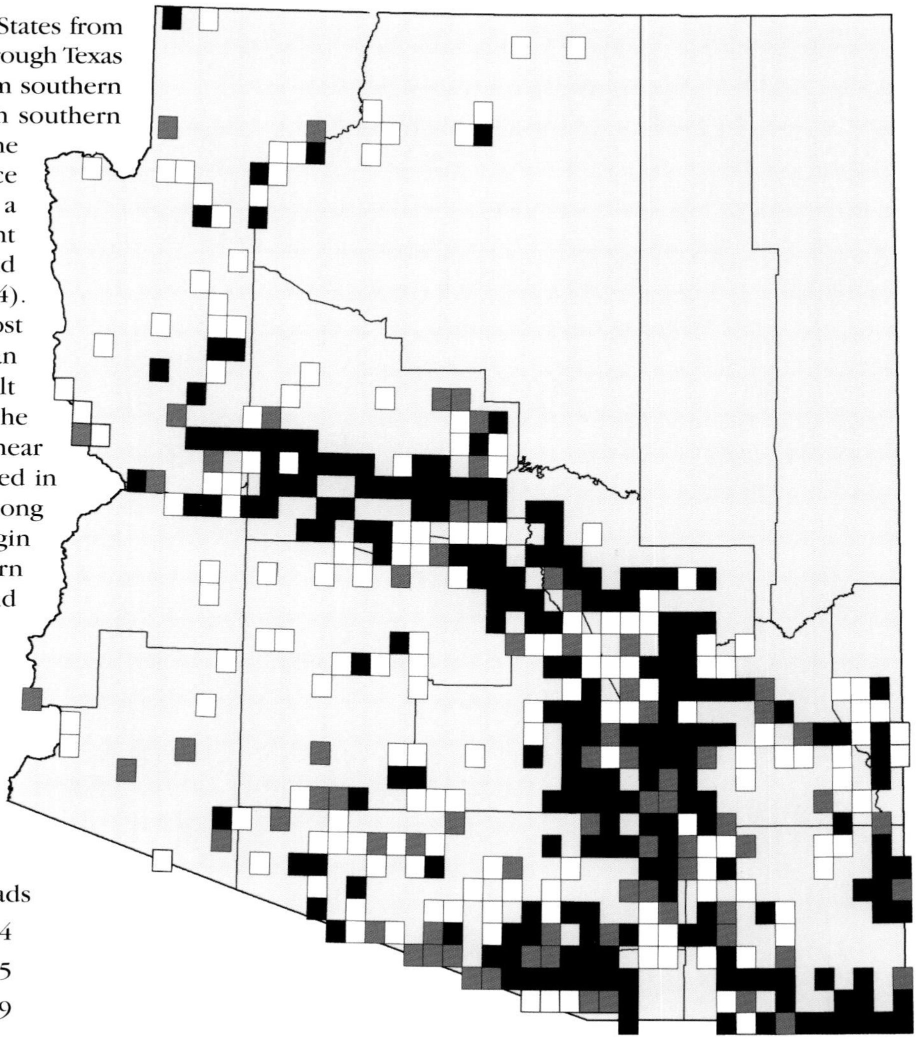

Bell's Vireo Breeding Evidence Reported in 407 (22%) of 1834 priority blocks

	Blocks	Quads
Possible	130 (32%)	164
Probable	74 (18%)	75
Confirmed	203 (50%)	209

Gray Vireo

by Troy E. Corman *Vireo vicinior*

With their relatively long tail raised and energetically thrown about, Gray Vireos typically prefer to forage and nest on dry, mid-elevation slopes dominated by open stands of junipers. Fairly active for vireos, these rather plain birds often sing from within the vegetation as they quickly move from tree to tree.

HABITAT

In Arizona, breeding Gray Vireos are typically found in relatively arid, open vegetative communities containing juniper, often on sloping terrain. Atlasers noted 69 percent of their observations from pinyon pine- and juniper-dominated habitats, including the adjacent cold-temperate grasslands with small scattered juniper stands (n = 305). Occupied locations often contain a scattered low woody shrub layer component that may include sagebrush, greasewood, cliffrose, and shrub live oak. On Black Mesa, LaRue (1994) found this species primarily in open pinyon pine and juniper-covered slopes and small canyons that support a scattered growth of Utah serviceberry. They are occasionally found in the same habitat as the similar Plumbeous Vireo; however, the latter typically prefers the taller and denser woodlands of pinyon pine and juniper, frequently at slightly higher elevations. An additional 10 percent of Gray Vireo records were documented on chaparral-covered slopes with scattered juniper and pinyon pine. Open Madrean evergreen oak woodlands with scattered juniper and pinyon pine accounted for an additional 9 percent of records.

BREEDING

In Arizona, Gray Vireos typically begin to arrive on their breeding grounds in late March or early April. The males arrive a few days before the females, and nest building can begin one to two days after pair formation (Barlow et al. 1999). Early nest construction begins by mid- to late April in Arizona, and atlasers first noted this activity on 22 April.

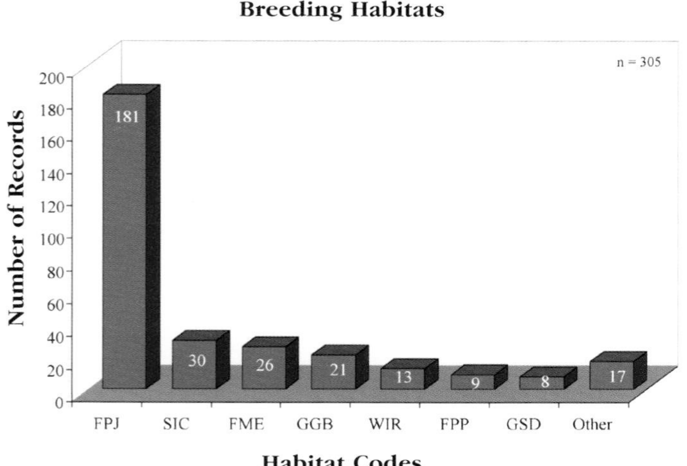

Based on atlas data, some early nests contain eggs by late April and early May. Gray Vireos were observed feeding fledglings by 31 May. Atlas data reveal the peak nesting period for Gray Vireos is from mid-May through late June, although some nesting activity continues into late summer. Atlasers reported the latest nest with young on 20 July and adults feeding fledglings through 13 August. Nests with eggs have been found as late as 2 August in Texas (Barlow et al. 1999). Fall migration begins in August, with individuals arriving on their wintering grounds in Arizona as early as 25 August (Phillips et al. 1964). Gray Vireos are rarely observed during migration in Arizona, but most records fall in September, with stragglers casually into October and November. They are short-distance migrants that winter locally in Sonoran Desert canyons of southwestern Arizona and Mexico, which often include elephant trees.

Both members of the pair construct the nest that takes 5–6 days for completion (Barlow et al. 1999). Of 33 Gray Vireo nests measured by atlasers, 20 (61 percent) were in either Utah or one-seeded juniper and 9 (27 percent) were in pinyon pine. The other nests were discovered in shrub live oak (2), Emory oak (1), and netleaf hackberry (1). The mean nest height of these nests was 7.5 ft (2.3 m) and the range was 3.3–17.1 ft (1.0–5.2 m).

Clutch sizes for Gray Vireos range from 2 to 4 eggs, which are incubated by both adults for 12–14 days, but primarily by the female (Barlow et al. 1999). Both parents feed the nestlings, which fledge in 13–14 days and are fed for 5–10 days following nest departure (Barlow et al. 1999). There is little information, but with the lengthy nesting season, Gray Vireos have the potential for successfully fledging two broods per year.

Atlasers documented only one incident of Brown-headed Cowbird brood parasitism. Adults were observed feeding a fledgling near a nest on 26 June 1997. Gray Vireos

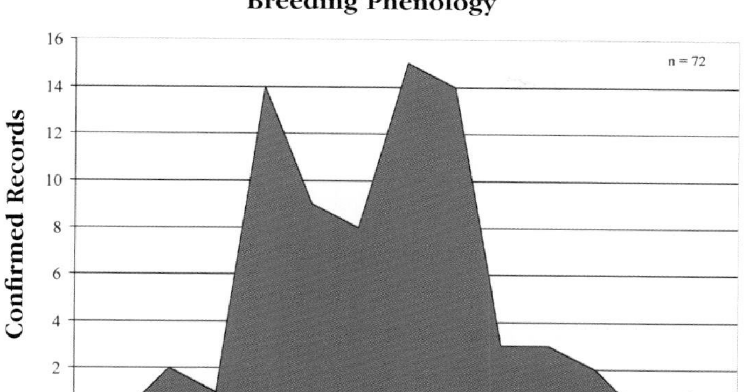

are known to abandon their nest following cowbird nest parasitism; therefore, successful fledging of cowbird young is infrequent (Barlow et al. 1999).

DISTRIBUTION AND STATUS

Gray Vireos nest from southern Utah and western Colorado, south to southern Nevada, Arizona, and New Mexico. Isolated populations also breed in southern California, western Texas, northern Baja California, and one locality in northern Coahuila. In Arizona, Gray Vireos have been described as a fairly common nesting species in northwestern and central Arizona, locally south to the Chiricahua Mountains (Phillips et al. 1964).

Before the mid-1980s, published accounts noted this vireo as absent in northeastern Arizona from the area east of the Grand Canyon and north of the Little Colorado River (Monson and Phillips 1981). However, Jacobs (1986) considered them uncommon summer residents on Navajo and Hope tribal lands, and LaRue (1994) reported Gray Vireos to be a fairly common summer resident on Black Mesa near Kayenta. Atlasers encountered them as far south as near Sanders.

Gray Vireos were documented nesting in Arizona at elevations ranging from 3500 to 6800 ft (1067–2073 m). Atlasers found Gray Vireos to be fairly common and widely distributed across northern Arizona, east to the foothills of the Carrizo and Chuska ranges in northern Apache County. They were noted as far west as the slopes of Mount Perkins and confirmed nesting as far south as the Hualapai and McCracken ranges. Gray Vireos were detected along the southern edge of the Mogollon Rim, south to the Superstition and Pinal mountain region. In southeastern Arizona, they were found fairly regularly from the Santa Teresa Mountains and Galiuro Mountains south to the Winchester Mountains. Gray Vireos were sparsely distributed on the eastern foothills of the Santa Catalina Mountains and southern reaches of the Pinaleno Mountains. They were detected very locally in the Dos Cabezas and Chiricahua ranges, possibly indicating a population decline from earlier accounts from this area (Phillips et al. 1964). However, observers discovered a pair of Gray Vireos near Guadalupe Canyon in extreme southeastern Arizona.

Although Arizona contains a significant proportion of the Gray Vireo's breeding range, population trends are basically unknown in the state. Drought conditions that began during the atlas period and the subsequent bark beetle infestations have recently killed extensive stands of pinyon pine and juniper woodlands across northern Arizona. This has raised significant concerns for the Gray Vireo and other primarily juniper dependent species.

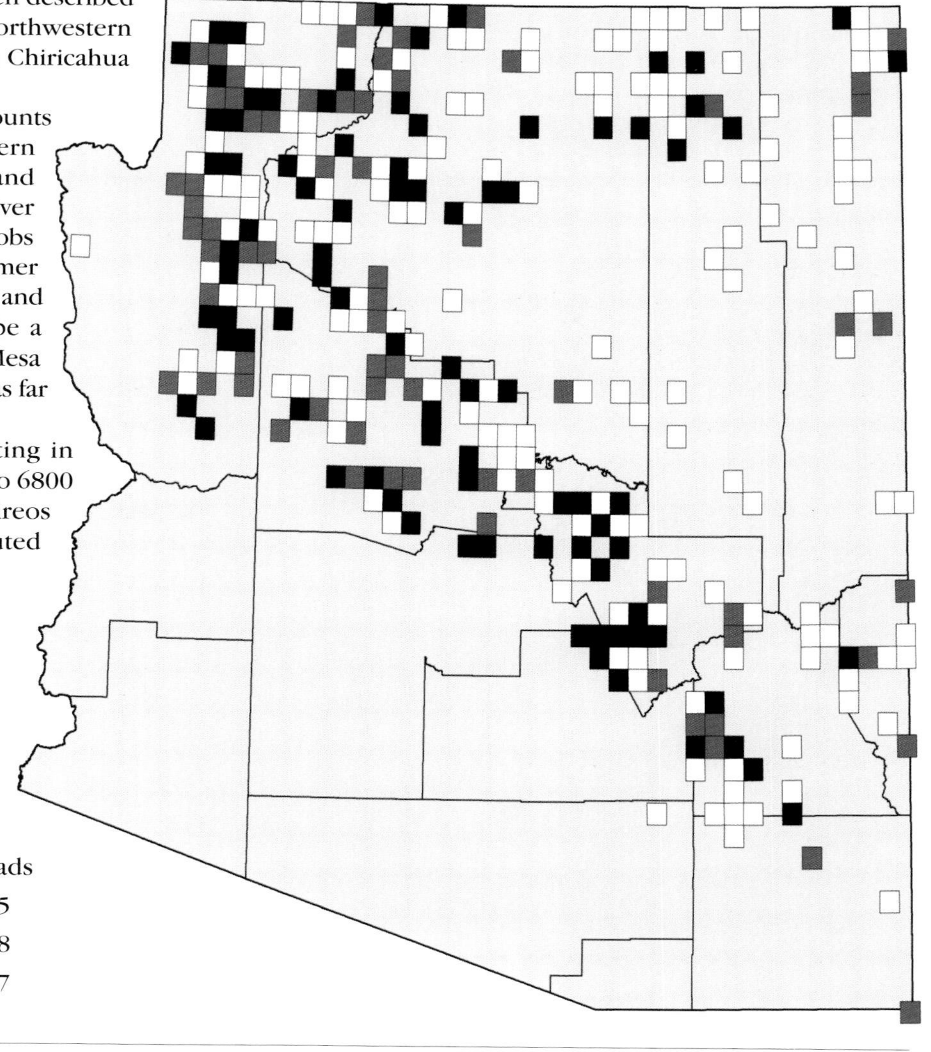

Gray Vireo Breeding Evidence Reported in 315 (17%) of 1834 priority blocks

	Blocks	Quads
Possible	160 (51%)	165
Probable	68 (22%)	68
Confirmed	87 (28%)	87

Plumbeous Vireo

by Cathryn Wise-Gervais *Vireo plumbeus*

In 1997, the American Ornithologists' Union split the familiar, white-spectacled Solitary Vireo into three species. Of these, the Plumbeous Vireo is the largest and dullest, and as its name suggests, has an overall gray appearance. Their familiar song can be heard throughout the summer in most of Arizona's heavily wooded forests.

JIM BURNS

HABITAT

Plumbeous Vireos are primarily a woodland species that often inhabits drier conifer forests and oak woodlands. In Arizona, they also commonly occur in dense pinyon pine–juniper woodlands and mountain riparian zones. Atlasers reported Plumbeous Vireos in fifteen vegetative communities. Approximately 38 percent of records were from forests largely dominated by ponderosa pine, including nearly pure stands to those associated with Gambel's oak or pinyon pine (n = 385). Plumbeous Vireos were found less frequently (12 percent of records) in high-elevation mixed-conifer forests containing firs, pines, and aspen and in the nearby cool montane drainages. Atlasers reported 21 percent of Plumbeous Vireo records in dense pinyon pine–juniper woodlands, but found that the birds were more common in woodlands offering extensive pinyon pine than in drier, juniper-dominated stands. South of the Mogollon Rim, they were regularly found nesting in Arizona sycamore dominated mountain drainages and atlasers reported nearly 16 percent of records in this habitat type. In southeastern Arizona's sky islands, atlasers also commonly encountered these vireos in Madrean evergreen oak woodlands and in Madrean pine-oak forests at higher elevations containing Apache, Chihuahuan, and ponderosa pines.

Breeding Habitats

n = 385

Habitat Codes	FPJ	WIR	FPO	FMP	FPP	FMM	FME	WMR	FMO	Other
Number of Records	81	60	57	45	43	29	19	18	11	22

BREEDING

Plumbeous Vireos winter in western Mexico and typically begin arriving in southern Arizona by late March or early April and by mid-April in the north. The birds begin singing immediately upon arrival to the breeding grounds, and nesting activities soon follow. Atlasers reported Plumbeous Vireos carrying nesting material and nest building on 30 April and 1 May, respectively. Observers located the earliest occupied nest likely containing eggs on 14 May and the first nest with young on 1 June. Atlas data suggest that Plumbeous Vireo breeding activities peak from mid-May through mid-June, with a second activity spike from late June to early July. These later nests are likely the renesting attempts of pairs that failed earlier in the season (Curson and Goguen 1998). Atlasers noted nests with young through 13 July and adults feeding dependent fledglings to 1 August. In Arizona, the first fall migrant Plumbeous Vireos are noted by early to mid-August. Peak passage is in early September and most have departed by late October. However, these birds winter in limited numbers in lowland riparian areas of southern Arizona.

Male Plumbeous Vireos lead their mates to prospective nest areas, and once the location has been chosen, the pair begins work on the nest together. However, the male's participation wanes after a few days (Curson and Goguen 1998). Although nest placement and site characteristics are known to vary depending on habitat and location, these vireos tend to place their nests relatively low and under dense cover (Curson and Goguen 1998). Atlasers took measurements at 26 Plumbeous Vireo nests in 12 tree species, with 70 percent in deciduous trees. The most commonly reported nest trees were oaks (10 nests), including Gambel's, Emory, silverleaf, and Arizona white. Other trees included pinyon pine, ponderosa pine, juniper, sycamore, ash, walnut, cottonwood, and boxelder. The median nest height was 9.8 ft (3.0 m) and ranged from 3.6 to 61.3 ft (1.1–18.7 m).

Like other vireos, Plumbeous nests are cup-shaped structures that typically hang from the fork of a branch. Most clutches consist of 4 eggs (range 3–5), and both adults incubate these for approximately 13–15 days (Curson and Goguen 1998). Both sexes feed the nestlings for 13–14 days

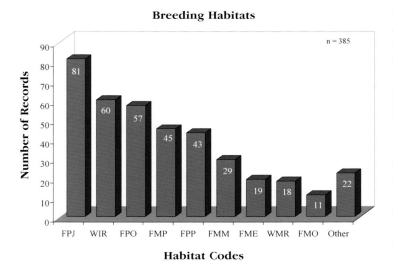

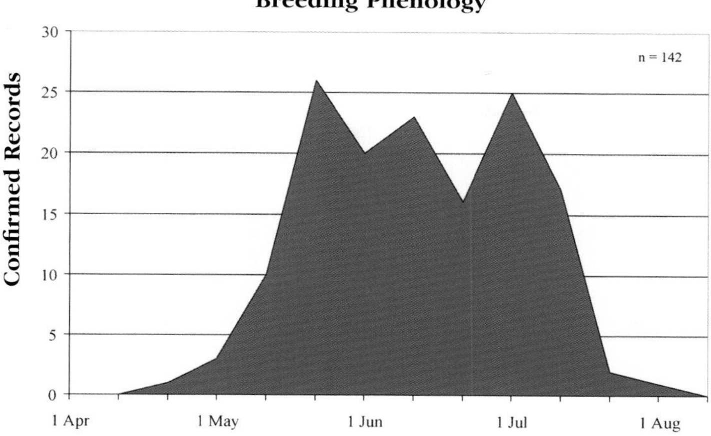

and for approximately 2 weeks following nest departure (Curson and Goguen 1998).

Plumbeous Vireos typically raise only a single brood but will renest if their first attempts fail (Curson and Goguen 1998). These vireos are common Brown-headed Cowbird hosts and atlasers reported seven incidents of brood parasitism, from 6 June to 18 July.

DISTRIBUTION AND STATUS

Plumbeous Vireos breed primarily from southern Idaho and Wyoming south through the highlands of Mexico to Honduras. They also nest locally in eastern California, Montana, South Dakota, and western Texas. In Arizona, Plumbeous Vireos have always been considered common summer residents in forests containing ponderosa pine, as well as denser pinyon pine–juniper and oak woodlands (Swarth 1914; Phillips et al. 1964). This species is typically a mid- to high-elevation bird rangewide, and in Arizona it was noted on priority blocks primarily from 4500 to 8800 ft (1372–2682 m). Several lower riparian nests were discovered however, including one at 3420 ft (1042 m).

Since Plumbeous Vireos sing periodically throughout the day and sometimes even from the nest, atlasers had little trouble detecting them during surveys. Atlas data reveal no real surprises in the distribution of Plumbeous Vireos in Arizona, but helped clarify their range in remote and infrequently visited areas. Atlasers regularly encountered these vireos in southeastern Arizona's forested mountains, including smaller ranges such as the Mule, Whetstone, and Winchester ranges. They were also noted locally to the west in the Atascosa Mountains and Baboquivari Mountains.

In central Arizona, Plumbeous Vireos were found throughout the White Mountains and Mogollon Rim regions, with records encircling the White Mountain Apache tribal lands. This bird undoubtedly occurs throughout these tribal lands, where atlas surveys could not be conducted. Toward the west, atlasers encountered these vireos on many of the higher ranges of the Arizona Strip region, including the Virgin Mountains. The westernmost records were in the isolated Hualapai Mountains and Cerbat Mountains. Atlasers obtained plentiful Plumbeous Vireo records in the heavily timbered regions of the Navajo and Hopi tribal lands, including Keams Canyon north through Black Mesa and from the Defiance Plateau north to the Carrizo Mountains.

Breeding Bird Survey (BBS) data suggest that northeastern Arizona has one of the highest densities of Plumbeous Vireos in the West. In addition, BBS data and other analysis suggest an increasing trend for this species in Arizona and New Mexico and stable status in Colorado (Sauer et al. 1996). Given this, it is likely that Arizona's most frequently encountered vireo will continue to be the Plumbeous.

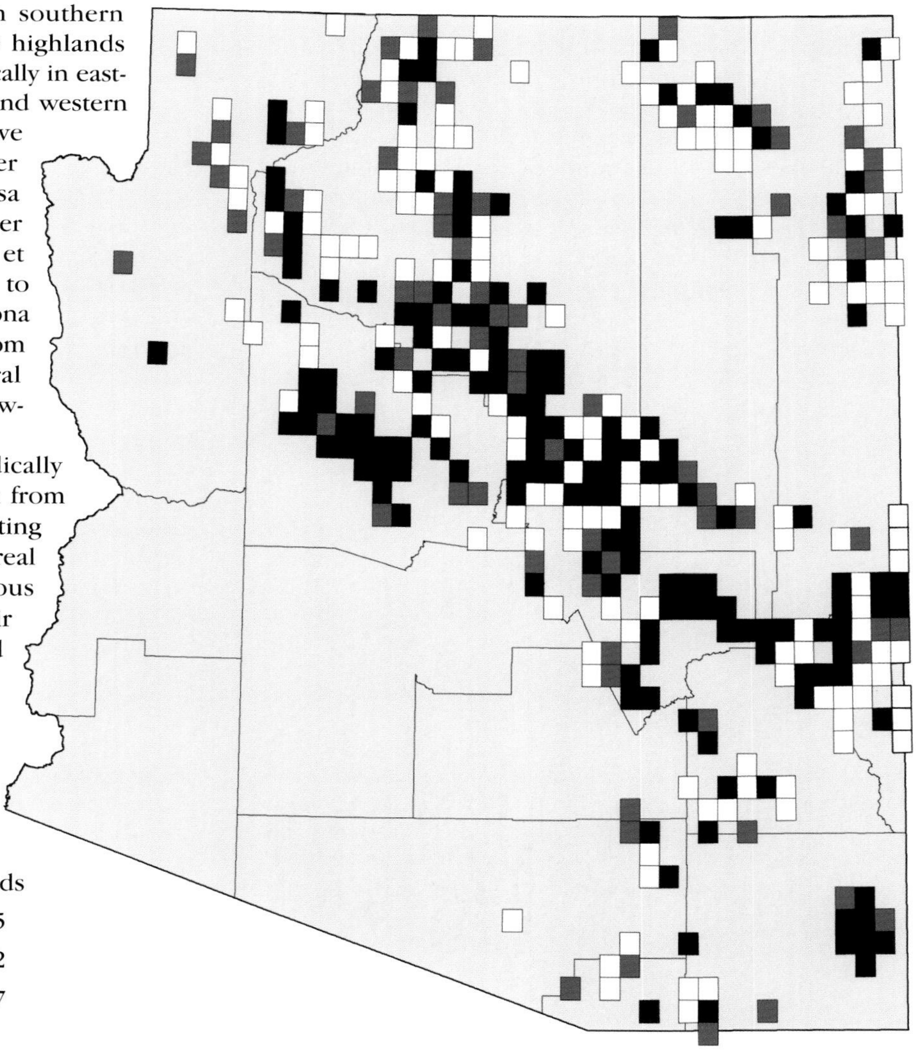

Plumbeous Vireo Breeding Evidence Reported in 369 (20%) of 1834 priority blocks

	Blocks	Quads
Possible	147 (40%)	155
Probable	69 (19%)	72
Confirmed	153 (41%)	157

Hutton's Vireo

by Troy E. Corman *Vireo huttoni*

The Hutton's Vireo is a small, retiring species that is easily overlooked and often mistaken for a Ruby-crowned Kinglet by the casual observer. Primarily resident in habitats associated with evergreen oaks throughout much of the state, their monotonous song or agitated whine typically gives this vireo's presence away.

DAN FISCHER

HABITAT

In Arizona, Hutton's Vireos closely associate with evergreen oaks and much of their breeding distribution parallels the range of these oak woodlands in the state. Typically, these vireos prefer tall, continuously canopied woodlands with large oaks and shade (Marshall 1957). Predictably, Hutton's Vireos were most commonly reported (36 percent of atlas records) in extensive stands of Madrean evergreen oak woodlands (n = 136). The adjacent foothill drainages and mountain canyon bottoms containing Arizona sycamore, and frequently a mixture of evergreen oaks, accounted for an additional 19 percent of the records. Madrean pine-oak forests, which often include oaks and junipers with a Chihuahuan, Apache, and ponderosa pine overstory, were also favored at higher elevations in the southeastern mountains and accounted for 12 percent of atlas records. In central Arizona, another 10 percent of Hutton's Vireo observations were noted in ponderosa pine–Gambel's oak forests, where the vegetation included some junipers and scrub live oaks. Atlasers also encountered Hutton's Vireos nesting very locally at lower elevations away from oaks in Fremont cottonwood– and Goodding willow–dominated riparian woodlands.

BREEDING

Hutton's Vireos are primarily a resident species throughout their range. However, some populations in northern Arizona are at least partially migratory, making seasonal movements to lower-elevation riparian groves and mesquite bosques. Males initiate singing by early February and their rather simple monotonous songs are frequently heard through late August in Arizona. Some resident Hutton's Vireos remain paired throughout the year, while others are typically paired by the end of March. Nest building by Hutton's Vireo pairs has recently been observed in Arizona as early as 9 March in lowland riparian woodlands. Atlasers noted these vireos constructing nests by 5 April at higher elevations. In Arizona, some egg clutches are likely laid as early as mid-March, but most are laid in April through July. Atlas data suggest that a peak nesting activity period occurs from mid-May through June. Adults were observed feeding fledged young from late April through mid-August.

In Arizona, Hutton's Vireos frequently construct their nests in a variety of evergreen oaks including silverleaf, Emory, Arizona white, and netleaf. Atlasers also found their often well-hidden nests in Arizona sycamore, Fremont cottonwood, velvet ash, and Gambel's oak. Atlas field crews took measurements at only three nests, which ranged from 4.3 to 39 ft (1.3–12 m) in height. Davis (1995) compiled height measurements for 102 nests from museums and Cornell's Nest Record Program and found the mean nest height to be 16 ft (4.9 m) with a range of 3–45 ft (0.9–13.7 m).

Hutton's Vireos typically lay 3–4 eggs, rarely 5 (Bent 1950). Both parents incubate the eggs for 14–16 days and feed the nestlings until they fledge approximately 14–17 days later (Van Fleet 1919; Harrison 1978). The adults have been observed feeding young up to 21 days after nest departure (Davis 1995). The lengthy breeding season and numerous late nesting records would suggest that Hutton's Vireos have more than one brood per season, although evidence is lacking and later nests could pertain to replacement nest from previous failed attempts.

Hutton's Vireos are considered an uncommon host of Brown-headed Cowbirds (Davis 1995) and the atlas only documented two cases during the project, both in mid-June. An atlaser documented a Hutton's Vireo feeding

Breeding Habitats

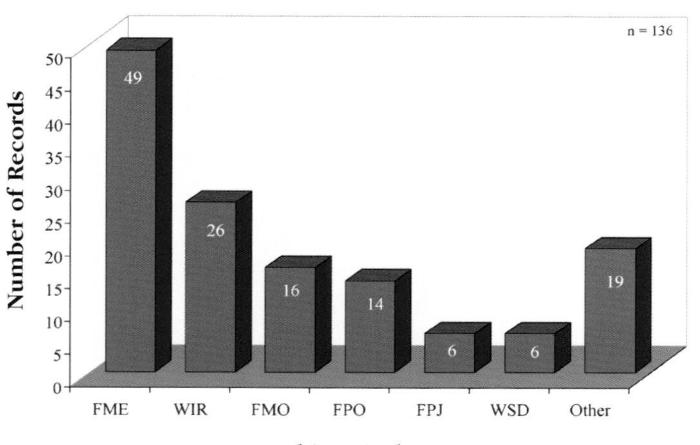

Breeding Phenology

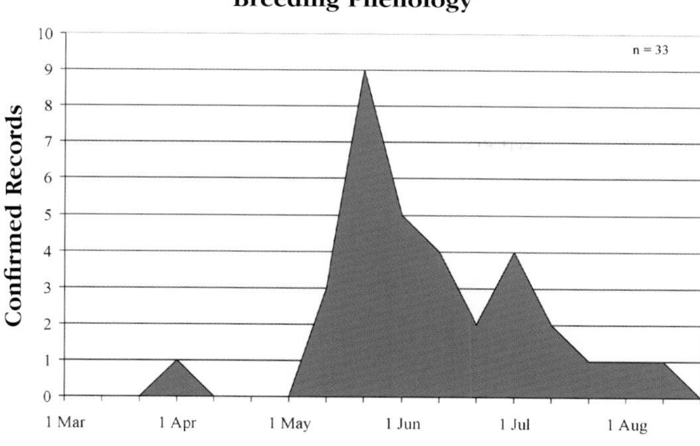

a fledgling Bronzed Cowbird on 22 June 1999 near Patagonia. This vireo was previously not noted as a host of the Bronzed Cowbird (Lowther 1995).

DISTRIBUTION AND STATUS

Hutton's Vireos are primarily a resident species of the Pacific Slope from southwestern British Columbia, south to northern Baja California. In the interior, this vireo ranges from central Arizona and the Big Bend region of Texas, south through the highlands of Mexico to Guatemala. The earliest distribution accounts for Hutton's Vireo in Arizona noted the species from southeastern mountain ranges (Swarth 1914) and later north sparingly to the Mazatzal Mountains, Sierra Ancha, and the Whiteriver–Ft. Apache area (Phillips et al. 1964). Monson and Phillips (1981) further extended their breeding range north locally to the Prescott region and west in southeastern Arizona to the Baboquivari-Quinlan Mountains. It is unknown if these previous accounts represent a steady range expansion to the north or if this unobtrusive vireo was simply overlooked at northern localities. The several fall Hutton's Vireo records from 1953 to 1960 within the lower Colorado River valley and Kofa Mountains suggest local dispersing or migrating individuals from northern outposts.

Atlasers found Hutton's Vireos to be rather common throughout their previously reported distribution in the state, typically from 3800 to 7500 ft (1158–2286 m). However, atlasers documented them nesting sparingly and possibly irregularly at lower-elevation riparian woodlands. This included a pair nest building near Boyce Thompson Arboretum along Queen Creek at 2520 ft (768 m) and an adult feeding a fledgling along the lower San Pedro River near Cascabel at 3020 ft (920 m). They have also been observed nest building at the Hassayampa River Preserve near Wickenburg at 1950 ft (594 m). During the atlas period, Hutton's Vireos were found north along the entire southern edge of the Mogollon Rim. Data are lacking, however, on White Mountain Apache tribal lands, where permits to conduct atlas surveys could not be obtained. These vireos undoubtedly continue to breed on these tribal lands. There are few records above the Mogollon Rim; however, one individual was observed in appropriate breeding habitat in an atlas block north of Escudilla Mountain, southwest of Springerville.

Atlasers discovered Hutton's Vireos ranging farther north than noted in previous literature. The most northern records were in the upper West Fork of Oak Creek Canyon north of Sedona and northwest to the Juniper Mountains south of Seligman. Based on earlier account of this species distribution in the state, it would appear that these little vireos have steadily extended their breeding range northwestward in the past forty years.

Hutton's Vireo Breeding Evidence Reported in 119 (7%) of 1834 priority blocks

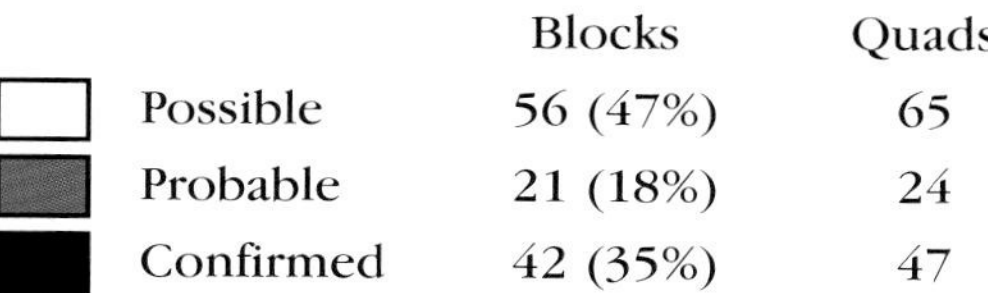

	Blocks	Quads
Possible	56 (47%)	65
Probable	21 (18%)	24
Confirmed	42 (35%)	47

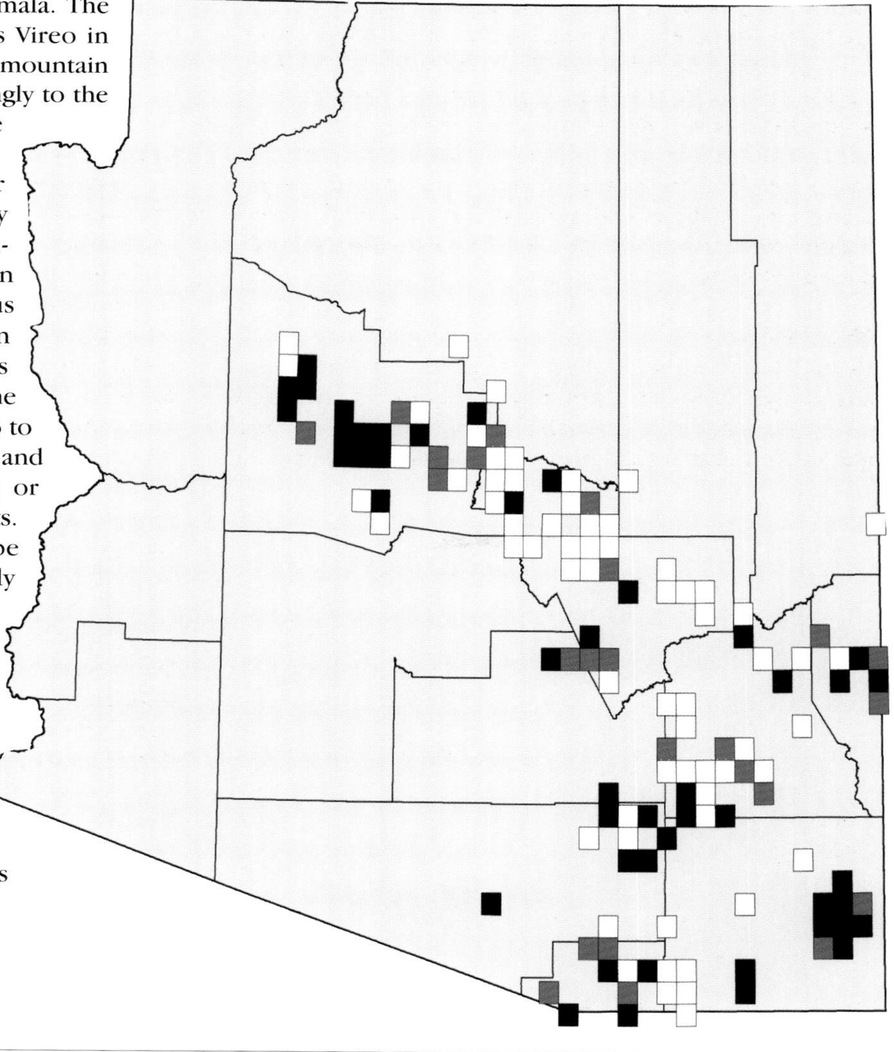

Warbling Vireo

by Annalaura Averill-Murray
and Troy E. Corman

Vireo gilvus

Found in many diverse habitats during migration, Warbling Vireos primarily breed in the mixed-conifer, deciduous, and riparian forests of Arizona's high country. This species' intricate, warbling song is exuberantly sung while well hidden within the tree canopy. Like most vireos, this species persistently sings, even from the nest.

JIM BURNS

HABITAT

Throughout their breeding range, Warbling Vireos are strongly associated with mature mixed deciduous forest and woodland, often along watercourses (Gardali and Ballard 2000). In Arizona, Warbling Vireos reach their highest breeding densities in montane forests with a strong quaking aspen component. However, they are also found nesting in forest and riparian woodland with other deciduous associations, such as Gambel's oak and sycamore. Atlasers reported 34 percent of 116 potential breeding records from mixed-conifer forest containing firs, pines, aspen, and Gambel's oak and an additional 22 percent from montane drainages containing aspen, maple, and alder. Warbling Vireos were also reported nesting in ponderosa pine–Gambel's oak associations (14 percent of atlas records). The relatively few atlas records from aspen-dominated forests likely relates to the limited distribution of this vegetation community in Arizona. Warbling Vireos are rarely reported breeding in pure coniferous forest, and few atlas records came from these forests. Atlasers also documented Warbling Vireos breeding locally in sycamore-lined drainages south of the Mogollon Rim and in a few tall cottonwood groves in northern Arizona.

BREEDING

Warbling Vireos typically arrive in southern Arizona in mid- to late March, but not until mid-April in the north. Their spring migration is quite protracted with individuals regularly passing through Arizona into mid-June. These late spring migrants, as well as those that begin returning south by mid-July, greatly complicate the determination of breeding status at some Arizona locations.

Atlasers noted Warbling Vireos singing within known breeding areas by late April and early May. There were two reports of adults either carrying food or feeding young in mid-May that likely pertain to courtship feeding rather than early nesting activity. Adults were observed carrying nesting material by 12 May; and occupied nests, likely containing eggs, were found by 20 May. Atlasers confirmed breeding in Arizona from mid-May through early August (n = 49), with the majority (76 percent) of confirmations from early June to mid-July. The latest occupied nest was found on 12 July, although nesting likely continued into August. Adult vireos were observed feeding fledglings as late as 5 August. As noted above, Warbling Vireos begin appearing in lowland riparian areas of Arizona in July, with peak passage in late August and September. Their abundance quickly declines in October and few individuals remain after mid-month.

Atlasers documented nesting substrates and compiled measurements at eight Warbling Vireo nests: three in Gambel's oak, two in quaking aspen, and one each in bigtooth maple, Fremont cottonwood, and New Mexico locust. Nests were typically constructed in large trees, 21–80 ft tall (6.4–24.4 m; n = 8), with a median height of 34 ft (10.4 m). Nest height ranged from 18.4 to 50.2 ft (5.6–15.3 m; n = 7), with a median of 27.9 ft (8.5 m). The recorded heights of 115 nests within the Mogollon Rim region of Arizona averaged 43.3 ft (13.2 m) and ranged from 7.5 to 121.4 ft (2.3–37 m) above the ground (Gardali and Ballard 2000).

Female Warbling Vireos typically construct the nest and both sexes incubate the clutch of 3–5 (typically 4) eggs for 12–14 days. Both adults share brooding and feeding duties until the young fledge at approximately 14 days after hatching (Baicich and Harrison 1997; Gardali and Ballard 2000). The number of broods per season is not well known, but double-brooding has been documented elsewhere (Gardali and Ballard 2000).

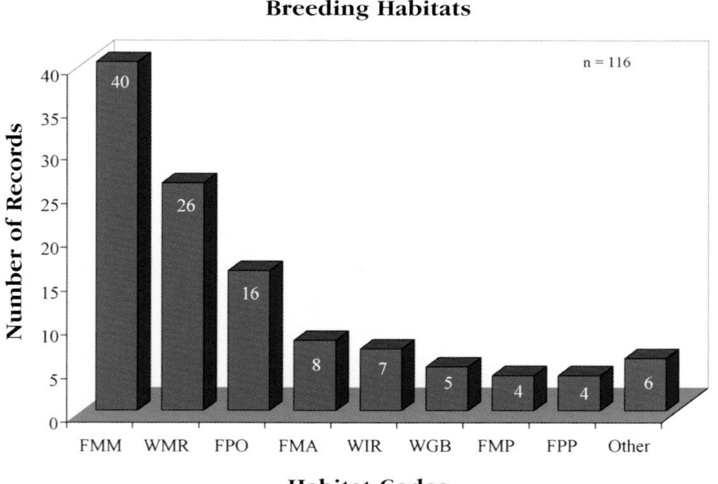

Breeding Phenology

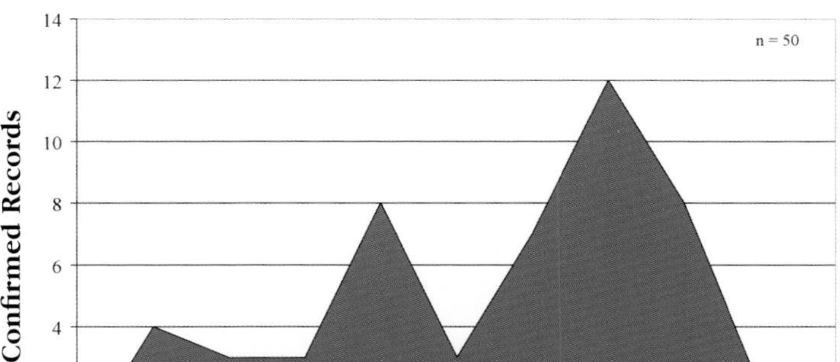

1 May 1 Jun 1 Jul 1 Aug

Atlasers documented one instance of a Warbling Vireo feeding a fledgling Brown-headed Cowbird. This species is a common host for the Brown-headed Cowbird (Friedmann 1963), with parasitism rates of up to 80 percent reported from other western locales (Gardali and Ballard 2000). During the atlas period, a Warbling Vireo was observed feeding a Bronzed Cowbird fledgling in the Huachuca Mountains (Gardali and Ballard 2000).

DISTRIBUTION AND STATUS

Warbling Vireos breed over much of western North America from southeast Alaska and northwest Canada south to the mountains of southern Mexico. To the east, they breed primarily from southern Canada south to Oklahoma, Mississippi, and the Appalachian region of North Carolina (Gardali and Ballard 2000). Warbling Vireos are a fairly common breeding species in the higher forested mountains and plateaus of Arizona (Phillips et al. 1964). Atlasers confirmed these vireos nesting in atlas blocks at elevations from 5700 ft (1737 m) to near 10,000 ft (3048 m).

In southeastern Arizona, atlasers documented Warbling Vireos only locally in the Santa Catalina and Huachuca mountains. However, this species was more commonly encountered in the larger Chiricahua and Pinaleno ranges. Historically, this species bred in the Rincon Mountains and possibly nested at higher elevations in the Santa Rita Mountains (Phillips et al. 1964). These two mountain ranges were not thoroughly surveyed during the atlas period, but suitable habitat for Warbling Vireos is very limited.

Warbling Vireos were frequently encountered on atlas blocks in the White Mountains and nearby Blue Range. They were less widespread to the west in the Mogollon Rim region, but they undoubtedly nest throughout the adjacent higher elevations of the unsurveyed White Mountain Apache tribal lands. On Navajo tribal lands in northeastern Arizona, atlasers documented these birds nesting locally on the Defiance Plateau, including upper Canyon de Chelly, and north through the Chuska to the Carrizo mountains. They were also encountered locally in the Tsegi Canyon drainage and on Black Mesa, where LaRue (1994) noted them as common summer residents in the aspen groves of the upper canyons. Warbling Vireos were widespread on the Kaibab Plateau and were noted in isolated ranges to the west, including the Virgin Mountains and Hualapai Mountains.

Based on previous knowledge, atlas data reveal little change in the distribution of Warbling Vireo populations in Arizona. Some populations may locally increase as forests recover from recent widespread forest fires. Gambel's oak and aspen are often the first to replace burned conifer stands and are readily inhabited by these forest vireos.

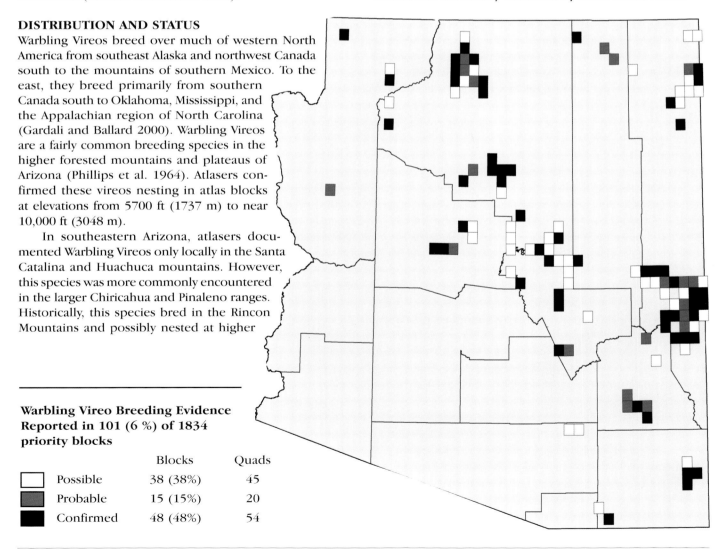

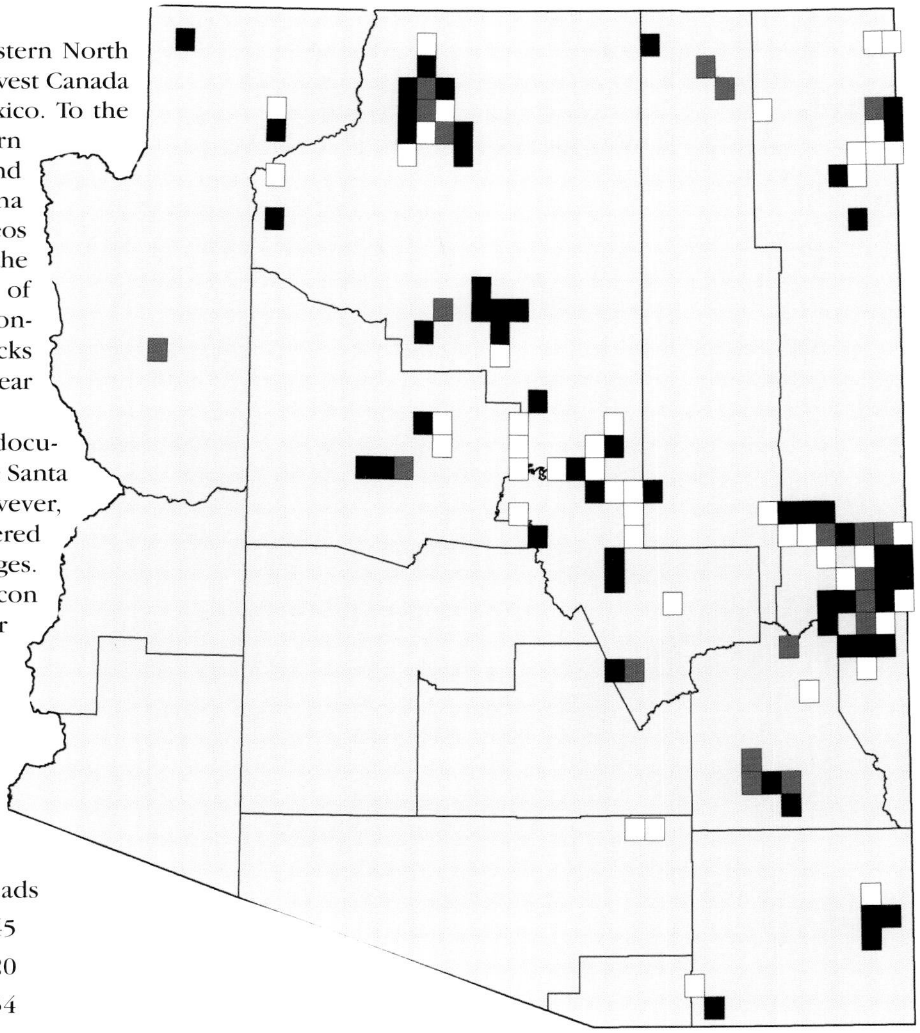

Warbling Vireo Breeding Evidence Reported in 101 (6 %) of 1834 priority blocks

	Blocks	Quads
Possible	38 (38%)	45
Probable	15 (15%)	20
Confirmed	48 (48%)	54

Gray Jay

by Troy E. Corman *Perisoreus canadensis*

Reaching their most southern limit in Arizona, inquisitive Gray Jays float slightly and quietly from tree to tree. Their fluffy appearance, obvious curiosity, and tameness often make them an interesting and welcome companion while hiking through cool spruce woods. But back at camp, some Arizonans consider them a nuisance because of their bold, thieving ways.

JIM BURNS

HABITAT

Gray Jays are spruce-loving birds and are typically missing in coniferous forests lacking spruce. Spruce-dominated forests are in short supply in Arizona, found only at the higher elevations affording the cool climate and relatively damp conditions they require. Atlasers reported Gray Jays primarily in Engelmann spruce–dominated forests or in forests containing a mixture of spruce (Engelmann and blue) and fir (corkbark, Douglas, and white). A scattering of quaking aspen can also be found at the lower elevational limits of this jay in Arizona. Atlasers found the Gray Jay on some of the higher mountain slopes at tree line, where Engelmann spruces are dwarfed by the persistent high winds and heavy snowpack and where the understory often includes common juniper. Within their deep forest domains, campgrounds and favorite campsites are frequent haunts of the opportunistic Gray Jay. Studies have found pairs occupy and defend a large, permanent all-purpose territory that averages approximately 148 ac (60 ha) in size (Winternitz 1998). They typically select forests with extensive closed canopy, but often forage near forest clearings and the edges of alpine meadows.

BREEDING

Unlike other populations to the north, Gray Jays are not known to undertake any altitudinal movements in Arizona. The small resident population in Arizona has attracted little attention from researchers and all aspects of their natural history in the state remains largely unknown. Atlasers were unable to gain much insight into the timing of nesting activity; therefore, we must rely on information from populations in Colorado. For a bird of the far north and high elevations, Gray Jays nest extraordinarily early, in late winter and early spring in often very cold and snowy conditions. Nest building typically takes place in February or March, approximately 3–4 weeks prior to the first egg being laid (Strickland and Ouellet 1993). In Colorado, nests with eggs have been reported from 17 March to 2 May (Bent 1946), with the young fledging in May and June. The only confirmation record during the atlas period was an observation of an adult feeding fledged young on 12 June.

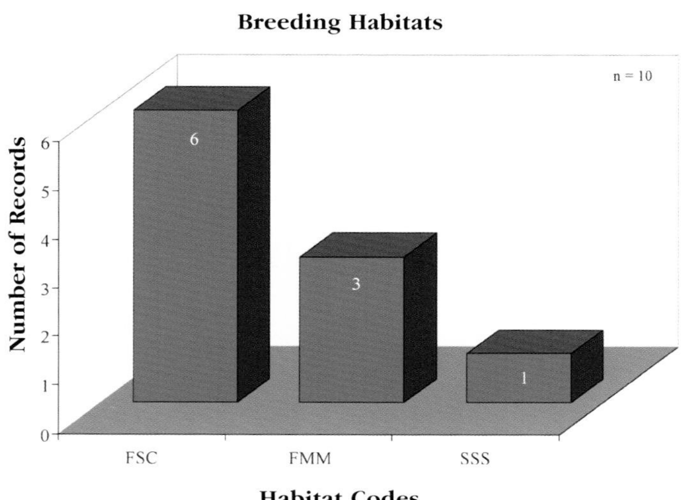

Constantly in visual and soft vocal contact, the Gray Jay pair usually remains together for life and shares the duties of nest construction. Nests are often placed only one or two trees north of the southern edge of a forest opening to increase the nest's southern exposure (Strickland and Ouellet 1993). For similar reasons, most nests are constructed on the south side of the tree and near or against the main trunk of a spruce or fir from 6 to 55 ft (1.8–16.8 m) above the ground (Strickland and Ouellet 1993). It is not uncommon to find incubating and brooding females with fresh snow accumulated beside her on the rim of the nest. These jays have also been observed incubating at temperatures as low as –22 F (–30 C) in Alaska (Brandt 1943). The typical clutch size is 3–4 eggs, but may range from 2 to 5 (Bent 1946). The female incubates the eggs for 18–19 days, and the pair feeds the nestlings, which leave the nest in 22–24 days (Strickland and Ouellet 1993). The family begins to travel as a group when the young have been out of the nest for nearly three weeks; several weeks later, the dominant juvenile expels its brood members from the natal territory (Strickland and Ouellet 1993). There is only one successful brood per season; however, Gray Jays will renest only if the failure occurs during the incubation period in April (Strickland and Ouellet 1993).

DISTRIBUTION AND STATUS

Gray Jays are resident in the boreal and subalpine coniferous forests of North America from Alaska and Canada, south locally to northern California and in the Rockies sparingly to New Mexico and Arizona. In the East, they are found as far south as northern Michigan and northern edges of New England. They reach their southernmost distribution in an isolated population at the higher elevations of the White Mountains in east-central Arizona (Phillips et al. 1964).

Atlasers noted Gray Jays at elevations ranging from 8750 to 11,000 ft (2667–3353 m). Prior accounts described Arizona's Gray Jay population as common residents (Phillips et al. 1964; Monson and Phillips 1981), a status that could not be assigned to them during the atlas period. In their limited range in Arizona, atlasers reported this jay to be local and rather sparse in numbers. They were found from Escudilla Mountain near the New Mexico border, west through the upper Black River drainage to just south of Big Lake. The largest population appears to be in the Mount Baldy vicinity, including the upper West Fork of the Little Colorado River drainage. Gray Jays can be found to the north to Greens Peak and near Whiting Knoll. Atlasers found them as far east as CC Cabin, approximately 3 mi (4.8 km) east of Greens Peak. The exact eastern limits of the Gray Jay in Arizona likely include the northeastern section of the White Mountain Apache tribal lands, where access to conduct atlas surveys was not granted. Within these tribal lands, they surely occupy the western and southern slopes of Mount Baldy and the upper White River drainage.

Gray Jays were not reported from adjacent Greenlee County during atlas surveys. However, habitat north of Hannagan Meadow suggests their presence there. Historically, they were reported to occupy the Blue Range, which would include northern Greenlee County (Phillips et al. 1964). Although still found with some regularity at several locations, especially in the vicinity of specific campgrounds, the obvious reduction in numbers and the possible reduced distribution is of concern. These quiet and unassuming jays of the spruce forests deserve much more attention in Arizona.

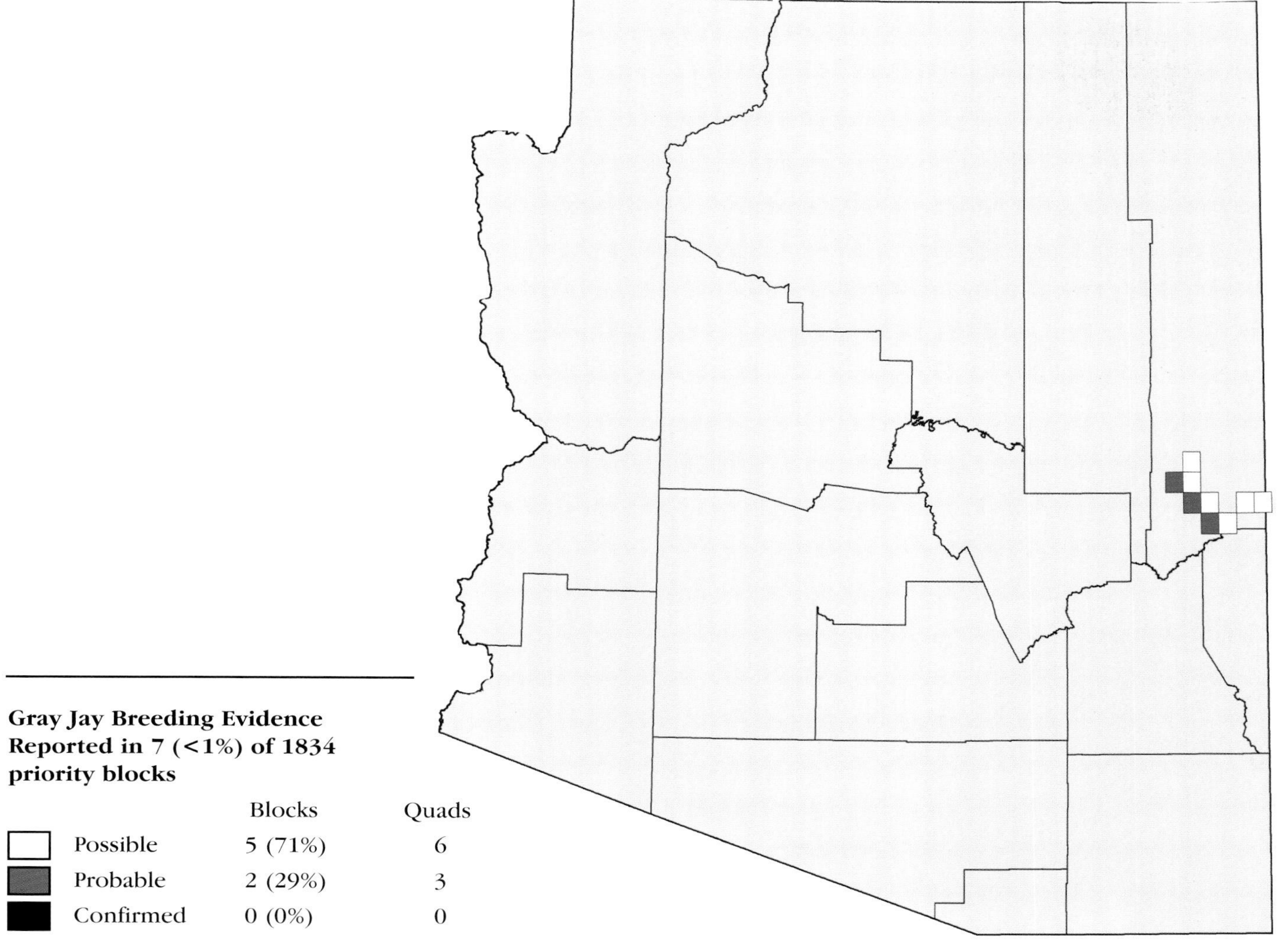

Gray Jay Breeding Evidence Reported in 7 (<1%) of 1834 priority blocks

	Blocks	Quads
Possible	5 (71%)	6
Probable	2 (29%)	3
Confirmed	0 (0%)	0

Steller's Jay

by Suzanne Sitko *Cyanocitta stelleri*

One of the more familiar birds in western coniferous forests and adjacent backyards, the Steller's Jay shows typical corvid family attributes—bold, intelligent, and opportunistic. Often raiding nests and dominating backyard bird feeders, Steller's Jays are prey for accipiters, much to the satisfaction of some backyard bird enthusiasts.

BRUCE TAUBERT

HABITAT

In Arizona, Steller's Jays inhabit almost any tall-timbered coniferous forests, either pure stands or those with a mixed deciduous component. Atlasers reported 66 percent of all records of these jays (n = 231) from the following three coniferous forest types: nearly pure stands of ponderosa pine (24 percent), ponderosa pine-Gambel's oak associations (22 percent), and mixed conifer containing various species of fir, pine, aspen, and oak (20 percent). Being opportunistic, Steller's Jays also were recorded in several other habitats during the breeding season. Pinyon pine–juniper woodlands with scattered ponderosa pines accounted for 15 percent of atlas records. In southeastern Arizona, Steller's Jays were also regularly encountered in Madrean pine-oak woodlands containing a mixture of Apache, Chihuahuan, and ponderosa pines with an alligator juniper and evergreen oak understory. They were reported less frequently in montane riparian woodlands with various species of pines, firs, aspen, and other deciduous trees. Steller's Jays were also noted as frequent inhabitants of Arizona's limited spruce-fir forests. In addition, Steller's Jays are regular visitors to residential parks, campgrounds, neighborhoods, and backyard feeders within or near these forests.

BREEDING

Steller's Jay's apparently maintain monogamous, long-term pair bonds and typically remain on territory throughout the year, with courtship and bond renewal occurring by late winter or early spring (Greene et al. 1998). Steller's Jays are uncharacteristically secretive in the vicinity of their nests, and very few active nests were discovered during the atlas period. Nests with young were first noted on 28 May; however, adults were already feeding a fledgling on that same date indicating egg laying by mid- to late April. Atlas data show that actual breeding activity in Arizona peaks between late May and mid-June. However, nests with young were noted as late as 16 July, and adults were observed feeding fledglings through 28 July. Brandt (1951) reported a late Arizona nest containing eggs on 20 July. Although basically nonmigratory, periodic fall irruptions bring individuals and small flocks (mainly young birds) of this jay into lowland areas and habitats not normally occupied, including desert riparian woodlands and neighborhoods.

For a species that spends so much time in the lofty canopy of tall pines, Steller's Jays typically select the dense cover of smaller trees for nest sites. They especially favor the small dense stands of 20–30 ft (6–9.1 m) conifers. Normally raucous, the breeding female becomes nearly silent and will not flush easily from her nest (Kaufman 1996; Greene et al. 1998), perhaps adding to the difficulty of atlasers locating their nests. Atlasers took measurement at only three active nests and all were in Douglas firs, which measured from 10.8 to 22.9 ft (3.3–7.0 m) high. The heights of these three nests ranged from 8.4 to 14.3 ft (2.6–4.4 m). Greene et al. (1998) noted that most nests are placed 9.8–16.4 ft (3–5 m) above the ground, but can range from ground level to 98.4 ft (30 m).

Steller's Jay pairs select nest sites and construct their nests together, although the female contributes the most to this activity (Greene et al. 1998). They typically choose a site on a horizontal tree limb near the trunk. Most clutches consist of 4–5 eggs, but can range from 2 to 6 (Baicich and Harrison 1997). The female incubates her clutch for approximately 16 days while receiving food from her mate (Goodwin 1976). Both parents feed the nestlings through nest departure in 16–18 days and continue feeding the fledglings for up to one month (Goodwin 1976). Only one brood is produced per year, but the pair will renest if earlier efforts have failed.

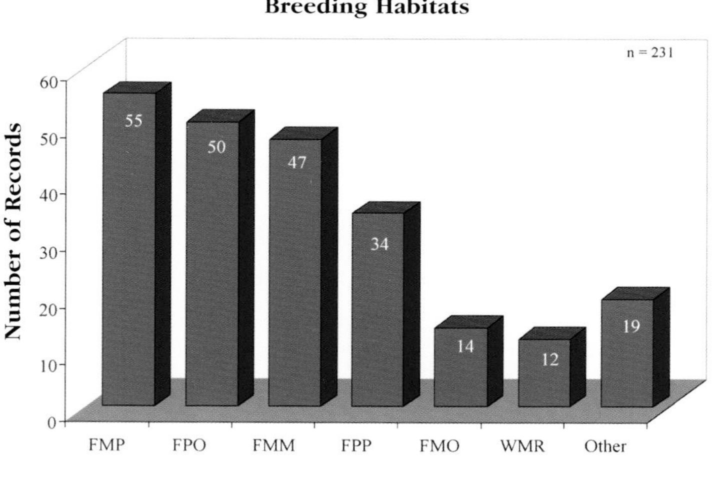

Breeding Phenology

Confirmed Records (0–9); n = 38; 1 May, 1 Jun, 1 Jul, 1 Aug

However, the limited appropriate habitat within these dry rugged mountains may not have been surveyed. Atlasers did detect them in several smaller ranges within this region including the Patagonia and Santa Teresa mountains.

As expected, Steller's Jays were widespread in the White Mountains and Mogollon Rim regions. While Atlas surveyors were not granted access on White Mountain Apache tribal lands for survey purposes, forest habitats on this unsurveyed reservation undoubtedly contain breeding populations of Steller's Jays as they do in adjacent regions. On Navajo tribal lands, they were found throughout the Defiance Plateau north to the Carrizo Mountains and along Black Mesa north to the Tsegi Canyon drainage. Westward, Steller's Jays were found fairly regularly on eastern Hualapai tribal lands north to Mounts Logan, Trumbull, and Dellenbaugh.

Long-term Breeding Bird Survey data suggest that overall Steller's Jay populations are apparently fairly stable. However, the extensive loss of ponderosa pine and other forests to large wildfires, recent drought, and subsequent bark beetles infestations in Arizona will likely have negative effects on these forest jays. Continued loss of undisturbed forest habitats from urban encroachment may also force these birds to utilize habitats not necessarily preferred for breeding, but it is apparent that Steller's Jays are adaptable and able to utilize a variety of habitats.

DISTRIBUTION AND STATUS

Common inhabitants of forests of western North America, Steller's Jays occupy coastal forests from southeast Alaska to central California. Inland, they occur in mountain and interior forests from the northern Rockies and Cascades south through the highlands of Mexico to western Nicaragua (Greene et al. 1998). The breeding distribution of Steller's Jays in Arizona is rather patchy, conforming to the location of tall coniferous forests on mountaintops, cool canyons, and higher-elevation plateaus and mesas. Atlasers documented these jays in the state at elevations from approximately 5300 to 11,000 ft (1615–3353 m).

Steller's Jays are typically quite vocal with a variety of loud distinctive calls that carry well through their forest territories. Consequently, atlasers usually had little trouble locating them on atlas block where they occurred. They were encountered in most of the higher mountain ranges of southeastern Arizona where previously reported by Phillips et al. (1964), although these jays were not found during atlas surveys conducted in the Galiuro Mountains.

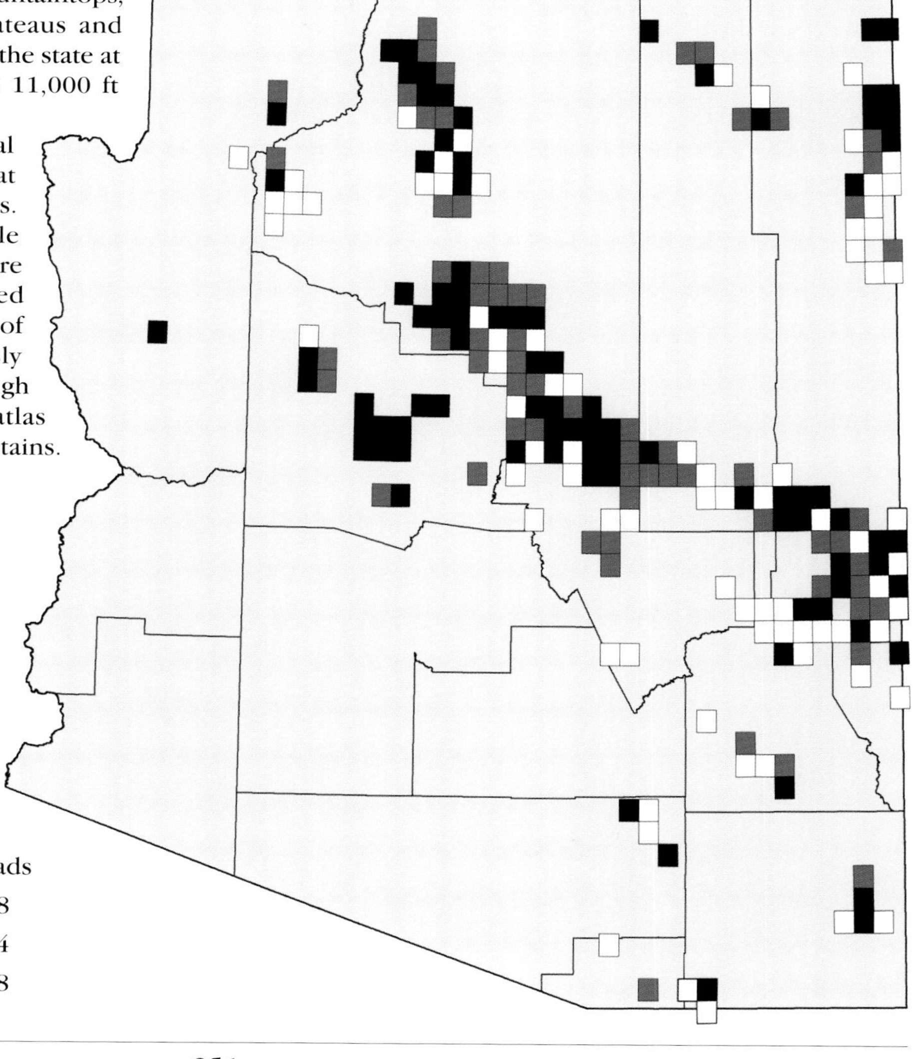

Steller's Jay Breeding Evidence Reported in 207 (11%) of 1834 priority blocks

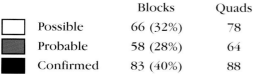

	Blocks	Quads
Possible	66 (32%)	78
Probable	58 (28%)	64
Confirmed	83 (40%)	88

Western Scrub-Jay

by Cathryn Wise-Gervais *Aphelocoma californica*

Western Scrub-Jays have the broadest geographic range of Arizona's jays, and occur in the widest range of habitats. These curious birds often announce themselves with harsh calls so are conspicuous wherever they occur. Western Scrub-Jays can also become quite tame and bold, especially when it comes to stealing a quick snack!

BRUCE TAUBERT

HABITAT

Western Scrub-Jays are found throughout Arizona in scrub oak thickets and chaparral-covered slopes as well as in open pinyon pine-juniper associations and even in some suburban neighborhoods. They generally prefer drier, more open habitats than other species of jays in the state, although there is some overlap between species. Western Scrub-Jays are also regularly found at lower elevations than are Arizona's other jays. Atlasers reported these birds in twenty-three different habitat types, but 47 percent of potential breeding records were in pinyon pine–juniper woodlands (n = 604). An additional 12 percent of the records were in the adjacent shrubby grasslands with scattered juniper and in pinyon pine–juniper stands with scattered ponderosa pine. Chaparral-dominated areas containing scrub live oak, scattered juniper, barberry, manzanita, and other woody shrubs accounted for 14 percent of atlas records, and 9 percent were from very open Madrean evergreen oak woodlands. Far fewer records were obtained in riparian woodlands and in brushy semiarid grasslands. Within all these habitats, these opportunistic jays will frequent backyard feeding stations and water features.

BREEDING

Western Scrub-Jays are primarily nonmigratory and often remain on territory in pairs throughout the year. Courtship and pair-bond renewal often occur in late winter and early spring and frequently includes courtship feeding. Courting males hop around the females with heads thrust upwards and tails fanned (Ehrlich et al. 1988). These jays can begin nest construction in late March or early April in Arizona. Atlasers first reported Western Scrub-Jays carrying nesting materials on 12 April, although a nest discovered with eggs on 15 April indicates earlier nest building activity. Observers located 11 Western Scrub-Jay nests with eggs from 15 April to 7 June and discovered eight nests with young from 7 May to 21 June. Researchers in coastal California reported slightly earlier breeding dates, as they found nests with eggs by mid-March and nestlings by early April (Curry et al. 2002). Atlas data suggest that Western Scrub-Jay breeding activity in Arizona peaks from early May to mid-June, but continues into early August (n = 69). Observers noted an adult carrying nesting material as late as 8 July and feeding fledged young through 26 July. Although typically a sedentary species in Arizona, hatchling-year Western Scrub-Jays periodically wander widely in large numbers to lowland deserts, riparian woodlands, and neighborhoods during fall and winter. These irregular irruption years may be based on food shortages within their typical range and often coincide with other corvid movements.

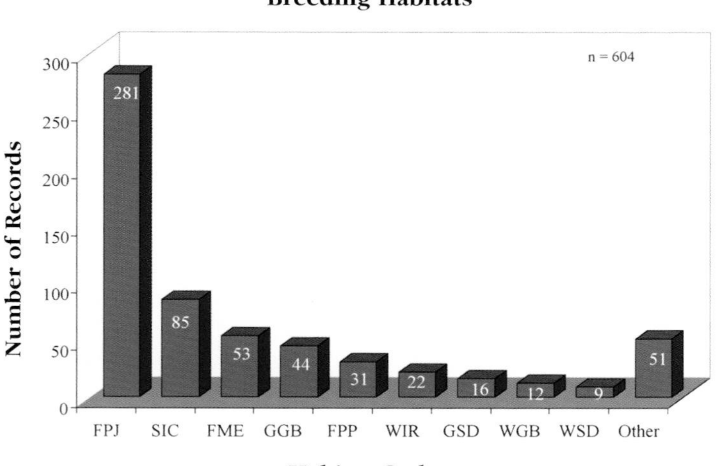

Western Scrub-Jays nest in fairly isolated pairs, and both sexes work together in constructing the typically well-concealed nest. This species generally nests fairly low in trees or shrubs, from 6.6 to 13.1 ft (2–4 m), although occasionally to 49.2 ft (15 m) above the ground in a pine or oak (Curry et al. 2002). Atlasers took measurements at ten Western Scrub-Jay nests, with five in juniper, two in pinyon, two in scrub live oak, and one in Wright silktassel. The median nest height of these nests was 5.9 ft (1.8 m) and ranged from 3.9 to 8.5 ft (1.2–2.6 m).

Typical Western Scrub-Jay clutches consist of 3–5 eggs (range 2–6), and the female incubates these for 17–19 days (Curry et al. 2002). Males feed females both before and during incubation, and both parents feed the young (Kaufman 1996). Young Western Scrub-Jays fledge at approximately 20–26 days, but parental care continues for approximately 34 days following nest departure (Ritter 1983). These jays typically rear one (rarely two) broods per season, but pairs are known to renest up to three times if earlier attempts fail (Ritter 1983).

Breeding Phenology

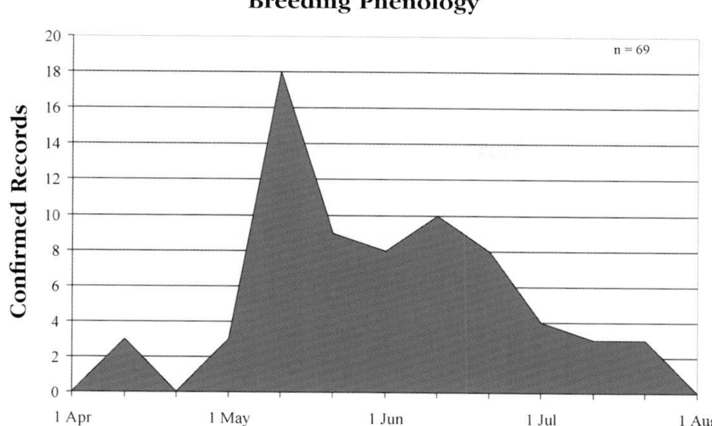

DISTRIBUTION AND STATUS

Western Scrub-Jays inhabit many regions of the western United States. They occur from western Washington south to the tip of Baja California and from southern Idaho and Wyoming southeast to central Texas and south to Oaxaca, Mexico. In Arizona, these jays have previously been noted as common and familiar residents in most mid-elevation brush and open woodlands from the state's eastern border west to the Hualapai Mountains in the north and to the Baboquivari Mountains in the southeast (Phillips et al. 1964). Within this range, atlasers regularly encountered Western Scrub-Jays on atlas blocks from approximately 3800 to 6800 ft (1158–2073 m). However, atlasers also found them nesting locally in some dry brushy foothill canyons down to 3300 ft (1006 m) and to the upper limits of pinyon pine–juniper and chaparral to 7800 ft (2377 m).

Atlas data reveal few surprises in the breeding distribution of Western Scrub-Jays in Arizona, but help define their limits within the state. As noted by Phillips et al. (1964), they were widespread, but more sparsely distributed in southeastern Arizona mountains and foothills than farther north. In central Arizona's White Mountains and Mogollon Rim regions, Western Scrub-Jays distribution was clearly defined surrounding the tall timbered forests and higher elevations. They were widespread within all pinyon pine–juniper associations of Navajo and Hopi tribal lands, but were largely absent to the south within the Little Colorado River valley between Saint Johns and Cameron.

Atlasers discovered Western Scrub-Jays nesting farther west in Arizona than previous literature suggested. The birds were confirmed breeding in higher elevations of the Black Mountains from approximately Mount Perkins south to Mount Nutt, and in the Cerbat Mountains. Atlasers also confirmed breeding in the Harquahala Mountains, where they were previously considered only as winter visitors (Monson and Phillips 1981), and found a pair of birds in suitable breeding habitat in the nearby Harcuvar Mountains.

Based on historical account of Western Scrub-Jays in Arizona, their distribution and abundance have changed little within the state. However, local populations of these familiar and adaptable jays may decline with the recent loss of many pinyon pine–juniper stands due to drought and subsequent bark beetle infestations.

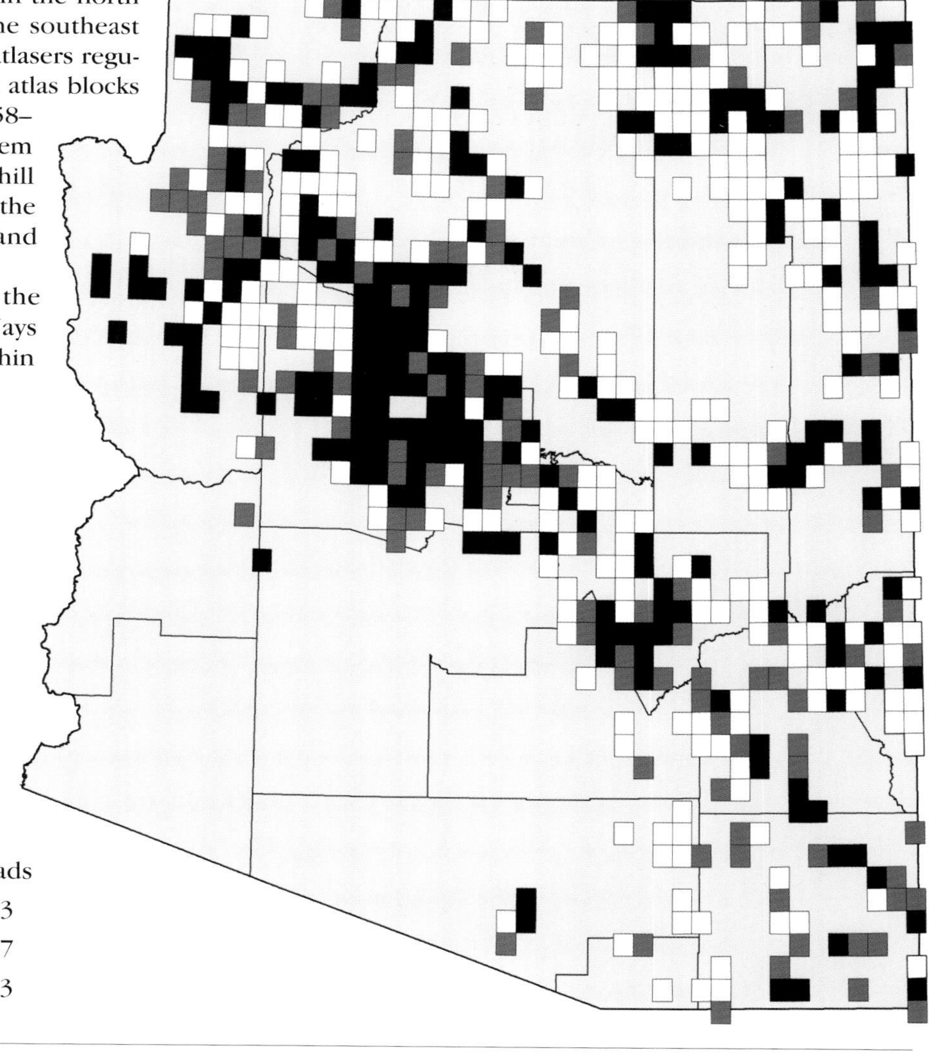

Western Scrub-Jay Breeding Evidence Reported in 608 (33%) of 1834 priority blocks

	Blocks	Quads
Possible	265 (44%)	273
Probable	123 (20%)	127
Confirmed	220 (36%)	223

Mexican Jay

by Cathryn Wise-Gervais *Aphelocoma ultramarina*

Formerly known as the Gray-breasted Jay, this highly social and conspicuous bird has a complex social organization. This species is nonmigratory and long-lived, and individuals have been recorded on the same territory for more than twenty years. There is little to no natal dispersal, so individuals in flocks are frequently all related to each other.

DAN FISCHER

HABITAT

Mexican Jays rely heavily on acorns, especially during the winter, so it is easy to see why they so favor oak woodlands. Although atlasers reported these jays in thirteen different habitat types, 48 percent of records were in Madrean evergreen oak woodlands (n = 144). Mixed oak species such as Emory, Arizona white, silverleaf, and others characterize this habitat type, and these are often intermingled with juniper and pinyon pine. Several adjacent oak-associated habitats were also noted harboring groups of these social jays. Atlasers reported 15 percent of records in drainages and canyons with tall sycamores, Arizona cypress, and oaks. Additionally, 10 percent of records were from the slightly higher Madrean pine-oak forests where evergreen oak, alligator juniper, and Arizona madrone stands intermingle with Apache, Chihuahuan, and ponderosa pines. Fewer Mexican Jays were reported from pinyon pine–juniper–Gambel's oak associations with varying densities of ponderosa pine. Many of these latter records were from northern populations below the Mogollon Rim.

BREEDING

Mexican Jays are Arizona residents that normally live in groups of 5–25 individuals throughout the year (Brown 1994). Mating systems are complex and variable, and within each flock there are typically 2–4 breeding females that breed more or less simultaneously (Brown 1994). Courtship activities are minimal, and paired birds are difficult to distinguish until actual nest building begins (Brown 1994). Mexican Jay breeding studies in the Chiricahua Mountains revealed that birds can initiate nest construction activities as early as mid-February or early March (Brown 1994). Atlasers did not report nest building until 2 April, however. In Arizona, most eggs are laid in April and early May, although Brown (1994) noted nests with eggs from 4 March to 26 June. Atlasers reported a fledgling on 15 April, suggesting a very early nesting effort, although most fledglings were not noted until after mid-May. Likely owing to the secretive nature of Mexican Jays around the nest, atlasers located few active nests, and most confirmations were from observations of adults feeding fledglings or juveniles in family groups. In southeastern Arizona, Brown (1994) noted that most nesting activity occurs from early April to late May. During the atlas project, nests with young were noted through 8 July, and adults were observed feeding fledgling to 15 August.

Breeding Habitats

n = 144

Habitat Codes	FME	WIR	FMO	FPP	FPJ	FPO	SIC	Other
Number of Records	69	22	14	9	6	5	4	15

Mexican Jays place their typically well-concealed nests in a wide variety of trees. Active nests can be challenging to find and atlasers took measurements at only two Mexican Jay nests, one each in Arizona white oak and Emory oak. Nest heights for these were 9.8 and 24 ft (3 and 7.3 m), respectively. This species' nesting habits have been extensively studied in the Chiricahua Mountains. Of 421 nests reported by Brown (1994), most were in Emory oak (33 percent), alligator juniper (22 percent), Arizona white oak (21 percent), and Chihuahuan pine (19 percent). The remaining 4 percent of nests were in various species of pines, firs, cypress, and oaks. The nests were usually placed in the top half of trees with a mean height of 20.3 ft (6.2 m) and range from 5.9 to 62 ft (1.8–18.9 m) above the ground (n = 443; Brown 1994).

The typical breeding arrangement for Mexican Jays in Arizona consists of one pair for each nest, although both members regularly copulate with other birds so broods are generally of mixed paternity (Brown 1994). Typical clutches

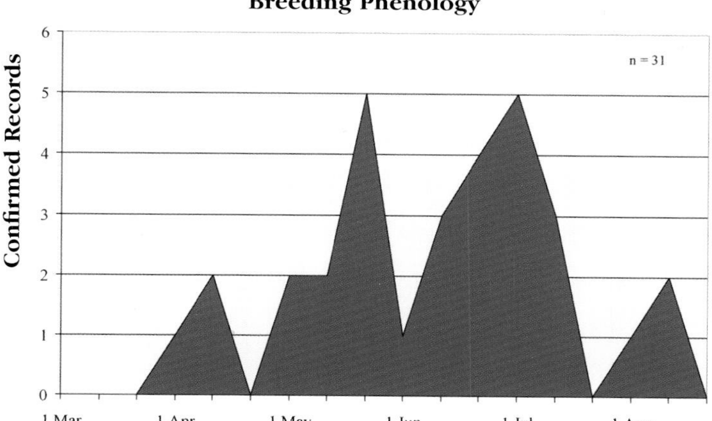

consist of 4 eggs (range 1–6) and are incubated by the female for approximately 18 days (Gross 1949). The male and other members of the flock feed the incubating and brooding female and also participate in feeding the nestlings, which fledge in about 25–28 days (Brown 1994). The parents and flock members continue feeding the young for several weeks following nest departure. Pairs typically raise only one brood per year but will renest if their first attempt fails (Brown 1994).

DISTRIBUTION AND STATUS

As their name suggests, these noisy jays are primarily found in Mexico and range northward into central Arizona, west-central New Mexico, and west Texas. In Mexico, they are found throughout the Sierra Madre Occidental and Oriental, and south to the volcanic belt (Howell and Webb 1995). Within Arizona, Mexican Jays are described as common residents in the evergreen oak woodlands of southeastern Arizona and north sparingly to below the Mogollon Rim (Swarth 1914; Phillips et al. 1964). Atlasers confirmed these jays breeding on priority blocks from approximately 3800 to 7200 ft (1006–2438 m).

As noted by others, Mexican Jays are widespread and familiar inhabitants of the oak woodland associations of southeastern Arizona, including many of the smaller mountain ranges. Atlasers documented them from Guadalupe Canyon and adjacent southern Peloncillo Mountains west to the Baboquivari Mountains. These jays were regularly encountered north through the Galiuro, Pinaleno, and Santa Teresa mountains to locally on nearby Lookout Mountain north of Aravaipa Canyon. Interestingly, atlasers did not detect Mexican Jays in the Pinal Mountains area, where Phillips et al. (1964) had previously noted them.

Although atlasers encountered Mexican Jays over a fairly wide area below the Mogollon Rim, population densities appeared to be much lower than farther south. The distribution of these jays undoubtedly continues across the southern slope of the Mogollon Rim, including within the White Mountain Apache tribal lands in western Gila and southern Navajo counties. Unfortunately, atlas data are lacking for this large reservation, on which access permits to conduct surveys could not be obtained. To the west, Mexican Jays were found south to the Sierra Ancha and Mazatzal Mountains. The birds were also found north sparingly through Strawberry to just north of Fossil Creek and within the Apache Maid Mountain vicinity south of Stoneman Lake.

Atlas data reveal that Mexican Jays still occur throughout most of their previously defined range in Arizona. Other than local habitat loss to wildfires, these jays face few threats and will likely continue to greet noisily those who venture into their oak woodland domains.

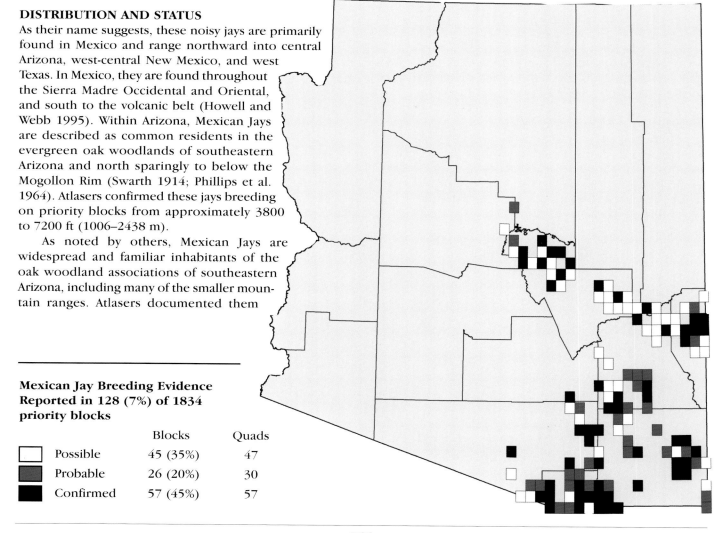

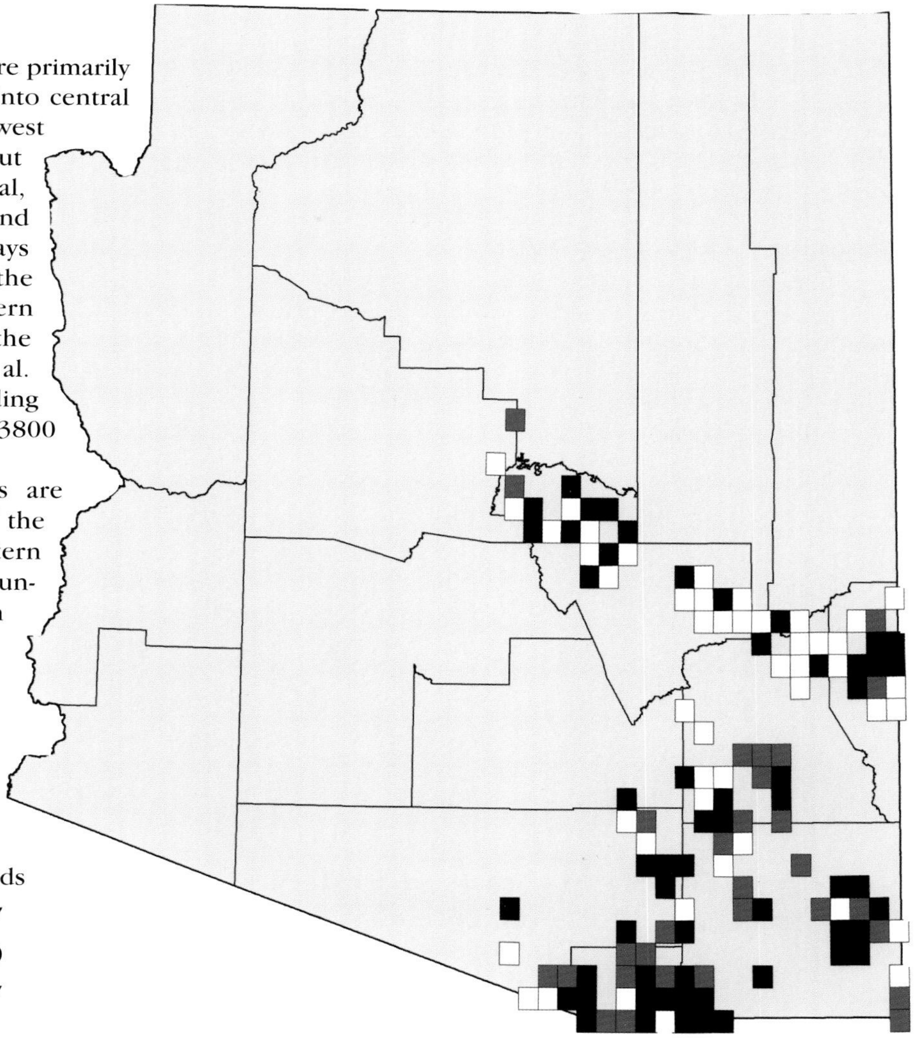

Mexican Jay Breeding Evidence Reported in 128 (7%) of 1834 priority blocks

	Blocks	Quads
Possible	45 (35%)	47
Probable	26 (20%)	30
Confirmed	57 (45%)	57

Pinyon Jay

by Jennifer L. Martin

Gymnorhinus cyanocephalus

The highly social Pinyon Jay has been the subject of extensive study in Arizona. Commonly named for its winter mainstay, the Pinyon Jay/pinyon pine relationship provides a beautiful illustration of coevolution. Jays feed on the nutrient-rich pine nuts and cache some for leaner times. Nuts that are missed often germinate to become the next generation of pinyon pines.

HABITAT

Pinyon Jays, the sole member of their genus, are closely associated with the pinyon pines and adjacent conifers of northern and central Arizona. Therefore, it was not surprising that atlasers reported 70 percent of Pinyon Jay records from pinyon pine–juniper woodlands (n = 340). An additional 11 percent of atlas records were from the adjacent grasslands with scattered stands of juniper and pinyon pine. At slightly higher elevations, atlasers noted 10 percent of their Pinyon Jay observations in pinyon-juniper associations with scattered stands of ponderosa pine. These birds wander widely in search of food and may account for the few records in sagebrush desertscrub, evergreen oak woodlands, ponderosa pine forest, and even mixed-conifer forests. The Pinyon Jay's omnivorous nature enables it to survive when nuts are scarce, and its powerful flight allows wide exploration in search of patchily distributed pine crops, berries, and larger insects.

BREEDING

Though considered nonmigratory, Pinyon Jays flocks wander erratically and irregularly in search of food. Most individuals spend their lives in their natal flocks, which often average between 100 and 200 birds (Balda 2002). Pair bonds are typically permanent and are made at any time during the year soon after the loss of a mate. Nest building activity is highly synchronized within a flock, but may vary among neighboring flocks and varies greatly among years (Balda 2002). Timing of nesting for the flock is largely based on the abundance of food and late snowfall levels, and nesting can begin by early February or not until mid-April (Balda 2002). Most eggs are laid in March and April. Atlasers often did not begin surveys within Pinyon Jay habitat until late April or early May; therefore, they typically missed early nesting efforts of this jay. Most atlas confirmations were of adults feeding fledglings or observations of fledglings within flocks beginning on 19 April. Atlasers discovered no nests with eggs, but noted several nests with young from 5 May to 10 July and noted adults feeding fledglings through 3 August.

Pinyon Jays are colonial nesters, with twenty-five or more pairs nesting in one woodland stand. They are also one of the earliest nesting passerines in the United States. The Pinyon Jay pair builds the nest together until they reach the final lining, which the female completes alone. Most nests are constructed in 5–9 days and are typically placed in ponderosa pine, pinyon pine, or juniper at heights ranging from approximately 3.3 to 114.8 ft (1–35 m) above the ground (Balda 2002). Atlasers measured five nests in junipers that ranged in height from 6.9 to 11.5 ft (2.1–3.5 m). In northern Arizona, nests are more frequently built on the south side of the tree (Balda and Bateman 1972; Marzluff and Balda 1992).

Egg laying begins approximately 3–8 days following completion of the nest construction, and most clutches consist of 3–5 eggs (Balda 2002). The female rarely leaves the nest for more than a few minutes during the 17-day incubation period and is fed solely by her mate (Bateman and Balda 1973; Marzluff and Balda 1992). Like breeding, feeding of incubating females is synchronized within the flock and is very noisy for the 45 seconds or so that it takes for the males to deliver

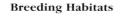

Breeding Habitats

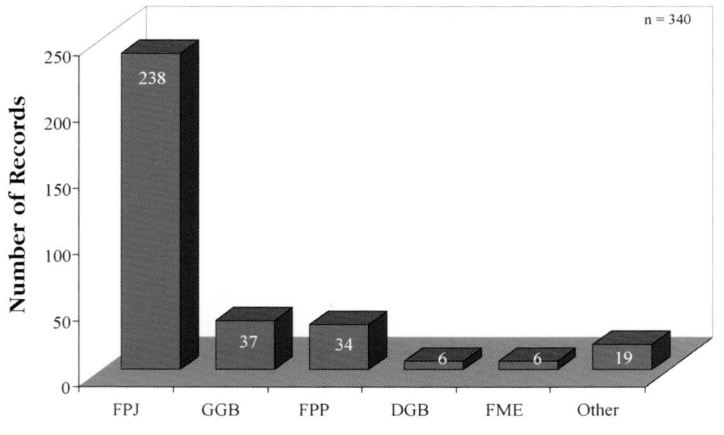

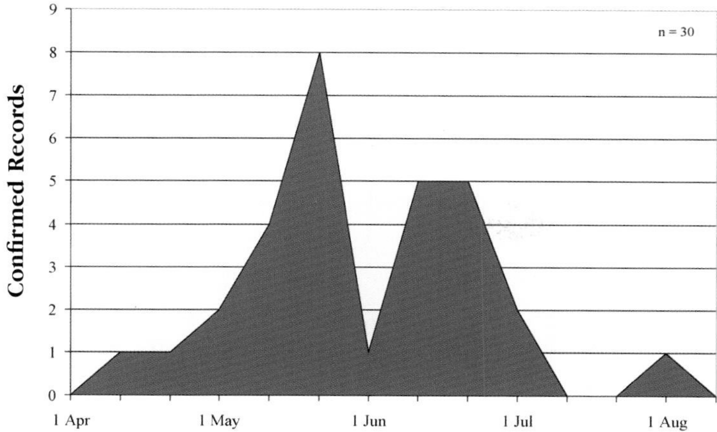

the food, after which the flock falls silent (Marzluff and Balda 1992). The young fledge at 21–23 days and gradually become nutritionally independent of their parents 6–8 weeks following nest departure (Balda 2002). Pinyon Jays produce only one brood per season, but will renest 5–6 times in one season if previous attempts fail (Balda 2002).

Beginning in late summer, the major behavior of the Pinyon Jay flock is to locate, harvest, transport, and cache pine nuts in individual sites. During the fall, numerous adjacent flocks may join to produce large and noisy roving groups of nearly 1000 individuals (Balda 2002).

DISTRIBUTION AND STATUS

Pinyon Jays are primarily resident in western North America from central Oregon and southern Montana south into New Mexico, central Arizona, and northern Baja California. They also breed locally in western South Dakota and Nebraska.

As noted by others, the distribution of Pinyon Jays in central and northern Arizona closely parallels the widespread distribution of Colorado pinyon pine. Atlasers documented these jays on priority blocks at elevations from approximately 4600 to 7800 ft (1402–2377 m), consistent with this bird's reputation as a mid-elevation species. They do not breed in the Mexican pinyon and other pines of southeast Arizona. However, when cone crops periodically fail in the north, Pinyon Jays (primarily yearlings) disperse widely in large fall and winter flocks, sometimes traveling to southeastern Arizona sky islands and beyond. Although found locally below the Mogollon Rim during surveys, atlasers were unable to confirm them nesting in these southern localities.

In northwestern Arizona, atlasers noted Pinyon Jays nesting west to the Cerbat Mountains northwest of Kingman and south to approximately Chino Valley. They were not detected in the Hualapai Mountains area, where Phillips et al. (1964) had previously noted them nesting. Pinyon Jays were also largely absent within the Little Colorado River drainage, where extensive stands of pinyon pine and juniper are lacking.

Though research has not been conducted to identify changes in gross distribution, vast areas of contiguous pinyon pine–juniper habitat were eradicated by governmental agencies between the 1940s and 1960s and may have caused shifts in the distribution of Pinyon Jays (Balda 2002). During this period, approximately 988,400 ac (400,000 ha) of these woodlands were removed and converted to grazing land in Arizona (Arnold et al. 1964). The recent extensive loss of pinyon pines in northern Arizona to drought and subsequent bark beetle infestations will undoubtedly also negatively affect populations of these fascinating jays within the state.

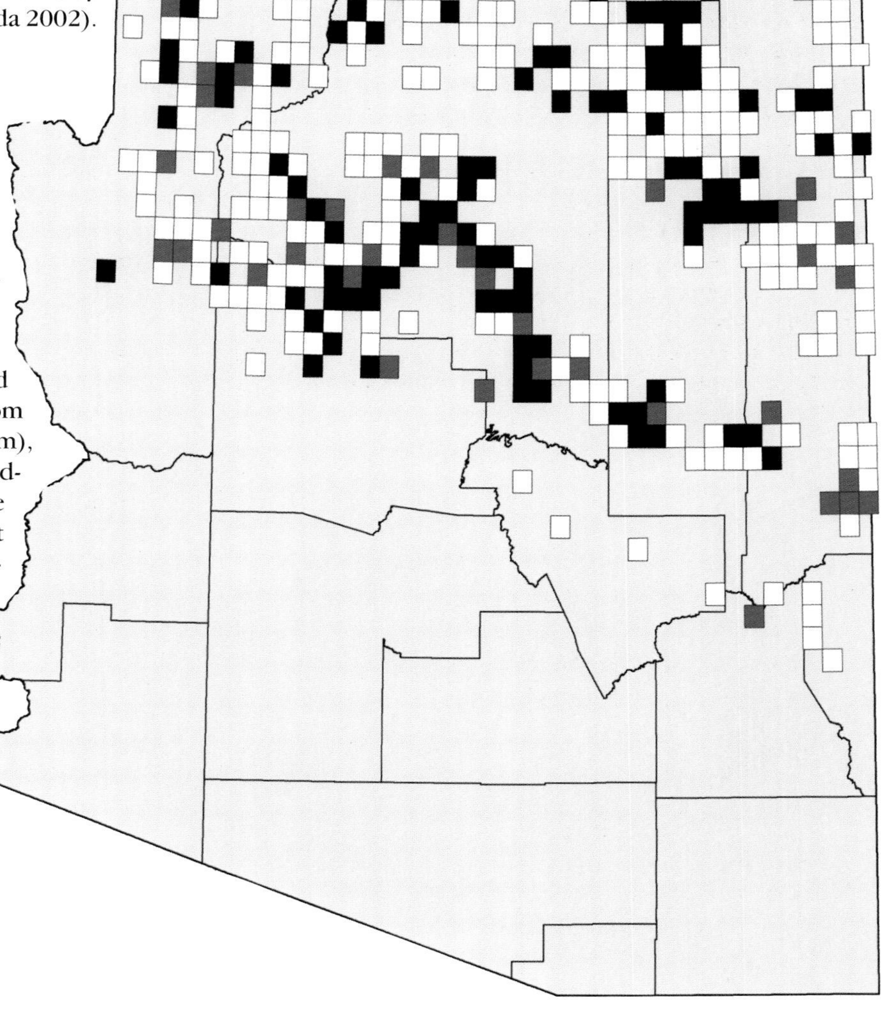

Pinyon Jay Breeding Evidence Reported in 338 (18%) of 1834 priority blocks

	Blocks	Quads
Possible	206 (61%)	211
Probable	38 (11%)	38
Confirmed	94 (28%)	95

Clark's Nutcracker

by Cathryn Wise-Gervais *Nucifraga columbiana*

Closely associated with cone-bearing trees, Clark's Nutcrackers transport multitudes of pine seeds to distant cache sites in a sublingual pouch. Forgotten seeds are thereby "planted," making these birds major players in the dispersal of several pine species. Like other corvids, these diligent birds often announce themselves with loud, grating calls.

JIM BURNS

HABITAT

Clark's Nutcrackers primarily occur in high-elevation coniferous forest associations. They are frequently observed on mountain ridges, forested canyon rims, or in tall trees near clearings and montane meadows. In northern Arizona, their diligent quest for pine seeds often takes them to forests containing one or more of the following pines: Colorado pinyon, limber, southwestern white, bristlecone, and ponderosa (Tomback 1998). Atlasers obtained 63 potential breeding records for this species, in nine vegetative communities. Of these, 54 percent were in mixed-conifer forests of Douglas fir, white fir, ponderosa pine, limber pine, and aspen. An additional 25 percent of records were in forests of primarily pure ponderosa pine or those with a Gambel's oak association. Fewer records were obtained from spruce-fir forests containing subalpine fir, Engelmann spruce, and blue spruce, although this is likely due to the limited distribution of this forest type in Arizona. During atlas surveys, Clark's Nutcrackers were also encountered occasionally in cool, forested montane drainages of fir, pine, aspen, maple, and other deciduous trees; aspen groves; and pinyon pine–juniper woodlands with scattered ponderosa pine.

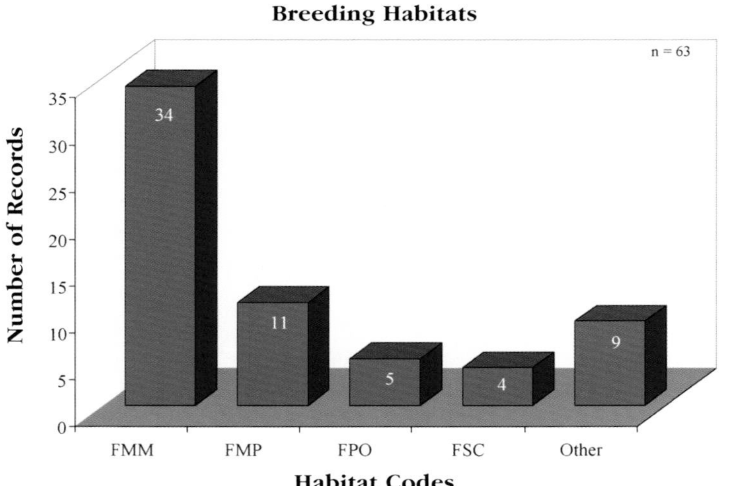

BREEDING

Clark's Nutcrackers reside year-round in Arizona and often initiate breeding activity in late winter or early spring. This early timetable probably ensures that young are independent when the typical seed-caching period begins in late summer (Vander Wall and Balda 1977; Tomback 1978). The timing of nesting can vary from several weeks to more than a month and is probably related to elevation, as well as annual snowpack levels and food availability (Tomback 1998). Throughout their range, nesting building typically occurs in March and April, the same period most egg clutches have been found (Tomback 1998). This is well before most atlasers initiated surveys within the higher-elevation forests Clark's Nutcrackers occupy. Atlasers obtained only ten confirmed breeding records for this species, and the earliest was an observation of adults feeding fledged young on 19 April. This would indicate that egg laying in this instance began by mid-March. Observers reported birds carrying nesting materials on the late date of 2 May and an occupied nest on 17 June. Fledglings have a lengthy parent dependency period that often last through early to mid-August (Tomback 1978).

Nest trees vary with geographic location, but some of the most commonly used substrates include pinyon pine, ponderosa pine, spruce, and Douglas fir. Atlasers did not measure any Clark's Nutcracker nests, but measurements from other parts of the species range indicate that nests are placed at a wide range of heights, from 6.6 to 16.4 ft (2–5 m) in pinyon pines and juniper (Bradbury 1917; Tomback 1977) to 5.9–78.8 ft (1.8–24 m) in taller pines, firs, and spruce (Mewaldt 1956; Tomback 1976). Nests are usually located near seed cache sites, on south-facing slopes or in canyon bottoms, and are often poorly concealed (Bradbury 1917; Mewaldt 1956; Tomback 1998). Both sexes collect nesting material and contribute to building the structure.

The typical Clark's Nutcracker clutch consists of 3 eggs (range 2–5), and both sexes incubate these for approximately 18–22 days (Skinner 1916; Mewaldt 1956). Both adults feed and brood the nestlings and the young remain in the nest for about 20 days. Fledglings remain dependent on food from parents for 3–4 months and begin caching their own pine seeds in late summer (Tomback 1978). Clark's Nutcrackers rear only one brood per year (Tomback 1998).

DISTRIBUTION AND STATUS

Clark's Nutcrackers are residents of the high-elevation mountain ranges of western North America, but periodically wander into lower elevations in fall and winter (Tomback 1998). The birds are found from the east slopes of Canada's coastal ranges south through the Cascades and Rocky Mountains to central Arizona and south-central New Mexico. They also occur in the high elevations of the Great Basin region and in California. In Arizona, Clark's Nutcrackers were previously described as common residents in the boreal zones of the White Mountains, San Francisco Mountains, Kaibab Plateau, and occasionally on the South Rim of the Grand Canyon (Phillips et al. 1964). They were later noted as possibly nesting in the Bill Williams Mountains and Chuska Mountains as well (Monson and Phillips 1981). Atlasers documented Clark's Nutcrackers on priority blocks from approximately 6600 ft (2011 m) to near timberline above 11,000 ft (3353 m) on Mount Baldy and the San Francisco Peaks. However many atlas confirmations may involve family groups far from their nesting site, as dependent fledglings are capable of extended flights (Winternitz 1998).

Atlasers encountered the raucous Clark's Nutcracker in most of the previous noted isolated regions of Arizona. They were especially widespread in the White Mountains and Blue Range regions. These corvids undoubtedly also occur in the similar adjacent forests of the White Mountain Apache tribal lands where surveys could not be conducted and atlas data are lacking. Clark's Nutcrackers were found only locally above the Mogollon Rim in southern Coconino County, where nesting has not been confirmed, but mixed-conifer forests are fairly widespread. They were also found in the San Francisco Peaks region north to Kendrick Peak and west to Sitgreaves Mountain near Williams. Atlasers noted them as fairly widespread on the Kaibab Plateau and only locally on the South Rim of the Grand Canyon and on Mount Trumbull.

On Navajo tribal lands, Jacobs (1986) described Clark's Nutcrackers as fairly common at elevations above 7000 ft (2136 m). Atlasers found these birds in several areas of Black Mesa where LaRue (1994) noted them as resident in the upper canyons. Clark's Nutcrackers were also found in the Carrizo and Chuska mountains, and south locally on the Defiance Plateau including upper Canyon de Chelly.

Atlas data reveal few surprises in the distribution of Clark's Nutcrackers in Arizona. Their status appears to be fairly stable, but populations fluctuate considerably from year to year, making it difficult to determine population trends.

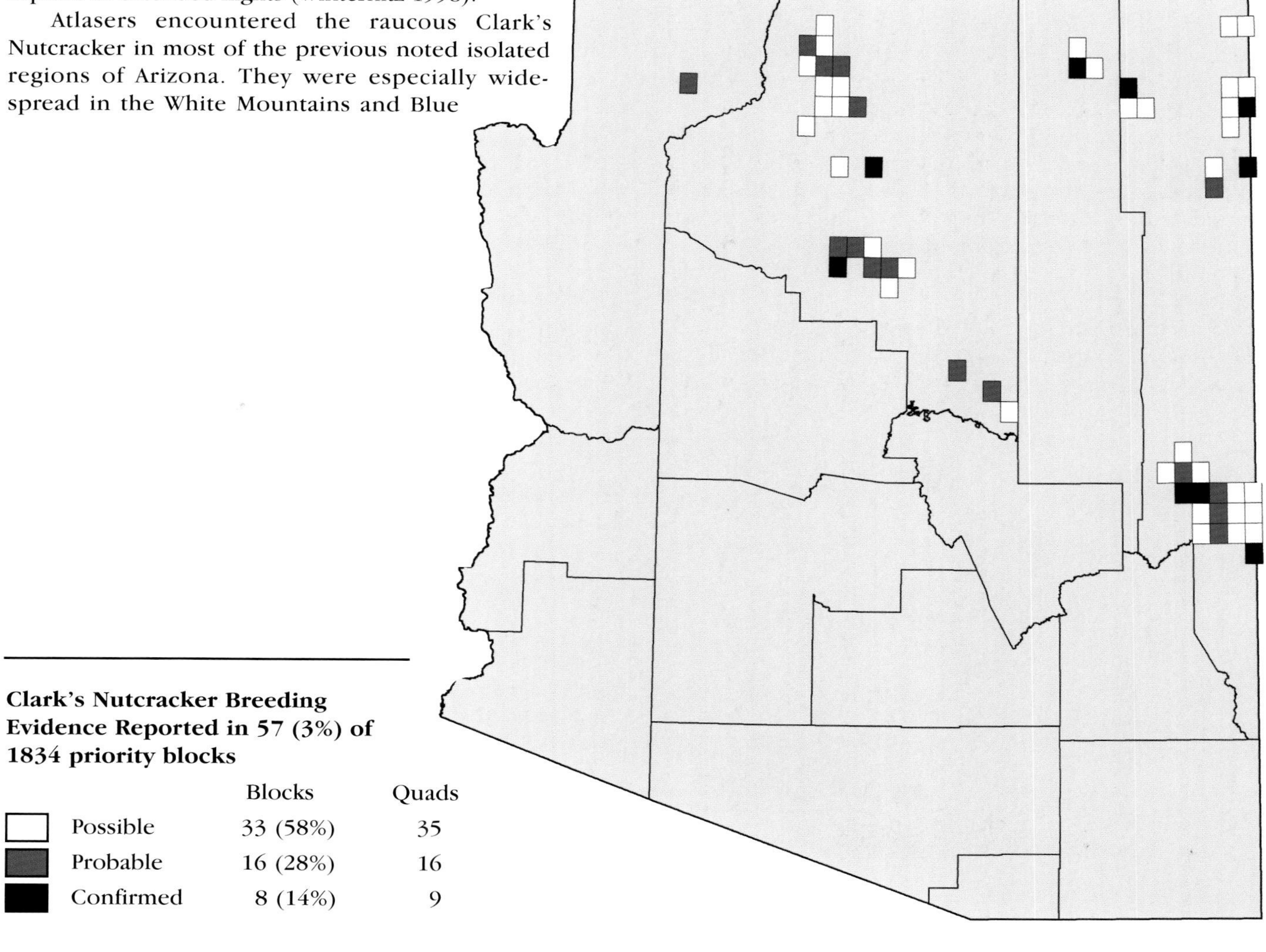

Clark's Nutcracker Breeding Evidence Reported in 57 (3%) of 1834 priority blocks

	Blocks	Quads
Possible	33 (58%)	35
Probable	16 (28%)	16
Confirmed	8 (14%)	9

Black-billed Magpie

by Troy E. Corman *Pica hudsonia*

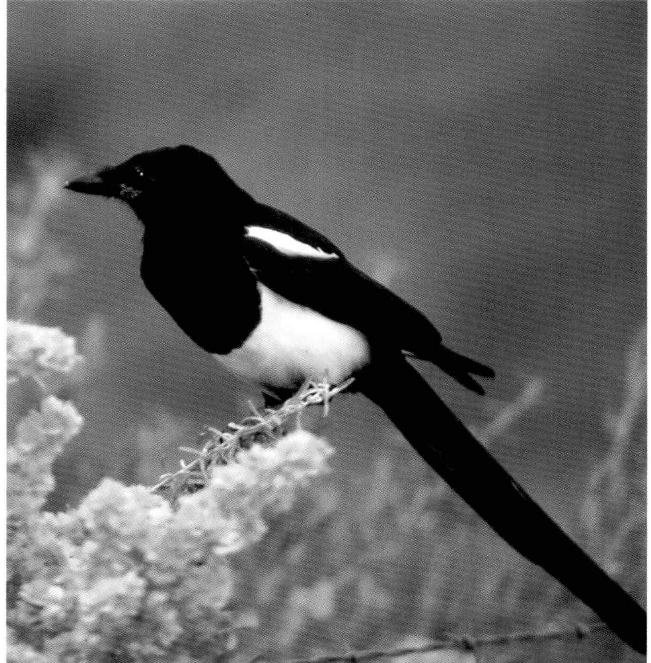
DAN FISCHER

With their large size, loud harsh calls, and bold black-and-white plumage, Black-billed Magpies rarely escape notice in the riparian edge habitats that they frequent in northeastern Arizona. Their large nests are unique, sturdy structures that can remain intact for several years and that are subsequently used for roosting and nesting by owls and hawks.

HABITAT

Throughout their range, Black-billed Magpies occupy semi-open landscapes from forest edges and linear riparian woodlands to scattered tree groves in agricultural and suburban settings. In Arizona, Black-billed Magpies are found primarily along perennial drainages, springs, and dry washes with stands of trees and taller shrubs. Fremont cottonwood woodlands are especially favored, but groves of exotic Russian olive and tamarisk are also locally frequented. Many of Arizona's occupied locations contain a mixture of cottonwoods and these nonnative trees. Black-billed Magpies often forage in nearby open sagebrush, fields, orchards, corrals, and around isolated habitations, but their long tails and slow flight require individuals to keep near cover to avoid raptors (Bent 1946). Thus, they typically avoid the widespread desert scrublands that surround many occupied localities in Arizona.

BREEDING

Owing to the local status of Black-billed Magpies in Arizona, there is little information available on the timing of nesting in the state. Pairs typically form while in nonbreeding flocks during fall and winter (Birkhead 1991). North of Arizona, nest building can begin on warm days in January and February, which are frequently interrupted by periods of colder and inclement weather (Trost 1999). In Utah and Colorado, eggs are laid between late March and early June, with some nests with young reported through the end of July (Bent 1946, Trost 1999). The only occupied nest reported during the atlas was on 5 May, with all other confirmed records obtained from the discovery of used nests and fledglings.

Black-billed Magpie nests are a unique domed structure made with a mass of sticks (often thorny) and typically include openings on both sides for access (Trost 1999). The males contribute more to the nest construction, at least to superstructure, while the female concentrates more on the mud nest bowl (which also helps hold the nest base together) and grass lining (Erpino 1968; Buitron 1988). Typically, their large nests take approximately six weeks to construct (Bent 1946). However, well-constructed nests can take as long as three months to finish and flimsy ones can be built in less than 1 week (Birkhead 1991). Black-billed Magpie nests are large bulky structures and thus need sturdy trees or larger shrubs for support. During atlas surveys, nests were located in the largest trees available in the region and included Fremont cottonwood, netleaf hackberry, boxelder, Russian olive, Gambel's oak, and tamarisk. The height of 12 nests measured by atlasers averaged 10.8 ft (3.3 m) with a range of 8–17.7 ft (2.4–5.4 m). Reuse of nests in subsequent years is quite variable (typically less than 25 percent) and it might not be the original pair that reuses the nest (Trost 1999).

There is a typical lag period between completion of the nest and the initiation of egg laying that can range from 7 to

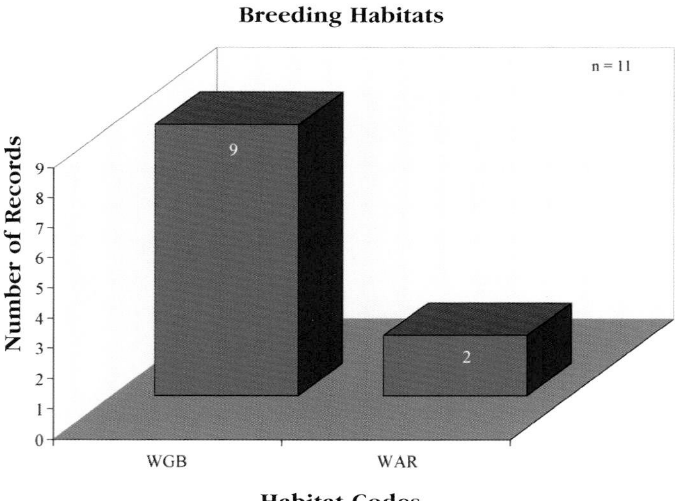

16 days (Erpino 1969). Black-billed Magpie clutches are typically large, containing 5–9 eggs, rarely up to 13 (Bent 1946; Reese and Kadlec 1985). The female incubated the eggs for approximately 18 days, but can range from 17 to 22 (Bent 1946). The male provides almost all food the female eats during this period (Mugaas and King 1981). Both parents feed the nestlings, which fledge in 24–30 days (Erpino 1968, Buitron 1988) and are dependent on their parent for food for up to 6–8 weeks following nest departure (Buitron 1988, Birkhead 1991). Black-billed Magpies only raise one brood per season, although the pair may renest two or three times if earlier attempts are unsuccessful (Trost 1999).

DISTRIBUTION AND STATUS

Because of their intolerance of extended periods of high heat or high humidity, Black-billed Magpies are restricted primarily to the interior of western North America (Hayworth and Weathers 1984). They are resident from southern Alaska, south through southwestern Canada, and range east to Minnesota, and south to northern Arizona and New Mexico.

Before 1885, Black-billed Magpies were considered to be common in parts of northeastern Arizona, where they were found nesting in 1873 as far south as Navajo Springs, which is just southeast of Navajo and the Puerco River (Phillips et al. 1964). Woodbury and Russell (1945) reported on the drastic decline of this species in Arizona to where it became only an infrequent visitor to the state (Phillips et al. 1964). However, since about 1970, they have once again become a common resident at Teec Nos Pos and southward along Chinle Wash to Many Farms (Monson and Phillips 1981). Black-billed Magpies have also been found to be an irregular fall and winter wandering species across the northern edge of Arizona from Mount Trumbull area and Fredonia east to Kayenta (Monson and Phillips 1981; C. LaRue, personal communication). Atlasers found Black-billed Magpies as a locally common nesting species in northern Apache County at elevations from approximately 4760 to 5800 ft (1451–1768 m). Most populations were along Chinle Wash and its tributaries from the Utah border south to Chinle. Tributaries included Laguna Creek to above Dennehotso, Walker Creek above Mexican Water, Hasbidito Creek, and Lukachukai Wash. They also continue to be rather common in the extreme northeast along Teec Nos Pos Wash, a tributary of the San Juan River. Recent breeding season reports from local residents in Fredonia were not verified by atlas efforts. However, riparian habitat along nearby Kanab Creek would appear ideal for this species.

Loss of cottonwoods along drainages due to fires, lowered water tables, and inappropriate grazing practices likely helps limit the breeding distribution of Black-billed Magpies in Arizona. Shooting may also be a local issue for the state's relatively small populations. Densities of these magpies are strongly influenced by adequate nesting substrate and food availability within an area (Trost 1999). Quite intelligent birds, they are very sensitive to nest disturbance, which often leads to reduced broods or abandonment. Several researchers have noted that when magpie populations are studied intensively over several years, the number of nesting pairs in the area frequently declines steadily (Trost 1999).

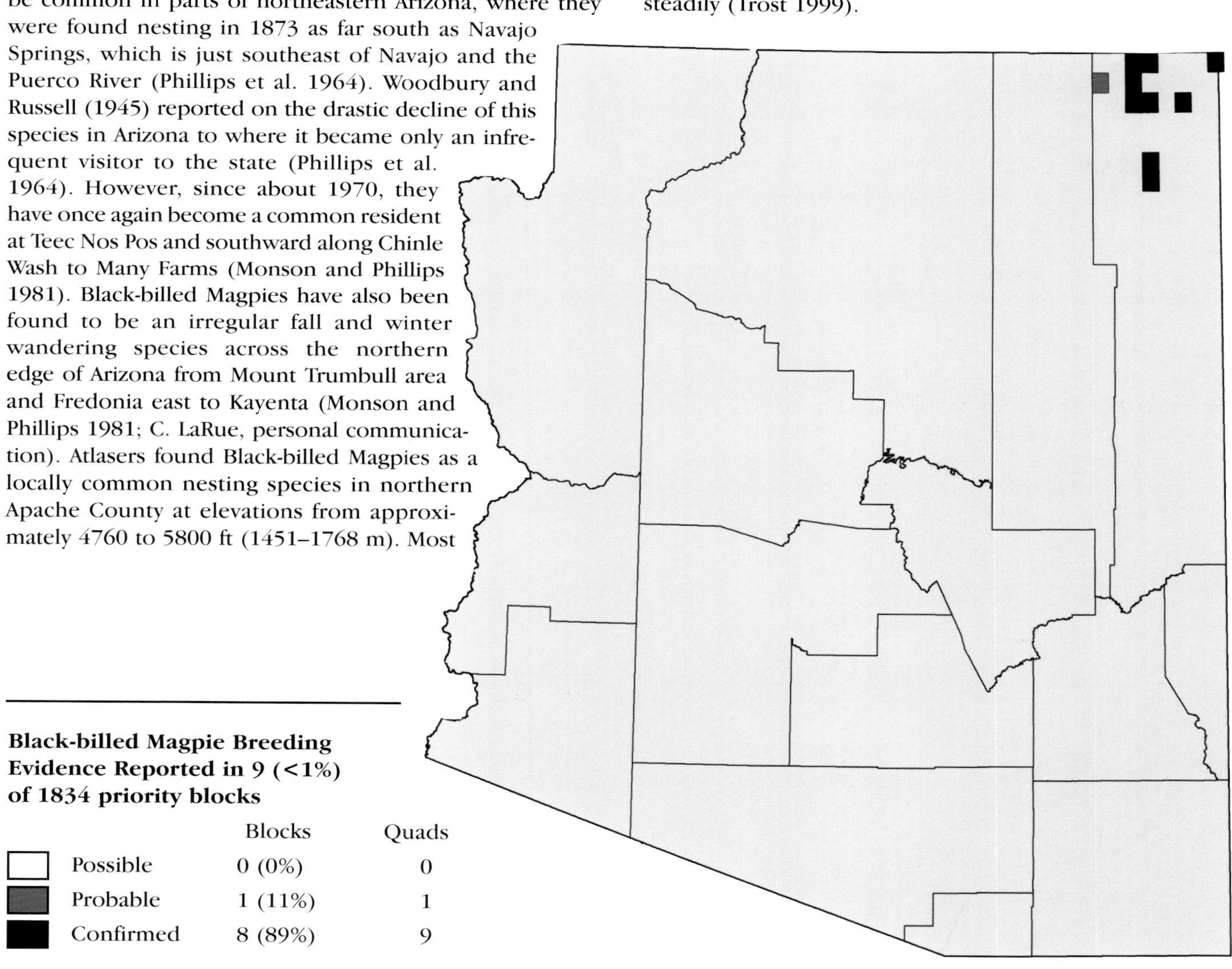

Black-billed Magpie Breeding Evidence Reported in 9 (<1%) of 1834 priority blocks

	Blocks	Quads
Possible	0 (0%)	0
Probable	1 (11%)	1
Confirmed	8 (89%)	9

American Crow

by Cathryn Wise-Gervais *Corvus brachyrhynchos*

American Crows are highly intelligent and opportunistic, and are both admired and hated for their resilience and resourcefulness. Tool use is well documented in this species, and adults are known to drop items such as clams or hard-shelled nuts from heights to open them. Although widespread in the East, they are restricted primarily to the northern highlands in Arizona.

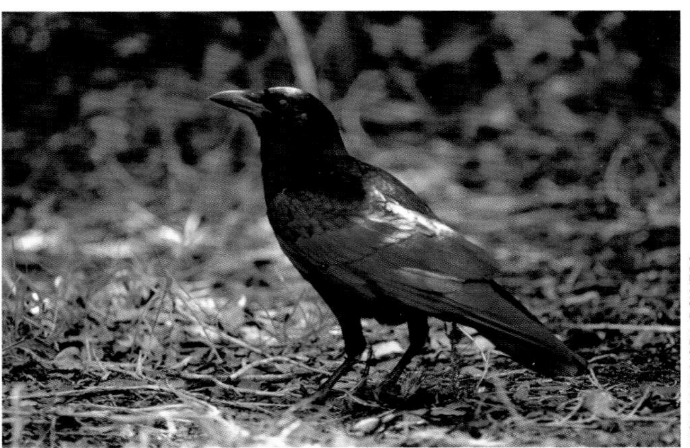
RICK AND NORA BOWERS

HABITAT

American Crows are one of North America's most widespread birds and occupy a wide range of habitats. In much of the country, American Crows are considered a common cropland pest, pilfering grain and other agricultural products. In Arizona however, this species is typically encountered during the breeding season only in open forests and woodland edges at mid- to higher elevations. This limited range is likely due to heat and aridity constraints, as the species does periodically occur in some lowland agricultural areas during the winter months. American Crows prefer settings that provide open areas for ground foraging coupled with scattered surrounding trees for nesting and cover (Verbeek and Caffrey 2002). Atlasers reported American Crows in twenty different habitat types. The greatest number of individual records (38 percent) were in forests containing ponderosa pine, from almost pure stands to those with a Gambel's oak or pinyon pine–juniper association (n = 91). Atlasers also discovered American Crows nesting very locally in pinyon pine–juniper woodlands. However, there were only fourteen atlas records reported within this widespread vegetative community, and this finding strongly suggests that it is not a preferred habitat within the state. Fewer records were noted in high-elevation mixed-conifer forests and the adjacent cool, forested drainages. American Crows were found very locally inhabiting riparian woodlands with tall stands of cottonwood.

Breeding Habitats

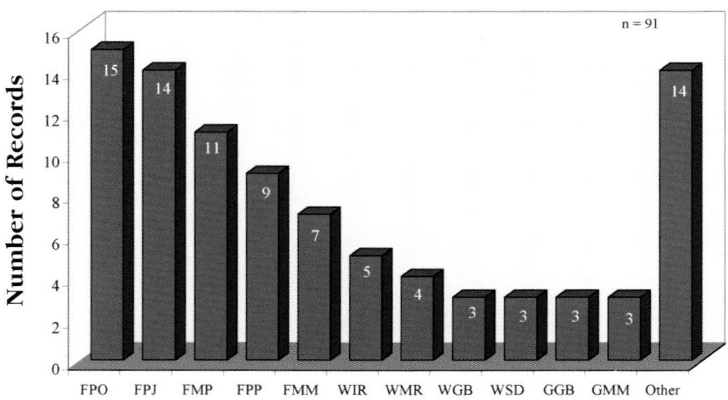

Habitat Codes

BREEDING

American Crows often roost communally during much of the year but are typically found in pairs or small family units during the breeding season. However, in some regions of their range, they maintain territories throughout the year. Pairs are thought to be monogamous and form bonds that may last until death (Verbeek and Caffrey 2002). Relatively few active American Crow nests were discovered during atlas surveys. Atlasers reported adults carrying nesting material from 21 March to 10 May and noted the first fledgling on 23 May. By backdating the earliest fledgling observation, observers estimated that egg laying likely occurred by late March. Atlasers discovered a late occupied nest on 11 June, likely indicating a renesting attempt. Observers noted adults feeding dependent young through 13 July and found the latest fledglings on 30 July. Verbeek and Caffrey (2002) reported that throughout their range, the general nesting period of American Crows extends from mid-March to mid-June. This time frame is very similar to the limited data collected by atlasers in Arizona.

American Crows typically place their well-hidden nests close to the tree trunk, and usually in the top one-third to one-quarter of the tree (Chamberlain-Auger et al. 1990). Nest heights are often related to tree heights and vary greatly across their range. In Arizona, these crows frequently nest in ponderosa pine with nests also noted in pinyon pine, juniper, cottonwood, and possibly Russian olive. Atlasers measured only one nest, and this was at 32.1 ft (9.8 m) in a juniper.

American Crow pairs construct the nest together, although the female handles much of the final lining of the nest bowl (Verbeek and Caffrey 2002). Most clutches consist of 4–5 eggs (range 3–7); only the female incubates these (Verbeek and Caffrey 2002). Researchers disagree on the exact length of incubation, but a general figure of 16–19 days seems likely and corresponds closely to other North American species of crows (Verbeek and Caffrey 2002). The male and one or more nest helpers (when present) may feed the female throughout incubation (Kilham 1989, Caffrey 1992). Eggs hatch asynchronously over 2–3 days; both parents and helpers feed the young. Young fledge at 28–35 days of age but continue to be fed by the adults for an additional 2–3 weeks (Verbeek and Caffrey 2002).

Breeding Phenology

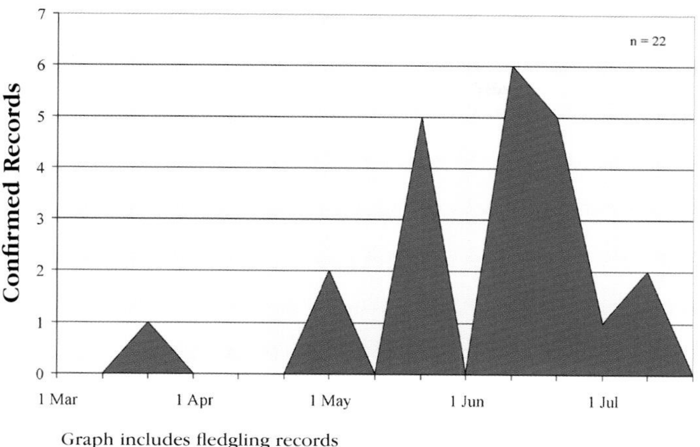

Graph includes fledgling records

DISTRIBUTION AND STATUS

American Crows occur throughout most of the central and eastern United States north to central Canada. In the West, they breed from British Columbia south through California to adjacent northern Baja California and in the interior south to northern Nevada, northern Utah, central Arizona, and south-central New Mexico. The species is notably absent from much of the arid southwestern desert regions during the breeding season. American Crows probably reach their highest breeding densities in the northeastern United States, and numbers have probably increased significantly since European settlement due to the clearing of forests and spread of farmlands.

In Arizona, American Crows are far outnumbered by their larger and more heat-tolerant relative, the Common Raven. Still, atlasers encountered them fairly regularly within the range previously described by Monson and Phillips (1981) at elevations primarily from 5200 to 9300 ft (1585–2835 m). Atlasers encountered American Crows in open regions of the Mogollon Plateau, including the White Mountains south into the lower Blue and San Francisco River drainages to Clifton. They were found locally in the adjacent San Carlos Apache tribal lands and undoubtedly also continue to nest in the unsurveyed White Mountain Apache tribal lands as atlas records nearly encircle this reservation. Their status in the lower Salt River drainage in Gila County remains unclear. Individuals and seemingly paired birds were noted in mid-July in lower riparian woodlands near the Roosevelt Lake inflows of both the Salt River and Tonto Creek.

American Crows were most widespread in the Mormon Lake-Flagstaff region and were found breeding north sparingly to the South Rim of the Grand Canyon and west to north of Seligman. They were also found nesting west to the Santa Maria Mountains, and it is likely that birds located near Prescott were nesting.

On Navajo and Hopi tribal lands, Jacobs (1986) considered American Crows locally common residents in the Chuska Mountains south to the Defiance Plateau. Atlasers also confirmed them breeding north to the adjacent Lukachukai Mountains and possibly west to Many Farms and Chinle areas in cottonwood groves. American Crows were noted in the Ganado area as well, and a pair of birds was found in Keams Canyon.

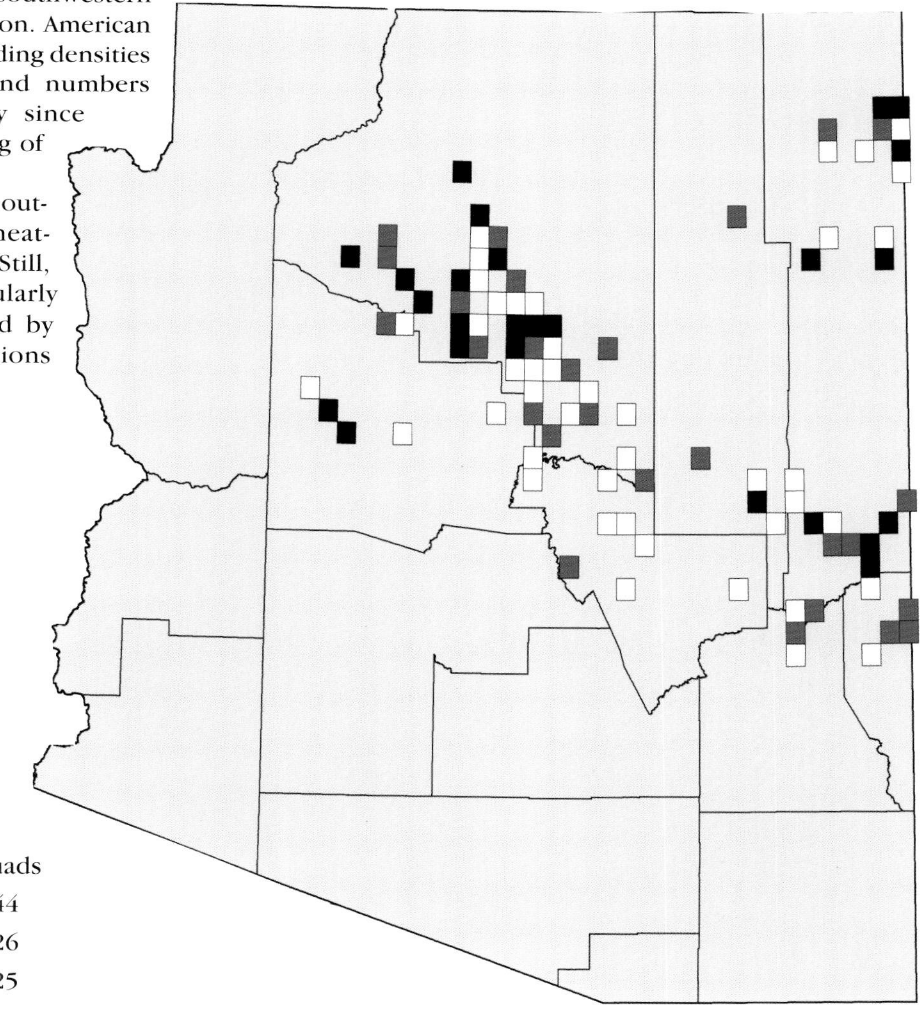

American Crow Breeding Evidence Reported in 89 (5%) of 1834 priority blocks

	Blocks	Quads
Possible	39 (44%)	44
Probable	25 (28%)	26
Confirmed	25 (28%)	25

Chihuahuan Raven

by Cathryn Wise-Gervais *Corvus cryptoleucus*

Intermediate in size between the Common Raven and American Crow, this gregarious species is commonly encountered in the Southwest's windswept grasslands and adjacent desert flats. Chihuahuan Ravens can be very challenging to identify in the field, but are best distinguished by snowy white base feathers on the neck, visible under windy conditions or while they are preening.

DAN FISCHER

HABITAT

Chihuahuan Ravens are more selective in their habitat choices than the widespread Common Raven, and are typically found in or near various grasslands and desert flats. This is a bird of open flat to gently rolling country, and they typically avoid mountains, canyons, and heavily forested regions. Atlasers reported Chihuahuan Ravens in fourteen habitat types, but 46 percent of the potential breeding records obtained were in semiarid grasslands (n = 137). This vegetative community is often characterized by mixed grasses, and scattered areas of mesquite, yucca, cholla, and prickly pear. Observers also reported 40 percent of records in the transition zone of this grassland with the Chihuahuan and Sonoran deserts. These areas typically contain soaptree yucca, velvet mesquite, creosote, and various species of acacia. Atlasers occasionally reported Chihuahuan Ravens in habitats adjacent to grasslands, including open cottonwood-willow riparian woodlands, dry desert washes, pastures, orchards, agricultural lands, and open foothill stringers of evergreen oaks.

BREEDING

Although Chihuahuan Ravens do not migrate in traditional sense, they do form large foraging congregations that roam locally from fall to early spring. Some individuals remain on their breeding grounds year-round, but those that leave typically return by March. Throughout much of their range, pairs form from March to early May (Aldous 1942), and at this time exhibit courtship behaviors such as billing, head-bobbing and fluffing neck feathers to reveal the white base (Bednarz and Raitt 2002). Many prior observers in Arizona and New Mexico noted that Chihuahuan Ravens typically lay eggs in May, with nestlings in June, and fledging occurring in July to early August (Bendire 1895; Aldous 1942; Bent 1946; Brandt 1951). Atlas data reveal that a proportion of Chihuahuan ravens initiate nesting activity slightly earlier in the spring and have a breeding season that lasts later in the fall than previously reported. Atlasers noted paired birds as early as 8 February and 1 March and observed nest building as early as 5 April. Numerous occupied nests were reported through late April, and many of these likely contained eggs. Atlasers first verified a nest with eggs on 1 May, but a nest with young noted on 13 May suggests that eggs were laid by mid- to late April. Atlas data reveal a breeding activity peak in late April to late May, and a lesser peak in mid-July (n = 68). Some late nesting activity continues into early fall in Arizona as atlasers discovered a Chihuahuan Raven nest with young on 3 September.

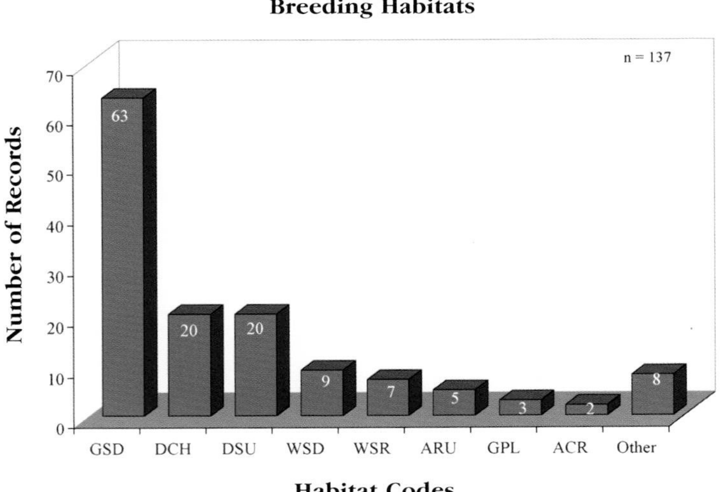

Chihuahuan Ravens nest in a wide array of both natural and artificial substrates in Arizona. Nesting substrates frequently include mesquite, soaptree yucca, cottonwood, windmills, power poles, and locally behind highway billboards. Nests are often placed in isolated trees or structures with a commanding view of their vast surroundings. These gregarious birds will sometimes nest in small clusters of 3–5 nests, separated from each other by several hundred meters or more (Bednarz and Raitt 2002). Nest heights range from 4.9 to 65.6 ft (1.5–20 m), but most are low between 6.6 and 13.1 ft (2–4 m) above ground (Bendire 1895; Aldous 1942; Bent 1946; Haydock and Ligon 1986). Atlasers measured only two Chihuahuan Raven nests, one each in Fremont cottonwood and in Goodding willow, at 26.2 ft and 17 ft (8 and 5.2 m), respectively. Early observations suggest that only the female constructs the nest, but more study is

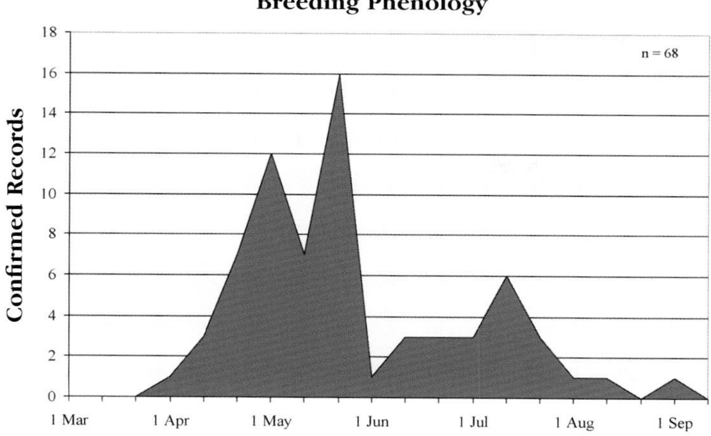

needed (Bednarz and Raitt 2002). Nest structures often comprise thorny sticks, such as from mesquite, and have a loose, messy appearance. Many nests are reused requiring only minor repairs (Bednarz and Raitt 2002).

Chihuahuan Ravens typically lay 5–6 eggs, but clutches can range from 3 to 8 (Mishaga 1974; Haydock and Ligon 1986). It is presumed that only the female incubates from 18 to 21 days, while the males perch nearby (Haydock and Ligon 1986; Bednarz and Raitt 2002). Nestlings are brooded and fed by both parents, and fledging typically occurs at 37–40 days of age (Haydock and Ligon 1986). It is unknown how long the young continue to be fed following nest departure, but they can remain in the area from 5 to 20 days (Bednarz and Raitt 2002). Most evidence suggests that only one brood is produced per year, but renesting is likely if earlier efforts fail.

DISTRIBUTION AND STATUS

The distribution of Chihuahuan Raven is poorly understood, primarily due to the difficulty in field identification where their range overlaps with Common Ravens. They breed in southeastern Colorado and southwestern Nebraska, south through west and south Texas to central Mexico. To the west they nest to south-central Arizona and northern Sonora. In Arizona, Chihuahuan Ravens were previously documented nesting in the mesquite-soaptree yucca grasslands of southeastern Arizona north to Safford and near Oracle westward possibly into the open, brushy Sonoran desertscrub of Tohono O'odham tribal lands (Phillips et al 1964).

During the atlas period, observers commonly reported Chihuahuan Ravens throughout most of their historic range in Arizona and helped define some distributional limits. They were discovered nesting on priority blocks from elevations of approximately 1880–5300 ft (573–1615 m). Observers obtained notable confirmed breeding records at locations marking the northern and western edges of this species' range. The westernmost record was in the upper Hickiwan Valley northwest of Hickiwan on Tohono O'odham tribal lands, where observers noted several pairs and used nests in mesquite. Atlasers extended the Chihuahuan Ravens nesting distribution slightly to the north into the brushy grasslands of San Carlos Apache tribal lands between the Gila and Natanes ranges.

Chihuahuan Ravens are likely the least-studied corvid in North America, and this species deserves more attention (Bednarz and Raitt 2002). Although the sample size of Breeding Bird Survey route data in Arizona is too small to determine population trends, atlas data suggest some local declines of these ravens in semiarid grasslands of eastern Pima and adjacent Pinal counties.

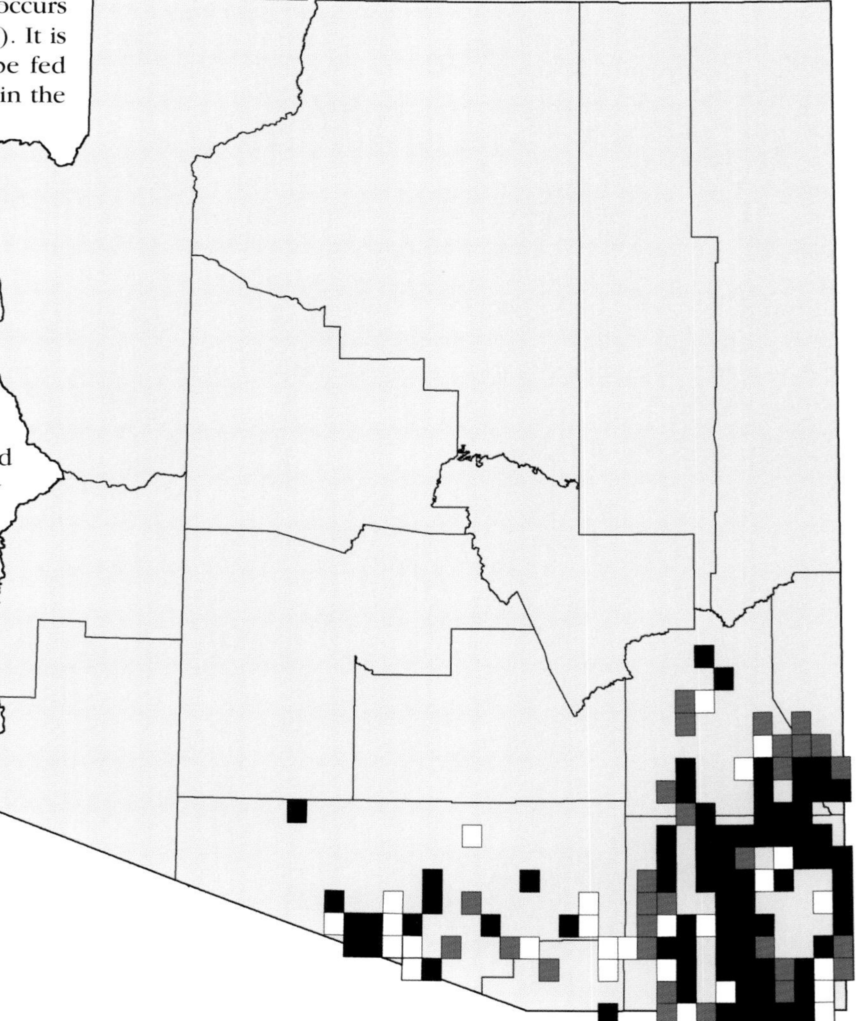

Chihuahuan Raven Breeding Evidence Reported in 127 (7%) of 1834 priority blocks

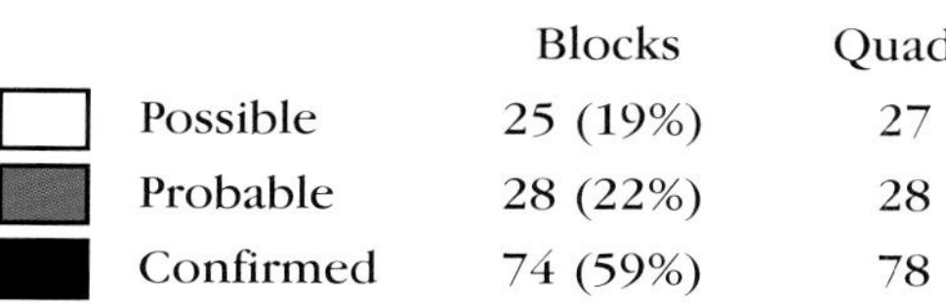

	Blocks	Quads
Possible	25 (19%)	27
Probable	28 (22%)	28
Confirmed	74 (59%)	78

Common Raven

by Cathryn Wise-Gervais *Corvus corvax*

Creator, messenger, trickster, thief: few birds are steeped in as much myth and mystery as the highly intelligent Common Raven. The bird's more favorable traits include a vast repertoire of calls and sounds and highly acrobatic flight. On the dark side, Common Ravens have a well-deserved reputation for eating gruesome and unappealing things.

RICHARD DITCH

HABITAT

Common Ravens are extremely adaptable and are able to carve out an existence even in the most inhospitable terrain. Relatively tall substrates for nesting and food availability appear to be their most limiting factors. They are found in nearly every habitat present within their extensive range, from tundra to desert. Common Ravens find Arizona's many cliffs and canyons much to their liking, and atlasers reported Common Ravens in thirty-six habitat types, including deserts, grasslands, and open woodlands. It was not surprising that observers reported most records from Sonoran desertscrub and in pinyon pine–juniper woodlands (23 percent and 18 percent of records, respectively; n = 1456), inasmuch as these are the two most widespread vegetative communities in the state. It is likely that these birds are simply making use of available terrain in these cases and are not selecting these areas for specific vegetation characteristics. Common Ravens generally avoided extensive dense forests and instead selected nearby open areas. Although the majority of records were obtained in more sparsely vegetated areas, observers did report Common Ravens in Mexican evergreen oak woodlands and in open ponderosa pine forests, as well as in diverse riparian areas statewide. Common Ravens were also regularly encountered in many rural, agricultural, and urban settings.

Breeding Habitats

BREEDING

Common Ravens are year-round residents throughout their North American range, and typically begin courtship displays and territory defense in late winter. Although Common Ravens are thought to mate for life, there are no data to back this statement, and extra-pair copulations are common (Boarman and Heinrich 1999). Atlasers reported paired birds as early as 17 February and observed Common Ravens nest building on 4 March. Observers reported the earliest nest with young on 9 March, indicating egg laying by early to mid-February. Atlas data suggest that Arizona's peak breeding period is from mid-May to mid-June. This corresponds with breeding dates reported range wide for nests with eggs from mid-February to mid-June and nests with young from mid-March to mid-July (Boarman and Heinrich 1999). Atlasers reported the latest occupied nest on 26 July and last observed adults with dependent fledglings on 9 August.

Given the Common Raven's versatility, it is not surprising that this species will nest in a variety of both natural and artificial substrates. Common Arizona substrates include cliff ledges, rock outcrops, canyon walls, transmission towers, cross beams of power poles, windmills, under bridges, and in many species of trees. Several nests were also found in saguaros, but these large cacti are surprisingly rarely used given their relatively widespread occurrence. Atlasers took at least partial measurements at sixty-nine nests, with thirty-eight in twelve species of tree or tall shrub, twenty-one on cliffs or rocky ledges, and eight on human-built structures. Nest heights ranged from 11.2 to 59 ft (3.4–18 m) with a median of 19.7 ft (6 m). Rangewide, nest heights vary considerably and are probably related to the height of available nest substrates. Common Ravens tend to nest toward the top of trees, but typically under the canopy (Boarman and Heinrich 1999).

Female Common Ravens are thought to do most of the actual nest building, but the male will bring nest materials and may help with the base construction (Harlow 1922, Jones 1935, Stiehl 1985). Common Raven nests are exceedingly messy and can contain a good deal of trash and debris. Adults and young regularly defecate off the nest rim, so nests are often smelly and heavily whitewashed. Typically clutches

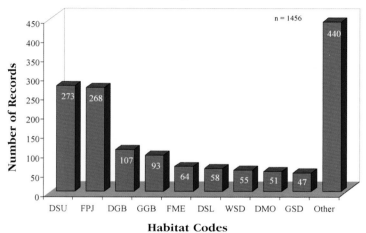

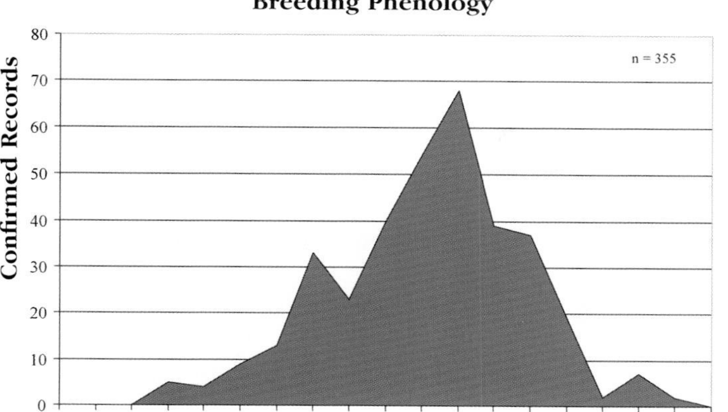

consist of 4–6 eggs (range 3–7) and are incubated by the female for 20–25 days (Harlow 1922; Stiehl 1985). Both parents feed the noisy nestlings, which have been described as "grotesque gargoyles" when young (Tyrrell 1945). Fledging occurs at 4–7 weeks of age, and the young are capable of short flights when they leave the nest. However, they continue to rely on their parents for food from 1 to 6 weeks following nest departure (Boarman and Heinrich 1999).

DISTRIBUTION AND STATUS

Common Ravens occur throughout Canada and Alaska, but in the eastern United States they are found only in the northern states and down the Appalachian Mountains to northern Georgia. The birds are common in the West, from the Rocky Mountain region west to the Pacific Coast and south through central Texas and Mexico to north Nicaragua.

Most literature describes the ubiquitous Common Raven as a fairly common to abundant resident throughout much of Arizona. Atlasers documented them breeding on survey blocks at elevations from approximately 160 to 9500 ft (49–2896 m). They were regularly encountered over much of the northern half of the state and fairly widespread in southeastern Arizona. Atlasers missed Common Ravens on many of southeastern Arizona's open grassland and desertscrub blocks, which were often occupied by the smaller Chihuahuan Ravens.

Previous observers noted that Common Ravens were sparsely distributed along the lower Colorado River valley (Phillips et al. 1964; Rosenberg et al. 1991). Atlas data support these earlier observations, with few records south of Lake Havasu. In the arid low deserts to the east of this river valley, Common Ravens were primarily limited to the higher desert mountain ranges. They were also sparsely distributed within the adjacent Gila River valley upstream to its confluence with the Salt River near Phoenix. Common Ravens have only recently begun to nest in the greater Phoenix area, with local pairs selecting to nest on tall building ledges, on billboard structures, and nearby cliffs. These adaptable urban populations are expected to increase.

Common Raven populations appear to be stable or locally increasing in Arizona. These opportunistic birds have greatly benefited from the introduction of transmission towers and power poles in many flat, treeless regions of the state. With their playful squabbles, aerial acrobatics, and delightfully varied calls, these large, intelligent birds will undoubtedly continue to grace the many varied landscapes of Arizona.

Common Raven Breeding Evidence Reported in 1442 (79%) of 1834 priority blocks

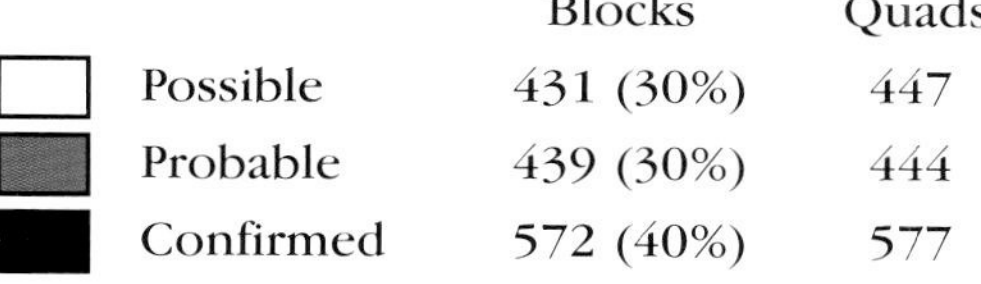

	Blocks	Quads
Possible	431 (30%)	447
Probable	439 (30%)	444
Confirmed	572 (40%)	577

Horned Lark

by Cathryn Wise-Gervais *Eremophila alpestris*

The handsome Horned Lark thrives in some of Arizona's bleakest landscapes. Named for its striking horn-shaped head feathers, this hardy species captivates observers with its tinkling song and ability to blend seamlessly into its surroundings.

JIM BURNS

HABITAT

Horned Larks are habitat generalists seeking little more than open, barren ground on flat to gently rolling terrain. In Arizona, this requirement is most often met in heavily grazed grasslands or in agricultural areas, but atlasers reported Horned Larks in a total of nineteen habitat types. Twenty-four percent of potential breeding records for Horned Larks were in northern Arizona's cold-temperate desertscrub, characterized by low-growing scattered shrubs such as sagebrush, blackbrush, and shadscale (n = 635). Arizona's varied grasslands accounted for 45 percent of all atlas records, from cold-temperate (18 percent) and Plains (15 percent) grasslands in the north to semiarid grasslands (10 percent) in the south. The remaining grassland records were primarily from montane grasslands and larger subalpine meadows. Following wet winters, Horned Larks were also encountered nesting in a few areas of western Arizona's sparsely vegetated lower Sonoran and Mojave desertscrub.

Atlasers also reported 17 percent of Horned Lark records from rural and agricultural settings that included pastures and fallow, barren, or stubble fields. This also included high-use areas for range livestock such as near artificial water sources (e.g., windmills, earthen tanks, runoff catchments). In fact, Horned Larks are considered one of the most abundant species using heavily grazed areas (Kantrud and Kologiski 1983; Bock and Webb 1984). They will not tolerate brushy areas and commonly move from barren fields as soon as vegetation sprouts and matures in late spring and summer (Beason 1970).

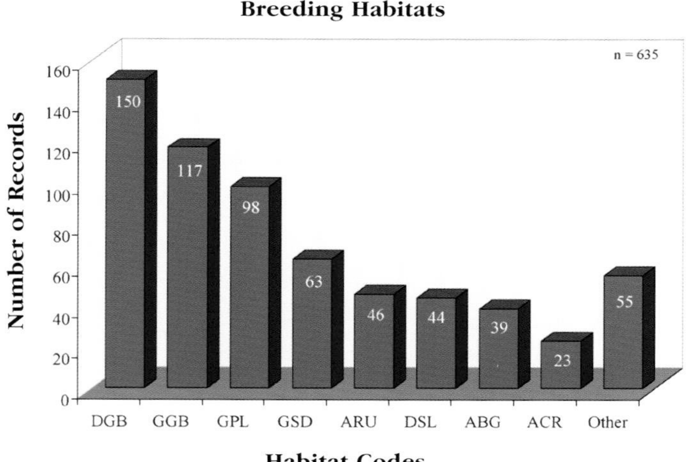

BREEDING

Various Horned Lark populations in Arizona are resident, while others are migratory and move into the lowlands to winter. Resident populations can begin courtship and pairing in late winter with some nesting beginning in February. Atlasers first reported Horned Larks nest building on 5 April, but it is likely the birds started nesting earlier in some southern Arizona populations prior to most atlas surveys. In fact, surveyors reported a fledgling Horned Lark on 9 April, indicating that in this instance, the eggs were laid by at least mid-March. Nesting activity begins several weeks to a month later at higher elevations and more northern localities in Arizona. Statewide atlas data suggest that the peak period of Horned Lark breeding activity is from late May to late June (n = 83). Some nesting activities continue through the summer however, with observers reporting adults feeding fledglings on 23 July and performing distraction display on 7 August. The latest fledgling was noted on 3 September. These records suggest a protracted breeding season, during which the birds typically raise two and sometimes three broods (Beason 1995).

Researchers believe that female Horned Larks select the ground nest site and build the nest without male assistance (Beason 1970). Despite the open conditions that Horned Larks prefer, their nests are extremely difficult to find. Not only are the small structures expertly concealed, but the adults also approach the nest area very cautiously. When approaching the nest, these birds typically drop to the ground over 50 ft (15.2 m) from the nest and walk the remainder of the way (Beason 1970). As a result of this stealthy behavior, atlasers found only seven Horned Lark nests and confirmed most birds by observing adults carrying nest materials or food, or by finding dependent fledglings. Of the nests reported, all were on the ground under various cover, including snakeweed, cholla, globemallow, unidentified grasses and forbs, a dead creosote bush, and under a mound of dried cow dung.

Horned Lark clutch size varies widely but is usually between 2 and 5 eggs (Beason 1995). The female incubates

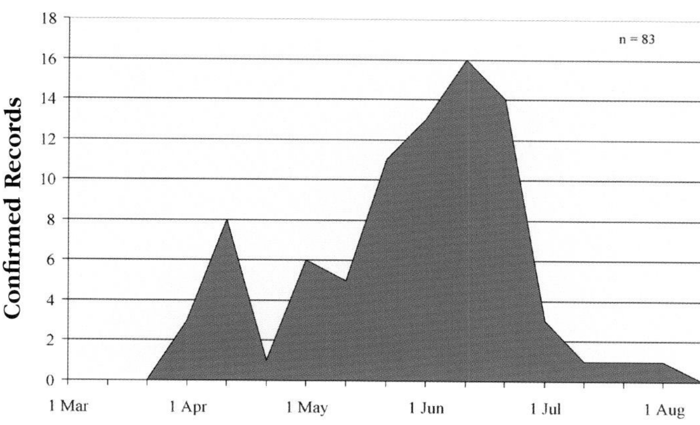

these for 11–13 days, and both parents assist with feeding the young (Beason 1995). The nestlings develop the ability to walk and run before they are able to fly and leave the nest at approximately 10 days of age. They are not independent of parents or capable of sustain flight until they are 3–4 weeks old, however (Cannings and Threlfall 1981).

Distribution

Horned Larks are a widespread species not only in North America but also in Eurasia as far as Siberia. In North America, they breed in most flat open, barren landscapes from Arctic tundra in Alaska and Canada south primarily to central Mexico. Many subspecies and geographic variations in plumage color occur rangewide, enabling the birds to match the soil of areas it inhabits. In Arizona alone, Phillips et al. (1964) described seven races statewide, with three of them nesting.

Horned Larks breed throughout Arizona where appropriate habitats exist, but are primarily absent in all brushy and wooded regions (Phillips et al. 1964). They inhabit a wide range of elevations, and atlasers noted them on priority blocks from approximately 90 to 9200 ft (27–2804 m). Atlasers also reported the birds statewide, but found them also predictably absent in rugged regions with relatively high topographic relief. In southeastern Arizona, Horned Larks were encountered throughout the Sulphur Springs, San Bernardino, and upper San Simon valleys, and were also commonly found breeding in the Sonoita and San Rafael grasslands. Atlasers found that breeding Horned Larks were primarily absent in the San Pedro River and Altar valleys, however. In the desert regions to the west, Horned Larks were encountered most regularly in extensive agricultural areas, but were also found locally and irregularly in desert creosote flats.

Atlasers reported most Horned Lark records in Northern Arizona, especially north of the forested Mogollon Rim region. In fact, this bird was one of the few species besides the Common Raven and Rock Wren that atlasers could reliably encounter in the most barren areas of Navajo and Hopi tribal lands or in the rangelands of the Little Colorado River watershed. They were also commonly encountered in the grasslands of Chino Valley, Coconino Plateau north of Seligman, and in the Arizona Strip region.

Undoubtedly, Horned Larks in Arizona have benefited from the clearing of desert areas for agriculture. These opportunistic birds are also one of the very few species benefiting from the widespread heavy grazing of grasslands within the state.

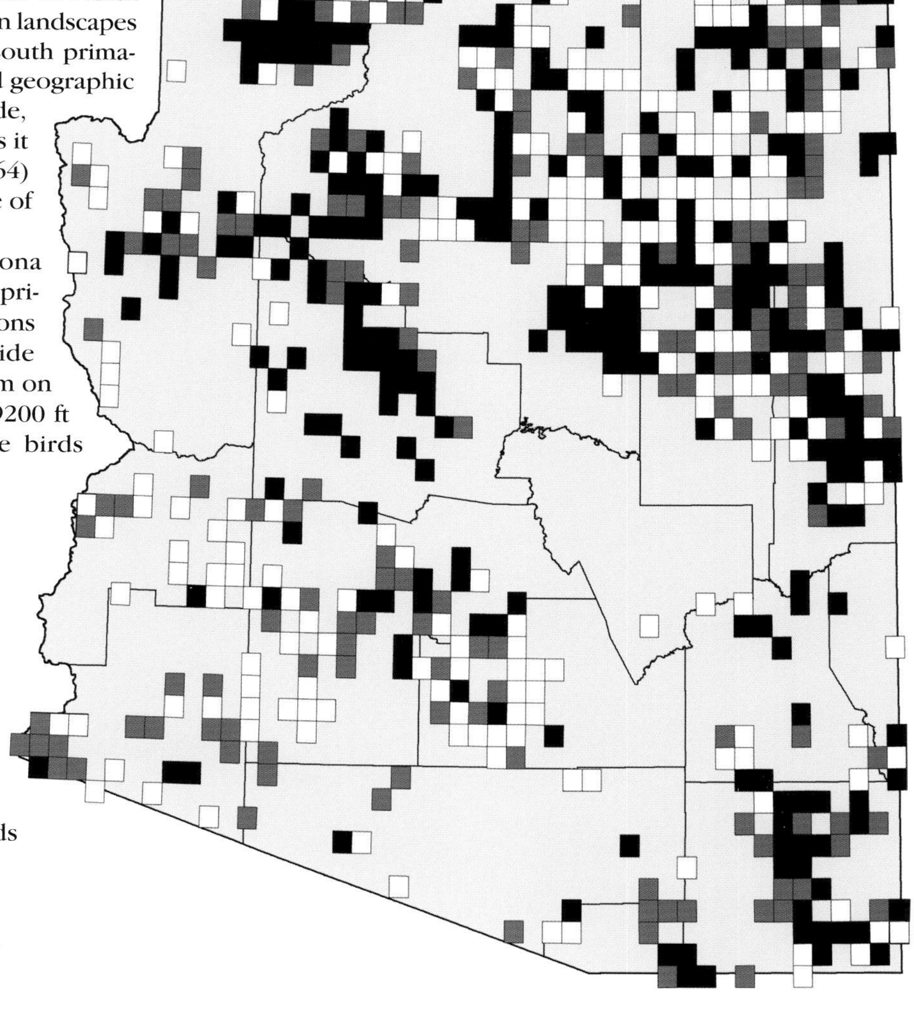

Horned Lark Breeding Evidence Reported in 641 (35%) of 1834 priority blocks

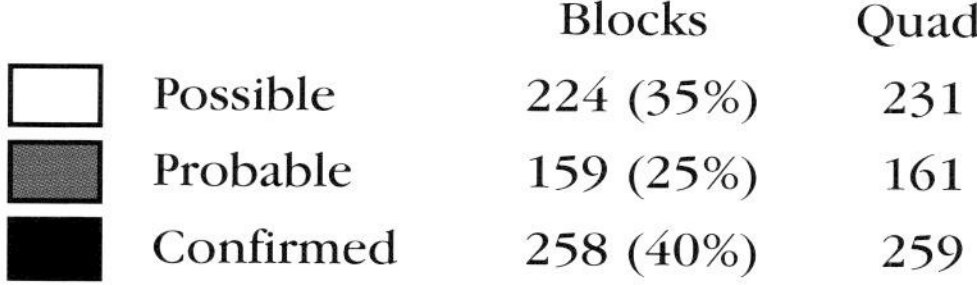

	Blocks	Quads
Possible	224 (35%)	231
Probable	159 (25%)	161
Confirmed	258 (40%)	259

Purple Martin

by Troy E. Corman *Progne subis*

Extremely popular and almost entirely dependent on humans for nesting structures throughout the East, Purple Martins nest almost exclusively in natural settings in the West. Arizona has two separate populations that are distinctly different in their choice of nesting habitats and breeding phenology, and there is still much to learn about these large, fascinating swallows.

HABITAT

There are two subspecies of Purple Martins in Arizona, with each breeding in quite different habitats and elevations. Atlasers reported the *hesperia* subspecies most frequently in more densely vegetated Sonoran desertscrub habitats where large saguaros with many cavities are in abundance. Nearly 49 percent of all atlas records were found in this vegetative community ($n = 125$). This includes the outskirts of Tucson, where the housing is sparse and the native desert habitat is largely intact. At higher elevations, populations of *arboricola* are found locally in forests with ponderosa pine (22 percent of all records). These forests ranged from nearly pure stands to those with a Gambel's oak, Madrean evergreen oak, or pinyon pine–juniper association. They were also found sparingly in mixed conifer with ponderosa pine, Douglas fir, and quaking aspen. In all habitats, they frequently take advantage of open water and are often found foraging over and drinking at rivers, lakes, ponds, and earthen stock tanks, often at considerable distances from nesting sites.

BREEDING

A few Purple Martins begin to arrive in Arizona in mid- to late April, casually as early as March, but do not become common in their breeding areas until after mid-May. At both high and low elevations, they waste little time in investigating potential nest sites with individuals observed entering cavities by 1 May. The timing of egg laying in Arizona is difficult to surmise owing to their lofty cavity abodes. There is also some evidence to suggest that higher-elevation nesting activity may begin three or more weeks earlier than in the desert. Montane forest populations had occupied nests by late May and nests with young by 7 July. This date would indicate egg laying no later than mid-June and likely earlier, inasmuch as an adult was observed feeding a recently fledged young on 4 July. The latest nest with young in the higher mountain populations was reported on 20 July.

In comparison, Stutchbury (1991) noted that desert-nesting Purple Martins did not lay eggs until early to mid-July near Tucson. She suggested that this was due to timing of the late summer monsoon season with its subsequent increase of flying insect prey. Most reports from atlasers of desert Purple Martins carrying nesting material and occupied nests from mid-May to late June likely pertained to potential nest investigations and multiple-cavity-guarding behavior instead of true nesting. However, some desert-nesting Purple Martins may periodically nest earlier when insect populations are high following wet winters and springs. In the desert, atlasers did not discover nests with young until 30 July, with the latest on 21 August. Purple Martins depart Arizona by late September or early October, casually through late October.

In Arizona, Purple Martins typically nest in cavities previously excavated by woodpeckers. However, locally they may also nest on cliffs. In 1996, more than 100 pairs were reported nesting in crevices of a sandstone cliff near Flagstaff (Brown 1997). Montane populations in Arizona frequently nest in pine cavities, especially in ponderosa snags, and less frequently in quaking aspen. The mean height of the six ponderosa pine nesting cavities measured by atlas field crews was 51.8 ft (15.8 m), with a range of 34.4–70.2 ft (10.5–21.4 m). Sonoran Desert populations in Arizona nest almost exclusively in large, living saguaros. Their nests average significantly lower than

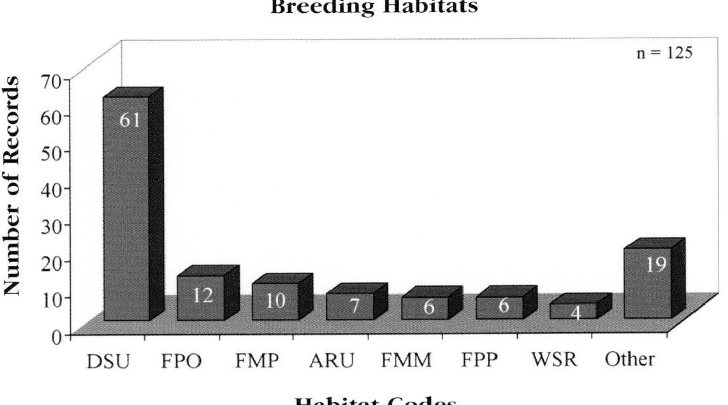

Breeding Phenology

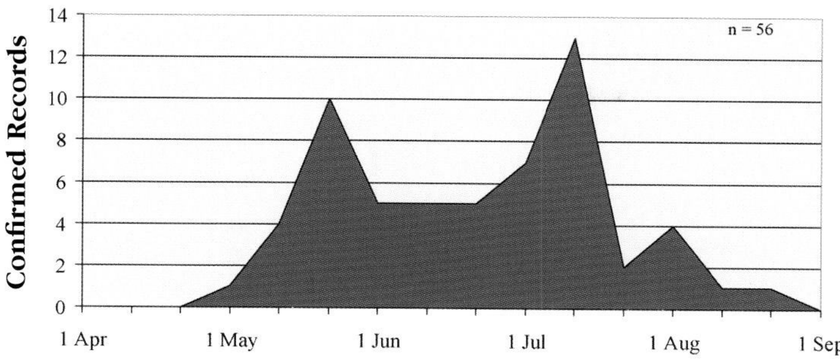

montane populations. Stutchbury (1991) measured 49 nests in saguaros with a mean nest height of 24.3 ft (7.4 m) and a range of 15.4–34.1 ft (4.7–10.4 m).

Female Purple Martins incubate the 3–5 eggs for 15–18 days, and both parents feed the nestlings for approximately 28–29 days (Allen and Nice 1952; Brown 1997). Typically only one brood is raised per year, but two broods have been documented (Brown 1997).

DISTRIBUTION AND STATUS

Purple Martins breed throughout eastern North America from southern Canada south through the Gulf States. West of the Rockies, populations are much more scattered, nesting very locally in British Columbia south to Baja California and from Utah and western Colorado, south to central Mexico. Purple Martins nest in the saguaro associations of south-central Arizona and throughout open forested areas above and below the Mogollon Rim, including the Prescott region, Sierra Ancha, and the Natanes Plateau (Phillips et al. 1964).

Atlasers found Purple Martins nesting in disjunct populations throughout much of their previously described distribution in the state. Forest martins were found nesting at elevations from 5560 to 9100 ft (1695–2774 m), while desert martins nested from 1800 to 4060 ft (549–1237 m). They were encountered nesting as far northwest as the Santa Maria Mountains and in scattered populations from Williams, just south of Flagstaff, and along the Mogollon Rim northeast of Payson. Purple Martins were more widespread in the southern White Mountain region from Luna Lake and Alpine down the Black River through northeastern San Carlos Apache tribal lands, including the Point of Pines area. They undoubtedly nest in the adjacent White Mountain Apache tribal land, where access to conduct surveys was not granted. Atlasers did not detect them in the Chiricahua Mountains, Hualapai Mountains, Mount Trumbull region, South Rim of the Grand Canyon, or Chuska Mountains, where they had previously been noted as breeding (Phillips et al. 1964; Monson and Phillips 1981; Jacobs 1986; Brown et al. 1987).

Atlasers found desert nesting Purple Martins from the Salt River Canyon and Roosevelt Lake area, south along the lower San Pedro River to near Cascabel. They were noted also near San Carlos Reservoir and locally east near Markham Creek northeast of Fort Thomas. They were found throughout much of Pima County west to Organ Pipe Cactus National Monument. During the atlas, Purple Martins were also discovered nesting for the first time in Maricopa County near the Sand Tank and Sauceda mountains.

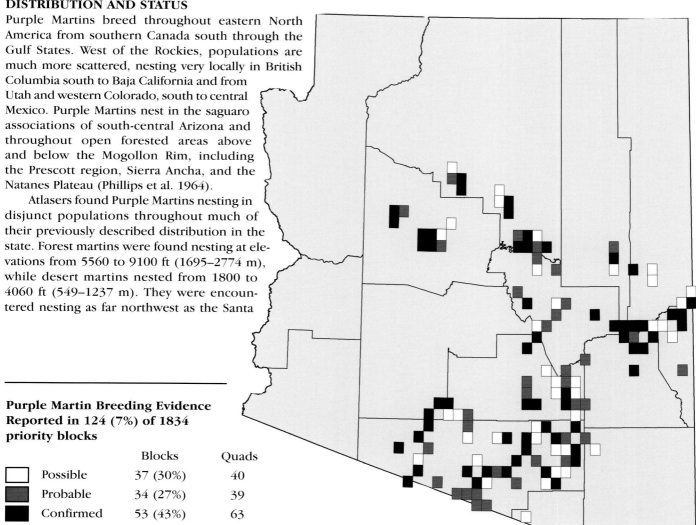

Purple Martin Breeding Evidence Reported in 124 (7%) of 1834 priority blocks

	Blocks	Quads
Possible	37 (30%)	40
Probable	34 (27%)	39
Confirmed	53 (43%)	63

Tree Swallow

by Troy E. Corman *Tachycineta bicolor*

One of the earliest spring arrivals in Arizona, Tree Swallows can be observed coursing their way north over agricultural fields and waterways by late January or early February. These sharp, blue-backed swallows are relatively recent and welcomed additions to Arizona's nesting avifauna, where their breeding distribution continues to expand.

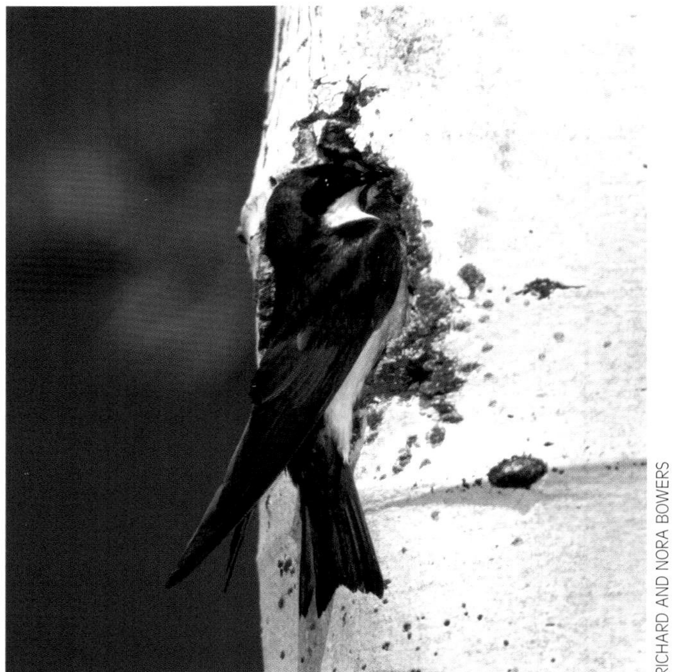
RICHARD AND NORA BOWERS

HABITAT

In Arizona, nesting Tree Swallows prefer high-elevation forest edges, which are often near open water sources. Cavities for nesting and nearby open foraging areas such as meadows, marshes, water bodies, or natural clearings are important habitat components for this swallow. They typically avoid nesting in extensive forest, preferring edges, clearings, or smaller tree groves. Most observations by atlasers were from mixed-conifer forests and montane wooded drainages containing Douglas fir, white fir, ponderosa pine, and quaking aspen stands. Tree Swallows were also reported along and over high-elevation marshes, ponds, lakes, and montane meadows, including those near spruce-fir forests. On several occasions, atlasers found these swallow nesting in primarily pure stands of aspen and in various ponderosa pine–dominated–habitats. Several reports also came from rural settings in which bluebird nest boxes were available, such as near scattered cabins, ranches, and parks. During the atlas period, a pair of Tree Swallows was also confirmed nesting at slightly lower elevations at a lakeside with tall Fremont cottonwoods.

BREEDING

Tree Swallows winter commonly only along the lower Colorado River in Arizona, where they roost in the extensive cattail and bulrush marshes. They rarely winter elsewhere in southern Arizona; however, spring migration can begin by late January, which helps to complicate their true winter status. Migration reaches a peak in February and March, with stragglers into May. Because this species nests sparingly and only relatively recently in Arizona, there is little information regarding when these swallow arrive on their breeding grounds in the state. However, atlasers reported individuals entering cavities by 4 May, suggesting arrival by late April. Tree Swallows were reported with occupied nests through 30 June and nests with young through 13 July. The latest atlas record pertained to an adult feeding a fledgling on 10 August. Early fall migrants can be observed by early July in Arizona lowlands, with a peak passage in late August and September. Stragglers are occasionally noted well into December.

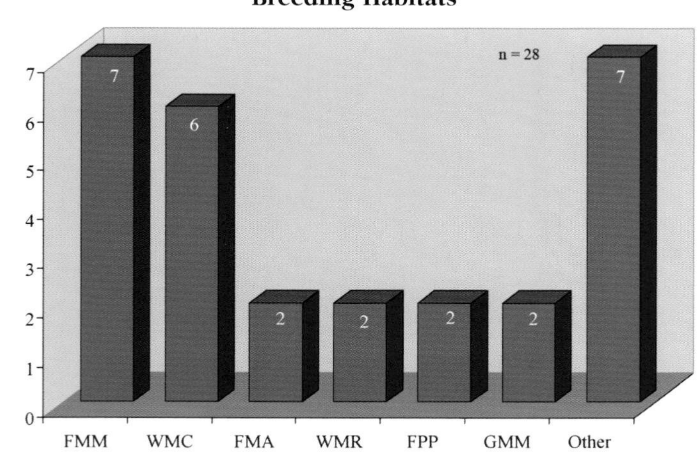

Male Tree Swallows typically arrive and begin defending nesting territory several days prior to the arrival of the female (Robertson et al. 1992). Appropriate nests sites are often limited, and competition for them is likely a driving force behind much of the breeding ecology and behavior of Tree Swallows (Robertson et al. 1992). These swallows are rather quarrelsome and frequently oust the more abundant Violet-green Swallow from nesting cavities (Sclater 1912). In Arizona, nests are typically placed in quaking aspen or conifer snag cavities. Atlasers also discovered Tree Swallows nesting locally in bluebird nest boxes near Flagstaff, Parks (east of Williams), and in the White Mountains region. Tree nest cavities are typically 3.3–32.8 ft (1–10 m) above the ground (Rendell and Robertson 1989). However, in Colorado, aspen nest cavities have been reported up to 60 ft (18 m) high (Pantle 1998).

Female Tree Swallows are the primary nest constructors, but during egg laying and incubation, the male frequently delivers feathers to the female, which she subsequently arranges in the nest (Cohen 1985). The typical clutch size is 4–7 eggs, but can range from 2 to 8 (Robertson et al. 1992). The female incubates the eggs for approximately 14–15 days

Breeding Phenology

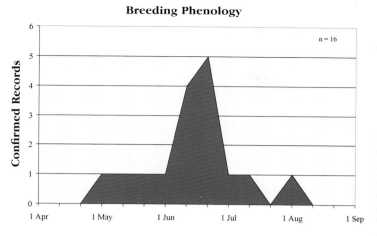

Confirmed Records

n = 16

0 1 2 3 4 5 6

1 Apr 1 May 1 Jun 1 Jul 1 Aug 1 Sep

(Kuerzi 1941). Both adults begin feeding nestlings as soon as they hatch and continue through nest departure in approximately 18–22 days (Robertson et al. 1992). The adults feed the fledglings for a minimum of three days following nest departure (Kuerzi 1941). Most evidence suggests that there is only one successful brood produced per season; however, Tree Swallows commonly renest if earlier attempts fail (Robertson et al. 1992).

DISTRIBUTION AND STATUS

Nesting as far north as the tree line limits in Alaska and Canada, Tree Swallows breed southward into California, Utah, Arizona, New Mexico, Arkansas, Tennessee, and northern Georgia. Early published information considered Tree Swallows as only a migrant and wintering species in Arizona, where it was noted as typically absent between mid-May and early July (Phillips et al. 1964). The first record of nesting in Arizona was not until July 1973, when two active nests were discovered on the Kaibab Plateau (Monson and Phillips 1981). Subsequently, additional nests were found in the White Mountains in the late 1970s and an individual was observed in appropriate nesting habitat in the Chuska Mountains in July 1980 (Monson and Phillips 1981).

Atlasers documented the Tree Swallows' continued breeding range expansion in Arizona, with most confirmations of nesting at elevations from 6100 to 9400 ft (1859–2865 m). However, during the atlas period, a pair of these swallows was discovered with fledglings on 28 June 1995 at Watson Lake near Prescott at an elevation of 5160 ft (1573 m). Atlasers discovered additional nesting locations in the White Mountains from Luna Lake to near Show Low. New nesting sites were also found along the Black River on San Carlos Apache tribal lands, upper Canyon Creek at the base of the Mogollon Rim, and in the Flagstaff area from Mormon Lake to Parks. Atlasers confirmed Tree Swallows nesting at the edges of subalpine meadows and lakes on the Kaibab Plateau, as well as in the Lukachukai Mountains and Chuska Mountains in northern Apache County. Owing to the many similar physical characteristics and nesting habits of the much more abundant Violet-green Swallow in Arizona, many additional breeding pairs of Tree Swallow may have gone undetected during atlas surveys. Also, based on habitat, elevation, and proximity to adjacent breeding location, this spirited swallow undoubtedly nests on White Mountain Apache tribal lands as well, where efforts to acquire permission to conduct atlas surveys were unsuccessful.

During the past thirty years, Tree Swallows have obviously expanded their breeding range southward to include Arizona as they have elsewhere in North America. This welcome trend is expected to continue within the state.

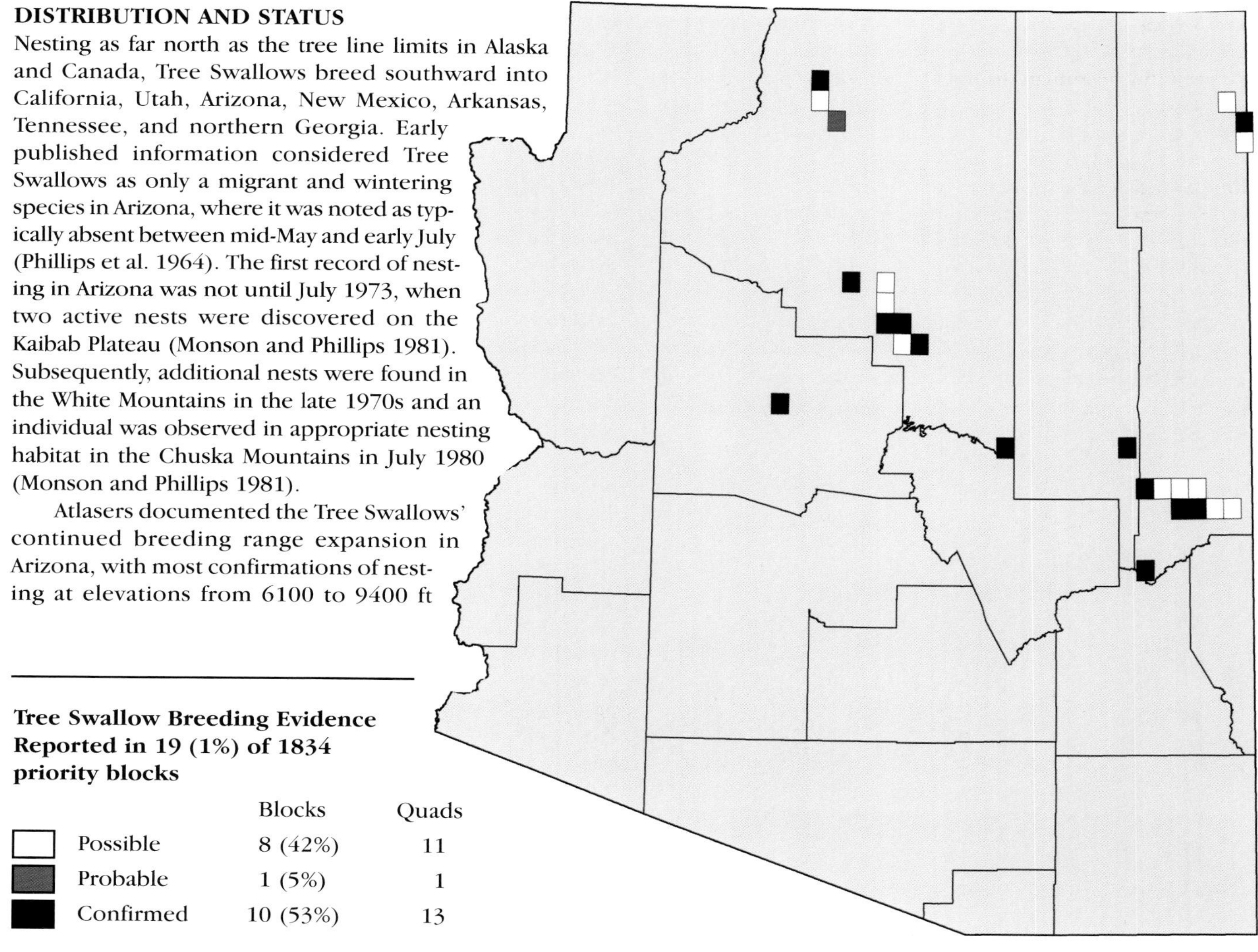

Tree Swallow Breeding Evidence Reported in 19 (1%) of 1834 priority blocks

	Blocks	Quads
Possible	8 (42%)	11
Probable	1 (5%)	1
Confirmed	10 (53%)	13

Violet-green Swallow

by Troy E. Corman *Tachycineta thalassina*

A true harbinger of spring in much of Arizona is the arrival of Violet-green Swallows, which often appear not in spring but midwinter. These flashy birds are regularly observed perched high on exposed tree branches or energetically chasing one another through forest clearings. They also frequently forage higher than other swallows, where they share the skies with White-throated Swifts.

HABITAT

Violet-green Swallows are common migrants over most habitats in Arizona, especially along waterways and over lakes, ponds, and irrigated lands. They frequently forage in small groups or loose flocks, skimming low over fields, forest openings, or water. At other times, they are found circling high above mountain peaks or darting along canyon walls and cliff faces. Nesting in a wide elevational range in Arizona, atlasers noted Violet-green Swallows in thirty different vegetative communities with none being exceptionally prevalent. However, atlasers reported most observations from forested habitats, including pinyon pine–juniper, ponderosa pine, mixed conifer, aspen, spruce-fir, and pine-oak. Within many of these forested habitats, tall snags appear to be very important to these swallows for nesting and perching. Violet-green Swallows were frequently found nesting along sycamore-lined drainages, in steep-walled canyons, and locally in towering cliffs above rivers and dams at lower elevations. Atlasers also discovered this species nesting very locally, and perhaps irregularly, in denser Sonoran Desert landscapes with an abundance of saguaros close to the Mexican border.

BREEDING

Often appearing first along the lower Colorado River by mid- to late January (Rosenberg et al. 1991), Violet-green Swallows typically arrive in other parts of the state in February and March. Locally in the Sonoran Desert, atlasers noted that some pairs likely begin nesting activity by late March as nests with young were discovered as early as 17 April in Organ Pipe Cactus National Monument. This early timing coincides well with breeding dates for desert nesting in Sonora (Russell and Monson 1998). In comparison, the bulk of Arizona's population initiates nesting activity approximately one month later with nest building observed by 21 April and nest with young reported by 21 May. Atlas data suggest that peak nesting activity is from mid-June through mid-July (n = 181), with nests with young reported into early August. Early southbound Violet-green Swallows begin to appear away from breeding areas in August. However, peak passage occurs in mid-September through mid-October, with few records after early November (Phillips et al. 1964).

Violet-green Swallows nest in holes, cavities, and crevices in a variety of situations, which are often reused in successive years (Bent 1942; Cohen 1982). With Arizona's many cliffs and canyons, they find an abundance of small cavities and cracks in which to nest. They also frequently nest in natural cavities and those constructed by woodpeckers in live trees and snags. In Arizona, the most common nesting tree species are ponderosa pine, quaking aspen, Douglas fir, Arizona sycamore, and very locally in large saguaros. Atlasers measured the height of thirty-three Violet-green Swallow nests, with twenty-four in tree cavities. The mean cavity height of the fifteen nests in ponderosa pine was 40.7 ft (12.4 m) with a range of 18.7–85.3 ft (5.7–26 m). Nests in quaking aspen (n = 8) had a mean cavity height of 35.8 ft (10.9 m) with a range of 14.8–65.6 ft (4.5–20 m). In northern Arizona, this swallow was also found nesting locally in dirt bank cavities, in a hole in a water tower beam, and in nest boxes placed high on trees and sides of buildings.

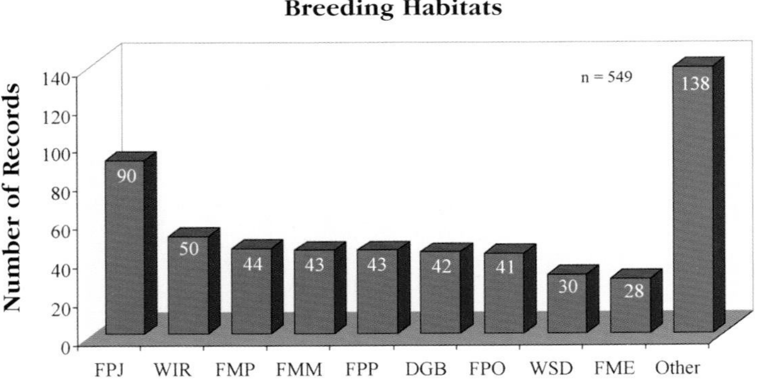

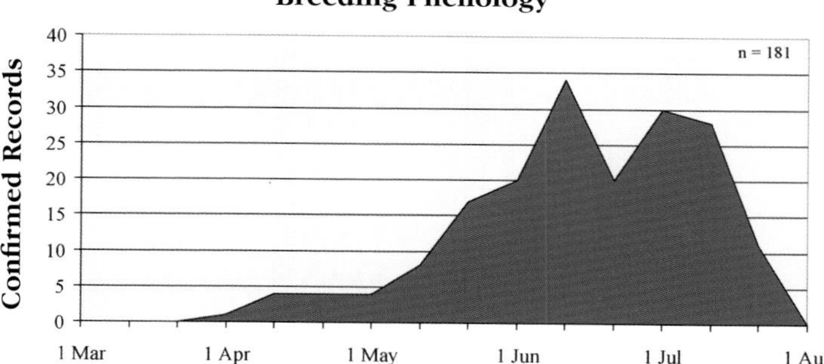

Although both males and females participate in nest construction, the females collect most of the nesting material (Combellack 1954). They typically lay 4–6 eggs, which are incubated for 14–15 days (Brown et al. 1992). Both parents feed the nestlings, which depart the nest 23–24 days after hatching and remain dependent on the adults for an unknown period thereafter (Edson 1943). Violet-green Swallows have been known to successfully fledge two broods in one season; however, most studies suggest that one brood per year is standard (Brown et al. 1992).

DISTRIBUTION AND STATUS

Violet-green Swallows breed in western North America from central Alaska south to central Mexico, and east to the Rocky Mountain region. Atlasers found these swallows nesting commonly from 3200 to 10,500+ ft (975–3200+ m) throughout northern, central, and eastern Arizona. However, they were also confirmed nesting locally as low as 1200 ft (366 m) below Alamo Dam. Atlasers did observe them throughout the nesting season along cliffs in the Bill William River delta area, where they have been found nesting in the past (Rosenberg et al. 1991). Monson (1949) noted Violet-green Swallows nesting at even lower elevations along the Colorado River at Parker Dam (on the California side) at approximately 450 ft (137 m).

As noted by Phillips et al. (1964), Violet-green Swallows are the common swallows of Arizona's mountain forests. They were found regularly throughout the wooded canyons and forested ranges of southeastern Arizona, locally west to the Baboquivari Mountains. To the north, these birds breed throughout the Mogollon Rim region and undoubtedly over much of the unsurveyed White Mountain Apache tribal lands. The accompanying distribution map for this swallow clearly emphasizes the unfortunate lack of atlas data from this diverse area of the state.

One of the most interesting finds during the atlas was the discovery of Violet-green Swallows nesting locally in saguaro cavities in Organ Pipe Cactus National Monument and one location on the Barry M. Goldwater Range in Maricopa County. This species had previously never been found nesting in saguaros in Arizona and these records likely pertain to the small subspecies *brachyptera*, which nests in giant cacti in Baja California and coastal Sonora. The preliminary surveys conducted during the atlas suggest that nesting in this habitat in the state may be of very local and irregular occurrence.

The abundance and distribution of Violet-green Swallows in Arizona appear to have changed very little when compared to previously published literature. This stability could be because many nest on the abundant cliffs and canyon walls found throughout much of the state.

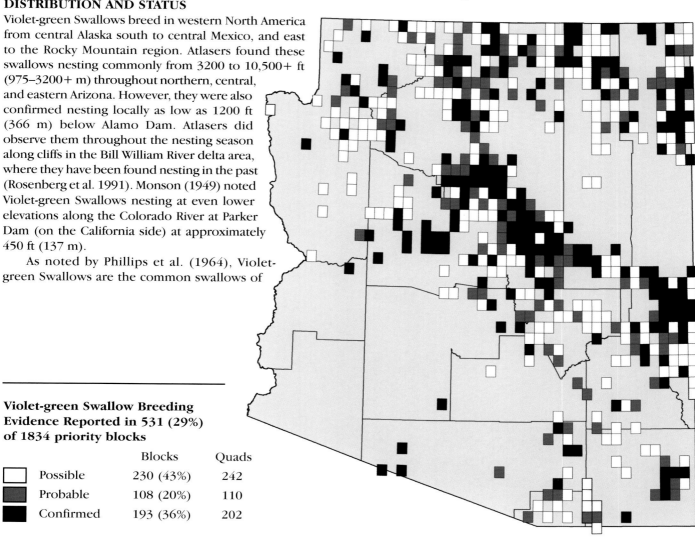

Violet-green Swallow Breeding Evidence Reported in 531 (29%) of 1834 priority blocks

	Blocks	Quads
Possible	230 (43%)	242
Probable	108 (20%)	110
Confirmed	193 (36%)	202

Northern Rough-winged Swallow

by Cathryn Wise-Gervais

Stelgidopteryx serripennis

Northern Rough-winged Swallows are small aerial acrobats that are often observed foraging over water or scooping insects from the water's surface. This bird was named for curious stiffened barbs on the outer flight feather edge. These structures are most pronounced on adult males, but their function remains unknown.

JIM BURNS

HABITAT

Arizona's nesting populations of Northern Rough-winged Swallows are generally found along open drainages and local dry washes with associated bank cavities. Most locations are in proximity to water, but this is not a requirement. Atlasers reported this species in twenty-nine habitat types, indicating a great deal of flexibility in habitat choice. However, approximately 41 percent of potential breeding records were from along lowland riparian areas including cottonwood-willow-mesquite associations, exotic tamarisk-dominated drainages, and the adjacent desert dry washes (n = 301). These birds take advantage of human-altered landscapes, and 15 percent of records were from irrigated agricultural and rural areas. Occupied locations in these settings included along canals, irrigation ditches, road cuts, stock ponds, and wastewater facilities. Atlasers reported fewer Northern Rough-winged Swallows in marshes and sycamore-dominated drainages than in other wetland environs. In addition, observers obtained some records in residential areas and in suburban parks with lakes and canals, indicating that the species tolerates some degree of human activity.

BREEDING

Northern Rough-winged Swallows typically winter in small numbers in southern Arizona, especially within the lower Colorado and Gila River valleys. Spring migration begins early, with individuals appearing away from wintering areas in late January and February. These swallows begin seeking nest cavities immediately upon arrival, sometimes by early February along the lower Colorado River (Rosenberg et al. 1991). Atlasers reported the first occupied Northern Rough-winged Swallow nest on 4 March. Observers had difficulty determining nest contents unless young were present, and the earliest nest with young was reported on 4 May. Backdating of this brood would indicate that egg laying likely occurred in early to mid-April. Atlas data suggest that the breeding activity peak for Arizona's Northern Rough-winged Swallows occurs in late April to early May, but continues through late June (n = 90). Late nesting activity included nest building on 17 July, a nest with young on 22 July, and fledglings reported into mid-August. Fall migration in Arizona typically begins in early August and continues through early November.

There is some debate regarding Northern Rough-winged Swallow nest excavation. Most researchers agree that the species takes up residence in existing burrows that were formerly excavated by other birds or rodents, but several observers have reported Northern Rough-winged Swallows actively engaged in excavating (Weydemeyer 1933; Dingle 1942). Researchers do agree that both sexes seek out potential sites, and meet prospective mates while in the process of "house shopping" (Dejong 1996). Common nest sites in Arizona are in banks along perennial drainages, lakes, earth-lined canals, and irrigation ditches. Atlasers also found this swallow nesting regularly in steeply eroded banks of dry washes at considerable distances from water, in cliff cavities, and even in human-built structures including buildings, bridges, and dams. Atlasers took measurements at ten nests, and all were in either dirt cutbanks or in rocky cliffs. The median height of these banks and cliffs was 28 ft (8.5 m) and ranged from 4.6 to 131 ft (1.4–40 m). The median nest cavity height was 6.2 ft (1.9 m) and ranged

Breeding Habitats

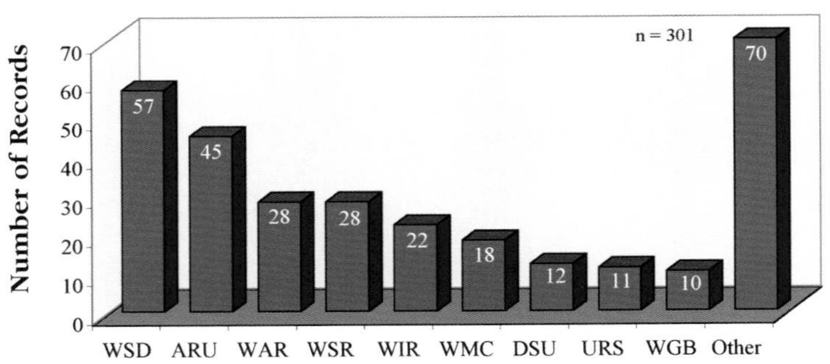

Habitat Codes

Breeding Phenology

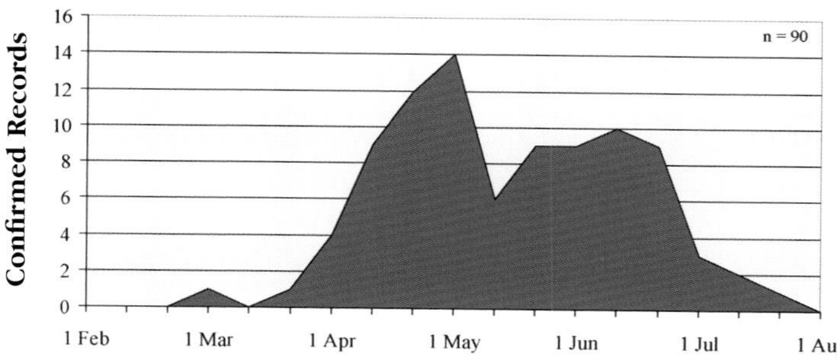

from 1.8 to 32.8 ft (0.6–10 m). Female Northern Rough-winged Swallows build nests within their cavities and these consist of a neat cup atop a rather messy foundation. The nest is typically constructed so the incubating female can view the cavity entrance (Dejong 1996).

The typical Northern Rough-winged Swallow clutch size varies geographically but ranges from 4 to 8 eggs (Ehrlich et al. 1988). The female alone incubates the eggs for approximately 16 days (Dejong 1996). Only the female feeds the young for the first 3 days, after which the male will assist. The young fledge at about 19 days of age but continue to be fed by parents for several weeks (Peterjohn 1989). Although the birds will renest if their first attempt fails, they are not known to raise more than one brood annually (Dejong 1996).

DISTRIBUTION AND STATUS

Found nesting throughout the continental United States, Northern Rough-winged Swallows breed north into southern Canada to central British Columbia and then south through Mexico to northern Panama. Phillips et al. (1964) described the Arizona range of this species as encompassing the Sonoran zones of the state, generally at elevations below 6500 ft (1981 m), and reported the birds nesting locally and irregularly at higher elevations, such as near Flagstaff. Atlasers encountered these birds breeding at elevations from approximately 90 ft (27 m) near Yuma to 8300 ft (2530 m) along upper Nutrioso Creek in the White Mountains.

Northern Rough-winged Swallows are a generally uncommon to common nesting species in Arizona, especially near perennial drainages. Atlasers found that the birds were more sparsely distributed in desert and grassland regions away from water sources. As expected, Northern Rough-winged Swallows were more numerous and regular along the larger drainages and tributaries of central and western Arizona, including the lower Colorado, Gila, Big Sandy, and Verde rivers. They were encountered regularly in the irrigated agricultural river valleys of the Gila and lower Santa Cruz. Except for the Virgin River area and the extreme lower Grand Canyon region, northern Arizona records were sparse and local. Within Navajo and Hopi tribal lands, these swallows nest in widely scattered pairs along arroyo banks in open alluvial valley floors (C. LaRue, personal communication).

Atlas data reconfirm the local distribution of nesting Northern Rough-winged Swallows in the Mogollon Rim and White Mountains regions. They undoubtedly also breed sparingly in the adjacent unsurveyed White Mountain Apache tribal lands. South of the Gila River, these swallows were encountered most regularly along the drainages of Arivaca and Sonoita creeks, as well as along the Santa Cruz and San Pedro rivers.

Local Northern Rough-winged Swallow populations in Arizona are largely influenced by the availability of nest sites and often by nearby water bodies for foraging. Therefore, annual fluctuations in breeding numbers at a given site are normal, especially during years of low precipitation.

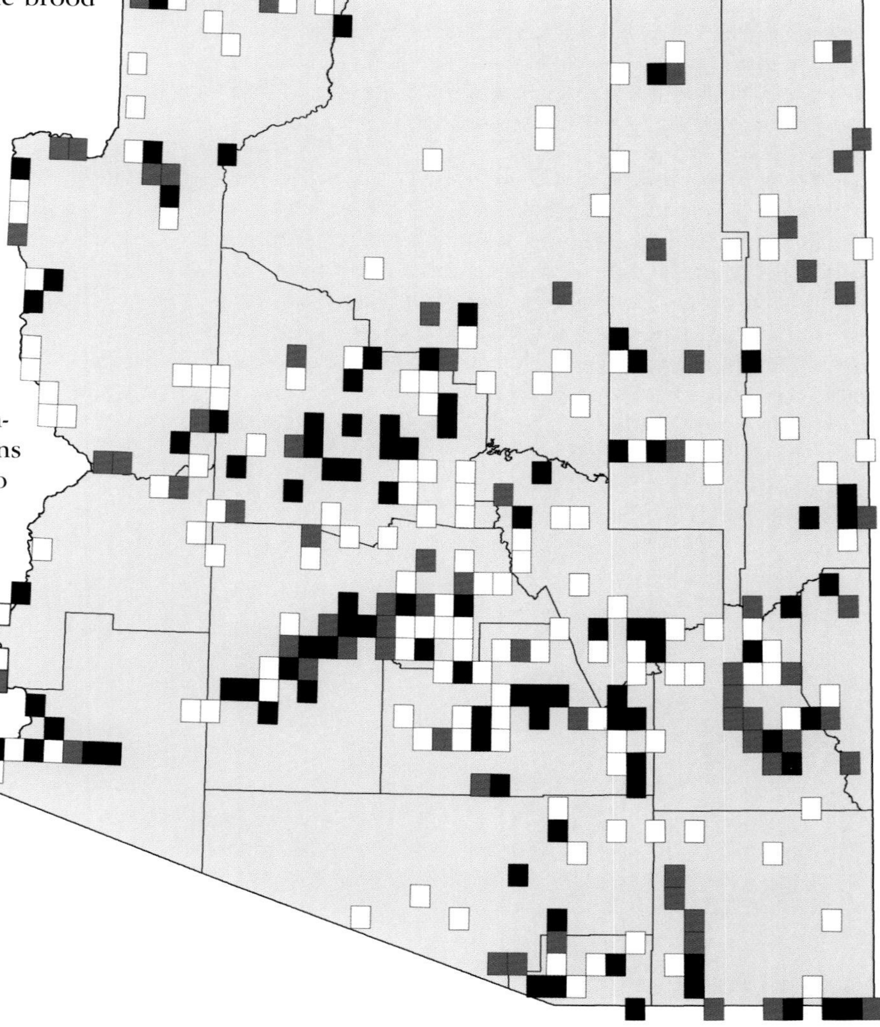

Northern Rough-winged Swallow Breeding Evidence Reported in 276 (15%) of 1834 priority blocks

	Blocks	Quads
Possible	135 (49%)	150
Probable	59 (21%)	67
Confirmed	82 (30%)	93

Cliff Swallow

by Cathryn Wise-Gervais *Hirundo pyrrhonota*

Cliff Swallows are best known for their distinctive gourd-shaped mud nests, and their adobe nest colonies can contain thousands of these highly gregarious birds. Sassy and acrobatic, Arizona's Cliff Swallows are most often observed on the wing, uttering shrill cries and creaks when intruders venture too close.

JIM BURNS

HABITAT

Rather than keying in on a particular vegetative community, Cliff Swallows generally select open areas that offer sources of mud for nest construction and either natural or artificial structures for nest placement. As the name suggests, these birds are commonly associated with cliffs or rocky outcrops, but they also frequently nest on bridges, dams, or buildings. During the atlas period, Cliff Swallows were reported in twenty-nine habitats, with the majority of records (22 percent) obtained in rural, agricultural, or urban areas, where they nest under human-built structures (n = 303). Sixteen percent of records were in cottonwood-willow riparian areas and a total of 26 percent of records were in various other riparian habitats throughout the state, including drainages dominated by sycamore and those containing primarily exotic tamarisk or Russian olive. These birds typically avoid heavily wooded areas, preferring instead open country such as grasslands, canyons, and deserts.

BREEDING

Phillips et al. (1964) described three Cliff Swallow races breeding in Arizona, which are distinguished by forehead color. Spring arrival dates for the two most prevalent races are quite different. The most common and widespread race, *tachina*, arrives on western and central Arizona breeding grounds between mid-February and mid-March. The most distinctive race, *melanogaster*, has a chestnut forehead, breeds primarily in the southeast, and typically does not arrive until mid-April.

Along the lower Colorado River, Cliff Swallows begin nest building by late February (Rosenberg et al. 1991), and slightly later throughout the rest of Arizona. Atlasers observed occupied Cliff Swallow nests as early as 11 March and recorded nest building on several priority blocks in the Phoenix vicinity in mid-March. Birds above the Mogollon Rim and in southeastern Arizona initiate breeding approximately one month later. Atlasers generally could not determine nest contents unless young were present, and did not report any nests with eggs. Observers reported adults feeding a fledgling on 7 May. Atlas data suggest that Cliff Swallow breeding activity peaks statewide from mid-May to mid-June. Atlasers noted nests with young regularly into early August and one late nest containing young was discovered on 1 September in southeastern Arizona. Fall migrants have been noted in Arizona as early as late June, but most birds migrate in August-September, with a few still traveling into early October.

Cliff Swallows build distinctive, gourd-shaped mud nests by plastering wet earth to over hanging surfaces and adjacent nests. Well-protected nests may last several seasons, but exposed nests tend to deteriorate fairly rapidly. Atlasers measured only nine Cliff Swallow nests and these ranged in height from 3.3 to 36 ft (1–11 m), with the lowest nests over water under canal bridges. Of the nest sites, four were on natural rock, one on a dirt bank, three on bridges, and one in a highway culvert. Cliff Swallows were also found nesting under high eaves and covered entranceways of buildings, as well as low under canal-regulating structures.

Both adults incubate their clutch, which typically consists of 4–5 eggs (range 1–6), and incubation takes 12–14 days (Bent 1942). Young fledge at 20–26 days and are fed by the parents for as much as an additional week after fledging (Brown and Brown 1995). Recent studies suggest that Cliff Swallow pairs produce only one brood per year, but they will renest if earlier attempts fail (Brown and Brown 1995). However, the lengthy nesting season in Arizona (March-August) would suggest more than one brood per season.

Breeding Habitats

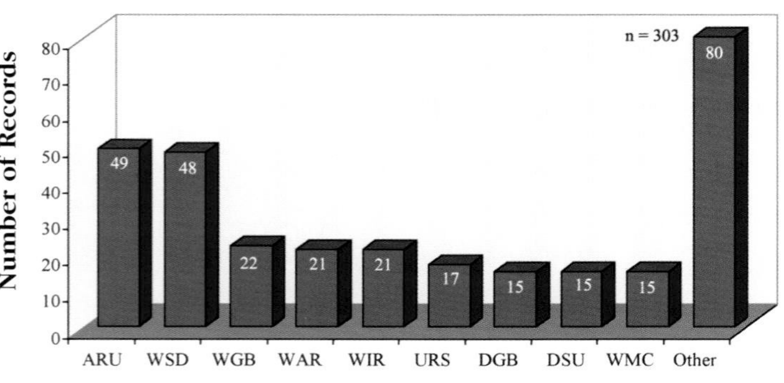

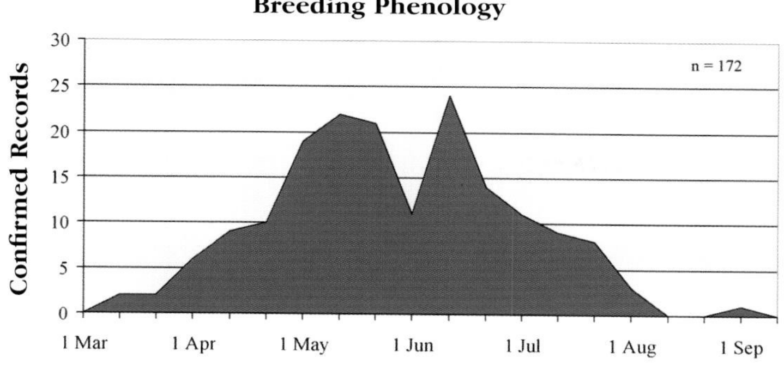

Several bird species will usurp Cliff Swallow dwellings, often expelling the original occupants. In urban and rural areas, the most common invader is the House Sparrow, which uses the nests for both nesting and roosting. Cliff Swallows are well known for regularly visiting unguarded neighbors' nests to deposit or physically transfer (with bill) their own eggs (Brown and Brown 1989). Researchers in Nebraska determined that 22–43 percent of nests contained at least one parasitic egg laid by another female (Brown and Brown 1989).

DISTRIBUTION

Cliff Swallows nest throughout much of North America from Alaska and Canada, south to central Mexico. It is unlikely that the species was ever very common in the northeastern states, and they were completely absent in the southeast. However, in the past 100–150 years these swallows have expanded their breeding range east and southeast due to widespread clearing of forests and con-struction of bridges, buildings, and culverts (Brown and Brown 1995). In Arizona, Phillips et al. (1964) reported that Cliff Swallows breed nearly statewide but noted their breeding colonies are localized by the need of mud.

Atlasers encountered Cliff Swallows throughout a vast range of elevations in Arizona, and confirmed the birds breeding on priority blocks from approximately 160 to 8340 ft (49–2542 m). Observers found these swallows to be common to locally abundant in many regions of the state with open perennial creek and river drainages, as well as at isolated springs and around earthen tanks created for range livestock. Atlasers confirmed breeding on only a few blocks around Tucson despite an abundance of seemingly suitable habitat, but found that the birds were widespread in the greater Phoenix area. Atlasers regularly reported and confirmed Cliff Swallows breeding in both the Gila and lower Colorado River valleys, but the birds remain absent in the Grand Canyon. The Glen Canyon Dam removes most of the sediments once used by Cliff Swallows for nest building, and the last documented nest colony was observed in 1975 at Marble Canyon (Brown et al. 1987).

Much like the Barn Swallow, this swallow's distribution in the arid Southwest is determined by the availability of mud for nest construction and nearby nesting cliffs or structures. Cliff Swallows are erratic in their faithfulness to nest sites, sometimes returning to the same colony site each year and other times not. Atlasers found many old, inactive Cliff Swallow structures in remote and isolated canyons. This unpredictability makes determining population trends difficult, inasmuch as absences can result from the bird's whimsy rather than from actual declines.

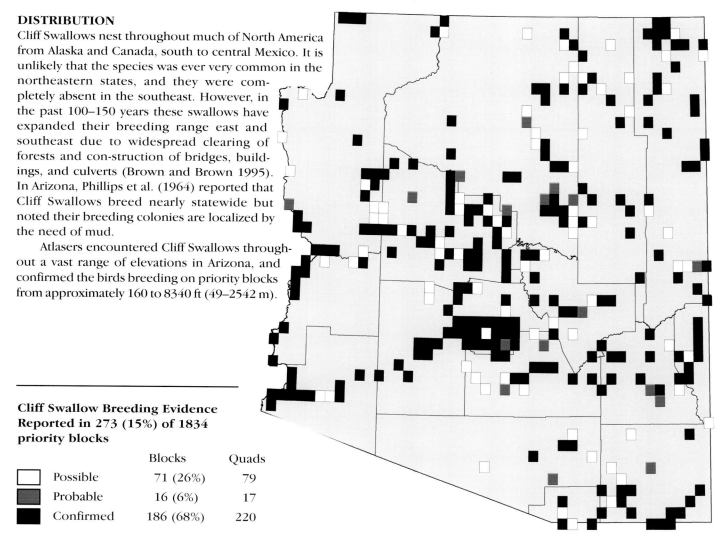

Cliff Swallow Breeding Evidence Reported in 273 (15%) of 1834 priority blocks

	Blocks	Quads
Possible	71 (26%)	79
Probable	16 (6%)	17
Confirmed	186 (68%)	220

Barn Swallow

by Troy E. Corman *Hirundo rustica*

The sights and sounds of the familiar Barn Swallow, dashing and wheeling through the air with a grace matched by few others, bring back a flood of summer memories for those who were raised in rural America. Their playful spirit rejuvenates the souls of many an admirer.

DAN FISCHER

HABITAT

Observed foraging over a wide variety of open habitats in Arizona, Barn Swallows rely primarily on built structures in which to construct their mud nests. Atlasers found this to be true, with 67 percent of all observation reported from rural or urban settings (n = 170). Within these environs, Barn Swallows frequently inhabit buildings, stadiums, parking garages, low bridges, and road culverts. Typically avoiding heavily wooded and extensive forest regions, these swallows require nearby open areas for foraging. Barn Swallows are frequently observed buoyantly winging their way over ball fields, irrigated farm fields, pastures, grasslands, wetlands, and open bodies of water. In the arid landscapes of Arizona, Barn Swallows are greatly limited by the availability of mud for nest construction.

BREEDING

In Arizona, most Barn Swallows typically arrive in March and April, occasionally earlier. Spring migration peaks from mid-April through mid-May with stragglers into early June. Pairing and nesting activity begins soon after returning to breeding localities, and studies have found that approximately 50 percent of first clutches are laid in nests from the previous year (Brown and Brown 1999). Atlasers noted occupied nests by 25 April, and the first nest with eggs was reported on 28 April. Nests with young were observed by 9 May, and atlas data suggest that the peak nesting period is from mid-May through early July. Barn Swallows were observed constructing nests as late as 18 July. In southeastern Arizona, nesting activity continues well into September.

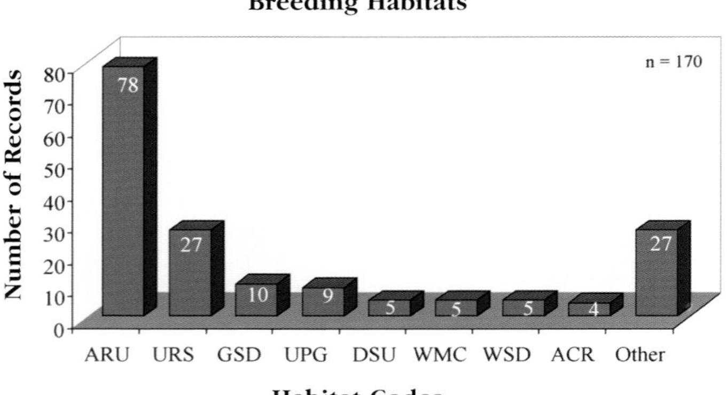

The latest nests with young were found at Saint David on 9 September and at Bisbee as late as 27 September. This is well after most atlas surveys had ended and the frequency of late season nesting is likely higher than atlas data reveal. Fall migration typically begins in mid-July and steadily increases, reaching a strong passage period in late September through mid-October. During this period, congregations of a thousand or more birds are periodically seen foraging over irrigated agricultural fields and open water. Numbers quickly diminish through November, with stragglers occasionally reported into late December.

The Barn Swallow pair works together to construct the mud nest, which is usually placed just underneath a horizontal overhang and either fastened to a vertical wall or built on top of a horizontal ledge or other substrate (Brown and Brown 1999). Barn Swallows nest singly or in small groups. In Arizona, nests are found under the eaves of buildings; under covered porches, patios, and entranceways; in farm and abandoned buildings; under low bridges and culverts; or under canal-regulating structures. The Barn Swallows' preference for low, dark nesting locations is probably due to their cave-nesting roots, and in Arizona this species typically avoids tall bridges and other well-lit structures commonly used by Cliff Swallows.

Both sexes incubate the 3–7 eggs for 13–15 days, but females do considerably more (Brown and Brown 1999). Barn Swallow nestlings are fed by both parents, which fledge in approximately 21 days, with a range of 15–24 days (Anthony and Ely 1976). However, the parents will lead young back to the nest to sleep for several days after fledging (Brown and Brown 1999). The parents continue to feed their young for several days to a week following nest departure and family groups have broken up entirely by two weeks after fledging (Medvin and Beecher 1986). Barn

Breeding Phenology

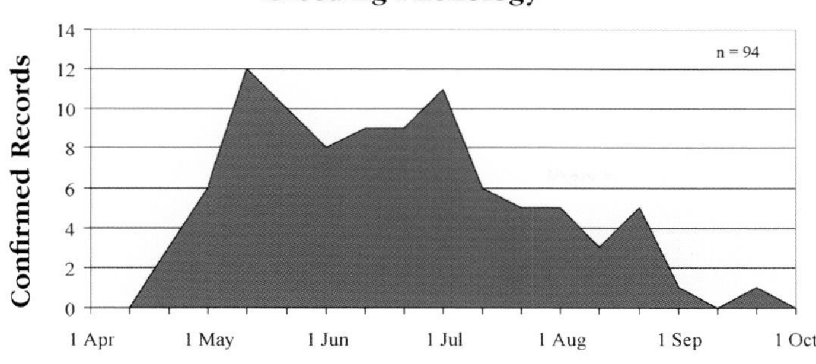

Swallows commonly rear two broods per season, often from the same nest (Bent 1942).

DISTRIBUTION AND STATUS

The Barn Swallow is the most widely distributed and abundant swallow in the world, nesting throughout much of the northern hemisphere (Brown and Brown 1999). In North America, they breed from southern Alaska and Canada, south to central Mexico. Phillips et al. (1964) described the nesting distribution of the Barn Swallow in Arizona as a local summer resident in the eastern half of the state from Nogales and Douglas, north to Show Low, Snowflake, and Holbrook. They also noted this swallow nesting irregularly in Sells and Tucson, and at Mayer in Yavapai County.

As they have elsewhere within North America, Barn Swallows have expanded their nesting range in Arizona and were documented nesting from approximately 1370 to 9200 ft (418–2804 m). Atlasers noted that this swallow's breeding distribution is still concentrated in the southeastern and east-central regions of the state, where it is fairly common. However, they also discovered many previously undocumented nesting locations and confirmed Barn Swallows nesting in every county but Yuma. In southeastern Arizona, they were confirmed nesting regularly west to Sasabe and were observed collecting nesting material as far west as Papago Farms on Tohono O'odham tribal lands. In Pinal County, Barn Swallows were discovered nesting under irrigation and canal regulating structures near the agricultural communities of Casa Grande and Coolidge.

Atlasers noted Barn Swallows nesting locally in the Flagstaff and Williams areas, northwest to Rose Well, Truxton, and northern Chino Valley. They were confirmed nesting for the first time in the extreme northeast at Tec Nos Pos and are suspected of nesting at several other localities on Navajo tribal lands. Above the Mogollon Rim, Barn Swallows were confirmed nesting from Heber to Luna Lake, and north to Saint Johns and at the Petrified Forest National Park headquarters. Atlasers found Barn Swallows nesting commonly under the many road culverts along Highway 70 between San Carlos and Thatcher. Much farther west, they also were discovered nesting locally in low culverts along Highway 60 between Salome and Aquila. At the latter locations, nearby irrigated agricultural fields and subsequent runoff likely accounted for the availability of mud for nest building in this otherwise arid region.

Many local nesting sites may be used only periodically following wet springs when mud is more readily available. Flying insect are also typically much more abundant during these high precipitation years, providing a plentiful food source for these seemingly carefree swallows and their young.

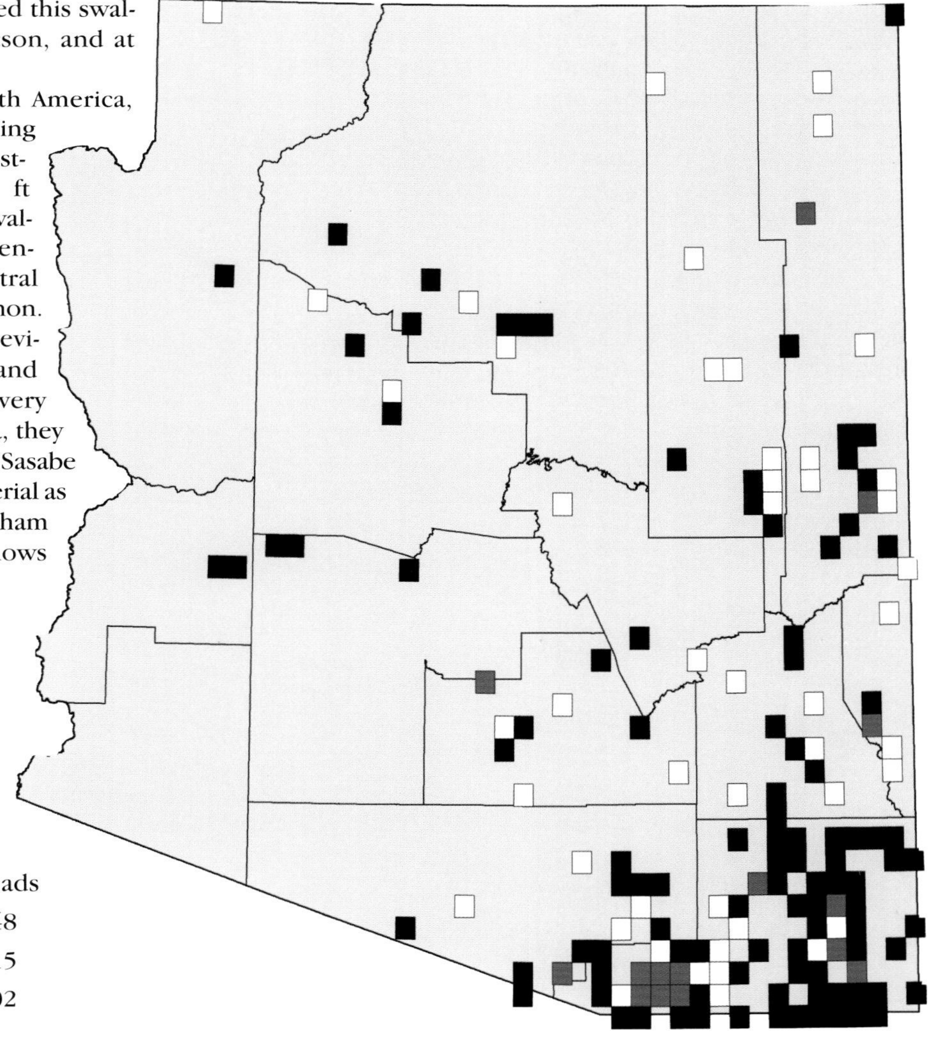

Barn Swallow Breeding Evidence Reported in 141 (8%) of 1834 priority blocks

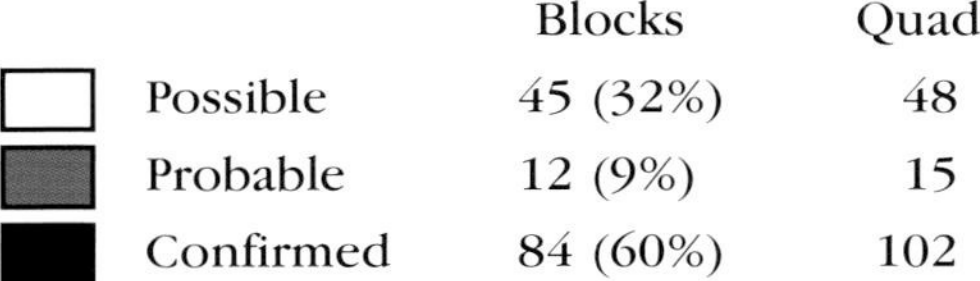

	Blocks	Quads
Possible	45 (32%)	48
Probable	12 (9%)	15
Confirmed	84 (60%)	102

Mountain Chickadee

by Suzanne Sitko *Poecile gambeli*

While the Black-capped Chickadee has been recognized as one of the nation's favorite birds, Arizona's counterpart, the Mountain Chickadee, is equally engaging, providing hours of entertainment at montane backyard feeders with its familiar calls and acrobatic antics. An omnivorous picker and gleaner, Mountain Chickadees forage through forest trees, capitalizing on any food source they can find.

BRUCE TAUBERT

HABITAT

Mountain Chickadees are widespread inhabitants of Arizona's conifer forests, occupying most forests containing ponderosa pine, from nearly pure stands to those with a Gambel's oak or pinyon pine-juniper associations. These three forest habitats accounted for 48 percent of atlas records ($n = 289$). At higher elevations, these chickadees are also common residents in the state's mixed-conifer forests containing Douglas fir, white fir, various pines, and aspen, as well as in subalpine spruce-fir forests. They reach their lower elevational limits in the denser and taller stands of pinyon pine–juniper woodlands, where atlasers reported a surprising 25 percent of all records for this species. Atlasers also found these energetic forest birds sparingly using several nearby habitats, including aspen groves, wooded montane drainages with a strong deciduous component, and evergreen oak woodlands.

Mountain Chickadees are very opportunistic, and upon discovering a well-stocked backyard feeding station, they may become permanent residents of yards and neighborhoods. Often these birds attract other small passerines, and one may find additional yard species thanks to the Mountain Chickadee.

BREEDING

Mountain Chickadees form breeding pairs between the late fall and early spring. Pairs begin breaking off from foraging flocks in late winter and early spring to begin inspecting potential nest cavities (McCallum et al. 1999). Atlasers first reported these chickadees carrying nesting material on 22 April; early Arizona nests likely contain eggs by mid- to late April. Mountain Chickadees were observed carrying food as early as 5 May, suggesting possible nestlings; however, this could not be determined since males also feed their incubating mates. The earliest reported nest with young was on 25 May, although fledglings were noted by 2 June, further supporting early May hatching dates. Statewide atlas data reveal a peak nesting period between early June and early July ($n = 120$), with a steady decline thereafter. However, breeding activity does continue into August, as atlasers reported a nest with young through 31 July and adults feeding fledglings into late August. Fledgling Mountain Chickadees remain with their parents for 2–3 weeks following nest departure and then often join mixed-species foraging flocks (McCallum et al. 1999).

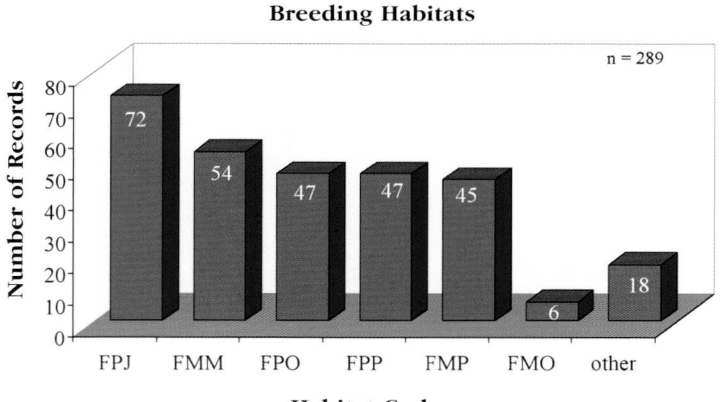

A cavity nester, the Mountain Chickadee will use old woodpecker nest holes or nest boxes, or it will excavate nest cavities in soft wood (Phillips et al. 1964). The female often selects the nest cavity, and both sexes help build the nest by filling the cavity with soft material including loose fur. Eight Mountain Chickadee nests in four tree species were measured during atlas surveys. Nest trees were Utah juniper (1), ponderosa pine (2), quaking aspen (1), and Gambel's oak (4). The median nest height was 9.4 ft (2.9 m) and ranged from 5.6 to 18 ft (1.7–5.5 m). In one central Arizona study, Li and Martin (1991) calculated an average nest height of 49 ft (15 m), with all but one of the twenty-nine nests in aspen.

Mountain Chickadees lay about 6–8 eggs on average, with the early eggs being buried with fur and other nesting materials by the female until incubation begins (McCallum et al. 1999). Only the female incubates the eggs, and the incubation period lasts for approximately 14–15 days. The male assists in feeding nestlings, with both sexes delivering whole

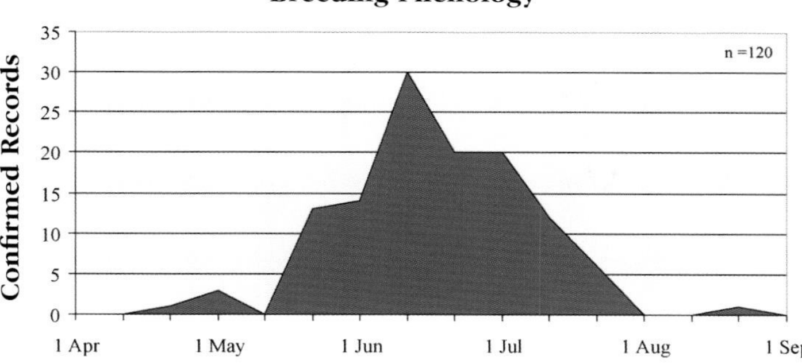

food. Mountain Chickadees sometimes produce a second brood, usually with fewer eggs (McCallum et. al 1999).

DISTRIBUTION AND STATUS

Mountain Chickadees are a signature species of western coniferous forests from southern Arizona, New Mexico, and even northern Baja California north through western Canada sparingly to the Yukon Territory (McCallum et. al 1999). Typically nonmigratory, Mountain Chickadees periodically move into lowland deciduous riparian drainages during years of low pine-seed production. Juveniles typically dominate these movements.

Atlasers found Mountain Chickadees fairly easy to detect on atlas blocks and documented them nesting at elevations from approximately 5500 to 10,500 ft (1676–3200 m) in Arizona. A widespread species, Mountain Chickadees have been described as common residents of conifer forests and locally in pinyon pine–juniper woodlands in central and northern Arizona (Phillips et al. 1964; Jacobs 1986; Brown et al. 1987). Although atlasers were not permitted to conduct atlas surveys on White Mountain Apache tribal lands, these chickadees undoubtedly breed throughout the diverse forest and woodland habitats of this reservation. During the atlas period, Mountain Chickadees were not detected in the Mazatzal Mountains in northeastern Maricopa County, where Witzeman et al. (1997) considered them fairly common residents. To the northwest, they were found in several isolated ranges including the Hualapai, Music, and Virgin mountains.

In southeastern Arizona, Mountain Chickadee populations are restricted to only a few isolated mountain ranges, most notably the Rincon, Santa Catalina, Pinaleno, and north to the Pinal mountains. Phillips et al. (1964) reported the absence of any chickadee species in the nearby Santa Rita and Huachuca ranges, where suitable habitat exists. Monson and Phillips (1981) later noted summer observations of Mountain Chickadees in the Huachuca Mountains during the early 1970s. During the atlas period, Mountain Chickadees were confirmed breeding for the first time in the Santa Rita Mountains. These unusual summer records may follow those periodic winters when numbers of these chickadees move south and may pertain to several pairs taking advantage of unoccupied breeding habitat in the Santa Rita and Huachuca mountains.

One of the more conspicuous birds in conifer forests in Arizona, the Mountain Chickadee is a good indicator of the diversity of forest habitat structure. Prior literature suggests that their distribution within the state has had little change, and the species remains common in most occupied forests. Still, it is unknown how local populations of these familiar songbirds will be affected by the recent loss of forests to widespread wildfires and drought-induced bark beetle infestations.

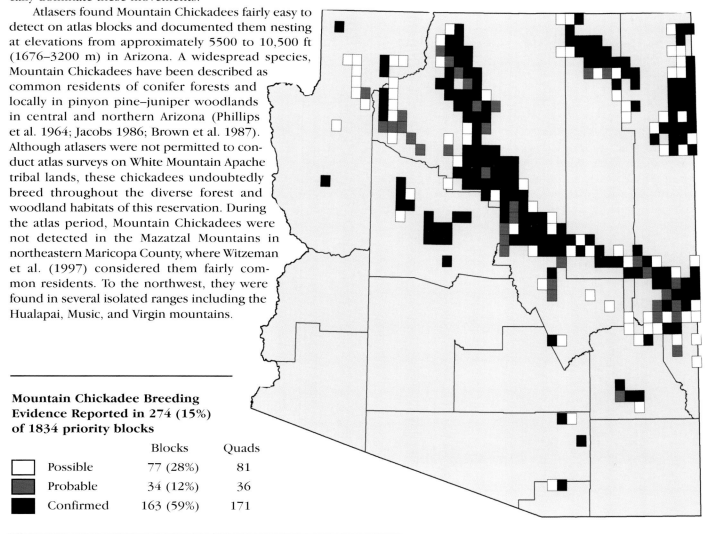

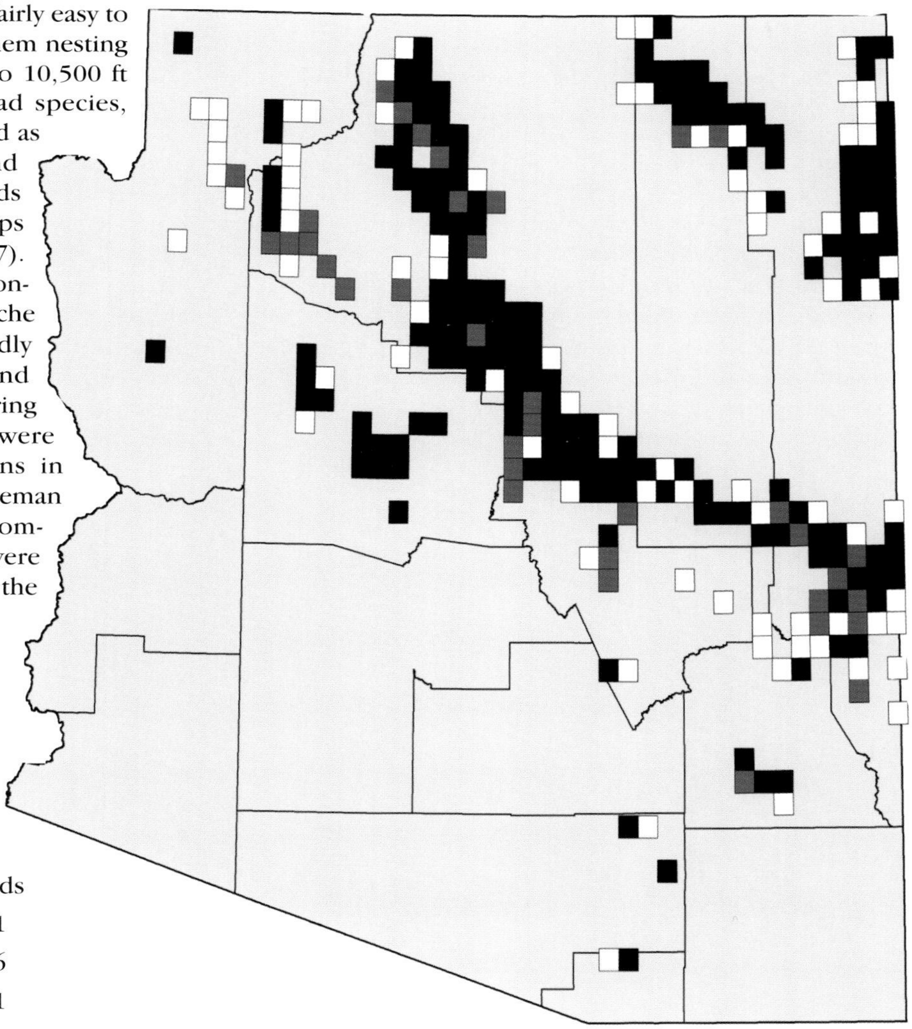

Mountain Chickadee Breeding Evidence Reported in 274 (15%) of 1834 priority blocks

	Blocks	Quads
Possible	77 (28%)	81
Probable	34 (12%)	36
Confirmed	163 (59%)	171

Mexican Chickadee

by Troy E. Corman *Poecile sclateri*

Among the conifer-forested slopes and canyons of the Chiricahua Mountains, an imitated whistle of a Northern Pygmy-Owl will often quickly attract a noisy mob of passerines, including the resident Mexican Chickadee. Much remains to be learned about the nesting affairs of these local inhabitants.

DAN FISCHER

HABITAT

Found in a wide variety of forested habitats in Mexico, Mexican Chickadees are primarily restricted to coniferous forests within their very limited Arizona range. Atlasers reported most observations from the higher edges of Madrean pine-oak woodlands dominated by mature tall stands of ponderosa, Chihuahuan, and Apache pines with an understory of scattered evergreen oaks and alligator juniper. However, Mexican Chickadees were found to be more common at higher elevations in the limited mixed-conifer forests and associated higher montane drainages. Dominant trees often include ponderosa pine, Douglas fir, white fir, and very locally on some north-facing slopes, Engelmann spruce.

During mid- to late summer, many family groups of Mexican Chickadees regularly travel down into the adjacent cool drainages and canyons (Marshall 1957). Here they can be encountered foraging through a mixture of pines, Douglas fir, Arizona cypress, bigtooth maple, Arizona sycamore, alligator juniper, Arizona madrone, and various evergreen oaks. During this period they often begin to join mixed-species foraging flocks. Hutto (1987) and others consider these chickadees a nuclear species, based on their presence in almost all mixed-species flocks, frequent calling, and sentinel behavior.

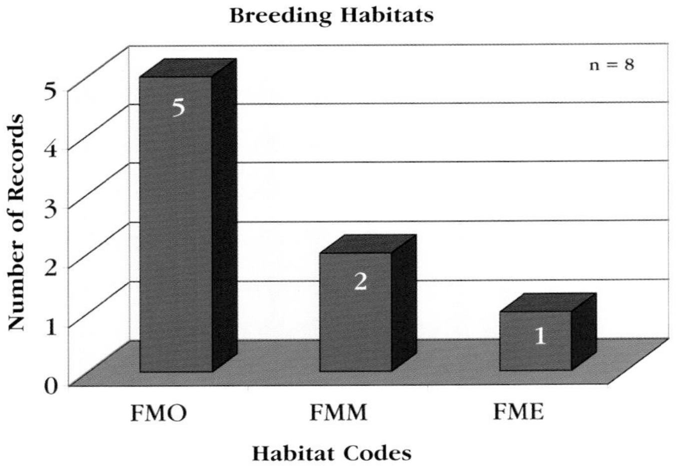

BREEDING

Mexican Chickadees become much more vocal in the early spring, especially at dawn (Dixon and Martin 1979). Very little is known about the nesting habits and phenology of the Mexican Chickadees in Arizona. Atlasers were unable to locate any active nests and collected minimal additional information to help solve the many nesting-ecology mysteries surrounding this chickadee. Much of what follows was compiled from the persistent endeavors of H. Brandt in the late 1940s (Brandt 1951). He noted that in Arizona, nest building commences in mid- to late April and continues well into May. Mexican Chickadees become much quieter and more retiring during the typical egg-laying period. Brandt discovered nests with fresh eggs from 10 to 28 May and suggested that egg laying may begin by 8 May, based on the occurrence of the first nest with young on 26 May. Atlasers did observed an adult carrying food on 27 May. The first fledglings are typically not observed until mid-June. However, atlasers noted a fledgling on 3 June, suggesting some pair may begin egg laying by late April. A report from an atlaser of a fledgling on 11 May could pertain to young from previous year, which occasionally remain with the adults and periodically perform begging behavior (Brant 1951). Atlasers observed adults feeding fledged young through 6 July.

In Arizona, Mexican Chickadees typically nest in cavities of conifers. Most of the few nests described have been in snags of ponderosa pine and Douglas fir, or more uniquely in cavities on the underside of large dead limbs at a height of 35–60 ft (10.6–18.3 m) above the ground (Brandt 1951; Ficken and Ficken 1987). However, these chickadees readily used nest boxes placed on conifers 12–16 ft (3.7–4.9 m) high (Brandt 1951). Most observations suggest that they are very secretive near the nest, especially during egg laying and incubation.

Excavation of the nest cavity has not been observed in this species as it has with other chickadees and titmice, but a pair was observed actively removing flakes of decaying wood that had been placed in a nest box (Brandt 1951). Only females construct the nest inside the cavity, which often entails bringing large amounts of nesting material that includes moss, grass, and especially fur. However, during her collecting forays her calling mate typically closely accompanies her. It can take the female nearly four weeks to construct the well-insulated nest (Brandt 1951).

Most egg clutches consist of 5–9 eggs and are incubated solely by the female for approximately 14 days (Brandt 1951). The male has been observed feeding the female near the nest during incubation, often calling when he arrives with food (Ficken and Nocedal 1992). Both parents feed the nestlings. The length of the nestling period is unknown, but is likely between 15 and 21 days as in other North American chickadee species. Family groups remain together throughout much of the summer, but the length of parent dependency is unknown. Most evidence suggests that only one brood is produced per season, but Mexican Chickadees will renest if earlier attempts have failed.

DISTRIBUTION AND STATUS

As its name implies, the primary distribution of the Mexican Chickadee lies south of the U.S. border. It is a resident species from Oaxaca, north to Sonora and Chihuahua and in disjunct populations in southern Coahuila and Nuevo Leon (Howell and Webb 1995). In the United States, Mexican Chickadees are found nesting only in two borderland sky island ranges, the Chiricahua Mountains in southeastern Arizona and the nearby Animas Mountains in southwestern New Mexico. As noted earlier, some individual descend to lower elevations in fall and winter. This Chickadee has been reported once on 20 January 1924 in the adjacent Swisshelm Mountains (Monson and Phillips 1981) and on 4 September 1987 in Guadalupe Canyon, southern Peloncillo Mountains. Brandt (1951) described the Mexican Chickadee as the third most abundant bird in the coniferous forests of the Chiricahua Mountains, where Phillips et al. (1964) also noted it as a common resident.

Atlasers encountered Mexican Chickadees typically at elevations ranging from 7000 to 9600 ft (2134–2926 m), but they also observed pairs and family groups in cool canyons down to 6000 ft (1829 m) during the summer. Atlasers found these chickadees fairly widespread in the higher elevations of the Chiricahua Mountains from Cochise Head, northeast of Chiricahua National Monument, and south to Swede Peak. They were found nesting down to the upper South Fork Cave Creek drainage on the eastern slope and as far west as Stanford Peak.

In the Chiricahua Mountains, Balda (1967) estimated the density of Mexican Chickadees at 1.7 pairs/25 ac (10 ha) in ponderosa pine dominated landscapes, and 6.4 pairs/25 ac (10 ha) at higher elevations in Douglas fir–spruce. However, populations seem to have declined in recent years, perhaps related to drought (Ficken and Nocedal 1992) and local habitat loss from wildfires. Given the genetic vulnerability of small isolated populations, there is concern about the long-term persistence of these chickadees in the United States (Ficken and Nocedal 1992). Mexican Chickadees deserve much more attention from researchers, and populations should be closely monitored in Arizona and New Mexico to gain insight into future trends.

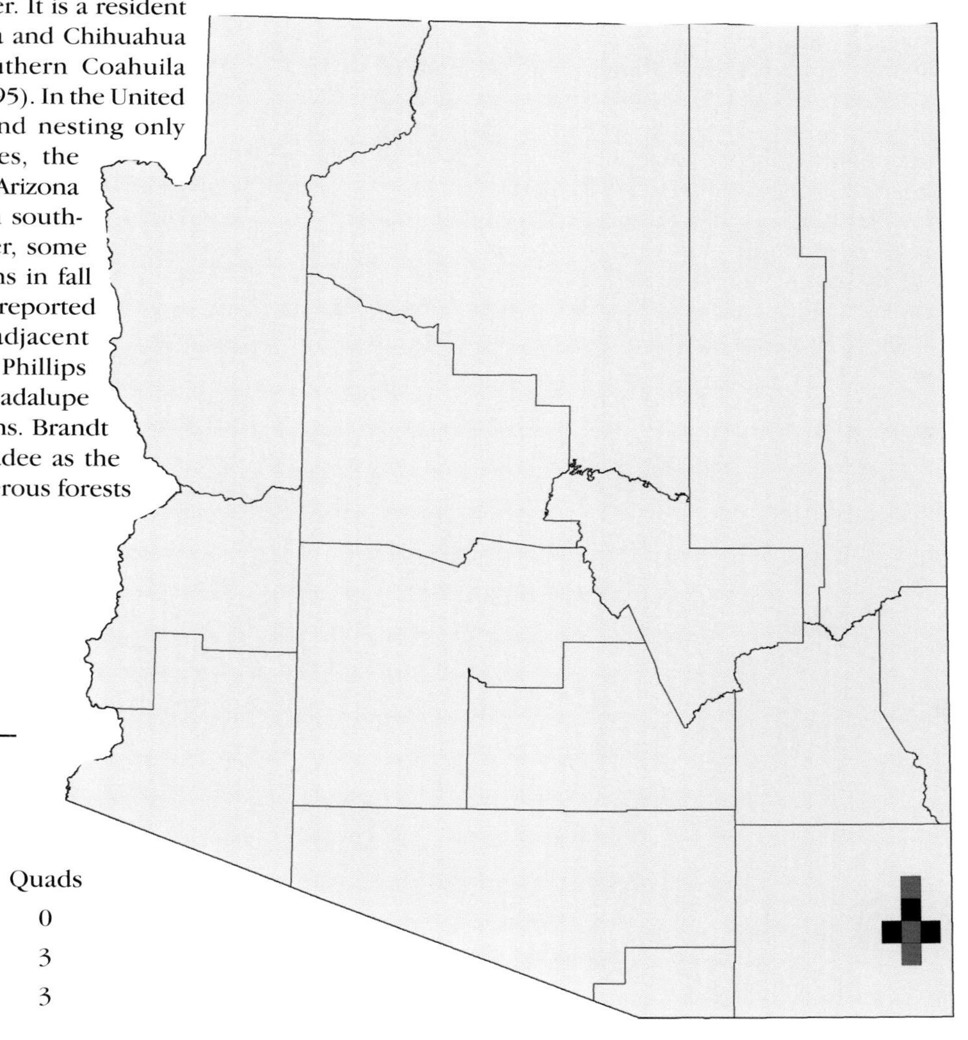

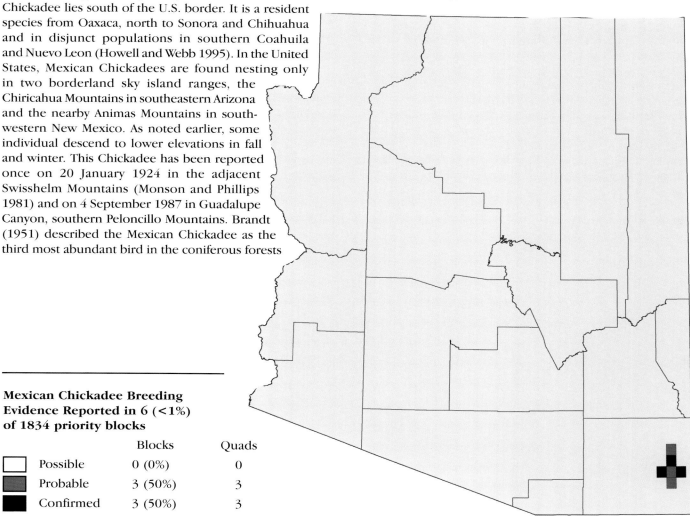

Mexican Chickadee Breeding Evidence Reported in 6 (<1%) of 1834 priority blocks

	Blocks	Quads
Possible	0 (0%)	0
Probable	3 (50%)	3
Confirmed	3 (50%)	3

Bridled Titmouse

by Troy E. Corman *Baeolophus wollweberi*

A rather quiet, foraging group of Bridled Titmice meticulously working their way through the oaks and sycamores can suddenly change to a noisy, confrontational gang when danger is perceived in their neighborhood. These admirable crested birds are a favorite of visiting birders to the wooded canyon of central and southeastern Arizona.

RICK AND NORA BOWERS

HABITAT

Bridled Titmice are typically encountered in pairs or small roving groups and often reach their highest Arizona densities in or near Madrean evergreen oak associations. They are characteristic inhabitants of the evergreen oak woodlands in the state, which often include extensive stands of Emory, Arizona white, netleaf, and silverleaf oaks. These woodlands accounted for 28 percent of all atlas records for this species (n = 218). However, most atlas records (34 percent) were noted in canyons and foothill drainages where these little crested birds are found among Arizona sycamores, often with some evergreen oak influence. Bridled Titmice were also encountered nesting locally within tall riparian woodlands below the oak zone, including larger gallery stands of cottonwood, willow, and velvet ash. They reach their highest elevation extreme on mountain slopes that, in southeastern Arizona, take them regularly into open Madrean pine-oak forests where evergreen oaks and alligator juniper have an overstory of ponderosa, Chihuahuan, and/or Apache pines. Similarly, in central Arizona, atlasers also reported Bridled Titmice occupying open ponderosa pine forests with pinyon pine, juniper, and Gambel's oak associations.

Breeding Habitats

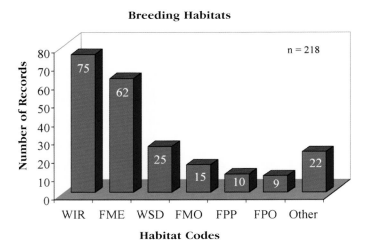

n = 218

Habitat Codes	Number of Records
WIR	75
FME	62
WSD	25
FMO	15
FPP	10
FPO	9
Other	22

BREEDING

Basically a resident species, Bridled Titmice often maintain pair bonds throughout the year. Courtship feeding is often initiated in March as the pair begins their inspection of potential nest cavities. Males continue to feed their mates through incubation. Nest construction within the selected cavity can begin by late March or early April in Arizona. Atlasers noted the earliest occupied nest on 4 April and detected nests with young by 26 April. These records indicate some Bridled Titmice initiate egg laying by early to mid-April. Statewide atlas data suggest that the nesting activity of these birds peaks between mid-May and mid-June, but continues well into the summer. Some nests contain young into at least late July and atlasers reported adults feeding fledglings through 28 August. There is no evidence of second clutches (Nocedal and Ficken 1998), and later nesting dates suggest renesting efforts following earlier failed attempts.

As a cavity nester, the resident Bridled Titmouse apparently prefers natural tree cavities to those excavated by woodpeckers. Oaks are often selected when they are available, but they also commonly use cavities in Arizona sycamore, velvet ash, and Fremont cottonwood at lower elevations. Bridled Titmice also readily take advantage of nest boxes (Nocedal and Ficken 1998). Nest height generally ranges from 1.5 to 33 ft (0.5–10 m) above the ground (Bent 1946; Brandt 1951).

The Bridled Titmouse pair works together in constructing the nest in preparation of the typical clutch of 5–7 eggs (range 4–8; Bent 1946). Most evidence suggests that the female does most of the incubation and that the male brings food to her during this nesting stage. However, males have been known to brood the young and have even developed a partial brood patch (Nocedal and Ficken 1998). There are no precise data, but estimates suggest that the incubation period lasts for 13–14 days (Nocedal and Ficken 1998). Both parents feed the nestlings, which depart the nest in approximately 18–20 days, with flight occurring when the young are 25–27 days old (Nocedal and Ficken 1998). Young Bridled Titmice often remain with their parents into the fall, at which time they may set off on their own to form small foraging groups with other juveniles.

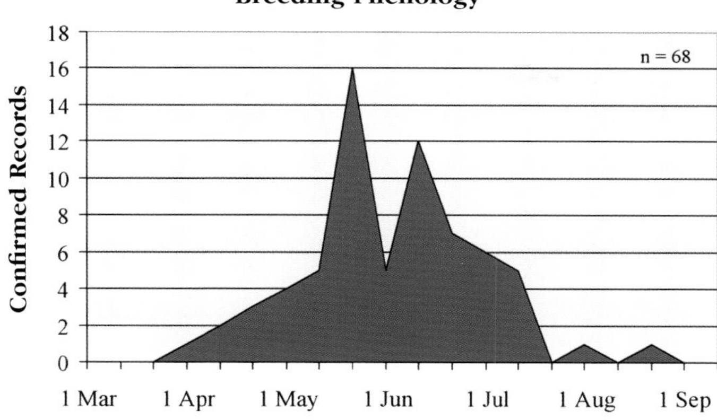

An interesting note is that nesting Bridled Titmouse pairs often have a single helper that actively feeds nestlings and fledglings, removes fecal sacs, and participates in mobbing potential predators (Nocedal and Ficken 1998). Cooperative breeding is apparently rare among chickadees and titmice, and the Bridled Titmouse seems to be the only North American parid in which helpers may be frequent (Nocedal and Ficken 1998).

DISTRIBUTION AND STATUS

Bridled Titmice occur from central Arizona and southwestern New Mexico south through the highlands of Mexico to central Oaxaca. In southeastern Arizona, they are found west to the Baboquivari Mountains. Their range extends northward to the southern edge of the Mogollon Rim and Oak Creek Canyon area north of Sedona, then west to the Juniper Mountains in Yavapai County (Phillips et al. 1964). Atlasers were able to extend this range slightly to the west to include the Trout Creek drainage of the Aquarius Mountains in southeastern Mohave County.

In Arizona, Bridled Titmice are common residents at elevations from approximately 4500 to 7000 ft (1372–2134 m) and locally down to 3600 ft (1220 m) in canyons and foothill drainages with sycamore. They are an uncommon breeding species in the larger and denser stands of lowland riparian woodlands along the Santa Cruz, Verde, and lower San Pedro rivers, where they nest as low as 1960 ft (6597 m) near Dudleyville and Winkelman. Rather perplexing is the fact that Bridled Titmice were not detected nesting on upper reaches of this same drainage within the San Pedro National Conservation Area until 1998 (Krueper 1999). Prior to that year, they were regarded as only a regular winter visitor and had been absent throughout the nesting season.

In late summer, Bridled Titmice occasionally wander to higher elevations and annually to lower riparian habitats in the fall and winter. During the winter, these feisty birds frequently forage in flocks of 6–10 individuals with reports of larger flock consisting of 20–25 titmice (Swarth 1904). Chickadees, vireos, warblers, kinglets, and nuthatches often loosely join foraging titmice flocks in Arizona, with the chattering titmice often determining the direction of travel.

The evergreen oak woodlands and sycamore-lined drainages that the Bridled Titmouse favors are not harvested to any great extent in Arizona. Titmouse populations appear to be fairly stable, and there is little concern for the overall population within the state. Therefore, these little acrobatic birds will undoubtedly continue to charm and entertain the many observers that encounter them.

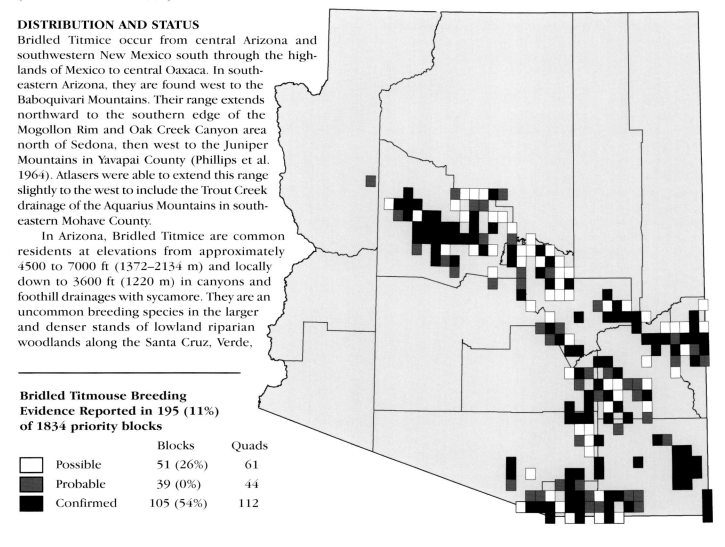

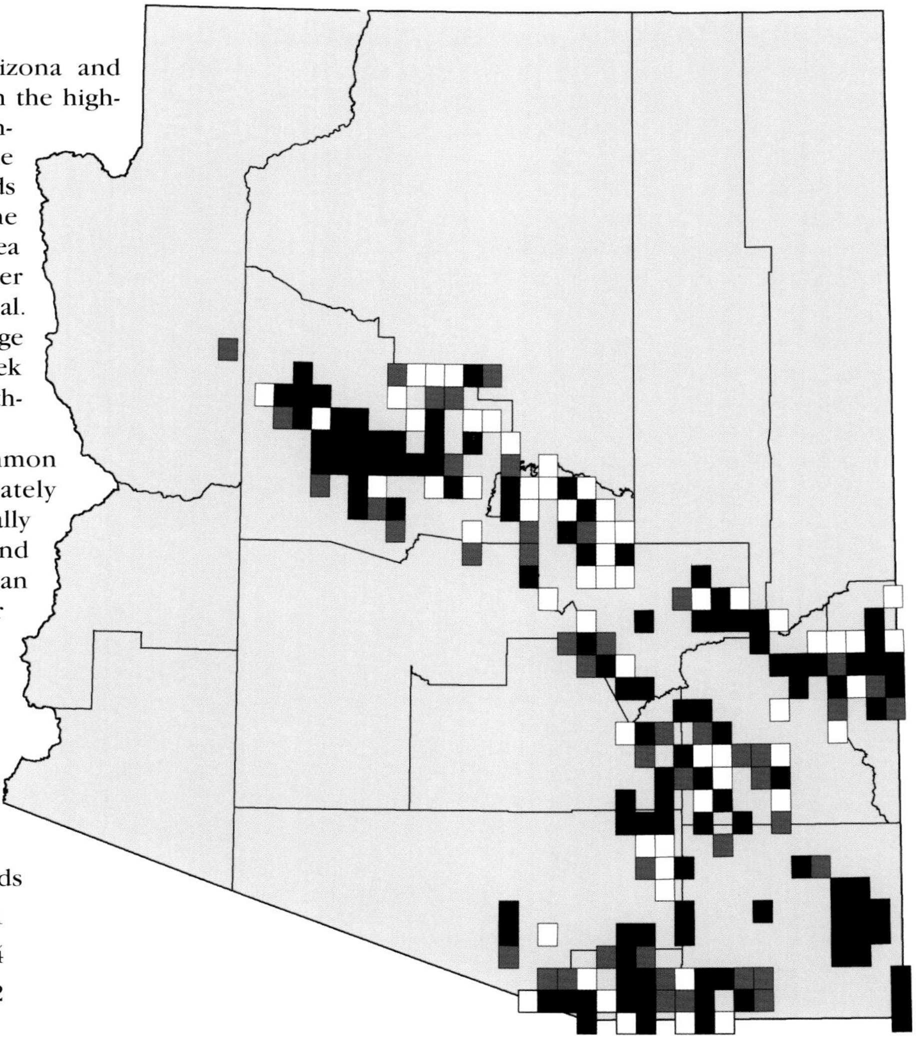

Bridled Titmouse Breeding Evidence Reported in 195 (11%) of 1834 priority blocks

	Blocks	Quads
Possible	51 (26%)	61
Probable	39 (0%)	44
Confirmed	105 (54%)	112

Juniper Titmouse

by Chuck LaRue *Baeolophus ridgwayi*

The Juniper Titmouse is an aptly named cavity-nesting inhabitant of semiarid woodlands containing junipers. A nondescript species that was formerly known as Plain Titmouse, it is a personable little spirit that adds it own spark to the often monotonous expanses of junipers across northern and eastern Arizona.

JIM BURNS

HABITAT

In Arizona, Juniper Titmice are closely associated with dry woodlands that contain Utah and one-seed junipers. Of the 526 breeding records obtained by atlasers, 62 percent were in pinyon pine-juniper woodlands and 25 percent were in three other vegetative communities with strong juniper components. These were Madrean evergreen oak–juniper woodlands, cold-temperate grasslands with scattered open stands of juniper, and pinyon pine–juniper woodlands interspersed with ponderosa pines. Juniper Titmice will frequently forage and occasionally nest at the edge of adjacent habitats in Arizona and may account for some of the nineteen other habitats this species was infrequently reported using. These include chaparral, open riparian woodlands with Arizona sycamores, and ponderosa pine–Gambel's oak associations. When available, the opportunistic Juniper Titmouse will also take full advantage of well-stocked backyard feeding stations, often becoming daily visitors.

BREEDING

Juniper Titmice are permanent residents, and there is little seasonal movement within their range to other habitats. Most evidence indicates they mate for life and maintain pair bonds throughout the year. Early nesting activity can begin by March in Arizona, and atlasers noted the first occupied nest (likely containing eggs) on 5 April. While it is not surprising that atlasers did not locate any nests with eggs for this little cavity-dweller, this factor does complicate determining the breeding phenology of this species in Arizona. Some Juniper Titmice may begin laying eggs in mid- to late March, based on a nest containing calling young discovered on 14 April and a fledgling reported on 21 April. Atlas data reveal that these small tufted birds continue to nest through the summer however, with a peak from mid-May to late June (n = 165). Occupied nests were discovered through 7 July, and Juniper Titmice were observed feeding fledglings through 2 August.

Atlasers took measurements at 16 Juniper Titmouse nests of which 12 (75 percent) were in either one-seed or Utah junipers. The remaining nests were in an Arizona walnut, pinyon pine, Arizona white oak, and Gambel's oak. These trees ranged from 9.8 to 59 ft (3–18 m) tall, with a median height of 17.8 ft (5.4 m). The nest cavities ranged from 3.7 to 14.4 ft (1.1–4.4 m), with a median of 10.5 ft. (3.2 m) above the ground. All but two of the nests were in live trees with the nests located in both old woodpecker holes and natural cavities. Grinnell and Miller (1944) reported that these titmice often place nests in crevices in twisted trunks of larger, older juniper trees. They will also readily use nest boxes (Cicero 2000).

More attention should be given to these little spunky gray birds. The natural history aspect of the Juniper Titmouse remains largely unknown and can only be inferred from prior studies conducted on its counterpart, the Oak Titmouse (*Baeolophus inornatus*). The Juniper Titmice female typically chooses the nest site, constructs the nest in 4–10 days, and incubates the eggs while being fed by the male (Cicero 2000). Most clutches consist of 5–6 eggs (range 4–7), and the incubation period lasts 14–16 days (Cicero 2000). Both parents feed the young, which remain in the nest for approximately 16–21 days. It is unknown how long fledglings remain dependent on their parents, but the brood starts breaking up approximately one month following nest departure (Cicero 2000). Juniper Titmice usually raise one brood each season, but a second brood may occasionally follow (Cicero 2000).

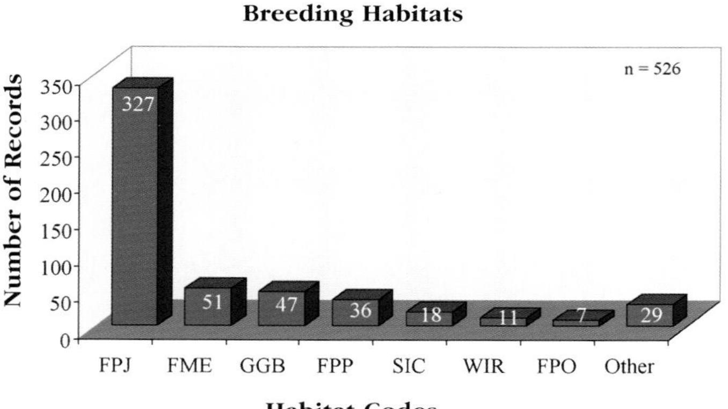

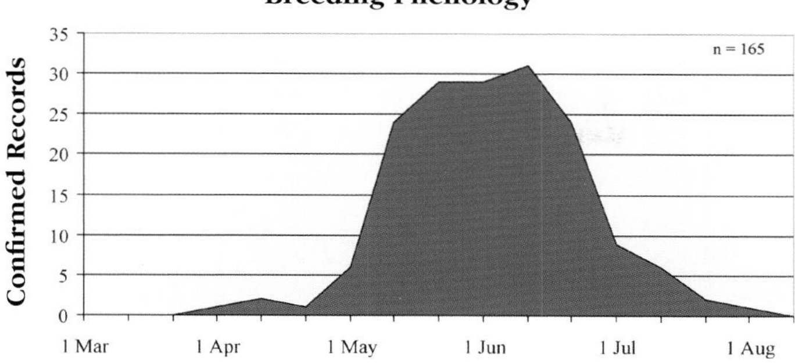

DISTRIBUTION AND STATUS

The Juniper Titmouse is a widespread resident of the Great Basin, Colorado Plateau, and intermountain region of the American West from southeastern Oregon and southwestern Wyoming south through Nevada, Utah, western Colorado to New Mexico and Arizona. The edges of this extensive range reach California, the Oklahoma panhandle, extreme west Texas, and the extreme northeast corner of Sonora, Mexico.

Because the Juniper Titmouse is so closely associated with habitats containing a juniper component, the species' range in Arizona is nearly identical to that of the distribution of junipers in central and northern regions of the state. Furthermore, because these are trees of mid-elevations, the Juniper Titmouse is a bird of habitats typically occurring from 4800 to 7500 ft (1463–2286 m) in most of its Arizona range. However, atlasers confirmed them nesting locally in junipers down to 3450 ft (1052 m). Although inhabiting semiarid woodlands, they avoid Arizona's low hot deserts and valleys lacking junipers. Likewise, the species is absent from the higher elevations of the state such as in the ponderosa pine-mantled Mogollon, Kaibab, and Defiance plateaus, and the San Francisco, White, and Chuska mountains. The southwest edge of its geographic range in Arizona is essentially the southwest flank of the Colorado Plateau. Small populations peripheral to this primary range are found in the foothills of some of the southeastern Arizona mountain ranges such as the Chiricahua, Pinaleno, Dragoon, Galiuro, Santa Catalina, and Rincon mountains. The occupation of mountain foothills in this region continues into extreme northeastern Sonora, Mexico, where they are known from the west slope of the Sierra San Luis (Russell and Monson 1998).

Juniper Titmouse populations in Arizona appear to be secure and stable. Although they are habitat specialists, their habitat appears to be secure at this time. Atlasers found the species in essentially the same areas noted by Phillips et al. (1964) and added one new breeding location in the Dragoon Mountains. This record was an occupied nest found at Cochise Stronghold on 14 May. Data from Breeding Bird Surveys from 1966–1999 show a very slight decrease in population levels rangewide that is probably not statistically significant. The Juniper Titmouse has certainly followed the spread of junipers into adjoining grasslands in Arizona over the past century. Likewise, the large-scale removal of pinyon pine–juniper woodlands during range conversion projects during the 1960s and 1970s certainly eliminated the species from local areas.

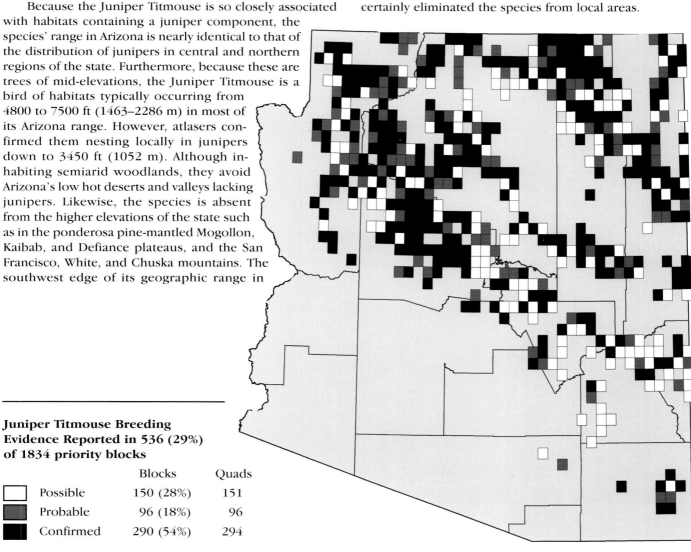

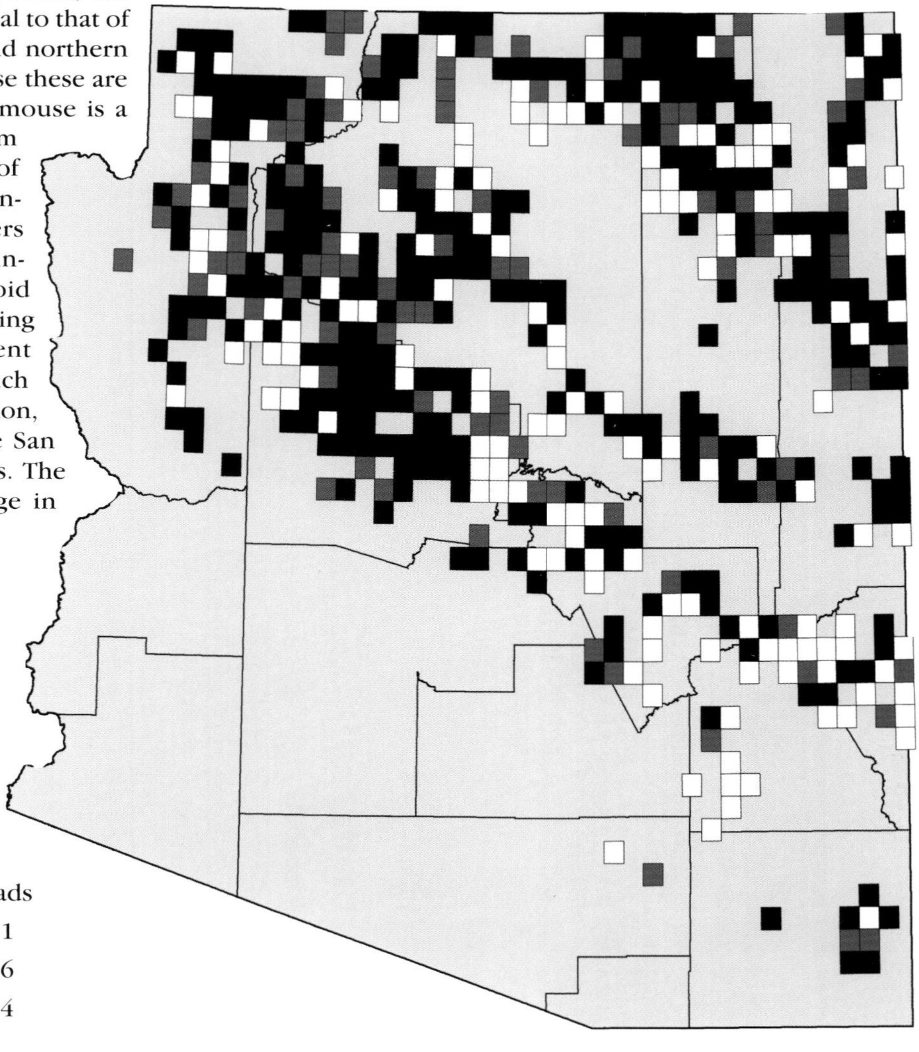

Juniper Titmouse Breeding Evidence Reported in 536 (29%) of 1834 priority blocks

	Blocks	Quads
Possible	150 (28%)	151
Probable	96 (18%)	96
Confirmed	290 (54%)	294

Verdin

by Cathryn Wise-Gervais *Auriparus flaviceps*

Verdins are yellow-faced desert-dwellers that are commonly encountered in southern Arizona. These tiny birds are readily observed flitting through thorny shrubs or tending their round spiky nests, alternately singing or scolding emphatically. Although primarily insectivorous, Verdins will also readily consume nectar, which they obtain by piercing tubular flowers or by visiting hummingbird feeders.

EARLE ROBINSON

HABITAT

Although Verdins are commonly associated with desert environments, atlasers reported these opportunistic birds in nineteen habitat types, including riparian edges, scrubby grasslands, and urban settings. As expected, most Verdin records were obtained in Sonoran desertscrub areas offering an abundance of thorny shrubs and trees including acacia, paloverde, mesquite, and ironwood (42 percent; n = 887). Verdins are also common inhabitants of desert washes and these drainages accounted for 27 percent of all atlas records. Atlasers regularly encountered Verdins in brushy semiarid grasslands with scattered yucca, agave, acacia, and mesquite, as well as in both Mojave and Chihuahuan desertscrub associations. Verdins typically avoid the interior of cottonwood-willow riparian woodlands and dense mesquite bosques, but frequently forage and nest at the edge of these habitats. These little desert birds are somewhat adaptable, and can be found regularly in rural landscapes and residential neighborhoods, both where native vegetation persists and in ornamental plantings. Within these settings, they may become frequent visitors to backyard flowers and hummingbird feeders.

BREEDING

Verdins are year-round desert residents in Arizona. They can initiate breeding early, as soon as resources allow. In the Sonoran Desert, Verdins become more territorial in mid-January, and pairs can form soon after (Taylor 1971). Atlasers reported the first nest with eggs on 28 February, although a nest with young was discovered on 9 March, indicating egg-laying initiation in mid-February. Atlas data reveal that nesting activity increases quickly after mid-March and reaches a peak between mid-April and mid-May (n = 535). Nesting effort decreased sharply there after, but continued into early August. Austin (1977) reported that only about 30–35 percent of Verdin nesting attempts in June and July were successful in fledging young. Atlasers reported nests with young through 8 August and fledglings as late as 2 September.

Verdin nests are sturdy structures that can persist for several years after use. As a result, these nests are a fixture of southern Arizona's desert regions, and are readily apparent on nearly any stroll through these arid landscapes. Verdin nests are intricately woven globes of sharp sticks, stoutly anchored to the nest tree or shrub. Males sometimes start building a "sample" nest that is then completed with help from the female, an activity thought to strengthen the pair bond (Webster 1999). Verdin nests are often constructed in fairly shaded localities under the canopy of low tree or shrub. Because of their distinct appearance, atlasers were able to easily detect and take measurements at 174 nests. The three most common nest plants were paloverde (36 percent), acacia (25 percent, including both catclaw and whitethorn), and ironwood (14 percent). The remaining nests were located in a variety of substrates, including mesquite, graythorn, hackberry, and cholla. Average nest substrate height was 14.4 ft (4.4 m) with a range of 4.1–39.3 ft (1.3–12 m). The average nest height was 6.4 ft (2 m) and range from 2.8 to 18 ft (0.9–5.5 m). The industrious Verdin will also build several roosting nests throughout the year. Summer roosts tend to be smaller structures (Webster 1999), compared to the thicker walled winter roosts (Gilman 1902). They often place winter roosts higher than breeding nests, possibly to take full advantage of the winter sun.

The average Verdin clutch consists of 4 eggs (range 3–6), which are incubated exclusively by the female for 14–18 days (Hensley 1959; Taylor 1971). Female Verdins

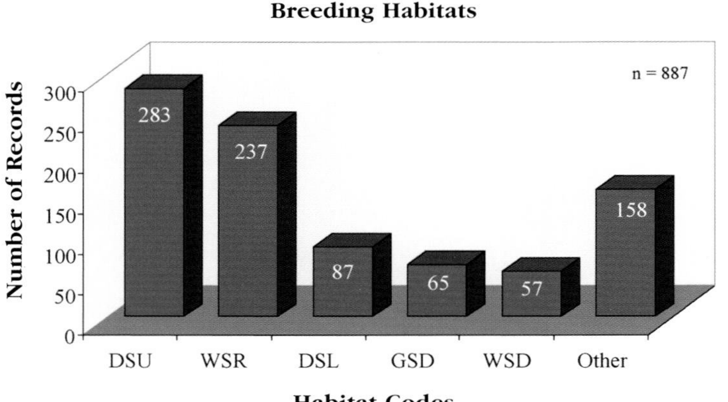

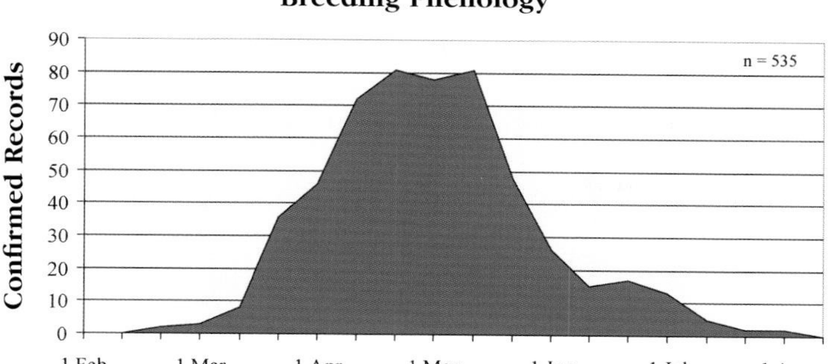

alone feed the young for the first 5–7 days after hatch and then the male will assist as the young begin vigorously calling (Webster 1999). The young leave the nest at 17–21 days after hatching, but parental care continues for about 18 days after fledging (Webster 1999). The sight of fledgling Verdins often befuddles beginning birders, as the young closely resemble short-tailed Bushtits. Several studies in Arizona have found that approximately half of the Verdin pairs attempt to raise two broods per year, and females may start laying their second clutch only two days after the first brood has fledged (Taylor 1971; Austin 1977). Juveniles build their own roosting nest soon after independence (Webster 1999).

DISTRIBUTION AND STATUS

Verdins are southwestern residents found from eastern California and southern Nevada south through Baja California, south-central Arizona, and southern New Mexico. They are found east through Texas and as far south as central Mexico. In Arizona, their range roughly follows that of mesquite, and Phillips et al. (1964) noted that this species had apparently increased with the spread of mesquite into grasslands and other habitats. Verdins are typically found at lower elevations in the state and were confirmed breeding on survey blocks from approximately 90–5200 ft (27–1585 m).

Verdins have always been considered a common resident in the desert regions of southern and western Arizona (Swarth 1914), and, unlike several other desert species, do not extend up the Colorado River into the Grand Canyon (Phillips et al. 1964). Atlasers indeed found the birds to be quite common and easily confirmed throughout their historic range, absent only from high-elevation areas, as expected. As noted by Brown et al. (1987), atlasers documented Verdins up the Colorado River through the Lake Mead National Recreation Area to at least Pearce Ferry, with one record in the lower Granite Gorge. They were also found north into the Virgin River area. Atlasers found Verdins up the Verde River drainage to Clarkdale and likely continue up the Salt River Canyon into the unsurveyed White Mountain Apache tribal lands.

Verdin populations are stable across their range, but habitat losses due to urban sprawl no doubt have had some adverse effects on these birds. Fortunately, Verdins tolerate close proximity to humans if provided with suitable ornamental plantings or, better yet, natural vegetation. The birds especially favor native, thorny trees such as paloverde and acacia, as well as tubular flowers such as chuparosa and penstemon.

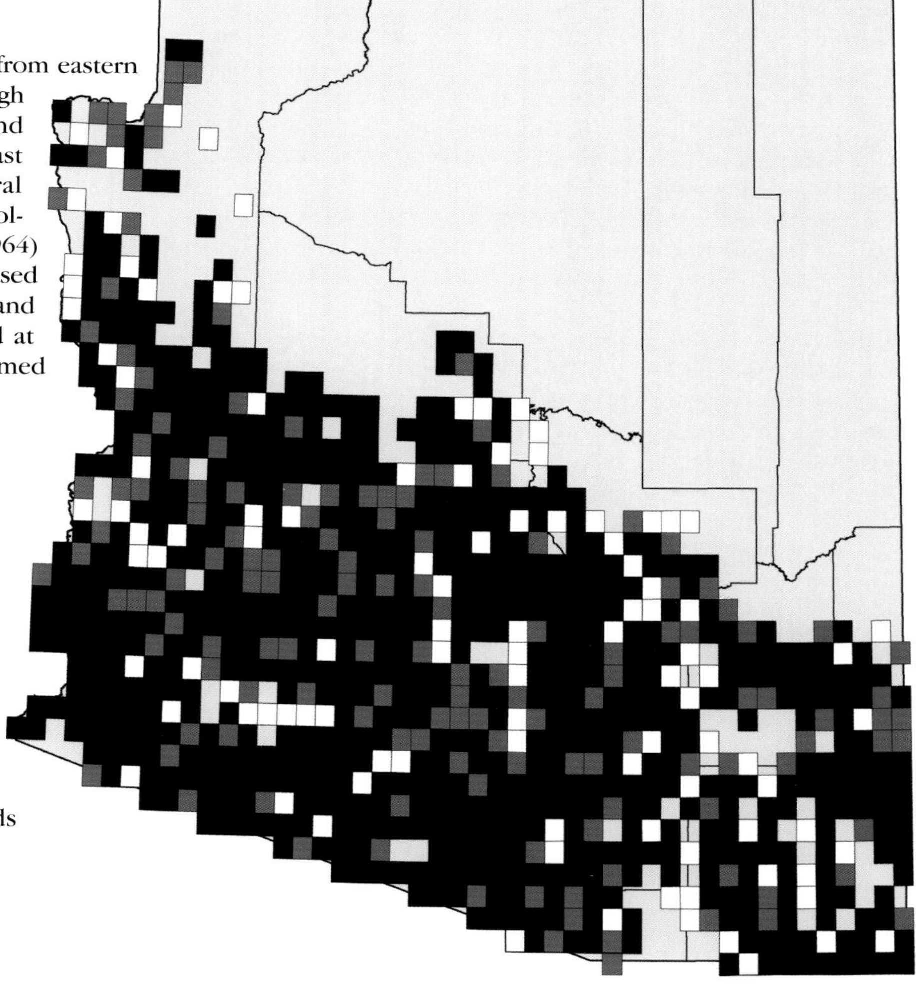

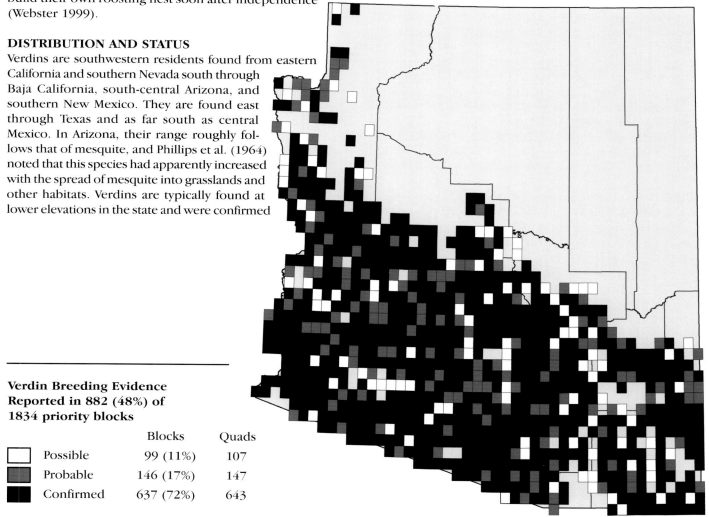

Verdin Breeding Evidence Reported in 882 (48%) of 1834 priority blocks

	Blocks	Quads
Possible	99 (11%)	107
Probable	146 (17%)	147
Confirmed	637 (72%)	643

Bushtit

by Cathryn Wise-Gervais *Psaltriparus minimus*

Small but spunky, this drab little bird makes itself conspicuous by traveling in noisy, chattering groups. Often seen foraging upside down chickadee-style, some Bushtit pairs have nonbreeding "helpers" that assist with all aspects of nesting. Although both sexes sport identical plumage, females have whitish-yellow irises, and males and juveniles have brown irises.

HABITAT

Bushtits are open woodland birds that are often observed energetically foraging through low trees and shrubs. In Arizona, they favor semiarid brushy landscapes from evergreen oak and pinyon-juniper woodlands to chaparral-covered slopes and open riparian groves. Atlasers obtained 43 percent of potential Bushtit breeding records in pinyon pine-juniper woodlands (n = 655). Atlasers also reported Bushtits in grasslands with scattered stands of juniper and in pinyon pine-juniper forests containing some ponderosa pine. These little gray birds were regularly encountered (11 percent of records) in Madrean evergreen oak woodlands, often with some pinyon pine and juniper influence. They were also found in southeastern Arizona's open Madrean pine-oak forests. Ten percent of Bushtit records were in chaparral associations and another 10 percent were from open riparian woodlands including foothill canyons with sycamore and higher-elevation reaches of cottonwood- and willow-dominated drainages. Atlasers noted that Arizona's roving Bushtit flocks wandered widely later in the summer, ascending to mixed-conifer forests and foraging down into nearby brushy mesquite thickets and washes.

BREEDING

Resident Bushtit flocks typically contain 10–40+ individuals, and the birds begin forming pairs in late January or early February (Sloane 2001). Nest site selection begins at this time, and atlasers first observed adults nest building on 26 February. Other researchers in Arizona reported nest building as early as late January (Sloane 2001) but noted that activity was sporadic and that cool inclement weather caused the birds to suspend nest construction and regroup into flocks (Addicott 1938). Bushtit nests are pendulous and are covered from above. This characteristic makes determining nest contents difficult and atlasers reported only three nests with eggs. Observers reported occupied nests by 20 March and adults feeding young on 5 April, indicating that, in this case, the birds laid eggs in mid- to late March. Atlas data suggest that the peak breeding period for Bushtits statewide is from mid-May to mid-June, but nesting activity continues throughout the summer months. Observers reported the latest nest with young on 6 August and noted fledglings as late as 26 August. By September most individuals (and young) have rejoined their flocks and these range over large areas, often straying from typical breeding habitats.

Breeding Habitats

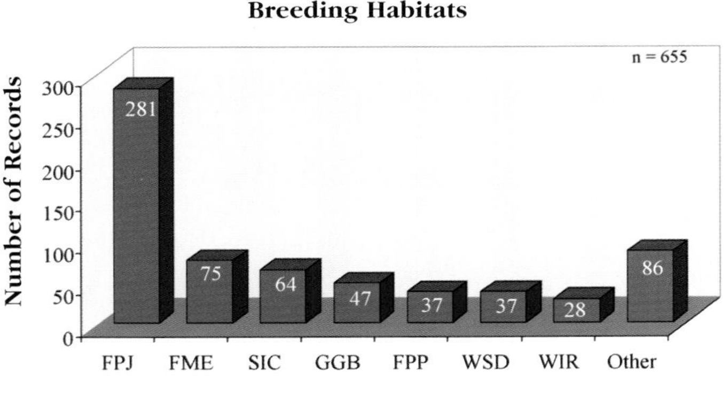

Habitat Codes

Bushtit nests are distinctive pendulous structures, often having the appearance of a wool sock hung in a tree. The birds enter and exit through a small hole near the top of their fully enclosed home. Atlasers took measurements at 47 Bushtit nests in eight tree and shrub species with 21 (46 percent) in juniper (including 2 in mistletoe clumps), 17 (36 percent) in pinyon pine, and 3 or fewer nests in cottonwood, scrub live oak, Goodding willow, barberry, ponderosa pine, and hackberry. The median nest height was 10.8 ft (3.3 m) and ranged from 4.6 to 34.4 ft (1.4–10.5 m). Atlasers found that there was considerable variation in nest placement relative to the center of the substrate tree, and reported nests both at the center as well as on distal branches.

Both sexes construct the nest; males help bring nest materials to the site and females usually place these and stretch them into the final, gourdlike shape (Sloane 2001). Soft, flexible nest materials allow the structure to stretch and accommodate the nesting pair, any helpers, and the

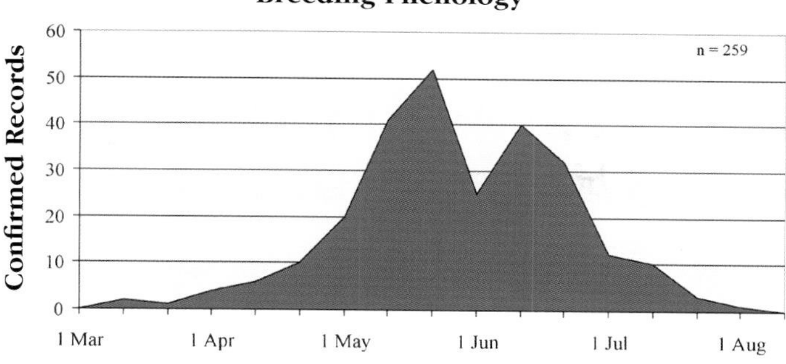

nestlings, all of which sleep within each evening (Sloane 2001). Sloane reported an Arizona nest that contained four adults and 10 nestlings!

Most Bushtit clutches consist of 5–6 eggs (range 3–10), which are incubated by both sexes for 12–13 days (Sloane 2001). All adults associated with the nest will feed the nestlings, and occasionally a second clutch of eggs is initiated in the same nest before the first brood has departed (Phillips et al. 1964). Nest helpers have been noted at fewer than half the occupied nests and can be observed at any stage of nesting. Helpers are usually unmated males, but can also be failed breeding pairs or the young of a previous brood (Sloane 2001).

Bushtits are rare Brown-headed Cowbird hosts (Ehrlich et al. 1988), and there are no records of them successfully rearing cowbirds (Sloane 2001). Atlasers observed one instance of adult Bushtits feeding a Brown-headed Cowbird fledgling on 5 August.

DISTRIBUTION AND STATUS

Bushtits are a western species found along the Pacific Coast from southwestern British Columbia south to Baja California. They also occur from eastern Oregon and Nevada, southeast to central Texas and south through the highlands of Mexico to Guatemala. Away from arid desert regions, Bushtits are found as common residents nearly statewide in Arizona (Phillips et al. 1964). Atlasers confirmed Bushtits breeding on priority blocks from approximately 3000 to 7500 ft (914–2286 m).

In southeastern Arizona, Bushtits breed regularly west to the Baboquivari Mountains and are absent as a nesting species primarily only in desertscrub, semiarid grasslands, and conifer forests on higher mountain slopes. They breed fairly commonly among the riparian woodlands on the upper San Pedro River, but are absent in similar habitat on the lower reaches of this drainage.

These little gray birds are widespread in central Arizona with noticeable absence primarily only in the higher-elevation coniferous forests. As noted by Phillips et al. (1964), Bushtits were encountered in the isolated Harquahala Mountains; atlasers also found them in the nearby Harcuvar Mountains and north of the Santa Maria River in the Arrastra Mountains. In northeastern Arizona, they were found commonly in most pinyon pine–juniper associations, but were largely lacking in the more arid Little Colorado River and Chile Wash watersheds.

Bushtit populations in Arizona appear to be fairly stable, although local densities can vary considerably from year to year, with weather a possible factor (Sloane 2001). Regardless, these little social birds will undoubtedly continue to roam the many brushy landscapes of Arizona.

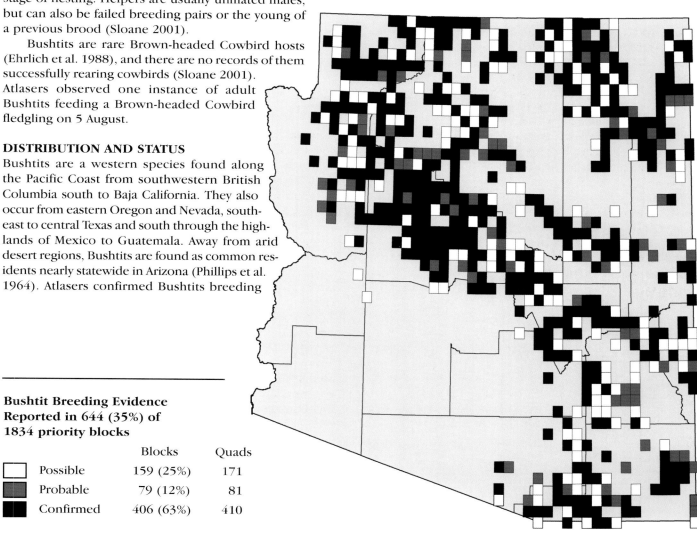

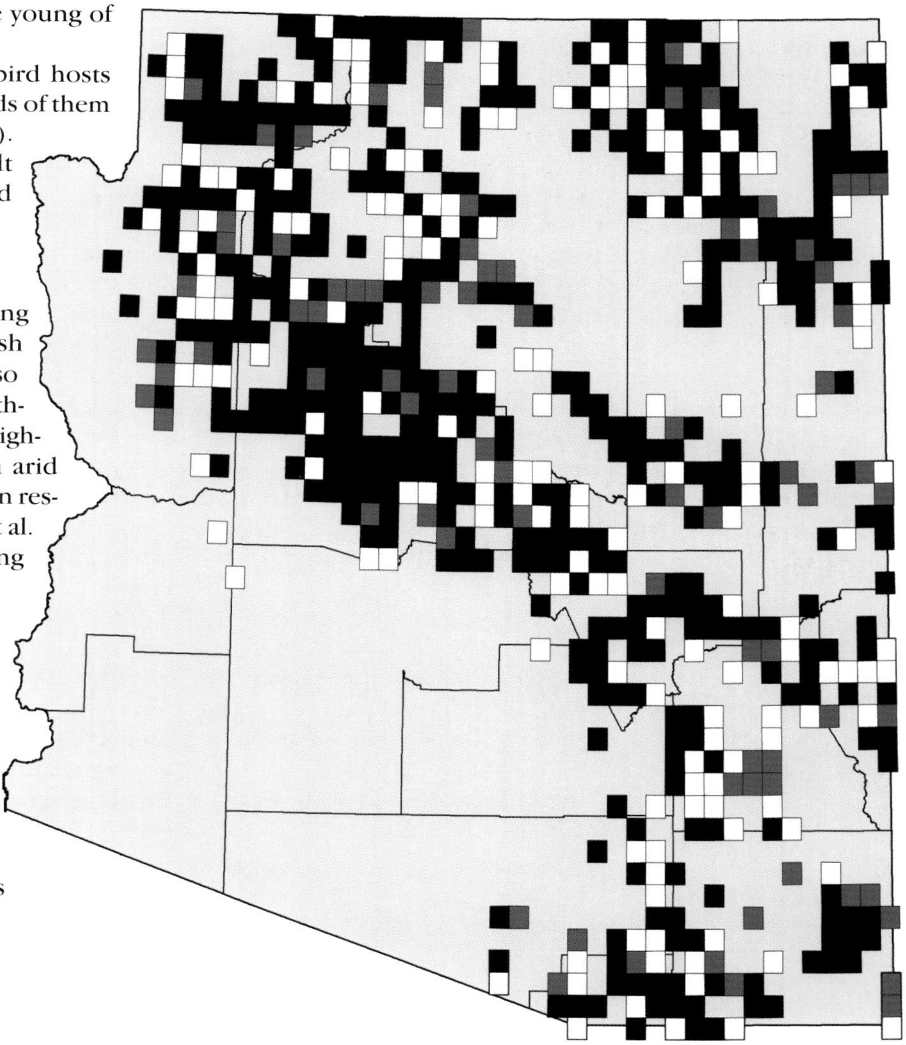

Bushtit Breeding Evidence Reported in 644 (35%) of 1834 priority blocks

	Blocks	Quads
Possible	159 (25%)	171
Probable	79 (12%)	81
Confirmed	406 (63%)	410

Red-breasted Nuthatch

by John R. Spence *Sitta canadensis*

Residents of high-elevation conifer forests, Red-breasted Nuthatches are active and agile birds that clamber over trees and branches, often upside down, while searching for insects. The nasal, tinny quality of the "yank yank" contact call between a pair is one of the most characteristic sounds of Arizona's cooler forests.

RICK AND NORA BOWERS

HABITAT

In Arizona, Red-breasted Nuthatches breed almost exclusively in high-elevation forests composed of conifers and aspen. The species favors forests with a mix of Douglas fir, white fir, spruces, and aspen. Other common trees in occupied locations include subalpine fir, Engelmann spruce, blue spruce, ponderosa pine, maple, and alder. During atlas surveys, Red-breasted Nuthatches were most commonly detected in mixed-conifer forests, where 56 percent of all records were obtained (n = 102). These nuthatches were also commonly encountered in the adjacent forested montane drainages and subalpine spruce-fir forests. They typically avoid nesting in the drier ponderosa pine dominated forests, but atlasers noted them locally in older stands and those with a Gambel's oak or aspen association. They require dead trees or snags as part of the forest composition for nesting and the species usually declines in response to extensive logging and clearing of snags.

BREEDING

Courtship commences early for Red-breasted Nuthatches, with paired males singing and dancing for their mates as early as mid-winter. Typically, unpaired males establish territories and start singing in March and April (Ghalambor and Martin 1999). These males may also initiate construction on several different cavities during this period. Atlasers reported the first occupied nest by 1 May, although early egg laying may begin by late April. Of 295 nests in central Arizona, the mean initiation date for egg laying was 19 May (Ghalambor and Martin 1999). In Arizona, atlas data suggest that peak breeding occurs in June, with occupied nests noted through 13 July. In years with large infestations of spruce budworm, the larvae are an important part of the Red-breasted Nuthatches diet. In July and early August fledglings were often seen accompanied and being fed by adults.

Although single males often start excavating nest cavities on their territories, the female selects the typically soft wood site and does most nest building. In much of the species' range in the West, aspen is a preferred nest substrate. Because of this species' preference for high remote dense forests, atlasers found relatively few nests. However, extensive data are available from studies conducted by Ghalambor and Martin (1999) from central Arizona forests. Both aspen and small firs with broken tops are preferred, with more than 90 percent of nests in completely dead trees or snags. Mean nest height was 33 ft (10 m), and varied from 2 to 105 ft (0.7–32 m).

During nest construction and egg laying, Red-breasted Nuthatches are highly aggressive, and typically exclude other species from nesting in the nest tree. However, one Arizona pair was noted nesting in the same tree as a pair of Northern Pygmy-Owls. Eventually, the male owl caught and killed the male nuthatch, feeding it to his mate (Ghalambor and Martin 1999). Clutch size is generally 5–6 eggs, but varies from 2 to 8, which the female incubates for about 12–13 days (Ghalambor and Martin 1999). The male feeds the female during incubation, and apparently may also roost in the cavity. Both parents feed the young through nest departure in 18–21 days (Baicich and Harrison 1997). After fledging, the young tend to remain with the adults for approximately two weeks, but sometimes remain with them much longer as family groups, sometimes joining other species in mixed flocks in fall and winter.

Red-breasted Nuthatches are unique among North American passerines in their behavior at the nest site. Both adults spend considerable amounts of time smearing sticky conifer resin around the nest entrance. Recent studies have shown that the resin repels House Wrens (Ghalambor and Martin 1999), and it is thought that this unusual behavior

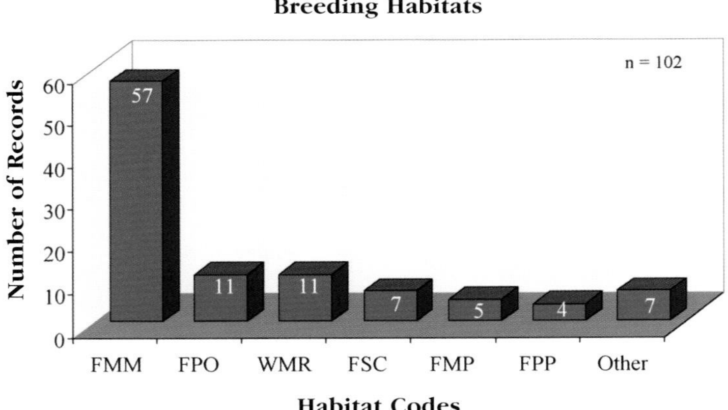

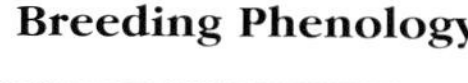

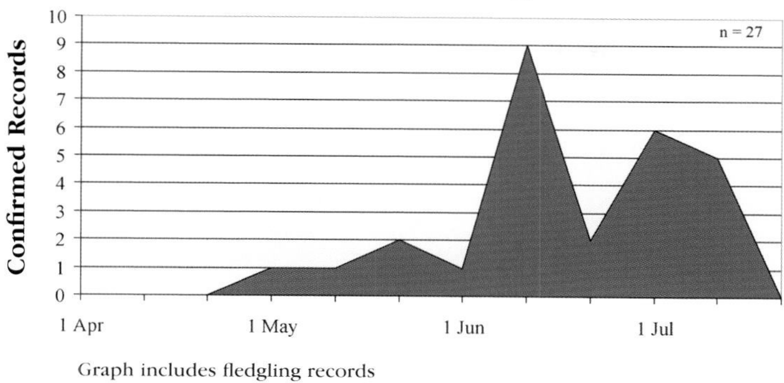

is a form of nest defense. Unfortunately, nuthatches are occasionally found dead trapped in the resin.

DISTRIBUTION AND STATUS

The Red-breasted Nuthatch is a widespread species in the higher-elevation and northern coniferous forests of western North America north to southern Alaska. Its distribution extends eastward through the boreal forests of Canada to the Atlantic Provinces, and south along the Appalachian Mountains to North Carolina. The southernmost breeding distribution of the species is in the mountains of southeastern Arizona and southern California. Red-breasted Nuthatches do not breed in the mountains of Mexico, where the species is known only as a winter vagrant (Russell and Monson 1998).

Throughout most of their range, Red-breasted Nuthatches are a common species with stable or increasing populations (Ghalambor and Martin 1999). They are known to be an "irruptive" species, with alternating years when large numbers of birds move south and down slope in late summer and fall, including desert regions.

Red-breasted Nuthatches were located on 102 quads scattered throughout the state, typically where mixed-conifer or spruce-fir forests occur. Most atlas observations were at elevations from 7500 to 10,000 ft (2286–3048 m). However, the species was documented on cool north-facing slopes and down montane drainages to approximately 6700 ft (2012 m) and can be found at upper timberlines as high as 11,500 ft (3505 m) in Arizona. Red-breasted Nuthatches are widespread in the White Mountains region, and their distribution undoubtedly continues west into the adjacent unsurveyed White Mountain Apache tribal lands. Atlasers frequently encountered Red-breasted Nuthatches elsewhere along the Mogollon Rim north to the San Francisco Mountains area. These nuthatches were noted locally west to the Hualapai and Virgin mountains, as well as on Mount Trumbull. On Navajo and Hopi tribal lands, atlasers found Red-breasted Nuthatches in cooler canyons of Black Mesa and from the Carrizo Mountains south to upper Canyon de Chelly.

In southeastern Arizona, Red-breasted Nuthatches were found in the Chiricahua, Pinaleno, Galiuro, and Santa Catalina mountains, and only locally in the cooler east slope canyons of the Huachuca Mountains. These nuthatches were not detected in the Santa Rita Mountains where they had been noted previously by Phillips et al. (1964). However, atlas surveys were very limited in the higher elevations of this range, where they may still occur.

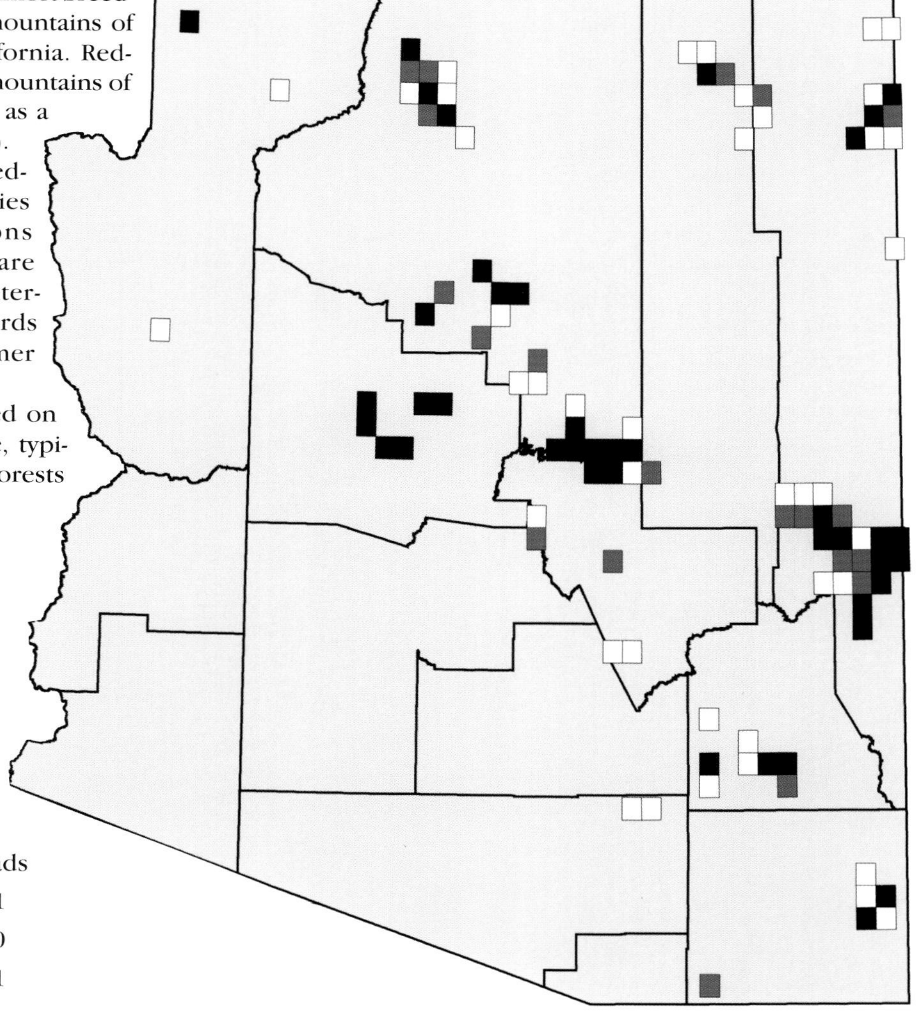

Red-breasted Nuthatch Breeding Evidence Reported in 85 (5%) of 1834 priority blocks

	Blocks	Quads
Possible	32 (38%)	41
Probable	15 (18%)	20
Confirmed	38 (45%)	41

White-breasted Nuthatch

by John R. Spence *Sitta carolinensis*

The White-breasted Nuthatch, dressed neatly in black, white, and gray, is an engaging permanent resident of most forests in Arizona. It habitually forages upside-down, walking down tree trunks, and it often clings to the undersides of branches. Although it is a common bird, surprisingly little is known about its breeding biology.

HABITAT

White-breasted Nuthatches breed throughout Arizona wherever forests and extensive woodlands occur, but typically below spruce-fir habitat associations. Atlasers reported these nuthatches most commonly (61 percent) in forests and woodlands dominated by either pinyon pine–juniper or ponderosa pine ($n = 422$). In ponderosa pine forests, White-breasted Nuthatches were most regularly encountered in pine stands with a Gambel's oak association. During atlas work the species was also commonly encountered in Madrean evergreen woodlands and Madrean pine-oak forests of southeastern Arizona. Atlasers noted the species fairly regularly in the more open and drier stands of mixed-conifer forests, but they were rarely detected in the cooler forested montane drainages. Although White-breasted Nuthatches commonly nest in canyons and foothill drainages containing Arizona sycamore, they are rather sparse and local summer inhabitants of cottonwood-willow dominated drainages. White-breasted Nuthatches tend to favor open forests and edges around clearings rather than denser forest interiors, and can tolerate a certain amount of logging and clearing (Szaro and Balda 1979). Throughout most of their breeding range in Arizona, they are generally found where there are conifers or oaks. Elsewhere in North America, they breed most commonly in deciduous forests, particularly in the East (Pravosudov and Grubb 1993), but in Colorado they were also found mostly in coniferous forests (Kuenning 1998).

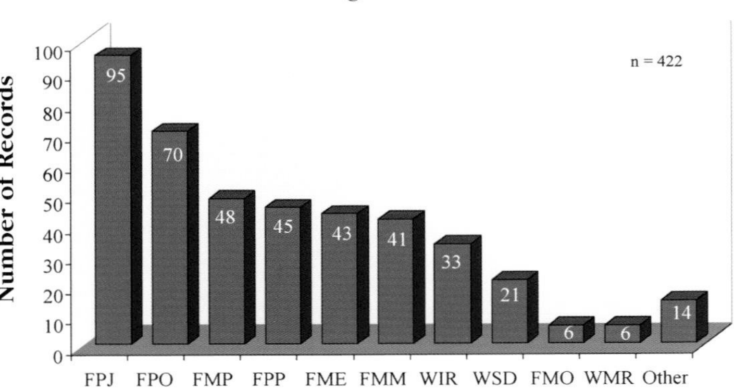

BREEDING

White-breasted Nuthatches are monogamous, often maintaining pair bonds and territories throughout the year. Courtship commences early, with males starting to sing in late winter, but usually not peaking until April and early May. Only the female White-breasted Nuthatch constructs the nest within the selected cavity. Although nest construction typically starts in April in Arizona, atlasers noted an individual carrying nesting material on the early date of 19 March. This was at a lower elevation in southern Arizona and may not be unusually early at these locations. Occupied nests were reported as early as 23 April and may have contained eggs by that time. Adult White-breasted nuthatches were observed feeding fledglings as early as 21 May, suggesting that some egg laying begins in early to mid-April in Arizona. Statewide atlas data reveal that peak breeding occurs in late May and June, with the latest occupied nest noted on 6 July. In Arizona, fledged young were observed being fed as late as 9 August, although most fledging and parental care occurs from mid-June through July.

Unlike the other two nuthatch species in the state, White-breasted Nuthatches do not excavate their own cavities, preferring to nest in woodpecker holes and natural cavities (Pravosudov and Grubb 1993). The nest cavity is usually in a snag or dead portion of a live tree, although the species will sometimes accept nest boxes. Atlasers took measurements at six nests of this nuthatch in ponderosa pine, Gambel's oak, and netleaf oak. The median substrate height was 38 ft (11.5 m). Median nest cavity height was 21 ft (6.4 m), but varied in height from 6 to 39.4 ft (1.8–12 m).

White-breasted Nuthatches have a unique behavior at the nest site known as "bill-sweeping." Both adults will sweep their bills around the entrance of the nest cavity. They usually hold an insect in their bill while performing the sweeping motions, typically an ant or beetle that exudes

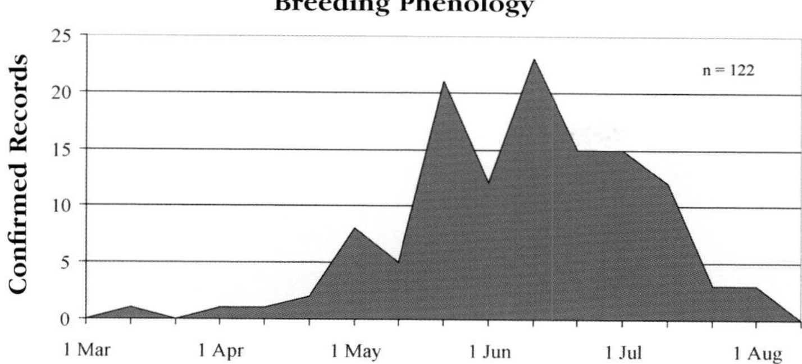

noxious and foul-smelling fluids. This behavior has been considered to be a form of nest defense, as it may deter potential predators from entering the nest (Kilham 1968).

The mean clutch size for White-breasted Nuthatches is 7 eggs, but this can vary from 5 to 9. The female incubates the eggs, while the male feeds her (Bent 1948). Hatching occurs at 12–14 days, and the young are brooded by the female and fed by both parents (Pravosudov and Grubb 1993). Young birds typically fledge at about 26 days and remain dependent on the adults for about two weeks (Pravosudov and Grubb 1993). Unlike Pygmy Nuthatches, there is no evidence of cooperative breeding in White-breasted Nuthatches. Following the breeding season the young disperse away from their natal territory, while the parents stay and join mixed-species flocks that wander through their territory.

DISTRIBUTION AND STATUS

In North America, the White-breasted Nuthatch is the most widely distributed of the four nuthatch species. It is found throughout the United States and southern Canada wherever forests occurs, and extends south through the highlands of Mexico as far as Oaxaca. The species is absent in the northern boreal forests and Alaska.

In Arizona, White-breasted Nuthatches are found throughout the state's forests, including those on isolated western ranges, such as the Hualapai, Cerbat, and Virgin mountains. Most prior literature considered them fairly common residents in Arizona (Swarth 1914; Phillips et al. 1964), and atlasers reported them nesting at elevations primarily from 3800 to 9600 ft (1158–2926 m). However, atlasers noted them nesting locally and in limited numbers in the cottonwood-willow riparian woodlands along the lower San Pedro River down to 2000 ft (610 m). The densest populations occur in the belt of pinyon pine–juniper, ponderosa pine, and mixed-conifer forests from the Kaibab Plateau south and east along the Mogollon Rim to the White Mountains. Atlas records nearly encircle the unsurveyed White Mountain Apache tribal lands, indicating that this nuthatch undoubtedly occurs throughout this diverse reservation. They are also common on the higher mesas of Navajo and Hopi tribal lands, and from the Carrizo Mountains south through the Defiance Plateau. White-breasted Nuthatches do not inhabit all of Arizona's extensive woodlands of pinyon pine and juniper, preferring those at higher elevations or taller and denser stands.

Based on Breeding Bird Survey data, some of the densest populations of White-breasted Nuthatch in the western United States occur in northern and central Arizona (Pravosudov and Grubb 1993). Although there are local fluctuations in number, the species is either stable or increasing throughout most of its range.

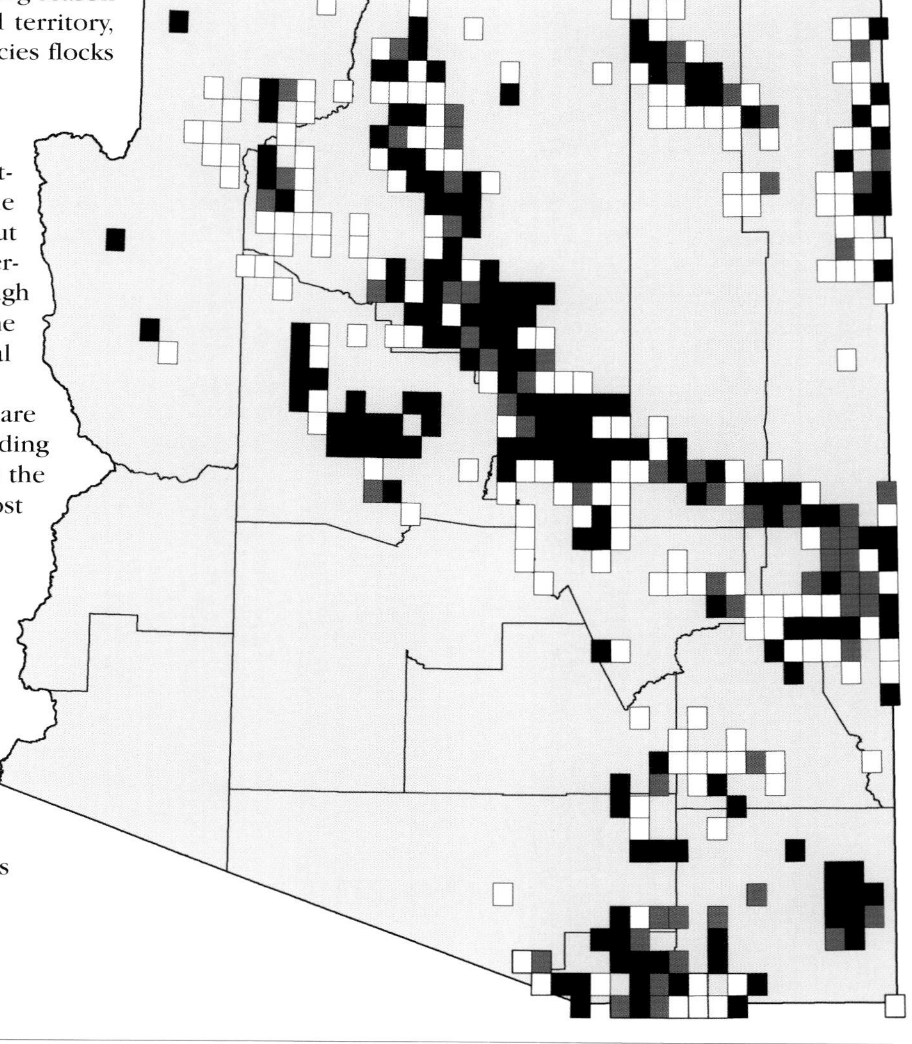

White-breasted Nuthatch Breeding Evidence Reported in 395 (22%) of 1834 priority blocks

	Blocks	Quads
Possible	170 (43%)	186
Probable	59 (15%)	60
Confirmed	166 (42%)	170

Pygmy Nuthatch

by John R. Spence *Sitta pygmaea*

The Pygmy Nuthatch is one of the few passerines in North America to breed cooperatively, with up to three helpers at the nest. It is also one of a handful of birds known to have used tools and is the only North American passerine that huddles in roosts and induces hypothermia to survive cold nights.

HABITAT

Pygmy Nuthatches breed primarily in pine forests and in Arizona favor those dominated by taller ponderosa pine. Seventy-eight percent of the 202 potential breeding records obtained by atlasers for this nuthatch were in either pure ponderosa pine forests or those with a Gambel's oak or pinyon pine–juniper association. Mixed-conifer forests with various species of firs, pines, and aspen accounted for an additional 16 percent of records. Atlasers reported Pygmy Nuthatches very infrequently in several adjacent habitats such as subalpine spruce-fir forests, aspen groves, and in the Madrean pine-oak forests of southeastern Arizona. They were also reported on a few blocks in nearby pinyon pine–juniper woodlands, where they forage and occasionally nest (Woodbury and Russell 1945; C. LaRue, personal communication). Pygmy Nuthatches tend to be more common in old-growth or at least seminatural pine forests compared with more intensively managed and logged forests, and their abundance is strongly related to snag density (Szaro and Balda 1979; Sydeman et al. 1988). Where habitat conditions are good, the species is typically one of the most abundant birds present.

BREEDING

Pygmy Nuthatches mate for life and are a highly social and cooperatively breeding species. Studies show that about 35–40 percent of pairs have from 1 to 3 helpers, typically yearlings from the pair's previous breeding season and almost always male (Kingery and Ghalambor 2001). Researchers have also determined that pairs with helpers fledge more young than pairs lacking helpers (Sydeman et al. 1988; Kingery and Ghalambor 2001). In early to mid-March, the adult male selects a site within the breeding territory. The pair, sometimes including the helpers, then begins excavation of a cavity, and this process can take several weeks. In some cases, nuthatches are known to reuse old cavities or those constructed by woodpeckers. They also readily accept nest boxes. In Arizona, the earliest active nest discovered during the atlas contained eggs on 5 April and adults have been observed feeding fledglings as early as 5 May. This suggests that some early egg laying may take place by late March. Atlasers located the majority of active nests from about mid-May through the end of June. Pygmy Nuthatches occasionally attempt to breed a second time, although these nesting attempts often fail (Kingery and Ghalambor 2001). Although atlasers did observe adults carrying food throughout the breeding period, these dates must be considered with caution as Pygmy Nuthatches cache seeds, so they may be storing food instead of feeding young. The latest active nest with young in Arizona was discovered on 18 July and adults were observed feeding fledglings through 25 August.

The nest is usually in a conifer snag or dead portion of a live tree and is often south-facing (Kingery and Ghalambor 2001). Most nests discovered by atlasers were in ponderosa snags, with two in Douglas fir snags. The median height of 10 nests was 24.6 ft (7.5 m) and ranged from 7.2 to 62 ft (2.2–18.9 m). Of 287 Pygmy Nuthatch nests within mixed-conifer forests on the Mogollon Rim, significantly more nests were discovered in aspen (64 percent) and fir (28 percent) than pine (T. Martin, personal communication). There can be fierce competition for cavities between Pygmy Nuthatches and other small species. They are strongly

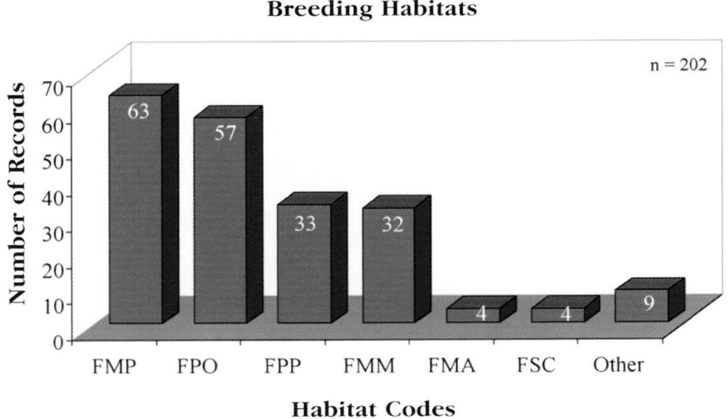

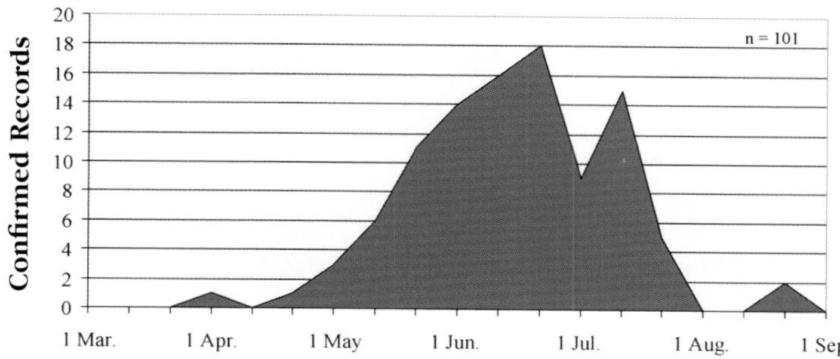

territorial toward their own kind, and typically exclude other Pygmy Nuthatches from the same snag. They are particularly aggressive toward House Wrens, which are known to destroy nuthatch eggs. The cavity is generally deeper than it is wide with a relatively small entrance that excludes most larger bird species.

Female Pygmy Nuthatches lay from 5 to 9 eggs and incubate these for 13–16 days (Kingery and Ghalambor 2001). While incubating, the female is fed by the male and any helpers. The length of time before young fledge is highly variable, but is generally between 14 and 22 days after hatching. Fledglings are dependent on adults and helpers for another 28–30 days, and often continue to beg for food well beyond this time (Kingery and Ghalambor 2001). Overall, this species has a long breeding period compared with other passerines. Following the breeding season, the family group, including adults, helpers and young, often flocks with other family groups.

DISTRIBUTION AND STATUS

The Pygmy Nuthatch is a fairly widespread species that occurs in disjunct populations in western North America. Its breeds from the mountains of southern British Columbia through California into northern Baja California, and from the Rocky Mountains south to central Mexico. Throughout its range, the species is basically sedentary.

The range of Pygmy Nuthatches in Arizona closely follows the distribution of ponderosa pine within the state; they were noted at elevations from 5200 to 9600 ft (1585–2926 m). Atlasers commonly found Pygmy Nuthatches in tall pines in northern Arizona, particularly in the extensive ponderosa-dominated forests north of the Mogollon Rim on the Colorado and Kaibab plateaus, from the North Rim of the Grand Canyon and Flagstaff south and east to the White Mountains. These little nuthatches undoubtedly nest throughout much of the unsurveyed White Mountain Apache tribal lands as well. Isolated populations were noted west to the Hualapai Mountains and Cerbat Mountains near Kingman.

Pygmy Nuthatches were also encountered in the Pinaleno, Santa Catalina, Huachuca, and Chiricahua mountains in southeastern Arizona. Historical records are known from the Santa Rita Mountains (Phillips et al. 1964), but Pygmy Nuthatches were not reported in this range during the atlas period. Preferred habitat is rather limited in the Santa Rita Mountains and may not have been surveyed by atlasers. They were also not detected in the Mazatzal Mountains of northeastern Maricopa County, where Witzeman et al. (1997) considered them uncommon residents.

Based on North American Breeding Bird Survey data, Pygmy Nuthatches are most abundant in Arizona and California, and this species' presence and abundance has often been used as an indicator of the health of pine forests in the western United States.

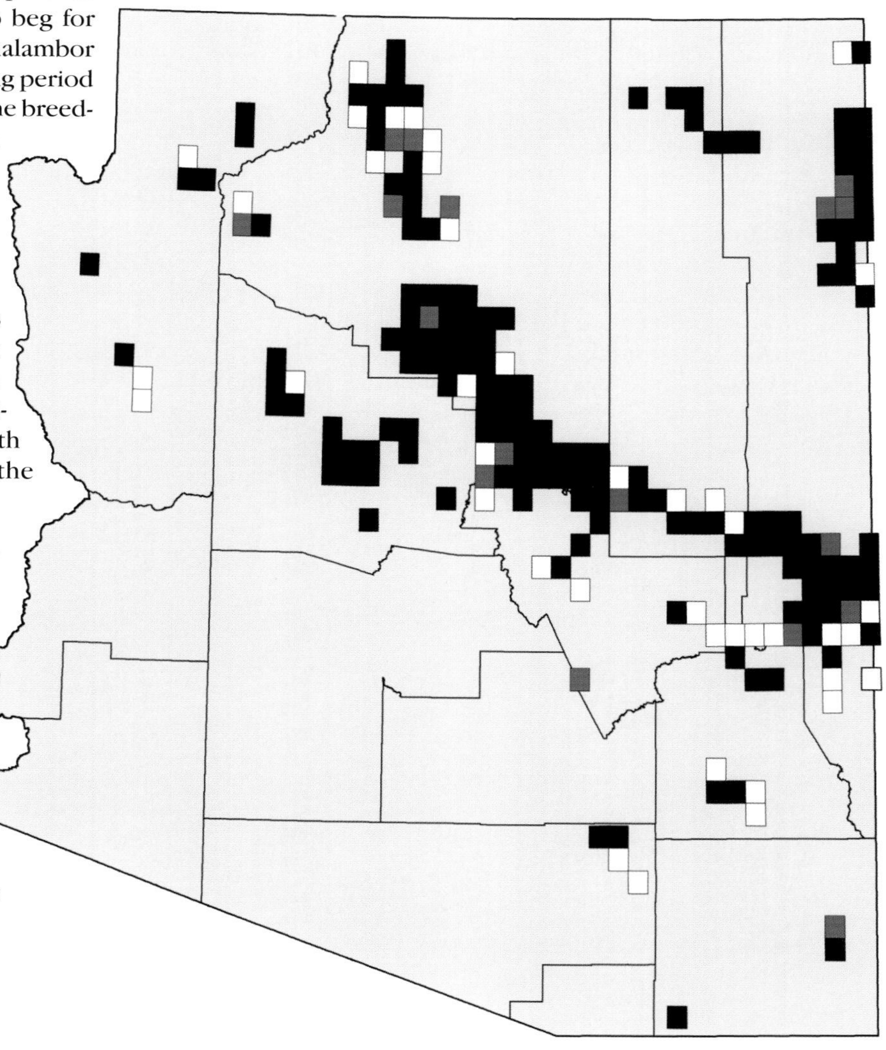

Pygmy Nuthatch Breeding Evidence Reported in 194 (11%) of 1834 priority blocks

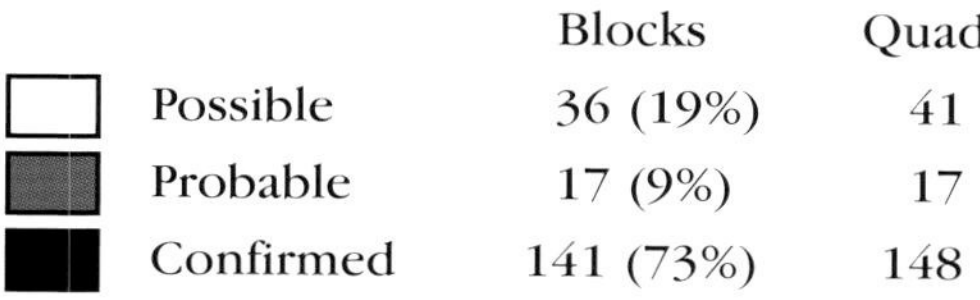

	Blocks	Quads
Possible	36 (19%)	41
Probable	17 (9%)	17
Confirmed	141 (73%)	148

Brown Creeper

by Peter Friederici *Certhia americana*

An inconspicuous forest dweller, the Brown Creeper is seldom found far from big trees. Its camouflaged plumage blends into the bark as it creeps up tree after tree, making high-pitched, easily overlooked calls and searching for invertebrate prey hidden in cracks and crevices.

DAN FISCHER

HABITAT

Breeding Brown Creepers have a very strong association with tall, montane coniferous forests located on northern Arizona's broad, high plateaus and southern Arizona's "sky island" ranges. The majority of the 153 atlas records were obtained from forests dominated by ponderosa pine (52 percent), including those with Gambel's oak and, less frequently, pinyon pine–juniper associations. They were encountered regularly in mixed-conifer forests (32 percent of all records) containing various pines, firs, aspen, and Gambel's oak. In southeastern Arizona, Brown Creepers also nest fairly commonly in Madrean pine-oak woodlands with Apache, Chihuahuan, and ponderosa pines. Fewer atlas records were obtained in subalpine spruce-fir forests, Madrean evergreen oak woodlands, and cool forested montane drainages. Components important for good breeding habitat in these forests include high vertical diversity and canopy cover and many large snags and living trees for nesting and foraging (Hejl et al. 2002). The presence of large, tall trees with furrowed and/or loose bark appears important to the species not only for nest sites, but also for optimum foraging habitat (Franzreb 1985, Siegel 1989).

BREEDING

Some Brown Creepers are resident year-round in parts of Arizona, and some migrate from elsewhere to winter in woodlands and lowland riparian groves in the state. Most individuals breeding in Arizona appear to arrive on their breeding grounds in late March and April (Phillips et al. 1964). The earliest reported occupied nest during the atlas project was noted on 30 April, although adults were observed feeding a fledgling on 18 May. This suggests that some egg laying in Arizona may begin in early to mid-April. Immediately following the atlas period, early nesting activity was also noted when a Brown Creeper was observed constructing a nest on 16 March in Oak Creek Canyon, north of Sedona (T. Corman, personal communication). However, atlas data reveal that most nesting activity occurs between late May and mid-July. Brown Creepers were also recorded nest building as late as 18 June, with occupied nests through 25 June and possibly to 23 July. Because the species has never been recorded raising more than one brood in a season (Hejl et al. 2002), these records likely represented later nesting attempts after nest failure. Atlasers reported adults feeding fledglings through 2 August. Although Brown Creepers begin moving locally to nearby habitats in August, migrants are rarely observed in Arizona lowlands before early October.

Although male Brown Creepers will bring some nesting material, females build the well-camouflaged nests. Nests are typically tucked behind the loose bark of large, old trees, especially snags, and they often have two entrances (Hejl et al. 2002). They are well hidden, and atlasers recorded measurements at only three nests—two in ponderosa pine snags, and one in a Douglas fir snag. Nests were built from 8.9 ft (2.7 m) to more than 33 ft (10 m) high. Siegel (1989) found 30 Brown Creeper nests on the Kaibab Plateau, 29 in ponderosa pine snags and 1 in a living ponderosa. Nest trees were large, averaging 22.4 in. (56.9 cm) in diameter, and nests averaged 27.3 ft (8.3 m) in height. Along the Mogollon Rim, most nests found during a long-running study have been in dead quaking aspens; others were in Douglas fir, white fir, and Gambel's oak (T. Martin in Hejl et al. 2002). The diameter of these nest trees averaged 16 in. (40.8 cm) and the average nest height of 77 nests was 22 ft (6.7 m) with a range of 3–60 ft (0.9–18.3 m).

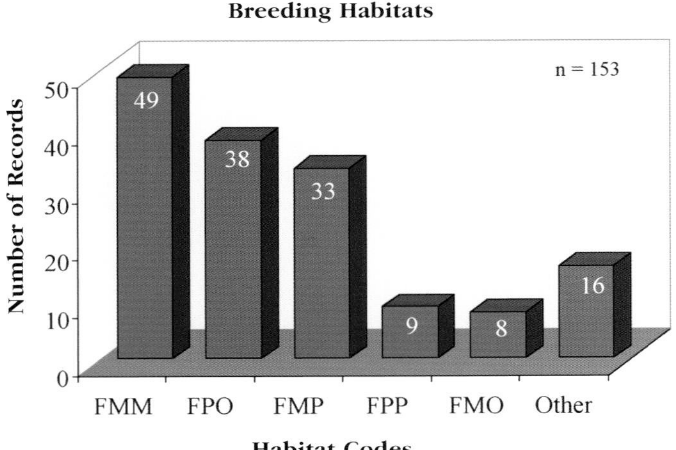

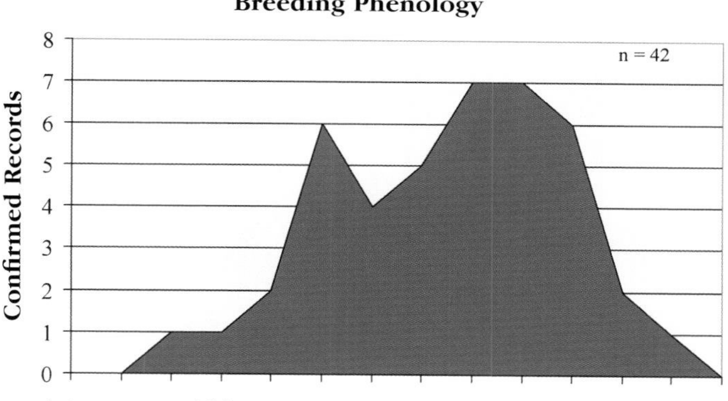

Only the female Brown Creeper incubates the average clutch of 5–6 eggs (range 3–8) for approximately 15 days, but the male will feed the female during this period (Hejl et al. 2002). Both parents gather food for nestlings. The young fledge at 14–20 days of age, but are typically cared for in family groups for another several weeks (Hejl et al. 2002). Davis (1978) noted that although the fledglings were primarily foraging and feeding on their own after two weeks, they were still begging and receiving food from parents at 17 days after nest departure.

DISTRIBUTION AND STATUS

Brown Creepers breed from southern Alaska and southern Canada south through northeastern United States and locally down the Appalachian Mountains to northern Georgia. In the West, they breed primarily in coniferous forests south through the highlands of Mexico to Nicaragua. Brown Creepers were long considered conspecific with creepers in the northern Old World (Hejl et al. 2002).

During the atlas period, Brown Creepers were fairly common in most locations that provide suitable forested habitat at elevations from 5400 to 10,500 ft (1646–3200 m). They were most widespread in forests of the Kaibab Plateau and Mogollon Rim country, including the White Mountains region. The species doubtless also occurs in the diverse forests of the adjacent unsurveyed White Mountain Apache tribal lands. Surveyors on Navajo tribal lands encountered these birds on northern Black Mesa and from the Carrizo Mountains south locally to the Defiance Plateau. In southeastern Arizona, atlasers noted Brown Creepers only in the higher ranges supporting rather large stands of tall conifers, including the Chiricahua, Huachuca, Pinaleno, Santa Catalina, Rincon, and Santa Rita mountains. They were found locally to the west on Hualapai tribal lands, Mount Trumbull, the Mount Dellenbaugh area, and, as suggested by Monson and Phillips (1981), in the Hualapai Mountains. Although encountered in the Mazatzal Mountains, Brown Creepers went unreported in northeastern Maricopa County, where Witzeman et al. (1997) described them as uncommon residents.

Brown Creeper abundance appears to be correlated with the presence of dense stands of large, old trees, including snags. They have likely declined in the western United States owing to twentieth-century forest management practices, especially the selective removal of snags and of large trees favored by these birds (Hejl et al. 2002). Few data exist to document trends in Arizona, but a review of studies in the Rocky Mountain region found that these birds were uniformly less abundant in logged than unlogged forests (Hejl et al. 1995).

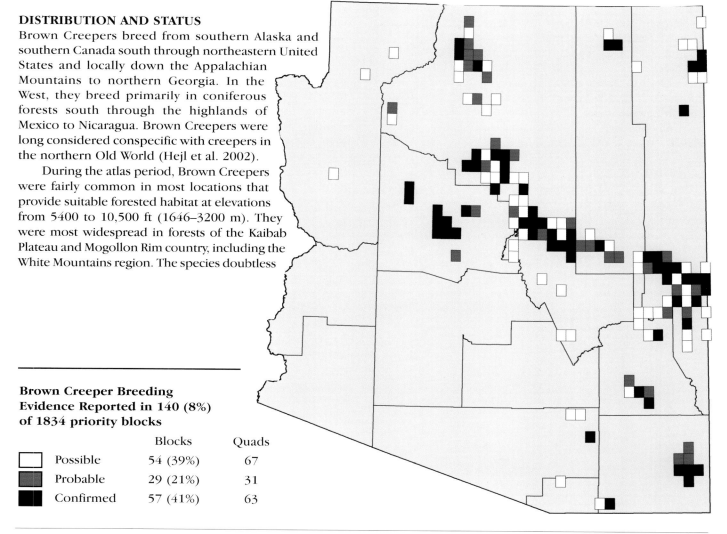

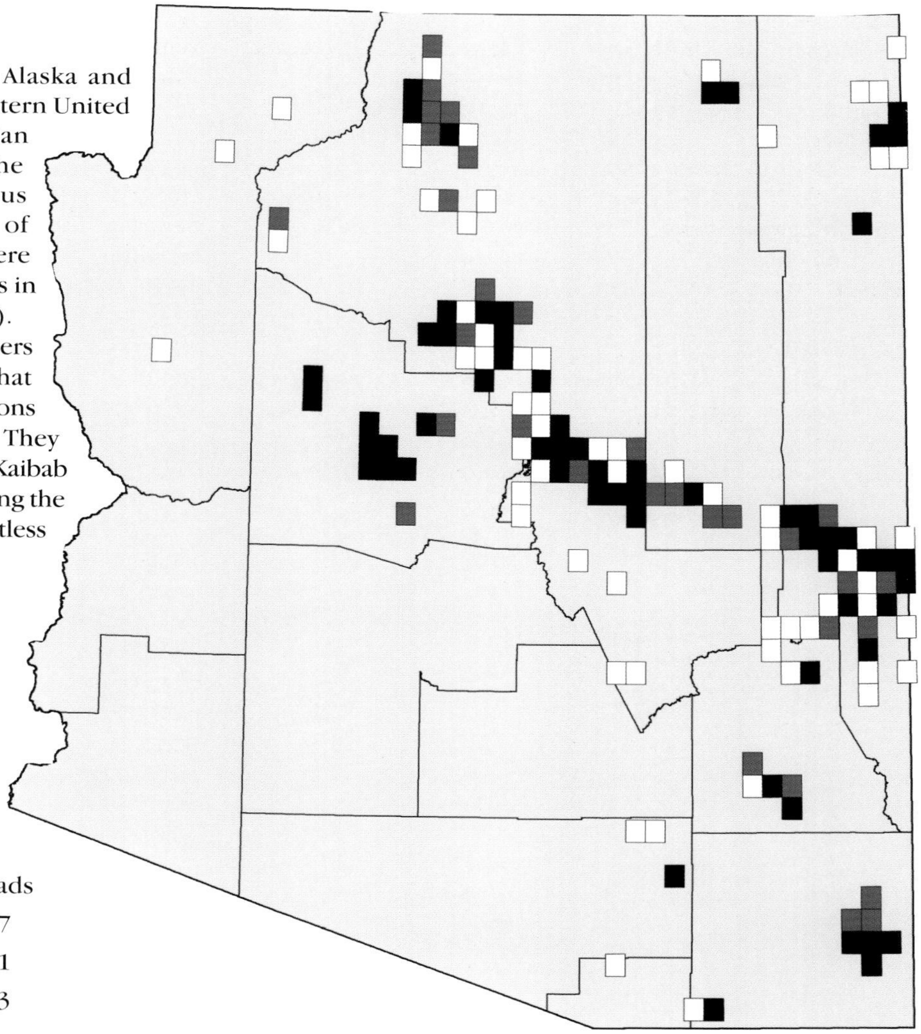

Brown Creeper Breeding Evidence Reported in 140 (8%) of 1834 priority blocks

	Blocks	Quads
Possible	54 (39%)	67
Probable	29 (21%)	31
Confirmed	57 (41%)	63

Cactus Wren

by Cathryn Wise-Gervais *Campylorhynchus brunneicapillus*

Bold and inquisitive, Cactus Wrens are the largest wrens in the United States and are conspicuous wherever they occur. Arizona's state bird has a characteristic "char-char-char" song that sounds much like someone trying to start an old car. Whether scolding cats or chattering at fledglings, this raucous species is easy to spot and entertaining to observe.

BRUCE TAUBERT

HABITAT

Cactus Wrens primarily inhabit arid regions and in Arizona are typically found in association with Sonoran, Chihuahuan, and Mojave desertscrub communities. They reach their highest densities in habitats containing an abundance of cholla, but these cacti are not a requirement for this adaptable bird. Cactus Wrens are true xenophiles that obtain nearly all the water needed for survival from food (Proudfoot et al. 2000). As a result, this large, familiar wren can thrive in even the driest, most inhospitable terrain. Atlasers obtained 942 potential breeding records for Cactus Wrens in twenty-one different habitats. Of these, 56 percent were in Sonoran desertscrub associations, including some of the drier, sparsely vegetated environments. An additional 15 percent were in semiarid grasslands characterized by scattered mesquite, agave, yucca, and cholla. Atlasers commonly encountered Cactus Wrens in Mojave and Chihuahuan desertscrub, as well as in desert dry washes. This wren's adaptable nature also allows it to nest regularly in residential neighborhoods and parks, especially if these are landscaped with cacti and thorny shrubs.

BREEDING

Cactus Wrens are nonmigratory and typically remain in pairs year-round. Observers noted that the frequency of both singing and nest building increases in January and February, but atlas surveys generally did not start in earnest until late February. Atlasers reported the earliest occupied nest on 5 March and a nest with young on 14 March. By backdating the latter observation, these eggs were laid by late February. Nest-initiation dates tend to vary considerably, however, depending on annual rainfall. In fact, atlasers noted that Cactus Wrens delayed egg laying by one or more months following winters with low precipitation. Atlas data include records from both wet and dry years and suggest that Cactus Wren breeding activity generally peaks in Arizona from mid-April through mid-May (n = 443). Observers noted a steep decline in breeding activity through the summer months, but reported the latest nest with young on 21 August. Adults were noted carrying food on 1 September, and dependent fledglings were reported through 19 September. Observers obtained the majority of late summer nesting records in southeastern Arizona, suggesting Cactus Wrens in this region enjoy a longer than normal breeding period thanks to a resource-rich summer monsoon period.

Cactus Wrens construct distinctive globular nests of long grass blades, weed stalks, and other flexible substances. They then line their nest interiors with softer materials, including feathers. The industrious adults can build as many as five alternate nest structures, and these are often used as roost sites and may also function secondarily as decoys for predators (Proudfoot et al. 2000). The Cactus Wren's covered nests are typically placed in the open rather than in the shade of a tree or shrub, seemingly an odd preference for a desert dweller. Atlasers took measurements at 143 Cactus Wren nests. The vast majority of nests were in various species of cholla (75 percent), but they were also found in other cacti such as prickly pear (8 percent) and saguaro (4 percent). The remaining 13 percent of nests were in yuccas and thorny trees including Joshua tree, paloverde, mesquite, ironwood, graythorn, and hackberry. The median substrate height for all nests measured was 5.6 ft (1.7 m) and height ranged from 2.5 to 39.4 ft (0.8–12 m). The median nest height was 4.6 ft (1.4 m), with a range of 1.7–14.4 ft (0.5–4.4 m).

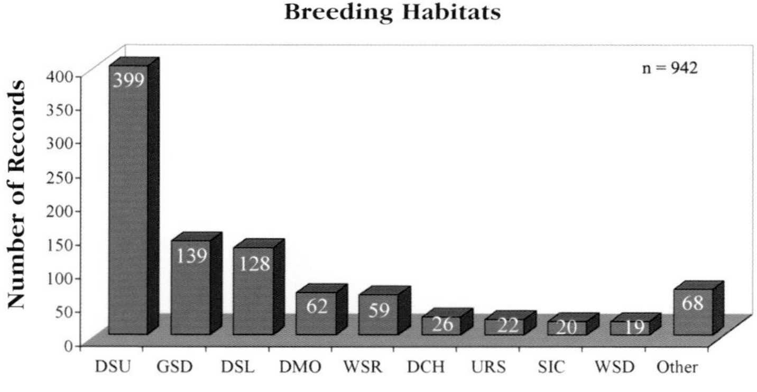

Breeding Phenology

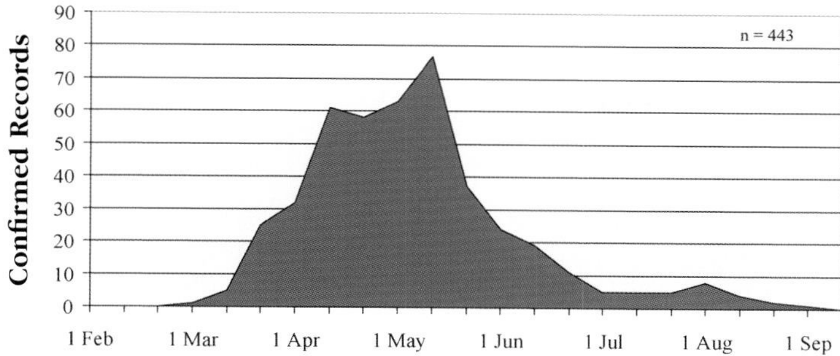

Typical Cactus Wren clutches consist of 3–5 eggs, and pairs often raise 2–3 broods per year in Arizona (Anderson and Anderson 1960). Females incubate for 16–17 days, while their nearby mates roost and defend the nest area. Both adults bring food to the nest, but only the female actually distributes it to the young (Anderson and Anderson 1960). Nestlings fledge at approximately 21 days of age (range 17–23) and are capable of flight by this time (Hensley 1959, Anderson and Anderson 1960; Ricklefs 1975). The young birds generally stay in the natal area after fledging and will often roost in their old nest at night. By this time, both parents have moved into their own separate roost nests, but they will continue feeding fledglings until the female lays her next clutch. The male will continue to feed the first brood alone while the female initiates the next clutch (Anderson and Anderson 1962), and parental dependency generally continues for 17–25 days after fledging (Proudfoot et al. 2000).

DISTRIBUTION AND STATUS

Cactus Wrens are birds of the arid Southwest and occur from southern California and Nevada east through central Texas and south to central Mexico. In Arizona, atlasers documented Cactus Wrens on survey blocks from approximately 80 to 5600 ft (24–1707 m).

Phillips et al. (1964) considered Cactus Wrens a common species in most desert regions below 4000 ft (1219 m) in Arizona. Although the species was previously noted as absent from the Colorado River above Lake Mead (Monson and Phillips 1981), atlasers reported and confirmed the birds almost continuously up into the lower Granite Gorge of the Grand Canyon. Elsewhere in northwestern Arizona, atlasers encountered Cactus Wrens fairly regularly west of the Shivwits Plateau and Virgin River drainage. Cactus Wrens were also found locally east along the Utah border to Hurricane Wash.

Cactus Wrens were historically absent in the upper Verde River valley (Phillips et al. 1964), but records began to increase upstream of Camp Verde by the mid-1970s (Monson and Phillips 1981). Atlasers documented this wren north to near Sedona and up the Verde River drainage to near Clarkdale. They were also encountered north to near Payson and up into the Salt River Canyon, where this wren's range likely continues into the lower elevations of the unsurveyed White Mountain Apache tribal lands. Cactus Wrens were largely lacking in the sparsely vegetated Yuma Desert of the Barry M. Goldwater Range and in the Mohawk Valley of the lower Gila River. Otherwise, these large wrens were common throughout their historical range.

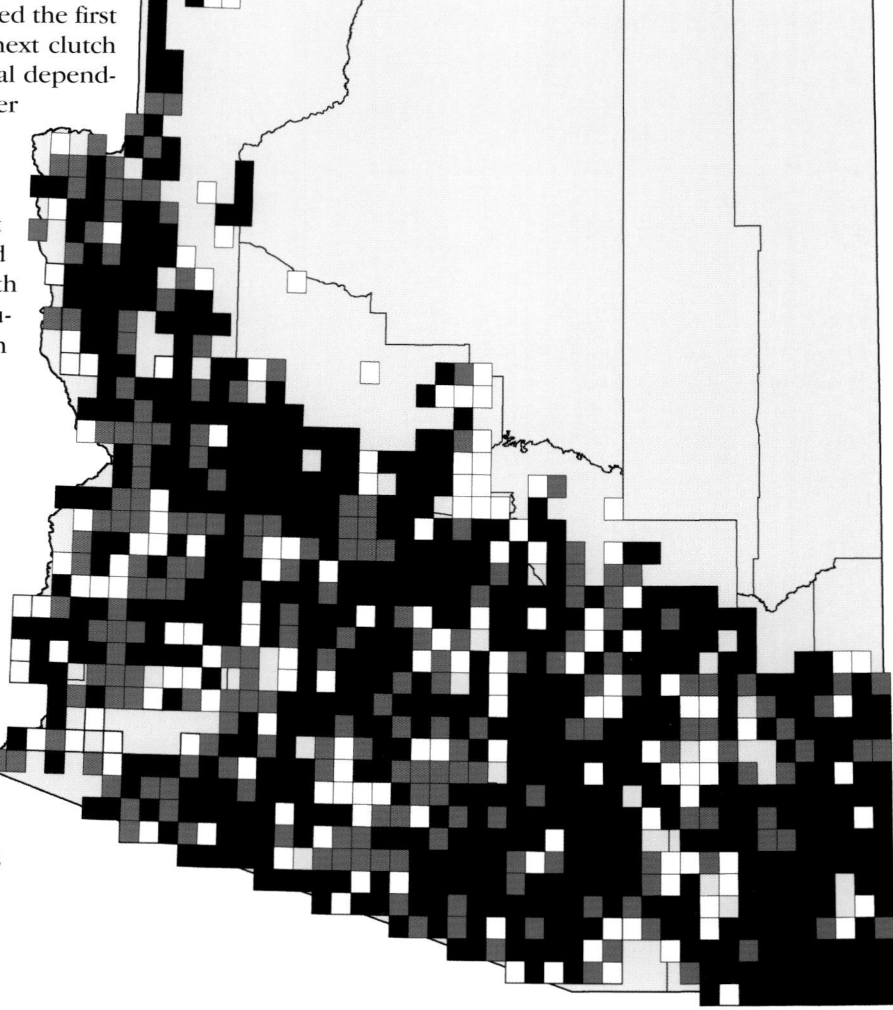

Cactus Wren Breeding Evidence Reported in 928 (51 %) of 1834 priority blocks

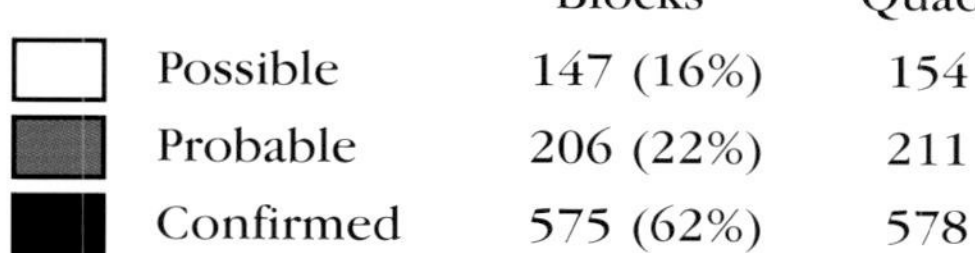

	Blocks	Quads
Possible	147 (16%)	154
Probable	206 (22%)	211
Confirmed	575 (62%)	578

Rock Wren

by Cathryn Wise-Gervais *Salpinctes obsoletus*

Arizona's Rock Wrens can thrive even in bleak, sun-baked areas that few other birds inhabit. In fact, this bird's cheerful song and distinctive "tick-ee" call can be the only bird sounds encountered in desolate canyons and on rock piles. Observers commonly see these pale little rock-hoppers bobbing energetically between boulders in their endless quest for insects.

JIM BURNS

HABITAT

As their name suggests, these wrens prefer open and often arid, rocky areas such as boulder fields, talus slopes, canyons, outcrops, rocky hillsides, and desert dry washes. Occupied barren sites can be found in or near almost any vegetative community and elevation in Arizona, as illustrated by atlasers reporting Rock Wrens in thirty-one habitat types. Because this species was found statewide, it is not surprising that the two most commonly reported habitat codes were also the two that cover the most area geographically. These were Sonoran desertscrub (26 percent of records) and open pinyon pine–juniper woodlands (17 percent of records; n = 1120). Birds of open environments, Rock Wrens were frequently encountered in most desertscrub and patchy grassland associations across the state. They were largely absent in heavily wooded or vegetated regions and in relatively flat landscapes lacking incised washes or rocky slopes. Only nine atlas records statewide were reported in agricultural or residential areas, indicating that this wren also generally avoids human settlements for nesting.

BREEDING

Rock Wrens reside in Arizona year-round, although northern and mountain populations migrate south or to lower elevations during the winter. Migrants return to breeding areas in March, but lowland desert residents initiate singing and pairing in February with nesting soon after. Atlasers observed birds nest building on 9 March, and also reported Rock Wren fledglings on 18 and 23 March. These latter records indicate that some birds began nesting in February. Atlasers reported nests with eggs from 27 March to 28 June and found nests with young from 30 March to 27 July. Atlas data suggest that, statewide, Rock Wren breeding activity peaks from mid-May to mid-June, but the birds continue to breed late into the summer months. Atlasers obtained the latest breeding confirmations of adults feeding fledglings on 11 August and noted fledglings through 6 September. Rock Wrens in Arizona begin dispersing to nonbreeding areas by late August or early September, with migrants arriving on wintering grounds through October.

Rock Wrens nest in small natural crevices and cavities in cliffs, outcrops, and among boulders, as well as in shallow abandoned rodent burrows in eroded banks and road cuts. Observers took measurements at fifty-one Rock Wren nests. Of these, only five were in substrates other than in rock cavities or drainage cutbanks. Atlasers discovered one nest each in cavities of an ironwood tree, a juniper stump, in the dead stalk of a yucca, in a pipe, and under a roof ledge. The median nest height for these nests was 2.6 ft (0.8 m) and ranged from 0 to 45.3 ft (0–13.8 m).

It is unclear which sex chooses the nest site, or if both birds accomplish this task together. It is well documented, however, that both members of the pair bring small stones, twigs, or other objects to the nest site (Lowther et al. 2000) and, with these materials, often build a curious walkway or path leading to the nest hole. After this entranceway is completed, the female Rock Wren will turn her attention to building a loose cup nest within the cavity. There she typically lays 5–6 eggs, but sometimes as many as 10 (Bent 1948). Only the females incubate for 12–14 days, and males will occasionally feed the sitting females (Merola 1995). Both adults feed the young, and these fledge at approximately 14–16 days. The parents often coax young from the

Breeding Habitats

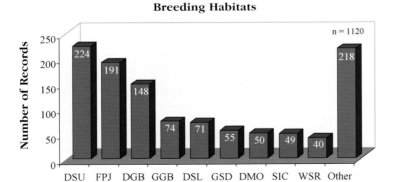

Habitat Codes

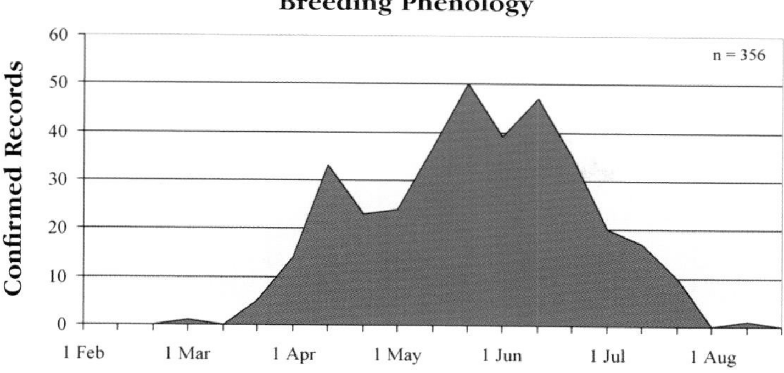

cavity using food and vocalizing (Merola 1995). The male continues to care for fledglings about one week following nest departure, but the young will remain on the parent's territory for about four weeks (Merola 1995). During this time, family groups forage together regularly. Rock Wrens typically produce 1–2 broods per year, but 3 have occasionally been reported (Lowther et al. 2000).

DISTRIBUTION AND STATUS

Rock Wrens are found primarily only in western North America, where northern populations are migratory. They breed from southern Canada to central Mexico, and south locally to Nicaragua. They are found east to central Kansas and Texas. Rock Wrens have the widest elevational breeding range of any bird in Arizona, from low, rocky desert foothills to above timberline on talus slopes of the highest peaks. Atlasers confirmed this species breeding at elevations from approximately 300 to 11,500 ft (91–3505 m).

Most prior literature described Rock Wrens as fairly common summer residents nearly statewide in Arizona, but noted that they can be rather local in distribution due to their habitat requirement of open, rocky terrain (Phillips et al. 1964; Jacobs 1986; Rosenberg et al. 1991). Atlasers reported Rock Wrens on nearly continuous quad maps in the central and northern parts of the state, with several larger gaps in the southwest, as noted by Phillips et al. It is likely these gaps result from areas of flat, open country that offer no hills or rocky substrates. Rock Wrens are also noticeably absent in the extensive irrigated agricultural lands in the Gila, lower Santa Cruz, and Colorado River valleys. Several other gaps are readily apparent on the atlas map, including along the heavily forested Mogollon Rim region, including the unsurveyed White Mountain Apace tribal lands. While much of this reservation is too densely forested for Rock Wrens, it is likely that some suitable habitat exists along exposed ridges and talus slopes.

Atlasers noted that Rock Wrens can become rather quiet during certain periods of the nesting cycle and could be easily missed in low wren density areas. Only the most intrepid surveyors made special efforts to locate silent wrens in their hot, rugged, and often treacherous domain.

Breeding Bird Survey (BBS) data indicate that Rock Wren densities are much higher in the northern quarter of Arizona than elsewhere within the state. Although BBS data suggest a declining trend for this species rangewide, populations in Arizona are apparently stable with few threats facing their rocky neighborhoods.

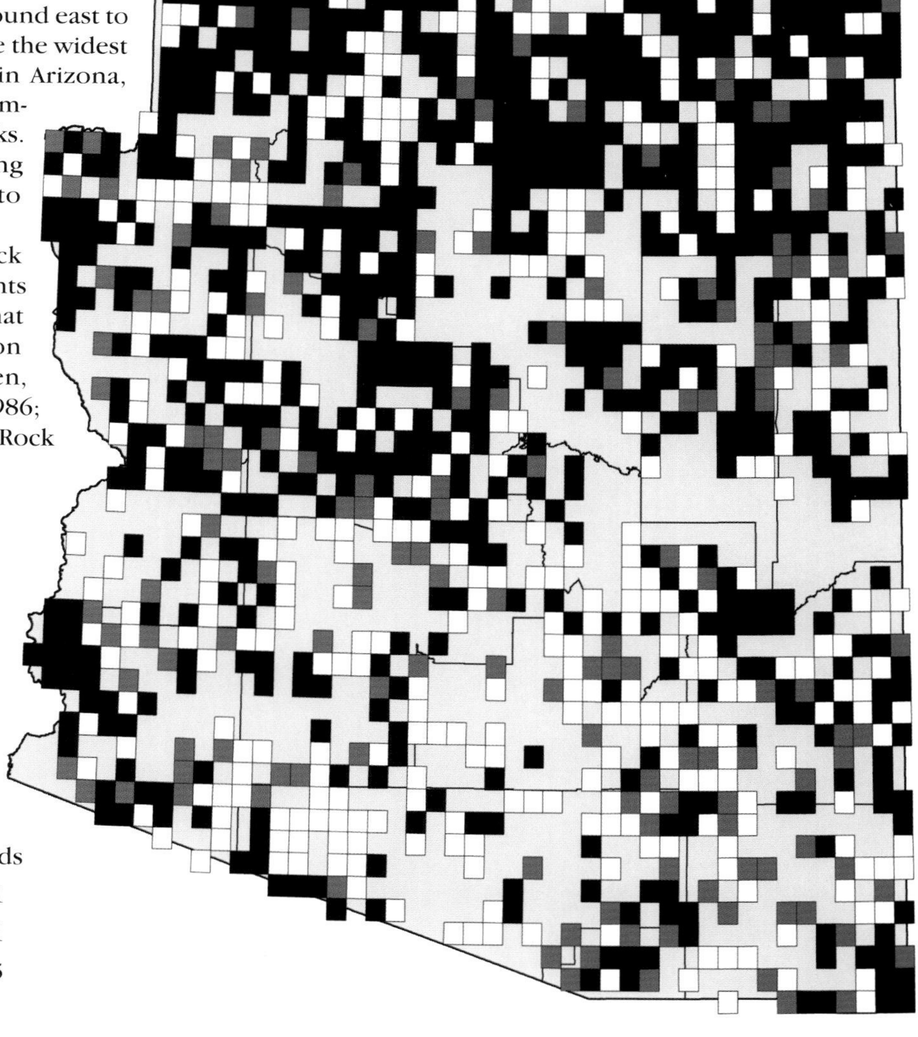

Rock Wren Breeding Evidence Reported in 1117 (61%) of 1834 priority blocks

	Blocks	Quads
Possible	351 (31%)	371
Probable	150 (13%)	151
Confirmed	616 (55%)	625

Canyon Wren

by Peter Friederici *Catherpes mexicanus*

RICK AND NORA BOWERS

A sweet singer of rugged lands, the Canyon Wren is more often heard than seen, sending its "gushing cadence of clear, curved notes tripping down the scale" (Peterson 1990) through canyons and along cliff faces. It lives wherever sheer rock creates habitats that are both difficult to reach and beautiful.

HABITAT

Canyon Wrens are not bound to any particular vegetation type. They are found, instead, wherever topography provides appropriate substrates for foraging and nesting—typically in the form of canyons, cliffs, large outcrops, and exposed, rocky ridgelines. Locally, they also occur among steep, boulder-covered slopes and canyon bottoms. The vegetation surrounding such rugged features can vary widely. Associations recorded during this atlas project ranged from arid lowland Sonoran desertscrub to montane mixed-conifer forests and riparian woodlands. Though often found near streams and rivers, Canyon Wrens can also be found in extremely arid mountain ranges that lack any perennial water. A useful rule of thumb is this: if rock-climbing skills are required to explore an area fully, Canyon Wrens are likely to be there. However, they were not encountered above timberline on the bare, windswept San Francisco Peaks. Though found close to towns and human habitations in Mexico (Phillips et al. 1964), Canyon Wrens are rather infrequently found in such places in Arizona; sightings in developed areas accounted for only seven atlas observations (n = 765).

BREEDING

Although they are occasionally heard singing during the late fall and early winter, Canyon Wrens greatly increase their singing efforts in February. Pairs often remain together throughout the year, and pair bonds may last for several years (Jones and Dieni 1995). The nesting season is protracted due to the wide range of elevations and habitats occupied in Arizona. In lowland Sonoran Desert habitats nest building was documented on 18 March, and an occupied nest as early as 10 March. The earliest fledglings were observed on 9 April, indicating that some clutches are laid by mid-March. The low percentage of confirmed records in the Sonoran Desert region is probably due to generally early atlas visits to these blocks, though it may also indicate some level of extraterritorial movement in early spring. At higher elevations, active nests were commonly observed through June. Canyon Wrens will raise more than one brood (Jones and Dieni 1995), and nests with young located on 27 July and 4 August probably represent renesting efforts or second broods. These wrens and their juvenile broods often descend to nearby canyon bottoms in late summer where individuals may remain to winter and forage among tree root tangles, accumulated flood debris, and boulder piles.

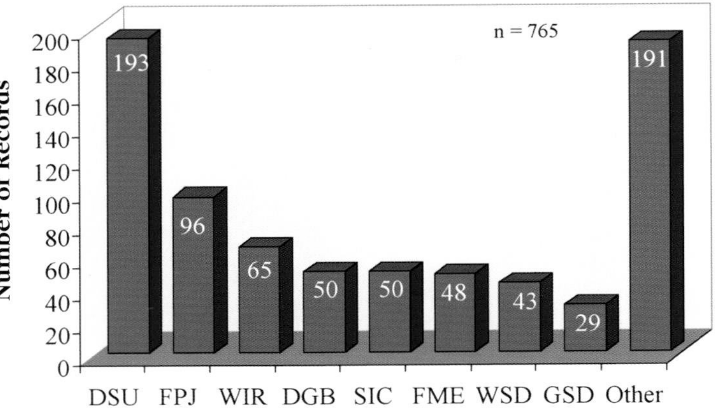

Most nests found during the atlas project were on natural substrates such as cliffs and rock outcrops, though Canyon Wrens have also been seen nesting on buildings at places such as the Hassayampa River Preserve. Nests are typically hidden in crevices, caves, and locally in mineshafts, adits, and old Cliff Swallow nests. Their nests are typically difficult to observe, and only adult activity or the begging sounds of the nestlings give away their locations. Male Canyon Wrens feed incubating females and, of course, nestlings, and their habit of singing near the nest before and after delivering food makes locating nests a bit easier. Nests are generally built of sticks and grasses, then lined with softer materials.

The median height of eighteen Canyon Wren nests measured during the atlas was 6.6 ft (2 m), but this figure masks a great deal of variability. The lowest nest measured was only 1.3 ft (0.4 m) high in a rocky stream bank, the highest an estimated 121.4 ft (37 m) on a cliff in the Grand Canyon region. Owing to nest inaccessibility, most confirmations for this species came from seeing recent fledglings or adults carrying food.

Canyon Wren clutches average 5 eggs (range 3–7), which are incubated by the female for 12–18 days. The nestling period averages 15 days (Jones and Dieni 1995). The adults continue to care for the fledglings actively for 5–10 days

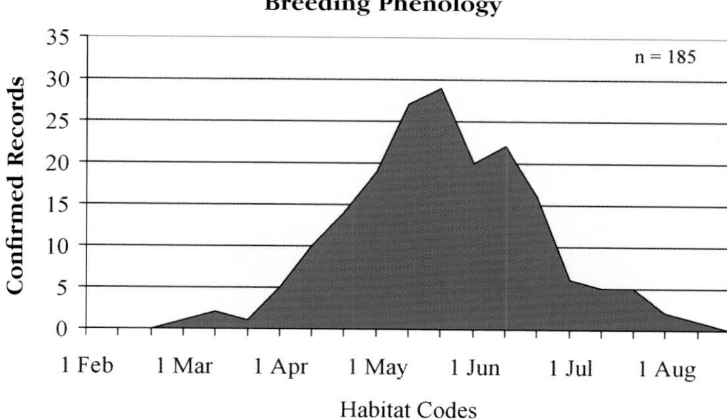

following nest departure, and then may remain within family groups for several months (Jones and Dieni 1995). Both adults and juveniles can often be observed foraging along rock faces and in crevices.

DISTRIBUTION AND STATUS

Canyon Wrens breed throughout the interior West from southern British Columbia to southern Mexico and from central Texas to the Pacific Coast. Though some birds wander a bit in winter, especially to lower elevations, most individuals are thought to maintain the same territories in summer and winter (Jones and Dieni 1995).

In Arizona, the Canyon Wren is most concentrated in the Mogollon Rim and Grand Canyon regions, but it is found fairly regularly statewide in appropriate habitat. Atlasers reported these wrens at elevations ranging from approximately 300 to 9000 ft (91–2743 m). These wrens undoubtedly occur among the many canyons and cliffs within the White Mountain Apache tribal lands, where atlas surveys were unfortunately not conducted. Populations grow sparse in parts of north-central and northeastern Arizona that lack appropriately steep, rugged topography, as well as in the lowlands of the Sonoran Desert. Though largely absent in the lower Colorado River valley (Rosenberg et al. 1991), atlasers did locate this species and confirm its breeding in mountainous areas on the Yuma Proving Ground just east of the river, as well as in arid ranges to the east and southeast of Yuma. It was also found more widely in the conifer zones than reported in Phillips et al. (1964). Breeding territories are apparently rather large (Phillips et al. 1964), and the species is never found in great densities.

Breeding Bird Survey data, though scanty, show a stable population for Canyon Wrens in Arizona. Recreational rock climbing may cause disturbance at a few nest sites (Jones and Dieni 1995), but the inaccessibility of most suitable nesting habitat makes both disturbance by humans and large-scale population declines unlikely. Thanks to the species' predilection for topographic rather than vegetation qualities, it has probably been affected less than most Arizona birds by human-induced habitat changes.

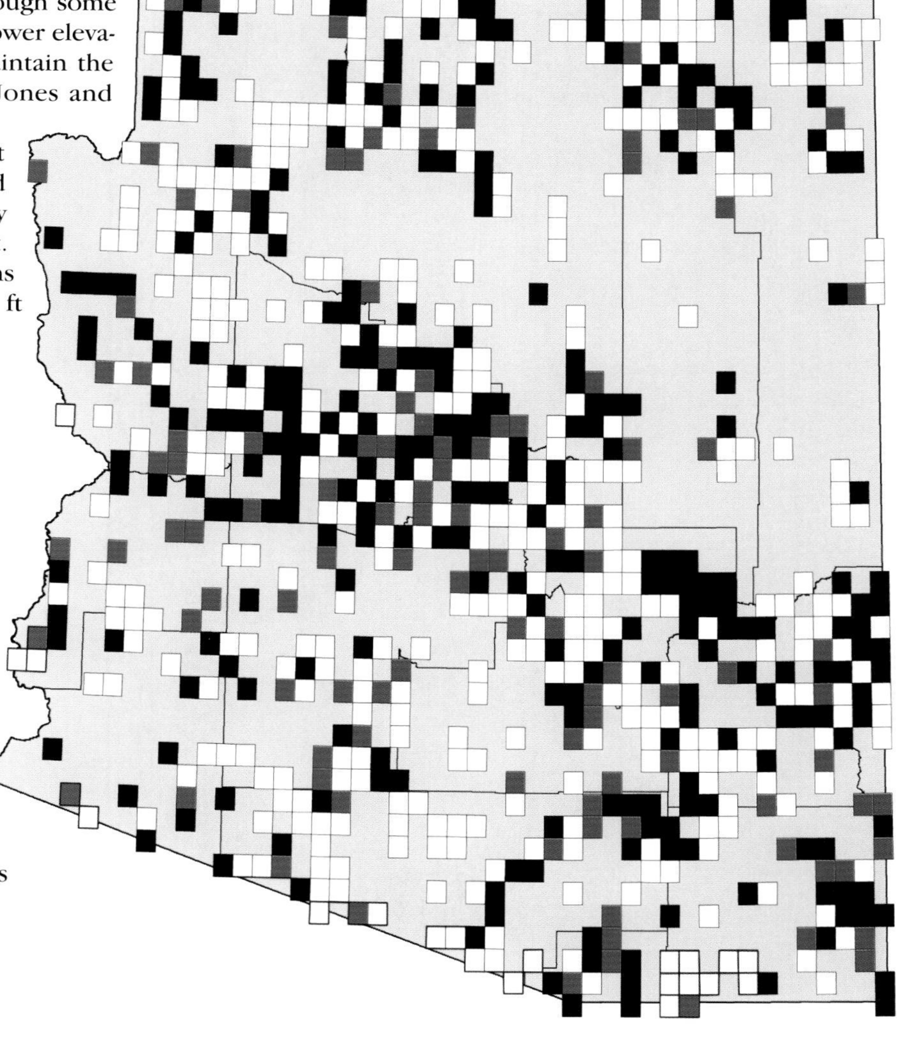

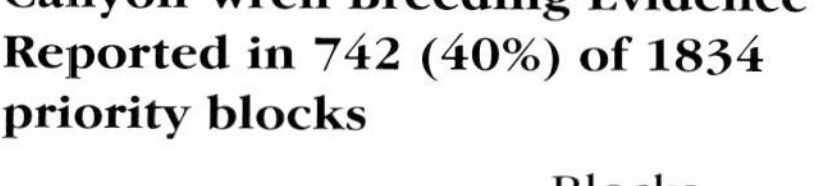

Canyon Wren Breeding Evidence Reported in 742 (40%) of 1834 priority blocks

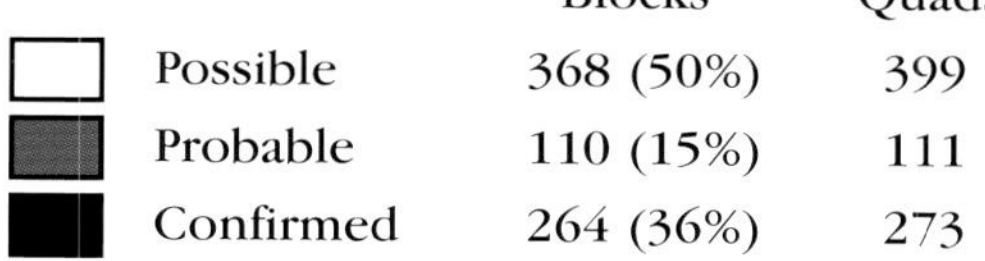

	Blocks	Quads
Possible	368 (50%)	399
Probable	110 (15%)	111
Confirmed	264 (36%)	273

Bewick's Wren

by Troy E. Corman *Thryomanes bewickii*

The ringing, "suweet peee" song of the Bewick's Wren is a common spring and summer component of woodlands in southern and central Arizona. In the northern third of the state however, these active birds sing a much longer, multiple phrased song that is surprisingly reminiscent of a Song Sparrow.

HABITAT

Inhabiting a wide variety of brushy wooded habitats in Arizona, Bewick's Wrens are often observed methodically probing tree trunks, limbs, and leaf litter in search of food. They are most abundant in vegetative communities containing juniper and oak, but range from desert foothills and riparian woodlands to chaparral and open pine covered slopes. Atlasers reported approximately 43 percent of observations in pinyon pine–juniper woodland associations ($n = 841$). This includes grasslands with small, local juniper stands and woodlands with scattered ponderosa pine. They favor riparian woodlands as well and were frequently encountered in canyons and foothill drainages with Arizona sycamore and along lowland drainages with cottonwood, willow, and mesquite. Within the Grand Canyon, Bewick's Wrens are also common inhabitants of tamarisk thickets. Evergreen oak woodlands are especially favored, and these slender wrens occur up into the Madrean pine-oak forests of southeastern Arizona. Locally, atlasers documented Bewick's Wrens nesting in heavily wooded desert dry washes, especially those containing dense stands of netleaf hackberry or mesquite.

BREEDING

Resident male Bewick's Wrens begin to sing in southern Arizona in late January or early February, prior to the departure of lowland wintering populations in March and early April. Actual nest construction may not begin until early March, however, and atlasers reported an occupied nest on 28 March. An adult Bewick's Wren was also observed feeding a fledgling on 23 April, further indicating that some eggs are laid by mid- to late March. Populations in northern Arizona and at higher elevations may not initiate nesting activity until April or even May. Based on the statewide atlas data, the breeding activity for Bewick's Wrens in Arizona reaches a peak from late May to late June ($n = 230$), although atlasers discovered nests with young through 27 July. Some adult wrens were also observed feeding fledged broods through August and as late as 2 September. These wrens typically begin arriving in lowland wintering area of Arizona in September.

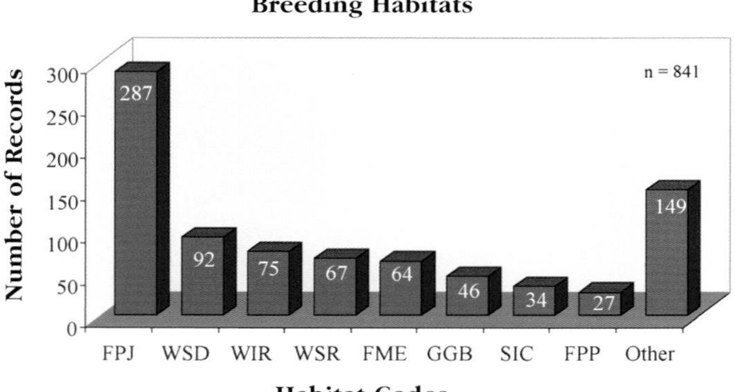

Bent (1948) noted that any suitable cavity or place of support will suit the Bewick's Wren for a nesting site. During the atlas period, most nests were found in natural tree cavities or those excavated by woodpeckers. Various juniper and oak species accounted for more than half of the twenty-nine documented nest trees. Nests were also noted in pinyon pine, netleaf hackberry, Arizona sycamore, Arizona walnut, catclaw acacia, crucifixion thorn, banana yucca, and one odd nest in a saguaro next to a wooded drainage. Nests were also found in a slash pile, fence post, and windmill pumphouse. Bewick's Wren nests have been built 0–33 ft (0–10 m) above the ground (Kennedy and White 1997). Of 29 nests measured during the atlas, the mean nest height was 5.9 ft (1.8 m) above the ground with a range of 2–24.6 ft (0.6–7.5 m).

Both sexes build the nest, although it is the industrious male that often initiated construction and builds much of the larger stick foundation (Kennedy and White 1997). Bewick's Wren clutches typically consists of 5–6 eggs, but can range from 3 to 8 (Kennedy and White 1997) and occasionally higher (Bent 1948). The female is the sole incubator for the 14–16 days it takes them to hatch, although the male often provides food for his incubating mate. Both parents feed the nestlings for 14–16 days and continue to feed the fledglings for an additional two weeks after nest departure (Kroodsma 1974; Kennedy and White 1997). This wren

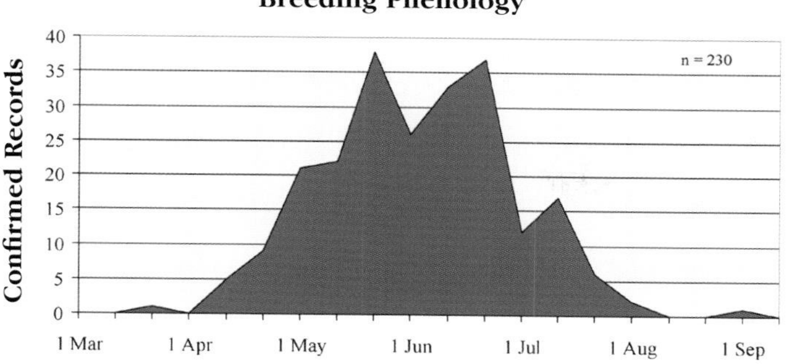

can successfully fledge two broods per season and the males may start the foundation for a second nest while the female incubates the eggs or tends nestlings of the first brood (Kennedy and White 1997).

DISTRIBUTION AND STATUS

Bewick's Wrens breed from southwestern British Columbia south into Baja California and from southern Wyoming and Kansas south to southern Mexico. Populations east of the Mississippi River have disappeared significantly, with only small pockets remaining in a few states (Kennedy and White 1997). Most evidence suggests these declines are related to the range expansion and competition with the nest-destroying House Wren (Kennedy and White 1997). Although there is some range overlap in Arizona, Bewick's Wrens tend to nest at lower elevations than do House Wrens.

This highly animated wren has been describes as an uncommon to common summer resident throughout eastern, central, and northern Arizona (Phillips et al. 1964). Atlasers recorded these birds throughout most of their prior described range at elevations from 480 to 7400 ft (146–2256 m) and helped delineate their limits within the state.

Summer records of Bewick's Wrens were evidently rare in the mid-1900s within the lower Colorado River valley, but Rosenberg et al. (1991) considered these birds as locally fairly common breeders in riparian habitats south to Cibola National Wildlife Refuge by the 1980s. Populations remain spotty within this valley, with the most southern atlas observation just south of Parker. Unexpected, was the discovery of these wrens nesting locally west of the Baboquivari Mountains on Tohono O'odham tribal lands. They were found breeding in Sonoran desertscrub, especially along densely wooded washes, and were confirmed nesting as far west as Papago Farms. Elsewhere in Arizona, they primarily enter Sonoran Desert associations only in riparian woodland corridors along perennial drainages.

Absent at higher elevation conifer forests, Bewick's Wrens were encountered regularly along the entire southern slope of the Mogollon Rim. Within this region of the state, this wren undoubtedly also nests throughout the unsurveyed White Mountain Apache tribal lands.

Unlike the critically dwindling populations in the East, the adaptable Bewick's Wren in Arizona has few threats that would greatly change their abundance or distribution. In fact, its distribution in the state has undoubtedly expanded in some areas as habitat becomes appropriate. Decades of inappropriate grazing practices and fire suppression of many open grasslands have led to heavy invasion of brushy mesquite or juniper, habitats now often occupied by these wrens.

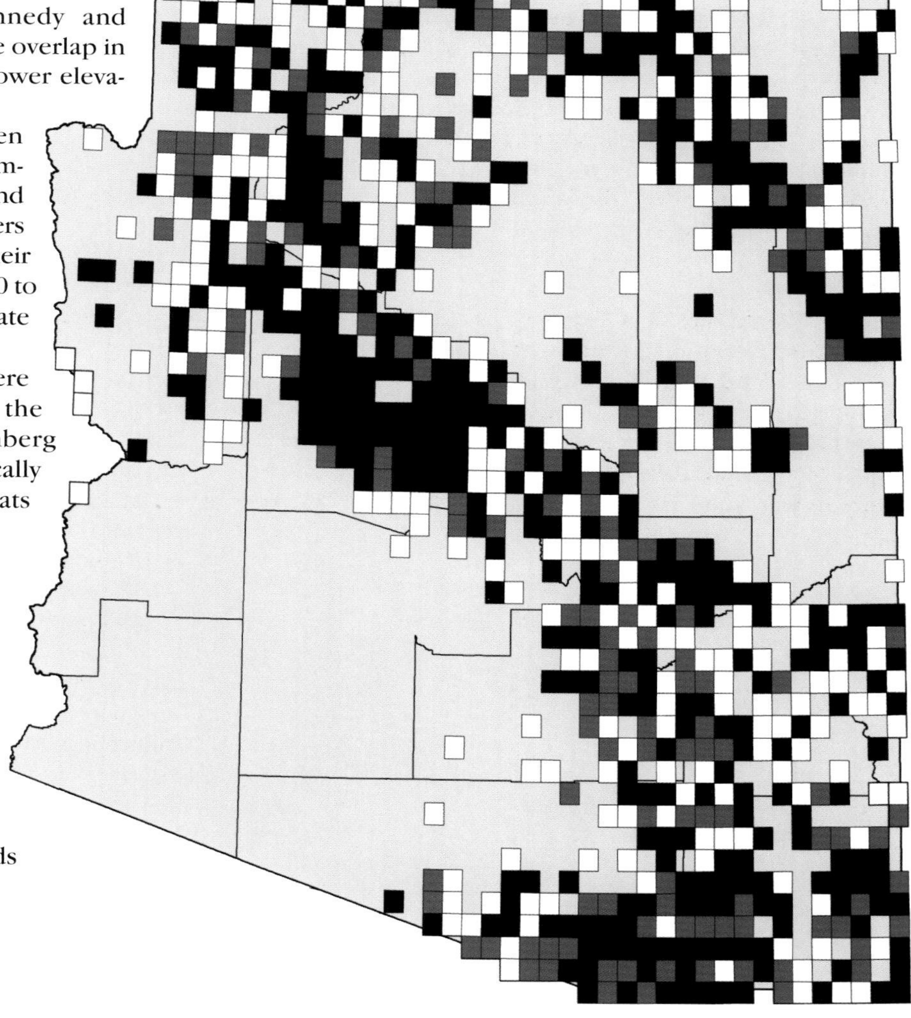

Bewick's Wren Breeding Evidence Reported in 822 (45%) of 1834 priority blocks

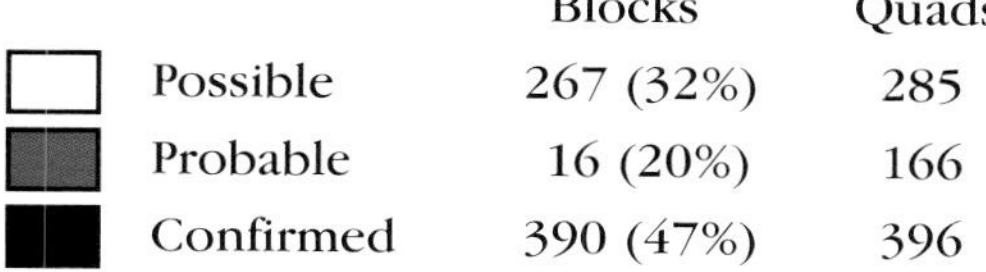

	Blocks	Quads
Possible	267 (32%)	285
Probable	16 (20%)	166
Confirmed	390 (47%)	396

House Wren

by Cathryn Wise-Gervais *Troglodytes aedon*

This North American songster's eastern range has expanded significantly over the last century due to the clearing of dense forests for agricultural and residential developments. These plain little wrens often destroy the eggs and nestlings of their neighbors, so are generally unpopular with other bird species and are regularly chased away from nests.

HABITAT

House Wrens are found primarily in open woodlands, along forest edges, in recovering burned areas, and in riparian corridors. Ground cover often consists of scattered shrubs and fallen trees. Although commonly occurring in suburban neighborhoods in the East, they are found only locally in such settings in Arizona. Atlasers reported House Wrens in fifteen vegetative communities, but most records were obtained in higher elevation riparian woodlands and forests, often with some deciduous component. Observers reported the highest percentage of records in cool, montane drainages comprised of tall mixture of deciduous and coniferous trees (20 percent; n = 161). Atlasers reported 19 percent of records in mixed-conifer forests consisting of Douglas fir, white fir, ponderosa pine, and often aspen and Gambel's oak. House Wrens were also frequently encountered in ponderosa pine–dominated forests from almost pure stands to those with a Gambel's oak and, less frequently, pinyon pine–juniper association (36 percent of records). These wrens breed down into some cooler mountain drainages containing sycamore, especially in southeastern Arizona. At higher elevations, they frequently inhabit groves of aspen and the edges of subalpine spruce-fir forests.

BREEDING

House Wrens begin arriving on their Arizona breeding grounds in late March or early April, with some lingering migrants still passing through into late May. Males arrive before females and begin establishing territories immediately. Females are thought to select males with the best territories, and these usually offer more than one potential nest site (Johnson 1998). Atlasers reported nest-building activity as early as 17 April. Atlas data are insufficient to determine when these wrens initiate egg laying in Arizona, but it is likely that they may begin by late April or early May at lower elevations. Atlasers reported House Wrens carrying food on 24 May. Males rarely feed females during incubation (Johnson 1998), so it is possible that this bird was bringing food to young in the nest. Atlasers reported several occupied nests (contents undetermined) in late May, and the earliest nest with young on 2 June. During the atlas project, most House Wren confirmation occurred in June through mid-July with nests with young reported through 26 July. The latest breeding record obtained during the atlas period was of an adult feeding a fledgling 18 August. Most House Wrens nest twice per season so it is likely that the later atlas records represent second broods or renesting attempts. House Wren populations are primarily migratory in Arizona, moving to lower elevations or south for the winter. Movements can begin by mid- to late August, with a peak passage in September and continuing into November.

House Wrens nest in cavities such as old woodpecker holes or natural crevices, but will also take up residence in nest boxes or other human-contrived artifacts including old boots, cow skulls hung for decoration, or laundry left on the clothesline (Johnson 1998). Atlasers took measurements at only eight House Wren nests. Three nests were in aspen, two were in Douglas fir, and one each was in cottonwood, sycamore, and ponderosa pine. The median height for these nests was 13 ft (3.9 m) and ranged from 6.9 to 32.8 ft (2.1–10 m). These values are considerably lower than the nest height mean of 29.5 ft (9 m) reported by Li and Martin (1991) for 115 Arizona nests. This discrepancy is probably due to the extremely small number of nests measured during the atlas period.

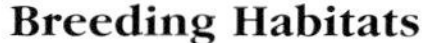

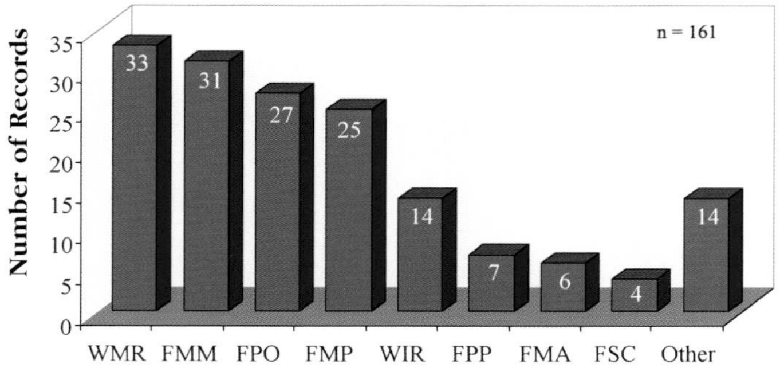

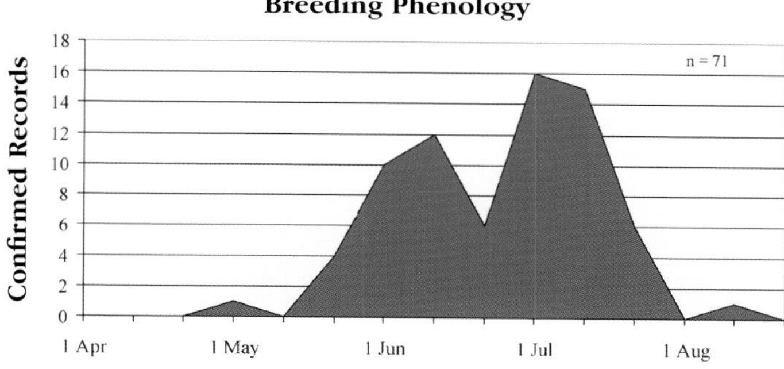

Males begin the official nest-building process by lining their cavity with sticks. Once paired, the female completes the nest, then lays 4–8 eggs and incubates these alone (Johnson 1998). The incubation period lasts for approximately 12 days, and this period shortens toward the end of the breeding season. The young fledge when approximately 16 days old and are fed by both parents for an additional 2 weeks after nest departure (Johnson 1998).

DISTRIBUTION AND STATUS

As currently recognized, House Wren have one of the most extensive ranges of any passerine in the Western Hemisphere, occurring from southern Canada to the southern tip of South America. In North America, they breed south to northern Georgia in the East and through the mountains of the West into southern Mexico. The House Wren is considered a common summer resident in the forested mountains and higher plateaus of Arizona (Phillips et al. 1964). Populations in several southeastern Arizona mountain ranges are often referred to as the Brown-throated Wren, a conspicuously buffier race occurring into Mexico.

Atlasers confirmed House Wrens breeding throughout their previously described range at elevations primarily from 5500 to 10,200 ft (1676–3109 m) and locally in drainages to 4600 ft (1402 m). They were found most consistently along the Mogollon Rim region from the White Mountains northwest to the Flagstaff and Williams areas. These wrens undoubtedly continue to nest within the diverse White Mountain Apache tribal lands where atlas surveys were not conducted. As reported by Jacobs (1986) and LaRue (1994), House Wrens were common in appropriate habitat on Navajo tribal lands. Atlasers encountered these wrens from the Carrizo Mountain south locally to the Defiance Plateau and in the aspen canyons of the Black Mesa and nearby Tsegi Canyon drainage. They were widespread on the Kaibab Plateau and were confirmed breeding at one location on the South Rim of the Grand Canyon as noted by Brown et al. (1987).

House Wrens were found nesting in many isolated mountain ranges, including in the Hualapai, Cerbat, and Virgin ranges in the west. In southeastern Arizona, House Wrens were encountered in most of the higher forested ranges, including one pair reported nesting near habitations at the Kitt Peak Observatory in the Quinlan Mountains.

House Wrens populations are considered stable in the United States and Canada, and Breeding Bird Survey data suggest increasing trends throughout the country, especially in the West. Population trend information is lacking specifically for Arizona, but the range of this wren has apparently changed little within the state.

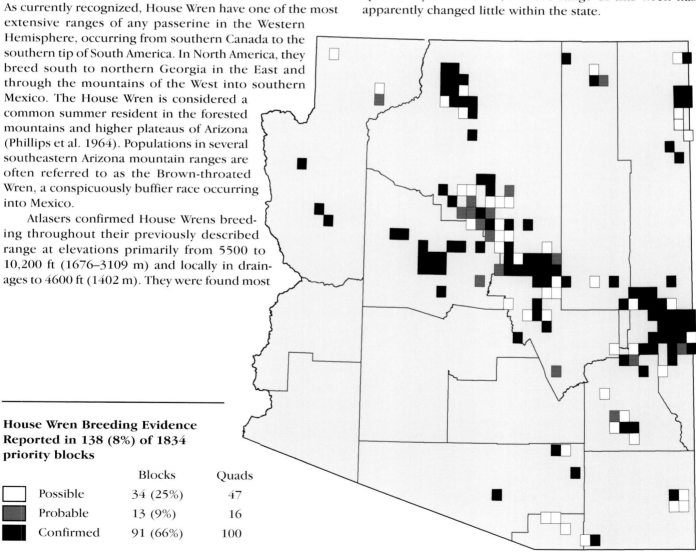

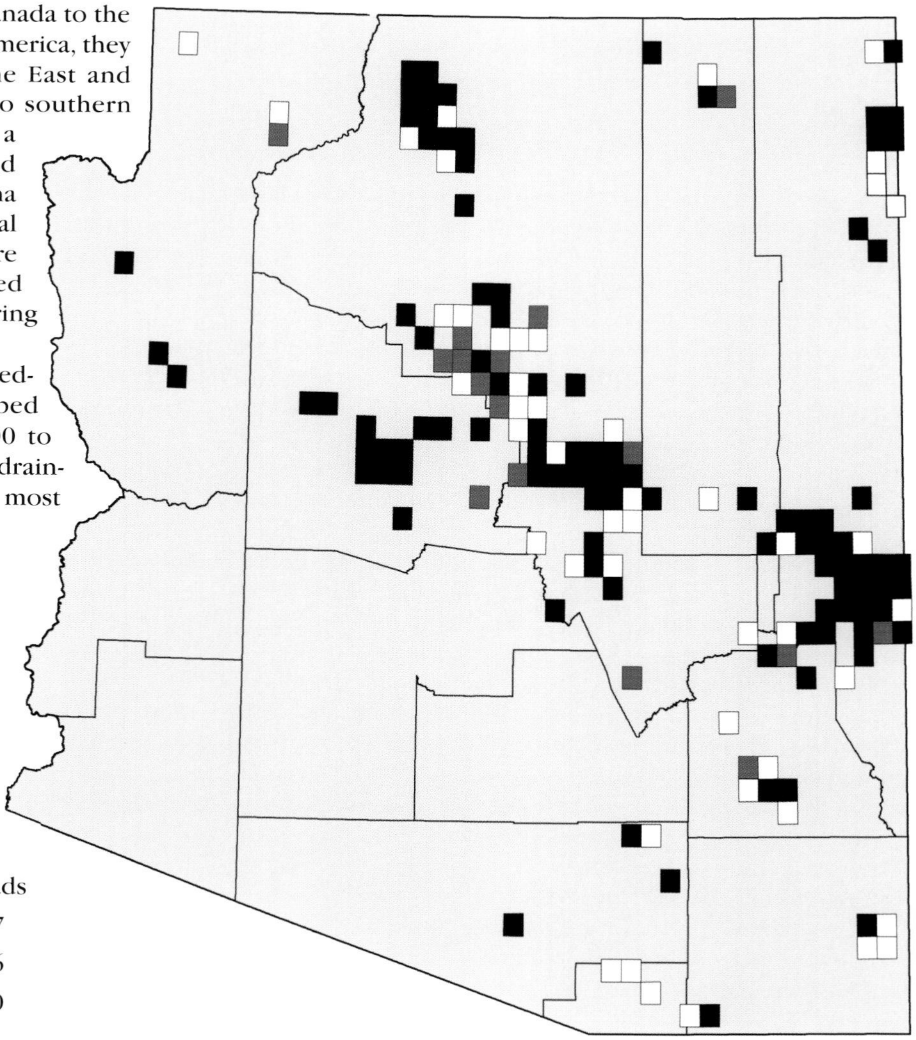

House Wren Breeding Evidence Reported in 138 (8%) of 1834 priority blocks

	Blocks	Quads
Possible	34 (25%)	47
Probable	13 (9%)	16
Confirmed	91 (66%)	100

Winter Wren

by Troy E. Corman *Troglodytes troglodytes*

The exuberant song of the Winter Wren is of such volume and penetrating quality that it seems quite unfitting a bird of such diminutive size. Like a tiny rodent, they secretively scamper low among exposed tree roots, streamside debris, or decaying timber. Encounters with these little forest wood nymphs are all too brief as they quickly appear and then retreat among the shadows.

BRIAN SMALL

HABITAT

The nesting habitat of the Winter Wren is typically cool and often damp, shadowy forest ravines along steep, narrow drainages with an abundance of fallen trees, rotting logs, stumps, limbs, and dense tangles. The four atlas records were all from small, cool, montane riparian drainages containing decadent stands of Douglas and white fir. Other dominant trees often included some ponderosa pine, Gambel's oak, and bigtooth maple. Understory typically consisted of downed trees, forest litter, and boulders, interspersed with patches of various ferns, moss, and forbs. Most localities discovered with Winter Wrens were in very narrow convoluted canyons with pockets and steep sided drainages that receive very little sunlight. These secluded areas remain very cool, damp, and dark, and appear to be especially favored by these shy little wrens.

BREEDING

Winter Wrens are typically sparse and very local winter residents of central and southern Arizona. However, the abundance and occupied localities often varies greatly from one year to the next. Most Winter Wrens have departed by March or early April to nesting areas well to the north of Arizona. Due to their local and only recent nesting discovery, atlasers collected little nesting information. Winter Wrens have been found in nesting areas of Arizona by 3 May, but males likely begin establishing territories by early April. Much of the following timing of breeding information is from research conducted by Hejl et al. (2002) in northern Idaho. Males begin singing in April and continue through July, but singing bouts are reduced during periods when they are feeding nestlings or fledglings. In Idaho, males have been observed nest building from late April to late July, with a peak in May and June. The first clutch of eggs is typically laid from late April to mid-May in Idaho, with later nests containing eggs through at least the end of July. The only confirmed record during the atlas was the observation of an agitated adult carrying food on 2 July. In Idaho, most young fledge by late July or early August. It is unknown if Arizona's nesting population is resident, but away from known breeding areas, Winter Wrens are rarely reported before mid-October or November.

The male Winter Wren selects nest sites and then constructs several nests built almost entirely by him. Females will typically choose one of the nests and begins to line it in preparation for egg laying (Hejl et al. 2002). The interval between beginning to line the inside of the nest and egg laying can vary between 3 and 18 days (Armstrong 1955). Favorite nest sites are among roots of upturned trees, but Winter Wrens also nest in or under streambanks or cliffs, old woodpecker cavities, and in decaying logs, stumps, and snags. Hejl et al. (2002) found the average nest height of ninety-seven nests measured in Idaho to be 3.9 ft (1.2 m), with a range from 0.3 to 26.9 ft (0.1–8.2 m) above the ground or stream.

Most Winter Wren clutches contain 5–7 eggs (range 1–9; Hejl et al. 2002). Only female wrens incubate and this period lasts 14–16 days (Van Horne 1995; Hejl et al. 2002). Unlike some wren species, male Winter Wrens rarely feed the female during incubation (Armstrong 1955). The female feeds the nestlings more than the male does, but his contribution increases as the nestlings become older (Hejl et al. 2002). Most evidence suggests that the young fledge when they are 16–18 days old. The adults continue feeding fledglings for an unknown period; second clutches are initiated 6–36 days later (Hejl et al. 2002).

DISTRIBUTION AND STATUS

Winter Wrens breed throughout much of the Northern Hemisphere. In North America they nest from coastal Alaska and southern Canada south to central California, northern Idaho, and the northeastern United States. They breed locally down the Appalachian Mountains to northern Georgia, but are perplexingly absent in the southern Rocky Mountains.

Winter Wrens were previously considered only a winter visitor in Arizona, but, beginning in 1985, there were irregular summer reports of singing Winter Wrens along the West Fork of Oak Creek Canyon north of Sedona (F. Brandt, personal communication). The closest known nesting area is within the Sierra Nevada of California. However, from mid-May through late July 1987, a singing territorial male was observed in the Jemez Mountains of Los Alamos County, New Mexico. This individual was also observed carrying nest material during this period. A territorial Winter Wren was again observed singing within this mountain range nearly every summer from 1995 to

1999 (S. Williams, personal communication). There have also been recent local summer records from Nevada (T. Floyd, personal communication).

Atlasers reported a singing Winter Wren approximately 2.5 mi (4 km) up the West Fork of Oak Creek from the confluence with Oak Creek on 25 June 1994. A very agitated individual was later observed in this area by atlasers on 26 June 1996, but no further evidence of breeding was obtained at this locality. On 2 July 1999, observers finally confirmed Winter Wrens nesting in Arizona. An agitated pair was observed, including one carrying food, in upper See Canyon just below the Mogollon Rim, north of the town of Christopher Creek (J. Rourke, personal communication). A third singing individual was also observed in this area. The following year, two more territorial Winter Wrens were found along canyons draining the Mogollon Rim several miles to the east. One singing individual was discovered in upper Canyon Creek on 12 July, the other singing and agitated individual south of the Gentry Lookout Tower on 28 May. All records were at elevations between 6100 and 6800 ft (1859–2073 m).

Though undoubtedly local, Winter Wrens could be a more widespread nesting species in Arizona than atlas data reveal. This is especially true along the southern base of the entire Mogollon Rim, where many unsurveyed canyon drainages exist. Birders rarely visit these isolated and often remote canyons during the summer, particularly by individuals familiar with the song of the Winter Wren. There are likely many dozens of narrow canyons draining the Mogollon Rim that contain microhabitat pockets of cool, shaded ravines that could harbor additional nesting pairs of this little skulking wren.

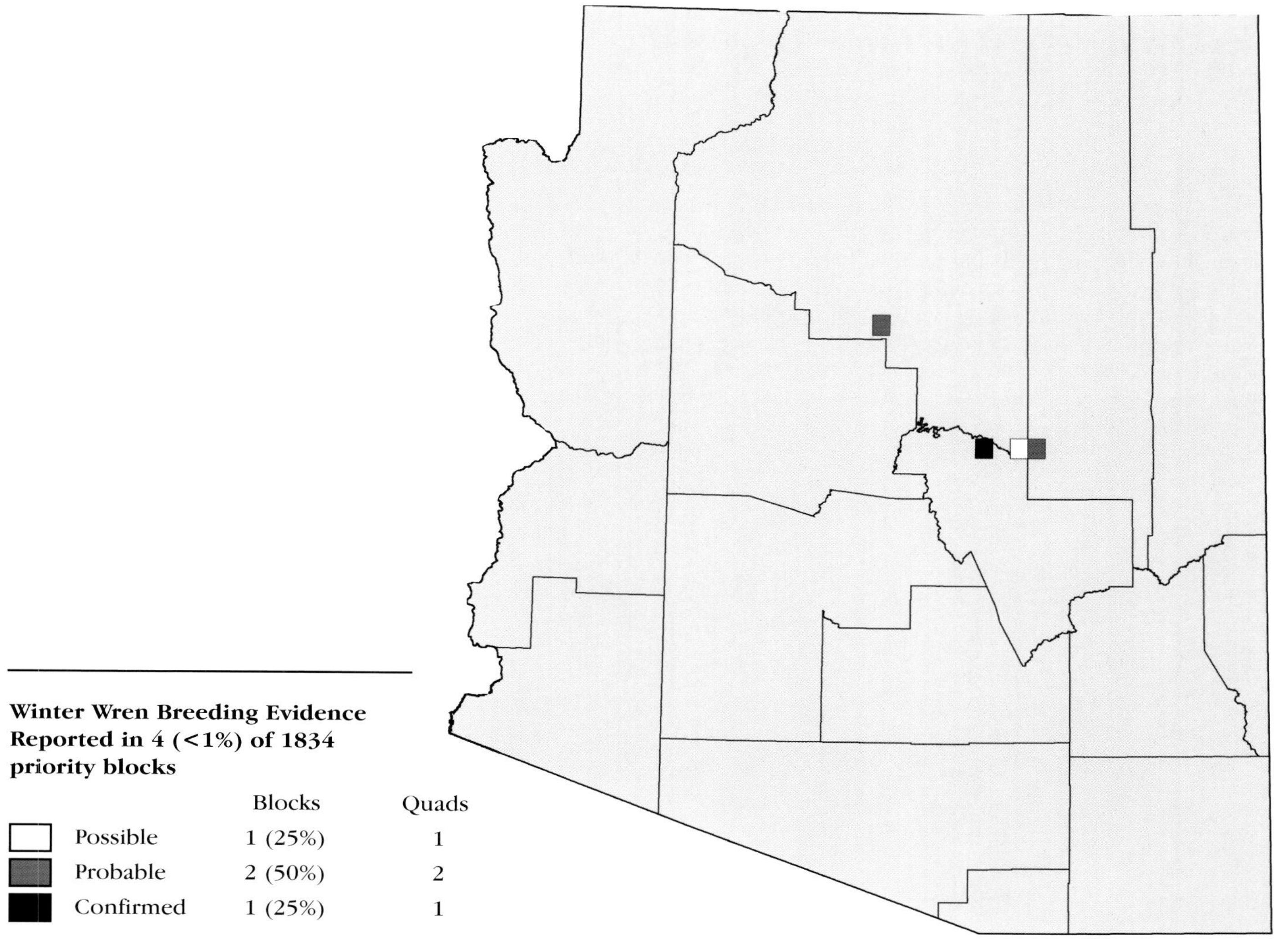

Winter Wren Breeding Evidence Reported in 4 (<1%) of 1834 priority blocks

	Blocks	Quads
Possible	1 (25%)	1
Probable	2 (50%)	2
Confirmed	1 (25%)	1

Marsh Wren

by Troy E. Corman *Cistothorus palustris*

JIM BURNS

With a sudden loud outburst of gurgles and sharp raspy notes, the merry song of the Marsh Wren can often invigorate a seemingly sleepy wetland. Male Marsh Wrens are the most diligent of nest builders, routinely constructing 7–15 nests in their territory in hopes of attracting one or more mates. Some industrious individuals construct more than twenty abodes.

HABITAT

As its name implies, the Marsh Wren is a bird of deep-water wetlands and during the breeding season, is seldom found in any other habitat. In Arizona, these wrens typically occur in very dense stands of cattails, bulrush, or a combination of both. Along the Colorado River, densities of Marsh Wrens were found to be lower in more open marshes or marshes dominated by common reed (Rosenberg et al. 1991). Atlasers reported 89 percent of Marsh Wrens within extensive cattail and bulrush stands primarily along the edges of lakes, pond, and reservoirs, as well as slower sections of rivers. However, some were found in nearby earthen irrigation ditches, canals, and runoff ponds in agricultural areas. The other 11 percent were found in scattered, open Fremont cottonwood–willow associations, typically with nearby emergent vegetation stands.

BREEDING

Though Arizona's breeding Marsh Wrens are thought to be primarily resident, migratory populations winter commonly in marshes and wet, weedy areas in western and southern Arizona. Spring migration occurs from March to mid-April, casually to mid-May. In Arizona, males will sing short songs on warm sunny days throughout the winter, but they begin to sing more earnestly in February and March. Observing the activity of Marsh Wrens is no easy task, and atlasers collected very little breeding information while conducting typical atlas surveys. Rosenberg et al. (1991) noted that Marsh Wrens nest from March to August along the lower Colorado River. The first nest-building activity reported by atlasers was on 14 May. An adult was observed carrying a fecal sac on 24 May, suggesting egg laying in early May. Nest-building activity was observed as late as 21 July. However, males build numerous nest structures, which are used as showcases to entice females into their territory and for roosting throughout the year. In Arizona, migrating Marsh Wrens begin to appear in nonbreeding areas by mid-August and September.

When entering a Marsh Wren's territory, females typically inspect the many nests while being escorted by the resident male (Kroodsma and Verner 1997). She often accepts one of his nests, then lines it with soft materials before laying eggs (Verner 1964). Alternatively, the female will initiate a new nest (Welter 1935). Studies have found that approximately 50 percent of the males of some populations have two or more mates within their territory (Kroodsma and Verner 1997). In Arizona, their globular nests are usually intricately woven to several stalks of cattails or bulrushes. Nest heights were not measured in Arizona, but in other state nests have ranged from 1.3 to 6.5 ft (0.4–2 m) in height above the ground or water (Bent 1948, Verner 1965).

Female Marsh Wrens lay an average clutch of 4–6 eggs; however, clutch sizes decline as the nesting season advances (Kroodsma and Verner 1997). Incubation can last from 12 to 16 days and is performed solely by the female (Welter 1935; Verner 1965). The female is also the primary caregiver to the nestlings, with the male often providing very little sustenance to the young until they fledge in 12–16 days (Kaufman 1996). Typically both parents feed the fledglings for an additional 12–14 days following nest departure (Verner 1965). Some Marsh Wren populations routinely attempt two broods per season, often initiating the second nesting approximately 2 weeks after the first young have fledged (Welter 1935).

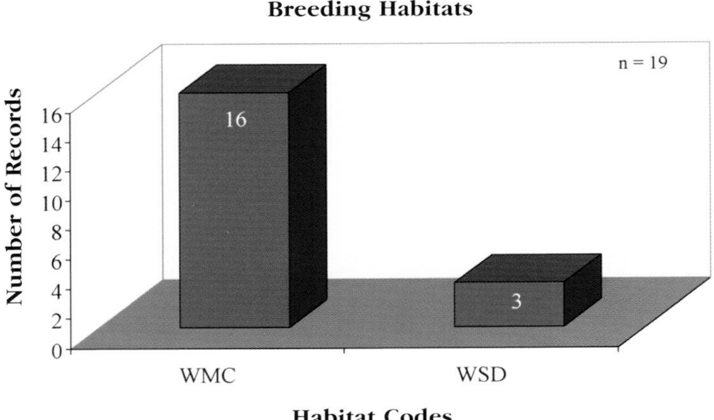

DISTRIBUTION AND STATUS

The breeding distribution of Marsh Wrens is often very spotty and irregular, nesting in southern Canada, north to northeastern British Columbia and then south throughout much of northern United States. They nest locally as far south as Arizona and California in the West and along the Gulf and East Coasts. There is also a disjunct population in central Mexico (Howell and Webb 1995). In Arizona, Marsh Wrens have been described as local residents along the lower Colorado River and in marshes of the lower Salt River (Phillips et al. 1964), as far upstream as Granite Reef Dam (Monson and Phillips 1981). Rosenberg et al. (1991) noted Marsh Wrens as locally common summer breeders along the lower Colorado River, with the largest populations at Topock Marsh, the Bill Williams River delta, and above Imperial Dam.

Atlasers encountered Marsh Wrens over most of the previously described breeding range in the state at elevations ranging from 100 to 950 ft (31–290 m). Along the Salt River, they were only found near the confluence of the Gila River. Lack of appropriate habitat likely extirpated the populations upstream to Granite Reef Dam. Atlasers did discover Marsh Wrens during the nesting season in several locations along the Gila River in the Arlington Valley and then downstream between Wellton and Tacna. Many of the extensive cattail and bulrush marshes along the Gila River are periodically eradicated by flood events. Such an event occurred in 1993 during the first year of the atlas. Although appropriate wetlands rapidly returned in subsequent years, Marsh Wren populations remain relatively low between the Arlington Valley and the confluence of the Salt River. The breeding race of Marsh Wren in Arizona is considered basically nonmigratory. There are now more than 75 mi (121 km) of unsuitable habitat separating populations on the middle Gila River from the larger populations on the Colorado River and this may hinder recruitment. Atlasers also discovered Marsh Wrens along the Bill Williams River, several miles upstream from the previously known population at the delta.

Several reports of nesting Marsh Wrens in the St. Johns region in southern Apache County could not be verified. This would represent a new disjunct nesting population in Arizona. However, specific follow-up surveys revealed no wrens and no evidence of nesting such as used nests. As elsewhere in their western range, the distribution of nesting Marsh Wrens in Arizona is not necessarily governed by the availability of cattail and bulrush marshes. There are hundreds if not thousands of acres of these emergent plants across the state that lack breeding populations of this small wetland wren.

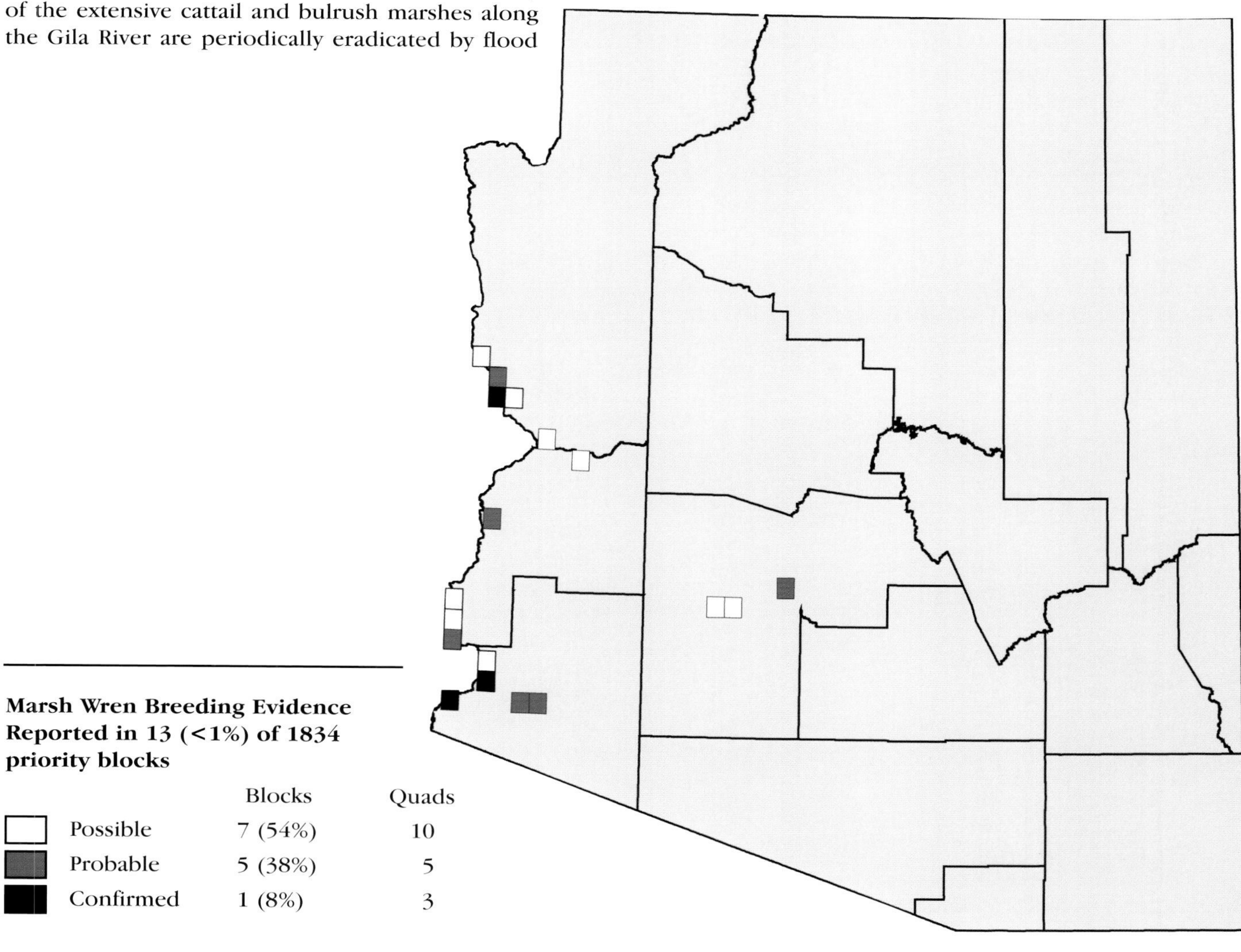
Marsh Wren Breeding Evidence Reported in 13 (<1%) of 1834 priority blocks

American Dipper

by Troy E. Corman *Cinclus mexicanus*

A unique passerine of clear, boulder-filled mountain streams, the American Dipper sings a loud melodious song that can be heard above an ambiance of swiftly flowing and cascading water. Dippers often survey their underwater surrounding by dunking their heads before diving into rapid currents and eddies in search of prey clinging to submerged rocks.

RICK AND NORA BOWERS

HABITAT

American Dippers are typically found along very clear and swift perennial drainages, often with an abundance of waterfalls and boulders. During the breeding season, a limiting factor is the availability of streamside nest sites in the form of large rocks, cliffs, and bridges with overhanging ledges and crevices. The vegetative habitat along drainage is not as important to the American Dipper as is the stream clarity, stream bottom composition for ease of foraging, and aquatic prey abundance. American Dippers prefer stream bottoms with an abundance of rocks, sand, and rubble (Kingery 1996). Drainages that contain these characteristics are found in several very different vegetative communities in Arizona. Of 26 atlas records, more than half were from cool montane drainages often containing a mixture of tall conifers, maple, alder, cottonwood, and sycamore. Within the Grand Canyon, American Dippers where noted at lower elevations where the characteristic vegetation included a scattered cottonwood, willow, seepwillow, and exotic tamarisk. They were also encountered nesting along high-elevation drainages dominated by thinleaf alder, coyote willow, and Geyer willow.

BREEDING

Some populations in Arizona move to lower elevations outside the breeding season, while others maintain resident territories. Nest building often begins early for American Dippers and is frequently initiated one to two weeks after they begin defending nesting territories (Kingery 1996). In Arizona, active nest constructing has been observed as early as 11 February (S. Barlow, personal communication). In the White Mountains region, atlasers observed nest building activity as late as 16 May, which could pertain to a second brood attempt. The earliest confirmed atlas record was of an adult feeding a fledgling on 25 April, indicating egg laying no later than the second week of March. Later nests may contain young into early or mid-July in Arizona, based on a nest with eggs discovered on 13 June.

Female American Dippers do most if not all the construction of the domed, mossy nest. Nests are built near water and most Arizona nests are on overhanging ledges, cliff crevices, and under bridges. They are also well known for nesting behind waterfalls, where the adults fly through the cascading water to reach their damp abode (Kingery 1996). American Dippers occasionally nest among exposed tree roots and under overhanging dirt banks (Kingery 1996). Atlasers measured the height of only one nest, which was on a ledge 7.9 ft (2.4 m) above the water. Kingery (1996) compiled nest height measurements from several sources, which suggested that the majority of nests are between 3.3 and 9.8 ft (1–3 m) above the stream but can range as high as 29.5 ft (9 m).

American Dippers typically have a clutch size of 4–5 eggs, which only the female incubates (Bent 1948). Males sometimes feed the incubating females, and both parents feed the nestlings that hatch in 14–17 days (Hann 1950; Price and Bock 1983). Nestlings normally depart the nest when they are 24–26 days old, at which time the parents often divide their brood between them and feed the fledglings for an additional 4–24 days (Kingery 1996). American Dippers produce one to two broods per season, frequently reusing their previous nest by removing the inner lining and then replacing it with fresh material (Kingery 1996).

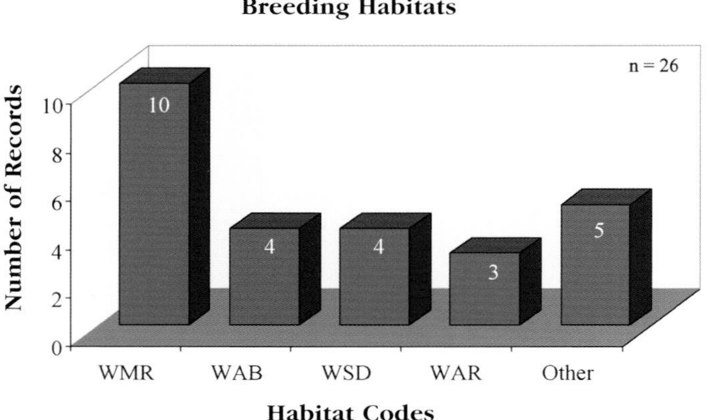

DISTRIBUTION AND STATUS

American Dippers nest in mountainous and some coastal regions of western North America from Alaska to Panama, often in isolated populations. In Arizona, they have previously been described as a fairly common resident along the

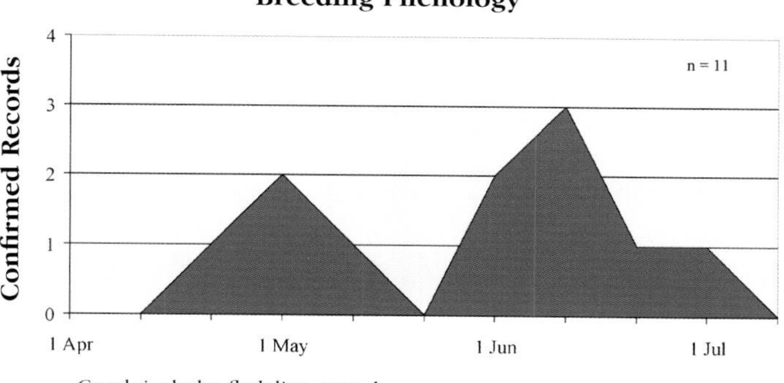

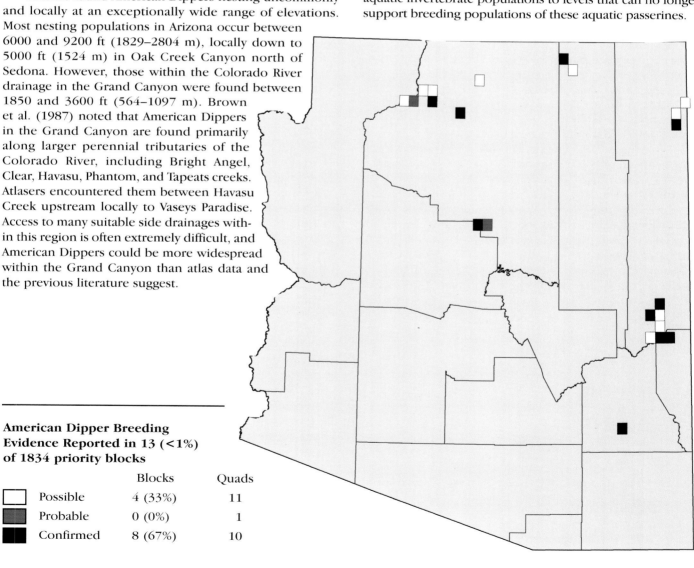

Graph includes fledgling records

southern rim of the Mogollon Plateau from Oak Creek east to the White Mountains and at the bottom of the Grand Canyon (Phillips et al. 1964). They were also reported nesting sparingly in the Sierra Ancha and Chuska mountains. An unsuccessful American Dipper nest with eggs was discovered in early May 1973 in Cave Creek Canyon, Chiricahua Mountains (Monson and Phillips 1981).

Atlasers found American Dippers nesting uncommonly and locally at an exceptionally wide range of elevations. Most nesting populations in Arizona occur between 6000 and 9200 ft (1829–2804 m), locally down to 5000 ft (1524 m) in Oak Creek Canyon north of Sedona. However, those within the Colorado River drainage in the Grand Canyon were found between 1850 and 3600 ft (564–1097 m). Brown et al. (1987) noted that American Dippers in the Grand Canyon are found primarily along larger perennial tributaries of the Colorado River, including Bright Angel, Clear, Havasu, Phantom, and Tapeats creeks. Atlasers encountered them between Havasu Creek upstream locally to Vaseys Paradise. Access to many suitable side drainages within this region is often extremely difficult, and American Dippers could be more widespread within the Grand Canyon than atlas data and the previous literature suggest.

On Navajo Tribal lands, atlasers found American Dippers nesting within the Tsaile Creek drainage in the Chuska Mountains and in the upper reaches of Canyon de Chelly as noted by Jacobs (1986). They were also confirmed nesting along upper Piute Creeks on the Shonto Plateau and were observed in the Tsegi Canyon drainages near the Betatakin Ruins.

The largest concentration of American Dippers in Arizona is within the White Mountains region, which likely continues east in the adjacent unsurveyed White Mountain Apache tribal lands. Atlasers finally confirmed American Dippers nesting in the Pinaleno Mountains along Ash Creek after many years of observations.

Atlasers were unable to document any evidence of American Dippers nesting along streams draining the southern slope of the Mogollon Rim between Strawberry and the Navajo County line, where they historically have bred. Outside the nesting season, American Dippers are regularly observed within this region along East Verde River and along Tonto, Christopher, Haigler, and Canyon creeks. Some evidence suggests that the recent widespread introduction of exotic crayfish in many of these drainages may have decimated the aquatic invertebrate populations to levels that can no longer support breeding populations of these aquatic passerines.

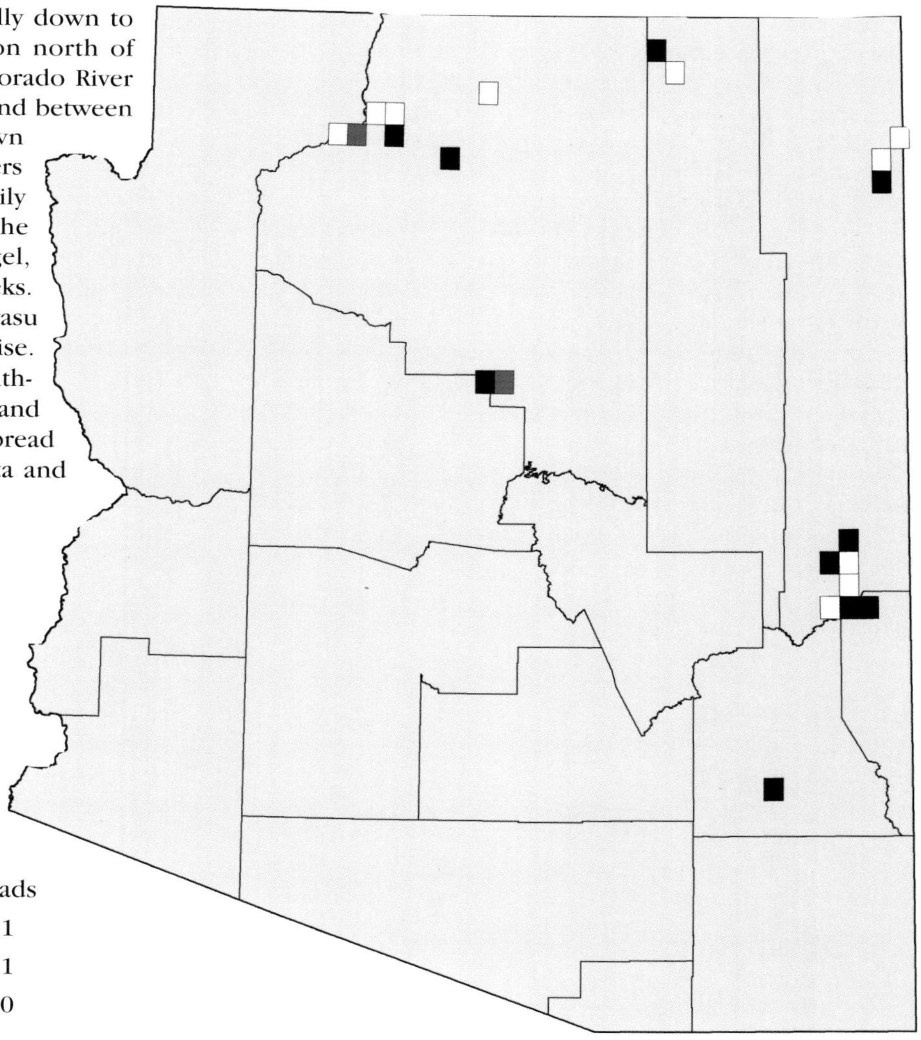

American Dipper Breeding Evidence Reported in 13 (<1%) of 1834 priority blocks

	Blocks	Quads
Possible	4 (33%)	11
Probable	0 (0%)	1
Confirmed	8 (67%)	10

Golden-crowned Kinglet

by Cathryn Wise-Gervais *Regulus satrapa*

Golden-crowned Kinglets fascinate ornithologists by their ability to withstand extremely low temperatures and thus winter in cold climates. This bird's diminutive size and striking facial pattern are diagnostic in the field, as is its thin, high-pitched call. They are primarily insect-eaters and, with their grooved soles, are specially adapted to forage from branch tips.

BRIAN SMALL

HABITAT

Golden-crowned Kinglets are most commonly associated with cool and often moist boreal spruce-fir forests, but they also nest locally in other conifer stands. This species and its preferred dense old-growth trees are sparsely distributed in Arizona, and atlasers reported only thirty-seven potential breeding records in five vegetative communities. Observers obtained 51 percent of Golden-crowned Kinglet records in mixed-conifer forests characterized by various species of firs and pine, typically with scattered aspen and Gambel's oak. In Arizona, these birds reach their highest densities in subalpine spruce-fir forests often containing Engelmann spruce, blue spruce, and subalpine fir, where 27 percent of records were obtained. Atlasers also encountered Golden-crowned Kinglets nesting locally down into cool montane drainages frequently containing various pines, firs, maple, oak, and aspen.

BREEDING

Arizona's breeding Golden-crowned Kinglets are primarily nonmigratory, although they occasionally descend slightly to adjacent forests during the winter (Phillips et al. 1964). Although nests have been reported as early as 19 March in Montana after a warm winter and early spring (Blackford 1955), a more typical time frame for early nest construction is in late April and May (Ingold and Galati 1997). Atlasers first observed a pair of Golden-crowned Kinglets in suitable breeding habitat on 11 May, which were noted carrying nesting material on 20 May. An adult was observed carrying food on 29 May, but it is possible that this sighting was actually a male carrying food to his incubating mate. Atlasers reported adult kinglets feeding fledglings from 23 June-2 August and noted the latest nest with young on 18 July. Atlasers obtained twenty-one confirmed records for this species, mostly of dependent fledglings, with 73 percent falling in July. Individuals and small groups are irregularly found in Arizona's lowland riparian woodlands between November and March, and evidence suggests that these individuals may be migrants from outside the state (Phillips et al. 1964).

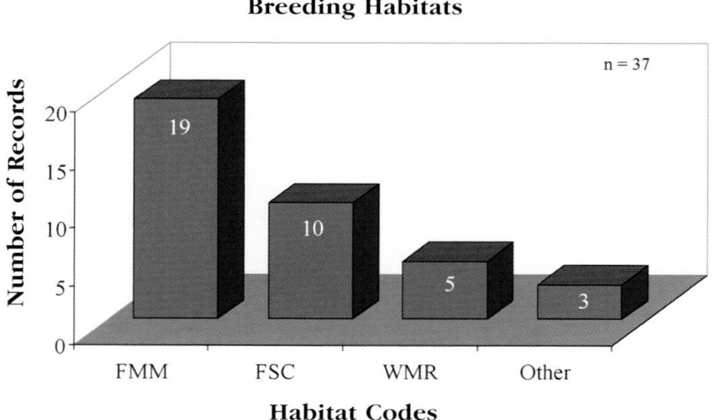

Golden-crowned Kinglet pairs build their well-concealed, semi-pendulant nests over a period of approximately five days (Ingold and Galati 1997) These nests are typically placed high in dense conifers, so can be difficult to locate. Atlasers took measurements of only two Golden-crowned Kinglet nests, both in Engelmann spruce at 12.5 and 23 ft (3.8 and 7.0 m) above the ground. Little can be inferred from such a small sample size, but these two nests were considerably lower than the mean of 50.2 ft (15.3 m) determined for nineteen Minnesota nests (Ingold and Galati 1997).

Golden-crowned Kinglets have large clutches relative to their small bodies, with typical nests containing 8–9 eggs, which can range from 5 to 11 (Ehrlich et al. 1988). This mass of eggs is sometimes arranged in two layers within the nest, probably to facilitate incubation by such a tiny body. Only the female incubates, but the male feeds her while she is on the eggs (Ingold and Galati 1997). The young hatch after approximately 15 days (Galati 1991) and are fed by both parents, although the male may initially bring more food to the nest as the female broods the newly hatched young. As the young grow, the female helps feed for a short period, then focuses her attention on building a new nest and incubating her second set of eggs. Fledging occurs at approximately 16–19 days, and earlier if the nestlings are disturbed (Ingold and Galati 1997). After about 2 weeks out of the nest, young are able to procure most of their own food, but still commonly beg from parents (Ingold and Galati 1997).

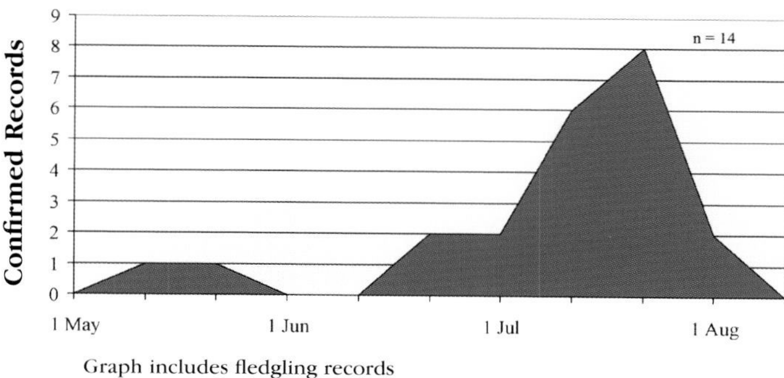

Graph includes fledgling records

DISTRIBUTION AND STATUS

Golden-crowned Kinglets breed from southern Alaska and southern Canada, south locally in the Appalachian Mountains to North Carolina. In the West, they nest along the Pacific Coast to northern California and in higher mountain ranges primarily east to Colorado and New Mexico. There are also isolated populations in Mexico and Guatemala. This species' distribution corresponds closely to the range of high-elevation spruce or mixed-conifer forests, especially in the arid Southwest. Atlasers confirmed Golden-crowned Kinglets breeding in Arizona at elevations from approximately 7000 to 10,600 ft (2134–3231 m).

In Arizona, Golden-crowned Kinglets are typically described as an uncommon to fairly common breeding species of most boreal forests within the state (Phillips et al. 1964; Monson and Phillips 1981). However, Brown et al. (1987) considered them a rare summer resident on the Kaibab Plateau. Given the availability of habitat, atlasers also found Golden-crowned Kinglets surprisingly sparse and local on this plateau. Golden-crowned Kinglets reach their highest density in the White Mountains and in the San Francisco Mountains area. These kinglets undoubtedly also nest fairly commonly in the higher elevations of the White Mountain Apache tribal lands, where atlas surveys could not be conducted. On the Mogollon Rim, Golden-crowned Kinglets were local, but fairly regularly detected in cool, snowmelt drainages. Atlasers also discovered a few pairs in upper Reynolds Creek in the Sierra Ancha.

In southeastern Arizona, atlasers had similar findings as Phillips et al. (1964) as they located nesting Golden-crowned Kinglets only in the higher elevations of Chiricahua, Pinaleno, and Santa Catalina mountains. Atlasers did not report Golden-crowned Kinglets in the Chuska Mountains on Navajo tribal lands, but Jacobs (1986) noted a summer record in this area previously.

Although Breeding Bird Survey data suggest significant declines in western Golden-crowned Kinglet numbers, eastern surveys show increasing trends from 1966 to 1994. These increases are believed to be due to spruce tree plantings (Ingold and Galati 1997), while western decreases are attributed to habitat loss due to fire and timber harvesting activities. Franzreb and Ohmart (1978) reported a significant density reduction of these kinglets after a mixed-conifer forest in Arizona had been selectively harvested. Atlasers reported Golden-crowned Kinglets throughout their previously described range in Arizona, suggesting some population stability; however, the relative abundance of these birds remains unknown in the state.

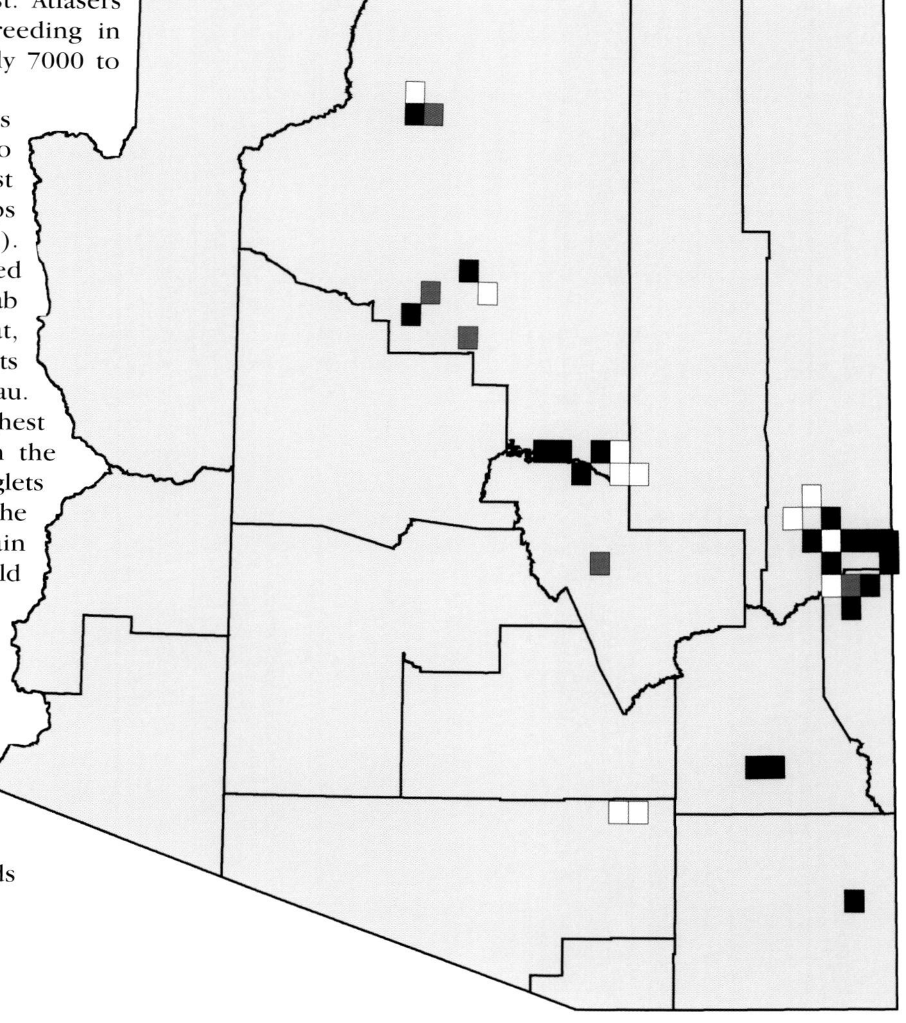

Golden-crowned Kinglet Breeding Evidence Reported in 29 (2%) of 1834 priority blocks

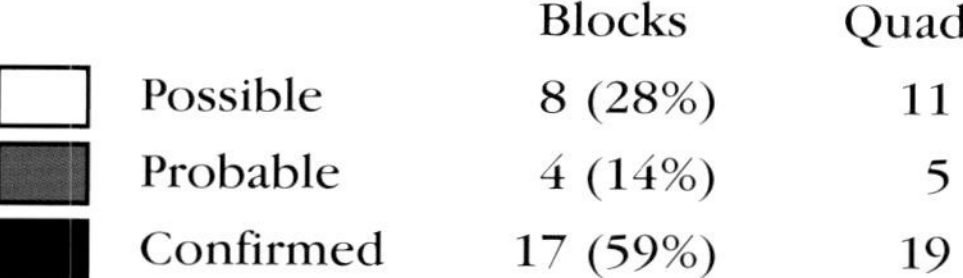

	Blocks	Quads
Possible	8 (28%)	11
Probable	4 (14%)	5
Confirmed	17 (59%)	19

Ruby-crowned Kinglet

by Cathryn Wise-Gervais *Regulus calendula*

RICK AND NORA BOWERS

Small and sprightly, Ruby-crowned Kinglets flit nervously from branch to branch in their seemingly endless quest for insects. Ironically, this bird was named for a striking characteristic that is infrequently revealed. Instead, the species can be quickly identified even from a distance by their tiny size and restless habit of constantly flicking their wings.

HABITAT

During the breeding season, Ruby-crowned Kinglets typically forage and nest in dense foliage high in the conifer forest treetops, often to the chagrin of researchers far below. Atlasers reported this species in eight habitat types, all of which are found at higher elevations. In Arizona, Ruby-crowned Kinglets reach their highest densities in mixed-conifer forests where 54 percent of the forty-eight potential breeding records were obtained. Within these forests, the birds are typically encountered nesting in Douglas fir and white fir, but also regularly forage in the associated ponderosa pine and aspen. They are also attracted to nearby cool, montane drainages often supporting firs, pines, and deciduous trees such as aspen, maple, Gambel's oak, and willow. Though spruce-fir forests are relatively limited in Arizona, Ruby-crowned Kinglets are characteristic summer inhabitant of the Engelmann spruce, blue spruce, and subalpine fir stands. Atlas data reveal that these kinglets are typically lacking in the widespread and drier ponderosa pine dominated forests of Arizona, but the birds may visit such areas if they are adjacent to cooler drainages and slopes containing firs.

BREEDING

Ruby-crowned Kinglets are less cold-hardy than their Golden-crowned relatives and are common to abundant during migration and as winter visitors in Arizona's lowlands. Spring migration begins in late March or early April in Arizona, with few transients remaining after early May. This species typically arrives on their high elevation breeding grounds in mid-April, and atlasers first reported birds singing in suitable breeding habitat on 19 April. Pair formation and breeding activities are thought to occur shortly after the birds arrive on their breeding grounds (Ingold and Wallace 1994). Nest building in the state likely begins in May, although atlasers did not report this activity until 10 June. Many high elevation atlas blocks were not visited until early June and early nesting activity was undoubtedly missed. In addition, Ruby-crowned Kinglet nests are difficult to locate, inasmuch as they are placed high in trees and are well concealed among dense foliage.

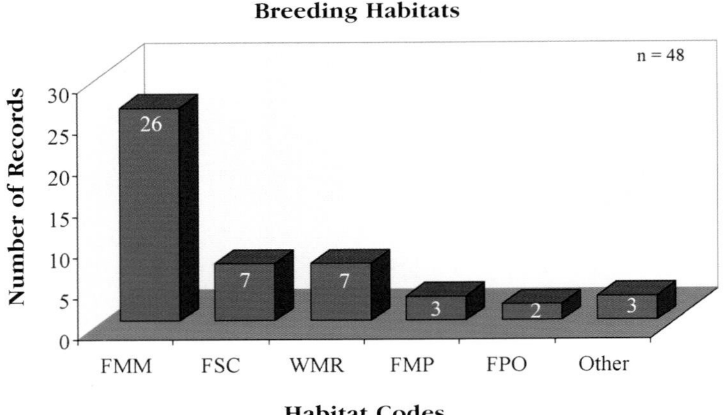

Observers obtained only sixteen confirmed breeding records for Ruby-crowned Kinglets, and none of these were nests with eggs or young. Atlasers did report adults carrying food and fecal sacs on 14 and 18 June, respectively, suggesting that egg laying in these cases occurred by late May or early June. In Colorado, active nests were noted from mid-May through July, with the latest nest containing young on 5 August (Barrett 1998). Most atlas confirmations for this species were of adults feeding fledglings in July, toward the end of the birds' breeding cycle. Observers reported adults carrying food through 2 August. Ruby-crowned Kinglets typically begin appearing outside their breeding habitats in early to mid-September in Arizona, with migration continuing into November.

Ruby-crowned Kinglets typically nest high in conifers, and this preference made nest finding exceedingly difficult for atlasers. In Arizona, most nests are constructed in various species of spruce and fir. Although atlasers did not locate any active nests, most nests are constructed 20–40 ft (6.1–12.2 m) high, with some lofty nests documented to near 90 ft (27.4 m) above the ground (Ingold and Wallace 1994).

Female Ruby-crowned Kinglets construct their well-concealed nests in approximately five days without male assistance (Harrison 1979; Ingold and Wallace 1994). Nests are comprised of soft materials and are protected from above by dense overhanging foliage (Ingold and Wallace 1994). Clutch sizes can be quite large, especially given the size of the bird, and typically consist of 7–9 eggs but can range from 5 to 12 (Harrison 1979). Incubating females are completely concealed within the nest and eggs hatch after

Breeding Phenology

Confirmed Records

n = 15

1 May 1 Jun 1 Jul 1 Aug

about 13–16 days (Ingold and Wallace 1994). Both adults feed the young, but only the female broods. Fledging occurs at approximately 16 days of age, and parental care continues for at least 10 days after the young leave the nest (Ingold and Wallace 1994).

DISTRIBUTION AND STATUS

Ruby-crowned Kinglets breed throughout most of boreal forests of Canada and Alaska, south to northern New York and Michigan in the East. In the West, they breed in higher mountain ranges south locally to southern California, southeastern Arizona, and central New Mexico. Ruby-crowned Kinglets are common summer residents of Arizona's more extensive boreal forest zones such as those found on the Mogollon and Kaibab plateaus, and very locally in higher southeastern ranges (Phillips et al. 1964). Atlasers regularly encountered the species in appropriate habitat at elevations from 6800 to 10,200 ft (2073–3109 m) and locally higher.

In Arizona, breeding Ruby-crowned Kinglets are most abundant and widespread on the Kaibab Plateau and in the White Mountains. Their nesting range undoubtedly continues west into the higher-elevation forests of the White Mountain Apache tribal lands, where atlas surveys could not be conducted. The birds were sparsely distributed on the Mogollon Rim west of this reservation and were discovered locally in the Sierra Ancha. These kinglets were regularly encountered in the San Francisco Mountains area and were found on the isolated Sitgreaves, Bill Williams, and Hualapai mountains as well.

On Navajo tribal lands, Jacobs (1986) considered Ruby-crowned Kinglets summer residents in the Lukachukai Mountains. Atlasers also noted them in the Carrizo Mountains and confirmed them nesting in the Chuska Mountains. LaRue (1994) noted that these kinglets were fairly common summer residents in upper canyons of Black Mesa, and observers made similar findings during atlas surveys.

Although nesting in the same southeastern Arizona mountains as Golden-crowned Kinglets, Ruby-crowns are far less abundant and very local within these ranges. Atlasers found them most common in the Pinaleno Mountains, very local in the Chiricahua Mountains, and missed them altogether in the Santa Catalina Mountains. In the latter range, summering singing birds have previously been noted in a subalpine fir stand on the north slope of the mountain summit (Phillips et al. 1964). Small and local populations of Ruby-crowned Kinglets could have easily been missed while conducting atlas surveys within the Santa Catalina Mountains.

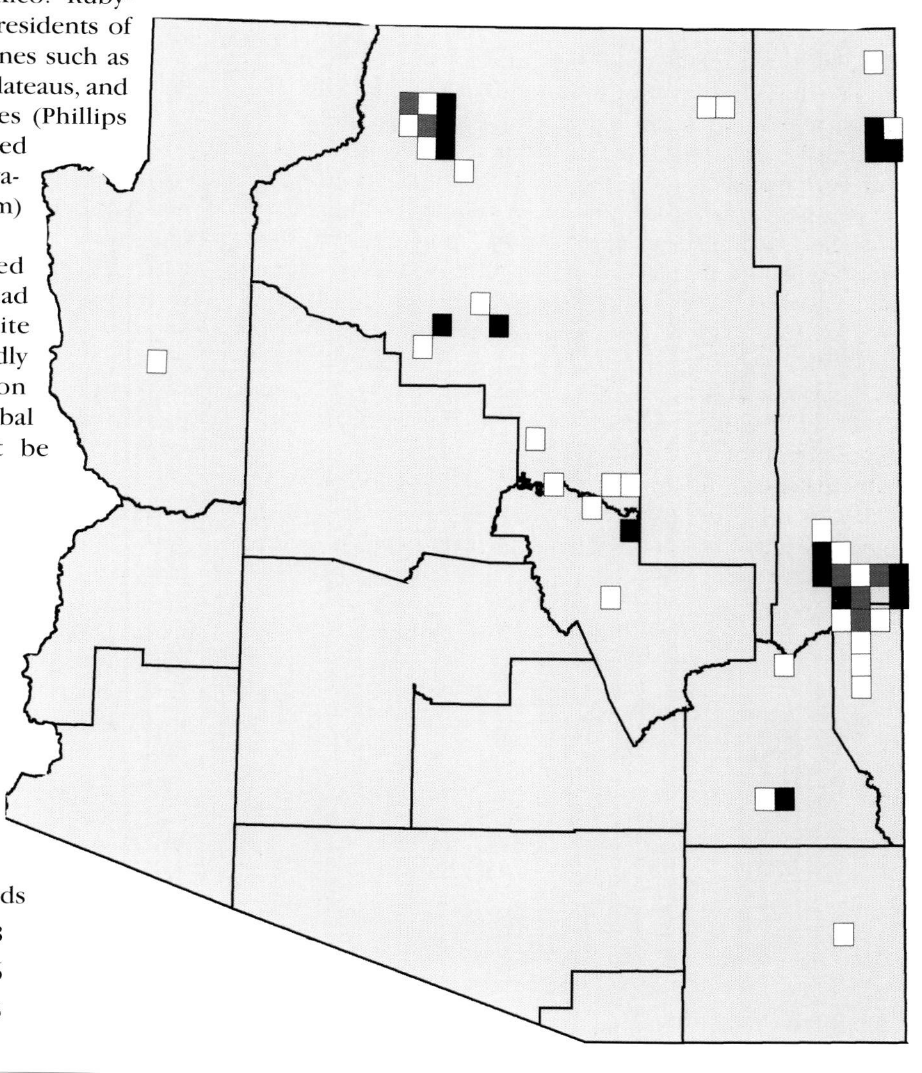

Ruby-crowned Kinglet Breeding Evidence Reported in 42 (2%) of 1834 priority blocks

	Blocks	Quads
Possible	24 (56%)	28
Probable	6 (15%)	6
Confirmed	12 (29%)	15

Blue-gray Gnatcatcher

by Cathryn Wise-Gervais *Polioptila caerulea*

The Blue-gray Gnatcatcher is aggressive for its small size and is known for its emphatic scolding. These birds eat small insects and spiders and glean these from the tips of branches or on foliage. They often flick their long tails while foraging, perhaps to scare up unseen prey.

HABITAT

In Arizona, Blue-gray Gnatcatchers are commonly encountered nesting in open woodlands, forest edges, brushy riparian corridors, and on shrub covered mountain slopes. Although atlasers reported this species in twenty-three vegetative communities, most records (40 percent) were obtained in the widespread pinyon pine–juniper woodlands (n = 491). They were found less frequently where these woodlands contained scattered ponderosa pine. Blue-gray Gnatcatchers are often noted in oak associations, and approximately 21 percent of atlas records were fairly evenly distributed between open Madrean evergreen oak woodlands and chaparral-influenced areas, often containing scrub live oak, manzanita, cliffrose, and other low woody shrubs. Atlasers also encountered these gnatcatchers nesting in several riparian habitats from canyons with sycamore down to mountain foothill drainages and even dry washes with dense stands of netleaf hackberry and mesquite. Within these lower elevations groves and thickets, their range overlaps locally with that of the resident Black-tailed Gnatcatcher.

BREEDING

Blue-gray Gnatcatchers begin to arrive on Arizona breeding grounds in mid- to late March, and immediately begin courting and establishing territory. These birds are believed to be monogamous, and the female will often accompany the male as he patrols their territory (Ellison 1992). Atlasers noted Blue-gray Gnatcatchers, one of the earlier nesting insectivorous songbirds, carrying nesting material on 14 April with numerous nest construction activities reported through mid-May. Egg laying can begin by late April in Arizona and atlasers noted the first nest with young on 11 May. Statewide atlas data reveal a nesting activity peak in late May, but nesting continues through late July. Observers discovered a late nest with eggs on 27 July, indicating that some nests may contain young into early to mid-August in Arizona. Blue-gray Gnatcatchers can begin their fall migration as early as mid-August, with peak passage in mid-September and continuing into October. Although numbers vary from year to year, they typically winter fairly commonly from south-central Arizona westward, particularly in lowland riparian woodlands and heavily wooded washes.

Both Blue-gray Gnatcatcher sexes take part in nest construction and build neat, high-walled cups on limbs far from the center trunk or saddled in the crotch of limbs (Ellison 1992). Atlasers took at least partial measurements at forty-one nests in sixteen tree or shrub species, including several juniper species (12), pinyon pine (6), cliffrose (6), and several oak species (4). Other nests were discovered in sagebrush (3), hackberry, mesquite, locust, and Joshua tree. The mean nest height for all nests was 8.2 ft (2.5 m), but ranged from 2.6 ft (0.8 m) in sagebrush to 26.6 ft (8.1 m) in a cottonwood. Blue-gray Gnatcatcher nests can be expertly camouflaged, which, coupled with their small size, can make them difficult to locate. They periodically change their minds about a given nest site, and the pair will sometimes completely dismantle the new abode and rebuild it elsewhere piece by piece.

Female Blue-gray Gnatcatchers lay 4–5 eggs (range 3–6), and both sexes incubate for approximately 13 days (range 11–15; Weston 1949). The adults will seldom leave their eggs uncovered during the incubation period (Ellison 1992), possibly to reduce the likelihood of brood parasitism. The sitting bird will call prior to leaving the nest, possibly in response to sighting the relieving mate, which

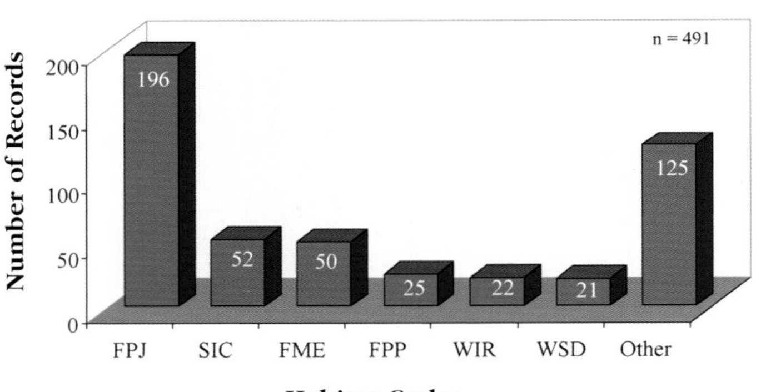

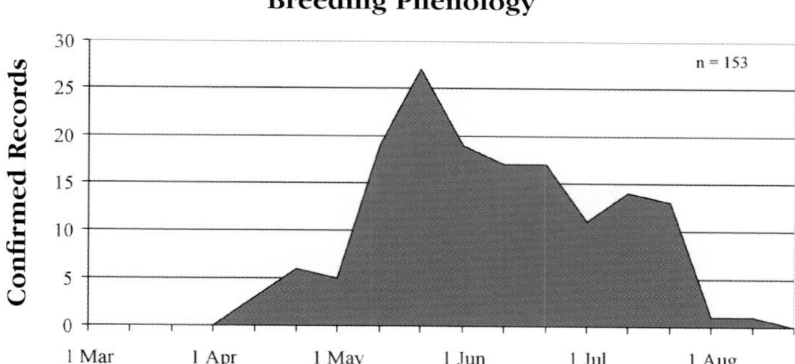

arrives silently and covers the eggs (Ellison 1992). Despite this bird's vigilant nest guarding, they are still regular victims of Brown-headed Cowbird parasitism, and atlasers reported nine instances of this from 23 May to 24 July.

Both parents feed the young, but the male makes more feeding trips early in the nestling period (days 1–4) as the female spends more time brooding (Ellison 1992). Young will leave the nest and sit in nearby branches by day 12 (Root 1969), and they fledge around day 13 (range 10–15 days; Ellison 1992). Parents will continue to provide food for approximately 16 days after fledging, and the young typically remain in the parents' territory for about a month before dispersing (Root 1969; Ellison 1992). Although most pairs produce only one brood per season, second brood attempts are not uncommon and are likely in Arizona, given the birds' 3–4 month nesting season in the state.

DISTRIBUTION AND STATUS

Blue-gray Gnatcatchers are the only truly migratory gnatcatcher in North America. They breed throughout the eastern half of the United States and adjacent Canada, as well as in the West from southwestern Oregon to southwestern Wyoming south through Mexico (including Baja California) to Guatemala. Phillips et al. (1964) considered Blue-gray Gnatcatchers to be common summer residents throughout much of the state, but noted them as very local in the southwest due to limited appropriate habitat. Atlasers confirmed these birds on atlas blocks primarily from 3000 to 7400 ft (366–2097 m), although they nest locally down to 1400 ft (366 m) along the Colorado River within the Grand Canyon.

Atlasers readily found Blue-gray Gnatcatchers in suitable habitat in northern and central Arizona, although in some regions they were curiously missed on survey blocks containing pinyon pine–juniper stands. This was especially notable between Springerville and Heber, where these woodlands are often quite extensive. Although they were found throughout the lower mountains and foothills of southeastern Arizona, Blue-gray Gnatcatchers breeding densities appear to be relatively low in many areas.

In the arid southwestern mountains, atlasers encountered these gnatcatchers in local scrub live oak thicket at higher elevations and in oak and Arizona rosewood–dominated foothill drainages. These included the Ajo, Kofa, and Harcuvar ranges. Atlasers did not detect them in the Harquahala, Castle Dome, and Mohave mountain ranges, as noted by Phillips et al. (1964), but additional surveys should find them nesting locally there.

Atlasers located Blue-gray Gnatcatchers regularly throughout most of their historical range, suggesting some population stability in the state. Habitat losses due to local urban sprawl no doubt have had some adverse effects on this small insectivore, but specific data documenting this are lacking.

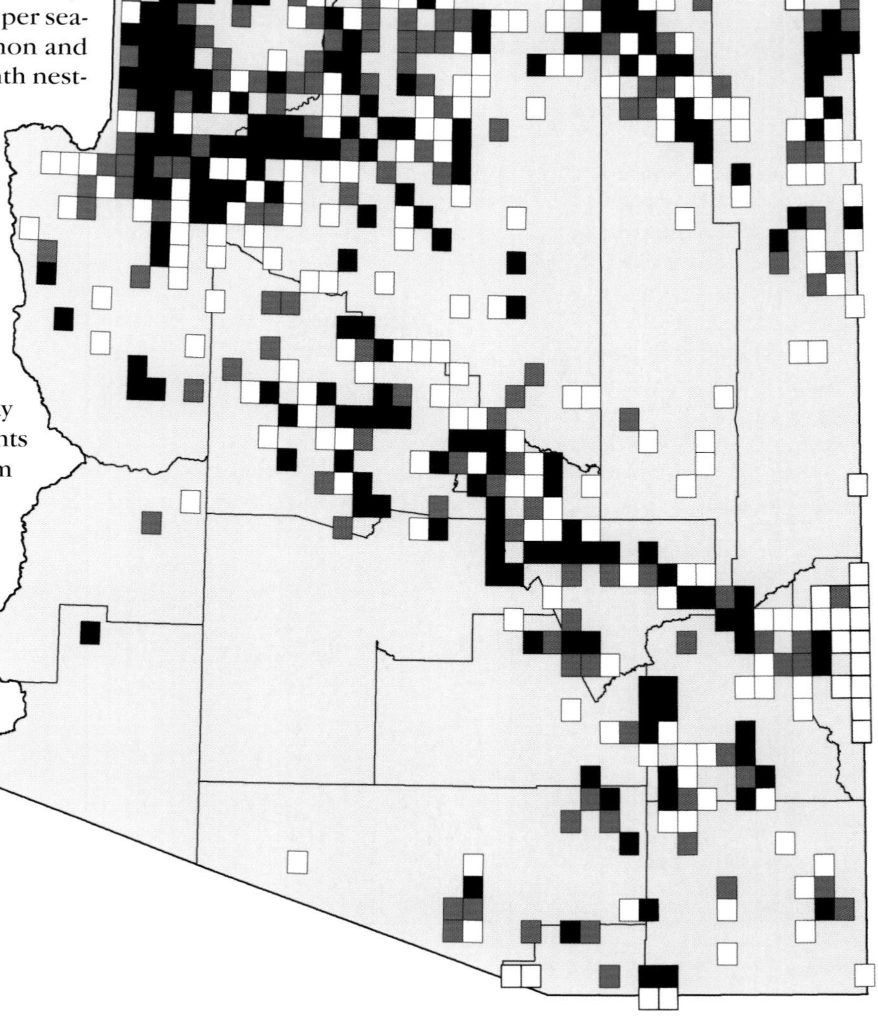

Blue-gray Gnatcatcher Breeding Evidence Reported in 477 (26%) of 1834 priority blocks

	Blocks	Quads
Possible	189 (39%)	203
Probable	117 (25%)	122
Confirmed	171 (36%)	183

Black-tailed Gnatcatcher

by Cathryn Wise-Gervais *Polioptila melanura*

Weighing only about five grams, Black-tailed Gnatcatchers are one of the smallest North American songbirds. These busybodies are capable of making far more noise than one would expect from such petite birds, and they are commonly heard before they are seen. Once spotted, these energetic desert dwellers are conspicuous as they flit through spiny trees and shrubs.

JIM BURNS

HABITAT

Black-tailed Gnatcatchers prefer arid lowlands and are primarily encountered in Sonoran, Mojave, and Chihuahuan desertscrub associations. Though atlasers reported them in nineteen breeding habitat types, inhabited areas were all generally in or near dry, low elevation locales that offered at least some degree of brushy cover for foraging and nesting. Atlasers reported 52 percent of potential breeding records in Sonoran desertscrub often containing various spiny legume trees, shrubs, and cacti (n = 774). Atlasers reported 27 percent of Black-tailed Gnatcatchers records in wooded dry washes that meandered through deserts. In addition, observers noted that Black-tailed Gnatcatchers commonly inhabit both Mojave and Chihuahuan desertscrub, as well as semiarid grasslands containing scattered mesquite, acacia, and yucca. These gnatcatchers were rarely reported in residential or rural settings and were typically found in such areas only when natural areas like preserves or parks were nearby.

BREEDING

Black-tailed Gnatcatchers are year-round residents in Arizona. Males acquire their black silky caps by late January or early February. These birds remain paired throughout the year and defend permanent territories (Bent 1949; Phillips et al. 1964). In the Sonoran Desert, these gnatcatchers initiate nesting activity early, with most broods fledging before the worst summer heat. Atlasers first reported a pair of Black-tailed Gnatcatchers investigating potential nest sites on 18 February and observed active nest building by 28 February. The earliest nest with eggs was reported on 2 March and a nest with young was noted by 18 March. Not including fledglings, atlasers obtained 378 breeding confirmations for this common and conspicuous species. These data suggest that Black-tailed Gnatcatcher breeding activity in Arizona peaks in mid- to late April, followed by a steep decline after mid-May. Observers continued to report active nests well into late summer, however, with the latest egg clutches noted on 8 August. Black-tailed Gnatcatchers were observed feeding fledglings through 7 September, well after most atlas surveys had ended for the season.

Black-tailed Gnatcatchers typically build their compact, cup-shaped nests fairly low in desert trees and shrubs and atlasers took measurements at 141 nests in 18 identifiable substrates. Fifty-five percent of nests measured were in two species of paloverde, illustrating a clear preference for these trees in the Sonoran Desert. Other common nest trees included mesquite (9 percent), various species of acacia (9 percent), and ironwood (5 percent). Atlasers found that Black-tailed Gnatcatcher nests were regularly constructed in mistletoe clumps. Several nests each were also discovered in wolfberry, smoketree, tamarisk, desert hackberry, and crucifixion thorn. Other, nest plants included jojoba, staghorn cholla, and banana yucca. The median height for all nests was 4.6 ft (1.4 m), but heights ranged from 1.6 to 26.2 ft (0.5–8 m).

Black-tailed Gnatcatchers pairs are thought to be monogamous and will work together to build their nest, typically placed in a fairly shaded fork formed by several branches (Farquhar and Ritchie 2002). Typical clutches consist of 4 eggs, but can range from 3 to 5 (Bent 1949). Pairs share incubation duties, which last approximately 14–15 days (Woods 1921). Both parents will feed the nestlings, and these will fledge at between 9–14 days of age (Woods 1921, 1928). Parental care outside the nest continues for approximately three weeks (Baicich and Harrison 1997).

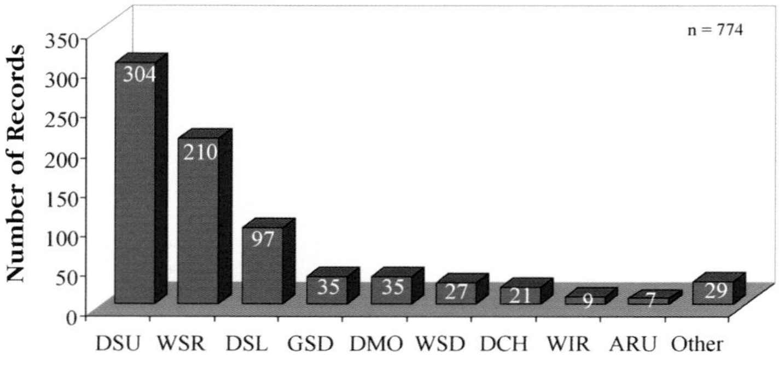

Breeding Phenology

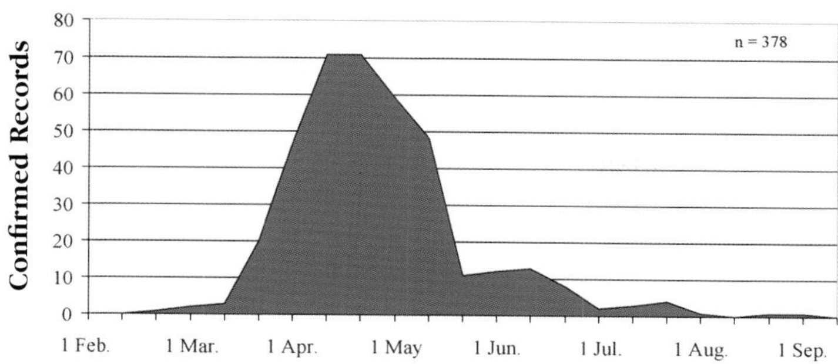

These gnatcatchers often produce two broods during the season and frequently renest if earlier efforts fail. They are often observed moving nest materials from one spot to another. Atlasers observed one pair dismantling a nest that contained a Brown-headed Cowbird egg. Black-tailed Gnatcatchers are common Brown-headed Cowbird hosts, and during the atlas period, atlasers reported twenty-three incidents of brood parasitism. The earliest record was of a nest containing a cowbird egg on 30 April, and the latest observation was of adults feeding a fledgling cowbird on 21 August.

DISTRIBUTION AND STATUS

Black-tailed Gnatcatchers occur primarily in the Southwest from southern Nevada to central Mexico and from southwestern Texas west to southeastern California. In Arizona, these gnatcatchers occur primarily in southern and western desert regions, where they reach their high density in Sonoran desertscrub associations. They are less abundant and more locally distributed east of the San Pedro River valley (Phillips et al. 1964), where they reach their highest elevation limits. Atlasers confirmed Black-tailed Gnatcatchers nesting at elevations from approximately 90 ft (27 m) south of Yuma to 5000 ft (1524 m) near Portal.

Phillips et al. (1964) noted that Black-tailed Gnatcatchers were absent within the Verde River valley, but atlasers reported them in desertscrub along this drainage north to near Camp Verde. Although primarily absent at the bottom of the Grand Canyon (Phillips et al 1964), Black-tailed Gnatcatchers were confirmed nesting within the upper reaches of Lake Mead and Grand Wash Cliff regions as noted by Monson and Phillips (1981). Black-tailed Gnatcatchers are primarily a sedentary species, so it is interesting to note that these birds are occasionally reported within the Grand Canyon as far upstream as Lees Ferry and up to near the South Rim and Toroweap Valley (Brown et al. 1987). It is likely that these wandering individuals are dispersing juveniles.

Atlasers discovered that Black-tailed Gnatcatchers are sparsely distributed north of Lake Mead, including in the Virgin River valley and at one locality in the Hurricane Wash vicinity near the Utah border. Their northern edge in eastern Arizona includes the lower San Francisco River near Clifton and in the Salt River Canyon, where they may possibly enter into the unsurveyed White Mountain Apache tribal lands.

Most prior survey data suggest that Black-tailed Gnatcatcher populations are fairly stable to slightly decreasing in Arizona. Atlasers found these feisty gnatcatchers very common and practically reliable on desert atlas blocks. They are sensitive to increased urbanization, however, and are one of the first desert dwellers to disappear with residential development, even when native vegetation remains (Germaine 1995).

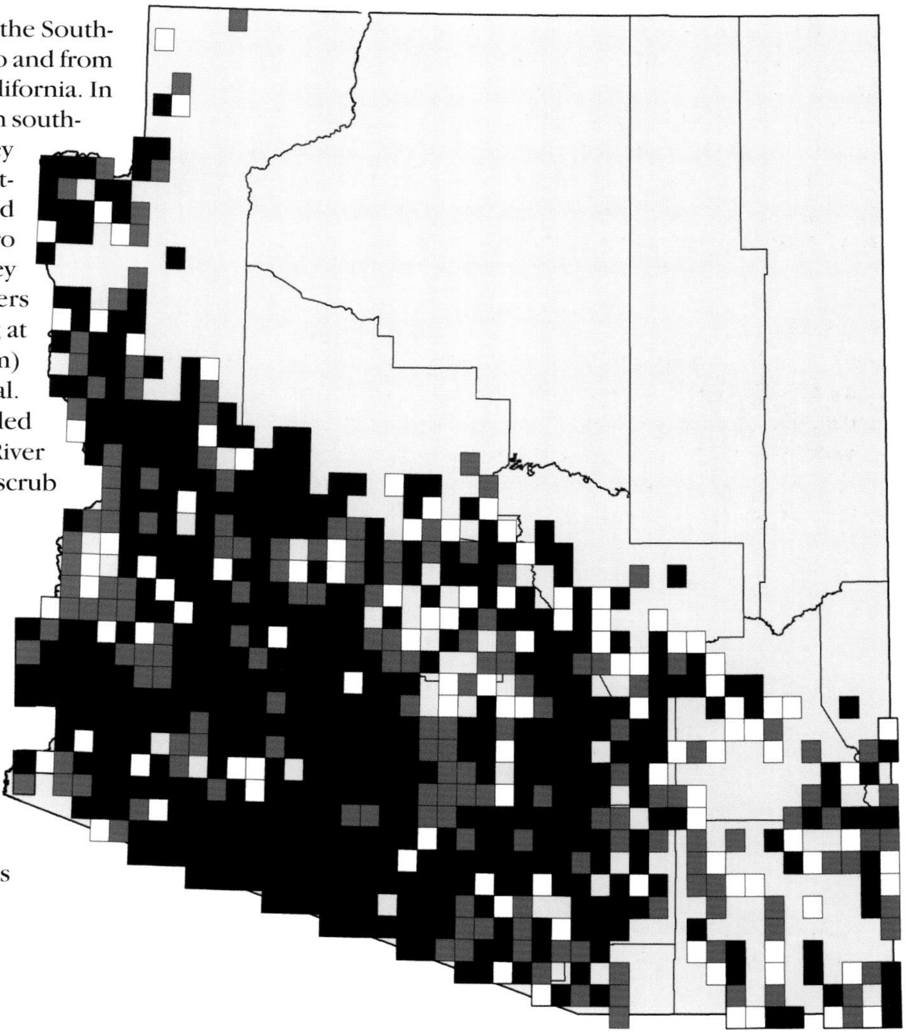

Black-tailed Gnatcatcher Breeding Evidence Reported in 760 (41%) of 1834 priority blocks

	Blocks	Quads
Possible	107 (14%)	111
Probable	167 (22%)	169
Confirmed	486 (64%)	490

Black-capped Gnatcatcher

by Troy E. Corman *Polioptila nigriceps*

Limited to only a few nesting localities in the United States, all in south-central Arizona, Black-capped Gnatcatchers are basically irregular visitors. The northern edge effect appears to limit the density and distribution of these silky-capped, "mewing" mites, for their preferred thorny thickets are in abundance within their local Arizona range.

HABITAT

Black-capped Gnatcatchers are typically found in arid and often dense thorny, scrub thickets along foothill dry washes, lower canyon slopes, or adjacent to riparian areas. Atlasers reported most observations from habitats dominated by taller and denser Sonoran Desert vegetation. In Arizona, they seem especially to favor areas with a combination of small groves of netleaf hackberry and velvet mesquite with nearby denser stands of catclaw acacia, hopbush, jojoba, and other low woody shrubs. Several others were reported in dry or intermittent drainages containing velvet mesquite and acacia thickets. They were also noted in a few open foothill drainages dominated by scattered Arizona sycamore and Fremont cottonwood, often with an understory of netleaf hackberry, mesquite, and Mexican elderberry. They are typically encountered nesting in taller and denser vegetation than Black-tailed Gnatcatchers and are easily overlooked unless detected by call.

BREEDING

Throughout most of their range, Black-capped Gnatcatchers are primarily a resident species. However, evidence suggests that some northern populations may migrate slightly south or wander to lower elevation during the winter. Often found in pairs throughout the year, the males acquire their silky black caps in February and March, during which time singing commences. The nesting period is rather lengthy for Black-capped Gnatcatchers, with early nest building activity initiated by mid-March in Arizona. Atlasers found an occupied nest on 27 April. An adult carrying a fecal sack from another nest on 5 May would suggest the initiation of egg laying no later than 20 April. Some of the earlier records in Arizona included nesting-building activity through late July and the latest nest fledging young by late August or early September. Russell and Monson (1998) noted that in adjacent Sonora, Black-capped Gnatcatchers begin nesting in March and have typically fledged their last broods by July. But Russell and Monson also mention that a pair was observed feeding a fledgling Brown-headed Cowbird in extreme southern Sonora on 31 August.

There is little published information on the breeding biology of Black-capped Gnatcatcher, but like other gnatcatchers, the pair shares the responsibility of nest construction. Nests are typically well hidden by small branches and foliage. Few nests have been found in Arizona, but the shrub of choice appears to be netleaf hackberry. Other nests in Arizona have been discovered in velvet mesquite and Arizona sycamore. The only nest measured during the atlas was constructed in a netleaf hackberry 17.1 ft (5.2 m) above the ground. The range of heights for several other nests measured in Arizona was 2.7 ft (0.8 m) and 5.5 ft (1.7 m) in a velvet mesquite and 7.5 ft (2.3 m) in a netleaf hackberry (T. Huels, personal communication).

In Arizona, most Black-capped Gnatcatcher clutches contained 3–4 eggs, incubated by both parents (Groschupf 1992). The incubation period is unknown for this species, but is assumed to be approximately 13–14 days as it is with the other two gnatcatchers in the state. Nestlings fledge in approximately 10–15 days and are fed by both parents for an unknown period following nest departure. They typically produce two broods per season, but one prolific pair in Arizona was known to fledge successfully at least eight young from three nests in 1981. Like other gnatcatchers, Black-capped Gnatcatchers in Arizona are frequent brood hosts of the Brown-headed Cowbird.

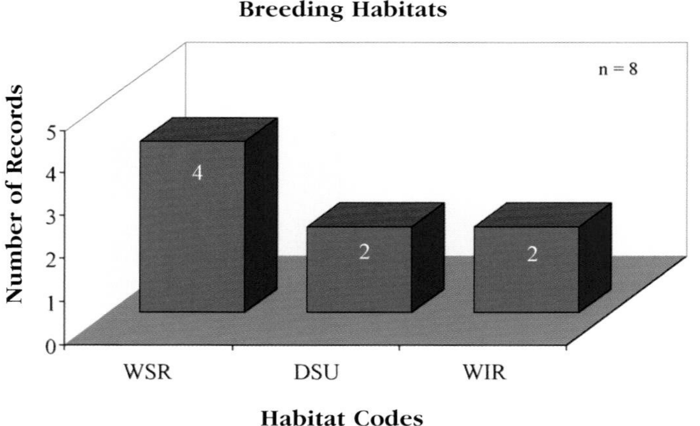

DISTRIBUTION AND STATUS

Primarily a Mexican species, Black-capped Gnatcatchers nest from extreme south-central Arizona south on the Pacific slope of Mexico to Colima (Dunn and Garrett 1987). Black-capped Gnatcatchers were first discovered in Arizona on 22 May 1971 along Sonoita Creek near the roadside rest area southwest of Patagonia (Phillips et al. 1973). The newly found pair fledged three nestlings on 19 June. Since their first discovery, Black-capped Gnatcatchers have been a very local and irregular nesting species in Arizona, with lengthy periods of no observations. Most records pertain to only singles or pairs. In March 1973, another pair was discovered along Sonoita Creek below the Patagonia Lake dam (Speich and Witzeman 1975). This species was not noted again in Arizona, until a pair was found nesting at Chino Canyon, Santa Rita Mountains, in 1981, which successfully fledging eight young from three different nests by late August (Rosenberg and Witzeman 1999). Observations of this gnatcatcher continued in Chino Canyon through 1986. Another pair was located near the Mexican border in Sycamore Canyon in the Pajarito Mountains in 1984, and the species was confirmed breeding here in 1986 (Rosenberg and Witzeman 1999).

During the atlas period, few Black-capped Gnatcatcher records were obtained through atlas surveys, with most reported as casual observations. All Arizona Black-capped Gnatcatcher records, including those during the atlas period, have occurred within a very narrow range of elevations from 3500 to 4000 ft (1066–1219 m). In adjacent Sonora, Russell and Monson (1998) noted that these gnatcatchers have been documented primarily below 2625 ft (800 m), but they occur locally on brushy slopes to approximately 4600 ft (1402 m).

During the atlas period, Black-capped Gnatcatchers were only reported in the state between 1996 and 2000. A female was discovered in Chino Canyon with a probable hybrid Black-capped/Black-tailed Gnatcatcher male on 31 March 1996 (J. Martin, personal communication). The following year, a male Black-capped Gnatcatcher was discovered in Brown Canyon on the eastern slope of the Baboquivari Mountains on 22 April (N. Crook and R. Taylor, personal communication). Other observers visited this location several days later and discovered a pair with a nest and a second pair farther down the canyon. In late May 1998, an individual was detected near the roadside rest stop just southwest of Patagonia (D. Stejskal and R. Taylor, personal communication). Atlasers discovered the westernmost Arizona record on 31 May 1998, when a male was observed feeding a fledgling in Sycamore Canyon on the western slope of the Baboquivari Mountains on Tohono O'odham tribal land. A Black-capped Gnatcatcher pair was discovered in California Gulch, southwestern Santa Cruz County, from 23 to 31 July 1999 (C. Benesh, personal communication). Atlasers also discovered a pair of Black-capped Gnatcatchers along Sonoita Creek below Patagonia Lake on 18 March 2000.

Black-capped Gnatcatcher populations appear to surge northward periodically very locally into Arizona, where they often remain for several years, only to contract once again, leaving few locations very reliable. In Arizona, these gnatcatchers are in such low densities that they are easily missed by typical atlas surveys. Without close scrutiny, they are also easily mistaken for the much more common Black-tailed Gnatcatchers. Identification is also complicated by the fact that Black-capped Gnatcatchers apparently occasionally hybridize with Black-tailed Gnatcatchers in Arizona, producing individuals with intermediate plumage and calls. Typically nesting at slightly lower elevations in Arizona than Blue-gray Gnatcatchers, atlasers found all three of Arizona's gnatcatcher species nesting adjacent to each other's territories in Chino Canyon.

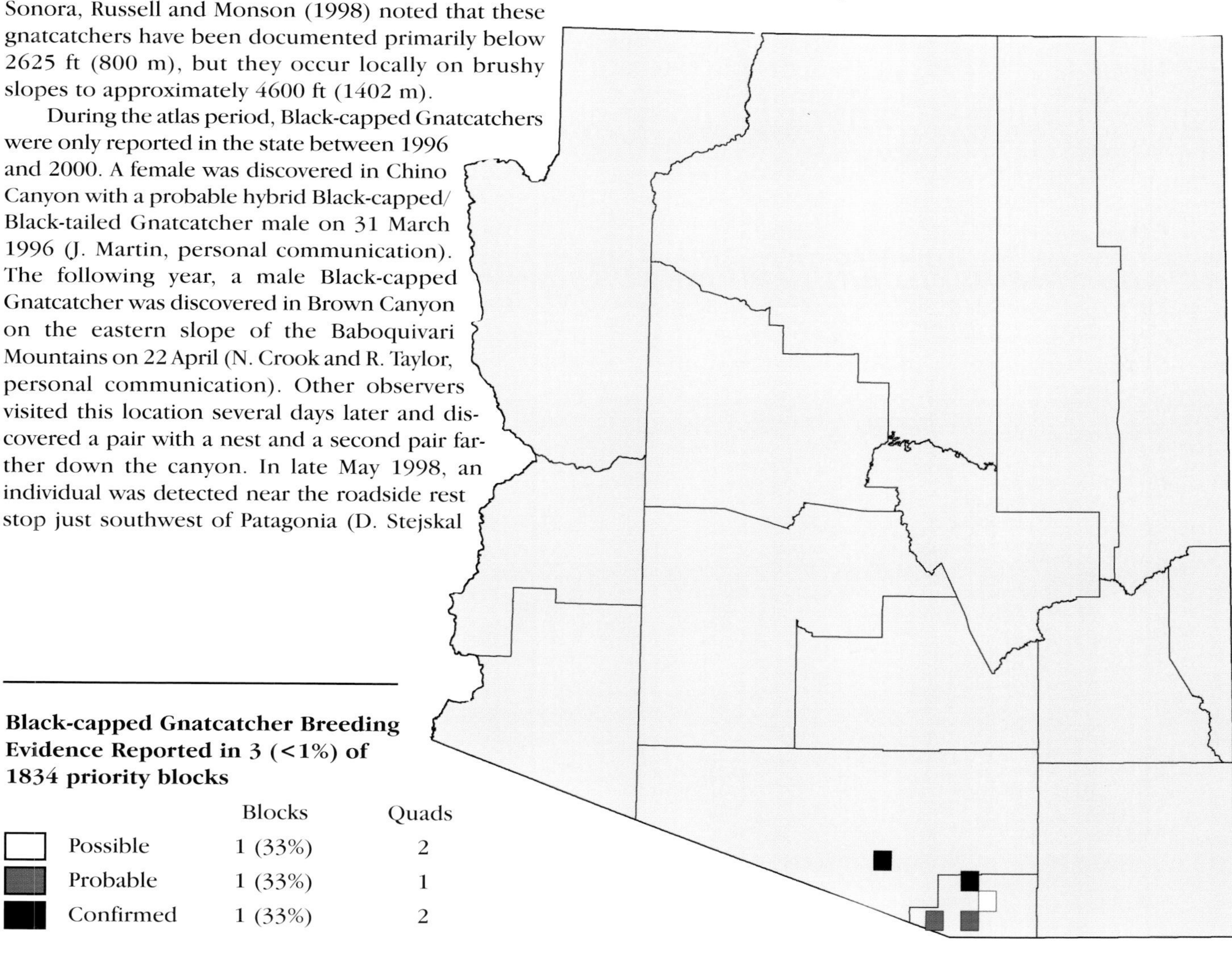

Black-capped Gnatcatcher Breeding Evidence Reported in 3 (<1%) of 1834 priority blocks

	Blocks	Quads
Possible	1 (33%)	2
Probable	1 (33%)	1
Confirmed	1 (33%)	2

Eastern Bluebird

by Troy E. Corman *Sialia sialis*

BRIAN SMALL

The resident Eastern Bluebird of southeastern Arizona, sometimes referred to as the Azure Bluebird, is a much paler subspecies than the nominate race to the East. With their whispering warbles and charming nature, Eastern Bluebirds are favorite research subjects in many parts of their range, although Arizona's local populations have been surprisingly little studied.

HABITAT

Inhabiting a wide variety of open woodlands and forest edge habitats across their range, Eastern Bluebirds prefer relatively open Madrean evergreen oak and pine-oak woodlands for nesting in Arizona. In southwestern populations, Marshall (1957) noted that savannah-like woodlands and forests must be extensive or clearings frequent in order to attract these bluebirds, and most localities typically have more than one nesting pair. Common tree species at occupied locations often include Emory, Arizona white, silverleaf, and Mexican blue oaks or a mixture of Chihuahuan, Apache, and ponderosa pines with oak at higher elevations. They can also be found nesting in foothill drainages with oaks and Arizona sycamores and have nested locally in Fremont cottonwoods, such as near Patagonia. Within these vegetative communities, they prefer fairly open understories and clearings with grassy to sparse ground cover and little in the way of woody brush and saplings. Historically, these open woodlands were established and maintained by infrequent burns (Marshall 1957). Eastern Bluebirds often sing and forage from exposed perches and drop gracefully from low snags or dead limbs in their pursuit of insects.

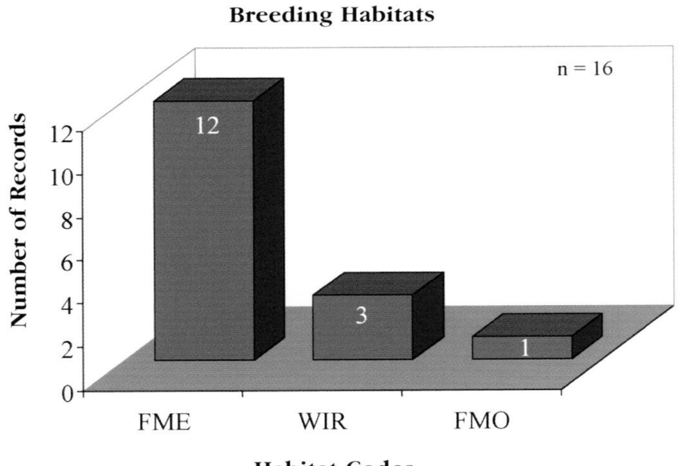

BREEDING

In Arizona, flocking Eastern Bluebirds will wander into adjacent habitats during the winter, but they typically return to nesting areas in early spring. They often maintain pair bonds throughout the year or acquire mates in nonbreeding season flocks. Nest construction may begin in March in southeastern Arizona and atlasers noted occupied nests by 2 April. Nesting activity continues through the summer, and observers reported the latest nest with young on 14 August. Due to their limited distribution in the state, atlas data are insufficient to determine any peak period of nesting. Russell and Monson (1998) noted that in Sonora, Eastern Bluebirds commonly initiate nesting in May and that many pairs are nesting in July after summer rains have begun.

As with other bluebirds, Eastern Bluebirds are primarily cavity nesters and will construct nests in natural cavities in fence posts and live or dead trees, or those constructed by woodpeckers. The height of nest cavity can range from 2 to 30 ft (0.6–9.1 m) above the ground (Robbins and Blom 1996). In Arizona, most nesting substrates include various species of oaks and pines, Arizona sycamore, and locally in Fremont cottonwood. They are also well known for their frequent use of nest boxes. Measurements were taken at only one active nest during the atlas period, which was in an Emory oak at a height of 16.1 ft (4.9 m) above the ground. Nest construction efforts may continue for as long as three weeks, with nests later in the season being completed in less than a week (Gowaty and Plissner 1998). The female alone builds the nest, often gathering the material from the ground. Males will sometimes be observed carrying nesting material; however, this is more for display than actually helping with the nest building process (Gowaty and Plissner 1998). Nests are a loosely constructed cup often made entirely of dried grasses, weed stems, or pine needles and lined with finer grasses (Bent 1949).

Eastern Bluebirds have an average clutch size of 5–6 (range 3–7) eggs (Bent 1949). Incubation averages about 14 days (range 11–19) and is performed solely by the female (Gowaty and Plissner 1998). Only females brood the nestlings as well, however both parents share the responsibility of feeding them. Nestlings fledge in 15–21 days, and both parents continue to feed them for another three weeks

(Gowaty and Plissner 1998). Eastern Bluebird pairs frequently produce 2–3 broods per year (Bent 1949), often reusing the same nest.

DISTRIBUTION AND STATUS

Eastern Bluebirds primarily breed from southeastern Canada south to central Texas and northern Florida, with northern populations migratory. Separate resident populations occur from southeastern Arizona south along the Sierra Madre Occidental in Mexico to northern Nicaragua.

First collected in Arizona in 1884 (Brewster 1885), the pale *fulva* subspecies of Eastern Bluebird was listed by Swarth (1914) as rare in summer in the Santa Rita and Huachuca Mountains of extreme southern Arizona. Phillips et al. (1964) also noted them as rare and local residents in these same mountain ranges and west beyond Nogales. They also were found nesting locally in the Chiricahua Mountains beginning in 1960 (Ligon 1969). Eastern Bluebirds expanded their range north in the 1970s with nesting along Sonoita Creek near Patagonia, in Happy Valley east of the Rincon Mountains, and in Bear Canyon, Santa Catalina Mountains, where it was considered an uncommon local resident (Monson and Phillips 1981).

Atlas data reveal that Eastern Bluebirds have retracted their range from the 1970s expansion. They are now locally an uncommon to fairly common resident from the Pajarito, Santa Rita, and Patagonia Mountains east to the Huachuca Mountain foothills and a very sparse resident in the Chiricahua Mountains. In the past, these bluebirds were encountered nesting at elevations from approximately 4000 ft (1219 m) along Sonoita Creek near Patagonia to 6300 ft (1920 m) in Sawmill Canyon, Huachuca Mountains.

Loss of nesting cavities and habitat alteration would appear to be the limiting factor of the Eastern Bluebird in Arizona. Uncontrolled fuelwood cutting in oak woodlands and the removal of large dead trees and dead branches results in loss of potential nest sites. Loss of grasses and forbs to heavy grazing likely reduces insect prey availability. However, where both fire and grazing have been excluded, heavy woody undergrowth and dense foliage may be responsible for the scarcity of this bird in Arizona (Ligon 1969). Bluebird nest-box programs have been extremely successful in the East, but they are rarely used in southeastern Arizona. In the Chiricahua Mountains, Ligon (1969) reported that a pair of Azure Bluebirds occupied a nest box within two days of box placement.

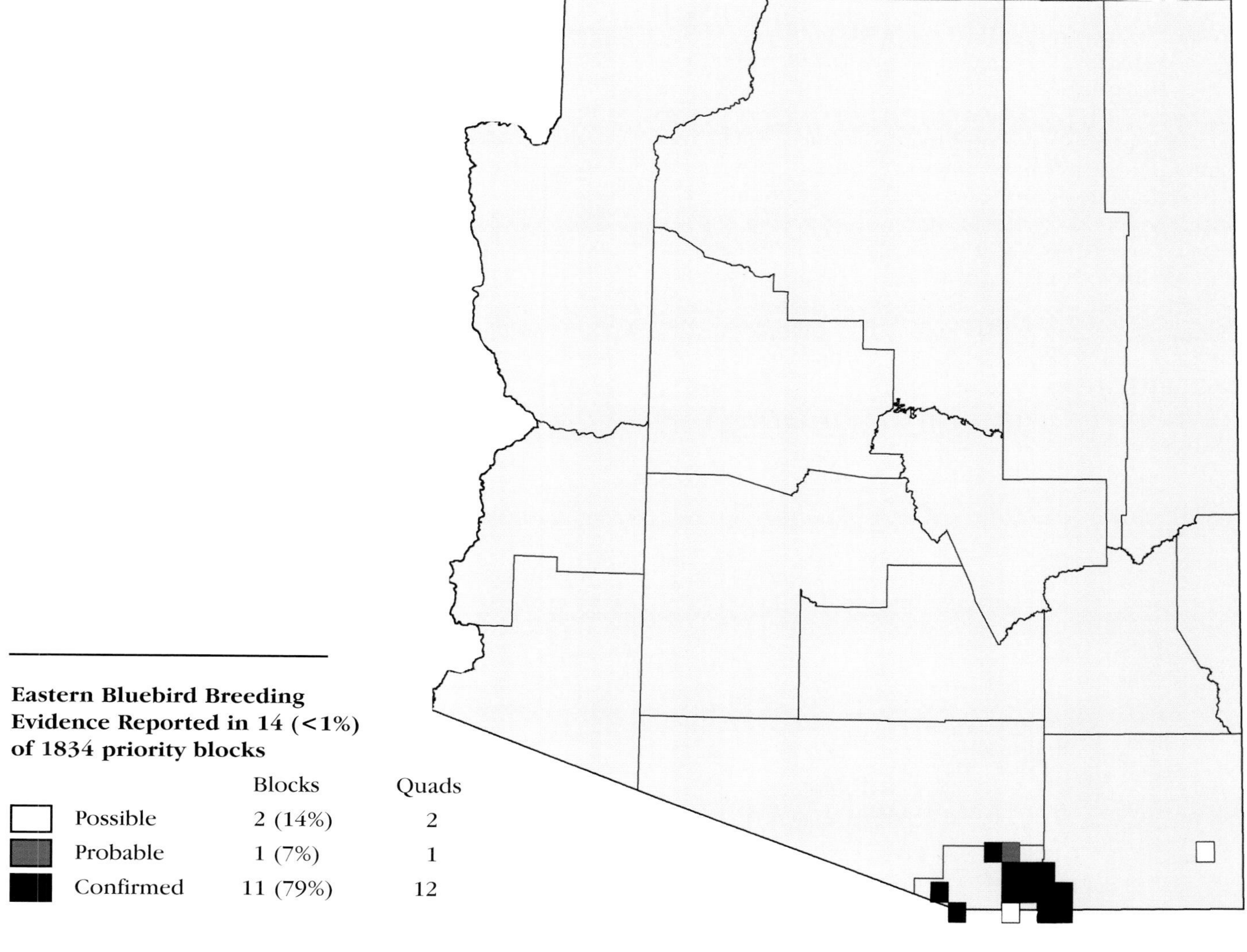

Eastern Bluebird Breeding Evidence Reported in 14 (<1%) of 1834 priority blocks

	Blocks	Quads
Possible	2 (14%)	2
Probable	1 (7%)	1
Confirmed	11 (79%)	12

Western Bluebird

by John R. Spence *Sialia mexicana*

A brilliant flash of blue and rust dropping to the ground from a low perch in a tree reveals the presence of a foraging Western Bluebird. One of the most beloved of native birds, Western Bluebirds are widespread denizens of open forest vegetation throughout much of Arizona.

DAN FISCHER

HABITAT

Western Bluebirds are common breeders in coniferous woodlands and forests throughout most of Arizona. The species prefers open stands of pinyon pines, junipers, and ponderosa pines, especially where snags are common (Szaro and Balda 1986; Rosenstock 1996). They generally forage in open forests, clearings, and along forest edges by perching low on a tree, shrub, or snag. In Arizona, they typically reach their highest breeding density in ponderosa pine–dominated forests from almost pure stands to those with a Gambel's oak or pinyon-juniper association. Approximately 43 percent of all atlas records were reported in these forests (*n* = 363). Taller and higher-elevation pinyon pine–juniper woodlands accounted for an additional 36 percent of atlas Western Bluebird records, including where these woodlands transition into grasslands. Fewer records were obtained in mixed-conifer forests often containing Douglas fir, white fir, ponderosa, and aspen. South of the Mogollon Rim, these bluebirds were also occasionally reported nesting in woodlands dominated by a mixture of Madrean evergreen oaks, pinyon pine, and juniper. Atlasers infrequently encountered Western Bluebirds nesting in adjacent riparian stands with cottonwoods.

BREEDING

In Arizona, Western Bluebirds start arriving on their breeding grounds in March or April. Pairs can form while in late winter flocks or on the breeding grounds, and the pair bond can last for years. Males often locate an area suitable for breeding as early as late winter, and they are known to check the site several times before the start of the breeding season. Competition for nest sites can be intense, and in many cases groups of Violet-green Swallows can evict Western Bluebirds from good snags, especially prior to egg laying (Brawn 1990). Nest construction can begin by early April in Arizona (Guinan et al. 2000), and atlasers reported the first occupied nest (likely containing eggs) on 29 April. Egg laying continues into June and early July at higher elevations. Peak nesting activity is from mid-May at lower elevations to late June at higher elevations. The latest active nest with young located by atlasers was on 26 July. Family groups and small flocks begin to form in August and may increase in size through the fall and winter as they wander widely in search of fruiting trees and mistletoe berries.

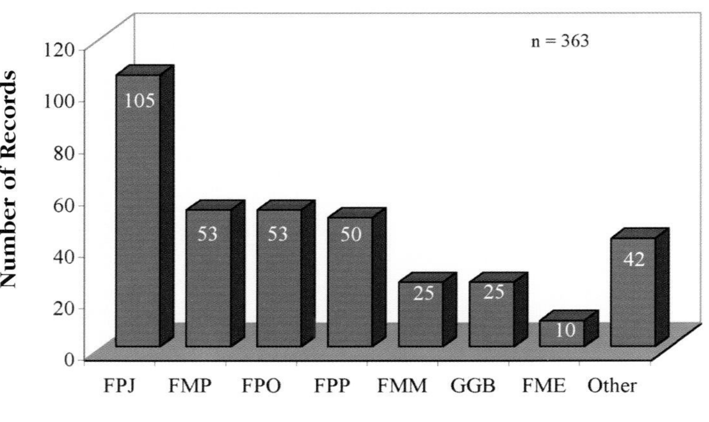

Western Bluebird nests are constructed by the female and typically placed in a natural or woodpecker excavated cavity in a snag or live tree. However, the species readily accepts nest boxes. Of forty-four nests discovered during atlas surveys, most were in ponderosa pine (17). The remaining nests were noted in pinyon pine (9), Gambel's oak (8), various species of juniper (6), quaking aspen (2), and one each in Fremont and narrowleaf cottonwoods. The average height of these nests was 18.7 ft (5.7 m) and ranged from 4.6 to 51.8 ft (1.4–15.8 m).

In Arizona, the typical Western Bluebird clutch consist of 4–5 eggs (range 1–6), incubated by the female for approximately 14 days (range 12–17 days; Guinan et al. 2000). The male feeds the incubating female and both adults feed the nestlings. Studies have found that typically less than 15 percent of pairs have helpers at the nests, consisting of other adults, typically males, or of young from previous broods (Guinan et al. 2000). An Arizona study noted that young fledge when they are 18–25 days old and typically remain dependent on adults for an additional two

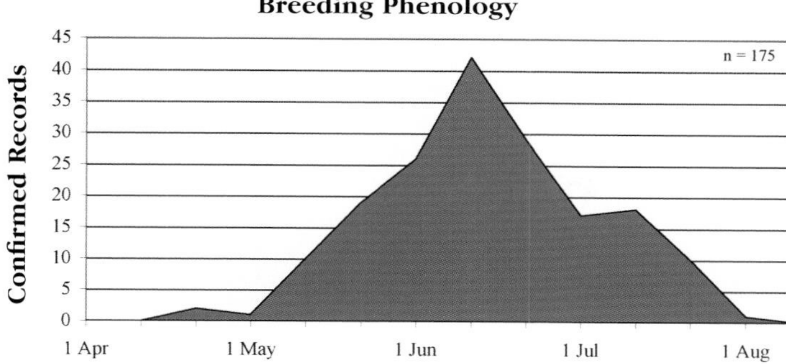

weeks. Western Bluebirds often initiate a second brood (Brawn 1991).

DISTRIBUTION AND STATUS

Western Bluebirds are widespread residents of western North America, although many northern populations are largely migratory. Breeding occurs from southern British Columbia and Alberta south through western Montana and Washington to northern Baja California. A large gap in their breeding range exists over much of Nevada, northern Utah, southern Idaho, and Wyoming. However, Western Bluebirds breed extensively in western Colorado and adjacent Utah south to the central highlands of Mexico.

In Arizona, Western Bluebirds are common summer residents of forests along the southern and western rim of the Colorado Plateau and northward, including Navajo and Hopi tribal lands and the Kaibab Plateau. Atlasers found them nesting at elevations from approximately 4800 to 9600 ft (1463–2926 m). They were regularly encountered in the White Mountains and along the Mogollon Rim region, with records nearly encircling the unsurveyed White Mountain Apache tribal lands. These bluebirds undoubtedly nest throughout this habitat diverse reservation. They were also confirmed nesting in the Bradshaw Mountains north through the Mingus and Juniper ranges and west to the isolated Hualapai Mountains. To the northwest, atlasers documented Western Bluebirds nesting at higher elevations of Hualapai tribal lands and within the Arizona Strip region, including the Virgin Mountains.

Populations are sparsely distributed and typically in lower densities in southern Arizona, where Western Bluebirds are generally described as rare to uncommon summer residents in isolated mountain ranges (Monson and Phillips 1981; Witzeman et al. 1997). Within this region, atlasers encountered them in the Mazatzal, Pinal, Pinaleno, Santa Catalina, Rincon, and Chiricahua mountains. Western Bluebirds were also previously noted nesting in the Huachuca Mountains, but they went unreported during atlas surveys within this range, where Eastern Bluebirds were found breeding.

Although Western Bluebirds are common in Arizona, they appear to have declined in recent decades based on Breeding Bird Survey data (Guinan et al. 2000). Principal factors for their decline include clear-cut logging, major stand-replacing fires, overgrazing, and loss of snags due to harvesting or competition from introduced European Starlings. Conservation measures that provide for natural burns that open up forests but preserve larger trees and snags, and include reductions in grazing intensity, should favor the species. Snag preservation is critical to maintaining healthy breeding populations. Nest boxes can also be used to increase breeding populations locally in the short term. For example, Brawn (1985) noted 300–400 percent increases in breeding density in logged forests after nest boxes were installed.

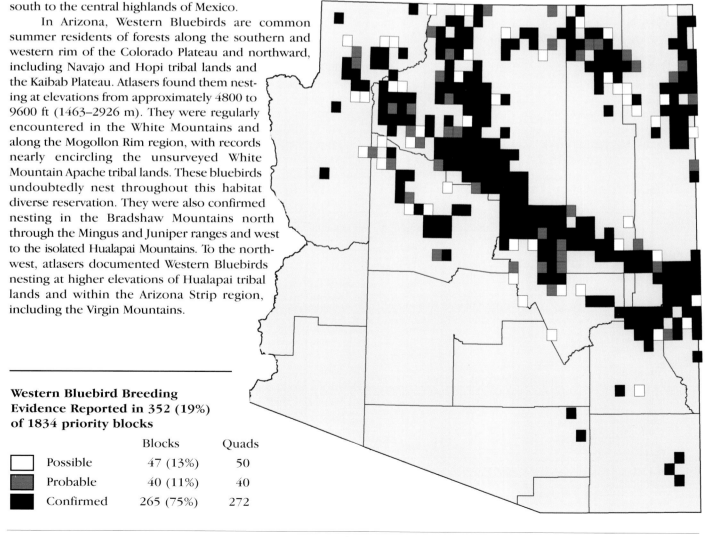

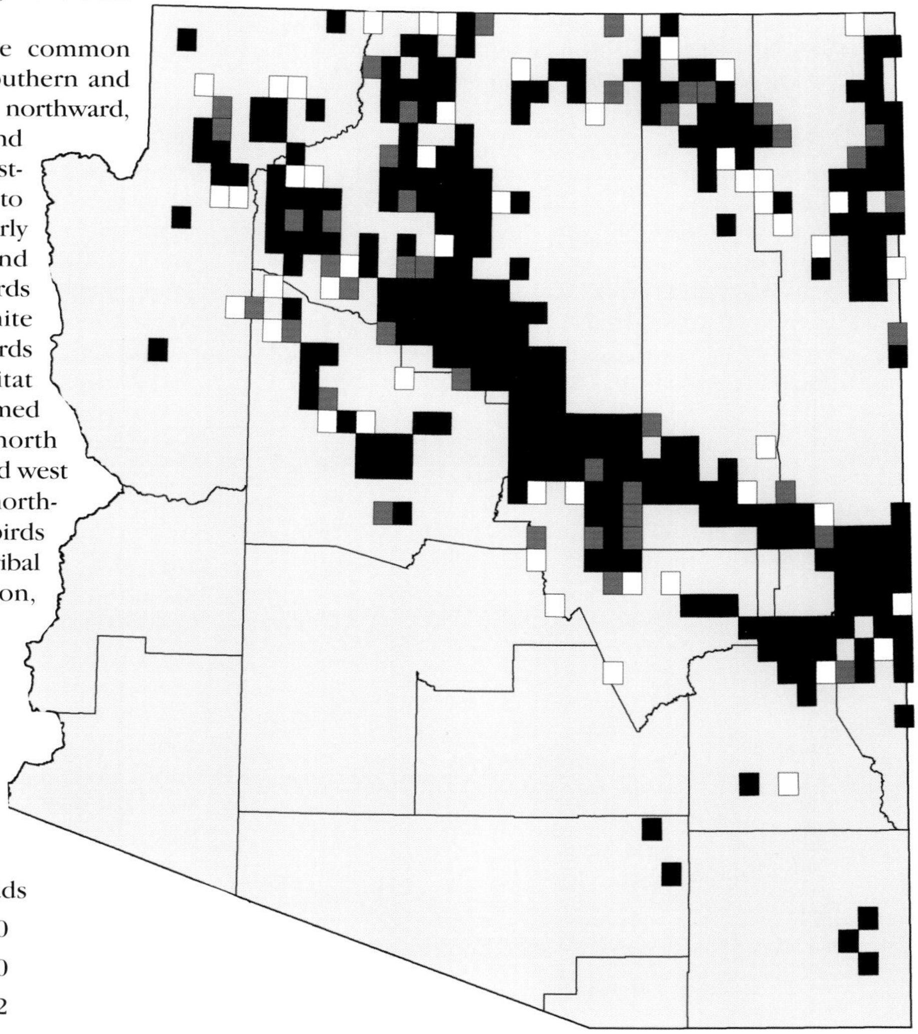

Western Bluebird Breeding Evidence Reported in 352 (19%) of 1834 priority blocks

	Blocks	Quads
Possible	47 (13%)	50
Probable	40 (11%)	40
Confirmed	265 (75%)	272

Mountain Bluebird

by John R. Spence *Sialia currucoides*

Considered by many birders to be one of the most beautiful birds in North America, the male Mountain Bluebird is an intense sky blue. This remarkable species behaves more like a flycatcher or kestrel than a thrush, and uses a variety of ground, perch, and hover foraging, as well as flycatching and hawking techniques.

JIM BURNS

HABITAT

Mountains Bluebirds breed along the edges of coniferous forests wherever meadows and clearings occur. They are most common in Arizona in open pinyon pine–juniper woodlands and in the adjacent grasslands or sagebrush with scattered trees, typically at elevations above 5000 ft (1524 m). These vegetative communities accounted for 70 percent of all atlas records (n = 222). At higher elevations in the state, Mountain Bluebirds are frequently encountered foraging over montane meadows, subalpine grasslands, and forest clearings, often using fence lines, wooden posts, and other low exposed perches. In these environments, they typically nest in the nearby forest edges of aspen, Gambel's oak, ponderosa pine, and Douglas fir. Atlasers also found these bluebirds occupying clearings around isolated cabins, ranches, corrals, and earthen livestock tanks. Phillips et al. (1964) also suggested that they nested up to timberline in Arizona. Mountain Bluebirds favor clearings and open forests, and expand rapidly into recently burned areas and logging clear-cuts. Areas supporting a mix of open ground or low herbaceous cover, a selection of short and medium height perches for foraging, and snags or scattered trees for nesting are favored.

BREEDING

Male Mountain Bluebirds arrive early on their breeding grounds, usually by March or April in Arizona. Females arrive fairly soon thereafter and select males in part based on the quality of the nest cavities he presents to her. Nest building typically commences in mid-April and extends into May for first broods. Early egg-laying initiation likely begins by late April in Arizona, based on nests with young reported by atlasers on 16 May. Atlas data reveal that most breeding in the state occurs from late May through the end of June, with some pairs attempting to breed a second time later in the summer (n = 87). The latest active nest reported during the atlas was a nest with young discovered on 31 July. Elsewhere within their range, Mountain Bluebirds are occasionally noted nesting through August (Powers and Lombardo 1996). Like Western Bluebirds, these birds form family groups and begin wandering in small flocks by August and September. Mountain Bluebirds can be found in northern Arizona throughout the winter, especially near fruiting junipers or Russian olive stands. They also descend irregularly to lowland agricultural areas and grasslands, sometimes in impressive numbers.

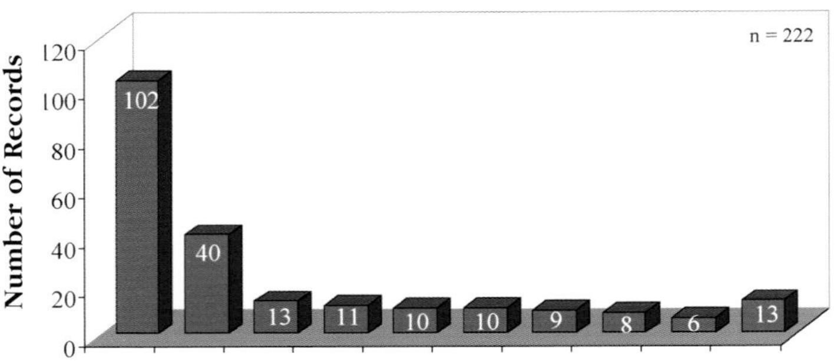

Secondary cavity nesters, Mountain Bluebirds often use cavities excavated by woodpeckers but will also nest in natural tree cavities, nest boxes, and built structures. In Arizona, nests have also been frequently discovered in holes in alluvial dirt banks and rocky cliffs (LaRue 1994). Competition is sometimes fierce between bluebirds and other cavity nesters such as swallows (Power and Lombardo 1996). Near urban areas, European Starlings and House Sparrows generally win over these bluebirds for nest cavities. Of twenty-three Mountain Bluebird nests described during the atlas surveys, fourteen were in various species of juniper. Nests were also noted in pinyon pines and in or on built structures such as a fence post, metal pipe, shed, and even a tin can placed in a juniper. The nest cavities were generally below 10 ft (3 m) in height, with a median of 4.7 ft (1.4 m) and a range of 2.0–24.9 ft (0.6–7.6 m; n = 22).

Only female Mountain Bluebirds construct the nest within the cavity, which can take from several days to less

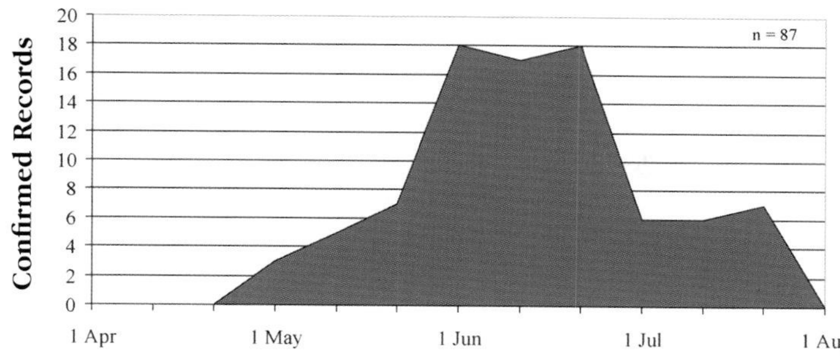

than a week (Power and Lombardo 1996). The typical clutch size is 5–6 eggs, but this can vary from 4 to 8 (Bent 1949). The female incubates the eggs for 12–14 days, while the male brings her food on the nest. Both sexes feed the young, although when present such as during brooding, the female forces the male to give her food items, which she then either consumes herself or transfers to the young (Power and Lombardo 1996). Young fledge at 18–21 days but remain dependent on the adults for another two weeks in most cases, but as long as two months in stressful years. High nestling and especially fledgling mortality occurs during lengthy stormy periods, when conditions are wet and cold and insect prey becomes dormant (Power and Lombardo 1996). Some studies have found that approximately half of the populations attempt a second brood (Power 1966), often in the same nest.

DISTRIBUTION AND STATUS

Mountain Bluebirds are widespread and fairly common breeders in western North America from central Alaska and central Manitoba south to central Arizona and south-central New Mexico. They nest sparingly in several mountain ranges of western Texas (Power and Lombardo 1996). The species is mostly found to the east of the Pacific Coastal ranges from British Columbia south to California.

In Arizona, Mountain Bluebirds breed commonly on the Colorado Plateau above and to the north of the Mogollon Rim, and in and around the White Mountains (Phillips et al. 1964). Atlasers encountered these bluebirds nesting within their historical range at elevations primarily from 5200 to 10,000 ft (1585–3048 m). Based on the availability of appropriate habitat, the species undoubtedly breeds within the unsurveyed White Mountain Apache tribal lands. Atlasers found them nesting as far south as northeastern San Carlos Apache tribal lands, just south of the Black River. In May 1981, a pair of Mountain Bluebirds was also discovered nesting in southeastern Arizona in grasslands near Sonoita (Church 1982).

These bluebirds were also found nesting east to the Juniper Mountains in northwestern Yavapai County and north rather locally to the Arizona Strip region. As noted by others, Mountain Bluebirds were widespread in appropriate habitat on Navajo and Hopi tribal lands.

In general, Mountain Bluebird populations appear to be stable throughout their range based on Breeding Bird Survey data (Power and Lombardo 1996). However, the loss of suitable nest sites is the primary cause of local declines (Power 1966), and placement of nest boxes would benefit these attractive birds.

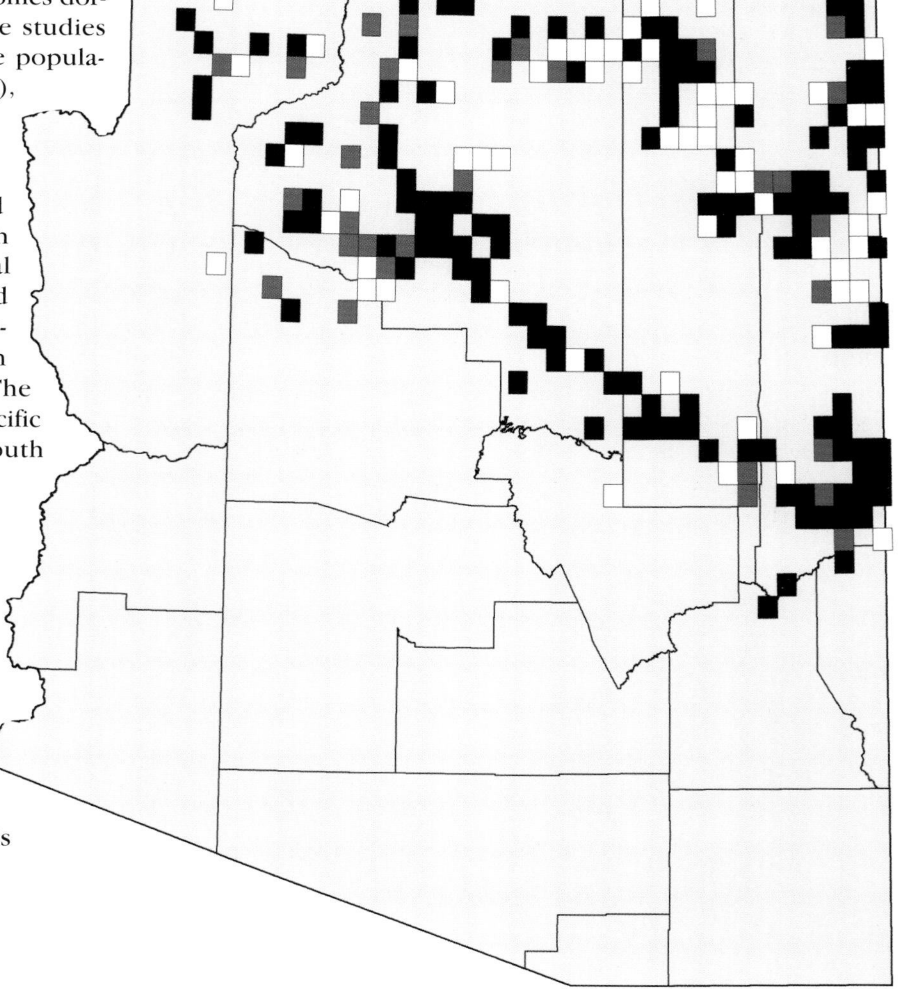

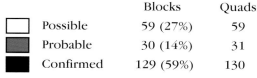

Mountain Bluebird Breeding Evidence Reported in 218 (12%) of 1834 priority blocks

	Blocks	Quads
Possible	59 (27%)	59
Probable	30 (14%)	31
Confirmed	129 (59%)	130

Townsend's Solitaire

by John R. Spence *Myadestes townsendi*

The subtly plumaged Townsend's Solitaire is a summer denizen of remote high-elevation forests and mountain slopes in Arizona. Although a shy and retiring bird, it signals its presence with a loud complex warbling song as well as distinctive far-reaching, squeaky call notes.

HABITAT

Townsend's Solitaires breed in high-elevation conifer forests in Arizona and are often encountered near mountain ridges or steeper slopes. They reach their highest density in mixed-conifer forests typically containing Douglas fir, white fir, ponderosa pine, and aspen. This cool vegetative community accounted for 29 percent of atlas records (n = 105). Although Townsend's Solitaires are usually found in lower abundance in ponderosa pine–dominated forests, approximately 50 percent of atlas records were reported in these typically drier forests, including those with a Gambel's oak and, less frequently, pinyon pine–juniper association. Atlasers also regularly encountered Townsend's Solitaires in cool montane drainages with a mixture of coniferous and deciduous trees, and in Arizona's relatively limited spruce-fir forests containing Engelmann spruce, blue spruce, and subalpine fir. This species prefers more open forests or stand edges rather than forests with a higher canopy closure (Bowen 1997; Levad 1998). Townsend's Solitaires often breed in thinned and logged forest edges, along successional stands resulting from wind and fire damage, as well as in undisturbed forests (Bowen 1997).

BREEDING

The breeding biology of the Townsend's Solitaire is less well known than its winter ecology. The species is unique among Arizona thrushes in that individuals vigorously defend winter territories rich in its preferred food, juniper berries. In early spring, these birds abandon their winter territories and begin moving toward their breeding grounds, although stragglers are occasionally reported in the lowlands into late May. Atlasers reported the first Townsend's Solitaires in breeding areas in early April with singing individuals by late April. They typically deliver their elaborate and often spirited songs from high on exposed treetops (Bowen 1997). The initiation of nest construction likely take place by early to mid-May in Arizona based on observations of adults feeding fledglings by 6 June. Atlasers had difficulty observing nesting behavior of this wary species with most confirmed records pertaining to spotted fledglings. Additional active nest records would be needed to determine the peak nesting period in Arizona. However, atlasers discovered nests with young through late July and reported dependent fledglings well into August. The bulk of the population in Arizona begin to vacate their breeding grounds in August and September, when they often move to lower elevation to feed on fruiting junipers, Russian olive, and mistletoe berries.

Townsend's Solitaire nests are typically placed in a hollow on or near the ground, often on a steep slope including road cuts and eroded drainage banks (Bowen 1997). In most cases the nests are concealed under an overhanging object such as a log, stump, rock, tree root, or low branch, which functions to protect the nest from weather and detection by predators. Only four nests were described during the course of the project, three on the ground under rock overhangs and one on an old road cut. The nest is constructed primarily by the female, and consists of a loosely woven twig "foundation," on which a finely woven cup nest is placed. Nest construction can take as little as two days or more than two weeks with lengthy periods of no building activity (Bowen 1997).

Typical Townsend's Solitaire clutches consist of 4 eggs, with a range of 3–5 (Baicich and Harrison 1997). Females incubate the eggs for 11–13 days, during which time the male provides her food. Incubating females rarely leaves the nest to forage on their own (Bowen 1997). Nestlings

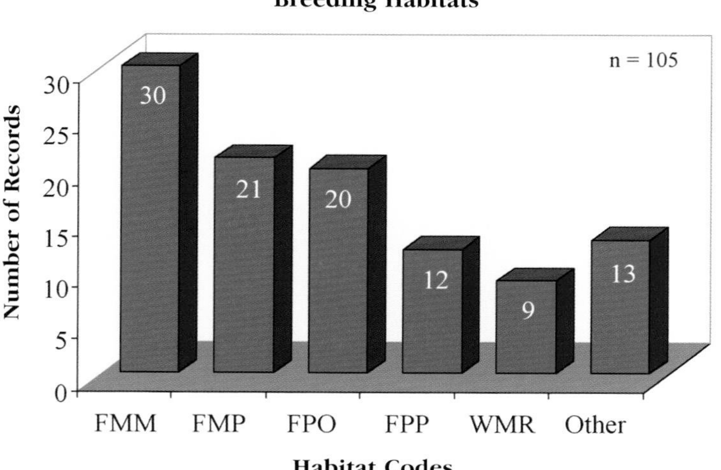

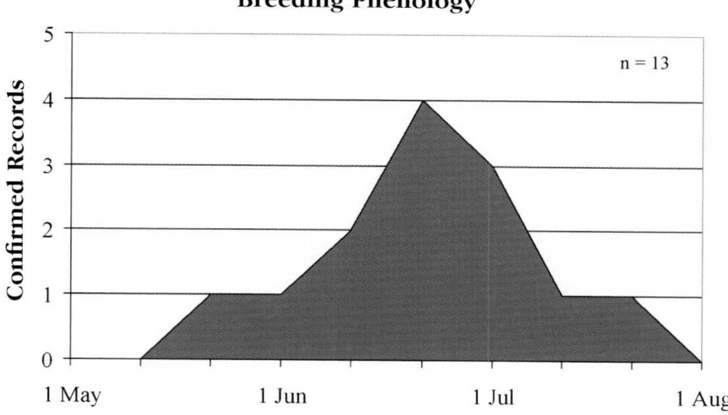

are fed by both parents, and grow rapidly, fledging 10–14 days after hatching (Bowen 1997). Townsend's Solitaires typically produce only one brood per season, but second broods are not unusual. Breeding pairs respond to nest predation by repeatedly renesting, making as many as four attempts per season (Bowen 1997).

DISTRIBUTION AND STATUS

The nominate subspecies of Townsend's Solitaire breeds from Alaska south through the mountains of the western United States as far as southern California and central Arizona and New Mexico. A second subspecies is resident in the higher elevations of the Sierra Madre Occidental of western Mexico. In Arizona, Phillips et al. (1964) considered the Townsend's Solitaire a rather common summer resident in northern Arizona.

Atlasers found Townsend's Solitaires to be relatively uncommon to locally common birds in northern and central Arizona at elevations ranging from approximately 6500 to 11,000 ft (1981–3353 m). The bulk of the state's breeding population is centered on the Kaibab Plateau and from Williams and the San Francisco Mountains regions east along the Mogollon Rim to the White Mountains, including the Blue Range. The species undoubtedly also breeds on White Mountain Apache tribal lands where unfortunately atlas surveys could not be conducted. Atlasers also confirmed Townsend's Solitaires nesting west to Mount Trumbull and possibly near Mount Floyd northeast of Seligman. They were found nesting throughout the higher elevations of Navajo tribal lands, including the upper canyons of Black Mesa and from the Carrizo Mountains south through the Defiance Plateau.

There are few documented Townsend's Solitaire breeding season records between the White Mountains of Arizona and the Sierra Huachinera of northern Sonora (Russell and Monson 1998). However, most have occurred in the Chiricahua and Huachuca mountains (Phillips et al. 1964; Taylor 1993, 1995). During the atlas, a pair was noted near Mt. Lemmon in the Santa Catalina Mountains on 24 June 1995, and several individuals were noted in the Chiricahua Mountains. There is still no evidence of breeding in southeastern Arizona, despite extensive suitable habitat. Further investigation may reveal that Townsend's Solitaires are local and possibly irregular breeding species in the higher mountain ranges of southeastern Arizona, particularly in the Pinaleno, Santa Catalina, and Chiricahua mountains.

The status of Townsend's Solitaire in Arizona is unclear, but studies elsewhere suggest that populations in the western United States and Canada are relatively stable or in some cases increasing (Bowen 1997). These unique, shy gray thrushes deserve much more attention in Arizona.

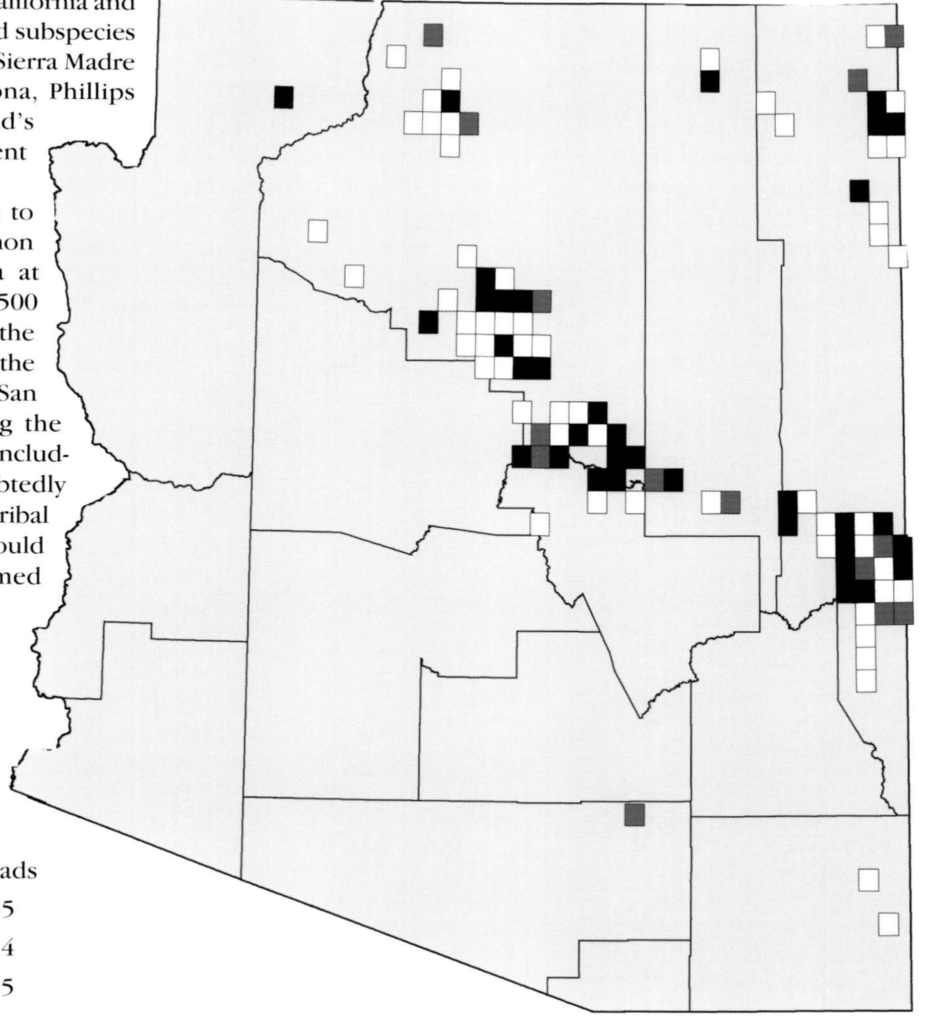

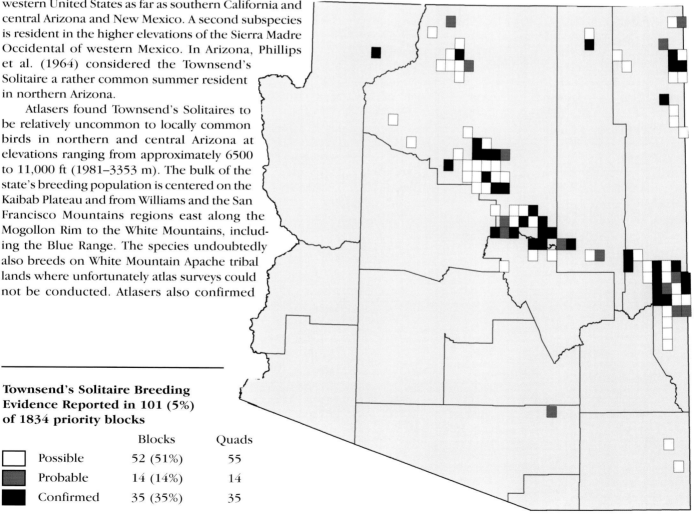

Townsend's Solitaire Breeding Evidence Reported in 101 (5%) of 1834 priority blocks

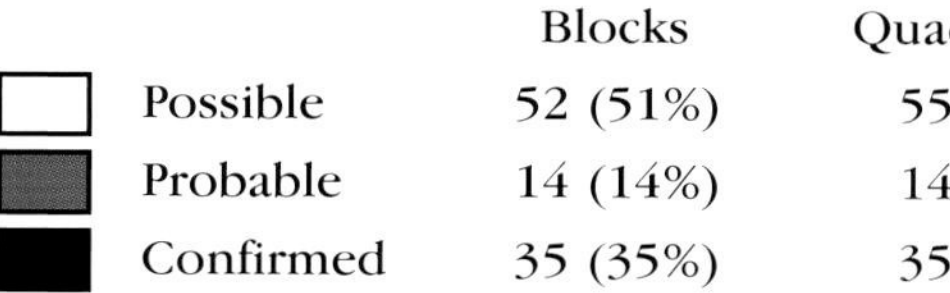

	Blocks	Quads
Possible	52 (51%)	55
Probable	14 (14%)	14
Confirmed	35 (35%)	35

Swainson's Thrush

by Troy E. Corman *Catharus ustulatus*

RICK AND NORA BOWERS

An uncommon migrant through the state, Swainson's Thrushes reach their southern nesting limits in Arizona, where few remain to breed. Seldom venturing into the open, these secretive thrushes often remain undercover. Their upward spiraling, flutelike song can be heard emanating at dawn and dusk from the woodland shadows.

HABITAT

Across their breeding range, Swainson's Thrushes inhabit a variety of coniferous forests and adjacent riparian woodlands and thickets. In general, canopy closure and tree density are often high in forests occupied by these thrushes. Even the small and very local populations in Arizona, can be found in quite different habitats. At higher elevations, atlasers noted these thrushes in mature spruce-fir forests dominated by Engelmann spruce, blue spruce, and subalpine fir. The understory frequently includes an abundance of young conifers, scattered deciduous shrubs, downed timber, ferns, and other low-light tolerant plants. Atlasers also found Swainson's Thrushes nesting very locally along wooded montane drainages with water birch, Rocky Mountain maple, and some conifers as well as in more open, but dense streamside alder-willow thickets. Occupied breeding locations in Arizona, are typically cooler and wetter than the surrounding areas often inhabited by Hermit Thrushes.

BREEDING

In Arizona, the first migrant Swainson's Thrushes appear in mid- to late April, with peak passage in early to mid-May. Stragglers are observed regularly into early June, but only casually through the end of the month. It is unknown when they first appear on their limited breeding grounds in Arizona, but atlas data suggest that they do so by at least mid- to late May. On breeding grounds, the duration of singing is relatively short and intense (Evans Mack and Yong 2000). Swainson's Thrushes are unusually quiet when they first arrive but begin singing in earnest upon nest initiation several weeks later (Evans Mack and Yong 2000). Nest construction in Arizona likely begins by at least late May, based on a nest with eggs discovered near Greer on 6 June. Another occupied nest was found in the Chuska Mountains on 12 July. Singing individuals were noted through 22 July. In Colorado, adults have been observed feeding fledglings through 31 July, with fledglings reported into mid-August (Pantle 1998). In Arizona, fall migration for Swainson's Thrush begins in early September and continues through mid-October, casually later into early November.

The well-hidden nests of Swainson's Thrushes are typically placed in understory vegetation, particularly in thickets of deciduous shrubs or conifer saplings (Evans Mack and Yong 2000). Of the two nests found during the atlas, one was in a water birch and the other in a shrub willow, either Bebb or Geyer. The latter nest was 3.9 ft (1.2 m) high in a 14.4 ft (4.4 m) willow. From multiple sources, Evans Mack and Yong (2000) compiled nest height measurements for 981 nests that ranged from 0 to 79 ft (0–24 m) in height, with 60 percent between 3.3 and 7.9 ft (1.0–2.4 m).

Only the female Swainson's Thrush constructs the nest, which takes approximately 4 days (Bent 1949). Typical clutches consists of 4 eggs, with a range of 1–5 (Evans Mack and Yong 2000). The female incubates the eggs for 10–14 days, while the male sings nearby and occasionally feeds her on the nest (Stanwood 1913). Both adults feed nestlings through nest departure of young in 10–14 day (Stanwood 1913) and for an unknown period following fledging. Most evidence suggest only one brood is produced per year, but they will renest if earlier attempts fail (Evans Mack and Yong 2000).

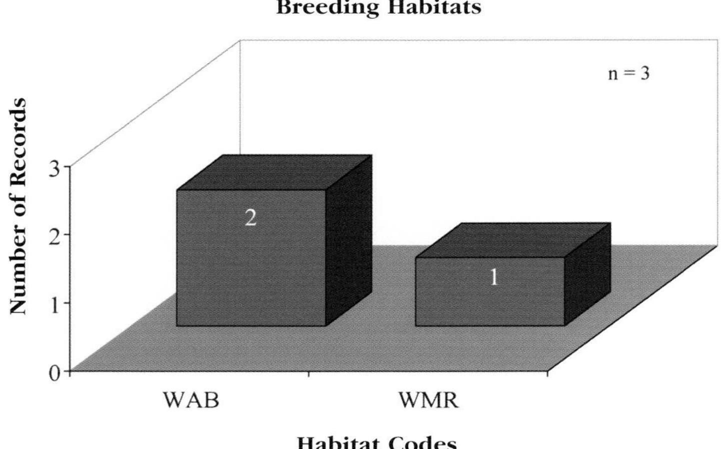

DISTRIBUTION AND STATUS

Swainson's Thrushes nest throughout much of southern Canada, south through northern New England, Wisconsin, and locally to West Virginia and possibly farther south in the

Appalachian Mountains. In the West, these thrushes are found from Alaska, south to the coast of southern California and locally in the interior to northern Arizona and New Mexico. Early summer accounts of Swainson's Thrushes in Arizona, noted them as rare summer residents only in fir forests of the San Francisco Peaks (Phillips et al. 1964). In the late 1970, these thrushes were also discovered singing in the White Mountains at several locations along the West Fork of the Little Colorado River from the headwaters near Mount Baldy down to the confluence with its South Fork west of Eagar (Monson and Phillips 1981). Swainson's Thrushes were periodically reported in these areas through the initiation of atlas surveys.

Atlasers found that the nesting status of Swainson's Thrushes has changed little, remaining rare and very local in the state. Singing individuals were detected in subalpine spruce-fir forests on the north slopes of the San Francisco Mountains and in the White Mountains at elevations from 9700 to 9800 ft (2957–2987 m). Nesting was confirmed along the West Fork of the Little Colorado River near Greer at an elevation of approximately 8300 ft (2530 m). Atlas surveys were not conducted upstream of Sheep Crossing in the West Fork of the Little Colorado River, where they had been noted through the early 1990s and likely continue to occur. At approximately 7800 ft (2377 m) elevation on Navajo tribal lands, atlasers also discovered two to three pairs of Swainson's Thrushes nesting along an upper side drainage of Tsaile Creek in the Chuska Mountains. This thrush had previously been noted only as a rare migrant on these tribal lands (Jacobs 1986).

The local populations of Swainson's Thrushes in Arizona are likely larger than the few historical and atlas records suggest. Many unsurveyed drainages and mountain slopes remain in adjacent remote and rugged areas. More thorough and timely surveys may reveal these secretive thrushes nesting in additional locations within the White Mountains region, and possibly the Chuska Mountains. This includes the higher elevations of the eastern White Mountain Apache tribal lands where atlas surveys could not be conducted.

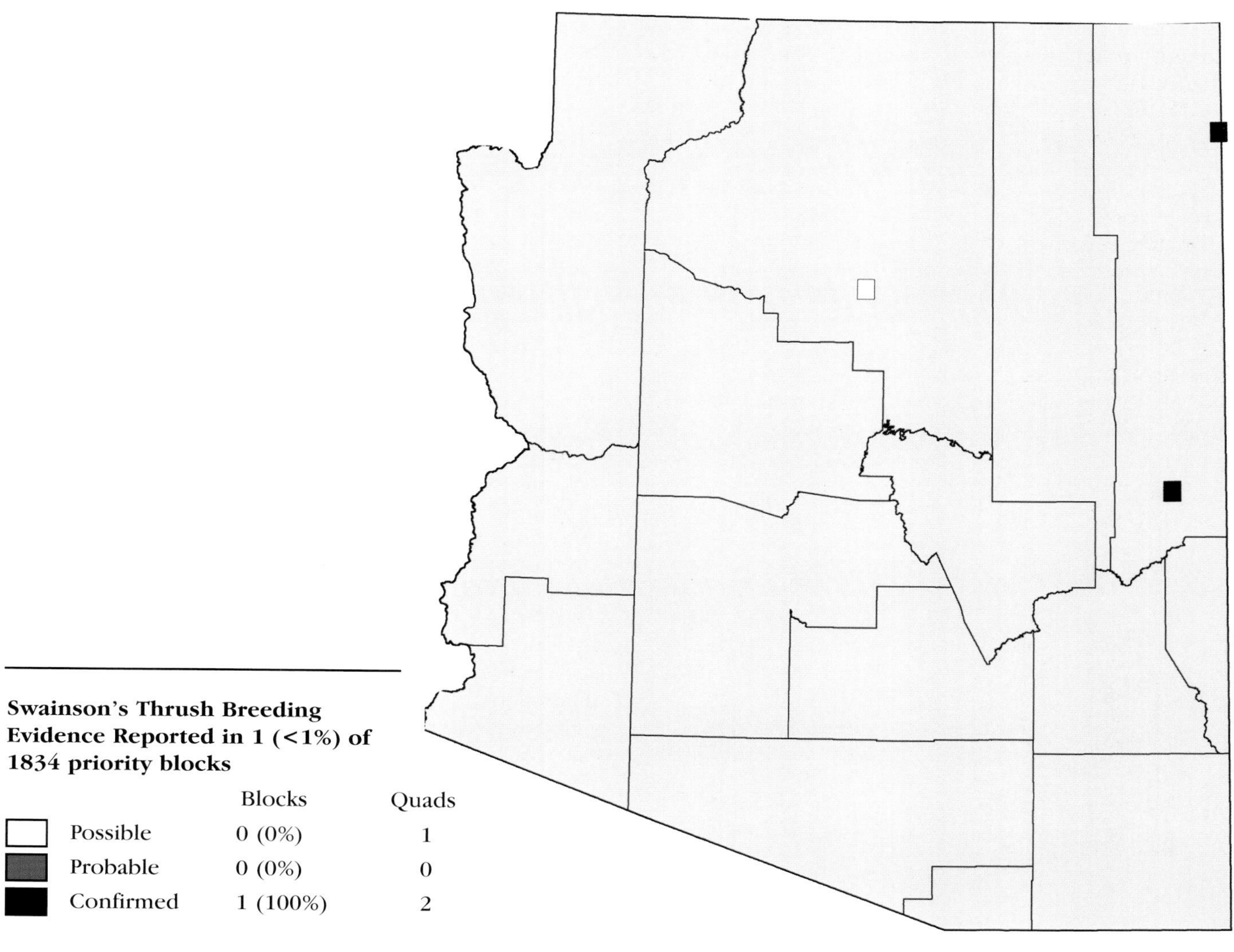

Swainson's Thrush Breeding Evidence Reported in 1 (<1%) of 1834 priority blocks

	Blocks	Quads
Possible	0 (0%)	1
Probable	0 (0%)	0
Confirmed	1 (100%)	2

Hermit Thrush

by John R. Spence *Catharus guttatus*

The ethereal, haunting song of the Hermit Thrush is commonly heard echoing throughout the conifer forests of Arizona. Considered by many birders to be the finest songster in North America, this thrush is a subtly plumaged, shy bird most often seen foraging among the shadows and leaf litter on the forest floor.

HABITAT

In Arizona, Hermit Thrushes breed most often in coniferous and mixed coniferous–deciduous forests, frequently with a fairly high canopy closure. They typically prefer cooler forests with scattered stands of saplings, smaller trees, and shrubs. Atlasers reported the species most frequently (42 percent of 161 records) in mixed-conifer forests with dominant trees consisting of Douglas fir, white fir, ponderosa pine, southwestern white pine, and aspen. Ponderosa pine forests with a Gambel's oak association accounted for an additional 19 percent of atlas records. However, in drier ponderosa pine–dominated forests, these thrushes are much more sparsely distributed and are often found on cooler north-facing slopes and drainages. In southeastern Arizona, Hermit Thrushes also nest in Madrean pine-oak forests consisting of Chihuahuan, Apache, and ponderosa pines with an understory of madrone, alligator juniper, and various Madrean evergreen oaks. They also regularly inhabit subalpine spruce-fir forests and in montane drainages with a mixture of firs, pines, and deciduous trees such as maple, alder, oak, and occasionally sycamore. There is some evidence in the literature that Hermit Thrushes are associated with interior edges, or small clearings, within forest vegetation (Jones and Donovan 1996).

BREEDING

The hardy Hermit Thrush can be found wintering throughout the state, but are most common in southern and western Arizona. They begin arriving on their higher-elevation breeding grounds in April, with males typically arriving first and establishing territories. They sing their beautiful advertisement song from exposed perches primarily in the early morning and evening, though sometimes throughout the day. At the beginning of the breeding season, males vigorously chase any females that enter their territory. After several days of wild chases, which become slower and more relaxed by days 3–4, the male finally accepts the presence of the female (Jones and Donovan 1996).

In Arizona, Hermit Thrushes can begin nest construction as early as 22 April. Atlasers reported the first Hermit Thrush nest with eggs on 20 May, but an adult feeding a recent fledgling on 26 May would indicate that egg laying occurred in late April or early May. In addition, Phillips et al. (1964) reported a female was collected in the Santa Catalina Mountains with large eggs in her oviduct on 22 April. Despite these early dates, atlas data suggest that the peak nesting period for this species in Arizona is from mid-June to mid-July. The latest active nest was a nest with young discovered on 28 July. Atlasers reported fledglings in southeastern Arizona as late as 2 September, suggesting some nesting activity well into August. Migrant Hermit Thrushes begin to appear in nonbreeding areas of Arizona in mid- to late September, with most arriving in October.

Hermit Thrush nests are typically placed low in a shrub or small tree, generally near the trunk. Although researchers on the Mogollon Rim report that very young white fir is the preferred nest substrate (Martin and Roper 1988), atlasers also found nests in Douglas fir, Engelmann spruce, Gambel's oak, ponderosa pine, and southwestern white pine. The mean nest height of 12 nests measured by atlasers was 7.9 ft (2.4 m) with a range of 3.0–15.7 ft (0.9–4.8 m). In comparison, Martin and Roper (1988) noted a mean nest height of only 3.6 ft (1.1 m) in a closely studied population in snowmelt drainages on the Mogollon Rim.

Breeding Habitats

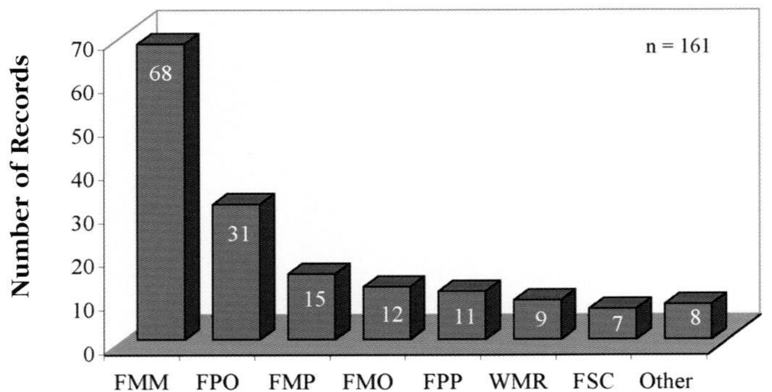

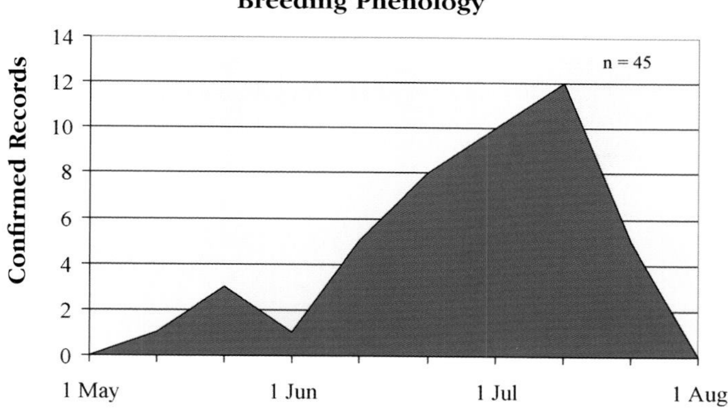

The female Hermit Thrush does all the construction work on the bulky nest, although the male may bring her nest material. The typical clutch size is 4, although it can vary from 3–6 (Martin and Li 1992). The male feeds the female during the 11–13 days she incubates (Bent 1949). Both parents feed the young, but the sexes divide the labor, with the male doing most of the food gathering, and the female most of the feeding (Bent 1949). Fledging occurs 10–15 days after hatching (Jones and Donovan 1996). Hermit Thrushes typically produce one brood per year, but two successful broods have been documented and three are possible (Martin and Li 1992).

DISTRIBUTION AND STATUS

Hermit Thrushes are the most widespread *Catharus* thrush in North America. They breed from western Alaska east in a broad band through the boreal forests of Canada, south through New England and the Appalachian Mountains to North Carolina. The species is also found throughout the mountains of the West, south to southern Arizona and New Mexico. Hermit Thrushes are not known to breed in adjacent Sonora, and are considered only winter visitors in Mexico (Russell and Monson 1998).

Atlasers found Hermit Thrushes to be common and fairly widespread in suitable habitat in the state, mostly at elevations from approximately 6200 to 10,000 ft (1829–3048 m). Locally, however, they were confirmed nesting in cool forested canyons down to 5200 ft (1585 m) and possibly to timberline. They are found in a broad band along the Mogollon Rim from the Flagstaff and Williams areas southeast to the White Mountains. They undoubtedly continue to nest on White Mountain Apache tribal land, where atlas surveys could not be conducted. Hermit Thrushes occurred fairly regularly elsewhere in northern Arizona including the Kaibab Plateau, Black Mesa, and from the Carrizo Mountains south to the Defiance Plateau.

Isolated Hermit Thrush populations were also documented west to the Prescott area, Hualapai Mountains, and Arizona Strip region in the northwest. In southeastern Arizona, they breed or are suspected of breeding on most of the higher sky island mountains and were also confirmed breeding locally in the Winchester and Santa Teresa mountains.

The Hermit Thrush is a common bird throughout most its range, and Breeding Bird Survey route data in western United States indicate that populations remain stable. Breeding Bird Survey routes in Arizona that occur in suitable habitat record fewer than five individuals per route except for the region around Flagstaff, the Kaibab Plateau, and the White Mountains, where routes detect from five to twenty birds.

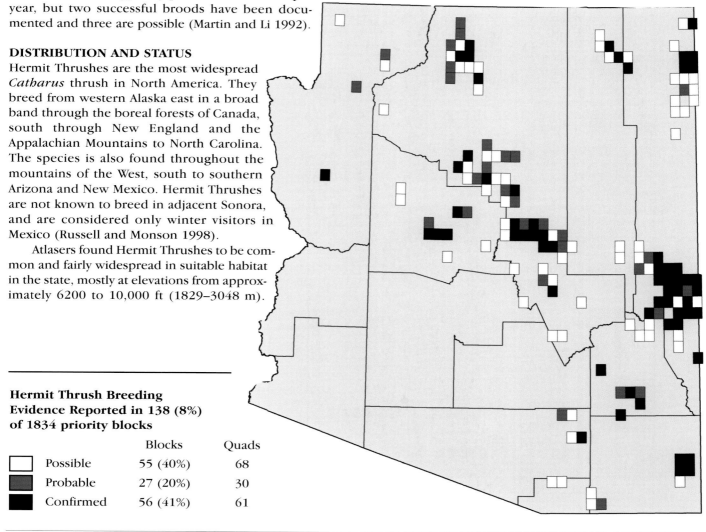

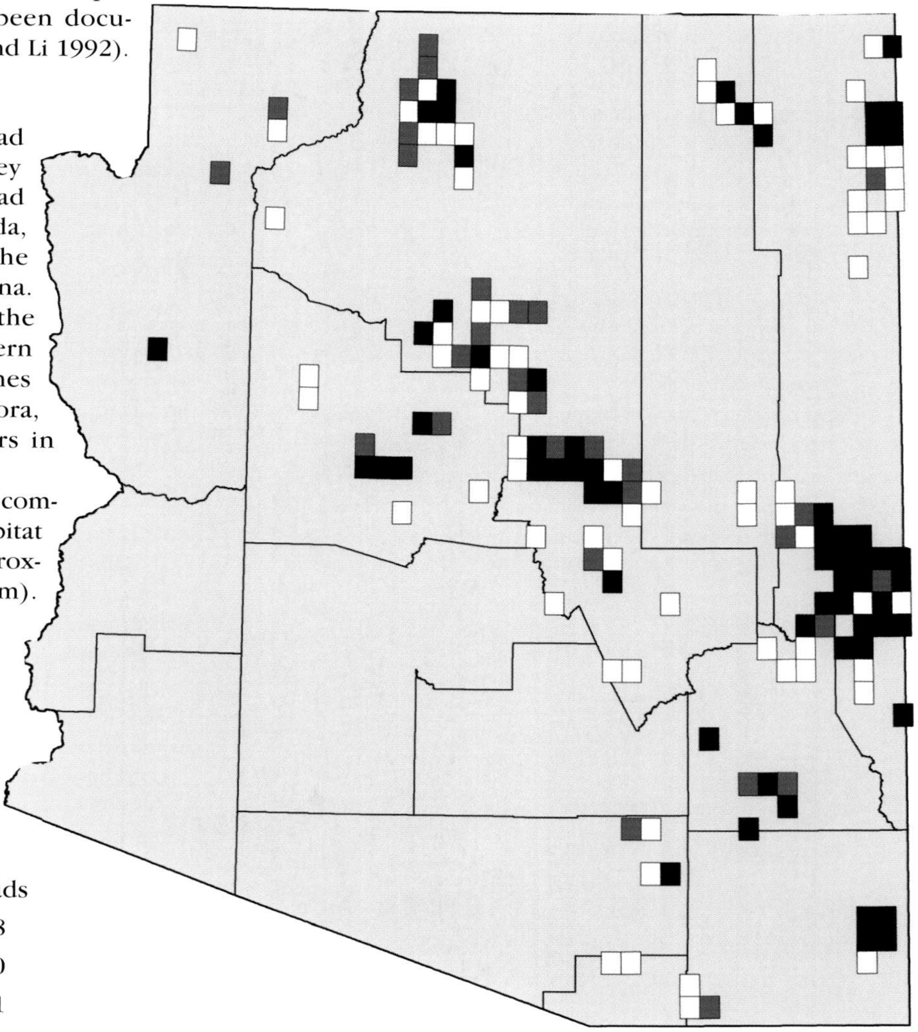

Hermit Thrush Breeding Evidence Reported in 138 (8%) of 1834 priority blocks

	Blocks	Quads
Possible	55 (40%)	68
Probable	27 (20%)	30
Confirmed	56 (41%)	61

American Robin

by Cathryn Wise-Gervais *Turdus migratorius*

The American Robin is one of the most familiar songbirds in the United States and Canada. Its tame nature, large size, and distinctive songs make this bird easy to observe. These birds migrate in large groups that collectively search for worm-rich damp soil in the spring and abundant berry crops in the fall.

DAN FISCHER

HABITAT

Throughout much of their range, American Robins are most common in suburban yards and gardens where they will forage on the ground and nest in ornamental shade and fruit trees. This species is also found in native habitats, however, and favors riparian woodlands and early successional mixed-conifer and deciduous forests. Breeding American Robins in Arizona are more common in natural rather than human-altered settings. Atlasers reported American Robins in twenty-four habitat types, from lowland riparian woodlands to high-elevations aspen and spruce-fir forests, indicating a degree of flexibility in habitat choice. However, observers obtained a roughly equal number of records in each of the five most commonly reported vegetative communities, accounting for 69 percent of atlas records (n = 305). These include mixed-conifer forests, ponderosa pine–dominated forests, and sycamore-lined drainages. Fewer records were obtained in montane riparian areas of mixed deciduous and coniferous trees, pinyon pine–juniper woodlands, Madrean evergreen oak woodlands, and cottonwood-willow riparian areas.

BREEDING

American Robins are considered the harbingers of spring in many regions of the United States, although they often winter throughout Arizona's middle and lower elevations. They begin arriving and singing in the state's breeding areas by March or April, and males typically appear several days before the females (Sallabanks and James 1999). In general, atlasers began reporting American Robins on breeding grounds by mid-April and noted an occupied nest by 22 April. Early egg laying is undoubtedly initiated by early to mid-April based on the observations of adults feeding fledglings by 15 May. Statewide atlas data suggest a peak in breeding activity in early to mid-June, but nesting continued through July. Observers reported nests with eggs as late as 20 July and a nest with young through 29 July, indicating dependent fledglings well into August. Arizona's American Robins typically begin moving from high elevations into the juniper belt by late July (Phillips et al. 1964) and begin appearing irregularly in other lowland wintering areas, including deserts and urban centers, in September and October.

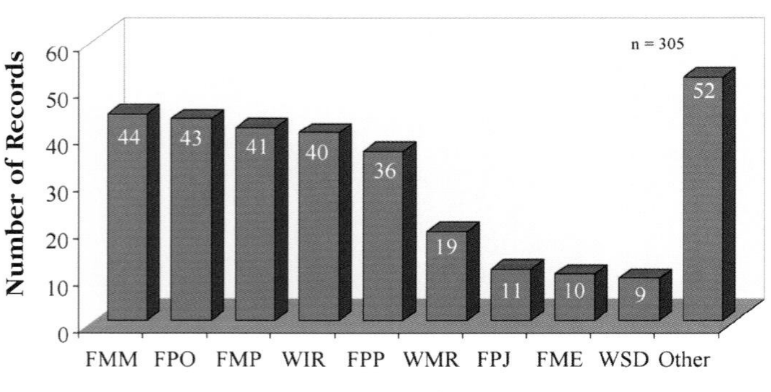

American Robins typically nest low in protected trees or shrubs, but will also nest in a wide variety of situations providing a shelf and some cover from above, including cliffs, cutbanks, buildings, and other structures (Bent 1949; Howell 1942). American Robin nests typically include generous amounts of mud, and the availability of this material often limits the breeding distribution of this bird in Arizona's many arid landscapes. Atlasers described nineteen American Robin nests, twelve in deciduous trees. Nearly half of the nests were discovered in alder, willow, and ponderosa pine, with others in Douglas fir, Gambel's oak, netleaf oak, box elder, sycamore, and locust. The median height of these nests was 8.2 ft (2.5 m), which range in height from 3.3 to 35.1 ft (1.0–10.7 m).

Although male American Robins may bring nest materials to their mates, it is the female that selects the final nest site and builds the nest, usually in 5–7 days (Sallabanks and James 1999). The American Robin's clutch typically consists of 3–4 eggs, rarely more (Sallabanks and James 1999), and the female incubates these for 12–14 days (Howell 1942). The female will continue to brood the young for approximately one week following hatching, and both adults feed the young. Fledging occurs at about 13 days of age, but

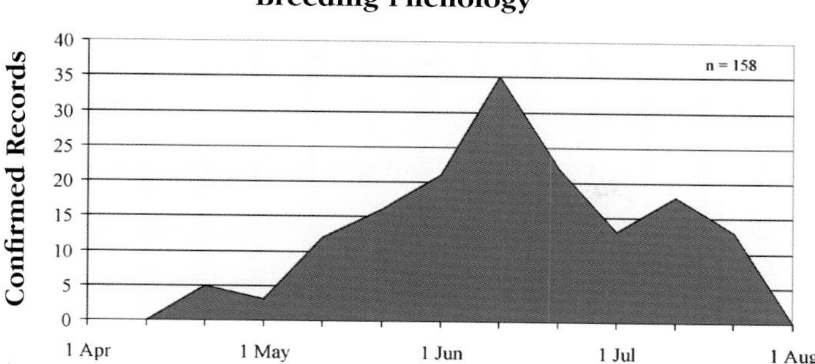

parental care continues for approximately 3 weeks after the young leave the nest (Sallabanks and James 1999). American Robins frequently rear two (rarely three) broods per season (Sallabanks and James 1999). They recognize and destroy Brown-headed Cowbird eggs (Friedmann 1929), and no incidents of brood parasitism were observed during the atlas period.

DISTRIBUTION AND STATUS

American Robins are the most widespread thrush in North America, found from coast to coast and from northern Alaska to central Mexico. Although breeding American Robins in Canada and Alaska travel south for the winter, not all populations are migratory. In many western regions, the species simply moves to lower elevations during the colder months. Such is the case in Arizona, where the species winters commonly (sometimes abundantly) in berry-rich juniper stands and fruiting Russian olive.

In Arizona, American Robins are known to nest commonly in open forests and woodlands in northern, central, and eastern Arizona; they are typically absent during the breeding season from the lower desert regions. Beginning in the mid-1960s, however, a few pairs of American Robins began nesting in shaded, irrigated suburban neighborhoods and parks in Tucson and later in Phoenix and near Yuma (Monson and Phillips 1981; Rosenberg et al. 1991). Nesting in these Sonoran Desert urban areas was not reported during the atlas period and atlasers confirmed American Robins breeding on priority blocks at elevations from approximately 3250 to 9500 ft (991–2896 m). However, they were encountered down to 1800 ft (549 m) near Littlefield where they have nested in the past. They were also confirmed nesting locally in pecan orchards and neighborhoods in Safford.

Atlasers confirmed American Robins breeding in a continuous band from the Kaibab Plateau south to the Bradshaw Mountains and Prescott area, and east along the Mogollon Rim to the White Mountains region. Although American Robins certainly breed within White Mountain Apache tribal lands, atlasers could not verify this, as atlas surveys were unfortunately not permitted on this habitat diverse reservation. In addition, atlasers regularly encountered American Robins nesting on the Navajo and Hopi tribal lands, including on higher mesas such as Black, Zilnez, and Balakai, and in the Carrizo Mountains south to the Defiance Plateau. They were also confirmed nesting west locally to the Hualapai Mountains.

Nesting American Robins were encountered throughout the forested mountains and main canyons of southeastern Arizona. They were noted west to the Nogales area and confirmed nesting in Guadalupe Canyon.

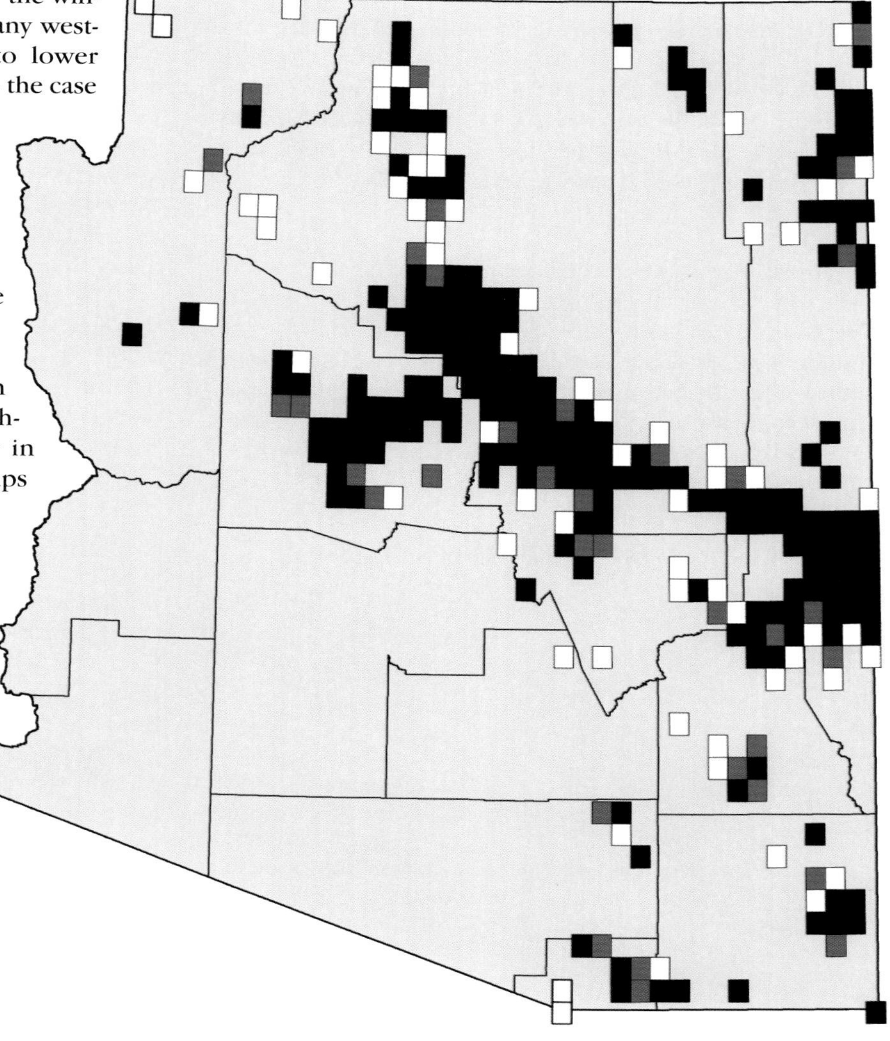

American Robin Breeding Evidence Reported in 273 (15%) of 1834 priority blocks

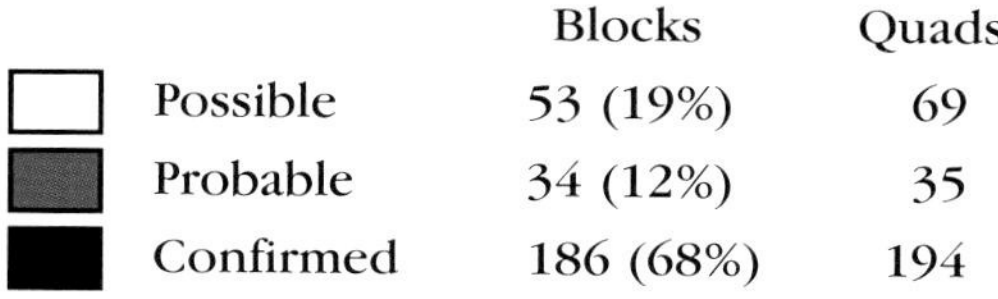

	Blocks	Quads
Possible	53 (19%)	69
Probable	34 (12%)	35
Confirmed	186 (68%)	194

Gray Catbird

by Troy E. Corman *Dumetella carolinensis*

Well known in eastern North America, Gray Catbirds have received very little attention across their western range. These shadow-colored birds often keep to the dark recesses of the dense thickets in which they frequent. They are such a retiring species that their varied babbling songs are often delivered from under the cover of their leafy domain.

JIM BURNS

HABITAT

Throughout their range, Gray Catbirds are typically found in or near low, dense woody thickets and tangles of shrubs, young trees, and briars. They are frequently found near streams, rivers, or woodland edges. In western North America, open streamside thickets appear to be the habitat of choice for Gray Catbirds. Atlasers found this species primarily only in high-elevation shrubby alder and willow thickets along small, low gradient creeks and rivers. Within their range in Arizona, beaver dam-building activity often enhances this habitat. Dominant shrubs along occupied drainage typically include thinleaf alder and several species of scrub willows, especially coyote, Geyer, and Bebb willows. Scattered cottonwoods are also found at some locations. Shrub stands are frequently dense and are typically 5–10 ft (1.5–3 m) high. Other shrubs may include cerro hawthorn, raspberry, gooseberry, shrubby cinquefoil, and red elderberry, with an understory and adjacent open areas of grasses, sedges, and many forbs.

BREEDING

In Arizona, Gray Catbirds begin to arrive in late April or May. Within their limited Arizona breeding range, the earliest observation during the atlas period was on 18 May. Singing commences upon arrival and continues until late in incubation of the first nest (Zimmerman 1963). Pair formation and nest construction take place shortly after the females return to their breeding grounds (Gross 1948).

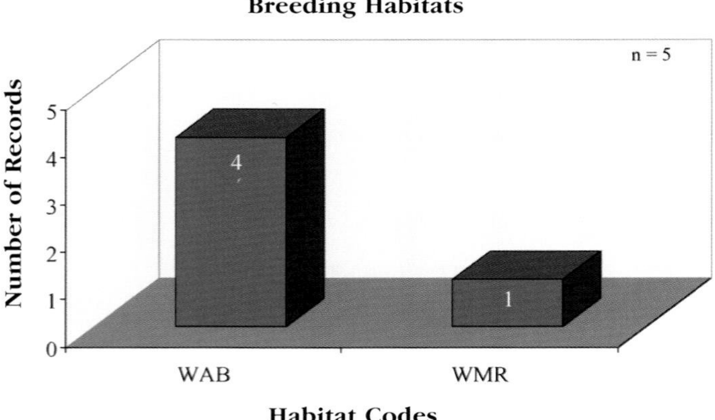

Due to Gray Catbird's retiring nature and limited range in Arizona, atlasers collected little breeding biology information. The earliest confirmed record reported by atlasers was of a pair feeding a bobbed-tailed fledgling on 30 June 1994 along the Little Colorado River at the Wenima Wildlife Area north of Springerville. This record would suggest nest construction initiation by late May or early June. Atlasers also discovered two nests with eggs in July, which likely pertain to renesting attempts after failed earlier efforts or a second nesting after fledging prior broods. One of these nests was along the headwaters of the San Francisco River near Alpine on 1 July 1993 and the other near Greer on the West Fork of the Little Colorado River on 10 July 1998. The later nest would suggest breeding activity continuing into early August when adults would be feeding fledglings. Gray Catbirds have been reported on their nesting grounds in Arizona as late as 14 September. Exceptional, was a report of a singing individual on 25 December 1980 near the confluence of the Little Colorado River with its South Fork east of Eagar (Monson and Phillips 1981). Gray Catbirds are casual migrants and winter visitors to the remainder of Arizona. However, there are records for every month of the year in southeastern Arizona.

The female Gray Catbird constructs most of the nest in 5–6 days (Gross 1948). Nests are typically well concealed, low in dense living shrubs, saplings, small trees, and vines (Cimprich and Moore 1995). Atlasers discovered nests in dense scrub willow thickets. Cimprich and Moore (1995) compiled nest measurements from many studies and noted the mean nest height of 4.9 ft (1.5 m). Gray Catbird egg clutches typically consist of 3–4 eggs, but can range from 1 to 5, rarely 6 (Gross 1948). The female incubates the clutch for 12–14 days (Cimprich and Moore 1995) and both parents feed the nestlings through nest departure when the young are 8–12 days old (Zimmerman 1963). The adults feed the fledglings for 12–24 days (Zimmerman 1963; Baicich and Harrison 1997). Throughout most of there breeding range, Gray Catbirds attempt two broods per year (Cimprich and Moore 1995). Gray Catbirds readily recognize Brown-headed Cowbird eggs and quickly remove them once they are discovered in the nest (Scott 1977).

DISTRIBUTION AND STATUS

Gray Catbirds breed throughout most of eastern and central United States and southern Canada, west through the southern Rocky Mountain region to southern British Columbia and northern Washington. They reach their southwestern limit of distribution in the White Mountains of east-central Arizona. Phillips et al. (1964) noted that Gray Catbirds also likely nested in Oak Creek Canyon north of Sedona, based on reports beginning in June 1955, and possibly on the west side of the Chuska Mountains. An individual was collected in the southern foothills of the Chuska Mountains on Wheatfield Creek on 25 June 1927 (Woodbury and Russell 1945), suggesting possible historical nesting in this area. A nest with young was also discovered at Show Low, Navajo County, in July 1937 (Phillips et al. 1964).

Atlasers found Gray Catbirds only in the White Mountains region of Apache County at elevations ranging from 6700 to 8500 ft (2042–2591 m). The largest population continues to be found along the upper Little Colorado River drainage. This includes the West Fork of the Little Colorado River as far upstream as Greer and downstream past the confluence of the South Fork. Atlasers found Gray Catbirds very locally along the Little Colorado River near Eagar and Springerville downstream to the Wenima Wildlife Area north of Springerville. They were also noted locally along Rudd Creek at the Sipe White Mountain Wildlife Area and along Nutrioso Creek near Nutrioso. The southernmost nesting record was along the San Francisco River just southeast of Alpine.

Within the past century, much of the riparian thicket habitat that Gray Catbirds depend on in the White Mountains region has been lost to urban development and inappropriate livestock grazing practices. More recently, grazing and browsing by elk in the area has greatly damaged this important habitat. Some appropriate riparian stands continue to exist along Show Low Creek in and around the town of Show Low, where Gray Catbirds had nested historically. However, this land is privately owned and was not surveyed during the atlas period.

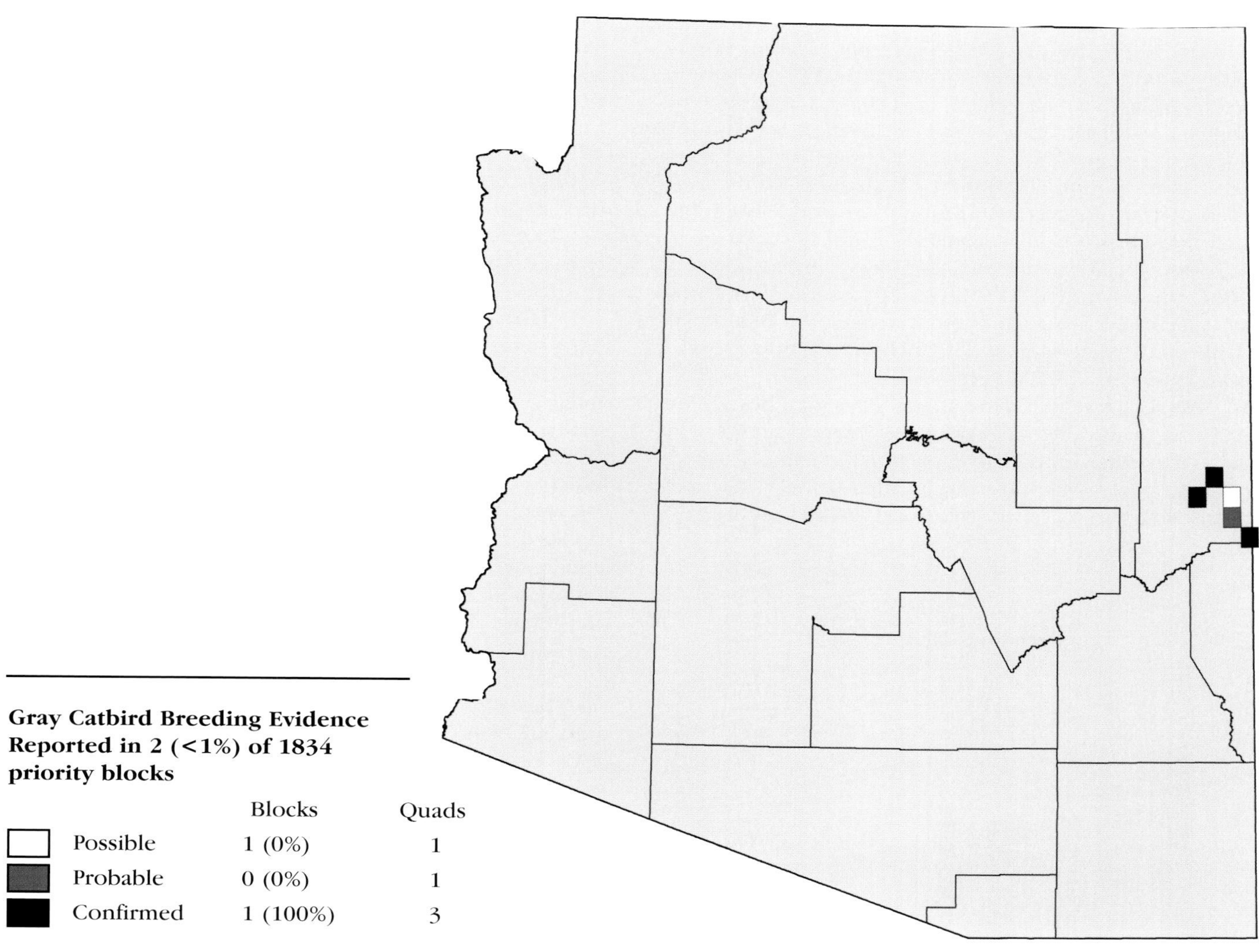

Northern Mockingbird

by Cathryn Wise-Gervais *Mimus polyglottos*

Despite the Northern Mockingbird's amazing repertoire, many an angry exclamation has been directed at this songster during his persistent midnight serenades. Notorious for their intimidating defense of young, these birds commonly dive-bomb other birds, cats, and even humans that stray too close to fledglings hidden nearby.

HABITAT

Northern Mockingbirds are familiar and commonplace throughout their North American range. As such, they occupy a wide variety of relatively open vegetative communities, typically with shrubby thickets and scattered trees. Atlasers reported this widespread species in thirty-two habitat types during the atlas period. The most commonly reported vegetative communities were also the most prevalent in Arizona: Sonoran desertscrub including wooded desert dry washes (34 percent of records) and open pinyon pine–juniper woodlands (13 percent of records; n = 1312). It is likely that these adaptable birds simply select appropriate vegetative structure within these widespread habitats. Atlasers also reported Northern Mockingbirds commonly inhabiting brushy grasslands, sagebrush dominated deserts, and riparian woodland edges. Their flexibility in habitat selections is notably apparent in their widespread use of exotic plantings in urban and rural neighborhoods and parks. Observers occasionally reported this species in Madrean evergreen oak woodlands but found that the birds generally avoided densely wooded areas, especially at higher elevations.

Atlas data reveal that the annual density of desert nesting Northern Mockingbirds can change dramatically from one year to the next based on winter precipitation. In fact, atlasers revisiting desert blocks during normal or dry years were surprised to find this species conspicuously absent in areas where it had not only been present, but abundant during the preceding year, which saw above-normal precipitation.

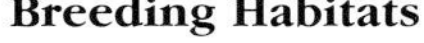

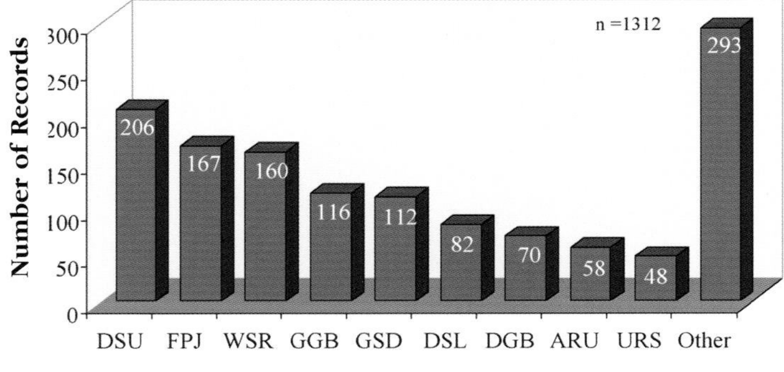

BREEDING

Northern Mockingbirds are resident throughout much of Arizona, but some populations depart to lower elevations and more southern localities during the winter. They normally begin returning to northern Arizona breeding areas by late March or early April. In the state's lowland desert regions, Northern Mockingbirds begin their nesting period in late winter to early spring. In the north and at higher elevations, nesting typically begins in late April or May. As courtship commences, adults hop on the ground and perform a curious wing flashing behavior that serves to reveal white wing patches. While the function of this activity has been debated, it is most likely a territorial display (Derrickson and Breitwisch 1992).

Atlasers reported Northern Mockingbirds nest building in the desert as early as 23 February, and located nests with eggs on 28 February. However, a nest with young was noted on 1 March indicating egg laying by mid-February. Statewide atlas data suggest that the peak of Northern Mockingbird breeding activity occurs from late May to late June (n = 459), but observers confirmed this species breeding throughout the summer. Nests with young were reported through 15 August and atlasers observed adults feeding fledglings as late as 4 September. Most of the later nesting pairs were noted in southeastern Arizona, where they may take advantage of the abundant insect food supply due to monsoon activity.

Northern Mockingbirds build and use several nests each breeding season (Derrickson and Breitwisch 1992); these are characteristically placed fairly low in a wide variety of brushy locations. Atlasers measured 134 Northern Mockingbird nests in 27 tree and shrub species. The most commonly reported nest plants were various juniper species (21 percent), followed by barberry (12 percent), various cholla species (12 percent), wolfberry (10 percent), and ironwood (10 percent). Other frequently used trees included tamarisk, pinyon pine, and mesquite. The median height of the 134 nests was 3.9 ft (1.2 m), with a range of 0.8–11.1 ft (0.3–3.4 m).

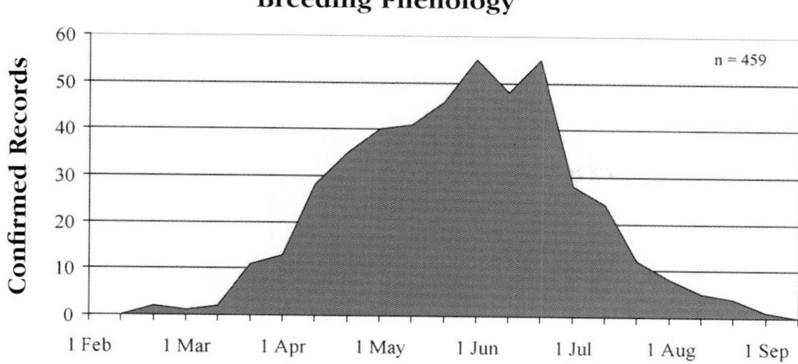

Male Northern Mockingbirds may build several nests before the female selects one for lining in preparation for her eggs (Derrickson and Breitwisch 1992). Typical clutches consist of 3–5 eggs (range 2–6) and are incubated by the female for approximately 12–13 days (Derrickson and Breitwisch 1992). Both parents feed the nestlings, but only the female broods them for the first 6 days (Breitwisch et al. 1984). The young fledge approximately 12 days after hatching (Laskey 1962), but are still fed by their parents for several days. Once the adults begin constructing a new nest for their second brood, they will feed their fledglings more sporadically. Northern Mockingbirds usually raise two, and sometimes three broods per season (Sprunt 1964; Breitwisch 1988; Derrickson 1989).

Northern Mockingbirds are infrequent cowbird hosts, but they are known as an "acceptor" species (Friedmann et al. 1977). Observers did not report any incidents of cowbird parasitism during the atlas period, however.

DISTRIBUTION AND STATUS

Northern Mockingbirds have an extensive range, and they nest throughout much of North America from coast to coast and from the southern Canadian border south throughout most of Mexico and the Caribbean. These birds breed nearly statewide in Arizona and are typically absent only at higher elevations, in densely wooded areas, or sparsely vegetated landscapes. Atlasers confirmed Northern Mockingbirds breeding on priority blocks at elevations from approximately 90 to 7800 ft (27–2377 m).

Phillips et al. (1964) considered Northern Mockingbirds common summer residents in open brushy areas throughout the state, noting that they were more sparsely distributed in the western deserts except in wet years. Atlas data reveal that most confirmed records obtained west of Tucson and Phoenix were reported during the wetter years of 1993, 1998, or 2000. For example, of the 32 confirmed records obtained in Yuma County, 24 (75 percent) were obtained during the three wet years of the atlas period. In Pinal County, 33 (62 percent) of the 53 confirmed records were obtained during wet years.

Brown et al. (1987) considered Northern Mockingbirds uncommon summer residents along the Colorado River within the Grand Canyon. Although seemingly appropriate habitat exists, surveys during the atlas period suggested this species is largely absent within the entire Canyon corridor.

The distribution and abundance of Northern Mockingbirds have likely increased locally in Arizona owing to pinyon pine and juniper encroachment in the northern grasslands, and the invasion of mesquite and other shrubs into the southeastern grasslands. These adaptable birds also readily take advantage of expanding urban development, irrigated landscapes, and exotic residential vegetation.

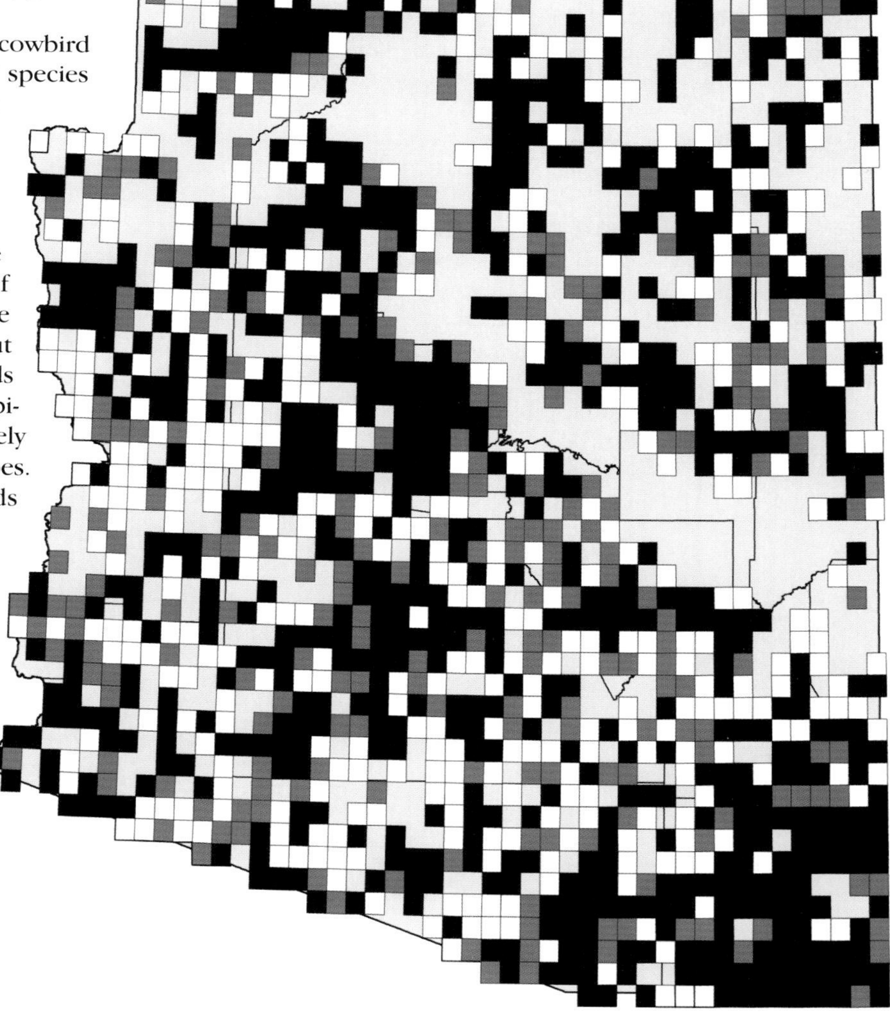

Northern Mockingbird Breeding Evidence Reported in 1320 (72%) of 1834 priority blocks

	Blocks	Quads
Possible	394 (30%)	403
Probable	241 (18%)	242
Confirmed	685 (52%)	689

Sage Thrasher

by Troy E. Corman *Oreoscoptes montanus*

Most birders in the state think of Sage Thrashers as migrants and wintering species in southern and central Arizona. However, the open sagebrush country of northern Arizona also harbors nesting populations of these small thrashers, whose melodious songs help ease the monotony of their shrubby, gray-green surroundings.

HABITAT

During the nesting season, Sage Thrashers are birds of open, flat, or gently sloping country, where continuous stands of sagebrush or similarly structured shrubs cover the landscape. In Arizona, this habitat typically occurs in wide drainage swales, plains, mesa tops, or gentle foothill slopes. North of the Grand Canyon, Sage Thrashers were often encountered where big sagebrush was the dominant shrub species. Other characteristic plants frequently included cliffrose, blackbrush, snakeweed, cholla, various grasses, and widely scattered junipers. South and east of the Grand Canyon, atlasers found these thrashers nesting not only in big sagebrush but also in a more diverse array of open shrublands that often did not include sagebrush. Four-winged saltbush, shadscale, and black greasewood were often the dominant plant species in occupied areas. Other low-growing shrubs sometimes found in this habitat included snakeweed, rabbitbrush, ephedra, Fremont barberry, cholla, sand sagebrush, Bigelow sage, and black sagebrush.

BREEDING

Because of food availability, the abundance and distribution of Sage Thrashers wintering in Arizona are quite variable from one year to the next. However, northbound migrants begin to move through southern Arizona as early as mid-January with a distinct peak in March. They typically arrive in their northern Arizona breeding areas by late February and March. Sage Thrashers sing most intently and consistently during territory establishment and courtship in late March and April. Song frequency then quickly decreases after the initiation of nest construction and they are noticeably quiet once the eggs are laid (Reynolds et al. 1999).

In Arizona, nest building and the initiation of egg laying likely occur in April, approximately 1–2 weeks after their arrival on the breeding grounds (Reynolds et al. 1999). Unfortunately, most atlas surveys were not conducted in their preferred habitats until May and June. Therefore, atlasers were unable to collect much information on the early nesting activity of this thrasher. The assumption that nesting begins by April in Arizona is supported by the fact that nests with eggs have been found in early to mid-April much farther north in Idaho and Washington (Reynolds et al. 1999). Also, atlasers discovered a nest with young on 17 May, which also supports egg laying in late April or early May. The latest nest with young reported by atlasers was on 27 June, although adults were observed carrying food as late as 22 July. Sage Thrashers begin dispersing in August with a peak southbound passage in September. They begin arriving in southern Arizona between mid-September and October. During years when junipers are heavily laden with berries, many remain to winter in open juniper woodlands, where dozens of these thrashers can be observed feasting in a single tree.

Very secretive in the vicinity of their nest, Sage Thrashers typically fly within 10–30 ft (3–9.1 m) of the nest then travel under dense cover the remainder of the way on the ground (Killpack 1970). Atlasers discovered these birds nesting in big sagebrush, sand sagebrush, four-winged saltbush, Fremont barberry, cholla, and cliffrose. In Arizona, they have also been reported nesting in black greasewood and juniper (C. LaRue, personal communication). The mean nest height of the five active nests measured during the atlas was 16 in. (40 cm) with a range of 9–33 in. (23–85 cm). North of Arizona, many nests have been found on the ground under dense sagebrush (Reynolds and Rich 1978).

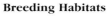

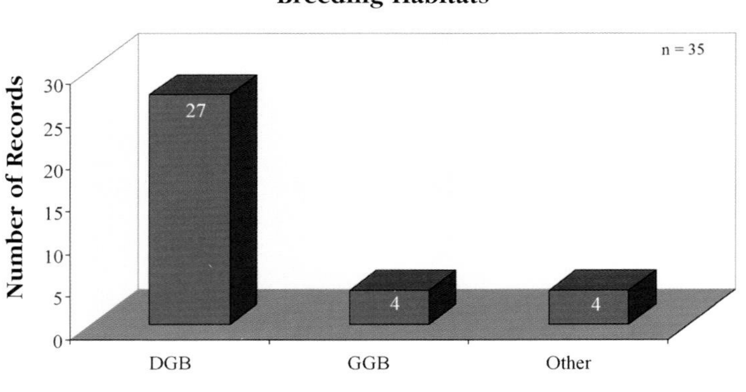

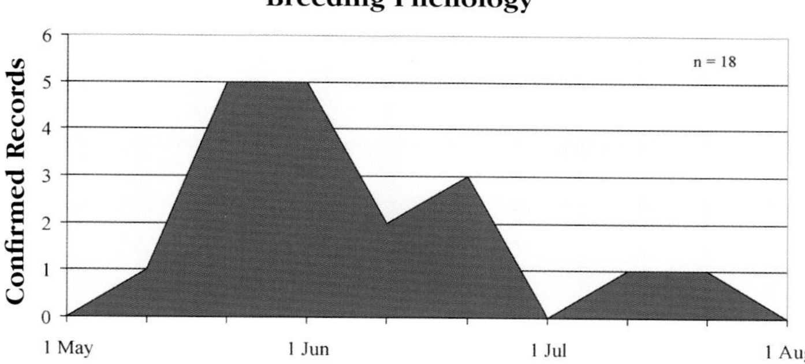

Nest placement tends to be just below the densest vegetation within the plant, often close to the center (Rich 1980). Some pairs construct intricate stick canopies above the nest to provide shade, and possibly to help conceal the nest from predators (Bent 1948; Rich 1985).

Sage Thrasher pairs share the duty of incubating the typical clutch of 4–5 eggs (Gilman 1907; Reynolds and Rich 1978). Incubation typically lasts from 11 to 15 days, and both parents feed the nestlings through fledging in approximately 11–14 days (Reynolds et al. 1999). Sage Thrashers are known to have as many as two broods per season (Rich 1978).

DISTRIBUTION AND STATUS

During the breeding season, Sage Thrashers nest in western North America from the southern edge of British Columbia, south through the Great Basin region to northern Arizona and New Mexico. They reach their southern nesting limits in the northern one-third of Arizona, where Phillips et al. (1964) noted them as fairly common summer residents in northeastern and possibly northwestern Arizona. Based on historical records, they also suggest nesting south possibly to Springerville. Even Brown et al. (1986) noted that this species possibly nested in northwestern Arizona, however there was still no evidence to support this.

There have been few avian studies in the preferred habitat of the Sage Thrasher in Arizona. Therefore, it was not surprising that atlasers documented Sage Thrashers as a much more widespread nesting species in northern Arizona than previous published literature had noted. In Arizona, these thrashers were found nesting at elevations from 4800 to 7200 ft (1463–2195 m). Phillips et al. (1964) reported Sage Thrashers nesting only in Apache and Navajo counties. Atlasers confirmed it nesting from the Arizona Strip region in northwestern Arizona, and to the east and southeast through northern Coconino County. They were encountered nesting for the first time south of the Grand Canyon, in shrublands east of Valle, Coconino County. Sage Thrashers were found in scattered localities throughout the Navajo and Hopi tribal lands. The most southern confirmed record was near St. Johns, Apache County.

As noted before, Sage Thrashers are rather quiet and secretive while nesting and can be easily overlooked. The sparse distribution of Sage Thrashers found during the atlas project may reflect the difficulty in detecting this species later in the breeding season. Additional surveys conducted in April, when males are singing much more frequently, may reveal a more accurate breeding distribution in the state.

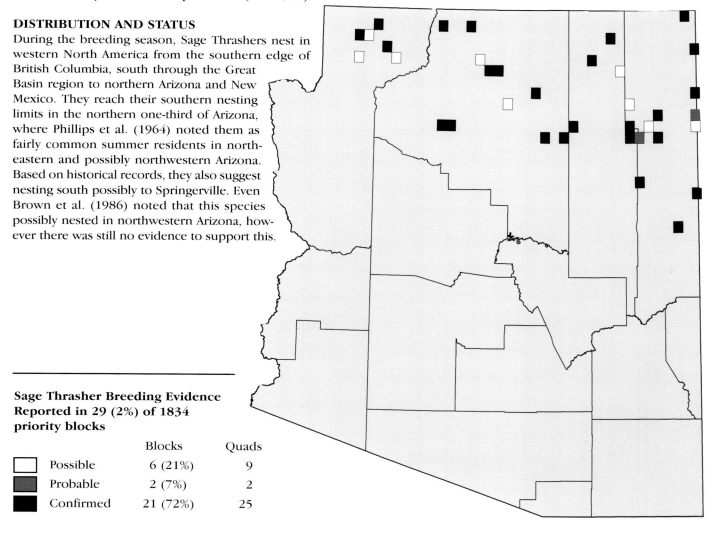

Sage Thrasher Breeding Evidence Reported in 29 (2%) of 1834 priority blocks

	Blocks	Quads
Possible	6 (21%)	9
Probable	2 (7%)	2
Confirmed	21 (72%)	25

Bendire's Thrasher

by Troy E. Corman *Toxostoma bendirei*

The rich, spirited song of the Bendire's Thrasher is unique in that it typically lacks the brief pauses frequently heard in the songs of other thrashers in Arizona. In the Sonoran Desert, their numbers appear to fluctuate considerably from one year to the next, becoming most abundant after winters with above normal rainfall.

JIM BURNS

HABITAT

More widespread in Arizona than any other thrasher, Bendire's Thrashers nest in a diverse array of flat to gently rolling open habitats across the state from desertscrub and brushy grasslands to neighborhood parks and rural settings. Approximately 50 percent of all potential atlas breeding records for this thrasher were reported in Sonoran desertscrub associations (n = 324). Here it typically favored an abundance of trees, shrubs, and cacti that were adjacent to more open areas. In sparsely vegetation desert areas, they were frequently encountered along dry washes with scattered trees and shrubs. In southeastern and central Arizona, Bendire's Thrashers were found in arid, brushy grasslands with scattered mesquite, acacia, and yucca. In the northwest, they were found in open brushy habitats with a Mojave desertscrub influence, where the habitats often contained blackbrush, and various species of saltbush, yucca, and cholla. Grassy and shrubby areas with scattered junipers and sagebrush were favored in northern Arizona, including the Arizona Strip region in the extreme northwest.

Bendire's Thrashers are also regularly found in rural situations such as shelterbelts, brushy field edges, shrubby trees along irrigation ditches, and along overgrown corrals and fence lines. Locally, atlasers also found them in open residential parks with a mixture of exotic and native desert tree, where they sometimes become rather tame. Phillips et al. (1964) noted that Bendire's Thrashers avoid all continuous, heavy vegetation and grasslands lacking shrubs.

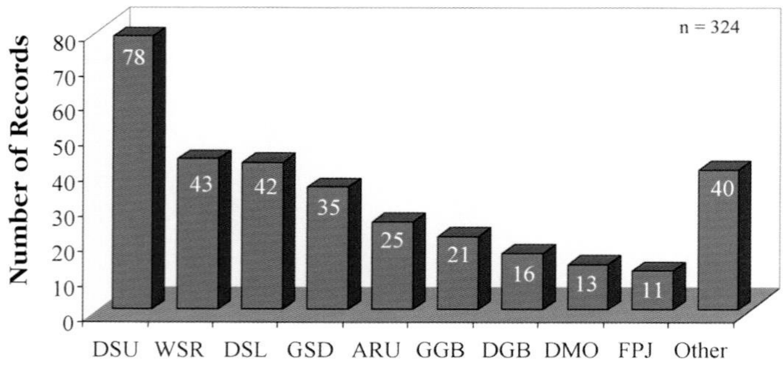

BREEDING

In south-central Arizona, some Bendire's Thrasher populations are resident, while they are primarily migratory elsewhere in the state. Migrants begin to arrive as early as late January in southern Arizona and late March and April in the north. Singing commences in January, reaching a peak in February and March, and continuing irregularly into August and early September.

Atlasers noted the first Bendire's Thrasher nest with eggs on 3 March, although Gilman (1909) discovered a nest with eggs as early as 19 February in Arizona. Atlas data suggest that the peak nesting period is in April, but nesting efforts continue fairly strongly through mid-June. Nests with eggs were found as late as 11 July, but an adult carrying a fecal sack, indicating a nest with young, was noted as late as 10 August. All nesting records in July and August were from south-central and southeastern Arizona, where late nesting could be influenced by the summer monsoon season in this region.

The stick nests of Bendire's Thrashers are constructed in a variety of shrubs, trees, and cacti. Field crews measured 24 active nests with a mean nest height of 5.2 ft (1.6 m) and a range of 1.9–9.8 ft (0.6–3.0 m). Atlas data suggest that blue and foothill paloverdes are especially favored as nest substrates in Arizona. Atlasers also found them nesting in velvet mesquite, catclaw acacia, sweet acacia, ironwood, desert hackberry, smoketree, crucifixion thorn, wolfberry, graythorn, cholla, and even a saguaro skeleton in the desert regions. Several nests were discovered in mistletoe clumps in larger desert trees. Nests were found in cliffrose, Utah juniper, and tamarisk at higher elevations and ornamental trees are also used in residential parks.

The typical clutch for Bendire's Thrasher consists of 3–4 eggs, rarely 5 (Brown 1901). Gilman (1909) found that Bendire's Thrashers frequently fledge two broods per year in Arizona, occasionally three. Near Sacaton, one pair of thrashers fledged young about 1 May, a second brood fledged 6 July, and the female was incubating a third set of eggs by 25 July (Gilman 1915). There is apparently little information on the length of incubation, but nestlings are reported to depart the nest when they are approximately 12 days old (England and Laudenslayer 1993).

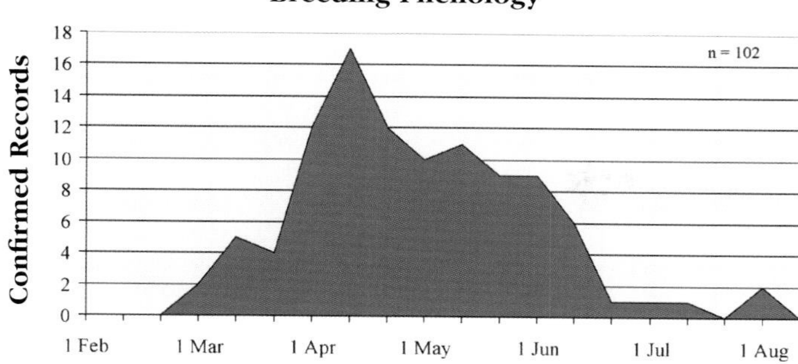

DISTRIBUTION AND STATUS

The Bendire's Thrasher has a relatively small breeding distribution centered in Arizona and also nest in adjacent California, Nevada, Utah, and New Mexico, south to Sonora and possibly northern Sinaloa. Phillips et al. (1964) reported Bendire's Thrashers as rather common to local summer residents in open habitats nearly statewide in Arizona.

During the atlas project, Bendire's Thrashers were noted as uncommon to locally common at elevations from approximately 500 ft (152 m) in southwestern Arizona to 6100 ft (1859 m) on the Colorado Plateau of the northeast. In general, atlasers found this thrasher much more sparsely distributed in northern Arizona than in the south. Bendire's Thrashers were found nesting most consistently in the Sonoran Desert uplands in Maricopa, Pinal, and Pima counties. Historically, this thrasher was unrecorded as a nesting species in the yucca grasslands of the Sulphur Springs Valley. They apparently took advantage of the massive invasion of scattered brush in the area (Phillips et al. 1964). First confirmed nesting in the Sulphur Springs Valley near Elfrida and Double Adobe in 1985, atlasers found them to be a widespread nesting species throughout this and the San Bernardino Valley.

Bendire's Thrashers were largely absent from the immediate river valleys of the San Pedro, lower Gila, and Colorado. They were also inexplicably undetected over a large area of Yavapai County and in adjacent Mohave and Coconino counties where habitat and elevation appear suitable. Because of the reduced numbers of this thrasher during years with below normal precipitation, atlasers may have missed this species in blocks that were surveyed only during dry years.

Prior to the atlas, there were no published records of Bendire's Thrasher in the Grand Canyon and Arizona Strip regions of the northwest (Monson and Phillips 1981; Brown et al. 1987). However, atlas surveys revealed this thrasher in numerous localities in this region. They are widespread, but apparently local nesting species north of the Mogollon Rim. Bendire's Thrashes have been described as fairly common summer residents in greasewood-dominated areas and open juniper savannas on Navajo and Hopi tribal lands (Jacobs 1986; LaRue 1994).

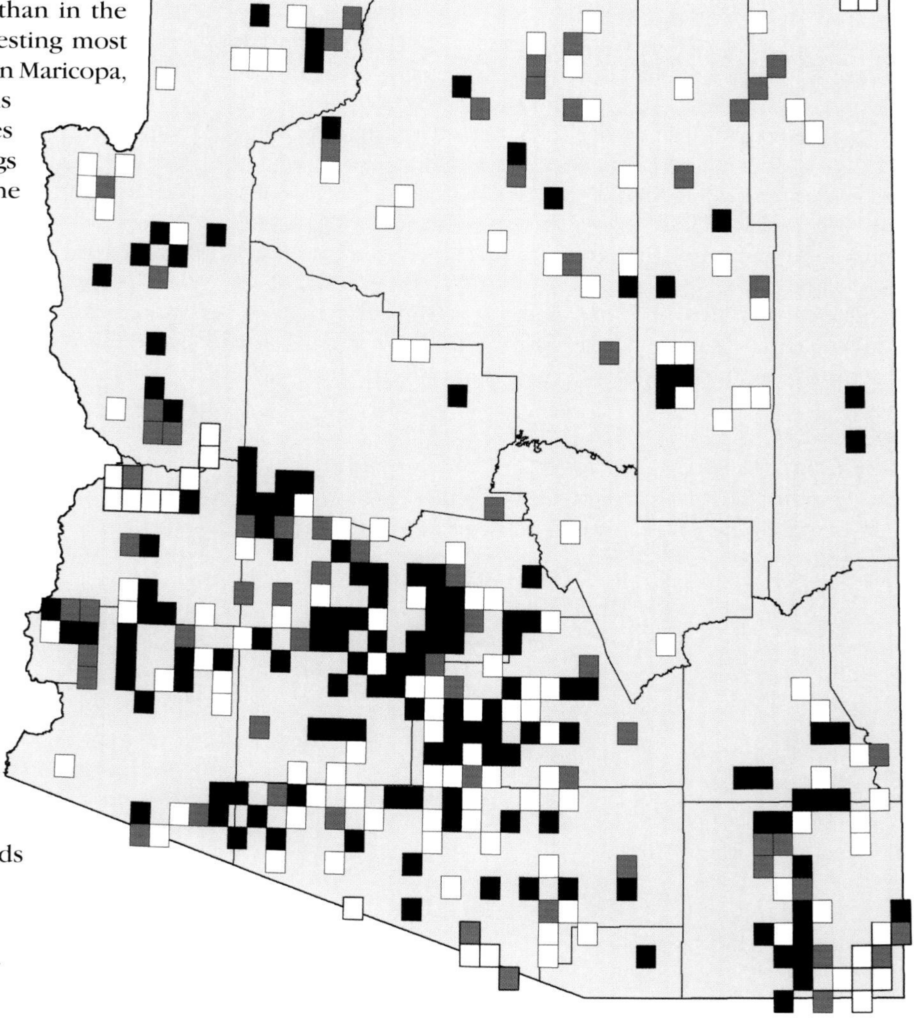

Bendire's Thrasher Breeding Evidence Reported in 321 (18%) of 1834 priority blocks

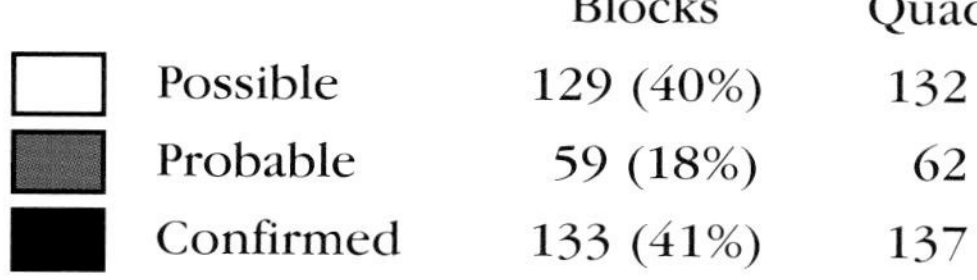

	Blocks	Quads
Possible	129 (40%)	132
Probable	59 (18%)	62
Confirmed	133 (41%)	137

Curve-billed Thrasher

by Troy E. Corman *Toxostoma curvirostre*

The loud, clear "whit-weet" whistle of the Curve-billed Thrasher is a commonly heard and easily recognized voice of the Sonoran Desert. Unlike other thrashers in Arizona, these adaptable desert inhabitants are frequently found in xeroscaped urban areas, where they become rather tame, often visiting watering and feeding stations.

DAN FISCHER

HABITAT

Typically desert inhabitants, Curve-billed Thrashers often occur in higher densities than other Arizona thrashers. Adaptable, they also frequent many urban settings typically shunned by other thrashers. Throughout much of their Arizona range, cholla is an important habitat component frequented by this noisy thrasher, although prickly pear or low, thorny shrubs will also suffice. They remain most abundant in more diversely vegetated Sonoran Desert landscapes, where 50 percent of all atlas records were reported (n = 672). The next most frequently reported vegetative community was semiarid grasslands, which accounted for 15 percent of all records. They occur much less frequently in sparsely vegetated Sonoran desertscrub areas lacking cholla or along densely vegetated dry washes and lowland riparian areas where other thrasher species are typically more abundant. Where desert habitats meet urban and rural settings, these familiar birds frequently inhabit desert landscaped yards and parks, especially those containing cacti and low shrubs. They were sparingly reported in Chihuahuan desertscrub associations, although this is likely due to the limited amount of this habitat in Arizona.

BREEDING

Like many thrashers, the length of the breeding season varies annually for Curve-billed Thrashers, as it is closely tied to precipitation amounts and duration during certain periods of the year. During years with normal or above normal winter precipitation, this thrasher may begin singing and courtship activity in December. During these years, nest building can begin as early as January. The earliest nesting record reported by atlasers was a nest with young on 31 January indicating clutch initiation by mid-month. Atlas data reveal a sharp increase in the number of active nests beginning in late March, with a distinct peak from mid-April through mid-May. Nesting activity sharply declines by mid-June, but atlasers noted active nests into early September. The latest nest with young was reported on 31 August, suggesting dependent young well into September. Abundant rainfall during the late summer monsoon period likely encourages the later nesting attempts in August, with most late records coming from the southeastern regions most influenced by these rains. Significantly fewer atlas surveys were conducted after mid-August, so late nesting activity is likely more frequent than the atlas data reveal.

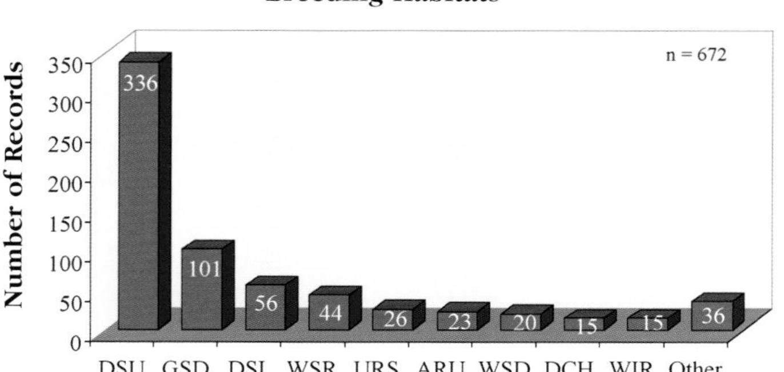

Atlasers noted that during years with below normal winter precipitation in the Sonoran Desert, egg laying may be delayed until April or even May. However, in urban settings where irrigated landscapes allow for more reliable annual food supplies, extremely dry years did little in delaying the nesting activity of Curve-billed Thrashers.

Atlasers took measurements at 87 nests of Curve-billed Thrashers, and 90 percent were constructed in cholla of six species. Of all the nests measured in cholla, 62 percent were identified as jumping or teddybear cholla. Atlasers also found Curve-billed Thrasher nests in saguaro, foothill paloverde, catclaw acacia, netleaf hackberry, and various species of prickly pear. For all nests, the mean height above the ground was 4.6 ft (1.4 m), but they ranged from 2.3 to 8.5 ft (0.7–2.6 m). The higher nests were all found on saguaros, typically on top of a lower arm, next to the saguaro trunk.

Both members of the pair help construct the bulky stick nest, which is frequently built on top of or adjacent to the nest from the previous year. The number of eggs laid is often dependent upon seasonal precipitation and subsequent abundance of insect prey. During winters with an abundance

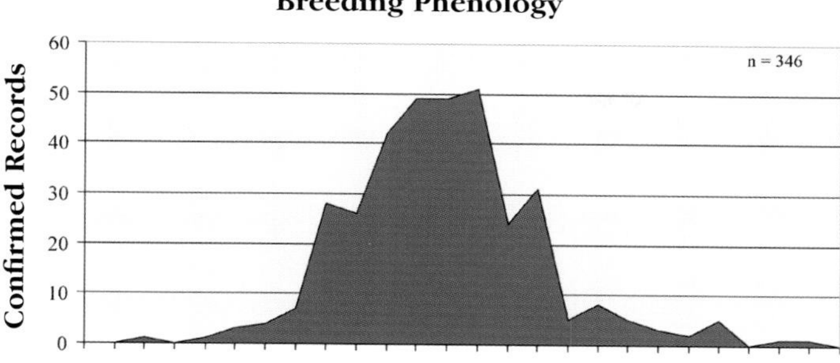

of precipitation, atlasers frequently noted Curve-billed Thrasher clutches of 3–4 eggs. However, during dry years, nests often contained only 1–2 eggs. Both parents help incubate the eggs for approximately 12–15 days and the young depart the nest in approximately 14 days (Fischer 1980). The fledglings continue to be fed by the parents until they are 3–5 weeks of age. With their lengthy nesting season in Arizona, these prolific thrashers can raise as many as four broods per year (Tweit 1996), although 2–3 broods are much more common. Second clutches are often laid in the same or new nest only 2–3 weeks following fledging of the first brood (Bent 1948). However, a pair built a second nest during the last three days of the nestling period of their first brood and laid the first egg only four days later (Pfister 1984).

DISTRIBUTION AND STATUS

Curve-billed Thrashers are resident from southern Mexico north through western Texas to southeastern Colorado and west to southern Arizona. Previous literature noted this thrasher as a very common resident in southern Arizona, west to the Growler and Kofa Mountains, and the Big Sandy River (Phillips et al. 1964). They were later considered uncommon to sparse west to the Cabeza Prieta Mountains (Monson and Phillips 1981).

Curve-billed Thrashers were found commonly throughout their previously described range at elevations from 600 to 5200 ft (183–1585 m). Most records above 4000 ft (1219 m) were from southeastern Arizona. Atlasers encountered them regularly west to the western slope of the Castle Dome Mountains on the Kofa National Wildlife Refuge, and to the eastern foothills of the Tinajas Altas Mountains west of the Cabeza Prieta National Wildlife Refuge. Typically avoiding the lower elevations of the Sonoran Desert, where vegetation is sparse and cholla is lacking, Curve-billed Thrashers were absent in the Colorado River valley and Gila River valley below Painted Rock Dam. They were noted slightly northwest of their previously described distribution in Arizona. The most northwestern records were near Chloride in the western foothills of the Cerbat Mountains, in the foothills of the Black Mountains near Oatman, and northeast of Davis Dam at Burns Spring.

In central Arizona, Curve-billed Thrashers were regularly encountered as far north as Prescott Valley and in the Verde River valley to near the Verde Hot Springs. At the northeastern edge of their range in the state, they were noted from the southern slope of the Natanes Mountains on San Carlos Apache tribal lands to just northwest of Morenci.

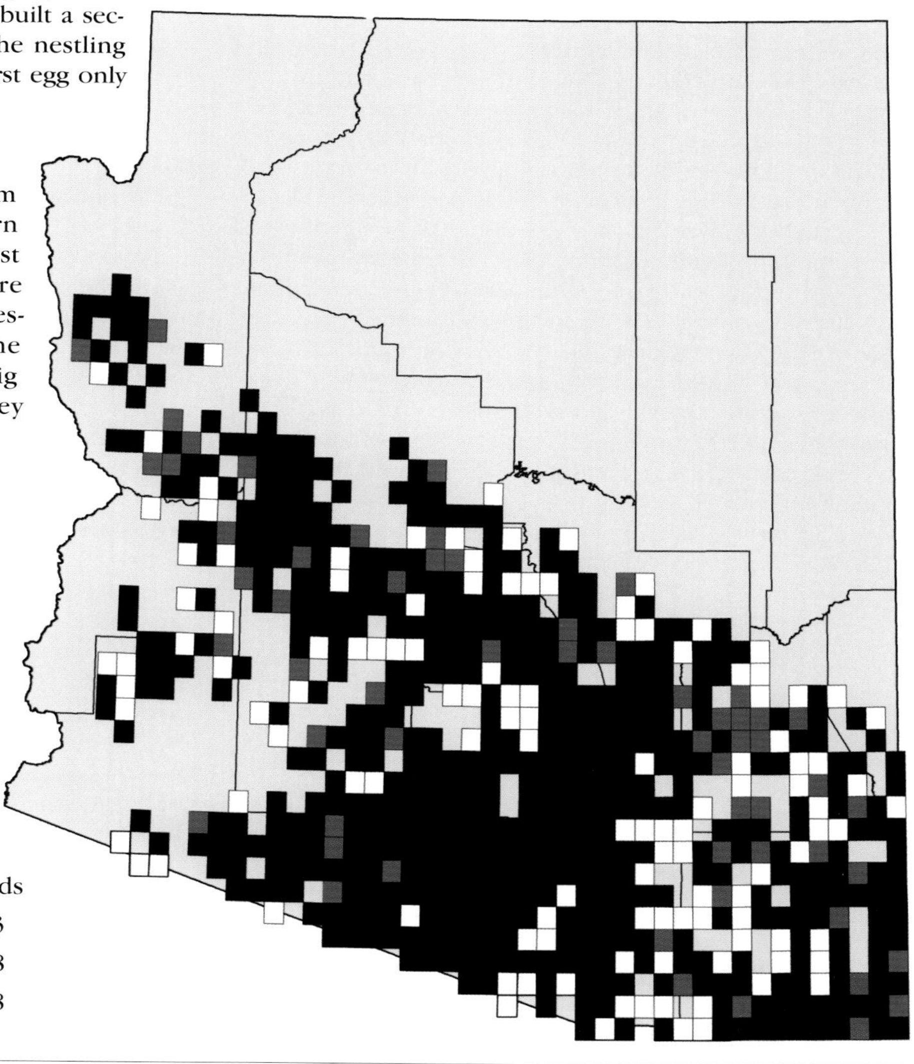

Curve-billed Thrasher
Breeding Evidence Reported in 659 (40%) of 1834 priority blocks

	Blocks	Quads
Possible	118 (18%)	123
Probable	58 (9%)	58
Confirmed	483 (73%)	488

Crissal Thrasher

by Troy E. Corman *Toxostoma crissale*

The wary Crissal Thrasher is a rusty-vented recluse of dense, brushy thickets in which it quickly vanishes at the slightest disturbance. Except for when it sings from the top of a shrub or low tree, satisfactory views of this skulker are few. The observer is often left with frustrating glimpses of a bird with a long, dark tail, dashing ahead between patches of underbrush.

HABITAT

Regardless of the habitat or elevation in which they occur, Crissal Thrashers characteristically associate with tall, dense brush and shrub thickets. Atlasers reported this thrasher most frequently (30 percent of all records) in heavily vegetated dry washes in open deserts and lower mountain foothill drainages and canyons (n = 571). Dominant trees and shrubs along these washes can be quite variable, but frequently included velvet mesquite, graythorn, wolfberry, hackberry, paloverde, and ironwood. Along lowland drainages, atlasers regularly encountered them in dense mesquite stands, exotic tamarisk thickets, and edges of Fremont cottonwood–willow riparian woodlands. Crissal Thrashers were also regularly reported on dry, chaparral covered mountain slopes, where manzanita, shrub live oak, and mountain mahogany have grown thick and dense.

At higher elevations, atlasers noted these shy thrashers ranging up to the edge of evergreen oak and pinyon pine–juniper woodlands. They prefer cold-temperate desertscrub associations in northern Arizona, where big sagebrush, cliffrose, scrub live oak, and Fremont barberry mix with scattered Utah juniper and pinyon pine. Crissal Thrashers avoid urban and residential habitats, but they sometimes take advantage of dense thickets of mesquite, tamarisk, and saltbush created by agricultural irrigation ditches and runoff.

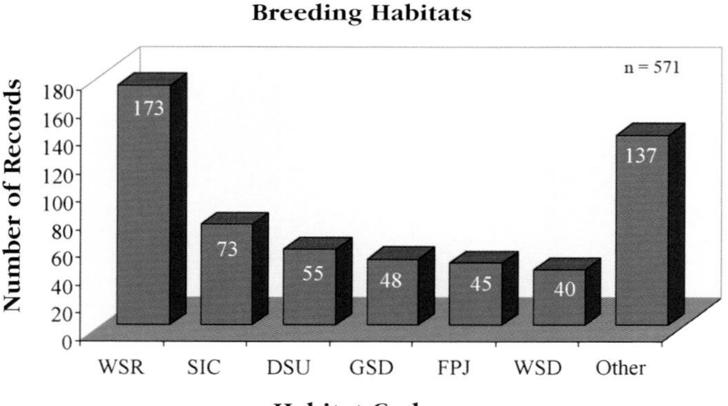

BREEDING

Primarily a resident species, Crissal Thrashers initiate nesting activity early and typically begin to sing in January and early February in southern Arizona. The earliest nest with eggs reported by atlasers was on 9 March. However, nests with eggs have been found in Arizona as early as 24 January along the middle Gila River (Gilman 1909) and 18 February near Camp Verde (Mearns 1886). Atlasers likely missed many early nesting attempts, inasmuch as most surveys were not conducted until late February or early March. The earliest nests with young were reported on 18 March. Atlas surveys revealed a slight peak in nesting activity for this thrasher in late March and then a significant peak in mid-May. This may reflect the fact that Crissal Thrashers often produce two broods per season. Most nesting activity is completed by mid-July, but an exceptionally late nest with eggs was discovered on 8 August near San Simon, Cochise County.

Nests of the Crissal Thrasher are typically constructed within the densest section of a tree or shrub and are difficult to locate. At the slightest disturbance, adults furtively slip off the hidden nest dropping down to the ground through the underbrush. In southern Arizona, atlas field crews discovered nests in various species of mesquite, blue paloverde, foothill paloverde, ironwood, wolfberry, graythorn, and a well-shaded cholla. At higher elevations and in northern Arizona, nests were noted most frequently in Utah juniper and shrub live oak, but also in big sagebrush, Fremont barberry, cliffrose, and skunkbush. The mean nest height of the twenty-nine active nests the field crew measured was 4.9 ft (1.5 m) above the ground, with a range of 1.6–7.5 ft (0.5–2.3 m).

The typical clutch size of Crissal Thrasher is 2–3 eggs with a range of 1–4 (Bent 1948). Both parents share the incubation duties for 14 days and feed the nestlings until they fledge 14–16 days later (Gilman 1909; Finch 1982). In Arizona, at least two broods are attempted each season, and three broods are likely during wetter years with an abundance of cover and food for the young (Gilman 1909).

DISTRIBUTION AND STATUS

Crissal Thrashers are primarily a resident species from southeastern California and southern Nevada southeast

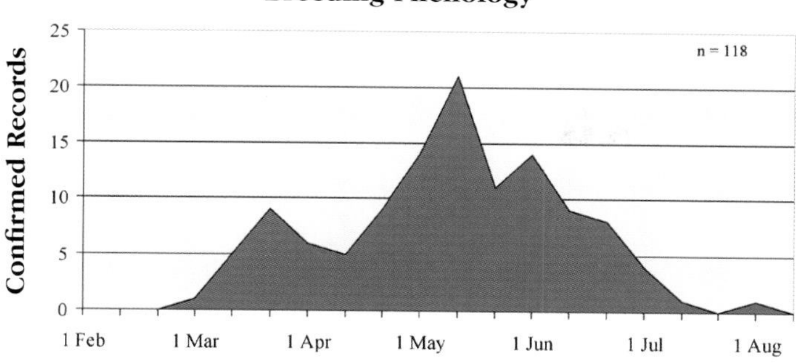

through Arizona, New Mexico, and western Texas. This thrasher's range continues into Mexico through Sonora and Chihuahua and south through the Mexican Plateau to Zacatecas and Hidalgo (Howell and Webb 1995). Prior literature considered Crissal Thrashers as common residents in Arizona, south and west of the Mogollon Rim and Coconino Plateau (Phillips et al. 1964). Monson and Phillips (1981) also noted them as being observed during the summer in the Toroweap Valley north of Grand Canyon National Park.

The presence of Crissal Thrashers is often revealed by their song or the periodically delivered "djurry-jurry" calls that are habitually given only when they are a safe distance away. Otherwise, these stealthy birds are much quieter than Curve-billed Thrashers and easily overlooked among the dense underbrush. Atlasers found Crissal Thrashers to be more widespread in Arizona than previous literature suggests. They were reported at elevations from approximately 100 ft (30 m) along the Colorado River near Gadsden to 6400 ft (1951m) on chaparral-shrouded slopes below the Mogollon Rim.

This thrasher was discovered nesting throughout the Arizona Strip region in the northwestern corner of the state, and east as far as House Rock Valley and Page. Atlasers also documented Crissal Thrashers nesting for the first time on the Coconino Plateau. The birds also breed east locally on Navajo tribal lands within the Little Colorado River valley, including Moenkopi Wash. Phillips et al. (1964) previously considered this thrasher an uncommon fall migrant near the South Rim of the Grand Canyon and within the Little Colorado River valley. However, Phillips et al. suggested that specimens and sight records near Shumway, Navajo County, and Concho, Apache County, might pertain to breeding individuals. Atlasers were able to document that Crissal Thrashers do nest locally throughout this region and that most of the historical records within the Little Colorado River valley likely pertain to resident individuals.

Atlasers discovered Crissal Thrashers nesting locally west of Growler Valley in western Pima County and throughout the Cabeza Prieta National Wildlife Refuge, where Phillips et al. (1964) reported this species to be absent. Because this species tends to shy away from urban development, Crissal Thrashers were found to be largely absent from the greater Phoenix and Tucson metropolitan areas. They were also sparsely distributed in the smaller rural and agricultural communities between Phoenix and Tucson. This timid thrasher will undoubtedly continue to lose habitat as residential and urban areas expand.

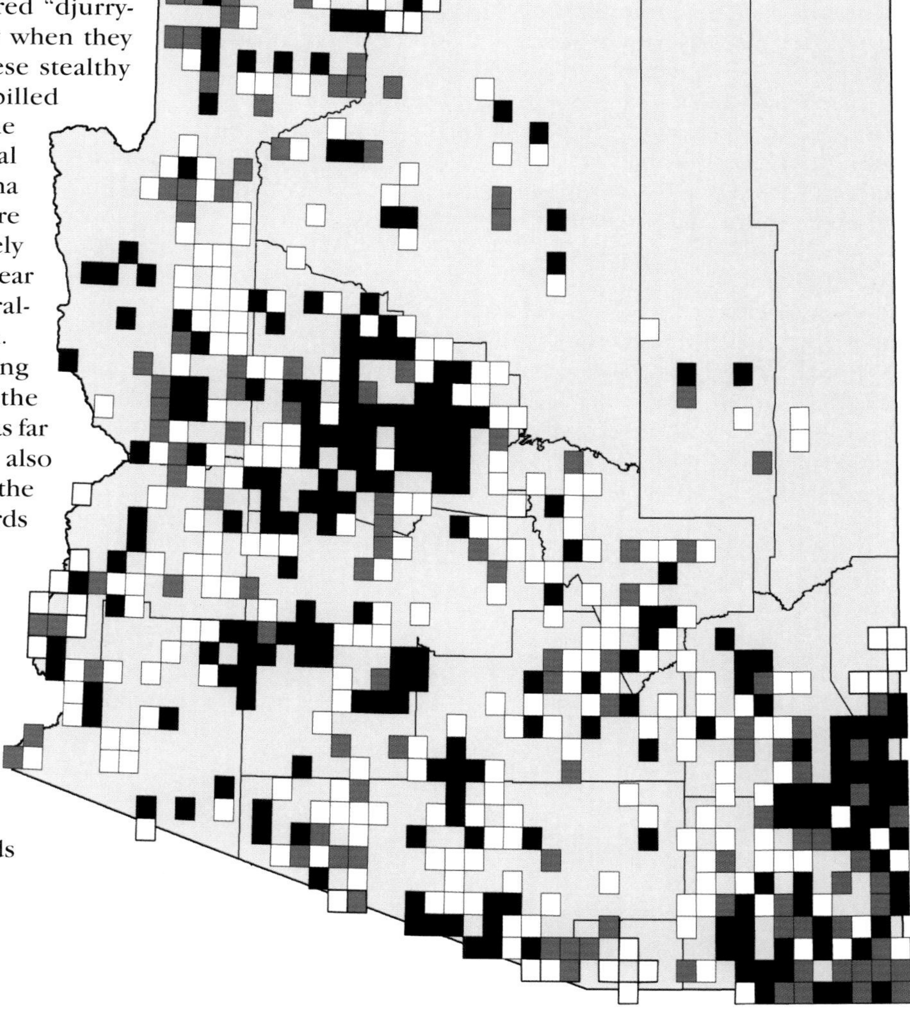

Crissal Thrasher Breeding Evidence Reported in 569 (32%) of 1834 priority blocks

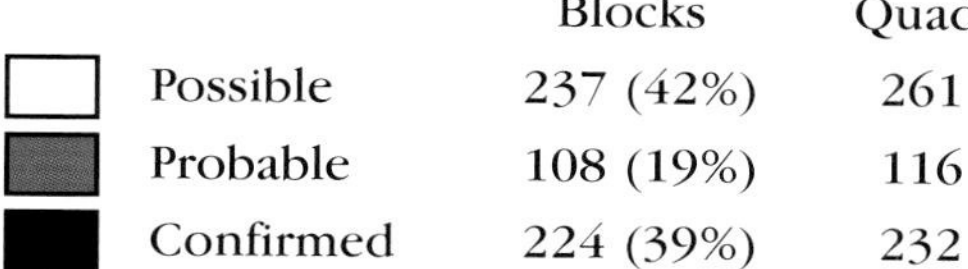

	Blocks	Quads
Possible	237 (42%)	261
Probable	108 (19%)	116
Confirmed	224 (39%)	232

Le Conte's Thrasher

by Troy E. Corman *Toxostoma lecontei*

The Le Conte's Thrasher is a stealthy denizen of some of the hottest, driest, and most desolate expansive desert habitat in Arizona. With tail cocked, it often prefers to run rather than fly, and has perfected the skill of staying out of sight despite its sparsely vegetated environment.

JIM BURNS

HABITAT

Le Conte's Thrashers are unique in Arizona in that their distribution is primarily confined to the most inhospitable and arid regions of the Sonoran Desert. Atlasers noted 87 percent of all Le Conte's Thrasher records were from the more sparsely vegetated lower Sonoran Desert region ($n = 62$). Typical desert habitat consists of open, flat to gently rolling hills and shallow braided washes with very sparse vegetation. In Arizona, common plants include scattered creosote and lower growing shrubs such as littleleaf saltbush, bursage, graythorn, and wolfberry. Trees and larger shrubs are usually very sparingly distributed and can include shrubby mesquite, paloverde, ironwood, ocotillo, or crucifixion thorn. Saguaros are typically absent from Sonoran Desert areas where Le Conte's Thrashers are found. Contrary to habitat descriptions for these thrashers within the deserts of California (Sheppard 1996), cholla is not commonly found in their Arizona range.

BREEDING

Le Conte's Thrashers remain on territory and pair bonds are maintained through constant daily contact with mate (Sheppard 1996). They periodically sing throughout the year, but singing bouts usually peak between December and February in the state. In extreme southwestern Arizona, Le Conte's Thrashers typically begin nest-building activity in late January and early February prior to most atlasers initiating their surveys. Atlasers reported nests with eggs from 2 March–26 May, which falls within the range of 21 February–24 June reported by Bent (1948). However, a very early post-atlas Le Conte's Thrasher nest with 3 eggs was discovered east of Tacna on 8 January (P. Lehman, personal communication). The earliest nest with young reported by atlasers was on 18 March. Since many early nesting efforts were likely missed by atlasers, the peak nesting period is difficult to determine from atlas data. As with other desert nesting thrashers, Le Conte's is influenced by the timing and amount of seasonal rains. These thrashers sing and nest more prevalently during years with higher than normal fall and winter rainfall in Arizona, and may delay nesting in low precipitation years.

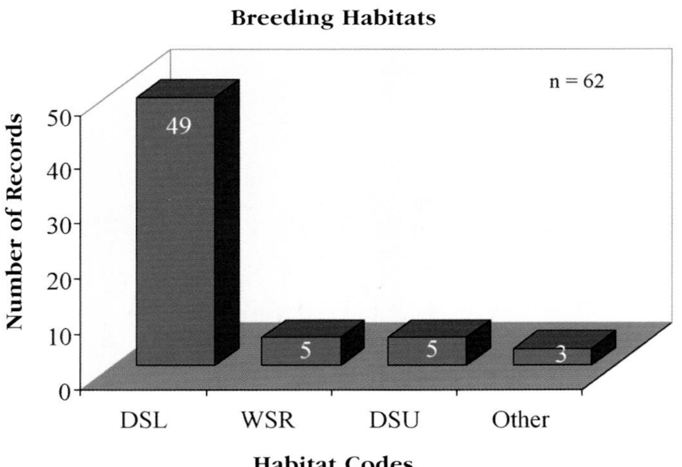

Although both sexes help build the nest, the degree of participation by the male is highly variable (Sheppard 1996). In Arizona, nests are usually built in isolated shrubby trees or large shrubs, which are densely vegetated and usually protected by thorns. These include honey and velvet mesquite, blue and foothill paloverde, ironwood, ocotillo, and crucifixion thorn. Several nests were discovered in dense wolfberry growing in the shade of a mesquite. In California, a high percentage of nests are found in cholla and saltbushes (Bent 1948; Sheppard 1996). However, only one of the 19 nests described by atlas field crews was in a cholla. The median height of these nests was 3.9 ft (1.2 m) and ranged from 1.8 to 6.3 ft (0.5–1.9 m). The nest of twigs cradles a distinctive, well-padded cup of pale, fuzzy plant seeds, leaves, or flowers, a unique trait not found in any other desert nesting thrasher species (Sheppard 1996). One or more nests from previous years, in various stages of disarray, are sometimes located in the same tree or shrub and are often near active nests.

Le Conte's Thrashers lay a typical egg clutch of 3–4 eggs (range 2–5; Sheppard 1996). Both sexes share the duty of incubation and intensive studies of this thrasher in

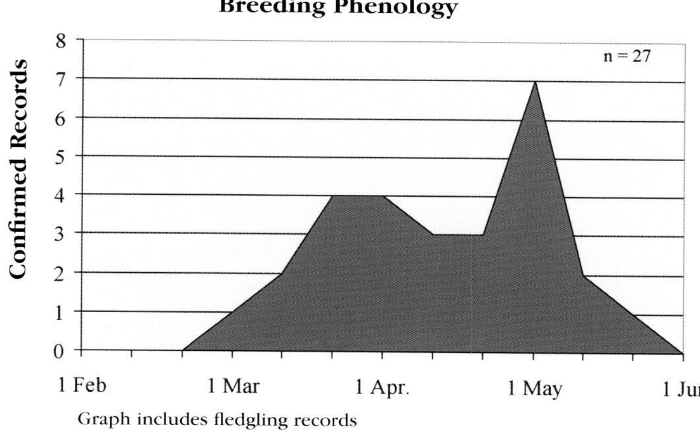

California revealed an incubating period of 14–19 days, with the young fledging approximately 15 days later (Sheppard 1996). Parents continue to feed the young for approximately 15–18 days after nest departure. Le Conte's Thrashers average 2–3 nesting attempts per year, with some pairs successfully fledgling young from all three broods (Sheppard 1996).

DISTRIBUTION AND STATUS

The Le Conte's Thrasher is resident from southeastern California, southern Nevada, and extreme southwestern Utah south to northeastern Baja California and western Sonora. In Arizona, it is found in extreme western and southwestern Arizona east up the Gila River valley to the Florence and Picacho Peak regions (Phillips et al. 1964). They were also previously reported in the Avra Valley of northern Pima County (Monson and Phillips 1981), although this thrasher has not been detected in this region since the 1980s. In the Sonoran Desert, atlasers found Le Conte's Thrasher at elevations ranging from 150 to 1500 ft (46–457 m), where it reaches the highest elevations at the eastern edge of its range near Florence and Picacho Reservoir.

Noteworthy discoveries during the atlas were of small, isolated populations of Le Conte's Thrashers in the Mojave Desert along the Sacramento Valley west of Kingman and within the lower Detrital Valley south of Lake Mead. These Mojave Desert populations were at higher elevations than those in the Sonoran Desert with an elevation range of 1800–3240 ft (550–990 m). In 1865, Elliott Coues collected the only specimen in this region, which previously had been considered a vagrant or migrant (Phillips et al. 1964). Atlasers were unable to document its continued occurrence in the extreme northwest near Littlefield, as noted by Phillips et al. (1964).

The largest populations of Le Conte's Thrashers in Arizona are found on the Cabeza Prieta National Wildlife Refuge and the Barry M. Goldwater Range, where there is limited human access and disturbance. However, the preferred habitat of these thrashers continues to be seriously threatened by urban sprawl and agriculture at the eastern edge of their range. Many populations in the middle Gila River valley are now confined to isolated pockets surrounded by agriculture and rapidly encroaching urban development. Phillips et al. (1964) noted that they are intolerant of man and his activities and had retreated from newly farmed areas of central Arizona. This area includes the Gila River Indian Community where Rea (1983) noted that if the tribe continued to permit more mechanized farming and other nontribal activities onto the reservation, this thrasher was bound to disappear.

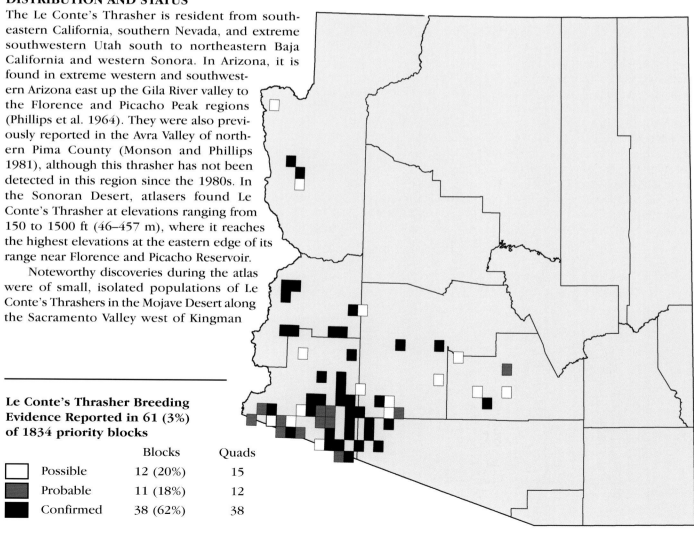

Le Conte's Thrasher Breeding Evidence Reported in 61 (3%) of 1834 priority blocks

	Blocks	Quads
Possible	12 (20%)	15
Probable	11 (18%)	12
Confirmed	38 (62%)	38

European Starling

by Cathryn Wise-Gervais *Sturnus vulgaris*

In 1890–1891, a hundred European Starlings were released in New York City's Central Park, no one suspecting that these adaptable birds would quickly spread across the continent. This noisy, aggressive species displaces native birds from nest cavities and destroys their eggs. As a result, European Starlings are considered an unwelcome pest wherever they occur.

HABITAT

Although found in a wide variety of habitats, European Starlings are most numerous in or near human settlements. These birds select areas that provide both open, short grassy localities for foraging and trees or human-made structures for roosting and nesting. Atlasers reported European Starlings in twenty-three habitat types, but they obtained 55 percent of records in rural, agricultural, and urban areas statewide (n = 348). Their close association with humans is also apparent in their native Europe (Cabe 1993). Adjacent to human settlements, observers reported European Starlings breeding in Sonoran desertscrub and along desert dry washes containing tall saguaros for nesting (22 percent of records). The birds also nest regularly in nearby open riparian woodlands containing tall deciduous trees with cavities, such as cottonwood, willow, and sycamore (13 percent of records). European Starlings generally avoid large expanses of undisturbed native vegetation, including deserts, forests, woodlands, and brushy areas; they prefer to forage in mowed or grazed fields, pastures, or lawns (Cabe 1993). In both urban and native landscapes in Arizona, European Starlings commonly nest in trees or saguaros by aggressively displacing resident woodpeckers and other cavity nesting birds. Urban nesting Gila Woodpeckers are particularly vulnerable.

BREEDING

European Starlings reside in Arizona year-round and can initiate breeding activities quite early. Males typically select nest sites and collect some material prior to acquiring mates (Cabe 1993). This activity may account for an atlas observation of an adult carrying nesting material on 16 January. Royall (1966) reported that pair formation begins by mid- to late February in Arizona when nest building begins in earnest. Most atlas surveys were not conducted until later in the spring so the earliest breeding records were probably not well represented. Atlasers did report the first European Starling fledgling on 1 April, suggesting that egg laying was initiated by late February. Occupied nests were noted by 12 March. Atlasers reported European Starling nests with young from 12 April to 1 July. Atlas data suggest that European Starling breeding activity in Arizona peaks in early May followed by a sharp decline into the summer months. One individual was observed carrying nesting material on 8 July, but only fledglings were reported thereafter into August. An occupied nest was reported on 10 September, but this observation was more likely a roosting bird.

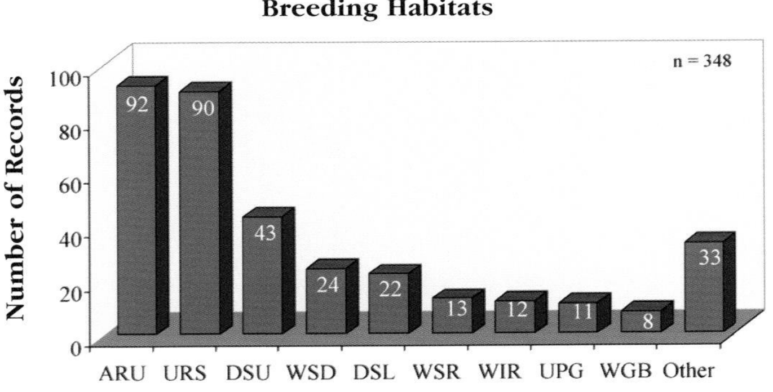

European Starlings are highly opportunistic in many aspects of their life history, including in their nest site choice. These birds will nest almost anywhere a cavity can be found, including in buildings or other human-made structures, nest boxes, and in tree or cliff cavities (Cabe 1993). In southern Arizona, they will also commonly nest among the frond bases of untrimmed palm trees and in saguaro cavities (Royall 1966). Rather social birds, three or more pairs may nest in one saguaro containing many cavities. Bent (1950) noted nests are commonly 10–25 ft (3–7.6 m) above ground, but can range to 60 ft (18.3 m). The female often removes nest material provided earlier by the male and begins afresh, with both sexes building together (Cabe 1993). European Starlings commonly usurp active nests of other species and in such instances will discard previous nest materials and destroy clutches.

Typical European Starlings clutches consist of 4–5 eggs and often engage in intraspecific egg dumping, especially if

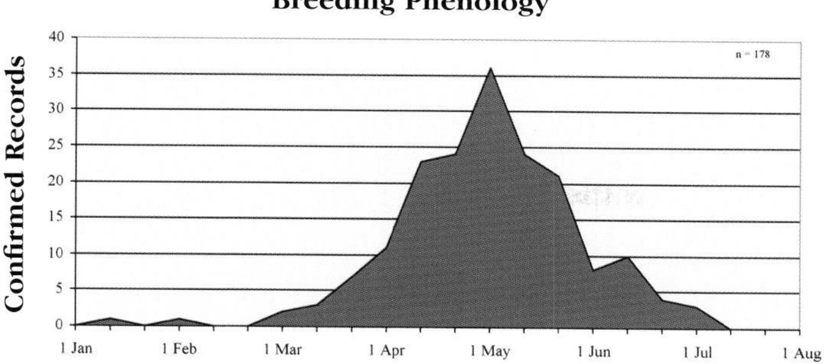

a nest is lost during egg laying (Feare 1991; Cabe 1993). Both sexes incubate the eggs for about 12 days, but the male's participation is typically less (Cabe 1993). In monogamous pairs, both parents brood and feed the young. Second mates of polygynous pairs feed alone, and males alone may feed young if their mate disappears (Cabe 1993). The young fledge at 21–23 days after hatching and continue to be fed by adults for up to 10–12 days (Feare 1984). European Starlings usually raise two broods per season (Cabe 1993). They aggressively defend their nest sites and are rare Brown-headed Cowbird hosts (Friedmann et al. 1977).

DISTRIBUTION AND STATUS

The European Starling's native breeding range covers much of Eurasia, with wintering areas extending into northern Africa. Amazingly, this species required little more than a century to colonize much of the North American continent and today is found from coast to coast. European Starlings are residents from southern Alaska and northern Canada south into northern Mexico, and may actually be expanding its range farther south into Mexico (Cabe 1993).

European Starlings were first reported in Arizona near Lupton in 1946, and the first nest in the state was in Glendale in 1954 (Phillips et al. 1964). They apparently did not become common in northern Arizona until after 1965 (Monson and Phillips 1981). In a relatively short period, the species colonized much of the state and today the species is commonly encountered in most rural and urban centers. Atlasers confirmed this adaptable species nesting over a wide range of elevations from approximately 100 to 8400 ft (30–2560 m). Although atlasers found that European Starlings reached their highest breeding density in and around Phoenix and Tucson, they also regularly found the birds in smaller towns, communities, and even in some isolated ranches and tribal villages. In addition, many smaller nesting populations were undoubtedly missed while conducting atlas surveys due to the location of randomly chosen priority blocks and the reluctance of atlasers to report them as casual observations. In many cases, observers simply ignored these birds outside of priority blocks! European Starlings were reported less frequently in the more sparsely populated northern third of the state. They went unreported in the Grand Canyon region where Brown et al. (1987) considered them common residents near permanently occupied human habitations.

Apparently increasing statewide, European Starlings will probably continue on an upward trend, given the rate of growth in the state. As human settlements appear and expand in previously undisturbed areas of Arizona, this aggressive and highly social invader will undoubtedly follow soon after.

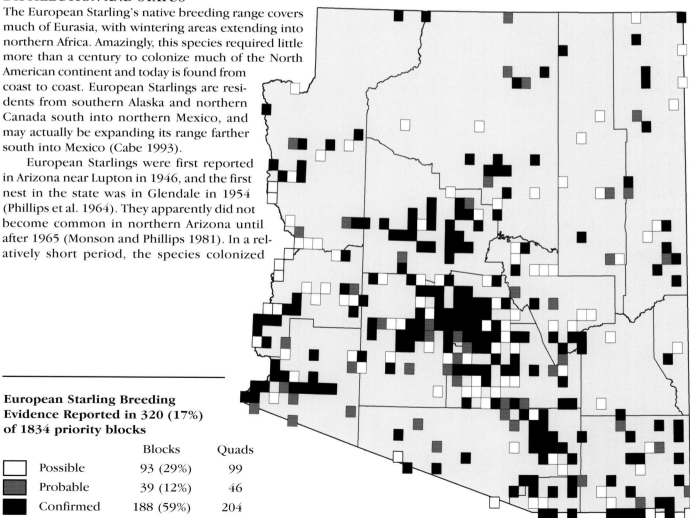

European Starling Breeding Evidence Reported in 320 (17%) of 1834 priority blocks

	Blocks	Quads
Possible	93 (29%)	99
Probable	39 (12%)	46
Confirmed	188 (59%)	204

Phainopepla

by Cathryn Wise-Gervais *Phainopepla nitens*

Phainopepla means, "shining robe" and refers to the male's silky black plumage. These ruby-eyed birds are closely associated with mistletoe, and regularly disperse this parasitic plant. Phainopeplas also have a dual breeding season and will nest in early spring in the desert and later in summer at higher elevations.

DAN FISCHER

HABITAT

Phainopeplas are southwestern birds that are closely tied to mistletoe during most of the year and have a curious breeding cycle that is still not well understood. They inhabit and nest in two distinctly different habitats annually in Arizona. These birds nest in the desert in late winter and early spring when mistletoe berry production peaks, and then nest in open woodlands at higher elevations in late spring and summer.

Atlasers reported Phainopeplas in twenty-eight habitat types across Arizona. The birds reach their highest breeding densities in desert washes characterized by dense stands of paloverde, mesquite, and ironwood. Occupied stands typically contain clumps of mistletoe and these arid wooded drainages accounted for 28 percent of the potential breeding records (n = 894). Observers reported an additional 30 percent of records in the surrounding Sonoran desertscrub where nesting trees are more scattered and the landscape is more open. Fifteen percent of atlas records were obtained in mesquite bosques and riparian woodland associations containing cottonwood, willow, ash, hackberry, and sycamore. Atlasers obtained fewer nesting records in pinyon pine–juniper woodlands, Madrean evergreen oak woodlands, semiarid grasslands, and in both Mojave and Chihuahuan desertscrub associations.

BREEDING

Phainopeplas reside year-round in Arizona, but make seasonal movements as mentioned above. Desert-nesting activities can begin as early as late February and continue through April and into May. As temperatures increase and mistletoe berry production decreases, the birds depart from the desert. They begin nesting in riparian and mountain foothill woodlands in May and continue through July and into August (Chu and Walsberg 1999). More research is needed to determine if all birds attempt to raise two broods or if two distinct populations exist, one nesting early in the deserts, the second nesting later in the woodlands.

Atlasers first reported an occupied Phainopepla nest on 15 February in the desert, and first reported breeding outside of lowland desert areas on 1 May, when adults were observed carrying nesting materials. Observers reported nests with eggs statewide from 16 March to 1 July and located nests with young from 14 March to 12 July. Atlas data suggest that Phainopepla breeding activities peak from mid- to late April and most of these records were of desert-nesting birds. Although breeding activity statewide during the atlas period continued until mid-August, atlasers did not obtain as many confirmations later in the season. It is unclear if this was because the birds are easier to confirm in the deserts compared to woodlands or if there are simply more Phainopeplas breeding in the former rather than the latter.

Male Phainopeplas select nest sites and construct much of the nests, sometimes even before finding a mate (Rand and Rand 1943). These nests are neat and compact cuplike structures and seem surprisingly small compared to the size of the bird. Common nest trees include paloverde, mesquite, acacia, oaks, and sycamore (Walsberg 1977). Atlasers took measurements at 121 Phainopepla nests in 17 tree species, including those listed above. The most commonly reported nest trees were in two species of paloverde (48 percent of nests), mesquite (17 percent), acacia (10 percent), and ironwood (9 percent). Other regularly used trees included juniper, pinyon pine, and walnut. Unusual nest sites included cholla and ponderosa pine. Thirteen of the nests (11 percent) were constructed within

Breeding Habitats

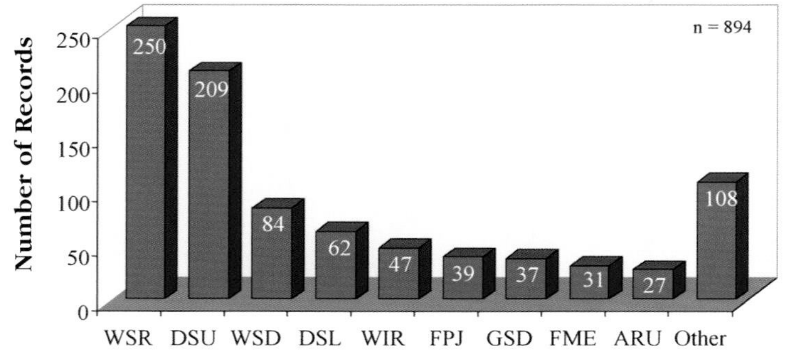

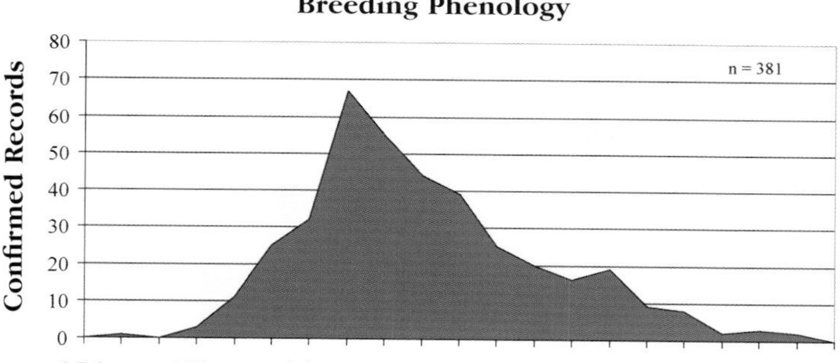

mistletoe clumps. The median nest height of 121 nests was 7.9 ft (2.4 m) and ranged from 3.3 to 32.8 ft (1–10 m).

Phainopeplas typically lay 2–3 eggs (range 2–4), and both adults share incubation duties for a period lasting approximately 14 days (Chu and Walsberg 1999). Both adults feed and brood the young, which remain in the nest for approximately 14–19 days (Chu and Walsberg 1999). Desert and woodland breeders both raise one brood each but will renest if their first attempt fails. Although the species is known as an uncommon Brown-headed Cowbird host, observers did not report any incidents of cowbird parasitism during the atlas period.

DISTRIBUTION AND STATUS

Phainopeplas occur primarily in the southwestern portion of North America primarily from northern California (where local) southeast through southern Nevada, Arizona, southern New Mexico and southwest Texas (Chu and Walsberg 1999). They breed south through the central plateau of Mexico, Sonora, and Baja California. In Arizona, atlasers took measurements at Phainopepla nests at elevations from 130 to 6380 ft (40–1945 m).

In describing the Phainopepla's range in Arizona, Phillips et al. (1964) stated that "Phainopeplas have no respect for the rules" and went on to describe two sometimes overlapping ranges, used in alternate seasons. They breed throughout southwestern Arizona east to Tucson in the spring and in the southeast and north to Sedona during the summer months (Monson and Phillips 1981). Scattered breeding records were previously reported near Snowflake, and possible breeding records have been obtained near Mount Trumbull (Monson and Phillips 1981).

Atlasers found the species to occur widely throughout southern and western Arizona at one time or another during the breeding season. However, the birds apparently do not adapt well to human-altered landscapes and were notably absent in extensive agricultural regions and in many urban areas in the state. Atlasers noted Phainopeplas breeding north along the lower San Francisco and Blue Rivers and into the Salt River Canyon. Nesting birds were found in northwestern Arizona near Williams, north of Seligman, and in the Mojave Desert region north to the Virgin River. During the atlas period, observers noted Phainopeplas regularly along the Colorado River in the Grand Canyon to above Lava Falls. Brown et al. (1987) considered this species as uncommon upstream to Phantom Ranch. They were encountered nesting sparingly north of the forested Mogollon Rim region and within the Little Colorado River valley.

Although atlasers regularly encountered Phainopeplas throughout their historic range, Breeding Bird Survey data suggest a declining trend in Arizona from 1980 to 1996. Nevertheless, these fascinating birds remain quite common and conspicuous in many regions of the state.

Phainopepla Breeding Evidence Reported in 882 (48%) of 1834 priority blocks

	Blocks	Quads
Possible	199 (23%)	214
Probable	186 (21%)	190
Confirmed	497 (56%)	500

Olive Warbler

by Troy E. Corman *Peucedramus taeniatus*

Those who do not know the songs and unique calls of the Olive Warbler may let many individuals pass by unnoticed. Pairs often forage loosely and constantly together, keeping themselves high in the upper canopy of pines and firs while frequently emitting soft contact calls. These mysterious passerines continue to keep many aspects of their life history a secret.

RICK AND NORA BOWERS

HABITAT

Olive Warblers are closely associated with open pine forests particularly those on mountain slopes and ridge containing ponderosa pine. Approximately 60 percent of all atlas records were reported in ponderosa pine–dominated forest, including those with a Gambel's oak component (n = 62). These warblers were also encountered fairly regularly in mixed-conifer forests containing various species of pines, Douglas fir, and white fir. In southeastern Arizona, atlasers reported Olive Warblers most frequently in Madrean pine-oak forests dominated by Chihuahuan, Apache, and ponderosa pine, with an understory of various species of Madrean evergreen oaks, alligator juniper, and Arizona madrone. Marshall (1956) found them more common in white fir than in pine in the Rincon Mountains.

BREEDING

In Arizona, the migratory populations of the Olive Warblers begin to arrive in March, peaking in early April when territories are quickly established. Males were heard singing from late March through the end of July. The earliest confirmed atlas record was nest-building activity on 13 April in southeastern Arizona. Atlasers reported an adult carrying food on 10 May, suggesting clutch initiation as early as late April. Likely because of the birds' lofty and well-concealed nesting location, atlasers reported few active nests and were unable to determine nest contents. In Arizona, most nests with eggs have previously been found from 23 May to 1 July, with nests with young observed through late July (Bent 1953; Lowther and Nocedal 1997). The first fledgling reported by atlasers was observed being fed by adults on 25 May, and this behavior was noted through 23 July. However, an extremely late nesting effort was suggested in the Huachuca Mountains when an adult pair was observed feeding a begging fledgling on 7 October (S. Healy, personal communication).

In Arizona, observations of Olive Warblers typically begin to diminish in late September. However, during late summer through winter, small groups of Olive Warblers can often be found associating in mixed foraging flocks that include other species of warblers, vireos, chickadees, nuthatches, and kinglets (Lowther and Nocedal 1997).

Apparently, the female Olive Warbler constructs the compact nest while the male accompanies her (Lowther and Nocedal 1997). In Arizona, nests are placed in conifers, including ponderosa pine, Chihuahuan pine, Apache pine, southwestern white pine, and Douglas fir. Nests are usually built in terminal needles of branch, well away from the trunk and 20–70 ft (6.1–21.3 m) above the ground (Brandt 1951; Bent 1953; Lowther and Nocedal 1997). Clumps of mistletoe are also often used for placing their nests (Bent 1953). Atlasers noted one female with an accompanying male collecting caterpillar webbing from a Gambel's oak.

Typical clutches consist of 3–4 eggs (Bent 1953), and most evidence suggests that only the female incubates. However, the male Olive Warbler has been observed feeding the incubating female (Lowther and Nocedal 1997). There is no information on the length of incubation or nestling stages, but the young are known to remain with their parents after fledging and often through the fall and winter (Lowther and Nocedal 1997). There are no records of second broods for Olive Warblers, although the lengthy nesting season would suggest that this is possible.

Previous literature noted that cowbird brood parasitism was unrecorded for Olive Warbler (Dunn and Garrett 1997; Lowther and Nocedal 1997). However, atlasers did observe

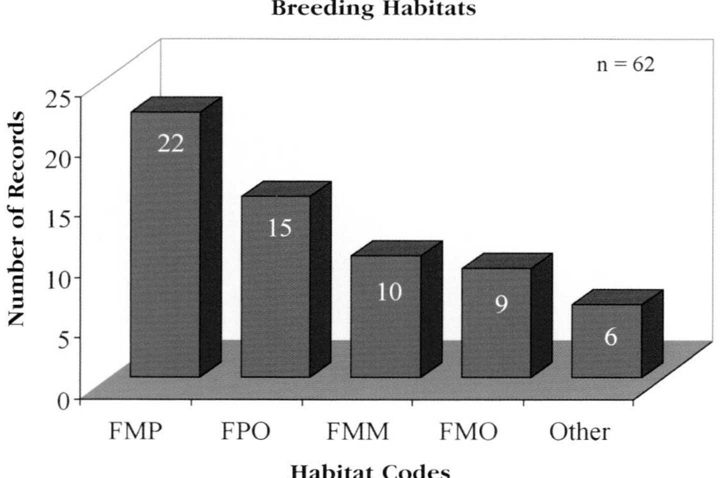

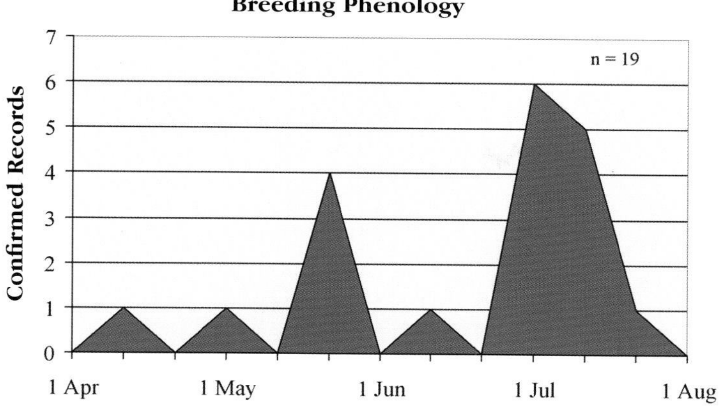

an adult feeding a Brown-headed Cowbird fledgling on 14 July 2000 along the Mogollon Rim west of Show Low.

DISTRIBUTION AND STATUS

The Olive Warbler is mainly a resident from central Arizona and southeastern New Mexico south to Nicaragua, but at least part (if not most) of Arizona's population migrates south of the state for the winter. Earlier accounts of this warbler in Arizona described it as a fairly common summer resident to the higher southeastern mountain ranges, north along the southern edge of the Mogollon Rim to near Payson (Phillips et al. 1964). Monson and Phillips (1981) later reported that the range of this species had expanded northwestward to include the Sierra Prieta just west of Prescott and Bill Williams Mountain south of Williams. This expanded distribution included the Bradshaw and Pinal mountains, as well as a single record from the San Francisco Mountains near Flagstaff, where they were previously noted as absent.

Atlasers found Olive Warblers to be fairly common summer residents at higher elevations between 6400 and 9500 ft (1951–2896 m) throughout their previous described range. Observers also encountered this warbler from the Santa Maria Mountains in northwestern Yavapai County to the San Francisco Mountains and Kendrick Peak area. Both these sites are farther northwest than previously reported, which supports the steady northern range expansion first noted in the mid-1970s (Monson and Phillips 1981). Atlas surveyors also documented this species in the Galiuro and Santa Teresa mountains in southeastern Graham County, where they previously had not been reported. These two isolated mountain ranges are difficult to access and have had few avian surveys.

Olive Warblers are likely more common along the entire Mogollon Rim region than atlas data suggest. However, they are apparently more local and much less common than Grace's and Yellow-rumped Warblers using the same habitat. It is also very likely that some atlasers were unfamiliar with its songs and calls and likely missed this unique species. Atlasers were unable to conduct surveys on the White Mountain Apache tribal lands in eastern Gila and southern Navajo and Apache counties, where the species undoubtedly breeds among the extensive conifer forests.

Olive Warblers are an adaptable species, and most populations in Arizona are likely stable or locally slightly increasing. Population densities appear to be much higher in ponderosa pine forests in southeastern Arizona, than farther north near Flagstaff. Balda (1969) found 5.6 pairs/25 ac (10 ha) in the Coronado National Forest, while Rosenstock (1996) reported less than 1 pair/25 ac (10 ha) in Coconino National Forest.

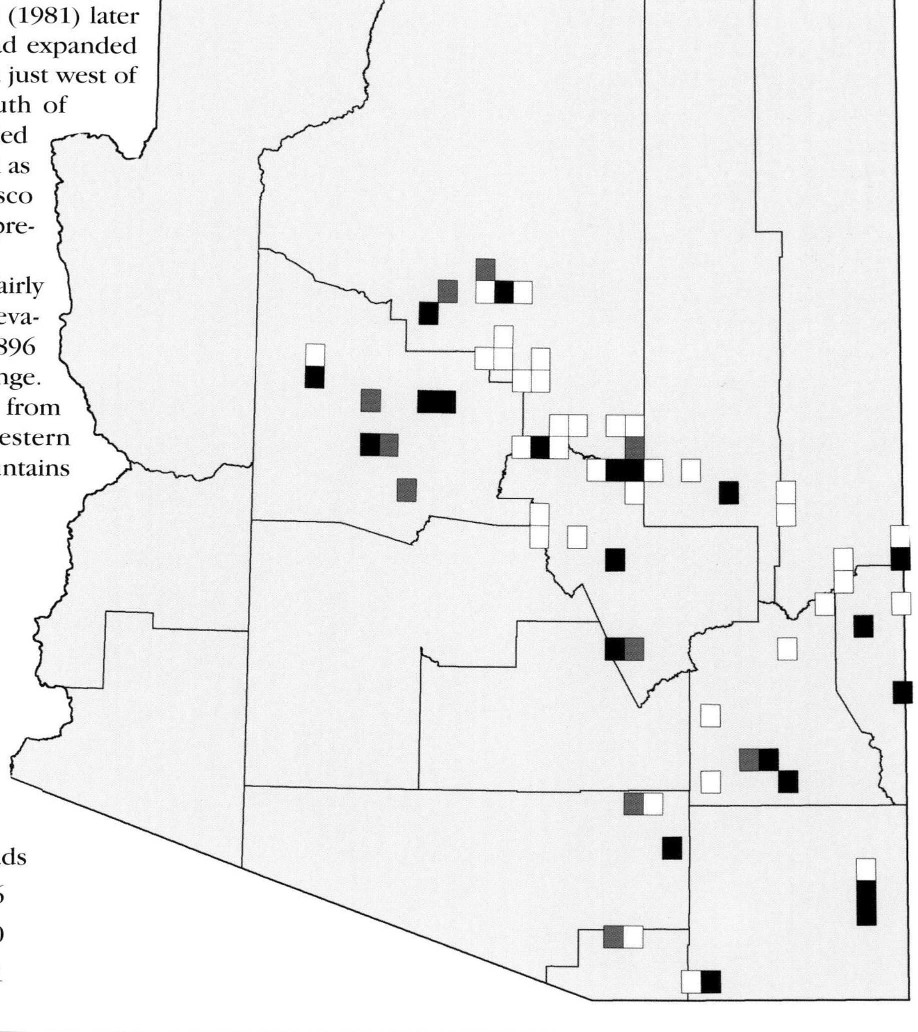

Olive Warbler Breeding Evidence Reported in 46 (3%) of 1834 priority blocks

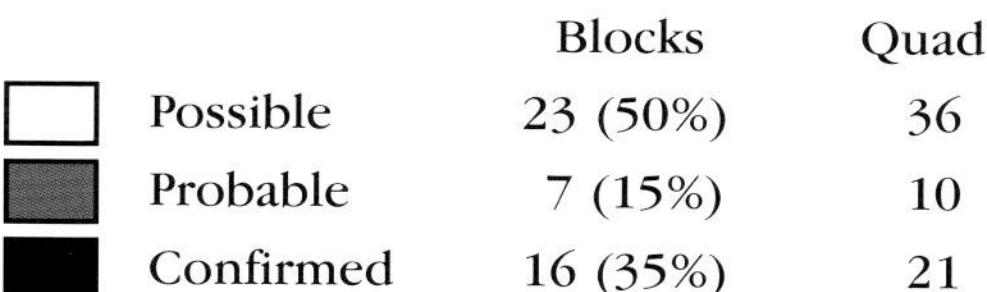

	Blocks	Quads
Possible	23 (50%)	36
Probable	7 (15%)	10
Confirmed	16 (35%)	21

Orange-crowned Warbler

by Troy E. Corman *Vermivora celata*

The brightly colored cap that gives the otherwise obscurely marked Orange-crowned Warbler its name is seldom visible. In Arizona, these hardy greenish warblers are nowhere numerous during the nesting season, but seasonally they become locally abundant during migration or as a winter resident in lowland riparian woodlands and thickets.

JIM BURNS

HABITAT

In Arizona, Orange-crowned Warblers prefer to nest in cooler, montane habitats with a significant deciduous tree and shrub component. Most breeding observations in the state are from mountain drainage bottoms, but they are also found nesting locally on moist, high-elevation slopes. Atlasers reported 64 percent of all Orange-crowned Warbler records in cool, moist mountain drainages and open mixed-conifer covered slopes dominated by quaking aspen, Douglas fir, white fir, Gambel's oak, bigtooth maple, and New Mexico locust (n = 28). They were also noted along higher boreal drainages adjacent to spruce-fir or mixed-conifer forests within dense thickets of Geyer willow, Bebb willow, and thinleaf alder.

Several additional atlas observations were from forest stands dominated by quaking aspen, open spruce-fir forests, and locally in large, dense stands of Gambel's oak and New Mexico locust. Similarly, atlasers encountered Orange-crowned Warblers defending dense thickets of deciduous montane shrubs, including oaks, locusts, and maples on steep mountain ridges and slopes recovering from past forest fires.

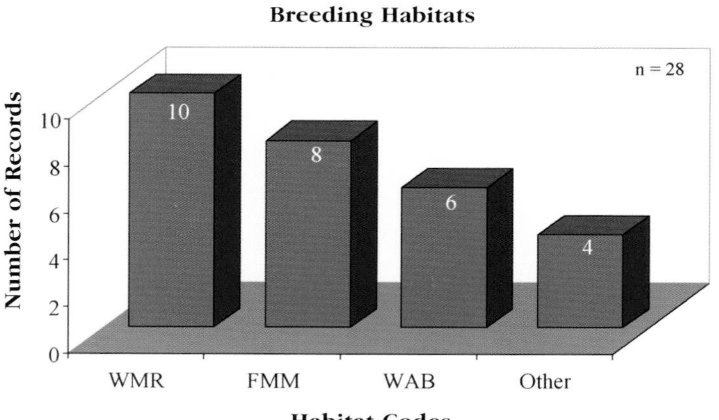

BREEDING

Generally an uncommon to common wintering species in southern and western Arizona, Orange-crowned Warblers begin migrating north in March, with a peak passage in April and stragglers well into May. They arrive on their breeding ground in the state by early to mid-April. Male Orange-crowned Warblers begin singing and establishing territories shortly after their arrival. In Arizona, nest construction can begin during the final days of April and in early May (Zyskowski 1993). Of 115 Orange-crowned Warbler nests discovered along the Mogollon Rim of Arizona, the mean date for the initiation of egg laying was 23 May, with a range from 3 May to 21 June (Zyskowski 1993). Peak nesting activity in Arizona likely occurs from mid-May through mid-June. The earliest atlas confirmation was of a nest with young discovered on 30 May. Atlasers observed adults feeding fledglings from 3 June to 12 July. Later nesting attempts likely fledge young in late July, with a few adults tending young into early August. In Arizona, Orange-crowned Warblers begin appearing away from nesting areas by early August, becoming common by late August and September. Stragglers are occasionally reported in northern Arizona through late November (C. LaRue, personal communication).

Nests of Orange-crowned Warblers are typically well concealed and on the ground, occasionally in a tree or shrub (Sogge et al. 1994). Little information can be gained from the single nest noted during the atlas period. However, from intensive research on the Mogollon Rim of Arizona, Zyskowski (1993) described the nest site selection of Orange-crowned Warblers. All but 3 of 138 nests were place on the ground, with most directly under woody plant stems. Fifty-nine percent were under bigtooth maple, 23 percent under New Mexico locust, and 18 percent under coniferous species. They were found using habitats with a higher humidity, greater pine density, and few fir saplings. The three nests above the ground were placed 0.6–10.5 ft (2–3.2 m) high on horizontal limbs of white fir and in a natural cavity of a maple.

The following nesting phenology was taken from studies conducted by Zyskowski (1993) and Sogge et al. (1994).

Female Orange-crowned Warblers construct their nests in approximately 3–5 days and usually lay the first egg 2–3 days after the nests are completed. The female incubates the typical clutch of 4–5 eggs for 12–14 days. Both parents feed the nestlings, which depart the nest in 12–13 days and continue feeding the young for an undermined period following fledging. Orange-crowned Warblers usually produce only one brood per season, but they will renest if earlier attempts have failed.

DISTRIBUTION AND STATUS

Orange-crowned Warblers nest across Canada and in western North America from Alaska, down the Rocky Mountains and other interior ranges and higher plateau to central Arizona and New Mexico. They reach their southern nesting limits in several southeastern Arizona and western Texas mountain ranges. Along the Pacific Coast, these warblers nest south to northern Baja California.

Earlier accounts of Orange-crowned Warblers in Arizona described them as a fairly common, local summer resident in the higher elevations of the White, Pinaleno, and Santa Catalina mountains (Phillips et al. 1964). Orange-crowned Warblers were later suspected of also nesting sparingly near Mormon Lake southeast of Flagstaff, and in the San Francisco, Chuska, Pinal, and Bill Williams mountains (Monson and Phillips 1981). These warblers were noted as fairly common summer residents in the upper canyons of Black Mesa south of Kayenta, where first confirmed nesting in 1983 (LaRue 1994). In the late 1980s, these warblers were also discovered nesting locally in snowmelt drainages flowing north from the Mogollon Rim, north of the town of Christopher Creek (T. Martin, personal communication).

Detected throughout most of their previously document nesting location in the state, atlasers found Orange-crowned Warblers to be local, but a more widespread nesting species than earlier literature suggests. They were noted nesting at elevations ranging from approximately 7000 ft (2133 m) to above 10,000 ft (3048 m) in the Inner Basin of the San Francisco Mountains. Atlasers detected multiple singing Orange-crowned Warblers in June along the southeast rim of the Kaibab Plateau near Saddle Mountain and locality on the western slope of this plateau near Big Springs. They were also encountered and suspected of breeding in the Carrizo Mountains in extreme northern Apache County. To the southwest, these warblers were detected on Sitgreaves Mountain northeast of Williams, and confirmed nesting in the upper West Fork of Oak Creek Canyon northwest of Sedona and near Mount Union in the Bradshaw Mountains.

In Arizona, most breeding populations of Orange-crowned Warblers appear to be rather small and quite local. Therefore, they could have been easily missed on atlas blocks while conducting surveys, particularly in rugged regions with many small canyons and steep slopes. Their rapid, trilling songs are also unremarkable and are easily lost among the chorus of other warblers in their preferred habitat. Orange-crowned Warblers likely breed in additional pockets of appropriate habitat in higher, remote mountain ranges and plateaus in northern Arizona, as well as in canyons and drainages along the Mogollon Rim. This includes within the White Mountain Apache tribal lands, where access to conduct atlas surveys was not granted.

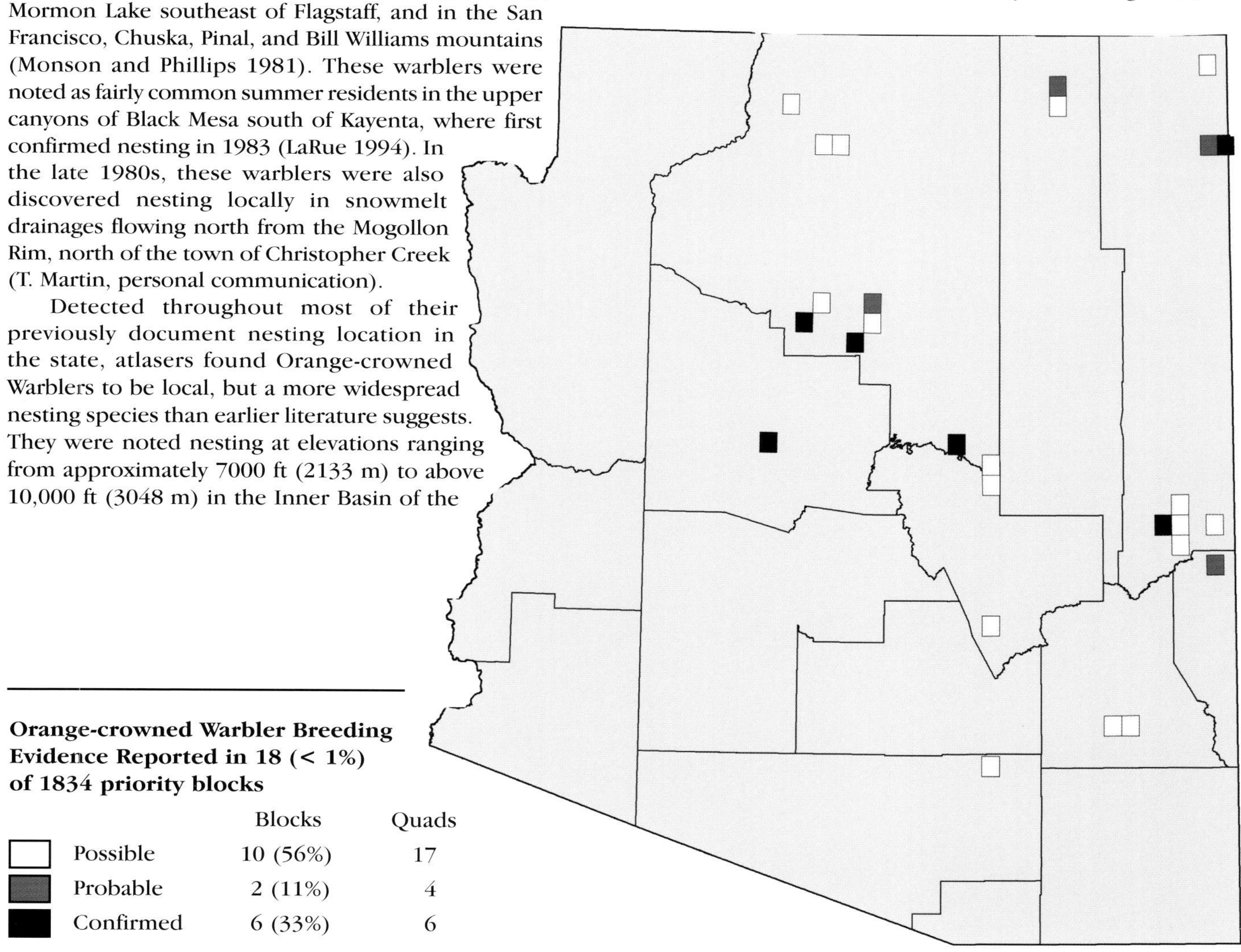

Orange-crowned Warbler Breeding Evidence Reported in 18 (< 1%) of 1834 priority blocks

	Blocks	Quads
Possible	10 (56%)	17
Probable	2 (11%)	4
Confirmed	6 (33%)	6

Virginia's Warbler

by Cathryn Wise-Gervais *Vermivora virginiae*

Dr. W. Anderson first discovered Virginia's Warblers in 1858, and the species was later named after his wife. Although Arizona birders commonly encounter this bird singing or foraging in mid-elevation woodlands and in steep, brushy canyons, there is still much to learn about this timid warbler's natural history.

HABITAT

Although Virginia's Warblers are known to occur in a variety of habitats, they are commonly thought of as a pinyon pine–juniper or mid-elevation oak woodland species. These birds rarely, if ever, breed in pure conifer forest and instead favor a scrubby deciduous component integrated into their preferred woodlands (Olson and Martin 1999). In Arizona, occupied habitats are often found within canyons, along drainages, or on steep mountain slopes and frequently have some oak component. Atlasers reported Virginia's Warblers in 18 different vegetative communities, with no more than 17 percent of records in any given habitat (n = 248). Approximately half of all atlas records were fairly evenly distributed within three forest habitats: mixed-conifer, ponderosa pine–oak, and montane riparian areas. These forests often include pines, firs, and deciduous trees such as Gambel's oak, New Mexico locust, and maple. South of the Mogollon Rim, Virginia's Warblers also frequently inhabit woodlands containing evergreen oaks, including brushy sycamore-lined drainages and the Madrean pine-oak forests of southeastern mountain ranges. Virginia's Warblers are also encountered on shrubby deciduous slopes within pinyon pine–juniper woodlands and in areas of dense chaparral. At higher elevations, these warblers tend to select open forests slopes and edges where light penetrates the shrubby understory they favor (Olson and Martin 1999). Virginia's Warblers were also confirmed nesting locally along boreal drainages in dense thickets of Geyer willow and alder.

Breeding Habitats

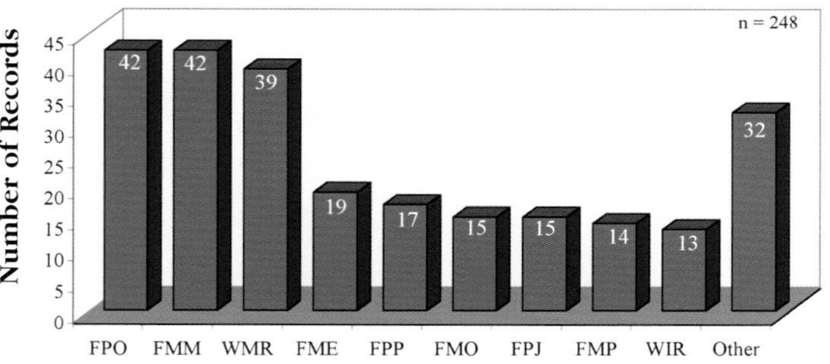

Habitat Codes

BREEDING

Virginia's Warblers begin arriving in southern Arizona in late March but do not reach the Mogollon Rim until late April (Olson and Martin 1999). Males typically arrive a week before the females to begin establishing territories, and pairing occurs as soon as females arrive. Atlasers first reported Virginia's Warblers singing in suitable breeding habitat in late March and early April. Observers noted birds carrying nesting material on 1 May, but nest construction can begin by late April in Arizona, with early egg-laying initiation by 30 April (Olson and Martin 1999). Atlasers first located a nest with young on 19 May and obtained sixty-one breeding confirmations for Virginia's Warblers, not including fledgling records. Active nests are difficult to find, and observers discovered only two nests with eggs and six nests with young from 19 May to 6 July. Atlas data suggest that breeding activities in Arizona peak in early June but continue through most of July. In keeping with atlas data, the mean clutch initiation date for 226 nests monitored on the Mogollon Rim in Arizona was 30 May (Olson and Martin 1999). Atlasers reported adults feeding fledglings through the end of July. Departure from Arizona breeding areas begins in late July with peak southbound passage occurring between mid-August and mid-September. Individuals rarely linger in Arizona past late September.

Virginia's Warblers nest on the ground, usually under a grass clump or in a woody shrub. Nests are frequently placed on sloping terrain. In Arizona, the birds often choose New Mexico locust- or oak-dominated sites, which indicate more open, drier, and warmer locations (Martin 1998). Atlasers described only five Virginia's Warbler nests, and two of these were placed beneath unidentified shrubs. The remaining nests were under a grass clump, alligator juniper, and silverleaf oak. Nests in Arizona have also been reported under maples, firs, oaks, or logs (Horton 1987; Martin 1998).

Both the male and female Virginia's Warblers are thought to select the nest site together, but it is the female that builds the nest (Olson and Martin 1999). Females usually lay 4 eggs (range 3–5) and incubate these for approximately 13 days (Olson and Martin 1999). Males feed the females infrequently during incubation and often accompany them when they leave the nest (Barber et al. 1998;

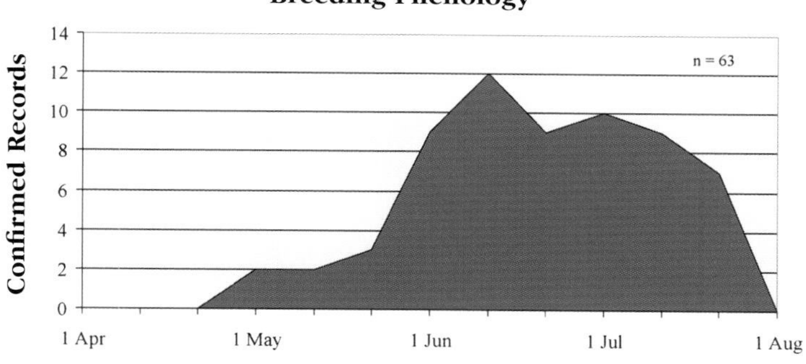

Martin and Ghalambor 1999). Both parents feed the young through the 10–14 day nestling period and then for at least 2 weeks following nest departure (Olson and Martin 1999).

Virginia's Warblers raise only one brood per season but will renest if earlier efforts fail (Olson and Martin 1999). In areas where Brown-headed Cowbirds are common, these warblers are frequent hosts; atlasers noted one adult warbler feeding a fledgling cowbird on 26 July.

DISTRIBUTION AND STATUS

Virginia's Warblers occur throughout the Intermountain West, primarily from Nevada, southern Idaho, and Wyoming south to southern Arizona, New Mexico, and locally in southwest Texas. In Arizona, these warblers are generally considered common summer residents (Phillips et al. 1964) and atlasers confirmed breeding on priority blocks at elevations from approximately 4800 to near 10,000 ft (1463–3048 m).

Observers reported Virginia's Warblers regularly in the Mogollon Rim region. The species undoubtedly continues to breed throughout much of the White Mountain Apache tribal lands, inasmuch as atlas records nearly encircle this unsurveyed reservation.

The Virginia's Warbler's breeding range extends west to isolated mountains in Mohave County, including the Hualapai, Cerbat, and Virgin ranges. This species was encountered frequently in the dense montane deciduous scrub habitats on the Kaibab Plateau, South Rim of the Grand Canyon, and on Navajo and Hopi tribal lands, including the Tsegi Canyon drainage, Black Mesa, and from the Carrizo Mountains to the Defiance Plateau.

Virginia's Warblers were commonly encountered in the higher sky islands of southeastern Arizona west to the Santa Rita and Santa Catalina ranges. They were also discovered locally in the smaller and infrequently visited Winchester and Santa Teresa mountains.

Atlasers regularly encountered Virginia's Warblers throughout their historic range in the state, and Breeding Bird Survey (BBS) data show that some of the highest Virginia's Warbler breeding concentrations occur in Arizona (Olson and Martin 1999). Although BBS data suggest increasing trends, these data should be used with caution due to small sample sizes. In addition, recent studies suggest that Virginia's Warblers are one of the few bird species that are severely affected by controlled burns. These warblers are closely associated with the brushy and highly combustible forest understory that forest managers seek to eliminate (Horton 1987).

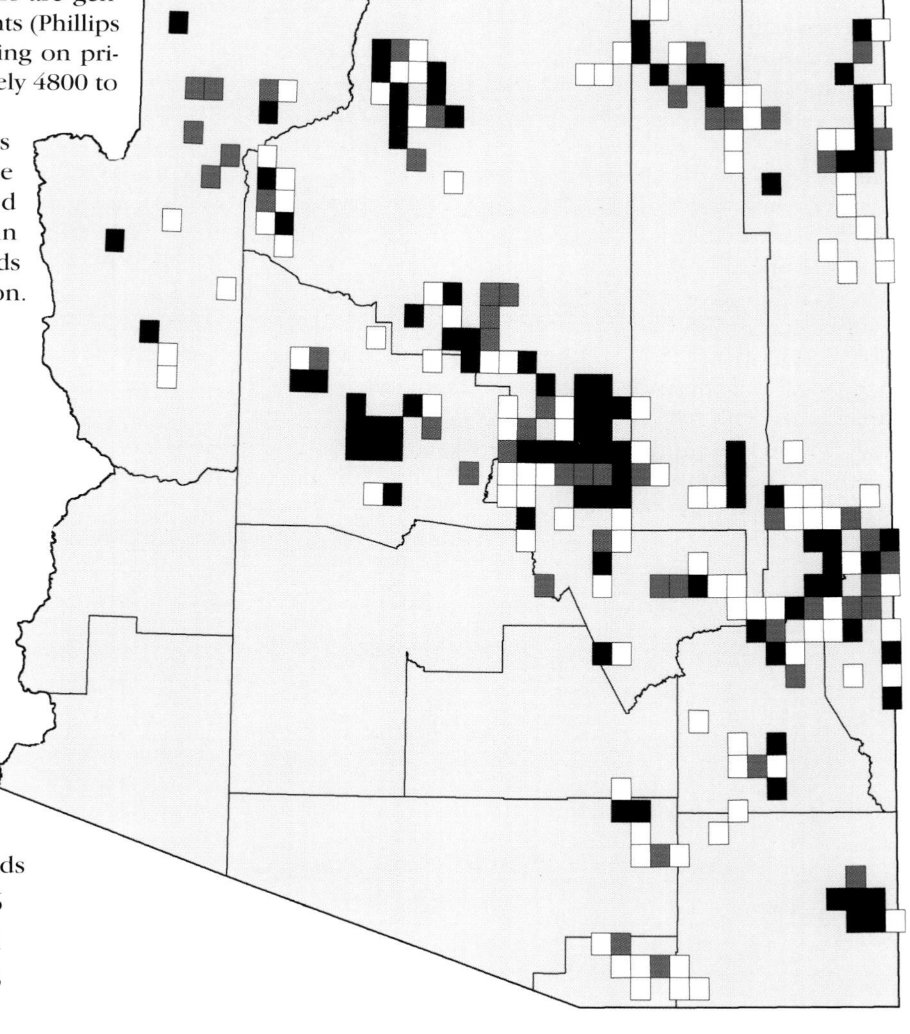

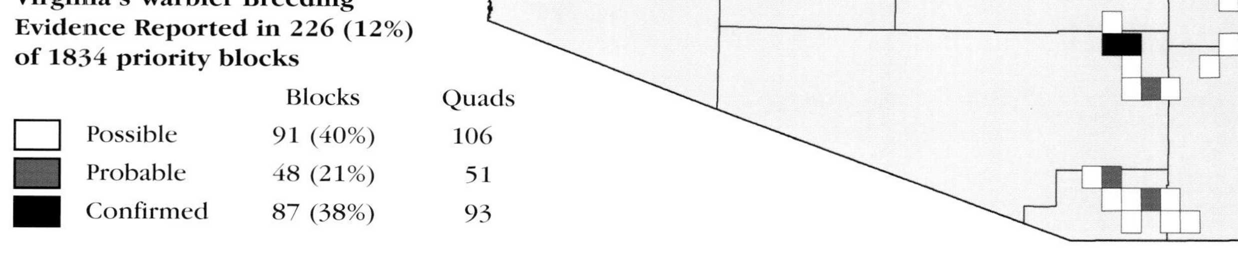

Virginia's Warbler Breeding Evidence Reported in 226 (12%) of 1834 priority blocks

	Blocks	Quads
Possible	91 (40%)	106
Probable	48 (21%)	51
Confirmed	87 (38%)	93

Lucy's Warbler

by Troy E. Corman *Vermivora luciae*

As the trees begin to leaf and bloom in early spring, the sweet song of the rusty-rumped Lucy's Warbler can be heard emanating from desert dry washes and riparian woodlands throughout Arizona's lowlands. A very large proportion of its breeding range is in Arizona, where, unlike other western warblers, it has a unique habit of nesting in cavities.

DAN FISCHER

HABITAT

Often found breeding in dryer conditions than other warblers in North America, Lucy's Warblers are most abundant along perennial or intermittently flooded drainages containing mesquite. Atlasers reported the majority of these warblers (54 percent of all records) from Sonoran Desert dry washes containing large mesquite, ironwood, and paloverde and in the immediately adjacent upland desertscrub (*n* = 725). However, in Arizona, they appear to reach their highest density in the few remaining large mesquite bosques and in dense cottonwood-willow riparian woodlands where 16 percent of all atlas records were reported. This lower percentage is likely related to the scarcity and local distribution of native lowland riparian areas compared to the more widespread and abundant desert washes. Atlasers also reported them in reduced numbers in netleaf hackberry thickets and at slightly higher elevation in foothill drainages dominated by Arizona sycamore, velvet ash, Arizona alder, and evergreen oaks. Locally atlasers also noted Lucy's Warbler using thickets of tamarisk, particularly those along the Colorado River and its tributaries within the Grand Canyon.

BREEDING

In Arizona, the first Lucy's Warblers typically arrive in early March, irregularly in late February, and exceptionally as early as 17 February. Nesting activity generally begins in early April, although atlasers discovered nests with young near Tucson on 5 April and 10 April. These records clearly indicate that some pairs begin nest construction and egg laying in mid- to late March. Statewide atlas records noted a peak nesting period from late April to mid-May with a significant decline after early June. During the atlas, the latest nesting activity observed was a nest being built on 30 June, with numerous reports of adults feeding fledglings through 27 July. Southbound migrations may begin as early as late June, with the bulk of the population vacating the state by late July or early August (Rosenberg et al. 1991; Johnson et al. 1997). Stragglers continue through much of September, exceptionally into October, with very few November and December records (Monson and Phillips 1981).

This is the only fairly consistent cavity-nesting warbler in western North America, and Lucy's Warblers choose a wide assortment of locations in which to construct their nests. Nests are typically placed in cavities in tree trunks, hollow limbs, or nestled among loose bark (Johnson et al. 1997). Atlasers found most Lucy's Warbler nests in trees or snags, included mesquite, cottonwood, willow, paloverde, ironwood, Arizona sycamore, netleaf hackberry, Arizona walnut, catclaw acacia, and Emory oak. Atlasers also discovered Lucy's Warbler nests in shallow cavities in cliffs and dirt banks, in an abandoned Cliff Swallow nests, among flood debris in trees, and among the rigid leaves of agave and yucca. Others have reported them nesting in saguaros and deserted Verdin nests (Gilman 1909; Bent 1953). Of 26 nests measured by atlas field crews, the median nest height was 8.7 ft (2.6 m) above the ground and ranged from 2.3 to 36.1 ft (0.7–11.0 m).

Gilman (1909) reported that the female constructs the nest; however, the male will sometimes accompany her to the nest site. Only the female incubates the typical clutch of 4–5 (range 3–7) eggs (Bent 1953). Brown (1994) estimated the incubation duration to be 12 days and the nestling stage to be 11 days. Both adults feed the nestlings and tend the fledglings for an unknown period (Johnson et al. 1997). Most evidence suggests that two broods are likely produced per season (Bent 1953, Johnson et al. 1997). There are numerous accounts of Brown-headed

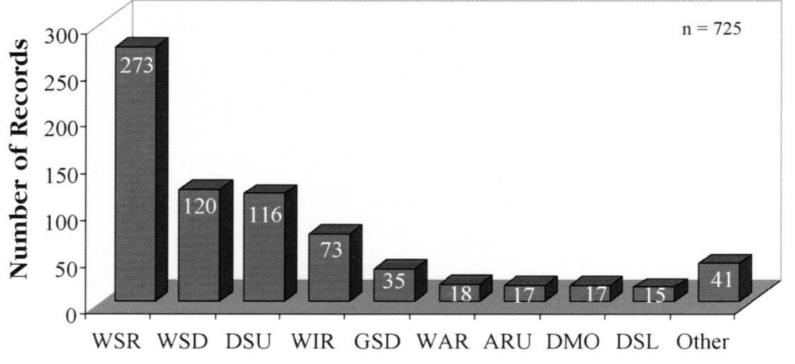

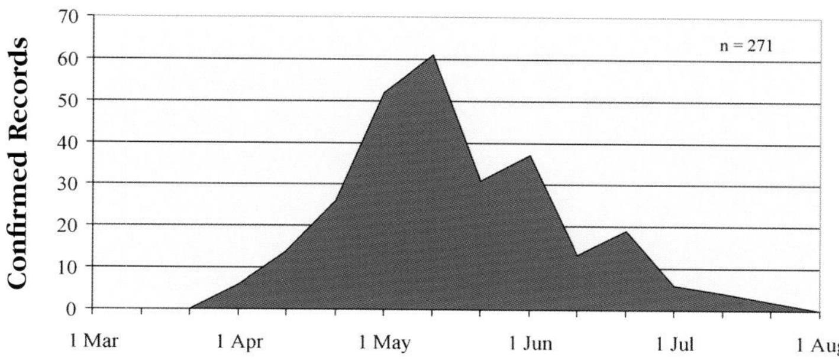

Cowbird brood parasitism on Lucy's Warblers (Friedmann et al. 1977), but atlasers did not note this.

DISTRIBUTION AND STATUS

Lucy's Warblers have a relatively small breeding range from extreme southern Utah and Nevada south to southeastern California and northern Sonora and east to New Mexico and extreme western Texas. Phillips et al. (1964) considered this warbler an abundant summer resident in southern and central Arizona and along the entire Colorado River, including within the Grand Canyon. Monson and Phillips (1981) also noted them in the Virgin River valley of extreme northwestern Arizona. Along the Colorado River within the Grand Canyon, Lucy's Warblers were once closely associated with areas of mesquite and acacia. However, since the construction of Glen Canyon Dam in 1963, populations have greatly increased and spread into the subsequent abundant thickets of tamarisk (Brown et al. 1987).

Atlasers found Lucy's Warblers common to abundant throughout much of their historical range in western, central, and southern Arizona at elevations between 140 and 4900 ft (43–1494 m). These small warblers were encountered north along drainages below the Mogollon Plateau including Oak Creek Canyon north of Sedona, the Salt River, and lower San Francisco River. They were not detected nesting south of Yuma, where this warbler had historically been reported, but they were found nesting sparingly in the more vegetated washes west of Pima County, where they had previously been noted as absent (Phillips et al. 1964). During the atlas period they were confirmed nesting for the first time along the Little Colorado River as far upstream as Cameron, along lower Kanab Creek, and along the Navajo Creek arm of Lake Powell. Lucy's Warblers were also discovered likely nesting along washes just north of Lake Mead National Recreation Area west of the Grand Wash Cliffs.

Lucy's Warblers were distinctly absent from much of the urban and agricultural areas in and around the greater Phoenix region south through western Pinal County, as well as in extensive agricultural areas in the lower Gila and Sulphur Springs valleys. Even though Lucy's Warblers remain locally abundant in Arizona, many populations have been extirpated or diminished by loss of native lowland riparian habitat throughout the state, especially mesquite bosques (Johnson et al. 1997). Reduced populations have been documented within the lower Colorado, Gila, and Santa Cruz river drainages.

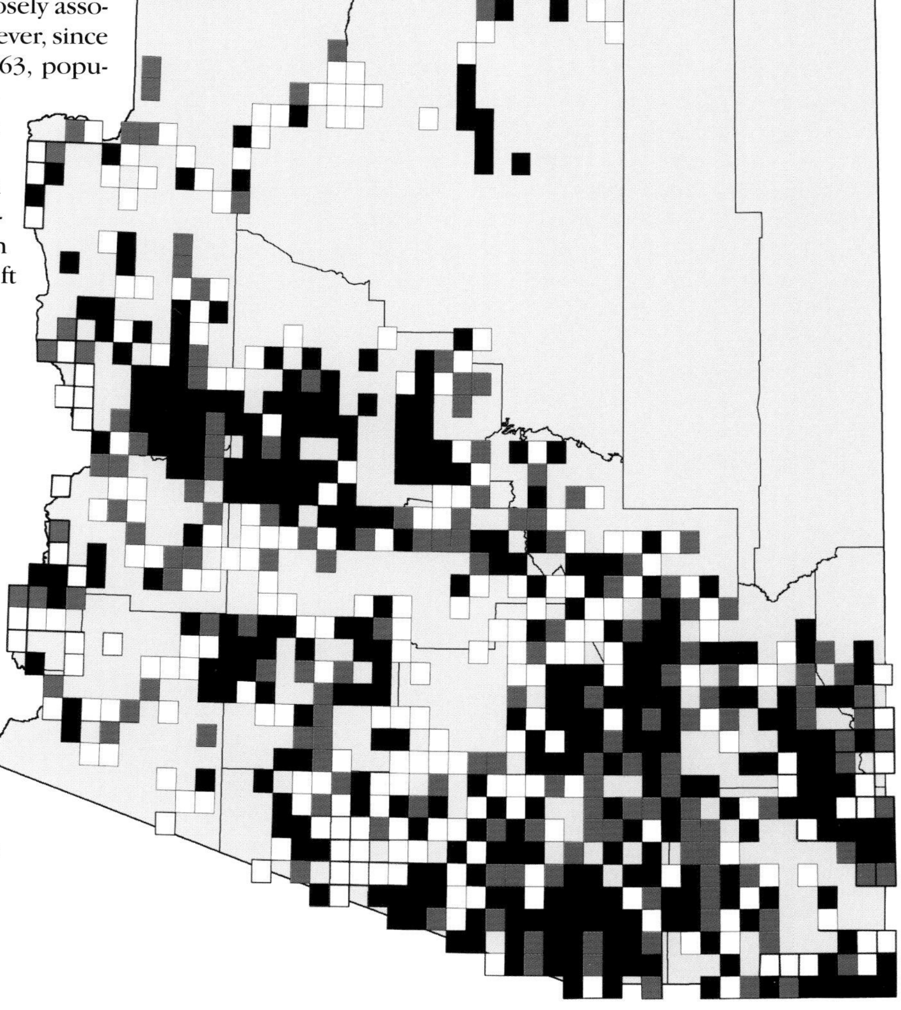

Lucy's Warbler Breeding Evidence Reported in 685 (37%) of 1834 priority blocks

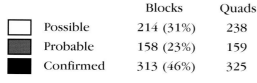

	Blocks	Quads
Possible	214 (31%)	238
Probable	158 (23%)	159
Confirmed	313 (46%)	325

Yellow Warbler

by Cathryn Wise-Gervais *Dendroica petechia*

Yellow Warblers are arguably Arizona's brightest warbler, and their gold plumage can be quite conspicuous in dark leafy riparian canopies. The genus name is derived from the Greek dendron, "tree," referring to the birds' arboreal lifestyle. The species name means "red spotted" and accurately describes the breast of the breeding male.

JIM BURNS

HABITAT

Yellow Warblers are closely associated with moisture-loving deciduous trees throughout much of their extensive North American range. In the arid West, this preference leads them primarily to cottonwood and willow dominated riparian areas. Atlasers reported the vast majority (86 percent) of Yellow Warbler observations in only two riparian woodland types across Arizona. Fifty-three percent of records were reported in Fremont cottonwood–willow associations, and these areas often included a dense understory of deciduous saplings, seepwillow, mesquite, and tamarisk (n = 283). This warbler also ranges up into lower canyons and mountain foothill drainages typically containing Arizona sycamore, cottonwood, ash, and willow, where an additional 33 percent of atlas records were obtained.

Very locally, atlasers also discovered Yellow Warblers nesting in tall, dense monotypic tamarisk thickets. However, there are hundreds of miles of rivers and streams in southwestern Arizona where the exotic tamarisk has completely displaced cottonwood and willow. The absence of breeding Yellow Warblers in these altered drainages strongly suggests that tamarisk does not typically provide suitable nesting habitat in the state.

BREEDING

Yellow Warblers begin arriving in southern Arizona breeding areas in mid-March and in northern Arizona by mid-April. Atlasers reported males singing on territory by 4 April with paired birds noted shortly thereafter. Nest construction can begin within several days of the arrival of the female (Lowther et al. 1999) and atlasers first noted this activity on 16 April. Although the contents of an occupied nest on 28 April could not be determined, early egg laying likely begins by late April in Arizona based on observations of nests with young by 9 May. Atlasers reported active Yellow Warbler nests from 28 April to 14 July. Atlas data suggest that Yellow Warbler nesting activity in Arizona picks up rapidly in early May and reaches a peak by mid-June, but atlasers continued confirming this bird throughout the summer. Observers reported adults feeding fledglings through 10 August. The initiation of nesting activity in Arizona is significantly earlier than reported elsewhere within the species range by Lowther et al. (1999). Arizona's Yellow Warblers begin appearing outside of nesting areas in late July and early August, but fall migration generally peaks in September and continues into mid-October.

Yellow Warbler nests are typically placed in upright tree forks, in a wide range of trees, shrubs, and heights. Willow is one of the most common trees used range wide, and five of the twelve nests described by atlasers were in Goodding willow. Other nests were found in Arizona sycamore, tamarisk, Fremont cottonwood, bigtooth maple, and velvet mesquite. The median height of the twelve nests reported by atlasers was 21.9 ft (6.7 m), and ranged from 12.8–42.0 ft (3.9–12.8 m). These values are considerably higher than those obtained in other parts of the country (Lowther et al. 1999), but little should be inferred from such a limited sample size.

Yellow Warbler females construct their nests with little or no assistance from the males (Bent 1953). They lay 4–5 eggs and the female incubates these for 11–12 days (Lowther et al. 1999). The male commonly feeds the incubating female and both adults feed the young, which depart from the nest at approximately 9–12 days after hatching (Baicich and Harrison 1997). Parental care continues outside the nest for another two weeks or so after fledging (Smith 1943). Yellow Warblers rarely attempt second broods, but will renest multiple times if earlier attempts fail (Lowther et al. 1999). However, the lengthy nesting period of this species in Arizona (April to August) suggests that multiple broods could be more frequent.

Breeding Habitats

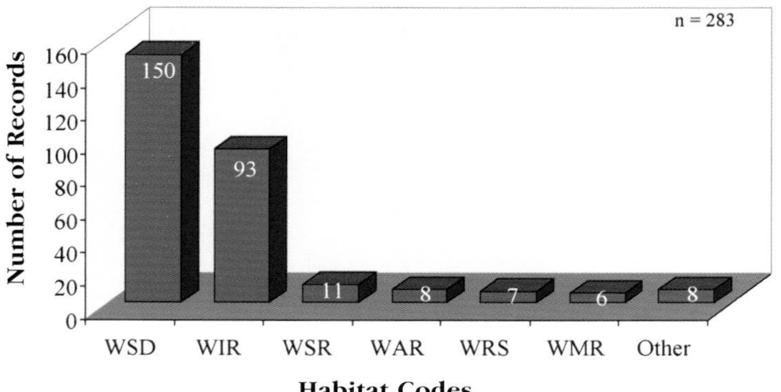

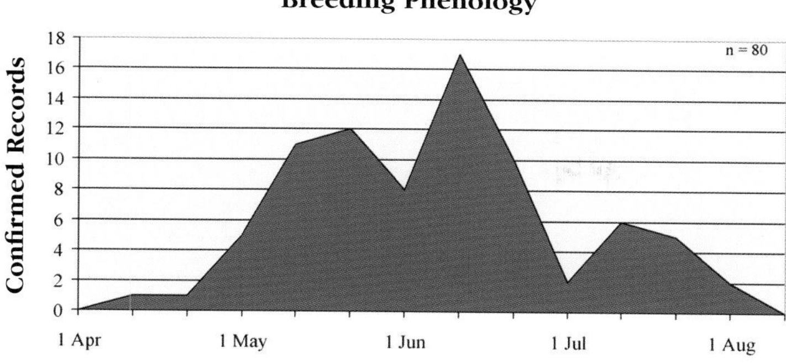

Yellow Warblers are common Brown-headed Cowbird hosts and have developed a strategy to discourage this persistent pest. Females sometimes cover a cowbird egg with new layers of nesting material, in essence banishing the alien to the "basement" then continue to lay eggs atop this. Yellow Warbler nests have been found with as many as six tiers, each containing at least one cowbird egg (Berger 1955). Atlasers reported fifteen incidents of cowbird brood parasitism during the atlas period, from 2 June to 21 July.

DISTRIBUTION AND STATUS

Migratory populations of Yellow Warblers have the broadest distribution of any of the *Dendroica* warblers (Lowther et al. 1999). They breed throughout most of Alaska and Canada south into the mid-latitude areas of the United States. In western North America, this species breeds south locally to central Mexico.

Throughout much of Arizona, Phillips et al. (1964) considered this warbler common in most perennial drainages below 6500 ft (1981 m) containing tall broadleaf trees, but the species was noted as conspicuously absent in surprising locations. Early naturalists considered Yellow Warblers an abundant summer resident along most of the lower Colorado River, where Grinnell (1914) estimated 1–4 singing males for every acre (0.4 ha) of cottonwood-willow habitat. Yellow Warblers disappeared from most of this drainage by the mid-1950s, primarily from extensive habitat loss and eventual heavy cowbird parasitism (Rosenberg et al. 1991).

Atlasers confirmed Yellow Warblers breeding on priority blocks ranging in elevation primarily from 480–5500 ft (146–1676 m). However, they were confirmed nesting locally to 7000 ft (2134 m) near Flagstaff and possibly to 7600 ft (2316 m) along Rudd Creek southeast of Eagar. Atlasers commonly found Yellow Warblers in central Arizona along most drainages below the Mogollon Rim and along lower perennial drainages in the southeast. In the north, these warblers were primarily found nesting in the Grand Canyon along the Colorado River and its immediate tributaries. They were noted very locally elsewhere in this region, including the Beaver Dam Wash confluence with the Virgin River and the lower Little Colorado River. Along the lower Colorado River, atlasers confirmed Yellow Warblers nesting locally only from Topock Marsh, south to the Bill Williams delta.

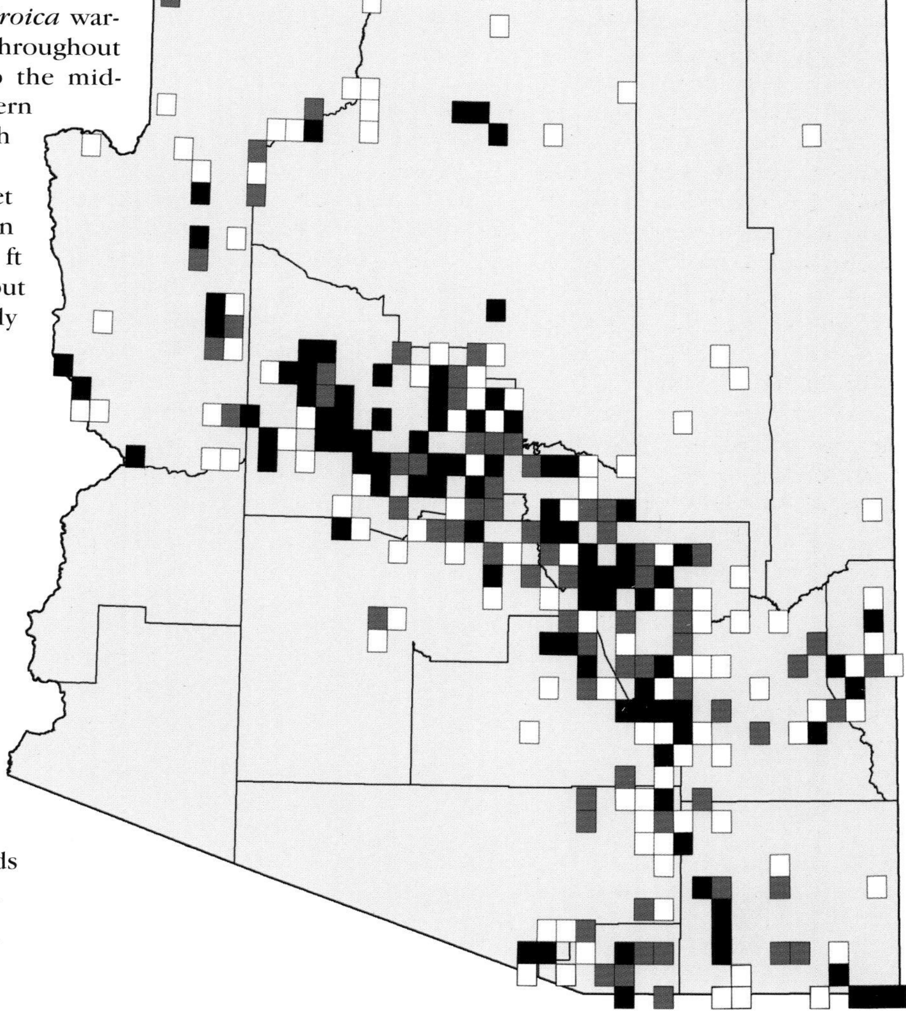

Yellow Warbler Breeding Evidence Reported in 214 (12%) of 1834 priority blocks

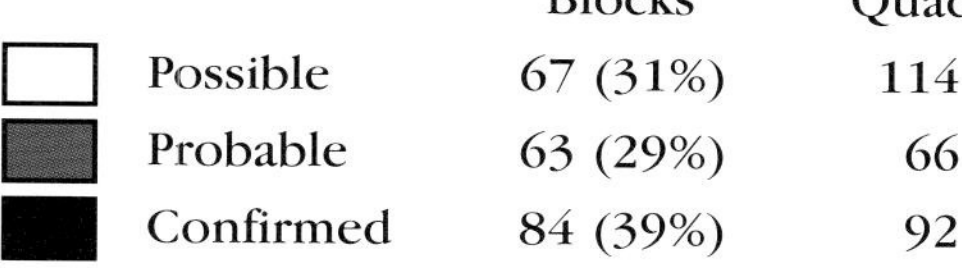

	Blocks	Quads
Possible	67 (31%)	114
Probable	63 (29%)	66
Confirmed	84 (39%)	92

Yellow-rumped Warbler

by Cathryn Wise-Gervais *Dendroica coronata*

Affectionately known as "butter-butts," Yellow-rumped Warblers are one of the few warblers that commonly both breed and winter in Arizona. These lovely little warblers nest in higher-elevation coniferous forests, where they spend much of their time singing, nesting, and foraging high in the canopy.

DAN FISCHER

HABITAT

Yellow-rumped Warblers in Arizona breed primarily in coniferous forests and in adjacent mountain drainages containing pines and firs. Atlasers reported these familiar warblers in eight vegetative communities, with the majority of observations (56 percent) in primarily pure ponderosa pine or mixed conifer–dominated forests (n = 157). Although the species commonly uses older stands of ponderosa pine in Arizona, these warblers reach their highest density in cool mixed-conifer forests that include Douglas fir, white fir, and aspen. This species is also abundant in spruce-fir forests containing subalpine fir and Engelmann spruce. Twenty-two percent of Yellow-rumped Warbler records were in Gambel's oak and ponderosa pine associations, and 11 percent were in pinyon pine–juniper woodlands with scattered ponderosa pine. Although atlas data seem to suggest that Yellow-rumped Warblers prefer nesting in forests containing ponderosa pine, this may reflect the fact that ponderosa dominates most tall conifer forests in Arizona.

BREEDING

Yellow-rumped Warblers are common winter residents in the lowlands of southern and western Arizona and begin to migrate to higher elevation nesting areas by early or mid-April. As with many other warblers, the males arrive about a week before the females and begin establishing territories. Nesting activity generally begins soon after the females arrive; the first instance of an adult carrying nesting material during the atlas period was on 17 May. The mean initiation date for egg laying of 130 Arizona nests on the Mogollon Rim was 30 May, and atlasers reported the earliest nest with young on 5 June. This record would suggest the initiation of egg laying no later than 20 May. Atlas data suggest a peak in breeding activity from late June to mid-July, followed by a sharp decline. The latest breeding records reported during the atlas period were of adults feeding fledged young on 2 and 3 August. Most Yellow-rumped Warblers migrate into Arizona's lowlands in October, but early individuals occasionally appear in late August and early September.

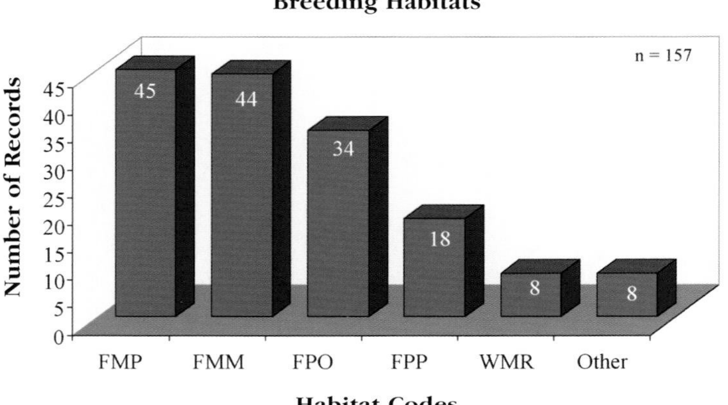

Yellow-rumped Warblers typically construct their cup-shaped nests on horizontal limbs of a wide variety of conifers (Harrison 1975), but also in deciduous trees in Arizona. Atlasers took measurements at only two Yellow-rumped Warbler nests, one in Douglas fir and the other in ponderosa pine. In another study in Arizona's snowmelt drainages above the Mogollon Rim, 155 nests were measured, with a mean nest height of 35 ft (10.7 m) and a range of 0–117.8 ft (0–35.9 m) above the ground (T. Martin, personal communication). These nests were found in Douglas fir (35 percent of all nests), bigtooth maple (29 percent), white fir (26 percent), southwestern white pine (5 percent), and Gambel's oak (5 percent).

Female Yellow-rumped Warblers construct the nest, a process that usually takes approximately 10 days (Knight 1908). A typical clutch consists of 4–5 eggs (Hunt and Flaspohler 1998), but 3–4 was the range of 14 Arizona nests (T. Martin, personal communication). The female does most of the incubation, but the male may assist occasionally during the 12–13 day period (Knight 1908, Bent 1953). Both adults feed the nestlings but it is usually the female that broods. The young fledge at approximately 10–14 days

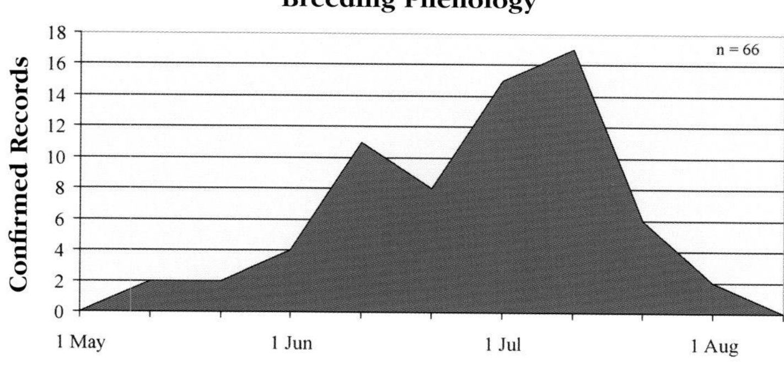

after hatching and their parents continue to feed them for approximately 14 days after nest departure (Hunt and Flaspohler 1998). Pairs typically raise one brood per season but will renest if their first attempt fails. Seconds broods after successful nesting attempts have been documented, but the frequency of this is still unknown.

Yellow-rumped Warblers are reported as regular Brown-headed Cowbird hosts, but none of twenty-nine nests studied in Arizona were parasitized (Martin 1992). Atlasers reported one adult feeding a cowbird fledgling on 3 August.

DISTRIBUTION AND STATUS

Yellow-rumped Warblers occur in northern and western North America, with the Myrtle form breeding primarily in Canada, Alaska, and in the northeastern United States. The Audubon form breeds from the Rocky Mountains west to the Pacific Coast and south to central Mexico. Phillips et al. (1964) considered Yellow-rumped Warblers to be common summer residents in conifer forests above 8500 ft (2591 m) in Arizona, and less common in the lower and drier ponderosa pine dominated forests. Atlasers confirmed Yellow-rumped Warblers breeding on priority blocks at elevations ranging from approximately 6100 to 10,500 ft (1859–3200 m).

Atlasers found Yellow-rumped Warblers to be most commonly and consistently distributed along the Mogollon Rim and White Mountains region northwest to Williams and the San Francisco Mountains region. As suggested by the accompanying distribution map, this warbler certainly breeds throughout much of the higher elevations on White Mountain Apache tribal lands, where atlas surveys could not be conducted and data are lacking. Sizable populations were also detected from the South Rim of the Grand Canyon north to the Kaibab Plateau. In northwestern Arizona, this warbler was documented nesting in isolated higher mountain ranges of the Arizona Strip region and locally on Hualapai tribal lands. Yellow-rumped Warblers were confirmed nesting to the northeast on Black Mesa and from the Defiance Plateau north to the Carrizo Mountains.

South of the Mogollon Rim, atlasers found Yellow-rumped Warbler distribution to be rather spotty. In Yavapai County, the species was detected primarily on Mingus Mountain and in the Bradshaw Mountain range. In southeastern Arizona, atlasers documented this warbler only in the Pinaleno, Santa Catalina, Rincon, and Chiricahua Mountains. Yellow-rumped Warblers were not detected in the Santa Rita and Huachuca Mountains, where they had previously been reported nesting (Phillips et al. 1964). However, appropriate nesting habitat remains very limited in these two mountain ranges, and atlasers could easily have overlooked the small numbers of Yellow-rumped Warblers that may continue to breed there.

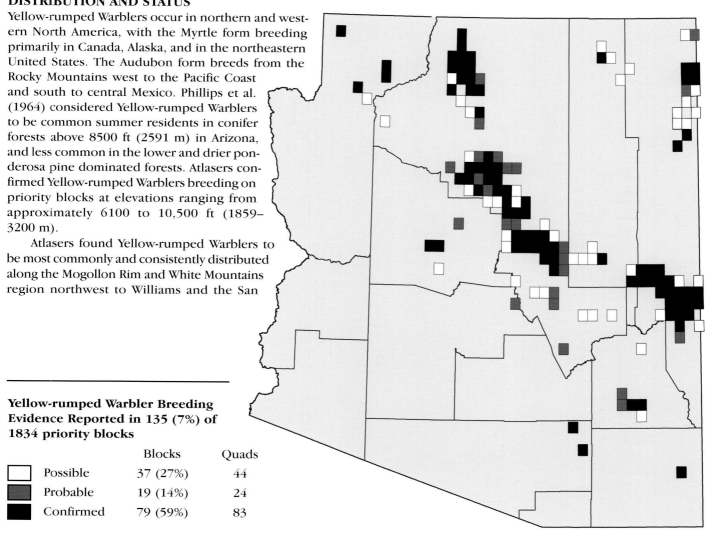

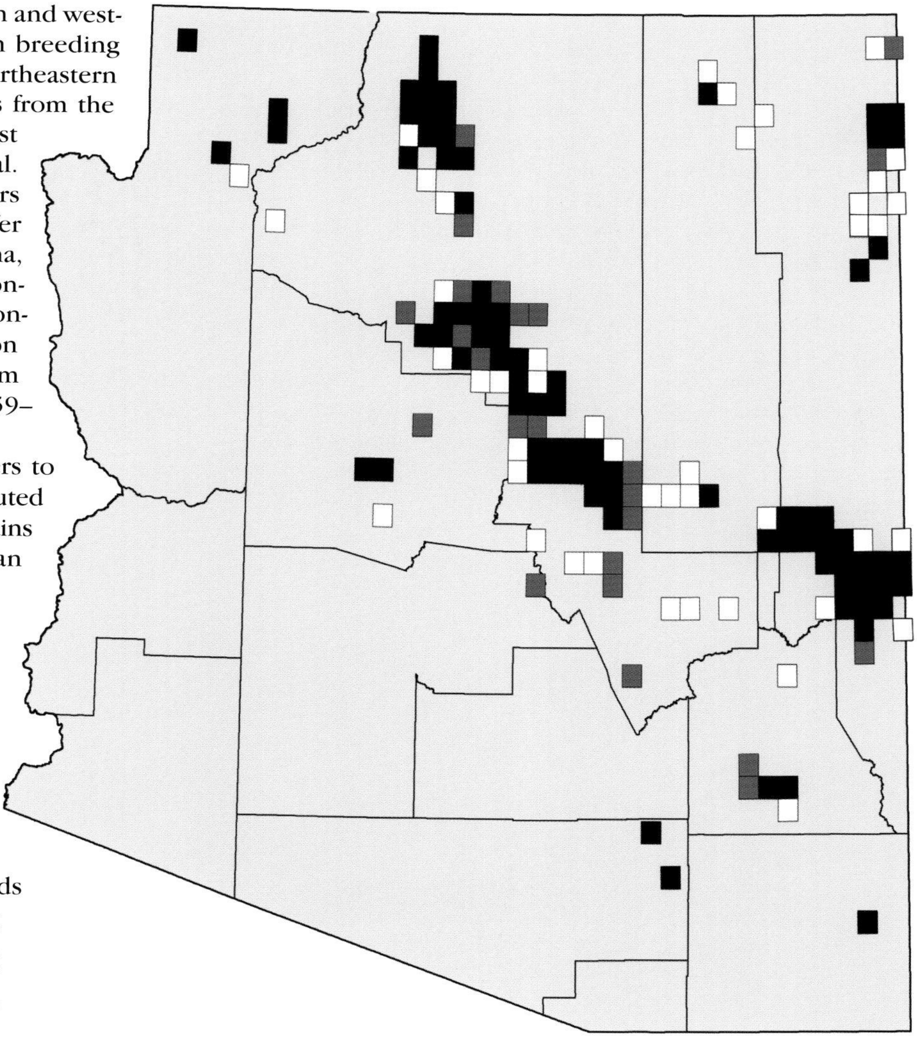

Yellow-rumped Warbler Breeding Evidence Reported in 135 (7%) of 1834 priority blocks

	Blocks	Quads
Possible	37 (27%)	44
Probable	19 (14%)	24
Confirmed	79 (59%)	83

Black-throated Gray Warbler

by Cathryn Wise-Gervais *Dendroica nigrescens*

Black-throated Gray Warblers lack the vibrant hues of most other warblers, but they are certainly no less handsome. Their crisp colors and distinctive, wheezy song set them apart from other mid-elevation songsters, and they are easy to observe thanks to their tame, inquisitive nature.

HABITAT

Black-throated Gray Warblers are western birds that favor open woodlands and are commonly encountered nesting in pinyon pine–juniper or oak woodland associations. In northern Arizona, this species clearly prefers pinyon pine–juniper woodlands above all other habitat types, and atlasers reported 46 percent of the potential breeding records in this widespread habitat alone (n = 363). Within these woodlands, this lovely little warbler was encountered much more frequently in taller stands at higher elevations that offered higher densities of mature pinyon pine. They were frequently absent in drier stands primarily comprising juniper, and atlasers regularly failed to locate the species in some extensive woodlands that superficially appeared to offer excellent conditions. As a result, Black-throated Gray Warbler habitat choice remains somewhat mysterious and is worthy of further study. At higher elevations, atlasers also found this species in pinyon–juniper stands with scattered ponderosa pine and in ponderosa pine–Gambel's oak associations.

South of the Mogollon Rim these warblers are commonly encountered in Madrean evergreen oak woodlands, where 18 percent of records were obtained. Black-throated Gray Warblers are also frequent inhabitants of the nearby sycamore-dominated drainages and range up into southeastern Arizona's Madrean pine-oak forests containing stands of Apache, Chihuahuan, and ponderosa pines.

Breeding Habitats

n = 363

Habitat Codes	Number of Records
FPJ	166
FME	65
FPP	34
FPO	25
FMO	18
WIR	14
Other	41

DAN FISCHER

BREEDING

Although limited numbers of Black-throated Gray Warblers winter in southern Arizona, most begin returning to the state in mid-March and arrive on breeding grounds in early to mid-April. Observers first reported paired birds on 27 April and observed nest building activity soon after on 29 April. The earliest occupied nest was located on 15 May, but adults were seen carrying food on 9 May and were reported feeding fledged young on 19 May. Both of these latter records suggest that the birds laid eggs in late April in these cases. Although atlasers obtained 111 confirmed records for this species, not including fledgling sightings, they found few active nests. Most confirmed records were of adults carrying food or feeding fledged young, and it is difficult to determine the peak nesting period from these activities. However, atlas data suggest that Black-throated Gray Warbler breeding activity peaks in Arizona from mid-June through early July and continues through the summer. The latest nest with young was discovered on 10 July, but adults were observed feeding fledglings through 30 July and performing distraction displays to 5 August. Black-throated gray Warblers sometimes begin their southerly migration by early August, but they are more commonly observed traveling through Arizona in September and early October.

Black-throated Gray Warblers have been known to nest in firs, oaks, and in pinyon pine (Guzy and Lowther 1997). Observers measured only five nests during the atlas period, three in juniper and two in oak. Of the nests in oak, one was in Arizona white oak and the other was in a mistletoe clump in a scrub live oak. The median nest height was 6.2 ft (1.9 m) with a range from 1.6 to 16.1 ft (0.5–4.9 m). This nest height value is considerably lower than the 24.6 ft (7.5 m) mean for seven southeastern Arizona nests reported by Harrison (1984). Clearly, more Arizona nest data should be collected before a solid nest height estimate can be obtained.

Female Black-throated Gray Warblers do most of the nest construction, with little assistance from their mates.

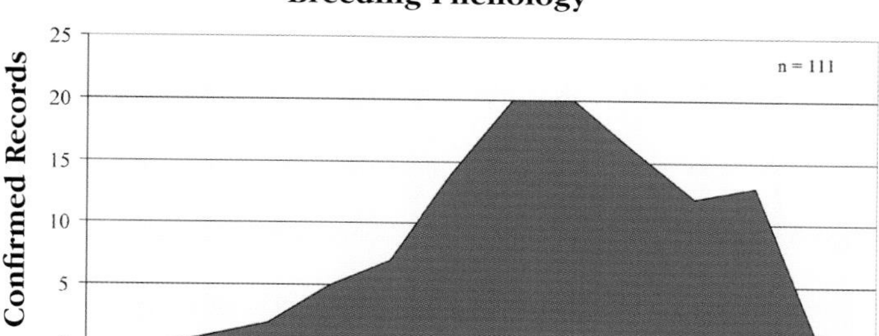

Instead, the male warbler sits idly nearby and scolds the female softly while she works! Nests are usually placed on a horizontal branch and appear as deep cups (Guzy and Lowther 1997). A notable feature of Black-throated Gray Warbler nests is that they are often lined with a thick layer of feathers, from a variety of bird species including Greater Roadrunners and Steller's Jays (Dawson 1923). Females usually lay 4 eggs (range 3–5; Bent 1953). It is likely that only females incubate (Pyle et al. 1997), but the length of incubation is unknown. Both adults feed their newly hatched young (Guzy and Lowther 1997) and continue to provide some food after fledging. More study is needed to determine the incubation period, the age when nestlings fledge, and the number of broods that the birds produce yearly.

Although Black-throated Gray Warblers are considered infrequent Brown-headed Cowbird hosts, observers reported ten incidents during the atlas period. These sightings were made statewide from 2 June to 24 July and include seven records of the warblers feeding cowbird fledglings.

DISTRIBUTION AND STATUS

Black-throated Gray Warblers breed only in western North America and occur from southwestern British Columbia south to northern Baja California. To the east, they nest from southern Idaho and central Wyoming south through New Mexico and Arizona to the highlands of northern Sonora. Range wide, the species is most common at mid-elevation woodland zones and such is true in Arizona as well. Atlasers encountered Black-throated Gray Warblers on priority blocks from approximately 4700 to 8200 ft (1432–2499 m).

Phillips et al. (1964) described Black-throated Gray Warblers as common summer residents in pinyon pine–juniper woodlands and other dense vegetation in eastern Arizona west to the Baboquivari and Bradshaw mountains and the South Rim of the Grand Canyon. The species was also confirmed breeding in the Hualapai Mountains in the late 1970s (Monson and Phillips 1981). Atlasers commonly located Black-throated Gray Warblers throughout these areas and found them to be fairly widespread in the northwest as well. Numerous records were obtained of this bird nesting along the slopes of the Kaibab Plateau, within the Arizona Strip region, and on Hualapai tribal lands. Atlasers reported the westernmost nesting locality in the Cerbat Mountains north of Kingman.

Atlasers also found that Black-throated Gray Warblers were widespread on mountain slopes and higher mesas within Navajo and Hopi tribal lands and along the southern slope of the Mogollon Rim. These warblers undoubtedly breed in portions of White Mountain Apache tribal lands, where atlas surveys were not conducted.

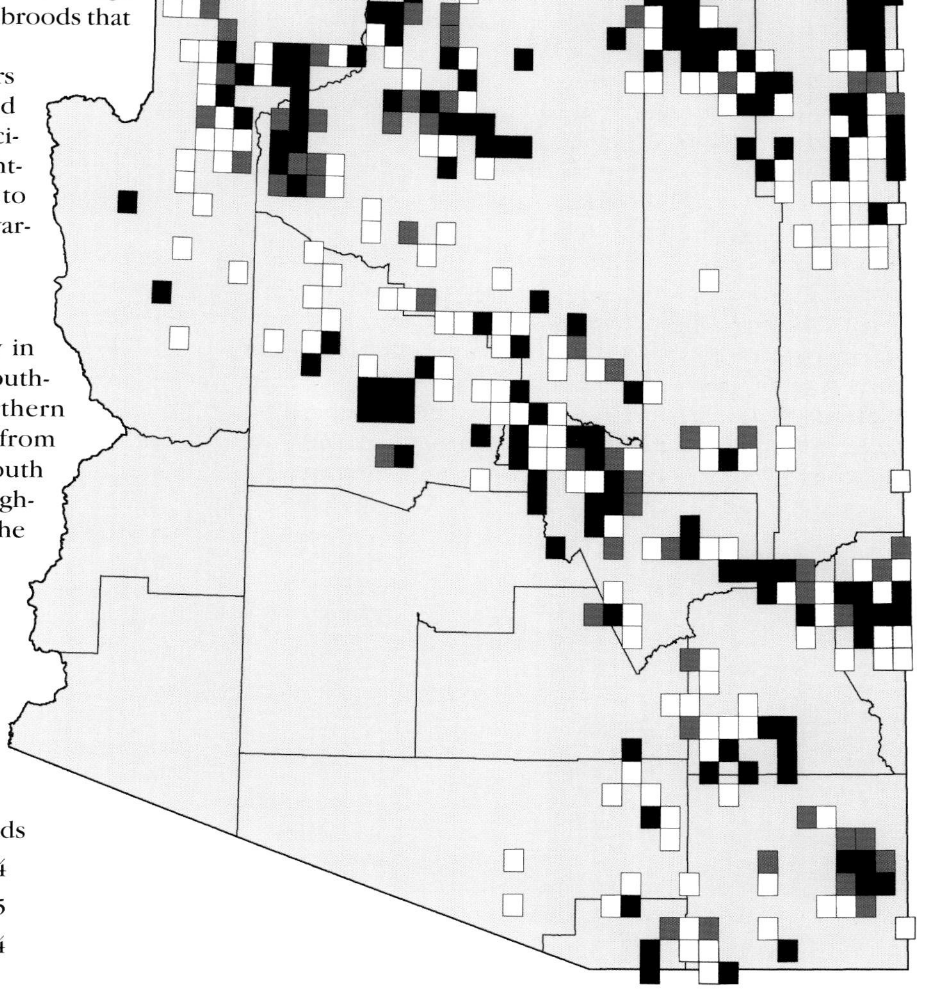

Black-throated Gray Warbler Breeding Evidence Reported in 343 (19%) of 1834 priority blocks

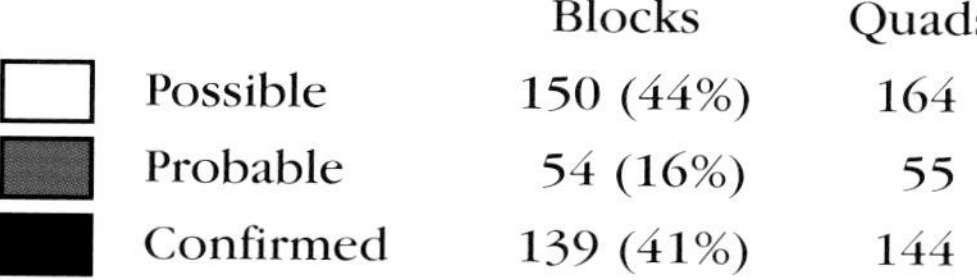

	Blocks	Quads
Possible	150 (44%)	164
Probable	54 (16%)	55
Confirmed	139 (41%)	144

Grace's Warbler

by Cathryn Wise-Gervais *Dendroica graciae*

Famous ornithologist Elliot Coues named this small western wood warbler after his sister, Grace. These lovely little birds conduct most of their daily activities high above the forest floor, so much of their natural history remains unknown.

DAN FISCHER

HABITAT

Grace's Warblers prefer parklike stands of mature trees and favor open conifer forests that are generally dominated by ponderosa or similar pines. These stands may also contain oaks, juniper, firs, and other trees, but these seem secondary to the presence of the larger pines. Although atlasers reported this species in eleven habitat types, 94 percent of all records were obtained in just five vegetative communities, all of which contain ponderosa pine. Observers found 31 percent of Grace's Warbler records in ponderosa pine–Gambel's oak associations and 25 percent in primarily pure ponderosa pine stands (n = 198). Sixteen percent of records were in pinyon pine–juniper woodlands with scattered ponderosa pine and 13 percent were in mixed-conifer forests of Douglas fir, white fir, ponderosa and other pines. In southeastern Arizona, observers commonly detected Grace's Warblers in Madrean pine-oak forests dominated by Chihuahuan, Apache, and ponderosa pines (11 percent of records). Only a handful of records were reported in habitats adjacent to pine-dominated forests, including Madrean evergreen oak woodlands and cool montane riparian areas characterized by a mixture of both coniferous and deciduous trees.

BREEDING

Grace's Warblers typically return to their southern Arizona breeding grounds in early April and to their northern breeding grounds in mid- to late April. Males arrive slightly earlier than females and begin singing immediately to establish territories and attract mates. Pairs form in mid- to late April, and nest construction soon follows. Although atlasers obtained eighty-six confirmed breeding records for Grace's Warblers, few of these were active nests, and so exact breeding chronology is still a bit unclear. Atlasers reported a nest with eggs on 10 May and noted the earliest adults carrying food on 27 May and feeding fledglings by 1 June. Atlas data suggest that Grace's Warbler breeding activity in Arizona peaks from mid-June to mid-July. However, because most confirmations were of adults carrying food or feeding fledglings, this period may simply indicate a peak for nests with young and dependent fledglings. The latest confirmed atlas observation was of an adult feeding fledged young on 14 August, indicating that at least some active nests persist into late July. Arizona's Grace's Warblers begin migrating south in late August, but most travel in September. Observers have reported only a few stragglers still migrating into mid-October.

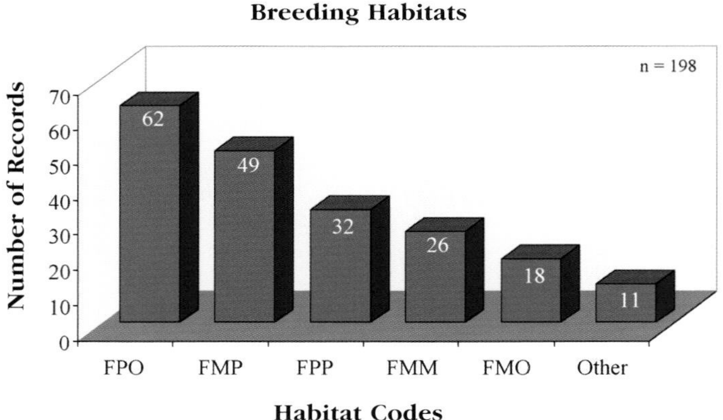

In Arizona, Grace's Warblers typically place their nests in needle clusters at branch ends or toward the top of tall ponderosa or other long-needled conifers such as Apache pine. Their nests are often constructed well away from the trunk and typically 25–40 ft (7.6–12.2 m) above the ground (Stacier and Guzy 2002). The cryptic nature of these nests as well as their height above ground makes their detection difficult, so it is not surprising that observers took measurements at only three Grace's Warbler nests during the atlas period. These nests ranged in height from 29.5 to 47.9 ft (9–14.6 m) above ground. Additional Arizona nests have ranged from 16.4 to 59.1 ft (5–18 m) in height (Stacier and Guzy 2002).

Female Grace's Warblers select the nest site and build the compact, cuplike nest while the male perches nearby and observes (Stacier and Guzy 2002). Females lay 3–4 eggs (Bent 1953) and incubate these without male assistance for 10–12 days. Only the female broods the young, but both sexes feed the nestlings (Stacier and Guzy 2002). The young grow quickly and depart the nest in approximately 9 days, and both parents continue feeding the fledglings for as many as 15 days following nest departure (Stacier and Guzy 2002).

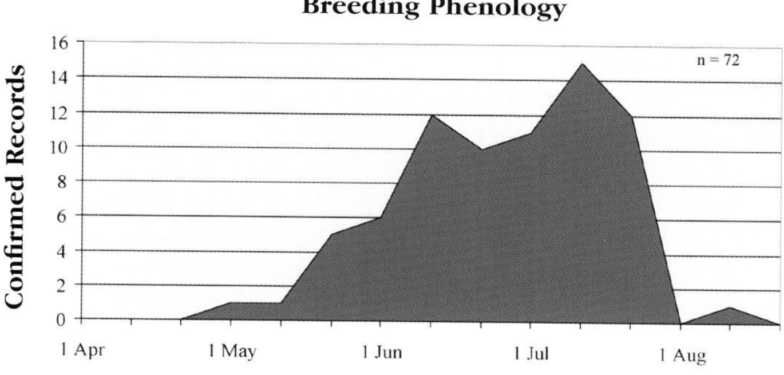

There is no evidence suggesting that Grace's Warblers produce more than one brood per season, but renesting efforts occur frequently following earlier nest failure and may explain a nest with eggs reported by atlasers on 1 July. Grace's Warblers are a regular Brown-headed Cowbird host, and atlasers reported five incidents of possible cowbird brood parasitism. All observations were of adult Grace's Warblers feeding fledgling cowbirds between 30 June and 11 July.

DISTRIBUTION AND STATUS

Grace's Warblers are primarily a southwestern species, closely related to the Yellow-throated Warbler of the East. Northern populations are migratory and the species breeds from southern Nevada, southern Utah, and southwestern Colorado south through the highlands and western Mexico to northern Nicaragua.

Phillips et al. (1964) described the Grace's Warbler breeding range in Arizona as including Transition Zone areas statewide, and considered the species a common summer resident in these forests. Similarly, atlasers discovered that the status and distribution of this little pine-inhabiting warbler has changed little in the state. Grace's Warblers were detected nesting at elevations ranging from approximately 5700 to 9200 ft (1737–2804 m). Predictably, this closely corresponds to the elevation limits of ponderosa pine in the state. Atlasers consistently encountered this warbler from the White Mountains and Mogollon Rim regions north through Flagstaff and Williams to the Kaibab Plateau. Although Grace's Warblers most certainly breed throughout much of the White Mountain Apache tribal lands, their presence in this area went undetected, as the tribe did not permit atlas surveys. This unfortunate fact is especially notable in the accompanying distribution map, with atlas records nearly surrounding the unsurveyed tribal lands.

On Navajo and Hopi tribal lands, observers commonly encountered Grace's Warblers on Black Mesa and from the Carrizo Mountains south to the Defiance Plateau. Atlas surveys also helped delineate the distribution of this warbler in northwestern Arizona. Observers in this remote region of the state reported Grace's Warblers locally west to the Hualapai, Cerbat, and Virgin mountains, as well as on Kaibab-Paiute tribal lands west of Fredonia and in several locations on Hualapai tribal lands. These warblers were also detected regularly in all of the southeastern Arizona mountains containing tall pines, including the Galiuro and Santa Teresa ranges, where few previous avian surveys have been conducted.

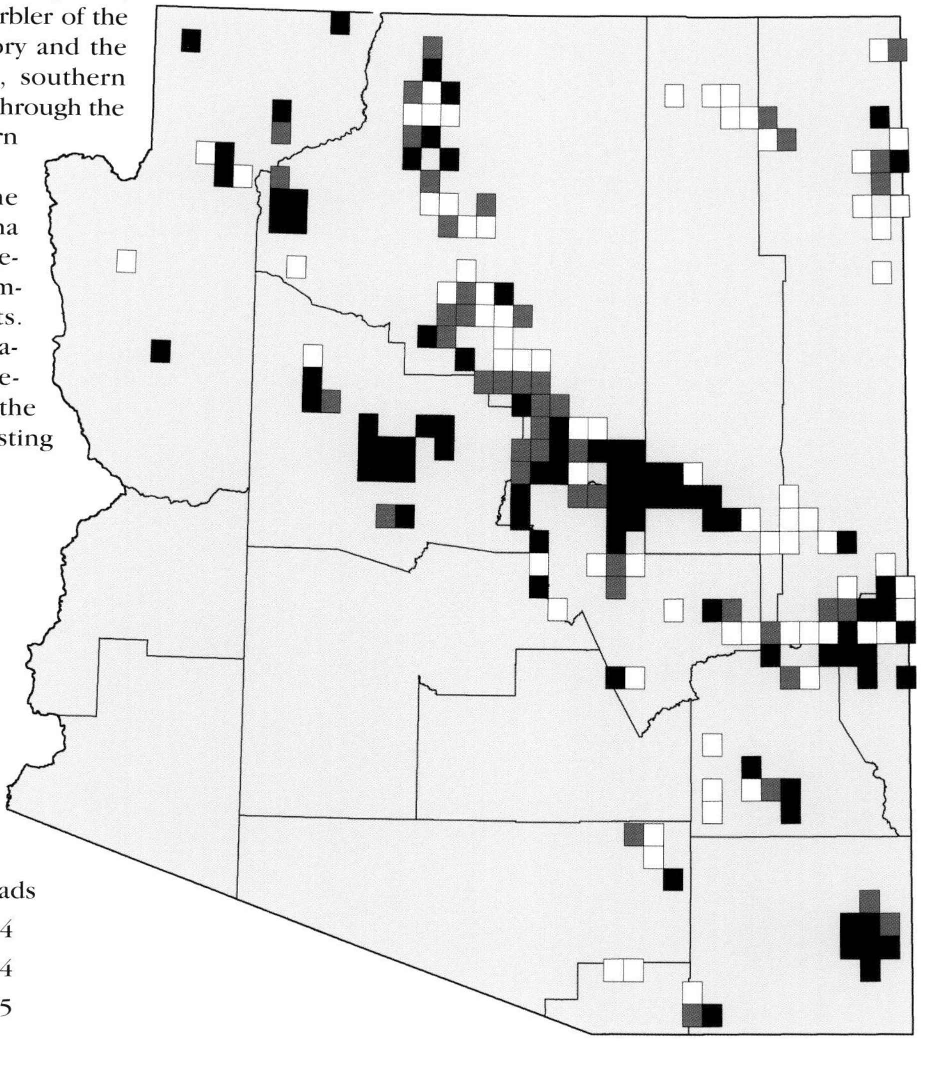

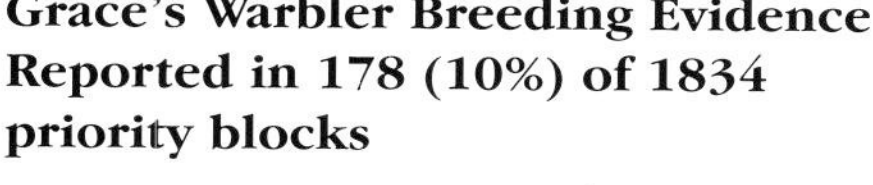

Grace's Warbler Breeding Evidence Reported in 178 (10%) of 1834 priority blocks

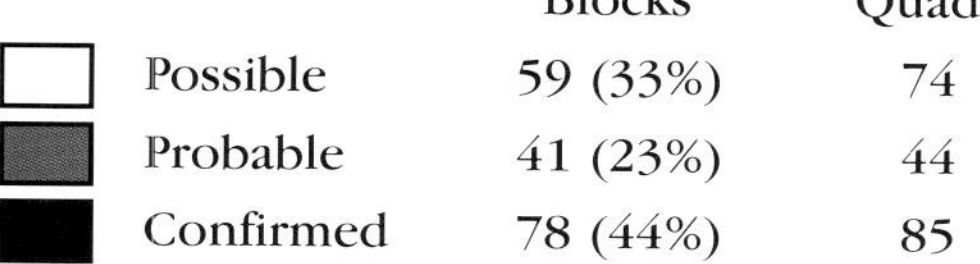

	Blocks	Quads
Possible	59 (33%)	74
Probable	41 (23%)	44
Confirmed	78 (44%)	85

MacGillivray's Warbler

by Tracy D. McCarthey *Oporornis tolmiei*

Nearing the southern edge of their nesting range, the distribution of MacGillivray's Warblers in Arizona remains patchy and very local. Apart from when males sing from exposed perches, these skulking warblers are typically encountered close to the ground foraging among the dense tangles of deciduous vegetation.

HABITAT

In Arizona, MacGillivray's Warblers are most frequently found nesting along or near mountain drainages, springs, or slopes with a mixture of coniferous and deciduous trees and shrubs. Atlas data reveal that nearly 70 percent of MacGillivray's Warblers were recorded in cool, montane riparian woodlands (n = 41). Typical habitat within these drainages and canyons often consists of varying combinations of Douglas fir, white fir, ponderosa pine, and quaking aspen with a fairly dense understory of young conifers, bigtooth maple, boxelder, New Mexico locust, Gambel's oak, gooseberry, and wildrose. Where creeks flow through subalpine meadows or adjacent to mixed-conifer and spruce-fir forests, MacGillivray's Warblers also nest among the dense thickets of thinleaf alder and shrubby Geyer and Bebb willows. They often frequent areas within these habitat types with early successional or short, scrubby vegetation. These areas can be extremely moist such as along drainages or relatively dry mountain slopes recovering from a fairly recent fire event with low dense stands of Gambel's oak, snowberry, and raspberry. Paramount, however, is the occurrence of short, dense vegetation available for nesting and foraging substrates, inasmuch as MacGillivray's Warblers rarely conduct any activities above the shrub layer.

BREEDING

MacGillivray's Warblers are common transients throughout Arizona, with early migrants arriving in mid- to late March.

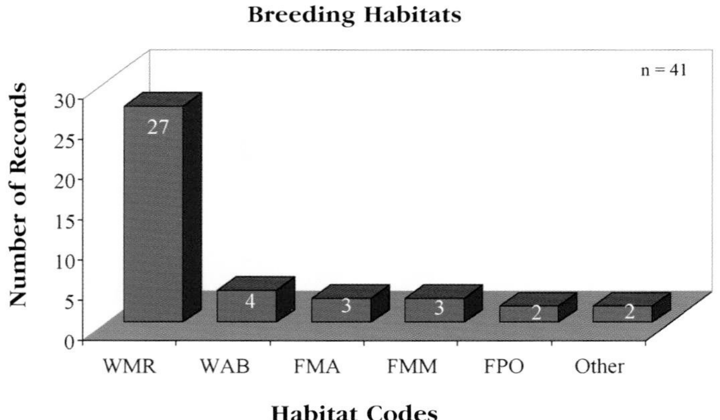

Peak passage is in April and early May with stragglers into early June. In Arizona, these warblers arrive on their breeding grounds in late April or early May to establish territories. The earliest confirmation during the atlas period was an individual carrying nesting material on 31 May. Nesting dates can vary depending on the amount of snow cover in an area. Atlas data suggest that peak breeding activity occurs from late June to mid-July; however, the sample size was relatively small. Studies on local populations on the Mogollon Rim in Arizona found the mean egg-laying initiation date of 8 June, with a range of 28 May–5 July (T. Martin, personal communication). Adults were observed carrying food through 26 July and may continue to feed later fledglings into early August. In Arizona, southbound migration typically begins in early August, with peak migration in late August and September. Stragglers continue into October and are rarely noted after mid-month.

Nests are typically placed low and under cover of dense vegetation. Atlasers took measurements at only one MacGillivray's Warbler nest, which was constructed in a snowberry only 5.5 in. (14 cm) above the ground. Of 150 MacGillivray's Warbler nests measured during research on the Mogollon Rim, the mean nest height was 22.4 in. (57 cm), but nests ranged in height from 0.0 to 4.9 ft (0.0–1.5 m) above the ground (T. Martin, personal communication). Nearly 88 percent of the nests discovered on the Mogollon Rim were placed in either young bigtooth maple or white fir, but nests were also found in Douglas fir saplings and thickets of raspberry, gooseberry, or young Gambel's oak. Along drainages in the White Mountains of Arizona, MacGillivray's Warblers also nest in dense thickets of various shrub willows and alder.

Most evidence suggests only female MacGillivray's Warblers construct the nest and incubates the eggs. Typically clutches consist of 4 eggs, but in Arizona ranges from 2–5 (T. Martin, personal communication). The incubation period is approximately 11–13 days (Pitocchelli 1995), and the young leave the nest after only 8–10 days (Baicich and Harrison 1997). Females predominantly feed the nestlings (Pitocchelli 1995) and both parents assist in tending to fledglings (Baicich and Harrison 1997). MacGillivray's Warblers are thought to produce only one brood per season (Pitocchelli 1995), although they will renest after a failed nesting attempt.

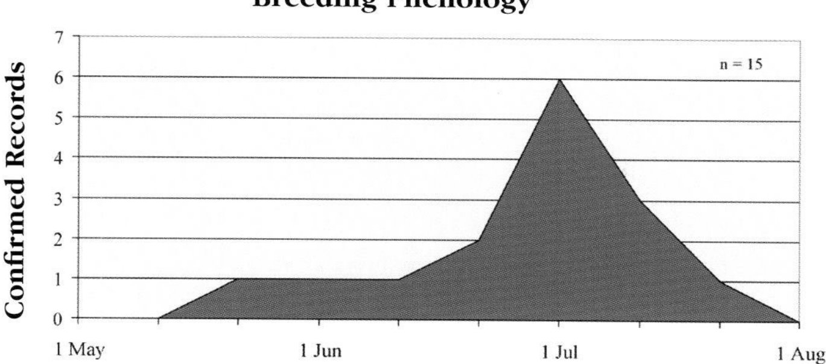

DISTRIBUTION AND STATUS

MacGillivray's Warblers primarily breed in western North America from southeastern Alaska and Yukon south to central California, Utah, and Colorado. At the southern edge of their breeding distribution in Arizona, New Mexico, and southern California, their range is patchy and very local.

In Arizona, Phillips et al. (1964) described MacGillivray's Warblers as fairly common summer residents along higher elevation drainages in the White and very locally, San Francisco mountains. By the mid-1970s, these warblers were also found nesting on Bill Williams Mountain and possibly near Happy Jack (Monson and Phillips 1981). Through the 1980s, additional nesting locations were discovered on the North Rim of the Grand Canyon (Brown et al. 1987), Black Mesa south of Kayenta (LaRue 1994), and possibly in the Carrizo and Chuska mountains in extreme northeastern Arizona (Jacobs 1986). MacGillivray's Warblers have been known to also nest locally in snowmelt drainages on the Mogollon Rim northeast of Payson since at least 1984 (T. Martin, personal communication).

Atlasers found MacGillivray's Warblers nesting in most of the previous noted sites and many additional locations at elevations ranging from approximately 5800 ft (1768 m) to near 10,000 ft (3048 m) in the Inner Basin of the San Francisco Mountains. The lowest elevation sites were discovered just below the Mogollon Rim along upper Canyon and Tonto creeks, and in side drainages of upper Oak Creek Canyon, including its West Fork. In addition, new localities for this species were documented in the far northwest region of the state in the Virgin Mountains and on Mount Logan. On the Kaibab Plateau, these warblers were more widespread than past records indicated. The southernmost nesting population of MacGillivray's Warblers was discovered in the Pinaleno Mountains. Additional populations likely occur on White Mountain Apache tribal lands, where atlas surveys could not be conducted.

With their low densities and limited distribution in Arizona, isolated populations of MacGillivray's Warblers are very susceptible to habitat alteration and loss. On the Mogollon Rim, researchers have documented localized extinctions of MacGillivray's Warblers, possibly due to a combination of factors leading to a decline in low, deciduous vegetation such as maple, oak, and aspen. These factors may include a recent decline in winter precipitation, heavy elk browsing, and local fire suppression resulting in a lack of early successional vegetation (T. Martin, personal communication).

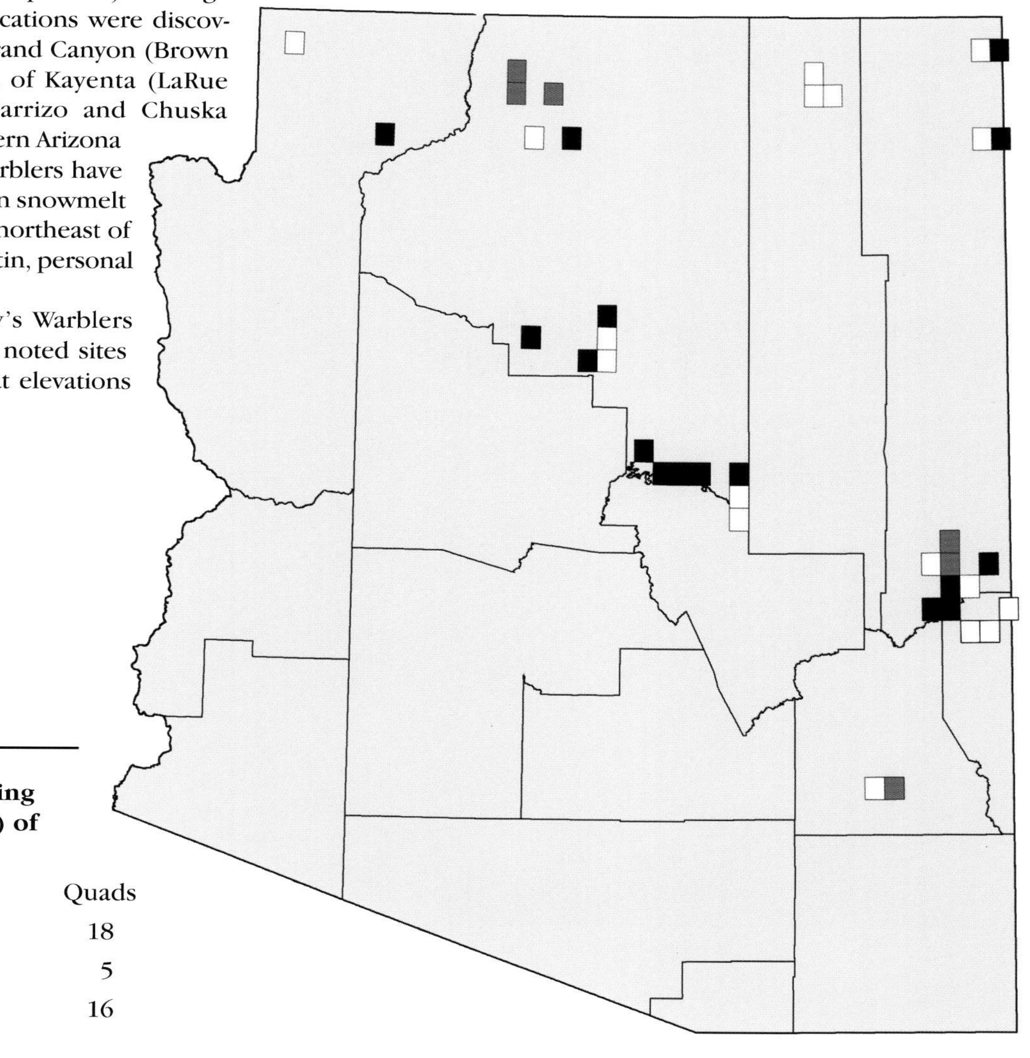

MacGillivray's Warbler Breeding Evidence Reported in 30 (2%) of 1834 priority blocks

	Blocks	Quads
Possible	11 (37%)	18
Probable	4 (13%)	5
Confirmed	15 (50%)	16

Common Yellowthroat

by Bill Burger *Geothlypis trichas*

The black-mask and "wichety wichety wichety" song of male Common Yellowthroats make them among the most easily identifiable warblers. Although commonly seen or heard, and despite being one of North Americas most widespread warblers, they are secretive around their nests and much about their breeding biology remains poorly known.

HABITAT

Common yellowthroats typically occur in damp areas with thick, low vegetation in a wide range of habitats. In Arizona, such dense vegetation is usually found in association with water; thus, yellowthroats are primarily found in wetlands or other riparian areas. Thirty-five percent of all atlas records of this warbler were in lowland riparian areas dominated by cottonwood, willow, mesquite, seepwillow, and other low vegetation (n = 214). Marshlands, cienegas, ponds, and lake edges typically dominated by bulrush, cattails, and/or sedges comprised another 29 percent of the atlas observations. A variety of other riparian-associated or wetland habitats made up the remainder of the records and included areas dominated by tamarisk, vegetation bordering sewage ponds or canals, agricultural runoff ditches, higher elevation stream courses, and areas of reeds or seepwillows. In southeastern Arizona, atlasers reported approximately three percent of Common Yellowthroat observations from semiarid grasslands. These records likely reflect this warbler's ability to take advantage of the wet, humid conditions and luxuriant dense vegetative growth enhanced by the late summer monsoon season. During the monsoon period, some individuals move from flooded riparian areas into adjacent giant sacaton and other grass-dominated swales and attempt late-season nesting.

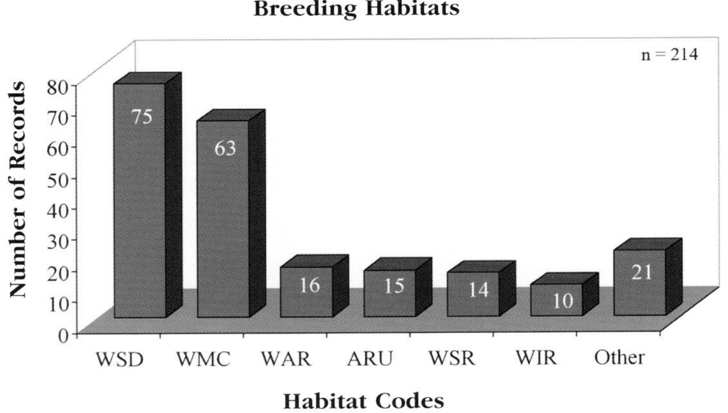

BREEDING

Common Yellowthroats winter in wetlands throughout southern and western Arizona; however, some evidence suggests many of the wintering birds breed north of the state (Phillips et al. 1964). Most migrants begin to arrive on territory in late February and March. Atlasers noted singing males by 31 March along the lower Colorado River and pairs by 2 April in the lower Gila River Valley. Common Yellowthroats are very secretive around their nests, and this is reflected in the few nests located. An adult was observed carrying food on 23 April near Patagonia suggesting nest building and egg laying in early April. The earliest fledgling was noted near Wickenburg on 2 May. Atlas data suggest two peak nesting periods in Arizona: late May to mid-June and mid-July to early August. This may pertain to two broods, or to those populations influenced by late summer monsoons. Adults were observed carrying food and feeding recently fledged young through 16 August. Atlasers reported singing males through 22 August in southeastern Arizona, which may indicate local nesting activity continuing well into August and after most atlas surveys had ended. Some Common Yellowthroats begin appearing in nonbreeding areas by late July or early August, indicating the start of fall migration.

Even though Common Yellowthroats are easily detected through their distinctive song, most atlas observations were left unconfirmed due to the dense vegetation and wet environments they inhabit. These warblers are also notoriously secretive around their well-concealed nests. Common Yellowthroat nests were not described during atlas fieldwork, but several nests in Arizona have been found in grass clumps adjacent to stands of threesquare bulrush and cattails at the edge of cienegas and small streams (T. Corman, personal communication). Nests are often on the ground in dry areas or in vegetation within about 4 in. (10 cm) of the ground in marshy or other wet areas. Common Yellowthroat nests are often supported by sedges, grasses, reeds, cattails, or other dense vegetation

Breeding Phenology

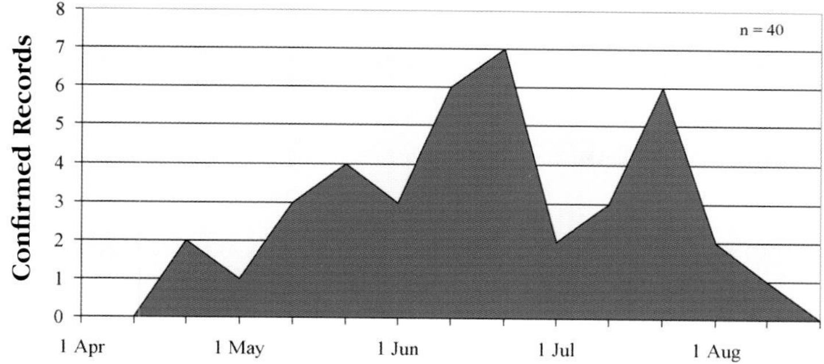

that provides concealment and protection from the sun (Guzy and Ritchison 1999).

Guzy and Ritchison (1999) summarize breeding information, though they caution that few studies of breeding biology of Common Yellowthroats have been conducted. Females choose the nest site and construct the nest, usually taking 4–5 days. Clutches typically consist of 3–4 eggs, but can range from 1 to 6 (Bent 1953). The female incubates the eggs for approximately 12 days. Both parents feed the nestlings, which develop rapidly and fledge in 10–12 days, becoming independent when they are about 30 days of age.

The overall range of egg dates for Common Yellowthroats suggests that second broods may be common throughout much of the breeding range, although this has been documented in only a few localities. Atlasers only noted one instance of Brown-headed Cowbird brood parasitism, but Common Yellowthroats are locally regular hosts in Arizona, with most observations pertaining to adults feeding cowbird fledglings.

DISTRIBUTION AND STATUS

Common Yellowthroats are one of North America's most widespread warblers, breeding throughout much of the United States and Canada, south into central Mexico. In much of the arid Southwest, populations are concentrated in wetlands and riparian areas, and therefore locally distributed. In Arizona, Common Yellowthroats have been described as common summer residents in much of the state below 6500 ft (1981 m) where appropriate habitat exists, and locally at higher elevations in the White Mountain region (Phillips et al. 1964).

Atlasers noted evidence of Common Yellowthroats likely nesting at elevations ranging from 100 ft (30 m) along the lower Colorado River to 8350 ft (2545 m) near Greer in the White Mountains. As the accompanying map indicates, Common Yellowthroats breed in suitable habitats throughout much of Arizona. They were prevalent in southeastern Arizona and along most perennial and intermittent river corridors in the state. Atlasers found few nesting localities in northern Arizona away from the Colorado River drainage, which likely pertains to the sparseness of wetland habitat in that region. Similarly, Common Yellowthroats were infrequently detected in the Sonoran Desert region of southwestern Arizona away from the Colorado and Gila River valleys.

Overall, Common Yellowthroats appear to be doing well in the state. During the atlas period, many city and town wastewater-treatment facilities created wetland habitats that were readily populated with nesting Common Yellowthroats. This has even occurred at locations surrounded by miles of open desert landscapes and far from other established populations. Additionally, there has been a gradual increase in the number of riparian areas protected and properly managed within the state where populations of this little wetland warbler have greatly increased.

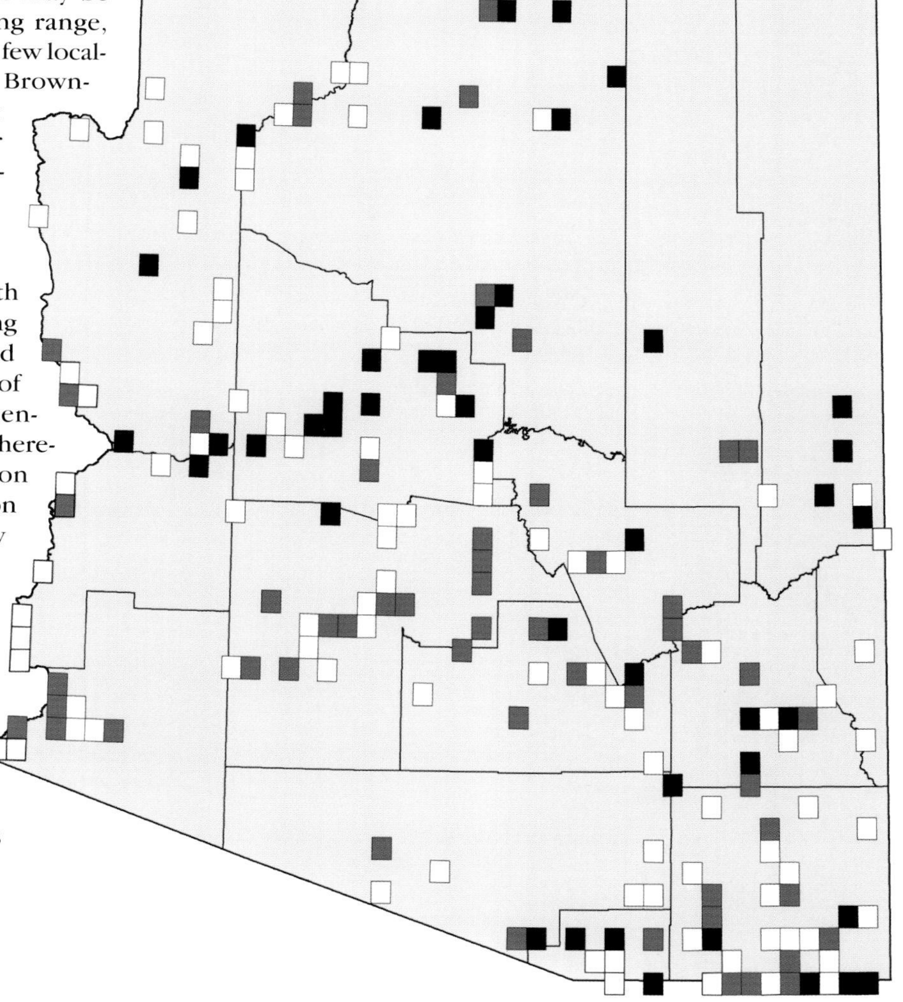

Common Yellowthroat Breeding Evidence Reported in 134 (7%) of 1834 priority blocks

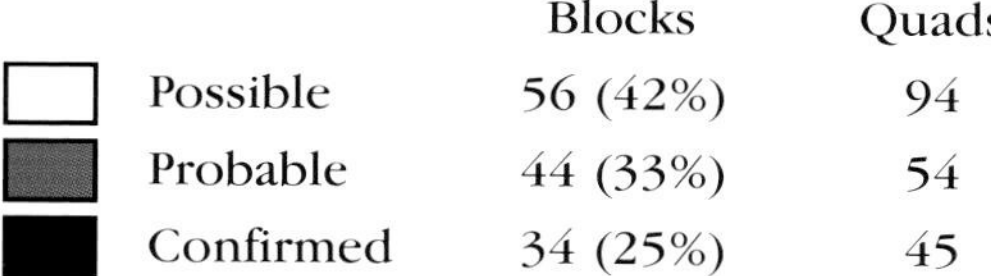

	Blocks	Quads
Possible	56 (42%)	94
Probable	44 (33%)	54
Confirmed	34 (25%)	45

Red-faced Warbler

by Troy E. Corman *Cardellina rubrifrons*

The white rump and deep crimson face of the strikingly handsome Red-faced Warbler often appear as tiny beacons as they flit among the dark green hues of the tall firs and pines they prefer. Seemingly bold and inquisitive, whistled imitations of a pygmy-owl call, may find the observer soon surrounded by a frenzy of these loudly chipping, ruby-fronted gems.

DAN FISCHER

HABITAT

Nesting in montane forests of Arizona, Red-faced Warblers reach their greatest abundance in or near deep, heavily forested canyons and cool, steeply sloping drainages. They become far less numerous in flatter terrain and are often absent in adjacent drier conifer forests. These attractive warblers are most frequently encountered in mixed-conifer forests and adjacent montane drainages where 60 percent of potential atlas breeding records were obtained ($n = 107$). These vegetative communities frequently contained Douglas fir, white fir, ponderosa pine, and aspen, often with an understory of Rocky Mountain maple, Gambel's oak, and other broadleaf trees or shrubs. Atlasers also encountered this species locally in drainages dominated by ponderosa pine, particularly if the forest has a Gambel's oak association. In the mountains of southeastern Arizona, Red-faced Warblers also frequent moist canyons containing Madrean pine-oak woodlands and mixed-conifer forests. Here the dominant trees often include Apache, Chihuahuan, ponderosa, and southwestern white pines with an understory of bigtooth maple, Gambel's oak, and various Madrean evergreen oaks. In the White and San Francisco mountains, this warbler locally approaches the lower reaches of Engelmann spruce and subalpine fir.

BREEDING

Red-faced Warblers typically begin arriving in Arizona in late April, rarely as early as 9 April, with nesting activity beginning soon after arrival on territory (Phillips et al. 1964). Nest building activity was not noted until 11 May, but Martin and Barber (1995) reported egg laying in southeastern Arizona as early as 4 May and on the Mogollon Rim as early as 8 May. Atlasers reported the earliest fledgling on 25 May, which would suggest egg laying in late April and incubation initiating no later than 1 May. Based on statewide atlas data, Red-faced Warbler nesting activity in Arizona increases in late May through much of June, with a significant increase in early July of adults feeding fledglings. Atlasers reported the latest nest with eggs on 12 July and adults were observed carrying food and feeding fledged young into late July and early August. Some individuals begin to depart the breeding grounds in July, with a peak passage in August and early September (Martin and Barber 1995). Stragglers have been observed into late September and exceptionally to 11 October (Phillips et al. 1964; Monson and Phillips 1981).

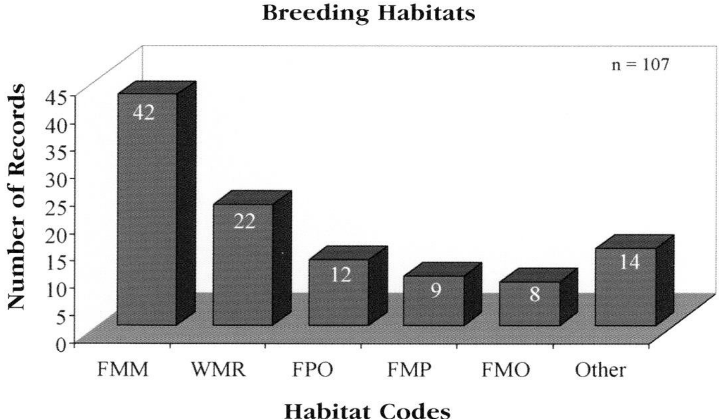

Only the female constructs the nest, which is placed on the ground, typically low on a steep slope, bank, or among forbs on rock faces (Martin and Barber 1995). Red-faced Warbler nests are often constructed at the base of a tree trunk, log, rock, shrub, or grass clump and are frequently well concealed by overhanging vegetation, dry leaves, or other forest debris (Bent 1953; Martin and Barber 1995).

The following Red-faced Warbler nesting information is from intensive work conducted and compiled by Martin and Barber (1995) in Arizona. Full clutches typically consists of 4–5 eggs (rarely 6), although occasionally only 3 eggs are laid later in the season. Only the female incubates and the incubation period lasts approximately 13 days. Both parents feed the nestlings through fledging in 11–13 days. The parents continue to feed the fledglings for an additional week or so following nest departure. Pairs usually renest following the failure of their first clutch, with some attempting to renest three and rarely four times.

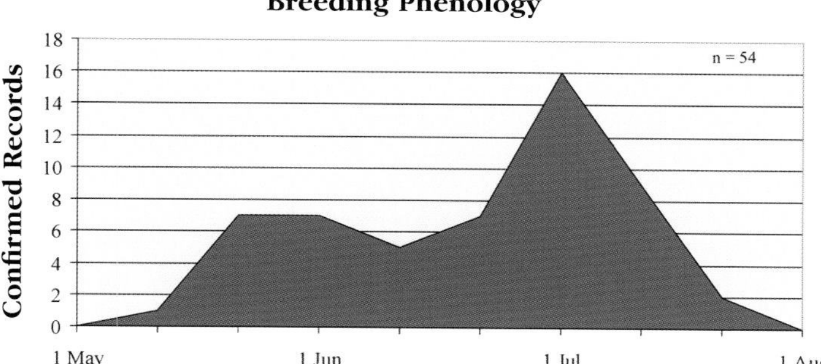

However, only one successful brood per season has ever been recorded.

Red-faced Warblers are considered rare Brown-headed Cowbird hosts (Martin and Barber 1995). Atlasers documented three instances of adult warblers feeding fledgling cowbirds between 19 June and 10 July.

DISTRIBUTION AND STATUS

Red-faced Warblers breed from north-central Arizona and west-central New Mexico, south to Durango, Mexico (Howell and Webb 1995). In Arizona, they were historically found only in the higher southeastern mountain ranges north to the base of the Mogollon Rim. Since the mid-1930s, observers began noting them above the Mogollon Rim and in the Flagstaff region (Phillips et al. 1964). By the 1980s the species was nesting north to the White Mountains and northwest to the Bill Williams and Hualapai mountains (Monson and Phillips 1981).

Atlasers commonly encountered Red-faced Warblers nesting throughout their previously documented range in Arizona at elevations from 6000 to 9200 ft (1829–2804 m). Locally, they were also found nesting as low as 5350 ft (1631 m) along the West Fork of Oak Creek Canyon. Based on the available habitat, these warblers undoubtedly continue to nest along the southern edge of the Mogollon Rim. This includes the forested White Mountain Apache tribal lands, where atlas surveys could not be conducted; as a result, data omitted from this area are obvious on the adjacent distribution map. During the atlas period, Red-faced Warblers were confirmed nesting for the first time in the Mazatzal Mountains of northeastern Maricopa County and first noted in the seldom-visited Santa Teresa Mountains in western Graham County.

Atlas data provide further evidence of the continued northern range expansion of the Red-faced Warblers in Arizona. Territorial birds were documented on Kendrick Peak northwest of Flagstaff and on Sitgreaves Mountain north of Parks, and both of these locations are slightly farther north than previously noted. Atlasers discovered a singing individual on the western slopes of the Kaibab Plateau near Big Springs, which may represent a spring overshoot. However, breeding habitat does exist locally on the plateau, and this record only adds to a growing number of summer observations since the mid-1970s in this vast, undersurveyed region (Brown et al. 1986).

Habitat loss and degradation from timber harvesting activity and wildfires appear to be the Red-faced Warblers greatest conservation concern in Arizona. Franzreb (1977) reported that their numbers diminish drastically or they vanished altogether as a consequence of logging on the breeding grounds. Similarly, in a study of a gradient of disturbed forest plots that ranged from clear-cut to selectively logged, this attractive warbler was present primarily only in untouched (control) areas (Szaro and Balda 1979).

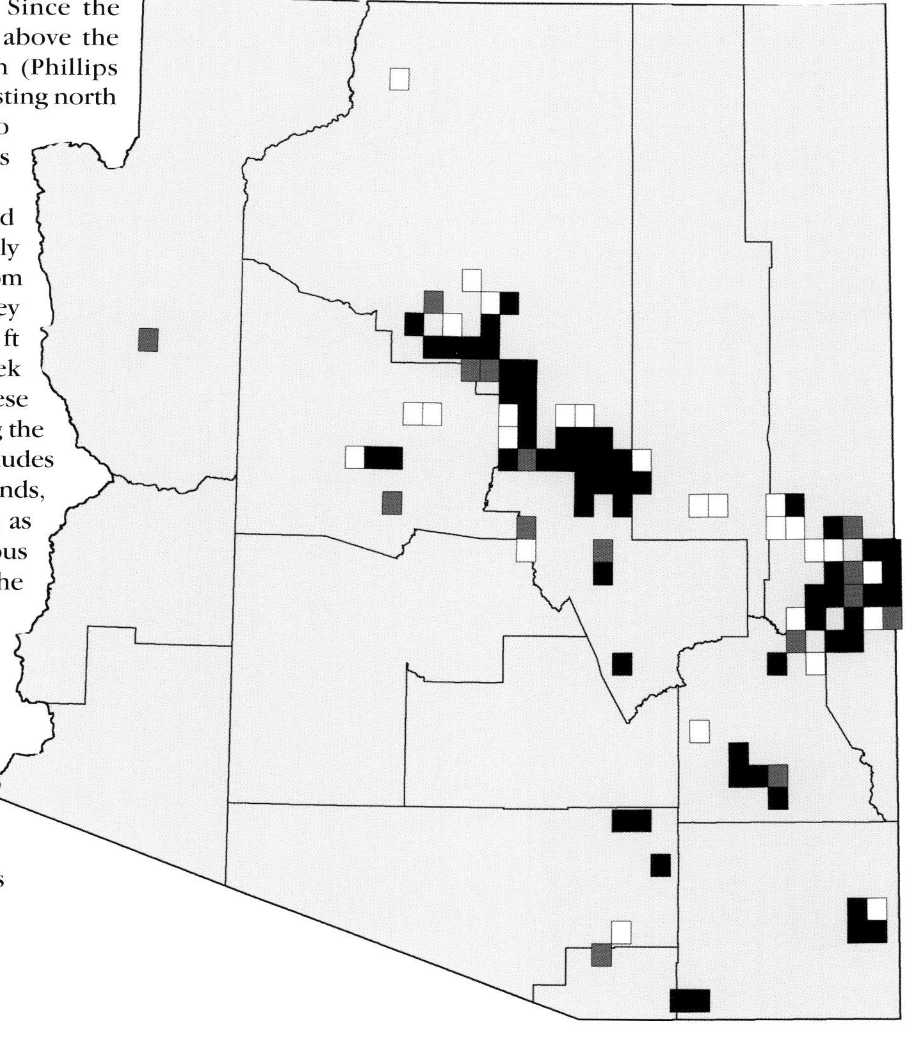

Red-faced Warbler Breeding Evidence Reported in 81 (4%) of 1834 priority blocks

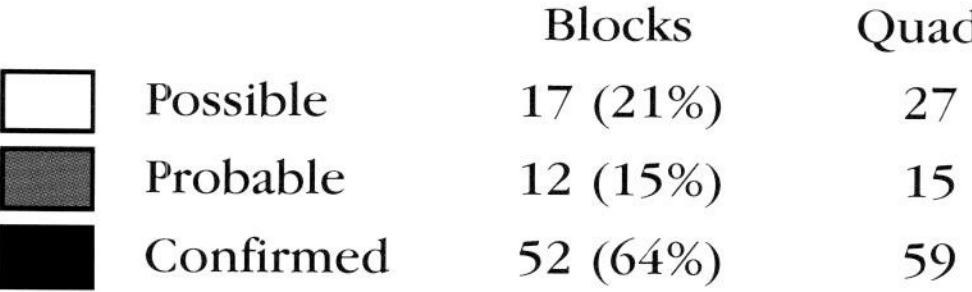

	Blocks	Quads
Possible	17 (21%)	27
Probable	12 (15%)	15
Confirmed	52 (64%)	59

Painted Redstart

by Troy E. Corman *Myioborus pictus*

Flashy, energetic woodland spirits, Painted Redstarts are common features in cool mountain canyons of central and southeastern Arizona. Foraging low in trees or along rocky streams, their perky, charming attitude attract the attention of even the most casual observer. They continuously pivot from side to side, emphasizing the patches of white on their spread wings and tail.

BRUCE TAUBERT

HABITAT

Painted Redstarts are characteristic birds of the pine-oak forests, especially where this habitat enters into canyon bottoms with perennial or intermittent water. These perky warblers are most frequently encountered in well-shaded, forested canyons and on mountain slopes with a high diversity of deciduous and coniferous trees. Atlasers reported Painted Redstarts most frequently in mountain drainages dominated by Arizona sycamore and evergreen oaks, which accounted for 30 percent of all atlas records (n = 109). An additional 17 percent were noted in higher drainages that often included Douglas fir, ponderosa pine, Gambel's oak, and maple. They were encountered fairly commonly in ponderosa pine forests south and west of the Mogollon Rim, particularly when Gambel's or other oaks were present. In southeastern Arizona, Painted Redstarts are frequent inhabitants of Madrean pine-oak forests, often containing Apache, Chihuahuan, and ponderosa pines with a fairly dense understory of various evergreen oaks, alligator juniper, and Arizona madrone. These warblers were also detected nesting locally and in reduced numbers along drier foothill drainages of almost pure evergreen oaks of various species. Within this habitat, the oaks were typically tall, dense, and frequently maintained a fairly closed canopy.

BREEDING

Although a few Painted Redstarts regularly winter in lower mountain canyons in southeastern Arizona, the majority of the state's breeding population begins arriving in early to mid-March and is widespread by April. Males often arrive 2–10 days before the females to establish territories (Marshall and Balda 1974). Pairs form shortly thereafter, with nest-building activity reported as early as 8 April. The earliest Painted Redstart nest with eggs discovered during the atlas was on 9 May. However, fledglings noted on 19 May would indicate that egg laying was initiated by late April. Statewide atlas data show that nesting efforts steadily increased through late May and June, with a sharp decrease after mid-July. Nests with eggs have been reported as late as 14 July in southeastern Arizona (Barber et al. 2000), and atlasers reported adults feeding fledglings through 5 August. Migration begins in late August and early September, with most individuals having departed the state by mid-October.

Breeding Habitats

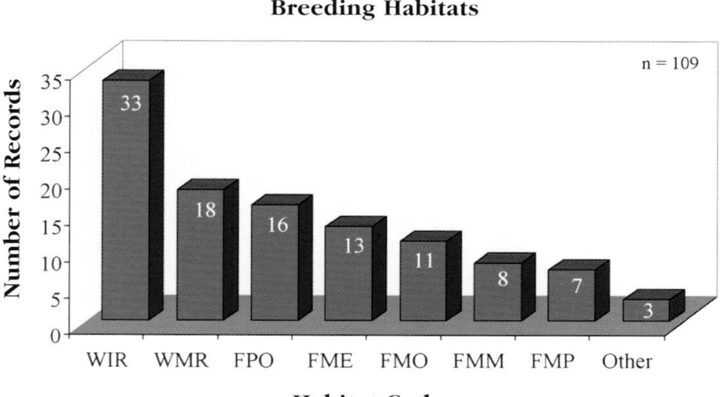

Habitat Codes

Painted Redstarts typically construct their nests on the ground in a sheltered area frequently on a steep slope of a canyon, creek embankment, or vertical rocky wall with scattered patches of grass and other low vegetation. The nest is well concealed and is often under tufts of grass, overhanging rocks, or forest litter. Atlasers also discovered Painted Redstart nests tucked away among the roots of fallen trees and several nests in Arizona have been discovered 10–20 ft (3.0–6.1 m) high in large shallow cavities of Arizona sycamore (Barber et al. 2000; S. Johnsen, personal communication).

Only the female constructs the nest and incubates the typical clutch of 3–4 eggs, sometimes 5 (Barber et al. 2000). The eggs hatch after an incubation period of 13–14 days, and both parents feed the nestlings until they fledge in their black and white plumage approximately 13 days later (Barber et al. 2000). The family group remains together for an additional 2–3 weeks, at which time the young begin feeding independently and often leave the territory (Marshall and Balda 1974). Painted Redstarts frequently produce two broods per season, with the later nests sometimes parasitized by Brown-headed, and less frequently, Bronzed cowbirds (Friedmann et al. 1977). However, atlasers reported no incidences of cowbird brood parasitism for this warbler.

Breeding Phenology

Confirmed Records

7 6 5 4 3 2 1 0

n = 38

1 Apr 1 May 1 Jun 1 Jul 1 Aug

DISTRIBUTION AND STATUS

Painted Redstarts breed primarily from central Arizona and New Mexico south through the highlands of Mexico and in disjunct populations to Nicaragua. In Arizona, Phillips et al. (1964) described this animated warbler as occurring commonly from southeastern and central Arizona, west to the Baboquivari Mountain, north to the Mogollon Rim, and northwest locally to the Hualapai Mountains.

Atlas surveys revealed that the breeding distribution of Painted Redstarts has basically remained unchanged in Arizona. Atlasers encountered them nesting throughout their historical range at elevations primarily between 5000 and 7500 ft (1524–2286 m). Painted Redstarts were also found nesting locally as low as 3900 ft (1189 m), such as along Sycamore Canyon in the Pajarito Mountains near the Mexico border. In southeastern Arizona, atlasers noted this flashy warbler nesting locally in some of the drier and lower ranges lacking many of the other mountain warblers. These included the Patagonia, Dragoon, Galiuro, Winchester, and Santa Teresa mountains. Additional surveys conducted in the similarly vegetated Mule Mountains may determine that this warbler nests there as well. Painted Redstarts were quite common in the higher mountains of southeastern Arizona and still fairly common farther north, such as along forested canyons and ridges along the southern slope of the Mogollon Rim.

Painted Redstarts are infrequently reported north of the Mogollon Rim and when they are, they usually pertain to spring overshoots or postbreeding dispersing adults or recently fledged young. Atlasers noted this warbler along the eastern edge of Pinal and Maricopa counties in the Pinal, Superstition, and Mazatzal mountains. The northwesternmost breeding outposts in Arizona were noted on Bill Williams Mountain south of Williams and in the Hualapai Mountains. In Yavapai County, atlasers noted that the breeding distribution of these warblers extends north from the Bradshaw Mountains to the Santa Maria and Mingus mountains. The basic breeding distribution of Painted Redstarts in central Arizona is not accurately portrayed on the accompanying map owing to lack of data from the White Mountain Apache tribal lands. This species undoubtedly nest throughout much of this habitat diverse reservation, where access permits to conduct atlas surveys could not be obtained.

Overall, populations of Painted Redstarts in Arizona appear to be fairly stable, although actual trend information is lacking for this species. South and west of the Mogollon Rim, they were encountered on most atlas blocks containing appropriate habitat and when present in an area, these showy, intensely active warblers rarely go unnoticed.

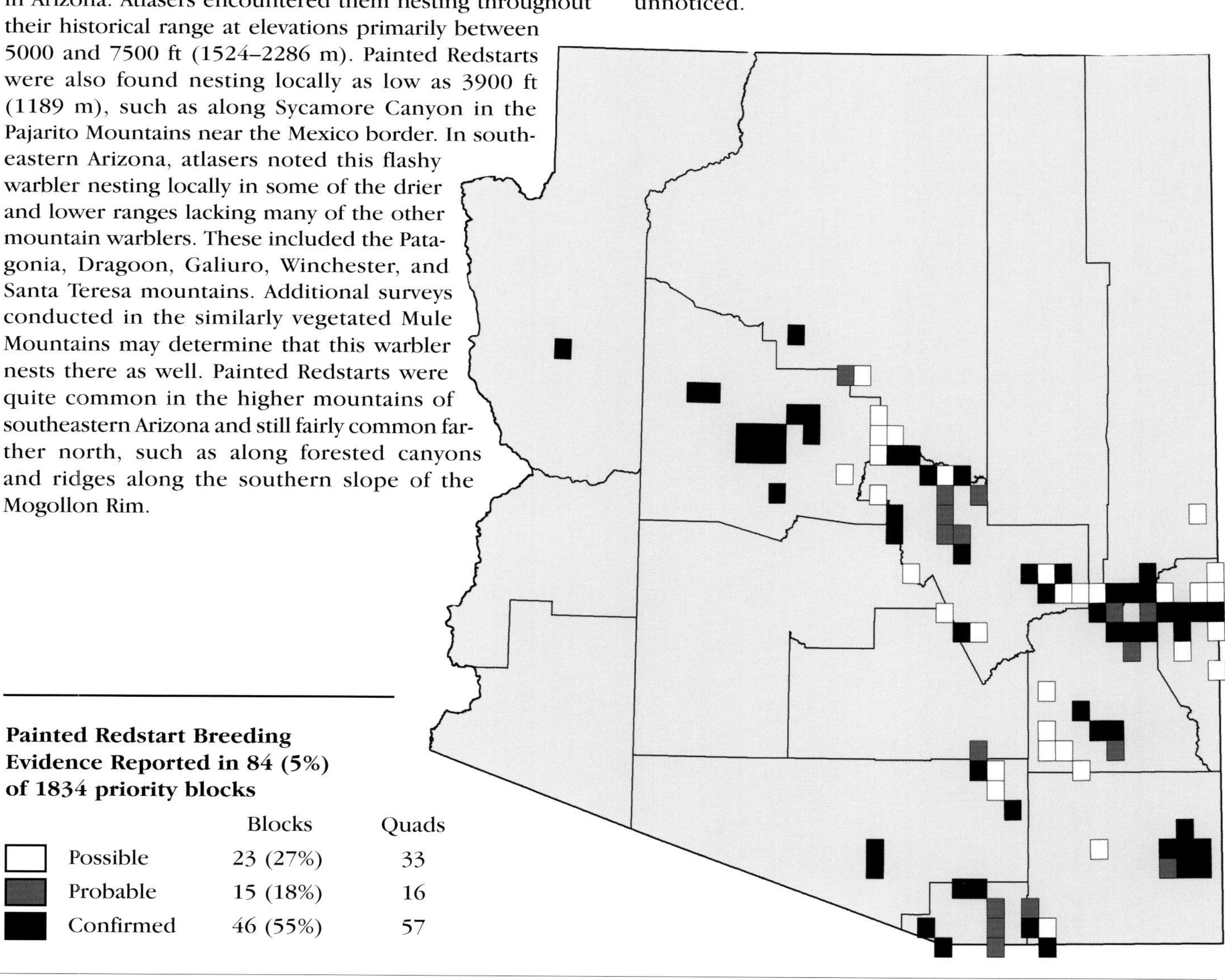

Painted Redstart Breeding Evidence Reported in 84 (5%) of 1834 priority blocks

	Blocks	Quads
Possible	23 (27%)	33
Probable	15 (18%)	16
Confirmed	46 (55%)	57

Yellow-breasted Chat

by Annalaura Averill-Murray and Troy E. Corman

Icteria virens

RICK AND NORA BOWERS

The eclectic song of these large, colorful warblers consists of a variety of unmusical notes and odd sounds that can be heard from dawn to well into the evening during the height of breeding season. Otherwise, Yellow-breasted Chats skulk amid dense, shrubby vegetation and are often difficult to detect.

HABITAT

Throughout their range, Yellow-breasted Chats are associated with dense, shrubby vegetation with an open canopy or subcanopy (Eckerle and Thompson 2001). In Arizona, this species is largely restricted to riparian deciduous woodlands or riparian scrub vegetation where 95 percent of all atlas records were reported (*n* = 266). Atlasers noted the majority of Yellow-breasted Chat observations (49 percent) from lowland riparian woodlands characterized by cottonwood and willow with a dense understory of mesquite, tamarisk, and other shrubs. Locally, they were also found nesting in adjacent large mesquite bosques. Additionally, 19 percent of records for this species were from lower mountain canyons and foothill riparian corridors dominated by Arizona sycamore. Fewer individuals were documented along lower intermittent drainages characterized by dense thickets of mesquite, arrowweed, seepwillow, and tamarisk.

The Yellow-breasted Chat is somewhat of a generalist in its use of available nesting habitat (Brown and Trosset 1989), as demonstrated by its ability to use mature tamarisk-dominated areas within the lower Colorado and other lowland river valleys. Atlasers recorded 4 percent of all observations for this species in riparian areas comprised largely of tamarisk. Although they will use tamarisk and mesquite-dominated riparian areas in Arizona, they appear to reach their highest breeding densities in cottonwood-willow woodlands (Rosenberg et al. 1991).

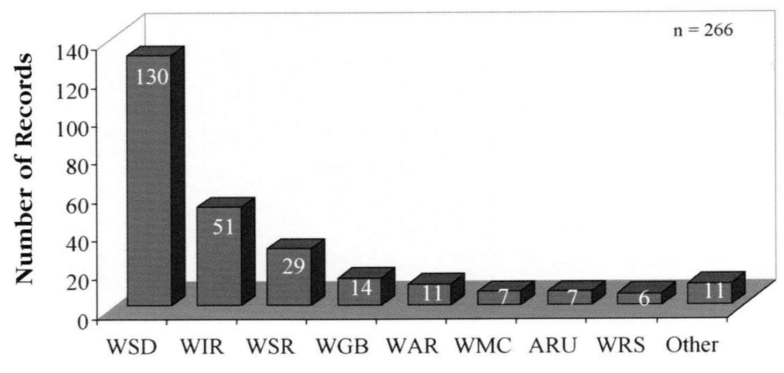

BREEDING

In Arizona, Yellow-breasted Chats typically begin arriving on their southern breeding grounds in mid-April, occasionally earlier, with most arriving later in the month or into early May. Pairs form shortly after females arrive, followed quickly by nest construction. Atlasers reported several very early nesting efforts, including a nest containing eggs on 22 April and fledglings on 10 May. Most nesting activity in Arizona begins in early May. Atlas data reveal a peak in Yellow-breasted Chat nesting activity in Arizona between late May and late June; however, breeding activity continued well into summer. Most late-nesting attempts were noted in the southeastern corner of the state, including an observation of nest building on 25 July and adults carrying food on 24 August. Like many other passerine birds in this region of the state, they may take advantage of abundant food and cover resources enhanced by late summer monsoon activity.

Migrating Yellow-breasted Chats are typically silent and difficult to detect in the dense cover they prefer. In Arizona, fall migration can begin by late August and peaks in September. Most individuals have departed Arizona by early October, with stragglers occasionally reported through the month.

Yellow-breasted Chat nests are typically placed within 3–4 ft (0.9–1.2 m) of the ground in a dense thicket or tangle of vegetation (Eckerle and Thompson 2001). Atlasers described five nest sites with a median nest height of 3.6 ft (1.1 m) and a range of 2.0–9.3 ft (0.6–2.8 m). Nests were located in seepwillow, mesquite, and Goodding willow. Along the lower Colorado and Bill Williams rivers, 63 percent of Yellow-breasted Chat nests were placed in tamarisk (*n* = 59; Averill 1996).

The female constructs the bulky cup nest and incubates the usual clutch of 3–5, sometimes 6, eggs (Eckerle and Thompson 2001). Incubation lasts for approximately 12 days, and young leave the nest 8–11 days after hatching (Baicich and Harrison 1997). Yellow-breasted Chats produce one to two broods per year, and renesting attempts following loss of earlier eggs or broods are frequent in this species.

Yellow-breasted Chats are considered a common host of the Brown-headed Cowbird (Friedmann 1963) and atlasers documented two instances of brood parasitism by

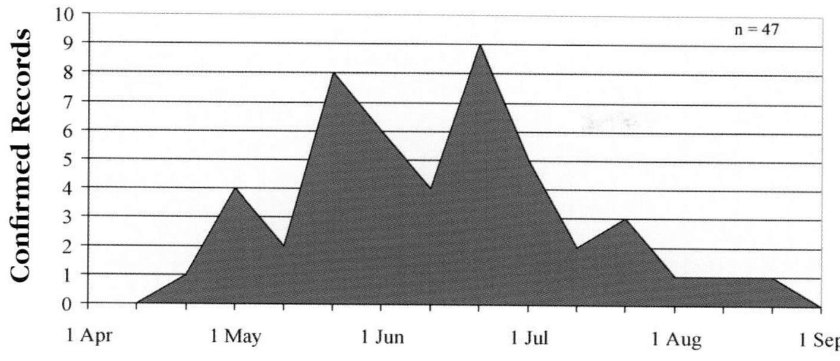

this cowbird. Parasitism rates of 5–91 percent have been recorded throughout their breeding range. Additionally, Bronzed Cowbirds are also known to parasitize Yellow-breasted Chat nests in Arizona. In 1985, one nest was discovered along Bonito Creek northeast of Safford that contained several eggs of both cowbird species. While these large warblers do incur some reproductive losses owing to cowbirds, they are typically able to raise both cowbirds and chats within the same nest, unlike some smaller host species (Thompson and Nolan 1973; Averill 1996; Burhans and Thompson 1999).

DISTRIBUTION AND STATUS

Yellow-breasted Chats breed throughout much of the United States and southern Canada, south to northern Mexico. Many populations, especially in the West, are isolated from one another owing to their preference for wooded riparian areas. In Arizona, Phillips et al. (1964) considered Yellow-breasted Chats as fairly common to very common along wooded rivers, streams, and ponds below 6500 ft (1981 m).

Similarly, atlasers noted Yellow-breasted Chats as a fairly common nesting species at scattered locations throughout much of the state, with the bulk of the population in central and southeastern Arizona. During the atlas project, these birds were found at elevations ranging from approximately 100 to 7440 ft (30–2268 m). This species is locally common along major watercourses such as the Colorado, Gila, Salt, Big Sandy, Verde, Agua Fria, San Pedro, and upper Santa Cruz rivers, including the adjacent tributaries. Atlasers noted this species as largely absent from the breeding avifauna of the arid deserts of southwestern Arizona. However, singing individuals were found in a select few locations along large, densely wooded washes and earthen tanks on Tohono O'odham tribal lands into at least mid-May. Later surveys were not conducted at these desert locations, and it is unknown if these individuals remained to nest.

Atlas data again emphasize the fact that Yellow-breasted Chats are very locally distributed north of the Mogollon Rim, likely owing to the very limited distribution of their preferred habitat. In northern Arizona, they were encountered along the Colorado River in the Grand Canyon, the adjacent Little Colorado River, at several locales on Navajo and Hopi tribal lands, and in the Virgin River watershed in extreme northwestern Arizona. Just north of the Mogollon Rim, atlasers found concentrations of Yellow-breasted Chats along East Clear and Chevelon creeks, and along the upper Little Colorado River from Eagar north to Saint Johns.

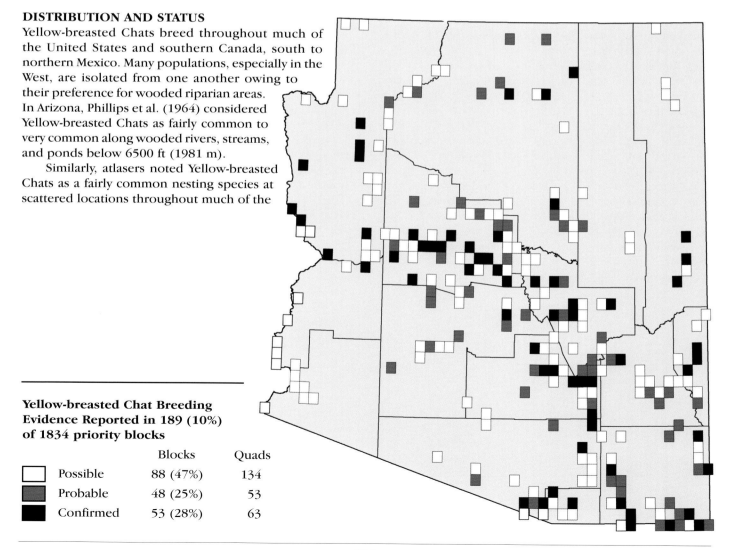

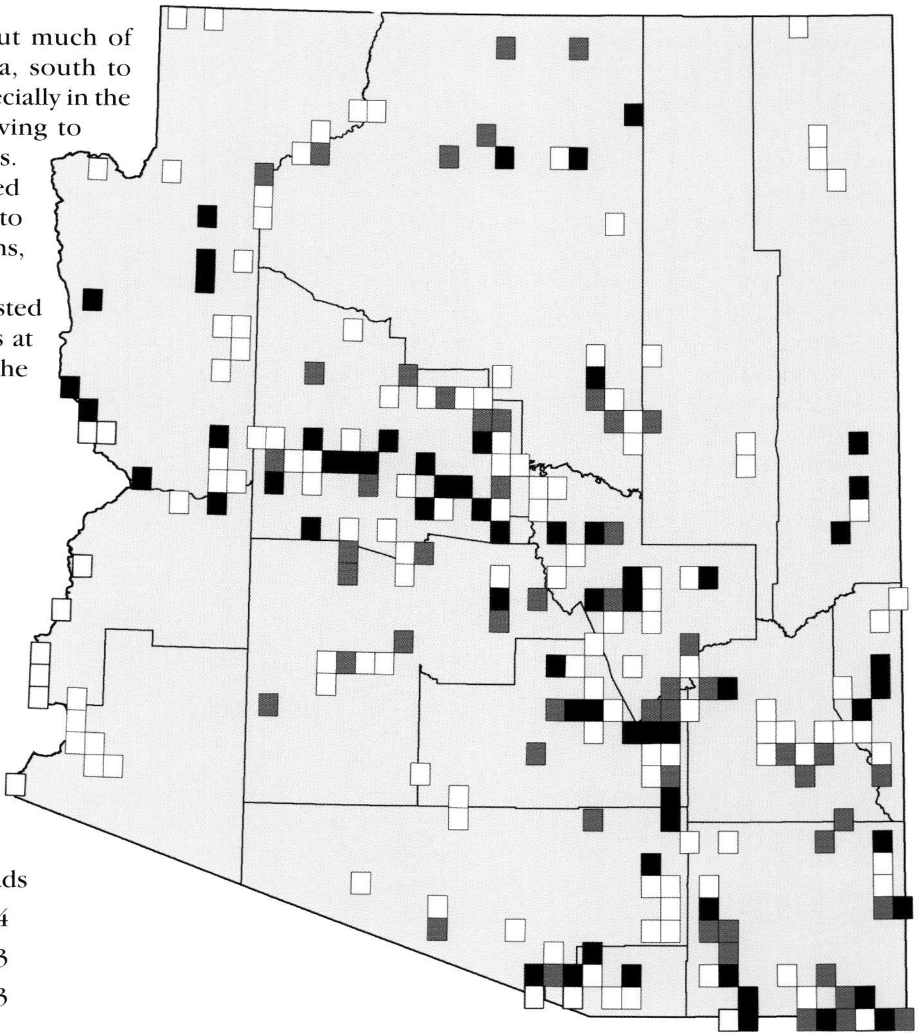

Yellow-breasted Chat Breeding Evidence Reported in 189 (10%) of 1834 priority blocks

	Blocks	Quads
Possible	88 (47%)	134
Probable	48 (25%)	53
Confirmed	53 (28%)	63

Hepatic Tanager

by Cathryn Wise-Gervais *Piranga flava*

RICK AND NORA BOWERS

Although less showy than other Arizona tanagers, the Hepatic Tanager possesses its own unique charm, and is commonly encountered in pine-oak woodlands as it forages methodically through the treetops. "Hepatic" means "related to the liver" and refers to the bird's grayish red plumage.

HABITAT

Hepatic Tanagers inhabit many different habitats across their extensive range, but generally occur in a variety open forests and woodlands in Arizona, including wooded drainages. The species reaches its highest density in pine-oak associations, especially in areas where several habitats merge (Marshall 1957). Atlasers reported 231 potential breeding records for the species in sixteen different vegetative communities, with no single habitat being especially prevalent. In the mountains and canyons of southeastern Arizona, these tanagers are especially common in woodlands containing mixed evergreen oaks and open stands of Apache, Chihuahuan, and/or ponderosa pines. They are also frequently encountered in canyons where this habitat merged with sycamore-dominated drainages, and atlasers reported 42 percent of records for the species in these areas.

In central and northwestern Arizona, Hepatic Tanagers were most often reported in open ponderosa pine forests with an understory of Gambel's oak, evergreen oak, or pinyon pine–juniper. They were reported less frequently in pure ponderosa pine stands and very locally in cooler forests containing Douglas fir. Atlasers also noted this tanager's widespread, but relatively patchy use of taller and denser woodlands of pinyon pine and juniper, especially if these forests contained scattered ponderosa pines. Approximately 24 percent of atlas records were reported in pinyon–juniper dominated woodlands.

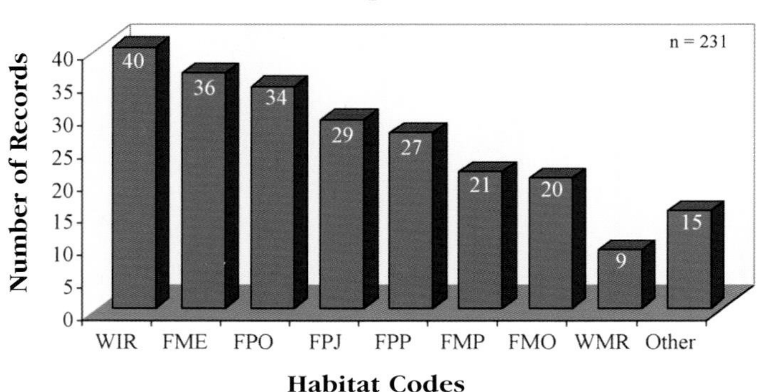

BREEDING

Most Hepatic Tanagers in Arizona are migratory and begin arriving in southern Arizona by late March or early April. Atlasers first reported these tanagers singing in suitable breeding habitat on 16 April. Pairing presumably occurs soon after arrival on territory and observers reported Hepatic Tanagers nest building on 3 May and an occupied nest (likely containing eggs) on 15 May. Due to their lofty nests, nests with eggs could not be determined, but atlasers reported adults feeding fledged young on 7 June indicating some nests contain eggs by early May in Arizona. Nest building and occupied nests were commonly reported from late May to early June, with most confirmations occurring from late June and mid-July when adults were feeding nestlings and fledglings. Atlasers continued confirming this species nesting through the summer with nests with young discovered on 6 August and adults feeding fledglings through 13 August. Although a few hardy Hepatic Tanagers remain to winter locally in southeastern Arizona canyons and foothills, most migrate south from late August through October.

Hepatic Tanager nests are shallow structures, typically placed in outer branches of both coniferous and deciduous trees (Baicich and Harrison 1997). Presumably the female does most of the nest building (Kaufman 1996), as is the case with other tanager species in Arizona. Observers collected measurements at eleven Hepatic Tanager nests during the atlas period. Five nests were in ponderosa pine, two were in sycamore, and one each was in Gambel's oak, Apache pine, Chihuahuan pine, and Utah juniper. The median nest tree height was 52 ft (16 m) and height ranged from 21.3 to 89 ft (6.5–27 m). The median nest height was 29.5 ft (9 m) and ranged from 10.8 to 65.6 ft (3.3–20 m).

Little is known of the Hepatic Tanager's life at the nest. The typical clutch consists of 4 eggs (range 3–5), and the female incubates these for approximately 13 days (Bent 1958). Both parents tend the young and feed them a diet primarily comprising insects. It is not known at what age the young fledge, but this probably occurs at approximately 13–15 days of age, as in Western Tanagers. Most evidence suggests Hepatic Tanagers typically raise only one brood per season (Baicich and Harrison 1997).

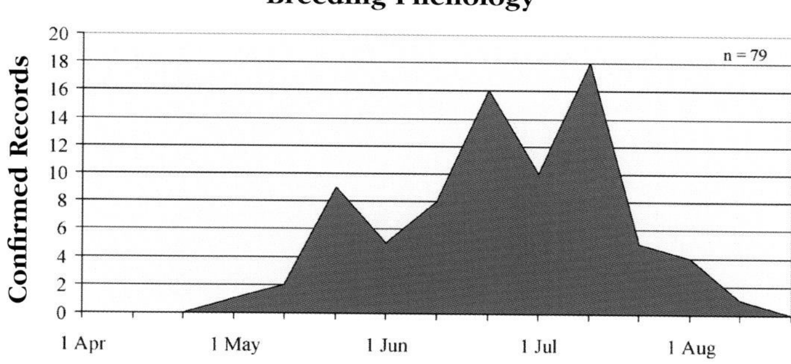

This tanager is considered a rare Bronzed Cowbird host (Bent 1958; Friedmann 1971). Atlasers reported one incident of a Hepatic Tanager feeding a fledgling Bronzed Cowbird on 12 July.

DISTRIBUTION

Hepatic Tanagers have an extensive breeding range south through Mexico and Central America to northern Argentina (Eddleman 2002). Within the United States, they are basically migratory and breed primarily in Arizona and New Mexico with small, local populations in southern Colorado, southwestern Texas, and southeastern California. In Arizona, this species is typically encountered at elevations from 5000 to 7500 ft (1524–2286 m), but atlasers confirmed them breeding locally down to 3800 ft (1158 m) in Sycamore Canyon in the Pajarito Mountains and pairs were noted over 9000 ft (2743 m) near Green's Peak in the White Mountains.

Hepatic Tanagers have previously been described as common to fairly common summer residents in southeastern and central Arizona northwest to Flagstaff, Williams, and the Hualapai Mountains (Phillips et al. 1964). Atlasers discovered that these tanagers have expanded their breeding range considerably to the north and northwest during the past 20–30 years. On Navajo tribal lands, nesting was confirmed in a canyon of northern Black Mesa and a pair was detected at the southern end of the Defiance Plateau. The birds were also noted north to near Tusayan. Hepatic Tanagers were encountered fairly regularly on Hualapai tribal lands, west locally to the Cerbat Mountains and north to the Mount Trumbull, Mount Logan, and Mount Dellenbaugh areas of the Arizona Strip region. Much of the occupied habitat in this region primarily consisted of pinyon-juniper woodland with scattered ponderosa pine in some areas.

Atlasers regularly located Hepatic Tanagers throughout the Mogollon Rim region and the species undoubtedly breeds within the unsurveyed White Mountain Apache tribal lands. In the mountains of southeastern Arizona, these tanagers are especially common and widespread west to the Baboquivari and Quinlan mountains. They were also found in many of the smaller ranges including the Patagonia, Mule, Whetstone, Dragoon, Winchester, and Santa Teresa mountains.

Hepatic Tanager populations appear to be fairly stable within their historical range in the state, and atlas data strongly suggest increasing and expanding populations in the north. Breeding Bird Survey data suggest a slight but statistically nonsignificant population increase from 1980 to 1999 on twenty-one routes sampled. These data should be used with caution, given the limited number of routes reporting these tanagers (Eddleman 2002).

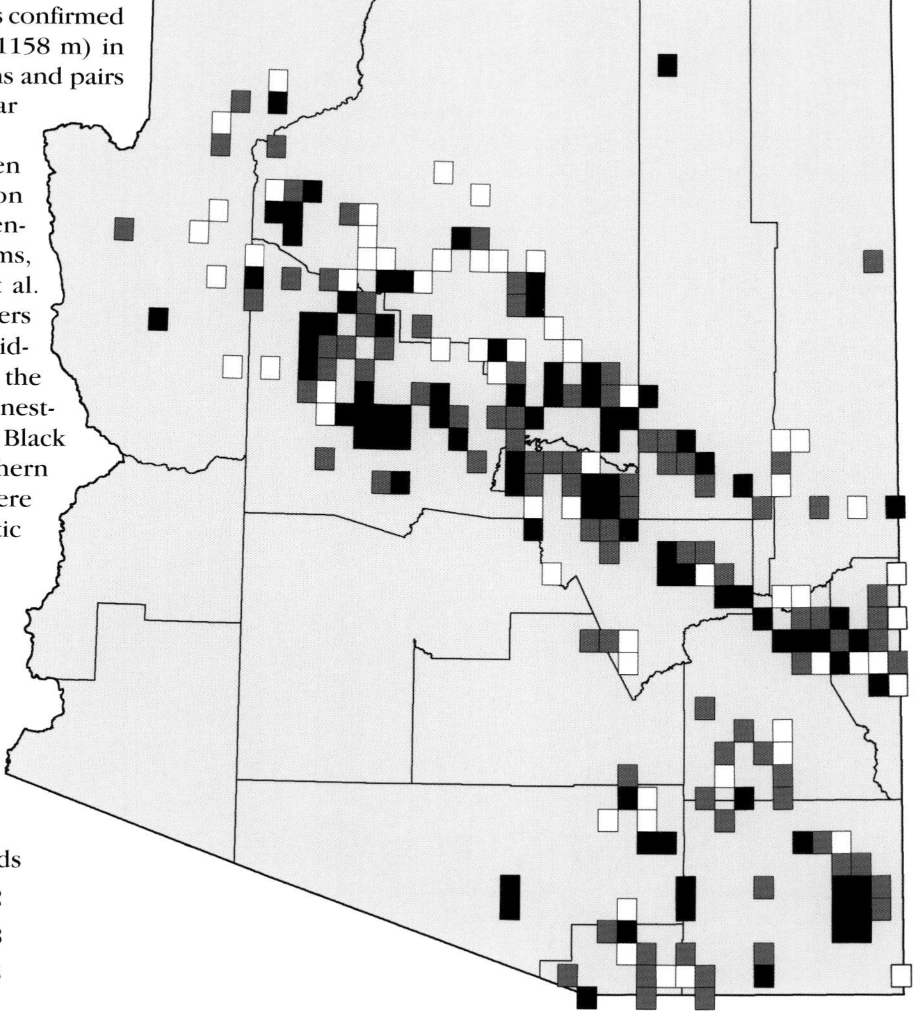

Hepatic Tanager Breeding Evidence Reported in 217 (12%) of 1834 priority blocks

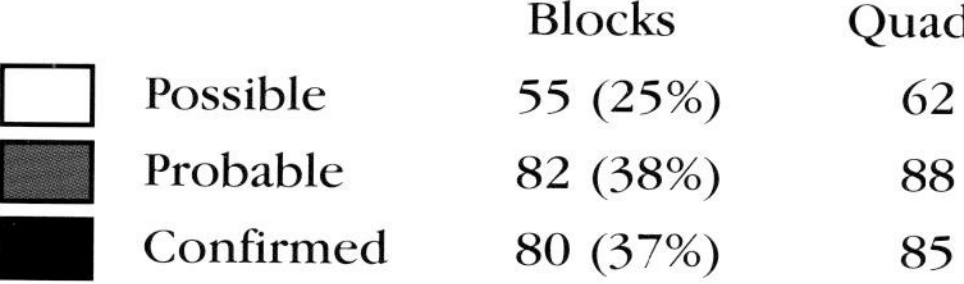

	Blocks	Quads
Possible	55 (25%)	62
Probable	82 (38%)	88
Confirmed	80 (37%)	85

Summer Tanager

by Troy E. Corman *Piranga rubra*

Even brilliant male Summer Tanagers can be surprisingly inconspicuous as they sing and forage high among the dense foliage of cottonwoods and willows. Their distinctive yet short, rapid call is a familiar summer sound for anyone who ventures into their shady, riparian retreats.

HABITAT

Favoring broadleaf woodlands, Summer Tanagers are riparian-obligate species in the arid Southwest. In Arizona, they breed primarily along lowland drainages with stands of native riparian vegetation greater than 35 ft (10.7 m) in height. Atlasers reported 84 percent of all records for this species in only two riparian communities (n = 306). They attain their highest densities along perennial drainages where continuous woodlands of large Fremont cottonwood and Goodding willow exist (46 percent of records). These lush stands may also contain velvet ash, Arizona walnut, exotic tamarisk, and mesquite. In fact, Summer Tanagers regularly frequent the adjacent mesquite bosques as well. In foothill drainages and lower mountain canyons, these birds are less common but regular inhabitants of sycamore-dominated areas (38 percent of records). However, they are typically sparse or absent as a nesting species at higher elevations were these same drainages transition into oak woodlands. These tanagers have nested locally in larger stands of athel tamarisk within the lower Colorado River valley, which Rosenberg et al. (1991) suggest may indicate that height of canopy may be more important than tree species to these birds. Atlasers also noted Summer Tanagers nesting sparsely along some dry washes in southeastern Arizona with dense, narrow woodlands of netleaf hackberry, ash, and mesquite.

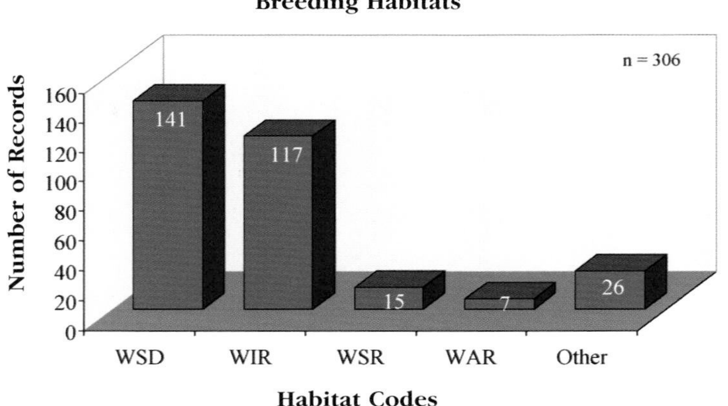

BREEDING

In Arizona, Summer Tanagers typically begin to arrive on their breeding ground in mid-April, with the earliest migrant reported by atlasers on 7 April. Males set up territories quickly and courtship begins immediately upon arrival of the females (Robinson 1996). Atlasers observed nest building activity by 27 April and the first clutch of eggs are likely laid in early to mid-May. The earliest nests with young were reported on 16 May and 19 May. In Arizona, statewide atlas data suggest that peak nesting activity occurs from mid-May to early July, with later attempts continuing well into August. The latest breeding activity observed was an adult feeding a fledged young on 11 September. Most Summer Tanagers have left their breeding grounds by late September with stragglers continuing through October. They are casually reported in November and through the winter in Arizona.

During nest building, the male Summer Tanager often accompanies the female to the nest site, but does not assist in the construction (Robinson 1996). Nests are typically placed on a horizontal limb among clusters of leaves and small branches (Robinson 1996). In Arizona, most nests are placed in cottonwoods or willows, but they also nest in walnut, ash, sycamore, athel tamarisk, and, locally, oak. Atlasers described the location of only two nests and these were reported in Fremont cottonwood and Arizona white oak. Previous literature reported Summer Tanager nests in the southwest at heights ranging from 15 to 50 ft (4.6–15 m) above the ground (Bent 1958; Rosenberg et al. 1991).

Nests of the Summer Tanager are sturdy and well constructed (Bent 1958; Robinson 1996). Typical clutch size consists of 3–4 eggs (range 2–5) and the female begins the 11–12 days of incubation the day that the last egg is laid (Bent 1958, Fitch and Fitch 1955). At least some males have been observed feeding the females throughout incubation (Fitch and Fitch 1955). Both parents feed the nestlings through fledging in 8–10 days after hatching and are attended by the adults for 3–4 weeks following nest departure (Robinson 1996). Rosenberg et al. (1991) noted that males immediately begin to sing again after the first brood fledged and that most pairs attempt a second brood.

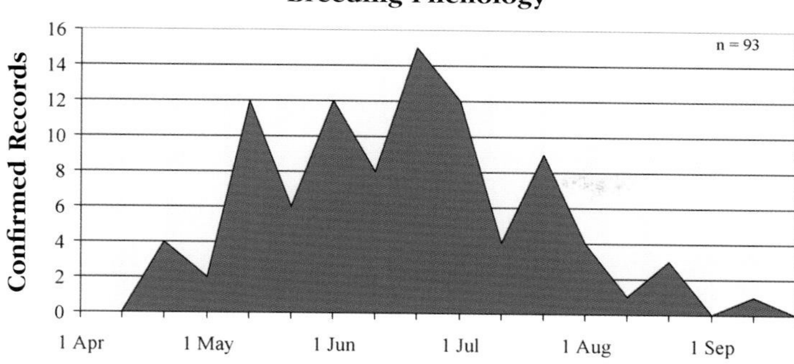

DISTRIBUTION AND STATUS

Summer Tanagers breeds throughout much of southeastern United States north to New Jersey, Ohio, and Iowa, and south through Texas and northern Mexico. In the Southwest, they are found primarily along riparian corridors of southeastern California, Arizona, and New Mexico, locally extending into southern Nevada and adjacent Utah.

Phillips et al. (1964) considered Summer Tanagers as common summer resident in most of the lowland broadleaf associations of southeastern and central Arizona, as well as along the lower Colorado River. They were later reported as nesting in the extreme northwest along the lower Beaver Dam Wash and locally at the bottom of the Grand Canyon (Monson and Phillips 1981).

Atlasers commonly encountered Summer Tanagers throughout their previously described range in that state at elevations primarily below 5600 ft (1707 m). They were widespread in appropriate habitat in southeastern Arizona west to canyons within the Baboquivari Mountains. To the north, these tanagers were regularly encountered along the lower Blue, Black, and Salt River drainages. Within the Gila River drainage, Summer Tanagers were found primarily only east of Florence, with a small local population just below the confluence of the Gila and Salt rivers southwest of Phoenix. They were also commonly noted along perennial drainages in central Arizona, west to the Big Sandy and Bill Williams rivers. They remain sparse and local along the lower Colorado River, as well as along this drainage within the Grand Canyon, upstream to near Page. Brown et al. (1987) noted that within the Grand Canyon, Summer Tanagers were primarily found nesting in the isolated cottonwood-willow associations, particularly within perennial side drainages of the Colorado River. Atlasers also noted this species continued presence at Beaver Dam Wash near its confluence with the Virgin River.

Historically noted as common breeding birds along the lower Colorado River north to Fort Mohave (Cooper 1861; Grinnell 1914), Summer Tanager numbers and their distribution had declined tremendously by 1976 owing to habitat loss (Rosenberg et al. 1991). Apparently by the early 1900s, this species had already been nearly extirpated along the middle Gila River for similar reasons (Rea 1983). However, where tall, native lowland riparian woodlands remain in the state, these attractive songsters readily inhabit them.

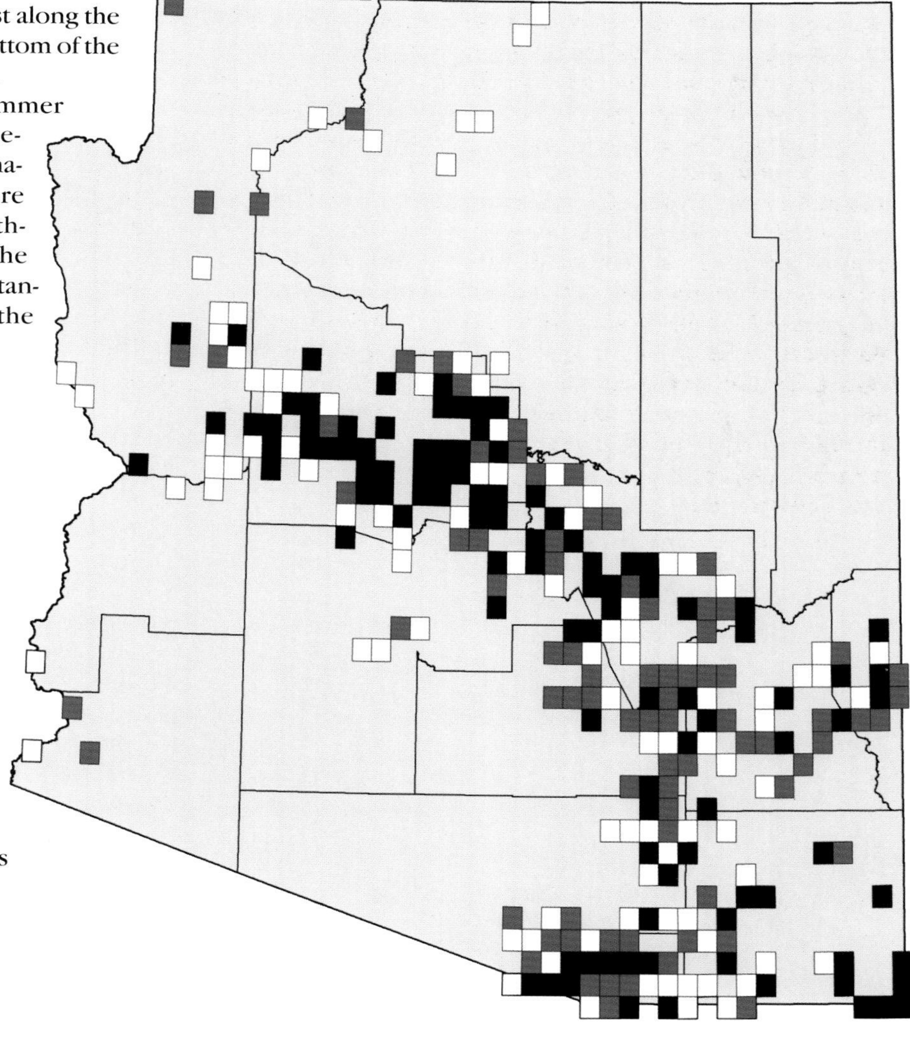

Summer Tanager Breeding Evidence Reported in 239 (13%) of 1834 priority blocks

	Blocks	Quads
Possible	64 (27%)	101
Probable	77 (32%)	82
Confirmed	98 (41%)	106

Western Tanager

by Amanda Moors and Troy E. Corman

Piranga ludoviciana

The Western Tanager is an astonishingly colorful bird with its flashy red, yellow, and black plumage, but, owing to its habit of staying high up in the conifers, it can be difficult to see. The males have quite a bit of variation in the amount of red coloring on the head, possibly due to their unique method of obtaining pigment.

DAN FISCHER

HABITAT

During migration in Arizona, Western Tanagers are encountered in almost any vegetative community in the state from deserts and grasslands to urban and rural shade trees. These colorful tanagers primarily nest in higher-elevation forests and woodlands containing tall conifers. Approximately 64 percent of 246 atlas records for this species were fairly evenly divided between three forest types: mixed-conifer, ponderosa pine, and ponderosa pine–Gambel's oak associations. They appear to reach their highest breeding density in the cool mixed-conifer forests and adjacent montane drainages that frequently include Douglas fir, white fir, aspen, oak, and various pine species, including ponderosa. Atlasers noted these tanagers nesting much less frequently in drier forests where pinyon pine–juniper woodlands merge with ponderosa pine stands. They do nest at the edge of Arizona's limited subalpine spruce-fir forests, but typically avoid the more extensive and denser stands. In the mountains and canyons of southeastern Arizona, Western Tanagers also nest in Madrean pine-oak woodlands containing evergreen oaks with Chihuahuan, Apache, and ponderosa pines, and where this vegetative community merges with sycamore-dominated drainages.

BREEDING

In southern Arizona, Western Tanagers typically begin arriving in mid-April, occasionally earlier, and in northern regions of the state by late April or early May. This tanager has a prolonged northbound migration that can extend well into June and southbound passage can begin by early to mid-July, which has led some people to believe that the birds breed in areas where they are only migrating through (Phillips et al. 1964).

Male Western Tanagers begin singing and actively establishing territories upon their arrival on breeding ground in late April and early May in Arizona. Atlasers noted nest construction activity by 12 May and occupied nests (likely containing eggs) by 21 May. Fledglings were reported as early as 11 June, indicating some early egg laying by mid-May in the state. Atlas data suggest that most Western Tanager nesting activity occurs from mid-June through mid-July, with the latest occupied nest noted on 17 July. However, adults were observed feeding fledglings through 13 August. As noted earlier, fall migration often begins by mid-July in Arizona, peaks in late August and September, with late passage individuals through late October.

Only female Western Tanagers construct the loosely woven nest, taking approximately 4–5 days to complete (Hudon 1999). Nests are often placed in a conifer at a fork of a horizontal branch far from the trunk (Ehrlich et al. 1988). Median nest height from the seven nests measured by atlasers was 23.2 ft (7.1 m) and ranged from 11.8 to 55.1 feet (3.6–16.8 m). Nests were found in ponderosa pine, white fir, Engelmann spruce, rocky mountain maple, and pinyon pine.

Western Tanager clutches typically consist of 3–4 eggs, but can range up to 5 (Bent 1958). Although the male occasionally feeds the incubating female during the approximate 13-day incubation period, he infrequently visits the nest during this period (Hudon 1999). Both parents feed nestlings that fledge in 11–15 days and continue to feed the young for 2–4 weeks following nest departure (Hudon 1999). Most evidence indicates only one brood is raised per season, but they will renest if earlier efforts have failed (Hudon 1999). Western Tanagers are typically considered

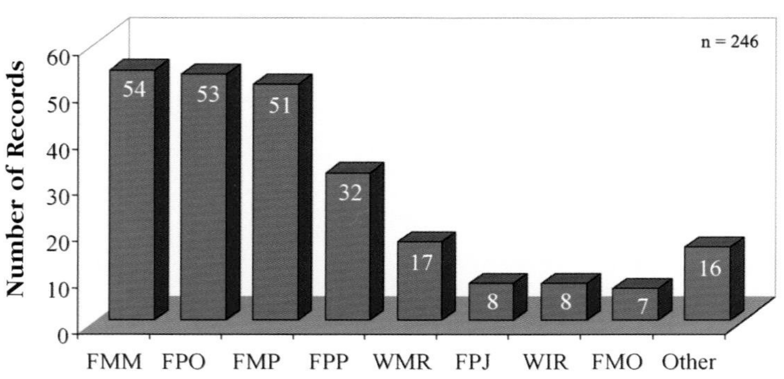

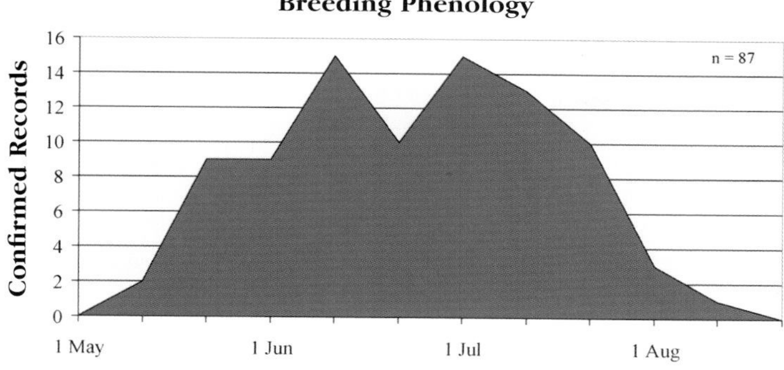

rare Brown-headed Cowbird host, but successful brood parasitism was frequent in one northeastern New Mexico study in pinyon pine–juniper woodlands (Hudon 1999).

DISTRIBUTION AND STATUS

As their name implies, Western Tanagers are found primarily in western North America. These attractive tanagers migrate north from Mexico and Central America wintering grounds to nest primarily from southeastern Alaska and western Canada south to Arizona and New Mexico. They also nest locally in the mountains of northern Baja California and southwestern Texas.

In Arizona, Western Tanagers commonly breed in taller coniferous forests throughout the state and locally even in smaller, isolated cool canyon stands containing Douglas fir. The latter habitat was most frequently used in drainages of the higher plateaus and mesas on Navajo and Hopi tribal lands. In this region, they were regularly noted in the Tsegi Canyon–Black Mesa areas and from the Carrizo Mountains south to the Defiance Plateau, including in Canyon de Chelly National Monument.

Surprisingly, Western Tanagers were previously reported as absent as a nesting species in the coniferous forests from the Prescott region northwest (Phillips et al. 1964; Monson and Phillips 1981). Atlasers encountered this species nesting at elevations ranging from approximately 5500 to 9600 ft (1676–2926 m), including regularly in the forests around Prescott. They were also discovered to the northwest on Hualapai tribal lands and in the Mounts Dellenbaugh, Trumbull, and Logan areas, as well as in isolated ranges to the west including the Hualapai, Cerbat, and Virgin mountains.

Western Tanagers were commonly recorded nesting along the Mogollon Rim from the White Mountains northwest to the Williams and Flagstaff areas and north to the Kaibab Plateau. Atlas data strongly suggest that these tanagers also nest in the adjacent forests of White Mountain Apache tribal lands, where atlas surveys could not be conducted and data are lacking. They were regularly encountered in the higher mountain and canyon forests of southeastern Arizona, where they reach their southern breeding limits. The species has not been found nesting in the mountains of adjacent Sonora (Russell and Monson 1998). In southeastern Arizona, Western Tanagers have previously been noted aggressively defending their territory against the rare Flame-colored Tanager (Morse and Monson 1985), where these two closely related species are increasingly hybridizing.

Western Tanager populations appear to be fairly stable in Arizona and their preference for open forests makes it relatively tolerant of some limited timber thinning practices. Atlasers regularly encountered these striking tanagers occupying appropriate coniferous forests throughout the state.

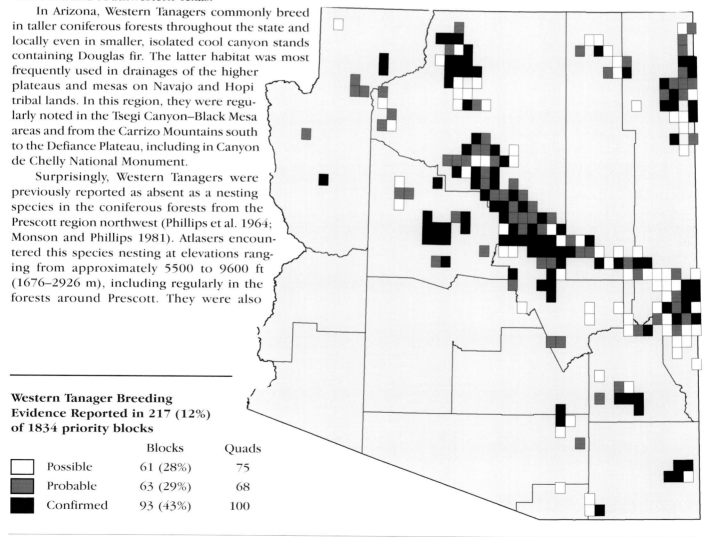

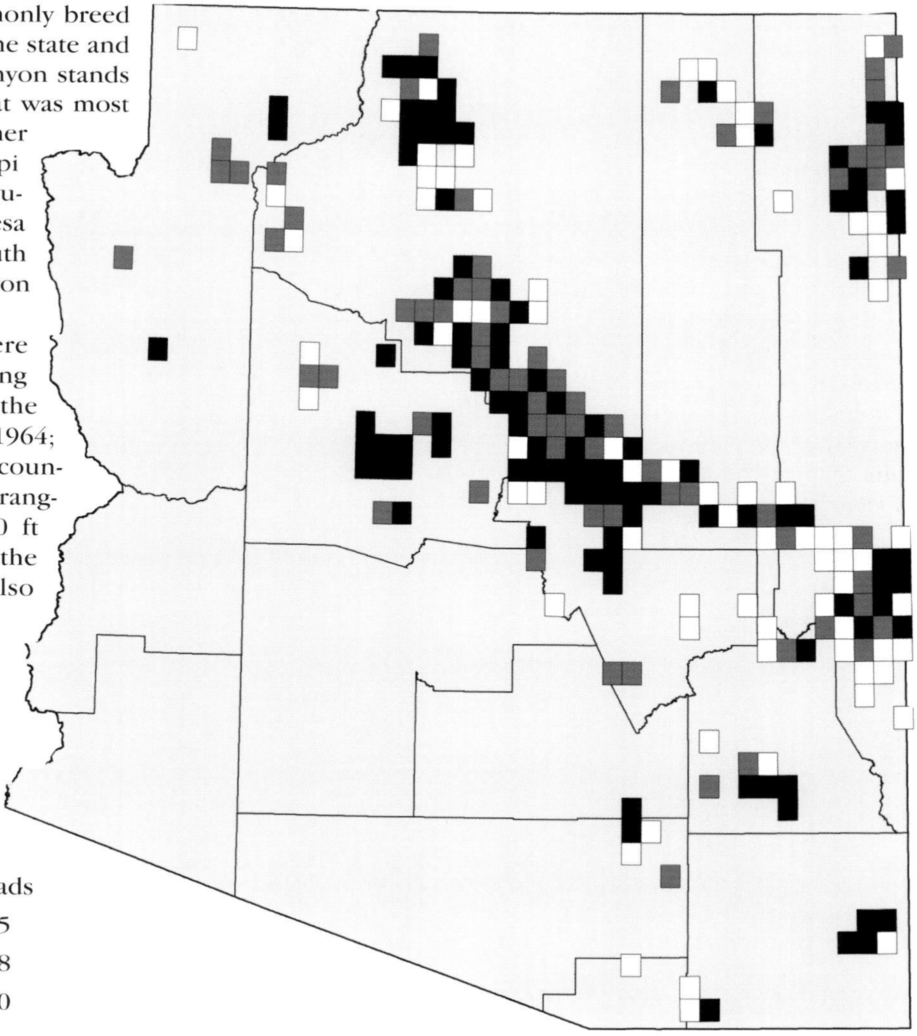

Western Tanager Breeding Evidence Reported in 217 (12%) of 1834 priority blocks

	Blocks	Quads
Possible	61 (28%)	75
Probable	63 (29%)	68
Confirmed	93 (43%)	100

Flame-colored Tanager

by Troy E. Corman *Piranga bidentata*

Welcome additions to Arizona's breeding avifauna, Flame-colored Tanagers are eagerly prized by visiting birders. These stunningly attractive tanagers have recently become almost regular but rare spring and summer visitors to several mountain ranges in the southeast. However, finding appropriate mates in their new northern frontier has proven to be rather difficult for this bold pioneer.

GARY ROSENBERG

HABITAT

Commonly observed foraging and singing high in the canopy of pine-oak forests, Flame-colored Tanagers descend infrequently to lower tree levels. In Arizona, they are often discovered in well-shaded mountain canyons with tall trees. Most records during the atlas were from drainages containing both deciduous and coniferous trees with dense, multilayered canopy levels. Deciduous trees in canyons often occupied by Flame-colored Tanagers include Arizona sycamore, Arizona walnut, bigtooth maple, Gambel's oak, and various species of Madrean evergreen oaks such as Emory, silverleaf, and netleaf. Additionally, Douglas fir, Arizona cypress, alligator juniper, and various pines, including ponderosa, Apache, and Chihuahuan, are regularly scattered throughout their canyon territories. However, these tanagers were also noted locally nesting in areas dominated by tall, dense stands of Madrean evergreen oaks adjacent to the immediate drainage or in lower sycamore-oak dominated drainages lacking tall conifers.

BREEDING

Flame-colored Tanagers are resident throughout most of their range and pairs are often observed together at all seasons. They are apparently migratory at the northern edge of their range, however, and have been found as early as 1 April in Arizona. Most records in the state suggest these attractive tanagers typically do not arrive in their breeding canyons until mid-April or later. Singing and courtship begin soon after arrival, with nest construction noted by early to mid-May. Observers reported a Flame-colored Tanager nest with young by the first week of June, suggesting egg laying by late May. Fledglings were reported as early as 15 June and a nest with young was noted as late as 26 June. Another observer reported a female Flame-colored Tanager defending fledglings into the third week of July. The year following the atlas period, a family group containing an adult male Flame-colored Tanager and apparently two hybrid fledglings, was noted on the late date of 22 August (M. Kehl, personal communication). Most Flame-colored Tanagers have departed Arizona by mid-August, with individuals occasionally lingering into early September.

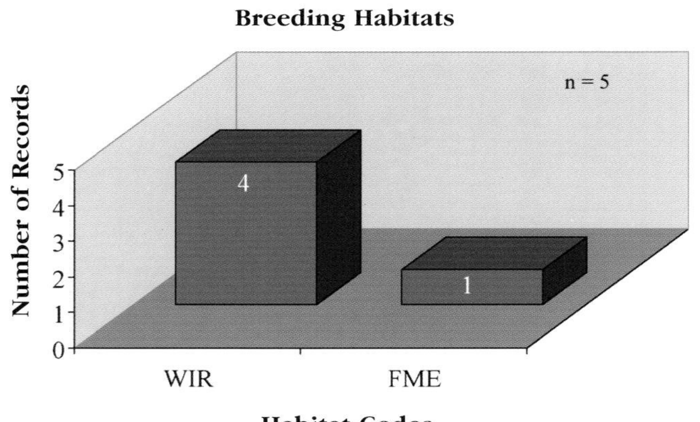

Flame-colored Tanager nests have been described as loosely constructed cups of stiff rootlets, slender twigs, and vine tendrils, which are later lined with fine grass stems (Stiles and Skutch 1989). During the atlas period, one female was observed collecting dried grass blades from the side of a forest trail. In Arizona, nests have been discovered in Arizona sycamore, various species of pines, and unidentified evergreen oaks. One nest was estimated to be approximately 35 ft (10.7 m) up a 90 ft- (27.4 m)-tall sycamore (R. Taylor, personal communication). The heights of the other few nests ever found in Arizona have not been reported, but Stiles and Skutch (1989) noted Flame-colored Tanager nests placed 16–35 ft (4.9–10.7 m) above the ground.

Females construct the nest and incubate the typical clutch of only 2–3 eggs (Stiles and Skutch 1989). The incubation period for Flame-colored Tanagers is unknown, but, as with several other closely related tanagers, is assumed to be 12–13 days. Both parents feed the nestlings, which likely fledge when they are approximately 14 days old. The adults presumably continue to feed the fledglings for about 2 additional weeks following nest departure. In Arizona,

1–2 broods are likely produced per year, with several renesting attempts if earlier efforts fail.

DISTRIBUTION AND STATUS

Flame-colored Tanagers are basically a resident tropical species from southern Sonora, south through the highlands of Mexico to western Panama. These tanagers are elusive and very infrequently observed in Sonora, where all accepted observations are from the southeast and there are no confirmed nesting records (Russell and Monson 1998). With southeastern Arizona observations increasing, the lack of records in the mountains of northeastern Sonora likely pertains to limited and very inconsistent observer coverage in the area. The first record of Flame-colored Tanagers north of Mexico was an adult male discovered in Cave Creek Canyon, Chiricahua Mountains in April 1985. This male paired with a female Western Tanager, reared one brood, and attempted a second nesting (Morse 1986). Flame-colored Tanagers were not found again in Arizona until April and May 1992, when pairs and individuals appeared in Madera Canyon, Santa Rita Mountains, and in Ramsey Canyon, Huachuca Mountains. The pair in Madera Canyon attempted to breed, but the nest was later abandoned.

Observations of Flame-colored Tanagers during the atlas period were all noted in the Chiricahua, Huachuca, and Santa Rita mountains at elevations ranging from 5300 to 7300 ft (1615–2225 m). With the very local and irregular distribution of Flame-colored Tanagers in Arizona, few records were obtained through atlas survey efforts. Most information for this species was compiled from casual observations reported by the many birders visiting occupied canyons through the breeding season. Most atlas-period breeding records were from the eastern slope of the Huachuca Mountains, where nesting attempts were documented in Miller and Ramsey canyons. Flame-colored Tanagers and/or possible hybrids were also noted in adjacent Carr and Garden canyons. Nesting activity was also confirmed in the Santa Rita Mountains in Madera Canyon on several occasions. During the atlas period, fewer Flame-colored Tanagers were noted in the Chiricahua Mountains. A male was observed in Cave Creek Canyon in 2001, and a female that was apparently paired with a Hepatic Tanager successfully fledged young from a nest in East Whitetail Canyon in 1998 (R. Taylor, personal communication).

During the atlas period, Flame-colored Tanagers were reported in southeastern Arizona nearly every year. Several males apparently returned to the same canyons to defend territories in successive years. However, some records may also have pertained to a returning Western/Flame-colored Tanager hybrid progeny. Throughout the atlas period, hybrid individuals in the population mired the credibility of some observations of Flame-colored Tanagers. Western Tanagers are not known to breed in Sonora (Russell and Monson 1998) or elsewhere to the south in Mexico. Therefore, the mountains of southeastern Arizona are the only known localities the breeding ranges of these two related tanagers periodically overlap. In Arizona, male Flame-colored Tanagers have successfully paired with female Western Tanagers and female Flame-colored Tanagers have paired with male Western Tanagers, hybrid tanagers, and apparently once even with a male Hepatic Tanager. Most hybrid individuals closely resemble Flame-colored Tanagers and are easily mistaken if not closely scrutinized. With so few individual of these striking birds appearing in Arizona each year, this unfortunate saga is likely to continue.

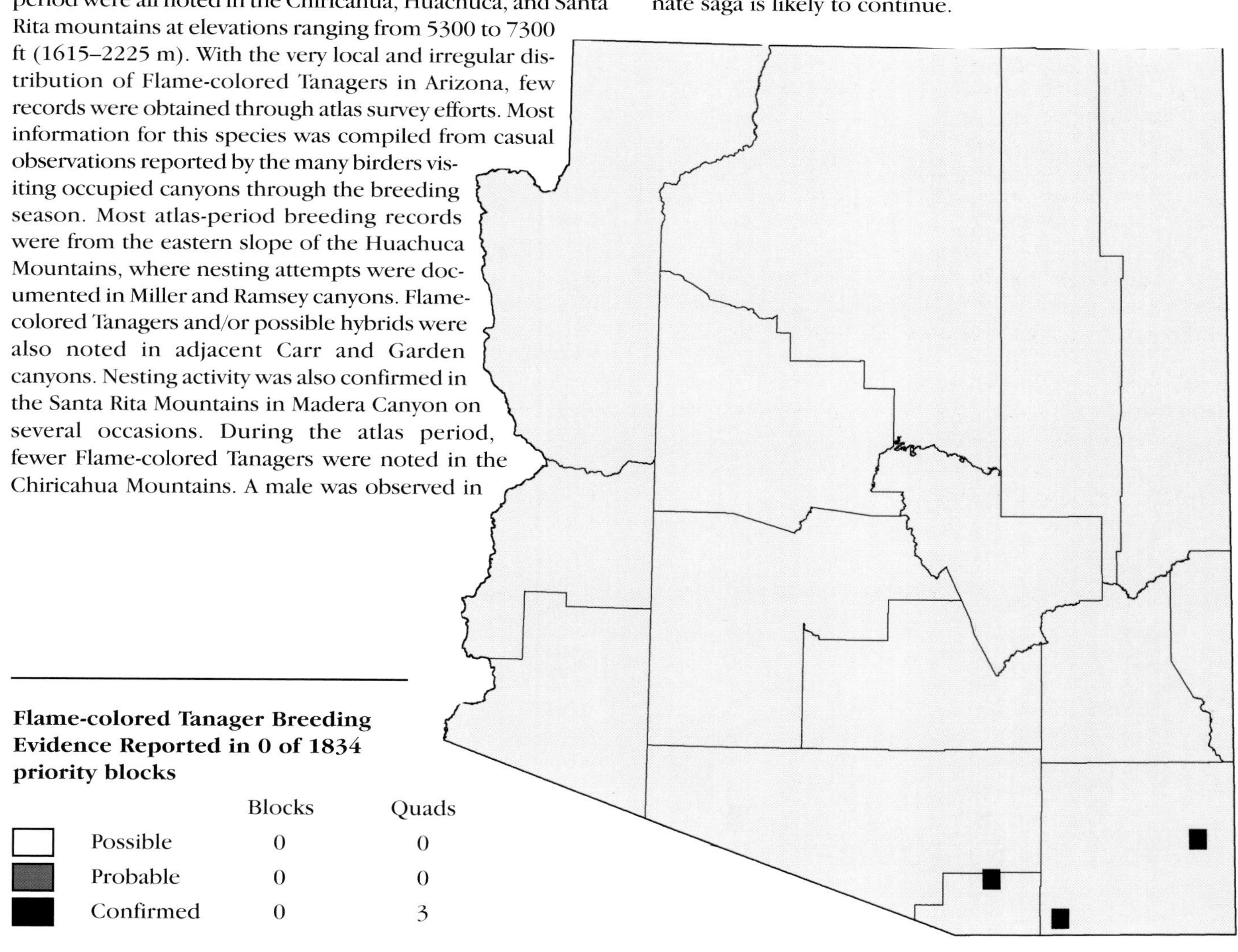

Flame-colored Tanager Breeding Evidence Reported in 0 of 1834 priority blocks

	Blocks	Quads
Possible	0	0
Probable	0	0
Confirmed	0	3

Green-tailed Towhee

by Troy E. Corman *Pipilo chlorurus*

RICK AND NORA BOWERS

Slipping through the underbrush, Green-tailed Towhees often respond to an observer's squeaking with soft "mews" as they creep higher in the dense tangles for an inquisitive view. During the summer in northern Arizona, this small, rufous-capped towhee can be found with its white throat reverberating from a rapid, buzzy song that is reminiscent of the Lark Sparrow.

HABITAT

For a fairly local nesting species in Arizona, Green-tailed Towhees are found nesting in a surprisingly wide array of habitats and successional stages, with many locations a combination of several vegetative communities. An important component appears to be habitats with low, dense woody vegetation. Atlasers noted this species most frequently (40 percent of records) nesting at higher elevations in openings and edges of mixed-conifer forests and montane riparian drainages (n = 42). Dominant vegetation often included low thickets of gooseberry, Gambel's oak, New Mexico locust, Rocky Mountain maple, and young conifers such as Douglas fir and white fir. This towhee commonly associates with burned and cleared areas in higher elevation coniferous forests, where suitable shrub habitats grow following the overstory removal (Franzreb and Ohmart 1978). Atlasers also found Green-tailed Towhees in high-elevation riparian thickets along small perennial drainages. These thickets typically range from 4 to 8 ft (1.2–2.4 m) high and frequently include thinleaf alder, Bebb willow, Geyer willow, cerro hawthorn, gooseberry, shrubby cinquefoil, and red elderberry. In northern Arizona, this towhee was also found nesting in scrublands containing a mixture of sagebrush and Gambel's oak and locally in tall stands of big sagebrush at higher elevations with very scattered pinyon pine and juniper.

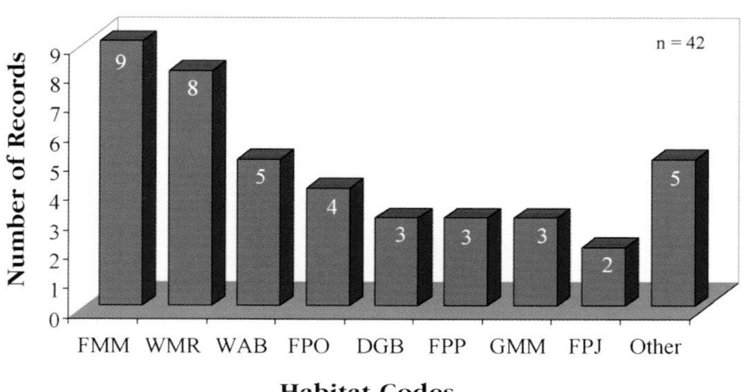

BREEDING

In Arizona, spring migration for Green-tailed Towhees begins in March, peaks in April and early May, with stragglers reported occasionally through mid-June. Although some individuals begin to sing during migration, singing increases once they reach their Arizona breeding areas beginning in late April or early May. Atlasers found few active nests and the earliest confirmed record was a nest with eggs on 3 June. However, on the Mogollon Rim of Arizona, researchers have discovered Green-tailed Towhee nests with eggs from 4 May to 10 July, with most first clutches initiated in late May (Dobbs et al. 1998). Atlasers observed adults carrying food by 6 June and feeding fledged young through 27 July. Later nests may still contain young into early August (Dobbs et al. 1998). Fall migration for these towhees in Arizona typically begins by mid-August, exceptionally as early as 30 July (Krueper 1999), and peaks in mid-September. Although numbers vary considerably from year to year, Green-tailed Towhees are often a common wintering species in brushy habitats of southern and western Arizona.

The female constructs the well-concealed nest in 2–5 days, which is typically placed on or near the ground (Dobbs et al. 1998). Atlasers found Green-tailed Towhee nests in rabbitbrush, big sagebrush, and white fir. On the Mogollon Rim, nests have also been found in Douglas fir, New Mexico locust, Rocky Mountain maple, gooseberry, and raspberry (Dobbs et al. 1998). The height of two nests measured by atlasers was 5 and 15 in. (13 and 39 cm) above the ground. The median height of 123 nests on the Mogollon Rim was 24.8 in. (63 cm; Dobbs et al. 1998).

Only the female Green-tailed Towhee incubates the 3–4 (range 2–5) eggs for 11–13 days (Martin 1995). Both parents feed the nestling, which typically depart the nest in 11–14 days (Dobbs et al. 1998) and feed the fledgling for a minimum of two weeks (Dotson 1971). Green-tailed Towhees are capable of fledging two broods per year, but there is no direct evidence of this (Dobbs et al. 1998). Studies on the Mogollon Rim have found that greater than 75 percent of nests are lost to predators and this towhee has been observed attempting to renest four to five times during a season (Martin 1993).

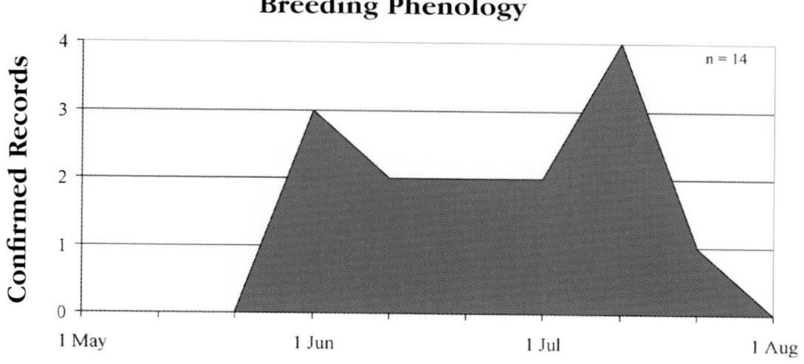

DISTRIBUTION AND STATUS

Green-tailed Towhees nest from Montana and southeastern Washington south through the mountains of California, Arizona, and New Mexico. There is also a disjunct nesting population in northern Baja California (Howell and Webb 1995) and they are known to nest irregularly in the Guadalupe and Chisos mountains of western Texas (Oberholser 1974). In Arizona, previous description of their breeding range noted them nesting only in the White Mountains region, San Francisco Mountains, and on the Kaibab Plateau (Phillips et al. 1964). In 1976, they were discovered nesting on Bill Williams Mountain (Monson and Phillips). In the 1980s, LaRue (1994) found Green-tailed Towhees nesting on northern Black Mesa southwest of Kayenta, and Jacobs (1986) reported them breeding in the Carrizo, Chuska, and Lukachukai mountains in the extreme northeast corner of the state. During the late 1980s, they were also found breeding just north of the Mogollon Rim northeast of Payson (T. Martin, personal communication).

Atlasers found that Green-tailed Towhees continue to nest fairly commonly in all previously noted locations at elevations ranging from 6400 to 10,500 ft (1951–3200 m). Atlasers also discovered them nesting and potentially nesting in many additional locations in northern Arizona. They were encountered singing in appropriate nesting habitat on Mt. Logan in northern Mohave County. Atlasers also noted then in several locations at lower elevations on the western slope of the Kaibab Plateau near Big Springs. In northern Apache County, atlasers discovered Green-tailed Towhees to be fairly widespread along drainages and high plateaus from the Carrizo Mountains, south locally on the Defiance Plateau to Lone Tule Wash northeast of Ganado. Breeding populations south of Canyon de Chelly were previously unknown. In the White Mountains, atlasers encountered them from just north of McNary east to Greer and Escudilla Mountain and south to the Hannagan Meadow area. Green-tailed Towhees also undoubtedly nest in the adjacent higher elevations of the White Mountain Apache tribal lands, where access permits to conduct atlas surveys could not be obtained.

Most evidence suggests that Green-tailed Towhee populations are fairly stable throughout their range (Dobbs et al. 1998). As forests along the Mogollon Rim and elsewhere begin to recover from recent extensive wildfires in Arizona, these small attractive towhees may eventually be found nesting at new localities among early successional woody thickets.

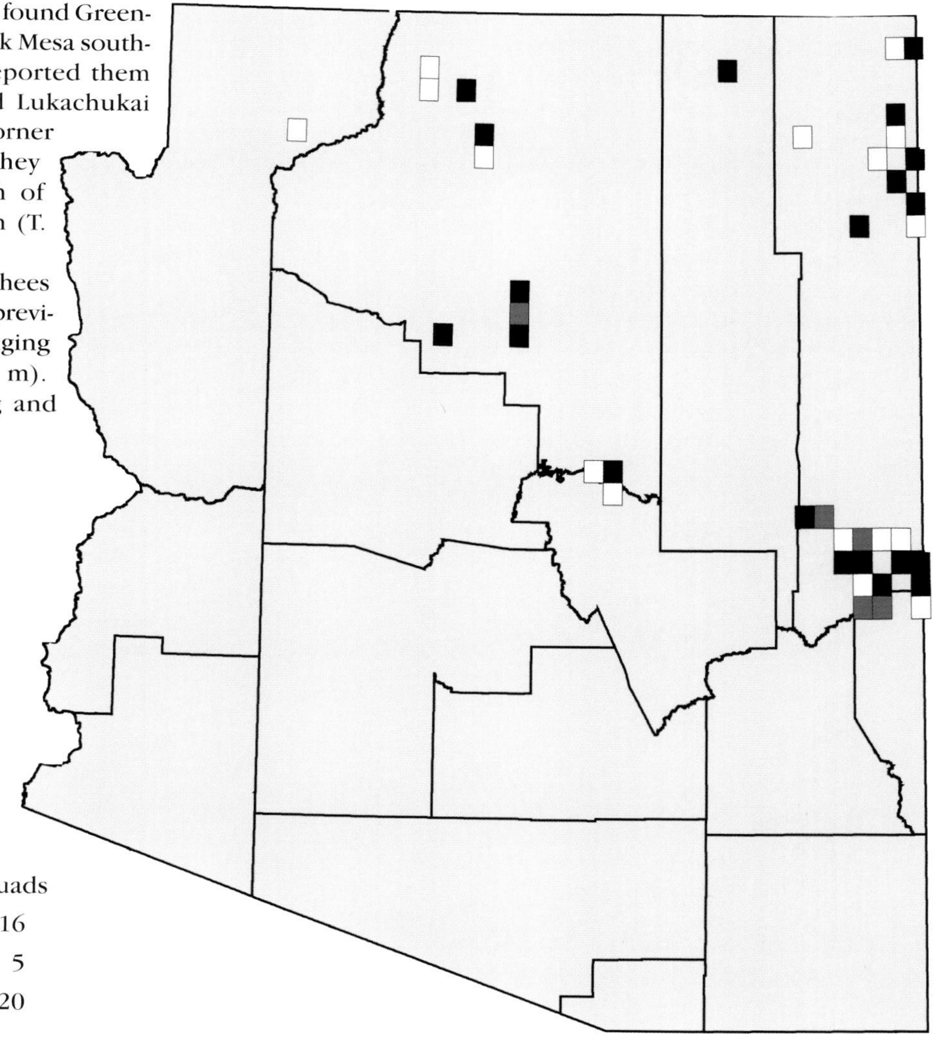

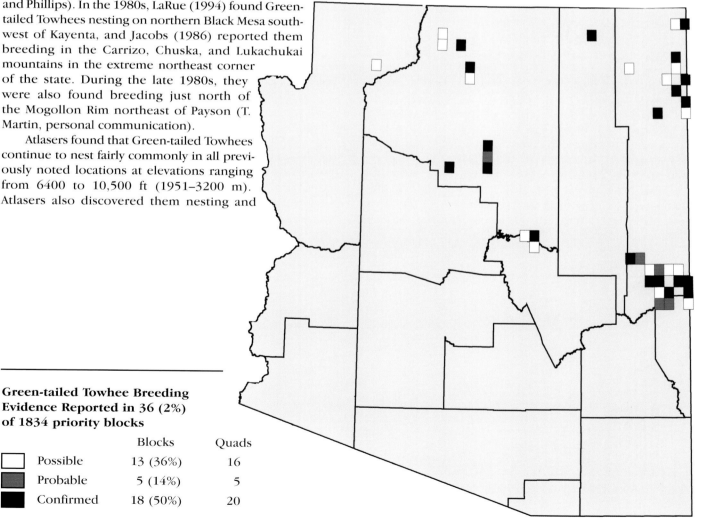

Green-tailed Towhee Breeding Evidence Reported in 36 (2%) of 1834 priority blocks

	Blocks	Quads
Possible	13 (36%)	16
Probable	5 (14%)	5
Confirmed	18 (50%)	20

Spotted Towhee

by Cathryn Wise-Gervais *Pipilo maculatus*

JIM BURNS

The Spotted Towhee's distinctive short and abrupt song is a familiar sound on brushy slopes and in open woodland scrub throughout Arizona. This chaparral dweller was formerly known as the Rufous-sided Towhee, and its ruby-red eyes and chestnut sides are diagnostic characteristics that set the bird apart from plainer ground-foraging birds.

HABITAT

Throughout their range, Spotted Towhees occur in dense and often semiarid scrubby thickets that offer low-growing woody shrubs. In Arizona, these conditions typically exist in open woodlands, on chaparral-covered slopes, and in brushy canyons. Atlasers reported Spotted Towhees in twenty-six different habitat types, but the majority of records (40 percent) were in the widespread pinyon pine–juniper woodlands, including stands containing scattered ponderosa pine (n = 584). They are especially common in chaparral-dominated areas (17 percent) and in Madrean evergreen oak woodlands (11 percent). Observers also regularly encountered Spotted Towhees in brushy canyons and foothill drainages containing sycamore, ash, and oaks. They were found less frequently in Gambel's oak–ponderosa pine associations and in sagebrush-juniper–dominated areas.

Spotted Towhees are often detected as they noisily forage beneath shrubs among dense leaf litter and debris with an odd hop forward then scratch back technique. Adequate leaf litter seems to be a vital component in habitat choice, along with shrubs offering screenlike cover beneath which to forage. In fact, researchers speculated that the dorsal white spotting on the bird is a form of camouflage mimicking sun-dappled shade at feeding areas (Sibley and West 1959).

Breeding Habitats

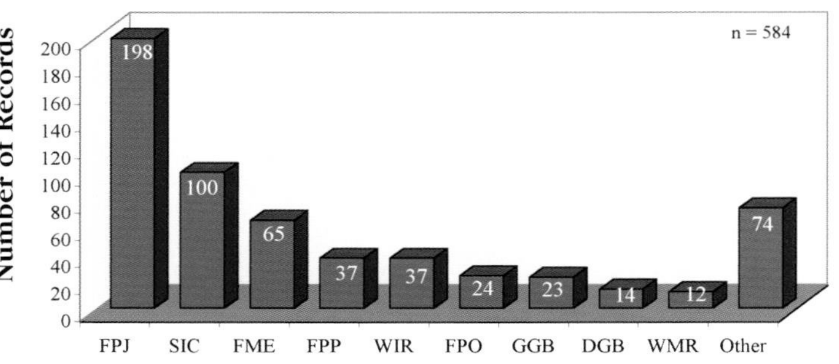

Habitat Codes

BREEDING

Spotted Towhees are year-round residents in Arizona, but will descend annually in varying numbers to lower-elevation desert washes and riparian thickets after the breeding season. Few individuals remain in these areas after mid-March. Atlasers noted paired birds by 6 April and observed an individual carrying nesting material on 26 April. However, early egg laying likely begins by mid-April in Arizona, based on a nest with young discovered on 6 May. Observers reported Spotted Towhee nests containing eggs from 5 May to 26 July. Atlas data suggest that breeding activity statewide in Arizona peaks in mid- to late June but continues into late summer. In southeastern Arizona, an observer noted an adult carrying nesting material on 15 August and prior records indicate some nesting continuing well into August in this region of the state (Bailey 1923). Atlasers reported Spotted Towhees feeding or accompanying recently fledged young on 22 and 24 August, respectively. Migrants typically begin arriving in lowland areas in October, occasionally in late September.

It is likely that female Spotted Towhees select the nest site, but data are lacking on this (Greenlaw 1996). Researchers do know that the female constructs the nest on her own, and usually places the structure on or very near the ground (Greenlaw 1996). Atlasers reported fourteen nests at elevations from 4800 to 7960 ft (1463–2426 m), all placed directly on the ground. Nests were constructed beneath a variety of trees and shrubs including juniper, oak, sagebrush, manzanita, and New Mexico locust. Nests on the ground are usually in a depression so that the rim of the nest is roughly equal to the level of the ground. The nest structure typically comprises an outer layer of coarse material such as bark strips and a softer interior cup.

Females typically lay 3–5 eggs (range 2–6; Greenlaw 1996) and incubate these without male assistance for 12–14 days (Baumann 1959; Davis 1960). During this time the male visits the nest regularly and may feed the female periodically (Greenlaw 1996). Both adults feed the young after hatching, but only the female broods. The nestlings fledge at 9–11 days, and parents continue feeding the youngsters for approximately one month (Baumann 1959).

Spotted Towhees typically raise one brood per season, but second broods are uncommonly produced in some populations. They will also regularly renest if their first attempt

Breeding Phenology

Confirmed Records

35
30
25
20
15
10
5
0

n = 146

1 Apr 1 May 1 Jun 1 Jul 1 Aug 1 Sep

fails. Spotted Towhees are known to be infrequent hosts of Brown-headed Cowbirds (Friedman 1963) and atlasers did not report any incidents of cowbird brood parasitism.

DISTRIBUTION AND STATUS

Although there are many recognized Spotted Towhee subspecies in western North America, only the large *montanus* race nests in Arizona and in adjacent southwestern states. Spotted Towhees occur from southern Canada to central Mexico and locally south to Guatemala. They range from the Pacific Coast (including northern Baja California) east to central South Dakota and southwest to Texas.

Most prior accounts considered Spotted Towhee common and widespread residents in eastern and northern Arizona's dense, mid-elevations brush (Swarth 1914; Phillips et al. 1964). Atlas surveys revealed similar findings and helped clarify this towhee's distribution in the state. Atlasers confirmed Spotted Towhees breeding on priority blocks from approximately 4100 to 8100 ft (1250–2469 m).

In southeastern Arizona, Spotted Towhees were encountered fairly regularly in appropriate habitat west to the Santa Catalina and Santa Rita foothills. Atlasers were surprised to find that the birds were sparsely distributed west to the Quinlan Mountains near Kitt Peak and were not detected in the Baboquivari Mountains, where seemingly appropriate habitat remains unoccupied. It is likely that additional surveys in high-elevation oak woodlands may reveal nesting populations in this rugged range.

Along the Mogollon Rim, atlas records nearly encircle the unsurveyed White Mountain Apache tribal lands where Spotted Towhees undoubtedly commonly nest. To the west, observers noted singing birds in the isolated chaparral uplands of the Harquahala Mountains, and it is likely that the birds breed here as well as in the nearby Harcuvar Mountains. Further surveys are needed to document breeding Spotted Towhees in both locations, however. Atlasers discovered that Spotted Towhees were fairly widespread breeders in northwestern Arizona. The birds were encountered throughout the Arizona Strip region and were confirmed nesting west to the Cerbat Mountains and locally near Mount Nutt in the Black Mountains west of Kingman.

Atlasers regularly reported Spotted Towhees throughout most of the appropriate habitat within the state. Breeding Bird Survey (BBS) data indicate that these towhees reach some of their highest densities in northwestern Arizona (Price et al. 1995). In addition, BBS population trend estimates (1968–1995) suggest statewide Spotted Towhee numbers have increased significantly (Greenlaw 1996).

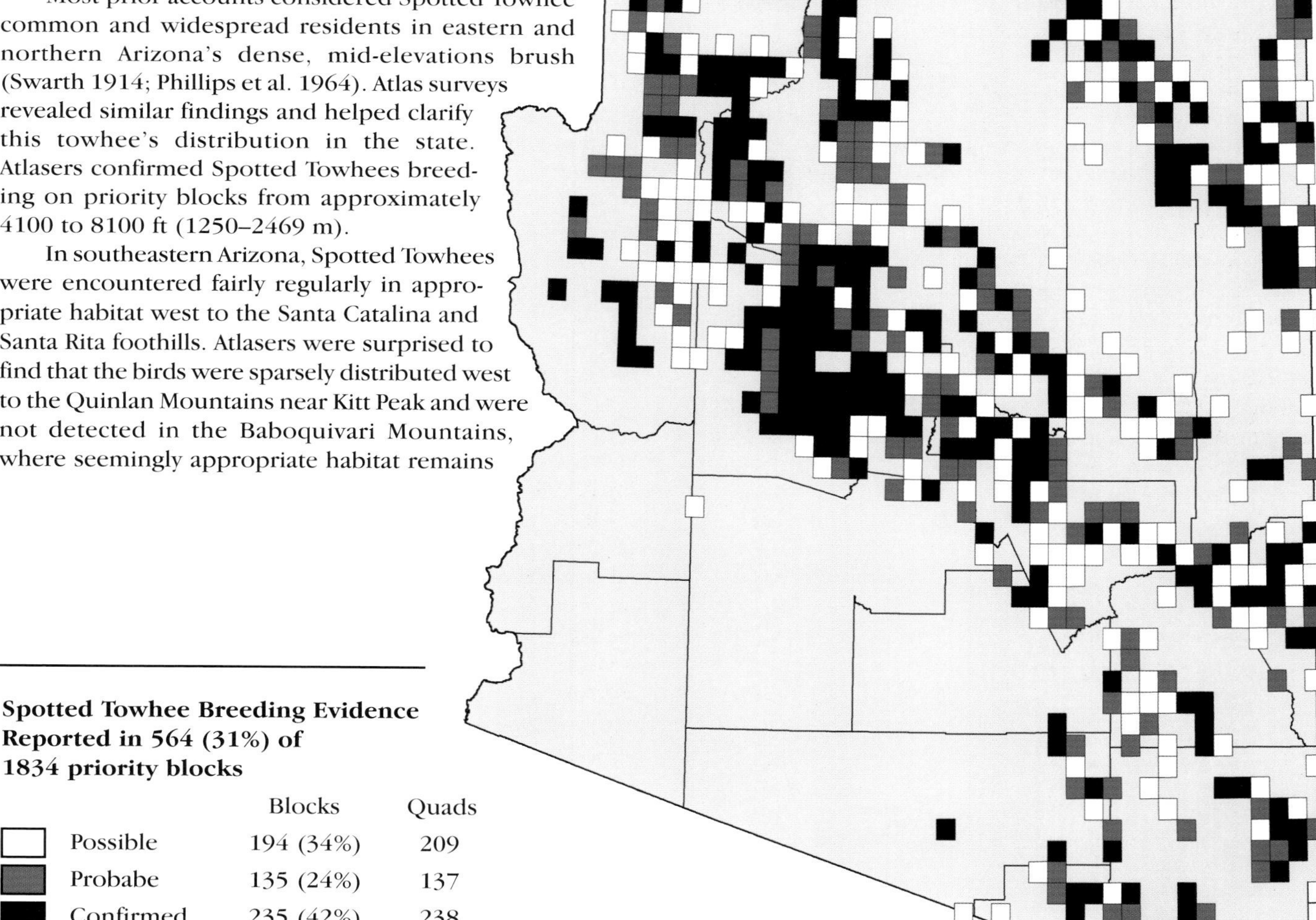

Spotted Towhee Breeding Evidence Reported in 564 (31%) of 1834 priority blocks

	Blocks	Quads
Possible	194 (34%)	209
Probabe	135 (24%)	137
Confirmed	235 (42%)	238

Canyon Towhee

by Troy E. Corman *Pipilo fuscus*

Familiar birds of lush deserts, dry washes, and brushy foothills, Canyon Towhees are often found in pairs throughout the year. When left undisturbed near human habitations, these adaptable birds often become rather tame, freely entering open doors and windows as they inquisitively inspect their surroundings.

JIM BURNS

HABITAT

In Arizona, Canyon Towhees are found in a variety of habitats that are characteristically arid and brushy. Atlasers reported them most frequently (44 percent of records) in Sonoran desertscrub associations with an abundance of trees, cacti, and dense, shrubby ground cover (n = 664). This includes the more heavily wooded dry washes and rocky, desert foothill slopes where brushy cover is also often in abundance. They clearly avoid the lower elevation Sonoran desertscrub, where shrub and cacti cover is typically sparse. In southeastern and central Arizona, Canyon Towhees were also commonly reported in semiarid grasslands with scattered, but dense shrubs including catclaw acacia, whitethorn acacia, velvet mesquite, beargrass, agave, and various species of yuccas (17 percent of records). At higher elevations they were noted fairly regularly in chaparral associations, open pinyon pine–juniper woodlands, and more open stands of evergreen oak woodlands. Less frequently, Canyon Towhees were reported along the edge of lowland riparian areas, typically with a mixture of Fremont cottonwood, Goodding willow, and velvet mesquite. This towhee is also quite adaptable and can be found around sparsely populated rural communities, ranches, and locally in residential areas with an abundance of native vegetation.

BREEDING

Canyon Towhees are primarily a nonmigratory resident in Arizona, although some descend locally to lower elevations during the winter. They can be heard singing throughout the year, but most frequently at dawn from late February to October. Atlasers reported Canyon Towhees nest building as early as 6 March. However, a nest with young found on 12 March indicates nest construction and clutch initiation by late February. Statewide atlas data note a strong peak in nesting activity from late April through mid-May, but nesting continues fairly regularly through early August. The latest Canyon Towhee nest with young was discovered by atlasers on 11 September, but adults were observed feeding fledglings as late as 25 September. Many of the active nests found in August and September were from southeastern Arizona, where late nesting activity is likely influenced by the late summer monsoon period.

Atlas field crews reported Canyon Towhees nesting in 23 different tree and shrub species, with no obvious preference for any one species. In the Sonoran Desert they were documented nesting in paloverde, ironwood, velvet mesquite, crucifixion thorn, desert hackberry, graythorn, wolfberry, cholla, and mistletoe clumps. In foothills and canyons they also nested in netleaf hackberry, jojoba, catclaw acacia, and sugar sumac. Soaptree yucca, cholla, and prickly pear were used in arid grasslands. At higher elevations, they nested in cliffrose, alligator juniper, scrub live oak, and various other species of oaks.

Of the 38 active Canyon Towhee nests measured, the mean nest height was 3.9 ft (1.2 m) above the ground with a range of 0.5–10.5 ft (0.15–3.2 m). The lowest nest was constructed in a clump of prickly pear cacti and the highest nest was noted in a Goodding willow snag, shaded by a living willow.

Canyon Towhee clutches typically consists of 3–4 eggs, incubated solely by the female (Marshall and Johnson 1968). The incubation period is not well documented, but Kaufman (1996) suggested approximately 11 days. They regularly produce two broods per season and three broods are quite possible in Arizona (Johnson and Haight 1996).

Canyon Towhees have a low incidence of Brown-headed and Bronzed Cowbird brood parasitism (Friedmann and Kiff

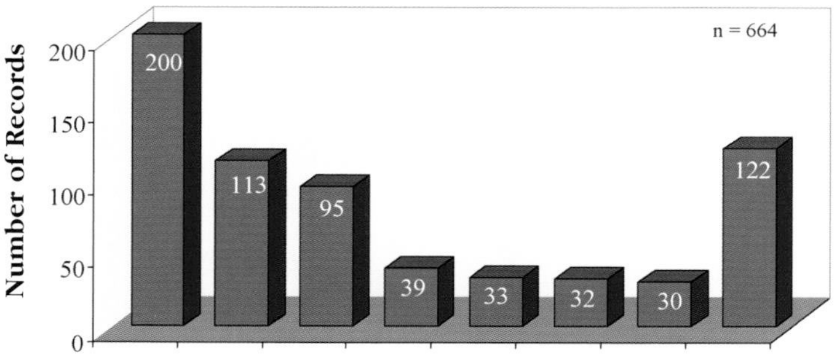

Breeding Phenology

Confirmed Records (0–45); n = 252; 1 Feb, 1 Mar, 1 Apr, 1 May, 1 Jun, 1 Jul, 1 Aug, 1 Sep, 1 Oct

1985). Atlasers reported only two cases pertaining to the Brown-headed Cowbird.

DISTRIBUTION AND STATUS

The range of the Canyon Towhee includes south-central Colorado, south through Arizona, New Mexico, and east to central Texas. In Mexico, they are found south through the Central Plateau to Oaxaca (Howell and Webb 1995). Phillips et al. (1964) considered Canyon Towhees to be rather common residents in appropriate habitat of southern, central, and northwestern Arizona. This included the higher elevations of the Kofa Mountains in southwestern Arizona. Phillips et al. also noted an isolated population in Apache County from Springerville area north to Lupton. In the mid-1970s, Canyon Towhees were also noted as far northwest as the upper Lake Mead area of the Colorado River (Brown et al. 1987).

During the atlas, Canyon Towhees were encountered commonly throughout their previously described range south and northwest of the Mogollon Rim at elevations ranging from 1000 to 6700 ft (305–2042 m). In southern Arizona, they were found west into the Cabeza Prieta National Wildlife Refuge to the Sierra Pinta foothills. Canyon Towhees were noted into the Salt River Canyon and they undoubtedly also occur in this region on the White Mountain Apache tribal lands where atlas surveys could not be conducted.

Atlasers found this towhee to be uncommon and much more sparsely distributed north of the Rim. In Apache County, they were found from the Springerville area north to Wide Ruin Wash near Klagetoh on Navajo tribal lands. Access to conduct atlas surveys in southern Navajo and Apache counties was often limited by private land issues. Therefore, Canyon Towhees could be more widely distributed than atlas records suggest in this region. A pair of birds was found east of Keams Canyon on Hopi tribal lands, where they are considered only casual transients (C. LaRue, personal communication). Atlasers discovered other new locations for Canyon Towhees just north and east of Aripine, Navajo County, and south of Wupatki National Monument, Coconino County.

There were several observations of Canyon Towhees on the South Rim of the Grand Canyon in the fall and winter of the 1930s and 1940s. However, these were felt to be casual visitors from populations well to the south (Brown et al. 1987). Atlasers documented Canyon Towhees in this same area during the nesting season and they likely pertain to small, sparsely distributed resident populations in this region.

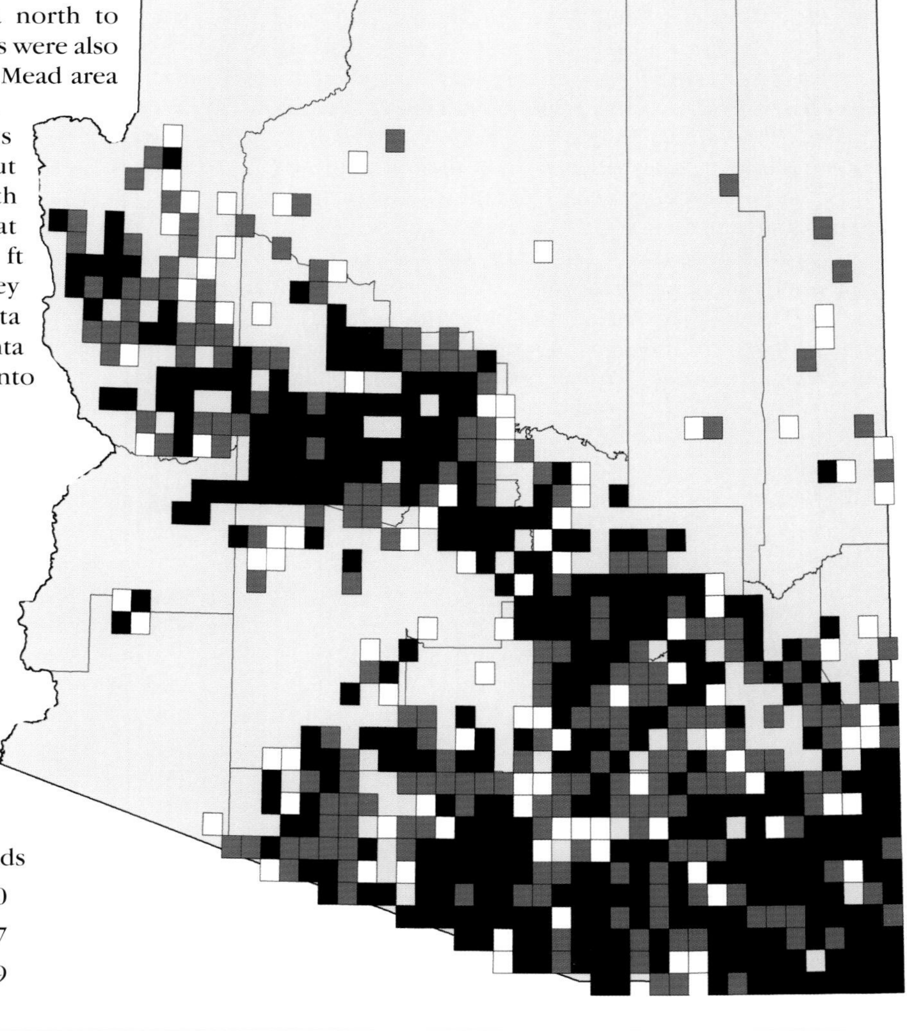

Canyon Towhee Breeding Evidence Reported in 662 (36%) of 1834 priority blocks

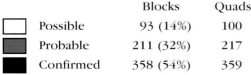

	Blocks	Quads
Possible	93 (14%)	100
Probable	211 (32%)	217
Confirmed	358 (54%)	359

Abert's Towhee

by Troy E. Corman *Pipilo aberti*

An exceptionally large proportion of the Abert's Towhee's entire range is found within Arizona, where they nest in many dense habitats from lowland riparian thickets to irrigated suburban backyards. Often observed in pairs, this rather timid towhee keeps to the shadows and, with a sharp, ringing "peenk," dashes for the nearest cover at the slightest disturbance.

JIM BURNS

HABITAT

Throughout their limited range, Abert's Towhees are typically encountered in or near habitats where the understory is dense and the soil is often damp. They reach their highest densities in lowland riparian thickets containing Fremont cottonwood, Goodding willow, seepwillow, and mesquite. Abert's Towhees also take advantage of the dense growth of adjacent desert dry washes that empty into these wetter drainages. These two habitats accounted for approximately 63 percent of all atlas record for this species (n = 310). Use of desert dry washes for nesting is much more prevalent following winters and springs with above average precipitation. During these periodic wet years, atlasers confirmed them nesting locally in limited numbers in larger and densely vegetated washes many miles from permanent water sources.

For a species that has a relatively restricted breeding range, Abert's Towhees are surprisingly adaptable. This is one of the few riparian species that has adapted fairly well to the monotypic thickets of exotic tamarisk now growing abundantly along many of Arizona's lowland waterways. Atlasers also found then nesting regularly in saltbush, mesquite, and other dense shrubs along irrigation ditches, canals, and runoff ponds in agricultural areas. In urban and rural settings, Abert's Towhees were frequently noted in irrigated parks and backyards with an abundance of cover such as hedgerows, gardens, and other dense ornamental plantings.

BREEDING

The nesting season for Abert's Towhees can begin as early as late January, with the earliest nest with eggs reported in Phoenix on 5 February 1965 (S. Demaree, personal communication). The earliest confirmed record for the atlas period was an adult feeding recently fledged young on 1 March, suggesting an early February clutch initiation. Atlas data suggest that nesting activity peaks from mid-April through late May, with some nesting continuing into September. The latest confirmed record during the atlas period was a nest with young discovered on 11 September.

The female constructs the bulky cup nest, which is typically placed in dense cover, low in trees or shrubs (Dawson 1968; Tweit and Finch 1994). Abert's Towhees are not too particular in selecting nest sites and in Arizona these include mesquite, wolfberry, graythorn, seepwillow, velvet ash, Mexican elderberry, cottonwood, willow, catclaw acacia, netleaf hackberry, and frequently in mistletoe clumps. Abert's Towhees also nest commonly in tamarisk and in many exotic plantings in urban settings. For nine nests measured by atlas field crews, the nest height ranged from 2.0 to 9.3 ft (0.6–2.8 m). An exceptionally high nest in Arizona was reported in a mistletoe clumps 30 ft (9.1 m) above the ground (Stevens 1878).

Abert's Towhee clutches typically contain 3 eggs, but can range from 1–5 (Dawson 1968). Females incubate the eggs for 14 days (Dawson 1968). Both parents feed the nestlings for 12–13 days and the fledglings for an additional 4–5 weeks (Finch 1984). Pairs regularly produce 1–2 broods per year, but are known to renest many times if earlier efforts fail (Tweit and Finch 1994).

Atlasers noted seven instances of Brown-headed Cowbird brood parasitism of Abert's Towhees, with the earliest nest with eggs reported on 1 April in north Phoenix. Finch (1983) found Brown-headed Cowbird brood parasitism extremely high along the Colorado River late in the breeding season. However, nests initiated before mid-April, were found to be largely free of cowbird eggs. Abert's Towhees have also been successfully parasitized by Bronzed Cowbirds in Phoenix, where nests with eggs and adults feeding recently fledged young have been observed (E. Hatcher, personal communication).

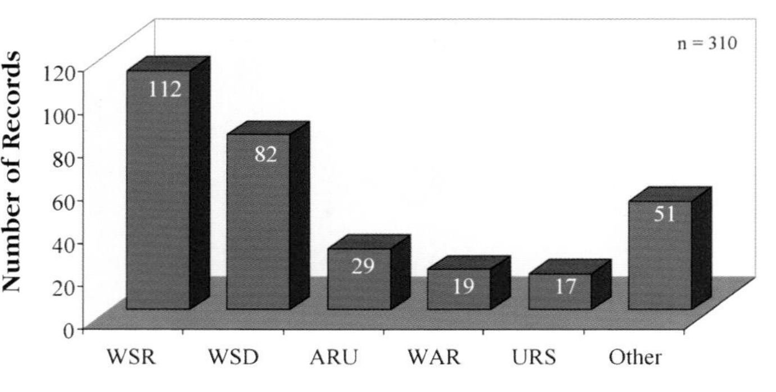

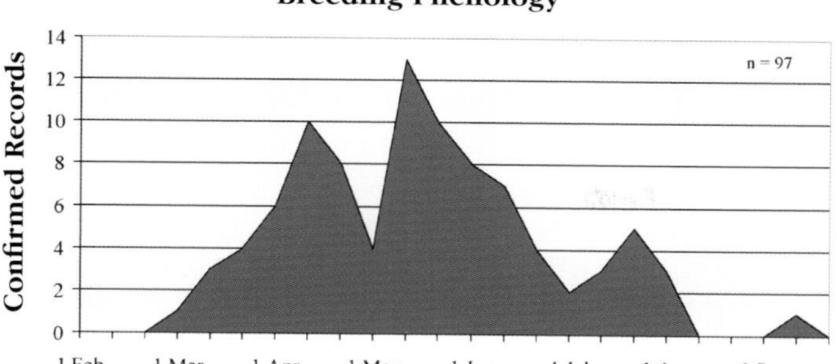

DISTRIBUTION AND STATUS

The resident Abert's Towhee has the distinction of having more than 80 percent of its entire range contained within Arizona, where atlasers found it nesting at elevations from near 80 to 4900 ft (24–1493 m). This species also edges into adjacent Nevada, Utah, California, and New Mexico and sparingly into Sonora and Baja California.

Phillips et al. (1964) noted Abert's Towhees as common along most lowland perennial drainages in western, southern, and central Arizona, including most of the Verde, Big Sandy, Gila, and San Pedro River drainages. Since the mid-1970s, they have expanded their range within the upper Santa Cruz River drainage to Nogales and upstream along Sonoita Creek to Patagonia (Christmas Bird Count data). Atlas data confirm their continued occurrence throughout much of their historical distribution within the state. Atlasers were able to document nesting at Portal and along the San Simon River drainage where Monson and Phillips (1981) noted Abert's Towhee only as a nonbreeding stray. Atlasers also found this species nesting for the first time along larger and denser vegetated washes of the Santa Rosa Valley within the Tohono O'odham tribal lands.

Although an isolated population of Abert's Towhees occurs within the Virgin River drainage in northwestern Arizona, atlasers did not detect it along the Colorado River north of the Fort Mojave tribal lands. Historically, this species had been recorded north to the Hoover Dam area (Phillips et al. 1964). Lack of atlas records may reflect the fact that habitat in this region is local and may not have been visited by surveyors. Abert's Towhees have not been found within the lower Grand Canyon where habitat and elevation would suggest it be there. However, the presence of the Lake Mead waterway and the lack of continuous habitat elsewhere in the region could limit expansion of this sedentary species into the canyon.

The loss of this towhee's preferred native riparian habitat throughout its range has likely reduced the overall population numbers. Exotic habitats such as tamarisk thickets and ornamental plantings in Phoenix and other urban settings have not fully replaced native habitat loss, and the population decline over the last 150 years has probably been extensive though poorly documented (Tweit and Finch 1994). Conversely, the increased irrigation of desert lands in Arizona undoubtedly has locally increased the amount of habitat suitable for these wary but adaptable towhees (Dawson 1968).

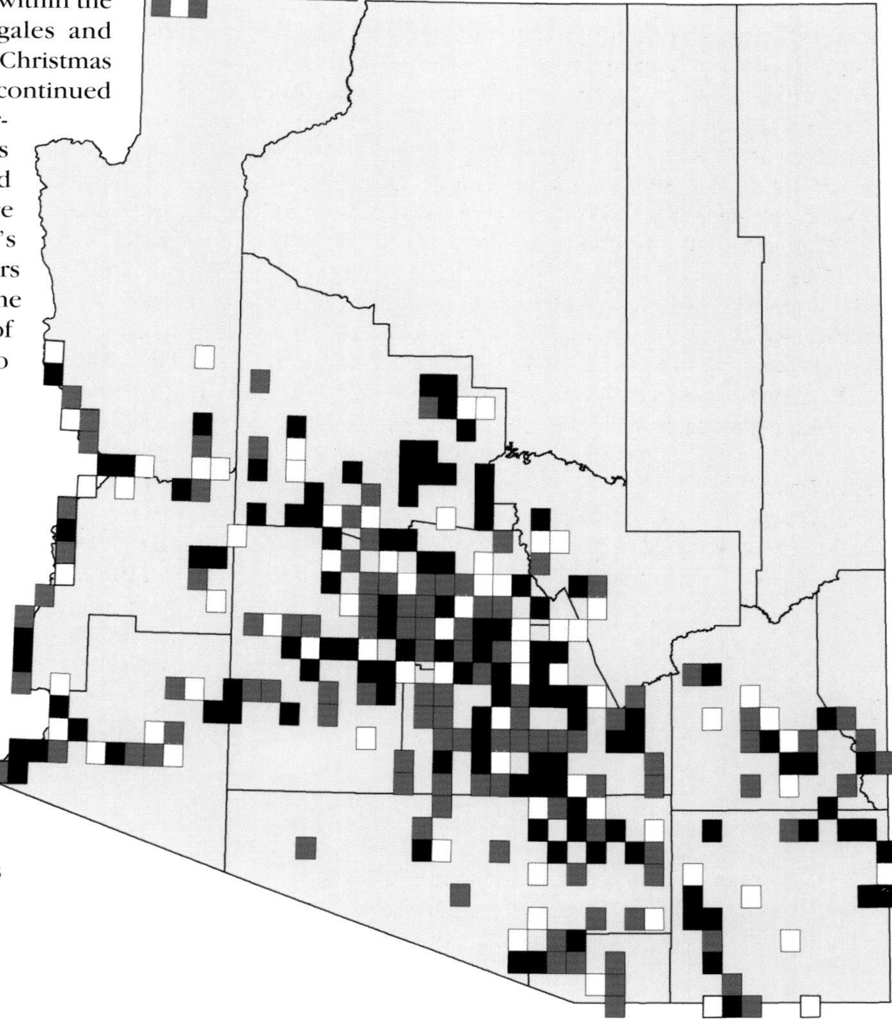

Abert's Towhee Breeding Evidence Reported in 262 (14 %) of 1834 priority blocks

	Blocks	Quads
Possible	53 (21%)	73
Probable	101 (38%)	109
Confirmed	108 (41%)	117

Rufous-winged Sparrow

by Troy E. Corman *Aimophila carpalis*

Well studied in Arizona, the Rufous-winged Sparrow is closely tied to rainfall for initiation of nesting activity. Their distinctive bouncing-ball song is a familiar sound to those who visit south-central Arizona deserts, especially during the late summer monsoon period.

DAN FISCHER

HABITAT

Rufous-winged Sparrows in Arizona favor habitats that combine scattered shrubs and trees from the Sonoran Desert with semiarid grasslands, typically on level or gently rolling terrain. Approximately 81 percent of all atlas records were noted in this habitat (n = 96). Atlasers found these sparrows most often inhabiting areas dominated by paloverde, velvet mesquite, acacia, desert hackberry, graythorn, ocotillo, prickly pear, and various species of cholla. Grasses are an essential ground cover component, and often include tobosa grass and false grama (Lowther et al. 1999). Atlasers also observed this sparrow at the edges of wooded washes and small groves of mesquite in and around earthen stock tanks and grassy swales. They were encountered locally at the edges of residential areas, particularly those where homes and businesses are interspersed with protected areas of native desert vegetation. Rufous-winged Sparrows typically avoid Sonoran desertscrub habitats where grasses are sparse or lacking.

BREEDING

Primarily a resident species that can be heard singing at various times year round; Rufous-winged Sparrows normally maintain territories throughout the year and remain paired for life (Lowther et al. 1999). This sparrow is highly dependent on periods of ample rainfall to stimulate nesting activity. They have been known to build a nest and lay the first egg in 5–6 days following the first rainfall in an area (Lowther et al. 1999). Most singing and nesting typically occur during the late summer monsoon period. However, most confirmed records by atlasers were collected during the spring. This is likely because in desert habitats, atlasers conducted many more surveys earlier in the breeding season than during the more uncomfortable hot, humid weather of late summer.

Spring nesting activity was previously noted only during years of above normal winter and early spring precipitation (Ohmart 1969). However, atlasers confirmed this sparrow nesting in spring in all but two years of the atlas. Many of these were years with below normal winter precipitation. In Arizona, spring nest construction can begin as early as late March (Lowther et al. 1999), and nests with eggs have been reported from 29 March to 11 September (Ohmart 1969; Wolf 1977). Atlasers noted the earliest occupied nest on 14 April and a nest with young on 23 April. Spring nesting efforts cease if vegetation dries but will resume with the initiation of summer monsoon rains (Lowther et al. 1999). The latest occupied nest reported by atlasers was on 27 August and fledglings were observed through 4 September. However, a very late nesting was noted in 1996, when adults were observed feeding older fledglings in Tucson on 15 October (Lowther et al. 1999). This nesting effort likely began in early to mid-September.

The bulky grass nest is constructed solely by the female and takes 3–4 days to complete (Ohmart 1969). Field crews took measurements at very few Rufous-winged Sparrow nests, but of 175 nests measured in the northern foothills of the Santa Rita Mountains, Lowther et al. (1999) noted a mean nest height of 3.9 ft (1.2 m) and a range of 1.6–9.8 ft (0.5–3.0 m). Atlasers found this sparrow nesting in jumping cholla, paloverde, velvet mesquite, desert hackberry, and in a mistletoe clump on a whitethorn acacia.

Rufous-winged Sparrows lay a typical clutch of 3–4 eggs (range 2–5), which the female incubates for 11–12 days

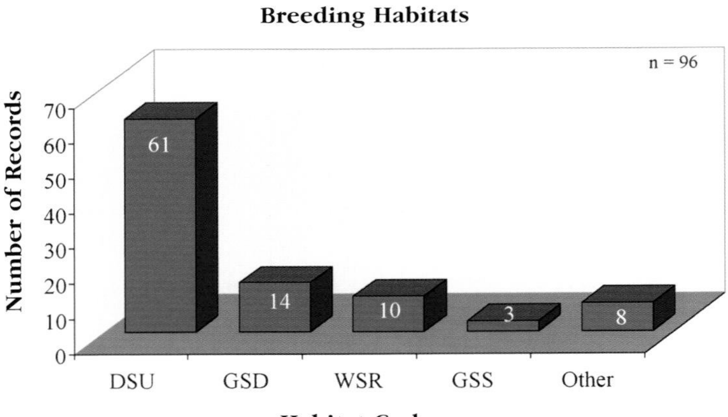

Breeding Phenology

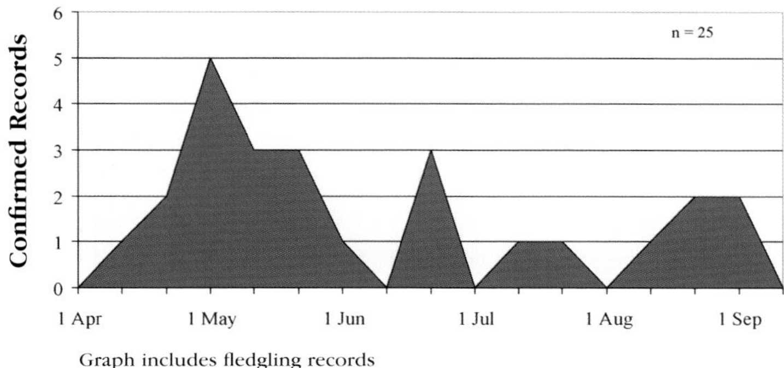

Graph includes fledgling records

(Ohmart 1969). Young remain in the nest for 7–10 days (usually 8 or 9) and are dependent on the parents for an additional three weeks following nest departure (Austin and Ricklefs 1977). If summer rains are sufficient and persist, breeding continues and true second broods are begun (Lowther et al. 1999). Brown-headed Cowbird brood parasitism has been reported fairly frequently in the past (Ohmart 1969; Lowther et al. 1999), but was not reported by atlasers.

DISTRIBUTION AND STATUS

Rufous-winged Sparrows have a limited distribution, and in the United States, are only found in south-central Arizona. However, most of the population is found in adjacent Mexico, where it occurs along the Pacific slope from Sonora to northern Sinaloa (Howell and Webb 1995).

The distribution of Rufous-winged Sparrows has fluctuated over the years in Arizona. Common when first discovered near Tucson in 1872, this sparrow disappeared from this area by the mid-1880s, apparently because of grazing pressures, and was not found near Tucson again for fifty years (Phillips et al. 1964). Phillips et al. mention the species as formerly more common and less local, but still considered it locally common from near Oracle and the Tucson region, west across much of the Tohono O'odham tribal lands. Monson and Phillips (1981) noted that during the 1970s, following ample summer rains they dispersed in winter and spring to other areas. These included the Tumacacori Mountains, Tombstone, Saint David, the east slope of the Santa Rita Mountains, the Nogales area, north to near Coolidge, and west as far as Quitobaquito Springs in Organ Pipe Cactus National Monument.

In general, atlasers encountered Rufous-winged Sparrows fairly commonly throughout much of their historical range where appropriate habitat still exists. However, likely in response to availability of grasses, the species is not evenly distributed with some local populations containing few individuals and pairs. These sparrows were found at elevations ranging from 2080 to 4100 ft (634–1250 m). Atlasers discovered that Rufous-winged Sparrows occurred locally within the lower San Pedro River valley from Mammoth north to Winkelman and near Cactus Forest, just southeast of Florence. During the atlas period, they were also found for the first time in Maricopa County near the Sand Tank Mountains on the Barry M. Goldwater Range. Atlasers noted the western limits of the Rufous-winged Sparrow's range were along wide washes and drainages just east of the Ajo Mountains. To the southeast, these sparrows were found near Rio Rico, the upper Cienega Creek drainage, and near Happy Valley on the east side of the Rincon Mountains. Atlasers also reported singing individuals northeast of Tombstone and near Sierra Vista, but nesting has never been confirmed in these outlying areas.

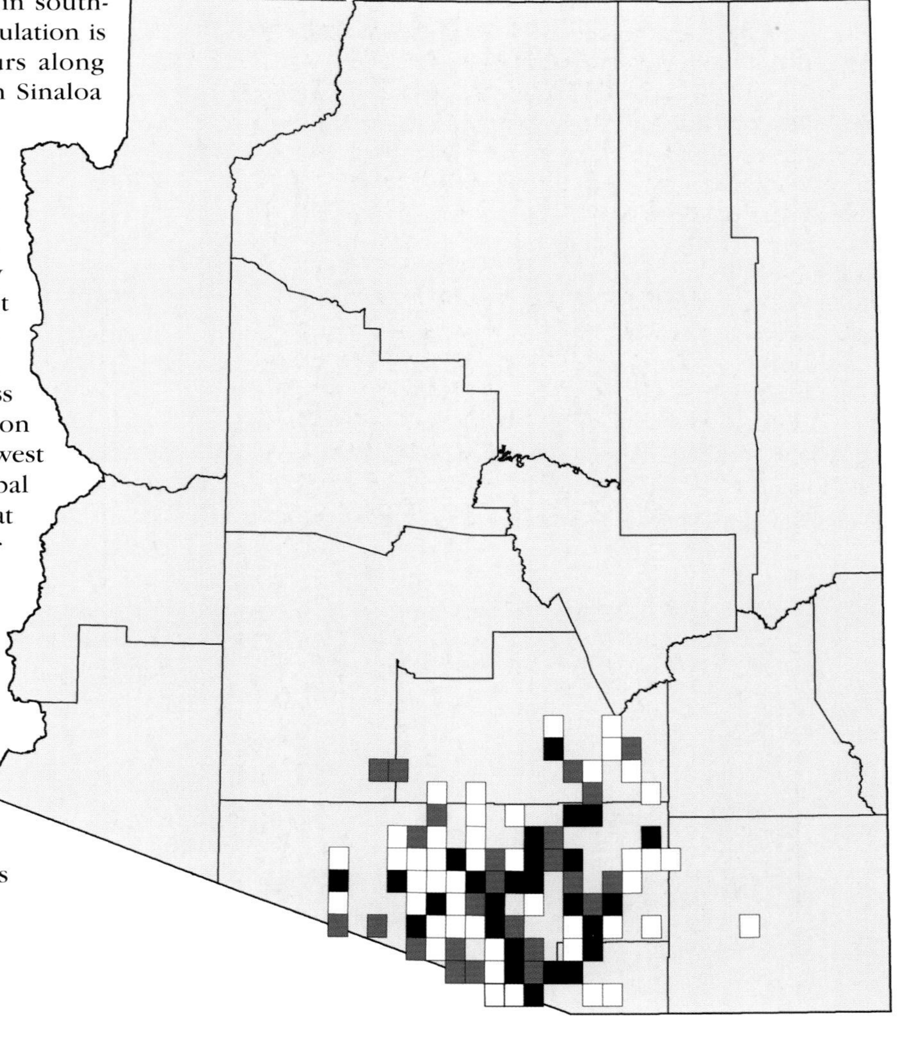

Rufous-winged Sparrow Breeding Evidence Reported in 89 (5%) of 1834 priority blocks

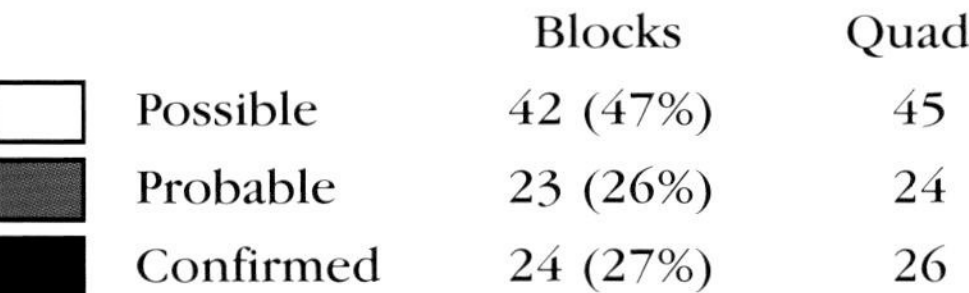

	Blocks	Quads
Possible	42 (47%)	45
Probable	23 (26%)	24
Confirmed	24 (27%)	26

Cassin's Sparrow

by Troy E. Corman *Aimophila cassinii*

Male Cassin's Sparrows deliver a uniquely sweet, yet melancholy song, which is often enhanced by skylarking performances. On trembling wings, they launch themselves skyward near the commencement of the song; then, on set wings, they float slowly downward to a low perch as the song concludes.

DAN FISCHER

HABITAT

In Arizona, Cassin's Sparrows prefer habitats with an abundance of tall grass and scattered low, woody shrubs. Atlasers reported 79 percent of all observations of this sparrow from semiarid grasslands (n = 108). Low, shrubby velvet mesquite frequently occurs in the grassland habitats this sparrow selects. However, other shrubs may include soaptree yucca, whitethorn acacia, catclaw acacia, ocotillo, creosote, prickly pear, and agave. Bock et al. (1986) noted that Cassin's Sparrows breed more abundantly in native Arizona grasslands compared to grasslands dominated by exotic lovegrasses. Atlasers encountered Cassin's Sparrows much less frequently in Sonoran savanna grasslands, a limited habitat in south-central Arizona with scattered ironwood, mesquite, and paloverde. Similarly, they were noted sparingly in both Sonoran and Chihuahuan desertscrub habitats containing patches of grass and weedy ground cover. Studies by Bock and Webb (1984) found that Cassin's Sparrows prefer lightly grazed or ungrazed upland grasslands to heavily grazed grasslands. These sparrows are also most abundant in unburned native grasslands with 50 percent brushy canopy cover (Bock and Bock 1992).

BREEDING

The abundance, movement, distribution, and breeding phenology of Cassin's Sparrows vary annually in Arizona, based on the timing and amount of local precipitation. Most nesting activity is concentrated in the late summer monsoon period. However, following winters and springs with above-normal precipitation, this sparrow can be heard singing locally in March and April, only to fall silent during the normally very dry period of May and June. An exception to this was noted on 9 April 1995, when an atlaser observed a Cassin's Sparrow nest building north of Douglas. The outcome of this nesting attempt was unknown, although birds continued to sing and skylark at this location through at least 28 May. This species had previously not been reported nesting in the spring in Arizona.

Atlasers reported Cassin's Sparrows singing irregularly and very locally in May and June, but most singing and breeding activity occurs primarily after the onset of monsoon rains in early July. It is thought that many perched singing males are unmated, especially those outside their typical breeding range. Based on recent studies, it was also found that males performing skylarking flight songs indicated paired status and nesting activity was likely (Schnase et al. 1991).

During the typical late summer breeding period, atlasers observed Cassin's Sparrows carrying nesting material as early as 12 July. Although observers were unsuccessful in discovering nests with eggs, they noted adults carrying food on 31 July, suggesting clutch initiation by mid-July. Atlasers reported adults feeding fledglings by 6 August and based on atlas data, peak nesting activity is from late July to late August. Nesting activity continues into September, with adults observed carrying food as late as 1 September and fledglings reported through 9 September. Since few atlasing surveys were conducted after mid-August, later nesting activity is likely more frequent than the data suggest. An unusually late nesting effort was documented in Arizona near Hereford in 1987, when a fledgling incapable of sustained flight was observed on 21 October and an adult was singing nearby.

Female Cassin's Sparrows construct their nests on or near the ground in a low shrub or grass clump (Dunning et al. 1999). Of twenty nests found in southeastern Arizona, eleven were in desert broom, five were in burroweed, and

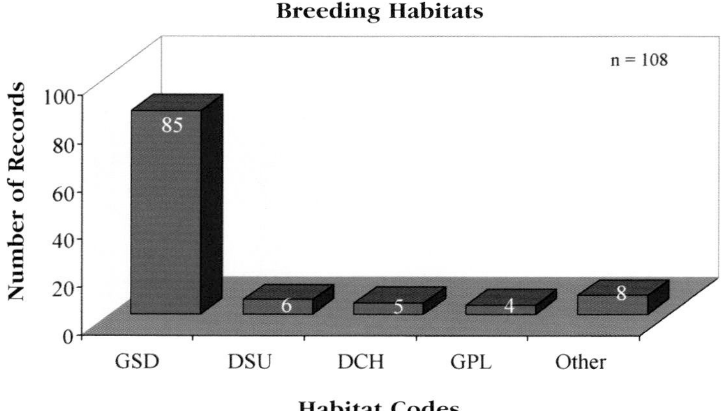

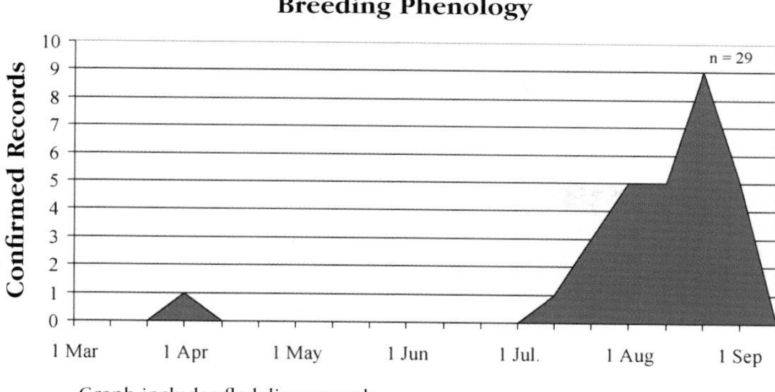

Graph includes fledgling records

the remaining in grass clumps with nest height ranging from 0.0 to 7.9 in (0.0–20.0 cm) above the ground (Dunning et al. 1999). The female incubates the typical 3–4 egg clutch for approximately 11 days, and both parents feed the nestlings, which fledge in approximately 9 days (Dunning et al. 1999). Cassin's Sparrows are capable of double brooding, but there is no clear evidence of this (Schnase et al. 1991).

DISTRIBUTION AND STATUS

Cassin's Sparrows typically nest from Nebraska, south through Texas and northern Mexico, west to southeastern Arizona. Erroneously reported as only a post-breeding and winter visitor in southeastern Arizona (Phillips et al. 1964), Cassin's Sparrows were not confirmed nesting in the state until 1965 near Tucson (Ohmart 1966). In the 1970s, nesting was suspected to the northwest in Yavapai County when a fledgling and an adult male were collected in Chino Valley and singing birds were found in the grasslands at Cordes Junction during the typical nesting period (Monson and Phillips 1981). Although nesting annually in southeastern Arizona, these rather nomadic sparrows breed irregularly and very locally elsewhere in the state.

In Arizona, most Cassin's Sparrows breed at elevations from 3000 to 5000 ft (914–1524 m), but atlasers encountered them from 2200 to 5600 ft (671–1707 m) in southeastern Arizona. They were noted as fairly common and widespread in the southeast, from just west of Sells, east to the New Mexico border and north to central Greenlee County between Duncan and Clifton. These sparrows were also found north to the southern edge of the Pinaleno Mountains. Monson and Phillips (1981) had previously noted these sparrows occurred north to the San Carlos tribal lands and beyond Globe. They were not detected in these regions of the state during the atlas period.

North of the Mogollon Rim, Cassin's Sparrows were only found at one location in grasslands east of Saint Johns at 6700 ft (2042 m). Birders rarely visit the extensive grasslands in this region during the late summer and additional surveys may reveal that these sparrows are an irregular nesting species. In Yavapai County, atlasers confirmed Cassin's Sparrows nesting for the first time near Camp Verde and in the grasslands west of Congress. They were also found singing in the semiarid grasslands near Cordes Junction.

Many potential breeding records for this wandering, rain-dependent sparrow were likely missed due to lack of sufficient surveys in shrubby grasslands and Chihuahuan desertscrub associations in late July and August. This is especially true if surveys were conducted only during years with low precipitation.

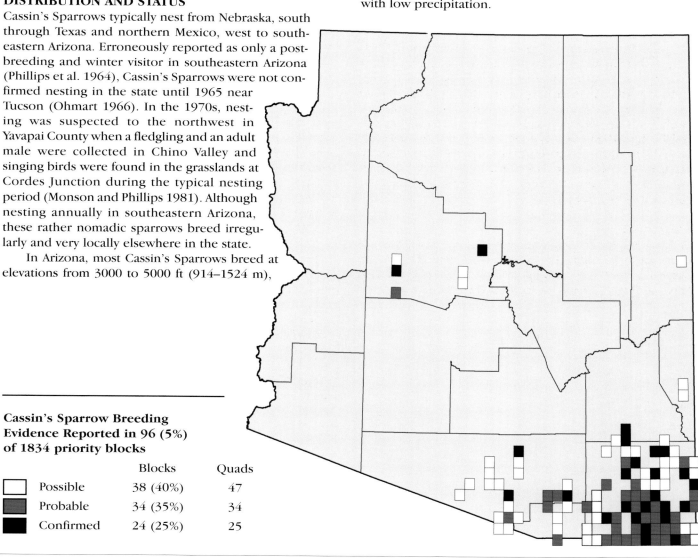

Cassin's Sparrow Breeding Evidence Reported in 96 (5%) of 1834 priority blocks

	Blocks	Quads
Possible	38 (40%)	47
Probable	34 (35%)	34
Confirmed	24 (25%)	25

Botteri's Sparrow

by Troy E. Corman *Aimophila botterii*

Unlike several other grassland sparrows in southeastern Arizona, Botteri's Sparrows will begin singing before the onset of the seasonal late summer rains. Their slightly darker coloration and redder tones help distinguish these sparrows, but it is their song that adds confidence when identifying this inhabitant of tall grasslands.

DAN FISCHER

HABITAT

Botteri's Sparrows are grassland specialists, and in Arizona they especially frequent areas with taller grasses. Their presence in an area is often first detected when male are noted singing from elevated perches such as tall bunchgrass clumps, fences, or low woody shrub. Approximately 90 percent of all atlas records for this sparrow were reported from semiarid grasslands, particularly in areas that transition into several other vegetative communities (n = 70). Botteri's Sparrows reach their greatest abundance in Arizona in grassy swales, floodplain bottoms, and lower canyon drainages that are periodically flooded and dominated by giant sacaton. This is especially true for dense, senescent sacaton stands reaching greater than 6.5 ft (2 m) in height (Webb and Bock 1990). They breed in sacaton bottoms of widely varying character, but only those bordered by grassy hillsides and gentle upland slopes, where they often forage (Webb and Bock 1996). They also nest in upland grasslands that are often interspersed with very scattered, low shrubs such as velvet mesquite, whitethorn acacia, catclaw acacia, ocotillo, and various low cacti. These sparrows were also encountered nesting locally in rolling grasslands intermixed with open stands of evergreen oaks. Botteri's Sparrows breed sparingly in grasslands dominated by soaptree yucca, exotic lovegrass, or alkali sacaton (Webb 1985).

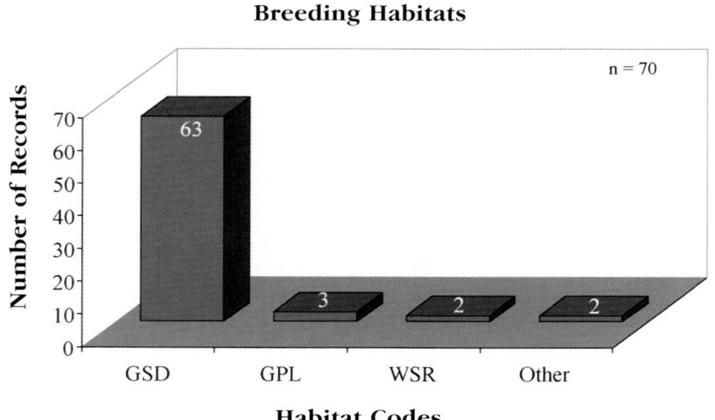

BREEDING

Some Botteri's Sparrows arrive in Arizona breeding areas by late April, although most do not appear until mid-May. The earliest singing male reported by atlasers was on 11 May. In Arizona, males typically sing full songs from early May through mid-September, with most singing activity in late June–early July just before the summer rainy season (Webb 1985). Egg laying initiation usually begins in mid-July, but Webb (1985) noted clutches from 17 June to 24 August. As would be expected for a tall-grassland specialist, atlasers discovered few nests, and nesting date information was supplemented by specific research conducted on this sparrow during the atlas period. The peak nesting period for Botteri's Sparrows in Arizona is from late July to mid-August. The earliest nest with young reported during the atlas period was 24 July, and the latest confirmation records were of fledglings on 7–8 September. Based on egg dates from other Arizona studies, some late nests likely contain young into mid-September (Webb and Bock 1996). Most Botteri's Sparrows have departed Arizona by late September, with stragglers occurring into mid-October.

Much of the following breeding biology for Botteri's Sparrows has been taken from intensive studies conducted at the Appleton-Whittell Audubon Research Ranch south of Sonoita in 1981–1983 (Webb 1985). Botteri's Sparrows construct their well-concealed nest on the ground in approximately six days. The nest site is almost always in a tall, thick, overhanging grass clump. They typically nest at the elevated edge of sacaton-dominated bottoms and to a lesser extent adjoining upland grassland slopes, which may reduce the risk of flood inundation (Webb and Bock 1990). Typical Botteri's Sparrow clutches consist of 3–4 eggs, but can range from 2–5. The eggs hatch after an incubation period by the female of 12–13 days. If the young are left undisturbed, they typically leave the nest when they are approximately 10 days old. The parents continue to feed the fledglings until gaining independence when they are 4–5 weeks old. In Arizona, Botteri's Sparrows are not known to double brood, but will renest if the first nest is destroyed before advanced brooding.

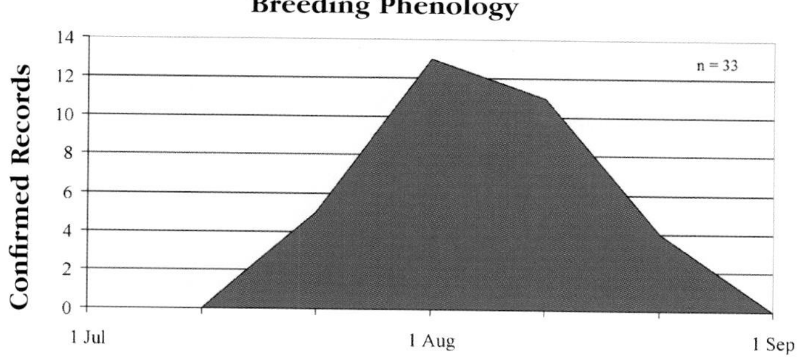

Likely owing to the difficulty in finding their nests in the tall grass they favor, these sparrows are very rare Brown-headed Cowbird hosts. Of twenty-four Botteri's Sparrow nests discovered by Webb (1985), only one contained a cowbird egg.

DISTRIBUTION AND STATUS

Botteri's Sparrows occur in disjunct populations from southeastern Arizona, southwestern New Mexico, and south Texas, south to northern Costa Rica. Only the extreme northern populations are migratory. They are highly susceptible to loss or alteration of grassland habitats, and, based on historical records, their distribution in Arizona has changed considerably. Before 1895, they were collected as far north as Fort Grant, Graham County, and near Oracle, Pinal County (Phillips et al. 1964). The northernmost records came from a specimen collected in 1876 at Goodwin Station, Graham County, which was possibly in the Gila River valley near present-day Geronimo (Webb 1985).

The western distribution of Botteri's Sparrows has contracted and expanded over the past century. Before 1895, they occurred as far west as the Altar Valley, but Phillips et al. (1964) noted that they were no longer present west of Sonoita. However, by 1967, Botteri's Sparrows were found just east of Nogales and later as far west as Arivaca (Monson and Phillips 1981). During the atlas, it was found once again to occupy the upper Altar Valley, likely in response to appropriate grassland habitat management at the Buenos Aires National Wildlife Refuge.

Atlasers found Botteri's Sparrows to be fairly common to locally common in grasslands at elevations from 3550 to 5200 ft (1082–1585 m). They were encountered from the San Bernardino Valley in extreme southeastern Arizona, west to the Buenos Aires National Wildlife Refuge. The northern edge of their current distribution is the foothills of Mount Fagan south of Vail, Pima County. In the San Pedro River valley, Botteri's Sparrows were found from the Mexico border north to just south of Saint David. In the Sulphur Spring Valley, atlasers detected them primarily south of Sunizona. Atlasers did not detect this sparrow near the Pinery Creek drainage west of Chiricahua National Monument, where Webb (1985) had reported them.

Botteri's Sparrow populations in southeastern Arizona are vulnerable to inappropriate grazing practices and other habitat disturbances. However, these grassland specialists can tolerate prescribed burning and moderate cattle grazing without extirpation, and their current status is considered fairly stable (Webb and Bock 1996). This is particularly true in protected and properly managed localities such as wildlife refuges, preserves, and conservation areas.

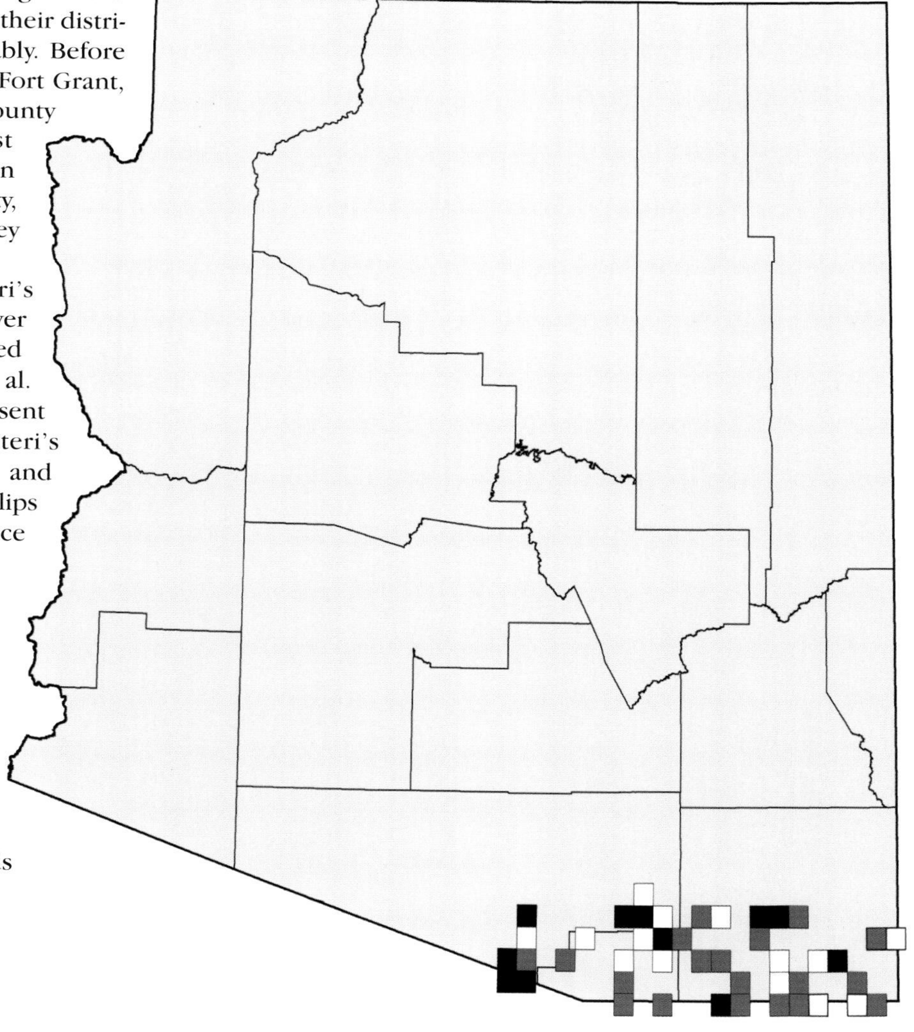

Botteri's Sparrow Breeding Evidence Reported in 40 (2 %) of 1834 priority blocks

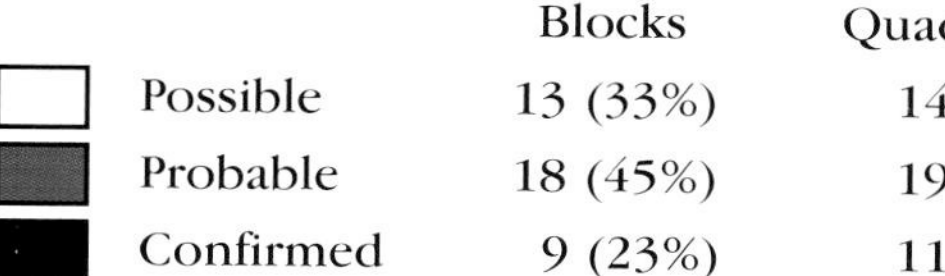

	Blocks	Quads
Possible	13 (33%)	14
Probable	18 (45%)	19
Confirmed	9 (23%)	11

Rufous-crowned Sparrow

by Troy E. Corman *Aimophila ruficeps*

The distinctive, rapid "dear, dear, dear" call emanating from a dry slope is often the first clue that a Rufous-crowned Sparrow is near. When singing, Rufous-crowned Sparrows often secure an exposed perch on a low shrub or rock, but they quickly vanish to their brushy and boulder-strewn world at the slightest disturbance.

JIM BURNS

HABITAT

In Arizona, characteristic habitat for Rufous-crowned Sparrows consists of arid rocky slopes, boulder fields, or outcrops with scattered low trees, shrubs, and grasses. Inhabited areas range from moderately sloping foothills and ravines to steep canyon sides. Throughout much of their distribution in Arizona, characteristic shrubs often include jojoba, yucca, agave, cacti, beargrass, and acacia. In northern Arizona, Fremont barberry, sagebrush, and shrub live oak are often dominant shrubs where Rufous-crowned Sparrows occur. They typically avoid similar habitat on relatively flat terrain. Atlasers reported Rufous-crowned Sparrows most frequently (20 percent of records) on slopes in semiarid grasslands (n = 348). Although they usually avoid dense, chaparral covered slopes, approximately 19 percent of atlas records were reported in open and scattered stands of this vegetative community. An additional 18 percent of potential atlas breeding records were from brushy, rocky slopes of Sonoran Desert mountain ranges. In southeastern Arizona, these sparrows were most frequently encountered on mountain slopes containing a combination of semiarid grassland and open Madrean oak woodlands. This habitat comprised 15 percent of the atlas records. Fewer atlas observations were noted in open pinyon pine–juniper woodlands and other desertscrub associations. At higher elevations, these sparrows can also be found locally on dry, open mountainsides adjacent to pine-oak woodlands.

Breeding Habitats

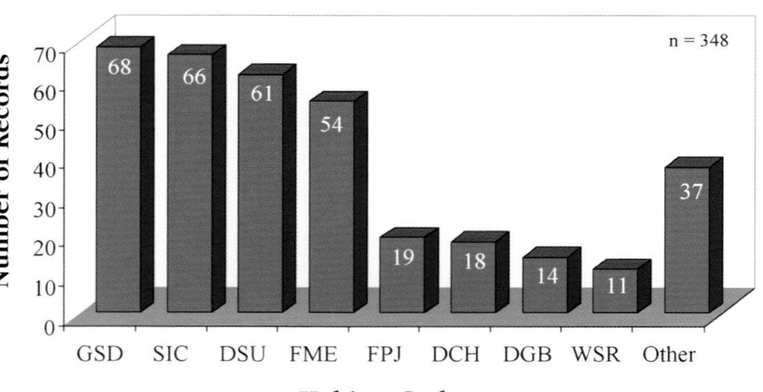

BREEDING

Primarily a resident species, there is little evidence to suggest that Rufous-crowned Sparrows do much other than some altitudinal movement to nearby lowlands during the winter. At least some pairs appear to remain together throughout the year. In Arizona, males begin to sing consistently in late February and March.

During the atlas project, Rufous-crowned Sparrows were observed nest building as early as 29 March. However, atlasers also witnessed adults carrying food on 10 April. This suggests that nest building can begin slightly earlier, with egg laying no later than late March. Spring nesting activity appears to peak from late April-early June. Atlas data reveal a possible lull in mid-June, with nesting activity peaking again in July and August. The typical late summer monsoon rains often contribute to the lush growth of grasses and annuals in southeastern Arizona. Like many other passerines in this region, Rufous-crowned Sparrows readily take advantage of the new abundance of cover and food for rearing late season broods. Adults were observed feeding fledglings as late as 28 August. In southeastern Arizona, nests with eggs have been found as late as 5 September (Phillips 1968).

Female Rufous-crowned Sparrows typically construct their well-hidden nest on the ground under overhanging vegetation, rocks, or other debris. Atlasers reported nests under logs, at base of grass clumps, under beargrass, and one nest 1.6 in. (4 cm) above the ground in a jojoba. The female incubates the typical clutch of 3–4 eggs for approximately 11–13 days (Collins 1999). Both parents feed the nestlings, which abandon the nest when they are 8–9 days old and move about under the cover of nearby shrubs and grasses (Collins 1999).

These sparrows typically produce one to two broods per season. Although two broods have only been documented in California (Collins 1999), successful second broods are likely routine at least in southeastern Arizona

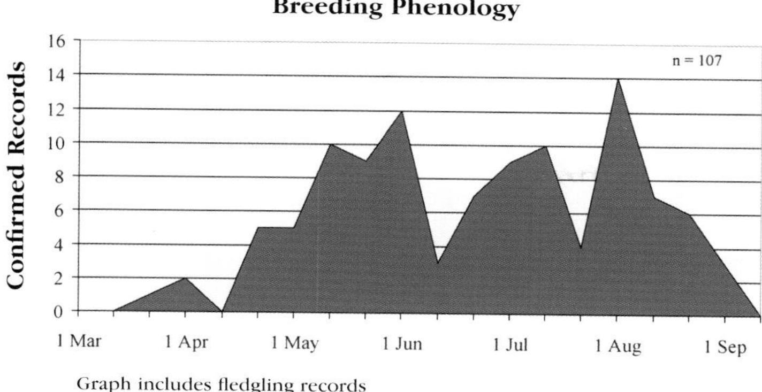

Graph includes fledgling records

during the late summer monsoon period. Rufous-crowned Sparrows are considered rare Brown-headed Cowbird hosts (Friedman 1971), likely owing to this sparrow's preferred habitat and typically well-concealed nests.

DISTRIBUTION AND STATUS

Rufous-crowned Sparrows are resident in disjunct populations from southwestern United Sates, south to Oaxaca, Mexico. In the United States, they occur as far north as central California and east to Kansas and Arkansas. Rufous-crowned Sparrows have been reported as common in southern Arizona, north sparingly along the slopes of the Mogollon Rim (Phillips et al. 1964). They also occur locally west to the Ajo and Kofa mountains, and sparingly along most of the Grand Canyon, where Phillips et al. (1964) described this sparrow's range and status as poorly known.

Atlas data reveal that Rufous-crowned Sparrows could still be found throughout their historical distribution in Arizona at elevations from approximately 2200 to 7000 ft (670–2134 m). Collins (1999) also noted these sparrows at elevations as high as 8000 ft (2438 m). Atlasers discovered Rufous-crowned Sparrows were much more widespread along the Mogollon Rim and in Mohave County than earlier literature suggested. Atlas surveys also helped delineate this sparrow's distribution along the rims of the Grand Canyon, but additional surveys are still needed before their status in this rugged and remote section of the state is clearly understood. Atlasers reported Rufous-crowned Sparrows for the first time along Kanab Creek and Snake Gulch on the western slope of the Kaibab Plateau. They were also noted east along the rims of Marble and Glen canyons to near Page and up the Little Colorado River Gorge west of Cameron. Isolated records in southern Navajo County were along Chevelon Canyon and near Snowflake along Silver Creek. Atlasers found them along the Black River drainage as far upstream as the Bear Wallow Creek confluence. Rufous-crowned Sparrows likely also occur throughout the lower mountain slopes and canyons within White Mountain Apache tribal lands, where access permits to conduct atlas surveys could not be obtained.

In southwestern Arizona, Rufous-crowned Sparrows were only found on slopes of the higher desert ranges such as the Harquahala, Harcuvar, Kofa, Ajo, Sauceda, Sand Tank, Santa Rosa, and Picacho mountains. Near Phoenix, these sparrows were encountered in the Sierra Estrella and South mountains. Likely owing to limited appropriate habitat in these arid ranges, Rufous-crowned Sparrows were typically present in low numbers and often found only on brushier, north-facing slopes.

Rufous-crowned Sparrow populations appear to be fairly stable in Arizona. There is little that threatens their preferred habitat, and recent drought and wildfires may temporarily open some habitats that have previously been too densely vegetated for this sparrow.

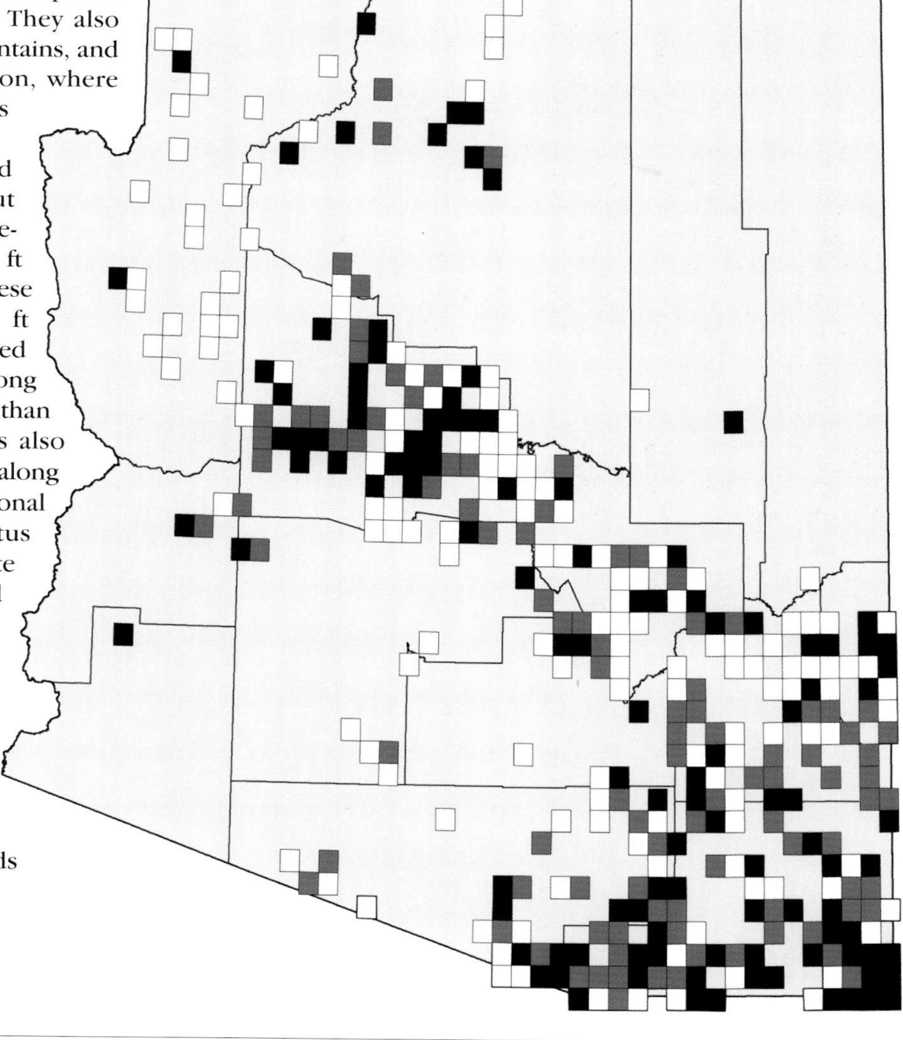

Rufous-crowned Sparrow Breeding Evidence Reported in 346 (19%) of 1834 priority blocks

	Blocks	Quads
Possible	137 (40%)	154
Probable	99 (28%)	103
Confirmed	110 (32%)	118

Five-striped Sparrow

by Troy E. Corman *Aimophila quinquestriata*

The Five-striped Sparrow is greatly prized by visiting birders to southeastern Arizona, for they know it breeds nowhere else in the United States. During the height of Arizona's late summer monsoon season, many hopeful visitors make the pilgrimage to the local arid, brushy slopes that this sparrow prefers.

DAN FISCHER

HABITAT

These attractive sparrows inhabit a variety of dense vegetative communities in Mexico, from arid and semiarid thornscrub to tropical deciduous forests. In Arizona, most localities occupied by Five-striped Sparrows can be characterized as fairly tall, dense, and often thorny brush with scattered grasses and forbs. They typically select steep, arid hillsides and slopes of primarily rocky desert canyons with some permanent water source nearby, often in the form of intermittent drainage pools or springs. Atlasers characterized the habitat as a mixture of Sonoran desertscrub and semiarid grassland. Shrubs that are often present in their preferred habitat regularly include catclaw acacia, velvet mesquite, netleaf hackberry, hopbush, yellow trumpet, desert honeysuckle, ocotillo, and Mexican kidneywood and are typically 3–7 ft (0.9–2.1 m) in height (Mills 1977). Density of the shrubs is apparently more important than plant species composition, and steep hillsides probably characterize the habitat of this dark stocky sparrow to the extent that they provide the necessary conditions for the correct vegetation structure (Mills 1977).

BREEDING

The migratory status of Five-striped Sparrows in Arizona is largely unknown. Phillips and Farfan (1993) noted that the northern race is largely migratory; however, this species has been irregularly noted in Arizona during the winter, when it is quiet and easily overlooked. Limited nesting information was collected during the atlas project, and much of what we know about the breeding phenology and behavior of the Five-striped Sparrow in Arizona comes from intensive studies conducted during the late 1970s (Mills et al. 1980). Unless noted differently, much of what follows is from this exhaustive work.

Most male Five-striped Sparrows apparently arrive in breeding areas in May and June and sing their high, tinkling song into September. However, recently these sparrows have been noted singing irregularly as early as April. It is unknown when pairs are formed, but birds are often already paired when they are first sighted on territory. The frequency and duration of singing bouts is greatest between June and September in Arizona (Groschupf 1992). There is an apparent influx of singing male Five-striped Sparrows after mid-July, which typically corresponds to the initiation of the late summer monsoon season. Some nest building activity has been observed during the last few days of May, but peak activity begins soon after the summer rains begin and often continues well into early September. In Arizona, nests with egg have been found from 4 June to 20 August, with significantly more clutches in July. Atlasers reported an adult feeding recently fledged young on 25 July. The latest nest with young reported in Arizona was in mid-September.

It takes the female Five-striped Sparrow approximately 3–5 days to construct the deep nest cup. Nests are placed within grass clumps or shrubs from 7 to 59 in. (19–150 cm) above the ground. They are usually hidden in heavy foliage of the nest plant or under the canopy of shrubby trees such as hackberry and mesquite. The female incubates the 3–4 eggs for 12–13 days and both parents feed the nestlings, which fledge when they are 9–10 days old. In Arizona, Five-striped Sparrows have been known to fledge three broods successfully within a season, and females can lay the first

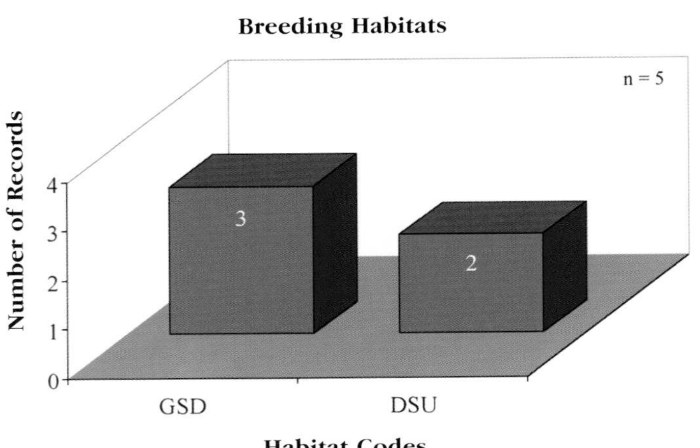

egg of a subsequent nest only 5–7 days following nest departure of the earlier brood. While the female initiates the next brood, the male takes on full responsibilities of feeding the fledgling of the first brood, which can continue up to 18 days. Brown-headed Cowbirds are known to parasitize the nests of this sparrow in Arizona readily, although this was not reported during the atlas period.

DISTRIBUTION AND STATUS

Five-striped Sparrows breed from extreme south-central Arizona south to north-central Jalisco, Mexico (Howell and Webb 1995). Russell and Monson (1998) consider this sparrow to be fairly common in appropriate habitat throughout much of Sonora. They were first reported in Arizona (and the United States) in 1957 just west of Madera Canyon in the Santa Rita Mountain foothills (Binford 1958). This sparrow was not found in the state again until 1969 near Patagonia when the first breeding record was obtained (Mills 1977). It has been found nesting locally in Arizona ever since, particularly in Mexico border canyons in southwestern Santa Cruz County.

All breeding populations of Five-striped Sparrows in Arizona have been found within a narrow elevation range of 3500–4000 ft (1067–1219 m). Atlasers confirmed that populations continued in a few specific canyons and drainages along the Mexico border of the Atascosa and Pajarito mountains. These include Sycamore, Tonto, and Holden canyons, and California Gulch. During the atlas period, two singing males were also detected in Baboquivari Canyon on the western slope of the Baboquivari Mountains (M. Stevenson, personal communication). This locality is on the Tohono O'odham tribal lands, and these sparrows were first noted there in 1978 (Monson and Phillips 1981). They were not relocated in historical breeding locations in Chino Canyon, Santa Rita Mountains, or above Sonoita Creek near Patagonia. However, a Five-striped Sparrow was reported in lower Madera Canyon, Santa Rita Mountains, during the 1996 breeding season. This individual was near potential breeding habitat, but may have been wandering due to the unseasonably hot and dry conditions during that period.

Recent surveys suggest a decline in the number of breeding Five-striped Sparrows in Arizona since the late 1970s (Groschupf 1994). Mills (1977) noted that the number of individuals within a population apparently fluctuates from year to year, and some local edge populations may periodically be extirpated only to become reestablished in later years. Population stability appears to be related to breeding success, which is apparently correlated to rainfall and habitat quality (Groschupf 1994). Additionally, there are many remote and rugged canyons in the southern Baboquivari Mountains that are seldom, if ever visited by individuals familiar with this sparrow. Future surveys may reveal additional small populations, particularly in brushy canyons with a permanent water source.

Arizona's limited populations of Five-striped Sparrows are potentially threatened by human activities. In occupied locations that are frequently visited by birders, the use of song playback has the potential to disrupt breeding activities and should be discouraged (Zimmer and Zimmer 1992). This is especially true for the small California Gulch population of Five-striped Sparrows, which is currently visited by birders almost daily during the nesting season. Inappropriate grazing practices, wildfires, mining exploration, Border Patrol activities, and road construction also have the potential to cause disturbance and habitat loss for this extremely local nesting sparrow in Arizona.

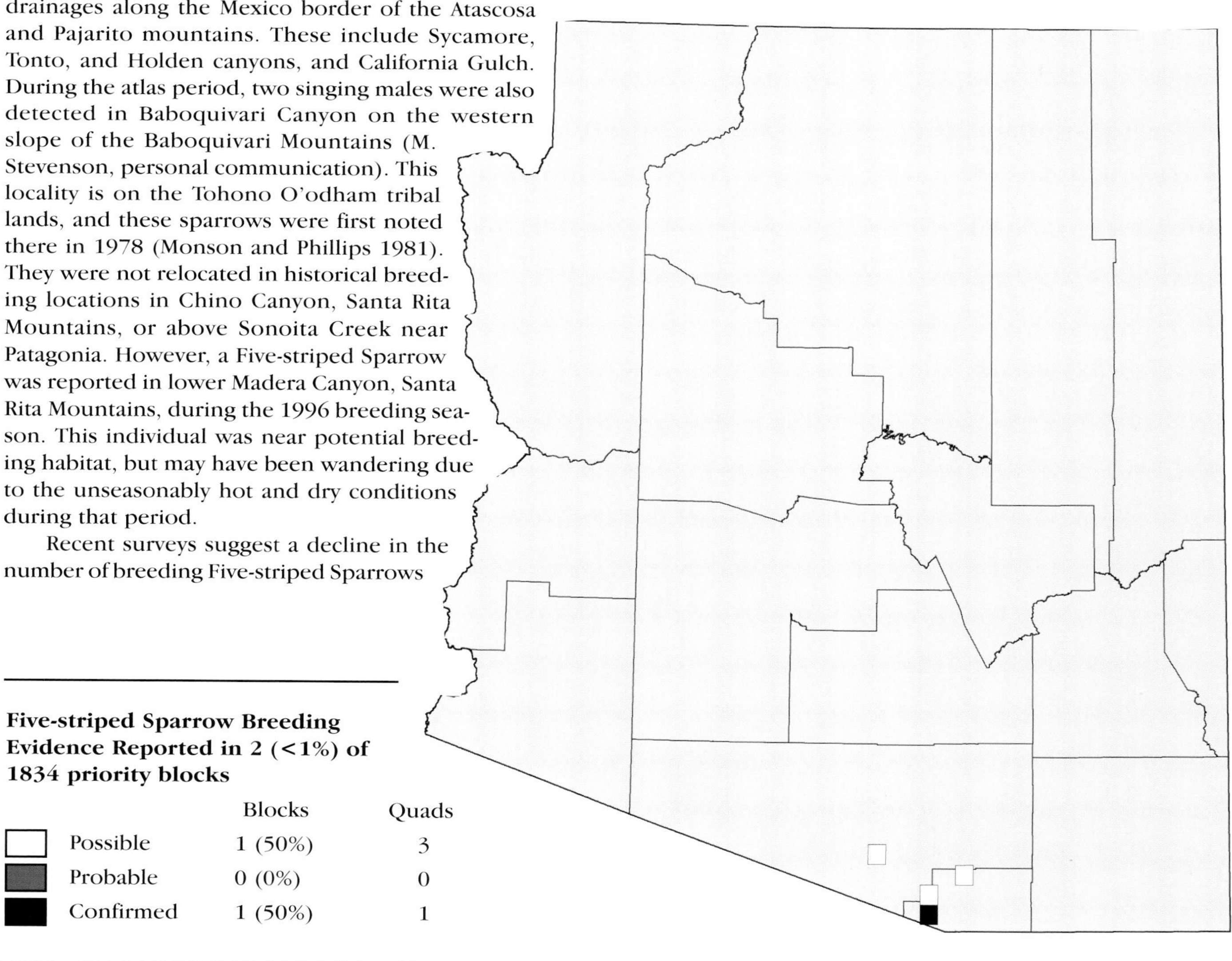

Five-striped Sparrow Breeding Evidence Reported in 2 (<1%) of 1834 priority blocks

	Blocks	Quads
Possible	1 (50%)	3
Probable	0 (0%)	0
Confirmed	1 (50%)	1

Chipping Sparrow

by Cathryn Wise-Gervais *Spizella passerina*

The Chipping Sparrow's distinctive song is a nonmusical, single-pitch trill that is commonly heard throughout the summer in northern Arizona's open woodlands. Chipping Sparrows eat primarily insects and seeds, and commonly feed on the ground close to cover. During fall and winter these birds will often forage in large, sometimes mixed-species flocks.

RICK AND NORA BOWERS

HABITAT

Chipping Sparrows are widely distributed throughout North America and their breeding habitats vary greatly depending upon geographic location. Unlike many of Arizona's sparrows that closely associate with grassland communities, these birds favor open woodlands, forest edges, and clearings. Atlasers reported Chipping Sparrows in twenty-five vegetative communities, indicating a good deal of habitat choice flexibility. The majority of atlas records were from pinyon pine-juniper woodlands (45 percent of records) and from pinyon-juniper transition areas containing grassland, sagebrush, or ponderosa pine (23 percent; *n* = 476). Approximately 16 percent of records were obtained in open ponderosa pine forests including stands with a Gambel's oak association. In addition, Chipping Sparrows were reported nesting locally in Madrean evergreen oak woodlands, open mixed-conifer forests, and even at the edge of subalpine meadows and spruce-fir forests. These adaptable birds also nest in central and northern Arizona's suburban parks and neighborhoods. In fact, Chipping Sparrows are thought to be more numerous now rangewide than during presettlement times, owing to their ability to use human-made environments (Stull 1968; Rising 1996).

BREEDING

Spring migration for Arizona's Chipping Sparrows typically begins in early March, and males initiate singing and establishing territories upon their arrival on breeding grounds by early April. Males arrive approximately one week before females (Walkinshaw 1944), and pairs form soon after the females appear. Nesting usually begins within two weeks of the female's arrival on the breeding grounds, but this can be delayed by cold weather (Middleton 1998). Atlasers first observed adults defending territory on 19 April and reported an individual carrying nesting material on 10 May. However, a fledgling was first noted on 17 May, indicating that some early nests contain eggs by mid- to late April. Observers found nests with eggs or young from 12 May to 26 July. Atlas data suggest that breeding activity statewide peaks from mid- to late June but continues through the summer. Adults were observed feeding fledglings as late as 29 August. Chipping Sparrow can begin southbound migration as early as late July in Arizona, but are more commonly observed in transit in September and October. They are widespread and locally abundant winter residents in southern and western Arizona, where they are often encountered foraging in large flocks near riparian woodlands and in large washes.

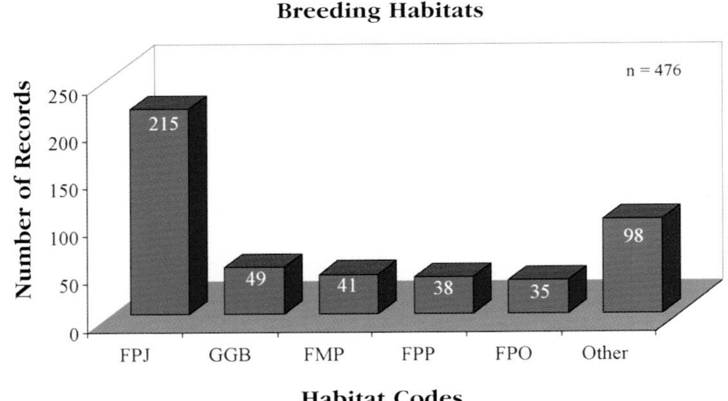

Female Chipping Sparrows construct their loosely woven cup nest without male assistance, and this structure is often so flimsy that light can be seen through it (Middleton 1998). Observers took measurements at twenty-seven nests during the atlas period. Ten nests were discovered in several species of juniper; the remaining nests were in big sagebrush (7), pinyon pine (5), ponderosa pine (3), and Fremont barberry (2). The median height of all nests measured was 5 ft (1.2 m) and height ranged from 1.8 to 25 ft (0.6–7.5 m).

A typical Chipping Sparrow clutch consists of 4 eggs (range 2–7), which the female will incubate exclusively for approximately 10–12 days (Middleton 1998). Upon hatching, the female broods while the male provides food for both the young and his mate (Middleton 1998). After three days, however, both parents feed nestlings. Most young depart the nest between the ages of 9–12 days, and parents continue to provide food for approximately 3 weeks while the young improve their flight and foraging skills (Middleton 1998). Many studies have reported Chipping Sparrows rearing two broods in one season. In such cases, the male will continue to care for the first batch of fledglings while the female renests (Middleton 1998).

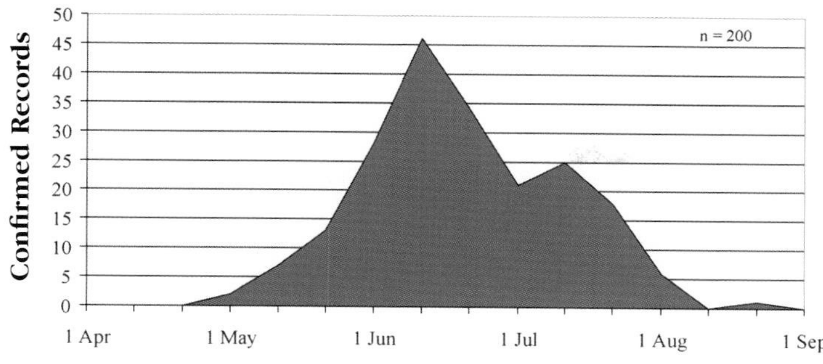

Chipping Sparrows are common Brown-headed Cowbird hosts throughout North America (Middleton 1998), but only one parasitism event was noted during the atlas. Observers reported a Chipping Sparrow nest containing a Brown-headed Cowbird egg on June 13.

DISTRIBUTION AND STATUS

Chipping Sparrows are found throughout North America, from eastern Alaska east to southern Newfoundland and south into Central America (Middleton 1998). Although they breed throughout much of the United States, they are largely absent in desert regions, the southern Great Plains, and along the Gulf of Mexico coastal areas. Chipping Sparrows have previously been described as common to abundant summer residents in central and northern Arizona's woodlands and open forests (Phillips et al. 1964). Although these birds most commonly breed in the state at elevations from 5500 to 8000 ft (1675–2438 m), atlasers confirmed Chipping Sparrows nesting on priority blocks from approximately 4200 to 9600 ft (1280–2926 m).

Atlas data reveal that Chipping Sparrows are widespread and common nesting birds from San Carlos Apache tribal lands northward. Atlasers found the species fairly easy to confirm, inasmuch as begging fledglings can be rather noisy. Confirmed breeding records nearly surround the White Mountain Apache tribal lands, indicating that these sparrows undoubtedly continue to nest throughout this unsurveyed reservation. To the west they were found nesting to the Hualapai Mountains and south to the Bradshaw Mountains.

Chipping Sparrows are apparently sparse and local breeders in the mountains of southeastern Arizona. Prior nesting records exist for the Huachuca and Chiricahua mountains and they were noted as possibly nesting in the Santa Catalina and Pinaleno ranges (Monson and Phillips 1981). During the atlas project, these birds were confirmed breeding in the Chiricahua Mountains and reported singing in June in the Pinaleno Mountains. Although suitable habitat exists, Chipping Sparrows went unreported as a potential nesting species in the other two ranges noted above. There are few breeding records in Sonora as well (Russell and Monson 1997).

Observers regularly reported Chipping Sparrows throughout most of their historic range during the atlas period, suggesting some degree of population stability in the state. Breeding Bird Survey data indicate that continental populations were fairly stable between 1966 and 1994, although some regional western populations have revealed significant declines (Middleton 1998).

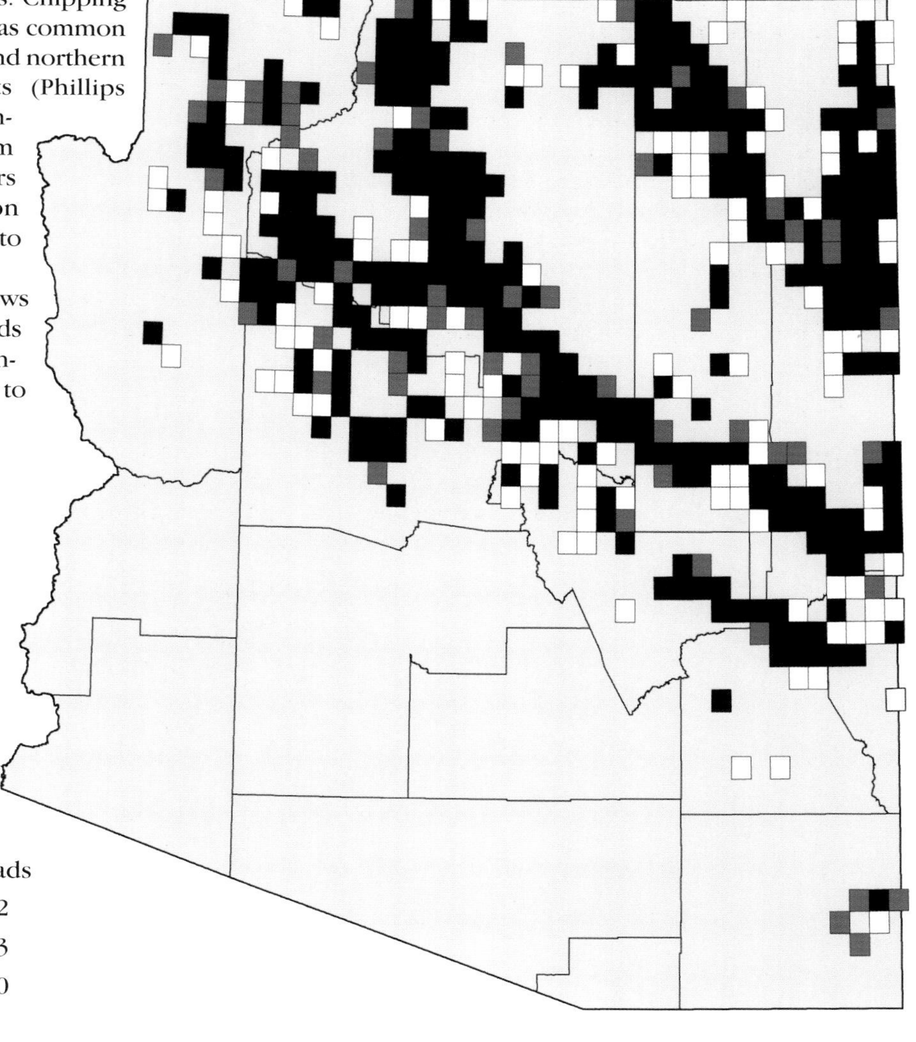

Chipping Sparrow Breeding Evidence Reported in 470 (26%) of 1834 priority blocks

	Blocks	Quads
Possible	115 (24%)	122
Probable	61 (13%)	63
Confirmed	294 (63%)	300

Brewer's Sparrow

by Cathryn Wise-Gervais *Spizella breweri*

Brewer's Sparrows are subtle in color and blend well with the mellow hues of the sagebrush plains and open desertscrub that they call home. Given its muted plumage, this small sparrow's buzzy and animated song—which has been likened to a Chipping Sparrow trying to sing like a canary—is perhaps its most distinctive quality.

JIM BURNS

HABITAT

Breeding in western shrublands, Brewer's Sparrows are strongly associated with open sagebrush country, including shrubby foothills and rolling brushy terrain. Although atlasers reported Brewer's Sparrows breeding in eight vegetative communities, 77 percent of records were from cold-temperate desertscrub-dominated landscapes (n = 128). Most occupied locations are characterized by big sagebrush and saltbush, but may also contain other sagebrush and low woody species with a mixture of native and nonnative grasses. These sparrows were also reported in adjacent grasslands comprised of scattered junipers and low woody shrubs (13 percent of records). The few remaining local records were in nearby areas where preferred shrublands merged with other adjacent habitats such as plains grasslands, very open pinyon pine-juniper woodlands, and high-elevation Mojave desertscrub. Rotenberry et al. (1999) noted that Brewer's Sparrows generally selected nesting substrates that were less than 5 ft (1.5 m) in height.

BREEDING

In Arizona, Brewer's Sparrows begin their spring migration in March-April, but some birds may still be traveling through the state well into May and casually later. Even during migration, these sparrows sing their cheerful song persistently in anticipation of the summer nesting season. Males arrive on their Arizona breeding grounds several days before the females and begin establishing territories immediately. Atlasers first reported a pair of Brewer's Sparrows in suitable breeding habitat on 16 April. In Arizona, early nest-building activity likely begins by late April, with egg laying in early May, based on a nest with young discovered on 17 May. Paine (1968) reported a nest with eggs as early as 19 April in California and similar early nesting would be expected in Arizona at the southern edge of Brewer's Sparrows breeding range. Most atlas surveys were not conducted in northern Arizona sagebrush country until May, so some earlier Brewer's Sparrows nesting activity may have been missed. Although observers reported adults feeding fledged young on 11 July and located dependent fledglings as late as 26 July, most breeding records were obtained in mid- to late June.

LaRue (1994) noted that Brewer's Sparrows in Arizona begin to form local flocks by late July. Small flocks typically begin arriving in southern Arizona by mid-August, but they do not become common in these winter areas until mid-September or October.

Brewer's Sparrows most commonly nest in big sagebrush range-wide (Rotenberry et al. 1999). Similarly, eleven of the thirteen Brewer's Sparrow nests described by atlasers were in sagebrush. The other nest plants were wolfberry and broom snakeweed. The median nest plant height for the 13 nests was 2.2 ft (0.7 m) and ranged from 1.4 to 5.0 ft (0.4–1.5 m). The median nest height was 1.0 ft (0.3 m) and ranged from 0.6 to 2.8 ft (0.2–0.9 m). These nest measurements correspond closely to those collected in other states (Rotenberry et al. 1999). For example, 90 percent of nests measured in Idaho were between 0.7 and 1.6 ft (0.2–0.5 m) high (n = 58; Petersen and Best 1985a).

Most evidence suggests that it is primarily the female Brewer's Sparrow that builds the neat and compact nest (Rotenberry et al. 1999). The typical clutch consists of 3–4 attractive eggs, but this can range from 2–5. Females do most of the incubating, although males occasionally assist

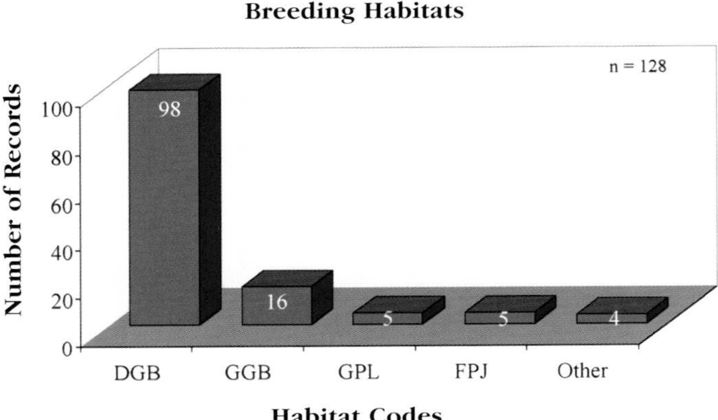

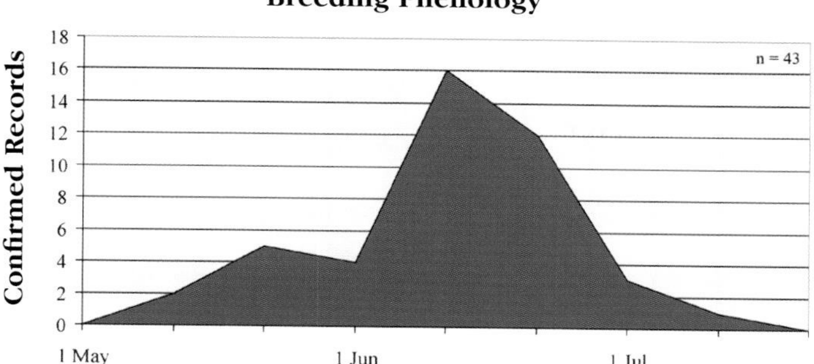

or bring food to incubating females (Rotenberry et al. 1999). The incubation period lasts for 10–12 days (Rising 1996), after which both parents feed the young until fledging at 6–9 days of age (Rotenberry et al. 1999). The young are flightless the first several days following nest departure and remain in nearby shrubs. Brewer's Sparrows will often renest if earlier efforts fail and may raise second broods if resources allow (Rotenberry et al. 1999).

DISTRIBUTION AND STATUS

Brewer's Sparrows breed in the interior of western North America primarily from southern Canada south through northern New Mexico and Arizona. There is also a disjunct population in northwestern Canada, and these birds typically occur in montane valleys and in areas above timberline (Rotenberry et al. 1999). In contrast, Brewer's Sparrows are typically found at mid-elevations throughout their breeding range, and atlasers confirmed breeding on priority blocks from approximately 4300 to 7400 ft (1311–2256 m).

Atlasers discovered Brewer's Sparrows nesting much more extensively in northern Arizona than previous literature indicated. Phillips et al. (1964) reported the species nesting only within the Navajo and Hopi tribal lands in northeastern Arizona. However, in 1975, Brewer's Sparrows were found nesting to an unknown extent farther west in the Toroweap Valley, just north of the Grand Canyon (Monson and Phillips 1981). Atlasers documented these sparrows throughout much of the Arizona Strip region and north and east of the Kaibab Plateau. They were also found nesting well south of the Grand Canyon, including on Hualapai tribal lands and on the Coconino Plateau, south to Seligman and locally in the Williamson Valley area north of Simmons (C. Tomoff, personal communication). Earlier omissions probably resulted from a lack of survey effort, as suitable sagebrush habitat is plentiful though often patchy in these areas. Brewer's Sparrows were also found nesting throughout a large portion of northeastern Arizona south locally to the Little Colorado River valley near Holbrook and Saint Johns.

Given the frequency with which Brewer's Sparrows were reported and the estimated abundance figures given by atlasers, it would appear that this species is fairly stable in Arizona, although the abundance of nesting populations within the Arizona Strip region can shift dramatically from one year to the next. Brewer's Sparrows are common nesters in appropriate habitat during wet or normal precipitation years, but they can be nearly absent when winter and spring precipitation is low (T. Corman, personal communication). Given this, further research would be required to determine long-term population trends at their southern limits in Arizona. Breeding Bird Survey data rangewide suggest a decreasing trend from 1966 to 1996, possibly owing to sagebrush habitat fragmentation and loss (Rotenberry et al. 1999).

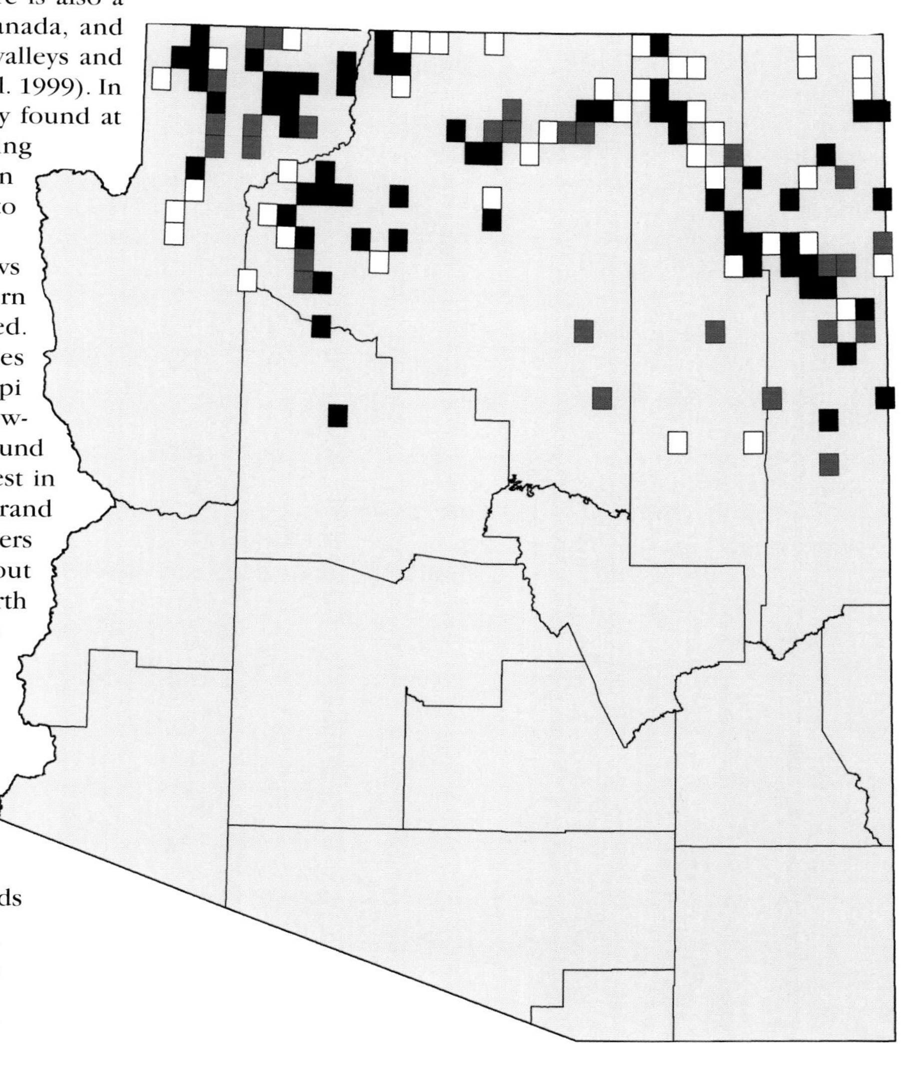

Brewer's Sparrow Breeding Evidence Reported in 126 (7%) of 1834 priority blocks

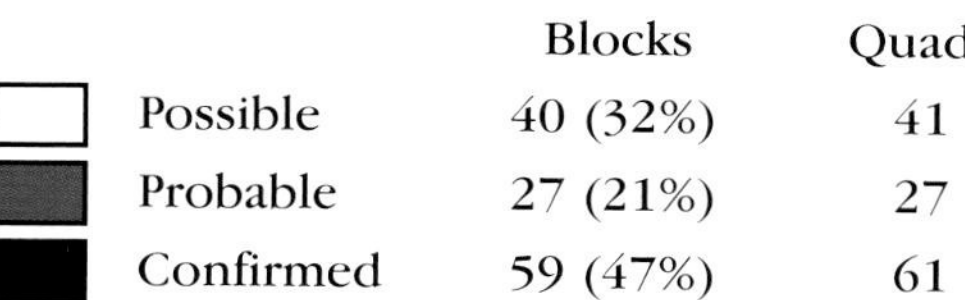

	Blocks	Quads
Possible	40 (32%)	41
Probable	27 (21%)	27
Confirmed	59 (47%)	61

Black-chinned Sparrow

by Troy E. Corman *Spizella atrogularis*

The unique and vibrant descending song of the Black-chinned Sparrow is a familiar spring and summer sound on arid brushy hills and chaparral-shrouded mountain slopes. Preferring habitats infrequently visited by birders, these attractive sparrows were found to be much more common and widespread than previously thought.

DAN FISCHER

HABITAT

Typically inhabiting mid-elevations in Arizona, Black-chinned Sparrows are encountered nesting in a variety of arid, brushy, and generally sloping habitats. Steep mountain slopes and remote ridges covered with dense chaparral vegetation are especially favored in central Arizona. Characteristic woody shrubs at these locations include shrub live oak, manzanita, mountain mahogany, and Apache plume. Chaparral associations accounted for 43 percent of all atlas records for this sparrow (n = 239). In the northwest corner of the state, Black-chinned Sparrows were found primarily on arid foothills and drainage slopes with tall, dense stands of big sagebrush, cliffrose, and Mormon tea. Pinyon pine and junipers were frequently found scattered through this habitat, which accounted for 27 percent of atlas records for this species. Populations of Black-chinned Sparrows were often much more locally distributed in southern Arizona. Here they were found most frequently on rocky, arid foothill slopes with thickets of acacia, beargrass, agave, yucca, and patches of various grasses with scattered juniper and evergreen oaks. Occasionally this sparrow was also encountered in dense, thickets at the bottom of dry, rocky canyons.

BREEDING

Arizona has both migratory and resident populations of Black-chinned Sparrows, with migratory birds arriving on their breeding grounds in March and April. They can begin singing on territory by early to mid-March in Arizona. The earliest atlas nesting records for this sparrow were of an occupied nest on 28 April, an adult carrying food on 8 May, and a nest with young on 9 May. These observations indicate that nest building begins as early as mid-April in Arizona, with the earliest eggs laid by the end of the month. Few nests were actually found during the atlas project, likely because of the rough terrain and dense brushy slopes this species prefers. Statewide atlas data suggest that the peak nesting period for Black-chinned Sparrows in Arizona is from late May to late June. The latest nesting activity reported by atlasers was of an adult feeding a fledgling on 6 August with fledglings noted through the end of August.

Migratory populations of Black-chinned Sparrows begin moving south or to lower elevation in late August or early September. However, these sparrows are rarely observed during migration and the distribution of Arizona's wintering populations is still poorly understood. Wintering birds are often found in lower canyons and brushy foothill washes.

Black-chinned Sparrow nests are typically well concealed and placed near the center of various dense shrubs (Tenney 1997), often near the edge of a dry wash or swale. Measurements were taken at only 8 nests during the atlas period. These nests averaged 2.7 ft (0.8 m) above the ground and ranged from 1.2 to 6.8 ft (0.4–2.1 m). During the atlas period, most nests were reported in sagebrush, but also in Utah juniper, low in grass clumps, and an odd, exposed nest in a cane cholla.

Black-chinned Sparrows clutches typically consist of 3–4 eggs, but this can range from 2–5 (Newman 1968). Females incubate the eggs for 12–13 days and often remain tight on the nest until closely approach (Tenney 1997). There is apparently little information on the length of the nestling stage; however, 9–12 days is likely. Both parents tend the nestlings and the fledglings (Tenney 1997). Most evidence suggests that only one brood is produced per season, but they regularly renest if earlier attempts fail (Tenney 1997).

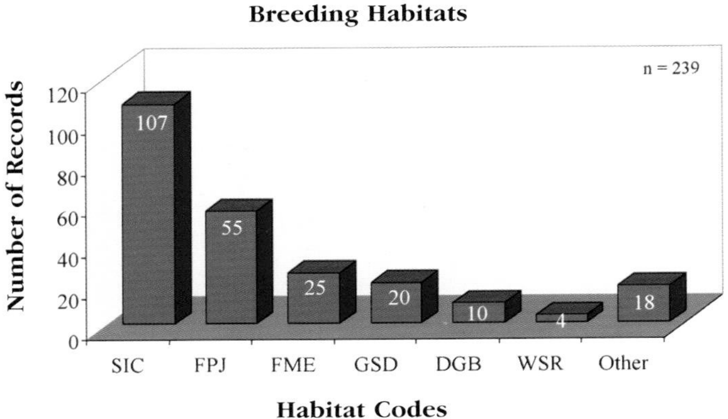

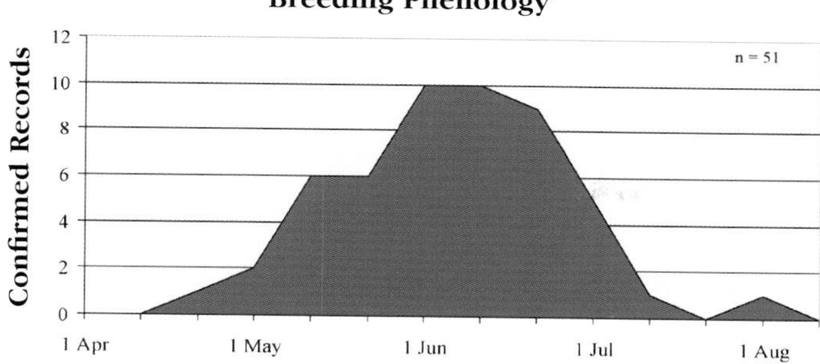

DISTRIBUTION AND STATUS

Black-chinned Sparrows breed in scattered localities in much of California south to northern Baja California, and east through southern Nevada, southwestern Utah, Arizona, New Mexico, and extreme western Texas. They breed in disjunct populations to central Mexico. Phillips et al. (1964) noted this sparrow to be fairly common in chaparral across Arizona below the Mogollon Rim from New Mexico west and northwest to the Hualapai Mountains. Black-chinned Sparrows were also noted breeding south very locally to the Chiricahua and Mule mountains. Monson and Phillips (1981) later described this sparrow's range to include the Grand Wash Cliffs and Toroweap Valley in northwestern Arizona, and possibly the southern end of the Huachuca Mountains.

Atlasers found Black-chinned Sparrows to be fairly common to locally common throughout their historical range in Arizona. These sparrows were also noted as more widespread than previous literature suggested, primarily at elevations between 3800 and 7720 ft (1158–2353 m). They were encountered for the first time on the western slope of the Kaibab Plateau, west through many areas of the Arizona Strip region. Black-chinned Sparrows were also discovered nesting in isolated populations on the northern slope of Gray Mountain, west of Cameron on Navajo tribal lands, and several were noted singing very locally on Black Mesa in northern Navajo County.

Black-chinned Sparrows were also found southwest of their previous known range in the higher elevations of the Harcuvar and Harquahala mountains and very locally in the shrub live oak patches of the Kofa Mountains near Signal Peak. Due to the limited habitat at the latter location, this sparrow may only nest there after exceptionally wet winters, which was the case when singing birds were located on 27–28 April 2001 and at least one pair on 31 May 2001. They were found singing in similar habitat on the eastern slope of the Ajo Mountains in late April, but later surveys were not conducted in this area. Therefore, it is unknown if these sparrows remained to nest. In Southeastern Arizona, Black-chinned Sparrows remained locally distributed, with observations in the Chiricahua, Mule, Huachuca, Whetstone, Dragoon, Baboquivari, Rincon, Santa Catalina, and Galiuro mountains.

Most evidence suggests Arizona populations of Black-chinned Sparrows are fairly stable. There are relatively few historical avian records northwest of the Grand Canyon. Therefore, it is unclear if the widespread occurrence of this attractive sparrow in the Arizona Strip region indicates a steady range expansion or simply overlooked populations in these relatively remote areas.

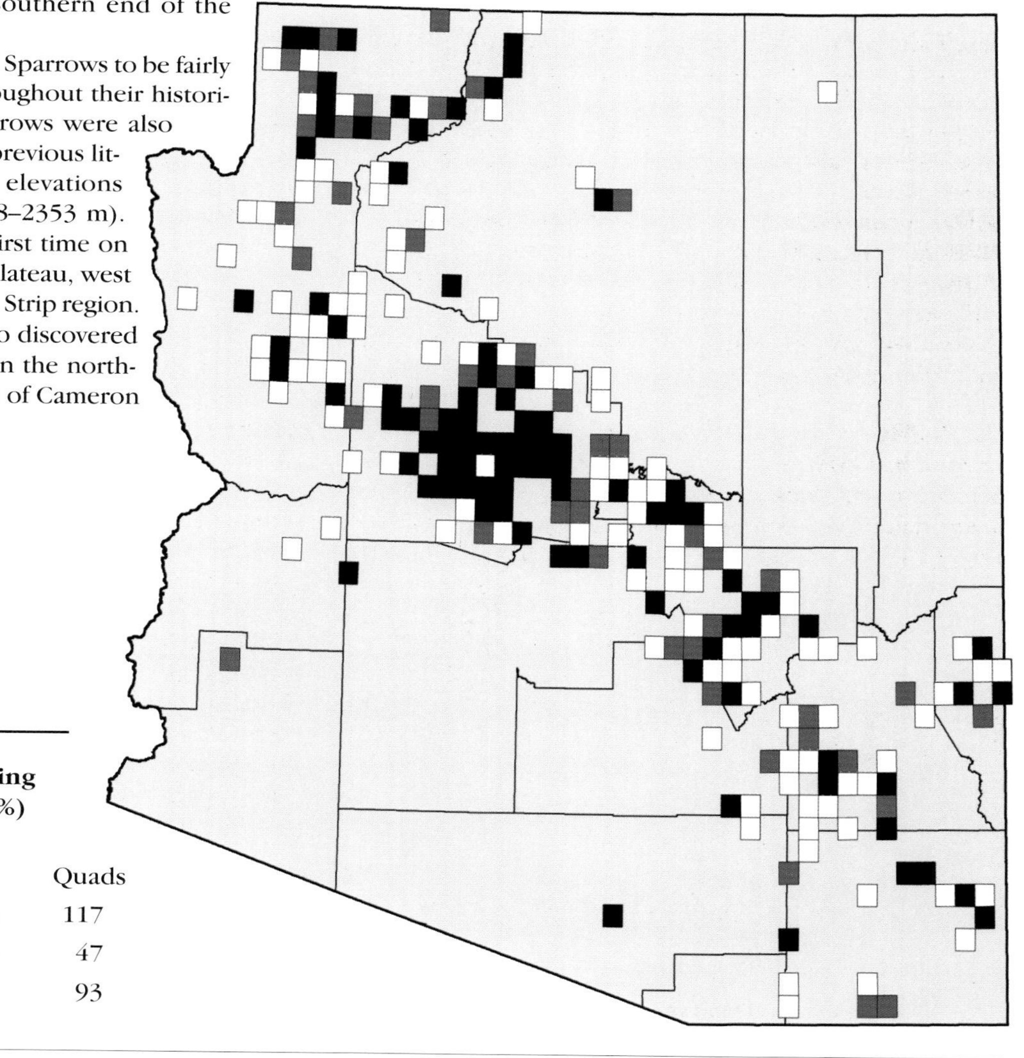

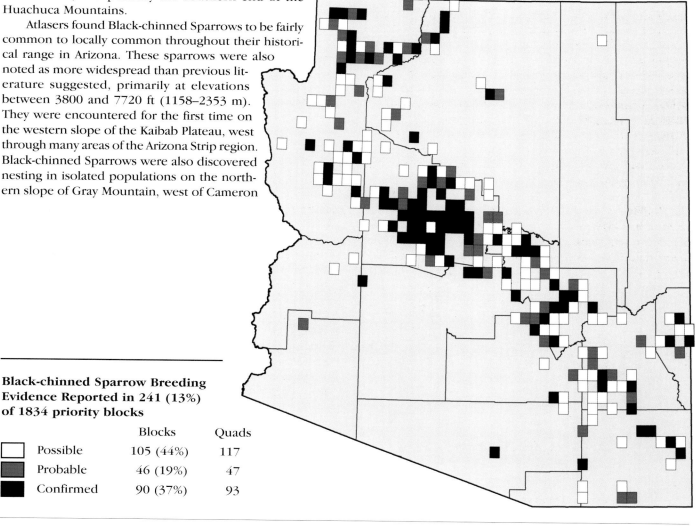

Black-chinned Sparrow Breeding Evidence Reported in 241 (13%) of 1834 priority blocks

	Blocks	Quads
Possible	105 (44%)	117
Probable	46 (19%)	47
Confirmed	90 (37%)	93

Vesper Sparrow

by Cathryn Wise-Gervais *Pooecetes gramineus*

The Vesper Sparrow's song is rapid and jingly, and is often given at sunset—fittingly, for "vesper" derives from the Latin word for "evening." Formerly known as the "Grass Finch" or "Bay-winged Sparrow," this streaky grassland species has a distinct white eye-ring and white outer tail feathers.

JIM BURNS

HABITAT

Vesper Sparrows are considered habitat generalists rangewide and are found in a variety of open areas offering low cover (Jones and Cornely 2002). Although Vesper Sparrows are commonly associated with dry grassland uplands, they use several other habitats in Arizona. Atlasers reported breeding Vesper Sparrows in ten habitat types, and 48 percent of records were in cold-temperate and plains grasslands often containing widely scattered junipers, low woody shrubs, various forbs, and mixed native and nonnative grasses (n = 122). Atlasers reported 34 percent of records in areas where grassland habitat merged with cold-temperate desertscrub and dominant vegetation included patchy low shrubs such as sagebrush and blackbrush. In the White Mountains and other high elevation areas of Arizona, Vesper sparrows were frequently encountered in montane meadows and subalpine grasslands. In all habitats, these sparrows prefer areas offering song perches such as fence posts, tall shrubs, or young scattered trees (Jones and Cornely 2002). Vesper Sparrows generally avoid wet or densely vegetated areas.

BREEDING

Vesper Sparrows winter south of the Mogollon Rim throughout most of western and southern Arizona, and their northward movements begin in early March. Males typically arrive on their Arizona breeding grounds in late March and early April, and atlasers first recorded birds paired in suitable breeding habitat on 6 April. Best and Rodenhouse (1984) found that males arrived approximately one week before females to establish territories.

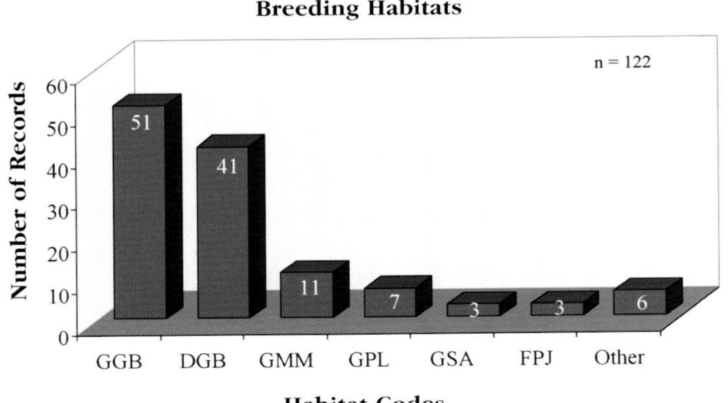

Nest construction likely begins by mid- to late April in Arizona, since nests with eggs have been found as early as 6 May (LaRue 1994). Owing to later survey efforts in northern Arizona, atlasers may have missed many early nesting efforts. The earliest confirmed breeding record obtained by atlasers was an adult Vesper Sparrow carrying food on 17 May. Observers had difficulty discovering the well-concealed nests of this sparrow and reported only three nests with eggs from 2 June to 18 July. Atlas data suggest that breeding activity in Arizona peaks in mid-June through early July then tapers off in late summer. Although Jones and Cornely (2002) reported active nests for this species range-wide from late March to early September, they noted the peak nesting period is from mid-May to late July. Atlasers reported the latest Vesper Sparrow fledgling on 15 August, and noted individuals in nonbreeding areas by late August. The typical peak of Vesper Sparrow fall migration in Arizona is in September and early October.

Vesper Sparrows nest on the ground, under grass clumps or near the base of shrubs. Atlasers described only two nests, one beneath a sagebrush and the other under a clump of grass.

Female Vesper Sparrows find a natural hollow or dig a shallow depression for their nests. They then construct the small cup-shaped structure by weaving together fine materials (Jones and Cornely 2002). Nests are usually well concealed and are only rarely placed in the open (Krueger 1981).

Vesper Sparrows typically lay 3–5 eggs per clutch, and the females incubate these for 11–14 days without male assistance (Jones and Cornely 2002). Both adults feed the nestlings but it is the female that primarily broods and shades the young. Atlasers occasionally noted adults performing distraction displays on the ground in an effort to lead the observers away from the nest or fledglings. The nestlings depart from the nest in approximately 10 days of age, but this can range from 7 to 14 days (Dawson and

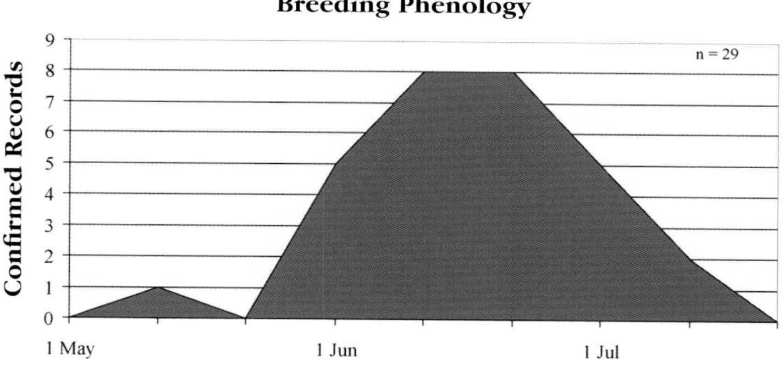

Evans 1960). The young are dependent on the adults for 20–29 days after fledging (Jones and Cornely 2002), and Vesper Sparrow pairs will typically raise one to two broods per year. When the birds undertake multiple breeding attempts, later broods are generally smaller (Berger 1968). Males have been known to take over feeding the first fledged brood while the female initiates the second clutch (Berger 1968).

DISTRIBUTION AND STATUS

Vesper Sparrows breed throughout the northern United States and southern Canada from the northeastern Atlantic seaboard, west to the Central Valley of California. In western North America, these sparrows are found nesting north through Alberta and south to central Arizona and New Mexico.

Phillips et al. (1964) considered Vesper Sparrows fairly common summer residents in Arizona north of the Mogollon Rim including on Navajo and Hopi tribal lands, in the White Mountains region, and in the open rangelands north of Flagstaff. Atlasers verified the occurrence of Vesper Sparrows throughout much of their known historical range in the state, and confirmed the species breeding on priority blocks at elevations ranging from approximately 5600 to 9500 ft (1707–2896 m).

Atlas data reveal that Vesper Sparrows were a fairly common to locally common nesting species throughout much of Apache County, but they were noticeably absent within the Little Colorado River valley downstream of the Saint Johns area. In addition, these sparrows were sparsely distributed on Black Mesa on Navajo tribal lands, just as LaRue (1994) described them. Atlasers found Vesper Sparrows nesting throughout the Coconino Plateau west and north of the Flagstaff area, as well as in the Aubrey Valley and on eastern Hualapai tribal lands. Observers also encountered Vesper Sparrows east of Mormon Lake to the Winslow and East Clear Creek areas. Brown et al. (1987) previously reported them nesting in the Toroweap Valley, and atlasers obtained one Vesper Sparrow nesting record on the Arizona Strip near Mount Dellenbaugh.

Vesper Sparrows are able to respond quickly to habitat changes and colonize new areas rapidly as habitat becomes suitable (Jones and Cornely 2002). In addition, they move around in response to rainfall so their breeding range probably expands and contracts slightly on an annual basis. Although atlas data suggest that Vesper Sparrows in Arizona still occupy much of their known historical range, habitat loss has undoubtedly occurred in the past 150 years from inappropriate grazing practices, dense shrub invasion, agriculture, and urban development. Population trend estimates using Breeding Bird Survey data suggest declining populations in Arizona (Sauer et al. 2001).

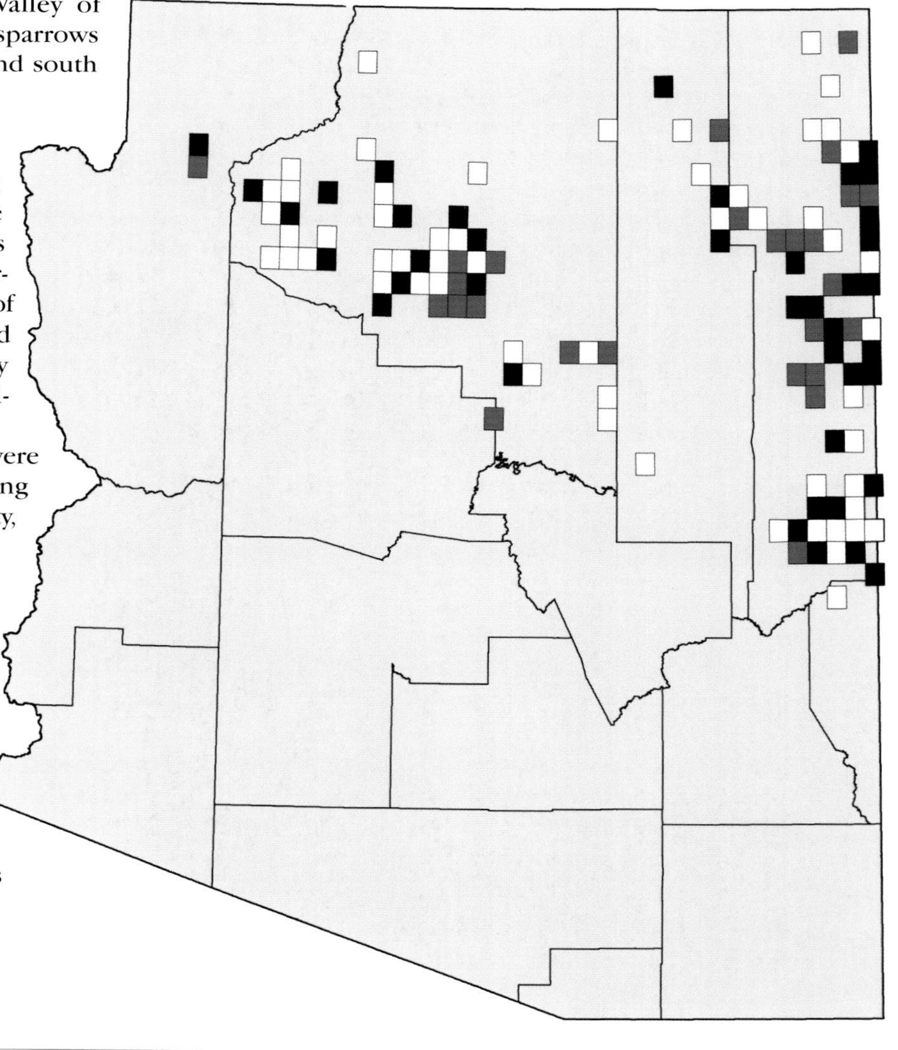

Vesper Sparrow Breeding Evidence Reported in 120 (7%) of 1834 priority blocks

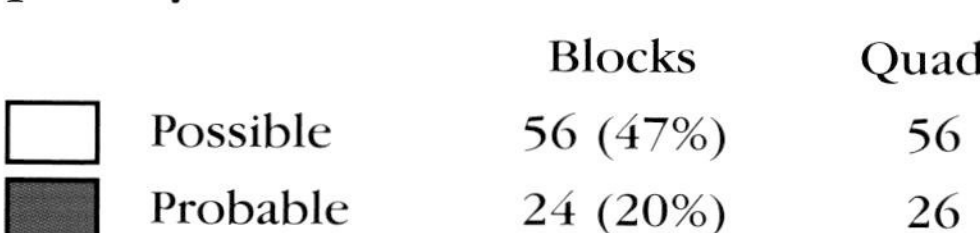

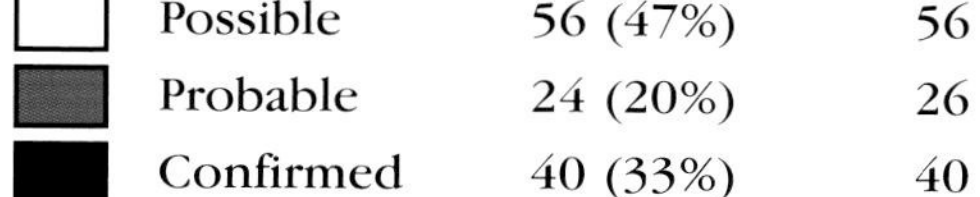

	Blocks	Quads
Possible	56 (47%)	56
Probable	24 (20%)	26
Confirmed	40 (33%)	40

Lark Sparrow

by Cathryn Wise-Gervais *Chondestes grammacus*

Given their unmistakable facial pattern and distinctive bubbling song, Lark Sparrows are probably one of the easiest of Arizona's sparrows to identify. Males engage in an unusual turkey-like courtship dance to attract females, during which they strut with tails cocked and wings drooping to the ground.

DAN FISCHER

HABITAT

Lark Sparrows favor open country with scattered trees and low shrubs. They are commonly found nesting in shrub-steppe associations, in mesquite grasslands, and along woodland edges. This species can be found in a variety of successive vegetative stages, including areas recovering from intensive grazing or crop production (Martin and Parrish 2000). Atlasers reported Lark Sparrows in thirty habitat types, indicating a fair degree of habitat choice flexibility. Most atlas records were obtained in northern regions of the state, and observers reported 44 percent of records in a mixed habitat comprising grassland and cold-temperate desertscrub vegetation (n = 648). These areas contained variable amounts of grasses, scattered juniper, sagebrush, greasewood, rabbitbrush, and other woody shrubs. In southeastern Arizona, Lark Sparrows were most commonly encountered (14 percent of records) in semiarid grasslands with scattered mesquite, acacia, and yucca, and were also found in areas where this habitat merged with open Madrean evergreen oak and pinyon pine–juniper associations. They were reported less frequently in open pinyon pine–juniper woodlands (12 percent of records). Observers also found Lark Sparrows nesting locally along brushy fallow fields, near earthen stock tanks with scattered tamarisk stands, and near isolated, abandoned ranches and homesteads. Rosenberg et al. (1991) noted that Lark Sparrows nested very irregularly and locally in citrus orchards and near other irrigated vegetation in the lower Colorado and Gila River valleys.

BREEDING

Lark Sparrows commonly winter in southern Arizona and begin arriving on their breeding grounds by late March or early April in full song. Males court females with a distinctive dance, and atlasers first observed paired birds on 19 April. They were observed carrying nesting material on 6 May, although some nest construction begins by late April in Arizona, based on observations of adults feeding a fledgling on 26 May. Atlasers reported twenty-three active Lark Sparrow nests with eggs or young from 14 May to 6 August, and atlas data from northern and central Arizona suggests a peak in breeding activity from mid- to late June.

In southeastern Arizona, however, atlas data reveal that Lark Sparrows breed very locally and irregularly in May, with nesting activities increasing in mid- to late June. Breeding activity peaked in this region of the state in early July; additional birds may begin arriving from elsewhere at the initiation of the monsoon season. Nesting continues through early August with adults observed carrying food through late August and accompanying dependent young to mid-September. Arizona's Lark Sparrows can begin dispersing in July, but most migrants are observed in August and September.

Female Lark Sparrows usually construct their grassy cup nest directly on the ground under cover, but will nest low in shrubs (Martin and Parrish 2000). Atlasers recorded measurements at twenty-one Lark Sparrow nest sites, with only four above ground level in junipers (3) and a saltbush. Ground nests were under snakeweed (6), sagebrush (5), juniper (3), and various other shrubs, grass, cholla, and wood debris.

Lark Sparrow clutches typically consist of 4 eggs (range 3–6), and only the female incubates these for 11–12 days (Martin and Parrish 2000). Both adults feed the nestlings, and the young fledge at 11–12 days of age. Lark Sparrows usually rear one brood per year, but two broods are not uncommon (Martin and Parrish 2000).

Lark Sparrows are regular Brown-headed Cowbird hosts. However, atlasers reported only one incident of a Lark Sparrow pair with a begging cowbird fledgling on 16 August.

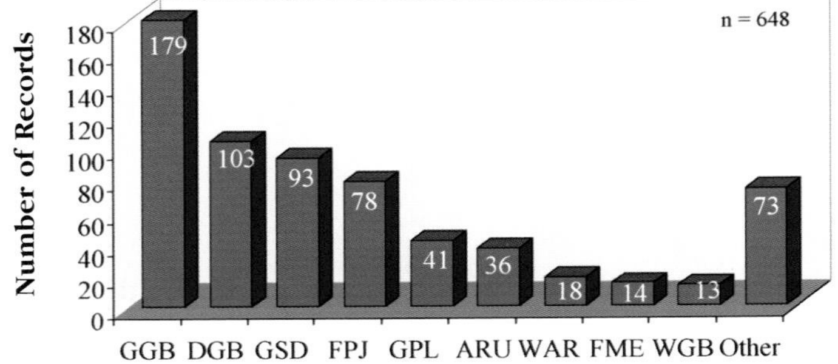

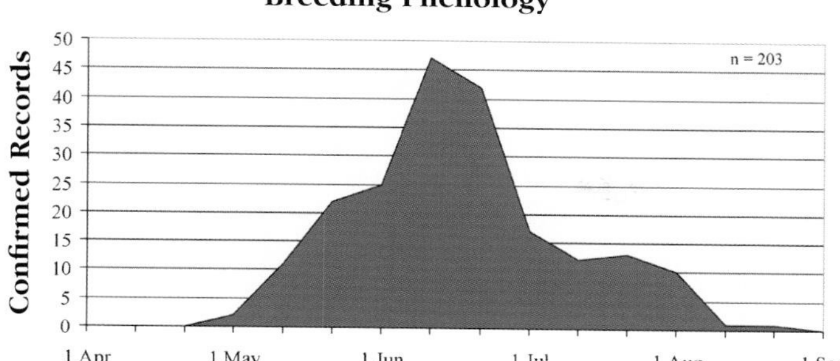

DISTRIBUTION AND STATUS

Lark Sparrows breed primarily in western and central North America from southern Saskatchewan south to north-central Mexico. Monson and Phillips (1981) considered Lark Sparrows fairly common summer residents in eastern Arizona, west to the Altar Valley in the south and Prescott region in the north. Brown et al. (1987) noted that these sparrows were uncommon summer residents in the Grand Canyon region, including on the Kaibab Plateau and the South Rim. Phillips et al. (1964) felt that the breeding range in southeastern Arizona was very spotty and believed that many of the singing birds encountered in this area were transients. Monson and Phillips (1981) later determined that Lark Sparrows were common residents in southeastern Arizona; atlas data reflect this determination, inasmuch as a significant number of confirmed breeding records were obtained from this region during the late summer.

Atlasers confirmed Lark Sparrows nesting on priority blocks at elevations from approximately 3400 to 7600 ft (1036–2316 m) and reported individuals that were probably nesting as low as 200 ft (61 m). As would be expected, this species was primarily absent from the arid desert regions of the south and west, and from forests and heavy woodlands throughout the state. Lark Sparrows were much more widespread and common in northern regions of the state. Here they were regularly encountered in the grasslands and open pinyon pine–juniper woodlands north of the Mogollon Rim, Arizona Strip region, and throughout the Navajo and Hopi tribal lands. In addition, atlasers discovered Lark Sparrows in appropriate habitats just south of the Mogollon Rim and on the rolling plains of the Coconino Plateau south to the southern slope of the Bradshaw Mountains. These sparrows were first discovered nesting locally near Parker, Yuma, and Tacna beginning in the late 1970s (Monson and Phillips 1981; Rosenberg et al. 1991). Atlasers report two probable breeding records in irrigated agricultural areas along the Gila River near Yuma and Tacna. Other local and irregular nesting sites in these river valleys may have been missed while conducting typical atlas surveys.

As previously noted, atlas data reveal that Lark Sparrows are more common and widespread than prior literature suggested. These attractive sparrows may have benefited from the widespread grassland invasion of juniper, mesquite, and other woody shrubs due to inappropriate grazing practices and fire suppression activities. Breeding Bird Survey data suggest that despite declining trends in the eastern United States, Lark Sparrows in the West are stable or slightly increasing (Martin and Parrish 2000).

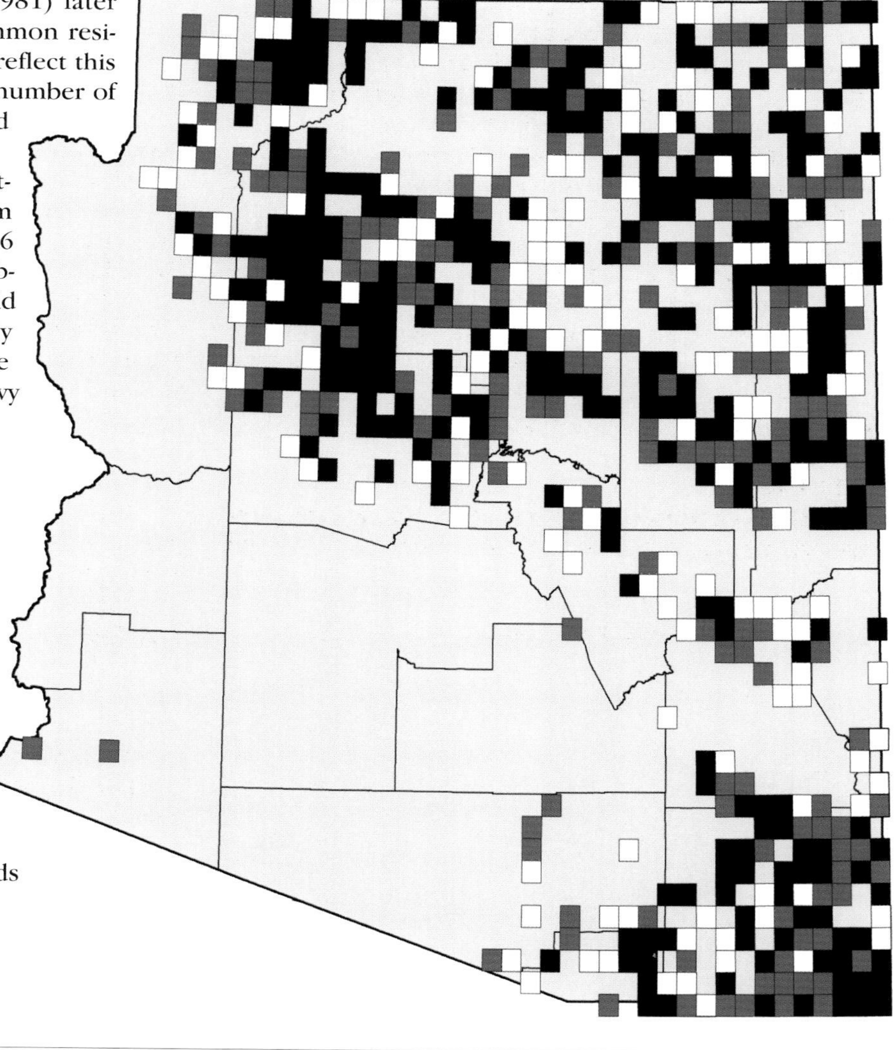

Lark Sparrow Breeding Evidence Reported in 650 (35 %) of 1834 priority blocks

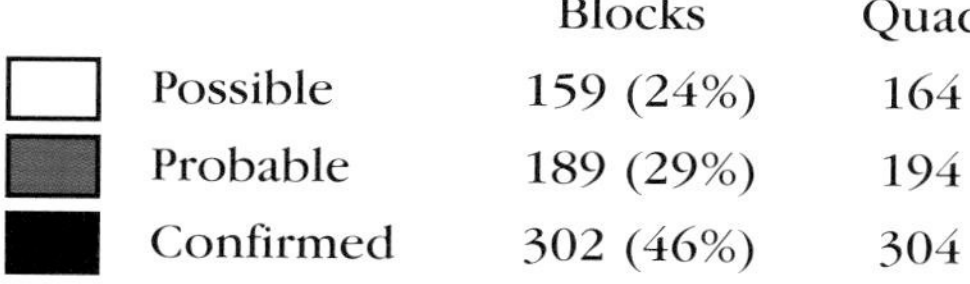

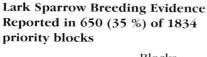

	Blocks	Quads
Possible	159 (24%)	164
Probable	189 (29%)	194
Confirmed	302 (46%)	304

Black-throated Sparrow

by Cathryn Wise-Gervais *Amphispiza bilineata*

Once appropriately named the "Desert Sparrow," the Black-throated Sparrow has a call and song with distinctive bell-like qualities. This striking bird occupies a variety of arid landscapes and is Arizona's most wide-spread nesting sparrow. During low precipitation years, resident populations commonly remain in small flocks and may delay nesting for many months.

DAN FISCHER

HABITAT

Black-throated Sparrows are birds of open, arid country. In Arizona, they will nest in a variety of low to mid-elevation shrubby habitats. In fact, atlasers reported these birds in no less than twenty vegetative communities during the atlas period. Observers most commonly reported Black-throated Sparrows in Sonoran desertscrub associations often characterized by saguaro, paloverde, creosote, cholla, ocotillo, and various other low shrubs and cacti (41 percent of records, $n = 1267$). Atlasers also regularly detected these attractive sparrows in Mojave and Chihuahuan desertscrub associations. In northern Arizona, these birds were most often encountered in cold-temperate desertscrub dominated by sagebrush, saltbush, shadscale, and greasewood and where this habitat merged with grasslands (22 percent of records). Approximately 13 percent of Black-throated Sparrow records were obtained from semiarid grasslands containing mixed grasses, yucca, acacia, and scattered mesquite. They were noted less frequently in open pinyon pine–juniper woodlands, desert dry washes, and along the edges of several riparian habitats.

BREEDING

Black-throated Sparrows are year-round residents throughout much of southern and western Arizona, and most of northern Arizona's populations arrive on their breeding grounds in mid-March to early April. Resident Black-throated Sparrows can initiate breeding quite early, sometimes in the late winter as long as sufficient resources exist. Food and nest cover are generally dependent on rainfall, so in low precipitation years these same birds may delay nesting until summer monsoons. During the atlas period, observers first reported Black-throated Sparrows nest building on 21 February and located a nest with young on 8 March. This would indicate that some egg laying occurs during the final week of February. Atlasers reported sixty-eight Black-throated Sparrow nests with eggs from 8 March to 24 August, and they located sixty nests with young from 8 March to 20 August.

Atlas data suggest that the peak breeding season for Black-throated Sparrows in Arizona is from mid-April through late June statewide, but nesting activity continues through the summer. The latest atlas breeding record was of adults feeding fledged young on 11 September; however, Phillips et al. (1964) noted a Black-throated Sparrow nest with eggs near Tucson on 14 September. This is well after most atlas surveys had ended. Northern Arizona's Black-throated Sparrow populations begin migrating in August, with few individuals remaining north of the Mogollon Rim after early September.

Black-throated Sparrows typically nest in low, dense shrubs (Johnson et al. 2002). Atlasers took measurements at eighty-five Black-throated Sparrow nests in twenty-six plant species. The most commonly reported nest plant was cholla (15 percent of records), followed by bursage (11 percent) and paloverde (8 percent). Other frequently used plants included sagebrush, ephedra, and snakeweed. The median nest height of these nests was 1.0 ft (0.3 m), and heights ranged from 0 to 6.2 ft (0–1.9 m).

Female Black-throated Sparrows usually do most of the nest construction, but occasionally the males will assist (Johnson et al. 2002). Typical Black-throated Sparrow clutches consist of 3–4 eggs (range 2–4; Rising 1996), and females incubate these for approximately 12 days (Johnson et al. 2002). Both adults feed the young, and these fledge before they are fully flighted, at about 10 days of age (Baicich and Harrison 1997). Parental care continues for another

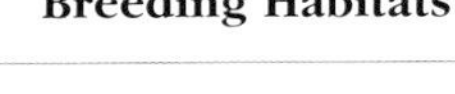

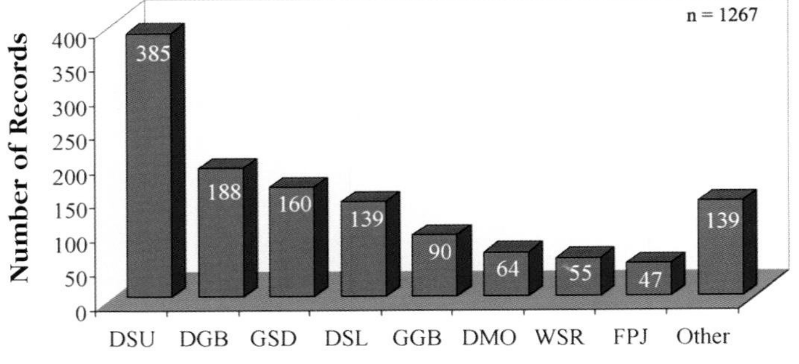

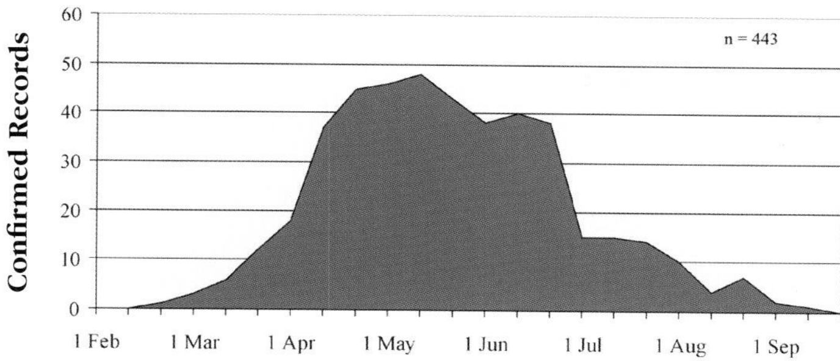

10–14 days after fledging (Johnson et al. 2002). Black-throated Sparrows generally attempt to raise at least two broods per year (Johnson et al. 2002), but three broods are possible during years with adequate precipitation and food.

Black-throated Sparrow are common Brown-headed Cowbird hosts, and observers reported twelve incidents during the atlas period. As would be expected, nests initiated later in breeding season are more likely to be parasitized (Johnson et al. 2002). In keeping with this, observers reported cowbird eggs or young in Black-throated Sparrow nests from 8 May to 30 July, and observed an adult Black-throated Sparrow feeding fledgling cowbirds as late as 11 September. One central Arizona study suggested that nests with nearby telephone lines or other such high perches were more likely to be parasitized, possibly because the female cowbirds were able to use the perches to locate Black-throated Sparrow nests (Johnson et al. 2002).

DISTRIBUTION AND STATUS

Black-throated Sparrows breed from southeastern Oregon, southeast to Colorado, then south to central Texas, central Mexico, and Baja California. Northern breeding populations are migratory, and will move south and/or to lower elevations during the winter, thus augmenting resident populations.

Phillips et al. (1964) considered Black-throated Sparrows common and widespread throughout Arizona's arid regions below 6500 ft (1981 m). Similarly, atlasers confirmed these sparrows nesting on priority blocks at elevations from approximately 150 to 6600 ft (46–2012 m). However, this species was also occasionally encountered on drier mesas in the northeast above 7000 ft (2134 m). Atlas data indicate that this species occupies nearly all the suitable habitat statewide, but observers noted that the birds were more sparsely distributed on northeastern Arizona's Colorado Plateau. As would be expected, Black-throated Sparrows were absent from forested mountains and heavily wooded plateaus of Arizona. They were also sparse or absent in extensive grassland regions, such as in the Chino Valley of Yavapai County and in the Sonoita–San Rafael grasslands of Santa Cruz County. In addition, atlasers found that Black-throated Sparrows generally avoided the heavily urbanized and extensive agricultural areas in southern desert regions, especially in the vicinity of Phoenix, Tucson, Parker, and Yuma.

Although Breeding Bird Survey data indicate that Black-throated Sparrows are on a slightly declining trend in Arizona, atlasers commonly encountered the species throughout their historical range, and the birds are still considered Arizona's most numerous and widespread sparrow. Black-throated Sparrows have lost a considerable amount of breeding habitat due to agriculture and urbanization, but it is likely that other habitat changes have offset some of these losses. For example, woodland clearing for grazing and other purposes probably benefits this species, as did shrub invasion of grasslands.

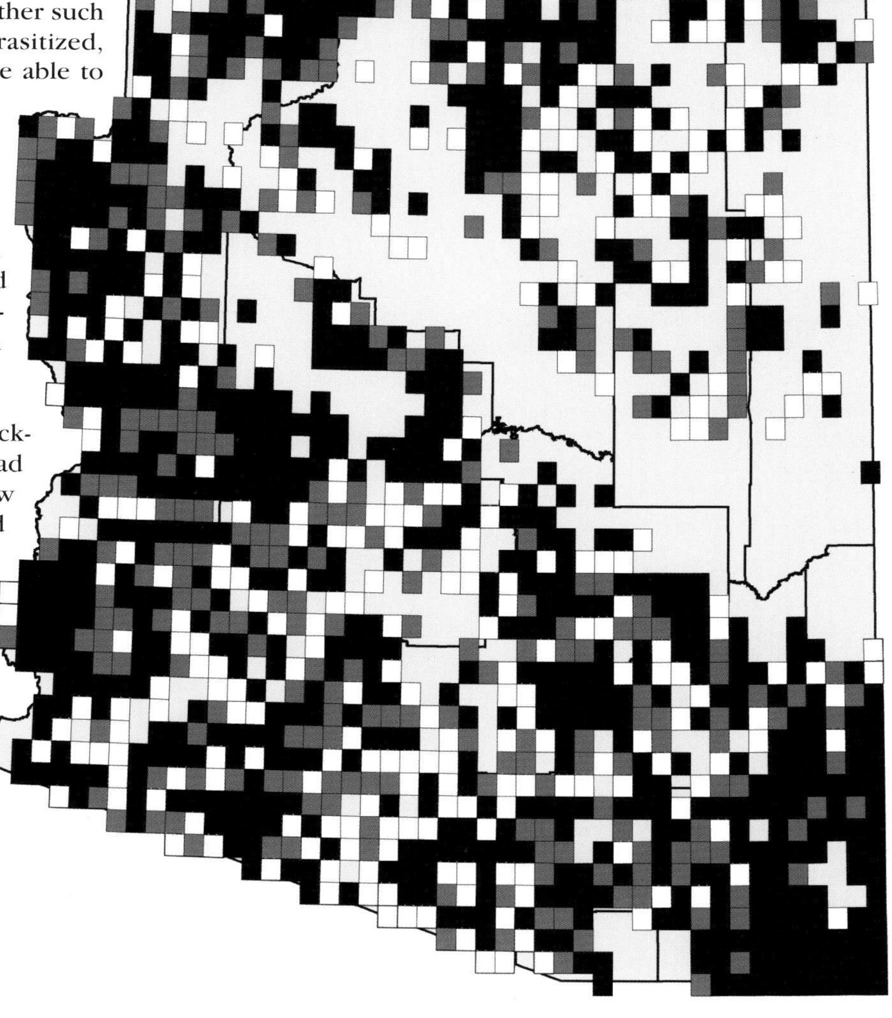

Black-throated Sparrow Breeding Evidence Reported in 1260 (69%) of 1834 priority blocks

	Blocks	Quads
Possible	279 (22%)	288
Probable	278 (22%)	282
Confirmed	703 (56%)	709

Sage Sparrow

by Troy E. Corman *Amphispiza belli*

Scurrying through the desert shrubs with tail cocked like a tiny roadrunner, Sage Sparrows prefer to run than fly when too closely approached. Their tails twitch nervously as they forage on the ground, or while perched on top of a shrub as they periodically monitor the intruder that has invaded their arid, shrubby domain.

JIM BURNS

HABITAT

As their name implies, Sage Sparrows are often found nesting in semi-open habitats where sagebrush or similar structured shrubs are conspicuous features. Studies have found that vertical structure, habitat patchiness, and vegetation density may be more important in habitat selection than specific shrub species (Martin and Carlson 1998). However, these sparrows are closely associated with big sagebrush throughout most of their nesting range (Rich 1978b). Of all records obtained from atlas surveys, 85 percents were noted in cold-temperate desertscrub associations typically dominated by big sagebrush and scattered stands of four-winged saltbush, rabbitbrush, blackbrush, or shadscale (*n* = 82). In Arizona, they appear to be most common in evenly spaced shrub stands that are 3–5 ft (0.9–1.5 m) in height. Fewer atlas records were noted in open grasslands intermixed with sand sagebrush and other low shrubs or in shrublands with very scattered junipers. Sage Sparrows typically avoid nearby open pinyon pine– and juniper-dominated habitats, even when big sagebrush is a common understory component.

BREEDING

Sage Sparrows are short-distance migrants that begin moving north from their Arizona wintering areas in late winter. They are observed in some northern nesting areas beginning in mid-February, with most individuals arriving on territory in March. Singing commences by late February and can be heard through early July. On Black Mesa in northern Navajo County, LaRue (1994) observed nesting building activity as early as 6 April. Few atlas surveys were conducted within this sparrow's nesting range prior to early May. Therefore, much of the early nesting activity was likely missed. The earliest confirmed breeding records collected during the atlas included a nest with young on 5 May and fledglings by 13 May. Atlas data reveal peak nesting activity in June, but this likely reflects the period most atlas surveys were conducted within the Sage Sparrow's nesting range. Adults were observed carrying food through 12 July, with fledglings noted through early August. In Arizona, Sage Sparrows begin appearing away from nesting areas in early to mid-September.

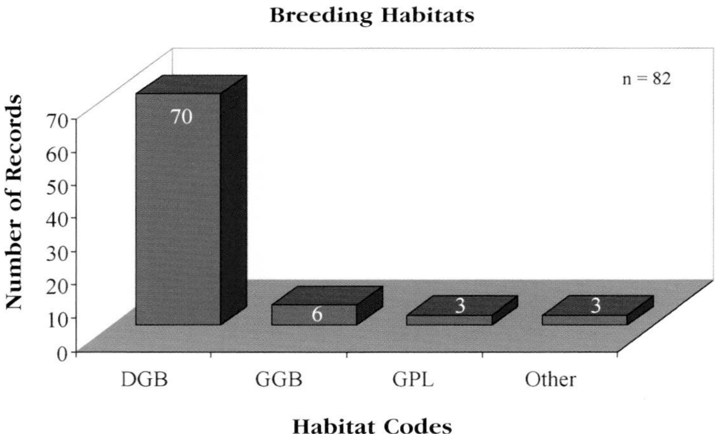

Female Sage Sparrows typically construct their nests in 1–2 days while the male sings from nearby shrubs. Most nests are built in woody shrubs and less often in grass clumps or on the ground at the base of a shrub (Martin and Carlson 1998). Studies by Winter and Best (1985) suggested that shrub height and microclimate may influence location of nests, with the sparrows preferring taller shrubs with larger canopies. Measurements were taken at only two nests during the atlas period, with one in a big sagebrush 11 in. (28 cm) above the ground and the other on the ground under a sagebrush. In Arizona, they also likely nest in saltbush and rabbitbrush as they do in adjacent states. North of Arizona, Sage Sparrow nests have been found as high as approximately 16 in. (40 cm) with a mean height of 13.4 (34 cm) above the ground (Petersen and Best 1985b).

The typical clutch size of the breeding race of Sage Sparrow in Arizona, *nevadensis*, is 2–3 eggs, but can range from 1–4. Incubation is conducted primarily by the female and lasts approximately 13 days (Miller 1968). Both parents feed the nestlings, which fledge in 9–10 days and are fed by both parents for an unknown period following nest departure (Petersen and Best 1986). Most interior Sage Sparrows raise two, and occasionally three, broods per year.

Breeding Phenology

Confirmed Records (0–6); n = 17; 1 Apr, 1 May, 1 Jun, 1 Jul

DISTRIBUTION AND STATUS

Sage Sparrows breed from eastern Washington, southeast to Wyoming, and south to north Arizona and New Mexico. These sparrows also nest from northern California south to central Baja California. Prior to the atlas project, the breeding distribution of Sage Sparrows in Arizona was described as limited only in the northeast corner of the state on Navajo and Hopi tribal lands (Phillips et al. 1964). They were considered common to abundant residents in this region north of the Puerco River valley and west to the Echo Cliffs. However, Phillips et al. (1964) did suggest that Sage Sparrows also nest in sagebrush habitat farther west. Brown et al. (1987) also noted that these sparrows may nest within the Grand Canyon region in the foothills of the Kaibab Plateau.

Atlasers found Sage Sparrows as common and sometimes local nesting species throughout their previously described range and significantly farther west than previously known. However, atlas surveys revealed that the distribution of these sparrows in Arizona is rather patchy, which likely reflects the irregular distribution of their preferred habitat. Atlasers encountered the majority of nesting Sage Sparrows at elevations between 5000 and 7000 ft (1524–2134 m), although they were noted nesting locally above and below these elevations. The most southern confirmed records were in the upper Puerco River valley near Chambers and Sanders, south locally to just north of Saint Johns.

Undoubtedly overlooked in the past, atlasers were finally able to document that Sage Sparrows nest over a fairly wide area west of Page. New localities include the northern Paria Plateau, House Rock Valley, and northern edge of the Kaibab Plateau to Fredonia. They were also discovered nesting locally to just south of the South Rim of the Grand Canyon. Atlasers encountered Sage Sparrows nesting in the Arizona Strip region from Kanab Creek west to the Hurricane Cliffs, including the Toroweap and Antelope valleys.

Reaching the southern edge of its interior nesting range in Arizona, very few avian studies in the state have included Sage Sparrows or their preferred habitat. Preliminary observations at the western edge of their range in Arizona also suggest that breeding populations of these brush-loving sparrows are greatly reduced or absent during years with below-normal precipitation. Therefore, they were easily missed if visits to these regions occurred only during dry years.

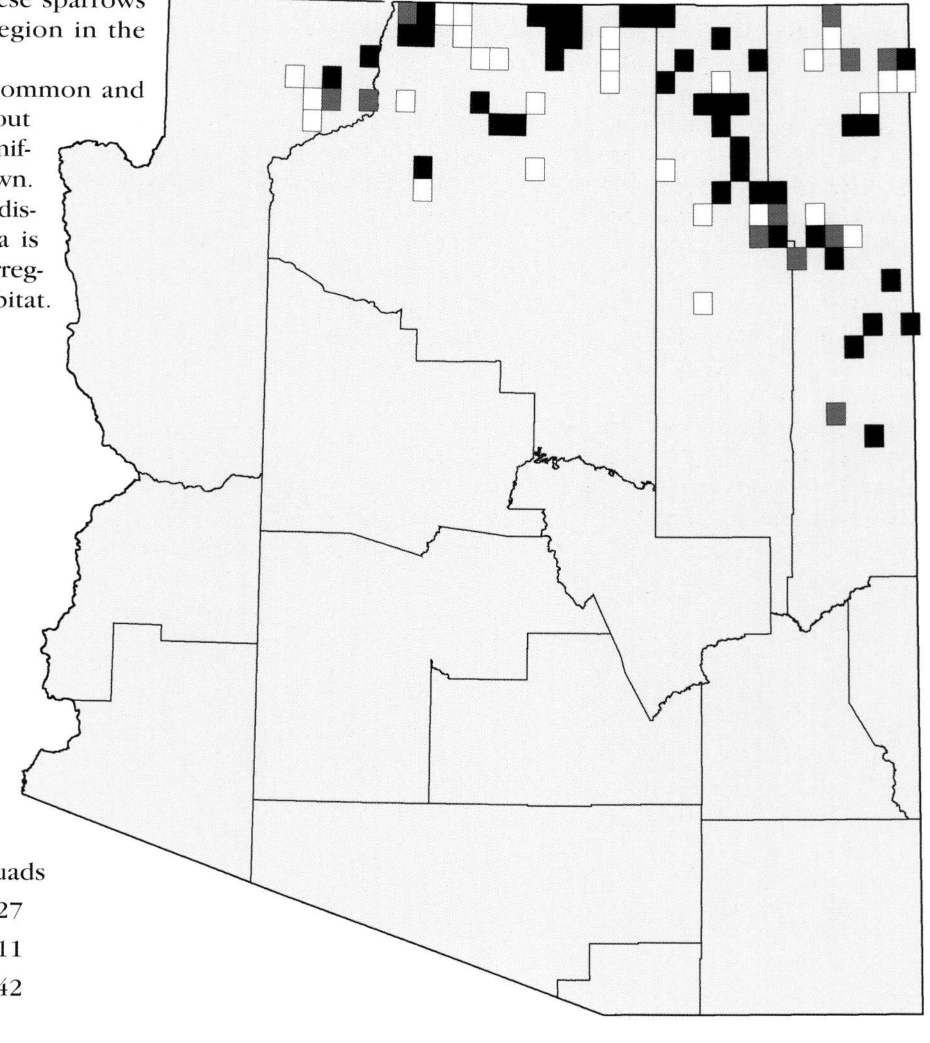

Sage Sparrow Breeding Evidence Reported in 78 (4%) of 1834 priority blocks

	Blocks	Quads
Possible	25 (32%)	27
Probable	11 (14%)	11
Confirmed	42 (54%)	42

Savannah Sparrow

by Troy E. Corman *Passerculus sandwichensis*

Small, heavily streaked passerines of open grassy landscapes, Savannah Sparrows are common and much more widespread as winter visitors in Arizona than they are as breeders. On their nesting territories, these grassland sparrows typically deliver their thin, buzzy song from an exposed perch close to the ground such as a fence line, post, weed stem, or rock.

DAN FISCHER

HABITAT

Although they were named for Savannah, Georgia, where the first specimen was collected, Savannah Sparrows are also well named for the open and often grassy habitats they prefer. The many subspecies can be found breeding in a diverse array of open, treeless environments across their range from salt marshes and agricultural field to mountain meadows and arctic tundra. However, in Arizona, these sparrows are found nesting locally only in high-elevation grasslands and larger mountain meadows. Most atlas records were from areas of dense ground cover consisting of short grasses, forbs, and sedges, typically where the soil was damp. Atlasers reported seven of eight potential breeding records for this sparrow from subalpine grasslands, often in areas with moister soil such as near lakes, ponds, and seeps. These preferred damp areas often have a wet meadow or wetland flora typically containing moisture loving grasses, sedges, and small rushes. The remaining atlas record was from a slightly lower elevation in a larger mountain meadow containing a variety of forbs and grasses.

BREEDING

Common and sometimes locally abundant winter residents of grasslands and agricultural fields in southern and western Arizona, Savannah Sparrows typically begin moving north in February and March. Spring migration in the state peaks in April, with stragglers casually to late May and early June. It is unknown when Savannah Sparrows first arrive in their breeding areas in Arizona, but likely soon after snowmelt at their high-elevation grasslands in April. With so few breeding locations in Arizona, atlasers were unable to collect much in the way of breeding phenology. Males typically arrive one to three weeks earlier than the females to set up territories (Potter 1972). The earliest atlas record was of singing males in mid-May. The only confirmed record was of a nest with young discovered on 25 June. This suggests nest building and egg laying by early June. Adults were observed in breeding areas through 30 July. In northern Arizona, Savannah Sparrows begin arriving in nonbreeding areas in early August, exceptionally by mid-July. South of the Mogollon Rim, individuals begin to arrive in mid- to late August.

Savannah Sparrows build their well-concealed, grassy nests on the ground and are constructed by the female in 1–3 days (Wheelwright and Rising 1993). The nest is typically built in dense grass clumps or near the base of forbs, and away from woody vegetation (Wheelwright and Rising 1993). The most common clutch size is 4 eggs, but can range from 2–6 (Austin 1968). Incubation is by the female only and a compilation of various populations studies across their range indicated the typically incubation period is from 11 to 13 days (Wheelwright and Rising 1993). Nestlings generally fledge when they are 10–12 days old, but any disturbance after day 8 often induces premature nestling departure (Wheelwright and Rising 1993). Both parents continue to feed the fledglings for 2–3 weeks. Female Savannah Sparrows often initiate second clutches approximately 2 weeks following the fledging of the first brood (Wheelwright and Rising 1993), with two and sometimes three broods successfully reared per season (Rising 1996).

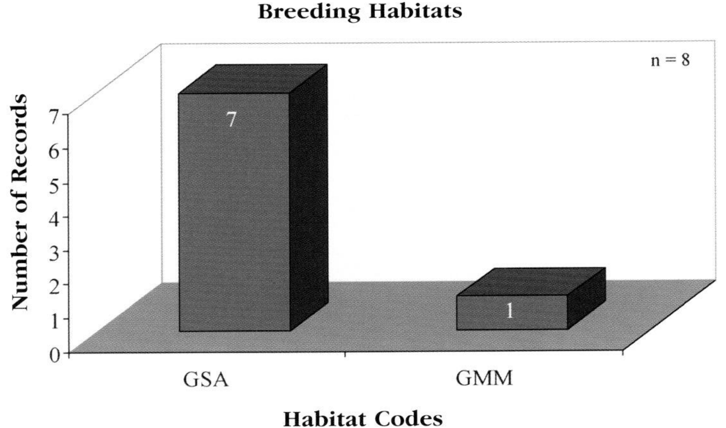

DISTRIBUTION AND STATUS

Found breeding throughout much of the northern half of North America, there are currently seventeen recognized subspecies of Savannah Sparrow (Wheelwright and Rising 1993). Migratory populations breed from Alaska and Canada south to central California, Arizona, and down the Appalachian Mountains to northern Georgia. There are also resident populations on the Central Plateau of Mexico and along the southwest coast primarily from central California, Baja California, and Sonora.

In Arizona, previous literature noted Savannah Sparrows were fairly common summer residents in the White Mountain region, including the Springerville area (Phillips et al. 1964). They also suggested that they possibly nest near Mormon Lake and formerly near Kayenta. The latter was assumed from individuals collected there in July and August, but likely pertains only to early migrants. During the late 1970s, Savannah Sparrows were repeatedly heard singing near Willcox and seen there as late as 4 June (Monson and Phillips 1981), but there was no further evidence of nesting activity.

Atlasers found nesting Savannah Sparrow at elevations primarily between 8700 and 9300 ft (2652–2835 m), but locally down to near 8000 ft (2438 m). As noted by others, Arizona's breeding populations were encountered primarily only in the White Mountains region where atlasers found Savannah Sparrows to be uncommon to locally common. They were noted from just west of Green's Peak, then southeast to near Sunrise Lake and White Mountain Reservoir and on to the Big Lake area. The most southern observations from atlasers came from just north of Greenlee County, including near Luna Lake. Savannah Sparrows likely also nest locally in similar habitat in the adjacent White Mountain Apache tribal lands where efforts to acquire access permits to conduct atlas surveys were unsuccessful. Atlasers did not detect this sparrow near Springerville, where it had previously been reported nesting (Phillips et al. 1964).

Away from the White Mountains populations, atlasers noted a pair of Savannah Sparrows in the De Motte Park grasslands on the Kaibab Plateau near the border of the Grand Canyon National Park (North Rim) and Kaibab National Forest. This high-elevation habitat is very similar to where this sparrow breeds in the White Mountains, and more intensive surveys may reveal it nesting there, at least irregularly. However, the annual livestock grazing pressure on the De Motte Park grasslands of the Kaibab National Forest may greatly reduce the available appropriate habitat there. This is particularly true during years of below normal precipitation and subsequent limited grass and forb growth. Drought conditions that plagued much of the atlas period may also have temporarily eliminated the moist grasslands favored by these sparrows along Mormon and other nearby lakes southeast of Flagstaff. These sparrows may nest irregularly near these lakes following winters and springs with normal or above normal precipitation.

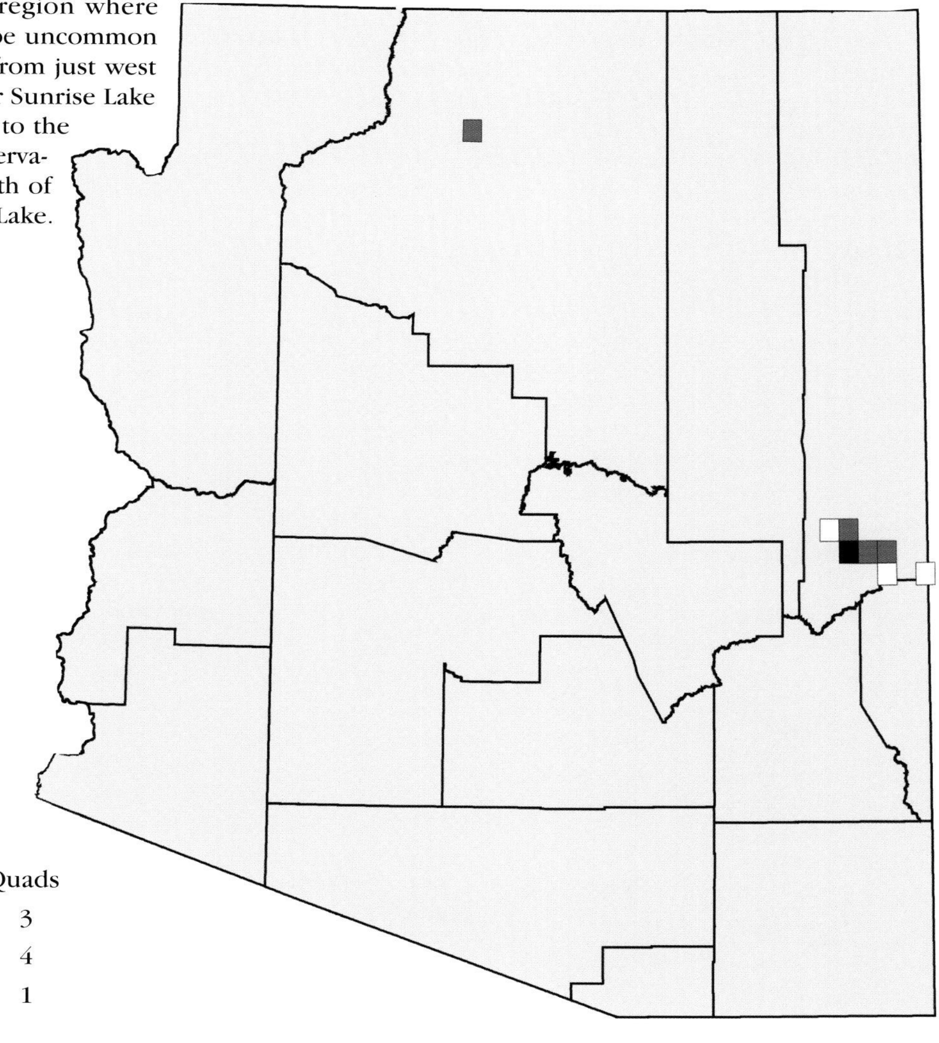

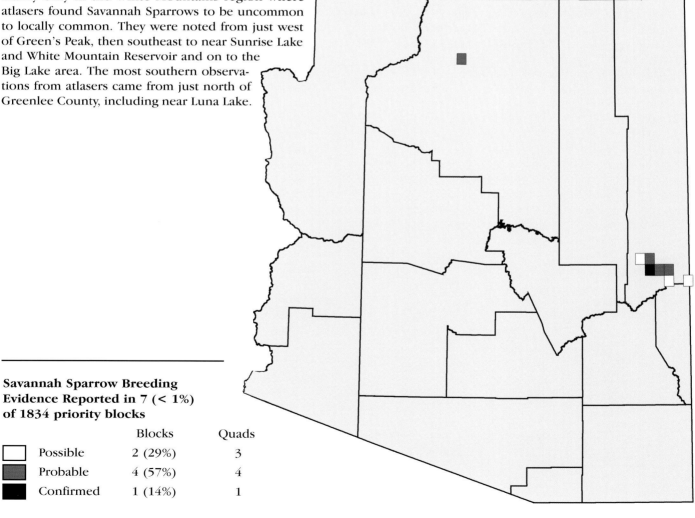

Savannah Sparrow Breeding Evidence Reported in 7 (< 1%) of 1834 priority blocks

	Blocks	Quads
Possible	2 (29%)	3
Probable	4 (57%)	4
Confirmed	1 (14%)	1

Grasshopper Sparrow

by Troy E. Corman *Ammodramus savannarum*

With the advent of the late summer rainy season, the inconspicuous Grasshopper Sparrow can be observed singing its insectlike song from a fence or isolated low shrub in a sea of windswept grass. Only those observers with the most acute hearing are able detect the staccato, high-pitched notes of this grassland inhabitant.

HABITAT

A grassland dependent species, Grasshopper Sparrows prefer large expanses of intermediate height grass for nesting. Occupied grasslands in Arizona often include some low, woody shrub component such as scattered young mesquite and mimosa. They nests primarily in semiarid grasslands within the state where atlasers reported 83 percent of potential breeding records (n = 24). These sparrows were reported at only a few grassland localities lacking woody shrubs, such as in the San Rafael Valley and along the edge of alfalfa fields. Herkert (1994) reported that larger and more continuous grasslands are occupied much more frequently by these birds than are smaller or more fragmented tracts (Herkert 1994). Bock and Webb (1984) characterized the Grasshopper Sparrow's habitat in southeastern Arizona as having nearly 75 percent ungrazed grass cover with the mean height of 12 in. (30 cm), 5 percent woody cover, and approximately 20 percent bare ground.

BREEDING

In southeastern Arizona, Grasshopper Sparrows are inconspicuous residents and go largely undetected until males begin to sing in July and continue into early September during the typical monsoon season. They are occasionally observed from April through June perched silently on low fence lines within their grassland domain. Periodically, atlasers reported a few singing and paired birds in late May and June. This unusual early breeding behavior may occur only during those irregular years with unseasonably wet springs. It is unknown if pairs occasionally attempt an early brood during these odd years. Atlasers first noted paired males singing in the isolated Chino Valley population in Yavapai County on 27 June. Late summer monsoon activity likely has limited influence on this population, which may routinely initiate breeding earlier than the southeastern Arizona populations. As with most ground-nesting grassland sparrows, Grasshopper Sparrow nests are difficult to locate, and this may explain the lack of active nest records in the atlas database. Much more research is needed to determine when nest construction and egg laying begins in Arizona's local nesting populations. All atlas confirmations were of adult Grasshopper Sparrows carrying food from 27 July to 31 August.

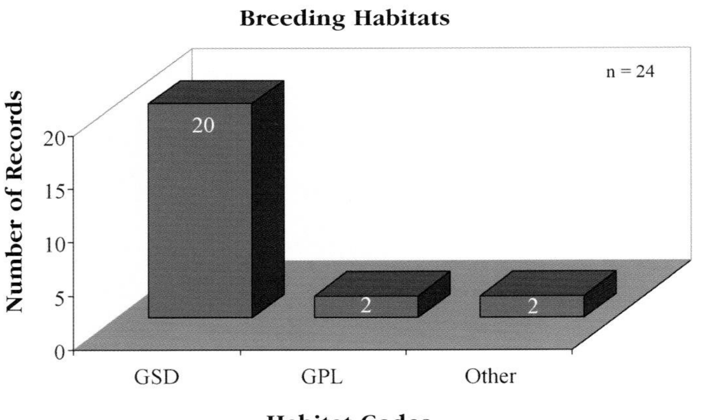

Grasshopper Sparrow nests are constructed only by the female in approximately 2–3 days and are placed on the ground, typically in a shallow hollow tucked at the base of a tuft of grass, forb, or shrub (Vickery 1996). The distinctive nests are usually well concealed by overhanging grasses or forbs and frequently domed in the back. The side entrance rim is usually level with or slightly above the ground (Harrison 1979). Adding to the difficulty in locating the cryptic nest, flushed female Grasshopper Sparrows slip off the nest and run a short distance through the vegetation before becoming airborne (Smith 1968). Returning birds also typically do not fly directly to the nest, but drop down at a distance, then approach on foot via several pathways (Smith 1968).

Most Grasshopper Sparrow clutches consist of 4–5 eggs (range 3–6) and are incubated solely by the female for approximately 11–13 days (Smith 1968). Both parents feed the nestlings that are incapable of flight when they depart the nest in 8–9 days, but are adept at scurrying through the vegetation during this period (Smith 1968). Parental care continues for a minimum of 1–2 weeks following nest departure before the female may begin construction of a second nest and raise another brood (Vickery 1996).

DISTRIBUTION AND STATUS

The Grasshopper Sparrow breeds from extreme southern Canada, south through most of the eastern United States, and they are much more locally distributed west of the Rocky Mountains. Small isolated resident populations also exist in southeastern Arizona, Florida, Mexico, Central America, and the Caribbean.

The reddish *ammolegus* subspecies of Grasshopper Sparrow nests only in southeastern Arizona, southwestern New Mexico, and extreme northern Sonora (Strong 1988). It was described from a series of breeding specimens collected in 1932 near the Huachuca Mountains (Oberholser 1942). Atlasers reported Grasshopper Sparrows as locally, fairly common at elevations between 3400 and 5200 ft (1036–1585 m). They were detected in many of the locations noted by Monson and Phillips (1981), including the grasslands of the San Bernardino, Babocomari, and San Rafael valleys, Sonoita Plains north to the upper Cienega Creek drainage, and the extreme upper San Pedro River drainage southeast of Sierra Vista. Atlasers also discovered that they were much more widespread in grasslands of the Sulphur Springs Valley north to Willcox, and in the Buenos Aires National Wildlife Refuge in the Altar Valley than previous literature suggests.

Monson and Phillips (1981) reported Grasshopper Sparrows occurring near Nogales and the Santa Rita Experimental Range. Grasshopper Sparrows were not reported occupying these areas during the atlas period. Historically, they also nested at least irregularly north to the Ft. Grant area in southern Graham County and possibly north to the Coyote Mountain region in the Altar Valley (Phillips et al. 1964). Several specimens indicate winter residency in southeastern Arizona; however, many individuals likely move south into Sonora for the winter (Phillips et al. 1964), particularly during years when grass cover and food resources are in short supply.

On 12 July 1973, a singing male Grasshopper Sparrow of the paler *perpallidus* subspecies was collected in Chino Valley, Yavapai County (Monson and Phillips 1981). Atlasers noted a small, precarious population continues to exit at this location. Singing birds were reported in late June 1993 at this isolated location and adults were observed carrying food on 10 August of that year. Otherwise, this subspecies is an inconspicuous sparse migrant statewide in April to early May and from mid-September (exceptionally August) to early November, and rare to uncommon local winter resident in grasslands and weedy agricultural areas of western and southern Arizona.

Grassland loss, fragmentation, and degradation are the primary reasons for Grasshopper Sparrow declines in North America (Vickery 1996). Extensive and intensive grazing in western North America has had negative impacts on this species (Bock and Webb 1984). Grazing practices that rotate pastures and allows periods of rest so that thatch can build up under bunchgrass would improve conditions for both breeding and wintering populations of Grasshopper Sparrows (Latta et al. 1999). Another critical threat to this species is conversion of grassland to ranchettes, vineyards, and other suburban development. Unfortunately, most of the Sonoita Plains, Chino Valley, and grasslands immediately west of the upper San Pedro River are privately owned and rapidly being developed.

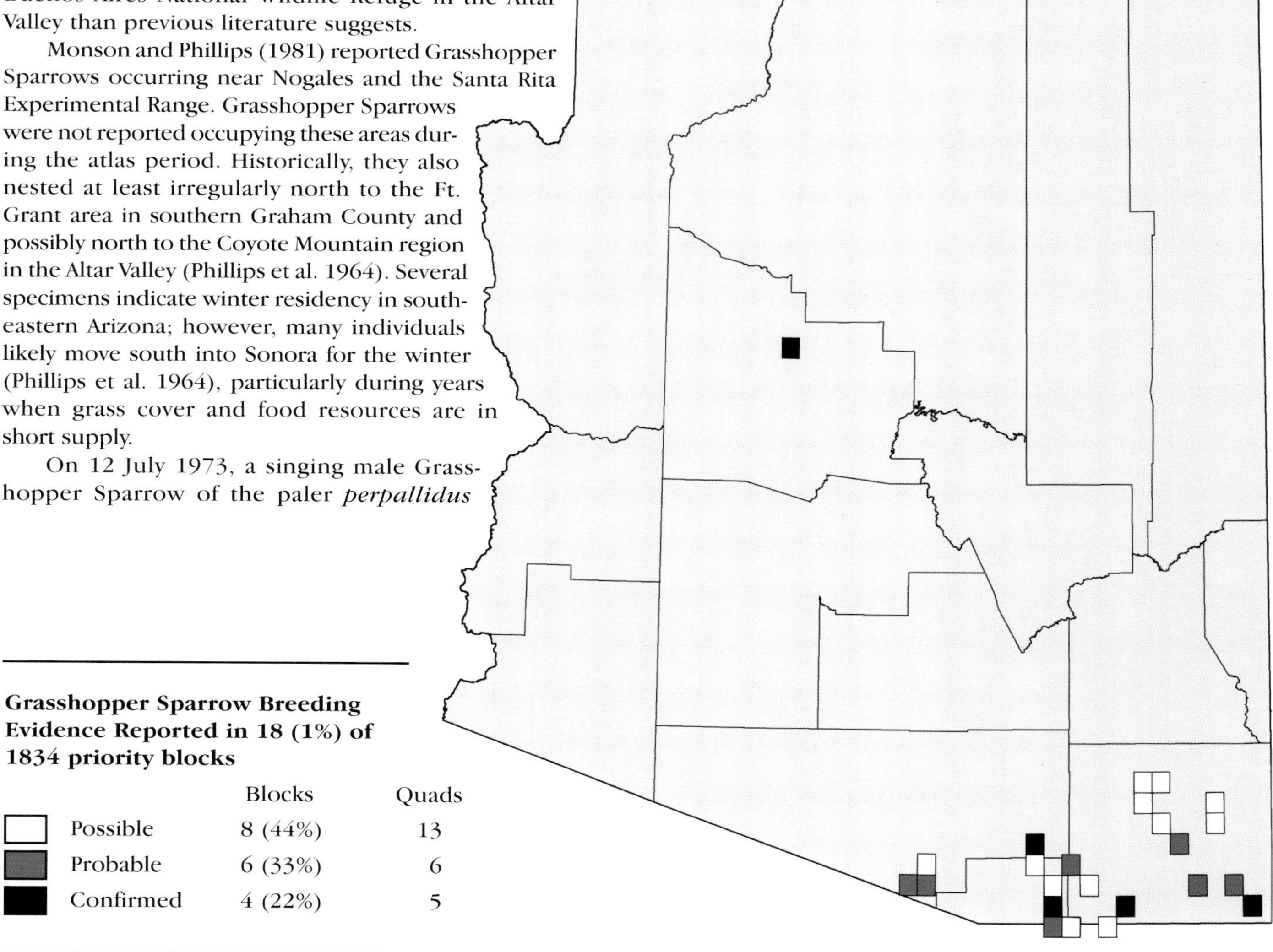

Grasshopper Sparrow Breeding Evidence Reported in 18 (1%) of 1834 priority blocks

	Blocks	Quads
Possible	8 (44%)	13
Probable	6 (33%)	6
Confirmed	4 (22%)	5

Song Sparrow

by Norm Shrout *Melospiza melodia*

In early spring, a distinctive and melodic song announces the presence of this skulking species. During the breeding season, Song Sparrows often appear suddenly from the dense riparian thicket with their long tail characteristically flipped to one side. They typically question your presence with diagnostic "chimp" call notes before disappearing back into cover.

RICHARD DITCH

HABITAT

The Song Sparrow is one of the most geographically variable species in North America and selects an equally diverse range of vegetative communities across its extensive range. However, key habitat components often include dense undergrowth near water or at least moisture. This is especially true in the arid Southwest, inasmuch as Song Sparrows are typically encountered near thickets along wetlands and low-gradient, perennial drainages. In Arizona, Song Sparrows reach their highest density in lowland riparian woodlands with a dense vegetative understory. Approximately 33 percent of all atlas records were reported from cottonwood-willow dominated drainages frequently containing thickets of young trees, seepwillow, tamarisk, and emergent vegetation (n = 181). Song Sparrows were also frequently reported (24 percent of records) along marshes, ponds, and river edges within stands of cattail, bulrush, and sedges. They quickly inhabit this vegetation at human-made sites as well, including wastewater treatment facility ponds, canals, irrigation ditches, and agricultural runoff ponds. These birds have also adapted to nesting in dense thickets of exotic tamarisk that now dominate many of Arizona's waterways and accounted for 12 percent of atlas records for this species. Song Sparrows were noted less frequently in higher elevation foothill drainages containing sycamore, cottonwood, ash, and willow. They continue to nest very locally in the White Mountains along boreal riparian thickets, often containing alder and various species of scrub willows.

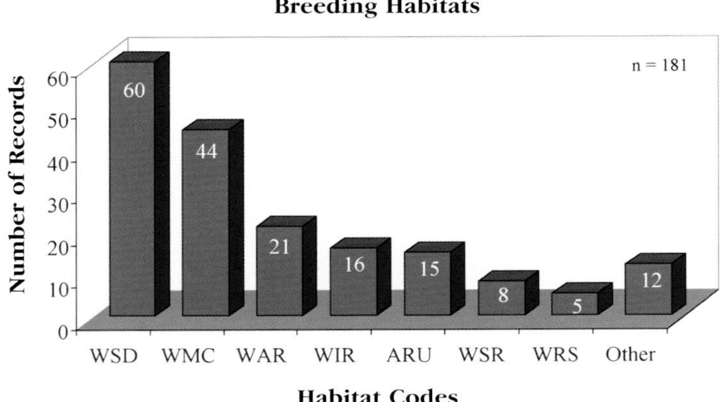

BREEDING

Song Sparrows are primarily resident throughout their range in Arizona, being joined in winter by migrating birds from the north. Males may initiate singing to reestablish territory boundaries as early as late January and February in Arizona. Nest building in Arizona likely begins in mid-March, based on atlas observations of nests with young by 15 April and reports of fledglings along the lower Colorado River by 17 April (Rosenberg et al. 1991). Although the sample size was relatively low, atlas data suggest that peak nesting in Arizona occurs in early May. Nesting activity likely continues into early August, however, in that atlasers noted an individual carrying nesting material as late as 12 July. Data from other western regions of the Song Sparrow range show similar nesting dates from late February through August (Arcese et al. 2002). Migrants begin appearing in nonbreeding areas of Arizona by late August and early September.

Song Sparrow females construct their well-hidden nests quietly and secretively over a period of 4–5 days (Arcese et al. 2002). Nests are typically placed on or near the ground in dense vegetation or debris. Atlas crews took measurements at six Song Sparrow nests, which ranged from 2.3 to 6.5 ft (0.7–2.0 m) in height, with a median height of 4.6 ft (1.4 m). These nests were discovered in wolfberry, Goodding willow, Fremont cottonwood, graythorn, and tamarisk. Nests closer to the ground are found under grass tufts, annuals, shrubs, and emergent vegetation (Austin 1968).

Song Sparrows typically lay 3–5 eggs and are incubated by the female for approximately 12–13 days, but this can range to 14–15 days when incubation coincides with cooler weather (Arcese et al. 2002). Both parents feed the nestlings until they fledge in 8–12 days (Arcese et al. 2002). If second broods are attempted, the male takes on more of the responsibility of feeding fledglings, which gain full independence at 24–30 days of age. Song Sparrows commonly produce 2–3 broods in a season (Byers et al. 1995).

Song Sparrows are commonly parasitized by Brown-headed Cowbirds (Friedmann 1963) and these sparrows are regularly observed feeding begging cowbird fledglings in Arizona. Atlasers had difficulty discovering the location

Breeding Phenology

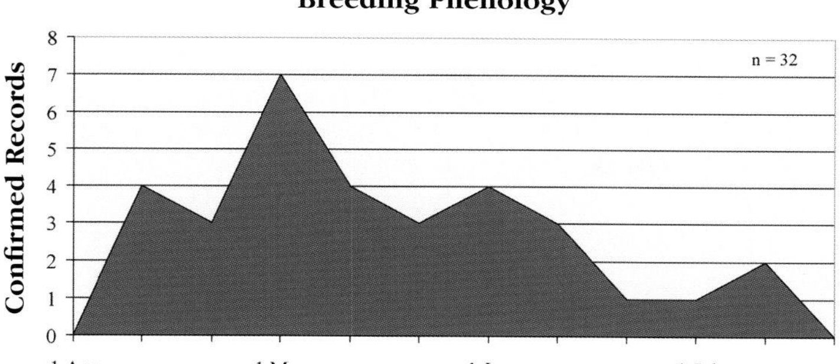

of Song Sparrow nest, but of ten nests with eggs or young reported, one contained a Brown-headed Cowbird egg.

DISTRIBUTION AND STATUS

Twenty-four recognized subspecies of Song Sparrow inhabit North America from Newfoundland to the Aleutian islands of Alaska south to isolated populations in central Mexico (Arcese et al. 2002). In the East, they breed south to northern Georgia and are largely absent as a nesting species in the southern Great Plains region and southeast. These sparrows breed south locally to northern Sonora and central Baja California in the West.

The distribution and abundance of breeding Song Sparrow populations in Arizona have been greatly modified during the past hundred years because of the human manipulation of water sources in the state. Locally, they are fairly common residents along perennial waterways, canals, ponds, and marshes of southern and western Arizona where sufficient vegetative cover exists (Phillip et al. 1964; Monson and Phillips 1981). Atlasers encountered these sparrows breeding primarily at elevations ranging from 90 to 5000 ft (27–1524 m). However, Song Sparrows were also confirmed nesting locally as high as 8320 ft (2536 m) near Greer. Other potential breeding records north of the Mogollon Rim were obtained near Mormon Lake, Show Low, and Luna Lake.

In western Arizona, Song Sparrows were noted locally along the lower Colorado, Gila, and Virgin River drainages. They were sparingly distributed in the Lake Mead and lower Grand Canyon region upstream to below Lava Falls. Surveys could not be conducted in Havasupai tribal lands, where Brown et al. (1987) noted Song Sparrows as uncommon summer residents along Havasu Creek.

Atlasers encountered Song Sparrows fairly regularly within the Gila, Verde, San Pedro, and upper Santa Cruz River drainages and tributaries. They were previously noted as nesting along the San Francisco River (Monson and Phillips 1981), but atlasers did not detect them there. In southeastern Arizona, these sparrows were found nesting west to the Arivaca area, and very locally west to artificial ponds near Papago Farms.

Following historical population declines as a consequence of drainage and habitat destruction in Arizona, Song Sparrow populations appear to be relatively stable (Rising 1996). These wetland sparrows quickly take advantage of available habitat. Following the removal of livestock from the upper San Pedro River in late 1987, Song Sparrow populations increased by 383 percent by 1990 (Krueper et al. 2003).

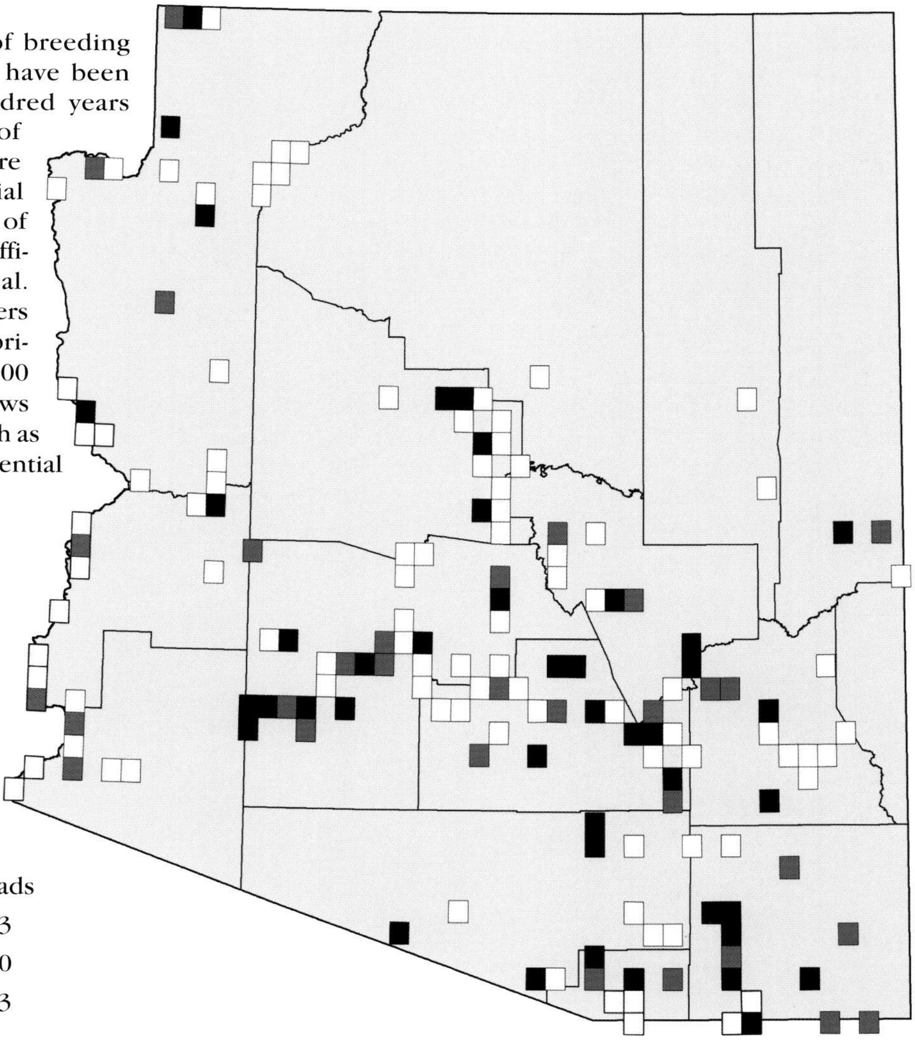

Song Sparrow Breeding Evidence Reported in 117 (6%) of 1834 priority blocks

	Blocks	Quads
Possible	61 (52%)	93
Probable	24 (21%)	30
Confirmed	32 (27%)	43

Lincoln's Sparrow

by Troy E. Corman *Melospiza lincolnii*

With its many hues of brown, buff, and gray, the secretive Lincoln's Sparrow is a notably handsome species. They reach their southern breeding limits in the few remaining higher elevation drainages and subalpine wetlands in Arizona, where their rich, bubbling trills can be heard on early summer mornings.

JIM BURNS

HABITAT

In Arizona, Lincoln's Sparrows nest only in high elevation riparian thickets and wetlands. These habitats are very limited in the state and primarily occur in moist subalpine meadows or along small perennial drainages near open subalpine conifer forests. Adjacent forest trees often include blue spruce, Engelmann spruce, and aspen. Dominant shrubs along occupied drainage typically include thinleaf alder and several species of scrub willows, particularly Geyer and Bebb willows. Shrub stands are often dense and regularly attain heights of 4–8 ft (1.2–2.4 m). Other commonly occurring shrubs are cerro hawthorn, gooseberry, red-osier dogwood, water birch, shrubby cinquefoil, and red elderberry. Understory ground cover and adjacent open areas frequently consist of grasses, sedges, and many forbs. In Arizona, this habitat is sometimes enhanced by beaver dam activity. Lincoln's Sparrows were also found nesting locally in Nebraska sedge and other low, dense wetland vegetation along grassy ponds in subalpine meadows.

BREEDING

Wintering throughout southern and western Arizona, Lincoln's Sparrows begin to migrate north in early to mid-February. Migration in the state peaks in March and April, with stragglers in May, exceptionally to early June. Lincoln's Sparrows begin singing from exposed perches on their Arizona breeding grounds in May. The males singing bouts decline considerably during nesting, and typically ceases entirely by the middle or late incubation period (Ammon 1995).

With so few breeding locations in Arizona, combined with the shy and elusive nature of Lincoln's Sparrows, atlasers were unable to collect much in the way of early nesting records. However, in Colorado, nest building was reported from 30 May to 13 June, with nest with eggs as early as 11 June (Versaw 1998). The earliest atlas record for Arizona was of an agitated pair on 17 June, which suggests an active nest or fledged young nearby. The earliest confirmed record was of an adult carrying food on 30 June and the latest was of an adult giving a distraction display on 29 July. Some late nesting activity likely continues into August. Fall migration for Lincoln's Sparrows in Arizona begins by late August, exceptionally mid-August, and continues through mid-November.

Female Lincoln's Sparrows typically construct their well-concealed nests on the ground in 2–3 days, often in a shallow depression under dense shrubs or among sedges, grasses, and forbs (Speirs and Speirs 1968). Nests are often placed in areas where the soil is damp or moist (Ammon 1995). The birds enter and depart the nest from a distinct nest-entrance tunnel through the adjacent ground vegetation (Ammon 1995). Saunders (1910) noted that when disturbed, females slip quietly from their nest and run through the vegetation without making a noise, behaving more like a mouse than a bird. Typical clutches consist of 3–5 eggs, which the female incubates for 10–13 days (Ammon 1995). Both parents feed the nestlings that depart the nest in 10–11 days and for an additional 1–2 weeks as fledglings (Speirs and Speirs 1968; Ammon 1995). The adults chip excitedly when an observer approaches a nest area and will feign injury in an attempt to lure intruders away. Lincoln's Sparrows typically rear one brood per season, but second broods have been observed during favorable years (Ammon 1995).

Breeding Habitats

n = 7

Habitat Codes	Number of Records
WAB	3
WMC	2
WMR	1
GSA	1

DISTRIBUTION AND STATUS

Lincoln's Sparrows nest in the boreal zones of Alaska and much of Canada, south to the extreme northern edge of eastern United States. In the West, they breed primarily in the higher mountainous regions south to southern California, central Arizona, and central New Mexico. Phillips et al. (1964) noted Lincoln's Sparrows nesting not uncommonly only within the higher elevations of the White Mountains region of Arizona. Phillips et al. also suggested possible nesting southeast of Flagstaff near Mormon Lake, based on several summer records from this area. Since 1969, Lincoln's Sparrows have also nested in the Inner Basin of the San Francisco Mountains near Flagstaff (Carothers et al. 1973; Monson and Phillips 1981).

Atlas surveys revealed that Lincoln's Sparrows continue to nest locally in the White and San Francisco mountains at elevations from 8300 to 10,000 ft (2530–3048 m). In the White Mountains, they were found nesting primarily only along the West Fork of the Little Colorado River and nearby tributaries from near Sheep Crossing downstream to Greer. Lincoln's Sparrows may also nest along similar high elevation drainages within the nearby White Mountain Apache tribal lands, on which access permits to conduct atlas surveys could not be obtained.

Atlasers also encountered these sparrows nesting for the first time on the Kaibab Plateau along permanent, subalpine meadow ponds. Specifically, they were confirmed nesting at Frank's and Crane lakes on the Kaibab National Forest. More intensive surveys on the Kaibab Plateau may find additional nesting sites within the National Forest and the nearby North Rim of Grand Canyon National Park. Another likely new nesting locality discovered by atlasers was along a perennial side drainage of Tsaile Creek in the Tunitcha-Chuska Mountains in northern Apache County. An agitated pair was found at this location at approximately 7800 ft (2377 m) elevation. Jacobs (1986) had previously suggested that Lincoln's Sparrows may nest in the Chuska Mountain or on the Defiance Plateau.

Lincoln's Sparrows require dense ground and shrub cover for successful nesting. Unfortunately, much of the specific riparian and wetland habitats these skulking sparrows depend on for nesting in Arizona are highly vulnerable owing to unnatural grazing and browsing pressure from elk and domestic livestock.

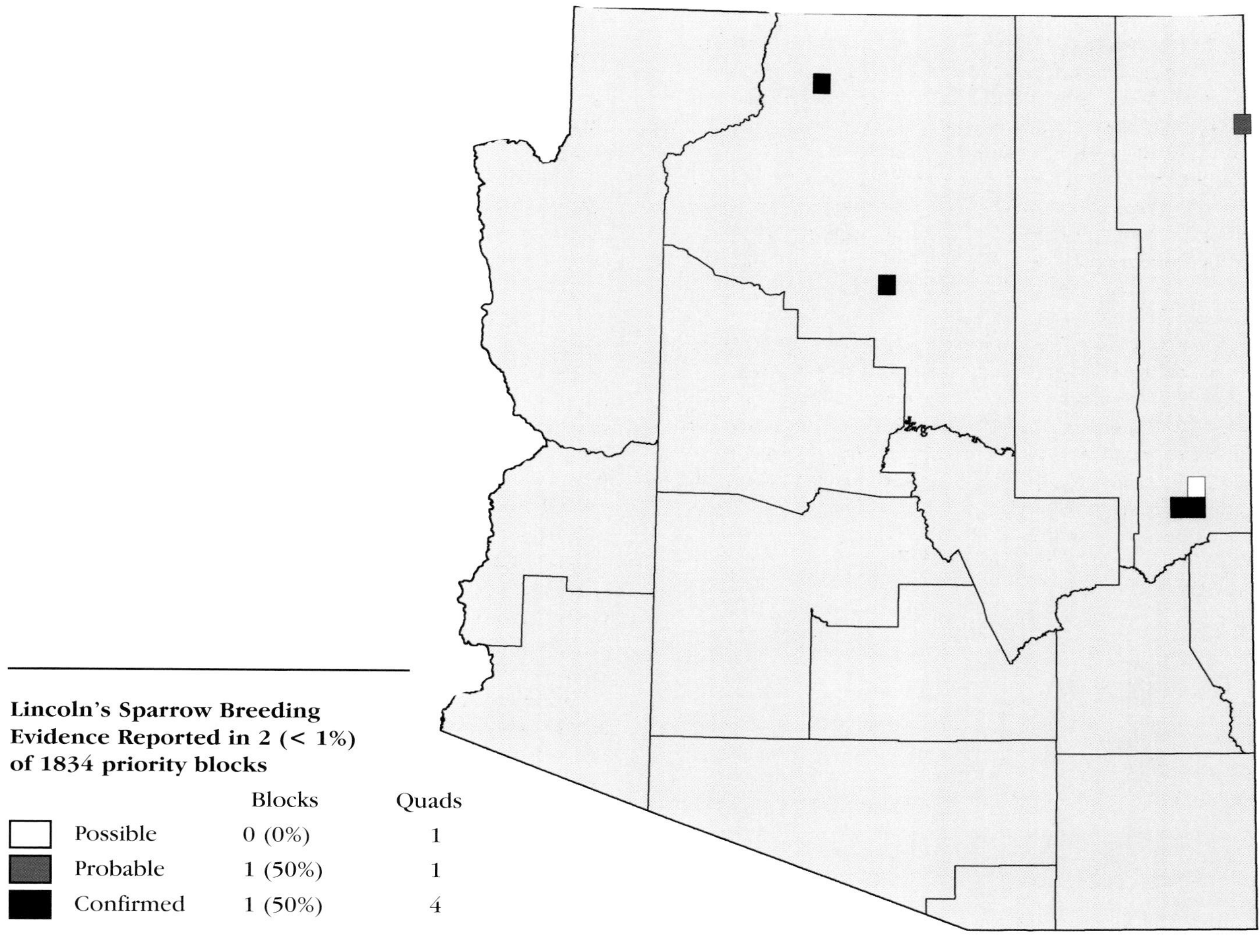

Lincoln's Sparrow Breeding Evidence Reported in 2 (< 1%) of 1834 priority blocks

	Blocks	Quads
Possible	0 (0%)	1
Probable	1 (50%)	1
Confirmed	1 (50%)	4

Dark-eyed Junco

by Chuck LaRue *Junco hyemalis*

JIM BURNS

The Dark-eyed Junco is a familiar and ubiquitous forest-dwelling sparrow of the higher uplands of central and northern Arizona. The two races that breed in Arizona —the widespread "Red-backed Junco" and, in the northeast on the Navajo Nation, the "Gray-headed Junco"—were formerly classified within a single species collectively known under the latter name.

HABITAT

Throughout their Arizona breeding range, Dark-eyed Juncos are closely associated with montane forests containing a ponderosa pine component. Atlasers found 51 percent of the potential breeding records for this species in two widespread forest types: primarily pure ponderosa pine and ponderosa pine–Gambel's oak associations (n = 178). Twenty-two percent of records were in mixed-conifer forests, and 12 percent of records were in pinyon pine–juniper woodlands with scattered ponderosa pines. They are also fairly common inhabitants of Arizona's relatively limited subalpine spruce-fir forests, aspen groves, and forest edges of montane grassland meadows. Dark-eyed Juncos were reported only locally at upper elevational limits of nearby pinyon pine–juniper woodlands and chaparral associations.

BREEDING

Several races of Dark–eyed Junco, such as "Oregon" and "Pink-sided Juncos," winter abundantly in Arizona and breed at northern latitudes. Arizona's breeding junco races undergo a limited, primarily altitudinal, migration (Phillips et al. 1964) and may remain in portions of their breeding ranges all year. It is likely that winter weather severity and vagaries of food supply determine such movements. In any event, they typically begin singing on Arizona territories by March, occasionally in February, and atlasers reported the earliest confirmed breeding date on 12 May, when adults were observed feeding fledglings. By backdating this record through the nestling and incubation periods, atlasers estimated that these fledglings hatched from eggs laid in mid-April. Thatcher (1968) reported nest building in Arizona as early as 24 March and young fledging from another nest on 28 April. Atlas data suggest that Dark-eyed Junco breeding efforts are bimodal, with peaks in the number of confirmed records in mid- to early June and again in July. The latest breeding confirmations were adults carrying food on 3 August and fledglings sighted through 25 August.

Dark-eyed Juncos place their nests low, and ten of twelve nests located by atlasers were on the ground, which is the typical pattern throughout the range of the species (Nolan et al. 2002). Atlasers found that nests were well hidden and were typically sheltered from above by plants and other materials such as shrubs, clumps of grass, rock, dirt banks, branches, and, in one case, a pipe. One nest was found in a juniper and another was found in an Engelmann spruce, 4.9 ft (1.5 m) and 3.6 ft (1.1 m) aboveground, respectively.

It appears that Dark-eyed Juncos are monogamous and all nest-building efforts are accomplished by the female (Nolan et al. 2002). The typical clutch size is 4, with 3- and 5-egg clutches also being frequent (Nolan et al. 2002). The female incubates the eggs for 12–13 days (Ehrlich et al. 1988), during which time the male aggressively defends the nest area from potential small predators (Nolan et al. 2002). Both adults tend the nestlings, and the young fledge at 9–13 days of age. The postfledging dependency period may last 3 weeks or more (Ehrlich et al. 1988; Baicich and Harrison 1997). The bimodal peak in confirmations clearly indicates that Dark-eyed Juncos raise two broods in Arizona. It is possible that three broods, previously reported in Arizona "Red-backed Juncos" (Thatched 1968), are raised when resources allow.

Dark-eyed Juncos are uncommon Brown-headed Cowbird hosts, and observers reported two instances of cowbird brood parasitism during the atlas period. Atlasers found Brown-headed Cowbird eggs in two Dark-eyed Junco nests, one near Hannagan Meadow on 13 June and the second south of Heber on 11 July.

Breeding Habitats

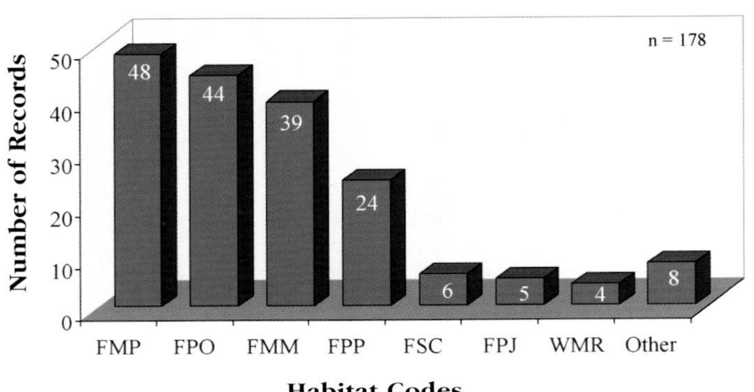

DISTRIBUTION AND STATUS

The various races of Dark-eyed Juncos breed in North America from Alaska east across much of Canada to the northeastern United States and south along the Appalachian cordillera to northern Georgia. In the West, the breeding

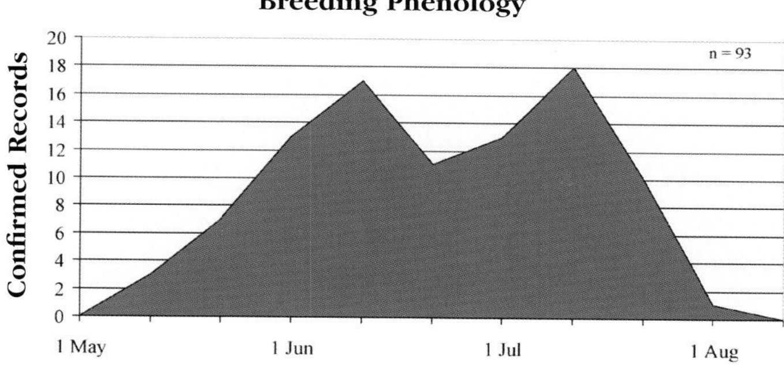

range encompasses most of the region from the Rocky Mountains to the Pacific Ocean south to southern California, central Arizona, southern New Mexico, and extreme west Texas (Nolan 2002).

The "Red-backed Junco" breeds from north central Arizona south and east across the state, through New Mexico to the Guadalupe Mountains of Texas. The breeding range of the "Gray-headed Junco" of the Navajo Nation uplands includes the eastern Great Basin, the Intermountain region, and the southern Rocky Mountains north to southern Idaho and southern Wyoming (Nolan 2002).

Atlasers found that Dark-eyed Juncos were present in suitable habitat throughout their previously described breeding range in Arizona. Most of the breeding records in the state were from 6000 to 8000 ft (1829–2438 m) but nesting activity ranges to near timberline at 11,200 feet (3414 m). Atlasers documented Dark-eyed Juncos breeding throughout all of the principal uplands of the state that were noted by Woodbury and Russell (1945), Phillips et al. (1964), Monson and Phillips (1981), and LaRue (1994). These included the Kaibab, Coconino, Mogollon, Natanes, Defiance and Shonto plateaus, the Hualapai, Bradshaw, Sierra Ancha, Mazatzal, White, and Chuska mountains, and northern Black Mesa. This forest bird undoubtedly also breeds throughout the White Mountain Apache tribal lands where surveys were unfortunately not conducted. Although breeding was not known conclusively for several of these areas prior to atlas fieldwork, breeding was documented for the first time in the Bradshaw, Hualapai, and Sierra Ancha mountains.

The atlas effort extended the known breeding range into a number of isolated locations to the north and west. These new breeding locations included the Virgin Mountains in the extreme northwest, the Mount Dellenbaugh area, the Uinkaret (Mount Trumbull) Mountains, and the Aubrey Cliffs area of the Hualapai Nation. Breeding was also confirmed in Carrizo Mountain in the extreme northeast.

Although some races have shown recent declines, the "Gray-headed Junco" has shown a trend of increasing numbers (Peterjohn et al. 1997). An ecologically successful generalist such as the Dark-eyed Junco is capable of withstanding a variety of ecological and habitat perturbations, and therefore this forest sparrow should be secure in Arizona.

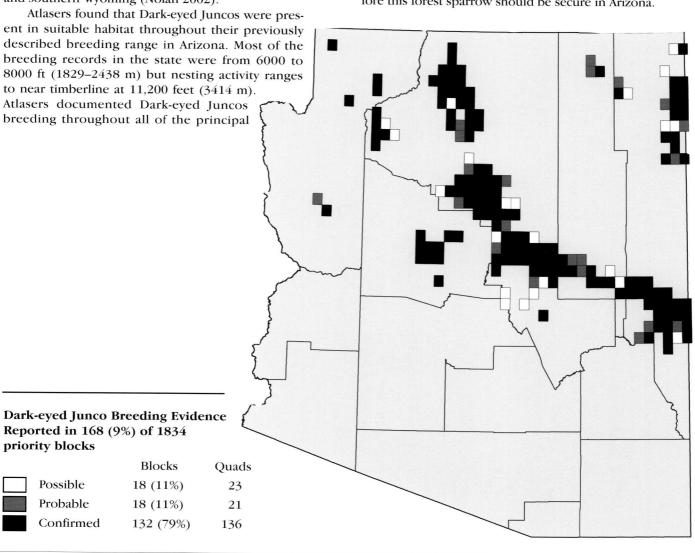

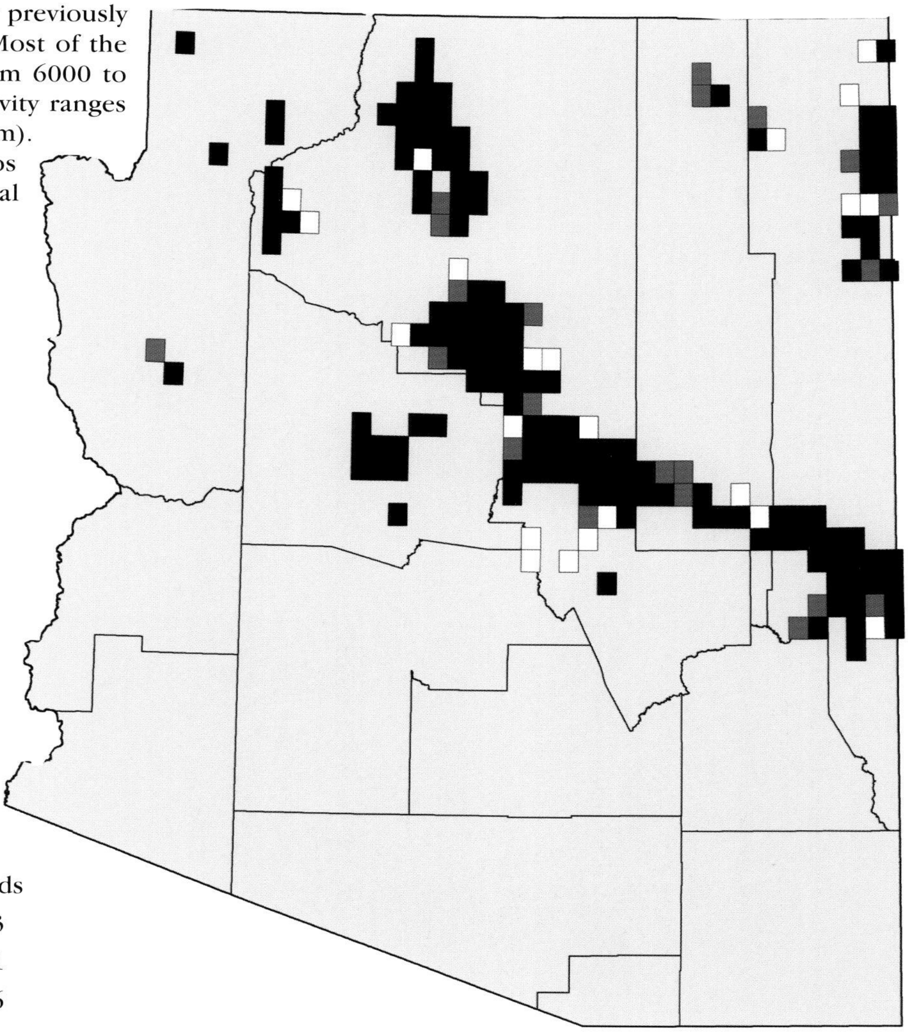

Dark-eyed Junco Breeding Evidence Reported in 168 (9%) of 1834 priority blocks

	Blocks	Quads
Possible	18 (11%)	23
Probable	18 (11%)	21
Confirmed	132 (79%)	136

Yellow-eyed Junco

by Troy E. Corman

Junco phaeonotus

JIM BURNS

With their bright golden eyes glowing as they forage among the shadows of the forest floor, Yellow-eyed Juncos are a favorite of visiting birders to southeastern Arizona. This junco's peculiar shuffling walk is notably different from the hopping gait of their closely related kin to the north.

HABITAT

Yellow-eyed Juncos inhabit many of the coniferous forest clad mountains and canyons of southeastern Arizona. They are most abundant in forests that are cooler, wetter, and more shaded, and are noticeably absent from the drier ranges. Ground cover in most occupied habitats typically consists of scattered grass clumps, small shrubs, forbs, ferns, downed trees, and an abundance of leaf litter in which to forage. Atlasers reported 45 percent of potential breeding records for this species from Madrean pine-oak forests often containing tall Chihuahuan, Apache, and ponderosa pines, with an understory of various evergreen oaks, alligator juniper, and Arizona madrone (n = 30). An additional 31 percent of the observations came from cooler slopes and shaded canyons containing mixed-conifer forests. These forests often include Douglas fir, white fir, ponderosa pine, and scattered quaking aspen stands. They were encountered much less frequently nesting in lower canyons where pine-oak forests transition into Arizona sycamore dominated drainages. Yellow-eyed Juncos were occasionally reported Madrean evergreen oak woodlands, various ponderosa pine dominated habitats, and subalpine coniferous forests containing Engelmann spruce.

BREEDING

Some Yellow-eyed Junco pairs remain together throughout the year and courtship typically takes place in mid- or late April (Austin 1968). Often observed on or near the ground, singing males are frequently encountered high on exposed limbs or near the tops of tall pines. Some singing can begin by late February, but the true complete song can be heard beginning in April and continuing throughout most of the nesting season. These juncos can initiate nest-building activity by early April, and atlasers noted an adult carrying nesting material as late as 3 July. Atlasers reported very few nests with eggs or young. However, egg clutches in Arizona have been found from 12 April to 1 August (Austin 1968; Sullivan 1999). Peak nesting activity is through much of June and into early July. The first fledged young reported by atlasers was observed being fed by an adult on 24 May, and Sullivan (1999) noted that some later nests contain young into mid-August. Yellow-eyed Juncos are basically nonmigratory, but they will descend in early fall to lower elevation forests and woodlands where they spend the winter months.

Yellow-eyed Junco females construct the well-concealed nest, which is typically placed on the ground, often on a slope. Nests are often hidden by tufts of grass, shrubs, small logs, forest debris, or overhanging rocks. Infrequently, nests have also been discovered 1–2 ft (0.3–0.6 m) high in dense shrubbery, young conifers, or yuccas (Swarth 1904; Willard 1923a). Nests in Arizona have also been reported very rarely 9–15 ft (2.7–4.6 m) high, such as in a cavity of a dead pine branch and in a dense young oak (Willard 1923a).

Females incubate the typical clutch of 3–4 eggs (range 1–5) for approximately 13 days (Weathers and Sullivan 1989). Both Yellow-eyed Junco parents help feed the nestlings, which leave the nest when they are 10–13 days old and are still incapable of sustained flight (Weathers and Sullivan 1991). The fledglings are fed for 2–3 weeks following nest departure, and at 3–4 weeks of age the male evicts the fledgling from the immediate natal territory (Sullivan 1999). However, juveniles remain near their natal territory until late August, when they begin moving downslope for winter (Sullivan 1999). In Arizona, Yellow-eyed Juncos have had as many as three successful broods per year (Weathers and Sullivan 1989).

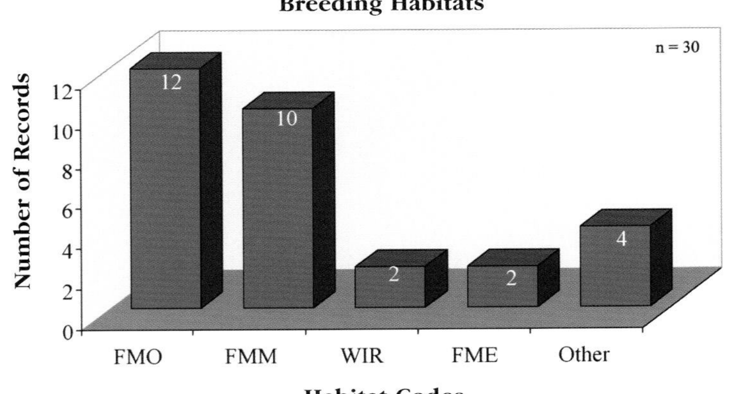

DISTRIBUTION AND STATUS

Yellow-eyed Juncos are resident from southeastern Arizona and southwestern New Mexico, south through the higher elevations of Mexico to central Oaxaca and locally to

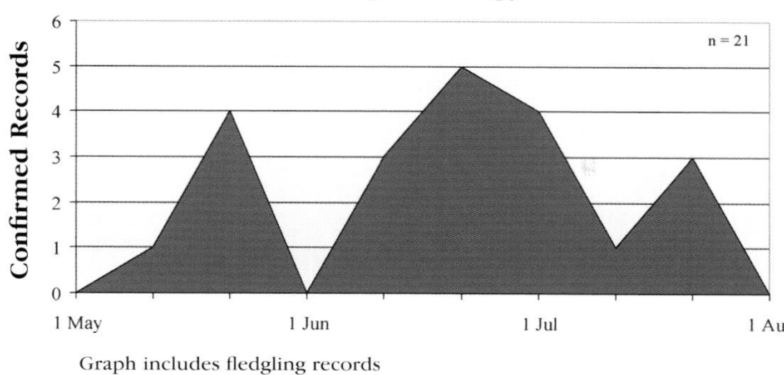

Guatemala. There is also a disjunct population, possibly a separate species, in the mountains of southern Baja California. In Arizona, Phillips et al. (1964) considered these charming juncos as abundant in the higher south-eastern mountain ranges from the Pinal, Santa Catalina, and Pinaleno mountains south.

Within their range, atlasers encountered Yellow-eyed Junco nesting commonly at elevations ranging from approximately 5900 ft (1798 m) to near 10,000 ft (3048 m) on the highest forested peaks of the Pinaleno Mountains. Monson and Phillips (1981) also noted them nesting locally as low as 5300 ft (1615 m) in cool canyons containing Arizona cypress.

The distribution of this junco has changed little from its previously described range in Arizona. The most northern population is in the Pinal Mountains in southern Gila County. They were found and often confirmed nesting throughout the higher elevations of the Pinaleno, Santa Catalina, Rincon, Santa Rita, and Chiricahua mountains. Yellow-eyed Juncos were found primarily only in the cooler drainages and watered canyon on the eastern slopes of the Huachuca Mountains and were noticeably absent on the drier slopes in the remainder of this range. This junco was confirmed nesting for the first time in the Mule Mountains, were previously only winter records existed. They were searched for in the Santa Teresa Mountains, and more thorough surveys in the remote, seldom-visited higher elevations of the Galiuro Mountains may find this species nesting there. However, this is a relatively dry range.

Nearly all of Arizona's Yellow-eyed Junco populations are within lands administered by the U.S. Forest Service and in areas timber harvesting is minimal. The greatest threat facing local populations of these unique juncos is catastrophic wildfire enhanced by past fire-suppression activities. They reveal little concern for most recreational activities and in fact are regularly encountered nesting near heavily used sites such as campgrounds, picnic areas, and trailhead parking areas. At these locations, Yellow-eyed Juncos become relatively tame and often allow close approach, especially when compared to their flighty dark-eyed relatives to the north.

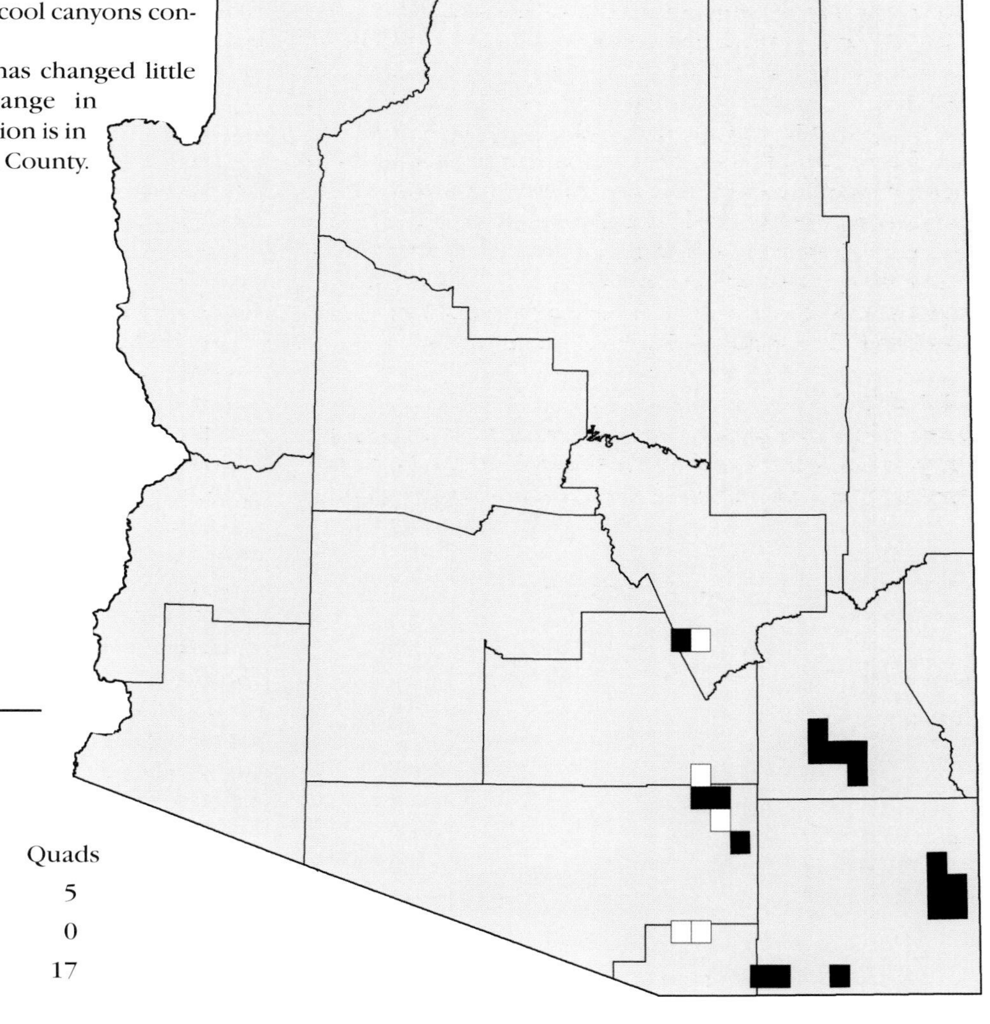

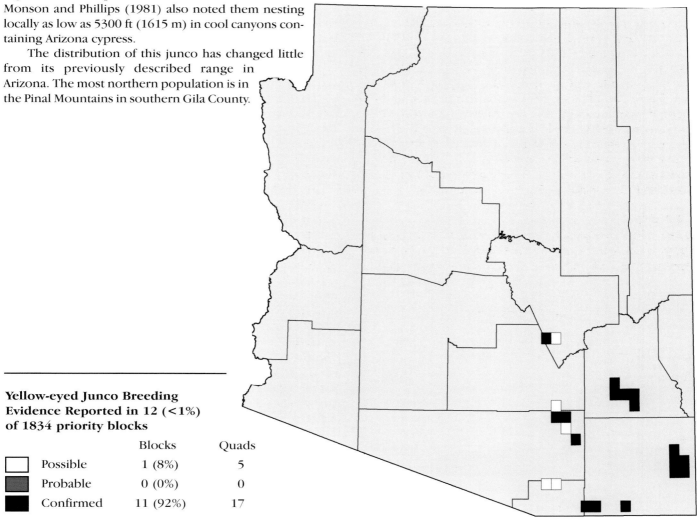

Yellow-eyed Junco Breeding Evidence Reported in 12 (<1%) of 1834 priority blocks

	Blocks	Quads
Possible	1 (8%)	5
Probable	0 (0%)	0
Confirmed	11 (92%)	17

Northern Cardinal

by Cathryn Wise-Gervais *Cardinalis cardinalis*

RICHARD DITCH

The brilliant male Northern Cardinal commands more attention at the bird feeder than nearly any other bird, and seven states have selected this robust songster as their state bird. Arizona visitors are generally surprised to encounter these familiar inhabitants of eastern deciduous woodlots in Sonoran Desert landscapes.

HABITAT

Northern Cardinals generally select habitats offering dense, low-growing shrubs for nesting and cover coupled with conspicuous perches for singing (Halkin and Linville 1999). Arizona's Northern Cardinals are primarily desert dwellers, but they also inhabit adjacent riparian areas. Atlasers reported Northern Cardinals in nineteen habitat types, although 49 percent of potential breeding records were in taller and denser Sonoran desertscrub associations, including heavily wooded dry washes characterized by mesquite, ironwood, and paloverde (n = 492). They were rarely reported in the drier and sparsely vegetated Sonoran desertscrub landscapes of western Arizona. These birds were also regularly encountered along cottonwood-willow or lower sycamore-dominated drainages, especially if mesquite, hackberry, or other dense shrubs were available (28 percent of records). Fewer records were obtained in brushy semiarid grasslands, oak woodland edges, chaparral associations, and rural and residential neighborhoods with native vegetation.

BREEDING

Northern Cardinals are year-round residents in Arizona and begin nesting in early spring. Some of these homebodies even stay in pairs on their breeding territories all year (Laskey 1944). Atlasers reported the birds carrying nesting material on 23 February, but did not discover a nest with eggs until 11 April. However, adults were already feeding fledglings by 12 April, indicating that some early egg laying is initiated by mid-March or earlier in Arizona. Observers located thirty-one Northern Cardinal nests with eggs, from 11 April to 4 August and fifteen nests with young, from 7 May to 20 July. Although atlas data suggest a peak in Northern Cardinal breeding activity in mid-May, observers continued confirming the species throughout the summer, and noted a second activity spike in mid-July. The majority of August and early September breeding records were from southeastern Arizona, and these midsummer records were likely in response to increased resource availability due to monsoon activity. Observers reported adults feeding fledglings through 7 September. These late records may represent second broods, as this species will raise two broods per season when resources allow.

It may seem ironic that a dapper bird such as the Northern Cardinal would build a messy nest, but such is true. Northern Cardinal nests are scraggly collections of stems and twigs and can be placed in numerous trees and shrubs. Atlasers took measurements at fourteen Northern Cardinal nests at elevations between 2600 and 4240 ft (792–1292 m). The nests were in seven identifiable plants and two were in unidentified shrubs. Nests were discovered in two species of hackberry (5), wolfberry (3), mesquite (2), and one each in desert broom, blue paloverde, shrub live oak, and graythorn. The median nest height was 5.9 ft (1.8 m) and heights ranged from 3 to 12.1 ft (0.9–3.7).

Female Northern Cardinals build their nests and incubate their eggs without male assistance. They lay 3–4 eggs (range 2–5) and incubate these for 11–13 days (Baicich and Harrison 1997). Females are known to sit tight on the nest or remain in the immediate nest area for the duration of the incubation period. This high degree of attentiveness probably discourages some cowbird parasitism. Males feed females on the nest and both parents feed the nestlings. The young depart the nest at approximately 9–10 days of age (Austin 1968) and continue to be fed at least occasionally by parents for 25–56 days after fledging (Halkin and Linville 1999).

Although Northern Cardinals are considered common Brown-headed Cowbird hosts, observers surprisingly did not report any incidents of parasitism during atlas fieldwork. Immediately following the atlas period, however, a Northern Cardinal was observed feeding a young cowbird

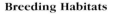

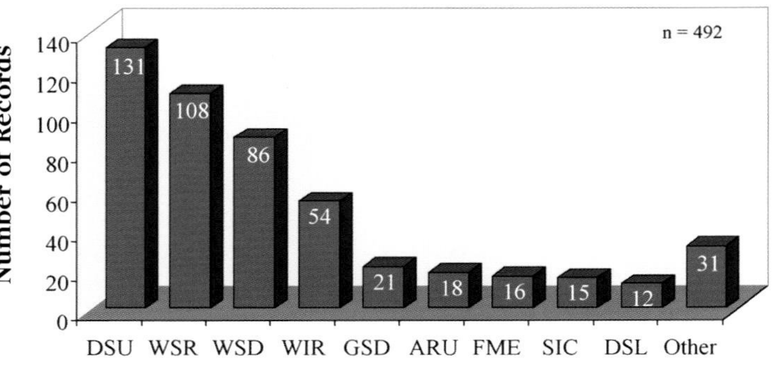

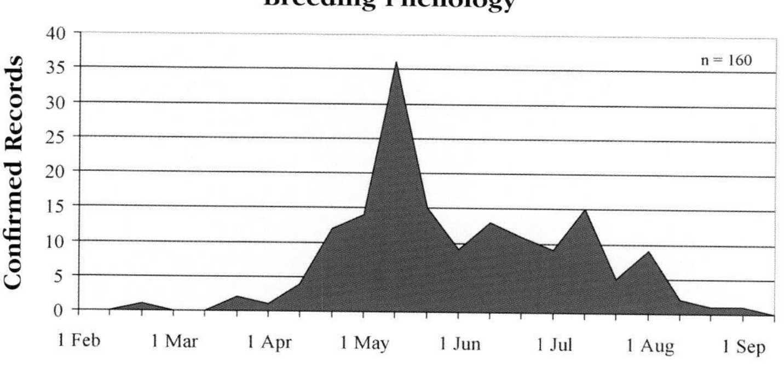

fledgling on the late date of 24 September (S. Johnson, personal communication).

DISTRIBUTION AND STATUS

Though Northern Cardinals occur in a few small and isolated locations in the Colorado River valley of southeastern California and Arizona, the species reaches the western edge of its range in west-central Arizona. Northern Cardinals are common throughout the eastern and central United States and adjacent Canada. They breed south to Belize, northern Guatemala, and to the Pacific Coast of southern Mexico.

This common resident has expanded its range considerably to the west and northwest in Arizona since the 1870s (Monson and Phillips 1981). Northern Cardinals reside throughout central and southern Arizona, west to Organ Pipe Cactus National Monument and north to the foot of the Mogollon plateau (Phillips et al 1964). Atlasers confirmed this species breeding on priority blocks from approximately 750 to 5700 ft (229–1737 m). Northern Cardinals were noted north throughout the upper Verde River drainage, including its headwaters in the Chino Valley near Paulden, and along Oak Creek near Sedona. Observers discovered Northern Cardinals regularly northwest through the Santa Maria Mountain foothills and into the upper Big Sandy River drainage, including Trout Creek and other Aquarius Mountain drainages.

Along the Bill Williams River, Northern Cardinals were encountered near Alamo Lake but were not detected in the Bill Williams River National Wildlife Refuge area and south to Parker where previously noted nesting (Van Rossem 1946; Monson 1949). Prior accounts considered the birds rare and local residents between Ehrenberg and the Bill Williams River delta (Rosenberg et al. 1991). Although atlasers failed to find them in this region, small, local populations could have easily been missed by typical atlas surveys. Northern Cardinals are casually reported south to Yuma (Rosenberg et al. 1991) and the only lower Colorado River valley atlas record was of a singing territorial male on the Imperial Reservoir block.

Other than within the lower Colorado River valley, atlasers commonly encountered Northern Cardinals throughout their previously described Arizona range, indicating some degree of stability. Researchers suggest that local expansions and contractions can occur independently of population size changes and that young birds are often "pioneers," moving into new areas as a result of dispersal pressures (Halkin and Linville 1999). Breeding Bird Survey data from eastern states indicate declines, but more data are needed to determine population status of this familiar bird in Arizona.

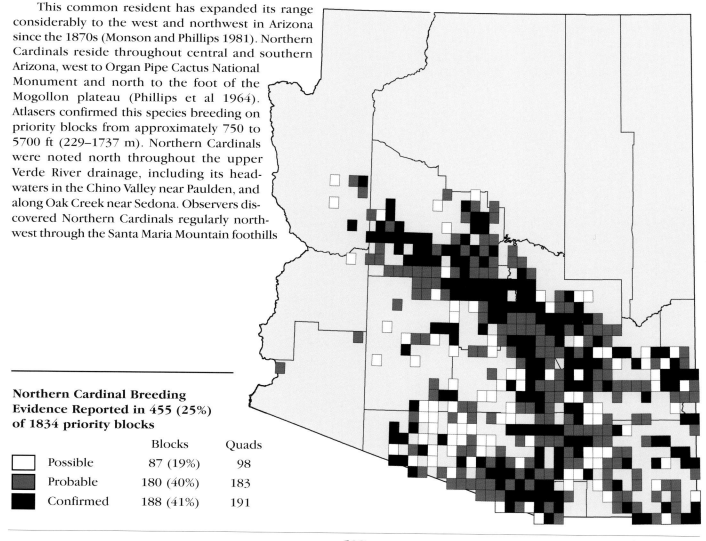

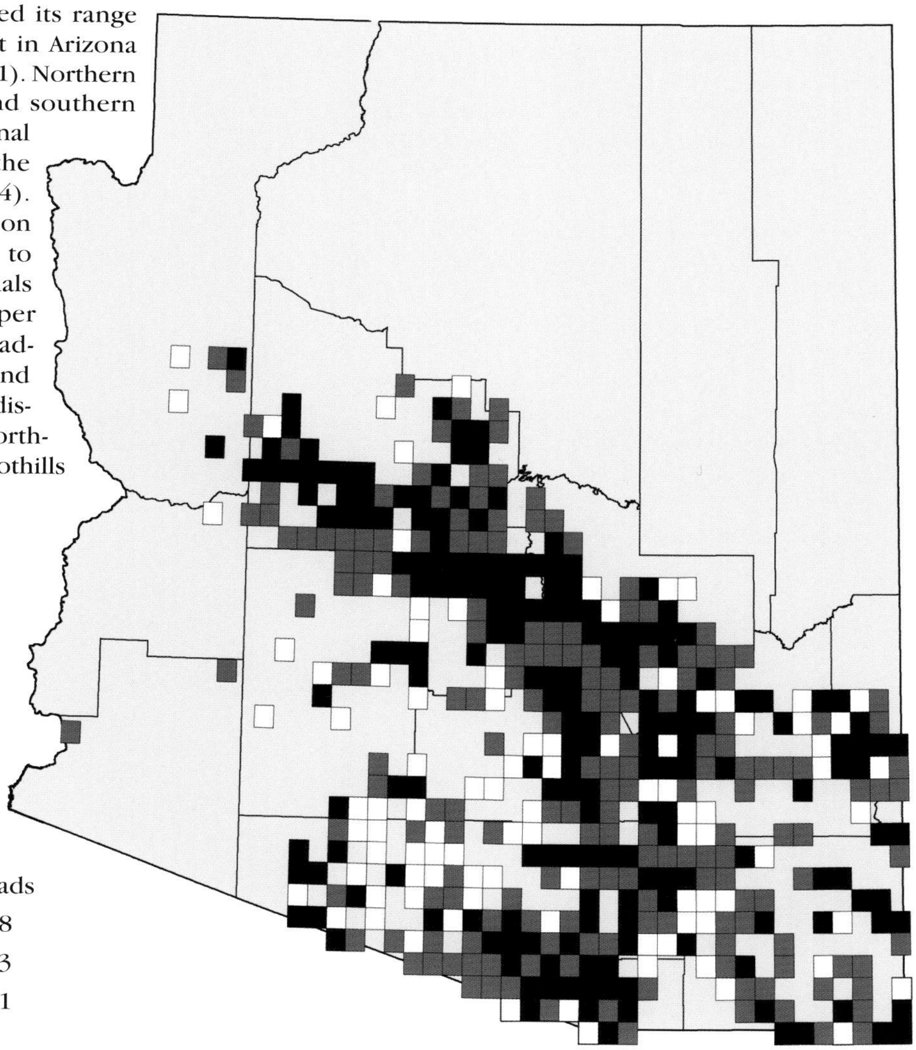

Northern Cardinal Breeding Evidence Reported in 455 (25%) of 1834 priority blocks

	Blocks	Quads
Possible	87 (19%)	98
Probable	180 (40%)	183
Confirmed	188 (41%)	191

Pyrrhuloxia

by Cathryn Wise-Gervais *Cardinalis sinuatus*

Pyrrhuloxias are related to the more common Northern Cardinal but have straw-colored bills and an overall grayer appearance than their close relative. Their exotic-sounding name is derived from the Greek "pyrrhula" meaning "flame-colored" and "loxuos" meaning "crooked," probably in reference to the bird's uniquely shaped beak.

GARY ROSENBERG

HABITAT

Pyrrhuloxias are primarily desert birds and are found in open, brushy landscapes offering areas with dense, low-growing foliage. Atlasers reported the species in thirteen habitat types, and 38 percent of potential breeding records were in Sonoran desertscrub associations characterized by saguaro, paloverde, and other cacti and legume trees ($n = 267$). They were also frequently reported in the wooded dry washes that meander their way through the desert and frequently contain taller stands of mesquite, paloverde, ironwood, and hackberry. These arid drainages accounted for 23 percent of atlas records. Atlasers reported 26 percent of Pyrrhuloxia records in semiarid grasslands and Chihuahuan desertscrub associations that often contain mixed grasses, scattered mesquite, acacia, soaptree yucca, and ocotillo. Fewer records were reported from brush near isolated ranches and farms, in mesquite thickets near earthen livestock tanks, and in brushy areas along riparian drainages. Though often encountered in the same habitats, Pyrrhuloxias regularly occur in more sparsely vegetated localities than Northern Cardinals (Tweit and Thompson 1999).

BREEDING

Most of Arizona's Pyrrhuloxias are year-round residents, but some individuals will locally disperse into lower river valleys and higher foothill locations during the cooler months. Territoriality and pairing begin in late February and March in Arizona with nest construction initiated later in the month. Atlasers reported the first occupied nest likely containing eggs on 7 April, but noted only thirteen Pyrrhuloxia nests with eggs from 14 April to 24 August. Atlas data suggest that the peak breeding period for Pyrrhuloxia in Arizona is in mid-May, with a lesser peak in early August. Later nesting records were primarily noted in areas prone to significant monsoon activities. Although the birds are not known to produce more than one brood per season, late nesting records indicate that the birds may initiate renesting attempts during the monsoon season. However, second broods are very possible in southeastern Arizona, and the nesting affairs of this species deserve more study. Observers reported an adult Pyrrhuloxia carrying nesting material on 4 September, but the fate of this late nesting attempt is unknown.

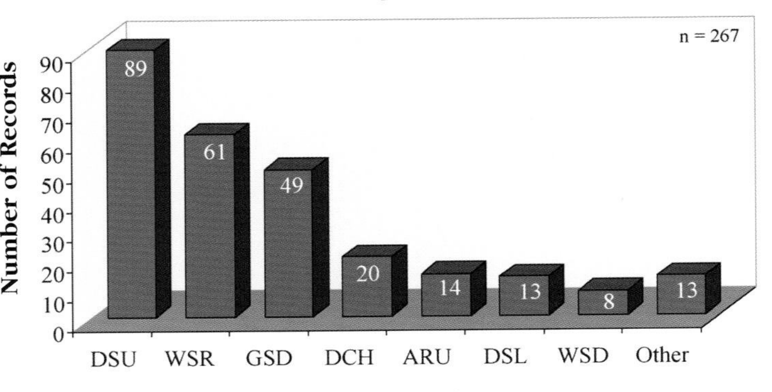

Pyrrhuloxias typically place their nests in dense, often thorny brush, such as in mesquite or graythorn and usually nest in more open habitats than Northern Cardinals (Tweit and Thompson 1999). Atlasers measured only three Pyrrhuloxia nests, one each in ironwood, foothill paloverde, and catclaw acacia. These ranged in height from 3.0 to 6.9 ft (0.9–2.1 m). Other Arizona studies reported an average nest height of 7.9 ft (2.4 m) with a range of 4.9–14.8 ft (1.5–4.5 m) aboveground ($n = 20$; Gould 1960). The female alone constructs the nest; meanwhile, the male stays among the trees singing (Gould 1961). Pyrrhuloxia nests are usually neater and slightly smaller than Northern Cardinal nests (Tweit and Thompson 1999).

Pyrrhuloxia typically lay 3 eggs (range 2–4), and the female incubates these for approximately 14 days (Gould 1961). The male occasionally feeds the incubating and brooding female and both parents provide food to nestlings (Tweit and Thompson 1999). The young fledge at approximately 10–13 days of age but are typically unable to fly well and often perch near the nest (Tweit and Thompson 1999). It is unclear how long fledglings receive food from their parents, but one female in southern Arizona was observed feeding a fledged youngster from 9 September to 12 October (Anderson and Anderson 1946). Juveniles often

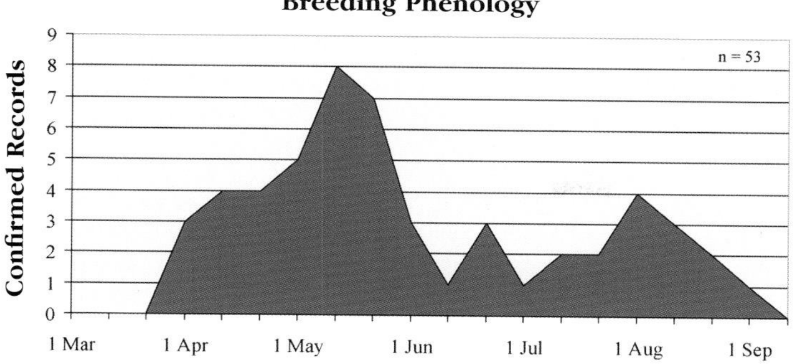

form small flocks at this stage, joined by postbreeding adults later in the fall (Tweit and Thompson 1999).

Pyrrhuloxias are known hosts for both Brown-headed and Bronzed Cowbirds (Friedmann 1971). However, observers did not report any incidents of brood parasitism during the atlas period.

DISTRIBUTION AND STATUS

Pyrrhuloxias reach the northern edge of their range in southern Arizona and New Mexico and are commonly found in higher densities throughout southern and western Texas (Tweit and Thompson 1999). These birds range into central Mexico, as far south as the southern tip of Baja California and northern Michoacan and Queretaro.

In Arizona, Pyrrhuloxias are encountered primarily from southeastern and south-central sections of the state west through the Tohono O'odham tribal lands to Ajo (Phillips et al. 1964). Within this historical range, atlasers confirmed the species breeding on priority blocks from approximately 1200 to 5500 ft (366–1676 m). Pyrrhuloxias also occasionally occur west to the Mohawk and Castle Dome mountains, and there are several summer records now for the lower Colorado River valley (Monson and Phillips 1981; Rosenberg et al. 1991). The westernmost atlas records were of individuals in the San Cristobal Valley and near the Tinajas Altas Mountains of southeastern Yuma County.

Monson and Phillips (1981) described the northern range for the Pyrrhuloxia as including the Gila River Indian tribal lands and within the southern San Simon and San Pedro River valleys. Atlas data reveal that these handsome birds have extended their breeding range northward to include the Rainbow Valley and Maricopa Mountains area, Boyce Thompson Arboretum vicinity, and lower San Pedro River valley to Winkelman. They were also discovered nesting sparingly in the Gila River valley from Ft. Thomas to Safford and near Duncan.

Before the atlas project, there was only one report of Pyrrhuloxias nesting near Wickenburg (Monson and Phillips 1981). Atlasers discovered a sizable isolated population in the scattered and patchy mesquite grasslands and desertscrub in this area. These birds were noted north to Yarnell, west to the Aguila Valley, and south into the Hassayampa Plain.

Atlasers encountered Pyrrhuloxias fairly commonly throughout their previously described range in Arizona and noted some obvious range expansions to the north. This would suggest some stability in populations and possibly even slight increases. Breeding Bird Survey data show that this attractive species occurs in higher densities in Texas than in Arizona, but no statistically significant population trends have been revealed (Price et al. 1995).

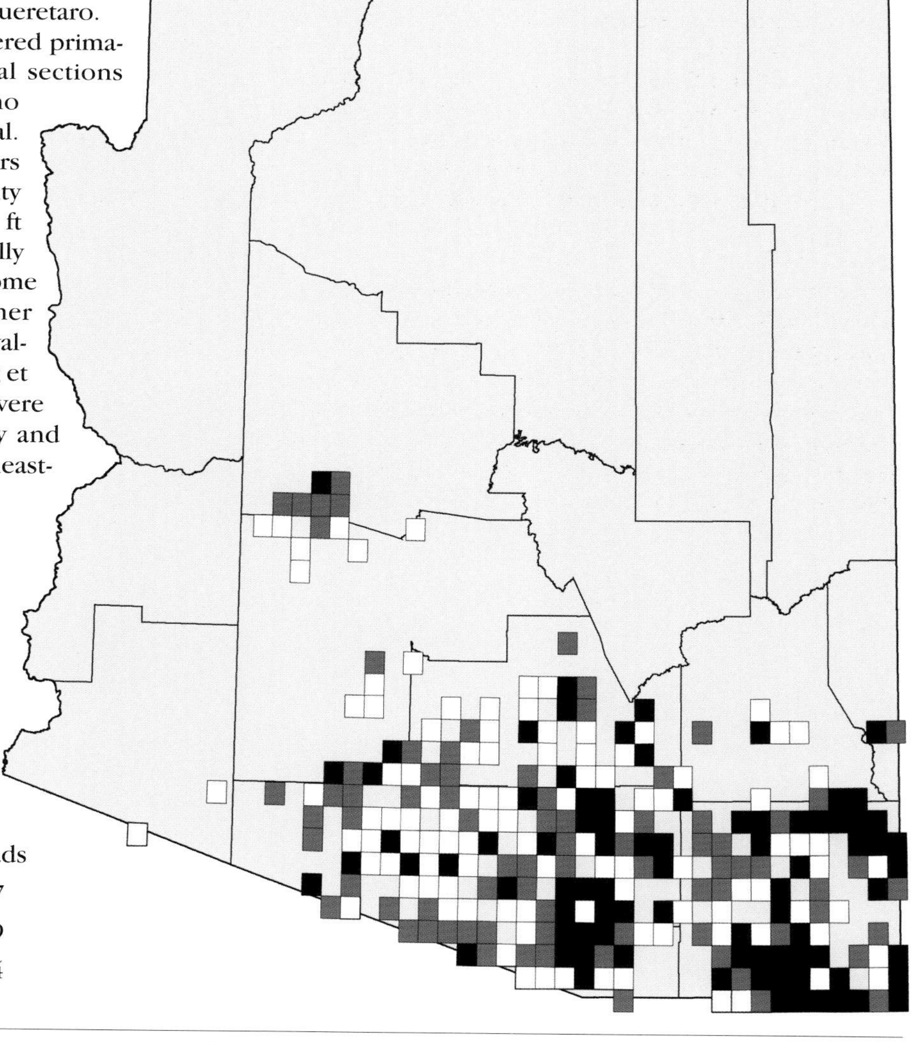

Pyrrhuloxia Breeding Evidence Reported in 262 (14%) of 1834 priority blocks

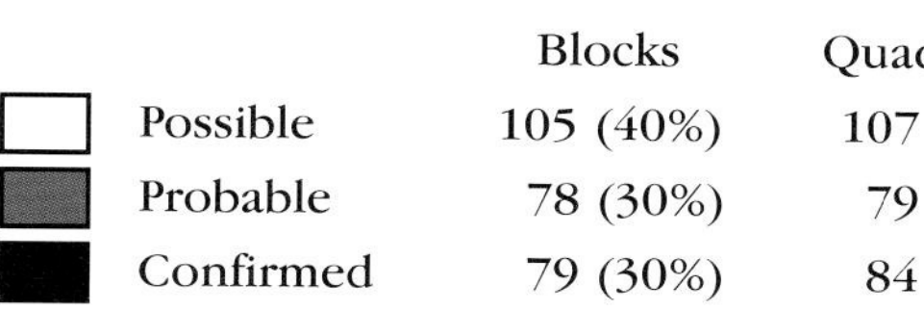

	Blocks	Quads
Possible	105 (40%)	107
Probable	78 (30%)	79
Confirmed	79 (30%)	84

Black-headed Grosbeak

by Cathryn Wise-Gervais

Pheucticus melanocephalus

Black-headed Grosbeaks are large-billed, heavy-bodied birds that are probably best known for their rich, melodious song. Although both sexes sing, even from the nest, the male's song is considerably more complex and is easy to recognize. This song is also a sure sign of spring throughout most of Arizona's forests.

BRUCE TAUBERT

HABITAT

Occurring in almost any habitat containing trees and shrubs during migration, Black-headed Grosbeaks breed in a wide array of woodland and forest communities in Arizona. They reach their highest densities in structurally diverse habitats with a strong deciduous component, but they will also occupy conifer-dominated woodlands. Black-headed Grosbeaks prefer open forests with clearings and are infrequently encountered in dense, closed canopy habitats. Atlasers located Black-headed Grosbeaks in twenty-three different vegetative communities, indicating a fair degree of habitat choice flexibility. Atlas data reveal no strong habitat preferences in Arizona for this species. Although 21 percent of potential atlas breeding records for this grosbeak were reported in pinyon pine–juniper woodlands, the number of actual records was relatively low compared to the availability of this widespread habitat in Arizona (n = 444). Black-headed Grosbeaks in central and northern Arizona are most often encountered nesting in open pine and Douglas fir forests with deciduous trees such as Gambel's oak, locust, maple, or aspen. They especially favor deciduous tree-dominated canyons and mountain drainages. South and west of the Mogollon Rim, these grosbeaks are also regular nesting inhabitants in foothill drainages and canyons with sycamore, alder, and walnut. In the mountains of southeastern Arizona, they are common summer residents of Madrean pine-oak forests and evergreen oak woodlands.

Breeding Habitats

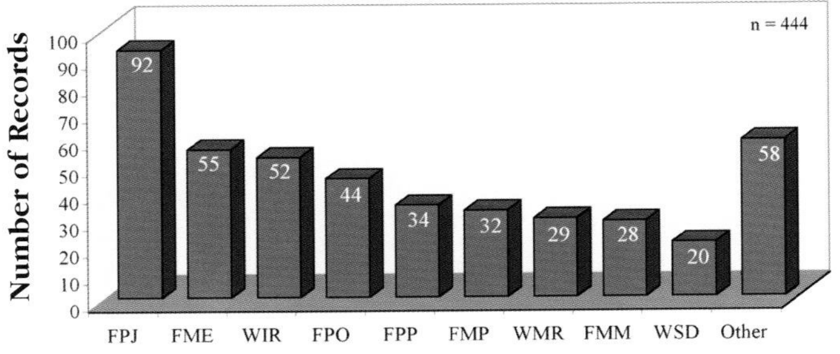

Habitat Codes

BREEDING

Black-headed Grosbeaks have a fairly protracted spring migration through Arizona, as early arrivals appear in late March and late migrants are noted through mid-June. Most individuals arrive on their Arizona breeding grounds in early to mid-April, however, and atlasers reported the earliest nest building activity on 26 April. Early egg-laying initiation may begin by late April and early May, as atlasers reported fledglings by 17 and 25 May in southeastern Arizona. Observers reported eight Black-headed Grosbeak nests with eggs from 19 May to 17 July and nine nests with young from 27 May to 1 August. Atlas data suggest that the peak breeding period for Black-headed Grosbeaks statewide is from mid-June through mid-July, with a steep decline in late July. As noted, however, nests with young were discovered through 1 August, and adults were observed feeding fledglings through the end of the month. In Arizona, many southbound Black-headed Grosbeaks begin appearing in lowland washes and riparian areas by early to mid-July, although peak passage is in August and September, with few remaining after mid-October.

Black-headed Grosbeaks typically construct their nests in the outer branches of small deciduous trees and shrubs (Weston 1947; Ritchison 1938). Nests are flimsy cup-shaped structures and are constructed primarily by the female (Hill 1995). Observers took measurements at fourteen Black-headed Grosbeak nest sites in nine tree and shrub species. Nests were placed in willow (3), pinyon pine (2), Gambel's oak (2), and one each in ponderosa pine, alder, barberry, Russian olive, Emory oak, and Arizona white oak. The median nest height was 10.8 ft (3.0 m) and ranged from 5.6 to 24.9 ft (1.7–7.6 m).

The typical Black-headed Grosbeak clutch consists of 3 eggs (range 2–5), which both sexes incubate. Only the female develops a full brood patch, suggesting that she may do more of the actual egg-warming, while males may sit on the eggs to relieve the female and to protect the nest from predators (Hill 1995). The incubation period lasts for 12–14

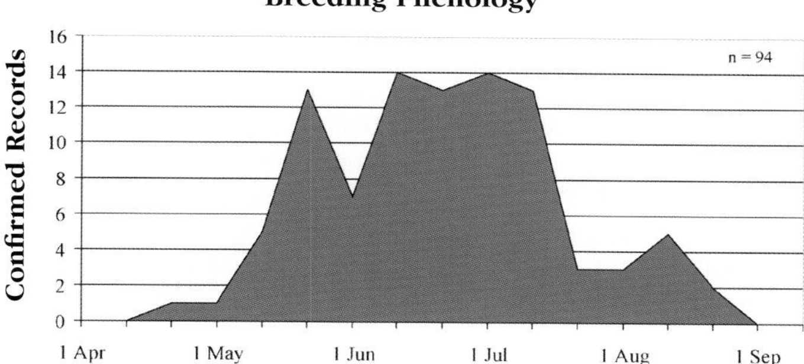

days (Weston 1947; Ritchison 1938), then both parents feed and brood the young. The young leave the nest at approximately 12 days old, before they are able to fly. For about 2 weeks, the fledglings perch silently in dense vegetation near the nest and are fed by their parents. The adults continue to feed the young for some time after fledging, and as the young become adept fliers, they frequently follow parents begging with a distinctive "whee-urr" call.

DISTRIBUTION AND STATUS

Black-headed Grosbeaks are neotropical migrants and do not winter regularly in great numbers anywhere north of the Mexican border. The species breeds from southwestern Canada to northern Baja California and Oaxaca and from coastal California east to central Kansas. They are primarily absent as a nesting species in the Mojave and Sonoran Desert regions of California and Arizona. They are common summer residents of mid-elevation forests and woodlands in eastern, central, and northern Arizona (Phillips et al. 1964). Atlasers confirmed this species breeding on atlas blocks primarily from 4200 to 9300 ft (1280–2835 m). However, they were discovered nesting locally in some sycamore-oak dominated canyons down to 3650 ft (1113 m).

Atlas surveys verified the presence of Black-headed Grosbeaks throughout their historical range and revealed new nesting localities. Atlasers documented these grosbeaks nesting throughout southeastern Arizona's mountains and foothills west to the Baboquivari-Quinlan Mountains. Although Black-headed Grosbeaks typically breed in foothill riparian woodlands containing sycamore, oaks, cottonwood, and willow in this region, they are typically absent as a nesting species in large cottonwood- and willow-dominated drainages such as the San Pedro and Santa Cruz rivers.

Widespread inhabitants in Arizona's Mogollon Rim and White Mountains regions, Black-headed Grosbeaks undoubtedly occur throughout much of the habitat diverse White Mountain Apache tribal lands, where atlas surveys could not be conducted. However, these birds were notably absent in higher elevation forests dominated by spruce-fir. They were encountered breeding west to the isolated Hualapai and Cerbat mountains and south to the Bradshaw Mountains. On Navajo and Hopi tribal lands, Black-headed Grosbeaks were noted nesting locally in the Tsegi Canyon and Black Mesa regions south to Balakai Mesa and locally to Keams Canyon. These birds were regularly detected from the Carrizo Mountains south to the Defiance Plateau, including in the Canyon de Chelly drainages.

Black-headed Grosbeaks were regularly encountered on surveyed blocks containing appropriate nesting habitat. Most evidence suggests fairly stable populations of these attractive grosbeaks in Arizona and across their range. This favorable status is probably aided by the bird's ability to use a wide array of habitats, not only for breeding, but during migration as well.

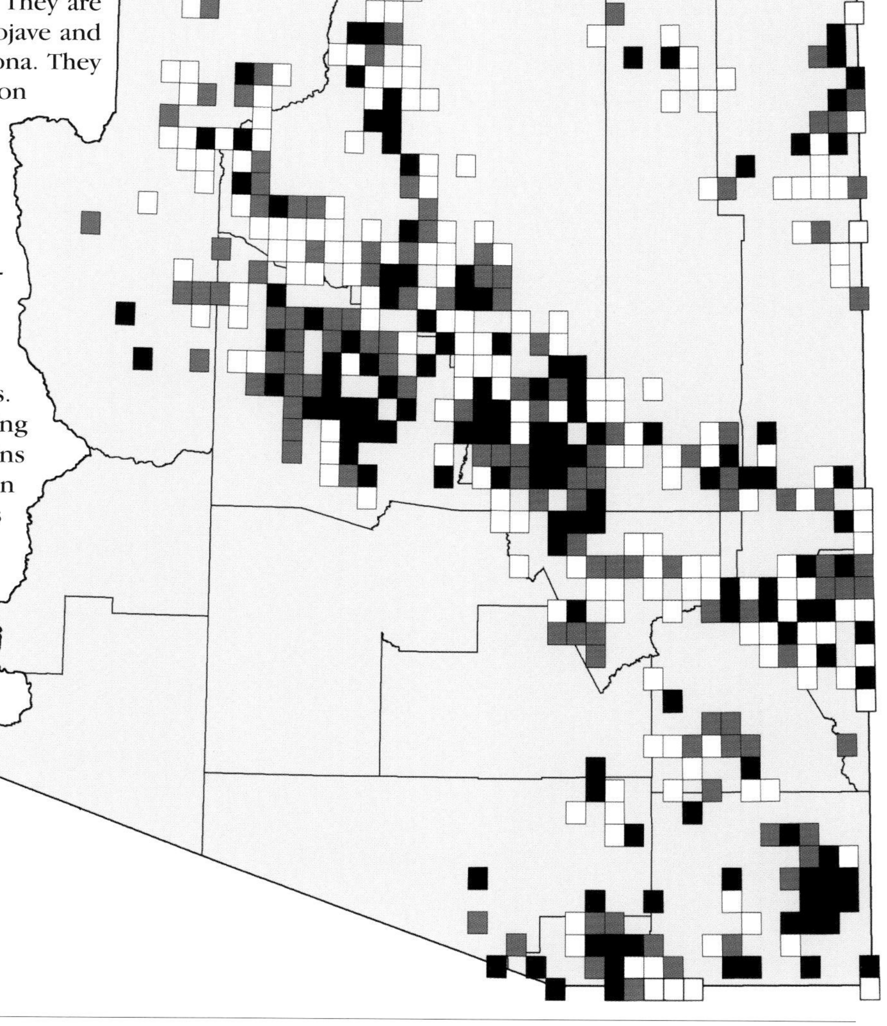

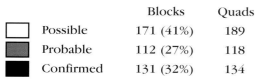

Black-headed Grosbeak Breeding Evidence Reported in 414 (23%) of 1834 priority blocks

	Blocks	Quads
Possible	171 (41%)	189
Probable	112 (27%)	118
Confirmed	131 (32%)	134

Blue Grosbeak

by Chuck LaRue *Passerina caerulea*

Blue Grosbeaks are large stocky buntings that grace riparian habitats and thickets throughout most of Arizona. The presence of these birds is often revealed by the loud rich song of the male or by the hard, distinctive "tink!" call that is given by both sexes.

HABITAT

In Arizona, Blue Grosbeaks are birds closely associated with riparian habitats, especially those containing scattered small to medium sized trees and dense thickets. Mesquite is a common component of habitats used in southern and western Arizona. Although they were found breeding in twenty-two vegetative communities, nearly 80 percent of the breeding records were from six habitats ($n = 433$). Over half of the breeding records obtained by atlasers were in three types: lowland riparian woodlands of cottonwood, willow, mesquite, and tamarisk (24 percent); foothill drainages with sycamore, cottonwood, ash, and mesquite (16 percent); and desert dry washes often dominated by mesquite and other low trees and shrubs (12 percent). Blue Grosbeaks also inhabit mesquite and hackberry thickets in semiarid grasslands, dense brush and low trees along irrigated agricultural lands, and riparian groves in northern Arizona, often containing cottonwood, Russian olive, and tamarisk. In fact, these adaptable birds can be found nesting in stands of exotic tamarisk throughout Arizona.

BREEDING

Blue Grosbeaks are summer residents in Arizona and are generally present from late April into October. They arrive first in western Arizona and do not become regular in the southeast and north until mid-May or even later. Early nest building typically begins in mid-May, and atlasers discovered nests with eggs by the end of the month. However, most of the breeding activity was documented from early July to early September, with a peak in early August. This suggests that this attractive bird is relying partly on food resources influenced by the late summer monsoon rains. Nest building activity has been observed as late as 4 September in southeastern Arizona. The latest breeding confirmation during the atlas period was of an adult feeding fledged young near Patagonia on 10 October (N. Crook, personal communication). These dates place this species among the latest breeders in the state. Most Blue Grosbeaks have departed Arizona by mid- to late October, although a few individuals winter irregularly in the southeast.

It is unknown if only the female Blue Grosbeak or both adults of the monogamous pair participate in the building of the cup type nest (Ehrlich et al. 1988). Nests are typically placed low in small trees, shrubs, or dense brush and in Arizona are often discovered at the edge of riparian stands in willow, tamarisk, and mesquite. Measurements were taken at only three Blue Grosbeak nests during the atlas project. These were in velvet ash, velvet mesquite, and acacia. As is typical of the species, the nests were placed relatively low, ranging from 6.9 to 8.2 ft (2.1–2.5 m) above the ground. The nest plants ranged from 9.2 to 18.7 ft (2.8–5.7 m) in height.

The Blue Grosbeak clutch size varies from 2 to 5 eggs, with 4 being average (Stabler 1959; Bent 1968). The female incubates for 11–12 days and the young fledge at 9–10 days of age (Stabler 1959). Both adults tend to the young (Erhlich et al. 1988), but there is apparently little information on how long parental dependency continues following nest departure. They commonly produce second broods in southern regions (Ingold 1993) and this is very likely in Arizona given the lengthy five-month nesting period. Studies have suggested there is typically a 2–3 week period between the first and second broods (Ingold 1933). Atlasers documented eight incidents of Brown-headed Cowbird brood parasitism from 31 May to 19 August suggesting that Blue Grosbeaks are frequent cowbird hosts in the state.

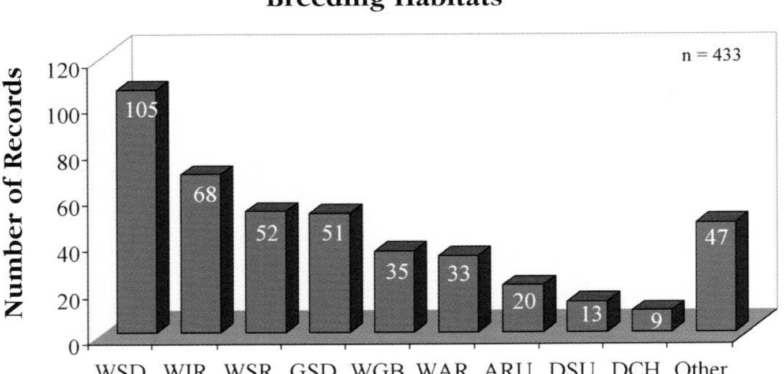

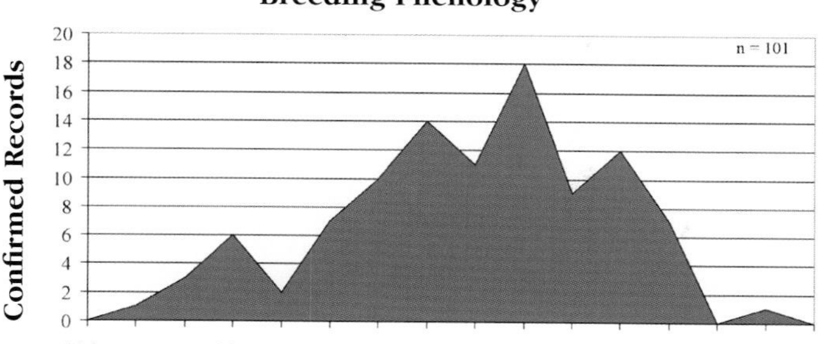

DISTRIBUTION AND STATUS

Blue Grosbeaks are widespread summer residents across much of the southern two thirds of the United States from central California to New Jersey and reaches its northernmost extent in the Great Plains to southern North Dakota. They also breed south to Costa Rica. In Arizona, atlasers documented territorial Blue Grosbeaks at elevations from approximately 90 ft (27 m) along the lower Colorado River to 7700 ft (2347 m) in the White Mountains. However, most of the confirmations were at middle elevations from 4000 to 6000 ft (1219–1829 m).

Atlasers found the Arizona distribution of the Blue Grosbeak to be nearly the same as that described by Phillips et al. (1964), but being perhaps more frequent across much of northern Arizona north of the Mogollon Rim. Two centers of abundance are clearly illustrated by the atlas distribution map. The larger of the two is in the extreme southeast from the Baboquivari Mountains east throughout most of Cochise County and north to the Gila, San Pedro, San Francisco, and Black River drainages. They are especially abundant in this region of the state where monsoon precipitation is typically very pronounced in July and August and likely influences these higher breeding densities. The second concentration area falls across most of Yavapai County in west-central Arizona.

Of all of Arizona's breeding birds, the Blue Grosbeak appears to most readily exploit the thickets of exotic tamarisk that have become so widely established in riparian areas throughout the state. Woodbury and Russell (1945) noted it breeding in tamarisk near Lees Ferry as early as 1938. Virtually all of the nesting pairs found by Bradfield (1974) on Oraibi Wash on Hopi tribal lands were breeding in tamarisk as were all of the pairs found by Sogge et al. (1998) on the Colorado River in the Grand Canyon. It was the most numerous breeding bird in the tamarisk thickets of Black Mesa near Kayenta (LaRue 1994). Rosenberg et al. (1991) called it "unique among midsummer-breeding, migratory insectivores in being able to breed in stands of pure saltcedar" in the lower Colorado River valley.

Breeding Bird Survey data suggest that populations of this large bunting are fairly stable in Arizona. Its ability to breed in tamarisk also suggests that it may have become more widespread and common, particularly in northern Arizona, as this exotic plant has become established and continues to spread. Consequently, the Blue Grosbeak appears to be secure as a breeding bird in Arizona's riparian communities.

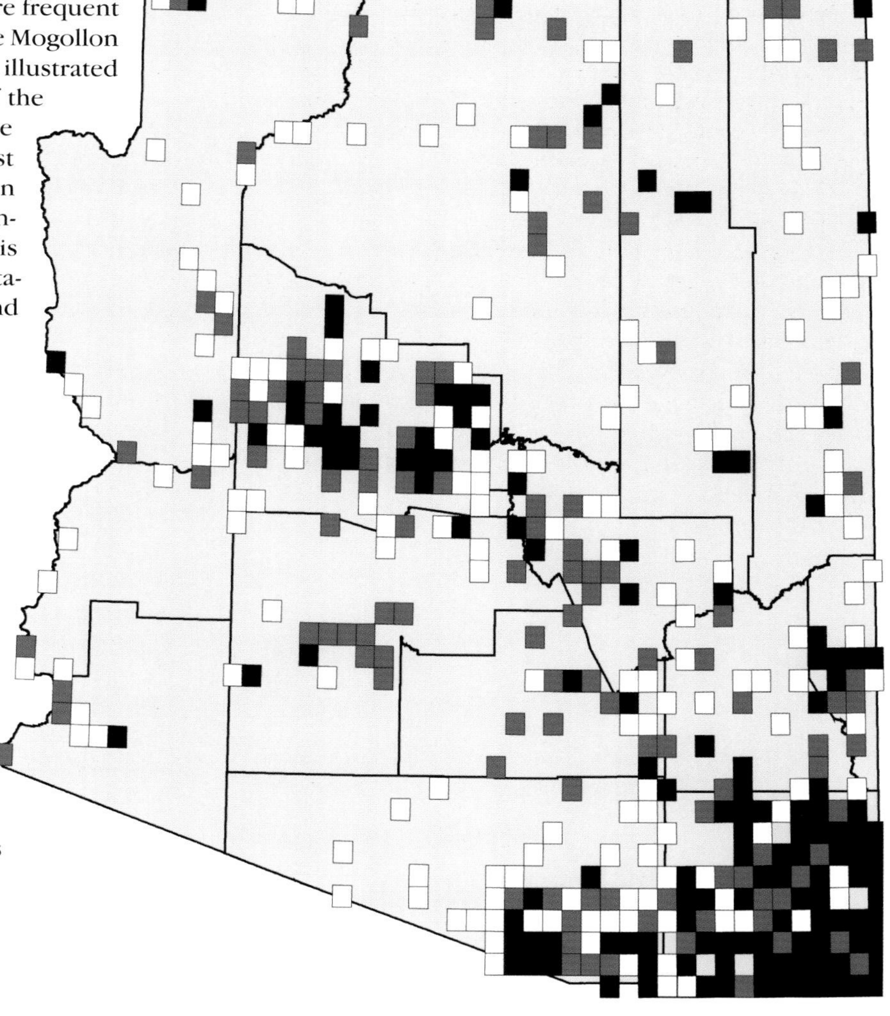

Blue Grosbeak Breeding Evidence Reported in 371 (20%) of 1834 priority blocks

	Blocks	Quads
Possible	133 (36%)	171
Probable	110 (29%)	116
Confirmed	128 (35%)	140

Lazuli Bunting

by Cathryn Wise-Gervais *Passerina amoena*

Lazuli Buntings were appropriately named for the gemstone lapis lazuli, and the male's brilliant blue and bronze plumage is truly unmistakable. Males of this species sing unique songs comprised of individualized phrases pieced together over an extended period of time, and males typically cannot attract mates until their second season.

HABITAT

Lazuli Buntings breed in a wide variety of brushy deciduous habitats throughout their range, from open forests to mountain slopes and canyons. They are especially fond of riparian woodlands and can be found even in dense growth at isolated springs. This adaptable species is quick to colonize new areas as suitable habitat appears, and has been observed in forests recovering from recent burns and in new growth at the bottom of dry reservoirs (Greene et al. 1996). Atlasers obtained only fifty-three widely scattered potential breeding records for this species in twelve vegetative communities. Sixty-six percent of atlas records were from three riparian communities dominated by either sycamore or cottonwood-willow and typically containing dense undergrowth. Other riparian trees often found in occupied locations were alder, oak, boxelder, ash, and occasionally aspen at higher elevations. In northern Arizona, these buntings also occur locally in open Gambel's oak and New Mexico locust thickets on mountain and canyon slopes. Atlasers encountered Lazuli Buntings nesting very locally and possibly irregularly in exotic Russian olive and tamarisk thickets.

BREEDING

Migrant Lazuli Buntings typically begin to arrive in southern regions of the state by late March or early April and later in April farther north. Males begin singing and establishing territories in late April or early May in Arizona. Females arrive approximately 4–6 days later than the males, and pairs form soon after the females appear (Greene et al. 1996). Female Lazuli Buntings are very secretive while nesting and often remain low in the underbrush, unlike the boldly singing male. Observers obtained only eleven confirmed breeding records for this species; the earliest of these was an observation of a female carrying nesting material on 14 May. Occupied nests have been discovered as early as 27 May (Witzeman et al. 1997), and atlasers reported adults feeding fledged young by 19 June. Additional Arizona breeding records would be needed before the peak nesting period can be determined for the state. However, the Lazuli Bunting's breeding season is quite protracted in Arizona, and atlasers reported nests with eggs as late as 15 August and adults feeding fledged young through 29 August.

Lazuli Buntings have only recently been discovered breeding in southeastern Arizona, and all nesting records in this region are concentrated during the late summer monsoon season. These buntings are typically absent from the area in June but begin arriving in riparian woodlands in early to mid-July. If rains have been sufficient, Lazuli Bunting males will begin singing and establishing territories. During the atlas period in this region, an occupied nest was discovered and adults were observed feeding fledglings in July and August. In 1988, adults were also noted tending fledglings into early September along the upper San Pedro River (T. Corman, personal communication).

Young (1991) reported that Lazuli Buntings begin staging in southeastern Arizona and adjacent regions in late August and September. Here they remain for approximately a month to complete a plumage molt before continuing to their wintering grounds in Mexico. Although small numbers of Lazuli Buntings winter irregularly in southeastern Arizona, most depart by mid-October.

While the male sings nearby, female Lazuli Buntings selects and constructs the cup-shaped nest that is typically concealed low in dense brush. Atlasers did not take measurements at any Lazuli Bunting nests, but data from other

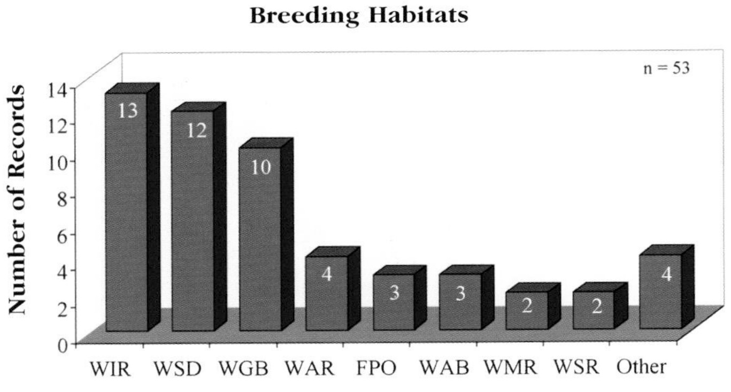

parts of the birds' range suggest that a wide variety of young trees, shrubs, and annuals are used for nesting (Greene et al. 1996). The average height of 125 nests measured in several western states was 3.6 ft (1.1 m; Green et al. 1996).

Lazuli Bunting clutches typically consist of 3–4 eggs (range 1–6), and their incubation period lasts approximately 12 days (Greene et al. 1996). Only the female incubates, and she remains in close proximity to the nest for the entire incubation and brooding period, leaving only to forage nearby. Both parents provide food for young during the nestling stage of 9–11 days and continue supplemental feedings for approximately 2 weeks after fledging (Greene et al. 1996). It is common for Lazuli Buntings to produce two broods per year in southern regions of their range, with the male providing all food to the first brood while the female incubates the second clutch (Greene et al. 1996).

Lazuli Buntings have recently become common Brown-headed Cowbird hosts, especially in riparian areas. In fact, researchers in Montana reported a 100 percent parasitism rate for Lazuli Bunting nests in riparian areas of the Bitterroot Valley (Greene et al. 1996). Although observers did not report any incidents of cowbird brood parasitism during the atlas period, this is likely due to the low number Lazuli Bunting nests they found.

DISTRIBUTION AND STATUS

The Lazuli Bunting's breeding range is restricted to western North America, extending from southern Canada south to coastal northern Baja California and southeastern Arizona. The species breeds east to central North Dakota, western Oklahoma, and possibly western Texas.

Most literature prior to the atlas project considered Lazuli Buntings to be uncommon to fairly common summer residents in central and northern Arizona only (Phillips et al. 1964; Monson and Phillips 1981; Jacobs 1986). This assumption was based on widely scattered breeding records from Prescott, Camp Verde, and the White Mountains northward. Atlasers further document this bunting's sparse and local distribution within the state, but they also encountered it in additional potential breeding areas at elevations ranging from approximately 1900 to 8400 ft (579–2560 m). Because of the secretive nature of the nesting females, observers had difficulty in confirming this species. However, atlasers were able to obtain numerous potential breeding records based on the presence of singing males on territory in June and July.

In the Grand Canyon region, Lazuli Buntings were noted locally on the western slope of the Kaibab Plateau near Big Springs and within the Canyon, where Brown et al. (1987) considered them uncommon breeders in tamarisk thickets and along perennial tributaries. They were encountered in several localities on Navajo and Hopi tribal lands, including Black Mesa, Keams Canyon, Canyon de Chelly, the Chuska Mountains, and Teec Nos Pos. Numerous scattered records were obtained in central Arizona from the White Mountains east to Flagstaff, Camp Verde, Oak Creek Canyon, Cottonwood, and Prescott. The westernmost confirmed nesting records were in the Hualapai, Cerbat, and Black mountains, where they were often detected near springs.

The late summer breeding populations of Lazuli Buntings in southeastern Arizona were confirmed nesting along the upper San Pedro River and near Arivaca. It is likely that these birds also nest locally along the upper Santa Cruz River and Sonoita Creek, as singing males and pairs were regularly encountered in these areas.

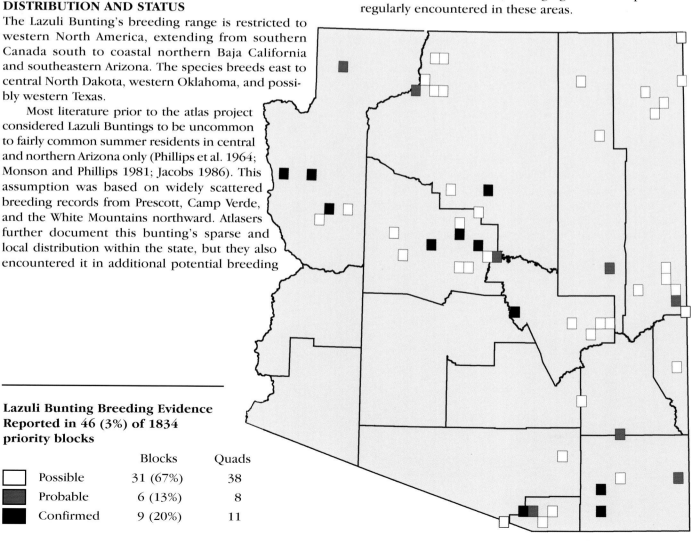

Lazuli Bunting Breeding Evidence Reported in 46 (3%) of 1834 priority blocks

	Blocks	Quads
Possible	31 (67%)	38
Probable	6 (13%)	8
Confirmed	9 (20%)	11

Indigo Bunting

by Troy E. Corman *Passerina cyanea*

A very familiar and common roadside bird in the East, Indigo Buntings began to invade the Southwest more than sixty years ago. These little, intensely blue passerines are widespread but very locally distributed in Arizona. This is likely because of their preference for dense, deciduous woodlands, a scarce habitat in the state.

JIM BURNS

HABITAT

Indigo Bunting territories typically contain areas with low shrubby growth or dense thickets in which to conceal their low nests and nearby tall, broadleaf deciduous trees that serve as singing perches. In Arizona, this combination can be found primarily only in riparian areas. Atlasers reported nearly 36 percent of all records from lowland riparian areas dominated by various willows, Fremont cottonwood, velvet ash, and mesquite (n = 59). Another 32 percent of the records were from foothill drainages and canyons dominated by Arizona sycamore and frequently containing Fremont cottonwood, Arizona walnut, or Arizona alder. North of the Mogollon Rim, Indigo Buntings were encountered locally along drainages containing scattered cottonwoods with thickets of thinleaf alder, Russian olive, or various species of scrub willows. At mid- and higher elevations, ground cover often included raspberry, Arizona rose, and gooseberry. Fewer observations were reported from montane riparian areas with aspen and maple and locally in tamarisk thickets within the Grand Canyon.

BREEDING

In Arizona, the first few Indigo Buntings arrive in late April, but most individuals do not appear until May. The earliest atlas record was of a singing male on 22 April. Pairing typically takes place within a few days of the female's arrival into the male's territory (Carey 1982). The earliest confirmations were of females carrying nesting material on 6 May and nest building on 15 May. Few nests were actually located during the atlas, but egg laying likely begins in mid- to late May. The first nest with eggs reported by atlasers was on 22 June and the first fledglings on 26 June. The peak nesting season of Indigo Buntings could not be determined by the few confirmed atlas records, but the majority of Arizona's nesting records fall between late June and late July. The latest confirmed atlas record was of an adult feeding a fledgling on 19 August and males were observed singing through 10 September in southeastern Arizona. Nesting activity appears to increase during the late summer monsoon period in southeastern Arizona, and some late nesting efforts likely continue through August and into September, well after most atlas surveys had ended. Fall migration in the state begins by September, with stragglers remaining regularly to early October and casually into early December.

Only the female Indigo Bunting builds the nest, but she is sometimes accompanied by the male, who takes no part in the nest construction (Payne 1992). Early in the breeding season a nest may be constructed in 8–10 days; however, some nests are completed in as little as 2 days later in the summer (Payne 1972). Few nests have been described in Arizona, and plants used to support the nest are likely quite varied. In other parts of its range, nests are typically constructed in dense cover 1.0–3.3 ft (0.3–1.0 m) above the ground, incorporating several vertical or oblique stems of a branching forb or shrub as support (Payne 1972).

Indigo Buntings lay a full clutch containing 3–4 eggs, which are incubated by the female for 12–13 days (Taber and Johnston 1968). At most nests, only the female feeds the nestlings until they depart the nest in 9–12 days. A few days after nest departure, males often take over the feeding of the fledglings, allowing the female to attempt a second brood quickly (Payne 1992). Such relief from caring for fledged young may be the male's main direct contribution to breeding success of the female on his territory (Payne 1992).

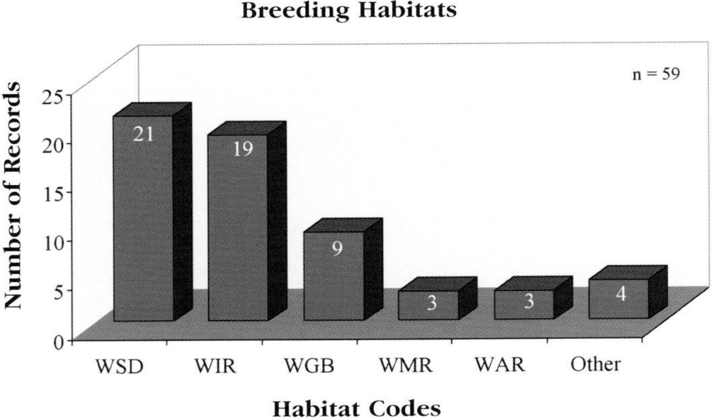

Throughout their range, many Indigo Bunting nests are parasitized by Brown-headed Cowbirds. Atlasers discovered a nest with a cowbird egg in Oak Creek Canyon on 22 June.

DISTRIBUTION AND STATUS

Indigo Buntings are found nesting throughout eastern United States and adjacent Canada, west throughout much of the Great Plains to the Rocky Mountains. Swarth (1918) obtained the first Arizona specimen of this bunting on 30 June 1917 in the Sierra Ancha northwest of Globe. However, populations began to expand noticeably into the southwest in the 1940s. Phillips et al. (1964) described Indigo Buntings as rare migrants, nesting locally at least in Oak Creek Canyon and Prescott areas, and possibly in the Sierra Ancha and along the White River in White Mountain Apache tribal land. Phillips et al. also suggested that it was unlikely that these buntings nested south of the Salt River. They were confirmed nesting in the bottom of the Grand Canyon in 1964 and in southeastern Arizona by 1967 (Monson and Phillips 1981). By the 1970s, Rosenberg et al. (1991) considered Indigo Buntings as uncommon but local summer residents in the lower Colorado River valley.

During the atlas period, Indigo Buntings were noted as widespread but a very local breeding species throughout much of northern, central, and eastern Arizona at elevations ranging from 480 to 7500 ft (146–2286 m). Atlas data suggest that these buntings could be found nesting throughout the state where patches of appropriate habitat exist. However, they were most consistently found in larger and more continuous stands of tall, deciduous trees such as along Arivaca, Sonoita, and Oak creeks, and within the San Pedro, Santa Cruz, Verde, Agua Fria, and Santa Maria river drainages. In the White Mountains, atlasers encountered Indigo Buntings primarily along the Little Colorado River, Blue River, and Nutrioso Creek. They likely continue to nest locally along other drainages within the adjacent White Mountain Apache tribal lands, but atlasers were unable to acquire access permits to conduct surveys on this reservation. Other than within the Grand Canyon, atlasers noted Indigo Buntings to be largely absent from drainages dominated by exotic tamarisk, such as along the lower Colorado, Salt, and Gila rivers.

Most atlas observations consisted of a bold, singing territorial male. The drab nesting females are much more secretive, often remaining low in dense cover, and therefore easily overlooked. Many localities contain just a single pair, but at least fifteen pairs were detected along a 5 mi (8 km) surveyed section of the Santa Cruz River south of Tubac in late July 2001. Where breeding territories overlap in Arizona, these buntings will hybridize with Lazuli Buntings.

Breeding populations of these attractive buntings will likely continue increasing in Arizona as more riparian areas are protected and enhanced within the state. However, groundwater withdrawal, inappropriate livestock grazing practices, and wildfires continue to threaten their preferred riparian habits in the state.

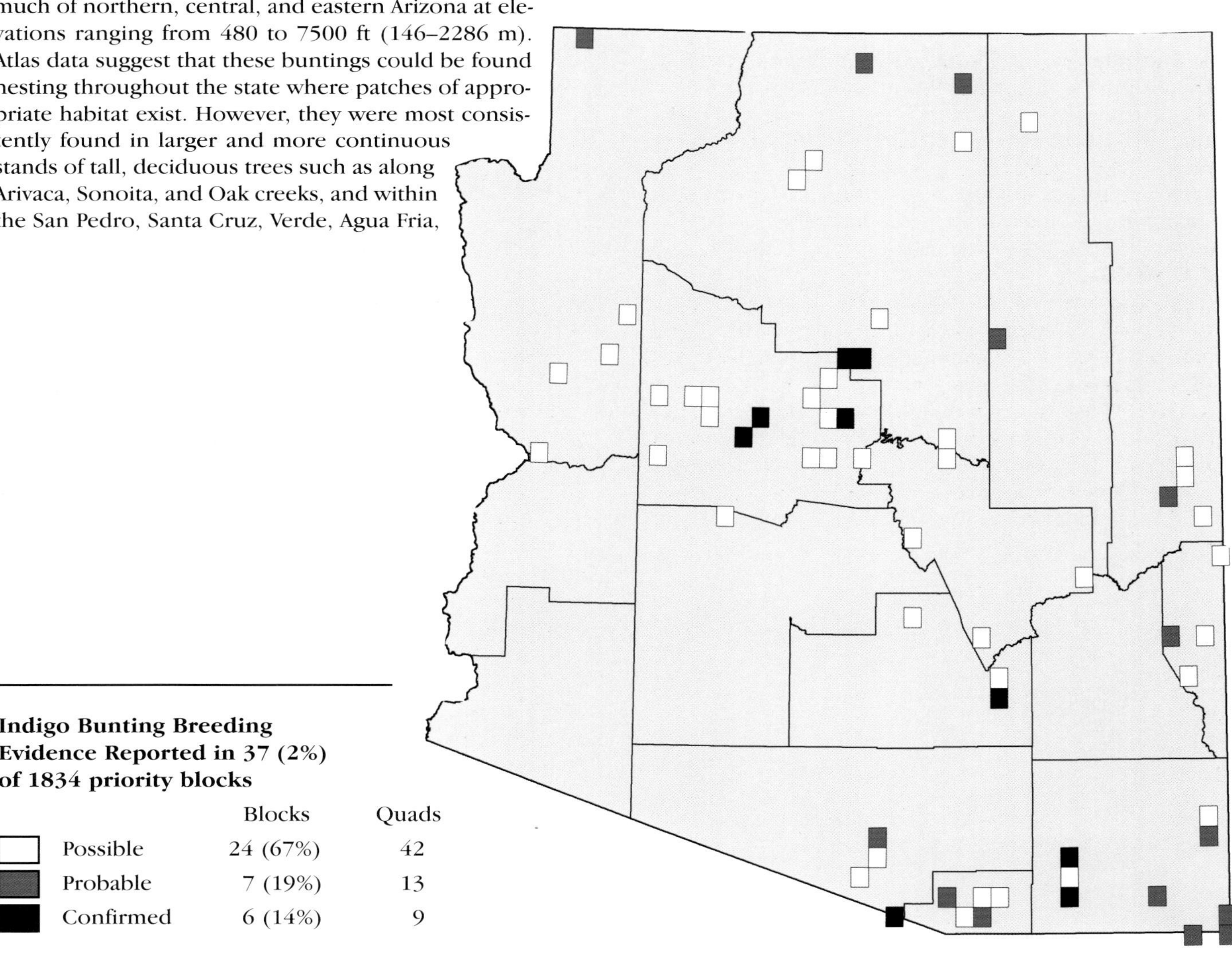

Indigo Bunting Breeding Evidence Reported in 37 (2%) of 1834 priority blocks

	Blocks	Quads
Possible	24 (67%)	42
Probable	7 (19%)	13
Confirmed	6 (14%)	9

Varied Bunting

by Troy E. Corman *Passerina versicolor*

Often appearing black at a distance, a male Varied Bunting under appropriate lighting conditions is a spectacular bird indeed, with its intense combination of purple, blue, and red. Although arriving in late spring in Arizona, it routinely postpones nesting activity until the initiation of the late summer monsoon season.

HABITAT

In Arizona, Varied Buntings typically inhabit brushy arid slopes, canyons, and dry washes. Approximately 71 percent of all atlas observations of this bunting were noted along drainage edges containing mesquite and netleaf hackberry, with or without a scattering of cottonwood, willow, ash, or sycamore (n = 73). They often spend much of their time on the adjacent arid slopes among dense thicket of shrubby mesquite, graythorn, ocotillo, hopbush, cacti, and other low, thorny shrubs. Locally, especially at the western edge of their range, atlasers noted Varied Buntings in dense Sonoran desertscrub vegetation, which often included mesquite, paloverde, ironwood, wolfberry, and saguaro. Atlasers also occasionally encountered this bunting in the dense mesquite thickets surrounding earthen livestock tanks, water catchments, and irrigation ditches.

BREEDING

Most Varied Buntings typically do not arrive in the state until the second week of May, although occasionally as early late April. Males arrive on territory just prior to the females and immediately initiate singing. The amount of song is initially high, then rapidly decreases as pair bonds and territories are reestablished (Groschupf and Thompson 1998). Singing typically does not resume until after the first significant late summer rainfall initiates the beginning of the monsoon season and nest building activity. However, highly unusual was a pair observed at the Boyce Thompson Arboretum just prior to the atlas project that constructed a nest and was incubating three eggs by 13 June 1992 (C. Tomoff, personal communication). This unusually early nesting was likely in response to an exceptionally wet winter and spring at this location, with above average rain continuing well into May when the birds arrived.

The earliest confirmed atlas breeding observation was an adult carrying a fecal sac (indicating a nest with young) on 25 July. This would suggest egg laying by mid-July. Studies have found that the initial egg laying coincides with the first significant summer rainstorm in an area and during poor rainfall years, this may be delayed until mid-August (Groschupf and Thompson 1998). Therefore, it is not unusual to have nesting activity continuing well into September. Atlasers observed adults feeding fledglings as late as 22 September and an exceptionally late nesting was noted near Patagonia in 1999, when an adult was observed feeding a fledgling on 9 October (N. Crook, personal communication). Most Varied Buntings have migrated south of Arizona by the end of September and are casually report into mid-October.

Presumably only the female constructs the nest. Located approximately 2.2–4.2 ft (0.7–1.27 m) above the ground, the nest is typically placed in dense cover of thorny shrubs near a wash or on the adjacent slope (Groschupf and Thompson 1998). In Arizona, nests are often constructed in velvet mesquite, desert hackberry, catclaw acacia, and graythorn. Varied Buntings lay a typical clutch of 3–4 eggs, with 3 being most common in Arizona (Groschupf and Thompson 1998). As in other North American buntings, the incubation period is approximately 13–14 days and is performed only by the drab female (Groschupf and Thompson 1998). The nestlings are fed by both parents and likely fledge in 12–14 days, but are capable of short flights and scurry along the ground at 10–11 days (Groschupf and Thompson 1998). Most evidence suggests these buntings produce only one brood per season, but will renest if earlier attempts fail.

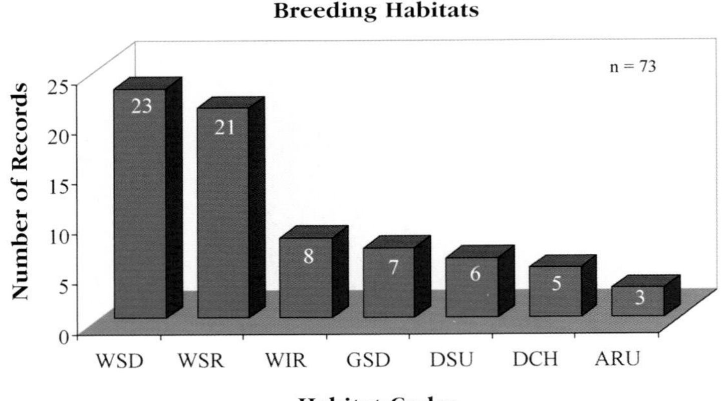

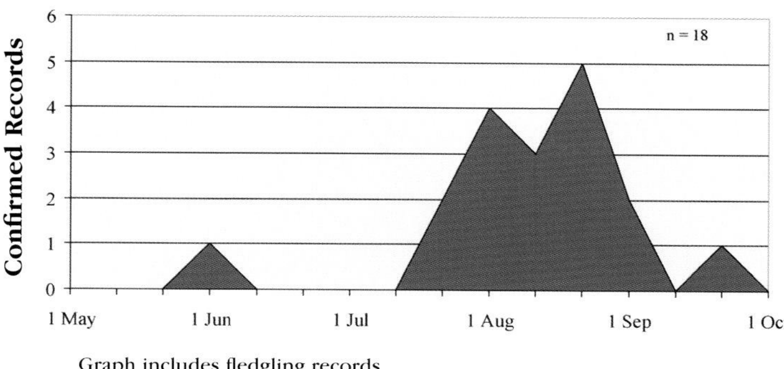

Graph includes fledgling records

Brown-headed Cowbirds brood parasitism is relatively frequent for this bunting in Arizona. As an example, Groschupf and Thompson (1998) reported a nest near Patagonia that held only three cowbird nestlings ready to fledge.

DISTRIBUTION AND STATUS

Varied Buntings breed along the southern borders of Arizona, New Mexico, and Texas, south through much of Mexico, with disjunct populations south to Guatemala. Only the more northern populations appear to be migratory. Once considered a very rare summer resident, Phillips et al. (1964) noted these buntings as locally uncommon in southern Arizona north to the Santa Catalina Mountains and west perhaps to the Ajo area and east to Patagonia and Guadalupe Canyon. By 1980, it was considered locally uncommon to common in the state, with singing males noted north to upper Aravaipa Canyon, Graham County, and west to near Portal (Monson and Phillips 1981). Since 1988, Varied Buntings have been found nesting irregularly at the Boyce Thompson Arboretum near Superior (C. Tomoff, personal communication), which represents Arizona's and the species' northernmost nesting locality.

Atlasers helped document the continued steady increase of the Varied Bunting's breeding distribution in Arizona, where it was found at elevations from 1350 to 5100 ft (411–1554 m). However, atlas blocks not surveyed after early July could have easily missed this late-nesting species. They were most abundant on the lower slopes of the Santa Rita Mountains, south to Patagonia and Nogales, and west along the Mexico border to the slopes of the Baboquivari Mountains. To the east, Varied Buntings were much more widespread than prior literature suggested, but populations are more local with fewer individuals. Here they were found along the upper San Pedro River from south of Saint David to Hereford, in the Mule Mountains near Bisbee, and as far north in the Sulphur Springs Valley as the Swisshelm Mountains and just south of Gleeson. They were fairly common along the Mexico border east of Douglas to Guadalupe Canyon and uncommon in the Portal area. In Graham County, a singing male was detected along the Gila River near San Jose.

Varied Buntings were found sparingly west of the Baboquivari Mountains through Tohono O'odham tribal lands to Organ Pipe Cactus National Monument at Bates Well. They were confirmed breeding locally along washes and in canyons of the Sauceda and Sand Tank mountains in southern Maricopa County. This handsome bunting was encountered at several locations along the southern and western slopes of the Santa Catalina and Rincon mountains and in Buehman Canyon on the eastern slope. The most northern potential nesting location remains at the Boyce Thompson Arboretum and nearby Whitlow Dam area.

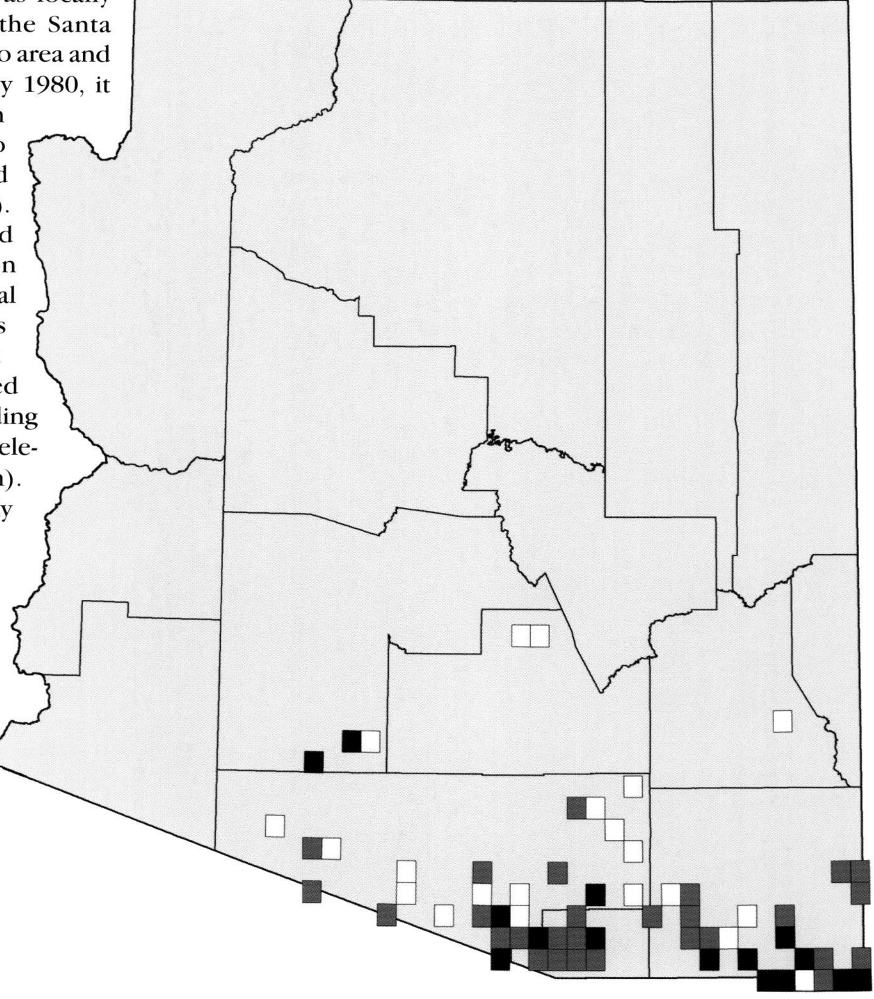

Varied Bunting Breeding Evidence Reported in 50 (3%) of 1834 priority blocks

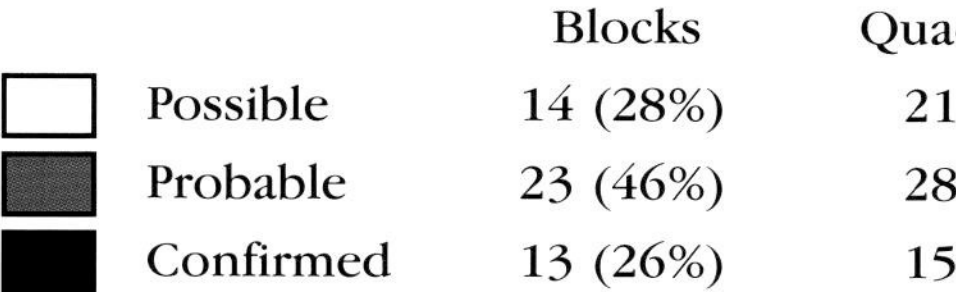

	Blocks	Quad
Possible	14 (28%)	21
Probable	23 (46%)	28
Confirmed	13 (26%)	15

Red-winged Blackbird

by Greg S. Clark *Agelaius phoeniceus*

The Red-winged Blackbird is one of the most numerous and well studied of North American songbirds. Taken for granted as a common bird, it has been invaluable to researchers to learn about bird territoriality, mate selection, and predator avoidance. There is much to admire about this widespread, adaptable bird.

HABITAT

Red-winged Blackbirds are highly gregarious birds that generally select dense cover for both nesting and roosting where rich food sources of either insects or seeds are available (Yasukawa and Searcy 1995). During the breeding season in Arizona, these blackbirds are strongly associated with emergent vegetation, riparian groves, and irrigated agricultural lands, where the males sing conspicuously from elevated perches. Of the 250 potential breeding records obtained by atlasers, approximately 50 percent were reported from marshes, ponds, lakes, and river edges containing cattails, bulrushes, or other emergent vegetation. This includes the open borders of cottonwood- and willow-dominated drainages. These adaptable birds readily take advantage of some human-modified habitats as well. Approximately 36 percent of atlas records for this species were reported in rural and agricultural settings that provide sufficient cover to meet nesting requirements. Within these environments, Red-winged Blackbirds were noted nesting in irrigated croplands such as alfalfa, hay, and grains, and among emergent vegetation in canals, ditches, irrigation holding ponds, and wetlands at wastewater treatment facilities. They were also noted nesting locally in flooded exotic tamarisk stands.

BREEDING

Although a proportion of the state's populations are year-round residents, many of Arizona's Red-winged Blackbirds are migratory birds that winter in the state in huge flocks. Spring migration begins in February and early March, approximately the same period when territorial singing commences in Arizona's lowland marshes. Atlasers reported the earliest nest building activity on 10 April, although they may locally begin in late March. The earliest nest with young was discovered on 21 April, indicating clutch initiation by early April. Based on statewide atlas data, breeding activity peaks from late May through mid-June but continues through the summer. Atlasers reported nests with eggs through 2 August and adults carrying food as late as 26 August. In general, the birds tend to begin nesting activity slightly later at higher elevations and more northern locations in Arizona. The timing of fall migration is difficult to determine due to widespread summer dispersal of individuals and flocks but apparently peaks in October in Arizona.

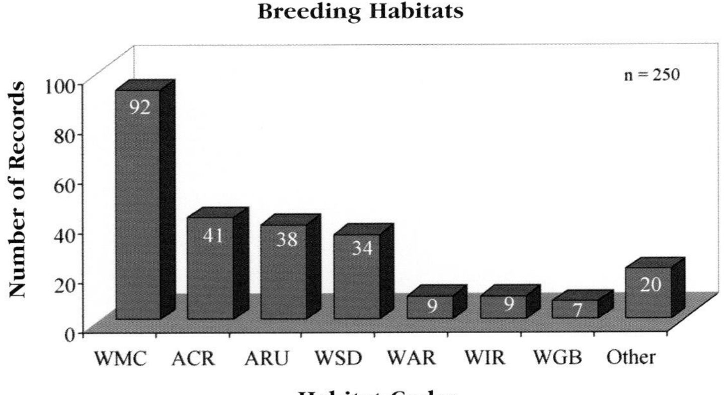

Nest sites are chosen by the female Red-winged Blackbird, and she alone constructs the open-cup nest (Yasukawa and Searcy 1995). Most nests are built over or adjacent to water in dense marsh vegetation, typically below 3 ft (0.9 m) in height. However, in irrigated agricultural areas, they use field crops such as wheat or alfalfa. These resourceful birds will also nest in flooded young trees and shrubs in Arizona such as willow, seepwillow, tamarisk, mesquite, and elderberry (Phillips et al. 1964). Three nests described by atlasers were all in cattail stands.

Typically nesting in large colonies, Red-winged Blackbirds are strongly polygynous, with males often having harems of five or more nesting females within a territory (Yasukawa and Searcy 1995). Most clutches consist of 3–4 eggs, but may range from 2 to 6 eggs (Ehrlich et al. 1988). Only the female incubates while the male performs predator vigilance, and incubation requires 11–13 days (Yasukawa and Searcy 1995). Both parents bring food to the nestlings, but typically the male brings a much smaller percentage due to other duties. However, there are examples where the male brings significantly more food, and this characteristic may vary with habitat type or geographic location (Yasukawa and Searcy 1995). Should the female be lost, the male is capable of rearing the brood alone. Nestlings depart the nest in 11–14 days (Ehrlich et al. 1988) and both parents, especially the female, will feed fledglings for up to two weeks on

Breeding Phenology

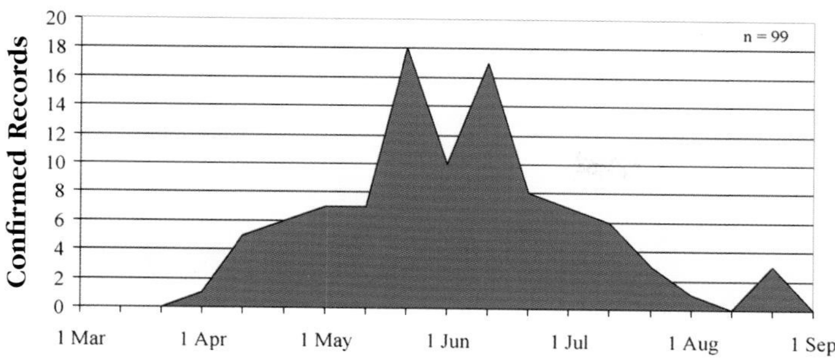

territory (Yasukawa and Searcy 1995). Red-winged Blackbirds often rear two broods per year, but occasionally three are produced (Ehrlich et al. 1988). They are considered to be frequent hosts for Brown-headed Cowbirds (Yasukawa and Searcy 1995), but atlasers reported no incidents of cowbird parasitism.

DISTRIBUTION AND STATUS

North America's most widespread and abundant blackbird, Red-winged Blackbirds nest from Alaska to Newfoundland and south through Mexico and locally to Costa Rica. Northern populations are primarily migratory. In Arizona, Red-winged Blackbirds nest in appropriate habitat nearly statewide and are often considered locally abundant in marshes and irrigated farmland (Phillips et al. 1964; Rosenberg et al. 1991). Observers reported the birds over a wide range of elevations and confirmed the species breeding on priority blocks from approximately 80 ft (24 m) along the lower Colorado River to 9200 ft (2804 m) at lakes in the White Mountains.

Red-winged Blackbirds appear to reach their highest breeding densities in agricultural river valleys of Arizona, where they find nesting and foraging habitat in abundance. They were encountered throughout the heavily farmed lower Colorado and Gila River valleys, where Breeding Bird Survey data also reveal their greatest abundance in the state (Price et al. 1995). Atlasers noted that these blackbirds were more locally distributed north of the Mogollon Rim, with concentrations in the White Mountains region north to Saint Johns and from Williams to the Mormon Lake area. Appropriate habitat is limited on the Navajo and Hopi tribal lands, but this species is routinely found nesting where emergent vegetation stands occur. Owing to the nature of priority block selection and atlas surveys, many local nesting sites such as at isolated farm or ranch ponds, were likely missed and are not represented on the accompanying map.

Many natural marshes, cienegas, and springs have been lost in Arizona due to water diversions, damming, groundwater pumping, and urban and agricultural development. However, numerous additional human-made habitats have been created that now harbor large nesting populations of Red-winged Blackbirds. Overall, populations appear to be fairly secure for these readily adaptable and resourceful birds in Arizona.

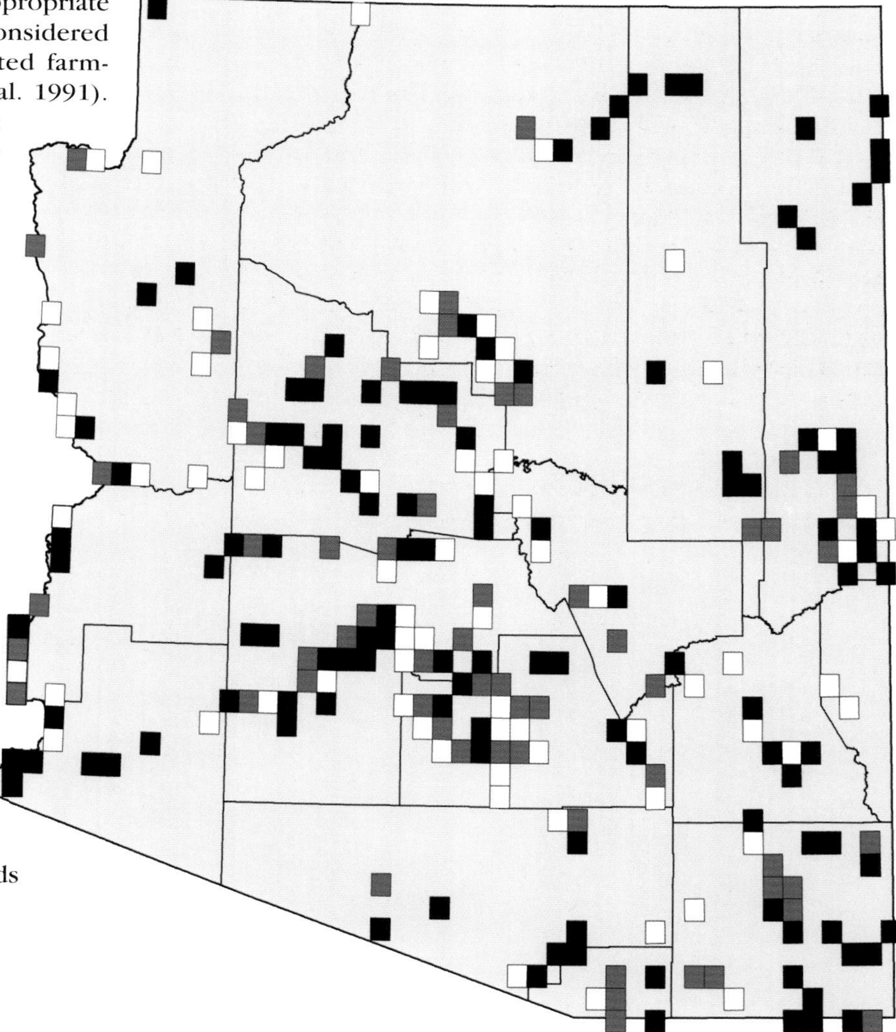

Red-winged Blackbird Breeding Evidence Reported in 205 (11%) of 1834 priority blocks

	Blocks	Quads
Possible	54 (26%)	71
Probable	47 (23%)	61
Confirmed	104 (51%)	123

Eastern Meadowlark

by Troy E. Corman *Sturnella magna*

Reaching its westernmost range in Arizona, the Eastern Meadowlark trills a sweet, lilting song that is a welcomed early spring sound in a variety of grasslands across the state. Also known as Lilian's Meadowlark, the pale race nesting in Arizona has extensive white outer tail feathers and noted by some authorities as a separate species.

JIM BURNS

HABITAT

Familiar birds of open grassy landscapes, Eastern Meadowlarks are often encountered as they sing from the top of an exposed low perch such as a fence post or low woody shrub. In Arizona, they reach their highest breeding abundance in semiarid grasslands of the southeast. This grassland community often includes scattered low shrubs such as young mesquite and acacia, and accounted for 44 percent of all potential atlas records for this species (n = 178). They rarely share their southeastern breeding habitat with their Western counterpart. On the contrary, in northern Arizona the Western Meadowlark can often be heard singing in many of the same open plains and cold-temperate grasslands that harbor Eastern Meadowlarks. Atlasers also regularly encountered these birds inhabiting the high mountain subalpine grasslands of east-central Arizona. Eastern Meadowlarks were reported infrequently in wet meadows and in adjacent agricultural fields of grain and alfalfa.

BREEDING

Atlas data indicate that Eastern Meadowlarks have a fairly long nesting season in Arizona, particularly in the southeast. Singing typically begins to escalate in February and pair bonding soon follows. The species is highly polygynous, and researchers have estimated that 50–80 percent of all male Eastern Meadowlarks have two (rarely three) mates concurrently (Lanyon 1995).

Early nest building and egg laying activity likely begins in March as adults were observed carrying food as early as 7 April in southeastern Arizona. Atlas data suggest that Eastern Meadowlarks that migrate to northern Arizona in March and April, may initiate breeding approximately a month later as the earliest confirmation was also of an adult carrying food on 18 May north of the San Francisco Mountains. Likely in response to late summer monsoon rains and the subsequent increase in insect prey abundance in southeastern Arizona, atlasers documented nesting activity regularly throughout August and into September. The latest nest with young reported by atlasers was found on 1 September and adults were observed carrying food as late as 8 September. However, they have been observed carrying food as late as 22 September in the southeast. Because most atlas surveys ended well before September, nesting activity this late in the season may be more common than atlas records indicate. Eastern Meadowlarks begin arriving in nonbreeding areas in September, but may linger in the north into November, occasionally later (Phillips et al. 1964).

The female Eastern Meadowlark alone constructs the often well-concealed nest, which is built on the ground in a shallow depression and typically includes a low arching grassy dome above (Bent 1958). The time required to build the nest varies from 4 to 8 days (Lanyon 1995). The depression is lined with fine grass blades, and the female constructs the dome with coarse dried grasses and forbs, which are generally interlaced with grasses and annuals growing next to the nest. This helps conceal the nest and protects the eggs and young from sun and rain (Bent 1958).

The female incubates the clutch of 4–5 (range 2–7) eggs for 13–15 days (Bent 1958). Both parents feed the nestlings for 10–12 days and the fledglings for an additional 2–3 weeks following nest departure (Lanyon 1995). The female has been known to begin constructing a second nest a few days after the young leave the first, and the male is left with full parental duty once she begins to incubate the second clutch (Bent 1958). Eastern Meadowlarks are not known to have more than two successful nestings per year;

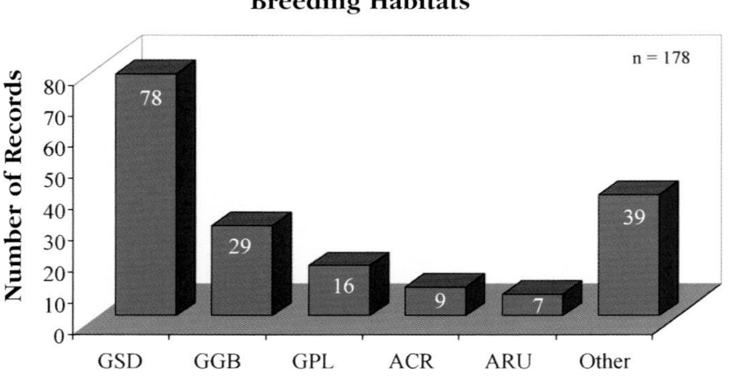

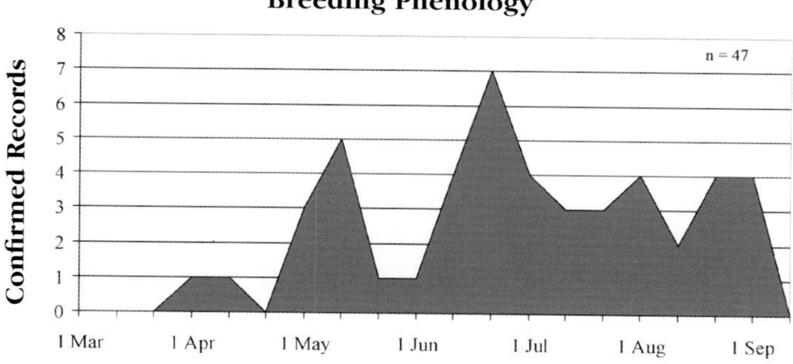

however, the lengthy breeding season of the little studied southeastern Arizona population may allow for a greater number of successful broods.

DISTRIBUTION AND STATUS

The Eastern Meadowlark has an extensive breeding range that includes southeastern Canada south through the eastern, central, and southwestern United States and on through Central America and northern South America (American Ornithologists' Union 1998). Phillips et al. (1964) described this meadowlark as a fairly common summer resident in southeastern, central, and northern Arizona. Northern populations are at least partially migratory and likely account for the individuals and small, local wintering flocks found in agricultural regions of the lower Gila and sparingly lower Colorado River valleys.

During the atlas period, Eastern Meadowlarks were commonly encountered nesting in the grasslands of southeastern Arizona. Within this region of the state, they breed at elevations ranging from 3500 to 5000 ft (1067–1524 m). They range west to the Altar Valley and basically north to the Sulphur Springs Valley in Graham County and just west of Duncan. Atlasers also encountered these meadowlarks nesting in the higher grasslands north of the Natanes Mountains on the San Carlos Apache tribal lands.

Eastern Meadowlarks were noted fairly commonly in the cooler subalpine grasslands of the White Mountains region, where they were confirmed nesting at elevations as high as 9000 ft (2743 m). They were also more widespread than previous literature suggested north of the White Mountains, where they were found as far north as Petrified Forest National Park and west to near Chevelon Creek in Coconino County. The westernmost breeding populations were noted from Prescott and Chino valleys north to the Coconino Plateau. They were previously unknown as a breeding bird west of Coconino County, but atlasers documented singing and calling birds into Mohave County near Peach Springs and Truxton. Although confirmed nesting west of Wupatki National Monument, these meadowlarks were not reported from the general Flagstaff-Mormon Lake areas, where they historically occurred.

Eastern Meadowlark populations appear to be relatively stable in Arizona and can still be found throughout most of their historical distribution within the state. However, like most other grassland dependent species in Arizona, their preferred habitat is threatened in many localities by urban development, inappropriate grazing practices, and many other human-influenced activities.

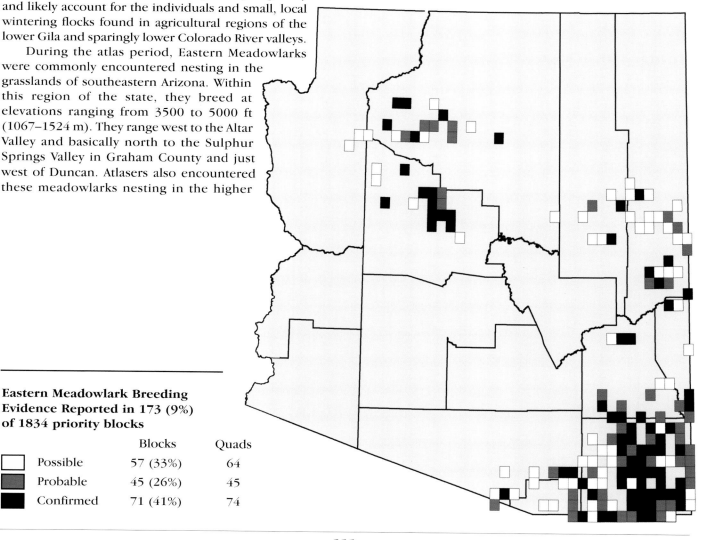

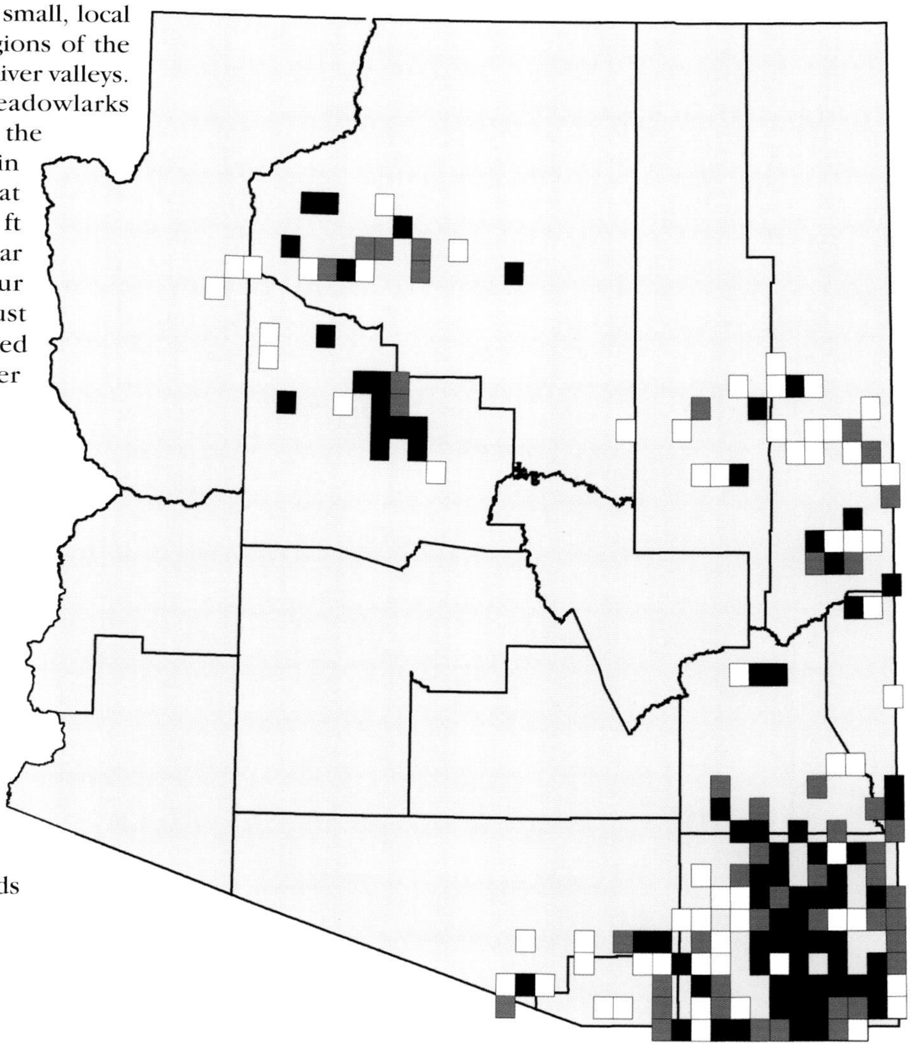

Eastern Meadowlark Breeding Evidence Reported in 173 (9%) of 1834 priority blocks

	Blocks	Quads
Possible	57 (33%)	64
Probable	45 (26%)	45
Confirmed	71 (41%)	74

Western Meadowlark

by Cathryn Wise-Gervais *Sturnella neglecta*

Western Meadowlarks are common along roadsides, where they will perch on fence posts to sing or simply survey the surrounding terrain. The "chuck" call and cheerful bubbling song of this yellow-breasted prairie dweller are distinctive, and they allow observers to discern Western from Eastern Meadowlarks quickly.

JIM BURNS

HABITAT

Western Meadowlarks are birds of open country that are typically encountered in grasslands, rural areas with pastures, fallow fields, croplands, and desert flats. Atlasers reported Western Meadowlarks in twenty-three vegetative communities, although 58 percent of records were from three grassland and desertscrub associations in the northern half of Arizona (n = 359). Typical occupied locations in this region of the state include rolling expanses of grasslands with varying amounts of low woody shrub such as sagebrush, saltbush, blackbrush, and occasional scattered juniper stands. Atlasers reported a total of 18 percent of Western Meadowlark records in several rural settings, including irrigated cropland such as alfalfa and grains fields, pastures, and fallow areas. Western Meadowlarks also nest locally in semiarid grasslands and in high-elevation montane meadows. As noted by Phillips et al. (1964), following winters with above normal precipitation, atlasers encountered these meadowlarks nesting irregularly and sparsely in desertscrub associations. Apparently, during these wetter years, some Western Meadowlarks take advantage of the lush spring growth of grasses and annuals (and elevated insect density) to nest in these typically unsuitable arid landscapes.

In many parts of the state, Western and Eastern Meadowlarks occur sympatrically, often to varying degrees from year to year. There seem to be no clear formulas describing the habitat preference of one species versus the other. However, Western Meadowlarks regularly occupy drier and less densely vegetated terrain than Eastern Meadowlarks and are typically absent as a nesting species in Arizona's southeastern grasslands.

Breeding Habitats

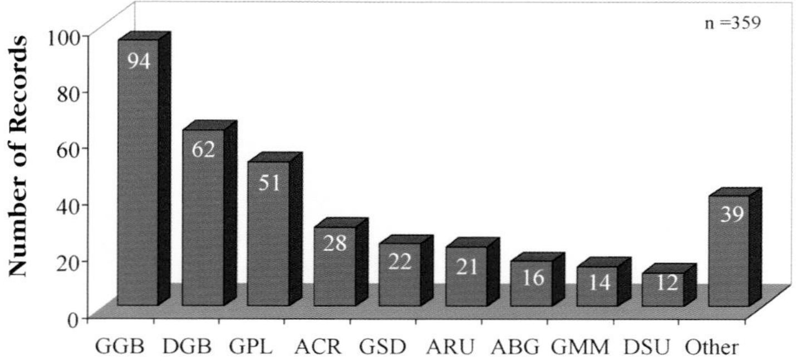

BREEDING

Western Meadowlarks occur year-round in Arizona, although migrants from the north augment winter populations. In lowland desert and agricultural regions, atlasers noted singing birds by mid-February and nest building activity by 27 March. An adult was observed carrying food on 12 April, indicating clutch initiation by late March as well. Atlas data suggest that nesting activity at higher elevations and more northern localities may begin a month or so later. Owing to the secretive nature of this species while nesting and the cryptic character of the nests, atlasers discovered few active nests. Statewide atlas data suggest that Western Meadowlark breeding activity peaks in mid-June, then tapers off, with minor levels of activities continuing to early August. However, most atlas breeding confirmations were of adults carrying food or feeding fledglings; therefore, this peak may only represent the seasonal height of nests with young and fledglings. Observers last reported adults with fledglings on 14 August. Fall migrants begin appearing in September, and the birds will form sizable wintering flocks at this time.

Western Meadowlarks build domed grass nests that, despite their considerable size, are well concealed and difficult to detect. Nests are comprised of grasses and stems and often are associated with elaborate entrance tunnels that can be several feet long (Lanyon 1994). Atlasers took measurements at only four nests, and all were placed on the ground under vegetation clumps. Overhanging plants included grasses, winterfat, and filaree. Females alone gather nesting material and build the nest, and males show no interest in either the nest or eggs (Lanyon 1994).

Females lay 3–7 eggs (Baicich and Harrison 1997) and incubate these for 13–14 days (Lanyon 1994). Both parents feed the young, but because males often have two mates,

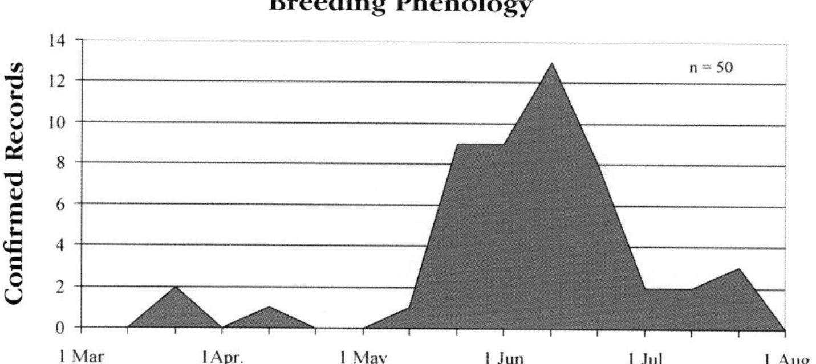

his level of involvement varies as he divides his time between multiple nests (Lanyon 1994). Young fledge at approximately 10–12 days, but parents continue feeding them for another two weeks after fledging (Lanyon 1994). Female Western Meadowlarks frequently attempt to produce two broods per year and will renest several times if earlier efforts fail (Lanyon 1994).

DISTRIBUTION AND STATUS

As their name implies, Western Meadowlarks breed primarily west of the Mississippi River, but also nest east through Michigan and southern Ontario. They range north to the prairie and plains regions of south-central Canada south to central Mexico and east from the Pacific Coast to central Texas. The species formerly bred only to the forest edge in Missouri, Illinois, and Wisconsin, but because of agricultural expansion in the twentieth century, Western Meadowlarks were able to expand their range east and north (Lanyon 1994).

Atlasers encountered Western Meadowlarks in suitable breeding habitat throughout their previously described range in Arizona (Phillips et al. 1964; Monson and Phillips 1981). Atlas data reveal that these birds establish breeding territories at elevations from approximately 120 ft (37 m) in agricultural lands south of Yuma to 9200 ft (2804 m) in montane grasslands in the White Mountains. In northern Arizona, they were fairly widespread in grassland associations north of the Mogollon Rim and south through Chino Valley and the Agua Fria National Monument. Toward the northwest, Western Meadowlarks were regularly encountered in the Arizona Strip region and south to the Sacramento, Detrital, and Hualapai valleys west and north of Kingman. These meadowlarks were previously not well documented as a nesting species in Mohave County, although Brown et al. (1987) considered them a fairly common summer resident in the Toroweap Valley. Western Meadowlarks were mostly absent in Cochise, Graham, and Santa Cruz counties, where Eastern Meadowlarks reach their highest densities in the state. However, Phillips et al. (1964) reported this species nesting at least once in an exceptionally wet year (1941) in the Sulphur Springs Valley.

In southwestern and south-central Arizona, Western Meadowlarks were detected primarily only within rural and agricultural dominated regions of the lower Colorado, Gila, and Santa Cruz River valleys. They were also regularly encountered in the extensive irrigated farmlands between Vicksburg and the Aguila Valley and Harquahala Plains.

Breeding Bird Survey data suggest a slightly declining trend for Western Meadowlarks rangewide. Atlasers reported this species throughout their known historical range and in additional locations as well, suggesting that this grassland songster is fairly secure in Arizona, but more study is need to determine population trends in the state.

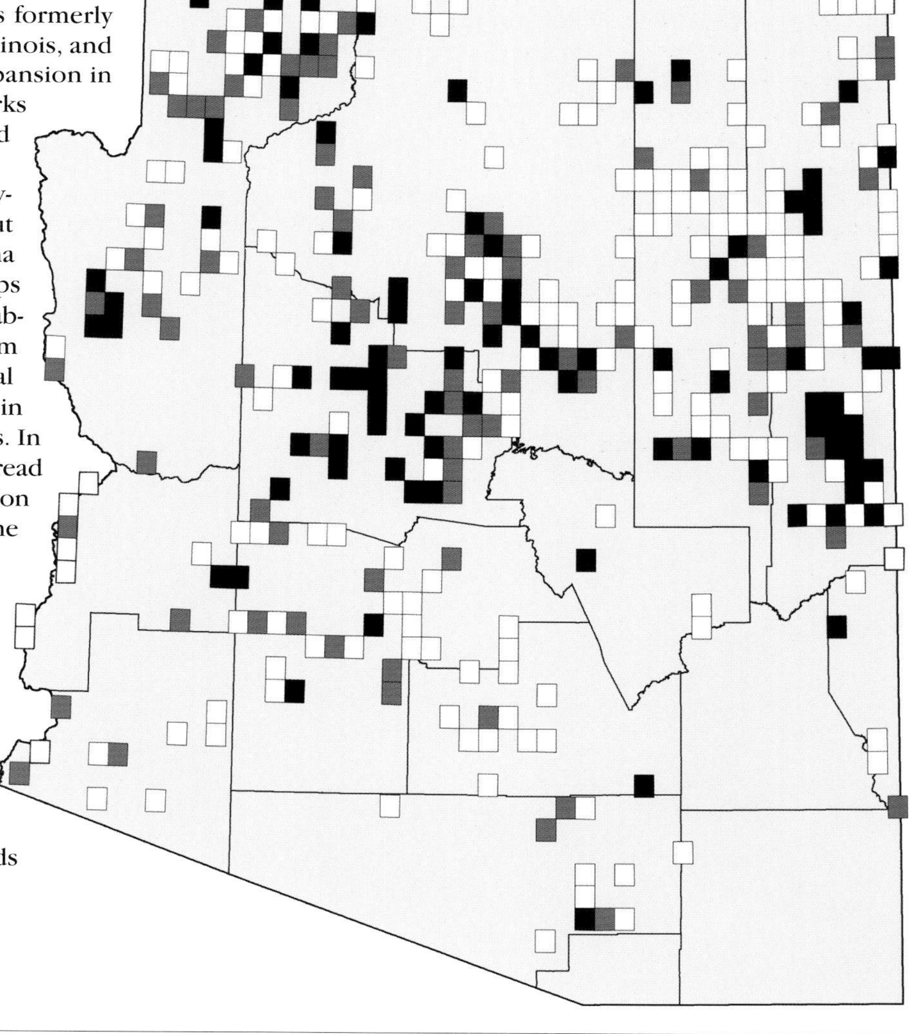

Western Meadowlark Breeding Evidence Reported in 370 (20 %) of 1834 priority blocks

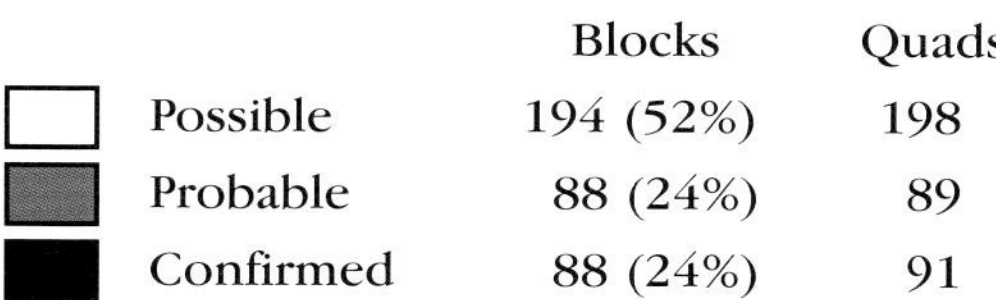

	Blocks	Quads
Possible	194 (52%)	198
Probable	88 (24%)	89
Confirmed	88 (24%)	91

Yellow-headed Blackbird

by Troy E. Corman

Xanthocephalus xanthocephalus

The grating series of gasps and screeches produced by the courting male Yellow-headed Blackbird is in sharp contrast to the strikingly handsome bird himself. A breathtaking winter experience is to witness the synchronized flight of thousands of these showy males as they repeatedly lift and settle over agricultural fields, flashes of brilliant yellow and white in a rolling sea of black.

GEORGE ANDREJKO

HABITAT

Typically encountered roosting and nesting in emergent wetland vegetation, Yellow-headed Blackbirds are not as ubiquitous in Arizona as their Red-winged counterparts. However, some nesting colonies in the state are quite large. Although stands of cattails and bulrushes are the most frequently used marshland vegetation for nesting, there are many localities within the state that provide extensive stands of this habitat but lack breeding populations of Yellow-headed Blackbirds. Atlasers also found these blackbirds nesting very locally in flooded shoreline trees such as willow and tamarisk. Nesting colonies were found along rivers, ponds, and lakes, including wetlands at wastewater facilities and irrigation runoff ponds in agricultural areas. Yellow-headed Blackbirds typically nest over deeper water, frequently in the densest and most shaded section of the stand. They often nest in the same wetlands as the more abundant Red-winged Blackbird, which are relegated to nest in emergent vegetation over shallower water by the more dominant Yellow-headed Blackbird (Orians and Willson 1964). During the nesting season, they forage almost exclusively within the wetlands when aquatic insects are abundant and in nearby irrigated agricultural fields when wetland insects are in short supply (Twedt and Crawford 1995).

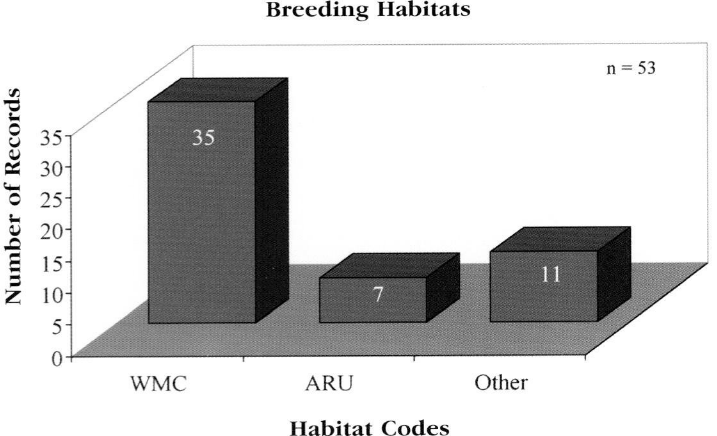

BREEDING

Male Yellow-headed Blackbirds typically begin to establish territories approximately 1–2 weeks before the arrival of the females. The earliest singing individual reported by atlasers was on 27 March. Atlasers noted nest building activity by 24 April and nest with eggs by 1 May. However, an adult observed carrying food by 5 May would suggest egg laying by late April. Similarly, a study along the lower Colorado River reported females nest building by mid-April and that most nests contained eggs by 22 April and the first nestling was noted on 29 April (Rosenberg et al. 1991). Likely because of the birds' deep wetland nesting sites, atlasers reported relatively few active nests. Most confirmations were observations of adults either carrying nesting material or food. Atlasers observed nest building activity through 24 June and reported adults feeding fledglings through 11 August.

Some adult male Yellow-headed Blackbirds initiated fall migration quite early, and begin to appear well away from nesting areas by late June and early July in Arizona. However, most individuals depart the higher elevation breeding grounds during late August and early September, with few remaining north of the Mogollon Rim after mid-October. Yellow-headed Blackbirds winter in large, primarily all-male flocks, in southern and western Arizona marshes, agricultural areas, and livestock feedlots. Most of the females winter much farther south in central Mexico (Phillips et al. 1964).

Male Yellow-headed Blackbirds are typically polygynous and generally have a harem of 2–6 females (Twedt and Crawford 1995). Nest construction is conducted solely by the female and can begin as early as three days after she arrives on territory (Twedt and Crawford 1995). Nest construction often takes 4–5 days to complete, but can range from 2–10 days (Ortega and Cruz 1991). In Arizona, nests are attached to cattails, bulrush, willow, and locally in tamarisk. The only nests measured during the atlas period were found in

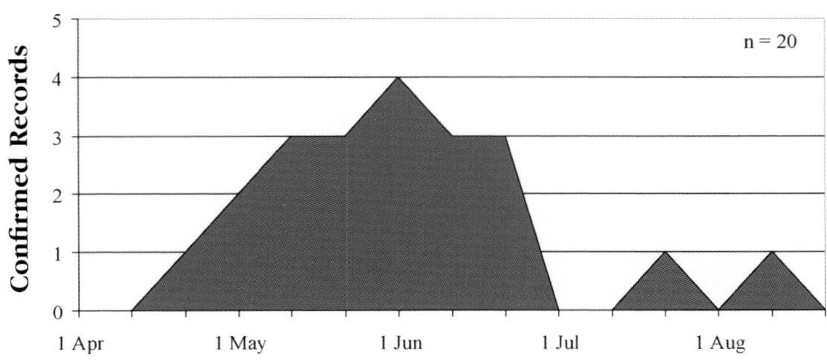

tamarisk at Ganado Lake in Apache County. They were 4.3 and 4.9 ft (1.3 and 1.5 m) above the water surface, although the lake level was steadily going down at the time.

Female Yellow-headed Blackbirds incubate the 2–5 egg clutch for 12–13 days, while the male maintains vigilance against territorial intruders (Twedt and Crawford 1995). Females feed the nestlings exclusively for at least the first four days and the male may help after that, but typically only at the primary nest (Twedt and Crawford 1995). The primary nest is the first nest initiated in his territory. Nestlings frequently fledge when 9–12 days old (Fautin 1941). Females do not raise second broods, but may renest with only two egg clutches if their first brood is lost (Twedt and Crawford 1995).

DISTRIBUTION AND STATUS

Breeding across western and central North America, Yellow-headed Blackbirds nest from British Columbia east locally to the Great Lakes region, and south locally in California, Arizona, New Mexico, and the Texas panhandle. They also breed in the adjacent Colorado River delta in Mexico. In Arizona, the breeding distribution of these spectacular blackbirds has always been patchy and rather limited, but has steadily increased over the years. Phillips et al. (1964) reported nesting populations only along the lower Colorado River and in small local colonies north of the Mogollon Rim. They were later noted nesting locally along the lower Gila River and found nesting in Chino Valley in 1976 (Monson and Phillips 1981).

Atlasers reported Yellow-headed Blackbirds nesting at wetlands at a great range of elevations in Arizona, from approximately 90 ft (27 m) along the Colorado River to above 9000 ft (2743 m) in the White Mountains. They were encountered throughout most of their previously described range and in several additional localities. Along the Colorado River, atlasers found them nesting north to Topock Marsh and along the adjacent Gila River upstream to Tacna. Elsewhere on the Gila River, they were noted nesting locally from near the confluence of the Salt River downstream through the Arlington Valley. Yellow-headed Blackbirds were also discovered nesting in agricultural ponds and ditches near Gladden and southwest of Tonopah in Maricopa County and near Kingman.

These blackbirds were also confirmed breeding locally north of the Mogollon Rim with concentrations of records at higher elevation lakes in the White Mountains and near Flagstaff southeast to Mormon and Kinnikinick lakes. Jacobs (1986) noted that Yellow-headed Blackbirds were locally common breeders on Navajo tribal lands, where atlasers confirmed them nesting near Sawmill and at Ganado, Cow Springs, and possibly Many Farms lakes. Owing to their local distribution, nesting colonies of these large, showy blackbirds were likely missed. This includes isolated ranch and farm ponds not visited by atlasers.

Yellow-headed Blackbird Breeding Evidence Reported in 39 (2%) of 1834 priority blocks

	Blocks	Quads
Possible	13 (33%)	16
Probable	4 (10%)	5
Confirmed	22 (56%)	26

Brewer's Blackbird

by Troy E. Corman *Euphagus cyanocephalus*

Iridescent, glossy blackbirds with shockingly bright yellow eyes, male Brewer's Blackbirds are always on the alert to defend their brown-eyed mates from other intruding males. Very adaptable, they take advantage of many human-modified habitats in urban and rural communities at higher elevations in Arizona.

GEORGE ANDREJKO

HABITAT

Brewer's Blackbirds nest in a wide range of habitats in Arizona, preferring cooler, higher elevation areas that are often near irrigated lands or other permanent water sources. Other crucial features for breeding areas appear to be suitable nest sites, guard perches, and short-grass foraging areas (Horn 1968). Many of Arizona's nests contain mud, which may help explain their consistent frequency of occurring near water sources in the arid southwest. Nearly 41 percent of all atlas Brewer's Blackbird records were reported from near a variety of the higher elevation wetland communities (n = 79). These include marshy meadows, springs, ponds, and lake edges with nearby scattered trees and shrubs to perennial drainages with various shrub willows, alder, cottonwood, aspen, Douglas fir, and ponderosa pine. Approximately 25 percent of all atlas records for these blackbirds were from open rural and residential settings with scattered watered lawns, parks, cemeteries, pastures, fencerows, shade trees, and shrubs. Less frequently, atlasers observed these blackbirds in open ponderosa pine woodlands, typically near human-made earthen livestock tanks or ponds. Brewer's Blackbirds were also regularly observed foraging in montane meadow grasslands with nearby low depression ponds typically filled and maintained by spring snowmelt.

BREEDING

Often encountered wintering in huge flock in agricultural areas and livestock feedlots south and west of the Mogollon Rim, Brewer's Blackbirds begin migrating north in early March, with stragglers occurring through mid-May. Males arrive first, and pairing commences quickly soon after females arrive in April. In Arizona, nest building is initiated in mid-April, and the first clutches of eggs are laid the end of April or early May. Atlasers observed nest-building activity through 25 June and nests with eggs as late as 1 July. Statewide atlas data suggest a peak in nesting activity from late May to mid-June. Atlasers noted the earliest dependent fledglings on 30 May, and the latest confirmed records were of adults feeding fledglings on 27 July. In Arizona, some Brewer's Blackbirds begin arriving in nonbreeding areas by mid- to late August, but often do not arrive in numbers to lowland wintering areas until late September or October.

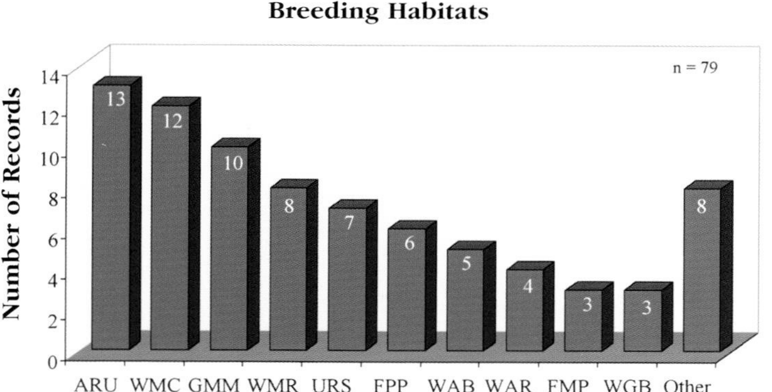

Like many other species of blackbirds in Arizona, Brewer's Blackbirds nest in loose colonies. The females defend a small territory from other females, which is typically restricted to the immediate vicinity of the nest, while the male constantly guards his mate from other approaching males and predators (Williams 1952). These blackbirds construct their nests in trees, shrubs, and even on the ground. In Arizona, nests have been located in various shrubby willows, boxelder, big sagebrush, tamarisk, ponderosa pine, Douglas fir, and several exotic trees and shrubs near homes and ranches. Atlasers also found several active nests on rocky ledges adjacent to a drainage or spring, with one actually constructed on top of a wet, dripping slab. Other nests were discovered on support beams under small, low bridges. The average height of the six nests measured during the atlas was 5.6 ft (1.7 m) and ranged from 3 to 6.9 ft (0.9–2.1 m) above the ground.

It takes approximately 5–10 days for female Brewer's Blackbirds to construct their nest (Williams 1952). The average clutch consists of 5 eggs, but can range from 3 to 7 (La Rivers 1944). The male sometimes feed the female while she

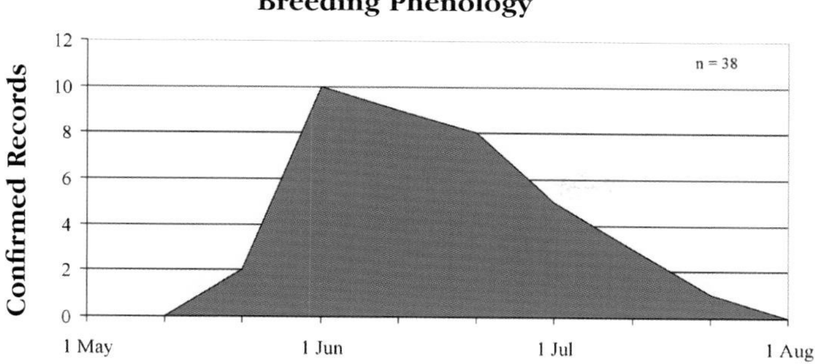

incubates the eggs for approximately 12–13 days (Williams 1952). Both parents feed the nestlings, which typically depart the nest when the young are 12–13 days old (Williams 1952). They continue feeding the fledglings until the young become independent at about 34–39 days of age (Martin 2002). Migratory Brewer's Blackbird populations typically produce only one brood per season, while many resident Pacific Coastal populations often produce two (Williams 1952). Atlasers reported one active Brewer's Blackbird nest that contained a single Brown-headed Cowbird egg.

DISTRIBUTION AND STATUS

Brewer's Blackbirds nest primarily in western North America from southern Canada, south to northern Baja California and central Arizona. Their breeding range has expanded east through the Great Lakes region. In Arizona, this blackbird has previously been described as a common summer resident on and just below the Mogollon Rim, west to the Flagstaff area and scarcer on the South Rim of the Grand Canyon, the Kaibab Plateau, and in the Chuska Mountains (Phillips et al 1964). Jacobs (1985) considered Brewer's Blackbirds as common summer residents in higher and wetter localities of Navajo tribal lands including the base of the northeastern mountain ranges. Similarly, LaRue (1994) noted that they also breed in low numbers on Black Mesa southwest of Kayenta.

Atlasers found Brewer's Blackbirds to be fairly common to common nesting species at elevations from 5800 to 9200 ft (1768–2804 m). They were encountered most consistently throughout much of the White Mountains region south to northern Greenlee County and north within the Little Colorado River drainage to Saint Johns. The southernmost records came from the Black River near West Poker Mountain and locally below the rim along upper Christopher and Canyon creeks. Brewer's Blackbirds undoubtedly breed locally within the adjacent White Mountain Apache tribal lands where access permits to conduct atlas surveys could not be obtained.

Atlasers confirmed Brewer's Blackbirds nesting from Happy Jack north through the Flagstaff area and west to near Williams in the Parks and Davenport Lake areas. On the Kaibab Plateau, they were encountered primarily along montane meadows and lakes, but also near Big Springs on the western slope. These blackbirds were reported by atlasers in several new localities on Navajo tribal lands including Ganado and Window Rock areas, north through the Defiance Plateau and upper reaches of Canyon de Chelly.

Based on historical literature, the distribution of Brewer's Blackbirds in Arizona has apparently changed very little. However, some populations have expanded into adjacent areas that have been altered by man. This is especially true in ever expanding residential areas, including the subsequent new development of nearby parks, ponds, and lakes.

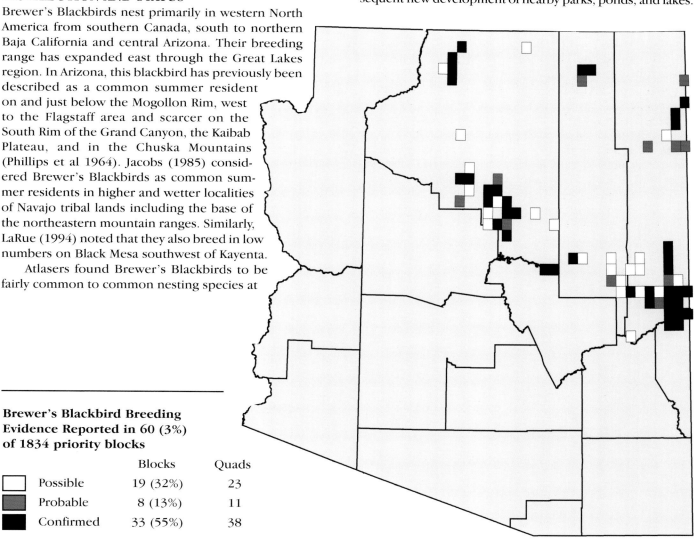

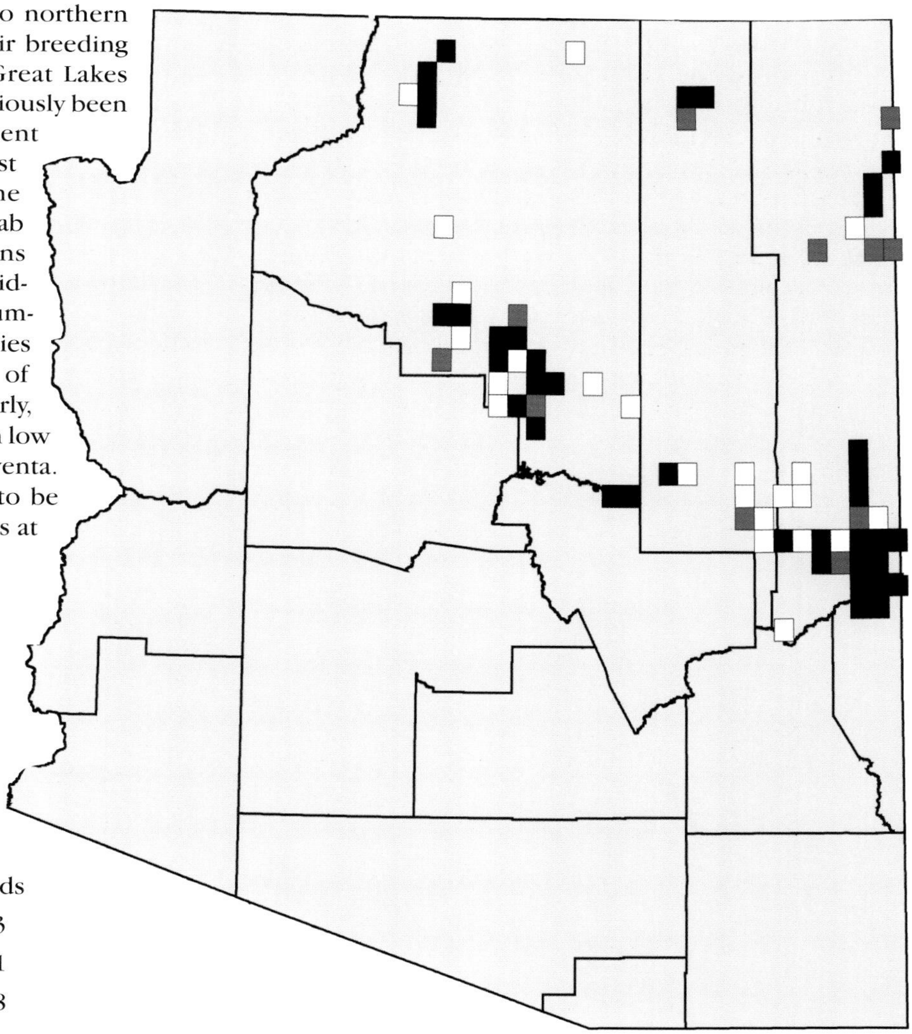

Brewer's Blackbird Breeding Evidence Reported in 60 (3%) of 1834 priority blocks

	Blocks	Quads
Possible	19 (32%)	23
Probable	8 (13%)	11
Confirmed	33 (55%)	38

Great-tailed Grackle

by Cathryn Wise-Gervais *Quiscalus mexicanus*

Decidedly tropical sounding, the conspicuous Great-tailed Grackle is capable of myriad vocalizations, from pleasant gurgling to sharp squawking. In the spring, the shiny black males strut around with long tails cocked and bills raised to the sky. These yellow-eyed suitors flutter their wings and trill to attract and captivate seemingly nonchalant females.

RICHARD DITCH

HABITAT

Great-tailed Grackles were historically found primarily south of the United States border in open areas offering scattered trees and reliable water sources. Such areas included marshlands, riparian woodlands, and in coastal scrub. During the twentieth century, this species expanded its North American range considerably in response to agricultural developments and urbanization. Irrigated lands and ornamental plantings offered many of the same components the birds were selecting in native settings. Today, Arizona's Great-tailed Grackles reach their highest density in or near human settlements and irrigated landscapes, and where 70 percent of potential breeding records were obtained (n = 283). They are typically common inhabitants of most urban and rural environments from city parks, golf courses, and neighborhoods to shade trees at ranches, farms, and smaller isolated communities. Great-tailed Grackles are particularly fond of water and are often observed wading and foraging through flooded lawns, pastures, and agricultural fields or along the shores of canals, ponds, lakes, and rivers. These resourceful blackbirds also take full advantage of open garbage cans and dumpsters. Approximately 20 percent of atlas records for this grackle were noted from waterways containing either emergent vegetation or trees such as cottonwood, willow, mesquite, and tamarisk.

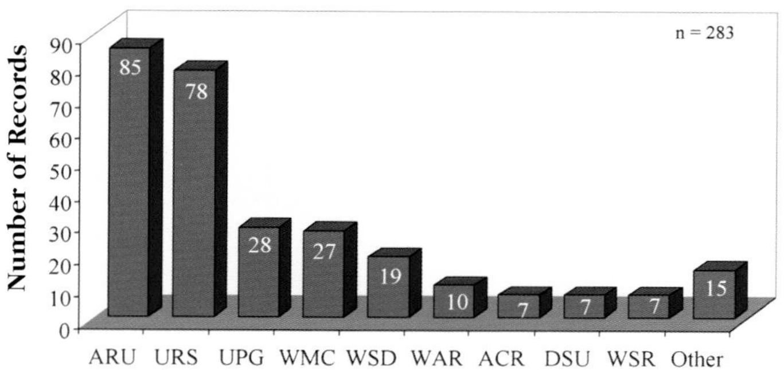

BREEDING

Great-tailed Grackles reside year-round in southern and western Arizona but are largely migratory in the north. The male's territory song is a variable combination of loud squawks, squeals, and whistles that are difficult to ignore from February through August in Arizona. In the lowlands of the state, nest construction begins by mid-March, and atlasers reported the earliest occupied nest likely containing egg on 31 March. Adults were feeding nestlings by 13 April further suggesting clutch initiation by late March. Atlasers reported 145 confirmations for this species, not including fledgling sightings. These data suggest that Great-tailed Grackle breeding activity in Arizona peaks in mid- to late May, then declines during the summer months. Atlasers reported nests with young through 8 August and adults feeding fledglings as late as 15 September. Researchers in Texas reported a very similar breeding season, as nesting was reported primarily from mid-March through mid-July (Johnson and Peer 2001). Postbreeding flocks begin forming in mid- to late summer.

Great-tailed Grackles typically nest in small colonies in a wide variety of settings, but nests are generally placed in close proximity to water and to open areas for foraging. The species is tolerant of nearby human activity and commonly nests in tall shade trees in yards and parks, with many active nests in a single tree. The grackles are not very particular in nest tree selection, and in Arizona are frequently found using exotics such as eucalyptus, athel tamarisk, aleppo pine, and mulberry. Native trees used include cottonwood, willow, and mesquite. Arizona's Great-tailed Grackles will also nest locally in marsh vegetation such as cattails and bulrush. Consequently, nests can range from 1.6 to 66+ ft (0.5–20+ m) in height (Johnson and Peer 2001), with lower nests typically above water.

Several Great-tailed Grackle males may defend territories in different sections of the same tree and may attract one or more females to each territory (Johnson and Peer 2001). Females select the site and build the nest, a structure that consists of woven plant material plastered with mud. Females will often pilfer materials from other unattended nearby grackle nests, and males will usually stand watch

Breeding Phenology

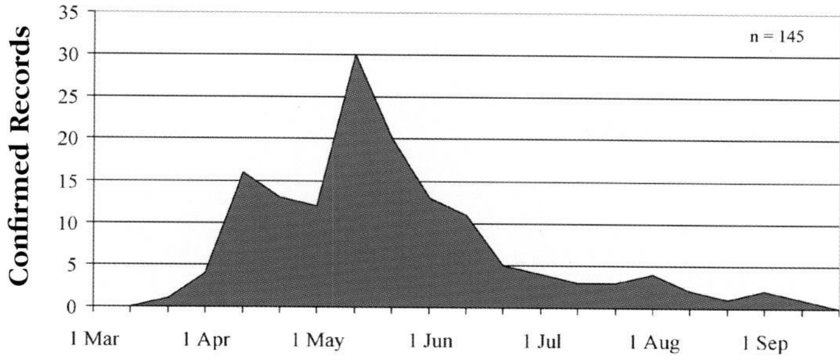

nearby. The typical Great-tailed Grackle clutch consists of 3–4 eggs (range 1–5; Teather and Weatherhead 1989), which females incubate for 13–14 days (Guillory et al. 1981). Under normal circumstances, only females brood and feed the nestlings, possibly because polygamous males are occupied with additional mates and territory defending duties. Fledging occurs at approximately 12 days, and one to two broods are raised per year (Johnson and Peer 2001).

DISTRIBUTION AND STATUS

Great-tailed Grackles are native to Mexico and Central America, with populations extending south along the coasts of northern South America. These adaptable blackbirds expanded into the southwestern United States in the early 1900s and their breeding range continues to expand northward. They currently breed regularly west of the Mississippi River from Missouri and Nebraska west to coastal southern California, and north locally to Oregon and northern Nevada.

Great-tailed Grackles first appeared in Safford in 1935 and nested there the following year, and their initial spread into Arizona has been well documented (Phillips 1950; Phillips et al. 1964; Monson and Phillips 1981). From the southeast, they spread west and north, with the birds first noted in the lower Colorado River valley in 1964, within the Grand Canyon in 1974, and in Flagstaff in 1977. During the atlas period, Great-tailed Grackles were confirmed breeding on priority blocks at elevations from approximately 90 to 7000 ft (27–2134 m) and were noted locally to 8000 ft (2438 m) near Luna Lake.

Atlasers commonly encountered Great-tailed Grackles throughout the urban and agricultural regions of southern and western Arizona, with the highest concentrations noted in the vicinity of Phoenix southeast to Tucson. The birds were also regularly reported breeding within the Gila, Verde, and lower Colorado River valleys and were widespread in the southeast.

Away from Flagstaff, Great-tailed Grackles were much more sparsely distributed north of the Mogollon Rim, as would be expected given the availability of appropriate habitat. Consequently, many small local nesting sites may have been missed while conducting atlas surveys. Great-tailed Grackles were first discovered on Navajo and Hopi tribal lands in 1978, where they are now considered a locally fairly common summer resident near lakes and some communities (C. LaRue, personal communication).

These noisy blackbirds are undoubtedly still expanding into new areas of Arizona, especially in the north, and can appear just about anywhere when dispersing. As urban and rural communities continue to grow and expand into previously undeveloped regions of the state, the adaptable Great-tailed Grackles will undoubtedly soon follow.

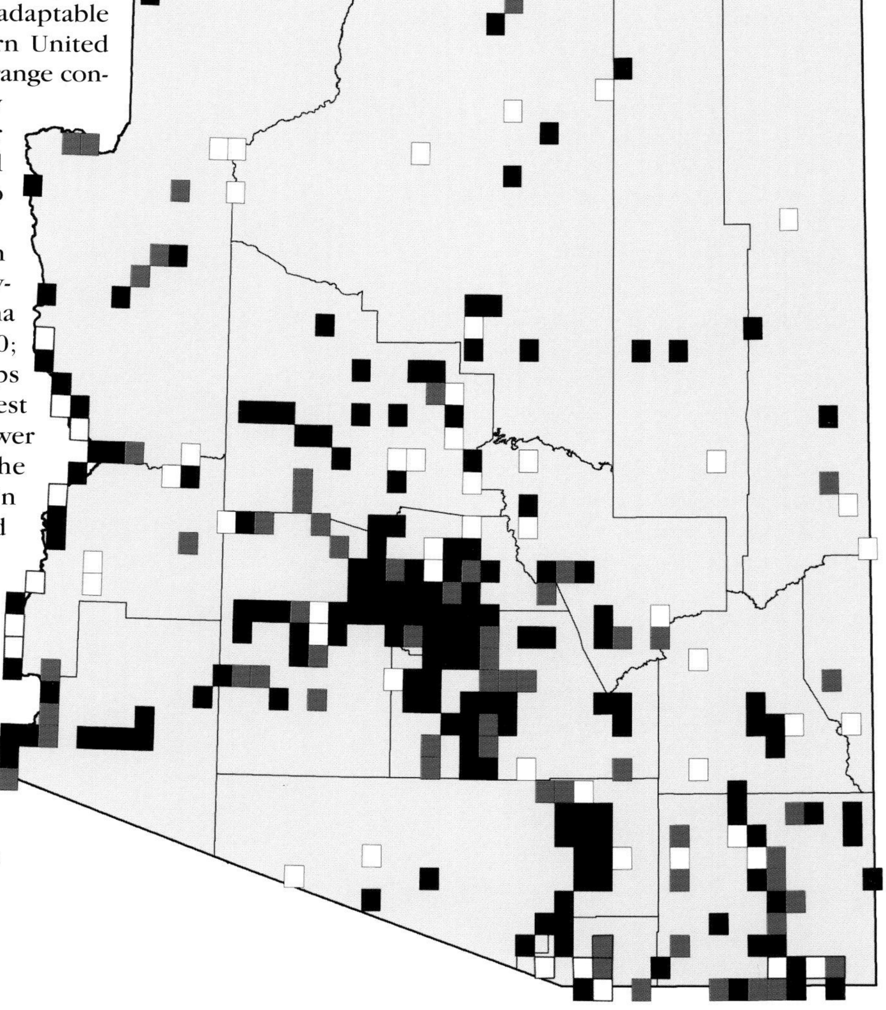

Great-tailed Grackle Breeding Evidence Reported in 230 (13%) of 1834 priority blocks

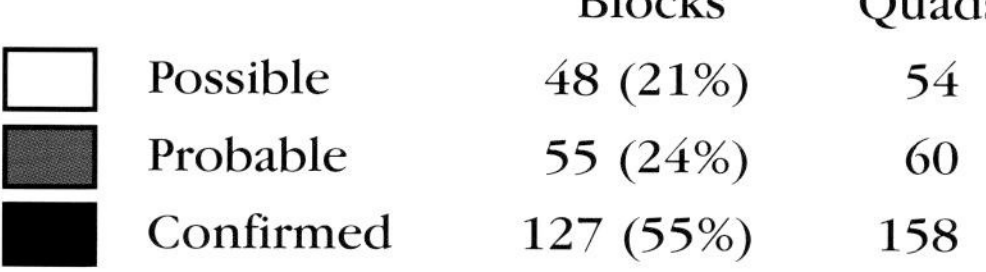

	Blocks	Quads
Possible	48 (21%)	54
Probable	55 (24%)	60
Confirmed	127 (55%)	158

Bronzed Cowbird

by Troy E. Corman *Molothrus aeneus*

Birders seem not to loathe the Bronzed Cowbird anywhere near as much as they do its Brown-headed counterpart. Indeed, with squeaky whistles and quivering wings, an amorous male vying for the attention of a seemingly aloof female is quite an entertaining spectacle. Orioles, especially Hooded, are the primary hosts of this fascinating red-eyed cowbird.

RICK AND NORA BOWERS

HABITAT

During the spring and summer, Bronzed Cowbirds can be found in a wide variety of habitats in Arizona. Atlasers encountered these birds most frequently (44 percent of 168 records) in rural and urban areas, including farm and ranch yards, irrigated pastures, and residential neighborhoods. In these settings, they are often observed foraging and courting on manicured grassy lawns, parks, cemeteries, and golf courses. An additional 38 percent of atlas records were from various riparian communities, with nesting orioles and other potential host species in abundance. These include lowland drainages with cottonwood, willow, and mesquite; densely wooded desert dry washes; and sycamore-lined drainages in mountain foothills and canyons. Bronzed Cowbirds were observed less commonly at higher elevations in Madrean evergreen oak and pine-oak woodlands.

BREEDING

Individuals and small groups of Bronzed Cowbirds typically begin to appear in breeding areas in mid-April in Arizona. However, atlasers reported pairs and individuals as early as 27 March. The male's elaborate courtship displays are typically performed from the ground and begin soon after their arrival. Displays include ruff extension, lowering of the head so bill touches its breast, leg bobbing, quivering wings, and bursts of its squeaky song as he advances toward the seemingly uninterested foraging female (Bent 1958). He then proceeds to launch himself periodically above the female, where he hovers over her with a fluttering flight. This amusing scene may be repeated several times. Some evidence suggests that once copulation has taken place, the male flies off without any further interaction with the female (Lowther 1995).

The earliest nest with eggs reported during the atlas was in a Northern Cardinal nest on 7 May. However, a fledgling was reported with an adult Hooded Oriole on 15 May, indicating that early egg laying begins by late April in Arizona. Atlasers reported very few active nests containing Bronzed Cowbird eggs or young; therefore, a peak egg-laying period could not be determined. The latest nest with eggs was in a Hooded Oriole nest on 7 August. Foster parents were reported feeding fledglings through 22 August. Phillips et al. (1964) noted that adults are typically gone from Arizona by early August, with the juveniles sometimes remaining to mid-September. Locally, individuals and small flocks are found wintering in the Tucson and Phoenix area, where they forage at feedlots, stables, and zoos.

Bronzed Cowbirds have been known to lay their eggs in the nests of eighty-two bird species (Lowther 1995). However, Friedmann (1929) noted they apparently favor *Icterus* orioles as hosts, with approximately 75 percent of all eggs laid in oriole nests. This was also true during the atlas in Arizona. Of twenty-two confirmed breeding observations where the host species was determined (Appendix D), fourteen were oriole species, with a large majority (10) noted as Hooded Orioles. Nine other host species were reported during the atlas: Bullock's Oriole, Scott's Oriole, Northern Cardinal, Hepatic Tanager, Summer Tanager, Hutton's Vireo, Lucy's Warbler, Yellow Warbler, and Black-tailed Gnatcatcher. Lowther (1995) did not list the latter four species as Bronzed Cowbird hosts. In 1985, a Yellow-breasted Chat nest containing eggs of the host and both cowbird species was also found along Bonito Creek in Graham County.

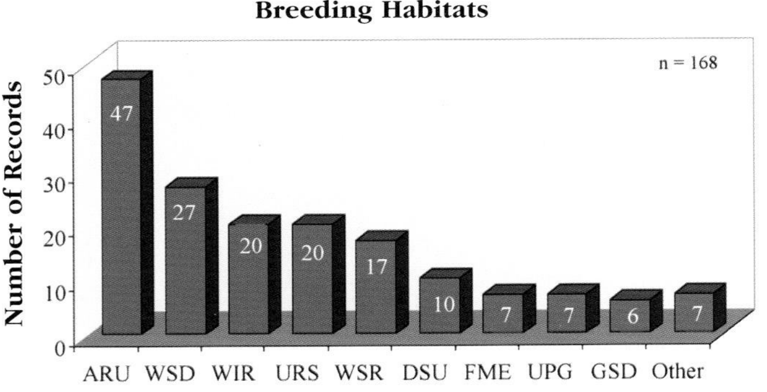

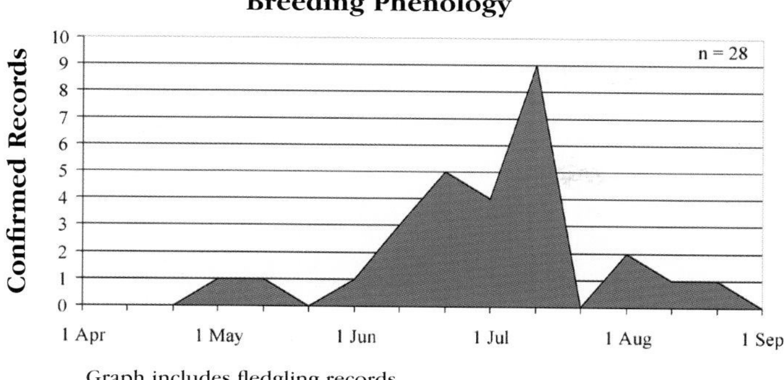

Carter (1986) noted that the eggs are laid at dawn and that more than one female may lay in the same nest. Near Sacaton, Pinal County, Gilman (1914) found a Hooded Oriole nest containing two Bronzed and four Brown-headed Cowbird eggs. Brandt (1951) also found a Hooded Oriole nest near Tucson with one oriole egg and six Bronzed Cowbird eggs. Female Bronzed Cowbirds often pierce the eggs that are already in the host nest (Carter 1986). Successful brood parasitism may closely depend on the timing of the host's egg laying; Carter (1986) found that none of the cowbirds that hatched more than 48 hours after their nestmates survived in the ten nests he was observing.

DISTRIBUTION AND STATUS

The Bronzed Cowbird breeds from central Arizona, southeastern California, southwestern New Mexico, southern Texas, and southeastern Louisiana on south through Mexico to Colombia. Breeding populations in the United States are thought to be at least partially migratory. The establishment of towns and cities and expansion of irrigated agricultural lands in the arid southwest likely influenced the initial occurrence of this species in Arizona. This species was first found in Arizona in 1907 at Sacaton and Tucson (Gilman 1909; Visher 1910). It was found regularly thereafter, and probably began to winter within a few years (Phillips et al. 1964). This species continued to expand rapidly in the state and was considered a common summer resident in southern and central Arizona north to Wickenburg (first noted in 1927) and west to Organ Pipe Cactus National Monument, rarely west to the Colorado River (Phillips et al. 1964). Since about 1970, Monson and Phillips (1981) also noted it to be rare to uncommon north to the base of the Mogollon Rim and northeast to Prescott. This cowbird is considered to be a rare local breeding species along the lower Colorado River valley (Rosenberg et al. 1991).

Atlasers encountered Bronzed Cowbirds throughout their previously described Arizona range at elevations between 110 and 6200 ft (34–1890 m) and documented their continued steady push to the northwest. These stocky cowbirds were confirmed nesting regularly along perennial drainages and canyons west and northwest of Prescott, including within the Hualapai Mountains. One individual was also observed as far northwest as Kingman. Not unexpectedly, this cowbird's distribution in the state closely mirrors the primary distribution of the Hooded Oriole, including following the oriole's range expansion in the northwest.

Current Bronzed Cowbird populations in Arizona remain relatively small and local, and they likely have little effect on the overall population of orioles. However, reduced numbers of nesting Hooded Orioles in larger metropolitan areas may be partially related to an increase in both cowbird species.

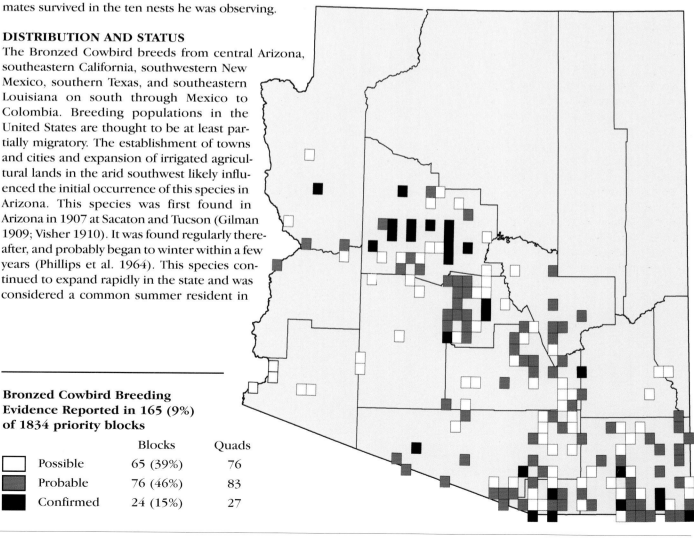

Bronzed Cowbird Breeding Evidence Reported in 165 (9%) of 1834 priority blocks

	Blocks	Quads
Possible	65 (39%)	76
Probable	76 (46%)	83
Confirmed	24 (15%)	27

Brown-headed Cowbird

by Annalaura Averill-Murray *Molothrus ater*

The Brown-headed Cowbird is Arizona's most common and ubiquitous brood parasite, typically laying its eggs in the nests of small or medium-sized open-nesting passerines. Brown-headed Cowbirds are known to parasitize more than 220 species, 144 of which have actually raised a cowbird nestling.

HABITAT

Brown-headed Cowbirds are commonly associated with human-modified, fragmented landscapes, reaching high densities in woodland edges and wood-field ecotones as opposed to extensive forests or grasslands. In Arizona, atlasers found Brown-headed Cowbirds in almost all of the potential vegetation communities, including desertscrub, riparian woodland, coniferous forest, grassland, agricultural lands, and residential areas.

Brown-headed Cowbird occurrence in any particular habitat type is likely a function of host species density and the accessibility of host nests. For example, atlasers frequently documented these cowbirds in riparian and wetland areas (29 percent of 1265 records), including wooded desert dry washes. This is likely because of the linear nature of these landscapes (high edge to interior forest ratio) and the high density of nesting songbirds. Sonoran upland desertscrub and pinyon pine–juniper woodlands accounted for 29 percent of atlas records for this cowbird. However, these are also the two most widely distributed vegetation communities in the state. Atlasers found Brown-headed Cowbirds more frequently in grassland with a scattered tree or shrub component (10 percent) than extensive, open grassland (2 percent). Phillips et al. (1964) described Brown-headed Cowbirds as scarce in pinyon pine–juniper woodlands and of uncertain breeding status in adjacent ponderosa pine associations. Although atlas records reflect presence and not abundance, it is possible that this cowbird species has become more pervasive and abundant in pinyon pine–juniper and ponderosa pine communities in recent years, perhaps because of increased forest fragmentation.

Breeding Habitats

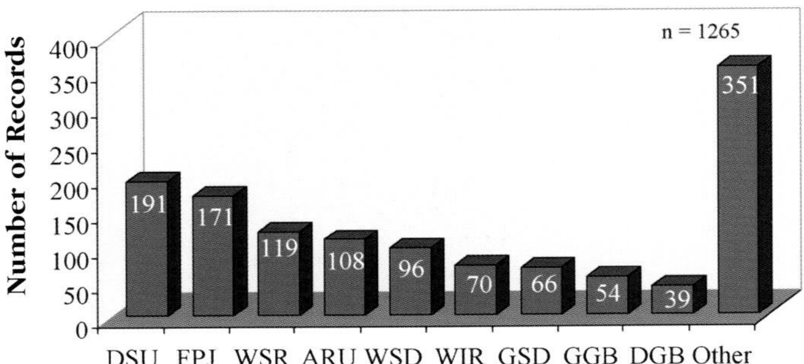

BREEDING

Brown-headed Cowbirds begin arriving on their southern Arizona breeding grounds in mid- to late March, but not until April in the north. Peak migration usually occurs in late April and early May. Eggs are typically deposited from April to mid-July (Rosenberg et al. 1991; Lowther 1993). The earliest breeding confirmation for this species was a nest with eggs on 14 April. Atlasers found the majority (89 percent) of Brown-headed Cowbird eggs and nestlings from early May to early August with a peak in mid-June. Late nesting records included two active nests with cowbird eggs found in mid-August. Atlasers observed host species feeding dependent Brown-headed Cowbird young through 11 September, and this activity is occasionally reported into late September in southeastern Arizona.

In mid- to late July, Brown-headed Cowbirds begin to form local foraging flocks of 100 or more individuals, often with juveniles. Brown-headed Cowbirds can be found wintering by the thousands with other blackbird species near livestock feed lots and irrigated agricultural lands in southern Arizona.

Atlasers documented forty-one host species for the Brown-headed Cowbird (Appendix D), including several species known to eject cowbird eggs from their nests. It is unknown whether all of these species successfully raised cowbird young. Of 161 parasitism events in which atlasers indicated host species identity, the Black-tailed Gnatcatcher (n = 20), Yellow Warbler (n = 14), Bell's Vireo (n = 13), Black-throated Gray Warbler (n = 11), and Black-throated Sparrow (n = 10) were the most commonly observed host species. Infrequently observed host species included Crissal Thrasher (n = 1), a species known to eject cowbird eggs from its nest (Finch 1982), and other species with few recorded parasitism events in the literature (Bushtit, Rufous-crowned

Breeding Phenology

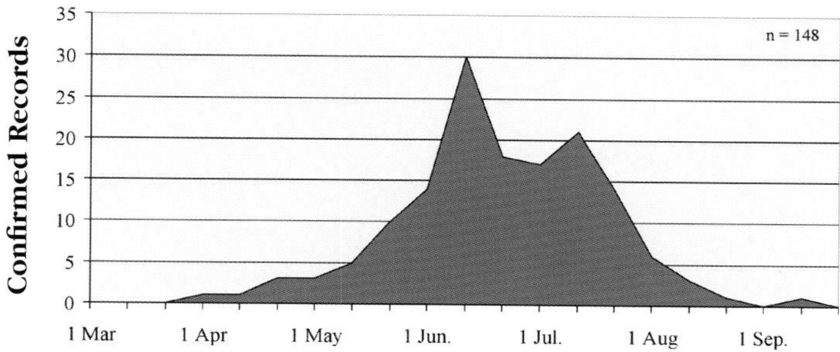

Sparrow, Grace's Warbler, Olive Warbler, Lucy's Warbler, and Red-faced Warbler). Bullock's Oriole was a relatively common host species ($n = 9$) despite the fact that it may eject or damage cowbird eggs and is, therefore, not an ideal host (Rothstein 1977). Atlasers also found a broken Brown-headed Cowbird egg below a Western Kingbird nest, possibly rejected by this potential host species.

A female Brown-headed Cowbird can lay 30–40 eggs per season (Lowther 1993; Baicich and Harrison 1997). The incubation period ranges from 10 to 13 days (Ehrlich et al. 1988), and cowbird eggs laid simultaneously with host eggs usually hatch first (Lowther 1993). Because of this, cowbird nestlings often outcompete host nestlings for food, decreasing survivorship of host nestlings (Lowther 1993). Brown-headed Cowbirds have been implicated in the decline of several songbird species in Arizona, particularly riparian obligates such as Willow Flycatcher, Bell's Vireo, and Yellow Warbler (Phillips et al. 1964; Rosenberg et al. 1991). Brown-headed Cowbirds fledge at 8–13 days after hatching and are fed by host parents for 2–4 weeks following nest departure (Woodward and Woodward 1979).

DISTRIBUTION AND STATUS

Before European settlement, the Brown-headed Cowbird was basically confined to the Great Plains region of North America (Mayfield 1965). They currently breed from southeastern Alaska and northern British Columbia south and east through much of western and southern Canada, the United States (except southern Florida), northern Baja California, and northern and central Mexico (Lowther 1993). In Arizona, Brown-headed Cowbirds are generally described as a common summer resident, and atlasers documented breeding activity for this species in survey blocks ranging from 90 to 9300 ft (33–3414 m) in elevation.

Atlasers documented Brown-headed Cowbirds throughout Arizona. However, this species was less frequently encountered in the western part of the state (Mohave, La Paz, and Yuma counties) where vegetation and breeding bird density is typically sparse. Similarly, their breeding distribution in the northeastern corner of the state appeared to be less uniform. Much of this area is also sparsely vegetated and has low avian species richness and abundance. Brown-headed Cowbird records encircle the White Mountain Apache tribal lands where atlas surveys could not be conducted.

Phillips et al. (1964) noted that Brown-headed Cowbirds had apparently become much more common and widespread in recent years. Breeding Bird Survey data suggest regional variation in population trends, with Arizona exhibiting an overall significant decline for this ubiquitous cowbird (Sauer et al. 2002).

Brown-headed Cowbird Breeding Evidence Reported in 1235 (67%) of 1834 priority blocks

	Blocks	Quads
Possible	524 (42%)	532
Probable	535 (43%)	548
Confirmed	176 (14%)	184

Hooded Oriole

by Troy E. Corman *Icterus cucullatus*

A familiar inhabitant of Arizona's native riparian woodlands, the brilliant Hooded Oriole often announces its presence by very characteristic chattering and "wink" calls. Common in much of Arizona, unfortunately, urban populations show early signs of decline, possibly due to heavy cowbird brood parasitism.

RICK AND NORA BOWERS

HABITAT

In Arizona, Hooded Orioles obtain their highest breeding densities in riparian communities containing tall stands of deciduous trees. During the atlas project, these slender orioles were reported most frequently in lowland drainages with Fremont cottonwoods, willows, and mesquite, and in lower canyons and foothills drainages dominated by Arizona sycamore, walnut, and ash. These two riparian communities accounted for 42 percent of 517 potential breeding records for the species. Although occurring in lower densities, Hooded Orioles were also encountered fairly regularly (31 percent of records) nesting along desert dry washes containing dense stands of netleaf hackberry, mesquite, paloverde, or ironwood. Occupied dry washes often include taller, older trees with an abundance of mistletoe in which they frequently construct their nest. These adaptable orioles are often found in rural desert communities and larger urban neighborhoods where exotic fan palms and shade trees have been introduced.

BREEDING

An early migrant in Arizona, Hooded Orioles typically begin to appear in early or mid-March, exceptionally in late February. Early nest building is initiated in late March or early April, as atlasers reported an occupied nest on 12 April and a nest with eggs on 17 April. Adults were observed feeding fledged young by 20 April and 23 April, further indicating that some nesting activity begins before April. Statewide atlas data reveal that Hooded Oriole nesting activity quickly reaches a peak in mid-May, then steadily declines through the summer. The latest nest with eggs was found on 8 August, and adults were observed feeding fledged young through 14 August. Most of Arizona's breeding population has left the state by mid-September, with individuals reported regularly through mid-October and rarely and irregularly into the winter. Wintering birds are most often found frequenting residential hummingbird feeders (Monson and Phillips 1981).

Nest construction takes approximately 3–6 days (Scott 1885) and is performed only by the female, although the male encourages the process by often follows her to the nest. The nests are a rather shallow cup for an oriole, often constructed of coarse material. However, the materials used to build the nest and the site chosen for their placement is quite variable (Pleasants and Albano 2001). When attached on the underside of the large leaves of fan palms, the nest is constructed primarily of long, sturdy strands of the palm leaf fibers. At such locations, the female works from below, using her bill to poke holes in the palm leaf and push fibers through as if it were sewn (Pleasants and Albano 2001). Away from palm trees, a common material is long dried fibers from the leaves of agave and yucca or sturdy grasses. Along favorite fishing holes, some nests are made almost entirely of discarded fishing line.

In rural and residential areas of Arizona, most nests are placed in fan palms, while along perennial drainages Hooded Orioles prefer Arizona sycamore, Fremont cottonwood, and velvet ash. Netleaf hackberry along dry washes is favored in semiarid grasslands and in the Sonoran Desert, nests are most frequently found in mistletoe clumps in paloverde, mesquite, and catclaw acacia along larger washes. Atlasers reported a number of odd nest locations, which included a nest attached to a porch lamp and several more under concrete highway bridges attached to dried sealant. Another nest was attached to the underside of the exposed sticks of an active Red-tailed Hawk nest placed more than 100 ft (30.5 m) above the ground on a transmission tower. Atlasers took measurements at twenty-three Hooded Oriole nests with a mean height of 20 ft (6.1 m) and range of 0.7–47.8 ft (0.2–14.5 m). The lowest nest measured held older young and was found dangling over a large pool of water in an Arizona alder. With every stiff breeze, the heavy nest would actually dip into the water, dousing the noisy nestlings!

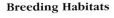

Breeding Habitats

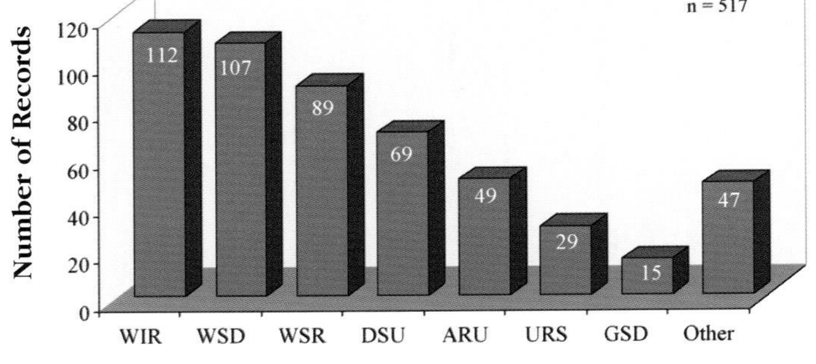

Habitat Codes

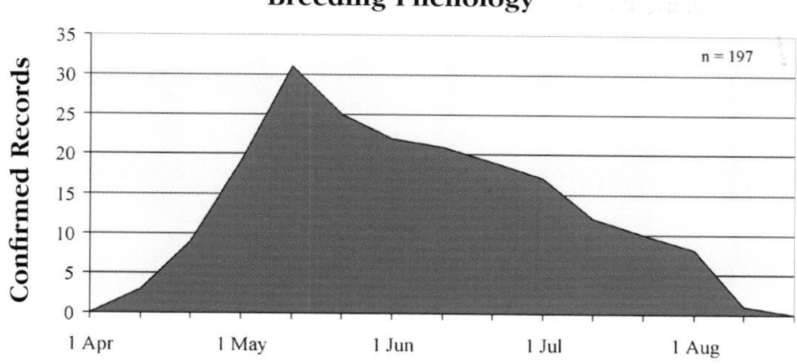

Hooded Orioles have a typical clutch size of 3–4 eggs with a range of 2–5 (Bent 1958). The female is the sole incubator, which lasts for 12–14 days (Bendire 1895). Both parents feed the young, and the length of the nestling stage is not well known; however, it is suggested as being approximately two weeks (Bent 1958). Hooded Orioles are known to produce 2–3 broods per season (Pleasants and Albano 2001). They are frequent hosts of both Brown-headed and Bronzed cowbirds in Arizona, with atlasers reporting ten parasitism records by the latter species.

DISTRIBUTION AND STATUS

Hooded Orioles have a fairly limited breeding range that extends from northern California through Baja California and from southern Nevada, Arizona, and New Mexico south through northwestern Mexico. They also range from southern Texas south along the Gulf Coast of Mexico to Belize.

Most prior literature considered Hooded Orioles as common summer resident across southern Arizona. In the early 1900s, this species began to spread northward as far as below Davis Dam along the Colorado River, Kingman, and the southern base of the Mogollon Rim (Phillips et al. 1964). By the 1940s, these orioles nested northwest to the Virgin River valley and Beaver Dam Wash (Monson and Phillips 1981). Hooded Orioles had reached the bottom of the Grand Canyon by 1974 (Brown et al. 1987). An out of range nesting pair on Navajo tribal lands was observed at Chinle in 1971 (Monson and Phillips 1981).

During the atlas period, Hooded Orioles were noted as fairly common to common throughout their previously described range. Rosenberg et al. (1991) considered the Hooded Oriole as a fairly common but local summer breeder within the lower Colorado River valley. Atlas data support these earlier findings. North of the Mogollon Rim, atlasers discovered these birds at several locations along the Little Colorado River between Leupp and Cameron and confirmed them nesting as far north as Page. Atlas data suggest possible local decline of these attractive orioles in the greater Tucson and Phoenix metropolitan areas. An increase in both cowbird species could be related to these local declines.

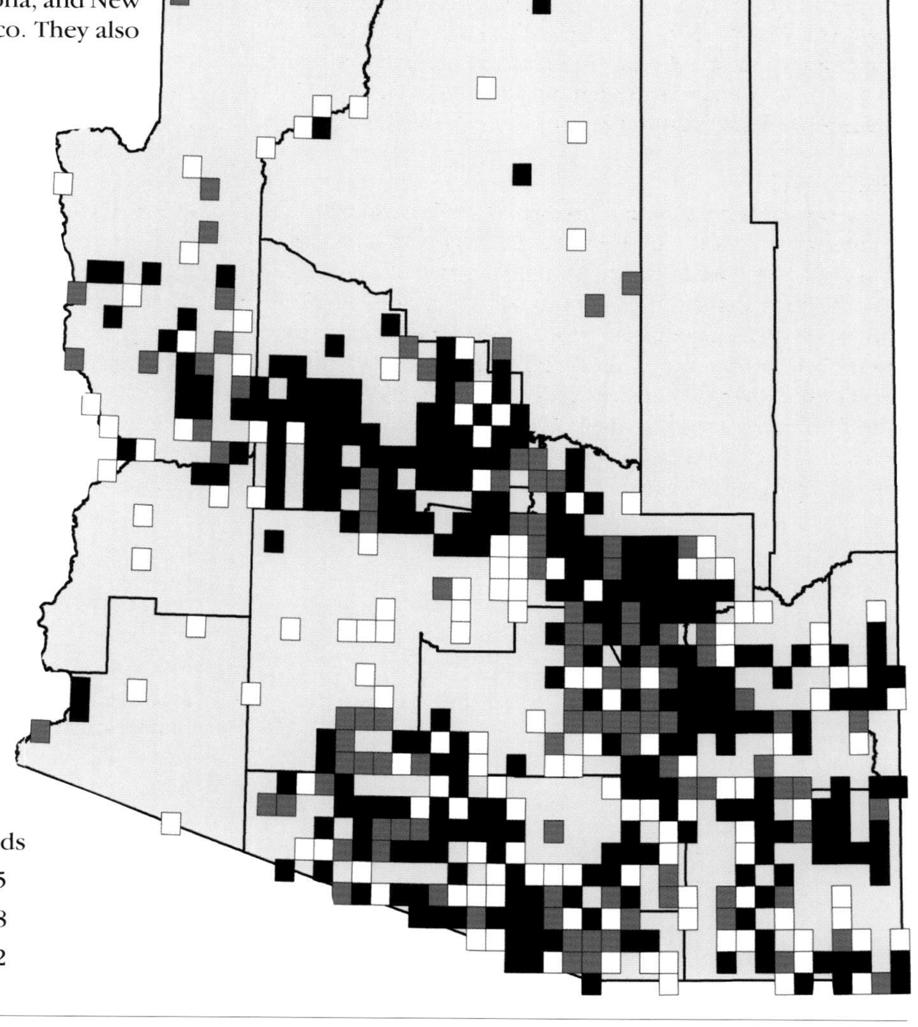

Hooded Oriole Breeding Evidence Reported in 491 (27%) of 1834 priority blocks

	Blocks	Quads
Possible	126 (26%)	145
Probable	103 (21%)	108
Confirmed	262 (53%)	272

Streak-backed Oriole

by Troy E. Corman *Icterus pustulatus*

Widespread and common south of Arizona, the stocky Streak-backed Oriole was first discovered nesting in Arizona, and the United States, through atlas surveys. These attractive orioles construct a conspicuous and large, dangling nest. Typically suspended from the tips of a slender branch, the nest sways with the slightest breeze.

TROY CORMAN

HABITAT

Found in a wide variety of woodlands and semi-open habitats throughout their range, Streak-backed Orioles prefer stands of tall deciduous trees for nesting. In Arizona, most local summer records are from lowland riparian woodlands, especially those containing tall Fremont cottonwoods. Dominant understory trees frequently include velvet mesquite, seepwillow, tamarisk, and scattered Goodding willow. Occupied cottonwood stands typically contain a fairly open midstory, where most nests are constructed above a relatively dense 8–10 ft (2.4–3.0 m) high understory. Atlasers also discovered Streak-backed Orioles nesting in an isolated grove of dead and dying pecan trees surrounded by cultivated fields. This abandoned grove was no longer irrigated and also had a dense understory of shrubby velvet mesquite.

BREEDING

There have been so few nesting pairs in Arizona, that the migratory status of Streak-backed Orioles is relatively unknown. However, some individuals have been found wintering near breeding areas in the state. In nearby Sonora, many but not all individuals from the northern portion of their range are migratory, departing in October and returning in March (Russell and Monson 1998). Some of these individuals may actually disperse northward, as most of Arizona's Streak-backed Oriole records fall between October and April, with a peak in December and January.

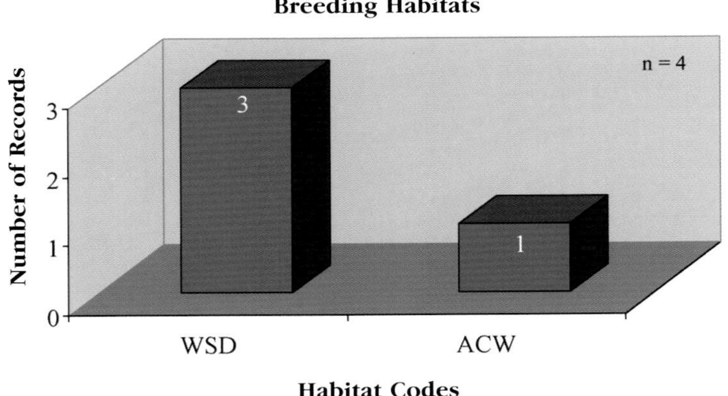

Little has been written on the breeding phenology of the Streak-backed Oriole. In nearby Sonora, nesting efforts are noted from May into September, with nesting activity peaking in July (Russell and Monson 1998). Several nesting pairs discovered during the atlas period were closely monitored, and much of the following information was taken from these observations. The timing of initial courtship and pairing has not been determined in Arizona. However, nest construction can begin by mid-May and continue well into June. In Arizona, most eggs are laid in late June to early July, possibly in association with the beginning of the summer monsoon season (Corman and Monson 1995). A female Streak-backed Oriole that lost her nest to high winds during the initial egg-laying period on 28 June began constructing a new nest on the same limb only two days later (G. Hentz, personal communication). Nest construction continued through mid-July until it was also lost to unknown causes. Atlasers reported nests with young from 9 July to 3 August, but nesting may continue well into August if earlier attempts have failed.

Only the female Streak-backed Oriole constructs the nest, but the male often accompanies his mate as she collects nesting material, then follows her back to the nest site. Nesting material used in Arizona includes long strips from the lining of cottonwood bark and grasses (Corman and Monson 1995). Nest building is a lengthy process, and it typically takes 3.5–4 weeks to complete the long, pendulous nests, which are often 15–20 in. (38–51 cm) in length. Most of the Streak-backed Oriole nests discovered in Arizona have been constructed in tall Fremont cottonwoods in a fairly open situation under the canopy. However, one female constructed her obvious nest in a leafless, dead pecan tree with no protection from the elements (G. Hentz, personal communication). The height of three nests measured during the atlas ranged from 20 to 25 ft (6.1–7.6 m) above the ground.

There is little information on clutch size for Streak-backed Orioles, but this likely ranges from 3 to 5 as in other closely related orioles. Incubation takes approximately 12–14 days and is conducted solely by the female (Corman and Monson 1995). Both parents feed the nestlings, and observations in Arizona suggest that the young fledge in approximately 14 days. The period of parental dependency following nest departure is unknown because nest monitors quickly lost track of the orioles when the young fledged.

Bronzed Cowbirds frequently parasitize the nests of this oriole in adjacent Sonora (Russell and Monson 1998), and they were often observed near and even entering nests under construction in Arizona (G. Hentz, personal communication). Observations in Arizona and Sonora suggest that some males could be polygynous (Corman and Monson 1995; Russell and Monson 1998).

DISTRIBUTION AND STATUS

Streak-backed Orioles are primarily a resident species from western Mexico to northwestern Costa Rica. Russell and Monson (1998) described this oriole as common to abundant throughout much of southern and east-central Sonora, where it is found at elevations primarily below 3280 ft (1000 m). In Arizona, Phillips et al. (1964) described Streak-backed Orioles as rare to casual winter visitors and transients only in the Tucson region. An individual was observed farther north at the confluence of the Gila and Salt rivers in early April 1976 (Monson and Phillips 1981). Since 1980, Streak-backed Orioles were also irregularly and locally reported during the fall through early spring in Green Valley, Cook's Lake south of Dudleyville in Pinal County, and even one to the far north at the bottom of the Grand Canyon (Rosenberg and Witzeman 1999).

Before the atlas discovery of Streak-backed Orioles nesting in Arizona, there were only two records of this oriole in the state between May and August. They were first found nesting along the lower San Pedro River near Dudleyville on 6 June 1993. Two pairs returned to this area to nest in 1994, and at least one pair nested every year within a few miles of this area throughout the atlas period. Also in 1994, a pair was discovered at an abandoned pecan grove northwest of Marana in Pima County (G. Hentz, personal communication). This pair was unsuccessful in their several nesting attempts and never returned. An adult male was also observed several times in June 1996 at a private residence along the San Pedro River near Cascabel in northwestern Cochise County. Finally, a nest was discovered after the 2001 breeding season in a small stand of cottonwoods just north of Cook's Lake near the San Pedro River. During the atlas period, Streak-backed Orioles were encountered at elevations ranging from 1890 to 3200 ft (576–975 m).

The nesting population of Streak-backed Orioles on the lower San Pedro River apparently remains extremely small and very local. However, there are many miles of appropriate nesting habitat along this river from Cascabel north. Much of it is inaccessible and privately owned and could harbor additional pairs of these attractive tropical orioles.

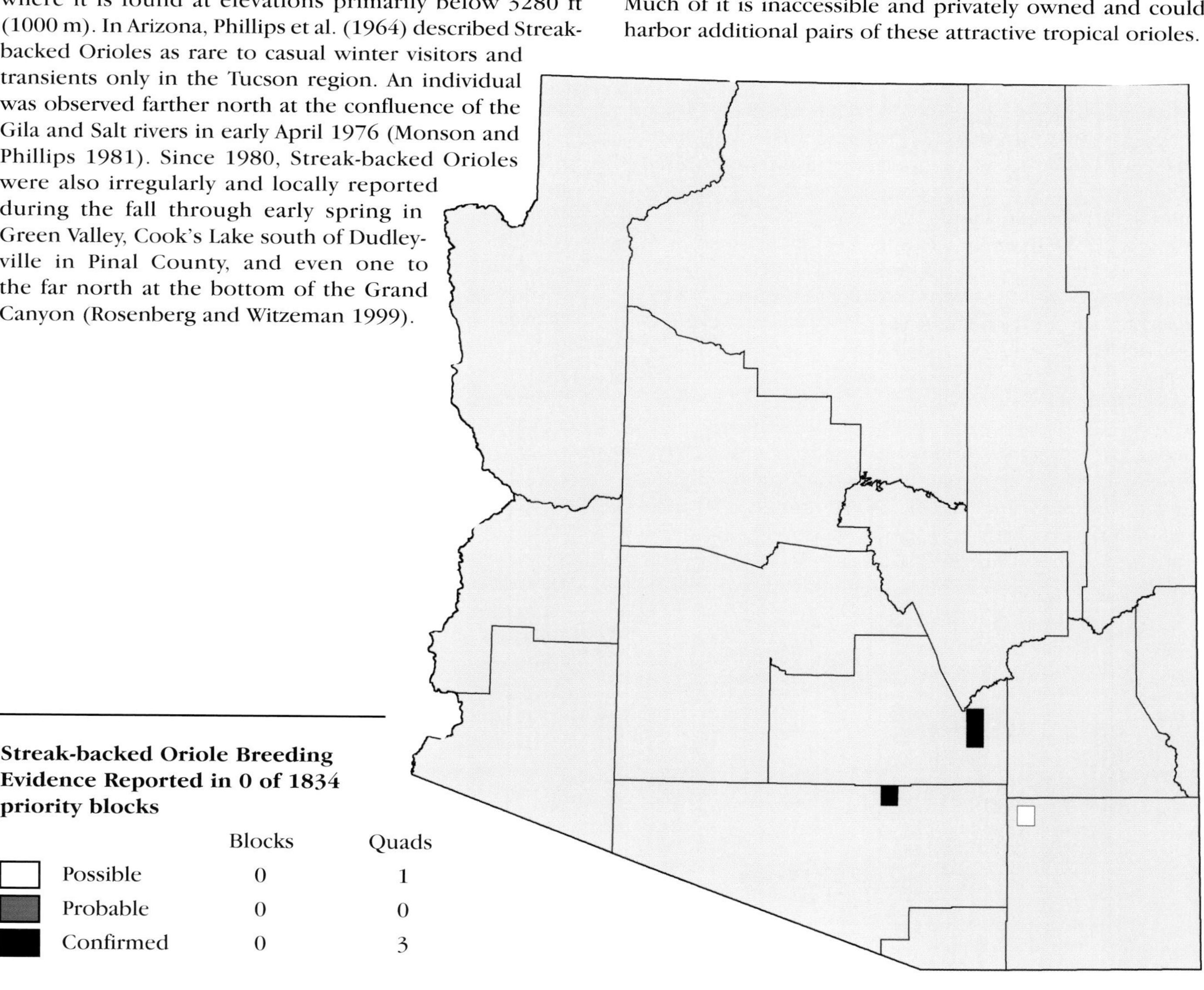

Streak-backed Oriole Breeding Evidence Reported in 0 of 1834 priority blocks

	Blocks	Quads
Possible	0	1
Probable	0	0
Confirmed	0	3

Bullock's Oriole

by Peter Friedericici *Icterus bullockii*

Once considered conspecific with the Baltimore Oriole of the East, Bullock's Oriole is once again a separate species and a characteristic bird of riparian woodlands throughout most of the western United States. Its bright colors, distinctive song, and hanging nest often make its summertime presence in the cool shade of these woodlands readily apparent.

DAN FISCHER

HABITAT

In Arizona, Bullock's Orioles are closely associated with a variety of riparian communities, but they also nest locally in deciduous shade trees. Atlasers most often encountered this species nesting in cottonwood-willow associations at low elevations, where it also occurs in fairly dense mesquite bosques and tamarisk thickets. Bullock's Orioles also commonly nest in the broad-leafed riparian woodlands of middle elevations and canyons, characterized by sycamores, walnuts, ashes, and other trees. These two riparian communities account for 38 percent of atlas records ($n = 447$). Cottonwood-dominated drainages, lakeshores, and springs are also commonly frequented in northern Arizona, including areas with just a few tall, isolated trees. The species takes advantage of some areas that have been heavily altered by human activity, where it breeds in smaller residential and rural areas that include the large deciduous shade trees it favors for nesting. The species sometimes breeds in somewhat drier habitats such as pinyon pine–juniper or evergreen oak woodlands and occasionally at higher elevations in montane riparian areas with alder, cottonwood, and boxelder.

BREEDING

Bullock's Oriole is a migratory species that rarely winters in Arizona. It begins to appear in the southwestern deserts in early to mid-March, but those individuals appear to be migrants bound for the Pacific Coast (Phillips et al. 1964). Arizona's nesting birds typically begin arriving in breeding areas in early to mid-April and into May in the north. Breeding activity begins about the middle of April, with the earliest active nest located by atlasers on 16 April. The earliest dates for fledgling observations were 8 May and 13 May, indicating clutch initiations in mid- to late April. Statewide atlas data suggest that breeding activity peaks from late May to mid-June, with a steady decline through the summer. Although many of Arizona's breeding Bullock's Orioles are on their way south by the end of July, some nesting activity continues in the southeastern corner of the state. A female was observed carrying nesting material on 28 July, and nests with young were noted on 8 August and the exceptionally late date of 11 September. These few late summer nesting records may be related to favorable conditions produced by strong monsoon activity in this region of the state; some pairs will produce two broods in southern Arizona (Rosenberg et al. 1991). Few individuals are noted in the state after late September.

Atlasers document Bullock's Orioles nesting commonly in such broad-leafed trees as cottonwoods, willow, and sycamores, with a few scattered records in netleaf hackberry, velvet ash, evergreen oaks, mesquite, catclaw acacia, and pinyon pine. Several nests were noted in mistletoe clumps. The species has also been recorded nesting in exotic tamarisk where these trees exceed 16.4 ft (5 m) in height (Rosenberg et al. 1991). Bullock's Orioles prefer larger trees, and the median height of nineteen nest trees measured during the atlas was 41 ft (12.5 m). The median nest height was 21.3 ft (6.5 m), but ranged from 9.5 to 42.7 ft (2.9–13 m). Nest density can be high and atlasers discovered two active nests in a single tree, with other nests in adjacent trees. Bent (1958) reported three nests in one tree.

Female Bullock's Orioles typically weave their pendulous nests without assistance of the male. Clutches average 4–5 eggs and are incubated by the female for approximately 11 days (Rising and Williams 1999). Both adults feed the nestlings through fledging at about two weeks of age and for an unknown period following nest departure (Rising and Williams 1999).

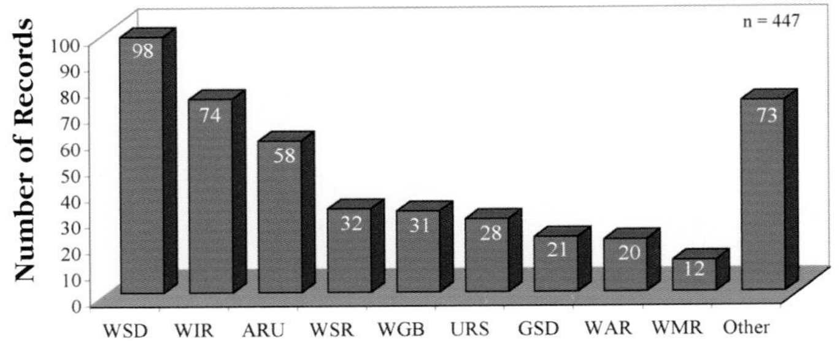

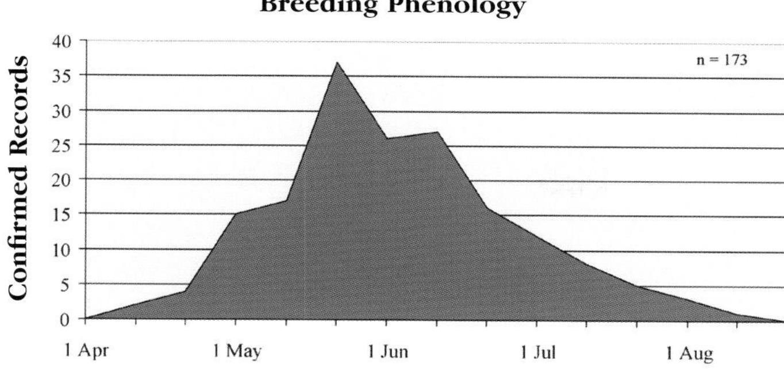

The species is parasitized by both Brown-headed and Bronzed Cowbirds, though it also has been recorded ejecting cowbird eggs from its nests (Rising and Williams 1999). Atlas workers recorded nine instances of successful brood parasitism by Brown-headed Cowbirds and three such instances by Bronzed Cowbirds.

DISTRIBUTION AND STATUS

The breeding range of Bullock's Oriole is restricted largely to the United States from the Great Plains west, and it barely enters southern Canada and northern Mexico as a breeding species. In Arizona, these orioles can be found almost anywhere on migration, and their breeding range extends throughout most of the state. However, the species is largely absent in desertscrub associations away from riparian or irrigated rural settings.

Most prior literature describes Bullock's Oriole as a common summer resident in Arizona. Atlasers reported these birds nesting at elevations from approximately 150 ft (46 m) along the lower Colorado River to 7700 ft (2347 m) in the White Mountains. The centers of abundance for this species in the state are in the southeastern corner and the mid-elevations of Yavapai County. Although previously noted as sparingly distributed along the Mexico border of southeastern Arizona (Phillips et al. 1964; Monson and Phillips 1981), atlasers confirmed these orioles nesting throughout this region. Bullock's Orioles are basically absent as a nesting species in heavily urbanized areas such as Phoenix and Tucson, even though cottonwoods and other tall shade trees are plentiful in city parks, golf courses, and some residential neighborhoods.

Bullock's Oriole records were quite scattered in the northern half of the state, where the species appears to be absent from many areas of suitable-looking habitat. This was especially notable on Navajo and Hopi tribal lands. As an example, they were not found nesting in the cottonwood groves of Canyon de Chelly National Monument. As noted by Brown et al. (1987), Bullock's Orioles were reported nesting sparingly within the Grand Canyon corridor, but commonly from Lees Ferry to Page.

Atlas data reveal Bullock's Orioles nesting commonly in most of historical locations within Arizona. The species appears much more tolerant of human alteration of riparian areas than many of the species with which it once shared such habitats (Rosenberg et al. 1991).

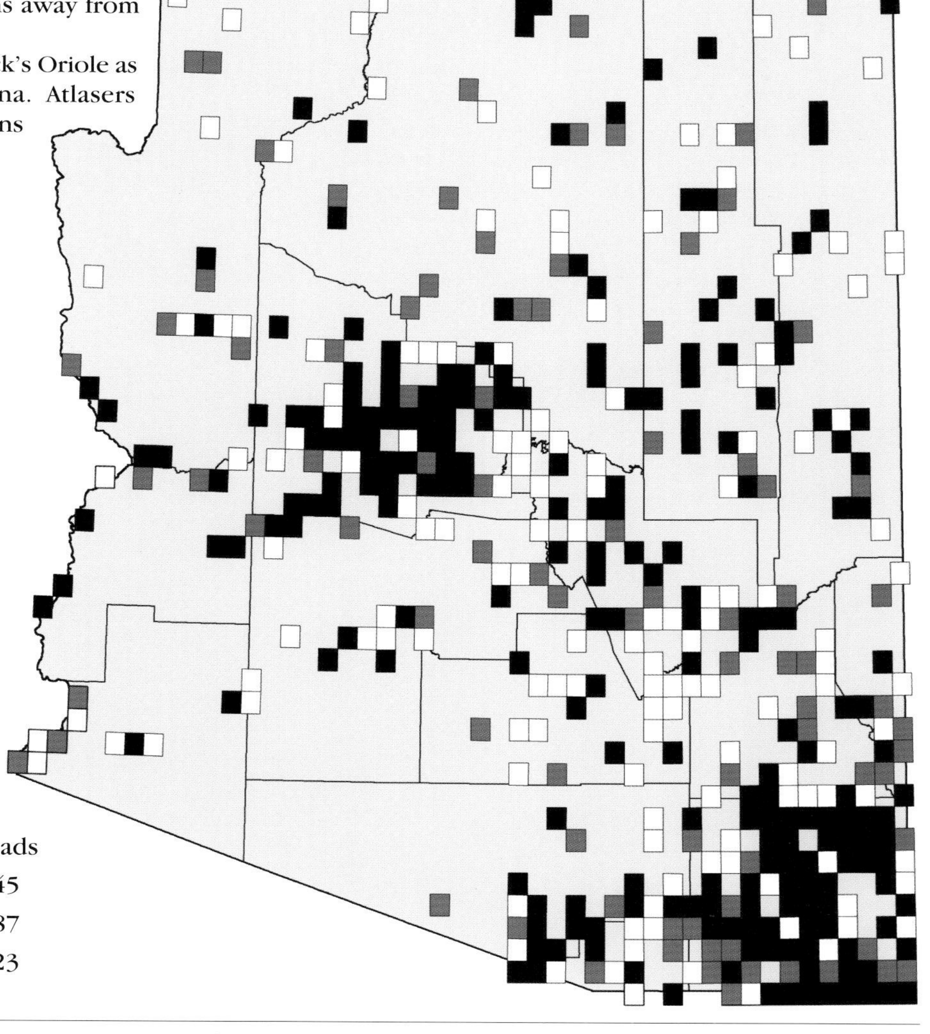

Bullock's Oriole Breeding Evidence Reported in 411 (22%) of 1834 priority blocks

	Blocks	Quads
Possible	122 (30%)	145
Probable	82 (20%)	87
Confirmed	207 (50%)	223

Scott's Oriole

by Troy E. Corman *Icterus parisorum*

The sudden, loud, and clearly whistled song of the Scott's Oriole often catches an observer's attention well before this striking bird is located inconspicuously on some elevated perch. This oriole's preference for drier and more arid environments than other orioles favor allows it to occur throughout much of Arizona.

HABITAT

In Arizona, Scott's Orioles breed in a much wider array of habitats than other orioles in the state and are typically encountered in arid scrub and open woodland landscapes. Atlasers reported this oriole in twenty-three different vegetative communities, from deserts and dry washes to chaparral and open wooded slopes. They were encountered much more frequently in the Sonoran desertscrub than previous literature suggested. Approximately 29 percent of all atlas records were from well-vegetated Sonoran Desert areas, including the desert foothill slopes and the wooded dry washes that meander through this arid landscape ($n = 747$). Dominant trees included velvet mesquite, paloverde, and ironwood, particularly those containing mistletoe clumps, where these orioles often construct their nests. Atlasers reported another 27 percent of observations in open pinyon pine–juniper woodlands, including cold-temperate grasslands with scattered junipers. Scott's Orioles were frequently encountered in semiarid grasslands and Chihuahuan desertscrub areas with soaptree and other yuccas. Other regularly used habitats included Madrean evergreen oak woodlands, interior chaparral, and Mojave desertscrub associations, particularly those with Joshua trees. They were occasionally found foraging and nesting in adjacent open cottonwood and sycamore-dominated drainages as well.

BREEDING

Although a few early male Scott's Orioles arrive in southern Arizona by the second week of March, most do not arrive on their breeding grounds until April. Atlasers observed nest-building activity in the Sonoran Desert as early as 8 April, and the first nest with eggs was discovered on 15 April. However, atlasers observed an adult carrying food on 17 April near Lukeville, suggesting nest building in late March and egg laying by the first few days of April. Based on atlas data, the peak nesting period is from late April through mid-May, with a second peak in mid-June. In southeastern Arizona, nest with eggs were found as late as 27 July, nests with young to 14 August, and adults feeding young through 20 August. These rather late nesting efforts may be correlated to these orioles' taking advantage of the abundant food resources during the typical late summer monsoon period in this region. In northern Arizona, most Scott's Orioles have departed by early August, with stragglers through early September. These orioles are rarely reported in the state after mid-September, although a few winter irregularly and very sparsely in southern Arizona (Monson and Phillips 1981).

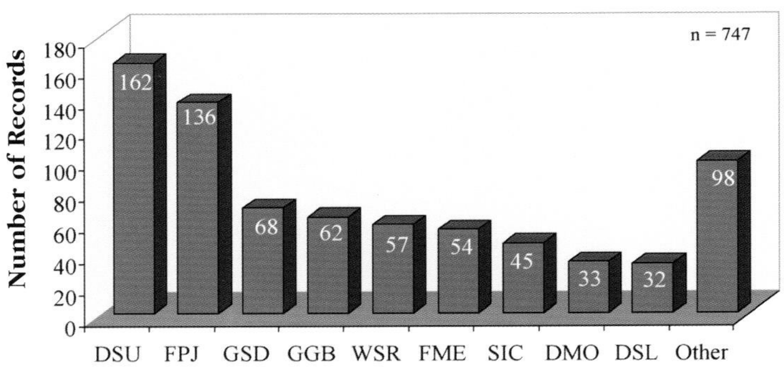

Only the female Scott's Oriole constructs the sturdy nest frequently made of narrow fibers taken from the edges of yucca and agave leaves. The mean height of thirty-eight nests measured by atlasers was 8.5 ft (2.6 m) above the ground, with a range of 4.6–20.0 ft (1.4–6.1 m). Because these orioles nest in such a wide range of habitats, nesting sites are also quite varied. In the Sonoran Desert, atlasers found nests most frequently in foothill or blue paloverdes, often in clumps of mistletoe. Other Sonoran Desert nests were found in crucifixion thorn and in mistletoe clumps growing on catclaw acacia, whitethorn acacia, and ironwood. One odd nest with eggs was also discovered 6.6 ft (2 m) high in a jumping cholla. Atlasers found Joshua tree and other yuccas the nest substrates of choice in the Mojave Desert. Similarly, in semiarid grasslands and the Chihuahuan Desert, they preferred soaptree yuccas. At higher elevations, such as southeastern Arizona mountain foothills and pinyon-juniper–dominated landscapes in the north, atlasers found Scott's Orioles nesting most frequently in various species of juniper and pinyon pine, but also in several species of

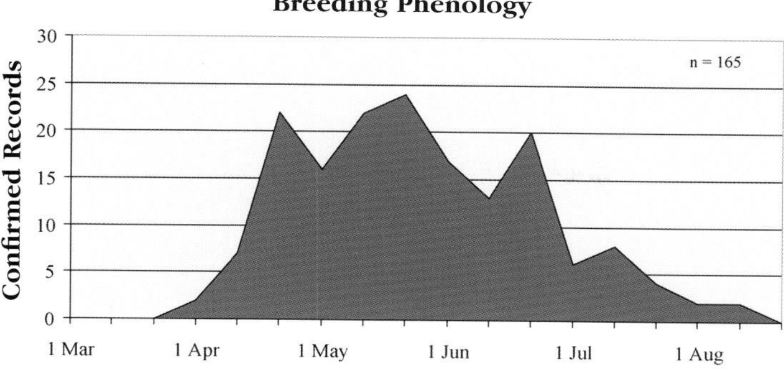

evergreen oaks, Fremont barberry, and yucca. Several nests were also found high in Arizona sycamore and Fremont cottonwood in riparian drainages.

Scott's Orioles lay a typical clutch of 3–4 eggs, but this can range from 1 to 5 (Flood 2002). The female incubates the eggs for approximately 13 days, ranging from 11 to 15 days (Flood 2002). Both parents feed the nestlings, which fledge at approximately 12 days of age (Bent 1958; Flood 2002). Scott's Orioles produce one to two broods per year and have been known to attempt three (Flood 2002). Atlasers found one nest with eggs in southeastern Arizona on 18 July, which also contained a Bronzed Cowbird egg.

DISTRIBUTION AND STATUS

Scott's Orioles breed from south-central Mexico and Baja California, north locally in southern California, extreme southern Wyoming, and east to central Texas. These orioles are typically described as common summer residents in Arizona, although they are considered uncommon and more sparsely distributed in the north and southwestern desert regions (Phillips et al. 1964).

Atlasers confirmed Scott's Orioles nesting at elevations ranging from 910 to 6940 ft (277–2115 m). They were encountered commonly and most regularly in southeastern Arizona, north to the southern slope of the Mogollon Rim, and throughout the northwest. This includes much of the Arizona Strip region, where few prior records existed. Atlasers reported Scott's Orioles fairly regularly on the slopes and foothills of the higher desert mountain ranges in southwestern Arizona. They were especially common throughout the relatively protected areas of the Cabeza Prieta National Wildlife Refuge, Organ Pipe Cactus National Monument, eastern Barry M. Goldwater Range, and immediately adjacent Tohono O'odham tribal lands. Scott's Orioles were widespread north of the Mogollon Rim in open pinyon pine and juniper woodlands, but they occurred sparingly and rather locally in this region of the state.

As noted by Rosenberg et al. (1991), Scott's Orioles were absent along the immediate lower Colorado River corridor, nesting as far west as the Dome Rock Mountains east of Ehrenberg. They were also primarily absent within the largely urban and agricultural regions of the lower Gila, lower Salt, and Santa Cruz river valleys.

The distribution of Scott's Orioles has apparently changed very little in Arizona, and populations of these striking birds appear to be fairly stable. Their clear, melodious songs are a pleasing feature of the state's many arid landscapes.

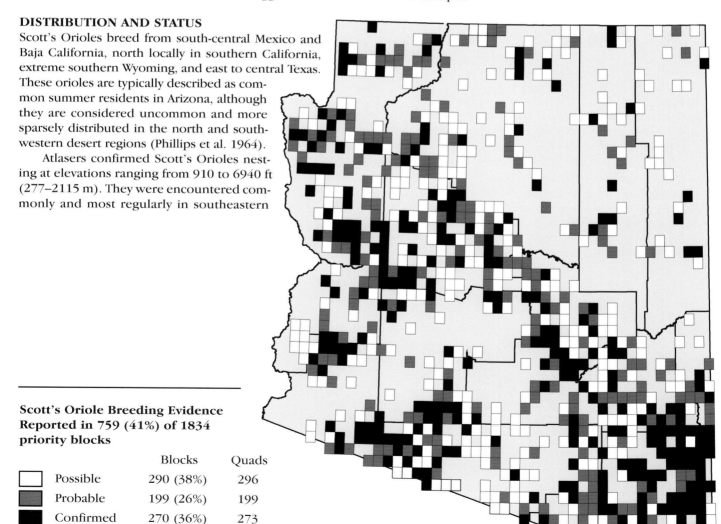

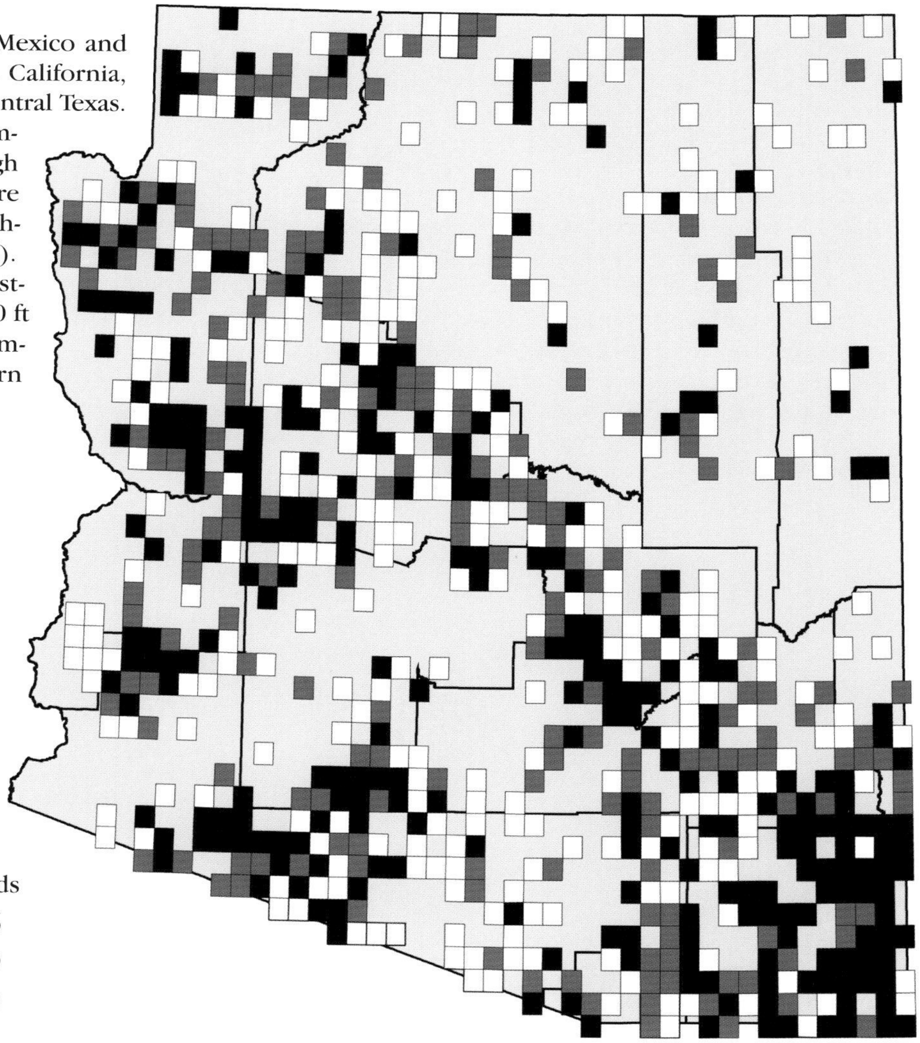

Scott's Oriole Breeding Evidence Reported in 759 (41%) of 1834 priority blocks

	Blocks	Quads
Possible	290 (38%)	296
Probable	199 (26%)	199
Confirmed	270 (36%)	273

Cassin's Finch

by Troy E. Corman *Carpodacus cassinii*

Found foraging for seeds on the forest floor or savoring buds high in the trees, Cassin's Finches are frequently much more common during migration and winter in Arizona than as a nesting species. Throughout the spring, males sing exuberantly from lofty perches or while on the wing, only to become quiet and inconspicuous later in the season.

DAN FISCHER

HABITAT

Throughout their range, Cassin's Finches typically nest in or near open, mature coniferous forests or woodlands and less often in adjacent stands of quaking aspen. Of 22 potential breeding records collected during the atlas period, 96 percent were noted in various forests containing ponderosa pine. In fact, ponderosa pine–dominated forests, including those with a Gambel's oak association, accounted for more than half the records. Cassin's Finches were also encountered within mixed-conifer forests containing Douglas fir, white fir, quaking aspen, and various species of pines. Only one atlas record was obtained from higher elevation spruce-fir forests containing Engelmann spruce and subalpine fir. Foraging pairs and small flocks are regularly observed foraging near forest clearings or at the edge of subalpine meadows.

BREEDING

The seasonal movement of Arizona's nesting Cassin's Finch populations is unclear, owing to the fall and winter influx of individuals from regions north of the state. Although some of the state's Cassin's Finches undoubtedly move to lower elevations during cooler months, they are cold-hardy birds, and many are resident in the forests in which they breed. In Arizona, spring migration may begin by March with a peak passage in April and stragglers well into May.

Atlasers noted singing males in known nesting areas by 19 April and observed courtship behavior by 10 May. From April to early June, Cassin's Finches engage in prolonged and vigorous singing bouts beginning at dawn and continuing throughout the day (Hahn 1996). Adult males are known to cease singing within one or two days of the onset of nest building by their mates and begin evicting intruding males from the vicinity of the females by chasing and threat displays (Samson 1976).

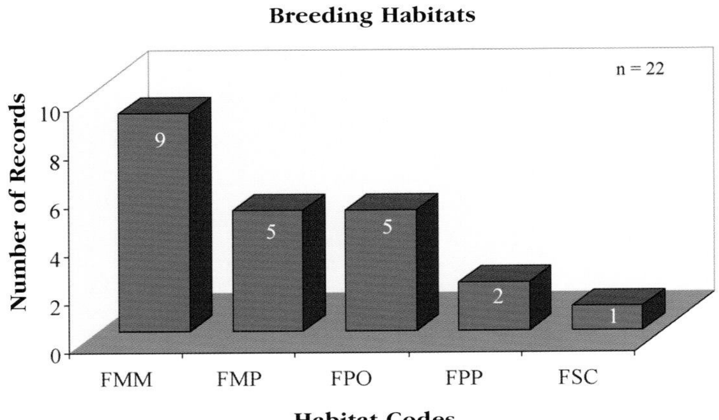

Atlasers had difficulty in locating Cassin's Finch nests, and very limited breeding data were obtained during the atlas period. However, in Colorado, where Cassin's Finches are a much more widespread breeding species, Winn (1998) reported nest building occurring from 8 May to 24 July. A similar nesting period would be expected in Arizona. The only confirmed atlas records were of several observations of fledglings from 27 June to 29 July, but in Colorado, adult Cassin's Finches have been observed feeding fledged young from 25 May to 24 August (Winn 1998). The fall and winter distribution and abundance of Cassin's Finches in Arizona is extremely variable from one year to the next. However, they often begin appearing away from nesting areas in late September and early October.

Some researchers suggest that these finches may nest semicolonially (Samson 1976; Hahn 1996). Few nests have been described in Arizona, but the vast majority of Cassin's Finch nests are placed in large conifers, usually well out on a lateral branch or near the trunk within 3.3 ft (1 m) of the top of the tree (Samson 1976). These finches are known to nest in a wide selection of pines and firs, and in Arizona they likely nest most commonly in ponderosa pine, Douglas fir, white fir, and much less frequently in quaking aspen. The nest placement height can also be quite variable across their range. Hahn (1996) compiled nest records from a number of sources and found the average nest height to be approximately 36 ft (11 m), with a range of 6.6–88.6 ft (2–27 m) above the ground.

Female Cassin's Finches apparently construct the rather loose and frail nest in just a few days (Samson 1976). Clutches range in size from 3 to 6, but typically consist of 4–5 eggs (Orr 1968). The female incubates the eggs for approximately 12 days, during which time the male feeds her and adopts a sentry position not far from the nest (Samson 1976). Both parents feed the nestlings (Orr 1968), until they fledge in approximately 16 days (Sullivan et al. 1986). The parents continue feeding the fledglings for an unknown period following nest departure. Cassin's Finches generally produce only one brood per season, but will renest if earlier attempts fail.

DISTRIBUTION AND STATUS

Cassin's Finches are found breeding throughout the forested regions of the interior West from southeastern British Columbia, south locally to southern California, northern Arizona, and north-central New Mexico. In Arizona, these finches have been described as common summer residents only on the Kaibab Plateau, then south uncommonly and infrequently to Flagstaff (Phillips et al. 1964; Monson and Phillips 1981). On Navajo tribal lands, summer observations of Cassin's Finches suggested nesting on Black Mesa south of Kayenta (LaRue 1994) and locally in the Chuska Mountains (Jacobs 1986).

Atlasers noted Cassin's Finches as rather uncommon and local on higher plateaus and mountains of extreme northern Arizona at elevations ranging from 6800 to 9500 ft (2073–2896 m). The largest continuous population of this finch in the state remains in the higher elevations of the Kaibab Plateau, including the North Rim of the Grand Canyon. Atlasers also documented Cassin's Finches locally on the South Rim of the Grand Canyon and to the northwest on Mount Trumbull and Mount Logan. Singing individuals were also noted in appropriate nesting habitat on Black Rock Mountain, near the Virgin Mountains in the extreme northwest corner of Arizona. On Navajo tribal lands, Cassin's Finches were confirmed nesting on Black Mesa and in the Lukachukai-Chuska Mountains. Appropriate habitat also exits in the nearby Carrizo Mountains to the north and more thorough surveys in this remote range may reveal them nesting there as well. During the atlas period, these finches were detected only once during the summer in the Flagstaff area.

The breeding distribution of Cassin's Finches in Arizona is not easily explained. The southern limits of their breeding range in the state are apparently not determined by the available habitat. Extensive and seemingly appropriate forest habitat remains unoccupied throughout central Arizona along the Mogollon Rim and White Mountain regions. This same region of the state is treated to small roving flocks of these attractive forest finches during migration and often through the winter, but curiously, they have never been known to nest there.

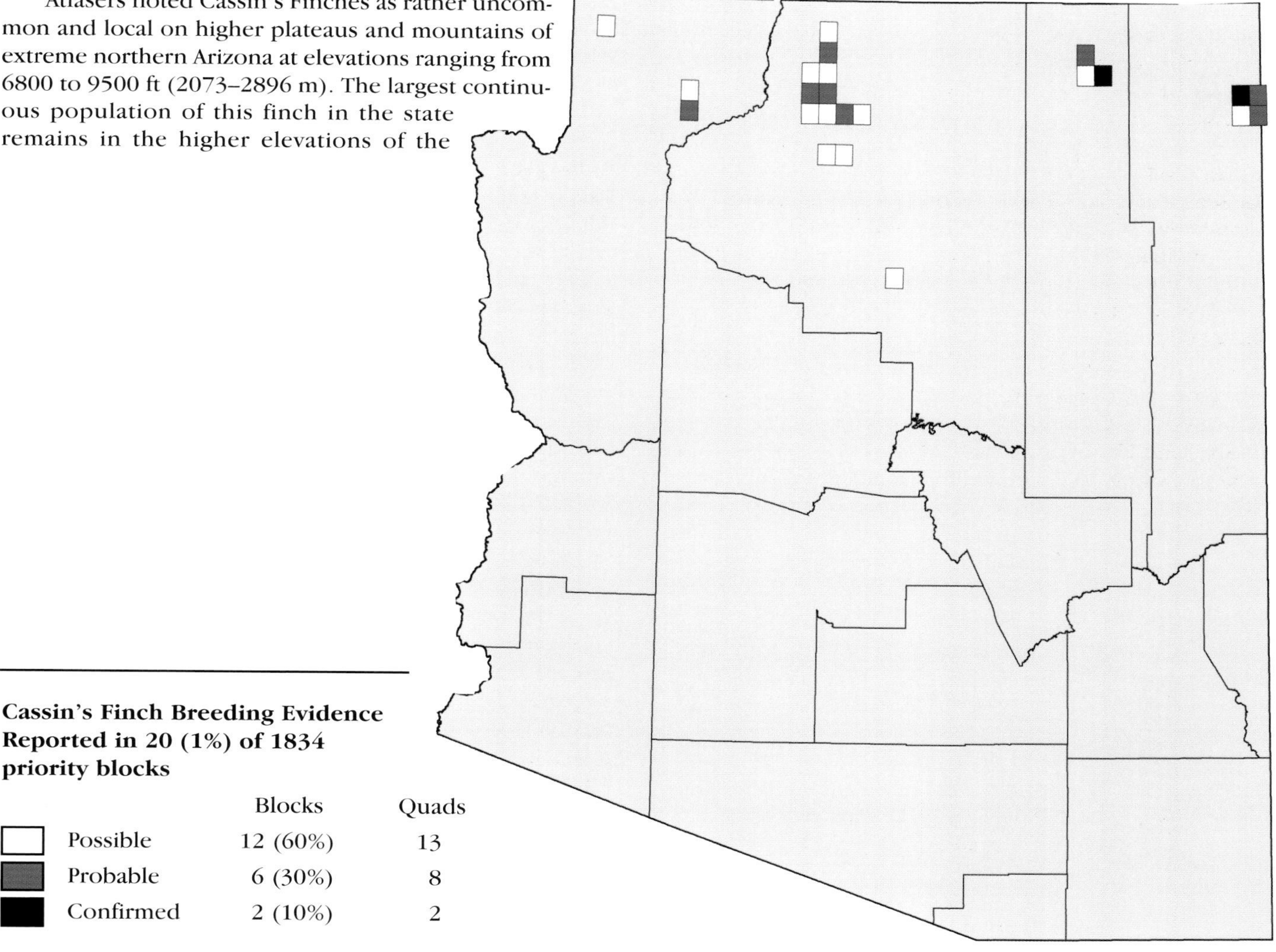

Cassin's Finch Breeding Evidence Reported in 20 (1%) of 1834 priority blocks

	Blocks	Quads
Possible	12 (60%)	13
Probable	6 (30%)	8
Confirmed	2 (10%)	2

House Finch

by Cathryn Wise-Gervais

Carpodacus mexicanus

One of Arizona's most widespread and abundant species, House Finches are familiar to even the most casual backyard observer. These adaptable and resourceful birds occupy many of the state's habitats, and males can vary considerably in color from pale yellow to red based on pigments they receive in food.

BRUCE TAUBERT

HABITAT

House Finches inhabit a wide variety of vegetative communities in Arizona including desertscrub, riparian areas, open woodlands, and grasslands with scattered trees. They reach some of their highest breeding densities in or near urban and rural settlements, where they readily take advantage of water, food, and nest sites found in conjunction with human habitations. Atlasers reported House Finches in twenty-five habitat types across Arizona (n = 1525). The two most commonly reported habitats used by this species, Sonoran desertscrub and pinyon pine–juniper woodlands, are also the two most widely distributed vegetative communities in Arizona. It is likely that these adaptable birds are not actively selecting these habitats over others but are instead simply making use of what is available. House Finches favor woodland edges and are commonly encountered nesting in many of the state's linear riparian stands from densely wooded desert washes to cottonwood-, willow-, and sycamore-dominated drainages. They also nest in drainage thickets of exotic tamarisk and Russian olive. Although atlasers found House Finches statewide, this species regularly avoids densely forested and higher elevation habitats.

BREEDING

House Finches are for the most part year-round residents throughout Arizona and can initiate nesting as early as mid-February in lowland desert and urban areas. Atlasers observed adults carrying nest material as early as 14 February, and early clutch initiation likely begins in late February or early March. However, observers did not report a nest with eggs until 15 March and the first nest with young on 25 March. Atlasers obtained 537 confirmed records for this species, excluding fledgling sightings. These data suggest that House Finch breeding activity peaks between mid-April and mid-May, then tapers off throughout the summer months. However, atlasers reported House Finch nests with eggs through 1 August, and adults were observed feeding fledglings through late August. Although migration is not well documented for House Finch, some birds do move locally to lower elevations and to abundant winter food resources, where they may form large flocks.

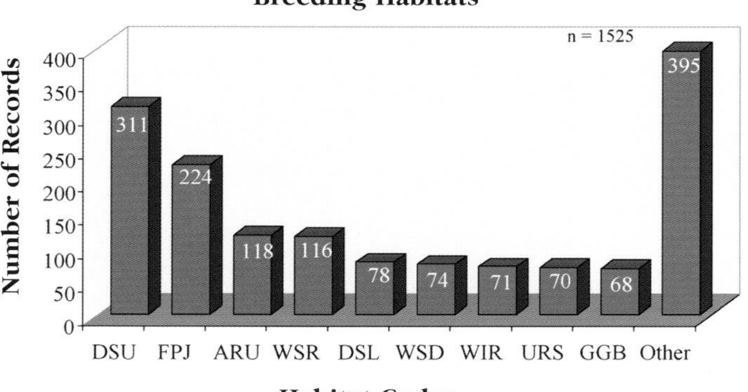

House Finches are known to nest in a variety of trees and shrubs, as well as on rock ledges, and human-built structures. Atlasers also located several nests in old Bullock's and Hooded Oriole nests. In fact, several lofty House Finch nests were discovered inside Hooded Oriole nests that were in turn attached to the underside of an active Red-tailed Hawk nest placed high on a transmission tower! Atlasers took measurements at 145 House Finch nests in 20 substrates. Forty-three percent of nests were in several species of cholla, 14 percent were in juniper, and 7 percent were in paloverde. House Finch nests were also regularly reported in saguaros, acacia, hackberry, ironwood, tamarisk, smoketree, and yucca. Two nests were observed on human-built structures, and one was on a cliff. The median nest height was 4.9 ft (1.5 m) and heights ranged from 1.9 to 39.4 ft (0.6–12 m; n = 145). In contrast, 278 nests in Michigan were often placed much higher, with a mean nest height of 15.7 ft (4.8 m; Hill 1993).

Female House Finches do most of the nest construction, but the males will often carry materials to the nest site (Evenden 1957; Thompson 1960). The typical clutch size in Arizona consists of 4 eggs, but ranges from 3 to 5 (Hensley 1959). The female does all the incubating but is fed by her mate while on the nest (Hill 1991). Incubation takes 12–14 days, slightly longer in cold weather (Hill 1993). Both adults feed the young and these fledge at approximately 12 days of age. Prior to fledging, the nest becomes quite soiled as nestlings commonly defecate on the rim. House Finch pairs are prolific and routinely produce three broods per year (Hill 1993).

House Finches are considered an infrequent Brown-headed Cowbird host (Hill 1993). During the atlas period,

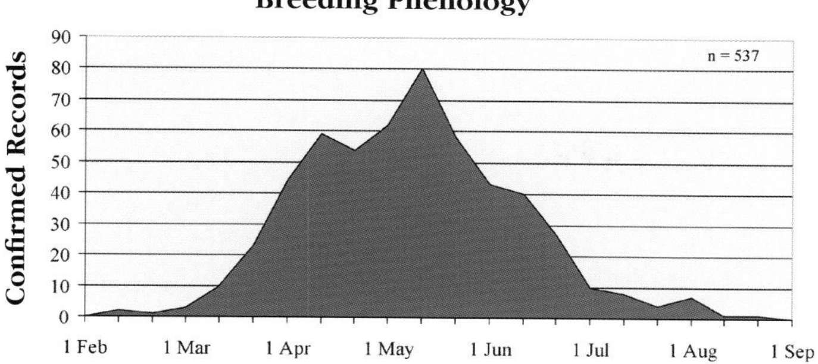

only three incidents of parasitism were reported between 27 May and 27 June.

DISTRIBUTION AND STATUS

Before 1945, House Finches were considered a western North American species and were found from California to central Texas and from southern British Columbia to southern Mexico. They were introduced to Long Island, New York, around 1940. These birds are now widespread in eastern North America from Nova Scotia to northern Florida and west to the Great Plains region, where their breeding range continues to expand west toward their native range. This adaptable species was able to expand its range rapidly due in part to backyard feeding stations. House Finches quickly inhabit newly available habitats. Furthermore, they occur over a wide range of elevations, and in Arizona they were confirmed breeding on priority blocks from approximately 100 to 7500 ft (30–2286 m).

Most prior Arizona literature describes House Finches as widespread and abundant, and atlas data support this status. Phillips et al. (1964) even noted that in the arid southwestern region of the state "there are few places in the desert where House Finches do not occur." The species nests in open ponderosa pine forests, especially near human habitations such as near Flagstaff and Payson, and very locally in higher forests. Atlasers reported the species statewide with the exceptions of densely forests areas and higher elevations such as above the Mogollon Rim, White Mountains region, and Kaibab Plateau. House Finches were also sparsely distributed in dry, desolate areas within the Little Colorado River valley and southern portions of Navajo and Hopi tribal lands.

As mentioned previously, atlasers noted House Finches in many habitats, including urban, rural, and wilderness settings. The frequency with which this species was encountered, coupled with the relative abundances atlasers reported, suggest that Arizona populations of this bird are certainly stable. In fact, these adaptable and ubiquitous finches could be locally increasing in the state as forests and woodlands are fragmented and urbanization continues.

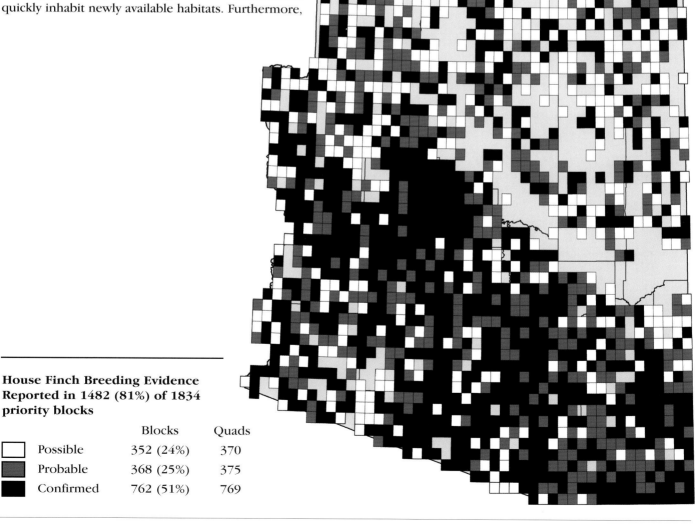

House Finch Breeding Evidence Reported in 1482 (81%) of 1834 priority blocks

	Blocks	Quads
Possible	352 (24%)	370
Probable	368 (25%)	375
Confirmed	762 (51%)	769

Red Crossbill

by Troy E. Corman *Loxia curvirostra*

Red Crossbills acrobatically clamber over pine limbs and often hang upside down as they use their unique bill to extract pine seeds from cones. Not following the norm of other mountain nesting passerines, these rather nomadic finches typically nest in winter and early spring, challenging atlasers to discover their occasionally snow-rimmed nests.

DAN FISCHER

HABITAT

Red Crossbills nest primarily in forests dominated by mature conifers. Atlasers reported 88 percent of all potential breeding records for this species from forests containing ponderosa pine (n = 105). In fact, they were encountered most frequently in ponderosa pine–dominated forests and in mixed-conifer forests containing Douglas fir, white fir, and various pine species. Atlasers reported significantly fewer Red Crossbill observations from pinyon pine–juniper dominated landscapes. Use of these woodlands for nesting may occur only during years producing an abundance of pinyon pine nuts. These birds were also noted fairly regularly in several locally distributed habitats, including spruce-fir forests and the Madrean pine-oak forests in southeastern Arizona ranges. During the irregular flight years when flocks of Red Crossbills invade lowland desert urban areas, they have infrequently been found nesting in exotic aleppo pine stands, such as those in city parks, cemeteries, and school grounds.

BREEDING

The abundance and distribution of Red Crossbills in Arizona can be quite varied from one year to the next, and these fluctuations are related to the abundance of pinecones and ultimately pine seeds in a given area. This principal food source is the most important factor influencing timing of nesting. Phillips et al. (1964) noted that male Red Crossbills are heard singing from frozen forests from November through the spring. The principal nesting season for these finches in western North America is in winter and occasionally in spring through late summer (Phillips et al. 1964). This fact may help explain the few nests discovered during atlas surveys and why most confirmations were of adults feeding fledged young or observations of fledglings. Most high-elevation surveys were conducted from May to July. The earliest confirmed atlas record was of a male feeding a female on the nest near the South Rim of the Grand Canyon on 7 February. Atlasers reported the first fledgling on 18 March; the only other occupied nest found by atlasers was on 30 April. Red Crossbills were observed feeding fledglings through 20 June, suggesting nest with young at least into mid-May. Atlasers reported streaked fledglings through 31 July. Nesting efforts may occur occasionally into the fall in Arizona, inasmuch as a recent fledgling was collected on 7 October 1948 on Hualapai tribal lands in Coconino County (Austin 1968).

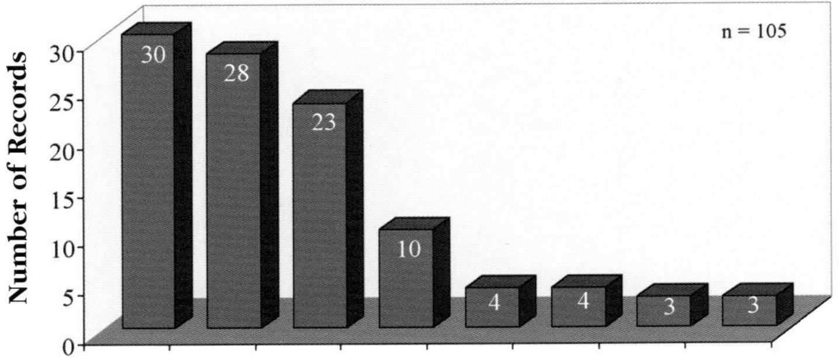

Female Red Crossbills construct the nest; however, males will sometimes collect nesting material (Austin 1968). Nests are well concealed in dense cover and usually well shaded by the trunk or branches, which may help limit snow accumulation and insulate the nest from the cold. In Arizona, most nests have been discovered in ponderosa pine, but Red Crossbills also likely nest in various other pines, spruce, and fir. The average nest height is approximately 25 ft (7.6 m), with a range of 10–40 ft (3–12 m) above the ground (Austin 1968).

Red Crossbills typically lay 3 eggs per clutch, but this can range from 2 to 4 (Bailey et al. 1953). Only the female incubates, and the male helps feed her while she is on the nest. The eggs hatch after an incubation period of 12–16 days, but most frequently in 14 days (Austin 1968). The female will brood the young almost continuously for the first 5 days after hatching (Bailey et al. 1953). Both parents feed the nestlings, which typically fledge when they are 15–25 days old and are fed up to a month following nest departure (Bailey et al. 1953). The male will take over sole

Breeding Phenology

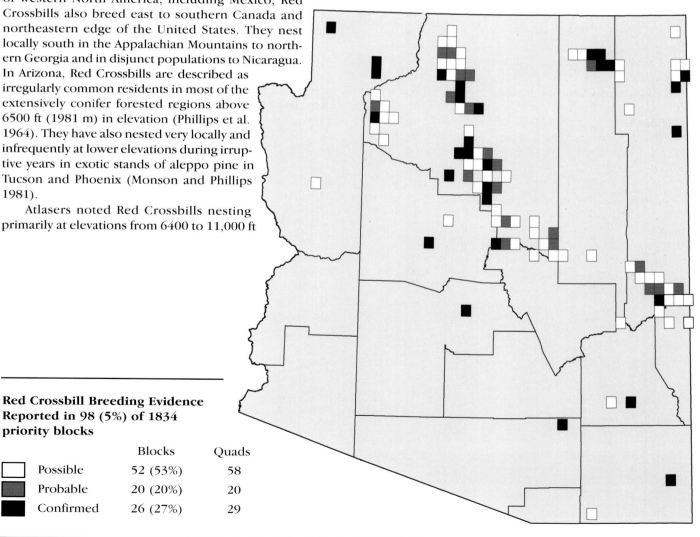

Graph includes fledgling records

responsibility for the fledglings of the first brood when the female begins incubating the next clutch. Such rapid multiple broods may result when local seed crop is exceptionally large (Bailey et al. 1953). Based on available pine seed crop, Red Crossbills likely produce 2–4 broods per year with some populations nesting almost continuously for 6–9 months (Adkisson 1996).

DISTRIBUTION AND STATUS

Nesting throughout much of the conifer-forested regions of western North America, including Mexico, Red Crossbills also breed east to southern Canada and northeastern edge of the United States. They nest locally south in the Appalachian Mountains to northern Georgia and in disjunct populations to Nicaragua. In Arizona, Red Crossbills are described as irregularly common residents in most of the extensively conifer forested regions above 6500 ft (1981 m) in elevation (Phillips et al. 1964). They have also nested very locally and infrequently at lower elevations during irruptive years in exotic stands of aleppo pine in Tucson and Phoenix (Monson and Phillips 1981).

Atlasers noted Red Crossbills nesting primarily at elevations from 6400 to 11,000 ft (1951–3353 m). One main exception to this was a recently fledged individual captured by a cat on 8 May 2001 in north Scottsdale at an elevation of 1380 ft (421 m). This heavily streaked individual had pin flight feathers, a very short tail, an obvious mouth gap, and basically uncrossed mandibles. This followed a large fall and winter invasion of Red Crossbills to the desert southwest.

Atlasers encountered Red Crossbills from the White Mountains northwest along the Mogollon Rim and through Flagstaff and Williams north to the Kaibab Plateau. This crossbill likely breeds throughout much of the adjacent White Mountain Apache tribal lands along the Mogollon Rim as well, but access permits to conduct surveys within this reservation could not be obtained. On Navajo and Hopi tribal lands, Red Crossbills were reported regularly on Black Mesa and from the Carrizo Mountains south locally to the Defiance Plateau.

Red Crossbills were also found in the higher elevations of the eastern Hualapai tribal lands. Elsewhere in the northwest, they were confirmed nesting on several isolated mountain ranges of the Arizona Strip region, including Mount Logan, Mount Trumbull, and Black Rock Mountain. In southeastern Arizona, atlasers encountered these unique finches sparingly in the Santa Catalina, Pinaleno, Chiricahua, and Huachuca mountains.

Red Crossbill Breeding Evidence Reported in 98 (5%) of 1834 priority blocks

	Blocks	Quads
Possible	52 (53%)	58
Probable	20 (20%)	20
Confirmed	26 (27%)	29

Pine Siskin

by Cathryn Wise-Gervais *Carduelis pinus*

Well known for their irruptive occurrences, these small, heavily streaked finches spend much of their time flitting high in the pines foraging for seeds or in weedy patches close to the ground. The Pine Siskin's narrow bill and buzzy vocalizations make him easy to distinguish from other, brighter *Carduelis* finches.

BRUCE TAUBERT

HABITAT

During the breeding season, Pine Siskins occur primarily in open coniferous forests with tall trees, but they can wander into many different settings the remainder of the year, especially following population irruptions. Atlasers reported Pine Siskins in thirteen habitat types containing various combinations of pines, firs, and spruce, with the highest percentage of records (33 percent) in mixed-conifer forests of Douglas and white fir, ponderosa pine, and scattered aspen (n = 108). Observers reported 26 percent of records in pure ponderosa pine forests and 13 percent in ponderosa pine–Gambel's oak associations. Pine Siskins were encountered infrequently in montane drainages containing various pines, firs, aspen, oak, and maple, as well as in drier pinyon pine–juniper woodlands with scattered ponderosa pine stands. Fewer records were obtained in high elevation forests of Engelmann spruce, blue spruce, and subalpine fir. However, this could be due to the relatively limited distribution of pure spruce-fir forests in Arizona, inasmuch as the species is commonly encountered in such forests in the state. Approximately 50 percent of the Pine Siskin records obtained during the Colorado Breeding Bird Atlas were in spruce-fir dominated forests (Barrett and Levad 1998).

BREEDING

Arizona's Pine Siskins are primarily year-round residents in or near their montane breeding range, but populations may disperse to other forests if local seed crops are poor. As a result, breeding phenology and particular breeding areas may change annually. During the atlas period, it is likely that many early nesting efforts were missed because atlas surveys in many coniferous forests often did not begin until late spring. Atlasers obtained only twenty-one confirmed breeding records for Pine Siskins, including fledgling sightings, and these observations were from 24 April to 27 July. The earliest confirmation was of nest-building activity, and the latest record was of an adult feeding a fledgling. Very few active nests were discovered during the atlas period, making it difficult to determine nesting chronology in the state. Nest-building activity in Colorado extends from early May to early August (Barrett and Levad 1998), indicating a fairly lengthy nesting season. It is likely that Arizona's birds follow a similar breeding pattern. In Arizona, Pine Siskins occasionally begin appearing in nonbreeding montane areas by late July or August, and in lowland weedy fields and riparian woodland in late September or October. However, their abundance and timing of arrival are highly variable from one year to the next.

In colder climates, Pine Siskins are believed to be successful early-season nesters, largely thanks to their well-insulated nests (Dawson 1997). Pine Siskins often nest in loose colonies and place their well-concealed nests on the distal limbs of conifers or less commonly in deciduous trees or shrubs (Dawson 1997). Although nest heights can range from approximately 3 to 50 ft (0.9–15.2 m) above the ground, the average height for forty-seven nests measured by various researchers throughout the bird's range was 19.3 ft (5.9 m; Dawson 1997).

Pine Siskins typically lay 3–4 eggs, and the female incubates these exclusively while being fed by the male (Dawson 1997). Her attentiveness to the eggs and unwillingness to leave them is thought to play an important role in nest success, especially in cold conditions. Incubation lasts approximately 13 days (Weaver and West 1943), but the female continues brooding until approximately the last 5–7 days of the nestling period (Dawson 1997). The male provides nearly all the food for his brood and mate, and the female typically

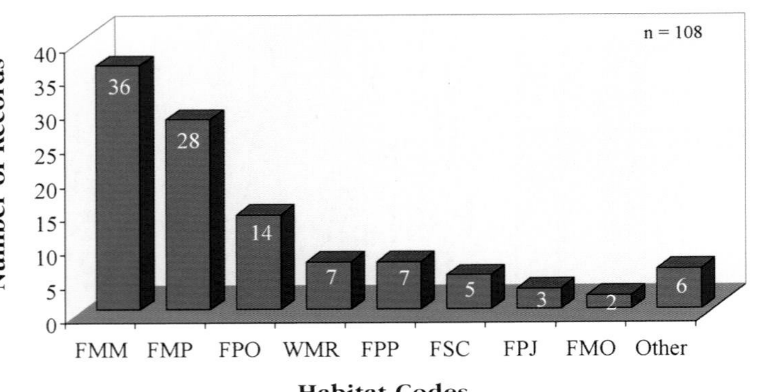

Breeding Phenology

Confirmed Records

0 1 2 3 4 5 6

n = 18

1 Apr 1 May 1 Jun 1 Jul 1 Aug

Graph includes fledgling records

does not assist with feedings until day 8 or 9 after hatching. The young fledge at 13–17 days and continue to depend on adults for an additional 3 weeks after leaving the nest (Dawson 1997). Pine Siskins are generally believed to be single-brooded, although some evidence suggests that the species may occasionally double-brood if resources allow.

DISTRIBUTION AND STATUS

In general, Pine Siskins nest from central Alaska east to southern Labrador and south in the East to northern New York and Michigan. In the West, they breed on the Pacific Coast south to northern California and in higher mountain ranges and plateaus south to central Mexico and locally to Guatemala. Because of irruptive tendencies, however, the species' abundance at particular localities varies considerably from year to year (Dawson 1997). There are also many local nesting records south of their typical eastern United States breeding range. In central and northern Arizona, Pine Siskins are considered common summer residents in coniferous forests from ponderosa pine up to timberline and rare to uncommon in southeastern ranges (Phillips et al. 1964). Atlasers confirmed this small finch breeding on priority blocks at elevations from approximately 5500 ft (1676 m) near Prescott to above 10,000 ft (3048 m) in the White and San Francisco mountains.

Pine Siskins were encountered regularly in central Arizona from the White Mountains and along the Mogollon Rim north to the San Francisco Mountains and west to the Prescott and Williams areas. In addition, these birds likely also breed in the adjacent White Mountain Apache tribal lands, but atlas surveys were not conducted there to verify this. Atlasers reported Pine Siskins locally south to the Mazatzal Mountains and the Sierra Ancha, and it is likely that these individuals were nesting.

Jacobs (1985) considered Pine Siskins common summer residents at higher-elevation forests on Navajo and Hopi tribal lands. During the atlas period, these birds were encountered regularly on Black Mesa and from the Carrizo Mountains south to the Defiance Plateau. Elsewhere in the north, Pine Siskins were widespread on the Kaibab Plateau and the South Rim of the Grand Canyon and were found locally on Wolf Hole Mountain in the northwest.

In southeastern Arizona, atlasers documented Pine Siskins locally throughout the summer in the higher elevations of the Santa Catalina, Pinaleno, and Chiricahua mountains, where, as noted by Phillips et al. (1964), they presumably breed. These small finches were not reported from the Santa Rita Mountains where nesting had previously been documented (Phillips et al. 1964).

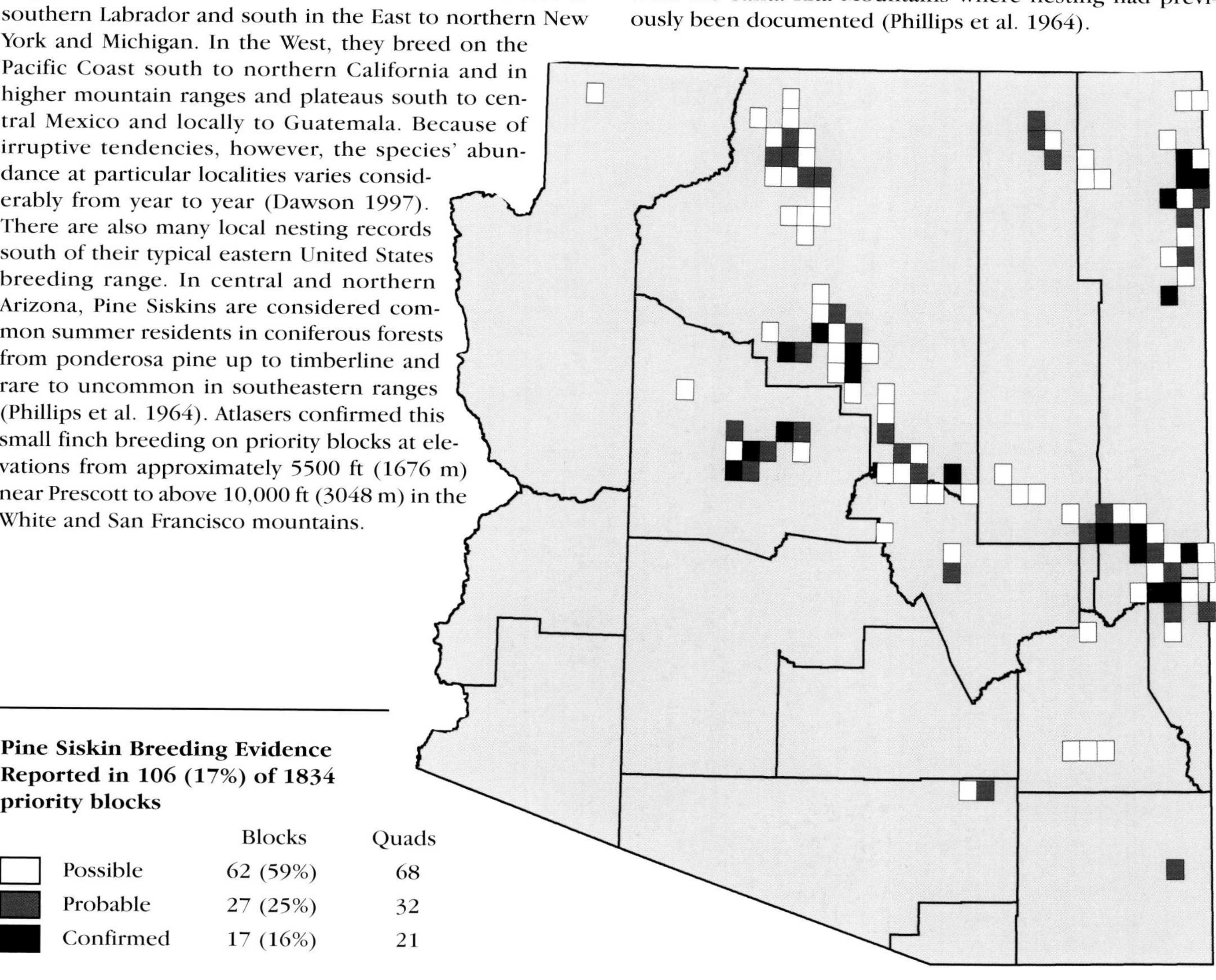

Pine Siskin Breeding Evidence Reported in 106 (17%) of 1834 priority blocks

	Blocks	Quads
Possible	62 (59%)	68
Probable	27 (25%)	32
Confirmed	17 (16%)	21

Lesser Goldfinch

by Cathryn Wise-Gervais *Carduelis psaltria*

The bright and sprightly Lesser Goldfinch is an accomplished songster, capable of mimicking dozens of avian species and even rock squirrels. Like yellow nomads, these petite finches often travel in flocks, and are frequently found near water feasting on grass and flower seeds.

HABITAT

Lesser Goldfinches occupy a wide variety of habitats throughout the western United States, but Arizona's birds are most frequently encountered in riparian settings. Although atlasers reported Lesser Goldfinches potentially nesting in twenty habitat types, 47 percent of all atlas records were noted in only two riparian woodland communities (n = 506). Observers reported 27 percent of records in lowland riparian areas characterized by cottonwood, willow, tamarisk, and mesquite. An additional 20 percent of records were from sycamore-dominated drainages and canyons also containing cottonwood, willow, ash, or alder. In northern Arizona, Lesser Goldfinches also nest in riparian areas containing cottonwoods and other deciduous trees, including small isolated stands at springs and along intermittent drainages.

Locally, these diminutive finches take advantage of deciduous shade trees and orchards in rural and residential settings, and can become regular visitors to gardens and seed feeders. They can also be found nesting locally in foothill desert washes containing stands of tall hackberry and in Madrean evergreen oak woodlands. Atlasers occasionally confirmed Lesser Goldfinches nesting in several conifer-dominated habitats as well, including pinyon pine–juniper woodlands and open ponderosa pine forests, with or without a Gambel's oak association.

BREEDING

Lesser Goldfinches are year-round residents throughout most of Arizona, but many northern and mountain populations typically disperse to lower elevations during the fall and winter in search of food. Where they are resident, Lesser Goldfinches can initiate breeding quite early, and their protracted breeding season is well known. In fact, it is likely that these birds are capable of nesting nearly year-round in southern Arizona. Phillips et al. (1964) noted that a juvenile Lesser Goldfinch was collected in Patagonia on 18 February and was thought to have hatched by mid-January. The earliest occupied nest reported by atlasers was on 5 February. Atlas data suggest that the peak period for breeding activity statewide is from mid-May to early June.

Atlasers reported active Lesser Goldfinch nests throughout the summer months, with the latest nest with eggs located on 29 August. Prior literature reported several instances of Lesser Goldfinches nesting occasionally into November in Arizona. During the atlas period, observers noted an adult feeding a fledgling on 15 November, and observers found that even at higher elevations, nesting activity can extend well into the fall. Near Luna Lake, an adult was observed feeding a fledgling on 4 October at an elevation of near 8000 ft (2438 m). Since most atlas surveys ended by mid-August, it is likely that many late breeding records for this species were missed.

Female Lesser Goldfinches select the nest site and focus intently on nest construction while males watch and do not assist (Watt and Willoughby 1999). Phillips et al. (1964) watched a female remove her dead mate's body from the nest she was constructing, then continue her activity. Apparently the male had been shot and had fallen into the nest. Nests are usually placed in a fork of multiple branches or in a clump of leaves providing cover (Watt and Willoughby 1999). Many species of trees and shrubs are used for nest placement in Arizona, but cottonwood, willow, and sycamore are the most frequently reported. Atlasers took measurements at only nine Lesser Goldfinch nests. Nest trees included tamarisk (3 nests), hackberry (2 nests), oak (2 nests), and one each in paloverde and walnut. The median height of these nests was 10.2 ft (3.1 m) and ranged from 4.3 to 26.2 ft (1.3–8.0 m). However, nests can range from 3 to 45 ft (0.9–13.7 m) above the ground (Watt and Willoughby 1999).

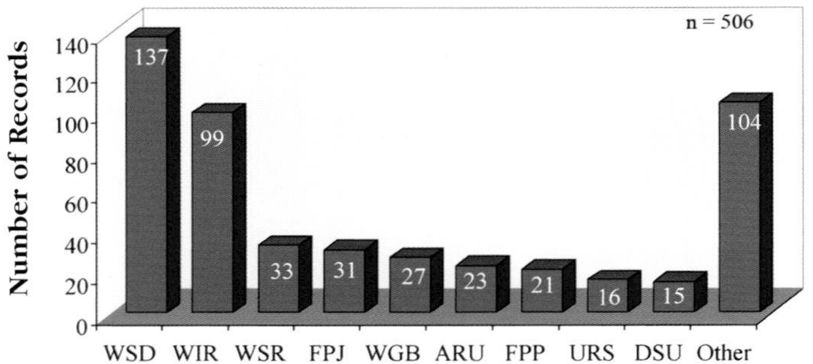

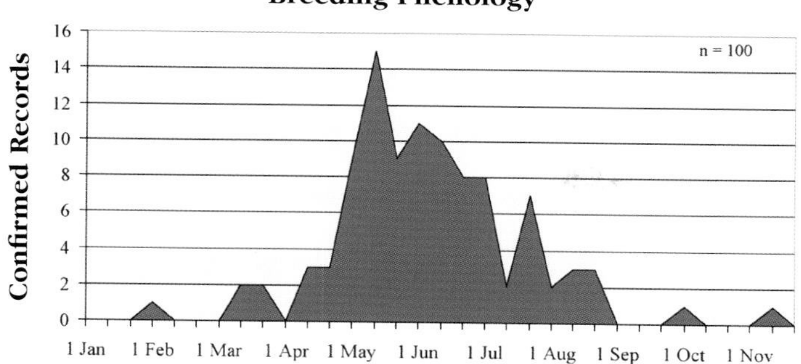

The typical Lesser Goldfinch clutch consists of four eggs (range 3–5; Linsdale 1968); the female incubates these for 12–13 days while being fed by the male (Coutlee 1968; Linsdale 1968). Both sexes feed the young through fledging in 11–12 days and for several weeks following nest departure (Baicich and Harrison 1997; Watt and Willoughby 1999). More studies are needed to determine if pairs produce multiple broods per year, but the lengthy nesting season suggests the possibility when resources allow.

DISTRIBUTION AND STATUS

Lesser Goldfinches breed primarily from Oregon to Colorado and Texas south through much of Mexico (including Baja California) and locally in Central America to Panama. In Arizona, Lesser Goldfinches are primarily absent as a nesting species in the arid Mojave and Sonoran desertscrub associations of the west and southwest, but otherwise are found nearly statewide in appropriate habitat. However, even in these desertscrub habitats nesting attempts occasionally occur as noted by Monson and Phillips (1981) and one observation by atlasers of nest building in a paloverde near the Harcuvar Mountains. Atlasers confirmed these small finches breeding on priority blocks from approximately 500 ft (259 m) at the Bill Williams River National Wildlife Refuge to 8200 ft (2438 m) near Nutrioso. However, they were also encountered locally within the lower Colorado River Valley at lower elevations near Yuma.

Most prior Arizona literature described Lesser Goldfinches as fairly common to common summer residents in riparian areas containing cottonwood, willow, or sycamore and locally in other deciduous trees up to the Transition Zone. Atlas data reveal that these goldfinches were more widespread and abundant south of the Mogollon Rim from the Prescott area to southeastern Arizona, as noted by Phillips et al. (1964).

Although appropriate habitat is more locally distributed in northern Arizona, atlasers routinely encountered Lesser Goldfinches where suitable habitat occurred. The birds were fairly widespread and locally common on Navajo and Hopi tribal lands as reported by Jacobs (1986) and LaRue (1994). These goldfinches were found intermittently along the Colorado River and its tributaries within the Grand Canyon, where Brown et al. (1987) considered them fairly common summer residents. As would be expected, these little finches were largely absent from heavily forested and higher elevations of the state, but were confirmed nesting in several localities in the Flagstaff area and White Mountains region.

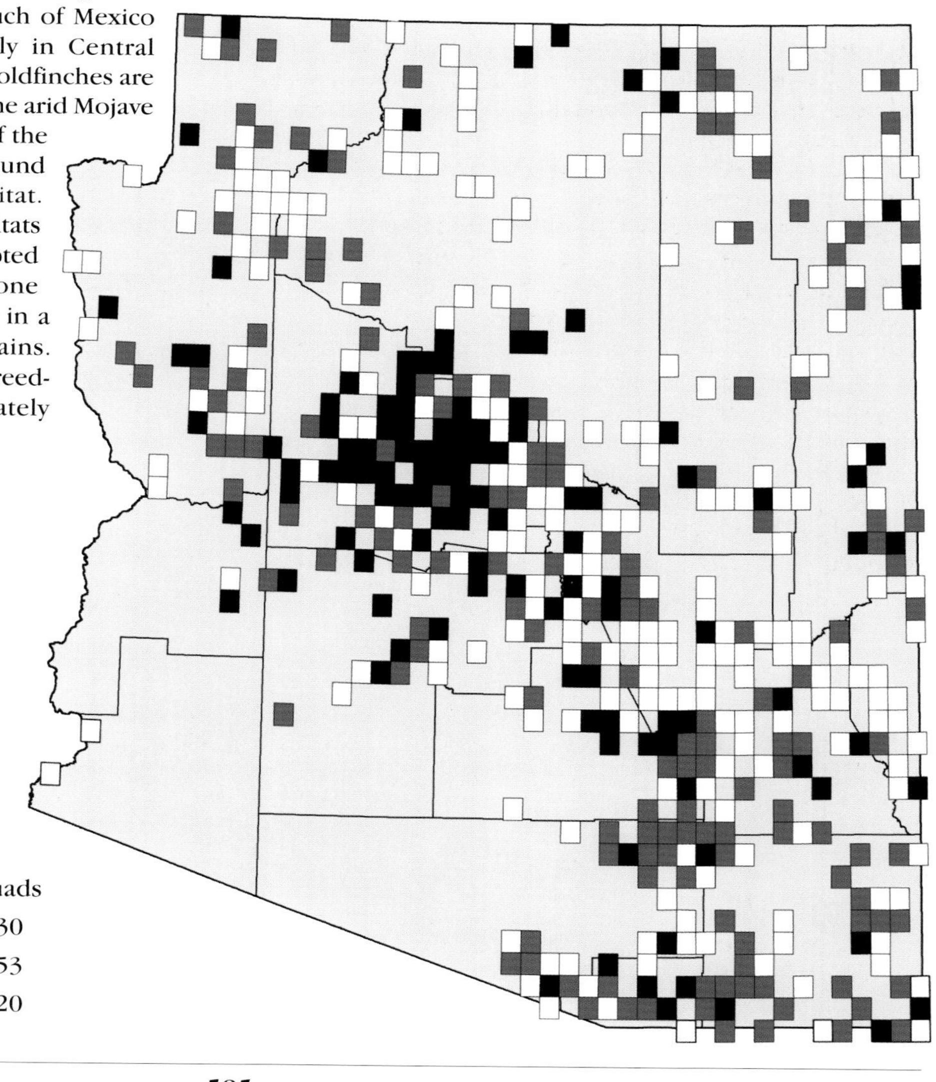

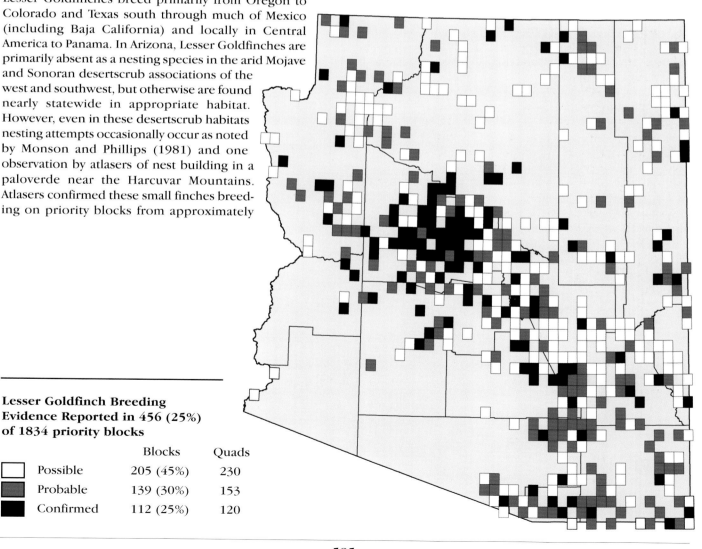

Lesser Goldfinch Breeding Evidence Reported in 456 (25%) of 1834 priority blocks

	Blocks	Quads
Possible	205 (45%)	230
Probable	139 (30%)	153
Confirmed	112 (25%)	120

Evening Grosbeak

by Troy E. Corman *Coccothraustes vespertinus*

Occurring in several widespread forest communities in Arizona, Evening Grosbeaks are surprisingly a very local nesting species in the state and are nowhere numerous. With their massive bills and handsome golden hued plumage, these stocky grosbeaks are all too infrequently encountered.

JIM BURNS

HABITAT

In Arizona, Evening Grosbeaks nest locally and apparently often erratically in coniferous forests that typically have a deciduous tree component. Atlasers reported ten of the nineteen potential breeding records for this species from mixed-conifer forests. These forests frequently contain Douglas fir, white fir, ponderosa pine, and quaking aspen with a scattered understory of bigtooth maple, Gambel's oak, or New Mexico locust. Other observations were from ponderosa pine–dominated forests and pure aspen stands in central and north Arizona. In southeastern Arizona mountains, Evening Grosbeaks were also encountered in Madrean pine-oak forests, often including various species of pines, such as Chihuahuan, Apache, and ponderosa, with an understory of alligator juniper, Gambel's oak, and various evergreen oaks. Evening Grosbeaks were reported only twice at high-elevation forests containing Engelmann spruce and subalpine fir. They were also noted locally visiting several residential feeding stations throughout the summer near Flagstaff and in the White Mountains.

BREEDING

Very little has been written on the breeding biology of the Evening Grosbeak in Arizona. Spring migrants are often reported in the state from mid-April through May and occasionally into early June. In Colorado, the colorful courtship displays and pair bonding for these birds begin in April, and pairs arrive on their breeding grounds in mid- to late May (Bekoff and Scott 1989). Evening Grosbeaks typically begin nest building soon after the pair arrives on territory, and atlasers noted an adult carrying nesting material on 21 May. However, an adult was reported feeding a fledgling near Greer on 5 June. This suggests that nest building initiated no later than late April and egg laying in early May. Phillips et al. (1964) also noted a nearly full-grown juvenile on 2 June in Arizona. Atlasers were unable to locate active nests of this local nesting species, although collectors in southeastern Arizona mountains, have found nest with eggs from mid-May through early July (Willard 1910a, Bent 1968). Atlasers reported fledglings as late as 14 July, and Swarth (1904) noted an adult feeding a large fledgling on 30 July in the Huachuca Mountains. From late summer to late spring, Evening Grosbeaks are very irregularly reported in the mountain foothills and lowlands of Arizona. During flight years, they occasionally congregate in local flocks of several hundred individuals. Peak fall migration for these birds in Arizona apparently occurs between mid-October and mid-December (Phillips et al. 1964).

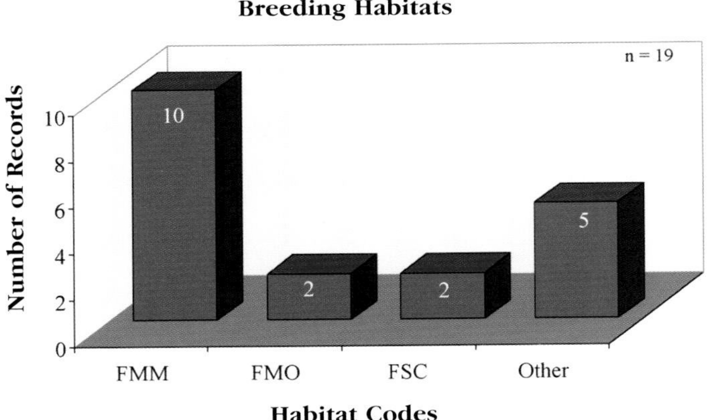

The nest is constructed almost entirely by the female Evening Grosbeak; however, the male frequently accompanies her to the nest (Scott and Bekoff 1991). Few nests have been found in Arizona, but they have been noted in various pines, firs, aspen, willows, and oaks (Swinburne 1888; Willard 1910a). In Arizona, nests have been reported at heights ranging from 15 to 86 ft (4.6–26.2 m) above the ground. The female is the sole incubator of the clutch of 3–5 eggs, which take 13–14 days to hatch (Scott and Bekoff 1991). The male often feeds the female while she incubates (Bekoff et al. 1987). Both parents feed the nestlings, which depart the nest when they are 13–14 day old (Baicich and Harrison 1997). Fledglings often remain near the nest for an additional 2–5 days (Scott and Bekoff 1991). Late-season broods have been reported, but many may represent renesting attempts after earlier failed efforts (Gillihan and Byers 2001). However, second broods have been documented in Colorado (Scott and Bekoff 1991) and are thus likely in more southern locations such as Arizona.

DISTRIBUTION AND STATUS

Evening Grosbeaks breed from southern Canada south to the northern edge of the central and northeastern United States, and, in the West, south in the mountains to California, Arizona, and New Mexico. There are disjunct populations in northern and south-central Mexico. Evening Grosbeaks have previously been described as rather uncommon and erratic summer residents at higher elevations of northern and eastern Arizona (Phillips et al. 1964). This includes the White Mountains region, both rims of the Grand Canyon, the Flagstaff area, the Bradshaw Mountains, the Sierra Ancha, and higher southeastern mountain ranges. These grosbeaks have also been noted occasionally during the summer on Bill Williams Mountain southwest of Williams (Monson and Phillips 1981) and in the Chuska Mountains of northeastern Arizona (Jacobs 1986).

Atlasers encountered Evening Grosbeaks at elevations ranging from approximately 6400 to 9100 ft (1951–2774 m) in Arizona. These birds continue to be generally uncommon and local in their distribution, and they were not detected in several locations where they had previously been noted. Small populations of these grosbeaks continue to exist on the Kaibab Plateau and in the San Francisco Mountains region from Kendrick Peak to Flagstaff. In the White Mountains region, Evening Grosbeaks were encountered locally from northern Greenlee County northwest to Show Low. They also undoubtedly nest on the adjacent White Mountain Apache tribal lands where permits to conduct atlas surveys could not be obtained. On Navajo tribal lands, they were found only in the Chuska Mountains.

Based on historical observation, the abundance and distribution of the *mexicanus* subspecies of Evening Grosbeaks in the southeastern mountain ranges have been greatly reduced. This scarcity was most obvious in the Santa Rita, Rincon, and Pinaleno mountains, where they had previously been found in summer but were not reported during the atlas period. Atlasers encountered this grosbeak only near Rose Canyon Lake in the Santa Catalina Mountains, near Rustler Park in the Chiricahua Mountains, and in Sawmill and Carr canyons in the Huachuca Mountains. Factors contributing to the apparent decline of nesting Evening Grosbeaks in this region of the state are unknown.

Evening Grosbeaks were not encountered in several other locations where they previously had been known to nest, which could be related to this species' erratic nature and relatively low breeding densities in Arizona. These forests birds are considerably more secretive during the breeding season and often spend much of their time foraging in the treetops. Consequently, atlasers who were unfamiliar with their calls might have missed many potential nesting pairs while conducting surveys on their blocks.

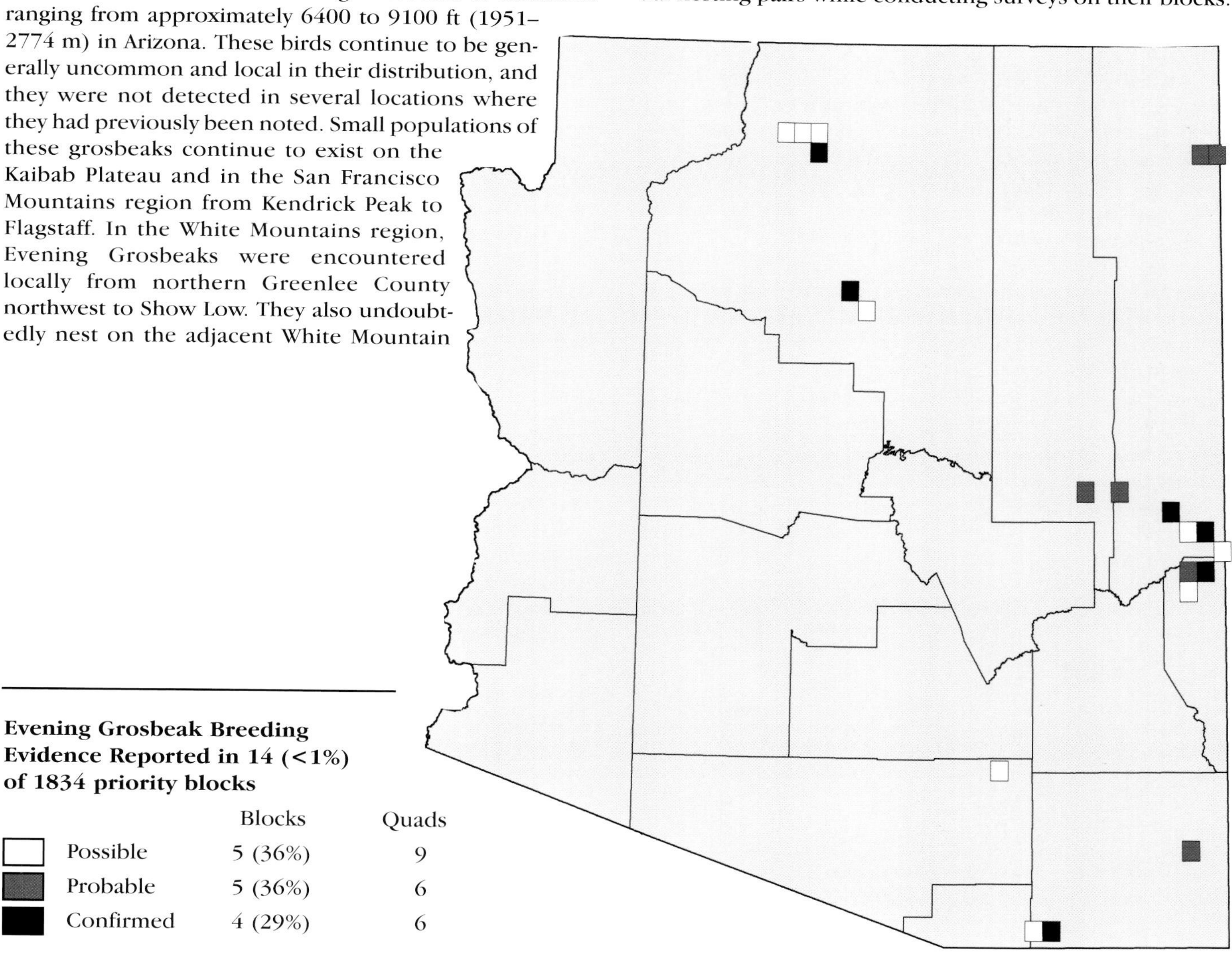

Evening Grosbeak Breeding Evidence Reported in 14 (<1%) of 1834 priority blocks

	Blocks	Quads
Possible	5 (36%)	9
Probable	5 (36%)	6
Confirmed	4 (29%)	6

House Sparrow

by Troy E. Corman *Passer domesticus*

Like feathered shadows, the all too familiar House Sparrow consistently follows and mirrors the distribution of human populations and the habitats they modify. These resourceful birds are persistent and prolific breeders, whose incessantly loud, cheerful voice can eventually become a tiresome drone.

HABITAT

The introduced House Sparrow is an abundant resident of cities and towns nearly worldwide in distribution. In Arizona as elsewhere, this species reaches its highest densities in and around urban and rural communities, where they are difficult to miss from backyards, parks, and heavily developed downtown districts to feedlots, stables, and farm buildings. Even remote and isolated ranches and small tribal villages with a number of buildings and shade trees typically have several pairs of these amazingly resourceful and adaptable sparrows. They also spread into adjacent agricultural lands where they find an abundance of food and nesting sites.

These omnivorous sparrows forage primarily on the ground, but also in trees and shrubs where it feeds on a wide variety of seeds, fruit, and insects. Of course, this resourceful bird greedily accepts almost any human handouts, and you would be hard pressed not to observe these ubiquitous birds eagerly foraging for inadvertently dropped morsels at the local fast-food establishment.

BREEDING

The breeding season begins early for the House Sparrow in Arizona, with the first nest-building activity starting in early to mid-February at some locations. During the atlas project, the earliest nest with young was reported on 18 March, which indicates egg laying beginning in late February. However, in Tucson, young capable of flight were observed as early as 9 March (Phillips et al. 1964), which suggests that some egg clutches are laid in early February in Arizona.

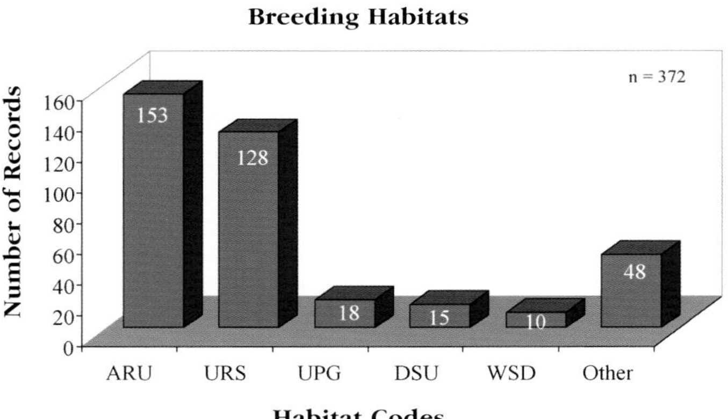

Statewide atlas data reveal that the nesting activity peak for these sparrows is in mid-May, with some efforts continuing into August. The latest nest with young reported was on 26 July, and adults were observed feeding fledglings as late as 10 August. However, late nesting activity likely continues well into September in Arizona, but few atlas surveys were conducted after mid-August. The nesting activities of this ubiquitous urban dweller typically receive little attention from the general birding public, and later seasonal activity likely goes unnoticed.

Although both sexes construct the messy nest, the male does most of the work. Female House Sparrows prefer hole-type nest sites to those constructed among tree branches (Cink 1976). They nest in almost any nook or cranny inside or on buildings and other structures, including nest boxes (Lowther and Cink 1992). Cavities of trees and saguaros are also frequently used in or near urban or rural settings in Arizona. The nest site typically offers an enclosed volume, which is more or less filled with nesting material (Lowther and Cink 1992). Less frequently, tree forks or dense branching provides an anchoring platform for their globular nests (Lowther and Cink 1992). Atlasers also found them regularly nesting in Cliff Swallow nests under bridges and overpasses.

In general, both members of the House Sparrow pair help incubate the 4–6 (range 1–8) eggs for approximately 11 (range 10–14) days (Lowther and Cink 1992). Both parents feed the nestlings, which fledge in about 14 days and are independent about 7–10 days after leaving the nest (Lowther and Cink 1992). Amazingly, House Sparrows can successfully fledge 3–4 broods within a season, with the female initiating the next clutch on an average of 8 (range 3–17) days after previous young fledge (Lowther and Cink 1992). House Sparrows also frequently reuse the same nest within and between seasons (Lowther and Cink 1992).

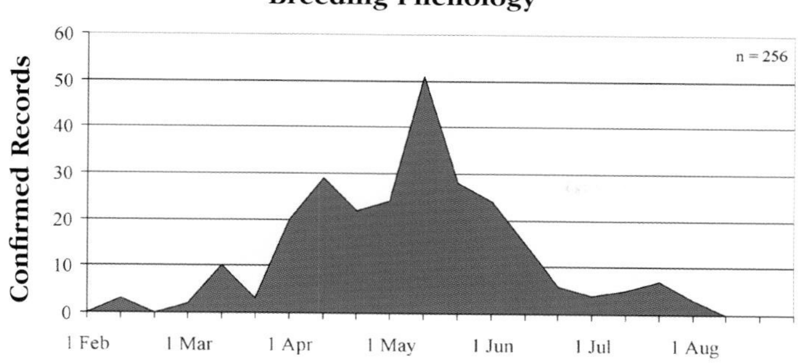

DISTRIBUTION AND STATUS

House Sparrows are native to much of Eurasia and first introduced to North America at Brooklyn, New York, in 1851–1852. From there they quickly spread westward, aided by additional transplants from established populations (Lowther and Cink 1992). They are now a widespread and abundant species throughout southern Canada, the United States (except Alaska), and Mexico. House Sparrows were never introduced to Arizona, but spread there from rapidly expanding eastern United States populations and those introduced in California and Utah in the early 1870s.

The first report of House Sparrows in Arizona was in Tucson in 1903–1904. They were established in all cities and towns throughout the state by 1915, possibly as early as 1910 (Phillips et al. 1964). As expected, atlasers found this sparrow to be widespread in the most heavily developed regions of the state, which included all cites and larger towns, the adjacent suburbs, and irrigated agricultural lands. Otherwise the survey blocks fell randomly, and not all included the small isolated populations of House Sparrows that are established across the state at ranches, smaller towns, or highway rest stops. Thus, as noted by Lowther and Cink (1992), within broad ecological limits, a sparse population of House Sparrows largely indicates a sparse population of humans.

The House Sparrow's ability to spread rapidly is illustrated by atlasers' observations of individuals or pairs of House Sparrows that suddenly appeared at isolated day camp sites in the open Sonoran Desert many miles from the nearest habitation. In one case, all that was present was a truck, several small tents, and a tarp for midday shade placed in a remote section of the Cabeza Prieta National Wildlife Refuge. On 24 April 1995, less than twenty-four hours after the campsite had been established, a panting individual materialized out of nowhere. This location was more than 15 mi (24.1 km) from the nearest established population of House Sparrows in Ajo!

Populations of House Sparrows will undoubtedly continue to grow and spread in Arizona as long as their very accommodating human hosts do the same. These aggressive birds are known to destroy the eggs and young of native birds and to take over the nests of Cliff and Barn Swallows (Bent 1958). However, owing to their urban and rural lifestyle, these admirably adaptable sparrows currently pose little if any significant threat to native bird populations in Arizona.

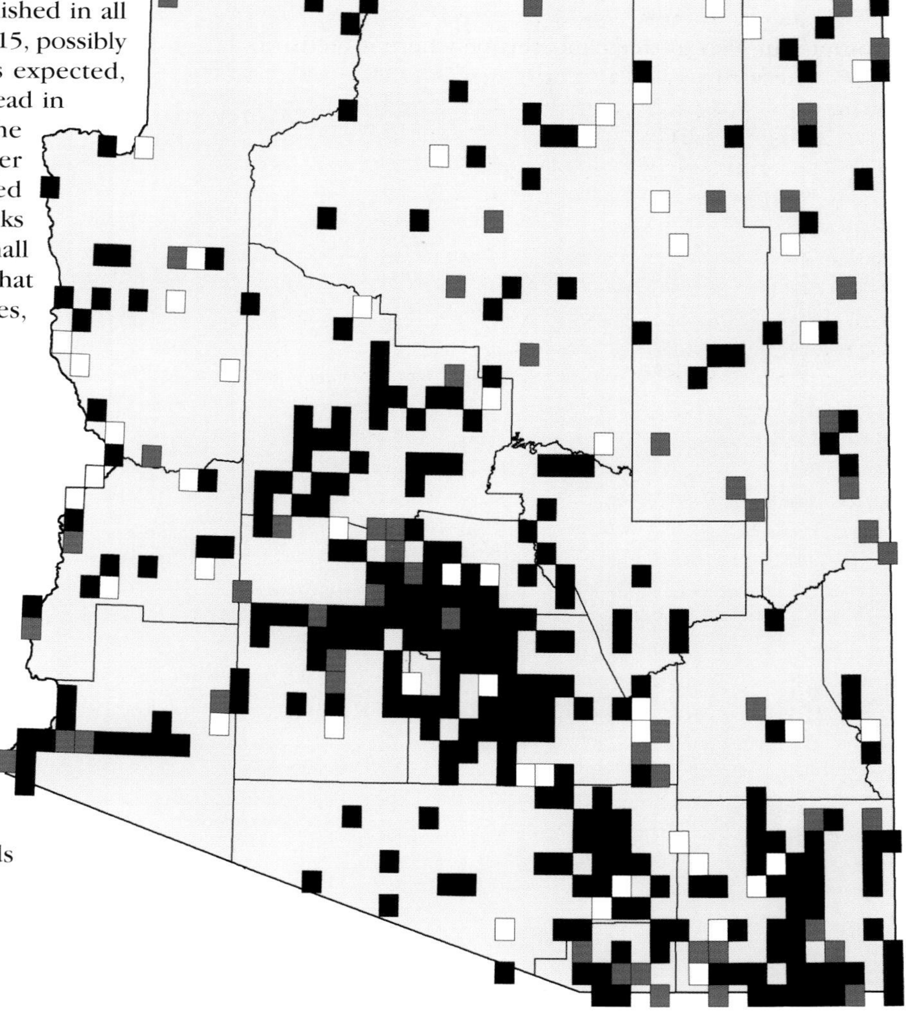

House Sparrow Breeding Evidence Reported in 341 (19%) of 1834 priority blocks

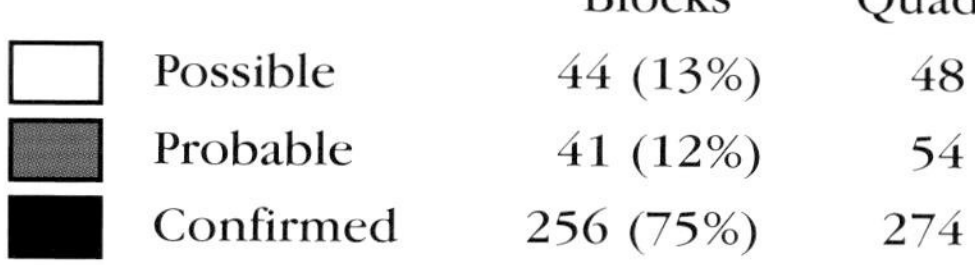

	Blocks	Quads
Possible	44 (13%)	48
Probable	41 (12%)	54
Confirmed	256 (75%)	274

Supplemental Species Accounts

by Troy E. Corman

The following forty-seven species are discussed under three fairly distinct categories. *Rare and Local Nesting Species* were confirmed breeding in Arizona during the atlas period, but were noted in only one or two localities in the state. *Possible and Probable Nesting Species* were also encountered in Arizona during the atlas period in appropriate nesting habitat during the proper season, but confirmed nesting activity was not reported. As noted earlier, eight of these species had previously been documented nesting in Arizona. *Historical Nesting Species* had been reported nesting in the state prior to the atlas project (1993), but were not suspected of nesting in Arizona during the atlas period.

RARE AND LOCAL NESTING SPECIES

WHITE-FACED IBIS *Plegadis chihi*

A common migrant and an increasing local winter resident in Arizona, the White-faced Ibis can be observed at almost any open, shallow water source in the state during migration. Wetlands, flooded fields, lakeshores, and various ponds appear to be especially favored for foraging and loafing. Spring migration begins in March and continues through much of May, with stragglers and nonbreeding individuals noted locally throughout the summer. A few southbound migrants begin to appear by at least early July, with peak passage in August and September. Late-migrating flocks are noted well into November in southern and western Arizona.

Prior to the atlas project, the White-faced Ibis was suspected of occasionally nesting in Arizona. White-faced Ibis nests with eggs were reported by a canoeist among the tules at Mormon Lake, southeast of Flagstaff, in 1992. Unfamiliar with the species, the observer described large, dark greenish-bronze birds with long curved bills, further describing the eggs as having an attractive blue-green color. Unfortunately, word of this observation came too late to be followed up and verified. This was one year before the initiation of atlas surveys. During the early atlas period, White-faced Ibises were noted at this lake in June on several occasions, but nesting was not documented. Water levels may not have been adequate at this shallow lake throughout much of the atlas period, which eventually dried up completely during the final few years of the project.

White-faced Ibis were finally confirmed as a nesting species in Arizona on June 21, 2000, when U.S. Fish and Wildlife Service biologists B. Zaun and K. King discovered a nesting colony within an island of bulrush. The location was on Cibola Lake, a backwater of the Colorado River within Cibola National Wildlife Refuge. The elevation of the lake is approximately 220 ft (67 m). Based on first hatching, egg laying probably began around June 14. Although approximately 1500 ibis used this 40 by 40 m stand of bulrush as a nightly roost site, only about seventy-five nests were observed. Nests were made entirely of bulrush stems, which were attached to standing bulrush 2–4 ft (0.6–1.2 m) above the water. Nineteen nests located along the perimeter were flagged and monitored weekly. The eggs began to hatch around 7 July. White-faced Ibises did not nest at this location the following year.

At the southern edge of their nesting range, near-optimal habitat conditions apparently must be met before White-faced Ibises attempt to breed in Arizona. Throughout much of the state, water levels at many of the potential nesting locations fluctuate greatly from one year to the next creating unreliable foraging and nesting habitat. Therefore, the White-faced Ibis will likely remain a very local and irregular nesting species in Arizona.

MOUNTAIN PLOVER *Charadrius montanus*

Primarily known as a rare to uncommon and very local fall and winter resident in southern Arizona, Mountain Plovers are typically observed in small flocks inhabiting barren agricultural fields or turf farms from late August to early March. However, during the atlas period, the open, shortgrass prairies of east-central Arizona were found to harbor a local nesting population of Mountain Plovers. First suspected of nesting in the state when small flocks were noted in August 1914 northeast of Springerville (Phillips et al. 1964). However, Tolle (1976) speculated that these birds might have been early migrants. Suspicions were brought to the forefront again when a nest with eggs of these plovers was found on 12 June 1978 in New Mexico, only 7 mi (11 km) from the Arizona border and approximately 23 mi (37 km) east of Springerville (Johnson and Spicer 1981). In a region of the state that has received very little biological attention, Johnson and Spicer further speculated Mountain Plovers might be scattered but locally common breeders in the shortgrass prairies from the Springerville region north and west to Holbrook.

Atlasers observed four adult Mountain Plovers in the grasslands just northwest of Springerville on 30 June 1994, but no further nesting evidence was noted. In late spring 1996, specific surveys for the Mountain Plover were conducted in the area, and the species was finally confirmed breeding in Arizona when a nest with three eggs was discovered and photographed on 15 May. At an elevation of approximately 6860 ft (2091 m), the nest and additional pairs were observed in heavily grazed, gently rolling areas dominated by a mosaic of bare earth, gravel, and short hummocks of blue grama. Nesting was also suspected in central Navajo County on Navajo tribal land, when atlasers observed a pair of Mountain Plovers between Dilkon and Winslow on 14 June 1995 at an elevation of 5360 ft (1634 m).

As Johnson and Spicer (1981) previously suggested, specific spring surveys for Mountain Plovers may reveal them to be a more widespread nesting species in Arizona than these few atlas records suggest. Most of the suitable habitat in southern Navajo and Apache counties remains unsurveyed because of private- and state-leased-land access restrictions. Most of the open grasslands in this area are heavily grazed and dominated by blue grama, which is characteristic of Mountain Plover breeding habitat throughout the Great Plains (Graul and Webster 1976).

LONG-BILLED CURLEW *Numenius americanus*

Prior to the atlas project, Long-billed Curlews were considered uncommon to locally common migrants in Arizona. Most records are concentrated primarily between mid-March to early May and then again from early July to late September. Observations of wintering flocks of Long-billed Curlews in agricultural areas of southern Arizona have also steadily increased.

During the atlas period, Long-billed Curlews were a rather unexpected addition to Arizona's nesting avifauna. On 21 June 1993, two adults with three half-grown young were observed in grasslands just west of Eagar, Apache County (D. Jones, personal communication). The elevation at this location was approximately 7140 ft (2176 m). Periodic summer observation of Long-billed Curlews in the area north to the Springerville-Eagar airport continued well into the atlas period. This included three adult curlews observed mobbing a Ferruginous Hawk flying over the grasslands near the airport. In 1915, Goldman (1926) observed a Long-billed Curlew at Big Lake in southern Apache County on 25 June. Atlasers also observed a pair of these curlews in the alpine grasslands north of Big Lake on 19 June 1993. This date suggests another possible nesting location in the White Mountains region. However, southbound migrants are regularly observed by late June in Arizona, and without additional breeding evidence these potential nesting records will remain questionable.

RED-SHOULDERED HAWK *Buteo lineatus*

Typically a very rare vagrant or migrant in Arizona, Red-shouldered Hawks are most often observed in or near riparian woodlands containing tall cottonwood, willow, and/or sycamore trees. Most observations are in fall and winter, but individuals have lingered well into the spring and occasionally throughout the summer.

Red-shouldered Hawks had been noted nesting in Arizona only one other time prior to the atlas project. In late spring 1970, a pair was discovered with a nest and two young in a Fremont cottonwood near the northern edge of Mittry Lake north of Yuma (Glinski 1982). The elevation at this location is approximately 120 ft (37 m). Arizona's second nesting attempt occurred during the atlas. Beginning on 22 April 1999, a Red-shouldered Hawk was periodically noted at the Hassayampa River Preserve near Wickenburg, Maricopa County, at an elevation of 1940 ft (591 m). By the spring of 2000, a pair of Red-shouldered Hawks was confirmed at this location, and nest construction in a cottonwood was observed by 20 April. The pair was observed incubating for over a month during late May and June. However, by late June, adult attendance at the nest had waned and the attempt was determined to have failed (R. Glinski, personal communication). This pair attempted to nest again in 2001, but the outcome was unknown.

JIM BURNS

Red-shouldered Hawk

The only other potential nesting record during the atlas period was of a Red-shouldered Hawk observed on 24 May near the confluence of Beaver Dam Wash and the Virgin River near Littlefield in extreme northwestern Arizona. Evidence suggests that California populations of the western race *elegans* of the Red-shouldered Hawk have increased and expanded into areas they had not inhabited historically (Wilbur 1975). This may help explain the steady increase of observations of this raptor in Arizona during the past several decades, and additional nesting attempts in the state are to be expected.

RINGED TURTLE-DOVE *Streptopelia risoria*

A common caged bird, the exotic Ringed Turtle-Dove has been found nesting locally in a few Tucson and Phoenix neighborhoods since at least the 1970s (Monson and Phillips 1981). These exotic doves apparently do not thrive well in the wild, and all populations have remained small, very local, and heavily reliant on nearby feeding stations.

Ringed Turtle-Doves went unreported by atlasers in the Tucson area, where Monson and Phillips (1981) noted the presence of this species since at least 1964. However, atlasers did detect a small population in the Sunnyslope area of north-central Phoenix, where an individual was observed carrying nesting material on 5 May 1995. The Ringed Turtle-Dove population in and around the Phoenix Zoo and adjacent Papago Park area has been greatly reduced from the high numbers observed in the late 1970s and early 1980s. However, atlasers still noted a few individuals in Papago Park and nearby Tempe through the end of the atlas period. Another population of Ringed Turtle-Doves is apparently thriving locally in a north Mesa neighborhood (T. Hildebrandt, personal communication).

MONK PARAKEET *Myiopsitta monachus*

Native to South America, Monk Parakeets are popular caged birds that have established local populations in a significant number of city parks and suburbs in North America. In South America, they nest in a wide range of habitats from open woodland, savanna, arid scrubland, riverine forest, cultivated lands, and orchards, especially around human habitations (American Ornithologists' Union 1998).

This gregarious nesting species can build massive stick structures with variable cavities for different pairs of nesting parakeets. In North America, nests are constructed in trees, including pines and palms, and electrical poles, especially those containing transformers.

Atlasers discovered a nesting colony of Monk Parakeets in Casa Grande on 17 June 2000. They were coming and going from a large bulky nest approximately 8 ft (2.4 m) in diameter in a date palm. One parakeet was observed breaking off a live mesquite branch then taking it to the nest, where it proceeded to work it into the structure. Local residents in the area noted this population in existence for at least a decade.

HAMMOND'S FLYCATCHER *Empidonax hammondii*

Another species reaching the southern limits of its breeding range in Arizona, Hammond's Flycatchers are common migrants throughout the state. These flycatchers also winter locally, primarily in lowland riparian woodlands in southeastern Arizona north sparingly to at least the lower Verde River. Hammond's Flycatchers have been documented nesting in the state only once prior to the atlas project. A pair with a nest was found in the Chuska Mountains of extreme northeastern Arizona on 4 July 1980 (Monson and Phillips 1981). The habitat was mixed-conifer with some spruce, and the nest was approximately 24.6 ft (7.5 m) high in a Douglas fir (Rosenberg and Terrill 1986). Throughout much of their range, these flycatchers apparently prefer horizontal limbs of conifers for nest placement, but nests have been found in adjacent broadleaf deciduous trees (Sedgwick 1994). Hammond's Flycatchers typically build their nests at a much greater height than do Dusky and Cordilleran Flycatchers in Arizona.

During the atlas period, Hammond's Flycatchers were confirmed nesting only once. An occupied nest of these flycatchers was discovered on 16 June 2001 in a mixed-conifer forest in the San Francisco Mountains north of Flagstaff at an elevation of approximately 8400 ft (2560 m). The habitat consisted primarily of white fir, Douglas fir, and quaking aspen with some ponderosa and limber pines. The nest was constructed at a height of 34.9 ft (10.6 m) in an approximately 60 ft (18.3 m)-tall ponderosa pine (C. LaRue, personal communication). An atlaser also discovered a singing flycatcher in very similar habitat near 9000 ft (2743 m) elevation in the White Mountains near Big Lake during the summer of 1993. Habitat, elevation, and habit of foraging high in conifers all suggested Hammond's Flycatcher; however, the observer was not positive of the identity.

Hammond's Flycatchers may be a very sparse and extremely local nesting species in Arizona. Nesting pairs could be easily overlooked among the similar and more common Dusky and Cordilleran Flycatchers nesting in higher elevation forested regions of the state. However, Dusky Flycatchers are most common in forested areas dominated by low and often dense deciduous trees, especially stands of saplings, willows, alder, and Gambel's oak. The White Mountains and Kaibab Plateau contain seemingly abundant breeding habitat for Hammond's Flycatcher, and the species should be looked for in these regions.

SCISSOR-TAILED FLYCATCHER *Tyrannus forficatus*

With their long elegant tail and habit of perching conspicuously on power lines, fences, or bare branches, Scissor-tailed Flycatchers are an easily observed and identified species. In Arizona, these showy flycatchers are typically casual to rare transients throughout the state with dates ranging from 20 April to 18 November, with the majority of observations from May to October.

Most observations of Scissor-tailed Flycatchers in Arizona are of single individuals, except for two noted together on 19 May 1990 near Portal, Cochise County (Rosenberg and Witzeman 1999). Nesting activity for this flycatcher had not been reported in Arizona prior to the atlas project. However, a female Scissor-tailed Flycatcher apparently paired with a Western Kingbird and attempted to nest across the Colorado River in Needles, California, from May to July 1979 (Rosenberg et al. 1991). During the atlas period, two Scissor-tailed Flycatchers were found together in a desert rural area near Gila Bend, Maricopa County, on 9 July 1994 (D. Kaplan, personal communication). The pair remained at this location through at least 28 August. The span of dates would suggest the possibility of nesting at or near this location, but nesting activity was not noted for this tantalizing observation.

However, a pair of Scissor-tailed Flycatchers was discovered near Dudleyville, Pinal County, on 23 June 1995. This pair remained in the area, and on 8 July several observers noted the female drop to the ground in a mesquite-shaded yard, pick up nesting material, and fly into another, more open yard with several scattered trees. The nesting materials were being taken to an exotic Tree of Heaven. Observations of one or more of these flycatchers continued into mid-July, but it was unknown if this, the first known nesting attempt in Arizona, was successful. The general location of this site was at the edge of upland

Scissor-tailed Flycatcher

Sonoran desertscrub vegetation and a velvet mesquite bosque within the lower San Pedro River corridor. The specific habitat included scattered houses, trailers, and outbuildings, with yards, fenced livestock, and other open areas. Dominant vegetation included velvet mesquite, saguaro, and scattered paloverde, with a mixture of some exotics such as athel tamarisk and Tree of Heaven.

AMERICAN PIPIT *Anthus rubescens*

American Pipits are common migrant throughout the state beginning in late August and are winter residents in southern and western Arizona in open areas near water or irrigated agricultural lands. In southern Arizona, few individuals are noted past the end of April; however, a few stragglers are occasionally noted into May and June in the north.

In Arizona, American Pipits are found nesting only above timberline, which greatly limits their distribution in the state. Phillips et al. (1964) noted the American Pipit nesting on the windswept, treeless talus slopes of the San Francisco Peaks and in the White Mountains. These hardy birds are the only avian species nesting at this elevation and habitat in Arizona. Atlasers confirmed American Pipits nesting only above 11,000 ft (3353 m) in the San Francisco Peaks. The only other likely nesting locality would be atop Arizona's second highest peak, Mount Baldy, in the White Mountains. However, the higher elevations of Mount Baldy are within the White Mountain Apache tribal lands, where access to conduct atlas surveys was not granted.

RUFOUS-CAPPED WARBLER *Basileuterus rufifrons*

Common to fairly common residents in the mountain and foothill of eastern Sonora (Russell and Monson 1998), Rufous-capped Warblers were very casually reported in southeastern Arizona prior to the atlas project. These active warblers are typically found in pairs throughout the year, where they often occupy dry, rocky situation at the edges of canyon bottoms, where riparian plants give way to those of dry hillsides (Russell and Monson 1998). The first state record was a singing individuals discovered in Cave Creek Canyon in the Chiricahua Mountains on 9 May 1977. A nest with eggs was discovered nearby on 19 July, but the nest failed and the adult was last observed that year on 23 July (Monson and Phillips 1980). It was never determined if a second bird was ever present at this location. The following year, likely the same warbler was observed near this site on 8 April (Monson and Phillips 1980). Intriguing reports of Rufous-capped Warblers in the Huachuca Mountains were also later noted on 14 August 1983 and 7 April 1985.

Rufous-capped Warblers were not reported in Arizona again until the beginning of the atlas period. In 1993, an individual was observed in California Gulch on 24 July, and the following year a singing individual was discovered in nearby lower Sycamore Canyon from 16 March, where it remained into at least June (Rosenberg and Witzeman 1999). On 25 May 1995, the discovery of a singing Rufous-capped Warbler in the seldom-visited Whetstone Mountains soon made French Joe Canyon a regular destination for birders. This rocky canyon contains several small springs and stands of various species of Madrean evergreen oaks, which are flanked by steep arid, slopes with thickets of spiny vegetation. Three days after the original discovery, a second singing individual was also found in the canyon where they were both irregularly reported into the fall of that year. One or more Rufous-capped Warblers were irregularly noted again in this canyon from spring through 11 September 1996. Rufous-capped Warblers were not found again in French Joe Canyon until 20 November 1999, where they remained through much of 2000.

Because of the presence of multiple individuals, nesting was suspected in previous years, but an obvious pair of Rufous-capped Warblers was first noted in French Joe Canyon in the spring of 2001. On 5 May and 14 June of that year, nest-building activity was observed, but no further

Rufous-capped Warbler

nesting evidence was noted until a nest with eggs was found on 7 August 2001. On 18 August, the adult pair was observed feeding recently fledged young. The adults continued feeding their begging young through 26 August. The three fledglings remained with the pair through at least 9 September. This was the first known successful nesting record of Rufous-capped Warblers north of Mexico.

In 2002, the year following the atlas, the pair of Rufous-capped Warblers in French Joe Canyon produced two broods. The first nesting likely began in April of that year, for a pair was observed feeding recently fledged young on 16 May. The adult pair continued feeding the fledglings through 7 June, as they began constructing a second nest. Two young fledged from the second nest by at least 6 August and were observed being fed through 30 August.

WHITE-CROWNED SPARROW *Zonotrichia leucophrys*

During migration and winter, White-crowned Sparrows are one of the most abundant and widespread birds in Arizona. Mearns (1890) reported these sparrows as apparently breeding in June at the base of the San Francisco Mountains, but they were never reported during the summer in this area again. However, in 1969, White-crowned Sparrows were confirmed nesting in Arizona, when a population was discovered in the Inner Basin of the San Francisco Mountains (Balda et al. 1970). This area was frequently visited during the summer by skilled ornithologists from the 1930s to the 1950s without any reports of this sparrow, suggesting fairly recent colonization (Carothers et al. 1973). Atlasers detected White-crowned Sparrows just below timberline in the San Francisco Mountains at elevation from approximately 10,800 to 11,500 ft (3292–3505 m). Adults were observed carrying food on 13 July. Habitat was steep talus slopes with patches of subalpine conifer scrublands often known as krummholz or elfinwoods. This unique habitat consists of dwarf junipers along with stunted and distorted Engelmann spruce and bristlecone pines, which have been dwarfed by frequent high winds, short growing season, and deep, long-lasting snow packs.

A singing individual was also collected near timberline near the summit of Mount Baldy in east-central Arizona on 11 July 1936 (Phillips et al. 1964). This sparrow was observed again in this area on 7 July 1976 (Monson and Phillips 1981). Atlasers also noted several singing White-crowned Sparrows at this location on 12 June 1999. During the summer of 1957, a fledgling White-crowned Sparrow was also found near the North Rim Ranger Station in Grand Canyon National Park (Brown et al. 1987). Atlasers did not detect this sparrow anywhere on the Kaibab Plateau during the summer. White-crowned Sparrows may nest irregularly and in very small numbers on Mount Baldy and the higher elevations of the Kaibab Plateau.

ROSE-BREASTED GROSBEAK *Pheucticus ludovicianus*

The eastern counterpart of the Black-headed Grosbeak, the brightly colored Rose-breasted Grosbeak is a rare but regular migrant throughout Arizona, especially in the spring. Atlasers noted Rose-breasted Grosbeaks from 18 April to 19 June. Most individuals are observed from mid-April through June and then again in late September through mid-November. However, Rose-breasted Grosbeaks have been noted every month of the year in the state (Monson and Phillips 1981).

Periodically in the spring, Rose-breasted Grosbeaks pass through Arizona in higher than normal numbers. One such flight through the lower Colorado River Valley in June 1977 was followed by a pair staying and reported nesting near Vidal, California (Rosenberg et al. 1991). This location is southwest of Parker and approximately 6 mi (10 km) from Arizona. Those that occasionally linger through the summer sometimes attract Black-headed Grosbeak mates. Such was the case of a male Rose-breasted Grosbeak that apparently paired with a female Black-headed Grosbeak. Both were observed occupying a nest near Portal in early June 1994, but evidence suggested that this nesting attempt failed.

AMERICAN GOLDFINCH *Carduelis tristis*

Very familiar to many bird enthusiasts in eastern North America, American Goldfinches are irregularly uncommon to common migrants and winter residents in Arizona. Most are observed between September and April, with stragglers into early June. Atlasers observed migrating American Goldfinches through 8 June.

In the arid West, American Goldfinches frequently nest at the edges of tall, deciduous riparian woodlands or similar habitat with an abundance of nearby weed seeds, especially composites. The only potential nesting record in Arizona prior to the atlas period was the observation of a female with an accompanying male, constructing a nest on 31 May 1978 at Teec Nos Pos in the extreme northeastern corner of the state (Monson and Phillips 1980) at approximately 5100 ft (1554 m). American Goldfinches are known to nest occasionally along the San Juan and Zuni rivers in nearby northwestern New Mexico and southeastern Utah, so this observation was not unexpected. Unfortunately, the outcome of this nest building endeavor is unknown. Nickell (1951) commented on the peculiar habit of American Goldfinches abandoning many nests before construction was completed, or at times after completion but before egg laying. However, Walkinshaw noted there was a period of rest between nest completion and egg laying of 2–27 days (Bent 1968). The pair shows so little attention during this rest period that a casual observer might well consider the nest abandoned (Bent 1968).

The only breeding confirmation of American Goldfinches during the atlas was west of Eagar, Apache County. On 24 July 1993, atlasers observed an adult male feeding a fledgling along the South Fork of the Little Colorado River at an elevation of approximately 7400 ft (2256 m). American Goldfinches had been observed or suspected of nesting in northern New Mexico on several occasions south to near Zuni in McKinley County. Nesting records in New Mexico span from mid-June to early August, with family groups and begging young noted as late as 1 October (S. Williams, personal communication). American Goldfinches may be a sparse, very irregular, and easily overlooked nesting species in Apache County.

ORANGE BISHOP *Euplectes franciscanus*

Several small populations of Orange Bishops, native to sub-Saharan central Africa, were discovered nesting locally in north-central Phoenix during the atlas period. Much of what follows is from information compiled by Gatz (2001). Like other populations established in southern California, it is assumed Arizona's Orange Bishops originated from escaped or illegally liberated cagebirds. First found in late summer 1998, they were confirmed nesting on 4 July 2000, when a male was observed carrying nesting material. In Africa, Orange Bishops inhabit open grasslands and dense weedy areas along wetlands and wet, irrigated agricultural fields. During the atlas period, they occupied a grassy, tree-lined, desert dry wash running through a residential neighborhood. The wash is partially channelized and edged with scattered blue paloverde, velvet mesquite, desert broom, and desert willow. Some irrigation and street runoff provided local and nearly permanent stands of shallow water and associated patches of wetland vegetation. The breeding season apparently begins in May and early June, when the male Orange Bishops appear in bright alternate plumage. Males have been observed displaying to females by mid- to late June, and this activity continues into September. Nest construction apparently begins at the advent of summer rains in early July. Their intricately woven grassy nests have been constructed in stands of cattails and exotic Johnson grass, which grow tall and thick during the late summer monsoon period. One nest was approximately 3.3 ft (1.0 m) above the water. Nesting activity continues through August, with one female observed feeding a fledgling in September. Orange Bishops continued nesting locally along this wash each summer through the end of the atlas period.

POSSIBLE AND PROBABLE NESTING SPECIES

LEAST GREBE *Tachybaptus dominicus*

Primarily breeding north to southern Sonora (Russell and Monson 1998), the little Least Grebe is a rare straggler to southern Arizona. Most records are from smaller and frequently isolated ponds with an abundance of emergent and overhanging vegetation. Many records pertain to fall and winter, suggesting northward postbreeding dispersal, although several individuals had lengthy stays that span several years. In adjacent Sonora, Least Grebes are noted nesting from March to September (Russell and Monson 1998), although they may nest any time of year throughout most of their range.

Before 1978, these tropical grebes had been encountered from Quitobaquito Springs in Organ Pipe Cactus National Monument east to the Santa Cruz River valley and north to Tucson. Monson and Phillips (1981) reported that one intermittently occupied pond held seven individuals on a single day in 1964, indicating that nesting had taken place.

During the atlas period, several individual Least Grebes were discovered between late summer and winter at Picacho Reservoir, at a pond in the western foothills of the Chiricahua Mountains, and at Willcox (Rosenberg and

JIM BURNS

Least Grebe

Witzeman 1998; Rosenberg 2001). An individual Least Grebe was also observed at the Sweetwater Wetlands in Tucson from early June through November 2000. Although apparently unmated, at one point this individual was observed carrying nesting material (M. Stevenson, personal communication).

NEOTROPIC CORMORANT *Phalacrocorax brasilianus*

The status of Neotropic Cormorants in Arizona has changed tremendously during the past several decades. The presence of this cormorant in the state was finally confirmed on 10 March 1961, when two individuals were found dead near a ranch south of Green Valley (Phillips et al. 1964). By 1980, Neotropic Cormorants were considered a rare but regular straggler to lakes, ponds, and drainages in the Santa Cruz River valley north to Tucson, occasionally east to southern Cochise County (Monson and Phillips 1981). They were also found once north to the Phoenix area and several individuals have been noted along the lower Colorado River north to Lake Havasu (Rosenberg et al. 1991). Most of these early records pertained to only one or two individuals, but observations ranged through all seasons.

Neotropic Cormorant observations in Arizona continued to accumulate steadily through the 1980s, then accelerated in the early 1990s and through the atlas period. By the end of the atlas project, these cormorants had become uncommon to locally common residents in the lower Salt River valley from the greater Phoenix area downstream to its confluence with the Gila River. Atlasers also noted Neotropic Cormorants farther down the Gila River to Gillespie and Painted Rock dams. These cormorants were encountered in several other potential nesting areas, including Patagonia Lake and Picacho Reservoir. However, the latter location was dry during the final years of the atlas project.

Neotropic Cormorant

In New Mexico, Neotropic Cormorants have nested in the lower and middle Rio Grande River valley since 1972 (Hudertmark 1974; Hubbard 1978). Nesting has not been documented in Arizona but is suspected to have taken place near the end of the atlas period. By the spring and summer of 2000, concentrations of Neotropic Cormorants along the lower Salt River contained 35–40 individuals and included adults with white filoplumes and juveniles. Neotropic Cormorants prefer to nest in small trees, live or dead, often overhanging water or on islands (Telfair and Morrison 1995). Dense stands of tamarisk, willow, and other trees line pools and channels of the lower Salt and middle Gila rivers, affording seemingly abundant nesting and foraging habitat. During the first few years of the atlas, several adult Neotropic Cormorants were also observed among nesting Double-crested Cormorants on a small tamarisk-covered island below Painted Rock Dam. However, nesting activity of the former could not be determined before this potential nesting location was abandoned as water levels dropped and the impoundment eventually dried.

American Wigeon

AMERICAN WIGEON *Anas americana*

American Wigeons are common migrants and winter statewide where water remains open. They often become locally abundant winter residents at urban lakes and ponds, particularly along manicured lawns and golf courses, where they frequently graze. Nonbreeding summering individuals can be found occasionally almost anywhere in the state (Phillips et al. 1964). Mearns (1890) suspected that these dabbling ducks first nested at Mormon Lake southeast of Flagstaff in 1887. They were later documented nesting occasionally in limited numbers at high elevation lakes in the Mogollon Rim region from the Mormon Lake area east to the White Mountains (Phillips et al. 1964; Piest and Sowls 1981; Myers 1982). However, American Wigeons may not breed annually in Arizona.

Waterfowl studies in the White Mountains of Arizona revealed that American Wigeons begin clutch initiation in early June, with duckling broods observed in July and August (Piest and Sowls 1981). The only potential breeding record obtained for this duck during the atlas period was of an adult noted at a lake near Green's Peak in the White Mountains on 28 June 1993.

NORTHERN SHOVELER *Anas clypeata*

Another common migrant and winter visiting duck to Arizona, Northern Shovelers are particularly fond of wastewater treatment ponds, where they often congregate in tremendous numbers during the winter. Here they use their specialized straining bills to filter out plankton and other organic matter from these otherwise barren ponds, which often lack vegetative cover.

Although Mearns (1890) noted Northern Shovelers as abundant in May and June on lakes in the San Francisco Mountains and Mormon Lake areas, he found no nests. Phillips et al. (1964) and later Monson and Phillips (1981) reported no definitive nesting records for Arizona. However, W. Fleming reported a hen with seven ducklings at Crescent Lake in the White Mountains in 1953 (Brown 1985), and a few broods were later noted at other lakes in the White Mountains and on Anderson Mesa near Flagstaff (Piest 1981; Myers 1982). Two Northern Shoveler broods were noted in June, suggesting clutch initiation in mid-May (L. Piest, personal communication).

Nonbreeding Northern Shovelers can be found occasionally as individuals or pairs statewide during the summer, making it difficult to determine their breeding status. Atlasers reported potential nesting pairs at Many Farms Lake on 9 June 1994, and a pair of Northern Shovelers was noted on 25 June 1994 at White Mountain Reservoir and an individual at Pintail Lake near Show Low on 25 July 1997.

CANVASBACK *Aythya valisineria*

Large diving ducks with distinctive head profiles, Canvasbacks are generally uncommonly distributed in small flocks throughout Arizona during migration, with larger concentrations on mountain lakes in the fall (Phillips et al. 1964). They can also winter fairly commonly in larger groups on lakes, ponds, and open sections of deeper rivers in the state.

Canvasbacks are very rarely reported during the summer months in Arizona and are typically considered a nonbreeding species in the state (Phillips et al. 1964). However, Piest (1981) noted several summering pairs and ducklings on higher-elevation lakes in the White Mountains. Of three broods discovered, the earliest was estimated to have been from a clutch laid in mid- to late June (L. Piest, personal communication). Atlasers discovered a pair of Canvasbacks at White Mountain Reservoir on 25 June 1994 and an individual at Luna Lake on 28 July 2000, but no further nesting evidence was obtained.

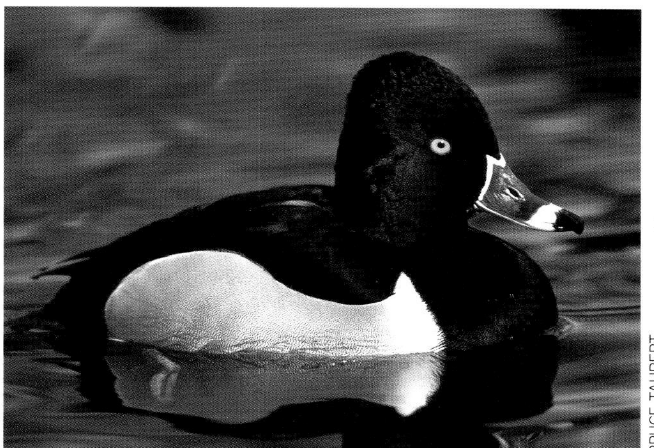
BRUCE TAUBERT

Ring-necked Duck

RING-NECKED DUCK *Aythya collaris*

In Arizona, Ring-necked Ducks are common migrants and winter residents at open water sources throughout the state. Although summering nonbreeding birds are occasionally found throughout Arizona, they nest fairly commonly on high-elevation lakes in the White Mountains region (Phillips et al. 1964). These ducks have also been noted nesting sparingly along lakes on Anderson Mesa near Flagstaff (Myers 1982). Jacobs (1986) reported that Ring-necked Ducks likely nest in many of the small lakes and ponds in the Chuska Mountains on Navajo tribal lands.

Nesting Ring-necked Ducks typically select lakes and ponds with both open water and an abundance of emergent vegetation, where they frequently construct their nests. Bulrush stands were especially favored for nesting in one Arizona study (Myers 1980). Although a few early Ring-necked Duck clutches are laid by late May or early June in Arizona, many nests are initiated much later in the summer (L. Piest, personal communication). In fact, L. Piest estimated more than half of the young remained flightless into early October (Brown 1985).

Ring-necked Ducks were unfortunately not confirmed as a nesting species during the atlas period, although pairs were reported throughout June in several lakes and reservoirs in the White Mountains region and locally in the Chuska Mountains. Drought conditions plagued Arizona during much of the atlas project, which led to record low water levels and many previously known nesting lakes drying completely in this region of the state. Timing of most atlas surveys at many of the potential nesting locations may also have hampered the detection of duckling broods with few conducted after late July or early August.

LESSER SCAUP *Aythya affinis*

Lesser Scaups are common to abundant migrants and winter residents in Arizona, with the largest concentrations at river reservoirs and below dams. A few nonbreeding birds are occasionally observed throughout the summer in the state (Monson and Phillips 1981). Jacobs (1985) noted that there were numerous June and July records of singles and pairs on Navajo and Hopi tribal lands, but breeding has not been documented. Brown (1985) reported that there were a few nesting records of Lesser Scaups in the White Mountains region, but provided no further details. The only potential breeding record during the atlas was an observation of a pair in a small, high-elevation lake in the Chuska Mountains on 30 May 1994.

SHORT-TAILED HAWK *Buteo brachyurus*

Small forest buteos, Short-tailed Hawks are widespread inhabitants from Mexico to South America. Their range is apparently extending northward, with the first observations in Sonora in 1982 (Russell and Monson 1998). Arizona obtained its first unconfirmed reports in the Chiricahua Mountains in August 1985 and the Huachuca Mountains in July 1988. This hawk was finally documented in the state when one of two individuals was photographed in late July and reported through early September 1999 in the Huachuca Mountains (Rosenberg 2001).

In 2001, during the final cleanup year of the atlas project, Short-tailed Hawks were discovered again in southeastern Arizona. In the upper Chiricahua Mountains, an adult with a buff-colored juvenile giving begging calls was observed from 5 August to 3 September, strongly suggesting local nesting. Similar observations have occurred following the atlas period, further supporting likely nesting efforts in Arizona. Most of Arizona's Short-tailed Hawk records are during the period from mid-July through early September. However, observations of recent fledglings by mid-July indicates clutch initiation by mid-May.

Short-tailed Hawks are considered one of the most aerial buteos, with virtually all daylight hours spent airborne (Wheeler 2003). Consequently, in Arizona they are most frequently encountered as they soar and kite on updrafts over mountain peaks and ridges. With set wings, these raptors will kite effortlessly in one position for lengthy periods. Typical foraging and suspected breeding habitats in the state include pine and pine-oak forests on mountain slopes and in upper canyons.

EARED QUETZAL *Euptilotis neoxenus*

Impressively attractive, Eared Quetzals are timid forest birds of Mexico that range rarely and erratically northward into Arizona. The discovery of up to four individuals in Cave Creek Canyon in the Chiricahua Mountains, beginning on 23 October 1977, provided the first record for Arizona and

JIM BURNS

Eared Quetzal

the United States (Rosenberg and Witzeman 1998). Before 1991, all observations of this species in the state were from canyons in the Chiricahua and Huachuca mountains. Occupied habitat in Arizona typically consists of Madrean pine-oak woodlands and adjacent cool drainages and canyons with various species of pine, Douglas fir, evergreen oak, juniper, Arizona madrone, maple, and scattered sycamore. Eared Quetzals typically nest at higher elevation forests above the sycamore-dominated canyons favored by Elegant Trogons.

A major influx of Eared Quetzals occurred in the state during the summer and fall of 1991, with singles and pairs totaling 8–12 individuals appearing in the Chiricahua, Huachuca, and Santa Rita mountains. During that same year, a pair in Ramsey Canyon in the Huachuca Mountains began nesting in a cavity of a large bigtooth maple snag in September and were observed feeding nestlings well into October (Williamson 1992). Unfortunately, this late nesting effort failed when a major storm on 26 October dropped the temperature dramatically in the canyon and the last of two chicks apparently succumbed to hypothermia. In northern Mexico, Eared Quetzal nesting activity can begin in late spring, but most pairs nest during the typical monsoon period from July to September (Williamson 1992).

Likely owing to the 1991 influx, individual Eared Quetzals were reported in June 1992 in widely scattered localities north to the Mogollon Rim near Hospital Ridge, along the Black River, and in the Sierra Ancha. A pair was also periodically reported in several canyons in the Huachuca Mountains through 1992 and into the first year of the atlas period in late May and June 1993. Other atlas period reports include a pair of Eared Trogons investigating a tree cavity near Rustler and Barfoot Parks high in the Chiricahua Mountains on 9–11 June 1994 and an individual noted on the Mogollon Rim on 18 June 1994.

EASTERN WOOD-PEWEE *Contopus virens*

It is common and widespread as a nesting species in eastern and central North American woodlands, but there are few confirmed records of the Eastern Wood-Pewee in Arizona. On 23 June 1998, a singing territorial male was discovered in Madera Canyon, Santa Rita Mountains, along an Arizona sycamore–lined section of the drainage. This determined individual defended his territory from adjacent Western Wood-Pewees through the summer, apparently without attracting a mate. It was last reported on 20 August.

YELLOW-THROATED VIREO *Vireo flavifrons*

Yellow-throated Vireos are rare vagrants to Arizona, with most records occurring between May and September. They commonly breed in open deciduous forests of eastern North America, where they favor forest edges and gallery forests along streams and rivers. One male Yellow-throated Vireo spent the late summer of 1992 singing and maintaining a territory among the willows and cottonwoods of the upper San Pedro River east of Sierra Vista. Apparently, this same individual returned during the first year of the atlas project in 1993 and sang periodically from 28 May through 20 September. A second individual could not be determined at this location, and this persistent bird was presumed unmated. This or another Yellow-throated Vireo was present in the same vicinity in June 1994.

YELLOW-GREEN VIREO *Vireo flavoviridis*

The Yellow-green Vireo is a tropical counterpart of the familiar and widespread Red-eyed Vireo of North America. It winters in northwestern South American and migrates north to breed from Panama north locally to southern Texas and southern Sonora. Russell and Monson (1998) suggested that this vireo's nesting season in Sonora is more closely tied to the summer monsoon season than is that of any other migratory species. Records indicate that Yellow-green Vireos arrive in southern Sonora in late May and establish territories in June. Nesting occurs in July, and they depart south by late August (Russell and Monson 1998).

Accordingly, most of Arizona's few Yellow-green Vireo records are from mid-May through mid-August. The majority of records are from along foothill drainages containing various combinations of sycamore, cottonwood, willow, ash, and hackberry.

During the last few years of the atlas project, singing Yellow-green Vireos were discovered along Sonoita Creek southwest of Patagonia between 21 and 24 July 1999 and in nearby Harshaw Canyon from 18 June to 20 September 2000. An intriguing atlas record was of a singing Yellow-green Vireo in Guadalupe Canyon in the extreme southeastern corner of the state, reported feeding a possible fledgling on 8 August. This observation could not be confirmed, and since the location was immediately adjacent to the Mexico border, it could not constitute the first Arizona breeding record. It is unclear if these records pertain to migratory overshoots or if the breeding range of Yellow-green Vireo is gradually extending north into southeastern Arizona.

BLACK-CAPPED CHICKADEE *Poecile atricapillus*

Black-capped Chickadees are familiar forest and woodland birds over much of the northern half of North America. In Arizona, they are casual fall and winter visitors to the extreme northern edge of the state, with the southernmost records along Chinle Wash near Many Farms. The only potential breeding record for Arizona pertains to two Black-capped Chickadees observed in Betatakin Canyon west of Kayenta on 25 May 2000. They were compared directly with the more expected Mountain Chickadees. This suggests breeding here and possibly elsewhere in similar isolated aspen stands in several other nearby Tsegi Canyon drainages (C. LaRue, personal communication).

CAROLINA WREN *Thryothorus ludovicianus*

The breeding range of the Carolina Wren has gradually expanded westward, and the species has recently been documented nesting locally in Colorado and New Mexico. A singing individual was discovered at Cook's Lake near the lower San Pedro River on 13 June 1999 (T. Koronkiewicz, personal communication), the first Arizona record. This solitary individual sang throughout the summer and remained to repeat the process through the spring of 2001.

RUFOUS-BACKED ROBIN *Turdus rufopalliatus*

Primarily endemic to western Mexico, Rufous-backed Robins are resident north to southern Sonora. In Sonora, they breed within lowland riparian woodlands, typically from late June to August during the summer monsoon season (Russell and Monson 1998). Unlike American Robins, these retiring birds are practically silent most of the year, and singing is concentrated into a brief period just prior to nesting activity (Russell and Monson 1998).

JIM BURNS

Rufous-backed Robin

Rufous-backed Robins are basically casual to rare fall and winter visitors to Arizona, with the earliest individuals arriving in early October. Wintering Rufous-backed Robins typically depart Arizona by early to mid-April. They are considered accidental visitors from May through July, with only one or two records for each of those months. Therefore, it was somewhat surprising when an individual was captured in a mist net on 5 June 1996 along the upper San Pedro River east of Sierra Vista. This individual was reported to have had a highly vascularized incubation/brooding patch, suggesting recent breeding activity (J. Whetstone, personal communication). In 1999, a Rufous-backed Robin lingered as late as 14 May near Peña Blanca Lake.

BOBOLINK *Dolichonyx oryzivorus*

Bobolinks are unique birds that typically prefer to nest in irrigated hay fields and damp, but not marshy meadows. These specific habitat attributes often greatly limit their breeding distribution, particularly in the more arid West. Furthermore, due to annual precipitation variation or crop rotations, some nesting localities could be appropriate one year but not the next.

There are very few nesting records for Bobolinks in Arizona, with most in the east-central region of the state. A small colony was reported near Show Low in 1937, and a pair was observed near Snowflake on 15–16 June 1968 (Monson and Phillips 1981). They were confirmed nesting in a damp field next to the Little Colorado River near Eagar in June and July 1979 and periodically reported at this locality into the 1980s. In 1983, several Bobolinks were also discovered nesting in a damp meadow near Payson.

During the atlas period, a male Bobolink was noted in appropriate nesting habitat near Eagar on 23 June 1994. Unfortunately, this observation was reported too late in the season, and the site was never visited again to determine if it pertained to a nesting effort.

COMMON GRACKLE *Quiscalus quiscula*

A widespread and familiar species of eastern and central North America, Common Grackles have steadily expanded their breeding range to the West during the twentieth century, a trend that apparently continues to this day (Peer and Bollinger 1997). Historically, they did not breed extensively west of the central Great Plains region, but habitat alterations such as agricultural shelterbelts and stands of shade trees in rural and urban areas have facilitated their westward expansion (Peer and Bollinger 1997). They arrived in New Mexico in 1951 and were discovered nesting as far northwest as Farmington by 1970 (Hubbard 1978). These grackles also nest locally in southwestern Colorado (Chace 1998). The first verified Arizona record was in 1980 (LaRue and Ellis 1992), and Common Grackles are now apparently sparse but almost regular migrants in northeastern Arizona (C. LaRue, personal communication). Based on prior records of other western states, Peer and Bollinger (1997) noted that increased occurrences of this grackle in a given region suggest that breeding may occur in the near future.

Common Grackles nest in open woodlands, forest edges, and in open areas with scattered trees such as are found in human-altered landscapes. On Navajo and Hopi tribal lands, fifteen scattered records span from late April to late July and from late September to late December (C. LaRue, personal communication). During the atlas period, a male Common Grackle was noted in Kayenta on 10 June 1994, and one to two individuals summered at Lees Ferry along the Colorado River from 28 May to 31 July 1997. With confirmed nesting activity in the adjacent four corners regions of New Mexico and Colorado, it is likely only a matter of time before Common Grackles will be discovered nesting in Arizona.

PINE GROSBEAK *Pinicola enucleator*

Pine Grosbeaks are large and amazingly unwary finches that frequently allow close approach when encountered. Nesting primarily in or near spruce-fir forests, their southernmost breeding distribution is a small, isolated population in the White Mountains of east-central Arizona. Although resident, even here they are very sparsely distributed and infrequently observed among the Engelmann spruce, subalpine fir, and scattered aspen at elevations above 9500 ft (2896 m). Most summer records are concentrated in the Sunrise Ski and Campground area of the White Mountain Apache tribal lands south to the Baldy Peak area and the headwaters of the West Fork of the Little Colorado River. There are very few breeding records within this limited population, and the only atlas period observation was of a pair of Pine Grosbeaks on 25 June 1994 near Sunrise Campground.

Throughout much of its range, the Pine Grosbeak's nesting activity begins in late May and early June (Adkisson 1999). Seemingly appropriate breeding habitat also exists in the fairly extensive subalpine spruce-fir forests in the San Francisco Mountains and higher elevations of the Kaibab Plateau. However, Pine Grosbeaks have been reported only once in the latter regions during the summer, during June and July 1929 (Phillips et al. 1964). In Colorado, Pine Grosbeaks prefer moist, open spruce-fir forest and are most common in wet valleys above 9800 ft (2987 m), where there are numerous openings in the forests such as near meandering brooks and associated alpine meadows (Adkisson 1999). This closely describes occupied habitat in the White Mountains, but perennial drainages are extremely limited at these elevations in the steeper-sloping San Francisco Mountains and the drier Kaibab Plateau. Preferring forest openings and edges, nesting Pine Grosbeaks are typically rare or absent in dense coniferous forests or those dominated by aspen (Adkisson 1999).

Elsewhere in Arizona, Pine Grosbeaks are primarily an irruptive species, occurring very infrequently and in limited numbers in coniferous forests between early November and mid-April, with stragglers reported exceptionally to early May. Most observations are in northern Arizona, although they have been reported at Prescott, in the Sierra Ancha, and in several southeastern ranges, including the Pinaleno, Santa Catalina, and Chiricahua mountains (Monson and Phillips 1981).

HISTORICAL NESTING SPECIES

AMERICAN BITTERN *Botaurus lentiginosus*

Throughout Arizona, American Bitterns are primarily a rare to locally uncommon migrant beginning in late August and wintering primarily along the lower Colorado and Gila rivers. Spring migration begins in March, with stragglers into early May. All observations of this bittern during the atlas period were along the lower Colorado River from 20 March to 25 April; these were considered migrants.

Historically, American Bitterns were noted nesting commonly at lakes and wetlands in the San Francisco Mountain region. They were considered especially abundant at the end of May among the tules at Mormon Lake southeast of Flagstaff (Mearns 1890). Individuals near Tucson on 26 May 1893 and one "pumping" near Prescott 7 June 1930 (Phillips et al. 1964) could have been very late migrants, but their presence also suggests possible nesting activity. In the White Mountains, a female American Bittern was collected near Big Lake on 16 June 1915. The date and the fact that this specimen had a slightly enlarged ovary also indicate likely nesting (Goldman 1926).

Along the lower Colorado River, Rosenberg et al. (1991) noted calling American Bitterns during the early summer period at Martinez Lake in 1978 and at the Bill Williams River delta in 1980, which suggests the possibility of breeding activity. Observations of American Bitterns in Arizona between mid-May and mid-August should be investigated to determine any nesting activity.

CALIFORNIA CONDOR *Gymnogyps californianus*

Many bone remains of California Condors have been found in caves within the Grand Canyon region. However, none of these bones has been dated as less than about 11,000 years old, roughly the time when many of the large mammals of the Pleistocene became extinct (Emslie 1987). It is commonly assumed the disappearance of the California Condor from much of its Pleistocene range was a direct result of these extinctions, inasmuch as condors presumably fed largely on carcasses of these creatures (Snyder and Rea 1998). However, California Condors were reported in Arizona as late as 1924 near Williams, Coconino County (Phillips et al. 1964). As human populations increased along the Pacific Coast of North America, condor numbers declined to the point that by the late 1930s they could be found only in California. Numbers of California Condors continued to drop due to human interactions (shooting, poisoning, and power-line collisions) that ultimately pushed the population to an all-time low of twenty-two individuals in 1982.

In December 1996, an experimental group of six young California Condors was released at the Vermilion Cliffs in northern Arizona. Subsequent releases continued through the end of the atlas period in 2001, building the free-flying population to twenty-two individuals. Pairing and breeding activity began as individuals matured with the first nesting attempt noted in Marble Canyon in 2001. Unfortunately this attempt and those that followed in 2002 were unsuccessful.

California Condor

However, a pair successfully fledged one nestling from a Grand Canyon cave on 5 November 2003, making it the first successful wild hatched and reared California Condor since 1984 and likely the first in Arizona in more than a century.

Courtship activity of the California Condors has been observed between January and April. Once paired, these large birds begin investigating remote nest caves on cliffs; in Arizona they have selected sites in Marble Canyon and Grand Canyon and on the Vermilion Cliffs. Although the sample size is low, California Condors in Arizona have been routinely laying their single egg in March. Both parents share the responsibility of incubation, which lasts for approximately 56 days. The young fledge when they are about six months of age.

WHITE-TAILED HAWK *Buteo albicaudatus*

The inclusion of the White-tailed Hawk as a historical nesting species in Arizona is dubious at best (Monson 1998). G. F. Breninger (1899) claimed to have taken an egg from a nest of this raptor between Florence and Red Rock, Pinal County, in 1897. Neither adult was collected, and the identification of the egg has been questioned. This is the only reference to this hawk's ever nesting in Arizona. Even in Sonora to the south, where a nest has yet to be found, this species is rare (Monson 1998). There is only one specimen, collected by Breninger at Phoenix in 1899, and only a handful of sight records for the White-tailed Hawk in Arizona.

APLOMADO FALCON *Falco femoralis*

Before 1890, the regal Aplomado Falcon was considered a fairly common resident of the semiarid grasslands of southeastern Arizona (Henshaw 1875; Bendire 1892). Aplomado Falcons were noted most frequently in areas of open grasslands with scattered stands of mesquite and soaptree yucca, or at the edge of riparian woodland that meander through the grasslands. Most records of these falcons were obtained from Cochise County north to Ft. Bowie, but they have been noted at least once near Tucson (Visher 1910). The nineteenth-century distribution of the Aplomado Falcon in Arizona was probably more extensive than the few published records suggest (Keddy-Hector 1998). Based on available historical habitat and their known distribution in New Mexico, these falcons may have ranged well north of present-day Interstate 10, perhaps as far as the Gila River valley and then west to the Santa Cruz River and Altar valleys (Keddy-Hector 1998).

Bendire (1892) describe the only Aplomado Falcon nesting records in Arizona, which were obtained from Lt. Harry C. Benson, who found five active nests in the spring of 1887 in the vicinity of Fort Huachuca. All the nests were placed low in mesquite trees, 7–15 ft (2.1–4.6 m) above the ground. These falcons apparently used old nests constructed in prior years by Chihuahuan Ravens. One nest contained three small nestlings on 25 April, suggesting that egg laying was initiated in late March. Other nests contained eggs on 28 April and 5 May. Two nests discovered with eggs on 14 May could have been replacement clutches for the previously collected broods.

There are very few published records of Aplomado Falcons in Arizona after 1900, and the latest accepted observations were near McNeal on 13 November 1939 and Saint David on 7 October 1940 (Phillips et al. 1964). Limited information on the Aplomado Falcon's natural history in Arizona leads to speculation as to the factors contributing to its almost abrupt extirpation from the state. However, heavy grazing pressure throughout the region during and following the 1880s, coupled with severe drought periods, likely reduced prey base abundance for these falcons. Continued grazing also reduced the natural frequency of fire in the grasslands of southeastern Arizona, which likely enhanced the proliferation of mesquite and other woody shrubs. With the widespread increase of shrubs in the open grasslands, appropriate foraging areas for these falcons were greatly reduced. Hector (1987) stated that hunting Aplomado Falcons often force fleeing birds into limited patches of thick ground cover or crowns of isolated trees. The falcons are agile enough to corner and capture such grounded prey.

Aplomado Falcon

However, he further noted that when potential prey fled into continuous forests, thick brush, or dense deep grass, the falcons tended to abandon pursuit quickly.

SANDHILL CRANE *Grus canadensis*

The only historical notes suggesting that Sandhill Cranes ever nested in Arizona was from Mearns (1890), who reported a few pairs breeding at Mormon Lake southeast of Flagstaff, where a Mormon settler took its eggs in 1886. In July 1910, a pair of Sandhill Cranes was observed near Reservation Ranch on White Mountain Apache tribal lands; the date suggests that they were breeding there as well (Leopold 1923).

In Arizona, Sandhill Cranes are now uncommon migrants and fairly common to locally abundant winter residents. These distinctive birds typically occur in the state from late September or early October through mid-March, with stragglers remaining into mid-April.

WILSON'S PHALAROPE *Phalaropus tricolor*

Common to abundant migrants in Arizona, Wilson's Phalaropes can be found locally throughout the summer in the state. Spring migration begins in late March or early April, with peak passage during early May. Stragglers are regularly observed into early June. Wilson's Phalaropes nest in sparse to dense vegetation of marshes, lakeshores, or nearby uplands. North of Arizona, nests with eggs are found from early May through late June. Adult female Wilson's Phalaropes begin returning south through Arizona as early as mid- to late June, with numbers of these shorebirds increasing in July and August. Many individuals and small flocks of phalaropes are obviously migrating through Arizona during the entire nesting period of May through July. It is therefore difficult to determine the true status of pairs and individual males observed during this period.

The only confirmed breeding records in Arizona were of several males tending nests with eggs on 15 June 1981, and then again on 2 June and 10 June 1982 at Pintail Lake near Show Low, Navajo County (Piest 1983). Since 1979, pairs have been irregularly observed near Springerville in seemingly appropriate nesting habitat in June (Rosenberg and Terrill 1986). On 13–14 June 2000, atlasers noted three pairs of Wilson's Phalaropes, including one pair with a slightly smaller juvenile along Ganado Lake on Navajo tribal lands. Lacking further nesting evidence and noting little available nesting habitat due to heavy grazing along the lakeshore, they were presumed to be early southbound migrants.

THICK-BILLED PARROT *Rhynchopsitta pachyrhyncha*

Historically, there is no definitive evidence that the nomadic Thick-billed Parrots ever nested among the lofty pine-clad ridges of Arizona. Most documented observations in the state were during the fall and winter when these gregarious noisy parrots traveled widely in search of substantial pinecone crops. At least in the Chiricahua Mountains, however, accounts of these parrots span all seasons and were observed nearly annually during the early 1900s; thus it seems likely they bred at least irregularly. Thick-billed Parrots ranged north centuries ago to at least Beaver Creek near Camp Verde, but were primarily found only in the higher southeastern Arizona mountain ranges after 1900. These included the Chiricahua, Dragoon, Pinaleno, Galiuro, Santa Catalina, Whetstone, Huachuca, Patagonia, and Santa Rita Mountains (Phillips et al. 1964). Numbers of parrots varied considerably both seasonally and annually. Some years none were reported, followed by events such as early fall 1917, when an estimated flock of 1000–1500 was noted in Rucker Canyon in the Chiricahua Mountains (Wetmore 1935). Visits north of Mexico by Thick-billed Parrots gradually diminished; the last reliable reports in Arizona were in 1922 and 1935 (Phillips et al. 1964). These parrots suffered heavily from shooting in the United States, and the species was very likely extirpated north of the border by this stress (Snyder et al. 1994). Populations of Thick-billed Parrots were also likely reduced by the destruction of pine forests within their mountain strongholds in the Sierra Madre Occidental of northwest Mexico from Chihuahua south to Durango.

Thick-billed Parrots still breeds within 50 mi (80 km) of the U.S. border in northwestern Chihuahua (Snyder et al. 1999). They initiate nesting in the summer, with most egg laying occurring from mid-June to late July. Nests with young are first noted in mid-July, and the nestlings fledge approximately two months later in September and October (Lanning and Shiflett 1983).

In an effort to reestablish a population in Arizona, twenty-nine Thick-billed Parrots confiscated from smugglers were released in the Chiricahua Mountains in 1986. Additional small groups were released through 1989 (Snyder et al. 1994). These parrots consistently wintered among the conifers at the top of the Chiricahua Mountains, where snow was deep and disturbance was minimal. Small flocks summered in the Chiricahuas as well as to the north among the pine forests along the Mogollon Rim in central Arizona. They possibly nested in 1987, and one or more young of the year were observed in 1988. In 1989, the three known Mogollon Rim nests failed as drought in the area greatly reduced the availability of pinecones. The final blow was a massive forest fire, which ravaged much of their summer retreat in 1990. The Thick-billed Parrot flocks scattered, and the few remaining disappeared by the end of that year, likely owing to predation.

CAVE SWALLOW *Hirundo fulva*

Cave Swallows are very casual visitors to Arizona. The first individual in the state was detected at a Cliff Swallow colony on the University of Arizona campus in Tucson on 11 May 1979 (Monson and Phillips 1981). Each year from 1979 to 1982 a lone individual was observed at this location and reported from mid-April through mid-June (Huels 1984). Two Cave Swallows appeared at this location during the 1983 nesting season. They nested in an old Cliff Swallow nest and fledged three young. By backdating, it was determined eggs were likely laid on or about 1 June and fledging the first young on 11 July (Huels 1984). One adult was last observed on 31 July.

VEERY *Catharus fuscescens*

Veerys were first collected on 3–4 July 1936 along the Little Colorado River near its South Fork west of Eagar in Apache County. These thrushes were found nesting at least irregularly in this area through 1980 (Monson and Phillips 1981). A few individuals were detected singing along this section of the Little Colorado River through 1987, but no further breeding activity has been noted.

NORTHERN PARULA *Parula americana*

Northern Parulas have become a rare but apparently increasing migrant throughout Arizona, with more individuals found locally wintering as well. These small warblers are casually reported in Arizona during the summer months, including one likely nesting record. On 10–11 July 1992, a singing male Northern Paula was observed with two fledglings along the Verde River south of Cottonwood (C. Tomoff, personal communication). Atlasers observed this warbler on three atlas blocks ranging in date from 8 May to 11 June, with no nesting activity observed.

BLACK-AND-WHITE-WARBLER *Mniotilta varia*

Rare migrants throughout Arizona, Black-and-White Warblers have also become sparse local winter visitors and are noted casually throughout the summer. Atlasers reported individuals on six atlas blocks ranging in date from 25 March to 2 July.

On 9 and 14 June 1990, a pair of Black-and-White Warblers was observed feeding two fledged downy young approximately 25 mi (40 km) west of Prescott in a side drainage of the Santa Maria River (R. Houser, personal communication). Arizona is significantly well outside their normal breeding range, and this discovery was unexpected.

AMERICAN REDSTART *Setophaga ruticilla*

Phillips et al. (1964) considered the American Redstart a probable rare summer resident along the Little Colorado River near Eagar since their initial discovery in 1936. One or two pairs nested at least irregularly near the confluence of the Little Colorado River and its South Fork into the mid-1980s (Rosenberg and Terrill 1986). American Redstarts were not reported at this local stronghold throughout the atlas period. This bird also attempted nesting once near Prescott in 1977 (Monson and Phillips 1981). Atlasers noted these flashy warblers on four different blocks that ranged in dates from 9 May to 29 June, but all were considered migrants or summering individuals.

LARK BUNTING *Calamospiza melanocorys*

Lark Buntings were detected nesting in Arizona in July 1973 near Chino Valley. A juvenile accompanied by five adult pairs was collected after striking a fence (Monson and Phillips 1981). They may also nest occasionally and locally on tribal lands of northeastern Arizona during exceptionally wet years. On 16 June 1992, P. Ryan observed four singing and displaying male Lark Buntings north of Highway 264 near Tselani (C. LaRue, personal communication). Otherwise, these birds are locally common to abundant winter visitors in southern Arizona, particularly in the southeast. Lingering spring migrants have been observed into early June, and returning fall migrants begin to appear in July. Nesting activity was not observed in Arizona during the atlas period. However, migrant Lark Buntings were encountered in a wide variety of desert and grassland habitats on nearly 100 blocks, with the vast majority observed during peak migration in April and August.

BALTIMORE ORIOLE *Icterus galbula*

Baltimore Orioles are casual transients in Arizona from early April through early June and from mid-August into mid-November. A male Baltimore Oriole paired with a female Bullock's Oriole and nested along the lower Verde River in June 1980 (Monson and Phillips 1981). A similar pair also attempted to nest in Chino Valley, Yavapai County, in the early 1980s.

LAWRENCE'S GOLDFINCH *Carduelis lawrencei*

Lawrence's Goldfinches are primarily an erratic and irregular fall and winter visitor to Arizona, sometimes locally concentrating in large numbers. During flight years, wintering populations of these fancy little finches begin migrating out of the state by mid- to late February. Most individuals and small flocks are gone by mid-March, but some regularly linger into April and sometimes May. However, there are Arizona records every month of the year, including several nesting records in La Paz and Maricopa counties.

The first nest of Lawrence's Goldfinch in Arizona was found along the Colorado River near Parker in 1952. Near the Bill Williams River delta, a pair of Lawrence's Goldfinches was also present from late May through June 1978 and were suspect of breeding. The following year, a nest in a tamarisk at the edge of a large cottonwood grove was found at this location on 18 April and contained three young by 12 May (Rosenberg et al. 1991).

To the east, Lawrence's Goldfinches have been found nesting on two different occasions along the lower Verde River east of Fountain Hills. These include a pair with fledglings on 10 April 1977 and two pairs with nests on 7 May 1978. Nesting was also suggested when juveniles were observed along the Hassayampa River near Wickenburg in late June 1980 (or 10 July). Some nesting events in Arizona followed flight years, but others did not. Therefore, it is unclear what stimulated these nomadic little finches to nest within the state occasionally. Atlasers detected Lawrence's Goldfinches on eight different blocks that ranged in dates from 8 March to 21 July, but none were suspected of nesting.

Appendix A:
List of Atlas Volunteers

The Arizona Breeding Bird Atlas project and this book would not have been possible without our dedicated volunteers. Their generous contributions of time and effort were truly monumental, and we express a great appreciation to all of them. Volunteers and the approximate number of priority blocks they completed are listed below:

50–60 BLOCKS
Arnold Moorhouse
Tim Price
Carl Tomoff

40–49 BLOCKS
Greg Clark
Troy Corman

30–39 BLOCKS
B. June Babcock

20–29 BLOCKS
Richard Hibbard
Chuck LaRue
David Mikesic
Lin Piest
Walter Thurber

10–19 BLOCKS
Bob Bradley
Mark Brown
Bob Henry
George Hentz
Celia Holm
Ron Kearns
Richard Leibold
Tracy McCarthey
Elaine Morrall
John Spence

4–9 BLOCKS
Ruth Amster
Steven Bahe
Mike Baker
Bob Barry
David Boyd
Bill Burger
Henry Detwiler
Mark Flippo
Michael Francis
Todd Furniss
Jim Gacey
Bill Grossi
Guy Hamman
Brian Heap
Susanna Henry
Debbie Hileman
Jennifer Holmes
Susi MacVean
Jonathan Manygoats
Robert Morse
Michael Plagens
Barbara Raulston
Jina Sagar
Karen Short
Mark Stevenson
Cathy Taylor
Douglas Tempel
Deb Treadway
Jack Whetstone

2–3 BLOCKS
Janie Agyagos
Harvey Beatty
Mary Ann Benoit
Melinda Berger
Frank Brandt
Terry Brodner
Walter Bull
Courtney Conway
Ted Cordery
Alan Craig
Rebecca Davis
John Dorio
Ron Engel-Wilson
Dan Fischer
Glenn Frederick
Peter Friederici
Virginia Gilmore
Dan Godec
Kate Gooby
John Grahame
Paul Gravatt
David Griffin
Diana Herron
J. David Hoerath
Nadine Holder
Kathleen Holt
Becca Hooker
Rob Hunt
Jim Keller
Jim Kelly
Dave Krueper
Richard Langley
Eugene Lewis
Stan Lilley
Nancy London
Deborah Lutch
Gabriel Martinez
Janine McCabe
Betsy McKellar
Grace McKernan
Chris Mehling
Henry Messing
Jack Meyer
Sandra Miller
Jean Moore
George Morrison
Laurie Nessel
John Nystedt
Jerry D. Orr
Bill Pelle
Dee Pfleger
Mike Pruss
Tim Reeves
Rich Richins
Ben Robles
Don Rosie
Susan Ruffini-Taylor
Stephen Rutkowski
Norm Shrout
Greg Slover
Christy Smith
Pat Sonneborn
Tim Tibbitts
Dick Tonder
Craig Wilcox
Karen Williams
Toni Williams
John Windes
Brenda Zaun

1 BLOCK
Carl Aalbers
Amber Alexander
Walt Anderson
Sharon Arnold
Annalaura Averill-Murray
John Bacourn
Scott Bailey
Albert Bammann
Patricia Beall
Lynne Beck
Chris Benesh
Erin Bibles
Deborah Bieber
Terrance Blows
Joan Braun
Ruth Breitmaier
Gerald Brink
Bryan Brown
Nikolle Brown
Sirena Brownlee
Jeff Buler
Carolyn Burdick
Scott Burge
Jim Burns
Joshua Burns
Barbara Cain
Eleanor R. Campbell
Barbara Carlson
Cheryl Carrothers
Jeff Casper
Jim Clark
Mary Coar
John Coons
Jeffrey Cooper
Sylvia Crisler
Tim Crisler
Doug Danforth
Dave Danskin
Salome Demaree
Carol Dewaard
Vanessa Dickinson
Louis Dombroski
George Drew
Louisa Evers
Dave Felley
Brad Fiero
Lisa Fitzner
Aaron Flesch
Emery Froelich
Earline Gardner
Eric Gardner
Gerry Gebhart
Rick Gerhart
Joe Hall
Jon Hanna
Homer Hansen
Elizabeth Hatcher
Gary Helbing
John Higgins
John Hildebrand
Tom Hildebrandt
Wesley Hochachka
Bob Hoffa
John Hoffman
Mike Holloran
Karen Horton
Roy Houser
Tricia Hurley
Ralph Irwin
Debbie James
Bud Johnson
Daniel Jones
Hollis Jones
Keith Jones
Joe Kahl
Melody Kehl
Carmen Kennedy
Ken Kingsley
Barbara Koenig
Ramsay Koury
Larry Langstaff
David Larson
Mark Larson
Margie Latta
Diane Laush
Tamara Lesh
Duane Longfellow
Anita MacFarlane
Randall Madding
Rob Magill
James Mann
David Mann
Beth McCauley
Bob McClow
Brain McKnight
Steve Messenger
Don Moniak
Randall Moore

1 BLOCK *(continued)*

Debbie Moyer
Clark Munger
Carol Munz
Chris Olson
Ruth Olsen
Wayne Paintner
Richard Palmer
Gabriel Paz
Mark Peterson
Jim Petterson
Barbara Phillips
Clive Pinnock
Jean Porter
Jenise Porter
Bonnie Pranter
Carol Rawlings
Scott Richardson
Mitch Ross
Brenda Russell
John Samuelson
Bob Scheibe
Robert Schroeder
Joan Scott
Mark Severson
Bob Shank
Albert Sillas
Devin Skinner
Dan Smith
Victor Smith
Pam Sponholtz
Cara Staab
Sam Stearman
Bart Stegman
Cheryl Stewert
Robert Sullivan
Bill Sutton
Paul Sweet
Sarah Swope
Billy Tarrant
Douglas Tookey
Martin Tuegel
John Unruh
Lyn Vanderwerf
Theona Vyvial
Jon Wangnild
Cynthia West
Hana West
Larry Wheatland
Russell R. Widner
Deanna Williams
John Williams
Randy Wilson
Barb Winterfield
Cathryn Wise-Gervais
Janet Witzeman
Joe Woodley
Lori Young

PRIORITY BLOCK HELPERS

Dennis Abbate
Frank Agyagos
Emily Alexander
Chris Amster
B. Anderson
Irma Andrews
Henry Apfel
Eric Atene
Roy Averill-Murray
Vic Bacon
Tara Bailey
Richard Bailowitz
Gwen Baluss
Jeanine Baker
Mary Bammann
Alison Banks
Bob Bates
Dana Bayer
Wade Beall
Greg Beatty
A. J. Beck
William Begay Jr.
Paul Beier
Dave Belitsky
Mabe Bendixen
Millie Bilotta
Scott Black
Yvonne Bloch
Sulojana Blows
Pat Boleyn
Dave Booth
Cass Boracci
Rick Bowers
Laurie Bowman
Linda Brandt
Stan Braun
Shauna Brown
Manuel Bravo
Mario Bravo
Bob Brawdy
Bill Breed
W. Breed
Carl Breitmaier
Mark Brennan
Deb Brewster
Betty Brink
Carol Briske
Rob Brodner
Scott Brownwood
Adam Burdick
Alex Burdick
Gene Burdick
Brenda Burger
Ed Burnett
Karla Burnly
Deva Burns
Joseph Busch
Chris Caldwell
Mark Cantrell
Dave Carrothers
Liz Carver
Donna Cellini
Tilly Chew
Dean Chickadonz
Pat Christgau
Barbara Clark
D. J. Clark
Michael Collier
Arlene Comon
Glenn Condon
Kathy Cook
Marnie Cook
Ken Cook
Kyle Cooper
Denise Copeland
Andrew Cordery
Cindy Cordery
Ian Cornelius
Donita Cotter
Al Creighton
Mary Creighton
D. Keith Crenshaw
Gary Cress
Cris Cristoffer
Nigel Crook
Pat Crouch
Sherry Crouch
Ernestine Culver
Chris Cutler
Natalie Danforth
Dorothy Danskin
Cecelia Dargan
Brian Dasilva
Carolyn Dearing
Tom Deecken
Tami Denette
Suzanne Derosier
Sonja Detsoi
Lara Dickson
Stacy Drasen
Nancy Drew
Diane Drobka
Charles Drost
C. Drowley
Brian Dykstra
Keeley Eaton
Judy Edison
Bruce Eierts
David Ellis
Dave Eshbaugh
Fred Esparza
Marty Fabritz
Robert Farley
Mary Ferguson-Carter
Georgian Ferrante
Jenny Fiero
Mike Fike
Tim Fletcher
Milton Foster
Jefford Francisco
Fitz Francisco
Terry Frederick
Tom Fresques
Donald Frink
Genice Froehlich
Toni Fudge
Mary Sue Fulks
Barbara Furniss
Amy Gaiennie
Ellis Gardner
Greg Garnett
Cameron Ghalambor
Eve Gill
Rob Gill
Wendy Glenn
Matt Goode
Alice Gravatt
Cavetta Green
Tom Greene
Alison Grinder
Cathy Groshek
Heidi Haas
Jim Hailey
Elaine Halbedel
Marvin Hall
Nancy Hall
Jennifer Hamilton
Karla Hansen
Danita Hardy
Paul Hardy
Marcia Harmon
Andrew Harris
Sylvia Harris
Jeff Hartin
Christine Hass
Ed Hayden
Cortney Hayflinger
Stuart Healy
Victoria Helbing
Don Henry
Linda Hensley
Nancy Herbert
William Herron
Annaliese Hibbard
Emily Hibbard
Ron Hileman
Earl Hill
Eric Hill
Steve Hill
Patrick Holcomb
Bill Holliman
Geoffrey Holm
Richard Holm
George Hoover
Ron Horeisi
Jim Horton
Brice Hoskin
Rose Houk
Barb Houser
Glynes Hummel
Signe Hurd
Mike Ingraldi
Ralph Irwin Jr.
E. Jeter
Enoch Johnson
Ginger Johnson
Kathy Johnson
Silvia Johnson
Jennifer Jollivette
Jill Jones
Justin Jones
Kingford Jones
Rod Jones
Roy Jones
Dorothy Jorgensen
Dale Julian
Dan Kaplan
Phyllis Kegley
Dale Keiser
Debra Keiser

PRIORITY BLOCK HELPERS *(continued)*

Tom Kennedy
Al Kersting
Ken Kertell
Dylan Kesler
John Koehler
Eric Koford
Lynn Kollar
Steve Kollar
Toni Krausman
R. Kreycik
Mia Labarbara
Sarah Lantz
Paula Larson
Annie LaRue
Joyce Lebowitz
Eulalia Lewis
M. Lieterman
Ries Lindley
Robert Link
Teresa Link
Val Little
John Lofgreen
Ardelle Loge
Marg Lomow
Ruby Longfellow
Rosita Lopez
Andy Loranger
Steve Lors
Eunice Lovejoy
Petra Lowe
Joann Loza
Carl Lutch
Ralph Mancke
Dean Manygoats
Silvio Marcario
John Martin
Paul Martin
Rick Martos
Bill Massey
Jim Mattson
Chris May
John May
Nora Mays
Matt McCarty
John McGehee
Steve McKellar
Craig McMullen
Josh Mehlen
C. Mehlus
M. Melius
David Mell
Ray Meyer
Bea Meyers
Phil Meza
Lyle Minard
David Moll
Karen Moniak
Catherine Moore
Narca Moore-Craig
Amanda Moors
Earl Moree
Sheryle Morris-Shank
Pete Moulton
Mary Muchowski
Mike Mueller
Amber Munig
Mike Neal
Jennifer Neale
Andrea Nesbitt
Judy Nestingen
Mike Nestingen
John Nichol
Matt Nichols
Eugene Nida
Robert Nieman
Catherine Nishida
Dan Nolan
Bob Norton
Erika Nowak
Annette Nystedt
Dave Olson
Gene Olson
Vanessa Olson
Joe Ondrejko
Cecelia Overby
Jen Owen
Bobby Paintner
Victor Parra Jr.
Frank Parsons
Arthur Payte
Dave Pearson
Nancy Pearson
Rebecca Peck
Don Perry
Andy Perry
Don Pollock
Ron Popowski
Les Porter
Patti Porzig
Dan Prieskorn
Glenn Proudfoot
Cadie Pruss
Shane Quasula
Roger Radd
Lee Rains
Donn Rawlings
Hugh Rieck
Amparo Rifa
Joe Rigney
Ryan Riley
N. Robb
Earle Robinson
Robin Roche
Jerry Roe
Gary Romig
Gary Rosenberg
Steve Rosenstock
Raeleen Rosie
Jean Ruhser
Jonathan Rupp
Nancy Rupp
Dorothy Russell
Ben Sacks
J. Saunders
Paul Saywer
Laurie Schaal
Jean Scheibe
Janine Schroeder
Ruby Schroeder
Bob Schumacher
Susan Sferra
Teresa Shaffer
Marnie Shepperd
Noel Sherwin
Arlene Shideler
Harold Shideler
Jim Shilling
Ruth Shilling
Jimmy Simmons
Stan Skousen
Alex Smith
Dave Smith
E. Linwood Smith
Tim Snow
Mark Sogge
Tina Sommers
Lia Spegiel
John Spencer
Joe Spitler
Shirley Spitler
Mary Jo Stegman
Kay Stephenson
Emerson Stiles
Dan Stoeker
Ed Stoll
Chris Straw
Georgette Sullivan
Don Swann
Elliot Swarthout
John Swett
Josh Tajz
E. Talgo
Lydell Tapijo
Jay Taylor
Robert Terry
John Thomas
N. Thomas
Bob Thomen
Campbell Thompson
Karen Thompson
Kari Thompson
Mary Thornton
Frances Thurber
Ron Tinseth
Sue Trachy
Darren Tucker
George Tucker
Diane Turret
Sandy Upsom
Sam Vacca
Anita Van Auken
Christie Van Cleve
Ron Van Ommeren
Karen Vandersall
Carlton Wahl
Gordon Wahl
Daniel Walters
Eric Walters
Peggy Wang
Dale Ward
Laurie Ward
Mike Ward
Lisa Warren
Barb Waters
John Waters
Teresa Weninger
Peg Wenrick
Jim Wesley
L. Whetstone
Wes Whiting
Barbara Wightman
Richard Wild
Cliff Williams
Joe Willy
Adam Wilson
Lou Winterfield
Ann Witham
Jim Witham
Bob Witzeman
Dick Wood
Cyndee Woodley
Diane Wright
David Wyant
Daniela Yellan
Ruth Yoder
Herb Young
Scott Zalaznik
Joe Zbyrowski
Heidie Zeigher
Norm Zimmerman
Barbara Zinn
Sue Zorkstruck

FIELD CREWS

The following intrepid individuals were members of the atlas field crews, which annually drove thousands of miles to all corners of Arizona and hiked hundreds of miles each through some of the most remote regions of the state.

Seth Ames
Annalaura Averill-Murray
Gwen Bauluss
Mike Collins
Troy Corman
Tami Denette
David Felley
Aaron Flesch
Peter Friederici
David Griffin
Megan Hall
Charley Land
Margie Latta
Tracy McCarthey
John McGehee
Lisa Miller
Karen Newlon
Judy Putera
Karen Short
Benny Thatcher
Bryant Ward
Cathryn Wise-Gervais

Although the following individuals were unable to help survey priority blocks, they contributed valuable Casual Observation records that were incorporated into the atlas database. Our apologies to anyone we may have overlooked.

Sandy Anderson
Mark Apel
Lorraine Avenetti
Charles Babbitt
Chris Bagnoli
William Baltosser
Bob Barsh
Jack Bartley
Jason Berkley
Brad Bergstrom
Brent Bibles
Barbara Bickel
Michael Bizzantz
Ned Boyajian
Marvin Burnam
Dave Cagle
Clifford Cathers
Matt Chew
Margorie Cole
Vince Costi
Kristin Covert
Gary Crandall
Richard Crossin
Jamey Driscoll
Laura Duncan
Russell Duncan
Elaine Fass
Karen Fawcett
Jay Follett
Steve Ganley
John Gassner
Tom Gatz
Rich Glinski
Caleb Gordon
Jodi Griffith
Robert Grimmond
Jan Hart
Gerald Hester
Steven Hopp
Ron Huettner
Rich Hoyer
David Irwin
Dave Jasper
Kenn Kaufman
Curt Kessler
John Koloszar
Carroll Lam
Ross Lein
Wade Leitner
Chip Lewis
Brandon Marette
Bryce Marshall
Rob Marshall
Tom Martin
Bill Matheny
Robert Mckernan
Bob Miller
Tim Miller
Gale Monson
L.B. Myers
Tom Newman
Eben Paxton
Tim Pender
Daniel Perry
Trevor Persons
John Puschock
Dave Quady
Liz Roberts
Armand Ramirez
Jerry Rather
Michael Rogers
Donna Roten
Jay Rourke
Michael Rupp
Steve Russell
Sue Sitko
Steven Speich
Rich Stallcup
Dave Stejskal
Mike Sumner
Norma Tapia-Luepka
Jesse Taylor
Jim Taylor
Rick Taylor
Darren Thome
Ross Timmons
Bob Tweit
Joan Tweit
Joelle Viau
Sheri Williamson
Blair Wolf
Tom Wood
Brian Wooldridge

Appendix B. Arizona Breeding Bird Atlas Project Funding, 1993–2003

The following graph depicts the monetary contributions by each funding source during the field survey period and most of the Atlas manuscript preparation period. The average annual funding for the Atlas project was approximately $120,000 during the first eight years, which supported two to three full-time staff and seasonal field crews (including transportation).

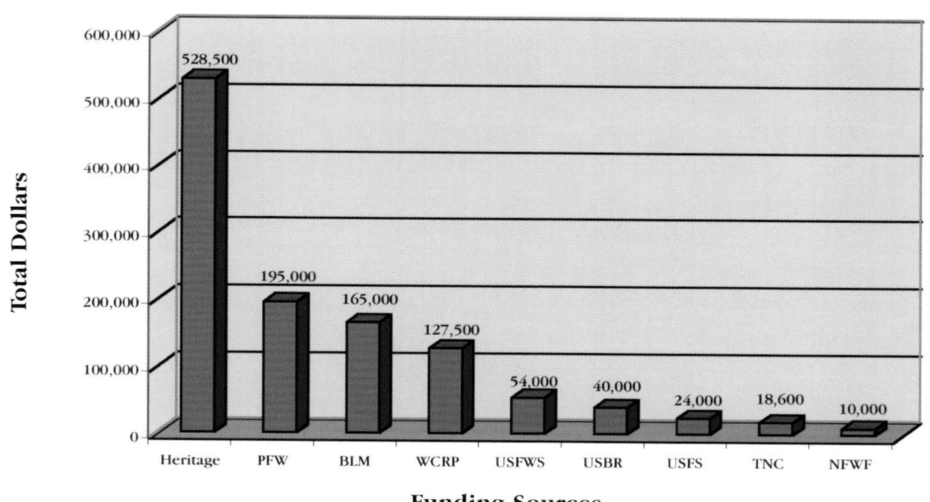

FUNDING SOURCE DEFINITIONS:

BLM	Bureau of Land Management
Heritage	Arizona Game and Fish Department Heritage Fund (State Lottery revenue)
NFWF	National Fish and Wildlife Foundation
PFW	Partnerships for Wildlife
TNC	The Nature Conservancy
USBR	U.S. Bureau of Reclamation
USFS	U.S. Forest Service
USFWS	U.S. Fish and Wildlife Service
WCRP	Wildlife Conservation Restoration Program

Appendix C. Common and Scientific Plant Names Used in the Text

Common Name	Scientific Name
acacia, catclaw	*Acacia greggii*
acacia, sweet	*Acacia farnesiana*
acacia, whitethorn	*Acacia constricta*
agave	*Agave* spp.
alder, Arizona	*Alnus oblongifolia*
alder, thinleaf	*Alnus incana tenuifolia*
alfalfa	*Medicago* spp.
allthorn	*Koeberlinia spinosa*
Apache plume	*Fallugia paradoxa*
arrowweed	*Pluchea sericea*
ash, velvet	*Fraxinus pennsylvanica*
aspen, quaking	*Populus tremuloides*
aster	*Aster* spp.
barberry, Fremont	*Mahonia fremontii*
beargrass	*Nolina* spp.
beavertail, prickly pear	*Opuntia basilaris*
birch, water	*Betula occidentalis*
bitterbrush	*Purshia* spp.
blackbrush	*Coleogyne ramosissima*
blackberry, Himalayan	*Rubus discolor*
blueberry	*Vaccinium* spp.
bluegrass	*Poa spp.*
boxelder	*Acer negundo*
brickelbush	*Brickellia* spp.
brittlebush, white	*Encelia farinosa*
brome, fringed	*Bromus ciliatus*
brome, nodding	*Bromus anomalus*
brome, red	*Bromus rubens*
broom, desert	*Baccharis sarothroides*
buckthorn, Fendler	*Ceanothus fendleri*
buckwheat	*Erogonum* spp.
buffaloberry, roundleaf	*Shepherdia rotundifolia*
buffalograss	*Buchloe dactyloides*
buffelgrass	*Pennesetum ciliare*
bulrush, California	*Schoenoplectus californicus*
bulrush, hardstem	*Schoenoplectus acutus*
bulrush, threesquare	*Schoenoplectus americanus*
burrobush, white	*Hymenoclea salsola*
bursage, white	*Ambrosia dumosa*
buttonbush	*Cephalanthus occidentalis*
cactus, barrel	*Ferocactus* spp.
cactus, organ pipe	*Stenocereus thurberi*
cattail	*Typha* spp.
cheatgrass	*Bromus tectorum*
chokecherry	*Prunus* spp.
cholla, cane	*Opuntia spinosior*
cholla, jumping	*Opuntia fulgida*
cholla, staghorn	*Opuntia versicolor*
cholla, teddybear	*Opuntia bigelovii*
chuparosa	*Justicia californica*
cinquefoil, shrubby	*Dasiphora floribunda*
cliffrose	*Purshia* spp.
clover	*Trifolium* spp.
clover, yellow sweet	*Melilotus officinalis*
coldenia	*Tiquilia* spp.
cottonwood, Fremont	*Populus fremontii*
cottonwood, narrowleaf	*Populus angustifolia*
creeper, thicket	*Parthenocissus vitacea*
creosotebush	*Larrea tridentata*
crucifixion thorn	*Canotia holacantha*
currant	*Ribes* spp.
cypress, Arizona	*Cupressus arizonica*
daisy fleabane	*Erigeron* spp.
desert holly	*Atriplex hymenelytra*
dogwood, red-osier	*Cornus sericea*
dropseed	*Sporobolus* spp.
elderberry, Mexican	*Sambucus nigra*
elderberry, red	*Sambucus racemosa*
elm, Siberian	*Ulmus pumila*
ephedra	*Ephedra* spp.
eucalyptus (or gum)	*Eucalyptus* spp.
fescue, alpine	*Festuca brachyphylla*
fescue, Arizona	*Festuca arizonica*
filaree	*Erodium cicutarium*
fir, corkbark	*Abies lasiocarpa var. arizonica*
fir, Douglas	*Pseudotsuga menziesii*
fir, subalpine	*Abies lasiocarpa*
fir, white	*Abies concolor*
fern, bracken	*Pteridium aquilinum*
galleta, big	*Pleuraphis rigida*
geranium	*Geranium* spp.
globemallow	*Sphaeralcea* spp.
gooseberry sp.	*Ribes* spp.
grama, blue	*Bouteloua gracilis*
grama, false	*Cathestecum erectum*
grama, hairy	*Bouteloua hirsuta*
grama, sideoats	*Bouteloua curtipendula*
grape, Arizona	*Vitis arizonica*
grass, Bermuda	*Cynodon dactylon*
grass, Johnson	*Sorghum halepense*
grass, salt	*Distichlis spicata*
graythorn	*Ziziphus obtusifolia*
greasewood, black	*Sarcobatus vermiculatus*
hackberry, desert	*Celtis pallida*
hackberry, netleaf	*Celtis laevigata var. reticulata*
hairgrass, tufted	*Deschampsia caespitosa*
hawthorn, cerro	*Crataegus erythropoda*
hopbush	*Dodonaea viscosa*
honeysuckle	*Anisacanthus thurberi*
honeysuckle, desert	*Lonicera* spp.
indigobush (dalea)	*Psorothamnus* spp.
iodine bush	*Allenrolfea occidentalis*
ironwood	*Olneya tesota*
jojoba	*Simmondsia chinesis*
Joshua tree	*Yucca brevifolia*
junegrass, prairie	*Koeleria macrantha*
juniper, alligator	*Juniperus deppeana*
juniper, common	*Juniperus communis*
juniper, one-seeded	*Juniperus monosperma*
juniper, Rocky Mountain	*Juniperus scopulorum*
juniper, Utah	*Juniperus osteosperma*
kidneywood, Mexican	*Eysenhardtia polystachya*
kinnikinnik	*Arctostaphylos uva-ursi*
locust, New Mexico	*Robinia neomexicana*

Common Name	Scientific Name
lovegrass, Lehmann	*Eragrostis lehmanniana*
lupine	*Lupinus* spp.
madrone, Arizona	*Arbutus arizonica*
mahogany, mountain	*Cercocarpus* spp.
manzanita	*Arctostaphylos* spp.
maple, bigtooth	*Acer grandidentatum*
maple, Rocky Mountain	*Acer glabrum*
mahonia, creeping (Oregon grape)	*Mahonia repens*
globemallow	*Sphaeralcea* spp.
mannagrass, northern	*Glyceria borealis*
marsh-purslane	*Ludwigia palustris*
mesquite, curly	*Hilaria belangeri*
mesquite, honey	*Prosopis glandulosa*
mesquite, velvet	*Prosopis velutina*
mesquite, vine	*Panicum obtusum*
mimosa	*Mimosa* spp.
mistletoe	*Phoradendron* spp.
mistletoe, dwarf	*Arceuthobium* spp.
Mormon tea	*Ephedra* spp.
mountain lover	*Paxistima myrsinites*
muhly, mountain	*Muhlenbergia montana*
mulberry, Texas	*Morus microphylla*
muttongrass	*Poa fendleriana*
needle and thread	*Hesperostipa comata*
Nolina (beargrass)	*Nolina* spp.
oak, Arizona white	*Quercus arizonica*
oak, Emory	*Quercus emoryi*
oak, Gambel's	*Quercus gambelii*
oak, Mexican blue	*Quercus oblongifolia*
oak, netleaf	*Quercus rugosa*
oak, sand (shinnery)	*Quercus havardii*
oak, scrub live	*Quercus turbinella*
oak, silverleaf	*Quercus hypoleucoides*
oak, wavyleaf	*Quercus pauciloba*
ocotillo	*Fouquieria splendens*
olive, desert	*Forestiera pubescens*
olive, Russian	*Elaeagnus angustifolia*
paintbrush, Indian	*Castilleja* spp.
paloverde, blue	*Parkinsonia florida*
paloverde, foothill	*Parkinsonia microphylla*
palm, California fan	*Washingtonia filifera*
palm, date	*Phoenix* spp.
pecan	*Carya illinoinensis*
persimmon, Texas	*Diospyros texana*
pine, Apache	*Pinus engelmannii*
pine, Arizona	*Pinus arizonica*
pine, aleppo	*Pinus halepensis*
pine, bristlecone	*Pinus aristata*
pine, Chihuahuan	*Pinus leiophylla var. chihuahuana*
pine, limber	*Pinus flexilis*
pine, ponderosa	*Pinus ponderosa*
pine, southwestern white	*Pinus strobiformis*
pinyon pine, Mexican	*Pinus cembroides*
pinyon pine, two-needle	*Pinus edulis*
prickly pear	*Opuntia* spp.
rabbitbrush	*Chrysothamnus* spp.
ragweed, canyon	*Ambrosia ambrosioides*
raspberry	*Rubus* spp.
redbud, western	*Cercis obiculata*
reed, common	*Phragmites australis*
ricegrass, Indian	*Achnatherum hymenoides*
rose, wild	*Rosa* spp.
rosewood, Arizona	*Vauquelinia californica*
rush	*Juncus* spp.
sacaton, alkali	*Sporobolus airoides*

Common Name	Scientific Name
sacaton, giant	*Sporobolus wrightii*
sage	*Salvia* spp.
sage, Bigelow	*Artemisia bigelovii*
sagebrush, big	*Artemisia tridentata*
sagebrush, black	*Artemisia nova*
sagebrush, sand	*Artemisia filifolia*
saguaro	*Carnegiea gigantea*
saltbush, fourwing	*Atriplex canescens*
saltbush, littleleaf	*Atriplex polycarpa*
schismus (Mediterranean grass)	*Schismus barbatus*
sedge, beaked	*Carex rostrata*
sedge, Nebraska	*Carex nebrascensis*
seepweed	*Sueda* spp.
seepwillow	*Baccharis salicifolia*
serviceberry, Utah	*Amelanchier utahensis*
shadscale	*Atriplex confertifolia*
sibbaldia, creeping	*Sibbaldia procumbenss*
silktassel, Wright	*Garrya wrightii*
skunkbush	*Rhus aromatica*
smartweed, water	*Polygonum amphibium*
smoketree	*Psorothamnus spinosus*
snakeweed	*Gutierrezia* spp.
snowberry	*Symphoricarpos* spp.
soapberry, western	*Sapindus saponaria*
sorghum	*Sorghum* spp.
sotol	*Dasylirion wheeleri*
spike trisetum	*Trisetum spicatum*
spikerush, common	*Eleocharis macrostachya*
spruce, blue	*Picea pungens*
spruce, Engelmann	*Picea engelmannii*
squirreltail	*Elymus elymoides*
sumac, smooth	*Rhus glabra*
sumac, sugar	*Rhus ovata*
sycamore, Arizona	*Platanus wrightii*
tamarisk	*Tamarix* spp.
tamarisk, athel	*Tamarix aphylla*
tanglehead	*Heteropogon* spp.
tarbush	*Flourensia cernua*
thistle, Russian	*Salsola tragus*
threeawn	*Aristida* spp.
timothy, alpine	*Phleum alpinum*
tobosagrass	*Pleuaphis mutica*
trumpet, yellow	*Tecoma stans*
vanclevea	*Vanclevea stylosa*
walnut, Arizona	*Juglans major*
watercress	*Rorippa nasturtium-aquaticum*
whortleberry	*Vaccinium myrtillus*
wheatgrass (wildrye)	*Elymus* spp.
wheatgrass, tall	*Agropyron elongatum*
willow, Bebb	*Salix bebbiana*
willow, coyote	*Salix exigua*
willow, desert	*Chilopsis linearis*
willow, Geyer	*Salix geyeriana*
willow, Goodding	*Salix gooddingii*
willow, Scouler	*Salix scouleriana*
willow, yellow	*Salix lutea*
wolfberry	*Lycium* spp.
yarrow, western	*Achillea millefolium*
yucca, banana	*Yucca baccata*
yucca, soaptree	*Yucca elata*

Appendix D. Cowbird Brood Parasitism

One component of nest data collection was to gain some knowledge into the extent and specifics of cowbird brood parasitism in Arizona. Specific natural history information for each of Arizona's two cowbird species is given in the species account, but some discussion is warranted regarding host species.

Brown-headed Cowbird

Observers reported 223 incidents of Brown-headed Cowbird parasitism on 202 quads and noted 41 host species. Atlasers identified the Brown-headed Cowbird hosts in 161 of the confirmed sightings for this species, with a single host identified in 158 sightings and multiple hosts noted in three sightings. Multiple hosts pertain to observations of two species of birds feeding the same individual cowbird fledging. Such events are not that uncommon. The most commonly reported host species were Black-tailed Gnatcatcher, Yellow Warbler, and Bell's Vireo (12 percent, 9 percent, and 8 percent of records, respectively). Several Brown-headed Cowbird host species identified by atlasers are considered rare cowbird hosts. These records include sightings of adults feeding young cowbirds outside of the nest. It is important to note that in some instances, these individuals may not be the same birds responsible for hatching and rearing the cowbird to fledging.

Brown-headed Cowbird Hosts

Host Species	Records	Host Species	Records
Black-tailed Gnatcatcher	20	Spotted Towhee	2
Yellow Warbler	14	Vermilion Flycatcher	2
Bell's Vireo	13	Western Wood-Pewee	2
Black-throated Gray Warbler	11	Brewer's Blackbird	1
Black-throated Sparrow	10	Bushtit	1
Blue-gray Gnatcatcher	9	Chipping Sparrow	1
Bullock's Oriole	8	Common Yellowthroat	1
Hooded Oriole	7	Crissal Thrasher	1
Plumbeous Vireo	7	Gray Flycatcher	1
Willow Flycatcher	7	Gray Vireo	1
Blue Grosbeak	6	Indigo Bunting	1
Grace's Warbler	5	Lark Sparrow	1
Abert's Towhee	4	Olive Warbler	1
House Finch	3	Phainopepla	1
Hutton's Vireo	3	Rufous-crowned Sparrow	1
Red-faced Warbler	3	Virginia's Warbler	1
Yellow-breasted Chat	3	Warbling Vireo	1
Canyon Towhee	2	Western Kingbird *	1
Dark-eyed Junco	2	Western Tanager	1
Lucy's Warbler	2	Yellow-rumped Warbler	1
Song Sparrow	2		

* broken cowbird egg found under nest.

Bronzed Cowbird

Atlasers also reported 30 incidents of Bronzed Cowbird brood parasitism on 29 quads and reported hosts for 22 of these observations. The most commonly reported Bronzed Cowbird hosts were Hooded Oriole (45 percent of records) and Bullock's Oriole (14 percent of records).

Bronzed Cowbird Hosts

Host Species	Records
Hooded Oriole	10
Bullock's Oriole	3
Northern Cardinal	2
Hutton's vireo	1
Black-tailed Gnatcatcher	1
Lucy's Warbler	1
Yellow Warbler	1
Hepatic Tanager	1
Summer Tanager	1
Scott's Oriole	1

Literature Cited

Abbott, C. G. 1907. Summer bird-life of the Newark, New Jersey marshes. *Auk* 24 (1):1–11.

Adams, D. A., and T. L. Quay. 1958. Ecology of the Clapper Rail in southeastern North Carolina. *J. Wildlife Management* 22:149–156.

Addicott, A. B. 1938. Behavior of the Bushtit in the breeding season. *Condor* 40:49–63.

Adkisson, C. S. 1996. Red Crossbill (*Loxia curvirostra*). In *Birds of North America* 256 (A. Poole and F. Gill, eds.). Philadelphia: Academy of Natural Sciences; Washington: American Ornithologists' Union.

Adkisson, C. S. 1999. Pine Grosbeak (*Pinicola enucleator*). In *Birds of North America* 456 (A. Poole and F. Gill, eds.). Philadelphia: Birds of North America.

Aldous, S. E. 1942. The White-necked Raven in relation to agriculture. US Fish and Wildlife Service Res. Rep. 5.

Alkon, P. U. 1982. Estimating the age of juvenile Chukars. *J. Wildlife Management* 15:265–275.

Allen, P. E. 1950. Roadrunner in eastern Oklahoma. *Condor* 52:43.

Allen, R. W., and M. M. Nice. 1952. A study of the breeding biology of the Purple Martin (*Progne subis*). *Am. Midl. Nat.* 47:606–665.

Altman, B. 1999. Nest success and habitat relationships of the Olive-sided Flycatcher in managed forests of northwestern Oregon. Report submitted to US Fish and Wildlife Service, Oregon State Office, Portland.

Altman, B., and R. Sallabanks. 2000. Olive-sided Flycatcher (*Contopus cooperi*). In *Birds of North America* 502 (A. Poole and F. Gill, eds.). Philadelphia: Birds of North America.

American Ornithologists' Union. 1998. *Check-list of North American Birds*, 6th ed. Washington, DC: American Ornithologists' Union.

Ammon, E. M. 1995. Lincoln's Sparrow (*Melospiza lincolnii*). In *Birds of North America* 191 (A. Poole and F. Gill, eds.). Philadelphia: Academy of Natural Sciences; Washington, DC: American Ornithologists' Union.

Anderson, A. H. 1933. The Arizona state list since 1914. *Condor* 36:78–83.

Anderson, A. H. 1972. *A Bibliography of Arizona Ornithology*. Tucson: University of Arizona Press.

Anderson, A. H., and A. Anderson. 1946. Late nesting of the Pyrrhuloxia at Tucson, Arizona. *Condor* 48:246.

Anderson, A. H., and A. Anderson. 1948a. Notes on two nests of the Beardless Flycatcher near Tucson, Arizona. *Condor* 50:163–164.

Anderson, A. H., and A. Anderson. 1948b. Observations on the Inca Dove at Tucson, Arizona. *Condor* 50:152–154.

Anderson, A. H., and A. Anderson. 1960. Life history of the Cactus Wren, pt. II: The beginning of nesting. *Condor* 61:186–205.

Anderson, B. W., and R. D. Ohmart. 1985. Habitat use by Clapper Rails in the lower Colorado River Valley. *Condor* 87:116–126.

Anderson, J. L. 1996. Floristic patterns on late Tertiary lacustrine deposits in the Arizona Sonoran Desert. *Madroño* 43:255–272.

Anderson, J. O., and G. Monson. 1981. Berylline Hummingbirds nest in Arizona. *Continental Birdlife* 2:56–61.

Anthony, L. W., and C. A. Ely. 1976. Breeding biology of Barn Swallows in west-central Kansas. *Bull. Kans. Ornithol. Soc.* 27:37–43.

Arcese, P., M. K. Sogge, A. B. Marr, and M. A. Patten. 2002. Song Sparrow (*Melospiza melodia*). In *Birds of North America* 704 (A. Poole and F. Gill, eds.). Philadelphia: Birds of North America.

Archer, T. J. 1996. Observations on nesting and display flights of the Vermilion Flycatcher in western Texas. *SW Naturalist* 41:443–444.

Arendt, W. J. 1988. Range expansion of the Cattle Egret (*Bubulcus ibis*) in the Great Caribbean Basin. *Colon. Waterbirds* 11:252–262.

Armstrong, E. A. 1955. *The Wren*. London: Collins.

Arnold, J. F., D. A. Jamison, and E. H. Reid. 1964. The pinyon-juniper type of Arizona: effects of grazing, fire, and tree control. USDA Prod. Res. Rep. 84.

Atwater, M. G. 1959. A study of renesting in Canada Geese in Montana. *J. Wildlife Management* 23:91–97.

Austin, G. T. 1977. Production and survival of the Verdin. *Wilson Bull.* 89:572–582.

Austin, G. T., and R. E. Ricklefs. 1977. Growth and development of the Rufous-winged Sparrow (*Aimophila carpalis*). *Condor* 79:37–50.

Austin, J. E., and M. R. Miller. 1995. Northern Pintail (*Anas acuta*). In *Birds of North America* 163 (A. Poole and F. Gill, eds.). Philadelphia: Academy of Natural Sciences; Washington, DC: American Ornithologists' Union.

Austin, O. L., Jr. 1968. Life histories of North American cardinals, grosbeaks, buntings, towhees, finches, sparrows, and allies, pt. 1–3. *US Nat. Mus. Bull.* 237.

Austing, G. R. 1964. *The World of the Red-tailed Hawk*. Philadelphia: Lippincott.

Averill, A. 1996. Brown-headed cowbird parasitism of neotropical migrant songbirds in riparian areas along the lower Colorado River. M.S. thesis, University of Arizona.

Averill-Murray, A., T. E. Corman, and C. J. Wise. 1997. Arizona breeding bird atlas project 1997 progress report. Nongame and Endangered Wildlife Program Tech. Report 128. Arizona Game and Fish Department, Phoenix.

Averill-Murray, A., S. Lynn, and M. L. Morrison. 1999. Cowbird parasitism of Arizona Bell's Vireos (*Vireo bellii arizonae*) in a desert riparian landscape: Implications for cowbird management and riparian restoration. In *Research and Management of the Brown-headed Cowbird in Western Landscapes* (M. L. Morrison, L. S. Hall, S. K. Robinson, S. I. Rothstein, D. C. Hahn, and T. D. Rich, eds.). Studies in Avian Biology 18.

Babcock, R. E. 1975. Another instance of incubation by a male Whip-poor-will. *Wilson Bull.* 87:284.

Baicich, P. J., and C. J. O. Harrison. 1997. *A Guide to the Nests, Eggs, and Nestlings of North American Birds*, 2d ed. San Diego: Academic Press.

Bailey, A. M., R. J. Niedrach, and A. L. Baily. 1953. The Red Crossbills of Colorado. Mus. Pictorial 9, Denver Mus. Nat. Hist.

Bailey, F. M. 1923. Birds recorded from the Santa Rita Mountains in southern Arizona. *Pac. Coast Avifauna* 15:1–60.

Baird, S. F. 1859. Birds of the Boundary. In *Report on the United States and Mexican Boundary Survey* by W. H. Emory. Vol. 2, part 2. 34th Cong., H. Ex. Doc. 135.

Baird, S. F. 1860. List of birds collected on the Colorado Expedition. In *Zoology: Report upon the Colorado River of the West* by Lt. J. C. Ives. Part 5, 36th Cong., S. Ex. Doc.

Balda, R. P. 1967. Ecological relationships of the breeding birds of the Chiricahua Mountains, Arizona. Ph.D. diss., University of Illinois, Urbana.

Balda, R. P. 1969. Foliage use by birds of the oak-juniper woodland and ponderosa pine forest in southeastern Arizona. *Condor* 71:399–412.

Balda, R. P. 2002. Pinyon Jay (*Gymnorhinus cyanocephalus*). In *Birds of North America* 605 (A. Poole and F. Gill, eds.). Philadelphia: Birds of North America.

Balda, R. P., and G. C. Bateman. 1972. The breeding biology of the Piñon Jay. *Living Bird* 11:5–42.

Balda, R. P., B. C. McKnight, and C. D. Johnson. 1975. Flammulated Owl migration in the southwestern United States. *Wilson Bull.* 87:520–533.

Balda, R. P., G. Weisenberger, and M. Strauss. 1970. White-crowned Sparrow (*Zonotrichia leucophrys*) breeding in Arizona. *Auk* 87(4):809.

Baltosser, W. H. 1980. A biological inventory of endangered species occurring in Guadalupe Canyon (Hidalgo County), New Mexico. New Mexico Department of Game and Fish, contract 519–68–06, final rep. 35–39.

Baltosser, W. H. 1989. Nectar availability and habitat selection by hummingbirds in Guadalupe Canyon. *Wilson Bull.* 101:559–578.

Baltosser, W. H., and S. M. Russell. 2000. Black-chinned Hummingbird (*Archilochus alexandri*). In *Birds of North America* 495 (A. Poole and F. Gill, eds.). Philadelphia: Academy of Natural Sciences; Washington, DC: American Ornithologists' Union.

Baltosser, W. H., and P. E. Scott. 1996. Costa's Hummingbird (*Calypte costae*). In *Birds of North America* 251 (A. Poole and F. Gill, eds.). Philadelphia: Academy of Natural Sciences; Washington, DC: American Ornithologists' Union.

Bannor, B. K., and E. Kiviat. 2002. Common Moorhen (*Gallinula chloropus*). In *Birds of North America* 685 (A. Poole and F. Gill, eds.). Philadelphia: Birds of North America.

Barber, D. R., P. M. Barber, and P. G. Jablonski. 2000. Painted Redstart (*Myioborus pictus*). In *Birds of North America* 528 (A. Poole and F. Gill, eds.). Philadelphia: Birds of North America.

Barber, P. M., T. E. Martin, and K. G. Smith. 1998. Pair interactions in Red-faced Warblers. *Condor* 100:512–518.

Barlow, J. C. 1962. Natural history of the Bell's Vireo, *Vireo bellii* Audubon. *Univ. Kansas Publ.* 12:241–296.

Barlow, J. C. 1980. Patterns of ecological interactions among migrant and resident vireos on the wintering grounds. In *Migrant Birds in the Neotropics: Ecology, Behavior, Distribution, and Conservation* (A. Keast and E. S. Morton, eds.). Washington, DC: Smithsonian Institution Press.

Barlow, J. C., S. N. Leckie, and C. T. Baril. 1999. Gray Vireo (*Vireo vicinior*). In *Birds of North America* 447 (A. Poole and F. Gill, eds.). Philadelphia: Birds of North America.

Barrett, N. M. 1998. Ruby-crowned Kinglet. In *Colorado Breeding Bird Atlas* (H. Kingery, ed.). Denver: Colorado Wildlife Heritage Foundation.

Barrett, N. M., and R. Levad. 1998. Pine Siskin. In *Colorado Breeding Bird Atlas* (H. Kingery, ed.). Denver: Colorado Wildlife Heritage Foundation.

Bateman, G. C., and R. P. Balda. 1973. Growth, development, and food habits of young Piñon Jays. *Auk* 90:39–61.

Baumann, S. A. 1959. The breeding cycle of the Rufous-sided Towhee *Pipilo erythrophthalmus* in central California. *Wasmann J. Biology* 17:161–220.

Beale, E. F. 1858. The report of the superintendent of the wagon road from Fort Defiance to the Colorado River. 35th Cong., 1st sess. H. Doc. 124.

Beason, R. C. 1970. The annual cycle of the Prairie Horned Lark in west-central Illinois. M.S. thesis, Western Illinois University, Macomb.

Beason, R. C. 1995. Horned Lark (*Eremophila alpestris*). In *Birds of North America* 195 (A. Poole and F. Gill, eds.). Philadelphia: Academy of Natural Sciences; Washington, DC: American Ornithologists' Union.

Bechard, M. J., and J. K. Schmutz. 1995. Ferruginous Hawk (*Buteo regalis*). In *Birds of North America* 172 (A. Poole and F. Gill, eds.). Philadelphia: Academy of Natural Sciences; Washington, DC: American Ornithologists' Union.

Bednarz, J. C. 1988. A comparative study of the breeding ecology of Harris' and Swainson's hawks in southeastern New Mexico. *Condor* 90:311–323.

Bednarz, J. C. 1995. Harris' Hawk (*Parabuteo unicinctus*). In *Birds of North America* 146 (A. Poole and F. Gill, eds.). Philadelphia: Academy of Natural Sciences; Washington, DC: American Ornithologists' Union.

Bednarz, J. C., and R. J. Raitt. 2002. Chihuahuan Raven (*Corvus cryptoleucus*). In *Birds of North America* 606 (A. Poole and F. Gill, eds.). Philadelphia: Birds of North America.

Bekoff, M., A. C. Scott, and D. A. Coner. 1987. Nonrandom nest site selection in Evening Grosbeaks. *Condor* 89:819–829.

Bellrose, F. C. 1976. *Ducks, Geese and Swans of North America*. Harrisburg: Stackpole Books.

Bemis, C., and J. D. Rising. 1999. Western Wood-Pewee (*Contopus sordidulus*). In *Birds of North America* 451 (A. Poole and F. Gill, eds.). Philadelphia: Birds of North America.

Bendire, C. E. 1892. Life histories of North American birds, vol. 1. *US Nat. Mus. Spec. Bull.* 1.

Bendire, C. E. 1895. Life histories of North American birds, vol. 2. *US Nat. Mus. Spec. Bull.* 1.

Bent, A. C. 1919. Life histories of North American diving birds. *US Nat. Mus. Bull.* 107.

Bent, A. C. 1923. Life histories of North American wildfowl, pt. 1. *US Nat. Mus. Bull.* 126.

Bent, A. C. 1925. Life histories of North American wildfowl, pt. 2. *US Nat. Mus. Bull.* 130C.

Bent, A. C. 1926. Life histories of North American marsh birds. *US Nat. Mus. Bull.* 135.

Bent, A. C. 1929. Life histories of North American shorebirds, pt. 2. *US Nat. Mus. Bull.* 146.

Bent, A. C. 1932. Life histories of North American gallinaceous birds. *US Nat. Mus. Bull.* 162.

Bent, A.C. 1937. Life histories of North American birds of prey, pt 1. *US Nat. Mus. Bull.* 167.

Bent, A. C. 1938. Life histories of North American birds of prey, pt 2. *US Nat. Mus. Bull.* 170.

Bent, A. C. 1939. Life histories of North American woodpeckers. *US Nat. Mus. Bull.* 174.

Bent, A. C. 1940. Life histories of North American cuckoos, goatsuckers, hummingbirds and their allies. *US Nat. Mus. Bull.* 176.

Bent, A. C. 1942. Life histories of North American flycatchers, larks, swallows, and their allies. *US Nat. Mus. Bull.* 179.

Bent, A. C. 1946. Life histories of North American jays, crows and titmice, pt. 1. *US Nat. Mus. Bull.* 191.

Bent, A. C. 1948. Life histories of North America nuthatches, wrens, thrushes, and their allies. *US Nat. Mus. Bull.* 195.

Bent, A. C. 1949. Life histories of North American thrushes, kinglets, and their allies. *US Nat. Mus. Bull.* 196.

Bent, A. C. 1950. Life histories of North American wagtails, shrikes, vireos, and their allies. *US Nat. Mus. Bull.* 197.

Bent, A. C. 1953. Life histories of North American wood warblers, *US Nat. Mus. Bull.* 203.

Bent, A. C. 1958. Life histories of North American blackbirds, orioles, tanagers, and allies. *US Nat. Mus. Bull.* 211.

Bent, A. C. 1968. Life histories of North American cardinals, grosbeaks, towhees, finches, sparrows, and allies, pt. 1. *US Nat. Mus. Bull.* 237.

Berger, A. J. 1955. Six-storied Yellow Warbler nest with 11 cowbird eggs. *Jack-Pine Warbler* 33:84.

Berger, A. J. 1968. Vesper Sparrow. In Life histories of north American cardinals, grosbeaks, buntings, towhees, finches, sparrows, and their allies, pt. 2 (O. L. Austin Jr., ed.). *US Nat. Mus. Bull.* 237.

Best, L. B., and N. L. Rodenhouse. 1984. Territory preference of Vesper Sparrows in cropland. *Wilson Bull.* 96:72–82.

Bibles, B. D. 1999. The relationship between productivity and habitat quality in Gray Hawks. Ph.D. diss., University of Arizona.

Bibles, B. D., R. L. Glinski, and R. R. Johnson. 2002. Gray Hawk (*Asturina nitida*). In *Birds of North America* 652 (A. Poole and F. Gill, eds.). Philadelphia: Birds of North America.

Bildstein, K. L., and K. Meyer. 2000. Sharp-shinned Hawk (*Accipiter striatus*). In *Birds of North America* 482 (A. Poole and F. Gill, eds.). Philadelphia: Academy of Natural Sciences; Washington, DC: American Ornithologists' Union.

Binford, L. 1958. First record of Five-striped Sparrow in the United States. *Auk* 75:103.

Bird, D. M., and R. S. Palmer. 1988. American Kestrel. *Handbook of American Birds*, vol. 5, *Diurnal Raptors* (R. S. Palmer, ed.). New Haven: Yale University Press.

Birkhead, T. R. 1991. *The Magpies: The Ecology and Behaviour of Black-billed and Yellow-billed Magpies*. London: Academic Press.

Bishop, R. A. 1964. The Mearn's Quail (*Cyrtonyx montezumae mearnsi*) in southern Arizona. M.S. thesis, University of Arizona.

Blackford, J. L. 1953. Breeding haunts of the Stephen's Whip-poor-will. *Condor* 55:281–286.

Blackford, J. L. 1955. Early nesting of Golden-crowned Kinglet. *Condor* 57:242–243.

Blair, D. L., and F. Schitoskey Jr. 1982. Breeding biology and diet of the Ferruginous Hawk in South Dakota. *Wilson Bull.* 94:46–54.

Blancher, P. J., and R. J. Robertson. 1984. Resource use by sympatric kingbirds. *Condor* 86:305–313.

Blancher, P. J., and R. J. Robertson. 1987. Effect of food supply on the breeding biology of Western Kingbirds. *Ecology* 68:723–732.

Boal, C. W. 1994. A photographic and behavioral guide to aging nestling Northern Goshawks. *Stud. Avian Biol.* 16:32–40.

Boarman, W. I., and B. Heinrich. 1999. Common Raven (*Corvus corvax*). In *Birds of North America* 78 (A. Poole and F. Gill, Eds.). Philadelphia: Academy of Natural Sciences; Washington, DC: American Ornithologists' Union.

Bock, C. E. 1970. The ecology and behavior of the Lewis' Woodpecker (*Asyndesmus lewis*). *University Calif. Publ. Zool.* 92:1–100.

Bock, C. E., and J. H. Bock. 1992. Response of birds to wildfire in native versus exotic Arizona grassland. *Southwestern Naturalist* 37:73–81.

Bock, C. E., J. H. Bock, K. L. Jepson, and J. C. Ortega. 1986. Ecological effects of planting African lovegrasses in Arizona. *National Geographic Research* 2:456–463.

Bock, C. E., and B. Webb. 1984. Birds as grazing indicator species in southeastern Arizona. *J. Wildlife Management* 48:1045–1049.

Boe, J. S. 1992. Wetland selection by Eared Grebes, *Podiceps nigricollis*, Minnesota. *Can. Field-Nat.* 106:480–488.

Bolen, E. G. 1967. Nesting boxes for black-bellied tree ducks. *J. Wildlife Management* 31:68–73.

Bolen, E. G., B. McDaniel, and C. Cottam. 1964. Natural history of the black-bellied whistling duck (*Dendrocygna autumnalis*) in southern Texas. *Southwestern Naturalist* 9:78–88.

Bowen, R. V. 1997. Townsend's Solitaire (*Myadestes townsendi*). In *Birds of North America* 269 (A. Poole and F. Gill, eds.). Philadelphia: Academy of Natural Sciences; Washington, DC: American Ornithologists' Union.

Bowers, J. E. 1982. Plant geography of southwestern sand dunes. *Desert Plants* 6:31–54.

Bowers, R. K. 1988. Western Screech-Owl (*Otus kennicottii*). In *Raptors of Arizona* (R. L. Glinski, ed.). Tucson: University of Arizona Press.

Bowers, R. K., and J. B. Dunning Jr. 1984. Nest parasitism by cowbirds on Buff-breasted Flycatchers, with comments on nest-site selection. *Wilson Bull.* 96:718–719.

Bowers, R. K. and J. B. Dunning Jr. 1994. Buff-breasted Flycatcher (*Empidonax fuvifrons*). In *Birds of North America* 125 (A. Poole and F. Gill, eds.). Philadelphia: Birds of North America.

Bowers, R. K., Jr., and J. B. Dunning Jr. 1997. Buff-collared Nightjar (*Caprimulgus ridgwayi*). In *Birds of North America* 267 (A. Poole and F. Gill, eds.). Philadelphia: Academy of Natural Sciences; Washington, DC: American Ornithologists' Union.

Bowman, R. 2002. Common Ground-Dove (*Columbina passerina*). In *Birds of North America* 645 (A. Poole and F. Gill, eds.). Philadelphia: Birds of North America.

Bowman, R., and G. E. Woolfenden. 1997. Nesting chronology of the Common Ground-Dove in Florida and Texas. *J. Field Ornithol.* 68:580–589.

Boyle, S. 1998a. Broad-tailed Hummingbird. In *Colorado Breeding Bird Atlas* (H. Kingery, ed.). Denver: Colorado Wildlife Heritage Foundation.

Boyle, S. 1998b. White-throated Swift (*Aeronautes saxatalis*). In *Colorado Breeding Bird Atlas* (H. Kingery, ed). Denver: Colorado Wildlife Heritage Foundation.

Bradbury, W. C. 1917. Notes on the nesting habits of the Clarke Nutcracker in Colorado. *Condor* 19:149–155.

Bradfield, M. 1974. *Birds of the Hopi Region, Their Hopi Names, and Notes on Ecology*. Flagstaff: Northern Arizona Society of Sciences and Art.

Brakhage, G. K. 1965. Biology and behavior of tub-nesting Canada Geese. *J. Wildlife Management* 29:751–771.

Brandt, H. 1943. *Alaska Bird Trails*. Cleveland: Bird Research Foundation.

Brandt, H. 1951. *Arizona and Its Bird Life*. Cleveland: Bird Research Foundation.

Brawn, J. D. 1985. Population biology, community structure, and habitat selection of birds in ponderosa pine habitat. Ph.D. dissertation, Northern Arizona University.

Brawn, J. D. 1990. Interspecific competition and social behavior in Violet-green Swallows. *Auk* 107:606–608.

Brawn, J. D. 1991. Environmental effects on variation and covariation in reproductive traits of Western Bluebirds. *Oecologia* 86:193–201.

Brawn, J. D., and R. P. Balda. 1988. The influence of silvicultural activities on ponderosa-pine forest bird communities in the southwestern United States. *Bird Conserv.* 3:3–21.

Breitwisch, R. 1988. Sex differences in the defense of eggs and nestlings by Northern Mockingbirds, *Mimus polyglottos*. *Animal Behavior* 36:62–72.

Breitwisch, R., P. G. Merritt, and G. H. Whitesides. 1984. Why do Northern Mockingbirds feed fruit to their nestlings? *Condor* 86:281–287.

Breninger, G. F. 1898. The ferruginous pygmy-owl. *Osprey* 2:128.

Breninger, G. F. 1899. White-tailed Hawk in Arizona. *Auk* 16:352.

Brennan, Leonard A. 1999. Northern Bobwhite (*Colinus virginianus*). In *Birds of North America* 1 (A. Poole and F. Gill, eds.). Philadelphia: Academy of Natural Sciences; Washington, DC: American Ornithologists' Union.

Brewster, W. 1885. Preliminary notes on some birds obtained in Arizona by Mr. F. Stephens in 1884. *Auk* 2:84–85.

Brisbin, I. L., Jr., and T. B. Mowbray. 2002. American Coot (*Fulica americana*). In *Birds of North America* 697 (A. Poole and F. Gill, eds.). Philadelphia: Birds of North America.

Brown, B. T. 1988. Breeding ecology of a willow flycatcher population in Grand Canyon, Arizona. *Western Birds* 19:25–33.

Brown, B. T. 1991. Abundance, distribution and ecology of nesting Peregrine Falcons in Grand Canyon National Park, Arizona. Final Report to Grand Canyon National Park, Contract CX8210–7–0009.

Brown, B. T. 1992. Nest chronology, density and habitat use of Black-chinned Hummingbirds along the Colorado River, Arizona. *J. of Field Ornithol.* 63:393–400.

Brown, B. T. 1993. Bell's Vireo (*Vireo bellii*). In *Birds of North America* 35 (A. Poole and F. Gill, eds.) Philadelphia: Academy of Natural Sciences; Washington, DC: American Ornithologists' Union.

Brown, B. T. 1994. Rates of brood parasitism by Brown-headed Cowbirds on riparian passerines in Arizona. *J. Field Ornithol.* 65:160–168.

Brown, B. T., S. W. Carothers, and R. R. Johnson. 1983. Breeding range expansion of Bell's Vireo in Grand Canyon, Arizona. *Condor* 85:499–500.

Brown, B. T., S. W. Carothers, and R. R. Johnson. 1987. *Grand Canyon birds: Historical Notes, Natural History, and Ecology*. Tucson: University of Arizona Press.

Brown, B. T., and M. W. Trosset. 1989. Nesting-habitat relationships of riparian birds along the Colorado River in Grand Canyon, Arizona. *Southwest Nat.* 34:260–270.

Brown, C. R. 1997. Purple Martin (*Progne subis*). In *Birds of North America* 287 (A. Poole and F. Gill, eds.). Philadelphia: Academy of Sciences; Washington, DC: American Ornithologists' Union.

Brown, C. R., and M. B. Brown. 1989. Behavioural dynamics of intraspecific brood parasitism in colonial Cliff Swallows. *Anim. Behav.* 37:777–796.

Brown, C. R., and M. B. Brown. 1995. Cliff Swallow (*Hirundo pyrrhonota*). In *Birds of North America* 149 (A. Poole and F. Gill, eds.). Philadelphia: Academy of Natural Sciences; Washington, DC: American Ornithologists' Union.

Brown, C.R., and M.B. Brown. 1999. Barn Swallow (*Hirundo rustica*). In *Birds of North America* 452 (A. Poole and F. Gill, eds.). Philadelphia: Birds of North America.

Brown, C. R., Knott, A. M., and E. J. Damrose. 1992. Violet-green Swallow. In *Birds of North America* 14 (A. Poole, P. Stettenheim, and F. Gill, eds.). Philadelphia: Academy of Natural Sciences; Washington, DC: American Ornithologists' Union.

Brown, D. E. (ed.).1982. Biotic communities of the American Southwest: United States and Mexico. *Desert Plants* 4:1–342.

Brown, D. E. 1985. *Arizona Wetlands and Waterfowl*. Tucson: University of Arizona Press.

Brown, D. E. 1989. *Arizona Game Birds*. Tucson: University of Arizona Press.

Brown, D. E., and D. H. Ellis. 1977. Masked Bobwhite recovery plan. US Fish and Wildlife Service Office of Endangered Species, Region 2, Albuquerque. Revised by S.W. Hoffman, 1984.

Brown, D. E., J. C. Hagelin, M. Taylor, and J. Galloway. 1998. Gambel's Quail (*Callipepla gambelii*). In *Birds of North America* 321 (A. Poole and F. Gill, eds.). Philadelphia: Academy of Natural Sciences; Washington, DC: American Ornithologists' Union.

Brown, H. 1901. Bendire's Thrasher. *Auk* 18:225–231.

Brown, H. 1904. Masked Bobwhite (*Colinus ridgwayi*). *Auk* 21:209–213.

Brown, J. L. 1994. Mexican Jay (*Aphelocoma ultramarina*). In *Birds of North America* 118 (A. Poole and F. Gill, eds.). Philadelphia: Academy of Natural Sciences; Washington, DC: American Ornithologists' Union.

Brown, L., and D. Amadon. 1989. *Eagles, Hawks and Falcons of the World*. New York: Wellfleet Press.

Brown, N. L. 1995. Notes on the winter roost and diet of Long-eared Owls in the Sonoran Desert. *J. of Raptor Research* 29(4):277–279.

Brua, R. B. 2001. Ruddy Duck (*Oxyura jamaicensis*). In *Birds of North America* 696 (A. Poole and F. Gill, eds.). Philadelphia: Birds of North America.

Brush, T. 1983. Cavity use by secondary cavity-nesting birds and response to manipulation. *Condor* 85:461–466.

Brush, T. 1999. Current status and recent nesting of Northern Beardless-Tyrannulet and Tropical Parula in the lower Rio Grande Valley. *Texas. Bull. Tex. Ornithol. Soc.* 32:3–12.

Buckley, N. J. 1999. Black Vulture (*Coragyps atratus*). In *Birds of North America* 411 (A. Poole and F. Gill, eds.). Philadelphia: Birds of North America.

Buitron, D. 1988. Female and male specialization in parental care and its consequences in Black-billed Magpies. *Condor* 90:29–39.

Bunn, D. S., A. B. Warburton, and R. D. S. Wilson. 1982. *The Barn Owl*. Vermilion, SD: Buteo Books.

Burhans, D. E., and F. R. Thompson III. 1999. Habitat patch size and nesting success of Yellow-breasted Chats. *Wilson Bull.* 111:210–215.

Burley, N. 1980. Clutch overlap and clutch size: Alternate and complementary tactics. *Amer. Natur.* 115:223–246.
Burns, F. L. 1915. Comparative periods of deposition and incubation of some North American birds. *Wilson Bull.* 27:275–286.
Burton, J. A. (ed.) 1984. Owls of the World. Dover, NH: Tanager Books.
Butler, R. W. 1992. Great Blue Heron (*Ardea herodias*). In *Birds of North America* 25 (A. Poole, P. Stettenheim, and F. Gill, eds.). Philadelphia: Academy of Natural Sciences; Washington, DC: American Ornithologists' Union.
Byers, C., U. Olsson, and J. Curson. 1995. *A Guide to the Buntings and North American Sparrows*. Sussex: Pica Press.
Cabe, P. R. 1993. European Starling (*Sturnus vulgaris*). In *Birds of North America* 48 (A. Poole and F. Gill, eds.). Philadelphia: Birds of North America.
Caffrey, C. 1992. Female-biased delayed dispersal and helping in American Crows. *Auk* 109:609–619.
Calder, W. A. 1973. Microhabitat selection during nesting of hummingbirds in the Rocky Mountains. *Ecology* 54:127–134.
Calder, W. A., and L. L. Calder. 1992. Broad-tailed Hummingbird. In *Birds of North America* 16 (A. Poole, P. Stettenheim, and F. Gill, Eds.). Philadelphia: Academy of Natural Sciences; Washington, DC: American Ornithologists' Union.
Calkins, J. D., J. C. Hagelin, and D. F. Lott. 1999. California Quail (*Callipepla californica*). In *Birds of North America* 473 (A. Poole and F. Gill, eds.). Philadelphia: Birds of North America.
Camou-Luders, G., W. P. Kuvlesky Jr., and F. S. Guthery. 1999. Rainfall and Masked Bobwhites in Sonora, Mexico. Proc. 9th US-Mexico Border Conf.
Cannings, R. J. 1987. The breeding biology of Northern Saw-whet Owls in southern British Columbia. In *Biology and Conservation of Northern Forest Owls* (R. W. Nero, R. J. Clark, R. J. Knapton, and R. H. Hamre, eds.). US Forest Service General Technical Report RM-142.
Cannings, R. J. 1993. Northern Saw-whet Owl (*Aegolius acadicus*). In *Birds of North America* 42 (A. Poole and F. Gill, eds.). Philadelphia: Academy of Natural Sciences; Washington, DC: American Ornithologists' Union.
Cannings, R. J., and T. Angell. 2001. Western Screech-Owl (*Otus kennicottii*). In *Birds of North America* 597 (A. Poole and F. Gill, eds.). Philadelphia: Birds of North America.
Cannings, R. J., and W. Threlfall. 1981. Horned Lark *Eremophila alpestris* breeding biology at Cape St. Marys, Newfoundland, Canada. *Wilson Bull.* 93:519–530.
Cardiff, S. W., and D. L. Dittmann. 2000. Brown-crested Flycatcher (*Myiarchus tyrannulus*). In *Birds of North America* 496 (A. Poole and F. Gill, eds.). Philadelphia: Birds of North America.
Cardiff, S. W., and D. L. Dittmann. 2002. Ash-throated Flycatcher (*Myiarchus cinerascens*). In *Birds of North America* 664 (A. Poole and F. Gill, eds.). Philadelphia: Birds of North America.
Carey, M. 1982. An analysis of factors governing pair bonding period and the onset of laying in Indigo Buntings. *J. Field Ornithol.* 53:240–248.
Carothers, S. W. 1974. Breeding ecology and time-energy budget of male Vermilion Flycatchers and comments on the social organization of southwestern riparian birds. Ph.D. diss., University of Illinois, Chicago.
Carothers, S. W., and B. T. Brown. 1991. *The Colorado River Through Grand Canyon: Natural History and Human Change*. Tucson: University of Arizona Press.
Carothers, S. W., J. R. Haldeman, and R. P. Balda. 1973. Breeding birds of the San Francisco Mountain area and the White Mountains, Arizona. Tech. Series 12. Flagstaff: Northern Arizona Society of Science and Art.
Carothers, S. W., and R. R. Johnson. 1976. The Mississippi Kite in Arizona: A second record. *Condor* 78:114–115.
Carroll, J. P., W. P. Kuvlesky Jr., S. A. Gall, and F. Garza-Salazar. 1994. Status of Mexican quails. Transactions of the North American Wildlife Natural Resources Conference.
Carter, M. D. 1984. The social organization and parasitic behavior of the Bronzed Cowbird in south Texas. Ph.D. diss., University of Minnesota.
Carter, M. D. 1986. The parasitic behavior of the Bronzed Cowbird in south Texas. *Condor* 88:11–25.
Cartron, J. E., W. S. Richardson, and G. A. Proudfoot. 2000. The Cactus Ferruginous Pygmy-Owl: taxonomy, distribution, and natural history. In *Ecology and conservation of the Cactus Ferruginous Pygmy-Owl in Arizona* (J. E. Cartron and D. M. Finch, eds.). Gen. Tech. Rep. RMRS-GTR-43. Ogden, UT: US Department of Agriculture, Forest Service, Rocky Mountain Research Station.
Chace, J. F. 1998. Common Grackle. In *The Colorado Breeding Bird Atlas* (H. Kingery, ed.). Denver: Colorado Wildlife Heritage Foundation.
Chace, J. F., and R. C. Tweit. 1999. Greater Pewee (*Contopus pertinax*). In *Birds of North America* 450 (A. Poole and F. Gill, eds.). Philadelphia: Academy of Natural Sciences; Washington, DC: American Ornithologists' Union.
Chamberlain-Auger, J. A., P. J. Auger, and E. G. Strauss. 1990. Breeding biology of American Crows. *Wilson Bull.* 102:615–622.
Chapin, E. A. 1925. Food habits of the vireos. *USDA Bull.* 1355.
Christensen, G. C. 1954. The Chukar Partridge in Nevada. *Nevada Fish and Game Comm. Biol. Bull.* 1.
Christensen, G. C. 1970. The Chukar Partridge: Its introductions, life history and management. *Nev. Fish and Game Dept. Biol. Bull.* 4.
Christensen, G. C. 1996. Chukar (*Alectoris chukar*). In *Birds of North America* 258 (A. Poole and F. Gill, eds.). Philadelphia: Academy of Natural Sciences; Washington, DC: American Ornithologists' Union.
Chu, M., and G. Walsberg. 1999. Phainopepla (*Phainopepla nitens*). In *Birds of North America* 415 (A. Poole and F. Gill, eds.). Philadelphia: Birds of North America.
Church, J. P. 1982. Southernmost nesting record for the Mountain Bluebird. *Western Birds* 13:35.
Cicero, C. 2000. Oak Titmouse (*Baeolophus inornatus*) and Juniper Titmouse (*Baeolophus ridgwayi*). In *Birds of North America* 485 (A. Poole and F. Gill, eds.). Philadelphia: Birds of North America.
Cimprich, D. A., and F. R. Moore. 1995. Gray Catbird (*Dumetella carolinensis*). In *Birds of North America* 167. (A. Poole and F. Gill, eds.). Philadelphia: Academy of Natural Sciences; Washington, DC: American Ornithologists' Union.
Cink, C. L. 1976. The influence of early learning on nest site selection in the House Sparrow. *Condor* 78:103–104.
Cink, C. L. 2002. Whip-poor-will (*Caprimulgus vociferous*). In *Birds of North America* 620 (A. Poole and F. Gill, eds.). Philadelphia: Birds of North America.
Clark, W. R., and T. R. Bogenschutz. 1999. Grassland habitat and reproductive success of Ring-necked Pheasants in northern Iowa. *J. Field Ornithol.* 79:380–392.
Clements, J. F. 2000. *Birds of the World: A Checklist*. Vista, CA: Ibis.
Cohen, R. R. 1982. A comparison of Violet-green Swallow and Tree Swallow breeding biology at high altitude in Colorado. *J. Colo.-Wyo. Acad. Sci.* 14:60.
Cohen, R. R. 1985. Capturing breeding male Tree Swallows with feathers. *N. Am. Bird Bander* 10:18–21.
Collins, C. T., K. Corey, J. Pike, and L. R. Hays. 1991. The status and management of the Least Bell's Vireo within the Prado Basin, California, 1986–1990. Final Rep. to Orange County Water District, Fountain Valley, CA.
Collins, P. W. 1999. Rufous-crowned Sparrow (*Aimophila ruficeps*). In *Birds of North America* 472 (A. Poole and F. Gill, eds.). Philadelphia: Birds of North America.
Combellack, C. R. B. 1954. A nesting of Violet-green Swallows. *Auk* 71:435–442.
Conway, C. J. 1990. Seasonal changes in movements and habitat use by three sympatric species of rails. M.S. thesis, University of Wyoming, Laramie.
Conway, C. J. 1995. Virginia Rail (*Rallus limicola*). In *Birds of North America* 173 (A. Poole and F. Gill, eds.). Philadelphia: Academy of Natural Sciences; Washington, DC: American Ornithologists' Union.
Conway, C. J., W. R. Eddleman, S. H. Anderson, and L. R. Hanebury. 1993. Seasonal changes in Yuma Clapper Rail vocalization rate and habitat use. *J. Wildlife Management* 57(2):282–290.
Conway, C. J., and C. Kirkpatrick. 2001. Population status, detection probability, and effects of fire on Buff-breasted Flycatchers. Final Report, Heritage Grant # I99028. Arizona Game and Fish Department, Phoenix.
Conway, C. J., and T. E. Martin. 1993. Habitat suitability for Williamson's Sapsuckers in mixed-conifer forests. *J. Wildlife Management* 57:322–328.
Conway, C. J., C. Sulzman, and B. E. Raulson. 2002. Population trends, distribution, and monitoring protocols for California Black Rails. Final Report. Heritage Program Grant I99010. Arizona Game and Fish Department, Phoenix.
Cooper, J. G., 1861. New Californian Animals. *Proc. Calif. Acad. Sci.* 2:118–123.

Corman, T. E., and G. Monson. 1995. First United States nesting records of the Streak-backed Oriole. *Western Birds* 26:49–53.
Corman, T. E., and R. T. Magill. 2000. Western yellow-billed cuckoo in Arizona:1998 and 1999 survey report. Nongame and Endangered Wildlife Program Technical Report 150. Arizona Game and Fish Department, Phoenix, Arizona.
Coues, E. 1866a. From Arizona to the Pacific. *Ibis* 12:259–275.
Coues, E. 1866b. List of the birds of Fort Whipple, Arizona. *Proc. Acad. Nat. Sci. Phila.* 18:39–100.
Coues, E. 1878. *Birds of the Colorado Valley.* Misc. Publ. 11, US Geological Survey.
Coutlee, E. L. 1968. Comparative breeding behavior of Lesser and Lawrence's Goldfinches. *Condor* 70:228–242.
Cramp, S. (ed.). 1985. *The Handbook of the Birds of Europe, the Middle East and North Africa: The Birds of the Western Palearctic*, vol. 4, *Terns to Woodpeckers*. New York: Oxford University Press.
Cramp, S., and K. E. L. Simmons (eds.). 1980. *The Birds of the Western Palearctic.* Oxford: Oxford University Press.
Crocker-Bedford, D. C., and B. Chaney. 1988. Characteristics of goshawk nesting stands. In *Southwest Raptor Management Symposium and Workshop* (R. Glinski et al., eds.). Washington, DC: National Wildlife Federation.
Crockett, A. B., and P. L. Hansley. 1977. Coition, nesting, and postfledging behavior of Williamson's Sapsucker in Colorado. *Living Bird* 16:7–19.
Csada, R. D., and R. M. Brigham. 1992. Common Poorwill (*Phalaenoptilus nuttallii*). In *Birds of North America* 32 (A. Poole and F. Gill, eds.). Philadelphia: Academy of Natural Sciences; Washington, DC: American Ornithologists' Union.
Cullen, S. A., J. R. Jehl Jr., and G. L. Nuechterlein. 1999. Eared Grebe (*Podiceps nigricollis*). In *Birds of North America* 433 (A. Poole and F. Gill, Eds.). Philadelphia: Academy of Natural Sciences; Washington, DC: American Ornithologists' Union.
Curry, R. L., A. T. Peterson, and T. A. Langen. 2002. Western Scrub-Jay (*Aphelocoma californica*). In *Birds of North America* 712 (A. Poole and F. Gill, eds.). Philadelphia: Birds of North America.
Curson, D. R., and C. B. Goguen. 1998. Plumbeous Vireo (*Vireo plumbeus*). In *Birds of North America* 366 (A. Poole and F. Gill, eds.). Philadelphia: Academy of Natural Sciences; Washington, DC: American Ornithologists' Union.
Cutler, T. L., M. L. Morrison, and D. J. Griffin. 1996. Final report: Wildlife use of Jose Juan Tank and Red Tail Tank, Cabeza Prieta National Wildlife Refuge, southwestern Arizona. US Dep. of Defense Contract N68711–93-LT-3026.
Davis, D. M. 1978. A nesting study of the Brown Creeper. *Living Bird* 17:237–263.
Davis, G. P., Jr. 1982. *Man and Wildlife: The American Exploration Period, 1824–1865* (N. B. Carmony and D. E. Brown, eds.). Phoenix: Arizona Game and Fish Department.
Davis, J. 1960. Nesting behavior of the Rufous-sided Towhee in coastal California. *Condor* 62:434–456.
Davis, J., G. F. Fisler, and B. S. Davis. 1963. The breeding biology of the Western Flycatcher. *Condor* 65:337–382.
Davis, J. N. 1995. Hutton's Vireo (*Vireo huttoni*). In *Birds of North America* 189 (A. Poole and F. Gill, eds.). Philadelphia: Academy of Natural Sciences; Washington, DC: American Ornithologists' Union.
Davis, W. E., Jr. 1986. Effects of old nests on nest-site selection in Black-crowned Night-Herons and Snowy Egrets. *Wilson Bull.* 98:300–303.
Davis, W. E., Jr. 1993. Black-crowned Night-Heron (*Nycticorax nycticorax*). In *Birds of North America* 340 (A. Poole and F. Gill, eds.). Philadelphia: Academy of Natural Sciences; Washington, DC: American Ornithologists' Union.
Davis, W. E., Jr., and J. A. Kushlan. 1994. Green Heron (*Butorides virescens*). In *Birds of North America* 129 (A. Poole and F. Gill, eds.). Philadelphia: Birds of North America.
Dawson, J. W. 1998a. Great Horned Owl (*Bubo virginianus*). In *Raptors of Arizona* (R. Glinski, ed.). Tucson: University of Arizona Press.
Dawson, J. W. 1998b. Harris' Hawk (*Parabuteo unicinctus*). In *Raptors of Arizona* (R. Glinski, ed.). Tucson: University of Arizona Press.
Dawson, J. W. 1998c. Prairie Falcon (*Falco mexicanus*). In *Raptors of Arizona* (R. Glinski, ed.). Tucson: University of Arizona Press.
Dawson, J. W., and R. W. Mannan. 1989. A comparison of two methods of estimating breeding group size in Harris' hawks. *Auk* 106:480–483.
Dawson, J. W., and R. W. Mannan. 1991. The role of territoriality in the social organization of Harris' hawks. *Auk* 108:661–672.
Dawson, W. L. 1923. *The Birds of California*. San Diego: Moulton.
Dawson, W. R. 1968. Life histories of North American cardinals, grosbeaks, buntings, towhees, finches, sparrows, and allies, pt. 2. (O. L. Austin Jr., ed.) *US Nat. Mus. Bull.* 237.
Dawson, W. R. 1997. Pine Siskin (*Carduelis pinus*). In *Birds of North America* 280 (A. Poole and F. Gill, eds.). Philadelphia: Academy of Natural Sciences; Washington, DC: American Ornithologists' Union.
Dawson, W. R., and F. C. Evans. 1960. Relation of growth and development to temperature regulation in nestling Vesper Sparrows. *Condor* 62:329–340.
DeGraaf, R. M., V. E. Scott, R. H. Hamre, L. Ernst, and S. H. Anderson. 1991. *Forest and Rangeland Birds of the United States: Natural History and Habitat Use.* Washington, DC: US Forest Service.
DeGroot, D. S. 1928. Record sets of eggs of California raptors. *Condor* 30:360–361.
Dejong, M. J. 1996. Northern Rough-winged Swallow (*Stelgidopteryx serripennis*). In *Birds of North America* 234 (A. Poole and F. Gill, eds.). Philadelphia: Academy of Natural Sciences; Washington, DC: American Ornithologists' Union.
Demaree, S. R. 1975. Observations on roof nesting Killdeers. *Condor* 77:487–488.
Derrickson, K. C. 1989. Bigamy in Northern Mockingbirds: circumventing female aggression. *Condor* 91:728–732.
Derrickson, K. C., and R. Breitwisch. 1992. Northern Mockingbird (*Mimus polyglottos*). In *Birds of North America* 7 (A. Poole and F. Gill, eds.). Philadelphia: Academy of Natural Sciences; Washington, DC: American Ornithologists' Union.
Dexter, C. 1998. Turkey Vulture (*Cathartes aura*). In *Colorado Breeding Bird Atlas* (H. Kingery, ed.). Denver: Colorado Wildlife Heritage Foundation.
Dickinson, V. M. 1996. Breeding biology of the Crested Caracara in south Texas. *Wilson Bull.* 108:516–523.
Dingle, E. 1942. Rough-winged Swallow. In Life histories of North American flycatchers, larks, swallows and their allies (A. Bent, ed.). *US Nat. Mus. Bull.* 179.
Dixon, K. L., and D. J. Martin. 1979. Notes on the vocalizations of the Mexican Chickadee *Parus sclateri*. *Condor* 81:421–423.
Dobbs, R. C., P. R. Martin, and T. E. Martin. 1998. Green-tailed Towhee (*Pipilo chlorurus*). In *Birds of North America* 368 (A. Poole and F. Gill, eds.). Philadelphia: Birds of North America.
Dobbs, R. C., T. E. Martin, and C. J. Conway. 1997. Williamson's Sapsucker (*Sphyrapicus thyroideus*). In *Birds of North America* 285 (A. Poole and F. Gill, eds.). Philadelphia: Academy of Natural Sciences; Washington, DC: American Ornithologists' Union.
Dodd, N. L., and J. R. Vahle. 1998. Osprey. In *Raptors of Arizona* (R. Glinski, ed.). Tucson: University of Arizona Press.
Dotson, R. A. 1971. The breeding biology and ethology of the Green-tailed Towhee. M.S. thesis, University of Utah.
Duebbert, H. F. 1966. Island nesting of the Gadwall in North Dakota. *Wilson Bull.* 78:12–25.
Duncan, D. C. 1987. Nest-site distribution and overland brood movements of Northern Pintails in Alberta. *J. Wildlife Management* 51:716–723.
Duncan, S. 1990. Auditory communication in breeding northern flickers (*Colaptes auratus*). Ph.D. dissertation, University of Wisconsin, Milwaukee.
Dunk, J. R. 1995. White-tailed Kite (*Elanus leucurus*). In *Birds of North America* 178 (A. Poole and F. Gill, eds.). Philadelphia: Academy of Natural Sciences; Washington, DC: American Ornithologists' Union.
Dunn, J., and K. Garrett. 1997. *A Field Guide to Warblers of North America*. Boston: Houghton Mifflin.
Dunn, J. L., and K. L. Garrett. 1987. The identification of North American gnatcatchers. *Birding* 19:17–29.
Dunne, P., D. Sibley, and C. Sutton. 1988. *Hawks in Flight: The Flight Identification of North American Migrant Raptors.* Boston: Houghton Mifflin.
Dunning, J .B., Jr., R. K. Bowers Jr., S. J. Suter, and C. E. Bock. 1999. Cassin's Sparrow (*Aimophila cassinii*). In *Birds of North America* 471 (A. Poole and F. Gill, eds.). Philadelphia: Birds of North America.
Eaton, Stephen W. 1992. Wild Turkey (*Meleagris gallopavo*). In *Birds of North America* 22 (A. Poole, P. Stettenheim, and F. Gill, eds.). Philadelphia: Academy of Natural Sciences; Washington, DC: American Ornithologists' Union.

Eckerle, K. P., and C. F. Thompson. 2001. Yellow-breasted Chat (*Icteria virens*). In *Birds of North America* 575 (A. Poole and F. Gill, eds.). Philadelphia: Academy of Natural Sciences; Washington, DC: American Ornithologists' Union.

Eddleman, W. R. 1989. Biology of the Yuma Clapper Rail in the southwestern US and northwestern Mexico. Final report, Intra-Agency Agreement 4-AA-30–02060, US Bureau of Reclamation, Yuma Project Office.

Eddleman, W. R. 2002. Hepatic Tanager (*Piranga flava*). In *Birds of North America* 655 (A. Poole and F. Gill, eds.). Philadelphia: Birds of North America.

Eddleman, W. R., and C. J. Conway. 1998. Clapper Rail (*Rallus longirostris*). In *Birds of North America* 340 (A. Poole and F. Gill, eds.). Philadelphia: Academy of Natural Sciences; Washington, DC: American Ornithologists' Union.

Eddleman, W. R., R. E. Flores, and M. L. Legare. 1994. Black Rail (*Laterallus jamaicensis*). In *Birds of North America* 123 (A. Poole and F. Gill, eds.). Philadelphia: Academy of Natural Sciences; Washington, DC: American Ornithologists' Union.

Edson, J. M. 1943. A study of the Violet-green Swallow. *Auk* 60:396–403.

Edwards, H. H., and G. D. Schnell. 2000. Gila Woodpecker (*Melanerpes uropygialis*). In *Birds of North America* 532 (A. Poole and F. Gill, eds.). Philadelphia: Academy of Natural Sciences; Washington, DC: American Ornithologists' Union.

Ehrlich, P. R., D. S. Dobkin, and D. Wheye. 1988. *The Birder's Handbook: A Field Guide to the Natural History of North American Birds*. New York: Simon & Schuster.

Ellison, W. G. 1992. Blue-gray Gnatcatcher (*Polioptila caerulea*). In *Birds of North America* 23 (A. Poole and F. Gill, Eds.). Philadelphia: Academy of Natural Sciences; Washington, DC: American Ornithologists' Union.

Emslie, S. D. 1987. Age and diet of fossil California Condors in Grand Canyon, Arizona. *Science* 237:768–770.

Enderson, J. H., S. A. Temple, and L. G. Swartz. 1973. Time-lapse photographic records of nesting Peregrine Falcons. *Living Bird* 11:113–128.

England, A. S., M. J. Bechard, and C. S. Houston. 1997. Swainson's Hawk (*Buteo swainsoni*). In *Birds of North America* 265 (A. Poole and F. Gill, eds.). Philadelphia: Academy of Natural Sciences; Washington, DC: American Ornithologists' Union.

England, A. S., and W. F. Laudenslayer Jr. 1993. Bendire's Thrasher (*Toxostoma bendirei*). In *Birds of North America* 71 (A. Poole and F. Gill, eds.). Philadelphia: Academy of Natural Sciences; Washington, DC: American Ornithologists' Union.

Erpino, M. J. 1968. Nest-related activities of Black-billed Magpies. *Condor* 70:154–165.

Erpino, M. J. 1969. Seasonal cycle of reproductive physiology in the Black-billed Magpie. *Condor* 71:267–279.

Evans Mack, D., and W. Yong. 2000. Swainson's Thrush (*Catharus ustulatus*). In *Birds of North America* 540 (A. Poole and F. Gill, eds.). Philadelphia: Birds of North America.

Evenden, F. G. 1957. Observations on nesting behavior of the House Finch. *Condor* 59:112–117.

Faanes, C. A., and R. J. Howard. 1987. Habitat suitability index models: Black-shouldered Kite. US Fish and Wildlife Service Biol. Rep. 82 (10.130).

Farquhar, C. C., and K. L. Richie. 2002. Black-tailed Gnatcatcher (*Polioptila melanura*). In *Birds of North America* 690 (A. Poole and F. Gill, eds.). Philadelphia: Birds of North America.

Fautin, R. W. 1941. Development of nestling Yellow-headed Blackbirds. *Auk* 58:215–232.

Feare, C. J. 1984. *The Starling*. Oxford: Oxford University Press.

Feare, C. J. 1991. Intraspecific nest parasitism in starlings *Sturnus vulgaris*: Effects of disturbance on laying females. *Ibis* 133:75–79.

Ficken, M., and J. Nocedal. 1992. Mexican Chickadee (*Parus sclateri*). In *Birds of North America* 8 (A. Poole, P. Stettenheim, and F. Gill, eds.). Philadelphia: Academy of Natural Sciences; Washington, DC: American Ornithologists' Union.

Ficken, M. S., and R. W. Ficken. 1987. Bill-sweeping behavior of a Mexican Chickadee. *Condor* 89:901–902.

Finch, D. M. 1982. Rejection of cowbird eggs by Crissal Thrashers. *Auk* 99:719–724.

Finch, D. M. 1983. Brood parasitism of the Abert's Towhee: Timing, frequency, and effects. *Condor* 85:355–359.

Finch, D. M. 1984. Some factors affecting productivity in the Abert's Towhee. *Wilson Bull.* 96:701–705.

Fischer, D. H. 1980. Breeding biology of Curve-billed Thrashers and Long-billed Thrashers in southern Texas. *Condor* 82:392–397.

Fischer, D. L. 2001. *Early Southwest Ornithologists, 1528–1900*. Tucson: University of Arizona Press.

Fisher, A. K. 1893. The hawks and owls of the United States in their relation to agriculture. *USDA Div. Ornithol. and Mammal. Bull.* 3:1–210.

Fitch, H. S., and V. R. Fitch. 1955. Observations on the Summer Tanager in northeastern Kansas. *Wilson Bull.* 67:45–54.

Fitzhugh, E. L. 1974. Chronology of calling, egg-laying, crop gland activity, and breeding among wild Band-tailed Pigeons in Arizona. Ph.D. diss., University of Arizona.

Fitzner, R. E. 1980. Behavioral Ecology of the Swainson's Hawk in Washington. Pac. NW Lab. PLN-2754.

Fleming, W. B. 1959. Migratory waterfowl in Arizona: A management study. *Ariz. Game and Fish Dept. Wildl. Bull.* 5:1–71.

Flood, N. J. 2002. Scott's Oriole (*Icterus parisorum*). In *Birds of North America* 608 (A. Poole and F. Gill, eds.). Philadelphia: Birds of North America.

Flores, R. E., and W. R. Eddleman. 1991. Ecology of the California Black Rail in southwestern Arizona. Final report, US Bureau of Reclamation, Yuma Project Office.

Flores, R. E., and W. R. Eddleman. 1993. Nesting biology of the California Black Rail in southwestern Arizona. *Western Birds* 24:81–88.

Flores, R. E., and W. R. Eddleman. 1995. California Black Rail use of habitat in southwestern Arizona. *J. Wildlife Management* 59:357–363.

Forshaw, J. M. 1989. *Parrots of the World*. 3rd ed. Melbourne: Lansdowne Editions.

Francis, W. J. 1965. Double broods in California Quail. *Condor* 67:541–542.

Franzreb, K. E. 1977. Bird population changes after timber harvesting of a mixed conifer forest in Arizona. US Dep. Agric. For. Ser. Res. Pap. RM-184. Rocky Mt. Forest and Range Exp. Sta., Fort Collins, CO.

Franzreb, K. E. 1985. Foraging ecology of Brown Creepers in a mixed-deciduous forest. *J. Field Ornithol.* 56:9–16.

Franzreb, K. E. 1989. Ecology and conservation of the endangered Least Bell's Vireo. Biol. Rep. 89, US Fish and Wildlife Service.

Franzreb, K. E., and R. D. Ohmart. 1978. The effects of timber harvesting on breeding birds in a mixed-coniferous forest. *Condor* 80:432–441.

Fredrickson, L. H. 1970. Breeding biology of American Coots in Iowa. *Wilson Bull.* 82:445–458.

Friedmann, H. 1929. *The Cowbirds: A Study in the Biology of Social Parasitism*. Springfield, IL: C. Thomas.

Friedmann, H. 1963. Host relations of the parasitic cowbird. *US Nat. Mus. Bull.* 233.

Friedmann, H., and L. F. Kiff. 1985. The parasitic cowbirds and their hosts. *West. Found. Vertebr. Zool.* 2:225–304.

Friedmann, H., L. F. Kiff, and S. J. Rothstein. 1977. A further contribution to knowledge of the host relations of the parasitic cowbirds. *Smithson. Contrib. Zool.* 235.

Galati, R. 1991. *Golden-crowned Kinglets*. Ames: Iowa State University Press.

Gamble, L. R., and T. M. Bergin. 1996. Western Kingbird (*Tyrannus verticalis*). In *Birds of North America* 227 (A. Poole and F. Gill, eds.) Philadelphia: Birds of North America.

Gammonley, J. H. 1996. Cinnamon Teal (*Anas cyanoptera*). In *Birds of North America* 209 (A. Poole and F. Gill, eds.). Philadelphia: Birds of North America.

Ganey, J. L. 1998. Spotted Owl (*Strix occidentalis*). In *Raptors of Arizona* (R. Glinski, ed.). Tucson: University of Arizona Press.

Ganey, J. L., and R. P. Balda. 1989. Home-range characteristics of Spotted Owls in northern Arizona. *J. Wildlife Management* 53:1159–1165.

Ganey, J. L., and R. P. Balda. 1994. Habitat selection by Mexican Spotted Owls in northern Arizona. *Auk* 111:162–169.

Gardali, T. and G. Ballard. 2000. Warbling Vireo (*Vireo gilvus*). In *Birds of North America* 551 (A. Poole and F. Gill, eds.) Philadelphia: Academy of Natural Sciences; Washington, DC: American Ornithologists' Union.

Gatz, T. A. 1998. White-tailed Kite. In *Raptors of Arizona* (R. Glinski, ed.). Tucson: University of Arizona Press.

Gatz, T. A. 2001. Orange Bishops breeding in Phoenix, Arizona. *Western Birds* 32:81–82.

Gatz, T. A., M. D. Jakle, R. L. Glinski, and G. Monson. 1985. First nesting records and current status of the Black-shouldered Kite in Arizona. *Western Birds* 16:57–61.
Gehlbach, F. R. 1994. *The Eastern Screech-Owl: Life History, Ecology, and Behavior in the Suburbs and Countryside*. College Station: Texas A&M University Press.
Gehlbach, F. R., and N. Y. Gehlbach. 2000. Whiskered Screech-Owl (*Otus trichopsis*). In *Birds of North America* 507 (A. Poole and F. Gill, eds.). Philadelphia: Academy of Natural Sciences; Washington, DC: American Ornithologists' Union.
Genelly, R. E. 1955. Annual cycle in a population of California Quail. *Condor* 57:263–285.
Germaine, S. S. 1995. Relationships of birds, lizards, and nocturnal rodents to their habitat in the greater Tucson area, Arizona. Arizona Game and Fish Department Technical Report 20.
Ghalambor, C. K., and T. E. Martin. 1999. Red-breasted Nuthatch (*Sitta canadensis*). In *Birds of North America* 459 (A. Poole and F. Gill, eds.). Philadelphia: Academy of Natural Sciences; Washington, DC: American Ornithologists' Union.
Gibbs, D., Barnes, E., and J. Cox. 2001. *Pigeons and Doves: A Guide to the Pigeons and Doves of the World*. New Haven: Yale University Press.
Gibbs, J.P., F. A. Reid, and S.M. Melvin. 1992. Least Bittern (*Ixobrychus exilis*). In *Birds of North America* 17 (A. Poole, P. Stettenheim, and F. Gill, Eds.). Philadelphia: Academy of Natural Sciences; Washington, DC: American Ornithologists' Union.
Gibson, F. 1971. The breeding biology of the American Avocet (*Recurvirostra americana*) in Oregon. *Condor* 73:444–454.
Gilliard, E. T. 1958. *Living Birds of the World*. New York: Doubleday.
Gillihan, S.W., and B. Byers. 2001. Evening Grosbeak (*Coccothraustes verspertinus*). In *Birds of North America* 599 (A. Poole and Fl Gill, eds.). Philadelphia: Birds of North America.
Gillory, H. D., J. H. Deshotels, and C. Guillory. 1981. Great-tailed Grackle reproduction in south central Louisiana. *J. Field Ornithol.* 52:325–331.
Gilman, M. F. 1902. Notes on the Verdin. *Condor* 4:88–89.
Gilman, M. F. 1907. Migration and nesting of the Sage Thrasher. *Condor* 9:42–44.
Gilman, M. F. 1909a. Among the thrashers in Arizona. *Condor* 11:49–54.
Gilman, M. F. 1909b. Nesting notes on the Lucy Warbler. *Condor* 11:166–168.
Gilman, M. F. 1909c. Red-eyed Cowbird at Sacaton, Arizona. *Condor* 11:173.
Gilman, M. F. 1909d. Some owls along the Gila River in Arizona. *Condor* 11:145–150.
Gilman, M. F. 1914. Breeding of the Bronzed Cowbird in Arizona. *Condor* 16:255–259.
Gilman, M. F. 1915a. A forty acre bird census at Sacaton, Arizona. *Condor* 17:86–90.
Gilman, M. F. 1915b. Woodpeckers of the Arizona lowlands. *Condor* 17:151–163.
Giudice, J. H., and J. T. Ratti 2001. Ring-necked Pheasant (*Phasianus colchicus*). In *Birds of North America* 572 (A. Poole and F. Gill, eds.). Philadelphia: Academy of Natural Sciences; Washington, DC: American Ornithologists' Union.
Glinski, R. L. 1982. The Red-shouldered Hawk (*Buteo lineatus*) in Arizona. *Am. Birds* 36:801–803.
Glinski, R. L. (ed.). 1998. *Raptors of Arizona*. Tucson: University of Arizona Press.
Glinski, R. L., and R. S. Hall. 1998. Swainson's Hawk (*Buteo swainsoni*). In *Raptors of Arizona* (R. Glinski, ed.). Tucson: University of Arizona Press.
Glinski, R. L., and R. D. Ohmart. 1983. Breeding ecology of the Mississippi Kite in Arizona. *Condor* 85:200–207.
Glinski, R. L., and R. D. Ohmart. 1984. Factors of reproduction and population densities in the Apache cicada (*Diceroprocta apache*). *Southwestern Naturalist* 29:73–79.
Glover, F. A. 1956. Nesting and production of the Blue-winged Teal (*Anas discors* Linnaeus) in northwest Iowa. *J. Wildlife Management* 20:28–46.
Goad, M. S. and R. W. Mannan. 1987. Nest site selection by Elf Owls in Saguaro National Monument, Arizona. *Condor* 89:659–662.
Goldman, E. A. 1926. Breeding birds of a White Mountains lake. *Condor* 28:159–164.
Goodwin, D. 1976. *Crows of the World*. Ithaca, NY: Cornell University Press.
Gorsuch, D. M. 1934. Life history of the Gambel's Quail in Arizona. *Univ. Arizona Bull.* 2:1–89.
Gould, P. J. 1960. Territorial relationships between cardinals and pyrrhuloxias. M.S. thesis, University of Arizona.
Gould, P. J. 1961. Territorial relationships between cardinals and pyrrhuloxias. *Condor* 63:246–256.
Gowaty, P. A., and J. H. Plissner. 1998. Eastern Bluebird (*Sialia sialis*). In *Birds of North America* 381 (A. Poole and F. Gill, eds.). Philadelphia: Birds of North America.
Grant, G. S. 1982. Avian incubation: egg temperature, nest humidity, and behavioral thermoregulation in a hot environment. *Ornithol. Monographs* 30.
Graul, W. D., and L. E. Webster. 1976. Breeding status of the Mountain Plover. *Condor* 78:265–267.
Green, R. E. 1988. Effects of environmental factors on the timing and success of breeding of Common Snipe *Gallinago gallinago* (Aves: Scolopacidae). *J. Applied Ecol.* 25:79–94.
Greene, E., W. Davison, and V. R. Muehter. 1998. Steller's Jay (*Cyanocitta stelleri*). In *Birds of North America* 343 (A. Poole and F. Gill, eds.). Philadelphia: Academy of Natural Sciences; Washington, DC: American Ornithologists' Union.
Greene, E., V. R. Muehter, and W. Davidson. 1996. Lazuli Bunting (*Passerina amoena*). In *Birds of North America* 232 (A. Poole and F. Gill, eds.). Philadelphia: Academy of Natural Sciences; Washington, DC: American Ornithologists' Union.
Greenlaw, J. S. 1996. Spotted Towhee (*Pipilo maculatus)*. In *Birds of North America* 263 (A. Poole and F. Gill, eds.). Philadelphia: Academy of Natural Sciences; Washington, DC: American Ornithologists' Union.
Grinnell, J. 1914. An account of the mammals and birds of the lower Colorado Valley with especial reference to the distributional problems presented. *Univ. Calif. Publ. Zool.* 12(4):51–294.
Grinnell, J., and A. H. Miller. 1944. The distribution of the birds of California. *Pac. Coast Avifauna* 27:1–617.
Groschupf, K. 1992. A closer look: Black-capped Gnatcatcher. *Birding* 24:160–164.
Groschupf, K. 1994. Current status of the Five-striped Sparrow in Arizona. *Western Birds* 25:192–197.
Groschupf, K. D., and C. W. Thompson. 1998. Varied Bunting (*Passerina versicolor*). In *Birds of North America* 351 (A. Poole and F. Gill, eds.). Philadelphia: Birds of North America.
Gross, A. O. 1948. *Dumetella carolinensis* (Linnaeus) Catbird. In Life histories of North American nuthatches, wrens, thrashers, and their allies (A. Bent, ed.). *US Nat. Mus. Bull.* 195.
Gross, A. O. 1949. Nesting of the Mexican Jay in the Santa Rita Mountains. *Condor* 51:241–249.
Grossman, M. L., and J. Hamlet. 1988. *Birds of Prey of the World*. New York: Bonanza Books.
Guinan, J. A., P. A. Gowaty, and E. K. Eltzroth. 2000. Western Bluebird (*Sialia mexicana*). In *Birds of North America* 510 (A. Poole and F. Gill, eds.). Philadelphia: Birds of North America.
Gullion, G. W. 1954. The reproductive cycle of American Coots in California. *Auk* 71:366–412.
Gutierrez, R. J., C. E. Braun, and T. P. Zapatka. 1975. Reproductive biology of the Band-tailed Pigeon in Colorado and New Mexico. *Auk* 92:665–677.
Gutierrez, R. J., A. B. Franklin, and W. S. Lahaye. 1995. Spotted Owl (*Strix occidentalis*). In *Birds of North America* 265 (A. Poole and F. Gill, eds.). Philadelphia: Academy of Natural Sciences; Washington, DC: American Ornithologists' Union.
Guzy, M. J., and P. E. Lowther. 1997. Black-throated Gray Warbler (*Dendroica nigrescens*). In *Birds of North America* 319 (A. Poole and F. Gill, eds.). Philadelphia: Academy of Natural Sciences; Washington, DC: American Ornithologists' Union.
Guzy, M. J., and G. Ritchison. 1999. Common Yellowthroat (*Geothlypis trichas*). In *Birds of North America* 448 (A. Poole and F. Gill, eds.). Philadelphia: Birds of North America.
Hahn, T. P. 1996. Cassin's Finch (*Carpodacus cassinii*). In *Birds of North America* 240 (A. Poole and F. Gill, eds.). Philadelphia: Academy of Natural Sciences; Washington, DC: American Ornithologists' Union.
Halkin, S. L., and S. U. Linville. 1999. Northern Cardinal (*Cardinalis cardinalis*). In *Birds of North America* 440 (A. Poole and F. Gill, eds.). Philadelphia: Birds of North America.
Hall, L. S. 1996. Habitat selection by the Elegant Trogon (*Trogon elegans*) at multiple scales. Ph.D. diss., University of Arizona.
Hall, L. S., and J. O. Karubian. 1996. Breeding behavior of Elegant Trogons in southeastern Arizona. *Auk* 113:143–150.

Halterman, M. D. 2001. Population status of the yellow-billed cuckoo at the Bill William's River NWR and Alamo Dam, Arizona, and southern Nevada: Summer 2000. Report for US Bureau of Reclamation Lower Colorado Regional Office, and US Fish and Wildlife Service.

Halterman, M. D., S. A. Lamon, and M. J. Whitfield. 1989. Status and distribution of the Elf Owl in California. *Western Birds* 20:71–80.

Hamas, M. J. 1994. Belted Kingfisher (*Ceryle alcyon*). In *Birds of North America* 84 (A. Poole and F. Gill, eds.). Philadelphia: Academy of Natural Sciences; Washington, DC: American Ornithologists' Union.

Hancock, J., and J. Kushlan. 1984. *The Heron Handbook*. New York: Harper & Row.

Hann, H. W. 1950. Nesting behavior of the American Dipper in Colorado. *Condor* 52:49–62.

Hanna, W. C. 1961. Turkey Vulture nesting in Pima County, Arizona. *Condor* 63:419.

Hardy, R. 1939. Nesting habits of the western Red-tailed Hawk. *Condor* 41:79–80.

Hargrave, L. L. 1940. Data on grouse and quail. Phoenix: Arizona Game and Fish Commission.

Harlow, R. C. 1922. The breeding habits of the Northern Raven in Pennsylvania. *Auk* 39:399–410.

Harrison, C. 1978. A field guide to the nests, eggs, and nestlings of North American birds. Collins, Glasgow, Scotland.

Harrison, H. H., 1979. *A Field Guide to Western Bird Nests*. Boston: Houghton Mifflin.

Hastings, J. R., and R. M. Turner. 1965. *The Changing Mile*. Tucson: University of Arizona Press.

Hatch, J. J., and D. V. Weseloh. 1999. Double-crested Cormorant (*Phalacrocorax auritus*). In *Birds of North America* 441 (A. Poole and F. Gill, eds.). Philadelphia: Birds of North America.

Haug, E. A., B. A. Millsap, and M. S. Martell. 1993. Burrowing Owl (*Speotyto cunicularia*). In *Birds of North America* 61 (A. Poole and F. Gill, eds.). Philadelphia: Academy of Natural Sciences; Washington, DC: American Ornithologists' Union.

Hawbecker, A. C. 1942. The nesting of the White-tailed Kite in southern Santa Cruz County, California. *Condor* 42:106–111.

Haydock, J., and J. D. Ligon. 1986. Brood reduction in the Chihuahuan Raven: An experimental study. *Ecology* 67:1197–1205.

Hayworth, A. M., and W. W. Weathers. 1984. Temperature regulation and climatic adaptation in Black-billed and Yellow-billed Magpies. *Condor* 86:19–26.

Head, A. 1903. Nesting habits of two flycatchers at Lake Tahoe. *Bird-Lore* 5:153–155.

Hector, D. P. 1987. The decline of the Aplomado Falcon in the United States. *Am. Birds* 41:381–389.

Heermann, A. L. 1859. Report upon birds collected on the Survey. In *Reports of Exploration and Surveys for a Railroad to the Pacific Ocean* by Lt. J. G. Park, 1:9–21.

Hejl, S. J., J. A. Holmes, and D. E. Kroodsma. 2002. Winter Wren (*Troglodytes troglodytes*). In *Birds of North America* 623 (A. Poole and F. Gill, eds.). Philadelphia: Birds of North America.

Hejl, S. J., R. L. Hutto, C. R. Preston, and D. M. Finch. 1995. Effects of silvicultural treatments in the Rocky Mountains. In *Ecology and Management of Neotropical Migratory Birds* (T. Martin and D. Finch, eds.). New York: Oxford University Press.

Hejl, S. J., K. R. Newlon, M. E. McFadden, J. S. Young, and C. K. Ghalambor. 2002. Brown Creeper (*Certhia americana*). In *Birds of North America* 669 (A. Poole and F. Gill, eds.). Philadelphia: Academy of Natural Sciences, and Washington, DC: American Ornithologists' Union.

Helm, R. N., D. N. Pashley, and P. J. Zwank. 1987. Notes on the nesting of the Common Moorhen and Purple Gallinule in southwestern Louisiana. *J. Field Ornithol.* 58:55–61.

Hendrickson, D. A., and W. L. Minckley. 1984. Cienegas: Vanishing climax communities of the American Southwest. *Desert Plants* 6:131–175.

Henny, C. J., and L. J. Blus. 1981. Artificial burrows provide new insight into Burrowing Owl nesting biology. *Raptor Res.* 15:82–85.

Henry, S. G. 1998. Elf Owl (*Micrathene whitneyi*). In *Raptors of Arizona* (R. Glinski, ed.). Tucson: University of Arizona Press.

Henry, S. G., and F. R. Gehlbach. 1999. Elf Owl (*Micrathene whitneyi*). In *Birds of North America* 413 (A. Poole and F. Gill, eds.). Philadelphia: Academy of Natural Sciences; Washington, DC: American Ornithologists' Union.

Henshaw, H. W. 1875. The Ornithological Collections. In *Zoology. Geog. & Geol. Expl. Sur. West 100th Meridian* 5(3):133–507.

Hensley, M. M. 1959. Notes on the nesting of selected species of birds of the Sonoran Desert. *Wilson Bull.* 71:86–92.

Hepp, G. R., R. A. Kennamer, and W. F. Harvey IV. 1990. Incubation as a reproductive cost in female Wood Ducks. *Auk* 107:756–764.

Herkert, J. R. 1994. The effects of habitat fragmentation on midwestern grassland bird communities. *J. Ecol. Appl.* 4:461–471.

Hill, G. E. 1991. Plumage coloration is a sexually selected indicator of male quality. *Nature* 350:337–339.

Hill, G. E. 1993. House Finch (*Carpodacus mexicanus*). In *Birds of North America* 46 (A. Poole and F. Gill, eds.). Philadelphia: Birds of North America.

Hill, G. E. 1995. Black-headed Grosbeak (*Pheucticus melanocephalus*). In *Birds of North America* 143 (A. Poole and F. Gill, eds.). Philadelphia: Academy of Natural Sciences; Washington, DC: American Ornithologists' Union.

Hill, W. L. 1986. Clutch overlap in American Coots. *Condor* 88:96–97.

Hilty, S. L., and W. L. Brown. 1986. *A Guide to the Birds of Colombia*. Princeton, NJ: Princeton University Press.

Hines, J. E., and G. J. Mitchell. 1983. Gadwall nest-site selection and nesting success. *J. Wildlife Management* 47:1063–1071.

Holt, D. W., and W. D. Norton. 1986. Observations of nesting Northern Pygmy-Owls. J. Raptor Res. 20:39–41.

Holt, D. W., and J. L. Petersen. 2000. Northern Pygmy-Owl (*Glaucidium gnoma*). In *Birds of North America* 494 (A. Poole and F. Gill, eds.). Philadelphia: Birds of North America.

Horn, H. S. 1968. The adaptive significance of colonial nesting in the Brewer's Blackbird (*Euphagus cyanocephalus*). *Ecology* 49:683–694.

Horton, S. P. 1987. Effects of prescribed burning on breeding birds in a ponderosa pine forest, Southeastern Arizona. M.S. thesis, University of Arizona.

Houston, C. S., D. G. Smith, and C. Rohner. 1998. Great Horned Owl (*Bubo virginianus*). In *Birds of North America* 372 (A. Poole and F. Gill, eds.). Philadelphia: Academy of Natural Sciences; Washington, DC: American Ornithologists' Union.

Houston, D. C. 1986. Scavenging efficiency of Turkey Vultures in tropical forest. *Condor* 88:318–323.

Howard, O. W. 1899. Some of the summer flycatchers of Arizona. *Bull. Cooper Ornithol. Club* 1:103–107.

Howard, O. W. 1904. The Coues Flycatcher as a guardian of the peace. *Condor* 6:79–80.

Howe, W. H. 1986. Status of the Yellow-billed Cuckoo (*Coccyzus americanus*) in New Mexico. New Mexico Department of Game and Fish. Contract 516.6–75–09.

Howell, J. C. 1942. Notes on the nesting habits of the American Robin (*Turdus migratorius* L.) *Am. Midl. Nat.* 28:259–603.

Howell, S. N. G. 2002. *Hummingbirds of North America: The Photographic Guide*. San Diego: Academic Press.

Howell, S. N. G., and S. Webb. 1995. *A Guide to the Birds of Mexico and Northern Central America*. New York: Oxford University Press.

Howell, T. R. 1952. Natural history and differentiation in the Yellow-bellied Sapsucker. *Condor* 54:237–282.

Hubbard, J. P. 1978. *Revised Check-list of the Birds of New Mexico*. Albuquerque: New Mexico Ornithological Society.

Hudertmark, C. A. 1974. Breeding range extensions of certain birds in New Mexico. *Wilson Bull.* 86:298–300.

Hudon, J. 1999. Western Tanager (*Piranga ludoviciana*). In *Birds of North America* 432 (A. Poole and F. Gill, eds.). Philadelphia: Birds of North America.

Huels, T. R. 1984. First record of Cave Swallows breeding in Arizona. *Am. Birds* 38:281–283.

Hughes, J. M. 1996. Greater Roadrunner (*Geococcyx californianus*). In *Birds of North America* 244 (A. Poole and F. Gill, eds.) Philadelphia: Academy of Natural Sciences; Washington, DC: American Ornithologists' Union.

Hughes, J. M. 1999. Yellow-billed Cuckoo (*Coccyzus americanus*). In *Birds of North America* 418 (A. Poole and F. Gill, eds.). Philadelphia: Birds of North America.

Hungerford, C. R. 1964. Vitamin A and productivity in Gambel's Quail. *J. Wildlife Management* 28:141–147.

Hunt, P. D., and D. J. Flaspohler. 1998. Yellow-rumped Warbler (*Dendroica coronata*). In *Birds of North America* 376 (A. Poole and F. Gill, eds.). Philadelphia: Birds of North America.

Hunt, W. G., D. E. Driscoll, E. W. Bianchi, and R. E. Jackman. 1992. Ecology of Bald Eagles in Arizona. Report to US Bureau of Reclamation, Contract 6-CS-30-04470. Santa Cruz, CA: BioSystems Analysis, Inc.

Hunt, W. G., R. E. Jackman, T. L. Brown, J. G. Gilardi, D. E. Driscoll, and L. Culp. 1995. A pilot Golden Eagle population study in the Altamont Pass Wind Resource Area, California. Report to National Renewable Energy Laboratory, Subcontract XCG-4-14200 to the Predatory Bird Research Group, University of California, Santa Cruz.

Hutto, R. L. 1987. A description of mixed-species insectivorous bird flocks in western Mexico. *Condor* 89:282–292.

Hutto, R. L. 1995. Composition of bird communities following stand-replacement fires in Northern Rocky Mountain (USA) conifer forests. *Conserv. Biol.* 9:1041–1058.

Ingold, J. L. 1993. Blue Grosbeak (*Guiraca caerulea*). In *Birds of North America* 79 (A. Poole and F. Gill, eds.). Philadelphia: Academy of Natural Sciences; Washington, DC: American Ornithologists' Union.

Ingold, J. L. and R. Galati. 1997. Golden-crowned Kinglet (*Regulus satrapa*). In *Birds of North America* 301 (A. Poole and F. Gill, eds.). Philadelphia: Academy of Natural Sciences; Washington, DC: American Ornithologists' Union.

Ingold, J. L., and G. E. Wallace. 1994. Ruby-crowned Kinglet (*Regulus calendula*). In *Birds of North America* 119 (A. Poole and F. Gill, eds.). Philadelphia: Academy of Natural Sciences; Washington, DC: American Ornithologists' Union.

Jackson, B. J. S., and J. A. Jackson. 2000. Killdeer (*Charadrius vociferus*). In *Birds of North America* 517 (A. Poole and F. Gill, eds.). Philadelphia: Birds of North America.

Jackson, J. A. 1976. How to determine the status of a woodpecker nest. *Living Bird* 15:205–221.

Jackson, J.A. 1983. Nesting phenology, nest site selection, and reproduction success of Black and Turkey Vultures. In *Vulture Biology and Management* (S. R. Wilbur and J. A. Jackson, eds.). Berkeley: University of California Press.

Jackson, J. A. 1988. American Black Vulture. In *Handbook of North American Birds*, vol. 4 (R. Palmer, ed.). New Haven: Yale University Press.

Jackson, J. A., and H. R. Ouellet. 2002. Downy Woodpecker (*Picoides pubescens*). In *Birds of North America* 613 (A. Poole and F. Gill, eds.). Philadelphia: Birds of North America.

Jackson, J. A., H. R. Ouellet, and B. J. S. Jackson. 2002. Hairy Woodpecker (*Picoides villosus*). In *Birds of North America* 702 (A. Poole and F. Gill, eds.). Philadelphia: Birds of North America.

Jacobs, B. 1986. *Birding on the Navajo and Hopi Reservations*. Sycamore, MO: Jacobs Publishing.

Jacot, E. C. 1934. An Arizona nest of the Ferruginous Rough-leg. *Condor* 36:84–85.

James, J. D., and J. E. Thompson. 2001. Black-bellied Whistling-Duck (*Dendrocygna autumnalis*). In *Birds of North America* 578 (A. Poole and F. Gill, eds.). Philadelphia: Birds of North America.

Johnsgard, P. A. 1975. *Waterfowl of North America*. Bloomington: Indiana University Press.

Johnsgard, P. A. 1978. *Ducks, Geese, and Swans of the World*. Lincoln: University of Nebraska Press.

Johnsgard, P. A. 1979. *Birds of the Great Plains*. Lincoln: University of Nebraska Press.

Johnsgard, P. A. 1983. *The Hummingbirds of North America*. Washington, DC: Smithsonian Institution Press.

Johnsgard. P. A. 1988. *North American Owls: Biology and Natural History*. Washington, DC: Smithsonian Institution Press.

Johnsgard, P. A. 1999. *The Pheasants of the World*. 2nd ed. Washington, DC: Smithsonian Institution Press.

Johnson, B. R., and R. A. Ryder. 1977. Breeding densities and migration periods of Common Snipe in Colorado. *Wilson Bull.* 89:116–121.

Johnson, K. 1995. Green-winged Teal (*Anas crecca*). In *Birds of North America* 193 (A. Poole and F. Gill, eds.). Philadelphia: Academy of Natural Sciences; Washington, DC: American Ornithologists' Union.

Johnson, K., and B. D. Peer. 2001. Great-tailed Grackle (*Quiscalus mexicanus*). In *Birds of North America* 576 (A. Poole and F. Gill, eds.). Philadelphia: Birds of North America.

Johnson, L. S. 1998. House Wren (*Troglodytes aedon*). In *Birds of North America* 380 (A. Poole and F. Gill, eds.). Philadelphia: Academy of Natural Sciences; Washington, DC: American Ornithologists' Union.

Johnson, M. J., C. Van Riper III, and K. M. Pearson. 2002. Black-throated Sparrow (*Amphispiza bilineata*). In *Birds of North America* 637 (A. Poole and F. Gill, eds.). Philadelphia: Birds of North America.

Johnson, R. R., J. E. Cartron, L. T. Haight, R. B. Duncan, and K. J. Kingsley. 2000. A historical perspective on the population decline of the Cactus Ferruginous Pygmy-Owl in Arizona. In *Ecology and Conservation of the Cactus Ferruginous Pygmy-Owl in Arizona* (J. E. Cartron and D. M. Finch, eds.). Gen. Tech. Rep. RMRS-GTR-43. Ogden, UT: US Department of Agriculture, Forest Service, Rocky Mountain Research Station.

Johnson, R. R., R. L. Glinski, and S. W. Matteson. 2000. Zone-tailed Hawk (*Buteo albonotatus*). In *Birds of North America* 529 (A. Poole and F. Gill, eds.). Philadelphia: Birds of North America.

Johnson, R. R., and L. T. Haight. 1996. Canyon Towhee (*Pipilo fuscus*). In *Birds of North America* 264 (A. Poole and F. Gill, eds.). Philadelphia: Academy of Natural Sciences; Washington, DC: American Ornithologists' Union.

Johnson, R. R., L. T. Haight, and J. D. Ligon. 1999. Strickland's Woodpecker (*Picoides stricklandi*). In *Birds of North America* 474 (A. Poole and F. Gill, eds.). Philadelphia: Birds of North America.

Johnson, R. R., L. T. Haight, and J. M. Simpson. 1979. Owl populations and species status in the southwestern United States. In *Owls of the West: Their Ecology and Conservation* (P. Schaeffer and S. Ehler, eds.). Tiburon, CA: George Whittel Education Center.

Johnson, R. R., and J. M. Simpson. 1971. Important birds from Blue Point Cottonwoods, Maricopa County, Arizona. *Condor* 73:379–380.

Johnson, R. R., H. K. Yard, and B. T. Brown. 1997. Lucy's Warbler (*Vermivora luciae*). In *Birds of North America* 318. (A. Poole and F. Gill, eds.). Philadelphia: Academy of Natural Sciences; Washington, DC: American Ornithologists' Union.

Johnson, S. J. 1986. Development of hunting and self-sufficiency in juvenile Red-tailed Hawks (*Buteo jamaicensis*). *Raptor Res.* 20:29–34.

Johnson, T. B., and R. B. Spicer. 1981. Mountain Plovers on the New Mexico-Arizona border. *Continental Birdlife* 2:69–73.

Johnston, R. F. 1960. Behavior of Inca Dove. *Condor* 62:7–24.

Johnston, R. F. 1992. Rock Dove (*Columbia livia*). In *Birds of North America* 13 (A. Poole, P. Stettenheim, and F. Gill, eds.). Philadelphia: Academy of Natural Sciences; Washington, DC: American Ornithologists' Union.

Johnston, R. F., and J. W. Hardy. 1959. The Ridgeway Whip-poor-will and its associated avifauna in southwestern New Mexico. *Condor* 61:206–209.

Jones, F. M. 1935. Nesting of the Northern Raven in Virginia. *Wilson Bull.* 45:188–191.

Jones, P. W., and T. M. Donovan. 1996. Hermit thrush (*Catharus guttatus*). In *Birds of North America* 261 (A. Poole and F. Gill, eds.). Philadelphia: Academy of Natural Sciences; Washington, DC: American Ornithologists' Union.

Jones, S. L., and J. E. Cornely. 2002. Vesper Sparrow (*Pooecetes gramineus*). In *Birds of North America* 194 (A. Poole and F. Gill, eds.). Philadelphia: Birds of North America.

Jones, S. L., and J. Scott Dieni. 1995. Canyon wren (*Catherpes mexicanus*). In *Birds of North America* 197 (A. Poole and F. Gill, eds.). Philadelphia: Academy of Natural Sciences, and Washington, DC: American Ornithologists' Union.

Jones, S. R. 1991. Distribution of small forest owls in Boulder County, Colorado. *J. Colo. Field Ornithol.* 25:55–70.

Kantrid, H. A., and R. L. Kologiski. 1983. Avian associations of the northern Great Plains grasslands. *J. Biogeogr.* 10:331–350

Kaufman, K. 1996. *Lives of North American Birds*. Boston: Houghton Mifflin.

Keddy-Hector, D. P. 1998. Aplomado Falcon (*Falco femoralis*). In *Raptors of Arizona* (R. Glinski, ed.). Tucson: University of Arizona Press.

Kelly, J. P. 1993. The effect of nest predation on habitat selection by Dusky Flycatchers in limber pine-juniper woodland. *Condor* 95:83–93.

Kelly, J. W. 1955. History of the nesting of an Anna Hummingbird. *Condor* 57:347–353.

Kennedy, E. D., and D. W. White. 1997. Bewick's Wren (*Thryomanes bewickii*). In *Birds of North America* 315 (A. Poole and F. Gill, eds.). Philadelphia: Academy of Natural Sciences; Washington, DC: American Ornithologists' Union.

Kennedy, P. L., D. E. Crowe, and T. F. Dean. 1995. Breeding biology of the Zone-tailed Hawk at the limit of its distribution. *J. Raptor Res.* 29:110–116.

Kennerly, C. B. R. 1859. Report on the birds of the route. In *Reports of Explorations and Surveys for a Railroad to the Pacific Ocean* vol. 10, no. 3, 19–35.

Keppie, D. M., and C. E. Braun. 2000. Band-tailed Pigeon (*Columba fasciata*). In *Birds of North America* 530 (A. Poole and F. Gill, eds.). Philadelphia: Birds of North America.

Kerpez, T. A., and N. S. Smith. 1990a. Competition between European Starlings and native woodpeckers for nest cavities in saguaros. *Auk* 107:367–375.

Kerpez, T. A., and N. S. Smith. 1990b. Nest-site selection and nest-cavity characteristics of Gila Woodpeckers and Northern Flickers. *Condor* 92:193–198.

Kilham, L. 1968. Reproductive behavior of White-breasted Nuthatches: Distraction display, bill-sweeping, and nest-hole defense. *Auk* 85:477–492.

Kilham, L. 1979. Three-week vs. four-week nestling periods in *Picoides* and other woodpeckers. *Wilson Bull.* 91:335–338.

Kilham, L. 1989. *The American Crow and the Common Raven*. College Station: Texas A&M University Press.

Killpack, M. L. 1970. Notes on Sage Thrasher nestlings in Colorado. *Condor* 72:486–488.

Kingery, H. E. 1996. American Dipper (*Cinclus mexicanus*). In *Birds of North America* 229. (A. Poole and F. Gill, eds.). Philadelphia: Academy of Natural Sciences; Washington, DC: American Ornithologists' Union.

Kingery, H. E., and C. K. Ghalambor. 2001. Pygmy Nuthatch (*Sitta pygmaea*). In *Birds of North America* 567 (A. Poole and F. Gill, eds.). Philadelphia: Academy of Natural Sciences; Washington, DC: American Ornithologists' Union.

Kirk, D. A., and M. J. Mossman. 1998. Turkey Vulture (*Cathartes aura*). In *Birds of North America* 339 (A. Poole and F. Gill, eds.). Philadelphia: Birds of North America.

Knight, O. W. 1908. *The Birds of Maine*. Bangor: Charles Glass.

Kochert, M. N., K. Steenhof, C. L. McIntyre, and E. H. Craig. 2002. Golden Eagle (*Aquila chrysaetos*). In *Birds of North America* 684 (A. Poole and F. Gill, eds.). Philadelphia: Birds of North America.

Koenig, W. D., P. B. Stacey, M. T. Stanback, and R. L. Mumme. 1995. Acorn Woodpecker. (*Melanerpes formicivorus*). In *Birds of North America* 194 (A. Poole and F. Gill, eds.). Philadelphia: Birds of North America.

Koloszar, J. G., and J. T. Driscoll. 2001. Arizona bald eagle 2001 nest survey. Nongame and Endangered Wildlife Program Technical Report 189. Phoenix: Arizona Game and Fish Department.

Koplin, J. R. 1969. The numerical response of woodpeckers to insect prey in a subalpine forest in Colorado. *Condor* 71:436–438.

Kozicky, E. L., and F. W. Schmidt. 1949. Nesting habits of the Clapper Rail in New Jersey. *Auk* 66:355–364.

Kroodsma, D. E. 1974. Song learning, dialects, and dispersal in the Bewick's Wren. *Z. Tierpsychol.* 35:352–380.

Kroodsma, D. E., and J. Verner. 1997. Marsh Wren (*Cistothorus palustris*). In *Birds of North America* 308 (A. Poole and F. Gill, eds.). Philadelphia: Academy of Natural Sciences; Washington, DC: American Ornithologists' Union.

Krueper, D. J. 1999. Annotated checklist to the birds of the upper San Pedro River Valley, Arizona. San Pedro Riparian Nat. Cons. Area. Bureau of Land Management, Sierra Vista, Arizona.

Krueper, D., J. Bart, and T. D. Rich. 2003. Response of vegetation and breeding birds to the removal of cattle on the San Pedro River, Arizona (USA). *Conserv. Biol.* 17(2):607–615.

Kuenning, R. R. 1998. White-breasted Nuthatch (*Sitta carolinensis*). In *Colorado Breeding Bird Atlas* (H. Kingery, ed.). Denver: Colorado Wildlife Heritage Foundation.

Kuerzi, R. G. 1941. Life history studies of the Tree Swallow. *Proc. Linn. Soc. N.Y.* 52–53:1–52.

Kunzmann, M. R., L. S. Hall, and R. R. Johnson. 1998. Elegant Trogon (*Trogon elegans*). In *Birds of North America* 357 (A. Poole and F. Gill, eds.). Philadelphia: Birds of North America.

Kuvlesky, W.P., Jr., S. A. Gall, S. J. Dobrott, S. Tolley, F. S. Guthery, S. A. DeStefano, N. King, K. R. Nolte, N. J. Silvy, J. C. Lewis, G. Gee, R. Engel-Wilson, and G. Camou-Lourdes. 1997. The status of Masked Bobwhite recovery in the United States and Mexico. In *Quail IV* (L. A. Brennan et al., eds.). Tallahassee: Tall Timbers Research Station.

La Rivers, I. 1944. Observations on the nesting mortality of the Brewer Blackbird, *Euphagus cyanocephalus*. *Am. Midl. Nat.* 32:417–437.

Landry, R. E. 1979. Growth and development of the Burrowing Owl. M.S. thesis, Calif. State University, Long Beach.

Lanning, D. V., and J. T. Shiflett. 1983. Nesting ecology of Thick-billed Parrots. *Condor* 85:66–73.

Lanyon, W. E. 1994. Western Meadowlark (*Sturnella neglecta*). In *Birds of North America* 104 (A. Poole and F. Gill, eds.). Philadelphia: Birds of North America.

Lanyon, W. E. 1995. Eastern Meadowlark (*Sturnella magna*). In *Birds of North America* 160 (A. Poole and F. Gill, eds.). Philadelphia: Academy of Natural Sciences; Washington, DC: American Ornithologists' Union.

LaRue, C. T. 1994. Birds of northern Black Mesa, Navajo County, Arizona. *Great Basin Naturalist* 54:1–63.

LaRue, C. T., and D. H. Ellis. 1992. The Common Grackle in Arizona: First specimen record and notes on occurrence. *Western Birds* 23:84–86.

Laskey, A. R. 1944. A study of the cardinal in Tennessee. *Wilson Bull.* 56:27–44.

Laskey, A. R. 1962. Breeding biology of mockingbirds. *Auk* 79:596–606.

Latta, M. J., C. J. Beardmore, and T. E. Corman. 1999. Arizona Partners in Flight Bird Conservation Plan. Version 1.0. Nongame Threatened and Endangered Wildlife Program Technical Report 142. Phoenix: Arizona Game and Fish Department.

Latta, S. C., and M. E. Baltz. 1997. Lesser Nighthawk (*Chordeiles acutipennis*). In *Birds of North America* 340 (A. Poole and F. Gill, eds.). Philadelphia: Academy of Natural Sciences; Washington, DC: American Ornithologists' Union.

Lawrence, L. K. 1967. A comparative life history study of four species of woodpeckers. *Ornithol. Monographs* 5:1–156.

Layman, S. A. 1987. Brown-headed Cowbirds in California: historical perspectives and management opportunities in riparian habitats. *Western Birds* 18:63–70.

Leberman, R. C. 1992. Common Snipe (*Gallinago gallinago*). In *Atlas of Breeding Birds in Pennsylvania* (D. W. Brauning, ed.). Pittsburgh: University of Pittsburgh Press.

LeCount, A. L. 1970. Fall food preferences of the Blue Grouse in the White Mountains of Arizona. M.S. thesis, University of Arizona.

Lemmon, C. R., G. Bugbee, and G. R. Stephens. 1994. Tree damage by nesting Double-crested Cormorants in Connecticut. *Connecticut Warbler* 14:27–30.

Lemon, W. C. 1991. Foraging behavior of a guild of Neotropical vultures. *Wilson Bull.* 103:698–702.

Lenington, S. 1980. Bi-parental care in Killdeer: an adaptive hypothesis. *Wilson Bull.* 92:8–20.

Leonard, D.L., Jr. 2001. Three-toed Woodpecker (*Picoides tridactylus*). In *Birds of North America* 588 (A. Poole and F. gill, eds.). Philadelphia: Birds of North America.

Leopold, N. F., Jr. 1923. Reason and instinct in bird migration. *Auk* 40:409–414.

LeSchack, C. R., S. K. McKnight, and G. R. Hepp. 1997. Gadwall (*Anas strepera*). In *Birds of North America* 283 (A. Poole and F. Gill, eds.). Philadelphia: Academy of Natural Sciences; Washington, DC: American Ornithologists' Union.

Lesh, T., P. C. Christgau, H. Green, and R. Miller. 1994. Nest search methods for Flammulated Owls (*Otus flammeolus*) on the Coconino National Forest, Arizona. Nongame and Endangered Wildlife Program Technical Report 40. Phoenix: Arizona Game and Fish Department.

Levad, R. 1998a. Common Snipe (*Gallinago gallinago*). In *Colorado Breeding Bird Atlas* (H. Kingery, ed.). Denver: Colorado Wildlife Heritage Foundation.

Levad, R. 1998b. Townsend's Solitaire (*Myadestes townsendi*). In *Colorado Breeding Bird Atlas* (H. Kingery, ed.). Denver: Colorado Wildlife Heritage Foundation.

Levy, S. H. 1959. Thick-billed Kingbird in the United States. *Auk* 76:92.

Levy, S. H. 1962. The Ridgeway Whip-poor-will in Arizona. *Condor* 64:161–162.

Levy, S. H. 1971. The Mississippi Kite in Arizona. *Condor* 73:476.

Levy, S. H. 1988a. Crested Caracara (*Caracara plancus*). In *Raptors of Arizona* (R. Glinski, ed.). Tucson: University of Arizona Press.

Levy, S. H. 1988b. Status and distribution of the Crested Caracara in Arizona. Unpub. report to Arizona Game and Fish Department.

Li, P., and T. E. Martin. 1991. Nest-site selection and nesting success of cavity-nesting birds in high elevation forests drainages. *Auk* 108:405–418.

Ligon, J. D. 1961. *New Mexico Birds and Where to Find Them*. Albuquerque: University of New Mexico Press.

Ligon, J. D. 1969. Factors influencing breeding range expansion of the Azure Bluebird. *Wilson Bull.* 81:104–105.

Ligon, J. D. 1971. Notes on the breeding of the Sulphur-bellied Flycatcher in Arizona. *Condor* 73:250–252.

Lindvall, M. L., and J. B. Low. 1982. Nesting ecology and production of Western Grebes at Bear River Migratory Bird Refuge, Utah. *Condor* 84:66–70.

Linsdale, J. M. 1968. *Spinus psaltria hesperophila* Green-backed Goldfinch. In Life histories of North American cardinals, grosbeaks, buntings, towhees, finches, sparrows and allies (O. L. Austin Jr., ed.). *US Nat. Mus. Bull.* 237.

Low, J. B. 1941. Nesting of the Ruddy Duck in Iowa. *Condor* 43:142–151.

Lowther, P. E. 1993. Brown-headed Cowbird (*Molothrus ater*). In *Birds of North America* 47 (A. Poole and F. Gill, eds.) Philadelphia: Academy of Natural Sciences; Washington, DC: American Ornithologists' Union.

Lowther, P. E. 1995. Bronzed Cowbird (*Molothrus aeneus*). In *Birds of North America* 144 (A. Poole and F. Gill, eds.). Philadelphia: Academy of Natural Sciences, and Washington, DC: American Ornithologists' Union.

Lowther, P. E. 2000. Cordilleran Flycatcher (*Empidonax occidentalis*). In *Birds of North America* 556 (A. Poole and F. Gill, eds.). Philadelphia: Birds of North America.

Lowther, P. E. 2001. Ladder-backed Woodpecker (*Picoides scalaris*). In *Birds of North America* 565 (A. Poole and F. Gill, eds.). Philadelphia: Birds of North America.

Lowther, P. E. 2002. Thick-billed Kingbird (*Tyrannus crassirostris*). In *Birds of North America* 604 (A. Poole and F. Gill, eds.). Philadelphia: Birds of North America.

Lowther, P. E., C. Celada, N.K. Klein, C.C. Rimmer, and D.A. Spector. 1999. Yellow Warbler (*Dendroica petechia*). In *Birds of North America* 454 (A. Poole and F. Gill, eds.). Philadelphia: Birds of North America.

Lowther, P. E., and C. L. Cink. 1992. House Sparrow (*Passer domesticus*). In *Birds of North America* 12 (A. Poole, P. Stettenheim, and F. Gill, eds.). Philadelphia: Academy of Natural Sciences; Washington, DC: American Ornithologists' Union.

Lowther, P. E., K. D. Groschupf, and S. M. Russell. 1999. Rufous-winged Sparrow (*Aimophila carpalis*). In *Birds of North America* 422 (A. Poole and F. Gill, eds.). Philadelphia: Birds of North America.

Lowther, P. E., D. E. Kroodsma, and G. H. Farley 2000. Rock Wren (*Salpinctes obsoletus*). In *Birds of North America* 486 (A. Poole and F. Gill, eds.). Philadelphia: Academy of Natural Sciences; Washington, DC: American Ornithologists' Union.

Lowther, P. E., and J. Nocedal. 1997. Olive Warbler (*Peucedramus taeniatus*). In *Birds of North America* 310 (A. Poole and F. Gill, eds.). Philadelphia: Academy of Natural Sciences; Washington, DC: American Ornithologists' Union.

Lusk, R. D. 1901. In the summer home of the Buff-breasted Flycatcher. *Condor* 9:38–41.

MacGregor, W. G., and M. Inlay. 1951. Observations on failure of Gambel's Quail to breed. Calif. Fish and Game 37:218–219.

Machie, R. J., and H. K. Buechner. 1963. The reproductive cycle of the Chukar. *J. Wildlife Management* 277:246–260.

MacWhirter, R. B. and Bildstein, K. L. 1996. Northern Harrier (*Circus cyaneus*). In *Birds of North America* 210 (A. Poole and F. Gill, eds.). Philadelphia: Academy of Natural Sciences; Washington, DC: American Ornithologists' Union.

Mader, W. J. 1975. Biology of the Harris' Hawk in southern Arizona. *Living Bird* 14:59–85.

Mader, W. J. 1978. A comparative nesting study of Red-tailed Hawks and Harris' Hawks in southern Arizona. *Auk* 95:327–337.

Maender, G.J., S. Bailey, and K. L. Hiett. 1996. Nesting Anna's Hummingbirds (*Calypte anna*) in urban Tucson, Arizona. *Western Birds* 27:78–80.

Mallory, M., and K. Metz. 1999. Common Merganser (*Mergus merganser*). In *Birds of North America* 442 (A. Poole and F. Gill, eds.). Philadelphia: Birds of North America.

Marks, J. S., D. L. Evans, and D. W. Holt. 1994. Long-eared Owl (*Asio otus*). In *Birds of North America* 133 (A. Poole and F. Gill, eds.). Philadelphia: Academy of Natural Sciences; Washington, DC: American Ornithologists' Union.

Marshall, J., and R. P. Balda. 1974. The breeding ecology of the Painted Redstart. *Condor* 76:89–101.

Marshall, J. T., and R. R. Johnson. 1968. *Pipilo fuscus mesoleucus*, Canyon Brown Towhee. In Life histories of North American cardinals, grosbeaks, buntings, towhees, finches, sparrows, and allies (O. L. Austin Jr., ed.). *US Nat. Mus. Bull.* 237, Part 2.

Marshall, J. T., Jr. 1956. Summer birds of the Rincon Mountains, Saguaro National Monument. *Condor* 58:81–97.

Marshall, J. T., Jr. 1957. Birds of pine-oak woodland in southern Arizona and adjacent Mexico. *Pac. Coast Avifauna* 32.

Marti, C. D. 1969. Renesting by Barn and Great Horned Owls. *Wilson Bull.* 81:467–468.

Marti, C. D. 1992. Barn Owl (*Tyto alba*). In *Birds of North America* 1 (A. Poole and F. Gill, eds.). Philadelphia: Academy of Natural Sciences; Washington, DC: American Ornithologists' Union.

Martin, D. J. 1973. Selected aspects of Burrowing Owl ecology and behavior in central New Mexico. *Condor* 75:446–456.

Martin, J. A., and M. L. Morrison. 1999. Distribution, abundance, and habitat characteristics of the Buff-breasted Flycatcher in Arizona. *Condor* 101:272–281.

Martin, J. W., and B. A. Carlson. 1998. Sage Sparrow (*Amphispiza belli*). In *Birds of North America* 326 (A. Poole and F. Gill, eds.). Philadelphia: Birds of North America.

Martin, J. W., and J. R. Parrish. 2000. Lark Sparrow (*Chondestes grammacus*). In *Birds of North America* 488 (A. Poole and F. Gill, eds.). Philadelphia: Birds of North America.

Martin, S. G. 2002. Brewer's Blackbird (*Euphagus cyanocephalus*). In *Birds of North America* 616 (A. Poole and F. Gill, eds.). Philadelphia: Birds of North America.

Martin, T. E. 1992. Breeding productivity considerations: What are the appropriate habitat features for management? In *Ecology and Conservation of Neotropical Migrant Landbirds* (J. Hagan and D. Johnson, eds.). Washington, DC: Smithsonian Institution Press.

Martin, T. E. 1993. Nest predation among vegetation layers and habitat types: revising the dogmas. Am. Nat. 141:897–913.

Martin, T. E. 1995. Avian life history evolution in relation to nest sites, nest predation, and food. Ecol. Monogr. 65:101–127.

Martin, T. E. 1998. Are microhabitat preferences of coexisting species under selection and adaptive? *Ecology* 79:656–670.

Martin, T. E., and P. M. Barber. 1995. Red-faced Warbler (*Cardellina rubrifrons*). In *Birds of North America* 152 (A. Poole and F. Gill, eds.). Philadelphia: Academy of Natural Sciences, and Washington, DC: American Ornithologists' Union.

Martin, T. E., and C. K. Ghalambor. 1999. Males feeding females during incubation. I. Required by microclimate or constrained by nest predation. *Am. Nat.* 153:131–139.

Martin, T. E., and P. Li. 1992. Life history traits of open- versus cavity-nesting birds. Ecology 73:579–592.

Martin, T. E., and J. J. Roper. 1988. Nest predation and nest-site selection of a western population of hermit thrush. *Condor* 90:51–57.

Marzluff, J. M., and R. P. Balda. 1992. *The Pinyon Jay: Behavioral Ecology of a Colonial and Cooperative Corvid*. London: Poyser.

Maxwell, G. R., II, and H. W. Kale, II. 1977. Breeding biology of five species of herons in coastal Florida. *Auk* 94:689–700.

Mayfield, H. F. 1965. The Brown-headed Cowbird, with old and new hosts. *Living Bird* 4:13–28.

McAllister, N. M. 1958. Courtship, hostile behavior, nest establishment and egg-laying in the Eared Grebe (*Podiceps caspicus*). *Auk* 75:290–311.

McCallum, D. A. 1994. Flammulated Owl (*Otus flammeolus*). In *Birds of North America* 93 (A. Poole and F. Gill, eds.). Philadelphia: Academy of Natural Sciences; Washington, DC: American Ornithologists' Union.

McCarthey, T. D., T. E. Corman, and M. J. Latta. 1994. Arizona breeding bird atlas project 1994 progress report. Nongame and Endangered Wildlife Program Technical Report 60. Arizona Game and Fish Department, Phoenix, Arizona.

McClaran, M. P., and T. R. Van Devender. 1995. *The Desert Grassland*. Tucson: University of Arizona Press.

McClelland, B. R., and P. T. McClelland. 2000. Red-naped Sapsucker nest trees in northern Rocky Mountain old-growth forest. *Wilson Bull.* 112:44–50.

McCrimmon, D. A., Jr., J. C. Ogden, and G. T. Bancroft. 2001. Great Egret (*Ardea alba*). In *Birds of North America* 570 (A. Poole and F. Gill, eds.). Philadelphia: Academy of Natural Sciences; Washington, DC: American Ornithologists' Union.

McCullum, D. A., R. Grundel, and D. L. Dahlsten. 1999. Mountain Chickadee (*Poecile gambeli*). In *Birds of North America* 453 (A. Poole and F. Gill, eds). Philadelphia: Academy of Natural Sciences; Washington, DC: American Ornithologists' Union.

McLaughlin, S. P. 1986. Floristic analysis of the southwestern United States. *Great Basin Naturalist* 46:46–65.

McLaughlin, S. P. 1989. Natural flostic areas of the western United States. *J. Biogeography* 16:239–248.

McLaughlin, S. P. 1992. Vascular flora of Buenos Aires National Wildlife Refuge, Pima County, Arizona. *Phytologia* 73(5):353–377.

Meanley, B. 1985. *The Marsh Hen: A Natural History of the Clapper Rail of the Atlantic Coast Marsh*. Centreville, MD: Tidewater.

Mearns, E. A. 1886. Some Arizona birds. *Auk* 3:60–73.

Mearns, E. A. 1890. Observations on the Avifauna of portions of Arizona. *Auk* 7:45–55, 251–264.

Medvin, M. B., and M. D. Beecher. 1986. Parent-offspring recognition in the Barn Swallow (*Hirundo rustica*). *Anim. Behav.* 34:1627–1639.

Melvin, S.M., and J.P. Gibbs. 1996. Sora (*Porzana carolina*). In *Birds of North America* 250 (A. Poole and F. Gill, eds.). Philadelphia: Academy of Natural Sciences; Washington, DC: American Ornithologists' Union.

Merola, M. 1995. Observations on the nesting and breeding behavior of the Rock Wren. *Condor* 97:585–587.

Merriam, C. H. 1890. Results of a biological survey of the San Francisco Mountains region and desert of the Little Colorado in Arizona. Washington, DC: US Department of Agriculture.

Mewaldt, L. R. 1956. Nesting behavior of the Clark Nutcracker. *Condor* 58:3–23.

Meyerriecks, A. J. 1962. Green Heron. In *Handbook of North American Birds*, vol. 1 (R. Palmer, ed.). New Haven: Yale University Press.

Middleton, A. L. A. 1998. Chipping Sparrow (*Spizella passerina*). In *Birds of North America* 334 (A. Poole and F. Gill, eds.). Philadelphia: Academy of Natural Sciences; Washington, DC: American Ornithologists' Union.

Mikesic, D. G., and R. B. Duncan. 2000. Historical reviews of Arizona's nesting Northern Harriers, including the most recent confirmed nesting in 1998. *Western Birds* 31:243–248.

Miller, A. H. 1937. The nuptial flight of the Texas Nighthawk. *Condor* 39:42–43.

Miller, A. H. 1968. Life histories of North American cardinals, grosbeaks, buntings, towhees, finches, sparrows, and allies, pt. II (O. L. Austin Jr., ed.). *US Nat. Mus. Bull.* 237.

Mills, A. M. 1986. The influence of moonlight on the behavior of goatsuckers (Caprimulgidae). *Auk* 103:370–378.

Mills, G. S. 1977. New locations for the Five-striped Sparrow in the United States. *Western Birds* 8:121–130.

Mills, G. S. 1998. American Kestrel (*Falco sparverius*). In Raptors of Arizona (R. Glinski, ed.). Tucson: University of Arizona Press.

Mills, S., J. Silliman, K. Groschupf, and S. Speich. 1980. Life history of the Five-striped Sparrow. *Living Bird* 18:95–110.

Millsap, B. A. 1981. Distributional status of falconiformes in west-central Arizona, with notes on ecology, reproductive success, and management. Tech. Note 355, US Department of Interior, Bureau Land Management, Denver, CO.

Millsap, B. A. 1998a. Barn Owl (*Tyto alba*). In *Raptors of Arizona* (R. Glinski, ed.). Tucson: University of Arizona Press.

Millsap, B. A. 1998b. Long-eared Owl (*Asio otus*). In *Raptors of Arizona* (R. Glinski, ed.). Tucson: University of Arizona Press.

Millsap, B. A., and R. R. Johnson. 1988. Status report: Ferruginous Pygmy-Owl. In Southwest Raptor Management Symposium and Workshop Proceedings (R. Glinski, B. Pendleton, M. Moss, M. La Franc Jr., B. Millsap, and S. Hoffman, eds.). Washington, DC: National Wildlife Federation.

Mirarchi, R. E., and T. S. Baskett. 1994. Mourning Dove (*Zenaida macroura*). In *Birds of North America* 117 (A. Poole and F. Gill, eds.). Philadelphia: Academy of Natural Sciences; Washington, DC: American Ornithologists' Union.

Mishaga, R. J. 1974. Notes on asynchronous hatching and nestling mortality in White-necked Ravens. *Wilson Bull.* 86:174–176.

Mitchell, R. M. 1977. Breeding biology of the Double-crested Cormorant on Utah lake. *Great Basin Naturalist* 37:1–23.

Mock, D. W. 1978. Pair-formation displays of the Great Egret. *Condor* 80:159–172.

Monson, G. 1948. Egrets nesting along Colorado River. *Auk* 65:603–607.

Monson, G. 1949. Recent notes from the lower Colorado River valley of Arizona and California. *Condor* 51:262–265.

Monson, G. 1972. Unique birds and mammals of the Coronado National Forest. Report prepared for Coronado National Forest, Tucson.

Monson, G. 1998a. Ferruginous Pygmy-Owl (*Glaucidium brasilianum*). In *Raptors of Arizona* (R. Glinski, ed.). Tucson: University of Arizona Press.

Monson, G. 1998b. Northern Pygmy-Owl (*Glaucidium gnoma*). In *Raptors of Arizona* (R. Glinski, ed.). Tucson: University of Arizona Press.

Monson, G. 1998c. Red-tailed Hawk (*Buteo jamaicensis*). In *Raptors of Arizona*. (R. Glinski, ed.) Tucson: University of Arizona Press.

Monson, G. 1998d. Whiskered Screech-Owl (*Otus trichopsis*). In *Raptors of Arizona* (R. Glinski, ed.). Tucson: University of Arizona Press.

Monson, G. 1998e. White-tailed Hawk (*Buteo albicaudatus*). In *Raptors of Arizona* (R. Glinski, ed.). Tucson: University of Arizona Press.

Monson, G., and A. Phillips. 1981. *Annotated Checklist of the Birds of Arizona*. Tucson: University of Arizona Press.

Moore, W. S. 1995. Northern Flicker (*Colaptes auratus*). In *Birds of North America* 166 (A. Poole and F. Gill, eds.). Philadelphia: Academy of Natural Sciences; Washington, DC: American Ornithologists' Union.

Moore, W. S., and W. D. Koenig. 1986. Comparative reproductive success of Yellow-shafted, Red-shafted, and hybrid flickers across a hybrid zone. *Auk* 103:42–51.

Morrison, J. L. 1996. Crested Caracara (*Caracara plancus*). In *Birds of North America* 249 (A. Poole and F. Gill, eds.). Philadelphia: Academy of Natural Sciences; Washington, DC: American Ornithologists' Union.

Morse, R. J. 1986. Fire in the pines. *Birding* 18(4):220–224.

Morse, R. J., and G. Monson. 1985. Flame-colored Tanager in Arizona. *Am. Birds* 39:843–844.

Moskoff, W. 2002. Green Kingfisher (*Chloroceryle americana*). In *Birds of North America* 621 (A. Poole and F. Gill, eds.). Philadelphia: Birds of North America.

Mowbray, T. B., C. R. Ely, J. S. Sedinger, and R. E. Trost. 2002. Canada Goose (*Branta canadensis*). In *Birds of North America* 682 (A. Poole and F. Gill, eds.). Philadelphia: Birds of North America.

Mueller, A. J. 1992. Inca Dove (*Columbina inca*). In *Birds of North America* 28 (A. Poole, P. Stettenheim, and F. Gill, eds.). Philadelphia: Academy of Natural Sciences; Washington, DC: American Ornithologists' Union.

Mueller, H. 1999. Common Snipe (*Gallinago gallinago*). In *Birds of North America* 417 (A. Poole and F. Gill, eds.). Philadelphia: Birds of North America.

Mugaas, J. N., and J. R. King. 1981. Annual variation of daily energy expenditure by the Black-billed Magpie: A study of thermal and behavioral energetics. *Stud. Avian Biol.* 5.

Muller, M. J., and R. W. Storer. 1999. Pied-billed Grebe (*Podilymbus podiceps*). In *Birds of North America* 410 (A. Poole and F. Gill, eds.). Philadelphia: Birds of North America.

Murphy, E. C., and W. A. Lehnhausen. 1998. Density and foraging ecology of woodpeckers following a stand-replacement fire. *J. Wildlife Management* 62:1359–1372.

Myers, T. L. 1980. Observations on the nesting of waterfowl at Coleman Lake (Coconino Co.), 1980. Arizona Cooperative Wildlife Research Unit, University of Arizona.

Myers, T. L. 1982. Ecology of nesting waterfowl on Anderson Mesa in north central Arizona. M.S. Thesis, University of Arizona.

Neff, J. A. 1940. Notes on nesting and other habits of the Western White-winged Dove. *J. Wildlife Management* 4:279–290.

Neff, J. A. 1947. Habits, food, and economic status of the Band-tailed Pigeon. US Fish and Wildlife Service North American Fauna 58.

Nelson, D. L. 1998. Snowy Plover (*Charadrius alexandrinus*). In *Colorado Breeding Bird Atlas* (H. Kingery, ed.). Denver: Colorado Wildlife Heritage Foundation.

Newman, J. D. 1968. Arizona Black-chinned Sparrow. In Life histories of cardinals, grosbeaks, buntings, towhees, finches, sparrows, and their allies (O. L. Austin Jr., ed.). *US Nat. Mus. Bull.* 237.

Newton, I. 1979. *Population Ecology of Raptors*. Vermilion, SD: Buteo Books.

Nice, M. M. 1962. Development of behavior in precocial bird. *Trans. Linn. Soc. N.Y.* 8:1–211.

Nicholson, D. J. 1937. Notes on the breeding of the ground dove in Florida. *Wilson Bull.* 49:101–114.

Nickell, W. P. 1951. Studies of habitats, territory and nests of the Eastern Goldfinch. *Auk* 68:447–470.

Nocedal, J., and M. S. Ficken. 1998. Bridled Titmouse (*Baeolophus wollweberi*). In *Birds of North America* 375 (A. Poole and F. Gill, eds.). Philadelphia: Birds of North America.

Nolan, V. 1960. Breeding behavior of the Bell's Vireo in southern Indiana. *Condor* 62:225–244.

Nolan, V., Jr., E. D. Ketterson, D. A. Cristol, C. M. Rogers, E. D. Clotfelter, R. C. Titus, S. J. Schoech, and E. Snajdr. 2002. Dark-eyed Junco (*Junco hyemalis*). In *Birds of North America* 716 (A. Poole and F. Gill, eds.). Philadelphia: Birds of North America.

Oberholser, H. C. 1942. Description of a new Arizona race of the grasshopper sparrow. *Proc. Biol. Soc. Washington* 55:15–16.

Oberholser, H. C. 1974. *The Bird Life of Texas*, vol. 1. Austin: University of Texas Press.

Ohmart, R. D. 1966. Breeding record of the Cassin Sparrow (*Aimophila cassinii*) in Arizona. *Condor* 68:400.

Ohmart, R. D. 1969. Physiological and ethological adaptations of the Rufous-winged Sparrow (*Aimophila carpalis*) to a desert environment. Ph.D. diss., University of Arizona, Tucson.

Ohmart, R. D. 1973. Observations on the breeding adaptations of the roadrunner. *Condor* 75:140–149.

Olson, C. R., and T. E. Martin. 1999. Virginia's Warbler (*Vermivora virginiae*). In *Birds of North America* 477 (A. Poole and F. Gill, eds.). Philadelphia: Birds of North America.

Orians, G. H., and M. F. Willson 1964. Interspecific territories of birds. *Ecology* 45:736–744.

Oring, L. W. 1964. Behavior and ecology of certain ducks during the postbreeding period. *J. Wildlife Management* 8:223–233.

Oring, L. W., E. M. Gray, and J. M Reed. 1997. Spotted Sandpiper (*Actitis macularia*). In *Birds of North America* 289 (A. Poole and F. Gill, eds.). Philadelphia: Academy of Natural Sciences.

Orr, R. T. 1968. Cassin's Finch. In Life histories of North American cardinals, grosbeaks, buntings, towhees, finches, sparrows, and allies, pt. 1 (O. L. Austin Jr., ed.). *US Nat. Mus. Bull.* 237.

Ortega, D. P., and A. Cruz. 1991. A comparative study of cowbird parasitism in Yellow-headed Blackbirds and Red-winged Blackbirds. *Auk* 108:16–24.

Overturf, J. E. 1979. The effects of forest fire on breeding bird populations of ponderosa pine forests of northern Arizona. M.S. thesis, Northern Arizona University, Flagstaff.

Owre, O. T., and P. O. Northington. 1961. Indication of the sense of smell in the Turkey Vulture, *Cathartes aura* (Linnaeus), from feeding tests. *Am. Midl. Nat.* 66:200–205.

Page, G. W., J. S. Warriner, J. C. Warriner, and P. W. C. Paton. 1995. Snowy Plover (*Charadrius alexandrinus*). In *Birds of North America* 154 (A. Poole and F. Gill, eds.). Philadelphia: Academy of Natural Sciences; Washington, DC: American Ornithologists' Union.

Paine, R. T. 1968. Brewer's Sparrow. In Life histories of North American cardinals, grosbeaks, buntings, towhees, finches, sparrows, and allies (O. L. Austin Jr., ed.). *US Nat. Mus. Bull.* 237, Pt. 2.

Palmer, R. S. 1962. *Handbook of North American Birds*, vol. 1. New Haven: Yale University Press.

Palmer, R. S. 1976. *Handbook of North American Birds*, vol. 3. New Haven: Yale University Press.

Palmer, R. S. 1988. *Handbook of North American Birds*, vol. 4. New Haven: Yale University Press.

Pantle, D. 1998a. Swainson's Thrush (*Catharus ustulatus*). In *Colorado Breeding Bird Atlas* (H. Kingery ed.). Denver: Colorado Wildlife Heritage Foundation.

Pantle, D. 1998b. Tree Swallow (*Tachycineta bicolor*). In *Colorado Breeding Bird Atlas* (H. Kingery, ed.). Denver: Colorado Wildlife Heritage Foundation.

Paradzick, C. E., R. F. Davidson, J. W. Rourke, M. W. Sumner, A. M. Wartell, and T. D. McCarthey. 2000. Southwestern willow flycatcher 1999 survey and nest monitoring report. Nongame and Endangered Wildlife Program Technical Report 151, Arizona Game and Fish Department.

Parker, J.W. 1999. Mississippi Kite (*Ictinia mississippiensis*). In *Birds of North America* 402 (A. Poole and F. Gill, eds.). Philadelphia: Birds of North America.

Parsons, K. C., and J. Burger. 1981. Nestling growth in early- and late-nesting Black-crowned Night-Herons. *Colonial Waterbirds* 4:120–125.

Parsons, K. C., and T. L. Master. 2000. Snowy egret (*Egretta thula*). In *Birds of North America* 489 (A. Poole and F. Gill, eds.). Philadelphia: Academy of Natural Sciences; Washington, DC: American Ornithologists' Union.

Paton, P. W. C. 1995. Breeding biology of Snowy Plovers at Great Salt Lake, Utah. *Wilson Bull.* 107:275–288.

Payne, R. B. 1992. Indigo Bunting (*Passerina cyanea*). In *Birds of North America* 4 (A. Poole, Peter Stettenheim, and F. Gill, eds.). Philadelphia: Academy of Natural Sciences; Washington, DC; American Ornithologists' Union.

Peck, G. K., and R. D. James. 1987. *Breeding Birds of Ontario: Nidology and Distribution*, vol. 2. Toronto: Royal Ontario Museum of Life Sciences.

Peer, B. D., and E. K. Bollinger. 1997. Common Grackle (*Quiscalus quiscula*). In *Birds of North America* 271. (A. Poole and F. Gill, eds.). Philadelphia: Academy of Natural Sciences; Washington, DC: American Ornithologists' Union.

Peterjohn, B. G. 1989. *The Birds of Ohio*. Bloomington: Indiana University Press.

Peterjohn, B. G., J. R. Sauer, and W. A. Link. 1996. The 1994 and 1995 summary of the North American Breeding Bird Survey. *Bird Popul.* 3:48–66.

Petersen, K. L., and L. B. Best. 1985a. Brewer's Sparrow nest-site characteristics in a sagebrush community. *J. Field Ornithol.* 56:23–27.

Petersen, K. L., and L. B. Best. 1985b. Nest-site selection by Sage Sparrows. *Condor* 87:217–221.

Petersen, K. L., and L. B. Best. 1986. Diets of nestling Sage Sparrows and Brewer's Sparrows in an Idaho sagebrush community. *J. Field Ornithol.* 57:283–294.

Pfister, R. 1984. Behavior of a breeding pair of Curve-billed Thrashers (*Toxostoma curvirostre*) and their progeny. Department of Ecology and Evolutionary Biology, University of Arizona.

Phillips, A., J. Marshall, and G. Monson. 1964. *The Birds of Arizona*. Tucson: University of Arizona Press.

Phillips, A. R. 1940. Two new breeding birds for the United States. *Auk* 57:117–118.

Phillips, A. R. 1950. The Great-tailed Grackles of the Southwest. *Condor* 52:78–81.

Phillips, A. R. 1968. Scott's Rufous-crowned Sparrow (*Aimophila ruficeps scottii*). In Life Histories of North American cardinals, grosbeaks, buntings, towhees, finches, sparrows, and allies, pt. 2 (O. L. Austin Jr., ed.). *US Nat. Mus. Bull.* 237.

Phillips, A. R., and R. P. Farfan. 1993. Distribution, migration, ecology, and relationships of the Five-striped Sparrow, *Aimophila quinquestriata*. *Western Birds* 24:65–72.

Phillips, A. R., Speich, S., and W. Harrison. 1973. Black-capped Gnatcatcher, a new breeding bird for the United States; with a key to the North American species of *Polioptila*. *Auk* 90:257–262.

Pickwell, G., and E. Smith. 1938. The Texas Nighthawk in its summer home. *Condor* 40:193–215.

Piest, L. A. 1981. Evaluation of waterfowl habitat improvements on the Apache-Sitgreaves National Forest, Arizona. Final Report. USDA Forest Service, Southwestern Region, Albuquerque.

Piest, L. A. 1982. Evaluation of waterfowl habitat improvements in the Apache-Sitgreaves National Forest, Arizona. M.S. thesis, University of Arizona.

Piest, L. A. 1983. First nesting records of Wilson's Phalarope in Arizona. *Western Birds* 14:111.

Piest, L. A., and L. K. Sowls 1981. Records of American Wigeon breeding in Arizona. *Western Birds* 12:54.

Piest, L. A., and L. K. Sowls. 1985. Breeding duck use of a sewage marsh in Arizona. *J. Wildlife Management* 49:580–585.

Pitelka, F. A. 1944. White-throated Swift breeding with Cliff Swallows at Berkeley, California. *Condor* 46:34–35.

Pitocchelli, J. 1995. MacGillivray's Warbler (*Oporornis tolmiei*). In *Birds of North America*. 159 (A. Poole and F. Gill, eds.). Philadelphia: Academy of Natural Sciences; Washington, DC: American Ornithologists' Union.

Platt, J. B. 1976. Sharp-shinned Hawk nesting and nest site selection in Utah. *Condor* 78:102–103.

Pleasants, B. Y., and D. J. Alba 2001. Hooded Oriole (*Icterus cucullatus*). In *Birds of North America* 568 (A. Poole and F. Gill, eds.). Philadelphia: Birds of North America.

Ponton, D. A. 1983. Nest site selection by Peregrine Falcons. *Raptor Res.* 17:27–28.

Poole, A. F., R. O. Bierregaard, and M. S. Martell. 2002. Osprey (*Pandion haliaetus*). In *Birds of North America* 683 (A. Poole and F. Gill, eds.). Philadelphia: Birds of North America.
Porter, D. K., M. A. Strong, J. B. Giezentanner, and R. A. Ryder. 1975. Nest ecology, productivity, and growth of the Loggerhead Shrike on the shortgrass prairie. *Southwestern Naturalist* 19:429–436.
Potter, K. M. 1998. Double-crested Cormorant. In *Colorado Breeding Bird Atlas*, (H. Kingery, ed.). Denver: Colorado Wildlife Heritage Foundation.
Potter, P. E. 1972. Territorial behavior in Savannah Sparrows in southeastern Michigan. *Wilson Bull.* 84:48–59.
Power, H. W. 1966. Biology of the Mountain Bluebird in Montana. *Condor* 68:351–371.
Power, H. W., and M. P. Lombardo. 1996. Mountain Bluebird (*Sialia currucoides*). In *Birds of North America*. 222 (A. Poole and F. Gill, eds.). Philadelphia: Academy of Natural Sciences; Washington, DC: American Ornithologists' Union.
Powers, D. R. 1996. Magnificent Hummingbird (*Eugenes fulgens*). In *Birds of North America* 221 (A. Poole and F. Gill, eds.). Philadelphia: Academy of Natural Sciences; Washington, DC: American Ornithologists' Union.
Powers, D. R., and S. M. Wethington. 1999. Broad-billed Hummingbird (*Cynanthus latirostris*). In *Birds of North America* 430 (A. Poole and F. Gill, eds.). Philadelphia: Birds of North America.
Pratt, H. M., and D. W. Winkler. 1985. Clutch size, timing of laying, and reproductive success in a colony of Great Blue Herons and Great Egrets. *Auk* 102:49–63.
Pravosudov, V. V., and T. C. Grubb Jr. 1993. White-breasted Nuthatch (*Sitta carolinensis*). In *Birds of North America* 54 (A. Poole and F. Gill, eds.). Philadelphia: Academy of Natural Sciences; Washington, DC: American Ornithologists' Union.
Price, F. E., and C. E. Bock 1983. Population ecology of the Dipper (*Cinclus mexicanus*) in the Front Range of Colorado. Stud. Avian Biol. 7.
Price, J., S. Droege, and A. Price. 1995. *The Summer Atlas of North American Birds*. London: Academic Press.
Price, J. T., and T. L. Root. 2001. Climate change and Neotropical migrants. *Transactions of the 66th North American Wildlife and Natural Resources Conference* 66:371–379.
Proudfoot, G. A. 1996. Natural history of the Cactus Ferruginous Pygmy-Owl. M.S. thesis, Texas A&M University–Kingsville.
Proudfoot, G. A., and R. R. Johnson. 2000. Ferruginous Pygmy-Owl (*Glaucidium brasilianum*). In *Birds of North America* 498 (A. Poole and F. Gill, eds.). Philadelphia: Birds of North America.
Proudfoot, G. A., D. A. Sherry, and S. Johnson. 2000. Cactus Wren (*Campylorhynchus brunneicapillys*). In *Birds of North America* 558 (A. Poole and F. Gill, eds.). Philadelphia: Birds of North America.
Pulich, W. M, Sr., and W. M. Pulich Jr. 1963. The nesting of the Lucifer Hummingbird in the United States. *Auk* 80:370–371.
Purdue, J. R. 1976a. Adaptations of the Snowy Plover on the Great Salt Plains. Oklahoma. Southwest Nat. 21:347–357.
Purdue, J. R. 1976b. Thermal environment of the nest and related parental behavior in Snowy Plovers, *Charadrius alexandrinus*. *Condor* 78:180–185.
Pyle, P., S. N. G. Howell, R. P. Yunick, and D. F. DeSante. 1987. *Identification Guide to North American Passerines*. Bolinas, CA: Slate Creek Press.
Rabenold, P. P. 1986. Family associations in communally roosting Black Vultures. *Auk* 103:32–41.
Radke, E. L., and J. Klimosewski. 1977. Late fledging date for Harris' Hawk. *Wilson Bull.* 89:470–471.
Rand, A. L., and R. M. Rand. 1943. Breeding notes on the Phainopepla. *Auk* 60:333–340.
Rashid, S. 1999. Northern Pygmy Owls in Rocky Mountain National Park. Colo. Field. Ornithol. 33:94–101.
Rea, A. M. 1983a. Cathartid affinities: A brief overview. In *Vulture Biology and Management* (S. R. Wilbur and J. A. Jackson, eds.) Berkeley: University of California Press.
Rea, A. M. 1983b. *Once a River: Bird Life and Habitat Change on the Middle Gila*. Tucson: University of Arizona Press.
Rea, A. M. 1998a. Black Vulture. In *Raptors of Arizona*, (R. Glinski, ed.). Tucson: University of Arizona Press.
Rea, A. M. 1998b. Turkey Vulture. In *Raptors of Arizona* (R. Glinski, ed.). Tucson: University of Arizona Press.
Reese, K. P., and J. A. Kadlec. 1985. Influence of high density and parental age on the habitat selection and reproduction of Black-billed Magpies. *Condor* 87:96–105.
Rendell, W. B., and R. J. Robertson. 1989. Nest-site characteristics, reproductive success and cavity availability for Tree Swallows breeding in natural cavities. *Condor* 91:875–885.
Repking, C. F. 1975. Distribution and habitat requirements of the Black Rail (*Laterallus jamaicensis*), along the lower Colorado River. M.S. Thesis, Arizona State University, Tempe.
Repking, C. F., and R. D. Ohmart. 1977. Distribution and density of Black Rail populations along the lower Colorado River. *Condor* 79:486–489.
Rett, E. Z. 1946. An unusual nest of the White-throated Swift. *Condor* 48:141.
Reynolds, R., and B. Linkhart. 1998. Flammulated Owl (*Otus flammeolus*). In *Raptors of Arizona* (R. Glinski, ed.). Tucson: University of Arizona Press.
Reynolds, R. T. 1983. Management of western coniferous forest habitat for nesting Accipiter hawks. USDA Forest Service Gen. Tech. Rep. RM-102.
Reynolds, R. T., S. M. Joy, and D. G. Leslie. 1994. Nest productivity, fidelity, and spacing of Northern Goshawks in northern Arizona. *Stud. Avian Biol.* 16:106–113.
Reynolds, R. T., E. C. Meslow, and H. M. Wight. 1982. Nesting habits of coexisting Accipiter in Oregon. *J. Wildlife Management* 46:124–138.
Reynolds, R. T., and T. D. Rich. 1978. Reproductive ecology of the Sage Thrasher (*Oreoscoptes montanus*) on the Snake River Plain in south-central Idaho. *Auk* 95:580–582.
Reynolds, R. T., T. D. Rich, and D. A. Stephens. 1999. Sage Thrasher (*Oreoscoptes montanus*). In *Birds of North America* 463 (A. Poole and F. Gill, eds.). Philadelphia: Birds of North America.
Reynolds, R. T., and H. M. Wight. 1978. Distribution, density and productivity of Accipiter hawks breeding in Oregon. *Wilson Bull.* 90:182–196.
Rich, T. D. 1978a. Nest placement in Sage Thrashers. *Wilson Bull.* 90:303.
Rich, T. D. 1978b. Cowbird parasitism of Sage and Brewer's sparrows. *Condor* 80:348.
Rich, T. D. 1980. Nest placement in Sage Thrashers, Sage Sparrow and Brewer's Sparrows. *Wilson Bull.* 92:362–368.
Rich, T. D. 1985. A Sage Thrasher nest with constructed shading platform. *Murrelet* 66:18–19.
Richinson, G. 1938. Breeding biology of the Black-headed Grosbeak in northern Utah. *Western Birds* 14:159–167.
Ricklefs, R. E. 1975. Patterns of growth in birds III. Growth and development of the Cactus Wren. *Condor* 77:34–45.
Rising, J. D. 1996. A guide to the identification and natural history of the Sparrows of the United States and Canada. San Diego: Academic Press.
Rising, J. D., and P. L. Williams. 1999. Bullock's Oriole (*Icterus bullockii*). In *Birds of North America* 416 (A. Poole and F. Gill, eds.). Philadelphia: Academy of Natural Sciences, and Washington, DC: American Ornithologists' Union.
Ritchison, G. 1999. *Downy Woodpecker*. Mechanicsburg, PA: Stackpole Books.
Ritter, L. V. 1983. Nesting ecology of Scrub-Jays in Chico, California. *Western Birds* 14:147–158.
Robbins, C. S., and E. A. T. Blom. 1996. *Atlas of the Breeding Birds of Maryland and the District of Columbia*. Pittsburgh: University of Pittsburgh Press.
Robbins, C. S., D. Bystrak, and P. H. Geissler. 1986. The breeding bird survey: Its first fifteen years, 1965–1979. Resource Publ. 157, US Fish and Wildlife Service.
Robertson, H. A. 1990. Breeding of collared doves *Streptopelia decaocto* in rural Oxfordshire, England. *Bird Study* 37:73–83.
Robertson, R. J., Stutchbury, B. J., and R. R. Cohen. 1992. Tree Swallow. In *Birds of North America* 11 (A. Poole, P. Stettenheim, and F. Gill, eds.). Philadelphia: Academy of Natural Sciences; Washington, DC: American Ornithologists' Union.
Robichaux, R. H. (ed). 1999. *Ecology of Sonoran Desert Plants and Plant Communities*. Tucson: University of Arizona Press.
Robinson, J. A., L. W. Oring, J. P. Skorupa, and R. Boettcher. 1997. American Avocet (*Recurvirostra americana*). In *Birds of North America* 275 (A. Poole and F. Gill, eds.). Philadelphia: Academy of Natural Sciences; Washington, DC: American Ornithologists' Union.
Robinson, J. A., J. M. Reed, J. P. Skorupa, and L. W. Oring. 1999. Black-necked Stilt (*Himantopus mexicanus*). In *Birds of North America* 449 (A. Poole and F. Gill, eds.). Philadelphia: Birds of North America.

Robinson, W. D. 1996. Summer Tanager (*Piranga rubra*). In *Birds of North America* 248 (A. Poole and F. Gill, eds.). Philadelphia: Academy of Natural Sciences; Washington, DC: American Ornithologists' Union.

Rohwer, F. C., W. P. Johnson, and E. R. Loos. 2002. Blue-winged Teal (*Anas discors*). In *Birds of North America* 625 (A. Poole and F. Gill, eds.). Philadelphia: Birds of North America.

Romagosa, C. M., and T. McEneaney. 1999. Eurasian Collared-Dove in North America and the Caribbean. North American Birds 53:348–353.

Root, R. B. 1969. The behavior and reproductive success of the Blue-gray Gnatcatcher. *Condor* 71:16–31.

Rosenberg, G. H. 2001. Arizona Bird Committee report:1996–1999 records. *Western Birds* 32:50–70.

Rosenberg, G. H., and J. L. Witzeman. 1998. Arizona Bird Committee report, 1974–1996: Part 1 (Nonpasserines). *Western Birds* 29:119–224.

Rosenberg, G. H., and J. L. Witzeman. 1999. Arizona Bird committee report, 1974–1996: Part 2 (Passerines). *Western Birds* 30:94–120.

Rosenberg, G. H., and S. B. Terrill. 1986. The avifauna of Apache County, Arizona. *Western Birds* 17:171–187.

Rosenberg, K. V., R. D. Ohmart, W. C. Hunter, and B. W. Anderson. 1991. *Birds of the Lower Colorado River Valley*. Tucson: University of Arizona Press.

Rosenfield, R. N., and J. Bielefeldt. 1993 Cooper's Hawk (*Accipiter cooperii*). In *Birds of North America* 75 (A. Poole and F. Gill, eds.). Philadelphia: Academy of Natural Sciences; Washington, DC: American Ornithologists' Union.

Rosenstock, S. S. 1996. Habitat relationships of breeding birds in northern Arizona ponderosa pine and pine-oak woodlands. Arizona Game and Fish Department, Technical Report 23.

Rotenberry, J. T., M. A. Patten, and K. L. Preston. 1999. Brewer's Sparrow (*Spizella breweri*). In *Birds of North America* 390 (A. Poole and F. Gill, eds.). Philadelphia: Academy of Natural Sciences; Washington, DC: American Ornithologists' Union.

Rothstein, S. I. 1977. Cowbird parasitism and egg recognition of the Northern Oriole. *Wilson Bull.* 89:21–32.

Rourke, J. W., T. D. McCarthey, R. F. Davidson, A. M. Santaniello. 1999. Southwestern willow flycatcher nest monitoring protocol. Nongame and Endangered Wildlife Program Technical Report 144, Arizona Game and Fish Department.

Rowley, J. S. 1962. Nesting of the birds of Morelos, Mexico. *Condor* 64:253–272.

Royall, W. C., Jr. 1966. Breeding of the Starling in central Arizona. *Condor* 68:195–205.

Russell, H. N., and A. M. Woodbury. 1941. Nesting of the Gray Flycatcher. *Auk* 58:28–37.

Russell, S. M. 1996. Anna's Hummingbird (*Calypte anna*). In *Birds of North America* 226 (A. Poole and F. Gill, eds.). Philadelphia: Academy of Natural Sciences; Washington, DC: American Ornithologists' Union.

Russell, S. M., and G. Monson. 1998. *The Birds of Sonora*. Tucson: University of Arizona Press.

Rust, H. J. 1947. Migration and nesting of nighthawks in northern Idaho. *Condor* 49:177–188.

Ryan, T. P., and C. T. Collins. 2000. White-throated Swift (*Aeronautes saxatalis*). In *Birds of North America* 526 (A. Poole and F. Gill, eds.). Philadelphia: Academy of Natural Sciences; Washington, DC: American Ornithologists' Union.

Ryder, R. A. 1998. Snowy Egret. In *Colorado Breeding Bird Atlas* (H. Kingery, ed.). Denver: Colorado Wildlife Heritage Foundation.

Ryser, F. A., Jr. 1985. *Birds of the Great Basin*. Reno: University of Nevada Press.

Salata, L. R. 1983. Status of the Least Bell's Vireo on Camp Pendleton, California: Research done in 1983. Final Rep., US Fish and Wildlife Service.

Sallabanks, R., and F. C. James. 1999. American Robin (*Turdus migratorius*). In *Birds of North America* 462 (A. Poole and F. Gill, eds.). Philadelphia: Birds of North America.

Samson, F. B. 1976. Territory, breeding density, and fall departure in Cassin's Finch. *Auk* 93:477–497.

Sauer, J. R., and S. Droege. 1990. Wood Duck population trends from the North American breeding bird survey. In *Proceedings of the 1988 North American Wood Duck Symposium* (L. Fredrickson et al., eds.). St. Louis.

Sauer, J. R., J. E. Hines, and J. Fallon. 2001. The North American Breeding Bird Survey Results and Analysis 1966–2000. Version 2001.2. Laurel, MD: Patuxent Wildlife Res. Center.

Sauer, J. R., J. E. Hines, and J. Fallon. 2002. The North American Breeding Bird Survey, Results and Analysis 1966–2001. Version 2002.1. Laurel, MD: Patuxent Wildlife Res. Center.

Sauer, J. R., S. Orsillo, and B. G. Peterjohn. 1995. Geographic patterns and population trends of breeding and wintering Loggerhead Shrikes in North America. *Proc. West. Found. Vert. Zool.* 6:128–141.

Sauer, J. R., B. G. Peterjohn, S. Schwartz, and J. E. Hines. 1996. The North American Breeding Bird Survey home page. Version 95.1. Laurel, MD: Patuxent Wildlife Res. Center.

Saunders, A. A. 1910. Bird notes from southwestern Montana. *Condor* 12:195–204.

Schemnitz, S. D. 1961. Ecology of the Scaled Quail in the Oklahoma panhandle. Wildl. Monogr. 8.

Schemnitz, S. D. 1994. Scaled Quail (*Callipepla squamata*). In *Birds of North America* 106 (A. Poole and F. Gill, eds.). Philadelphia: Academy of Natural Sciences; Washington, DC: American Ornithologists' Union.

Schmid, M. K., and G. F. Rogers. 1988. Trends in fire occurrence in the Arizona upland subdivisions of the Sonoran Desert, 1955–1983. *Southwestern Naturalist* 33:437–444.

Schnase, J. L., W. E. Grant, T. C. Maxwell, and J. J. Leggett. 1991. Time and energy budgets of Cassin's Sparrow (*Aimophila cassinii*) during the breeding season: Evaluation through modelling. *Ecol. Modelling* 55:285–319.

Schnell, J. H. 1979. Black Hawk (*Buteogallus anthracinus*). Tech Note TN-329. US Department of Interior, Bureau of Land Management, Denver.

Schnell, J. H. 1994. Common Black-Hawk (*Buteogallus anthracinus*). In *Birds of North America* 122 (A. Poole and F. Gill, eds.). Philadelphia: Academy of Natural Sciences; Washington, DC: American Ornithologists' Union.

Schnell, J. H. 1998. Common Black-Hawk (*Buteo anthracinus*). In *Raptors of Arizona* (R. Glinski, ed.) Tucson: University of Arizona Press.

Schukman, J. M., and B. O. Wolf. 1998. Say's Phoebe (*Sayornis saya*). In *Birds of North America* 374 (A. Poole and F. Gill, eds.). Philadelphia: Birds of North America.

Schwertner, T. W., H. A. Mathewson, J. A. Roberson, M. Small, and G. L Waggerman. 2002. White-winged Dove (*Zenaida asiatica*). In *Birds of North America* 710 (A. Poole and F. Gill, eds.). Philadelphia: Birds of North America.

Sclater, W. H. 1912. *A History of the Birds of Colorado*. London: Witherby and Co.

Scott, A. C., and M. Bekoff. 1991. Breeding behavior of Evening Grosbeaks. *Condor* 93:71–81.

Scott, D. M. 1977. Cowbird parasitism on the Gray Catbird at London, Ontario. *Auk* 94:18–27.

Scott, P. E. 1993. A closer look: Lucifer Hummingbird. *Birding* 25:245–251.

Scott, P. E. 1994a. Impact on Costa's Hummingbird of extended flowering by *Justicia californica*. Abstracts of 1994 N. Am. Ornithol. Conf., Missoula, MT.

Scott, P. E. 1994b. Lucifer Hummingbird (*Calothorax lucifer*). In *Birds of North America* 134 (A. Poole and F. Gill, eds.). Philadelphia: Academy of Natural Sciences; Washington, DC: American Ornithologists' Union.

Scott, W. E. D. 1885. On the breeding habits of some Arizona birds. *Auk* 2:159–165.

Sedgwick, J. A. 1993. Dusky Flycatcher (*Empidonax oberholseri*). In *Birds of North America* 78 (A. Poole and F. Gill, eds.). Philadelphia: Academy of Natural Sciences; Washington, DC: American Ornithologists' Union.

Sedgwick, J. A. 1994. Hammond's Flycatcher (*Empidonax hammondii*). In *Birds of North America* 109 (A. Poole and F. Gill, eds.). Philadelphia: Academy of Natural Sciences; Washington, DC: American Ornithologists' Union.

Sheppard, J. M. 1996. Le Conte's Thrasher (*Toxostoma lecontei*). In *Birds of North America* 230 (A. Poole and F. Gill, eds.). Philadelphia: Academy of Natural Sciences; Washington, DC: American Ornithologists' Union.

Short, L. L. 1971. Systematics and behavior of some North American woodpeckers, genus *Picoides* (Aves). *Bull. Am. Mus. Nat. Hist.* 145.

Short, L. L. 1974a. Habits and interactions of North American Three-toed Woodpeckers (*Picoides arcticus* and *Picoides tridactylus*). *Am. Mus. Novit.* 2547:1–42.

Short, L. L. 1974b. Nesting of southern Sonoran birds during the summer rainy season. *Condor* 76:21–32.

Short, L. L. 1982. *Woodpeckers of the World*. Monogr. Ser. 4, Delaware Museum of Natural History, Greenville.

Sibley, C. G., and D. A. West. 1959. Hybridization in the Rufous-sided Towhees of the Great Plains. *Auk* 76:326–338.

Siegel, J. J. 1989. An evaluation of the minimum habitat quality standards for birds in old-growth ponderosa pine forests, northern Arizona. M.S. thesis, University of Arizona.

Simpson, J. M., and J. R. Werner. 1958. Some recent bird records from the Salt River Valley, central Arizona. *Condor* 60:68–70.

Skinner, M. P. 1916. The nutcrackers of Yellowstone Park. *Condor* 18:62–64.

Skutch, A. F. 1945. Incubation and nestling periods of birds. *Auk* 62:8–37.

Skutch, A. F. 1954. Life history of the Tropical Kingbird. *Proc. Linn. Soc. N.Y.* 63–65:21–38.

Skutch, A. F. 1960. Life histories of Central American birds II. *Pac. Coast Avifauna* 34.

Skutch, A. F. 1983. *Birds of Tropical America*. Austin: University of Texas Press.

Sloane, S. A. 2001. Bushtit (*Psaltriparus minimus*). In *Birds of North America* 598 (A. Poole and F. Gill, eds.). Philadelphia: Birds of North America.

Smallwood, J. A., and D. M. Bird. 2002. American Kestrel (*Falco sparverius*). In *Birds of North America* 602 (A. Poole and F. Gill, eds.). Philadelphia: Birds of North America.

Smith, A. P. 1908. Some data and records from the Whetstone Mountains, Arizona. *Condor* 10:75–78.

Smith, C. (ed.). 1990. *Handbook for Atlasing American Breeding Birds*. Woodstock, VT: Vermont Institute of Natural Science.

Smith, D. G., and J. R. Murphy. 1978. Biology of the Ferruginous Hawk in central Utah. *Sociobiology* 3:79–98.

Smith, D. G., C. R. Wilson, and H. H. Frost. 1974. History and ecology of a colony of barn owls in Utah. *Condor* 76:131–136.

Smith, D. G., J. R. Murphy, and N. D. Woffinden. 1981. Relationships between jackrabbit abundance and Ferruginous Hawk reproduction. *Condor* 83:52–56.

Smith, K. G. 1982. On habitat selection of Williamson's and "Red-naped" Yellow-bellied Sapsuckers. *Southwestern Naturalist* 27:464–466.

Smith, P. W. 1987. The Eurasian Collared-Dove arrives in the Americas. *American Birds* 41:1370–1379.

Smith, R. L. 1968. Grasshopper Sparrow. In Life histories of North American cardinals, grosbeaks, bunting, towhees, finches, sparrows and allies, pt. 2 (O. L. Austin Jr., ed.). *US Nat. Mus. Bull.* 237.

Smith, R. L., and L. D. Flake. 1985. Movements and habitats of brood-rearing Wood Ducks on a prairie river. *J. Wildlife Management* 49:437–442.

Smith, V. A. 1992. Notes on nesting Three-toed Woodpeckers in northern Utah. *Utah Birds* 8:61–65.

Smith, W. P. 1943. Some Yellow Warbler observations. *Bird-Banding* 14:57–63.

Snyder, H. A. 1998. Northern Harrier (*Circus cyaneus*). In *Raptors of Arizona* (R. Glinski, ed.) Tucson: University of Arizona Press.

Snyder, H. A. 1998. Zone-tailed Hawk (*Buteo albonotatus*). In *Raptors of Arizona* (R. Glinski, ed.) Tucson: University of Arizona Press.

Snyder, H. A., and R. L. Glinski. 1988. Zone-tailed Hawk. In *Proceedings of the Southwest Raptor Management Symposium and Workshops* (R. L. Glinski, B. G. Pendleton, M. B. Moss, M. N. LeFranc Jr., B. A. Millsap, and S. W. Hoffman, eds.). Washington, DC: National Wildlife Federation.

Snyder, N., and H. Snyder. 1991. *Birds of Prey: Natural History and Conservation of North American Raptors*. Stillwater, MN: Voyageur Press.

Snyder, N. F. R., E. C. Enkerlin-Hoeflich, and M.A. Cruz-Nieto. 1999. Thick-billed Parrot (*Rhynchopsitta pachyrhyncha*). In *Birds of North America* 406 (A. Poole and F. Gill, eds.). Philadelphia: Birds of North America.

Snyder, N. F. R., S. Koenig, J. Koschmann, H. A. Snyder, and T. B. Johnson. 1994. Thick-billed Parrot releases in Arizona. *Condor* 96:845–862.

Snyder, N. F. R., and A. M. Rea. 1998. California Condor (*Gymnogyps californianus*). In *Raptors of Arizona* (R. Glinski, ed.). Tucson: University of Arizona Press.

Snyder, N. F. R., and H. A. Snyder. 1998ba Cooper's Hawk (*Accipiter cooperii*). In *Raptors of Arizona* (R. Glinski, ed.). Tucson: University of Arizona Press.

Snyder, N. F. R., and H. A. Snyder. 1998b. Northern Goshawk (*Accipiter gentiles*). In *Raptors of Arizona* (R. Glinski, ed.). Tucson: University of Arizona Press.

Snyder, N. F. R., and H. A. Snyder. 1998c. Sharp-shinned Hawk (*Accipiter striatus*). In *Raptors of Arizona*. (R. Glinski, ed.). Tucson: University of Arizona Press.

Snyder, N. F. R., and J. W. Wiley. 1976. Sexual size dimorphism in hawks and owls of North America. *Ornithol. Monographs* 20:1–96.

Sogge, M. K., D. Felley, and M. Wotawa. 1998. Annotated species list and summary. In *Riparian Bird Community Ecology in the Grand Canyon*. Flagstaff: US Geological Survey, Colorado Plateau Field Station.

Sogge, M. K., W. M. Gilbert, and C. Van Riper III. 1994. Orange-crowned Warbler (*Vermivora celata*). In *Birds of North America* 101 (A. Poole and F. Gill, eds.). Philadelphia: Academy of Natural Sciences; Washington, DC: American Ornithologists' Union.

Sordahl, T. A. 1980. Antipredator behavior and parental care in the American Avocet and Black-necked Stilt. Ph.D. diss., Utah State University, Logan.

Sorenson, M. D. 1991. The functional significance of parasitic egg laying and typical nesting in Redhead ducks: An analysis of individual behaviour. *Anim. Behav.* 42:771

Soulliere, G. J. 1990. Review of Wood Duck nest-cavity characteristics. In *Proceedings of the 1988 North American Wood Duck Symposium* (L. Fredrickson et al., eds.). St. Louis.

Sowls, L. K., and P. M. Smith. 1990. Canada Goose transplants in Arizona. In *Proceedings of the symposium for Managing Wildlife in the Southwest* (P. R. Krausman and N. S. Smith, eds.). Tucson.

Speich, S. M., and J. L. Witzeman. 1975. Arizona bird records, 1973, with additional notes. *Western Birds* 6:145–155.

Speirs, J. M., and D. H. Speirs. 1968. *Melospiza lincolnii lincolnii*, Lincoln's Sparrow. In Life histories of North American cardinals, grosbeaks, buntings, towhees, finches, sparrows, and allies, pt. 3 (A. Bent, ed.). *US Nat. Mus. Bull.* 237.

Sprunt, A. 1964. *Mimus polyglottos polyglottos*. Eastern Mockingbird. In Life histories of North American nuthatches, wrens, thrashers and their allies. (A. Bent, ed.). New York: Dover.

Squires, J. R. and R. T. Reynolds. 1997. Northern Goshawk (*Accipiter gentilis*). In *Birds of North America* 298 (A. Poole and F. Gill, eds.). Philadelphia: Academy of Natural Sciences; Washington, DC: American Ornithologists' Union.

Stabler, R. M. 1959. Nesting of the Blue Grosbeak in Colorado. *Condor* 61:46–48.

Stacey, P. B., and C. E. Bock. 1978. Social plasticity in the Acorn Woodpecker. *Science* 202:1298–1300.

Stacey, P. B. and J. D. Ligon. 1987. Territory quality and dispersal options in the Acorn Woodpecker and a challenge to the habitat saturation model of cooperative breeding. *Am. Nat.* 130:654–676.

Stacier, C. A., and M. J. Guzy. 2002. Grace's Warbler (*Dendroica graciae*). In *Birds of North America* 677 (A. Poole and F. Gill, eds.). Philadelphia: Birds of North America.

Stager, K. 1964. The role of olfaction in food location by the Turkey Vulture (*Cathartes aura*). *Los Angeles County Mus. Contrib. Science* 81:1–63.

Stanwood, C. J. 1913. The olive-backed thrush (*Hylocichla ustulata swainsoni*) at his summer home. *Wilson Bull.* 25:118–137.

Steenhof, K. 1998. Prairie Falcon (*Falco mexicanus*). In *Birds of North America* 346 (A. Poole and F. Gill, eds.). Philadelphia: Birds of North America.

Stendell, R. C. 1972. The occurrence, food habits, and nesting strategy of White-tailed Kites in relation to a fluctuating vole population. Ph.D. diss., University of California, Berkeley.

Sterling, J. C. 1999. Gray Flycatcher (*Empidonax wrightii*). In *Birds of North America* 458 (A. Poole and F. Gill, eds.). Philadelphia: Birds of North America.

Stevens, F. 1878. Notes on a few birds observed in New Mexico and Arizona in 1876. *Bull. Nuttall Ornithol. Club* 3:92–94.

Stewart, P. A. 1974. A nesting of Black Vultures. *Auk* 91:595–600.

Stewart, P. A. 1983. The biology and communal behaviour of American Black Vultures. *Vulture News* 9–10:14–36.

Stewart, R. E., and H. A. Kantrud. 1974. Breeding waterfowl populations in the prairie pothole region of North Dakota. *Condor* 76:70–79.

Stiehl, R. B. 1985. Brood chronography of the common raven *Corvus corvax*. *Wilson Bull.* 103:83–92.

Stiles, F. G., and A. F. Skutch. 1989. *A Guide to the Birds of Costa Rica*. Ithaca, NY: Cornell University Press.
Storer, R. W., and G. L. Nuechterlein. 1992. Western Grebe (*Aechmophorus occidentalis*) and Clark's Grebe (*Aechmophorus clarkii*). In *Birds of North America* 26 (A. Poole and F. Gill, eds.). Philadelphia: Academy of Natural Sciences; Washington, DC: American Ornithologists' Union.
Stouffer, P. C., and R. T. Chesser. 1998. Tropical Kingbird (*Tyrannus melancholicus*). In *Birds of North America* 358 (A. Poole and F. Gill, eds.). Philadelphia: Birds of North America.
Strickland, D., and H. Ouellet. 1993. Gray Jay (*Perisoreus canadensis*). In *Birds of North America* 40 (A. Poole, P. Stettenheim, and F. Gill, eds.). Philadelphia: Academy of Natural Sciences; Washington, DC: American Ornithologists' Union.
Stromberg, M. R. 2000. Montezuma Quail (*Cyrtonyx montezumae*). In *Birds of North America* 524 (A. Poole and F. Gill, eds.). Philadelphia: Birds of North America.
Strong, T. R. 1988. Status of thr Arizona Grasshopper Sparrow (*Ammodramus savannarum ammolegus*). Project E-3 completion report. Phoenix: Arizona Game and Fish Department, and Albuquerque: U.S. Fish and Wildlife Service.
Stull, W. D. 1968. *Spizella passerina* (Bechstein): Eastern and Canadian Chipping Sparrow. In Life histories of North American cardinals, grosbeaks, buntings, towhees, finches, sparrows and allies, pt. 2 (O. L. Austin Jr., ed.). *US Nat. Mus. Bull.* 237.
Stutchbury, B. J. 1991. Coloniality and breeding biology of Purple Martins (*Progne subis hesperia*) in saguaro cacti. *Condor* 93:666–675.
Stutchbury, B. J., and R. J. Robertson. 1988. Within-season and age-related patterns of reproductive performance in female Tree Swallows (*Tachycineta bicolor*). *Can. J. Zool.* 66:827–834.
Sullivan, K. A. 1999. Yellow-eyed Junco (*Junco phaeonotus*). In *Birds of North America* 464 (A. Poole and F. Gill, eds.). Philadelphia: Birds of North America.
Sullivan, S. L., W. H. Pyle, and S. G. Herman. 1986. Cassin's Finch nesting in big sagebrush. *Condor* 88:378–379.
Sumner, E. L., Jr. 1929. Comparative studies in the growth of young raptors. *Condor* 31:85–111.
Sutton, G. M. 1940. Roadrunner. In Life histories of North American cuckoos, goatsuckers, hummingbirds, and their allies (A. C. Bent, ed.). *US Nat. Mus. Bull.* 176.
Sutton, G. M., and A. R. Phillips 1942. June bird life of the Papago Indian Reservation, Arizona. *Condor* 44:57–65.
Swainson, G. A., M. I. Meyer, and J. R. Serie. 1974. Feeding ecology of breeding Blue-winged Teals. *J. Wildlife Management* 38:396–407.
Swarbrick, B. M. 1975. Ecology of the Mexican Duck in the Sulphur Springs Valley of Arizona. M.S. thesis, University of Arizona.
Swarth, H. S. 1904. Birds of the Huachuca Mountains, Arizona. *Pac. Coast Avifauna* 4.
Swarth, H. S. 1905. Summer birds of the Papago Indian Reservation and of the Santa Rita Mountains, Arizona. *Condor* 7:23–28, 47–50, 77–82.
Swarth, H. S. 1909. Distribution and molt of the Mearns Quail. *Condor* 11:39–43.
Swarth, H. S. 1914. A distributional list of the birds of Arizona. *Pac. Coast Avifauna* 10.
Swarth, H. S. 1918. Notes on some birds from central Arizona. *Condor* 20:20–24.
Swenson, J. E., and P. Hendricks. 1983. Chick movements in Common Poorwills. *Wilson Bull.* 95:309–310.
Swinburne, J. 1888. Breeding of Evening Grosbeaks in the White Mountains of Arizona. *Auk* 5:113–114.
Sydeman, W. J., M. Güntert, and R. P. Balda. 1988. Annual reproductive yield in the cooperative Pygmy Nuthatch (*Sitta pygmaea*). *Auk* 105:70–77.
Szaro, R. C., and R. P. Balda. 1979a. Bird community dynamics in a ponderosa pine forest. *Studies in Avian Biology* 3.
Szaro, R. C., and R. P. Balda. 1979b. Effects of harvesting ponderosa pine on nongame bird populations. USDA Forest Service Research Paper RM–212, Rocky Mt. and Range Exp. Sta., Fort Collins, CO.
Szaro, R. C., and R. P. Balda. 1986. Relationships among weather, habitat structure and ponderosa pine forest birds. *J. Wildlife Management* 50:253–260.
Taber, R. D. 1949. Observations on the breeding behavior of the Ring-necked Pheasant. *Condor* 51:153–175.
Taber, W., and D. W. Johnston. 1968. Indigo Bunting *Passerina cyanea*. In Life histories of North American cardinals, grosbeaks, buntings, towhees, finches, sparrows, and allies, pt. 1 (O. L. Austin Jr., ed.). *US Nat. Mus. Bull.* 237.
Taylor, R. C. 1980. *The Coppery-tailed Trogon: Arizona's "Bird of Paradise."* Tucson: Borderline Productions.
Taylor, R. C. 1993. *Location Checklist to the Birds of the Chiricahua Mountains*. Tucson: Borderline Productions.
Taylor, R. C. 1994. *Trogons of the Arizona Borderlands*. Tucson: Treasure Chest.
Taylor, R. C. 1995. *Location Checklist to Birds of the Huachuca Mountains and the Upper San Pedro River*. Tucson: Borderline Productions.
Taylor, W. K. 1971. A breeding biology study of the Verdin, *Auriparus flaviceps* (Sundevall) in Arizona. *Am. Midl. Nat.* 85:289–328.
Teather, K. L., and P. J. Weatherhead. 1989. Sex-specific mortality in nestling Great-tailed Grackles. *Ecology* 70:1485–1493.
Teitler, R. 1988. *Taming and Training Lovebirds*. Neptune City, NJ: TFH Publications.
Telfair, R. C. 1994. Cattle Egret (*Bulbulcus ibis*). In *Birds of North America* 113 (A. Poole and F. Gill, Eds.). Philadelphia: Academy of Natural Sciences; Washington, DC: American Ornithologists' Union.
Telfair, R. C., II, and M. L. Morrison. 1995. Neotropic Cormorant (*Phalacrocorax brasilianus*). In *Birds of North America* 137 (A. Poole and F. Gill, eds.). Philadelphia: Academy of Natural Sciences; Washington, DC: American Ornithologists' Union.
Tenney, C. R. 1997. Black-chinned Sparrow (*Spizella atrogularis*). In *Birds of North America* 270 (A. Poole and F. Gill, eds.). Philadelphia: Academy of Natural Sciences; Washington, DC: American Ornithologists' Union.
Tenney, C. R. 2000. Northern Beardless-Tyrannulet (*Camptostoma imberbe*). In *Birds of North America* 519 (A. Poole and F. Gill, eds.). Philadelphia: Birds of North America.
Terres, J. K. 1996. *The Audubon Society Encyclopedia of North American Birds*. New York: Random House.
Thatcher, D. M. 1968. Gray-headed Junco. Pp 1098–1126 in Life histories of North American cardinals, grosbeaks, buntings, towhees, finches, sparrows, and their allies, pt. 2 (O. L. Austin Jr., ed.). *US Nat. Mus. Bull.* 237.
Thompson, C. F., and V. Nolan Jr. 1973. Population biology of the Yellow-breasted Chat (*Icteria virens L.*) in southern Indiana. *Ecol. Monographs* 43:145–171.
Thompson, W. L. 1960. Agonistic behavior in the House Finch. Part I: Annual cycle and display patterns. *Condor* 62:245–271.
Thomsen, L. 1971. Behavior and ecology of Burrowing Owls on the Oakland municipal airport. *Condor* 73:177–192.
Tobalske, B. W. 1992. Evaluating habitat suitability using relative abundance and fledging success of Red-naped Sapsuckers. *Condor* 94:550–553.
Tobalske, B. W. 1997. Lewis' Woodpecker (*Melanerpes lewis*). In *Birds of North America* 284 (A. Poole and F. Gill, eds.). Philadelphia: Academy of Natural Sciences; Washington, DC: American Ornithologists' Union.
Todd, R. L. 1986. A saltwater marsh hen in Arizona: a history of the Yuma Clapper Rail (*Rallus longirostris yumanensis*). Completion Report, Fed. Aid Proj. W-95-R, Arizona Game and Fish Department.
Tolle, D. A. 1976. A westward extension in the breeding range of the Mountain Plover. *Wilson Bull.* 88:358–359.
Tomback, D. F. 1976. A late nesting attempt by Clark's Nutcracker. *Wilson Bull.* 88:499–500.
Tomback, D. F. 1977. The behavioral ecology of Clark's Nutcracker (*Nucifraga columbiana)* in the eastern Sierra Nevada. Ph.D. diss., University of California, Santa Barbara.
Tomback, D. F. 1978. Foraging strategies of Clark's Nutcracker. *Living Bird* 16:123–161.
Tomback, D. F. 1998. Clark's Nutcracker (*Nucifraga columbiana*). In *Birds of North America* 331 (A. Poole and F. Gill, eds.). Philadelphia: Birds of North America.
Tomlinson, R. 1972. Current status of the endangered Masked Bobwhite Quail. *Transactions of the Thirty-seventh North American Wildlife and Natural Resources Conference*. Washington, DC: Wildlife Management Institute.
Travis, J. R. 1992. *Atlas of the Breeding birds of Los Alamos County, New Mexico*. Los Alamos: Los Alamos National Laboratory.

Trost, C. H. 1999. Black-billed Magpie (*Pica pica*). In *Birds of North America* 389 (A. Poole and F. Gill, eds.). Philadelphia: Birds of North America.

Tuck, L. M. 1972. *The Snipes: A Study of the Genus Capella*. Toronto: Canadian Wildlife Service.

Tucson Audubon Society. 1995. *Finding Birds in Southeastern Arizona*. Tucson: Tucson Audubon Society.

Twedt, D. J., and R. D. Crawford. 1995. Yellow-headed Blackbird (*Xanthocephalus xanthocephalus*). In *Birds of North America* 192 (A. Poole and F. Gill, eds.). Philadelphia: Academy of Natural Sciences; Washington, DC: American Ornithologists' Union.

Tweit, R. C. 1996. Curve-billed Thrasher (*Toxostoma curvirostre*). In *Birds of North America* 235 (A. Poole and F. Gill, eds). Philadelphia: Academy of Natural Sciences; Washington, DC: American Ornithologists' Union.

Tweit, R. C., and D. M. Finch. 1994. Abert's Towhee (*Pipilo aberti*). In *Birds of North America* 111 (A. Poole and F. Gill, Eds.). Philadelphia: Academy of Natural Sciences; Washington, DC: American Ornithologists' Union.

Tweit, R. C., and C. W. Thompson. 1999. Pyrrhuloxia (*Cardinalis sinuatus*). In *Birds of North America* 391 (A. Poole and F. Gill, eds.). Philadelphia: Birds of North America.

Tweit, R. C., and J. C. Tweit. 2000. Cassin's Kingbird (*Tyrannus vociferus*). In *Birds of North America* 534 (A. Poole and F. Gill, eds.). Philadelphia: Birds of North America.

Tweit, R. C., and J. C. Tweit. 2002. Dusky-capped Flycatcher (*Myiarchus tuberculifer*). In *Birds of North America* 631 (A. Poole and F. Gill, eds.). Philadelphia: Birds of North America.

US Fish and Wildlife Service. 1999. Endangered and threatened wildlife and plants; proposed rule to remove the bald eagle in the lower 48 states from the list of endangered and threatened wildlife; proposed rule. Federal Register 64(128):36454–64.

Vahle, J. R., and G. L. Beatty. 1995. Osprey nest site survey and monitoring on the Alpine and Springerville Ranger Districts of the Apache-Sitgreaves National Forest. Nongame and Endangered Wildlife Program Technical Report 61, Arizona Game and Fish Department.

Vahle, J. R., N. L. Dodd, and S. Nagiller. 1988. Osprey. In *Proceedings of the Southwest Raptor Management Symposium and Workshop* (R. L. Glinski, B. G. Pendleton, M. B. Moss, M. N. LeFranc Jr., B. A. Millsap, and S. W. Hoffman, eds.). Washington, DC: National Wildlife Federation.

Van Fleet, C. C. 1919. A short paper on the Hutton Vireo. *Condor* 21:162–165.

Van Horne, B. 1995. Assessing vocal variety in the Winter Wren, a bird with a complex repertoire. *Condor* 97:39–49.

Van Rossem, A. J. 1946. An isolated colony of the Arizona Cardinal in Arizona and California. *Condor* 48:247–248.

Vander Wall, S. B., and R. P. Balda. 1977. Coadaptations of the Clark's Nutcracker and piñon pine for efficient seed harvest and dispersal. *Ecol. Monographs* 47:89–111.

Verbeek, N. A. M., and C. Caffrey. 2002. American Crow (*Corvus brachyrhynchos*). In *Birds of North America* 647 (A. Poole and F. Gill, eds.). Philadelphia: Birds of North America.

Verner, J. 1964. Evolution of polygamy in the Long-billed Marsh Wren. *Evolution* 18:252–261.

Verner, J. 1965. Breeding biology of the Long-billed Marsh Wren. *Condor* 67:6–30.

Versaw, A. E. 1998. Lincoln's Sparrow. In *Colorado Breeding Bird Atlas* (H. Kingery, ed.) Denver: Colorado Wildlife Heritage Foundation.

Vickery, P. D. 1996. Grasshopper Sparrow (*Ammadramus savannarum*). In *Birds of North America* 239 (A. Poole and F. Gill, eds.). Philadelphia: Academy of Natural Sciences; Washington, DC: American Ornithologists' Union.

Visher, S. S. 1910. Notes on the birds of Pima County, Arizona. *Auk* 27:279–288.

Voss-Roberts, K. A. 1984. Nest-site characteristics and source of egg loss in Yellow-headed Blackbird (*Xanthocephalus xanthocephalus*). M.S. thesis, Arizona State University.

Wakeling, B. F. 1991. Population and nesting characteristics of Merriam's turkey along the Mogollon Rim in Arizona. Arizona Game and Fish Department Tech. Rpt. 7.

Wakeling, B. F., and H. G. Shaw. 1994. Characteristics of managed forest habitat selected for nesting by Merriam's turkey. In *Sustainable Ecological Systems: Implementing an Ecological Approach to Land Management*. US Forest Service Gen. Tech. Rep. RM–247.

Wakeling, B. F., S. R. Boe, M. M. Koloszar, and T. D. Rogers. 2001. Gould's turkey survival and habitat selection modeling in southeastern Arizona. *Proceedings of the National Wild Turkey Symposium* 8:101–108.

Walkinshaw, L. H. 1940. Summer life of the Sora Rail. *Auk* 57:153–168.

Walkinshaw, L. H. 1944. The Eastern Chipping Sparrow in Michigan. *Wilson Bull.* 56:193–205.

Wallmo, O. C. 1954. Nesting of Mearns Quail in southeastern Arizona. *Condor* 56:125–128.

Walsberg, G. E. 1977. Ecology and energetics of contrasting social systems in the Phainopepla (Aves: Ptilogonatidae). *Univ. Calif. Publ. Zool.* 108:1–63.

Walsberg, G. E., and K. A. Voss-Roberts. 1983. Incubation in desert nesting doves: Mechanisms for egg cooling. *Physiol. Zool.* 56:88–93.

Walters, E. L., E. H. Miller, and P. E. Lowther. 2002. Red-breasted Sapsucker (*Sphyrapicus rubber*) and Red-naped Sapsucker (*Sphyrapicus nuchalis*). In *Birds of North America* 663 (A. Poole and F. Gill, eds.). Philadelphia: Birds of North America.

Ward, L. Z. 1993. Arizona Peregrine Falcon reproductive survey:1992 report. Phoenix: Arizona Game and Fish Department.

Warnock, N., and L. W. Oring. 1996. Nocturnal nest attendance of Killdeers: more than meets the eye. *Auk* 113:502–504.

Warriner, J. S., J. C. Warriner, G. W. Page, and L. E. Stenzel. 1986. Mating system and reproductive success of a small population of polygamous Snowy Plovers. *Wilson Bull.* 98:15–37.

Waser, N. M. 1976. Food supply and nest-timing of Broad-tailed Hummingbirds in the Rocky Mountains. *Condor* 78:133–135.

Watt, D. J., and E. J. Willoughby. 1999. Lesser Goldfinch (*Carduelis psaltria*). In *Birds of North America* 392 (A. Poole and F. Gill, eds.). Philadelphia: Academy of Natural Sciences; Washington, DC: American Ornithologists' Union.

Wauer, R. H. 1968. Northern range extension of the Wied's Crested Flycatcher. *Condor* 70:88.

Weathers, W. W., and K. A. Sullivan. 1989. Juvenile foraging proficiency, parental effort, and avian reproductive success. *Ecol. Monographs* 59:223–246.

Weathers, W. W., and K. A. Sullivan. 1991. Growth and energetics of nestling Yellow-eyed Juncos. *Condor* 93:138–146.

Weaver, R. L. and F. H. West 1943. Notes on the breeding of the Pine Siskin. *Auk* 60:492–504.

Webb, E. A. 1985. Distribution, habitat and breeding biology of the Botteri's Sparrow (*Aimophila botterii arizonae*). Master's thesis, University of Colorado, Boulder.

Webb, E. A., and C. E. Bock. 1990. Relationship of the Botteri's Sparrow to sacaton grassland in southeastern Arizona. In *Managing Wildlife in the Southwest: Proceedings of the Symposium* (P. R. Krausman and N. S. Smith, eds.). Tucson: Arizona Chapter, National Wildlife Society.

Webb, E. A., and C. E. Bock. 1996. Botteri's Sparrow (*Aimophila botterii*). In *Birds of North America* 216 (A. Poole and F. Gill, eds.). Philadelphia: Academy of Natural Sciences, and Washington, DC: American Ornithologists' Union.

Webb, P. M. 1958. A study of the introduction, release and survival of Chukar Partridge, Sand Grouse, and other game species. F. A. Compl. Rept. W-58, R-6. Arizona Game and Fish Department.

Webb, P. M., and R. Robeck. 1962. Statewide wildlife restocking project. F. A. Compl. Rept. Proj. W-11-D. Arizona Game and Fish Department.

Webster, C., and S. DeStefa 2001. Distribution and habitat of Greater Roadrunners in the metropolitan area of Tucson, Arizona. Final report to the Arizona Game and Fish Department, Phoenix.

Webster, M. D. 1999. Verdin (*Auriparus flaviceps*). In *Birds of North America* 470 (A. Poole and F. Gill, eds.). Philadelphia: Academy of Natural Sciences; Washington, DC: American Ornithologists' Union.

Weller, M. W. 1958. Observations of the incubation behavior of a Common Nighthawk. *Auk* 75:48–59.

Weller, M.W. 1961. Breeding biology of the Least Bittern. *Wilson Bull.* 73:11–35.

Welter 1935. The natural history of the Long-billed Marsh Wren. *Wilson Bull.* 47:3–34.

Weston, F. M. 1949. Blue-gray Gnatcatcher. In Life histories of North American thrushes, kinglets and their allies. *US Nat. Mus. Bull.* 196.

Weston, H. G. 1947. Breeding behavior of the Black-headed Grosbeak. *Condor* 49:54–73.

Wetmore, A. 1925. Food of American phalaropes, avocets, and stilts. *USDA Bull.* 1359.

Wetmore, A. 1935. The Thick-billed Parrot in southern Arizona. *Condor* 37:18–21.

Weydemeyer, W. 1933. Nesting of the Rough-winged Swallow in Montana. *Auk* 50:362–363.

Whaley, W. H. 1986. Population ecology of the Harris' Hawk in Arizona. *Raptor Res.* 20:1–15.

Wheeler, B. K. 2003. *Raptors of Western North America.* Princeton, NJ: Princeton University Press.

Wheelwright, N. T., and J. D. Rising. 1993. Savannah Sparrow (*Passerculus sandwichensis*). In *Birds of North America* 45 (A. Poole and F. Gill, eds.). Philadelphia: Academy of Natural Sciences; Washington, DC: American Ornithologists' Union.

White, C. M., N. J. Clum, T. J. Cade, and W. G. Hunt. 2002. Peregrine Falcon (*Falco peregrinus*). In *Birds of North America* 660 (A. Poole and F. Gill, eds.). Philadelphia: Birds of North America.

Whitmer, M. C., and R. E. Patrick. 1987. Continuous breeding of a Barn Owl in Texas. *Southwestern Naturalist* 32:402–403

Whitmore, R. C. 1980. Reclaimed surface mines as avian habitat islands in the eastern forest. *Am. Birds* 34:13–14.

Whitson, M. A. 1975. Courtship behavior of the Greater Roadrunner. *Living Bird* 14:215–255.

Whittaker, R. H., and W. A. Niering. 1965. Vegetation of the Santa Catalina Mountains, Arizona: a gradient analysis of the south slope. *Ecology* 46:429–452.

Wilbur, S. R. 1973. The Red-shouldered Hawk in the western United States. *Western Birds* 4:15–22.

Wiley, J. W. 1975. The nesting and reproductive success of Red-tailed hawks and Red-shouldered Hawks in Orange County, California, 1973. *Condor* 77:133–139.

Willard, F. C. 1910a. Nesting of the Western Evening Grosbeak (*Hesperiphona vespertina montana*). *Condor* 12:60–62.

Willard, F. C. 1910b. Seen on a day's outing in southern Arizona. *Condor* 8:110.

Willard, F. C. 1911. The Blue-throated Hummingbird. *Condor* 13:46–49.

Willard, F. C. 1913. Some late nesting notes from the Huachuca Mountains, Arizona. *Condor* 15:41.

Willard, F. C. 1923a. Some unusual nesting sites of several Arizona birds. *Condor* 25:121–125.

Willard, F. C. 1923b. The Buff-breasted Flycatcher in the Huachucas. *Condor* 25:189–194.

Willey, D. W. 1993. Home-range characteristics and juvenile dispersal ecology of Mexican Spotted Owls in southern Utah. Final report 1992–93. Flagstaff, AZ: High Desert Research Collective.

Williams, L. 1952. Breeding behavior of the Brewer's Blackbird. *Condor* 54:3–47.

Williamson, S. L. 1992. The Eared Trogon in Arizona: behavior, management, and ecology of the "Northern Quetzal." In *Proceedings of the Chiricahua Mountains Research Symposium*, 15–16 March 1992. Tucson: Southwest Parks and Monuments Association.

Williamson, S. L. 2000. Blue-throated Hummingbird (*Lampornis clemenciae*). In *Birds of North America* 531 (A. Poole and F. Gill, eds.). Philadelphia: Birds of North America.

Williamson, S. L. 2001. *A Field Guide to Hummingbirds of North America.* Boston: Houghton Mifflin.

Winn, R. 1998. Cassin's Finch (*Carpodacs cassinii*). In *Colorado Breeding Bird Atlas* (H. Kingery, ed.). Denver: Colorado Wildlife Heritage Foundation.

Winship, G. P. 1892–1893. The Coronado Expedition, 1540–1542. US Bureau Ethnology, 14th Ann. Rpt. Washington, DC

Winter, B. M., and L. B. Best. 1985. Effects of prescribed burning on placement of Sage Sparrow nests. *Condor* 87:294–295.

Winternitz, B. L. 1998a. Clark's Nutcracker (*Nucifraga columbiana*). In *Colorado Breeding Bird Atlas* (H. Kingery, ed.). Denver: Colorado Wildlife Heritage Foundation.

Winternitz, B. L. 1998b. Gray Jay (*Perisoreus canadensis*). In *Colorado Breeding Bird Atlas* (H. Kingery, ed.). Denver: Colorado Wildlife Heritage Foundation.

Witzeman, J., and D. Stejskal. 1984. The summer season, June 1–July 31, 1984. *Am. Birds* 38:1048.

Witzeman, J. L., S. R. Demaree, and E. L. Radke. 1997. *Birds of Phoenix and Maricopa County, Arizona.* Phoenix: Maricopa Audubon Society.

Wolf, B. O. 1997. Black Phoebe (*Sayornis nigricans*). In *Birds of North America* 268 (A. Poole and F. Gill, eds.). Philadelphia: Academy of Natural Sciences; Washington, DC: American Ornithologists' Union.

Wolf, B. O., and S. L. Jones. 2000. Vermilion Flycatcher (*Pyrocephalus rubinus*). In *Birds of North America* 484 (A. Poole and F. Gill, eds.) Philadelphia: Academy of Natural Sciences; Washington, DC: American Ornithologists' Union.

Wolfe, L. R. 1931. The breeding Limicolae of Utah. *Condor* 33:51–59.

Wood, C. W., Jr., and T. N. Nash III. 1976. Copper smelter effluent effects on Sonoran Desert vegetation. *Ecology* 57:1311–1316.

Woodbury, A. M., and H. N. Russell Jr. 1945. Birds of the Navajo Country. *Bull. Univ. Utah* 35.

Woodhouse, S. W. 1853. Report on the Natural History. In *Report of an Expedition down the Zuni and the Colorado Rivers in 1851* by Capt. L. Sitgreaves. Washington, DC.

Woodin, M. C., and T. C. Michot. 2002. Redhead (*Aythya americana*). In *Birds of North America* 695 (A. Poole and F. Gill, eds.). Philadelphia: Birds of North America.

Woods, R. S. 1921. Home life of the Black-tailed Gnatcatcher. *Condor* 23:173–178.

Woods, R. S. 1924. Notes on the life history of the Texas Nighthawk. *Condor* 26:3–6.

Woods, R. S. 1928. Nesting of the Black-tailed Gnatcatcher. *Condor* 30:139–143.

Woodward, P. W., and J. C. Woodward. 1979. Survival of fledgling Brown-headed Cowbirds. *Bird-Banding* 50:66–68.

Wright, J. M. 1997. Olive-sided Flycatchers in central Alaska, 1994–1996. Juneau: Alaska Department of Fish and Game.

Yasukawa, K., and W. A. Searcy. 1995. Red-winged Blackbird (*Agelaius phoeniceus*). In *Birds of North America* 184 (A. Poole and F. Gill, eds.). Philadelphia: Academy of Natural Sciences; Washington, DC: American Ornithologists' Union.

Yosef, R. 1996. Loggerhead Shrike (*Lanius ludovicianus*). In *Birds of North America* 231 (A. Poole and F. Gill, eds.). Philadelphia: Academy of Natural Sciences; Washington, DC: American Ornithologists' Union.

Young, B. E. 1991. Annual molts and interruption of the fall migration for molting in Lazuli Buntings. *Condor* 93:236–250.

Zimmer, B., and K. J. Zimmer. 1992. Point/counterpoint: Using bird tapes. *Birding* 24:168–173.

Zimmerman, D. A. 1960. Thick-billed Kingbird nesting in New Mexico. *Auk* 77:92–94.

Zimmerman, D. A., and S. H. Levy. 1960. Violet-crowned hummingbird nesting in Arizona and New Mexico. *Auk* 77:470.

Zimmerman, J. L. 1963. A nesting study of the Catbird in southern Michigan. *Jack-Pine Warbler* 41:142–160.

Zwickel, F. C. 1992. Blue Grouse (*Dendragapus obscurus*). In *Birds of North America* 15 (A. Poole and F. Gill, eds.). Philadelphia: Academy of Natural Sciences; Washington, DC: American Ornithologists' Union.

Zwickel, F. C., and A. N. Lance. 1965. Renesting in Blue Grouse. *J. Wildlife Management* 29:402–404.

Zyskowski, K. 1993. Nest-site selection in Orange-crowned and Virginia's warblers in high-elevation forests of the Mogollon Rim (Arizona): Variation in nest placement, phenology, and microclimate. Fayetteville: Arkansas Department of Fish and Wildlife.

Index of English Bird Names

Avocet, American, 178–79

Becard, Rose-throated, 334–35
Bishop, Orange, 14, 18, 595
Bittern, American, 600
Least, 18, 102–3
Blackbird, Brewer's, 560–61
Red-winged, 552–53
Yellow-headed, 558–59
Bluebird, Eastern, 18, 428–29
Mountain, 432–33
Western, 430–31
Bobolink, 14, 599
Bobwhite, Northern, 88–89
Bunting, Indigo, 548–49
Lark, 603
Lazuli, 546–47
Varied, 550–51
Bushtit, 392–93

Canvasback, 14, 596
Caracara, Crested, 152–53
Cardinal, Northern, 538–39
Catbird, Gray, 442–43
Chat, Yellow-breasted, 484–85
Chickadee, Black-capped, 599
Mexican, 384–85
Mountain, 382–83
Chukar, 14, 74–75
Coot, American, 170–71
Condor, California, 600
Cormorant, Double-crested, 18, 100–101
Neotropic, 18, 595
Cowbird, Bronzed, 564–65, 613
Brown-headed, 16, 566–67, 612
Creeper, Brown, 400–401
Crane, Sandhill, 602
Crossbill, Red, 580–81
Crow, American, 362–63
Cuckoo, Yellow-billed, 2, 14, 202–3
Curlew, Long-billed, 14, 18, 591

Dipper, American, 18, 416–17
Dove, Common Ground-, 196–97
Eurasian Collared-, 18, 188–89
Inca, 194–95
Mourning, 16, 192–93
Ringed Turtle-, 591
Ruddy Ground-, 16, 18, 198–99
White-winged, 190–91
Duck, Black-bellied Whistling-, 50–51
Ring-necked, 14, 597
Ruddy, 72–73
Wood, 18, 54–55

Eagle, Bald, 2, 126–27
Golden, 150–51
Egret, Cattle, 18, 110–11
Great, 106–7
Snowy, 108–9

Falcon, Aplomado, 24, 601
Peregrine, 2, 18, 27, 156–57
Prairie, 18, 158–59
Finch, Cassin's, 576–77
House, 16, 578–79
Flicker, Gilded, 292–93
Northern, 290–91
Flycatcher, Ash-throated, 16, 320–21
Brown-crested, 322–23
Buff-breasted, 2, 18, 24, 310–11
Cordilleran, 308–9
Dusky, 18, 306–7
Dusky-capped, 18, 318–19
Gray, 18, 304–5
Hammond's, 14, 592
Olive-sided, 296–97
Scissor-tailed, 18, 592
Sulphur-bellied, 18, 324–25
Vermilion, 316–17
Willow, 2, 302–3

Gadwall, 56–57
Gnatcatcher, Black-capped, 18, 426–27
Black-tailed, 424–25
Blue-gray, 422–23
Goldfinch, American, 14, 594
Lawrence's, 603
Lesser, 584–85
Goose, Canada, 52–53
Goshawk, Northern, 2, 134–35
Grackle, Common, 599
Great-tailed, 562–63
Grebe, Clark's, 98–99
Eared, 94–95
Least, 14, 595
Pied-billed, 92–93
Western, 96–97
Grosbeak, Black-headed, 542–43
Blue, 544–45
Evening, 18, 586–87
Pine, 14, 18, 600
Rose-breasted, 14, 594
Grouse, Blue, 78–79

Harrier, Northern, 14, 128–29
Hawk, Common Black-, 138–39
Cooper's, 132–33
Gray, 18, 136–37
Harris's, 140–41
Ferruginous, 148–49
Red-tailed, 16, 146–47
Red-shouldered, 591
Sharp-shinned, 130–31
Short-tailed, 597
Swainson's, 142–43
White-tailed, 48, 601
Zone-tailed, 18, 144–45
Heron, Black-crowned Night-, 114–15
Great Blue, 104–5
Green, 112–13
Hummingbird, Anna's, 258–59
Berylline, 14, 18, 246–47
Black-chinned, 256–57
Blue-throated, 250–51
Broad-billed, 242–43
Broad-tailed, 262–63
Costa's, 260–61
Lucifer, 18, 254–55
Magnificent, 252–53
Violet-crowned, 248–49
White-eared, 14, 18, 244–45
Ibis, White-faced, 14, 18, 590

Jay, Gray, 14, 18, 348–49
Mexican, 354–55
Pinyon, 356–57
Steller's, 350–51
Western Scrub-, 352–53
Junco, Dark-eyed, 534–35
Yellow-eyed, 536–37

Kestrel, American, 16, 154–55
Killdeer, 174–75
Kingbird, Cassin's, 328–29
Thick-billed, 330–31
Tropical, 18, 326–27
Western, 16, 332–33
Kingfisher, Belted, 18, 266–67
Green, 268–69
Kinglet, Golden-crowned, 418–19
Ruby-crowned, 420–21
Kite, Mississippi, 14, 124–25
White-tailed, 122–23

Lark, Horned, 10, 368–69
Lovebird, Peach-faced, 200–201

Magpie, Black-billed, 360–61
Mallard, 58–59
Martin, Purple, 370–71
Meadowlark, Eastern, 554–55
Western, 10, 556–57
Merganser, Common, 70–71
Mockingbird, Northern, 10, 16, 444–45
Moorhen, Common, 168–69

Nighthawk, Common, 16, 232–33
Lesser, 16, 230–31
Nightjar, Buff-collared, 14, 236–37
Nutcracker, Clark's, 358–59
Nuthatch, Pygmy, 398–99
Red-breasted, 394–95
White-breasted, 396–97

Oriole, Baltimore, 603
Bullock's, 572–73
Hooded, 568–69
Scott's, 574–75
Streak-backed, 14, 16, 18, 570–71
Osprey, 18, 120–21
Owl, Barn, 206–7
Burrowing, 222–23
Elf, 45, 220–21
Ferruginous Pygmy-, 2, 7, 218–19
Flammulated, 16, 27, 208–9
Great Horned, 16, 214–15
Long-eared, 10, 226–27
Northern Pygmy-, 16, 216–17
Northern Saw-whet, 16, 228–29
Spotted, 2, 7, 224–25
Western Screech-, 16, 210–11
Whiskered Screech-, 14, 212–13

Parakeet, Monk, 14, 18, 592
Parrot, Thick-billed, 602
Parula, Northern, 603
Pewee, Eastern Wood-, 598
Greater, 298–99
Western Wood-, 300–301
Pheasant, Ring-necked, 76–77
Phainopepla, 10, 16, 458–59
Phalarope, Wilson's, 602
Phoebe, Black, 312–13
Say's, 16, 314–15
Pigeon, Band-tailed, 186–87
Rock, 184–85
Pintail, Northern, 64–65
Pipit, American, 14, 593
Plover, Mountain, 14, 18, 590
Snowy, 172–73
Poorwill, Common, 16, 234–35
Pyrrhuloxia, 18, 540–41

Quail, California, 84–85
Gambel's, 16, 86–87
Montezuma, 18, 90–91
Scaled, 82–83
Quetzal, Eared, 14, 597

Rail, Black, 2, 14, 160–61
Clapper, 2, 162–63
Virginia, 164–65
Raven, Chihuahuan, 364–65
Common, 16, 366–67
Redhead, 68–69
Redstart, American, 603
Painted, 482–83
Roadrunner, Greater, 204–5
Robin, American, 440–41
Rufous-backed, 599

Sandpiper, Spotted, 180–81
Sapsucker, Red-naped, 278–79
Williamson's, 276–77
Scaup, Lesser, 597
Shoveler, Northern, 14, 596
Shrike, Loggerhead, 10, 16, 336–37
Siskin, Pine, 582–83
Snipe, Wilson's, 182–83
Solitaire, Townsend's, 434–35
Sora, 166-167
Sparrow, Black-chinned, 516–17
Black-throated, 16, 522–23
Botteri's, 506–7
Brewer's, 18, 514–15
Cassin's, 504–5
Chipping, 512–13
Five-striped, 510–11
Grasshopper, 18, 528–29
House, 588–89
Lark, 520–21
Lincoln's, 532–33
Rufous-crowned, 508–9
Rufous-winged, 45, 502–3
Sage, 18, 524–25
Savannah, 526–27
Song, 530–31
Vesper, 518–19
White-crowned, 14, 594
Starling, European, 456–57
Stilt, Black-necked, 176–77
Swallow, Barn, 10, 380–81
Cave, 602
Cliff, 378–79
Northern Rough-winged, 376–77
Tree, 18, 372–73
Violet-green, 374–75
Swift, White-throated, 27, 45, 240–41

Tanager, Flame-colored, 14, 18, 492–93
Hepatic, 18, 486–87
Summer, 488–89
Western, 490–91
Teal, Blue-winged, 60–61
Cinnamon, 62–63
Green-winged, 66–67
Thrasher, Bendire's, 45, 448–49
Crissal, 18, 45, 452–53
Curve-billed, 450–51
Le Conte's, 454–55
Sage, 18, 446–47
Thrush, Hermit, 438–39
Swainson's, 436–37
Titmouse, Bridled, 386–87
Juniper, 388–89
Towhee, Abert's, 44, 500–501
Canyon, 498–99
Green-tailed, 494–95
Spotted, 496–97
Trogon, Elegant, 2, 264–65
Turkey, Wild, 80–81
Tyrannulet, Northern Beardless-, 18, 294–95

Veery, 603
Verdin, 10, 16, 390–91
Vireo, Bell's, 338–39
Gray, 18, 340–41
Hutton's, 344–45
Plumbeous, 342–43
Warbling, 346–47
Yellow-green, 598
Yellow-throated, 598
Vulture, Black, 116–17
Turkey, 16, 118–19

Warbler, Black-and-white, 603
Black-throated Gray, 472–73
Grace's, 474–75
Lucy's, 45, 466–67
MacGillivray's, 18, 476–77
Olive, 460–61
Orange-crowned, 462–63
Red-faced, 480–81
Rufous-capped, 18, 593
Virginia's, 464–65
Yellow, 468–69
Yellow-rumped, 470–71
Whip-poor-will, 238–39
Wigeon, American, 14, 596
Woodpecker, Acorn, 272–73
American Three-toed, 288–89
Arizona, 286–87
Downy, 282–83
Gila, 274–75
Hairy, 284–85
Ladder-backed, 280–81
Lewis's, 270–71
Wren, Bewick's, 16, 408–9
Cactus, 16, 402–3
Canyon, 27, 406–7
Carolina, 599
House, 410–11
Marsh, 414–15
Rock, 16, 404–5
Winter, 18, 412–13

Yellowthroat, Common, 478–79

Atlas Author Biographies

ANNALAURA AVERILL-MURRAY is a Habitat Specialist for the Arizona Game and Fish Department, Tucson Regional Office. She began birding in Arizona in 1994, after moving from California to start a M.S. program at the University of Arizona. For her M.S. thesis, she investigated cowbird nest-site selection and parasitism rates of Neotropical migratory songbirds along the lower Colorado River in Arizona. She was the Arizona Game and Fish Department's Atlas field crew leader from 1998 to 2000, participating in surveys on many blocks throughout the state.

ROBERT BRADLEY has been a serious birder and avid lister for thirty years. His interest in birds has taken him around the globe, including several visits to South America, Europe and Africa. Robert participated in his first Arizona Christmas Bird Count (CBC) in 1971 and since then has not missed a single year. He assisted with the establishment of the Salt-Verde Rivers CBC in 1985, and this continues to be a popular and productive count. An Arizona resident for more than thirty years, Robert and his family now reside in Colorado.

BILL BURGER is the Region VI Nongame Specialist for Arizona Game and Fish Department and works on a wide variety of projects with birds, mammals, and herps. His work with birds in Arizona has included surveying for Clapper Rails, Willow Flycatchers, and Ferruginous Pygmy-Owls. With the help of others in Region VI, Bill completed eleven Atlas blocks. He especially enjoyed the Atlas field work since it combined his enthusiasm for hiking and exploring with learning more about Arizona's breeding birds and contributing to an important project.

GREG CLARK became a birder in 1994 during the Arizona Breeding Bird Atlas project, and atlasing then consumed all his weekends from March to August until the fieldwork was completed in 2000. His interests quickly expanded to include bird photography, sound recording, and educational projects involving birds. Having noticed that few Burrowing Owls were found on Atlas blocks, he is now involved with building new habitat and relocating displaced Burrowing Owls to areas where they will thrive.

TROY E. CORMAN has been an avid birder since high school. Raised in rural south-central Pennsylvania, he moved to Arizona in 1980 to pursue higher education and new adventures. For several years he conducted wildlife inventories on the upper San Pedro River for the Bureau of Land Management. He has worked for the Nongame Branch of the Arizona Game and Fish Department since 1990, conducting surveys and coordinating projects for species of concern. He coordinated the Arizona Breeding Bird Atlas project from its inception. His passion for birds has taken him as far away as Peru and East Africa, and he plans to increase his world travels.

JAMEY DRISCOLL is the Bald Eagle Management Coordinator for the Arizona Game and Fish Department. A graduate of Purdue University in 1991, he has worked on studies of Ospreys, Golden Eagles, and Northern Goshawks, and he has banded nearly 200 Bald Eagle nestlings. Jamey has studied raptor species in Alaska, California, and Indiana as well as Arizona.

DAN L. FISCHER makes his home in the western foothills of the Chiricahua Mountains of southeastern Arizona. He has a passion for the conservation of wildlife, particularly when it comes to birds. In addition, he is also an avid photographer and writer and in recent years has expanded his interest to the historical aspect of ornithology by authoring *Early Southwest Ornithologists, 1528–1900* (University of Arizona Press, 2001).

PETER FRIEDERICI encountered his share of flat tires, rattlesnakes, mosquitoes, and other perils during his seven years as a Breeding Bird Atlas field crew member. He now works as an editor at Northern Arizona University, where his work keeps him from birding as much as he'd like—though he does get to watch Cordilleran Flycatchers and Lewis's Woodpeckers from his office window. He is the author or editor of several books, including *The Suburban Wild* (University of Georgia Press, 1999) and *Ecological Restoration of Southwestern Ponderosa Pine Forests* (Island Press, 2003).

BILL GROSSI is a wildlife biologist for the Bureau of Land Management (BLM) and has lived in Arizona for sixteen years. He has served as the wildlife program leader in the BLM State Office in Phoenix for the past twelve years, and was able to lend his support to the Atlas Breeding Bird Atlas project by obtaining federal funding for the effort. His statewide responsibilities, plus interests in camping, hunting, and traveling complement his desire to visit and bird the far corners of Arizona and North America. He is particularly thankful for his understanding spouse, Mary.

CHUCK LARUE has been chasing birds across the mesas and through the canyons of northern Arizona and the Four Corners region since 1966. The Arizona Breeding Bird Atlas project allowed him to combine his twin passions of hiking and birding in his favorite landscape. He has been involved in the study of birds along the Colorado River corridor in Glen and Grand canyons and throughout the varied lands of the Navajo and Hopi Nations. He lives in Flagstaff with his family and is planning many future birding adventures.

MARGIE LATTA began her wildlife biology career in 1994 as an Arizona Breeding Bird Atlas field crew member. As a lover of the outdoors, birding throughout Arizona was a great way to start her biology career. From 1996 to 2000 she was the Arizona Partners in Flight State Coordinator, where she directed the creation of the Arizona Bird Conservation Plan. She has since worked for the Arizona Game and Fish Department, conducting land acquisitions and management of Department lands and her current Department work focuses on wildlife and natural resource conservation projects on private lands throughout Arizona.

JENNIFER L. MARTIN was once most frequently found in a cluttered office where she worked as the Arizona Bird Conservation Initiative Coordinator for the Nongame Branch of Arizona Game and Fish Department. In October of 2003 she gave birth to a healthy baby boy named Justice. She now juggles infant care with her work as a freelance technical writer, and tries to find time to enjoy scenic trails, traditional music festivals, and used bookstores.

TRACY MCCARTHEY recounts that her love for birds began when she worked as a biological technician on an avian research study on the Mogollon Rim in central Arizona. It was here that she learned how to interpret the behavioral clues associated with nesting birds and how to enjoy the challenge of locating bird nests. After a brief sojourn at the University of Arkansas working on a small mammal project, she spent four field seasons traveling Arizona, camping, backpacking, and documenting breeding birds as an Atlas project technician. She now works as a biological consultant for Archaeological Consulting Services, Ltd.

AMANDA MOORS has lived and worked in Arizona since 1994, before which she worked on avian research projects in New England. As biologist for the San Carlos Apache Tribe, she conducted surveys for big game as well as for nongame species and assisted the Atlas field crews with surveys on San Carlos Apache tribal lands for several years. In 1999, she started a consulting business and currently conducts Mexican Spotted Owl surveys for the U.S. Forest Service in the Santa Catalina Mountains and for the San Carlos Apache Tribe.

LIN PIEST began his birding career in Arizona by studying nesting waterfowl in the White Mountains as a graduate student at the University of Arizona. He started working for the Arizona Game and Fish Department in 1984 in Flagstaff. He worked his way downstream to the Phoenix and Yuma offices, where he is currently involved with surveys and management for birds along the lower Colorado River. He continues to marvel that he was actually paid for much of the birding he did for the Atlas project.

NORM SHROUT, a seasoned food service director, has been gradually shifting focus from food to his real passion: birding. He grew up in New York with just enough time to investigate the eastern birds and graduate from Cornell University before heading southwest to Phoenix. He has spent many years participating in research, fieldwork, conservation, fundraising and birding adventures for his hometown Bird Club, Audubon Society, U.S. Geological Survey, and the Arizona Game and Fish Department. His greatest interest is birding by ear, and he is constantly working to increase his repertoire.

SUE SITKO has worked for wildlife and natural resource conservation nearly twenty years, most recently as the White Mountains Program Manager for The Nature Conservancy in Arizona. This and previous positions with the Arizona Game and Fish Department, Minnesota Department of Natural Resources, and Pima County Parks have allowed her to help conserve species such as the Peregrine Falcon, Bald Eagle, Desert Tortoise, Blanding's Turtle, and even a rare cactus or two. She has been watching and observing birds since high school, when she realized she wanted to find a job that would pay her to watch birds. On rare occasions, her dream comes true.

JOHN SPENCE, born and raised in Utah, started birding at the age of twelve. He moved to Page, Arizona, after obtaining an M.Sc. in plant ecology from Utah State University and a Ph.D. in botany from University of British Columbia. He now works for the National Park Service at Glen Canyon National Recreation Area as an ecologist. He has completed water birds surveys on Lake Powell, breeding bird inventories and monitoring projects in the Grand Canyon, and has conducted research on plants in many parts of the world. His most recent interest is butterflies, and he can be often seen running after them through wildflower meadows.

CATHY WISE-GERVAIS probably changed a lifetime's worth of tires during her six field seasons on the Atlas crew, but her backcountry adventures during the project more than made up for it. She was a wildlife biologist for the Arizona Game and Fish Department for seven years during the Atlas project and as an avid backpacker and climber, thoroughly enjoyed the experience. She graduated from UC Davis with a degree in avian sciences, then studied birds for thirteen years in California, Utah, and Arizona. She is now a freelance writer/naturalist and, along with her husband Joe, is raising her family and five breeds of fancy chickens in Cave Creek, Arizona.